General Chair's Welcome Message

It is my great pleasure to welcome you to Utah and the 23rd Annual International Conference on Mobile Computing and Networking – MobiCom 2017.

The MobiCom conference series serves as a highly selective, premier international forum addressing networks, systems, algorithms, and applications that support mobile computers and wireless networks. MobiCom 2017 continues this tradition with a full and exciting program. Our main technical program features the latest research in mobile computing and wireless and mobile networking. We look forward to keynote addresses by Prof. Hari Balakrishnan from M.I.T. and Cambridge Mobile Telematics, and by Dr. Thyaga Nandagopal from the National Science Foundation. We are pleased that we can host an address by the 2017 SIGMOBILE RockStar winner, Shyam Gollakota, and that 2017 ACM SIGMOBILE Test-of-Time Paper awardee, Giuseppe Bianchi, receives his award at MobiCom. In addition to these main conference events, MobiCom 2017 includes eight co-located workshops, the Mobile App Competition, the MobiCom Student Research Competition, a panel session on Macro Trends in Wireless Research and Experimentation, an N2Women event, and the second edition of the MobiJob student career event.

Heartfelt thanks go to all members of the organizing committee for helping to make MobiCom 2017 a success. TPC co-chairs Ben Greenstein and Kannan Srinivasan assembled and led a world-class program committee to review and select papers for the main technical program. Workshop co-chairs Tam Vu and Bozidar Radunovic were responsible for selecting and organizing the eight co-located workshops. Domenico Giustiniano and Kirk Webb served as demo co-chairs to bring us an exciting set of demos. Poster co-chairs Ioannis Pefkianakis and Kate Ching-Ju Lin ran the poster selection process and worked with Dimitrios Koutsonikolas to select contributions for the student research competition. Eric Eide was our diligent finance chair, while Robert Ricci expertly served as local arrangements chair. (And the pair served as advisors to and in overall support of the general chair.) Our three publicity chairs, Ahmed Elmokashfi, Chunyi Peng and JeongGil (John) Ko, faithfully publicized MobiCom information throughout the whole process. Kyungmin Lee did an amazing job continuously updating the MobiCom website, while Ali Rostami took care of MobiCom's social media presence. Lenin Ravindranath Sivalingam and Long Lu took care of the 5th Mobile App competition. Mike Wittie and Feng Qian obtained a student travel grant from NSF and oversaw the grant application process. As registration chair Eugene Chai worked with RegOnline to implement all our registration options. Younki Lee and Neal Patwari served as MobiCom app co-chairs to bring conference details to your smartphones. Finally, Vijay Gopalakrishnan served as MobiJob chair to organize our student career event.

Special thanks go to our SIG sponsor, ACM SIGMOBILE, as well as our financial sponsors: the National Science Foundation (student travel grants); Samsung (gold sponsor); Microsoft (silver sponsor); Google and NEC Labs (bronze sponsors). Additional financial support was provided by EntryPoint and Lucidchart. The support of these organizations is crucial to MobiCom's continued success.

A final word of thanks goes to the MobiCom Steering Committee, Victor Bahl (Chair), Suman Banerjee, Ramesh Govindan, David B. Johnson, Kang Shin and Heather Zheng. Their trust, support and guidance are greatly appreciated.

It is my hope that your stay in Utah's Wasatch Mountains will be enjoyable and that the first MobiCom to be held in the heart of Silicon Slopes will be a memorable and inspiring event.

Kobus Van der Merwe

General Chair
University of Utah

Technical Program Committee Chairs' Message

Welcome to ACM MobiCom '17, the 23nd Annual International Conference on Mobile Computing and Networking.

MobiCom is the premier forum for cutting-edge research in mobile systems and wireless networks. This year's technical program features 35 outstanding papers, covering a wide variety of topics:

- Wireless access and backhaul
- Cellular systems
- Light communication
- Near field communication
- Localization
- RFID
- Wireless privacy and security
- IoT and wearables
- Data management
- Virtual reality
- Mobile applications and Web

This year's call for papers brought in 307 abstract registrations -- and 186 turned into qualified submissions from Asia, Europe, and the United States.

We again had a heavy PC (30 members) and a light PC (30 members). The two-tiered PC balanced the goals of broader inclusivity and running an effective TPC meeting. The TPC was made up of experts from diverse research areas, and TPC selection also took into account gender, seniority, institution, country, expertise, and academic or industrial background. The TPC included researchers from 10 countries: France, India, Italy, Singapore, South Korea, Sweden, Switzerland, Taiwan, U.K., and the U.S. Twenty percent of the TPC members were female. The TPC also had broad industry participation, with members from Cisco, Google, IBM, Microsoft, and NEC.

The paper review process was double-blind. It was carried out in three phases: First, each paper was reviewed by at least three TPC members, and the top 107 papers were advanced to the second phase. Review scores, in addition to reviewer confidence and normalization with respect to other papers by the same reviewer, were considered in the selection process. In the second phase, each paper was reviewed by at least two more reviewers, followed by an online discussion; that produced 68 papers for the TPC meeting on June 1 and 2 in Seattle, which was the final phase. These 68 papers were discussed at length at the meeting. Eventually, 35 papers were conditionally accepted into the program. The heavy PC participated in all three phases; the light TPC participated only in the first phase.

Each of the 35 papers was assigned a shepherd from the heavy PC. Shepherds' identities were provided to authors, unlike in the previous year. Reviewers remained anonymous. Shepherds coordinated with reviewers to address the review comments and they approved the final versions for publication. The result of this process is a strong and diverse technical program consisting of 35 high-quality papers.

October 16-20, 2017
Snowbird, UT, USA

Association for
Computing Machinery

Advancing Computing as a Science & Profession

MobiCom '17

Proceedings of the 23rd Annual International Conference on Mobile Computing and Networking

Sponsored by:

ACM SIGMOBILE

Supported by:

National Science Foundation, Samsung, Microsoft, Google, NEC Labs, EntryPoint & Lucidchart

Association for
Computing Machinery

Advancing Computing as a Science & Profession

The Association for Computing Machinery
2 Penn Plaza, Suite 701
New York, New York 10121-0701

Notice to Past Authors of ACM-Published Articles
ACM intends to create a complete electronic archive of all articles and/or other material previously published by ACM. If you have written a work that has been previously published by ACM in any journal or conference proceedings prior to 1978, or any SIG Newsletter at any time, and you do NOT want this work to appear in the ACM Digital Library, please inform permissions@acm.org, stating the title of the work, the author(s), and where and when published.

ISBN: 978-1-4503-4916-1 (Digital)

ISBN: 978-1-4503-5676-3 (Print)

Additional copies may be ordered prepaid from:

ACM Order Department
PO Box 30777
New York, NY 10087-0777, USA

Phone: 1-800-342-6626 (USA and Canada)
+1-212-626-0500 (Global)
Fax: +1-212-944-1318
E-mail: acmhelp@acm.org
Hours of Operation: 8:30 am – 4:30 pm ET

As TPC Co-Chairs, we would like to express our sincere gratitude to everyone who made this technical program possible. We thank all the authors who submitted their great research work to the conference. We are grateful to all the TPC members – their enthusiasm and hard work produced this strong technical program. We also want to thank the entire MobiCom '17 team, especially our General Chair, Kobus Van der Merwe, for his tremendous support and behind-the-scenes effort. We also are grateful to Google for hosting the TPC meeting at its office. Finally, we extend our thanks and appreciation to the MobiCom Steering Committee for their guidance and wisdom.

We hope that you will find the program exciting and thought-provoking.

Ben Greenstein
Technical Program Co-Chair
Google, USA

Kannan Srinivasan
Technical Program Co-Chair
The Ohio State University, USA

Table of Contents

Paper Session IV: Aurora Borealis

SIGMOBILE RockStar Award

Paper Session V: Location! Location! Location!

Paper Session VI: Tag, You're It!

Paper Session VII: Leaks, Plugs, Alice and Bob

Keynote Address

Paper Session VIII: Frameworks and Such

Paper Session IX: Better, Faster Apps and Web

Demonstrations

Posters

MobiCom 2017 Conference Organization

General Chair:	Kobus Van der Merwe (University of Utah)
Program Co-Chairs:	Ben Greenstein (Google, USA) Kannan Srinivasan (Ohio State University, USA)
Workshops Co-Chairs:	Tam Vu (University of Colorado, Denver, USA) Bozidar Radunovic (Microsoft Research, Cambridge, UK)
Demo Co-Chairs:	Domenico Giustiniano (IMDEA Networks Institute, Spain) Kirk Webb (University of Utah, USA)
Posters Co-Chairs:	Ioannis Pefkianakis (Hewlett Packard Labs, USA) Kate Ching-Ju Lin (National Chiao Tung University, Taiwan)
SRC Chair:	Dimitrios Koutsonikolas (University at Buffalo, USA)
Finance Chair:	Eric Eide (University of Utah, USA)
Publicity Co-Chairs:	Ahmed Elmokashfi (Simula Research Laboratory, Norway) Chunyi Peng (Ohio State University, USA) JeongGil (John) Ko (Ajou University, South Korea)
Web Chair:	Kyungmin Lee (Facebook, USA)
Local Arrangements Chair:	Robert Ricci (University of Utah, USA)
Social-media Chair:	Ali Rostami (Rutgers University, USA)
App Competition Co-Chairs:	Lenin Ravindranath Sivalingam (Microsoft Research, Redmond, USA) Long Lu (Stony Brook University, USA)
Student Travel Grants Co-Chairs:	Mike Wittie (Montana State University, USA) Feng Qian (Indiana University, USA)
Registration Chair:	Eugene Chai (NEC Labs, USA)
App Co-Chairs:	Youngki Lee (Singapore Management University, Singapore) Neal Patwari (University of Utah, USA)
MobiJob Chair:	Vijay Gopalakrishnan (AT&T Labs – Research)
Steering Committee:	Victor Bahl (Chair) (Microsoft Research, USA) Suman Banerjee (University of Wisconsin-Madison, USA) Ramesh Govindan (University of Southern California, USA) David B. Johnson (Rice University, USA) Kang Shin (University of Michigan, USA) Heather Zheng (University of California, Santa Barbara, USA)

Technical Program Committee: Fadel Adib (Massachusetts Institute of Technology)
Sharad Agarwal (Microsoft Research Redmond)
Victor Bahl (Microsoft Research Redmond)
Aruna Balasubramanian (Stony Brook University)
Tarun Bansal (Google)
Elizabeth Belding (University of California, Santa Barbara)
Srdjan Capkun (ETH Zurich, Switzerland)
Geoffrey Challen (University at Buffalo)
Ranveer Chandra (Microsoft Research Redmond)
Bo Chen (Cisco Meraki)
Yingying Chen (Stevens Institute of Technology)
David Chu (Google)
Samir Das (Stony Brook University)
Christina Fragouli (University of California, Los Angeles)
Mario Gerla (University of California, Los Angeles)
Shyamnath Gollakota (University of Washington)
Marco Gruteser (Rutgers University)
Haitham Hassanieh (University of Illinois, Urbana Champaign)
Tian He (University of Minnesota)
Wenjun Hu (Yale University)
Y. Charlie Hu (Purdue University)
Polly Huang (National Taiwan University, Taiwan)
Kyle Jamieson (Princeton University)
Sneha Kasera (University of Utah)
Dimitrios Koutsonikolas (University at Buffalo)
Robin Kravets (University of Illinois, Urbana Champaign)
Srikanth Krishnamurthy (University of California, Riverside)
Swarun Kumar (Carnegie Mellon University)
Sung-Ju Lee (Korea Advanced Institute of Science & Technology, South Korea)
Mo Li Nanyang (Technological University, Singapore)
Robert LiKamWa (Arizona State University)
Songwu Lu (University of California, Los Angeles)
Thomas Moscibroda (Microsoft Research Asia)
Thyaga Nandagopal (National Science Foundation)
Vishnu Navda (Microsoft Research India)
Srihari Nelakuditi (University of South Carolina)
Jason Nieh (Columbia University)
Panos Papadimitratos (KTH Royal Institute of Technology in Stockholm, Sweden)
Giovanni Pau (Laboratoire d'Informatique de Paris 6, France)
Chunyi Peng (Ohio State University)
Chiara Petriolli (University of Rome, Italy)
Matthai Philipose (Microsoft Research Redmond)
Lili Qiu (University of Texas at Austin)
Bozidar Radunovic (Microsoft Research Cambridge, UK)

Technical Program Committee (continued):

Eric Rozner (IBM Research Austin)
Ashutosh Sabarwal (Rice University)
Souvik Sen (Google)
Prasun Sinha (Ohio State University)
Raghupathy Sivakumar (Georgia Institute of Technology)
Josh Smith (University of Washington)
Lakshmi Subramanian (New York University)
Karthik Sundaresan (NEC Laboratories)
Andreas Terzis (Google)
He Wang (Purdue University)
Matt Welsh (Google)
Jie Xiong (Singapore Management University, Singapore)
Xinyu Zhang (University of Wisconsin)
Heather Zheng (University of California, Santa Barbara)
Lin Zhong (Rice University)
Xia Zhou (Dartmouth College)

MobiCom 2017 Sponsors & Supporters

SIG Sponsor:

Student Travel Grants:

Silver Sponsor:

Bronze Sponsors:

Other Supporters:

Making Roads Safer by Making Drivers Better

Hari Balakrishnan
M.I.T. and Cambridge Mobile Telematics
Cambridge, MA
hari@csail.mit.edu

ABSTRACT

The world's roads see over 50 million injuries and 1.25 million fatalities every year; road accidents are the leading cause of death among people between the ages of 15 to 30. This talk will describe how mobile sensing (especially using smartphones), signal processing, machine learning, and behavioral science can improve road safety by making people better drivers. I'll discuss several challenges in achieving this goal, as well as learnings from successful deployments in multiple countries. Interesting problems include inferring vehicular dynamics from noisy sensor data; accurate drive detection; detecting and discouraging distracted driving; designing good incentives for safe-driving; and the design of new sensing platforms to augment smartphone sensors.

CCS Concepts/ACM Classifiers

• General and reference ~ General literature

Author Keywords

Vehicle safety; Mobile sensing; Signal Processing; Machine Learning; Behavioral Science

BIOGRAPHY

Hari Balakrishnan is the Fujitsu Professor of Computer Science and a Director of MIT's Center for Wireless Networks and Mobile Computing. His research is in networked computer systems, with current interests in networking, data management, and sensing for a world of "truly mobile" devices connected to cloud services running in large datacenters. Based on the CarTel research project, he co-founded Cambridge Mobile Telematics (CMT), a company that develops mobile sensing, inferencing, and data analytics technologies to change driver behavior and make roads safer around the world. He is an alumnus of UC Berkeley (PhD, 1998, winner of the ACM doctoral dissertation award) and IIT Madras (1993), which named him a distinguished alumnus in 2013. He was inducted to the National Academy of Engineering in 2015 and to the American Academy of Arts and Sciences in 2017 for his contributions to networks and distributed systems. He has also received "test of time" awards from SIGCOMM, SIGMOBILE, SIGOPS, and SIGMOD.

MobiCom'17, October 16-20, 2017, Snowbird, UT, USA.

ACM ISBN 978-1-4503-4916-1/17/10.
DOI: https://doi.org/10.1145/3117811.3117847

WEBee: Physical-Layer Cross-Technology Communication via Emulation

Zhijun Li*
University of Minnesota
Minneapolis, MN
lizhijun.hit@gmail.com

Tian He†
University of Minnesota
Minneapolis, MN
tianhe@umn.edu

ABSTRACT

Recent advances in Cross-Technology Communication (CTC) have improved efficient coexistence and cooperation among heterogeneous wireless devices (e.g., WiFi, ZigBee, and Bluetooth) operating in the same ISM band. However, until now the effectiveness of existing CTCs, which rely on packet-level modulation, is limited due to their low throughput (e.g., tens of bps). Our work, named WEBee, opens a promising direction for high-throughput CTC via physical-level emulation. WEBee uses a high-speed wireless radio (e.g., WiFi OFDM) to emulate the desired signals of a low-speed radio (e.g., ZigBee). Our unique emulation technique manipulates only the payload of WiFi packets, requiring neither hardware nor firmware changes in commodity technologies – a feature allowing zero-cost fast deployment on existing WiFi infrastructure. We designed and implemented WEBee with commodity devices (Atheros AR2425 WiFi card and MicaZ CC2420) and the USRP-N210 platform (for PHY layer evaluation). Our comprehensive evaluation reveals that WEBee can achieve a more than 99% reliable parallel CTC between WiFi and ZigBee with 126 Kbps in noisy environments, a throughput about 16,000x faster than current state-of-the-art CTCs.

CCS CONCEPTS

• **Networks** → Wireless Networks;

KEYWORDS

Cross Technology Communication; Signal Emulation; WiFi OFDM; ZigBee OQPSK, DSSS

1 INTRODUCTION

According to Gartner [15], the number of Internet of Things (IoT) devices connected wirelessly will reach 20 billion by 2020, leading to the intense coexistence of wireless technologies.

For spectrum efficiency under dense deployment, many of today's wireless technologies are designed to share the unlicensed spectrum (e.g., ISM bands), including such popular technologies as WiFi, Bluetooth, and ZigBee. Despite the common belief that coexistence of wireless technologies leads harmful interference, it in fact offers new opportunities for those technologies to collaborate. Recent research shows that cross-technology communication (CTC), defined as direct communication (i.e., message/data exchange) among heterogeneous wireless devices, can bring about many benefits. For example, ZiFi [50] can significantly reduce the standby energy of WiFi devices when a low-power ZigBee radio is used to wake up the WiFi NIC whenever it detects the existence of WiFi APs, and FreeBee [23] can reduce this by 58% more if the open/private setting of a WiFi AP is conveyed through CTC. Furthermore, CTC will provide more efficient channel coordination by exchanging global RTS/CTS and TDMA messages *explicitly* among coexisting heterogeneous devices, in replace of *implicit* clear channel assessment (CCA).

Traditionally, bridging wireless technologies was achieved indirectly through multi-radio gateways, which introduce extra hardware cost, deployment complexity, and doubling the traffic into and out from these gateways. To avoid these drawbacks, a few pioneering works [5, 9, 20, 23] support CTC among heterogeneous wireless devices despite their incompatible physical layer modulation. We note that existing CTCs use packet-level modulation – embedding symbols using the packet length [5], timing [23], and sequence patterns [20, 43]. For example in [43], a sender transmits a sequence of long and short Wi-Fi packets to construct Morse codes, which can be decoded by receivers through RSSI energy sensing. With packet-level modulation, a packet can express at most a few bits in CTC [5], as opposed to thousands of bits if the packet were used for intra-technology communication [18]. Furthermore, early solutions [9, 49] require sending dummy packets for CTC, which wastefully occupy the channel, leading to further inefficiency.

In this paper, we introduce a new direction for high-throughput CTC, a physical-level emulation technique named WEBee (for WiFi Emulated ZigBee). In a nut-shell, WEBee chooses the payload of a WiFi frame in such a way as a portion of this WiFi frame is recognized by commodity ZigBee devices transparently as a legitimate ZigBee frame. Since we modify neither the firmware nor hardware of the WiFi transmitter, this WiFi frame can also be legitimately received by WiFi receivers. We note that the pioneering work [19] produces RFID AM signals using Wi-Fi devices, which inspires us to create physical-level cross-technology communication that is dual standard compliance (i.e., ZigBee and WiFi).

*Zhijun Li is a visiting professor at the University of Minnesota and officially affiliated with Harbin Institute of Technology, China.
†Tian He is the corresponding author.

MobiCom '17, October 16–20, 2017, Snowbird, UT, USA

ACM ISBN 978-1-4503-4916-1/17/10...$15.00
https://doi.org/10.1145/3117811.3117816

Table 1: Motivation of the WEBee

	Cost	Spectrum Efficiency	Throughput	Parallel CTCs
Gateway	Median	Median	High	Not Support
FreeBee[23]	Low	Median	Low	Not Support
Esense[5]	Low	Low	Low	Not Support
B^2W^2[9]	Low	Low	Low	Not Support
WEBee	**Low**	**High**	**High**	**Support**

To support CTC, a WiFi transmitter needs to emulate the ZigBee time-domain waveform closely enough so that it can pass ZigBee preamble detection and allow successful OQPSK demodulation. With such signal emulation, WEBee conceptually can achieve a 250Kbps data rate from WiFi to ZigBee, the ceiling speed of standard ZigBee communications. In practice, after accommodating emulation errors, a WEBee WiFi transmitter achieves a 99.9% symbol reception ratio at 63Kbps data rate, which is more than 8,000 times faster than the reliable free-channel rate (7.5bps@99%) reported by FreeBee [23]. Moreover, since WiFi occupies a much wider bandwidth (20MHz) than ZigBee (2MHz), WEBee can successfully emulate two ZigBee frames under different frequencies within a single WiFi frame, resulting in a 16,000x throughput and a higher spectrum efficiency.

This paper presents the first emulation-based CTC design from WiFi to ZigBee specifically. However, the features we provide and the challenges we address in this emulation-based design are indeed generic and applicable to a whole set of future physical-layer CTCs. Specifically, the major contributions of WEBee are as follows:

- We design WEBee, a CTC technique that emulates ZigBee frames with the payload of WiFi frames. Without modifying the firmware or hardware of both WiFi and ZigBee devices, WEBee is a transparent design that be can easily deployed in existing WiFi infrastructure with broad applicability.
- To extend the range, we address a few unique challenges, which include (i) optimized ZigBee signal emulation using the WiFi OFDM modulation, (ii) reverse WiFi channel coding mapping, (iii) pilot/null subcarrier avoidance, (iv) parallel CTC, and (v) link-level reliability. These techniques provide general guidances for range extension of emulation-based CTC designs.
- We implement and evaluate WEBee on commodity devices (Atheros AR2425 WiFi NIC and MicaZ CC2420) and the USRP-N210 platform (for PHY-layer evaluation). Our extensive evaluation demonstrates that WEBee can achieve a fast, robust, and parallel CTC performance under a full range of wireless configurations, including stationary, mobile, long-distance, and duty-cycled settings. In all these settings, the frame reception ratio (FRR) reaches above 99% with six retransmissions, and throughput is orders of magnitude larger than existing CTC solutions [5, 9, 23, 43]. We have also embedded WEBee into Nexus 5 smart phones with BCM4330 WiFi chips to control Zigbee Smart bulb directly, indicating WEBee is applicable in today's mainstream devices as well [27].

2 MOTIVATION

Spectrum efficiency calls for sharing within the unlicensed bands. Between 2014-2016, the FCC [12–14] opened the spectrum in 600MHz, 5GHz, and 7GHz, bringing in new ISM standards, including LTE-U (by T-Mobile and Verizon Wireless [33]) and 802.11ah (i.e., WiFi HaLow [41]). Such coexisting environments necessitate explicit information exchange among heterogeneous wireless devices to support channel coordination and cross-technology collaboration. Information can be exchanged through either multi-radio gateways or cross-technology communication (CTC). In this section, we examine the limitations of existing solutions and summarize the benefits of WEBee in Table 1.

Limitation of Gateways: Clearly, multi-radio gateways can serve as translators among heterogeneous wireless devices with incompatible physical layers. However, this solution is inherently limited in several aspects. First, gateways incur extra hardware costs and deployment complexity, in which the density and physical locations of the gateways noticeably impact network performance. Second, gateway-based approaches induce significant traffic overhead flowing in and out from the gateway, which further intensifies interference, especially in multi-hop scenarios. Third, gateways have to be deployed in advance in the situations where CTCs are required, making it difficult to support mobile and ad hoc scenarios.

Limitation of Packet-Level CTC: The inherent limitation of the packet-level CTCs is their throughput. Usually, the duration of a wireless packet is in the range of milliseconds. Embedding CTC symbols with sparse packet-level information (i.e., the packet Tx timing in FreeBee [23], the packet RSSI duration in Esense [5]) limits the bandwidth. For example, in ZigBee devices, the packet-level RSSI information is sampled at only 31.25KHz, while the phase-shift is obtained at 4MHz by the ZigBee PHY for (de)modulation. In other words, the throughput of packet-level CTCs is inherently bounded by a low sampling rate (e.g., KHz) in contrast to hundreds of Kbps for native ZigBee communication.

Another limitation of the packet-level CTCs is that they fail to utilize bandwidth fully. A single WiFi transmission occupies 20-40MHz channels, while ZigBee receivers only obtain packet-level information within a 2MHz-wide ZigBee channel. We note that this is an inherent limitation of packet-level CTCs because the packet-level information (e.g., packet Tx timing) perceived by ZigBee at different channels is the same, making parallel symbol transmission infeasible at the packet level.

Advantage of Physical-Level CTC: As summarized in Table 1, WEBee resolves the limitation of gateways by offering direct connectivity. For example, it allows a WiFi AP to control all IoT devices equipped with low-power ZigBee radios in a smart home without a gateway. Instead of depending on sparse packet-level information,

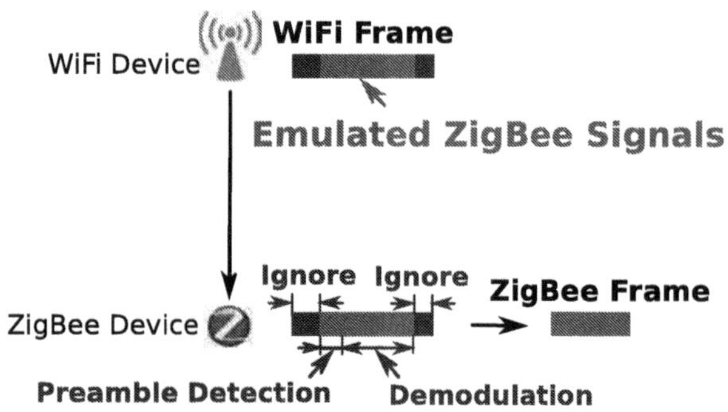

Figure 1: The Architecture of the WEBee

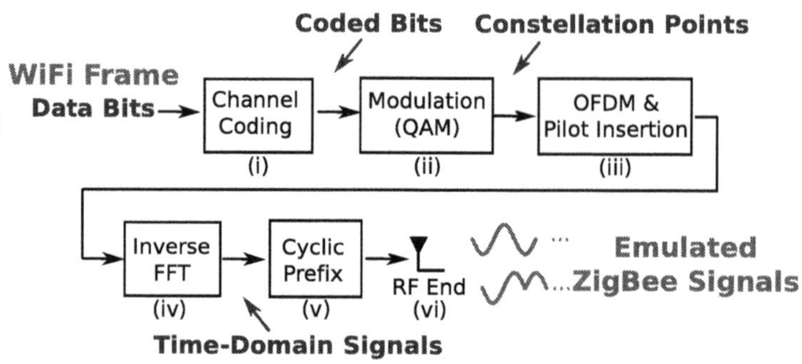

Figure 2: How WiFi Transmitter Works

WEBee achieves a throughput close to that of the ZigBee standard by emulating time-domain ZigBee signals. Parallel CTCs become feasible by emulating multiple time-domain ZigBee signals at different frequency bands, further boosting the total throughput.

3 OVERVIEW OF THE WEBEE DESIGN

Figure 1 illustrates how WEBee works: a WiFi device transmits a frame with a *selected* payload that can be recognized by a ZigBee receiver as a *legitimate* ZigBee frame. More specifically, WEBee constructs the payload of a WiFi frame *elaborately* so that the RF waveform of the payload resembles that of ZigBee signals. When such a WiFi frame is transmitted into the air through the front end of the WiFi RF, the WiFi header, preamble, and trailer are ignored by ZigBee receivers as noise, while the payload will successfully pass the ZigBee preamble detection and the emulated ZigBee frame will be then demodulated at the ZigBee receiver. We note that WEBee is indeed a *transparent* design, in the sense that a ZigBee receiver cannot differentiate whether the sender is a ZigBee or a WiFi device. Moreover, time-domain waveforms of multiple ZigBee frames can be modulated into one WiFi frame because of the wider band of WiFi transmissions. Multiple ZigBee receivers working on different channels can detect and demodulate different emulated ZigBee frames simultaneously and independently.

3.1 Background

To explain WEBee, it is necessary to first introduce how WiFi transmitters and ZigBee receivers work. Although our description is specific, our approach is generically applicable to future emulation-based CTCs.

3.1.1 How a WiFi Transmitter Works. Figure 2 shows how a WiFi transmitter (802.11g/n) works, from step (i) to step (vi). (i) The channeling coding module encodes the data bits in a WiFi frame into redundant coded bits for robustness. (ii) Then these coded bits are mapped into a set of constellation points based on selected modulation schemes, typically Quadrature Amplitude Modulation (QAM). (iii) By using Orthogonal Frequency Division Multiplexing (OFDM), these constellation points are modulated into 48 data subcarriers, while additional pseudo-random pilot symbols are modulated into pilot subcarriers for channel estimation at the WiFi receivers. (iv) After that, Inverse Fast Fourier Transform (IFFT) combines all these subcarriers and turns them into a time-domain signal. (v) The WiFi time-domain signal is then processed by the cyclic prefix module, which prefixes a WiFi symbol with a repetition of the end. By cyclic prefixing, a guard 0.8us interval is formed to eliminate inter-symbol interference. (vi) Finally, a whole WiFi symbol with a $4\mu s$ duration is generated at the WiFi sender and is sent by the WiFi RF radio.

The objective of WEBee is to create time-domain waveforms that can be recognized by ZigBee receivers. To emulate ZigBee waveforms, WEBee proceeds with a reverse direction from step (vi) to step (i) as shown in Figure 2. To transmit the desired time-domain ZigBee RF signals at step (vi) from the commodity WiFi radios, at step (iii) WEBee needs to choose corresponding frequency components, which are mapped from the set of constellation points (complex numbers) selected at step (ii). These constellation points are controlled by the source bits of the WiFi payload.

In other words, source bits in a *selected* WiFi payload determine the QAM constellation points after the WiFi modulator. When a specific combination of constellation points are fed into the IFFT, the desired time-domain signals are emulated and transmitted from the commodity WiFi radios. With such signal emulation, the commodity ZigBee radios can demodulate and decode the "frame" sent from the WiFi to achieve CTC. It is noted that WEBee does not change the WiFi modulator, and therefore QAM-based emulation contains an intrinsic error because only a limited number of discrete QAM constellation points are available for emulation.

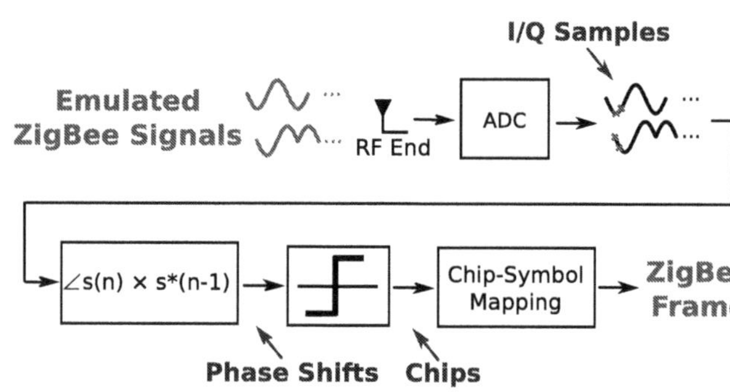

Figure 3: How ZigBee Receiver Works

3.1.2 How a ZigBee Receiver Works. WEBee sends WiFi frames to commodity ZigBee devices. The physical layer of ZigBee receivers is shown in Figure 3. Because of sharing the same ISM wireless band (e.g., 2.4GHz), the waveform emulated by WiFi can be sampled by ZigBee devices. To receive a frame, a ZigBee RX Radio down-converts the received WiFi passband waveforms to baseband and digitalizes them into in-phase and quadrature (I/Q) samples using ADC.

The modulation of ZigBee is Offset Quadrature Phase-Shift Keying (OQPSK), in which the phase shifts between the consecutive I/Q samples are used to demodulate the ZigBee symbols. Specifically, the phase shift between two consecutive complex samples $s(n)$ and $s(n-1)$ is computed by $arctan(s(n) \times s^*(n-1))$, where $s^*(n-1)$ is the conjugate of $s(n-1)$. With thresholding, ZigBee outputs the chip value "1" if the phase shift is bigger than $0°$ and otherwise outputs the chip value "0". After collecting 32 chips, ZigBee maps these chips into four bits (i.e., a ZigBee symbol in frame), according to the predefined symbol-to-chip spreading relationship in the direct sequence spread spectrum (DSSS) process.

3.1.3 Why Emulation is Feasible. In ZigBee (i.e., IEEE 802.15.4), direct sequence spread spectrum (DSSS) is used to improve protection against interference and noise by multiplying original bits with a pseudo random noise spreading code. Specifically, a ZigBee symbol (i.e., 4-bits) are mapped into a 32-chip sequence. In DSSS, a correlation threshold is defined to control the maximum Hamming distance between the received 32-chip sequence and the predefined chip sequence that the receiver can tolerate. A none-zero threshold means that ZigBee receivers inherently can tolerate a certain number of errors in chip sequences. Normally, 12 is the default threshold, i.e., 12 chip errors can be recovered by the ZigBee DSSS technique. In some scenarios, this threshold is set more loosely to adapt to environments with high interference and noise. For example, in [28], the default of such a threshold is set to 20 for ZigBee frames to survive WiFi interference. As mentioned early, QAM-based emulation could introduce errors in chip sequences. However, such errors are mediated by DSSS, and the emulated ZigBee symbols can be decoded by ZigBee successfully with a high probability.

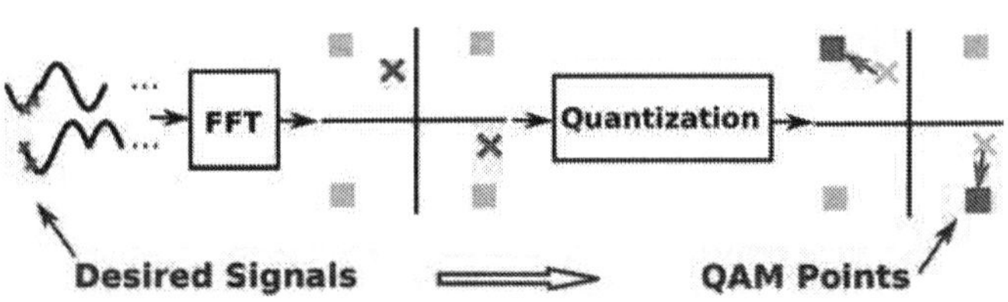

Figure 4: The Basic Process of QAM Emulation.

3.2 QAM Emulation

QAM emulation is the core of the WEBee design. Figure 4 shows that the QAM selection is done in the reverse direction, where the desired ZigBee time-domain signals are fed into the FFT to select corresponding QAM constellation points. The challenging issue of QAM emulation is that because the QAM points in WiFi OFDM are predefined and discrete, the frequency components of the desired time-domain signals might not match the discrete QAM points perfectly, as shown in Figure 4, leading to intrinsic QAM quantization errors.

In Fourier transform analyses, the Parseval's theorem [42]states an equation of energy in the time-domain and frequency-domain. Combined with the linear property of Fourier transform, we have the following equation for the errors introduced by frequency-domain quantization, i.e.,

$$\int_{t=-T/2}^{T/2} |u(t) - v(t)|^2 dt = T \sum_{k} |U[k] - V[k]|^2, \qquad (1)$$

where $u(t)$ is the desired time domain signal, $v(t)$ is the time domain signal after QAM quantization, and $U[k]$ and $V[k]$ are corresponding DFTs.

The difference-energy equation shows that minimizing the signal distortion in the time-domain under energy metric is equivalent to minimizing the total deviation of frequency components after QAM quantization. Therefore QAM emulation is essentially an optimization process to choose the closest k QAM points in term of total Euclidean distance to each of k FFT points of desired signals as shown in Figure 4, which can be done easily in $O(k)$.

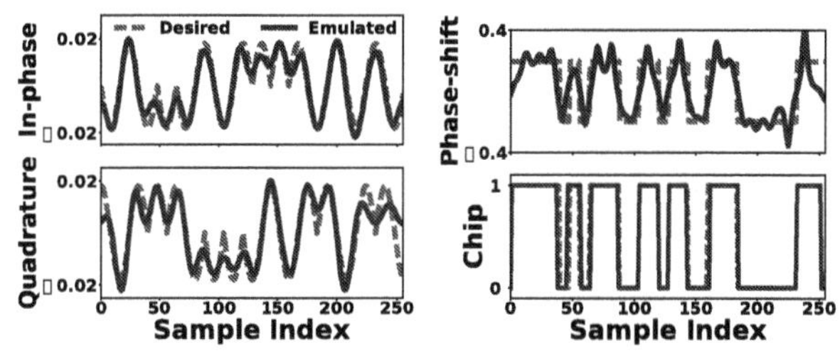

(a) Emulated time-domain signal (b) Phase shifts of emulated signal

Figure 5: Comparison between WiFi QAM Emulated Signal and the Desired ZigBee Signal

As a proof of concept example, an emulated ZigBee symbol "5" is emulated according to the process shown in Figure 4, where the 64-QAM constellation points in IEEE 802.11g standard are utilized for emulation. After the IFFT, the emulated time-domain signal is shown in Figure 5a, where the real/imaginary parts of the emulated time-domain signal are compared with the desired In-phase/Quadrature (or I/Q) signal of the ZigBee symbol. It is easy to see that the desired ZigBee signals are approximated well by the emulated WiFi signal, with some tolerable distortion.

Furthermore, the phase shifts of the emulated signal (and corresponding chip values) are calculated and shown in Figure 5b. The results prove that the emulated signal can be decoded by ZigBee successfully.

3.3 Emulation under Hardware Constraints

For the sake of clarity, the QAM emulation illustrated in Figures 4 and 11 are introduced without mentioning hardware constraints. Clearly, to support cross-technology communication from WiFi to ZigBee in commodity devices, WEBee needs to handle a few challenging issues. Figure 6 shows the detailed transmission path of WiFi OFDM. In addition to QAM emulation, we need to support two additional types of emulation: (i) channel coding emulation and (ii) post-QAM emulation. The challenges related to each of these emulations are discussed in section 4 and section 5, respectively.

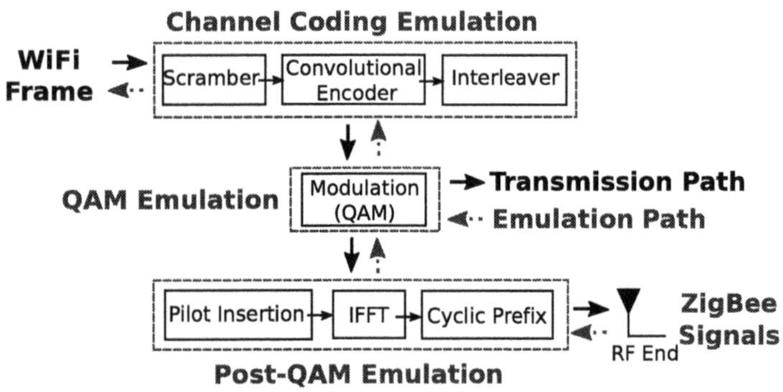

Figure 6: Complete WEBee Emulation Procedure.

4 CHANNEL CODING EMULATION

It is known that channel coding (convolutional encoding) makes WiFi OFDM communications more resilient to noise and interference by introducing redundancy (extra bits). But this imposes a challenge for emulation from the reverse direction because we can map source bits in the WiFi payload into only a *constrained* set of coded bits to activate QAM points for OFDM subcarrier modulation.

More specifically, in WiFi 64-QAM, six coded-bits are used to map one QAM point. Given 48 QAM points, a total of 288 ($= 48\times 6$) coded bits are used. Given a channel coding rate of 3/4, we use the 216 ($= 288 \times \frac{3}{4}$) bits in the WiFi payload to generate the 288 coded bits.

If matrices in Galois field GF(2) are used to define the relationship between the source bits X and the coded bits Y, it is easy to model the convolutional encoding as a matrix M satisfying the following equation:

$$M \times_{GF(2)} X = Y \tag{2}$$

For any Y, finding the X satisfying the equation (2) is equivalent to finding the inverse of M under GF(2). If M is full row-rank and square, the inverse of M can be calculated easily by Gaussian Elimination.

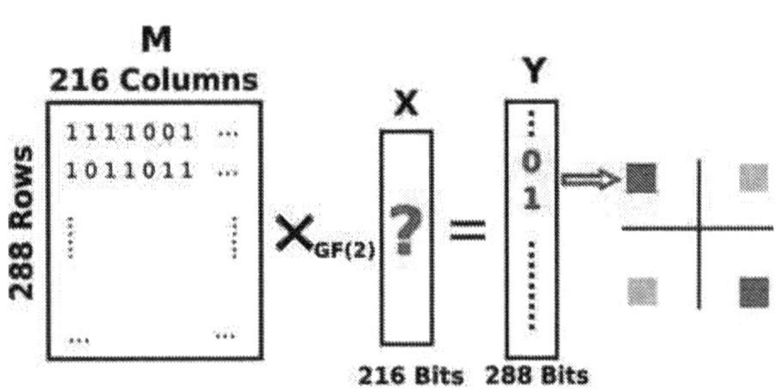

Figure 7: Invertible QAM Points under Constraints of WiFi Channel Coding

However, as shown in Figure 7, to map 216 source bits in X to 288 coded bits in Y, convolutional encoding uses a 288-by-216 matrix M. Since M is not full row-rank (row:288 > column:216), the matrix equation is an overdetermined system (i.e., more equations than unknowns). In other words, WEBee cannot emulate an arbitrary combination of 48 QAM points using 216 source bits.

But luckily, we note, ZigBee signals occupy only a 2MHz band, covering 7 WiFi subcarriers with a 312.5KHz bandwidth each. To emulate ZigBee signals, WEBee needs to control only 7 WiFi QAM points (14 QAM points in the parallel case) instead of all 48 QAM points. According to Equation 2, WEBee needs to control only 84 bits (14 ×6 bits) of Y by manipulating the X. Let Y' be the 84-bits subvector of Y and M' be the corresponding submatrix, we have,

$$M' \times_{GF(2)} X = Y'. \tag{3}$$

Given M' is now a full row-rank matrix (row:84 < column:216), for arbitrary coded bits Y, the matrix equation (3) is an underdetermined system with multiple solutions of X. In other words, WEBee can emulate an arbitrary combination of 14 QAM points with 216 source bits in multiple ways.

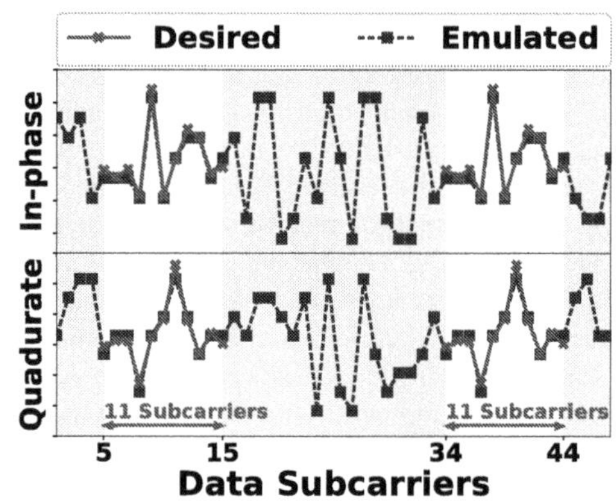

Figure 8: An Example of QAM Approximation by Controlling a Subset of Subcarriers

Our experiment in Figure 8 indicates that WEBee emulates ZigBee closely in two subregions of 11 subcarriers (7 data + 4 guard subcarriers) using 216 source bits. These two subregions overlapped with 2MHz ZigBee channels with 625KHz guarding bands on each side. Since we cannot control all 48 QAM points, additional signals are introduced in non-overlapped subcarriers, as shown in Figure 8, which is fine because ZigBee does not sample these subcarriers for demodulation.

To investigate the emulation capacity of source bits further, we increase the total bandwidth of desired subcarriers. When the total bandwidth becomes wider (i.e., the number of elements in Y become larger), the row rank of M increases. Theoretically, when M becomes square and full row-rank, WEBee can control up to 36 subcarriers (216 bits) with a total bandwidth of 11.25MHz, which is much larger than twice the ZigBee bandwidth (2Mhz). It is noted that since we can choose arbitrary elements in Y, WEBee is capable of controlling non-continuous bands of subcarriers, paving the way for parallel CTC.

Scrambler and interleaver: In addition to channel coding, the data scrambling in WiFi OFDM is performed by XORing the incoming source bits with the output of a 7-bit linear feedback shift register. Since the scrambler is a one-to-one mapping from the source bits to the scrambled bits, it is easy to reverse the scrambler by

XORing the scrambled bits with the same output of the shift register once the scrambling seed is known. We can read the scrambling seed from many commodity WiFi radios. For instances, in ath5k supported WiFi cards (e.g., Atheros AR5112 and AR2425), we can fix the scrambling seed by setting the GEN_SCRAMBLER field in the AR5K_PHY_CTL register of the driver. For BCM4330 WiFi chips used by LG Nexus 5, the scrambling seed has been fixed at 8. In other Atheros chipsets (e.g., AR9580 and AR5001G), the scrambling seed is incremented by one between frames, which is easy to track [19]. Similarly, the interleaver is also a one-to-one mapping from the coded bits to the permuted coded bits. This permutation is known in the WiFi standard and can be reversed easily.

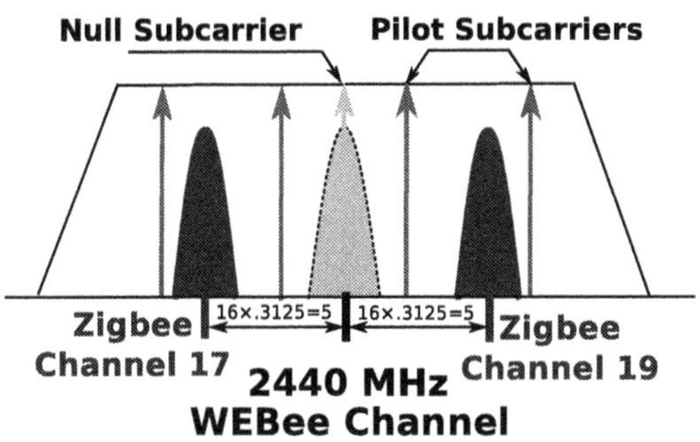

Figure 9: Channels Mapping for Pilot Avoidance

5 POST-QAM EMULATION

This section addresses challenges due to hardware constraints, such as pilot/null subcarrier avoidance, boundary flipping, and cyclic prefixing.

5.1 Pilot/Null Subcarrier Avoidance

In WiFi OFDM, each 20 MHz channel is composed of 64 subcarriers: 48 subcarriers for data, 4 subcarriers as pilot subcarriers for channel state estimation, and 12 null subcarriers. Without hardware modification, the WiFi signals transmitted in the pilot/null subcarrier cannot be controlled by software. Therefore, if the pilot subcarriers overlap with the frequency bands of ZigBee devices, WEBee cannot work properly. In WEBee, channel mapping is necessary to avoid the collision with the pilot/null subcarriers in WiFi OFDM.

Figure 9 shows a channel mapping scheme for pilot subcarrier avoidance. For example, once the central frequency of a WEBee channel is set as 2440MHz, the two regions of WiFi OFDM data subcarriers [-21, -7] and [7, 21]) can be utilized to achieve two parallel WEBee cross-technology communications in standard ZigBee channel 17 and channel 19. We note many commodity WiFi radios (e.g., Atheros AR9485, AR5112, and AR2425) can set their central frequency.

5.2 Post-QAM Challenges

We introduce the high-level idea of QAM evaluation in Section 3.2. In this section, we discuss a few research challenges imposed by the post-QAM process.

Challenge I: Non-continuity after Segmentation: Compared with the 16μ duration of a ZigBee symbol, a WiFi symbol occupies

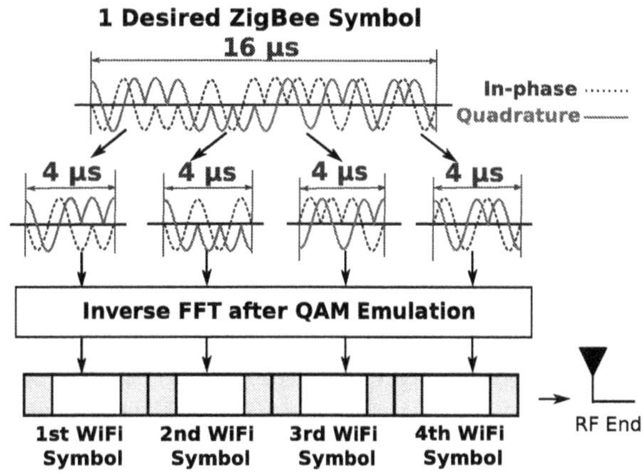

Figure 10: Emulate OQPSK with WiFi QAM.

$4\mu s$. Therefore, a full ZigBee symbol has to be segmented before emulated by four individual WiFi symbols , as shown in Figure 10. Such segmentation will introduce emulation error without further processing.

Technically, QAM points used by a WiFi symbol are selected by feeding the time-domain signal of one-fourth of a ZigBee symbol into Discrete Fourier transform (DFT). In DFT, the sampling in the frequency domain leads to the replicates of time domain signals; specifically, the signal $\hat{x}(n)$ recovered from the DFT samples via the following synthesis equation

$$\hat{x}(n) = \frac{1}{N}\sum_{k}(\sum_{n} x(n)e^{-j2\pi nk/N})e^{j2\pi kn/N} \tag{4}$$

$\hat{x}(n)$ is a periodic signal that consists of a sum of shifted replicates of the discrete time signal $x(n)$.

On one hand, the DFT treats the time-domain data by assuming they were periodic by concatenating with the shifted replicates of themselves. On the other hand, at the ZigBee receiver, Offset Quadrature Phase-Shift Keying(OQPSK) modulation adds a $\pi/2$ phase offset to the quadrature signals of the ZigBee symbol, which makes concatenated replicates noncontinuous, as shown in Figure 11a. This non-continuity introduces signal boundary errors, when the QAM emulation is used for an individual WiFi symbol, each emulating one-fourth of the *supposedly* continuous ZigBee symbol.

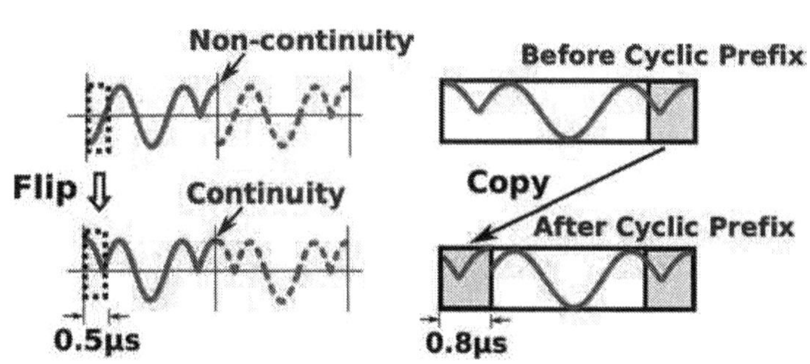

(a) Flipping Effect (b) Boundary with CP

Figure 11: Effects of Flipping and Cyclic Prefix

Challenge II: Cyclic Prefixing (CP): Another source of error comes from the WiFi cyclic prefixing, a technique to eliminate inter-symbol interference (ISI). As illustrated in Figure 11b, with cyclic prefixing, a guard interval lasting 0.8μs in each WiFi symbol is copied from the right of WiFi symbol and pasted into (overwrite) the left of the symbol . As a result, the front segment and the end segment of WiFi signals are the same. However, ZigBee I/Q signals do not have such repetition. Because of the cyclic prefix enforced by WiFi modulation, we have a segment of signals with 0.8μs duration which is *out of our control* in signal emulation.

Solution: Selective boundary flipping: Since WEBee does not modify the hardware used, we cannot completely remove these two sources of errors, but we can mediate them. Before feeding one-fourth of the desired ZigBee Q signal to FFT, we build a continuous shifted replicated signal Q' by flipping a half-chip of Q at the boundaries as illustrated in Figure 11a. We note that flipping the desired signal is done in software for the emulation purpose, and thus no hardware changes are involved. Since the duration of a half chip of Q is 0.5μs less than that of a cyclic prefix (i.e., 0.8μs), boundary flipping can mediate errors due to noncontinuity without penalty given the constraint of cyclic prefixing.

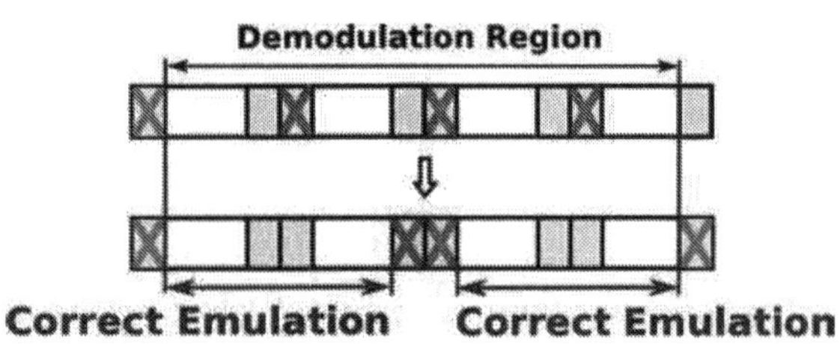

Figure 12: Flipping Boundary Selection

As Figure 12 shows, four WiFi symbols have eight boundaries, among which the left/right-most boundaries are not used by OQPSK demodulation [37]. A naive selection would be flipping only left(right) boundaries of ZigBee signal segments. The upper part of Figure 12 shows the number of regions corrupted by cyclic prefix is 3. But if we choose boundary flipping wisely, as shown in the lower part of Figure 12, the number of regions corrupted by cyclic prefix is reduced to 2, leading to a better demodulation.

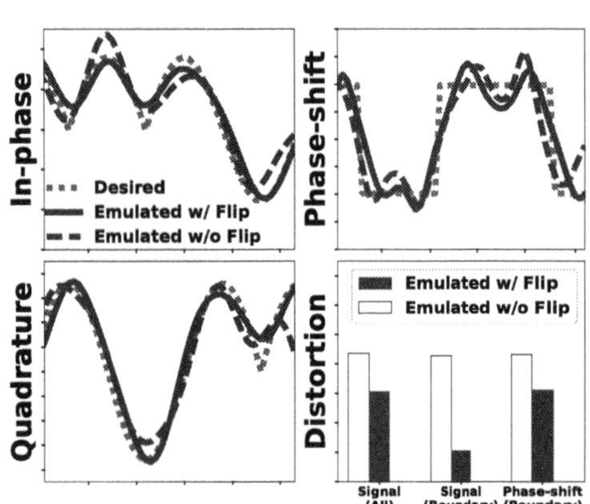

Figure 13: The Effects of Boundary Flip.

Experimentally evaluating our design, Figure 13 shows the emulated signal generated by QAM emulation with selective boundary flip resembles the desired ZigBee signal closely. For example, the phase-shift distortion is significantly lower with selective boundary flip, leading to better chip demodulation performance.

About Robustness of DSSS: It is noted that selective boundary flipping can mediate but not eliminate signal distortion completely. However, thanks to the use of DSSS, the ZigBee symbol can tolerate a certain number of chip errors, leading to a high symbol-level reliability (above 97%), as proven in our testbed later.

6 RELIABLE WEBEE

Due to the intrinsic discrepancy between WiFi and ZigBee, signal distortion cannot be avoided completely during emulation, even with DSSS. Therefore, we need additional high-level mechanisms to achieve highly reliable CTC (e.g., 99% and above).

6.1 Interference and Multipath Effect

In essence, WEBee is a genuine WiFi device. Therefore, WEBee avoids interference from other ISM-band devices (e.g.,WiFi, ZigBee, and BlueTooth) using the standard WiFi CSMA/CA mechanism. The advanced co-existence designs for WiFi [17, 28, 44–46] can be directly applied to WEBee to improve its reliability. Also interestingly, since WEBee emulates the low-bit-rate ZigBee, it can nicely reduce the inter-symbol interference caused by multipath propagation.

6.2 Repeated Transmission for Reliability

For higher reliability, WEBee can simply transmit WiFi frames (i.e., multiple copies of an emulated ZigBee frame) repeatedly. Note that this mechanism is transparent because that a ZigBee receiver cannot tell whether the sender is a WiFi or ZigBee device, and the no special decoding process is required at the ZigBee receiver.

Given the frame reception ratio (FRR), the reception probability of one WEBee frame after m repeated transmission is

$$1 - (1 - FRR)^m. \tag{5}$$

Our later experiment in Section 7.1.3 will show that WEBee's FRR is between 40% and 60%. Accordingly, the reliability is between 95.3% and 99.5% after six retransmissions, as validated by our experiments. Although retransmission is considered inefficient in intra-technology communication, it is acceptable for CTC, given that it is mostly used for low-volume control and coordination. Moreover, in duty-cycled ZigBee networks, it is a common practice to transmit a train of the same frames to wake up the receivers [11, 30].

6.3 Link-layer FEC for Reliability

Beside simple retransmission, WEBee also supports a FEC scheme with two design elements: preamble protection and payload coding. It is not a completely transparent design as retransmission, but it has a better spectrum efficiency with 90 ~ 99% FRR as shown in evaluation.

6.3.1 Preamble Protection with Repetition. The preamble of an emulated ZigBee frame is a constant string of some symbols '0' followed by a symbol '7A'. Such frame synchronization cannot be protected by a coding mechanism. WEBee, therefore, provides a repeated frame synchronization mechanism. As shown in Figure 14, preamble repetition improves the chances of successful preamble detection. If the first preamble is identified successfully, WEBee discards the second.

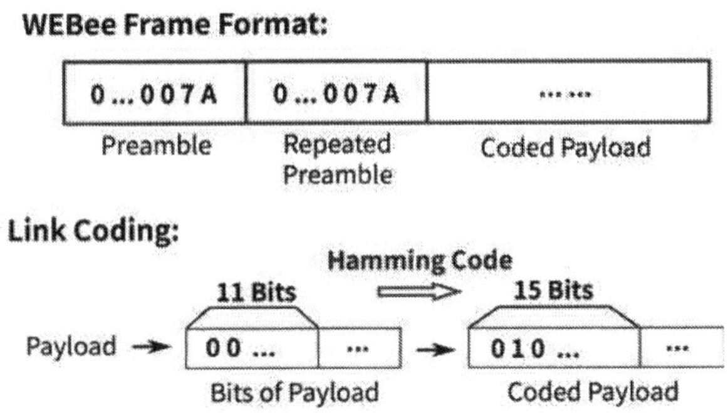

Figure 14: Reliable CTC with Link Coding

6.3.2 Payload Coding. To protect content of an emulated ZigBee frame, we use the computational efficient binary Hamming Code. Since the errors caused by the signal emulation are at the symbol level, while the binary Hamming codes work at the bit level, we employ a simple interleaver scattering the bits in corrupted symbol before applying hamming coding as shown in Figure 14.

The parameter of Hamming Code is determined based on the symbol reception ratio of WEBee, which is higher than 95%. The Hamming Code (15, 11) has the capability of error detection rate of 1/11, which is sufficient to handle the 5% symbol error rate.

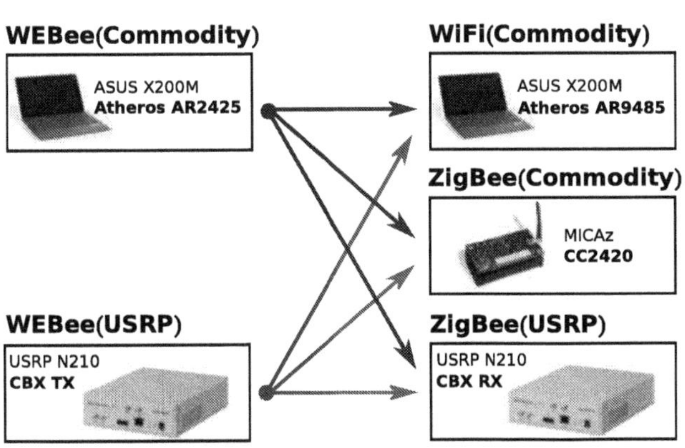

Figure 15: Experiment Setting for WEBee

7 PERFORMANCE EVALUATION

As shown in Figure 15, the WEBee testbed consists of two types of senders: (i) the USRP-N210 platform with 802.11 b/g PHY [3],(ii) a commodity WiFi card Atheros AR2425 as well as three types of receivers: (i) a commodity ZigBee receiver (i.e., MICAz); (ii) a commodity WiFi receiver (i.e., Atheros AR9485); and (iii) a USRP-N210 with 802.15.4 PHY [37].

We note that WEBee CTC is supported directly among commodity devices and USRP-N210 devices are used only for evaluation purposes to measure low-level PHY information, such as the distortion of phase and symbol error rate, which are inaccessible by commodity devices. For the frame reception rate and other high-level metrics, the performance of WEBee in USRP and the WEBee are very similar. With WEBee, a broadcast frame from an Atheros AR2425 WiFi card (or USRP-N210) can be simultaneously received by the MICAz and Atheros AR9485 receivers, indicating this frame is indeed both WiFi-compliant and ZigBee-compliant. It is noted that we also implemented WEBee on LG Nexus 5 smart phones with BCM4330 WiFi chips, indicating our technology is applicable in today's mainstream devices.

During experiments, we fix the scramble seed and configure the mode of transmitter. By adjusting the MTU, each emulated frame consists of a 32-bit preamble, and a default frame payload of 25 bytes, resulting in about a 1ms duration, which is the typical length of payload for ZigBee communications. To ensure statistical validity, we obtain the average result of 10 experiments, each of which sends 1,000 WEBee frames under a wide range of settings including indoor/outdoor, short/long distance, mobile, and duty-cycled scenarios.

7.1 Experimental Results

Our evaluation starts from PHY-layer measurements (i.e., time-domain signal, symbol error rate (SER)) to link-layer statistics (i.e., frame reception ratio (FRR) and throughput). Our study also covers multiple scenarios, including (i) stationary, (ii) long-range, (iii) mobile, (iv) duty-cycled, and (v) parallel CTC.

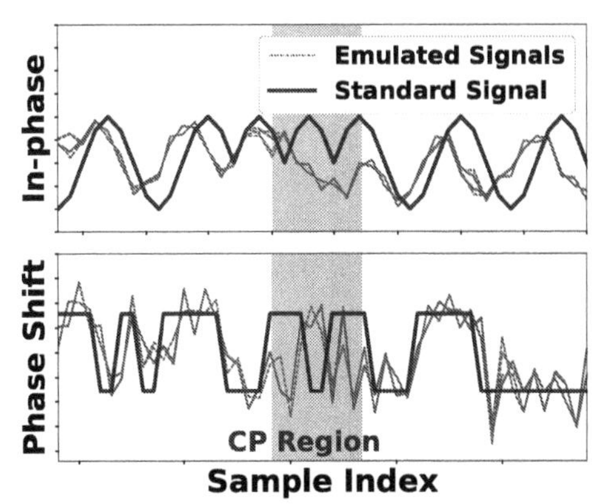

Figure 16: Phase Shifts of Emulated Signals.

7.1.1 Emulated Signals. To ensure reception, the RF waveform of the WiFi payload needs to emulate that of ZigBee signals as closely as possible. It is known that the ZigBee OQPSK demodulation is based on the phase shift, i.e., the angle between two consecutive complex samples. The chip value is decoded as "1" if the phase shift is positive, and otherwise as "0". Figure 16 shows the phase shifts of the received signals by ZigBee (red line) and by ideal standard signal (blue line). Although these two lines are not perfectly aligned, they have the same positive or negative signs, allowing successful chip decoding. After collecting 32 chips, ZigBee converts these chips to a ZigBee symbol with smallest chip Hamming distances. Using the USRP receiver, we measure the distribution of chip Hamming distances between emulated ZigBee and intended ZigBee symbols. Figure 17 shows that the Hamming distances of emulated symbols are mainly concentrated in the region of [7,12], especially in [8,9].

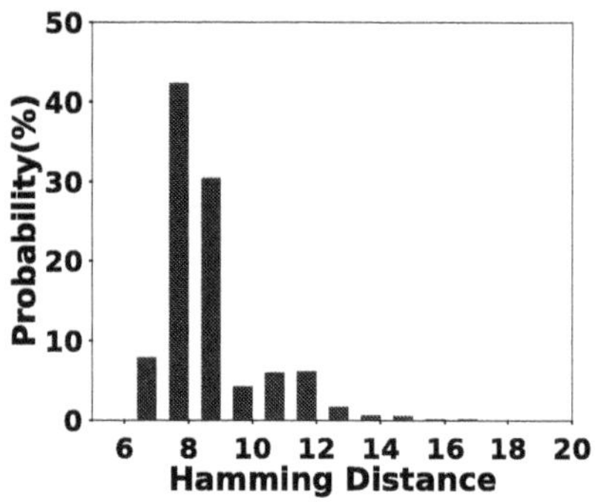

Figure 17: H-Distance of Emulated Signals.

Figure 16 also shows that for all emulated symbols, the central segments of emulated signals always present significant distortions in phase shifts. This phenomenon is a direct result of selective boundary flipping, shown in Figure 12. Because of this emulation constraint, the Hamming distances of emulated signals are always larger than some specific number, such as 6 shown in Figure 17. Thanks to the inherent redundancy in DSSS, such Hamming distances can be tolerated by ZigBee decoding, leading to a low symbol error rate (< 3%).

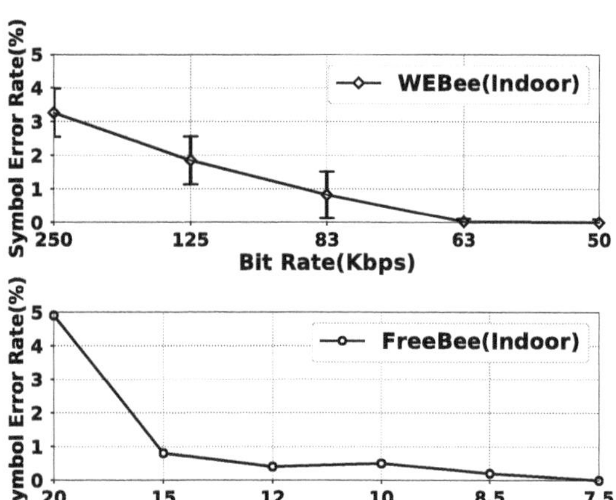

Figure 18: SER of WEBee vs. FreeBee

7.1.2 Symbol Error Rate (SER). Figure 18 shows the main result of this work, comparing the symbol error rate (SER) of WEBee and FreeBee [23]. In WEBee, the symbol is standard ZigBee symbol where each symbol stands for 4 data bits, while the symbol in FreeBee is an interval of consecutive WiFi beacon frames and represents $\lfloor log_2(100) \rfloor = 6$ data bits. The symbol error rates of both WEBee and FreeBee depend on the number of repetition, a parameter to trade off between throughput and reliability. Figure 18 illustrates the SERs under different throughputs: WEBee reaches a 99.9% symbol success rate when the frames are sent at a rate of 63Kbps, while FreeBee achieves a 99.9% symbol success rate with bit rate 7.5bps. Under the same success rate, the throughput of WEBee is more than 8,000 times of that of FreeBee. We note that FreeBee could achieve theoretically 1.4Kbps when it saturates the channel with non-stop beaconing and ignores symbol errors due to interference. We do not compare WEBee with this case as FreeBee is supposed to be a free channel design.

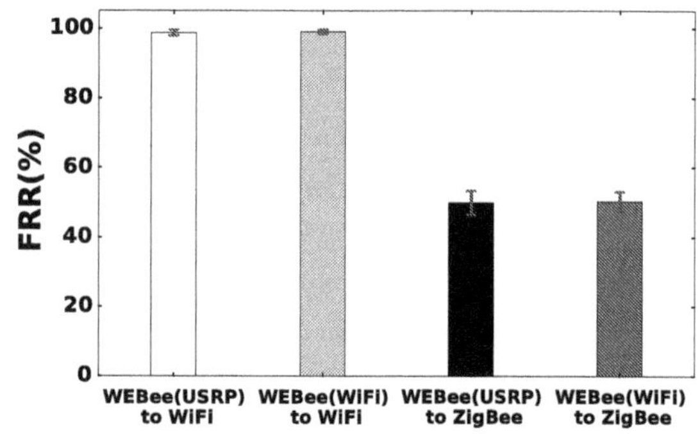

Figure 19: Frame Reception Ratio under Four Settings

7.1.3 Frame Reception Ratio (WiFi vs. ZigBee). WEBee embeds a ZigBee frame into an authentic WiFi frame. To confirm and evaluate such embedding, we conduct experiments using the testbed in Figure 15, where a WEBee sender (either USRP or Atheros AR2425) broadcasts WEBee frames to Atheros AR9485, MICAz CC2420 and USRP N210. Figure 19 shows that the WiFi card Atheros AR9485 receives more than 99% of the frames from both USRP and Atheros AR2425, while the ZigBee CC2420 receives about 50% of the frames.[1] This performance is expected because the WEBee sender indeed transmits a WiFi frame to WiFi receivers, while the WiFi payload cannot emulate ZigBee symbols perfectly. The last bar of Figure 19 shows from the commodity wifi card Atheros AR2425 to the commodity ZigBee CC2420, WEBee achieve around 50% frame reception Ratio (FRR). A similar FRR is achieved using USRP N210 as a sender as shown in the third bar of Figure 19.

Interestingly, this experiment also indicates WEBee can support *cross-technology-broadcast* if we allocate portions of payload to ZigBee and WiFi, separately, because ZigBee naturally ignores non-compliant RF waveforms, while WiFi can decode the whole frame.

Figure 20: Lab

Figure 21: Hallway

[1] As a frame consists of many symbols, a single symbol error would lead to a frame loss.

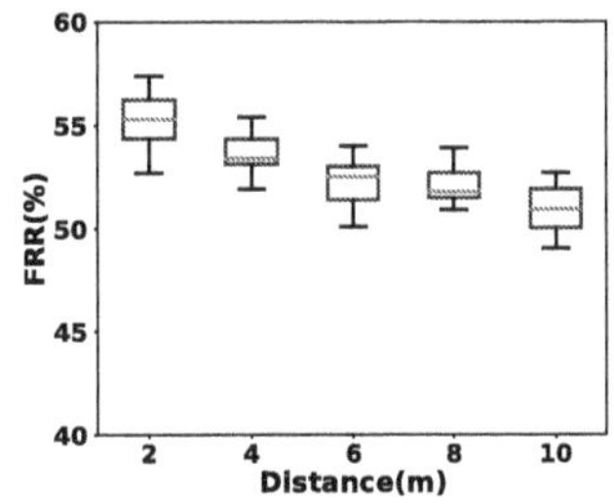

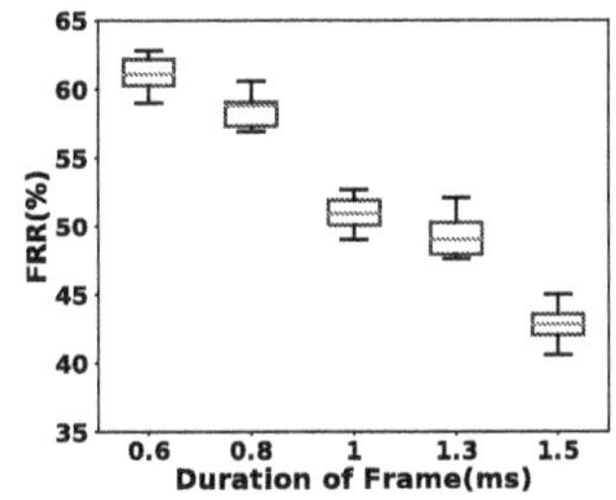

Figure 22: Frame Reception Ratio with Distances (Lab). **Figure 23: Frame Reception Ratio with Durations (Lab).**

7.1.4 WEBee Performance (Indoor vs. Outdoor). We evaluate the indoor performance of WEBee in two sits: (i)a laboratory room (Figure 20) and a hallway (Figure 21). We set the transmission power at 10dBm. Figure 22 shows those frame reception ratios (FRR) between the WEBee sender and the ZigBee receiver under varying distances. With increasing distances from 2 to 10 meters, the FRR drops slowly to 50%, indicating that signal attenuation will not significantly degrade WEBee's reliability.

Figure 23 plots the frame reception ratios with different frame lengths. As expected, the FRRs decrease when the durations of the emulated ZigBee frames increases. Figure 23 also shows that WEBee demonstrates an acceptable performance (>40%) for all the packet lengths that ZigBee normally uses.

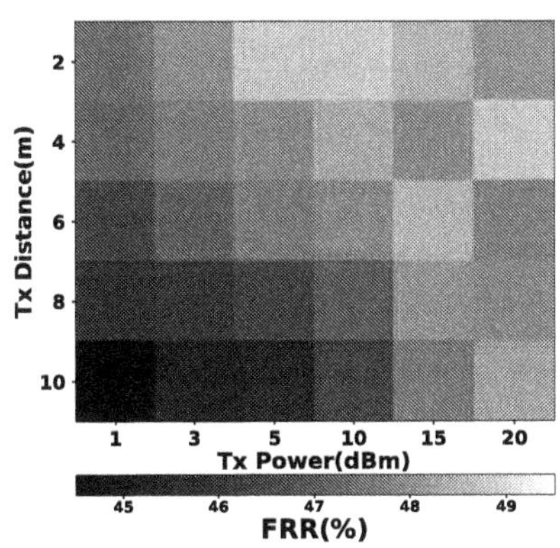

Figure 24: Frame Reception Ratio vs. Tx Powers & Distances

The transmission power also impacts the performance of the signal emulation. Figure 24 shows that the FRRs concentrate in the region between 45% and 55% with different combinations of transmission power and distance settings. When the transmission power of WiFi is set as 20 dBm[2], the FRR of WEBee stays stable at any distance less than 10 meters. This occurs because the signal attenuation has been compensated for by a higher transmission power.

We note that WEBee has a much longer range than that of ZigBee-to-ZigBee communication since WiFi devices normally operate at 20dBm, while ZigBee devices operate at 0dBm. Since energy is less a concern for WiFi devices than for ZigBee devices, this feature is very useful in allowing a WiFi AP to control all IoT devices equipped with low-power ZigBee radios in a large residential area.

[2]the maximum transmitter output power allowed by FCC under ISM band is 30dBm

Figure 25: Outdoor Site

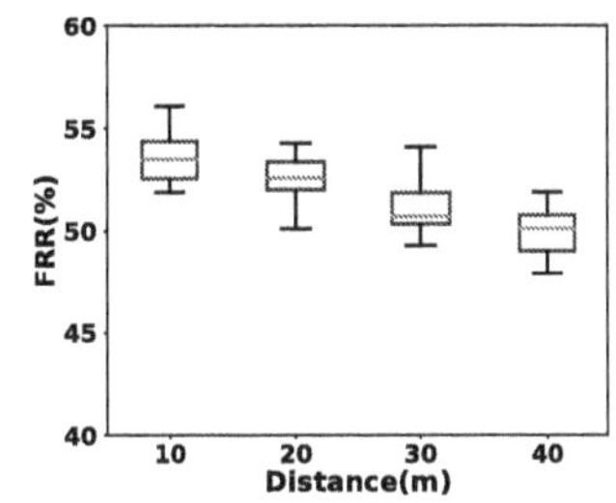

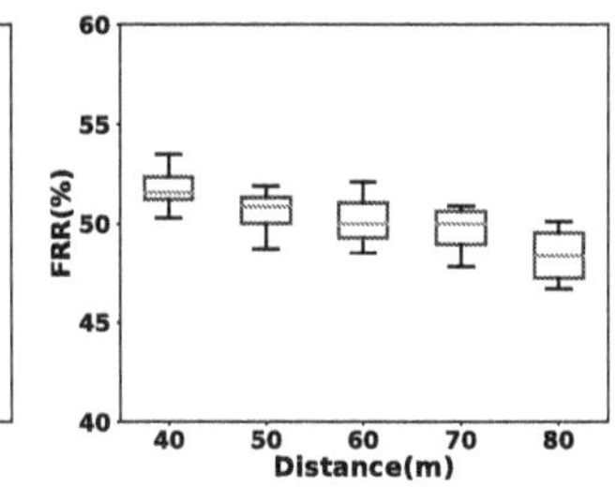

Figure 26: Frame Reception Ratio with Dist. (Hallway) **Figure 27: Frame Reception Ratio with Dist. (Outdoor)**

To validate, Figures 26 and 27 show the FRR of WEBee with long-distance transmissions at an indoor hallway(Figure 21) and at an outdoor site (Figure 25) where the transmission power are all set as 20dBm. The experimental results show that WEBee achieves the FRRs between 45% and 55% from 10 to 80 meters, which is much further than that of ZigBee-to-ZigBee communication.

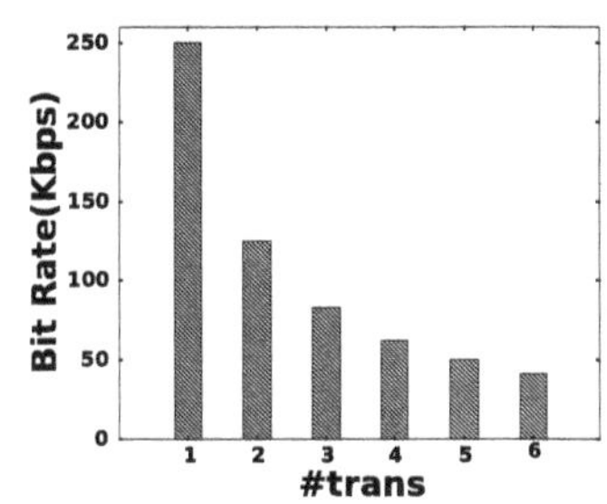

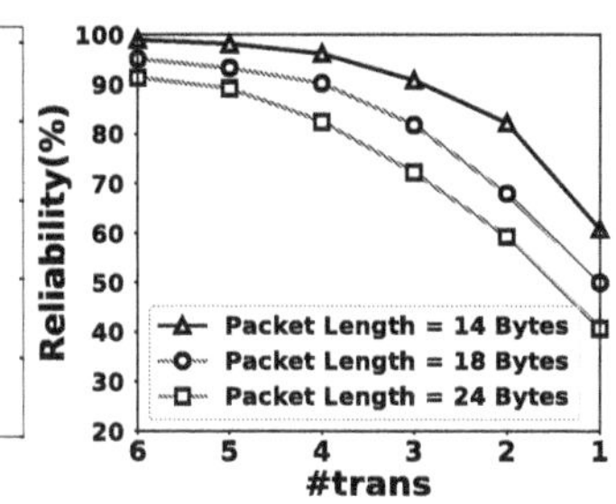

Figure 28: Bit Rates with the number of Trans. **Figure 29: Reliability with the number of Trans.**

7.1.5 Repeated Transmission. We show that WEBee can achieve between 45% and 55% FRR with one transmission. To make it reliable enough for practical CTC, we can retransmit the same frame multiple times. We note that retransmission improves the reliability but at the cost of effective throughput, i.e., the bit rate of WEBee CTC drops when #trans become larger. For example, Figure 28 shows that with #trans = 1, WEBee achieves 250Kbps,the bit rate of standard ZigBee, and with #trans = 2, WEBee achieves 125Kbps.

Figure 29 illustrates the reliability of reception with varying #trans and frame lengths. For example, when the emulated frame length is 14 bytes, the reliability of reception is above 99% when the WEBee transmission is repeated 6 times.

The performance of repeated transmission under different distances is also evaluated in Figure 30, where transmission distance is set to 10 meters and frame length is fixed as 18 bytes. From this figure, we can see that repeated transmission has a stable performance when the distance changes.

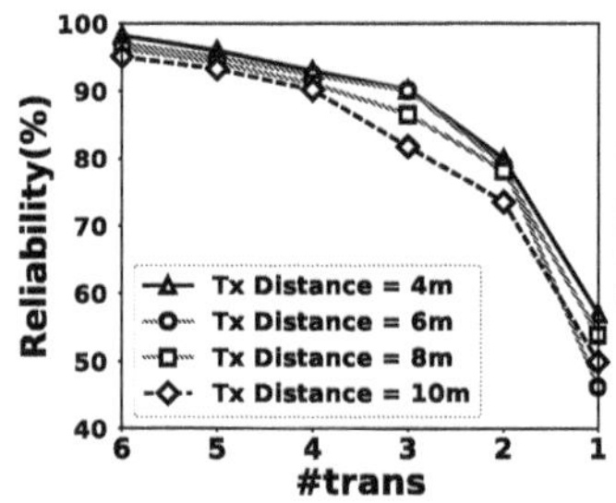

Figure 30: Reliability of Repeated Transmission under Different Tx Dist.

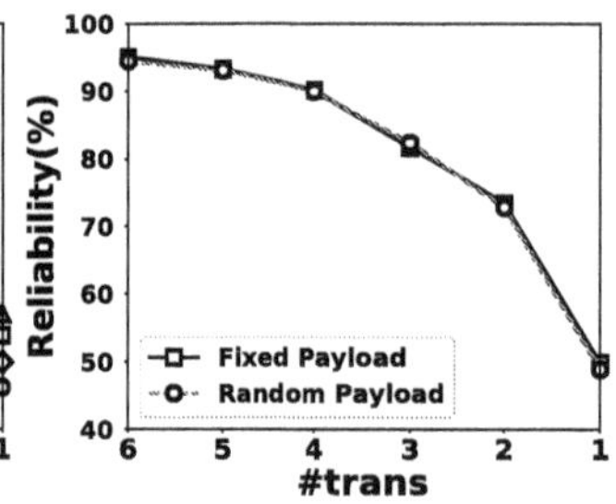

Figure 31: Reliability of Repeated Transmission under Different Payloads.

The impact of different symbols in the emulated ZigBee frames is also evaluated. In the experiment, the transmission distance is set to 10 meters, and the fixed frame length is set to 18 bytes. Figure 31 illustrates the FRRs are very stable, regardless the WiFi frame carry a payload to emulate same ZigBee symbols or a payload to emulate random ZigBee symbols. In summary, repeated transmission is a simple, transparent, and robust mechanism that makes WEBee work well in real wireless environments.

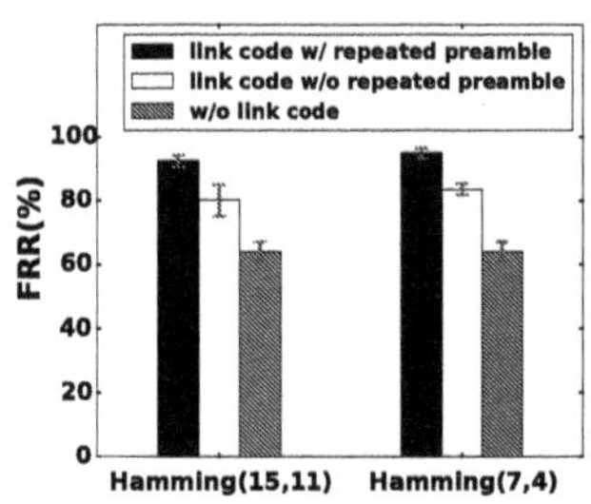

Figure 32: Frame Reception Ratio under 0.5ms Duration

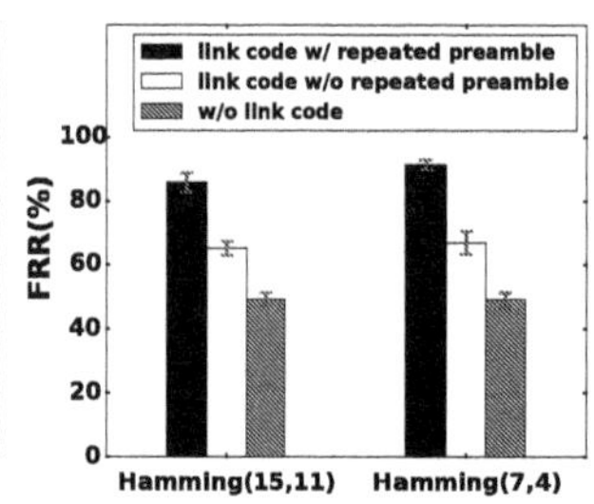

Figure 33: Frame Reception Ratio under 1ms Duration

7.1.6 Link Coding/Decoding. Link coding requires that ZigBee receivers understand the format of link coding, and hence is not as transparent a design as retransmission. On the other hand, WEBee's link coding design can improve reliability more efficiently. Figures 32 and 33 illustrate the performance of WEBee with repeated preamble and link coding. Two types of link coding mechanisms, i.e., Hamming code (15,11) and Hamming code (7,4), are evaluated in this experiment. At the same time, the impact of different frame lengths is also investigated in Figures 32 and 33.

As they show, when the link coding mechanism is utilized, the corruption of a few emulated symbols can be recovered, so the FRR of WEBee is improved shown as Figures 32 and 33. But if the preamble is corrupted, the link coding is not effective. When link coding is combined with repeated preamble, the FRR of WEBee can reach 99% when the frame duration is about 0.5ms, as shown in Figure 32 and above 90% with the 1ms frame duration.

The difference between Hamming (7,4) and Hamming (15,11) is very small if the frame length is short, and such a difference would slightly increase when the frame length becomes larger. It is the effect of low symbol error rate in WEBee, the Hamming (15,11) has enough capability to recover such errors.

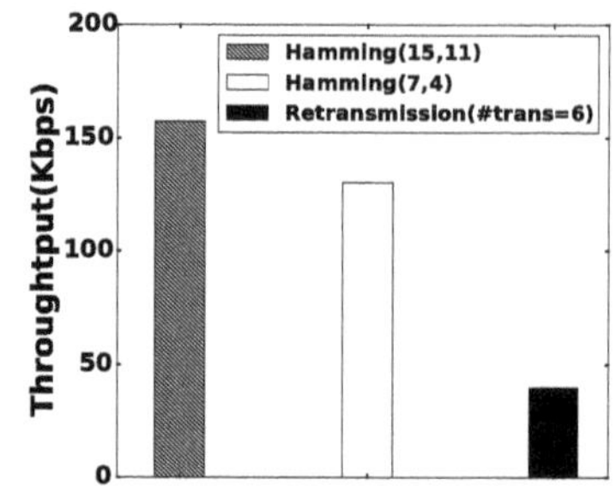

Figure 34: Throughput Coding vs. Retransmission

Furthermore, Figure 34 compares the throughput of the link coding and retransmission. As shown, the link coding obtains a high reliability with good throughput while retransmission only gain a high reliability with the cost of decreasing the effective throughput. This is a tradeoff between the receiver transparency and throughput.

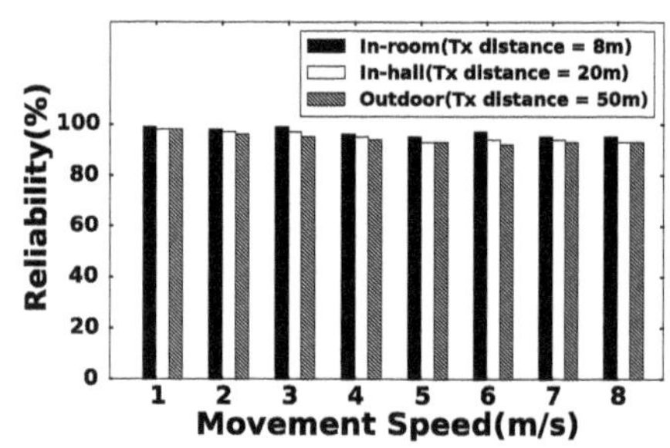

Figure 35: Reliability under Mobility.

7.1.7 Performance under Mobilitity. We also evaluate WEBee with a mobile ZigBee receiver at three sites (i.e., room, hallway, and outdoor). In this experiment, each WEBee frame is retransmitted 8 times and the interval between consecutive frames is set as 8ms. The speeds are set between 1m/s and 8m/s, respectively. Figure 35 shows that WEBee works well under different wireless environments and different levels of mobilities.

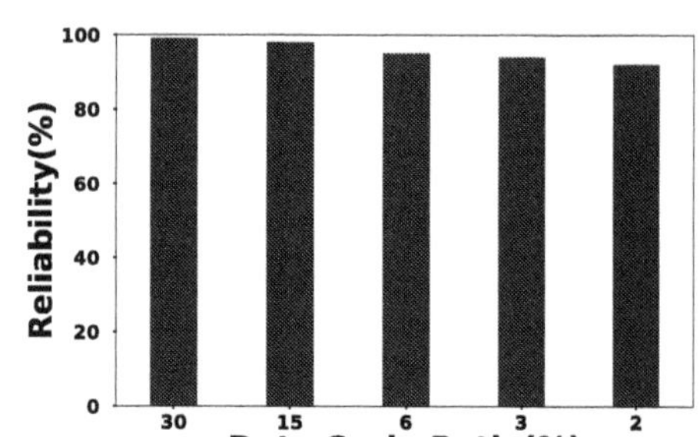

Figure 36: Reliability under Low Duty-Cycle.

7.1.8 Performance under Low Duty-Cycles. WEBee is also evaluated using low-duty-cycle ZigBee receivers, which sleep most of the time and wake up periodically to check for radioactivity. In this case, a sender needs to transmit a train of repeated frames to wake up the receiver [11, 30]. In our experiments, each WEBee frame is retransmitted 100 times. The duty-cycle ratios are set as 30%, 15%, 6%, 3%, and 2%, respectively. The results in Figure 39 show that the WEBee can work well under a wide range of duty-cycle settings.

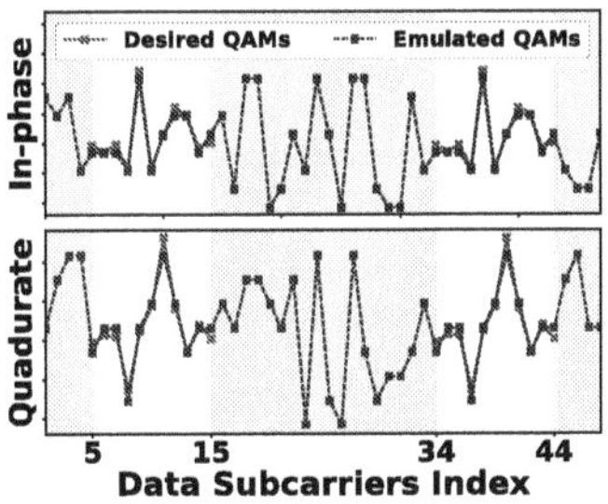

Figure 37: QAM Points in Data Subcarriers for Parallel Communication.

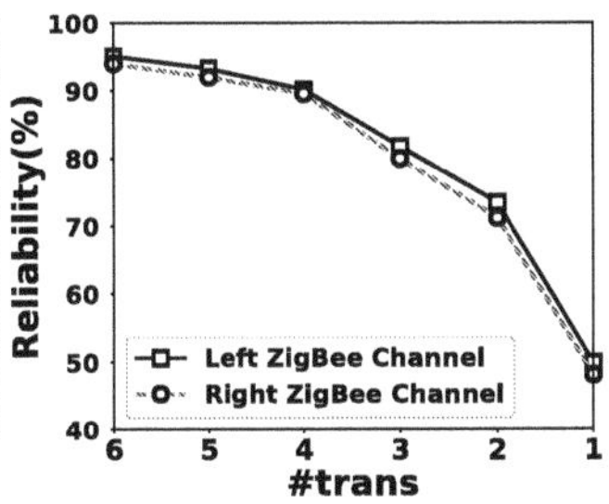

Figure 38: Frame Reception Ratio on Different Parallel ZigBee Channels.

7.1.9 *Parallel Communication.* Here we show that WEBee can support two parallel communications from WiFi to ZigBee. Using the channel mapping, as shown in Figure 9, WEBee sends two ZigBee frames with two different subcarrier regions (11 data subcarriers each) in WiFi as shown in Figure 37. Figure 38 compares the performance of WEBee between the left and right ZigBee channels when repeated transmission is utilized. In this experiment, the transmission distance is 10 meters, and the frame length is 18 bytes.

Figure 38 shows that the FRRs of WEBee are above 93% under different parallel ZigBee channels. At the same time, the FRR at one channel is slightly worse than the FRR at another channel overall. The reason for this phenomenon is the diversity of the channel quality under different channels. With two parallel channels, the aggregate throughput of WEBee can be more than 16,000x faster than that of packet-level CTCs.

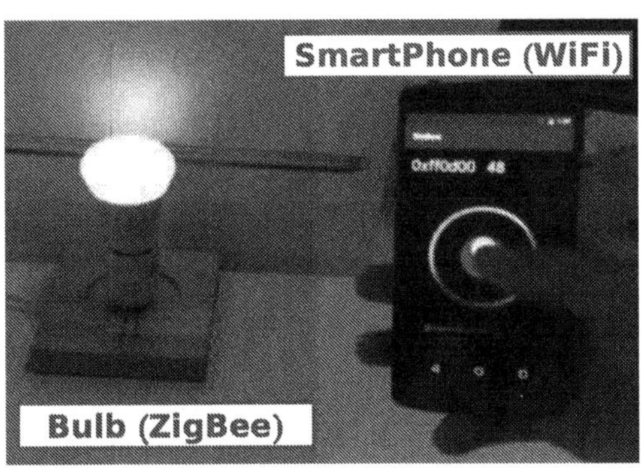

Figure 39: WEBee Smart Light Control

7.1.10 *Application: Smart Light Control.* The last experiment shows that WEBee can be used in real-life settings. We embed WEBee into an LG Nexus 5 smart phone equipped with a Broadcom BCM4330 WiFi chip. Without making any hardware modification on either side, we tunnel Zigbee control packets through the WEBee link to control light intensity, color and on/off status of ZigBee bulbs. All control operations were successful during the experiments. Our solution eliminates the need for expensive ZigBee gateways (e.g., WINK Hub), hence reduces the cost of light control in smart environments. The related videos can be found at [24, 25] and the technical support for WEBee is available at [10].

8 RELATED WORKS

In its early days, research on wireless coexistence focused mostly on cross-technology inference avoidance, cancellation, and detection [1, 2, 6–8, 16, 21, 29, 31, 34–36, 38–40, 45–48, 50–52]. Recently, cross-technology communications (CTC) have emerged as a mechanism for explicit coordination and collaboration. FreeBee[23] establishes CTC by modulating the interval of WiFi Beacons. Esense [5] establishes communication channels from WiFi to ZigBee by modulating the lengths of WiFi frames. HoWiES [49] extends the Esense mechanism to convey data with combinations of WiFi frames. GSense [48] uses gaps embedded between the customized preamble to deliver cross-technology communications. In comparison with these packet-level CTC [5, 9, 23, 48, 49], WEBee is the first work to implement the CTC based on physical signal emulation, leading to 16,000x throughput improvement. Also, WEBee is the first work to achieve parallel CTC, which is infeasible using packet-level modulations (e.g., RSSI and timing).

The WEBee's concept of signal emulation is inspired by several recent works [4, 19, 22, 26, 32] that implement the signal manipulation. The research in [22] produces standard WiFi signals by controlling the backscatter. The work in [19] provides an amplitude modulated pulse signal that could be detected by RFID using WiFi devices. The work in [4] generates WiFi CTS frame from the LTE devices, which is no longer a LTE-complaint MAC frame.

Uniquely, WEBee has the capability to emulate ZigBee signals with WiFi payloads without any hardware and firmware modification. Its dual-standard compliance (i.e., ZigBee and WiFi) enables many interesting designs, such as WiFi-ZigBee dual payloads for cross-technology broadcast, cross-technology-encapsulation (i.e., encapsulating ZigBee frames for multi-hop networked control over IP). These features are not supported in existing works [4, 19, 22].

9 CONCLUSION

This work presents WEBee, a physical-level cross-technology communication design based on signal emulation. Using multiple subcarrier regions, WEBee is the first to offer parallel cross-technology communication. Our extensive experiments show that WEBee achieves bit rates more than 16,000x those of the current state of the art with 99% symbol reliability.

Our experiments also demonstrate that WEBee can work well under long-distance, mobile, and low duty-cycle scenarios. As future work, our recent development indicates that enhanced versions of WEBee can support bi-directional communication and the MIMO OFDM modulation under 802.11n, offering more opportunities for high-level cross-technology coordination in the ISM band. Last, we note that the vision of Software Defined Radio (SDR) allows a single transceiver to adapt as needed, but its pure software-based design requires significant cost, energy, and computational complexity. WEBee, in contrast, opens a new pathway to achieve SDR through emulation, striking a nice balance among reliability, flexibility, deployability, and complexity.

ACKNOWLEDGEMENT

This work was supported in part by the NSF CNS-1444021, NSF CNS-1718456 and NSF China 61672196. We sincerely thank our shepherd Shyam Gollakota and anonymous reviewers for their valuable comments and feedback.

REFERENCES

[1] Fadel Adib, Swarun Kumar, Omid Aryan, Shyamnath Gollakota, and Dina Katabi. 2013. Interference alignment by motion. In *MobiCom '13*. ACM, 279–290.

[2] Paramvir Bahl, Ranveer Chandra, Thomas Moscibroda, Rohan Murty, and Matt Welsh. 2009. White space networking with wi-fi like connectivity. *ACM SIGCOMM Computer Communication Review* 39, 4 (2009), 27–38.

[3] B. Bloessl, M. Segata, C. Sommer, and F. Dressler. 2013. An IEEE 802.11a/g/p OFDM Receiver for GNU Radio. In *In ACM SIGCOMM 2013, 2nd ACM SIGCOMM Workshop of Software Radio Implementation Forum (SRIF 2013)*.

[4] Eugene Chai, Karthik Sundaresan, Mohammad A Khojastepour, and Sampath Rangarajan. 2016. LTE in unlicensed spectrum: are we there yet?. In *MobiCom '16*. ACM, 135–148.

[5] Kameswari Chebrolu and Ashutosh Dhekne. 2009. Esense: Communication through energy sensing. In *MobiCom '09*. ACM, 85–96.

[6] Bo Chen, Yue Qiao, Ouyang Zhang, and Kannan Srinivasan. 2015. Airexpress: Enabling seamless in-band wireless multi-hop transmission. In *MobiCom '15*. ACM, 566–577.

[7] Bo Chen, Vivek Yenamandra, and Kannan Srinivasan. 2015. Interference alignment using shadow channel. In *INFOCOM 2015*. IEEE, 2128–2136.

[8] Lin Chen, Ruolin Fan, Kaigui Bian, Mario Gerla, Tao Wang, and Xiaoming Li. 2015. On heterogeneous neighbor discovery in wireless sensor networks. In *INFOCOM '15*. IEEE, 693–701.

[9] Zicheng Chi, Yan Li, Hongyu Sun, Yao Yao, Zheng Lu, and Ting Zhu. 2016. B2W2: N-Way Concurrent Communication for IoT Devices. In *Proceedings of the 14th ACM Conference on Embedded Network Sensor Systems CD-ROM*. ACM, 245–258.

[10] "The Minnesota Networks Data and System Group". 2017. Cross-Technology-Communication. (2017). Available at http://tianhe.cs.umn.edu/CTC.

[11] Adam Dunkels. 2011. The contikimac radio duty cycling protocol. (2011).

[12] FCC. 2014. Increased Availability of Spectrum for Unlicensed Uses in the 5 GHz Band. (2014). Available at https://www.fcc.gov/document/fcc-increases-5ghz-spectrum-wi-fi-other-unlicensed-uses.

[13] FCC. 2015. Rules for unlicensed operations in the TV and the 600 MHz band. (2015). Available at https://www.fcc.gov/document/fcc-adopts-rules-unlicensed-services-tv-and-600-mhz-bands.

[14] FCC. 2016. *Fact Sheet: Spectrum Frontiers Order To Identify, Open Up Vast Amounts Of New High-Band Spectrum For Next Generation (5g) Wireless Broadband*. Available at https://apps.fcc.gov/edocs_public/attachmatch/DOC-340310A1.pdf.

[15] Inc Gartner. 2016. *Gartner Report*. Available at http://cloudtimes.org/2013/12/20/gartner-theinternet-of-things-will-grow-30-times-to-26-billion-by-2020/.

[16] Tian Hao, Ruogu Zhou, Guoliang Xing, Matt W Mutka, and Jiming Chen. 2014. Wizsync: Exploiting wi-fi infrastructure for clock synchronization in wireless sensor networks. *IEEE Transactions on mobile computing* 13, 6 (2014), 1379–1392.

[17] A. C. Hsu, D. S. L. Wei, and C. C. J. Kuo. 2015.. Coexistence WiFi MAC design for mitigating interference caused by collocated bluetooth.. In *IEEE Trans. Computers, 64(2):342-352,*.

[18] Texas Instruments. 2006.. 2.4 GHz IEEE 802.15.4 / ZigBee-ready RF Transceiver.

[19] Vikram Iyer, Vamsi Talla, Bryce Kellogg, Shyamnath Gollakota, and Joshua Smith. 2016. Inter-technology backscatter: Towards internet connectivity for implanted devices. In *Proceedings of the 2016 conference on ACM SIGCOMM 2016 Conference*. ACM, 356–369.

[20] Wenchao Jiang, Zhimeng Yin, Song Min Kim, and Tian He. 2017. Transparent Cross-technology Communication over Data Traffic. In *INFOCOM 2017*.

[21] Tao Jin, Guevara Noubir, and Bo Sheng. 2011. Wizi-cloud: Application-transparent dual zigbee-wifi radios for low power internet access. In *INFOCOM, 2011 Proceedings IEEE*. IEEE, 1593–1601.

[22] Bryce Kellogg, Vamsi Talla, Shyamnath Gollakota, and Joshua R Smith. 2016. Passive wi-fi: Bringing low power to wi-fi transmissions. In *NSDI '16*. USENIX Association, 151–164.

[23] Song Min Kim and Tian He. 2015. FreeBee: Cross-technology Communication via Free Side-channel. In *MobiCom '15 (MobiCom '15)*. ACM, New York, NY, USA, 317–330. https://doi.org/10.1145/2789168.2790098

[24] Zhijun Li, Ling Liu, and Tian He. 2017. WEBEE Demo and Smartligh Control. (2017). Available at https://youtu.be/eHVDn20FOqM.

[25] Zhijun Li, Ling Liu, and Tian He. 2017. WEBee Smartligh Control. (2017). Available at https://youtu.be/Nf9ng1E2Dj0.

[26] Zhenjiang Li, Yaxiong Xie, Mo Li, and Kyle Jamieson. 2015. Recitation: Rehearsing wireless packet reception in software. In *MobiCom '15*. ACM, 291–303.

[27] Zhijun Li, Zhimeng Yin, Ruofeng Liu, Ling Liu, and Tian He. 2017. Demo: WEBee: Physical-Layer Cross-Technology. In *MobiCom 2017*.

[28] Chieh Jan Mike Liang, Nissanka Bodhi Priyantha, Jie Liu, and Andreas Terzis. 2010. Surviving WiFi Interference in Low Power ZigBee Networks. In *SenSys '10*.

[29] Rajesh Mahindra, Hari Viswanathan, Karthik Sundaresan, Mustafa Y Arslan, and Sampath Rangarajan. 2014. A practical traffic management system for integrated LTE-WiFi networks. In *Proceedings of the 20th annual international conference on Mobile computing and networking*. ACM, 189–200.

[30] David Moss and Philip Levis. 2008. BoX-MACs: Exploiting physical and link layer boundaries in low-power networking. (2008).

[31] Georgios Nikolaidis, Mark Handley, Kyle Jamieson, and Brad Karp. 2015. COPA: cooperative power allocation for interfering wireless networks. In *Proceedings of the 11th ACM Conference on Emerging Networking Experiments and Technologies*. ACM, 18.

[32] Jiajue Ou, Yuanqing Zheng, and Mo Li. 2014. MISC: Merging incorrect symbols using constellation diversity for 802.11 retransmission. In *INFOCOM 2014*. IEEE, 2472–2480.

[33] Qualcomm Technologies, Inc. 2014. *LTE Advanced in unlicensed spectrum*. Qualcomm Technologies, Inc. Available at http://www.qualcomm.com/solutions/wireless-networks/technologies/lte-unlicensed.

[34] Božidar Radunović, Ranveer Chandra, and Dinan Gunawardena. 2012. Weeble: Enabling low-power nodes to coexist with high-power nodes in white space networks. In *Proceedings of the 8th international conference on Emerging networking experiments and technologies*. ACM, 205–216.

[35] Saravana Rathinakumar, Bozidar Radunovic, and Mahesh K Marina. 2016. CPRecycle: Recycling Cyclic Prefix for Versatile Interference Mitigation in OFDM based Wireless Systems. In *Proceedings of the 12th International on Conference on emerging Networking EXperiments and Technologies*. ACM, 67–81.

[36] Abusayeed Saifullah, Mahbubur Rahman, Dali Ismail, Chenyang Lu, Ranveer Chandra, and Jie Liu. 2016. SNOW: Sensor network over white spaces. In *Proceedings of the International Conference on Embedded Networked Sensor Systems (ACM SenSys)*.

[37] T Schmid. 2005. *Gnu radio 802.15. 4 en-and decoding*. Technical report, UCLA NESL (2005).

[38] Souvik Sen, Romit Roy Choudhury, and Srihari Nelakuditi. 2011. No time to countdown: Migrating backoff to the frequency domain. In *MobiCom '11*. ACM, 241–252.

[39] Souvik Sen, Naveen Santhapuri, Romit Roy Choudhury, and Srihari Nelakuditi. 2013. Successive interference cancellation: Carving out MAC layer opportunities. *IEEE Transactions on Mobile Computing* 12, 2 (2013), 346–357.

[40] Karthikeyan Sundaresan, Srikanth V Krishnamurthy, Xinyu Zhang, Amir Khojastepour, Sampath Rangarajan, et al. 2015. TRINITY: A Practical Transmitter Cooperation Framework to Handle Heterogeneous User Profiles in Wireless Networks. In *MobiHoc '15*. ACM, 297–306.

[41] Wi-Fi Alliance. 2016. Wi-Fi HaLow. (2016). Available at http://www.wi-fi.org/discover-wi-fi/wi-fi-halow.

[42] Eric W. Weisstein. 2000. Parseval's Theorem. (2000). Available at http://mathworld.wolfram.com/ParsevalsTheorem.html.

[43] Zhimeng Yin, Wenchao Jiang, Song Min Kim, and Tian He. 2017. C-Morse: Cross-technology Communication with Transparent Morse Coding. In *INFOCOM 2017*.

[44] Sangki Yun, Daehyeok Kim, and Lili Qiu. 2013. Fine-grained spectrum adaptation in wifi networks. In *MobiCom '13*. ACM, 327–338.

[45] Sangki Yun and Lili Qiu. 2015. Supporting WiFi and LTE co-existence. In *Computer Communications (INFOCOM), 2015 IEEE Conference on*. IEEE, 810–818.

[46] Xinyu Zhang and Kang G Shin. 2011. Enabling coexistence of heterogeneous wireless systems: Case for ZigBee and WiFi. In *MobiHoc '11*. ACM, 6.

[47] Xinyu Zhang and Kamg G Shin. 2013. Cooperative carrier signaling: Harmonizing coexisting WPAN and WLAN devices. *IEEE/ACM Transactions on Networking* 21, 2 (2013), 426–439.

[48] Xinyu Zhang and Kang G Shin. 2013. Gap sense: Lightweight coordination of heterogeneous wireless devices. In *INFOCOM, 2013 Proceedings IEEE*. IEEE, 3094–3101.

[49] Yifan Zhang and Qun Li. 2013. HoWiES: A holistic approach to ZigBee assisted WiFi energy savings in mobile devices. In *INFOCOM, 2013 Proceedings IEEE*. IEEE, 1366–1374.

[50] Ruogu Zhou, Yongping Xiong, Guoliang Xing, Limin Sun, and Jian Ma. 2010. ZiFi: wireless LAN discovery via ZigBee interference signatures. In *Proceedings of the sixteenth annual international conference on Mobile computing and networking*. ACM, 49–60.

[51] Wenjie Zhou, Tarun Bansal, Prasun Sinha, and Kannan Srinivasan. 2014. Bbn: throughput scaling in dense enterprise wlans with bind beamforming and nulling. In *MobiCom '14*. ACM, 165–176.

[52] Wenjie Zhou, Tanmoy Das, Lu Chen, Kannan Srinivasan, and Prasun Sinha. 2016. BASIC: backbone-assisted successive interference cancellation. In *MobiCom '16*. ACM, 149–161.

Stateful Inter-Packet Signal Processing for Wireless Networking

Shangqing Zhao†, Zhengping Luo†, Zhuo Lu†, Xiang Lu‡, and Yao Liu†

† University of South Florida, Tampa FL, USA.
‡ Institute of Information Engineering, Chinese Academy of Sciences (CAS), and University of CAS, Beijing, China.
Emails: {shangqing@mail., zhengpingluo@mail., zhuolu@}usf.edu, luxiang@iie.ac.cn, yliu@cse.usf.edu.

ABSTRACT

Traditional signal processing design (e.g., frequency offset and channel estimation) at a receiver treats each packet arrival as an independent process to facilitate decoding and interpreting packet data. In this paper, we enhance the performance of this process in the wireless network domain. We propose STAteful inter-Packet signaL procEssing (STAPLE), a framework of *stateful* signal processing residing between the physical and link layers. STAPLE transforms the signal processing procedure into a lightweight stateful process that caches in a small-sized memory table physical and link layer header fields as packet state information. The similarity of such information among packets serves as prior knowledge to further enhance the reliability of signal processing and thus improve the wireless network performance. We implement STAPLE on USRP X300-series devices with adapted configurations for 802.11a/b/g/n/ac and 802.15.4. The STAPLE prototype is of low processing complexity and does not change any wireless standard specification. Comprehensive experimental results show that the benefit from STAPLE is universal in various wireless networks.

KEYWORDS

Wireless networking; Signal processing; Estimation and decoding; Wireless link performance; Software radio system and protocol

1 INTRODUCTION

In a wireless network, signal processing is an essential procedure at a receiver during packet reception. It includes three major steps: timing/frequency synchronization, channel estimation, and equalization [1–4]. These together are generally treated as an independent process, serving as the foundation towards data decoding and higher layer protocol management [5–10].

This paper demonstrates that leveraging common protocol information across network packets can substantially improve the signal processing performance in a wireless network. Our motivation is that in a realistic network scenario, packets are not transmitted with uniformly random in-packet settings, such as date rate, packet size, source and destination addresses in the physical (PHY) or medium access control (MAC) fields. There exist common PHY and MAC header fields across different packets. For example in a WiFi network: a station only receives data from the access point (AP), indicating that the packets it cares about always have the same source address; and packets for data-intensive applications usually have the same packet size (i.e., the maximum allowable size). Such commonness of in-packet settings can serve as prior knowledge to improve the signal processing performance.

Hence, if we take signal processing out of its traditional domain and place it in a practical wireless network, there is indeed a lot of prior knowledge that can be used to boost its performance. The underlying challenge is how we are able to harness all possible common information and piece everything together to re-design signal processing with limited overhead for practical use in the wireless network domain.

In this paper, we propose the STAteful inter-Packet signaL procEssing (STAPLE) framework, which is a generic design to improve the performance of signal processing for wireless networking. Rather than designing signal processing in its traditional domain, we make signal processing stateful within the network domain. In particular, the key design in STAPLE is that a receiver maintains a small-sized state table, whose entry includes bit values of selected PHY/MAC fields from successfully decoded packets, such as MAC addresses, packet length and data rate, depending on a standard. These bit values constitute the state of a packet.

When a new packet arrives and decoding error happens, STAPLE performs state association (i.e., matching the bit values of its header fields with a known entry to restore the packet to a previous state). If the association succeeds, STAPLE considers the state of the packet is known (i.e., a part, if not all, of PHY/MAC information is known). Then, such known knowledge serves for the same purpose of "training sequence" (also known as "preamble" in many standards [11, 12]). Therefore, the restored state is combined with the original preamble in the packet to form a longer preamble. STAPLE re-performs signal processing on this longer preamble. Because more "prior" information is fetched for signal processing, STAPLE can obtain better frequency and channel estimates, which helps packet decoding and accordingly improves the network link performance.

To the best of our knowledge, there is no comprehensive system study in the literature to utilize the "prior knowledge" extracted

Corresponding authors: Zhuo Lu (University of South Florida) and Xiang Lu (CAS).

MobiCom'17, October 16–20, 2017, Snowbird, UT, USA.
 ISBN 978-1-4503-4916-1/17/10...$15.00
DOI: http://dx.doi.org/10.1145/3117811.3117846

from packet headers to improve the signal processing performance in wireless networks. We propose STAPLE as a general software radio system framework, then explore the feasibility and evaluate effectiveness of such a framework. In particular, we design and implement STAPLE with adapted configurations for 802.11a/b/g/n/ac and 802.15.4 on USRP X300 devices. The features of STAPLE are as follows: (i) lightweight processing and low overhead with a very small state table size (as experimental results suggest that it is sufficient to store 2-5 states at a station and 12-20 at the AP); (ii) a universal framework that benefits a wide range of wireless networks; (iii) no modification to any wireless standard; (iv) orthogonality to existing packet data decoding mechanisms (e.g., partial packet recovery [13–15]).

We conduct comprehensive experiments to show the benefits of STAPLE for different wireless standards. Our main contributions are summarized as follows: (i) We propose to improve signal processing within the network domain. We introduce the concept of the state of a packet as the bit values of selected PHY and MAC fields, and demonstrate that state-associating a packet to a previous state and re-performing signal processing in STAPLE improve the wireless network performance. (ii) We design, implement and configure the STAPLE prototypes for 802.11b/g/n/ac and 802.15.4. STAPLE is lightweight, effective and brings universal performance benefit to the packet reception process for wireless networks. Comprehensive experimental results show that STAPLE improves the packet delivery ratio by up to 20.8% under various conditions.

2 PRELIMINARIES

In this section, we describe preliminaries about signal processing and packet decoding in wireless networks.

2.1 Packet Specifications in Wireless Networks

Figure 1: Generic packet structure viewed at the PHY and MAC layers.

In today's wireless networks, elements for data exchange are packets that contain both standard-specified information and user data. Figure 1 illustrates a generic packet format viewed at the PHY and MAC layers. As shown in Figure 1, a packet consists of the preamble, the PHY header, and the PHY payload that includes the MAC header and payload.

The preamble is specified in a wireless standard and known to the public. It is also called as pilot or training sequence [16] for energy detection, timing/frequency synchronization and channel estimation [17]. The PHY header usually provides specific PHY layer information for decoding the PHY payload. Depending on a wireless standard, such information may include packet length, modulation type, and data rate. The PHY header may also contain a checksum field, such as cyclic redundancy check (CRC) in 802.11b, to verify the successful decoding of the PHY header. The MAC header facilitates the functionality of coordinating multi-access of network nodes to share the wireless channel. It generally includes the source and destination MAC addresses, and packet type information, such as acknowledgement (ACK), beacon, and data packets in 802.11a/b/g/n/ac [11]. MAC payload is the actual data at the MAC layer, including high-layer protocol information and the user's data at the application layer. In today's wireless networks, this payload is usually encrypted [11, 12].

When a packet is transmitted by a sender to a receiver in a wireless network, the increase of the energy level at the receiver triggers the packet reception process.

2.2 Packet Reception in Wireless Networks

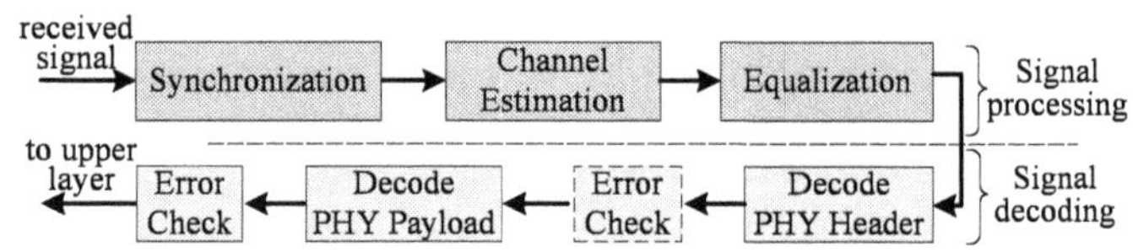

Figure 2: Packet reception at a receiver.

The packet reception process consists of two relatively independent procedures: signal processing and signal decoding, as shown in Figure 2. The signal processing procedure is used to prepare all necessary pre-decoding steps before decoding the packet data at the receiver. These steps generally happen in sequence as synchronization, channel estimation and equalization. The signal decoding procedure is to first decode the PHY header to obtain essential PHY information, which is then used to decode the PHY payload, including the MAC header and the MAC payload.

Signal Processing: Because the radio wave propagating through the wireless channel is a complicated phenomenon characterized by various environmental factors, such as the multi-path fading and the doppler effect [17], the signal processing procedure estimates and compensates those factors before the signal is decoded into data bits. Generally, signal processing contains three major steps: synchronization, channel estimation, and equalization, as shown in Figure 2. All these steps are based on the known preamble with length n in the packet, denoted by $\mathbf{x} = [x_1, x_2, \cdots, x_n]$, where x_i is the i-th baseband symbol in the preamble.

Synchronization includes timing synchronization and frequency synchronization. Timing synchronization is triggered by energy detection, and is to find the start position of the first PHY layer symbol in a packet [18] such that the later processing on the symbols in the packet is aligned. After timing synchronization, the received signal of the preamble in the packet is represented as a vector $\mathbf{s} = [s_1, s_2, \cdots, s_n]$. Frequency synchronization is to estimate and compensate the frequency offset Δf between the transmitter and the receiver [17] from the received preamble signal $\mathbf{s}$ based on the knowledge of the preamble $\mathbf{x}$.

After frequency offset compensation, the received signal vector of the preamble $\mathbf{s} = [s_1, s_2, \cdots, s_n]$ has been compensated to a new vector $\mathbf{s}' = [s'_1, s'_2, \cdots, s'_n]$ [4], based on which channel estimation is performed to estimate the channel state information (CSI).

The maximum-likelihood (ML) algorithm that minimizes the estimation error on the flat-fading channel [17] is

$$\hat{h} = (\mathbf{x}^H\mathbf{x})^{-1}\mathbf{x}^H\mathbf{s}', \quad (1)$$

where $(\cdot)^H$ and $(\cdot)^{-1}$ denote the matrix conjugate transpose and inverse, respectively. ML channel estimation for frequency-selective channels [3], orthogonal frequency-division multiplexing (OFDM) [1] or multiple-input and multiple-output (MIMO) channels [19] are performed in a similar linear[1] process to (1).

Once the receiver obtains the estimated CSI $\hat{h}$, it performs channel equalization [20] to compensate the channel effect to support coherent demodulation. Note that OFDM has been widely adopted in today's wireless standards, such as in 802.11a/g/n/ac [11], because it significantly simplifies the channel equalization process by transforming a frequency-selective wireless channel into multiple parallel flat-fading ones.

Signal Decoding: Signal decoding follows immediately once signal processing is finished. As a packet may have different modulation and coding schemes in the PHY header and payload (e.g., in 802.11a/g/n/ac), the receiver first demodulates and decodes the PHY header and obtains the data rate information (i.e., the modulation and error-correction coding information) about the PHY payload, along with other necessary information. As shown in Figure 2, if a checksum (e.g., CRC or parity) exists in the PHY header and the decoded header does not pass the error check, the receiver has to drop the packet (when there is no other error recovery option); otherwise, the receiver uses the data rate information in the PHY header to demodulate and decode the PHY payload, obtaining the MAC header and the MAC payload. If the receiver verifies the checksum of the MAC payload, it passes the payload data to the upper layer for protocol management and data delivery.

Demodulation and error-correction decoding during the signal decoding process have been well studied in the wireless communication domain [21, 22].

3 DESIGN MOTIVATION BEHIND STAPLE

In this section, we introduce the intuition behind stateful signal processing, then use real-world measurements to validate our intuition. Finally present our basic design of the STAPLE mechanism.

3.1 Basic Intuition and Observations

Traditionally, the entire packet reception is treated as an independent process at a receiver. Recent studies have focused on enhancing the signal decoding procedure to improve wireless link performance, such as partial packet recovery [7, 9, 14, 15, 23, 24]. Little attention has been focused on re-designing the signal processing procedure for wireless packet reception, even in the signal processing community, because synchronization, channel estimation and equalization are all well explored in the literature [1, 2, 4, 16, 17, 25].

In this paper, we take a closer look at the signal processing procedure. Intuitively, such a procedure must be treated as an independent process for each packet arrival. For example, upon arrival of a packet, the receiver estimates the frequency offset and the CSI from the preamble, compensates their effects on the received signal for decoding. As the frequency offset and the CSI are time-varying and hard to predict [4], the receiver has to estimate and compensate their effects again when a new packet arrives.

[1]Note that although the matrix inverse operation in (1) is nonlinear, the preamble $\mathbf{x}$ is known to the public and accordingly $(\mathbf{x}^H\mathbf{x})^{-1}\mathbf{x}^H$ in (1) can be pre-computed.

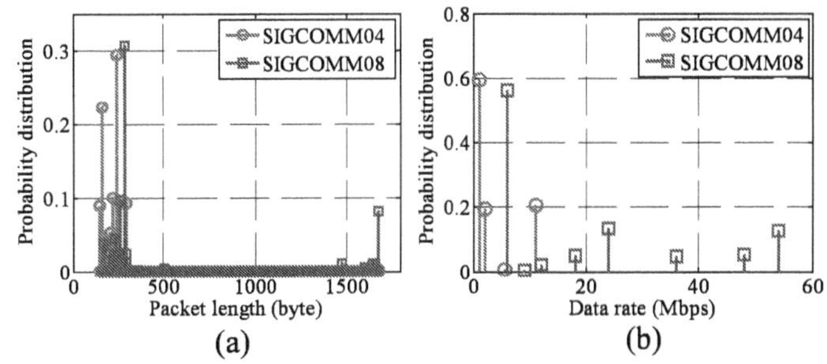

Figure 3: Distributions of (a) packet length and (b) data rate in SIGCOMM04/08 datasets.

It is difficult to further improve a well-established signal processing algorithm in practice. Our design intuition is that if we place signal processing in the network domain, we should be able to boost its performance if we can leverage the common information across different packets. In a wireless network, packets indeed have some common information, which can serve as prior knowledge during packet arrival. We analyze the realistic packet trace datasets SIGCOMM04 [26] and SIGCOMM08 [27] to see whether common information exists between packets in typical WiFi network usages. Figure 3(a) shows the packet length distributions in the datasets. We observe that the distribution in each dataset is extremely uneven and consists of two regions: the first region includes small packet lengths (1-250 byes), indicating control or short data packets; and the second is around the maximum allowable packet size (1400-1600 bytes), indicating packets for data-intensive applications. Similarly, uneven distributions of data rates in packets are shown in Figure 3(b). Given an AP in SIGCOMM08, we also find that on average 4.2 nodes sent 51.7 packets to the AP within one-second period. Those packets have the same PHY/MAC field values with high probability. The quantitative evaluation on each of these fields will be detailed in Section 5.

3.2 Basic Design of STAPLE

The preliminary observations show that there exists common (but maybe scattered) information among packets, which can serve as prior knowledge for signal processing during packet reception. If we look at such prior information solely within the signal processing domain, a traditional way is to perform profiling/training among all PHY/MAC fields in collected packets to build the prior distributions of such fields, and then integrate these distributions into a maximum a posteriori (MAP) framework [17] to improve signal processing.

Nonetheless, such a method faces two practical issues: (i) Profiling empirical distributions is always practically cumbersome due to its heavy dependencies on variable factors, such as physical environments, the number of users, and how they use the network, all of which cannot be easily predicted from time to time. (ii) Different data fields in packets are very likely to exhibit distinct distributions and also have correlations. Integrating these distributions into a unified framework is challenging. Moreover, the design must be lightweight and efficient to ensure low overhead and timely signal processing.

Thus, we avoid designing this method solely in the signal processing domain. Rather, we look at it from the network perspective. A core idea in network management is to maintain a network state, such as the backoff state at the MAC layer or the congestion control state in TCP. When a sender transmits a packet, we can use its header field values to form its state. Formally, we define the state of a packet as follows.

Definition 3.1. The state of a packet is a bit sequence concatenated by one or more bit strings in the PHY and MAC header fields in the packet.

All PHY/MAC header fields in a packet can be combined to represent a state. In this way, the state space of a packet might be very large in theory. In practice, we can carefully select a few fields that are very likely to have the same value across packets to form the state (as indicated in our packet trace analysis). Hence, our motivation is to introduce state management into signal processing in a network context. Figure 4 draws the sketch of STAPLE, which consists of three major steps.

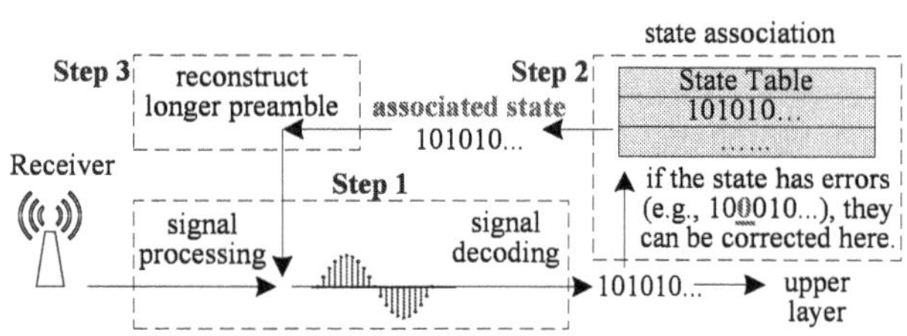

Figure 4: Sketch of STAPLE.

1) When a receiver receives a packet, it first goes through signal processing and decoding. If no error happens, the receiver can directly send the data to the MAC and higher layers, finishing the packet reception.

2) When errors happen, STAPLE tries to associate the corrupted packet with a previous state. Specifically, it compares the PHY/MAC fields in the corrupted packet with a state table that stores those fields from successfully decoded packets, which finds the closest state to the packet and recover it into that state. As shown in Step 2 of Figure 4, when the state of the packet has errors, they can be then corrected after state association; when the state contains no error and exactly matches a previous one, other parts of the packet, such as the packet payload, should have errors leading to decoding failure. In both cases, the state of the packet is associated.

3) At this point, the PHY/MAC header fields in the packet state can be considered as prior knowledge. This indicates that the information can be combined with the original preamble in the packet to form a longer preamble to re-perform the signal processing, which can yield better estimates for frequency offset and CSI (as estimation errors in signal processing generally decrease with the preamble length increasing [1, 2, 28, 29]). Then, the receiver re-performs the signal decoding using these better estimates. They can improve the performance of decoding the payload because it usually has a higher modulation/coding rate than the packet header, and accordingly requires more accurate frequency offset and CSI estimates.

STAPLE transforms prior information in a wireless network into the concept of packet state. In this way, prior information is recovered by state association, and is then used to construct a longer preamble. This new preamble is in turn used to re-do the signal processing to obtain better frequency offset and CSI estimates, which is called signal re-processing in this paper.

4 ARCHITECTURE AND COMPONENTS

In this section, we turn the basic concept of STAPLE into detailed design. We first present the STAPLE architecture, and then elaborate its key components.

4.1 STAPLE Architecture

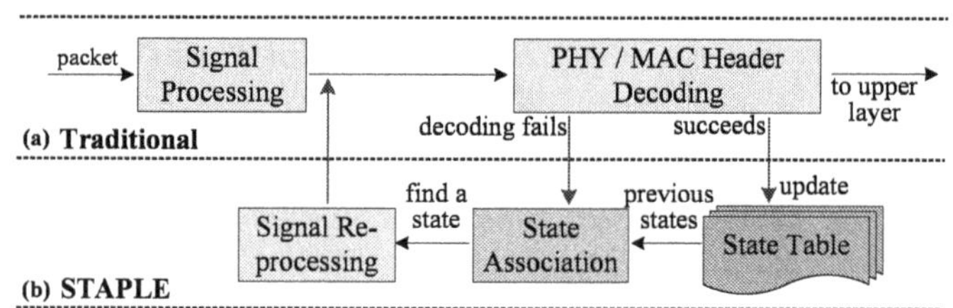

Figure 5: Architecture of STAPLE.

STAPLE can be regarded as a module (as shown in Figure 5(b)) flexibly attached to the traditional architecture of a wireless receiver (as shown in Figure 5(a)).

There are three key components in STAPLE: state association, signal re-processing, and state table management. To provide a generic framework, we decouple the design of STAPLE into two independent parts: (i) designing STAPLE components (i.e., state association and signal re-processing) and (ii) constructing the state of a packet from PHY/MAC fields. In the following, we describe the first part, which is standard-independent. The second part answers what PHY/MAC fields are used to construct the state of a packet and will be discussed based on wireless standards in Section 5.

4.2 State Association

State association is triggered when the decoding of a packet P fails. From Definition 3.1, we know that the state of a packet is the bit combination of several selected PHY/MAC fields. Thus, STAPLE can read the state of the packet $S(P)$ by combining the decoded bit values in certain PHY/MAC fields in P, as shown in Figure 6. Note that even upon failure of decoding an entire packet, the bit values in its PHY/MAC fields can still be decoded (with potential errors), and then fetched into state association for state look-up and comparison.

After obtaining $S(P)$, STAPLE associates it with a previous state in the state table, which stores a set of previous states, denoted by $\mathcal{S} = \{S_1, S_2, \cdots, S_{|\mathcal{S}|}\}$, where $|\mathcal{S}|$ denotes the cardinality of $\mathcal{S}$.

As P is a corrupted packet, any bit in P can be erroneous. However, if we can find a state in $\mathcal{S}$ that resembles $S(P)$, it is very likely

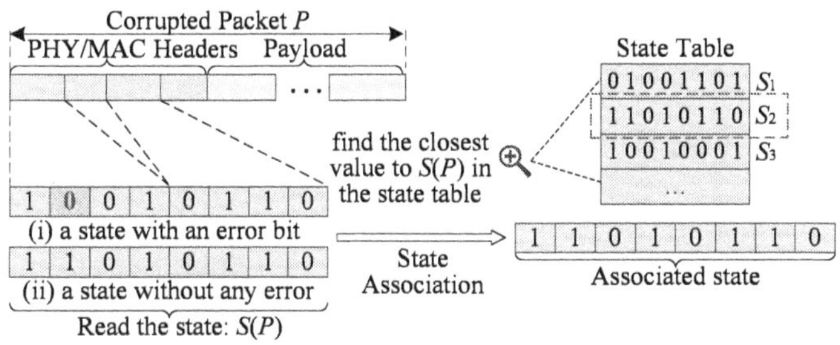

Figure 6: State association in STAPLE.

that $S(P)$ should be equal to that state, but may exhibit another value because of noise or interference during the reception of P. This is from our observations in packet trace analysis: a node is found to send packets to another node with limited variations of bit values in PHY/MAC headers, therefore exhibiting a limited set of most frequent states. If these states are all stored in the table, the state of a corrupted packet is very likely stored in the state table.

As a result, the state association component in STAPLE finds the stored state closest to $S(P)$ in the state table. The measure of "being closest" is by the Hamming distance, which is defined as the number of bit differences between two bit sequences. Accordingly, the association algorithm can be written as

$$\text{Objective}: \quad \hat{S}(P) = \arg\min_{s \in \mathcal{S}} H(s, S(P)) \tag{2}$$

$$\text{Subject to}: \quad H(S(P), \hat{S}(P)) < d_{\text{th}}, \tag{3}$$

where $H(\cdot, \cdot)$ denotes the Hamming distance between two bit sequences, and the objective (2) is to re-associate the packet P with a new state $\hat{S}(P) \in \mathcal{S}$ that is the closest to the original state $S(P)$. A constraint (3) also exists to make sure that the Hamming distance between $\hat{S}(P)$ and $S(P)$ must be smaller than a threshold d_{th}. This is because the real state of P does not always exist in the state table. A large value of $H(S(P), \hat{S}(P))$ indicates that (i) packet P was transmitted with a completely different state that was never stored in the state table; (ii) too many bit errors happened because of low signal quality. In both cases, STAPLE stops state association and simply drops the packet P.

It is also possible that the corrupted packet P is associated to a wrong state $\hat{S}(P)$, which can happen when the Hamming distances among some pairs of states stored in the table are very small. STAPLE makes best efforts to associate P with a previous state. When P is indeed associated to a wrong state, STAPLE is not likely to recover P by signal re-processing. But this only reduces the gain from STAPLE and does not degrade the performance as P is already corrupted. Wrong association can be mitigated by carefully choosing PHY/MAC fields to construct the state of a packet, which is detailed in Section 5. A smaller threshold d_{th} can also mitigate wrong association from happening. We will evaluate the impacts of d_{th} in experiments in Section 6.

Figure 6 shows two simple examples of how state association works: (i) when a corrupted packet P has a state with one error bit $S(P) = 10010110$, state association is performed based on (2) with threshold $d_{\text{th}} = 2$ to obtain $\hat{S}(P) = S_2 = 11010110$ because their Hamming distance $H(S(P), S_2) = 1$. This indicates that the second bit in $S(P)$ is likely an error, and is corrected from 0 to 1. Then, the state of P is associated to a new one $\hat{S}(P) = 11010110$. (ii) When P has a state without any error bit $S(P) = 11010110$, obviously $\hat{S}(P) = S(P) = S_2 = 11010110$ after state association.

When the header is coded in some standards (e.g., convolutional coding is used for 802.11g/n/ac headers), state association can be performed on the coded data and thus the Hamming distance comparison will not be affected by the coding scheme.

Note that the performance benefits of STAPLE do not come solely from error-correcting a part of the PHY/MAC header in a packet during state association. More importantly, STAPLE helps improve the performance when the payload, not the header, is decoded with errors. This is because the payload usually has a higher modulation/coding rate than the header, therefore requires more accurate frequency offset and CSI estimates that STAPLE can provide based on a longer preamble formed by the conventional preamble and the state of a packet. Overall, state association serves as the first essential step for this generic framework to improve the signal processing performance.

4.3 Signal Re-processing

Given the corrupted packet P as the input, the output of state association is the associated state $\hat{S}(P)$. Then, STAPLE performs signal re-processing, which consists of two steps as shown in Figure 7.

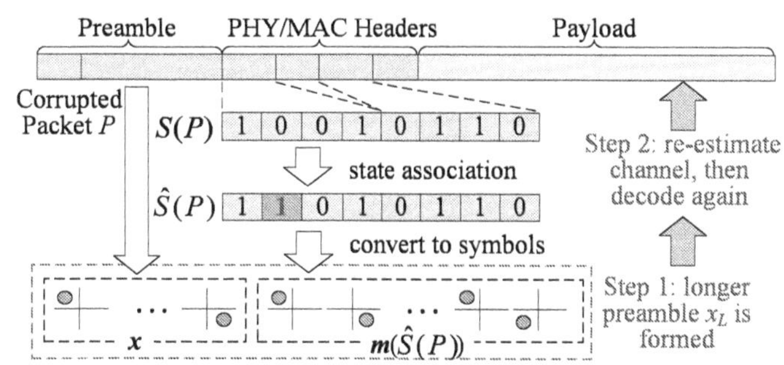

Figure 7: Signal re-processing in STAPLE.

First, STAPLE converts $\hat{S}(P)$ that represents the recovered bits from PHY/MAC fields in packet P to physical layer symbols, which is done by re-modulating $\hat{S}(P)$. If a header is interleaved or/and coded (e.g., 1/2 convolutional coding in WiFi signal), STAPLE re-interleaves or/and re-encodes, then re-modulates $\hat{S}(P)$. Denote by $\mathbf{m}(\hat{S}(P))$ the symbol vector of re-modulated symbols from $\hat{S}(P)$. The longer preamble is constructed as $\mathbf{x}_L = [\mathbf{x}\ \mathbf{m}(\hat{S}(P))]$, where $\mathbf{x}$ is the original preamble described in Section 2.2.

Second, given the newly constructed preamble $\mathbf{x}_L$, we can improve both frequency synchronization and channel estimation during signal processing, as shown in Figure 2: (i) Frequency synchronization for low complexity processing must leverage a special repetitive structure (e.g., two same consecutive symbols in 802.11 a/g/n/ac) in the preamble. The longer preamble $\mathbf{x}_L$ does not generally result in such a repetitive structure, leading to a non-convex optimization problem in [1, 2]. (ii) In contrast, channel estimation is usually a linear process (as discussed in Section 2.2). A longer preamble in general results in a more accurate CSI estimate.

As performing signal re-processing requires a tradeoff between performance and complexity, and we wish to ensure low complexity in the STAPLE implementation, we choose to perform signal re-processing only based on channel estimation, and avoid solving the non-convex optimization to re-estimate the frequency offset at the receiver. Thus, given $\mathbf{x}_L$, STAPLE re-estimates the CSI as

$$\hat{h}_L = (\mathbf{x}_L^H \mathbf{x}_L)^{-1} \mathbf{x}_L^H \mathbf{s}'_L, \quad (4)$$

where $\mathbf{s}'_L$ is the vector combined by the received symbols from the original preamble part and from the PHY/MAC fields in the received signal of packet P at the receiver.

After obtaining a better CSI estimate $\hat{h}_L$, STAPLE re-demodulates and re-decodes the corrupted packet P in order to recover it. The implementation for this step can be optimized to minimize the processing complexity for a wireless standard. We will analyze the implementation complexity for 802.11ac in Section 6.2.1.

If there are pilot signals in the payload of the packet P (e.g., pilot subcarriers in 802.11 a/g/n/ac), because more information is obtained by STAPLE, it can yield a better initial channel estimate $\hat{h}_L$, which can be based on to track the channel change using these pilots [16] in a fast fading wireless channel environment.

Although $(\mathbf{x}_L^H \mathbf{x}_L)^{-1}$ is not a linear operation in (4), in OFDM equalization for many wireless standards, $\mathbf{x}_L^H \mathbf{x}_L$ is a complex number and $(\mathbf{x}_L^H \mathbf{x}_L)^{-1}$ only incurs a division operation in the complex domain. In addition, the value of $(\mathbf{x}_L^H \mathbf{x}_L)^{-1}$ can always be precomputed during state update and stored along with its associated state in the state table.

4.4 Table Management Policies

The state table (shown in Figure 5(b)) is used to store the states of successfully decoded packets. We design two table update policies.

1) Timestamp-based policy, which uses packet arrival time as an indicator to update the table. Each state is stored with a timestamp. Once the most recent packet is decoded successfully, STAPLE updates the state's timestamp if the state is already in the table, or otherwise replaces the oldest state with this new one.

2) Frequency-based policy, which stores a timestamp and a usage count with each state in the table. Similar to the previous policy, the timestamp is used to indicate the last update time of a state. Once a packet is decoded, STAPLE updates the state's timestamp and increments the usage count if the state is already in the table. Otherwise, STAPLE replaces the state that has the smallest count with the new state. If several states have the same count number, STAPLE chooses the oldest state for replacement. This policy also zeros out the count of a state if the state's timestamp is too old (i.e., larger than a given threshold).

When the table size is sufficiently large, the two policies should have no evident performance difference. However, if the table size is small, the downlink performance may not be affected significantly because a station, as the receiver, always receives data solely from the AP. The uplink performance of the station that transmits more data (than others) to the AP may be boosted because the state of its packets can always be stored in the AP's table. Therefore, the AP should choose a larger table size than a station in practice. The impacts of state table parameter configurations and policy setups will be evaluated in experiments in Section 6.

5 CONFIGURING THE STAPLE SYSTEM

We have designed the major components in STAPLE. Another key question left is which PHY/MAC fields constitute the state of a packet, which is standard-dependent. In this section, we configure STAPLE for 802.11a/b/g/n/ac and 802.15.4 by specifying how to construct the state of a packet in such networks.

5.1 Methodology for Configurations

The motivation to develop STAPLE is from the observation that there exist most frequently appeared values of PHY/MAC header fields in packets. Thus, we aim to select those fields exhibiting little randomness to form the state of a packet. In particular, we use Shannon entropy [30] per bit to quantitatively measure the randomness of each PHY/MAC field in packet trace data and choose those fields with low entropies. We choose the SIGCOMM04/08 datasets for 802.11b/g and our own datasets STAPLEn/STAPLEac for 802.11n/ac, respectively. These datasets can represent typical WiFi scenarios in a conference, a campus or a residential place.

STAPLEn is a dataset collected from a campus WiFi network and STAPLEac from a residential WiFi network. Unlike 802.11b/g packet capturing, it is not always possible for a third-party to correctly capture and decode all 802.11n/ac data packets because of beamforming between individual stations and the AP [31]. Hence, we place four laptops at different locations and capture packets individually in the networks. We then aggregate all packets to measure the entropy of each header field. We find that the 802.11ac network did not run in the multi-user MIMO (MU-MIMO) mode because the GroupID field in all collected packets was set to 0. Thus, our collection and measurement can reflect how PHY/MAC fields in packets are set up for routine WiFi use in a non-MU-MIMO 802.11ac network.

Note that wireless standards adopt different coding schemes for the PHY/MAC headers, which can affect the complexity of the signal re-processing component in STAPLE. We categorize a coding scheme into one of three types: plaintext (P), interleaving and coding (I/C) data, and encryption (E). Type-P indicates no coding is used for a header field (e.g., PHY/MAC headers of 802.11b); Type-I/C means that data fields in a header are interleaved and error-correction coded (e.g., MAC headers of 802.11a/g/n/ac); Type-E indicates that data fields in a header are all encrypted (e.g., MAC headers of 802.15.4). Generally, we avoid choosing Type-E fields and select Type-P or Type-I/C fields based on their entropy values for our implementation.

Constructing the state of a packet is not unique. In our STAPLE configurations for 802.11a/b/g/n/ac and 802.15.4, we target a lightweight design that balances between performance benefits and costs of storage and computation in typical wireless networks with normal usages. It is certainly feasible to add additional fields to (or remove existing fields from) our configurations to optimize STAPLE along certain direction.

Because a newer 802.11 standard usually extends and relies on previous ones, we configure STAPLE starting from 802.11b (legacy) to 802.11ac (state-of-the-art) for the sake of clear presentation. Our implementation and evaluation are focused on 802.11ac in Section 6. We also minimize the description of a wireless standard, which is well documented.

5.2 Configurations for Wireless Standards

Configurations for 802.11b: We start from 802.11b, which is a legacy WiFi standard but still backward supported in many WiFi networks. Figure 8 shows a typical structure of physical protocol data unit (PPDU) for 802.11b, including the PHY Layer Convergence Procedure (PLCP) preamble, PLCP header, and PLCP Service Data Unit (PSDU) that contains the MAC header and the MAC payload.

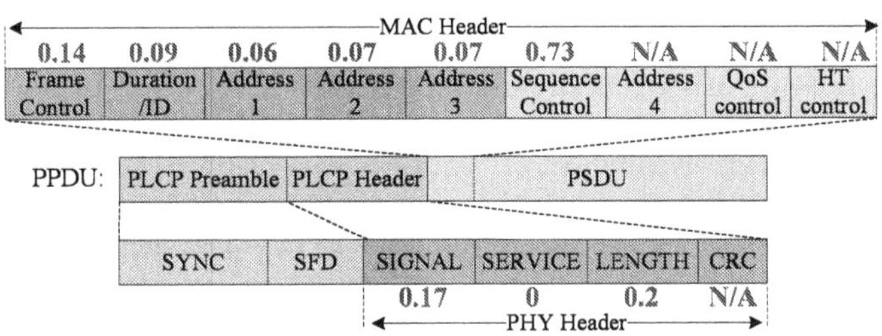

Figure 8: Typical format of an 802.11b data packet and measured entropies of field values inside PHY and MAC headers.

As shown in Figure 8, the PLCP header represents the PHY header including four fields of Type-P: SIGNAL, SERVICE, LENGTH, and CRC, where SIGNAL denotes the modulation scheme, LENGTH is the payload length, SERVICE contains three bits to represent the PHY configuration and the rest of bits are reserved and default to 0. The 802.11b MAC header at the beginning of PSDU consists of a set of fields.

According to the measured entropy in each PHY/MAC field in Figure 8, we choose SIGNAL, SERVICE, LENGTH at the PHY header and Frame Control, Duration/ID, Addr.1, Addr.2, and Addr.3 in the MAC header to form the state of a packet because of their low entropies. We also include CRC in the PHY header because CRC directly depends on other fields. Once these fields are known, we can simply calculate the CRC. Including CRC increases the length of the state of a packet, and accordingly can further improve the signal processing reliability because more data is used for signal processing. Thus, for a packet P, its state $S(P)$ is written as $S(P)$ = SIGNAL|SERVICE|LENGTH|CRC|Frame Control|Duration/ID|Addr.1|Addr.2|Addr.3 in our STAPLE configuration for 802.11b.

Configurations for 802.11a/g: 802.11a/g uses OFDM to combat multipath fading. Figure 9 shows a typical format of the PPDU including the PLCP preamble, PLCP header, PSDU and others. Different from 802.11b, all the data except for the PLCP preamble is of Type-I/C in an 802.11a/g packet.

The PLCP header includes the SIGNAL field that occupies one single OFDM symbol and the Service field that exists in the next symbol. SIGNAL contains a number of fields of Type-I/C to represent packet information like the data rate and packet length. We

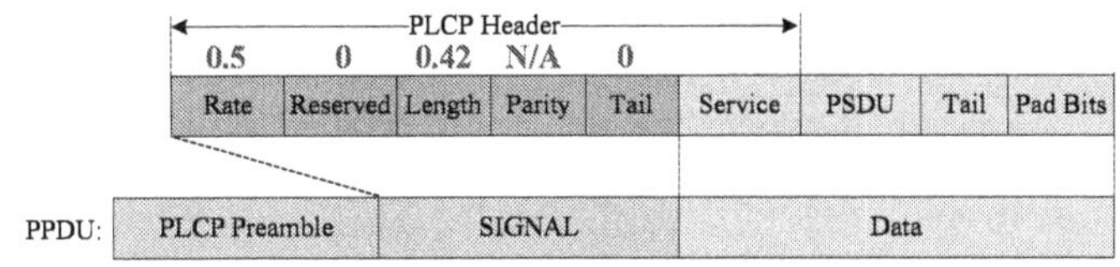

Figure 9: Typical structure of an 802.11a/g packet and measured entropies in SIGNAL.

measure the entropy of each field in SIGNAL, also shown in Figure 9. All entropies are small therefore we include the entire SIGNAL field in the state of a packet. Note that the Parity field can be directly computed given other fields, therefore we do not need to measure its entropy.

The Service field is used to synchronize the descrambler shown in Figure 9. All bits in Service are constantly set to 0. The MAC header at the beginning of PSDU follows Service. The 802.11a/g MAC header structure is exactly the same as that of 802.11b. However, Service and the MAC header together do not exactly occupy one OFDM symbol. This means that they are interleaved and coded with other data then OFDM-modulated, which can be difficult (if not impossible) for STAPLE's signal re-processing to accurately extract Service and parts of the MAC header from interleaved and coded OFDM symbols. Therefore, Service and all MAC fields can be used for state association, but not for signal re-processing in STAPLE. As we aim at a lightweight design, we avoid using any of these fields to reduce the size of the state table. Therefore, the state $S(P)$ for packet P in our STAPLE configuration for 802.11a/g is $S(P)$ = SIGNAL.

Configurations for 802.11n/ac: 802.11n and 802.11ac are the state-of-the-art WiFi standards leveraging MIMO technologies with more complicated packet formats.

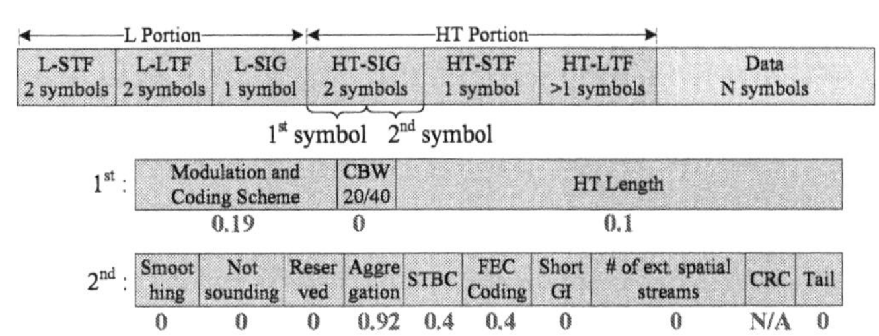

Figure 10: Typical packet format in 802.11n and measured entropies of field values inside HT-SIG.

Figure 10 depicts a typical packet structure of 802.11n which contains two portions: legacy (L) and high throughput (HT). The L portion is for backward compatibility, and the HT portion is specified to support MIMO communication. The L-SFT and L-LFT fields at the beginning of the L portion are legacy preambles. The HT-SFT and HT-LFT fields in the HT portion are preambles for MIMO training. The L-SIG of Type-I/C is exactly the same as the SIGNAL field in 802.11a/g. Hence, we use the entire L-SIG field for STAPLE. HT-SIG of Type-I/C is at the beginning of the HT portion and consists of 2 OFDM symbols with a number of fields. We measure the entropy of each field from packet trace data, as shown in Figure 10. Most fields have small entropies, therefore we include the entire HT-SIG field. Note that the single-bit Aggregation field indicates whether multiple payloads are combined together into a single packet with a unique PHY header, and it is almost random with entropy close to 1. However, we cannot exclude this bit because it is interleaved and coded with other fields in exactly one OFDM symbol. We find that the high entropy of this single bit always happens in the downlink. It does not have substantial impact on the performance but the size of the state table needs to be slightly increased at the downlink. Therefore, we still include it to represent the state of a packet. As a result, the state $S(P)$ for packet P in our configuration for 802.11n is $S(P)$ = L-SIG|HT-SIG.

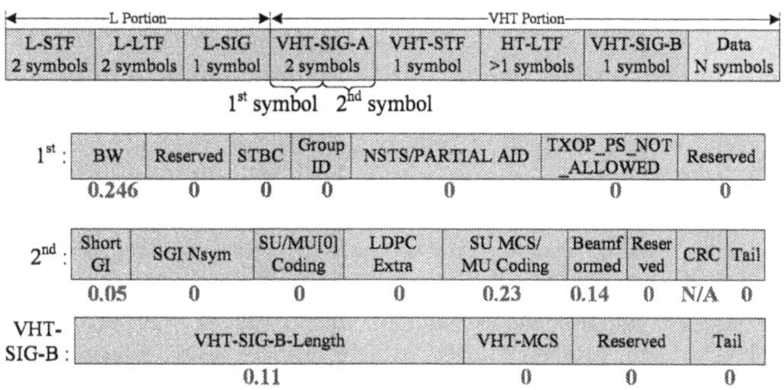

Figure 11: Typical packet format in 802.11ac and measured entropies of field values inside VHT-SIG-A and VHT-SIG-B.

Figure 11 plots the typical packet format in 802.11ac, which has a very similar structure to 802.11n: the HT portion becomes the very HT (VHT) portion. Similarly, based on the measured entropies from packet trace data shown in Figure 11, we include L-SIG and VHT-SIG to represent the state of a packet. In addition, we find the entropies of fields in the VHT-SIG-B are also small. Thus, we set the state as $S(P)$ = L-SIG|VHT-SIG|VHT-SIG-B in our configuration for 802.11ac.

Configurations for 802.15.4: IEEE 802.15.4 is the basis for ZigBee towards low-cost, low-speed ubiquitous communication. We configure STAPLE for offset-QPSK (O-QPSK) based ZigBee, whose typical packet format is shown in Figure 12.

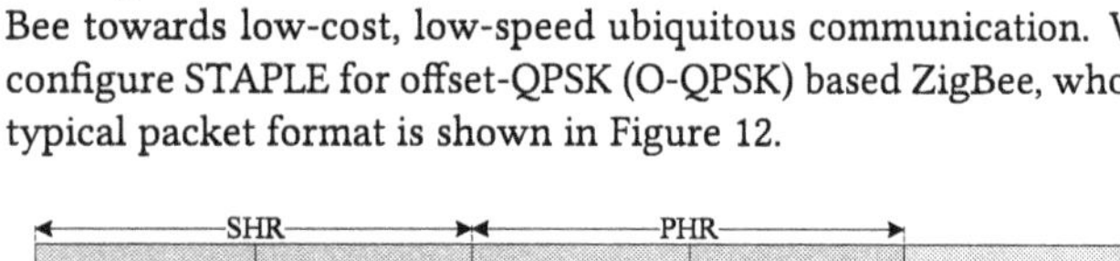

Figure 12: Typical 802.15.4 packet format.

As shown in Figure 12, the PHY header (PHR) of 802.15.4 contains only two Type-P fields: Length and Reserved, which indicate the length of the packet and reserved bits (set to all 0s), respectively. The MAC header is contained in PSDU, which is however of Type-E. To reduce the complexity, our STAPLE configuration avoids any Type-E data during signal re-processing, therefore choosing to include only Length and Reserved for the state of a packet P, i.e., $S(P)$ = Length|Reserved.

6 EXPERIMENTAL EVALUATION

In this section, we implement STAPLE with adapted configurations for 802.11b/g/n/ac and 802.15.4. We first describe our implementation and experiment setups, then focus on presenting experimental evaluation of STAPLE in 802.11ac, and finally describe experimental results on other standards.

6.1 Implementation and Setups

Platform and Implementation: STAPLE requires modifications of a conventional wireless receiver. We choose the X300 USRP with CBX daughterboards [32] as the implementation platform. We synchronize multiple USRPs using OctoClock-G [32] when performing MIMO experiments with 2 - 8 antennas.

We implement a generic software radio platform that covers the basic designs of 802.11b/g/n/ac and 802.15.4 transceivers. We adopt BPSK, QPSK, and 16QAM for 802.11b/g/n/ac, and O-QPSK for 802.15.4. For 802.11n/ac, we implement the Alamouti code [33] based MIMO transmission schemes. In 802.11g/n/ac implementations, the header and data payload of a packet use 1/2 and 3/4 convolutional coding schemes, respectively. We also implement a CSMA/CA scheme with uniform random backoff (i.e., the contention window for random backoff is always fixed [34, 35]) at the MAC layer for all standards. Note that it is challenging and time-consuming to implement a comprehensive USRP-based system fully compatible with all 802.11 PHY/MAC standards. To balance the efficiency of fast prototyping and the cost of high-fidelity evaluation, our implementation is a proof of concept one with a subset of fundamental STAPLE-related PHY functionalities, serving the purpose of evaluating the benefits of STAPLE brought to practical wireless scenarios with different system setups and conditions. As mentioned in Section 4.3, our STAPLE implementation does not improve frequency offset estimation but improves the channel estimation in signal re-processing.

Also note that we implement a subset of modulation and coding schemes. However, our experiments generate packets according to packet trace data. This means the PHY field that denotes the data rate in some generated packets may indicate a higher rate scheme that we do not implement. In this case, we choose 16QAM as the scheme to modulate and demodulate. This does not give an advantage to STAPLE during performance evaluation, since we still allow all possible values in the data rate field of a packet, which affect state association and state table update of STAPLE in practice.

Experimental setups: We conduct experiments in a realistic indoor environment shown in Figure 13 as the scenario reflects how STAPLE can help improve the wireless link performance in an office environment with typical WiFi usages. Network nodes are placed at different locations for performance evaluation with limited transmit power. In our network experiments, packets are generated with PHY/MAC field values according to the SIGCOMM04/08 and STAPLEn/ac datasets.

In STAPLE, the default threshold for state association (2) is set to 12. The default size of the state table for a station in the downlink

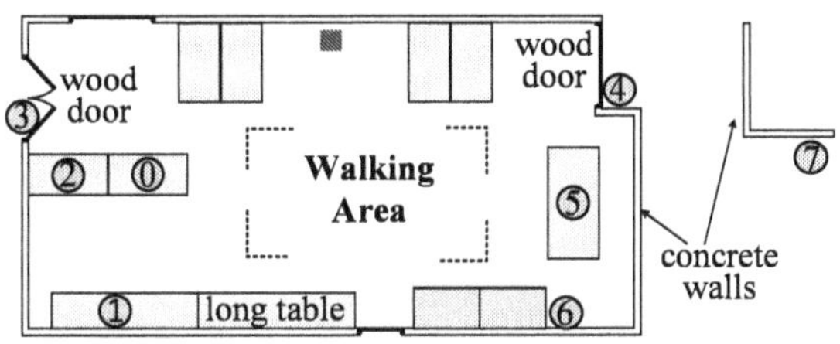

Figure 13: Environment for experiments.

is set to 5; and that for the AP in the uplink is 15. The default table update policy is frequency-based. In experiments, we change table setups to evaluate the impact of STAPLE parameters on the performance. We use the construction of the packet state for each standard given in Section 5.

Performance Metrics: Packet dropping due to decoding errors only happens at the PHY layer and STAPLE is a method to improve the PHY layer performance. Thus, it is natural to use the performance metric at the PHY layer to directly see the benefits of STAPLE without involving other potential affecting factors at higher layers. In experiments, we measure the packet delivery ratio (PDR) with and without STAPLE, where PDR is defined as the ratio of the number of successfully decoded PHY packets at a node to the total number of PHY packets transmitted to the node. We measure the benefit of STAPLE by using the performance gain ratio, which is defined as

$$\text{Performance gain ratio} = \frac{\text{PDR with STAPLE}}{\text{PDR with traditional design}} - 1.$$

6.2 STAPLE for 802.11ac Networks

We focus on performance evaluation on 802.11ac because it is a state-of-the-art WiFi standard. We consider two types of scenarios in experiments: single-link evaluation, in which a two-antenna transmitter sends packets to a receiver with 2 – 8 antennas; (ii) network evaluation, in which we set up two clock-synchronized USRPs as a single 802.11ac AP, and six USRPs as stations communicating with the AP.

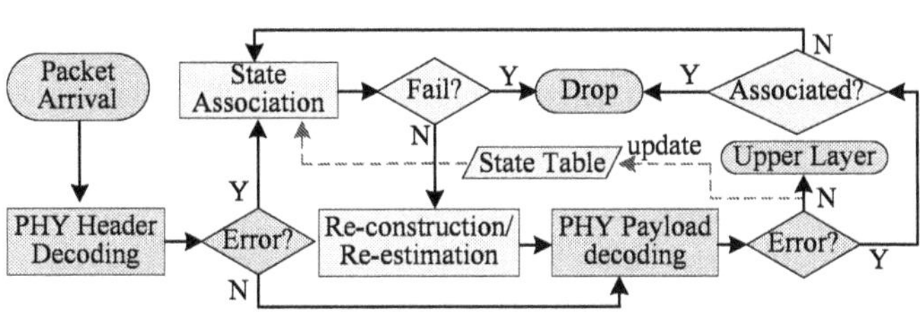

Figure 14: Implementation of 802.11ac.

6.2.1 Implementation Complexity for 802.11ac. Figure 14 shows the flowchart of our STAPLE implementation for 802.11ac. the extra storage due to STAPLE is mainly the memory used for the state table, whose size is 5 states for stations and 15 states for the AP as default values. In terms of extra processing complexity, if errors are detected in the PHY layer, extra procedures including state association, preamble reconstruction, and CSI re-estimation are introduced by STAPLE. All these procedures are linear, which will not incur much overhead. If errors occur in the data payload, re-decoding the payload is needed. The re-decoding complexity is not linear and depends on the decoding algorithm that is usually polynomial. However, thanks to the PHY payload check, this case does not quite often happen in today's WiFi networks.

Table 1: Complexity of STAPLE for 802.11ac.

Situation	Extra processing
1) No error in a packet	none
2) Error first detected in PHY header	state association, preamble reconstruction and CSI re-estimation
3) Error not detected in header but payload	extra processing in 2), and re-decoding of PHY payload

6.2.2 Single-Link Performance Evaluation. In our single-link performance evaluation, we fix the modulation scheme for packets and measure the link performance between two nodes to evaluate how STAPLE helps improve the single-link performance.

Varying locations: We first compare the single-link performance between a traditional receiver and STAPLE at different locations. We fix the transmitter at location 1 as shown in Figure 13, and place the receiver at location 0, 3, 4, or 5, which represents the short-distance line of sight (S-LoS), short-distance Non-LoS (S-NLoS), long-distance NLoS (L-NLoS), or long-distance LoS (L-LoS) channel condition, respectively. The transmitter and receiver are both equipped with 2 antennas.

Figure 15 depicts the performance gain ratios at different locations under BPSK, QPSK, and 16QAM. We can observe that the performance of STAPLE is uniformly better than the performance of traditional signal reception for most cases. There is no performance improvement at locations 0 and 5 (both LoS cases) for the BPSK modulation because the packet delivery ratio is 100%. We also find that at location 4 (L-NLoS), STAPLE substantially improves the packet delivery ratio for 16QAM from 80% to 95% (a performance gain ratio of 17.6% shown in Figure 15). This is because communication with higher data rate is less error-tolerant, thus demanding more accurate CSI estimation, which STAPLE provides. We can conclude from Figure 15 that STAPLE improves the performance in NLoS cases more than that in LoS cases.

Varying packet lengths: We then evaluate the effect of packet length on the performance gain of STAPLE. During this experiment, the transmitter always sends packets with a fixed length. Table 2 shows the packet delivery ratios on a 2×4 MIMO link from location 1 to location 5 with QPSK modulation for varying packet lengths. It is noted from Table 2 that transmitting shorter packets results in better packet delivery ratios. For example, traditional signal reception and STAPLE achieve almost 100% packet delivery ratio when the packet length is no larger than 100 bytes. As the packet length increases, STAPLE gradually outperforms traditional signal reception, and improves the packet delivery ratio

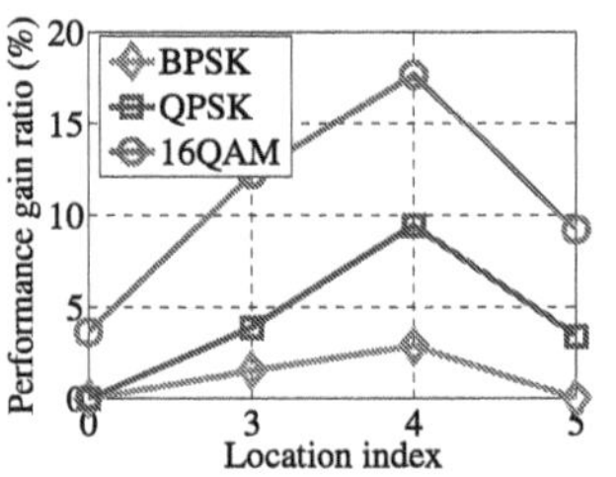

Figure 15: Performance gain ratios under different locations.

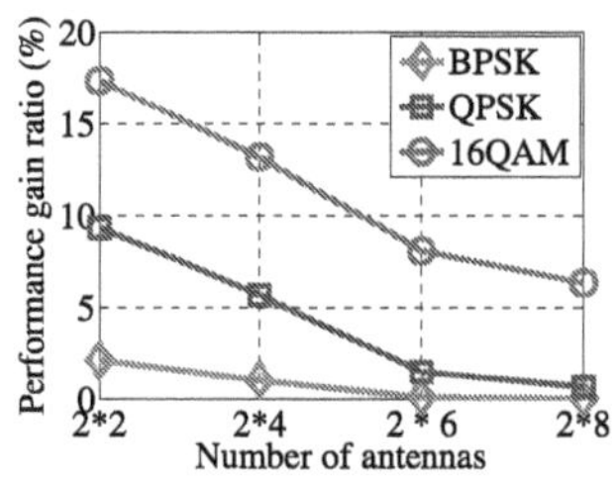

Figure 16: Performance gain ratios in single-link with 2×2–8 MIMO.

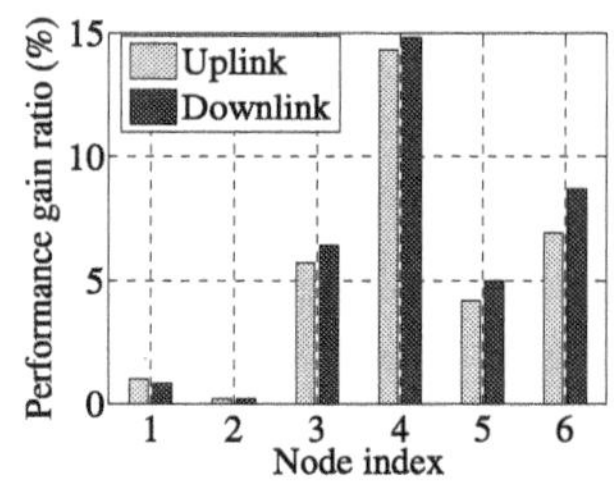

Figure 17: Performance gain ratios of STAPLE for 802.11ac (uplink and downlink).

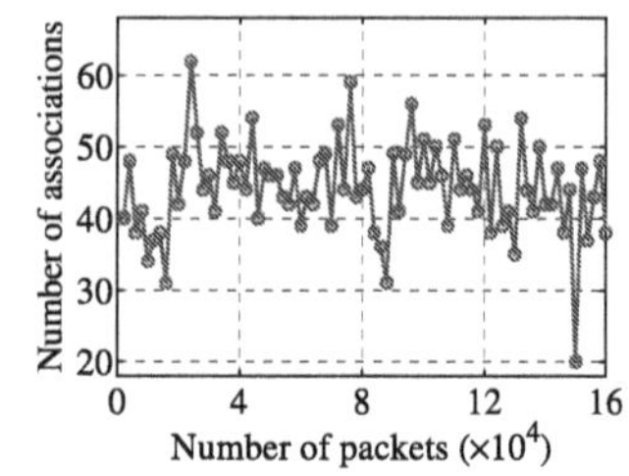

Figure 18: Number of state associations for every 2000 packets.

Table 2: Packet delivery ratios with different packet lengths (in bytes) on 2×4 MIMO.

	10	100	500	1000	1500
Traditional	99.9%	99.9%	98.3%	93.5%	91.5%
STAPLE	100%	100%	99.9%	99.7%	98.3%

Table 3: Performance gain ratios from STAPLE under noisy MIMO channels at location 7.

	BPSK	QPSK	16QAM
2 × 4	20.2%	N/A	N/A
2 × 6	16.6%	20.4%	N/A
2 × 8	11.4%	18.9%	20.8%

from 91.5% to 98.3% (a performance gain ratio of 7.4%) when the length is 1500 bytes.

Varying numbers of antennas: We also measure the performance benefits from STAPLE for 2×2–8 MIMO links. Figure 16 plots the performance gain ratios of STAPLE on 2×2, 2×4, 2×6, and 2×8 MIMO links under different modulation schemes. The transmitter and the receiver are placed at locations 1 and 4, respectively, as shown in Figure 13. We can observe from Figure 16 that STAPLE generally improves the performance more as the number of antennas decreases. For example, under 16QAM, STAPLE achieves a 17.6% performance gain ratio in the 2×2 scenario and a 6.0% ratio for the 2×8 scenario. Similarly, the performance gain ratio for QPSK reduces from 9.4% to only 0.6% when the number of receive antennas increases from 2 to 8. This is due to more link reliability from more antennas.

We then move the receiver to location 7 in Figure 13 to test the performance in an L-NLoS MIMO channel. Table 3 shows the performance gain ratios of STAPLE on 2×4, 2×6, and 2×8 MIMO links. We find that location 7 is beyond the limit of the 2×4 MIMO link under QPSK and 16QAM, and beyond the limit of the 2×6 MIMO link under 16QAM. In these cases, the receiver cannot reliably decode any packet with or without STAPLE. In other cases, we always observe that STAPLE substantially improves the link reliability, with the maximum gain ratio achieved at 20.8% for the 2×8 MIMO link under 16QAM. Consequently, we conclude that STAPLE brings more benefits in noisy channel environments.

6.2.3 Network Performance Evaluation. Next, we evaluate the performance gain of STAPLE in an 802.11ac network environment. In our testing network, the AP and stations are equipped with 4 and 2 antennas, respectively. In the single-link evaluation, we always fix the modulation scheme for a packet to test the performance of a single link. In our network performance evaluation, all the values in the PHY/MAC fields of a packet (e.g. packet size and modulation scheme) are generated according to 802.11ac packet trace data. This creates a much more dynamic environment especially in uplink scenarios. We place the AP at location 0, and also place other stations, named nodes 1–6, at locations 1–6, respectively, as illustrated in Figure 13.

Overall performance: Figure 17 shows the overall performance gain ratios under uplink and downlink scenarios. Similar to the single-link case, STAPLE always improves the packet delivery ratio. We find in Figure 17 that there are very slight performance gains for nodes 1 and 2. This is because these two nodes have very good LoS channels to the AP and corrupted packet at these nodes are mostly due to collisions in the network. STAPLE is not a mechanism to resolve packet collisions. If there is no collision, the single-link packet delivery ratio for nodes 1 and 2 are close to 100%. Thus, there is little room for STAPLE to improve the performance.

As Figure 17 illustrates, the maximum performance gain ratios for the uplink and downlink are 14.3% and 14.8%, respectively, both observed at node 4, which is the furthest away from the AP in the network. This shows the capability of STAPLE to boost the link performance under noisy conditions.

We also demonstrate the dynamics of state associations inside STAPLE at the AP. We compute the number of successful state associations for every 2000 packets received. Figure 18 plots this number as a function of the total number of received packets at the AP. It is seen that most of the time, STAPLE needs to perform signal re-processing on 30-60 packets for every 2000 packets, and packet corruption events are uniformly distributed over time in our testing environment.

Impacts of threshold in state association: In state association (2), a pre-set threshold d_{th} is needed to associate a corrupted packet with a previous state. We test the impact of different thresholds on

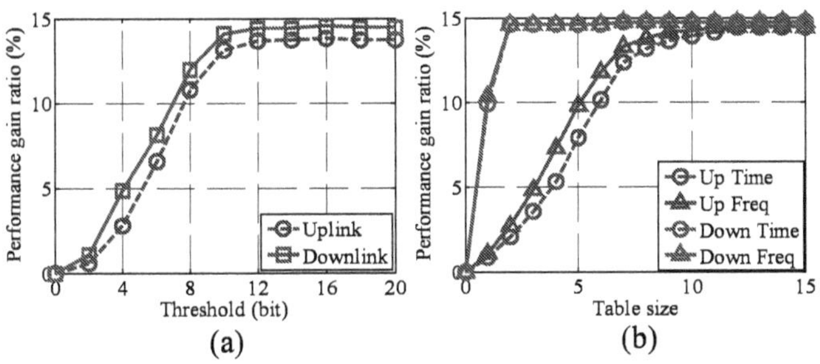

Figure 19: The impacts of (a) threshold in state association and (b) state table size.

the performance gain ratio of STAPLE at node 4. Figure 19(a) illustrates the uplink and downlink performance gain ratios with different thresholds. We can observe that the performance gain ratio of STAPLE first increases then remains approximately the same as the threshold d_{th} keeps increasing. This means that a larger d_{th} is desirable to maximize the performance gain from STAPLE in practice. But a larger d_{th} may indicate that STAPLE tries to recover heavily corrupted packets that may be not recoverable with signal re-processing, incurring more wrong associations and processing overhead. Therefore, the optimal value of d_{th} for STAPLE to balance the performance gain and complexity is 12-20 bits, as observed in Figure 19(a).

Impacts of state table setups: We also evaluate the impacts of the state table size and update policy on the performance gain of STAPLE at node 4 in the network.

Figure 19(b) shows the comparison of performance gain ratios of timestamp-based and frequency-based table update policies for different table sizes. From Figure 19(b), the frequency-based policy exhibits slightly better performance than the timestamp-based policy. The difference is negligible for both uplink and downlink when the table size is large.

We also see from Figure 19(b) that the state table size has more impacts on the performance benefits of STAPLE. For the downlink, as a station only cares about the packets from the AP, a small table maintaining 2-5 states is sufficient to increase the performance gain ratio to approximately 15%. For the uplink, the AP requires a larger table size because it has to communicate with a number of nodes. Figure 19(b) shows that a table with the size of 12-15 states at the AP is sufficient for the testing network to achieve a nearly 15% performance gain ratio.

6.3 STAPLE for Other Standards

During our experiments with 802.11ac, we find that STAPLE always improves the packet delivery by up to 20.8% and 15% in single-link and network evaluations, respectively. In the following, we show the benefits of STAPLE brought to 802.11b/g/n and 802.15.4.

802.11b/g/n network setups: We use the previous network scenario and default STAPLE parameters to set up the 802.11b/g/n testing network with the AP placed at location 0, and nodes 1-6 placed at locations 1-6, respectively, as shown in Figure 13.

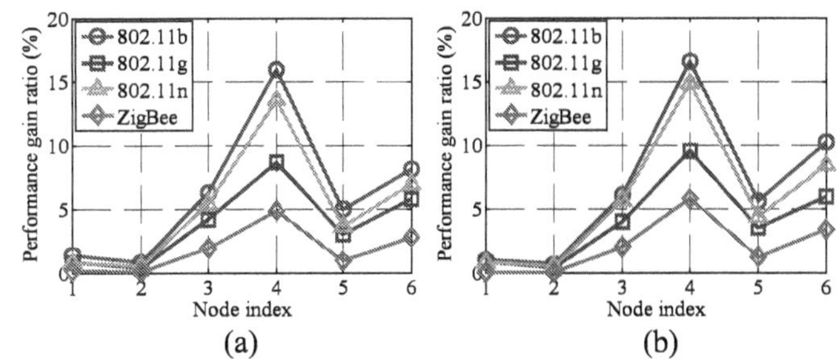

Figure 20: Network-level performance gain ratios: (a) uplink and (b) downlink.

802.15.4 network setups: The network topology is the same as the one in 802.11 scenarios: the network coordinator is placed at location 0, and nodes 1-6 placed at locations 1-6, respectively. Nodes 1-6 are communicating with the coordinator in the network. We obtain two ZigBee datasets [36] and [37]. The packets in [36] have 7 different lengths and packets in [37] always have the same length. We generate data packets according to [36]. The state table size is set to 5 for all nodes.

Experimental Results: Figure 20 shows the performance gain ratios of STAPLE in the uplink and downlink scenarios, respectively. Similar to Figure 17, nodes 1 and 2 gain slight benefits from STAPLE because of their good LoS channels to the AP; and node 4 has the highest performance gain ratios among all nodes.

It is observed at node 4 that the highest performance gain ratio (15.9% in uplink or 16.6% in downlink) is achieved under 802.11b and the lowest (4.9% in uplink or 5.8% in downlink) is under 802.15.4. This is because the packet state sizes in 802.11b and 802.15.4 are the largest and smallest in our STAPLE configurations (in Section 5.2), respectively. A large packet state size means that STAPLE can construct a longer preamble for signal re-processing, therefore generally indicating better performance gain. The experimental results from Figure 20 also demonstrate that STAPLE can benefit a wide range of wireless networks.

6.4 Discussions and Limitations

6.4.1 Discussions. In our performance evaluation, the downlink performance is found always slightly better than the uplink performance. This is because all nodes in the network transmit packets with limited power, leading to a minor hidden terminal problem. For example, as shown in Figure 13, with the AP being placed at location 0, node 1 (at location 1) has a small probability of not accurately sensing the transmission from node 4 (at location 4), and vice versa. This only results in minor asymmetric uplink and downlink performance, and does not affect the evaluation of the performance gains from STAPLE.

During our experiments, the size of the state table in STAPLE is chosen and evaluated empirically according to the distributions of PHY/MAC header fields in real-world 802.11 datasets. Therefore, the choice of 2-5 states for stations and 12-20 for the AP should be practically suitable for a normal WiFi network environment. The table size may have to be increased in a network with a large number of users using data-intensive applications. An under-designed table size may only reduce the performance gain of STAPLE, but does not degrade the network performance. In addition, the advantage of STAPLE is that the downlink requires much smaller table size than the uplink, which significantly benefits network users.

For 802.11ac, our packet collection and evaluation are based on the non-MU-MIMO mode. The MU-MIMO mode does not affect the uplink and is for the downlink only [11]. In addition, MU-MIMO related PHY fields (e.g., GroupID) usually remain constant if a user does not change his/her location dramatically. Thus, a low-overhead STAPLE design is expected to be still effective when used for the MU-MIMO mode in 802.11ac.

6.4.2 Limitations. In this paper, configurations for STAPLE are based on packet trace analysis for typical wireless network scenarios (e.g., a typical residential WiFi network). When a network has a large number of users, the size of the state table should be increased at least for the uplink in order to accommodate more users' packet information. As a result, configurations for STAPLE may need to be adapted accordingly for the scenarios with a large number of users and intensive network usages.

STAPLE can be considered as a way to push the performance limit of signal processing for wireless networking. Experimental results show that overall, STAPLE achieves moderate performance improvements in different evaluation scenarios. Thus, it is important to minimize the complexity of the STAPLE implementation and configuration for a practical scenario to avoid excessive energy overhead, which is proportional to the processing complexity.

STAPLE is designed as a general software radio architecture to improve the signal processing performance on a wireless link. STAPLE is shown effective to improve the link performance under long-distance or severe channel fading scenarios. However, STAPLE cannot resolve any packet corruption due to collisions in wireless networks. This may limit its use in the scenarios with congested network traffic under good channel conditions, where the wireless packet collisions are the dominate performance bottleneck.

7 RELATED WORK

In this section, we discuss existing works related to the research efforts in this paper.

Wireless signal processing: Timing/frequency synchronization and channel estimation have been well explored in the signal processing and wireless communication communities under a wide range of algorithmic settings and channel conditions [1, 2, 4, 25, 29, 38, 39], thereby establishing a relatively mature research area. Essential signal processing procedures for traditional packet reception remain generally unchanged. STAPLE takes signal processing out of the traditional domain and places it in the network domain, then demonstrates a new perspective of re-designing the signal processing procedure to improve the performance during packet reception at a wireless receiver.

Partial packet recovery: STAPLE is related to partial packet recovery (PPR) that attempts to recover a corrupted packet using a number of approaches, such as automatic repeat request (ARQ), forward error correction (FEC) [6–10, 14, 24, 40–42]. In particular, hybrid-ARQ (HARQ) [7, 9, 24] has become a widely-used technique to combine the information from multiple packets to improve the wireless link performance. STAPLE differs from H-ARQ in the following aspects: (i) H-ARQ focuses on repairing corrupted packets with the cooperation from the transmitter. STAPLE is designed as a new architecture of signal processing only residing at the receiver without any cooperation at the receiver; (ii) H-ARQ combines the retransmitted packet (including the redundant code) with the originally corrupted packet for error correction to help decoding. On the contrary, STAPLE does not directly touch upon signal decoding, but leverages low-entropy packet header information to construct a longer preamble to improve the signal processing accuracy, which in turn enhances the decoding performance.

To the best of our knowledge, STAPLE is designed as a new way to provide better signal processing performance, which is orthogonal to H-ARQ and other existing partial packet recovery mechanisms. Therefore, STAPLE can be integrated with these mechanisms to further improve the wireless network performance.

Link quality improvement: Research efforts [21, 22, 42–45] have been devoted to improving the wireless link quality. For example, [22, 43] focus on resolving the problem of packets collisions. Channel prediction is proposed in [46] to facilitate rate selection in 802.11 networks. An architecture is designed in [47] to flexibly support multiple radio frequency link chains. In addition, a few recent efforts focus on improving the MU-MIMO performance from various aspects [19, 48–50]. STAPLE is also related to [21] that leverages protocol signatures to improve the packet decoding performance based on modifications to the 802.11 PHY layer.

In contrast, STAPLE focuses on a different domain to improve the signal processing performance during packet reception and does not modify any standard. Hence, STAPLE is also complementary to these efforts and is broadly applicable to wireless networks.

8 CONCLUSION

This paper presents STAPLE, which is a lightweight, efficient mechanism to improve the signal processing performance for wireless networking. The core idea of STAPLE is to collect common header information to form the state of a packet, and use state association to recover a corrupted packet back to a previous state for constructing a longer preamble to further enhance the reliability of signal processing. We implement STAPLE on USRP X300 devices with adapted configurations for 802.11a/b/g/n/ac and 802.15.4. Experimental results show that STAPLE improves the wireless network performance under various conditions.

ACKNOWLEDGEMENT

The authors would like to thank the shepherd Dr. Bo Chen and the anonymous reviewers for the insightful comments and feedback. The work at University of South Florida in this paper was supported in part by NSF under grants CNS-1527144, CNS-1553304, and CNS-1701394, and ARO under grant W911NF-14-1-0324.

REFERENCES

[1] J.-J. Van de Beek, M. Sandell, and P. O. Borjesson, "ML estimation of time and frequency offset in OFDM systems," *IEEE Trans. Signal Process.*, vol. 45, pp. 1800–1805, 1997.

[2] P. H. Moose, "A technique for orthogonal frequency division multiplexing frequency offset correction," *IEEE Trans. Commun.*, vol. 42, pp. 2908–2914, 1994.

[3] L. M. Davis, I. B. Collings, and P. Hoeher, "Joint MAP equalization and channel estimation for frequency-selective and frequency-flat fast-fading channels," *IEEE Trans. Commun.*, vol. 49, pp. 2106–2114, 2001.
[4] T. M. Schmidl and D. C. Cox, "Robust frequency and timing synchronization for OFDM," *IEEE trans. commun.*, vol. 45, pp. 1613–1621, 1997.
[5] M.-A. Badiu, G. E. Kirkelund, C. N. Manchón, E. Riegler, and B. H. Fleury, "Message-passing algorithms for channel estimation and decoding using approximate inference," in *Prof. of IEEE ISIT*, 2012.
[6] G. Angelopoulos, M. Medard, and A. Chandrakasan, "Harnessing partial packets in wireless networks: Throughput and energy benefits," *IEEE Trans. Wireless Commun.*, 2016.
[7] P. Larsson, L. K. Rasmussen, and M. Skoglund, "Throughput analysis of hybrid-AQR–a matrix exponential distribution approach," *IEEE Trans. Commun.*, vol. 64, pp. 416–428, 2016.
[8] Y. Wang, W. Li, and S. Lu, "The capability of error correction for burst-noise channels using error estimating code," in *Prof. of IEEE SECON*, 2016.
[9] D. Jia, Z. Fei, J. Yuan, S. Tian, and J. Kuang, "A hybrid EF/DF protocol with rateless coded network code for two-way relay channels," *IEEE Trans.Commun.*, vol. 64, pp. 3133–3147, 2016.
[10] M. S. Mohammadi, Q. Zhang, and E. Dutkiewicz, "Reading damaged scripts: partial packet recovery based on compressive sensing for efficient random linear coded transmission," *IEEE Trans. Commun.*, vol. 64, pp. 3296–3310, 2016.
[11] "Wireless LAN medium access control (MAC) and physical layer (PHY) specifications," *IEEE Std 802.11*, 2013.
[12] "Low-rate wireless personal area networks (LR-WPANs)," *IEEE Std 802.15.4*, 2011.
[13] M. Gowda, S. Sen, R. R. Choudhury, and S.-J. Lee, "Cooperative packet recovery in enterprise WLANs," in *Prof. of IEEE INFOCOM*, 2013.
[14] B. Han, A. Schulman, F. Gringoli, N. Spring, B. Bhattacharjee, L. Nava, L. Ji, S. Lee, and R. R. Miller, "Maranello: Practical partial packet recovery for 802.11." in *Prof. of NSDI*, 2010.
[15] M.-H. Lu, P. Steenkiste, and T. Chen, "Design, implementation and evaluation of an efficient opportunistic retransmission protocol," in *Prof. of ACM MobiCom*, 2009.
[16] S. Noh, M. D. Zoltowski, Y. Sung, and D. J. Love, "Pilot beam pattern design for channel estimation in massive MIMO systems," *IEEE J. Sel. Topics Signal Process.*, vol. 8, pp. 787–801, 2014.
[17] A. Goldsmith, *Wireless communications*. Cambridge university press, 2005.
[18] D. Tse and P. Viswanath, *Fundamentals of wireless communication*. Cambridge university press, 2005.
[19] X. Xie, E. Chai, X. Zhang, K. Sundaresan, A. Khojastepour, and S. Rangarajan, "Hekaton: Efficient and practical large-scale MIMO," in *Prof. of ACM MobiCom*, 2015.
[20] Y. Chen, X. Liu, Y. Cui, J. Zou, and S. Yang, "A multiwinding transformer cell-to-cell active equalization method for lithium-ion batteries with reduced number of driving circuits," *IEEE Trans. Power Electron.*, vol. 31, pp. 4916–4929, 2016.
[21] J. Huang, Y. Wang, and G. Xing, "LEAD: leveraging protocol signatures for improving wireless link performance," in *Prof. of ACM MobiSys*, 2013.
[22] S. Gollakota and D. Katabi, "Zigzag decoding: combating hidden terminals in wireless networks," in *Prof. of ACM SIGCOMM*, 2008.
[23] P. Larsson, L. K. Rasmussen, and M. Skoglund, "Throughput analysis of ARQ schemes in Gaussian block fading channels," *IEEE Trans. Commun.*, vol. 62, pp. 2569–2588, 2014.
[24] A. Chelli, E. Zedini, M.-S. Alouini, J. R. Barry, and M. Pätzold, "Performance and delay analysis of hybrid ARQ with incremental redundancy over double Rayleigh fading channels," *IEEE Trans. Wireless Commun.*, vol. 13, pp. 6245–6258, 2014.
[25] M.-A. Badiu, C. N. Manchón, and B. H. Fleury, "Message-passing receiver architecture with reduced-complexity channel estimation," *IEEE Commun. Lett.*, vol. 17, pp. 1404–1407, 2013.
[26] M. Rodrig, C. Reis, R. Mahajan, D. Wetherall, J. Zahorjan, and E. Lazowska, "CRAWDAD dataset uw/sigcomm2004 (v. 2006-10-17)," Downloaded from http://crawdad.org/uw/sigcomm2004/20061017, Oct. 2006.
[27] A. Schulman, D. Levin, and N. Spring, "CRAWDAD dataset umd/sigcomm2008 (v. 2009-03-02)," Downloaded from http://crawdad.org/umd/sigcomm2008/20090302, Mar. 2009.
[28] O. Besson and P. Stoica, "On parameter estimation of MIMO flat-fading channels with frequency offsets," *IEEE Trans. Signal Process.*, vol. 51, pp. 602–613, 2003.
[29] Q. Li, K. C. Teh, and K. H. Li, "Low-complexity channel estimation and turbo equalisation for high frequency channels," *IET Commun.*, vol. 7, pp. 980–987, 2013.
[30] T. M. Cover and J. A. Thomas, *Elements of information theory*. John Wiley & Sons, 2012.
[31] "Monitoring 802.11n and 802.11ac networks," http://www.tamos.com/htmlhelp/commwifi/monitoring_802_11n_networks.htm.
[32] M. Ettus, "USRP user's and developer's guide," *Ettus Research LLC*, 2005.
[33] S. M. Alamouti, "A simple transmit diversity technique for wireless communications," *IEEE J. Sel. Areas Commun.*, vol. 16, pp. 1451–1458, 1998.
[34] S. Sen, R. R. Choudhury, and S. Nelakuditi, "CSMA/CN: carrier sense multiple access with collision notification," *IEEE/ACM Trans. Netw.*, vol. 20, pp. 544–556, 2012.
[35] S. Sen, R. Roy Choudhury, and S. Nelakuditi, "No time to countdown: Migrating backoff to the frequency domain," in *Prof. of ACM MobiCom*, 2011.
[36] S. Fu and Y. Zhang, "CRAWDAD dataset due/packet-delivery (v. 2015-04-01)," Downloaded from http://crawdad.org/due/packet-delivery/20150401/packet-metadata, Apr. 2015, traceset: packet-metadata.
[37] A. Iqbal, K. Shahzad, S. A. Khayam, and Y. Cho, "CRAWDAD dataset niit/bit_errors (v. 2008-07-08)," Downloaded from http://crawdad.org/niit/bit_errors/20080708/802.15.4, Jul. 2008, traceset: 802.15.4.
[38] G. Liu, L. Zeng, H. Li, L. Xu, and Z. Wang, "Adaptive interpolation for pilot-aided channel estimator in OFDM system," *IEEE Trans. Broadcast.*, vol. 60, pp. 486–498, 2014.
[39] A. Movahedian and M. McGuire, "On the capacity of iteratively estimated channels using LMMSE estimators," *IEEE Trans. Veh. Technol.*, vol. 64, pp. 97–107, 2015.
[40] J. Xie, W. Hu, and Z. Zhang, "Revisiting partial packet recovery in 802.11 wireless LANs," in *Prof. of ACM MobiSys*, 2011.
[41] Y. Xie, Z. Li, M. Li, and K. Jamieson, "Augmenting wide-band 802.11 transmissions via unequal packet bit protection," in *Prof. of IEEE INFOCOM*, 2016.
[42] J. Huang, G. Xing, J. Niu, and S. Lin, "CodeRepair: PHY-layer partial packet recovery without the pain," in *Prof. of IEEE INFOCOM*, 2015.
[43] L. Kong and X. Liu, "mZig: Enabling multi-packet reception in ZigBee," in *Prof. of ACM MobiCom*, 2015.
[44] X. Xie, X. Zhang, S. Kumar, and L. E. Li, "piStream: Physical layer informed adaptive video streaming over LTE," in *Prof. of ACM MobiCom*, 2015.
[45] B. Kellogg, V. Talla, S. Gollakota, and J. R. Smith, "Passive Wi-Fi: Bringing low power to Wi-Fi transmissions," in *Prof. of NSDI*, 2016.
[46] D. Halperin, W. Hu, A. Sheth, and D. Wetherall, "Predictable 802.11 packet delivery from wireless channel measurements," in *Prof. of ACM SIGCOMM*, 2010.
[47] B. Chen, V. Yenamandra, and K. Srinivasan, "Flexradio: Fully flexible radios and networks," in *Prof. of NSDI*, 2015.
[48] A. B. Flores, S. Quadri, and E. W. Knightly, "A scalable multi-user uplink for Wi-Fi," in *Prof. of NSDI*, 2016.
[49] C. Shepard, A. Javed, and L. Zhong, "Control channel design for many-antenna MU-MIMO," in *Prof. of ACM MobiCom*, 2015.
[50] E. Hamed, H. Rahul, M. A. Abdelghany, and D. Katabi, "Real-time distributed MIMO systems," in *Proc. of ACM SIGCOMM*, 2016, pp. 412–425.

WiFi-Assisted 60 GHz Wireless Networks

Sanjib Sur[∞,*], Ioannis Pefkianakis[¬], Xinyu Zhang[▷], Kyu-Han Kim[¬]
University of Wisconsin-Madison[∞], Hewlett Packard Labs[¬], University of California San Diego[▷]
sur2@wisc.edu, ioannis.pefkianakis@hpe.com, xiz368@eng.ucsd.edu, kyu-han.kim@hpe.com

ABSTRACT

Despite years of innovative research and development, gigabit-speed 60 GHz wireless networks are still not mainstream. The main concern for network operators and vendors is the unfavorable propagation characteristics due to short wavelength and high directionality, which renders the 60 GHz links highly vulnerable to blockage and mobility. However, the advent of multi-band chipsets opens the possibility of leveraging the more robust WiFi technology to assist 60 GHz in order to provide seamless, Gbps connectivity. In this paper, we design and implement *MUST*, an IEEE 802.11-compliant system that provides seamless, high-speed connectivity over multi-band 60 GHz and WiFi devices. *MUST* has two key design components: (1) a WiFi-assisted 60 GHz link adaptation algorithm, which can instantaneously predict the best beam and PHY rate setting, with zero probing overhead; and (2) a proactive blockage detection and switching algorithm which can re-direct ongoing user traffic to the robust interface within sub-10 ms latency. Our experiments with off-the-shelf 802.11 hardware show that *MUST* can achieve 25-60% throughput gain over state-of-the-art solutions, while bringing almost 2 orders of magnitude cross-band switching latency improvement.

CCS CONCEPTS

• **Networks → Wireless access networks; Network protocol design;**

KEYWORDS

60 GHz; Millimeter-Wave; IEEE 802.11ad; Session Transfer

1 INTRODUCTION

The multi-GHz unlicensed spectrum at the 60 GHz millimeter-wave frequency band promises to shift current WiFi-experience from "Wireless" to Gbps "Wire-like". With up to 14 GHz of free spectrum [1], 60 GHz offers a foundation for next-generation bandwidth-intensive applications, such as uncompressed video streaming, snap wireless file synchronization, wireless virtual and augmented reality, wireless data centers, and Gbps Internet access. Multiple standardization efforts such as IEEE 802.11ad [24], 802.15.3c [12], ECMA [20] and millimeter-wave products [48] are tailored to support such applications, and promise upto 7 Gbps of wireless bit-rate. These advances and research demonstrations [23, 54, 63] have also led millimeter-wave technology to be recommended as a key enabler for multi-Gbps 5G cellular networks [1–3].

However, the short wavelength (5 mm at 60 GHz) and weak reflection characteristics (compared to LTE/WiFi signals) render 60 GHz links highly vulnerable to channel propagation loss [51, 60]. In the same environment, a 60 GHz link suffers from around 1000× higher signal strength loss compared to typical LTE/WiFi [53]. Millimeter-wave devices overcome such challenge by focusing RF energy towards narrow spatial direction through beamforming using phased-array antennas. Maintaining beams from access point (AP)/base station toward mobile users is a challenging task and 60 GHz links formed via such narrow beams get highly affected during mobility and human blockage [15, 47, 53, 54].

Our experiments with off-the-shelf IEEE 802.11ad platform in indoor settings show the potential of incorporating 60 GHz links in enterprise networks, but also expose its limitations. While a few of the observations are broadly expected, our measurement study quantifies the benefit and limitations of adopting 60 GHz in today's enterprises. In static, Line-Of-Sight (LOS) settings, 60 GHz can achieve 2.5 Gbps throughput, which is 4× higher than state-of-the-art WiFi (IEEE 802.11ac)[1]. However, during blockage and mobility where WiFi can transmit at full speed, 60 GHz links may occasionally get fully disconnected for several hundred milliseconds. Although IEEE 802.11ad transmitter and receiver can recover from such dynamics by searching for the best signal-strength beam at runtime, our experiments show that the search algorithm itself takes hundreds of ms to converge. Recent research proposals [6, 35, 47, 54] seek to minimize the convergence time to the best beam. However, such approaches either assume quasi-stationary 60 GHz links, or have limitations to find the settings at low cost, in dynamic scenarios with today's commodity devices. Even if an "Oracle" could instantaneously find the best beam, our results show multiple occasions where 60 GHz link establishment is not feasible, due to the fundamental physics of the millimeter-wave communication. Deploying denser APs [58, 64] or reflectors [5] could improve but does not guarantee robust 60 GHz connectivity despite the high deployment cost.

Fortunately, the advent of multi-band WiFi chipsets [59] opens the possibility of leveraging the more robust WiFi interface in those scenarios where 60 GHz fundamentally performs poorly, to enable robust connectivity. Specifically, WiFi's omni-directional view of the wireless channel could be leveraged to design highly-adaptive 60 GHz beam and PHY rate selection. In the scenarios where a 60 GHz link cannot be established due to obstacles, WiFi could provide admittedly lower speeds, but still a robust communication anchor.

Designing WiFi-assisted millimeter-wave communication is a challenging problem for *three* key reasons. *First*, while omni-directional WiFi Channel State Information (CSI) could provide a hint to the

*Sanjib Sur interned at Hewlett Packard Labs, Palo Alto during this work.

MobiCom '17, October 16–20, 2017, Snowbird, UT, USA

ACM ISBN 978-1-4503-4916-1/17/10...$15.00
https://doi.org/10.1145/3117811.3117817

[1]In this paper, we use 60 GHz or IEEE 802.11ad, and WiFi or IEEE 802.11ac interchangeably.

most dominant propagation path (and hence to the best 60 GHz beam), it is coarse grained estimation, and often leads to erroneous beam selection, as shown by our experiments. *Second*, simultaneously transmitting data over multiple interfaces with highly heterogeneous speeds (*i.e.* 60 GHz and WiFi) degrades application performance over TCP, compared to a single-interface transmission. To our surprise, we have observed that TCP throughput can drop by up to 5×, when both 60 GHz and WiFi are used simultaneously. *Finally*, designing seamless 60 GHz-WiFi interface switching, which meets the sub-10 ms latency requirements of many real-time applications, remains an open problem. Existing off-the-shelf multi-band devices adopt a reactive interface switching approach, which requires multiple seconds to identify and switch to the best interface.

In this paper, we present *MUST* (*MU*lti-band fast *S*ession *T*ransfer), an IEEE 802.11-compliant system which provides high-speed, robust connectivity over 60 GHz and WiFi multi-band devices, in dynamic indoor environments. *MUST* achieves its objective by introducing *two* key design components: (1) *Fast link adaptation:* A WiFi-assisted 60 GHz link adaptation module that can instantaneously predict the best 60 GHz beam and PHY rate setting, with zero 60 GHz probing, under blockage and mobility; (2) *Seamless switching:* A low-latency (sub-10 ms), proactive switching algorithm to reroute traffic from highly fragile 60 GHz links to WiFi, without breaking the existing connection. *MUST* design is built upon *two* key observations: (1) Human mobility and blockage affect the dominating path of the 60 GHz channel and thus best beam, at much slower pace (order of 100s of ms). While a small scale variation can still affect channel quality of the best beam, it does not necessarily change the entire best beam direction in a practical system. Thus, instead of relying on the existing method of link adaptation that itself can take hundreds of ms to converge, *MUST* uses out-of-band information with appropriate modeling that provides the hint for the 60 GHz channel's most dominating path and best link settings. (2) When LOS is blocked, 60 GHz suffers from highly dynamic, occasional zero-throughput connectivity that eventually degrades upper layer performance. In order to achieve smooth real-time response, it is far better to proactively move to WiFi interface to survive blockage.

We implement *MUST* in an off-the-shelf IEEE 802.11ad/ac multi-band AP platform without any modifications to the end-user device or additional standards support. Different from existing efforts, which focus on a single aspect of 60 GHz communication (*e.g.* link adaptation [6, 35, 47, 54]), *MUST* is a full-fledged system design which introduces optimizations across the protocol stack, considering system-level constraints and overheads. Our experiments show that *MUST* can accurately approximate the best performance link settings under various channel dynamics in enterprise environment. Even after including all out-of-band probing and interface switching related overheads, it stays within 10% of the optimum and achieves 25-60% throughput gain over state-of-the-art solutions. While proactively switching to WiFi can occasionally incur performance loss (less than 6% on average), *MUST* improves the switching latency by almost 2 orders of magnitude.

2 BACKGROUND

2.1 IEEE 802.11ad and 802.11ac

60 GHz: IEEE 802.11ad [24] devices operate on the 60 GHz unlicensed spectrum, which uses 2.16 GHz of channel bandwidth per link, with peak PHY rate upto 7 Gbps (the commodity IEEE 802.11ad devices in our experiments support upto 4.62 Gbps). IEEE 802.11ad devices can overcome the high channel propagation loss of 60 GHz signal, by using multi-antenna phased-array to steer RF energy towards narrow spatial direction (*i.e.*, beamforming). Specifically, they use analog amplitude and phase shifters that are configured according to a predefined codebook of beamforming coefficients, with each codebook entry generating a *sector* (or beam). Due to the small form factor of 60 GHz RF components and antennas, large phased-arrays can be integrated into mobile devices.

IEEE 802.11ad supports a beamforming training (BFT) process to discover the highest signal strength Tx and Rx beams between a pair of devices. BFT comprises of a mandatory Sector Level Sweep (SLS) phase, and an optional Beam Refinement Phase (BRP), which hierarchically evaluate the Tx and Rx beam combinations, to identify the best one [24, 53].

WiFi: IEEE 802.11ac [25] devices operate on the 5 GHz band, with up to 160 MHz of channel bandwidth. Although the highest 802.11ac PHY rate is 6.9 Gbps, the rates which are used by typical off-the-shelf WiFi devices are up to 866.7 Mbps. This is because mobile user devices do not support more than 2-stream MIMO due to energy and antenna size constraints. Moreover, 160 MHz channels are often disabled by AP vendors in enterprise and campus settings due to mutual interferences with legacy 802.11a/n devices.

2.2 Fast Session Transfer

To enable seamless transition to IEEE 802.11ac interface on the same device, IEEE 802.11ad supports an optional Fast Session Transfer (FST) feature [24]. Specifically, IEEE 802.11ad specifies the MAC-level control and coordination procedures between the AP and user, which allows traffic to migrate in between the WiFi and 60 GHz interfaces, transparent to higher layer protocols.

3 MEASUREMENTS ON OFF-THE-SHELF HARDWARE

In this section, we conduct experiments with off-the-shelf hardware to understand how 60 GHz compares with WiFi in various indoor settings. While few of the measurement observations are broadly expected, our goal here is to assess the benefits and limitations of incorporating 60 GHz in typical enterprise settings. The findings of this section form the basis of our arguments behind WiFi-assisted 60 GHz wireless networks.

3.1 Experimental Platform and Methodology

Platform. We conduct all our experiments using commodity APs and end-user devices (Figure 1(*b*)) that integrate both 60 GHz and WiFi radios on the same device. The 60 GHz radio at AP consists of a baseband chipset that supports 2.16 GHz channel bandwidth and up to 16-QAM modulation level, with 4.62 Gbps peak PHY rate. In addition, a separate RFIC controls an integrated 32-element phased-array antenna (arranged in a 4×8 matrix), that can generate directional beams in three-dimensional space. The spatial direction

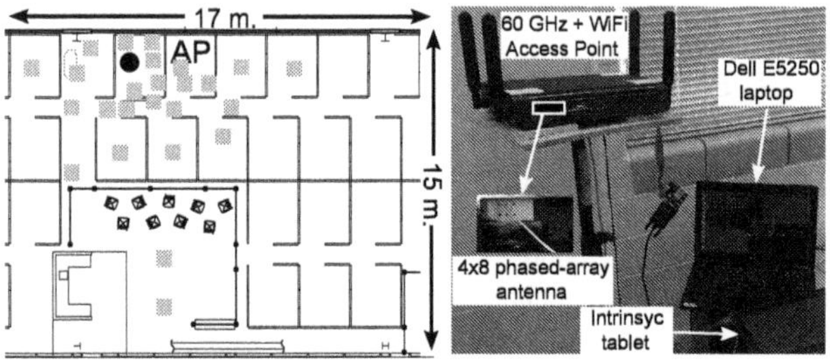

Figure 1: (*a*) Experimental floorplan. Square boxes represent static users' position. (*b*) Experimental platform.

of the beams depends on the phased-array antenna configurations, and have been optimized by the vendor to minimize the overlap, and hence to maximize spatial coverage. Several example transmit beam directions in our platform are shown in Figure 5(*a*), where each dot represents the strongest direction of the beam. The azimuth and elevation angles of the beams can span within {-87.5°, 90°} and {-45°, 45°} respectively[2]. Phased-array beamforming training and rate adaptation algorithms are implemented at the firmware of the baseband chipset, which sends the control signals to the RFIC, to steer the beam directions.

Our AP platform's WiFi interface supports 3 antennas, upto 80 MHz bandwidth and MU-MIMO technology. Its peak PHY rate is 866.7 Mbps. Both the 60 GHz and WiFi radios are connected to a general-purpose System-on-Chip (*a.k.a.* host) via PCIe bus, which uses a dual-core 1.7 GHz CPU with a 512 MB DDR3 memory, and runs OpenWrt [4]. The host system implements legacy functionalities including processing and forwarding packets from backhaul Ethernet to the radios. An off-the-shelf platform with similar hardware-software architecture is available here [30]. At the user side, we use Dell laptops [17] and Intrinsyc tablets [27] that also integrate the 60 GHz and WiFi chipsets on the same device. User devices have the same 60 GHz radio as the AP, but their WiFi interfaces only have 2 antennas.

Methodology. For our experiments, we modified the kernel and firmware of our AP, to periodically collect fine-grained statistics such as throughput, PHY rate, beam directions, for each connected user device. Using our testbed, we conduct experiments in an enterprise and a campus building.

3.2 Performance in Multiple Settings

We start our measurement study by comparing 60 GHz and WiFi throughput in the building floor shown in Figure 1(*a*). For our experiments, we generate saturated TCP traffic from an AP to a user, in controlled settings, without external channel interferences, or perturbations in the physical environment.

Static settings. We place the AP at two different heights from the floor (2.6 ft table and 9 ft tripod), and a user at 25 different spots (represented by rectangles) in Figure 1(*a*). Figure 2(*a*) shows the distribution of the 60 GHz and WiFi throughput difference ($Thr_{60} - Thr_{WiFi}$) for the two AP placements. While 60 GHz can achieve up to 1.7 Gbps higher throughput than today's state-of-the-art WiFi, it is typically better in LOS settings. Overall, 60 GHz outperforms WiFi in more settings when the AP is placed higher, because more non-blocking links can be established. When an obstacle blocks the LOS, WiFi can achieve up to 405 Mbps higher throughput (Figure 2(*a*)). In most of the settings where WiFi performs better, 60 GHz link achieves almost zero throughput, or it gets disconnected. Figure 2(*c*) further shows that in open LOS, 60 GHz can achieve more than 1.5 Gbps throughput even beyond 10 m from the AP (typical AP separation distance in today's enterprise). However, obstacle blockage may disconnect 60 GHz links, and even beam searching and steering may not be able to establish any connection in Non-Line-Of-Sight (NLOS). WiFi on the other hand provides more stable and robust connection in NLOS.

Spatial and temporal dynamics. 60 GHz channel is more dynamic than WiFi in both space and time, because of its higher wireless frequency [45]. The dynamic performance of 60 GHz channel in various static and pedestrian mobility settings is shown in the boxplot throughput distribution of Figure 2(*b*) within the experimental area in Figure 1(*a*). While 60 GHz throughput can reach upto 2.2 Gbps in the aforementioned settings, more than 25% of the links show no connection. WiFi links never disconnect and the throughput ranges from 80 to 480 Mbps.

Summary. 60 GHz communication shows high potential to achieve multi-Gbps speed with today's off-the-shelf IEEE 802.11ad hardware, which can outperform state-of-the-art WiFi by more than 1 Gbps in LOS. However, WiFi is robust under blockage. *Thus, 60 GHz and WiFi can be complimentary to each other in a typical indoor setting.*

3.3 Convergence to the Best-Speed Setting

The 60 GHz poor performance instances shown by our experiments are not only attributed to channel dynamics (*e.g.*, blockage), but also to the slow convergence to the best-throughput beam and rate settings [53, 64]. We conduct controlled experiments to quantify such overhead. Specifically, a static LOS user device is placed 50 cm away from the AP, and a human body intentionally blocks in between. We monitor the SNR change of the current transmit beam at every 1 ms interval and measure the time elapsed between removing the blockage and returning to the best beam and rate (that is used before blockage occurrence). Figure 2(*d*) shows the distribution of 60 GHz link recovery time for 50 blockage scenarios. We observe very high convergence times, varying from 10 ms to 910 ms, with a median of 295 ms.

The reason behind such long convergence time is that, existing design lacks effective mechanisms to determine when to trigger beam searching, which is left as an open option in IEEE 802.11ad. For example, our platform collects the Packet-Error-Rate (PER) statistics over multiple probe packets to evaluate the reliability of a beam [40]. It will trigger a beam search only if the beam's "reliability" drops below a threshold, which leads to poor responsiveness. Although recent research proposals hold potential for fast convergence, they either assume quasi-stationary 60 GHz links [54] or require constant customized probing [32, 47]. After triggering the beam searching process, beam scan for small-sized phased-array (32 elements) is a fast operation. Our AP's IEEE 802.11ad radio can perform SLS and BRP scans in 1.25 ms. However, for larger phased-array platforms (*e.g.* 1000-elements), the IEEE 802.11ad SLS and BRP procedure can still be on the order of seconds [53, 64].

[2]Note that, range of the elevation angle is typically smaller due to restricted vertical movement of the user devices.

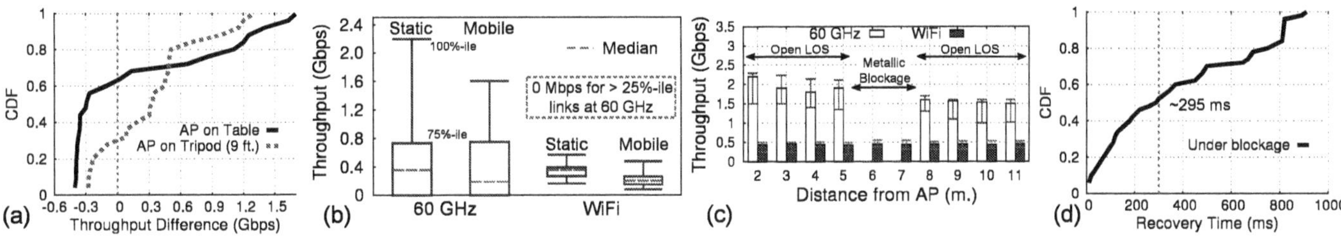

Figure 2: (*a*) Throughput difference between 60 GHz and WiFi links for two AP heights across 25 static locations. (*b*) Spatial and temporal dynamics. (*c*) 60 GHz and WiFi throughput in open LOS and NLOS. (*d*) Distribution of 60 GHz static link recovery time across 50 LOS blockage scenarios.

Summary: Probing-based 60 GHz beam and rate adaptation algorithms result in long convergence time in dynamic settings, even for a small-sized phased-array. *A probe-less fast link adaptation approach is desired to utilize the 60 GHz channel capacity, under channel dynamics.*

3.4 Joint 60 GHz and WiFi Operation

3.4.1 Enabling Single vs. Multiple Interfaces

Our experimental results corroborate the use of both 60 GHz and WiFi to achieve high-speed and robust connectivity. Indeed, existing schemes [29, 38, 41–43] have already considered simultaneously leveraging all the network interfaces (*e.g.* LTE and WiFi) to boost performance. We seek to understand if such approaches can work in our 60 GHz and WiFi settings. We conduct controlled experiments in static, open LOS, where the AP generates TCP traffic to one user device in two scenarios: (1) AP and user communicate only through 60 GHz, and (2) AP enables parallel transmissions over both 60 GHz and WiFi. In the latter scenario, our AP uses the open source Linux bonding driver [16] to bond 60 GHz and WiFi, and expose a single virtual IP/MAC address towards the network stack. We modified the bonding driver to push packets in parallel at both interfaces. Figure 3(*a*) shows the average (min/max) throughput for both scenarios, and for various 60 GHz link performance settings, as indicated by the 60 GHz PHY rates[3]. To our surprise, we observe that the TCP throughput drops by up to 5× when both interfaces are used in parallel! While the 60 GHz interface alone can achieve more than 2.5 Gbps, parallel 60 GHz & WiFi transmissions barely achieve 500 Mbps.

Root cause. The above experimental result is surprising to say the least. The root cause turned out to be hidden inside the TCP's congestion control. Specifically, due to highly heterogeneous speed links, we observe almost 50% of the TCP packets to arrive at the receiver out-of-order. Out-of-order packets result in duplicate ACKs and trigger the *Fast Retransmit* at the TCP sender [14], which results in unnecessary retransmissions. Further, limited receiver buffer space causes incomplete TCP packets that arrived early from the faster 60 GHz interface, to be frequently dropped due to buffer overflow. Both issues cause the sender to reduce the TCP congestion window (cwnd). Figure 3(*b*) shows the evolution of cwnd over time during a 1 GB downlink TCP transfer, for both single and parallel transmissions[4]. When both interfaces are used, the cwnd is severely affected and

[3]Rates 1251 and 2502 Mbps are hardware-disabled in our platform.
[4]Our AP implements TCP CUBIC [26], default option for Linux.

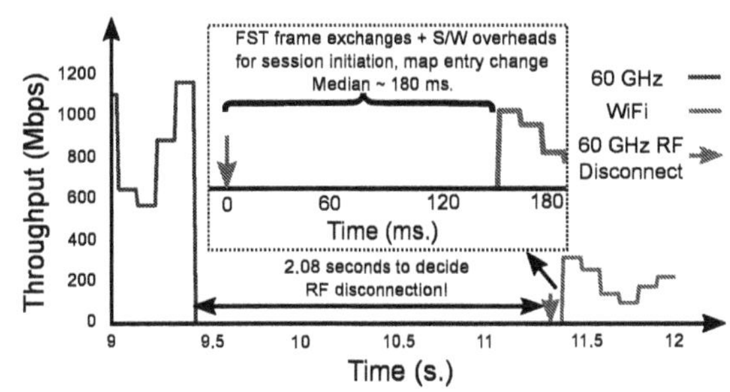

Figure 4: Temporal analysis of our platform's FST.

always remains smaller than 250 packets. However, under the same setup when packets are sent solely through 60 GHz, the cwnd quickly converges to approximately 2900 packets and consumes almost 4× less time to finish the transfer.

Does MPTCP help? At first blush, it may seem that the problem can be solved by enabling flow control over both paths using multipath TCP (MPTCP) [18]. Unfortunately, independent studies [21, 43] have shown that MPTCP performs poorly over heterogeneous paths, even for stable Gbps data-center links. This is because out-of-order TCP packets and limited receiver buffer size similarly affect MPTCP's performance. Our experiments also verify that using the 60 GHz interface alone achieves 7% to 45% higher throughput compared to MPTCP over 60 GHz and WiFi. The authors in [43] proposed extensive modifications to MPTCP for heterogeneous-speed paths, by opportunistically retransmitting TCP sequences over the highest-speed path, or by reducing congestion window over slow paths. However, both approaches waste network resources. Allocating larger buffer size at the receiver may reduce buffer overflow, but it does not prevent out-of-order packet reception. Besides, large receiver buffer size severely affects TCP's response to real-time mobile applications such as VR video streaming.

Summary: *Simultaneously transmitting through the 60 GHz and WiFi interfaces can severely affect TCP performance. Therefore, we opt to select one interface at a time, to accommodate individual user's traffic and switch to the best interface without breaking the existing connection.* We next evaluate the cost associated with such interface switching.

3.4.2 Interface Switching Overheads

IEEE 802.11ad FST overheads. Our platform implements the IEEE 802.11ad FST feature (Section 2.2, [24]), to allow for IEEE 802.11-compliant interface switching. The latency related to FST control

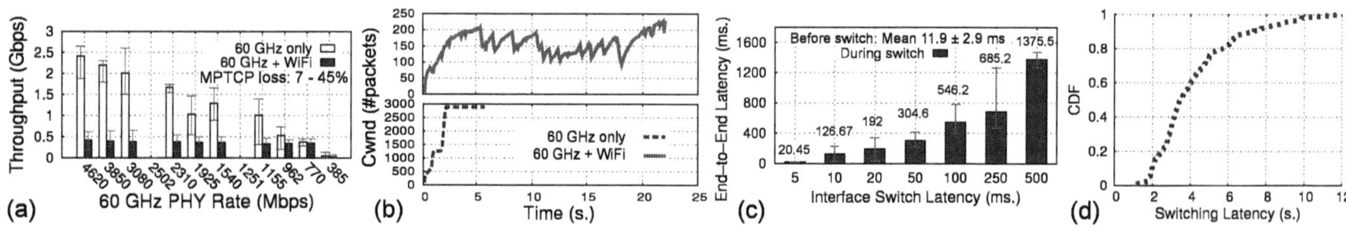

Figure 3: TCP's behavior under parallel transmission: (a) Throughput under various 60 GHz PHY rates. (b) Congestion window evolution for 1 GB downlink transmission. (c) TCP end-to-end latency under varying interface switch latency. (d) Distribution of switching latency in reactive FST.

packet and coordination handshake overhead at the radio is typically less than 2 ms. The implemented FST manager is a user level daemon, which runs on top of the kernel's bonding driver and triggers interface switching upon 60 GHz link disconnection. Our measurements show that the time elapsed between FST trigger and completion is on median 180 ms in our platform. This high latency is specific to the off-the-shelf platform and mainly attributed to the overheads of initiating a new session, various OS and firmware level message exchanges and under-optimized software implementation.

Impact of overheads on TCP. Unfortunately, such interface switching cost can severely degrade TCP performance. We experimentally evaluate the impact, by modifying our kernel's bonding driver to artificially add controlled delays, when switching between interfaces. Figure 3(c) shows how TCP's end-to-end latency is affected by various interface switching latencies. While the increase of the TCP's end-to-end latency after introducing 5 ms switching latency is almost negligible, we observe that TCP performs poorly when the switching latency goes beyond 10 ms. For example, a 100 ms switching latency can exacerbate end-to-end latency by more than 500 ms. This is because all the TCP packets are dropped during interface switching, resulting in packet retransmissions and congestion window shrinkage.

Limitations of reactive FST. Besides minimizing interface switching costs, an important design decision is when to trigger FST. The off-the-shelf platform takes a reactive approach and switches to WiFi, only after 60 GHz link gets disconnected based on a link timeout. For example, Figure 4 shows the switching procedure of our platform's FST, in a scenario where 60 GHz link breaks, before the 9.5^{th} second. It takes approximately 2.26 seconds for the FST to switch to WiFi. Specifically, the 60 GHz firmware and RF front-end needs 2.08 seconds to decide the link disconnection, and send the disconnection event to the FST daemon. Upon disconnection, the switching cost is approximately 180 ms. Our experiments in 200 mobile scenarios show that, our platform's FST switching latency from 60 GHz to WiFi takes 1.2 to 11.7 seconds (*c.f.* Figure 3(d)). The median latency is 3.5 seconds, which is prohibitive for delay-sensitive applications. While an aggressive timeout may improve the switching latency, it will still suffer from high oscillation between interfaces. Besides, in a reactive approach, such timeout needs to be at least greater than the total time for 60 GHz link convergence.

Summary: High switching latencies ($\geq$ 10 ms) and reactive FST-trigger approaches can severely limit the adoption of 60 GHz in today's enterprise settings. *A proactive switching algorithm that can achieve sub-10 ms latency in switching is required for seamless, high-throughput connection.*

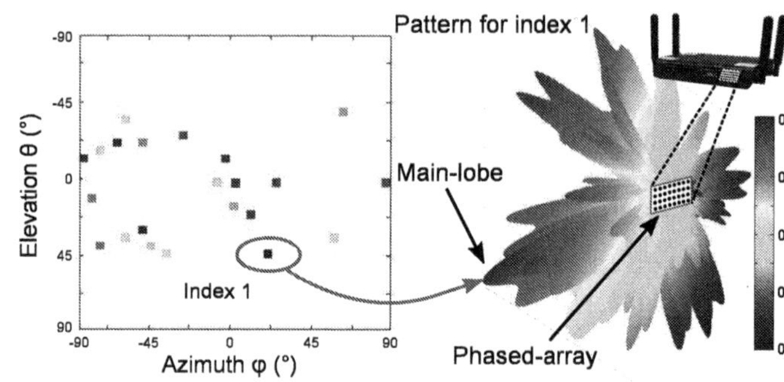

Figure 5: (a) Phased-array beam directions. (b) Measured 3D radiation pattern of beam index 1 ($G_1(\phi, \theta)$).

4 MUST DESIGN

MUST is an 802.11-compliant system that provides seamless, high-speed connectivity in dynamic indoor wireless networks. To overcome the limitations of existing designs, *MUST* sets 3 design goals. (1) *Fast 60 GHz link adaptation: MUST* seeks to instantaneously identify the best link setting at 60 GHz (beam and PHY rate) with zero probing overhead, thus evading the high link convergence time. (2) *Seamless, low-latency interface switching: MUST* aims to *proactively* migrate flows to WiFi, when 60 GHz link establishment is not feasible due to blockage, ensuring robust connectivity. It targets for seamless, sub-10 ms interface switching latency, to prevent disruptions of latency-sensitive applications. (3) *Standard compatibility:* Commodity 60 GHz and WiFi devices provide limited access/control of low-layers, and the protocol/hardware design represents a compromise between cost and performance. *MUST* thus needs to be lightweight and respect the standard constraints.

In the next sections, we describe *MUST* link adaptation (Section 4.2.1) and seamless interface switching algorithms (Section 4.2.2). We first start with a primer on 60 GHz phased-array beamforming on off-the-shelf platforms.

4.1 A Primer on Phased-Array Beamforming

A phased-array consists of a set of quasi-omni planar antenna elements arranged in a geometrical pattern (linear or rectangular). Different sets of antenna configuration weights are applied to the elements to form directional beam patterns. For example, consider a 1-D linear array of N antenna elements (with uniform separation of d between them) that can generate K beam patterns. The pattern of the kth beam is characterized by its *array-factor* (gain at azimuth direction ϕ) [56] and can be expressed as:

$$G_k(\phi) = \sum_{n=1}^{N} c(n,k) \cdot e^{(j2\pi n d cos\phi/\lambda)} \quad (1)$$

where λ is the wavelength of the wireless signal and $c(n,k)$ denotes the configuration weight (discrete phase and amplitude) applied to the nth element to generate k^{th} beam. The weights are designed to boost the signal strength towards a desired azimuth direction through phase-construction, while canceling signals towards unintended directions [56]. Note that, each of the *beam pattern* $G_k(\phi)$ is known and fixed once the phased-array antenna and weights are designed.

Since our 60 GHz AP platform supports a 2-D phased array (4×8 matrix), it allows directional beam generation towards various azimuth (ϕ) and elevation (θ) directions, each with gain pattern $G_k(\phi, \theta)$. For example, Figure 5(a) shows the strongest directions (*i.e.* main lobe) for a few beams in our AP. Each dot in the figure represents the desired direction of the beams (obtained from vendor's datasheet), where azimuth 0° and elevation 0° represent the orthogonal direction to the phased-array antenna's plane. Different from common perception, the beams generated via discrete antenna configurations cannot achieve perfect cone shapes. To keep the 60 GHz hardware design simple and cost-effective [47, 56, 61], practical phased arrays only employ limited phase granularity control on each element[5], which limits their ability to appropriately cancel signals towards unintended directions. To understand this issue, we followed the procedure in [34] and used an off-the-shelf 60 GHz signal strength sniffer (Vubiq PEM-003 with 3° horn antenna [36]) to measure the beam radiation pattern. We connect the AP to a 3 m away user in open LOS and place the sniffer 1.5 m from the AP. We further modified the 60 GHz kernel driver in the AP to use only transmit beam index 1 for communication. Then, we rotate the AP along azimuth and elevation plane at 3° interval. Along each interval, we generate saturated TCP traffic and measured strength of emitted signal from AP. Figure 5(b) shows measured 3D beam pattern for the beam index 1. Although the main lobe points to desired 20° azimuth and 45° elevation, there are multiple side-lobes that emit strong spurious signals to several unintended directions.

Phased-array and 60 GHz channel interaction. 60 GHz wireless channel is known to be sparse, consisting of a single dominating LOS path, and very few weak reflection paths between the transmitter and receiver [9, 44, 46, 51, 54, 60]. The former is often orders of magnitude stronger [47, 54, 64].

The phased-array beam pattern (*e.g.* Figure 5(b)) simply acts as a directional amplifier of the 60 GHz channel. When a peak lobe of the beam $G_k(\phi, \theta)$ aligns with the dominating path, the strongest channel can be created. So, the best beam k^* is the one that amplifies the channel either through its main lobe or side lobes, *i.e.*,

$$k^* = \underset{k \in \{1...K\}}{argmax} \; \sum_{\phi,\theta} G_k(\phi, \theta) \cdot D(\phi, \theta) \quad (2)$$

[5] Phased-array on our AP allows 2-bit phase control per elements that can generate 4 possible phase values *i.e.* {0°, 90°, 180°, 270°}.

where $D(\phi, \theta)$ denotes the complex channel gain along azimuth ϕ and elevation θ, *w.r.t.* AP's phased-array. Whenever the dominating path between AP and user changes either due to mobility or blockage, they need to find the new best beam k^*.

4.2 Predictable 60 GHz Performance

4.2.1 Tracking the Best Beam

Unlike existing millimeter-wave channel estimation approaches [6, 47, 54], the key goal of *MUST* is to track the dominating path between the 60 GHz transmitter and receiver, without requiring any additional 60 GHz probing, or any modifications to the off-the-shelf hardware. *MUST* predictability stems from the observation that other paths, when present, are order of magnitude weaker than the dominating path [47, 54, 64]. Thus, by simply tracking the change in the dominating path, *MUST* can predict the best beam direction and strength with reasonable accuracy. *MUST* further employs an error tracking mechanism for the prediction and LOS path blockage detection in order to maintain robust connection.

To understand how the prediction works, suppose the peak dominating path lies at azimuth ϕ and elevation θ. The channel gain at (ϕ, θ) is $D(\phi, \theta)$. Then, consider that the device's motion causes the dominating path to shift by $(\Delta\phi, \Delta\theta)$ *w.r.t.* AP. As long as we can reliably estimate the shifts, we can predict the best beam by convolving the known beam patterns $G_k(\phi, \theta)$ with the new shifted dominating path. Formally, denote $D'(\phi + \Delta\phi, \theta + \Delta\theta)$ as the channel gain of the new dominating path, then *MUST* can find the best beam as:

$$k^* = \underset{k \in \{1...K\}}{argmax} \; \sum_{\phi,\theta} G_k(\phi, \theta) \cdot D'(\phi + \Delta\phi, \theta + \Delta\theta) \quad (3)$$

But *how to identify the shifted 60 GHz channel $D'(\phi + \Delta\phi, \theta + \Delta\theta)$, given that we can only measure the channel response of the current beam in use?* One possible solution is to use the out-of-band channel information from the WiFi antennas co-located in the same AP, as proposed in BBS [35]. At a high level, BBS uses WiFi CSI to estimate the absolute (ϕ, θ), which corresponds to the angle with the dominating path. Then, it selects the best beam whose main lobe is geometrically closest to (ϕ, θ). But BBS assumes a one-to-one mapping between the angular channel profile of the WiFi and 60 GHz channels, which works fine when 60 GHz devices use mechanical horn antennas [35]. However, this assumption does not hold in practical 60 GHz systems that use phased-array antennas. This is because, the 60 GHz beam direction closest to the dominating path does not necessarily yield the strongest channel. For example, the signal strength map in Figure 6(a) (top) computed by MUSIC [49] from WiFi CSI samples collected in our 3-antenna AP shows the dominating path at azimuth -64° and elevation 2°. However, the best 60 GHz beam lies at azimuth -87° and elevation -11°, as shown in Figure 6(c) (bottom), where each dot represents the main direction of the 60 GHz beam and color is its signal strength. This is because the dominating path of 60 GHz channel may not completely align with any of the available beams' main lobes, but may align with arbitrary side-lobes (Figure 5(b)), which creates the best beam spatially away from dominating direction. Also, searching for the best beam within a cluster of angular positions specified by WiFi's angular profile may not yield the best beam either.

MUST adopts a different principle: it tries to identify the angular shift of the 60 GHz dominating path from the successive time-domain spatial snapshots of the WiFi channel, and then find the 60 GHz best beam using Eq. (3). Following the foregoing example, Figure 6(b) shows the WiFi signal strength map when the device's azimuth shifts by 30° *w.r.t.* AP. Then, the successive analysis of the WiFi spatial snapshots (Figures 6(a) and 6(b)) can be used to potentially estimate the shift of 30° in the azimuth direction. Specifically, if W_1 denotes the WiFi angular profile at time t_1 and W_2 at time t_2, then the device's angular shift (equivalent to the shift of dominating path) is:

$$\{\Delta\phi, \Delta\theta\} = \underset{\Delta\phi,\Delta\theta}{argmin} \quad |W_1(\phi,\theta) - W_2(\phi+\Delta\phi, \theta+\Delta\theta)|^2$$

i.e., the angular shift can be derived from the translation of the second angular profile W_2 that best matches the first one W_1. In order to avoid abrupt error from measurement of WiFi spatial channel, *MUST* applies a time-domain linear filter on the estimated azimuth shift (with α = 0.3), *i.e.*,

$$\Delta\phi(t+1) = \alpha \cdot \Delta\phi(t) + (1-\alpha) \cdot \Delta\phi(t+1)$$

A same filter is applied on the estimated elevation shift as well. Note that, the shift of the dominating direction is not enough to find the best beam, since the strength of the dominating direction may also have changed. *MUST* applies a "reverse engineering" model on the current beam's measured gain, to detect such gain change. Specifically, if $|h_k|$ is the measured gain of the current beam k, and $|h_k^m|$ is the modeled response with the shifted dominating path, then *MUST* finds the new gain of the dominating path:

$$\begin{aligned} D'^{*}(\phi+\Delta\phi, \theta+\Delta\theta) &= \underset{D'}{argmin} ||h_k| - |h_k^m||^2 \\ |h_k^m| &= |\textstyle\sum_{\phi,\theta} G_k(\phi,\theta) \cdot D'(\phi+\Delta\phi, \theta+\Delta\theta)| \end{aligned} \tag{4}$$

Said differently, with the shifted dominating direction, *MUST* searches through the possible gain change in the direction by modeling the current beam's gain and matching with the measured gain. Finally, after estimating $D'^{*}(\phi+\Delta\phi, \theta+\Delta\theta)$ it applies Eq. (3) to identify the best beam and the SNR.

Dealing with multiple dominating paths. Our design builds upon the fundamental principle of 60 GHz channel sparsity [9, 46, 51, 54, 57] and assumes one dominating LOS path, while the side paths have order of magnitude lower signal strength. The same assumption has been adopted and validated by existing beam searching algorithm [47]. Occasionally, in open LOS, there could be additional 1 or 2 paths from strong reflectors near to the device (*e.g.* side concrete wall). Since, *MUST* uses an approximate single path model to find the best beam, it may result in inaccurate prediction. Thus, *MUST* introduces an error tracking mechanism in its prediction. Specifically, it tracks the difference between the current beam's gain h_k with the predicted gain h_k^m as: $\epsilon = ||h_k| - |h_k^m||^2$ (from Eq. (4)). When our prediction error exceeds a threshold ($\epsilon > E_t$) – *e.g.* in the presence of multiple dominant paths – then *MUST* will trigger an IEEE 802.11ad scan to recover the best beam. We empirically set the threshold E_t to 1.5 dB, which is the average SNR separation between two PHY rate options [24]. Our model has limitation to find the best beam, when

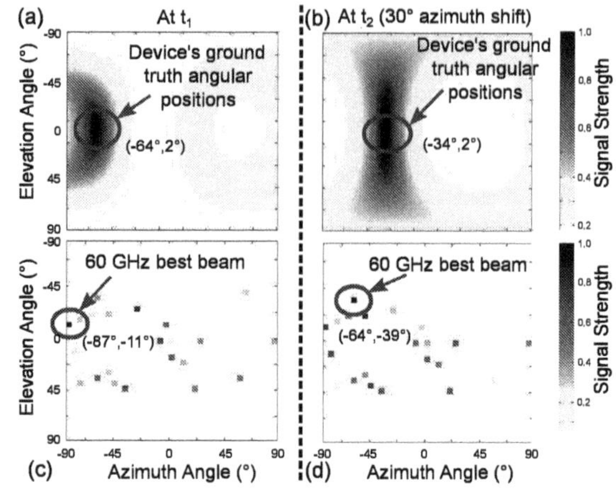

Figure 6: WiFi (top) and 60 GHz (bottom) spatial maps.

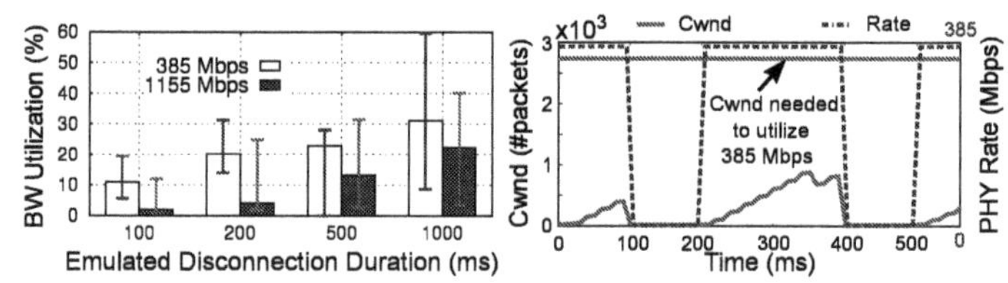

Figure 7: TCP's reaction under occassional disconnections: (a) BW utilization. (b) Congestion window evolution.

60 GHz LOS path is blocked. Typically, in such cases, 60 GHz performance drops by multiple Gbps, with rampant link disconnections. *MUST* devises a proactive blockage adaptation scheme to address this challenge, as we discuss next.

4.2.2 Proactive LOS Blockage Adaptation

When LOS blockage occurs at 60 GHz, multiple reflection paths may exist, but even the beam with the strongest channel *does not guarantee that the 60 GHz link can sustain the connection* (*c.f.* Section 3, [54, 64]). Thus, *MUST* isolates the NLOS case and handles it separately. It applies a probabilistic blockage model to identify a hint of LOS blockage, and switches to WiFi without wasting time, scanning for alternative 60 GHz beams.

LOS blockage reaction. The above design choice is based on our measurement observation that, during LOS blockage, even if 60 GHz link may intermittently offer higher PHY rate than WiFi, it is highly unstable and can have rampant disconnections with zero throughput lasting several hundred ms. Such instability is more harmful to higher layer protocols than a mediocre or even congested but stable WiFi link.

To understand this issue in detail, we set up a controlled experiment, where the AP sends saturated TCP traffic to a user over 60 GHz. Then, we emulate occasional 60 GHz link disconnections by dropping packets for a controlled time-duration at the radio. Figure 7(a) shows the effective bandwidth utilization (*i.e.* ratio of the achieved throughput over the max throughput) of TCP, under such disconnections. For occasional 100 ms disconnections, TCP's bandwidth utilization is hardly 10%, when 60 GHz rate varies from 385 Mbps (minimum PHY rate at 60 GHz) to 0 Mbps. The utilization further drops below 2%, when the rate shows a large drop from 1155 Mbps to 0 Mbps.

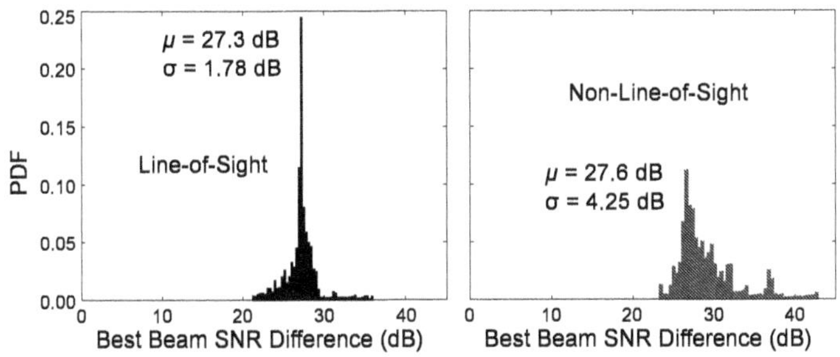

Figure 8: PDF of SNR difference between 60 GHz best beam and WiFi best path: (*a*) 300 LOS; (*b*) 150 NLOS locations.

Such poor performance in NLOS is attributed to TCP's congestion window adaptation (Figure 7(*b*)), which does not get enough time to explore the available bandwidth when the link becomes open. For example, Figure 7(*b*) shows that to utilize the 385 Mbps open link, the congestion window need to converge to approximately 2900 packets. However, link gets fully disconnected by the time it reaches hardly 800 packets. We next show how to proactively detect such blockage and switch to WiFi, to achieve a smooth real-time response at the upper layer.

LOS blockage detection. *MUST* LOS blockage detection scheme is based on the findings in [10, 53], which show that the same obstacles and NLOS reflectors have a distinct effect on signal strength change of 60 GHz and WiFi because of the frequency difference. This is also resonated in our measurements, presented in Figure 8. When the LOS is open, the signal strength difference distribution (shown in Figure 8(*a*)) between 60 GHz best beam and WiFi best path closely matches the hardware power budget difference of 27 dB that includes transmit power, beamforming gain and noise power difference between 60 GHz and WiFi interface. However, when the LOS is blocked, the difference shows higher variations (Figure 8(*b*)). This is because: (1) The same obstacle attenuates the signal strength of 60 GHz and WiFi differently, and (2) The same NLOS reflector causes distinct reflection loss on 60 GHz and WiFi signal, due to the disparate wavelengths and penetration/scattering properties [10].

MUST can identify LOS blockage by comparing the SNR between the 60 GHz beam and the best WiFi path. Once strong blockage occurs, the SNR difference diverges significantly from the hardware link budget difference, creating a signature for such blockage effect. Algorithm 1 formalizes the detection procedure. Specifically, *MUST* tracks the difference of the SNR of 60 GHz best beam and WiFi best path for a small interval Δt. To calculate the best path strength at WiFi, *MUST* selects the CSI of the WiFi antenna that is physically closest to the 60 GHz phased-array antenna, and uses the strongest tap strength of its power-delay profile. Ideally, in open LOS this difference should follow the fixed hardware link budget difference with a high probability. *MUST* thus tracks this difference and declares *LOS blockage* when the difference rises beyond a threshold σ (empirically set to 3 dB). To prevent false blockage detection, *MUST* further monitors the 60 GHz PHY rate, where an average rate below minimum PHY rate is an additional blockage hint.

Addressing false switching. *MUST* blockage detection scheme may falsely trigger interface switching. For example, Algorithm 1 may falsely switch a user to WiFi, when the 60 GHz dominant LOS path is blocked, while reflection paths from strong reflectors allows 60 GHz to outperform WiFi. Further, such false positive may also occur when multipath at WiFi cancel each other and the difference between 60 GHz beam and WiFi best path becomes significantly lower than the hardware link budget. However, *MUST* can rapidly recover from false positives, by intermittently performing IEEE 802.11ad beam scan while serving the user at WiFi. When IEEE 802.11ad scans indicate high 60 GHz performance, *MUST* will switch user to 60 GHz. Furthermore, we will later show that average performance loss due to the false switching is very low (less than 6% on average) mainly due to the fact 60 GHz is worse than WiFi most of the time, when the LOS is blocked.

Algorithm 1 *LOS Blockage Detection*

1: Parameters: α = 385 Mbps; Δt = 5 ms; μ = 27 dB; σ = 3 dB;
2: [] —— *During each interval* Δt *I do:*
3: Best beam SNR $B_k \leftarrow$ *MUST* prediction;
4: Best path SNR P_k of WiFi $\leftarrow$ *max IFFT*(CSI_{WiFi});
5: $C \leftarrow C \cup |\mu - |B_k - P_k||$;
6: Measure average PHY rate $\widehat{R}$;
7: [] —— *At the end of interval I do:*
8: **if** $\widehat{R} < \alpha$ **and** *mean*(C) $> \sigma$ **then** Switch to WiFi;
9: **else** $C \leftarrow \Phi$; Continue from 2;

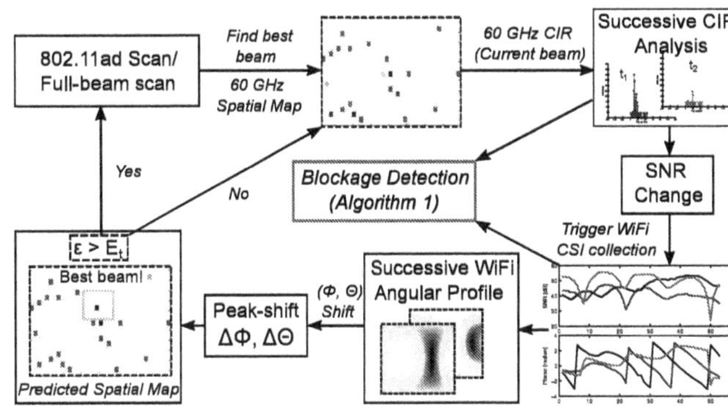

Figure 9: *MUST* prediction flow.

4.3 Practical Interface Switching

Leveraging its prediction model, *MUST* allows the 60 GHz link to *instantaneously* converge to the best beam and rate setting and *proactively* switch to the WiFi interface before the link suffers from catastrophic degradation. Figure 9 summarizes the entire prediction flow for *MUST*. At run-time, *MUST* starts with existing IEEE 802.11ad beam scan to identify the single dominating LOS path and use the best beam for communication with the user device. When the performance of the current beam in use changes (*e.g.* as indicated by SNR change of the beam), *MUST* triggers to collect the out-of-band WiFi channel information. It sends probe packets to the user from the WiFi interface and measures the channel response of the received ACK. Since a probe packet is small (less than 50 bytes), the average time to probe and collect WiFi CSI from ACK is typically 1∼2 ms. Then, *MUST* uses its prediction model to identify the best beam direction and strength. Further, it employs the error tracking mechanism to

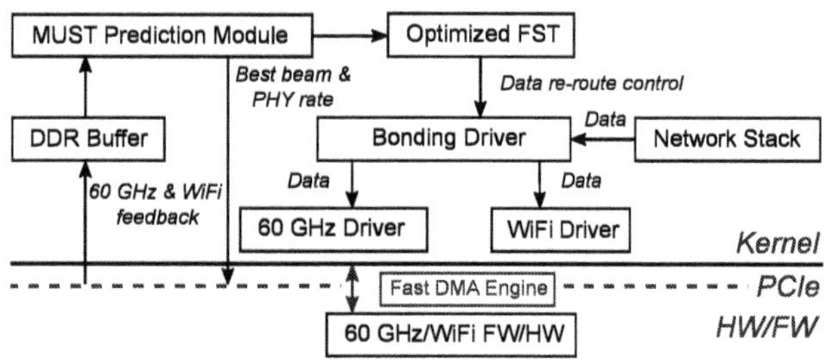

Figure 10: *MUST* system architecture.

recover from inaccurate prediction. In parallel, *MUST* employs Algorithm 1 to detect LOS blockage at 60 GHz and switch to WiFi. While operating at WiFi, *MUST* relies on existing IEEE 802.11ad beam-searching to switch traffic flows to the 60 GHz interface. Current *MUST* design is focused on AP-side adaptation, since the enterprise networks are mainly downlink (AP to user) dominated. Further, enterprise 60 GHz user devices use quasi-omni broad beams for data reception to reduce sensitivity. However, a similar adaptation can also be applied from the user side to adapt its own beam direction.

Optimizing FST. The actual flow migration between the 60 GHz and WiFi interface is realized by adopting and optimizing the IEEE 802.11ad FST feature (*c.f.* Section 2.2), which can avoid breaking the existing connections. Our platform implements IEEE 802.11ad FST over Linux's bonding driver [16], to expose a single virtual IP/MAC address towards the network stack. While the entire FST protocol to switch from 60 GHz to WiFi (including coordination and handshake) can finish within 1.5-2 ms, our measurements show that the platform requires approximately 180 ms (*c.f.* Section 3.4.2) for such operation. This is for two reasons: (1) On disconnection from 60 GHz RF front-end, current under-optimized firmware-kernel implementation still takes additional median 120 ms for message exchanges, hardware and software queuing delays and trigger FST daemon; (2) On trigger and completion of FST protocol, the daemon takes additional 60 ms to complete the virtual MAC switch at the Linux bonding driver, and reroute the packets to WiFi interface. This latency further degrades TCP's end-to-end latency (Section 3.4.2). We optimize the FST daemon and bonding driver to overcome this latency. Specifically, we generate software interrupt to the FST daemon, when Algorithm 1 detects the signature of blockage without waiting for RF disconnection from 60 GHz firmware. We further modified the bonding driver and use WiFi as backup slave instead of rehauling the virtual MAC of the active slave (*i.e.* 60 GHz). We will evaluate the effectiveness of our optimized FST with *MUST* proactive switch in Section 6.1.3. Note that, both the 60 GHz and WiFi radios employ their own power adaptation and sleep scheduling to reduce total power consumptions. An aggressive power adaptation from the user device may affect the completion time of IEEE 802.11ad FST control and coordination handshake procedure, though we found little variation throughout our experiments. We leave the detailed study of the power adaptation on *MUST* system design as our future work.

5 IMPLEMENTATION

We implement *MUST* on the commodity 60 GHz and WiFi AP without any modification to the end-user devices. Our implementation spreads across our AP's kernel and firmware, as shown in Figure 10. *MUST* software architecture is built on top of the existing open source OpenWrt [4] design, while the hardware architecture of our platform including the 60 GHz RF front-end (Section 3.1) is similar to all existing off-the-shelf tri-band platforms (*e.g.* [30]). Thus, our *MUST* design and implementation can be directly extended to any off-the-shelf tri-band platforms. The most important modifications are as follows: (1) We added suitable hooks to both kernel and firmware sides to read periodic stats from both 60 GHz and WiFi radios, and extract them in DDR buffer. The stats feed our *MUST* prediction module. We further launch adaptation commands to commit the selected beam and rate, to the 60 GHz firmware and hardware. (2) We modified our AP's existing FST daemon to handle the software interrupt from Algorithm 1, and appropriately modified the Linux's bonding driver to incorporate the practical interface switching. Note that, our platform does not allow us to trigger IEEE 802.11ad scans efficiently in real-time, which is required by our prediction algorithm. Hence, we compute the best beam and rate offline and then use the selected setting for our evaluation. We further replayed the PHY layer traces and prediction results in our platform to evaluate the switching algorithm, optimized FST and bonding driver implementation in real-time.

CPU core affinity: *MUST* runs on a multi-radio, multi-core CPU system architecture. Each wireless interface triggers interrupt request (IRQ) to notify the CPU, when a packet need to be served. The packets are copied in the kernel and user buffer for further processing. IRQ and packet processing affinity to CPU cores are critical to achieve optimal system's performance. *MUST* implements CPU core affinity based on the principle of minimizing communication required among cores, while keeping the cache hit ratio high for IRQ and packet processing modules' code and data [28]. Thus, *MUST* serves 60 GHz and WiFi packets at different cores, while assigning both IRQ and packet processing modules of an interface in the same core. We illustrate the importance of such "balanced" core affinity, by comparing it with an allocation where both 60 GHz and WiFi packet queues are processed by the same core and all IRQs are handled by another core. In our experiment, we generate saturated TCP traffic from an AP to a user at 60 GHz, while WiFi remains idle. Figure 11(a) shows the throughput (averaged over 500 ms intervals) distribution for "balanced" and "unbalanced" core affinity, where median throughput improvement is 47.3% under the former. Further, "balanced" distribution allows for more efficient CPU utilization and IRQs servicing. Figure 11(b) shows the CPU utilization and the IRQs serviced at 60 GHz, where "balanced" distribution improves utilization by average 12.8% and IRQ servicing by 54.8%.

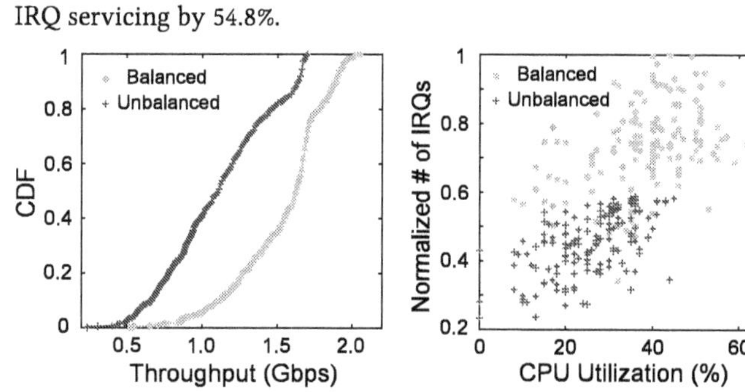

Figure 11: Effect of optimizing core affinity. (a) Throughput performance. (b) CPU utilization and serviced IRQs.

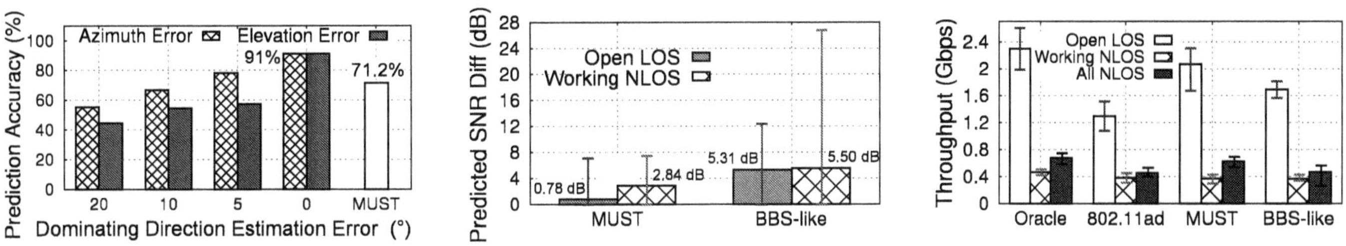

Figure 12: (a) **Best throughput beam prediction under dominating path estimation error and with *MUST*.** (b) **Predicted SNR difference of *MUST* and BBS under open LOS and working NLOS *w.r.t.* Oracle.** (c) **Throughput comparison under LOS (static and mobile), working NLOS (*i.e.* 60 GHz works) and all NLOS.**

6 EVALUATION

In this section, we evaluate *MUST* in various settings using testbed experiments and large-scale trace-driven emulation. We compare *MUST* with our platform's beam and rate selection algorithm (named as "802.11ad"), and with BBS [35]. We also compare *MUST* prediction with an "Oracle" solution which instantaneously converges to the best setting.

6.1 Micro-benchmarks

We first evaluate *MUST* along *three* key performance metrics: (1) How *accurately MUST* can predict the best quality beam? (2) How much *performance improvement MUST* can bring to 60 GHz link? (3) How *accurately MUST* can detect blockage and how *fast* it can switch from 60 GHz to WiFi?

6.1.1 Prediction Accuracy

Identifying best beam. We first evaluate how accurately *MUST* can zero in on the best quality beam, defined as the one which maximizes receiver's SNR. For our experiments, we mounted our AP on a 9 ft high tripod in the same enterprise setting, and placed a user device within 10×10 m^2 area (Figure 1). Then, we compare *MUST*'s beam prediction with Oracle, in multiple static, LOS and NLOS scenarios. We find the Oracle (optimal) beam, by scanning every transmit beam for each static point, and pick the one with highest receiver's SNR. Figure 12(a) shows that *MUST* can predict the best beam with 71.2% accuracy compared to Oracle. The root causes for inaccurate prediction are twofold. First, *MUST* may not always precisely track the 60 GHz dominant path, and may end up converging to suboptimal beams. We investigate how such tracking errors affect prediction accuracy, by artificially introducing errors (*i.e.* shift in azimuth and elevation direction) in the measured dominating direction which varies from 5° to 20°. Figure 12(a) shows even an error of 10° can drop the overall prediction accuracy by over 30%. This is because the dominating direction itself typically spans over a small angular spread of <10° [60]. Second, *MUST* approximates the entire 60 GHz channel using a single dominating direction. Even an accurate dominant direction tracking (0° error) that models single path, can at best achieve 91% accuracy. However, *MUST* error tracking and blockage detection mechanisms can recover such inaccurate predictions.

Beam quality prediction. We further evaluate how accurately *MUST* can predict user's SNR compared to Oracle, for the LOS and NLOS settings described above. Figure 12(b) shows that in LOS, *MUST* average prediction error lies within 0.78 dB. Since, 60 GHz PHY rate options are on average separated by 1.5 dB signal strength, this error has a negligible effect on achievable throughput performance of *MUST*, as we will show later. We further compare BBS [35] under the same setup. Since, BBS can not directly predict the signal strength, we calibrate the WiFi peak direction signal strength with the hardware link budget difference between 60 GHz and WiFi. BBS's prediction error is significantly higher and exceeds 5 dB on average for both LOS and NLOS settings, resulting in erroneous rate selection. In NLOS, the error from *MUST* prediction can be higher (average 2.84 dB), however, in most NLOS cases it will trigger IEEE 802.11ad scans to recover from such errors.

6.1.2 Throughput Gain from Prediction

We next evaluate the throughput gains of *MUST* over 802.11ad and BBS achieved from selecting best beam and rate. Since BBS does not specify any rate adaptation algorithm, we use our platform's default one. To perform a fair comparison, we assume that BBS will switch to WiFi when 60 GHz PHY rate drops below minimum PHY rate. Figure 12(c) shows that *MUST* achieves on average 25% and 60% gains over BBS and 802.11ad in LOS, while it remains close to 10% to Oracle. In working NLOS cases (where 60 GHz is still the best interface), *MUST* performs similar to BBS and 802.11ad, and achieves within 20% from the Oracle. This is because in such scenarios, the existence of multiple dominating paths may lead to inaccurate beam and rate prediction, and thus *MUST* will frequently fallback to 802.11ad. In all NLOS, including where 60 GHz links are blocked, all algorithms will eventually switch to WiFi. *MUST* can almost instantaneously switch to WiFi achieving 34% and 39% throughput gains over BBS and 802.11ad, respectively. Note that, original BBS as described in [35] does not have such interface switching capability, and thus in practice it will achieve zero throughput, when 60 GHz links break.

6.1.3 Blockage Detection and Fast Switching

We now evaluate efficacy of *MUST* to detect LOS blockage (Algorithm 1) and switch to WiFi.

Accuracy and false detection. We conduct a simple experiment with TCP traffic from an AP to a user device. The user moves along a fixed trajectory for 15 seconds within the 10×10 m^2 area. The trajectory consists of approximately 1/3 blockage and 2/3 open LOS to the AP. Since, finding the optimal performing interface in mobile scenario is difficult, we emulate the mobility by statically positioning the user device along the fixed trajectory and measure the maximum throughput achieved from both 60 GHz and WiFi interfaces. Then we run Algorithm 1 to decide the best performing interface. We define accurate decision as the cases in which *MUST* chose the highest

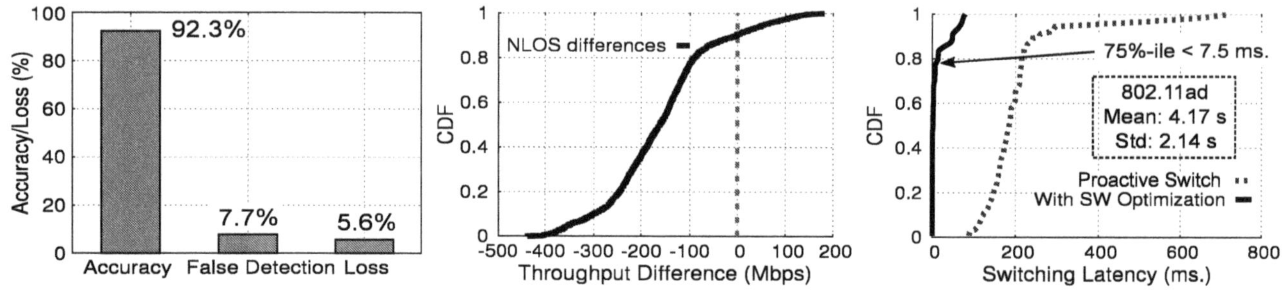

Figure 13: **Blockage detection & switching:** (*a*) **Accuracy, false detection and throughput loss.** (*b*) **Throughput difference between 60 GHz and WiFi in all NLOS.** (*c*) **Interface switching latency under proactive switch and with software optimization.**

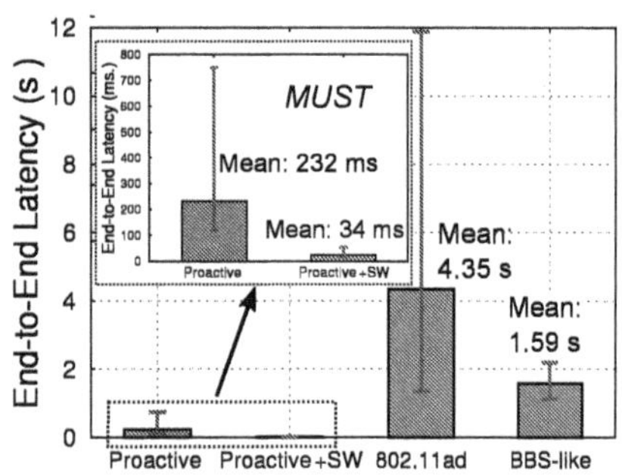

Figure 15: TCP end-to-end latency with *MUST*.

throughput interface. Figure 13(*a*) shows that in 92.3% of the cases, *MUST* can accurately detect the best performing interface. Although, the heuristic nature of Algorithm 1 can result in average 7.7% false detections, the average throughput loss is below 6% compared to Oracle. This is because, in NLOS, 60 GHz performs worse than WiFi most of the times. Specifically, we observe that in less than 10% of the NLOS (out of more than 200 NLOS locations), 60 GHz outperforms WiFi as shown in Figure 13(*b*). *MUST* never falsely switches to WiFi in open LOS, since it monitors the 60 GHz PHY rate, which remains well above 385 Mbps in LOS (*c.f.* Algorithm 1).

Switching latency improvement. Blockage detection triggers optimized FST of *MUST*. We next evaluate the switching latency of our fast switching (described in Section 4.3) in multiple blockage scenarios. Figure 13(*c*) shows that switching latency is bounded by 7.5 ms in 75%-ile of the cases with standard deviation of 1.46 ms. The latency deviation is attributed to our platform's OS and firmware related idiosyncrasies[6]. We believe this latency can be further minimized with tighter control over 60 GHz firmware which is currently unavailable in the platform. *MUST* achieves almost 2 orders of magnitude improvement from off-the-shelf 802.11ad solution that has an average 4.17 s switching latency.

TCP performance under fast switch. The proactive, low-latency FST of *MUST* design brings benefit to the higher layer applications. We measure TCP's end-to-end latency for *MUST*, 802.11ad and BBS. End-to-end latency is measured as *RTT*/2 for the single hop connection. Figure 15 shows that *MUST* proactive interface switching (without the FST software optimization) reduces the 802.11ad solution's average TCP end-to-end latency from 4.35 s to 232 ms. The

[6]Proactive switch without the software optimization still suffers from high latency (median 180 ms) due to the off-the-shelf platforms' poor driver implementation (*c.f.* dotted line in Figure 13(c)).

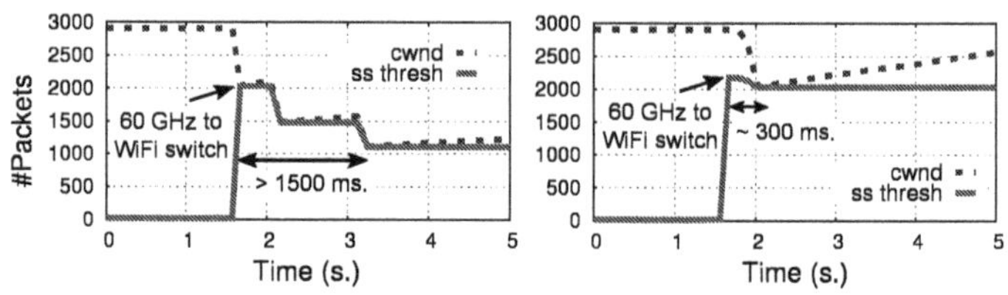

Figure 16: TCP congestion window and slow start threshold under: (*a*) **Proactive switch.** (*b*) **With software optimization.**

software optimization brings additional benefit to *MUST*, and further drops the average end-to-end latency to 34 ms. The additional benefit is further reflected in TCP's congestion window adaptation. Specifically, Figure 16(*a*) shows that, the additional latency introduced by the non-optimized switch, will increase TCP dropped packets, and will affect the TCP congestion window and slow start threshold. While under an optimized switch (Figure 16(*b*)), congestion window can quickly start to converge within 300 ms, non-optimized implementation introduces larger delay (> 1.5 s).

6.2 Field Trials

Our experiments so far have been focused on single AP-user settings. We next evaluate *MUST* in more realistic field trials conducted in an enterprise (Figure 1) and campus buildings, where various sources of dynamics including environment mobility and WiFi interferences coexist in a complex manner.

TCP throughput. Figure 14(*a*) compares *MUST*, BBS and 802.11ad in settings where an AP generates saturated downlink TCP traffic to a varying number (one to three) of static and mobile users with pedestrian walking speed (xU/yM implies y mobile out of the total x users). Our results show that *MUST* throughput gains increase during users' mobility. When all the users are mobile (1U/1M, 2U/2M & 3U/3M), *MUST* achieves on average 45% and 48% throughput gains over BBS and 802.11ad, respectively. However, for static LOS users, BBS and 802.11ad can converge to the best beam and rate setting, reducing *MUST* gains.

We further elaborate on *MUST* gains under mobility, by monitoring a user's TCP throughput in a 15 s mobile trace, presented in Figure 14(*b*). Initially, all the algorithms operate on 60 GHz and achieve more than 1.6 Gbps average throughput. Between 6th and 6.5^{th} second, 60 GHz link breaks. While *MUST* instantaneously switches to WiFi, BBS and 802.11ad require roughly 3.5 s to switch interface, achieving zero throughput during the switch.

UDP gains. We further compare *MUST* with BBS and 802.11ad in our field-trial settings with saturated UDP traffic. In order to effectively

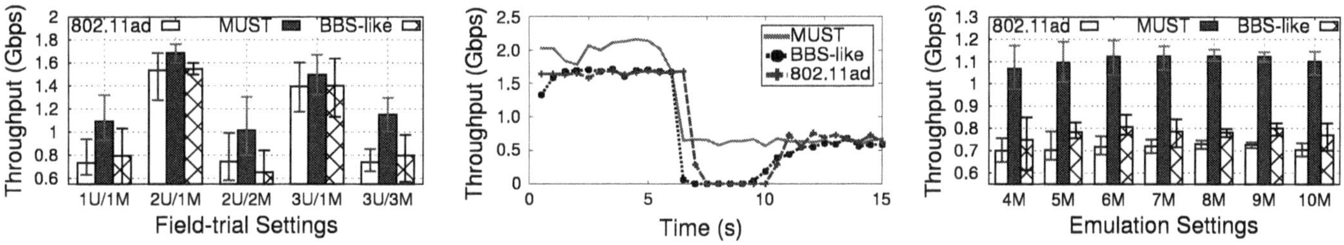

Figure 14: *MUST*, BBS and 802.11ad comparison in field-trial and trace-driven emulation: (*a*) Field-trial throughput with static and mobile users. (*b*) Example mobility trace for a 15 s walk (pedestrian speed). (*c*) Emulated multi-user throughput performance.

Algorithm Comparison	Gain (%) Median	Max	Min
vs. 802.11ad	49.3	58.0	43.8
vs. BBS-like	45.6	57.7	28.3

Table 1: *MUST* UDP gains in the field-trial settings.

use the Gbps 60 GHz link speed, we configure the UDP settings at both AP and user side to support jumbo frames and larger transport layer socket buffer following [33]. *MUST* achieves 49.3% and 45.6% median UDP throughput gain over the 802.11ad and BBS respectively (Table 1). Similar to TCP, *MUST* achieves highest gain during mobility due to faster link adaptation and WiFi switching.

Trace-driven emulation. We finally resort to trace-driven emulation to evaluate larger topologies with up to 10 users. We consider mobile users or moving obstacles in users' physical environment. Figure 14(*c*) shows that *MUST* achieves on average 42% and 55% TCP throughput gains over BBS and 802.11ad across all the settings. Moreover, we observe that in such dynamic environments, the number of users connected to the AP does not considerably affect *MUST* gains.

7 RELATED WORK

Millimeter-wave measurements and modeling. Properties of the millimeter-wave wireless channel, including the effects of environmental reflection and human blockage have been well studied through measurements or statistical models [9, 10, 15, 22]. It has been observed that the millimeter-wave channel is sparse, *i.e.*, there exist only a few paths between the transmitter and receiver. Such sparsity results in fragile 60 GHz links, during blockage and mobility [51, 53, 54, 64]. However, it creates a unique opportunity for a predictive model of link performance, as shown in *MUST*.

Cross-band channel prediction. Recent works [50, 55] harnessed wireless channel correlation across frequency bands to predict channel quality. For example, CSpy [50] built a machine learning model that implicitly captures such correlation to infer best quality alternative WiFi channel without probing. R2-F2 [55] enables LTE base stations to infer the downlink channel by observing the uplink channels from the same user. BBS [35] leveraged the WiFi channel to narrow down 60 GHz beam search space, which works fine for systems using mechanical horn antennas. *MUST* on the other hand can instantaneously predict the best beam and PHY rate settings for practical 60 GHz systems employing phased-array beamforming.

60 GHz link adaptation. Many millimeter-wave systems [6, 47, 54] explored ways of estimating 60 GHz beam quality, with minimum measurement overhead. BeamSpy [54] models the 60 GHz channel using a discrete set of signal paths and can instantaneously predict the best alternative beam under blockage. But it is applicable only for quasi-stationary links. AgileLink [6] hashes the beam directions, and quickly identifies the best path by tracking how the energy changes across different hash functions. However, it requires fine-grained phase control over the antenna elements, whereas standard off-the-shelf 60 GHz devices (including our platform) only support 2-4 bit phase control [47]. Compressive sensing based approaches have also been proposed for tracking the 60 GHz paths [32, 47, 62], but they require customized beaconing signals, and the high computational latency may neutralize the saving of beam searching overhead.

Multi-radio collaboration. Existing work on multi-radio collaboration at lower frequency bands has been focused on: traffic management among interfaces (*e.g.*, data offloading across LTE and WiFi) [11, 13, 29, 31, 41], mobility management [42], energy efficiency [7, 37–39], and routing in multi-band mesh networks [8, 19, 52]. Different from these efforts, *MUST* is the first one to explore the principles of coordination between two completely disparate technologies: 60 GHz and WiFi. The huge bit-rate gaps, signal coverage patterns and distinct sensitivities to blockage and mobility together render traditional solutions (*e.g.*, MPTCP, probe-and-adapt) ineffective.

8 CONCLUSION

In this paper, we explore the possibility of leveraging the existing WiFi technology to design high-performance, robust 60 GHz wireless networks. To this end, we design and implement *MUST* using standard, off-the-shelf hardware that provides seamless, high-speed connectivity in highly dynamic 60 GHz indoor environments. *MUST* introduces a WiFi-assisted 60 GHz link adaptation module that can instantaneously predict the best 60 GHz beam and PHY rate setting. It further designs a proactive switching algorithm to achieve sub-10 ms switch to WiFi, allowing latency-sensitive traffic to run seamlessly over existing network stack. Our experimental results confirm high gain of *MUST* over state-of-the-art solutions. We consider *MUST* to be a key building block of 60 GHz WLANs, and an important component of next-generation 5G networks, which will consist of dense picocellular millimeter-wave deployments, alongside WiFi/LTE.

ACKNOWLEDGEMENT

We sincerely thank the anonymous reviewers and our shepherd David Chu for their valuable comments and feedback. Sanjib Sur and Xinyu Zhang were partially supported by the NSF under Grant CNS-1617321, CNS-1506657, CNS-1518728, CNS-1343363, and CNS-1350039 during this work.

REFERENCES

[1] FCC Promotes Higher Frequency Spectrum for Future Wireless Technology. https://apps.fcc.gov. 2015.

[2] Verizon applauds FCC chairman's move to 5G spectrum. http://www.fiercewireless.com/tech/verizon-applauds-fcc-chairman-s-move-to-5g-spectrum. 2015.

[3] Unlocking the Promise of Broadband for All Americans. https://obamawhitehouse.archives.gov/blog/2016/07/15/unlocking-promise-broadband-generate-gains-all-americans. 2016.

[4] OpenWrt Wireless Freedom. https://openwrt.org/. 2017.

[5] Omid Abari, Dinesh Bharadia, Austin Duffield, and Dina Katabi. Cutting the Cord in Virtual Reality. In *Proc. of ACM HotNets-XV.* 2016.

[6] Omid Abari, Haitham Hassanieh, Michael Rodreguez, and Dina Katabi. Millimeter Wave Communications: From Point-to-Point Links to Agile Network Connections. In *Proc. of ACM HotNets-XV.* 2016.

[7] Yuvraj Agarwal, Trevor Pering, Roy Want, and Rajesh Gupta. SwitchR: Reducing System Power Consumption in a Multi-Client, Multi-Radio Environment. In *IEEE International Symposium on Wearable Computers.* 2008.

[8] Mansoor Alicherry, Randeep Bhatia, and Li Erran Li. Joint Channel Assignment and Routing for Throughput Optimization in Multiradio Wireless Mesh Networks. *IEEE Journal on Selected Areas in Communications* Vol. 24, No. 11. 2006.

[9] C.R. Anderson and T.S. Rappaport. In-Building Wideband Partition Loss Measurements at 2.5 and 60 GHz. *IEEE Transactions on Wireless Communications* Vol. 3, No. 3. 2004.

[10] Christopher R. Anderson, Theodore S. Rappaport, Kyung Bae, Alex Verstak, Naren Ramakrishnan, William H. Tranter, Clifford A. Shaffer, and Layne T. Watson. In-Building Wideband Multipath Characteristics at 2.5 & 60 GHz. In *Proc. of IEEE VTC.* 2002.

[11] Aruba Networks, Inc. Carrier-Class Public WiFi for 3G/4G Offload. http://www.arubanetworks.com/pdf/solutions/SB_Offload.pdf. 2012.

[12] IEEE Standards Association. IEEE Standards 802.15.3c-2009: Millimeter-wave-based Alternate Physical Layer Extension. 2009.

[13] Mehdi Bennis, Meryem Simsek, Andreas Czylwik, Walid Saad, Stefan Valentin, and Merouane Debbah. When Cellular Meets WiFi in Wireless Small Cell Networks. *IEEE Communications Magazine* Vol. 51, No. 6. 2013.

[14] Ethan Blanton and Mark Allman. On Making TCP More Robust to Packet Reordering. In *Proc. of ACM SIGCOMM.* 2002.

[15] Sylvain Collonge, Gheorghe Zaharia, and Ghais El Zein. Influence of the Human Activity on Wide-Band Characteristics of the 60 GHz Indoor Radio Channel. *IEEE Transactions on Wireless Communications* Vol. 3, No. 6. 2004.

[16] Thomas Davis. Linux Ethernet Bonding Driver HOWTO. www.kernel.org. 2011.

[17] Dell Inc. Latitude 12 5000 Series (E5250). http://www.dell.com/en-us/work/shop/productdetails/latitude-e5250-laptop. 2016.

[18] Shuo Deng, Ravi Netravali, Anirudh Sivaraman, and Hari Balakrishnan. WiFi, LTE, or Both? Measuring Multi-Homed Wireless Internet Performance. In *Proc. of ACM IMC.* 2014.

[19] Richard Draves, Jitendra Padhye, and Brian Zill. Routing in Multi-Radio, Multi-Hop Wireless Mesh Networks. In *Proc. of ACM MobiCom.* 2004.

[20] ECMA International. Standard ECMA-387: High Rate 60 GHz PHY, MAC and PALs. 2010.

[21] Simone Ferlin, Thomas Dreibholz, and Ozg Alay. Multi-Path Transport Over Heterogeneous Wireless Networks: Does It Really Pay Off?. In *Proc. of IEEE Globecom.* 2014.

[22] Nadir Hakem, Gilles Delisle, and Yacouba Coulibaly. Radio-Wave Propagation into an Underground mine environment at 2.4 GHz, 5.8 GHz and 60 GHz. In *European Conference on Antennas and Propagation (EuCAP).* 2014.

[23] Daniel Halperin, Srikanth Kandula, Jitendra Padhye, Paramvir Bahl, and David Wetherall. Augmenting Data Center Networks with Multi-gigabit Wireless Links. In *Proc. of ACM SIGCOMM.* 2011.

[24] IEEE Standards Association. IEEE Standards 802.11ad-2012, Amendment 3: Enhancements for Very High Throughput in the 60 GHz Band. 2012.

[25] IEEE Standards Association. IEEE Standards 802.11ac-2013: Enhancements for Very High Throughput for Operation in Bands below 6 GHz. 2013.

[26] Injong Rhee and Lisong Xu and Sangtae Ha and Alexander Zimmermann and Lars Eggert and Richard Scheffenegger. CUBIC for Fast Long-Distance Networks. In *Internet-Draft.* 2015.

[27] Intrinsyc Software International, Inc. Mobile Development Platform Tablet. https://www.intrinsyc.com/press-release/intrinsyc-announces-development-platforms-featuring-new-high-performance-qualcomm-snapdragon-820-processor/. 2016.

[28] Hye-Churn Jang and Hyun-Wook Jin. MiAMI: Multi-core Aware Processor Affinity for TCP/IP over Multiple Network Interfaces. In *IEEE Symposium on High Performance Interconnects.* 2009.

[29] Xavier Lagrange. Very Tight Coupling between LTE and Wi-Fi for Advanced Offloading Procedures. In *IEEE Wireless Communications and Networking Conference Workshops.* 2014.

[30] TP-LINK Technologies Co. Ltd. Wi-Fi Routers | AD7200. http://www.tp-link.com/us/products/details/cat-5506_AD7200.html. 2016.

[31] Rajesh Mahindra, Hari Viswanathan, Karthik Sundaresan, Mustafa Y. Arslan, and Sampath Rangarajan. A Practical Traffic Management System for Integrated LTE-WiFi Networks. In *Proc. of ACM MobiCom.* 2014.

[32] Zhinus Marzi, Dinesh Ramasamy, and Upamanyu Madhow. Compressive Channel Estimation and Tracking for Large Arrays in mm-Wave Picocells. Vol. 10, No. 3. 2016.

[33] Energy Sciences Network. UDP Tuning. https://fasterdata.es.net/network-tuning/udp-tuning. 2012.

[34] Thomas Nitsche, Guillermo Bielsa, Irene Tejado, Adrian Loch, and Joerg Widmer. Boon and Bane of 60 GHz Networks: Practical Insights into Beamforming, Interference, and Frame Level Operation. In *Proc. of ACM CoNEXT.* 2015.

[35] Thomas Nitsche, Adriana B. Flores, Edward W. Knightly, and Joerg Widmer. Steering with Eyes Closed: mm-Wave Beam Steering without In-Band Measurement. In *Proc. of IEEE INFOCOM.* 2015.

[36] Pasternack. 60 GHz Transmit/Receive (Tx/Rx) Development System. https://www.pasternack.com. 2013.

[37] Ioannis Pefkianakis, Jaideep Chandrashekar, and Henrik Lundgren. User-Driven Idle Energy Save for 802.11x Mobile Devices. In *Proc. of IEEE MASS.* 2014.

[38] Trevor Pering, Yuvraj Agarwal, Rajesh Gupta, and Roy Want. CoolSpots: Reducing the Power Consumption of Wireless Mobile Devices with Multiple Radio Interfaces. In *Proc. of ACM MobiSys.* 2006.

[39] Christopher Pluntke, Lars Eggert, and Niko Kiukkonen. Saving Mobile Device Energy with Multipath TCP. In *Proc. of ACM MobiArch.* 2011.

[40] Qualcomm Incorporated. Techniques for Rate Selection in Millimeter-Wave Communication Systems. In *US Patent 9,312,985.* 2016.

[41] Qualcomm Technologies, Inc. LTE and Wi-Fi Convergence: Leveraging Both to Meet Capacity Demand. https://www.qualcomm.com/news/onq/2014/02/18/lte-and-wi-fi-convergence-leveraging-both-meet-capacity-demand. 2014.

[42] Costin Raiciu, Dragos Niculescu, Marcelo Bagnulo, and Mark James Handley. Opportunistic Mobility with Multipath TCP. In *Proc. of ACM MobiArch.* 2011.

[43] Costin Raiciu, Christoph Paasch, Sebastien Barre, Alan Ford, Michio Honda, Fabien Duchene, Olivier Bonaventure, and Mark Handley. How Hard Can It Be? Designing and Implementing a Deployable Multipath TCP. In *Proc. of USENIX NSDI.* 2012.

[44] T.S. Rappaport, F. Gutierrez, E. Ben-Dor, J.N. Murdock, Yijun Qiao, and J.I. Tamir. Broadband Millimeter-Wave Propagation Measurements and Models Using Adaptive-Beam Antennas for Outdoor Urban Cellular Communications. *IEEE Transactions on Antennas and Propagation* Vol. 61, No. 4. 2013.

[45] T.S. Rappaport, Shu Sun, R. Mayzus, Hang Zhao, Y. Azar, K. Wang, G.N. Wong, J.K. Schulz, M. Samimi, and F. Gutierrez. Millimeter Wave Mobile Communications for 5G Cellular: It Will Work! *IEEE Access* 1. 2013.

[46] Theodore S. Rappaport, Eshar Ben-Dor, James N. Murdock, and Yijun Qiao. 38 GHz and 60 GHz Angle-Dependent Propagation for Cellular and Peer-to-Peer Wireless Communications. In *Proc. of IEEE ICC.* 2012.

[47] Maryam Eslami Rasekh, Zhinus Marzi, Yanzi Zhu, Upamanyu Madhow, and Haitao Zheng. Noncoherent mmWave Path Tracking. In *Proc. of ACM HotMobile.* 2017.

[48] Grand View Research Report. Wireless Gigabit (WiGig) Market Size To Reach $7.42 Billion By 2024. http://www.grandviewresearch.com/press-release/global-wireless-gigabit-wigig-market. 2016.

[49] Ralph O. Schmidt. Multiple Emitter Location and Signal Parameter Estimation. *IEEE Transactions on Antennas and Propagation* Vol. 34, No. 3. 1986.

[50] Souvik Sen, Bozidar Radunovic, Jeongkeun Lee, and Kyu-Han Kim. CSpy: Finding the Best Quality Channel without Probing. In *Proc. of ACM MobiCom.* 2013.

[51] Peter F. M. Smulders. Statistical Characterization of 60-GHz Indoor Radio Channels. *IEEE Transactions on Antennas and Propagation* Vol. 57, No. 10. 2009.

[52] Anand Prabhu Subramanian, Himanshu Gupta, Samir R. Das, and Jing Cao. Minimum Interference Channel Assignment in Multiradio Wireless Mesh Networks. *IEEE Transactions on Mobile Computing* Vol. 7, No. 12. 2008.

[53] Sanjib Sur, Vignesh Venkateswaran, Xinyu Zhang, and Parmesh Ramanathan. 60 GHz Indoor Networking through Flexible Beams: A Link-Level Profiling. In *Proc. of ACM SIGMETRICS.* 2015.

[54] Sanjib Sur, Xinyu Zhang, Parmesh Ramanathan, and Ranveer Chandra. BeamSpy: Enabling Robust 60 GHz Links Under Blockage. In *Proc. of USENIX NSDI.* 2016.

[55] Deepak Vasisht, Swarun Kumar, Hariharan Rahul, and Dina Katabi. Eliminating Channel Feedback in Next-Generation Cellular Networks. In *Proc. of ACM SIGCOMM.* 2016.

[56] Junyi Wang, Zhou Lan, Chin-Sean Sum, Chang-Woo Pyo, Jing Gao, Tuncer Baykas, Azizur Rahman, Ryuhei Funada, Fumihide Kojima, Ismail Lakkis, Hiroshi Harada, and Shuzo Kato. Beamforming Codebook Design and Performance Evaluation for 60GHz Wideband WPANs. In *Proc. of IEEE VTC.* 2009.

[57] Teng Wei and Xinyu Zhang. Facilitating Robust 60 GHz Network Deployment By Sensing Ambient Reflectors. In *Proc. of USENIX NSDI.* 2017.

[58] Teng Wei and Xinyu Zhang. Pose Information Assisted 60 GHz Networks: Towards Seamless Coverage and Mobility Support. In *Proc. of ACM MobiCom.* 2017.

[59] www.qualcomm.com. Qualcomm Atheros and Wilocity Announce Tri-band Wi-Fi: Industry's First Standards-compliant, Multi-Gigabit Wireless

Chipset. https://www.qualcomm.com/news/releases/2011/05/31/qualcomm-atheros-and-wilocity-announce-tri-band-wi-fi-industrys-first. 2011.
[60] Hao Xu, Vikas Kukshya, and Theodore S. Rappaport. Spatial and Temporal Characteristics of 60-GHz Indoor Channels. *IEEE Journal on Selected Areas in Communications* Vol. 20, No. 3. 2002.
[61] Jialiang Zhang, Xinyu Zhang, Pushkar Kulkarni, and Parameswaran Ramanathan. OpenMili: A 60 GHz Software Radio Platform with a Reconfigurable Phased-Array Antenna. In *Proc. of ACM MobiCom*. 2016.
[62] Anfu Zhou, Xinyu Zhang, and Huadong Ma. Beam-forecast: Facilitating Mobile 60 GHz Networks via Model-driven Beam Steering. In *Proc. of IEEE INFOCOM*. 2016.
[63] Xia Zhou, Zengbin Zhang, Yibo Zhu, Yubo Li, Saipriya Kumar, Amin Vahdat, Ben Y. Zhao, and Haitao Zheng. Mirror Mirror on the Ceiling: Flexible Wireless Links for Data Centers. In *Proc. of ACM SIGCOMM*. 2012.
[64] Yibo Zhu, Zengbin Zhang, Zhinus Marzi, Chris Nelson, Upamanyu Madhow, Ben Y. Zhao, and Haitao Zheng. Demystifying 60GHz Outdoor Picocells. In *Proc. of ACM MobiCom*. 2014.

Pose Information Assisted 60 GHz Networks: Towards Seamless Coverage and Mobility Support

Teng Wei
University of Wisconsin - Madison
twei7@wisc.edu

Xinyu Zhang
University of California San Diego
xiz368@eng.ucsd.edu

ABSTRACT

60 GHz millimeter-wave networking has emerged as the next frontier technology to provide multi-Gbps wireless connectivity. However, the intrinsic directionality and limited field-of-view of 60 GHz antennas make the links extremely sensitive to user mobility and orientation change. Hence, seamless coverage, even at room level, becomes challenging. In this paper, we propose Pia, a robust 60 GHz network architecture that can provide seamless coverage and mobility support at multi-Gbps bitrate. Pia comprises multiple cooperating access points (APs). It leverages the pose information on mobile clients to proactively select the AP and manage multi-link spatial reuse. These decisions require a model of the pose/location of the APs and ambient reflectors. We address these challenges through a set of AP-pose sensing and compressive angle estimation algorithms that fuse the pose measurement with link quality measurement on the client. We have implemented Pia using commodity 60 GHz platforms. Our experiments show that Pia reduces the occurrence of link outage by 6.3× and improves the spatial sharing capacity by 76%, compared to conventional schemes that only use in-band information for adaptation.

CCS CONCEPTS

•**Hardware** →*Digital signal processing; Networking hardware; Wireless devices; Beamforming;* •**Networks** →*Network experimentation; Network mobility;*

KEYWORDS

60 GHz; Multi-AP; Mobility; Location; Orientation; Pose sensing

1 INTRODUCTION

The millimeter-wave (mmWave) wireless technology is emerging as a disruptive networking paradigm to provide multi-Gbps connectivity for demanding applications, such as wireless backhaul [19], cordless virtual reality (VR) [7], wireless fiber-to-home [15], mobile-to-screen video cast [6], *etc.* FCC's recent policy to release 14 GHz of unlicensed spectrum, along with standardization activities such as the IEEE 802.11ad [26], 802.15.3c [1] and 802.11ay [5], have spawned many consumer grade mobile devices on the 60 GHz mmWave band. For example, TPCAST [59], a 60 GHz adapter, can replace the cables between a VR headset and its PC host. Recent

MobiCom'17, October 16–20, 2017, Snowbird, UT, USA.
© 2017 ACM. ISBN 978-1-4503-4916-1/17/10...$15.00
DOI: dx.doi.org/10.1145/3117811.3117832

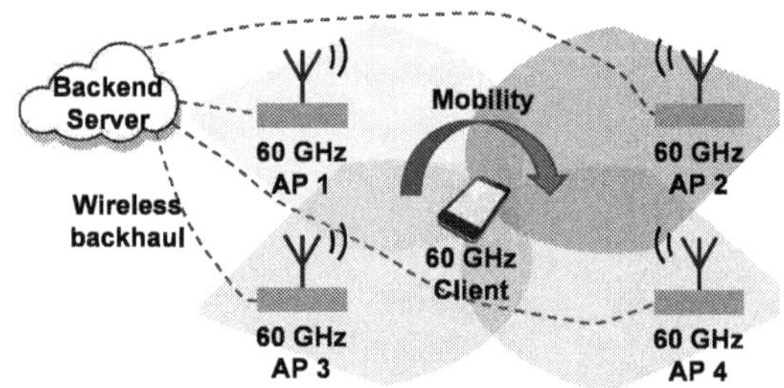

Figure 1: Multi-AP networks: APs are partially overlapped and connected to a backend server via wireless backhaul.

60 GHz capable smartphones and laptops [49] can stream Gbps uncompressed videos to an external display.

Ideally, one would anticipate the 60 GHz technology as the next-frontier for mobile broadband, to replace the current WiFi. However, to date, the use cases of the 60 GHz wireless technology have mostly been focusing on point-to-point, stationary links. To enable seamless coverage and mobility support, 60 GHz networks need to overcome fundamental barriers that do not exist in the prior low-frequency counterparts. To compensate for the intrinsic attenuation losses due to short signal wavelengths, 60 GHz radios adopt phased-array antennas which comprise many planar patch elements to form directional beam patterns. Although these beams are electronically steerable, their joint coverage is still limited due to the inherent half-space coverage of patch antennas [46]. So the phased-array bears a limited field-of-view (FoV), much like a camera. And the signal strength largely depends on whether the receiver falls in the transmitter's FoV. Consequently, achieving stable 60 GHz connectivity, even at room-level, becomes a nontrivial task.

In this paper, we propose Pia, a robust 60 GHz network architecture that can provide room-scale coverage at multi-Gbps bit-rate. Pia is tailored for emerging applications such as wireless virtual-reality [7], augmented-reality [42], uncompressed miracast [6], all requiring Gbps connectivity between a mobile device and a backend server for computational offloading or graphical rendering. Our basic idea is to deploy multiple cooperating APs (*e.g.*, at the corners of the room), each covering a "picocell" region that can complement others' blind spots. No matter how the client device moves and rotates, it is likely to fall in the FoV of at least one of the APs (Fig. 1). The APs can be 802.11ad-compatible access points or dedicated relaying devices [7], which connect to a backend server through Ethernet cables or fixed-beam wireless backhaul [19].

The idea of multi-AP coordination has been investigated extensively in legacy WiFi or cellular networks [22, 39, 44, 51, 52], and the key problem is to determine which AP to connect to, based on signal strength, traffic load, *etc.* But the new characteristics of 60 GHz bring unique dimensions to the problem. Since each 60 GHz AP may possess hundreds of beam directions, a straightforward way of selecting the AP will entail trial-and-error probing across all

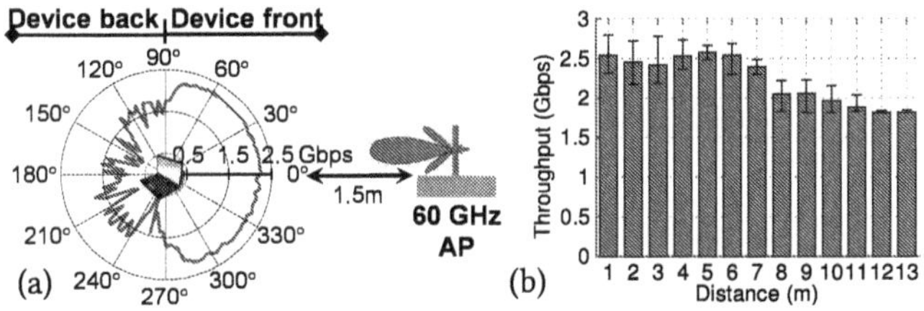

Figure 2: FoV and performance of the commercial 60 GHz laptop in our measurement. Varying (a) client device's azimuth orientation, (b) AP-to-client distance (azimuth = 0°).

these directions for all APs. When multiple clients coexist, multiple iterations of probing are needed to negotiate the best spatial reuse, which compounds the overhead. Most critically, the probing needs to be done not only when a client changes its location, but also its orientation. Consequently, the probing overhead may overwhelm normal data transmission.

Pia overcomes this issue by leveraging the 5-DoF pose information (x, y, z position and polar/azimuth orientation) that is available on many mobile devices (*e.g.*, VR headsets [25] and smartphones/tablets with visual-inertial sensing capabilities [23, 36]). More specifically, Pia employs a model-driven approach to predict the best AP based on a client's pose, and to assign the best beam pattern each AP should use to maximize the spatial reuse among multiple clients. To this end, we identify 4 unique design challenges.

First, our measurements indicate that the 60 GHz throughput often experiences a catastrophic drop as a client moves out of the AP's FoV, so the conventional multi-AP protocols that react after throughput change can no longer sustain robust connectivity. We thus design a *pose-assisted link predictor* that allows the client to proactively switch to a new AP, before the current link quality drops to an intolerable level. This decision builds on a prediction of the client's short-term pose change, paired with a simple model of the AP's coverage which does not require probing all beam patterns.

Second, a vast literature in directional-antenna networking at low-frequency bands assumed cone-shaped beams [11]. In contrast, practical 60 GHz phased-arrays have imperfect directional beam patterns that often comprise multiple sidelobes, causing irregular interference patterns across spatial angles. Pia addresses this challenge using a *pose-assisted spatial sharing* mechanism, which jointly optimizes the AP selection and beam assignment, to maximize the concurrent transmission opportunity when multiple clients coexist.

Third, the above two mechanisms assume Pia knows the AP's relative position and orientation within the client's coordinate. However, the actual APs are often placed in an ad-hoc manner. To meet this challenge, we design a statistical algorithm, called *AP-pose sensing (APS)*, that can estimate the AP's pose based on a random set of link-quality measurement at the client side.

Finally, Pia's interference management mainly models the line-of-sight (LOS) link quality. But the model can be occasionally disturbed by non-line-of-sight (NLOS) reflections from close-by objects (*e.g.*, concrete walls or metal cabinet). We design a novel *compressive angle estimation* method, that fuses the pose information with the link quality measurement, so as to discriminate the reflection paths and model their impacts separately.

The contributions of Pia can be summarized as follows.

(i) We propose to use pose information as a fundamental primitive, and identify the associated challenges/opportunities to facilitate robust connectivity within a 60 GHz multi-AP architecture.

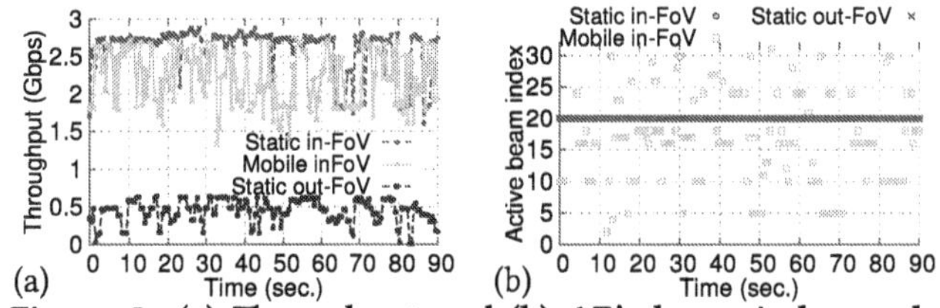

Figure 3: (a) Throughput and (b) AP's beam index under static/mobile in-FoV and static out-FoV.

(ii) We design pose-assisted link prediction, spatial sharing, and AP-pose sensing mechanisms, to enable efficient link/interference management for practical 60 GHz clients.

(iii) We implement Pia on a COTS testbed with 4 60 GHz radios each with a 4×8 phased array. Our experiments show that Pia's pose-assisted AP switching effectively reduces the hazard times (catastrophic throughput drops) by 4.2~6.3×, and the spatial sharing enhances the network capacity by 76% compared to the 802.11ad.

2 BACKGROUND AND OVERVIEW

2.1 Limited FoV of the 60 GHz Radio

Impact of FoV alignment on link quality. Early studies of 60 GHz phased-array [46] indicated that its coverage is often limited to less than half-space. To elucidate the problem, we set up two 802.11ad laptops, as AP and client, respectively; both equipped with the Qualcomm QCA6300 series chipset [45]. We measure the link throughput when rotating the client in front of the AP which is 1.5 m away and facing to the client directly (more details of the setup are in Sec. 5). From the results (Fig. 2(a)), we can make two observations. *First*, the client's high-throughput coverage area forms an angular sector (around 170°), which we refer to as its *FoV*. Once the AP falls outside the client's FoV, the throughput drops sharply, from 2.2 Gbps to several hundred Mbps. Note that *the antenna's FoV is different from its beam pattern*. Each beam pattern is much narrower than the FoV itself (more in Sec. 4.1). *Second*, there is no 'notch' inside the FoV—all the beam patterns together can fully cover the FoV, ensuring a consistently high throughput.

The limited FoV practically exists in all 60 GHz devices, because the phased array's front-side comprises many planar antenna elements, each having a FoV of 80° to 180° [46, 71]. The backside has very weak signal emissions, because it is grounded by a metal plane, and often faces inward the host device which causes strong attenuation. Following this common practice, 802.11ad-compatible laptops (*e.g.*, Acer P446 and Dell Latitude E7240) typically install the phased array close to the outer surface of the lid. The TPCAST [59] 60 GHz adapter is mounted atop a VR headset, with the phased array pointing towards the ceiling. For smartphones, antennas are recommended to be placed on the top or bottom surface [48].

Note that, besides the host device itself, the human user can further block the phased array. In this work, we assume the user of the device always falls outside the phased array's FoV, *i.e.*, blocking the backside only. This is a valid assumption considering the antenna placement principle [57] (in the most unobstructed zone during regular use), and also the fact that the user moves synchronously with the device in practical applications, *e.g.*, mobile gaming and wireless VR. Blockage of other users can be alleviated by careful AP deployment/planning, which will be discussed in Sec. 7.

Fig. 2 (b) also plots the measured throughput as link distance increases, with client and AP falling in each other's FoV. We find the

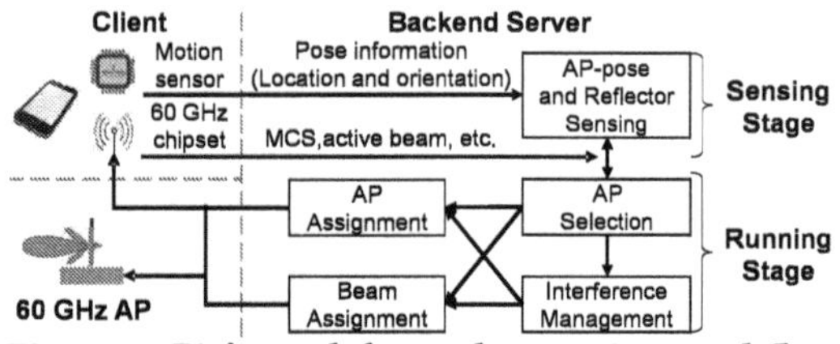

Figure 4: Pia's modules and operation workflow.

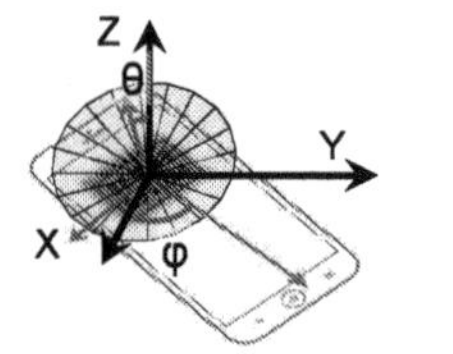

Figure 5: 5-DoF pose of the phased array.

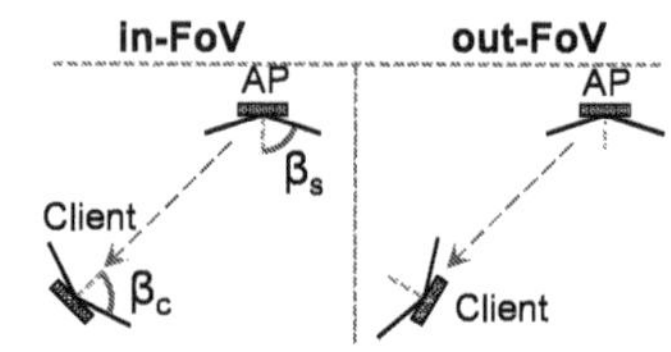

Figure 6: Link status prediction based on the poses.

link can sustain a high throughput over a reasonably long distance. Even at 13 m, the throughput remains at 1.8 Gbps, much higher than the out-of-FoV case. This range is consistent with previous measurements [40, 76]. It indicates that *the devices' orientation, which determines FoV alignment, plays a more critical role than link distance in maintaining robust room-level connectivity.*

Profiling the beam-steering under mobility. Can the beam steering on commercial 802.11ad radios be fast enough to adapt to the user movement? To answer this question, we walk inside the network area, holding the client device with natural pose variations, but keeping it within the FoV to an AP. Fig. 3(a) further plots the throughput measurement over time. Although the throughput shows higher variations, the mobile in-FoV case can still maintain 50% at worst and 80% on average compared to the stationary case, and 3~5× higher than the out-of-FoV case. The beam index changes rapidly in the mobile case (Fig. 3 (b)), indicating the real-time beam adaption of 802.11ad can accommodate user mobility with reasonable efficiency, at least at walking speed. So *the in or out of FoV relation becomes the dominant factor that determines link throughput.*

2.2 Pia Operations

To facilitate seamless coverage and mobility support for 60 GHz networks, Pia adopts a two-stage workflow (Fig. 4). The *sensing stage* takes the 60 GHz link status information, *i.e.*, modulation and coding scheme (MCS) and beam index, along with the pose information from the mobile client as input, and runs the *AP-pose sensing (APS)* algorithm (Sec. 3.2) to estimate the APs' pose within the client's coordinate system. With the same input, Pia also runs a compressive angle estimation algorithm to estimate the location/orientation of major reflectors that may affect the network performance (Sec. 4.2). Both schemes are one-time initialization procedures that run before putting the network into use. They need to be repeated only when the APs are redeployed or the environment changes significantly.

During the *running stage*, each client periodically feeds back its pose information to the *backend server*, using its current AP as a relay. The server runs the link prediction (Sec. 3.1) and interference management (Sec. 4) algorithms, and returns the decisions to the APs/clients. Pia's decision-making mechanisms are proactive in nature, based on a prediction of the long-term (> 500 ms) pose (Sec. 3.1.2). The pose sampling period and feedback latency are relatively negligible compared with the look-ahead time.

3 PIA DESIGN

3.1 AP Selection

We first consider a single mobile client and focus on how to dynamically select the AP to maintain high link throughput. This issue resembles the classical AP handoff problem in WiFi [22, 39, 44, 51, 52]. A common solution is to probe each AP and select the one with highest potential throughput. However, such approaches are reactive, and more critically, the many-beam phased-arrays in 60 GHz networks will cause huge probing overhead. For example, to probe all possible beams, an 802.11ad client needs to wait for the beam training beacon, which occurs only once per beacon period (typically 100 ms) [41]. By the time a proper AP is identified, the link may have already suffered from a long period of outage. Pia adopts a different design principle. It *predicts* the best AP based on the client's pose, without explicit probing. It proactively decides on *which AP* the client should switch to, and *when*. The AP/beam selection algorithms will execute each time when a new pose data arrives. Pia will inform AP the new beam selection only when algorithm's output changes. We now describe the mechanisms in detail.

3.1.1 Pose-Assisted Link Predictor. In Pia, each pose sample, denoted as $P = [x, y, z, \theta, \varphi]$, represents the 3D location, polar and azimuth angle of the norm of the phased array in a spherical coordinate system (Fig. 5). We can ignore the rotation angle around the antenna's norm direction because such rotation does not change the FoV alignment relation between the client and AP.

Based on the empirical insights in Sec. 2.1, each client discriminates the APs using a binary metric 0/1, denoting whether an AP is estimated to be within or out of FoV. It should be noted that this binary metric is only applied for AP selection purposes. Finer-grained metrics will be used for multi-client interference management (Sec. 4.1). In addition, for picocell coverage within a room area, the power budget of commodity 60 GHz devices already provides consistently high throughput for the in-FoV case (Sec. 2.1). For larger scale networks such as outdoor small-cells, the AP-to-client distance may have a non-negligible impact, but can be easily modeled in Pia given the location information.

The predictor takes the AP's and client's poses as input. It predicts the link status as 1 if they mutually fall within each other's FoV (Fig. 6), and 0 otherwise. We define the FoV angle as from the antenna norm to the edge of its coverage (β_s and β_c in Fig. 6). For example, the FoV of our device is 85°, measured in Fig. 2. A device's FoV is generally available from its antenna specifications, or can be manually measured following Sec. 2.1.

Let $\mathbf{P_c} = [x_c, y_c, z_c, \theta_c, \varphi_c]$ and $\mathbf{P_s} = [x_s, y_s, z_s, \theta_s, \varphi_s]$ be poses of client and AP, respectively. Pia computes two vectors $\mathbf{V_s}$ and $\mathbf{V_{sc}}$ that point to the norm of AP's antenna and the direction from AP to client, following 3D geometry:

$$\mathbf{V_s} = \mathbf{R_y}(\theta_s)\mathbf{R_z}(\varphi_s)[0, 0, 1]^{\mathrm{T}} \quad (1)$$

$$\mathbf{V_{sc}} = [x_c, y_c, z_c]^T - [x_s, y_s, z_s]^{\mathrm{T}} \quad (2)$$

where $(\cdot)^{\mathrm{T}}$ denotes transpose operator. $\mathbf{R_y}(\alpha)$ and $\mathbf{R_z}(\alpha)$ are the 3D rotation matrices [65] that rotate a point relative to the origin along Y-axis and Z-axis by an angle of α respectively. Eq. (1) converts the orientation of AP's antenna into a vector format. Then Pia can determine the angle ϕ_s between vectors $\mathbf{V_s}$ and $\mathbf{V_{sc}}$ by:

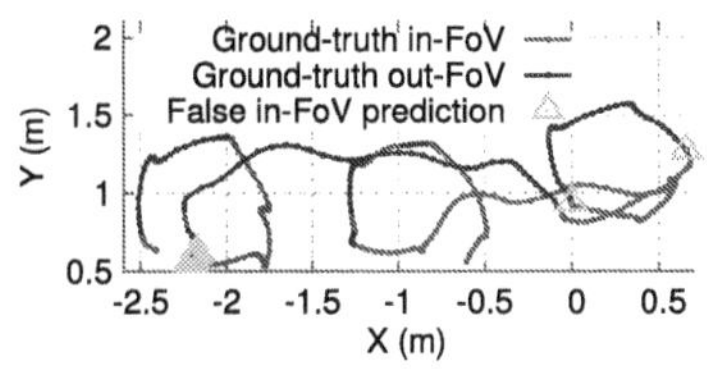

Figure 7: Link status prediction error in a sample walking: false in-FoV prediction is highlighted by green triangle. The dense cluster implies multiple errors occur consecutively.

$$\phi_s = atan2(||\mathbf{V_s} \times \mathbf{V_{sc}}||_2, \mathbf{V_s}^T \mathbf{V_{sc}}) \quad (3)$$

where function *atan2(·)* calculates the four-quadrant inverse tangent [66]. Similarly, Pia computes the angle ϕ_c between the norm of client's antenna and $-\mathbf{V_{sc}}$, and checks if ϕ_s and ϕ_c are smaller than the AP's FoV β_s and client's FoV β_c:

$$\text{Link\_State} = \begin{cases} 1, & \phi_s \le \beta_s \quad \phi_c \le \beta_c \\ 0, & \text{Otherwise} \end{cases} \quad (4)$$

Fig. 7 plots an example trace of the link predictor, as the client walks within a 2×3 m^2 region with natural orientation changes (More setup details are available in Sec. 6). To obtain the ground-truth link state, we measure the link throughput corresponding to each pose sample, and then convert it into 1/0, using a threshold of 1.6 Gbps that can reliably distinguish the in-FoV and out-FoV (Sec. 2.1). We highlight the false in-FoV predictions (*i.e.*, out-FoV predicted as in-FoV) which mislead the client to switch to a low-throughput AP. We find the prediction error is only 9.11% across all the 1324 pose samples. More importantly, the errors mostly concentrate on the boundary area *i.e.*, when transiting from in/out-FoV to out/in-FoV. We will show that such errors have marginal impacts because Pia reacts well before the transition occurs (Sec. 3.1.3).

3.1.2 Pose Predictor. Pia needs to estimate the link status for the near future based on a prediction of the client's pose. For simplicity, it adopts a classical kinematic model, Continuous White Noise Acceleration (CWNA) [10], for pose prediction, although other kinematic models can be applied as well. CWNA assumes zero acceleration, *i.e.*, both the linear and angular velocities are stable within a very short duration. Thus, the pose $\hat{\mathbf{P_c}}$ at time $t+1$ can be predicted as:

$$\hat{\mathbf{P_c}}(t+1) = \mathbf{P_c}(t) + \Delta\hat{\mathbf{P_c}}(t),$$
$$\Delta\hat{\mathbf{P_c}}(t+1) = \Delta\mathbf{P_c}(t),$$

where $\Delta\mathbf{P_c}(t) = \mathbf{P_c}(t+1) - \mathbf{P_c}(t)$ is the pose velocity.

A key question here is how far should Pia predict ahead of time. Let L denotes the look-ahead time. L should be long enough to ensure the AP switching can finish timely, yet not too long to make the prediction unreliable. In our Pia implementation (Sec. 5), the AP switching time is negligible (< 10 ms), so we empirically set L to 500 ms, roughly the scale where human movement velocity remains coherent [10].

3.1.3 AP Switcher. To avoid the adversarial impact of false in-FoV predictions (Sec. 3.1.1), Pia leverages the *transition area* where different APs' FoVs partially overlap (Fig. 8 (a)). It makes AP switching decision ahead of time before the link status of current AP degrades, so as to avoid the boundary region vulnerable to false prediction. To realize seamless switching, the APs should be deployed with partially overlapping FoVs. However, we will empirically verify that, even when this requirement is not satisfied, Pia's AP switcher can still minimize the client's outage duration (Sec. 6.2).

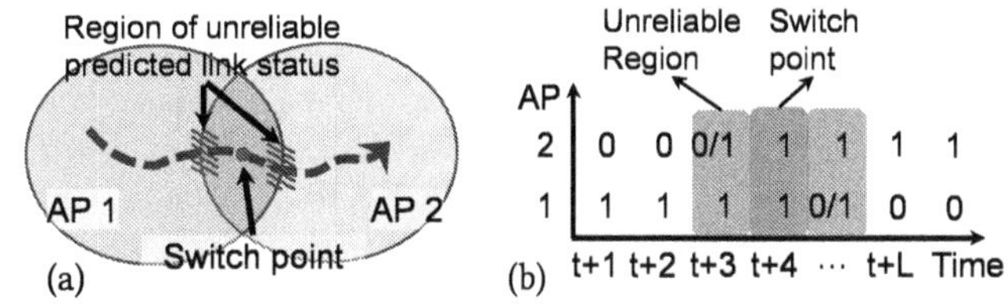

Figure 8: (a) AP switching during the transition area. (b) Table of predicted link status for two APs.

To determine the desired AP and appropriate switching time, Pia's AP switcher takes the predicted link status for all APs from time $t+1$ to $t+L$ as input. Fig. 8(b) shows an example time series of link status (0/1) prediction for two APs, computed based on the pose data of headset and AP using Eq. (4). Such information forms a table-like data structure. Pia then makes the switching decision following three basic rules: *(i)* Prepare a switching only if the current AP has at least one 0 value in the table. Otherwise, the AP will remain in the client's FoV in the look-ahead duration L and switching is unnecessary. *(ii)* Look for other APs that have overlapped 1s with current AP in the predicted time span, and select the AP with smallest AP-to-client distance as the AP to switch to. This essentially enables Pia to react within the transition area, and choose an alternative AP with potentially strongest RSS. *(iii)* Choose the center of overlapped 1s as the switching time, so as to avoid the boundary regions vulnerable to prediction errors (Fig. 8).

There are two exceptional cases that Pia needs to handle in order to minimize the impact of potential link outage: *(i)* When no other APs have any 1s, Pia needs to stick to the current AP. *(ii)* When no overlapped 1s exist, Pia will switch to the AP that has the earliest 1 in the predicted time span.

3.2 AP-Pose Sensing

The above link predictor assumes the APs' poses are known. Ideally, a user can measure APs' poses during deployment. However, in practice, the phased array antenna is commonly sealed inside the device, and the exact direction where its FoV points to is invisible to the end user. Pia's APS algorithm overcomes this barrier by automatically estimating each AP's pose, which will account for the antenna array placement inside the device. Although certain localization schemes [28] may help obtain the AP's (x_s, y_s, z_s) coordinate, they require at least three reference devices. Pia's use cases typically do not satisfy this requirement because only one reference device, *i.e.*, the mobile client, exists with known position. Besides, these schemes need access to fine-grained PHY-layer information such as phase, and often require precise carrier clock calibration between the transmitter and receiver, which is not viable on commodity 60 GHz hardware. To enable 5-DoF AP-pose sensing for a wider range of 60 GHz devices, we devise *a statistical algorithm that only needs the link throughput measurement as input.*

Collecting the sensing data. APS is called during the sensing stage of Pia, when the user randomly walks within the network coverage. Meanwhile, the client device records its pose and link throughput with respect to a connected AP. Then, Pia converts the link throughput into binary link status in the same way as the experiments in Fig. 7. Since a client device can estimate the link throughput for multiple APs simultaneously, a user only needs to collect the sensing data for all APs with a single walk. Besides, the user's walking trace needs not cover every spot in the area.

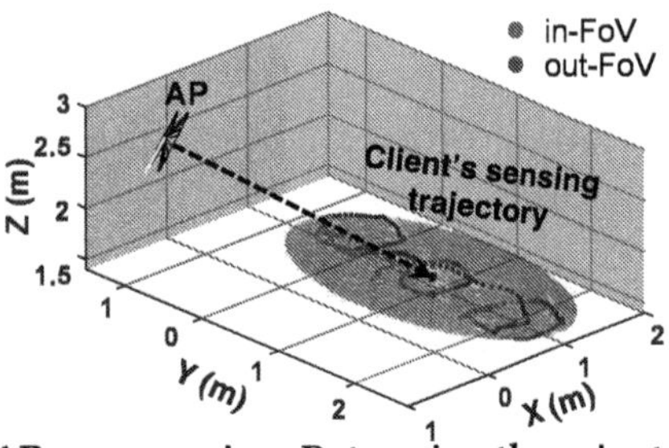

Figure 9: AP-pose sensing: Determine the orientation from a 3D ellipsoid that covers all client's poses in the AP's FoV.

Statistical estimation of the AP pose. Let S_s denote a set that contains all legitimate AP's pose values, and S_t be the pose samples in the sensing trajectory. Then the optimal estimation of the AP pose should result in the minimum error in matching the measured in-FoV/out-FoV samples. We formulate this optimal estimation P^* as one that minimizes the weighted false in-FoV errors (w_{FI}) and false out-FoV errors (w_{FO}) for a given set of samples:

$$P^* = \arg\min_{P_i \in S_s} w_{FI} \sum_{j=1}^{|S_t|} inFoV(P_i, P_j) * (1 - t_j) + w_{FO} \sum_{j=1}^{|S_t|} (1 - inFoV(P_i, P_j)) * t_j, \tag{5}$$

where $|S_t|$ represents the number of samples in S_t, and t_j is the ground-truth link status (0/1 value). Function $inFoV(\cdot)$ determines if the client and AP are within each other's FoV (Eq. 4) and returns a binary (0/1) indicator. P_i denotes the AP's pose and is the only variable we need to solve. We choose to minimize the weighted error because the false in-FoV error is more harmful to the link stability than the false out-FoV error (Sec. 3.1). Thus, it deserves a larger weight in the optimization (w_{FI}:w_{FO} = 4:1 in Pia).

However, Eq. (5) is non-convex, and solving it directly will be computationally expensive due to the large space of S_s. Suppose we partition locations in the unit of 10 cm and rotations in 3°. Then the number of candidate poses for a typical-size room (120 m^3) will be 2^{28}.

Algorithm 1 AP-Pose Sensing

```
procedure APPOSESENSING(S_t, T_t, w_FI, w_FO)
    [x_d, y_d, z_d] = ellipsoidCenter(S_t)            ▷ Find the sweet spot
    D = APLocList(S_t)               ▷ Generate list of legitimate AP locations
    vMin ← inf, P* ← NULL                             ▷ Initialize variables
    for [x_s, y_s, z_s] ∈ D do
        [θ_s, φ_s] = toAngle([x_s, y_s, z_s], [x_d, y_d, z_d]) ▷ To orientation
        P_i ← [x_s, y_s, z_s, θ_s, φ_s], v ← 0          ▷ Candidate AP pose
        for P_j ∈ S_t, t_j ∈ T_t do
            v = v + inFoV(P_i, P_j) * (1 − t_j) * w_FI
+(1 − inFoV(P_i, P_j)) * t_j * w_FO                     ▷ Eq. (5)
        end for
        if v < vMin then                        ▷ Minimize weighted error
            vMin ← v, P* ← P
        end if
    end for
    return P*                            ▷ Return the estimated AP's pose
end procedure
```

To prune the search space, we leverage a sweet spot where the axial direction of the AP's FoV passes through. At this location spot, the in-FoV estimation should have a minimal error. To locate such a spot, consider an example trace of sensing data in Fig. 9, where we mark all locations with "in-FoV" link status as red dots. Using the approach in [58], Pia finds a 3D ellipsoid of minimum volume covering all the red dots. The ellipsoid's center is identified as the sweet spot because steering the AP's FoV to it will maximize the number of red dots the AP covers. Afterward, Pia searches over the 3D space using Eq. (5) to determine the AP's location. The search space becomes much smaller because it only involves 3-DoF. Since the sweet spot uniquely specifies the axial direction of the AP's FoV, the AP's orientation can be directly determined for a given location without searching. Algorithm 1 summarizes the above procedure of APS. Moreover, Pia can detect the AP position change after initial sensing, because an inaccurate AP pose will significantly reduce the AP selection accuracy (Sec. 6.1). When the AP selection reliability degrades below a certain threshold, Pia will notify the user to recalibrate the AP's pose.

4 POSE-ASSISTED INTERFERENCE MANAGEMENT

Despite the 7 GHz of spectrum for 802.11ad, there only exist 4 orthogonal channels. Multiple clients sharing the same channel can become inevitable in dense networks, and when the AP-to-server wireless backhaul needs dedicated channels. The 802.11ad standard [26] specifies a spatial sharing mechanism, where directional links can sense their mutual interference. Concurrent transmissions are allowed only among interference-free directional links. However, to allow other links to sense its interference, each link needs to first transmit in an exclusive service period [26]. This repeats whenever its beam changes, which ultimately reduces spatial reuse, especially when there are multiple mobile links. We now describe how Pia overcomes the challenge.

4.1 Improving the Spatial Sharing Opportunity

4.1.1 Beam Strength Vector. Pia uses *beam strength vector* (BSV) as the core data structure to arbitrate the AP beam assignment for multi-client scenarios. BSV is defined as a vector characterizing the RSS values (*w.r.t.* the AP) across different transmit beam patterns. An example BSV is shown in Fig. 10 (a), measured using our 60 GHz AP and a customized software radio (Sec. 5) separated by 2 m. To obtain the BSV in commodity 60 GHz devices, there are two approaches:

Measurement from radio. First, one can leverage 802.11ad's built-in beam training protocol. At the beginning of each beacon interval (BI), the AP transmits multiple beacon frames, each using a different beam pattern. The client can record the RSS of each transmit beam pattern, which forms the BSV. This approach doesn't rely on the pose information and can be applied to general scenarios.

Prediction from pose. However, an AP sends out beacon frames at a fixed time interval, e.g., 100 ms, which is too long for delay-sensitive VR applications. Instead of waiting until the beginning of a BI, Pia chooses to leverage the pose information to directly derive the BSV. It first calculates the polar/azimuth angle looking from the AP's pose to the client's position (similar to Eq. (2) and (3)). It then looks up the gains of all beam patterns in the view-angle direction. The angular beam pattern can be obtained from the phased-array datasheet or using a one-time measurement (Sec. 5). Fig. 10 (b) illustrates a 2D example of this procedure, where the left plots the gains of different beam pattern indexes at different angles, and the right shows the corresponding BSV at angle -36°.

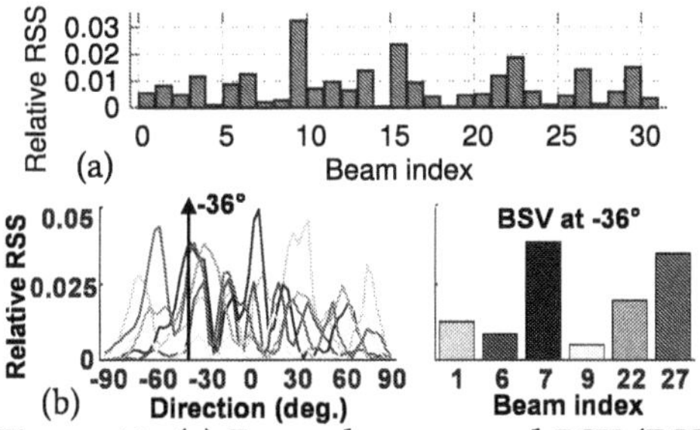

Figure 10: (a) Example measured BSV (RSS across all beam patterns for a given angle.) (b) Derive BSV from beam patterns at -36°.

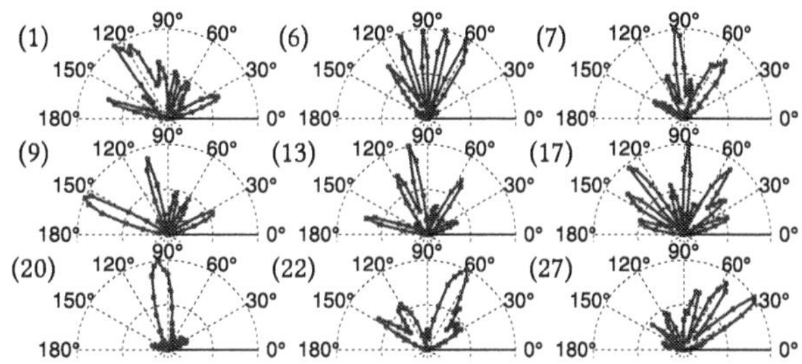

Figure 11: Samples of measured beam patterns of the phased array antenna. Left-top number is the beam index.

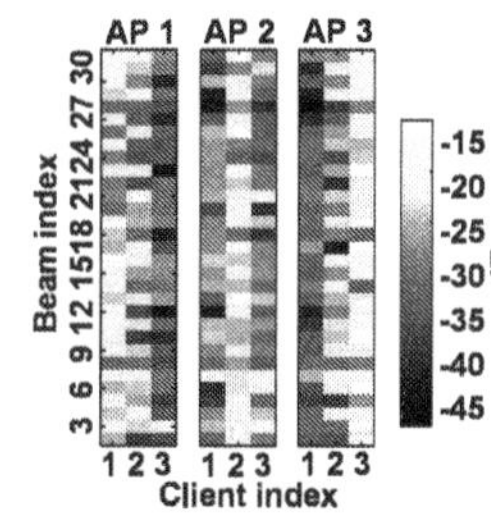

Figure 12: An example BSM for 3 APs and 3 clients.

4.1.2 *Pose-Assisted Spatial Sharing.* To enhance the spatial reuse opportunity, we introduce a novel interference management framework, which leverages the pose information to simultaneously determine the *best AP and beam pattern* for each client. Our key insight is that practical phased-arrays are not perfectly directional. Due to the use of discretized beamforming weights (*i.e.*, codebook entries) [46], each beam pattern may bear a main lobe along with multiple weaker side lobes. Fig. 11 illustrates example beam patterns of our AP device, measured using a software radio (Sec. 5)[1]. The results are consistent with previous measurement study [40] using similar hardware. Therefore, instead of greedily choosing the beam with strongest main lobe for each link and then measure whether the links can coexist without interference as specified by 802.11ad [26], Pia can judiciously assign beams with weaker lobes, which may sacrifice the RSS of certain links but create more spatial reuse opportunities for them.

We formulate this basic idea as a joint AP selection and beam selection problem. For clarity, we will focus on the downlink and optimize the AP's beam selection because the downlink traffic will be the dominance in the VR application. However, the extension to uplink and client-side optimization can follow the same principle since the client's pose is available. Our objective is to find the optimal AP and beam assignment that maximizes the overall link quality using *beam strength map (BSM)*, a data structure that aggregates the BSVs between each pair of AP and client. Each row of BSM is a BSV for a client and an AP. Fig. 12 plots an example measured using our 3-AP 3-client testbed (Sec. 5). To account for the signal attenuation over distance, Pia subtracts the predicted BSV by the pathloss of Frii's model [64] which takes the AP-to-client distance as input. Note that Pia does not need to predict client's absolute RSS because the spatial sharing mechanism only relies on the ratio between BSVs.

Suppose there are N_c clients and N_s APs. Let $\mathbf{A}(i)$ and $\mathbf{B}(i)$ be the AP and beam assignment for client i. Ideally, to maximize network capacity via spatial reuse, Pia should maximize the *signal-to-interference-ratio (SIR)* of all clients:

$$\max_{\mathbf{A},\mathbf{B}} \frac{1}{N_c} \sum_{i=1}^{N_c} \frac{BSM[\mathbf{A}(i), i, \mathbf{B}(i)]}{\sum_{j=1}^{N_s} INF_{max}(j, i)}, \tag{6}$$

[1]Practical phased-array beam patterns deviate from the horn shape because: *(i)* The OEM codebook does not account for the electromagnetic impact from peripheral electronic components on the phased array. *(ii)* To reduce the manufacturing cost, the 60 GHz phased-arrays only have limited phase-shift resolution (2-bit for each antenna element on the Qualcomm platform we use, *i.e.*, switching among 0°, 90°, 180°, and 270°). *(iii)* Our radio uses the same beam pattern for both beacon frames and data frames. The former is expected to have more diverse and wider beams[26].

where $BSM[\hat{a}, i, \hat{b}]$ denotes the signal strength from AP $\hat{a}$ to client i using beam $\hat{b}$, and function $INF_{max}(\hat{a}, i)$ calculates the maximum interference that AP $\hat{a}$ can cause to client i, which is given by:

$$INF_{max}(\hat{a}, i) = \max_{j, \mathbf{A}(j)=\hat{a}} INF(j, i),$$

$$INF(j, i) = \begin{cases} BSM[\mathbf{A}(j), i, \mathbf{B}(j)], & \mathbf{A}(j) \neq \mathbf{A}(i) \\ 0, & \mathbf{A}(j) = \mathbf{A}(i). \end{cases}$$

However, directly solving Eq. (6) entails a high computational complexity of $O((N_s N_b)^{N_c})$, where N_b is the number of beam patterns in the phased array. This above SIR-based solution is not scalable to the client number. Moreover, in our evaluation (Sec. 5), we found it cannot process the pose input in real time for even two clients. Instead, we design a lightweight algorithm that maximizes the *signal-to-leakage-ratio (SLR)*. The leakage is defined as the signal strength sent by an AP and received by an undesired client. SLR computes the ratio of desired client's RSS to leakage. Maximizing the SLR will also enhance the SIR because it minimizes the leakage that causes interference to others. SLR reduces the optimization complexity by decomposing the dependency between clients in AP assignment and beam assignment.

Algorithm 2 SLR-based AP and Beam Assignment

procedure *ASSIGNSLR*($BSM[]$, N_c)
  for $i = 1 : N_c$ **do**
    $\mathbf{A}(i) \leftarrow$ *indexOfMax*(*mean*($BSM[:, i, :].'$)) ▷ Assign AP
  end for
  for $i = 1 : N_c$ **do**
    for $j = 1 : N_c$ **do**
      $SLR[j, :] \leftarrow \frac{BSM[\mathbf{A}(i), i, :]}{BSM[\mathbf{A}(i), j, :]}$ ▷ Leakage from client i to j
    end for
    $\mathbf{B}(i) \leftarrow$ *indexOfMax*(*min*($SLR[:, :]$)) ▷ Assign beam
  end for
  return A and B ▷ Return AP and beam assignment
end procedure

(i) AP assignment. To maximize the SLR, it is best to assign the client to an in-FoV AP at closest distance, because it maximizes the RSS while minimizing the leakage from other APs. Pia thus assigns the client to an AP with the maximum average BSV across all beam indexes (*e.g.*, client 1 is assigned to AP 1 in Fig. 12). When assigned to the same AP, clients can work under the 802.11ad TDMA mode.

(ii) Beam assignment. Upon a new client assignment, the AP first iterates through each beam index, and calculates the RSS of current client and maximum leakage signal strength to other clients, which forms the SLR. The AP then chooses the beam assignment that has

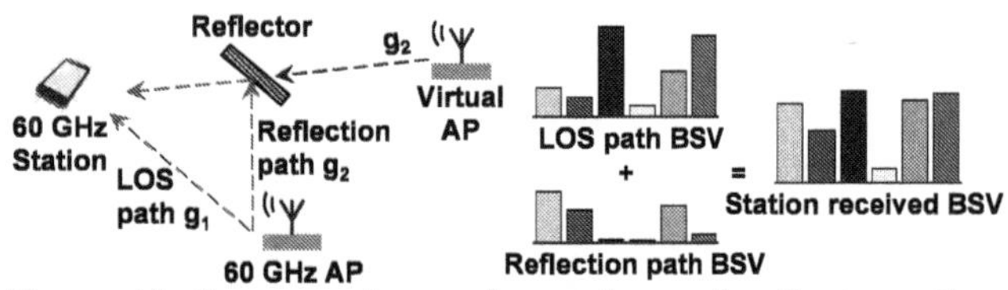

Figure 13: Compressive angle sensing and reflector estimation: measured BSV is the sum of BSVs along two paths.

the maximum SLR value. Finally, it examines whether the resulting SIR for each client exceeds its packet decoding threshold; if not, it assigns a dedicated time slot for it. Algorithm 2 summarizes the SLR-based algorithm. Its runtime complexity can be straightforwardly derived as $O(N_c N_b (N_s + N_c))$, and it is efficient enough to run in real time. Though the SLR-based algorithm is suboptimal, our evaluation shows its performance is close to the SIR-based algorithm.

4.2 Dealing With the Environmental Reflectors

The above scheme geometrically models the interference coming from transmitters within direct LOS. In practice, when the transmitters become close to strong ambient reflectors, their beams may be redirected, causing NLOS interference. To account for such effects, Pia incorporates a novel reflector sensing scheme which enhances the model in Sec. 4.1.2. It requires the user to conduct a one-time environment learning, by placing the 60 GHz client device near each strong reflector (typically concrete walls and large metal furniture [35]). Due to the well-known sparsity of 60 GHz channel [55], from 60 GHz radio's eyes, there are only a few dominant reflectors, which can account for more than 95% of the total energy that can be received by the radio in a typical indoor environment [62]. The selective scanning reduces the human labor and accelerates the sensing process by avoiding many unnecessary positions. However, we cannot let the user directly input the reflector coordinate since the reflectivity is unknown. Pia uses a novel signal angle sensing algorithm (Sec. 4.2.1), which fuses the pose sensor measurements with the BSV measurement, to estimate the relative location/orientation of reflectors. During the SLR estimation, Pia accounts for the NLOS interference from each reflector by modeling it as a virtual transmitter (Sec. 4.2.2). Moreover, strong reflectors unlikely move frequently due to the size and weight. We only need to rerun environment learning when their positions change.

4.2.1 Pose-Assisted Compressive Angle Estimation. The key idea in our NLOS interference model is to reverse engineer the reflectors' impact by tracing back NLOS signals' angle of departure (AoD) and angle of arrival (AoA). Such signal angles may be measured using a cone-shaped antenna with perfect directionality [77]. However, our goal is to enable angle sensing in practical 60 GHz devices which have imperfect beam patterns (Fig. 11). Our solution originates from a key observation: Whenever the reflector's impact becomes non-negligible, the measured BSV will deviate from the one predicted by using the LOS model (Sec. 4.1.2), and become the superposition of two BSVs along the LOS path and reflection path (Fig. 13).

Following the same approach as Sec. 4.1.1, Pia first obtains the measured BSV, from which it then *estimates the number of paths and their angles*, based on a statistical optimization model. For simplicity of exposition, we focus on the AoD estimation, but the AoA applies in the same way. We first uniformly divide the AP-to-client view angles (θ, φ) into N_p pairs following the geodesic grid [67]. Let $\mathbf{V}(\theta_i, \varphi_i)$ denote the predicted BSV (Sec. 4.1.1) for the ith pair of direction (θ_i, φ_i), and g_i be the unknown channel gain along the BSV direction. The measured BSV $\mathbf{V}_r$ can be expressed as the sum of BSVs from all directions multiplied by their associated gains: $\mathbf{V}_r = \sum_{i=1}^{N_p} \mathbf{V}(\theta_i, \varphi_i) g_i$. Thus, we may estimate the AoD by solving g_i in the system of equations:

$$\mathbf{V}_r - \sum_{i=1}^{N_p} \mathbf{V}(\theta_i, \varphi_i) g_i = 0 \tag{7}$$

where the direction (θ_i, φ_i) associated with a non-zero g_i will be the AoD of one path.

The problem (7) is under constrained because $N_p > N_b$. For example, to achieve an AoD estimation granularity of 8°, we need to uniformly divide the 3D view angle into 337 directions according to the geodesic grid [67]. Yet, for a phased-array of 32 elements, the number of beam patterns is only 64 following the standard practice of codebook design [61]. To address this problem, we harness the channel sparsity of the 60 GHz channel [55], *i.e.*, most AoD directions have close to zero gain (*i.e.*, $g_i \approx 0$), and only those corresponding to the LOS and a few strong reflection paths are non-negligible. We thus stack the g_i into an $N_p \times 1$ column vector $\mathrm{G} = [g_1, \ldots, g_{N_p}]^T$, which is now sparse. Thus, we can reformulate Eq. (7) into a compressive sensing problem that minimizes the l_1 norm of the sparse vector G,

$$\min ||\mathrm{G}||_1 \ \textit{subject to} \ ||\mathbf{V}_r - \hat{\mathbf{V}}\mathrm{G}||_2 \le \varepsilon \tag{8}$$

where $\hat{\mathbf{V}} = [\mathbf{V}(\theta_1, \varphi_1), \ldots, \mathbf{V}(\theta_{N_p}, \varphi_{N_p})]$ is an $N_b \times N_p$ matrix, and ε is determined by the radio's noise power in BSV measurement. Eq. (8) can be solved efficiently in polynomial time using the ℓ_1-MAGIC [12] or CVX [24] toolbox.

4.2.2 Modeling the Reflector Impact. Given the AoA/AoD, Pia can back-trace the departure and arrival paths, and locate the intersection points as the estimated reflector positions. Let $\mathbf{P_c} = [x_c, y_c, z_c, \theta_c, \varphi_c]$ and $\mathbf{P_s} = [x_s, y_s, z_s, \theta_s, \varphi_s]$ be the poses of client and AP, and (θ_a, φ_a) and (θ_d, φ_d) be the estimated AoA and AoD. The AP's pose can be estimated by the APS algorithm (Sec. 3.2). The AoA path travels along a series of points with coordinate:

$$\mathbf{K_a}(l_a) = \mathbf{R_y}(\theta_c)\mathbf{R_z}(\varphi_c) \begin{bmatrix} \cos(\varphi_a)\sin(\theta_a) l_a \\ \sin(\varphi_a)\sin(\theta_a) l_a \\ \cos(\theta_a) l_a \end{bmatrix} + \begin{bmatrix} x_c \\ y_c \\ z_c \end{bmatrix} \tag{9}$$

Eq. (9) first rotates a point at the AoA angle (θ_a, φ_a) *w.r.t.* the origin by an offset of client's orientation (θ_c, φ_c), and then translates the coordinate by an offset of client's location $[x_c, y_c, z_c]$. The only unknown variable in Eq. (9) is l_a that controls the distance between point $\mathbf{K_a}(l_a)$ and $[x_c, y_c, z_c]$. In a similar way, we back trace the AoD path and form a series of points with coordinate $\mathbf{K_d}(l_d)$ with l_d as the variable.

In practice, the AoA and AoD paths might not intersect in 3D space due to the residual error of angle sensing. Pia will select a point with closest distance to the two paths. Toward this goal, Pia determines the two points $\mathbf{K_a}(l_a^*)$ and $\mathbf{K_d}(l_d^*)$ with l_a^* and l_d^* that minimize the distance between them:

$$(l_a^*, l_d^*) = \underset{(l_a, l_d)}{\arg\min} ||\mathbf{K_a}(l_a) - \mathbf{K_d}(l_d)||_2. \tag{10}$$

The closest intersection point, *i.e.*, the estimated reflector position, $\mathbf{K_r}$ is their median center: $\mathbf{K_r} = (\mathbf{K_a}(l_a^*) + \mathbf{K_d}(l_d^*))/2$.

To capture the reflector's impact, Pia adopts the concept of virtual AP (vAP) – a virtual signal source that mirrors the position of real AP relative to the reflector (Fig. 13). This idea is inspired by the 60 GHz ray-tracing method [17, 18, 33], which has proven to

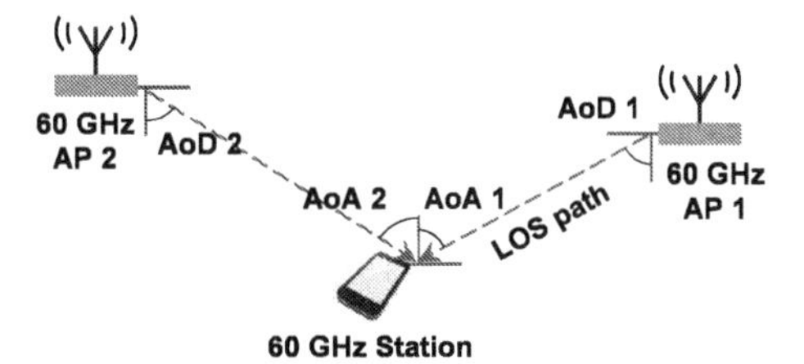

Figure 14: Estimate the initial pose of the client using compressive angle sensing.

predict the 60 GHz signal propagation reasonably close to real measurement. A reflector will redirect the signals so that they look like emitting from the vAP. Given the client position $\mathbf{K_c} = [x_c, y_c, z_c]^T$ and reflector position $\mathbf{K_r}$, the vAP position $\mathbf{K_v}$ can be derived from geometry (Fig. 13), by moving from the reflector position along the AoA direction over distance l_d^*:

$$\mathbf{K_v} = \frac{l_d^*(\mathbf{K_r} - \mathbf{K_c})}{l_a^*} + \mathbf{K_r}. \quad (11)$$

To determine the vAP's orientation (θ_v, φ_v), Pia solves equation:

$$\mathrm{R_y}(\theta_v)\mathrm{R_z}(\varphi_v)\begin{bmatrix}\cos(-\varphi_d)\sin(\theta_d)\\ \sin(-\varphi_d)\sin(\theta_d)\\ \cos(\theta_d)\end{bmatrix} = \frac{\mathbf{K_c} - \mathbf{K_r}}{l_a^*}, \quad (12)$$

where the left side forms a unit vector from vAP's orientation (θ_v, φ_v) toward vAP's AoD direction $(\theta_d, -\varphi_d)$. The unit vector should be at the same direction as the one from reflector's position to client's position (*i.e.*, right side). The azimuth angle of vAP's AoD is negative because it is the mirror symmetry of the real AP.

Once the pose of vAP is determined, it will be used in Pia's spatial sharing module (Sec. 4.1.2) in the same way as a real AP, except that vAP should account for the reflection loss of reflector (estimated in the channel gain g_i). This procedure of vAP localization should be repeated for each reflector during the sensing stage.

4.3 Calibrating the Client's Pose Offset

Since the outputs of APS and reflector sensing will be used by other client devices, in order for Pia to operate correctly, each later joined client that does not run the sensing stage, needs a one-time calibration for its pose. The pose information on mobile devices may contain an unknown initial offset *w.r.t.* the AP's coordinate due to two reasons. *(i)* Not all devices are capable of reporting absolute location/orientation. Many accurate and mature indoor navigation technologies [23, 31, 32, 50, 63] can only measure relative location/orientation change based on visual-inertial sensors. *(ii)* The pose, especially orientation, of a phased array antenna may not be the same as the pose of its host device.

Therefore, Pia needs to estimate an initial pose for each newly joined client *w.r.t.* the AP's coordinate, so that it does not need to rerun the APS and reflector sensing. Our solution is designed upon the compressive angle estimation (Sec. 4.2.1), following two steps:

(i) Determining the in-FoV APs. When a client first enters the network area and moves around, it searches for two nearby APs within the FoV. There are multiple ways to determine if an AP is in the FoV. For example, the client can estimate the link throughput by sending data to the backend server and using the throughput thresholding heuristic in Sec. 2.1. Alternatively, the client can estimate the RSS from the beacon frames. Then, the client estimates the AoAs and AoDs *w.r.t.* the LOS APs (Fig. 14). Note that the sensed angle is relative to the device's phased array antenna rather than the AP's coordinate. Then, the two APs share their pose information (estimated from APS) with the client. *(ii) Determining the initial pose.* The two LOS paths originating from two APs intersect at the client's location (Fig. 14). Given the APs' locations and the AoD of the LOS paths, a simple geometrical calculation can pinpoint the client's location. Pia can determine the client's orientation in the AP's coordinate, in a similar way as finding the vAP's orientation in Sec. 4.2.2. The estimated location and orientation together form the initial pose of the client. It is worth noting that the initial pose estimation requires the AP fall in the client's FoV. Thus, it cannot be applied to assist the network operations, such as AP switching.

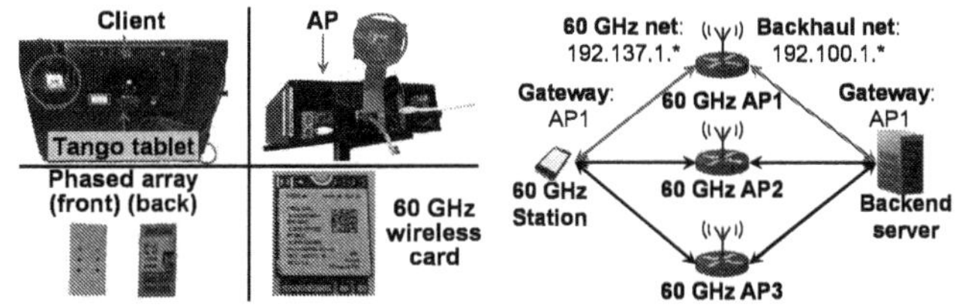

Figure 15: (Left) Pia's hardware components, phased-array in the red circle. (Right) Multi-AP configuration.

5 IMPLEMENTATION

Multi-AP 60 GHz network testbed. We prototype Pia based on a multi-AP 60 GHz testbed, as shown in Fig. 15. The testbed consists of three APs and one client, all equipped with the Qualcomm 60 GHz wireless network interface card (with QCA6310 32-element phased array/RF front-end and QCA6320 MAC/baseband). Each AP is a small PC which interfaces the card through an M.2-to-PCIe adapter. We mount the phased array antenna on a flat panel that can adjust its tilt angle. Each client is a laptop (Acer P446-M59BB) with the phased array built in the outer side of the laptop's cover.

Although the server-to-AP backhaul links can use 60 GHz interfaces with fixed beams, our prototype implements them using 10 Gbps Ethernet with a NETGEAR XS708E switch. We configure the two-hop network into two subnets, and the APs simply act as relays between client and the backend server (Fig. 15). To switch the AP, Pia modifies their gateway, and the data will be forwarded along the new AP. The switching latency is less than 5 ms (Sec. 6.2).

Extracting radio information from Linux driver. We use the latest wil6210 driver [34] for the 60 GHz wireless adapters. Since the firmware (wil6210.fw) and phased array codebook (wil7210.brd) are still unavailable in the Linux firmware library, we port them from a Windows driver (Atheros Sparrow 11ad) released by Acer. We modify the wil6210 driver and make it quickly (131 entries/second) export the low-layer information to user space, including instant (Tx/Rx) throughput, signal quality, active (Tx/Rx) beam index, and (Tx/Rx) MCS. Such information is used as input to Pia's modules.

Client pose. We attach a Google Tango tablet [23] to the laptop's outer surface, which can track the laptop's relative pose at cm-level and degree-level accuracy [14, 21] with less than 80 ms latency [3]. We will evaluate the impact of pose errors in Sec. 6. We develop an Android application that converts the quaternion rotation into pose (Sec. 3.1.1) and streams it to the laptop via USB at 297 entries/second.

Pia components. We implement the major design components (AP selection, APS, spatial sharing, signal angle sensing) in Matlab and C. The algorithms run on the back-end server (Fig. 1) which is a commodity PC with i7-3770k CPU and 16 GB memory. To achieve millisecond AP switching latency, many legacy 802.11 drivers (*e.g.*, ath5k, ath9k, ath10k [2] and iwlwifi) support mac80211 VIF [4] which allows one client to maintain multiple virtual interfaces to different APs [13, 30], thus eliminating the re-authentication and re-association that account for the major overhead in AP switching. Since such support is still under development in wil6210, we achieve rapid AP switching through reverse-tethering, *i.e.*, configuring the AP into the managed mode and client into the AP mode, which allows the laptop to maintain connections to multiple senders.

Measuring beam patterns. Pia's interference management requires the phased array's beam patterns (Sec. 4). Since our 60 GHz radio's hardware specifications are not public, we measure them using the same 60 GHz software radio as in [55, 62, 73]. We place a receiver radio (with a 20° horn antenna) 2 m away from an AP and point its antenna center to the AP's phased array. We mount the AP on a 3D motion controller that can rotate its azimuth/elevation angle at a step of 3°, allowing us to measure the RSS from different directions (*i.e.*, angular beam pattern). Since the beam switching on the 60 GHz wireless card is controlled by closed-source firmware, we are currently unable to switch the phased array's beam directly. In order to obtain the beam patterns for all beam indexes (31 in total), we measure the RSS values of beacon frames at the beginning of each beacon interval, which are sent sequentially by the AP, each using a different beam pattern, following the 802.11ad standard [26, 41]. We predict the BSV using pose data from the measured beam patterns. Besides, we find that in our platform the beacon frames share the same codebook as the data frames. Even though they may be different in other radios, we can still follow the same principle and measure beam patterns of the data frame.

6 EVALUATION

Methodology: We deploy the 60 GHz testbed in a 7×8 m^2 office environment, with 3 APs mounted on stands (2 m height) near the corner of the room, forming a triangle and facing 45° towards the ground. We choose the corner positions because of the physical constraints and convenience, just like the placement of typical home routers. Besides, it is also the best way to stress-test our system's capability since the client needs to perform AP switching more frequently. Pia can easily scale to a larger space with more APs.

To bootstrap the system, we first generate a set of legitimate AP poses to feed APS (Sec. 3.2). Pia creates a bounding box using the rouge room size input by the user, and then partitions the possible AP coordinate by a step of 10 cm. Further increasing the granularity will not improve the AP-pose sensing accuracy because it is already close to the system limit (Sec. 6.1). We then execute the AP switching in real time (Sec. 3.1). The current Qualcomm firmware does not support real-time beam control and RSS feedback for each beacon frame. To evaluate the interference management (Sec. 4.1), we collect BSV data over 100 random client poses for the commodity 60 GHz AP using our customized 60 GHz Rx (Sec. 5). We then use the BSV data as input to evaluate the performance of Pia's spatial reuse, angle sensing, and reflector estimation, which best approximate the end-effect of an actual device.

Metrics: In the micro benchmarks, we focus on metrics directly related to the design modules' performance, *e.g.*, AP selection accuracy, pose error, SIR, and angle sensing error. The system level tests will focus on network-level metrics: throughput, latency, and reliability. We measure the achievable throughput by iperf3 [27] and the network latency by sending back-to-back ping packets. By default, error bars in all results denote the 90-percentile error.

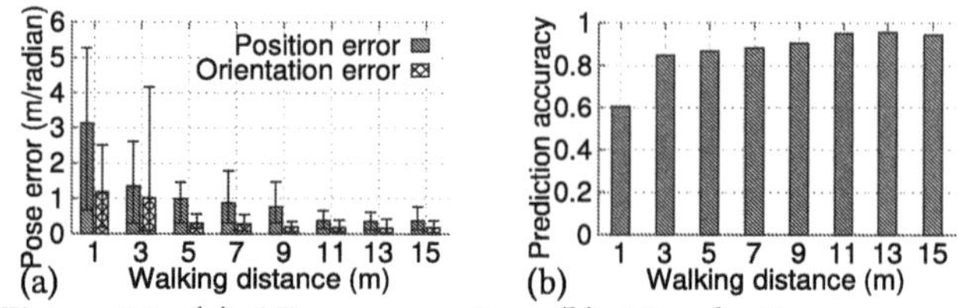

Figure 16: (a) AP-pose sensing, (b) AP selection accuracy, over user's training effort—walking distance.

6.1 Micro Benchmarks

6.1.1 Effectiveness of APS and AP Selection. **Impact of training.** We first evaluate how the sensing stage affects APS (Sec. 3.2) by collecting training data while walking randomly over 15 meters, which only takes a user less than one minute to walk through. We partition the collected data into multiple sizes to evaluate the impact of data size on the sensing accuracy. Fig. 16 (a) shows that both the location error and orientation error decrease dramatically over longer walking traces. When the walking distance is <5 meters, the estimation error tends to be large, because Pia doesn't gather sufficient data to statistically filter out erroneous locations. With >11 m training, the AP's pose error stabilizes at 0.29 m and 0.17 radian (*i.e.*, 9.7°), which indicates *the APS algorithm can quickly estimate AP's pose with minimal training efforts.*

We then use the collected data onwards for Pia's link predictor. Fig. 16 (b) shows that with distance >11 m, *Pia's AP selection reliability (i.e., choosing an in-FoV AP) can maintain at 94.4%.* Pia can achieve a high prediction accuracy using relative small training efforts because it exploits the geometrical structure of the FoV.

Impact of client's pose information error. We then inject Gaussian noise to the collected data, and vary the mean from mm to decimeter-level, consistent with the range of pose errors on mobile devices (Sec. 7). The resulting APS location estimation error (Fig. 17 (a)) grows linearly with the client's pose error. Fortunately, since many recent mobile location tracking schemes [60, 70, 75] can already provide at least 10~30 cm accuracy, the estimated AP pose is sufficient for reliable AP selection. Besides, since the APS is a one-time initialization, specialized tracking devices such as Tango can be used to ensure high precision. In addition, the APS orientation is not sensitive to client's pose error because the sweet spot of ellipsoid center (Sec. 3.2) averages out the deviation.

Fig. 17 (b) plots the impact of pose error on link prediction. The location error has a limited impact—even for 1.21 m client position error, Pia's link prediction accuracy only decreases by 2.1% Yet, 0.52 radians (30°) of orientation error reduces the prediction accuracy by more than 10%, because orientation error more easily deviates the radio's FoV. Fortunately, recent 3D orientation tracking systems can maintain the error below <5° [74], as accurate as Tango. Therefore, Pia can run on mobile devices with more than 90% AP selection accuracy.

AP switching latency. To verify if the client can seamlessly switch across APs, we force it to switch between two APs per second. Fig. 19 plots the round-trip latency between the client and backend server, from which we observe three patterns. The latency is less than 1 ms when measure occurs in a beacon interval (BI), and increases to 3 ms at the beginning of BI due to the beaconing overhead. The 3 ms latency follows the 100 ms periodicity that well matches with the AP's beacon interval. The AP switching causes additional 10~25 ms packet latency, because of the beam training

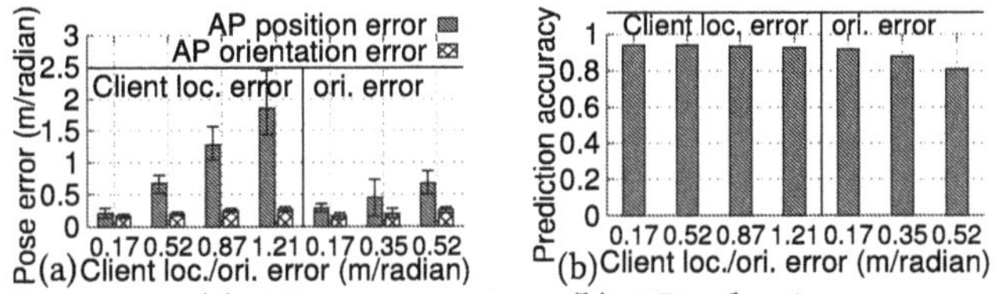

Figure 17: (a) AP-pose sensing, (b) AP selection accuracy, over client's pose error.

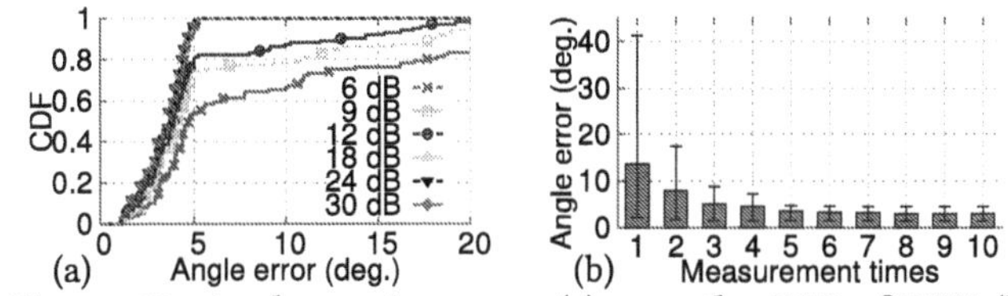

Figure 18: Angle sensing error (a) over the SNR of BSV, (b) using multiple BSVs (SNR=6 dB).

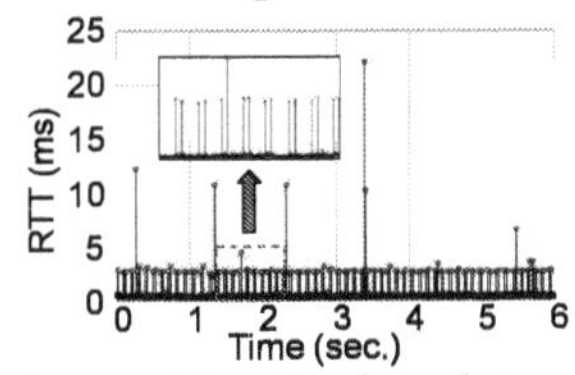

Figure 19: Packet latency during the AP switching.

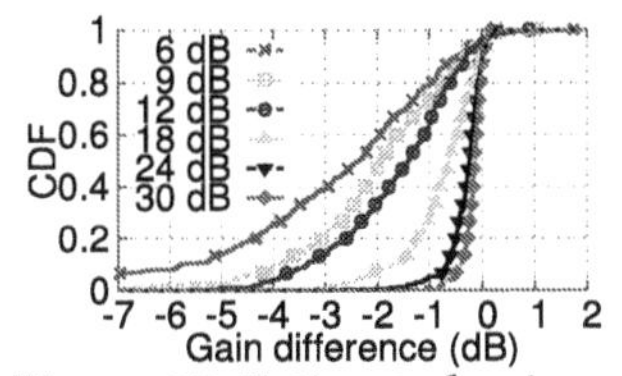

Figure 20: Estimated gain error over SNR of BSV.

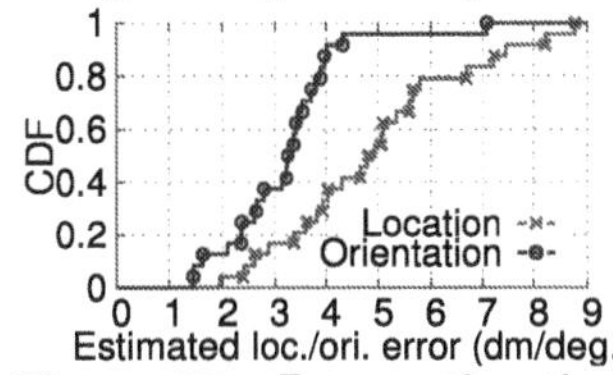

Figure 21: Pose estimation error using angle sensing.

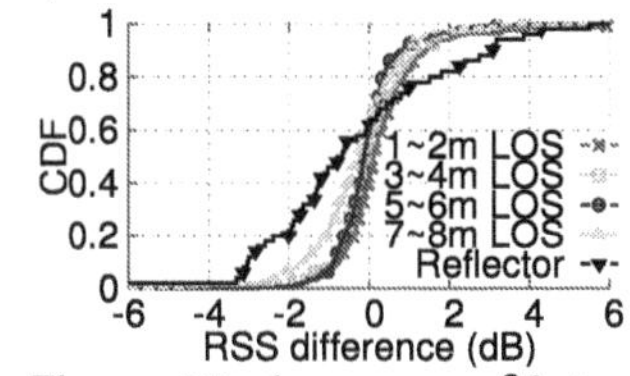

Figure 22: Accuracy of interference prediction.

overhead with the new AP. Yet, every time it only affects a single packet. Besides, the pose information can be exploited to reduce the beam adaptation overhead, which we leave for future work.

6.1.2 Effectiveness of Compressive Angle Estimation and Interference Prediction. **Accuracy of signal angle sensing.** The performance of Pia's compressive angle estimation (Sec. 4.2) is determined by the SNR of BSV measurement. To evaluate the impact, we first measure BSV under higher SNR (>30 dB). Since BSVs are obtained by measuring the detailed waveform of beacon frames, we can add Gaussian noise to the original waveform and create BSVs for different SNRs. The CDF plot in Fig. 18 (a) shows an average angle estimation error of less than 5° when SNR is high (*e.g.*, >9 dB). Residual errors are caused by discretization of the view angles (Sec. 4.2). The angle error may drift a lot under low SNR, when the BSV is significantly distorted by noise. However, by simply repeating the BSV measurement by 5 times and averaging out, angle error can be reduced to less than 5° (Fig. 18 (b)). Such repetitive measurements add little extra sensing time (only 5 BIs for 5 measurements).

Pia's angle sensing can also estimate each path's channel gain (Sec. 4.2.1). Fig. 20 plots the CDF of estimation error, where we obtain the ground-truth by dividing the measured BSV by the predicted one (Sec. 4.1.1). A higher SNR leads to more accurate gain estimation (error <3.4 dB when SNR >9 dB). Notably, the estimated gain is generally smaller than the ground-truth because compressive sensing solver spreads the energy to other directions to minimize the residual error.

Accuracy of client-pose and reflector estimation. Since the client's pose estimation and reflector estimation rely on the compressive angle estimation, we run them consecutively. We first repeat the former at 20 random spots and compare it with ground-truth that measures *w.r.t.* AP's coordinate using a laser range-finder. The result (Fig. 21) shows a mean position offset of 0.5 m. We further place a strong reflector (metal sheet) and randomly vary its position around the Tx/Rx from 1 to 3 m. The reflector position estimation shows similar accuracy, albeit requiring 5 BSV measurements due to low SNR (reflected signal is 10~15 dB weaker than LOS). Notably, the positioning accuracy is comparable to state-of-the-art indoor localization systems [50, 70, 72, 75], and the orientation accuracy < 5° suffices for Pia to run reliably (Fig. 17 (b)).

Interference prediction accuracy. Pia estimates the interference using predicted BSV (Sec. 4.1.2). To verify its accuracy, we calculate the signal strength difference between the collected BSV data and the predicted one subtracted by the pathloss of Frii's model (Sec. 4.1.2). We found Pia can reliably predict the strength of LOS paths based on their poses and active beam indexes regardless of the client-to-AP distance, with a small average error of 0.74 dB (Fig. 22). The prediction error over reflected paths is larger (<4 dB) due to extra errors from reflector estimation. Yet, Pia can tolerate this residual prediction error by using a more conservative decodable threshold (Sec. 4.1.2).

Performance of SLR-based assignment. The SLR-based algorithm evades exponential searching space for optimal AP and beam assignment (Sec. 4.1.2). Fig. 23 (a) and Fig. 23 (b) plot the SIR and Jain's fairness [29] difference between the SLR algorithm and the optimum (*i.e.*, maximizing average SIR). We found at least 50% of the SLR outputs are the optimal assignment (*i.e.*, zero SIR difference), and 90% have <3 dB difference, implying the SLR-based algorithm performs close to the optimum. Furthermore, for those suboptimal assignments, the SLR-based algorithm more likely gives better fairness (*i.e.*, negative fairness difference), because the optimal solution may sacrifice fairness to maximize the SIR.

Since we do not have real-time control over the radio's transmit beam index, we cannot quantify the impact of client's moving speed. The beam selection (Sec. 4.1.2) may not catch up, for instance, if the large pose estimation delay (*i.e.*, time between when pose changes and when estimation changes) is large compared to moving speed. In this case, the radio may have to fall back to the 802.11ad standard. However, for the VR system, since pose information feedback is also used for graphics rendering, we believe the pose estimation delay is sufficiently small for Pia to operate correctly under the VR-motion speed. We will have more exploration in the future work once the hardware grants us a better control.

6.2 System Level Tests

6.2.1 Network Robustness by AP Switching. We conduct a system-level test of the AP switching by emulating the wireless VR scenario, where the client follows a random walk and pan/tilt change. The backend server streams a real-time uncompressed video (1280×720 at 75 FPS, approximately 1.58 Gbps bit-rate) via the APs to clients. Owing to the channel fading, throughput measurement will show small fluctuations even when the link is stationary. The small

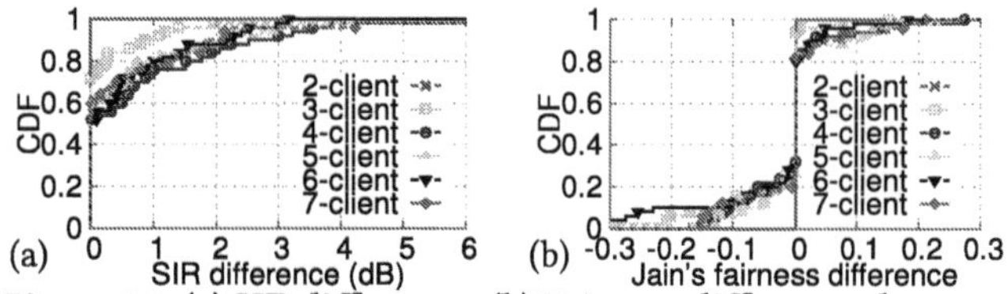

Figure 23: (a) SIR difference, (b) Fairness difference, between SLR-based and SIR-based assignment.

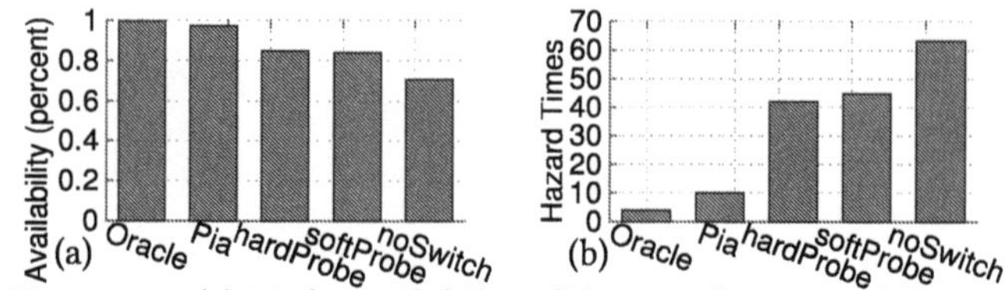

Figure 24: (a) Link availability, (b) Hazard times, of five AP switching schemes.

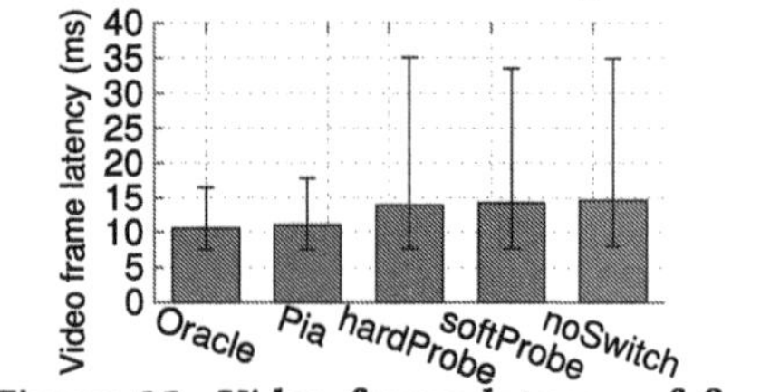

Figure 25: Video frame latency of five AP switching schemes.

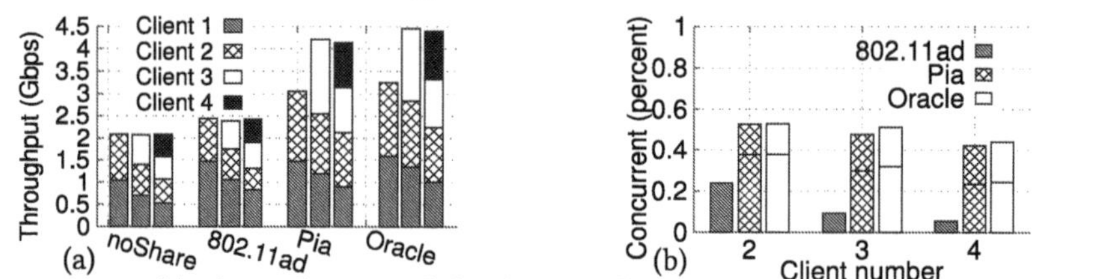

Figure 26: (a) Throughput, and (b) chance of concurrency, by four spatial sharing schemes.

throughput variations do not affect the video transmission reliability, but will falsely trigger many bad link indications if we threshold the link state by the video bitrate. Thus, we choose the threshold as 95% of the video bitrate and consider video frames cannot be delivered reliably when the network throughput drops below $T = 1.50$ Gbps. We run Pia against 4 schemes:

(i) noSwitch: Client connects to a single fixed AP. *(ii) hardProbe:* Client sequentially probes each AP (once per second) by temporarily switching to it and sending a few packets to have the MCS stabilized. If the probed AP's link quality is better, the client will stay with it. *(iii) softProbe:* Client measures network throughput every 0.5s, and probes for the best one only if the throughput drops below T. *(iv) oracle:* Switch AP based on the known throughput in the trace data without counting any overhead.

Link availability. Fig. 24 (a) plots the *link availability, i.e.*, percentage of time that throughput exceeds T. Pia's availability is 97.3%, close to the *oracle* (99.6%) whose availability is below 100% due to certain blind spots not covered by any AP. This can be addressed by proper deployment or adding more APs. The availabilities of other schemes are much lower (< 84.9%). Even *hardProbe* and *softProbe* show low availability due to the AP probing overhead.

Hazard times. Fig. 24 (b) plots hazard times, *i.e.*, the number of occurrences that link throughput drops below T in a 5-minute test. Compared with *noSwitch*, *softProbe*, and *hardProbe*, Pia reduces the hazard times by 6.3×, 4.5× and 4.2×. The extra hazard times over the *oracle* is caused by occasional wrong AP selection. The unavailability, *i.e.*, 1-availability, divided by hazard times gives the average duration of each drop. *Pia can not only quickly recover from wrong predictions, but also prevent most throughput drops by proactively switching the AP.*

Video frame latency. Fig. 25 plots the measured video frame latency. The mean and 90-percentile latency of Pia (11.0 ms and 17.8 ms) are close to the oracle (10.6 ms and 16.4 ms), and much lower other schemes (90-percentile about 40 ms). Note that the latency can be reduced substantially under higher PHY bit-rates (802.11ad supports up to 6.7 Gbps, whereas the Qualcomm radio can only reach 2.5 Gbps).

6.2.2 *Multi-client Spatial Sharing.*

We conduct trace-based emulation to evaluate Pia's spatial sharing mechanism. We reuse the BSV trace collected in Sec. 6.1, calculate the SIRs of clients in concurrent transmission, and map them to the achievable bitrate following a standard 802.11ad rate table [55]. The impact of reflectors is modeled through the vAPs (Sec. 4.2). We determine the AP and beam selection for each client using Pia and 3 baselines: *(i) noShare:* The transmission opportunity is randomly assigned to one client at a time. Each client finds the best AP and beam based on the 802.11ad AP discovery and beam training. *(ii) 802.11ad:* Clients run interference sensing, each in a dedicated BI, to determine the concurrent transmission feasibility (Sec. 4.1). Afterward, they transmit concurrently in next 5 BIs. *(iii) oracle:* Maximizing the clients' SIRs (Eq. (6)).

Throughput gain. Fig. 26 (a) plots the achievable throughput over the number of clients. All clients achieve similar throughput in *noShare*, since it roughly splits the time equally. *802.11ad* improves throughput by 17.3% compared to *noShare*. Yet, clients suffer from unfairness—client1's throughput is 75.7% higher than others, because client1 is at a position causing asymmetric interference that starves others, a well-known problem in directional networks [38]. Pia performs closely to the oracle, with 1.47× and 2× gain over *noShare* for 2 and 3 client cases, respectively, and offers higher fairness. Note that the throughput stops increasing as client number reaches 4 because spatial reuse saturates.

Concurrent transmission opportunity. Fig. 26 (b) plots percentage of successful concurrent transmissions for client1 and client2. Although the percentage gradually decreases as more clients join, Pia improves the concurrent transmission opportunity by 28% and 36.7% for 2-client and 4-client respectively compared to *802.11ad*. The stacked bars represent a breakdown of the source of gain, from selecting beams with weaker signal leakage (bottom) and eliminating interference sensing overhead (top), which together verify the effectiveness of Pia's pose-assisted spatial reuse mechanism.

7 DISCUSSION

60 GHz AP deployment. Based on our experiments, we identified 3 general guidelines to maximize the coverage and effectiveness of Pia in a multi-AP network. *(i)* Deploying the APs higher than typical human heights, such as ceiling, that will maximize the AP's FoV to the client and minimize blockage of other passing-by people.

(ii) However, placing the AP to the ceiling cannot prevent the link blockage. When a user walks away from the AP's beneath center, the client's FoV is still prone to moving out of the AP's FoV. To ensure multi-Gbps coverage everywhere, the APs should be densely deployed. *(iii)* The FoV of APs should be partially overlapped to minimize the number of blind spots. Besides, it is worth noting that Pia is not tied to any specific ways of AP deployment.

Pose information availability. Our evaluation results show Pia can tolerate 0.5 m location error and 0.35 radians orientation error. Current mobile devices, combining motion sensors, light sensor, camera, *etc.*, can already provide accurate pose tracking. A^3 [74] can estimate 3D orientation <5° using accelerometer and magnetometer. Many mobile localization systems [31, 32, 37, 50, 63] can track users at centimeter to decimeter accuracy. Commercial products such as Google Tango [23] can provide the 6-DoF tracking at cm-level accuracy, by using motion sensors and a depth-camera. VR headsets like HTC Vive [25] can tracking user motion at mm-level precision[20], which is the ideal candidate for our system. All of these systems suffice to support Pia's pose-assisted design principle.

Extension to general mobile 60 GHz networks. In this work, we tailored the system design to match a typical wireless VR setup in a constrained room environment. However, the design principles can be extended to general millimeter-wave networks to support mobility and seamless coverage. Although the absolute location tracking technologies for mobile devices may not be sufficiently accurate and reliable, the relative motion tracking (*e.g.*, rotation change and moving offset) using built-in visual-initial sensors can suffice for Pia. To alleviate the accumulated drift of relative tracking, Pia may periodically apply the pose calibration (Sec. 4.3). Moreover, to mitigate the initial training overhead, we could deploy APs to known locations and develop an online-sensing method to infer the phased array's orientation (inside the AP) and reflectors' poses during usage. Though it may trigger many error predictions at the beginning, the accuracy could improve over more collected data, which we will leave for our future work.

8 RELATED WORK

Pia is most closely related with the following domains:

Robust 60 GHz networks. To make 60 GHz networks robust against human blockage and movement, prior research primarily focused on minimizing the beam searching overhead, so that the 60 GHz links can efficiently recover from disruption. Existing systems leveraged the correlation between beams [56] or used out-of-band channel [7, 54] to estimate the best beam at low overhead. However, when blockage occurs, the reflection path may be either weak or non-existent [55]. To ensure better coverage, MoVR [7] adopted a customized 60 GHz relay to amplify and forward the AP's signals. To maximize the beam alignment, MoVR also leverages the pose to guide the AP/mirror's beam steering. Pia shares similar spirit—the multiple APs act as relays for the client. Yet, Pia focuses on the more general problems of AP selection/switching and spatial reuse, harnessing the pose information on client devices. Pia is compatible with 802.11ad or any future 60 GHz base stations, and does not need dedicated analog signal forwarders as in [7].

The general idea of using smartphone sensors to improve network performance has been examined in [47], which proposed to synthesize various motion sensor hints to adapt protocol primitives such as bit-rate adaptation. Sani *et al.* [8] conducted an empirical study and showed that, by judiciously choosing among multiple directional antennas on a mobile device based on motion sensor information, the WiFi link SNR can be improved by 3 dB. In contrast, new challenges emerge in 60 GHz networks due to vulnerability to blockage and limited FoV. Meanwhile, the electronically steerable beams bring new opportunities to spatial reuse. Yang *et al.* [69] designed a sensor-assisted multi-level codebook for efficient beam searching under mobility. Pia, in contrast, harnesses the 5-DoF pose information to address the network-level problems arising from multiple APs and clients.

AP handover and selection. Numerous solutions have been proposed to curtail the AP handover/reassociation overhead in WiFi networks. The most viable idea is to fork multiple virtual network interfaces [13, 30]. Although the switching mechanism itself is still applicable, the decision metrics for switching (*e.g.*, signal strength, distance [39, 52] and location [22, 44, 51]) in low-frequency networks are no longer applicable to the 60 GHz network due to orientation sensitivity. Alternative machine-learning based selection algorithms [16, 53, 68]) have been explored. However, such learning algorithms require dense training, and the accuracy is still much lower compared with Pia's geometry-model based algorithm (Sec. 6.1). Athanasiou *et al.* [9] proposed an asymptotically optimal algorithm to balance and ensure fair client association in 60 GHz networks. In contrast, Pia is the first work from an architecture/systems perspective that optimizes the 60 GHz link quality and reliability via AP/beam switching using the pose information.

Spatial reuse of 60 GHz networks. Directional antennas are known for achieving spatial reuse and alleviating interference. A vast literature [11] explored the MAC issues in directional networks. DIRC [38] further accounted for the impact of irregular interference with imperfect directionality. These systems focus on static radios, with a cone-shaped antenna model, which differs dramatically from the beam shape of practical 60 GHz phased arrays (Sec. 4.1). Park *et al.* [43] proposed a null-forming technique that can create specific null points to avoid interfering peer devices, but this requires arbitrary control of the antenna weights, whereas practical 60 GHz phased arrays can only use a set of fixed beamforming weights which form a codebook.

9 CONCLUSION

Whereas the "laser-like" beam of millimeter-wave radios has triggered many doubts about their coverage, we have demonstrated the high potential of Pia to address the concern. Pia employs the 5-DoF pose information on mobile devices, together with a multi-AP network architecture, to achieve seamless coverage under mobility and user's orientation change. Pia can be applied to meet the needs of demanding Gbps applications such as wireless VR. Its design principle of pose-assisted mobility 60 GHz networking can also be extended to general mmWave pico-cell/small-cell networks with dense AP deployment.

ACKNOWLEDGEMENTS

We appreciate the insightful feedback from the anonymous reviewers and our shepherd Professor Haitham Hassanieh who helped improving this work. This project is supported in part by the NSF under Grant CNS-1506657, CNS-1518728, CNS-1343363, CNS-1350039, and CNS-1617321.

REFERENCES

[1] 2009. IEEE Standards 802.15.3c. (2009).

[2] 2014. Virtual STA and AP Interfaces with ath5k, ath9k and ath10k. http://www.candelatech.com/vsta.php. (2014).

[3] 2015. Google Wants to Use Tango Tech for VR, But Admits Current Dev Kits Arenfit Optimized. http://www.roadtovr.com/google-wants-to-use-tango-tech-for-vr-but-admits-current-dev-kits-arent-optimized/. (2015).

[4] 2015. mac80211 Multiple Virtual Interface (vif) Support. https://wireless.wiki.kernel.org/en/users/documentation/iw/vif. (2015).

[5] 2016. IEEE 802.11ay Study Group. http://www.ieee802.org/11/Reports/tgay_update.htm. (2016).

[6] 2016. Miracast. http://www.wi-fi.org/wi-fi-certified-miracast/. (2016).

[7] Omid Abari, Dinesh Bharadia, Austin Duffield, and Dina Katabi. 2016. Cutting the Cord in Virtual Reality. In *Proceedings of the ACM Workshop on Hot Topics in Networks (HotNets)*.

[8] Ardalan Amiri Sani, Lin Zhong, and Ashutosh Sabharwal. 2010. Directional Antenna Diversity for Mobile Devices: Characterizations and Solutions. In *Proceedings of the International Conference on Mobile Computing and Networking (MobiCom)*.

[9] George Athanasiou, Pradeep Chathuranga Weeraddana, Carlo Fischione, and Leandros Tassiulas. 2015. Optimizing client association for load balancing and fairness in millimeter-wave wireless networks. *IEEE/ACM Transactions on Networking* (2015).

[10] Yaakov Bar-Shalom, X Rong Li, and Thiagalingam Kirubarajan. 2004. *Estimation With Applications to Tracking and Navigation: Theory Algorithms and Software.* John Wiley & Sons.

[11] O. Bazan and M. Jaseemuddin. 2012. A Survey On MAC Protocols for Wireless Adhoc Networks with Beamforming Antennas. *IEEE Communications Surveys Tutorials* 14, 2 (2012).

[12] Emmanuel Candes and Justin Romberg. 2005. L1-Magic: Recovery of Sparse Signals via Convex Programming. *URL: www. acm. caltech. edu/l1magic/downloads/l1magic. pdf* (2005).

[13] Ranveer Chandra and Paramvir Bahl. 2004. MultiNet: Connecting to Multiple IEEE 802.11 Networks Using a Single Wireless Card. In *INFOCOM 2004. Twenty-third AnnualJoint Conference of the IEEE Computer and Communications Societies.* IEEE.

[14] Matthew Costi and Robert Dabrowski. 2014. Mobile Motion Capture. (2014).

[15] Bao Linh Dang, M Garcia Larrode, R Venkatesha Prasad, Ignas Niemegeers, and AMJ Koonen. 2007. Radio-Over-Fiber Based Architecture for Seamless Wireless Indoor Communication in the 60GHz Band. *Computer communications* (2007).

[16] Manpreet Singh Dang, Amol Prakash, Dinesh K Anvekar, D Kapoor, and Rajeev Shorey. 2000. Fuzzy Logic Based Handoff in Wireless Networks. In *Vehicular Technology Conference Proceedings, 2000. VTC 2000-Spring Tokyo. 2000 IEEE 51st*, Vol. 3. IEEE.

[17] Eric De Groot, Tamal Bose, Clint Cooper, and Matt Kruse. 2014. Remote Transmitter Tracking with Raytraced Fingerprint Database. In *IEEE MILCOM*.

[18] Degli-Esposti and etc. 2014. Ray-Tracing-Based mm-Wave Beamforming Assessment. *IEEE Access* (2014).

[19] Cedric Dehos, Jose Luis González, Antonio De Domenico, Dimitri Kténas, and Laurent Dussopt. 2014. Millimeter-Wave Access and Backhauling: The Solution to the Exponential Data Traffic Increase in 5G Mobile Communications Systems? *IEEE Communications Magazine* (2014).

[20] Doc-Ok.org. 2016. Lighthouse Tracking Examined. http://doc-ok.org/?p=1478. (2016).

[21] Eberhard Glch. 2016. Investigations on Google Tango Development Kit for Personal Indoor Mapping. https://agile-online.org/conference_paper/cds/agile_2016/posters/102_Paper_in_PDF.pdf. (2016).

[22] Kristian Evensen, Andreas Petlund, Haakon Riiser, Paul Vigmostad, Dominik Kaspar, Carsten Griwodz, and Pål Halvorsen. 2011. Mobile Video Streaming Using Location-based Network Prediction and Transparent Handover. In *International Workshop on Network and Operating Systems Support for Digital Audio and Video (NOSSDAV)*.

[23] Google. 2014. Tango. https://get.google.com/tango/. (2014).

[24] Michael Grant and Stephen Boyd. 2014. CVX: Matlab Software for Disciplined Convex Programming, version 2.1. http://cvxr.com/cvx. (March 2014).

[25] HTC. 2016. Vive. https://www.vive.com/us/. (2016).

[26] IEEE Standards Association. 2012. IEEE Standards 802.11ad-2012: Enhancements for Very High Throughput in the 60 GHz Band. (2012).

[27] iPerf. 2015. The Ultimate Speed Test Tool for TCP, UDP and SCTP. https://iperf.fr/. (2015).

[28] Ahmadreza Jafari, Julien Sarrazin, David Lautru, Aziz Benlarbi-Delai, Luca Petrillo, and Philippe De Doncker. 2013. NLOS Influence on 60 GHz Indoor Localization Based on a New TDOA Extraction Approach. In *Microwave Conference (EuMC), 2013 European.* IEEE.

[29] Raj Jain, Dah-Ming Chiu, and William R Hawe. 1984. *A Quantitative Measure of Fairness and Discrimination for Resource Allocation in Shared Computer System.* Eastern Research Laboratory, Digital Equipment Corporation Hudson, MA.

[30] Srikanth Kandula, Kate Ching-Ju Lin, Tural Badirkhanli, and Dina Katabi. 2008. FatVAP: Aggregating AP Backhaul Capacity to Maximize Throughput. In *USENIX NSDI*.

[31] Wonho Kang and Youngnam Han. 2015. SmartPDR: Smartphone-Based Pedestrian Dead Reckoning for Indoor Localization. *IEEE Sensors journal* (2015).

[32] Wonho Kang, Seongho Nam, Youngnam Han, and Sookjin Lee. 2012. Improved Heading Estimation for Smartphone-Based Indoor Positioning Systems. In *Personal Indoor and Mobile Radio Communications (PIMRC), 2012 IEEE 23rd International Symposium on.* IEEE.

[33] A Khafaji, R Saadane, J El Abbadi, and M Belkasmi. 2008. Ray Tracing Technique based 60 GHz Band Propagation Modeling and Influence of People Shadowing. *IJECSE* (2008).

[34] Kvalo. 2016. Linux wil6210 Driver. http://git.kernel.org/pub/scm/linux/kernel/git-/kvalo/ath.git/. (2016).

[35] B Langen, G Lober, and W+ Herzig. 1994. Reflection and Transmission Behaviour of Building Materials at 60 Ghz. In *Personal, Indoor and Mobile Radio Communications, 1994. Wireless Networks-Catching the Mobile Future., 5th IEEE International Symposium on.* IEEE.

[36] Lenovo. 2016. Phab 2 Pro With Tango. http://shop.lenovo.com/us/en/tango/. (2016).

[37] Kaikai Liu, Xinxin Liu, and Xiaolin Li. 2013. Guoguo: Enabling Fine-Grained Indoor Localization via Smartphone. In *MobiSys.* ACM.

[38] Xi Liu, Anmol Sheth, Michael Kaminsky, Konstantina Papagiannaki, Srinivasan Seshan, and Peter Steenkiste. 2009. DIRC: Increasing Indoor Wireless Capacity Using Directional Antennas. *ACM SIGCOMM Computer Communication Review* (2009).

[39] Anthony J Nicholson, Yatin Chawathe, Mike Y Chen, Brian D Noble, and David Wetherall. 2006. Improved Access Point Selection. In *Proceedings of the 4th international conference on Mobile systems, applications and services.* ACM.

[40] Thomas Nitsche, Guillermo Bielsa, Irene Tejado, Adrian Loch, and Joerg Widmer. 2015. Boon and Bane of 60 GHz Networks: Practical Insights Into Beamforming, Interference, and Frame Level Operation. In *Proceedings of the 11th ACM Conference on Emerging Networking Experiments and Technologies.* ACM.

[41] Thomas Nitsche, Carlos Cordeiro, Adriana Flores, Edward W Knightly, Eldad Perahia, and Joerg C Widmer. 2014. IEEE 802.11 ad: Directional 60 GHz Communication for Multi-Gbps Wi-Fi. (2014).

[42] Sergio Orts-Escolano, Christoph Rhemann, Sean Fanello, Wayne Chang, Adarsh Kowdle, Yury Degtyarev, David Kim, Philip L. Davidson, Sameh Khamis, Mingsong Dou, Vladimir Tankovich, Charles Loop, Qin Cai, Philip A. Chou, Sarah Mennicken, Julien Valentin, Vivek Pradeep, Shenlong Wang, Sing Bing Kang, Pushmeet Kohli, Yuliya Lutchyn, Cem Keskin, and Shahram Izadi. 2016. Holoportation: Virtual 3D Teleportation in Real-time. In *Proceedings of ACM Symposium on User Interface Software and Technology (UIST)*.

[43] Minyoung Park, Praveen Gopalakrishnan, and Richard Roberts. 2009. Interference Mitigation Techniques in 60 GHz Wireless Networks. *IEEE Communications Magazine* (2009).

[44] V. Pichapati, H. Kowshik, A. P. Subramanian, R. Kokku, and M. Chetlur. 2014. Location Assisted Handoffs in Dense Cellular Networks. In *IEEE International Conference on Sensing, Communication, and Networking (SECON)*.

[45] Qualcomm. 2016. Qualcomm 802.11ad Products to Lead the Way for Multi-band Wi-Fi Ecosystem. https://www.qualcomm.com/news/releases/2016/01/05/qualcomm-80211ad-products-lead-way-multi-band-wi-fi-ecosystem. (2016).

[46] Kishore Ramachandran, Narayan Prasad, Kenichi Hosoya, Kenichi Maruhashi, and Sampath Rangarajan. 2010. Adaptive Beamforming for 60 GHz Radios: Challenges and Preliminary Solutions. In *Proceedings of the ACM International Workshop on mmWave Communications: From Circuits to Networks (mmCom)*.

[47] Lenin Ravindranath, Calvin Newport, Hari Balakrishnan, and Samuel Madden. 2011. Improving Wireless Network Performance Using Sensor Hints. In *Proc. of USENIX NSDI*.

[48] Corbett Rowell and Edmund Y Lam. 2012. Mobile-phone antenna design. *IEEE Antennas and Propagation Magazine* (2012).

[49] Swetank Kumar Saha, Viral Vijay Vira, Anuj Garg, and Dimitrios Koutsonikolas. 2015. 60 GHz Multi-Gigabit Indoor WLANs: Dream or Reality? *arXiv preprint arXiv:1509.04274* (2015).

[50] Yuanchao Shu, Kang G Shin, Tian He, and Jiming Chen. 2015. Last-Mile Navigation Using Smartphones. In *Proceedings of the 21st Annual International Conference on Mobile Computing and Networking.* ACM.

[51] Wee-Seng Soh and H. S. Kim. 2003. QoS Provisioning in Cellular Networks Based on Mobility Prediction Techniques. *IEEE Communications Magazine* 41, 1 (2003).

[52] Ivan Stojmenovic. 2003. *Handbook of Wireless Networks and Mobile Computing.* John Wiley & Sons.

[53] Raungrong Suleesathira and Sunisa Kunarak. 2005. Neural Network Handoff in Shadow-Rayleigh Fading. In *Circuits and Systems, 2005. ISCAS 2005. IEEE International Symposium on.* IEEE.

[54] Sanjib Sur, Ioannis Pefkianakis, Xinyu Zhang, and Kyu-Han Kim. 2017. WiFi-Assisted 60 GHz Wireless Networks. In *Proc. of ACM MobiCom.*

[55] Sanjib Sur, V. Venkateswaran, X. Zhang, and P. Ramanathan. 2015. 60 GHz Indoor Networking through Flexible Beams: A Link-Level Profiling. In *Proceedings of ACM SIGMETRICS.*

[56] Sanjib Sur, Xinyu Zhang, Parmesh Ramanathan, and Ranveer Chandra. 2016. BeamSpy: Enabling Robust 60 GHz Links Under Blockage. In *13th USENIX*

Symposium on Networked Systems Design and Implementation (NSDI 16).
[57] Guhapriyan Thanikachalam Tapan Pattnayak. 2016. Antenna Design and RF Layout Guidelines. Cypress Semiconductor. (2016).
[58] Michael J Todd and E Alper Yıldırım. 2007. On Khachiyan's algorithm for the computation of minimum-volume enclosing ellipsoids. *Discrete Applied Mathematics* (2007).
[59] TPCAST. 2016. HTC VIVE Wireless Upgrade Kit. http://www.tpcast.cn/h_en/index.html. (2016).
[60] Deepak Vasisht, Swarun Kumar, and Dina Katabi. 2016. Decimeter-level Localization With a Single WiFi Access Point. In *Proceedings of Usenix Conference on Networked Systems Design and Implementation (NSDI).*
[61] Junyi Wang, Zhou Lan, Chin-Sean Sum, Chang-Woo Pyo, Jing Gao, Tuncer Baykas, Azizur Rahman, Ryuhei Funada, Fumihide Kojima, Ismail Lakkis, and others. 2009. Beamforming Codebook Design and Performance Evaluation for 60GHz Wideband WPANs. In *IEEE Trans. on Vehicular Technology.*
[62] Teng Wei and Xinyu Zhang. 2017. Facilitating Robust 60 GHz Network Deployment By Sensing Ambient Reflectors. In *USENIX NSDI.*
[63] Martin Werner, Moritz Kessel, and Chadly Marouane. 2011. Indoor Positioning Using Smartphone Camera. In *Indoor Positioning and Indoor Navigation (IPIN), 2011 International Conference on.* IEEE.
[64] Wikipedia. 2016. Friis Transmission Equation. https://en.wikipedia.org/wiki/Friis_transmission_equation. (2016).
[65] Wikipedia. 2016. Rotation Matrix in 3D. https://en.wikipedia.org/wiki/Rotation_matrix. (2016).
[66] Wikipedia. 2017. Four-Quadrant Inverse Tangent. https://en.wikipedia.org/wiki/Atan2. (2017).
[67] Wikipedia. 2017. Geodesic Grid. https://en.wikipedia.org/wiki/Geodesic_grid. (2017).
[68] K Daniel Wong and Donald C Cox. 2000. A Pattern Recognition System for Handoff Algorithms. *IEEE Journal on selected areas in communications* (2000).
[69] Zhicheng Yang, Parth H Pathak, Yunze Zeng, and Prasant Mohapatra. 2015. Sensor-Assisted Codebook-Based Beamforming for Mobility Management in 60 Ghz WLANs. In *IEEE International Conference on Mobile Ad Hoc and Sensor Systems (MASS).*
[70] Chi Zhang and Xinyu Zhang. 2016. LiTell: robust Indoor Localization Using Unmodified Light Fixtures. In *Proceedings of the 22nd Annual International Conference on Mobile Computing and Networking.*
[71] Jialiang Zhang, Xinyu Zhang, Pushkar Kulkarni, and Parameswaran Ramanathan. 2016. OpenMili: A 60 GHz Software Radio Platform with a Reconfigurable Phased-Array Antenna. In *Proceedings of ACM MobiCom.*
[72] Yuanqing Zheng, Guobin Shen, Liqun Li, Chunshui Zhao, Mo Li, and Feng Zhao. 2014. Travi-Navi: Self-Deployable Indoor Navigation System. In *Proceedings of the 20th annual international conference on Mobile computing and networking.* ACM.
[73] Anfu Zhou, Xinyu Zhang, and Huadong Ma. 2016. Beam-forecast: Facilitating Mobile 60 GHz Networks via Model-driven Beam Steering. In *Proc. of IEEE INFOCOM.*
[74] Pengfei Zhou, Mo Li, and Guobin Shen. 2014. Use It Free: Instantly Knowing Your Phone Attitude. In *Proceedings of the 20th annual international conference on Mobile computing and networking.* ACM.
[75] Shilin Zhu and Xinyu Zhang. 2017. Enabling High-Precision Visible Light Localization in Today's Buildings. In *Proc. of ACM MobiSys.*
[76] Yibo Zhu, Zengbin Zhang, Zhinus Marzi, Chris Nelson, Upamanyu Madhow, Ben Y Zhao, and Haitao Zheng. 2014. Demystifying 60GHz Outdoor Picocells. In *Proceedings of ACM MobiCom.*
[77] Yanzi Zhu, Yibo Zhu, Ben Y. Zhao, and Haitao Zheng. 2015. Reusing 60GHz Radios for Mobile Radar Imaging. In *Proc. of ACM MobiCom.*

A Control-Plane Perspective on Reducing Data Access Latency in LTE Networks

Yuanjie Li*
University of California, Los Angeles
Los Angeles, CA
yuanjie.li@cs.ucla.edu

Zengwen Yuan*
University of California, Los Angeles
Los Angeles, CA
zyuan@cs.ucla.edu

Chunyi Peng
Purdue University
West Lafayette, IN
chunyi@purdue.edu

ABSTRACT

Control-plane operations are indispensable to providing data access to mobile devices in the 4G LTE networks. They provision necessary control states at the device and network nodes to enable data access. However, the current design may suffer from long data access latency even under good radio conditions. The fundamental problem is that, data-plane packet delivery cannot start or resume until all control-plane procedures are completed, and these control procedures run *sequentially* by design. We show both are *more than necessary* under popular use cases. We design DPCM, which reduces data access latency through parallel processing approaches and exploiting device-side state replica. We implement DPCM and validate its effectiveness with extensive evaluations.

KEYWORDS

4G/5G network, control plane, latency, parallel processing, device-side state replica

1 INTRODUCTION

Mobile users want always-on, low-latency network services. When accessing the Internet, we want data services available immediately. When we move, we expect negligible service suspension in mobility. This demand will be more pressing with the emerging delay-sensitive services, such as real-time virtual reality, safe autonomous driving, remote healthcare monitoring, etc.

In achieving this, the control plane operations play a vital role on providing users data access in the state-of-art mobile network (4G LTE). To establish data access to the Internet, the control plane must first create a service *session* (aka. connectivity) for each device. This session will install states at the device and all involved network nodes (base station, gateway, and mobility controller). When the device moves, it should retain the data access by migrating the ongoing session states to the user's new location. Upon transient failures (radio link outage, or rejected requests during control procedure), the session needs to be recovered or recreated. In all cases, these control procedures are well justified, since they provision necessary states to enable mobile data access. In fact, they need to be successfully completed before starting/resuming the data-plane packet delivery. This leads to user-perceived data access latency.

Unfortunately, we find that the current LTE control-plane operations are slow. Our 19-month user study over four major US carriers shows that, such control functions result in frequent impact on latency. For each device, the session establishment happens every 106.9s on average. The control functions contributes 72.5–999.6 ms latency to *every* session establishment, resulting in aggregated negative impacts. Such control functions result in the average latency of 168.7ms, 901.6ms and 0.8–3.0s (up to 1.1s, 1.9s, 11.0s) in *every* service establishment, wide-area roaming via location update and service access upon various failures (§2).

The fundamental reason is that, these procedures are mandated to run in globally *sequential* order. While intuitive and straightforward, this is inefficient for three reasons: (1) Some control procedures are not mandatory to starting/resuming data service, but they have to be completed first; (2) Some control procedures could run in parallel, but they are mandated to run sequentially; and (3) In presence of failures, the entire control sequence would be blocked, thus prolonging the latency. While discovered 4G LTE, such sequential execution design is a common practice, and still continues in various ongoing 5G standardization proposals [18].

We propose DPCM, a paradigm that reduces data access latency by accelerating the control-plane operations. The key observation is that, data-plane forwarding can start *without* waiting for *all* the control procedures to be completed. DPCM treats the control procedures as a state management problem, and accelerates the data access with three techniques. It first bypasses certain sequence of control procedures, and substitute them with equivalent, faster operations. To this end, we leverage the state replicas that are already available at the device, retrieve them early and install them at the nodes of interest. Second, we pipeline certain control-plane signaling procedures with the data-plane packet delivery. Last, DPCM parallelizes control procedures that are mandatory to retaining data service. We implement DPCM as a modular extension of OpenAirInterface [4], a software-defined cellular protocol stack. Our evaluation shows that, for every session establishment, wide-area roaming and various failure handling, on average DPCM achieves 88.7ms (2.1×), 735.4ms (5.8×) and 580.8ms–2.6s (7.8×–11.5×) latency reduction, respectively. On average, it reduces the video loading time from 9.8s to 5.7s (1.7×), and web loading from 1.5s to 0.7s (2.1×).

*The first two authors contribute equally to this work.

MobiCom '17, October 16–20, 2017, Snowbird, UT, USA

ACM ISBN 978-1-4503-4916-1/17/10...$15.00
https://doi.org/10.1145/3117811.3117838

2 MEASURING LATENCY

We motivate our work with an experimental study of user-perceived data latency in operational 4G networks. Our latency study covers

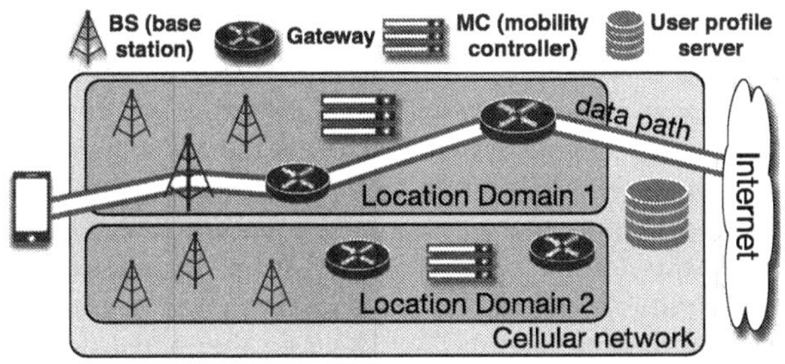

Figure 1: LTE network architecture.

	AT&T	T-Mobile	Sprint	Verizon	Total
Message#	290,677	692,916	144,868	94,212	1,222,673
Record#	24,053	51,620	9,632	9,752	95,057

Table 1: Dataset in the user study.

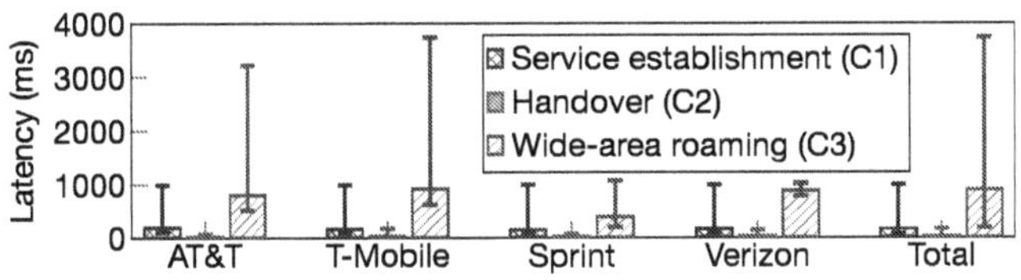

Figure 2: Latency measured in major U.S. LTE operators.

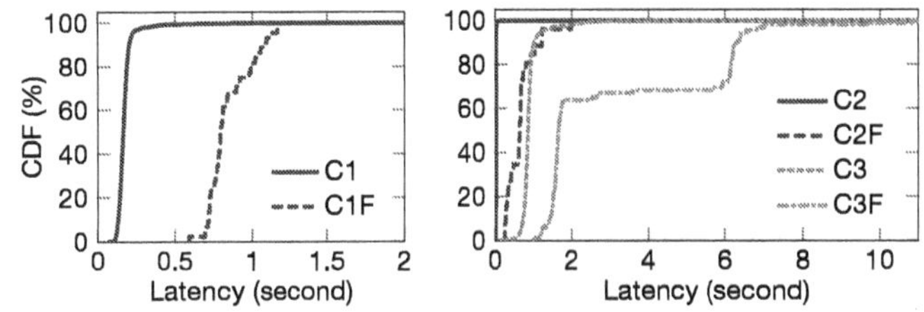

Figure 3: CDF of latency measured in all cases.

	C1	C1F	C2	C2F	C3	C3F
Record#	81,285	44	9,665	106	2840	141
avg (ms)	168.7	846.9	24.7	670.1	901.6	3004.5
50th (ms)	161.7	791.7	23.9	639.9	855.9	1647.8
95th (ms)	219.9	1138.0	37.8	1381.9	1235.1	6545.4
min (ms)	72.5	591.9	13.7	252.5	193.8	1167.5
max (ms)	999.6	1165.0	177.5	1995.0	3740.5	11019.0

Table 2: Statistics of latency measured.

three main usage cases: establishing data access (C1), retaining data access upon handover (C2) and wide-area roaming (C3).

Background: 4G LTE network. Figure 1 depicts a simplified LTE network architecture, consisting of four types of nodes: the base station (BS), the gateways (GWs), the mobility controller (MC), and the user profile server[1]. Similar to the Internet, the LTE performs both control and data plane operations. On the data plane, IP packets are delivered between the device and the Internet or between devices. The BS offers radio access to the device, while the gateways deliver data packets over the core infrastructure. On the control plane, various functions are provided to facilitate data delivery, including radio resource allocation, session management, mobility support, billing, and security, etc.

To support user mobility, the 4G network infrastructure is divided into multiple location domains. Each domain has multiple BSes and gateways, and is managed by an MC. Retaining data service in mobility has two cases: (1) *handover* within a domain, and (2) wide-area roaming (via *location update*) across domains.

Methodology and Dataset. We invited 15 volunteers (students, faculty members and company employees) using 23 phones, to sporadically participate in the user study during the 19-month period from 07/31/2015 to 02/28/2017. This study uses seven Android models (Google Pixel, Huawei Nexus 6P, Motorola Nexus 6, Samsung Galaxy S4/S5, LG Optimus 2, and LG Tribute) and two iPhone models (iPhone 5 and iPhone 6s Plus), over all four major US carriers.

We measure latency by analyzing control-plane messages collected by MobileInsight [3, 38], an open-source tool that enables the collection of fine-grained 4G protocol messages inside the phones. To identify the latency of each control procedure, we correlate each with our traces by following LTE standards [8, 11, 14]. We extract data access establishment and mobility records (each as a sequence of cellular messages, see Figure 4). For each record, we locate the messages to indicate the start/end events to retrieve latency (response/suspension/interruption time). As data services are initiated or resumed until these control functions finish, latency perceived by users is no shorter than the duration signified by the signaling messages. We thus measure the lower bound. We further preserve user privacy by not collecting user/phone identities or other phone logs. Our dataset includes 1,222,673 4G signaling messages, from which 95,057 session establishments/migrations are extracted (Table 1).

Figure 2, Figure 3 and Table 2 show the latency in all three cases without/with transient failures. The results are consistent across network carriers with different phone models.

C1: Latency in establishing new data service. We calculate the time elapsed from issuing the data service request to accessing the data service. Our result shows that, it takes 168.7 ms on average, ranging from 72.5 ms to 999.6 ms. Note that this latency is observed by every data session whenever a user starts. It is frequently experienced by users in reality. In the user study of 81,285 session establishments, a new data access is seen every 106.9 seconds. In the presence of transient radio outage (2.8% probability among all the requests), the latency is prolonged by 591.9–1165.0 ms in each establishment (C1F). The average delay increases to 846.9 ms (5.0×).

C2: Latency in retaining data service in handover. With an ongoing data, when the user moves to a different BS in the same location domain, the radio signal to the old base station turns weak, and handover is triggered. Our user study shows that, handover occurs every 70.0 s on average in walking scenarios. Normally, handover provides seamless mobility support, and small suspension is observed (24.7ms on average). However, transient radio outage may occur during handovers. We have observed 1.1% (106 out of 9,771) such failure instances. In such cases, transient outage incurs 670.1 ms delay on average, ranging between [252.5 ms, 1.9s].

[1]In 4G LTE jargons, they are eNodeB, serving gateway and packet data network gateway, mobility management entity, and home subscriber server, respectively.

C3: Latency in wide-area roaming. As the user roams in wide areas (e.g., during driving) across location domains, mobility support via location update is needed. The data service will be suspended, as the LTE core network has to migrate the user's data session states from the old location domain to the new domain. It is less frequent than handover, since it only occurs when the device crosses the location domain. Our study indicates that, 75% of location updates are triggered with less than 14 handoffs. Once it occurs, however, its impact on latency is larger. It takes 901.6ms on average to resume the service, in the range of [193.8ms, 3.7s]. Though C3 is not as frequent as starting new data access (C1), its impact on user's service disruption is more visible. We have observed 2,840 events with 5.3x disruption time on average.

Moreover, wide-area roaming is failure prone. Roaming failures are often caused by location update reject events. Upon such failures, service disruption latency is significantly prolonged (C3F). Our user study has found 141 C3F instances, which count 4.7% of all wide-area roaming events. Each failure incurs 3.0s delay on average, with 2.1s more service disruption than the failure-free case (C3).

3 UNDERSTANDING LATENCY

We next analyze where the above latency stems from. We show the control-plane operations are major latency contributors. The fundamental problem is that, to enforce correct data service, 4G LTE runs control procedures *sequentially*, thus satisfying the sequential consistency model. While intuitive and straightforward, such design is at the cost of long latency. We examine how control procedures are performed and viewed from a state management perspective, and gain insights on how to reduce their latency.

3.1 Service Establishment (C1)

The service establishment (C1) is initiated on a per-data-session basis. It is invoked once the device wants to access cellular data but has no active radio connectivity (idle mode). Prior study [52] shows that the device enters the idle mode after about 10 ± 0.5 seconds of inactivity. Consequently, C1 is activated frequently in practice.

Figure 4a plots the procedures for data session establishment in LTE. It shows that the control-plane procedures *precede* the data-plane delivery; this is mandated by the 3GPP standards [11, 14, 15].

For uplink, before data delivery starts, the control-plane procedures P1–P5 have to be completed *sequentially*. Such procedures involve four network nodes: BS, the gateways, MC, and the user profile server. The device first establishes radio connectivity with BS in P1, BS then sends a service request to MC in P2, MC performs authentication and security functions with the profile server in P3, MC sends the context setup request to BS in P4, and BS establishes radio bearer with the device in P5. Note that P1, P3, and P5 involve multiple rounds of message exchanges.

For downlink access, three more control procedures P6, P7, and P8 need to be completed before data delivery starts. They help the gateway to notify the device. Specifically, the gateway notifies MC on downlink data in P6, MC sends the paging message to BS and BS relays it to the device in P7. The gateway obtains the route through bearer modification in P8. After that, downlink data forwarding can start through the gateway, BS, and the device.

State management perspective. The above operations manage the control-plane states across network nodes via message passing. We next show that, data delivery can be started earlier, once all the needed control-plane states are available at those involved network nodes. This sheds light on how to reduce data access latency.

Distributed state management addresses three key issues: (1) What are the states to be managed? (2) What operations are performed on the states? (3) How such operations are realized in the distributed network setting? We focus on the *shared* states that need to be propagated across nodes, since *local* states do not need message passing between nodes.

We have analyzed the LTE standards [7, 8, 11, 13, 14] and identified six control-plane *states* required for data delivery over LTE: (S1) radio access list (RACL), which regulates radio access control between the device and BS; (S2) user's security context, including symmetric keys; (S3) user's billing policy; (S4) QoS policy on the user's service; (S5) user's location (represented as IDs of serving BS and GW on the route); and (S6) the device's IP address. Besides, LTE also defines other local/internal states (e.g. temporary identifiers). We have validated that they are either dynamically generated based on above states, or not mandatory for data forwarding.

For data delivery, the prerequisite on states is as follows. For uplink data, the device must have states S1–S6 [8, 14], the BS must have states S1–S5 [14, 15] and the gateway must have states S3 and S4 [7, 11]. Each state should keep the same value at different nodes. For downlink data, the gateway further needs S5.

Given these states, four basic state operations can be abstracted: Create, Delete, Update, Copy. The first three define the actions at a single node, and the last one defines the state transfer from one node to another. For instance, $\mathsf{Copy}_{X\rightarrow Y}[S]$ represents a copy action on state S from node X to node Y; $\mathsf{OP}_X[S]$ denotes one of the three single-node operations on state S at X. In LTE, these operations are realized with the control procedures in Figure 4 (standardized in [7, 8, 14, 15, 15]). The functionalities after these operations are the same as the standardized ones in LTE.

The control-plane procedures in LTE can be viewed accordingly. Table 3 lists all state operations in each control procedure used in C1–C3 based on 3GPP standards. Note that, MC generally plays a central role, since it usually keeps the primary copy of the states. Initially, upon powering on or disabling the airplane mode, each device performs the *attach* procedure. This is to register the device and bootstrap the access. When this procedure completes, MC has a complete copy of all states S1–S6, and propagates them to the BS and the device. These states stored at the device and the MC remain unchanged, unless being explicitly deleted when the device *detaches* from the network. Among them, only S2 can be regularly updated whenever the procedure P3 is invoked. The gateway always keeps S3 and S4, until the device changes its gateway (e.g., due to roaming to another location domain). The BS may delete the states for an associated device if the device stays inactive (say, after 10 ± 0.5s).

For uplink service establishment in C1, the state operations are as follows. S5 (BS ID here) is stored at BS but copied from BS to MC in P2; P3 updates S2 at MC, the user profile server and the device (a new key pair is created to replace the old one). In P4, S1–S4 are copied from MC to BS and S3-S4 are copied from MC to BS, where S1, S3 and S4 are stored at MC since the attach procedure. Afterwards, BS has all needed states (S1–S5) and GW has states

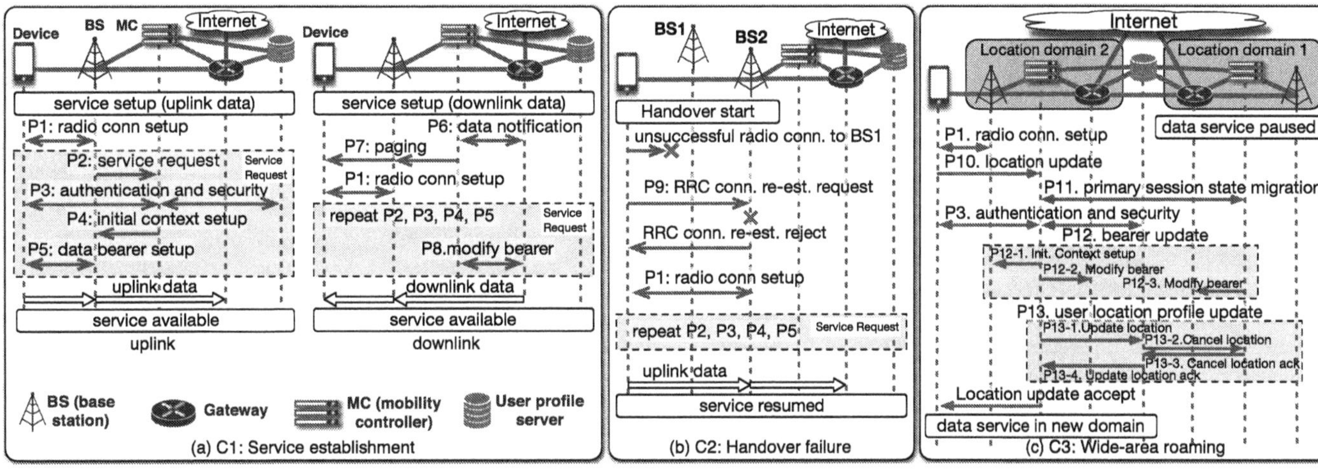

Figure 4: Control-plane procedures and data-plane forwarding for three cases (C1, C2, C3).

Procedure [Standard]	LTE-stack messages	States	State operations
P1: Radio conn. setup[14]	RRC connection setup	S5	$\text{copy}_{UE\rightarrow BS}$
P2: Service request[8]	NAS service request	S5	$\text{copy}_{BS\rightarrow MC}$
P3: Auth. and security[6, 19]	RRC security command	S2	update_{UE}, update_{MC}
P4: Initial context setup[15]	S1AP initial context setup	S1, S2, S3, S4	$\text{copy}_{MC\rightarrow BS}$
P5: Data bearer setup[14]	RRC connection reconfiguration	–	–
P6: Data notification[7, 11]	Downlink data notification	–	–
P7: Paging messages[8]	Paging message	–	–
P8: Modify bearer[8]	Modify bearer request	S5	$\text{copy}_{MC\rightarrow GW}$
P9: Radio conn. re-establishment[14]	RRC connection re-establishment	–	–
P10: Location update[8]	Tracking area update request	S5	$\text{copy}_{UE\rightarrow MC2}$
P11: Primary state transfer[7, 11]	Context request/response	S1, S2, S3, S4, S5, S6	$\text{copy}_{MC1\rightarrow MC2}$ [S1,S2,S3,S4,S6], $\text{copy}_{MC2\rightarrow MC1}$ [S5], delete_{MC1} [S1,S2,S3,S4,S6]
P12: Bearer update[7, 11]	Create session/Modify bearer request	S1, S2, S3, S4, S5	$\text{copy}_{MC2\rightarrow BS2}$ [S1,S2,S3,S4,S5], $\text{copy}_{MC2\rightarrow GW2}$ [S3,S4,S5], $\text{copy}_{MC1\rightarrow GW1}$ [S5]
P13: User location profile update[12]	Update/Cancel location request	S5	$\text{copy}_{MC2\rightarrow s}$, delete_{MC2}
P0: Attach	Bootstrap phase	S1, S2, S3, S4, S5, S6	not shown here

Table 3: LTE control procedures and their state operations in C1–C3 (UE: device, s: profile server).

(S3, S4), thus ready for data delivery. For downlink access in C1, S5 is copied from MC to the gateways in P8 to meet the additional requirements for downlink data delivery. Note that, the device already has a local copy of S1–S6 before the service establishment; only S2 is updated in P3.

Insights. We make two observations:

(I1) Control-plane procedures are done sequentially, mostly through MC. They block data service until completion. Data-plane forwarding cannot start until all control procedures are over. The LTE standards mandate sequential operations on control-plane procedures. They are to ensure *correctness* of state operations. Most such procedures are done through MC, which holds the primary copy of states.

(I2) Not all the sequential operations are necessary. For example, P2 is not mandatory to start uplink data, because data can be forwarded regardless of whether the location state S5 is updated at MC or not.

Guidelines. The above implies two guidelines to reduce latency.

(G1) The existing state replica at the device can be leveraged to accelerate some control procedures. Once attached, the device retains a copy of all S1–S6. We can leverage such state replica to bypass certain operations among LTE nodes. For example, without copying states from MC, BS copies states from the device-side replica directly in P1, thus bypassing P4.

(G2) State operations can be accelerated through piggybacked signaling exchanges. We can copy the needed states, and piggyback them in the existing signaling messages exchanged among nodes. For example, we may piggyback the device-side replica in the message from the device to BS in P1.

3.2 Handover (C2)

Handover is a common control-plane procedure triggered by user mobility. It is initiated by the network, if the device is at active state (when it remains active in data transfer). It retains the established data service. Ideally a successful handover should incur negligible latency on data-plane forwarding. Data delivery continues with the old BS when the network initiates handover. Data forwarding proceeds with the new BS after the handover. Interestingly, handover is initiated by the device if at the idle mode.

We examine latency in handover upon state operation failures (C2F). Figure 4b plots an example incurred by transient radio outage. Assume the planned handover for the device is to BS1. However, if the signal suddenly turns weak, this handover to the new BS1 will not succeed. Due to this handover failure and its lost connectivity with the old BS upon handover, the device selects another new BS2 (with strong radio signal) for handover. Radio connectivity to BS2 then needs to be reestablished for data access in P9. However, such a RRC re-establishment request would be rejected, because the device has never established radio connectivity with BS2 *a priori*. It thus incurs a control-plane operation failure. To cope with such a failure, the device has to run the entire sequence of service establishment procedures (C1) from P1 to P5, and the data service will be suspended in between. Moreover, our user study shows that, this type of transient radio link outage is regularly observed in operational LTE networks.

State management perspective. The long delay is actually caused by running the needed state operations sequentially. When the newly selected BS2 receives the RRC data service request in P9, it needs to have necessary states (S1–S5) to provide services. Without such states, BS2 has to reject the request and report a failure. However, copying states (S1–S5) from BS1 to BS2 is not supported by the current LTE standards. Copying from the old BS is neither an option, since it may have deleted all states after the planned handover to BS1. So BS2 has to let the device initiate the service establishment process (C1), to *copy* those states from MC. It can only start to offer data access after completing all operations.

Insight. We make another observation:

(I3) Lengthy control-plane operations can be triggered by transient radio link outage, thus incurring prolonged latency. The link outage during handover invokes the connectivity re-establishment request from the device (P9), which is rejected by BS2. The rejection further incurs lengthy operations P1–P5 and extra latency.

Guideline. We come up with another design rule:

(G3) State replica can help to avoid state operation failures. The available state replica at the device may help to eliminate control operation failures. In this case, the connection reestablishment fails since BS2 cannot copy the connectivity state from BS1. Instead, the newly selected BS2 can obtain the correct state replica from the device via the connection reestablishment request. This way, BS2 offers service immediately.

3.3 Wide-Area Roaming (C3)

In C3, location update is invoked when the user moves to a new location domain. In this case, a sequence of control-plane procedures are executed to resume its data service in the new domain, as shown in Figure 4c. Upon radio connectivity setup in P1, the device reports its arrival to the new MC (i.e., MC2) in P10. The new MC migrates states from the old MC, and notifies the device's location to the old MC in P11. Authentication and security procedure (P3) is applied again to the device. To resume data service, a data bearer (spanning the new BS/gateways, and old gateways) is sequentially updated in P12: The new MC initializes the bearer context at the new BS (P12-1), and modifies the new gateway's bearer (P12-2). Afterwards, the old MC also reconfigures the old gateway (P12-3), which then can relay its buffered downlink data to the device (via tunneling). The user's latest location is recorded at the profile server and deleted at the old MC in P13: The new MC updates the profile server (P13-1), which then notifies the old MC to delete the device's location (P13-2/3) and acknowledges to the new MC (P13-4).

State management perspective. To resume data delivery, the new BS must have states (S1–S5) identical to the device's ones, and the new gateway should know S3 and S4 (and S5 for downlink access). Moreover, the old gateway should also know the latest S5 so that it can relay the buffered downlink data to the device. In P11, all states except location (S5) are deleted at the old MC after being copied to the new MC, and the new MC copies S5 to the old MC. This leads to state migration between two MCs. In P12, states S1–S5 and S3–S5 are copied from the new MC to the new BS and the new gateways, and state S5 is copied from the old MC to the old gateways. In P13, S5 is copied to the user profile server, and deleted by the old MC. These operations are still done sequentially, but some are unnecessary.

Insights. We make two new observations:

(I4) Certain control-plane operations are conservative and time consuming. When updating the route, the new MC distributes the states to the new BS and new gateways in P12. Current LTE performs state-copying *sequentially* to each node.

(I5) Data-plane forwarding path is ready before the entire control state operations are completed. Similar to I1, the forwarding path is updated and available after bearer update (P12). However, data service is suspended until the location profile update (P13) is done.

Guidelines. We make two more guidelines:

(G4) Sequential state copy can be made parallel. The state-copying operations in P12 are safe to parallelize without write conflicts. We thus reduce latency by *parallelizing* state copy to all involved nodes.

(G5) Control-plane state operations and data-plane packet forwarding can be pipelined. Given that P13 does not involve any node on the forwarding path, we can concurrently perform location update to the profile server along with data forwarding. This way, service resumption delay is reduced.

3.4 Summary

In summary, the control-plane operations are major latency contributors for all three cases. On one hand, these procedures are fully warranted, since they provision necessary states (Table 3) to enable mobile data access. On the other hand, they take sequential operations among network nodes and the device. They are ineffective in three aspects: (A1) Certain procedures are ordered and required to run in a sequence, thus incurring long latency (see G1–G3); (A2) Some procedures are not mandatory to starting/resuming data service, but they have to be completed first (see G5); (A3) Some could be run in parallel, but are mandated to run sequentially (see G4).

4 DPCM DESIGN

We present DPCM, which reduces data access latency due to control-plane operations and retains the same functionalities as 4G LTE. Following the observations in §3, DPCM departs from the MC-centric, sequential design on the control plane. Instead, we leverage the state replicas available at the device and other nodes. We thus exploit short side-paths, parallelize certain control procedures, and pipeline the control-plane and data-plane operations without violating correctness. This results in three concrete techniques.

• **Bypassing:** To address A1, we first bypass certain existing sequence of control procedures, and substitute with equivalent, faster operations. Through these substituted operations, all required states at the device, the BS, and the gateway should be installed before data-plane forwarding. Therefore, such equivalent side-paths enable us to install states at the involved nodes earlier, thus establishing/resuming data services faster.

To realize bypassing, we seek to retrieve state replica *early* and install them at the nodes of interest. The key enabler is that, state replicas are already available for use. Such replicas exist at the device and other network nodes, once the device is attached to the network (see §3.1). Specifically, states S1–S6 are already stored at the device. They remain always available, even during the device's idle mode, unless the device is explicitly detached. In reality, their values remain largely unchanged (§4.4) except for S2. Note that, S2 is updated each time P3 is executed. However, it is used for encryption over the air transfer between the device and the BS. We can delegate this key generation of S2 from the MC to the device. We run local key agreement procedure (by following P3) at the device, produce updated S2 for the device and BS, and later notify the MC of this S2 update. We will elaborate on how to use it to reduce latency in C1–C3, and how to ensure correctness in §4.4.

• **Pipelining control-data:** We further pipeline certain control-plane signaling procedures with the data-plane packet delivery. The key premise is that, data-plane forwarding can start *without* waiting for the entire sequence of control procedures to be completed (A2). Therefore, we pipeline data delivery with those latter-stage control procedures. This way, data access latency is reduced. To realize control-data pipelining, we exploit the technique of in-band signaling. The idea is to piggyback the control-plane states and messages with the forwarded data packets. As data packets traverse BSes and gateways, control actions are also taken at these nodes.

• **Parallelizing control procedures:** DPCM last parallelizes certain control procedures that are mandatory to retaining data service. This addresses A3, where these control procedures are executed sequentially but could be run in parallel (e.g., route update at gateways and BS in C3). We thus perform concurrent state operations by leveraging multiple replicas at different nodes.

We next show how these three techniques are applied to handle all cases C1–C3. When potential conflicts arise due to parallel and concurrent state operations (which are deemed rather rare), we further present designs to cope with them all in §4.4.

4.1 Service Establishment (C1)

We first use bypassing to accelerate service establishment (G1, G2). We replace the existing procedures P1–P5 with two new ones P1′ and P13′ while retaining the original control functions. Note that, P13′ can be run in parallel with the data-plane forwarding, and only P1′ needs to be completed before data delivery starts. P1′ keeps the same rounds of message exchanges in P1, but augments them by piggybacking needed control states. This is made possible by

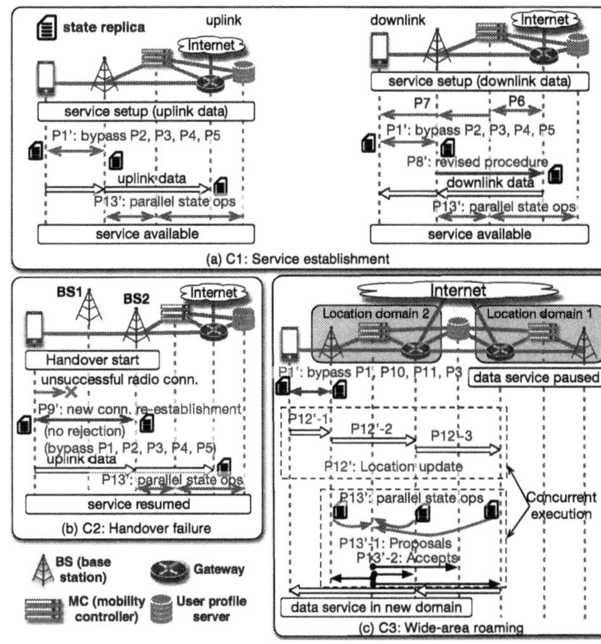

Figure 5: Solution sketch for C1, C2 and C3.

leveraging the available state replica at the device. Moreover, given the new P1′, P5 can be merged with it. P13′ synchronizes state updates at the BS, the MC and the profile server. P8 is also revised to transfer the needed states to the gateways for downlink access.

Uplink data. We skip the state copy action from MC to BS. In the new procedure P1′ (Figure 5a), we copy the device-side state replica to BS (following G1), by piggybacking it in the existing messages of P1 (following G2). P1′ thus installs all required states S1–S5 at the BS. To retain security of P3 (authentication and security), P1′ runs *local* key agreement procedure during the radio connectivity setup (§4.4). Upon completing P1′, the device has all S1–S6 and the BS has all S1–S5. Uplink data can be started immediately. Meanwhile, to notify the MC and the profile server on the device's security context (S2) and location (S5), a new procedure P13′ (elaborated in §4.3) runs in parallel with data forwarding. P13′ does not block the data service, since (1) MC and the profile server are not responsible for data forwarding; (2) MC has delegated the security key generation of S2 to the BS, thus approving the BS's local security context.

Downlink data. The downlink design (Figure 5a) is similar to that for uplink, except for P8. We still use the procedure P1′ to install states at the BS. Before downlink data forwarding starts, however, LTE still needs the gateway to have the latest state S5 (location/route information to the device). This is done by P8 in the original design. In DPCM, P8 is revised to P8′, which is initiated by BS once P1′ completes. P8′ copies the latest state S5 directly from BS, and sends it to the gateway. Upon receiving S5 in P8′, the gateway is notified about the user's downlink data endpoint. The downlink service can start *immediately* thereafter. Similar to the uplink case, the procedure P13′ will update MC and the profile server in parallel with the data forwarding.

Latency reduction analysis. Our solution bypasses P2, P3, P4 and P5, which perform state copy operations from MC. Since we have used the device-side replica, the BS gets the correct states needed to start data service after P1′. Therefore, all subsequent control procedures P2, P3, P4, and P5 are saved. Given that P13′ excutes in parallel with data forwarding, it does not contribute to data access latency. This applies to both uplink and downlink service establishments since the same procedures P1–P5 are involved. Moreover, such bypassing piggybacks the states within the existing device-to-BS message exchanges, which are mandatory for radio connectivity setup. P1′ suppresses the time for all non-radio signaling exchanges for uplink access, thus pushing its service establishment latency to the minimum (validated in §6.2).

Handling transient radio failures. DPCM also reduces latencies by tolerating radio failures. Upon transient radio link failures, the device re-initiates the service establishment procedure. Our solution also requires to perform recovery operations upon such failures. But our design is still faster, since it eliminates P2–P5 each time.

Handling rejections by data plane. Sometimes the data-plane nodes (gateways and BSes) may reject the connection (e.g. due to congestion). In this case, DPCM still retains the same functionality as legacy LTE, by dropping the data and stopping the forwarding. The uplink data will be dropped by the base station, while the downlink data will not be send by the gateway. The same mechanism also applies to handover and wide-area roaming below.

4.2 Handover (C2)

We focus on the unsuccessful handover attempt under transient radio link outage (§3.2). Long service suspension is then incurred to the device. Following I3, the root cause for the latency is that, the new BS has no proper states S1–S5; it has to initiate the service establishment from scratch according to standards [14]. Note that a successful handover incurs negligible latency on data-plane forwarding (caused by inevitable radio link switching to handover).

Figure 5b shows our solution. To install states at the new BS2, we still leverage the device-side state replica, and piggyback necessary states to skip the state copy operation from MC (following G5), similar to that of P1′ for C1. Consequently, it avoids repeating P1–P5 triggered by handover failure to BS1. We thus design a new connectivity re-establishment procedure P9′ to bypass unnecessary control procedures. As a result, the new BS2 will receive the correct control states S1–S5, and reconnection reject will not happen at the first place. This design effectively eliminates rerunning P1–P5. Similar to the service establishment (C1), the new procedure P13′ will run in parallel with the data forwarding to notify the MC and the profile server of the security context (S2) and location (S5).

Latency reduction analysis. Our design avoids the latency in handling the handover reject. Therefore, the service suspension latency caused by procedures P1 + P2 + P3 + P4 + P5 (procedures in C1), plus the RRC connection re-establishment reject and local operations (here, cell re-scanning at the device side), is saved.

4.3 Wide-Area Roaming (C3)

For wide-area roaming, we apply bypassing (similar to P1′ in C1), pipelining (following G5), and parallelization (following G4).

Figure 5c shows how DPCM achieves them. DPCM first applies P1′ to copy device-side state replica to the new BS (§4.1). Then a new procedure P12′ is defined to replace P12. Note that, the device knows the IP address of its old gateway (stored inside its local state replica). Given this information, it is possible for the device to deliver IP packets to the old gateway via the new BS and new gateway. Based on this, P12′ constructs an IP packet, which carries the device-side state replica. The destination for this IP packet is set as the old gateway. It can implicitly update the device's location and bearer along the route. If the device has the pending uplink data, it can send these data packets immediately after this update packet. Upon receiving this packet, the new BS copies the device-side state replica in P12′-1. It then forwards the packet to the new gateway based on the destination IP (P12′-2, equivalent to P12-2). The new gateway also copies states, and forwards the packet to the old gateway (P12′-3, equivalent to P12-3). Afterwards, the new BS has all S1–S5, the new gateway has S3–S5, and the old gateway has the updated location S5. Therefore, data forwarding can start for uplink delivery to the Internet. The old gateway can use S5 to relay its buffered downlink data to the device.

Meanwhile, we need to synchronize the state updates at the new BS, the new gateway, the old gateway, the new MC, and the profile server. This is done by the new procedure P13′. Note that there is no need to update the old MC, which only notifies the old gateway (done in P12′). In P13′, we use parallel state updates. This may lead to conflicts. To handle it, DPCM follows the current 4G design rule: the new MC determines the final state value. In P13′, the new MC has final say on states S1-S6 except S2 (delegated to the new BS).

Specifically, in P13′-1, nodes with state replica (e.g., the new BS, new gateway, etc.) can *propose* the states to the new MC. In P13′-2, The new MC decides whether the proposed state replica need to be updated or not, since it has the final authority on the state values. If the state is valid, the new MC broadcasts a confirmation message (Accept) to the new gateway, the new BS, the old gateway and the user profile server. If the state replica need to be updated, the new MC broadcasts an Update message with the correct states. More details of Update will be elaborated in §4.4.

Tolerating failures. Upon transient radio failures, our latency reduction will be even bigger than that for service establishment in C1. This is because DPCM prevents external radio failures from propagating to the control plane. It also tolerates internal control-plane operation failures by using multiple state replicas. In particular, the device-side replica is *always available* before it is detached (e.g., powers off or airplane mode), which offers a baseline assurance.

4.4 Handling State Conflicts

Control states may be updated by either the device or the MC in LTE, thus possibly leading to inconsistent replicas at nodes. However, our user study shows that such updates, with their consequent conflicts, are rare in practice. We find that state "write" operations are infrequent in reality. We count the number of "read" (copy) and "write" (create and update) operations in our user study. The "write" operations account for only 1.3% (15,412 out of 247,842 operations).

When conflicts do arise, DPCM aims to ensure the same correctness as the current LTE. We devise domain-specific schemes to detect and resolve them. Upon conflicts, DPCM guarantees the worst-case latency is no larger than 4G. To this end, it adopts the premise similar to LTE: the MC has the final say on the state updates. In leveraging the state replicas, DPCM disallows other nodes to locally modify the state value, thus mitigating the potential inconsistencies. Therefore, in DPCM, the MC has final say on S1–S6 except S2. For S2, MC delegates it to the device and BS. This is reasonable, since S2 is responsible for the encryption key for the air transfer between the device and the BS. The device and the BS can decide on it.

Concurrent updates by device. Bypassing works under the premise that state replicas are identical. When the malicious or selfish device modifies the control states (e.g., increasing the QoS level), potential conflicts may arise between the device and other nodes. However, this can be detected and resolved in DPCM.

In DPCM, each state (S1, S3–S6) is originally distributed by the MC similar to the current LTE. Moreover, the state replica is signed with a fingerprint, which includes a hash of the states and a signature by MC. At runtime, both the states and the fingerprint are carried in the messages. The network nodes can thus verify whether the session states are issued by MC (with the correct signature), and whether they are modified since their distribution (with the hash).

When the cheating or compromised device modifies states, such state changes can be detected by network nodes via mismatched fingerprint for the new state replica. Then network nodes roll back to the LTE legacy design by asking a copy directly from MC. While simple, such rollback is correct in LTE due to the following fact: Without the connectivity states, no control procedures can run.

Concurrent updates by MC. Another conflict may arise when the MC updates certain state values. For example, when a prepaid user runs out of his data credits, the MC may update his radio access control list (S1) to forbid further access. When the MC wants to modify certain control states, it can use Update (in C1–C3) or 4G's modification procedures [8] (after C1–C3) to notify the involved device, the BS and the gateway.

However, transient period exists where the nodes use the out-dated state values to forward data, when the MC are updating these nodes. DPCM prevents it by using domain-specific conflict resolution dependent on specific states S1–S6. Specifically the user location (S5) does not pose problems, since all nodes are always notified with the latest device location by the device and BS (§4.3). For IP address (S6), no issues arise in common scenarios because it remains the same after attach (in both LTE and DPCM). Note that the dynamic change of gateway/IP assignment can still be supported by DPCM. To do so, the mobility controller (MC) first determines the potential change of gateway/IP, and then rollbacks DPCM to 4G LTE to run the legacy procedures. This ensures that, DPCM retains the same complexity and scalability as 4G LTE.

∘ *S1: Radio access control list (RACL).* RACL over LTE turns out to be *group based*, following the 3GPP standards [8, 13]. That is, a group of users may have the same access rights (e.g., "international roaming users") and may share the group access signature. Therefore, a device that was originally in an access group but later revoked by the MC, may still pass the authorization using the old signature. It thus gains radio access. To prevent this, DPCM requires the MC to initiate the delete operation only after successful C1–C3. The revoked device consequently cannot gain radio access. The incurred latency is no worse than the current LTE.

∘ *S2: Security context.* DPCM delegates the security key generation of S2 from MC to BS. For the first-time registration (attach), DPCM still requires the legacy 4G mechanism (no accelerations). Afterwards, it runs the key negotiation between the device and the BS during the connectivity setup (P1′). In this process, DPCM retains the same security level as 4G LTE (elaborated in Appendix).

To this end, DPCM adopts the Diffie-Hellman protocol [40] for local security key negotiation, and binds it to the unclonable group identification [29] in group-based radio access authorization. For each radio access group, the profile server generates a key pair $\langle K_{pub}^{UE}, K_{pri}^{UE} \rangle$. The public key K_{pub}^{UE} has been pre-distributed to all BSes, while the private key K_{pri}^{UE} is only pre-stored in the user profile server. For each service establishment or handover or location update, the device calculates the one-time signature $Cert_{UE}$ based on $\hat{K}_{pri}^{UE}$ and the current device-side timestamp T_{UE}. Upon receiving them, the BS uses K_{pub}^{UE} to verify whether the signature $Cert_{UE}$ is derived from K_{pri}^{UE}, and performs similar derivation of signature $Cert_{NW}$ for mutual authentication. Then it runs the Diffe-Hellman protocol to compute the key. It is resilient to man-in-the-middle attacks since the mutual authentication has been completed.

∘ *S3: Billing policy.* DPCM retains correct data billing by *decoupling* packet counting (accounting) from charging rule updates (pricing). At runtime, the gateway correctly counts packets *without* charging rules. The bill remains correct, as long as the gateway uses the same packet counter for billing with the charging rule retrieved later.

∘ *S4: QoS.* DPCM retains correct QoS by regulating its update before the successful connectivity establishment. Downgraded QoS is only allowed after successful C1–C3. Data forwarding is still no worse than LTE, which mandates the same rule during this period.

5 IMPLEMENTATION

We have implemented DPCM as an extension of OpenAirInterface [45], a software-defined 4G control/data-plane protocol stack. Figure 6 shows its two parts: DPCM-enabled network nodes and DPCM-enabled devices. Our implementation seeks to support *incremental deployment* on existing 4G network infrastructure, and *backward compatibility* with commodity phones.

Network Nodes. Each network node realizes DPCM with a modular virtualization layer under the control-plane protocol stacks, without changes on existing 4G protocols. It supports incremental deployability and backward compatibility: It retains the illusion of sequential control to upper 4G protocol stacks, but re-intercepting 4G signaling and data messages to achieve DPCM's functionalities (summarized in Table 4). It also supports legacy 4G devices, by relaying their messages to the upper 4G protocols. Such virtualization-based implementation reduces control-plane complexity, facilitates network management via modularity, and ensures correctness for other LTE functions by retaining the illusion of sequential control.

(1) Bypassing. DPCM piggybacks necessary state replicas to achieve the bypassing. To leverage the device-side state replica, we use the `criticalExtensionsFuture` container in 4G RRC connectivity setup messages [14] to piggyback the necessary states.

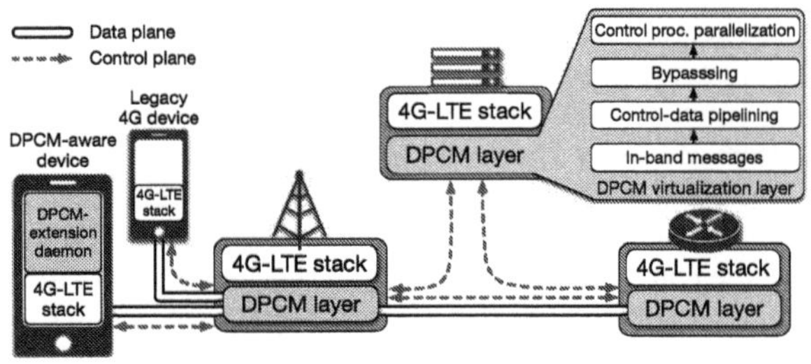

Figure 6: DPCM's system components.

LTE-stack messages	DPCM-layer action
P1: Radio conn. setup	Relay to LTE stack. Run bypassing with its piggybacked info.
P2: Service request	Locally acknowledge LTE stack with the state from the bypassing.
P3: Auth. and security	Immediately acknowledge LTE stack with local key agreement and radio access control group identification.
P4: Initial context setup	Locally acknowledge LTE's requests. Bypassing has achieved the same function.
P5: Data bearer setup	Relay to LTE stack.
P6: Data notification	Relay to LTE stack.
P7: Paging messages	Relay to LTE stack.
P8: Modify bearer	Locally acknowledge LTE stack. In-band pipelining has achieved the same function.
P9: Radio connectivity reestablishment	Relay to LTE stack. Run bypassing with its piggybacked info
P10: Location update	Relay to LTE stack.
P11: Primary state transfer	Locally acknowledge LTE stack. Bypassing and parallelization have achieved the same function.
P12: Bearer update	Locally acknowledge LTE stack. In-band pipelining has achieved the same function.
P13: User profile update	Relay to LTE stack.

Table 4: DPCM virtualizes 4G control procedures.

These fields are only visible to DPCM layer, and are removed when the message is delivered to the upper 4G protocols.

(2) Pipelining Control-Data. We implement DPCM's in-band pipelining by overloading the standardized cellular data tunnel (GTP-U [13]). The signaling messages are piggybacked as payloads (together with normal data) of the GTP-U packets. On receipt of them, the DPCM layer will extract the signaling messages, push them to acceleration components, and hold the normal data until mandatory control procedures are completed.

(3) Control-control parallelization. The DPCM layer implements concurrent operations to parallelize sequential control procedures.The state replica proposed from the device to network nodes is carried within the data-plane (via GTP-U tunnels [13]). The state replica proposed by network nodes is piggybacked inside the standardized messages from control interfaces (S1-AP [15] between the BS and MC, and GTP-C [7] between the MC and gateways). Once the the network nodes install the correct states and resolve the state conflicts, DPCM locally acknowledges 4G protocols' pending procedures without waiting for legacy state migrations.

(4) Handling conflicts. It is realized as follows.

○ *Radio access control (S1) and security (S2).* DPCM uses the PBC library [1] to implement the group identification for radio access control, and key negotiation through the Diffe-Hellman protocol.

○ *Data Billing (S3).* DPCM retains the correct data billing by decoupling packet counting from charging rule. The granularity of counting packets depends on whether per-flow or per-device billing is applied (based on pre-purchased data plan). The base station learns it by checking the device's charging group (using group identification). For per-flow billing, the gateway temporarily records the flow ID for every packet.

○ *QoS (S4).* With unclonable group identification above, the gateway learns the device's QoS class, which offers further information on packet delay/loss/priority. For the non-class QoS metrics, only the minimum QoS (e.g., best-effort service) is offered before session state is migrated. This forwarding under QoS is still no worse than 4G: Under the same condition, 4G will not enable any data access to the device at the same time.

Device-side support. To benefit from DPCM, the devices should be upgraded to support it. DPCM can be incrementally deployed as a software daemon, without changing the hardware modem. It pre-stores device-side session states in the reserved fields of the SIM card (standardized in [9]). Note that only the critical states S1–S6 should be stored on the client side. To retain the same security level as 4G LTE, these states are associated with the fingerprints (§4.4) stored in the SIM card. It extends the existing device-side state replica for bypassing control procedures using radio connectivity setup (P1). This is realized with the ENVELOPE commands [10] from OS to SIM card (e.g., via Android Telephony [2]). Then it generates DPCM-aware in-band messages (§4.1–§4.3). It uses Android's VPN interface `oip` [31] to redirect packets to a separate tunnel at OS level, re-encapsulates it with piggybacked device-side states, and then forward them to the LTE air interface.

6 EVALUATION

We assess DPCM's overall latency reduction (§6.1), effectiveness of its components (§6.2), benefits on apps (§6.3) and its overhead (§6.4).

Experiment setup. To approximate the operational networks, we deploy DPCM in a testbed, configure it with the parameters observed from real-world operational networks and run evaluation experiments.

The testbed consists of three servers (Dell PowerEdge T320, 2.7 GHz 6-core Intel Xeon E5-2420V2 CPU, 8 GB RAM and three 1 Gbps Ethernet ports) with the network topology shown in Figure 4c. One server runs the user profile database, while others emulate two location domains by running multiple machines each serving as the software-defined BS, gateway and MC separately. Each virtual machine installs Ubuntu 14.04, OpenAirInterface [45] and DPCM. We use `oaisim` from OpenAirInterface to emulate the mobile device and the radio link. We configure the testbed with parameters and round-trips observed from the user study logs over operational networks (§2). In each log, we retrieve signaling messages and quantify the elapsed time between successive messages in each control procedure. We then configure the radio latency in `oaisim` as the round-trip time of 4G radio connectivity setup procedure, and the round-trip delay for each procedure in OpenAirInterface as the breakdown results (using `tc` command). To assess the failure handling, we inject the state migration failures between the MC and gateways/BS/profile server, and transient radio link failures. Our approximation of radio transmission time might be

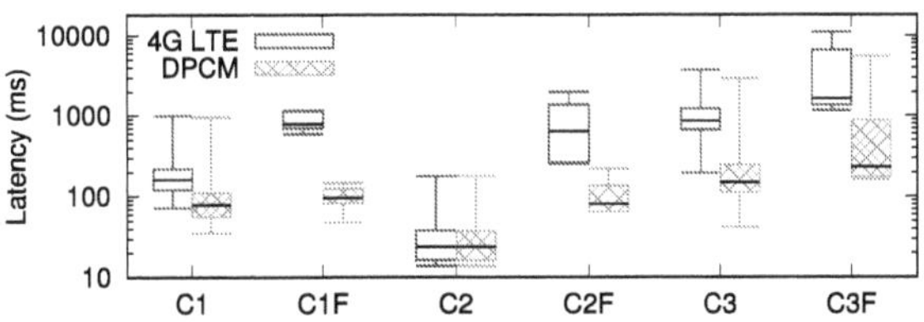

Figure 7: DPCM's overall latency reduction.

		C1	C1F	C2	C2F	C3	C3F
DPCM (ms)	Avg	80.0	98.2	24.7	89.3	166.2	359.1
	Min	35.0	47.5	13.7	63.9	41.2	160.0
	95th	112.5	124.3	37.8	135.3	245.0	887.3
	Max	957.1	146.0	177.5	220.6	2927.0	5546.8
Δ (ms)	Avg	88.7	748.7	0	580.8	735.4	2645.4
	Min	29.4	483.2	0	153.7	132.0	961.1
	95th	132.7	1026.1	0	1300.0	988.8	6130.7
	Max	928.3	1081.2	0	1881.2	2887.5	10835.0
η	Avg	2.1×	8.9×	1×	7.8×	5.8×	11.5×
	Min	1.04×	5.4×	1×	2.5×	1.2×	1.2×
	95th	3.0×	13.3×	1×	16.7×	7.5×	26.2×
	Max	16.9×	22.1×	1×	17.5×	13.9×	59.9×

Table 5: Statistics of latency reduction. For each round, Δ = 4G - DPCM, η = 4G/DPCM.

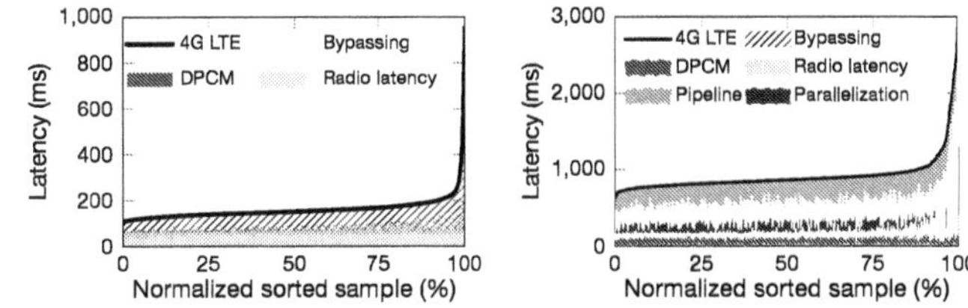

(a) Service establishment (C1) (b) Location update (C3)

Figure 8: DPCM's latency reduction breakdown.

Reduction over 4G (ms)		C1	C1F	C2F	C3	C3F
Bypassing	50th	83.2	694.8	561.0	34.9	99.7
	95th	132.7	1026.1	1300.0	126.2	222.5
	max	928.3	1081.2	1881.2	473.8	227.7
	avg	88.7	748.7	580.8	51.5	129.8
Pipelining/ Parallelization	50th	N/A	N/A	N/A	664.0	1317.9
	95th	N/A	N/A	N/A	940.2	5915.5
	max	N/A	N/A	N/A	2773.8	10632.0
	avg	N/A	N/A	N/A	683.9	2515.6

Table 6: DPCM's latency reduction breakdown.

slightly optimistic without taking into account of the time needed for transferring extra bytes piggybacked (312 byte in §6.4).

6.1 Overall Performance

We examine how much control-plane latency DPCM could reduce compared with 4G LTE. In each round, we configure the test bed with the parameters and round-trips observed from the operational 4G, and compare DPCM with 4G under two metrics: $\Delta = 4G - DPCM$ and $\eta = 4G/DPCM$. Figure 7 and Table 5 show the results in all the normal/failure scenarios in §2–3. We have three observations.

First, DPCM reduces control-plane latency in all the scenarios except C2. On average, it reduces latency to 80.0ms (4G: 168.7ms), 98.2ms (4G: 846.9ms), 89.3ms (4G: 670.1ms), 166.2ms (4G: 901.6ms), and 359.1ms (4G: 3004.5ms) in C1, C1F, C2F, C3 and C3F, respectively. Note that for legacy LTE, all scenarios' results conform to our studies in §2. For each run, we define Δ as DPCM's latency reduction over 4G, and η as the ratio of 4G's latency over DPCM. Table 5 shows that, the minimal reduction is 29.4ms, 483.2ms, 153.7ms, 132.0ms and 961.1ms in C1, C1F, C2F, C3 and C3F. On average, DPCM achieves 2.1×, 8.9×, 7.8×, 5.8×, and 11.5× reduction, respectively.

Second, DPCM saves more latency in mobility scenario. On average, DPCM saves 646.7ms more latency in C3 than C1 (no failures). The reason is that, the mobile scenario involves more control procedures (Figure 4) and thus more opportunities for latency reduction.

Third, DPCM further reduces latencies by handling failures. Latency reductions (Δ) are more significant in the failure cases (C1F, C2F and C3F). This is because DPCM helps to carry needed states in in-band signaling messages and thus largely avoid further failures. In fact, DPCM is resilient to transient failures and it induces low latency in all the cases, regardless of failures or not.

6.2 Micro Benchmark

We next assess the latency reduction in each DPCM's component. For each round of the above test, we quantify DPCM's latency reductions over 4G from its components. Figure 8 and Table 6 show the results.

Efficiency in control latency reduction. We show that DPCM is efficient in reducing the control-plane latency. Note that the total latency can be divided into radio and non-radio latency. Radio latency is inevitable since message passing between the device and the network (the BS) is mandatory for any control function. In fact, DPCM aims to cut off non-radio latency caused by sequential execution of control procedures. Figure 8 shows that, DPCM latency is close to the radio link latency. This implies that DPCM has approximated the lower bound of the control latency reduction without radio-link latency reduction. Our solution can gain bigger reduction in 5G due to the radio link latency reduction (e.g. up to 1ms [35, 43]). Then the saving gain from DPCM will be relatively larger.

Bypassing. The bypassing helps reduce latencies for all scenarios except C2. For service establishment (C1/C1F) and handover with failures (C2F), the bypassing contributes all of the latency reduction (shown in Figure 7). It reduces 88.7ms on average, and 928.3ms at maximum in C1. Upon failures, it reduces more, i.e. 748.7ms and 580.8ms on average in C1F and C2F. This is because bypassing carries the states needed and thus the request will not be rejected in DPCM when the device attempts to re-establish connectivity after transient radio outrage. For wide-area roaming (C3), it reduces 51.5 ms on average and 473.8ms at maximum. It contributes to 7.0% of DPCM's total reduction on average.

We next evaluate its overhead. The bypassing may incur the processing delay for the group identification for radio access control for authorization, and the cryptographic key agreement ($P1 \longrightarrow P1'$ in §4–5); For the processing latency, Figure 9 plots the result under different key sizes (each has 500 runs). For the key size less than 512-bit, both procedures incur marginal latency. For the group identification, the maximum observed verification time is 3.9 ms with the 512-bit key, accounting for 4.8% extra latencies in C1 and 2.3% in C3. For key agreements, using keys less than 512-bit incurs the maximum computation latency of 3.7 ms. The key negotiation's computation overhead is much smaller than group identification, since it uses symmetric keys instead of the public/private key pair.

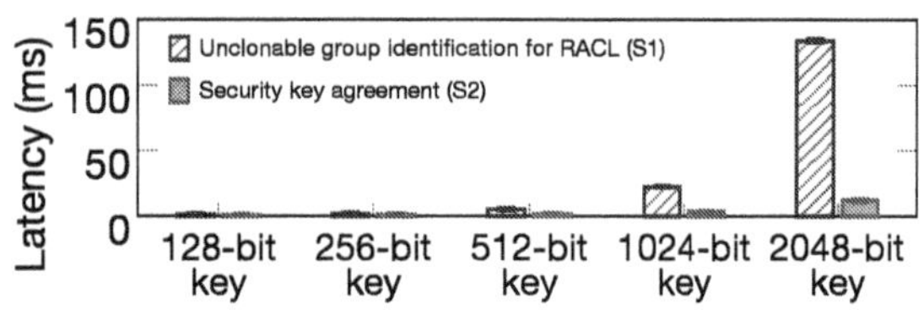

Figure 9: DPCM's bypassing's extra processing latency vs. cryptographical key size.

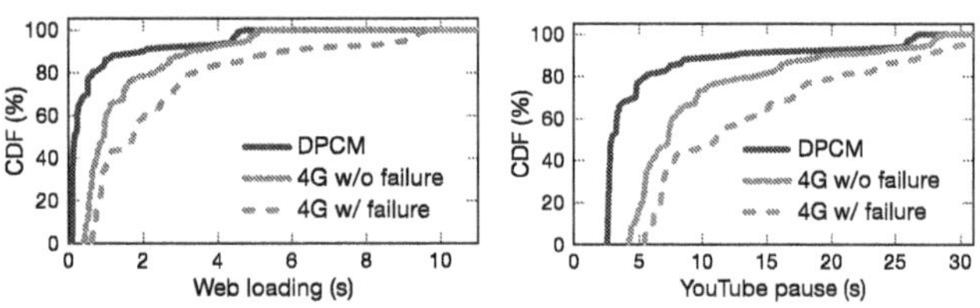

(a) Web (b) YouTube

Figure 10: Web/YouTube latency improvements in DPCM.

Pipelining and parallelization. DPCM's pipelining and parallelization help reduce latencies in wide-area roaming (C3/C3F). While not applicable to C1 and C2, they are critical components for wide-area roaming. In failure-free case (C3), the pipelining and parallelization reduce 683.9 ms on average and 2.7 s at maximum. They contribute 93.0% of DPCM's total latency reduction on average. With failures (C3F), they reduce 2.5s latency and contribute 95.1% reduction on average. The reason is that, the wide-area roaming involves more control procedures among more network nodes. This offers more room for DPCM to reduce the latency.

6.3 Benefits on Applications

We next quantify how DPCM helps reduce app-level delay. In this experiment, we run the Web page (via `wget`) and Youtube video (via `youtube-dl` [5]) request in two settings: static case to test the service establishment, and mobility case to test wide-area roaming. These applications first issue requests via cellular protocols in our test bed (by redirecting them to OpenAirInterface's built-in virtual interface `oip1`). They further trigger the responses of webpage and video streaming, with which we measure their loading times. We repeat this experiment with/without failures for 100 times.

Figure 10 shows the results in mobility cases with/without failures. Both apps experience longer delay than the data service suspension (Table 5). They are not resumed immediately due to the imperfect adaptation to the varying network. Without failures, DPCM reduces the average web loading from 1.5s to 0.7s (2.1×), and the average video loading from 9.8s to 5.7s (1.7×). With failures, DPCM achieves 3.7× reduction for web (from 2.5s to 0.7s) and 2.1× reduction for video (from 12.3s to 5.7s). In static settings without failures (C1), DPCM reduces the web loading from 417.0ms to 290.8ms (1.4×), and reduces video loading from 4.2s to 3.5s (1.2×) on average. With failures (C1F), DPCM achieves 2.2× reduction for web (from 637.9ms to 290.8ms) and 1.5× reduction for video (from 5.4s to 3.5s).

6.4 System Overhead

Signaling overhead. DPCM retains comparable signaling overhead to 4G. First, DPCM uses piggyback to avoid introducing more messages, but it needs extra bytes inside the signaling messages to piggyback the states. Our prototype piggybacks 312 more bytes for messages between device and network (including states and signatures), and 56 more bytes for other signaling messages inside the network (states only). Note that these signaling messages are physically delivered over the shared channel of data and signaling (PUSCH for uplink, PDSCH for downlink [20]). It may incur marginal transmission delay (e.g., 312B/1Mbps=2.5ms). Second, in the location update (C3), DPCM needs extra messages for parallelization and conflicts handling. For each location update, it exchanges 12 messages in the worst case with conflicts, which it is less than 4G (≥14 messages) since it bypasses multiple control procedures.

CPU and memory. DPCM demands marginal CPU and negligible memory. In all our experiments, the maximum CPU utilization is 1.3% on each network node, and 0.1% on the device (`oaisim` in our current prototype). The maximum memory consumption observed is 53.9MB on network nodes, and 3.5MB on the device.

Energy consumption. Our prototype emulates device with `oaisim`, so currently we cannot directly measure DPCM's power consumption on the device. We gauge that it is negligible, because DPCM reuses 4G's existing communication mechanisms, and only needs marginal processing (key agreement and the signature).

7 DISCUSSION

Hints for future 5G (and beyond). While designed for 4G LTE, DPCM is applicable to the future mobile network (e.g., 5G and beyond). Note that, the fundamental problem of sequential procedure execution is not unique to LTE. It will probably carry over to the 5G, since various ongoing 5G standardization proposals (listed in [18]) are reusing the current control-plane designs with modifications. With extensive efforts in reducing the 5G radio latency (targeting at ≤1 ms [34, 35, 43]), the control-plane operations will be likely the next major latency bottleneck. Our work offers an early alarm, and contributes new solutions for 5G and beyond. Assuming the 5G radio latency as 1 ms, our estimation (by running the experiments in §6) shows that on average, DPCM achieves 13.4× overall latency reduction in service establishment (C1), and 88.9× reduction in wide-area roaming (C3) over existing the control-plane design.

More problem/solution spaces for the future design. DPCM is our first effort to seek the alternative control-plane in the mobile network. We believe that, more improvements are possible by further exploring the problem and solution spaces. At the problem level, the data access latency may be further reduced, by generalizing DPCM from the control plane to the management plane and physical layers. In these contexts, we believe that the general idea of DPCM and its virtualization-based implementation can be generalized. At the solution level, other approaches are possible, such as a clean-slate redesign of control-plane protocols with built-in bypassing/parallelization/pipelining features.

Benefits on other applications. Besides the apps in §6.3, DPCM can also benefits others with varying latency reductions. For apps with continuous stream data (e.g., video streaming, virtual/augmented reality), DPCM reduces the first packet's latency. For bursty traffic (e.g., Web and instant messaging), DPCM benefits more because of their on-off traffic patterns and thus frequent connectivity establishment/migration.

8 RELATED WORK

In recent years, extensive efforts have been made to improve the performance of 4G LTE networks. They include improving the wireless access [25, 53, 57] and management [33, 60], cross-layer optimization of transport protocols [44, 61, 65] and apps [24, 26, 62, 63] to name a few. We study a different topic of how control-plane operations affect data access latency. At the control plane, several optimizations for specific control procedures (notably fast handoffs) are proposed, including the pre-tunneling [41, 64], mitigating the authentication time [22, 32, 55], modifying the signaling messages [28, 66], parameter tunings[21, 49, 50], etc. DPCM differs from them, since it studies a broader set of control procedures, and parallelizes them for low data access latency. Several recent efforts seek to simplify the cellular infrastructure using software-defined [36, 42, 58] and virtualization [27, 46, 47] approaches. Our work differs from them in two dimensions. First, we focus on a unique issue of latency deficiency (i.e. the sequential control). Second, DPCM leverages the client-side state replica to latency reduction, which has not been explored by prior efforts.

There have been several recent studies on the Internet control plane [30, 37, 39, 51, 56], in the context of software-defined networking. They examine how to perform consistent state update [39, 51], state migration in middle-boxes [30, 37, 54], and conflict resolution over shared states [56], etc. Instead, we study how to accelerate 4G control-plane operations, which are much more complex than their Internet counterpart.

9 CONCLUSION

It has become increasingly important to offer always-on, low-latency network service to the mobile users. In this work, we show that current LTE control-plane operations create a major bottleneck for reducing latency for mobile data access. On one hand, they are well justified since they provision necessary states at the device and network nodes to start or retain data service. On the other hand, their design does not account for efficient operations in the 4G/5G era. In fact, they are required to run sequentially and have to be all completed before starting/resuming data-plane packet delivery. In this work, we analyze their latency root causes and apply parallel computing techniques to speed it up.

Our work can be understood in a broader context. Like other distributed systems, LTE network should balance the latency and consistency in its control-plane operations. This problem is largely unaddressed, and leads to large delay at the user side. While the community has made extensive efforts on improving data-plane wireless access, issues on the control-plane have been overlooked to certain extent. On the solution side, our initial attempt to accelerate the control functions yields promising results. Our study may stimulate more community interests on applying the rich insights from distributed system context to revamp the 4G/5G design.

APPENDIX: SECURITY ANALYSIS

We show how DPCM retains the same security level as 4G LTE. This nails down to three goals: (1) for threats that can be defended by 4G (specified in standards [16, 17]), DPCM should also defend it; (2) for threats that cannot be defended by 4G (e.g., DoS), DPCM should not further ease or amplify them; (3) new threats should not be made possible by DPCM itself. We next analyze how DPCM satisfies them by exploring the possible attacks.

Authentication/authorization/accounting. DPCM offers mutual authentication and authorization with Diffe-Hellman protocol bound with group identification (§4.4), and correct accounting by decoupling packet counting from policy updates.

Over-the-air confidentiality and integrity. DPCM encrypts user's data and signaling over the air. It replaces 4G's key agreements with a variant of Diffe-Hellman protocol (§4.4).

Defenses to man-in-the-middle attacks. Two threats exist. The first is the IMSI catcher, which fakes the base station and sniffs the device behaviors. DPCM defenses this with mutual authentication, and encrypts user data and signaling over the air. The second is the Diffe-Hellman protocol for key agreement, whose original version can be exploited to fake the negotiated keys in the middle. DPCM defends it by binding the key agreement after the group-based authentication, thus detecting the faked device or network nodes.

Denial-of-service attacks. 4G LTE is vulnerable to DoS attacks *by design*. Previous works [23, 48, 59] have shown that, the malicious devices can exploit the radio resource scheduling and signaling messages, and launch radio jamming and DDoS attacks to base stations and mobility controllers. The 4G standards [16, 17] choose not to fully address DoS because of the high cost. Similar attacks can also appear in DPCM, which however does not ease or amplify them. With piggyback mechanisms, DPCM does not incur more signaling messages between device and network than 4G LTE.

Local device attacks. This is a new potential threat in DPCM. Since DPCM leverages device-side information, a selfish device may modify its local states and affect the control procedures for its own benefit (e.g. increase its QoS level). To defend it, DPCM lets network nodes detect the device's state modification (which is disallowed in DPCM). Once the modification is detected, DPCM rolls back to 4G's network-only control procedures, which guarantees the same 4G security level. Note that, the device-side states are initialized and distributed by the MC during the session state/migration. In DPCM, the state is distributed together with a fingerprint issued by the network nodes for integrity verification. The fingerprint includes a hash of the session states, and a signature issued by the mobility controller using the group identification key. At runtime, the device should carry the states *and* the fingerprint in the in-band messages. Then the network nodes can verify whether the session state is issued by the mobility controller (with the signature), and whether the states are modified since distribution (with the hash).

Acknowledgments: We greatly appreciate our shepherd, Dr. Eric Rozner, and the anonymous reviewers for their constructive comments. This work at its early stage was partially supported by NSF Grants: CNS-1526985, CNS-1526456, CNS-1423576 and CNS-1421440.

REFERENCES

[1] 2013. PBC Library. https://crypto.stanford.edu/pbc/. (2013).
[2] 2017. Android TelephonyManager class. http://developer.android.com/reference/android/telephony/TelephonyManager.html. (2017).
[3] 2017. MobileInsight. http://www.mobileinsight.net. (2017).
[4] 2017. OpenAirInterface project. https://gitlab.eurecom.fr/oai/openairinterface5g/wikis/home. (2017).
[5] 2017. Youtube-dl library. (2017). https://rg3.github.io/youtube-dl/.

[6] 3GPP. 2006. TS25.331: Radio Resource Control (RRC). (2006). http://www.3gpp.org/ftp/Specs/html-info/25331.htm
[7] 3GPP. 2012. TS29.274: 3GPP Evolved Packet System (EPS); Evolved General Packet Radio Service Tunneling Protocol for Control plane (GTPv2-C); Stage 3. (Sep. 2012). http://www.3gpp.org/DynaReport/29274.htm
[8] 3GPP. 2013. TS24.301: Non-Access-Stratum (NAS) for EPS; . (Jun. 2013). http://www.3gpp.org/ftp/Specs/html-info/24301.htm
[9] 3GPP. 2013. TS31.102: Characteristics of the Universal Subscriber Identity Module (USIM) application. (Sep. 2013). http://www.3gpp.org/DynaReport/31102.htm
[10] 3GPP. 2014. TS31.111: Universal Subscriber Identity Module (USIM); Application Toolkit (USAT). (Dec. 2014). http://www.3gpp.org/DynaReport/31111.htm
[11] 3GPP. 2015. TS23.401: General Packet Radio Service enhancements for Evolved Universal Terrestrial Radio Access Network (E-UTRAN) access. (Dec. 2015). http://www.3gpp.org/ftp/Specs/html-info/23401.htm
[12] 3GPP. 2015. TS29.272: Mobility Management Entity and and Serving GPRS Support Node related interfaces based on Diameter protocol. (Mar. 2015). http://www.3gpp.org/ftp/Specs/html-info/36331.htm
[13] 3GPP. 2015. TS29.281: 3GPP Evolved Packet System (EPS); Evolved General Packet Radio Service Tunneling Protocol for User Plane (GTPv1-U); Stage 3. (Sep. 2015). http://www.3gpp.org/DynaReport/29281.htm
[14] 3GPP. 2015. TS36.331: Radio Resource Control (RRC). (Mar. 2015). http://www.3gpp.org/ftp/Specs/html-info/36331.htm
[15] 3GPP. 2015. TS36.413: S1 Application Protocol (S1AP). (Jun. 2015). http://www.3gpp.org/ftp/Specs/html-info/36413.htm
[16] 3GPP. 2016. TS33.401: 3GPP System Architecture Evolution (SAE); Security architecture. (2016).
[17] 3GPP. 2016. TS33.401: Service requirements for the Evolved Packet System (EPS). (Jun. 2016).
[18] 3GPP. 2017. 3GPP 5G New Radio Working Group: Radio Interface architecture and protocols. (2017). http://www.3gpp.org/Specifications-groups/ran-plenary/46-ran2-radio-layer-2-and-radio-layer
[19] 3GPP. 2017. TS33.203: 3G security; Access security for IP-based services. (2017).
[20] 3GPP. 2017. TS36.211: Evolved Universal Terrestrial Radio Access (E-UTRA); Physical channels and modulation. (2017).
[21] Yair Amir, Claudiu Danilov, Michael Hilsdale, Raluca Musaloiu-Elefteri, and Nilo Rivera. 2006. Fast handoff for seamless wireless mesh networks. In *Proceedings of the 4th international conference on Mobile systems, applications and services*. ACM.
[22] Mortaza S Bargh, RJ Hulsebosch, EH Eertink, A Prasad, Hu Wang, and Peter Schoo. 2004. Fast authentication methods for handovers between IEEE 802.11 wireless LANs. In *Proceedings of the 2nd ACM international workshop on Wireless mobile applications and services on WLAN hotspots*. ACM, 51–60.
[23] Ramzi Bassil, Ali Chehab, Imad Elhajj, and Ayman Kayssi. 2012. Signaling oriented denial of service on LTE networks. In *Proceedings of the 10th ACM international symposium on Mobility management and wireless access*. ACM, 153–158.
[24] Kevin Boos, David Chu, and Eduardo Cuervo. 2016. Flashback: Immersive virtual reality on mobile devices via rendering memoization. In *Proceedings of the 14th Annual International Conference on Mobile Systems, Applications, and Services*. ACM, 291–304.
[25] Eugene Chai, Karthik Sundaresan, Mohammad A Khojastepour, and Sampath Rangarajan. 2016. LTE in unlicensed spectrum: are we there yet?. In *Proceedings of the 22nd Annual International Conference on Mobile Computing and Networking*. ACM, 135–148.
[26] Abhijnan Chakraborty, Vishnu Navda, Venkata N Padmanabhan, and Ramachandran Ramjee. 2013. Coordinating cellular background transfers using loadsense. In *The 19th Annual International Conference on Mobile Computing and Networking (MobiCom)*. ACM, 63–74.
[27] Junguk Cho, Karthikeyan Sundaresan, Rajesh Mahindra, Jacobus Van der Merwe, and Sampath Rangarajan. 2016. ACACIA: Context-aware Edge Computing for Continuous Interactive Applications over Mobile Networks. In *Proceedings of the 12th International on Conference on emerging Networking EXperiments and Technologies*. ACM, 375–389.
[28] Mostafa Zaman Chowdhury, Won Ryu, Eunjun Rhee, and Yeong Min Jang. 2009. Handover between Macrocell and Femtocell for UMTS Based Networks. In *IEEE ICACT*.
[29] Ivan Damgård, Kasper Dupont, and Michael Østergaard Pedersen. 2006. Unclonable group identification. In *Advances in Cryptology-EUROCRYPT*. Vol. 4004. Springer, 555–572.
[30] Aaron Gember-Jacobson, Raajay Viswanathan, Chaithan Prakash, Robert Grandl, Junaid Khalid, Sourav Das, and Aditya Akella. 2015. OpenNF: Enabling innovation in network function control. *ACM SIGCOMM Computer Communication Review* 44, 4 (2015), 163–174.
[31] Google. 2017. VpnService. https://developer.android.com/reference/android/net/VpnService.html. (2017).
[32] Robert Hsieh, Zhe Guang Zhou, and Aruna Seneviratne. 2003. S-MIP: A seamless handoff architecture for mobile IP. In *INFOCOM 2003. Twenty-Second Annual Joint Conference of the IEEE Computer and Communications*. IEEE.
[33] Junxian Huang, Feng Qian, Z Morley Mao, Subhabrata Sen, and Oliver Spatscheck. 2014. RadioProphet: Intelligent radio resource deallocation for cellular networks. In *Passive and Active Measurement*. Springer, 1–11.
[34] Huawei. 2013. 5G: A Technology Vision. http://www.huawei.com/5gwhitepaper/. (2013).
[35] GSMA Intelligence. 2014. Understanding 5G: Perspectives on future technological advancements in mobile. https://www.gsmaintelligence.com/research/?file=141208-5g.pdf&download. (Dec. 2014).
[36] Xin Jin, Li Erran Li, Laurent Vanbever, and Jennifer Rexford. 2013. SoftCell: scalable and flexible cellular core network architecture. In *CoNEXT 2013*.
[37] Junaid Khalid, Aaron Gember-Jacobson, Roney Michael, Anubhavnidhi Abhashkumar, and Aditya Akella. 2016. Paving the Way for NFV: Simplifying Middlebox Modifications using StateAlyzr. In *13th USENIX Symposium on Networked Systems Design and Implementation (NSDI 16)*. 239–253.
[38] Yuanjie Li, Chunyi Peng, Zengwen Yuan, Jiayao Li, Haotian Deng, and Tao Wang. [n. d.]. Mobileinsight: Extracting and Analyzing Cellular Network Information on Smartphones. In *Proceedings of the 22nd Annual International Conference on Mobile Computing and Networking (MobiCom '16)*. ACM.
[39] Hongqiang Harry Liu, Xin Wu, Ming Zhang, Lihua Yuan, Roger Wattenhofer, and David Maltz. 2013. zUpdate: Updating data center networks with zero loss. *ACM SIGCOMM Computer Communication Review* 43, 4 (2013), 411–422.
[40] Ralph C Merkle. 1978. Secure communications over insecure channels. *Commun. ACM* 21, 4 (1978), 294–299.
[41] Shantidev Mohanty and Ian F Akyildiz. 2006. A cross-layer (layer 2+ 3) handoff management protocol for next-generation wireless systems. *IEEE Transactions on Mobile Computing* 5, 10 (2006), 1347–1360.
[42] Mehrdad Moradi, Wenfei Wu, Li Erran Li, and Z. Morley Mao. 2014. SoftMoW: A Dynamic and Scalable Software Defined Architecture for Cellular WANs. In *ACM CoNext*.
[43] NGMN. 2015. NGMN 5G white paper. https://www.ngmn.org/uploads/media/NGMN_5G_White_Paper_V1_0.pdf. (2015).
[44] Binh Nguyen, Arijit Banerjee, Vijay Gopalakrishnan, Sneha Kasera, Seungjoon Lee, Aman Shaikh, and Jacobus Van der Merwe. 2014. Towards Understanding TCP Performance on LTE/EPC Mobile Networks. In *Proceedings of the 4th Workshop on All Things Cellular: Operations, Applications, and Challenges (AllThingsCellular'14)*. ACM.
[45] Navid Nikaein, Mahesh K Marina, Saravana Manickam, Alex Dawson, Raymond Knopp, and Christian Bonnet. 2014. OpenAirInterface: A Flexible Platform for 5G Research. *ACM SIGCOMM Computer Communication Review* 44, 5 (2014), 33–38.
[46] Shoumik Palkar, Chang Lan, Sangjin Han, Keon Jang, Aurojit Panda, Sylvia Ratnasamy, Luigi Rizzo, and Scott Shenker. 2015. E2: a framework for NFV applications. In *Proceedings of the 25th Symposium on Operating Systems Principles*. ACM, 121–136.
[47] Zafar Qazi, Melvin Walls, Aurojit Panda, Vyas Sekar, Sylvia Ratnasamy, and Scott Shenker. 2017. A High Performance Packet Core for Next Generation Cellular Networks. In *Proceedings of the 2017 ACM Conference on Special Interest Group on Data Communication (SIGCOMM'17)*. ACM.
[48] Radmilo Racic, Denys Ma, Hao Chen, and Xin Liu. 2008. Exploiting Opportunistic Scheduling in Cellular Data Networks. In *NDSS 2008*.
[49] Ishwar Ramani and Stefan Savage. 2005. SyncScan: practical fast handoff for 802.11 infrastructure networks. In *Proceedings IEEE 24th Annual Joint Conference of the IEEE Computer and Communications Societies.*, Vol. 1. IEEE, 675–684.
[50] Ayaskant Rath and Shivendra Panwar. 2012. Fast handover in cellular networks with femtocells. In *Communications (ICC), 2012 IEEE International Conference on*. IEEE, 2752–2757.
[51] Mark Reitblatt, Nate Foster, Jennifer Rexford, Cole Schlesinger, and David Walker. 2012. Abstractions for network update. In *Proceedings of the ACM SIGCOMM 2012 conference on Applications, technologies, architectures, and protocols for computer communication (SIGCOMM)*. ACM, 323–334.
[52] Sanae Rosen, Haokun Luo, Qi Alfred Chen, Z Morley Mao, Jie Hui, Aaron Drake, and Kevin Lau. 2014. Discovering fine-grained RRC state dynamics and performance impacts in cellular networks. In *The 20th Annual International Conference on Mobile Computing and Networking (MobiCom'14)*. ACM.
[53] Paul Schmitt, Daniel Iland, Mariya Zheleva, and Elizabeth Belding. 2016. HybridCell: Cellular connectivity on the fringes with demand-driven local cells. In *Computer Communications, IEEE INFOCOM 2016-The 35th Annual IEEE International Conference on*. IEEE, 1–9.
[54] Justine Sherry, Peter Xiang Gao, Soumya Basu, Aurojit Panda, Arvind Krishnamurthy, Christian Maciocco, Maziar Manesh, João Martins, Sylvia Ratnasamy, and Luigi Rizzo. 2015. Rollback-Recovery for Middleboxes. In *Proceedings of the 2015 ACM Conference on Special Interest Group on Data Communication*. ACM, 227–240.
[55] H. Soliman, C. Castelluccia, K. ElMalki, and L. Bellier. 1999. Hierarchical Mobile IPv6 (HMIPv6) Mobility Management. (1999). RFC 5380.
[56] Peng Sun, Ratul Mahajan, Jennifer Rexford, Lihua Yuan, Ming Zhang, and Ahsan Arefin. 2015. A network-state management service. *ACM SIGCOMM Computer Communication Review* 44, 4 (2015), 563–574.

[57] Sanjib Sur, Xinyu Zhang, Parmesh Ramanathan, and Ranveer Chandra. 2016. BeamSpy: enabling robust 60 GHz links under blockage. In *13th USENIX Symposium on Networked Systems Design and Implementation (NSDI 16)*. USENIX Association, 193–206.

[58] Aisha Syed and Jacobus Van der Merwe. 2016. Proteus: a network service control platform for service evolution in a mobile software defined infrastructure. In *Proceedings of the 22nd Annual International Conference on Mobile Computing and Networking*. ACM, 257–270.

[59] Patrick Traynor, Michael Lin, Machigar Ongtang, Vikhyath Rao, Trent Jaeger, Patrick McDaniel, and Thomas La Porta. 2009. On cellular botnets: measuring the impact of malicious devices on a cellular network core. In *Proceedings of the 16th ACM conference on Computer and communications security*. ACM, 223–234.

[60] Deepak Vasisht, Swarun Kumar, Hariharan Rahul, and Dina Katabi. 2016. Eliminating Channel Feedback in Next-Generation Cellular Networks. In *Proceedings of the 2016 conference on ACM SIGCOMM 2016 Conference*. ACM, 398–411.

[61] Keith Winstein, Anirudh Sivaraman, Hari Balakrishnan, et al. 2013. Stochastic Forecasts Achieve High Throughput and Low Delay over Cellular Networks.. In *Proceedings of the 10th USENIX conference on Networked Systems Design and Implementation (NSDI)*. 459–471.

[62] Xiufeng Xie, Xinyu Zhang, Swarun Kumar, and Li Erran Li. 2015. piStream: Physical Layer Informed Adaptive Video Streaming Over LTE. In *The 21st Annual International Conference on Mobile Computing and Networking (MobiCom)*. ACM, 413–425.

[63] Xiufeng Xie, Xinyu Zhang, and Shilin Zhu. 2017. Accelerating Mobile Web Loading Using Cellular Link Information. In *In ACM International Conference on Mobile Systems, Applications, and Services (MobiSys'17)*. ACM.

[64] Hidetoshi Yokota, Akira Idoue, Toru Hasegawa, and Toshihiko Kato. 2002. Link layer assisted mobile IP fast handoff method over wireless LAN networks. In *Proceedings of the 8th annual international conference on Mobile computing and networking*. ACM, 131–139.

[65] Yasir Zaki, Thomas Pötsch, Jay Chen, Lakshminarayanan Subramanian, and Carmelita Görg. 2015. Adaptive Congestion Control for Unpredictable Cellular Networks. In *Proceedings of the 2015 ACM Conference on Special Interest Group on Data Communication (SIGCOMM'15)*. ACM, 509–522.

[66] Haijun Zhang, Xiangming Wen, Bo Wang, Wei Zheng, and Yong Sun. 2010. A novel handover mechanism between femtocell and macrocell for LTE based networks. In *Communication Software and Networks, 2010. ICCSN'10.*

Experience: An Open Platform for Experimentation with Commercial Mobile Broadband Networks

Özgü Alay[1], Andra Lutu[1], Miguel Peón-Quirós[2], Vincenzo Mancuso[2], Thomas Hirsch[3], Kristian Evensen[3], Audun Hansen[3], Stefan Alfredsson[4], Jonas Karlsson[4], Anna Brunstrom[4], Ali Safari Khatouni[5], Marco Mellia[5], Marco Ajmone Marsan[2,5]

[1] Simula Research Laboratory, Norway [2] IMDEA Networks Institute, Spain
[3] Celerway Communications, Norway [4] Karlstad University, Sweden [5] Politecnico di Torino, Italy

ABSTRACT

Open experimentation with operational Mobile Broadband (MBB) networks in the wild is currently a fundamental requirement of the research community in its endeavor to address the need of innovative solutions for mobile communications. Even more, there is a strong need for objective data about stability and performance of MBB (e.g., 3G/4G) networks, and for tools that rigorously and scientifically assess their status. In this paper, we introduce the MONROE measurement platform: an open access and flexible hardware-based platform for measurements and custom experimentation on operational MBB networks. The MONROE platform enables accurate, realistic and meaningful assessment of the performance and reliability of 11 MBB networks in Europe. We report on our experience designing, implementing and testing the solution we propose for the platform. We detail the challenges we overcame while building and testing the MONROE testbed and argue our design and implementation choices accordingly. We describe and exemplify the capabilities of the platform and the wide variety of experiments that external users already perform using the system.

1 INTRODUCTION

Mobile broadband (MBB) networks have become the key infrastructure for people to stay connected everywhere they go and while on the move. Society's increased reliance on MBB networks motivates researchers and engineers to enhance the capabilities of mobile networks by designing new technologies to cater for a plethora of new applications and services, growth in traffic volume and a wide variety of user devices. In this dynamic ecosystem, there is a strong need for both open objective data about the performance and reliability of commercial operators, as well as open platforms for experimentation with operational MBB providers.

In this paper, we introduce ***MONROE**: the first open access hardware-based platform for independent, multihomed, large-scale experimentation in MBB heterogeneous environments.* MONROE comprises a large set of custom hardware devices, both mobile (e.g., via hardware operating aboard public transport vehicles) and stationary (e.g., volunteers hosting the equipment in their homes), all multihomed to three operators using commercial grade subscriptions.

Thorough systematic repeatable end-to-end measurements are essential for evaluating network performance, assessing the quality experienced by end users and experimenting with novel protocols. While existing experimental platforms, such as Planetlab [29], RIPE Atlas [31] or CAIDA Ark [3], meet these requirements, they are limited to fixed broadband networks and are not multihomed. MONROE is a one-of-a-kind platform that enables controlled experimentation with different commercial mobile carriers. It enables users to run custom experiments and to schedule experimental campaigns to collect data from operational MBB and WiFi networks, together with full context information (metadata). For example, MONROE can accommodate performance evaluation of different applications (e.g., web and video) over different networks or testing different protocols and solutions under the same conditions.

Objective performance data is essential for regulators to ensure transparency and the general quality level of the basic Internet access service [24]. Several regulators responded to this need with ongoing nationwide efforts [6]. Often, they do not open the solutions to the research community to allow for custom experimentation, nor do they grant free access to the measurement results and methodology. MONROE aims to fill this gap and offers free access to custom experimentation. The MONROE project selected 27 different external users to deploy their own custom experiments on the MONROE system with the purpose of testing and further improving the platform based on their feedback.

A common alternative to using controlled testbeds such as MONROE is to rely on end users and their devices to run tests by visiting a website [26] or running a special application [13]. The main advantage of such crowdsourcing techniques is scalability: it can collect millions of measurements from different regions, networks and user equipment types [10]. However, repeatability is challenging and one can only collect measurements at users' own will, with no possibility of either monitoring or controlling the measurement process. Mostly due to privacy reasons, crowd measurements do not always provide important context information (e.g., location, type of user equipment, type of subscription, and connection status (2G/3G/4G and WiFi)). MONROE is complementary to crowdsourcing approaches and the control over the measurement environment tackles the shortcomings of crowd data, though at the cost of a smaller geographical footprint [8]. Furthermore, MONROE supports the deployment of different applications and protocols, and enables benchmarking tools and methodologies.

MobiCom '17, October 16–20, 2017, Snowbird, UT, USA.
© 2017 ACM. ISBN 978-1-4503-4916-1/17/10...$15.00
DOI: https://doi.org/10.1145/3117811.3117812

In the rest of the paper, we report on our experience designing, implementing and using the platform. We detail the design considerations and demonstrate the versatility of our approach (Section 2). We explain how we cater for the requirements of experimenters and enable them to deploy myriad measurements on operational commercial MBB networks. The MONROE measurement node (hereinafter, the node or the MONROE node) sits in the center of the system and is the most important element, conditioning the proper functionality of the measurement system. We describe our experience with the MONROE system implementation and detail the hardware selection for the MONROE measurement node (Section 3). We forged the node to be flexible and powerful enough to run a wide range of measurement and experimental tasks, including demanding applications like adaptive video streaming. In the same time, we ensured that the node software design translates into a robust implementation (Section 4) that is also easily evolved and upgraded in order to sustain the most recent technological innovations. We further present the user access and scheduling solution we offer experimenters for exploiting the available resources of the platform in a fair manner (Section 5). Finally, we demonstrate that the MONROE system is a fitting solution to conduct a wide range of experiments over commercial cellular networks. To showcase its capabilities, we describe different categories of experiments MONROE supports (Section 6), which give an overview of the main categories of experiments MONROE users are conducting at the time of writing. Additionally, we expand on our experience interacting with the external users (Section 7).

2 SYSTEM DESIGN

Throughout the design process of MONROE, we interacted with the users of the platform (e.g., universities, research centers, industry and SMEs) and collected their feedback on requirements for platform functionality. This allowed us to gauge experimenters' expectations and use them to sketch the platform specifications.

2.1 Requirements

We summarize the main requirements as follows.

Large scale and Diversity: To give a representative view of the characteristics of an entire network, we need to collect measurements from a large number of vantage points. Furthermore, we should strive to collect measurements under diverse geographical settings, from major cities to remote islands.

Mobility: Mobility is what makes MBB networks unique compared to other wireless networks. To provide insight into the mobility dimension of MBB networks, it is imperative that the platform integrates a deployment under realistic mobility scenarios.

Fully programmable nodes: To accommodate the wide range of experiments users contemplate to run on the platform, we should forge measurement devices that are flexible, powerful and robust.

Multihoming support: To compare different mobile operators and/or different wireless technologies under the same conditions, the same node should connect to multiple providers at the same time (multihoming support). This further makes the platform particularly well suited for experimentation with methods that exploit aggregation of multiple connections.

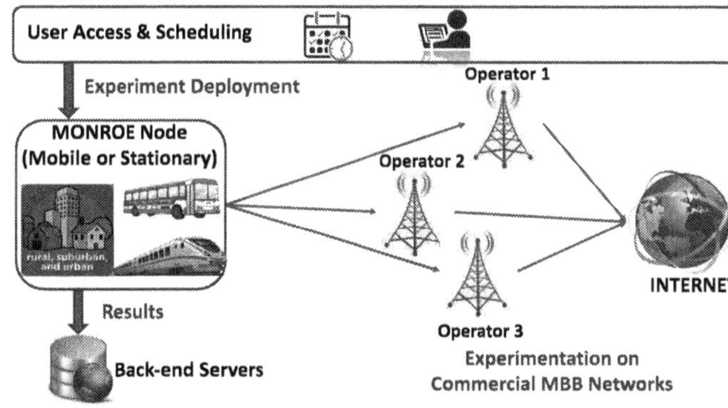

Figure 1: The MONROE platform: MONROE Nodes operate in trains, buses or inside homes and each connects to three commercial mobile operators in each country with MONROE presence. Users access the available resources and deploy their experiments via the User Access and Scheduling. Measurement results synchronize to external repositories operating in the back-end.

Rich context information: While analyzing the measurements, context information is crucial. The platform should monitor the network conditions, the time and location of the experiment, as well as the metadata from the modems, including, for example, cell ID, signal strength and connection mode.

Easy to use platform: It is crucial to make it easy for users to access the system and deploy experiments on all or a selected subset of nodes. This requires a user friendly interface together with a well managed and fair scheduling system.

2.2 Design Overview

We shaped the main building blocks of the MONROE platform such that we can meet the above-mentioned requirements. Note that while implementing different components of the platform, operational aspects also impacted the design choices, which we will discuss in detail in Sections 4-5. Next, we give an overview of the purpose and functionality of the main building blocks of the MONROE system, which we illustrate in Figure 1. All the software components of the MONROE system are open source [17].

MONROE Node: MONROE operates 150 nodes in 4 countries in Europe (Spain, Italy, Sweden and Norway). The measurement node resides at the core of our platform. Its design comprises two main notions, namely the hardware configuration, and the software ecosystem. In terms of hardware, each node has a main board that is a small programmable computer and supports (at least) 4 interfaces: three 3G/4G modems and one Wifi modem. To cover a diverse set of mobility scenarios, we customize a portion of the nodes (i.e., 95 out of 150 total nodes) to operate on public transport vehicles (buses and trains) and also in delivery trucks. In Section 3, we detail the choices for the node hardware implementation and our experience with running two node prototypes.

The node software is based on a Linux Debian "stretch" distribution to ensure compatibility with multiple hardware configurations and to enable a large set of experiments. Furthermore, especially considering the experimentation on protocols, Linux is the only operating system with sufficient hardware support for research and implementation of transport protocols due to the accessibility of the source code, flexibility and community maintenance to ensure operability with other systems. On top of the operating system, the nodes run: (i) *the management software* that performs the normal jobs expected on any mobile device, (ii) *the maintenance software* that monitors the operational status of the nodes and diminishes manual maintenance intervention and (iii) *the experimentation enablers*, that enable experiment deployment (via the scheduler client) and feed rich context information to the experiments. To provide agile reconfiguration and access for the experimenter to different software components, the experiments run in the Docker lightweight virtualized environment. This also ensures containment of external actions in the node system. We periodically transfer the results of the experiments from the nodes to a remote repository. We further detail in Section 4 the node software ecosystem and present our evaluation of potential node internal performance overheads.

User access and scheduling: MONROE enables access to platform resources through a user-friendly web portal [19] that allows authenticated users to use the MONROE scheduler to deploy their experiments. The MONROE Scheduler facilitates exclusive access to the nodes (i.e., no two experiments run on the node at the same time) while ensuring fairness among users by accounting data quotas. We provide the details and the implementation choices for the user access and scheduling policies in Section 5.

3 HARDWARE IMPLEMENTATION

Given the requirements we drew from MONROE stakeholders (Section 2), the measurement device needs to be small, able to function in different environments (buses, trains, homes), affordable, robust, sufficiently powerful and should support the mainline Linux kernel. The size and price constraints limited us to evaluate different Single Board Computers (SBCs). There is a large amount of different SBCs available to the consumer public, with different CPU architectures and hardware configurations. However, most contain hardware requiring the use of proprietary drivers, thus restricting us to old kernels or making it impossible to compile custom kernels. We evaluated several options, including popular ones such as Raspberry Pi [30], Odroid [25], Beaglebone [1] and we selected PC Engines APU [28]. We chose the APU because it provides sufficient processing power, storage and memory for the foreseeable future at a reasonable cost. APUs integrate a 1Ghz 64 bit quad core processor, 4GB of RAM and a 16GB HDD. APUs have 3 miniPCI express slots, two of which support 3G/4G modems.

Modem Selection: To multihome to three mobile operators and a WiFi hotspot, we initially equipped the PC Engines APU board with an Yepkit self-powered USB hub [38], three USB-based CAT4 MF910 MiFis [42] and one WiFi card [4]. The reason we chose the MF910 MiFi is because, at the time we selected the hardware, it was the most modern device sold by operators we measured.

In the prototype validation phase, this implementation presented some major obstacles. While the APUs proved to be very stable, the MiFis proved more challenging than expected. First of all, in the last quarter of 2016, the MiFis' vendor issued a forced update to the firmware. The update was applied despite the fact that we took special care to configure the devices not to receive automatic updates. As a result of the forced update, all our MiFis became inaccessible for the MONROE system. Furthermore, the MiFis themselves were prone to resets or to enter a working state (transparent PPP) from which we could only restore them to normal operation by draining their batteries, or performing a manual reboot by pushing the power button. Finally, after 6 months of operation, some of the MiFis showed clear signs of swollen batteries. This problem brought serious safety concerns for the nodes operating in places other than our own (controlled) premises (e.g., public transport vehicles). We thus modified the hardware configuration to use internal modems operating in the miniPCIe slots of the APU board.

Current Node Configuration: We decided to increase the control over the MONROE node and base its implementation on a dual-APU system. One of the two APUs in each node has two MC7455 miniPCI express (USB 3.0) modems [33], while the other has one MC7455 modem and a WiFi card. We chose Sierra Wireless MC7455 as our 4G modem since, at the time of the upgrade, it was supporting the most recent category (CAT6) an industrial grade modem could provide. This design eliminates the risk brought on by the use of batteries, avoids any forced updates (the new modems are not routers), simplifies resets (no draining of battery) and increases our overall control over the system.

Takeaways: APUs showed very stable performance, while repurposing the MiFis to behave as simple modems presented major challenges (e.g., forced updates and swollen battery problems). We thus bring forward a more compact and robust node configuration that relies on internal modems operating in miniPCIe slots. This also simplifies the node since we avoid potential NAT and routing issues the MiFis might trigger.

4 NODE SOFTWARE IMPLEMENTATION

In this section, we describe in detail the node software ecosystem and present the justification for our implementation choices.

4.1 Software Ecosystem

Figure 2 presents the elements that coexist in the MONROE node software ecosystem, namely the node management software, the node maintenance software and the experimentation enablers.

The **node management software** integrates a set of core components that run continuously in the background. They perform low-level work in line with the normal jobs expected on any mobile device or computer. These include (i) a *Device Listener*, which detects, configures and connects network devices, (ii) a *Routing Daemon*, which acquires an IP address through DHCP, sets up routing tables, (iii) a *Network Monitor*, which monitors interface state, checks the connectivity of the different interfaces and configures default routes. The node operates behind a firewall, which we configure with strict rules to increase node security.

The **node maintenance software** integrates components that monitor the node status and trigger actions to repair or reinstall when malfunctioning. A *system-wide watchdog* ensures that all core components (node management) are running. However, during the first few months, we experienced loss of connection to nodes because of problems that watchdogs could not tackle, such as file system corruptions which can occur due to frequent sudden power loss in mobile nodes. Thus, we defined and implemented a robust

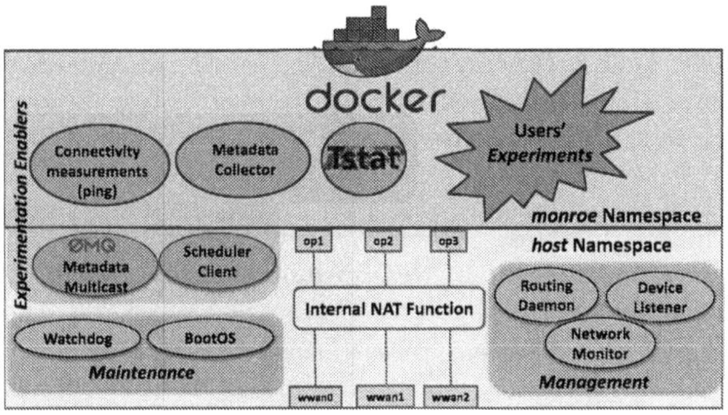

Figure 2: Node Software Ecosystem.

node recovery method, called BootOS, that enables a hard restart of the node (i.e., a reinstallation of the operating system to a known working baseline). This method allows us to recover both from file system errors that prevent system boot-ups, and software configurations that may lead to loss of connectivity. To achieve this goal, we trigger a two-stage boot loader process at node start-up. In the first stage, we start the BootOS, which resides entirely in RAM and only uses read-only hard-drive access for its normal operation. The BootOS verifies that the filesystem of the APU is not corrupt, and that no forced reinstallation has been requested. It then proceeds to boot the MainOS, which contains the MONROE system software. If the filesystem is corrupt, or in case of a forced reinstallation, the BootOS reinstalls an image of a known working installation.

The **experimentation enablers** include the scheduling client, the default experiments, and the services for external experiments. Within the node software ecosystem, we differentiate between the user experiments and the management and maintenance software by configuring a separate *monroe network namespace* where experiments run. This increases our control over the ecosystem and limits the impact external users can have on the node. This separation further allows us to account (as part of the scheduling system) the traffic volume each user consumes. We require that each experiment runs inside a virtualized environment (Docker container) to ensure separation and containment of processes. The *Scheduling Client* communicates with the Scheduler to enable experiment deployment per user request. It periodically checks for new experiment containers to run in the node and deploys them in advance to their scheduled execution time. Section 5 offers more details on the scheduling system. The *metadata broadcasting service* runs continuously in the background and relays metadata through ZeroMQ [41] in JSON [12] format to experiment containers. The nodes periodically run connectivity measurements (e.g., ping), and this together with metadata allow us to monitor the node's state and the overall health of the platform. Furthermore, the *Tstat* [9] passive probe provides insights on the traffic patterns at both the network and the transport levels, offering additional information on the traffic each interface exchanged during an experiment.

Takeaways: Containment of users activity in the node is paramount to avoid security risks, node malfunctioning events, unreliable results and, more severely, node loss. We prevent foreign unauthorized access to the node with a strict firewall. Then, continuous monitoring of the platform is crucial and we enable it by implementing monitoring functions in the node management software. Node maintenance is expensive, so it is important to forge the node as a self-healing system. We implement this functionality in the node maintenance software that takes automatic actions when the node malfunctions.

4.2 Experiment Containment

Docker Virtualization. The node design we propose mandates that MONROE users execute their experiments inside Docker containers, which provide isolation from the host node. This is true both for default monitoring measurements and external users experiments. Docker containers are based on a layered file system, where a container can reuse layers shared with other containers.

MONROE provides the default base image for the experiment containers, which integrates the base operating system installation with default tools that are potentially useful for many experiments. The lightweight containers provide just the contents that are unique for the particular experiment, significantly reducing the download and deployment time overhead and accountable traffic volume. Experiments running inside a container have access to the experimental network interfaces. They can read and write on their own file system, overlaid over that of the base MONROE image. Finally, there are specific paths (e.g., `/MONROE/results/`) where the experiments can write their results and that the node automatically transfers to the MONROE servers. Our public software repositories contain all the files necessary to build new user experiments, as well as experiment templates and examples.

Internal NAT Function. To ensure the minimum impact of user experiments gone wrong, we define the *monroe network namespace* where experiment containers run. For each physical interface that the network-listener detects as available, we create a virtualized ethernet, `veth`, interface pair, and move one end to the monroe namespace. We then add routing rules in the network namespace to allow routing by interface. In order to allow the network devices in the host namespace to communicate with the ones in the monroe network namespace, we define an internal Network Address Translation (NAT) function. We use `iptables` NAT masquerading rules in the host namespace to configure the NAT function. Finally, we add the corresponding routing rules to map each `veth` interface to the correct physical interface.

Overhead Quantification. The internal network design introduces two potential overheads that might impact performance measurements: (i) the internal NAT function that connects the network devices in the host namespace with their corresponding duplicates in the monroe namespace, and (ii) the Docker containers we use to separate the processes that correspond to a certain experiment that runs inside the container. Thus, prior to detailing the measurement results of different commercial MBB operators, we focus here on these two design overheads and aim to quantify their impact (if any) on performance measurement results. More specifically, we quantify the delay overhead by running ICMP ping measurements, and the impact on throughput by running HTTP downloads.

To instrument our system benchmarking measurements we use a single APU node running the Debian "stretch" MONROE image with a local Fast Ethernet link. Using a local link allows us to minimize the impact of the network on our measurements, and focus on the impact of the system overheads. We run http download measurements with `curl` and ICMP ping measurements with `fping`

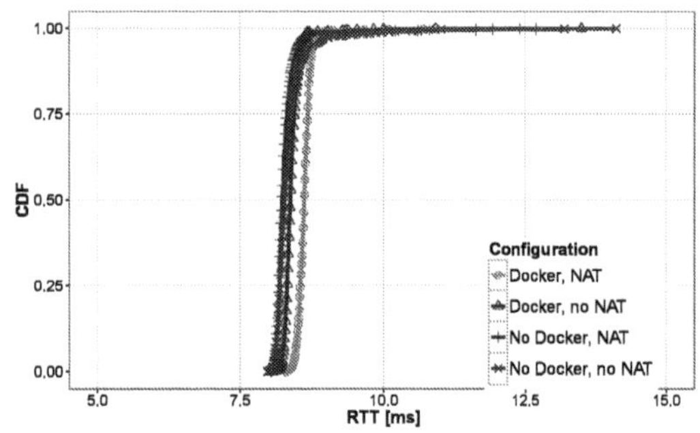

Figure 3: CDFs of ICMP RTTs [ms] measured against 8.8.8.8 per testing configuration over Fast Ethernet link.

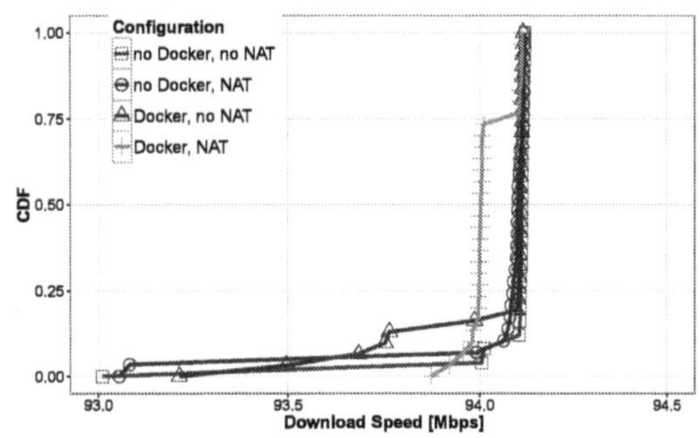

Figure 4: CDFs of Downloads Speed [Mbps] measured per testing configuration over Fast Ethernet link.

to quantify the impact of the internal NAT function and of the Docker virtualization. We focus on four configurations for our testing setup, namely: no NAT and no Docker (experiments run in host namespace), no NAT but Docker (experiments run inside a Docker container in the host namespace), internal NAT and no Docker (experiments run in the monroe namespace) and internal NAT and Docker (experiments run inside a Docker container in the monroe namespace).

To quantify the delay overhead, we collect 1,000 RTT samples against the Google DNS server 8.8.8.8 on the Ethernet connection on all four configurations. Figure 3 shows the results of the measurements. We conclude that the overhead of the NAT function internal to the node is insignificant. In average, we see a penalty in the order of 0.1ms, (i.e., in the range of clock granularity in Linux systems). We note that the Docker and NAT combination introduces a slight delay, which is not overwhelming.

For the throughput measurements, we download 1GB of data from a server configured in the local network. We collect 30 samples for each testing configuration. In Figure 4 we show the cumulative distribution of download speed per namespace and operator, for each of the different targets. We find that there is a 1% performance penalty that using the internal NAT function and the Docker virtualization introduces in average. We report no direct impact of using the Docker containers, which we expected, since the purpose of the Docker virtualization is purely for experiment containment.

Takeaways: Our priority in the node software implementation phase is keeping the nodes within normal functioning parameters for as long as possible and limiting direct maintenance intervention, while allowing external users to run a wide range of complex measurements with minimum interference. To achieve this, we separate the network namespace where users can run their experiments from the host namespace, where the monitoring and management software runs. This introduces two potential overheads in the system, which we quantify and show to have little or no impact.

5 USER ACCESS AND SCHEDULING

We provide access to the MONROE platform through a user-friendly interface consisting of an AngularJS-based web portal [19]. As part of the MONROE federation with the Fed4FIRE [7] initiative, the user access follows the Fed4FIRE specifications in terms of authentication and resource provisioning. Through the portal, experimenters interact with the scheduler and deploy their experiments without accessing directly the nodes. The scheduler API is accessible to enable experiment deployment automation. The scheduler prevents conflicts between experiments (i.e., only one user can run an experiment on a certain node at a time) and assigns resources to each user based on their requirements and resource availability.

Given the challenging scenarios we aim to cover in our testbed, nodes in MONROE have potentially unreliable connectivity and low bandwidth. This is the norm for node in buses, trains and trucks, which follow the schedule of the host vehicle. Experiment scheduling therefore accounts for two factors: (i) the node may not have connectivity at the time of the experiment and (ii) a high lead time when deploying containers means that experiments should be deployed early. Furthermore, experimenters may require to run synchronous measurements on multiple nodes. The common approach to task scheduling and decentralized computing, which deploys jobs to registered nodes based on their availability, struggles with these constraints. Therefore, for the MONROE scheduler, we follow a calendar-based approach, assigning time slots to experiments. Deployment of experiments takes place up to 24 hours in advance, as soon as the node retrieves information about the assigned task. This allows both immediate scheduling on nodes that are not otherwise occupied, and scheduling synchronous experiments on low availability nodes well in advance. It also allows synchronizing experiment runtime with vehicle schedules when available.

In addition to managing the time resource, the scheduler handles data quotas assigned by the contracts with the MBB operators. We assign each experimenter a fix data quota. In addition, we may assign users a quota on computing time (i.e., maximum time the users can run experiments on the node). We designed the quota system to provide fair usage of the available resources. An important factor to ensure fairness in day-to-day usage, is that a certain data quota is reserved by the experimenter in advance, and subtracted from the user quota for the duration of the experiment. Experimenters may subsequently refund the remaining quota. Hence, it is not possible to block large quantities of resources without having been assigned the necessary budget, even if the resources are not actually used.

From March 2016 until March 2017, the MONROE scheduler has been actively used by 30 users. A total of 75,002 experiments have successfully ran on the platform, while 7,972 scheduled experiments failed. There are many different reasons for failed experiments, for example that the container exits unexpectedly or the data quota is exceeded. Note that these failures are expected especially for the new users that are trying to familiarize themselves with the platform. We are running an open conversation with our users, gathering feedback from them and updating the user access and scheduling policies accordingly.

Takeaways: Resource allocation and experiment scheduling on MONROE is challenging because nodes have potentially unreliable connectivity (e.g., nodes in mobility scenarios) and limited data quota due to commercial-grade subscriptions. A calendar-based approach for scheduling addresses these requirements by taking into account per user and per node data quota, and synchronized experiment start time.

6 OPEN EXPERIMENTATION

Starting from the platform design phase, we have been working together with our stakeholders to understand their requirements from the MONROE system and which experiments have the highest appeal (Section 2). We then took this process further and, throughout 2016 and 2017, the MONROE consortium organized two open calls for external experimenters. After a thorough selection process based on peer-review, we funded 27 different projects (12 projects in May 2016 from the first open call (OC1) and 15 projects in February 2017 from the second open call (OC2)) to be among the first users of the MONROE system.

The experiments that these projects proposed are very diverse and cover a wide range of scenarios, from simple network performance measurements to innovative protocols evaluation to application performance assessment. All experimenters were encouraged to propose SW extensions to the platform (e.g., measurement packages that can be offered to the MONROE community) as well as HW extensions to the infrastructure (e.g., deploying MONROE nodes in locations with no previous MONROE coverage, or increasing the density of MONROE nodes in locations with MONROE coverage).

6.1 MONROE Experiments

We report next on our experience accommodating the 12 OC1 measurement campaigns on the platform[1], together with the base experiments deployed by the consortium. We are currently offering to the community a series of experiments [18], which any external users can deploy on their own. This goes toward achieving our goal of shaping MONROE into an Experimentation as a Service (EaaS) platform. We group all these experiments in three main categories: Mobile Broadband Performance, Service Oriented QoE and Innovative Protocols and Services. These categories also fit to the range of measurements that our users are currently curating and have been already actively deploying. The distribution of experiment runs on the MONROE platform to the time of writing among these categories is: Mobile Broadband Performance (19%), Service Oriented QoE (36%) and Innovative Protocols and Services (45%). The volume of data that experiments in different categories consume varies, with Service Oriented QoE taking the largest quota (60%), while Innovative Protocols and Services are the least demanding (10%), despite registering the largest number of experiment runs. We further detail each category and provide examples of experiments and analysis one can perform using MONROE.

[1]We mention that, at the time of writing, only the 12 projects from OC1 are actively using the MONROE platform. Though already approved, the additional 15 projects from OC2 have not started actively using the MONROE system.

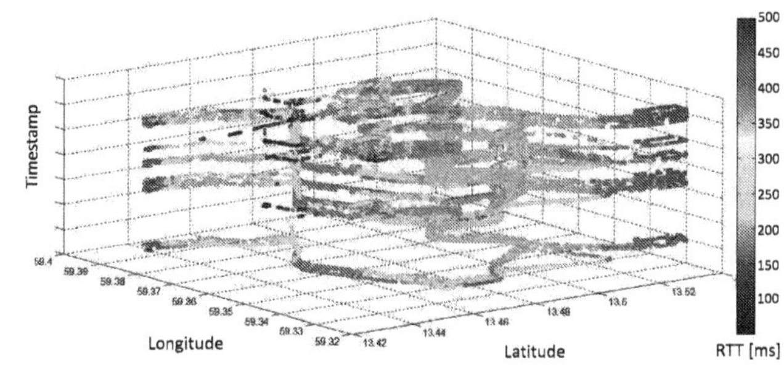

Figure 5: 3D graph average RTT for an operator in Sweden. Multiple laps are shown using the Y-axis offset based on relative timestamps to visually show the different trips.

6.1.1 Mobile Broadband Performance. To measure a mobile network in a reliable and fair way, it is important to identify the metrics that accurately capture its performance. Different stakeholders have different metrics of interest and we argue that MONROE is able to cater all of them. For example, regulators need connectivity, coverage and speed information to monitor whether operators meet their advertised services. Operators are interested in spatio-temporal data reporting the operational connectivity information to further identify instability and anomalies.

One important feature of the MONROE platform is that its deployment in public transportation vehicles allows users to evaluate MBB performance in diverse and complex urban mobility environments. A unique characteristic of this deployment is the repeatability of measurements obtained by many runs on the same route, at different hours. For example, Figure 5 shows RTT (ICMP ping) measurements for an operator in Sweden, as measured by the node operating aboard the same bus during several working days. In the figure, dot colors encode the range of values for the measured RTTs and we observe variations in RTT among different trips through the same location. Repeated measurements provide high confidence and diminish noise in the data, whereas measurement samples at the same location but at different hours allow for the analysis on the time-of-the-day effect (e.g., rush hour versus normal hours).

6.1.2 Service Oriented Quality of Experience. An important measurement dimension to explore comes from the great interest in how users perceive individual services and applications over different terminals (e.g., mobile phones, tablets, and computers). The recent proliferation of user-centric measurement tools (such as Netalyzr [13]) to complement available network centric measurements validates the increasing interest in integrating the end user layer in network performance optimization. MONROE enables experimentation with essential services and applications, including video streaming, web browsing, real-time voice and video, and file transfer services. The service oriented measurements give a good basis for investigating the mapping from Quality of Service to Quality of Experience. With such a mapping, operators can gain better understanding of how their customers perceive the services delivered by their network. From the end users and service providers perspective, they could acquire more knowledge of the performance over different MBBs and then choose the network that delivers the best quality for services that are of interest to them. Furthermore, application developers (e.g., Youtube, Netflix and Spotify) heavily

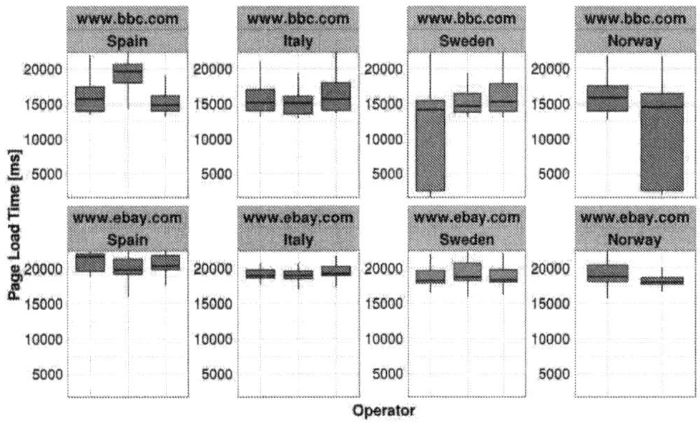

Figure 6: Page download time for 11 operators using data from 37 MONROE nodes in Spain, Italy, Sweden and Norway while fetching `www.bbc.com` and `www.ebay.com`; each subplot corresponds to a country-target pair, and each boxplot to a unique operator in each country.

rely on the underlying network characteristics while optimizing their services for the best user's experience.

To showcase the capabilities of the platform, Figure 6 reports the page load time (PLT) measured in the MONROE platform using a headless [21] browser to fetch two popular websites (www.bbc.com and www.ebay.com) from 37 nodes in four countries with MONROE coverage. If we focus on the PLT as an objective indicator for the quality of experience and track it in comparison with metadata information, we further enable the analysis of the mapping between QoS metrics to the end-user experience.

6.1.3 Innovative Protocols and Services. Another significant use case for MONROE is investigating the impact of middleboxes in the current Internet ecosystem. These range from address and port translators (NATs) to security devices to performance enhancing TCP proxies. Middleboxes are known to introduce a series of issues and hinder the evolution of protocols such as TCP. Since middleboxes are ubiquitous in MBB networks [34, 36, 37], in collaboration with the H2020 MAMI project [16] we aim to observe and characterize middlebox operations in the context of real-world MBB deployments. MONROE further enables assessment of existing protocols, paving the way for protocol innovation.

As an example in this category, we investigated whether the operators measured with MONROE use Performance Enhancement Proxy (PEP) [2] to improve end-users' quality of experience. These proxies provide higher performance and faster error recovery [5, 11, 23]. We ran throughput tests (http downloads) from all the MONROE nodes on different ports against the same responder, where we also run an instance of Tstat on server. We then cross-compared the Tstat analysis logs on the nodes (client-side) with the server-side logs to examine if the proxy splits the TCP connection. Table 1 shows the global view of operators. Yes, Yes*, and No in the table mean always, sometimes, or never. The third column indicates the usage of NAT in the operator network. For instance, op2 in Italy always uses NAT, and sometimes connections are routed through a PEP. On the contrary, op1 sometimes assigns public IP addresses, but HTTP traffic always goes through a PEP device. The forth column indicates if the performance seen on the client and server side are different. A mismatch hints for the presence of a PEP. The fifth column reports the number of public IPs seen in server-side traces (i.e., the "size" of the PEP boxes). The last column shows if the PEP changes the TCP headers (e.g., removing/adding/changing options), and on which ports. Overall, the picture varies with different PEP configurations for different operators.

Table 1: The summary of the operators and their settings.

	OP	NAT	PEP	# IP	L4 mangling
IT	op0	No	Yes	262	80
	op1	Yes*	Yes	129	80,443,8080
	op2	Yes	Yes*	1484	No
ES	op0	Yes	No	272	No
	op1	Yes	No	244	No
	op2	No	Yes	-	80
SE	op0	Yes*	Yes*	1652	No
	op1	No	Yes	3486	No
	op2	No	Yes*	4679	No
NO	op0	No	Yes*	472	No
	op1	Yes*	Yes*	46	No

6.2 External Projects Overview

The OC1 experiments focus mainly on Service Oriented Quality of Experience and assessing the QoE for popular applications, such as interactive video-conferencing (e.g., webRTC) or popular video-on-demand (VoD) application (e.g., YouTube) across multiple mobile carriers. There are 5 out of 12 such projects currently funded from OC1. Their number decreased to only one among the projects funded in OC2. A notable example in this category is a project that integrated the YoMoApp tool [35] with MONROE to monitor the QoE for YouTube. The resulting Yomo-Monroe [32] has two components: Yomo-docker and Yomo-browser-plugin. *Yomo-docker* [40] container provides features to estimate YouTube's "Quality of Experience." For this purpose, the docker container independently performs experiments and monitors the quality at the end-user side. *Yomo-browser-plugin* [39] monitors the quality of YouTube video streaming in the browser. This experiment is a software extension of MONROE and will be available as MONROE EaaS.

Three OC1 projects leverage MONROE data (from base experiments and metadata collection) to build and run anomaly detection algorithms or LTE performance benchmarking across multiple carriers. One particular OC1 project focuses on emergency communications and tests different protocol innovations. The project customized MONROE nodes with mobile, Ethernet connections, fixed point-to-point wireless links, low-band radio interfaces and satellite broadband – all classes of links that are used routinely in disaster situations to provide communications. The project proposes an application use-case for emergency communications in disaster situations. This is based on IP multi-homed support that enables resilient differentiated services, and allows an application to select the best available transport path. The users produced PATHspider-monroe [14, 27], a version of the PATHspider tool [15] adapted for running on MONROE nodes. PATHspider is a tool for A/B testing of path transparency to certain features in the Internet. We note that this experiment is also available as MONROE software extension and will be available as MONROE EaaS.

In OC2, the projects funded shifted mainly towards cloud and smart cities experimentation, with 8 out of 15 proposals active in these topics (e.g., smart city security monitoring with MONROE, analysis of latency-critical connected vehicle applications). The OC2 external users have strong proposals for understanding the synergies between mobile carriers and popular cloud service providers (e.g., characterizing mobile content providers in the wild or tackling net neutrality in MBB networks). A couple of OC2 users aim to use the MONROE platform and the data we produce to device machine learning algorithms for informing self-organizing networks (SON).

7 EXTERNAL USERS EXPERIENCE

In this section, we present a summary of our interaction with the external users while supporting them in the process of using the platform for experimentation. The OC1 experimenters had exclusive access to the prototype platform. Thus, we relied upon their feedback to refine the platform to its current version. We collected this feedback in the form of a report the users provided, which integrated a grading system for different components of the platform. The experimenters we selected through OC2 have access to a more mature version of the MONROE platform, which we aim to further improve pending their additional feedback.

7.1 External Users Feedback

Users reported that the documentation we provided in the MONROE User Manual [20] is very useful, receiving a score of 4.5/5 and that the MONROE experiment templates and examples are easy to reuse (4.2/5). The virtualization method based on Docker containers was very well received, with a mark of 5/5. However, our users strongly suggested to create more multimedia material to complement the written user manual, particularly showing the complete life cycle of an experiment from container creation to scheduling and retrieval of results. Access to metadata was also seen as easy and useful (4.5/5).

As expected when accessing a prototype platform, our users saw some issues at the beginning, giving a mark for easiness and usability of 3.6/5. Regarding scheduling of experiments, in general our users had some troubles understanding all the details of the scheduling process, pointing towards the need for more step-by-step instructions such as the requested multimedia material. Some topics that were particularly troubling for the platform users were the binding to specific interfaces in a multihomed platform and the optimization of the size of the Docker containers.

We provided important additions based on users feedback. First, by opening the scheduler API for command-line tools, we enable submission of experiments programmatically (indeed, a tool for that purpose was released openly by one of the users). Second, we enable SSH access to containers in testing nodes for debugging purposes. The users reported that debugging in batch mode was otherwise very complex and tedious since every debug run had to wait for scheduling, execution and retrieval of results. Finally, the user access and scheduler system now supports rescheduling of the past experiments on the same or different nodes.

7.2 Lessons Learned

To achieve the goals of the external users, we learned that the large availability of experimental resources in MONROE is mandatory, while still giving experimenters strong control of the testing environment. For this reason, each user had access to a series of development nodes (for building the measurement tools in the lab) and testing nodes (for testing the measurement tools in a limited portion of the actual platform). We further decided to guarantee our external users exclusive usage of reserved resources.

Apart from offering experimenters a system ready to accommodate their measurements, we also encouraged external users to propose hardware extensions and enhancements to the platform. This allows us to grow the platform, increase its geographical footprint and engage with the stakeholders to create a relevant product. Fostering a community around the MONROE platform also means producing a rich variety of software measurement tools. Apart from the experiments we maintain withing the consortium, we also encouraged external users to bring software extensions to the platform and contribute to the MONROE EaaS initiative. Numerous of our external users responded positively to this initiative and integrated new measurements software packages with MONROE, which they offer openly to the community. Finally, the MONROE platform aims to be complementary to other measurement infrastructure. Thus, it has been an important goal for us to be able to deploy measurement tools that also run on other hardware-based platforms or in crowd-sourcing platforms. Furthermore, we collaborate with other publicly funded projects in need of mobile measurement infrastructure. An example for this is the Horizon 2020 project NEAT [22] that is planning to use MONROE to evaluate their software and API for optimized transport protocol and network selection.

8 CONCLUSIONS

In this paper, we reported on our experience designing an open large-scale measurement platform for experimentation with commercial MBB networks. MONROE is a completely open system allowing authenticated users to deploy their own custom experiments and conduct their research in the wild. The platform is crucial to understand, validate and ultimately improve how current operational MBB networks perform towards providing guidelines to the design of future 5G architectures. We described our experience with the MONROE system implementation and detailed the hardware selection for the MONROE measurement node, its software ecosystem and the user access and scheduling solution. We emphasized the versatility of the design we propose, both for the overall platform and, more specifically, for the measurement nodes. In fact, the node software design is compatible with a number of different hardware implementations, given that it can run on any Linux-compatible multihomed system. Our current hardware solution is the most fitting for the set of requirements and the predicted usage of MONROE, which we evaluated based on our discussions and interaction with the platform's users.

ACKNOWLEDGMENTS

This work is funded by the EU H2020 research and innovation programme under grant agreement No. 644399 (MONROE), and by the Norwegian Research Council RFF project No. 245698 (NIMBUS). For more information, visit https://www.monroe-project.eu/. The authors would like to express their gratitude to the reviewers and, particularly, to Aruna Balasubramanian, for their invaluable advices to improve this work.

REFERENCES

[1] Beagleboard.org. http://beagleboard.org.

[2] J. Border, M. Kojo, J. Griner, G. Montenegro, and Z. Shelby. 2001. Performance Enhancing Proxies Intended to Mitigate Link-Related Degradations. (2001).

[3] CAIDA. Archipelago (Ark) Measurement Infrastructure. http://www.caida.org/projects/ark/

[4] Compex. WLE600VX. http://www.pcengines.ch/wle600vx.htm

[5] Viktor Farkas, Balázs Héder, and Szabolcs Nováczki. 2012. A Split Connection TCP Proxy in LTE Networks. In *Information and Communication Technologies*. Springer, 263–274.

[6] FCC. 2013. *2013 Measuring Broadband America February Report.* Technical Report. FCC's Office of Engineering and Technology and Consumer and Governmental Affairs Bureau.

[7] FED4FIRE. http://www.fed4fire.eu/.

[8] Mah-Rukh Fida, Andra Lutu, Mahesh Marina, and Ozgu Alay. 2017. ZipWeave: Towards Efficient and Reliable Measurement based Mobile Coverage Maps. *Proc. IEEE INFOCOM* (May 2017).

[9] A. Finamore, M. Mellia, M. Meo, M. M. Munafo, P. D. Torino, and D. Rossi. 2011. Experiences of Internet traffic monitoring with tstat. *IEEE Network* 25, 3 (May 2011), 8–14. DOI: https://doi.org/10.1109/MNET.2011.5772055

[10] Matthias Hirth, Tobias Hobfeld, Marco Mellia, Christian Schwartz, and Frank Lehrieder. 2015. Crowdsourced network measurements: Benefits and best practices. *Computer Networks* 90 (2015), 85–98.

[11] M. Ivanovich, P. W. Bickerdike, and J. C. Li. 2008. On TCP performance enhancing proxies in a wireless environment. *IEEE Communications Magazine* 46, 9 (September 2008), 76–83. DOI: https://doi.org/10.1109/MCOM.2008.4623710

[12] JSON. http://www.json.org/.

[13] Christian Kreibich, Nicholas Weaver, Boris Nechaev, and Vern Paxson. 2010. Netalyzr: illuminating the edge network. In *Proceedings of the 10th ACM SIGCOMM conference on Internet measurement.* ACM, 246–259.

[14] Iain R. Learmonth, Andra Lutu, Gorry Fairhurst, David Ros, and Özgü Alay. 2017. Path Transparency Measurements from the Mobile Edge with PATHspider. In *Proc. of the IEEE/IFIP Workshop on Mobile Network Measurement.*

[15] Iain R. Learmonth, Brian Trammell, Mirja Kühlewind, and Gorry Fairhurst. 2016. PATHspider: A tool for active measurement of path transparency. In *Proceedings of the 2016 Applied Networking Research Workshop.* 62–64.

[16] H2020 MAMI Project. Measurement and Architecture for a Middleboxed Internet. https://mami-project.eu/

[17] MONROE. Open Source Code. https://github.com/MONROE-PROJECT

[18] MONROE. Open-Source Experiments. https://github.com/MONROE-PROJECT/Experiments

[19] MONROE. User Access Portal. https://www.monroe-system.eu

[20] MONROE. User Manual. https://github.com/MONROE-PROJECT/UserManual

[21] MONROE. WebWorks Experiment. https://github.com/MONROE-PROJECT/Experiments/tree/master/experiments/WebWorks

[22] H2020 NEAT Project. A New, Evolutive API and Transport-Layer Architecture for the Internet. https://www.neat-project.org/

[23] Marc C. Necker, Michael Scharf, and Andreas Weber. 2005. *Performance of Different Proxy Concepts in UMTS Networks.* Springer Berlin Heidelberg, Berlin, Heidelberg, 36–51. DOI: https://doi.org/10.1007/978-3-540-31963-4_4

[24] networld2020. 2016. Service Level Awareness and open multi-service internetworking - Principles and potentials of an evolved Internet ecosystem. (2016).

[25] Odroid. http://www.hardkernel.com.

[26] OOKLA. http://www.speedtest.net/.

[27] PATHspider-monroe. https://github.com/mami-project/pathspider-monroe.

[28] PC Engines. APU2C4. https://www.pcengines.ch/apu2c4.htm

[29] Planetlab. https://www.planet-lab.org/.

[30] RaspberryPi. http://www.raspberrypi.org.

[31] RIPE Atlas. https://atlas.ripe.net/.

[32] Anika Schwind, Michael Seufert, Özgü Alay, Pedro Casas, Phuoc Tran-Gia, and Florian Wamser. 2017. Concept and Implementation of Video QoE Measurements in a Mobile Broadband Testbed. In *Proc. of the IEEE/IFIP Workshop on Mobile Network Measurement.*

[33] Sierra-Wireless. MC7455 miniPCI express (USB 3.0) modem. https://www.sierrawireless.com/products-and-solutions/embedded-solutions/products/mc7455/

[34] Narseo Vallina-Rodriguez, Srikanth Sundaresan, Christian Kreibich, Nicholas Weaver, and Vern Paxson. 2015. Beyond the radio: Illuminating the higher layers of mobile networks. In *Proceedings of the 13th Annual International Conference on Mobile Systems, Applications, and Services.* ACM, 375–387.

[35] Florian Wamser, Michael Seufert, Pedro Casas, Ralf Irmer, Phuoc Tran-Gia, and Raimund Schatz. 2015. YoMoApp: A Tool for Analyzing QoE of YouTube HTTP Adaptive Streaming in Mobile Networks. In *European Conference on Networks and Communications (EuCNC).*

[36] Zhaoguang Wang, Zhiyun Qian, Qiang Xu, Zhuoqing Mao, and Ming Zhang. 2011. An untold story of middleboxes in cellular networks. In *Proc. of SIGCOMM.*

[37] Xing Xu, Yurong Jiang, Tobias Flach, Ethan Katz-Bassett, David Choffnes, and Ramesh Govindan. 2015. Investigating Transparent Web Proxies in Cellular Networks. In *Proc. of Passive and Active Measurement.*

[38] Yepkit. USB Switchable Hub YKUSH Homepage. https://www.yepkit.com/products/ykush

[39] Yomo-browser-plugin. https://github.com/lsinfo3/yomo-browser-plugin.git.

[40] Yomo-docker. https://github.com/lsinfo3/yomo-docker.git.

[41] ZeroMQ. http://zeromq.org/.

[42] ZTE. USB-based CAT4 MF910 MiFi, product specification. http://www.ztemobiles.com.au/downloads/User_guides/MF910_Help1.0.pdf

Automating Diagnosis of Cellular Radio Access Network Problems

Anand Padmanabha Iyer
University of California, Berkeley
api@cs.berkeley.edu

Li Erran Li*
Uber Technologies
erranlli@gmail.com

Ion Stoica
University of California, Berkeley
istoica@cs.berkeley.edu

ABSTRACT

In an increasingly mobile connected world, our user experience of mobile applications more and more depends on the performance of cellular radio access networks (RAN). To achieve high quality of experience for the user, it is imperative that operators identify and diagnose performance problems quickly. In this paper, we describe our experience in understanding the challenges in automating the diagnosis of RAN performance problems. Working with a major cellular network operator on a part of their RAN that services more than 2 million users, we demonstrate that fine-grained modeling and analysis could be the key towards this goal. We describe our methodology in analyzing RAN problems, and highlight a few of our findings, some previously unknown. We also discuss lessons from our attempt at building automated diagnosis solutions.

1 INTRODUCTION

Cellular Radio Access Networks (RAN) form the backbone of connectivity on the move for billions of Internet users everyday. Being such a crucial component in their network infrastructure, cellular network operators are constantly striving to operate RANs optimally so as to provide high quality of user experience (QoE) to their subscribers. To achieve high performance in RANs, it is imperative that operators understand the impacting factors and can diagnose performance problems quickly.

RAN performance diagnosis is hard. Factors impacting RAN performance include user mobility, traffic pattern, interference, coverage, unoptimized configuration parameters, inefficient algorithms, equipment failures, software bugs and protocol errors [9, 23, 24]. It is very challenging to diagnose these problems due to the fact that the performance of multiple base stations are coupled by the shared radio access media and user mobility. Existing systems [4, 11] for troubleshooting perform their function by monitoring key performance indicators (KPIs), i.e., aggregate counters such as connection drop rate and throughput per cell, over a several-minute time window. Persistent poor KPIs of base stations or base station clusters trigger mostly manual root cause analysis. This process is slow and ineffective. Often times there are disagreements on who should handle the trouble ticket, such as the RF team, the call processing team or the modem team. In addition, many of these tickets conclude that the problem occurred due to reasons already discovered by earlier analyses[1] *after* extensive troubleshooting. Even worse, a large number of these problems reoccur after fixing several times.

Can cellular network operators automate the detection and diagnosis of RAN performance problems? In this paper, we attempt to answer this question by reporting our experience working with a major cellular network operator. We have studied a portion of this operator's RAN that servers over 2 million subscribers for a period of over a year. During this tenure, we have seen the network experience thousands of problems, and the effort spent by the operator in solving them. Based on this experience, we propose a new methodology to diagnose RAN problems in a better fashion. Our approach is also amenable to automation.

A key problem of current systems stems from relying on aggregate KPIs, making it hard to isolate the many root causes contributing to the observed poor KPI. The natural solution to this problem is to use fine-grained information to do such diagnosis. However, it is infeasible to continuously log metadata for every transmission in the physical layer (e.g., SINR) or for every frame in the MAC layer (e.g., block error rate), or for every packet in the IP layer (e.g., headers). Instead, in this work, we propose using connection (bearer) level traces which can be feasibly collected in current operational networks. A bearer is a connection between a UE and the cellular network. Bearer level traces contain per-procedure (e.g., initial attach) information and aggregate data per bearer (e.g., total physical resources allocated, average uplink SINR).

Our methodology first segregates RAN performance problems based on the broad underlying root causes, and then builds detailed performance models at the bearer level. Assigning the problems to broad buckets allows us to generalize the approach to diagnose them. We distinguish two types of performance metrics. For *event-based* performance metrics such as connection failures and drops, we use classification techniques in machine learning, such as decision trees, to build models that explain the problem. For *volume-based* performance metrics such as radio link layer throughput, we build detailed information theoretic regression models based on physical and MAC layer information. Building these models are non-trivial due to the availability of only aggregate information at the bearer level and because the model needs to consider protocols in several layers. We further derive cell-level KPI models from bearer-level models. This enables us to attribute the root causes affecting bearer-level to their impact on KPIs at the cell-level (§3).

To validate our proposal, we have applied our methodology to the data collected at the operator's RAN, where it revealed several

*Li was involved in this work prior to joining Uber.

MobiCom '17, October 16–20, 2017, Snowbird, UT, USA

ACM ISBN 978-1-4503-4916-1/17/10...$15.00
https://doi.org/10.1145/3117811.3117813

[1] e.g., we found multiple tickets that concluded that a particular device model caused load-balancing issues

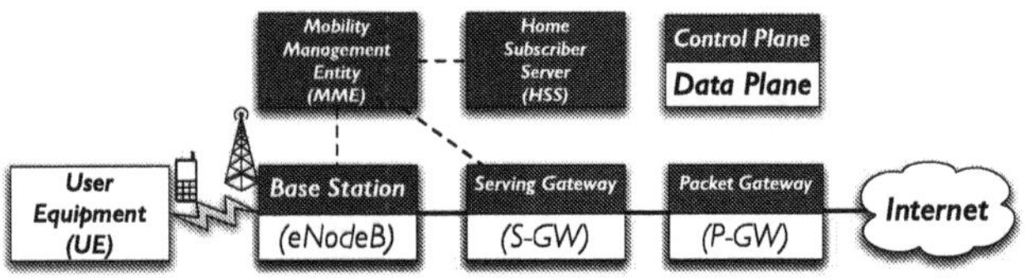

Figure 1: LTE network architecture

interesting insights (§4). First, we found that the detection of periodic channel quality indicator (P-CQI) feedbacks in the physical layer is unreliable. When the feedbacks are transmitted through uplink control channel, they are not protected by CRC. Since the base station only performs threshold-based detection, it could decode arbitrary values once the signal passes the threshold. Without the CRC, there is no way of knowing whether the decoded P-CQI is spurious or not. Coding redundancy can be applied to avoid most of these problems. However, we observed that these spurious P-CQIs are not negligible and causes many ongoing connections to drop. Second, the link adaptation algorithm in the physical layer is not efficient and results in poor throughput. Third, many connection failure alarms can be explained by known root causes. Some of these insights were not previously known.

Finally, while developing the diagnosis methodology and applying it on an operational network, we learned that while fine-grained analysis is tremendously useful, a fully automated diagnosis solution suitable for the next generation cellular networks requires solving several research and engineering challenges (§5).

2 BACKGROUND

In this section, we briefly review the LTE network architecture and its data collection mechanism to familiarize the reader with the basic entities in the network and the characteristics of the data available for RAN diagnosis. We also discuss how existing state-of-the-art RAN diagnosis systems function.

2.1 LTE Network Architecture & Protocols

LTE networks enable User Equipments (UEs) such as smartphones to access the Internet. The LTE network architecture is shown in fig. 1, which consists of several network entities. When a UE is in idle mode, it does not have an active connection to the network. To communicate with the Internet, a UE requests the network to establish a communication channel between itself and the Packet Data Network Gateway (P-GW). This involves message exchanges between the UE and the Mobility Management Entity (MME). The MME may contact the Home Subscriber Server (HSS) to obtain UE capability and credentials. To enable the communication between the UE and MME, a radio connection called radio bearer between the UE and the base station is established. GPRS Tunneling Protocol (GTP) tunnels are established between the base station and the Serving Gateway (S-GW), and between the S-GW and the P-GW through message exchanges involving these entities and the MME. The radio bearer and the two GTP tunnels make up the the communication channel between the UE and the P-GW called Evolved Packet System (EPS) bearer (or simply bearer in short).

When an active UE moves across a base station boundary, its connections will be handed off to the new base station. There are several different types of handoffs: handoffs that require the bearer to be handled by a new S-GW, a new MME, or handoffs that require the change of radio frequency or radio technology (e.g. from LTE to 3G). Some of these procedures are very involved. For an active UE, the network knows its current associated base station. For an idle UE, the network knows its current tracking area. A tracking area is a set of base stations that are geographically nearby.

S-GWs are mainly used as mobility anchors to provide seamless mobility. P-GW centralizes most network functions like content filter, firewalls, lawful intercepts, etc. P-GWs sit at the boundary of the cellular networks and the Internet. A typical LTE network can cover a very large geographic area and can have a pool of MMEs, S-GWs and P-GWs for reliability and load balancing purposes.

From a UE's perspective, LTE network protocols consist of protocols between the UE and MME, and between the UE and the base station. When a UE powers up, it initiates the attach procedure with MME. When a UE has data to send, it initiates a service request with the MME. These procedures trigger the radio resource control (RRC) connection setup procedure which involves several message exchanges with the base station. When the network has data to send to a UE when it is idle, a paging procedure is invoked.

2.2 Data Collection

Due to the sheer traffic volume, LTE networks do not continuously collect packet traces[2]. LTE networks continuously collect the following types of data.

Bearer and signaling procedure records A UE communicates with the network by establishing one or more bearers. Each bearer may have a different QoS profile or connect to a different IP network. Multiple TCP connections can be carried in one bearer. LTE networks keep track of a rich set of bearer statistics at the procedure level, like (1) transmitted and retransmitted bytes in the RLC sublayer of the data link layer, (2) number of transmissions and retransmissions in the MAC sublayer of the data link layer, (3) physical radio resources allocated, radio channel quality known as CQI, in the physical layer, (4) bearer success or failure reasons, (5) associated base station, S-GW, P-GW, MME, (6) bearer start and end time. LTE networks also collect data on many signaling procedures such as initial attach request, service request, handoff, paging (wake up a UE to receive incoming traffic). Data is collected at MMEs and base stations and is organized as records. Each record can have *several hundred* fields. In a LTE network, there is a pool of MMEs, S-GWs and P-GWs. A base station can communicate with multiple MMEs. Hence bearer level records need to be merged across MMEs.

Network element records Network elements such as base stations, MMEs have operational statistics such as aggregate downlink frame transmitted per time window and number of bearers failed per time window. These records are collected continuously. Data accumulated for each time window are sent to the operation center. Cellular analytics systems [3, 4, 10] at these centers use the data and configuration information of network elements and subscriber profiles for network monitoring, troubleshooting, trending analysis, planning and network optimization.

Figure 2 shows the number of active daily users and the amount of RLC layer traffic per hour during the peak hours from 4PM to 8PM in a typical week in the network we study. We define active

[2]Packets may be collected for a duration to enable fine-grained troubleshooting.

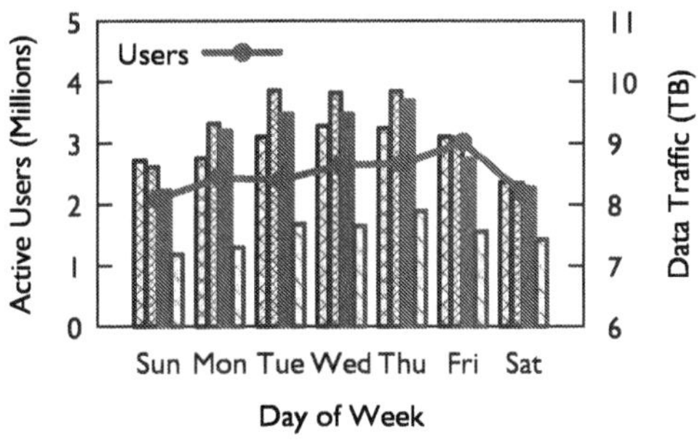

Figure 2: Active users and RLC layer traffic volume per peak hour (4PM to 8PM). Each bar represents the average for one peak hour.

users as those who used the network at least once in a given day. The portion of the network we studied serves over 2 million active subscribers using over 14,000 base stations, each with multiple cells. The volume is more than 6 TB per hour. We collected data for over a year, resulting in several 100s of TB of data.

2.3 RAN Performance Troubleshooting

Operators monitor a large number of KPIs per cell or per cluster of cells. These KPIs are classified into:

- *Accessibility.* Captures how available the RAN is. Includes attach and RRC connection failure rates.
- *Retainability.* Captures how well the network can complete the connection. It includes total bearer drop rate.
- Uplink and downlink *physical layer throughput.*
- *Quality.* Downlink & uplink block error rate (BLER).
- *Traffic volume.* Captures the uplink and downlink radio link layer traffic volume.
- *Connected user counts.* This include average RRC connected users and maximum RRC connected users.
- *Mobility.* Includes failure rates of various handoff types, tracking area update failure rate and paging success rate.

Existing practice, adopted by most major cellular network operators, is to use performance counters to derive these KPIs. The derived KPIs are then monitored by domain experts, aggregated over certain pre-defined time window. Based on domain knowledge and operational experience, these KPIs have service level agreements (SLA) to meet. For instance, an operator may have designed the network to have no more than 0.5% call drops in a 10 minute window. When a KPI that is being monitored crosses the threshold, an alarm is raised and a ticket created. This ticket is then handled by experts who investigate the cause of the problem. Our conversation with the network administrators revealed that such investigations can extend for several months, and may require expensive field trials. We have also confirmed with the experts that many of such alarms have known causes, but it is not possible to quickly conclude so due of the use of aggregated counters in deriving the KPIs.

3 METHODOLOGY

Our work focuses on access network problems. While there are other factors that affect application performance (e.g., poor interaction of the network with TCP [14] and buffer bloat [16]), they are orthogonal to our work since they do not originate in the RAN. Access network problems are among the hardest to diagnose because of the inherent nature of wireless networks; it is hard to capture the intricate details of the numerous procedures in an LTE network.

The path towards problem diagnosis starts with detecting whether a problem exists. This can be done in two ways: *passively,* where the operator comes to realize the problem when affected end-users report them, or *actively,* where the operator continuously monitors the network for problem detection before they become worse. Since passive approaches significantly degrade user experience, most cellular network operators actively monitor their networks. For this purpose, they define and monitor a number of performance metrics, which are termed Key Performance Indicators (KPI). We focus on access network KPIs for the rest of this paper.

3.1 Problem Isolation to RAN

Our quality of user experience can be impacted by many factors in the client side, cellular network and the Internet server side. The first step in analyzing performance issues is to isolate problems related to the access network. We achieve this by eliminating known non-RAN problems and modeling exogenous factors as noise.

Problems in the core network will impact a large number base stations. For example, if the Serving Gateway (S-GW) is overloaded, all base stations communicating with the S-GW will be impacted. Similarly, if a router in the core network has problems, it will impact all base stations that route through it. Although not common, core network problems do occur [9]. For example, we found a case where AS prepending was not configured properly, and caused reachability problem which impacted many base stations. However, due to their larger footprint, core network problems are relatively easy to detect.

Problems in the client side can also adversely impact access network KPIs. During conversations with network experts, we learned that there were cases where known phone models caused significant degradation of access network KPIs. We model other exogenous factors at the client side, Internet and server side as the noise impacting access network KPIs. These factors typically do not contribute to the KPIs problems of a large number of cells. However, they may be the main factor for a small number of cells. For example, if many users attached to a cell access the same overloaded server, then the throughput KPI will be adversely impacted.

Manually isolating the problem to RAN is cumbersome and infeasible to scale. Fortunately, there already exists a system for problem reporting and resolution, albeit manual, in the form of trouble tickets. We leverage this ticket system to automatically isolate problems to RAN. For instance, when a problem is detected, we can make sure that there are no core network problems by checking the ticket system. Similarly, we can ensure there is no significant correlation between KPI degradation to avoid device specific problems. We further use years of ticket resolution history and expertise of the network operator to form filtering rules.

3.2 Classification of RAN Problems

In the second step, we classify the access network problems, obtained as described earlier, into different categories. Classifying them into broad bins lets us analyze *classes* of problems rather than *individual* issues. In addition to letting us focus on the important problems, this also helps us with our goal of developing diagnosis methods that can be automated. We broadly classify problems into

LTE Physical Layer Parameters	
Name	*Description*
RSRP	Reference Signal Received Power: Average of reference signal power (in watts) across a specified bandwidth. Used for cell selection and handoff.
RSRQ	Reference Signal Received Quality: Indicator of interference experienced by the UE. Derived from RSRP and interference metrics.
CQI	Channel Quality Indicator: Carries information on how good/bad communication channel quality is.
SINR	Signal to Interference plus Noise Ratio: The ratio of the power of the signal to the interference power and background noise.
BLER	Block Error Ratio/Rate: Ratio of the number of erroneous blocks received to the total blocks sent.
PRB	Physical Resource Block: The specific number of subcarriers allocated for a predetermined amount of time for a user.

Table 1: A description of key parameters in LTE physical layer

the following, in the order of importance, based on our discussions with domain experts:

Coverage: Coverage represents one of the worst problems. Poor coverage can even lead to network inaccessibility, which often frustrates users. Unfortunately, such issues are hard to diagnose because traces cannot be generated when there is absolutely no coverage. However, it is possible to obtain insights on problems related to *poor* coverage using physical layer measurements. The primary physical layer parameter that influences coverage is RSRP (table 1).

Interference: Another major factor impacting user experience is interference. A user can be in an area with great coverage but still not be able to use the network due to the interference from nearby cells and/or users. This is especially true in LTE networks which is fundamentally designed for channel reuse. The amount of interference is influenced by the physical layer parameters RSRQ, CQI and SINR (table 1).

Congestion: While coverage and interference are characteristics of the user location, other factors also affect end-user experience. For instance, a base station can be overloaded. Congestion impacts many access network KPIs.

Configuration: Base stations have hundreds of configuration parameters, many of which are created and managed manually. It is easy to envision errors in these configurations, leading to many problems. For example, incorrect neighbor list or PCI configuration can adversely affect KPIs.

Network State Changes: Operators frequently update their networks (e.g., new releases and/or features). During the upgrades, problems can occur due to conflicts in software and/or because of compatibility issues.

Others: Software bugs, protocol implementation problems and hardware malfunction are some of the many other reasons for problems occurring in the RAN.

3.3 Root Cause Diagnosis

In the third step, we diagnose the root cause for these problems.

3.3.1 ***Issues with Cell-Level Metrics.*** Existing RAN troubleshooting techniques are based on *cell-level* metrics. Specifically, these methods build cell-level KPIs using aggregated counters. For example, the operator may create the RSRP histogram for each cell in each time window (e.g., every 10 minutes). Unfortunately, aggregating information at the cell-level results in major shortcomings due to its coarse-grained nature. Not only does aggregation result in many problems not being detected, the mixing of several bearers' RSRP in the aggregate counter makes it impossible to identify the impact of root causes in detected problems.

3.3.2 ***Modeling Bearer-Level Metrics.*** Our approach is to *model* performance metrics at the *bearer-level* using physical and MAC layer parameters. The use of bearer-level metrics eliminates the problems with cell-level metrics; and having a model lets us explain *why* things happened, thus diagnosing the problem. Our diagnosis methodology starts with eliminating known root causes, such as call admission control failures. Based on the classification of RAN problems, we distinguish two types of performance metrics:

Event Metrics: Several of the key performance metrics in RAN are discrete events. For instance, failures and drops are based on binary outcome. These metrics present a natural fit for models based on classification models, hence we use them. In particular, we describe a model for call drops using decision trees in §4.1.

Non-event/Volume Metrics: For continuous variables such as bearer throughput, we use the underlying information-theory model. §4.2 describes a regression model to diagnose throughput problems.

We describe the bearer-level modeling in detail in the next section. While our models are based on bearer-level, it may be useful to analyze problems at the cell level. For instance, the operator may wish to isolate cells that are consistently bad, or compare cells for troubleshooting. Our bearer-level approach makes this easy to do.

3.3.3 ***Computing Cell-Level Models.*** Given a bearer-level model, $Y = f(X)$, we can compute the cell-level model. We have two cases. First, Y is an event-based metric, e.g., RRC failure. The cell-level failure rate Z for time window j can be modeled as:

$$z_j = \frac{1}{N_j}\sum_{i=1}^{N_j} y_i = \frac{1}{N_j}\sum_{i=1}^{N_j} f(x_i) \qquad (1)$$

N_j is the number of bearers that start in time window j. z_j is estimated failure rate in time window j. If X is RSRP, then f is a multi-step function. If we only have RSRP histogram information (and not bearer-level information) in time window j, it will be very hard to model fit the histogram with failure rate.

Second, Y is a transmission-based metric, e.g., bearer throughput. The cell-level aggregate throughput Z at time window j is:

$$z_j = \frac{1}{T_j}\sum_{i=1}^{N_j} y_i \times \tau_i = \frac{1}{T_j}\sum_{i=1}^{N_j} f(x_i)\tau_i \qquad (2)$$

T_j is the total non-idle time of the cell and N_j is the number of bearers fall into time window j. τ_i is the fraction of scheduled time that is in time window j.

Comparing Cell-Level Models: If all the cells in the network are identical, the model we derive is equivalent to a per-RAN model that will apply across all cells. However, performance characteristic vary across cells. For example, we have learned that different cells may configure different number of retries in the random access procedure. Intuitively, for the same RSRP, a cell with a high number of retries will lead to fewer RRC failures and vice-versa. Our methodology can accommodate clustering cells based on their

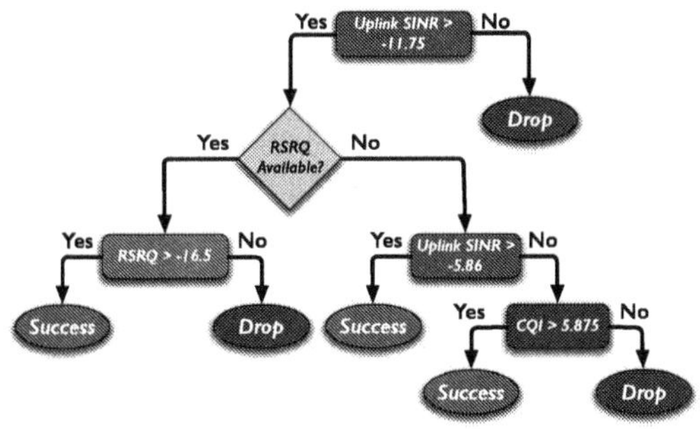

Figure 3: A sample decision tree used to explain drops. A random forest might provide better accuracy, but understanding the reason behind the drop is crucial for operators.

model similarity (§5). This helps in comparing these clusters in terms of configuration parameters and base station capabilities.

4 BEARER-LEVEL MODELING

In this section, we discuss bearer-level modeling in detail using two key bearer performance metrics, *connection drops* and *throughput*. These represent the two types of metrics our work aims to model. To build models for each of these metrics, we leverage protocol details in the physical, link and MAC layers.

4.1 Connection Drops Model

One of the core performance metrics for the cellular network operator is *retainability*, which captures how well the network can complete the connection. The retainability KPI is affected by RRC connection drop events, and are thus crucial for end-user QoE. Our traces give us ground truth (they indicate drops, but not the reason).

For certain drop events, we have known root causes recorded in the data, e.g., call admission control failure or access denied. We filter these out. This pre-processing step helps us avoid false alarms during troubleshooting. For example, one ticket showed that the connection failure KPI degradation of one cell was actually due to an unauthorized UE repeatedly trying to access the network. Note that the network can not block a UE from trying to access it because the UE can make an emergency call without subscription.

4.1.1 ***Decision Trees for Modeling Event Metrics.*** Due to the intricate nature of the wireless medium, connection drops are influenced by a combination of the underlying layer parameters instead of any single one. Such a setting, along with the availability of tremendous amounts of data lends itself a good fit for machine learning (ML) techniques [18]. Since we are interested in event metrics, we leverage classification techniques in ML.

In particular, we use decision trees to model event metrics. While there are several other, more sophisticated, techniques such as random forests [12], our primary goal is to obtain a model that can *reason* about the model decision. A decision tree is simple to understand, and directly provides us the underlying reason for a classification it makes. We use the collected data to train supervised decision trees (since we know the ground truth). The features for the learning are all those that fall into our broad categories. We also leverage domain knowledge for feature engineering. For instance, connection drops are affected directly by uplink and downlink channel conditions. Decoding probability depends on SINR. Hence

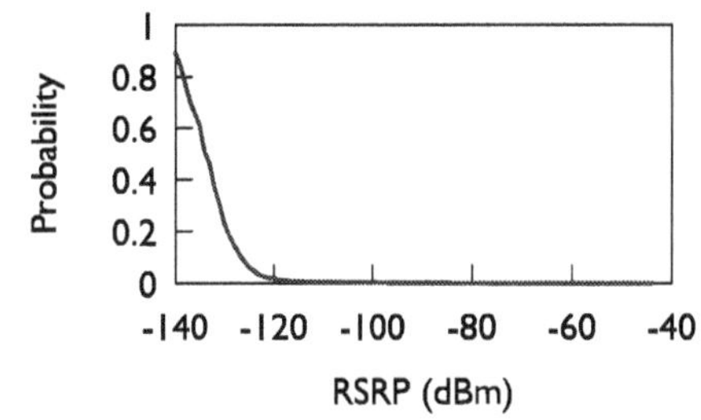

Figure 4: Impact of coverage on connection drops

we consider uplink and downlink SINR, which are available as raw features in the data. For downlink, we convert raw CQI to engineered feature, SINR.

An example of a learned decision tree is shown in fig. 3. As we can see, it first classifies based on uplink SINR, and then makes use of RSRQ if available. Otherwise, it uses uplink SINR and CQI. Experts confirm that the model agrees with their manual, labor intensive troubleshooting experience. In many of this network's cells, connection drops are mainly due to interference. Uplink SINR is more unpredictable because the interference comes from subscribers associated with neighboring base stations. In contrast, downlink interference is from neighboring base stations. This model achieved an accuracy of 92.1% with a cross-validation error of 10.1%.

4.1.2 ***Findings from Per-Root Cause Analysis.*** We were surprised by the decision tree models built by our approach, such as the one depicted in fig. 3, for many cells in this operator's network. Intuitively, we would have associated connection drops with poor coverage (RSRP). However, the model ignored RSRP and picked interference instead as the primary reason for drops. In addition, the model distinguishes between downlink RSRQ and CQI, which should affect interference similarly in theory.

To understand why our approach built this model, we studied the impact of each underlying root-cause (§3.2) *individually.* We plot the probability distribution of connection drops against physical layer parameters. This resulted in interesting insights.

Coverage Physical layer parameter RSRP is the received signal power of reference signals from the base station which can act as an indication of coverage. We plot the emperical distribution of connection drop with respect to RSRP in fig. 4. Areas with $RSRP < -130$ dBm experience high drops, but are relatively less in number.

Uplink Interference As shown in fig. 5, the drop probability for uplink SINR has a rather steep slope and peaks at -17dB. This is because the scheduler stops allocating grants at this threshold. If conditions do not improve, the connection will be dropped.

Downlink Interference There are two metrics to consider: RSRQ and downlink CQI. RSRQ is only reported when the UE might need to handoff. CQI is available independent of handoffs. Under normal circumstances, they should have identical shape. But from fig. 6 and fig. 7, we see that is not the case. To reveal the difference of these two distribution, we converted them to a common base, SINR. To convert CQI, we just use the standard CQI to SINR table. To convert RSRQ, we use the formula derived in [22], $SINR = \frac{1}{\frac{1}{12RSRQ} - \rho}$, where ρ depends on subcarrier utilization. For two antennas, it is between 1/3 and 5/3. For connection failure cases, we show the emperical distribution of their SINR differences with

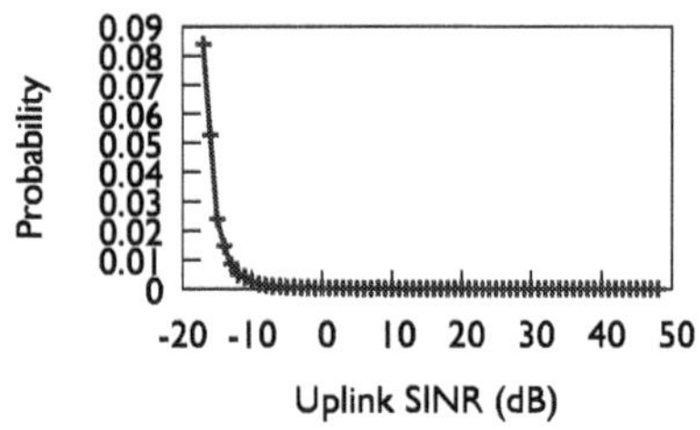

Figure 5: Impact of UL SINR on drops

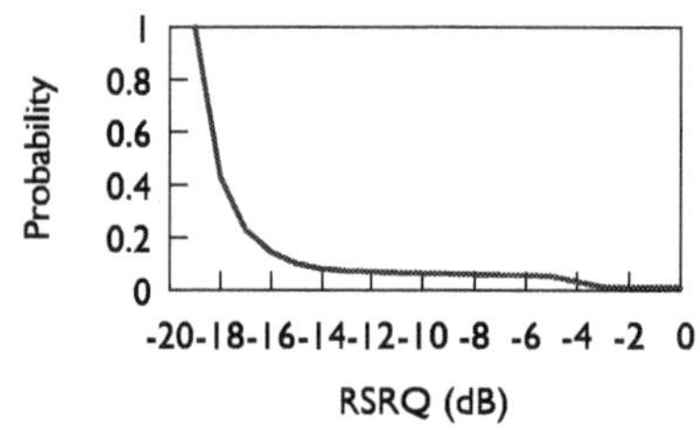

Figure 6: Impact of DL RSRQ on drops

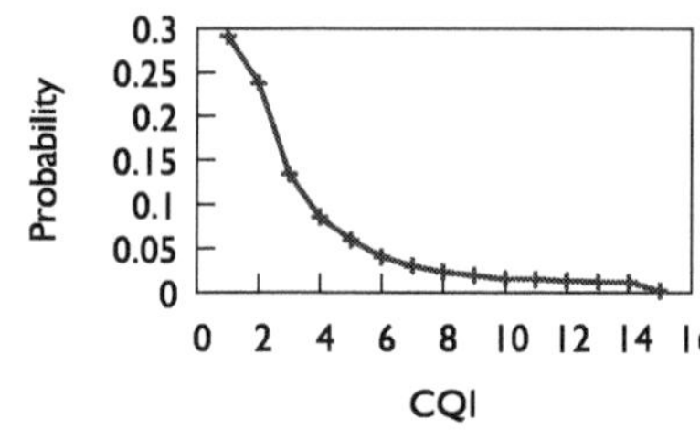

Figure 7: Impact of DL CQI on drops

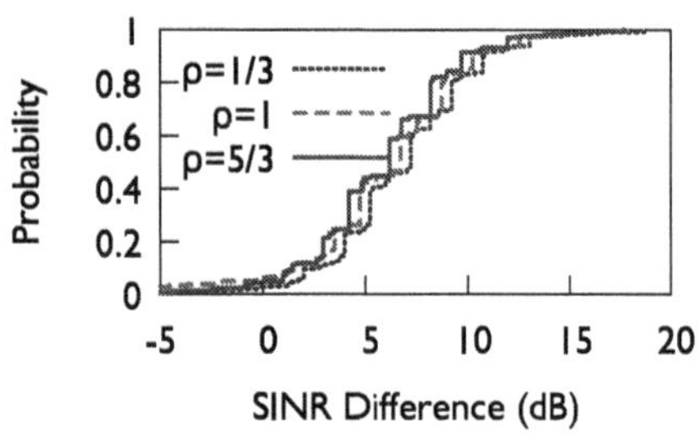

Figure 8: SINR gap between CQI and RSRQ

0%, 50% and 100% subcarrier utilization in fig. 8. We see that 10% has a SINR difference of 10 dB. This large discrepancy cannot be explained by hardware dependency or channel variations during our averaging time window.

Finding Insight: After talking to experts, we learned that P-CQI feedbacks through physical uplink control channel are not CRC protected. Correct decoding requires setting a threshold for received signal strengths under different channel conditions. It seems that the adaptation is problematic sometimes. P-CQI passing detection threshold can not be decoded correctly. Since there is no CRC, some spurious P-CQI will be used by the physical layer link adaption algorithm. This can cause high BLER leading to connection drops.

4.2 Throughput Model

RLC layer throughput is another important KPI in RAN.

4.2.1 ***Regression for Modeling Volume Metrics.*** Since volume / non-event metrics are continuous values, regression techniques in machine learning provides an attractive option to use to build diagnostic models. Regression models can output continuous values, and thus can be used to *predict* volume metrics based on input features. For instance, we can form an information-theoretic regression model that predicts throughput based on metrics. Our traces report the transmitted and retransmitted bits, and the total transmission time per bearer at the RLC sub-layer. Thus, we know the RLC throughput as the ground truth. When the predicted values and the actual values match (when the model is accurate), the regression model provides us the reasoning, in the form of weights on the input features, for why a particular throughput was achieved.

However, building an information-theoretic model is non-trivial because we need to account for the overhead in different layers (e.g., physical layer control channel overhead, MAC layer retransmission overhead). We again leverage domain knowledge and feature engineering to obtain a model for throughput prediction:

SINR Estimation Base stations have two antennas capable of MIMO spatial multiplexing (two streams) or transmit diversity. For both type of transmissions, each UE reports its two wideband CQIs, one per antenna. We use the CQI to SINR mapping table used at the base station scheduler to convert CQI to SINR. For transmission diversity, we convert the two CQIs to a single SINR: First we convert both CQIs to SINR, then we compute the two spectrum efficiencies (bits/sec/Hz) using Shannon capacity. We average the two spectrum efficiencies and convert it back to SINR. We then add a 3dB transmission diversity gain to achieve the final SINR. For spatial multiplexing, we convert the two CQIs to SINRs.

Account for PRB Control Overhead and BLER Target Each PRB is 180 KHz, but not all of it is used for transmission. For transmit diversity, a 29% overhead for each PRB exists on average because of resources allocated to physical downlink control channel, physical broadcast channel and reference signals. The physical layer has a BLER target of 10%.

Account for MAC Sub-layer Retransmissions The MAC sub-layer performs retransmissions. We denote the MAC efficiency as β_{MAC}. It is computed as the ratio of total first transmissions over total transmissions. We compute β_{MAC} using our traces. The predicted throughput due to transmit diversity is calculated as:

$$\begin{aligned} tput_{RLCdiv} &= (1.0 - \beta_{MAC}) \times 0.9 \times (1 - 0.29) \times 180 \times \\ &\quad PRB_{div} \times log2(1 + SINR_{div})/TxTime_{div} \end{aligned}$$

PRB_{div} denotes the total PRBs allocated for transmit diversity. $TxTime_{div}$ is the total transmission time for transmit diversity. Similarly we can calculate the predicted throughput due to spatial multiplexing. We then properly weigh the two by their respective fraction of transmission time to derive the final RLC throughput.

Account for Link Adaptation The base station does not use the SINR corresponding to the UE reported CQI directly. It performs link adaptation to achieve the desired BLER of 10%. If the observed BLER is higher than target, it will adjust the SINR by subtracting a few dB. If the observed BLER is lower than the target, it will adjust the SINR by adding a few dB. To increase the speed of converging to the BLER target, the feedback offset is computed differently according to deviation to the target BLER. For large deviations, the large step power offset is applied so that BLER can converge faster to the long term adaptation area. This adaptation is necessary since the propagation channel is subject to several conditions that vary in space and time, e.g., path loss, fast fading, UE speed and location. Since the base station adjusts a maximum of 6dB, we adjust the SINR used in our prediction by -6dB to compute the lower bound and +6dB to compute the upper bound. We compute the prediction error as follows. If the actual throughput is within the two bounds,

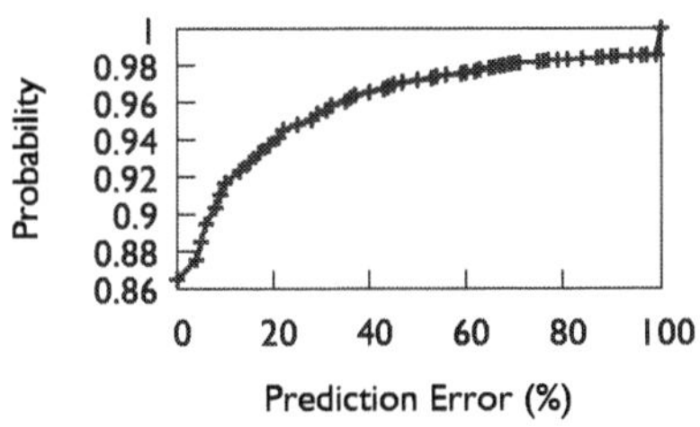

Figure 9: Actual vs predicted throughput

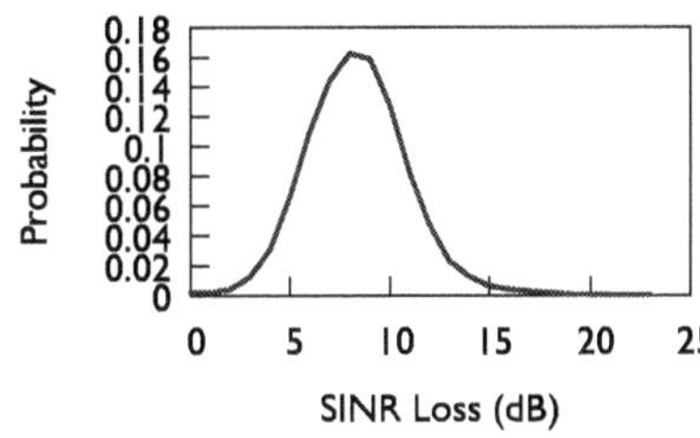

Figure 10: Loss of efficiency (dB)

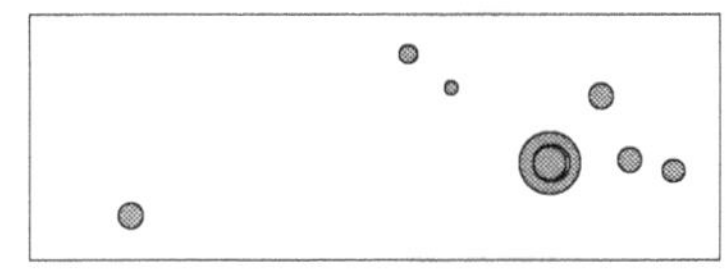

Figure 11: Geographic location (not to scale) of cells by aggregated dB loss shows losses are concentrated on a few cells.

the error is zero. Otherwise, the error is the distance to the closest bounds. The CDF in fig. 9 shows that our model is very accurate.

4.2.2 ***Finding: Loss of Efficiency.*** We characterized the difference between predicted throughput and actual throughput in terms of loss in dB. To compute this, we first convert the actual throughput into SINR. We then substract the SINR from the one used for throughput prediction. Figure 10 shows the distribution. It has a peak around 8dB. As we can see, around 20% of the bearers have a loss of efficiency of more than 10 dB.

To obtain insights on these high losses, we analyzed them aggregated by the cell in which the loss was experienced. Figure 11 presents the results of this analysis. For the purpose of anonymity, we do not provide the actual location of the cell, but only show the relative locations scaled by a constant factor. We find that a few cells contribute to many of the losses. Further, two cells from the same base station contribute to as much as 5 times the losses experienced by any single cell (including cells not shown).

We further investigated if the loss is a characteristic of the user. The first question is whether these losses are experienced by the same user. We find that this is not the case. While users tend to experience the loss continuously as long as they are in a cell and are actively utilizing the network, the aggregate loss is contributed by many users. A second suspect is the device model. Different manufacturers use different radio chipsets, and hence the measurements made by the device may differ. We find that most of the losses occur in Apple iPhones. But they are also the most used devices in our network, so we do not conclude that model contributes to losses.

Finding Insight: Due to the high fraction of bearers with high dB loss, we posit that the link adaptation algorithm is slow to adapt to changing conditions. We validate this based on two evidences. First, the link adaptation algorithm uses moving average SINR, which is a slow mechanism to adapt. Second, field experts confirmed our observations by replicating them in lab tests.

4.3 Detecting False Positives of KPI Changes

Our models can significantly reduce operator's troubleshooting efforts. For instance, it can help remove false positives of significant cell level KPI changes. We show this using drop rate. To do so, we apply the decision tree in §4.1 on a week worth of data divided into 10 minute windows. We used this window length since it matches closely with an interval that is usually used by the operators for monitoring drop rates. In every window, we predict the number of drops using our technique. The predicted drops are explainable, because we know precisely why those drops happened. We use a threshold of 0.5% for the drop rate (operator's SLA), hence anything

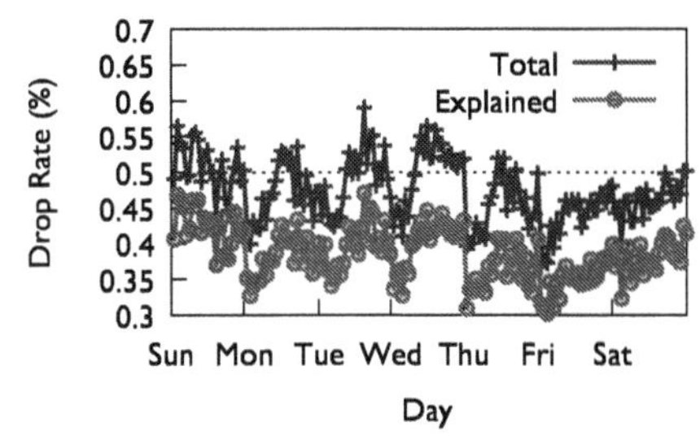

Figure 12: Our method can detect false positives in alarms, thus relieving the operator from re-investigating known problems.

above this threshold is marked as an anomaly. The results from this experiment is depicted in fig. 12. At numerous places the threshold is exceeded. Normally, these would have to be investigated by an expert but more than 80% of the drops are explained by our model.

To estimate the confidence, we analyzed our prediction results during the occurrence of these anomalies. We consider each connection drop or complete event as a Bernoulli random variable X with probability p (from decision tree). A sequence of n connection events follow a binomial distribution. The 95% confidence interval is approximated by $np \pm 2\sqrt{np(1-p)}$. We determine that the alarm is false if X is within the confidence interval. The bound was found to be (0.7958665, 0.8610155), which is within acceptable range.

4.4 Summary

To summarize our approach, we began by isolating problems to the RAN by leveraging the operator's existing ticket resolution system to filter our non-RAN related problems. We then classified problems into broad categories based on underlying root causes, each of which could be influenced by physical or mac layer parameters. Then we proposed building bearer-level models for key performance metrics for root cause diagnosis. For event metrics, we build decision tree models and for volume metrics we build information-theoretic regression models, in both leveraging domain knowledge for feature engineering. These models helped us unearth interesting insights. Finally, we show how the operator could leverage these models to reduce troubleshooting efforts.

5 DISCUSSION & FUTURE WORK

In this work, we discussed how using fine-grained, bearer level information could be beneficial in diagnosing performance problems in RANs. Based on this, we proposed models for RAN diagnostics that are amenable to automation. During the course of this work, we learned several valuable lessons and future work opportunities.

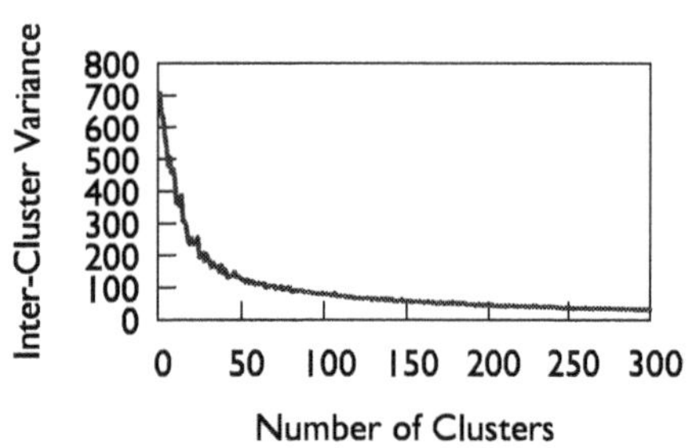

Figure 13: Number of clusters are small even when the number of cells are large (>50k).

First, fully automating diagnostics requires building models for several categories of metrics. Due to the large number of base stations in a RAN, this results in several thousands of models. Building and managing them can easily be a bottleneck, and requires engineering efforts to scale as generating models are compute-intensive. We plan on leveraging advancements in big-data machine learning.

Second, we found that due to the spatio-temporal nature of the wireless medium, the performance characteristics and thus the accuracy of the models are also highly spatio-temporal. This means that the automation system should be able to update the models it builds periodically. Unfortunately, this is not just a scalability challenge. Since failures are rare in a relative sense, building *effective and accurate* models is a research challenge. In our current system, we rebuild the models manually, which is not ideal.

We have made some progress towards these challenges. Specifically, we found that cells exhibit performance similarity. If we build a model $Y = f(X)$ for performance metric Y in terms of root cause X, we can order the predicted Y values as a vector and then use the vector distance between cells in a K-mean clustering algorithm. Figure 13 shows the variance between clusters with varying number of K. We see that the number of clusters can be small even with a large number of cells (>50k in our case). As an example, clustering on uplink SINR shows just 10 dominant clusters (fig. 14). The difference of clusters can be due to different base station releases (thus may have different algorithms e.g., link adaptation), different hardware capability (e.g., receiver sensitivity), the number of retries configured in the random access procedure. This indicates that it may be possible to use a single model for a group of cells.

Finally, with the industry moving towards software-defined cellular networks [1, 2], network operators must be able to support RAN performance diagnostics in *real-time*. The methodology we discussed here has the potential to be a real-time solution, and can even go further by predicting *potential future problems* because of its use of models. An open research challenge is in building and updating the models in real-time in a scalable fashion. We plan on leveraging learnings from our work on real-time analytics on cellular networks [15] for addressing some of these challenges.

6 RELATED WORK

Cellular Network Monitoring and Troubleshooting A number of cellular network monitoring and diagnosis systems exist [3–5, 8, 11]. AT&T GigaScope [8] and Alcatel-Lucent Wireless Network Guardian (WNG) [3] generates per IP flow records and monitors many performance metrics such as aggregate per-cell TCP throughput, delay and loss. Because these tools tap interfaces in the core networks, they lack information at the RAN. Systems targeting RAN [4, 11] typically monitor aggregate KPIs and per-bearer records separately. Their root cause analysis of KPI problems correlates with aggregation air interface metrics such as SINR histograms and configuration data. Since they rely on aggregates, it is hard for them to provide fine-grained diagnosis. Several studies [6, 14, 16, 19, 21, 26] focus on the interaction between applications and cellular networks. They are orthogonal to our work.

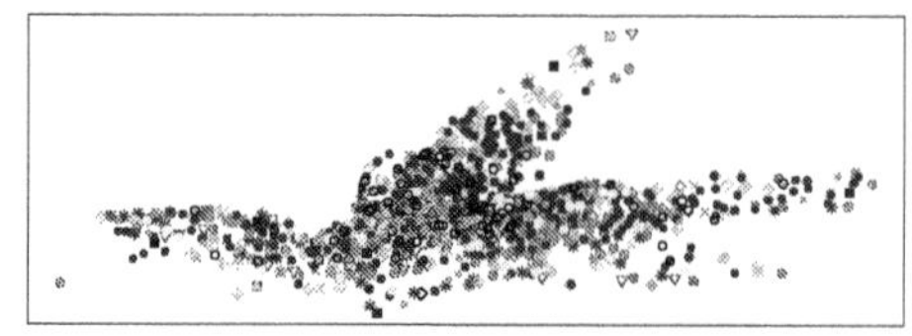

Figure 14: Geographic locations of cells clustered by model (color) shows they share performance characteristics (best viewed in color).

Modeling and Diagnosis Techniques Diagnosing problems in cellular networks has been explored in the literature in various forms [7, 13, 17, 20, 25], where the focus has either been detecting faults or finding the root cause of specific failures. A probabilistic system for auto-diagnosing faults in RAN is presented in [7]. It relies on KPIs. However, KPIs are not capable of providing diagnosis at high granularity. Moreover, it is unclear how their proposals capture complex dependencies between different components in RAN. An automated approach to locating anomalous events on hierarchical operational networks was proposed in [13] based on hierarchical heavy hitter based anomaly detection. It is unclear how their proposals carry over to RAN. Adding autonomous capabilities to alarm based fault detection is discussed in [17]. While their techniques can help systems auto-heal faults, correlation based fault detection is insufficient for fine granularity detection and diagnosis of faults. [20] looks at detecting call connection faults due to load imbalances. In [27], a technique to detect and localize anomalies from an ISP point of view is proposed. Finally, [25] uses machine learning to predict impending call drops and duration.

7 CONCLUSION

In this paper, we share our experience working with a major cellular network operator in answering the question of whether it is possible to develop automated solutions for problem detection and diagnosis in RANs. We show that fine-grained analysis is the key, and propose a bearer-level modeling methodology for RAN diagnostics. During this process, we were able to unearth several insights from the operator's RAN, some previously unknown. We learned that automatic detection and diagnosis of RAN problems in real-time requires answering several research challenges. We are currently pursuing many of them.

ACKNOWLEDGMENTS

We would like to thank the Mobicom reviewers and our shepherd, Chunyi Peng, for their valuable feedback. This research is supported in part by DHS Award HSHQDC-16-3-00083, NSF CISE Expeditions Award CCF-1139158, and gifts from Ant Financial, Amazon Web Services, CapitalOne, Ericsson, GE, Google, Huawei, Intel, IBM, Microsoft and VMware.

REFERENCES

[1] 2017. Bringing SDN to the RAN. https://www.sdxcentral.com/articles/news/cord-partners-xran-bring-sdn-ran/2017/02/. (2017).

[2] 3gpp. 2016. Self-Organizing Networks SON Policy Network Resource Model (NRM) Integration Reference Point (IRP). http://www.3gpp.org/ftp/Specs/archive/32_series/32.521/. (2016).

[3] Alcatel Lucent. 2013. 9900 Wireless Network Guardian. http://www.alcatel-lucent.com/products/9900-wireless-network-guardian. (2013).

[4] Alcatel Lucent. 2014. 9959 Network Performance Optimizer. http://www.alcatel-lucent.com/products/9959-network-performance-optimizer. (2014).

[5] Alcatel Lucent. 2014. Motive Big Network Analytics. http://www.alcatel-lucent.com/solutions/motive-big-network-analytics. (2014).

[6] Athula Balachandran, Vaneet Aggarwal, Emir Halepovic, Jeffrey Pang, Srinivasan Seshan, Shobha Venkataraman, and He Yan. 2014. Modeling Web Quality-of-experience on Cellular Networks. In *Proceedings of the 20th Annual International Conference on Mobile Computing and Networking (MobiCom '14)*. ACM, New York, NY, USA, 213–224. https://doi.org/10.1145/2639108.2639137

[7] Raquel Barco, Volker Wille, Luis Díez, and Matías Toril. 2010. Learning of Model Parameters for Fault Diagnosis in Wireless Networks. *Wirel. Netw.* 16, 1 (Jan. 2010), 255–271. https://doi.org/10.1007/s11276-008-0128-z

[8] Chuck Cranor, Theodore Johnson, Oliver Spataschek, and Vladislav Shkapenyuk. 2003. Gigascope: a stream database for network applications. In *Proceedings of the 2003 ACM SIGMOD international conference on Management of data (SIGMOD '03)*. ACM, New York, NY, USA, 647–651. https://doi.org/10.1145/872757.872838

[9] Bassam Eljaam. 2005. Customer satisfaction with cellular network performance: Issues and analysis. (2005).

[10] Ericsson. 2012. Ericsson RAN Analyzer Overview. http://www.optxview.com/Optimi_Ericsson/RANAnalyser.pdf. (2012).

[11] Ericsson. 2014. Ericsson RAN Analyzer. http://www.ericsson.com/ourportfolio/products/ran-analyzer. (2014).

[12] Tin Kam Ho. 1995. Random Decision Forests. In *Proceedings of the Third International Conference on Document Analysis and Recognition (Volume 1) - Volume 1 (ICDAR '95)*. IEEE Computer Society, Washington, DC, USA, 278–. http://dl.acm.org/citation.cfm?id=844379.844681

[13] Chi-Yao Hong, Matthew Caesar, Nick Duffield, and Jia Wang. 2012. Tiresias: Online Anomaly Detection for Hierarchical Operational Network Data. In *Proceedings of the 2012 IEEE 32Nd International Conference on Distributed Computing Systems (ICDCS '12)*. IEEE Computer Society, Washington, DC, USA, 173–182. https://doi.org/10.1109/ICDCS.2012.30

[14] Junxian Huang, Feng Qian, Yihua Guo, Yuanyuan Zhou, Qiang Xu, Z. Morley Mao, Subhabrata Sen, and Oliver Spatscheck. 2013. An In-depth Study of LTE: Effect of Network Protocol and Application Behavior on Performance. In *Proceedings of the ACM SIGCOMM 2013 Conference on SIGCOMM (SIGCOMM '13)*. ACM, New York, NY, USA, 363–374. https://doi.org/10.1145/2486001.2486006

[15] Anand Iyer, Li Erran Li, and Ion Stoica. 2015. CellIQ : Real-Time Cellular Network Analytics at Scale. In *12th USENIX Symposium on Networked Systems Design and Implementation (NSDI 15)*. USENIX Association, Oakland, CA, 309–322. https://www.usenix.org/conference/nsdi15/technical-sessions/presentation/iyer

[16] Haiqing Jiang, Yaogong Wang, Kyunghan Lee, and Injong Rhee. 2012. Tackling Bufferbloat in 3G/4G Networks. In *Proceedings of the 2012 ACM Conference on Internet Measurement Conference (IMC '12)*. ACM, New York, NY, USA, 329–342. https://doi.org/10.1145/2398776.2398810

[17] Yan Liu, Jing Zhang, M. Jiang, D. Raymer, and J. Strassner. 2008. A model-based approach to adding autonomic capabilities to network fault management system. In *Network Operations and Management Symposium, 2008. NOMS 2008. IEEE.* 859–862. https://doi.org/10.1109/NOMS.2008.4575232

[18] Kevin P Murphy. 2012. *Machine learning: a probabilistic perspective.* MIT press.

[19] Feng Qian, Zhaoguang Wang, Alexandre Gerber, Zhuoqing Mao, Subhabrata Sen, and Oliver Spatscheck. 2011. Profiling Resource Usage for Mobile Applications: A Cross-layer Approach. In *Proceedings of the 9th International Conference on Mobile Systems, Applications, and Services (MobiSys '11)*. ACM, New York, NY, USA, 321–334. https://doi.org/10.1145/1999995.2000026

[20] Sudarshan Rao. 2006. Operational Fault Detection in Cellular Wireless Base-stations. *IEEE Trans. on Netw. and Serv. Manag.* 3, 2 (April 2006), 1–11. https://doi.org/10.1109/TNSM.2006.4798311

[21] Sanae Rosen, Haokun Luo, Qi Alfred Chen, Z. Morley Mao, Jie Hui, Aaron Drake, and Kevin Lau. 2014. Discovering Fine-grained RRC State Dynamics and Performance Impacts in Cellular Networks. In *Proceedings of the 20th Annual International Conference on Mobile Computing and Networking (MobiCom '14)*. ACM, New York, NY, USA, 177–188. https://doi.org/10.1145/2639108.2639115

[22] Jari Salo. 2013. Mobility Parameter Planning for 3GPP LTE: Basic Concepts and Intra-Layer Mobility. www.lteexpert.com/lte_mobility_wp1_10June2013.pdf. (2013).

[23] Muhammad Zubair Shafiq, Jeffrey Erman, Lusheng Ji, Alex X. Liu, Jeffrey Pang, and Jia Wang. 2014. Understanding the Impact of Network Dynamics on Mobile Video User Engagement. In *The 2014 ACM International Conference on Measurement and Modeling of Computer Systems (SIGMETRICS '14)*. ACM, New York, NY, USA, 367–379. https://doi.org/10.1145/2591971.2591975

[24] Muhammad Zubair Shafiq, Lusheng Ji, Alex X. Liu, Jeffrey Pang, Shobha Venkataraman, and Jia Wang. 2013. A First Look at Cellular Network Performance During Crowded Events. In *Proceedings of the ACM SIGMETRICS/International Conference on Measurement and Modeling of Computer Systems (SIGMETRICS '13)*. ACM, New York, NY, USA, 17–28. https://doi.org/10.1145/2465529.2465754

[25] Nawanol Theera-Ampornpunt, Saurabh Bagchi, Kaustubh R. Joshi, and Rajesh K. Panta. 2013. Using Big Data for More Dependability: A Cellular Network Tale. In *Proceedings of the 9th Workshop on Hot Topics in Dependable Systems (HotDep '13)*. ACM, New York, NY, USA, Article 2, 5 pages. https://doi.org/10.1145/2524224.2524227

[26] Guan-Hua Tu, Yuanjie Li, Chunyi Peng, Chi-Yu Li, Hongyi Wang, and Songwu Lu. 2014. Control-plane Protocol Interactions in Cellular Networks. In *Proceedings of the 2014 ACM Conference on SIGCOMM (SIGCOMM '14)*. ACM, New York, NY, USA, 223–234. https://doi.org/10.1145/2619239.2626302

[27] He Yan, A. Flavel, Zihui Ge, A. Gerber, D. Massey, C. Papadopoulos, H. Shah, and J. Yates. 2012. Argus: End-to-end service anomaly detection and localization from an ISP's point of view. In *INFOCOM, 2012 Proceedings IEEE*. 2756–2760. https://doi.org/10.1109/INFCOM.2012.6195694

Adding the Next Nine: an Investigation of Mobile Broadband Networks Availability

Ahmed Elmokashfi, Dong Zhou, Džiugas Baltrūnas
Simula Research Laboratory, Fornebu, Norway
ahmed@simula.no,dong@simula.no,dziugas@simula.no

ABSTRACT

The near ubiquitous availability and success of mobile broadband networks has motivated verticals that range from public safety communication to intelligent transportation systems and beyond to consider choosing them as the communication mean of choice. Several of these verticals, however, expect high availability of multiple nines. This paper leverages end-to-end measurements to investigate the potential of current mobile broadband networks to support these expectations. We conduct a large-scale measurement study of network availability in four networks in Norway. This study is based on three years of measurements from hundreds of stationary measurement nodes and several months of measurements from four mobile nodes. We find that the mobile network centralized architecture and infrastructure sharing between operators are responsible for a non-trivial fraction of network failures. Most episodes of degraded availability, however, are uncorrelated. We also find that using two networks simultaneously can result in more than five nines of availability for stationary nodes and three nines of availability for mobile nodes. Our findings point to potential avenues for enhancing the availability of future mobile networks.

CCS CONCEPTS

• **Networks** → **Network measurement**; **Network reliability**; **Mobile networks**;

KEYWORDS

Interdependent networks; correlation networks; ultra-reliable communication

1 INTRODUCTION

Mobile Broadband (MBB) is becoming increasingly ubiquitous and an economic boon with mobile data traffic projected to increase by almost tenfold between 2015 and 2020 [11]. This success has encouraged industries that range from public safety communication to transportation systems to retail and beyond to use or consider using MBB for their communications. Many of these industries, however, expect carrier-grade availability of multiple nines, but present commercial MBB networks are hardly able to guarantee more than two nines [4, 35]. The need for a high level of availability and reliability is likely to become even more central as services like smart grid communication, intelligent transportation systems, driver-less cars, and tactile Internet become mainstream [18, 20].

Today, use cases with strict availability requirements largely opt for operating their own communciation networks. For example, most countries use specialized Terrestrial Trunked Radio (TETRA) and TETRAPOL networks to facilitate public safety communications [45, 46]. Well designed TETRA networks provide up to 99.95% availability [28] but are expensive to build, use specialized handsets, and are narrow band. These limitations have prompted governments around the world to seek alternatives. The US and Canada have decided to build dedicated national LTE networks [1, 19]. The UK has followed a more radical approach by deciding to depend on a commercial MBB operator starting from mid-2017 [21]. Building a specialized MBB network, while suitable in some cases, will not scale to cater for all services with tight availability budget. Also, many service providers will not be able to build such specialized networks, potentially stifling innovation. This has motivated industry and academia to put offering ultra high availability as one of 5G key targets [33, 37].

In this paper, we leverage end-to-end measurements to investigate the potential of current MBB networks to support services with high availability expectations, i.e., at least 99.9%. Our goal is threefold: (1) provide an empirical evaluation of the availability offered by today's commercial networks, which can inform vertical industries and developers; (2) highlight potential areas for improvement as an input to the ongoing discourse for defining 5G; and (3) contribute a methodology that can be leveraged for quantifying the availability of mobile networks.

Assessing MBB availability is a non-trivial task for two main reasons. First, there is no single metric that fully captures MBB availability and reliability. Hence, we need to use several metrics like data session stability, packet loss, and end-to-end delay to be able to characterize MBB availability. Second, MBB networks tend to share infrastructure, for historical and practical reasons, forming a complex temporal-spatial network of networks. This sharing can range from national roaming where an operator uses another operator's network in areas where it does not have base stations to the sharing of regional or long-haul transport infrastructure. The impact of these dependencies is often hard to gauge, since most of what is shared are physical links that can not be probed using traditional IP measurement tools like ping and traceroute. Furthermore, infrastructure sharing extends the task of assessing MBB availability beyond a single network.

We conduct a large-scale measurement study of network availability and show how it is influenced by infrastructure sharing.

MobiCom '17, October 16–20, 2017, Snowbird, UT, USA

ACM ISBN 978-1-4503-4916-1/17/10...$15.00
https://doi.org/10.1145/3117811.3117842

We also explore the potential of using several operators simultaneously to increase the overall availability even when operators share infrastructure. We focus on two metrics for characterizing availability: the stability of user equipment (UE) data connectivity to the mobile network and packet loss. Measurements used in this study are conducted using the NorNet Edge (NNE) measurements infrastructure [30]. NNE consists of hundreds of nodes for measuring MBB networks in Norway. Each node is connected to up to five operators. These nodes are stationary and hosted in places like schools and government offices. They are distributed to be representative for (indoor and stationary) users in urban/suburban areas. Measurements used in this study span three years from 2014 to 2017. The size and spread of NNE allow us to correlate measurements from different locations and networks in order to gain insights into interdependent failures. In addition, we use a set of mobile nodes on trains to evaluate the potential of using several operators when users are moving.

Our findings confirm the viability of end-to-end measurements in assessing network availability. We find that the centralized architecture of MBB networks is a major cause of correlated service outages within a single operator. We also find that causes of correlated packet loss episodes often lie in the mobile core network and the Internet. Overall, shared infrastructure contributes minimally to unavailability in MBB networks, but it can also result in outages that impact a large geographical area. Consequently, we find that combining connections from different operators can greatly boost MBB availability. In summary, we make the following contributions:

- We present, to the best of our knowledge, the most comprehensive study of MBB availability both in terms of duration and number of measurement probes. Further, we present a first attempt on studying the impact of shared infrastructure on MBB availability.
- We show that correlating measurements from geographically diverse probes can be leveraged for inferring interdependencies between operators.
- We quantify the benefit of combining two operators for both stationary and moving cases.
- We suggest possible ways for enhancing MBB connections availability — a key target of 5G.

2 MBB AVAILABILITY

Mobile networks are stateful, meaning that a user equipment (UE) must establish a data session to the mobile core network before it engages in any data exchange. This data session is a virtual tunnel between the UE and the packet gateway in the core network and is called a Packet Data Protocol (PDP) context and Evolved Packer System (EPS) bearer in UMTS and LTE networks, respectively. A data session is established on demand in UMTS. LTE is, however, an all-IP network. Thus, an attached UE keeps a default EPS bearer always established. Accordingly, the most basic measure of mobile service availability is the ability to maintain a stable data session. Once the data session is established, the next measure is the ability to reliably send data over it. The latter can be extended further to evaluate whether the network is able to offer a predictable and acceptable level of performance for a specific application [26]. In this paper, we focus on data session stability and packet loss as key metrics for assessing MBB reliability.

2.1 Causes of data session downtime and packet loss

A UE can experience packet loss or a complete loss of network connectivity for a number of reasons. Degraded wireless link performance may trigger the radio access network (RAN) to disconnect attached UEs. This can also happen when the UE and the network fail to successfully complete a horizontal handover (i.e. between different cells or basestations), inter-frequency handover (e.g. a handover from LTE-800MHz to LTE-2600MHz), or inter-RAT handover (e.g. a handover from UMTS to LTE). Failures of RAN and transport equipment as well as congestion in the RAN and transport can also lead to connection failures. Furthermore, outages that involve central components in the core network, like the packet or signaling gateways, can result in many users losing their connectivity.

Outages impact, in terms of affected users and duration, varies depending on underlying root causes. A poor wireless link impacts a few users. A failure at the Home Subscriber Server (HSS) can prevent many UEs from attaching to the network causing a large scale denial of service [48]. A fiber cut or a failure of an optical cross connect in the transport network can isolate a number of base stations. This can also affect customers of several MBB operators when the affected infrastructure is shared [12, 34]. The impact on user experience varies depending on outages duration. For example, a TCP session can recover by resending lost segments, if an outage lasts less than its retransmission timer (RTO). Note that the minimum RTO value is 1 second. However, longer outages result in TCP timeouts that can last up to 1 minute [40]

2.2 Metrics and approach

Data session downtime, which we refer to in the following as *downtime*, reports on MBB data session stability, while packet loss measures the usability of an established data connection. We combine these two metrics to quantify the *overall availability* (OA) of an MBB data connection. *OA* is defined as follows:

$$OA = 100 * (1 - c) * (1 - p) \quad (1)$$

Where c is the fraction of time the data connection is down and p is the fraction of lost packets. In this paper, we focus on downtime, packet loss, and OA as key metrics for assessing MBB availability. We base our assessment on three-years worth of measurements of four commercial Norwegian MBB operators. These measurements were collected by a large number of measurement nodes that are spread across Norway. We describe the measurement setup in the subsequent section.

3 MEASUREMENT INFRASTRUCTURE

This section describes the measurement setup and methodology.

3.1 NorNet Edge

NNE is a unique dedicated infrastructure for the measurement and experimentation with MBB networks. It comprises over a hundred stationary measurement nodes that are geographically spread in more than 100 municipalities all over Norway as well as set of

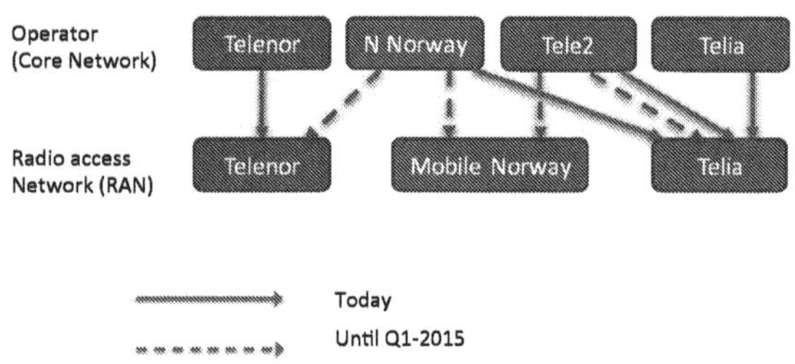

Figure 1: The measured networks.

backend servers. The nodes distribution reflects the population distribution with bias towards urban areas. More than half of the nodes are deployed in the three largest cities in Norway where a quarter of the population lives. This infrastructure has been operational since July 2013 [1].

A NNE node is a custom-made single board computer with one Fast Ethernet port, and 7 on-board USB ports. It runs a standard Debian Linux and a set of customer tools to manage connectivity to MBB networks. Each node is connected to up to four UMTS/LTE operators and one CDMA2000 1x Ev-Do network [2], using standard subscriptions. For the UMTS/LTE operators, the connections were, in the early days of NNE, through E3131 and E353 Huawei USB modems which support up to HSPA+. Later as LTE deployment picked up, NNE moved to using E392 Huawei USB modems which support LTE. Almost all NNE modems have supported LTE since the end of 2015. The modems are configured to prefer the best supported radio access technology (RAT). In addition, there are seven NNE nodes that are placed aboard NSB [3] regional and inter-city trains. The routes followed by these trains traverse a reasonable mix of urban and rural areas. The measurements collected aboard the trains closely mimic the user experience of the train passengers. We use the GPS location data from the train's fleet management system to identify the location of NNE measurement nodes and train speed during the measurements. The GPS locations are updated every 10 to 15 seconds in the fleet management system. In this paper, we only use measurements from trains to quantify multihoming benefits when UEs are moving (see Sec. 7). For more details about the measurement setup on trains please refer to our previous work [6]. The NNE backend contains the server side of the measurements. It also includes of a set of servers for managing and monitoring the nodes, and for storing measurement data.

3.2 Measured networks

Nodes in the NNE platform are connected to up to four UMTS/LTE networks, which are Telenor, Telia, Tele2 and Network Norway. These networks are not completely independent, they rather have a set of intricate dependencies as depicted in Fig. 1. All four operators maintain independent core networks but vary in their RAN footprint and transport connectivity, i.e., the physical network that interconnects the RAN and the core network. Next, we describe the intricate dependencies that bind these networks.

- *Telenor* maintains a nation-wide radio access network (RAN), a set of regional transport networks, and a nation-wide IP core network that consists of two identical yet separate fiber rings [17]. The transport networks interconnects Telenor's base station with its core IP network which interconnects them with the mobile core network.
- *Telia* [4] maintains a nation-wide RAN, but uses Telenor's transport and IP core networks for interconnecting its RAN and mobile core network.
- Before Q1 2015 *Tele2 and Network Norway* together owned and operated a RAN called Mobile Norway. This RAN did not have a nation-wide coverage. When outside their home network, Tele2 customers used Telia's RAN and Network Norway customers used Telenor's RAN. Mobile Norway mainly used a transport and core IP network called Broadnet for interconnecting its base stations and mobile core. Telia acquired Tele2 in Q1 2015 resulting in the decommissioning of Mobile Norway and Tele2 brand. Further, Network Norway switched to completely using Telia's RAN. These changes are illustrated by the dashed and solid lines in Fig. 1.

These complex relationships together with the multi-homed nature of NNE present a unique opportunity for assessing correlated failures and thus the impact of infrastructure sharing.

3.3 Measurement methodology and data set

A NNE node attempts to maintain an active data session at all times and immediately attempts to restore failed sessions. For measuring downtime, we record all timestamps where an active data session fails as well as all corresponding restoration timestamps. For measuring packet loss, an NNE node sends a 20-byte UDP packet every second to an echo server that is part of the NNE backend which echoes the packet back to the node. A packet is considered lost, if no reply is received within 60 seconds [5]. We inspect the server side's system logs to remove all loss episodes that are caused by system artifacts, e.g., server reboots. We also disregard loss episodes that are likely caused by congestion and failures in the NNE backend upstream provider's network. More specifically, we remove all loss episodes that simultaneously impact 10% of connections or more to three different operators. We also remove all downtime events that are related to nodes maintenance activities or node-specific artifacts like reboots and hardware failures.

Software running on the nodes also collects various metadata attributes (e.g. RAT, signal strength, etc) from the modems and periodically sends them to the NNE backend. This metadata is important for contextualizing the collected measurements. Our measurement period spans three years from the 1st of January 2014 to the 31st of December 2016. Overall, we collect measurements from 277 distinct measurement nodes and 545 MBB connections.

Our analysis, unless mentioned otherwise, is based on measurements from stationary nodes. Unlike when nodes are moving, the stationary scenario allows us to focus on characterizing MBB availability under relatively static conditions. Not only does this help

[1]A realtime visualization of NNE measurements is available at http://robustenett.no/map.
[2]We only focus on measurements from the UMTS/LTE operators, since we do not have the necessary logs to measure the CDMA2000 network downtime.
[3]NSB is a publicly-owned railway company operating most passenger trains in Norway.
[4]Formerly known as Netcom.
[5]NNE connections do not generally experience extreme delays. Measured RTTs to the backend servers are below 100 msec in 99.5% of the cases.

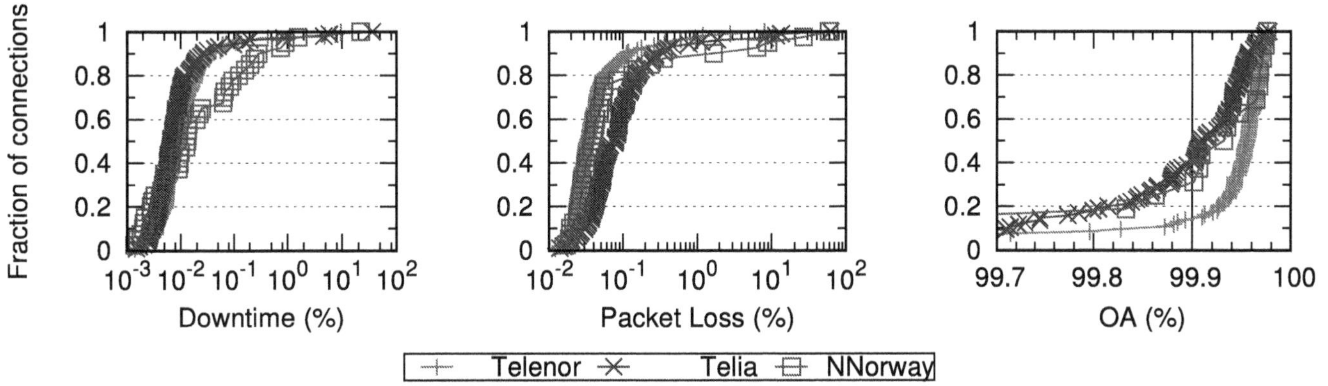

Figure 2: The distribution of downtime (left), packet loss (middle), and overall availability (right) in 2016. A considerable fraction of connections exhibits three nines of availability.

characterizing basic MBB availability, but also resembles many actual application scenarios that require high availability and are stationary like M2M communciation.

4 MEASURING AVAILABILITY

The plots in Fig. 2 show the distribution of downtime, packet loss, and OA for Telenor, Telia, and Network Norway (NNorway) stationary connections in 2016 [6]. The line in the OA distribution marks an OA of 99.9%, that is unavailability of 86.4 seconds per day on average. Note that by connections here were refer to the measured subscriptions.

The measured networks exhibit a high level of availability as measured by different metrics. However, there are clear differences between operators. More than 80% of Telenor connections achieve an OA of three nines or more, while only 60% and 70% of Telia and NNorway connections, respectively, achieve the same feat. Most of the unavailability in Telia can be attributed to packet loss since there are no major differences between downtime distributions for Telia and Telenor. Differences between NNorway and the other operators in OA can be traced back to differences in both downtime and packet loss. Note that stationary connections availability is an upper bound on MBB availability. Moving connections are subject to repeated handovers resulting in downtime and packet loss that are several times higher than the stationary case [6, 47].

We compare received signal quality across operators to verify whether the observed differences are a byproduct of NNE nodes placement. In particular, we measure the reference signals received power (RSRP) for each connection every minute in the first two weeks of June 2016. Then calculate the average RSRP. We focus on RSRP because it is a suitable measure of signal quality in LTE [13]. Recall that most of the measured connections are LTE. Figure 3 shows the average RSRP for all measured connections from the three operators above. Across networks, over 80% of connections receive a reasonably strong signal; over -100 dBm. Further, there are no clear difference between the three operators. This shows that the observed differences in downtime and packet loss can not be attributed to differences in coverage quality.

[6]Tele2 is not present on these graphs since it was decommissioned in Q2 2015.

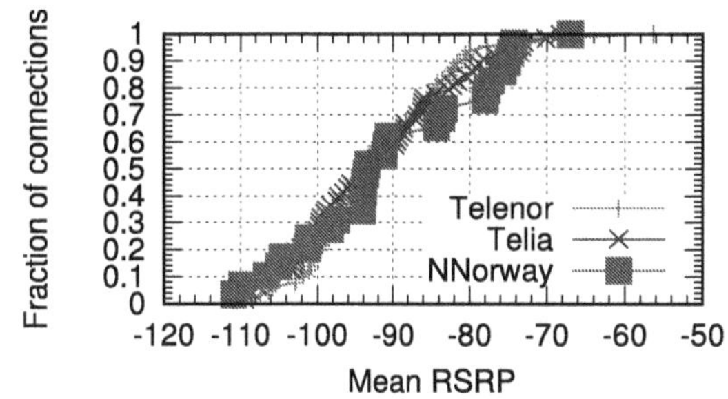

Figure 3: Mean RSRP. Most connections receive a reasonable signal quality.

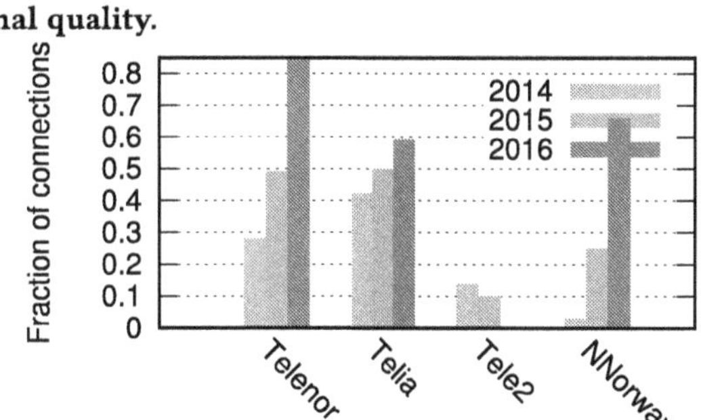

Figure 4: The fraction of connections with 99.9% OA over time.

4.1 Availability over time

Having seen that today's commercial MBB networks are characterized by a high level of OA, we now turn to investigating how OA has changed over time and causes of differences between operators. To this end, we measure the fraction of connections that have a 99.9% OA in each year in the study period, which we present in Fig. 4. All operators, except Tele2, have exhibited a positive trend in OA, with Telenor outperforming the other operators. Telenor connections with 99.9% OA have increased from less than a third in 2014 to over 80% in 2016.

We believe that the main cause of this positive trend is LTE roll-out. LTE is known to outperform UMTS on several performance metrics [7, 24, 25]. There is less packet loss in LTE thanks to the more robust air interface, the minimal state machine and flatter network architecture [13]. To check whether the differences between the operators can be attributed to differences in LTE deployment, we quantify LTE deployments as seen by the measurement nodes at

Table 1: LTE deployment as seen by NNE nodes

	Telenor	Telia	NNorway
2014	28% (4.3%)	31% (13.4%)	25% (17.5%)
2015	80% (3.2%)	55% (28%)	72% (10.6%)
2016	93% (3.4%)	70% (17.8%)	89% (5.2%)

the end of each studied year. Using the metadata collected by NNE nodes, we breakdown the life time of each connection according to time spent on different RATs. To monitor the change in LTE deployment over time, we perform this breakdown for two weeks every year one in mid-June and the other in mid-December. We classify a connection as predominantly LTE, if it has spent 90% of the measured week on LTE. Further, we label a connection as mixed-LTE, if it reports less than 90% LTE coverage.

Table 1 shows, for each operator, the percentage of predominantly LTE connections as well as mixed-LTE connections in December of every year [7]. The latter is inside the parentheses. When summing these numbers, we find that each operator's LTE coverage has doubled over the measurement period. We, however, note that Telia, compared to the other operators, has less predominantly LTE connections and more mixed-LTE connections. This hints that differences in time spent on LTE can be a plausible explanation for the differences in packet loss between Telia and the other operators in Fig. 2. To check this hypothesis, we perform the following simple test. For all Telenor and Telia connections, we identify all time periods, in December 2016, where these connection were exclusively on LTE [8]. We then compare packet loss for these periods. If the difference between the two operators persists then it can not be explained by the time spent on LTE. Figure 5 shows the measured packet loss distribution. Unlike in Fig. 2, Telia exhibits a lower packet loss which supports our hypothesis.

A closer look at Telia connections' metadata shows that, unlike other operators, Telia does not implement a seamless inter-RAT handover from UMTS to LTE. Once in UMTS, a Telia connection must become idle or in a paging radio state before going back to LTE. NNE nodes send data every second which does not allow these conditions to be realized. We, hence, find that Telia connections return to LTE only when they detach and reattach to the network. Note that the lack of such implementation may not adversely affect smart phones, since they tend to become idle when users are not using them. It, however, affects users with active data sessions while on UMTS. This highlights the importance of properly implementing inter-RAT handover from UMTS to LTE to ensure that UEs are always attached to the best available RAT.

Takeaways. The overall availability of stationary MBB connections has significantly improved over time, but it is still far from the carrier-grade availability of five-nines or more. The improved availability can be largely attributed to the stability brought by LTE. The observed differences between operators highlights the importance of independent long-term performance benchmarking of mobile networks.

[7] June results are consistent with the trend in the table.
[8] Other months show similar results.

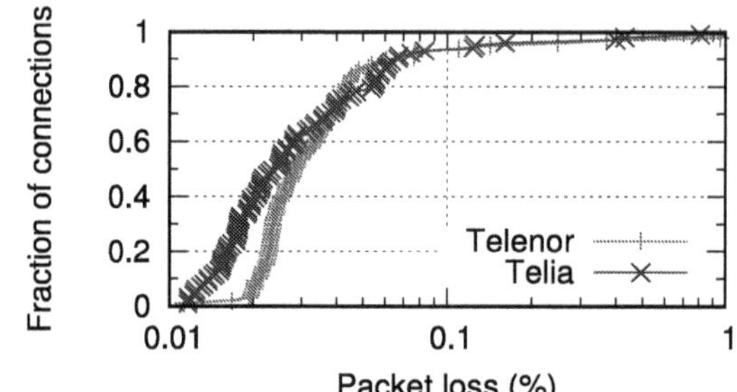

Figure 5: Comparing loss while on LTE. Telia loss is clearly lower.

5 CORRELATION OF OUTAGES

As Sec. 2.1 explains, there are numerous causes for unavailability (outages). Some of them are hard to pinpoint, especially those triggered by failures in shared infrastructure. In this section, we investigate whether end-to-end measurements can accurately discern infrastructure sharing. To this end, we employ a simple correlation-based approach that leverages the scale of NNE and the geographic spread of its nodes. Then gauge the suitability of end-to-end measurements by cross-checking the observed correlations with the known dependencies between operators (see Fig. 1). If end-to-end measurements prove successful, we can divide outages into correlated and uncorrelated and thus be able to assess the role of shared infrastructure. This will allow to quantify contributions of different classes of outages thus pointing to possible directions for increasing the OA.

5.1 Correlating downtime and loss

We divide each connection's lifetime into a time series of five-minute bins. We then build a binary downtime time series, where we set the time series value to one for bins where connections experience downtime and to zero otherwise. If a downtime spans multiple consecutive bins, we set all of them to one. We also construct packet loss time series by calculating the packet loss rate in each bin. We divide our time series into quarterly time series (i.e. 3 months long) giving us a total of up to 12 quarterly time series per connection. This division is important for observing changes in correlations over time. We then calculate the Pearson's correlation coefficient for every pair of downtime time series and for every pair of packet loss time series [9]. Pearson's correlation is a measure of linear dependence (i.e. whether the two time series exhibit similar and simultaneous changes). We include only pairs of time series that overlap for at least one day. On average, we have 52 days overlap between time series pairs.

To avoid spurious correlations due to short and excessively long downtimes, we only consider downtime outages that last for between 1 minute and 1 hour. We also only consider packet loss that is greater than 3%, i.e., losing 9 packets in a five-minute bin, to avoid spurious correlation due to random loss. If loss is lower than 3%, we set it to zero. Note that packet loss is measured only when the connection is up. Correlating downtime and packet loss may lead to different conclusions, as these metrics can give insights into different types of root causes. Downtime involves root causes that lie between the measurement node and the mobile core network.

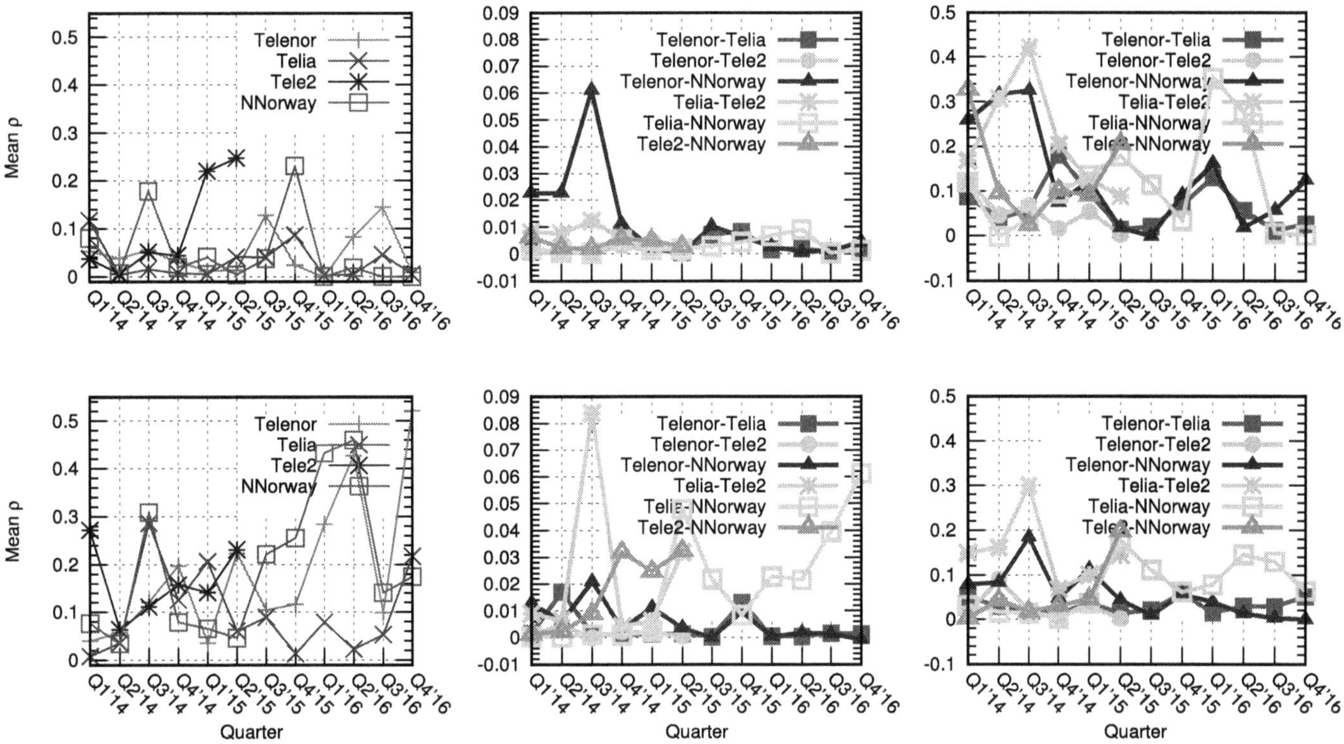

Figure 6: The average correlation coefficient between connections from the same network (intra-operator), connections from different networks (inter-operator), and connections to different networks that terminate at the same measurement node for downtime (top) and packet loss (bottom).

Packet loss, however, may involve root causes that lie in the Internet between the mobile core and NNE servers.

We divide the connection pairs into three groups. *1) Intra-operator,* for measuring correlations within a single operator. These correlations can be caused by shared transport as well as centralized components. *2) Inter-operator,* for measuring correlations between different operators. These correlations are caused by shared infrastructures and thus are expected to be higher for pairs that are geographically close to each other. *3) Diagonal pairs,* which are inter-operator pairs that are connected to the same measurement node, i.e., present at the same location. These pairs correspond to the highest geographic proximity. Hence, we expect diagonal pairs to exhibit much higher correlations compared to the average inter-operator pair. The six panels in Fig. 6 show the average correlation coefficient $\bar{\rho}$ over time for the different groups for both downtime and packet loss.

Intra-operator correlations are erratic, varying widely from a quarter to another. This indicates that the underlying causes do not follow a specific trend, e.g., correlation did not decrease as LTE deployment picked up.

Inter-operator correlation averages are about an order of magnitude lower than the *intra-operator* ones, but they are characterized by evident trends and changes. The difference in absolute values of $\bar{\rho}$ hints that inter-operator failures due to shared infrastructures are less frequent than their intra-operator counterparts. As expected, operators that use the same RAN (e.g. Telenor and NNorway; and Telia and Tele2 before Q1'2015) are more correlated. The observed correlations *match well* the changes in the relationship between the measured networks which we described in Sec. 3. For example, the correlation between Telenor and NNorway has dropped since early 2015, while the correlation between Telia and NNorway has picked up since then. Operators that only share transport, i.e., Telenor and Telia exhibit lower correlation. This correlation, however, jumps in some quarters, e.g., downtime Q4'15 and packet loss in Q2'14 and Q4'15, to take values comparable to operators that share RAN. Furthermore, Operators without significant infrastructure sharing like Telenor and Tele2 exhibit extremely low correlation.

The correlation between operators that share infrastructure is very evident when looking at *diagonal pairs*; $\bar{\rho}$ is an order of magnitude higher compared to all pairs. This high difference suggests that access and regional transport networks, and perhaps co-located cell sites, are key contributors to correlated failures. Note that we observe no difference in $\bar{\rho}$, when looking at diagonal pairs, for operators without significant sharing, e.g., Telenor and Tele2. This confirms that the the observed high diagonal correlations are not caused by artifacts at the measurement nodes.

5.2 Correlation and geography

In order to gain insights into causes of observed correlations, we next investigate whether the presence of correlation is related to the geographic distance between nodes. For each pair of connections with non-zero correlation, we compute the p-value for the measured correlation using a permutation test [22]. Our goal is to test the null hypothesis that the pair are not correlated. We fix

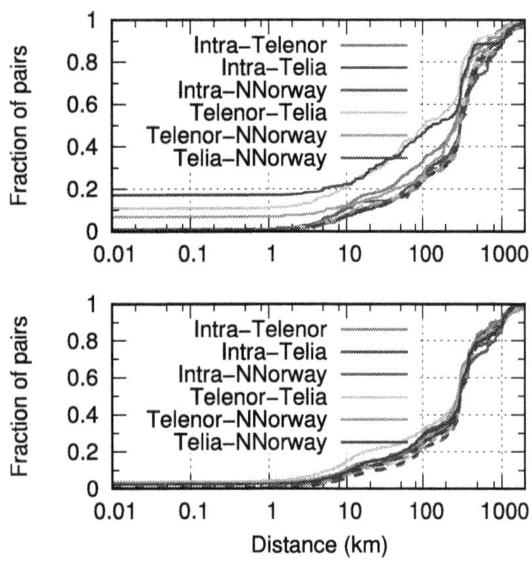

Figure 7: CDF of distances between node pairs for downtime (left) and packet loss (right). Solid lines (correlated) and dash lines (uncorrelated).

one of the time series and shuffle the other time series 1000 times, calculate the correlation coefficient for each of these 1000 pairs, and use these values to construct an empirical distribution of shuffled data correlation coefficient. Then, we compute the p-value for the measured correlation as its probability according to the shuffled data distribution. We reject the null hypothesis if the $p\text{-value} < 0.05$. In other words, a pair is label as correlated, if the chance that the measured correlation is due to randomness is less than 0.05. Note that we do not use a fixed correlation threshold, e.g., greater than 0.5, to label a pair as strongly correlated. Instead, we determine whether an observed non-zero correlation is down to randomness; if not we label a pair as correlated.

Figure 7 shows the distribution of distances between correlated pairs (solid lines) and uncorrelated pairs (dashed lines) for both downtime and loss and a set of operator combinations. These distribution are based on correlation measurements from all quarters. Inter-operator pairs, that are correlated with respect to downtime, are generally separated by a shorter distance compared to uncorrelated pairs [9]. Half of correlated Telenor-Telia and Telia-NNorway pairs are separated by 100km or less compared to 300km for uncorrelated pairs. Further, apart from intra-Telenor, curves for correlated intra-operator downtime pairs collapse onto uncorrelated pairs. All packet loss curves, apart from a slight difference by Telenor-Telia pairs, collapse onto each other.

The expected distance between any pair of connections is 300km, which is a byproduct of the way NNE nodes are placed, i.e., mostly in the three major cities in Norway. Hence, for uncorrelated pairs, the mode at 300km in Fig. 7 just reflects nodes' placement. For correlated pairs, however, it means that these correlations are independent of geography and are thus likely caused by shared central components. Further, the prevalence of shorter distances between correlated inter-operator downtime pairs points to causes in nodes' geographic proximity. These include components in the access and regional networks as well as co-located sites. The absence of a strong correspondence between packet loss correlations and distance suggests that these correlations are dominated by packet loss that occurs in the core network and beyond. This indicates that whereas the RAN and transport are well provisioned, Internet paths from the mobile core are less so.

5.3 Correlation observability and sensitivity

This subsection assesses the robustness and sensitivity of the measured correlations. These correlations can be influenced by a number of factors including the thresholds we use for defining failures, the number and placement of measurement nodes, and the nature of the underlying failures.

Impact of thresholds. We start by investigating the thresholds we use in Sec 5.1 to construct the binary downtime and packet loss time series. Recall that in Sec 5.1, we only correlate connection downtime events that last between 1 min and 1 hour and packet loss that is at least 3%. We lower the minimum downtime duration to 30 seconds and recompute $\bar{\rho}$ for all quarters. We also measure $\bar{\rho}$ for packet loss for two new minimum packet loss thresholds which are 1% and 5%. We then compute the percentage change in $\bar{\rho}$. Packet loss correlations show a slight decrease when lowering the threshold and a slight increase when increasing it; both are less than 5%. In the worst case, downtime correlation decreases by 46% when lowering the minimum duration, which means that failures shorter than 1 minutes are mostly uncorrelated. There are also much fewer correlated downtime instances compared to packet loss which makes downtime correlation susceptible to perturbations brought by adding uncorrelated instances. These findings indicate that choosing conservative minimum thresholds results in avoiding spurious correlations and consequently observing otherwise difficult to spot correlations. This supports our decision to focus on non-trivial minimum downtime and packet loss values when constructing the respective time series.

Impact of measurements nodes placement. We now turn to analyzing the impact of measurements nodes placement on observed correlations. In other words, our goal is to check whether these correlations and corresponding trends can be attributed to a small subset of connection pairs, namely highly correlated pairs. We investigate the impact of nodes placement by removing all diagonal inter-operator pairs, i.e., nodes that have connection to both operators. Recall that the average correlation between diagonal pairs is an order of magnitude higher than the average inter-operator pair. We repeat this test for all quarters. Across quarters, removing diagonal pairs halves the downtime correlations but has no impact on packet loss. The impact of diagonal pairs is in agreement with the previous observations that inter-operator downtime correlations seem to stem from failures in access and regional transport infrastructure and that packet loss correlations seem to be related to failures in the mobile core and the Internet. However, the removal of these pairs does not produce a qualitative difference in observed correlation trends. This stability can be explained by the presence of many non-diagonal connections in the geographic proximity of each other. For instance, in Q4 2016 one fifth of Telenor-Telia pairs, excluding diagonal pairs, are within 100km from each other. As

[9]This distinction is less evident for Telenor-NNorway since these two shared infrastructure for only the third of the study period.

Fig. 7 shows the presence of such nodes helps spotting correlations due to shared access and regional networks.

Takeaways. Correlating end-to-end measurements from geographically spread nodes proves powerful in capturing interdependencies between operators. We find that the causes of correlations in packet loss and intra-operator downtime seem to mostly lie in the mobile core and beyond. This involves the mobile core and the portion of the Internet between the mobile core and NNE servers for the former and the mobile core for the latter. Correlations in inter-operator downtime is caused by shared infrastructure, close to the edge. These findings suggest that operators need to follow different strategies to reduce correlations, 1) minimize infrastructure sharing for reducing inter-operator downtime correlations 2) diversify the mobile core for reducing intra-operator correlations 3) focus on the performance of paths from the mobile core to various destinations in the Internet for reducing packet loss correlations.

6 CHARACTERISTICS OF OUTAGES

Having established that end-to-end measurements capture interdependencies between operators reasonably well, we now take a closer look at the characteristics of correlated outages. We are interested in quantifying outages' magnitude and the extent and role of shared infrastructure.

6.1 Outages' magnitude

An outage size in terms of simultaneously impacted measurement nodes can give insights into root causes of outages. For instance, a large number of nodes at diverse geographic locations are likely to be impacted when a central network element fails. Outage size statistics help assessing operators vulnerability to large outages, i.e., the extent of centralization within an operator's network. For characterizing outages, we first need to group individual connections' outages into correlated failure events.

Grouping outages into events. We assume that all connections which experience downtime (packet loss) in the same five-minute bin are impacted by a common underlying outage. While this approach is admittedly simplistic, we believe it is adequate for our analysis since we are interested in building a qualitative understanding of outages' magnitude. Next, we refine this grouping by verifying that the involved connections are significantly correlated. A pair is significantly correlated if the measured correlation is positive and is associated with a p-value ≤ 0.05 (see Sec. 5).

Constructing intra-operator events. After identifying all connections that experience an outage in the same time bin, we go through all these pairs and divide them to one or more subgroups of significantly correlated pairs. The rationale here is to only group connections that have proved significantly correlated over the entire quarter. These subgroups are constructed as follows. We start with an empty graph that includes all initially identified connections but no links. Then we add a link between all significantly correlated connection pairs. Next, we pick an arbitrary connection N and build a directed acyclic graph (DAG) [8], that is rooted at N, following a depth-first search approach. We essentially identify all connections that N is significantly correlated with and add them to the DAG, then identify their neighbors, i.e., all connections that they are significantly correlated with, and add them to the DAG

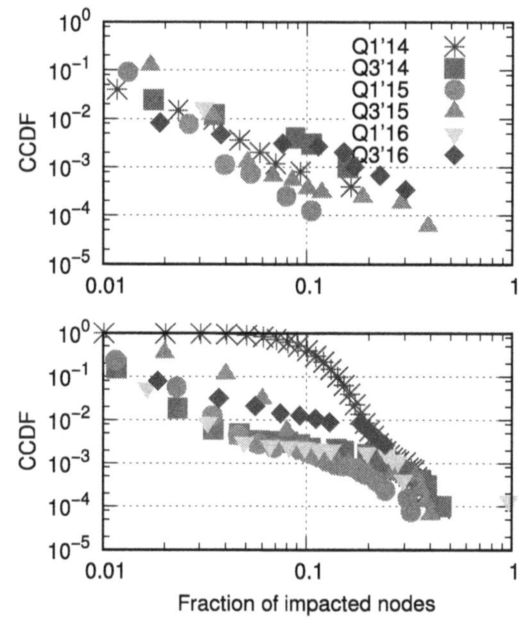

Figure 8: Intra-operator outages' size distribution for connection downtime (top) and packet loss (bottom) in Telenor.

and so on until there are no more connections to add. We remove the constructed DAG and repeat the same process until no connection is left. This process may result in multiple DAGs, which we consider as groups of nodes impacted by simultaneously occurring but separate events. Note that, by construction, any connection belongs to only one of the constructed DAGs. The outage size is the number of connections in each DAG divided by all connections that are available in the time bin of the outage.

Constructing inter-operator events. We identify all connections, from the two operators in question, that experience an outage in the same time bin and place them in two sets; one per operator. Then we start constructing a bipartite graph [8] by adding a link between pairs with significant correlation. Note that by a pair here, we mean two connections from two distinct operators. Finally, we traverse the bipartite graph and identify all connected bipartite sub-graphs which we consider as groups of nodes impacted by separate events. Note that, by construction, any connection belongs to only one of the constructed bipartite sub-graphs.

Intra-operator outage sizes. The panels in Fig. 8 show the CCDF of downtime and packet loss outage sizes for Telenor for different quarters. *Downtime* size distributions span a couple orders of magnitude and mostly collapse onto each other. These distributions appear to be consistent with a power-law distribution; a simple ordinary least square fitting yields a power law exponent $\alpha \approx 2\pm0.2$ indicating an undefined second moment, i.e., very high variability. The largest observed event impacted $\approx$ 40% of connections. Other operators show qualitatively similar results.*Packet loss* outage size distributions span also two orders of magnitude, but large outages that impact more than 10% of the connections are more likely. The distribution for Q1'2014 differs markedly from the other five quarters. In the first half of 2014, Telenor was suffering a mis-configuration that resulted in frequent packet loss events [10]. This misconfiguration resulted in a large extent of spurious correlation which increased the fraction of outages with large sizes. This high spurious correlation is due to the fact that the mis-configuration affected all connections. Hence, this spurious correlation is introduced by legitimate external factors and does not reflect a methodological weakness. To sum up, the long tail nature of outage sizes distributions confirms that the centralized MBB architecture is a major cause of correlated control and data plane outages.

Inter-operator outage sizes. The majority of correlated inter-operator downtime events have small impact. There is only four events that impact more than 5% of Telenor and Telia connections simultaneously. There are, however, more packet loss events that impact more than 5% of Telenor and Telia connections. Excluding outages that happened in the first half of 2014, there are 48 such events. These outages can be related to congestion and dynamics in the transport network and on shared Internet paths towards NNE servers. The former may not necessarily result in downtime if it does not last long enough for respective connection management timers to expire, which explains the difference between downtime and packet loss above. Looking at other inter-operator combinations, we note that for both metrics, the likelihood and extent of large simultaneous outages increase as the degree of infrastructure sharing increases. Operators that share the entire RAN are ≈ 8 to 10 times likelier to experience large simultaneous outages compared to operators that only share the core transport network.

Case studies. Next, we present and describe three outages demonstrating that the spread and scale of NNE yield a decent explanatory power.

1. Intra-Telenor downtime. At noon local time on 23/11/2015, 23 Telenor connections went down; this amounts to 27% of all active connections at the time. The first impacted and the last impacted connections experienced the outage within 43 seconds from each other. This is expected since EPS bearer tearing down is controlled by inactivity timers which are not synchronized across connections. The outage lasted for about 2 minutes. Except for three connections, all involved connections were hosted in and within 100 km from Oslo. Hence, the likely cause of this failure is either a failure of a network function in the CN that manages connections around Oslo, or the failure in the interconnect between Telenor's regional transport and its IP core. Note that it is unlikely that the base stations serving these connections share the same transport links, since they are located in different directions around Oslo [11].

2. Telenor-Telia downtime. At 02:19 AM on 26/11/2015, eight, eleven, and three Telenor, Telia, and NNorway connections respectively went down. Six affected nodes included both Telenor and Telia connections, which went down. The outage lasted about one minute. All the impacted connections are in Oslo or within 100 km from it. Hence, as in above the likely cause is the failure at the interconnect between Telenor's regional transport and its IP core. This outage highlights a possible weakness in the transport topology.

[10] 3G connections were erroneously forced to an idle state even when they were actively exchanging data. Please refer to [5, 15] for more details.

[11] Fiber in Norway is mostly laid next to railroad, highways, and power lines.

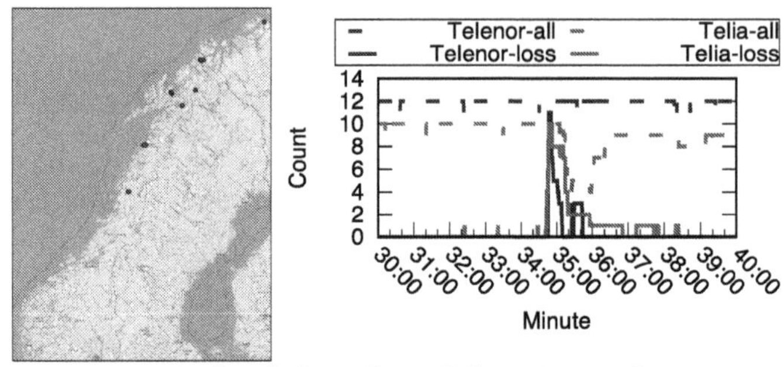

Figure 9: Correlated data plane failure in northern Norway. Geo-locations of impacted connections (left) and outage timeline (right).

3. Telenor-Telia packet loss. At 10:34 AM on 27/01/ 2016, eleven, ten, and two Telenor, Telia, and NNorway connections respectively experienced 100% packet loss for between 5 and 20 seconds depending on the operator. These connections are spread across the northern part of the country as illustrated on the map in Fig. 9. The same figure also shows how the number of available connections and those experiencing packet loss have changed in a 10-min period that includes the outage. The outage hit the two operators at about the same time. Soon, however, half of Telia connections disconnected, while Telenor recovered. This highlights that operators are using different inactivity timer values for managing the life time of data sessions. We also noticed that almost all connections suffered a sharp increase in RTT, up to seven times, in the two seconds preceding the outage. This hints that the underlying cause can be a reroute or a sudden congestion event at a central component in the transport network. Telenor runs a ring of two fiber backbones to cover the north of Norway. This ring starts in Tromsø and ends in Trondheim (See page 6 in [17]). Based on the location of affected connections, we expect them to be connected to different sides of the ring. Hence, the root cause most likely lies at one of the meeting points. Although this outage was short, it highlights a major weakness in the resilience of the MBB ecosystem in northern Norway.

Validating inferred outages. We validate all inferred intra-operator outages, that took place since Q3 2015, through direct communications with the affected operators. We have also leveraged publicly available fiber topology maps [17, 23, 36] together with the location of our nodes to verify whether a pair of nodes are likely to use the same fiber segments. This lends extra information to contextualize the identified outages (see case study 3 above). We plan to conduct a thorough validation in our future work.

6.2 Correlation graph

The measured correlations can be used for constructing a graph, i.e., a correlation network, by adding a link between correlated pairs. The primarily goal of constructing a correlation graph is to identify areas with high interdependence. For this to yield meaningful insights, observed correlations need to imply causation. To this end, we construct a simple hypothesis test.

The first idea behind our test is that correlation is a decreasing function of distance between measurement node pairs. The farther the two nodes are the less infrastructure they share. The second idea is that a non spurious correlation between remote nodes has to be caused by outages closer to the mobile core network or systematic network-wide outages. These outages will also impact other remote nodes because of the hierarchical structure of the network.

We start by assuming that correlation between nodes that are spaced by less than X km implies causation. For other significantly correlated node pairs, which are spaced by more than X km, we check how many other nodes each pair is commonly correlated with. We then accept that the correlation between a node pair implies causation if they are commonly correlated with at least one node. This low threshold is reasonable given that we use a two-stage verification process, i.e., the permutation test in Sec. 5 and this test.

We use the constructed graph to assess how tightly coupled the investigated networks by computing the maximum correlation distance η, which is the largest great circle distance between causally correlated pairs. We experiment with a few values of X in the range from 25 to 100 km. The choice of X has a little impact on intra-operator correlation network. X's value influences η for inter-operator downtime correlation network, because many inter-operator pairs do not have nodes in common. This spareness is a consequence to the fact that NNE nodes have a mixed configuration when it comes to the attached networks. We plan to study the interplay between measurement infrastructure layout and the ability to discern causation in our future work.

The map in Fig. 10 gives an example of the inferred causally correlated networks for Telenor-Telia downtime pairs in 2015. It shows that nodes are grouped into distinct clusters that follow geography. This confirms that the observed correlation between Telenor and Telia is mainly caused by outages in access and regional networks. These dependencies can extend to tens of kilometers though, indicating the presence of a non-trivial level of centralization in the transport network. Similar maps for intra-operator downtime pairs and inter/intra-operator packet loss mostly consist of a single giant component denoting a country-wide correlation.

The other plots in Fig. 10 show η for different combinations of operators when setting X to 25 km. Intra-operator pairs demonstrate η values around 1000 Km. Inter-operator downtime pairs are characterized by a relatively shorter η. These, however, can reach up to 100 km, which correspond to the diameter of a large metropolitan. Inter-operator loss pairs exhibit higher η values matching our previous observations. We also note that η follows closely interdependencies between operators. η for Telenor-NNorway packet loss pairs dropped in Q2 2015, which corresponds to the time frame that NNorway stopped roaming on Telenor. We also observe an increase in η for Telia-NNorway packet loss pairs starting from Q1 2015, which corresponds to the time that NNorway started roaming on Telia.

Takeaways. We have shown that correlating outages from a geographically diverse set of vantage points can give insights into the extent of underlying events. Furthermore, combining the correlations with knowledge about placement of the measurement nodes can help identifying regions with shared dependencies. Our analysis also shows that shared infrastructure can result in outages with non-trivial magnitude in terms of geographical impact, e.g., case study 3.

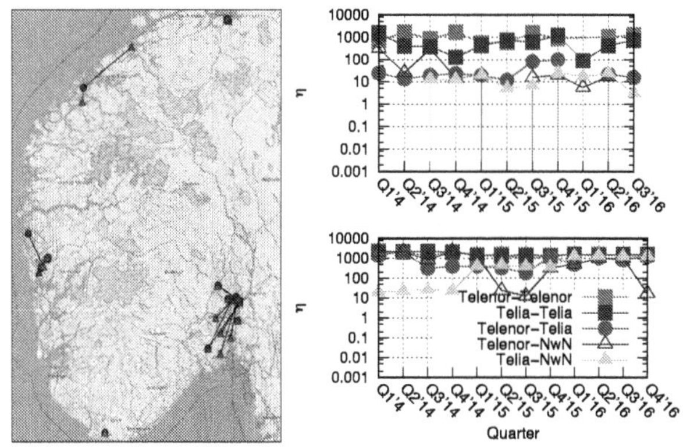

Figure 10: The identified correlation network when correlating Telenor and Telia in 2015 (left), the correlation distance η for downtime (top-right), and for packet loss (bottom-right).

7 CORRELATED OUTAGES IMPACT AND OPPORTUNITIES

Having seen that downtime and packet loss outages can sometimes simultaneously impact a non-trivial fraction of connections, we now turn to assess their contribution to the overall downtime and packet loss that is experienced by individual connections. This is important, since it can point to concrete avenues for boosting availability.

7.1 How bad are large and correlated failures?

We start by identifying for each connection all downtime and loss outages that correspond to the following: 1) *Large failures,* which we define as outages that affect at least 5% of all connections simultaneously, and 2) *Correlated failures,* which are failures that are simultaneously experienced with at least one significantly correlated connection; this set includes also large failures. These two groups of outages correspond to large scale failures and limited failures, respectively. Then, we examine the distributions of downtime and packet loss when excluding outages related that belong to these two categories. Figure 11 shows these distributions for intra-Telenor and Telenor-Telia downtime in 2016 [12]. Downtime decreases when removing intra-operator large and correlated outages. Connections with low downtime benefit the most from removing correlated failures. For instance, across operators the fraction of connections with 5 nines availability, i.e., *downtime* $\leq 0.001\%$ at least doubles. Removing large and correlated *inter-operator outages* has a negligible effect. However, removing these events lead to a visible increase in uptime for operator-pairs that share the RAN. Packet loss exhibits qualitatively similar results. According to the aforementioned observations, improving the availability of the majority of connections requires reducing uncorrelated failures.

Pinpointing the exact causes of uncorrelated failures requires collecting additional logs from the UEs (e.g. physical and MAC layer messages) and the network-side. Instead we perform a high level investigation of differences between connections that achieve 4 nines uptime and those do not, using measurements from the 1st week of June and the 1st week of December of 2016 for both Telia and Telenor. We compare the number of handovers and the

[12] We omit plots for other combinations and years due to space limitation.

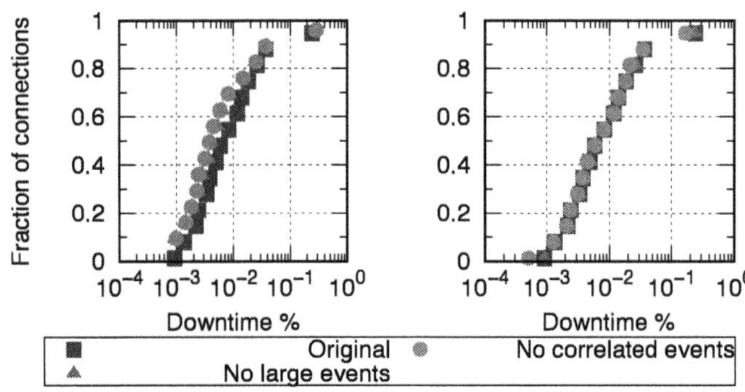

Figure 11: Breaking downtime into correlated and uncorrelated for intra-Telenor (left) and inter-Telenor-Telia (right)

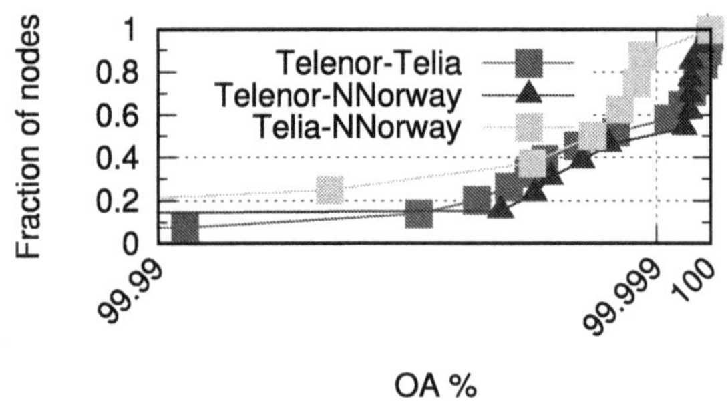

Figure 12: Increasing availability through multi-connectivity.

average RSRP. These two metrics evaluate the radio stability and signal quality respectively. The median RSRP for connections with 4 nines ≤ uptime is higher by between 3 to 7 dBm depending on the operator. Also, connections with 4 nines ≤ uptime experience a median of 10 handovers per week, an order of magnitude lower than connection with 4 nines ≥ uptime. These hint that better coverage as well as better radio planning and UE mobility management are key to increasing availability.

7.2 Leveraging multi-connectivity

Motivated by the observations above about the contribution of inter-operator correlated failures to overall downtime and packet loss, we next quantify the potential availability boost when combining connections from two different operators. We perform our evaluations for both stationary and moving connections.

7.3 Stationary connections

We consider all connection pairs that are present at each measurement node. Note that each measurement node includes up to four connections and at most one connection per operator. This gives a total of 101 pairs in 2016. We then perform a simple intersection operation between downtime time series of the two connections that constitute each pair to identify periods where both connections were experiencing an outage. To repeat the same for packet loss, we check whether packets that are sent in the same second are echoed back or not. Recall that the packet loss measurements are based on sending a small UDP packet every second over each connection.

Figure 12 shows the distribution of the OA when combining three operators; two at a time. As in Sec. 4, the overall uptime is calculated by multiplying the connection uptime by the fraction of successfully echoed packets. Multi-connectivity boosts the OA by an order of magnitude. Almost all connections are at least 4 nines available (i.e. a max of 8.64 seconds of unavailability per day) compared to 2 nines for individual connections (see Fig. 2). Furthermore, about half of Telenor-Telia and Telenor-NNorway combinations are at least 5 nines available. The benefit is less when combining operators that share the RAN, i.e., Telia and NNorway. Breaking the overall uptime to its constituents shows that it is mainly decided by the correlations in downtime since almost all packet loss pairs achieve five nines of availability or more. This essentially means that almost all packet loss less than 3% (i.e less than the qualification threshold in Sec. 5) is uncorrelated. In other words, its root causes must lie on the air interface or individual operator's core network. Hence, to increase the fraction of 5-nines connections, we need to reduce correlations in downtime. In practical terms, this translates to enhancing the reliability of access and regional transport networks.

Table 2: Multi-connectivity on the move

Node	Telenor	Telia	Combined
1	99.88%	99.95%	99.99%
2	97.94%	98.55%	99.47%
3	99.73%	99.65%	99.91%
4	99.76%	99.82%	99.94%

7.4 Moving connections

To quantify whether multi-connectivity benefits extend to the mobile case, we use measurements from four nodes aboard regional trains. We, however, only focus on measurements that are collected within Oslo metropolitan area because railroad stretches beyond this area suffer patchy coverage. Each node is connected to both Telenor and Telia. Our measurements span the period from the 1st of September to the 8th of December 2015, and comprise a total of 139 days worth of train driving time. We calculate the uptime experienced by each connection on these nodes and the overall uptime when combining them. Table 2 shows these values. Multi-connectivity has the potential to greatly improve MBB uptime on the move. Looking closer at the outages experienced by the moving connections, we find that they are mostly related to coverage holes and unsuccessful handovers. The huge benefit of connectivity is because operators coverage holes are not identical. Node 2 is placed on a train serving the southeastern part of Oslo and runs through a track with several tunnels and coverage holes.

Takeaways. Reducing correlated and large outages can boost the availability of already stable connections. Improving the availability of the majority of connections, however, requires addressing uncorrelated outages. Simultaneously using connections from two operators, that do not share the RAN, gives 5 nines availability in half of the measured cases. It also boosts moving connections availability to 3 nines.

8 RELATED WORK

Measurements of mobile networks. Recently there has been a growing interest in measuring and quantifying the performance and reliability of MBB networks. Several studies investigated the extent and causes of packet loss in MBB networks. Many of them identified RRC state transitions as a major cause of packet loss, e.g., [5, 38, 39]. Chen et. al performed a RAN level analysis of delays and packet loss in UMTS networks and attributed most periods with degraded performance to congestion and overloaded basestations [10]. A study by Huang et al. showed that physical layer retransmissions are behind most transport layer packet loss [25]. Other studies investigated packet loss under mobility and established that handovers are the main culprit [6, 31]. Shafiq et al. [41] characterized the operational MBB performance during two high profile crowded events in 2012 using using network-side traces. To the best of our knowledge, this paper is the first to use end-to-end measurements to investigate how shared infrastructure impacts MBB networks availability.

Ultra reliable cellular communciation. The growing interest in supporting machine type communciation (MTC) with stringent reliability requirements have motivated many to investigate possible approaches for achieving this. Popovski [37] has identified five major impairments for wireless reliability that are centered around channel quality, availability of resources, and equipment failure.

Several proposals have focused on leveraging transmission diversity either by using network coding or through double association with a macro and micro cell, e.g., [29, 43]. Other efforts have focused on optimizing cellular scheduling for latency and loss sensitive applications, e.g., [49]. Our work compliments these efforts by providing an empirical evaluation of today's networks and showing that multi-homing can boost availability significantly.

Infrastructure sharing. Investigating the reliability of the Internet physical infrastructure has been the subject of several previous works. Durairajan et al. [14] investigated the impact of infrastructure sharing in the US long-haul fiber optic network. Other articles investigated the vulnerability of the Internet to physical failures as well as the resiliency of optical networks to localized failures [2, 50]. This paper takes a first step towards investigating the impact of physical infrastructure sharing on MBB networks.

9 DISCUSSION AND CONCLUSIONS

In this paper we use end-to-end measurements to study the availability of today's MBB networks. Building on longitudinal data set from a geographically spread measurements infrastructure, we investigate the impact of infrastructure sharing on MBB reliability. In the following we discuss our findings, their implications, and the limitations of this paper.

MBB availability. This study shows that MBB availability and reliability are improving over time. The fraction of connections with three nines of availability has almost tripled over the study period. MBB networks, however, remain far from providing predictable and consistent availability. Most of degraded periods are uncorrelated which reinforces the common wisdom about the role of the mobile air interface. Accordingly, today's networks are far from being able to support services that require ultra-reliable communication, key to many 5G-visions [3, 33]. Supporting such services will thus require enhancing the reliability of the air interface. Existing proposals include increasing the spatial diversity, downlink and uplink decoupling, and coordinated multipoint transmission [16, 27, 42, 44]. In addition, we believe that there is a need for radically rethinking connectivity by devising solutions to seamlessly and simultaneously combining multiple operators.

Interdependencies between operators. We have shown that end-to-end measurements can help illuminating interdependencies between operators. Outages due to infrastructure sharing contribute minimally to the overall downtime experienced by individual connections. We, however, find that failures of shared components can isolate large geographic areas. While these outages are generally rare, their specter is alarming given the rising worries about targeted cyber-attacks. We believe that the regulatory bodies need to draft policies that regulate infrastructure sharing. Governments have already started recognizing vulnerabilities due to infrastructure sharing as a major threat [32].

Deriving additional metrics for reliability. Correlating outages seen by a diverse set of vantage points can help devising a set of new metrics to assess MBB reliability. More specifically, we have shown that two relevant metrics can be extracted form the measured correlations. The extent of centralization, which is measured by estimating the distribution of intra-operator events sizes. Ideally, operators should aim for engineering their networks to produce narrower outage size distributions. We have also proposed a simple hypothesis test to check whether measured correlations imply causation. We then construct a correlation network that interconnects all pairs with causal relationships. This graph can be used to measure, among other things, the extent of centralization and impact radius of infrastructure-sharing.

Leveraging multihoming. We have shown that combining connections from multiple operators can enhance MBB availability to a carrier-grade level. Implementing this, however, remains challenging. Existing business models and technology do not allow simultaneously using multiple operators via a single SIM card, which necessitates using two radios. Further, multi-path transport protocols like CMT-SCTP and MPTCP are by definition closed-loop protocols meaning that re-transmitting a lost packet may take one round trip time or more. This can potentially be solved by open-loop schedulers that leverage cross-layer communciation, e.g., using MAC messages to detect link-layer retransmissions. Also, efficient network coding schemes can help reconstructing lost data segments.

Limitations. This study has two main limitations. First, packet loss is measured against a single server, which may lead to spurious correlations. We have applied a set of filters to remove loss because of failures in the NNE backend and within NNE upstream provider, Uninett. Outages that are caused by failures in the interconnect between individual operators and Uninett will translate into network-wide events. Going forward, measuring packet loss to other destinations can reduce correlations due to interconnect failures. Augmenting packet loss measurements with traceroute tests may help locating failures. Second, NNE nodes deployment is relatively sparse which may lead to overestimating spurious correlations. Having a denser deployment would further help identifying causal links.

ACKNOWLEDGMENTS

This work was supported by the Research Council of Norway grants 240850 and 209954. We thank our shepherd, Bozidar Radunovic, and the anonymous reviewers for their thoughtful feedback; and Amund Kvalbein and Olav Lysne for their feedback on earlier drafts.

REFERENCES

[1] Action700. 700 MHz Broadband for Mission Critical Public Safety Data. http://www.citig.ca/action700.aspx, 2015.

[2] P. K. Agarwal, A. Efrat, S. K. Ganjugunte, D. Hay, S. Sankararaman, and G. Zussman. The resilience of wdm networks to probabilistic geographical failures. *IEEE/ACM Transactions on Networking (TON)*, 21(5):1525–1538, 2013.

[3] N. Alliance. NGMN 5G white paper. *White paper, Feb*, 2015.

[4] D. Baltrunas, A. Elmokashfi, and A. Kvalbein. Measuring the reliability of mobile broadband networks. In *Proceedings of the 2014 Conference on Internet Measurement Conference*, IMC '14, pages 45–58, New York, NY, USA, 2014. ACM. ISBN 978-1-4503-3213-2. doi: 10.1145/2663716.2663725. URL http://doi.acm.org/10.1145/2663716.2663725.

[5] D. Baltrūnas, A. Elmokashfi, and A. Kvalbein. Dissecting Packet Loss in Mobile Broadband Networks from the Edge. In *Proc. of INFOCOM*, 2015.

[6] D. Baltrunas, A. Elmokashfi, A. Kvalbein, and Ö. Alay. Investigating Packet Loss in Mobile Broadband Networks under Mobility. In *Proceddigns of IFIP Networking conference*, May 2016.

[7] N. Becker, A. Rizk, and M. Fidler. A measurement study on the application-level performance of LTE. In *Networking Conference, 2014 IFIP*, pages 1–9. IEEE, 2014.

[8] G. Chartrand and P. Zhang. *A first course in graph theory*. Courier Corporation, 2012.

[9] C. Chatfield. *The Analysis of Time Series: An Introduction, Sixth Edition*. Chapman & Hall/CRC Texts in Statistical Science. CRC Press, 2016. ISBN 9780203491683. URL https://books.google.no/books?id=qKzyAbdaDFAC.

[10] Y. Chen, N. Duffield, P. Haffner, W. ling Hsu, G. Jacobson, Y. Jin, S. Sen, S. Venkataraman, and Z. li Zhang. Understanding the Complexity of 3G UMTS Network Performance. In *IFIP Networking Conference*, 2013.

[11] *Cisco visual networking index Mobile Forecast, 2015 - 2020*. Cisco Systems, Inc., February 2016.

[12] CNN. *Why a massive cell phone outage hit the Southeast*, 2015. https://goo.gl/lp4Cr1.

[13] C. Cox. *An Introduction to LTE*. John Wiley & Sons Ltd., 1st edition, 2012. ISBN 9781119970385.

[14] R. Durairajan, P. Barford, J. Sommers, and W. Willinger. InterTubes: A study of the US long-haul fiber-optic infrastructure. In *ACM SIGCOMM Computer Communication Review*, volume 45, pages 565–578. ACM, 2015.

[15] A. Elmokashfi, A. Kvalbein, D. Baltrunas, J. Werme, and E. Arge. Robusthet i norske mobilnett tilstandsrapport 2014. Technical report, Oslo, 04/2015 2015.

[16] H. Elshaer, F. Boccardi, M. Dohler, and R. Irmer. Downlink and uplink decoupling: A disruptive architectural design for 5g networks. In *Global Communications Conference (GLOBECOM), 2014 IEEE*, pages 1798–1803. IEEE, 2014.

[17] T. Faremo. Telenor's Landsdekkende nett. In Fiberoptikk 2015, Trondheim, Norway, November 2015.

[18] G. P. Fettweis. The Tactile Internet: Applications and challenges. *IEEE Vehicular Technology Magazine*, 9(1):64–70, mar 2014. ISSN 1556-6072.

[19] FirstNet. http://www.firstnet.gov/.

[20] S. Forge, R. Horvitz, and C. Blackman. Is Commercial Cellular Suitable for Mission Critical Broadband? Technical report, European Comission, 2014.

[21] M. Garwood. EE wins lucrative emergency services contract. http://www.mobilenewscwp.co.uk/2015/12/10/ee-wins-7-billion-emergency-services-contract/, December 2015.

[22] P. I. Good. *Permutation, Parametric, and Bootstrap Tests of Hypotheses (Springer Series in Statistics)*. Springer-Verlag New York, Inc., Secaucus, NJ, USA, 2004. ISBN 038720279X.

[23] G. A. Hansen. Telenett i nordområdene - spesielle utfordringer. In Telecom World 2013, Longyearbyen, Norway, February 2013.

[24] J. Huang, F. Qian, A. Gerber, Z. M. Mao, S. Sen, and O. Spatscheck. A close examination of performance and power characteristics of 4G LTE networks. In *Proceedings of the 10th international conference on Mobile systems, applications, and services*, pages 225–238. ACM, 2012.

[25] J. Huang, F. Qian, Y. Guo, Y. Zhou, Q. Xu, Z. M. Mao, S. Sen, and O. Spatscheck. An In-depth Study of LTE: Effect of Network Protocol and Application Behavior on Performance. In *Proc. of SIGCOMM*, 2013.

[26] ICT-317669 METIS project. Deliverable D1.1 Scenarios, requirements and KPIs for 5G mobile and wireless system? https://www.metis2020.com/documents/deliverables/, 2013.

[27] R. Irmer, H. Droste, P. Marsch, M. Grieger, G. Fettweis, S. Brueck, H.-P. Mayer, L. Thiele, and V. Jungnickel. Coordinated multipoint: Concepts, performance, and field trial results. *IEEE Communications Magazine*, 49(2):102–111, 2011.

[28] P. Kelly. Mobile Broadband & the Future of Public Safety Networks from a Tetra Operator Perspective, April 2013. URL http://m.eu2013.ie/media/eupresidency/content/documents/Presentation-8.-15.50-Mobile-Broadband1.pptx.

[29] D. M. Kim and P. Popovski. Reliable uplink communication through double association in wireless heterogeneous networks. *IEEE Wireless Communications Letters*, 5(3):312–315, 2016.

[30] A. Kvalbein, D. Baltrūnas, J. Xiang, K. R. Evensen, A. Elmokashfi, and S. Ferlin-Oliveira. The Nornet Edge platform for mobile broadband measurements. *Elsevier Computer Networks special issue on Future Internet Testbeds*, 2014.

[31] L. Li, K. Xu, D. Wang, C. Peng, Q. Xiao, and R. Mijumbi. A Measurement Study on TCP Behaviors in HSPA+ Networks on High-speed Rails. In *Proc. of INFOCOM*, 2015.

[32] Lysneutvalget. Digital sårbarhet–sikkert samfunn, 2015.

[33] Nokia. 5G use cases and requirements, 2014.

[34] NRK. *Halve Norge var uten mobiltelefon*, 2011. https://goo.gl/E0WFKp.

[35] OpenSignal. The state of LTE. http://opensignal.com/reports/2015/09/state-of-lte-q3-2015/, September 2015.

[36] Osloeconomics. Konsekvensutredning - Alternativer for styrket robusthet i landsdekkende kjernenett. https://www.regjeringen.no/contentassets/fe88e9ea8a354bd1b63bc0022469f644/no/sved/3.pdf, August 2015.

[37] P. Popovski. Ultra-Reliable Communication in 5G Wireless Systems. In M. Latva-aho, R. Tafazolli, N. Rajatheva, L. M. Correia, and T. Rasheed, editors, *5GU*, pages 146–151. ICST, 2014. ISBN 978-1-63190-055-6. URL http://dblp.uni-trier.de/db/conf/5gu/5gu2014.html.

[38] F. Qian, Z. Wang, A. Gerber, Z. M. Mao, S. Sen, and O. Spatscheck. Characterizing Radio Resource Allocation for 3G Networks. In *Proc. of IMC*, 2010.

[39] S. Rosen, H. Luo, Q. A. Chen, Z. M. Mao, J. Hui, A. Drake, and K. Lau. Discovering Fine-grained RRC State Dynamics and Performance Impacts in Cellular Networks. In *Proc. of Mobicom*, 2014.

[40] S. Schütz, L. Eggert, S. Schmid, and M. Brunner. Protocol enhancements for intermittently connected hosts. *ACM SIGCOMM Computer Communication Review*, 35(3):5–18, 2005.

[41] M. Z. Shafiq, L. Ji, A. X. Liu, J. Pang, S. Venkataraman, and J. Wang. A first look at cellular network performance during crowded events. In *Proc. of SIGMETRICS*, 2013.

[42] B. Singh, Z. Li, O. Tirkkonen, M. A. Uusitalo, and P. Mogensen. Ultra-reliable communication in a factory environment for 5G wireless networks: link level and deployment study. In *Personal, Indoor, and Mobile Radio Communications (PIMRC), 2016 IEEE 27th Annual International Symposium on*, pages 1–5. IEEE, 2016.

[43] V. N. Swamy, P. Rigge, G. Ranade, A. Sahai, and B. Nikolić. Network coding for high-reliability low-latency wireless control. In *Wireless Communications and Networking Conference (WCNC), 2016 IEEE*, pages 1–7. IEEE, 2016.

[44] W. Tärneberg, M. Karaca, A. Robertsson, F. Tufvesson, and M. Kihl. Utilizing Massive MIMO for the Tactile Internet: Advantages and Trade-offs. In *IEEE SECON Workshops-Robotic Wireless Networks*. IEEE–Institute of Electrical and Electronics Engineers Inc., 2017.

[45] TETRA. https://tandcca.com/.

[46] TETRAPOL. http://www.tetrapol.com/.

[47] F. P. Tso, J. Teng, W. Jia, and D. Xuan. Mobility: A Double-Edged Sword for HSPA Networks. In *Proc. of MobiHoc*, 2010.

[48] Wirelesse2e. *Another Outage / More Lessons: Geo-redundancy Couldn't Prevent Verizon LTE Service Disruption*, 2011. https://goo.gl/Yv0IjH.

[49] Y. Xu and C. Fischione. Real-time scheduling in LTE for smart grids. In *Communications Control and Signal Processing (ISCCSP), 2012 5th International Symposium on*, pages 1–6. IEEE, 2012.

[50] L. Zhou. Vulnerability analysis of the physical part of the internet. *International journal of critical infrastructures*, 6(4):402–420, 2010.

The *Tick* Programmable Low-Latency SDR System

Haoyang Wu†, Tao Wang†, Zengwen Yuan‡, Chunyi Peng¶, Zhiwei Li†, Zhaowei Tan‡,

Boyan Ding†, Xiaoguang Li†, Yuanjie Li‡, Jun Liu†, Songwu Lu‡

†Peking University, ‡University of California, Los Angeles, ¶Purdue University

ABSTRACT

Tick is a new SDR system that provides programmability and ensures low latency at both PHY and MAC. It supports modular design and element-based programming, similar to the Click router framework [23]. It uses an accelerator-rich architecture, where an embedded processor executes control flows and handles various MAC events. User-defined accelerators offload those tasks, which are either computation-intensive or communication-heavy, or require fine-grained timing control, from the processor, and accelerate them in hardware. *Tick* applies a number of hardware and software co-design techniques to ensure low latency, including multi-clock-domain pipelining, field-based processing pipeline, separation of data and control flows, etc. We have implemented *Tick* and validated its effectiveness through extensive evaluations as well as two prototypes of 802.11ac SISO/MIMO and 802.11a/g full-duplex.

1 INTRODUCTION

Software-defined radio (SDR) allows users to build flexible and configurable wireless communication systems. A number of SDR platforms are already available for use for months or even years [2, 27, 32–35, 40]. However, today's requirements on SDR are different, given the latest technology push (e.g., 5G, wireless edge computing) and user demand pull (e.g., low-latency VR/AR applications, runtime control on drones and robotics). Consequently, the new challenge is to both offer sufficient programmability and ensure high performance; it has to be for both physical (PHY) and medium access control (MAC) layers. Unfortunately, we have found it hard to achieve both in the existing SDR systems.

The domain-specific challenge is that, wireless PHY and MAC differ in their data-flow and control-flow operations: (a) PHY is heavy in data-flow processing but lightweight on control flows; MAC needs complex control but little on data processing. (b) PHY works with simple pipeline stages for processing, whereas MAC needs complex branch instructions to perform event handling and control functions. (c) PHY is dominated by processing latency, whereas MAC is sensitive to timing. No existing software architecture nor hardware design solely addresses *all* these challenges to ensure both low latency and good programmability. We thus make a case for exploring software and hardware co-design solutions.

In this work, we describe the design and prototype of *Tick*. *Tick* is a new SDR system that seeks to the best of both worlds. On one hand, it provides a simple programming abstraction via graph of processing elements. Users write individual elements, which implement simple data processing or control-flow functions at PHY and MAC. Complete SDR system is built by connecting elements into the graph. This is made possible by adopting a novel accelerator-rich architecture, which consists of an embedded processor plus a number of user-defined accelerators. The processor focuses on control flows and various MAC event handling. Accelerators offload intensive computation, massive data transfer, fine-grained timing control from the processor, and accelerate these tasks in hardware.

Tick delivers high performance in low latency and high processing throughput using a number of software and hardware techniques. They include multi-clock-domain pipelining, field-based (rather than frame-based) processing pipeline, separation of data and control flows, and shadow registers for control flow and status report.

We have prototyped *Tick* on both PHY and MAC at a medium-priced FPGA development board. The implementation of *Tick* takes three-year efforts and includes PHY and MAC libraries offering 28 elements for PHY and 12 accelerators for MAC. We prototyped an 802.11ac SISO over an 80 MHz channel in *Tick* on Xilinx Kintex-7 FPGA kit. The measured latencies are 1.86 µs for PHY transmitter (Tx), 21.62 µs for PHY receiver (Rx), 17 µs for MAC Tx and 3 µs for MAC Rx. Compared with a simple reference design, *Tick* reduces latency by as much as 1.12 µs for PHY Tx (1.6× reduction, from 2.98 µs to 1.86 µs[1]), 26.39 µs for PHY Rx (2.2× reduction, from 48.01 µs to 21.62 µs), 8920 µs for MAC Tx (497× reduction, from 8938 µs to 18 µs) and 8926 µs for MAC Rx (2976×, from 8929 µs to 3 µs). While achieving low latency, *Tick* consumes moderate amount of FPGA resources (less than 30%). Our case studies of 802.11ac 2×2 MIMO and 802.11a/g full-duplex prototypes further confirm the programmability and latency performance of *Tick*.

2 A REFERENCE DESIGN FOR SDR

In this section, after introducing SDR, we describe a simple reference design. This reference adopts popular architectural choices at both PHY and MAC [22, 26, 33, 40]. We show that this popular design cannot meet the latency requirements of high-end wireless networking systems, e.g., 802.11ac [6].

[1]The latency reduction factor is defined as the reference design latency divided by the *Tick* latency. For example, we denote a reduction factor of 1.6 (2.98 µs/1.86 µs) as a 1.6× reduction for simplicity.

MobiCom '17, October 16–20, 2017, Snowbird, UT, USA

ACM ISBN 978-1-4503-4916-1/17/10...$15.00
https://doi.org/10.1145/3117811.3117834

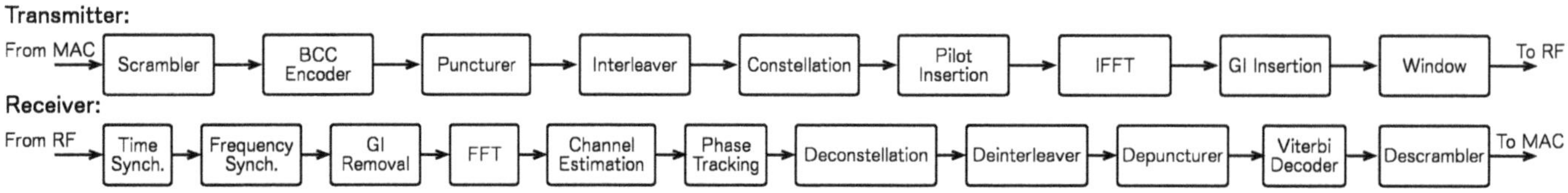

Figure 1: Transmitter and receiver modules for 802.11ac (SISO).

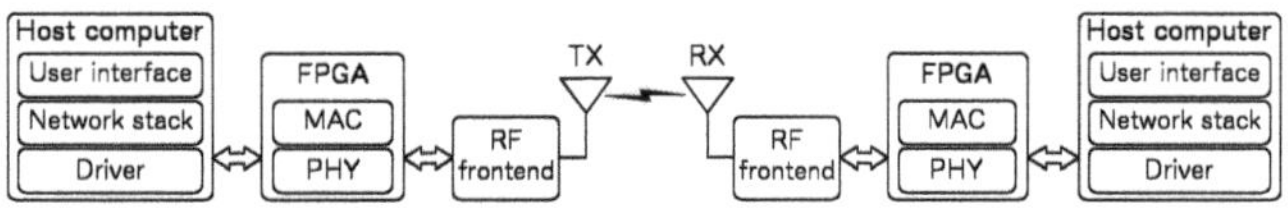

Figure 2: A typical SDR system: Transmitter and Receiver

2.1 SDR Primer

Shown in Figure 2, a typical SDR transmitter/receiver consists of four subsystems: a radio front-end (RF) that transmits/receives radio signals through antenna(s), the physical-layer (PHY) processing unit that uses PHY algorithms to convert the radio waveform into information bits or vice versa, the medium access control (MAC) processing unit that regulates transmissions over the shared wireless channel, and the interface to host computer that delivers higher-layer data packets to MAC or receives data from MAC.

We next briefly review both PHY and MAC. We use the 802.11ac SISO mode [6] as the reference for description. Note that practical wireless systems typically share similar design and algorithms, particularly at PHY.

PHY. PHY transforms information bits into a radio waveform, or vice versa. PHY has both control and data flows. The control flow is relatively simple. It sets configuration parameters. The data flow is more complex. It processes data using multiple functional blocks, which are pipelined together (illustrated in Figure 1). Data traverse these blocks. Each block performs certain computation on the transceived symbols. When the data rate is high (say, 433.3Mbps for 802.11ac SISO over 80 MHz channel, when using 256-QAM modulation type [6]), these PHY blocks require intensive processing power. Moreover, they operate on different types of data at different rates. In 802.11ac SISO, the scrambler works with one bit, while constellation maps each 6-bit block onto a complex symbol that uses two 16-bit numbers for 64-QAM.

From the latency standpoint, processing latency dominates the PHY unit. The required computation also increases with the communication speed.

MAC. MAC arbitrates channel access among all transceivers. Compared with PHY, MAC has more complex control flow but relatively simple data flow processing (e.g., CRC and (de)framing).

For its control flow, MAC needs to issue/accept various events and process each. Moreover, most MAC designs require timely response to critical events. Some even require accurate timing control at the granularity of microseconds. For example, in 802.11 CSMA/CA, short inter-frame spacing (SIFS) is needed between a DATA frame and an ACK frame. The current 802.11ac standard mandates SIFS to be 16 microseconds (μs) [6]. Fine-grained timing poses another challenge at MAC.

In summary, PHY and MAC differ in their data- and control-flow operations: (1) PHY is heavy in data flow processing but lightweight in control flow; in contrast, MAC needs complex control but is lightweight in data processing; (2) PHY typically uses simple pipeline stages for data processing, whereas MAC needs complex branch instructions to perform event handling; (3) PHY is dominated by processing latency, whereas MAC is sensitive to timing.

2.2 A Reference Design

Given the diverse requirements by PHY and MAC, people have explored different architectural techniques. In this section, we include them in a simple reference system. The goal is to (in)validate whether these existing ideas [22, 26, 33, 40] are effective to meet the latency requirements from 802.11ac.

Our reference design is for the 802.11ac SISO mode of Figure 1. At PHY, we use the pipelined modules, which all use a single global clock. Therefore, they form a single clock domain. This is the most popular technique used [22, 26, 40]. Moreover, processing is frame based. The entire frame traverses all pipeline stages. This is another popular technique reported by [22, 26, 33, 40].

At MAC, the reference uses the embedded processor based architecture. The processor handles all related event processing, including backoff, collision handling, timing control (SIFS, DIFS, etc.). More details on the reference are in §7.

2.3 Latency Performance

We next present the latency-related measurement results on the reference design. The 802.11ac standards [6] mandate the air transmission time for PHY, and SIFS between DATA and ACK frames. SIFS thus accounts for latency in both MAC and PHY. These timing requirements pose challenges to both PHY and MAC designs. Our experimental results show that, current reference SDR design cannot meet the stipulated timing requirements.

PHY. We test the 802.11ac prototype operating at 80 MHz channel width, using 64-QAM at 3/4 rate, for both the transmitter (Tx) and the receiver (Rx). Tx works at the maximum clock frequency 90 MHz, and Rx at the maximum clock frequency 45 MHz. We record the latency and the processing time for each frame. The latency is defined as the duration from the time the first incoming bit is received to the instant this first bit is processed and sent out. The processing delay is defined as the time it takes to process a whole frame.

The results are shown in Table 1. We make two observations. First, long latency is observed at the Rx side. It takes 48.01 μs for the first bit to be processed. However, latency at Tx is much shorter. Second, PHY receiver cannot meet the air transmission time deadline. Under 80 MHz channel, the air transmission time for a 100 B frame takes 44 μs, while a 1500 B frame (the maximum transmission unit size, MTU) takes 88 μs. To continuously process the stream of incoming frames, the PHY Rx should process each frame at least faster than the air transmission time plus SIFS. However, neither (1500 B) MTU-sized frame nor larger aggregated frame can catch up with the incoming speed. The (100 B) frame reception seems fine.

Reference Design	PHY		MAC	
	Tx	Rx	Tx	Rx
100 B:				
Latency	2.98 µs	48.01 µs	613 µs	604 µs
Proc. time[a]	23.85 µs	57.91 µs	615 µs	605 µs
1500 B:				
Latency	2.98 µs	48.01 µs	8938 µs	8929 µs
Proc. time[b]	44.88 µs	195.52 µs	8954 µs	8938 µs

[a] PHY air transmission time for 100 B is 44 µs.
[b] PHY air transmission time for 1500 B is 88 µs.

Table 1: Timing performance for the reference design.

However, when sending ACK to the sender (that needs 2.98 µs to prepare the first bit at PHY), the receiver does not have any budget left for its MAC (57.91 µs + 2.98 µs > 44 µs + 16 µs).

MAC. We show that the reference MAC, which relies on the embedded processor for processing, cannot meet the timing deadline. We test the CSMA/CA MAC using the MicroBlaze processor. We record the latency and the processing time for each frame at the MAC layer (Table 1).

We first observe long latency at both Tx and Rx. It takes more than 613 µs for the first byte to be processed for the small frame, and nearly 8938 µs for the MTU-sized frame. Second, SIFS timing cannot be met. MAC and PHY together substantially exceed SIFS (18.68 µs + 604 µs + 2.98 µs + 1 µs = 626.66 µs > 16 µs, details in §8). Furthermore, MAC alone contributes at least 604 µs. We thus make a case for exploring new architectural ideas for low-latency SDR.

3 ARCHITECTURE

In this section, we describe the architecture of *Tick*. *Tick* seeks to achieve low latency in SDR by applying hardware and software co-design techniques.

3.1 Components

We next introduce the main components in *Tick*.

Hardware Components. *Tick* uses two hardware components in its architecture: an FPGA board for PHY and MAC, and a commodity wide-band RF board. The FPGA-based prototyping offers maximum flexibility to explore hardware and software co-design ideas. The RF front-end offers a well-defined interface between digital and analog. It contains A/D, D/A, etc. It further supports single or multiple antennas, which enables SISO and MIMO operations.

Tick has two communication interfaces. One is between the host computer and FGPA using USB 3.0 or PCIe. The other is from the vendor's FMC interface to connect PHY and RF in low latency.

Software Components. The software stack in *Tick* provides the programming support and systems services for implementing various PHY and MAC protocols (Figure 3). The communication module facilitates massive data exchanges with the upper-layer IP protocol and the RF unit. Moreover, *Tick* provides a number of techniques to greatly improve the programmability and latency performance of PHY and MAC processing. To this end, the PHY and MAC libraries offer commonly used functions. The PHY and MAC runtime support allows for users to code, compile, and run their customized functions at ease.

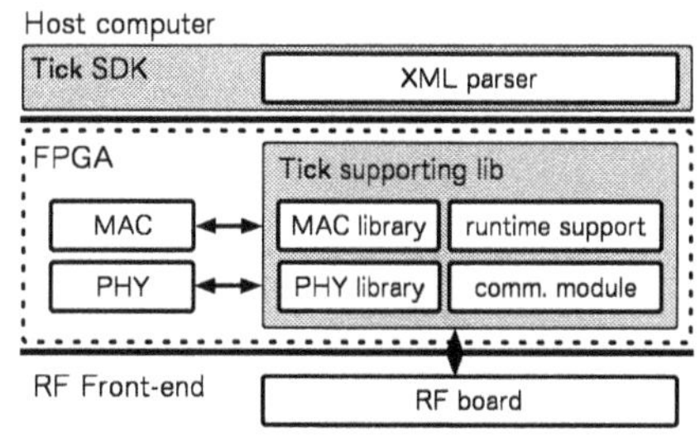

Figure 3: *Tick* software stack.

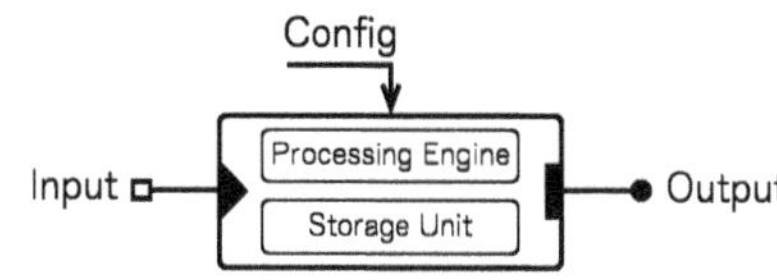

Figure 4: An *element* in *Tick*.

3.2 Programming *Tick*

To write a complete SDR system with both PHY and MAC, *Tick* provides a simple programming abstraction of "a graph of elements". A new wireless design is configured as a directed graph of elements. An element is the basic unit for modular programming in *Tick*. Each *element* represents a processing unit or function. All processing actions performed inside a function are encapsulated in an element. The edge, or connection, between two elements represents the route for message transfer from one element to the other. Therefore, the graph resembles the flowchart, with connections denoting message flow, and elements being actual objects that process messages.

Each element can have at most four components (Figure 4): the input and output ports, the processing engine (PE), the storage/memory unit, and the configurations. Ports are the endpoints of connections between elements, and each element can have a small number of ports for input and output. Messages are passed among elements via ports. PE implements the computation and processing needed by the element. The storage unit buffers the data or control information. Configurations enable us to set parameters and configurations for an element.

Elements are connected via ports. The connection is unidirectional. Each output port of an upstream element is thus connected to the input port of a downstream element. For simplicity, each port is only allowed for connect once. To offer flexibility, *Tick* provides special elements of multiplexer and demultiplexer for input merge and output split. In addition, an element without an input port is called a source, while an element without an outport port is a sink.

The embedded processor operates at the MAC layer only. It handles MAC event processing, offloads processing-heavy or communication-intensive tasks to MAC accelerators (a special class of elements to be elaborated next), and provides control and configurations on accelerators. However, it does not process MAC data frame directly.

Tick lets programmers use the standard XML language to perform several tasks for an element: connection of elements, memory/storage size, and parameters of interest. The coding of PE can be in high-level programming language HLS (High-Level Synthesis) C++ or in low-level language Verilog for FPGA.

Programming PHY is to write each PHY element in HLS C++ or Verilog, and interconnects them to form the pipeline. Users can use either XML file or our IDE (its GUI similar to GNU Radio) to specify

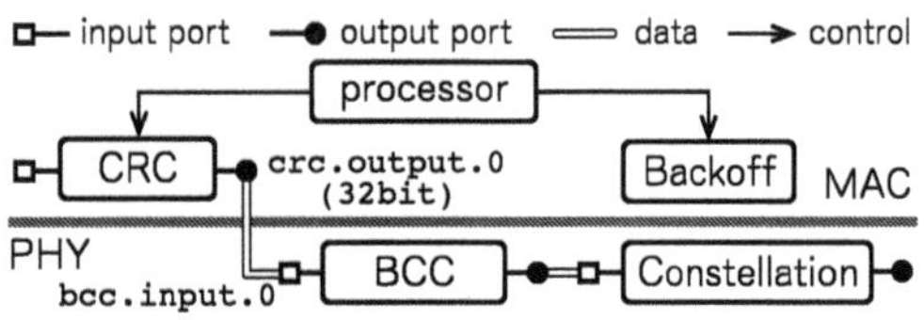

Figure 5: A toy example using *Tick*.

Program Snippet 1 Defining a BCC Encoder *element*

```
<name>bcc</name>
<input> <id>0</id> <width>32</width> </input>
<output> <id>0</id> <width>64</width> </output>
<configuration> <name>rate</name> <width>16</width> </configuration>
```

Program Snippet 2 Interconnecting MAC and PHY *elements*

```
<!-- interconnect elements in PHY -->
<connect>
    <port>bcc.output.0</port>
    <port>constellation.input.0</port>
</connect>
<!-- interconnection between MAC CRC and PHY BCC -->
<connect>
    <port>crc.output.0</port>
    <port>bcc.input.0</port>
</connect>
```

the configuration for interconnetion. Programming MAC needs to work with both the embedded processor and accelerators. Coding the embedded processor using API is straightforward (details in §7). Users write event-handling programs for MAC in C. An accelerator is also a special class of element. Programming it can be in HLS C++ or Verilog. Users can call common and systems accelerators (e.g., CRC, random backoff, timer). The configurations for accelerators are also via XML.

An Illustrative Example. We use a toy example (Figure 5) to show how to program the MAC and PHY chain. Assume the user builds a simple SDR transmitter, which has the following functions: if not in MAC backoff, the sender starts CRC computation and sends the frame to PHY, which has two pipeline stages of BCC encoding and constellation mapping.

The MAC layer in the resulting design consists of the embedded processor, a CRC accelerator, and a Backoff accelerator; The PHY layer has a BCC Encoder element and a Constellation element. Given this model, the user needs to take three steps.

First, the user populates *elements* using the template provided by *Tick*. It is done by defining `input`, `output` and `configuration` for the *element*. Program Snippet 1 shows the definition for the BCC Encoder. It defines the *element* name, input, output and one parameter (`rate`). The data widths are defined accordingly. *Tick* will automatically generate the corresponding Verilog module code, while the user uses either Verilog or HLS C++ to code the PE. The Constellation, CRC, and Backoff elements are defined similarly.

Second, the user interconnects the *elements* to make a working pipeline. It is also done using XML, as shown in Program Snippet 2. Note that all MAC accelerators are connected to the embedded processor by default.

Finally, the user implements proper MAC event-handling branch instructions within the processor. It thus interacts with each accelerator via reading and writing to corresponding registers (called CSR) through API, as shown in Program Snippet 3.

Program Snippet 3 MAC processor control logic

```
Reg_interrupt(INT_BackoffDone, handle_backoff); // register a Backoff
Write_CSR(backoffReqAddr, 1); // start Backoff
Write_CSR(crcReqAddr, 1); // calculate CRC

void handle_backoff() { // backoff interruption handler routine
  Write_CSR(backoffReqAddr, 0); // reset Backoff
  Write_CSR(sendToPHYReqAddr, 1); // send out CRC
}
```

4 DESIGN OVERVIEW

In this section, we provide a design overview for *Tick*.

4.1 Design for Programmability

Tick supports high programmability at both PHY and MAC. The overall idea is to carefully instrument an element, so that it balances latency performance and modular design.

PHY. Proper design of PHY elements enables a user to readily program PHY via the pipelined operation of such elements.

A PHY element uses its input/out ports to separate data flow (message passing) from control flow (configurations, or dynamic parameters such as frame size for the current frame). Each port needs to specify its bit-width (i.e., how much bits are needed). Control flow uses a small number of bits, and can be stored internally using the shadow control and status registers (CSRs). They *shadow* the CSRs from a special PHY accelerator, which passes information between MAC and PHY; see Figure 6 for an illustration.

Data flow needs a large number of bits. They are transferred between two connected elements via asynchronous FIFO (aFIFO). aFIFO provides the data queue for an upstream element and a downstream one; see Figure 7 for an illustration. It can also be viewed as a special element, which the user does not need to be aware of. It is automatically generated between elements by *Tick*'s runtime support.

Each PHY element has a special configuration parameter, i.e., its operating clock. This parameter enables multi-clock-domain pipeline, as elaborated in §5.

MAC. The embedded processor commands the control flow and configurations for accelerators. However, it does not process data messages directly. Accelerators offload computing, communication, and timing tasks from the processor. They directly work with data messages. Data are passed among involved accelerators via DMA, thus bypassing the processor.

An accelerator is a special class of element. It has all four components of an element. Each accelerator can also run on its own local clock. The embedded processor is a general-purpose processor, and we use MicroBlaze in our prototype. By default configuration, all accelerators are connected to the processor.

Passing Information between MAC and PHY. MAC and PHY need to pass critical information at runtime for efficient processing, e.g., current frame size. This is done by implementing an accelerator element in *Tick*. Therefore, the processor operates at the MAC layer only, but uses the special accelerator to pass information between MAC and PHY.

4.2 Design for Low Latency

Tick explores several software and hardware co-design techniques, to reduce latency and sustain high processing throughput. At PHY,

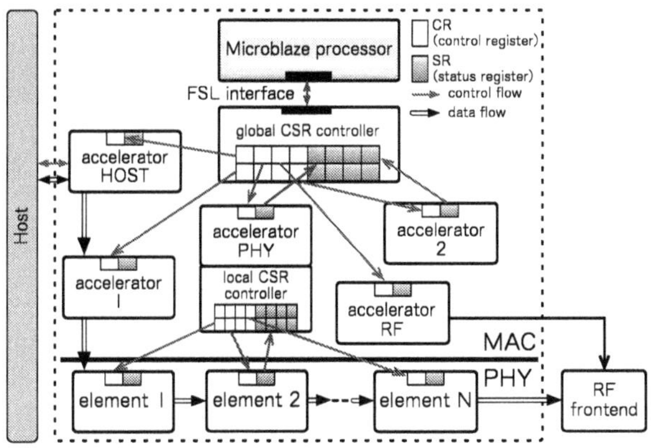

Figure 6: Control flow for both MAC and PHY in *Tick*.

two ideas are applied. First, multi-clock-domain pipelining (MCDP) lets each element on the pipeline operates with its separately generated clock. This greatly simplifies the global clock distribution, which is quite challenging to realize for ultra-high-speed PHY processing. Second, we apply field-based, rather than frame-based, processing to further reduce latency. It can customize the processing pipeline for different fields of the PHY frame. No all fields need to traverse the entire pipeline, thus reducing overall latency.

At MAC, we propose the accelerator-rich, embedded processor-aided design. It efficiently handles various events while meeting the timing deadline defined in tens of microseconds (e.g., SIFS) in modern wireless systems.

4.3 Aiming at the Best of Both Worlds

Tick is designed to be easily programmable and readily extendable, while simultaneously ensuring low latency. It differs from all existing SDR platforms, which do not aim to achieve both goals. Take the popular WARP system as an example. On one hand, the hardware-centric design by WARP (say, 802.11n) can meet the SIFS/DIFS timing requirements [36]. However, such fine-tuned, carefully instrumented designs tightly couple the PHY function blocks at the cost of easy programmability. Modification would not be easy, if impossible at all, without precise estimation on the entire signal processing flow. On the other hand, WARP offers a highly programmable option for PHY via WARPLab. However, WARPLab cannot meet the stringent 802.11 timing requirement, as concurred by several independent studies [21, 37, 37, 39, 41]. Consequently, it is even more challenging, if not feasible at all, to extend the current 802.11n design to the next-generation 802.11ac family.

Tick overcomes this dilemma by aiming at both goals. It introduces aFIFO to enable multiple-clock-domain pipeline (details in §5). Each aFIFO does incur small latency, which is, however, offset by the benefits gained from loosely-coupled modules and flexibilities to update anyone. Moreover, field-based processing significantly reduces the efforts to bypass bottleneck modules, e.g., IFFT. In contrast, a hardwired SDR design saves little on the aFIFO-incurred latency between modules, but results in high cost on diminished flexibility, extendability, and programmability.

We next elaborate on the design details in §5 and §6.

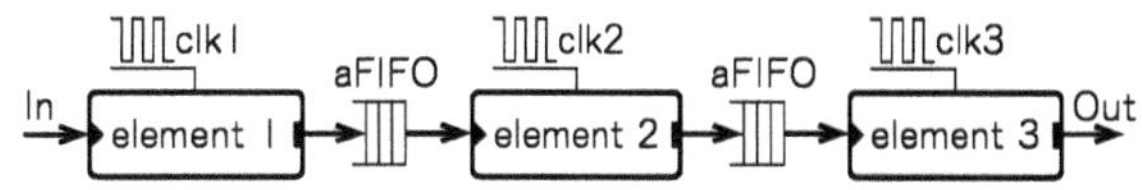

Figure 7: Multi-clock-domain pipeline (MCDP) in PHY.

5 MINIMIZING LATENCY AT PHY

We now describe the two techniques at PHY: multi-clock-domain pipeline and field-based pipeline processing.

5.1 Multi-Clock-Domain Pipeline (MCDP)

The first technique is multi-clock-domain pipeline (MCDP) [28, 30] of elements (Figure 7). In a nutshell, MCDP uses a globally-asynchronous, locally-synchronous clocking style [20]. Each element operates with its clock. Multiple adjacent elements can use the same clock to form a domain. Synchronous design can be used in each domain. Finally, all elements are interconnected to form the cross-domain PHY pipeline.

The choice of MCDP is motivated by the SDR PHY. First, it accommodates the diversity in computing workload of different elements at PHY. Second, it enables to customize the PHY pipeline stages to the operation demands of individual elements. Third, it offers better modular design at PHY. The design of each domain is no longer constrained. It can optimize the tradeoffs among clock speed, latency, and exploitation of element-level parallelism.

Our experience shows that, MCDP is not very effective at the transmitter of 802.11ac (Figure 1). This is because the IFFT module poses as the single processing bottleneck; adjusting clocks at other modules does not lead to sizable latency reduction. However, MCDP is quite effective at the receiver. The elements of Viterbi Decoder, FFT, and Time Synchronization all pose as processing bottlenecks. Using local clocks helps to adjust and match the bottleneck speeds.

We need to address three issues for MCDP: (1) How to enable message passing among elements across domains? (2) How to further reduce the latency overhead due to too many domains? (3) How to reduce latency when MAC exchanges information with PHY elements in different clock domains? We next elaborate on our solution to each.

Asynchronous FIFO for Inter-Domain Communication. Inter-domain communications in MCDP use explicit message-passing channels to communicate messages between elements in different domains.

In this work, we leverage the low-latency aFIFO for asynchronous communication across domains [10]. The design uses full and empty signals to indicate the occupancy of the FIFO. The empty and full signals are generated by FIFO itself. The empty signal is synchronized to the consumer's clock, while the full signal is synchronized to the producer's clock.

Grouping to Reduce Clock Domains. Inter-domain synchronization via aFIFO increases the number of clock cycles in MCDP. The issue becomes severe, if each element runs at its own clock and many aFIFOs are used.

Our solution gathers multiple adjacent elements together to form a group. Elements in a group operate at the same clock. This way, we can reduce the number of aFIFOs. Grouping balances the tradeoff among processing capability of each element, the communication delay due to aFIFO, and the number of pipeline bottlenecks.

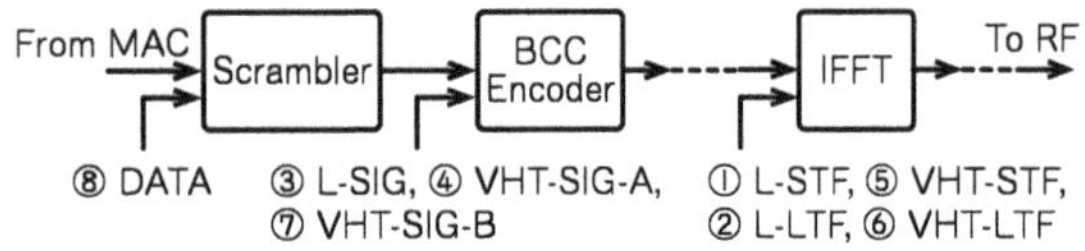

Figure 8: Field-based processing in 802.11ac PHY.

We automate the process of grouping elements. We compute the overall latency with grouping (i.e., reduced aFIFO but increased latency at elements in a group) and without grouping (minimal latency at each element but increased latency due to more aFIFOs). Whenever the grouped latency is smaller, we merge the element to the group; otherwise, we start a new group for the element.

Latency on PHY and MAC Interactions. We exploit shadow registers for efficient information exchange between PHY and MAC. The shadow register design provides the ability to load or shadow the contents of a primary CSR into a shadow CSR at the completion of a stored instruction. This is accomplished in 6 to 8 clock cycles (far below 1 µs given our clock frequency), with all registers being shadowed. We defer the discussion of CSRs to §6.

5.2 Field-Based Pipeline Processing

The next technique is to exploit the field-based, rather than frame-based, pipeline at PHY. Given the different fields of PHY data, we customize the pipeline (both which stages and the number of stages) to speed up computation. Therefore, only the data will go through the entire pipeline, while other PHY fields (headers and signals) only traverse a portion of the pipeline stages. We apply this technique at both the transmitter and the receiver of software radio.

The field-based pipelining is based on the observation that different fields play different roles at PHY processing. For example, the long/short training fields are used for channel estimation and training purpose only, and the content of these bits is not needed. Therefore, they do not need to traverse all stages of the entire pipeline. Instead, they can bypass certain stages, thus reducing latency. Moreover, this further enables concurrent processing along different parallel paths for different fields, contributing to further latency optimization. Figure 8 illustrates an example.

Customized Pipeline Stages for Fields. We apply domain knowledge to customize the pipeline at both Tx and Rx.

Take 802.11ac SISO of Figure 8 as an example. Note that PHY in many other wireless technologies share similar features. At the transmitter, both long and short training sequences enter the pipeline from IFFT, signals enter from the BCC encoder, but data will traverse the entire pipeline starting from the Scrambler. At the receiver, the short training sequence exits the pipeline after the Frequency-offset element, while the long training sequence exits after Channel-estimation. The signals exit after the Viterbi-decoder element, while the data go through the entire pipeline.

Control Flow for Fields. Compared with frame-based processing, field-based pipeline reduces processing latency but at the cost of finer-grained control flow at the field (but not the frame) level. The specific control information to enable field-based pipelining includes: how many fields in the frame, the order of fields, the starting point of a field and the field length, and the modulation type for each field.

To facilitate field-based processing, *Tick* automates the generation of control flow for fields. To this end, a user only needs to fill in the configuration table for PHY fields. Such configuration parameters are passed to each related element. The customized pipeline can then be constructed for each field of the PHY frame.

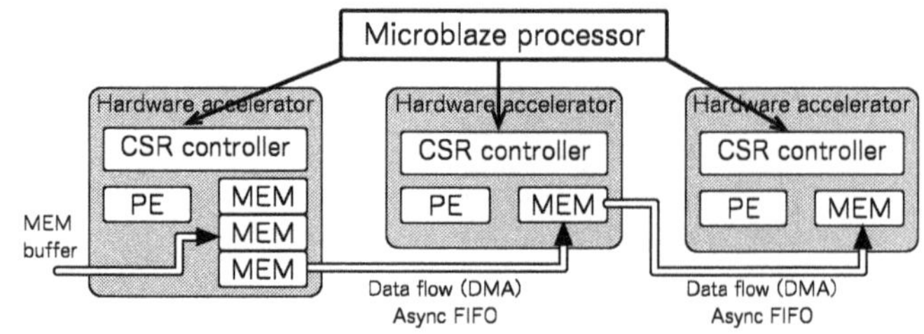

Figure 9: MAC layer accelerators architecture.

6 DESIGN FOR LOW-LATENCY MAC

We now describe our efforts to reduce MAC latency. Following the industry practice, we first split MAC functions into two portions. The high MAC implements functions of accepting frames from higher-layer IP modules, adding frame headers, and handling management frames (beacons, etc.). It is non-time-critical, thus being implemented in the device driver on the host computer. The low MAC copes with timing-critical functions; this is the focus here.

We adopt the accelerator-rich design [11, 24], aided by an embedded processor (Figure 9). The processor is definitely needed, to preserve programmability on event-based handling at MAC. However, as we have seen in §2.3, the embedded processor only design cannot ensure low latency. Offloading computation-intensive tasks from the processor does help to reduce latency. However, it is not sufficient. We further explore the idea of decoupling control and data flows as elaborated next.

Decoupling Control and Data Flows. We separate the control and data flows at the MAC layer. The control-flow communication between the processor and an accelerator is done by read and write operations on CSRs. The embedded processor works with the global CSRs only via the FSL (Fast Simplex Link) interface, while each accelerator retains a copy of shadow CSRs locally. See Figure 6 for an illustration. For a control register (CR) within CSRs, the embedded processor performs write operation only, whereas the accelerator executes read operation only. In contrast, given a status register (SR), the processor performs read operation only, while the accelerator runs write operation only. Given the separation of CRs and SRs, no read/write conflicts are possible for the control flow between the processor and each accelerator. Given the low volume of control flow, no sizable latency is observed.

Figure 6 further shows that, we have three levels of CSRs. The local CSRs at each accelerator shadow the global CSRs, and the CSRs at any PHY element further shadows the CSRs at the PHY accelerator (that handles information passing between MAC and PHY layers).

As illustrated in Figure 9, data flow among accelerators leverages the memory unit in each accelerator. Message exchanges are pipelined between communicating accelerators. While the data is read from the memory of the previous accelerator, data are concurrently written into the next accelerator. Therefore, the accelerator is not blocked in processing by the massive data exchanges via DMA. When accelerators use multi-clock domains, data exchange can also be done via the asynchronous FIFOs.

Program Snippet 4 *Tick* API for low MAC

```
// write value to the control register
void Write_CSR(unsigned int addr, unsigned int val);

// return value stored in the status register
int Read_CSR(unsigned int addr);
```

7 IMPLEMENTATION

We first present *Tick*'s baseline implementation, and then provide more details on PHY, MAC and other issues.

Prototype Environment. We prototype *Tick* with both PHY and low MAC, with the 802.11ac [6] SISO as our base implementation. It is done on the Xilinx Kintex-7 FPGA KC705 Evaluation Kit [38]. The embedded processor is MicroBlaze. The interfaces between host computer and the FPGA board include both USB 3.0 (converted by CYUSB3KIT-003 explorer kit [14, 15] to FMC interface) and PCIe [17, 18]. We select a commodity RF board using AD9371 [1] with the FMC interface. The RF front-end is capable of transmitting and receiving two 80 MHz channels within the frequency range from 300 MHz to 6 GHz. Figure 10 shows the *Tick* system (without the host computer).

The *Tick* library is programmed on Ubuntu 14.04. Our implementation results in 18 098 lines-of-code (LoC) in Verilog for PHY (8267 LoC for PHY Tx, 9831 LoC for PHY Rx), and 214 LoC in XML (96 LoC for connection and 118 for module definition. The MAC consists of 7412 LoC in Verilog HDL for accelerators, and another 2034 LoC in C for the embedded processor logic. To support connectivity and programmability, the *Tick* library has 4226 lines of driver code in C to communicate with the host driver and 1253 LoC in Python for the XML parser.

Runtime Support. *Tick* is offered as a standalone library to users. In PHY modules, *Tick* provides 28 standard elements written in Verilog to support 802.11a/g [5], 802.11n [5] and 802.11ac [6] protocols. They follow algorithms/specifications from the wireless standards. For example, we provide FFT-64, FFT-128, FFT-256, Viterbi Decoder, and Channel Estimation elements. In MAC modules, *Tick* provides 12 accelerators to support programmable MAC, including CRC-32, Backoff, Global Timer, communication accelerators that interact with PHY, RF and host computer, etc.

As a result, programmers only need to use XML configuration files to call PHY elements/MAC accelerators from the *Tick* library and interconnect them, similar to Program Snippet 2. We implement an XML parser in Python to convert user-defined configurations into Verilog HDL code for the elements/accelerators. Users can use Vivado Logic Analyzer provided by Xilinx to debug their implementation.

API. *Tick* provides two levels of APIs, one for low MAC and the other for host control logic. The API for low MAC controls element/accelerator via CSR, as Program Snippet 4 shows two example cases. The API for host-level control has three aspects, including API for data (e.g., send data frames from host to MAC using DMA), API for interrupts (e.g., register an interrupt at host), and API for control (e.g., get/set config parameters).

7.1 PHY Issues

Implementing an Element. In addition to the default PHY elements provided by current *Tick*, users can readily customize their own ones. They can create a template in XML, fill in the various parameters, and write PE in Verilog or HLS C++.

(MHz)	Scrambler	BCC	Puncture	Interleaver	Constellation	Insert	IFFT	GI
Max	500	600	600	430	650	460	90	430
Tick	500	500	500	400	500	400	90	400

(a) PHY Tx

(MHz)	Time sync.	Freq. offset	GI	FFT	Channel est.	Phase	Decons-tell.	Deint-leaver	Depunc-turer	Viterbi	Descr-ambler
Max	45	120	710	100	340	460	420	460	510	170	710
Tick	45	100	500	100	333	333	333	333	500	167	510

(b) PHY Rx

Table 2: Working frequencies for *Tick*-PHY using MCDP.

Choosing Clock Frequencies for MCDP. We implement MCDP by providing maximum clock frequency that each element can run on the given FPGA board. Due to FPGA resource and layout constraints, the working clock frequency may not reach the ideal maximum value. The clock frequencies *Tick* used on our FPGA board are listed in Table 2.

Eliminating Jitter Incurred by aFIFO. Another challenge comes from the strict timing requirement to send a frame over the air. For example, full-duplex system must be aligned for each I/Q sample [4, 8, 12, 21]. However, the aFIFO between elements introduces an uncertain latency jitter, which can be up to $\pm$ 0.15 μs. We eliminate this jitter in *Tick* by leveraging the global clock timer provided by MAC. Jitter-sensitive aFIFOs will fetch a timestamp from the global clock when the data can be sent out. The jitter is thus cancelled since the aFIFO's sending times are aligned.

Grouping Elements to Avoid Resource Overuse. Due to the clock resource constraint, the user may not use a separate clock for every element. *Tick* automatically analyzes adjacent elements to determine whether they should be grouped together. The elements in the same group use the same clock.

Handling Field-Based Processing. The field-based processing follows the configuration table specified by users. Such a table is two-dimensional, specifying field length and how it should be processed by each element. Next, our XML parser automatically generates a corresponding table in FPGA and creates shadow registers in each element. The element works immediately, once the corresponding field of incoming data is ready.

A challenge is to guarantee correct ordering. We adopt the "stop-and-wait" strategy in processing fields. The configuration table also regulates the field order. The later fields must wait until the early fields have been processed.

7.2 MAC Issues

Global Controller via CSRs. In our accelerator-rich architecture, the embedded processor controls each accelerator via CSRs. To provide scalable control over multiple accelerators, we define shared control registers in the global CSRs. The shared control registers can be read by multiple accelerators, so that global parameters can be distributed efficiently.

The control-flow latency mainly comes from the delay of reading/writing a register, which costs 5 to 6 clock cycles. We reduce such latency between embedded processor and CSR to 2 to 3 clock cycles, by reading/writing to consecutive addresses. Taking the latency caused by aFIFO between global CSR and shadow CSR into consideration (6 to 8 clock cycles). The entire control-flow latency between embedded processor and CSR in *Tick* is 11 to 14 clock cycles.

Implementing Accelerators. We implement four types of accelerators in MAC: computation-intensive accelerators (e.g., CRC checksum), timing-critical accelerators (e.g., Backoff), interface processing accelerators (e.g., interact with Host/PHY layer), and accelerators for grouped small modules (e.g., assemble ACK).

1. Computation-intensive accelerators. We offload computationally intensive CRC checksum in *Tick* to accelerators, so that the processor does not get stuck in fetching large data.

2. Timing-critical accelerators. We provide timing-related accelerators with access to a shared global clock and timestamp. For the processor, *Tick* uses a dedicated bus to reduce the latency of reading the timer value. Such a timing control mechanism avoids the significant delay and timing errors if reading the clock from the register.

The timeout notification from one accelerator to another is done through timestamp passing. The source accelerator first increments the global timer value it reads to the expected timeout value, and passes it to the processor as a timestamp. The processor then passes the timestamp to the timeout accelerator. Finally, when the timeout accelerator counts to the expected timestamp, it starts to alarm an event. The clock calibration unit in each time-related accelerator is also implemented using timestamp passing. It computes the latency offset based on the value it reads.

3. Interface processing accelerators. We next implement the accelerator for communicating with the host and with PHY. The host accelerator *prefetches* data from the host computer. It thus needs large memory to buffer data, and *Tick* sets eight frames as its buffer memory size. We also implement the PHY accelerator to provide isolation and control at the MAC layer. It communicates with the CSRs in each PHY element.

4. Accelerator for grouped small elements. Finally we use an accelerator for grouped small elements to reduce control overhead. Due to their relatively simple logic, one accelerator suffices to handle. We put assemble ACK, frame check, set retry bit into this accelerator in *Tick*.

7.3 Other Issues

Choosing Interface between RF and PHY Boards. Different RF boards introduce different latencies because they use different interfaces. For example, USRP N210 [16] uses the Ethernet interface, which incurs over 10 µs delay due to the Ethernet protocol. Therefore, we choose AD9371 [1] that adopts the FMC interface (a low-latency parallel data bus).

Choosing Interface between Host and MAC Board. Different interfaces between host and MAC introduce different latency. We have considered both PCIe and USB 3.0; they both provide sufficient throughput to 802.11. Our experiment shows that, the average latency of the PCIe interface (15.76 µs) is lower than that of USB 3.0 (53.25 µs). Since we implement a host accelerator which prefetches data from the host, the latency effect is offset. We thus choose USB 3.0, which is more accessible for laptops or even tablet PCs.

Dual-Interface Driver. We implement two interfaces when developing the *Tick* driver at the host, one to the user space and the other to the TCP/IP stack. The user-space interface provides direct access to FPGA at the user space for debugging. The network interface connects to the host's mac80211 interface (link-layer driver) in the kernel, so that the *Tick* can be used as an 802.11 device.

	Tick	PHY Tx	PHY Rx
SISO:			
Latency		1.86 µs	21.62 µs
Proc. time		21.26 µs	24.32 µs
MIMO:			
Latency		1.85 µs	23.57 µs
Proc. time		23.14 µs	26.28 µs

(a) 100 B

	Tick	PHY Tx	PHY Rx
SISO:			
Latency		1.86 µs	21.62 µs
Proc. time		42.07 µs	61.85 µs
MIMO:			
Latency		1.85 µs	23.57 µs
Proc. time		32.56 µs	43.55 µs

(b) 1500 B

Table 3: PHY latency and processing time of *Tick* 802.11ac.

8 EVALUATION

We first demonstrate that *Tick* achieves low-latency using benchmarks on PHY (§8.1), MAC (§8.2) and software and hardware interfaces (§8.3). Next, we assess the overall performance of *Tick* with latency, throughput, correctness, resource consumption, coding effort and comparison with state-of-the-art SDRs (§8.4). In this section, we mainly use 802.11ac SISO. More assessment of *Tick*'s extension for two case studies of 802.11ac MIMO and full duplex is presented in §9.

8.1 PHY

We implement and evaluate *Tick*-PHY design using the same configuration as the reference 802.11ac SISO design (§2). We have 9 elements in PHY Tx and 11 elements in PHY Rx. Our PHY implementation uses 64-QAM at 3/4 rate operating over 80 MHz channel for both Tx and Rx. We test two frame sizes: 100 B and 1500 B.

MCDP Performance. We first gauge MDCP performance at PHY. With MCDP, the overall latency and the processing time are reduced for both Tx and Rx at PHY (see SISO in Table 3).

For PHY Rx, the latency decreases from 48.01 µs (reference design in §2) to 21.62 µs, about 2.2× reduction. Note that, this latency remains identical for both frame sizes, because it takes the same amount of time for the first bit to be received and processed. *Tick* reduces processing time using MCDP as well. For small frame (100 B), the processing time decreases from 57.91 µs to 24.32 µs, 2.4× reduction. The reduction is even greater for the MTU frame (1500 B), from 195.52 µs to 61.85 µs (3.2× reduction).

For PHY Tx, *Tick* drops the latency from 2.98 µs to 2.49 µs (1.2× reduction). For small frames, the processing time changes from 23.85 µs to 21.89 µs (1.1× reduction). For MTU-sized frames, the processing time reduces from 44.88 µs to 42.70 µs (1.1× reduction).

MCDP Latency Reduction Analysis. The latency reduction achieved by MCDP is mainly through clock frequency speed up on elements. Specifically, there are three bottleneck elements in PHY Rx: time synchronization, FFT and Viterbi decoder, whose processing clock cycles are an-order-of-magnitude more than other elements. In the reference design, all three work at the lowest frequency (45 MHz). Using *Tick*, clock frequency for FFT is 100 MHz (2.2× speedup), and Viterbi decoder uses 167 MHz (3.7× speedup), as shown in Table 2b. For PHY Tx, latency reduction is also achieved through clock frequency speed up. However, PHY TX only has a single bottleneck in IFFT. Therefore, latency reduction at Tx is not as much as at Rx.

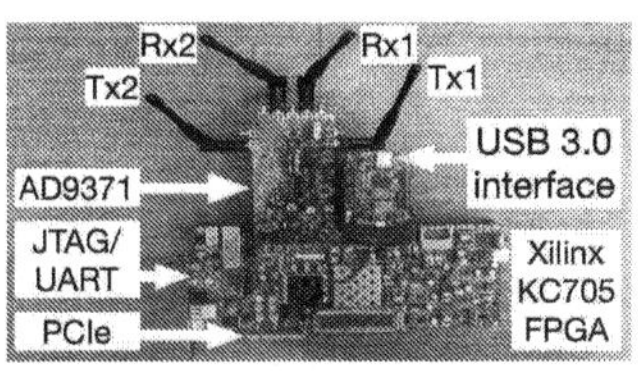

Figure 10: *Tick* system (w/o host computer).

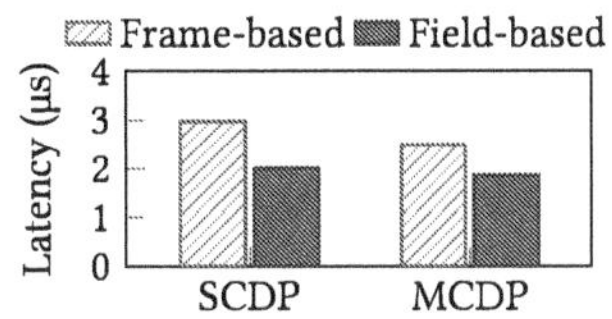

Figure 11: Field-based processing reduces latency (PHY Tx).

Tick	MAC Tx	MAC Rx
Latency	17 μs	3 μs
Proc. time	18 μs	4 μs

(a) 100 B

Tick	MAC Tx	MAC Rx
Latency	18 μs	3 μs
Proc. time	34 μs	19 μs

(b) 1500 B

Table 4: MAC latency and processing time w/ accelerators.

Field-Based Processing. Field-based processing further reduces latency over frame-based processing. We test both SCDP and MCDP in *Tick*. Figure 11 shows that, using field-based processing, the latency reduction is 0.97 μs (2.98 μs to 2.01 μs) for SCDP design. For MCDP, it reduces 0.63 μs (2.49 μs to 1.86 μs) for latency. The latency reduction is the same for both frame sizes.

Field-Based Processing Latency Reduction Analysis. In 802.11ac, field-based processing can start only as early as IFFT. The latency of the upstream elements is thus reduced. In 802.11ac, the reduced latency is visible but not significant. This is because IFFT, being the main latency contributor, is not skipped. Other 802.11 variants, e.g., 802.11a/g, may observe larger reduction by applying field-based processing, if the latency bottleneck element can be skipped. To meet the stringent SIFS timing requirement, every latency reduction factor matters. As an optimization technique, field-based processing further pushes latency reduction at PHY to the limit.

8.2 MAC

Accelerator-Based Latency Reduction. With the accelerator-based MAC architecture, *Tick* successfully reduces latency by more than *two orders of magnitude*. Table 4 summarizes the results.

For the Rx chain, the overall latency drops from 604 μs to 3 μs (201× reduction) for a small frame (100 B). *Tick* achieves 151× reduction (from 605 μs to 4 μs) in processing a complete frame. For MTU frame (1500 B), the overall latency reduction is 2976×, from 8929 μs to 3 μs. The processing time decreases from 8938 μs to 19 μs (470× reduction) in processing a full frame.

On the Tx chain for small frame (100 B), the overall latency drops from 613 μs to 17 μs (36× reduction); the processing time for a full frame drops from 615 μs to 18 μs (34× reduction). For MTU frame (1500 B), the overall latency decreases 497×, from 8938 μs to 18 μs. The processing delay for a full frame changes from 8954 μs to 34 μs (263× reduction).

Latency Reduction Analysis. The accelerator-rich architecture of *Tick*, which supports and coordinates multiple accelerators, is also the key enabler for low latency. Table 5 shows the latency breakdown for the reference design (§2). For both Tx and Rx, the latency has five factors: (L1) control flow latency at the interface between MAC and host (Tx)/PHY (Rx); (L2) processing time on the MAC frame header in the processor; (L3) the time to load data to the processor via DMA; (L4) the time to compute CRC checksum in the processor; and (L5) the time to send the frame to PHY (Tx), or to the host (Rx) . Among them, L1 and L5 are necessary overheads to control MAC and send data to the next stage. *Tick* does not effectively reduce these two factors. However, the two accelerators we implemented in *Tick* reduce L2, L3, and L4, effectively. The frame header accelerator modifies/checkes the header for data frame and reduces L2. The CRC accelerator offloads calculation from the processor, thus reducing the latency for L3 and L4.

Latency Breakdown	Tx		Rx	
	100 B	1500 B	100 B	1500 B
L1. Control information to MAC	12 μs	12 μs	<1 μs	<1 μs
L2. Frame header processing	10 μs	10 μs	12 μs	12 μs
L3. DMA data to processor	31 μs	447 μs	32 μs	448 μs
L4. CRC checksum calculation	560 μs	8469 μs	560 μs	8469 μs
L5. Transfer to PHY(Tx)/Host (Rx)	2 μs	16 μs	1 μs	15 μs

Table 5: MAC latency breakdown of the reference design.

In the reference design, L2, L3, and L4 together form the major latency bottleneck (at least 600 μs for the small frame and 8900 μs for the MTU-sized frame). Using accelerators, *Tick* reduces them to <6 μs for Tx and <3 μs for Rx (compared with Table 4). Note that, ad hoc design practice which accelerates CRC or frame header alone, still cannot meet the SIFS timing requirement.

8.3 Software and Hardware Co-design

Latency Overhead. The interfaces between MAC and PHY, PHY and RF front-end are two factors contributing to potentially large latency overhead. However, neither is an issue in *Tick*. The latency between PHY and MAC comes from aFIFO, which takes 6 to 8 clock cycles to feed the data from MAC to PHY. Under the maximum clock frequency (100 MHz) that aFIFO runs, it takes less than 0.08 μs for PHY to receive a data bit sent from MAC. For the AD9371 RF board, the latency at the RF front-end is less than 1 μs.

Note that, the interface between the host and FPGA also incurs communication latency. However, it does not affect timing-critical functions at MAC (e.g., DIFS, backoff, SIFS), because we implement a host accelerator, which prefetches data from the host. To support sufficient throughput for 802.11, both PCIe (15.76 μs latency on average) and USB 3.0 (53.25 μs latency on average) are viable choices.

SIFS Timing Requirement. The time interval between the DATA frame and an ACK frame should be smaller than SIFS. This interval consists of four components: (a) the delay at PHY Rx, from receiving the last frame sample at RF, to delivering the last byte of the frame to MAC; (b) the delay at MAC, from receiving the last byte from PHY Rx, to delivering the first byte of ACK to PHY Tx, after MAC finishes all Rx and Tx processing; (c) the delay at PHY Tx, from receiving the first byte of ACK from MAC to sending its first sample to RF; and (d) the communication delay, including PHY-MAC interface delay and the RF delay.

Following the above breakdown analysis, we show that, software and hardware co-design of *Tick* meets the SIFS timing requirement. We make three observations. First, the latency in *Tick*-PHY alone does not exceed the SIFS timing bound. In *Tick* PHY, Rx latency for (a) (4.84 μs) + Tx latency for (c) (1.86 μs) < SIFS (16 μs for 802.11ac [6]). Second, the MAC latency alone in *Tick* does not exceed the SIFS timing bound. With accelerators, the MAC latency of

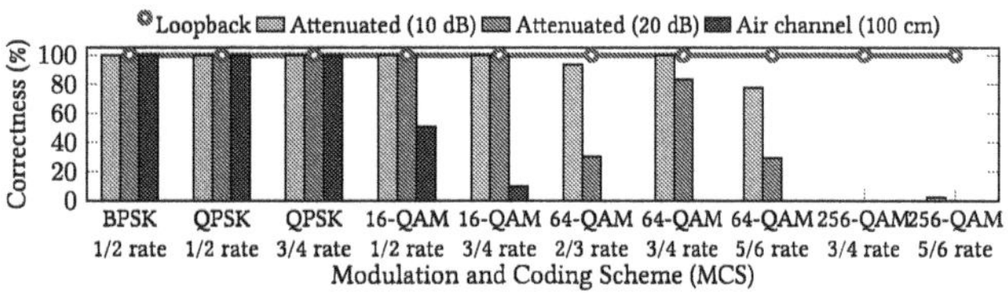

Figure 12: Correctness of *Tick* under different channels.

Frame Size	100 B	500 B	1000 B	1500 B	2000 B	3000 B	4000 B
Latency (μs)	334	356	382	404	415	449	489

Table 6: Overall latency in *Tick*.

processing the ACK frame is 7 μs (3 μs counts for MAC Rx, and 4 μs counts for ACK processing and MAC Tx). This latency corresponds to (2); it is smaller than the SIFS bound. Finally, the SIFS timing bound is satisfied by PHY and MAC together in *Tick*. This is valid because 6.70 μs + 7 μs + 1 μs (interface latency) < 16 μs.

8.4 Overall Performance

Overall Latency. We first gauge the overall latency of 802.11ac SISO on *Tick*. It is measured end-to-end, starting from the data frame generated by host computer, until it is received by the host computer. This latency consists of interface latency (USB 3.0 interface between host and Tx/Rx chain), Tx/Rx chain processing latency, air transmission time, and host processing time. We vary the frame length from 100B to 4000B and show the results in Table 6. *Tick* achieves overall latency at hundreds of μs, compared with 2500 μs latency in WARP [3]. We also notice that latency slightly grows with the frame length (334 μs for 100B, 489 μs for 4000B). This is because the air transmission time for a larger frame is longer.

Correctness. We also evaluate correctness under the following three scenarios: (1) ideal: we loopback the output waveform created by Tx into Rx, without traversing any channel. (2) controlled: we connect Tx and Rx through an attenuator (10 dB and 20 dB attenuation here) which emulates the wireless channel over the air. (3) real: we set RF frontends for Tx and Rx apart (1 m here) and run tests over the noisy radio channel; We also use a power amplifier (Mini-Circuits ZRL-2400LN+ [25]) to amplify radio signals. We send 1500 B frames consecutively at various fixed rates (aka, modulation and coding schemes (MCS)) and measure the percentage of correctly received frames at the Rx host. Figure 12 shows the results for 10 MCSes (from BPSK to 256-QAM) under different coding rates. We make three observations. First, our implementation is logically correct as it achieves 100% correctness in the ideal case. Second, correctness is sensitive to channel quality and MCS. *Tick* achieves 100% correctness for BPSK and QPSK, but turns difficult to support 256-QAM in both controlled and real-world experiments. This matches our expectation. Last, we also notice the gap between the controlled test and the real-world experiment. This is mainly caused by the used power amplifier; the radio signal is still too weak to support high MCS value. More efforts are clearly needed; this is part of our future work.

Consumed FPGA Resource. Table 7 shows the resource utilization on the Xilinx KC705 FPGA board. We count the amount of flip-flop (FF), lookup table (LUT) and block RAM (BRAM) used by PHY and MAC together. *Tick* consumes a modest amount of FPGA resources (less than 28% of each resource for SISO). We notice that

	Tick-Tx			*Tick*-Rx		
	FF	LUT	BRAM	FF	LUT	BRAM
Total Available	407 600	203 800	445	407 600	203 800	445
SISO:						
Used	24 869	37 020	69	29 407	56 890	75
Utilization (%)	6.1	18.2	15.5	7.2	27.9	16.9
MIMO:						
Used	38 359	43 457	133.5	59 501	133 173	136.5
Utilization (%)	9.4	21.3	29.9	14.6	65.3	30.6

Table 7: FPGA resource usage of *Tick* 802.11ac.

	With *Tick*		Without *Tick*	
	Language	LoC	Language	LoC
Element definition	XML	4	Verilog	151
Element connection	XML	8	Verilog	80
Algorithm implementation	Verilog	160	Verilog	160
Total LoC	XML & Verilog	172	Verilog	391

Table 8: Lines-of-code needed to program a BCC element.

Work	Metric	WARP	*Tick*	Note
WURC [3]	overall latency bandwidth	2.5 ms 10 MHz	334 μs 80 MHz	
MIDU [4]	transmission delay bandwidth	50 ms 500 kHz	100 μs 80 MHz	delay between consecutive frames
Duplex [21]	processing latency ACK latency bandwidth	11 μs 75 μs 10 MHz	4.91 μs 9.85 μs 20 MHz	Duplex modifies hardware code and cannot meet SIFS (>16 μs)

Table 9: Comparison of WARPLab and *Tick*.

LUT on the Rx side may become the main bottleneck, especially when it runs MIMO (details later in §9.1). This supplies a reference estimate for *Tick* implementation on other FPGA boards.

Coding Effort and Programmability. *Tick* requires less coding effort which implies nice programmability. Table 8 compares the LoC to program a BCC Encoder element (from the toy example) with/without *Tick*. With *Tick*, the LoC is merely half of that without *Tick*. Moreover, as the library usually implements the elements (the cost is inevitable and usually comparable across various SDR platforms), *Tick* users only need to define and configure elements in most cases. Since it uses XML, the cost is much lower (12 LoC vs. 231 LoC). In fact, the PHY implementation for the 802.11ac SISO in *Tick* has 18 312 LoC in total, including 18 098 LoC for the PHY library. Only 214 LoC is for element configuration and connection. Compared with the reference implementation without *Tick*, which uses 23 706 LoC in Verilog, the total coding cost reduces by 22.8%; Moreover, excluding the efforts for the basic PHY blocks, the programming efforts reduce from 5608 LoC to 214 LoC (26.2× reduction).

Comparison with the State-of-the-Art SDR. We compare *Tick* with WARP [22]. We consider both WARP's reference design and WARPLab, where the former is designed for low latency and the latter is designed for good programmability, as discussed in §4.3. For WARP's 802.11n reference design, its latency for data processing (2.48 μs, 802.11n) is comparable to *Tick* (2.48 μs, 802.11ac). However, it is hard to program over the WARP's 802.11n reference design. We further compare *Tick* with several representative studies using WARPLab [3, 4, 21] with latency results. We evaluate *Tick* under similar or even more stringent settings. Table 9 summarizes the key performance metrics. As a programmable SDR platform, *Tick* reduces latency by around one-order-of-magnitude (even two

	PHY Tx	PHY Rx	MAC Tx	MAC Rx
Latency	1.86 µs	21.62 µs	18 µs	3 µs
Proc. time[a]	15 101 µs	26 731 µs	10 504 µs	10 489 µs

[a] PHY air transmission time is 31 908 µs.

Table 10: Latency and processing time for A-MPDU in *Tick*.

orders of magnitude in [4]) than WARPLab, and supports higher bandwidth. Moreover, *Tick* is easy to program and extend. *Tick* supports 802.11ac and full duplex (see §9). The WARPLab's incapability of satisfying the timing constraints has been reported in the full-duplex [21], MIMO [37, 41] and 802.11ac [37, 39] cases.

9 CASE STUDIES

We use *Tick* to implement two case studies: 802.11ac (SISO, 2×2 MIMO) and full-duplex 802.11a/g, and assess their performances. The former is to demonstrate the performance merits of *Tick*, whereas the latter validates its programmability.

9.1 802.11ac SISO and MIMO

Implementation in *Tick*. For 802.11ac SISO, we follow the implementation for PHY and MAC in §7 and evaluate it in §8. Here we focus on 802.11ac 2x2 MIMO.

For 802.11ac 2×2 MIMO, we use the same MAC prototype as 802.11ac SISO. For MIMO, we have multiple spatial streams in PHY. We thus duplicate the data pipeline to implement multiple streams. Figure 13 shows the PHY block diagram. The PHY streams in MIMO will merge and split (via parser). We use Multiplexer and Demultiplexer elements to enable merge and parser operations. We also implement the multi-input multi-output element to process MIMO decoding.

Evaluation. We first assess the MAC performance. Since our 802.11ac MIMO and SISO prototypes use the same MAC, it achieves the same reduction in latency and processing time (Table 4).

We next look at PHY latency reduction (summarized in Table 3).. Note that our 802.11ac 2×2 MIMO prototype does not support frame aggregation and block ACK, but applies both MCDP and field-base processing as 802.11ac SISO. We can see that, 802.11ac 2×2 MIMO achieves latency and processing delay similar to 802.11ac SISO. In particular, it achieves microsecond-level latency at PHY Tx (1.85 µs). Regarding processing time, it is slightly faster than 802.11ac SISO for a large frame (say, 1500 B). Tx reduces latency from 42.07 µs to 32.56 µs, and Rx latency reduces from 61.85 µs to 43.55 µs. This is because MIMO supports two streams and certain processing functions are run in parallel. Based on the used air transmission time, the timing requirement for SIFS can also be met following the analysis similar to §7.

We also test the latency and processing delay of the maximum A-MPDU length frame (1 048 575 B) for the 802.11ac protocol. Table 10 shows the results. The PHY latency is the same as 802.11ac SISO, but processing time is significantly longer due to more data frames being sent out.

Since the MIMO implementation approximately doubles the used elements compared with SISO, the consumed resources also roughly double, as shown in Table 7.

Finally, we measure the maximum data processing capacity (measured in Mbps) that *Tick* PHY can support. SISO Tx supports up to 556.55Mbps and SISO Rx supports up to 314.09Mbps. Both exceed the throughput maximum stipulated by the standards [6] (263.3Mbps using 64-QAM[2]). MIMO Tx supports up to 1113.1Mbps and MIMO Rx supports up to 632.4Mbps. The throughput requirement from the standard (526.5Mbps using 64-QAM[2]) is also met.

Note that, to further boost performance, users do not need to change the SDR architecture. They just need to focus on optimizing the algorithm of a module or upgrade the FPGA capacity.

9.2 Full-Duplex 802.11a/g

Implementation in *Tick*. We implement a full-duplex 802.11a/g to demonstrate the programmability of *Tick*. Figure 14 shows its PHY function blocks. To support the channel estimation (self-interference channel and target channel) , we introduce a customized new preamble field to the 802.11a/g frame. This field is critical to fully realize full-duplex 802.11a/g. We observe that, using frame-based processing without *Tick*, one would have to rewrite every standard module to accommodate the newly added field. In contrast, with *Tick*, only lightweight effort is required to modify or customize some elements provided by the *Tick* library (marked in Figure 14). In particular, our implementation results in a full-duplex PHY with 22 elements, consisting of 25 740 lines of code. Among these elements, 15 elements are the standard ones *without* any modification (e.g., Interleaver, IFFT, Viterbi Decoder) provided by the Tick PHY library. We modified four elements from the library, i.e., Pilot Insertion, Channel Estimation, Timing Synchronization, and Phase Tracking. We customized three elements: Preamble Insertion, Tx-Rx Path and Self-Interference Cancellation. As a result, the time and invested human effort are reduced.

We further implement a simple MAC for full duplex with five accelerators. We use CRC-32 and RF communication accelerators from the *Tick* MAC library. We have customized accelerators of MAC-PHY configuration, Timing Control and Customized ACK.

Evaluation. We have also discovered the major gain by using field-based processing with full-duplex 802.11 a/g. *Tick* achieves the smallest latency (0.07 µs) for PHY Tx, which further reduces 1.79 µs (27× reduction) compared with 802.11ac. This latency is smaller than that for 802.11ac PHY, because the used preamble is fixed for every frame. Therefore, we precompute this field and bypass the bottleneck IFFT element in our field-based processing. The measured PHY latency and processing delay for the *Tick*-enabled full-duplex 802.11a/g are summarized in Table 11.

The maximum data processing capacity achieved by both half-duplex Tx and Rx are 122.73Mbps, following the previous definition. Therefore, our full-duplex 802.11a/g supports up to 245.46Mbps, which exceeds double throughput of the 802.11a/g protocol, which is 108Mbps.

Finally, Table 12 shows the FPGA resource utilization. Our implementation of full-duplex 802.11a/g consumes the amount of resources on KC705 FPGA with less than 10% on Tx and less than 20% on Rx.

[2]When using the long GI mode.

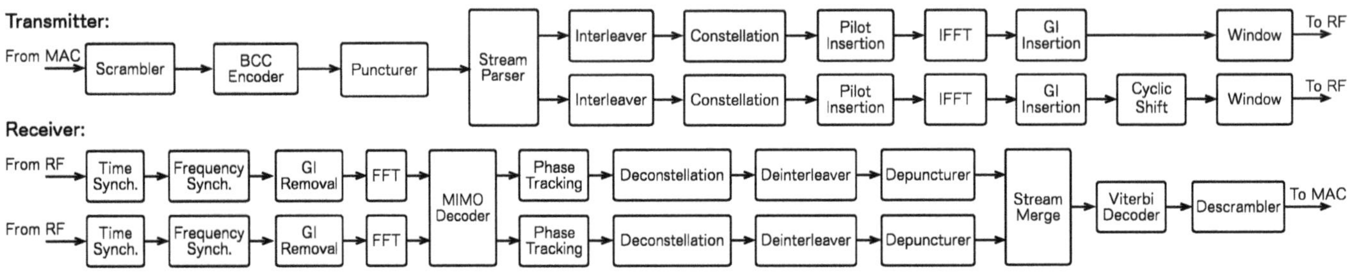

Figure 13: Transmitter and receiver modules for 802.11ac (MIMO).

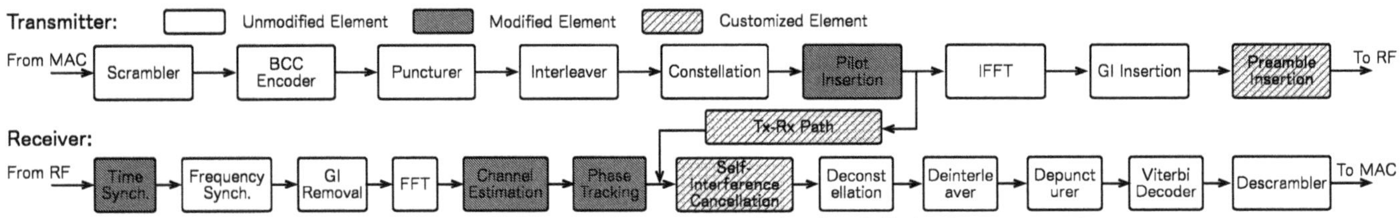

Figure 14: Transmitter and receiver modules for full-duplex 802.11a/g.

	PHY		MAC	
	Tx	Rx	Tx	Rx
100 B:				
Latency	0.07 µs	13.86 µs	0.25 µs	1.14 µs
Proc. time[a]	13.88 µs	49.79 µs	1.92 µs	2.17 µs
1500 B:				
Latency	0.07 µs	13.86 µs	0.25 µs	1.14 µs
Proc. time[b]	92.50 µs	115.57 µs	23.37 µs	28.18 µs

[a] PHY air transmission time for 100 B is 120 µs.
[b] PHY air transmission time for 1500 B is 328 µs.

Table 11: Latency and processing time of *Tick* full-duplex 802.11a/g.

	Tick-Tx			*Tick*-Rx		
	FF	LUT	BRAM	FF	LUT	BRAM
Total Available	407 600	203 800	445	407 600	203 800	445
Used	8111	19 552	41.5	22 773	40 820	93.5
Utilization (%)	2.0	9.6	9.3	5.6	20.0	21.0

Table 12: FPGA resource usage of *Tick* full-duplex 802.11a/g.

10 RELATED WORK

A number of software-defined radio (SDR) platforms have been well documented in recent years [2, 7, 22, 26, 27, 31–35, 40]. They achieve different goals following different designs. The software-centric design like GNU Radio [34] or Sora [33] offers good programmability at the cost of latency guarantee and fine-grained timing control, since they rely heavily on CPU computations. Atomix [7] proposes a modular software framework targeting DSP, which cannot meet the timing requirement of 802.11a. Ziria [31] designs a domain-specific programming language for SDR, but it is limited to PHY only. An alternative solution is to take the hardware-centric design approach, such as AirBlue [26], WARP [22] or OpenMili [40]. Proposals in this category ensure higher processing capacity and lower latency. However, they do not offer good programmability support at both MAC and PHY, due to the intricacy of hardware programming. None can achieve both low latency and good programmability.

Tick explores software and hardware codesign approaches. Its modular design is inspired by the Click router [23], but applies domain-specific optimizations at wireless PHY and MAC to boost performance. Our multi-clock-domain pipelining leverages design ideas from the architecture field [9, 29]. We adapt it to speed up the PHY pipeline. Accelerator-based architecture in FPGA has been applied for data centers [13, 19]. Our accelerator works on a different problem domain. It offloads computation and communication from the embedded processor at MAC.

11 CONCLUSION

Building highly programmable SDR systems with low latency performance can be challenging; no existing systems can achieve both. Of course, there are a number of technical challenges for both PHY and MAC. However, it is still conceptually feasible. In the SDR context, software techniques are great to promote programmability, while hardware can ensure high performance in terms of low latency and accurate timing control. This makes a case for us to explore software and hardware codesign techniques. The outcome is the *Tick* SDR platform reported in this paper.

The design and prototype of *Tick* is a three-year effort with many ups and downs. Many seemingly nice techniques turn out to be ineffective. They force us to explore new solution ideas, thus producing *Tick*. To date, it has been under internal use and tests at three university and research sites for over three months. On one hand, we hope it can eventually yield a reliable SDR platform with low latency and programmability for us and the broad research community. On the other hand, we are using it to explore domain-specific architecture designs for wireless networking systems in the long run. Along this general direction, we are just starting.

ACKNOWLEDGMENTS

The authors would like to thank their shepherd, Dr. Božidar Radunović, and the anonymous reviewers for their valuable comments and helpful suggestions. This work is also supported in part by NSF awards (CNS-1423576 and CNS-1526985) and in part by National Natural Science Foundation of China (NSFC) Grants 61370056 and 61531004.

REFERENCES

[1] Analog Devices. 2017. AD9371 Transceivers. https://www.digikey.com/en/product-highlight/a/analog-devices/ad9371-transceivers. (February 2017).

[2] Narendra Anand, Ehsan Aryafar, and Edward W Knightly. 2010. WARPlab: a flexible framework for rapid physical layer design. In *Proceedings of the 2010 ACM workshop on Wireless of the students, by the students, for the students (S3 '10)*. ACM, 53–56.

[3] Narendra Anand, Ryan E Guerra, and Edward W Knightly. 2014. The case for UHF-band MU-MIMO. In *Proceedings of the 20th Annual International Conference on Mobile Computing and Networking (MobiCom '14)*. ACM, 29–40.

[4] Ehsan Aryafar, Mohammad Amir Khojastepour, Karthikeyan Sundaresan, Sampath Rangarajan, and Mung Chiang. 2012. MIDU: Enabling MIMO full duplex. In *Proceedings of the 18th Annual International Conference on Mobile Computing and Networking (MobiCom '12)*. ACM, 257–268.

[5] IEEE Standards Association. 2012. IEEE Standard 802.11-2012: Wireless LAN Medium Access Control (MAC) and Physical Layer (PHY) Specifications. *IEEE Std.* 802 (2012).

[6] IEEE Standards Association. 2013. IEEE Standard 802.11ac-2013: Enhancements for Very High Throughput for Operation in Bands below 6 GHz. *IEEE Std.* 802 (2013).

[7] Manu Bansal, Aaron Schulman, and Sachin Katti. 2015. Atomix: A framework for deploying signal processing applications on wireless infrastructure. In *Proceedings of the 12th USENIX Symposium on Networked Systems Design and Implementation (NSDI '15)*. USENIX Association, Oakland, CA, 173–188.

[8] Dinesh Bharadia, Emily McMilin, and Sachin Katti. 2013. Full duplex radios. *ACM SIGCOMM Computer Communication Review* 43, 4 (2013), 375–386.

[9] S Casale Brunet, Endri Bezati, Claudio Alberti, Marco Mattavelli, Edoardo Amaldi, and Jörn W Janneck. 2013. Partitioning and optimization of high level stream applications for multi clock domain architectures. In *Proceedings of the 2013 IEEE Workshop on Signal Processing Systems (SiPS '13)*. IEEE, 177–182.

[10] Tiberiu Chelcea and Steven M. Nowick. 2000. Low-latency asynchronous FIFO's using token rings. In *Proceedings of the 6th International Symposium on Advanced Research in Asynchronous Circuits and Systems (ASYNC '00)*. 210–220.

[11] Tao Chen and G Edward Suh. 2016. Efficient data supply for hardware accelerators with prefetching and access/execute decoupling. In *Proceedings of the 49th Annual IEEE/ACM International Symposium on Microarchitecture (MICRO-49)*. IEEE, 1–12.

[12] Jung Il Choi, Mayank Jain, Kannan Srinivasan, Phil Levis, and Sachin Katti. 2010. Achieving single channel, full duplex wireless communication. In *Proceedings of the 16th Annual International Conference on Mobile Computing and Networking (MobiCom '10)*. ACM, 1–12.

[13] Jason Cong, Zhenman Fang, Yuchen Hao, and Reinman Glenn. 2017. Supporting address translation for accelerator-centric architectures. In *Proceedings of the 23rd IEEE Symposium on High Performance Computer Architecture (HPCA '17)*. IEEE, IEEE, Austin, TX, USA.

[14] Cypress. 2014. CYUSB3ACC-005 FMC Interconnect Board. http://www.cypress.com/documentation/development-kitsboards/cyusb3acc-005-fmc-interconnect-board-ez-usb-fx3-superspeed. (October 2014).

[15] Cypress. 2017. CYUSB3KIT-003 SuperSpeed Explorer Kit. http://www.cypress.com/documentation/development-kitsboards/cyusb3kit-003-ez-usb-fx3-superspeed-explorer-kit. (June 2017).

[16] Ettus. 2017. USRP Family of Products. https://www.ettus.com/product. (March 2017).

[17] Jian Gong, Jiahua Chen, Haoyang Wu, Fan Ye, Songwu Lu, Jason Cong, and Tao Wang. 2014. EPEE: An efficient PCIe communication library with easy-host-integration property for FPGA accelerators. In *Proceedings of the 2014 ACM/SIGDA International Symposium on Field-Programmable Gate Arrays (FPGA '14)*. ACM, 255–255.

[18] Jian Gong, Tao Wang, Jiahua Chen, Haoyang Wu, Fan Ye, Songwu Lu, and Jason Cong. 2014. An efficient and flexible host-FPGA PCIe communication library. In *Proceedings of the 24th International Conference on Field Programmable Logic and Applications (FPL '14)*. IEEE, 1–6.

[19] Muhuan Huang, Di Wu, Cody Hao Yu, Zhenman Fang, Matteo Interlandi, Tyson Condie, and Jason Cong. 2016. Programming and runtime support to Blaze FPGA accelerator deployment at datacenter scale. In *Proceedings of the 7th ACM Symposium on Cloud Computing (SoCC '16)*. ACM, 456–469.

[20] Anoop Iyer and Diana Marculescu. 2002. Power and performance evaluation of globally asynchronous locally synchronous processors. In *Proceedings of the 29th Annual International Symposium on Computer Architecture (ISCA '02)*. IEEE, 158–168.

[21] Mayank Jain, Jung Il Choi, Taemin Kim, Dinesh Bharadia, Siddharth Seth, Kannan Srinivasan, Philip Levis, Sachin Katti, and Prasun Sinha. 2011. Practical, real-time, full duplex wireless. In *Proceedings of the 17th Annual International Conference on Mobile Computing and Networking (MobiCom '11)*. ACM, 301–312.

[22] Ahmed Khattab, Joseph Camp, Chris Hunter, Patrick Murphy, Ashutosh Sabharwal, and Edward W Knightly. 2008. WARP: a flexible platform for clean-slate wireless medium access protocol design. *ACM SIGMOBILE Mobile Computing and Communications Review* 12, 1 (2008), 56–58.

[23] Eddie Kohler, Robert Morris, Benjie Chen, John Jannotti, and M Frans Kaashoek. 2000. The Click modular router. *ACM Transactions on Computer Systems (TOCS)* 18, 3 (2000), 263–297.

[24] Yunsup Lee, Rimas Avizienis, Alex Bishara, Richard Xia, Derek Lockhart, Christopher Batten, and Krste Asanović. 2011. Exploring the tradeoffs between programmability and efficiency in data-parallel accelerators. In *Proceedings of the 38th Annual International Symposium on Computer Architecture (ISCA '11)*, Vol. 39. ACM, San Jose, California, USA, 129–140.

[25] Mini-Circuits. 2017. ZRL-2400LN+. https://www.minicircuits.com/WebStore/dashboard.html?model=ZRL-2400LN%2B. (February 2017).

[26] Man Cheuk Ng, Kermin Elliott Fleming, Mythili Vutukuru, Samuel Gross, Arvind, and Hari Balakrishnan. 2010. Airblue: A system for cross-layer wireless protocol development. In *Proceedings of the 6th ACM/IEEE Symposium on Architectures for Networking and Communications Systems (ANCS '10)*. ACM, 4:1–4:11.

[27] Rishiyur Nikhil. 2004. Bluespec system verilog: Efficient, correct RTL from high-level specifications. In *Proceedings of the 2nd ACM and IEEE International Conference on Formal Methods and Models for Co-Design (MEMOCODE '04)*. IEEE, 69–70.

[28] John Oliver, Ravishankar Rao, Paul Sultana, Jedidiah Crandall, Erik Czernikowski, LW Jones, Diana Franklin, Venkatesh Akella, and Frederic T Chong. 2004. Synchroscalar: A multiple clock domain, power-aware, tile-based embedded processor. In *Proceedings of the 31st Annual International Symposium on Computer Architecture (ISCA '04)*. IEEE, 150–161.

[29] Greg Semeraro, David H Albonesi, Steven G Dropsho, Grigorios Magklis, Sandhya Dwarkadas, and Michael L Scott. 2002. Dynamic frequency and voltage control for a multiple clock domain microarchitecture. In *Proceedings of the 35th Annual IEEE/ACM International Symposium on Microarchitecture (MICRO-35)*. IEEE, 356–367.

[30] Greg Semeraro, Grigorios Magklis, Rajeev Balasubramonian, David H Albonesi, Sandhya Dwarkadas, and Michael L Scott. 2002. Energy-efficient processor design using multiple clock domains with dynamic voltage and frequency scaling. In *Proceedings of the 8th International Symposium on High-Performance Computer Architecture (HPCA '02)*. IEEE, 29–40.

[31] Gordon Stewart, Mahanth Gowda, Geoffrey Mainland, Bozidar Radunovic, Dimitrios Vytiniotis, and Cristina Luengo Agullo. 2015. Ziria: A DSL for wireless systems programming. In *Proceedings of the 20th International Conference on Architectural Support for Programming Languages and Operating Systems (ASPLOS '15)*, Vol. 50. ACM, 415–428.

[32] Paul D Sutton, Jorg Lotze, Hicham Lahlou, Suhaib A Fahmy, Keith E Nolan, Baris Ozgul, Thomas W Rondeau, Juanjo Noguera, and Linda E Doyle. 2010. Iris: An architecture for cognitive radio networking testbeds. *IEEE communications magazine* 48, 9 (2010).

[33] Kun Tan, He Liu, Jiansong Zhang, Yongguang Zhang, Ji Fang, and Geoffrey M Voelker. 2011. Sora: high-performance software radio using general-purpose multi-core processors. *Commun. ACM* 54, 1 (2011), 99–107.

[34] The GNU Radio Foundation. 2017. GNU Radio. http://www.gnuradio.org/. (March 2017).

[35] Artem Tkachenko, Danijela Cabric, and Robert W Brodersen. 2007. Cyclostationary feature detector experiments using reconfigurable BEE2. In *Proceedings of the 2nd IEEE International Symposium on New Frontiers in Dynamic Spectrum Access Networks (DySPAN '07)*. IEEE, 216–219.

[36] WARP Project. 2013. IFS calibration and benchmarks. http://warpproject.org/trac/wiki/802.11/Benchmarks/IFS. (November 2013).

[37] Xiufeng Xie, Xinyu Zhang, and Karthikeyan Sundaresan. 2013. Adaptive feedback compression for MIMO networks. In *Proceedings of the 19th Annual International Conference on Mobile Computing and Networking (MobiCom '13)*. ACM, 477–488.

[38] Xilinx. 2017. Xilinx Kintex-7 FPGA KC705 Evaluation Kit. https://www.xilinx.com/products/boards-and-kits/ek-k7-kc705-g.html. (July 2017).

[39] Hang Yu, Oscar Bejarano, and Lin Zhong. 2014. Combating inter-cell interference in 802.11ac-based multi-user MIMO networks. In *Proceedings of the 20th Annual International Conference on Mobile Computing and Networking (MobiCom '14)*. ACM, 141–152.

[40] Jialiang Zhang, Xinyu Zhang, Pushkar Kulkarni, and Parameswaran Ramanathan. 2016. OpenMili: A 60 GHz software radio platform with a reconfigurable phased-array antenna. In *Proceedings of the 22nd Annual International Conference on Mobile Computing and Networking (MobiCom '16)*. ACM, 162–175.

[41] Xinyu Zhang, Karthikeyan Sundaresan, Mohammad A Amir Khojastepour, Sampath Rangarajan, and Kang G Shin. 2013. NEMOx: Scalable network MIMO for wireless networks. In *Proceedings of the 19th Annual International Conference on Mobile Computing and Networking (MobiCom '13)*. ACM, 453–464.

BiPass: Enabling End-to-End Full Duplex

Lu Chen[⋆†], Fei Wu[⋆†], Jiaqi Xu[⋆†], Kannan Srinivasan[⋆], Ness Shroff[⋆⋄]
[⋆]Department of Computer Science and Engineering, [⋄] Electrical and Computer Engineering
The Ohio State University, Columbus, OH, 43210
{chen.4728, wu.1973, xu.1629, srinivasan.115, shroff.11}@osu.edu
[†] Co-primary authors

ABSTRACT

Full duplex techniques can potentially double the channel capacity and achieve lower delays by empowering two radios to simultaneously transmit in the same frequency band. However, full duplex is only available between two adjacent nodes within the communication range. In this paper, we present BiPass to break this limitation. With the help of full duplex capable relays, we enable simultaneous bidirectional in-band cut-through transmissions between two far apart nodes, so they can do full duplex communications as if they were within each other's transmission range. To design such a system, we analyze interference patterns and propose a loop-back interference cancellation strategy. We identify the power amplification problem at relay nodes and develop an algorithm to solve it. We also develop a routing algorithm, an opportunistic forwarding scheme, and a real-time feedback strategy to leverage this system in ad-hoc networks. To evaluate the real world performance of BiPass, we build a prototype and conduct experiments using software defined radios. We show that BiPass can achieve 1.6x median throughput gain over state-of-the-art one-way cut-through systems, and 4.09x gain over the decode-and-forward scheme. Our simulations further reveal that even when the data traffic is not bidirectional, BiPass has 1.36x throughput gain and 47% delay reduction over one-way cut-through systems in large networks.

CCS CONCEPTS

• **Networks** → *Wireless access networks*;

KEYWORDS

Full duplex; interference cancellation; multi-hop; relay

1 INTRODUCTION

Full duplex is a promising technique for enhancing future communication systems. Full duplex techniques allow radios to transmit and receive packets simultaneously in the same frequency band, which usually means higher spectrum efficiency and lower packet delays [5, 6, 8, 9, 13]. However, full duplex can only be activated between two adjacent nodes due to the fact that any radio has a limited communication range.

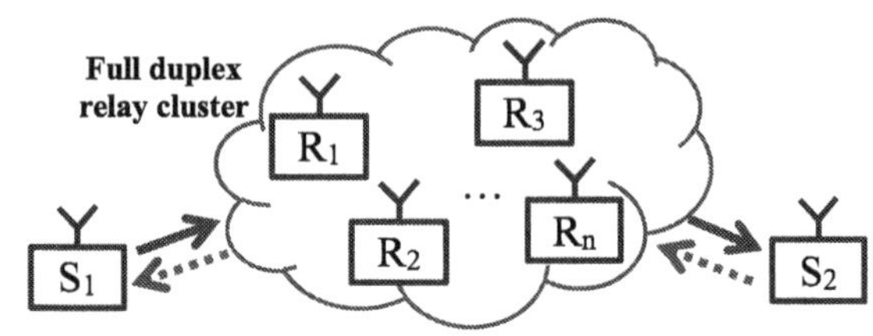

Figure 1: Source nodes S_1 and S_2 want to exchange information. Is it possible to enable bidirectional cut-through transmissions via relays between them?

Traditionally, relays have been employed to extend the communication range. Correspondingly, full duplex capable relays have been designed, which can forward the received signal while receiving [4, 7, 12]. Recent works [7, 17] have enabled one-way cut-through transmissions by leveraging the power of full duplex relays. Specifically, a source node can transmit packets to a far away destination node via full duplex relays almost instantly. Cut-through originates from network switch, with which a switch directly forwards a packet without decoding. However, full duplex, in its nature, is about in-band simultaneous bidirectional transmissions. This leads us to ask: ***Is it even possible to enable end-to-end full duplex via multiple full duplex relays***?

Consider the setup shown in Fig. 1. Two full duplex source nodes[1] S_1 and S_2 want to exchange data but are out of direct communication range. We want to enable simultaneous bidirectional in-band cut-through transmissions with full duplex relays between them. In other words, design a system that can enable S_1 and S_2 to do *end-to-end transmissions as if they were in direct communication range.*

This *end-to-end full duplex transmission* problem is an open problem. One could ask why state-of-the-art end-to-end single direction cut-through technique [7] ($S_1 \rightarrow S_2$) cannot naturally support bidirectional transmissions ($S_1 \leftrightarrow S_2$). The reason is that such a system is designed to cancel interference from one direction. Specifically, [7] measures the channels starting from S_2 backwards towards S_1 to measure all the causal channels and later use them to cancel such interference to enable $S_1 \rightarrow S_2$. Thus, to enable the reverse directional flow ($S_2 \rightarrow S_1$) simultaneously, [7] would need to measure the channels starting from S_1. These channels are different from the channels measured from S_2. Thus, the state-of-the-art

[1]Note that source nodes are also destination nodes in this setting. We also refer to them as end nodes in this paper.

MobiCom '17, October 16–20, 2017, Snowbird, UT, USA

ACM ISBN 978-1-4503-4916-1/17/10...$15.00
https://doi.org/10.1145/3117811.3117826

single direction cut-through system will not work for bi-directional end-to-end cut-through transmissions or end-to-end full duplex transmissions. More details on this aspect and power control follow in Sec. 3. This is a fundamental issue in enabling end-to-end full duplex traffic.

In this paper, we solve this open problem and present BiPass to realize the end-to-end full duplex system. There are many benefits of such a system. **Lower delay:** Compared with decode-and-forward (D&F) based solutions, our system does not need to forward packets hop by hop. Instead, packets can be exchanged as if they were close by. Compared with the state-of-the-art one-way cut-through systems [7, 17], the destination node in our system can transmit immediately without waiting for the end of the incoming stream, so it is likely to experience a much lower delay. **Throughput gain:** It has already been shown that one-way cut-through systems have throughput gain over traditional systems [7]. Similar to full duplex systems compared with half duplex systems, the throughput can potentially be further doubled in BiPass.

Despite the benefits it can potentially bring, there are multiple challenges in implementing BiPass to realize the above benefits.

Interference management. Due to the shared nature of the wireless medium, a transmission may be overheard by many other nodes. Since full duplex relays will forward signals that have been received, signals may keep looping among these relays. It has been shown that the interference in one-way cut-through systems is already difficult to analyze [7], and the problem is further exacerbated by the more complex interference pattern in the bidirectional setup.

Power amplification. Even if we can solve the interference problem, without a proper power amplification setting for the relays, the signal may gradually fade before reaching the target node, or suffer from nonlinear distortions due to over-amplification. Properly assigning power amplification coefficients is a problem that needs to be addressed.

Utilize BiPass in networks. In a wireless network, many relays are available to be employed to form a route. Selecting proper participating relay nodes is not an easy problem. Further, a network may have limited or even no bidirectional traffic flows. How to utilize BiPass efficiently in a network with mismatched traffic load is a question that entails further investigations.

This paper makes the following contributions:

- We propose a loop-back interference cancellation strategy and a power amplification algorithm as key solutions to address interference management and power amplification challenges above and realize the system in practice.
- We propose a routing selection algorithm, an opportunistic forwarding scheme, and a real-time feedback strategy to take full advantage of BiPass in large networks. Specifically, we relax the need for the entire path between S_1 and S_2 to be available and allow transmissions to still make progress towards their destinations. Thus, S_1 and S_2 in our framework need not be final destinations. Furthermore, the reverse flow could be end-to-end acknowledgements instead of data. This is vital for end-to-end recovery and data rate management.
- To the best of our knowledge, we are the first to propose and realize a system that enables simultaneous bidirectional in-band wireless cut-through transmissions via multiple full duplex relays. We implement our system with software defined radios, demonstrating its practicality and gains over the traditional decode-and-forward scheme, as well as the state-of-the-art one-way cut-through system.

2 RELATED WORK

Full duplex and full duplex relay: By cancelling self interference, a full duplex capable node can transmit and receive simultaneously in the same frequency band. Point-to-point full duplex systems have been well researched and successfully implemented. Specifically, [9, 13] propose antenna cancellation and analog cancellation technique respectively, [6] enables full duplex with single antenna, [3, 5, 8] show that MIMO is also possible for full duplex transmissions. Full duplex capability also holds for a relay node: it can amplify and forward the received samples almost immediately after receiving them. Full duplex relays have been successfully used in many recent works [4, 7, 12, 16].

One-way cut-through transmissions: Empowered by full duplex capable relays, one-way cut-through transmission has been shown to be possible. FastForward [4] enables constructive addition of signals from direct and relayed paths at the destination node, so that the received signal power is maximized. The authors in [12] propose a delay and forward system where relays also decode packets to avoid noise propagation problem. [1] uses full duplex relay at 60 GHz and applies it to virtual reality applications. However, these systems can only work for two-hop networks and are generally hard to directly extend to multi-hop cases. AirExpress [7] enables one-way cut-through transmissions via multiple relays by doing interference cancellation. The authors in [17] propose a scheduling scheme for one-way cut-through in networks. However, these systems can only support single direction transmissions, while BiPass can support bidirectional communications.

Bidirectional transmissions: Network coding is a strategy to improve the performance in bidirectional transmissions. There are several variations of network coding schemes including MAC-layer [2], physical-layer [18] and analog network coding [14]. The basic idea of network coding is to leverage the fact that each source node knows its own packets already, hence, a combined version of the information is enough for them to decode each other's information. In this sense, BiPass is also inspired by this idea. In fact, we think BiPass can be considered as *a generalization of the analog network coding* from one-relay networks to general multi-relay networks. In the design of [14], multi-hop is achieved by time division fashion scheduling. In contrast, BiPass is a coherent design for multi-hop networks, and has no requirement on interference range. Generally, current design of network coding techniques usually have stringent requirements such as negligible cross-hop interference, sophisticated power control, strict time/frequency synchronization, etc. In contrast, BiPass can be easily implemented in the real world without these requirements even for multi-hop communications. Also, compared with network coding, BiPass could potentially achieve larger throughput and lower delay since it has no concept of time slot, while network coding requires time division medium access. For example, 3 time slots are needed in a one-relay network with MAC-layer network coding.

3 THE DESIGN OF BIPASS

In this section, we discuss the design details of BiPass. All relay nodes in our system have two modes: *training mode* and *full duplex relay mode*. In the training mode, a node will transmit and receive simultaneously but without digital cancellation. It sends out a signal and estimates the channel with the received signal. In full duplex relay mode, a node will amplify and forward the signals that are being received, while performing interference cancellation using the channel estimation results from the training mode. Source nodes have the same *training mode* and *source mode*. In source mode, a source node will decode the signal after interference cancellation while transmitting its own packet.

3.1 Interference cancellation

To design a system that supports multi-hop bidirectional cut-through transmissions, the first question one may ask is: can we simply put several full duplex relays (doing only self interference cancellation) between source and destination? Unfortunately, this will lead to an unstable system due to an infinite signal loop problem. Conceptually, full duplex relays can be treated as special reflectors: they can amplify and retransmit whatever has been received. If no additional controls are performed, two full duplex relays may form an infinite loop: signals keep bouncing between them and signal strength may keep increasing until saturation due to the amplification made by relays. We call a system that is free from this infinite loop as a **stable system**.

3.1.1 Sequential training. We first define ***loop-back interference*** as: the signals (interference) received by a node that originated from itself, possibly having gone through other relays. Loop-back interference has an important feature: *a node can cancel its own loop-back interference.* This is because, similar to self interference cancellation, if a node knows what has been transmitted and the channels of the loop-back paths, it can construct the expected loop-back interference, and subtract it from the ensemble of the received signals. Intuitively, we want to cancel some of the loop-back interference to eliminate infinite loops in the system. We propose sequential training as a solution to get a stable system.

Sequential training procedure: Let $Ts = [R_1, R_2, ..., R_n, S_2, S_1]$ be a sequence in which nodes train for loop-back interference one after another. Once a relay node finishes training and is able to estimate its channel, it switches to full duplex relay mode to forward the signals it receives. Note that besides the self interference channel, $\boldsymbol{h}$ will also capture the channels of the relaying paths through those trained earlier than the node. Loop-back interference cancellation based on $\boldsymbol{h}$ and proper power amplification are performed while forwarding. Source nodes S_i $(i = 1, 2)$ do training similarly after all relays have finished this procedure, and then change back to source mode. In the following, we refer the sequence Ts as *training sequence.*

Although our solution bears similarities to the backward training process proposed in [7], it is very different in principle. One of our key finding is: *the sequential training can be performed with any sequence, in order to get a stable system.* In [7], the authors imply that the training will take place starting from the relay closest to the destination node, then move towards the source node. However, in the bidirectional case, both sides are source nodes and destination nodes. There is no concept of forward or backward direction. We believe that our views of loop-back interference differ sharply from the views on interference in [7], where the authors categorized the interference into forwarder interference, cross-hop interference, causal interference, non-causal interference etc.

In the following explanation of why this sequential training works, we assume that correct power amplification has been applied and no noise or residual interference is present in the system.

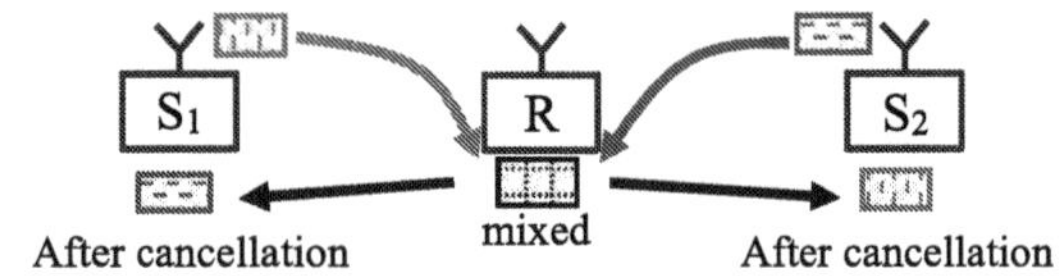

Figure 2: A one-relay system that supports simultaneous bidirectional cut-through transmissions.

Consider the one-relay system shown in Fig. 2. Following the training procedure, relay R will first perform channel estimation. In this case, it is same as traditional self interference estimation since there are no other relays to forward the signal. After this, it changes its mode to full duplex relay. Then source nodes perform training. Without loss of generality, we assume source node S_2 first starts this process. For S_2, besides self interference, it also receives a copy from relay R. These signals together form loop-back interference, which can be canceled at S_2. After the other source node S_1 undertakes the same process, S_1 and S_2 start data transmissions concurrently in the same frequency band.

R receives a mix of the two signals, which will then be amplified and transmitted by R. Thanks to the loop-back interference cancellation performed at the source nodes, S_1 will get only the signal from S_2 after cancellation and vice versa.

Now we extend the analysis to the multiple relays scenario using induction. Note that one-relay system is a stable system. Assume that there is a stable system cluster C with n $(n \geq 1)$ relays, as illustrated in Fig. 3. We introduce the $(n+1)$-th relay R_{n+1} to the system, and perform the sequential training process after C, namely the training sequence $Ts = [C, R_{n+1}, S_i]$, we want to show that this system is still a stable system.

Recall that a stable system means no infinite loops inside the system. Therefore each sample input to the n-relay cluster C will leave it within a certain time. Based on this observation, the relay cluster can be treated as a single relay. As shown in Fig. 3 with solid blue lines, for a given input directly from source nodes $S_i, i = 1, 2$, the cluster C will give a certain output. This output, together with signals directly from source nodes (solid yellow line), will act as input to R_{n+1}. These signals get amplified and forwarded by R_{n+1}, which become another input to C. As shown with dashed green line, C will give a corresponding output for this input. It must be noted that after the signal reaches R_{n+1} for the first time, either from path $S_i \rightarrow R_{n+1}$ or $S_i \rightarrow C \rightarrow R_{n+1}$, it will get canceled at R_{n+1} after the signal travels back again, thanks to the training and cancellation process. Because of this loop-back interference cancellation, the newly introduced relay R_{n+1} does not bring any infinite loop and thus this $(n+1)$-relay system is still a stable system, which again can be treated as a single relay. By induction, we conclude that BiPass is always a stable system by doing sequential training.

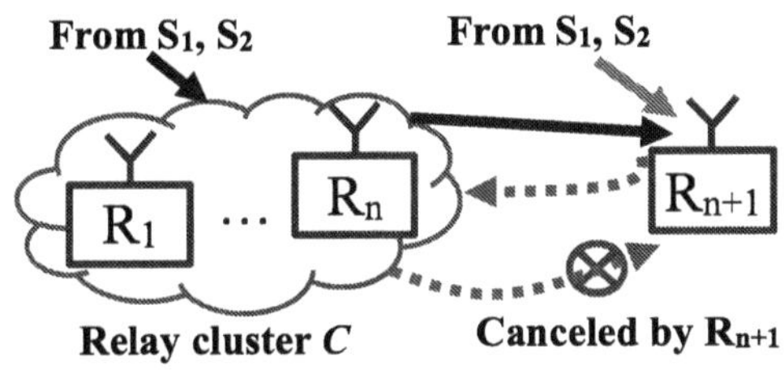

Figure 3: Putting one more relay to a stable system still yields a stable system. All possible signal propagation paths are shown in the figure.

Note that we made no assumptions on the physical locations of the relays in the above analysis. This leads to our key observation: *any training sequence can result in a stable system by doing sequential training.*

3.1.2 Valid paths. Since BiPass is a stable system that contains no loops, we can list all the possible paths from one side to another. In fact, for Fig. 3, all 6 possible paths from S_i to S_j $(i, j = 1, 2, i \neq j)$ can be listed as: $S_i \rightarrow S_j$, $S_i \rightarrow C \rightarrow S_j$, $S_i \rightarrow R_{n+1} \rightarrow S_j$, $S_i \rightarrow C \rightarrow R_{n+1} \rightarrow S_j$, $S_i \rightarrow R_{n+1} \rightarrow C \rightarrow S_j$, and $S_i \rightarrow C \rightarrow R_{n+1} \rightarrow C \rightarrow S_j$. We call these paths *valid paths*. One can thus recursively list all valid paths in BiPass with any number of relays. Note that due to cancellation, not all combinations of nodes give valid paths. For example, $S_i \rightarrow R_{n+1} \rightarrow C \rightarrow R_{n+1} \rightarrow S_j$ is *invalid*.

Longest valid path: If the delay spread is larger than the cyclic prefix (CP) length, inter-symbol interference (ISI) will be observed. Hence, delay spread is worth investigating since it limits the number of relays for a given CP length (and symbol length if we keep the CP ratio the same). Consider the worst case where all nodes are in a single collision domain, the longest valid path (in terms of number of hops) will determine the delay spread since the fastest link is the direct link from one source to another.

In fact, from the above analysis, one may notice that by adding a new relay, the longest valid path changes from $S_i \rightarrow Longest(C) \rightarrow S_j$ to $S_i \rightarrow Longest(C) \rightarrow R_{n+1} \rightarrow Longest(C) \rightarrow S_j$, where $Longest(C)$ contains the longest path that goes through C. In other words, each time a new relay node is added to the system, a signal can go through all the possible paths again after visiting this newly added node. This means that the length of longest path will be doubled. Generally, the delay spread via n relay nodes is

$$T_d = (2^n - 1)\Delta t, \quad (1)$$

where Δt is the latency introduced at each relay node.

This indeed limits the number of relays that can be used in a route. However, in practice, the longer paths may be too weak to make a difference. For example, in the above mentioned longest path, the path loss between R_1 and S_2 may be relatively high (otherwise there is no need to choose R_2 and R_3 as additional relays), so the power delivered by this path is deemed to be relatively low. In fact, if we assume that each node has a limited interference range of 2 hops, for example, node R_1 may only be able to reach R_3 directly but not R_4, then we find that $T_d = O(n^2)$. Even if we consider all paths, with $\Delta t = 50$ *ns* [4] and acceptable threshold be 0.8 μs (based on 802.11 standard CP length), we can support up to 4 relays without introducing any ISI based on Eq. 1. To employ more relays, one may use longer OFDM symbols to cover the delay spread.

3.2 Power Amplification

We have shown that one can get a stable system by doing sequential training. However, a full duplex relay needs to amplify the signal before forwarding in practice. Otherwise, the transmitted signal tends to be too weak for the other side to receive. We find that choosing this amplification coefficient is not an easy task.

3.2.1 Target and challenges. Assume that a relay receives signal $y = hx + n$, where hx is the intended signal after cancellation and n is the noise. It will multiply the signal by a real number $\sqrt{A}$ and transmit $b = \sqrt{A} \cdot y$. We call this A as the amplification coefficient. A must be chosen in a way that maximizes the throughput of the link, while subject to the following two constraints:

Constraint 1. $|b|$ has an upper limit. Usually there is a maximum magnitude limit on the signal a node can transmit. Each signal sample that is beyond the saturation limit suffers from clipping or other non-linear distortions, which in turn affects the decoding BER at the destination node. It has been shown that a larger clipping ratio can result in orders of increase in BER at the decoder [15]. In the following discussions, we assume the equivalent power constraint is 20 dBm.

Constraint 2. A shall be fixed once set. One may think of a dynamic adaptation scheme to keep adjusting the value of A to meet the above requirement. However, this approach can be hard to implement. To see the problem, assume a relay R_1 trains first followed by nodes R_i. If R_1 changes its A on the go, unless we somehow inform *all* R_i of this change, the cancellation performed at R_i will fail since it has the same effect as the channel suddenly changes. Also, this approach may introduce large overhead and long converge time.

Next we consider two naive solutions with the network shown in Fig. 4. For ease of explanation, in the following discussions, we assume 1) the received signal power is dominated by the strongest signal strength; 2) a node can only reach one-hop away nodes and cause no interference to others. Even with these strong assumptions, how to properly assign amplification coefficients turns out to be a nontrivial problem as we will see below due to the above constrains. We will remove these assumptions in our solution presented in Sec. 3.2.3. We assume R_1 trains before R_2 in Fig. 4 and the maximum transmission power is 20 dBm. The path loss between nodes are shown in the figure.

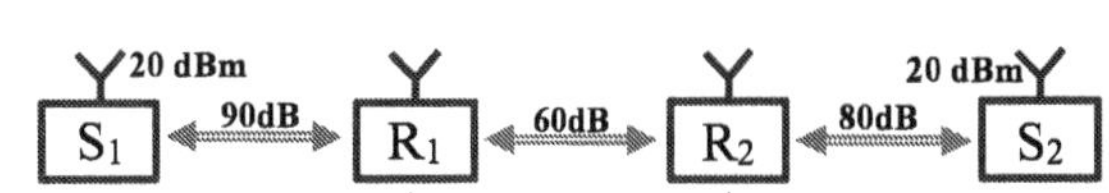

Figure 4: A 3-hop network with path loss shown. Naive solutions will not provide optimal solutions in this toy example, as summarized in Table 1.

Naive solution 1: One-side dependency. We first consider the one-side dependency scheme presented in [7]: a node should only consider its neighbor node on one side. For example, R_1 should only consider S_1 and R_2 should only consider R_1. As a result, $A_1 = 90$

Table 1: Settings and results of possible solutions

Solution	A_1	A_2	Comments
One-side	90 dB	60 dB	R_1 Tx at 30 dBm.
Two-side	60 dB	60 dB	20 dB SNR loss.
Our solution	60 dB	80 dB	R_1 trains first.
Our solution	80 dB	60 dB	R_2 trains first.

dB and A_2 = 60 dB. While this may work for one-way cut-through transmissions, it is not a practical solution for bidirectional scenario. For example, consider the transmitting power at R_1 from S_2 to S_1, it can be calculated as 20 dBm - 80 dB + 60 dB - 60 dB + 90 dB = 30 dBm, which obviously violates Constraint 1.

Naive solution 2: Two-side dependency. To solve the problem of one-side dependency, one may think a node should consider both its neighbors and set the amplification coefficient based on the strongest link. In the toy example illustrated in Fig. 4, this scheme will lead to $A_1 = A_2 = 60$ dB. However, it turns out that this solution is a very conservative suboptimal solution, which will result in SNR loss. For example, consider the path from S_1 to S_2, the signal strength received at S_2 is -90 dBm, while our solution in Sec. 3.2.3 can give -70 dBm signal strength.

3.2.2 Insight: effects of training sequence. While maximizing throughput is our target, it is not easy to achieve directly. This is because signal strength and noise power are coupled in this system. Thus, we relax our target to maximize the signal strength received at intended node. We will maximize SNR by a route selection algorithm in Sec. 4.1 and investigate noise propagation in Sec. 5.1.

Intuitively, to get a better signal strength at the end nodes, the relays should always use their maximum transmitting power. Thus, if a node receives a total power equal to P_{rx}, the amplification coefficient A should be chosen such that

$$A \cdot P_{rx} = P_{max}. \tag{2}$$

As a result, the task is mapped into identifying the received power at relay nodes. However, it is not easy. For a relay node, the received power is also affected by the choice of A of the other nodes. Interference cancellation performed at relays further complicates the analysis. To see the problem, consider the topology shown in Fig. 4 and assume R_1 trains before R_2. Then node R_2 in fact intrinsically has an advantage: it will cancel the loop-back interference before amplification. This means that the path $R_2 \rightarrow R_1 \rightarrow R_2$ should not be considered when deciding the amplification coefficient of R_2. Instead, all valid paths from source nodes to R_2 that need to be taken into account are $S_1 \rightarrow R_1 \rightarrow R_2$ and $S_2 \rightarrow R_2$. By adding up the power of these two paths, we get P_{rx2}, and thus A_2. However, it must be noted that before assigning A_2 to R_2, we need to know the amplification coefficient A_1 at R_1 since it affects the received power from path $S_1 \rightarrow R_1 \rightarrow R_2$. For node R_1, on the other hand, it needs to consider paths including $S_1 \rightarrow R_1$, $S_2 \rightarrow R_2 \rightarrow R_1$ and $S_1 \rightarrow R_1 \rightarrow R_2 \rightarrow R_1$. Again, we need the value of A_2 in order to decide A_1. It looks like we have a dilemma: the choice of A_1 and A_2 depend on each other.

Our key insight is that *we can first assume that some nodes have already configured their amplification coefficients properly based on Eq. 2.* In this example, if we first assume A_2 has been set such that R_2 transmits at P_{max}, then for R_1, R_2 can be treated as a source node (R_2 will no longer relay signals). To get A_1, we consider paths $S_1 \rightarrow R_1$ and $R_2 \rightarrow R_1$ (S_2 has no path to R_1 since R_2 is no longer relay). As a result, we get A_1 = 60 dB. Then we can get A_2 = 80 dB with A_1 in hand, with which R_2 indeed transmits at P_{max}.

It is not hard to see that when setting A_i, we can only assume that nodes trained later than R_i have properly configured their amplification coefficients due to interference cancellation. In other words, the setting of A_i should follow the same sequence Ts. This implies that *the training sequence makes a difference on the choice of A.* In fact, if the training sequence is $[R_2, R_1]$ in this example, then A_1 = 80 dB and A_2 = 60 dB. A summary of power setting schemes and results are listed in Table 1. We will further investigate the effects of training sequence on system performance in Sec. 5.2.

Algorithm 1: Amplification setting algorithm

```
1 Input: a) Training sequence Ts = {R1, ..., Rn, S2, S1}; b) Channel gains
  between any pair of participating nodes.
2 for i ∈ [1, n] do
3     Paths ← findPaths(src = Ts[i + 1, i + 2, ...],
        relay = Ts[1, ..., i − 1], dest = Ts[i]);
4     Prx ← receivedPower(Paths) ;
      // A vector of received power from each path
5     Prx.extend([ni, Ii]) ;
      // Noise and residual interference
6     Ai ← Pmax/∑ Prx ;
```

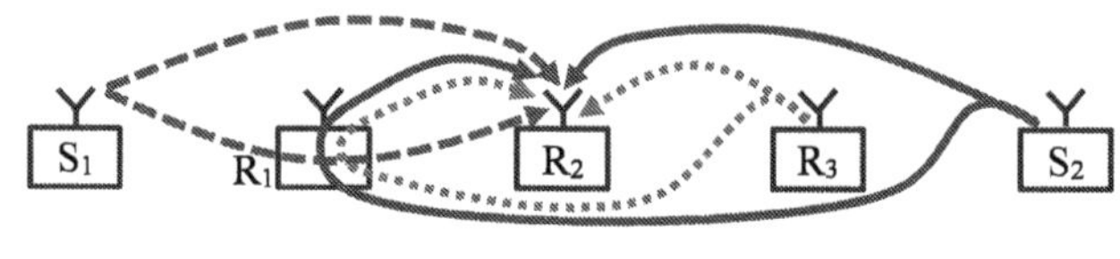

Figure 5: A 4-hop network. The paths used to calculate A_2 for R_2 are shown. S_1, S_2 and R_3 are considered as source nodes and R_1 as relay.

3.2.3 Our solution. Based on these observations and analysis, we propose a simple and practical solution to the amplification setting problem, as shown in Alg. 1. As an illustration, we consider the 4-hop network as shown in Fig. 5 and focus on the setting of A_2 for R_2.

According to the training sequence Ts, we start the training process from the first relay node in Ts to the last one. For each relay R_i, it first find all valid paths from nodes that have not yet performed training ($R_{i+1}, R_{i+2}, ..., R_n$) as well as the source nodes to itself R_i (Line 3). For example, assume $Ts = [R_1, R_2, R_3]$ and R_1 has finished this process and configured A_1 accordingly, Fig. 5 plots all the paths for R_2 that need to be taken into account to set power amplification. In this case, S_1, S_2 and R_3 are treated as source nodes and R_1 as relay.

Once a node gets these paths, it can calculate the received power from each of these paths (Line 4). Note that all source nodes are assumed to have the maximum transmission power P_{max}. For example, the received power at R_2 from the path $R_3 \rightarrow R_1 \rightarrow R_2$ in Fig. 5 can be calculated as $P_{max} L_{R_3,R_1} A_1 L_{R_1,R_2}$, where L_{R_i,R_j} is the path loss from node R_i to node R_j.

A node also need to take noise and residual interference at each relay into consideration since they also contribute to the received power (Line 5).

Finally, a node set its amplification coefficient based on the total received power (Line 6). Now in Fig. 5, we have A_1 and A_2 calculated. After this, R_3 start to repeat this process.

3.2.4 Overhead analysis. **Communication overhead:** Once the training process is finished and the link is established, multiple packets can be exchanged for a long time. Thus, the training overhead is amortized. **Computation overhead:** In practice, the number of relays in a system is limited. This is mainly because the noise propagation issue as we analyze in Sec. 5.1, especially when interference cancellation is not perfect, which increases the noise floor at each node. Also, a large number of relays require very long OFDM symbols as mentioned in Sec. 3.1.2, which may not be desired in practice, especially when we want to make the system standard compliant. Besides, not all nodes are connected in reality due to the large path loss. This will reduce the number of paths on Line 3. For these reasons, computation overhead is not a primary concern in practice.

4 HARNESSING BIPASS IN NETWORKS

In previous sections, bidirectional cut-through transmissions are made possible via interference management and power amplification algorithms. In this section, we investigate how to harness BiPass in wireless networks.

4.1 Routing selection

In traditional wireless routing designs (e.g., [10]), information can only be forwarded from the source to the destination via relays hop by hop. The feasibility of cut-through breaks this basic assumption, and thus leads to an interesting open problem: *How can we select the relays such that the end-to-end throughput is maximized in a cut-through enabled wireless network?*

The problem has been challenging when only a single pair of nodes S_1 and S_2 are considered. Given a set of relays $\mathcal{R}$, there can be a large number of valid paths from S_1 to S_2 via $\mathcal{R}$, which jointly determine the end-to-end SNR. To make the problem tractable, we leverage the analytical results in Sec. 5 that, for a given relay set $\mathcal{R}$, the end-to-end SNR from S_1 to S_2 can be approximated by the strongest valid path via $\mathcal{R}$. Note that the signal strength along a given path is bottlenecked by the weakest link along that path. Then, the end-to-end SNR via a relay set $\mathcal{R}$ can be given by Eq. 3.

$$SNR(\mathcal{R}) = \max_{path \in \sigma(\mathcal{R} \bigcup \{S_1, S_2\})} \min_{(N_i, N_j) \in path} G_{N_i, N_j}, \quad (3)$$

where $\sigma(\cdot)$ denotes the set of all permutations of $\mathcal{R}$ with S_1 and S_2 as the first and last elements respectively, $N_i \in \mathcal{R} \bigcup \{S_1, S_2\}$, and G_{N_i,N_j} donates the SNR between node N_i and node N_j.

For a single transmission pair (S_1, S_2), maximizing the throughput is equivalent to maximizing the end-to-end SNR. Therefore, the **Max-SNR** routing selection for (S_1, S_2) can be formulated as follows.

$$\max_{\mathcal{R}} SNR(\mathcal{R}). \quad (4)$$

When there are many concurrent transmission pairs in the network, MaxSNR routing can be problematic. From Eqs. 3 and 4, it can be observed that many relay sets $\mathcal{R}$ could potentially maximize Eq. 4 and the number of active relays is not necessarily minimized. This leads to two drawbacks: 1) one cut-through route may incur large interference to other ongoing transmissions; 2) The increase in delay spread may cause inter-symbol interference.

To address the above issues, we propose **MaxSNR-MinHop** routing, which could achieve at most a small constant SNR gap to the Max-SNR routing but at the same time minimizes the number of active relays.

In MaxSNR-MinHop, each node N_i maintains a routing table Γ_{N_i} to all other nodes in the network. The key idea of MaxSNR-MinHop is that the routing tables are constructed for a set of discrete SNR thresholds. Each SNR thresholds ideally corresponds to the minimum SNR required for successful decoding for a given transmission rate in the physical layer. In practice, each SNR threshold could be set slight higher than the ideal SNR threshold to allow imperfect interference cancellation. As will be shown in Sec. 6, the practical SNR threshold is very close to the ideal case. For a destination N_j and a given SNR threshold SNR_{thres}, node N_i stores the next-hop forwarder, denoted by $\Gamma_{N_i}(N_j, SNR_{thres})$, which minimizes the number of hops from node N_i to node N_j such that the end-to-end SNR is no less than the threshold SNR_{thres}. To illustrate the idea precisely, let $\Psi_{N_i}(SRN_{thres})$ denote the set of neighboring nodes of N_i such that the SNR between N_i and N_j is above SNR_{thres}.

$$\Psi_{N_i}(SRN_{thres}) \triangleq \left\{N_j | P_{max} G_{N_i,N_j} \geq SNR_{thres}\right\}.$$

Then, based on Eq. (3), the next-hop forwarder of node N_i must be in $\Psi_{N_i}(SRN_{thres})$, and thus $\Gamma_{N_i}(N_j, SNR_{thres})$ can be given by

$$\Gamma_{N_i}(N_j, SNR_{thres}) = \begin{cases} Null & \text{if } \forall N_k \in \Psi_{N_i}(SRN_{thres}), \\ & \Gamma_{N_k}(N_j, SNR_{thres}) = Null. \\ \arg\min_{N_k \in \Psi_{N_i}(SRN_{thres})} & \Gamma_{N_k}(N_j, SNR_{thres}) \quad \text{otherwise.} \end{cases} \quad (5)$$

Given the routing tables constructed (distributed construction of the routing table will be discussed), a source node S_1 could first check the maximum SNR threshold such that S_2 can be reached. Then S_1 starts constructing the route to S_2 by communicating the corresponding next-hop forwarder for the SNR threshold. The SNR threshold must also be sent to the forwarder such that the route to the destination can be constructed recursively hop by hop. Note that by increasing the number of SNR thresholds, the achieved SNR is within an arbitrarily small constant gap to the maximum SNR given by Eq. 4, the correctly constructed routing tables allows us to approximate MaxSNR routing with minimum number of hops. The key question left is how to construct the routing tables?

Distributed routing table construction: The major step in MaxSNR-MinHop is to construct the routing tables at each node in a distributed manner. Initially, each node only knows the list of neighboring nodes and their corresponding SNR thresholds. All the nodes periodically broadcast their routing tables to neighboring nodes. Once a new routing table is received from a neighbor N_j, the node N_i updates its routing table as follows. For a destination N_k and a threshold SNR_{thres}, if the total number of hops from N_i

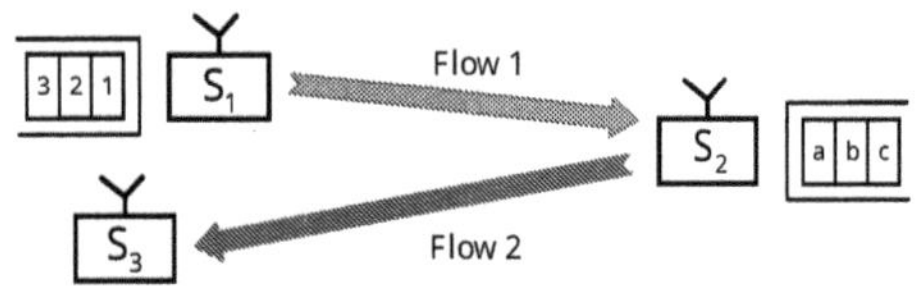

(a) S_1 want to transmit to S_2 while S_2 has data for S_3.

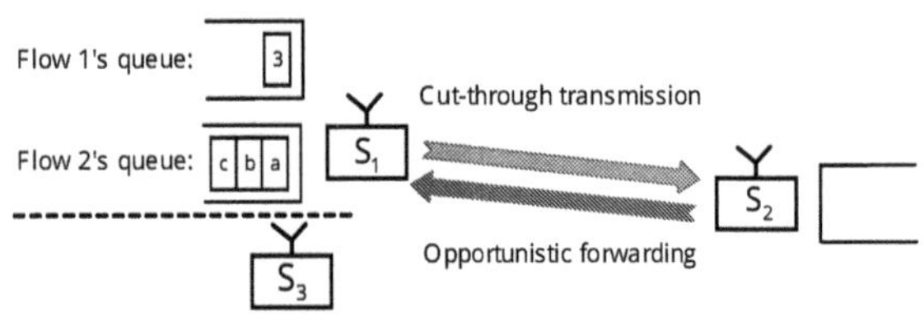

(b) S_2 opportunistically forward its packet to S_3.

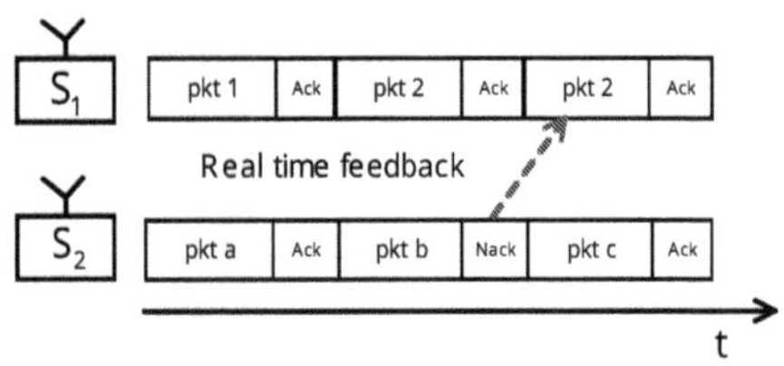

(c) Real-time feedback enables more timely error controls.

Figure 6: Illustration of opportunistic forwarding and real-time feedback.

to N_j and from N_j to N_k is smaller than the known minimum hops from N_i to N_k for SNR_{thres}, in the routing table of node N_i, the next-hop to node N_k for threshold SNR_{thres} can be updated by the next-hop to node N_j for threshold SNR_{thres}. The routing tables are exchanged among the nodes until all the routing tables converge. Although to maintain a small gap to the maximum SNR, more SNR thresholds are desirable, we note that the communication overhead of routing table construction in MaxSNR-MinHop increases linearly with the number of SNR thresholds. Fortunately, the communication overhead is not a major problem for two reasons: 1) in practice, there are only a limited number of feasible transmission rates, and thus a small number of SNR thresholds are sufficient; 2) since the routing tables need to be constructed only once, the communication overhead is amortized for the time when the network topology remains static.

Route establishment: The above route selection process is also a notification process: the relays will know whether it is selected to participate in the route. Similar to the designs in [7], once the route is determined, training and power setting process can start from the node closet to destination node since it has the information of all the participating relays.

4.2 Leveraging bidirectional transmissions

Compared with one-way cut-through, bidirectional cut-through brings most throughput and delay gains when the data traffic flows are also bidirectional. Then a natural question arises: *In a wireless network with limited or no bidirectional traffic flows, can we still achieve throughput and delay gains by leveraging bidirectional cut-through?* We answer the question affirmatively by proposing opportunistic forwarding and real-time feedback schemes, which will be illustrated through an example as shown in Fig. 6. In Fig. 6(a), there are two traffic flows in the network, where S_1, S_2 need to send streams of packets to S_2 and S_3, respectively.

4.2.1 Opportunistic forwarding. During the cut-through transmission from S_1 to S_2, S_2 checks its buffer, if there is any packet such that it is "closer" to the destination node from S_1 than that from S_2, S_2 forwards the packet to S_1. In the example shown in Fig. 6(b), S_2 forwards its packets to S_1 which is closer to S_3. Specifically in our scheme, we select our distance metric between two nodes S_2 and S_3 as the end-to-end SNR given by Eq. 4. Note that the distance from S_2 to S_3 is stored in the routing table of S_2, thus S_2 only needs to query S_1's routing table about the distance from S_1 to S_3. Since bidirectional cut-through transmission is enabled between S_1 and S_2, such a query takes zero overhead. With opportunistic forwarding, bidirectional cut-through can be utilized to increase the capacity of the network without the constraint of bidirectional traffic flows. As will be shown in the simulations in Sec. 6.3.2, the throughput gain can be substantial compared with one-way cut-through.

4.2.2 Real-time feedback. Bidirectional cut-through enables real-time feedback for the traffic in both directions. For example, in Fig. 6(c), the packet *pkt* 2 in the transmission from S_1 to S_2 is not successfully recovered at S_2. With real-time feedback, S_2 could piggyback a NACK instantly to S_1 such that S_1 could re-send *pkt* 2 with minimum delay. In comparison, in one-way cut-through, the lost packets cannot be recovered until the dedicated feedback slot after transmitting a block of packets. To mitigate routing establishment overhead, a large block size may be used in one-way cut-through. Thus, when there are packet losses, bidirectional cut-through can achieve a significant delay gain over one-way cut-through. The delay gain is more evident in real-time applications such as video streaming or gaming, where one received packet cannot be considered useful unless all packets with smaller indices have been successfully received. Furthermore, real-time feedback can also be utilized to dynamically adjust the data rates for both directions.

5 SYSTEM ANALYSIS

To better understand BiPass, in this section, we investigate some problems of the system.

5.1 Noise propagation

Noise at relays will get amplified together with the signals. A natural concern is that the noise accumulated from different paths at the end nodes may be too high to decode packets. In this section, we look into the problem of noise propagation in BiPass.

Consider the 2-relay topology shown in Fig. 7. Since source nodes S_1 and S_2 do not introduce additional noise at other nodes when transmitting, we assume they are in receiving-only mode so that we can focus on noise propagation. We also assume that the relays have set the amplification coefficients based on Alg. 1, and are in full duplex relay mode. Note that in this setting, each relay will transmit noise with power $A_i n_0$, where n_0 is the noise floor and A_i is its amplification coefficient. We want to know how much noise can be observed at the end nodes in this scenario.

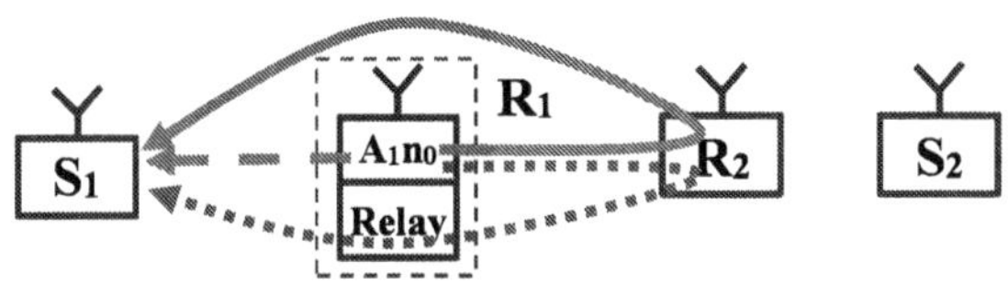

Figure 7: All possible three paths from R_1 to S_1 are shown. They are the reverse of paths from S_1 to R_1.

We first make the following **observation**: If channel reciprocity[2] holds between any two nodes without this system[3], then channel reciprocity holds between any two nodes when BiPass is set up and running. For example, in our system, if S_1 transmits at power P_{tx} and the received signal power at R_1 is P_{rx}, then if R_1 transmits at power P_{tx}, S_1 will receive signal with power P_{rx}. The key insight is that all the paths from one node to the other node are exactly the reverse of all paths from the other node to this node. Since the path loss and amplifications are the same for all the path pairs, we get the above conclusion.

Recall that the amplification coefficient A at relays are chosen based on the total power of received signals P_{rx}[4] as shown in Eq. 2. In other words, A can be treated as the total signal power loss from two end nodes to this relay node. Now if a relay transmits noise with power An_0, the sum power received at two end nodes will be $(An_0)/A = n_0$. Since noise from different relays are uncorrelated, the above analysis can be performed for each relay. We get the following conclusion: the total additional noise power introduced at the end nodes

$$n_{add} = \sum_i n_i, \tag{6}$$

where n_i is the noise floor at relay R_i. This conclusion implies that incorporating more relays, while it may increase signal strength, will also increase the noise floor at the end nodes.

Eq. 6 gives the total additional noise increase at both end nodes. For each relay R_i , it can be shown that the noise distribution is the same as the received signal power from source nodes at that relay. For example, assume at relay R_i, the received signal power from S_1 and S_2 is α_i and β_i, respectively, then the additional noise due to R_i observed at S_1 will be $\frac{\alpha_i}{\alpha_i+\beta_i}n_i$ and S_2 be $\frac{\beta_i}{\alpha_i+\beta_i}n_i$. We represent this ratio as $\phi_i := \alpha_i/\beta_i$.

5.2 Effects of training sequence

In Sec. 3.1.1, we conclude that any training sequence can yield a *stable* system. Later in Sec. 3.2.2 we analyze the effects of different training sequences on amplification coefficient selection of relay nodes. It seems that different training sequences may lead to different SNR of received signal at end nodes. Surprisingly, we find that training sequence has no effect on the received SNR at end nodes.

We first focus on noise propagation in a two-relay system, as shown in Fig. 8. We concluded in Sec. 5.1 that the total noise introduced at the two end nodes by each relay is equal to the noise floor n_i at that node. Also, the distribution n_i is same as the received signal power components ratio ϕ_i from source nodes. We want to show that ratio ϕ_i does not vary with different training sequences.

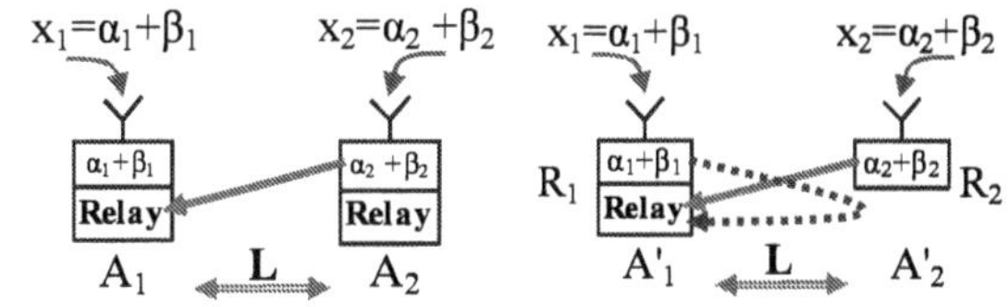

(a) Sequence $[R_2, R_1]$. (b) Sequence $[R_1, R_2]$.

Figure 8: Received signal components at R_1 with different training sequences.

Assume $x_i = \alpha_i + \beta_i$ is the external signal power (from source nodes in this case) received at relay i, where α_i and β_i represents the signal power components from S_1 and S_2, respectively. The path loss between R_1 and R_2 is assumed to be L. With training sequence $[R_2, R_1]$ as shown in Fig. 8(a), assume Alg. 1 gives A_i as the amplification coefficient for R_i; and with $[R_1, R_2]$ in Fig. 8(b), amplification coefficients are A'_i. Then the received signal power at R_1 in these two cases are

$$\begin{cases} P_{rx1} = x_1 + LA_2x_2 & (7a) \\ P'_{rx1} = x_1 + LA'_2x_2 + L^2A'_2A'_1x_1. & (7b) \end{cases}$$

Similarly, we can get the representations for R_2. Note that with Eq. 2, Eq. 7b can be rewritten as $P'_{rx1} = x_1 + LA'_2P'_{rx2} = x_1 + LP_{max}$.

The key insight here is that A_i and A'_i are related. Together with Eq. 2, we get

$$\begin{cases} P_{max} = A_2P_{rx2} = A_2(x_2 + LP_{max}) & (8a) \\ P_{max} = A'_1P'_{rx1} = A'_1(x_1 + LP_{max}) & (8b) \\ P_{max} = A'_2P'_{rx2} = A'_2(x_2 + LA'_1x_1). & (8c) \end{cases}$$

Plug the representations of x_2 and x_1 from Eq. 8a and Eq. 8b to Eq. 8c, we get $A'_2 = A_2(1+L^2A'_2A'_1)$. Substituting A'_2 in the second term of Eq. 7b, we get

$$P'_{rx1} = (1 + L^2A'_2A'_1)(x_1 + LA_2x_2). \tag{9}$$

Compared with Eq. 7a, Eq. 9 shows that the received signal at R_1 is simply scaled by $(1 + L^2A'_2A'_1)$ and thus maintains the same signal components and power ratio ϕ. A similar reasoning can be performed for R_2. We conclude that *changing the training sequence in this system does not change the noise power observed at end nodes.*

Now we consider the received signal strength at end nodes. In fact, due to the amplification taken by relays, the output of R_1 based on Eqs. 7a and 9 are the same since they have the same signal components and output power P_{max}. Similarly, the output of R_2 also remains the same. So *the training sequence also has no effect on signal power received at end nodes.*

Extending to multiple relays scenario is straight forward. By treating this 2-relay system as a whole, the above analysis reveals that its output is same regardless of training sequence for a given external input (from source nodes and other relays). In other words, swapping the training sequence between R_i and R_{i+1} in a n-relay system does not affect the other nodes in the system. Since swapping can be performed between any two consecutive nodes in T_s,

[2]Here we only consider the channel gain.

[3]Especially with the single-antenna full duplex design [6], this assumption can be easily met.

[4]We also consider the noise n_0 at the relays (Line 5 of Alg. 1), but we ignore noise here since in most cases $P_{rx} \gg n_0$. The conclusion in Eq. 6 thus acts as an upper bound.

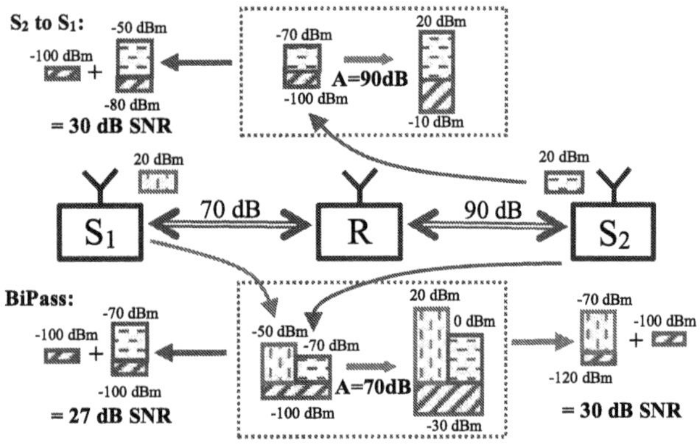

Figure 9: A one-relay system with signal propagation process illustrated. For one-way transmission from S_2 to S_1, although a 20 dB higher A is used at R, the SNR at S_1 only increases by 3 dB.

we conclude that **the training sequence has no effect on SNR at end nodes**.

5.3 Are we doubling the capacity?

Another question is: compared with one-way cut-through systems, can BiPass double the channel capacity? Consider the one-relay network as shown in Fig. 9. We assume that the noise floor at all nodes are -100 dBm. For one-way cut-through, based on the one-side dependency scheme used in [7], when S_1 wants to transmit packets to S_2, we set $A = 70$ dB; for the direction S_2 to S_1, $A = 90$ dB. However, in the bidirectional case, R can only give approximately 70 dB amplification (69.96 dB to be precise due to power addition) for both directions based on Alg. 1. *Does this mean we have a 20 dB SNR loss in the direction S_2 to S_1?*

In fact, in both systems, SNR is limited by the weakest link. As shown in Fig. 9, for S_2 to S_1 one-way transmission, R receives a signal with -70 dBm power (30 dB SNR). Recall that in the amplification process, noise is also amplified. So, although S_1 receives -50 dBm signal but it also receives -80 dBm noise. The SNR at S_1 is thus still limited by 30 dB. Similarly, we can see S_2 can also have a 30 dB SNR for the direction S_1 to S_2. While in our system, we get 30 dB SNR at S_2 and 27 dB SNR at S_1 due to the increase of noise floor.

We make the following **observations**: 1) SNR is basically limited by the weakest link in the path for both one-way and bidirectional transmissions, a larger A does not necessarily mean a large SNR increase. 2) Our system can not exactly double the channel capacity compared with one-way cut-through full duplex systems, but close to double. This is due to the noise accumulation problem that we analyzed in Sec. 5.1.

5.4 Additional Issues

Synchronization: Clearly, we do not need time synchronization. For frequency synchronization, previous work [7] has shown that a signal goes through a full duplex relay will remain the same frequency. Thus frequency offset is also not a problem, which usually entails careful processing [19].

Imperfect cancellation: It is possible that due to reasons including channel estimation errors, channel changes, etc, the cancellation at relays or end nodes are imperfect in reality. Since residual interference can be treated as noise, it will have a similar behavior as our analysis in Sec. 5.1. So, imperfect cancellation will only result in noise floor increase at end nodes.

Data rate selection: Feedback based scheme, the de facto rate selection scheme used today, is clearly one option for our system. Based on the packet reception rate, the source node can adjust its rate accordingly. In fact, since real-time feedback is possible in our system, a much faster reaction is expected than traditional half duplex systems. Alternatively, one can take advantage of the training process performed by the other source node to decide the data rate.

6 EVALUATIONS

To evaluate the performance of BiPass in the real world, we build a prototype with NI PXIe-1082 software defined radio platform with NI-5791 RF front end. Experiments are performed in a large office with 24 metallic cubicles inside. The carrier frequency is set to be 2.57 GHz to avoid external interference and the bandwidth used is 10 MHz. Our full duplex implementation follows the design in [13], a node has two antennas for dedicated transmitting and receiving. We think the design in [6], which uses one antenna for both transmitting and receiving, as well as considering nonlinear signal distortions, may further improve the performance of BiPass. The symbol size of OFDM is set to be 1024 samples (subcarriers) and CP ratio 0.2. We make it larger than 802.11 standard since our platform introduce a larger latency ($\sim 0.8\ \mu s$) when act as full duplex relays. The transmission power is set to be 0 dBm. Up to 3 relays are used in our experiments. Similar to the previous sections, we name the source nodes as S_i and relay nodes as R_i.

6.1 Micro-benchmark

6.1.1 Power amplification. In Sec. 3.2.3, we propose an algorithm for setting the power amplification coefficient of each relay in BiPass. In this section, we investigate the performance of this algorithm, compared with the two naive solutions (one-side and two-side dependency) mentioned in Sec. 3.2.1.

Fig. 10 shows the CDF of the transmitting power used by all the relays in 3-relay systems with different power setting schemes. We find that with the one-side dependency scheme, the power at relays can easily go beyond the limit which means signal clipping happens very often, thus resulting in an increasing BER at decoder [15]. We also observe the cases where amplification is so high that it exceeds our hardware limitation, in turn results in an unstable system. We utilize 20 dBm as transmission power to represent these cases in the figure. For two-side dependency solution, the transmitted power is conservative in all experiments. We observe the cases where relays use power 17 dB less power for transmission, which means large SNR loss as we analyzed in Sec. 3.2.1. With our proposed solution in Alg. 1, the transmitting power at relays are within ± 2 dB to its maximum power which is tolerant in reality. The small variances are mainly caused by path loss estimation errors, uncalibrated analog power amplifier, etc.

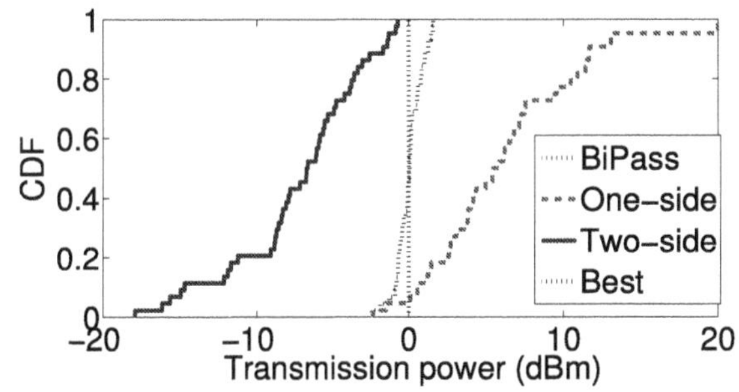

Figure 10: Transmission power used at relay nodes in a 3-relay system with different power schemes.

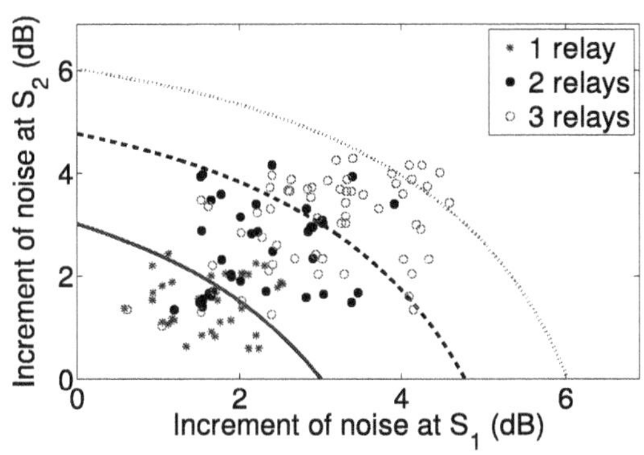

Figure 11: Increment of noise floor at each end node. The lines represent the theoretical values.

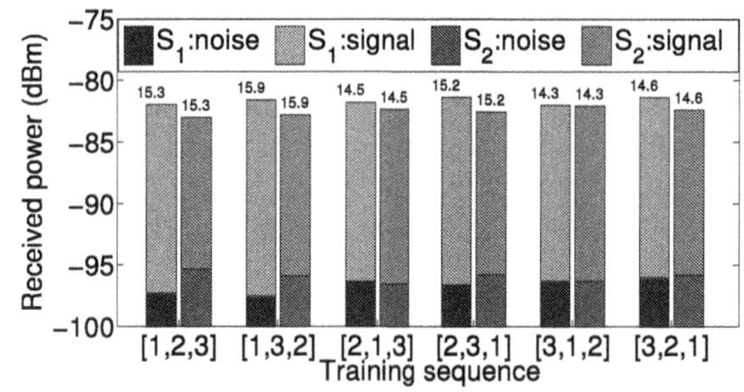

Figure 12: Signal and noise power at end nodes with different Ts. SNR values are indicated on top.

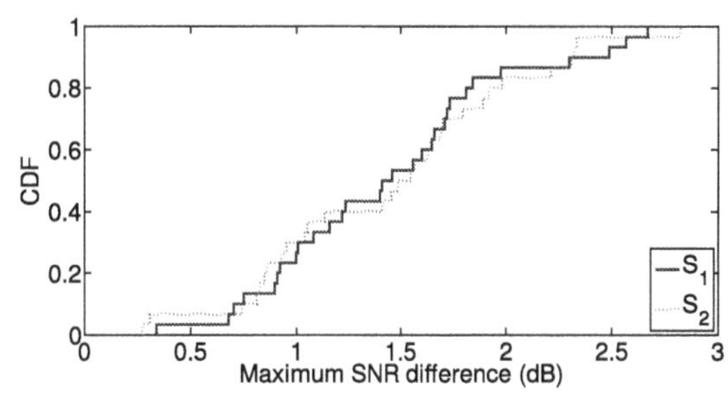

Figure 13: Maximum SNR difference at end nodes with different Ts.

6.1.2 Noise propagation. In this part, we do experiments to record the noise floor increase observed at the end nodes. For each experiment, we set up the link using sequential training procedure and set amplification coefficients with Alg. 1, end nodes are in receiving-only mode without transmitting any signal. We record the noise floor before and after the link set up and calculate the noise increase. Fig. 11 shows this noise increase observed by each end node with 1 to 3 relays in between. We also plot the theoretical values based on Eq. 6. Note that in our implementation, each node contains two antennas for dedicated transmission and reception, which means the channel reciprocity assumption made in Sec. 5.1 is not fulfilled. Even in this case, we can observe that the noise floor at end nodes increases with the number of employed relays, and the difference between theoretical values are within several dB.

6.1.3 Effects of the training sequence. To evaluate the effects of the training sequence, we record the SNR observed at end nodes with different training sequences in 3-relay systems. Fig. 12 shows the signal strength and noise power at end nodes in a typical trace. Again because of our two-antenna node design, we can see signal strength and noise power differences with different training sequences. Otherwise the signal strength observed by both end nodes should be the same with the same training sequence based on our channel reciprocity observation in Sec. 5.1. And for the same token, we observe that the signal and noise power tends to change in a correlated way. Nevertheless, the SNR difference is only within 2 dB in this experiment.

We further repeat the experiment for 30 times and record the largest difference between SNR values observed at end nodes with different training sequences. Fig. 13 shows that the difference is limited by 3 dB. This result implies that training sequence plays an insignificant role even without the channel reciprocity assumption we made in Sec. 5.2.

Table 2: Decoding possibilities at relay nodes

Relay Node	R_1	R_2	R_3
Decoding rate	0/30	0/30	0/30

6.1.4 Relay decodability. Since relay nodes receive packets from both sides, they tend to have a much lower chance to decode packets. To validate this, we do experiments with 3-relay systems and try to decode packets at relay using successive interference cancellation. Table 2 shows that relays can not decode any packet in all experiments. However, in one-way cut-through system, the relays can 100 percent decode all the packets. This result is expected since signals at relays are mixed from two source nodes in two-way system. The decoder experiences troubles on packet detection and channel estimation. Since data rate is selected based on the target node, the interference at relays results in much higher BER because of reduced SNR. Similar to network coding based schemes, we think this feature of our system can be further explored for security applications.

6.2 System throughput

In this section, we compare the achievable throughput of BiPass with both half duplex *D&F* scheme and AirExpress. We run experiments in a total of 90 randomly chosen topologies with 1 to 3 relays being employed. In each experiment, we apply BiPass, AirExpress and *D&F* for comparisons. In the case of AirExpress and *D&F*, we enable data transfer of each direction separately. For *D&F*, we iterate all possible routes and choose the path that can maximize its throughput. For each scheme, we use the highest achievable physical layer data rates which can be supported by the system. In each experiments, 200 packets are transmitted. The communication overhead for training is excluded in the calculation of throughput.

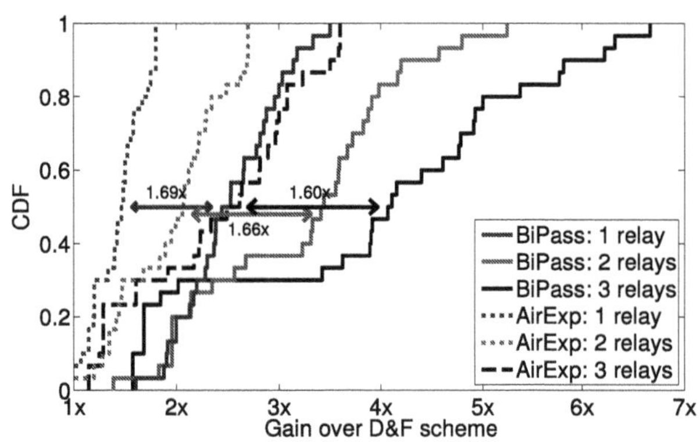

Figure 14: Throughput gain over half duplex *D&F* scheme with BiPass and AirExpress. BiPass shows over 1.6x median gain over AirExpress.

Fig. 14 shows the result of the throughput gain over *D&F* with AirExpress and BiPass. As we can see, both one-way and two-way systems can achieve a significant gain over *D&F*, and the gain increases with more relays. Specifically, BiPass shows median gains of 2.48x, 3.43x, and 4.09x over *D&F* with 1 to 3 relays in the system. Also, BiPass shows higher throughput over AirExpress since transmissions can happen in both directions concurrently with BiPass. We observe 1.69x, 1.66x and 1.6x median gain over AirExpress with 1 to 3 relays. The gain slightly decreases with number of relays due to the noise accumulation problem we analyzed in Sec. 5.1. Also, there is small residual interference after cancellation in our system, which further increases the noise floor at end nodes.

6.3 BiPass in networks

In order to understand the benefits of bidirectional cut-through in large wireless networks, we evaluate BiPass via simulations. In the simulations, 100 nodes are randomly placed in a $1000m \times 1000m$ field. Since one can expect that BiPass leads to a higher throughput gain when flows are always in both directions between a pair of nodes, we set up a challenging scenario for BiPass, where 10 traffic flows are generated between randomly picked nodes such that most of the traffic is not bidirectional. For BiPass, the power amplification is controlled by Alg. 1, while in other schemes each radio operates at its maximum power 20 dBm. 8 discrete data rates from 802.11g are used in the simulations. The residual interference due to imperfect cancellation and noise propagation are measured from the experiments and then fed into the simulator. To compare BiPass with existing techniques, we implement two benchmark schemes, i.e., the traditional *D&F* scheme with half duplex radios [10] and the one-way cut-through scheme AirExpress [7]. To avoid inter-symbol interference, the maximum number of relays for both BiPass and AirExpress is set to be 4. Throughout the simulations, the MAC layer employs a simple CSMA mechanism such that two routes/flows can be transmitted concurrently only when their mutual interference is marginal. We apply 100 random topologies in each of the following network simulations.

6.3.1 Different routing schemes. To study the performance of routing selection algorithms, we implement MinHop routing [10], our proposed MaxSNR routing and MaxSNR-MinHop routing algorithms. In MinHop routing, the routes are selected to minimize the expected number of hops.

Fig. 16 shows the impact of different routing algorithms on BiPass. It can be observed that the performance of MinHop is very bad for BiPass. This is because the routes selected by MinHop do not maximize the end-to-end SNR and thus is a poor metric for bidirectional cut-through. Compared with MaxSNR routing, MaxSNR-MinHop could achieve an additional 14% throughput gain. The major reason is that by minimizing the number of active relays, one transmission incurs less interference to the network and there might be more concurrent transmissions in the network.

6.3.2 Throughput gain of BiPass. In Fig. 15, we compare the achievable throughput of BiPass with AirExpress and the traditional *D&F* schemes. First, AirExpress and BiPass could achieve much higher throughput than *D&F*. The reason is that in *D&F*, when a node is transmitting, all its neighbor nodes cannot transmit to avoid incurring interference. As a result, the interference constraint greatly limit the achievable throughput of *D&F*. Second, BiPass achieves a median throughput gain of 1.36x over AirExpress. The throughput gain comes from two factors: 1) BiPass is able to leverage opportunistic forwarding while AirExpress could not; 2) BiPass uses a better routing selection algorithm than AirExpress. Our results suggest that even when the traffic flows are not bidirectional, BiPass still leads to substantial throughput improvement.

6.3.3 Delay performance of BiPass. Fig. 17 shows the delay performance of BiPass, AirExpress and *D&F*. First, the delay of AirExpress and BiPass is much lower than that of *D&F*. The reason is that in *D&F*, the delay of packets quickly accumulate hop by hop, while one cut-through transmission can cross multiple hops. Second, attributed to the opportunistic forwarding, BiPass achieves much lower delay than AirExpress. Specifically, the median delay reduction is 47%.

6.3.4 Delay gain v.s. block size. To mitigate the communication overhead of establishing a route, it is reasonable to assume that packets are transmitted in blocks for both AirExpress and BiPass. Fig. 18 plots the in-order delay performance in a network with a single traffic flow. In-order delay means a received packet cannot be considered useful unless all packets with smaller indices have been successfully received. The end-to-end packet loss probability is 0.1. Fig. 18 reveals that with real-time feedback enabled by BiPass, the in-order delay of BiPass is a constant independent of the block

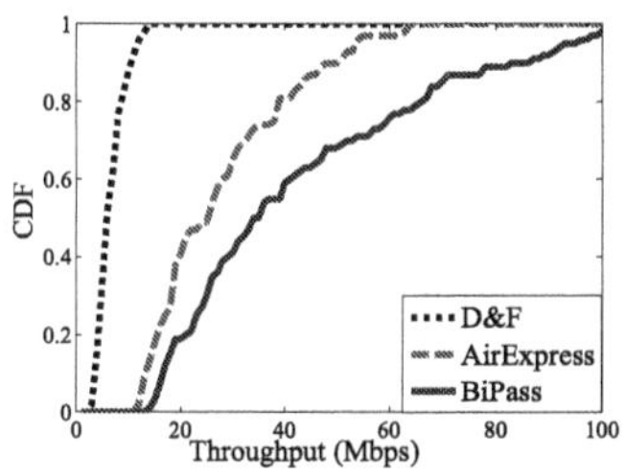

Figure 15: Throughput gain of BiPass over AirExpress and *D&F* schemes.

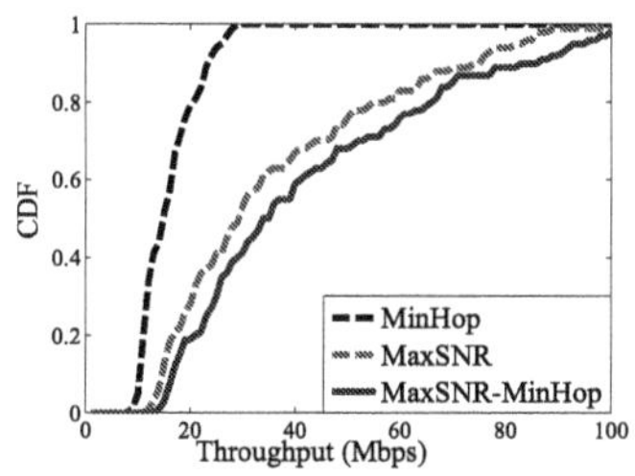

Figure 16: Throughput of BiPass with different routing selection schemes.

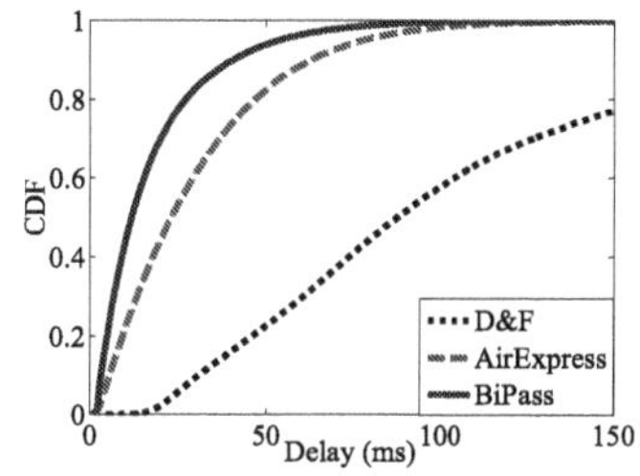

Figure 17: Delay gain of BiPass over AirExpress and *D&F* schemes.

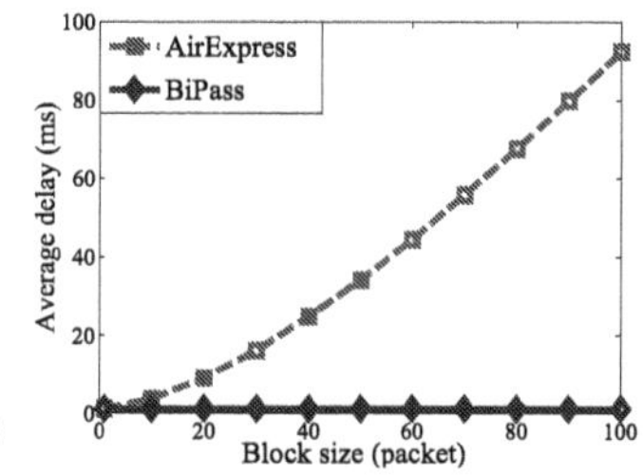

Figure 18: In-order delay performance when packets are transmitted in blocks.

size. Note that the delay of BiPass in Fig. 18 is much less than that in Fig. 17, this is because there is only a single flow in this new scenario, thus there are no contention latencies. On the other hand, for AirExpress, since feedback is only available after transmitting the whole block of packets, the delay increases significantly with the block size. This suggests that BiPass is much more appropriate for real-time applications such as video streaming or gaming.

7 DISCUSSION

In this section, we discuss some practical issues with BiPass and how we can further improve its performance.

Integrating with MIMO: MIMO can significantly improve the performance of wireless systems by transmitting multiple streams simultaneously. Full duplex MIMO has been shown possible in [3, 5]. By carefully choosing relays, or using relays with multiple antennas, we think BiPass can be extended to use MIMO.

More general topologies: Our current design works for two end nodes to exchange information. As extensions of our work, more general scenarios can be considered. For example, to support multiple nodes on each side, or to allow multiple simultaneous flows on overlapped paths. We think possible directions to realize these scenarios are using multiple antennas, multiple channel bands, etc.

Mobile scenario: Our current design considers only static environment. A possible extension of our work is to consider mobile scenario. Clearly, with our current design, a node would need to estimate channels frequently in this scenario, which means high overhead. It is possible that some of the nodes do not need to retrain when only one node moves, how to take advantage of this fact may help to extend BiPass to mobile scenario.

Other forwarding schemes: In our design of BiPass, amplify-and-forward is essentially implemented. Other forwarding schemes such as quantize-map-forward [11] may be explored to mitigate issues like noise propagation. However, how to do interference cancellation with these schemes is challenging.

Scheduling in networks: In our current network design, flows are CSMA based. We think how to optimally schedule flows in networks, especially considering inter-flow interference, is an open problem to solve.

8 CONCLUSION

In this paper, we present BiPass, the first system that supports simultaneous bidirectional cut-through transmissions in the same frequency band via multiple full duplex relays. Our end-to-end full duplex system can be treated as a generalized version of the current full duplex system, where we enable full duplex communications between two far away nodes. While our system focus on WiFi settings, the same approach can be extended to LTE, 60 GHz, etc. We believe that our design will inspire more researches and act as an enabling technique for many more exciting applications in the future. For example, [1] utilizes a full duplex relay at 60 GHZ to improve performance of virtual reality. Our system may further boost the performance by enabling multiple such relays.

ACKNOWLEDGEMENTS

We would like to thank our reviewers for their comments and suggestions to improve our paper. This work has been partially supported by NSF grants CNS-1254032, CNS-1302620, EARS-1547306, CNS-1514260, CNS-1314538, CNS-1518829, Army Research Office W911NF-14-1-0368, and Office of Naval Research N00014-15-1-2166.

REFERENCES

[1] Omid Abari, Dinesh Bharadia, Austin Duffield, and Dina Katabi. 2016. Cutting the cord in virtual reality. In *Proceedings of the 15th ACM Workshop on Hot Topics in Networks*. ACM, 162–168.
[2] Rudolf Ahlswede, Ning Cai, S-YR Li, and Raymond W Yeung. 2000. Network information flow. *IEEE Transactions on information theory* 46, 4 (2000), 1204–1216.
[3] Ehsan Aryafar, Mohammad Amir Khojastepour, Karthikeyan Sundaresan, Sampath Rangarajan, and Mung Chiang. 2012. MIDU: enabling MIMO full duplex. In *Proceedings of the 18th annual international conference on Mobile computing and networking*. ACM, 257–268.
[4] Dinesh Bharadia and Sachin Katti. 2014. FastForward: fast and constructive full duplex relays. In *ACM SIGCOMM Computer Communication Review*, Vol. 44. ACM, 199–210.
[5] Dinesh Bharadia and Sachin Katti. 2014. Full duplex MIMO radios. In *11th USENIX Symposium on Networked Systems Design and Implementation (NSDI 14)*. 359–372.
[6] Dinesh Bharadia, Emily McMilin, and Sachin Katti. 2013. Full duplex radios. In *ACM SIGCOMM Computer Communication Review*, Vol. 43. ACM, 375–386.
[7] Bo Chen, Yue Qiao, Ouyang Zhang, and Kannan Srinivasan. 2015. AirExpress: Enabling Seamless In-band Wireless Multi-hop Transmission. In *Proceedings of the 21st Annual International Conference on Mobile Computing and Networking*. ACM, 566–577.
[8] Bo Chen, Vivek Yenamandra, and Kannan Srinivasan. 2015. FlexRadio: Fully Flexible Radios and Networks.. In *NSDI*. 205–218.
[9] Jung Il Choi, Mayank Jain, Kannan Srinivasan, Phil Levis, and Sachin Katti. 2010. Achieving single channel, full duplex wireless communication. In *Proceedings of the sixteenth annual international conference on Mobile computing and networking*. ACM, 1–12.
[10] Douglas SJ De Couto. 2004. *High-throughput routing for multi-hop wireless networks*. Ph.D. Dissertation. Massachusetts Institute of Technology.
[11] Melissa Duarte, Ayan Sengupta, Siddhartha Brahma, Christina Fragouli, and Suhas Diggavi. 2013. Quantize-map-forward (QMF) relaying: An experimental study. In *Proceedings of the fourteenth ACM international symposium on Mobile ad hoc networking and computing*. ACM, 227–236.

[12] Kai-Cheng Hsu, Kate Ching-Ju Lin, and Hung-Yu Wei. 2016. Full-duplex delay-and-forward relaying. In *Proceedings of the 17th ACM International Symposium on Mobile Ad Hoc Networking and Computing*. ACM, 221–230.

[13] Mayank Jain, Jung Il Choi, Taemin Kim, Dinesh Bharadia, Siddharth Seth, Kannan Srinivasan, Philip Levis, Sachin Katti, and Prasun Sinha. 2011. Practical, real-time, full duplex wireless. In *Proceedings of the 17th annual international conference on Mobile computing and networking*. ACM, 301–312.

[14] Sachin Katti, Shyamnath Gollakota, and Dina Katabi. 2007. Embracing wireless interference: Analog network coding. *ACM SIGCOMM Computer Communication Review* 37, 4 (2007), 397–408.

[15] Xiaodong Li and Leonard J Cimini. 1997. Effects of clipping and filtering on the performance of OFDM. In *Vehicular Technology Conference, 1997, IEEE 47th*, Vol. 3. IEEE, 1634–1638.

[16] Yue Qiao, Ouyang Zhang, Wenjie Zhou, Kannan Srinivasan, and Anish Arora. 2016. PhyCloak: obfuscating sensing from communication signals. In *2016 USENIX Annual Technical Conference (USENIX ATC 16)*. USENIX Association.

[17] Yang Yang and Ness B Shroff. 2015. Scheduling in wireless networks with full-duplex cut-through transmission. In *2015 IEEE Conference on Computer Communications (INFOCOM)*. IEEE, 2164–2172.

[18] Shengli Zhang, Soung Chang Liew, and Patrick P Lam. 2006. Hot topic: Physical-layer network coding. In *Proceedings of the 12th annual international conference on Mobile computing and networking*. ACM, 358–365.

[19] Wenjie Zhou, Tanmoy Das, Lu Chen, Kannan Srinivasan, and Prasun Sinha. 2016. BASIC: backbone-assisted successive interference cancellation.. In *MobiCom*. 149–161.

Orion: RAN Slicing for a Flexible and Cost-Effective Multi-Service Mobile Network Architecture

Xenofon Foukas
The University of Edinburgh
x.foukas@ed.ac.uk

Mahesh K. Marina
The University of Edinburgh
mahesh@ed.ac.uk

Kimon Kontovasilis
NCSR "Demokritos"
kkont@iit.demokritos.gr

ABSTRACT

Emerging 5G mobile networks are envisioned to become multi-service environments, enabling the dynamic deployment of services with a diverse set of performance requirements, accommodating the needs of mobile network operators, verticals and over-the-top (OTT) service providers. Virtualizing the mobile network in a flexible way is of paramount importance for a cost-effective realization of this vision. While virtualization has been extensively studied in the case of the mobile core, virtualizing the radio access network (RAN) is still at its infancy. In this paper, we present Orion, a novel RAN slicing system that enables the dynamic on-the-fly virtualization of base stations, the flexible customization of slices to meet their respective service needs and which can be used in an end-to-end network slicing setting. Orion guarantees the functional and performance isolation of slices, while allowing for the efficient use of RAN resources among them. We present a concrete prototype implementation of Orion for LTE, with experimental results, considering alternative RAN slicing approaches, indicating its efficiency and highlighting its isolation capabilities. We also present an extension to Orion for accommodating the needs of OTT providers.

KEYWORDS

5G mobile networks; network architecture; RAN slicing; RAN virtualization; abstractions

1 INTRODUCTION

5G is on the horizon. There is an evolutionary dimension to 5G aimed at significantly scaling up and improving the efficiency of mobile networks to meet the demanding requirements such as 1000x increase in capacity via new radio access technologies and spectrum bands (e.g., massive MIMO, millimeter waves). On the other hand, an alternative and complementary *service-oriented* vision for 5G presents a significant opportunity to innovate on the architectural front with several resulting benefits (ease in service creation, network sharing, reduce capex/opex costs, enhance user experience, realize a more energy-efficient mobile network infrastructure, etc.). The idea underlying this service-oriented view is for the network to support a wide range of services, differing significantly in their service requirements and device types (including machine-type devices). For example, ITU [29] identifies three broad classes of 5G services (enhanced mobile broadband, massive machine type communications, ultra-reliable and low latency communications) and several specific services within these three service classes.

As a one-size fits all architecture is unlikely to be suitable for such diverse use cases, realizing the service-oriented 5G vision in a cost-effective manner necessitates a flexible mobile network architecture that can turn the physical infrastructure into multiple logical networks or *slices*, one per service instance. Each slice in such an architecture is an end-to-end virtualized network instance, spanning both the core and radio access network (RAN), and is tailored in terms of resources to meet the requirements of the service in question. Here resources comprise of different types including computing, network, storage, radio, access hardware and virtual network functions (VNFs). Unsurprisingly, most prominent 5G architectural visions embrace slicing [7, 16, 49, 52, 60, 61], building on its earlier success in multi-experiment testbed infrastructures such as PlanetLab [12] and multi-tenant data centers. As virtualization and softwarization (via software-defined networking (SDN) and network function virtualization (NFV)) are key slicing enablers, research prototypes and operational systems using virtualization technologies and SDN/NFV principles have started to appear, especially in the mobile core [9, 19, 30, 42, 46, 57, 58]. In fact, an early form of core slicing called dedicated core networks (DECOR) is already specified by the 3GPP standards [2].

In this paper, our focus is on RAN slicing which refers to the ability to dynamically create and manage virtual RANs, each customized to meet the requirements of an end-to-end service. RAN slicing is a challenging problem that is only starting to receive attention. The key difficulty is that the RAN virtualization and apportionment into different slices should satisfy two key objectives: (1) to ensure slice independence (functional isolation) so that tenants maintain full control of their slices to be able to tailor them to meet the respective service requirements; (2) to flexibly and adaptively share RAN resources (radio, processing, memory, networking), among different slice owners (or tenants), so that the RAN infrastructure is used as efficiently as possible, *without* violating objective (1).

Previous work on RAN slicing, as elaborated in the next section, represents extreme points in the design space and therefore has managed to only partially address the aforementioned objectives. One approach originating in RAN sharing focuses mainly on efficient sharing of radio resources with no support for functional isolation, giving the infrastructure provider full visibility and control over slices [18, 19, 50]. The other approach puts the isolation at the center stage without considering the efficient use of resources [47, 48].

In this paper, we present Orion, which to our knowledge is the first RAN slicing system that provides functional isolation among slices while facilitating efficient sharing of the RAN resources. The design of Orion makes an explicit distinction between the infrastructure

MobiCom '17, October 16–20, 2017, Snowbird, UT, USA.
 ISBN 978-1-4503-4916-1/17/10...$15.00
DOI: https://doi.org/10.1145/3117811.3117831

provider and service providers (slice owners), providing mechanisms that allow flexible and adaptive provisioning of resources to slices based on their requirements. Each slice can manipulate its allocated resources in a virtualized form completely independently, and similarly customize its control plane as per the service needs. The `Base Station Hypervisor` in Orion plays a key role in achieving this by virtualizing the radio resources via a novel set of abstractions introduced in this work and by having the control plane of each slice operating in an isolated container over it. Moreover, Orion's design allows the control planes of slices to be composed flexibly and independently, employing different levels of centralization, effectively leading to a more efficient utilization of the RAN resources and simplifying the coordination of base stations where and when required.

In summary, this paper makes the following contributions:

- (Sections 3 and 4) Present a realizable RAN slicing design in the form of Orion, that enables both the functional isolation among slices, as well as the efficient utilization of the underlying RAN resources via the novel `Hypervisor` component and by facilitating the flexible composition of the control planes of individual slices.
- (Section 4) Introduce a novel set of abstractions for the virtualization of the radio resources that is applicable to both current (LTE) and future (5G New Radio) RANs.
- (Sections 4, 5 and 6) Provide a concrete implementation of Orion over the OpenAirInterface (OAI) LTE platform [51] along with a detailed experimental evaluation of the various aspects of the system that highlight its performance and scalability as well as its various capabilities compared to the state-of-the-art solutions.
- (Section 7) Present an extended form of Orion that supports over-the-top (OTT) service providers and demonstrating its benefits.

2 RELATED WORK

RAN Slicing. State of the art on RAN slicing can be traced back to the earlier works on active RAN sharing [13, 22, 53, 63, 70]. Broadly speaking, two approaches under the names of Multi-Operator Core Networks (MOCN) and Multi-Operator RAN (MORAN) have been considered. While both approaches imply the use of separate core networks for each participating operator, MOCN allows for spectrum sharing among operators while MORAN requires dedicated spectrum for each. Relatively, more attention has been given in the literature to the MOCN approach (e.g., [26, 35, 41]), which has been standardized for LTE in Release 8. NVS [35] is a representative example. Note that the use of the term virtualization in some of these works is somewhat misleading as it refers only to the UE perceived performance isolation (i.e. throughput) among operators sharing the RAN radio resources and not on the functional isolation and corresponding performance isolation of the slices' virtual network functions in terms of the required computing resources (processing, memory, networking). As indicated at the outset, functional isolation is additionally essential in the RAN slicing context. The major focus of these works is on the design of efficient radio resource scheduling algorithms while considering certain guarantees for operators. The fact that radio resource sharing is also relevant for efficient RAN slicing is reflected in the more recent algorithmic work in this thread [11, 23, 32, 43]. This body of work is complementary to our focus on systems support for RAN slicing. In fact, we employ the NVS scheduling algorithm in our prototype to highlight the efficient radio resource use feature of Orion.

From a systems perspective, RAN sharing oriented slicing (with no functional isolation among slices) has been explored through the use of the FlexRAN software-defined RAN platform [18, 19, 36, 50], which we include in our comparative evaluations. FlexRAN decouples the control from the data plane of base stations using a custom-tailored southbound API and introduces a flexible and programmable control plane. Network slicing is enabled with FlexRAN by programmatically defining the way in which the radio resources need to be allocated among the connected UEs based on the requirements of the slice they belong to. A unified control plane, which is controlled by a single entity (usually the infrastructure provider), is responsible to perform the corresponding control operations. This approach can be limiting, since the capabilities of the slices are fully dependent on the types of control functions that are bundled in the control plane of FlexRAN. In contrast, Orion allows independent and fully customizable control planes for each slice so that slice owners can flexibly introduce their own functionality in the RAN and tailor their slice as per the needs of their service.

To accommodate this need for slice customizability, the other RAN slicing approach taken in the literature seeks full isolation (by running the virtual base station instance of a slice within a Docker container for example) but assumes dedicated radio hardware and spectrum per slice [47, 48], bearing some similarity to the MORAN form of RAN sharing in that resource sharing among slices is limited at best to computing, memory and storage resources. This has the downside of inefficient use of radio resources and foregoing potential statistical multiplexing gains. The work presented in [52] also takes the same approach, although the focus there is on the idea of a network store for VNFs to aid in dynamic network slicing. On a more general note, wireless virtualization overview and position papers like [5, 25, 39, 69] advocate functional isolation, which strengthen the motivation for the approach we take in Orion to have an isolated and customizable control plane for each slice.

In terms of radio resource virtualization, recent works in the domain of RAN slicing [24, 25, 36, 39] have advocated the need for abstractions that decouple the control plane decisions from the physical radio resource grid. However, the abstractions presented in these works are high-level and do not consider the constraints that can be imposed by the physical layer (e.g., frequency-dependencies in scheduling). The abstractions introduced in Orion for radio resource virtualization not only overcome these limitations but are also generic in that they are applicable to both current LTE and future 5G-NR air interface technologies.

Core Slicing. There has been significant progress on mobile core slicing to the point that it is fairly mature and also made its way into 3GPP standards in a basic form under the name of DECOR [2]. Virtualization of core network functions combined with the use of mature virtualization technologies (e.g., KVM [34], LXC [27], Docker [44], VLANs [8, 64]) have led to systems that realize core network slicing [33, 48, 52]. Even the possibility of EPC as a service over the cloud has been explored [66]. Several research proposals leveraging NFV in the core appeared in the recent past, aimed at its optimization for better scalability (e.g., [9]), customization for particular use cases (e.g., [67]) and in general making it more flexible (e.g., [58]).

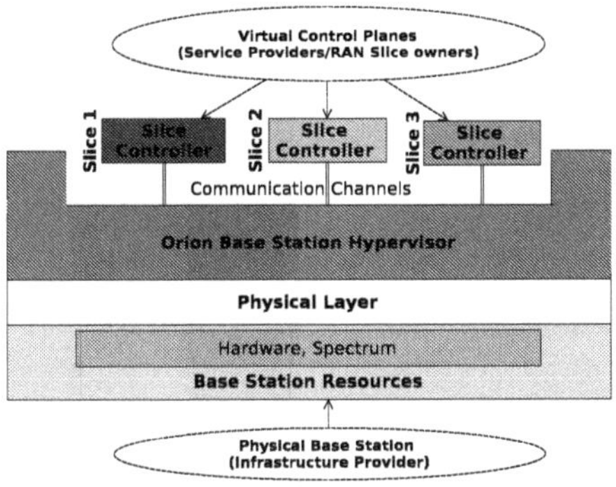

Figure 1: High-level architecture of Orion.

Management and Network Orchestration (MANO). The end-to-end nature of services create the need for a MANO entity responsible for realizing end-to-end slices spanning the core and the RAN as well as their life-cycle management to ensure compliance with their service requirements. This has led to MANO oriented research work [65] and several open-source MANO framework implementations (e.g., OSM [17], ONAP [40]). More pertinent to our work, the authors of Proteus [65] acknowledge the lack of a flexible RAN slicing solution and therefore consider use cases that focus on innovations around the mobile core. Orion fills this void. We present how Orion can be used in an end-to-end slicing context by interfacing with any of the MANO solutions mentioned above.

3 ORION OVERVIEW

The core contribution of this paper, Orion, is a novel RAN slicing system design that is in line with the spirit of network slicing and the needs of a flexible and cost-effective multi-service mobile network architecture – isolation among multiple virtual networks provides the necessary flexibility to customize and control a slice, whereas efficient sharing of the underlying physical infrastructure allows supporting diverse services in a cost-effective manner. Simultaneously being able to satisfy both these concerns of functional isolation between slices and efficient resource use in the context of the RAN is the main, as yet unresolved, challenge addressed by Orion.

Towards this end, Orion's design (Fig. 1) explicitly distinguishes the infrastructure provider from the service providers (the slice owners). The infrastructure provider is the owner of physical base stations, comprising of hardware resources (i.e., radio equipment, processing, memory, and network) and a chunk of spectrum. While it can be realized either via dedicated specialized hardware or in a cloud environment using re-programmable hardware (e.g., C-RAN baseband processing unit and remote radio heads), each physical base station in our model supports a single Radio Access Technology (RAT), meaning that all radio and spectrum resources available at the base station can be exploited through a *shared* physical layer. Note that, for concreteness in the description of Orion's design and implementation, we consider LTE as the underlying RAT and downlink scheduling as a running example throughout.

The `Base Station Hypervisor` that sits over the physical layer is the heart of Orion's design. It is the component used for managing RAN slices, for ensuring their full isolation – control logic for functional isolation and resources for performance isolation, as well as facilitating efficient sharing of underlying physical resources. Essentially, the `Hypervisor` binds the individual and isolated slices to the physical infrastructure, providing them with a virtual view of the underlying radio resources via a novel set of abstractions and the data plane state as well as applying their state changes over the physical data plane by mapping virtual to physical resources. The `Hypervisor` is part of the infrastructure provider's software infrastructure to support RAN slicing. The infrastructure provider is also responsible for admission control.

Service providers (e.g., MVNOs and verticals) in Orion realize their RAN slices through the creation of virtual base stations over the `Hypervisor`. Each virtual base station is a composition of a virtual control plane, responsible for managing data plane state that is revealed to it by the `Hypervisor`. The virtual control plane of a slice is effectively a local RAN-level slice controller running as a *separate process*, responsible to tailor the functionality and manage the allocation of resources to mobile devices (UEs) associated with the slice as if it was operating using its own dedicated infrastructure. The virtual control plane is also responsible for implementing the control protocols required for the communication and coordination of the virtual base station with the rest of the mobile infrastructure (e.g., S1 and X2 interfaces in LTE). This means that all operations defined for a given mobile network architecture can be supported by slices (including roaming) so long as the appropriate interfaces and messages are implemented as part of the respective virtual control planes. Note that although we discuss the data plane aspect both in our design and implementation, our primary focus expectedly is on the control plane. Following SDN principles, our design assumes control-data plane separation that is now widely accepted in the mobile networking domain [19, 37, 57, 68].

The communication of the slices' virtual control planes with the `Hypervisor` is message-based and happens through independent physical/virtual communication channels. This approach allows the deployment of slices either over the same physical machine as their `Hypervisor` or over separate physical machines. It also gives the flexibility to slice owners to compose their control planes using different levels of centralization to enable coordination based on their services' needs, independently of other slices.

The design of Orion provides strong isolation guarantees while allowing efficient resource sharing. First, since each of the slice controllers is running as a separate process, isolation among controllers in terms of memory and CPU can be achieved by employing well known OS and process virtualization techniques, like virtual machines (e.g., KVM) or containers (e.g., LXD and Docker). Second, the `Hypervisor` is the sole entity responsible for handling actual radio resources which it distributes among slices after virtualizing them, ensuring isolation from a radio resource perspective. Third, it can internally facilitate efficient resource use via a suitable allocation algorithm that also considers slices SLAs and underlying physical conditions. Additionally, from a UE perspective, the whole slicing operation is transparent, with each slice appearing as a different MVNO as in RAN sharing.

4 SYSTEM DESIGN & IMPLEMENTATION

This section details the key components of Orion: `Base Station Hypervisor` and `Virtual Control Plane` of a slice.

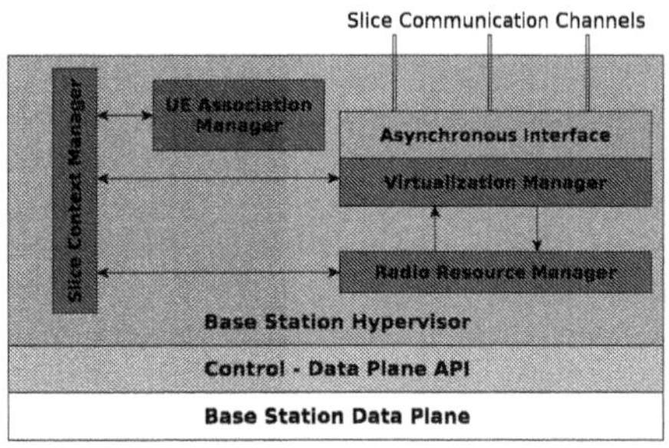

Figure 2: Architecture of the Orion Base Station Hypervisor.

4.1 Base Station Hypervisor

The `Base Station Hypervisor` (Fig. 2) acts as the intermediary between the data plane of the physical base station and the virtual control planes of slices. The `Hypervisor` communicates with the data plane via an API to access and modify the data plane state (e.g., obtain signal quality measurements and transmission queue sizes of UEs, apply scheduling decisions, etc.). The `Hypervisor` is responsible for allocating physical radio resources to slices with respect to their SLAs, transforms them into virtualized resources that are revealed to virtual control planes of slices in an isolated manner. On the other direction, slices use the provided virtual resources for their control plane operations and send their commands (e.g., scheduling decisions) back to the `Hypervisor`, which then translates them to a physical representation and applies them to the data plane. We now detail the internals of the `Hypervisor`.

4.1.1 Slice Context Manager. Prior to a slice's creation, the slice owner comes to an agreement on the required service type with the infrastructure provider, subject to admission control. This is formally translated into a *slice service description* that includes two elements:

A Service Level Agreement (SLA) that identifies the service requirements of the slice owner (e.g., average throughput, resource blocks). Orion does not restrict the SLA parameters and instead provides a flexible framework to implement suitably tailored mechanisms for admission control and fine-grained resource allocation.

A list of User Equipment (UE) identifiers required for the mapping of UEs to slices. Any unique identifier provided by the UE during the attachment process could be used.

The `Slice Context Manager` (Fig. 2) is responsible for the life-cycle management of slices at the base station. Each slice is associated with a context (Table 1) capturing the slice's capabilities and current state. Apart from the slice's SLA, this context keeps track of the active UEs on the slice, stores the configuration of the communication channel between the `Hypervisor` and the slice's virtual control plane, and all data structures for bookkeeping operations related to the use of physical resources by the slice in the past and present. The `Slice Context Manager` can obtain the identifiers of the UEs belonging to the slice from the management plane through a lookup function, further explained in Section 4.3.

Upon request for creation of a new slice, the `Slice Context Manager` does admission control. By checking the number of active slices, their SLAs and activity (through their context), and using an admission control policy adopted by the infrastructure provider (e.g., along the lines of [35]), either the slice is admitted with a corresponding context created, or rejected due to insufficient resources.

Slice Context
Slice id
UE identifier lookup function
Current slice SLA/policy settings
UEs currently connected to the slice
Communication channel configuration to slice local controller
Bookkeeping on usage of physical resources

Table 1: Per slice context maintained by the Hypervisor.

4.1.2 Radio Resource Manager. The `Radio Resource Manager` is responsible for the allocation of physical radio resources among co-located slices in a flexible and efficient manner, while ensuring slice isolation. While this is dependent on the nature of each resource, Orion adopts the principle that any physical radio resource meant for individual UEs can also be allocated among slices in an isolated fashion, because, by definition, they can be quantized and assigned to specific UEs. Such resources include radio resources allocated for downlink/uplink user and control traffic as well as for paging.

As an example, consider downlink LTE scheduling, involving two types of radio resources: (i) Resource Blocks (RB) for transmission of user traffic and (ii) Control Channel Elements (CCE, essentially a set of OFDM symbols) for transmission of the corresponding scheduling decisions. Due to their nature, these resources can be dynamically allocated to individual slices based on various criteria, like their SLAs, the channel conditions experienced by UEs in the slice etc. On the other hand, physical resources used either for the transmission of cell-related information (e.g., broadcast) or in a contention-based manner (e.g., random access) should not be allocated to slices because concurrent modifications from multiple slice control planes could lead to conflicts. Such resources are exclusively managed by the `Hypervisor` as discussed later in this section.

Orion provides a generic framework for the dynamic allocation of radio resources, which allows the implementation of different radio resource allocation mechanisms to fulfill different types of SLAs. Any allocation algorithm implemented in Orion would have inputs in the form of the physical radio resource grid and the context information of the active slices. The radio resource allocation process occurs periodically once every *allocation window* of duration t. At the beginning of each window, the `Radio Resource Manager` obtains the bookkeeping information and the SLAs of all the active slices from the `Slice Context Manager`. Through this information, and with the current cell configuration and allocation mechanism implemented, the `Radio Resource Manager` decides a splitting of the available radio resources among slices for the upcoming window. For each type of partition-able radio resource, it fills a two dimensional array that expresses the slice assignments of resources through a generic representation of the resource in the time and frequency domain. As an example, Fig. 3 illustrates LTE downlink scheduling for 2 slices. Each column represents a 1ms LTE subframe in Transmission Time Interval (TTI) units and each row the corresponding resource in the frequency domain (RBs in Fig. 3a and OFDM symbols in Fig. 3b). The tabulated numbers correspond to the ids of the slices to which the resources were allocated.

The decision of the `Radio Resource Manager` is forwarded to the `Slice Context Manager` to update the context of slices with allocated resources. Note that the `Slice Context Manager` and `Radio`

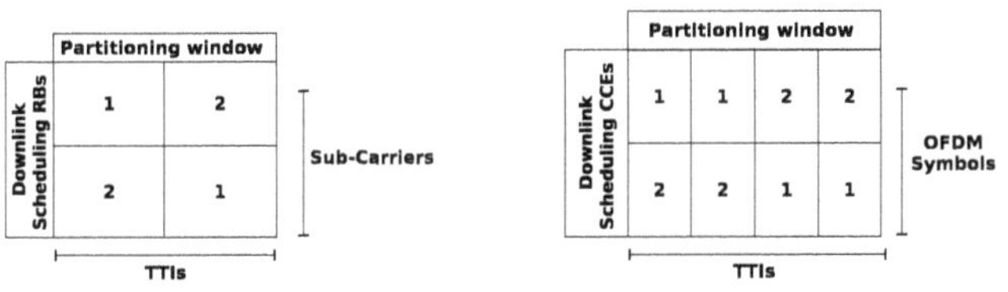

(a) Resource Blocks (b) Control Channel Elements

Figure 3: Resource partitioning between 2 slices for the LTE downlink scheduling example.

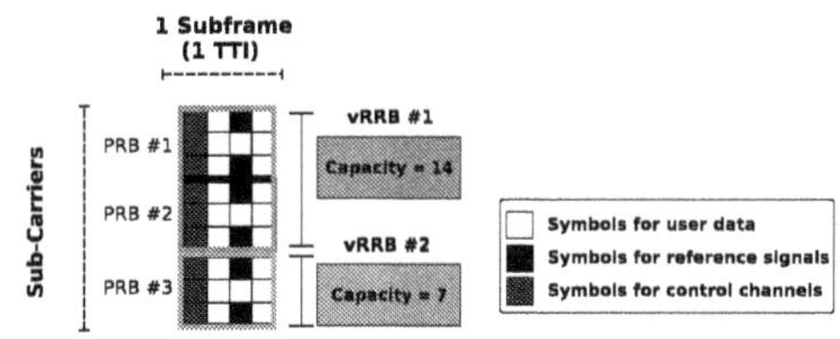

Figure 4: Mapping of PRBs to vRRBs in the context of LTE.

`Resource Manager` can be seen to provide the functionality of the 5G network slice broker introduced in the context of the 3GPP network sharing management architecture in [63]. When the slices' control planes make the scheduling decisions based on a virtualized and isolated form of their allocated resources via the `Virtualization Manager`, the `Radio Resource Manager` translates and updates the base station data plane state through the control-data plane API, and keeps track of the physical resources used by slices (via context updates) to inform the allocation in upcoming windows.

4.1.3 Virtualization Manager. The `Virtualization Manager` (Fig. 2) directly interacts with the virtual control plane of slices, maintaining slice isolation in terms of physical network resources. The interaction occurs through dedicated slice communication channels managed by an asynchronous interface. Besides, the `Virtualization Manager` undertakes two main tasks: (i) presenting an abstract view of radio resources to slices by mapping physical to/from virtual resources at runtime; (ii) presenting a virtual/abstract view of the data plane state to slices. The challenge for this component is to realize these tasks in a manner that does not compromise slice isolation.

Abstracting radio resources To ensure radio resource isolation, the `Virtualization Manager`, creates a virtualized view of the radio resources tailored to each slice, by obtaining the map of resources assigned by the `Radio Resource Manager` from the slice contexts. This virtualized view omits all resources not dedicated to a slice, including resources for random access, broadcasting, resources used only by the physical layer (e.g., for reference signals) and those allocated to other slices. It also omits the exact placement of the resources in the resource grid along the frequency dimension and instead reveals an abstract representation to the slices' control planes. On one hand, this allows the control planes of slices to directly and independently view and control the radio resources allocated to them, which can be dynamically re-assigned to different slices over time. On the other hand, by withholding the frequency dimension, potential inference and manipulation of resources allocated to a slice by other slices is prevented, keeping in mind that different tenants could in fact be direct competitors. It should be noted that this inference issue is not present in RAN sharing or in a static radio resources allocation setup. In the RAN sharing case, a single entity (the infrastructure provider) performs all the control operations and thus the exact usage of the resources is 'hidden' from the slice owners, while in the other case, the radio resources are statically assigned to slices, providing no visibility to the resources of other co-located slices.

For the case of downlink/uplink UE data transmissions, one of the main challenges is how to reveal the virtualized radio resources to slices so that they can be allocated to the UEs in the most flexible way and keeping in mind that the slices must be completely unaware of the physical resource grid layout, while at the same time respecting the allocation constraints imposed by the physical layer. Such constraints include group-based allocations, where more than one physical resource block (PRB) must be used as the minimum allocation unit for a UE (e.g., as specified in some types of LTE allocations [4]). Other constraints include frequency dependencies that might arise in the radio resource allocation process, where the use of a certain PRB limits the scheduling of a UE to only a subset of all the available resources. Such frequency dependencies are very common in many radio resource allocation schemes, like for example in the type 1 downlink resource allocation of LTE [4] or in scheduling schemes where frequency hopping is employed for frequency diversity gains (e.g., in some types of LTE uplink allocation [4]).

In order to deal with these issues, `Orion` introduces two abstractions for the virtualization of the radio resources, i.e., the *virtual Radio Resource Block (vRRB)* and the *vRRB pool*.

The vRRB is the fundamental radio resource abstraction employed by `Orion`. Each vRRB is characterized by a *capacity*, used to indicate the amount of data that it can hold. Capacity is expressed as the number of OFDM symbols contained in the vRRB and can be directly translated into a number of bits by the virtual control planes of slices based on the modulation and coding scheme (MCS) used. A vRRB can aggregate the OFDM symbols of one or more PRBs, after omitting symbols used for control channels and reference signals. This aggregation allows `Orion` to group together PRBs that must be used as a single unit, meaning that the capacity among different vRRBs can vary, as illustrated in Fig. 4 (vRRBs of one or two PRBs).

The `Hypervisor` aggregates and reveals the vRRBs to slices in the form of *vRRB pools*, where different sets of pools exist for the uplink and downlink. In each subframe, each slice can be assigned zero, one or more pools for downlink and correspondingly for uplink, each containing at least one vRRB. For example, in Fig. 5a, slice 1 has two vRRB pools, while slice 2 has only one. A slice can only view and allocate the vRRBs that are available in its pools (Fig. 5b), with the only constraint being that a UE can only be allocated vRRBs from the same pool. For example, in Fig. 5, a UE belonging to slice 1 can only be allocated resources from the red or yellow pool, but not both. The aggregation of vRRBs to pools captures the aforementioned frequency dependencies, since RBs that are mutually exclusive for a UE are assigned to different pools by the `Hypervisor`.

It should be noted that the abstractions of `Orion` are suitable both for current LTE as well as for future 5G New Radio (NR) networks, since both are based on OFDM and have the same fundamental frame structure [59]. The main difference is that NR is expected to support a more flexible resource grid, in which the number of TTIs and the

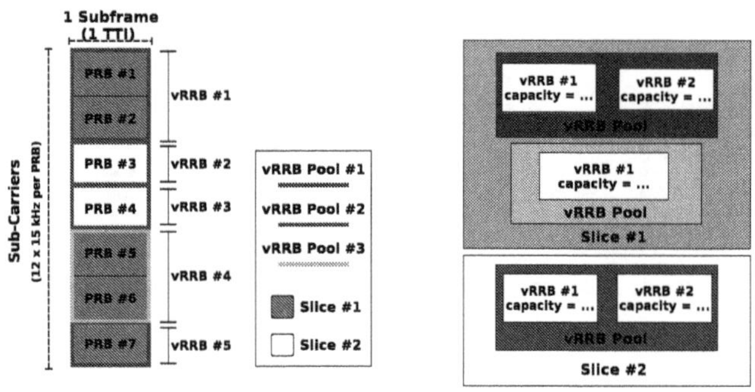

(a) vRRB and vRRB pool abstractions for LTE resource grid

(b) Abstractions of Fig. 5a from the slices' point of view

Figure 5: Illustration of Orion uplink/downlink radio resource virtualization abstractions in the context of LTE.

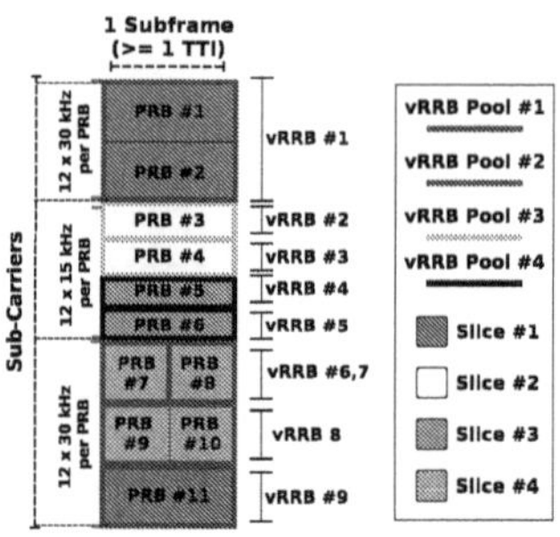

Figure 6: Orion uplink/downlink radio resource virtualization abstractions in the context of 5G NR – Flexible TTI and sub-carrier spacing numerology.

sub-carrier spacing of the RBs in a subframe can vary (Fig. 6) to support the diverse requirements of services and to provide support for mmWave communications [56]. In this context, the physical grid layout of the radio resources is one additional dimension that the `Hypervisor` should consider for mapping the physical resources to vRRBs. For example, for the FDD downlink grid presented in Fig. 6, a low data rate service without latency constraints should be allocated vRRBs 2 to 5 by the `Hypervisor` to maximize efficiency, while a low-latency service should be allocated vRRBs 6 and 7.

In contrast to the resources used for user traffic, control resources are provided in a simpler form, where the `Hypervisor` indicates to the virtual control planes of slices the role and amount of the assigned control resources through a message-based API. On the downlink, a virtual control plane can find out through this API how many CCEs are available for transmitting the scheduling decisions of its UEs, the resources available for sending uplink power control instructions as well as the resources available for uplink resource grants. On the uplink, this involves the TTIs in which a UE of the slice could report its signal measurements, so that it can be configured correspondingly by the higher layers of its virtual control plane (e.g., RRC).

The `Virtualization Manager`, besides presenting virtualized resources to slices, also performs the reverse mapping from slices' decisions over virtual resources to their physical counterparts. This involves consulting the context of the slices and performing all transformations required so that a command issued by the virtual control plane of a slice can be realized by the physical layer. Referring again to the example of LTE downlink scheduling, this mapping would involve a modification of the virtual control plane's scheduling decision to convert the vRRB allocation into a physical one, and the merging of the scheduling decisions from different slices into a single scheduling decision for the physical layer. Similarly, it would require the conversion of CCEs from the virtual to the physical form.

Virtualizing the data plane state To apply its control logic, a slice must be aware of its data plane state besides the resources allocated to it. Another task for the `Virtualization Manager` is to reveal the relevant data plane state to slices in an isolated manner, guaranteeing that any type of information related to specific UEs or their flows will be reported only to the corresponding slice. This virtualization in the data plane state ensures the isolation of data plane operations among slices, since the control plane of each slice is unaware of the data plane aspects that are relevant to the UEs of other co-located slices. Examples of relevant UE information include signal quality measurements, transmission queue sizes and number of flows (bearers in LTE) as well as event notifications like the (de)activation of a UE, the establishment of new flows, scheduling requests, etc. Given that the frequency domain is abstracted from the resource grid of slices, any UE-specific information related to the frequency domain is reported to the slice in an abstract form. As an example, relating to signal quality measurements and to the more fine-grained sub-band CQI reports that LTE can provide, the `Virtualization Manager` furnishes the measurements in the context of the vRRBs rather than the actual frequencies, through suitable mapping.

Apart from UE specific information, the `Virtualization Manager` also informs slices about cell-related configuration information like resource block sizes, supported transmission modes, nominal transmission power of base station, etc. Since all slices need to be aware of this information and in order to ensure a conflict-free operation of the physical base station, all such cell-related information is provided to slices in a read-only form, while the infrastructure provider retains the exclusive privilege for making changes, when needed.

4.1.4 UE Association Manager. The `UE Association Manager` (Fig. 2) associates UEs with slices in two steps: (i) the discovery of slices by UEs via the physical base station; (ii) the mapping of UEs to slices. To achieve this, the `UE Association Manager` interacts with the broadcast and random access processes of the base station, which are internal to the `Hypervisor` and not revealed to slices.

To aid in discovery, the `UE Association Manager` obtains the active slices from the `Slice Context Manager`. This information is then broadcasted by the base station. In the context of LTE, this can be done as in RAN sharing, where the base station broadcasts the list of PLMN ids, indicating all the MVNOs that are present. When a UE discovers a cell from its slice, it initiates the random access process. If successful, the attachment process begins and the UE is expected to send a unique identification (e.g., IMSI in LTE). Using this unique identifier, the `UE Association Manager` maps the UE to the appropriate slice by consulting the UE lookup function (Table 1) available for each slice through the `Slice Context Manager`. Once the correct slice is identified, the `UE Association Manager` updates the list of active UEs in the context of that slice. The corresponding virtual control plane is notified about the event through the

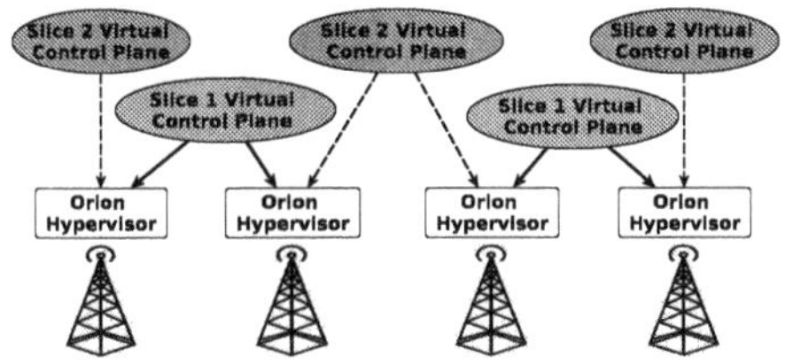

Figure 7: Flexible control plane composition enabled by Orion.

`Virtualization Manager` and from that point on takes up control of the UE (authentication, establishment of flows, scheduling, etc.). The attachment process is fully transparent to UEs in the sense that no changes are required to the protocols and signaling messages used for the interaction between the base station and the UEs.

4.2 Virtual Control Plane

As already alluded to in Section 3, Orion isolates memory and processing resources of slices by separating their virtual control planes from each other and the `Hypervisor`, thereby achieves functional isolation. Virtual control planes of slices in Orion are separate processes that exchange messages with the `Hypervisor` through dedicated communication channels. This separation allows slice deployment in a fully isolated manner using OS virtualization technologies, like containers and virtual machines, to enforce limits in terms of the allocated amount of memory and CPU.

A virtual control plane of a slice can be associated with multiple physical base stations (through their `Hypervisors`). Thus, the virtual control planes of individual slices can be composed independently and flexibly, like in the example of Fig. 7 for the case of two slices. As it can be seen, control plane centralization can be introduced into different regions of the RAN for each of the slices, based on the corresponding service's needs. This approach gives the flexibility to slice owners to enable RAN coordination (for load balancing, improved mobility management, etc.) when and where required. At the same time, it also enables an efficient utilization of the available computing resources for the placement of the slices' virtual control planes as demonstrated later through experiments in Section 5.2.

The communication between the virtual control plane of a slice and the `Hypervisor` is asynchronous (Fig. 8). To perform its operations, the control plane obtains the state of the virtual data plane and resources from the `Hypervisor` and stores it locally in a virtual RAN Information Base (vRIB). In its simplest form, the vRIB contains data structures with a raw representation of the virtual data plane state.

The vRIB can be both read and written by the slice's control plane, so changes due to control operations are first reflected in the vRIB. To maintain its consistency, the vRIB state is periodically synchronized with the `Hypervisor` via its `Virtualization Manager` and an asynchronous interface. Since the virtual control plane of slices and the `Hypervisor` can be deployed either on the same or on separate physical machines, depending on the setup and the available resources, the synchronization frequency of the vRIB can be tuned to the characteristics of the communication channel.

4.3 End-to-End Network Slicing

We now discuss how Orion can be integrated in an end-to-end network slicing setting. The virtualization of various components making

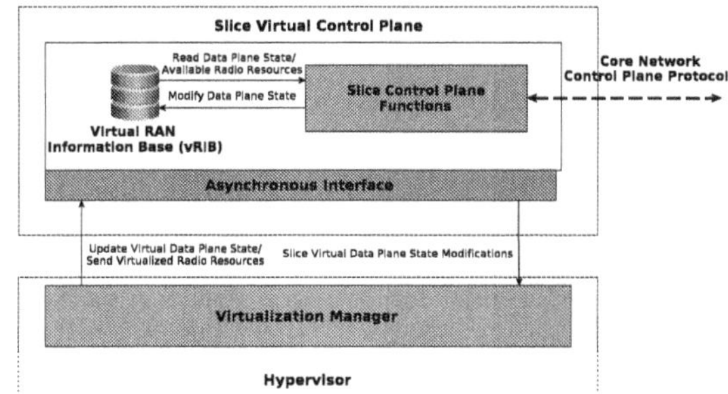

Figure 8: Virtual control plane of a slice in Orion.

up the slice (including network functions) is key to enabling flexible component placement over the network infrastructure through a MANO entity, based on the needs of the service corresponding to the end-to-end slice. This is certainly not a hurdle for Orion as its components can be turned into VNFs. For a complete solution, it is also very important to investigate the interactions of the Orion components with the management plane and with the other components making up the slice. These interactions and the entities involved are depicted in Fig. 9, where each number-annotated arrow represents an interaction required for the right instantiation, operation and management of a slice throughout its life-cycle.

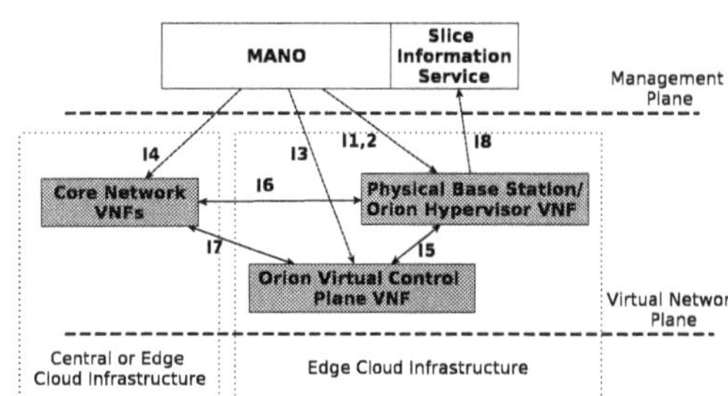

Figure 9: Interactions among components involved in an end-to-end network slicing setting.

Starting from the RAN and before the deployment of any slice, the MANO must deploy the VNFs of the physical base stations and the Orion `Hypervisor` for the RAT of choice (`I1`). This VNF is expected to outlive the slices' VNFs. Management of slices should occur through an appropriate interface between the MANO and the `Hypervisor` (`I2`). The orchestration of a slice by the MANO involves the creation, migration and destruction of the Orion virtual control plane VNF (`I3`), as well as of the core network VNFs (`I4`) (e.g., LTE EPC components). While a slice is active, its core network VNFs interact with the `Hypervisor` for the user plane (`I6`) and with the virtual control plane for the control plane operations (`I7`), while the `Hypervisor` VNF also communicates with the slice's virtual control plane (`I5`). A *Slice Information Service* is required on the management plane, so that the `Slice Context Manager` in the `Hypervisor` can locate the information required for the mapping of UEs to slices (`I8`). This resembles the role of the HSS in LTE, but storing slice-related registration information instead.

Fig. 9 also illustrates that the Orion VNFs are deployed over an edge cloud near the RF front-end, while the core network VNFs can be deployed either at the edge or in a central cloud, depending on the slice's requirements. For example, control plane VNFs (e.g., MME) could be centralized to simplify control/management, while data plane VNFs (e.g., S-GW) could be placed closer to the user [15]. Similarly, different slices could employ different core network VNF setups, optimized for their particular use case (e.g., as in [67] for MTC traffic). The flexible placement of VNFs, coupled with the capabilities offered by Orion for the customization of the RAN, allow the creation of flexible slices adapted to the service needs.

4.4 Implementation

We developed a prototype implementation of Orion, following the design described so far in this section and considering LTE as the RAT. The Orion `Hypervisor` was implemented from scratch in C. For the interaction of the `Hypervisor` with the base station data plane, we leveraged the control–data plane API of the publicly available FlexRAN platform [1], which in turn is based on an open-source software implementation of LTE called OpenAirInterface (OAI) [54].

Our implementation provides full support for the virtualization of downlink radio resources, with the `Hypervisor` creating a single vRRB pool per slice in each subframe (equal to a TTI of 1ms in LTE), with each of its vRRBs corresponding to a group of physical resource blocks (2, 3 or 4 based on the bandwidth of the cell). This is because OAI currently supports resource allocation type 0 on the downlink, in which, based on the LTE specification [4], resource blocks can be assigned to UEs only in groups of 2, 3 or 4 blocks depending on the available spectrum.

The identifier used for mapping UEs to slices is the IMSI stored in the SIM card of UEs. This is sent to the MME of the network by UEs during their attachment using the Non-Access Stratum (NAS) protocols of LTE and is normally not visible to the eNodeB. Therefore, the RRC layer of OAI was modified to capture the relevant signaling messages, obtain these ids and pass them to the `UE Association Manager` of the `Hypervisor`. OAI was further modified to allow core networks (EPCs) of different slices to be connected over the same eNodeB. This required enabling the association of the MMEs, HSSs and S/P-GWs of different slices with the same eNodeB as well as the redirection of newly attached UEs to the correct core network by the `UE Association Manager` both for signaling and user traffic. Once a UE completes the random access process, its signaling messages are directed to the correct MME so that it can be authenticated by the corresponding slice's HSS and a bearer can be established with the slice's S/P-GW. From that point on, all the UE traffic goes through the core network of the hosting slice.

The current implementation allows expressing the SLA parameters stored in the context of active slices (Table 1) in three ways: (i) a fixed allocation of resource blocks; (ii) an average of the aggregate amount of resource blocks allocated to the slice over a window of 100ms; and (iii) an average target throughput for the slice over a window of 100ms. For the second and the third case, the current implementation uses the NVS radio resource allocation algorithm [35].

To realize the virtual control plane of slices, we implemented a modified version of the FlexRAN controller that operates over the abstract virtual resources presented by the `Hypervisor` and also with an enhanced RIB structure that supports write primitives. Given that the virtual control planes of slices can be deployed either locally or over a networked setting, we implemented two types of channels for message exchanges with the `Hypervisor`: one TCP-based channel optimized for a minimum message exchange delay in a network setting and one optimized for inter-process communication using ZeroMQ [28]. The appropriate type is specified in the slice's service description during the creation of the slice and the proper communication channel is deployed accordingly. Moreover, depending on the type of deployment, the synchronization of the `Hypervisor` with the vRIB must also be optimized. Towards this end, in the current implementation with inter-process communication the vRIB is fully synchronized with the Hypervisor every 1ms, while in a networked setting, only the time critical parts of the vRIB (virtual resource allocations, time synchronization in subframes) are synchronized at this rate, with the rest synchronized infrequently every 4ms.

Finally, we created VNFs for the `Hypervisor` and the virtual control plane of Orion using Juju charms, enabling their deployment over an OpenStack-based environment and allowing usage of Orion with any OpenStack-compatible MANO framework (e.g., OSM).

5 EVALUATION

In this section, we quantitatively study Orion's resource consumption in different scenarios and benchmark it against other proposed RAN slicing solutions. We also examine the impact of the communication channel between the `Hypervisor` and the slice control plane. For the experiments, we used 2 Intel Xeon machines (E3-1245 @ 3.4GHz, 16GB RAM each) and 1 Intel i7 machine (5557U @ 3.10GHz, 8GB of RAM) for deploying physical base stations, the Orion Hypervisor and the virtual control planes of slices, depending on the specific experiment. All machines have Ubuntu 16.04 with a low-latency kernel and had support for Docker v1.13.1 [44], allowing the Orion components (Hypervisor, slice control planes) to be deployed in isolated containers. The core part of the network was deployed on an additional Intel-based machine (i7-4770R @ 3.2GHz, 8GB RAM), running the openair-cn open source EPC implementation [6]. For the RF front-end of physical base station, we used Ettus USRP B210 SDR boards and for UEs, up to 4 physical units (LG Nexus 5 and Samsung Galaxy Note 4 and 2 Huawei E3372 LTE dongles).

5.1 Scalability

Here we quantify how Orion scales in terms of the processing and memory requirements. To assess the overhead incurred for the virtualization operations performed by the Orion `Hypervisor`, we used a setup where each slice had 20 assigned (emulated) UEs and the available spectrum was saturated with TCP traffic. The results in Fig. 10a show that, apart from the initial overhead associated with the first slice, the addition of extra slices incurs a small and almost constant incremental overhead, both in terms of CPU and memory. This increase is mainly due to the `Hypervisor`'s `Virtualization Manager` operations (construction of the virtual resource grids of slices, synchronization with slices' virtual control planes). The initial bigger increase observed after the creation of the first slice is due to the activation of the asynchronous interface as well as the periodic execution of the `Radio Resource Manager` for the allocation of resources to slices, which is inactive when there are no slices. The actual number of slices that can be supported by a physical base station depends both on the `Hypervisor` overhead presented here and

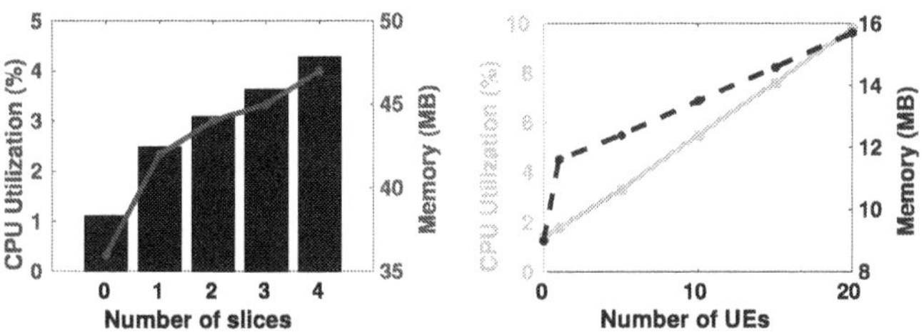

(a) Hypervisor overhead (4-core CPU and 20 UEs/slice)

(b) Virtual control plane overhead (2-core CPU)

Figure 10: Orion CPU and memory consumption scaling.

# Slices \ System	FLARE	FlexRAN	Orion
1	5MHz	5MHz	5MHz
2	5MHz/slice	10MHz	10MHz
3	5MHz for slices 1,2 10MHz for slice 3	20MHz	20MHz

Table 2: Allocation of channel bandwidth among slices. Both Orion and FlexRAN use shared spectrum for all slices.

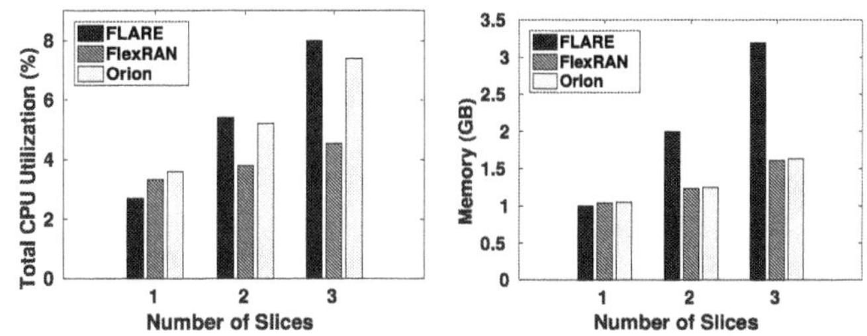

(a) CPU Utilization (10 cores)

(b) Memory footprint

Figure 11: Comparison of Orion with FLARE and FlexRAN with varying number of slices.

on the physical layer requirements, which can greatly vary depending on where the most demanding physical layer operations occur (e.g., at the baseband processing unit or at a remote radio head).

Next we turn our attention to the virtual control plane of a slice and quantify its overhead with a varying number of UEs (0 to 20) which increases linearly with the number attached UEs (Fig. 10b). The increases in the memory consumption are mainly due to the additional information stored in the vRIB as more UEs get attached and the memory required for the message exchanges with the Hypervisor. The initial sharp rise in the memory consumption is due to the creation of the UE-related part of the vRIB, once the first UE gets attached. The rise in CPU utilization is a result of the communication with the Hypervisor for the synchronization of the vRIB and from the scheduling of the attached UEs. However, the overhead is still fairly modest, meaning that the virtual control planes of multiple slices could be deployed side-by-side over the same physical machine (e.g., over an edge cloud data-center) without scaling issues. For example, in the commodity machine used for these experiments, at least eight slice control planes could be deployed without any issues.

5.2 Comparison with the State-of-the-Art

Here we compare the overall memory and processing requirements of Orion versus the state-of-the-art virtualization and RAN sharing solutions from the literature. One representative approach is *FLARE*, the RAN slicing solution proposed in [47, 48], which ensures isolation by deploying different instances of OAI over Docker containers and each slice is *statically* assigned a dedicated chunk of spectrum. The other alternative approach is represented by FlexRAN [18, 19, 50] that has been shown to provide RAN slicing capabilities following a RAN sharing approach but without functional isolation. It should be noted that, like Orion, both FLARE and FlexRAN are built using OAI as their basis. Therefore, any performance differences among them come mainly from the design choices of each system regarding how to perform RAN slicing; a fact that makes this comparison fair.

We design an experiment to compare Orion with these two alternatives for a varying number of slices, where each slice has TCP traffic (mimicking an aggregate demand from a set of UEs) to a single physical UE. Each slice was allocated spectrum according to the configuration of Table 2 for fairness. Three physical machines were used for this experiment as compute nodes for the various components required for each architecture. To capture the overall system performance, we measured the aggregate resources required for all the RAN components of each architecture across all physical machines. For the CPU utilization, this meant measuring the jiffies allocated to the RAN-related processes of each architecture over a constant number of 10 CPU cores (the total number of cores of all physical machines) and dividing this value with the total jiffies of all the CPUs for all system processes during the course of the experiment.

We see from Fig. 11a that Orion has relatively higher CPU requirements compared to FlexRAN, which is expected due to the Hypervisor's operation and the unavoidable cost to pay for the additional control plane processes that must be deployed as new slices are added. On the other hand, Orion starts with higher CPU requirements than FLARE, but soon becomes more lightweight, due to the fact that each new FLARE slice requires the deployment of a complete protocol stack, including the very demanding (CPU-wise) physical layer. Since in Orion all slices share the same physical layer, its overhead comes mainly from the Hypervisor and the slices' virtual control planes, which, as shown earlier, are fairly lightweight. The same observations and for the same reasons can be made for the memory consumption (Fig. 11b), with Orion performing significantly better compared to FLARE and marginally worse compared to FlexRAN.

Since both Orion and FlexRAN are composed of a number of different network functions (Hypervisor/physical layer and virtual control planes in Orion; Agent/data plane and controller in FlexRAN), it is insightful to break down the results of Fig.11 in order to understand their differences. This is illustrated in Fig.12a for three slices. As it can be observed, the Orion virtual control planes and the FlexRAN controller consume a negligible amount of memory. On the other hand, in terms of CPU utilization, Orion's biggest impact comes from the physical layer and the Hypervisor, but, in contrast to memory, a significant contribution is also made from the virtual control planes of slices. In the case of FlexRAN, the base station network function (FlexRAN Agent and data plane) has the biggest CPU utilization, also with a significant contribution from the controller.

One important thing to notice is that while some components of both systems, namely the Orion Hypervisor and the FlexRAN Agent, are placed near the base station and are effectively monolithic components regardless of the number of deployed slices, this analogy is not carried over to the other network functions. While in the case

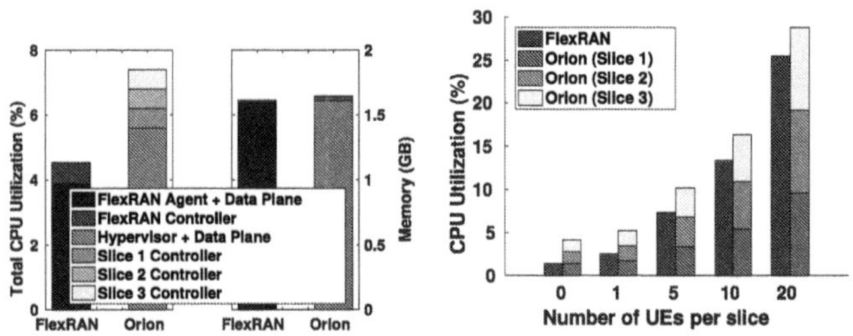

(a) Comparison of Orion and FlexRAN for 3 slices (1 UE/slice)

(b) Control plane CPU Utilization (2 cores)

Figure 12: Breakdown of resource requirements for Orion vs FlexRAN.

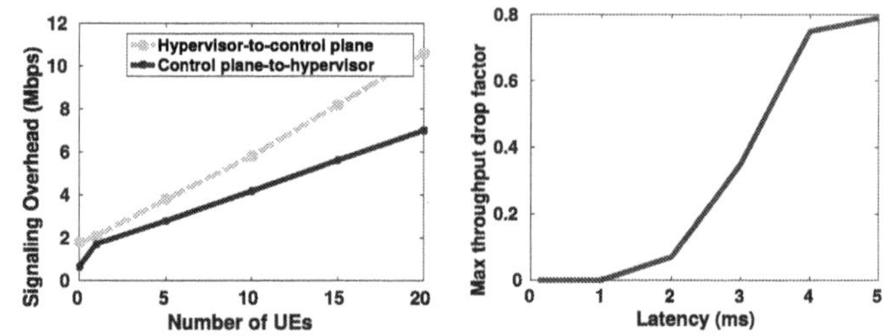

(a) Signaling bandwidth requirements

(b) Effect of signaling latency on maximum throughput

Figure 13: Network requirements for the interaction of the Hypervisor with the virtual control plane when not co-located.

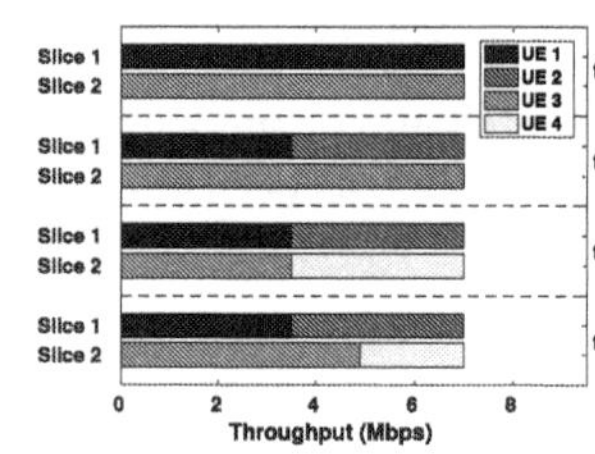

Figure 14: Isolation of RAN slices in terms of radio resources and control functions (scheduling).

of FlexRAN the controller is also a monolithic component, Orion provides individual control planes to slices. Apart from the functional isolation that this ensures, it also enables a better utilization of the underlying resources through the flexible placement of the control plane functions over the available compute nodes. We illustrate this point through an experiment in which three slices are deployed using Orion and FlexRAN and the overall control plane CPU utilization is measured for a varying number of UEs per slice. Results shown in Fig.12b indicate that Orion always performs slightly worse than FlexRAN, however this overhead is compensated by the fact that the control plane can be broken down into three functions that can be flexibly placed over different CPU cores or even completely different compute nodes; something that FlexRAN is unable to do.

5.3 Impact of Communication Channel

We now assess Orion's requirements for the communication between a slice control plane and the `Hypervisor` (in terms of bandwidth and latency) for their deployment in a networked setting. Understanding these requirements is very important from an end-to-end perspective for deploying the components of Orion as VNFs, since the orchestration entity needs to be aware of the physical constraints regarding their placement as part of the overall network service description.

To measure the bandwidth requirements of the control channel, we varied the number of UEs for a slice over the physical base station with 5MHz spectrum. In this experiment, UEs continuously had traffic to keep the slice at full load. The highest overhead was incurred for messages sent by the Hypervisor towards the control plane of the slice (Fig. 13a), for the synchronization of the vRIB and for the provision of the slice with virtual radio resources. The overall bandwidth requirements for this setup did not exceed 20Mbps, implying that such a scenario is feasible in practice.

To study latency constraints, we used a similar setup but with a single COTS UE attached to the slice. We used *netem* [21] to set the latency between the Hypervisor and the slice's virtual control plane and measured the drop in the maximum achievable throughput for the UE compared to a co-located deployment. Fig. 13b shows that networked deployment of Orion is efficient only when the latency remains below 2ms. This constraint could be relaxed to an extent with some optimizations (e.g., HARQ reporting optimizations) but a co-located deployment is preferable if possible. The slice controller could also be made distributed and hierarchical, so that time-critical scheduling operations can be handled at or near the physical base station, while other operations can be placed flexibly at other locations.

6 CASE STUDIES

6.1 Isolation Capabilities

We demonstrate the ability of Orion to provide radio resource and functional isolation, which is not possible with RAN sharing oriented slicing approaches [18, 19]. In this experiment, 2 slices with proportional fair downlink schedulers were created and statically allocated 5MHz of spectrum in equal shares by the `Hypervisor`. Initially, we connected 2 physical UEs (one per slice) and performed a throughput measurement to both using iperf, ensuring ideal channel conditions. As shown in instance $t1$ of Fig. 14, the `Hypervisor` guarantees the radio resource isolation so that each slice can obtain only half of the available radio resources, leading to an equal throughput for the UEs. Further aspects of this isolation of radio resources are demonstrated in instances $t2$ and $t3$ of Fig. 14 where more UEs are added to the slices and where each UE is constrained by the `Hypervisor` to the radio resources allocated within its slice. For example, in instance $t2$ the performance of UE3 remains unaffected by the addition of UE2 since UE2 belongs to a different slice.

Finally, the inter-slice functional isolation is illustrated in instance $t4$ of Fig. 14. The scheduler in the virtual control plane of slice 2 was replaced with a class-based scheduler allocating 70% of the resources to UEs in class 1 and the rest to class 2. In the experiment, UE3 and UE4 were assigned to class 1 and class 2, respectively. As shown in Fig. 14, the change in the control plane of slice 2 only affects the throughput of the UEs belonging to that slice, leaving the control plane and the UEs of slice 1 completely oblivious.

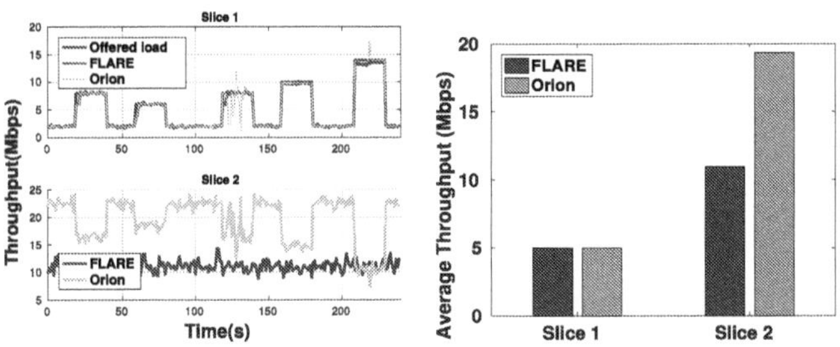

(a) Instantaneous slice throughput in static (FLARE) vs dynamic resource allocation (Orion).

(b) Average throughput achieved through static and dynamic spectrum use.

Figure 15: Benefit of Orion's flexible radio resource allocation.

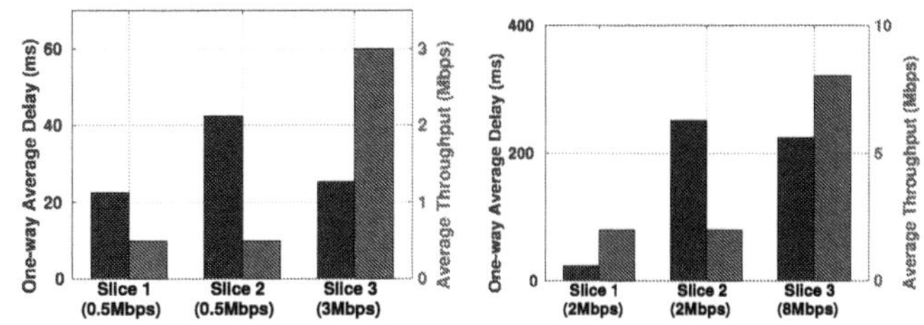

(a) Low offered load

(b) High offered load

Figure 16: Performance impact of Core-eNodeB latency and radio resource allocation policy/guarantees for low and high offered loads (load values in parentheses on x-axis).

6.2 Flexible Radio Resource Allocation

We now demonstrate the flexibility offered by Orion for dynamic radio resource allocation and how it can be used for efficiently utilizing the spectrum among co-existing slices. We created 2 slices, each with an average aggregate throughput requirement of 14Mbps. As a baseline, we considered FLARE, with each slice statically allocated 5MHz of spectrum. For the same scenario, we employed Orion with a pool of 10MHz for both slices and implemented the radio resource allocation using the algorithm of [35]. In the beginning of each allocation window, the resources were allocated to slices based on their effective traffic rate and on their average throughput requirement.

We connected 1 UE on slice 1 and 3 UEs on slice 2 and we used the D-ITG traffic generator [10] to generate TCP flows in slice 1. Specifically, we created a TCP flow with a constant rate of 2Mbps. On top of it, we sporadically created some short-lived flows (20s each), capable of attaining various rates (4-12Mbps). In slice 2, all the connected UEs accessed a DASH-based video streaming service to stream a video offering a wide range of bitrates. Using this setup, we measured the instantaneous (Fig. 15a) and the average (Fig. 15b) aggregate throughput achieved by each slice in FLARE and Orion for a period of 240s. As observed, for slice 1, both FLARE and Orion give similar results, fully covering the offered load and respecting the SLA of slice 1 for up to 14Mbps of *average* aggregate throughput.

For slice 2, however, Orion is seen to perform much better than FLARE, dynamically reallocating the idle resources from slice 1 and allowing the UEs in slice 2 to stream videos with a higher bitrate. FLARE, unlike Orion, is spectrum-limited and cannot go beyond 14Mbps at any point in time, irrespectively of what happens in slice 1. The flexibility of Orion comes without compromising slice SLAs. When slice 1 requires all of its expected resources (e.g., 210-230s in Fig. 15a), the `Radio Resource Manager` allocates fewer radio resources to slice 2, so the aggregate throughput of this slice drops.

6.3 Deployment in an End-to-End Setting

Here we highlight the capability of Orion to be deployed in an end-to-end network slicing setting and the effect of the slice configuration to overall performance in terms of throughput and delay. For this experiment we created 3 slices, each composed of VNFs for an EPC (HSS, MME, S/P-GW) and a virtual base station deployed over Orion. For slices 1 and 3, the S/P-GW VNFs of the EPC were placed on hosts 1 hop away from the eNodeB, to reduce the delay of the EPC–eNodeB communication as much as possible (less than 0.3ms). For slice 2, we deployed the S/P-GW VNF on a host connected to the eNodeB through a 20ms delay link (emulated with netem [21]) to reflect the placement of the mobile core functionality far from the eNodeB (e.g., in a central cloud). The eNodeB in this experiment was allocated 5MHz of spectrum, supporting a total rate of 14Mbps in ideal channel conditions. Finally, the `Orion Hypervisor` was configured so that slice 1 was guaranteed a static allocation of 4 resource blocks per subframe (maximum achievable throughput of 2Mbps) while slices 2 and 3 were guaranteed an average throughput of 2 and 8Mbps respectively, performing the allocation using the algorithm in [35].

In this setup, we used the D-ITG traffic generator [10] to generate downlink UDP traffic with exponentially distributed packet inter-arrival times and measured slice performance in terms of average throughput and delay. Initially, the load offered to slices was kept low, compared to the slices' SLA guarantees, and all slices manage to support the traffic demand (Fig. 16a). Moreover, we can observe that the average packet delay for slice 2 was higher than that of slices 1 and 3 by about 20ms, something expected considering the (emulated) 'far from eNodeB' placement of the core functions for slice 2.

Next, we re-run the experiment, increasing the load offered to slices to reach their limit (Fig. 16b). As we can observe, all slices still achieve an average throughput close to their offered load, which was expected since their load remains within the guaranteed limits. However, while the average delay of slice 1 stays at the same level, the average delay of slices 2 and 3 is over 200ms. The reason is that the static allocation used for slice 1, although inflexible, ensures stricter delay guarantees, as arriving packets could always be served without queuing for long. On the other hand, the flexible dynamic allocation of radio resources to the other slices guarantees the average throughput, but this was done over 100 ms windows (as described in Section 4.4), rather than per subframe. In such almost saturating traffic conditions the packets are more likely to experience a longer waiting time in the slice queues, increasing the average delay.

7 MULTI-SERVICE SLICES EXTENSION

The design of Orion enables RAN slicing in cases where the UE has a 1:1 relationship with the slice (e.g., MVNOs and verticals). However, deployment of Over-The-Top (OTT) services as distinct slices breaks this assumption and control decisions among slices cannot be guaranteed to be conflict-free. To overcome this, we propose an extension to Orion in the form of *service containers*, which targets slices offering multi-service capabilities (e.g., an MVNO with OTT services).

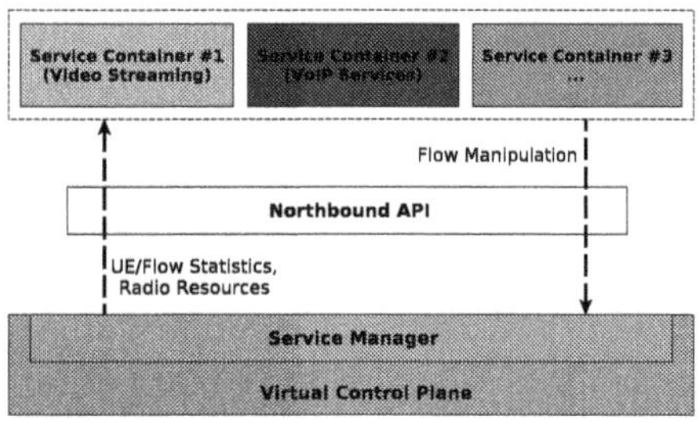

Figure 17: Extension of Orion to support multi-service slices.

The idea behind service containers is that an OTT service provider agrees with an MVNO to assume control of the flows corresponding to its service through its own isolated functions deployed over the virtual control plane of the slice. This concept is similar in spirit to the 3GPP Service Capability Exposure Function (SCEF) [3] and with research works like [62], where an API is defined for the interaction of applications with the mobile network to modify the service level or to obtain information about the network state. The deployment of service containers over the base stations of MVNOs can enhance this model with *real-time* control and monitoring capabilities, enabling the further optimization of OTT applications.

The design of this extension (Fig. 17) inherits the design principles discussed in Section 4. Service containers are deployed as processes over the virtual control plane of a slice, each with its own isolated memory and processing resources. The virtual control plane of the slice is extended with a Northbound API, enabling the exchange of information between the MVNO and the service provider. Using the API, a service can obtain information about the flows of UEs assigned to it (available UE flows, transmission queue sizes, signal quality etc.), as well as about the (abstracted) radio resources available for it. On the other direction, the service can issue scheduling decisions, indicating how its allocated resources should be distributed among its flows. A `Service Manager` sitting between the virtual control plane of the MVNO and the Northbound API is responsible to map flows to services, distribute the abstract radio resources to the containers and perform access control, ensuring that service containers can only access information and radio resources related to their serving flows.

In order to demonstrate the benefits of service containers, we consider the example of a DASH-based adaptive bitrate video streaming service provider for which a service container was developed and deployed over Orion for monitoring and scheduling the video flows of streaming UEs. The control function of this container is composed of a monitoring and a scheduling component. The monitoring component observes the CQI of the UEs that are streaming videos and provides real-time feedback to the video streaming client about the maximum sustainable bitrate that a UE can achieve given its CQI. Based on that feedback, the client readjusts the bitrate of the video to avoid freezes. The scheduling component makes the scheduling decisions (priority and MCS) for the video flows of the UEs by communicating with the video streaming clients every second and observing the buffer size of each video stream. Flows of video streams with lower buffer sizes are given a higher priority, on the premise that such flows need faster treatment to avoid buffer freezes.

For our evaluation, we considered a scenario with 2 UEs streaming a video [45] using the DASH reference client [14]. UE 1 had a fixed optimal signal quality and for UE 2 we introduced a big drop of the signal quality at $t = 35$s and then a big increase at $t = 75$s. Results obtained when the service container was active and managing the video flows (Fig. 18b) are compared against the regular non-assisted DASH service with the MVNO being responsible for scheduling all flows through a proportional-fair scheduler (Fig. 18a). When the signal quality of UE 2 changes suddenly, the non-assisted mechanism fails to adapt fast, leading to buffer freezes. In comparison, the cross-layer optimized control of flows enabled by the service containers allowed the bitrate to adjust more appropriately and to avoid stalls in the video stream, thus improving the overall quality of the service.

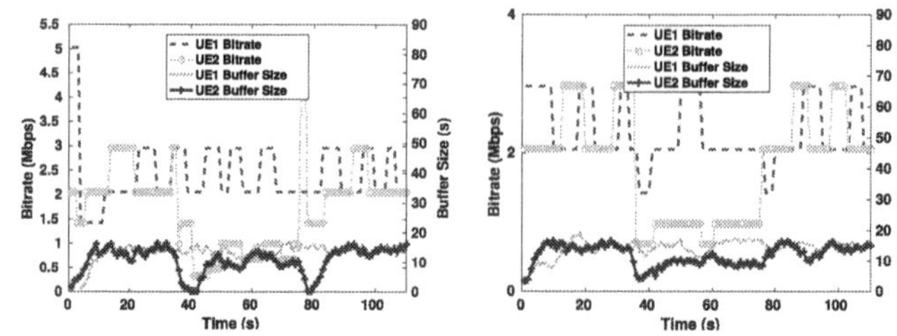

(a) MVNO managed **(b) OTT cross-layer optimized**

Figure 18: Video streaming performance in MVNO-managed vs. OTT-optimized control of flows.

This example is merely intended to demonstrate the capabilities enabled by service containers for OTTs, by allowing them to make control decisions using information unavailable to a non application-aware MVNO. More sophisticated control mechanisms could also be employed, like the cross-layer optimization mechanism for video delivery in [31] or the content-aware schedulers in [38] and [55].

8 CONCLUSIONS

We have presented Orion, a flexible RAN slicing architecture. Orion slices can be deployed dynamically over the network infrastructure, co-existing in a fully isolated manner in terms of radio resources and control functions. At the same time, Orion facilitates efficient radio resource sharing among slices. A prototype implementation of Orion was developed for LTE, with the performance evaluation indicating that it is a lightweight and flexible RAN virtualization solution. Orion's capabilites were highlighted through a number of use cases, revealing its suitability for future multi-service mobile networks.

The virtualization capabilities enabled by Orion can be seen as a concrete step towards realizing the so-called RAN-as-a-Service (RaaS) paradigm, where virtual RAN instances can be dynamically created over a cloud infrastructure. However, apart from virtualization, another significant aspect of the RaaS paradigm is the capability to perform a dynamic functional split of the RAN in terms of control and data plane operations, enabling a more flexible composition of RAN instances. Extending the design of Orion to accommodate this need, while retaining its virtualization capabilites is a natural next step. Another important aspect in the context of 5G is the efficient virtualization of radio resources in multi-RAT settings. Orion is currently designed for single-RAT settings, however investigating the feasibility of extending its capabilities for multi-RAT is a significant topic for future work. These and other future work issues are discussed further in [20].

ACKNOWLEDGEMENTS

We thank our shepherd Songwu Lu and the anonymous reviewers for the helpful suggestions on improving the paper.

REFERENCES

[1] 2017. FlexRAN. http://networks.inf.ed.ac.uk/flexran. (2017).

[2] 3GPP. 2017. Architecture enhancements for dedicated core networks. TS 23.707. (2017).

[3] 3GPP. 2017. Architecture Enhancements to Facilitate Communications with Packet Data Networks and Applications. TS 23.682. (2017).

[4] 3GPP. 2017. Evolved Universal Terrestrial Radio Access (E-UTRA); Physical layer procedures. TS 36.213. (2017).

[5] Ian F Akyildiz, Pu Wang, and Shih-Chun Lin. 2015. SoftAir: A software defined networking architecture for 5G wireless systems. *Computer Networks* 85 (2015), 1–18.

[6] OpenAirInterface Software Alliance. 2017. Openair-cn repository. https://gitlab.eurecom.fr/oai/openair-cn. (2017).

[7] Xueli An et al. 2016. On end to end network slicing for 5G communication systems. *Transactions on Emerging Telecommunications Technologies* (2016).

[8] Unknown Author. 2005. IEEE 802.1q – IEEE standard for local and metropolitan area networks virtual bridged local area networks. *IEEE Computer Society* (2005).

[9] Arijit Banerjee et al. 2015. Scaling the LTE Control-Plane for Future Mobile Access. In *Proceedings of the 11th ACM CoNEXT*. ACM, 19.

[10] Alessio Botta, Alberto Dainotti, and Antonio Pescapè. 2012. A tool for the generation of realistic network workload for emerging networking scenarios. *Computer Networks* 56, 15 (2012), 3531–3547.

[11] Pablo Caballero et al. 2017. Network slicing games: Enabling customization in multi-tenent networks. In *Proceedings of IEEE INFOCOM 2017*. IEEE.

[12] Brent Chun et al. 2003. Planetlab: An Overlay Testbed for Broad-Coverage Services. *ACM SIGCOMM Computer Communication Review* 33, 3 (2003), 3–12.

[13] Xavier Costa-Pérez et al. 2013. Radio Access Network Virtualization for Future Mobile Carrier Networks. *IEEE Communications Magazine* 51, 7 (2013), 27–35.

[14] DASH Industry Forum. 2017. DASH Reference Client. http://dashif.org/reference/players/javascript/v2.4.1/samples/dash-if-reference-player/index.html. (2017).

[15] Ericsson. 2016. A Vision of the 5G Core: Flexibility for New Business Opportunities. (2016).

[16] Ericsson. 2017. 5G Systems - Enabling the Transformation of Industry and Society. (Jan 2017).

[17] ETSI. 2017. Open Source MANO. https://osm.etsi.org/. (2017).

[18] Eurecom. 2017. Demo at MWC 2017:5G Cloud RAN slice. https://insights.ubuntu.com/event/mobile-world-congress-2017/. (2017).

[19] Xenofon Foukas et al. 2016. FlexRAN: A Flexible and Programmable Platform for Software-Defined Radio Access Networks. In *Proceedings of the 12th ACM CoNEXT*. ACM, 427–441.

[20] Xenofon Foukas et al. 2017. Network Slicing in 5G: Survey and Challenges. *IEEE Communications Magazine* 55, 5 (2017), 94–100.

[21] Linux Foundation. 2017. NetEm Linux network emulator. https://wiki.linuxfoundation.org/networking/netem. (2017).

[22] Thomas Frisanco et al. 2008. Infrastructure Sharing and Shared Operations for Mobile Network Operators from a Deployment and Operations View. In *Proceedings of IEEE NOMS 2008*. IEEE, 129–136.

[23] Pablo Caballero Garcés et al. 2015. RMSC: A Cell Slicing Controller for Virtualized Multi-tenant Mobile Networks. In *Vehicular Technology Conference (VTC Spring), 2015 IEEE 81st*. IEEE, 1–6.

[24] Anteneh A Gebremariam et al. 2017. Resource pooling via dynamic spectrum-level slicing across heterogeneous networks. In *14th IEEE annual consumer communications and networking conference (CCNC)*.

[25] Aditya Gudipati, Li Erran Li, and Sachin Katti. 2014. RadioVisor: A Slicing Plane for Radio Access Networks. In *Proceedings of the third workshop on Hot topics in software defined networking*. ACM, 237–238.

[26] Jun He and Wei Song. 2015. AppRAN: Application-Oriented Radio Access Network Sharing in Mobile Networks. In *Proceedings of IEEE International Conference on Communications (ICC)*. IEEE, 3788–3794.

[27] Matt Helsley. 2009. LXC: Linux container tools. *IBM devloperWorks Technical Library* (2009), 11.

[28] Pieter Hintjens. 2013. *ZeroMQ: Messaging for Many Applications*. O'Reilly Media, Inc.

[29] ITU-R. 2015. IMT Vision – Framework and overall objectives of the future development of IMT for 2020 and beyond. (Sept 2015).

[30] Xin Jin et al. 2013. Softcell: Scalable and Flexible Cellular Core Network Architecture. In *Proceedings of the ninth ACM CoNEXT*. ACM, 163–174.

[31] Vinay Joseph and Gustavo de Veciana. 2014. NOVA: QoE-Driven Optimization of DASH-based Video Delivery in Networks. In *Proceedings of IEEE INFOCOM*. IEEE, 82–90.

[32] Mahmoud I Kamel, Long Bao Le, and André Girard. 2014. LTE Wireless Network Virtualization: Dynamic Slicing via Flexible Scheduling. In *Vehicular Technology Conference (VTC Fall), 2014 IEEE 80th*. IEEE, 1–5.

[33] Young Han Kim et al. 2014. Slicing the Next Mobile Packet Core Network. In *Wireless Communications Systems (ISWCS), 2014 11th International Symposium on*. IEEE, 901–904.

[34] Avi Kivity et al. 2007. kvm: the Linux virtual machine monitor. In *Proceedings of the Linux symposium*, Vol. 1. 225–230.

[35] Ravi Kokku et al. 2012. NVS: A Substrate for Virtualizing Wireless Resources in Cellular Networks. *IEEE/ACM Transactions on Networking (TON)* 20, 5 (2012), 1333–1346.

[36] Adlen Ksentini and Navid Nikaein. 2017. Toward Enforcing Network Slicing on RAN: Flexibility and Resources Abstraction. *IEEE Communications Magazine* 55, 6 (2017), 102–108.

[37] Li Erran Li, Z Morley Mao, and Jennifer Rexford. 2012. Toward Software-Defined Cellular Networks. In *Proceedings of 2012 European Workshop on Software Defined Networking (EWSDN)*. IEEE, 7–12.

[38] Yan Li et al. 2008. Content-Aware Playout and Packet Scheduling for Video Streaming over Wireless Links. *IEEE Transactions on Multimedia* 10, 5 (2008), 885–895.

[39] Chengchao Liang and F Richard Yu. 2015. Wireless Virtualization for Next Generation Mobile Cellular Networks. *IEEE Wireless Communications* 22, 1 (2015), 61–69.

[40] Linux Foundation. 2017. ONAP. https://www.onap.org/. (2017).

[41] Rajesh Mahindra et al. 2013. Radio Access Network Sharing in Cellular Networks. In *Proceedings of 21st IEEE International Conference on Network Protocols (ICNP)*. IEEE, 1–10.

[42] Toktam Mahmoodi and Srini Seetharaman. 2014. Traffic Jam: Handling the Increasing Volume of Mobile Data Traffic. *IEEE Vehicular Technology Magazine* 9, 3 (2014), 56–62.

[43] Ilaria Malanchini, Stefan Valentin, and Osman Aydin. 2014. Generalized Resource Sharing for Multiple Operators in Cellular Wireless Networks. In *Wireless Communications and Mobile Computing Conference (IWCMC), 2014 International*. IEEE, 803–808.

[44] Dirk Merkel. 2014. Docker: lightweight linux containers for consistent development and deployment. *Linux Journal* 2014, 239 (2014), 2.

[45] Microsoft Test Content. 2017. DASH Sample Video. http://wams.edgesuite.net/media/MPTExpressionData02/BigBuckBunny_1080p24_IYUV_2ch.ism/manifest(format=mpd-time-csf). (2017).

[46] Mehrdad Moradi et al. 2014. SoftMoW: Recursive and Reconfigurable Cellular WAN Architecture. In *Proceedings of the 10th ACM CoNEXT*. ACM, 377–390.

[47] Akihiro Nakao et al. 2016. Demo at ITU FG IMT-2020 Workshop:Softwarized LTE in FLARE network slices. http://www.itu.int/en/ITU-T/Workshops-and-Seminars/201612/Pages/Programme.aspx. (Dec 2016).

[48] Akihiro Nakao, Ping Du, Yoshiaki Kiriha, Fabrizio Granelli, Anteneh Atumo Gebremariam, Tarik Taleb, and Miloud Bagaa. 2017. End-to-end Network Slicing for 5G Mobile Networks. *Journal of Information Processing* 25 (2017), 153–163.

[49] NGMN-Alliance. 2015. 5G White Paper. (Feb 2015).

[50] Navid Nikaein. 2017. FlexRAN tutorial on RAN sharing. https://gitlab.eurecom.fr/mosaic-5g/mosaic-5g/wikis/ran-sharing. (2017).

[51] Navid Nikaein et al. 2014. OpenAirInterface: A flexible platform for 5G research. *ACM SIGCOMM Computer Communication Review* 44, 5 (2014), 33–38.

[52] Navid Nikaein et al. 2015. Network store: Exploring slicing in future 5G networks. In *Proc. 10th ACM International Workshop on Mobility in the Evolving Internet Architecture (MobiArch'15)*. 8–13.

[53] Nokia. 2014. Network Sharing: Delivering mobile broadband more efficiently and at lower cost. http://resources.alcatel-lucent.com/asset/200192. (2014).

[54] OpenAirInterface Software Alliance. 2017. OpenAirInterface repository. https://gitlab.eurecom.fr/oai/openairinterface5g. (2017).

[55] Peshala Pahalawatta et al. 2007. Content-Aware Resource Allocation and Packet Scheduling for Video Transmission over Wireless Networks. *IEEE Journal on Selected Areas in Communications* 25, 4 (2007).

[56] Klaus I Pedersen et al. 2016. A Flexible 5G Frame Structure Design for Frequency-Division Duplex Cases. *IEEE Communications Magazine* 54, 3 (2016), 53–59.

[57] Kostas Pentikousis, Yan Wang, and Weihua Hu. 2013. Mobileflow: Toward Software-Defined Mobile Networks. *IEEE Communications magazine* 51, 7 (2013), 44–53.

[58] Zafar Ayyub Qazi et al. 2016. KLEIN: A Minimally Disruptive Design for an Elastic Cellular Core. In *Proceedings of the Symposium on SDN Research*. ACM, 2.

[59] Qualcomm. 2016. Making 5G NR a reality. (Dec 2016).

[60] Peter Rost et al. 2016. Mobile Network Architecture Evolution Toward 5G. *IEEE Communications* 54, 5 (2016).

[61] Peter Rost et al. 2017. Network Slicing to Enable Scalability and Flexibility in 5G Mobile Networks. *IEEE Communications magazine* (2017).

[62] Konstantinos Samdanis et al. 2013. Service Boost: Towards on-demand QoS enhancements for OTT apps in LTE. In *Network Protocols (ICNP), 2013 21st IEEE International Conference on*. IEEE, 1–6.

[63] Konstantinos Samdanis, Xavier Costa-Perez, and Vincenzo Sciancalepore. 2016. From Network Sharing to Multi-Tenancy: The 5G Network Slice Broker. *IEEE*

Communications 54, 7 (2016).
[64] Rob Sherwood et al. 2009. FlowVisor: A Network Virtualization Layer. *OpenFlow Switch Consortium, Tech. Rep* (2009), 1–13.
[65] Aisha Syed and Jacobus Van der Merwe. 2016. Proteus: A Network Service Control Platform for Service Evolution in a Mobile Software Defined Infrastructure. In *Proceedings of the 22nd ACM MobiCom*. ACM, 257–270.
[66] Tarik Taleb et al. 2015. EASE: EPC as a Service to Ease Mobile Core Network Deployment over Cloud. *IEEE Network* 29, 2 (2015), 78–88.
[67] Tarik Taleb, Adlen Ksentini, and Abdellatif Kobbane. 2014. Lightweight Mobile Core Networks for Machine Type Communications. *IEEE Access* 2 (2014), 1128–1137.
[68] Volkan Yazıcı, Ulas C Kozat, and M Oguz Sunay. 2014. A New Control Plane for 5G Network Architecture with a Case Study on Unified Handoff, Mobility, and Routing Management. *IEEE Communications Magazine* 52, 11 (2014), 76–85.
[69] Yasir Zaki et al. 2011. LTE Mobile Network Virtualization. *Mobile Networks and Applications* 16, 4 (2011), 424–432.
[70] Liang Zhao et al. 2011. LTE virtualization: From Theoretical Gain to Practical Solution. In *Proceedings of the 23rd International Teletraffic Congress*. International Teletraffic Congress, 71–78.

Accelerating Multipath Transport Through Balanced Subflow Completion

Yihua Ethan Guo, Ashkan Nikravesh, Z. Morley Mao, Feng Qian[†], Subhabrata Sen[‡]

University of Michigan [†]Indiana University [‡]AT&T Labs – Research
{yhguo, ashnik, zmao}@umich.edu fengqian@indiana.edu sen@research.att.com

ABSTRACT

Simultaneously using multiple network paths (*e.g.*, WiFi and cellular) is an attractive feature on mobile devices. A key component in a multipath system such as MPTCP is the scheduler, which determines how to distribute the traffic over multiple paths. In this paper, we propose DEMS, a new multipath scheduler aiming at reducing the data chunk download time. DEMS consists of three key design decisions: (1) being aware of the chunk boundary and strategically decoupling the paths for chunk delivery, (2) ensuring simultaneous subflow completion at the receiver side, and (3) allowing a path to trade a small amount of redundant data for performance. We have implemented DEMS on smartphones and evaluated it over both emulated and real cellular/WiFi networks. DEMS is robust to diverse network conditions and brings significant performance boost compared to the default MPTCP scheduler (*e.g.*, median download time reduction of 33%–48% for fetching files and median loading time reduction of 6%–43% for fetching web pages), and even more benefits compared to other state-of-the-art schedulers.

1 INTRODUCTION

Simultaneously using multiple network paths such as cellular and WiFi to accelerate data transfer is an attractive feature on mobile devices. It is supported by many commercial products such as Apple Siri [4], Gigapath by Korean Telecom [1], and Samsung Download Booster [2]. Researchers have also devised multipath strategies for applications such as file download [24, 29], web browsing [15, 16], and video streaming [9, 17, 38]. Currently the most widely used multipath solution is MPTCP [12], which enables unmodified applications to leverage multipath by adding a shim layer to the TCP interface. MPTCP establishes a *subflow* over each network path. The MPTCP sender distributes the data onto the subflows; the receiver reassembles the data into the original byte stream and delivers it to the app transparently.

MPTCP (or any transport-layer multipath scheme) has a complex protocol stack. In this work, we focus on optimizing the *schedulers*, which determine how the data is distributed onto the subflows. MPTCP supports different types of schedulers. For example, the *MinRTT* scheduler attempts to deliver the data as soon as possible by choosing a subflow with the smallest RTT unless its congestion window is full; the *ReMP* scheduler [13] boosts the reliability by duplicating packets over all subflows. There also exist schedulers that consider other dimensions such as energy efficiency [36], path priority [17] and receiver buffer occupancy [25].

Despite these efforts, we found that the multipath scheduler design is far from being optimal. In a pilot experiment conducted in §3, we observe that surprisingly, under representative WiFi/LTE network conditions, the MinRTT scheduler inflates the download time for a medium-sized file by up to 33% compared to the optimal scheduling decision derived offline. In real-world networks with fluctuating bandwidth or latency, MinRTT may perform even worse (up to 7.5x download time increase, 49% median increase compared to optimal scheduling) as shown in §7. Regarding the root cause, our key insight is that for such a file download, oftentimes the subflows do *not* complete at the same time at the *receiver* side. This inevitably leads to suboptimal performance: if Subflow A completes earlier than Subflow B, one could achieve a shorter overall download time by offloading some of the traffic from Subflow B to A. Therefore, achieving simultaneous subflow completion is a necessary condition for minimizing the data transfer time.

The key contribution of this paper is the design, implementation, and evaluation of DEMS (**DE**coupled **M**ultipath **S**cheduler[1]), a new multipath packet scheduler aiming at reducing the data chunk download time over multiple paths. A *data chunk* is simply a block of application-defined bytes, which is a very common data transfer workload in a wide range of applications, *e.g.*, fetching an image, JavaScript, MP3 file, or video chunk. The key idea behind DEMS is to *achieve simultaneous subflow completion at the receiver side through strategic packet scheduling over decoupled subflows* in order to minimize the chunk download time. Accomplishing this seemingly straightforward task, however, faces several challenges. First, MPTCP by default treats the user data as a continuous stream without even knowing the chunk boundary, letting alone performing any optimization for it. Second, the scheduler works at the sender side while we need to balance the flow completion time at the receiver side so there exists a "visibility gap" between the sender and receiver. Third, the task is further complicated by the fluctuating network conditions in wireless networks. Our judicious design addresses all above challenges as follows.

- As a first prerequisite for optimizing the chunk download time, DEMS is aware of the boundary of a chunk. Since how the data within a chunk is delivered does not matter (as long as the chunk can

[1]Note here "decoupled scheduling" is different from the decoupled congestion control in MPTCP.

MobiCom '17, October 16–20, 2017, Snowbird, UT, USA

ACM ISBN 978-1-4503-4916-1/17/10...$15.00
https://doi.org/10.1145/3117811.3117829

be reassembled correctly), DEMS can employfl exible and efficient schemes to split the chunk over subflows. For example, if only two paths are involved, one path can send data from the beginning in the forward direction, and the other path sends data from the end in the backward direction. Doing so simplifies our design and facilitates the performance by decoupling the subflows (§4.1).

• We devise a technique to ensure simultaneous subflow completion on the receiver side. To achieve this, at the *sender* side, DEMS strategically introduces a timing offset between the two subflows with different RTTs so that the last packets across all subflows will arrive at the receiver at the same time. The timing offset is dynamically determined based on the network latency and bandwidth dynamics (§4.2).

• Thefl uctuation of bandwidth and latency may still cause some differences in completion times across the subflows. To minimize this negative performance impact, DEMS performs data *reinjection*: if one subflowfi nishes earlier, it can "help" other subflows by transmitting a small portion of data (typically towards the end of the chunk download) that was already assigned to another subflow. Such data may be redundant (*i.e.,* transferred twice over two subflows) but it helps further reduce the overall download time (§4.3). We develop a method that adaptively determines the amount of the redundant data to strike a sweet spot between the performance and the additional data transmission due to reinjection (§4.4).

DEMS can work with any data transfer size and/or traffic pattern. The ideal workload on which DEMS yields the highest benefits is downloading application data chunks, which are very common to mobile traffic workloads. A wide range of mobile applications such as web browsing and video streaming involve downloading such data chunks (*e.g.,* an HTTP object or a video segment).

We integrated the DEMS components into a holistic system (§5) and implemented it on commodity mobile devices (§6). We conducted extensive evaluations over both emulated and real cellular/WiFi networks. The results indicate that DEMS is robust to diverse network conditions (including challenging multipath environments) and oftentimes brings significant performance boost compared to the state-of-the-art. Below highlights some key results.

• In stable network conditions, compared to MinRTT, DEMS reduces download time by up to 74%, 57% and 21% for 256KB, 1MB and 4MB download, respectively, under different combinations of delay/bandwidth of the paths. DEMS exhibits even better performance compared to ReMP, round-robin, and the best single path approach (§7.2, §7.5).

• In changing network conditions, DEMS reduces the median download time of 256KB and 1MBfi les by 12% to 46%, compared to MinRTT. Meanwhile, our adaptive reinjection scheme effectively reduces the redundant bytes by 48% to 86% compared to the naïve reinjection scheme while maintaining similar performance (§7.3).

• We conductedfi eld tests at 5 real-world locations such as a parking lot and a grocery store. DEMS reduces the download time by up to 88%, 83% and 77% for 256KB, 1MB and 4MBfi le, respectively, compared to MinRTT (the median reductions are 33%, 48%, and 42%, respectively). The real-world results are even better than the in-lab emulation results. Compared to wired networks, wireless networks like WiFi and cellular can sometimes exhibit high delay and bandwidth dynamics [22, 23]. Our evaluation demonstrates that compared to existing multipath schedulers, DEMS is able to robustly handle such environments (§7.4).

• DEMS reduces the median web page load time (across 10 popular websites) by 6% to 43% (median: 25%) under real network conditions, compared to MinRTT (§7.6).

Overall, ourfi ndings indicate that *strategically performing decoupled packet scheduling with balanced subflow completion can significantly improve the multipath transport performance,* which translates into better user QoE and improved energy efficiency (due to shortened radio-on time [21]). The remaining sections will focus on the motivation (§3), algorithm design (§4), system integration (§5), implementation (§6), and evaluation (§7) of DEMS. We discuss related work in §2 and limitations in §8.

2 RELATED WORK

Characterization of Mobile Multipath. Several prior efforts focus on characterizing the multipath performance over mobile networks. Chen *et al.* [6] studied thefi le download performance using MPTCP over 3G/4G and WiFi. Deng *et al.* [11] compared the performance between single-path and multipath in the mobile context. Han *et al.* [15] investigated the interaction between MPTCP and web protocols such as HTTP/1.1 and SPDY. Nika *et al.* [28] characterized the energy efficiency and performance of radio bundling (*i.e.,* multipath) in outdoor environments. Some other recent studies examined MPTCP performance [8] and its impact on applications [29] through crowd-sourced measurements.

Multipath Schedulers have been experimentally shown to affect download performance [28, 30, 31]. Several multipath scheduling algorithms have been proposed for different application scenarios. ECF makes scheduling decision using both congestion window size and RTT to avoid undesirable idle transmission periods and achieve higher aggregate throughput [26]. Compared to ECF, DEMS relies on chunk-based data transfer to decouple subflows and employs adaptive reinjection to combat variable network conditions. MPRTP focuses on real-time content delivery over multipath by adapting to the changing path characteristics [34]. DAPS aims at reducing receiver's buffer blocking time over multiple wireless networks [25]. ReMP duplicates the same packet onto all paths to reduce latency and to improve reliability [13]. eMPTCP takes energy consumption into consideration when making scheduling decisions [36]. Another energy-aware MPTCP scheduling algorithm was proposed in [32]. Compared to the above work, DEMS aims at reducing the download time for data chunks through a set of novel techniques.

Applications of Mobile Multipath. Previous studies have leveraged the MPTCP API extension to support enhanced socket options [18],fi ne-grained control on transport behavior [19], and multipath over UDP [5]. Some other studies investigated how to better use multipath for different applications, such as video streaming [7, 9, 17, 38], web browsing [16], smooth handover [10], and traffic sharing across users [27]. In contrast, DEMS is a general-purpose multipath scheduler that can benefit a wide range of applications.

3 BACKGROUND AND MOTIVATION

After providing necessary background in §3.1, we reveal the performance inefficiency caused by MPTCP's scheduling algorithm in §3.2, which leads to the key principle of DEMS in §3.3: ensure simultaneous subflow completion.

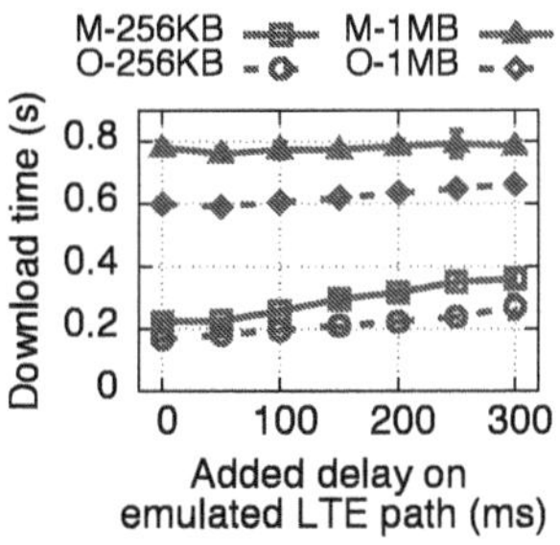

Figure 1: Compare chunk download time (M: MinRTT, O: Optimal).

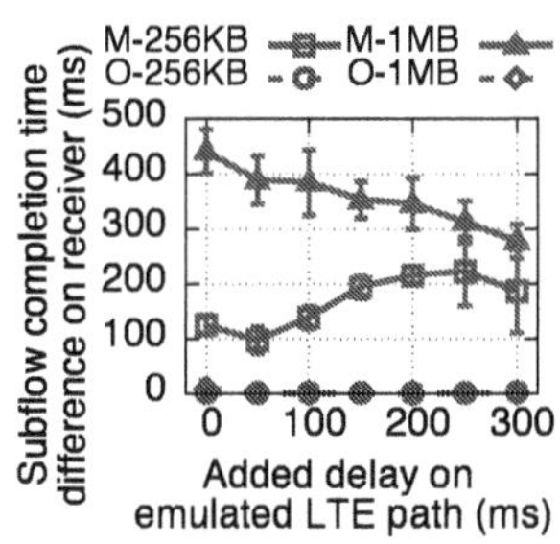

Figure 2: Compare subflow completion time on receiver.

3.1 Multipath TCP and its Schedulers

Multipath TCP (MPTCP [12]) enables simultaneous usage of multiple network paths (*a.k.a.* subflows). In the remainder of this paper, we primarily focus on two paths, as they correspond to the most common mobile multipath usage scenarios: jointly using WiFi and cellular on a smartphone or WiFi and Bluetooth on a wearable. We discuss how DEMS can be extended to more than two paths in §8.

MPTCP has a complex transport protocol stack consisting of several components: subflow management, packet scheduling, congestion control,fl ow control, *etc.*, among which we focus on optimizing the *schedulers*. A multipath scheduler takes packets from applications (stored in the "meta buffer") and determines on which subflow to transmit each packet. MPTCP currently supports three schedulers: round-robin, ReMP (sending the same data to all subflows for better reliability), and MinRTT. Among them, MinRTT is the default scheduler aiming at reducing the overall data transfer time. As long as the congestion window allows, MinRTT favors the subflow with the smallest RTT so that the packet can be delivered as soon as possible. The MinRTT scheduler is simple and robust, and has registered wide usage in practical systems [1, 4].

3.2 Can We Further Improve MinRTT?

Consider the common task of downloading a data chunk, which can be an image, a Javascript, an audio snippet, or a video chunk, over multipath. Our apparent goal is to minimize the download time. We conduct a pilot experiment to demonstrate (1) the impact of the scheduler on the download time, and (2) the potential room for improving MinRTT.

The experiment was conducted on a laptop with both WiFi and Ethernet connectivity, which emulate WiFi and LTE networks respectively using Linux `tc`. The network characteristics were chosen based on recent large-scale measurements of metropolitan LTE [22] and WiFi [35] users[2]. We use our user-level MPTCP testbed (to be described in §6) to provide the multipath support for the laptop.

We use the above setting to download a medium-sizedfi le of {256KB, 1MB} using the MinRTT scheduler and an optimal scheduling computed offline as follows. We download $p\%$ of thefi le over WiFi and $1 - p\%$ over cellular. Tofi nd the best p that leads to the shortest (*i.e.*, optimal) download time, we perform an "exhaustive search" by conducting many experiments covering the full range of $p \in [0, 100]$. We also vary the latency difference between the two paths by inflating the emulated LTE path, as it is common to have diverse path characteristics in mobile networks [11]. Note that except for the scheduling algorithm, the MinRTT and the optimal schemes share the same configurations (*e.g.*, the initial congestion window and congestion control algorithm) to ensure apples-to-apples comparison.

The results are shown in Figure 1. As shown, the scheduling decision clearly impacts the performance. Surprisingly, compared to the optimal case, MinRTT increases the download time by up to 33%. Note our experiment assumes stable network condition, whereas in real-world networks withfl uctuating bandwidth or latency, the gap between MinRTT and the optimal case can be even larger (up to 7.5x download time increase, 49% median increase compared to optimal scheduling) (§7). Also note that researchers have proposed other MPTCP schedulers such as deadline-aware scheduler [17], energy-efficient scheduler [36], real-time content scheduler [34] and buffer-blocking-aware scheduler [25]. They usually sacrifice chunk download time performance for other properties such as path priority and energy consumption, so we do not compare with them here.

By examining the results at the packet timing level, we identified a key reason why MPTCP yields suboptimal performance to be that the subflows do not complete at the same time at the receiver side. Figure 2 plots the two subflows' completion time difference when using the two schedulers. For MinRTT, the difference ranges from 100ms to 450ms while in the optimal scheme, the last bytes on the two subflows almost always arrive at the receiver simultaneously.

3.3 Ensuring Simultaneous Subflow Completion and its Challenges

Having all subflows complete at the same time at the receiver side is a necessary condition for achieving the optimal performance. The reason can be easily shown through *proof by contradiction*: suppose in an optimal scheme, Subflow Afi nishes earlier than Subflow B; in that case Subflow B can further "offload" some bytes to Subflow A, leading to an even shorter download time. But why cannot the MinRTT scheduler achieve this same-time-completion property? The reasons are multi-fold as explained below.

- When making a scheduling decision, MinRTT only considers the latency of each subflow without taking into consideration the bandwidth. Oftentimes, despite one subflow having a higher RTT than other subflows or even having a full congestion window (so it is temporarily unavailable), its higher bandwidth allows it to drain data from its sender buffer quickly. As a result, choosing the higher-RTT subflow can actually lead to lower end-to-end latency.
- Under practical network conditions (wireless in particular), the RTT and bandwidth are often highlyfl uctuating, leading to unbalanced subflow completion time. This factor is largely not taken into account by MinRTT.
- MinRTT is stateless in that the scheduling decision of the current packet does not explicitly depend on the previous packets. We will show that by strategically leveraging the information of previously transmitted packets, the scheduling decisions and thus the overall performance can be improved.

[2]WiFi: uplink 2020kbps, downlink 7040kbps, RTT 50ms;
LTE: uplink 2286kbps, downlink 9185kbps, RTT 70ms.

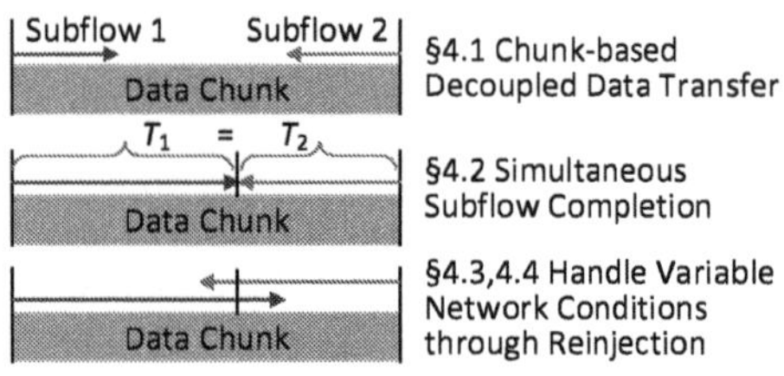

Figure 3: Key design decisions of DEMS.

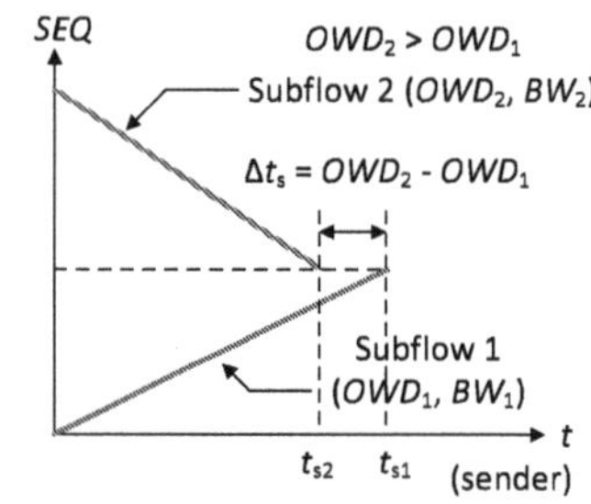

Figure 4: Achieve simultaneous subflow completion (sender-side view).

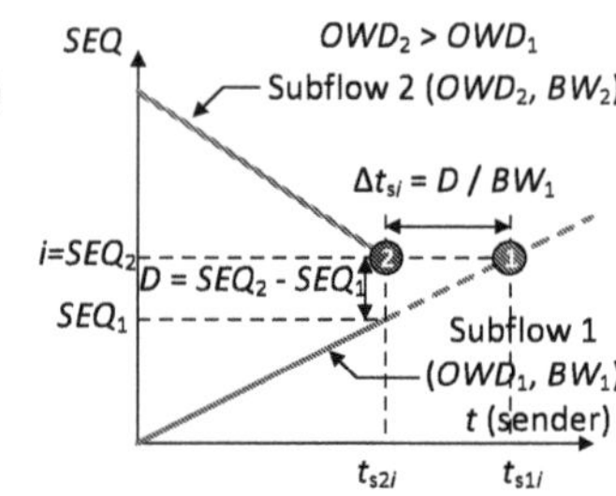

Figure 5: Choose a subflow with an earlier estimated data arrival time (sender-side view).

4 THE DEMS ALGORITHM

We propose DEMS, a new scheduling algorithm for reducing the data chunk download time over multipath. As shown in Figure 3, the key design decisions of DEMS include the following. (1) DEMS is aware of the chunk boundary, and it strategically decouples the paths for chunk delivery (§4.1). (2) DEMS ensures simultaneous subflow completion at the receiver side (§4.2). (3) DEMS allows a path to trade a small amount of redundant data for performance (§4.3, §4.4). We next elaborate them in this section.

4.1 Chunk-based Data Transfer

In DEMS, by default, data is delivered to the application on a *per-chunk* basis. A (data) chunk consists of a block of bytes defined by the application, which can be, for example, an image, a Javascript, an audio snippet, or a video chunk. At the sender side, after the sender app pushes the chunk to the multipath meta buffer, DEMS treats all data in the meta buffer as a chunk by default, thus being fully transparent to applications. At the receiver side, when the chunk is fully received, it is then delivered to the application. We will describe in §5 implementation alternatives for making DEMS aware of the chunk boundaries informed by applications through a simple API.

As long as a chunk can be correctly reassembled, bytes within the chunk can be delivered in any order. The data chunk is thus split into different parts that are distributed onto different paths for delivery. For the common scenario involving two paths, we design a "two-way" splitting approach: the two paths transfer the data in opposite directions, one from the beginning and the other from the end; when they "meet" each other, the chunk is fully downloaded. This approach is intuitive and parameterless. Furthermore, it helps improve the multipath performance by *decoupling* the two subflows. In conventional MPTCP, subflows are tightly coupled; a stall (*e.g.*, due to packet loss) in one subflow may slow down other subflows due to their limited and shared meta receive window whose size is difficult to set [29]. DEMS, on the other hand, decouples the two subflows by allowing each subflow to freely and independently transfer the data until the very end when subflows meet and merge. The receive window (16 MB by default) is configured to be larger than a typical chunk size so it will not become a performance bottleneck during a chunk transmission [29]. In rare cases when the application data is larger than the receive window, the data will be split into multiple chunks for transmission.

4.2 Simultaneous Subflow Completion

Now let us consider how to simultaneously complete subflows at the receiver side. Recall that the high-level idea is to introduce a timing offset at the sender to compensate the heterogeneous delay across both subflows.

Let usfi rst assume that the one-way delay (OWD) of both subflows can be accurately predicted. Let OWD_1 and OWD_2 be the OWD of Subflow 1 and 2, respectively, where $OWD_2 > OWD_1$. Let t_{s1} and t_{s2} be the time when the last byte is transmitted over Subflow 1 and 2, respectively. Let t_{r1} and t_{r2} be the time when Subflow 1 and 2 receives the last byte, respectively, *i.e.*, the subflow completion time at the receiver. If no packet reordering or loss happens, we have:

$$t_{r1} - t_{s1} = OWD_1 + t_{\text{offset}} \quad (1)$$

$$t_{r2} - t_{s2} = OWD_2 + t_{\text{offset}} \quad (2)$$

where t_{offset} is the clock difference between the sender and receiver (handling network conditionfl uctuation caused by packet losses/reordering will be discussed in §4.3 and §4.4). Thus, the subflow completion time difference is:

$$t_{r2} - t_{r1} = (t_{s2} - t_{s1}) + (OWD_2 - OWD_1) \quad (3)$$

Clearly the receiver-side subflow completion time difference depends on both the sender-side transmission completion time difference denoted as $\Delta t_s = t_{s2} - t_{s1}$ and the forward-path one-way delay difference denoted as $\Delta OWD = OWD_2 - OWD_1$. To ensure simultaneous subflow completion *i.e.*, $t_{r2} = t_{r1}$, we need:

$$t_{s1} - t_{s2} = OWD_2 - OWD_1 = \Delta OWD \quad (4)$$

Namely, at sender side, the subflow with a larger OWD mustfinish transmission ΔOWD earlier than the other subflow.

Recall that DEMS employs the "two-way" data split scheme where the two subflows start from the two ends of the chunk and move towards each other. This process is illustrated in Figure 4, which plots the *sender-side* view of the data transfer progresses at both subflows (the X axis is time and Y axis is the sequence number). Assuming the constant bandwidth, the data transfer curves are linear. Subflow 2 stops transmission at t_{s2}. Subflow 1 then spends ΔOWD time to transmit all its data,fi nishing at t_{s1}. To translate this into the *receiver-side* view is easy: by shifting the two curves towards the right by OWD_1 and OWD_2 respectively, they will meet at $t_{s1} + OWD_1 = t_{s2} + OWD_2$, indicating they complete simultaneously at the receiver side.

Now we describe how to incorporate the above idea into the DEMS scheduler design, which needs to handle two tasks: assigning each packet (with its byte range) to a subflow and deciding when

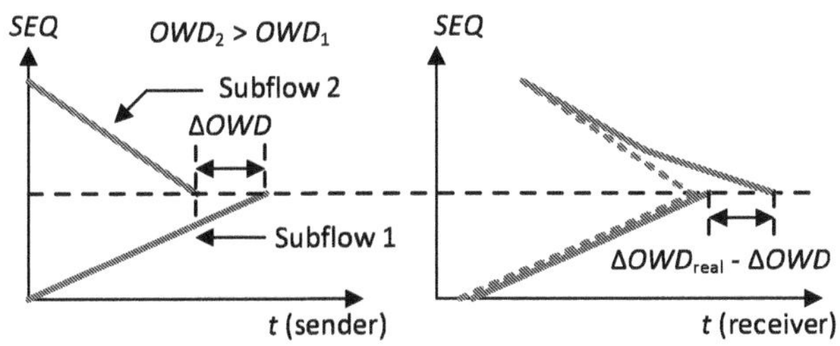

(a) Sender-side subflow balancing with ΔOWD

(b) Receiver-side view with actual $\Delta OWD_{real} > \Delta OWD$

Figure 6: Impact of inaccurate ΔOWD estimation.

to stop a subflow at the sender. The former is trivial as the chunk has already been split in "two-way". So we focus on the latter task. The basic idea is as follows. When the subflow with a larger OWD can transmit a packet over the network, we estimate its arrival time over both subflows, and then choose the subflow with an *earlier* packet arrival time for actual transmission. We next show that this strategy will make the large-OWD subflow stop transmission when Equation (4) holds, thus resulting in simultaneous subflow completion shown in Figure 4.

Consider a general scenario depicted in Figure 5 where Subflow 2 with a larger OWD can now transmit a byte whose sequence number is $i = SEQ_2$. Should this byte be immediately transmitted over Subflow 2 (marked as ❷) or later over Subflow 1 (marked as ❶) so that Subflow 2 can stop now? If we choose Subflow 2, the byte's estimated arrival time at the receiver side is:

$$est(t_{r2i}) = t_{s2i} + OWD_{2i} + t_{\text{offset}} \tag{5}$$

where t_{s2i} is the current sender-side timestamp and OWD_{2i} is the current estimation of OWD_2. Now consider choosing Subflow 1 to transmit SEQ_2. Since Subflow 1 is currently working on a byte with a smaller sequence number SEQ_1, SEQ_2 has to be buffered in the meta buffer and gets transmitted at ❶ after all bytes from SEQ_1 to $SEQ_2 - 1$ are transmitted (over Subflow 1). Therefore, the estimated arrival time of SEQ_2 over Subflow 1 is:

$$est(t_{r1i}) = t_{s2i} + \Delta t_{\text{si}} + OWD_{1i} + t_{\text{offset}} \tag{6}$$

The buffering delay, Δt_{si}, is computed as:

$$\Delta t_{\text{si}} = \frac{SEQ_2 - SEQ_1}{BW_{1i}} \tag{7}$$

where BW_{1i} is Subflow 1's current bandwidth estimation.

As said, we stop Subflow 2 and choose Subflow 1 when the estimated byte arrival time of the larger-OWD subflow (Subflow 2) is later than the smaller-OWD subflow (Subflow 1) *i.e.*, $est(t_{r2i}) > est(t_{r1i})$. In this situation, we have:

$$\Delta t_{\text{si}} = t_{s1i} - t_{s2i} < OWD_{2i} - OWD_{1i} \tag{8}$$

This is the same criteria as that in Equation (4), which guarantees the same receiver-side subflow completion time. Next, plugging Equation (7) into (8) yields:

$$D = SEQ_2 - SEQ_1 < (OWD_{2i} - OWD_{1i})BW_{1i} \tag{9}$$

D corresponds to the number of bytes remaining to be transmitted in the meta buffer (imagine SEQ_1 and SEQ_2 as two "pointers" moving towards each other). We use Equation (9) in our system to

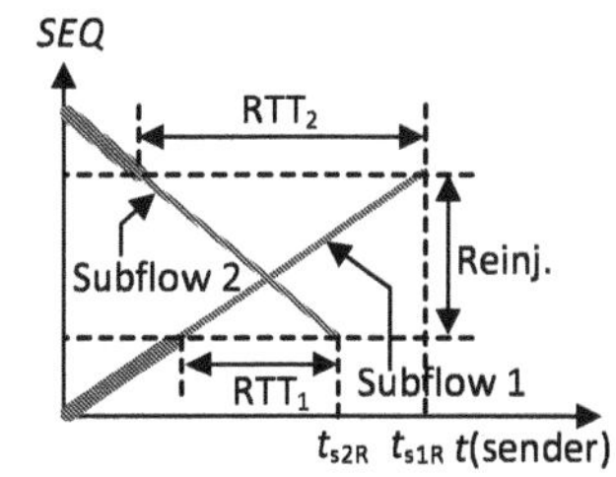

Figure 7: A simple reinjection scheme.

determine when to stop the transmission for the larger-OWD subflow as the two-way chunk download approaches to its end. Note the small-OWD subflow can always transmit new packets before meeting with the large-OWD subflow, as long as the congestion window allows.

4.3 Handling Variable Network Conditions

So far we assume that both subflows' OWD and the smaller-OWD subflow's bandwidth (*i.e.*, those on the right-hand side of Equation (9)) can be accurately predicted. Apparently this assumption does not always hold in practice in particular for wireless networks. Figure 6 illustrates the impact of inaccurate network condition estimation. At the sender side shown in Figure 6(a), DEMS makes scheduling decisions based on its estimated ΔOWD. Now assume Subflow 2's OWD increases over time, causing the sender to underestimate ΔOWD. In consequence, at the receiver side shown in Figure 6(b), the actual data reception time over Subflow 2 (in solid line) deviates from the expected time shown in the dashed line. As a result, Subflow 1 completes early than Subflow 2, leading to suboptimal chunk download time. Similar reasoning can be made for ΔOWD overestimation and inaccurate bandwidth estimation.

DEMS tolerates unbalanced completion of subflows under variable network conditions. It also takes a key design decision of performing *reinjection*: instead of having a full stop when all bytes of a chunk are transmitted, a subflow may further "overshoot" its portion by sending a small number of bytes that are beyond the meeting point of the two subflows, as illustrated in Figure 7. These bytes are redundant because they have already been transmitted over the other subflow. The purpose of reinjection is to trade redundant data for better performance: under uncertain network conditions, if the reinjected (redundant) data arrives earlier than its original copy, the overall download time is reduced.

A key challenge here is to carefully control how many bytes to reinject: reinjecting too little data incurs suboptimal performance, while reinjecting too much causes unnecessary battery drain or data plan usage (for cellular networks). In the extreme case adopted by MPTCP's redundant scheduler (ReMP) that duplicates *every* byte onto the secondaryfl ow, MPTCP falls back to the "best single path" approach.

In DEMS, reinjection only occurs near subflows' meeting point. Wefi rst present a simple reinjection approach that gives a reasonable "upper bound" for the number of reinjected bytes. In this approach, after the two subflows meet, they perform reinjection in their corresponding directions until all bytes of the chunk are either acknowledged or reinjected. As shown in Figure 7, Subflow 2 keeps reinjecting data until t_{s2R} when it hits the byte that was

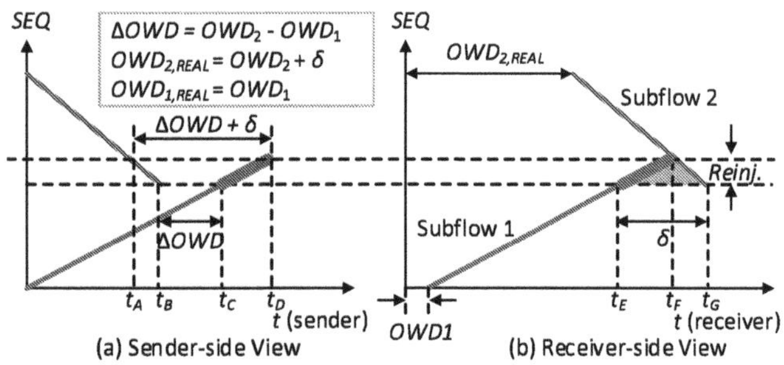

Figure 8: The adaptive reinjection scheme. All OWD values are exaggerated in the plot for illustration purpose.

transmitted and acknowledged over Subflow 1 (it takes RTT_1 for the ACK to arrive). Similarly, Subflow 1 stops reinjection at t_{s1R} when the remaining data has been acknowledged by Subflow 2. At t_{s1R}, any byte within the chunk has either been acknowledged (shown as thick lines in Figure 7, or has a redundant copy infl ight (shown as thin lines). By analyzing the "X" shape in Figure 7 (assuming the last byte on each subflow is not lost or reordered), we can compute the total number of reinjected bytes to be:

$$Reinj = \frac{BW_1 BW_2}{BW_1 + BW_2}(RTT_1 + RTT_2) \tag{10}$$

where BW_1 and BW_2 are the bandwidth of the subflows. Note they are the slopes of the two lines in Figure 7.

Equation (10) gives a reasonable upper bound of the reinjection overhead, which however is still too high as to be evaluated in §7. More importantly, this reinjection approach is not adaptive in that the reinjection behavior remains the same regardless of the network conditionfl uctuation. Ideally, when thefl uctuation is low (high), we should reinject less (more) data given that the subflow completion time balancing technique introduced in §4.2 is more (less) reliable.

4.4 Adaptive Reinjection

We design a scheme that performs adaptive reinjection while maintaining good performance. Let usfi rst consider a scenario where ΔOWD is underestimated: its real value, denoted as ΔOWD_{REAL}, is ΔOWD (the estimated version) plus δ. We use OWD_1 and OWD_2 to denote the estimated OWD for each subflow, and use $OWD_{1,\text{REAL}}$ and $OWD_{2,\text{REAL}}$ to denote their real values, respectively. Since what really matters is the prediction accuracy of the *difference* between OWDs (*i.e.*, ΔOWD), without loss of generality we assume $OWD_{1,\text{REAL}} = OWD_1$ and $OWD_{2,\text{REAL}} = OWD_2 + \delta$, for the ease of presentation.

Under the above setting, let usfi rst examine the sender side illustrated in Figure 8(a). Based on the completion time balancing technique introduced in §4.2, Subflow 1 and 2 would stop at t_C and t_B respectively where $t_C - t_B = \Delta OWD$. However, ΔOWD is underestimated. As a result, if we switch to the receiver's view in Figure 8(b), we will see that Subflow 1 completes δ time units before Subflow 2. This is because (assuming there is no clock drift between sender and receiver) $t_E = t_C + OWD_1$ and $t_G = t_B + OWD_{2,\text{REAL}}$, so $t_G - t_E = (OWD_{2,\text{REAL}} - OWD_1) - (t_C - t_B) = \delta$. Now let us consider how to perform reinjection. In Figure 8(b), to minimize the download time, Subflow 1 only needs to keep reinjecting data until it meets Subflow 2. The reinjected portion is highlighted in bold.

Now we derive the sender-side reinjection policy by shifting the reinjected portion back to Figure 8(a). When Subflow 1 reinjects the last byte at t_D, the byte's original transmission time (by Subflow 2) is t_A. As shown, $t_D - t_A = (t_B - t_A) + (t_C - t_B) + (t_D - t_C) = (t_G - t_F) + (t_C - t_B) + (t_F - t_E) = \Delta OWD + \delta$, which is the threshold for stopping reinjection. In other words, when ΔOWD is *underestimated* by δ, the *smaller-OWD* subflow keeps reinjection until the to-be-reinjected byte was transmitted more than $\Delta OWD + \delta$ time units ago. That is (using the notions introduced in §4.2):

$$\Delta t_{si} = t_{s1i} - t_{s2i} > OWD_{2i} - OWD_{1i} + \delta \tag{11}$$

Let the number of the reinjected bytes be r. By examining the gray triangle in Figure 8(b), we have $r/BW_1 + r/BW_2 = \delta$, which leads to $r = \delta BW_1 BW_2/(BW_1 + BW_2)$ where BW_1 and BW_2 are the subflows' bandwidth.

The counterpart scenario of ΔOWD overestimation can be derived in a similar way (proof omitted): when ΔOWD is *overestimated* by δ, the *larger-OWD* subflow keeps doing reinjection until the to-be-reinjected byte was transmitted less than $\Delta OWD - \delta$ time units ago, which is:

$$\Delta t_{si} = t_{s1i} - t_{s2i} < OWD_{2i} - OWD_{1i} - \delta \tag{12}$$

The reinjection overhead is also $r = \delta BW_1 BW_2/(BW_1 + BW_2)$. In reality we can only estimate (with a certain level of confidence) that ΔOWD_{REAL} falls in the range of $[\Delta OWD - \delta, \Delta OWD + \delta]$. DEMS thus lets both subflows to reinject according to Equation (11) and (12). The overall reinjection overhead is:

$$Reinj = 2\delta \frac{BW_1 BW_2}{BW_1 + BW_2} \tag{13}$$

These redundant bytes also help tolerate the inaccurate bandwidth prediction for the smaller-OWD subflow, as well as help recover from packet losses (within the reinjected byte range) quickly. Compared to (10), Equation (13) is usually much smaller. It is also adaptive as it is a function of δ that can be configured based on the predictability of the network condition. For example, δ can be set to $k \cdot StdDev(\Delta OWD)$.

4.5 Put Everything Together

We now walk through Algorithm 1, which combines chunk-based transfer (§4.1), subflow completion time balancing (§4.2), and adaptive reinjection (§4.4). The scheduling algorithm works at the sender side (the receiver-side logic is trivial). The input consists of the two network paths and a meta buffer that stores the packetized chunk data to be transmitted. The algorithm is invoked whenever either subflow can transmit a packet (*i.e.*, has some empty congestion window space). It makes a decision of transmitting a new packet, reinjecting a previously transmitted packet, or withholding transmission. Also note it only processes unacknowledged packets.

Line 7–13 handles the subflow with a smaller OWD. Recall that in §4.2, the default behavior is to always transmit a new packet over a small-OWD subflow whenever possible. Line 11–13 deals with the reinjection scenario according to Equation (11). Line 15–18 processes the subflow with a larger OWD. According to Equation (9), we may need to skip the large-OWD subflow to achieve simultaneous subflow completion. Line 16 performs adaptive reinjection over the large-OWD subflow according to Equation (12).

Algorithm 1: The DEMS scheduling algorithm

```
Input: subflow i ∈ {1, 2} that can transmit packet, packets in the meta buffer
       metaBuf[j], j ∈ [0, m].
Output: packet packet to transmit over subflow i.
1  packet ← GetNextUnAckedPacketOnThisSubflow(i);
2  smallOwdNo ← GetSmallOWDSubflowNo();
3  largeOwdNo ← GetLargeOWDSubflowNo();
4  ΔOWD ← GetΔOWD();
5  δ ← GetΔOWDVar();
6  trans ← false;
7  if i == smallOwdNo then
8      if not packet.tx [i] then
9          trans ← true;
10     else
11         delay ← ts − packet.ts [largeOwdNo];
12         if delay ≤ ΔOWD + δ then
13             trans ← true;
14 else
15     bw ← GetSubflowBW(smallOwdNo);
16     thres ← (ΔOWD − δ) ∗ bw;
17     if GetUntransmittedSize(metaBuf) ≥ thres then
18         trans ← true;
19 if trans then
20     Transmit(packet);
21     packet.ts [i] ← GetCurrTimestamp();
22 else
23     packet ← NULL;
```

5 SYSTEM DESIGN

We now elaborate on how to integrate the DEMS algorithm into a real system. Figure 9 plots the system diagram. At the sender side (right), the chunk data coming from the application is stored in the meta buffer, and is then split, scheduled, and transmitted by the packet scheduler. Working with the packet scheduler, the reinjection manager keeps track of packets' transmission states and makes decisions on adaptive reinjection. We also design a module for measuring and predicting network conditions (ΔOWD and bandwidth). The application can also optionally specify the chunk size through an API (to be elaborated next). The receiver side logic is much simpler. It passively receives/acknowledges the data, reassembles it in the receiver-side meta buffer, and delivers the in-order data to the application. Note that data over the (decoupled) subflows are acknowledged separately using the per-subflow ACK numbers. Meanwhile, similar to MPTCP, at the receiver meta buffer, the global sequence number carried by each packet is used to mark which portion within the chunk has been received. While Figure 9 illustrates one-way data transfer, our system supports full-duplex data transmission.

Interaction with Applications. DEMS provides applications with an optional hint API (through a socket option) to specify the chunk boundary, allowing DEMS to work on the chunks sequentially and to minimize the download time for each of them. Alternatively, if no hint is provided, DEMS leverages a heuristic that treats all data in the meta buffer as a single chunk. One issue here is that more data may arrive at the tail of the meta buffer from the app when the transmission is in progress. To handle this, we modify the packet fetch function (Line 1 in Algorithm 1) to let one subflow always fetch unacknowledged packets from the head of the meta buffer and the other subflow fetch from the tail of the meta buffer. The meta buffer is realized using a circular queue to allow efficient space reuse. In this way, DEMS is fully transparent to both the client-side and server-side applications. When there are multiple connections transmitting data simultaneously, DEMS can use a separate meta buffer for each connection and take bytes from each meta buffer in a round robin manner so that each connection is given a fair share of the network bandwidth. Other scheduling strategies such asfl ow prioritization can also be realized in DEMS.

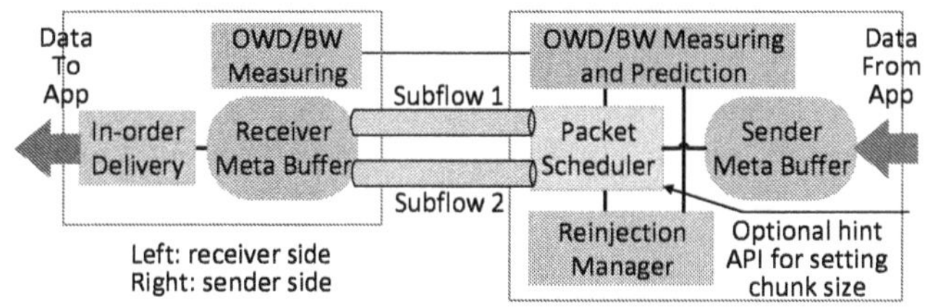

Figure 9: System diagram of DEMS.

ΔOWD Measurement and Prediction. OWD measurement requires cooperation between the sender and the receiver. The sender records the timestamp of each outgoing packet; the receiver records the reception time and sends it and the sequence number back to the sender through an encapsulated control message (§6). OWD is then estimated at the sender using exponential weighted moving average (EWMA) with α empirically chosen to be 0.25. Note that estimated OWD contains the sender-receiver clock drift, which is nevertheless cancelled out when a ΔOWD sample is calculated. Also, in wireless networks (cellular in particular), network latency is often correlated with the number of bytes-in-flight (BIF) [14, 23, 39]. We thus bin OWD samples for each subflow separately using measured BIF with a bin size of 10KB. The samples in each bin are processed separately using EWMA to facilitate a more accurate OWD estimation for each subflow at different BIF levels. We set δ, the parameter controlling adaptive reinjection (§4.4), to be the standard deviation of ΔOWD. The subflow bandwidth is also estimated using EWMA over measured samples. Note DEMS only needs the bandwidth estimation for the subflow with a smaller OWD (see Equation (9)). DEMS can also incorporate more sophisticated prediction methods (*e.g.*, those taking special consideration of network uncertainties [20]) to improve the prediction accuracy.

Congestion Control and Packet Losses. DEMS is compatible to any congestion control (CC) algorithm such as decoupled CC, LIA [37] and OLIA [24]. In our experiments we use decoupled CC that mobile multipath typically uses [15, 29]. Also, DEMS is robust to packet losses. Since the network condition prediction is performed in an online manner, delay or bandwidthfluctuation caused by (real or spurious) packet losses can be quickly picked up and reflected in the scheduling decision changes. We demonstrate in §7.4 that DEMS works well under diverse real-world scenarios including those with poor network conditions.

6 IMPLEMENTATION

DEMS can be directly integrated into MPTCP as a new scheduler. However, from the perspective of conducting real-world evaluations, MPTCP has two issues:fi rst, most of today's commercial Internet servers do not yet support MPTCP, making testing real workload difficult; second, MPTCP uses special TCP options that are often blocked by commercial cellular middleboxes [29].

To facilitate real-world test, we implemented a multipath TCP proxy infrastructure in C/C++. Between the proxy and the client host, multipath is realized as multiple conventional TCP connections each corresponding to a subflow established over a network path. For uplink traffic, at the client side, an application TCP connection's data is transparently split over the subflows using a custom light-weight encapsulation protocol (as opposed to using special TCP options); the data is then merged at the proxy and delivered to the server over conventional single-path TCP to ensure server transparency (assuming the client-proxy paths are the bottleneck). The downlink traffic is handled symmetrically. We have replicated MPTCP's three schedulers: MinRTT, round-robin, and ReMP by precisely following their algorithms. Compared to MPTCP, our proxy-based approach offers the same performance (based on our lab test[3]) while providing server transparency and middlebox friendliness.

We then implemented DEMS on our multipath proxy infrastructure. Most of the scheduling logic is implemented in the user space. Some low-level functionalities such as OWD/bandwidth measuring and prediction are implemented in the kernel through a light kernel module. Overall DEMS is lightweight: our implementation (not including the base proxy system) consists of 970 LoC (450 LoC for the scheduler and 520 LoC for network condition measurement/prediction). DEMS is generally compatible with Linux-based systems.

7 EVALUATION

We systematically evaluate DEMS under various settings including different network setups (emulated vs. real networks), different network conditions (stable vs. fluctuating), different workload (raw chunk download vs. real application workload), different clients (smartphone vs. laptop), *etc.*

7.1 Experimental Setup and Methodology

We study three variants of DEMS: DEMS-B, DEMS-S, and DEMS-F. They all employ chunk-based data transfer, decouple the subflows in the "two-way" manner, and attempt to ensure simultaneous subflow completion (§4.1 and §4.2). Their differences are the reinjection policy. DEMS-B ("Basic") does not perform reinjection; DEMS-S ("Simple reinjection") employs the naïve reinjection strategy described in §4.3; DEMS-F ("Full") performs the adaptive reinjection described in §4.4.

Our evaluation focuses on file download (upload can be handled by DEMS symmetrically). We set up our multipath proxy (developed in §6) on a commodity server with 4-core 3.6GHz CPU, 16GB memory, and 64-bit Ubuntu 16.04. The meta buffers at both the proxy and the receiver side are configured to be sufficiently large to avoid performance degradation due to limited buffer size. For apples-to-apples comparison, all schedulers use the same decoupled TCP congestion control (TCP CUBIC) and same subflow-level TCP send/receiver buffer sizes (8MB by default). Unless otherwise noted, the application server (hosting a file or web contents) is near the proxy, and uses only single-path. The RTT between the proxy and the app server is configured to be 4ms, which is the median RTT between a mobile ISP gateway (where our proxy can be deployed) and 30 popular content providers' servers based on a recent measurement study [33]. The client-proxy paths covering the "last-mile" wireless hops are thus the bottleneck.

We evaluated DEMS over both emulated and real multipath environments of WiFi and cellular. For emulation, we use Linux `tc` to throttle the bandwidth and to add extra delay on the client-proxy paths. By default, we use the network condition profiles from large-scale measurements of metropolitan LTE [22] and WiFi [35] users (same numbers as those used in §3.2). To emulate in-network buffering, we keep a 50ms bottleneck buffer for WiFi and a 500ms bottleneck buffer for LTE (set based on [23]) using `tc`.

We use two devices for evaluation: a laptop and a smartphone. The laptop is an HP EliteBook 840 with 1.90GHz dual-core CPU and 8GB memory, running Linux 3.18. When doing emulations over the laptop, we use Ethernet to emulate the LTE network, and use WiFi as it is. The smartphone is a Nexus 6p running Android 7.0 on Linux 3.10. We use its WiFi and cellular interfaces for experiments.

Recall in §5 that an application can interact with DEMS either using or not using a hint API. We adopt the non-API mode so DEMS is fully transparent to our applications. Finally, note that all evaluations were conducted on our multipath proxy infrastructure instead of MPTCP (recall in §6 that we replicated all MPTCP's schedulers on our infrastructure).

7.2 Stable Network Conditions

We first study the performance of DEMS under stable network conditions using emulation. The workload is file download. For each test, we repeat the download for 10 times and report the average value. We consider different delay differences and bandwidth of the two paths. Unless otherwise noted, we use MinRTT, the default MPTCP scheduler, as the comparison baseline.

Different Delay Differences. Figure 10 compares the download time across the three DEMS variants and MinRTT for different file sizes. We consider three RTT combinations to cover different subflow delay differences. All three DEMS variants outperform MinRTT. Among the three variants, DEMS-S achieves the highest download time reduction (15% to 38% compared to MinRTT) for medium-sized files (128KB to 1MB) due to its aggressive reinjection behavior. The performance gain brought by DEMS-F decreases slightly in most cases. However, Figure 11, which compares the size of reinjected data incurred by DEMS-S and DEMS-F, clearly indicates that DEMS-F strikes a much better balance between the performance and the reinjection overhead: compared to DEMS-S, DEMS-F reduces the reinjected data size by 23% to 100%. Regarding DEMS-B, it slightly falls behind DEMS-F by up to 8%. The difference is small because the network conditions are stable here.

Figure 10 indicates that DEMS brings more download time reduction as the two paths' RTT difference becomes larger. This is because a larger RTT difference usually indicates a larger ΔOWD that leads to more room for DEMS to balance the subflow completion time. Figure 10 also shows that DEMS's benefits are maximized when the file size is small or medium. For large files such as 8MB, all four schemes exhibit similar performance. The reason, as mentioned in §8, is that the subflow completion time difference is dwarfed

[3] In the test, the server is co-located with the proxy to ensure MPTCP and our approach traverses the same network paths.

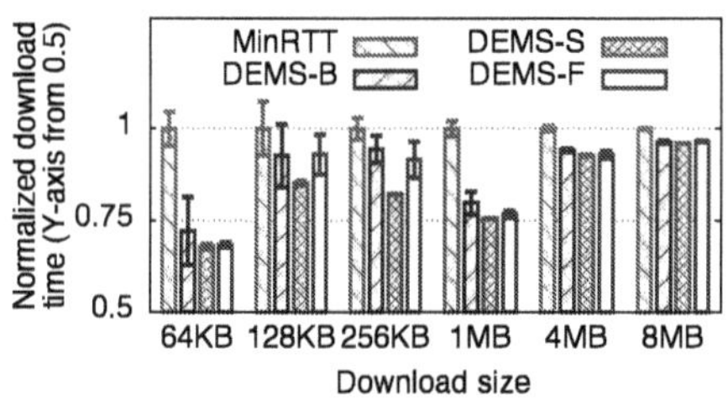

(a) WiFi RTT 50ms, LTE RTT 70ms

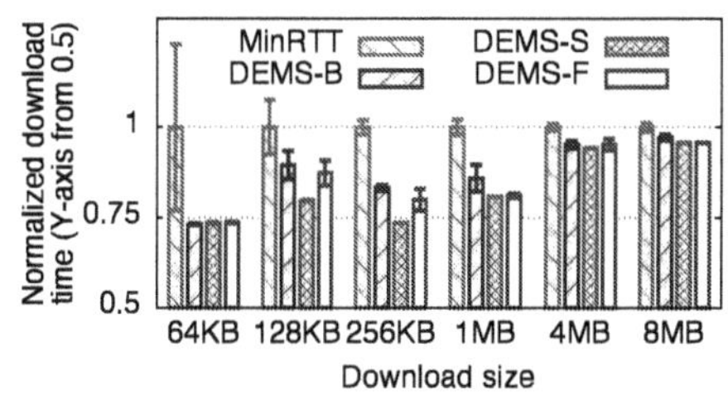

(b) WiFi RTT 50ms, LTE RTT 270ms

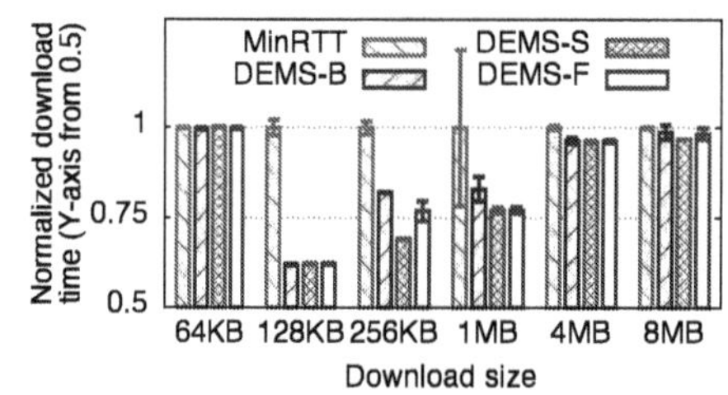

(c) WiFi RTT 50ms, LTE RTT 470ms

Figure 10: Compare performance between DEMS and MinRTT on downloading files with different sizes (laptop, emulation). The WiFi and LTE bandwidth are 7040kbps and 9185kbps respectively.

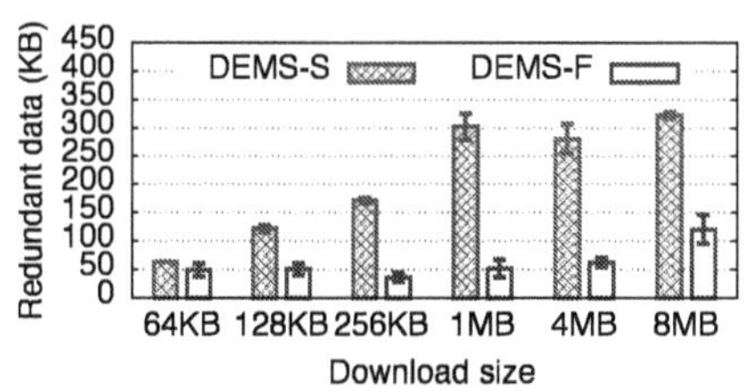

(a) WiFi 50ms, LTE 70ms

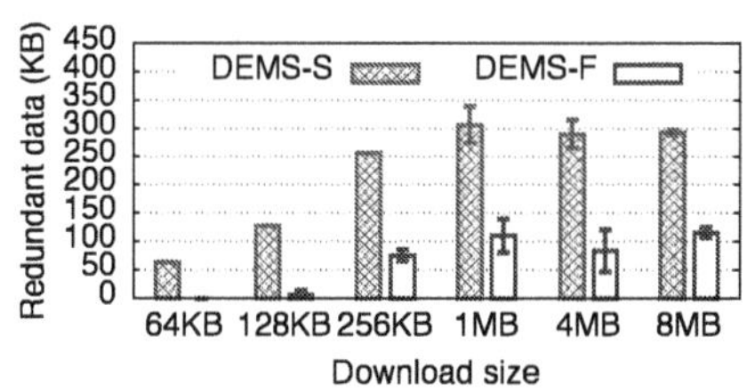

(b) WiFi 50ms, LTE 270ms

Figure 11: Compare redundant data between DEMS-S and DEMS-F (laptop, emulation).

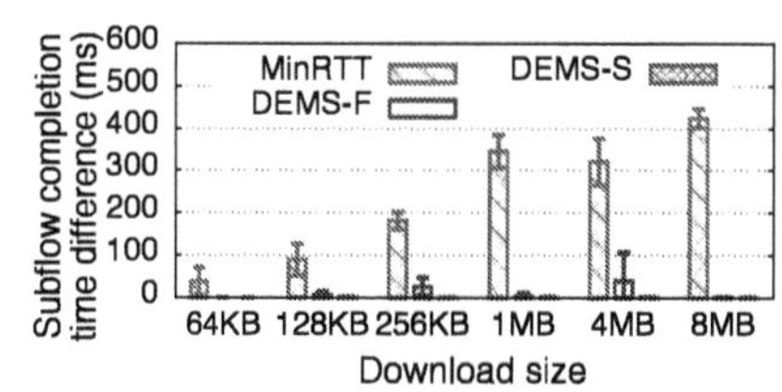

Figure 12: Compare subflow completion time difference (laptop, emulation, WiFi RTT 50ms, LTE RTT 270ms).

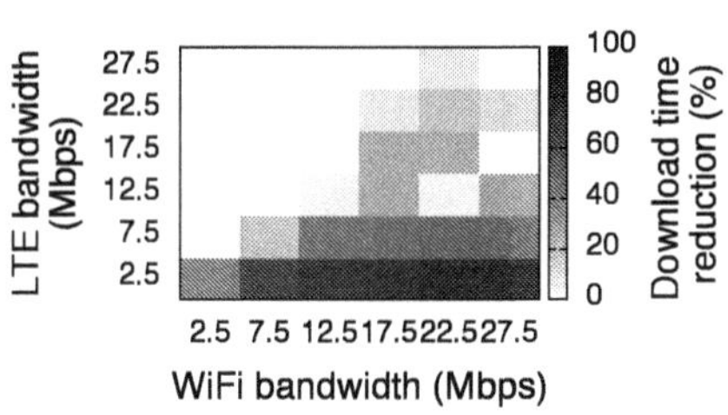

(a) 256KB download

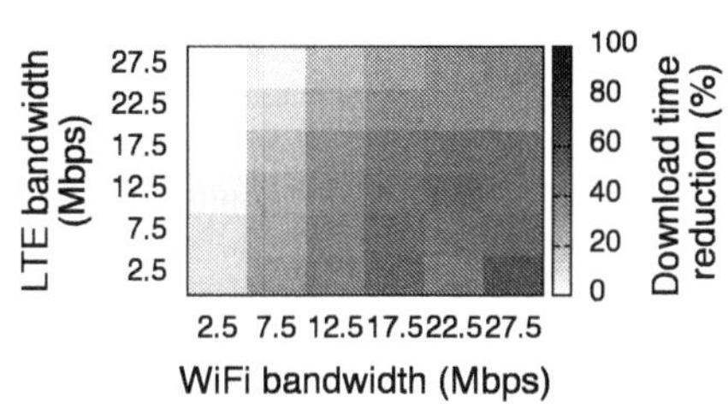

(b) 1MB download

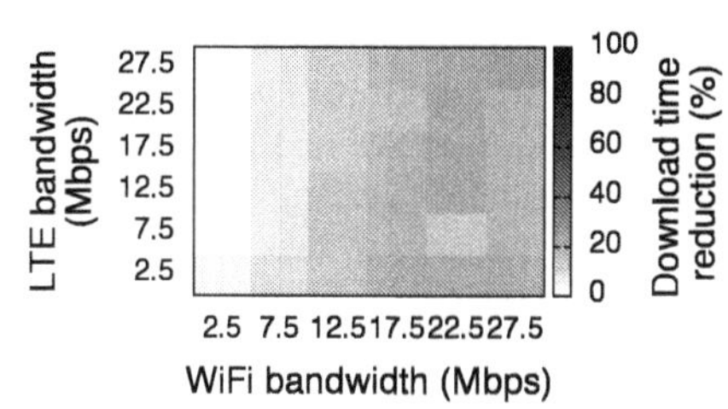

(c) 4MB download

Figure 13: Download time reduction brought by DEMS-F compared to MinRTT under 36 bandwidth combinations (laptop, emulation, WiFi RTT 50ms, LTE RTT 70ms).

by the long download duration. Nevertheless, we do expect that for future faster networks such as 5G network, DEMS will benefit large transfers. For the 64KB file download in Figure 10(c), all four schemes have the same performance because in this case the best strategy is to use the best single path.

Figure 12 plots the subflow completion time difference (measured at the receiver) between the two paths when three schedulers are used. It confirms that our algorithm in §4.2 effectively achieves simultaneous subflow completion, which leads to shorter chunk download time compared to MinRTT.

Different Bandwidth Combinations. To understand the impact of the paths' bandwidth on DEMS, We compare the download time of DEMS-F and MinRTT under 6*6=36 bandwidth combinations of WiFi and emulated LTE networks, for three file sizes (256KB, 1MB, and 4MB). The bandwidth of each path varies from 2.5Mbps to 27.5Mbps. The heat maps in Figure 13 visualize the download time reduction brought by DEMS-F compared to MinRTT. We observe two trends. First, as the WiFi bandwidth increases, the overall download time decreases. Therefore the optimizable portion of DEMS (*i.e.,* the two subflows' completion time difference) becomes more prominent, leading to more perceived performance enhancement. Second, increasing the LTE bandwidth also shortens the download time. However, it also reduces the in-network queuing delay and henceforth reduces ΔOWD. Therefore when fixing the WiFi bandwidth and increasing the LTE bandwidth, the download time reduction incurred by DEMS is not prominent. Overall, DEMS-F achieves up to 74%, 57%, and 21% of download time reduction for 256KB, 1MB and 4MB download, respectively, compared to MinRTT.

7.3 Varying Network Conditions

We next evaluate how DEMS performs under changing network conditions. We consider fluctuating latency and bandwidth separately.

Varying Latency. We conduct experiments at a location on our campus where the RTTs of both WiFi and LTE experience high variance (the *stddev* of RTT is up to 40% and 50% of the mean for WiFi and LTE, respectively) while the bandwidth is sufficiently

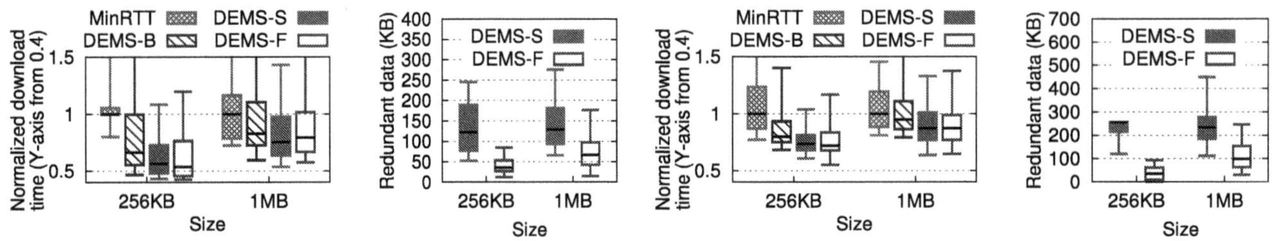

(a) BW Profile 1: download time (b) Profile 1: redundant data (c) BW Profile 2: download time (d) Profile 2: redundant data

Figure 14: Compare different scheduling algorithms under varying network conditions (laptop, trace-driven emulation).

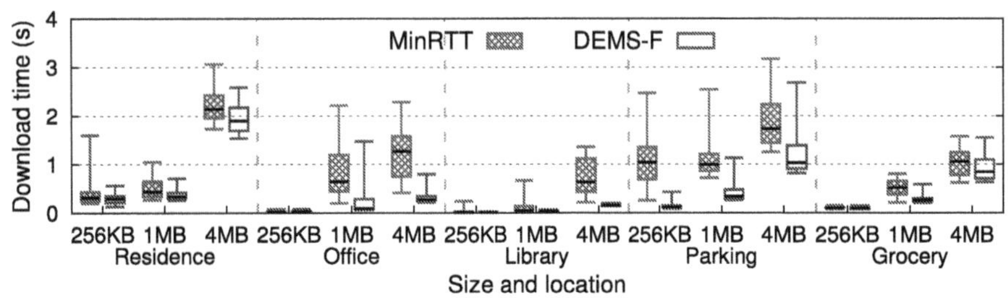

Figure 15: Compare performance of different scheduling algorithms (smartphone, real WiFi/LTE atfi ve locations).

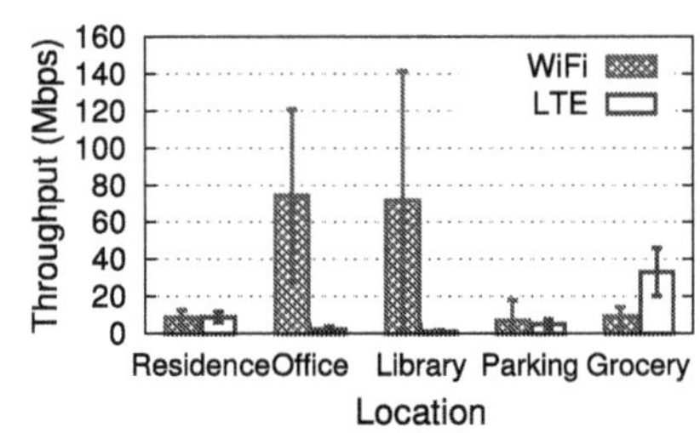

Figure 16: Downlink throughput of real WiFi and LTE atfi ve locations.

high. We then throttle the bandwidth to 7040kbps and 9185kbps for WiFi and cellular respectively before launching thefi le download experiments (256KB and 1MB, each repeating 10 times). The results are the following (figure not shown). DEMS-F and DEMS-S achieve similar download time that is 14% to 27% lower compared to MinRTT, respectively. However the reinjected data incurred by DEMS-F is much smaller – only 15% to 53% compared to DEMS-S. Also DEMS-B's download time is 12% worse compared to DEMS-F due to the reinjection performed by DEMS-F, which is particularly useful when it is difficult to accurately predict the network condition.

Varying Bandwidth. We take a "record and replay" approach to realistically emulate the varying bandwidth. We collect 5-minute bandwidth traces of both paths from two campus locations. The bandwidth at both locations is highly variable, with their *stddev* being up to 54% and 92% of the mean bandwidth for WiFi and LTE, respectively. Thefi rst location has overall lower bandwidth compared to the second. We then replay (emulate) the two bandwidth traces in our lab while maintaining stable baseline RTT. The results are plotted in Figure 14. Compared to MinRTT, DEMS-F reduces the median download time by 12% to 46% for the two bandwidth profiles, as shown in subplot (a) and (c). DEMS-S only marginally outperforms DEMS-F, at the cost of reinjecting much more data (1.9x to 7.1x) as shown in subplot (b) and (d). Also both DEMS-F and DEMS-S yield better results than DEMS-B, again because reinjection helps absorb the uncertainty of the varying network conditions.

7.4 Field Test under Real-World Settings

We now performfi eld test to assess DEMS under real-world settings. We went tofi ve locations: residential apartment, office, campus library, parking lot, and grocery store to conduct experiments of downloadingfi les of different size (256KB, 1MB, and 4MB). For eachfi le size, we used the Nexus 6p smartphone to repeatedly performfi le download using DEMS-F and MinRTT back to back for 5 minutes over multipath (cellular network provided by a large U.S. carrier and commercial WiFi). The results are shown in Figure 15, which indicates that the network conditions at thefi ve locations are indeed very diverse. Overall we obtained encouraging results: compared to MinRTT, DEMS-F reduces the download time by up to 88%, 83%, and 77% for 256KB, 1MB and 4MB download, respectively; the median download time reduction is 33%, 48%, and 42%, respectively. The download time variance is also reduced by DEMS-F.

The above improvements are attributed to the different path characteristics between WiFi and cellular networks that are not handled well by MPTCP. Compared to wired networks, wireless networks like WiFi and cellular can sometimes exhibit high delay and bandwidth dynamics [22, 23] that pose challenges to multipath schedulers. To illustrate this, Figure 16 shows the downlink throughput of each subflow calculated every 200ms when downloading 4MBfi les. As shown, at many locations, WiFi and LTE networks exhibit different and highly variable bandwidth that can affect their OWD and the OWD prediction accuracy. As shown in Figure 17, oftentimes the relative OWD of WiFi and LTE are indeed highly variable, and largerfi le downloads have even higher variabilities. Thefl uctuation of bandwidth and delay makes it hard to accurately predict OWD. For example, when downloading 4MB files at the *Residence* location, the relative OWD of LTE ranges from 100ms to 1.3s, causing its prediction error to reach up to 800ms. DEMS does not fully rely on such predictions and instead employs adaptive reinjection described in §4.4 to more robustly handle the performance variability of many wireless network settings.

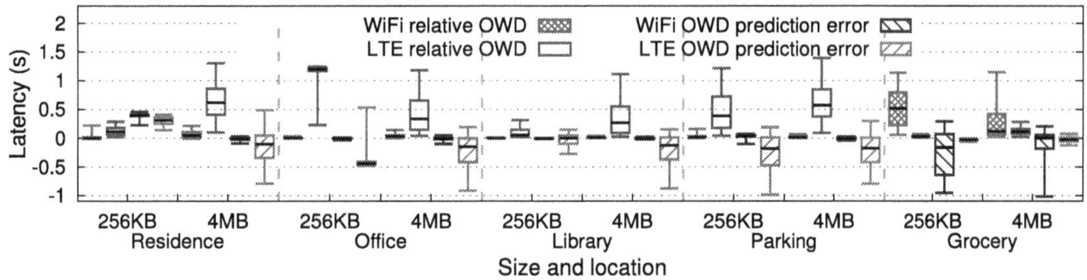

Figure 17: Relative OWD and prediction error of real WiFi and LTE networks afi ve locations.

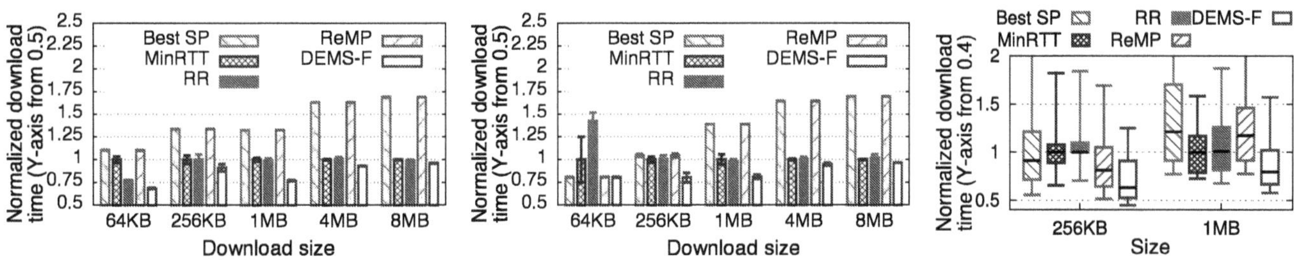

(a) Stable condition: WiFi 50ms, LTE 70ms

(b) Stable condition: WiFi 50ms, LTE 270ms

(c) Replay Bandwidth Profile 1

Figure 18: Compare performance among DEMS-F and four other schedulers (laptop, emulation).

7.5 Compare with Other Schedulers

Besides studying MinRTT, We further compare DEMS-F with three other scheduling approaches: round-robin, ReMP [13], and using the best single path to download afi le. Figure 18(a) and (b) compare the file download time using thefi ve schemes for two emulated stable network conditions. Figure 18(c) conducts a similar comparison under varying network condition (replaying Bandwidth Profile 1 collected in §7.3).

We observe that DEMS-F outperforms all other four schedulers. Besides this, in most cases, MinRTT achieves similar performance compared to round-robin (RR). This is likely explained by two reasons. First, in our implementation, the round-robin selection starts with the low-RTT path; starting from the high-RTT path will inflate the download time for smallfi les. Second, since we are performing bulk data transfer, it is unlikely that *both* paths have empty congestion window space at the same time. So during most of the time both MinRTT and RR have only one choice for path selection. Figure 18 also indicates the apparent limitation of the best single-path approach: compared to using multipath, using only one path significantly inflates the download time due to insufficient bandwidth. Regarding ReMP, it blindly duplicates *every* byte onto all subflows, making it essentially fall back to the "online" version of the best single-path approach. While ReMP and DEMS-F both transmit redundant data, DEMS-F's reinjection strategy is much more adaptive and strategic. For a 4MBfi le transfer, DEMS-F only transmits 2% of the redundant bytes sent by ReMP.

7.6 Web Browsing Performance

All experiments so far usefi le (raw data chunk) download as the workload. We now investigate how DEMS helps improve the QoE of web browsing, one of the most popular applications on mobile devices. A typical web page may consist of tens of objects, and downloading them faster would improve the QoE. We conduct web page loading experiments using off-the-shelf Chrome browser (53.0.2785.124) on our Nexus 6p smartphone. We picked 10 popular websites and use their mobile-version landing pages as the target web pages. The 10 websites cover diverse categories including news, education, travel, shopping, and government. We use the page load time (PLT), which is programmatically measured by the Chrome debugging interface, as the QoE metric. To make the experiments reproducible, we use Google Page Replay [3] to take a snapshot of each landing page and host it on our web server that is near the multipath proxy (§7.1). We compare the PLT of the 10 landing pages loaded by DEMS-F and by MinRTT under real-world network condition. The experiments were performed at a location on our campus where the RTTs and bandwidths of both WiFi and LTE experience high variance, similar to the network condition described in §7.3. We load each web page for 10 times and report the median PLT. As shown in Figure 19, compared to MinRTT, DEMS brings the per-page median PLT reduction of 6% to 43% across the 10 pages (median: 25%). The results indicate that DEMS can significantly improve the web QoE under real-world settings.

To understand why DEMS helps reduce the PLT, we take a closer took at the web object transmission pattern. Figure 20 exemplifies two waterfall diagrams for the same webpage when MinRTT and DEMS-F are used as the multipath scheduler. As shown, DEMS-F effectively reduces the reception duration (*i.e.*, download time) for many objects. Since many of them are on the critical path for web page loading, the overall PLT is effectively reduced. Also note that one key difference betweenfi le download and web page loading is that for the latter, computation and network activities are interleaved. Therefore, although the entire web page may be large, the web server has to intermittently feed data to the transport layer.

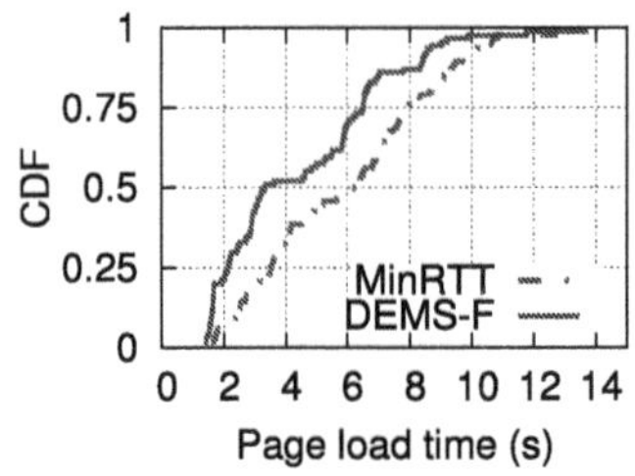

Figure 19: Compare web page load time when using DEMS-F and MinRTT (smartphone, real WiFi/LTE).

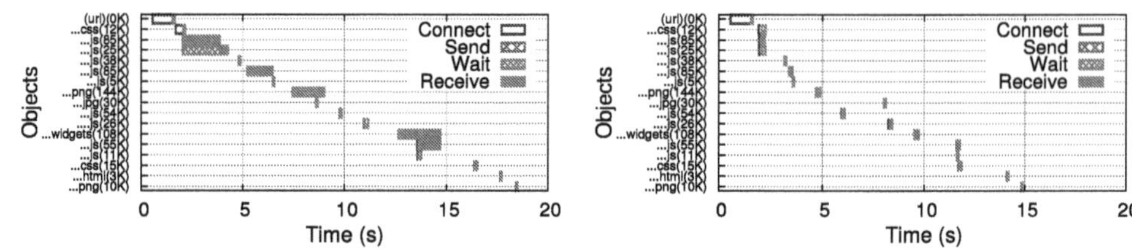

(a) MinRTT (b) DEMS-F

Figure 20: Example waterfall diagrams for MinRTT and DEMS-F (some objects are omitted for better illustration).

This naturally forms many small/medium-sized chunks that can be well optimized by DEMS.

Recall in §5 that an application can interact with DEMS either using or not using a hint API. Since it is challenging to modify the Chrome browser source code, we adopt the non-API mode in our experiments. In reality, since an HTTP(S) persistent connection may carry multiple web objects back to back, we thus envision that using the hint API to inform DEMS of the boundary between objects can provide additional benefits of minimizing the delivery time of each object. We leave this as future work[4].

7.7 System Overhead

We compared CPU utilization across the three schedulers: DEMS-F, MinRTT, and ReMP by running them on the smartphone. The workload is to upload a largefi le as fast as possible, with the aggregated bandwidth being around 50Mbps. Compared to the other two simpler schedulers, the additional CPU overhead incurred by DEMS-F is unnoticeable. For download traffic, since the mobile device acts as a receiver, the overhead is even more negligible.

8 DISCUSSIONS

Integration with MPTCP. While we implement DEMS on our own multipath TCP proxy infrastructure, DEMS can also be directly integrated into MPTCP. Since MPTCP provides a modular scheduler framework [30], the core logic of DEMS can be implemented as a new scheduler module. To facilitate OWD measurement (§5), the receiver side can leverage MPTCP options in TCP headers to carry necessary information used for estimating OWD at the sender side. The network prediction functionality can be implemented as a general API in MPTCP for all schedulers to use.

Applicability. DEMS can work with diverse traffic patterns and transfer sizes despite the ideal usage scenario being chunked data transfer, a very common workload as mentioned in §1. As DEMS shows the most promise for small-to-medium-size downloads, it can benefit a wide range of today's mobile applications (*e.g.*, video streaming) that involve downloading chunks from a few hundreds KBs to a few MBs. For very largefi les (*e.g.*, tens of MBs), when the network bandwidth is limited (a few Mbps), the subflow completion time difference is dwarfed by the long download duration, leading to overall small relative improvement brought by DEMS. Nevertheless, we do expect for future faster networks such as 5G with bandwidth of hundreds of Mbps, DEMS will significantly benefit large transfers.

Limitation. We discuss some limitations of DEMS. First, our current design focuses on two subflows. This was driven by realistically the most common mobile multipath use cases today. Nevertheless, the core concepts of DEMS (*e.g.*, chunk-based transfer, simultaneousfl ow completion, and adaptive reinjection) are also applicable to more than two paths, though involving more complexities. For example, instead of using the "two-way" splitting, each subflow can transmit packets in an interleaved (but still decoupled) manner. To achieve simultaneous subflow completion, a subflow can decide to stop transmission if the remaining data in the meta buffer can be delivered earlier by some other subflows with smaller OWD (some coordination algorithms need to be developed). In this way, at the sender side, the subflow with the largest and the smallest OWD will be thefi rst and the lastfi nishing subflow, respectively. This can compensate the delay differences among the subflows, leading to simultaneous subflow completion at the receiver side. We leave fleshing out the details on this to future work.

Second, the current DEMS design focuses primarily on improving download time, a critical factor impacting user QoE. In the future, we plan to explore additional dimensions like energy and limiting data usage on a particular subflow. This could possibly be done by adopting concepts from other special-purpose schedulers such as energy-aware [36] and subflow-priority-aware [17] schedulers.

9 CONCLUSION

Compared to single-path, multipath transport brings more complexities due to not only more involved paths but also their sophisticated interactions. Through judicious algorithm design, system integration, and extensive evaluation, we demonstrate that by strategically scheduling the packets, we can improve the multipath performance significantly (*e.g.*, median download time reduction of 33%–48% for fetchingfi les and median loading time reduction of 6%–43% for fetching web pages under real-world settings compared to MinRTT). In our future work, we plan to extend DEMS in several aspects (§8).

ACKNOWLEDGEMENTS

We would like to thank our shepherd, Professor Prasun Sinha, and the anonymous reviewers for their valuable comments and suggestions. This research was supported in part by the National Science Foundation under grants CCF-1438996, CCF-1629347, CNS-1345226, and CNS-1566331.

[4] In HTTP/2, objects might be multiplexed together. To handle this, multiplexed objects can be treated as one chunk.

REFERENCES

[1] 2015. In Korean, Multipath TCP is pronounced GIGA Path. http://blog.multipath-tcp.org/blog/html/2015/07/24/korea.html. (2015).

[2] 2016. Samsung Download Booster. http://www.samsung.com/uk/support/skp/faq/1061358. (2016).

[3] 2017. Google Web Page Replay Tool. https://github.com/chromium/web-page-replay. (2017).

[4] 2017. iOS: Multipath TCP Support in iOS 7. https://support.apple.com/en-us/HT201373. (2017).

[5] Maciej Bednarek, Guillermo Barrenetxea, Mirja Kühlewind, and Brian Trammell. 2016. Multipath Bonding at Layer 3. In *Proceedings of the 2016 Applied Networking Research Workshop*.

[6] Yung-Chih Chen, Yeon-Sup Lim, Richard J. Gibbens, Erich M. Nahum, Ramin Khalili, and Don Towsley. 2013. A Measurement-based Study of MultiPath TCP Performance over Wireless Networks. In *ACM IMC 2013*.

[7] Yung-Chih Chen, Don Towsley, and Ramin Khalili. 2014. MSPlayer: Multi-Source and multi-Path LeverAged YoutubER. In *ACM CoNEXT 2014*.

[8] Quentin De Coninck, Matthieu Baerts, Benjamin Hesmans, and Olivier Bonaventure. 2016. A First Analysis of Multipath TCP on Smartphones. In *PAM 2016*. Springer.

[9] Xavier Corbillon, Ramon Aparicio-Pardo, Nicolas Kuhn, Géraldine Texier, and Gwendal Simon. 2016. Cross-layer Scheduler for Video Streaming over MPTCP. In *ACM MMSys 2016*.

[10] Andrei Croitoru, Dragoş Niculescu, and Costin Raiciu. 2015. Towards WiFi Mobility without Fast Handover. In *USENIX NSDI 2015*.

[11] Shuo Deng, Ravi Netravali, Anirudh Sivaraman, and Hari Balakrishnan. 2014. WiFi, LTE, or Both? Measuring Multi-homed Wireless Internet Performance. In *ACM IMC 2014*.

[12] Alan Ford, Costin Raiciu, Mark Handley, and Olivier Bonaventure. 2013. TCP Extensions for Multipath Operation with Multiple Addresses. RFC 6824. (2013).

[13] Alexander Frömmgen, Tobias Erbshauser, Alejandro P. Buchmann, Torsten Zimmermann, and Klaus Wehrle. 2016. ReMP TCP: Low Latency Multipath TCP. In *IEEE ICC 2016*.

[14] Yihua Guo, Feng Qian, Qi Alfred Chen, Zhuoqing Morley Mao, and Subhabrata Sen. 2016. Understanding On-device Bufferbloat for Cellular Upload. In *ACM IMC 2016*.

[15] Bo Han, Feng Qian, Shuai Hao, and Lusheng Ji. 2015. An Anatomy of Mobile Web Performance over Multipath TCP. In *ACM CoNEXT 2015*.

[16] Bo Han, Feng Qian, and Lusheng Ji. 2016. When Should We Surf the Mobile Web Using Both Wifi and Cellular?. In *ACM All Things Cellular Workshop 2016*.

[17] Bo Han, Feng Qian, Lusheng Ji, and Vijay Gopalakrishnan. 2016. MP-DASH: Adaptive Video Streaming Over Preference-Aware Multipath. In *ACM CoNEXT 2016*.

[18] Benjamin Hesmans and Olivier Bonaventure. 2016. An Enhanced Socket API for Multipath TCP. In *Proceedings of the 2016 Applied Networking Research Workshop*.

[19] Benjamin Hesmans, Gregory Detal, Raphaël Bauduin, Olivier Bonaventure, et al. 2015. SMAPP: Towards Smart Multipath TCP-enabled APPlications. In *ACM CoNEXT 2015*.

[20] Brett D Higgins, Kyungmin Lee, Jason Flinn, Thomas J Giuli, Brian Noble, and Christopher Peplin. 2014. The Future is Cloudy: Reflecting Prediction Error in Mobile Applications. In *MobiCASE 2014*.

[21] Junxian Huang, Feng Qian, Alexandre Gerber, Z Morley Mao, Subhabrata Sen, and Oliver Spatscheck. 2012. A Close Examination of Performance and Power Characteristics of 4G LTE Networks. In *ACM MobiSys 2012*.

[22] Junxian Huang, Feng Qian, Yihua Guo, Yuanyuan Zhou, Qiang Xu, Z Morley Mao, Subhabrata Sen, and Oliver Spatscheck. 2013. An In-depth Study of LTE: Effect of Network Protocol and Application Behavior on Performance. In *ACM SIGCOMM 2013*.

[23] Haiqing Jiang, Yaogong Wang, Kyunghan Lee, and Injong Rhee. 2012. Tackling Bufferbloat in 3G/4G Networks. In *ACM IMC 2012*.

[24] Ramin Khalili, Nicolas Gast, Miroslav Popovic, Utkarsh Upadhyay, and Jean-Yves Le Boudec. 2012. MPTCP is Not Pareto-optimal: Performance Issues and a Possible Solution. In *ACM CoNEXT 2012*.

[25] Nicolas Kuhn, Emmanuel Lochin, Ahlem Mifdaoui, Golam Sarwar, Olivier Mehani, and Roksana Boreli. 2014. DAPS: Intelligent Delay-aware Packet Scheduling for Multipath Transport. In *IEEE ICC 2014*.

[26] Yeon-sup Lim, Erich M Nahum, Don Towsley, and Richard J Gibbens. 2017. ECF: An MPTCP Path Scheduler to Manage Heterogeneous Paths. In *ACM SIGMETRICS 2017 Abstracts*.

[27] Catalin Nicutar, Dragos Niculescu, and Costin Raiciu. 2014. Using Cooperation for Low Power Low Latency Cellular Connectivity. In *ACM CoNEXT 2014*.

[28] Ana Nika, Yibo Zhu, Ning Ding, Abhilash Jindal, Y. Charlie Hu, Xia Zhou, Ben Y. Zhao, and Haitao Zheng. 2015. Energy and Performance of Smartphone Radio Bundling in Outdoor Environments. In *Proceedings of the 24th International Conference on World Wide Web*.

[29] Ashkan Nikravesh, Yihua Guo, Feng Qian, Z. Morley Mao, and Subhabrata Sen. 2016. An In-depth Understanding of Multipath TCP on Mobile Devices: Measurement and System Design. In *ACM MobiCom 2016*.

[30] Christoph Paasch, Simone Ferlin, Ozgu Alay, and Olivier Bonaventure. 2014. Experimental Evaluation of Multipath TCP Schedulers. In *ACM SIGCOMM Capacity Sharing Workshop (CSWS) 2014*.

[31] Bahar Partov and Douglas J Leith. 2016. Experimental Evaluation of Multi-path Schedulers for LTE/wifi Devices. In *Proceedings of the Tenth ACM International Workshop on Wireless Network Testbeds, Experimental Evaluation, and Characterization*.

[32] Qiuyu Peng, Minghua Chen, Anwar Walid, and Steven Low. 2014. Energy Efficient Multipath TCP for Mobile Devices. In *ACM MobiHoc 2014*.

[33] Feng Qian, Vijay Gopalakrishnan, Emir Halepovic, Subhabrata Sen, and Oliver Spatscheck. 2015. TM3: Flexible Transport-layer Multi-pipe Multiplexing Middlebox without Head-of-line Blocking. In *ACM CoNEXT 2015*.

[34] Varun Singh, Saba Ahsan, and Jörg Ott. 2013. MPRTP: Multipath Considerations for Real-time Media. In *ACM MMSys 2013*.

[35] Joel Sommers and Paul Barford. 2012. Cell vs. WiFi: On the Performance of Metro Area Mobile Connections. In *ACM IMC 2012*.

[36] Yeon sup Lim, Yung-Chih Chen, Erich M. Nahum, Don Towsley, Richard J. Gibbens, and Emmanuel Cecchet. 2015. Design, Implementation and Evaluation of Energy-Aware Multi-Path TCP. In *ACM CoNEXT 2015*.

[37] Damon Wischik, Costin Raiciu, Adam Greenhalgh, and Mark Handley. 2011. Design, Implementation and Evaluation of Congestion Control for Multipath TCP. In *USENIX NSDI 2012*.

[38] Jiyan Wu, Chau Yuen, Bo Cheng, Ming Wang, and Jun-Liang Chen. 2016. Streaming High-quality Mobile Video with Multipath TCP in Heterogeneous Wireless Networks. *IEEE Transactions on Mobile Computing* 15, 9 (2016), 2345–2361.

[39] Yasir Zaki, Thomas Pötsch, Jay Chen, Lakshminarayanan Subramanian, and Carmelita Görg. 2015. Adaptive Congestion Control for Unpredictable Cellular Networks. In *ACM SIGCOMM Computer Communication Review*, Vol. 45. 509–522.

FSONet: A Wireless Backhaul for Multi-Gigabit Picocells Using Steerable Free Space Optics

Max Curran§, Md. Shaifur Rahman§, Himanshu Gupta, Kai Zheng, Jon Longtin, Samir R. Das, Thanvir Mohamed
Stony Brook University
Stony Brook, NY

ABSTRACT

Expected increase in cellular demand has pushed recent interest in picocell networks which have reduced cell sizes (100-200m or less). For ease of deployment of such networks, a wireless backhaul network is highly desired. Since RF-based technologies are unlikely to provide the desired multi-gigabit data rates, we motivate and explore use of free space optics (FSO) for picocell backhaul. In particular, we present a novel network architecture based on steerable links and sufficiently many robust short-range links, to help circumvent the key challenge of outdoor effects in reliable operation of outdoor FSO links. Our architecture is motivated by the fact that, due to the high density of picocells, many short-range links will occur naturally in a picocell backhaul. Moreover, use of steerable FSO links facilitates networks with sufficient redundancy while using only a small number of interfaces per node. We address the key problems that arise in the context of such a backhaul architecture, viz., an FSO link design with desired characteristics, and related network design and management problems. We develop and evaluate a robust 100m FSO link prototype, and simulate the proposed architecture in many metro US cities while show its viability via evaluation of key performance metrics.

CCS CONCEPTS

• **Networks** → **Network design and planning algorithms**; • **Hardware** → *Emerging optical and photonic technologies*;

KEYWORDS

Small Cells, Backhaul, Free Space Optics, Reconfigurable Networks

1 INTRODUCTION

It is widely expected that the explosion of mobile broadband data consumption will continue unabated. Some projections estimate a 1000-fold increase in capacity demand within a decade [32]. Researchers have been addressing this impending 'capacity crunch' using various mechanisms. These include improving spectral efficiency, developing shared spectrum regimes (e.g., white spaces), and utilizing very high frequency spectrum bands (e.g., 30-300 GHz). While all these mechanisms are bringing dividends, it is well understood that to keep up with the anticipated capacity demand, *spatial reuse* of wireless spectrum must improve dramatically. Spatial reuse has indeed been one of the key strategies used — e.g., cell radius have fallen steadily from tens of kms in the 1980s to just a few kms currently [32].

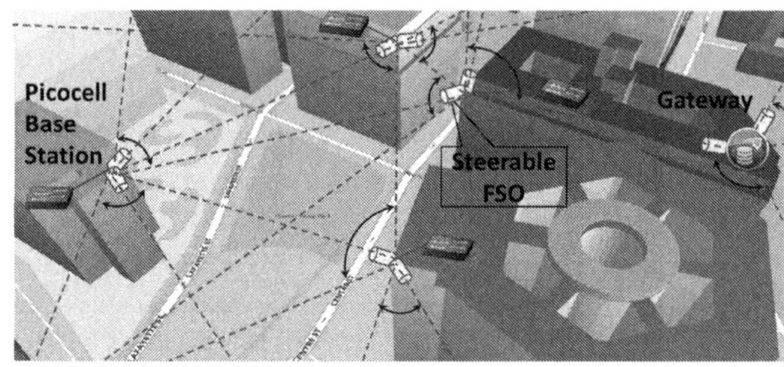

Figure 1: FSO-based backhaul network for picocells. Each base station has a network switch connecting steerable FSO devices.

Picocells' Backhaul Network. The above trend of reduced cell sizes has recently led to a significant interest in *picocells* with ranges of around 100–200 m or even less, specifically using the millimeter wave bands (30–300 GHz) [37, 65, 68]. Recent research also anticipates multi-Gbps capacity of such picocells [63, 68]. One significant concern in deployment of such networks is backhauling of the base stations to a close-by "gateway" for further connectivity. Given the high capacity requirement of the backhaul network, optical fiber communication is often the technology of choice as it can deliver very high data rates over long ranges. However, deploying optical fibers for such dense outdoor picocells can be significantly expensive; thus, a wireless solution is desired. Unfortunately, the existing or upcoming RF[1] based solutions are unlikely to be able to provide the required data rates of 10Gbps or more (see §2.1) at desired ranges (100–200 m and more).

FSO-based Backhaul Solution. Use of free-space optical (FSO) communications can have a strong potential in creating a wireless backhaul for picocells. FSO communication is similar in principle

§ Co-first student authors.

MobiCom '17, October 16–20, 2017, Snowbird, UT, USA

ACM ISBN 978-1-4503-4916-1/17/10...$15.00
https://doi.org/10.1145/3117811.3129239

[1]Including Sub 6 and traditional (6–42 GHz) microwave, licensed (70–95 GHz) and unlicensed mmWave (60 GHz).

to (wired) optical fiber communication, except that in FSO, the laser beam travels in free space instead of being enclosed in an optical fiber. In general, FSO links can provide very high data rates—even up to ≈100 Gbps—over long distances (≈kms) [39, 56]. Such tremendous speeds are enabled by high frequencies of lightwaves and absence of regulatory restrictions. However, while the FSO technology itself is not new, its commercial use has been quite limited [15]. This is because significant engineering efforts must be spent in overcoming outdoor effects, especially for long ranges. While short range (≈100 m or below) communication can simplify some of these efforts, so far no demanding applications existed to commercialize the short-range use.

Picocells offer a unique setting for FSO-based networks: short-range links arise naturally in densely deployed picocells and robust short-range links with sufficient "link margin" can handle most outdoor effects. To provide sufficient network redundancy with minimal number of FSO interfaces per node, we propose use of *steerable* FSO devices which can be steered with low latency to enable many links and thus create a "dynamic" network. See Fig. 1. Our overall approach (called FSONet) to designing an FSO-based backhaul that can provide desired network availability is based on the following multipronged strategy: (i) Use of steerable FSO links, creating a "dynamic" network with sufficient network redundancy, (ii) Having a sufficient number of robust short-range links that can handle most weather effects, and additional longer links for improved hop-count and network capacity in favorable conditions.

Our Contributions. To implement the above proposed vision, we make the following contributions:

1. We propose a novel FSO network architecture, based on robust short links and steerable FSO links, that can offer sufficient network availability in face of outdoor effects (§2).
2. We design and evaluate a 100m link prototype with active tracking and pointing (§3) with desired link margin and tolerance requirements, using commodity hardware.
3. We address the key problem of base station placement and dynamic network design that arises in our context. Since the problem is intractable, we design an efficient multi-step heuristic that delivers good quality network solutions in real settings (§4).
4. For the runtime operation of FSONet, we address the network reconfiguration problem which selects a network topology and flow-routes at runtime, in response to changing traffic and/or link failures (§5).

Finally, we conduct extensive simulations to demonstrate the effectiveness of our techniques (§6).

2 MOTIVATION, CHALLENGES AND PROPOSED ARCHITECTURE

Picocell networks are highly dense, with coverage range of about 100–200 m or less [68]. The nodes (base stations)[2] are connected to a small number of gateways for external connectivity, through a backhaul network. As mentioned before, a wired backhaul network can be very expensive to deploy. Thus, a wireless backhaul network is desired. Below, we make a case for an FSO-based backhaul network.

2.1 Case for FSO-based Backhaul for Picocells

Why not a point-to-point network? Creating point-to-point wireless links from each base station to a gateway may be technically plausible via FSO links, but unlikely to be practical for multiple reasons: (i) FSO links require a clear line of sight that is harder to obtain for long links. (ii) Number of transceivers needed at each gateway would be prohibitively high, due to many more nodes than gateways. (iii) The reliability of long-range FSO links is generally not satisfactory due to outdoor effects (discussed later).

Why not an RF-wireless mesh network? The capacity of links in a mesh network must be multiples of the capacity of individual base stations due to traffic aggregation. Given that the individual picocell base stations are expected to provide multi-gigabit capacity through mmWave bands [68], we need backhaul links capable of supporting up to 10 Gbps, perhaps even 40 Gbps, depending on the network topology. No known RF technology can provide such data rates at ranges of ≈100–200 m.[3]

Why FSO? Free-space optical (FSO) communication [51] links use modulated visible or infrared (IR) laser beams in the free space. Laser beams are very narrow, which eliminates crosstalk interference, and optical spectrum is also unregulated. Thus, FSO links can easily offer Gbps-Tbps of bitrates at long distances (several kms) using relatively low transmit power [39, 56]. However, at long ranges, FSO links can suffer transient failure due to various outdoor effects (discussed below). Fortunately, most of these attenuation problems become manageable at shorter links—in particular, short-range links with sufficient link "margin" can withstand most outdoor effects. Due to the high density of picocell networks, short links will arise naturally in a backhaul network connecting these base stations. In §2.3, we describe an FSO-based architecture based on robust short-range links and other characteristics such that it can provide high network availability.

Why Steerable FSO? For better handling of outdoor effects, we should create a mesh network with sufficient redundancy which requires each node to have more than a few links in the network. This would require many transceivers (perhaps, even ten or more) per node for a network with a few thousand nodes, since the strong directivity of FSO beams entails one transceiver per link. However, equipping a node with more than a few FSO transceivers is likely infeasible due to cost and size constraints. Thus, we propose the use of steerable FSO devices. A steerable FSO device can essentially steer the FSO beam to any one of many intended receivers—thus, creating a "dynamic" network, where the network topology can be controlled at runtime. Such flexibility also helps in efficient runtime handling of moving hotspots (see below). Finally, the steering mechanism is also leveraged in designing the tracking and pointing system (§3.2).

Demonstrating Changing Hotspots. There is some evidence in literature that cellular traffic does not peak in many base stations at

[2] We use the word *node* interchangeably with *base station* throughout the description.

[3] While THz technology may be able to achieve such data rates, it is relatively immature at this time and has limited outdoor range due to high atmospheric attenuation [29]. Massive MIMO in the mmwave bands can hypothetically deliver 10–40 Gbps at these distances, but the needed signal processing at such frequencies is very challenging.

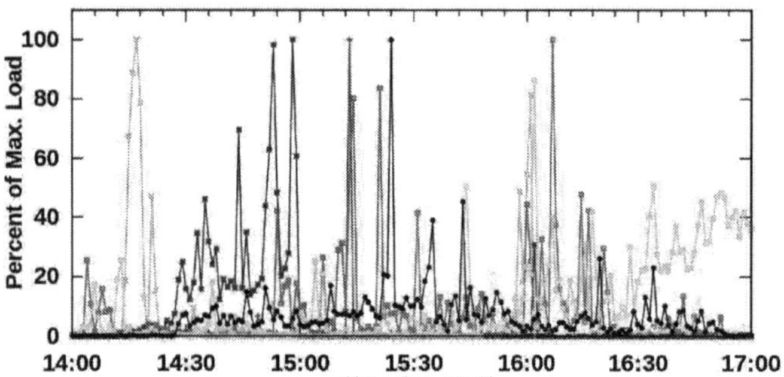

Figure 2: Time series of load seen on different sniffers (shown by different colors).

Cause (rate)	Attenuation (db/km)
Building Movement (without tracking)	40-100 [34]
Dense Fog (40-70 m visibility)	143-250 [33]
Thick Fog (70-250 m visibility)	40-143 [33]
Moderate Fog (250-500 m visibility)	20-40 [33]
Light Fog (500-1000 m visibility)	10-20 [33]
Snow (light to whiteout)	3-30 [33, 67]
Rain (25 to 150 mm/hour)	6-35 [33]
Scintillation (clear day)	5-13 [34]

Figure 3: Link attenuations due to outdoor factors.

exactly the same moment [59, 60]. To understand this effect in WiFi traffic in densely populated areas (which is perhaps most reflective of future picocellular networks), we ran the following measurement study: we deployed 7 time-synchronized sniffers in our building in a dense and active WiFi network of 30+ access points used by 200+ faculty and PhD students and many transient users. Post-processing the captured traces reveals that (i) only 1-2 out of 7 locations carry a significant fraction of the load at any moment, and (ii) these "hotspot" locations are different at different times. See Fig. 2.

2.2 Key FSO Challenge: Outdoor Effects

One concern with use of an FSO-based network in an urban setting is the presence of many high buildings which may limit the number of FSO inks as they require a clear line-of-sight; we alleviate this concern by simulating FSONet over many metro US cities (see §6). The other key concern is the attenuation of FSO signal due to various outdoor effects. We discuss these effects below by dividing them into four categories.

- Building Movements: Since FSO links require precise alignment of transceivers, minor movements of deployment platforms can result in significant signal attenuation [34], depending on the movement and link design. See Fig. 3. Solutions include active tracking and pointing and/or wider beams [18].
- Weather Effects: The signal attenuation from weather effects can be anywhere from 10 to 250 dB/km [33]. Among these, fog causes the worst attenuating factor, since the size of fog particles is comparable to the optical wavelengths. Note that attenuation from snow is generally less severe than from fog.
- Turbulence Effects: These include scintillation, beam wander, and beam spreading. For ranges up to 1km [66], beam spreading is negligible while beam wander is minimal (beam deviation of at most 2-3cm at 1km). Scintillation (optical intensity changes due to temperature variations) happens only when the weather is clear and results in minimal attenuation for links smaller than 500m [34].
- Blockage: Finally, since FSO links require a clear line of sight, obstructions such as birds can result in transient failures; these have generally been handled by using multiple beamlets [35].

In the following subsection, we present our approaches to handle each of the above effects.

2.3 FSONet Backhaul Architecture

We envision a dense picocell network, with each picocell having a range of about 100–200 m and capable of providing multi-gigabit (2-5 Gbps or more) peak capacity [68]. Picocell base stations themselves may be co-located indoors or outdoors for appropriate coverage requirements. We assume that indoor picocells have a fiber extended to an outdoor location to facilitate a line-of-sight backhaul connection to other picocells. Our goal is to create an FSO mesh network that connects the picocells base stations to a small number of gateways. *Note that the availability requirement of picocells is less stringent than "5 nines" and is generally 99 to 99.9% due to the default availability of macrocells in urban areas [27].* To that end, we design FSONet, a picocell backhaul with the following features:

1. Each base station has a network switch (see Fig. 1) connected to a small number of FSO devices. The FSO devices enable steerable bi-directional (either via two wavelengths on the same optical path [8] or via two separate optical paths) links. This creates a "dynamic" network.
2. We restrict the maximum range of links to about 500m,[4] and classify them into two categories: short ($\leq$ 100m) and longer (100-500m) links.
   (a) All links have an optical power *budget*[5] of about 30dB (to allow for SFP-based prototypes 3).
   (b) Each short ($\leq$ 100m) link has about 15dB link margin allocated specifically to withstand weather effects; we refer to such links as *robust short links.* Such links should have an availability of more than 99.5% in most US cities (see below).
   (c) All links handle building movements via the link's movement tolerance and an active tracking and pointing (TP) mechanism (§3).
3. The network contains a subnetwork called a *backbone* that (i) comprises solely of robust short links, and (ii) provides coverage, and connectivity from backbone nodes to gateways (§4).

[4]Links much longer than 500m are unlikely to be useful in a dense picocell network or even feasible in an urban area due to obstructions. In addition, links much longer than 500m can suffer significant scintillation effect.

[5]Optical budget is TX power minus RX sensitivity. If the path loss is higher than the budget, the link may still remain operational albiet at a lower data rate [31]. However, for simplicity, we implicitly assume the link to be non-operational when the path loss exceeds the optical budget.

Thus, in unfavorable weather conditions, the network availability is maintained (albeit, at a lower capacity than the full network) via a backbone whose robust short links can handle weather effects. In favorable weather conditions, the full network (including longer links) is operational. From (2b) above, this guarantees at least 99.5% network availability.

4. We can handle transient link outages due to blockages etc. by retransmission or rerouting flows by exploiting network redundancy (§5).

Link Budget Analysis. In short links, of the total 30dB budget, we allocate about 15dB margin for weather effects, and 10–15dB for *geometric* losses (due to beam divergence and limited receiver aperture) and link's movement tolerance. For longer links, we allocate about 25dB margin for geometric losses and movement tolerance and 2-5dB for any scintillation effects. The movement tolerance accounted above is needed to support the TP mechanism (see §3.2). We anticipate only minimal (0-2dB) coupling and optical system losses.

Tolerance to Weather Effects. Based on the fog attenuation model in [33], a 100m link with XdB link margin can withstand fog conditions that have a visibility of greater than $(1.3/X)$ km; thus, a 100m link with 15dB (13dB) can withstand fog with > 85m (100m) visibility. The visibility data of 20 US cities [52] implies that most cities have a 99.5% chance of having more than 250m visibility. As non-fog weather factors have much less attenuation, a 100m link with 13-15dB should should have an availability of much more than 99.5% in most US cities. Note that, as mentioned before, the availability requirement of picocells is generally 99 to 99.9% due to a macrocells [27].

Commercial FSO Link Solutions. Commercially available FSO links are fixed (i.e., do not steer), are bulky (up to 2 cubic feet [6, 15]) and expensive ($6K-25K for a device [14]); this is because their objective is to provide highly robust singular links for longer ranges (e.g., multiple kms). They achieve this by using multiple transmitters per link, and bulky TP mechanisms [53]. On the other hand, we envision lightweight and less expensive solutions by targeting smaller ranges (at most 500m) and embedding redundancy in the overall network rather than individual links; the combination of these factors allow us to use simpler solutions to handle outdoor effects (e.g., a lightweight TP solution).

3 FSO LINK DESIGN IN FSONET

In this section, we design and develop FSO link prototypes with desired characteristics for FSONet. In particular, we build a 3-node steerable link network, design a lightweight tracking and pointing (TP) mechanism, and develop and evaluate a prototype of a 100m link with the TP mechanism. We start with an introduction to SFPs and SFP-based FSO links.

SFPs. An SFP (small form-factor pluggable) transceiver is a small $(1/2'' \times 1/2'' \times 2'')$ and compact commodity optical transceiver [9], widely used to interface optical fibers with network switches. An SFP contains a laser source and a photodetector, for transmission and receiving respectively. In a traditional (wired) optical link, the transmitter SFP modulates the incoming bits onto the laser and launches the laser beam into the fiber; the beam is captured by the photodectector of the receiver SFP where it is demodulated.

SFPs are available with a variety of laser sources, varying in the wavelength (typically, between 800nm to 1550nm) of the emitted beam as well as the supported data rate (anywhere from 10Mbps to recent variants called CFPs with 100Gpbs [1]). SFP+ refers to an enhanced version of the SFP that supports data rates up to 16Gbps. *Bidirectional* SFPs transmit two beams at different wavelengths one in each direction on the same optical fiber. In an SFP-based wireless link, wireless interference is handled by collimation, as described below.

SFP-based FSO Links. We build our FSO link prototypes using SFP transceivers, as in prior works [38, 46, 47]. Our approach of using commodity SFPs is driven by convenience, as it serves our objectives without the need to use independent laser, photodetector, and modulation/demodulation logic. Moreover, SFP-based prototypes demonstrate feasibility of a form-factor manageable and cost-effective FSO link, as well as eye-safety since SFPs are classified as Class 1 safe [13, 26]. SFP+ (i.e., 10Gbps SFPs) with 30dB budget are readily available [2–4].

To create an FSO link using SFPs, the beam emanating from the transmitter SFP is channeled into a short optical fiber which feeds into a collimator. The collimated beam is then launched into free space towards the receiving SFP, where it is captured by another collimating lens and focused back into an optical fiber connected to the receiving SFP. Wireless interference is implicitly handled via two mechanisms: (i) First, a collimated beam is very narrow with minimal divergence, and is thus received only by the intended receiver; (ii) Second, in reconfigurable networks such as ours wherein a beam may be steered to different receivers, appropriate reconfiguration logic must ensure that a receiver receives beam signal from only one transmitter. Note that, in a real system, the received beam can be focused directly to an exposed photodetector (of about 30μm diameter for 10Gbps [34]) rather than an optical fiber; we compensate for this discrepancy by using a short 50μm multimode fiber at the receiver.[6]

3.1 Steerable FSO Links

We first discuss our choice of steering mechanism.

Galvo Mirrors as Steering Mechanism. We desire a steering mechanism that can steer a beam to an intended target with minimal latency. Several steering solutions [57] exist, but most are not commodity yet. Prior works [46, 47] on reconfigurable FSO networks have explored switchable mirrors, Galvo mirrors (GMs), and digital micromirror devices (DMDs). Switchable mirrors have high latency (10-20 msecs) and DMDs have a very low angular range ($\approx 6°$) unless intricate mirror assemblies are used [46]. On the other hand, GMs [23] have high angular range (up to 40°) with latency (small angle) of a fraction of a msec. Thus, we use GMs as our choice of steering mechanism. GMs also support much higher beam widths (up to 50mm [11]) than DMDs, and have an angular accuracy of 10μrad or less. A typical GM essentially consists of one or two mirrors at right angles, each of which can be independently rotated using an electrical signal. A laser beam can be steered using

[6]Intermodal dispersion in the fiber is not an issue [7], as we can use a very short fiber (a few cms).

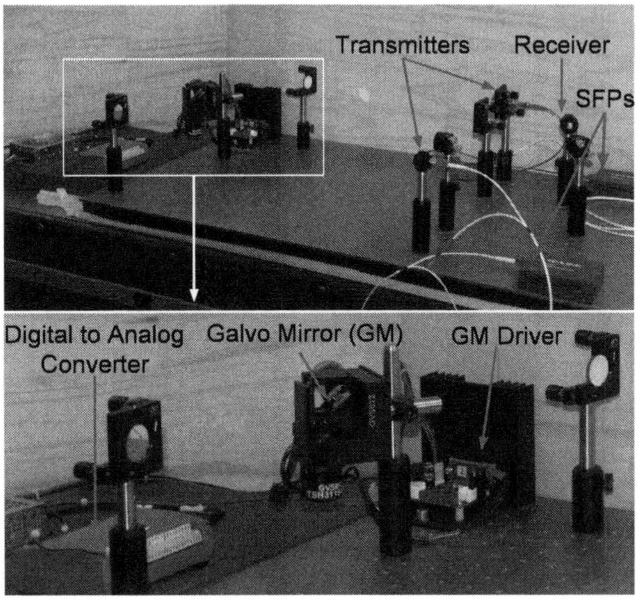

Figure 4: (Top) Three node experimental setup on an optical bench demonstrating FSO steering, (Bottom) Zoomed in to show the Galvo Mirror related set-up.

a GM by reflecting off its mirrors; in effect, a GM with two mirrors can steer a beam towards any target within a predetermined rectangular cone (called *coverage cone*). MEMS [41] are conceptually similar to GMs, with reduced latency at the cost of limited angular range and/or smaller mirrors [17]; small mirrors limit link range (due to small beam-width and higher divergence).

Steerable Link Prototype. Though steerable FSO links have been proposed before [41, 46, 47], but no prior work has actually built and evaluated a steerable link prototype, to the best of our knowledge. We have recently built a three-node prototype to evaluate GM's performance in steering an FSO link. See Fig. 4. Each node in the prototype is an FSO end-point using a bidirectional SFP+ connected to a computer. One node acts as a receiver (RX), while the other two act as senders (TX1 and TX2). To evaluate any throughput loss due to steering, we send 16KB UDP packets as fast as possible from TX1 and TX2 to the single receiver RX, while using the GM (GVS012 [23]) to switch the FSO link between TX1-RX and TX2-RX at varying rates (1-50 Hz). *Results:* We observe that the aggregate throughput for a steerable

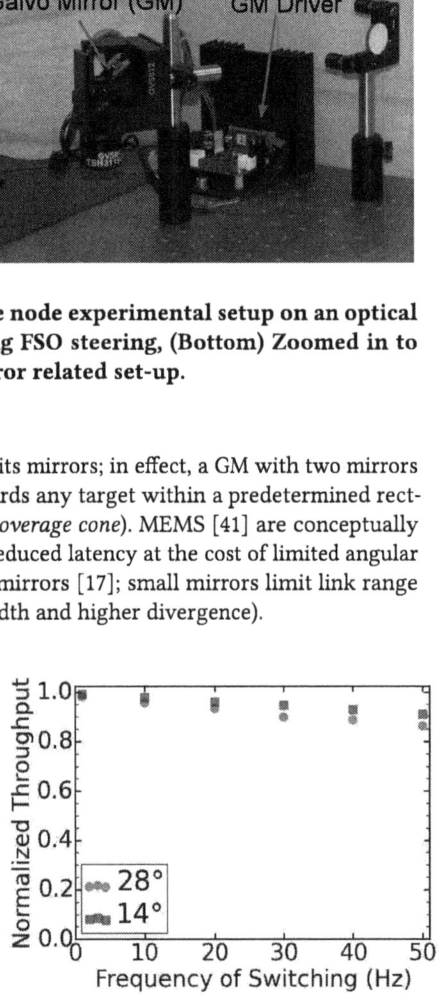

Figure 5: Normalized throughput vs. switching frequency at different steering angles.

link is only 1-2% less (vs. a fixed link) for a steering rate of 1 Hz, and about 8% less at 50 Hz. Large part of throughput loss is due to the recovery of the optical physical/link layers in the SFPs [46], and should not manifest in a real system not based on SFPs. In a non-SFP real system, the throughput loss should be closer to 2% at 50Hz, since our GM's switching latency is only about 400μm [23].

3.2 Active Tracking and Pointing (TP)

To keep an FSO link aligned in an event of building/tower (deployment platform) motion, we need to have a active tracking and pointing (TP) mechanism to *track* the movement of terminal(s) and a *pointing* mechanism to realign the link in real-time. We start with discussing the requirements of such a system in FSONet.

Angular Speed Requirements due to Building Motions. The fundamental reason for link misalignment is the movement of the beam at the receiver plane (due to the movement of the TX and/or RX assemblies). The tracking and pointing (TP) mechanism at the TX corrects any misalignment by moving the TX beam appropriately. Since any correction mechanism incurs a non-zero latency, a TP system can only be effective up to a certain *speed* of RX beam movement. To relate the RX beam movement to building motions that cause the beam movement, we map the movement speed of the RX beam to the most dominant[7] building motion in our context, viz., the angular movement speed of the TX assembly. Accordingly, we measure effectiveness of the TP mechanism in terms of the angular speed (i.e., rotation rate) of TX assembly (or building motion) that the TP mechanism is able to handle.

Prior studies suggest that building motions rarely have an angular speed of more than a few mrad/sec. In particular, based on the motion frequencies, building motions can be roughly divided into three categories [35]: (i) Vibrations can have a high frequency (1-10Hz), but rarely exceed 0.5mrad [35] in amplitude; (ii) Moderate frequency (fraction of a Hz) motions due to wind, etc. can have an amplitude of up to a few milliradians [34, 58]; (iii) Motion due to thermal variations have very low frequency (periods from minutes to months). Maximum angular speed (frequency times amplitude) across the above categories is at most a few mrad/sec. Below, we demonstrate that our link prototype is able to handle angular speeds of up to 15 mrad/sec, which is more than sufficient to handle any expected building motions.

Link Tolerance Requirements. To ensure link's operation at all times, the link should have an "angular tolerance" of more than the building motion that is possible within the TP system's latency; here, the link's *angular tolerance* is defined as the maximum angular motion of TX that can be tolerated (*absence of a TP system*) without losing the link. Due to our choice of GM as the pointing mechanism, we expect the TP latency to be of the order of few msecs. Thus, to handle building motion speeds of say 5 mrads/sec using a TP system with latency (to correct the link "sufficiently") of say 5 msecs, we need the link's angular tolerance to be at least 0.025 mrad. To be conservative and to account for other factors (e.g., noise), we aim for link's tolerance of 0.05–0.1 mrad.

[7] RX beam movement due to angular movement at TX depends on the link range, and thus can be significant (few 10s of cms) at 100m range. In contrast, RX beam movement due to linear movement of RX or TX does not depend on the link range, and is expected to be much less. Rotation of the RX assembly causes only slight misalignment.

TP based on GMs and Photodiodes. Typical TP mechanisms [48, 50] include a fast steering mirror or gimbal controlled by digital servos [54, 64, 69] for pointing, along with some tracking detectors to track the target or beam. Common tracking detectors include positioning sensing diodes [64] (e.g., CCDs [54], photodiode arrays [42]), accelerometers, cameras, GPS [69], etc.[8] In our context, it is natural to leverage our steering mechanism GMs as also the pointing mechanism. The pointing accuracy of GMs (10μrad) is much less than 1/8 of the beam divergence (about 280μrad) of our collimator [10], and thus should guarantee a less than 0.5dB tracking error [54]. For beam tracking, we use photodiodes, due to relatively short range (< 500m) of our links which entails minimal intensity fluctuations in outdoors [34, 66].

In particular, we locate four long-wavelength photo detectors in a quadrant around the circumference of receiving lens assembly. With the beam perfectly aligned for an operational link, we record the light intensity at the detectors. When the beam moves, the intensity on each detector will change independently; this variation is then used to provide a correction signal to the GMs at the transmitter terminal. We use the following control algorithm: First, we build a table that contains four-tuple diode readings for different 2D deviations of the TX from the initial (aligned) position; for a 100m link, 10k table entries sufficed. Then, to correct a misaligned link, we do a "reverse" look up in the table, i.e., find the deviation that would have resulted in (close to) the current diode readings, and use it to move the beam back via the GM at TX. In our prototype, we also added an integral term [22] (with a 0.1 coefficient) to the correction. The above control strategy can stabilize the link in minimal number of iterations and is fast enough, as discussed in §3.3. Tracking feedback can be transmitted across terminals over an in-band or an out-of-band (e.g., macrocellular) control channel. The above mechanism can also be used for the initial acquisition of the receiver, and thus, yielding a complete ATP (acquisition, tracking, and pointing) mechanism.

3.3 Robust 100m Link Prototype with TP

We now describe and evaluate our SFP-based 100m link prototype with the above described TP mechanism. The link prototype satisfies our stated requirements of sufficient link margin to handle weather effects, and the TP mechanism is effective in handling expected building motions. We also analyze longer links.

We set up our SFP-based 100m link in a long hallway. At 100m range, our indoor link prototype should exhibit similar performance as an outdoor link in clear weather; as mentioned in §2.2, atmospheric effects are negligible at these ranges. We address weather effects by demonstrating a sufficient link margin; as mentioned in §2.3, a 100m link with 13-15dB margin can withstand most weather effects. We use the 10G 1550nm SFP+ [4] with a 10GBASE-ZR interface[9], a transmission power of 0-4dBm and a receiver sensitivity of -25dBm yielding a total optical budget of 25-29dB. We use a uni-directional FSO link for simplicity, as it is sufficient for our objectives, with the other direction of the SFPs connected by an optical fiber. We use a GM at TX, and surround the RX's collimator by four photodiodes. See Figure 6(a)-(c). For photodiodes, we use Thorlabs' InGaAs variable-gain photodiodes [21] which have a low (70ns) rise time and include an amplifier in a compact package. Each of the photodiodes is covered by a bandpass optical filter [5] to minimize errors from stray light. The diodes are read via a DAQ [19] which can sample at up to 250k/sec. We address noise in the diode readings by increasing the gain of the diodes appropriately and also by taking an average of 100 samples per diode over a few milliseconds. The collimator [10] has a divergence of 0.28mrad and generates a beam of diameter 29mm at 100m which, being larger than the 25mm collimator, falls partially on the photodiodes at RX. The entire TX assembly is placed on a motorized rotational stage [16] to enable fine angular movement of the TX assembly at varying speeds, to simulate building motions.

[8]For very short links, simpler techniques can be used, e.g., [41] uses photodetector at *transmitter* with a reflective film at RX for a 1m link, but incurs a latency of several hundreds of msecs due to scanning.

[9]The physical layer standard used by 10GBASE-ZR interfaces is proprietary and not specified under IEEE 802.3ae.

Link Margin and Tolerance. At best alignment, the link's received power was around -12dBm, yielding a link margin of 13dB. We note that most of this path loss of 12-16dB in our prototype is alignment/pointing loss from manual alignment at the RX terminal, and can be reduced significantly with a more sophisticated alignment mechanism. In Fig. 7(a), we present reduction in RX power due to angular movement (tilt) of the TX, with or without active TP. Without TP, we move the TX slowly and observe that the RX power reduces minimally at 0.1 mrad tilt, and remains less than the initial link margin (13dB) up to a tilt of 0.2 mrad—implying an angular tolerance of a bit more than 0.2 mrad. With active TP, we use the motorized rotation stage to provide an angular movement at 5 mrad/sec, and observe that the RX power remains relatively stable with a reduction of a few dB over a wide range (up to 100 mrad; figure shows only up to 5mrad) of angular movement. Here, we use a USB-interfaced power meter [24] which logs power received every 3-5 msec.

TCP Throughput for Varying Angular Speeds. To demonstrate the link operation during continuous terminal movement, we compute the CDF of link's TCP throughput with TP active and TX rotating at varying angular speeds: 0–20 mrad/sec, using a motorized rotational stage, with an amplitude of 100 mrad. See Figure 7(b). Here, each run is over a 10 minute period, with throughput measured over every second. We observe that the throughput CDFs for speeds $\leq$ 15 mrad/sec are near-identical to that of the fixed link, with an average throughput of about 9.4 Gbps. The throughput deteriorates somewhat for 17.5 and 20 mrad/sec. We also logged RX power every 3-5 msec using [24] and observed that it remained around -15dBm for 0-15 mrad/sec speeds; this implies a link margin of 10dB and thus ability to handle fog conditions with visibility more than 130m even *during* 15 mrad/s motions.

TP Latency. The latency incurred in one iteration of the TP mechanism is around 6 msecs. Reading 100 samples from the diodes takes about 4 msecs, while the remaining tasks (feedback transfer, correction computation, GM latency) take about 2 msecs. The link usually regains operational alignment within a single iteration.

Analyzing Longer (200-500m) Links. Creating longer (200-500m) link prototypes is beyond the scope of this current work. Instead, we model an FSO link in Zemax [25] based on given optical elements and estimate link's signal loss (assuming perfect alignment) at various ranges. Zemax is an optical design software platform

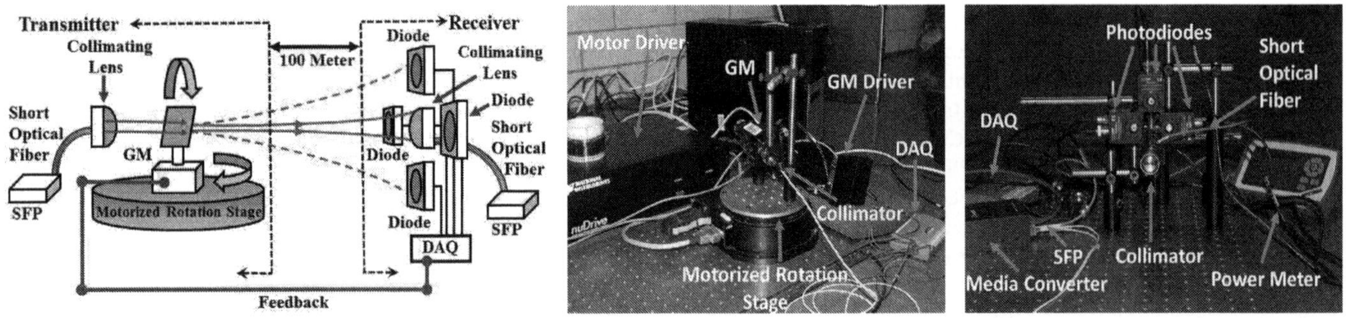

Figure 6: (a) Schematic diagram of the 100m link prototype, (b) Transmitter assembly with GM and motorized rotational stage, and (c) Receiver assembly with 4 photodiodes around the collimator.

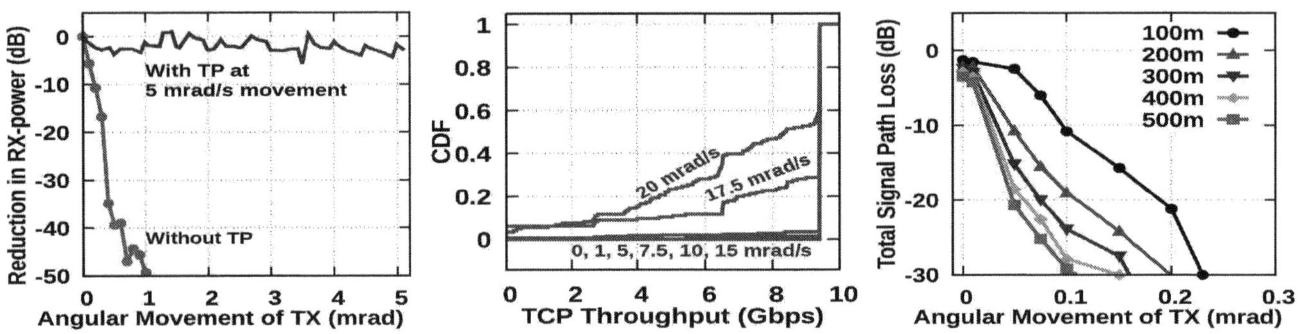

Figure 7: (a) Reduction in received power, with and without TP, (b) CDF of the link's TCP throughput for varying angular speeds of the TX assembly, (c) Path loss estimates based on Zemax for varying angular tilts and ranges.

widely used by optical engineers to analyze, simulate and optimize optical systems. Recall that, for links longer than 100m, we don't allocate any link margin for weather effects—so, the link should just have sufficient angular tolerance to support the active TP mechanism to handle expected building motions. Fig.7(c) shows that, assuming an optical budget of about 30dB, the angular tolerance is approximately 0.23 mrad for 100m, 0.15 mrad for 300m, 0.1 mrad for 500m, etc. Based on the performance results (Fig. 7(b)) of the 100m link prototype, the 0.1 mrad angular tolerance of a 500m link should suffice to handle motions of 5–7.5 mrad/sec angular speeds. Note that angular tolerance can be further improved by creating wider beams at RX [18], via a custom optical design, at the cost of slight power loss at perfect alignment. E.g., increasing the collimator divergence to 0.78 mrad improves the angular tolerance of 500m link to 0.2 mrad, while decreasing the power at perfect alignment by 1.5dB at 100m and 2dB at 500m.

4 DYNAMIC BACKHAUL-NETWORK DESIGN (DBND)

In our context, the network design problem entails placement of picocells and creating "potential" FSO links over the located picocells, given a geographical area to which we wish to provide picocell coverage to. Creation of potential FSO links in turn entails orientation of GMs associated with the FSO devices. We start with borrowing a few definitions from [47].

Candidate Links, Dynamic Network, Realizable Topologies. In our context, each picocell/node has a coverage area associated with it. To provide backhaul connectivity to gateways, each node is connected to a small number of steerable FSO devices via a network switch. For steerability, each FSO is equipped with a GM which is preconfigured to a coverage cone within which the FSO can steer its beam. See Figure 1. A link can be potentially established between two FSOs if there is a clear line of sight between them and each is contained in the coverage cone of the others' GMs. We refer to such links as *candidate link.* The set of all candidate links forms what is called a *dynamic network.* At runtime, the network is "reconfigured" to activate a subset of candidate links (by steering the beams appropriately) such that each only one candidate link per FSO is active; this network reconfiguration is done based on the prevailing traffic and state, and is discussed in the following section. A subset of candidate links that can be active simultaneously forms a *realizable topology* of the given dynamic network.

DBND Problem. Given a geographical area, which needs picocell coverage, potential locations where picocells can be placed, and locations of a few fixed gateways connected to the outside network, the DBND problem is to design a dynamic network. This entails determining (a) locations to place picocell nodes, and (b) candidate links (with clear line-of-sight) over these placed nodes by orienting the GMs associated with the nodes' FSOs. The created dynamic network $\mathcal{D}$ must have a realizable topology τ called backbone such that (i) τ consists solely of short links (i.e., $\leq$ 100 m), (ii) the set of nodes of τ provides full coverage to the given area, and (iii) each node i in τ is connected to a gateway via a path in τ. See Fig. 8(c)-(d). The purpose of the backbone is to maintain network availability (i.e., area coverage) in most adverse outdoor conditions, by ensuring its short links have sufficient link margin. To constrain infrastructure cost, we can impose constraints on the total number of nodes as well as the number of FSOs per node in $\mathcal{D}$.

DBND's Optimization Objective. At a high-level, we wish to create a "flexible" dynamic network $\mathcal{D}$ that has a rich set of realizable topologies sufficient to "handle" most of the anticipated traffic patterns. As observed in §2.1, we are particularly interested in traffic patterns with only a small number of hotspot nodes. Thus, a reasonable optimization objective is as follows. Let X be the fixed number of expected hotspots, and let $\mathcal{P}$ be the set of all possible X-size subsets of nodes in $\mathcal{D}$. Then, the *average-hotspot-flow (AHF)* optimization objective is to *maximize* the following:

$\text{avg}_{p \in \mathcal{P}} \max_\tau$ (max-flow from p to gateways, in a realizable topology τ of $\mathcal{D}$) (1)

Essentially, the above objective is to maximize the average (across all possible sets of hotspots) network-flow from the hotspots to the gateways; note that the objective implicitly also depends on the path lengths from hotspots to the gateways. The above objective is somewhat related but quite different from the *dynamic bisection bandwidth* (DBW) objective [47] for dynamic networks in data centers; DBW is not a suitable metric in FSONet due to two different node categories, viz., base stations and gateways, and traffic flows only between basestations and gateways.

Intractability, and Proposed Heuristic (FSH). It is easy to see that the DBND problem is NP-hard via a straightforward reduction from the set cover or Steiner tree problem. The closest known problem is the *Group Steiner Tree* (GST) problem [12], which, in our context, represents the "partial" problem of constructing the smallest backbone without the node degree constraint. The known approximation algorithms [12, 45] for GST, though polynomial, are very inefficient [12] to be useful here. The key challenges in solving the complete DBND problem arise from the node degree constraint and the network dynamicity which requires an intricate objective function. Even an Integer Linear Program (ILP) requires an exponential number of equations for the above objective function. Even in practice, a "good" solution can be challenging to achieve due to a limited number of potential node locations (e.g., building corners, roof tops, towers) and links (limited line-of-sight). We propose the following multi-step heuristic (referred as the *Four-Step Heuristic (FSH)*) that delivers good quality network solutions in real settings as shown in §6. The basic idea (see Fig. 8) is to first construct a backbone with minimal number of nodes, and then, augment it with additional nodes and links to optimize the objective.

1. Select a minimal number of nodes n_c to cover the given area, using a set-cover like greedy approach.
2. Connect each of the nodes in n_c to a gateway using only short-range links and possibly, additional nodes; this "Steiner-forest" problem is a slight variation of the well-known Steiner-tree problem [44]. This yields a backbone subnetwork with the desired properties.
3. Minimize the maximum degree of a node, by an iterative "exchange" of links (using a slight variation of the Furer-Raghavchari's trick [43]), following by a reconstruction phase as described below. This step addresses the constraint on number of FSOs per node.
4. Finally, we augment the above backbone with additional nodes and links to introduce dynamicity and improve its objective value. We do this by iteratively adding a "path" of nodes that most improves the objective.

Steps Details. For the first step, we partition the given area into "atomic" area-elements such that each area-element is either fully covered or fully uncovered by a node. Then, we greedily select nodes in the order of the number of yet-uncovered area-elements they cover.

In the second step, we construct a "Steiner forest" over the gateways and the nodes n_c selected in the first step. Similar to the standard 2-approx. Steiner tree algorithm [44], we start with the forest of just the gateway nodes and iteratively grow the forest by connecting a not-yet-connected node i of n_c to the current forest. To choose i, we pick the node that has the shortest path p_i of short links to the forest.

In the third step, to minimize the maximum node degree, we iteratively search for a triplet of nodes (u, v, w) such that u, v, w are nodes in the forest, (u, v) is a short-link not in the forest, degree of w is at least 2 more than the maximum degree of u and v, and w is either on the cycle created by adding (u, v) to the forest or w is an ancestor of u or v. See Fig. 9. On finding such a triplet, we replace a link of w by (u, v) — this maintains the backbone properties but reduces a node degree. We iterate until no such triplet exists. If the above still leaves certain nodes with degree higher than the node degree constraint δ, then we apply the following reconstruction step. We remove links to bound the maximum node degree by δ, connect the disconnected components to the gateways using minimal *additional* nodes, and redo the third step if needed (i.e., if a node degree is higher than δ). After sufficiently many iterations, if node-degree constraint is still not satisfied, we either reject the instance or move on to the next step with the backbone found till now with least violations.

Backbone. At the end of the third step, we have a backbone with minimal number of nodes and bounded node degree. For each node in the backbone: we equip it with d FSOs, where d is the node's degree, and associate one FSO per link. This essentially creates a dynamic network with the backbone as its realizable topology.

Fourth Step. We now augment the dynamic network with additional nodes and links, within the given constraints, to improve its objective value. To begin with, we add any possible candidate links *between* the backbone nodes — associating these new links with already existing FSOs at the nodes. Next, we iteratively add a node or a path of nodes to improve the AHF objective. Since the AHF objective considers all hotspots uniformly, we improve the objective simply by treating the entire dynamic network as a traditional (static) network and improving the max-flow between nodes to gateways as follows. We connect all nodes to a super-source and all gateways to a super-sink, compute the max-flow, and consider the final residual network $\widehat{R}$. Note that, in $\widehat{R}$, no node has a path to any gateway. We then connect a node to a gateway in $\widehat{R}$ (and thus $\mathcal{D}$) by adding a new path. More specifically, we add the path that yields the most increase in flow per added node. We iterate on the above, until all the allowed number of nodes have been added.

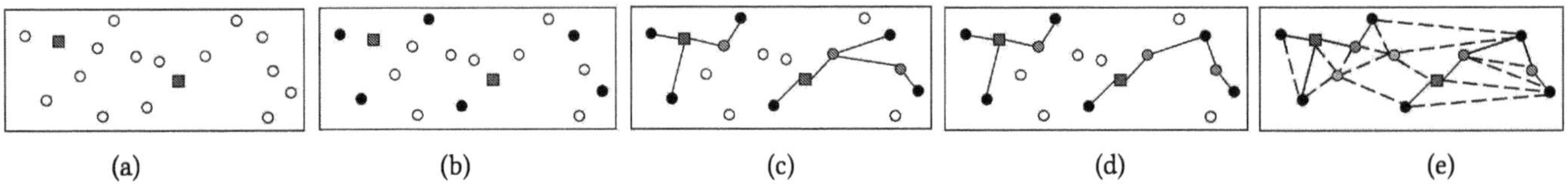

Figure 8: Four-Step Heuristic. (a) Given a geographic area (the rectangle), set of potential locations, and gateways (red). (b) Set of nodes n_c chosen to cover the area. (c) Steiner forest connecting the nodes n_c to the gateways. (d) Reduction of the maximum node (non-gateway) degree, (e) Augmenting the backbone with additional nodes (yellow) and links (dashed).

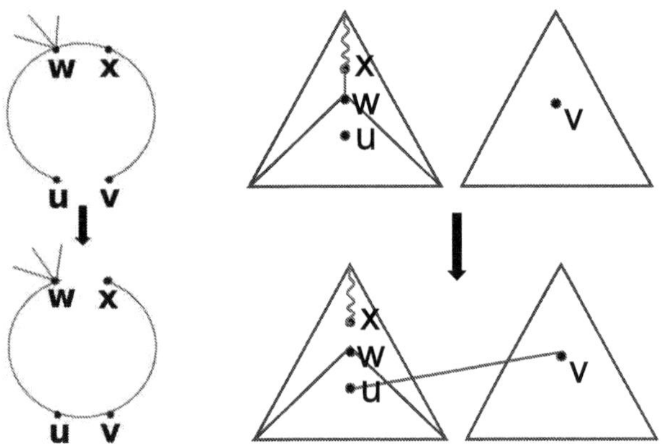

Figure 9: Transformations used to minimize the maximum node degree in FSH's 3rd step.

5 RUNTIME NETWORK MANAGEMENT

We now address the runtime reconfiguration of the network, which requires us to select a realizable (runtime) topology from the given dynamic network and compute routes for the flows over the selected topology, based on the prevailing traffic and network state. Optimization objective could be to maximize the total traffic demand satisfied. Since reconfiguration happens at runtime, we must design very fast algorithms.

Network Management Overview. We leverage software-defined networking (SDN) [30, 36, 40] in designing the network management layer. The network switches, which connect the FSO devices at each node, are envisioned to be SDN-capable receiving configurations (i.e., steering commands, routing table entries, etc.) from a logically centralized controller. The controller continually receives the status of the entire network status (e.g., link status, traffic patterns) from the SDN-enabled switches [40] via a control channel. The key component of the controller is the *reconfiguration engine* as described below. We preserve network connectivity and consistency during reconfigurations [47, 61] via techniques from [47] except that we execute reconfigurations one at a time rather than concurrently as they are expected to involve more links but occur less frequently in our context.

FSONet's Reconfiguration Engine. We reconfigure FSONet in response to certain network events of interest. In the context of a picocell network, the main event of interest is an arrival of a new high-demand flow. Infrequently, we also reconfigure the *entire* network periodically based on global information. We model a *flow* as arriving at a certain node with a *bandwidth-demand*. Bandwidth-demand may be application dependent and/or may reflect the SLAs associated with the flow type. We assume it can be estimated by analyzing very early part of the flow; accurate estimation will benefit performance, but is not critical in our context. An effective reconfiguration strategy should be infrequent, fast (run in a few tens of milliseconds), and incremental (incur minimal topology and routing-table changes so that the impact to the existing traffic is minimal). We allow multi-path routing. The *triggered* reconfiguration scheme from [47], for dynamic networks in data centers, is simple and fast, but effective only in very dense networks. Likewise, the matching-based scheme of [46], though decentralized, is suited for complete networks. In FSONet, the network is much sparser and all flows are to/from a small number of gateway nodes; thus, we instead employ the following scheme which is simple/fast, somewhat localized, and done only when "beneficial."

- If the bandwidth-demand is below a certain threshold (e.g., 100Mbps, in our simulations) *or* the current network configuration (i.e., runtime topology and the generic rules in the routing tables) is able to satisfy 90% of the bandwidth demand of the flow F, then we route F using the current generic rules.
- Else, we compute the multi-path route r (using max-flow) for the flow F, without changing the existing flow routes or topology. If r results in 90% of the bandwidth-demand of F being satisfied, then we add r as the flow-route for F in the routing tables.
- Else, we reconfigure FSONet by changing its runtime topology as well some of the existing flow-routes as follows. First, we find the shortest-path P in the dynamic network such that (a) P involves at least one inactive link, (b) Activation of links on path P entails neither deactivation of any "heavily-used" links[10] nor disconnection of any node from the gateways. Then, we activate/deactivate links to add P to the current runtime topology, and route affected traffic and F appropriately on the new runtime topology. If the above still doesn't satisfy 90% of F's bandwidth-demand, then we don't reconfigure at all and just route F as best as possible in the current configuration.

To minimize the computation time, we can precompute the reconfiguration for all possible parameter (e.g., F's arrival node and bandwidth-demand) values for a given network. For periodic reconfiguration based on global information, we adopt a greedy approach

[10]Note that activation of a link may require deactivation of other links, since each FSO can only have at most one active link incident on it.

of iteratively activating a path of links from a node to a gateway, in order of nodes' bandwidth demands.

Link/Network Outages. Link outages can be handled based on their duration: (i) retransmit dropped packets for very short outages (e.g., due to bird blockage), (ii) reroute flows for longer outages, (iii) reconfigure network (as above, since a link failure can be modelled as a flow arrival) for a semi-permanent link failure (e.g., bad weather). Finally, in case of extreme conditions where even the backbone fails, the traffic can be routed to the back-up macrocellular network.

6 EVALUATION

Having already established the performance of link prototype in §3, we now evaluate the "quality" of the FSONet networks created for many metropolitan US cities.

US Cities Data. In our simulation study, we create FSONet networks to provide *outdoor* coverage in 14 of the top US metro cities. We use topographical data from [20] which contains locations and 2D footprints of the buildings in the cities. We use building corners (at a uniform height) as the *potential locations* for picocell base stations. For determination of line-of-sight between two locations, we conservatively assume each building to be high-enough to be an obstruction.

Parameter Values. We vary the (ground) coverage radius of a node from 100 to 200 meters, with 100 m as the default value. We allow 3 to 6 FSOs per base station, with 4 as the default; note that only a low number is practical. We use ≈ 5% of the expected size of FSONet network as the number of gateways, and locate them randomly over the given locations. To constrain the total number of nodes: note that the first three steps of FSH attempt to create a small size backbone — an *essential* part of a FSONet network. Thus, we constrain only the number of nodes added in the fourth step of FSH; we allow at most $n_b/10$ nodes to be added in the fourth step, where n_b is the created backbone size.

FSONet Network Quality. Given the above set-up, we create FSONet networks in 14 of the top US cities, and focus on evaluating (i) the number of nodes n_b in the backbones and (ii) the average-hotspot-flow (AHF) objective, in the created FSONet networks.

Backbone Size (n_b) and Related Ratios. Recall that the backbone subnetwork is an essential part of FSONet network, and hence represents the smallest FSONet network possible using our techniques. First, we observe that the backbone size n_b varies from about 50 to 750 nodes across the cities, for default coverage radius of 100m. See Table 1. Delving in deeper, we observe that the n_c, the number of nodes selected in FSH's first step to provide coverage, is only about 2 to 2.8 times more than the loose lower bound (= total coverage area divided by $\pi 100^2$) which ignores both the coverage area's irregularity and the limited locations available to place nodes. Moreover, we observe that ratio of n_b to n_c is 2 to 3.5; this essentially represents the cost of enforcing the backbone condition (the key aspect of FSONet). Note that the n_b to n_c ratio is expected to be at least 2, as the backbone links can be at most 100m.

Average-Hotspot-Flow (AHF) Comparison. To evaluate the quality of the created FSONet networks, we *estimate* their AHF values and compare them to that of a representative "static" (i.e., with no steering FSO capability) network as well as a loose upper-bound. In particular, for a FSONet network $\mathcal{D}$, we compare its AHF value with the static network that contains $\mathcal{D}$'s backbone subnetwork, has the same number of nodes as $\mathcal{D}$, and wherein each node's degree is at most the number of FSOs per node in $\mathcal{D}$. To estimate the AHF value, we use Eqn.(1) with $X = 5$ and consider about 200 random subsets p of size 5. See Table 1. We make two observations about the AHF estimate of FSONet networks: (i) it is about 1.5 to 2.4 times the AHF estimate of the corresponding static graph—confirming the benefit of steerability/dynamicity in a network, (ii) it is about 0.5 to 0.7 of the trivial upper bound of 200 Gbps (= number of hotspots *times* the maximum number of FSOs per node *times* 10Gbps link capacity)—suggesting the effectiveness of our techniques.

City	Back-bone (n_b)	Coverage Factor (n_c/lower-bound)	Conn. Factor (n_b/n_c)	AHF Ratios	
				FSONet/ Static	FSONet/ upper-bound
NYC	752	2.38	3.434	2.53	0.63
Chicago	626	2.346	3.421	2.16	0.60
Seattle	533	2.278	3.25	1.99	0.62
SFO	503	2.284	3.288	1.82	0.62
DC	404	2.364	3.108	1.74	0.63
Boston	321	2.319	2.945	1.76	0.70
Portland	305	2.14	2.85	1.73	0.66
Baltimore	269	2.196	2.663	1.74	0.65
Philly	275	2.245	2.311	1.75	0.65
Houston	220	2.116	2.418	1.68	0.70
Denver	145	2.067	2.339	1.69	0.72
Detroit	139	2.179	2.279	1.62	0.73
Dallas	62	2.8	2.214	1.61	0.74
Miami	58	2.5	1.933	1.52	0.72

Table 1: Statistics for FSONet networks for 14 US cities, with default parameter values.

Table 2 shows range of statistics across cities for other values of coverage radius and # of FSOs/node, and we observe similar statistics except that the n_b/n_c ratio increases with the coverage radius, as expected.

Online Performance. To evaluate the online performance of the created FSONet networks (for default radius 100m and 4 FSOs/node), we run traffic simulations over the networks and measure appropriate performance metrics. In particular, we consider the traffic model wherein arrival of flows in the network is modelled as a Poisson process with rate varying from 5k to 100k (default being 10k) per second; each flow is randomly assigned to arrive at a network node. The flow's size is modelled as a Pareto random variable α in the range 10 KB to 1 TB; the default value of α is 1 so that 90% of the flows are less than 100KB. We assign bandwidth-demand to a flow as follows: with a 10% probability we pick a random rate between 100Mbps and 6Gbps, and with the remaining 90% probability, we assign the bandwidth-demand increasingly based on the size (e.g., 10-10,000KB flows get 100Mbps, 10-100MB get 500Mbps, and so

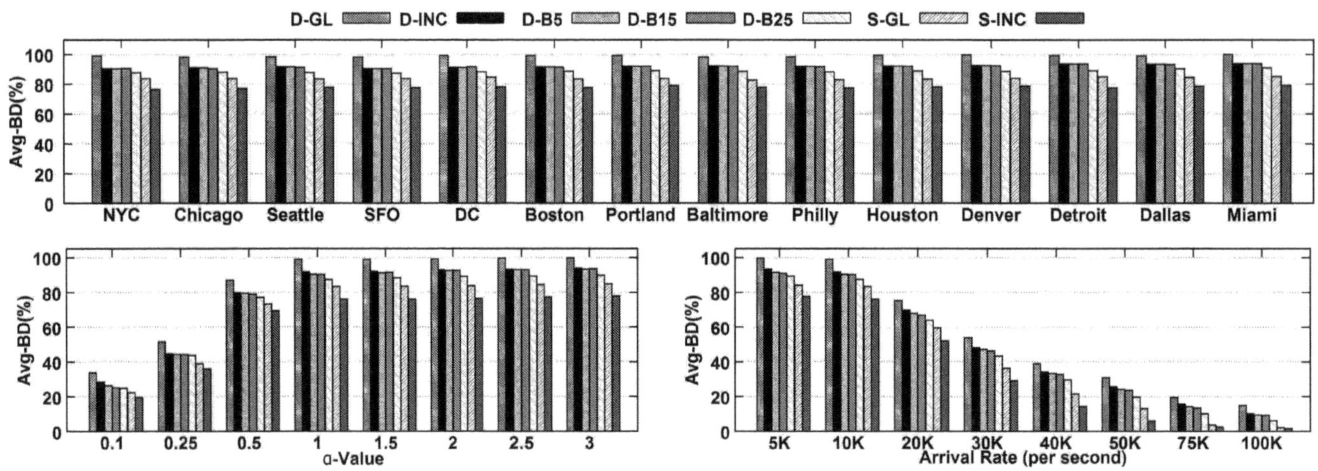

Figure 10: Performance (Avg-BD value) of various reconfiguration schemes in FSONet and its corresponding static picocell networks. (a) In FSONet networks of various cities for $\alpha = 1$ and flow arrival rate of 10,000/sec, (b) In Manhattan's FSONet network for varying α with flow arrival rate of 10,000/sec. (c) In Manhattan's FSONet network for varying flow arrival rates with $\alpha = 1$.

(Coverage, FSO/node)	Back-bone (n_b)	Coverage Factor (n_c/lower-bound)	Conn. Factor (n_b/n_c)	AHF Ratios FSONet/ Static	AHF Ratios FSONet/ upper-bound
(100m, 3)	58-752	2.08-2.80	1.93-3.43	1.58-2.68	0.64-0.76
(100m, 4)	58-752	2.08-2.80	1.93-3.43	1.52-2.53	0.6-0.74
(100m, 5)	58-752	2.08-2.80	1.93-3.43	1.50-2.42	0.58-0.73
(100m, 6)	58-752	2.08-2.80	1.93-3.43	1.47-2.27	0.56-0.72
(150m, 3)	42-632	2.43-3.00	3.00-5.80	1.54-2.61	0.62-0.78
(150m, 4)	42-632	2.43-3.00	3.00-5.80	1.51-2.47	0.61-0.77
(150m, 5)	42-632	2.43-3.00	3.00-5.80	1.58-2.38	0.59-0.75
(150m, 6)	42-632	2.43-3.00	3.00-5.80	1.45-2.24	0.58-0.72
(200m, 3)	36-584	2.46-3.00	4.50-8.99	1.55-2.56	0.63-0.78
(200m, 4)	36-584	2.46-3.00	4.50-8.99	1.50-2.39	0.62-0.76
(200m, 5)	36-584	2.46-3.00	4.50-8.99	1.56-2.31	0.59-0.75
(200m, 6)	36-584	2.46-3.00	4.50-8.99	1.44-2.19	0.58-0.73

Table 2: Range of values of different statistics across FSONet networks of 14 cities, for different values of picocell coverage radius and # of FSOs per node.

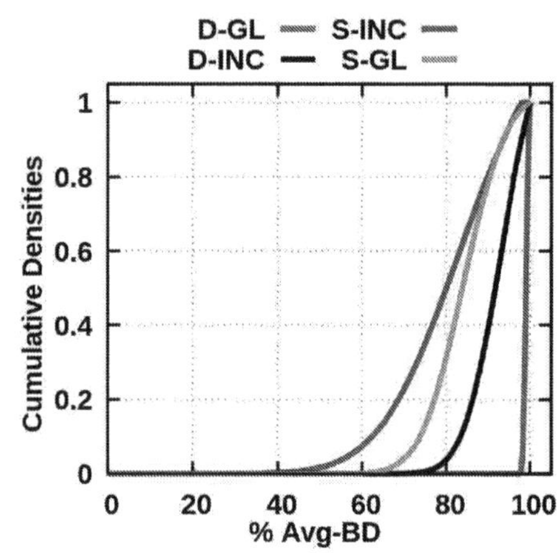

Figure 11: CDF plot for the Avg-BD metric in NYC FSONet.

on). The latter can be implemented by increasing the bandwidth-demand as more and more of the flow size is routed and discovered. The maximum values of size and bandwidth-demand roughly correspond to high-resolution multi-hour movies.

We consider the following reconfiguration schemes: (i) INC: the (incremental) approach from §5 executed for every large flow (i.e., > 100Mbps bandwidth-demand), (ii) GL: the global periodic-reconfiguration of §5 executed at the arrival and completion of every large flow, (iii) Bn: the slightly-modified INC approach executed for every "batch" of arrival of n large flows. Note that the GL approach is impractical due to high computation time and global changes to the network but serves as an apt comparison benchmark (upper-bound). We prefix the above acronyms with D- or S- for FSONet and static networks (as defined above) respectively.

We run the simulation for sufficient time to reach a steady state and measure, at each time instant, the total bandwidth-demand satisfied as a percentage of the total requested by all the flows at that time, and then average it over time. We use Avg-BD to refer to this average metric, and use it for comparison. See Fig. 10(a). Key observations: (i) D-INC performs quite close to D-GL (91-94% vs. 98-99%), (ii) D-INC (black bars in figure) performs significantly better than S-INC (red bars), i.e., 91-94% vs. 76-78%, and (iii) the D-Bn approaches perform almost same as the D-INC approach for $n = 5$ and 15, but worse for larger n. Since S-INC outperforms S-Bn approaches, they are not shown in Fig. 10 for clarity. Figure 10(b)-(c) plot the Avg-BD metric for varying α parameter of the Pareto distribution and flow-arrival rate, for the NYC network. As expected, the Avg-BD values decrease due to increase in the arrival rate and decrease in the α (since smaller α makes larger flow more likely)—but the relative performances of the approaches remain similar to before. We also plot the CDF of the Avg-BD metric for the NYC FSONet for $\alpha = 1$ and flow arrival rate of 10,000/sec. See Fig. 11; for clarity, we show only the main approaches viz., D-GL, D-INC, S-GL, and S-INC. We observe that the relative performance of the schemes is similar to that observed in Fig. 10(a), and that the CDFs show minimal tail effect.

Updates, Time. In Fig. 12, we compare the number of routing table entries changed per reconfiguration across schemes for NYC network. Less changes results in less network-update time, and facilitates concurrent reconfigurations [47]. We observe that the D-Bn approaches incur less changes than the D-INC approach, which incurs only about 0.25% of the changes incurred by GL (the GL approach needs to change *all* the entries). Note that the number of reconfigurations in a D-Bn approach is $(1/n)^{th}$ of that in D-INC. Thus, overall, the D-B15 approach seems to be most efficient since it performs very close to D-INC, but incur much less reconfigurations routing table changes. Finally, we note that the computation times of D-INC and D-Bn approaches were of the order of 0.1 msec while that of the GL approach was 10-20 msecs.

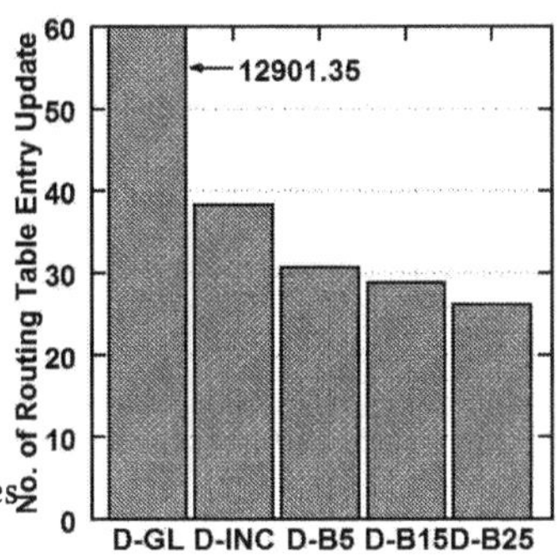

Figure 12: Number of routing table changes per reconfiguration, for various schemes.

Network Redundancy. To evaluate and compare network redundancy for FSONet and corresponding static networks: We delete a number of links randomly from the static network and delete the *same* set of links from FSONet, and measure the above defined Avg-BD metric for each, and compare the "performance deterioration." We define the *performance deterioration* as $(a - b)/b$ where b and a are the Avg-BD values of the network before and after deletion of links. See Fig. 13. We observe that the NYC FSONet network exhibit much less deterioration in performance than its static network.

7 RELATED WORK

Backhaul of picocell networks is a key challenge, and recent works have explored various solutions. Among wireless backhaul solutions, [49] addresses resource (power and scheduling) allocation in backhaul solutions with shared wireless channels, [62] presents beamforming techniques to overcome outdoor challenges in an mm wave based solution, and [55] explores a microwave-based backhaul solution. However, low frequency radio (below 6GHz) is limited in terms of data rates due to interference problems, and high frequency radio (mm and microwave from 6 to 300 GHz) are limited in range and data rates (e.g., mmwave can only deliver upto 1-2Gbps over 100-200m). Recently, free space optics technology (FSO) has emerged as an attractive alternative. E.g., [31] explores use of FSO flying platforms to create a backhaul network with vertical point-to-point FSO links; their motivation for vertical links is to circumvent the line-of-sight issue in dense urban areas. In addition, to handle outdoor effects, some works have explored hybrid RF/FSO [28, 70] or wired/FSO [70] solutions. Instead, we alleviate the line-of-sight concern by a simulation study over many metropolitan US cities, and circumvent the outdoor challenges in an FSO-based backhaul by using many short links and embedding redundancy in the network via steerable links.

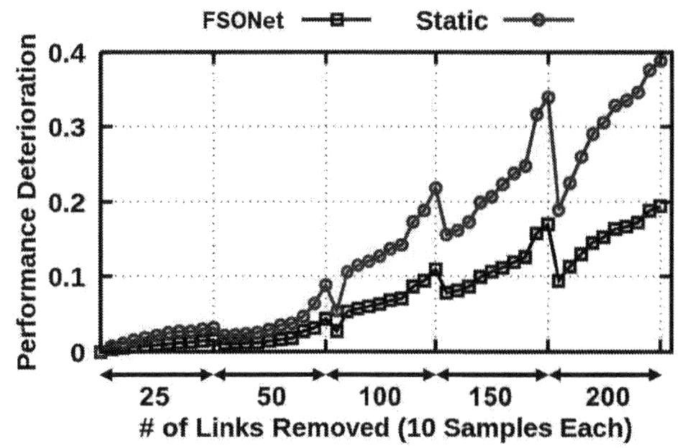

Figure 13: Performance deterioration of NYC's FSONet and static networks for varying number of link failures.

Our work is inspired by recent works on use of steerable FSO links for dynamic data center networks [46, 47]. In our context, the outdoor setting bring new challenges in FSO link engineering and network design. E.g., in a data center as the FSO devices are placed on top of racks, there is no placement problem. Moreover, in [47], a simple random network worked well as the dynamic network [47] as the racks were treated uniformly and the line of sight issue was circumvented by placing a full ceiling mirror. Similarly, in [46], use of a large number of intricate mirror assemblies allowed a complete dynamic network. In our context, the relative sparsity of network and specialized traffic pattern due to gateways calls for different reconfiguration strategies as discussed in §5.

8 CONCLUSIONS

We have developed FSONet, a wireless backhaul or multi-gigabit picocells based on steerable FSO links. To the best of our knowledge, this is the first work targeting multi-gigabit wireless solutions for picocell backhauls. We have explored one viable solution and addressed design challenges therein. However, there is room for much improvements and alternative choices in architecture design and techniques, e.g., to comprehensively address key cost-performance trade-offs. Could we design efficient FSO *networks* tailored to different weather and outdoor conditions? A somewhat generalization of FSONet's approach could be to design multi-tier FSO networks with say high-bandwidth but less-reliable subnetwork backed up a low-bandwidth but very reliable subnetwork. These directions form the basis of our future research.

ACKNOWLEDGMENTS

This work was partially supported by NSF grant 1514017.

REFERENCES

[1] 100G CFP Optical Transceivers. https://edgeoptic.com/cfp-optical-transceiver-the-basics/.
[2] 10G BiDi SFP+ Transceiver. https://tinyurl.com/zqwggq9.
[3] 10G BiDi XFP 100km Transceiver. https://www.alibaba.com/product-detail/XFP-module-10G-Tx-1490-Rx_60536576254.html.
[4] 10G SFP+ 1550nm 100km DOM Transceivers. http://www.fs.com/products/29799.html.
[5] 1550nm Bandpass Filter. https://www.thorlabs.com/thorproduct.cfm?partnumber=FB1550-12.
[6] Artolink 10G FSO Link Specs. http://artolink.com/page/products/free_space_optics_Artolink_10Gbps/.
[7] BER and Eye-Diagram of 10Gpbs signal over multi-mode fiber. https://www.youtube.com/watch?v=Ab2h1oqZ-GA.
[8] Bi-directional 10G SFP+. http://www.fs.com/products/31028.html.
[9] Cisco 10GBASE SFP+ modules. http://www.cisco.com/c/en/us/products/collateral/interfaces-modules/transceiver-modules/data_sheet_c78-455693.pdf.
[10] F810FC-1550 Collimation Package from Thorlabs. https://www.thorlabs.com/thorproduct.cfm?partnumber=F810FC-1550.
[11] GMs from Cambridge Technology. http://www.cambridgetechnology.com/products/galvanometer-xy-sets.
[12] Group Steiner Tree Problem. http://theory.cs.uni-bonn.de/info5/steinerkompendium/node30.html.
[13] Laser safety information. https://www.lia.org/subscriptions/safety_bulletin/laser_safety_information.
[14] LightPointe FSO Link Cost. http://tinyurl.com/k86o2vh.
[15] Lightpointe FSO Links. http://www.lightpointe.com.
[16] Micos. http://www.micosusa.com/product/subview.cfm_firstlevel=1&sublevel=17.htm.
[17] Mirrorcle technologies MEMS mirrors: Technical overview. http://www.mirrorcletech.com/pdf/Mirrorcle%20Technologies%20MEMS%20Mirrors%20-%20Technical%20Overview.pdf.
[18] Mounting stability in fso deployments. http://www.fsona.com/tech/app_notes/fSONA-APPNOTE-Mounting_Stability.pdf.
[19] Multifunction USB Data Acquisition Device. http://www.mccdaq.com/usb-data-acquisition/USB-1608G.aspx.
[20] Openstreetmap foundation. http://www.openstreetmap.org.
[21] Photodetector. https://www.thorlabs.com/thorproduct.cfm?partnumber=PDA20CS.
[22] PID Controller. https://en.wikipedia.org/wiki/PID_controller.
[23] Thorlabs galvo mirrors. http://tinyurl.com/haymezj.
[24] Thorlabs PM100D Power Meter. https://www.thorlabs.com/thorproduct.cfm?partnumber=PM100D.
[25] Zemax. https://www.zemax.com.
[26] *Safety of Laser Products – Part 1: Equipment classification, requirements and users guide, International Electrotechnical Commission (IEC) Standard 60825-1.* 2007.
[27] Small cell backhaul requirements. http://tinyurl.com/h8fomey, 2012. NGMN Alliance, White paper.
[28] Ahmed Douik et al. Hybrid radio/free-space optical design for next generation backhaul systems. *CoRR*, 2015.
[29] I. Akyildiz et al. Terahertz band: Next frontier for wireless communications. *Physical Communication*, 2014.
[30] M. Al-Fares et al. Hedera: Dynamic flow scheduling for data center networks. In *NSDI*, 2010.
[31] M. Alzenad, M. Z. Shakir, H. Yanikomeroglu, and M. Alouini. FSO-based vertical backhaul/fronthaul framework for 5G+ wireless networks. *CoRR*, abs/1607.01472, 2016.
[32] J. Andrews et al. What will 5G be? *IEEE JSAC*, 2014.
[33] M. Awan et al. Characterization of fog and snow attenuations for free-space optical propagation. *Journal of Communications*, 4(8), 2009.
[34] S. Bloom. The physics of free space optics. http://tinyurl.com/zyy3l5k, 2002. White paper.
[35] S. Bloom, E. Korevaar, J. Schuster, and H. Willebrand. Understanding the performance of free-space optics [invited]. *Journal of optical Networking*, 2(6):178–200, 2003.
[36] M. Casado et al. Ethane: Taking control of the enterprise. In *Proc. SIGCOMM*, 2007.
[37] K. Chandra et al. CogCell: Cognitive Interplay between 60GHz Picocells and 2.4/5GHz Hotspots in the 5G Era. *CoRR*, 2015.
[38] M. Chowdhury, M. Kavehrad, W. Zhang, and P. Deng. Combined CATV and very-high-speed data transmission over a 1550-nm wavelength indoor optical wireless link. In *Proc. of SPIE*, 2014.
[39] E. Ciaramella et al. 1.28-Tb/s free-space optical WDM transmission system. *IEEE Photonics Tech. Letters*, 2009.
[40] A. R. Curtis, J. C. Mogul, J. Tourrilhes, P. Yalagandula, P. Sharma, and S. Banerjee. Devoflow: Scaling flow management for high-performance networks. In *SIGCOMM*, 2011.
[41] P. Deng, M. Kavehrad, and Y. Lou. MEMS-based beam steerable free space optical communication link for reconfigurable wireless data center. In *Proc. of SPIE Vol*, volume 10128, pages 1012805–1, 2017.
[42] M. S. Ferraro, W. R. Clark, W. S. Rabinovich, R. Mahon, J. L. Murphy, P. G. Goetz, L. M. Thomas, H. R. Burris, C. I. Moore, W. D. Waters, K. Vaccaro, and B. D. Krejca. Inalas/ingaas avalanche photodiode arrays for free space optical communication. *Appl. Opt.*, 54(31), Nov 2015.
[43] M. Fürer and B. Raghavachari. Approximating the minimum-degree steiner tree to within one of optimal. *J. Algorithms*, 17(3), 1994.
[44] M. R. Garey and D. S. Johnson. *Computers and Intractability: A Guide to the Theory of NP-Completeness.* 1979.
[45] N. Garg, G. Konjevod, and R. Ravi. A polylogarithmic approximation algorithm for the group steiner tree problem. In *Proceedings of the Ninth Annual ACM-SIAM Symposium on Discrete Algorithms*, SODA '98, 1998.
[46] M. Ghobadi, R. Mahajan, A. Phanishayee, N. Devanur, J. Kulkarni, G. Ranade, P.-A. Blanche, H. Rastegarfar, M. Glick, and D. Kilper. Projector: Agile reconfigurable data center interconnect. In *Proceedings of the 2016 Conference on ACM SIGCOMM 2016 Conference*, SIGCOMM '16, 2016.
[47] N. Hamedazimi et al. FireFly: A reconfigurable wireless data center fabric using free-space optics. In *SIGCOMM*, 2014.
[48] T.-H. Ho. *Pointing, Acquisition, and Tracking Systems for Free-Space Optical Communication Links.* PhD thesis, University of Maryland, College Park, 2007.
[49] I. Maric et al. Resource allocation for constrained backhaul in picocell networks. In *Info. Theory and App. Workshop*, 2011.
[50] S. V. Kartalopoulos. *Free Space Optical Networks for Ultra-Broad Band Services.* John Wiley and Sons, 2001.
[51] D. Kedar and S. Arnon. Urban optical wireless communication networks: The main challenges and possible solutions. *IEEE Communications Magazine*, 2004.
[52] I. I. Kim and E. J. Korevaar. Availability of free-space optics and hybrid FSO/RF systems. In *Proc. SPIE*, 2001.
[53] S. G. Lambert and W. L. Casey. *Laser communication in space.* Artech House, 1995.
[54] C. Lv, H. Jiang, and S. Tong. Implementation of FTA with high bandwidth and tracking accuracy in FSO. In *2012 2nd International Conference on Consumer Electronics, Communications and Networks (CECNet)*, 2012.
[55] M. Coldrey et al. Non-line-of-sight microwave backhaul in heterogeneous networks. In *IEEE VTC*, 2013.
[56] A. K. Majumdar. *Advanced Free Space Optics (FSO): A Systems Approach.* Springer New York, 2015.
[57] P. F. McManamon et al. A review of phased array steering for narrow-band electrooptical systems. *Proc. of the IEEE*, 2009.
[58] A. G. A. Muthalif, K. K. Turahim, and S. A. Rahim. Active vibration isolation system to improve free space optics communication. In *Proceedings of the 2012 International Conference on Information Technology & Computing Intelligence*, pages 369–378. Springer, 2013.
[59] A. Nika et al. Understanding and predicting data hotspots in cellular networks. *Mobile Networks and Applications*, 2015.
[60] U. Paul et al. Understanding traffic dynamics in cellular data networks. In *INFOCOM*, 2011.
[61] M. Reitblatt, N. Foster, J. Rexford, C. Schlesinger, and D. Walker. Abstractions for Network Update. In *Proc. SIGCOMM*, 2012.
[62] S. Hur et al. Millimeter wave beamforming for wireless backhaul and access in small cell networks. *IEEE Trans. on Comm.*, 2013.
[63] S. Saha et al. 60 GHz Multi-Gigabit Indoor WLANs: Dream or Reality?
[64] M. K. A.-A. H. R. J. J. Sluss. A tracking system for mobile FSO. In *SPIE Proceedings Vol. 6877*, 2009.
[65] T. S. Rappaport et al. Millimeter wave mobile communications for 5G cellular: It will work! *IEEE Access*, 2013.
[66] H. Weichel. *Laser Beam Propagation in the Atmosphere.* SPIE Press, 1990. Chapter 5.
[67] H. Willebrand and B. Ghuman. *Free Space Optics: Enabling Optical Connectivity in Today's Networks.* Sams, 2001.
[68] Y. Zhu et al. Demystifying 60GHz outdoor picocells. In *MobiCom*, 2014.
[69] T. Yamashita, M. Morita, M. Shimizu, D. Eto, K. Shiratama, and S. Murata. The new tracking control system for free-space optical communications. In *2011 International Conference on Space Optical Systems and Applications (ICSOS)*, 2011.
[70] Yuan Li et al. Optimization of free space optical wireless network for cellular backhauling. *IEEE JSAC*, 2015.

MagneComm: Magnetometer-based Near-Field Communication

Hao Pan
Shanghai Jiao Tong University
panh09@sjtu.edu.cn

Yi-Chao Chen
Shanghai Jiao Tong University
yichao@utexas.edu

Guangtao Xue
Shanghai Jiao Tong University
gt_xue@sjtu.edu.cn

Xiaoyu Ji
Zhejiang University
xji@zju.edu.cn

ABSTRACT

Near-field communication (NFC) plays a crucial role in the operation of mobile devices to enhance applications such as payment, social networks, private communication, gaming, and etc. Despite of the convenience, existing NFC standards like ISO-13157 require additional hardware (*e.g.*, loop antenna and dedicated chip) and thereby hindering their wide-scale applications. In this work, we seek to propose a novel near-field communication protocol, *MagneComm*, which utilizes Magnetic Induction (MI) signals emitted from CPUs and captured by magnetometers on mobile devices for communication. Since CPUs and magnetometers are readily available components in mobile devices, *MagneComm* eliminates the requirement for special hardware and complements existing near-field communication protocols by providing additional bandwidth. We systematically analyze the characteristics of magnetic signals of CPUs and facilitate *MagneComm* with one-way communication, full-duplex communication, and multi-transmitter schemes in accordance with the hardware availability on devices. We prototype *MagneComm* on both laptops and smartphones. Extensive evaluation results show that *MagneComm* achieves up to 110 *bps* within 10 *cm*.

CCS CONCEPTS

• **Human-centered computing → Mobile computing; Ubiquitous and mobile computing systems and tools;** • **Security and privacy →** *Mobile and wireless security;*

KEYWORDS

near-field communication; magnetic induction; full-duplex

MobiCom '17, October 16-20, 2017, Snowbird, UT, USA

ACM ISBN 978-1-4503-4916-1/17/10...$15.00
https://doi.org/.1145/3117811.3117824

1 INTRODUCTION

Near-field communication (NFC) has been attracting considerable attention in recent years as it is facilitating a wide range of applications, including mobile payment, social networks, interactive gaming and etc. Nowadays, even the NFC module is integrated on major-brand smartphones, there is still a large portion of them without NFC due to the stringent requirement of NFC chips. Current NFC implementation is based on the ISO-13157 [19] standard which requires dedicated hardware, i.e. the NFC chip module consisting of an antenna and electric circuits for coding and decoding. The need for NFC chip, however, incurs extra costs and enlarges volume to size-limited smarthones and therefore greatly limits the applicability of NFC. On the other hand, even for NFC-capable devices, the NFC function is sometimes limited, e.g., NFC on iPhones only supports Apple Pay.

A number of alternative methods have been devised to alleviate the pain brought by the standard NFC implementation. Typical examples are Bluetooth, acoustic [15, 27], visible light [17, 21, 25] and etc. Most of these approaches rely on commodity hardware or built-in sensors. Among them, Bluetooth is a popular technique and applied for short-range communication on mobile devices. However, existing alternative implementations of NFC also face problems. First, they are vulnerable to security issues. For example, Bluetooth works in a relatively longer communication range than the standard NFC and it is easy for attackers to eavesdrop the transmitted information. Second, the communication channels endure noise and interference, *e.g.*, Bluetooth is easily interfered with WiFi signals, not to mention the acoustic and the visible-light approaches. Therefore, existing alternative NFC implementations fail to satisfy both the security and performance requirements.

In this paper, we try to provide an NFC implementation scheme without dedicated hardware while keeping the security and performance concerns in mind. We adopt Magnetic Induction (MI) signal emitted from mobile devices as a communication channel and exploit the build-in magnetometer for signal reception. Specifically, we elaborately control the CPU module for transmission of MI signals, and the magnetometers equipped on commodity mobile devices for signal decoding. By carefully regulating the MI signals emitted from CPUs, and sensing it with the magnetometers on devices, two devices are able to communicate in a near-field manner. We develop this concept into a full-duplex communication system (referred to as *MagneComm*) using techniques such as pulse width and

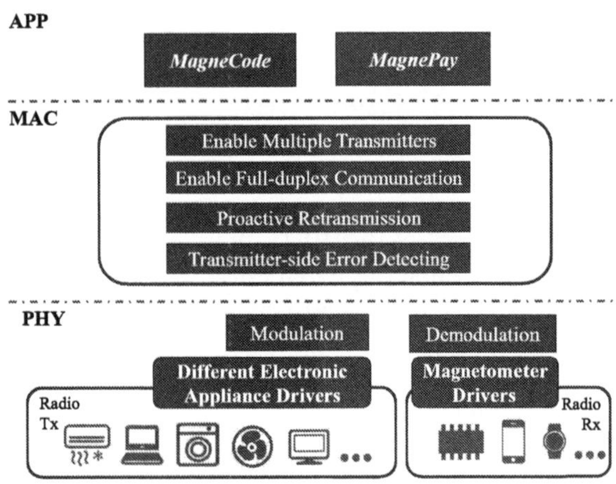

Figure 1: MagneComm Architecture.

amplitude modulation, channel estimation, proactive retransmission, and self-signal cancellation. The overall architecture of MagneComm is shown in Fig. 1 from a layered perceptive.

The design of MagneComm poses a number of difficult challenges. First, precise control over CPU by job scheduling in operation systems (OS) to generate suitable MI signals is complicated. With this constraint, complex modulation schemes, such as OFDM (orthogonal frequency division multiplexing) are essentially infeasible. We first investigate the characteristics of MI signals from extensive experiments and finally combine the pulse width with amplitude modulation as the fundamental modulation scheme to strike a balance between transmission speed and accuracy. Second, concurrent running jobs on CPUs bring about interference during the transmission process, and thus increase confusion when detecting CPU's MI signals. To guarantee the quality of transmission in noisy environments, we design a preamble for signal detection and and a retransmission scheme. The retransmission scheme monitors the real-time CPU usage and the bit error distribution, and retransmits the previous corrupted packet if necessary. Third, to overcome the low sampling rate of the magnetometers on mobile devices, we adopt multiple transmitters in order to improve the transmission rate. We also exploit signal cancellation technique and design a subtraction algorithm to realize full-duplex communication, when both the two devices are equipped with magnetometers.

We implement the MagneComm prototype and evaluate the communication between laptops and smartphones, as well as between two laptops. The coded MI signals can be successfully captured and decoded by the magnetometers on smartphones and laptops. When MagneComm is applied between two laptops, a self-signal cancellation algorithm is applied at the terminal of the transmitter to counterbalance MI signals from its own CPU, thereby enabling dual-duplex communication. In our experiments, MagneComm is able to achieve throughput of up to 110 *bps* in average between two laptops, 12 *bps* between a laptop and a smartphone. Our prototype supports an operating range of up to 10 centimeters between devices.

MagneComm can flourish abundant applications. For example, the designed MagneCode built upon MagneComm can enable an extended screen to obtain more information on mobile devices. The details of applications and their implementations are discussed in Sec. 7. The main contribution of this work can be summarized as follows:

- We propose MagneComm, a novel implementation scheme of NFC which eliminates the need for dedicated hardware by embedding data stream into the MI signals of a CPU without affecting the normal function of the device.
- A variety of communication schemes are devised using this system, including one-way, full-duplex and multiple transmitter communication to take full advantage of the functionality of the communication devices.
- We prototype the communication system between a laptop and a smartphone as well as between two laptops. Evaluation results demonstrate the efficacy of MagneComm.

The rest of this paper is organized as follows: In Sec. 2, we introduce the working principle of the magnetometer and CPU. In Sec. 3, we outline the characteristics of the MI signals generated by CPUs. In Sec. 4, we present the proposed transmission and reception protocols. The prototypes on smartphones and laptops are described in Sec. 5 and evaluations are described in Sec. 6. Future implementations of the proposed system are outlined in Sec. 7. Conclusions are drawn in Sec. 9.

2 BACKGROUND

In this section, we outline the working principle of magnetometers and the emission of Magnetic Induction (MI) signals from laptops. These are the fundamental issues related to the design of MagneComm.

2.1 Magnetometer

A magnetometer is an instrument that measures the magnetization of materials or the strength and direction of the magnetic field at a point in space. The most common magnetic sensors are Hall effect sensors and fluxgate sensors. Hall effect sensors are small and cheap while the sensitivity is low ($\leq 5mV/mT$). They are commonly employed with the gyroscopes and accelerometers used for motion tracking in mobile devices. As illustrated in Fig. 2(a), the voltage develops in a direction transverse to the current flow in p-type semiconductor in a magnetic field owing to Lorentz Force [16]. Hall effect magnetometers utilize the varying output voltage as the indicator to the magnetic field.

Fluxgate magnetometers provide greater sensitivity than Hall effect sensors. They are commonly used to measure DC or high-frequency magnetic field vectors. A fluxgate sensor employs a saturable inductor to sense the field produced by an external current. As shown in Fig. 2(b), a fluxgate magnetic sensor comprises a fluxgate sensor (sensing coil) with sensor conditioning and a compensation coil to internally close the control loop. The fluxgate sensor is repeatedly driven in and out of saturation, thereby enabling hysteresis-free operation with a high degree of accuracy. The internal compensation coil ensures stable gain and high linearity.

In this study, in additional to using built-in Hall effect magnetometers in mobile devices, we also employ a high-performance

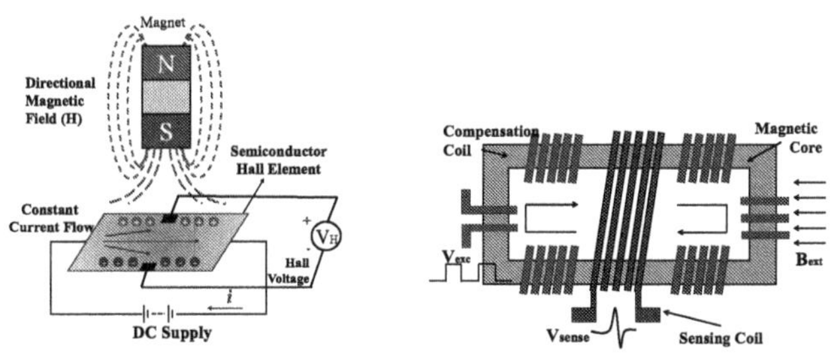

(a) Hall effect sensor. (b) Fluxgate sensor.

Figure 2: The working principle of two types of magnetometers.

fluxgate sensor, DRV425 from TI [7], to understand the impact of various magnetometers. The output analog signals from DRV425 are sampled by an ADC chip (ADC7606) controlled through STM32F107 Microcontroller Unit. The sampling rate of the ADC is set to $10KHz$ with 12-bit output resolution (up to $0.15nT$ per bit). Although higher sampling rates (up to $50KHz$) are possible, Magnetic Induction signals from the CPU presents little between $10KHz$ and $50KHz$ so a higher sampling rate would only increase the burden of data analysis without providing any benefit.

2.2 Magnetic Induction from Laptops

A laptop is a complex device with numerous electronic units, such as a CPU, GPU, electronic fan, speaker, hard disk, and battery. Theoretically, any of these units could be used to generate Magnetic Induction signals. By carefully controlling the working pattern of these units, we can embed a data stream in the generated MI signals. For example, the normal working power of a CPU ranges from 20 to $90W$. As shown in Fig. 3(a), the strength of Magnetic Induction signals can be adjusted by controlling the usage of the CPU. In addition, electronic fans consume around $3W$ power. Fig. 3(b) presents MI signals generated by a computer fan in the form of sine waves. Controlling the rotation speed of the fan to vary the phases and frequencies of these sine waves makes it possible to embed information in the MI signals.

Despite the multiple choices, we focus primarily on the Magnetic Induction signals generated by CPUs in this work. One advantage of using CPUs is that CPU usage can be easily controlled using loop and *sleep* commands, which are available for most programming languages and operating systems. In contrast, for example, controlling the fan may require specific drivers or APIs and is only supported by a few programming languages. Furthermore, it is easier to monitor CPU usage in real-time in order to estimate channel conditions. Finally, the multiple cores in a CPU can be used to design a multiple-transmitter communication protocol. The details of the protocols are discussed in Section 4.

3 MAGNETIC INDUCTION FROM CPU

The precise control over CPUs and emitted Magnetic Induction (MI) signals is the key to realize MagneComm. In this section,

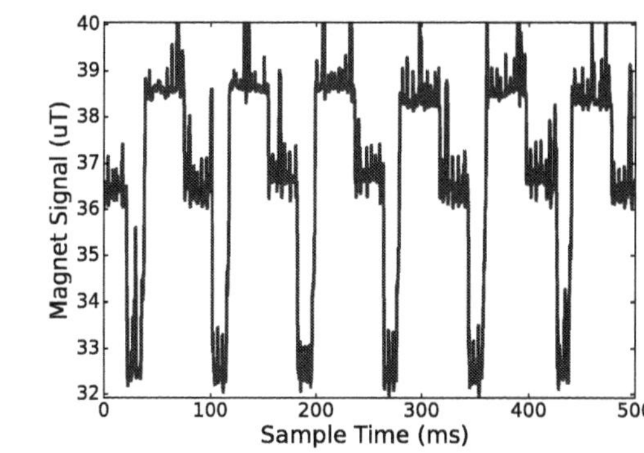

(a) CPU.

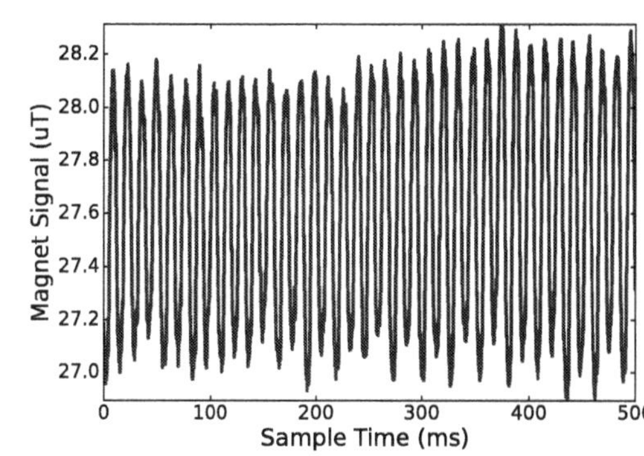

(b) Fan.

Figure 3: Magnetic Induction siganls emitted from CPU and fan.

we investigate the characteristics of the MI signals from CPUs and explore the design space of modulating data bits.

3.1 Characteristics

MI signals generated from a CPU are affected by many factors.

Multi-core CPU: multi-core CPUs (*i.e.*, CPUs with two or more independent processing units, called "cores") are common in recent mobile devices. Multiple cores make it possible to run multiple instructions in parallel. Unless otherwise specified in the program or OS, a program with multiple threads may attempt to use all of the cores at once. The fact that each core emits its own MI signals means that the MI signals from a CPU is actual the superposition of all of the cores.

CPU working status: different instructions can lead to different patterns in the MI signals, which can be identified by magnetometers with a high sampling rate (> $1.7\ MHz$) [8]. The sampling rate of the magnetometers used in most mobile devices ranges from 10 to $200\ Hz$. Based on experiment results, this type of magnetometer is able to determine whether a CPU is working or idle, but little else. As shown in Fig. 4, we run a program including four instructions: addition (+), subtraction (-), multiplication (*), division (/), and then a command for *sleep*. Omitting the glitch signal leaves only two levels of

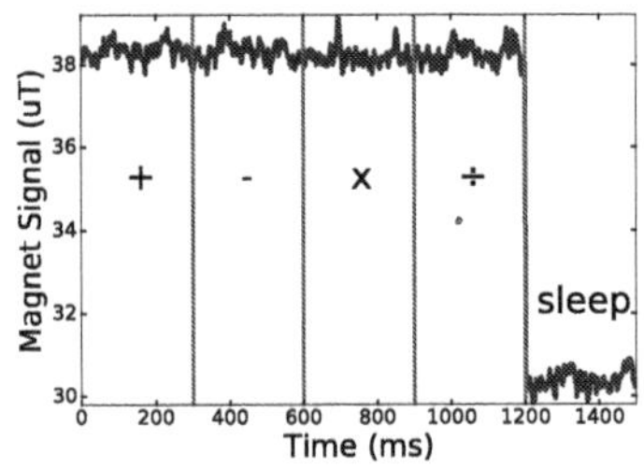

Figure 4: Emitted MI signals while CPU executing various instructions.

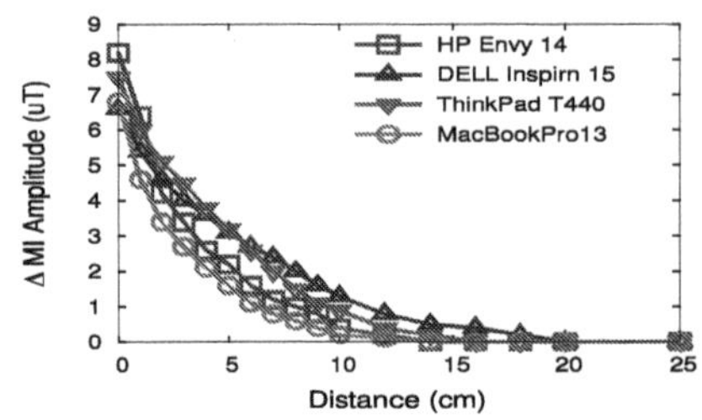

Figure 5: The amplitude change of MI signals of one CPU core at different distances.

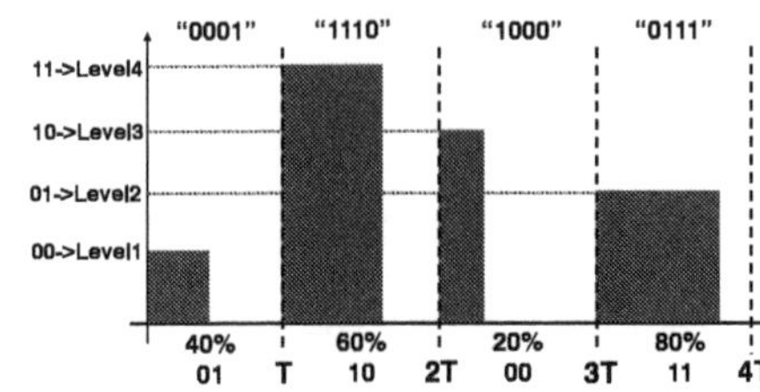

Figure 6: Example of PWAM data symbols.

magnitude in the MI signals, corresponding to the status of the machine (working and idle).

Distance: the magnitude of the MI signal is inversely proportional to the cube of the distance traveled. Furthermore, the material with which the case of the mobile device is constructed may also affect the magnitude, due to the shielding effect. Fig. 5 shows the changes in the magnitude of MI signals over distance, as measured using various types of laptops. At each distance, we measure MI signals when the CPU is in working and idle states, and calculate the magnitude difference between two states. We can see that at distances exceeding $10\ cm$, the magnitude change becomes too small to be distinguished by DRV425 magnetometer with the sensitivity of $0.16\ uT$.

3.2 Controlling Magnetic Induction Signals

In the following, we examine the methods used to control Magnetic Induction and modulate data.

Modulation: regular magnetometers can only measure the working and idle status of a CPU core; therefore, one intuitive way to embed data is to use On-Off Keying. That is, we switch a CPU core between idle and working to represent 0 and 1, respectively. For a $200Hz$ magnetometer, switching CPU status every 5ms would enable a data transmission rate of $200bps$. However, in most practical situations, it is difficult to control the CPU in this manner. Furthermore, On-Off keying is subject to noise generated by background programs.

We therefore selected Pulse Width and Amplitude Modulation (PWAM) which combines the Pulse Width Modulation (PWM) and Pulse Amplitude Modulation (PAM) to modulate data. Specifically, each data symbol has period T and is presented using the proportion of CPU working time during that period. A data symbol consists of $M+N$ data bits, where M bits are translated to a set of pre-defined 2^M levels of amplitude of CPU magnetic induction signals (PAM), N bits are translated to a set of pre-defined 2^N levels of CPU working percentage (PWM). Take Fig. 6 as an example, each data symbol is 30ms long and consists of 4 bits. The amplitude of each symbol could be $1, 4, 3, 2$ which represents data bits: 00, 11, 10 and 01. The CPU working percentage of each symbol could be 40%, 60%, 20%, 80% which represents bits: 01, 10, 01 and 11, respectively. We can adjust T, M and N according to the current channel condition as well as how precise we can control a CPU core.

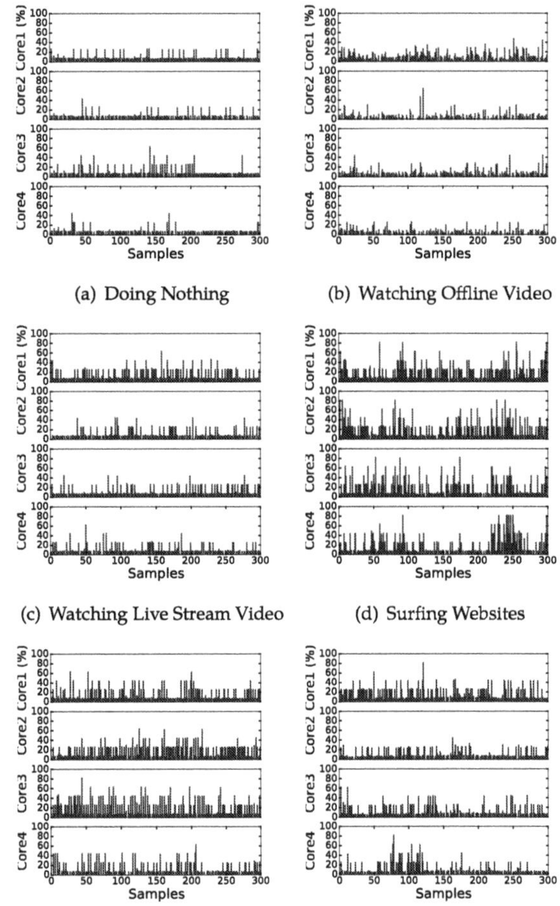

(a) Doing Nothing (b) Watching Offline Video

(c) Watching Live Stream Video (d) Surfing Websites

(e) Playing Games (f) Using Office Word

Figure 7: CPU usage of each core recorded every $50ms$ under various conditions.

Multiple cores: modern OSes optimize the scheduling of tasks specifically for multi-core CPUs to ensure efficiency in the execution of commands. The OS maintains queues of global tasks, which can be assigned to any core with free resources. In controlling specific CPU cores to generate a desired magnetic signal, processor affinity [26] can be used to bind a given process to a specific CPU core. As shown in Fig. 3(a), multiple cores can be used to generate the same PWAM symbols in order to increase transmission range, or generate different PWAM symbols for parallel communication. Most operating

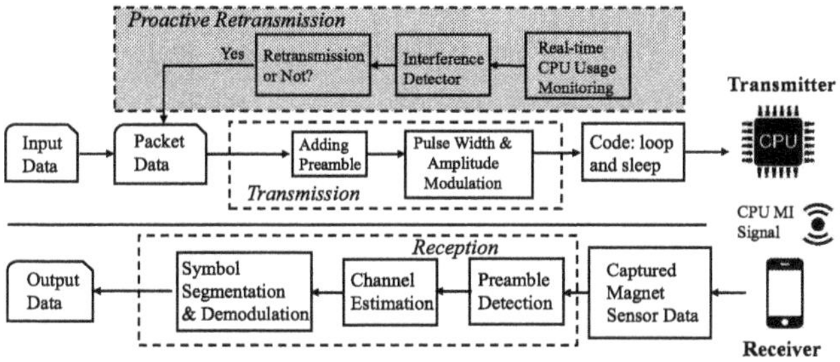

Figure 8: MagneComm operation flow.

systems feature processor affinity. In our prototype, we implemented it in Windows 7, 8, 10, Ubuntu14, MacOS X, and Android 6 and 7.

3.3 Noise from Running Programs

It is inevitable that the CPU will be used by the user and/or the OS during the transmission of data. CPU usage from other programs introduces noise to the signals used for communication. We seek to characterize this noise by collecting traces of MI signals while a user performs various activities, including watching offline videos of various resolutions and various video codecs, watching online streaming content, surfing websites, playing games, as well as doing nothing. Fig. 7 shows the corresponding CPU usage on each core. The CPU usage patterns vary little while watching videos and streaming, regardless of the resolution and codec. Thus, this data has been omitted due to space limitations. It is observed that when the computer is not used, the OS continues accessing the CPU for brief periods in the processing of background apps. This indicates that a mechanism is required for the detection of packet corruption and the retransmission of data due to the interference. We also observed that watching videos and streaming only occasionally increase the CPU usage, whereas surfing websites and playing games greatly affect CPU usage. Nonetheless, even for CPU intensive operations, there are numerous intervals of low CPU usage, which could be used for communication.

4 TRANSMISSION AND RECEPTION

4.1 System Overview

MagneComm is designed using the off-the-shelf laptops and smartphones. Fig. 8 illustrates the system architecture which comprises of two parts: a sender (*e.g.*, a laptop's CPU) and a receiver (*e.g.*, a smartphone's magnetometer). The sender embeds data with the Magnetic Induction (MI) signals generated by CPU in the laptop. The magnetometer on the phone captures the MI signals and decodes it to extract the transmitted data. The details of each step are described in this section.

4.2 Transmitter Design

MI signals can be generated by controlling the working or idle status of the CPU. In this section, we demonstrate the modulation of data bits while enabling the reliable transmission in the presence of noise caused by other background programs.

4.2.1 Preamble. Preamble is used for two purposes. One is to synchronize the sender and the receiver. An unique MI pattern

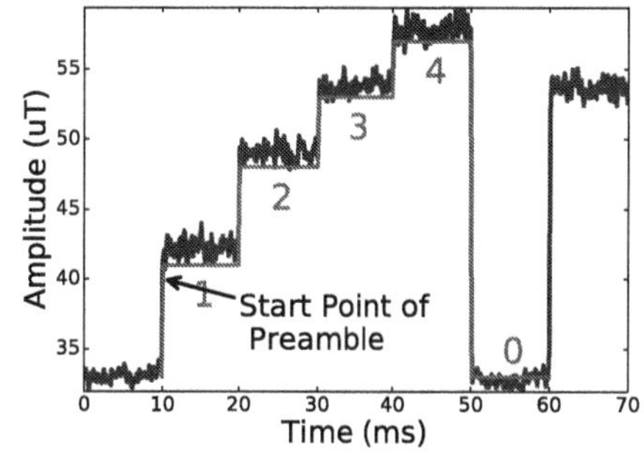

(a) Preamble Design.

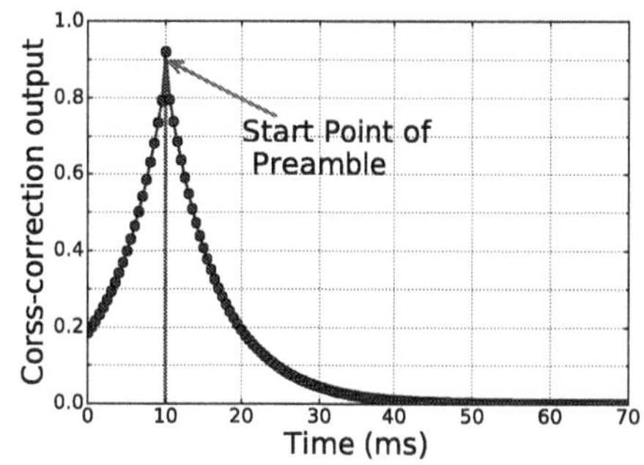

(b) Corss Correlation.

Figure 9: Preamble design and detection.

is introduced as the preamble at the beginning of each data frame, thereby allowing the receiver to use cross-correlation to identify the start time of each transmission. The other purpose is to enable the receiver to estimate channel conditions. Because the amplitude of MI signals varies when a different number of CPU cores are being used as well as under different channel conditions. The receiver must be aware of different amplitude values of a PWAM symbol in order to decode it. As shown in Fig. 9, the preamble is designed as a sequence of $[1, 2, 3, 4, 0]$ using four CPU cores, whose communication parameter M is set as 2. We evaluate the effectiveness of our preamble in Sec. 6.1.

4.2.2 Modulation. We opted for PWAM for the modulation of data bits due to its effectiveness and robustness to noise over On-Off Keying. The choice of T, M and N depends on the precision of controlling and the precision of CPU monitoring.

Single CPU core control precision: Fig. 10(a) shows the single CPU core control precision under various T and N. The control precision is defined as: $Prec_{control} = \frac{|U_{real} - U_{desired}|}{[1/(2^N - 1)]}$, where $U_{desired}$ is the desired CPU core usage, U_{real} is the actual CPU core usage generated, and $1/(2^N - 1)$ is the interval between 2^N levels (*e.g.*, when $N = 2$, the interval between 4 levels of CPU core usage is 33%). The closer the value of $Prec_{control}$ is to 0, the more preciously we can control the CPU cores. And from the Fig. 10(a) we can see that the smaller T and larger N reduces CPU controlling precision. The minimal symbol length T we can choose is $10ms$ with $N = 1$ bit per symbol.

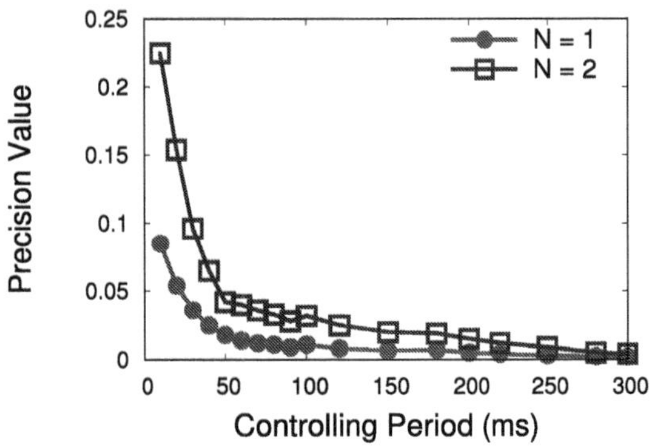

(a) CPU Controlling Error.

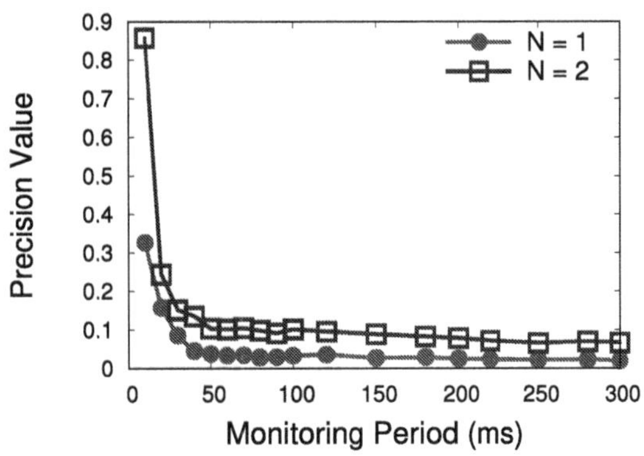

(b) CPU Monitoring Error.

Figure 10: The precision of CPU control and monitor

Single CPU core monitor precision: the transmitter must continuously monitor CPU usage ensure that packets are transmitted correctly. Thus, the precision with which the CPU core usage is monitored also limits the selection of T and N. We use MI measurements as a proxy for CPU usage and define monitoring precision in a similar manner: $Prec_{monitor} = \frac{|U_{sensor} - U_{monitor}|}{[1/(2^N - 1)]}$, where U_{sensor} is the CPU core usage estimated using measured MI signal by sensor, and $U_{monitor}$ is the monitored CPU core usage by OS itself. The results are shown in Fig. 10(b). We can see that the minimal symbol length can be correctly monitored is $20ms$. So after combining the limitation of CPU controlling and monitoring, we will select $T = 20ms, N = 2$ as our fastest transmission rate to modulate the information data bits.

4.2.3 Proactive Retransmission. In the scenarios where only the receiver has the magnetometer, the transmitter is not able to get acknowledgement from the receiver to check if a packet is successfully transmitted. Therefore, a corruption detection mechanism on transmitter is important to enable one-way communication in such scenarios. Fortunately, due to the near-field communication property, the major noise is actually generated by background programs. By continuously monitoring the CPU usage on all cores, the transmitter can know if a packet is corrupted due to the noise. Algorithm 1 shows our Proactive Retransmission mechanism.

Algorithm 1 Proactive retransmission on transmitter.

```
function RETRANSMISSION
    while packet x is sent do
        SymbolNoise_j ← Σ_{core i} Usage_i
        ReFlag_x ← Σ_{symbol j} Rule(SymbolNoise[j])
        if ReFlag_x ≠ 0 then
            Retransmit(packet x)
        else
            Transmit(packet x + 1)
        end if
    end while
end function
```

The transmitter controller monitors the real-time CPU usage on all cores with the same period of PWAM symbols, and after transmitting one packet, it uses the history experience to determine whether existed interfered symbols in the packet. For example, when over two non-transmitter CPU cores have more than 20% usage, the transmitter controller classifies this symbol into the interfered category and $Rule(SymbolNoise[j])$ would be set as 1. Because we did not employ error correction schemes, the transmitter retransmits the whole packet for any corrupted symbol. The throughput can be further improved if erasure coding [22] or partial packet recovery schemes [14] are introduced.

4.3 Receiver Design

The receiver performs preamble detection for use in synchronization and signal strength estimation. Following the segmentation of symbols, they are demodulated for the extraction of data bits.

Preamble Detection: a preamble is used to locate the start of a packet. The receiver applies cross-correlation to locate the preamble pattern accurately, and as mentioned above, channel estimation must be performed prior to the extraction of symbols.

Symbol Segementation: after preamble detection, the data embedded in MI signals can be accurately located. The receiver can easily segment the symbols after preamble with the fixed PWAM length known in advance. And after channel estimation, the receiver determines the amplitude and width information in each symbol, whereupon the original data bits can be recovered.

4.4 Enabling Multiple Transmitters

In wireless communication, multiple-antenna systems are generally known to outperform single-antenna system by increasing the transmission bandwidth and effectively countering the multipath and interference. In *MagneComm*, we employ the same idea and use multi-core CPU to serve as multiple transmitters. For example, in a laptop with the eight-core CPU, one core group consisting of two cores can be treated as the first transmitter, while the other core group consisting of six cores can be treated as the second transmitter. Two core groups can send data concurrently to increase the throughput.

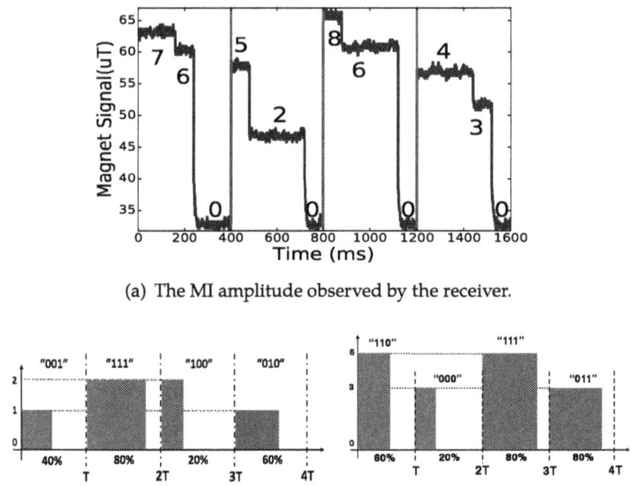

(a) The MI amplitude observed by the receiver.

(b) Transmitter I PWAM symbols. (c) Transmitter II PWAM symbols.

Figure 11: The working principle for multiple transmitters.

In the transmitter, we rely on process affinity for the generation of PWAM symbols using different CPU cores. However, in the receiver, we need a mechanism to distinguish PWAM symbols from different transmitters.

Our solution is based on a simple idea: each transmitter uses different number of CPU cores so the amplitude values of PWAM symbols from different transmitters are different. In the previous example, we allocate two cores to Transmitter one with $M = 2$, so it can generate MI signals with amplitudes $[0, 1, 2]$; we allocate six cores to Transmitter two with $M = 2$, so it generates $[0, 3, 6]$ amplitudes. And the superposition of amplitude values are shown in Table. 1. The mixed MI amplitude corresponds to only one pair <$Tx1$ signal, $Tx2$ signal>. So the receiver can easily to separate the mixed signals into two signals from Table. 1. Fig. 11 shows a two-transmitter example. When two transmitters are transmitting data bits simultaneously, the first transmitter uses two CPU cores to generate PWAM symbols, with the parameters are: $T = 300ms$, $M = 1$ and $N = 2$, and the second transmitter uses six CPU cores with the same parameters. When the receiver receive PWAM symbol, it detects the amplitude level of each period using the preamble signal as reference, and in this condition the preamble is designed as $[1, 2, 3, 4, 5, 6, 7, 8, 0]$. After obtaining the amplitude levels of each symbol, the receiver checks Table. 1 and rebuilds $Tx1$ and $Tx2$ signals to extract data bits separately.

Table 1: MI amplitudes observed by receivers when two transmitters are transmitting concurrently using different number of cores.

Mixed MI Signal	0	1	2	3	4	5	6	7	8
Tx 1 MI Signal	0	1	2	0	1	2	0	1	2
Tx 2 MI Signal	0	0	0	3	3	3	6	6	6

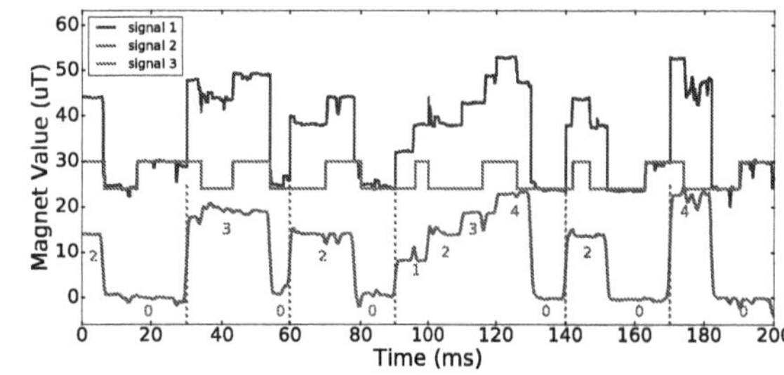

Figure 12: The cancellation principle of full-duplex communication: signal 1 plotted in blue represents the mixed MI signals, signal 2 in red represents the estimated MI signals generated by itself, and signal 3 in green represents the targeted MI signals after cancellation

4.5 Enabling Full-Duplex Communication

Full-duplex communication can be achieved when both mobile devices are equipped with magnetometers (*i.e.*, communication between two mobile phones.) The challenge of enabling full-duplex communication is that, when a mobile device is transmitting and receiving data at the same time, the received PWAM symbol is a linear combination of its own transmitted PWAM symbol and targeted PWAM symbol to decode. Fortunately, since the device knows what it is transmitting and has ability to estimate the amplitude of its own PWAM symbol, the device can subtract the transmitted PWAM symbol from the received one and recover the the targeted PWAM symbol. Fig. 12 shows an example to perform full-duplex communication. Considering that the magnetometers equipped on the smartphones are not sensitive enough to capture the other smartphone CPU's MI signals, we use two laptops both equipped with DRV425 magnet sensors to verify the feasibility of our full-duplex design. Specifically, one laptop sets the transmission parameters to: $T = 30ms$, $M = 0$, $N = 2$, while the other sets it to: $T = 30ms$, $M = 2$, $N = 2$.

5 SYSTEM PROTOTYPE

Two sets of prototypes are implemented to evaluate *MagneComm*.

Prototype I: Laptop and Phone. The first prototype employs transmitters on laptops running Windows, Ubuntu, or MacOS X, while the receiver is an Android phone. Laptops are equipped with Intel Core CPU (4 or 8 cores). The Android phone is a Huawei Nexus 6P equipped with a Hall effect magnetometer operating at a sampling rate of 50 Hz. In this prototype, we implement one-way communication with multiple-transmitter enabled. All experiments in Section 6 are repeated using all laptops.

Prototype II: Laptops with Magnetometers. The second prototype employs transmitters and receivers on two laptops with external magnetometers (DRV425) attached. In this system, we used the same set of laptops that were used in the first prototype. The magnetometer is a fluxgate sensor with sampling rate of 200 KHz. This prototype involves full-duplex communication with multiple-transmitter enabled.

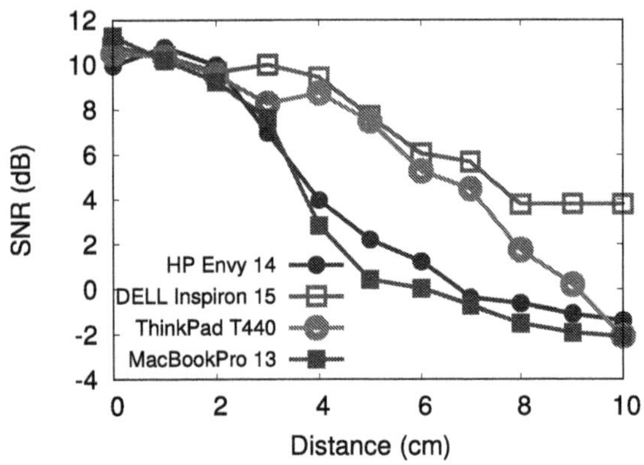

Figure 13: SNR vs. distance using different models of laptops.

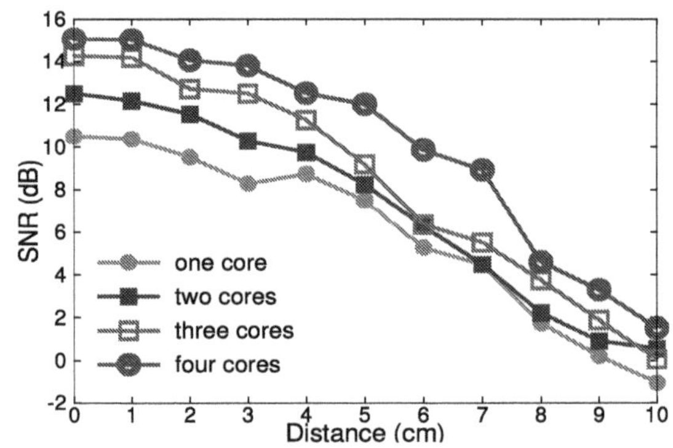

Figure 14: SNR vs. number of working CPU cores.

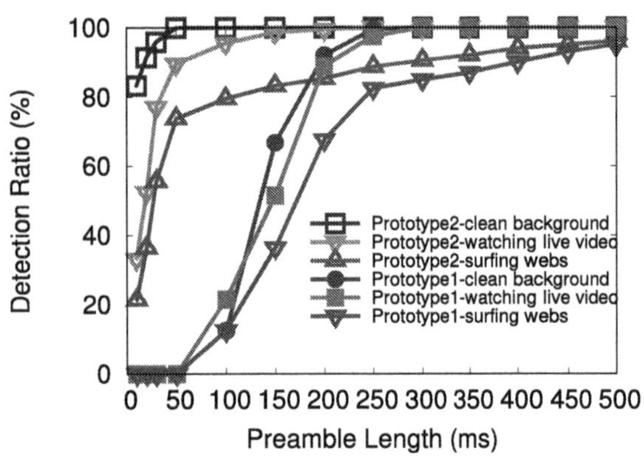

Figure 15: Preamble detection accuracy under various preamble lengths with $M = 2$.

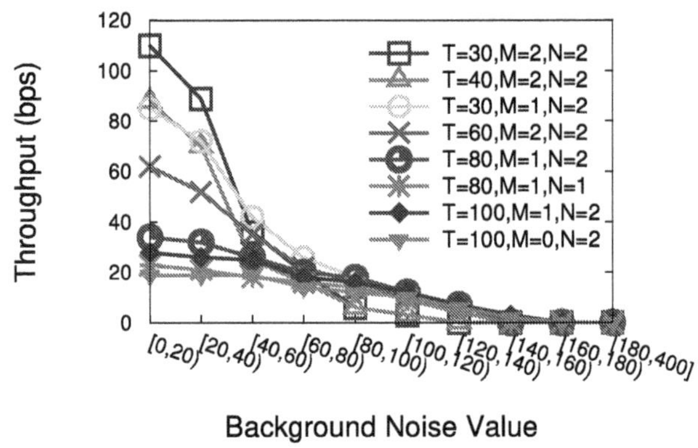

Figure 16: Throughput vs. levels of noise under various symbol length T.

6 EVALUATION

6.1 Micro Benchmark

Communication Distance : we first use Prototype II where two laptops equipped with external magnetometers to examine the valid communication ranges. Fig. 13 shows the SNR under various transmission distances using four different laptops. We can observe that SNR is similar for all laptops when distance is shorter than 3 *cm*. SNR for HP Envy 14 and MacBookPro 13 drops quickly after 3 *cm* while that from DELL Inspiron 15 remains high at 10 *cm*.

We can boost the transmission distance by utilizing multiple CPU cores. As shown in Fig. 14, the more CPUs used, the higher SNR we can get. At the distance of 5 *cm*, increasing the number of CPU cores from 1 to 4 increases SNR by 4 *dB*.

Device Orientation : to verify the impact of the device orientation to the communication, we change the angles of the receiver by 15°, 30°, 45°, 60°, and 75° while being placed at the same location. The results show that the device orientation has no influence to the observed MI signals. It's because that there are three orthogonal magnet sensors on a magnetometer and we calculate the square root of sum of the magnetism from three dimensions so it becomes independent to the device orientation.

Preamble Length : a longer preamble makes it easier to control CPU cores to generate the desired preamble pattern and is more robust against the noise. However, the longer preamble also results in the larger communication overhead. To obtain the best preamble length for MagneComm while background noise exists, we vary the preamble length and use Prototype I and II to test the ratio where preambles are correctly detected. Fig. 15 shows the results. We can see that 80% – 100% of preambles can be correctly detected when the length is 300 *ms* in Prototype I, and 50 *ms* in Prototype II.

PWAM parameters : In Sec. 4.2 we show that the symbol length T needs to be 20 *ms* or longer in order to precisely control and monitor the CPU usage. Nonetheless, channel condition also has impact to the selection of T. A shorter symbol period implies a higher data rate while it can also be more fragile to the noise. To find the best parameters for PWAM modulation, we vary T, M, N under different levels of noise using Prototype II. The level of noise is defined as the CPU usage caused by background programs. Each experiment lasts for 10 minutes. The corresponding throughputs are shown in Fig. 16.

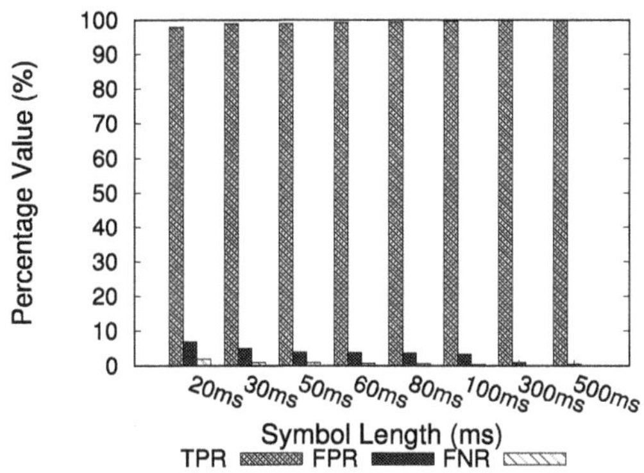

Figure 17: Corruption detection performance on the transmitter.

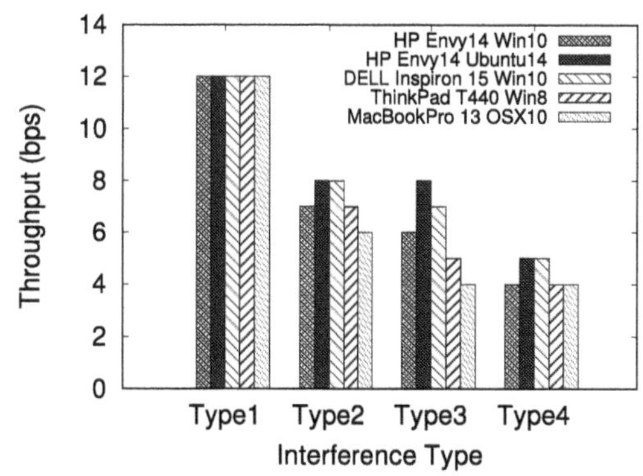

(a) Prototype I: throughput vs. scenarios.

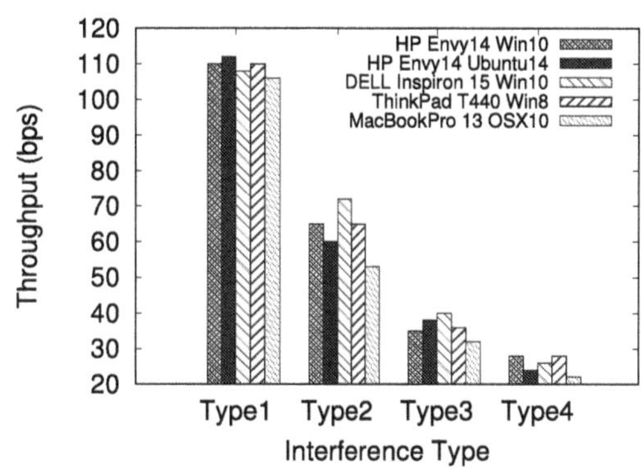

(b) Prototype II: throughput vs. scenarios.

Figure 18: Throughput under various scenarios for one-way communication. In Prototype I, $T = 300ms$, $M = 2$, $N = 2$. In Prototype II, $T = 30ms$, $M = 2$, $N = 2$. All laptops use 4 CPU cores for transmission. Scenario type 1 to 4 correspond to that the user is doing nothing, watching live video, surfing websites, and playing games, respectively.

We can observe that when the noise is small, using shorter symbol period T yields a larger throughput, as expected. When the noise value is 40% or larger, lower data rates with larger T start to out-perform because they can tolerate more noise. The results suggest that we can design a rate adaptation and use a look-up table to decide the best data rate for the current channel condition. We focus on the basic design of *MagneComm* in this work and leave the rate adaptation as the future work.

Corruption Detection from Transmitter: the success of one-way communication relies on that if a transmitter can correctly detect and retransmit corrupted packets. We transmit PWM symbols with T varying from 20 to 500 *ms* and $N = 2$ *bits* for 10 minutes in Prototype II, and evaluate the corruption detection accuracy.

The results are shown in Fig. 17. True Positive Rate (TPR) represents the number of symbols which are actually corrupted and are detected as corrupted to the number of actually corrupted symbol. False Positive Rate (FPR) represents the number of symbols which are correct but are detected as corrupted to the number of actually correct symbol. False Negative Rate (FNR) represents the number of symbols which are actually corrupted but are detected as correct symbol to the number of actually corrupted symbols. We can see that TPR is 99.6% or higher while FNR is 0.5% or lower when the symbol length is 30 *ms* or longer, which indicates that our corruption detection algorithm on transmitter can correctly detect corrupted symbols. Therefore, in our following experiments, we select the 30 *ms* as the fastest transmission rate instead of 20 *ms*.

6.2 One-Way Communication Performance

We evaluate the one-way communication performance using two prototypes described in Sec. 5. In Prototype I where a laptop is the transmitter and the mobile phone (Nexus 6P) is the receiver, PWAM symbol length is set to $200ms$ and each symbol contains 4 bits ($M = N = 2$). In Prototype II where one laptop acts as the transmitter and the other laptop acts as the receiver, the symbol length is set to 30 *ms* and each symbol contains 4 bits ($M = N = 2$). Each experiment lasts for 10 minutes and is repeated for 10 times. The average throughput is reported.

Fig. 18(b) and Fig. 18(a) first show how *MagneComm* perform while using different laptops as transmitters. The 4 laptops have various OSes (Win8, Win10, Ubuntu14 and MacOSX10) and CPU models (Intel i5 with 4 cores and i7 with 8 cores). When there is no other program running, *MagneComm* achieves 12 *bps* in Prototype I and 110 *bps* in Prototype II. While the noise is present, the throughput decreases. For example, while the user is surfing websites, the throughputs drop to 7 *bps* and 60 *bps*, respectively.

Fig. 19(b) and Fig. 19(a) show the throughput under various transmission ranges when there is no background noise. We make several observations. First, the throughput remains high for all types of transmitters when the range is 3 *cm*. Second, due to the SNR drops over distance, the valid communication for all transmitters is 5 *cm* and 8 *cm* for Prototype I and II, respectively. Finally, after 3 *cm*, the throughput of different transmitters varies significantly. More specifically, the throughput of ThinkPad T440 and DELL Inspiron 15 only drops by 26% at the distance of 5 *cm* while that of other laptops drops by more than 60% at the same distance.

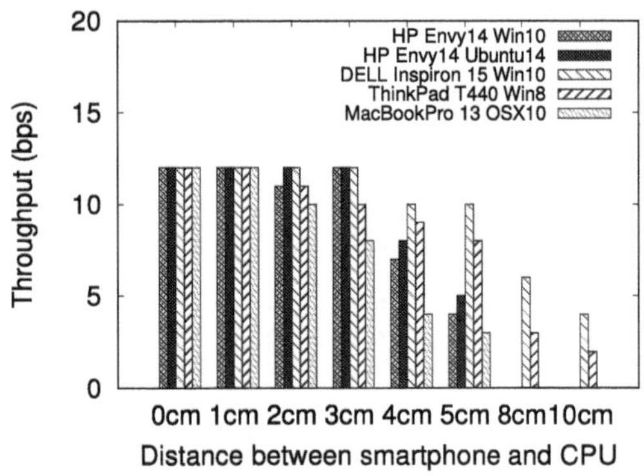

(a) Prototype I: throughput vs. distances.

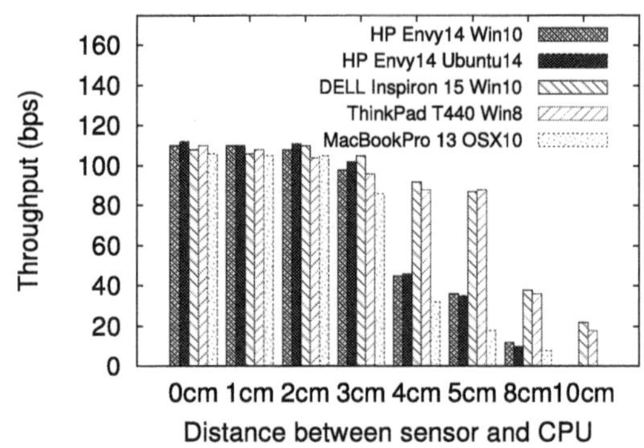

(b) Prototype II: throughput vs. distances.

Figure 19: Throughput under various distances for one-way communication. In Prototype I, $T = 300ms$, $M = 2$, $N = 2$. In Prototype II, $T = 30ms$, $M = 2$, $N = 2$. All laptops use 4 CPU cores for transmission.

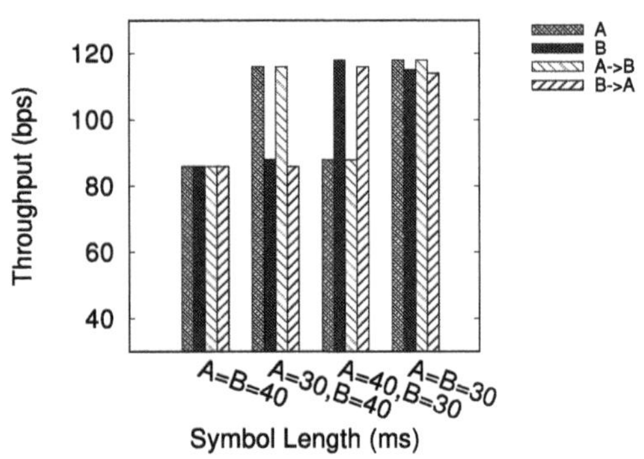

Figure 20: Full-duplex Performance Analysis. A->B means laptop A transmit data to B. Similar definition is also applied to B->A.

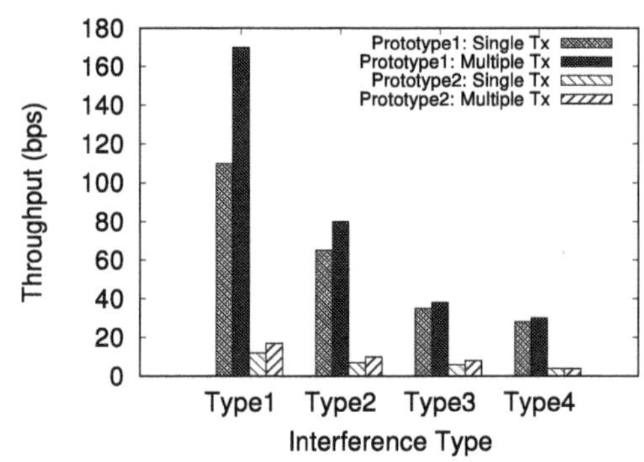

Figure 21: Multiple Transmitters performance analysis. Scenario type 1 to 4 correspond to that when the user is doing nothing, watching live video, surfing websites, and playing games, respectively.

In additional to Prototype I and II, we also implement another prototype where an Android phone acts as the transmitter and a laptop with an external magnetometer acts as the receiver. The Android phone is a Huawei Nexus 6P equipped with a Octa-core CPU, and the laptop is equipped with an external magnetometer. One-way communication is installed in this prototype with the throughput of 95 *bps* and maximal communication range of 4 *cm*. We exclude the details of evaluation due to the page limit.

6.3 Full-Duplex Communication Performance

We evaluate the full-duplex communication performance using Prototype II where two laptops are equipped with magnetometers and transmit data at the same time. Two laptops' CPUs are 3 *cm* away from each other. In Fig. 20, we show the throughput of two transmission directions in full-duplex communication and the throughput in one-way communication. Note that *A* and *B* represents the throughput in one-way communication where *A* and *B* acts as the receiver, respectively. *A->B* represents the throughput in full-duplex communication where *A* transmits data to *B*. We can see that when the total throughput in full-duplex communication (*i.e.*, *A->B* + *A<-B*) is 195.5% of that in one-way communication. It implies that our cancellation mechanism works effectively so the total throughput is almost doubled.

6.4 Multiple Transmitters Performance

We evaluate the performance of Multiple Transmitters protocol using both prototypes under one-way communication. Fig. 21 shows the results. By increasing the number of tx antennas (*i.e.*, the number of cores) from 1 to 2, the throughput is increased by 141.6% and 154.5% in Prototype I and II under the clean background, respectively. In noisy scenarios, the performance of the Multiple Transmitters protocol decreases because using multiple cores increases the risk of being interfered by the noise.

6.5 Energy Consumption

We measure the power consumption of *MagneComm* when HP Envy 14-j 104TX with Intel Core i7 6700HQ CPU acts as the transmitter and DRV425 magnetometer acts as the receiver.

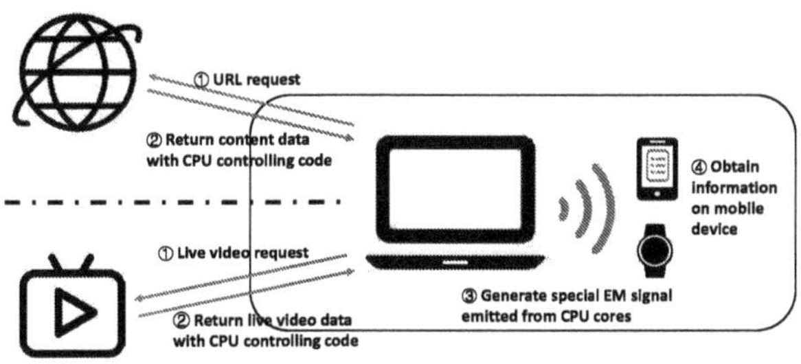

Figure 22: *MagneCode* and Expanded Screen.

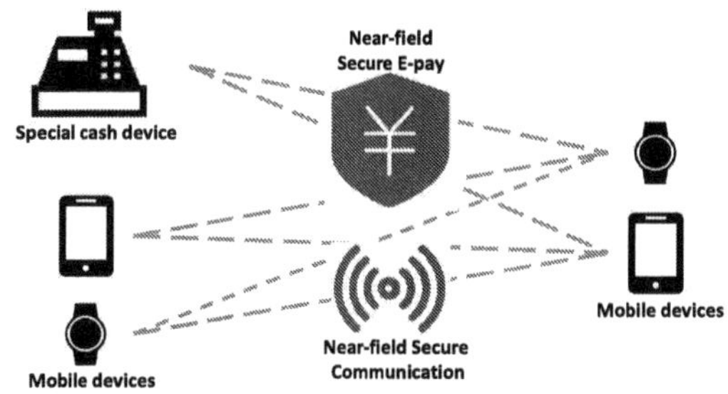

Figure 23: *MagnePay*.

The transmitter uses one core to generate one-way traffic for 1.5 hours. The average power consumption is reported in the Table. 2. For comparison, we also estimated the energy consumption of the Bluetooth 4.0 (BLE) [1], Wi-Fi (IEEE 802.11ac) [24], NFC (ISO-13157) [19], and Pulse [13]. Although the energy consumption of *MagneComm* is higher than other protocols, its capability of providing additional bandwidth using existing hardware is still valuable. Moreover, there are many techniques which can potentially reduce the power consumption of *MagneComm*, which includes using finer granularity of CPU duty cycle, reducing the maximal CPU usage level, applying error correction to improve the throughput, and etc. We leave it as our future work.

Table 2: Energy consumption of various communication protocols.

Protocols	Throughput	Watt	J/bit
BLE	$0.27Mbps$	$0.5W$	1.9×10^{-6}
802.11ac	$350Mbps$	$2.4W$	6.8×10^{-9}
NFC	$424kbps$	$0.6W$	1.4×10^{-6}
Pulse	$44bps$	$8.3 \times 10^{-4}W$	1.9×10^{-5}
MagneComm	$110bps$	$5.2W$	4.8×10^{-2}

7 DISCUSSION AND APPLICATIONS

In this section, we discuss a number of potential applications for *MagneComm*.

7.1 MagneCode & Expanded Screen

When using a laptop or mobile device, it is common nowadays to obtain information using a QRCode; however, this is not always possible when using a smaller mobile device, such as a smart watch, because they may not have a camera. Nonetheless, even the smallest devises are equipped with a magnetometer for e-compass functionality.

A magnetometer can be used to extract data embedded in MI signals. Thus, MagneCode can serve as an alternative to QRCode when camera is not available. As shown in Fig. 22, when a user wants to use a mobile device to obtain additional information, they first request the URL, which returns the controlling code that allows the laptop to generate MagneCode.

Moreover, MagneCode can be used to add background information, such as player statistics or advertisements, to the video content being viewed by the user and shown on an expanded screen without interfering with the original content.

7.2 MagnePay

NFC and RFID are mainstays of the near-field wireless communication systems used for e-commerce. Both of these technologies allow convenient e-payment; however, not all mobile devices are equipped with NFC. Furthermore, most payment cards are suitable for only one payment scenario; that is, unified e-payment systems have yet to be implemented. *MagneComm* technology could be used to fill this vacancy, based on the fact that magnetometers are used in nearly all mobile devices. When NFC and RFID becomes increasingly available, *MagneComm* can still complement them by providing extra bandwidth or empowering those old mobile devices.

Therefore, we propose an unified, safe, and convenient e-payment system called MagnePay. As shown in Fig. 23, we develop a device capable of generating an MI signals specific for businesses. The device can be used to embed business-related information within an MI signals, which can be accessed by customers on a mobile device (smartphone or smartwatch). This could also be used to make payments for friends, wherein one smartphone is used to generate the special MI signals and acts as a transmitter, while the other smartphone acts as a receiver, without the need for any special device.

8 RELATED WORK

Near-field wireless communication has attracted considerable attention due to the richness of the potential applications. Numerous techniques have been developed using a variety of media to enable the communications.

Visual: Visible light communication (VLC) provides over bandwidth 10K x greater than that of the common radio spectra. Due to its directionality and containment, VLC is also a good candidate for near-field communication [17]. In [21], the researchers proposed a novel near-field communication system for smartphones based on visible light, wherein data is encoded using different colors. Unfortunately, VLC generates redundant light pollution and its line of sight characteristics means that it cannot pass through obstacles. [25] presented a method by which to use VLC in dark environments; however, the LED drivers currently available are unable to modulate data bits into light pulse, and replacing existing LEDs would be very expensive.

Quick Response Codes (QRCodes) and other 2D barcodes, also belong to visual near-field communication. QRCodes are widely used in advertising and payments. Strata [11] proposed a layered coding scheme to enable visual communications and improve the scalability of QRCodes. Strata can dynamically adjust the transmission rates corresponding to a diversity of operating conditions, such as camera resolution and frame rates. Unfortunately, camera sensors are still not available on most wearable mobile devices. Moreover, the information embedded in QRCodes is fixed, and does not support streaming.

Vibration: Ripple [18, 23] explored the possibility of using physical vibrations as a mode of wireless communication. When implemented on two mobile devices in which the transmitter regulated vibrations and the receiver sensed them using accelerometers, Ripple achieved data transmission rates of 80bps on Android smartphones [23]. Ripple II [18] featured a redesigned receiver and the microphone is used to sense vibrations. Following the application of OFDM to the design of the physical layer, Ripple II achieved a transmission rate of 30Kbps. An ideal application of vibration communication would be in the development of body networks, where human bone could be used to transfer vibration signals. Unfortunately, in other scenarios, noise caused by the vibration limits applicability.

Audio: Acoustic communication over speaker-microphone links has also been explored for near-field communication. Dolphin [27] is a real-time acoustic-based dual-channel communication system in which a speaker is used as a transmitter and microphones are used as receivers. Data signals can be embedded within the original audio signal (as with the audio signal of TV shows), without any perceived difference in the original audio signal. This method has achieved data transmission rates of 500bps on smartphones. In [15], a near-ultrasound communication system was developed using the speakers of TVs and the microphone on a smartphone. This system is able to transmit data at 15 bps in a typical TV-watching environment.

Magnet: NFC Standards are mature short-range communication technologies based on magnetic induction. These systems rely on near-field coupling (approximately 5cm) without the need for a discovery mechanism. NFC can achieve data rates of up to 424kbps. Pulse [13] is a system that avoids the need for specialized hardware on the receiver. Rather, it uses two solenoids as transmitters (generating a modulated magnetic signal), and the magnetometer on mobile phones are used to decode the magnetic signals. The key advantage of Pulse is its use of a magnetometer, which is common on current smartphones. Nonetheless, Pulse still requires a purpose-built solenoid for use as a transmitter. A number of commercial products based on magnetic communication, such as LibertyLink docker [28] and FreeLinc's Near Field Magnetic Induction [20], have been implemented in situations requiring a secure and reliable communications channel. However, the need for antennas or coils limits their popularity.

MagneComm enables magnetic communication using components that are already available in almost all mobile devices. Thus, implementation requires only software for the transmitter and receiver. We have also developed a one-way communication protocol for scenarios in which transmitters are not equipped with a magnetometer. *MagneComm* also works in full-duplex mode while making full use of the transmitter hardware.

Other Magnet Application: One of the most common applications for magnet sensing is localization. In [6, 12], features of the Earth's magnetic field were used to implement indoor navigation systems. [12] proposed an unique cloud platform that runs disruptive geomagnetic positioning in its core to accurately pinpoint locations within a building using the magnetometer in smartphones. [6] demonstrated the feasibility of using an array of e-compasses to measure disturbances in the Earth's magnetic field caused by structural steel elements for use in indoor localization applications.

Devices with currents inside their electronic units produce magnetic field is also a well-known fact and explored for many applications. [9, 10, 29, 30] utilize magnetometers to track Electromagnetic changes emitted from different CPU operations and infer private information. Finexus [4] and uTrack [3] proposed to use the change in magnetic field to track motions of multiple fingertips. DOSE [5] used time-varying electromagnetic interference to monitor the operating states of appliance and infer human activities. uTouch [2] enabled touch interaction on a non-touch LCD by sensing electromagnetic interference when a user brings their hand near or touches the LCD's front panel. These applications are different from our work and focus on utilizing magnetic field in security domain or explore the usage for human-computer interaction.

9 CONCLUSION

In this paper, we present a novel approach for near-field communication using Magnetic Induction signals. The proposed system, called *MagneComm*, is implemented on laptops and smartphones. Systematic analysis of the characteristics of MI signals emitted from the CPU opens the door to using independent CPU cores to transmit data. *MagneComm* can be used for one-way communication with proactive retransmission to ensure the reliability of communication. It can also be used for full-duplex communication as long as the transmitter and receiver are both equipped with a magnetometer and both have the ability to generate an MI signal. The efficacy of this approach is demonstrated in experiments where *MagneComm* achieves throughput of $110\ bps$ over a distance of up to $10\ cm$ between devices. Between a laptop computer and smart phone, we achieve throughput of $12\ bps$. *MagneComm* complements existing near-field communication protocols with dedicated hardware by providing additional bandwidth. In the future, we will focus on boosting data rate with sophisticated data modulation and rate adaptation schemes, as well as developing the wide range of applications to which the *MagneComm* system could be applied.

Acknowledgements

We are grateful to our shepherd Swarun Kumar and anonymous reviewers for their constructive feedback. This work was supported by NSFC grant 61572324, Shanghai Talent Development Fund, and Fundamental Research Funds for the Central Universities 2017QNA4017.

REFERENCES

[1] Bluetooth Low Energy 2017. Bluetooth 4.0 BLE. (2017). https://en.m.wikipedia.org/wiki/Bluetooth_Low_Energy.

[2] K. Chen, G. A. Cohn, S. Gupta, and S. N. Patel. 2013. uTouch: Sensing Touch Gestures on Unmodified LCDs. In *Proceedings of the SIGCHI Conference on Human Factors in Computing Systems (CHI '13)*. ACM, New York, NY, USA, 2581–2584. https://doi.org/10.1145/2470654.2481356

[3] K. Chen, K. Lyons, S. White, and S. Patel. 2013. uTrack: 3D Input Using Two Magnetic Sensors. In *Proceedings of the 26th Annual ACM Symposium on User Interface Software and Technology (UIST '13)*. ACM, New York, NY, USA, 237–244. https://doi.org/10.1145/2501988.2502035

[4] K. Chen, S. N. Patel, and S. Keller. 2016. Finexus: Tracking Precise Motions of Multiple Fingertips Using Magnetic Sensing. In *Proceedings of the 2016 CHI Conference on Human Factors in Computing Systems (CHI '16)*. ACM, New York, NY, USA, 1504–1514. https://doi.org/10.1145/2858036.2858125

[5] K. Y. Chen, S. Gupta, E. C. Larson, and S. Patel. 2015. DOSE: Detecting user-driven operating states of electronic devices from a single sensing point. In *2015 IEEE International Conference on Pervasive Computing and Communications (PerCom)*. 46–54. https://doi.org/10.1109/PERCOM.2015.7146508

[6] J. Chung, M. Donahoe, C. Schmandt, I. Kim, P. Razavai, and M. Wiseman. 2011. Indoor Location Sensing Using Geo-magnetism. In *Proceedings of the 9th International Conference on Mobile Systems, Applications, and Services (MobiSys '11)*. ACM, 141–154.

[7] DRV425 2016. Integrated Fluxgate Magnetic Sensor IC for Open-Loop Applications. (2016). https://www.ti.com/product/DRV425.

[8] D. Genkin, L. Pachmanov, I. Pipman, and E. Tromer. 2015. Stealing Keys from PCs Using a Radio: Cheap Electromagnetic Attacks on Windowed Exponentiation.. In *CHES (Lecture Notes in Computer Science)*, Vol. 9293. Springer, 207–228.

[9] D. Genkin, I. Pipman, and E. Tromer. 2015. Get your hands off my laptop: physical side-channel key-extraction attacks on PCs - Extended version. *J. Cryptographic Engineering* 5, 2 (2015), 95–112. http://dblp.uni-trier.de/db/journals/jce/jce5.html#GenkinPT15

[10] W. Gu, Z. Yang, L. Shangguan, X. Ji, and Y. Zhao. 2014. ToAuth: Towards Automatic Near Field Authentication for Smartphones. In *2014 IEEE 13th International Conference on Trust, Security and Privacy in Computing and Communications*. 229–236. https://doi.org/10.1109/TrustCom.2014.34

[11] W. Hu, J. Mao, Z. Huang, Y. Xue, J. She, K. Bian, and G. Shen. 2014. Strata: Layered Coding for Scalable Visual Communication. In *Proceedings of the 20th Annual International Conference on Mobile Computing and Networking (MobiCom '14)*. ACM, 79–90.

[12] IndoorAtlas 2017. IndoorAtlas. (2017). http://www.indooratlas.com.

[13] W. Jiang, D. Ferreira, J. Ylioja, J. Goncalves, and V. Kostakos. 2014. Pulse: Low Bitrate Wireless Magnetic Communication for Smartphones. In *Proceedings of the 2014 ACM International Joint Conference on Pervasive and Ubiquitous Computing (UbiComp '14)*. ACM, 261–265.

[14] H. Balakrishnan K. Jamieson. 2007. PPR: partial packet recovery for wireless networks. In *ACM SIGCOMM Computer Communication Review*. ACM, 409–429.

[15] S. Ka, T. H. Kim, J. Y. Ha, S. H. Lim, S. C. Shin, J. W. Choi, C. Kwak, and S. Choi. 2016. Near-ultrasound Communication for TV's 2Nd Screen Services. In *Proceedings of the 22Nd Annual International Conference on Mobile Computing and Networking (MobiCom '16)*. ACM, 42–54.

[16] Lorentz force 2017. Lorentz force. (2017). https://en.wikipedia.org/wiki/Lorentz_force.

[17] M. Kavehrad N. Chi, H. Haas and T.D. Little. 2015. Visible light communications: demands factors, benefits and opportunities. In *IEEE Wireless Communications*.

[18] R.R. Choudhury N. Roy. 2016. Ripple II: Faster Communication through Physical Vibration. In *13th USENIX Symposium on Networked Systems Design and Implementation (NSDI 15)*. USENIX Association.

[19] NFC ISO 13157 2017. NFC ISO 13157. (2017). https://en.wikipedia.org/wiki/Near_field_communication.

[20] NFMI 2017. NFMI by FreeLinc. (2017). http://www.freelinc.com/technology.

[21] J. Niu, W. Song, C. Liu, L. Shu, and C. Chen. 2014. NECAS: Near field communication system for smartphones based on visible light. In *IEEE Wireless Communications and Networking Conference, WCNC 2014, Istanbul, Turkey, April 6-9, 2014*. 2426–2431.

[22] Luigi Rizzo. 1997. Effective erasure codes for reliable computer communication protocols. In *ACM SIGCOMM Computer Communication Review*. ACM, 24–36.

[23] N. Roy, M. Gowda, and R. R. Choudhury. 2015. Ripple: Communicating through Physical Vibration. In *12th USENIX Symposium on Networked Systems Design and Implementation (NSDI 15)*. USENIX Association, Oakland, CA, 265–278.

[24] P. P. Inamdar S. K. Saha, P. Deshpande. 2015. Power-throughput tradeoffs of 802.11n/ac in smartphones. In *IEEE Conference on Computer Communications (INFOCOM)*. IEEE.

[25] K. Wright T. Zhao and Z. Xia. 2016. The DarkLight Rises: Visible Light Communication in the Dark. In *In Proc. of MobiCom*.

[26] TMurgent Technologies. 2003. *White Paper: Processor Affinity*. TMurgent Technologies.

[27] Q. Wang, K. Ren, M. Zhou, T. Lei, D. Koutsonikolas, and L. Su. 2016. Messages Behind the Sound: Real-time Hidden Acoustic Signal Capture with Smartphones. In *Proceedings of the 22Nd Annual International Conference on Mobile Computing and Networking (MobiCom '16)*. ACM, 29–41.

[28] Dan Wolfson. 2003. The LibertyLink Docker Wireless Headset. *Computing Unplugged* (December 2003).

[29] A. Zajic and M. Prvulovic. 2014. Experimental Demonstration of Electromagnetic Information Leakage From Modern Processor-Memory Systems. *IEEE Transactions on Electromagnetic Compatibility* 56, 4 (Aug 2014), 885–893. https://doi.org/10.1109/TEMC.2014.2300139

[30] Z. Zhu, H. Pan, Y. Chen, X. Ji, F. Zhang, and C. You. 2016. MagAttack: Remote App Sensing with Your Phone. In *Proceedings of the 2016 ACM International Joint Conference on Pervasive and Ubiquitous Computing: Adjunct (UbiComp '16)*. ACM, New York, NY, USA, 241–244. https://doi.org/10.1145/2968219.2971404

PassiveVLC: Enabling Practical Visible Light Backscatter Communication for Battery-free IoT Applications

Xieyang Xu†, Yang Shen†, Junrui Yang♯, Chenren Xu†, Guobin Shen§, Guojun Chen†, Yunzhe Ni†*

†Peking University ♯Stanford University §Zepp Labs, Inc.
{xy.xu, sy2006, chenren, leochan, yunzhe.ni}@pku.edu.cn jackiey@stanford.edu jackyshen@zepplabs.com

ABSTRACT

This paper investigates the feasibility of practical backscatter communication using visible light for battery-free IoT applications. Based on the idea of modulating the light retroreflection with a commercial LCD shutter, we effectively synthesize these off-the-shelf optical components into a sub-*mW* low power visible light passive transmitter along with a retroreflecting uplink design dedicated for power constrained mobile/IoT devices. On top of that, we design, implement and evaluate PassiveVLC, a novel visible light backscatter communication system. PassiveVLC system enables a battery-free tag device to perform passive communication with the illuminating LEDs over the same light carrier and thus offers several favorable features including battery-free, sniff-proof, and biologically friendly for human-centric use cases. Experimental results from our prototyped system show that PassiveVLC is flexible with tag orientation, robust to ambient lighting conditions, and can achieve up to 1 *kbps* uplink speed. Link budget analysis and two proof-of-concept applications are developed to demonstrate PassiveVLC's efficacy and practicality.

CCS CONCEPTS

• **Hardware** → **Wireless devices**; • **Computer systems organization** → *Embedded systems*;

KEYWORDS

Visible Light Communication, Passive Communication, Backscatter, Battery-free, Internet of Things, Retroreflector

1 INTRODUCTION

The grand vision of Internet-of-Things (IoT) – bring everything to the Internet to better sense, understand and actuate the real world – is turning into reality at a quick pace. Indeed, most new generation of devices, ranging from externally powered home appliances [6, 32], mobile objects with large batteries [4], to miniature implantable sensors [42], thin and flexible wearables [15, 35], *etc.*, have claimed "IoT-capable". However, to fully realize the IoT vision, far larger amount of smart devices are yet to be deployed. Such devices are likely to be of small form factor, wireless communication and untethered when operating. Thus, energy consumption naturally becomes an obstacle. Analysis reveals that communication takes a significant portion of the overall energy consumption for typical IoT sensing devices. In consequence, how to enable extremely energy efficient wireless communication has become an active research front.

Recently, research efforts have shown that radio backscatter communication [23, 50] can effectively offer near zero-power (orders of μW) connectivity to small sensor devices and thus becomes a competitive communication paradigm in the IoT era. The major idea behind radio backscattering is to leverage existing infrastructures, such as TV band [31], FM radio [46] and WiFi channel [11, 22, 23, 49]. Along the line but exploring a different infrastructure – the lighting infrastructure, some previous work have demonstrated the possibility of backscattering the visible light for communications [28, 41].

Using light as the transmission medium, visible light communication (VLC) systems natively possess certain compelling merits, such as sniffing-proof and biological friendliness, over radio communication in human-centric applications. However, it is nontrivial to build a visible light backscatter system. Several issues need to be solved. First of all, in contrast to omni-directional radio propagation, the light is highly directional. While this property contributes to the favorable sniffing-proof feature, it requires precise mutual pointing between two communicating ends, which further demands the system to have accurate (relative) positioning capability and steerable optical components for proper alignment.

Secondly, unlike radio backscatter systems where the antenna coupling is highly efficient for their narrow specific spectrum band, the efficiency of optical coupling is typically very low (*e.g.* usually less than 20% via solar panels) as the visible light takes extremely wide spectrum. Direct optical coupling could neither harvest enough energy (*e.g.* hundreds of μW in indoor environments) to power up a high power LED (typically with hundreds of *mW* budget), nor its on/off state could effectively affect (hence directly modulate) the visible light transmission. Note that optical light concentrating components may help, but, again, it would require precise pointing and additional cost.

RetroVLC [28] solves these issues by exploiting the very nature of a retroreflector, *i.e.* reflecting the light back almost exactly along its incoming path, which not only achieves all-the-time precise pointing but also naturally concentrates the light energy for a point

*X.Xu, Y.Shen and J.Yang are the co-primary student authors. J.Yang was working on this project as part of his Bachelor thesis when he was with Peking University.

MobiCom '17, October 16–20, 2017, Snowbird, UT, USA

ACM ISBN 978-1-4503-4916-1/17/10...$15.00
https://doi.org/10.1145/3117811.3117843

light source. The prototyped system uses common retroflector fabrics and adopts On-off keying (OOK) communication for the uplink with a MCU-controlled LCD shutter, which however fundamentally limits the data rate – the fixed response time (*e.g.* a few milliseconds) of the commercial LCD when manufactured throttles its highest switching rate for OOK modulation. In addition, the nonlinear responses of LCD state to voltage changes makes it very difficult to produce precise multi-level signals, especially in the context of IoT devices. With these observations, the authors in [41] extended the idea of RetroVLC and resorted to use a plural of retroreflectors and LCD shutters to improve the data rate. A reflector and a LCD shutter form a 'pixel', each pixel can be switched on/off independently, and pulse amplitude modulation (PAM) is adopted to increase the rate in proportional to the number of pixels.

In this paper, we seek to improve the data rate of RetroVLC from the very heart of any communication system – the coding and modulation schemes. In particular, we make two key observations. Firstly, the Manchester coding used in RetroVLC is not optimized for bandwidth efficiency. Secondly, it is not necessary to "fully" switch on/off the LCD to convey a signal. When an LCD is charged or discharged, its transparency will change continuously and leads to a trend of increasing or decreasing signal strength at the receiver side. As long as this trend is distinguishable, we may stop the charing or discharging process early. Note that the distinguishability depends on the communication range and SNR, and should be set according to typical working range in practice. In addition, different LCD shutters may have different turn-over rate, but this observation remains valid as it is based on the intrinsic properties of LCD.

With these observations, we renovate the RetroVLC design with two major innovations: 1) We replace Manchester coding with Miller code, which doubles the bandwidth utilization and is still immune to the clock drift. This essentially yields 2x data rate improvement in theory; 2) We design a *trend-based* modulation and *code-assisted* demodulation scheme. This design effectively reduces the modulation time, hence directly translates to an increase in data rate. In our prototype, we managed to reduce the modulation time from 4 *ms* to 1 *ms*, which gives another 4x boost in data rate. It is nontrivial to achieve this change in demodulation as the dependencies between symbols and restrictions from coding scheme have to be taken into consideration. We formulate it as an optimization problem and solve it with dynamic programming. Note that the increased complexity solely happens at the reader side, and the tag (*i.e.* the IoT device) is not affected. As a remark, our innovation is orthogonal to that in [41] – the two can be combined to further improve the data rate.

In the following, we present the design, implementation and evaluation of PassiveVLC– a practical visible light backscatter communication subsystem for low-power IoT applications. We have prototyped PassiveVLC to demonstrate its practicality for deployments – the battery-free ViTag is approximately the size of a credit card and the ViReader could be organically integrated into normal LED-based illuminating infrastructure (*e.g.* flashlights or lamps), as shown in Fig. 1. We benchmarked our system under different ambient lighting conditions such as office environments, outdoor daytime/night and dark chamber. Experiments show that our ViTag prototype can achieve up to 1 *kbps* uplink speed, which is ~8x in

(a) ViTag Front (b) ViTag Back (c) ViReader

Figure 1: PassiveVLC system prototypes.

practice speedup as compared to our implementation of RetroVLC, with a 120° flexible orientation under sub-*mW* power budget.

To better understand the design tradeoff (form factor, working range, *etc.*) among various components in PassiveVLC, based on the benchmark data, we derive and verify a joint link budget analysis for the downlink and uplink, which can serve as a guidance for developing PassiveVLC-enabled applications. Finally, we have built two proof-of-concept applications that illustrate the potential of PassiveVLC in real-world IoT applications. The first application is a smart check-in system where a ViReader-enabled door will automatically grant the access when a ViTag-bearing user walks into its working range. The second is an optical IoT networking solution where a ViReader-capable lighting LED infrastructure interrogates multiple ViTag-bearing IoT devices for streaming sensor readings.

Contributions.

- We design, implement and evaluate PassiveVLC, a practical visible light backscatter communication subsystem for battery-free IoT applications. With our optimized trend-based modulation and code-assisted demodulation design (§4), PassiveVLC achieves ~8x data rate improvement over the state-of-art (§5).
- We perform the joint link budget analysis (§6) for PassiveVLC's downlink and uplink, and experimentally verify the relationship between ViTag's form factor and desired communication range.
- We built two proof-of-concept applications for smart check-in system and optical IoT networks (§7) and demonstrated the practicality of PassiveVLC.

2 BACKGROUND

2.1 Design Considerations

PassiveVLC is essentially a two-way communication link using visible light, while fulfills the following two basic requirements:

- **Efficiency:** Operate under a low-power budget, *e.g.*, can work on a battery-free mobile/IoT end that harvests light energy from the illumination LED.
- **Practicality:** Impose as little constraints as possible on actual use. This implies a practical working range in normal indoor situations, flexible tag orientation, and small size of the device.

These requirements immediately exclude a symmetric design, *i.e.*, using a LED to establish the uplink to the reader because a practical working range would require a high power LED which is not quite

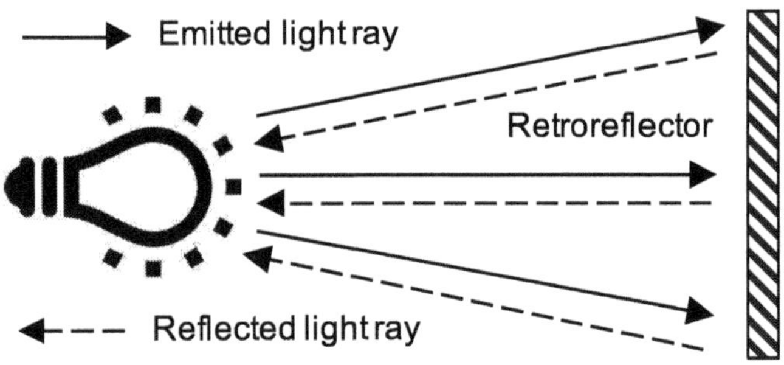

Figure 2: Energy concentrating property of a retroreflector when light source emits omni-directionally.

affordable by a small IoT device. It also excludes the adoption of optical light concentration component such as laser (to extend the working range) or mirror (to save the power for transmission power) as they would incur the overhead of precise pointing, a consequence of aforementioned directional propagation property of light. Inspired by free space laser communication systems [37], we use a *retroreflector* to meet both requirements.

2.2 Retroreflector and LCD Shutter

We introduce the principles and some (favorable) properties of the retroreflector and LCD.

2.2.1 Retroreflector As a Backscatter. A retroreflector is a device or surface that, unlike mirrors, *reflects light back to its source along almost exactly the same incoming direction with little scattering [8].* A retroreflector can be produced using spherical lenses or a corner reflector with three mutually perpendicular reflective surfaces. A large yet relatively thin retroreflector is possible by combining many small corner reflectors, using the standard triangular tiling. Cheap retroreflector material are readily available, *e.g.* the 3M Scotchlite Reflective Material Fabrics [1], and are widely used on road signs, bicycles, and clothing for road safety, especially at night.

The ability to bounce back light from any incidence angle to its source leads to a favorable *energy concentration* property of the retroreflector, as is illustrated in Fig. 2: light energy from a point light source being shed onto the surface area of a retroflector will be reflected back and concentrated to nearby the point light source.

2.2.2 Modulation with LCD Shutter. While retroreflectors can be used to modulate information bits, *e.g.*, by electronically controlling the reflection or absorption state using micro-electromechanical systems (MEMS) [12, 19, 33, 52] or semiconductor multiple quantum wells (MQW) technologies [21, 38], we hope to use off-the-shelf retroreflector fabrics for its thinness, flexibility and low cost. To modulate the lights reflected by such fabric, an LCD shutter that can pass or block light under the control of electrical field is adopted.

An LCD has a multi-layer sandwich structure. At the two ends of the LCD panel are two polarizer films whose polarization direction is fixed (often perpendicular to each other). In the middle are two glass electrodes that encompass a layer of nematic phase liquid crystal. Depending on the actual twisted or untwisted state of liquid crystal molecules, the polarity of passing light may be altered (called optical rotation [17]) or keep untouched, which will further cause

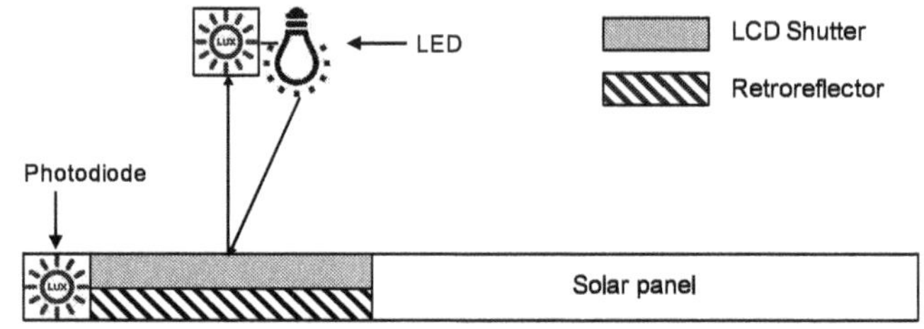

Figure 3: RetroVLC/PassiveVLC design illustration.

the light to pass or be blocked by the polarizer film. We thus can toggle the pass/block state of the whole LCD by imposing an electric field (through the two surrounding glass electrodes) on the liquid crystal layer. Note the liquid crystal molecules cannot instantly toggle between twisted and untwisted state. It typically takes in the range of few milliseconds, or termed as "response time", which fundamentally limits the data rate of OOK-based system [28].

3 SYSTEM DESIGN

The design of PassiveVLC overlaps with RetroVLC in its system architecture (§3.1) and circuit implementation (§3.2), but optimizes the software (de)modulation part of the retroreflecting link in terms of improving data rate (§4). In this section, we stay in the high level to recap the key components of RetroVLC/PassiveVLC.

3.1 Overview

The basic design of PassiveVLC is to backscatter the incoming light using a retroreflective fabric and to modulate it with an LCD shutter, as shown in Fig. 3. The overall system consists of a reader (ViReader) residing in the lighting infrastructure and tags (ViTags) integrated in mobile/IoT devices. A ViTag contains a light sensor, a retroreflective fabric, a transparent LCD shutter, solar panels and the control circuits, while a ViReader is a typical VLC device similar to [25, 29, 30, 43]. At a high level as shown in Fig. 4, PassiveVLC works as follows. For the downlink, the LED in ViReader switches on and off at a high frequency (*e.g.* 1 MHz, to avoid a human perceptible flickering), turning the illuminating light into a communication carrier. Information bits are carried using a certain modulation method and the light signals are picked up by the light sensor on ViTag and decoded therein. For the uplink, the same carrier is leveraged via reflection. The ViTag uses retroreflector to retrospectively reflect the light from lighting source and further carry information bits by remodulating this retroreflecting link – a solar-powered MCU electronically controls the state (pass/block) of the LCD shutter atop to realize OOK-trend based retrocommunication. The modulated reflected light carrier is then picked up by a photodiode on the ViReader and further demodulated and decoded.

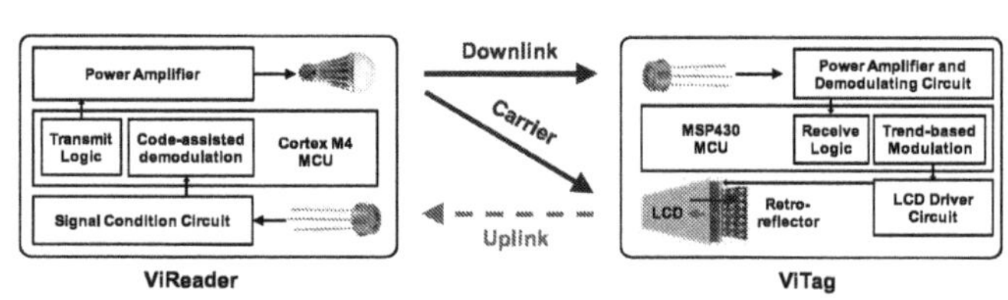

Figure 4: PassiveVLC system block diagram.

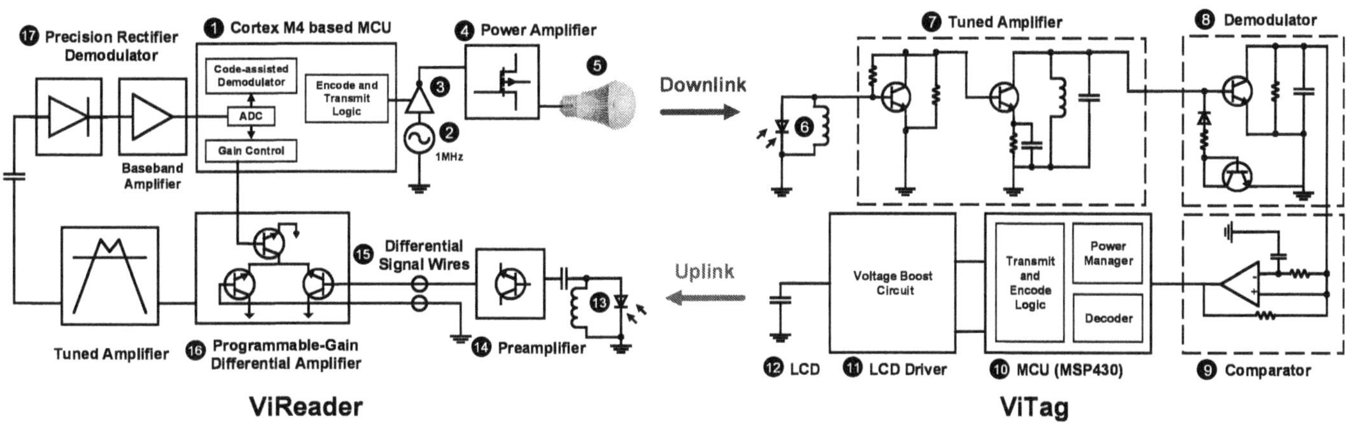

Figure 5: PassiveVLC circuit diagram: For ViReader-Tx, the information bits are first encoded by MCU ❶ into (clock period) coded signal while the carrier is generated by the oscillator ❷. The signal is then modulated by an amplifier ❸ and handed over to the power amplifier ❹ to drive the LED ❺ for transmitting the signal using visible light as the medium. For ViTag-Rx, the incoming light is first captured by the photodiode ❻ and turned in to electrical signal, which is then amplified and filtered by the tuned amplifier (for bandpass filtering) ❼. The demodulator ❽ extracts the baseband signal from the carrier. Then the signal is digitalized by a comparator ❾ before it is fed into the MCU ❿. For ViTag-Tx, the MCU ❿ performs (Miller) encoding and controls the LCD driver ⓫ to toggle the LCD ⓬ for modulating the reflected light. On the ViReader-Rx, the photodiode ⓭ captures the signal from the retroreflecting link, and the photocurrent is then amplified by preamplifier ⓮ to prepare for later transmission on wires ⓯. After that the signal is fed to the internal differential amplifier ⓰ through a pair of wires, such design suppresses the noises incurred by the long wires. The resulting signal is further demodulated ⓱ from the carrier and amplified before being into the ADC of MCU for code-assisted demodulation and decoding ❶.

3.2 Circuit Design

The circuit design of PassiveVLC is similar to RetroVLC [28] except for a minor change: we replaced the RC oscillator with a crystal oscillator. This change incurs a small energy consumption overhead on MCU from 23 μW to 26 μW, but significantly reduces system's clock drift, and thus improves link reliability, especially under temperature changes. Fig. 5 provides a detailed description of the overall operational flow of PassiveVLC and the functionality of each module in circuit level.

4 RETROREFLECTING LINK DESIGN

The key to PassiveVLC's design is the retroreflecting link. While the current circuit design addresses the challenges rooted from detecting the extremely weak and noisy reflected signal as well as the low power (sub- mW) requirement [28], one of the key contribution in this paper is the trend-based modulation and code-assisted demodulation design for optimizing the link speed of the retroreflecting link. In the rest of this section, we will elaborate the design of our modulation and coding schemes as well as their interaction.

4.1 Trend-based Modulation

The nonlinearity nature of the LCD shutter makes OOK the most feasible solution when it is used as the modulator [41]. In other words, LCD is turned on/off completely when in use [28, 41]. The potential inefficiency of this solution is that we will have to wait until the LCD completely change its on/off state before modulating the next symbol. Therefore the minimum interval for modulation or modulation bandwidth is highly limited by the response time of the LCD T_r – time needed for the LCD to switch between on and off

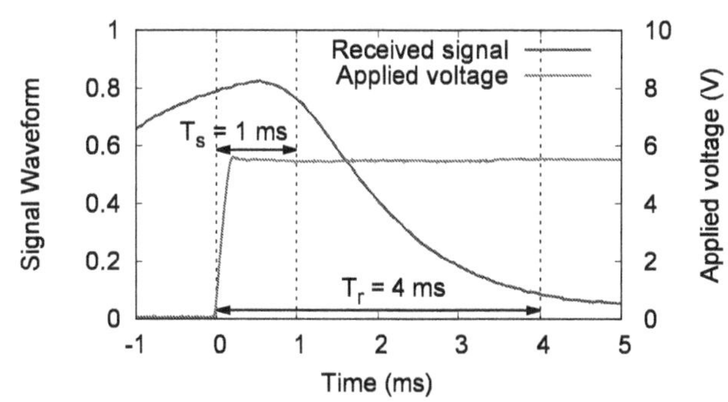

Figure 6: LCD signal in response to applied voltage.

states when we change the voltage applied to it. According to the measurements in our ViTag, it takes about $T_r = 4\ ms$ to completely change the state in response to the voltage change.

To boost bandwidth, we observe that as soon as the LCD is charged or discharged, even if incompletely, the level of its transparency will change over short time. The resulting *trend* of the voltage change on the receiver side already conveys the information. As shown in Fig. 6, a $T_s = 1\ ms$ period after voltage change is long enough to produce a distinguishable decreasing trend on the receiver side, which means that 1 ms can be used as a minimum modulation interval to deliver 1 $kbps$ data rate theoretically and 4x larger bandwidth in our case.

Specifically, while modulating a symbol '0', we discharge the LCD to increase its transparency level, resulting in an increase trend in the received waveform at ViReader-Rx. Similarly while modulating a symbol '1', we charge the LCD to decrease its transparency level, which leads to a decrease trend in the received waveform.

However, such trend-based modulation scheme has its weakness – it does not allow long consecutive '0' or '1' sequence since such sequence will generate a DC component in the received signal after the LCD is turned on or off completely, which is hard to catch by conventional amplifiers and vulnerable to ambient light shifts. Therefore, the design or choice of the coding scheme is critical in solving this issue.

4.2 Coding

As discussed earlier (§4.1), the coding design needs to accommodate the situation when a long stream of ones or zeros are to be sent. In RetroVLC [28], the use of Manchester coding solve this issue because it ensures that no more than 2 consecutive symbols of same type appear in the encoded symbol sequence. However, it consume up to approximately twice the bandwidth of the original signal under the same minimum modulation interval. Therefore, we utilize Miller encoding, which maintains the property of accommodating long stream of ones or zeros, but without compromising the data rate. As shown in Fig. 7: A bit '0' is modulated to two identical symbols. These symbols are of the same type to the previous symbol if the previous bit is '1', otherwise a different type is used for these two symbols. A bit '1' is modulated to two different symbols. The first one is of the same type to the previous symbol.

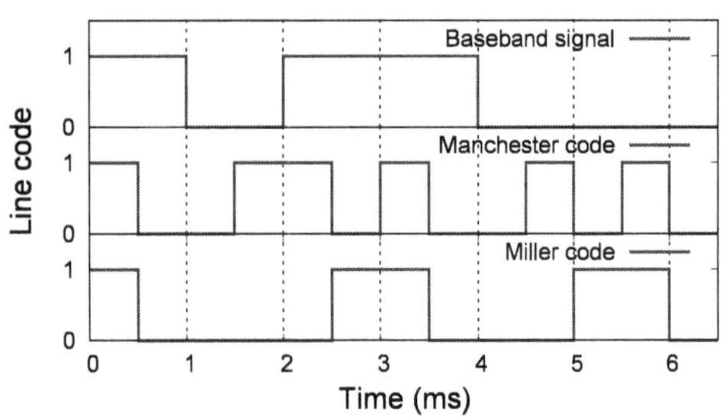

Figure 7: Example of Manchester coding and Miller coding.

Miller encoding has a property that only 2, 3 or 4 consecutive symbols of same type will appear in the encoded symbol sequence, which, on the one hand solves the problem of consecutive same-type symbols, and on the other hand, requires no smaller modulation interval compared to directly sending the information bits (though double the symbol rate).

To make the property mentioned above still holds for the very first symbol, a meaningless symbol '0' is padded before the symbol sequence, and the first symbol of the first bit is set to '0'. Besides, a special waveform is transmitted before the symbol sequence as preamble, helping to determine the precise timing of the symbol sequence as well as the signal strength.

The decoder for Miller encoding is simple as follows. We first drop the very first padding symbol. In the rest, every 2 symbols represent a bit – two identical symbols produce a '0' in the bit sequence, while two different symbols produce an '1'.

4.3 Code-assisted Demodulation

Demodulation is the process to recover the symbol sequence from the received and sampled waveform. In most cases, demodulation is straightforward as each symbol can be demodulated independently. However, in our case, we use a specially designed modulation scheme, which makes demodulation more complicated:

- Symbols are not independent with each other. The waveform of a symbol is affected by the previous ones.
- The waveform of a symbol is also related to the state of the LCD. For example, modulating an symbol '1' to an LCD in the fully off state will not cause the voltage on the receiver side to drop any more.
- Due to the coding scheme, not all possible symbol sequence is valid. We should take advantage of this property, producing only valid symbol sequence as output of the demodulation algorithm.

Conventional demodulation methods demodulate each symbol independently and thus fail to cooperate with trend-based modulation we use here, especially at high data rate when the trend is short and it is relatively challenging for symbol recognition. In contrast, by embracing these properties above, we aim to develop a novel demodulation design for our system to boost the link speed.

4.3.1 Demodulation at Sequence-Level. The straightforward way to independently demodulate each symbol has weaknesses:

- *It can't take advantage of the dependency between symbols.* As an example, the 5th symbol in Fig. 8 is more likely to be '0' when treated independently. But it's actually an '1' which can be easily identified when we take the previous and the next symbol into consideration.
- *It can't guarantee a valid output sequence.* As an example, the fact that at most 4 consecutive symbol '0' can occur in a valid symbol sequence could have saved us from regarding the 5th symbol in Fig. 8 as '0'. By demodulating each symbol independently, we lost the last chance to do so.

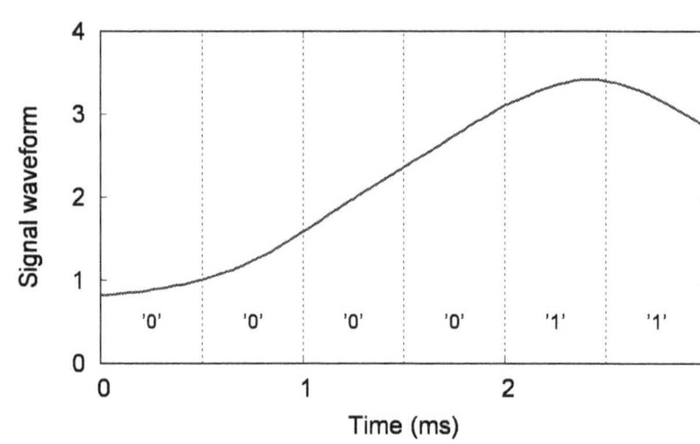

Figure 8: Waveform that fails conventional methods.

In order to overcome these weaknesses, we need to demodulate at sequence level instead of individual symbols. Inspired by Dynamic Time Warping (DTW) [10], we can formulate the demodulation problem as an optimization problem for multistage decision processes rather than several independent decision problems, to take symbol dependencies into consideration as well as the restrictions exerted by sequence validity.

Here, we demodulate by "optimally" (§4.3.2) decomposing the received waveform into segments where each segment represents consecutive symbols of same type. According to the properties mentioned in §4.2, some restrictions apply: Each segment should consists of 2, 3 or 4 symbols; Segment of 4 symbols can only occur after even number of symbols in the symbol sequence. In addition, minor error in timing should be to tolerated in case of possible clock skew and clock drift. That is, we should allow segments to overlap or separate a little bit in our decomposition.

4.3.2 Optimality of Decomposition. In §4.3.1 we formulate the demodulation problem as an optimization problem. But the definition of optimality remains unclear. To define optimality, a quantitative index for how likely that a decomposition is correct for a certain waveform is critical. Therefore we proposed *Match Score.*

The *Match Score* for a certain decomposition is defined as the sum of all its segments' *Match Score.* The *Match Score* of a segment is defined as the similarity of its waveform to the corresponding reference waveform.

But how to quantify the similarity of two given waveforms **X** and Y, both of the length n? In some existing systems like CDMA, correlation coefficient corr(**X**, Y) is used. But this is not suitable for us since we need to sum up the *Match Score* of segments, while the sum of correlation coefficients is meaningless, especially when segments are of different length. Therefore, we decide to develop a new 'addable' index.

An intuitive idea is to use the following formula:

$$NaiveSim\,(\mathbf{X},\mathrm{Y}) = \sum_{i=1}^{n} (\mathbf{X}[i] - \mathrm{Y}[i])^2$$

However, this formula is not practical because: It does not take into account the fact that the amplitude and mean of the waveform may vary from symbol to symbol. Therefore, the following formula, in which a scale factor a and an offset b are applied to adaptively adjust the amplitude and mean of the waveform, is used to address this problem. In other words, we normalize the two waveforms in a way that minimize the *Match Score.*

$$\begin{aligned} Sim\,(\mathbf{X},\mathrm{Y}) &= \min_{a\geq a_{\min},\, b} NaiveSim(a\mathbf{X}+b,\mathrm{Y}) \\ &= \min_{a\geq a_{\min},\, b} \sum_{i=1}^{n} (a\mathbf{X}[i] + b - \mathrm{Y}[i])^2 \end{aligned}$$

where $a_{\min}$ denotes the minimum scale allowed to prevent the waveform from degrading or flipping, which is a positive number usually set proportionally to the scale we obtained from preamble. As we calculate, the minimum value of the formula can be obtained when

$$a = \max\left(\frac{n\sum \mathbf{X}[i]\mathrm{Y}[i] - \sum \mathbf{X}[i]\sum \mathrm{Y}[i]}{n\sum \mathbf{X}[i]^2 - (\sum \mathbf{X}[i])^2}, a_{\min}\right)$$
$$b = \frac{1}{n}\left(\sum \mathrm{Y}[i] - \sum a\mathbf{X}[i]\right)$$

Fig. 9 gives an example of how it works, where **X** denotes a possible waveform of consecutive symbol '1', **Y** denotes the corresponding reference waveform, $a\mathbf{X}+b$ denotes the normalized waveform of **X**. In this case, $a = 3.4240, b = -4.2567, Sim\,(\mathbf{X},\mathrm{Y}) = 1.0786$.

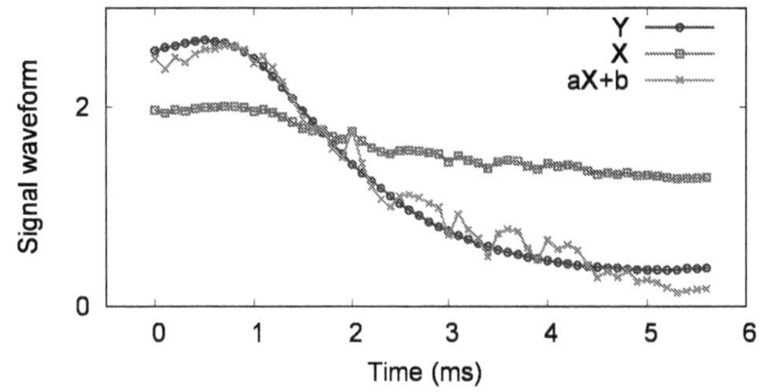

Figure 9: An example illustrating the effect of a and b.

Now we can formally define the *Match Score* of a segment as the *Sim* value of its waveform and the corresponding reference waveform. More specifically, let l_{sym} be the waveform length of a single symbol, n_{seg} be the number of symbols in the segment, **W** be the waveform of the segment, $\mathrm{R}(t, n_{\mathrm{seg}})$ be the reference waveform of n_{seg} consecutive symbol of type t ($t = 0, 1$), then the *Match Score* of the segment being n_{seg} consecutive symbols of type t is defined as:

$$MatchScore(\mathbf{W}, t, n_{\mathrm{seg}}) = Sim(\mathbf{W}, \mathrm{R}(t, n_{\mathrm{seg}}))$$

Note that the LCD may reach a fully on/off state, producing a level part (approximately) in the end of the waveform. These level parts should not be taken account in the calculation of *Match Score.*

4.3.3 Problem Formalization. Now let's formally define the optimization problem for demodulation. Let S be the received waveform, n be the number of symbols to demodulate, l_{sym} be the waveform length of a single symbol, *err* be the maximum timing error allowed in samples (which is usually set proportionally to l_{sym}), *Start* be the position where the symbol sequence start (which can be obtained by searching preamble), the optimization problem can be formulated as:

$$\begin{aligned} \min_{p_i, s_i, m} \quad & \sum_{i=0}^{m-1} MatchScore(\mathrm{S}[p_i \dots p_i + s_i l_{\mathrm{sym}} - 1], i \bmod 2, s_i) \\ \text{s.t.} \quad & -err \leq p_0 - Start \leq err \\ & -err \leq p_i - p_{i-1} + s_{i-1} l_{\mathrm{sym}} \leq err \quad (1 \leq i < m) \\ & 2 \leq s_i \leq 3 \quad \left(\textstyle\sum_{j<i} s_i \text{ is even}\right) \\ & 2 \leq s_i \leq 4 \quad \left(\textstyle\sum_{j<i} s_i \text{ is odd}\right) \\ & n = \sum_{i=0}^{m-1} s_i \end{aligned}$$

where m denotes the number of segments, s_i denotes the number of symbols in the ith segment, p_i denotes the very first sample of the ith segment.

(a) Indoor office: 200 lx (b) Outdoor cloudy day: 2000 lx (c) Outdoor night: 10 lx

Figure 10: Evaluation testbed setup with a pair of ViReader and ViTag.

4.3.4 *Solving the Optimization Problem.* So far we formulate the demodulation problem to an optimization problem for multistage decision processes. This problem can be solved using Dynamic Programming. The symbol sequence can be constructed through the process of dynamic programming.

While implementing the dynamic programming algorithm, an optimization is used to speed up the calculation: Instead of running the algorithm after all symbols are sampled, we solve a subproblem as soon as the required sample values for that subproblem are sampled. As measured in §5.3.2, the time required to solve all the subproblems related to a symbol is less than the time of a symbol, resulting in an almost real-time demodulation.

5 EVALUATION

In this section, we present the experimental results from our prototyped PassiveVLC– a 3 W modified flashlight as ViReader and a battery-free ViTag. Here are the highlighted results:

- **Link performance:** ViTag operates at up to 1 $kbps$ on a loss-free uplink when it is within 1 m from ViReader. PassiveVLC works for a flexible range of ViTag orientations up to $\pm 60°$ and under different ambient light condition (from dark chamber, outdoor night, indoor office to day light).
- **Energy Consumption:** PassiveVLC adapts to different data rate (0.25, 0.5 and 1 $kbps$) under a 150 μW power budget and achieves sub-μJ per bit.

5.1 Prototype Implementation

We implemented PassiveVLC system shown in Fig. 1. The ViTag is battery-free – it harvests light energy from the on-board solar panel. The size of ViTag is 8.2×5.2 cm, same as a credit card. About two-thirds area is used for solar cells and the rest for the LCD and retroreflector. The ViReader is modified from a flashlight which uses a 3 W white LED as the transmitter. Three photodetectors are used in serial to improve the SNR. The overall cost of each ViTag is about $8 and even less when in mass production.

5.2 Experimental Setup

We evaluate PassiveVLC using our prototype implementation with a testbed shown in Fig. 16. We carried most of the experiments in typical office environments, where the ambient light is maintained in a comfortable range around 200 lx. As ViReader is externally powered and the downlink signals are strong[1], we have thus focused on measuring the *bottleneck uplink performance.* We mount our system on a robot and programmably control the movement of our ViTag or ViReader to the desired position and orientation. The system parameters include distance (between ViTag and ViReader), incidence angle (ViTag), irradiation angle (ViReader), data rate (uplink), packet length (uplink) and FoV (reader). The default setting is summarized in Tab. 1. For each parameter setting, the ViTag continuously sends 100 packets (4-*byte* ID data for each) to ViReader with a constant rate and we take the average to report our results.

5.3 Micro-benchmarks

5.3.1 *How reliable is the retroreflecting link?* We use the packet loss rate (PLR) as the primary metric to answer this question. For VLC, the received signal strength is mainly affected by two factors, *i.e.* the distance between ViTag and ViReader and the incidence angle [29]. In addition, we would also like to see whether the packet length or ambient light condition will affect the link reliability.

Distance. We first measure the impact of distance on PLR by varying the Line-of-Sight (LoS) distance between ViReader and ViTag. We count the number of packets correctly received at ViReader under different data rate. From Fig. 11(a), we make two observations: First, when ViTag is sending bits faster, it also has a higher PLR. This is because when the LCD is not fully "open" or "close", the resulting low on/off ratio effect will decrease the signal strength. Second, under a fixed bit rate, ViTag maintains a fairly stable loss-free uplink until reaching a certain distance. This is because a lowest SNR, which is often called as sensitivity, is needed for ViReader-Rx to

[1] We used a 2.5 $kbps$ downlink in our experiments.

Parameter	Value	Note
Distance	1 m	Line-of-Sight
Incidence angle	0°	See Fig. 3 for illustration
Irradiation angle	0°	See Fig. 3 for illustration
Data rate	0.25 $kbps$	Baseline value in our test
Packet length	32 bits	Typical value for RFID tag
ViReader's FoV	4°	Default manufacture setting

Table 1: Default parameter setting for experiments.

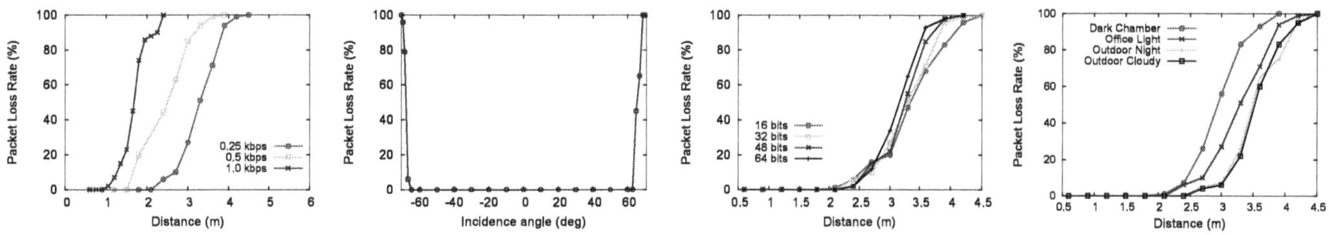

(a) Uplink bit rate (b) Orientation of ViTag (c) Packet payload length (d) Ambient light condition

Figure 11: The performance of packet loss rate (PLR).

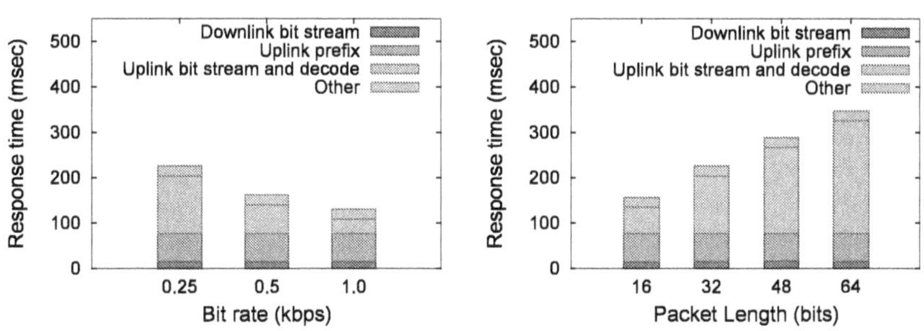

(a) Bite rate (b) Packet length

Figure 12: The performance of response time.

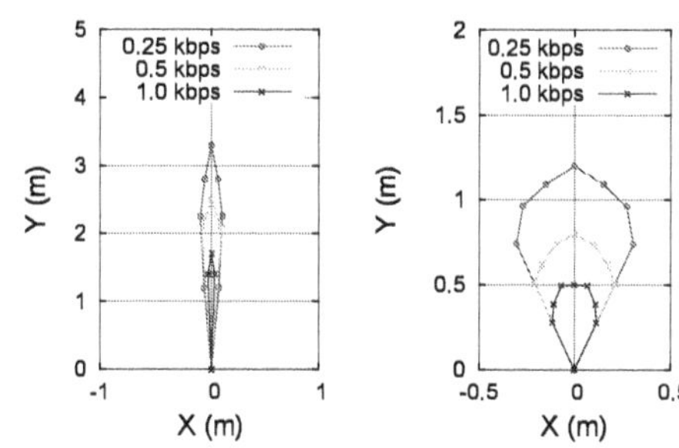

(a) Focus FoV (b) Wide FoV

Figure 13: Working range.

demodulate the backscattered signal. And with longer distance, the backscattered signal will suffer from a higher channel loss, which will be discussed further in §6.

Incidence Angle. We then evaluate the PLR under different incidence angles corresponding to the orientation of ViTag. In this experiment, we fixed the distance between ViReader and the ViTag at 1 *m*, and varied the orientation of the ViTag. The purpose of this experiment is to evaluate how flexible ViTag's orientation can be while maintaining a reliable link. Fig. 11(b) shows that when ViTag maintains a loss-free uplink when its incidence angle is between -60°and 60°. Thanks to the high coefficient of retroreflection on our retroreflector, it is able to concentrate the reflected light automatically and thus has a high gain in a wide range of orientations. Once the harvested energy is below the sensitivity level (± 65°or so in our case), the PLR drops to 100% in a sharp manner.

Packet Length. Packet length is another variable of interests regarding to PLR as it represents the needs of different IoT applications, such as identification, sensor data, *etc.*. In Fig. 11(c), we observe that a longer packet results in higher PLR in general. However, when ViTag is close to ViReader (< 2.7 *m*, typical distance between illuminating infrastructure and IoT devices in indoor environments), the PLR difference is marginal (< 5%). This is a desirable outcome because it illustrates that despite a long packet increases the bit error rate in theory, the length does not play a key role in increasing PLR when the link is relatively short, as in most cases.

Environmental Impact. So far in our experiments, the ambient lighting conditions are limited to office environments. In typical VLC systems, ambient light only plays a "negative" role – a strong lighting source can easily saturate the light sensor and make the receiver fail. Interestingly, there is such a trade-off in PassiveVLC system: on the one hand, the ambient light introduces the same challenge to the optical receiver side; on the other hand, a higher energy harvesting efficiency can potentially reduce the ViTag size or increase the communication range. We measure the PLR under different ambient light conditions. As shown in Fig. 11(d), we obtain the best results (in terms of the lowest PLR under same distance) in outdoor daytime and the worst in a dark chamber, as expected. Interestingly, we observe that the results from outdoor night outperform the ones from office environments. This is because we often have more lighting infrastructure in the vicinity which can bring unexpected noise. Overall, we demonstrate that PassiveVLC performs almost equally well under a variety of ambient lighting conditions. Note that PassiveVLC can't work when either ViTag or ViReader is under direct sunlight. However, this is a general problem with VLC, not unique to our system.

5.3.2 *Response Time.* Response time is defined as the time from the ViReader issuing a query to receiving a response from the ViTag. Therefore, a series of components in the downlink and uplink (encoding, prefix, preamble, bit stream, decoding) account for the response time in order. We experimentally segment these modules, report the timing breakdown results in Fig. 12. Note that we only show part of the components which are highly relevant to the uplink design. The rest accounts for only 10% of the total response time. In Fig. 12, we observe that the time spent on uplink bit stream is linearly proportional to the bit rate and the packet length, which is expected. Note that our current design has a relatively long constant delay (63 *ms*) for uplink prefix. This is because the downlink transmission causes a huge impulse in the on-board power supply module and other signal lines. Within several stages of amplification, the impulse will cause saturation in the last stage amplifier, which means that the reader cannot process any signal during that time. As a result, we add a fixed pattern of prefix before the uplink payload. The prefix also serves as the timing initialization in the decode process. We plan to improve our hardware design to reduce its impact in the future. Finally, we acknowledge that the current design of PassiveVLC is not very efficient in terms of response time – the ViReader can only issue at most 10 queries per second at the highest rate (1 *kbps*) we achieved. We have a dedicated discussion on that in §8.

5.3.3 Working Range. Another important question to ask is: how far the ViTag can be away from the ViReader while still maintain an acceptable data link. Here we define the working range as the area within which the ViTag can harvest enough energy and talk with the ViReader with a chance above 50%, *i.e.*, PLR is less than 50%, and measure the working range in office environments. Specifically, in this experiment we also adjust the FoV of the flashlight to its maximum (35°) therefore it is expected to work in a wider but shorter range. The working range in Fig. 13 is the area within the closed curve. First, we observe that a lower data rate link leads to a larger working distance in terms of both depth and breadth, and the reason is similar as discussed in §5.3.1. With an upright orientation of the ViTag, the maximum working distance is up to 3.3 *m*. Second, the angle of the working range is roughly equal to the FoV of the lighting source. This is to be expected and in fact is a favorable feature because based on it we can predict and control the "width" of the working range. We note that PassiveVLC's working range can be further extended with more energy harvested. A emulation-based analysis is provided in §6.

5.4 Energy Consumption

Measuring the energy consumption is always critical for understanding the design trade-off (data rate, form factor, *etc.* in our study) and finding optimization opportunities. In this experiment, we disconnect the solar panel from our tag and use Monsoon [5] to measure its power consumption. We power ViTag at 2 *V* because it's the minimum and safe operating voltage for the on-board MCU to work. We operate the PassiveVLC as usual and shows the time-series power consumption snapshot on the ViTag in Fig. 14. We can see that in each query, ViTag spends 23 *ms* in listening, which accounts for 678 μW and 15.6 μJ in total. This part of the energy is mostly spent on the static current of the analog circuit for signal detection. In other words, the receiving circuit is always on because ViTag never knows when it is expecting an incoming signal. We can address this deficiency with an efficient MAC protocol design. Then the ViTag receives the downlink bit stream and encodes the content to response, which consumes 373 μW. After that it turns off the receiving circuit and starts to transmit. In the transmission stage, ViTag spends less than 117 μW on average at the highest bit rate, which is much lower than mW-level LED-based transmission. We also see that ViTag spent more power in transmission but less energy per bit when it operates at a higher bit rate.

Overall, we demonstrate that with such a low energy budget, we are able to drive it by harvesting light energy using only small solar cells (a more detailed analysis is provided in §5.5). We summarize the break-down power/energy consumption for each query in Tab. 2.

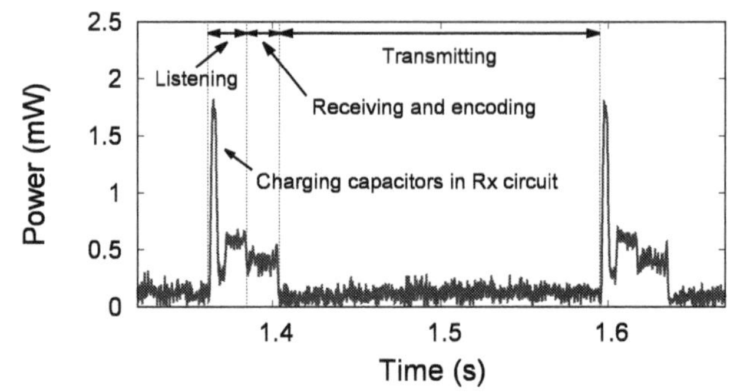

Figure 14: Snapshot of power consumption on ViTag.

Component \ Bit rate	0.25 *kbps*	0.5 *kbps*	1.0 *kbps*
Backscattering state	95 μW	108 μW	117 μW
Receiving state	373 μW	398 μW	408 μW
Average power	97 μW	113 μW	152 μW
Energy per bit	0.38 μJ	0.22 μJ	0.12 μJ

Table 2: Energy consumption of ViTag per query.

5.5 Size Tradeoff

In our ViTag implementation, we dedicate two-thirds of the area to solar cell and one-third to retroreflector. It is natural to ask: is this ratio the right choice or even the golden rule?

From Tab. 2, we observe that in the process of a query, peak power happens in the receiving state. In addition, the passive nature of PassiveVLC determines that the receiving phase is ahead of the backscattering phase, which results in a more challenging requirement for energy harvesting. For instance, in the case of 0.25 *kbps*, the power provided by solar panel needs to meet the requirement of the peak power (373 μW) instead of the (much lower) average power (97 μW).

Our measurements show that in the dark chamber, the LED flashlight casts 240 *lux* at the solar panel from a distance of 5 *m* away. In turn, one single solar cell (at the size of 54×27 *mm*) is able to provide 196 μW at 1.98 *V*. Therefore, the two cells we use are able to provide 392 μW to cover the required energy consumption. Note that this energy harvesting measurement is conservative – the ambient light intensity is often larger than 200 *lux* and thus more energy can be harvested for powering ViTag. To this end, our experimental measurements justify the ratio in our prototype.

Furthermore, the aforementioned scenario assumes a continuous communication is required. If the communication process can be intermittent, then the power requirements can be relaxed because in practice it just takes the solar panel more time to harvest the energy to reach the operating voltage.

6 LINK BUDGET ANALYSIS

Much like the link budget analysis on RF links [7], it is desirable to perform similar analysis for PassiveVLC to understand the relationship and trade-off among the involved key factors such as device's form-factor size, transmitted power of the illuminating infrastructure and the communication distance. For instance, when

Symbol	Parameter
P_t	Transmission power of the light source
G_t	Directional gain of the light source
G_{re}	Directional gain of the retroreflector
L_m	Loss through LCD modulator
A_{re}	Projected area of retroreflector
A_r	Projected area of photodiode in ViReader-Rx
R	Communication distance
θ	Irradiation angle, see Fig. 15 for illustration
α	Observation angle, see Fig. 15 for illustration
β	Incidence angle, see Fig. 15 for illustration

Table 3: Parameters in link budget analysis.

our ViReader is integrated into car's headlight for the purpose of recognizing road sign or pedestrian at least 30 *m* away, what's the required minimum size of ViTag? As another example, when a ViReader-enabled ceiling light wants to talk to the IoT devices placed in indoor environments, what is the suggested transmission power of the lighting infrastructure? Intuitively, a small increase in range will lead to a significant increase in path loss. To compensate for that, one simple solution is to adopt a larger retroreflector-LCD suite to concentrate more energy for the uplink budget. However, a larger LCD comes with more energy consumption, and in turn needs a larger solar panel. Hence, a systematic analysis would provide insights for guiding real application deployment.

For a retroreflector-based visible light backscatter communication system with LCD modulators, we propose a model (with all the parameter definition in Tab. 3) to count in the transmission power of the light source and all the factors of the gains and losses from the transmitter and the visible channel medium (downlink, retroreflector, LCD, *etc.*). The energy received by the photodiodes of ViReader is as follows:

$$P_r = P_t G_t \frac{A_{re}}{4\pi R^2} G_{re} L_m \frac{A_r}{4\pi R^2}$$

In this equation, there are six factors contributing to the two critical phases which we will elaborate in the rest of this section.

6.1 Power budget of Passive/Retro Transmitter

The transmission power of the uplink actually originates from ViReader-Tx. The radiated on-path light energy is determined by P_t and $G_t(\theta)$ (transmission power and directional characteristics of the light source) often modeled by Lambertian model [9]. In other words, these two factors together indicate how strong the downlink light beam is emitted towards the ViTag.

The third factor characterizes the downlink path loss and how much energy can be collected by the retroreflector of area A_{re} at a distance of R from ViReader-Tx, which is similar to Friis free space equation in radio propagation. In our case, thanks to its energy concentration property (Fig. 2), a larger retroreflector can harvest more energy for backscattering and thus improve the SNR of the received signal and potentially increase the communication distance. However, we note that it is not always practical to reply on increasing the retroreflector's area to extend the distance. The linearity can be easily overwhelmed by the square factor in power attenuation, let alone the attenuation factor becomes quadratic when considering the uplink together.

6.2 Path Loss of Retrocommunication

The first three factors compute the amount of energy captured by ViTag. The next step is to determine how much the backscattered energy can reach at the photodiodes or light sensor in ViReader-Rx.

Typical omni-directional antenna has relatively low directional gain because the energy disperses in all directions. However, thanks to the auto-focus feature of retroreflectors, it is possible to meet both high gain and wide angular range at the same time. G_{re}, the directional gain of the retroreflector, plays a key role here. To be more specific, G_{re} is equal to $R_A(\alpha, \beta)$, the retroreflection coefficient of the material, which determines how much energy it can concentrate for retroreflection given the incident light beam at a certain incidence angle β, to a certain observation angle (towards to the light sensor) α, deviated from the incident light. [2] While α is determined by the communication distance once the relative position of led and photodiode is fixed, β is directly associated with how flexible the orientation of ViTag can be when point to ViReader. For visible light backscatter systems, it is desired to have such material with a high R_A and it is insensitive to β at the same time. For the commodity retroreflectors [1] we use, it has an R_A of 500 $cd \cdot lx^{-1} \cdot m^{-2}$ ($\beta = 5°, \alpha = 0.2°$), which leads to a G_{re} of 27 *dBi*. In addition, R_A only attenuates 5 dB as β reaches to 40°. Our evaluation shows that at $\beta = 60°$, the gain is still sufficient to support an uplink transmission in 1 m. On the other hand, when β is fixed, R_A stays high only within a small α (typically less than 1°) and attenuates sharply as α rises above 1.5°. In Fig. 15, we show the illustration of the energy distribution of the reflected in gray scale. The resulting concentrated and narrow reflected beam suggested the placement of the light sensor is crucial in improving the SNR of the uplink.

L_m, the energy loss when light passes through the LCD modulator, also impacts the backscattered signal strength. In our system, the incidence light will pass through the LCD twice, before and after the retroreflection. Due to the polarizing nature of the LCD [2], a beam of non-polarized light becomes polarized after passing through and lost 50% power. Coupled with other factors (such

[2] An illustration of these angles can be found in Fig. 15.

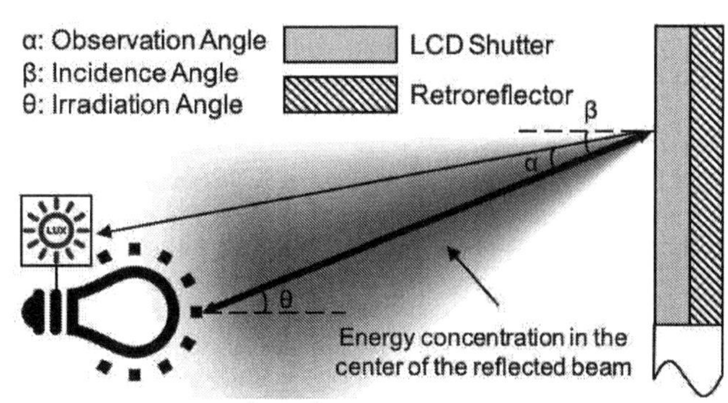

Figure 15: Reflected energy concentrates in a narrow observation angle of about 1.5°.

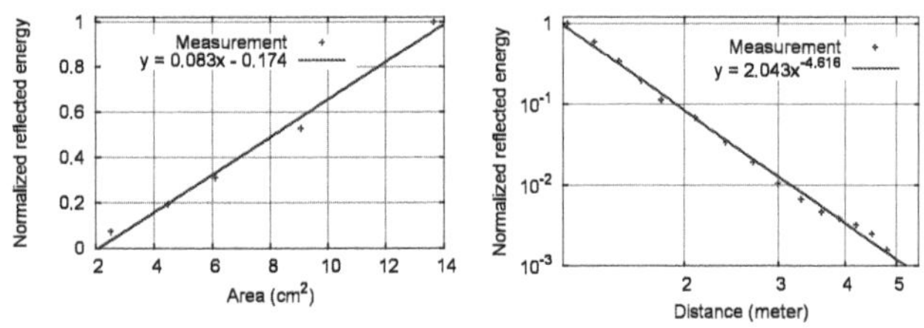

(a) Area of retroreflector (b) Communication distance

Figure 16: Model fitting for link budget analysis.

as absorption of liquid crystal), our measurements show that the power loss for the first time passing through the LCD is approximately 65%. The case of the second time is much more complicated because the retroreflector may change the polarization direction of the light, and it is challenging to measure the loss because the incident and outgoing light beams overlap in space. We estimate this loss as 50%[3] and thus L_m is approximately -7.6 dB. In addition, L_m also is also relevant to the data rate because when the LCD (dis)charging time is reduced, the amplitude of the modulated signal is "attenuated"as well. In our measurements, compared with the case of 0.25 *kbps*, the extra loss at a rate of 0.5 *kbps* and 1.0 *kbps* is 7.7 dB and 20.4 dB respectively. Note that this measurement is based on our ViReader-Rx module, and thus it includes the impact of the variant frequency response in our circuit implementation when ViTag operates at different data rate.

We have conducted several controlled experiments to verify our analysis. First, we change the area of retroreflector A_{re} and fix other parameters. The results shown in Fig. 16(a) demonstrate that received signal strength (square of the ADC voltage reading) is linearly proportional to A_{re} with R^2 of 0.9886. Next, we fix A_{re} and change the communication distance R and plot the results in Fig. 16(b). We make a linear fit of the received signal strength and the distance in log scale. The results show that the received signal strength is inversely proportional to 4.6th power of the distance, which fits our model well with R^2 of 0.9953. Note that our measurement starts at 1.2 m because the ADC is saturated from a closer location. However, PassiveVLC can still work at the distance of [0.6,1.2] m as long as we operate the average voltage when trend-based modulation is applied away from the saturation region.

7 PROOF-OF-CONCEPT APPLICATIONS

We evaluate two proof-of-concept applications to show how PassiveVLC applies to real world scenarios.

7.1 Smart Check-in System

Most existing smart check-in systems use RFID card, fingerprint or iris based identification techniques which requires a user in proximity. We argue that when bearing with ViTag a badge, PassiveVLC users can potentially enjoy a seamless experience when passing by different check-in points – a ViReader-enabled door will automatically grant the access when a authenticated PassiveVLC user is heading up into its working range, *e.g.*, from 2 m away. Thanks to the directionality of light, PassiveVLC can mitigate the false positives in RFID's case.

To evaluate the usability of PassiveVLC system in such scenario, we mount our ViReader prototype on the ceiling at 2 m in front of a door with a dip angle of 40 ° to ensure a 0.5 m of working range on the floor derived from the analysis of ground projection of the light cone. The number of 0.5 m is chosen to account for both PassiveVLC's response time (225 ms) and human walking speed (1 m/s). We ask five male and female subjects to wear our ViTag badge at different height (1, 1.05, 1.1, 1.15, 1.2 m) and head up towards the door at their natural walking speed. We count a test "successful" as ViReader is able to receive the ViTag's response without issuing retries. We conduct 100 tests in total and our experimental results show PassiveVLC achieve 90% of success rate.

7.2 Optical IoT/Sensor Networking

The second use case we present is optical IoT/sensor networking. Home/office sensors (motion, temperature, humidity *et al.*) can be integrated into ViTag and their sensory readings can be streamed to a ViReader-capable lighting LED infrastructure. PassiveVLC brings two benefits in this scenario: Firstly, it reduces the deployment cost because of its battery-free property. Secondly, it avoids the interference with other existing RF-based devices.

We instrument a wide FoV ceiling lamp of with our ViReader and place 1 to 5 ViTags in different locations (table, chair, TV, *etc.*) but still within ViReader's view. Each ViTag is assigned a unique ID and will response to ViReader's ID-based interrogation with 4-byte sensor data. The time to finish polling all the present ViTags are 0.225, 0.45, 0.675, 0.9 and 1.125 *sec* when 1 to 5 ViTags deployed respectively. We observe this "perfect" linearity because PassiveVLC is not running any operating system and thus all the operations can be scheduled into cycles precisely. We note that a complete PassiveVLC polling system requires a scanning/initialization phase as well as a MAC protocol, which we leave for future work.

8 DISCUSSION

Non-Line-of-Sight (NLoS). Due to the directional propagation property of light, PassiveVLC gains certain intrinsic security benefit such as sniff-proof, but it also suffers from an intrinsic limitation - it cannot work in NLoS situations, as any VLC system does.

Data Rate. The data rate or response time of PassiveVLC is doomed by the LCD shutter's turn-over rate, which may further limit its application to those low data rate IoT applications. There are several handy ways to improve the data rate to some extent. For example, instead of using a black-white LCD, color LCDs can be used to enable more communication channels. Accordingly, color filters should be added on the receiver side to distinguish different channels. As another example, one can use a plural of retroflectors and LCD shutters to achieve almost linearly increasing data rate, as evidenced in [41]. We further believe, once the technology is widely adopted, the market demand will stimulate the production of faster LCD shutters. Finally, devices other than LCD, e.g., digital micromirror device (DMD) can be treated as a promising modulator candidate – it can achieve tens of *kbps* with 100 mW power budget

[3] When the linearly polarized light is reflected by the retroreflector, the orientation of the polarized light is evenly distributed in all directions. Therefore the polarizer will decrease the reflected light intensity by about 50%.

[3], and it can be useful for IoT device with a larger surface, such as road sign, cloth fabrics *etc.*

Networked Operation. We have primarily focused on the communication aspects of a single ViTag-ViReader pair. When many of these devices (both ViTag and ViReader) are in range of each other, we need mechanisms to arbitrate the channel access. We have designed a simple query-response MAC similar to that of RFID and applied in the second proof-of-concept application. Unlike RFID which is completely passive, the solar panel can continuously harvest light energy from ambient light, it may initiate a communication session to the reader. Thus, the MAC needs to be slightly modified to accommodate this new situation. We have omitted this part for sake of space constraint.

9 RELATED WORK

PassiveVLC is inspired by the idea of (radio) backscatter communication but differ from that by using visible light as the medium to achieve low power communication.

Visible Light Communication Systems. There have been many efforts exploring communication mediums wherein visible lights carry information. Most works, however, either deal with only one-way communication without an uplink [14, 24, 26, 45], or go in a two-way fashion with both sides supplied by battery [13, 16, 27], which limit the practicality for real-world deployment. Specifically, LED-to-phone systems [25, 29, 39] only support downlink transmissions, targeted at phone localization. LED-to-LED systems [40, 47] consider visible light networks, where each end is not meant to be mobile, and is not battery-free. Until recently, the idea of visible light passive communication has been introduced and exercised in [28, 41, 48]. Specifically, by using the incoming light from the existing indoor lighting infrastructure as the carrier, RetroVLC [28] uses the retroreflector fabric to backscatter the encoded information modulated by a LCD shutter and achieve 0.125 *kbps* using OOK modulation and Manchester coding[4]. PassiveVLC is built on the RetroVLC framework but achieves 1 *kbps* (8x over RetroVLC) using the same LCD shutter based on an optimized trend-based modulation and code-assisted demodulation design. The authors in [41] extends this idea by proposing a pixelated VLC backscatter, which uses multiple smaller reflectors and LCD shutters to form numbers of pixels and improves the link throughput proportionally from 200 *bps* to 600 *bps* by using three pixels. However, one potential limitation is that it only works when the communication distance is fixed. On the other hand, instead of modulating light sources, the author in [48] embed data as various grayscale seamless patterns into reflective surface objects. An optical receiver can leverage its relative mobility to the object to scan the time series of the photodiode sensor reading of the reflected optical pulse from the unmodulated ambient light signals to realize mobile data communication. PassiveVLC, by contrast, is able to dynamically changes the data to send on the reflecting link and thus is more suitable for IoT applications.

Radio Backscatter Communication Systems. Backscattering is a way to provide transmission capability for extremely low-power devices, substituting the need for devices actively generating signals. The technique has been primarily used by RFID tags [20, 44]. Recently, TV-based [31, 36] and Wi-Fi [11, 22, 23, 49] systems started employing and advancing this technique. Our system shares the same design principles – achieve low energy communication by establishing a backscatter link. Although the current implementation of PassiveVLC is inferior to most radio backscatter system in terms of transmission rate (1 *kbps* versus several *kbps* [18, 22, 31, 46, 50] and even orders of *Mbps* [11, 23, 36, 49]) by a few orders of magnitude, our work has several advantages over RF-based approach in general: First, PassiveVLC is based on visible light, and thus completely immune to the interference from RF spectrum which is already crowded with "default" LAN and PAN technologies such as WiFi, BLE. Second, because of the backscattering nature, these RF-based systems tend to expose their transmissions to a wide surrounding area, leaving a good chance for side readers to overhear the information being transmitted. In contrast, ViTag relies on VLC, which implies that eavesdroppers are easily discernible. The use of retroreflectors further constraints the uplink transmission to stick along the tag-reader path. As a result, PassiveVLC comes with a good security property inherently, while other systems have to enhance their security with extra efforts [34, 51].

10 CONCLUSION

This paper present a first comprehensive attempt to the design, implementation, evaluation, demonstration and understanding of a practical backscattering communication system exploiting the visible light medium. With the proposed trend-based modulation and code-assisted demodulation design, we built a battery-free visible light backscatter tag and achieved up to 1 *kbps* uplink data rate, using commercially off-the-shelf retroreflector fabric and LCD shutter. While this technology is still in its infant stage, we believe this paper sheds light on new ways of thinking machine to machine communication in those scenarios where battery-free, sniff-proof, biologically friendly and spectral efficiency are much desired.

ACKNOWLEDGMENTS

We are grateful to the MobiCom reviewers for their constructive critique, and our shepherd, Dr. Yingying Chen in particular, for her valuable comments, all of which have helped us greatly improve this paper. We also thank Pan Hu, Liqun Li, Chao Sun, Xinyu Zhang, Chunshui Zhao and Lin Zhong for their thoughtful input and suggestions based on an early version of the work. This work is supported in part by National Key Research and Development Plan, China (Grant No. 2016YFB1001200), Science and Technology Innovation Project of Foshan City, China (Grant No. 2015IT100095) and Science and Technology Planning Project of Guangdong Province, China (Grant No. 2016B010108002).

[4]This result is carried out by implementing RetroVLC on the same hardware as PassiveVLC. The LCD used in RetroVLC [28] has a significantly shorter response time and thus achieves 0.5 *kbps*.

REFERENCES

[1] [n. d.]. 3M Scotchlite 8906 Silver Fabric Trim. http://solutions.3m.com/wps/portal/3M/en_US/ScotchliteNA/Scotchlite/Products/~/8906-Silver-Fabric-Trim. ([n. d.]).
[2] [n. d.]. Basic Working Principle of LCD Panel. http://qxwujoey.tripod.com/lcd.htm. ([n. d.]).
[3] [n. d.]. DLP7000DLP®0.7 XGA 2x LVDS Type A DMD. http://www.ti.com/lit/ds/symlink/dlp7000.pdf. ([n. d.]).
[4] [n. d.]. Mobike. http://mobike.com/. ([n. d.]).
[5] [n. d.]. Monsoon power monitor. http://www.msoon.com/LabEquipment/PowerMonitor. ([n. d.]).
[6] Yuvraj Agarwal, Bharathan Balaji, Seemanta Dutta, Rajesh K Gupta, and Thomas Weng. 2011. Duty-cycling buildings aggressively: The next frontier in HVAC control. In *Proc. ACM/IEEE IPSN*.
[7] Alejandro Aragon-Zavala. 2008. *Antennas and propagation for wireless communication systems*. John Wiley & Sons.
[8] Harrison H Barrett and Stephen F Jacobs. 1979. Retroreflective arrays as approximate phase conjugators. *Optics letters* 4, 6 (1979).
[9] Ronen Basri and David W Jacobs. 2003. Lambertian reflectance and linear subspaces. *IEEE transactions on pattern analysis and machine intelligence* 25, 2 (2003).
[10] Donald J Berndt and James Clifford. 1994. Using dynamic time warping to find patterns in time series.. In *Proc. ACM KDD workshop*, Vol. 10.
[11] Dinesh Bharadia, Kiran Raj Joshi, Manikanta Kotaru, and Sachin Katti. 2015. Backfi: High throughput wifi backscatter. In *Proc. ACM SIGCOMM*.
[12] Trevor K Chan and Joseph E Ford. 2006. Retroreflecting optical modulator using an MEMS deformable micromirror array. *IEEE Journal of lightwave technology* 24, 1 (2006).
[13] CW Chow, CH Yeh, YF Liu, and Y Liu. 2011. Improved modulation speed of LED visible light communication system integrated to main electricity network. *Electronics letters* 47, 15 (2011).
[14] Kaiyun Cui, Gang Chen, Zhengyuan Xu, and Richard D Roberts. 2010. Line-of-sight visible light communication system design and demonstration. In *Proc. IEEE CSNDSP*.
[15] Biyi Fang, Nicholas D Lane, Mi Zhang, Aidan Boran, and Fahim Kawsar. 2016. BodyScan: Enabling radio-based sensing on wearable devices for contactless activity and vital sign monitoring. In *Proc. ACM MobiSys*.
[16] D. Giustiniano, N. O. Tippenhauer, and S. Mangold. 2012. Low-complexity visible light networking with led-to-led communication. In *IFIP Wireless Days*.
[17] John Frederick William Herschel. 1820. On the Rotation Impressed by Plates of Rock Crystal on the Planes of Polarization of the Rays of Light, as Connected with Certain Peculiarities in Its Crystallization. *Transactions of the Cambridge Philosophical Society* 1 (1820).
[18] Pan Hu, Pengyu Zhang, and Deepak Ganesan. 2015. Laissez-faire: Fully asymmetric backscatter communication. In *Proc. ACM SIGCOMM*.
[19] Colin Jenkins, J Gordon Brown, Lijie Li, Walter Johnstone, and Deepak Uttamchandani. 2007. MEMS retro-phase-modulator for free-space coherent optical communications. *IEEE Journal of Selected Topics in Quantum Electronics* 13, 2 (2007).
[20] S Jeon, Y Yu, and J Choi. 2006. Dual-band slot-coupled dipole antenna for 900 MHz and 2.45 GHz RFID tag application. *Electronics letters* 42, 22 (2006).
[21] Stephane Junique, Daniel Agren, Qin Wang, Susanne Almqvist, Bertrand Noharet, and Jan Y Andersson. 2006. A modulating retro-reflector for free-space optical communication. *IEEE photonics technology letters* 18, 1 (2006).
[22] Bryce Kellogg, Aaron Parks, Shyamnath Gollakota, Joshua R Smith, and David Wetherall. 2015. Wi-fi backscatter: internet connectivity for RF-powered devices. In *Proc. ACM SIGCOMM*.
[23] Bryce Kellogg, Vamsi Talla, Shyamnath Gollakota, and Joshua R Smith. 2016. Passive Wi-Fi: bringing low power to Wi-Fi transmissions. In *Proc. USENIX NSDI*.
[24] Toshihiko Komine and Masao Nakagawa. 2003. Integrated system of white LED visible-light communication and power-line communication. *IEEE Transactions on Consumer Electronics* 49, 1 (2003).
[25] Ye-Sheng Kuo, Pat Pannuto, Ko-Jen Hsiao, and Prabal Dutta. 2014. Luxapose: Indoor positioning with mobile phones and visible light. In *Proc. ACM MobiCom*.
[26] Hoa Le Minh, Dominic O'Brien, Grahame Faulkner, Lubin Zeng, Kyungwoo Lee, Daekwang Jung, YunJe Oh, and Eun Tae Won. 2009. 100-Mb/s NRZ visible light communications using a postequalized white LED. *IEEE Photonics Technology Letters* 21, 15 (2009).
[27] Hongdi Li, Yaqiang Liu, Tao Xing, Yu Wang, Jorge Uribe, Hossain Baghaei, Shuping Xie, Soonseok Kim, Rocio Ramirez, and Wai-Hoi Wong. 2003. An instantaneous photomultiplier gain calibration method for PET or gamma camera detectors using an LED network. In *IEEE Nuclear Science Symposium Conference Record*.
[28] Jiangtao Li, Angli Liu, Guobin Shen, Liqun Li, Chao Sun, and Feng Zhao. 2015. Retro-VLC: Enabling battery-free duplex visible light communication for mobile and iot applications. In *Proc. ACM HotMobile*.
[29] Liqun Li, Pan Hu, Chunyi Peng, Guobin Shen, and Feng Zhao. 2014. Epsilon: A visible light based positioning system. In *Proc. USENIX NSDI*.
[30] Tianxing Li, Chuankai An, Zhao Tian, Andrew T Campbell, and Xia Zhou. 2015. Human sensing using visible light communication. In *Proc. ACM MobiCom*.
[31] Vincent Liu, Aaron Parks, Vamsi Talla, Shyamnath Gollakota, David Wetherall, and Joshua R Smith. 2013. Ambient backscatter: wireless communication out of thin air. In *Proc. ACM SIGCOMM*.
[32] Jiakang Lu, Tamim Sookoor, Vijay Srinivasan, Ge Gao, Brian Holben, John Stankovic, Eric Field, and Kamin Whitehouse. 2010. The smart thermostat: using occupancy sensors to save energy in homes. In *Proc. ACM SenSys*.
[33] Changping Luo and KW Goossen. 2004. Optical microelectromechanical system array for free-space retrocommunication. *IEEE Photonics Technology Letters* 16, 9 (2004).
[34] Rajalakshmi Nandakumar, Krishna Kant Chintalapudi, Venkat Padmanabhan, and Ramarathnam Venkatesan. 2013. Dhwani: secure peer-to-peer acoustic NFC. In *Proc. ACM SIGCOMM*.
[35] Anh Nguyen, Raghda Alqurashi, Zohreh Raghebi, Farnoush Banaei-kashani, Ann C Halbower, and Tam Vu. 2016. A Lightweight And Inexpensive In-ear Sensing System For Automatic Whole-night Sleep Stage Monitoring. In *Proc. ACM SenSys*.
[36] Aaron N Parks, Angli Liu, Shyamnath Gollakota, and Joshua R Smith. 2014. Turbocharging ambient backscatter communication. In *Proc. ACM SIGCOMM*.
[37] G Goetz Peter, S Rabinovich William, Rita Mahon, L Murphy James, S Ferraro Mike, R Suite Michele, R Smith Walter, B Xu Ben, R Burris Harris, I Moore Christopher, et al. 2010. Modulating retro-reflector lasercom systems at the Naval Research Laboratory. In *Proc. IEEE Milcom*.
[38] William S Rabinovich, R Mahon, PG Goetz, E Waluschka, DS Katzer, SC Binari, and GC Gilbreath. 2003. A cat's eye multiple quantum-well modulating retro-reflector. *IEEE Photonics Technology Letters* 15, 3 (2003).
[39] Niranjini Rajagopal, Patrick Lazik, and Anthony Rowe. 2014. Visual light landmarks for mobile devices. In *Proc. ACM/IEEE IPSN*.
[40] Stefan Schmid, Giorgio Corbellini, Stefan Mangold, and Thomas R Gross. 2013. LED-to-LED visible light communication networks. In *Proc. ACM MobiHoc*.
[41] Sihua Shao, Abdallah Khreishah, and Hany Elgala. 2016. Pixelated VLC-backscattering for Self-charging Indoor IoT Devices. *IEEE Photonics Technology Letters* (2016).
[42] Marc C Shults, Rathbun K Rhodes, Stuart J Updike, Barbara J Gilligan, and William N Reining. 1994. A telemetry-instrumentation system for monitoring multiple subcutaneously implanted glucose sensors. *IEEE Transactions on Biomedical Engineering* 41, 10 (1994).
[43] Zhao Tian, Kevin Wright, and Xia Zhou. 2016. The DarkLight rises: Visible light communication in the dark. In *Proc. ACM MobiCom*.
[44] Leena Ukkonen, Marijke Schaffrath, Daniel W Engels, L Sydanheimo, and Markku Kivikoski. 2006. Operability of folded microstrip patch-type tag antenna in the UHF RFID bands within 865-928 MHz. *IEEE Antennas and Wireless Propagation Letters* 5, 1 (2006).
[45] Jelena Vučić, Christoph Kottke, Stefan Nerreter, Klaus-Dieter Langer, and Joachim W Walewski. 2010. 513 Mbit/s visible light communications link based on DMT-modulation of a white LED. *IEEE Journal of lightwave technology* 28, 24 (2010).
[46] Anran Wang, Vikram Iyer, Vamsi Talla, Joshua R Smith, and Shyamnath Gollakota. 2017. FM Backscatter: Enabling Connected Cities and Smart Fabrics. In *Proc. USENIX NSDI*.
[47] Qing Wang, Domenico Giustiniano, and Daniele Puccinelli. 2014. OpenVLC: software-defined visible light embedded networks. In *Proc. ACM VLCS*.
[48] Qing Wang, Marco Zuniga, and Domenico Giustiniano. 2016. Passive Communication with Ambient Light. In *Proc. ACM CoNEXT*.
[49] Pengyu Zhang, Dinesh Bharadia, Kiran Joshi, and Sachin Katti. 2016. Hitchhike: Practical backscatter using commodity wifi. In *Proc. ACM SenSys*.
[50] Pengyu Zhang, Mohammad Rostami, Pan Hu, and Deepak Ganesan. 2016. Enabling practical backscatter communication for on-body sensors. In *Proc. ACM SIGCOMM*.
[51] Ruogu Zhou and Guoliang Xing. 2014. nShield: a noninvasive NFC security system for mobiledevices. In *Proc. ACM MobiSys*.
[52] Leah Ziph-Schatzberg, Thomas Bifano, Steven Cornelissen, Jason Stewart, and Zvi Bleier. 2009. Secure optical communication system utilizing deformable MEMS mirrors. In *Proc. SPIE*.

ReflexCode: Coding with Superposed Reflection Light for LED-Camera Communication

Yanbing Yang, Jiangtian Nie, Jun Luo
School of Computer Science and Engineering, Nanyang Technological University
Singapore
{yyang017,jnie001,junluo}@ntu.edu.sg

ABSTRACT

As a popular approach to implementing *Visible Light Communication* (VLC) on commercial-off-the-shelf devices, LED-Camera VLC has attracted substantial attention recently. While such systems initially used reflected light as the communication media, direct light becomes the dominant media for the purpose of combating interference. Nonetheless, the data rate achievable by direct light LED-Camera VLC systems has hit its bottleneck: the dimension of the transmitters. In order to further improve the performance, we revisit the reflected light approach and we innovate in converting the potentially destructive interferences into collaborative transmissions. Essentially, our ReflexCode system codes information by superposing light emissions from multiple transmitters. It combines traditional amplitude demodulation with slope detection to "decode" the grayscale modulated signal, and it tunes decoding thresholds dynamically depending on the spatial symbol distribution. In addition, ReflexCode re-engineers the balanced codes to avoid flicker from individual transmitters. We implement ReflexCode as two prototypes and demonstrate that it can achieve a throughput up to 3.2kb/s at a distance of 3m.

CCS CONCEPTS

• **Computer systems organization** → **Special purpose systems**; • **Networks** → *Wireless access networks*; • **Hardware** → **Design reuse and communication-based design**; • **Human-centered computing** → **Mobile computing**; • **Theory of computation** → Error-correcting codes;

KEYWORDS

Visible Light Communication; Collaborative Transmissions; Grayscale Modulation

1 INTRODUCTION

Deemed as a potential "role" in the 5G era, *Visible Light Communication* (VLC), using visible light spectrum as the communication media, has been attracting increasing attentions. While high-power *Light Emitting Diodes* (LEDs) and high-sensitivity *Photo-Diodes* (PD) may achieve a data rate at Gbit/s level within very short distance [17], readily deployable VLC systems need to be based on *commercial-off-the-shelf* (COTS) devices such as LED luminaires, screens, and smartphone cameras [13–16, 19, 20, 23, 34]. They are mostly applied for low-rate data communication services such as information broadcasting, where availability, efficiency, and reliability are more important than channel capacity. Among the latter category, the LED-Camera communication is particularly promising thanks to the widespread usage of LED lighting and smartphones [13, 14, 19, 20]. On one hand, LED luminaires, of high efficiency and long lifespan, are becoming a mainstream lighting apparatus [37] and are thus good choices of VLC transmitters. On the other hand, smartphone cameras, with the rolling-shutter effect [9], are deemed as convenient VLC receivers. More importantly, as a smartphone camera has a limited angle-of-view, using it as a receiver can largely avoid interference that severely challenges the potential deployment of LED-PD VLC [45].

Many innovative systems have been proposed for realizing LED-Camera VLC [9, 13, 14, 19, 20, 28]. These systems initially made use of reflected light as their communication media, but reflections may blend emissions from various interfering LED transmitters and hence these early systems were confined to a single transmitter [9, 28]. Recent developments shifted to direct light, i.e., taking photos of LED luminaires directly, in order to avoid interference [19, 20] and also to take the advantage of collaborative transmissions [13, 14]. We illustrate and compare these two approaches qualitatively in Figure 1; it shows the spatial division advantage of direct light. However, direct light LED-Camera VLC

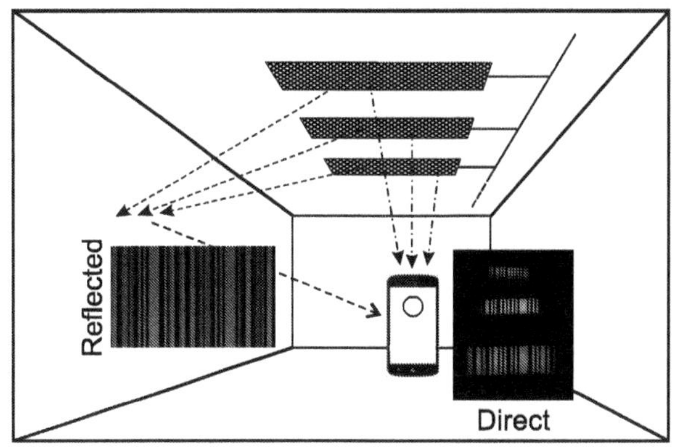

Figure 1: Two approaches of LED-Camera VLC: reflected vs. direct. One major difference is that, under direct light, the transmitters have a natural spatial division on the receiver side, i.e., the frame captured by a camera.

MobiCom '17, October 16-20, 2017, Snowbird, UT, USA

ACM ISBN 978-1-4503-4916-1/17/10...$15.00
https://doi.org/.1145/3117811.3117836

has already hit its bottleneck of data rate [13]: as the data rate is strongly affected by the dimension of a transmitter, achieving a kbit/s level of data rate at a reasonable distance would require a luminaire dimensionally similar to the outdated fluorescent tube. Reflected light, on the contrary, does not depend on the dimension of the transmitter, so it has the potential to serve as the stepping-stone for achieving higher data rates.

From a practical point of view, down light LED illumination faces severe issues with user experiences due to its glaring effect that may cause stress and anxiety [18, 32]. Although modifying the structure of LED may partially alleviate glare [8, 24], raising smartphones towards luminaires (hence directly looking at them) can hardly be a comfortable action and thus may discourage users from using such a VLC service. At the meantime, reflected light LED illumination has been gaining momentum in commercial usage [1, 4], thanks to its lower cost and aesthetical pleasingness. As a result, an LED-Camera VLC system, in particular its camera-based receiver, has to be fully functional under scenarios where the indoor environment is partially or even totally lit by reflected LED lighting.

Nevertheless, using reflected light as the communication media poses two significant challenges to a VLC system design: severe interference and low SNR (Signal-to-Noise Ratio). Because reflected light blends multiple transmissions and other light emissions together, specific mechanisms are needed to cope with the resulting mess. Solutions for *Radio-Frequency* (RF), such as FD (Frequency Division) and TD (Time Division), may not work, given that LED-Camera VLC can only support an optical clock rate at no more than 8kHz [13, 20]: FD entails a color-dependent channelization that significantly reduces signal strength and hence the transmission range [14], while TD effectively reduces the time sharing for individual luminaires, hence substantially lowering the already limited data rates. One may borrow the conventional cell-based design from cellular networks (as theoretical proposals for LED-PD VLC do [45]), yet a cellular partition successfully constructed for reflected light LED-Camera VLC would allow only a single transmission in each cell, and a single transmitter suffers a low SNR inherent to reflected VLC [13]. If the interfering co-cell transmissions can be made constructive, SNR may be elevated to support a reasonable transmission distance.

Therefore, we intend to answer the following question in our paper: *would it be possible to constructively use the multiple transmissions within a cell of a reflected light LED-Camera VLC system?* Apparently, a satisfactory answer would boost data rate for individual cells while extending the system to cover a large area in an interference-free manner through cell partition. To this end, we propose ReflexCode that codes information by superposing light emissions from multiple transmitters. With a close synchronization among these transmitters, the new modulation, termed *Grayscale-Shift Keying* (GSK), achieves a higher bit-per-symbol ratio than the commonly used *On-OFF Keying* (OOK), thus potentially resulting in a higher bit rate. In other words, ReflexCode aims to convert the originally destructive interferences into constructive signals. However, this idea has further imposed on us several challenges.

First of all, demodulating GSK with a high symbol rate is highly non-trivial even under ideal reflection. Experiments show that when the transmitting frequency reaches 5kHz or above, a symbol can barely maintain stable before changing to the next one, producing "blurred" boundaries between consecutive symbols. Secondly, the tonal range of grayscale may vary spatially within a frame captured by the camera due to the spatial distribution of the transmitters; this further complicates the demodulation as one cannot use fixed thresholds to identify respective symbols. Last but not least, as our higher order modulation renders the traditional run-length limited or DC balanced codes for OOK not applicable anymore, flicker may appear even under a high transmitting frequency due to the potentially introduced low-frequency components.

To cope with these issues, we devise a robust demodulation scheme to extract bits from a frame accurately: it combines traditional amplitude demodulation with slope detection to tackle the "boundary-blur" issue, and it also computes decoding thresholds dynamically depending on the spatial symbol distributions within a frame. In addition, we re-engineer balanced codes so as to suppress flicker for individual transmitters while maintaining the efficiency of GSK. In summary, our contributions can be summarized as:

- The innovative idea of GSK to constructively use multiple LED transmissions for boosting data rate.
- A robust demodulation algorithm to effectively extract information from GSK modulated transmissions.
- Novel balanced codes adapted to GSK for flicker mitigation and reliability improvement.
- Two prototypes for validating the effectiveness of ReflexCode, and extensive field experiments to showcase the promising performance of ReflexCode.

The remainder of our paper is organized as follows. We first set up the background for the design of ReflexCode in Section 2. Then we describe the system architecture of ReflexCode, as well as its major components, in Section 3. The extensive evaluations on ReflexCode prototypes are reported in Section 4. We survey related literature in Section 5 and finally conclude the paper in Section 6.

2 PRELIMINARY AND MOTIVATION

We set up the background for developing ReflexCode in this section. We first briefly introduce the rolling-shutter effect of a CMOS camera. Then we explain the advantage of the reflected light VLC in detail, followed by the basics of GSK.

2.1 Rolling Shutter

The rolling shutter effect stems from the sequential exposure of CMOS cameras. As the pixels are exposed and sampled in a column-by-column manner, they may record time-varying information [9, 20]. In particular, if the light emitted from an LED luminaire (transmitter hereafter) flickers in a high frequency unnoticeable by human users, the rolling shutter will lead to bright-dark bands in a frame depending on the ON-OFF state of the transmitters when individual columns are exposed. How a transmitter flickers is dictated by the modulation scheme, for which OOK (where bright band stands for "1" and dark one for "0") is widely used thanks to its simplicity and robustness. The bit rate of such a transmission depends on several factors including the signal frequency and the camera features, mostly importantly on the *Region of Interest* (RoI) [7]. As shown in Figure 2, direct light LED-Camera VLC has spatially separated RoIs, yet the dimensions of individual RoIs are determined by those

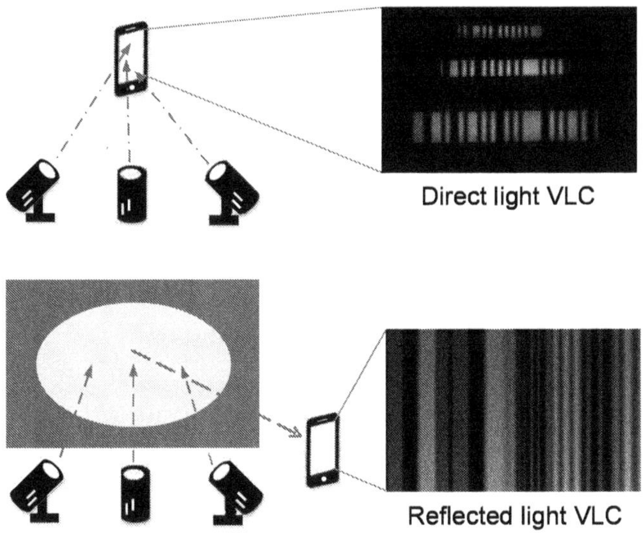

Figure 2: Rolling shutter under both direct and reflected VLCs.

of the transmitters and their distances from the receiver [13]. This makes it quite easy to handle interference but extremely difficult to scale-up data rate.

2.2 Reflection Advantage

As RoI is the major bottleneck to improve data rate, increasing RoI serves as a quick solution for boosting VLC performance. According to Figure 3, for a given camera (receiver hereafter) with a fixed *Angle-of-View* (AoV) characterized by β, we have the relation between the dimension of an RoI s_{RoI} and that of the transmitter s_{tx} by neglecting the small value of focal length:

$$s_{\text{RoI}} \propto s_{\text{tx}}/d_c, \quad (1)$$

where d_c is the distance from the transmitter to the receiver. Apparently, increasing s_{RoI} can be achieved by increasing s_{tx} and/or decreasing d_c. Nevertheless, as we discussed in Section 1, none of these values can be easily manipulated as they are determined by common lighting constraints. Fortunately, we may achieve both through reflected light VLC. Again according to Figure 3, the image of the transmitter on a reflector (e.g., wall or ceiling free of major blockage) is amplified due to the *Field of View* (FoV) of the transmitter, characterized by the angle α. In particular, we have another relation between the dimension of this image s_{image} and s_{tx}:

$$s_{\text{image}} = s_{\text{tx}} + 2d_r \times \tan\alpha,$$

where d_r is the distance from the transmitter to the reflector. Now, if we replace s_{tx} in (1) with s_{image}, we would have an increase in s_{RoI} as $\Delta s_{\text{RoI}} \propto 2d_r \tan\alpha/d_c$. Note that d_c now becomes the distance between the reflector and the receiver, which may be controlled (thus reduced) by a user. Based on our experience, this increase can easily amplify the RoI to the full width of the receiver (i.e., the camera width), allowing us to obtain the maximum achievable data rate for LED-Camera VLC. However, this amplification comes at two major costs: i) signal attenuation due to the long propagation distance and the absorption of the reflector, and ii) the interference from other transmitters due to the absence of spatial division: the "barcodes" could be a mess as shown in Figure 2. As we briefly explained in Section 1, both low SNR and interference demand special attention and are thus the major target of this paper.

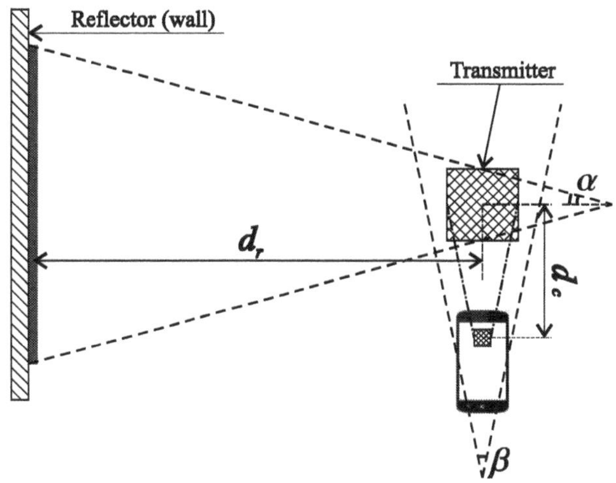

Figure 3: Amplifying RoI with reflected VLC.

2.3 Grayscale-Shift Keying (GSK)

Though omitted in Section 2.1, the brightness of the bands within an RoI can actually be individually controlled: the brightness of a given band is proportional to the light intensity when the band is exposed. Using the level of brightness (hence grayscale in digital image) to form symbols, a special *Amplitude-Shift Keying* (ASK) can be constructed. We term this modulation Grayscale-Shift Keying (GSK); it extends OOK to have a higher bit-per-symbol ratio. Although GSK applies to direct light VLC, it can be more complicated and less robust than OOK. However, as shown in Figure 2, the mutual-interfering transmissions under reflected light VLC naturally form bands with a various grayscale, albeit too messy to be demodulated without coordination. If we can constructively superpose these transmissions by re-designing the modulations for individual transmitters, we may end up with a GSK that potentially leads to a higher data rate, due to its higher SNR [44] and modulation order. Note that, in order to successfully superpose multiple transmissions on a reflector, the usable image size $\hat{s}_{\text{image}}$ has to be the overlap of all images of the concerned transmitters, which is smaller than individual s_{image}. Nonetheless, $\hat{s}_{\text{image}}$ could still generate a sufficiently large RoI at the receiver if the "amplifier" $(2d_r \tan\alpha)/d_c$ is large enough, which should be guaranteed within a single cell (i.e., a small area). Therefore, we hereafter focus only one single-cell VLC, where we convert destructive transmissions from multiple co-cell transmitters into GSK modulation.

3 ReflexCode: MODULATION BY SUPERPOSING TRANSMISSIONS

In this section, we first briefly introduce the overall design of ReflexCode, then we discuss its individual components in detail.

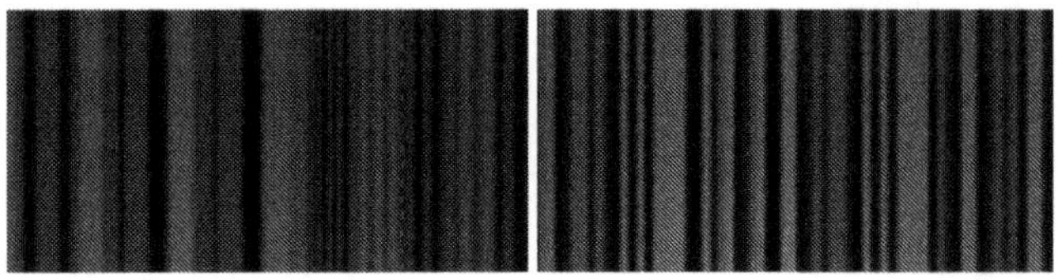

Figure 4: Superposition under asynchronous transmissions (left) and that under synchronized transmissions (right).

3.1 Overview of ReflexCode

The system is partitioned by default into two parts, namely transmitter and receiver. As shown in Figure 2 (the lower part), the transmitter consists of a group of coordinated LED luminaires, while the receiver uses a smartphone camera as its front-end. Although the reflector is part of the communication media, we do not involve it in the design of ReflexCode, yet we shall evaluate ReflexCode against various reflector colors and textures in Section 4.5.

On the transmitter side, GSK is obtained by superposing different ON-OFF states of the synchronized transmitters. Moreover, the emissions from individual transmitters have to be first encoded to achieve DC-balance and bounded disparity, so as to confine bit errors and avoid flicker. Finally, FEC is added to combat possible packet loss. On the receiver side, demodulation is proceeded by a tonal range identification process; this calibration is needed to cope with the nonuniform tone distribution. The demodulation process takes the dynamically calibrated thresholds and the local differentials as input to convert grayscale bands into bits.

3.2 GSK from Synchronized Emissions

Considering a common area on a reflector lit by N transmitters. Depending on how many transmitters are ON at a given moment, the reflected light intensity has $N + 1$ scales due to superposition. In conventional VLC systems, these transmitters may not be closely synchronized, hence the resulting superposition may not be decodable. However, synchronizing these transmitters is rather straightforward as they are connected to a common power grid [26]. In our prototypes, these transmitters share the same drivers and are thus inherently synchronized. Consequently, each grayscale lasts for a fixed amount of time, causing a determined width of a band on the receiver side. Therefore, we can treat each distinct grayscale as a symbol. We compare an asynchronous superposition with a synchronized one (hence GSK) in Figure 4. Although GSK may still lead to variations in the widths of bands due to consecutive identical symbols, asynchronous superposition results in a high variance in width and also very blurred boundaries between bands, making it almost impossible to demodulate.

As GSK encodes bits to these $N + 1$ symbols, the bit-per-symbol ratio is $b = \log_2(N + 1)$ in theory. Note that b does not have to be an integer. For example, if $N = 2$, we can code information in a ternary system instead of binary. However, we currently only consider the cases where b is an integer, so as to simplify the system design. In particular, our prototypes involve three transmitters to form at most a 4-GSK, with each symbol representing 2 bits in the following manner:

i) All three transmitters OFF to generate a totally dark band for 00, i.e., symbol-0 (or S-0),
ii) The middle transmitter tx_2 ON while others OFF for 01, i.e., symbol-1 (or S-1),
iii) The complement of symbol-1 (tx_1 and tx_3 ON and tx_2 OFF) for 10, i.e., symbol-2 (or S-2), and
iv) All ON to form symbol-3 (or S-3) for 11.

This balanced allocation aims to produce a symmetric tonal range within an RoI, thus facilitating the demodulation. The principle behind this allocation scheme can be readily extended to a larger N, yet we shall not dwell on this technique detail as we would most probably not have a very large N under normal lighting constraints.

3.3 Encoding with Flicker Mitigation

As a communication channel, DC balancing and bounding bit disparity are important to VLC, and a DC balance code is also crucial for mitigating visible flicker (one of the major side effects of LED-VLC). The existing *Run-Length Limited* (RLL) codes (as recommended in IEEE 802.15.7 [30]) are not designed for our collaborative transmissions that lead to GSK, as they are based on the assumption of a single transmitter with OOK modulation (2-GSK under our framework). However, ReflexCode employs a higher order GSK, so it is highly nontrivial to keep the overall brightness energy balanced and thus the transmitters free from flicker. In ReflexCode, the flicker can be caused at both symbol and transmitter levels, due to its superposing nature. For example, as shown in Figure 5, if we drive the transmitters by GSK symbols directly mapped from the original data bits, flicker may appear due to, for example, symbol stream of S-3, S-1, S-3, S-1 (marked in red) forces tx_2 to stay ON during successive four time slots.

To this end, we propose N's-complement (NC) coding to mitigate flicker at both symbol and transmitter levels based on the following definitions.

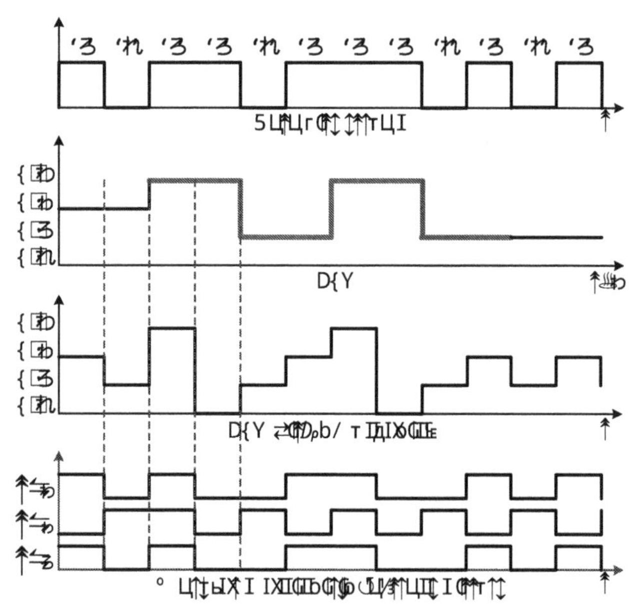

Figure 5: NC coding for flicker mitigation.

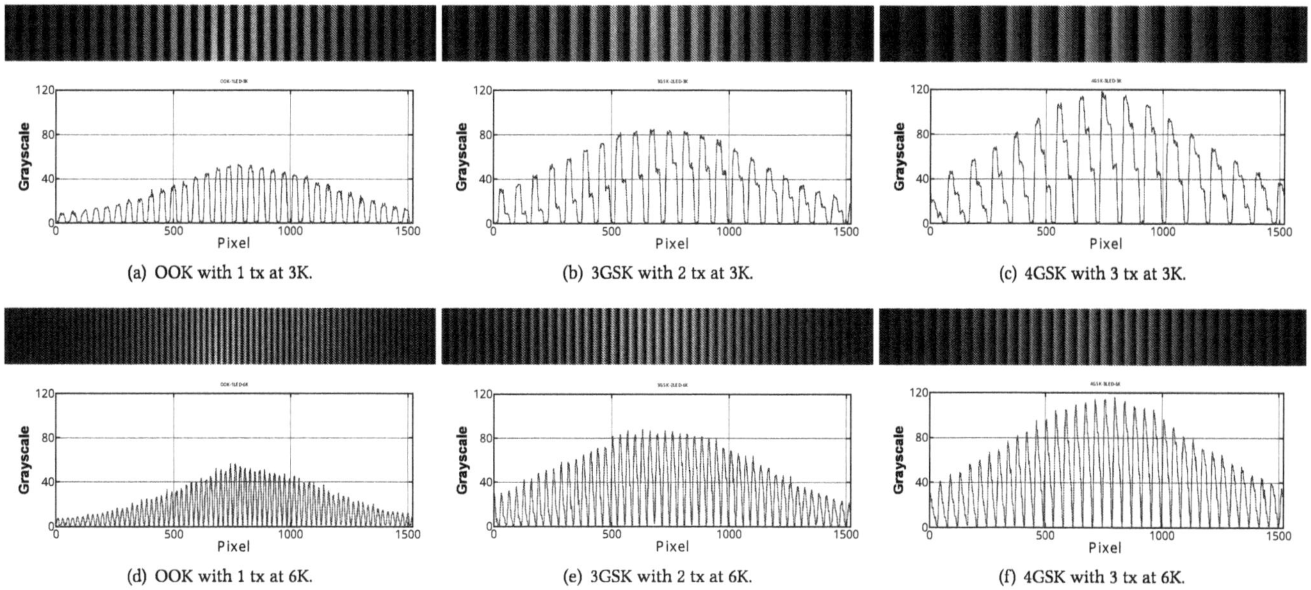

(a) OOK with 1 tx at 3K. (b) 3GSK with 2 tx at 3K. (c) 4GSK with 3 tx at 3K.

(d) OOK with 1 tx at 6K. (e) 3GSK with 2 tx at 6K. (f) 4GSK with 3 tx at 6K.

Figure 6: GSK with order varying from 2 to 4 under two different frequencies.

Definition 3.1. Given symbol S-n produced by putting n transmitters ON, the *complement* of S-n, $\overline{\text{S-n}}$, is produced by turning the original n transmitters OFF while switching the remaining $N - n$ transmitters ON.

The NC coding essentially splits a symbol into a pair of original and complement symbols to maintain a symbol level energy balance. At the transmitter level, this scheme reduces to normal Manchester coding at individual transmitters, as shown in Figure 5. We did a user study with 10 volunteers to observe the flicker of LED luminaires, and the results show no perceivable flicker on both individual transmitters and the superposed reflection. We omit the report of this user study in Section 4 due to its simplicity.

3.4 FEC to Combat Data Loss

Due to lack of feedback channel, LED-Camera VLC offers only one-way communication. Moreover, high data loss of LED-Camera VLC due to, for example, the inter-frame loss of a camera has been verified in [20]. All these necessitate a *Forward Error Correction* (FEC) scheme. We adopt rateless codes, in particular Raptor codes [31], as FEC for ReflexCode, due to their recent successful application to VLC [13, 40]. Under Raptor coding, a message with k original packets will generate $\gamma \times k$ encoded packets, where γ is the encoding overhead fixed as $\gamma = 1.25$ empirically. Therefore, ReflexCode divides an arbitrary message into blocks with k packets and generates Raptor encoded packets, for further modulated into GSK symbols for transmission.

Remarks: The aforementioned modules allow us to construct ReflexCode transmitter, whose outcomes are illustrated in Figure 6. To demodulate these symbols, we face two major challenges: i) the nonuniform tonal range distribution due to the spatial distribution of transmitters, and ii) the transience of intermediate symbols especially under high frequency.

3.5 Adapting to Nonuniform Distribution

As ReflexCode is devised for using reflected light, existing ambient light from other non-VLC luminaires or the sun (through windows) may shine upon the reflector affecting on ReflexCode's demodulation. Therefor, we employ a high-pass filter to remove low-frequency noises before demodulation. Moreover, the tonal range of grayscale symbol stream within a received frame is not uniformly distributed due to the spatial distribution of the transmitters. Basically, the reflection causes a brightest frame center and a gradual reduction of brightness on both sides as shown in Figure 6, which makes it difficult to set thresholds for detecting symbols with varying spatial location in a frame. Earlier proposals suggest using polynomial regression to fit the change of tonal range [9], yet it is too computational intensive for COTS VLC.

In ReflexCode, we dynamically measure the tonal range for each symbol so as to properly set the thresholds. Inspired by the pilot channel of CDMA, we put a few successive S-N ($N = 3$ in our current implementations) in a packet header. This acts as reference for measuring the tonal range, as a header represents the brightest pixels of a tonal range locally. Having multiple headers in a frame further enables us to detect the tonal range variation across the frame. ReflexCode starts by identifying headers, using a rough threshold determined by brightest pixels of a frame (the header closest to the center) and those at both edges of the frame, as shown by Figure 7(a). Upon locating all headers in a frame (according to their special width and the rough threshold), ReflexCode uses their brightness levels to determine a piecewise linear function as the envelope of the tonal range across the frame, as shown in Figure 7(b) (the envelope). And the thresholds (i.e., lower bounds) are set as 92%, 62%, 25%, and 0 for S-3, S-2, S-1, and S-0, respectively. We determine these thresholds empirically to minimize the error rate.

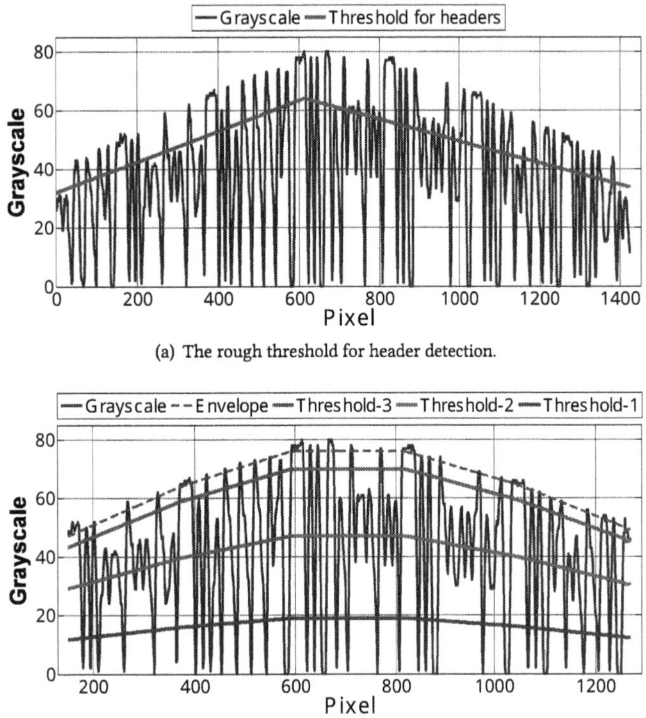

(a) The rough threshold for header detection.

(b) Determine the demodulation thresholds.

Figure 7: Determine thresholds for demodulating GSK coded packets.

3.6 Demodulation Driven by Differential

In addition to the demodulation thresholds, the procedure explained in Section 3.5 also extracts individual packets out of a frame. In the following, we present the core demodulation process to retrieve the data bits from a certain packet.

3.6.1 Width-Driven Demodulation: A Baseline. Existing LED-Camera VLC systems mostly apply OOK and demodulate it by examining the widths of grayscale bands in a frame [9, 13, 14, 20], while detecting the width of a band using a bisection threshold. In addition, by reasoning on the widths of bright/dark bands in a combinatorial manner, [13] is able to well handle the blooming effect, i.e., brighter gets wider while darker gets thinner. However, the GSK demodulated by ReflexCode is fundamentally different, as shown by the comparison in Figure 6. Essentially, the higher order nature of GSK makes the symbols more prone to the blooming effect, hence the symbol width and boundary become very vague for detection. Therefore, a width-driven demodulation may fail when facing a cluster of bands with various brightness levels; it is likely to deem bands for intermediate symbols as noise and hence discard them. This issue is particularly evident under a higher frequency, where intermediate symbols can hardly get stable before transiting to the next brightness level. As a result, we seek to obtain a precise symbol detection by examining the brightness gradient and the relation between consecutive symbols.

Algorithm 1: Judging Point Determination

Data: $G(i)$, x_{gap}, $y_{\text{gap}}(i)$
Result: J
begin
  $J \leftarrow \emptyset$; bLevel $\leftarrow 0$;
  while $i < m$ **do**
    Criterion 1: $G'(i-1) \times G'(i+1) < 0$
    Criterion 2: $G'(j) > 0, j \in [i-1, i+1]$ **and** $G''(j) \leq 0, j \in [i-1, i]$ **and** $G''(j) \geq 0, j \in [i, i+1]$
    Criterion 3: $G'(j) < 0, j \in [i-1, i+1]$ **and** $G''(j) \geq 0, j \in [i-1, i]$ **and** $G''(j) \leq 0, j \in [i, i+1]$
    if *i satisfies any criterion* **then**
      if $\left|\frac{G(i)-\text{bLevel}}{\text{bLevel}}\right| > y_{\text{gap}}(i)$ **then**
        $J \leftarrow J \cup \{i\}$;
      bLevel $\leftarrow G(i)$; $i \leftarrow i + x_{\text{gap}}$;

3.6.2 Judging Points Determination. With the thresholds obtained in Section 3.5, we still need to determine how to correctly sample pixels for comparing against the thresholds. For example, if we send S-0 and S-3 consecutively, there must exist some pixels with brightness levels equal to S-1 and/or S-2. Therefore, if we directly apply the thresholds throughout a whole frame, there would be a large number of detection errors. A correct logic should first determine where to sample pixels that can be part of a symbol, then use these pixels for demodulation by comparing them against the three thresholds.

Let us consider the function $G(i), i = 1, 2...m$ of pixel brightness in a frame, where m is the horizontal pixel size and G returns the average pixel brightness for a given column. Theoretically, the first-order derivative of $G(\cdot)$ should go to zero where a certain symbol appears. In reality, the value may not be exactly zero due to the transience of intermediate symbols under a high frequency. Moreover, G is discrete given pixels as input, so we should detect where the value of the finite difference of $G(i)$ goes across zero. We denote the indices of such pixels as *judging points*, and use **Algorithm 1** for their determination. Basically, the algorithm makes use of **Criterion 1** (i.e., first-order derivative crossing zero) to detect the local minimal and maximal, which potentially representing S-0 and S-3, and it utilizes the other two criteria (i.e., second -order derivative crossing zero) to detect positive and negative inflection points, which are candidates for S-1 and S-2. Here the derivatives are computed by finite differences. As one symbol may cause a couple of separated judging points that are still close to each other, the algorithm filters such redundant judging points belonging to the same symbol using two thresholds: i) $y_{\text{gap}}(i)$ varying with the tonal range, and fixed x_{gap} representing the minimum width of a grayscale band. Examples of the determined judging points in a packet are illustrated in Figure 8.

3.6.3 ReflexCode Demodulation. Given the thresholds and judging points determined in Section 3.5 and 3.6.2, ReflexCode may better handle the intermediate symbols that cannot be dealt with by the baseline width-driven demodulation mentioned in Section 3.6.1. Essentially, ReflexCode first locates all headers using brightness and

Algorithm 2: NC Error Correction

Data: J, $G(i)$, symStream, C_b
Result: ct_symStream
begin
  ct_symSream $\leftarrow \emptyset$; flag $\leftarrow$ **true**; $i \leftarrow 1$;
  while $i < |J|$ **do**
    if $[\text{symStream}_i, \text{symStream}_{i+1}] \in C_b$ **then**
      $\text{ct\_symStream}_i \leftarrow \text{symStream}_i$;
      $\text{ct\_symStream}_{i+1} \leftarrow \text{symStream}_{i+1}$;
    else
      ratio $\leftarrow G(J_i)/G(J_{j+1})$;
      [flag, sym_1, sym_2] $\leftarrow$ correct(ratio, C_b);
      if flag = **true then**
        $\text{ct\_symStream}_i \leftarrow \text{sym}_1$;
        $\text{ct\_symStream}_{i+1} \leftarrow \text{sym}_2$;
      else
        ct_symSream $\leftarrow \emptyset$; **return**
    $i \leftarrow i + 2$;

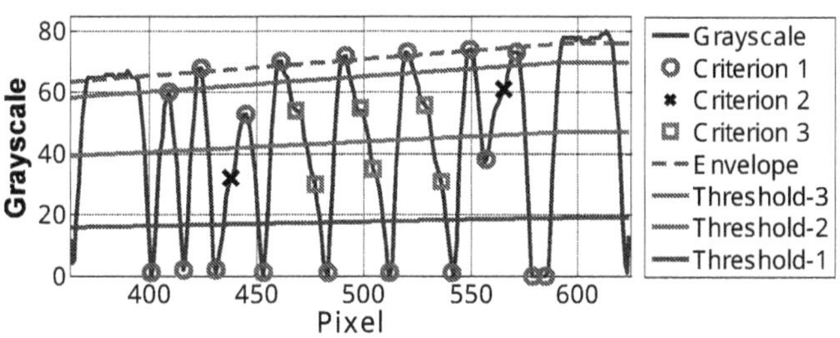

Figure 8: Illustrating for determined judging points in a packet.

width information, which results in the potential packets between two consecutive headers. For each potential packet, ReflexCode scans through judging points and demodulates them into bits by comparing them against thresholds. The resulting candidate packets are then given to Raptor decoding for recovering the original packet stream.

However, demodulation faces a challenge incurred by the inherent nonlinear variance of the tonal range across a frame and the piecewise linear thresholds used to approximate this nonlinearity. For example, the second judging point from the left identified in Figure 8 is actually representing S-3, but it gets wrongly demodulated to S-2 due to a local variance in tonal range (thus its value barely missing the threshold). Fortunately, the wrongly demodulated symbol stream becomes S-0, S-2, S-0, $\cdots$, yet based on the NC coding explained in Section 3.3, the only possible combination would be S-0, S-3, $\cdots$. Therefore, ReflexCode's NC coding has the ability to rectify these symbol errors.

More generally, ReflexCode checks every pair of symbols based on the property of NC coding to correct potential errors, using **Algorithm 2**. As NC coding results in a finite number possible combinations of two consecutive symbols (4 under $N = 3$), we take the set of these combinations C_b as an input. The algorithm checks though every two symbols sequentially: it accepts a pair if

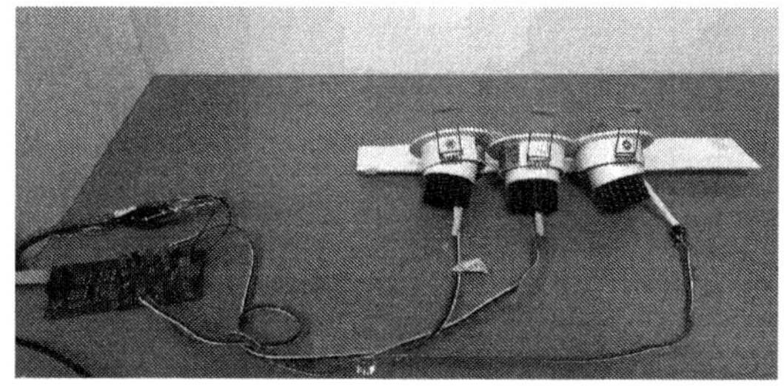

(a) Small-scale prototype.

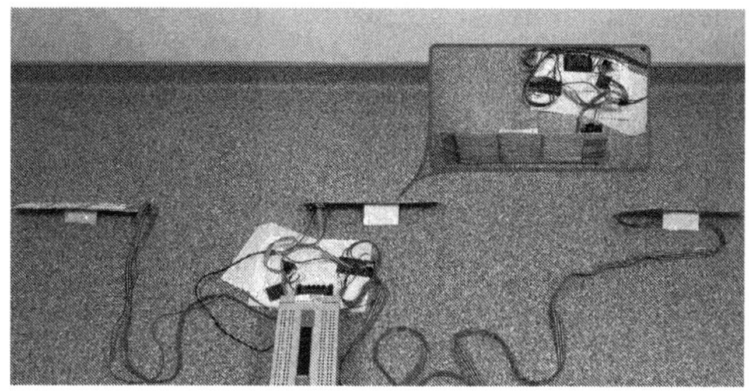

(b) Large-scale prototype.

Figure 9: Two prototypes of ReflexCode.

this pair belongs to C_b; otherwise symbol correction is needed. The correction procedure correct takes the ratio between the brightness levels of the two symbols as input (retrieved from G), and it searches for the closest symbol pair in C_b as the candidate. In our implementation, this whole algorithm is merged with the demodulation procedure, avoiding the need to go through every packet twice: the checking and correction take place upon every pair of symbols are identified but before translating them to bits.

4 PERFORMANCE EVALUATIONS

In this section, we evaluate the performance of ReflexCode using two prototypes shown in Figure 9.

4.1 Experimental Setup

We build two prototypes so as to put our evaluations into more realistic perspective:

- SS We construct this small-scale prototype using three LED spotlights [2], as shown in Figure 9(a). This prototype is meant to emulate the reflected lighting [1, 4], as the spotlights are facing directly to the reflector (a billboard). Due to the small dimension and the facing direction of these spotlights, direct light VLC is impossible, which is exactly the scenario where ReflexCode is supposed to work. Our current fixture puts those three spotlights at an adjacent distance of 7cm and a 20cm distance from the wall.
- LS This large-scale prototype, shown in Figure 9(b), is mimicking a normal direct lit room ($3.4 \times 3.2 \times 3\text{m}^3$ in dimension), where direct light VLC is possible but throughput confined by the dimension of the luminaires. Applying ReflexCode to

this scenario demonstrates the advantage of reflected VLC even under direct lit environments. We put the 3 LED luminaries on the ground and receive data through the reflected light on the wall; this has exactly the same effect as putting the luminaries on the ceiling but it allows for our easy access to the system for debugging. We assemble each luminaire using COTS LED strips [3]: it is made of 144 LED chips with an overall dimension of $30 \times 8\text{cm}^2$. The luminaires are arranged in a row with an 80cm adjacent distance and a 100cm distance from the wall.

For both prototypes, we employ the self-built LED driver consisting of low-cost transistors and a MSP430 MCU to drive the LED luminaires. We fix the transmitter-reflector distance as it is not a parameter to be controlled by our VLC service that piggybacks on an existing lighting infrastructure.

The two prototypes share most system parameters, in particular packet size and transmission frequency (up to 6kHz). A ReflexCode packet has a preamble of five successive S-3 and a single S-0 to indicate the header, followed by 24 data bits (8-bit packet sequence number and 16-bit payload), and finally ends with a S-0. We employ a Nexus 6 smartphone as the receiver, and build demodulation/decoding into an Android application. Basically, we configure the Nexus 6's camera to work in the preview mode so as to capture banded frames at a rate of 30fps. We fix the exposure time to 1/7500s. Beside throughput, we also evaluate ReflexCode in terms of *Packet Reception Ratio* (PRR) and *Packet Error Rate* (PER): while the former is the ratio between the successfully identified packets (those between two consecutive headers) and total transmitted ones, the latter is the percentage of wrongly demodulated packets out of all successfully identified ones. Each experiment consists of 10 sessions and every session contains 300 packets (before FEC); we report the average outcome over all sessions, except for throughput where maximum values are reported too.

4.2 Frequency Impact on Demodulation

As mentioned in 3.2, a higher transmission frequency (thus a higher symbol rate) may yield a higher data rate because one frame/RoI can carry more data bits. However, higher frequency complicates demodulation due to the significantly shrunk width of bands, as shown in Figure 6. Therefore, we first evaluate performance of ReflexCode under different frequency in terms of PRR and PER

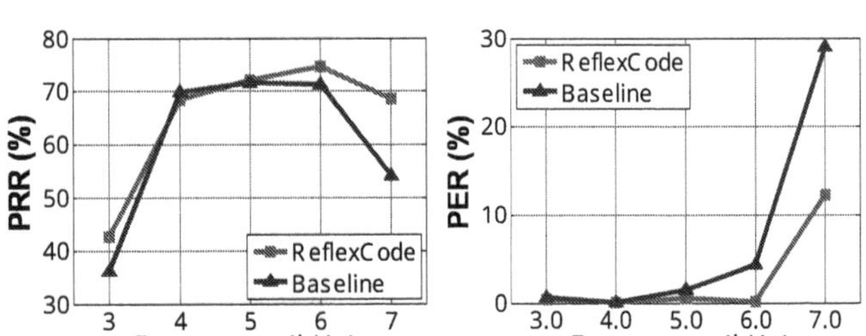

Figure 10: PRR and PER with a varying transmission frequency under SS.

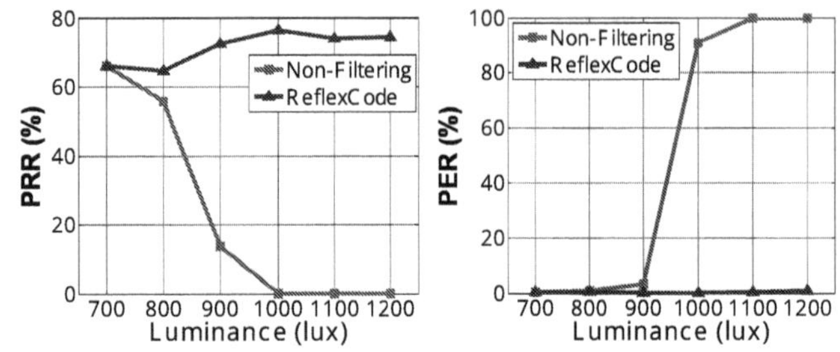

Figure 11: PRR and PER with a varying ambient light under SS.

with SS. We vary the frequency from 3kHz to 7kHz. We compare the results of ReflexCode with that obtained by a baseline of width-driven scheme described in Section 3.6, and comparisons are shown in Figure 10.

Whereas it is understandable that increasing frequency may cause complications in decoding individual symbols and hence result in a reduced PRR, it is less intuitive that lowering frequency may again reduce PRR. In fact, lowering frequency can reduce the chance of capturing a whole packet within a frame due to the widened symbols and the temporal asynchrony between transmitters and receivers. Consequently, the number of incompletely received packets get increased and thus causing a lower PRR, though decoding individual symbols are made easier. The joint effect of these two aspects causes the concave shape of PRR as shown in Figure 10(a). PER increases with the frequency due to the increased transience of the symbols, yet ReflexCode manages to maintain a relative low PER even at 7kHz. In general, ReflexCode outperforms the baseline especially at a higher frequency. We fix the transmission frequency at 6kHz hereafter.

4.3 Performance under Ambient Light

As variance in ambient light (caused by sunlight through window or other non-VLC luminaires) may affect the contrast of a frame, we study the impact of ambient light on the performance of ReflexCode by introducing an extra lumninaire beside SS. We vary the illuminance from 700lux (ReflexCode only) to 1200lux (combined effect of ReflexCode and the extra luminaire), which is monitored by a smartphone with a light meter [12] at a 40cm distance from the reflector. Adopting a common method to deal with ambient light in VLC, ReflexCode employs a high-pass filter to filter low frequency noises (in particular the DC component) caused by ambient light as mentioned in Section 3.5. We compare the results with and without such a filter and report PRR and PER in Figure 11. Apparently, using the high-pass filter makes ReflexCode largely insensitive to the interference of ambient light.

4.4 Effect of Transmitter Spacing

Since the light overlapping area on the reflector is crucial to the quality of GSK, we study how the adjacent distance between the transmitters affects the performance of ReflexCode based on LS. We vary the adjacent distance between transmitters from 0.2m to 0.8m,

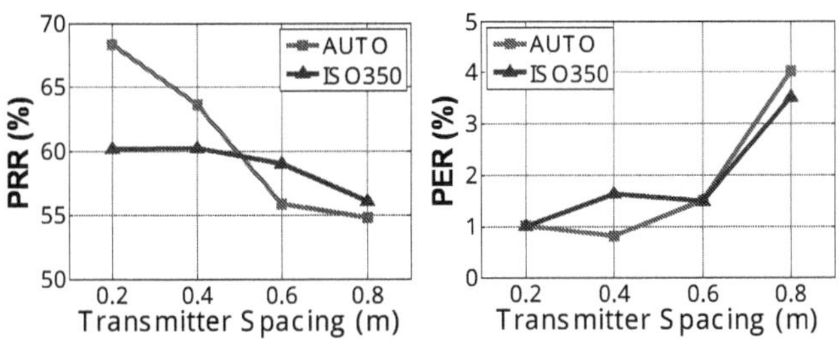

(a) PRR. (b) PER.

Figure 12: PRR and PER with a varying transmitter spacing under LS.

while the receiver is fixed at a 2.0m distance from the reflector. We also compare camera auto-ISO with a constant 350 ISO. Intuitively, Both PRR and PER degrade slightly due to the increased propagation distance from side transmitters (thus a reduced signal strength). These intuitions are fully corroborated by the results shown in Figure 12. Though a denser deployment may potential achieve a higher throughput, we hereafter fix the adjacent distance of LS to 0.6m to closely emulate a real indoor scenario.

4.5 Impact of Various Reflectors

In this section we test the robustness of ReflexCode against various reflectors, as realistic scenarios may not always offer us a plain-white reflector, although a ReflexCode user is recommended to properly choose a reflector (e.g., wall or ceiling) free of major blockage. We fix the receiver at a 40cm distance from the reflector for SS, and we compare camera auto-ISO with a constant 120 ISO.

We first test ReflexCode under five typical colors for the reflector, namely light green (LG), pink (PK), sky blue (SB), white (WH) and yellow (YL). As shown in Figure 13, ReflexCode is quite robust against color differences from WH except PK (much less common in our daily life), which seems to suggest that the red tone is particularly harmful to the tonal range in grayscale. In addition, auto-ISO always outperforms the fixed ISO, suggesting that auto-ISO is maintaining the maximum tonal range in a frame under various colors.

We then test ReflexCode with a textured reflector by attaching strips with various colors on the white reflector. In particular, we arrange those strips into six typical patterns, namely horizontal

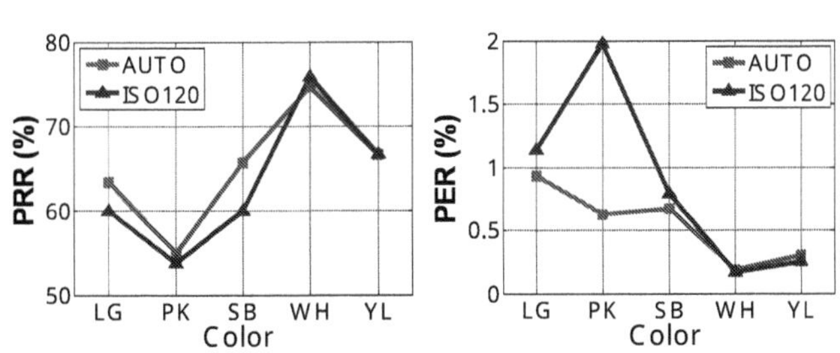

(a) PRR. (b) PER.

Figure 13: PRR and PER with various reflector colors under SS.

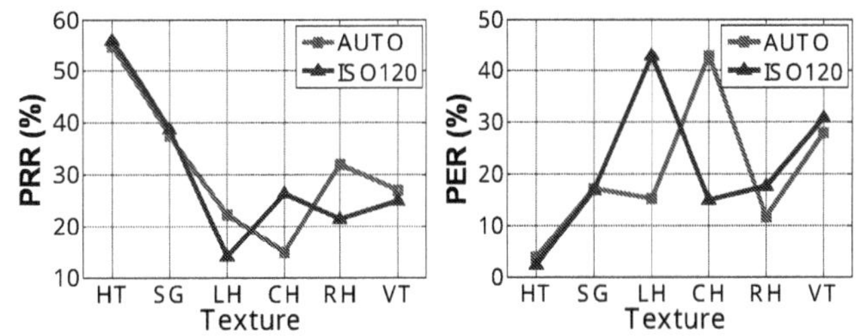

(a) PRR. (b) PER.

Figure 14: PRR and PER with various reflector textures under SS.

(HT), square grid (SG), left hatching (LH), cross hatching (CH) and right hatching (RH) and vertical (VT). The results reported in Figure 14 are rather intuitive concerning HT and VT: ReflexCode is insensitive to HT but is subject to the interference from VT, as GSK's grayscale bands are inherently vertical. The performances under the three hatching patterns are more curious and hence tricky to interpret: they seem to be strongly affected by the ISO setting, and we suspect that this might be an artifact introduced by individual camera designs. In general, ReflexCode should avoid operating under a reflector with visible textures to guarantee its VLC service quality, although it can still manage to transmit data at a lower rate with the help of Raptor coding.

4.6 Channel Property

Based on the standard settings determined by the aforementioned studies, we hereby investigate ReflexCode's channel property (in

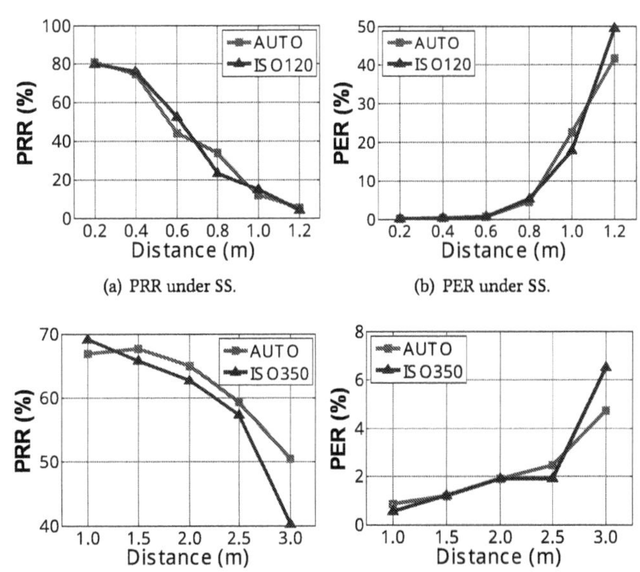

(a) PRR under SS. (b) PER under SS.

(c) PRR under LS. (d) PER under LS.

Figure 15: Channel property with a varying distance under both SS and LS.

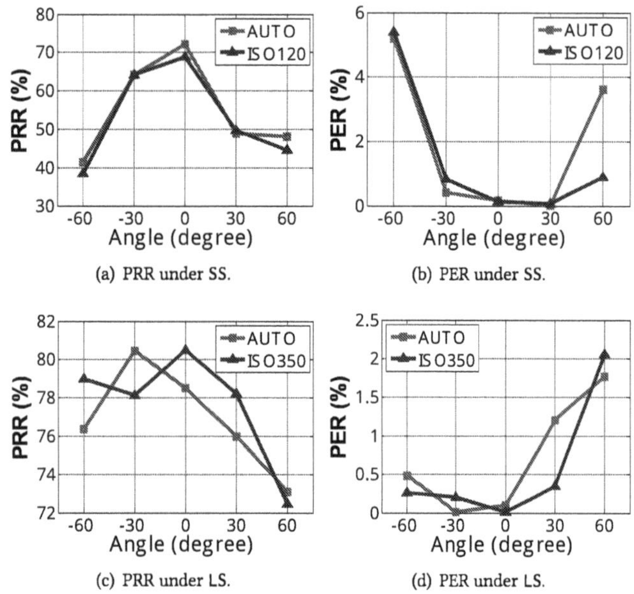

(a) PRR under SS. (b) PER under SS.

(c) PRR under LS. (d) PER under LS.

Figure 16: PRR and PER with a varying viewing angle of the receiver under both SS and LS.

terms of PRR and PER) against the transmission distance and viewing angle, using both SS and LS.

4.6.1 Attenuation in Distance. We first evaluate the channel property against the transmission distance using both prototypes. As the transmitter-reflector distance is fixed, we vary the reflector-receiver distance from 0.2m to 1.2m for SS and from 1m to 3m for LS, and the results in terms of PRR and PER are shown in Figure 15. As the reflected light attenuates with distance, a longer distance causes a lower signal strength at the receiver and hence shrinks the dimension of effective RoI. Consequently, it is natural to observe that the performance of ReflexCode degrades with an increased distance for both prototypes. Since LS employs more powerful transmitters, the performance degradation is made less severe, allowing the transmission distance to reach up to 3m. The performance of ReflexCode does not appear to be obviously sensitive to ISO settings, possibly because that the tonal range decreases with distance in a rather consistent manner.

4.6.2 Degradation with Viewing Angle. We test the performance of ReflexCode by varying the viewing angle between $[-60, 60]^\circ$ yet maintaining the same distance from the reflector center (0.4m for SS and 1.5m for LS), emulating realistic scenarios where a user may not face the reflector perpendicularly. As we would expect, Figure 16 shows that the channel quality degrades due to the deformed RoI that in turn affects the quality of the grayscale symbols. As the transmitters of LS offer a higher signal strength, this degradation appears to be minor for LS but becomes rather prominent in SS. The asymmetry of both PRR and PER may be caused by the minor inconsistency in deploying the transmitters and also in positioning the receiver during a test. Generally, we could conclude that ReflexCode maintains a rather good channel quality within a wide viewing angle. In reality, users may not bother to make a few more steps if they feel uncomfortable with the system performance.

4.7 Throughput

We finally investigate the throughput offered by ReflexCode. Whereas the channel property is evaluated right after the demodulation, the throughput is studied from the application perspective: it is calculated as totally recovered data bits after Raptor decoding divided by the total transmission time. The transmission time is defined as the time span from receiving the first frame till all data bits of a message get decoded. We conduct experiments with $k = 26$ and $k = 50$ for Raptor coding, and report both peak and average throughput for each experiment. We also compare the performance of ReflexCode (RC) with a baseline (BL) in which all three transmitters transmit identical Raptor coded packets synchronously with OOK/Manchester modulation at a frequency of 6kHz. We refrain from comparing ReflexCode with direct LED-Camera VLC systems, because the outcome is very expectable: the dimension of an LED transmitter used in ReflexCode is rather small, leading to a very low data rate under LS or even unsuccessful communications under SS, according to the throughput computed in [40]. Since there is no obvious difference between auto-ISO and a fixed ISO during the previous studies, we adopt auto-ISO in all the following tests.

4.7.1 Throughput vs. Distance. We first evaluate the throughput of ReflexCode under a varying distance for both SS and LS, and we report the results in Figure 17. It is expectable that both ReflexCode and the baseline have their throughput (both peak and average) reduced with an increasing distance, which accords with the trend of channel quality reported in Section 4.6.1. ReflexCode can achieve a maximum throughput of 3.5kb/s and 3.8kb/s under

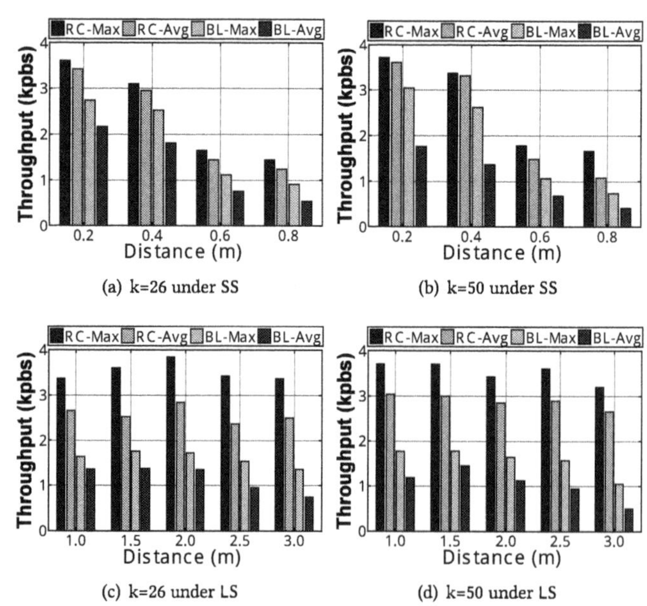

(a) k=26 under SS (b) k=50 under SS

(c) k=26 under LS (d) k=50 under LS

Figure 17: Throughput with a varying distance under both SS and LS.

both SS and LS, respectively, which are significantly higher than the corresponding values achieved by the OOK baseline. Moreover, the benefits of GSK over OOK become more evident with a larger distance, possibly because the higher bit-per-symbol ratio of GSK shortens the packet length that in turn allows more packets in one RoI. Again due to the more powerful transmitters, LS maintains a rather stable throughput with an increasing distance, whereas SS has a more evident decrease in throughput. Nevertheless, SS has a lower variance in performance (peak and average throughputs are close to each other) at a fixed distance, thanks to the better light focusing offered by the optical condenser used in the spotlight transmitters. We also observe that the throughput of ReflexCode with $k = 50$ is slightly higher than that with $k = 26$, indicating that the error rate of ReflexCode's demodulation is good enough to allow for a less aggressive FEC setting. Overall, ReflexCode can deliver an average throughput up to 3kb/s in a room scale scenario, strongly demonstrating its potential for realistic LED-Camera VLC applications, such as advertisement/coupon delivery in a shopping mall or emergence message broadcast in an indoor public area.

4.7.2 Throughput vs. Viewing Angle. We then report in Figure 18 the evaluation results under a varying viewing angle. Similar to what we have observed with a varying distance, we have the following observations from this set of experiments: i) the outcome agrees with the channel property studied in Section 4.6.2, ii) LS is much more robust than SS against the viewing angle due to the more powerful transmitters and the resulting larger reflecting area, and iii) more importantly, ReflexCode significantly outperforms the baseline under all viewing angles. We actually observe some abnormal trends in throughput that appear to be counter-intuitive: Figure 18(c) shows a slightly lower throughput at zero viewing angle (counter-intuitive results in a similar vein appear in Figure 17(c) too). We believe that this anomaly may be caused by the auto-ISO setting that can potentially respond to lighting variation in an unpredictable manner. Nevertheless, we would still recommend using auto-ISO as it does not really cause a major problem to ReflexCode, and we believe that the manufacturers should have configured it for delivering the best overall performance.

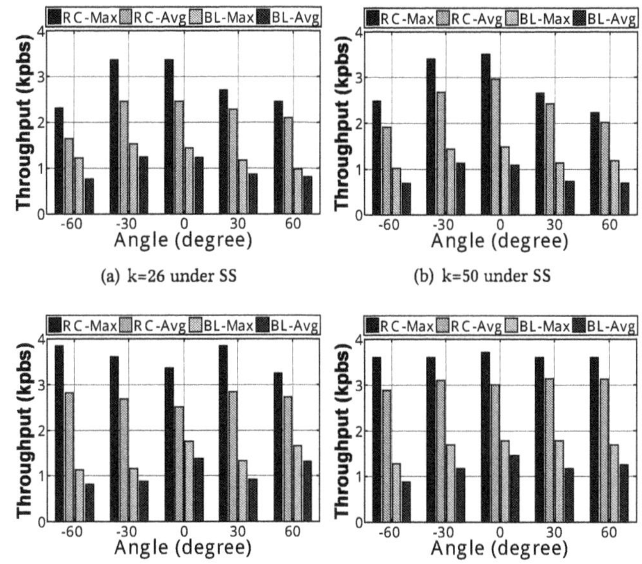

(a) k=26 under SS

(b) k=50 under SS

(c) k=26 under LS

(d) k=50 under LS

Figure 18: Throughput with a varying viewing angle of the receiver under both SS and LS.

5 RELATED WORK

There are mainly two trends of COTS-based VLC from the system development perspective, namely Screen-Camera [10, 11, 16, 23, 34, 35, 42] and LED-Camera [9, 13, 14, 19, 20, 40]. Whereas the former requires a specific device, the screen, but has a potential to achieve a higher throughput (at a cost of a reduced communication range), the latter only requires pervasively available lighting infrastructure. Due to the fundamental differences between them, we only focus our discussions on the latter that is relevant to ReflexCode. Note that, although the theoretically well-studied LED-PD VLC has got a few system avatars recently [6, 21, 33], we do not count them as COTS-based VLC because interfacing PD to COTS user devices (e.g., smartphones) is nontrivial beyond receiving simple messages [21].

LED-Camera VLC started with reflected light as the communication media [9, 28]. These seminal systems make use of only one LED transmitter to illuminate a reflector, and the applied modulation scheme (OOK in particular) is rather rudimentary. These lead to a very low data rate at around 100bps. Note that these earlier proposals also noticed the nonuniform distribution of reflected tonal range within a frame, yet they resort to polynomial regression to fit envelope, entailing unnecessary computational cost at the receiver side. Later proposals turned to direct light as an alternative. RollingLight [20] pioneered in demonstrating the possibility of constructing such a system, inspired by Luxapose [19] devised as a position system. To further improve the data rate, ColorBars [14] proposes to modulate data with Color-Shift Keying (CSK) at a cost of shortened communication range, while CeilingCast [13] suggests to combine multiple transmissions using rateless codes and also derives a simple model to characterize the performance bound of LED-Camera VLC.

As a communication system, coding and signal processing are crucial to VLC. Unlike LED-PD VLC where sophisticated RF techniques such as MIMO and UWB can be applied [6, 33], LED-Camera VLC is largely confined by the ability of its receiver (the rolling shutter camera). As a result, CSK [14] and GSK used by ReflexCode appear to be two major upgrading schemes from basic OOK. Another aspect of coding is DC balance. As VLC systems are piggybacking on existing lighting infrastructure, one has to guarantee that VLC transmission would not break lighting constraints, especially not to cause flicker. As the RLL codes recommended by IEEE 802.15.7 [30] are taken from existing RF systems, recent proposals aim to improve the performance of RLL for VLC: while [36] and [25] explore the serial concatenation of RLL and FEC codes to have a unified coding solution, [27] applies finite state machines to designing RLL codes so as to simultaneously achieve coding gain and flicker mitigation. Unfortunately, RLL codes may not always apply to a realistic VLC system. For example, Colorbars [14] still needs specially white light as inserted illumination symbols to make up for color offset resulted from the random combination of symbols, even when different symbols are distributed with the same proportion. Similarly, ReflexCode's GSK faces flicker at both symbol and transmitter levels, necessitating the need for a new coding mechanism.

Instead of acting as a data service, VLC finds its applications in other areas such as indoor localization [19, 21, 29, 38] and motion tracking [22, 41, 43]. In fact, the Visible Light Positioning (VLP) systems can be deemed as basic VLC systems from the communication perspective, as light beacons used by VLP are transmitting data at a relatively low rate to identify themselves. Therefore, the innovations of VLP lie in their ability of deriving the receiver's location based on the received messages from multiple beacons. As ReflexCode does not require any down light beacons, it has a potential to extend VLP. Motion tracking actually utilizes on the dual of VLC, namely Visible Light Sensing (VLS) [22, 41, 43]: it receives transmissions modulated by the variance in communication media and deduces information from them. Existing proposals all sense the direct light, so the advantage in reflected light taken by ReflexCode may broaden the scope of VLS applications.

6 CONCLUSION

In this paper, we have presented ReflexCode, a novel yet practical LED-Camera VLC system that adopts reflected light as its communication media. Compared with the existing peers, Reflex has improved on throughput substantially, mainly due to its innovation on exploiting collaborative transmissions to form GSK, a modulation scheme based on grayscale. In order to mitigate flicker and also to demodulate GSK efficiently, we have equipped ReflexCode with a new DC balanced coding adapting to GSK and a robust demodulation scheme driven by local variations in grayscale. Using two prototypes with different scales, we have validated the practicality of ReflexCode under various application scenarios, and we have also demonstrated its efficacy in throughput: it achieves a peak rate of almost 4kb/s at 2m distance and maintains an average rate of around 3kb/s at various distances up to 3m.

We are on the way to test higher order GSKs for further boosting data rate. However, one needs to be careful here, because a higher-order modulation means more LED luminaires in a VLC cell, which, on one hand, may not be very realistic and the other hand, increases the distance from some LED transmitters to the reflector. This latter effect causes a lower SNR and a higher error rate in demodulation. Therefore, although it is theoretically sound to raise the modulation order, we would anticipate such a system to be more complicated and also offers a much shorter transmission distance between the reflector and the receiver.

Two other issues remain on our agenda to further study: i) energy efficiency and ii) mobility support. While the transmitter side is known to be energy efficient, camera-based VLC is known to have a relatively high consumption on the receiver side. However, as LED-Camera VLC is not using the full functionality of the camera (as opposed to Screen-Camera VLC), there is a room for optimizing the energy consumption by only activating those necessary functions. As a wireless communication technology, VLC must also offer mobility support [5, 39]. Since ReflexCode is supposed to collaboratively operate multiple transmitters within a cell, mobility cross cell boundaries requires an adequate handover. We are planning to deploy a large testbed with multiple ReflexCode prototypes to facilitate our investigation on supporting mobility under VLC.

ACKNOWLEDGEMENT

The authors would like to thank the anonymous reviewers for their constructive feedback and valuable input. Special thanks to our shepherd, Prof. Zhang Xinyu, for his insights and time. This work was supported in part by the AcRF Tier 2 Grant MOE2016-T2-2-022 and the DSAIR Center at NTU.

REFERENCES

[1] *DELTA LIGHT.* http://www.deltalight.com/en/light-topics/indirect-lighting.
[2] *Low Cost LED Lamp.* https://item.taobao.com/item.htm?spm=a1z09.2.0.0.rUBQRc&id=520120735357&_u=95plk56ee7c.
[3] *LUXEON XF-3535L.* http://www.lumileds.com/products/matrix-platform/luxeon-xf-3535l.
[4] *Paulmann.* http://www.paulmann.com/en/all/all-about-light/led-strips/indirect-lighting.html.
[5] 2011. *IEEE Standard for Local and Metropolitan Area Networks–Part 15.7: Short-Range Wireless Optical Communication Using Visible Light.* IEEE Standard 802.15.7-2011. 1–309 pages.
[6] J.C. Chau, C. Morales, and T. D.C. Little. 2016. Using Spatial Light Modulators in MIMO Visible Light Communication Receivers to Dynamically Control the Optical Channel. In *Proc. of the 13th ACM EWSN.* 347–352.
[7] G. Corbellini, K. Aksit, S. Schmid, S. Mangold, and T. Gross. 2014. Connecting Networks of Toys and Smartphones with Visible Light Communication. *IEEE Communications Magazine* 52, 7 (2014), 72–78.
[8] H. Daicho, T. Iwasaki, K. Enomoto, Y. Sasaki, Y. Maeno, Y. Shinomiya, S. Aoyagi, E. Nishibori, M. Sakata, H. Sawa, and et al. 2012. A Novel Phosphor for Glareless White Light-Emitting Diodes. *Nature Communications* 3 (2012), 1132.
[9] C. Danakis, M. Afgani, G. Povey, I. Underwood, and H. Haas. 2012. Using a CMOS Camera Sensor for Visible Light Communication. In *Proc. of the 31th IEEE GLOBECOM Workshop.* 1244–1248.
[10] W. Du, J. C. Liando, and M. Li. 2016. SoftLight: Adaptive visible light communication over screen-camera links. In *Proc. of the 35th IEEE INFOCOM.* 1–9.
[11] W. Du, J. C. Liando, and M. Li. 2017. Soft Hint Enabled Adaptive Visible Light Communication over Screen-Camera Links. *IEEE Transactions on Mobile Computing* (2017), 527–537.
[12] A. Duque, R. Stanica, H. Rivano, and A. Desportes. 2016. Unleashing the Power of LED-to-Camera Communications for IoT Devices. In *Proc. of the 3rd ACM VLCS.* 55–60.
[13] J. Hao, Y. Yang, and J. Luo. 2016. CeilingCast: Energy Efficient and Location-bound Broadcast through LED-Camera Communication. In *Proc. of the 35th IEEE INFOCOM.* 1629–1637.
[14] P. Hu, P. H. Pathak, X. Feng, H. Fu, and P. Mohapatra. 2015. Colorbars: Increasing Data Rate of LED-to-Camera Communication Using Color Shift Keying. In *Proc. of the 11th ACM CoNEXT.* 12.
[15] W. Hu, H. Gu, and Q. Pu. 2013. Lightsync: Unsynchronized Visual Communication over Screen-Camera Links. In *Proc. of the 19th ACM MobiCom.* 15–26.
[16] W. Hu, Z. Huang J. Mao, Y. Xue, K. Bian J. She, and G. Shen. 2014. Strata: Layered Coding for Scalable Visual Communication. In *Proc. of the 20th ACM MobiCom.* 79–90.
[17] X. Huang, Z. Wang, J. Shi, Y. Wang, and N. Chi. 2015. 1.6 Gbit/s Phosphorescent White LED based VLC Transmission Using A Cascaded Pre-Equalization Circuit and A Differential Outputs PIN Receiver. *OSA Optics Express* 23, 17 (2015), 22034–22042.
[18] T. Kasahara, D. Aizawa, T. Irikura, T. Moriyama, T. Masahiro, and M. Iwamoto. 2006. Discomfort Glare Caused by White LED Light Sources. *J-STAGE Journal of Light & Visual Environment* 30, 2 (2006), 95–103.
[19] Y.-S. Kuo, P. Pannuto, K.-J. Hsiao, and P. Dutta. 2014. Luxapose: Indoor Positioning with Mobile Phones and Visible Light. In *Proc. of the 20th ACM MobiCom.* 447–458.
[20] H. Lee, H. Lin, Y. L. Wei, H. I. Wu, H. M. Tsai, and K. Lin. 2015. RollingLight: Enabling Line-of-Sight Light-to-Camera Communications. In *Proc. of 13th ACM MobiSys.* 167–180.
[21] L. Li, P. Hu, C. Peng, G. Shen, and F. Zhao. 2014. Epsilon: A Visible Light Based Positioning System. In *Proc. of 11th USENIX/ACM NSDI.* 331–343.
[22] T. Li, C. An, Z. Tian, A. T. Campbell, and X. Zhou. 2015. Human Sensing Using Visible Light Communication. In *Proc. of the 21st ACM MobiCom.* 331–344.
[23] T. Li, C. An, X. Xiao, A. T. Campbell, and X. Zhou. 2015. Real-time Screen-Camera Communication Behind Any Scene. In *Proc. of the 13th ACM MobiSys.* 197–211.

[24] R. J. Lin, M.-S. Tsai, and C.-C. Sun. 2015. Novel Optical Lens Design with a Light Scattering Freeform Inner Surface for LED Down Light Illumination. *OSA Optics Express* 23, 13 (2015), 16715–16722.

[25] X. Lu and J.L. Tiffany. 2016. Achieving FEC and RLL for VLC: A Concatenated Convolutional-Miller Coding Mechanism. *IEEE Photonics Technology Letters* 28, 9 (2016), 1030–1033.

[26] H. Ma, L. Lampe, and S. Hranilovic. 2013. Integration of Indoor Visible Light and Power Line Communication Systems. In *Proc. of 17th IEEE ISPLC.* 291–296.

[27] C. E. Mejia, C. N. Georghiades, M. M. Abdallah, and Y. Albadarneh. 2017. Code Design for Flicker Mitigation in Visible Light Communications Using Finite State Machines. *IEEE Transactions on Communications* (2017).

[28] N. Rajagopal, P. Lazik, and A. Rowe. 2014. Hybrid Visible Light Communication for Cameras and Low-Power Embedded Devices. In *Proc. of the 1st ACM VLCS.* 33–38.

[29] N. Rajagopal, P. Lazik, and A. Rowe. 2014. Visual Light Landmarks for Mobile Devices. In *Proc. of the 13th ACM IPSN.* 249–260.

[30] S. Rajagopal, R.D. Roberts, and S.K. Lim. 2012. IEEE 802.15. 7 Visible Light Communication: Modulation Schemes and Dimming Support. *IEEE Communications Magazine* 50, 3 (2012), 72–82.

[31] A. Shokrollahi. 2006. Raptor Codes. *IEEE Transactions on Information Theory* 52, 6 (2006), 2551–2567.

[32] T. Tashiro, S. Kawanobe, T. Kimura-Minoda, T. Ishikawa S. Kohko, and M. Ayama. 2015. Discomfort Glare for White LED Light Sources with Different Spatial Arrangements. *SAGE Lighting Research & Technology* 47, 3 (2015), 316–337.

[33] Z. Tian, K. Wright, and X. Zhou. 2016. The DarkLight Rises: Visible Light Communication in the Dark. In *Proc. of the 22nd ACM MobiCom.* 2–15.

[34] A. Wang, Z. Li, C. Peng, G. Shen, G. Fang, and B. Zeng. 2015. Inframe++: Achieve Simultaneous Screen-Human Viewing and Hidden Screen-Camera Communication. In *Proc. of the 13th ACM MobiSys.* 181–195.

[35] A. Wang, S. Ma, C. Hu, J. Huai, C. Peng, and G. Shen. 2014. Enhancing Reliability to Boost The Throughput over Screen-Camera Links. In *Proc. of the 20th ACM MobiCom.* 41–52.

[36] H. Wang and S. Kim. 2015. New RLL Decoding Algorithm for Multiple Candidates in Visible Light Communication. *IEEE Photon. Technol. Lett.* 27, 1 (2015), 15–17.

[37] B. Weir. 2012. Driving The 21st Century's Lights. *IEEE Spectrum* 49, 3 (2012).

[38] B. Xie, G. Tan, and T. He. 2015. SpinLight: A High Accuracy and Robust Light Positioning System for Indoor Applications. In *Proc. of the 13th ACM SenSys.* 211–223.

[39] Y. Yang. 2017. Practical Visible Light Communication System Utilizing LED Sensing. In *Proc. of the 15th IEEE PerCom Workshops.* 109–110.

[40] Y. Yang, J. Hao, and J. Luo. 2017. CeilingTalk: Lightweight Indoor Broadcast Through LED-Camera Communication. *IEEE Transactions on Mobile Computing (to appear)* (2017). https://doi.org/10.1109/TMC.2017.2694834

[41] Y. Yang, J. Hao, J. Luo, and S. J. Pan. 2017. CeilingSee: Device-free Occupancy Inference Through Lighting Infrastructure Based LED Sensing. In *Proc. of the 15th IEEE PerCom.* 247–256.

[42] Z. Yang, Y. Bao, C. Luo, X. Zhao, S. Zhu, C. Peng, Y. Liu, and X. Wang. 2016. ARTcode: Preserve Art and Code in Any Image. In *Proc. of the ACM UbiComp'16.* 904–915.

[43] C. Zhang, J. Tabor, J. Zhang, and X. Zhang. 2015. Extending Mobile Interaction Through Near-Field Visible Light Sensing. In *Proc. the 21st ACM MobiCom.* 345–357.

[44] J. Zhang, C. Zhang, X. Zhang, and S. Banerjee. 2016. Towards a Visible Light Network Architecture for Continuous Communication and Localization. In *Proc. of the 3rd ACM VLCS.* 49–54.

[45] R. Zhang, H. Claussen, H. Haas, and L. Hanzo. 2016. Energy Efficient Visible Light Communications Relying on Amorphous Cells. *IEEE Journal on Selected Areas in Communications* 34, 4 (2016), 894–906.

Shyam Gollakota - Winner of the 2017 ACM SIGMOBILE RockStar Award

Shyam Gollakota is the winner of the 2017 ACM SIGMOBILE RockStar Award. ACM SIGMOBILE's RockStar Award Committee selected Shyam in recognition of his outstanding early-career contributions and impact on our field. The RockStar Award is our community's acknowledgement of the depth, impact, and novelty of Shyam's research.

Prof. Shyam Gollakota is a creative force in his field of wireless computer networks who has developed new technologies that are disrupting the field. In only four years as a faculty member, Shyam has already carried out several new research efforts that are technically innovative and whose results are surprising.

Basically, in today's world of ubiquitous computing, small, powerful mobile devices communicate with each other over wireless networks – in your home, at work, at play, on airplane flights, and soon, even in your body. Shyam's work has focused on making wireless communication more effective, but more exciting, he's imagining new uses for wireless signals.

As a first example consider Shyam's invention of "ambient backscatter," which has created significant excitement inside and outside of the field. The context for this work is the world of ubiquitous sensors. Microscopic computing devices are increasingly being embedded in sensors that are implanted in structures (such as bridges), in homes (e.g., moisture detectors in the walls), or even in our bodies (e.g., in implanted medical devices or contact lenses). These devices need to communicate with each other and with the outside world. A particular problem is that the act of communicating (broadcasting messages) is a very power hungry activity: how can these tiny devices communicate, then, if they have little power, or even no power at all

In a technical tour-de-force, Shyam has shown how sensor devices can communicate with each other *without* having any source of power. Instead of batteries or wires, these devices pull power for communications "out of thin air." At a high level, while you're reading this message, you are being bombarded by radio waves from nearby TV and cell phone towers. Shyam's devices draw energy from the radio waves, storing up small amounts of energy to run the processor and sensors. The devices then use a technique that Shyam calls *ambient backscatter* for communication; basically, the battery-free device communicates by *reflecting and modulating* incoming radio waves (e.g., a TV or WiFi signal) in a slightly modified way that can be detected as a message by other sensors that are listening nearby.

As a second example, consider another of Shyam's projects in human-computer interfaces. Previous work on gesture recognition systems allows people to control devices through movements of their hands, arms, or bodies; e.g., Microsoft Kinect uses computer vision and 3D cameras in the space, while other systems (like the Nintendo Wii) use sensor devices held or worn by the user. Shyam developed the first whole-home gesture recognition system *without* user instrumentation or cameras. Instead, he used WiFi signals in the environment.

In a nutshell, Shyam's research tackles both longstanding problems and completely new (and unanticipated) applications of wireless networks. The significance of his research has already been widely recognized by the research community in the form of multiple best paper awards. Shyam's work is creative, technically deep, often surprising, and likely to have enormous practical impact in our world of ubiquitous computing and IoT devices.

Navigating the Chasm between Curiosity and Impact-Driven Research

Shyam Gollakota
University of Washington and Jeeva Wireless, Inc.
Seattle, WA
gshyam@cs.washington.edu

ABSTRACT

Being in academia provides a unique opportunity to explore one's curiosity and build cool systems that advance human understanding of engineering and science. System researchers however also have a responsibility to build systems that can impact practice in the near-term and perhaps, even create a brand new industry. In my talk, I will focus on my efforts so far navigating this chasm between curiosity and impact driven research. Specifically, I will share two research themes I have been working on as an assistant professor at UW CSE, where what initially began as curiosity-driven projects were transformed by the urge to make immediate practical impact as well as be unique. In particular, I will first talk about our journey going from a science-driven project on ambient backscatter (Sigcomm'13) to building wireless backscatter systems that work reliably and address a key pain-point in the industry. Next, I will talk about how we shifted gears from working on wireless gesture recognition (WiSee, Mobicom'13) to addressing a medical need of millions of people in the United States that go undiagnosed from sleep apnea (ApneaApp, Mobisys'15) and our experience licensing our technology to a multi-national medical corporation. Finally, I will share my thoughts on how our research community can help us better navigate this chasm.

CCS Concepts/ACM Classifiers
E.0 [General]

Author Keywords
Ambient backscatter; wireless gestures; Sleep apnea; passive Wi-Fi

MobiCom'17, October 16-20, 2017, Snowbird, UT, USA.

ACM ISBN 978-1-4503-4916-1/17/10.
DOI: https://doi.org/10.1145/3117811.3129240

BIOGRAPHY

Shyamnath Gollakota is an Associate Professor of the Department of Computer Science & Engineering at the University of Washington where he leads the Networks and Mobile Systems Lab. He is also the President of Jeeva Wireless Inc. His research covers a range of topics, including computer networks, human-computer interaction, battery-free computing and mobile health. His work on backscatter is being commercialized at Jeeva Wireless Inc. and ResMed Inc. has licensed his work on sleep apnea.

He is the recipient of a 2015 National Science Foundation Career Award and an Alfred P. Sloan Fellowship. He was named as MIT Technology Review's 35 Innovators Under 35, Popular Science 'brilliant 10' and twice to the Forbes' 30 Under 30 list. His research has earned Best Paper awards at SIGCOMM, MOBICOM, NSDI and CHI and named as a MIT Technology Review Breakthrough technology of 2016 as well as Popular Science top innovations in 2015. He is an alumnus of MIT (Ph.D., 2013, winner of ACM doctoral dissertation award) and IIT Madras (2012).

Pulsar: Towards Ubiquitous Visible Light Localization

Chi Zhang
University of Wisconsin-Madison
czhang296@wisc.edu

Xinyu Zhang
University of California San Diego
xiz368@eng.ucsd.edu

ABSTRACT

The past decade's research in visible light positioning (VLP) has led to technologies with high location precision. However, existing VLP systems either require specialized LEDs which hinder large-scale deployment, or need cameras which preclude continuous localization because of high power consumption and short coverage. In this paper, we propose Pulsar, which uses a compact photodiode sensor, readily fit into a mobile device, to discriminate existing ceiling lights—either fluorescent lights or conventional LEDs—based on their intrinsic optical emission features. To overcome the photodiode's lack of spatial resolution, we design a novel sparse photogrammetry mechanism, which resolves the light source's angle-of-arrival, and triangulates the device's 3D location and even orientation. To facilitate ubiquitous deployment, we further develop a light registration mechanism that automatically registers the ceiling lights' locations as landmarks on a building's floor map. Our experiments demonstrate that Pulsar can reliably achieve decimeter precision in both controlled environment and large-scale buildings.

CCS CONCEPTS

• **Computer systems organization → Special purpose systems**; • **Hardware → Signal processing systems; Sensors and actuators; Sensor applications and deployments; Sensor devices and platforms**;

KEYWORDS

Visible light sensing; Indoor localization; Signal processing; Sensor; Angle of arrival; Photodiode

1 INTRODUCTION

Indoor localization represents the enabling technology behind a huge space of location-based services, including human/robot navigation, targeted advertisement, inventory control, healthcare monitoring, augmented reality, *etc.* Recent research has led to solutions that deliver decimeter level accuracy under controlled experimental settings [24, 26]. Unfortunately, none of such solutions has widely penetrated the real-world. A recent pilot study of state-of-the-art indoor localization systems [33] concluded that indoor localization

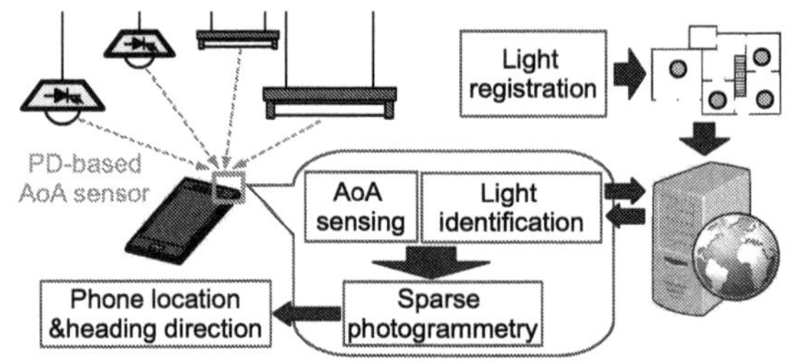

Figure 1: Pulsar's architecture.

persists as a grand challenge, primarily because no existing solution simultaneously satisfies desired properties of *high accuracy, reliability* and *low cost.*

The visible light positioning (VLP) technology has shown potential to fill the gap. VLP employs "smart LEDs" as location landmarks, and photodiodes (PDs) [31, 55, 66] or cameras [26, 40, 58, 64] as sensors. The dense overhead deployment of light fixtures, and multipath-free propagation profile, together enable VLP's high spatial resolution and resilience to environmental dynamics. Existing VLP technologies have achieved meter [31, 40] or decimeter precision [26, 58, 64], when using PD and camera, respectively.

However, two fundamental limitations have been impeding the adoption of VLP: *(i)* Requirement for specially designed smart LED bulbs, which modulate the light signals to create unique beacon IDs. Such bulbs are substantially more costly and bulkier than commercial LEDs or fluorescent lights (FLs) [48], which hinders near-term mass deployment. In fact, even the basic LEDs only make up around 7% of commercial/industrial lighting, and may take 10+ years towards wide penetration [49], mainly because FL fixtures have already dominated the market and retrofitting/updating cost is formidable. *(ii)* Dependence on regular light shape and angular response. VLP systems that employ RSS-based light propagation models commonly assume Lambertian radiation patterns [3, 31], which are applicable only to round-shaped LED bulbs (Sec. 2.1). A camera offers high spatial resolution and can unleash VLP from RSS models [26, 64]. A recent camera-based VLP system, LiTell [64], works even for conventional FLs. But the camera's narrow field-of-view (FoV), high power consumption (~2 watts [64]) and high processing latency (~2 seconds [64]) prevent it from supporting pervasive, real-time, energy efficient location tracking. The limitation to FLs also makes LiTell a transition solution as LEDs will eventually take over.

In order to overcome the limitations of conventional VLP systems, we introduce Pulsar in this paper. Pulsar builds on recent measurement observations [64] which identified the intrinsic high-frequency flickering patterns inside FLs using cameras. Yet Pulsar targets more ambitious design goals that are conducive to ubiquitous location-based services: *(i)* working under both LEDs and incumbent FLs in existing buildings; *(ii)* using energy-efficient "single-pixel" PDs, but still able to resolve 3D location with similar

MobiCom '17, October 16-20, 2017, Snowbird, UT, USA

ACM ISBN 978-1-4503-4916-1/17/10...$15.00
https://doi.org/10.1145/3117811.3117821

precision as the million-pixel cameras [64]; *(iii)* realizing *continuous, seamless coverage* as users roam around in practical building environment; *(iv)* allowing easy integration with mobile applications, and easy deployment with minimal bootstrapping overhead.

Fig. 1 illustrates the main components and workflow of Pulsar. Pulsar uses PD as its light sensor, which reduces the power consumption by several folds compared with camera-based VLP systems. In addition, owing to PDs' much higher dynamic range, Pulsar can capture LEDs' intrinsic frequencies that are much weaker than FLs', and even when the LEDs are more than 9m away (Sec. 3), in contrast to camera-based solutions [64] that only work within a range of 2.5m even for FLs. This salient property enables Pulsar to capture multiple lights simultaneously even when the lights are sparsely deployed on high ceilings, and obtain location fixes virtually without any blind spots.

Unfortunately, such benefits come with new challenges: *(i) Near-far interference.* The frequency features of faraway lights often mix with the weak side-peak artifacts of close-by lights and get masked, making it hard to distinguish collocated lights. *(ii) Lack of spatial resolution.* In contrast to the million-pixel camera, the PD is a single-pixel intensity sensor, which provides no spatial resolution and cannot easily identify its geometrical relation with different lights.

Pulsar's key solution principle lies in a novel mechanism, referred to as *sparse photogrammetry*, which resolves the light source's angle-of-arrival (AoA) using a compact light sensor. Pulsar's light sensor comprises two PDs with different FoVs[1], and hence different angular response patterns. The differential response between the two PDs follows a nonlinear function with the AoA, which can be calibrated and known at manufacturing time. At runtime, Pulsar can measure the differential response and map it back to the light source's AoA. By using AoA instead of RSS, Pulsar also circumvents the Lambertian model, enabling localization with lights of any shape. By combining the AoA of adjacent light sources, Pulsar can pinpoint the device's 3D location through a triangulation model. When more than 3 lights fall in its FoV, the Pulsar sensor can even compute its orientation angles. On the other hand, to solve the near-far problem, we observe that all frequency components of the same light have the same AoA, which allows us to single out a light's intrinsic frequency, even when it is immersed in other nearby lights' frequency components.

Full deployment of an indoor localization system requires knowing the landmarks' locations *a priori*, a problem often overlooked by existing localization systems. Pulsar uses a *light registration* mechanism to greatly simplify the issue: it only requires a one-time bootstrapping procedure, where a surveyor walks across the lights inside a building, while the lights' frequency features are captured by Pulsar, and lights' locations automatically registered on a publicly available floor map and stored in a database. Following any subsequent change of light fixtures, the database can be incrementally updated based on user devices' feedback.

We have conducted a full-fledged implementation of Pulsar. The Pulsar sensor is prototyped as a USB dongle, plugged in an Android phone that runs the localization algorithms. Owing to the use of lightweight PDs, we expect Pulsar can readily augment new generations of smartphones, robots or low-power IoT devices that need location-based services [4, 25, 29, 36]. We have further implemented the light registration mechanism along with a simple user interface.

Our experiments verify Pulsar's high accuracy, robustness, and usability. In controlled setups similar to many existing VLP systems [26, 31, 40, 58], Pulsar can achieve 10 cm of median location precision. In practical building environments, Pulsar can easily detect 3 or more lights within its FoV, achieving a median localization error of 0.6 m and heading direction error of 4° while walking. More importantly, Pulsar is robust to typical usage dynamics, such as the device's orientation variation and ambient sunlight interference. Our prototype implementation incurs a response latency of 840 ms, ready for real-time location queries, and a low power consumption of 150 mW even without duty-cycling.

To summarize, our contributions in Pulsar include: *(i)* A *sparse photogrammetry* mechanism that enables single-pixel PDs to sense a light source's AoA, and then pinpoint their own locations and heading direction. *(ii)* A light identification framework that enables a PD to discriminate LEDs/FLs whose frequency features interfere with each other; *(iii)* Validation of Pulsar based on a full-fledged implementation including an automatic landmark registration scheme.

2 AUGMENTING PHOTODIODES WITH AOA SENSING

2.1 Why AoA?

Prior PD based VLP systems [3, 31] commonly adopt round LED bulbs whose angular emission pattern follows a Lambertian model, but commercial light fixtures present several key barriers to such RSS-based models: *(i)* The light fixtures are commonly tube/rectangular shaped, yielding different channel responses along different directions. So the RSS modeling will need the PD's location in the first place. *(ii)* The light fixture may have complicated reflective structures and covers which reshape the emission pattern [41]. *(iii)* Static and dynamic blockages such as ceiling decorators and people passing by may partially block the light, causing unpredictable deviation in RSS. In addition, due to aging and inevitable hardware deviation, different lights' emission power can vary, even among the same type of lights [5, 37, 41, 57]. All these factors render RSS propagation modeling unusable in real indoor environments.

To understand these challenges, we use our light sensor prototype (Sec. 6) to measure the RSS of light sources across different irradiance angles (defined in Fig. 2), at 1m distance. We measure two representative tube lights (with and without the diffuser cover, shown in Fig. 3), commonly used in commercial buildings. We then measure the light intensity with sensor facing towards the light, and normalize it against intensity at 0°. From the results in Fig. 4, we see that the Lambertian model deviates from the measured RSS by up to 6dB, which translates into a few meters of error when the PD is a few meters away from the light [31]. Worse still, the angular response of the same light can change with viewing angle, meaning that a precise RSS propagation model requires the location/orientation of the PD *a priori*.

In summary, for robustness and ubiquity, the VLP system should work independently from lights' emission characteristics such as angular response and intensity. However, this almost forbids the

[1]Defined as the double-sided incident angle where RSS is halved in comparison to RSS at 0°. Unlike cameras, a PD can still sense light sources outside its FoV.

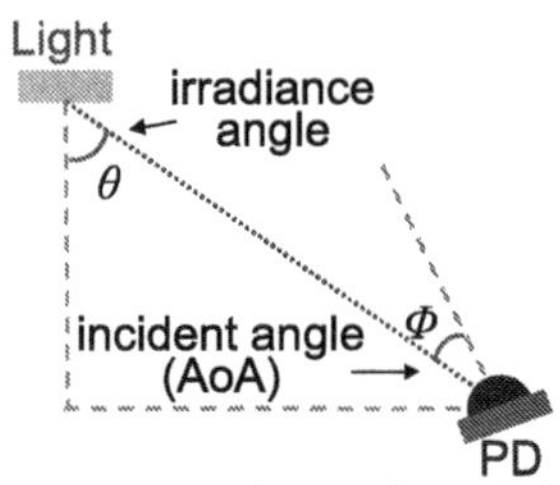

Figure 2: Channel model from light to PD.

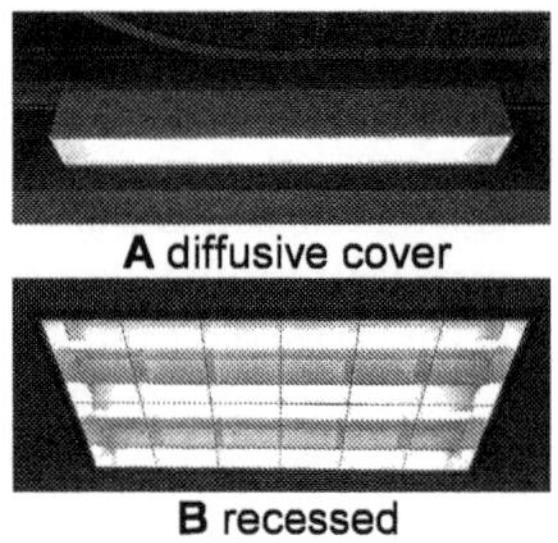

Figure 3: Two representative FLs.

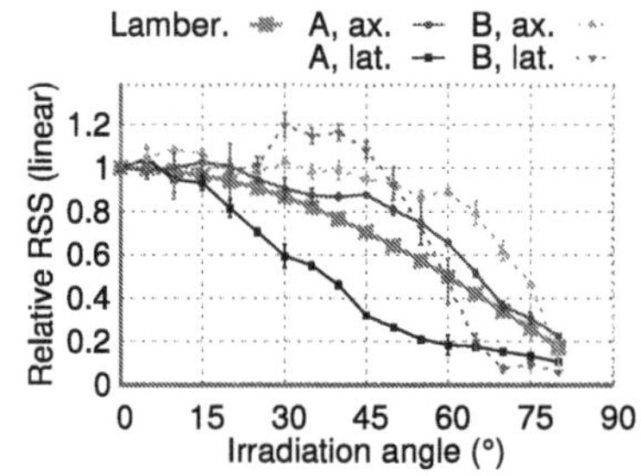

Figure 4: Axial/lateral Angular response of 2 tube fixtures, at 1m distance.

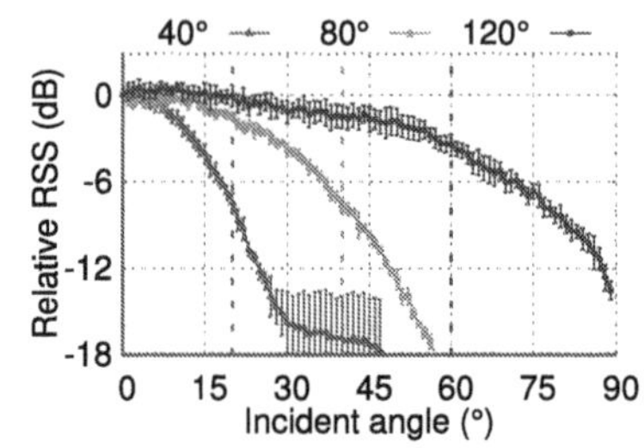

Figure 5: Angular response of 3 PDs. Dotted lines mark half-angle FoV from datasheets.

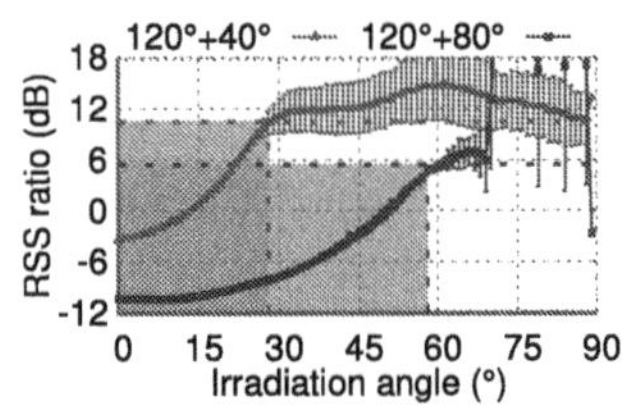

Figure 6: Composite angular response of 2 PD combinations.

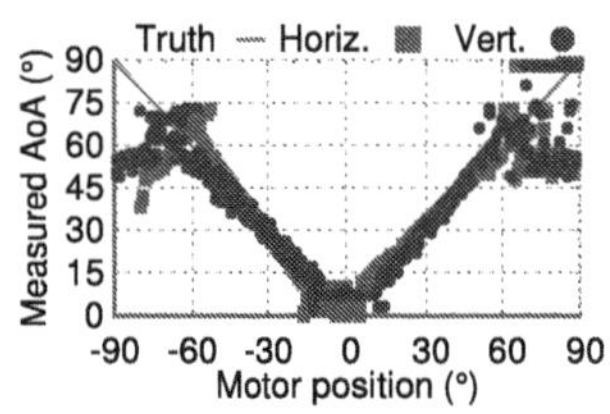

Figure 7: AoA accuracy for horizontally and vertically placed sensor.

use of RSS modeling. An AoA model can naturally avoid such problems, because it approximates the light as a point source, whose irradiation angle is unaffected by its shape, partial occlusion, and intensity variation.

2.2 Pulsar's AoA Sensing: Model and Principles

Harnessing the million-pixel sensors and high spatial resolution, a camera can easily extrapolate the physical geometries of multiple luminaries in an overhead scene image into 2-dimensional AoA information. This so-called *photogrammetry* technique [26] can arguably provide the most accurate and reliable geometrical information [3], albeit at the cost of higher power consumption, limited FoV, *etc.* In this section, we describe how Pulsar uses single-pixel PDs to obtain AoA while overcoming camera's inherent limitations (Sec. 1).

2.2.1 AoA Sensing Using Single-Pixel PDs. The key innovation of Pulsar lies in a *dual-PD light sensor.* Pulsar uses the differential angular responses between the 2 PDs to obtain 1-D AoA (*i.e.*, incident angle between incoming light and the PD's center axis, illustrated in Fig. 2), which will in turn feed Pulsar's sparse photogrammetry localization algorithm (to be discussed in Sec. 4).

More specifically, the RSS between each light source and the PDs follows a generic channel model [31, 63]:

$$\begin{aligned} \mathrm{RSS}_1 &= P_t A_t(\theta_1)\alpha(r_1)A_{r1}(\phi_1) \\ \mathrm{RSS}_2 &= P_t A_t(\theta_2)\alpha(r_2)A_{r2}(\phi_2) \end{aligned} \quad (1)$$

where P_t is the emission power of the light. $A_t(\theta)$ is the irradiance angular response at irradiance angle θ; $\alpha(r)$ is the propagation loss at distance r, and $A_{ri}(\phi)$ is the incident angular response of the i-th PD at incident angle ϕ [2]. Since the 2 PDs are most likely co-located on a mobile device, with negligible separation compared with r, we can safely assume $\theta_1 = \theta_2$, $r_1 = r_2$ and $\phi_1 = \phi_2 = \phi$. *By dividing the linear RSS observed by the 2 PDs, all other factors related to the emission/intensity characteristics of the light will cancel out:*

$$\frac{\mathrm{RSS}_1}{\mathrm{RSS}_2} = \frac{A_{r1}(\phi)}{A_{r2}(\phi)} = A_c(\phi) \quad (2)$$

Inverting Eq. (2) and we can obtain the 1-D AoA or incident angle:

$$\phi = A_c^{-1}\left(\frac{\mathrm{RSS}_1}{\mathrm{RSS}_2}\right) \quad (3)$$

Note that RSS_i can be measured in real-time by each PD at each frequency. The *composite angular response* $A_c = A_{r1}/A_{r2}$ is essentially a function that maps AoA to the differential response between the 2 PDs. Each PD's response function A_{ri} is fixed and is known through data-sheet or a one-time factory calibration, which in turn allows us to derive A_c as a static lookup table.

The above model builds on three approximations: *(i)* For A_c^{-1} to be a valid function, A_c needs to be *monotonic*, at least within a range of AoA. *(ii)* The two PDs bear the same AoA relative to a light source. *(iii)* The light source can be approximated as a point source from the PDs' perspective in terms of area. We now validate these approximations through measurements.

2.2.2 Accuracy of AoA model. We first verify the monotonic relation between AoA and A_c, using different PD combinations. We test 3 PDs with different FoVs: 40°(Vishay BPV10), 80°(Everlight PD333) and 120°(OSRAM BPW34). Fig. 5 plots the actual angular responses of the PDs, measured by rotating the PD using a programmable motion controller [12] while illuminated by a LED. Note that the measured FoV often deviates from the nominal rating in the datasheet, which necessitates a one-time factory calibration of the angular response.

To verify the AoA model, we measure the composite angular response A_c of different narrow+wide PD combinations: BPW34 + BPV10 and BPW34 + PD333, respectively. Fig. 6 shows that A_c indeed grows monotonically with AoA up to a certain threshold, beyond which it starts to drop, making A_c^{-1} ambiguous. The threshold AoA equals 28° and 57°, translating to usable FoV of 56° and 114° for the two combinations, which is much wider than most smartphone cameras (around 70° [2]). For both combinations, the monotonic region is slightly larger than the FoV of the PD with narrower FoV. In practice, *to ensure a one-to-one mapping between AoA and A_c, Pulsar only uses A_c when it falls in the monotonic region.*

We also notice a tradeoff between FoV and spatial resolution for the dual-PD sensor. The wider-FoV combination BPW34 + PD333 has lower spatial resolution — the composite angular response A_c is flat at near-zero AoA region, which can induce ambiguities. This

[2]Note that $A_{ri}(\phi) = \cos\phi$ only when the receiver follows the ideal Lambertian model and has 120° FoV.

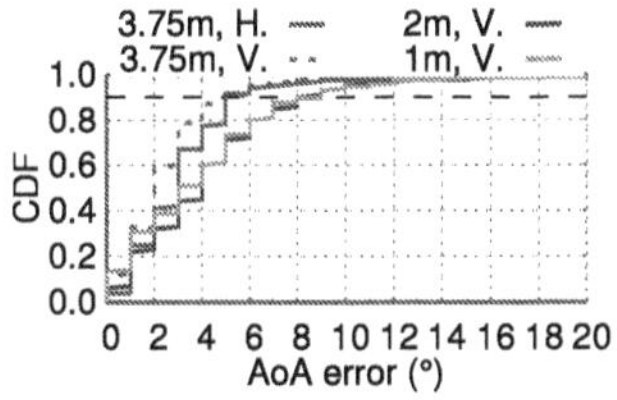

Figure 8: CDF of AoA sensing error.

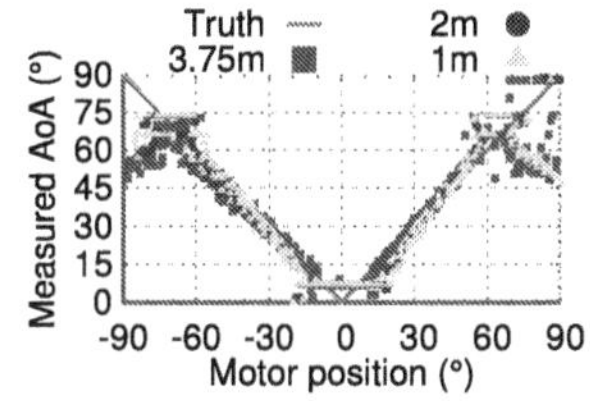

Figure 9: AoA accuracy vs light-to-sensor distance.

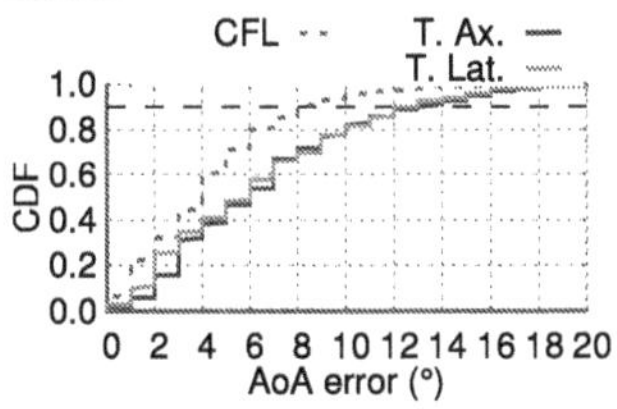

Figure 10: CDF of AoA error for tube FLs, along axial and lateral direction.

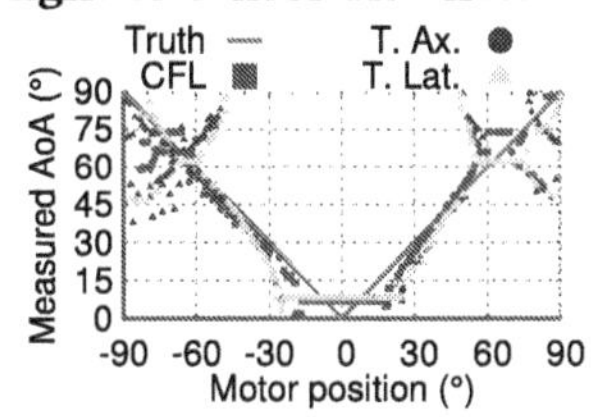

Figure 11: AoA sensing accuracy of tube FLs, along axial and lateral direction.

is because PDs with larger FoV have flatter angular response at lower AoA values. We expect combining 3 or more PDs can make a better tradeoff and provide even larger FoV. For simplicity, the rest of paper will use the BPW34 + PD333 combination, and leave other possibilities for future work.

2.2.3 Impact of PD Arrangement. Our AoA model assumes the two PDs are arbitrarily close and experience the same optical channel. But in practice, they have to be physically separated, inducing certain anisotropy. To evaluate the impact on AoA sensing, we place Pulsar's dual-PD sensor 3 m below a ceiling light, and rotate it to 500 random but known directions using the motion controller. Since the PDs have a very small form-factor, they are placed approximately 5 mm apart. The scatter plot in Fig. 7 and CDF in Fig. 8 indicate that the 90-percentile errors are less than 5° within the ambiguity-free region for all cases. This implies *the dual-PD can be abstracted as a single sensor, receiving lights isotropically.*

2.2.4 Point-source Approximation. When using a PD to sense a large light fixture (*e.g.*, tube lights in a rectangular housing) at close distance, the light spans across a large range of incident angles. The equivalent angular response will be a smoothed version of the original one, which may break the point-source approximation and introduce error in AoA.

To quantify the ultimate impact, we place a CFL lamp at various distances, leading to different levels of response smoothing. Using the same measurement methods as in Fig. 7, we found that even in the extreme case with 1m distance, the mean AoA error is only 4° (Figs. 8 and 9). And it reduces to 3° and 2° at 2m and 3.75m, respectively.

Further, we repeat the experiments with tube FLs (T8 type, Fig. 3A). The results (Figs. 10 and 11) show that when placed 2 m below the ceiling, Pulsar's mean AoA sensing error is below 6°, and 90-th percentile below 13°. Interestingly, the error does not change with direction (Sec. 2.2.3), as the amount of smoothing in the PD's angular response does not vary. Overall, *the point-source assumption well approximates reality.*

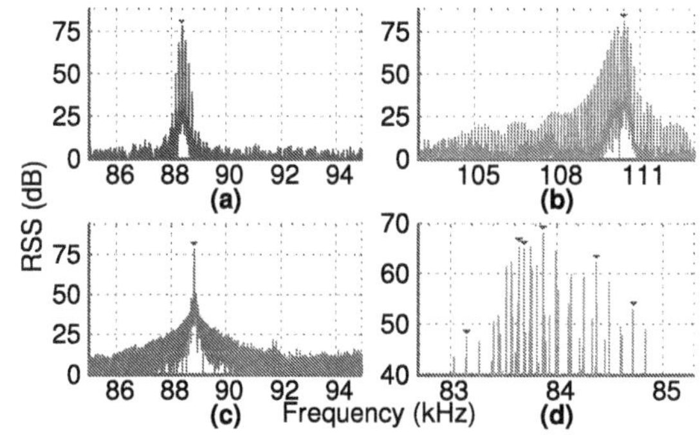

Figure 12: Characteristic frequency (CF) and side peaks for typical commercial lights: (a) T8 tube FL, (b) CFL bulb, (c) commercial LED, (d) signals from multiple tube FLs added together. Green triangles mark CFs.

3 DISCRIMINATING LIGHT LANDMARKS USING FREQUENCY FEATURES

Since 3-D localization requires 1-D AoA information from multiple landmarks, Pulsar's sensor must be able to *simultaneously discriminate the lights and compute the AoA of each.* This requires adjacent light fixtures to emit uniquely identifiable signals that do not interfere with each other when captured by the PD. Most existing VLP systems use modified LEDs which modulate the optical signals to meet these requirements [26, 31, 58]. Meanwhile, LiTell [64] proposed a way to discriminate unmodified FLs, based on the fact that their driver works by oscillating [35, 43, 51], and manufacturing tolerance [45] leads to unique interference-free oscillating frequencies, referred to as *characteristic frequencies* (CFs).

As in LiTell, Pulsar aims to discriminate the lights using their CFs as features. When capturing multiple lights simultaneously, LiTell can isolate the lights' signals because their locations differ on the camera image. In contrast, the use of single-pixel PDs brings two unique challenges to Pulsar. *(i) Near-far interference.* A light's emission spectrum comprises not only the CF, but also various spurious frequencies. The spurious signals from nearby/brighter lights can overwhelm the CF features from further/dimmer ones, making them unidentifiable. *(ii) Lack of spatial resolution.* Previous work [64] utilizes relation between consecutively located lights to facilitate error correction, while Pulsar's sensor cannot resolve spatial relation. This limits Pulsar's light identifying accuracy when collision happens. In the following sections, we describe how Pulsar meets these challenges.

3.1 Light Feature Extraction

To elucidate the near-far interference problem, we use a PD sensor (Sec. 6) to sample and analyze the frequency-domain spectrum of representative luminaries offline, including tube FL, compact FL (CFL), and LED. From the plots in Fig. 12(a)-(c), we see that each type of light manifests a peak CF, but accompanied by numerous side peaks [3]. Fig. 12(d) further shows the mixed light spectrum in an office room, with tube FL fixtures separated 1.2m apart on the ceiling. The PD sensor has 120° FoV, faces upwards and sits 4m below the ceiling. The ground-truth CF is measured by turning on each light separately. We can see that the PD captures the CFs

[3] Diversity of CFs within each model of light has been validated by [64].

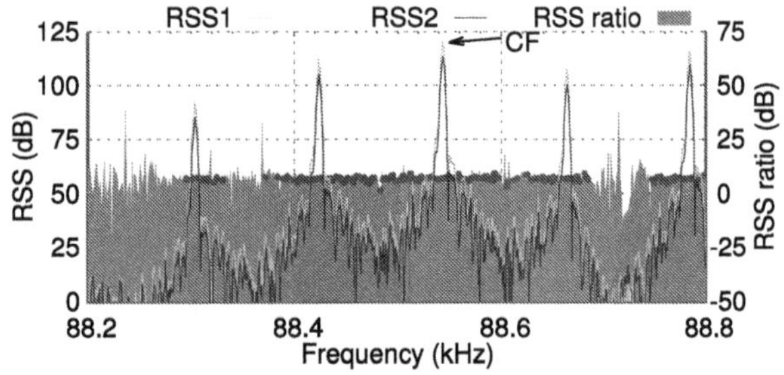

Figure 13: Artifacts in a single light's spectrum and corresponding RSS ratio. Dots show ratio with sufficient RSS.

Algorithm 1: Algorithm for light extraction.

input : $\mathcal{P}$ – spectrum peaks with sufficient RSS; ϵ_{AoA} – tolerance (minimum difference in AoA/RSS-ratio)

output : $\mathcal{L}$ – CFs

sortByRSS($\mathcal{P}$)

$\mathcal{L} \leftarrow \varnothing$

for $p \in \mathcal{P}$ **do**

  $\mathcal{L}$.add(p), $\mathcal{P}$.remove(p)

  for $q \in \mathcal{P}$ **do**

    if $|q.AoA - p.AoA| < \epsilon_{AoA}$ **then**

      $\mathcal{P}$.remove(q)

of 6 lights simultaneously. However, the faraway lights' CFs are immersed in the spurious peaks caused by close-by lights. Thus, unlike camera-based LiTell system [64] which only needs to extract the single strongest peak in the spectrum, we cannot single out every frequency by picking the strongest frequency components. In effect, there is even no easy way to identify the number of lights within the spectrum.

To overcome this challenge, note that we can use the model in Sec. 2.2 to compute the AoA of the signals corresponding to each individual frequency peak. We observe that *if different frequency peaks have the same AoA, it is likely that they originated from the same light source.* Therefore, we first sort the peaks in the spectrum by their AoAs, and then pick the strongest peak for each unique AoA, which corresponds to the true CF of one light. We repeat this until the remaining peaks become negligible (likely to be noise).

To verify the feasibility of this AoA-based light extraction, we set up one tube FL inside a darkroom. We then use our AoA sensor to receive the light signal, while moving the sensor up and down, just like walking. Fig. 13 shows that the RSS ratio is indeed consistent across different frequency components from the same light, as long as RSS's from both PDs are sufficient.

Alg. 1 summarizes the procedure of CF extraction in Pulsar. Note that since the AoA value is derived from RSS difference from 2 PDs, a slight difference in frequency responses of the 2 amplifiers may cause slightly different AoAs to be observed at each frequency. As a result, we empirically set a tolerance to the RSS ratio (0.5dB in our experiments) when merging spectrum peaks with similar AoAs, according to experimental results for a single light in the dark room. Meanwhile, when 2 lights have similar AoAs, the weaker one will be removed. Such similar AoAs often come from co-located lights, and thus will not reduce the number of effective lights.

Occasionally, frequency components of 2 different lights may collide (fall within 2 FFT bins), which may distort the AoA. However, it will only result in spurious detection under the following additional conditions: *(i) Both lights have sufficient RSS and their perceived RSS ratio is distorted by more than 0.5dB.* Either their RSS at the colliding frequency is comparable[4], or a different light dominates each PD. *(ii) RSS at the colliding frequency is higher than any other lights with similar perceived AoA.* In practice, we find this situation to be rare throughout our experiments.

3.2 Identifying Multiple Lights without Spatial Knowledge

Despite the diversity of the CF, occasionally there exist remotely separated luminaries with barely distinguishable CF values. LiTell [64] mitigated such CF collisions by combining two consecutively sampled lights, which provides a form of spatial error correction and greatly lowers possibility of CF feature collision. But it requires the user to travel across at least 2 lights, thus precluding instantaneous location fix without any user intervention. In contrast, Pulsar's PD-based sensor can resolve a group of lights' CFs simultaneously, which enhances feature diversity without user intervention, but entails a new challenge. Unlike camera [64], PD has no spatial resolution and cannot recognize whether two lights are adjacent.

To overcome this barrier, for each measurement observation of the light signals, Pulsar uses all the CFs it extracts (Sec. 3.1) as a feature collection, denoted as $\mathcal{L}$. It then searches for the set of lights in the database whose CFs are closest to $\mathcal{L}$ in terms of Euclidean distance. Given the large number of lights in each building, a brute-force search among all possible group combinations is infeasible. However, we can prune the search space based on two observations: *(i) Frequency error of each light.* Existing measurement study [64] showed that the CF feature is highly diverse even among lights in the same building (99% of the lights have CFs separated more than 20Hz). It is also stable, varying only by tens of Hz across weeks. Therefore, for each element in $\mathcal{L}$, it suffices to put the few database candidates with closest CF into the search space. *(ii) Physical distance between each identified light.* Since within each observation the sensor should see lights which are near each other, groups that have candidates with large distance (computed with the candidates' registered locations) are also likely to be incorrect matches. We thus combine these two factors into a score that describes how likely a match is valid. These two factors can be weighted and we empirically give them equal weight when values are in kHz and meters. In addition, we use the score as a *confidence* value for each light, which is later used for optimizing the reliability of localization (Sec. 4). Alg. 2 summarizes the above procedure which identifies the group of lights in one measurement observation.

3.3 Sensitivity and Coverage

Ideally, Pulsar needs to ensure multiple lights' CF features are detectable to realize blind-spot free location sensing. Existing work re-purposed smartphone cameras to extrapolate the lights' CFs [64]. Due to their narrow FoV [2] and low dynamic range, a camera can only capture a *single light* in office buildings with typical light

[4]If RSS's of the 2 lights are within 9dB, the summed RSS would be higher than *both* lights by more than 0.5dB, and the error in RSS ratio *may* exceed 0.5dB.

Algorithm 2: Algorithm for group light matching.

```
input  : 𝓛 – CFs; ϵ = 500Hz – maximum CF error; N = 2 –
         number of candidates; 𝓑 – CF database
output : 𝓔 – light identities
for l ∈ 𝓛 do
    l.candidates ← {b ∈ 𝓑 | ϵ > |l.CF − 𝓑.CF|}
    sortByError(l.candidates)
    truncate(l.candidates, N)
C ← candidateCombinations(𝓛)
for 𝓓 ∈ C do
    score(𝓛, 𝓓)
𝓔 ← {𝓓 ∈ C | 𝓓 has lowest score}
Procedure score(features 𝓛, candidates 𝓓)
    ϵ_d ← 0, ϵ_f ← 0
    for d ∈ 𝓓 do
        ϵ_d ← ϵ_d + meanDistance(d, {d' ≠ d ∈ 𝓛})
    for l ∈ 𝓛, d ∈ 𝓓 do
        ϵ_f ← ϵ_f + |l.CF − d.CF|
    𝓓.score = (ϵ_d + ϵ_f)/|𝓛|
```

density/height [64]. In contrast, Pulsar's PD sensor, owing to wider FoV and higher dynamic range (typically 30dB higher than CMOS cameras [38, 61]), should easily observe more than 3 lights in the same environment (see measurement results in Sec. 3.3). We now conduct experiments to verify how close Pulsar can be to this ideal.

Impact of distance. How far need the light/PD to be separated to ensure detectable CF? We answer the question by experimenting with two PDs of different FoVs (40° and 120°), and a GE CFL with 15W power, which is conservative compared with most commercial lighting fixtures (20W - 78W [50]). We also set up a Philips 8.5W LED bulb, with the same 800-lumen output as the CFL. To isolate the impact of incident angle, we pose the PD and lights so that they face each other directly. Then we measure the signal-to-noise ratio (SNR) between the CF component and the noise floor on the received light spectrum. The results in Fig. 14 show that the CFL's SNR decreases over distance, but remains above 26dB even at a distance of 8m. Considering the much higher emission power and high density of commercial tube FLs [50], we expect Pulsar to easily capture multiple lights' CF features simultaneously in real-world buildings. Note that the narrower PD has higher SNR due to higher angular gain.

The LEDs' CF feature is relatively weaker, but still 16dB above the noise floor at 8m distance. The weaker feature is due to the fact that LEDs are driven by DC and manufacturers usually employ filters on outputs of LED drivers to suppress flicker. As a contrast, we note that the camera-based CF detection system [64] only works for FL, and its SNR drops close to 0dB even at a short distance of 2.5m. In addition, we have followed the methodology in [64], and tested the CF diversity in a college building with 179 LEDs, which is the only large-scale LED deployment nearby. There are 2 different light models. The first covers 120 LEDs whose CFs roughly follow a distribution $\mathcal{N}(89.092, 0.831)$ kHz, while the CFs of the other model are scattered between 18 and 77 kHz. We found the LEDs exhibit diverse CFs just as the FLs measured in [64], albeit at weaker SNR which is not discernible by cameras.

Joint impact of ceiling height and light density. The actual number of lights Pulsar can capture in practical indoor environments depends on not only the lights' height/density, but also relative angle to the PD sensor. Since it is infeasible to test all buildings, we synthetically generate different height/density configurations, and use the SNR-to-distance trace in the foregoing experiment to compute the number of CFL bulbs visible to a PD. In addition to distance, the signal intensity is also scaled by the angular gains due to the light's irradiation angle (from the bulb) and incidental angle (into the PD), assuming the PD faces upwards and each light source has roughly 20 W power. For simplicity but without loss of generality, we only simulate round-shaped CFL with known gain patterns. A bulb is considered visible to the PD if the signal corresponding to its CF exceeds an SNR of 3dB.

From the results (Fig. 16), we observe that the number of observable lights increases with higher light density (smaller spacing). It also grows with ceiling height despite the increase in propagation loss. By analyzing the data, we observe that as long as the PD sensor has $> 80^\circ$ FoV (which is quite common for commodity PDs), it can observe 3+ lights in most practical settings (spacing $<$ 4m, height $>$ 2m).

Impact of ambient light interference. Sunlight may affect VLP when it operates near the window or under skylights. To test whether Pulsar can work under strong ambient light, we place its sensor dongle (Sec. 6) by a west-facing window on a sunny day, 2m below a tube FL. We started measurements at 1:30 PM when the sunlight starts to shine through the window, and stop at 7:00 PM close to sunset. The sensor dongle has its TIA gain configured to a low value of 1kΩ to avoid saturation, and the second stage gain is set to 300$\times$. Fig. 15 shows that the sensor remains at high SNR and does not saturate even under direct sunlight (approx. 35 kLux). Since the sunlight has no flicking frequency, it does not interfere Pulsar as long as saturation does not occur. This is salient property is harnessed in Pulsar's 2-stage amplifier design (Sec. 6) that is only sensitive to flickering light.

4 LOCALIZATION WITH SPARSE PHOTOGRAMMETRY

Once Pulsar identifies multiple lights within its sensor's FoV (Section 3) and computes the AoA relative to each light (Section 2), it uses simple geometrical models to derive the sensor's location. We now introduce how the models work, under common light density (3+ lights within FoV) and extremely sparse deployment.

4.1 3D Location Fix with 3+ Lights

Without loss of generality, we assume Pulsar's dual-PD to be installed on a smartphone's front-face, just like the current light sensor and front-camera. Denote the phone's location as $K = (x, y, -h)$, where (x, y) is its 2D coordinate and h the vertical distance to the ceiling. The light i's location $L_i = (x_i, y_i, 0)$ is known from Pulsar's light registration mechanism (Sec. 5), and stored in an online database. Further, denote the unit normal vector of the phone's surface as $\mathrm{N} = (a, b, c)$, which can be measured by standard smartphone motion sensors (compass, gyroscope, and accelerometer) [67]. The

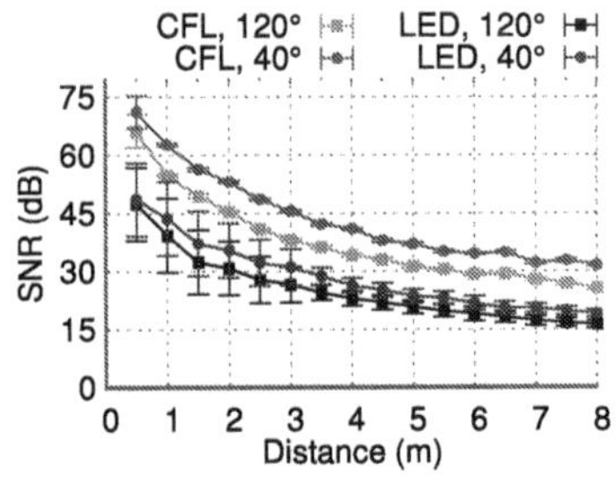

Figure 14: RSS vs distance for PDs with wide and narrow FoV.

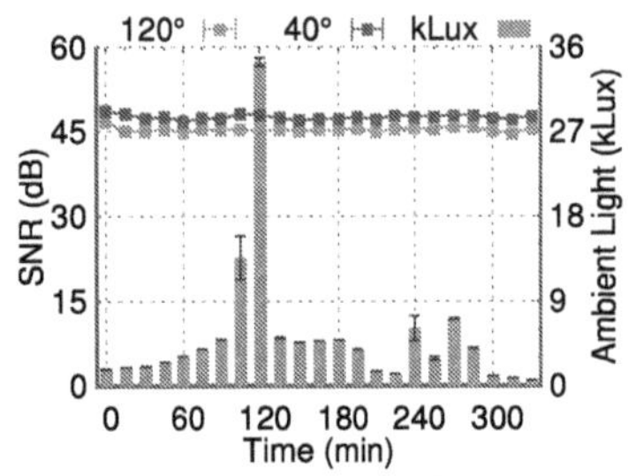

Figure 15: Impact of ambient light on SNR for PDs with narrow and wide FoV.

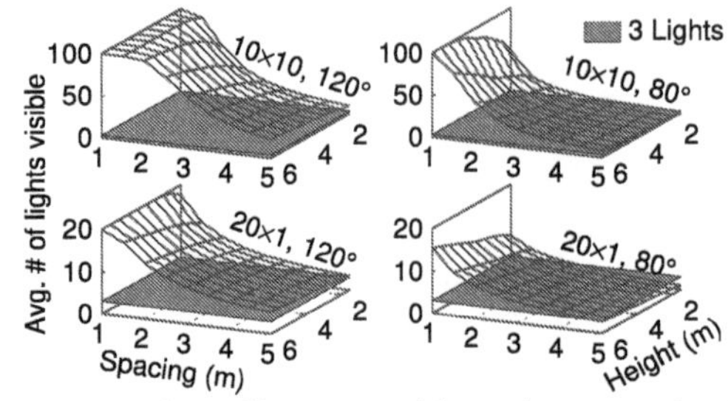

Figure 16: Number of lamps visible to the PD under different ceiling height and lamp density, with matrix (10×10) and array (20×1) configurations.

line vector from phone to light $\mathbf{PL_i} = (x_i - x, y_i - y, h)$ is parallel to the direction of incoming light beam. By definition, the AoA ϕ_i is the angle between the light beam and the normal vector of the phone's surface (Fig. 2), so we have:

$$\cos\phi_i = \frac{\mathbf{N} \cdot \mathbf{PL_i}}{|\mathbf{N}||\mathbf{PL_i}|} = \frac{a(x_i - x) + b(y_i - y) + ch}{\sqrt{(x_i - x)^2 + (y_i - y)^2 + h^2}} \quad (4)$$

since $|\mathbf{N}| = 1$ by design.

Eq. (4) is the core equation that enables Pulsar's sparse photogrammetry localization. To resolve the 3 unknowns representing the phone's location, we need AoA measurements from at least 3 lights to form a system of equations. When $n > 3$ lights are sensed, we can turn the *equation solving* into a *minimization problem*:

$$K = \underset{h>0}{\operatorname{argmin}} \sum_{i=0}^{n} w_i \left(\frac{\mathbf{N} \cdot \mathbf{PL_i}}{|\mathbf{N}||\mathbf{PL_i}|} - \cos\phi_i \right)^2 \quad (5)$$

which essentially finds the location vector that best fits the AoA measurements to all lights. Here w_i represents the matching confidence for light i (Sec. 3.2), which acts as a weight to prevent occasionally mismatched lights from disturbing the location computation.

4.2 Circumventing Unreliable Compass Information Using 4+ Lights

Compasses can measure the phone's azimuth angle, but are notorious for its poor accuracy indoor due to magnetic interferences from metal structures [13, 42, 60]. To overcome this limitation, Pulsar can treat azimuth as a variable in the system of Eq. (4), and use 4 or more lights to solve for both 3D location and azimuth. To this end, we note that the normal vector $\mathbf{N}$ can be rewritten as a function of azimuth α, roll β and pitch γ based on rotation matrix[5]:

$$\begin{aligned} \mathbf{N} = (&\cos\alpha \sin\gamma + \cos\gamma \sin\beta \sin\alpha, \\ &-\sin\gamma \sin\alpha + \cos\gamma \cos\alpha \sin\beta, \\ &\cos\gamma \cos\beta) \end{aligned} \quad (6)$$

The pitch γ and roll β angles are measured by the accelerometers relative to the direction of gravity. They have proven to be reliable in indoor environment [42, 67]. So we only solve for the azimuth variable α along with x, y, h, following the same minimization problem in Eq. (5). More generally, given 6 or more lights, we may even resolve the γ and β without any motion sensors, achieving both 3D location and 3D orientation sensing. But this entails ultra-high density light deployment and will not be covered in our experiments.

[5]The rotation matrix has many forms depending on definition of the axis and order of the rotation. Here we use the version that matches the Android API [19].

4.3 Identifying the Nearest of 2 Lights

Pulsar can fall back to coarse-grained light-cell level localization when insufficient number (≤ 2) of lights are simultaneously visible to populate the system of Eq. (4). This fallback mode requires Pulsar to identify the light closest to the phone, which can still afford meter-scale location granularity, depending on the light density.

Far-away lights have larger irradiance angle and hence lower angular gain, as well as higher propagation loss. However, the nearest light does not necessarily yield the highest RSS. Ambiguities can be introduced by variations of lights' output power and PD's angular response, as evident from the channel model in Eq. (1). The former effect is negligible compared to the distance attenuation [57], especially because most buildings prefer homogeneous light sources. To combat the latter variation (*i.e.*, RSS uncertainty due to PD's orientation), we leverage the PD's known angular response *w.r.t.* the measured AoA ϕ_i of the light i. More specifically, we can compensate for the angular response to obtain the true RSS: $RSS' = RSS/A_{r1}(\phi_i)$. Then the light with the highest RSS' always has the shortest distance to the PD.

In Pulsar, the cell-level location is also used to seed the initial point of the nonlinear minimization problem in Eq. (5) and accelerate its convergence. It also helps identify each overhead lights in the light registration process (Sec. 5).

5 LIGHT REGISTRATION ON MAP

Ubiquitous deployment of VLP requires a scalable way of surveying the landmark locations in the first place. Prior VLP systems [3, 26, 31, 40] assume *a priori* knowledge of the light fixtures' locations, but actually, even the "smart" LEDs do not know their own locations. The lights' locations and identities have to be associated manually, either by programming the bulbs or via a separate database. Pulsar's *light registration* scheme solves this problem. Simply put, it requires a one-time survey of the lights inside a building, which automatically registers the lights' locations on the building's floor plan image, and stores the results in Pulsar's database, eliminating the need for physically measuring the location of each light. The lights' locations can be translated into physical locations given the scale of the floor map.

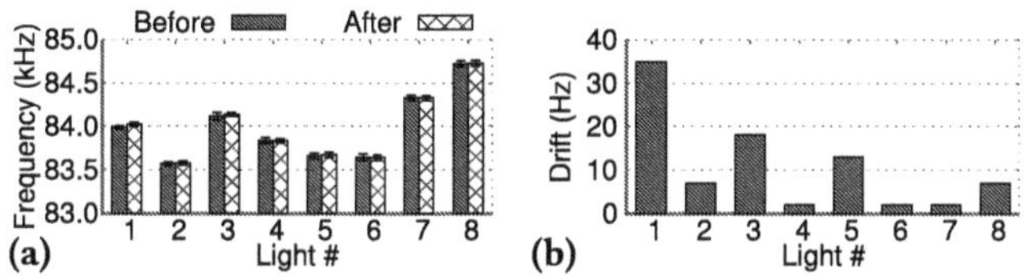

Figure 17: (a) Monthly mean and *std.* and (b) drift of CF before and after 1 year for 8 office tube FLs.

More specifically, a surveyor needs to start under a light with known location (on the map), hold a Pulsar receiver and walk across each of the ceiling lights inside the target building. Meanwhile, the surveyor's walking trajectory is tracked using existing inertial-tracking methods. When Pulsar detects a light (manifested by an RSS peak), it records the light's CF and marks its 2D location the same as the surveyor's current location (ceiling height is assumed known).

Our Pulsar prototype employs Google's Tango tablet to track the surveyor's trajectory. Tango combines cameras and inertial sensors to achieve decimeter precision [16] with its visual-inertial odometry (VIO). Due to inevitable drift of the inertial sensors, Tango's precision degrades over long distances. So we partition the surveying process into sections, each starting from a light with known location on map. The residual errors are small and can be compensated through manual adjustment on the map, considering the ceiling lights have highly regular separations. The compensation can also be automated through geometrical fitting and computer vision, but this is beyond the scope of our current work. We note that Pulsar is not tied to the Tango device — advances in robotics have enabled high-precision VIO using commodity smartphone cameras and motion sensors [8, 28].

We emphasize that the VIO methods work under several assumptions that are tolerable for controlled one-time surveying, but cannot substitute Pulsar's real-time localization: certain anchor points exist whose locations are known to the user device; the surrounding environment scene is static; the walking speed is low and needs to be regular. In addition, the camera operations incur high power consumption and are unsuitable for continuous localization battery-powered devices.

Further, note that the CF features depend on the lights' hardware and have shown to be highly stable over multiple weeks [64]. We have also conducted a year-long measurement of 8 randomly sampled lights in an office building. We found that the CFs are also stable at annual scale, with monthly and year-to-year average drift less than 10 Hz for most of the lights, as shown in Fig. 17, which is stable enough for reliable long-term identification [64]. In the longer term, a light's CF feature may change due to failure, aging or replacement. Such changes will manifest as a consistent single-light mismatch when users run the light identification algorithm (Section 3). Therefore, Pulsar can detect such outage events, and update its light database automatically, keeping the overhead of re-registration to a minimum.

Finally, the light registration should not be confused with the fingerprinting procedure in signature-based localization systems [44, 59]. The fingerprinting entails extensive survey of all *locations*, whereas Pulsar only needs a one-time walk-through of all light *landmarks* which are much sparser.

6 IMPLEMENTATION

Dual-PD light sensor. We design a custom light sensor that can be plugged into mobile devices with USB ports (Fig. 18). The sensor contains an `STM32F103C8T6` microcontroller, which samples the signals from 2 PDs (`BPW34` and `PD333`). The `MCP6024` quad operational amplifier is used to form 2 transimpedance amplifiers and 2 voltage amplifiers, which condition the signals before they enter the microcontroller. The entire prototype costs around $30, while a production version built into the phone (Sec. 8) will be significantly cheaper.

The firmware running on the microcontroller uses DMA and timer to drive 2 internal ADCs, which sample 2 PDs simultaneously at 300Ksps with 8-bit depth. Since the ADCs are directly timed by the hardware timer, jitter and artifacts in sampling are kept to a minimum, ensuring highly accurate spectrum analysis. The sampled data are buffered in a 16 KB ring buffer before being transferred to the mobile device via 12 Mbps USB 2.0 full speed. We use a rigid USB OTG adapter so Euler angles of the device and the dongle are kept the same.

Android app and registration software. As illustrated in Fig. 19, the Pulsar Android app comprises a few modules: UI (map/location display), 3-D position solver, database, light identification, signal processing and dongle communication. The light identification first runs FFT on the samples (streamed from the dongle) to obtain the spectrum, and then simultaneously extracts multiple lights' CFs and match their identities, following Sec. 3. The app then looks up a local database that maps each light's CF to its location. Then, the RSS of each light's CF feature feeds the differential channel response, which is mapped to the light's AoA (Sec. 2). Finally, Pulsar computes the sensor's 3D location and heading direction (Sec. 4), and presents the information in the UI.

We implement the dongle driver part in native C code with JNI to allow best real-time performance and avoid discontinuities in samples, which can introduce severe artifacts in spectrum analysis. We use a modified version of `libusb` [14] together with Android's USB Host API to provide access to the USB dongle in C code without requiring root privilege. Some of the signal processing and the location solver are also implemented in C since they require functions such as nonlinear minimization from a numerical library. We pick GNU Scientific Library (GSL) [17] as our numerical library and have ported it to Android. The database and PDs' calibration data are stored in pure text, providing the lights' identification number, CF, and physical locations. All other components are implemented in Java with standard Android API.

The inertial tracking for the light registration process (Sec. 5) is provided by the Tango tablet [20] since it has a complete and ready-to-use visual-inertial odometry (VIO) implementation. Many other monocular VIO techniques emerged recently in the robotic navigation field [8, 16], which have shown comparable tracking precision as Tango. But the implementations are either kept in private or constrained to a specific smartphone model. We have also implemented a graphical application on PC that allows the surveyor to fit the motion trace to floor plans and save the results as the database (Fig. 20).

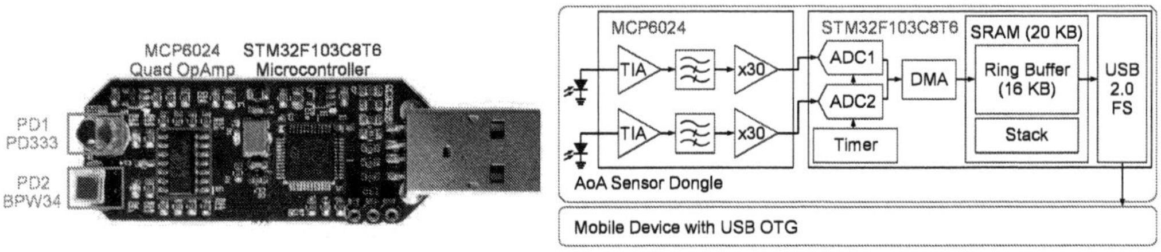

Figure 18: Photo and diagram of the customized AoA sensor.

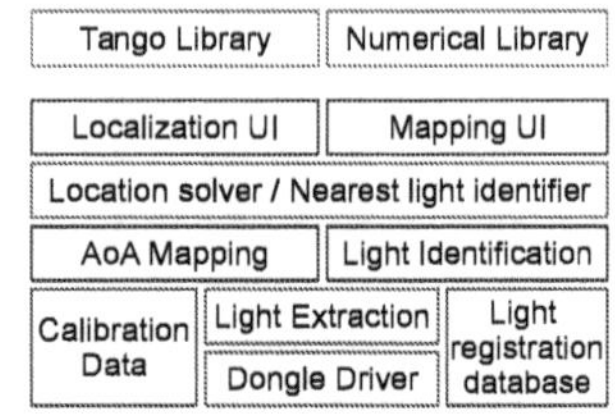

Figure 19: Architecture of the Pulsar Android app.

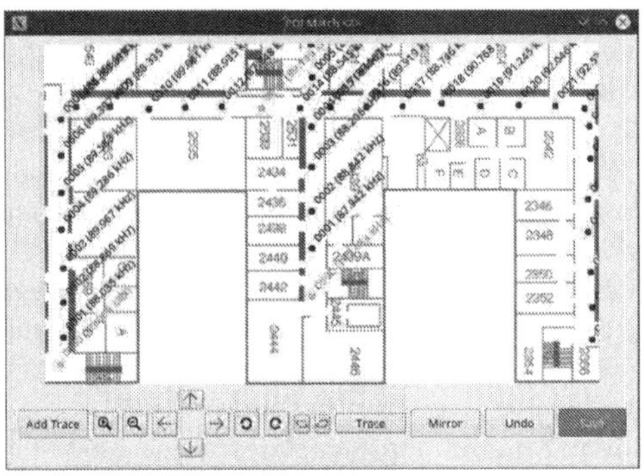

Figure 20: Light registration application running on a PC, generating the light database.

Figure 21: Photos of test venues: aisles with tube FLs (upper); an atrium with CFLs (lower).

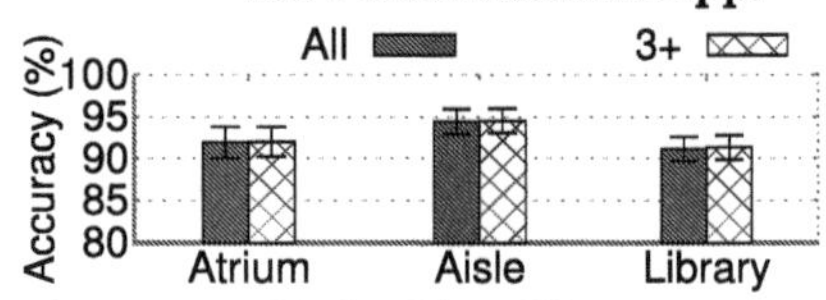

Figure 22: Light identification accuracy for 3 different types of areas, error bars show *std*.

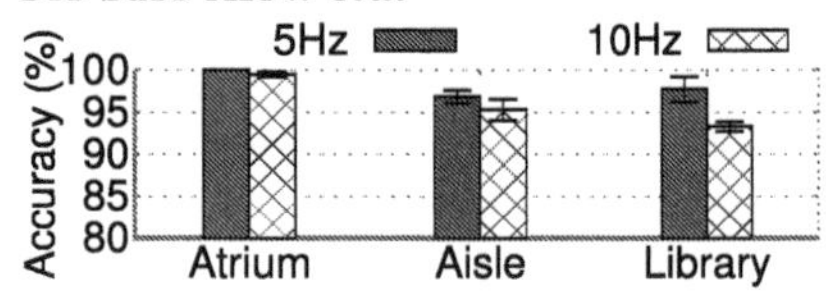

Figure 23: Light identification accuracy for smart bulbs.

Table 1: A comparison between LiTell and Pulsar.

	Ceiling height [a]	Coverage [b]	ID accuracy [c]	Battery life [d]	Latency	Light registration	Orientation	Requires tube FLs
LiTell	≈ 1m	57.1%	80.5%	2.45 hrs	1.62s [e]	Manual	Compass and light	Yes
Pulsar	> 9m	99.8%	94.4%	6.67 hrs	0.84s [f]	Automatic	Compass or light	No

[a] From phone to a 15W cabinet tube FL. [b] By area in an office building aisle. [c] For single measurement with tube FLs. [d] Nexus 5, full battery cycle, screen turned off, maximum update rate. Active idling alone last ≈11 hrs. [e] 7 pictures, ≈ 5 Hz spectral resolution. [f] 100,000-point FFT, 3 Hz resolution.

7 PERFORMANCE EVALUATION

We evaluate Pulsar's performance both through controlled experiments like existing VLP systems [26, 31], and through field tests in two environments: the aisles of an office building and the atrium of an activity center (Fig. 21). The aisles have tube FLs arranged linearly, 4.5m apart on 3m ceiling, while the atrium has 2 rings of CFLs spaced 1.5m apart on a 4m ceiling. For the light identification test, we include an additional library setting with densely deployed tube FLs on 2.8m ceiling. All computations are performed on the smartphone, with the self-contained Pulsar App. For the light registration mechanism, its landmark location precision depends on the external inertial tracking mechanism and can be manually adjusted during bootstrapping (Sec. 5). So we omit the tests for it.

7.1 Accuracy of Light Identification

We run Pulsar's multi-light identification algorithm over databases built for the test venues with light registration. The aisle, atrium, and library involve 64, 110 and 157 lights, each with 2-3 models of lights [6], respectively. For each venue, we hold the sensor, move to 1000 random locations, and compare the identification results with the database ground-truth. Further, we simulate the identification for smart LEDs with randomly allocated frequencies, with frequency drifts following $N(0, 5)$ Hz and $N(0, 10)$ Hz distribution, since we could not find a building with smart-bulbs deployed in large scale. We observed that the number of lights that Pulsar captures within its FoV varies from 3 to 6 in each measurement. In addition, with incumbent lights, in 92.5% of the time, Pulsar's light identification mechanism matches every single light correctly (Fig. 22, label 'All'). In 92.6% of the cases, Pulsar can identify at least 3 lights correctly (Fig. 22, label '3+'). If smart-bulbs are employed, the accuracy further rises to 93% - 100% (Fig. 23), depending on the number of lights and allocated bandwidth. The identification accuracy also shows high consistency across measurements, primarily owing to the homogeneous light layout in most buildings. Note that the wrongly matched lights in one capture are usually deemphasized by low weights (Sec. 4.1), which lessens their impact on the final localization result.

[6] CF range: aisle 88∼93 and 137∼148 kHz; atrium 81∼86, 103∼114 and 129∼134 kHz; library 58∼65 and 88∼90 kHz.

7.2 Accuracy of Sparse Photogrammetry

To receive from multiple lights, Pulsar's sensor must be able to extract frequency and AoA information from sources with highly diverse RSS simultaneously. Therefore, the sensor must work under a wide range of RSS. Its FoV and ambiguity-free range (Sec. 2) also needs to guarantee that it can "see" enough number of lights under low ceiling, sparse deployment scenarios. In the following experiments, we set up a controlled environment similar to existing VLP systems [26, 31] to evaluate Pulsar's performance under different settings. Specifically, we arrange 23W CFLs in a linear array, whose spacing and height (*w.r.t.* the sensor) can be flexibly adjusted. Unless

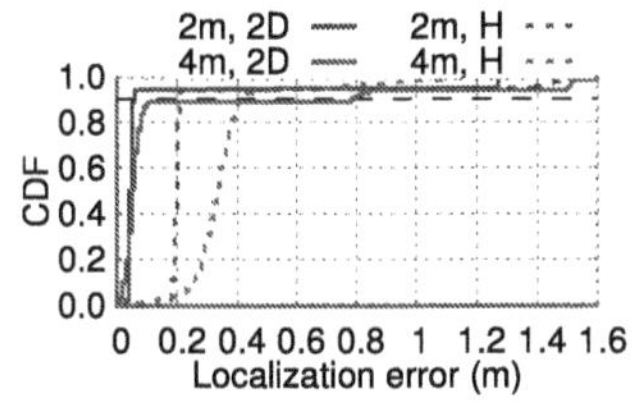

Figure 24: CDF of localization error vs. ceiling height.

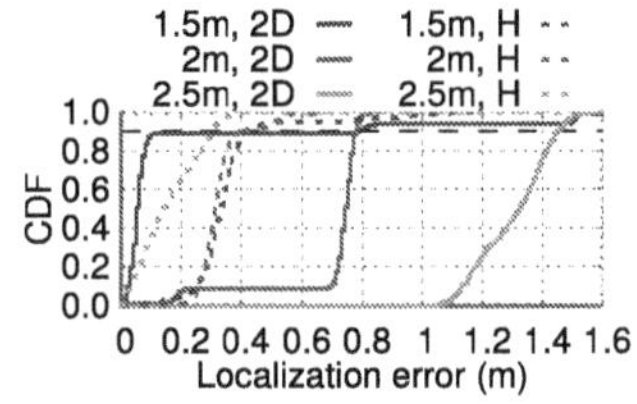

Figure 25: CDF of localization error vs. light spacing.

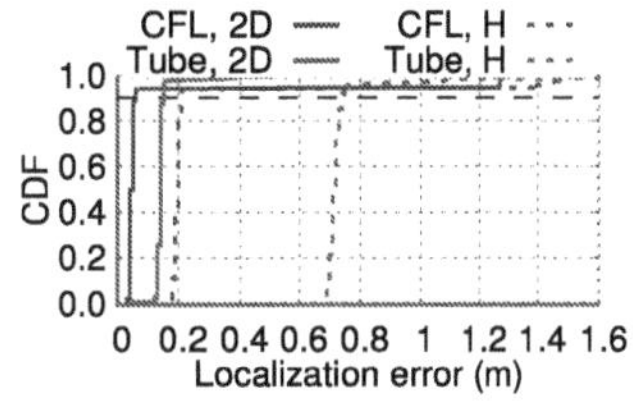

Figure 26: CDF of localization error vs. fixture type.

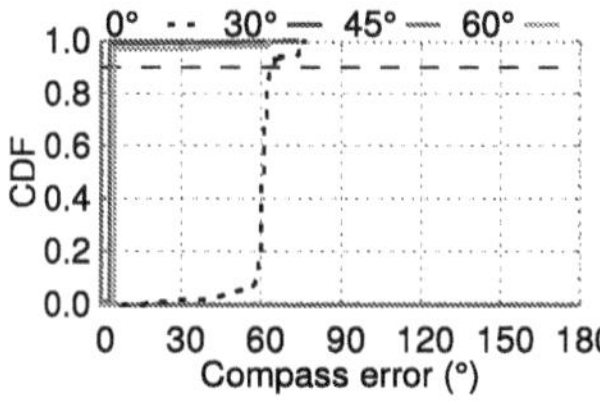

Figure 27: CDF of screen orientation error.

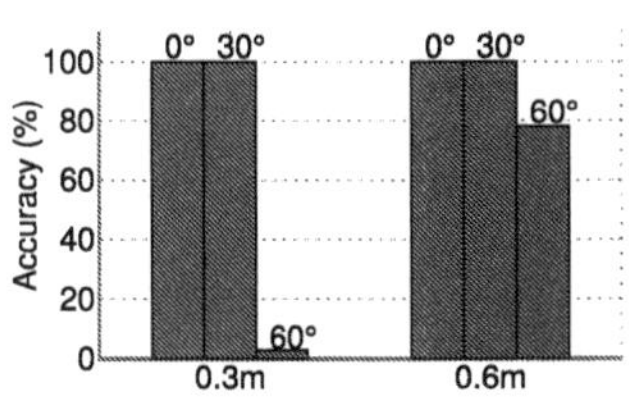

Figure 28: Accuracy of nearest light identification.

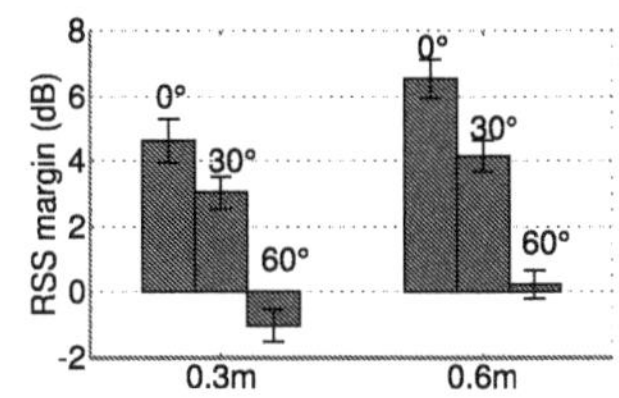

Figure 29: Margin of *RSS'* between near/far lights.

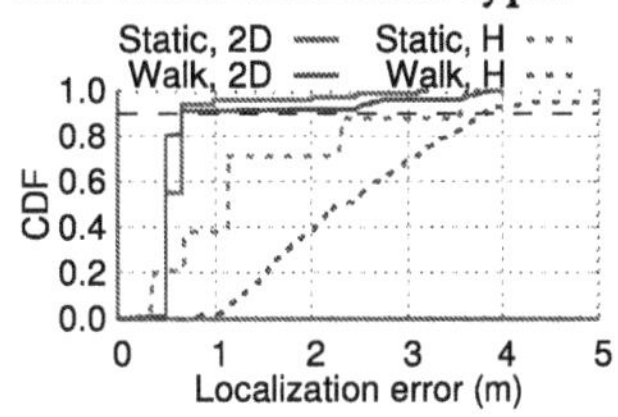

Figure 30: Localization error of static and walking user.

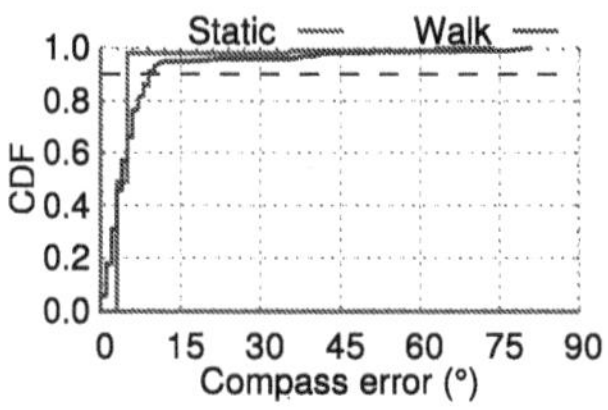

Figure 31: Orientation error of static and walking user.

noted otherwise, we repeat the experiment 500 times under each configuration.

3D localization accuracy. Fig. 24 shows Pulsar's localization performance across different ceiling heights, with 4 CFLs placed 1.5m apart and sensor placed flat. Pulsar achieves very high precision for both 2D and height localization (label 'H'), thanks to its AoA-based sensing scheme. The median error is 5cm for 2D localization (x, y) and 20cm for height (h), when the sensor is held 2m below the ceiling. The result is highly consistent across experiments, with 90-th percentile error close to the mean, due to the determinism and multipath-free propagation profile of visible lights. Under a high ceiling height of 4m, due to weaker RSS, the median error increases slightly, to 6cm and 31cm, for (x, y) and h, respectively. In an extreme test where the height grows to 6 m, we observe a large systematic error–the estimated locations are relatively tightly packed, but deviate from ground truth for more than 1m. However, note that typical commercial lights [50] use much higher emission power than our CFLs. Therefore, we expect Pulsar's sparse photogrammetry can provide accurate sub-light level localization under common luminaires and ceiling height settings.

Fig. 25 shows Pulsar's localization accuracy under different separations of the 4 CFLs, while height is maintained at 4m. We notice that Pulsar's localization error in h remains roughly the same, whereas the 2D localization precision degrades as the separation increases (median error 0.07m, 0.72m, and 1.27m, for 1.5m, 2m, and 2.5m separation, respectively). Further analysis shows the major source of error comes from the lateral direction *w.r.t.* the light array, as the RSS becomes much weaker from lights near the tail.

To verify that Pulsar behaves consistently for different types of lights, we compare Pulsar's localization accuracy between 4 CFLs and 4 T8 tube FLs. The tube FLs are enclosed in diffusive covers, arranged with 1.2m separation in between. Pulsar's sensor is placed 2m below the ceiling. Fig. 26 shows that Pulsar's 2D localization performance degrades by only about 10cm when we switch from CFL to tube FL, although the area of the light is larger by at least 10×. This echoes the micro-benchmark in Sec. 2.2.4. It further verifies that Pulsar's point source assumption holds in practical scenarios and does not become the bottleneck in location accuracy.

Pulsar's 3D localization mechanism requires at least 3 lights. Ideally, adding more lights should improve accuracy. However, since the visible light channel is very deterministic and AoA sensor suffers from very little interference, we observed that increasing the number of lights does not improve the accuracy significantly across our experiments.

Accuracy of heading direction estimation. When there are 4+ lights available within FoV, Pulsar can derive the sensor's normal vector (same as the smartphone's), which can substitute the compass and be used to derive the user's heading direction (Sec. 4.2). To evaluate the accuracy of heading solving, we hold the sensor in $\sim 0°$ (roughly flat), 30°, 45° and 60° inclinations under one row of 0.45m-long tube FLs spaced 0.8m apart, with a sensor-to-ceiling distance of 1.5m. We take 200 samples and compare the error with ground truth obtained relative to the floor-plan. Fig. 27 shows that the 90-th percentile error is only $3° \sim 5°$, when the sensor is not laid flat. When the sensor is paralleling to the ceiling, however, orientation of the smartphone no longer affects AoA, which means the orientation can be resolved to arbitrary value, yielding huge errors, while 3D localization results are correct. Since users normally will not hold the smartphone completely parallel to the ceiling, we expect this to be a corner case.

Accuracy of nearest light identification. To evaluate the effectiveness of Pulsar's nearest light identification, we place 2 CFLs 1.5m apart, and the sensor 2m below. As a stress test, we put the sensor near the center of the 2 lights' (x, y) projection, but slightly biased to one of them by a short distance of 0.3m to 0.6m. We then gradually rotate the sensor to the other light and see how often it is mistaken for the nearest one. To evaluate the reliability in discrimination, we use the margin in the compensated RSS (*RSS'* in Sec. 4.3), *i.e.*, difference between the compensated RSS of the nearest light and that of the other light. Each configuration takes 75 trials. From Figs. 28 and 29, we notice that Pulsar can identify the nearest light with close to 100% reliability when both lights fall roughly within the sensor's ambiguity-free range (Sec. 2.2.2). Once the nearest light is far out of the ambiguity-free range, error in identification is likely to happen, especially when the sensor is close to the center of the 2 lights. Since such extreme case should remain minority, and localization error caused by wrong identification is limited since

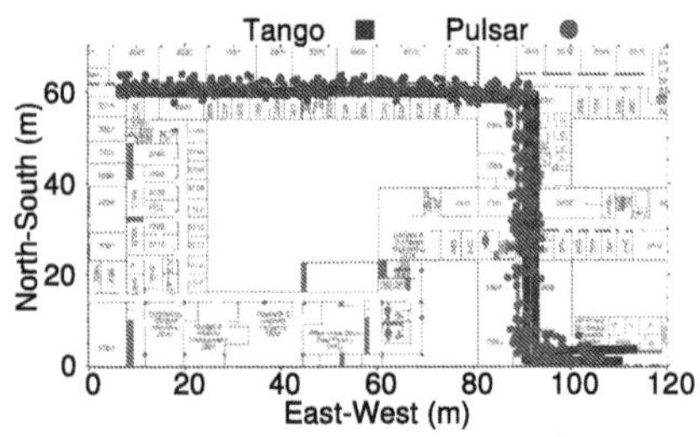

Figure 32: Localization accuracy within aisles of an office building.

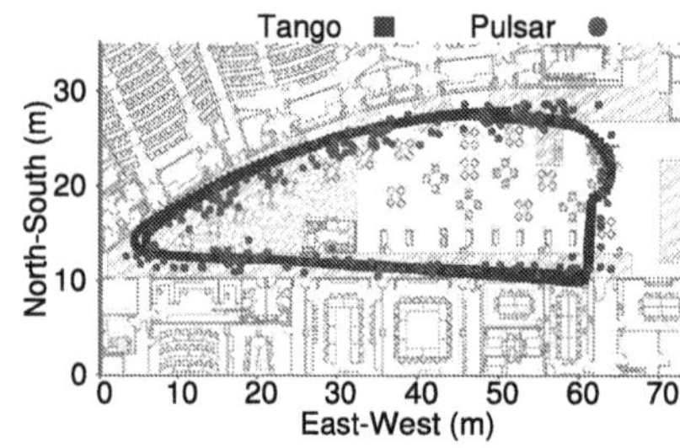

Figure 33: Localization accuracy within an atrium.

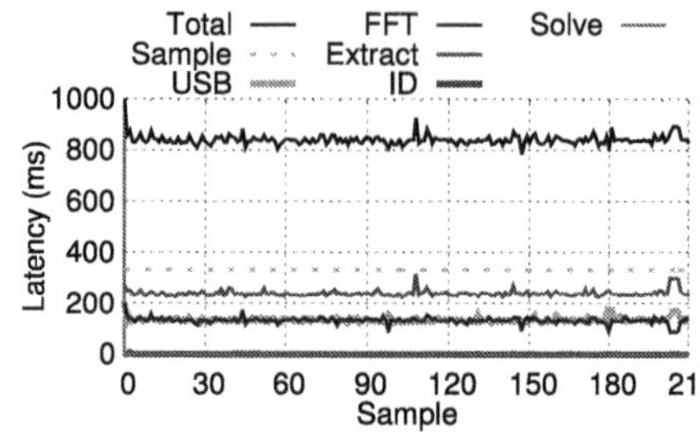

Figure 34: Pulsar's localization latency.

the receiver is close to the center between 2 lights, we conclude that Pulsar's nearest light identification is sufficient as a fallback mechanism to achieve cell-level location granularity.

Impact of human motion. We evaluate impact of user's movement with a compact setup, which includes one row of 0.45m-long tube FLs spaced 0.8m apart, placed 1.5m above the sensor. The sensor is first mounted on a tripod with 30°, 45° and 60° inclinations, and then is held by a user walking in the same spot, with device naturally rotated while walking. Fig. 30 shows that Pulsar's 2D localization accuracy does not degrade significantly under user's motion, while height estimation does show increased error. In addition, 90-th percentile error of heading estimation only increased slightly, from 5° to 9°. We thus conclude Pulsar is robust against normal user motion, as long as during each sampling period the AoA remains relatively constant.

7.3 Large-Scale, Real-time Field Tests

In this section, we verify Pulsar's localization performance in uncontrolled environment in real-time. For each test venue, we found the light registration process takes only about 10 to 20 minutes per 100 lights, since we just need to sample each light once. We walk across each venue following a marked route, and then compare the location traces generated by Pulsar and by Tango's visual-inertial odometry algorithm (shown to have sub-meter precision [16]). For a fair comparison, both run on the same Tango tablet simultaneously.

Fig. 32 and Fig. 33 depict Pulsar's performance in the aisles of the office building and the atrium, respectively, with background showing the floor-plan annotated by Pulsar's light registration application. Pulsar shows overall median and 90-th percentile accuracy of 0.6m and 1.6m, respectively. Its real-world performance is comparable to the VIO method which, despite the high precision, runs costly image processing and can only track relative movement (Sec. 5). In addition, unlike VIO, Pulsar does not suffer from sensor drift, thanks to deterministic light propagation and robust AoA sensing. Note that a few missing spots exist in the location traces, because of occasional shadowing or location solver failure. These problems can be avoided by enlarging the FoV and ambiguity-free range of the sensor (Sec. 2.2.2) and employing better minimization algorithms (Sec. 4.1) in future.

We have also measured Pulsar's processing latency within its Android app. Fig. 34 shows that the end-to-end localization latency is around 840ms across most of the location queries, which allows real-time 3D location fix. USB transfer and FFT all contribute to latency substantially, each making up 16% of total latency. Latency in extraction process is dominated by peak finding. Both the light extraction and location solving run efficiently, costing only up to tens of milliseconds. Integrating the sensor into smartphones and eliminating the USB interface, along with sparse spectrum recovery (Sec. 8) can potentially reduce 1/3 of the latency.

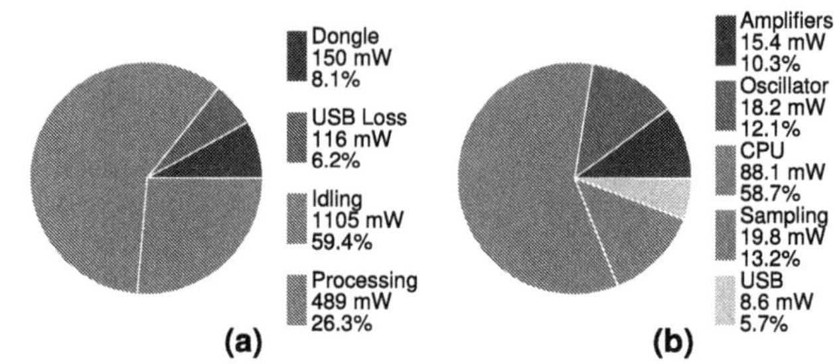

Figure 35: Power consumption breakdown for (a) the whole system and (b) the sensor dongle alone.

7.4 Power Consumption

We measure Pulsar's end-to-end energy consumption/battery life through the sysfs interface [39], and further break the power consumption down by disabling/disconnecting each component. Fig. 35(a) shows a system-wide breakdown, where "USB Loss" is caused by converting the battery voltage up to the USB's 5V and then back down to the dongle's 3.3V; and "Idling" means active idling with adb over Wi-Fi running. Fig. 35(b) further analyzes the sensor dongle, where "Sampling" includes ADC, timing, and DMA, which copies sampled data to the dongle's buffer. The microcontroller CPU of the dongle is responsible for copying data to the USB interface, whereas it busy waits when the sampling is in progress since we have not implemented any power-management. The dongle only consumes about 45mA of current when sampling (less than 150mW since it takes 3.3V power), which is even lower than WiFi's idle listening power [65]. From an end-to-end perspective, it is clear that Pulsar's PD-based solution avoids energy-hungry camera sensors and image processing, which leads to a power consumption of less than half of camera's power end-to-end (Table 1), despite that there still exist substantial spaces for optimization (Sec. 8).

8 DISCUSSION

Integrating the AoA sensor into COTS phones. With the microlens technology that is widely used in CMOS cameras [15], it is possible to integrate multiple PDs onto a compact and low-cost chip, much like the ambient light and proximity sensors used on today's smartphones. These sensors usually contain at least 2 PDs [53], with the proximity sensor already operating at tens to hundreds of kHz [23]. Unfortunately, due to hardware design and sometimes merely firmware/software limitation, fine-grained samples from these sensors are usually not available to applications. We envision future smartphones can easily integrate such AoA sensors much like the ambient light sensor, enabling more accurate localization as well as many other applications.

Further improving energy efficiency. Although the Pulsar prototype is significantly more energy efficient than camera-based counterparts[26, 64, 68], its high sampling rate (300 Ksps) provides a large space for optimization. To achieve reasonable (3 Hz) spectral resolution, Pulsar runs FFT with a long sample length (100,000 points), which wastes energy. Sparse spectrum recovery techniques such as bandpass sampling and sFFT [21] can significantly reduce computational loads, resulting in less power consumption. With such optimizations, Pulsar may be able to run entirely on energy-efficient microcontrollers.

Pulsar's hardware prototype also has space for polishing, such as integrating the sensor into smartphones to eliminate the costly USB interfaces, and adopting better hardware components. For example, a newer version of the microcontroller used [46] consumes less than 1/3 of the power while providing more computational power. With proper hardware implementations, Pulsar's sensor can be extremely low power and support continuously localization for battery-operated devices.

9 RELATED WORK

Existing localization schemes broadly fall into two categories: *(i)* Fingerprinting approaches that associate each location spot to a set of features provided by images [8, 16, 18], acoustics [47], magnetic field [11], RF signals [9, 62], or a mix of them [6]. Real-world tests showed that such features lack stability in the presence of human activities and environmental changes, and are often not discriminative enough to offer fine location granularity [32]. More crucially, they require blanket fingerprinting of all location spots, which entails huge bootstrapping and maintenance overhead. *(ii)* Model-driven approaches that calculate the distance between user devices and infrastructure landmarks, through models of received signal strength (RSS) [7, 10], phase [24, 56] or propagation time [34]. To achieve high location precision, such models often require specialized hardware like antenna arrays; they tend to be disturbed by multipath reflections from human bodies and ambient objects [1, 32].

Motion sensors (accelerometer, gyroscope, and magnetometer) can track a user's relative movement via step counting [30], but need to be calibrated by other approaches that provide absolute location fixes [52]. State-of-the-art robotic systems often integrate such sensors with a camera to realize visual-inertial odometry, which can simultaneously map the environment while tracking user movement [16]. But the performance suffers in homogeneous environment (*e.g.*, office hallways) and dynamic environment (*e.g.*, retail stores) [8]. The use of cameras entails heavy sensing and computational power, hence unsuitable for long-term mobile usage.

Compared with these approaches, VLP has several inherent advantages, especially in its dense overhead anchoring points and line-of-sight propagation profile that evade interferences from ambient environment. Most existing VLP systems employ *modulated* LEDs as anchor points to emit beacons. The receiver can either be a PD or a camera. The key challenge for PD based VLP lies in low spatial resolution. Existing work either uses multi-light trilateration or requires controlled user movement to resolve the spatial ambiguities [31]. Trilateration schemes assume LEDs' Lambertian radiation pattern, which no longer holds when collimating or diffusing optics are used for uniform illumination [54]. On the other hand, controlled device movement disturbs user experience and precludes continuous, real-time localization operations. Camera-based VLP systems [26, 27] can achieve decimeter precision through *photogrammetry*, which maps the geometrical relation between LED luminaries on a camera image to the camera's physical location/orientation [26]. Other systems [55, 58] use physical rotation or electronic polarization to create spatial diversity and simplify the sensor-side workload. All these modulated VLP systems require customized LEDs with a beaconing circuitry, which adds to the already high retrofitting cost of LEDs compared with FLs.

Our work was inspired by LiTell [64], which obviates the need for specialized LEDs. Yet LiTell only works for FLs whose CF features can be extrapolated from camera images. It is not applicable to LEDs, which have much weaker CFs, or light fixtures with small areas that will not leave enough samples in the image. More critically, cameras' low dynamic range limits LiTell's working range to around 2.5 meters, and their narrow FoV causes many blind spots where the ceiling lights are not directly visible. All these factors, along with other limitations (Table. 1), hinder continuous localization services. IDyLL [57] harnesses the regular separation of ceiling lights to calibrate motion sensors, thus improving dead-reckoning accuracy. But it needs users to walk in straight lines, and can only track relative movement. Fiatlux [5] extracts location fingerprints from minor intensity differences among incumbent lights, yet the fingerprints vary over time and are sensitive to ambient light and the sensor's orientation.

Despite more than a decade of research [22], VLP has not reached real-world users. By overcoming the high cost [26, 31, 40, 58], high power consumption [26, 64], and intermittent coverage [26, 64] in traditional VLP technologies, Pulsar can significantly accelerate the penetration of VLP.

10 CONCLUSION

To our knowledge, Pulsar represents the first VLP system that employs incumbent FLs/LEDs and lightweight PDs to achieve continuous 3D localization with sub-meter precision. It marks a new step in enabling the ubiquitous deployment of VLP, by solving three problems: discriminating co-located LEDs/FLs, sensing AoA and hence 3D location using single-pixel PDs, automatically registering light landmarks. We believe Pulsar's salient advantages will enable a wide range of location-based services, including robotic navigation, physical analytics and augmented reality.

ACKNOWLEDGEMENT

We would like to thank the anonymous reviewers and our shepherd Xia Zhou for their valuable comments and feedback. This project was partially supported by the NSF under Grant CNS-1343363, CNS-1350039, CNS-1506657, CNS-1518728, and CNS-1617321.

REFERENCES

[1] S. Adler, S. Schmitt, and M. Kyas. 2014. Path Loss and Multipath Effects in a Real World Indoor Localization Scenario. In *11th Workshop on Positioning, Navigation and Communication (WPNC)*.

[2] AnandTech. 2013. Understanding Camera Optics & Smartphone Camera Trends. http://www.anandtech.com/show/6777. (2013).

[3] J. Armstrong, Y. A. Sekercioglu, and A. Neild. 2013. Visible light positioning: a roadmap for international standardization. *IEEE Communications Magazine* 51, 12 (2013), 68–73.

[4] Luigi Atzori, Antonio Iera, and Giacomo Morabito. 2010. The internet of things: A survey. *Computer networks* 54, 15 (2010), 2787–2805.

[5] Martin Azizyan, Ionut Constandache, and Romit Roy Choudhury. 2007. Fiatlux: Fingerprinting Rooms Using Light Intensity. In *Proc. of Pervasive*.

[6] Martin Azizyan, Ionut Constandache, and Romit Roy Choudhury. 2009. SurroundSense: Mobile Phone Localization via Ambience Fingerprinting. In *Proc. of ACM MobiCom*.

[7] P. Bahl and V.N. Padmanabhan. 2000. RADAR: an In-Building RF-Based User Location and Tracking System. In *Proc. of IEEE INFOCOM*, Vol. 2.

[8] Cesar Cadena, Luca Carlone, Henry Carrillo, Yasir Latif, Davide Scaramuzza, José Neira, Ian D. Reid, and John J. Leonard. 2016. Simultaneous Localization And Mapping: Present, Future, and the Robust-Perception Age. *CoRR* abs/1606.05830 (2016).

[9] Yin Chen, Dimitrios Lymberopoulos, Jie Liu, and Bodhi Priyantha. 2012. FM-based Indoor Localization. In *Proc. of ACM MobiSys*.

[10] Krishna Chintalapudi, Anand Padmanabha Iyer, and Venkata N. Padmanabhan. 2010. Indoor Localization Without the Pain. In *Proc. of ACM MobiCom*.

[11] Jaewoo Chung, Matt Donahoe, Chris Schmandt, Ig-Jae Kim, Pedram Razavai, and Micaela Wiseman. 2011. Indoor Location Sensing Using Geo-magnetism. In *Proc. of ACM MobiSys*.

[12] Cinetics. 2017. Axis360 Pro. https://cinetics.com/kit/axis360. (2017).

[13] Ionut Constandache, Xuan Bao, Martin Azizyan, and Romit Roy Choudhury. 2010. Did You See Bob?: Human Localization Using Mobile Phones. In *Proc. of ACM MobiCom*.

[14] Kuldeep Singh Dhaka. 2017. libusb (modified version). https://github.com/kuldeepdhaka/libusb/tree/android-open2. (2017).

[15] Abbas El Gamal and Helmy Eltoukhy. 2005. CMOS image sensors. *IEEE Circuits and Devices Magazine* 21, 3 (2005), 6–20.

[16] Christian Forster, Luca Carlone, Frank Dellaert, and Davide Scaramuzza. 2016. On-Manifold Preintegration for Real-Time Visual-Inertial Odometry. *IEEE Transactions on Robotics* (2016).

[17] Free Software Foundation, Inc. 2017. GNU Scientific Library. https://www.gnu.org/software/gsl/. (2017).

[18] R. Gao, Y. Tian, F. Ye, G. Luo, K. Bian, Y. Wang, T. Wang, and X. Li. 2016. Sextant: Towards Ubiquitous Indoor Localization Service by Photo-Taking of the Environment. *IEEE Transactions on Mobile Computing* 15, 2 (2016).

[19] Google. 2017. Android Sensor Manager. https://developer.android.com/reference/android/hardware/SensorManager.html. (2017).

[20] Google Inc. 2017. Tango. https://get.google.com/tango/. (2017).

[21] Haitham Hassanieh, Piotr Indyk, Dina Katabi, and Eric Price. 2012. Simple and practical algorithm for sparse Fourier transform. In *Proc. of ACM-SIAM SODA*. 1183–1194.

[22] Shuhei Horikawa, Toshihiko Komine, Shinichiro Haruyama, and Masao Nakagawa. 2004. Pervasive Visible Light Positioning System using White LED Lighting. *Technical report of IEICE. DSP* 103, 719 (2004).

[23] Intersil Americas LLC. 2014. Digital Ambient Light Sensor and Proximity Sensor with Interrupt Function. http://www.intersil.com/content/dam/Intersil/documents/isl2/isl29011.pdf. (2014).

[24] Manikanta Kotaru, Kiran Joshi, Dinesh Bharadia, and Sachin Katti. 2015. SpotFi: Decimeter Level Localization Using WiFi. In *Proc. of ACM SIGCOMM*.

[25] Tomáš Krajník, Vojtěch Vonásek, Daniel Fišer, and Jan Faigl. 2011. AR-drone as a platform for robotic research and education. In *International Conference on Research and Education in Robotics*. 172–186.

[26] Ye-Sheng Kuo, Pat Pannuto, Ko-Jen Hsiao, and Prabal Dutta. 2014. Luxapose: Indoor Positioning with Mobile Phones and Visible Light. In *Proc. of ACM MobiCom*.

[27] Hui-Yu Lee, Hao-Min Lin, Yu-Lin Wei, Hsin-I Wu, Hsin-Mu Tsai, and Kate Ching-Ju Lin. 2015. RollingLight: Enabling Line-of-Sight Light-to-Camera Communications. In *Proc. of ACM MobiSys*.

[28] Lenovo. 2017. Lenovo Phab 2 Pro. http://www3.lenovo.com/in/en/tablets/android-tablets/tablet-phab-series/Lenovo-Phab-2-Pro/p/WMD00000220. (2017).

[29] J. J. Leonard and H. F. Durrant-Whyte. 1991. Mobile robot localization by tracking geometric beacons. *IEEE Transactions on Robotics and Automation* 7, 3 (1991), 376–382.

[30] Fan Li, Chunshui Zhao, Guanzhong Ding, Jian Gong, Chenxing Liu, and Feng Zhao. 2012. A Reliable and Accurate Indoor Localization Method Using Phone Inertial Sensors. In *Proc. of ACM Conference on Ubiquitous Computing (UbiComp)*.

[31] Liqun Li, Pan Hu, Chunyi Peng, Guobin Shen, and Feng Zhao. 2014. Epsilon: A Visible Light Based Positioning System. In *Proc. of USENIX NSDI*.

[32] Hongbo Liu, Yu Gan, Jie Yang, Simon Sidhom, Yan Wang, Yingying Chen, and Fan Ye. 2012. Push the Limit of WiFi Based Localization for Smartphones. In *Proc. of ACM MobiCom*.

[33] Dimitrios Lymberopoulos, Jie Liu, Xue Yang, Romit Roy Choudhury, Vlado Handziski, and Souvik Sen. 2015. A Realistic Evaluation and Comparison of Indoor Location Technologies: Experiences and Lessons Learned. In *Proc. of ACM/IEEE IPSN*.

[34] Andreas Marcaletti, Maurizio Rea, Domenico Giustiniano, Vincent Lenders, and Aymen Fakhreddine. 2014. Filtering Noisy 802.11 Time-of-Flight Ranging Measurements. In *ACM International on Conference on Emerging Networking Experiments and Technologies (CoNEXT)*.

[35] Maxim Integrated Products, Inc. 2004. Why Drive White LEDs with Constant Current? https://www.maximintegrated.com/en/app-notes/index.mvp/id/3256. (2004).

[36] Daniele Miorandi, Sabrina Sicari, Francesco De Pellegrini, and Imrich Chlamtac. 2012. Internet of things: Vision, applications and research challenges. *Ad Hoc Networks* 10, 7 (2012), 1497–1516.

[37] N. Narendran and Y. Gu. 2005. Life of LED-based white light sources. *Journal of Display Technology* 1, 1 (2005), 167–171.

[38] OSI Optoelectronics. 2013. Basic PIN Photodiode Characteristics. http://www.osioptoelectronics.com/technology-corner/frequently-asked-questions/basic-pin-photodiode-characteristics.aspx#06. (2013).

[39] Kevin Parker. 2011. Getting the battery current values for the Android Phone. https://stackoverflow.com/a/7031032/6520528. (2011).

[40] Niranjini Rajagopal, Patrick Lazik, and Anthony Rowe. 2014. Visual Light Landmarks for Mobile Devices. In *Proc. of ACM/IEEE IPSN*.

[41] Julian Randall, Oliver Amft, Jürgen Bohn, and Martin Burri. 2007. LuxTrace: Indoor Positioning Using Building Illumination. *Personal Ubiquitous Computing* 11, 6 (2007).

[42] Nirupam Roy, He Wang, and Romit Roy Choudhury. 2014. I Am a Smartphone and I Can Tell My User's Walking Direction. In *Proc. of ACM MobiSys*.

[43] Reid Iwao Sasaki. 1994. *The impact of electronic ballast compact fluorescent lighting on power distribution systems*. Purdue University School of Electrical Engineering.

[44] Souvik Sen, Božidar Radunovic, Romit Roy Choudhury, and Tom Minka. 2012. You Are Facing the Mona Lisa: Spot Localization Using PHY Layer Information. In *Proc. of ACM MobiSys*.

[45] Robert Spence and Randeep Singh Soin. 1988. *Tolerance design of electronic circuits*. World Scientific.

[46] STMicroelectronics. 2017. STM32L433CB. http://www.st.com/en/microcontrollers/stm32l433cb.html. (2017).

[47] Stephen P. Tarzia, Peter A. Dinda, Robert P. Dick, and Gokhan Memik. 2011. Indoor Localization Without Infrastructure Using the Acoustic Background Spectrum. In *Proc. of ACM MobiSys*.

[48] The Wall Street Journal. 2015. More Companies Are Outfitting Warehouses With Smart Lights. (2015).

[49] U.S. Department of Energy. 2014. Energy Savings Forecast of Solid-State Lighting in General Illumination Applications. (2014).

[50] U.S. Department of Energy. 2015. Adoption of Light-Emitting Diodes in Common Lighting Applications. (2015).

[51] H. van der Broeck, G. Sauerlander, and M. Wendt. 2007. Power driver topologies and control schemes for LEDs. In *IEEE APEC*.

[52] He Wang, Souvik Sen, Ahmed Elgohary, Moustafa Farid, Moustafa Youssef, and Romit Roy Choudhury. 2012. No Need to War-drive: Unsupervised Indoor Localization. In *Proc. of ACM MobiSys*.

[53] Elliott Wen, Winston Seah, Bryan Ng, Xuefeng Liu, and Jiannong Cao. 2016. UbiTouch: ubiquitous smartphone touchpads using built-in proximity and ambient light sensors. In *Proc. of ACM UbiComp*.

[54] A. J. W. Whang, Y. Y. Chen, and Y. T. Teng. 2009. Designing Uniform Illumination Systems by Surface-Tailored Lens and Configurations of LED Arrays. *Journal of Display Technology* 5, 3 (2009).

[55] Bo Xie, Guang Tan, and Tian He. 2015. SpinLight: A High Accuracy and Robust Light Positioning System for Indoor Applications. In *Prof. of ACM SenSys*.

[56] Jie Xiong and Kyle Jamieson. 2013. ArrayTrack: A Fine-grained Indoor Location System. In *Proc. of USENIX NSDI*.

[57] Qiang Xu, Rong Zheng, and Steve Hranilovic. 2015. IDyLL: Indoor Localization Using Inertial and Light Sensors on Smartphones. In *Proc. of ACM UbiComp*.

[58] Zhice Yang, Zeyu Wang, Jiansong Zhang, Chenyu Huang, and Qian Zhang. 2015. Wearables Can Afford: Light-weight Indoor Positioning with Visible Light. In *Proc. of ACM MobiSys*.

[59] Zheng Yang, Chenshu Wu, and Yunhao Liu. 2012. Locating in Fingerprint Space: Wireless Indoor Localization with Little Human Intervention. In *Proc. of ACM MobiCom*.

[60] Zheng Yang, Chenshu Wu, Zimu Zhou, Xinglin Zhang, Xu Wang, and Yunhao Liu. 2015. Mobility Increases Localizability: A Survey on Wireless Indoor Localization Using Inertial Sensors. *ACM Comput. Surv.* 47, 3 (2015), 54:1–54:34.

[61] Timothy York and Raj Jain. 2011. Fundamentals of Image Sensor Performance. http://www.cse.wustl.edu/~jain/cse567-11/ftp/imgsens/index.html. (2011).

[62] Moustafa Youssef and Ashok Agrawala. 2005. The Horus WLAN Location Determination System. In *Proc. of ACM MobiSys.*

[63] Chi Zhang, Joshua Tabor, Jialiang Zhang, and Xinyu Zhang. 2015. Extending Mobile Interaction Through Near-Field Visible Light Sensing. In *Proc. of ACM MobiCom.*

[64] Chi Zhang. and Xinyu Zhang. 2016. LiTell: Robust Indoor Localization Using Unmodified Light Fixtures. In *Proc. of ACM MobiCom.*

[65] Chi Zhang, Xinyu Zhang, and Ranveer Chandra. 2015. Energy Efficient WiFi Display. In *Proc. of ACM MobiSys.*

[66] Jialiang Zhang, Chi Zhang, Xinyu Zhang, and Suman Banerjee. 2016. Towards a Visible Light Network Architecture for Continuous Communication and Localization. In *Proc. of ACM VLCS.*

[67] Pengfei Zhou, Mo Li, and Guobin Shen. 2014. Use it free: Instantly knowing your phone attitude. In *Proc. of ACM MobiCom.*

[68] Shilin Zhu and Xinyu Zhang. 2017. Enabling High-Precision Visible Light Localization in Today's Buildings. In *Proc. of ACM MobiSys.*

RF-Echo: A Non-Line-of-Sight Indoor Localization System Using a Low-Power Active RF Reflector ASIC Tag

Li-Xuan Chuo, Zhihong Luo, Dennis Sylvester, David Blaauw, Hun-Seok Kim
University of Michigan
{lxchuo,zhluo,dmcs,blaauw,hunseok}@umich.edu

ABSTRACT

Long-range low-power localization is a key technology that enables a host of new applications of wireless sensor nodes. We present *RF-Echo*, a new low-power RF localization solution that achieves decimeter accuracy in long range indoor non-line-of-sight (NLOS) scenarios. RF-Echo introduces a custom-designed active RF reflector ASIC (application specific integrated circuit) fabricated in a 180nm CMOS process which echoes a frequency-shifted orthogonal frequency division multiplexing (OFDM) signal originally generated from an anchor. The proposed technique is based on time-of-flight (ToF) estimation in the frequency domain that effectively eliminates inter-carrier and inter-symbol interference in multipath-rich indoor NLOS channels. RF-Echo uses a relatively narrow bandwidth of ≤80 MHz which does not require an expensive very high sampling rate analog-to-digital converter (ADC). Unlike ultra-wideband (UWB) systems, the active reflection scheme is designed to operate at a relatively low carrier frequency that can penetrate building walls and other blocking objects for challenging NLOS scenarios. Since the bandwidth at lower frequencies (2.4 GHz and sub-1 GHz) is severely limited, we propose novel signal processing algorithms as well as machine learning techniques to significantly enhance the localization resolution given the bandwidth constraint of the proposed system. The newly fabricated tag IC consumes 62.8 mW active power. The software defined radio (SDR) based anchor prototype is rapidly deployable without the need for accurate synchronization among anchors and tags. Field trials conducted in a university building confirm up to 85 m operation with decimeter accuracy for robust 2D localization.

CCS CONCEPTS

• **Information systems** → **Location based services**; • **Computing methodologies** → **Machine learning**; • **Hardware** → **Wireless devices**; **Application specific integrated circuits**; **Hardware test**;

KEYWORDS

Indoor localization; Multipath; Non Line-of-sight; ASIC; RF reflection; Time-of-arrival; Neural network classification

MobiCom'17, , October 16–20, 2017, Snowbird, UT, USA.

ACM ISBN ISBN 978-1-4503-4916-1/17/10…$15.00
https://doi.org/10.1145/3117811.3117840

1 INTRODUCTION

Long-range low-power NLOS indoor localization can enable a host of location-aware Internet-of-Things (IoT) applications. Indoor navigation of public safety officials inside a building is a primary example. The localization tag built in wearable devices would significantly enhance the effectiveness of emergency evacuation, search and rescue operations. Intelligent warehouses and factories can be realized by tracking accurate locations of pallets, equipment, robots, and people in real-time to eliminate potential safety hazards while maximizing logistics efficiency. In hospitals, tracking of equipment, patients, and personnel can identify and eliminate infectious vectors, addressing a major health care issue. We envision ubiquitous localization-ready wireless tags to enable real-time tracking and logging of medical personnel / equipment interaction with patients.

A mobile tag for everyday IoT applications must be small, low power, low cost, and rapidly deployable without heavy infrastructure investment. We target a stringent power budget of <100μW in average (duty-cycled) and <100 mW peak power to fully integrate the solution in a centimeter-scale wearable tag. The localization accuracy requirement for a wide class of IoT applications is in the decimeter (10 cm) order and it must be functional in large (up to 100 m per dimension) indoor environments where NLOS scenarios are dominant with multipath-rich RF propagation. To date, there are few existing solutions that adequately address this set of challenging specifications which is critical to a wide set of localization based applications. Low-cost global positioning system (GPS) receivers [21], for example, cannot establish enough SNR to achieve better than several meters accuracy in indoor settings. WiFi or Bluetooth based indoor localization solutions are available today but their operating range is quite limited (<20 m) and their accuracy is in the order of a few meters that is insufficient to satisfy stringent public safety localization application requirements.

We introduce *RF-Echo*, a new approach in RF localization that utilizes a frequency-shifting active reflector on the tag that echoes the orthogonal frequency division multiplexing (OFDM) [26] ranging signal generated from an anchor. A frequency conversion based full duplex approach enhances the localization range and accuracy beyond the level achievable by conventional narrowband RF localization systems. We implemented the low power tag by fabricating a new custom ASIC in a 180nm CMOS technology. The anchor prototype is based on the USRP X310 [39] software defined radio (SDR) platform. Figure 1 shows the fabricated tag ASIC, the tag board, and the USRP based anchor. The tag ASIC area is 1.9×2.7mm^2 and its active power consumption at the maximum gain setting is 62.8mW. The proposed system has the following capabilities:

- **Decimeter accuracy with up to 85m localization range:** We propose a frequency domain signal processing technique

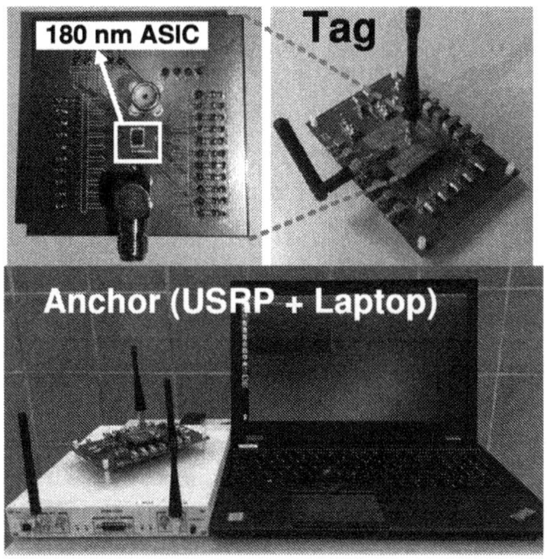

Figure 1: RF-Echo: The tag ASIC fabricated in 180nm CMOS (top), and the USRP based anchor (bottom)

that combines OFDM and neural network to accurately estimate the RF signal ToF in the frequency domain. Our measurement results show that decimeter accuracy is achievable over a ≤85 m operational distance indoor. Neural network training is based on extensive synthesized data, thus it does not require retraining after deploying the system in the field.

- **Low cost, small form factor, and low power for wearable tags:** The active reflector on the tag has a very simple architecture with minimal RF components comprising only a low noise amplifier (LNA), a bandpass filter, a frequency converter, and a power amplifier (PA). The tag does not require power-demanding high accuracy time / frequency references or sophisticated digital signal processing (DSP). The proposed technique eliminates the need for a phase-lock-loop (PLL) [30] or a crystal frequency reference for the tag IC, thus significantly lower the tag manufacturing cost.
- **Operable in NLOS and multipath-rich environments:** We investigate effective bandwidth enhancement techniques such as neural network based timing interpolation. This technique significantly enhances the effective bandwidth to analyze a multipath channel response profile in a finer resolution that is beyond the limit given in the literature [36] [7] for a narrowband system. Operating with a modest bandwidth (≤80 MHz), the proposed technique will provide sufficient resolution to distinguish line-of-sight (LOS) and NLOS paths, thus revealing the direct path distance to the target tag. This low bandwidth requirement is the key to allow RF-Echo to operate in ≤2.4GHz ISM bands. The bandwidth utilization is much lower than that of a conventional UWB system. The lower frequency signal penetrates walls better and experiences less multipath interference than conventional UWB systems.
- **Rapidly deployable, low complexity infrastructure anchors:** The bandwidth of the proposed localization signal can be easily supported by many low cost commercial off-the-shelf (COTS) RF transceivers (e.g., USRP [39]) for anchor prototyping. In addition, we eliminated the need for synchronization among anchors, while many other localization systems (e.g., [23]) require a common frequency and/or time reference among anchors. In the proposed scheme, infrastructure anchors are rapidly deployable by simply pulling them into outlets since ranging between an anchor and a tag can be performed independently without interaction among each other. Time synchronization between a tag and an anchor is also unnecessary for RF-Echo.

This paper presents the RF-Echo system architecture, algorithm, tag ASIC design, anchor implementation, and localization field trial results conducted in a university campus building. The feasibility of a narrowband decimeter-accuracy NLOS indoor localization system is demonstrated with a low-power custom ASIC implementing a low complexity analog-only architecture without a PLL or clock reference crystal. A neural network based ToF-enhancement technique is introduced to improve the reliability and accuracy of RF-Echo without an excessive bandwidth requirement. Despite the limited (1mW) transmit power available at the low-power tag, RF-Echo exhibits up to 85 m and 49 m ranging distance in realistic multipath-rich LOS and NLOS indoor scenarios respectively.

2 BACKGROUND

Before we describe RF-Echo in depth, we first briefly introduce a conventional time-of-flight (ToF) ranging method in this section. The 1-dimensional (1D) distance estimation process between the anchor and the tag is denoted by ranging. Higher dimensional localization is conducted by combining 1D ranging results from multiple anchors through multilateration process discussed in Section 3.

The ToF or time-of-arrival (ToA) based ranging techniques rely on measurements of signal travel time between an anchor and a tag with a goal to distinguish the shortest direct path arrival time from any subsequent (NLOS) multipaths [23] [15]. When sufficiently wide signal bandwidth is given, the ToF/ToA can be determined with high accuracy and since direct path always precedes the NLOS multipath, the two can be distinguished. One approach is to use an impulse-radio UWB system where very short (order of a nano second or less) pulses are transmitted and the arrival time of each pulse is estimated at the receiver to obtain the ToF of the transmitted signal [15] [41] [47] [25]. The bandwidth of an UWB pulse is inversely proportional to the pulse width and narrower pulses are preferred to obtain finer time resolution in ToF / ToA estimation. Since the RF signal travels at the speed of light, the time of flight directly maps to the distance with the relationship that 1 ns in ToF is equivalent to 30 cm in distance. The distance of the direct path in NLOS multipath-rich environments can be resolved by analyzing the first arrival signal time, not the strongest. One of key challenges to achieve decimeter level accuracy in ToF / ToA based ranging is to realize sub-nano second time resolution. In a conventional approach where the signal is sampled and then processed in the digital domain, this would require an ADC with >1G samples per second. However, such high-speed ADCs are extremely power hungry. Furthermore, as [23] shows, their cost increases exponentially with the sampling rate beyond 10MHz. Operating ADC at or above Nyquist

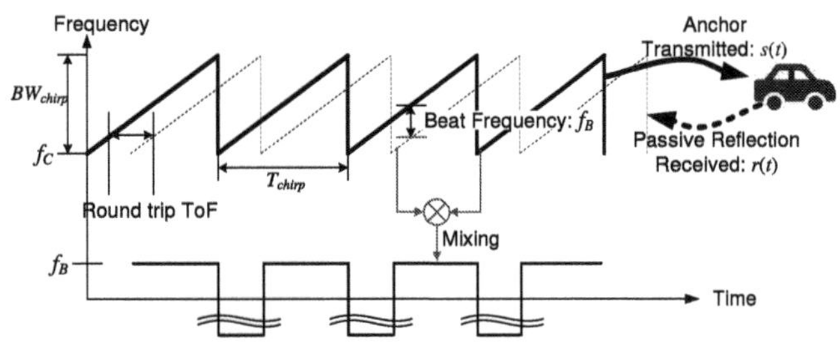

Figure 2: Operating principle of the FMCW radar. The time of flight (ToF) is proportional to the beat frequency f_B.

sampling rate (>1GHz for UWB signals) is, therefore, impractical for many low-power low-cost wireless sensor node localization applications.

While the UWB is beneficial to obtain the pulse arrival time in finer resolution, the wider bandwidth is prone to interference from different frequency bands. Relatively strong interference signals that might be present anywhere in the ultra-wide bandwidth can saturate UWB receiver amplifiers. A highly linear RF circuit for UWB is very power demanding, whereas the limited linearity of the amplifier could constraint the UWB receiver operability in the presence of in-band interferers. Moreover, due to its ultra-wide bandwidth, operating at a higher carrier frequency (typically >4GHz) is inevitable where signals experience worse pathloss and wall penetration loss, lowering its signal-to-noise ratio (SNR). According to the free-space Friis equation, 4 GHz carrier suffers 13 dB worse pathloss than a 900MHz carrier, which translates to more than 4× decrease in distance (6 dB SNR corresponds to 2× distance).

The frequency-modulated continuous-wave (FMCW) based ranging [36] [7] is a method widely used in radar systems to estimate ToF in the frequency domain. In conventional FMCW systems, the radar (i.e., anchor) transmits frequency-modulated chirp signals. The FMCW radar transmit signal, $s(t)$, is represented by equation (1) where f_c is the carrier frequency, s_f is the frequency chirp slope, and T_{chirp} is the chirp duration. The chirp bandwidth is defined as $BW_{chirp} = s_f T_{chirp}$. The operating principle of the FMCW radar is illustrated in Figure 2 .

$$s(t) = e^{j2\pi t(f_c + \frac{s_f t}{2})} \quad (1)$$

The FMCW radar estimates the distance to an object by analyzing the received signal $r(t)$ that is *passively reflected* by an object. The passively reflected signal $r(t)$ is a time-delayed (due to round-trip ToF) version of the transmitted signal. The $r(t)$ can be denoted by $h(t) * s(t) + n(t)$ where $*$ stands for convolution, $n(t)$ is the noise induced at the receiver and $h(t)$ is the round-trip channel impulse response in time domain. Note that the round-trip ToF and the ranging distance have the relationship (2), where τ_0 is the one way time-of-flight, c is the speed of light, and d is the distance to an object.

$$Roundtrip\ ToF = 2d/c = 2\tau_0 \quad (2)$$

For now, let us assume $h(t) = \delta(t - 2\tau_0)$ (i.e., non-multipath channel without delay spread). When the received reflection signal is mixed with the transmitted chirp signal, $r^*(t)s(t)$, a constant *beat* frequency, f_B, is observed in the down-converted (and low-pass filtered) baseband signal as in (3) (see Figure 2 for illustration). This constant beat frequency indicates the distance d to an object, as it is proportional to the round-trip ToF of the signal.

$$LPF\{r^*(t)s(t)\} = e^{j2\pi f_B t} + \tilde{n}(t),\ f_B = s_f d/c\tau_0 \quad (3)$$

3 PROPOSED SYSTEM: RF-ECHO

RF-Echo uses a full-duplex active RF reflector to estimate the range based on the round-trip ToF in frequency domain. The anchor transmits a 2.4 GHz carrier frequency ranging signal to the tag, which concurrently (in a full duplex fashion) relays the ranging signal back to the anchor with carrier frequency down-conversion to 900 MHz. Unlike a conventional RF radar, which relies on passive reflections, this active reflection with the frequency shifting approach allows full-duplex tag design without incurring complexity overhead to cancel the self-interference in the same frequency. Realizing a full-duplex system with the same transmit and receive frequency is technically challenging [4]. We have dramatically reduced the active reflector tag design complexity by intentionally shifting the reflection carrier frequency at the tag for full-duplex operation.

The main advantages of RF-Echo using a new active reflector tag are summarized as follows: 1) Increased range due to signal amplification at the tag IC. 2) Distinction between the tag reflection at 900MHz and non-targets passive reflection at 2.4 GHz. 3) Flexibility of the ranging signal scheme, allowing for application-specific waveform design. 4) Simplicity in the RF and analog tag IC design without discrete time sampling or DSP circuitry, resulting in low power, smaller chip area, low cost, and deterministic delay. 5) Lower signal pathloss and better wall penetration for the returning path from the tag because of the lowered (from 2.4GHz to 900MHz) carrier frequency.

The carrier frequency selection for the RF-Echo system is based on the trade-off study considering the tag power consumption, signal pathloss, wall penetration characteristic, and FCC regulations for different carrier frequency options. The 2.4 GHz ISM band for anchor transmission allows relatively high TX power over a wide bandwidth (80MHz). The 900 MHz band reflection is selected because of the maximum signal level specified in the FCC regulation which is the highest among sub-GHz bands for the continuous 80MHz bandwidth.

Figure 3 shows the RF-Echo system block diagram. The anchor consists of an off-the-shelf USRP SDR [39] that transmits a ≤80 MHz bandwidth ranging signal at 2.4 GHz. The tag receives this signal, shifts the carrier frequency to 900 MHz, and echoes it with a *deterministic delay*. Transmission and reception occur *concurrently at the anchor and tag*. The 2.4 GHz ISM band operation of the anchor allows up to 4W transmit equivalent isotropically radiated power (EIRP). On the other hand, the returning signal power from the tag is much lower, ≤1mW. This asymmetric power level is because of the FCC regulation (5000μV/m @ 3m at 900 MHz) and the low power constraint at the tag. RF-Echo allows a mechanism to adjust the transmit power from the anchor to limit the reflection power from the tag at 900 MHz to be under the FCC limit. Although the returning signal power is low, the sub-GHz frequency signal penetrates walls better and experiences less multipath interference than higher frequency signals.

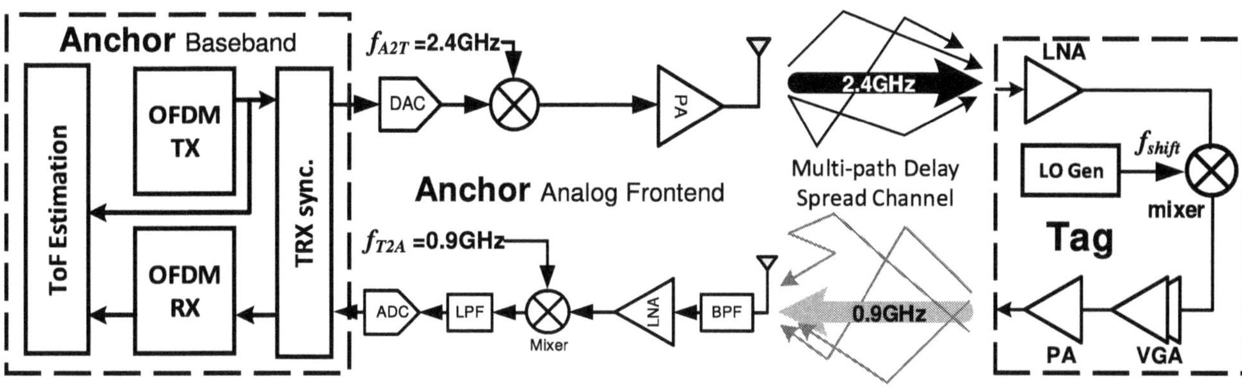

Figure 3: The overall RF-Echo system diagram. The channel impulse response is estimated in frequency domain using OFDM waveforms. The anchor broadcasts ≤80MHz OFDM signals at the 2.4GHz carrier frequency and the active reflector IC, fabricated in an 180nm CMOS process, echoes the OFDM signal with frequency down-conversion to the 900MHz carrier in a full duplex fashion.

Operating with a modest bandwidth of ≤ 80 MHz, the proposed system specification can be easily met by many low cost commercial off-the-shelf (COTS) RF transceivers and SDRs such as USRP [39] for anchor prototyping. In addition, we eliminated the need for synchronization among anchors in our scheme, while many other localization systems (e.g., [23]) require a common (i.e., cabled) frequency and/or time reference among anchors. In our scheme, infrastructure anchors are rapidly deployable since ranging between an anchor and a tag can be performed independently without interaction among each other. In fact, making anchors rapidly deployable is very crucial in some applications such as fire fighter location tracking. Time synchronization between a tag and an anchor is also unnecessary for RF-Echo.

3.1 OFDM based Ranging Waveform

The FMCW waveform discussed in Section 2 has a fundamental limit in estimating ToF when the channel has severe multipaths. Each multipath signal has a different arrival time at the anchor, thus unequal beat frequencies of random phase and magnitude multipath signals are mixed together resulting in the inter-carrier interference. Conventional FMCW systems use ultra-wide bandwidth to separate multiple beat frequencies in a high resolution [7]. To efficiently eliminate inter-carrier interference from multipaths without an excessive bandwidth requirement, we propose an OFDM based ranging signal using the datapath shown in Figure 4.

The transmitted OFDM symbol in frequency domain is defined by an $N \times 1$ complex valued vector $\mathbf{X} = [X[0], X[1], ..., X[N-1]]$ where $X[n]$ is a complex valued constellation point for the subcarrier n, and N is the number of subcarriers in the signal bandwidth (BW). The IFFT output of $\mathbf{x}$ is an $N \times 1$ complex valued vector $\mathbf{x} = [x[0], x[1], ..., x[N-1]]$, where $x[n]$ is the time domain complex sample at the time index n with Nyquist sampling rate of 1/BW (complex valued signal). To mitigate the inter-symbol interference (ISI) from the multipath delay spread, a cyclic prefix (CP) guard interval is appended to each OFDM symbol. Note that the CP guard interval must be longer than the worst case delay spread from multipaths. The CP appended signal $\mathbf{x}$ is converted to the continuous time domain signal $x(t)$ and then up-converted to 2.4 GHz for anchor transmission. This 2.4 GHz passband anchor transmit signal is denoted by $x_{A2T}(t) = x(t)e^{j2\pi f_{A2T}t}$, where f_{A2T} =2.4 GHz, as shown in Figure 3.

Accurately estimating the distance from the anchor to the tag is the central objective of RF-Echo. When the distance is d, the channel impulse response $h_{A2T}(t)$ from the anchor to the tag can be modeled as (4), where L_{A2T} is the number of multipaths, $\tau_0 = d/c$ is the one-way ToF of the RF signal to travel the distance d in the shortest path, and $h_{A2T,0}$ is the corresponding channel gain (complex valued). Other terms $h_{A2T,i}\delta(t - \tau_{A2T,i})$ are from multipath reflections satisfying $\tau_{A2T,i} > \tau_0$ with $i \geq 1$. The shortest path channel gain could be much weaker than those of other multipaths, $|h_{A2T,0}| \ll |h_{A2T,i}|$, $i > 0$, especially in NLOS conditions. Estimating τ_0 is our goal.

$$\begin{aligned} h_{A2T}(t) &= h_{A2T,0}\delta(t-\tau_0) + \sum_{i=1}^{L_{A2T}} h_{A2T,i}\delta(t-\tau_{A2T,i}), \\ h_{T2A}(t) &= h_{T2A,0}\delta(t-\tau_0) + \sum_{i=1}^{L_{T2A}} h_{T2A,i}\delta(t-\tau_{T2A,i}) \end{aligned} \tag{4}$$

Using $h_{A2T}(t)$, the received signal at the tag is denoted by $r_{tag}(t) = h_{A2T}(t) * x_{A2T}(t) + n_{tag}(t)$ where $n_{tag}(t)$ is noise added at the tag receiver front-end and the operator $*$ stands for convolution. We propose *active reflection* at the tag, where the received signal is frequency converted to 900 MHz band and sent back to the anchor in a full frequency duplex fashion. The reflected signal can be written as $x_{T2A}(t) = r_{tag}(t)e^{-2\pi f_{shift}t}$ where $f_{shift} = f_{A2T} - f_{T2A}$, and f_{T2A} =900 MHz. Here we ignore the deterministic delay of

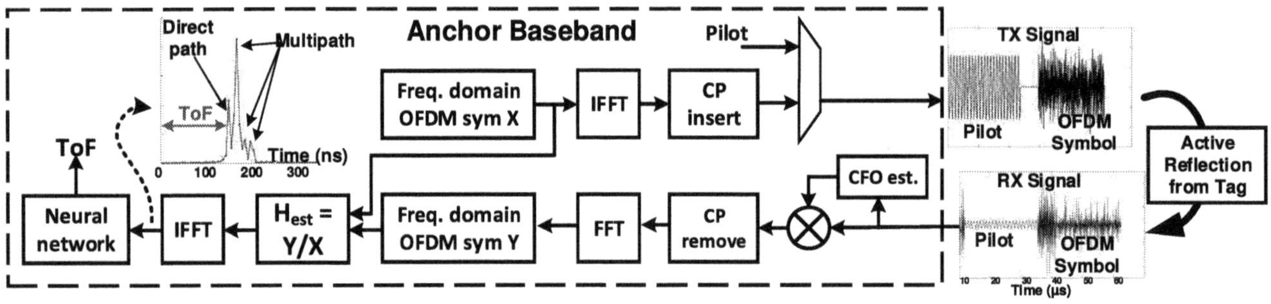

Figure 4: The OFDM based ToF estimation datapath. The OFDM ranging waveform eliminates inter-symbol and inter-carrier interferences to estimate the ToF in frequency domain. The obtained channel impulse response is fed into the neural network that extracts the ToF information from the channel impulse response.

the tag analog processing, which can be easily calibrated out at the anchor. The $x_{A2T}(t)$ reception and $x_{T2A}(t)$ transmission occur simultaneously at the tag (and at the anchor too). Unlike conventional digital systems, the active reflection tag employs *all-analog* processing as depicted in Figure 3. This approach allows the anchor to estimate the ToF τ_0 without ambiguity associated with the tag processing delay. The reflected signal $x_{T2A}(t)$ from the tag experiences channel impulse response $h_{T2A}(t)$ (4), which is different from $h_{A2T}(t)$ because of the carrier frequency difference. However, the shortest path ToF, τ_0, is common for both $h_{A2T}(t)$ and $h_{T2A}(t)$ as indicated in (4). The anchor receiver performs frequency mixing by $e^{-j2\pi f_{T2A}t}$ to bring the signal back to baseband. The baseband received signal at the anchor, therefore, can be represented by $y(t) = h_{A2T}(t) * h_{T2A}(t) * x(t) + n_{anchor}(t)$ where $n_{anchor}(t)$ is the equivalent noise at the anchor. In the frequency domain, (5) holds where $Y(f)$, $H_{A2T}(f)$, $H_{T2A}(f)$, $X(f)$ and $n_{anchor}(f)$ are Fourier transform representations of $y(t)$, $h_{A2T}(t)$, $h_{T2A}(t)$, $x(t)$, and $n_{anchor}(t)$ respectively. Before further processing, the guard interval is removed from $y(t)$ to mitigate the ISI as in conventional OFDM systems [26].

$$Y(f) = H_{A2T}(f)H_{T2A}(f)X(f) + n_{anchor}(f) \tag{5}$$

Note that the baseband signal $x(t)$ and $y(t)$ are sampled *simultaneously using the same local clock* of the anchor. By taking FFT on Nyquist sampled $y(t)$, the frequency domain received OFDM vector symbol $\mathrm{Y} = [Y[0], Y[1], \text{fi}, Y[N-1]]$ is obtained. Based on (5), channel estimation $\mathrm{H_{est}}$ in the frequency domain can be computed by (6). Unlike conventional FMCW, our method using OFDM does not suffer from inter-subcarrier interference in $\mathrm{H_{est}}$ computation. That is, $\frac{Y[j]}{X[j]}$ can be computed without interference from $i \neq j$ subcarriers because of inherent orthogonality among subcarriers in OFDM signaling [26]. The discrete time domain channel impulse response estimate $\mathrm{h_{est}} = [h[0], h[1], ..., h[N-1]]$ is obtained by taking IFFT on $\mathrm{H_{est}}$. Note that $\mathrm{h_{est}}$ is sampled at the rate of 1/BW. Our proposed system obtains the ToF τ_0 by analyzing the interpolated signal $h_{est}(t)$ of the discrete time channel impulse response such that $h_{est}(t) = h_{A2T}(t) * h_{T2A}(t) \approx interpolation(\mathrm{h_{est}})$. $h_{est}(t)$ reveals the round-trip ToF $2\tau_0$ as illustrated in Figure 4 top-left.

$$\mathrm{H_{est}} = \left[\frac{Y[0]}{X[0]}, \frac{Y[1]}{X[1]}, ..., \frac{Y[N-1]}{X[N-1]}\right] \tag{6}$$

3.2 Synchronization with Crystal-less Tags

The proposed active reflector based approach eliminates the need for time synchronization between the anchor and tag. The active reflector in the tag echoes the received signal to the anchor with a deterministic delay. All-analog design of the tag (Section 4) does not incur any sampling time ambiguity or sampling frequency offset that are inevitable in all discrete time based signal processing. Eliminating the notion of discretized time during the active reflection at the tag allows a tag design without a reference crystal to lower its manufacturing cost. Moreover, we propose a carrier frequency offset (CFO) self-calibration scheme to eliminate the conventional phase-lock loop (PLL) [30] for carrier frequency generation at the tag to further reduce its power consumption. Thus we demonstrate the feasibility of a *PLL-less and crystal-free* tag design for extremely cost-sensitive low-power tags.

The proposed CFO self-calibration is performed by sending a pilot tone, $p_{A2T}(t) = e^{j2\pi f_{pilot}t}$, before the OFDM signal $x(t)$ transmission (Figure 4, right). Any frequency mismatch f_{CFO} in the free-running LC oscillator (without a PLL) of the tag will alter the frequency of the received pilot signal (ignoring noise) to $p_{T2A}(t) = e^{j2\pi(f_{pilot}-f_{CFO})t+j\phi}$, where ϕ is the random phase mismatch. The frequency offset is estimated at the anchor by the frequency of the mixed signal; $p_{A2T}(t)p^*_{T2A}(t) = e^{j\phi}e^{j2\pi f_{CFO}t}$. The random phase offset ϕ can be ignored for ToF ranging. To validate this concept, the proposed tag IC (Section 4) is fabricated employing a free-running LC-oscillator circuit without a PLL or a reference crystal clock for frequency (f_{shift}) generation.

3.3 Neural Network based ToF Estimation

In contrast to the conventional UWB time domain ToF estimation where >1 GHz bandwidth is required to achieve cm-scale accuracy, we utilize a modest ≤80 MHz bandwidth OFDM signal and analyze the reflected signal in the frequency domain to reconstruct the time-domain channel impulse response. This ≤80 MHz constraint is from the 2.4 GHz ISM band restriction. Nyquist sampling rate

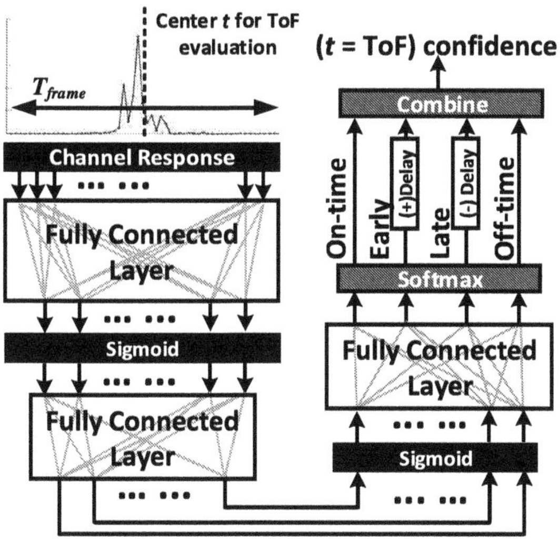

Figure 5: The proposed feedforward neural network structure. Input vector length T_{frame}=134ns (107 samples when BW = 80MHz and 10× interpolation are used). The first and second hidden layer have 48 and 16 neurons respectively. T_{offset} = 20ns for early and late neurons.

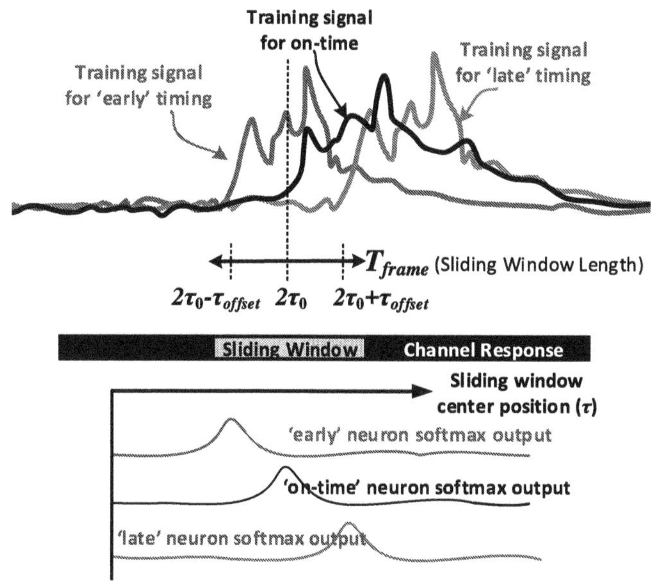

Figure 6: The proposed bootstrap aggregating method. The neural network is trained with early, on-time, and late channel impulse responses. The on-time training signal is centered at ToF $2\tau_0$. The early and late training signal are centered with a $\pm T_{offset}$ offset from ToF.

(=1/BW for a complex signal) of 80 MHz bandwidth signal indicates that the time resolution is only 12.5 ns. This is equivalent to 3.75 meter resolution for the RF signal that travels at the speed of light c, which would severely limit the accuracy of the ToF based ranging.

The accuracy limitation of this relatively low signal bandwidth of RF-Echo is overcome by a neural network based ToF estimator employed at the anchor. The proposed neural network has a fully connected feed-forward structure [17] with two hidden layers as shown in Figure 5. The neural network is trained with many (>500 k) multipath channel impulse response (CIR) training examples $h_{est}^{train}(t) = h_{A2T}^{train}(t) * h_{T2A}^{train}(t)$ that are synthesized (simulated) in Matlab. In other words, the neural network training *does not necessarily require real-world channel impulse response dataset* which is typically unavailable when RF-Echo is deployed in unknown environments. Extensive training dataset are generated using an ITU indoor channel model [20] with exponential delay profiles, randomly generated multipath taps, and random delay spreads to cover various NLOS channel scenarios. Based on the simulated dataset, feed-forward network weights are trained using a back-propagation method [17]. The neural network output is the confidence value that is (statistically) maximized when the input channel impulse response is well-aligned with the *representative shape* of the training dataset waveforms that are all centered at the ground-truth round-trip ToF. The training dataset $h_{est}^{train}(t)$ and the CIR estimation $h_{est}(t)$ signals are the interpolated (by a factor of ≥10×) version of the discrete time channel impulse response sampled at Nyquist rate. For neural network training and evaluation, we use the dB representation of the signal amplitude $20log_{10}(|h_{est}^{train}(t)|)$ and $20log_{10}(|h_{est}(t)|)$, respectively.

The training signal $h_{est}^{train}(t)$ is trimmed for the time span $t \in [2\tau_0 - \frac{T_{frame}}{2}, 2\tau_0 + \frac{T_{frame}}{2}]$, which is centered around the ground-truth round-trip ToF $2\tau_0$. T_{frame} is the training signal window size as shown in Figure 5 and 6. Note that the training signal window size is much shorter than the entire CIR time span because the neural network is only trained for the *CIR shape around the shortest ToF point.* For ToF estimation, the estimated channel impulse response $h_{est}(t)$ is fed into the trained neural network in a sliding window fashion as shown in Figure 6. When the sliding window position is τ, the $h_{est}(t)$ input window span is $t \in [2\tau - \frac{T_{frame}}{2}, 2\tau + \frac{T_{frame}}{2}]$ and the neural network evaluates if this windowed signal resembles the training dataset. The neural network output is (statistically) maximized when τ is the same as the ground-truth ToF $2\tau_0$, as illustrated in Figure 6.

To further improve the accuracy of the neural network based ToF estimation, we apply the *bootstrap aggregating* method [17] [6]. The idea is to train the neural network with several different models separately, then have all the models vote on the output to accurately estimate ToF from the $h_{est}(t)$ signal. In our proposed solution, we train the neural network not only with the training signal that is centered around the ground-truth $2\tau_0$ (i.e., *on-time* dataset) but also with other (independently generated) training dataset with a time offset τ_{offset} in ToF. The training dataset with the *early* and *late* offset has the signal span of $[2\tau_0 - \tau_{offset} - \frac{T_{frame}}{2}, 2\tau_0 - \tau_{offset} + \frac{T_{frame}}{2}]$ and $[2\tau_0 + \tau_{offset} - \frac{T_{frame}}{2}, 2\tau_0 + \tau_{offset} + \frac{T_{frame}}{2}]$ respectively as depicted in Figure 6. As the sliding window

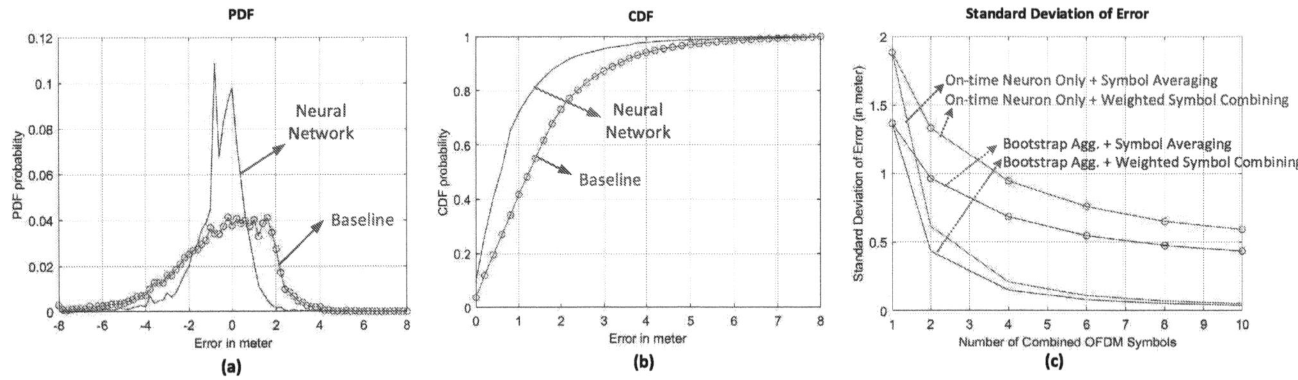

Figure 7: Ranging accuracy simulated in Matlab with 50ns delay spread multipath channels: (a) Probability density function (PDF) of errors from the proposed neural network method vs. baseline algorithm; (b) Cumulative density function (CDF) of errors, neural network vs. baseline algorithm; (c) Standard deviation of errors from multiple OFDM symbol combining: bootstrap aggregation vs. on-time neuron only, and averaging vs. confidence weighted symbol combining

position τ of the neural network input $h_{est}(t)$ changes from 0 to the maximum ToF, the neuron trained with *early* offset would generate a high confidence output first. As the slide window position τ passes by $2\tau_0$ and $2\tau_0 + \tau_{offset}$, we expect to observe a high confidence output sequentially from the *on-time* trained neuron and then from the *late* offset neuron. By combining these three confidence outputs with proper time delays, the accuracy of ToF estimate significantly improves compared to the case with *on-time* training dataset only.

Figure 7 shows the accuracy improvement from the proposed neural network algorithm compared to a hand-designed baseline algorithm. In the baseline algorithm, ToF is estimated by the timing when the power of the sample exceeds a dynamically set threshold level that is proportional to the first peak level in the channel impulse response. The threshold of the baseline algorithm is optimized over an extensive dataset for fair comparison. The Matlab simulation results in Figure 7 (a) and (b) confirm that, in a challenging 50m NLOS scenario, the neural network algorithm (error standard deviation e_{std} = 1.45m) outperforms the baseline (e_{std} = 2.09m). This result is from the single 20μs long OFDM symbol based ranging. The ranging accuracy of the neural network algorithm is further improved by the confidence-weighted symbol combining technique discussed in the next section.

3.4 Symbol Combining

The operating range target of RF-Echo is up to 100 m, which exceeds the typical operating range of popular ISM band communication standards such as WiFi. The operating range is constrained by the FCC regulation that limits the RF power transmission to be under 4W EIRP for 2.4 GHz ISM band and $\leq$5000μV/m @ 3 m for the 900 MHz returning path. Our tag ASIC maximum transmit power is limited to 0 dBm (1 mW). Although the 80 MHz bandwidth is significantly lower than that of UWB radios, it is still 4× wider than the legacy WiFi specification. Enhancing SNR for 80 MHz operation is critical to achieve $\approx$100 m range in indoor scenarios.

For RF-Echo, the complicated band-stitching technique [33] [32] can be replaced by a simple coherent signal combining of multiple OFDM symbols to enhance SNR. Although the tag and anchor are unsynchronized, a coherent channel estimation process is realized at the anchor by the *self-phase aligned processing*. That is, both transmit and receive signals are sampled using the *same local anchor clock* while the reflection delay of the tag is deterministic and constant. The frequency domain channel estimation from the i-th OFDM symbol can be represented by $\mathbf{H}_{\mathbf{est,i}} = \mathbf{H}_{\mathbf{est}} + \mathbf{n_i}$ where $\mathbf{H}_{\mathbf{est}}$ is the true channel response and $\mathbf{n_i}$ is the noise vector in frequency domain. As long as the channel is stationary for multiple consecutive OFDM symbols, combining K channel estimations from consecutive OFDM symbols would increase the effective SNR by a factor of K because channel estimation from multiple measurement would add constructively (due to the self-phase aligned coherent channel estimation) while the independent noises are combined incoherently; $\sum_{i=1}^{K} \mathbf{H}_{\mathbf{est,i}} = K\mathbf{H}_{\mathbf{est}} + \sum_{i=1}^{K} \mathbf{n_i}$. That is, $\| K\mathbf{H}_{\mathbf{est}} \|_2^2 = K^2 \| \mathbf{H}_{\mathbf{est}} \|_2^2$ while $\mathrm{E}\left\{\| \sum_{i=1}^{K} \mathbf{n_i} \|_2^2\right\} = K\mathrm{E}\left\{\| \mathbf{n_i} \|_2^2\right\}$. The OFDM symbol duration is in the order of 10s of μs. Therefore, combining $\leq$10 OFDM symbols per localization fix does not incur unacceptable delay, while it provides up to 10dB SNR improvement.

It is also possible to combine multiple ToF estimates from the neural network output. A naive way of combining multiple ToF estimates is to use arithmetic averaging of estimated distances. The proposed neural network approach allows combining multiple ToF estimates by weighted combination using the confidence output of the final neuron. Since the activation function of the final layer of the neural network is the soft-max function, we can interpret the neural network output as the confidence weight associated with each ToF estimate. The simulation results in Figure 7 (c) show the comparison between arithmetic averaging and the weighted combining. It also shows the performance gain of the proposed bootstrap aggregation (using early, on-time and late neurons) compared to the conventional case where only on-time neuron is used. The standard deviation of 1D ranging error (e_{std}) is reduced (Matlab simulation results) from 1.45m to <0.085m by applying the confidence weighted combining of $\geq$6 OFDM symbols (20μs each) in a 50ns delay spread NLOS channel. The actual measurement data using the fabricated IC is presented in Section 5.

3.5 Multilateration for 2D / 3D localization

The 2D or 3D coordinate of the tag is obtained by the multilateration process [5,8,9,38], which combines 1D ranging results from at least three anchors. It is the same process used by GPS geolocation. Given the distance estimate $\hat{d}_j$ from the j-th anchor to the tag, the tag location coordinate estimate $\mathbf{p}^*$ can be obtained by solving the optimization problem (7) [5] where $\mathbf{p}_j^{\text{anchor}}$ is the known coordinate of the j-th anchor, and J is the number of anchors. The optimization problem can be generalized to 2D or 3D coordinate localization cases with at least three anchors.

$$\mathbf{p}^* = \underset{\mathbf{p}}{\text{argmin}} \sum_{j=1}^{J} \left(\| \mathbf{p}_j^{\text{anchor}} - \mathbf{p} \|_2 - \hat{d}_j \right)^2 \tag{7}$$

The optimization problem (7) is non-convex. However, it can be efficiently solved by algorithms summarized in [8,9,38]. Closed form solutions are also available [5]. The accuracy of the multilateration is directly affected by the reliability of 1D ranging performed at each individual anchor.

4 IMPLEMENTATION

4.1 Active Reflector Tag IC

The proposed active reflector tag ASIC is fabricated in a CMOS 180nm process technology. Figure 8 (a) and (b) show the schematic of the proposed tag IC. It consists of a transformer-based differential low-noise amplifier (LNA), frequency down-conversion circuits, variable gain control units (VGA), and a class-AB power amplifier (PA). Figure 8 (c) shows the fabricated chip micrograph with each component indicated. The tag IC supports a gain dynamic range of 60 dB to adjust to the received signal strength at different distances. The frequency down conversion improves the pathloss of the return path (i.e., 900 MHz reflection rather than 2.4 GHz), which lessens the transmit burden at the low power reflector, while also solving the TX/RX self-interference issue for full duplex operation. The proposed asymmetric reflective architecture simplifies tag design by shifting all signal processing complexity to the anchor and eliminating the need for time synchronization between the anchor and the tag. The transmit power is also asymmetric between the anchor and tag. Given a gain setting at the tag, the anchor can adjust its transmit power so that the returning signal power from the tag at 900 MHz is under the FCC mask.

The tag IC is designed to support a >10 dB peak-to-average-power ratio for an 80 MHz bandwidth OFDM signal with 15 – 60 dB of variable total gain. The transformer-based input matched LNA performs inherent single-ended to differential conversion, providing the doubled-balanced mixer input. This architecture is suitable for compact input matching for the 80 MHz bandwidth target [11]. To minimize the power consumption and dimension on the tag, we eliminate the usage of a crystal oscillator and the phase-locked loop (PLL) for generating the shifting frequency (f_{shift}). Instead, it uses an LC-based free-running voltage controlled oscillator (VCO) as the local oscillator (LO) and a current-commuting mixer [30] with transformer load as shown in Figure 8. PLL-less LO generation

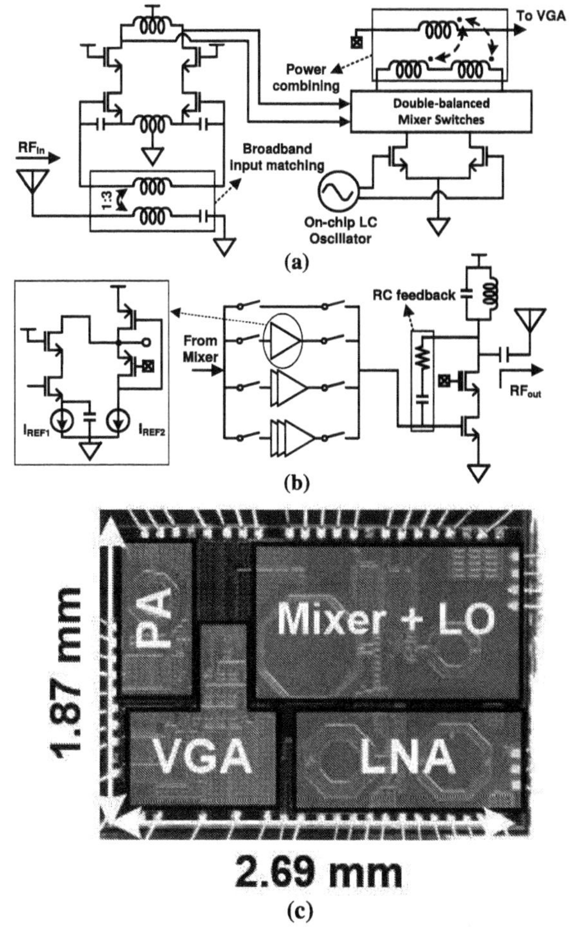

Figure 8: The active reflector ASIC: (a) LNA and mixer circuit schematic; (b) VGA and PA circuit schematic; (c) the chip die photo (fabricated in 180nm CMOS technology).

enables low power design of the tag but it is inevitable to have an inherent carrier frequency offset (CFO) that is slowly drifting over time from the target frequency. We tackle this issue using the CFO estimation/compensation technique described in Section 3. The pilot tone does not have to be inserted for every OFDM symbol as the CFO drifts slowly (at least in the order of millisecond) over time.

The transformer at the mixer output acts as a filter and a power combiner. The mixer is designed to directly drive the PA in the bypass mode with sufficient linearity. The variable gain amplifier (VGA) provides a high dynamic range and consists of 4 gain paths: high gain, mid gain, low gain, and bypass. Because of the required peak gain (60 dB) at 900 MHz and the limited on-chip area, an active inductor is used to boost the gain. The last stage is a single-ended class-AB PA with RC feedback to increase the linearity and stability.

By eliminating the off-chip crystal oscillator and PLL, the cost, complexity, and power consumption of the tag IC is significantly reduced. The measured power consumption of the tag IC is 62.8 mW when it operates with the maximum (60 dB) gain for active

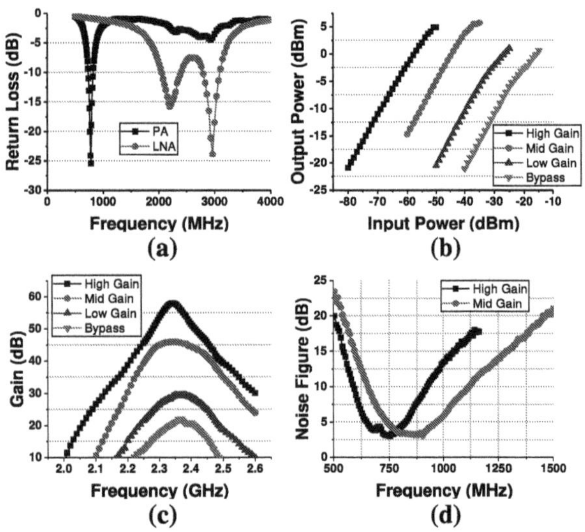

Figure 9: ASIC tag performance: (a) Input/Output impedance matching; (b) Different gain mode setting and the corresponding compression point. (c) Frequency response, showing the tag supports ≤80 MHz bandwidth at different gain modes; (d) Noise figure of the tag in high and mid gain mode.

full-duplex reflection. With a 30μs long ranging symbol (10μs pilot plus a 20μs OFDM symbol), the tag energy consumption per 1D ranging translates to 1.8μJ.

4.2 Anchor Design

For the anchor prototype (Figure 1), we use an USRP X310 [39] with an SBX-120 RF card [35] to enable the full duplex transmit and receive operation at the same time. The precise timing of the baseband OFDM transmit and receive signal sampling is controlled by a common 200 MHz main clock on the USRP FPGA. The global time stamp on the FPGA allows initiating both transmit and receive paths at the same time for the self-aligned time synchronization. The maximum OFDM signal bandwidth supported by the anchor prototype is 100 MHz. The baseband OFDM waveform generation, OFDM signal reception, pilot insertion, carrier frequency offset tracking, and neural network based post-processing are all performed on a laptop running GNU Radio [16] and Matlab software.

The 2D or 3D localization requires multiple anchors operating in a time multiplexed fashion. The accurate time synchronization among anchors, however, is not required as long as the ranging OFDM signal does not collide during the shared medium access. Each anchor can operate with a simple carrier sensing collision avoidance scheme for the medium access control. Accurate carrier frequency synchronization among anchors is also unnecessary. Any carrier frequency offset between an anchor and a tag will be resolved locally at each anchor. Without needs for accurate synchronization, anchors are rapidly deployable by simply pulling them into outlets. The 1D ranging between an anchor and a tag can be performed independently without interaction among each other. The 2D/3D localization coordinate of the target tag is established by sharing 1D

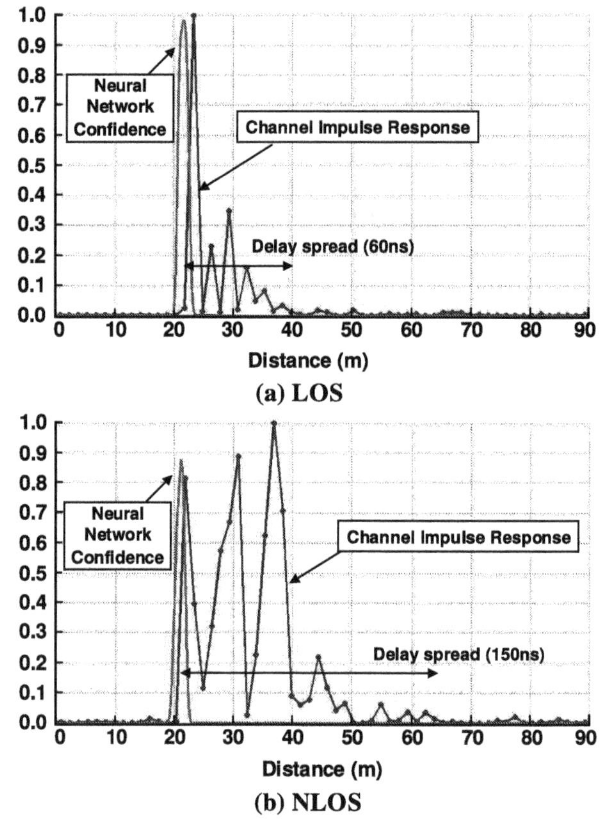

Figure 10: The anchor reconstructed channel impulse response and the neural network output confidence. For x-axis, time is converted to distance using $d/c = t$; (a) a LOS channel response; (b) a NLOS channel response.

ranging results among anchors and performing the multilateration process.

5 EVALUATION

The measured tag sensitivity is -73 dBm when SNR is 10 dB at the anchor, which is sufficient for reconstructing the channel impulse response at 85 m LOS. The 1-dB compression point of the tag is -60 / -42 / -31 / -22 dBm for high / mid / low / bypass gain mode, respectively (Figure 9).

Figure 10 shows examples of the reconstructed impulse response $H_{est}(t)$ wirelessly captured in the field-trial with 80MHz bandwidth. Note that $H_{est}(t)$ is plotted as a function of distance (not time) by using the relationship $d/c = t$. Figure 10 (a) and (b) are channel instances in a university building for LOS and NLOS scenarios at 21.75 and 21.3 m distances respectively. Notice the severe multipath delay spread in these channel impulse responses. It also shows the neural network confidence output that accurately estimates the ToF distance 21.7 m and 21.1 m at the maximum confidence of 0.97 and 0.87 (in the scale of 0.0 – 1.0) in LOS and NLOS scenarios.

Figure 11 summarizes the RF-Echo field-trial results for ≤85.6 m LOS and ≤39.3 m NLOS indoor 1D ranging conducted in a university

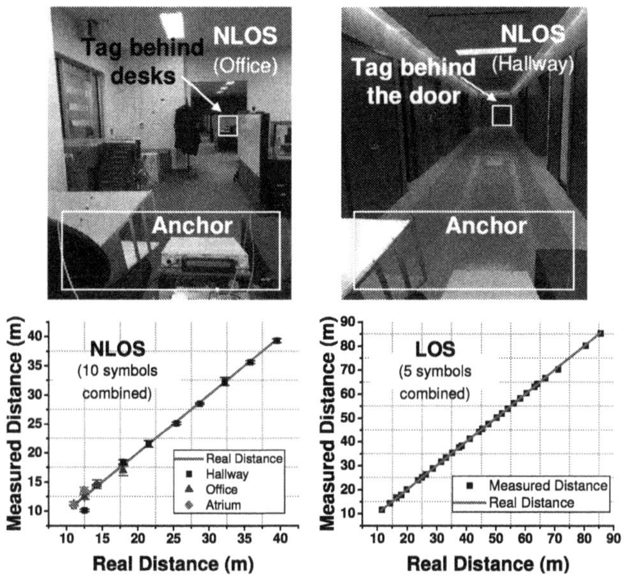

Figure 11: NLOS testing setups and the 1D LOS/NLOS ranging test results in various environments including Atrium, Office, and Hallway. The OFDM symbol length is 20μs.

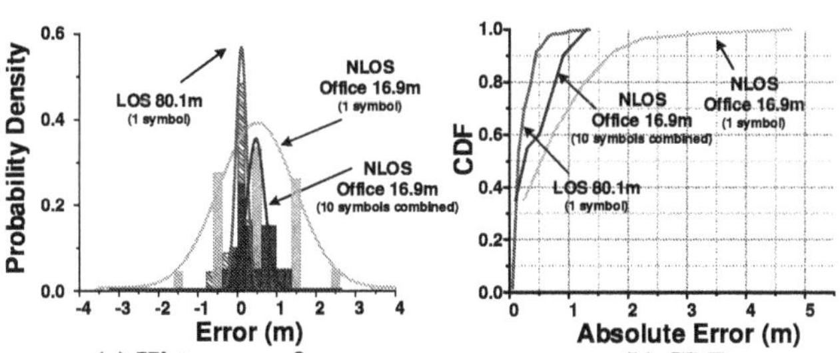

(a) Histogram of error (b) CDF

Figure 12: The 1D ranging error PDF and CDF for data points in Figure 11: (a) The error PDF with one or ten confidence-weighted OFDM symbols combining. Each symbol is 20μs long; (b) The CDF for same scenarios.

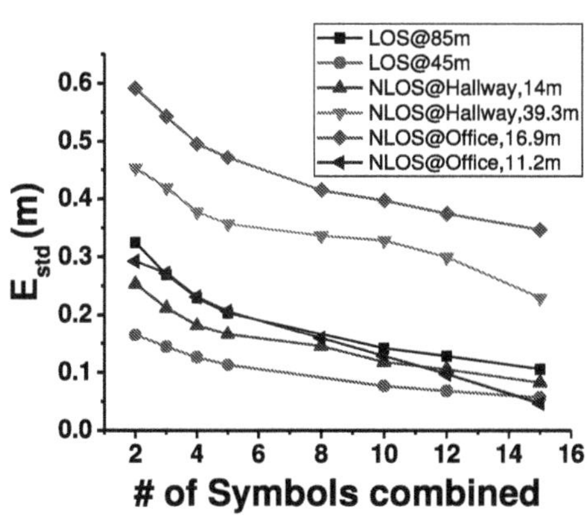

Figure 13: Error standard deviation as a function of the number of OFDM symbols combined.

campus building with testing setups shown in the same figure (top). The anchor has 30 dBm TX power and -90 dBm RX sensitivity. The operable ranging distance is limited by the tag IC reflection power $\leq$ 1mW (0dBm). The 1D ranging error histogram and the error standard deviation (e_{std}) of the same field-trials are presented in Figure 12 and 13, where the impact of neural network confidence-weighted symbol combining is shown. Each OFDM symbol is 20μs long with 1024 subcarriers.

Figure 14 shows the 2D localization map obtained from a 30×20m^2 university campus building space. The error CDF results are also shown. Anchors are black stars labeled with A_1 – A_6. The red triangles are the ground-truth tag locations, and the blue dots are estimated tag locations. Each tag location uses 10 OFDM symbols combined per estimate, and each test point has 10 estimations. Note that only A_1 – A_4 anchors are used to locate the LOS trajectory marked in the blue line. Whereas only A_4 – A_6 anchors are used to perform the NLOS localization inside a large classroom. Walls in this building are made of thick concrete and bricks. The cluster of blue dots shows the error deviation of each estimation. The error of LOS trajectory is small and almost invisible except the location around T_{14} on the map. 90th percentile LOS absolute error is $\leq$ 40cm. As the tag location extends in x-dimension, the angle difference from A_1 – A_4 anchors to the tag diminishes, making the accuracy at T_{14} worse in y-dimension. This artifact is known as the dilution of precision (DOP) in a GPS system [21]. NLOS localization capability (through thick concrete walls) is demonstrated via A_4 – A_6 anchors only to locate tags (T_{15} – T_{17}) in a large classroom. Note that A_4 is outside the classroom while A_5 and A_6 are in another classroom separated by a thick concrete wall. The error of this NLOS localization is small and unrecognizable on the map.

6 RELATED WORK

One of the conventional approaches to perform RF signal based ranging is to use received signal strength indicator (RSSI) [3, 28, 34, 46]. The pathloss expression of RF signal propagation directly maps the RSSI to a distance using an inverse-square law. Due to simplicity of measuring RSSI, it has been widely adopted in WiFi or Bluetooth for ranging. Unfortunately, in NLOS or multipath-rich environments, signal fading results in large deviation in RSSI from the theoretical pathloss equation. The RSSI statistically follows a Rayleigh or log-normal distribution [29] in many practical multipath scenarios, which indicates large errors (at least a few meters) in ranging.

The angle-of-arrival (AoA) or direction-of-arrival (DoA) approach has been studied in the literature as an alternative localization method [10, 14, 27, 44]. The AoA approach performs coherent signal processing extracting the phase information of the received RF carrier signal at different antenna locations. The phase difference at different locations reveals the angle-of-arrival. Multiple AoA estimations obtained from three or more anchors provide the tag location through multilateration. Its performance, in theory, is insensitive to signal strength variation and potentially more robust than the RSSI-based method. However, employing multiple antenna arrays for AoA estimation increases the system cost, size, and complexity. Moreover, when severe multipaths exist and their signal strength is higher than or comparable to the LOS signal strength,

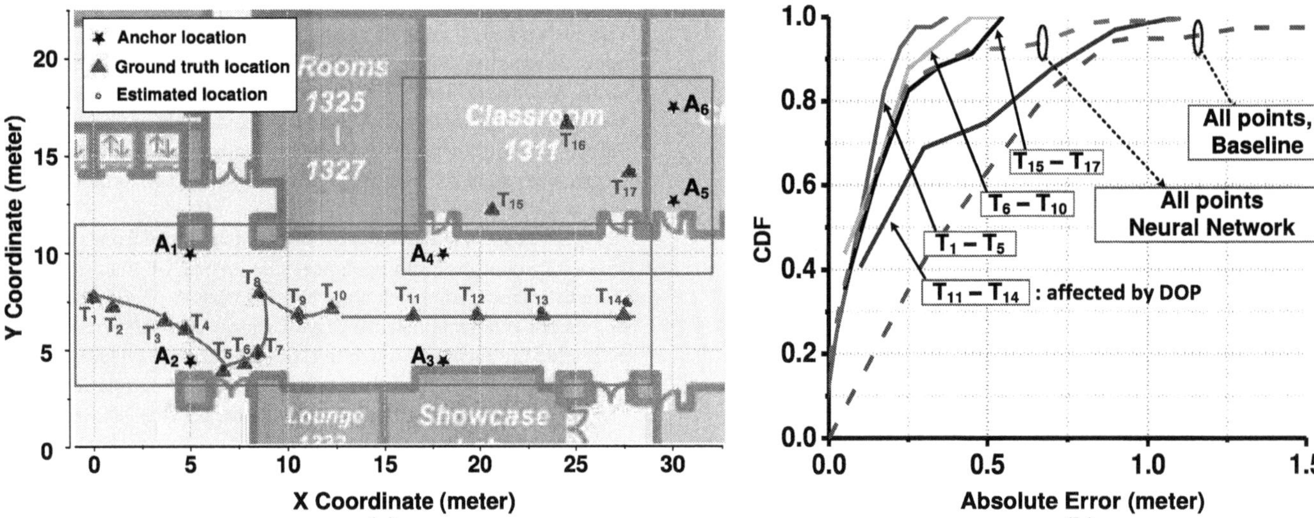

(a) (b)

Figure 14: The 2D localization map in a 30×20m^2 university building: (a) Only A_1 – A_4 anchors are used to localize T_1 – T_{15} along the blue trajectory. Only A_4 – A_6 are used to localize the NLOS positions (T_{15} – T_{17}); (b) The CDF of the 2D localization error. The T_{11} – T_{14} has higher errors due to the diminishing differences of angles from anchors (A_1 – A_4) to the tag (dilution of precision, DOP). The comparison of the proposed neural network algorithm and the baseline algorithm is shown for T_1 to T_{14}.

AoA estimation could easily fail. This vulnerability to multipaths makes AoA-based methods inappropriate for many indoor localization applications. Recently, a novel synthetic aperture radar (SAR) localization system [24] is proposed to demonstrate feasibility of indoor localization in multipath environments using a commodity mobile device (a tablet PC). However, the mobile device in [24] requires accelerometer data with several seconds of motion. Its relatively low energy efficiency, high manufacturing cost per tag, and slow localization update rate limit its application for ultra-low cost, massively deployed low power tags.

With ToA / ToF based ranging capabilities, UWB radio technologies have been gaining interests since their usage in the 3.1 to 10.6 GHz band was approved by the FCC in 2002. DecaWave DW1000 [13] [12] is a commercial off-the-shelf 802.15.4a (UWB) compliant radio chipset that supports pairwise ranging between transceivers. The chipset's architecture and algorithm are not released in public. Unlike our solution, a stringent ≈10 ppm carrier frequency offset is required for system operation. The transceiver draws 393mW [13] of active power during transmit and advertises a ranging accuracy of 10 cm. Localization is performed in a packet basis with a maximum 6.8Mb/s data rate. At this data rate and a 512-byte (half of the maximum) packet length, its energy per 1D ranging is 237μJ. The tag energy in RF-Echo is only 18μJ per 1D ranging with a conservative 10 OFDM symbols combining (including the pilot, 20μs per OFDM symbol).

Other ASIC solutions [19] [31] [37] published recently are all focusing on high-power and high-accuracy LOS applications such as radar or UWB ranging. [19] uses a time-extension method to avoid the high-speed ADC needed in the UWB ranging. Although [19] achieves decent accuracy without using a GHz-ADC, this solution requires strict timing synchronization between TX and RX, severely limiting the maximum operation range. [31] utilizes careful frequency planning and sub-sampling of the incoming signal to eliminate the need for high-speed ADC. However, this paper shares a common local oscillator (LO) between the TX and RX, bypassing the issue of synchronization. [37] realizes the phase domain successive-approximation radar (SAR) with a mm-wave frequency single-carrier. This approach requires a stringent TX-RX phase-locking (homodyne detection) and results in excessive power consumption of 457 mW with 4.38 mm^2 chip area.

WASP [33] is a relatively narrow band (125MHz) ToA-based system that reports up to 30 m indoor operation with 50 cm accuracy (with a tracking algorithm from a sequential measurement). Its COTS components based design utilizes high performance RF datapath whose power consumption is at least 2 Watts. Harmonium [23] introduces a compact (1.5cm^3) low-power (75mW) tag for UWB TDoA ranging with a unique frequency-stepped receiver architecture. However, its tight timing synchronization requirement between anchors (wire-connected to each other) limits its usability for large dimension operations. All evaluation in [23] was conducted in a rather small 4.6×7.2×2.7 m^3 room space.

Chronos [40] uses channel impulse response estimation available from commodity WiFi devices for indoor localization. It stitches multiple 802.11 WiFi bands to expand the effective signal bandwidth in order to achieve higher resolution and to resolve the multipath profile using non-uniform Discrete Fourier Transform (NDFT). The proposed solution, however, assumes certain signal sparsity which might not be guaranteed in multipath-rich NLOS indoor environments. Unlike RF-Echo, Chronos requires a WiFi compliant chipset on a tag device, which would increase the tag manufacturing cost and power consumption compared to the RF-Echo tag. Its operation is based on 35 WiFi channel band stitching with 5MHz minimum

System	Technology	LOS Accuracy	NLOS Accuracy	Testing Environment Dimension	Tag Power	System Bandwidth	Signal Type	Time per Localization Fix	Energy per Localization
H. Han et al. [19]	65nm ASIC: Real time-sampling	1.9 mm	N/A	LOS: < 1m	70 mW @ 1m 320 mW @ 2.1m	500 MHz	Impulse	100 μs	32 μJ @ 2.1m
T. Redant et al. [31]	40nm ASIC: Equivalent time-sampling	4 mm	N/A	LOS: 3.6m	195 mW	2 GHz	Multi tones	20 μs	3.9 μJ @ 3.6m
Tang et al. [37]	65nm ASIC: Frequency sweep	4 mm	N/A	LOS: < 1m	457 mW	1.7 GHz	Sub-carrier SAR (Phase)	2 μs	0.9 μJ @ <1m
WiTrack [2]	FMCW ToF	31 cm (90%)	40 cm (90%)	LOS: 3-11m NLOS: $6 \times 5m^2$	No tag	1.69 GHz	FMCW	At least 2.5 ms	N/A
Harmonium [23]	UWB TDoA	31 cm (90%)	42 cm (90%)	LOS: $4.6 \times 7.2 \times 2.7m^3$ NLOS: $4.6 \times 7.2 \times 2.7m^3$	75 mW	3.5 GHz	Impulse	52 ms	3900 μJ
PolyPoint [22]	UWB ToF (DecaWave chipset)	140 cm (90%)	N/A	LOS: $20 \times 20m^2$	150 mW	N/A	Impulse	62 ms	9300 μJ
TimeDomain [1]	UWB Two-way ToF	2.1 cm	N/A	N/A	1.8 W	2.2 GHz	Impulse	6.6 ms	11880 μJ
Ubicarse [24]	SAR + Motion sensor	39 cm (median)	59 cm*** (median)	LOS: $15 \times 10m^2$ NLOS: $15 \times 10m^2$	N/A	N/A	WiFi	100 ms	N/A
PinIt [42]	RFID SAR	16 cm (90%)	16 cm (90%)	LOS: $6 \times 5 \times 2.2m^3$ NLOS: $6 \times 5 \times 2.2m^3$ (200 tags with 15 cm spaced)	Passive	6 MHz (UHF)	UHF RFID	5.4 s****	N/A
Tagoram [45]	RFID SAR	12 cm (median)	N/A	LOS: $1 \times 2m^2$	Passive	6 MHz (UHF)	UHF RFID	At least 33 ms	N/A
WASP [33]	Narrow band ToA	50 cm (85%)	50 cm (65%)	LOS: 10m NLOS: $15 \times 15m^2$	2-2.5 W	125 MHz	OFDM	100 ms	200000 - 250000 μJ
FILA [43]	802.11 RSSI + CSI*	45 cm (median)	180 cm (90%)	LOS: $5 \times 8m^2$ NLOS: $32.5 \times 10m^2$	1.6 W**	80 MHz	OFDM	16 ms	25600 μJ
Chronos [40]	802.11 WiFi + Band-stitching	14.1 cm (median)	20.7 cm (median)	LOS: $20 \times 20m^2$ NLOS: $20 \times 20m^2$	1.6 W**	20MHz × 35 overlapped ch.	OFDM	84 ms	134400 μJ
RF-Echo	**180nm ASIC: Active reflection + Neural network estimation**	**26 cm (90%)**	**46 cm (90%)**	**LOS: $7 \times 90m^2$** **NLOS: $30 \times 20m^2$**	**62.8 mW**	**80 MHz**	**OFDM**	**20 μs per symbol**	**18 μJ (Pilot tone + 10 symbols)**

* CSI is Channel State Information on each subcarrier of 802.11 PHY layer ** Calculated based on Intel WiFi Link 5300 in RX mode [18]

*** Calculated based on reported x, y, z error **** Including computational time

Table 1: Comparison of accuracy, dimension of field trial environment, tag power, update rate, and energy consumption per localization for a representative sampling of recently published indoor RF localization systems.

spacing, which results in a relatively slow update rate of 84 ms per measurement and the theoretical limit of ≤60 meter ranging.

Table 1 summarizes comparison between our RF-Echo system and other ASIC / COTS based systems. RF-Echo's localization accuracy, tag power, energy efficiency, tag complexity (i.e., tag cost), localization update rate, and NLOS operable range all compare favorably to other prior arts summarized in Table 1.

7 CONCLUSION

In this paper, we proposed RF-Echo, a new RF localization solution with unprecedented accuracy and energy efficiency for indoor applications. A newly fabricated active reflector ASIC is introduced to demonstrate the feasibility of low-power wireless tags that are small, low cost, and rapidly deployable without heavy infrastructure investment. The proposed approach uses OFDM signaling that effectively mitigates inter-carrier and inter-symbol interference which are common in wide bandwidth RF localization systems. Unlike conventional ToF based systems, our solution does not require strict timing and/or frequency synchronization among anchors and tags. Instead, each individual anchor uses a self-aligned timing and on-the-fly CFO tracking. This enables ultra-low cost design for the tag without a conventional PLL and clock reference crystal. The modest bandwidth of the OFDM signal allows the system to operate in 2.4 GHz and sub-1GHz bands in which the signal penetrates indoor walls better compared to the signal at a higher frequency for UWB systems. We overcome the limitation of the relative low signal bandwidth by using a neural network based ToF estimation technique. Power consumption of the active reflector tag IC is only 62.8 mW. The anchor prototype is implemented on a USRP SDR platform. Field trials conducted in a university campus building confirm that the proposed system can operate up to 85 m distance in LOS scenarios and it can provide <40 cm standard deviation of error for 1D ranging in challenging indoor NLOS scenarios. Accurate multilateration field trail results (26 cm location error in LOS and 46 cm location error in NLOS, 90% CDF) are provided to demonstrate the usability of the proposed system for various applications including indoor navigation, public safety search and rescue operations.

8 ACKNOWLEDGMENTS

The authors thank the reviewers and shepherd for their comments and feedback. This work was supported in part by TerraSwarm – an SRC program sponsored by MARCO and DARPA. This work was also supported in part by the NIST Public Safety Innovation Accelerator Program (PSIAP) Grant #70NANB17H163.

REFERENCES

[1] Time Domain PulsON 400 RCM. Online.
[2] F. Adib, Z. Kabelac, D. Katabi, and R. C. Miller. 3d tracking via body radio reflections. In *Proceedings of the 11th USENIX Conference on Networked Systems Design and Implementation*, NSDI'14, pages 317–329, Berkeley, CA, USA, 2014. USENIX Association.
[3] K. Benkic, M. Malajner, P. Planinsic, and Z. Cucej. Using rssi value for distance estimation in wireless sensor networks based on zigbee. In *2008 15th International Conference on Systems, Signals and Image Processing*, pages 303–306, June 2008.
[4] D. Bharadia, E. McMilin, and S. Katti. Full duplex radios. In *Proceedings of the ACM SIGCOMM 2013 Conference on SIGCOMM*, pages 375–386, New York, NY, USA, 2013. ACM.
[5] M. S. Brandstein, J. E. Adcock, and H. F. Silverman. A closed-form location estimator for use with room environment microphone arrays. *Speech and Audio Processing, IEEE Transactions on*, 5(1):45–50, 1997.
[6] L. Breiman. Bagging predictors. *Mach. Learn.*, 24(2):123–140, Aug. 1996.
[7] G. M. Brooker. Understanding millimetre wave fmcw radars.
[8] R. Bucher and D. Misra. A synthesizable VHDL model of the exact solution for three-dimensional hyperbolic positioning system. *Vlsi Design*, 15(2):507–520, 2002.
[9] Y. Chan and K. Ho. A simple and efficient estimator for hyperbolic location. *Signal Processing, IEEE Transactions on*, 42(8):1905–1915, 1994.
[10] H. C. Chen, T. H. Lin, H. T. Kung, C. K. Lin, and Y. Gwon. Determining rf angle of arrival using cots antenna arrays: A field evaluation. In *MILCOM 2012 - 2012 IEEE Military Communications Conference*, pages 1–6, Oct 2012.
[11] H. S. Chen, H. Y. Tsai, L. X. Chuo, Y. K. Tsai, and L. H. Lu. A 5.2-ghz full-integrated rf front-end by t/r switch, lna, and pa co-design with 3.2-db nf and +25.9-dbm output power. In *2015 IEEE Asian Solid-State Circuits Conference (A-SSCC)*, pages 1–4, Nov 2015.
[12] DecaWave. Application note: APS007. Online.
[13] DecaWave. ScenSor DW1000. Online.
[14] E. Elnahrawy, J. Austen-Francisco, and R. P. Ma. Adding angle of arrival modality to basic rss location management techniques. In *2007 2nd International Symposium on Wireless Pervasive Computing*, Feb 2007.
[15] S. Gezici, Z. Tian, G. B. Giannakis, H. Kobayashi, A. F. Molisch, H. V. Poor, and Z. Sahinoglu. Localization via ultra-wideband radios: a look at positioning aspects for future sensor networks. *IEEE Signal Processing Magazine*, 22(4):70–84, July 2005.
[16] GNU Radio Website. Online, accessed December 2014.
[17] I. Goodfellow, Y. Bengio, and A. Courville. *Deep Learning*. MIT Press, 2016.
[18] D. Halperin, B. Greenstein, A. Sheth, and D. Wetherall. Demystifying 802.11n power consumption. In *Proceedings of the 2010 International Conference on Power Aware Computing and Systems*, HotPower'10, pages 1–, Berkeley, CA, USA, 2010. USENIX Association.
[19] H. G. Han, B. G. Yu, and T. W. Kim. 19.6 a 1.9mm-precision 20gs/s real-time sampling receiver using time-extension method for indoor localization. In *2015 IEEE International Solid-State Circuits Conference - (ISSCC) Digest of Technical Papers*, pages 1–3, Feb 2015.
[20] International Telecommunication Union. Propagation data and prediction methods for the planning of indoor radiocommunication systems and radio local area networks in the frequency range 900 MHz to 100 GHz. Online.
[21] E. Kaplan and C. Hegarty. *Understanding GPS: principles and applications*. Artech house, 2005.
[22] B. Kempke, P. Pannuto, and P. Dutta. Polypoint: Guiding indoor quadrotors with ultra-wideband localization. In *Proceedings of the 2Nd International Workshop on Hot Topics in Wireless*, HotWireless '15, pages 16–20, New York, NY, USA, 2015. ACM.
[23] B. Kempke, P. Pannuto, and P. Dutta. Harmonium: Asymmetric, bandstitched uwb for fast, accurate, and robust indoor localization. In *2016 15th ACM/IEEE International Conference on Information Processing in Sensor Networks (IPSN)*, pages 1–12, April 2016.
[24] S. Kumar, S. Gil, D. Katabi, and D. Rus. Accurate indoor localization with zero start-up cost. In *Proceedings of the 20th Annual International Conference on Mobile Computing and Networking*, MobiCom '14, pages 483–494, New York, NY, USA, 2014. ACM.
[25] Z. Li, W. Dehaene, and G. Gielen. A 3-tier uwb-based indoor localization system for ultra-low-power sensor networks. *IEEE Transactions on Wireless Communications*, 8(6):2813–2818, June 2009.
[26] R. v. Nee and R. Prasad. *OFDM for Wireless Multimedia Communications*. Artech House, Inc., Norwood, MA, USA, 1st edition, 2000.
[27] R. P and M. L. Sichitiu. Angle of arrival localization for wireless sensor networks. In *2006 3rd Annual IEEE Communications Society on Sensor and Ad Hoc Communications and Networks*, volume 1, pages 374–382, Sept 2006.
[28] C. Papamanthou, F. P. Preparata, and R. Tamassia. Algorithmic aspects of wireless sensor networks. chapter Algorithms for Location Estimation Based on RSSI Sampling, pages 72–86. Springer-Verlag, Berlin, Heidelberg, 2008.
[29] T. Rappaport. *Wireless Communications: Principles and Practice*. Prentice Hall PTR, Upper Saddle River, NJ, USA, 2nd edition, 2001.
[30] B. Razavi. *RF Microelectronics*. Prentice-Hall, Inc., Upper Saddle River, NJ, USA, 1998.
[31] T. Redant, T. Ayhan, N. D. Clercq, M. Verhelst, P. Reynaert, and W. Dehaene. 20.1 a 40nm cmos receiver for 60ghz discrete-carrier indoor localization achieving mm-precision at 4m range. In *2014 IEEE International Solid-State Circuits Conference Digest of Technical Papers (ISSCC)*, pages 342–343, Feb 2014.
[32] E. Saberinia and A. H. Tewfik. Enhanced localization in wireless personal area networks. In *Global Telecommunications Conference, 2004. GLOBECOM '04. IEEE*, volume 4, pages 2429–2434 Vol.4, Nov 2004.
[33] T. Sathyan, D. Humphrey, and M. Hedley. WASP: A system and algorithms for accurate radio localization using low-cost hardware. *IEEE Transactions on Systems, Man, and Cybernetics – Part C*, 41(2), Mar. 2011.
[34] M. Saxena, P. Gupta, and B. N. Jain. Experimental analysis of rssi-based location estimation in wireless sensor networks. In *Communication Systems Software and Middleware and Workshops, 2008. COMSWARE 2008. 3rd International Conference on*, pages 503–510, Jan 2008.
[35] SBX 120 Daughterboard, Ettus Research LLC. . Online.
[36] A. G. Stove. Linear fmcw radar techniques. *IEE Proceedings F - Radar and Signal Processing*, 139(5):343–350, Oct 1992.
[37] A. Tang, G. Virbila, D. Murphy, F. Hsiao, Y. H. Wang, Q. J. Gu, Z. Xu, Y. Wu, M. Zhu, and M. C. F. Chang. A 144ghz 0.76cm-resolution sub-carrier sar phase radar for 3d imaging in 65nm cmos. In *2012 IEEE International Solid-State Circuits Conference*, pages 264–266, Feb 2012.
[38] D. Z. Thai, M. Trinkle, A. Hashemi-Sakhtsari, and T. Pattison. Speaker localisation using time difference of arrival. Technical report, DTIC Document, 2008.
[39] Universal Software Radio Peripheral (USRP), Ettus Research LLC. Online.
[40] D. Vasisht, S. Kumar, and D. Katabi. Decimeter-level localization with a single wifi access point. In *13th USENIX Symposium on Networked Systems Design and Implementation (NSDI 16)*, pages 165–178, Santa Clara, CA, 2016. USENIX Assoc.
[41] M. Verhelst, N. V. Helleputte, G. Gielen, and W. Dehaene. A reconfigurable, 0.13um cmos 110pj/pulse, fully integrated ir-uwb receiver for communication and sub-cm ranging. In *2009 IEEE International Solid-State Circuits Conference - Digest of Technical Papers*, pages 250–251,251a, Feb 2009.
[42] J. Wang and D. Katabi. Dude, where's my card?: Rfid positioning that works with multipath and non-line of sight. In *Proceedings of the ACM SIGCOMM 2013 Conference on SIGCOMM*, pages 51–62, New York, NY, USA, 2013. ACM.
[43] K. Wu, J. Xiao, Y. Yi, M. Gao, and L. M. Ni. Fila: Fine-grained indoor localization. In *2012 Proceedings IEEE INFOCOM*, pages 2210–2218, March 2012.
[44] J. Xiong and K. Jamieson. Arraytrack: A fine-grained indoor location system. In *Proceedings of the 10th USENIX Conference on Networked Systems Design and Implementation*, nsdi'13, pages 71–84, Berkeley, CA, USA, 2013. USENIX Association.
[45] L. Yang, Y. Chen, X.-Y. Li, C. Xiao, M. Li, and Y. Liu. Tagoram: Real-time tracking of mobile rfid tags to high precision using cots devices. In *Proceedings of the 20th Annual International Conference on Mobile Computing and Networking*, MobiCom '14, pages 237–248, New York, NY, USA, 2014. ACM.
[46] G. Zanca, F. Zorzi, A. Zanella, and M. Zorzi. Experimental comparison of rssi-based localization algorithms for indoor wireless sensor networks. In *Proceedings of the Workshop on Real-world Wireless Sensor Networks*, REALWSN '08, pages 1–5, New York, NY, USA, 2008. ACM.
[47] Y. Zheng, M. A. Arasu, K. W. Wong, Y. J. The, A. P. H. Suan, D. D. Tran, W. G. Yeoh, and D. L. Kwong. A 0.18um cmos 802.15.4a uwb transceiver for communication and localization. In *2008 IEEE International Solid-State Circuits Conference - Digest of Technical Papers*, pages 118–600, Feb 2008.

Simultaneous Power-Based Localization of Transmitters for Crowdsourced Spectrum Monitoring

Mojgan Khaledi
University of Utah
mojgankh@cs.utah.edu

Mehrdad Khaledi
Rensselaer Polytechnic Institute
khalem@rpi.edu

Shamik Sarkar
University of Utah
shamik.sarkar@utah.edu

Sneha Kasera
University of Utah
kasera@cs.utah.edu

Neal Patwari
University of Utah
npatwari@ece.utah.edu

Kurt Derr
Idaho National Labs
kurt.derr@inl.gov

Samuel Ramirez
Idaho National Labs
samuel.ramirez@inl.gov

ABSTRACT

The current mechanisms for locating spectrum offenders are time consuming, human-intensive, and expensive. In this paper, we propose a novel approach to locate spectrum offenders using crowdsourcing. In such a participatory sensing system, privacy and bandwidth concerns preclude distributed mobile sensing devices from reporting raw signal samples to a central agency; instead, devices would be limited to measurements of received power. However, this limit enables a smart attacker to evade localization by simultaneously transmitting from multiple infected devices. Existing localization methods are insufficient or incapable of locating multiple sources when the powers from each source cannot be separated at the receivers. In this paper, we first propose a simple and efficient method that simultaneously locates multiple transmitters using the received power measurements from mobile devices. Second, we build sampling approaches to select mobile sensing devices required for localization. Next, we enhance our sampling to also take into account incentives for participation in crowdsourcing. We experimentally evaluate our localization framework under a variety of settings and find that we are able to localize multiple sources transmitting simultaneously with reasonably high accuracy in a timely manner.

1 INTRODUCTION

When software defined radios (SDRs) become ubiquitous, i.e., in the hands and pockets of average people, it will be easy for a selfish user to alter his radio(s) to transmit and receive data on unauthorized spectrum, for example, using an off-limits band, or transmitting/receiving on a channel when another device has priority. In addition, SDRs infected by a computer virus or malware could exhibit illegal spectrum use without the user's awareness. Cheap jamming devices are already being used for illegal activities and this trend is likely to grow [3]. The U.S. Federal Communications Commission has an enforcement bureau which detects spectrum violations via complaints and extensive manual investigation. The mechanisms used currently for locating spectrum offenders are time consuming, human-intensive, and expensive. A violator's illegal spectrum use can be too temporary and mobile to be detected and located using existing processes. We envision a novel approach that crowdsources

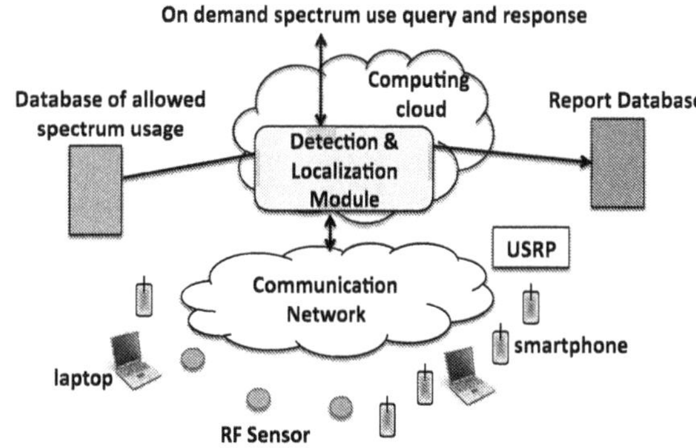

Figure 1: Enabling Distributed Set of Wireless Devices to Detect and Locate Spectrum Offenders.

the sensing and localization of spectrum offenders. We assume a distributed set of wireless devices, e.g., smartphones, radio frequency (RF) sensor nodes, laptops, access points and modems, etc., will participate by *sensing* the use of different bands of the spectrum over time and space and share their measurements with a detection and localization module on a (cloud) server, as shown in Figure 1. Our crowdsourced approach is expected to monitor a wide range of frequencies using a mix of SDR and non-SDR devices[1]. The detection and localization module requests and collects spectrum usage information from a variety of sensors. It compares the spectrum usage with the allowed spectrum usage information (spectrum policies and regulations, frequency bands, locations, etc.) available in a database to determine and locate spectrum offenders. This

[1]By 2020, the number of SDR devices is likely to be almost twice the number in 2014 [4].

MobiCom '17, October 16–20, 2017, Snowbird, UT, USA.
 ISBN 978-1-4503-4916-1/17/10...$15.00
DOI: https://doi.org/10.1145/3117811.3117845

spectrum usage database is akin to the whitespace database (e.g., an FCC-approved database that contains information on available whitespaces and their locations).

Towards the fulfillment of this vision, in this paper, we focus on crowdsourced localization of spectrum offenders. Due to privacy concerns and bandwidth and energy constraints, it is undesirable for mobile sensing devices to share raw signal samples with a central server, and hence, in our work, devices collect only received power measurements. Our mobile sensing devices do not decode any signals. A key challenge in localizing spectrum offenders is that of simultaneous localization of multiple transmitters[2]. We develop a simple, yet efficient and accurate approach that simultaneously localizes multiple transmitters using the power of the sum of all signals received at the selected wireless devices. While localization of a transmitter based on power measurements taken by a network of sensors has been widely studied (see [30] for a survey), we argue that the existing work on WSNs cannot be simply adapted for localization of multiple transmitters using crowdsourcing. If two devices transmit at the same time, the received signal is a phasor sum of the signals from both. Simultaneous transmission in the same channel can be a consequence of an attacker's violation of spectrum access rules or an intentional effort to jam. In either case, the signals may be impossible to separate, particularly when receivers report only power measurements to the server. Furthermore, it is important for crowdsourcing-based localization to account for the mobility and changing availability of user devices.

Many existing methods assume that if multiple transmitters are to be located, their signals can be separated at the receivers [30]. Note that even if all receivers were sophisticated enough to perform this blind source separation, a smart adversary could simply transmit signals that are not blind separable. When multiple signals cannot be separated, the few published methods [23, 25, 26] that are able to localize multiple transmitters from power measurements have high time complexity and do not consider the mobility and temporal availability of transmitters and receivers. For example, Quasi EM [26], a statistical approach to localize multiple transmitters, assumes that the transmitters and receivers are static and that the number of transmitters is known a priori. There is existing work on locating multiple transmitters using mobile robots [22]. However, this work is not applicable in our setting where mobile users move without network control. We need a localization algorithm which minimizes time complexity without significantly compromising the localization accuracy in dynamic environments in order to detect and locate unauthorized transmitters.

We present a method for simultaneous power-based localization of transmitters (SPLOT) for crowdsourced spectrum monitoring. We consider the temporal availability and mobility of both receivers and transmitters and make no assumptions about the number of transmitters. Our approach relies on the fact that, even when multiple transmissions overlap, typically the vast majority of power received by a receiver is from the nearest transmitter. Therefore, by finding local maxima in the spatially distributed received signal strength (RSS) measurements, we can approximate the region of presence of each transmitter. We can then convert the problem of simultaneous multiple transmitter localization to a set of single transmitter localization problems and use a matrix inversion approach to find the location of each transmitter. Notably, we only consider an approximate region of each transmitter that is confined to the area around each local maximum and thus, achieve fast, accurate, and scalable localization.

Next, we build sampling approaches to select mobile sensing devices required for RSS measurements. Our goal is to select a set of wireless devices that provides maximum coverage for the monitored area considering mobility of both the sensing and the offending devices as well as possible erroneous or missed measurements. In this paper, we define and use a new metric called *degree expansion*, that represents the amount of overlap in the sensing ranges of mobile sensing devices. Using this metric, we propose two sampling approaches: 1) Greedy sampling, and 2) Metropolis sampling. While good Samaritans can be recruited for monitoring spectrum, mobile users need not participate in crowdsourcing for selfish reasons (including depletion of batteries and use of their processing resources) unless they receive some payoff as a compensation. We enhance our sampling approach to incentivize mobile users such that we select nodes that maximize coverage but minimize the total payoff. Furthermore, our incentive mechanisms motivate mobile sensing devices to act truthfully. Our *truthful sampling* considers both the budget limit and mobility of mobile sensing devices.

We experimentally evaluate our approach in two different settings: 1) an open environment with non-uniformly distributed receivers in the Orbit testbed [34] using USRP2 nodes for transmitting and receiving signals, and 2) a cluttered office with 44 uniformly distributed sensors [31]. Our experimental results show that using SPLOT we are able to localize multiple transmitters with high accuracy and in a timely manner. The highest average localization error using SPLOT measured in the open environment is 1.16 meters for up to 4 simultaneously transmitting transmitters, and the highest average localization error in the cluttered office with mobile transceivers is 2.14 meters. In comparison, the highest average localization error in Quasi EM measured in the open environment is above 6 meters. Our results also show that SPLOT is tens of minutes faster than Quasi EM. We also implement SPLOT on commodity devices and perform multi-transmitter localization in a variety of indoor and outdoor experiments. We find SPLOT to significantly outperform Quasi EM in these settings as well.

2 LOCALIZATION

In this section, we describe our approach to simultaneously locating multiple transmitters in the areas near the mobile sensing devices (also referred to here as receivers). The localization problem considered here is challenging for several reasons. First, there may be multiple transmitters, and the number of transmitters is unknown. Second, each measurement of received power is an unknown combination of the received powers from each transmitter. Third, the number and the locations of both transmitters and receivers might change from one sample to the next. Fourth, each link from transmitter to receiver experiences multipath fading, which is known to complicate RSS-based localization. We do not use time-of-arrival (TOA) methods because they require recording and sharing users' sampled signals, which violates our privacy model. We do not use

[2]For instance, a malware-based attack could simultaneously cause many devices to violate rules or jam the spectrum.

angle-of-arrival (AOA) methods because they require additional RF hardware. We require an efficient and accurate localization approach that can locate all available transmitters in a dynamic environment using only power measurements.

2.1 Methodology

Our localization methodology assumes that receivers (mobile sensing devices) have been selected using our sampling approaches and that these receivers are spread geographically across the monitored area. Let K denote the unknown number of transmitters and $\theta = \{\theta_1, \theta_2, \ldots, \theta_K\}$ represent their unknown two-dimensional locations. Our problem is to determine K and θ based on observed received powers reported by L receivers, $y = \{y_1, y_2, \ldots, y_L\}$.

Our localization approach relies on two observations. First, receivers that are located near the transmitter observe generally higher power than the receivers that are distant from the transmitter. The second observation is that the observed RSS at each receiver is primarily affected by the nearest transmitter. To validate this observation, we compare the RSSs observed in selected receivers when there is no transmitter, when there is only one transmitter, and when we add multiple transmitters in different locations. Our results show that when there is a transmitter near a receiver, the RSS observed by this receiver increases substantially. However, there is a small growth on the observed RSS by the receiver when adding more transmitters at more distant locations.

These two observations allow us to reduce the problem of locating multiple, unknown number of transmitters to that of localizing a set of single transmitters as follows. First, we find the local maxima of RSSs observed by receivers that are greater than a predefined threshold. The predefined threshold is set to the minimum RSS that a receiver observes when there is a transmitter near it. By defining this threshold, we are able to separate the local maxima due to the presence of a transmitter from the local maxima due to the different fade levels at nearby receivers.

With the knowledge of the local maxima, our localization problem can be reduced to finding K transmitters, where K is equal to the number of local maxima. Instead of locating K transmitters in the entire monitored area, we divide the problem into K single transmitter localizations. For each local maximum, we locate a single transmitter. However, we confine the area to the small area around the local maximum and only use the RSSs that are observed by the receivers in this area for localization. Restricting the area to the small area around the local maximum reduces the time complexity of localization approach, and more importantly, confines the localization area and thus increases the accuracy of localization. This is because the noise in the measurements at receivers in other areas has little impact.

After reducing the multiple transmitter localization problem to a set of single transmitter localization, we locate each single transmitter in a small area around the local maximum using a single transmitter localization method. Specifically, we use a matrix inversion approach for single transmitter localization designed for higher efficiency and localization accuracy (see Section 5.3).

2.1.1 Single transmitter localization. In this section, we apply a linear model and perform inversion to localize the transmitted power. Our approach is designed to accurately locate a source with unknown transmit power. In this linear model, we estimate the power field, i.e., the power transmitted vs. position. This power field is then used to find the location of an unknown transmitter.

Given a local maximum of RSSs observed by receivers, we find a transmitter located in a confined area around the local maximum. The confined area is a circle of radius R from the local maximum. Let vector $y = [y_1, y_2, \ldots, y_L]$ be the received powers (in linear units of Watts) observed by L receivers located in the confined area. Also, let $x = [x_1, x_2, \ldots, x_Q]$ be the power field, where x_i represents the transmit power sent by a transmitter in voxel i. We select a grid of Q voxels that fill the confined area. We have a forward model for y,

$$y = Wx + n, \tag{1}$$

where n is an $L \times 1$ vector that represents the noise and fading contributing to the L RSS measurements, and W is an $L \times Q$ matrix where W_{ij} indicates the gain that would be experienced on the channel between a transmitter at voxel j and receiver i, if there is a transmitter in voxel j. The weight value W_{ij} is inversely related to the distance of the voxel and the receiver. We model the weight as,

$$W_{ij} = \begin{cases} d_{ij}^{-n_p}, & d > minPL \\ minPL^{-n_p}, & \text{otherwise} \end{cases} \tag{2}$$

Here, d_{ij} is the Euclidean distance from the center of voxel j to the receiver i. n_p is the path loss exponent and $minPL$ is a minimum path length.

A power field estimate $\hat{x}$ is estimated from y. However, finding $\hat{x}$ is, in general, an ill-posed inverse problem. We use a regularized least squares approach to compute an estimate,

$$\hat{x} = \Pi y \tag{3}$$

$$\Pi = \left(W^T W + \sigma_N^2 C_x^{-1}\right)^{-1} W^T, \tag{4}$$

where σ_N^2 is the noise variance, W^T is the transpose of matrix W, and the prior covariance matrix C_x is obtained by using an exponential spatial decay function,

$$[C_x]_{jl} = \sigma_x^2 e^{-f_{jl}/\delta_c}. \tag{5}$$

Correlation distance constant δ_c describes the distance at which two voxels have correlation coefficient $1/e$, σ_x^2 is the variance of the transmit power field, and f_{jl} is the length of the line between the centers of voxels j and l.

Finally, the transmitter location is estimated to be the center of voxel with maximum value of $\hat{x}$.

2.1.2 Dynamic Localization. We also address the problem of locating mobile transmitters. We consider two dynamic cases: 1) the number and locations of transmitters are changing; and 2) the number and location of both transmitters and receivers are changing.

One approach to locate these dynamic cases is to repeat the multiple transmitter localization procedure every time new received power measurements are made. This approach is not efficient since changes are likely to be small from one time interval to the next. Thus, in this section, we present methods to use the coordinates from the previous estimate in the current localization problem.

Dynamic transmitters: When changes happen only in the number and location of *transmitters*, our dynamic localization works as follows.

The localization module uses three data sources at time t: 1) the RSS measurements of the selected receivers in time $t-1$, which we denote y^{t-1}; 2) the RSS measurements of the receivers in time t, y^t; and 3) the locations of detected transmitters in time $t-1$, which we denote θ^{t-1}. The first step is to estimate the number of transmitters, which we accomplish by comparing y^{t-1} with y^t. If there is no significant change, the localization module sets $\theta^t = \theta^{t-1}$. If the RSS increases significantly for some of the receivers, the localization module performs multiple transmitter localization for the area that is covered by these receivers to find new transmitters. If the RSS decreases significantly for some receivers, the localization module removes previous transmitters if there are receivers with significant decrease in the RSS within the confined area (circle of radius r) around the previous transmitters. The set of transmitters at time t, θ^t is the union of the remaining transmitters from the previous time and the newly added transmitters.

Note that by significant change, increase or decrease, in RSS, we mean any changes in the RSS that is greater than a predefined threshold. The predefined threshold is determined by the localization module depending on the environment. This predefined threshold is equal to the minimum change in the RSS measurements of receivers when at least one transmitter is added to or removed from the environment.

One drawback of the above approach is the propagation of error. Since the localization module estimates current transmitter locations using the previous results, the error can be carried forward from one time interval to the next, and after some time, the detected transmitters may be far from the actual transmitters. To deal with this problem, we periodically reinitialize by performing the multiple transmitter localization algorithm without any previous time estimates.

Dynamic transmitters and receivers: When the number and the location of receivers also change over time, we cannot compare two consecutive RSS measurements on the same link, as the change in receiver position will cause significant RSS changes. Even by mapping the receivers in the previous time, $t-1$, to the nearest receiver available in time t and inversely relating the RSS to the distance between mapped receivers, we are not able to compare the RSSs in two consecutive time slots. This is due to the fact that RSS may be different for receivers with the same distance from the transmitter due to both shadowing and small-scale fading. Therefore, while the number or locations of receivers are changing, we perform multiple transmitter localization without using the previous time information. However, we limit the recalculation to at most every T seconds.

3 SAMPLING

An important aspect of offender localization is the task of selecting a set of mobile sensing devices for RSS measurements. The selection approach must consider the following: (i) maximum spatial coverage of the monitored area, and (ii) computational efficiency, i.e., select the nodes in a timely manner.

To select mobile sensing devices to maximize coverage, we define a new metric called *degree expansion*. A high degree expansion amounts to selecting receivers from new uncovered geographic areas and thus maximizing coverage.

Algorithm 1: Greedy Algorithm

input : $G = (V, E, W)$
    S // cardinality constraint
output: A // selected mobile sensing devices

$A = \emptyset$;
$v = argmax_{v \in G} d_G(v)$;// the mobile sensing device with maximum degree is selected first
$A = A \cup v$;
while $|A| < S$ **do**
    Select new node $v \in V - A$ where
    $v \in argmax_{i \in V - A_{j-1}} m_{i|A_{j-1}}$
    $A = A \cup v$;
end

We develop two selection algorithms namely *Greedy* and *Metropolis*, to select a set of mobile sensing devices with high degree of expansion in a timely manner.

3.1 Preliminaries

We assume that the mobile sensing devices know their locations. Let T be the time interval (same as in Section 2) after which the sampling is repeated. At the beginning of each time interval T, the central controller sends the sensing request for that time interval to the mobile sensing devices. Then, mobile sensing devices voluntarily inform the central controller about their current locations and their sensing ranges. The sensing range of a mobile sensing device is the maximum radius around their current location for a given transmit power that they are able to measure. Given the current locations of mobile sensing devices, the central controller constructs a weighted graph $G = (V, E, W)$ where $v \in V$ represents a mobile sensing device (node), $e_{i,j} \in E$ denotes a link between node i and node j, and $w_{i,j} \in W$ represents the weight of link $e_{i,j}$. There is a link between node i and node j, $e_{i,j} \in E$, if their sensing ranges overlap. $w_{i,j} \in [0, 1]$ shows the amount of overlap between the sensing range of node i and node j and is obtained from the following formula:

$$w_{i,j} = \begin{cases} \frac{(r_i + r_j - d_{i,j})}{(r_i + r_j)} & d_{i,j} \le r_i + r_j \\ 0 & otherwise \end{cases} \tag{6}$$

Here, r_i and r_j are parameters related to the sensing ranges of node i and node j respectively. $d_{i,j}$ denotes the Euclidean distance between two nodes. We define the following:

- S is a set of nodes where $S \subset V$.
- $N(S)$ is the *neighborhood* of S that includes all nodes in $V - S$ that have a link to S.
- $d_G(v)$ is *degree* of node v in graph G. $d_G(v)$ is equal to sum of the weights of links that connect to v.
- The degree expansion, $DX(S)$, of a set S is $DX(S) = \sum_{i \in N(S)} \min_{j \in S} w_{i,j}$.

To select mobile sensing devices that maximize the coverage, we develop algorithms for solving the optimization problem below:

$$\arg\max_{S \subset V} DX(S) \tag{7}$$

Algorithm 2: Metropolis Algorithm

```
input  : G = (V, E, W)
         S, M // cardinality constraint and number of
         iterations
output : A_opt // selected mobile sensing devices
// Initial sample, S nodes selected randomly.
A_current = random(V, S);
A_opt = A_current;
for i = 1 to M do
    v = rand(A_current, 1);
    w = rand(V - A_current, 1);
    A_new = {A_current - v} ∪ {w};
    α ∈ rand[0, 1];
    if α < q(A_new) / q(A_current) then
        A_current = A_new;
        if q(A_current) > q(A_opt) then
            A_opt = A_current;
        end
    end
end
```

where, S is the cardinality constraint. This optimization problem is NP-hard. It can be reduced to the *set cover* problem [14]. In the following sections, we propose two algorithms to obtain approximate solutions.

3.2 Greedy Algorithm

The greedy approach is shown in Algorithm 1. In the greedy algorithm, the selection is based on a greedy heuristic that selects the mobile sensing devices based on their marginal contributions to the degree expansion. The mobile sensing device with maximum degree expansion is selected first. Then, the mobile sensing devices are selected one by one iteratively based on their marginal contributions on degree expansion until S mobile sensing devices are selected. By iteration j, $j-1$ mobile sensing devices are selected (denoted by A_{j-1}), and the marginal contribution of mobile sensing device $i \in V - A_{j-1}$, if represented by $m_{i|A_{j-1}}$ is equal to $d_G(i) - \sum_{j \in N(A_{j-1}) \cup A_{j-1}} w_{i,j} - \sum_{j \in A_{j-1}} w_{i,j}$. The mobile sensing device with maximum marginal contribution to the degree expansion is selected as the winner of the j iteration. I.e., $v \in argmax_{i \in V - A_{j-1}} m_{i|A_{j-1}}$. To simplify the notation, we replace $m_{i|A_{j-1}}$ by m_i in the rest of this paper.

3.3 Metropolis Algorithm

Metropolis is a Markov Chain Monte Carlo (MCMC) method to sample and evaluate probability distributions [24]. Recently, Metropolis sampling has been applied to subgraph sampling [18]. In this section, we use the idea of subgraph sampling to approximate the optimization problem of Equation 7.

Overview: Given a graph $G = (V, E, W)$, the idea of Metropolis algorithm is to create a subgraph of size $S < |V|$ in each iteration. The first set of mobile sensing devices is selected randomly and the subsequent sets of mobile sensing devices are constructed by removing a node from and adding a new node to the subgraph. We choose a *quality measure*, described below, to quantify the degree expansion of samples. The acceptance or rejection of new mobile sensing devices is based on this quality measure. By selecting mobile sensing devices until convergence is achieved while keeping the selected mobile sensing devices with the maximum quality measure, we obtain a subgraph (selection of S mobile sensing devices out of N users) that approximately optimizes the degree expansion. We describe the pseudo-code of Metropolis in Algorithm 2.

Quality metric: Given a selected mobile sensing device A, the maximum possible degree expansion of graph $G = (V, E, W)$ is $\sum_{v \in V-A} d_G(v)$. This implies that the selected nodes, A, have links to all the other nodes, $V - A$ (i.e., $N(A) = V - A$). As a result, a normalized quality measure is equal to: $q(A) = \frac{DX(A)}{\sum_{v \in V-A} d_G(v)}$. The quality measure determines the degree expansion. A higher quality measure corresponds to a higher degree expansion.

4 TRUTHFUL SAMPLING

A naive way to provide incentives for the mobile sensing devices is to reward them such that the reward amount is greater than their declared cost of participation. The problem with this approach is that mobile sensing devices can over-report their costs and receive higher rewards. Therefore, the algorithm for selecting mobile sensing devices should also motivate them to truthfully report their costs. In this section, we enhance the greedy algorithm to consider both cost and degree expansion in selecting mobile sensing devices and add truthfulness. We design a time efficient payment mechanism for the case where the sampling is not optimal. Then, we propose the budget feasible version of the greedy algorithm. Finally, we propose a truthful mobility aware sampling approach that prevents selfish mobile sensing devices from cheating with regards to their availability for the sampling task. In truthful sampling, in addition to location and the measuring range, the mobile sensing devices also inform the central controller about their bids that can be equal or greater than their actual costs of collecting data, c_i.

Given graph $G = (V, E, W)$, and a cardinality or a budget constraint, the central controller selects winners and determines the payment, p_i, for each winner. We assume that all mobile sensing devices act rationally and selfishly, and their main goal is to maximize their own profits, not to harm others. Also, each user has a utility of $p_i - c_i > 0$ if selected and 0 otherwise.

4.1 Truthful Greedy Algorithm

Given the cardinality constraint S, the central controller wants to select S mobile sensing devices that maximize the degree expansion and minimize cost while considering individual rationality (provides the required incentives for selfish players to participate in the game) and incentive compatibility (truthfulness). This amounts to solving the following optimization problem.

$$\max_{S \in V} \sum_{i \in S} \frac{m_i}{c_i}$$

$$s.t.$$

$$\forall i, c_i', p_i(c_i) - c_i \geq p_i(c_i') - c_i \quad (8)$$

$$\forall i, p_i(c_i) - c_i \geq 0 \quad (9)$$

Here, Constraints 8 and 9 provide incentive compatibility and individual rationality.

Our allocation mechanism must consider both cost and the degree expansion. Our payment mechanism must ensure both incentive compatibility (IC) and individual rationality (IR). The best known payment mechanism for providing IC and IR is the well-known Vickrey-Clarke-Groves (VCG) mechanism [5]. Unfortunately, VCG fails to provide IC and IR when the allocation mechanism is not optimal. The problem of selecting a set of mobile sensing devices that maximize the total weight is equivalent to *set-cover* problem which is NP-hard. We use a Greedy algorithm to approximate the optimal solution. However, we still need a truthful payment mechanism that employs an approximated greedy algorithm to select mobile sensing devices. Towards this goal, we rely on Myerson's characterization of truthful mechanisms [21].

THEOREM 4.1. ***(Myerson 1981).*** *A mechanism with allocation mechanism A and payment mechanism P is truthful if and only if the following holds:*

- ***A is monotone:*** *The allocation mechanism keeps selecting the mobile sensing device i as a winner if it independently decreases its declared cost,* c_i.
- ***P pays winners the threshold amounts:*** *Paying each winner the maximum declared cost.*

First, we need to show the sub-modularity for $\frac{m_i}{c_i}$ which implies that:

$$\frac{m_1}{c_1} \geq \frac{m_2}{c_2} \geq \ldots \geq \frac{m_S}{c_S} \tag{10}$$

We show the sub-modularity by contradiction. Suppose mobile sensing device i and mobile sensing device l are selected by the central controller where $i < l$, i.e., the mobile sensing device i is selected before the mobile sensing device l. Let us assume that $\frac{m_i}{c_i} < \frac{m_l}{c_l}$. According to the sampling mechanism, $[i] = argmax_{j \in V - A_{i-1}} \frac{m_j}{c_j}$. That means $\frac{m_{i|A_{i-1}}}{c_i} \geq \frac{m_{l|A_{i-1}}}{c_l}$. Given that $A_{i-1} \subset A_{l-1}$, $m_{l|A_{i-1}} \geq m_{l|A_{l-1}}$. Therefore, we have $\frac{m_{i|A_{i-1}}}{c_i} \geq \frac{m_{l|A_{i-1}}}{c_l} \geq \frac{m_{l|A_{l-1}}}{c_l}$, which is a contradiction with our assumption. As a result, Equation 10 is true. Next, we determine the payment using the Myerson's conditions. The key point is that we have to find the maximum value for the cost that a mobile node can declare and still win. We can find this threshold amount for each winner i by setting $V' = V - \{i\}$ and run the greedy algorithm until i is no longer selected. Let k be the index of the last mobile sensing device where $\frac{m_k}{c_k} < \frac{m_i}{c_i}$. Then, we obtain the payment to mobile sensing device i from the following formula:

$$p_i(c_i) = max_{1 \leq j \leq k} \frac{c_j m_i^j}{m_j} \tag{11}$$

where m_i^j is the marginal contribution of mobile sensing device i on the degree expansion in iteration j.

LEMMA 4.2. *The payment mechanism provides individual rationality.*

PROOF. If a mobile sensing device is selected by the sampling mechanism, then the utility is equal to $\frac{c_j m_i^j}{m_j} - c_i$. Given that $\frac{m_i^j}{c_i} \geq \frac{m_j}{c_j}$, the utility of the winner is always positive. Also, if the mobile sensing device is not selected by the sampling mechanism, the utility of the device is zero. □

LEMMA 4.3. *The payment mechanism provides incentive compatibility for the declared cost.*

PROOF. Let c_i, c_i' be the declared cost of mobile sensing device i when it is being truthful and not truthful, respectively. We must consider four cases here. First, if mobile sensing device i is the winner, it is still selected even by over-reporting, $c_i' > c_i$, or under-reporting, $c_i' < c_i$, its cost. In this case, the utility of the mobile sensing device decreases. Thus, the mobile sensing device has no incentive to lie. Second, if the mobile sensing device i is a loser it is still not selected even if it over-reports or under-reports its cost. Then, the utility is still zero and once again there is no incentive to lie. Third, if mobile sensing device i is a winner, is not selected by over-reporting its cost. Then, the utility will be zero. Thus, the mobile sensing device has no incentive to lie. Fourth, if the mobile sensing device i is a loser and it is not selected by over-reporting its cost. Otherwise, it contradicts the sub-modularity. However, the mobile sensing device can be selected by under-reporting its cost. Let assume that the mobile sensing device l is selected by the greedy algorithm when the mobile sensing device i acts truthfully. This means $\frac{m_l}{c_l} \geq \frac{m_i}{c_i}$. Since the maximum threshold for the mobile sensing device i is at least $\frac{m_l}{c_l}$, the payment to player i is at least $\frac{m_i^l c_l}{m_l}$ meaning that the utility is at most zero. □

4.2 Budget-feasible Truthful Greedy Algorithm

We now consider a limit, B, on the total budget available to the controller. Given this limit, we must select a set of mobile sensing devices that maximize the marginal contribution on degree expansion. To select the mobile sensing devices with the budget limit constraint, similar to [38], we check the following condition at each iteration of the greedy algorithm, and stop the algorithm whenever the following condition no longer holds.

$$c_i \leq B \frac{m_i^j}{\sum_{j \in A_j} m_j} \tag{12}$$

Let $\{1, \ldots, k\}$ be the largest subset that respects condition 12. To find the amount of payment for mobile sensing device $i \leq k$, we remove this player from the set of mobile sensing devices, $V' = V - \{i\}$, and then run the greedy algorithm. In each iteration of greedy algorithm, we check the budget limit constraint, Equation 12. Let k' be the last iteration of the greedy algorithm for $V' = V - \{i\}$ that Equation 12 holds and mobile sensing device i is still a winner, $\frac{m_{k'}}{c_{k'}} \leq \frac{m_i^{k'}}{c_i}$. To simplify the notation, we write the proportional share of mobile sensing device i in iteration j, $\rho_i(j) = B\frac{m_i^j}{\sum_{j \in A_j} m_j}$ and $c_i(j) = \frac{c_j m_i^j}{m_j}$. The payment for user i in the budget feasible mechanism is:

$$p_i = max_{j \leq k'}(min(\rho_i(j), c_i(j))) \tag{13}$$

LEMMA 4.4. *The Budget feasible mechanism provides individual rationality.*

PROOF. Since the payment has the maximum value, we need to show the following for a $j \leq k'$.

(1) $c_i \leq \rho_i(j)$

(2) $c_i \leq c_i(j)$

The first condition is the budget limit constraint, Equation 12, that holds. The second condition is related to the threshold payment and shows that the mobile sensing device i is still winner. Otherwise, the mobile sensing device i is not selected □

Lemma 4.5. *The budget feasible mechanism provides incentive compatibility for the declared cost.*

Proof. To prove incentive compatibility, we need to show that p_i is the maximum cost that mobile sensing device i can declare and still be selected by the allocation mechanism. Let r be the index in $j \leq k'$ such that $min(\rho_i(j), c_i(j))$ is maximized. For the case where $\rho_i(r) < c_i(r)$, declaring higher cost puts the mobile sensing device i after first k' users, therefore, the mobile sensing device i will not be selected by the sampling mechanism. Otherwise, if there is a j where $j \leq k'$ such that $\rho_i(j) > \rho_i(r)$, considering the maximality of r, $c_i(j) < \rho_i(r) < \rho_i(j)$. This implies that mobile sensing device i by increasing its cost gets placed after mobile sensing device j and thus, will not be selected. If $\rho_i(r) \geq c_i(r)$, a higher cost places the mobile sensing device i after r and since r is the maximum index in k', mobile sensing device i will not be selected. Otherwise, if there is a j, $j < k'$ where $c_i(j) > c_i(r)$, by maximality we have $c_i(j) > \rho_i(j)$. i will not be selected because of the budget limit constraint, Equation 12. □

4.3 Mobility Aware Budget-feasible Truthful Greedy Algorithm

In this section, we consider mobile sensing devices that can frequently change their locations. We propose a truthful mobility aware sampling that prevents the selfish mobile sensing devices from lying about their availability for the sensing task. In this setting, when the central controller probes the nearby mobile sensing devices for sampling over the time interval T, the mobile sensing devices reply by declaring their locations, costs, and their availability. Based on this information, the central controller selects a set of mobile sensing devices that maximize the marginal degree contribution under the budget limit and also are available during the time interval T. By providing incentives for the mobile sensing devices to declare the availability truthfully, the controller only selects among those devices that are available over the time interval T.

The sampling approach in the mobility-aware truthful mechanism is the same as one in the previous subsection. However, in the mobility aware approach, the central controller first selects the mobile sensing devices that are available during the time interval T and then applies the greedy budget limit on the available mobile sensing devices. The payment mechanism in this case should provide incentive for mobile sensing devices to declare their availability times truthfully. Therefore, in the mobility aware truthful mechanism, the threshold payment depends on cost and the availability time of mobile sensing devices. Let t be index of a time interval that mobile sensing device i participates in the sampling, then the payment to mobile sensing device i is the maximum of threshold payments for each time slot T. Formally,

$$p_i = max_t(p_i(t)) \tag{14}$$

The above payment ensures the truthfulness of mobile arrival and departure times by removing the time dependency. Let a_i, d_i denote the arrival and departure times of device i, respectively. Let a'_i, d'_i be the declared arrival and departure time for the mobile sensing device i. Considering the fact that the mobile sensing device cannot declare early arrival and late departure, $[a'_i, d'_i] \in [a_i, d_i]$. Thus, the mobile sensing device i can only decrease the value of t. Since we take the maximum among all threshold payments, the payment to mobile sensing device i when it lies about the availability time is no greater than that when it reports truthfully.

4.4 Time complexity

Now, we show that truthful sampling can be done in polynomial time. For the Greedy algorithm, the time complexity is $O(S \log N)$. Recall that, S, N denote the cardinality constraints and the number of available mobile sensing devices, respectively. For the greedy truthful algorithm, the sampling time complexity is $O(S \log N)$. We also need to run the sampling mechanism S more times for payment determination. Thus, the time complexity is $O(S^2 \log N)$. This time complexity is the same for the budget-feasible algorithm. Finally, for the mobility-aware algorithm, the payment is the maximum threshold payment for each time slot. Therefore, the overall time complexity is $O(tS^2 \log N)$ where t is number of time intervals T that mobile sensing devices are available.

5 EXPERIMENTAL SETUP

To evaluate our sampling and localization approaches, we conduct experiments in two different areas: an open environment, and a cluttered office area. In this section, we describe these two areas and the mobility settings for transmitters and receivers. We also explain the evaluation metrics. The values of parameters used in our localization and sampling are listed in Table 1.

5.1 Test Environment

Open environment: In the open environment, there are no objects or obstructions in the area. This experiment is performed on the Orbit testbed [34], using the USRP2 nodes to transmit and receive signals. In this experiment, 14 receivers and 4 transmitters are placed non-uniformly inside of a 20 by 20 m area. The transmitters send a sinusoidal continuous wave (CW) signal, and the receivers measure received signal strength (RSS) at the same frequency.

Cluttered office: The office area is cluttered with desks, bookcases, filing cabinets, computers, and equipment. The collected data is a public data set [31]. In this experiment, 44 sensors are placed randomly in a 14 by 13 (m) area. Here, the transmitters are transmitting sequentially; and as this is a previously collected public experimental data set, we cannot change it to have multiple transmitters transmitting simultaneously. To approximate what the RSS would have been if multiple transmitters had transmitted simultaneously, we use the sum of linear received powers measured from each transmitter when transmitting sequentially. We justify this approximation as follows. First, we note that the expected value of the power of the sum of multiple signals is the sum of the powers of those individual signals [33]. Second, we perform a validation experiment in the Orbit testbed. For this validation, we randomly select two USRP2s and set them to transmit. We denote

Table 1: Evaluation parameters.

Parameters	Values	Descriptions
δ_p	1.5	Pixel width(m)
σ_x^2	0.5	Voxels variance(dB)
δ_c	1	Correlation coefficient
$minPL$	1.5	Minimum path length(m)
n_p	2	Path loss exponent
R	4	Confined area radius(m)
k	20	Number of iterations in Metropolis

the receiver linear power measurements as RSS(TX1) and RSS(TX2) when the transmitters transmit sequentially, and RSS(TX1,TX2) when they transmit simultaneously. Figure 2 shows the comparison of RSS(TX1)+RSS(TX2) vs. RSS(TX1,TX2). The data shows, in fact, that the linear approximation is very accurate, almost always within 0.5 dB.

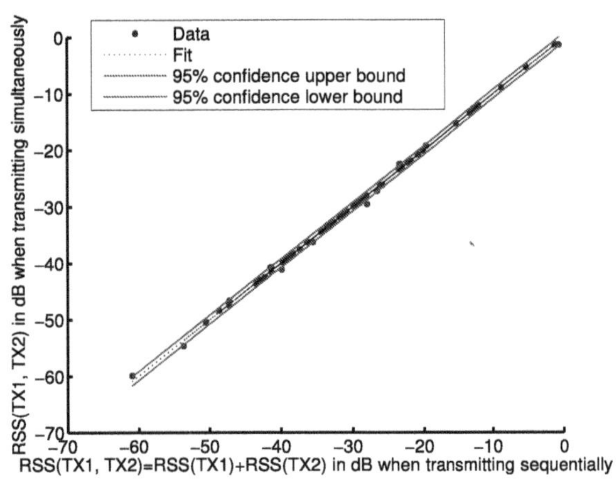

Figure 2: Correlation between the RSS received by receivers when transmitting simultaneously and when transmitting sequentially in the Orbit testbed.

Changes in Number and Locations of Transmitters and Receivers: To approximate mobility despite the fixed locations of mobile sensing devices in the two testbeds, we turn on and off the mobile sensing devices in the open environment and the cluttered office. To model the on and off states of each transmitter, we use a two state continuous time Markov chain that is able to model the bursts of device availability (on state) [29], with state 0 indicating off (or not transmitting) and state 1 indicating on (transmitting).

5.2 Evaluation Metrics

(1) *Localization error:* The localization error, ϵ_l, is equal to the root mean squared error of the best assignment between estimated and actual transmitter locations [17].

$$\epsilon_l(\theta, \hat{\theta}) = \frac{1}{|\hat{\theta}|} \min_{a \in A} \left(\sum_{i=1}^{|\theta|} \sum_{j=1}^{|\hat{\theta}|} a_{i,j} d(\theta_i, \hat{\theta}_j)^2 \right)^{\frac{1}{2}} \quad (15)$$

where A is the set of all permutations between the set of actual transmitter locations θ and the set of estimated transmitter locations $\hat{\theta}$, and $d(\theta_i, \hat{\theta}_j)$ is Euclidean distance between the ith actual and jth estimated transmitter locations.

(2) *Cardinality error:* The cardinality error, ϵ_c, is the fraction of time during which the number of estimated transmitters differs from the actual number of transmitters [7].

(3) *OSPA metric:* The optimal sub-pattern assignment (OSPA) metric, ϵ_p, penalizes the error in the number of estimated transmitters with a constant g that is measured in meters [36]. The OSPA metric is obtained by the following formula when $|\theta| \leq |\hat{\theta}|$,

$$\epsilon_p(\theta, \hat{\theta}) = \left(\frac{1}{|\hat{\theta}|} \min_{a \in A} \sum_{i=1}^{|\theta|} d^g(\theta_i, \hat{\theta}_{a_i})^2 + g^2 \left(|\hat{\theta}| - |\theta| \right) \right)^{\frac{1}{2}}, \quad (16)$$

where $d^g(\theta, \hat{\theta}) = \min(g, d(\theta, \hat{\theta}))$. When $|\theta| > |\hat{\theta}|$, the OSPA metric is obtained by inverting θ and $\hat{\theta}$ in (16).

5.3 Results

As mentioned in Section 2, after finding the local maxima, we perform localization in each sub area using the matrix inversion. This approach is simple and efficient in terms of time complexity. Based on our evaluation, the running time of the matrix inversion approach for a single transmitter in the open environment is 0.1 second, however, the running time of the well-known maximum likelihood estimator (MLE) [30] is around 1 second. In this section, we evaluate the matrix inversion approach in terms of the localization error. We compare the localization error of the matrix inversion approach with that obtained from the MLE. Table 2 shows the localization error in the open environment for each transmitter. As shown in this table, the matrix inversion approach preforms better in terms of the localization error. The average localization error of matrix inversion is 1.11 meters. In comparison, the average error of the MLE approach is 2.02 meters. Also, the variance of the localization error of the MLE approach is 4.1 square meters which is much higher than 0.18 square meters, the variance of the localization error of the matrix inversion approach. We also evaluate the localization error of one transmitter in the cluttered office. We find that the average and variance of localization error among all possible single transmitters are 1.6 meters and 0.61 square meters, respectively, in the matrix inversion approach. However, the average and variance of the localization error in the MLE approach are 1.77 meters and 1.55 square meters, respectively. Given the benefits of the matrix inversion approach in terms of both time complexity and the localization error, we select this approach to localize a single transmitter.

Next, we analyze the performance of SPLOT for multiple transmitters. To create the changes in number and locations of transmitters, we use the two state continuous time Markov chain and find the on and off states of each transmitter for 1000 seconds. The results are obtained by taking average of 100 different trials of transmitters in on and off states over 1000 seconds. We assume that only one transmitter is turned on at any instant, although once turned on at different time instants, multiple transmitters can be transmitting simultaneously. However, we do consider the scenarios where multiple transmitters can be simultaneously turned off.

Table 2: Localization error in Matrix inversion and MLE approaches for one transmitter in the open environment with no mobility.

Transmitter	Localization error(m)	
	Matrix inversion	MLE approach
TX1	1.41	1.01
TX2	0.5	1.03
TX3	1.11	0.97
TX4	1.41	5.08

Number of transmitters: We consider the impact of maximum number of transmitters on the performance of SPLOT. We set the maximum number of transmitters to 1, 2, 3, and 4 in the open environment. Figure 3 shows the changes in the average localization error of SPLOT and Quasi EM with the maximum number of transmitters in open environment. To find the localization error of Quasi EM, we provide the actual number of transmitters as an input parameter. Also to find the average localization error, we run 1000 trials of Quasi EM and take the average over these trials. The average localization errors shown in Figure 3 are over different combinations of transmitters in the open environment.

Figure 3 shows that the average localization error increases substantially with the increase in the number of transmitters in the Quasi EM approach. However, the average localization error of SPLOT is at or less than 1 meter, even though SPLOT also estimates the number of transmitters (unlike Quasi EM, SPLOT is not provided the number of transmitters as an input). Interestingly, we do not observe any penalty for increasing the number of transmitters being located.

Next, we compare the running time of SPLOT with that of Quasi EM in the open environment. Table 3 shows the running time of these two approaches for a trial of 100 seconds of the transmitters being in the on and off states. The Quasi EM is run only for one time. Table 3 shows that the running time of SPLOT is around 0.5 second. However, the running time of Quasi EM is above 200 seconds and the increase in the maximum number of transmitters substantially degrades the running time of Quasi EM degrades. We also expect the running time of Quasi EM to degrade more with increasing number of mobile sensing devices.

We also evaluate SPLOT in terms of average cardinality error and average OSPA error. Table 4 shows the average OSPA error and the average cardinality error of SPLOT with increasing maximum number of transmitters. This table shows that an increase in the maximum number of transmitters increases the average cardinality error. The average cardinality error in the worst case is around 0.14 when the maximum number of transmitters is 4. The OSPA metric considers both the localization error and the cardinality error in one metric. Table 4 shows that the average OSPA error increases by a very small amount even when the cardinality penalty is set to a very high value ($g = 5m$). This is because the fraction of times that the number of estimated transmitters $|\hat{\theta}|$ and the number of actual transmitters $|\theta|$ differ is very small.

Impact of transmitters' locations: Next, we analyse the effect of transmitter locations on the localization approach. To find the impact of transmitter locations, we use the cluttered office data with the maximum number of transmitters equal to 2. We consider different combinations of two transmitters such that the Euclidean distance between two transmitters varies from 3.5 meters to 18 meters. Figure 4 shows the relationship between the transmitters' Euclidean distance and the average localization error. Here, each data point is obtained by averaging over 100 different trials, each with its own randomly generated transmitter on and off chains. Also, note the different scales on the y-axes of the two plots. Figure 4 shows a linear correlation between the the transmitters distance and the localization error in the Quasi EM approach. However, in SPLOT, there is no apparent correlation between the distance between transmitters and the localization error. The correlation coefficients between distance and average localization error in the Quasi EM and SPLOT are 0.72 and −0.02, respectively.

Regarding the cardinality error, there is a small correlation between the distance between transmitters and the cardinality error in SPLOT. Our evaluations show that the correlation coefficient of distance and average cardinality error in SPLOT is around −0.35. With increasing distance, SPLOT is more successful in finding the local maxima and converting the multiple transmitters localization to a set of single transmitter localizations. Therefore, the average cardinality error decreases with increasing distance between transmitters. Similarly, there is also a small correlation of −0.1 between the distance and the OSPA error.

Table 3: Running time of SPLOT and Quasi EM in the open environment.

Maximum number of transmitters	Running time (second)	
	SPLOT	Quasi EM
1	0.5	211
2	0.5	985
3	0.7	2281
4	0.6	4169

Table 4: $\bar{\epsilon_p}(m)$, and $\bar{\epsilon_c}$, of SPLOT in the open environment.

Maximum number of transmitters	$\bar{\epsilon_p}(m)$			$\bar{\epsilon_c}$
	$g = 1$	$g = 2$	$g = 5$	
1	0.79	1.01	1.01	0
2	0.91	1.17	1.17	0
3	1.04	1.36	1.45	0.05
4	1.14	1.51	1.74	0.14

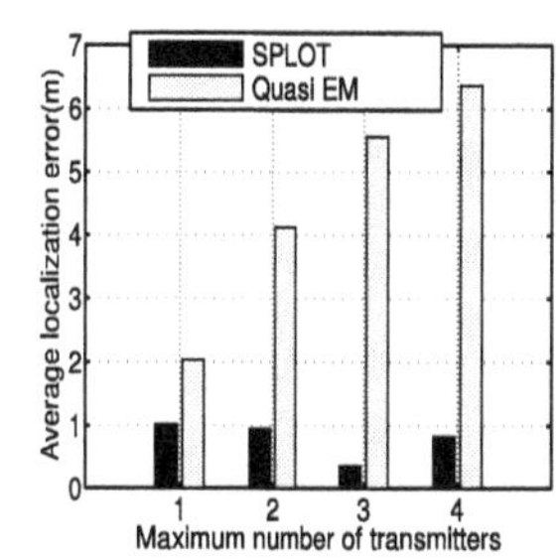

Figure 3: Average localization error versus the maximum number of transmitters in the open environment for Quasi EM and SPLOT.

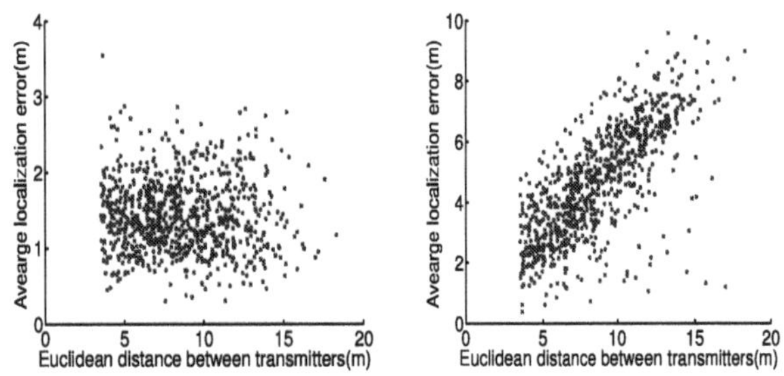

(a) (b)

Figure 4: Impact of transmitters' locations in cluttered office (a) SPLOT, (b) Quasi EM.

Impact of number of mobile sensing devices: The number of available mobile sensing devices plays a key role in our localization approach. Selecting a large number of mobile sensing devices for measurement increases the communication overhead between the mobile sensing devices and the localization module. It also increases the time taken and the energy consumption. On the other hand, selecting a very small number of mobile sensing devices decreases the accuracy of our localization approach in terms of the localization error, the cardinality error, and the OSPA error. In this section, we examine the impact of the number of mobile sensing devices on efficiency of our localization approach and show how we can maintain the localization accuracy by using a suitable sampling approach to select mobile sensing devices among all available mobile sensing devices.

Table 5 shows the average localization error and the average cardinality error when the maximum number of transmitters is 3 in the open environment with the number of mobile sensing devices reduced from 14 to 12, 9, and 6 for three sampling approaches for selecting mobile sensing devices (Random, Greedy, and Metropolis). We make the following observations. First, the average localization error changes by about 0.25 meters when reducing the number of mobile sensing devices from 12 to 6 for all sampling approaches and the average localization error is close to 1 meter even for 6 mobile sensing devices (see Table 5). The Table 5 also shows that the average localization error does not change too much by selecting mobile sensing devices randomly. This table also shows that the average cardinality error increases with reduction in the number of mobile sensing devices. This is possibly because the number of selected mobile sensing devices is not enough to cover the whole area and the localization approach is not able to detect the transmitters located in the uncovered area. Moreover, the results of random sampling in Table 5 show that the location of mobile sensing devices directly effects the cardinality error. In other words, we need to have enough mobile sensing devices to cover the whole area to be able to detect all available transmitters. Third, the results of average cardinality error for Greedy sampling show that by reducing the number of mobile sensing devices and selecting a good sampling approach, we can still have a small cardinality error. Finally, this table also shows that for the open environment where nodes are distributed non-uniformly, the Greedy sampling preforms better than the Metropolis sampling approach.

Table 5: $\bar{\epsilon_l}(m)$, and $\bar{\epsilon_c}$, of SPLOT with different numbers of mobile sensing devices and three transmitters in the open environment.

Number of mobile sensing devices	Random $\bar{\epsilon_l}(m)$	Random $\bar{\epsilon_c}$	Greedy $\bar{\epsilon_l}(m)$	Greedy $\bar{\epsilon_c}$	Metropolis $\bar{\epsilon_l}(m)$	Metropolis $\bar{\epsilon_c}$
14	0.35	0.05	0.35	0.05	0.35	0.05
12	0.89	0.04	0.86	0.02	0.89	0.03
9	0.95	0.14	1.03	0.05	0.97	0.09
6	1.16	0.33	1.09	0.07	1.12	0.23

Table 6: $\bar{\epsilon_l}(m)$, and $\bar{\epsilon_c}$, with different numbers of mobile sensing devices and two transmitters in the cluttered office.

Number of mobile	sensing devices	40	35	30	25	20	15	10	5
Greedy	$\bar{\epsilon_l}(m)$	1.47	1.64	1.90	2.14	2.01	1.96	2.02	2.24
	$\bar{\epsilon_c}$	0.03	0.04	0.04	0.07	0.1	0.23	0.36	0.49
Metropolis	$\bar{\epsilon_l}(m)$	1.47	1.57	1.68	1.79	1.89	1.98	2.02	1.96
	$\bar{\epsilon_c}$	0.02	0.03	0.04	0.06	0.1	0.16	0.25	0.43

Next, we evaluate the impact of number of mobile sensing devices in the cluttered office. The maximum number of transmitters is 2 and we vary the number of mobile sensing devices between 5 to 40 with increments of 5. Table 6 shows average localization and cardinality errors in the cluttered office. We make the following observations. First, the average localization error varies from 1.42 to 2.24 meters. However, the average cardinality error increases relatively substantially with reduction in the number of mobile sensing devices. Second, for the cluttered office area where the mobile sensing devices are located uniformly in the environment, Metropolis sampling preforms slightly better than greedy sampling. Third, Table 6 shows that by reducing the number of mobile sensing devices from 42 to 25 and using either of Metropolis or greedy sampling approaches, we can keep the localization error close to 2 meters and the cardinality error to about 0.06. Fourth, the results of Table 6 shows that 5 mobile sensing devices are not enough to cover the whole area in the cluttered office environment. As this table shows, even by selecting the Metropolis sampling the average cardinality error is 0.43 if we only select 5 mobile sensing devices. As we discussed earlier, the determination of the number of mobile sensing devices required is done by the localization module. Generally, there is always a trade off between the accuracy of the localization algorithm, and the communication and processing overheads. Depending on the importance of each of these parameters and the localization results, the localization module makes a decision about the number of required mobile sensing devices.

Comparison of SPLOT and Quasi EM in the cluttered office: With the help of our experimental results, we have shown, earlier in this section, that SPLOT preforms better than Quasi EM in the open environment. However, the number of transmitters and mobile sensing devices in the open environment is small and there is no significant noise or obstruction in the environment. In this section, we compare SPLOT with the Quasi EM in the cluttered office environment, where we have 44 nodes that are located uniformly in the cluttered office and we can select any of these nodes as a transmitter or a mobile sensing device. Figure 5 shows the CDF of average localization error in the cluttered office for different combinations of transmitters with maximum number of two transmitters. The average localization error on the x-axis corresponds to the localization error for each combination of transmitters obtained by averaging over 100 different trails. Figure 5 shows that the average localization error of SPLOT is significantly less than that of Quasi EM. Furthermore, the average localization error for any combinations of transmitters is 4.54 meters in Quasi EM which is much higher than the average localization error in SPLOT.

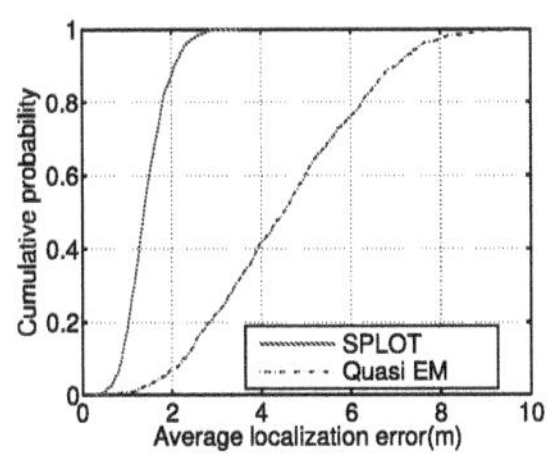

Figure 5: CDF of average localization error (m) in the cluttered office with maximum two transmitters.

6 IMPLEMENTATION

To further investigate its accuracy, we use commodity devices to implement SPLOT. Our mobile sensing device consists of a commodity smartphone/tablet that connects to an inexpensive Realtek dongle (RTL-SDR) [1] via a USB cable. The RTL-SDR acts as a mobile sensing device and collects raw In-phase/Quadrature(I/Q) samples. It operates in 25MHz-1750MHz with a sample rate up to 2.4MHz. We use BaoFeng BF-F8HP (BF) [2] transmitters that transmits VHF in 136MHz-174MHz and UHF in 400MHz-520MHz with up to 8W power. We build an Android smartphone/tablet app that measures spectrum in real time for a specified frequency range and sampling rate. Our app records the I/Q samples obtained from the RTL-SDR and computes the RSS values. In our set up, the app generates a (time, location, RSS) tuple every second. The location is the GPS coordinates for outdoor experiments. For indoor experiments, the app finds the location by indoor location fingerprinting [6].

Data Gathering. We have 30 users participate in our experiments for carrying both the transmitters and mobile sensing devices. Each user has their own Android mobile sensing device with our app installed on it. We collect data in different indoor and outdoor areas with at least two transmitters. The areas of our experiments are at least 30 m by 30 m[3] in size.

To determine the location and the transmission time of transmitters, each user that carries a transmitter, also carries a mobile sensing device. Our app, on the device, records the transmission time and the transmitter location every second. In some experiments, the transmitters transmit continuously, while in the other experiments, we give the transmitters a transcript for transmission that shows the time of transmission for each transmitter. We create the transcript to allows us to experiment with different number of active transmitters at different times. In all experiments, we configure the transmit power to 1W and the frequency band to 443MHz.

[3]We make the experiment area small to evaluate SPLOT in an environment where sensing devices receive signals from both transmitters and the interference is strong.

Test Environment. We preform different indoor, outdoor experiments for both stationary and mobile scenarios.

Engineering Building- We preform two experiments on the third floor of an engineering building. In both experiments, there are at most 8 mobile sensing devices[4] that are placed in four corridors of a square area of 40 m by 40 m. Two transmitters are located in two opposite corridors. In the first experiment (Experiment A), the mobile sensing devices are static while the transmitters transmit continuously and move along the corridors for 7 minutes at normal walking speed. In the second experiment (Experiment B), the mobile sensing devices move randomly in different corridors and the transmitters use a transcript for transmission.

Food Court-We preform two experiments in an indoor 30 m by 50 m university food court area. In both experiments, there are 6 mobile sensing devices located uniformly along the food court and both the transmitters and the mobile sensing devices are static. Also, in both experiments the transmitters use a transcript for transmission. In the first experiment (Experiment C), there are two transmitters that are located on two ends of the food court at first. Then, we gradually reduce the distance between the transmitters. In the second experiment (Experiment D), there are three transmitters located in three different corners of the food court.

Outdoor Area-We preform two experiments in an outdoor area of size 30 m by 50 m that is a part of a campus where both static (buildings, trees) and mobile obstacles (pedestrians) are present during the experiment. In both experiment there are at most 8 mobile sensing devices. In the first experiment (Experiment E), both transmitters and mobile sensing devices are static and the transmitters use a transcript for transmission. In the second experiment (Experiment F), both transmitters and mobile sensing devices are moving. The transmitters transmit continuously and move around a circle for 7 minutes at normal walking speed. The mobile sensing devices also move around the circle while maintaining a distance from the transmitters.

Results. We evaluate SPLOT using the data from our implementation[5] and compare its performance with that of Quasi EM. Figure 6(a) shows the average localization error of SPLOT and Quasi EM in experiments A to F. Figure 6(a) shows that the average localization error of SPLOT is substantially less than the Quasi EM. The average localization error decreases in both SPLOT and Quasi EM when both transmitters and the mobile sensing devices are static (Experiment C, D, E). The average localization error of Quasi EM increases significantly when transmitters and mobile sensing devices are mobile (Experiment A, B, F). In comparison, the average localization error of SPLOT is less than 5 meters.

Table 7 shows the average OSPA error and the average cardinality error of SPLOT for experiments A to F. This table shows that the average cardinality error increases when both transmitters and mobile sensing devices are mobile. Also, the average cardinality error in Experiment D is greater than that in Experiments C and E because of an increase in the number of transmitters. Table 7 also shows that the average OSPA error increases by a very small amount even with high cardinality penalty ($g = 5m$).

[4]Users are not able to run the app for the duration of the experiment for different reasons such as a battery issue, etc.

[5]We are not able to evaluate our sampling approaches using this data because of the small number of mobile sensing devices.

Table 7: $\bar{\epsilon_p}(m)$, $g = 5m$, and $\bar{\epsilon_c}$, of SPLOT for experiments A to F.

Experiment	A	B	C	D	E	F
$\bar{\epsilon_p}(m)$	5.39	5.05	4.19	5.03	3.79	6.38
$\bar{\epsilon_c}$	0.18	0.11	0.04	0.16	0	0.06

Table 8: $\bar{\epsilon_l}(m)$, of SPLOT and Quasi EM versus distance between two transmitters in experiment C.

	Distance (m)	45	41	36	29	18	9	6
$\bar{\epsilon_l}(m)$	SPLOT	3.38	3.82	3.67	4.92	2.9	3.68	1.16
	Quasi EM	18.72	17.34	14.43	11.31	8.7	4.96	5.66

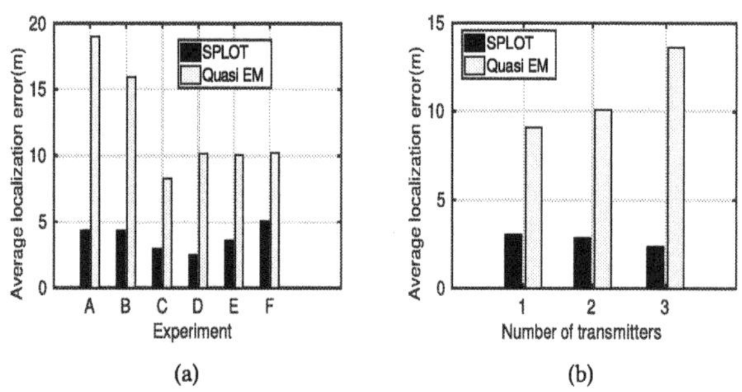

Figure 6: (a) Average localization error in experiments A to F (b) Impact of number of transmitters in the experiment D.

Figure 6(b) shows the changes in the average localization error of SPLOT and Quasi EM for different number of transmitters in Experiment D. Figure 6(b) shows that the average localization error increases with the increase in the number of transmitters in the Quasi EM approach. However, the average localization error of SPLOT is at or less than 4 meters, even though SPLOT also estimates the number of transmitters (recall that Quasi EM assumes that the number of transmitters is known).

Finally, we analyse the effect of transmitter locations on the localization approach using Experiment C with the number of transmitters equal to 2. We change the location of one transmitter such that the Euclidean distance between two transmitters varies from 6 meters to 45 meters. Table 8 shows the relationship between the transmitters' Euclidean distance and the localization error. Table 8 shows that there is no apparent correlation between the distance between transmitters and the localization error in SPLOT. However, the localization error decreases in the Quasi EM with decreasing distance between transmitters. This is because Quasi EM estimates the locations of both transmitters close to one of the transmitters.

7 RELATED WORK

Localization of multiple transmitters has been studied in existing work [22, 23, 25, 26, 30]. However, to the best of our knowledge, this paper is the first to develop and evaluate a localization approach that minimizes time complexity without significantly compromising localization accuracy in order to simultaneously locate unauthorized transmitters.

There are a great number of works that have focused on selecting a set of sensor nodes to provide the maximum coverage in wireless sensor networks (e.g., [8, 11, 39]). There are also a few existing works that consider both incentive and the coverage problem [15, 20, 40]. However, unlike our work, none of these existing works consider mobility, truthfulness, and the coverage problem all together. While [16] attempts to maximize the expected coverage for long-term participation, it does not apply to mobile environments where mobile sensing devices can be too temporary.

Recently, crowdsourcing using low-cost commodity radios has been used for spectrum monitoring (e.g., using RTL-SDR and smartphone [10, 28, 42], RTL-SDR and Raspberry Pi [32]), white space detection [35], and spectrum data decoding [9]. A few recent works on low-cost spectrum monitoring focus on transmitter identification [12, 43] and localization for detection of spectrum offenders [27, 41]. However, these existing works do not address the problems of multiple transmitters localization, sampling, and incentives, that we collectively address in our paper. The localization approach in [27] can only locate single static transmitters. However, our proposed localization approach, SPLOT, is able to locate multiple static or mobile transmitters. There is also some existing work on detection of spectrum misuse using only specialized hardware (e.g., USRPs [37] or spectrum analyzers [19]). However, this existing work, like [13], focuses on only monitoring spectrum usage and not on locating spectrum offenders.

8 CONCLUSION AND FUTURE WORK

We presented and evaluated a framework to locate multiple transmitters using crowdsourced measurements of received power. We addressed two main challenges in this framework. First, we presented a simple yet efficient and accurate method, SPLOT, for simultaneous localization of multiple transmitters using the received power measured by the selected mobile sensing devices. Second, we presented a sampling approach that determined the number and locations of required mobile sensing devices for measurement. Next, we enhanced our sampling to provide incentives for mobile sensing devices. We experimentally evaluated our framework and methods, and our results demonstrated the efficiency and accuracy of our approach.

Our work can proceed in the following directions. While evaluating our methodology, we have not explicitly evaluated how well the transmit power is estimated. We will perform this evaluation as future work. Very importantly, we will also investigate the effect of MIMO/beamforming as well as directional antennas on our localization methodology. Our approach assumes that mobile devices report RSS measurements and location information correctly. We will enhance our approach to make it robust against misreporting, malicious or erroneous, of RSS and device locations. While we use different smartphones and tablets, they all have the same RTL/SDR devices. In the future, we plan to study the impact of device heterogeneity on the quality of collected RSS measurements and its aggregation.

ACKNOWLEDGMENT

This material is based upon work supported by the National Science Foundation under Grant No. 1564287.

REFERENCES

[1] http://sdr.osmocom.org/trac/wiki/rtl-sdr.
[2] https://baofengtech.com/bf-f8hp.
[3] GPS Under Attack as Crooks, Rogue Workers Wage Electronic War. http://www.nbcnews.com/news/us-news/gps-under-attack-crooks-rogue-workers-wage-electronic-war-n618761.
[4] Software-Defined-Radio Market Sees Increased Growth. http://www.mwrf.com/software/software-defined-radio-market-sees-increased-growth.
[5] L. Anderegg and S. Eidenbenz. Ad hoc-VCG: A Truthful and Cost-Efficient Routing Protocol for Mobile Ad Hoc Networks with Selfish Agents. In *MobiCom*, 2003.
[6] P. Bahl and V. N. Padmanabhan. RADAR: An In-building RF-based User Location and Tracking System. In *IEEE INFOCOM*, 2000.
[7] M. Bocca, O. Kaltiokallio, N. Patwari, and S. Venkatasubramanian. Multiple Target Tracking with RF Sensor Networks. *IEEE Trans. Mobile Computing*, PP(99), 2013.
[8] J. Braams. A Node Scheduling Scheme for Energy Conservation in Large Wireless Sensor Networks. *Wirel. Comm. Mobile Comput*, 3(2), 2003.
[9] R. Calvo-Palomino, D. Giustiniano, V. Lenders, and A. Fakhreddine. Crowdsourcing Spectrum Data Decoding. In *IEEE INFOCOM*, 2017.
[10] A. Chakraborty, M. Rahman, H. Gupta, and S. R. Das. Specsense: Crowdsensing for Efficient Querying of Spectrum Occupancy. In *IEEE INFOCOM*, 2017.
[11] B. Cărbunar, A. Grama, J. Vitek, and O. Cflrbunar. Redundancy and Coverage Detection in Sensor Networks. *ACM Trans. Sen. Netw.*, 2(1), 2006.
[12] A. Dutta and M. Chiang. "See Something, Say Something" Crowd- sourced Enforcement of Spectrum Policies. *IEEE Transactions on Wireless Communications*, 2016.
[13] O. Fatemieh, R. Chandra, and C. Gunter. Secure Collaborative Sensing for Crowdsourcing Spectrum Data in White Space Networks. In *IEEE DySPAN*, 2010.
[14] U. Feige. A threshold of ln n for approximating set cover. *Journal of the ACM*, 1998.
[15] Z. Feng, Y. Zhu, Q. Zhang, L. M. Ni, and A. V. Vasilakos. Trac:Truthful Auction for Location-aware Collaborative Sensing in Mobile Crowdsourcing. In *IEEE INFOCOM*, 2014.
[16] L. Gao, F. Hou, and J. Huang. Providing Long-Term Participatory Incentive in Participatory Sensing. In *INFOCOM*, 2015.
[17] J. Hoffman and R. Mahler. Multitarget Miss Distance Via Optimal Assignment. *IEEE Trans. on Systems, Man and Cybernetics Part A: Systems and Humans*, 2004.
[18] C. Hubler, H. P. Kriegel, K. Borgwardt, and Z. Ghahramani. Metropolis Algorithms for Representative Subgraph Sampling. In *ICDM'08*, 2008.
[19] A. P. Iyer, K. Chintalapudi, V. Navda, R. Ramjee, V. N. Padmanabhan, and C. R. Murthy. SpecNet: Spectrum Sensing Sans Frontirs. In *NSDI*, 2011.
[20] L. G. Jaimes, I. Vergara-Laurens, and M. A. Labrador. A Location-Based Incentive Mechanism for Participatory Sensing Systems with Budget Constraints. In *IEEE PerCom*, 2012.
[21] C. Kim, D. Song, Y. Xu, J. Yi, and X. Wu. Optimal Auction Design. *Mathematics of operations research*, 1981.
[22] C. Kim, D. Song, Y. Xu, J. Yi, and X. Wu. Cooperative Search of Multiple Unknown Transient Radio Sources Using Multiple Paired Mobile Robots. *IEEE Transactions on Robotics (T-RO)*, 2014.
[23] R. Martin and R. Thomas. Algorithms and Bounds for Estimating Location, Directionality, and Environmental Parameters of Primary Spectrum Users. *IEEE Trans. Wireless Commun.*, 2009.
[24] N. Metropolis, M. N. Rosenbluth, A. H. Teller, and E. Telle. Equation of State Calculations by Fast Computing Machines. *J. Chem. Phys.*, 1953.
[25] A. Nasif and B. Mark. Collaborative opportunistic spectrum sharing in the presence of multiple transmitters. In *IEEE Globecom'08*, 2008.
[26] J. K. Nelson, M. R. Gupta, J. E. Almodovar, and W. H. Mortensen. A Quasi EM Method for Estimating Multiple Transmitter Locations. *IEEE Signal Processing Letters*, 16(8), 2009.
[27] A. Nika, Z. Li, Y. Zhu, Y. Zhu, B. Y. Zhao, X. Zhou, and H. Zheng. Empirical Validation of Commodity Spectrum Monitoring. In *ACM SenSys'16*, 2016.
[28] A. Nika, Z. Zhang, X. Zhou, B. Y. Zhao, and H. Zheng. Towards Commoditized Real-time Spectrum Monitoring. In *HotWireless*, 2014.
[29] J. Nonnenmacher, E. Biersack, and D. Towsley. Parity-based Loss Recovery for Reliable Multicast Transmission. *SIGCOMM Comput. Commun. Rev.*, 27(4), 1997.
[30] N. Patwari, J. N. Ash, S. Kyperountas, A. O. Hero III, R. L. Moses, and N. S. Correal. Locating the Nodes. *IEEE Signal Processing Magazine*, 22(4), 2005.
[31] N. Patwari, A. O. H. III, M. Perkins, N. S. Correal, and R. J. OfiDea. Relative Location Estimation in Wireless Sensor Networks. *IEEE Trans. on Signal Processing*, 2003.
[32] D. Pfammatter, D. Giustiniano, and V. Lenders. A Software-defined Sensor Architecture for Large-scale Wideband Spectrum Monitoring. In *IEEE/ACM IPSN'15*, 2015.
[33] T. Rappaport. *Wireless Communications: Principles and Practice.*
[34] D. Raychaudhuri, I. Seskar, M. Ott, S. Ganu, K. Ramachandran, and H. Kremo. Overview of the ORBIT Radio Grid Testbed for Evaluation of Next-Generation Wireless Network Protocols. In *IEEE WCNC*, 2005.
[35] A. Saeed, A. Harras, E. Zegura, and M. Ammar. Local and Low-Cost White Space Detection. In *ICDCS*, 2017.
[36] D. Schuhmacher, V. Ba-Tuong, and V. Ba-Ngu. A Consistent Metric for Performance Evaluation of Multi-Object Filters. *IEEE Trans. on Signal Processing*, 2008.
[37] L. Shi, P. Bahl, and D. Katabi. Beyond sensing: Multi-GHz Realtime Spectrum Analytics. In *NSDI*, 2015.
[38] Y. Singer. Budget Feasible Mechanisms. In *FOCS*, 2010.
[39] G. Xing, X. Wang, Y. Zhang, C. Lu, R. Pless, and C. Gill. Integrated Coverage and Connectivity Configuration for Energy Conservation in Sensor Networks. *ACM Trans. Sen. Netw.*, 1(1), 2005.
[40] X. Ying, S. Roy, and R. Poovendran. Incentivizing Crowdsourcing for Radio Environment Mapping with Statistical Interpolation. In *IEEE DySpan*, 2015.
[41] T. Zhang and S. Banerjee. A Vehicle-based Measurement Framework for Enhancing Whitespace Spectrum Databases. In *ACM MobiCom*, 2014.
[42] T. Zhang, A. Patro, N. Leng, and S. Banerjee. A Wireless Spectrum Analyzer in Your Pocket. In *HotMobile'15*, 2015.
[43] M. Zheleva, R. Chandra, A. Chowdhery, A. Kapoor, and P. Garnett. Txminer: Identifying transmitters in Real-world Spectrum Measurements. In *IEEE DySPAN*, 2015.

Minding the Billions: Ultra-wideband Localization for Deployed RFID Tags

Yunfei Ma, Nicholas Selby, Fadel Adib
Massachusetts Institute of Technology
{yunfeima,nselby,fadel}@mit.edu

ABSTRACT

State-of-the-art RFID localization systems fall under two categories. The first category operates with off-the-shelf narrowband RFID tags but makes restrictive assumptions on the environment or the tag's movement patterns. The second category does not make such restrictive assumptions; however, it requires designing new ultra-wideband hardware for RFIDs and uses the large bandwidth to directly compute a tag's 3D location. Hence, while the first category is restrictive, the second one requires replacing the billions of RFIDs already produced and deployed annually.

This paper presents RFind, a new technology that brings the benefits of ultra-wideband localization to the billions of RFIDs in today's world. RFind does not require changing today's passive narrowband RFID tags. Instead, it leverages their underlying physical properties to emulate a very large bandwidth and uses it for localization. Our empirical results demonstrate that RFind can emulate over 220MHz of bandwidth on tags designed with a communication bandwidth of only tens to hundreds of kHz, while remaining compliant with FCC regulations. This, combined with a new super-resolution algorithm over this bandwidth, enables RFind to perform 3D localization with sub-centimeter accuracy in each of the x/y/z dimensions, without making any restrictive assumptions on the tag's motion or the environment.

CCS CONCEPTS

• **Networks** → **Cyber-physical networks**; *Mobile networks*; *Sensor networks*;

KEYWORDS

RFID; Localization; Battery-free; UWB; Smart Environments

ACM Reference format:
Yunfei Ma, Nicholas Selby, Fadel Adib. 2017. Minding the Billions: Ultra-wideband Localization for Deployed RFID Tags. In *Proceedings of MobiCom '17, Snowbird, UT, USA, October 16–20, 2017*, 13 pages.
https://doi.org/10.1145/3117811.3117833

ACM ISBN 978-1-4503-4916-1/17/10...$15.00
https://doi.org/10.1145/3117811.3117833

1 INTRODUCTION

Accurate RFID localization can be a game-changer for many industries ranging from virtual reality to factory automation. For example, virtual reality systems, like the HTC Vive [28] and Facebook's Occulus Rift [44], rely on relatively large trackers like handheld motion controllers. Accurate RFID localization would enable us to replace these handheld trackers with on-body RFID stickers that can track multiple user limbs. Another application that can benefit from fine-grained RFID localization is packaging quality control in factories and warehouses. For example, today's packaging control ends once a box is sealed. However, since many of today's packaged items are already tagged with RFIDs, accurate RFID localization would enable employees to check the number of items in a box or whether the right item is in the right box even after the box is sealed. More generally, absolute RFID localization can enable many applications in retail stores, factories & warehouses, virtual & augmented reality, and smart environments.

Indeed, the topic of RFID localization has gained much attention from the academic community over the past decade [31, 41, 48, 52, 53, 57]. However, none of the past proposals can enable ubiquitous localization and deliver on the applications described above. In particular, early proposals in this space relied on measuring the received signal strength (RSS) [16, 18, 38, 41, 59] and the angle of arrival (AoA) [14, 32, 60] and demonstrated a median accuracy of the order of tens of centimeters. Recent proposals have demonstrated finer centimeter-scale localization accuracy. However, these proposals either require furnishing the environment with a dense, surveyed grid of reference tags and localize by matching to reference tags [17, 53], and/or they require the tag or the reader to move over multiple wavelengths on a predefined trajectory at a predefined speed [40, 48, 57].

In this paper, we investigate whether we can achieve sub-centimeter RFID localization by measuring the time-of-flight (TOF) – i.e., the time it takes the signal to travel between a reader and an RFID. Accurate TOF measurements would allow us to localize RFIDs without reference tags and without prior trajectory knowledge. In particular, the TOF can be mapped to the distance traveled by taking into account the speed at which the RF signals travel.

The fundamental challenge in realizing this goal, however, is that accurate TOF-based localization hinges on the ability to measure time at a very fine granularity. In particular, achieving centimeter-scale localization would require hardware that can support very high sampling rate or very large bandwidth, often multiple GHz of bandwidth [11, 19, 34].[1] In contrast, RFIDs communicate at only tens of kHz, i.e., five orders of magnitude lower than such systems. Hence, TOF-based localization with such a communication

[1] Time resolution is inversely proportional to the bandwidth.

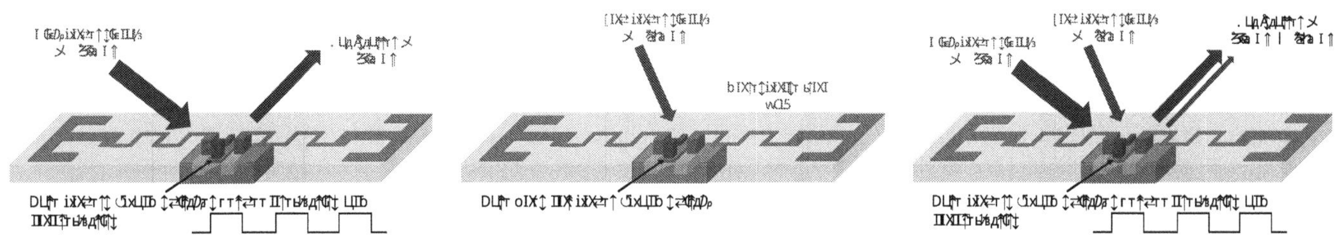

(a) Today's RFIDs backscatter ISM frequencies (b) Weak signal outside ISM can't power up RFID (c) RFind decouples sensing and power delivery

Figure 1: RFind leverages the physics underlying RFID switching. For simplicity, the figure only shows an RFID's frontend circuitry, consisting of an antenna inlay and a switching transistor. (a) An RFID powers up when the reader transmits a high power signal in the ISM band, e.g., at 915MHz. To respond, it modulates the voltage of the switching transistor, resulting in two backscatter states: reflective and non-reflective. (b) An RFID cannot power up when a reader transmits an extremely low power signal outside ISM. (c) Decoupling power delivery and sensing: When a reader transmits both a high power signal in ISM and an extremely low power signal outside ISM, the RFID powers up (due to ISM-frequency) and reflects both frequencies simultaneously, allowing RFind to sense the channel even outside the ISM band.

bandwidth would result in an accuracy of multiple kilometers. One option to overcome this challenge is to design new RFIDs that have large enough bandwidth to enable accurate localization [20, 23, 37]. Not only would such an approach require designing new hardware for RFID tags – making them significantly more expensive and non-compliant with today's FCC regulations and RFID communication protocols – but it would also leave out the billions of RFIDs already deployed in today's world [39].

We present RFind, a system that can achieve sub-centimeter RFID localization by directly measuring the time-of-flight *without any hardware modification to passive narrowband RFID tags* and despite their bandwidth limitations. Using a single antenna, RFind can compute the exact distance to an RFID tag. To achieve 2D or 3D localization, it uses two or three antennas respectively in close proximity to the first.

RFind's localization algorithm is based on a realization that RFID modulation is *frequency agnostic.* Specifically, RFIDs communicate with a wireless device called a reader through backscatter technology. In backscatter systems, the reader transmits a continuous wave at some frequency, and the RFID switches its internal impedance between two states – reflective and non-reflective – to communicate bits to the reader, as shown in Fig. 1(a). By sensing subtle changes in the reflected signal due to the RFID's impedance changes, a reader can decode the bits communicated by an RFID tag. RFind's realization is that such impedance changes may also be sensed at various frequencies. This is because reflectivity is fundamentally a physical process, similar to turning a mirror on and off.

RFind harnesses the above realization to generate a *virtual* localization bandwidth that can be multiple orders of magnitude larger than the bandwidth of RFID communication. In particular, rather than transmitting a continuous wave at a single frequency, RFind transmits continuous waves at multiple frequencies, as shown in Fig. 1(c). When an RFID switches its internal impedance to "reflective", it will reflect all the transmitted frequencies. On the other hand, when it changes its internal impedance to "non-reflective", it would absorb all the frequencies.[2] This effectively enables RFind's reader to estimate the RFID's channel at *all* the reflected frequencies. A large bandwidth enables the reader to compute the time-of-flight and use it to localize the RFID tag.

[2]Note that the amount of reflection/absorption can vary over frequency and is taken into account in RFind's design.

Translating this high level idea into a practical system, faces multiple challenges:

- First, the ISM band for UHF RFID is only 26 MHz wide [9]. Hence, even if a reader transmits at all of the frequencies within the ISM band, it would still be much smaller than the GHz-wide bandwidth necessary for centimeter-scale localization [11, 19, 34]. On the other hand, if it wishes to transmit outside the ISM band, it must limit itself to extremely low power due to FCC regulations; such power would not be sufficient to power up the tag as shown in Fig. 1(b).
- Second, transmitting and receiving over such a large bandwidth would require expensive hardware (high-speed ADCs, high-throughput I/Os, etc.) that can support Giga-samples/sec throughput.
- Finally, an RFID tag's signal does not arrive on a single path to the reader, but rather bounces off many reflectors in the environment before it arrives at the reader. This results in a classical challenge called multi-path, where an RF device receives several copies of the signal from the various reflectors. To overcome this challenge, past techniques require deploying a dense, surveyed grid of reference tags and localize by matching to the reference tags [53].

RFind introduces multiple innovations that enable it to deal with the above challenges:

- First, it decouples the frequency for communication from that for localization. Specifically, it only uses frequencies within the ISM band for communication and powering up, and at the same time, it transmits very low power (sub-milliWatt) frequencies outside the ISM band, as shown in Fig. 1(c). This allows it to measure the channel over a large bandwidth while remaining compliant to FCC regulations.
- Second, instead of acquiring the entire bandwidth at once, it performs frequency hopping to emulate a large *virtual* localization bandwidth in the time domain. In particular, at every point in time, it only transmits at two frequencies (one inside the ISM

and another outside the ISM band). Over time, it varies the carrier wave of the sensing frequency and estimates the channel at that frequency. Then, it stitches the channels at the various frequencies obtained from an RFID over time.[3] This enables it to transmit at a very narrow bandwidth at every point in time and operate entirely within the bandwidth (and sampling rate) capabilities of RFID readers on the market.

- Finally, it leverages the large virtual localization bandwidth to tease apart the various multi-paths in the environment (recall that time resolution is inversely proportional to bandwidth), and identify the path that arrives earliest in time as the line-of-sight path for localization. Then, it incorporates a super-resolution technique that enables it zoom in on the line-of-sight path to achieve sub-centimeter localization accuracy.

We implemented a prototype of RFind using USRP N210 software radios [8] and off-the-shelf Alien Squiggle RFID tags [12]. Our results demonstrate that RFind can emulate over 220 MHz of bandwidth on passive RFIDs. Combined with RFind's super-resolution algorithm, this bandwidth enables it to perform 3D localization with median and 90th percentile errors less than 1 cm and 3 cm respectively in each of the $x/y/z$ dimensions. Such accuracy matches or exceeds those reported by past state-of-the-art techniques [37, 53, 57]; however, in contrast to these past techniques, RFind does not require any reference tags and does not require any assumptions about the tag's motion.

RFind has few additional desirable features. First, it is modulation independent – i.e., it can work with any backscatter modulation: FM0, Miller-8, etc. [3]. Second, it is fully compliant with the RFID communication protocol (the EPC Gen2 [3]). And third, it can operate in both line-of-sight and non-line-of-sight environments. However, one drawback of our current implementation is that it requires few seconds in order to localize. We would also like to note that, similar to any RFID reader, even though RFind's reader is FCC compliant, marketing it commercially requires formal FCC certification [10].

Contributions: This paper presents RFind, the first system that can emulate a large bandwidth on passive narrowband RFIDs. RFind's design introduces two key innovations: first, it introduces a technique that decouples the frequencies for power delivery and sensing in RFID communications; second, it presents a new super-resolution algorithm that operates over a large emulated bandwidth enabling RFind to achieve very high accuracy in 3D localization. The paper also presents a prototype implementation and evaluation of RFind demonstrating its accuracy in localizing RFIDs in multipath-rich environments, without reference tags and without requiring tag or reader motion.

2 RFIND OVERVIEW

RFind is a system that enables sub-centimeter localization of UHF (ultra-high frequency) RFIDs. RFind's localization works in line-of-sight, non-line-of-sight, and highly cluttered settings. As a result, it can operate in multipath-rich indoor environments. Moreover, RFind is fully compliant with today's standard UHF RFID protocol (the EPC-Gen2) as well as with FCC regulations for consumer electronics.

At a high level, RFind operates by estimating the time-of-flight from an RFID reader to an RFID tag. It then maps the time-of-flight to distance by taking into account the propagation speed of RF signals. To perform 1D localization, RFind leverages one receive antenna. To enable 2D or 3D localization, it employs two or three antennas respectively and performs trilateration.

RFind's time-of-flight estimation has two components:

- **Emulating a Large Bandwidth on RFIDs:** The first component consists of a technique that enables RFind to emulate a large bandwidth on off-the-shelf RFIDs. The technique operates by decoupling the frequencies for power delivery and sensing in RFID communication. By varying the carrier wave of the sensing frequency over time, RFind can estimate the channel at each of these carriers. Then, it stitches the channel estimates at the various frequencies obtained from an RFID over time, realizing a large virtual bandwidth.
- **Localization by Multi-path Suppression and Super-resolution:** The second component of RFind is an algorithm that accurately localizes RFIDs using the large virtual bandwidth. The algorithm first identifies the line-of-sight path from RFind's reader to an RFID, and eliminates multi-path reflections. Then, it zooms in on the line-of-sight path through a super-resolution algorithm to achieve sub-centimeter localization accuracy.

In §3 and §4, we describe the above components in details.

3 EMULATING A LARGE BANDWIDTH ON NARROWBAND RFIDS

In this section, we explain how RFind can emulate a large bandwidth on passive RFIDs.

3.1 Frequency Agnostic Modulation

We start by providing intuition into why RFID backscatter is frequency agnostic, then delve into how RFind leverages this property to emulate a large bandwidth on passive RFIDs. We describe the different states of RFID modulation at a high level and refer the reader to [22] for a more detailed explanation. Fig. 2(a) shows the components of a typical RFID tag with an antenna, an impedance switch, and a power harvesting unit.[4] The switch is controlled by the RFID's logic (sequence of 0's and 1's), resulting in two states:

- *Non-reflective.* When the switch is off (i.e., logic=0), it acts as an open terminal as shown in Fig. 2(b). Since the input impedance of the power harvesting unit is designed to match the antenna, the received signal can flow into the circuit, enabling the tag to harvest as much power as possible. In this state, the RFID is absorptive or non-reflective.
- *Reflective.* When the switch is on (i.e., logic=1), it acts as a short terminal as shown in Fig. 2(c). Hence, the antenna is connected to ground rather than to a matched circuit.[5] Since the impedance is not matched, there is electromagnetic inhomogeneity which

[3] This is possible because there is no carrier frequency offset (CFO) across time measurements since passive tags don't generate their own RF signal but rather reflect the reader's signal.

[4] The impedance switch is usually implemented as a transistor between the antenna and the analog ground.

[5] Recall from basic circuit principles that the equivalent impedance of a circuit in parallel with ground is zero [25].

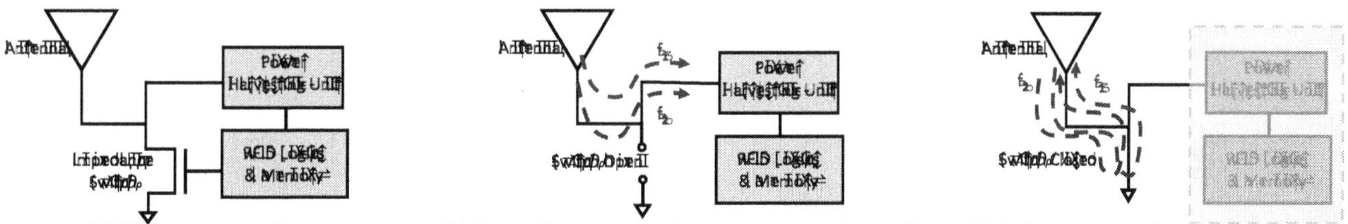

(a) RFID tag system diagram　(b) Non-reflective state when antenna switch is "off"　(c) Reflective state when antenna switch is on

Figure 2: RFID tag antenna impedance control by antenna switch. (a) RFID tag circuit diagram consisting of an antenna, antenna switch, power harvesting unit, and logic & memory circuitry. (b) RFID tag in non-reflective state. Antenna switch is turned "off", resulting in an open terminal. RF power flows into the power harvesting unit. (c) RFID tag in reflective state. Antenna switch is turned "on", resulting in a short terminal. RF power gets reflected by the ground.

results in total reflection. In this state, the RFID is reflective, and all received power by the antenna is reflected (re-radiated) back to the reader.

In the above discussion, we described the two states as perfectly reflective or perfectly absorptive. In practice, however, the matching is not perfect. As a result, an RFID switches between more-reflective and less-reflective states. Nonetheless, the fact that an RFID switches between two states holds, and is sufficient for RFind to sense the channel at different frequencies. We call this the *frequency agnostic* property of backscatter modulation. RFind extends this concept to sensing reflectivity changes in the *complex* domain rather than only in the amount of reflection power, as we describe in detail in Appendix A.

3.2 Decoupling Sensing & Power Delivery

RFind leverages the frequency agnostic property of RFID modulation to estimate a tag's channel over a wide bandwidth. Specifically, rather than transmitting a single frequency f_1 as in today's RFID protocol, it transmits at multiple frequencies, e.g., f_1 and f_2. When the switch is open, the tag absorbs both frequencies as shown in Fig. 2(b); when it is closed, the tag reflects both frequencies as shown in Fig. 2(c). In what follows, we describe how RFind expands on this idea to emulate a very large bandwidth on passive RFIDs.

3.2.1 *How large of a bandwidth can RFind sense?*

A natural question is: over how large of a bandwidth can RFind communicate with an off-the-shelf RFID? Traditionally, due to FCC regulations, this bandwidth is limited to only 26 MHz. Specifically, recall that passive RFIDs are batteryless and harness power from the reader's RF signal to power up and communicate. To deliver sufficient power, today's RFID readers transmit around 36dBm in the ISM band [9].

Outside the ISM band, however, this power is limited to -13.3 dBm and 6.7 dBm for average and peak power respectively,[6] i.e., $1,000\times$ lower than the peak power of frequencies within the ISM band and $100,000\times$ lower than their allowed average power as shown in Fig. 3.

To overcome this bandwidth limitation, RFind decouples RFID power delivery and sensing. In particular, it transmits at two frequencies simultaneously: f_p inside the ISM band (to power up the tag) and f_s outside the ISM band (at much lower power) as shown in Fig. 3. An RFind reader uses f_p to power up the tag, and f_s to sense the tag's backscatter reflection. RFind exploits the fact that RFID backscatter is frequency agnostic to sense the channel at f_s despite its very low power. Finally, in order to sense the channel over a wide bandwidth, RFind varies f_s over time and collects channel measurements.

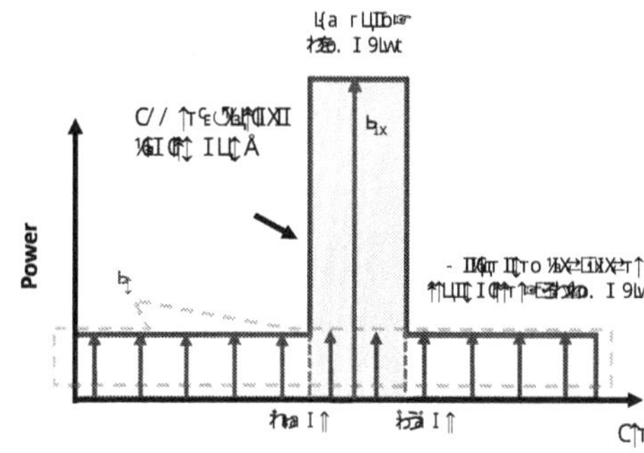

Figure 3: Decoupling Sensing and Power Delivery. By decoupling the frequencies of sensing and power delivery, RFind can transmit at an extremely low-power sensing frequency f_s outside the ISM band. This enables it to emulate a large bandwidth while remaining complaint to FCC regulations.

To investigate the feasibility of this idea, we run an experiment where we transmit at one high-power frequency and sweep the low-power sensing frequency f_s over 300 MHz. In this experiment, the tag is in direct line-of-sight of RFind's antenna. Fig. 4 shows the output of our experiment in blue when we plot the SNR (Signal-to-Noise Ratio) over the sensing frequency. We make few observations about this figure:

- First, RFind can sense the channel over a bandwidth of over 300 MHz, i.e., around $10\times$ larger than the ISM band for UHF communication, despite the low-power sensing frequency f_s.
- Second, the SNR is highest at the ISM band (between 902-926 MHz). Such result is expected since an RFID tag's antenna and matching circuit are designed to be flat over this frequency range. Outside this frequency range, the SNR fluctuates since the RFID's circuitry is not matched.
- Third, despite the fact that f_s is more than 30 dB lower than f_p in the ISM band, the SNR degradation can be relatively insignificant in some parts of the spectrum. For example, at 950 MHz, the SNR is the same as within the ISM band, despite the significantly lower-power signal. The underlying reason is that by

[6]FCC Part 15.231 rules that the average radiation limits for unlicensed low-power transmitter shall not exceed $12{,}500\mu V/m$ at 3 meter distance, so in SI base units, the EIRP $= 0.3 \times E^2 = -13.3$ dBm [1]. The peak power can be higher when applying duty cycle, with a maximum 20dB peak-to-average ratio as ruled by Part 15.35 [9].

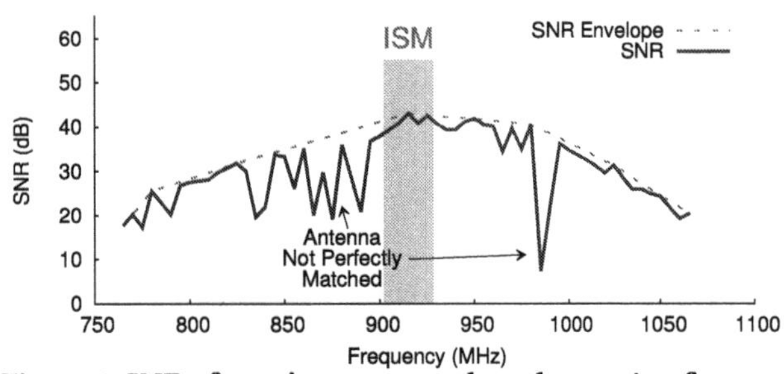

Figure 4: SNR of a tag's response when the sensing frequency is varied over a wide bandwidth. The SNR (in blue) is consistently higher than 10dB over more than 300 MHz despite that f_s is extremely lower power outside the ISM band.

reducing the transmit power at f_s, an RFind reader also experiences significantly less noise. This owes to the fact that the main source of noise in RFID readers is the phase noise induced by the self-leakage of the transmitted signal [37].[7] In particular, recall that RFID readers are full-duplex systems, and they transmit and receive on the same frequency. Moreover, the power of the phase noise due to self-leakage is proportional to the power of the transmitted signal itself.[8] This is why the noise floor is reduced by the same ratio as the sensing frequency f_s, resulting in negligible SNR degradation over certain parts of the spectrum.

- Finally, we observe that the envelope of the SNR (red line in Fig. 4) degrades as we move further from the ISM band. This owes primarily to the beam pattern of the antennas of the RFID and the reader.

3.2.2 Channel Estimation

Now that RFind has a mechanism to sense the tag's response at different sensing frequencies, it can apply standard channel estimation techniques to recover the channels at each of these frequencies. In particular, it uses the known preamble p_t of the tag's response y_t to obtain an estimate of the channel h_k at a given sensing frequency f_k as follows:

$$h_k = \sum_t y_t p_t^* \tag{1}$$

By repeating this operation over different sensing frequencies, RFind can obtain channel estimates $\{h_1 \ldots h_K\}$ over a wide bandwidth.

3.2.3 Integrating with the EPC-Gen2 Protocol

Next, we describe how RFind integrates its dual-frequency approach into the EPC-Gen2 Protocol. Fig. 5 shows the different stages of RFID communication:

(1) A reader initiates a session by transmitting a continuous wave on a high-power signal at some frequency f_p in the ISM band. The tag harnesses power from the signal to power up and start decoding.
(2) Then, the reader sends a Query command at f_p to the tag providing it with communication information (modulation, data rate, etc.). After a tag successfully decodes the Query, it starts modulating its antenna impedance to transmit a 16-bit number called RN16.
(3) At this moment, the reader transmits continuous waves at two frequencies f_p and f_s. As discussed in the previous section, because the backscatter modulation is frequency agnostic, both frequencies are reflected by the RFID. The reader calculates the channel at both frequencies
(4) Then, the reader sends an ACK at f_p and proceeds with the remainder of the communication session exactly as per today's EPC-Gen2 protocol [3].

[7] In today's RFID receivers, the phase noise floor is more than 80dB higher than its thermal noise floor [29, 33].

[8] In our implementation, we also filter out f_p in the analog domain at the receiver, which eliminates its effect on the phase noise.

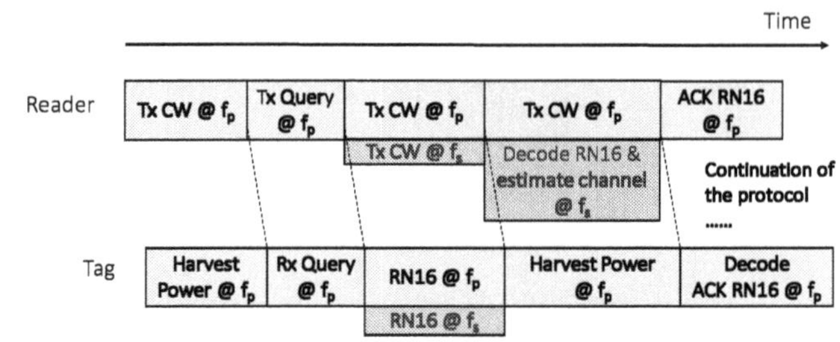

Figure 5: RFind is compatible with the RFID communication protocol. To incorporate RFind into the EPC-Gen2 protocol, a reader only needs to transmit at two frequencies rather than one at the third stage of a communication session.

Note that the fundamental difference between the above procedure and today's RFID protocol is that during the RFID backscatter stage (i.e., step 3), the reader transmits at two frequencies (f_p and f_s) rather than at just one frequency (f_p). One might wonder if transmitting at f_s might be sufficient during this stage if all the reader needs is to measure the channel at f_s. Recall, however, the tag still needs to harvest power when it is in the absorptive (or non-reflective) state of its backscatter modulation as described in §3.1. In fact, our experiments demonstrated that without transmitting at f_p, the communication session is interrupted since the tag runs out of power during the backscatter stage. This is why the reader should transmit at both frequencies during the stage of backscatter modulation.

3.2.4 Putting it together

RFind's technique to emulate a large bandwidth on passive RFIDs operates in three key stages:

- The first is a dual-frequency excitation technique, whereby the reader transmits at both a frequency f_p inside the ISM band and another extremely low power frequency f_s outside the ISM band. It uses f_p to power up the tag and communicate with it, and it uses f_s to estimate the channel of the tag at the corresponding frequency.
- Second, RFind repeats the above operation at different f_s carrier waves. In our implementation, RFind hops f_s over K consecutive carriers $\{f_1, f_2, \cdots, f_K\}$ as depicted in Fig. 3, where the spacing between adjacent carriers is equal to Δf. However, our technique is more general and can be used with a randomized hopping pattern.
- Finally, RFind leverages the fact that there is no carrier frequency offset (CFO) across the measurements. Hence, it can juxtapose the channel measurements obtained at different points in time

with the assumption that they were captured simultaneously.[9] This enables it to measure a large bandwidth of 300 MHz on off-the-shelf RFIDs.

It is worth noting that despite its large bandwidth of operation, incorporating RFind's design in today's readers likely requires only firmware modifications. Specifically, even though RFID readers can only transmit at a very narrow communication bandwidth, the center frequency of their communication can be varied over more than 100 MHz. This is because RFID readers are designed to accommodate for differences in regulations on the UHF band across regions and countries [3]. For example, while the UHF ISM band in the US is 902-928 MHz, China assigns two bands: 840.25-844.75 MHz and 920.25-924.75 MHz. In fact, this is also why RFID tag antennas are designed to be wideband despite that passive RFIDs can only support very narrow communication bandwidth of tens to hundreds of kHz. These underlying design properties make RFind amenable to practical use with today's passive RFIDs and readers.

4 LOCALIZATION USING LARGE VIRTUAL BANDWIDTH

So far, we have demonstrated how RFind can emulate a large bandwidth on passive off-the-shelf RFID tags. Next, we discuss how RFind uses the large bandwidth in order to localize an RFID tag. In this section, we focus on how it can localize a single tag. However, the technique generalizes to any number of tags in the environment.

RFind's localization algorithm operates in two stages. First, it leverages the bandwidth to tease apart the different paths traversed between an RFID and the reader, and identify the line-of-sight (LOS) path. Second, it zooms into the LOS path through super-resolution technique to achieve sub-centimeter localization accuracy.

4.1 Identifying the LOS path

In indoor environments, RF signals bounce off different obstacles (such as ceilings, walls, and furniture) before arriving at a receiver. This phenomenon is called the multipath effect. In order for RFind to localize an RFID, it first needs to identify the LOS path among all these paths. Below, we describe how RFind can identify the LOS path and obtain a rough time-of-flight estimate of that path.

Recall from §3.2.4 that RFind obtains the channel estimates in the frequency domain. To identify the LOS path, RFind needs to transform the channels from the frequency domain to the time domain, i.e., it needs to perform an inverse fourier transform. While there are various ways to implement an inverse fourier transform, RFind leverages the Inverse Fractional Fourier Transform (IFRFT) [15] since it incorporates an interpolation mechanism; hence, it provides RFind with a finer-granularity initial estimate of the time-of-flight.

Mathematically, let us denote the channel estimates as $h_1, \cdots, h_K$ at K different carrier frequencies. To obtain the time domain representation, RFind performs the following IFRFT operation:

$$S(\tau) = \sum_{k=1}^{K} h_k e^{j2\pi(k-1)\Delta f \tau} \quad (2)$$

where τ denotes the delay in the time domain. The solid black line in Fig. 6 shows the output of this operation when it is performed over

[9] In contrast, this assumption does not hold for WiFi transmissions. Hence, past WiFi-based proposals that perform frequency hopping introduce various techniques to address offsets such as packet detection delay and CFO [51, 55, 56].

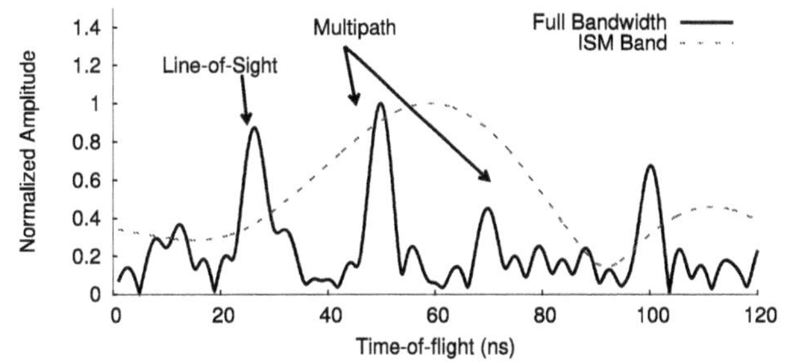

Figure 6: Delay profiles at different bandwidths. The delay profile computed with 220 MHz of bandwidth (in black) enables RFind to tease apart the different channel taps and identify the LOS as the path that arrives earliest in time. In contrast, a delay profile computed only with the 26 MHz ISM band does not provide sufficient resolution in isolating the paths.

an emulated bandwidth of 220 MHz. The figure plots the power as a function of the delay τ. The delay profile exhibits multiple peaks, each of which corresponds to a different path traversed by the RFID's signal. To identify the LOS path, RFind leverages the fact that the LOS arrives earliest in time, since all multi-path reflections traverse indirect paths as they bounce off reflectors, hence traversing a longer distance and experiencing a longer delay. It then uses the delay corresponding to the first peak as an initial estimate for the distance to an RFID.

To demonstrate the significance of a large bandwidth, we repeat the IFRFT operation over only the 26MHz ISM band and plot the delay profile as a dashed red line in Fig. 6. The plot shows that with such a small bandwidth, we are unable to tease apart the LOS path from the indirect paths. Intuitively, this is because when the bandwidth is smaller, the different paths merge into each other. Mathematically, at the output of an inverse fourier transform, each path is convolved with a sinc function whose width is inversely proportional to the bandwidth. Specifically, if there are L paths with delays $\{\tau_1 \dots \tau_L\}$, we can write the output of the IFRFT as:

$$\sum_{i=1}^{L} a_i sinc\left(B(t-\tau_i)\right) \quad (3)$$

where B is the bandwidth and a_i is the complex amplitude of the corresponding path. Hence, larger B results in fatter sinc functions. In particular, the resolution in separating multipath is the width of the sinc function main-lobe, given by [11]:

$$\text{Multipath Separability} = 1/B \quad (4)$$

Note that the final resolution in estimating each of the paths can be much finer, and is a function of the SNR and the sparsity of multipath [24]. In §6, we empirically evaluate the performance of RFind as a function of the sensing bandwidth.

4.2 Super-resolution Algorithm

In the previous section, we described how RFind can identify the LOS path and provide an initial distance estimate. However, this estimate is biased by noise and by leakage from other multipath components (due to the sinc effect described in §4.1). Below, we describe how RFind refines the initial estimate using a super-resolution algorithm.

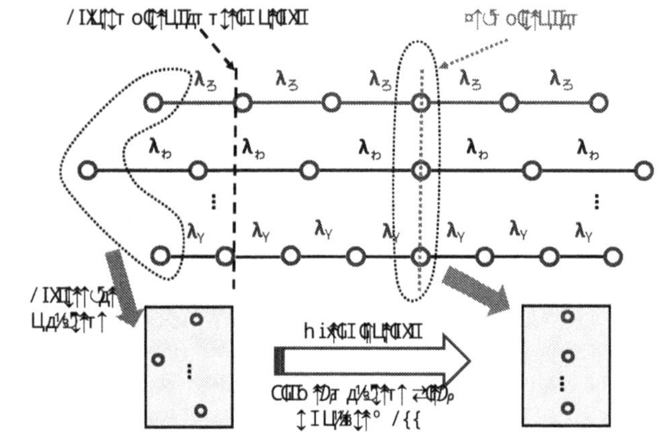

Figure 7: RFind's super-resolution technique consists of a clustering algorithm that resolves phase cycle ambiguity. It constructs a cluster by choosing one potential distance from each frequency and then finds the cluster which has the minimum WCSS.

To refine the distance estimate, we would like to leverage phase information. In particular, in the presence of a single LOS path, the phase ϕ_k on the k-th carrier can be written as a direct function of the distance d:

$$\phi_k = \frac{2\pi}{\lambda_k} d \mod 2\pi \quad (5)$$

Leveraging this phase, however, is complicated by multiple factors. First, the phase can only be measured mod 2π; this creates ambiguity in resolving the distance (mod λ). Second, the above equation assumes a single LOS path and ignores both noise multipath.

RFind's solution to these challenges consists of two steps. First, it uses the initial distance estimate from §4.1 as a filter to mitigate the impact of multipath and recover a phase estimate that can be approximated by Eq. 5 at each of the frequencies f_k. Second, it performs an optimization algorithm across the approximate phases calculated at the different frequencies to mitigate the impact of residual noise and leakage. In what follows, we explain these steps in details.

4.2.1 *Obtaining Filtered Phase Estimates*

Recall that by performing an inverse fourier transform, RFind moves the channel estimates from the frequency domain to the time domain. In doing so, it loses the structure of the phase information at each of the subcarriers according to Eq. 5. In order to recover that information, it needs to transform the delay profile back to the frequency domain, while mitigating multipath.

To recover phase estimates at each of the frequencies f_k while mitigating multipath, RFind constructs a transform that exploits the LOS estimate of the distance $\tilde{d}_0^c$ as a filter. Specifically, it projects the channels h_K at the different frequencies on its estimate of the channel caused by the LOS path. In Appendix B, we demonstrate that such projection can be realized through the following operation:

$$\theta_k = \angle \sum_{i=1}^{K} h_k e^{j\frac{2\pi}{c}(f_i - f_k)\tilde{d}_0^c} \quad (6)$$

where c is the speed of propagation. Effectively, this operation reinforces the signal strength on line-of-sight path and suppresses the leakage from the multi-path reflections.

4.2.2 *Combining Estimates Across Frequencies*

Now that we have the filtered phases at different frequencies, we formulate an optimization function that combines them in order to resolve phase ambiguity. RFind's optimization algorithm is inspired by past work that leverage multi-frequency techniques for localization [37, 51, 56]. In contrast to past algorithms, RFind takes advantage of the fact that it already has an initial distance estimate.

Specifically, RFind's search is bounded by Eq. 4 which limits the potential candidate distances to within a search range of c/B. Rather than searching over an infinite number of potential candidate distances due to the 2π ambiguity of Eq. 5, the number of potential candidates from each θ_k is:

$$\#\ \text{candidates} = \frac{c}{B\lambda} \quad (7)$$

Since RFind can emulate a bandwidth over $B = 220$ MHz on UHF RFIDs (whose λ is 33 cm), its search is limited to five candidate distances from each frequency k.

Fig. 7 demonstrates the intuition underlying RFind's optimization function. The figure shows the five candidate distances at each λ_k (or frequency f_k). The potential candidates can be clustered into different groups. Finally, the cluster that has the smallest width would correspond to the true location, since it is the one most robust to noise and leakage. Mathematically, RFind constructs different clusters $\boldsymbol{C}$, each of which consists of one distance estimate from each frequency. Then, it selects the cluster that has the minimum within-cluster sum of squares (WCSS). We can formulate the optimization function as follows:

$$\arg\min_{\boldsymbol{C}} \sum_{\hat{d} \in \boldsymbol{C}} |\hat{d} - \mu|^2 \quad (8)$$

where μ is the cluster center. The optimization function can be solved in linear time by exploiting the fact that the unwrapping function is monotonic across λ_k. Said differently, a given candidate at λ_{k+1} can be mapped to the closest unwrapped candidate at λ_k.

After identifying the minimum WCSS cluster, the super-resolution distance estimate can be expressed as:

$$\tilde{d}_0^s = \mu \quad (9)$$

The above algorithm enables RFind to find the distance from a tag to a single receiving antenna, which determines a circle in 2D and a sphere with a fixed radius in 3D space. To obtain 2D or 3D locations, RFind leverages two or three antennas respectively and performs trilateration.

5 IMPLEMENTATION & EVALUATION

We implement a prototype of RFind using USRP N210 software radios [8] and test it with a variety of commercial RFID tags [12, 45, 49].

Reader Implementation. We adapt a USRP RFID reader developed in [30] and integrate RFind's design into the EPC Gen2 protocol as described in §3.2.3. RFind's transmit-side implementation of an RFID reader uses two USRPs with SBX daughterboards [7]: the first USRP transmits at 30 dBm at a frequency f_p for power delivery and communication[10] and the second USRP transmits a sensing frequency f_s at extremely low power (with an average radiation

[10] f_p can be inside the ISM band (902-928 MHz) or in white spaces.

power at −15dBm and a peak power at −3dBm[11]) and sweeps it over 220MHz bandwidth. These transmit powers are complaint to FCC regulations for consumer electronics [9]. The two USRPs are synchronized by an external clock [2].

To perform 3D localization, RFind's receive-side implementation uses three USRP N210, each with a patch antenna [6], an external receive chain, and an LFRX daughterboard [5]. We design RFind's external receive chain such that it performs coherent decoding similar to an off-the-shelf reader. The receive chain consists of a filter, a variable gain low noise amplifier (LNA), and an I/Q mixer. The filter eliminates strong leakage from the power delivery carrier f_p, and is essential to mitigate self-jamming and reduce the phase noise induced by the high-power self-leakage from f_p. After filtering, the received signal is amplified by an LNA and down-converted to baseband by mixing with the sensing frequency f_s through an I/Q mixer that feeds to an LFRX daughterboard of the USRP. The USRPs samples baseband I/Q signals which are postprocessed in MATLAB.

Our MATLAB implementation incorporates a Chebyshev-I digital bandpass filter that rejects residual low-frequency noise then performs matched filtering to recover the channel estimates. We perform a one-time calibration step to account for over-the-wire offsets and for changes in the reflection coefficient at different frequencies. In our evaluation, the estimated channels are divided by those acquired during the calibration step. The channels are then processed according to the algorithms described in §4 to obtain a tag's 3D location.

Latency. Our current implementation requires around 6.4 seconds to output a location. This latency is primarily due to RFind's frequency hopping pattern (i.e., the second step of §3.2.4) as it sweeps over 220 MHz. Specifically, we set Δf to 10 MHz, and the USRP-based reader requires around 130 ms to switch and lock to a new sensing frequency f_s in order to collect channels at that frequency. Note that this latency could be decreased by increasing the hopping step Δf; however, increasing Δf may result in time-domain aliasing of the channel taps in multi-path rich environments. This is because increasing Δf results in sub-sampling the frequency domain, which leads to aliasing in the time domain. The super-resolution algorithm latency is sub-millisecond.

Commercial RFID tags. Unless otherwise noted, our experiments are performed with the most widely deployed type of passive RFIDs: the Alien Squiggle RFIDs [12]. Each of these tags costs 5-10 cents. To demonstrate the generality of RFind's techniques, we also tested a variety of other commercial tags such as the Omni-ID Exo tag [45] and the Smartrac tag [49].

Evaluation. We evaluate RFind in multi-path rich indoor environments, and test it in both LOS and NLOS settings. Our experiments are performed in an office building with different types of indoor reflectors including tables, chairs, computers, ceilings, and walls. The experimental environment consists of an office lounge that spans an area of $10m \times 12m$, and we performed localization experiments in multiple sites against different multipath backgrounds. The area includes office cubicles that are separated by dividers consisting of 20cm thick 2m-tall separators made of two layers of wood. For NLOS experiments, these separators ensure that there is no LOS path between RFind's antennas and the localized RFIDs. Finally, unless otherwise noted, RFind's receive antennas are separated by a distance of 20 cm in the x/y/z dimensions from its transmit antenna.

[11]Note that f_s is heavily duty-cycled due to the hopping pattern.

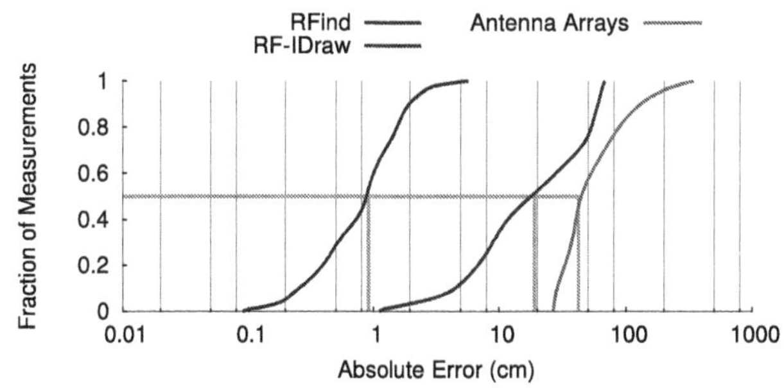

Figure 8: CDF of 2D Localization Accuracy. The figure shows 2D accuracy CDFs of RFind (blue), RFIDraw (red), and AoA (green).

Baselines. We compare RFind to state-of-the-art RFID localization schemes. Our baselines are: RFIDraw [54] and the AoA [14]. Similar to RFind, these state-of-the-art schemes do not require reference tags or reader/tag motion.[12] We implement RFIDraw and AoA with 8 antennas spanning an area of $2m \times 2m$, following the antenna patterns described in the respective papers. We implement RFind with only three receive antennas, placed within 20 cm of the transmit antenna.

Ground Truth. To obtain accurate ground truth RFID locations, we use the Bosch GLM 35 Laser Measure [4], which enables us to measure distances with sub-millimeter precision. Such precision is necessary since RFind achieves millimeter-scale ranging accuracy.

6 RESULTS

6.1 Comparison to State-of-the-Art

We start by comparing RFind's localization accuracy to the state-of-the-art techniques described in §5: RFIDraw and AoA. In fairness to these past techniques, we focus on 2D localization since both RF-IDraw and AoA are evaluated in 2D. In §6.2, we evaluate RFind's 3D localization accuracy.

We performed 150 experimental trials. In each trial, an RFID tag was placed randomly within the evaluation environment described in §5. Since the read range of off-the-shelf RFIDs is constrained by the ability to power them up at distances larger than 5-6 m, we discard instances where the RFIDs do not respond. Fig. 8 plots the CDF of 2D localization error for RFind, RFIDraw, and AoA. We observe the following:

- RFind achieves a median accuracy of 0.91cm and a 90th percentile accuracy of 1.92cm in 2D localization. In contrast, RFIDraw's median and 90th percentile accuracy is 19cm and 61.6cm; these results are comparable to RFIDraw's implementation which also reports a median localization accuracy of 19 cm.[13] This demonstrates that RFind achieves 21× improvement for the median accuracy and more than 32× improvement for the 90th percentile accuracy over state-of-the-art localization systems that do not

[12]In contrast, past proposals that can achieve higher accuracy require moving the tag or the reader on a predefined trajectory at a predefined speed [40, 48, 57].
[13][54] calls this the initial position accuracy.

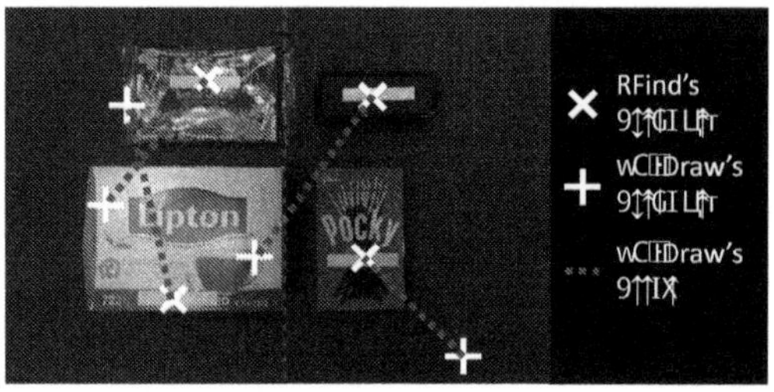

Figure 9: Sample output of the estimated RFID locations by RFind and RFIDraw. RFind's location estimations (indicated by crosses) enable pinpointing the location of the items they tag whereas RFIDraw's estimations (indicated by x's) cannot assign an RFID's location to the item it tags.

require reference tags or motion. Moreover, RFind can achieve this improvement despite the fact that it operates with only three closely-spaced receive antennas in contrast to RFIDraw which needs 8 antennas that are separated by 2 m. Such improvement is expected since RFind incorporates mechanisms to directly estimate the time-of-flight on off-the-shelf tags.

- Both RFind and RFIDraw outperform AoA approaches, which achieve a median accuracy of 42.4cm and a 90th percentile error of 129cm.
- Finally, to demonstrate the significance of such accuracy, we show one of our experimental results in Fig. 9. The figure shows four RFID-tagged items placed on a mat and overlays the estimated locations by RFind and RFIDraw. The figure demonstrates that RFind can pin down the locations of these items while RFIDraw lacks the ability to assign the RFID to the location of the item it tags. These results demonstrate that RFind can be used for localization applications requiring high accuracy such as in supply chains, factories, and retail stores.

6.2 3D Localization Accuracy

Next, we evaluate RFind's 3D localization accuracy in both LOS and NLOS settings. In our evaluation, we place two of RFind's receive antennas on the ground, separated by 80 cm and elevate a third antenna by 60 cm above the ground. We evaluate RFind's performance by placing an RFID at different 3D locations throughout the experimental environment described in §5. We also vary the location of the reader setup throughout the evaluation area. Since the read range of off-the-shelf RFIDs is constrained by the ability to power them up from a distance, we discard instances where the RFIDs do not respond. For NLOS experiments, the reader's antennas are separated from the RFID by 20 cm-think office dividers made of two layers of wood. Similar to past RFID literature [14, 42, 52, 54], we cannot do cross-room validation since a reader cannot power an RFID from another room.

We run 80 experimental trials and plot the CDF of accuracy along the x/y/z dimensions for the LOS and NLOS scenarios in Figs. 10(a) and (b) respectively. The figures reveal the following findings:

- In both LOS and NLOS settings, the median error is less than 1.1 cm along each of the x, y, and z dimensions. Moreover, even the 90th percentile error is less than 2 cm in x/y and less than 4 cm in the z dimension.
- The accuracy in LOS is higher than in NLOS settings. Such a result is expected since the SNR of the line-of-sight path degrades in NLOS, resulting in lower accuracy.
- The accuracy is higher in x/y than in the z dimensions. This is due to the fact that in our 3D evaluation experiments, the RFID was oriented vertically; hence, it is longer along the z dimension than along the x/y.
- Finally, we note that our discussion in §4.1 assumes that in NLOS settings, the direct path is not completely blocked (e.g., by metal) yet it may be significantly attenuated by an obstacle. To generalize to scenarios where the direct path is completely blocked, RFind can add additional antennas and perform clustering and outlier rejection (similar to past localization proposals, e.g., [56]).

6.3 Accuracy vs. Different Parameters

Next, we would like to evaluate RFind's localization accuracy as a function of different system parameters: distance, bandwidth, and antenna separation:

Accuracy vs. Distance. First, we evaluate RFind's localization accuracy as a function of distance. For simplicity, we focus on 1D localization, and repeat the above experiments at 1 m increments. The ground truth is reported using the laser measure described in §5. Fig. 11(a) shows the median and 10th and 90th percentile errors as a function of distance from the receive antenna. The figure demonstrates that the median error increases gradually with distance, but remains about 1cm even at 6m. The 90th percentile at 6 m degrades to around 17 cm; this is due to the fact that at this distance, the SNR drops below the 3 dB threshold for a large number of frequencies, forgoing the benefits of a large bandwidth. Finally, note that beyond 6 m the RFID reader is unable to reliably power up an RFID tag similar to past reported work with USRP readers [53].

Accuracy vs. Bandwidth. Next, we evaluate RFind's localization accuracy as a function of emulated bandwidth. Recall that RFind's localization accuracy comes from its unique ability to emulate a large bandwidth on today's off-the-shelf RFID tags. To understand the influence of bandwidth on localization accuracy, we vary the bandwidth of sensing frequencies provided to RFind's localization algorithm described in §4. We use the same dataset from §6.2 but focus on 1D accuracy for simplicity.

Fig. 11(b) shows the impact of bandwidth on localization accuracy. The plot demonstrates that the localization accuracy monotonically improves with increased bandwidth. Specifically, if RFind only uses frequencies within the 26MHz ISM band, the median errors before and after super resolution are 73 cm and 33 cm respectively and the 90th percentile is over 3 m. The median error quickly decreases with bandwidth and drops below 1 cm for bandwidths larger than 120MHz. This is because increased bandwidth provides finer granularity in teasing apart the LOS path from the multipath. Note, however, due to the stochastic nature of indoor multi-paths, achieving sub-centimeter accuracy at the 90th is only realized when the bandwidth exceeds 200 MHz.

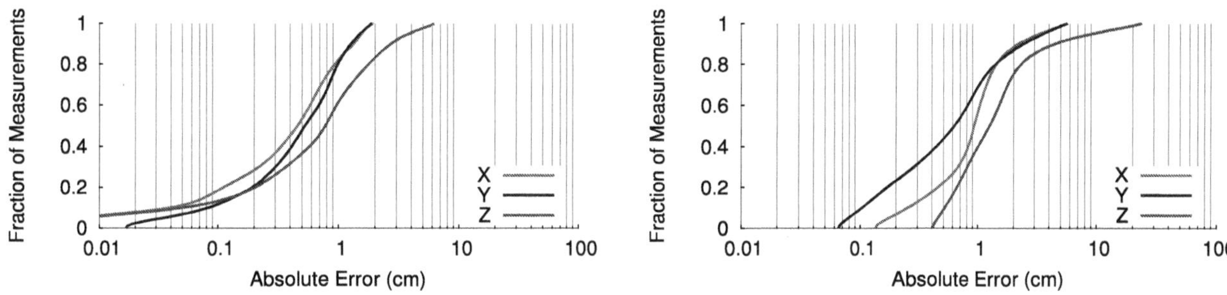

(a) 3D Accuracy in Line-of-Sight (b) 3D Accuracy in Non-Line-of-Sight

Figure 10: 3D Localization Accuracy in LOS & NLOS (a) shows RFind's localization error in LOS in each of the x/y/z dimensions. (b) shows RFind's localization error in NLOS in each dimension.

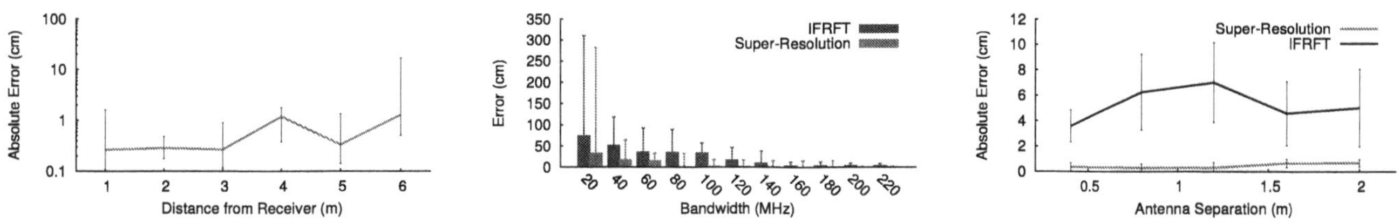

(a) 1D Error vs. Distance (b) 1D Error vs. Bandwidth (c) 2D Error vs. Antenna Separation

Figure 11: Micro-benchmarks. (a) shows that RFind's accuracy gradually decreases with distance but the median error remains about 1 cm even at 6 m from the receiver. (b) shows that RFind's accuracy increases with increased bandwidth both before and after super-resolution. (c) shows the independence of RFind's accuracy from antenna separation. In each figure, error bars indicate 10th and 90th percentile accuracy.

Accuracy vs. Antenna Span. In past antenna array-based localization systems such as RFIDraw [54], a large antenna span (or aperture) is critical to achieve high accuracy since a larger aperture results in a narrower beamwidth. Hence, these systems require separating their antennas by more than 2 m. In contrast to these past systems, RFind can directly measure the time-of-flight; hence, we expect the antenna span to have less impact on its performance.

To evaluate the impact of antenna separation on RFind's accuracy, we perform 2D localization experiments by gradually increasing the separation between RFind's receive antennas. We run 50 experimental trials and plot the output in Fig. 11(c). The figure shows the median and 90th percentile accuracy as the antenna span is varied from 40 cm to 2 m. The figure demonstrates that the antenna span has minimal impact on 2D localization accuracy. In fact, RFind can achieve sub-centimeter localization accuracy even with 40cm antenna span. This is due to the fact that RFind can directly compute 1D estimates with sub-centimeter accuracy. Interestingly, the accuracy is slightly higher when the antenna span is smaller. This owes to a slight improvement in SNR when the antennas are closer to the RFID of interest with a smaller aperture. This ability to perform accurate localization using a small antenna span suggests that RFind's design can enable compact and mobile RFID localization system.

7 RFIND IN APPLICATIONS

Finally, we would like to qualitatively test RFind in a number of real-world applications. Fig. 12 shows multiple instantiations of RFind for various applications. In each row of Fig. 12, the first column shows the test setup, the second column shows RFind's output, and the last two columns overlay the output over the real-world images. Across all these applications, RFind could achieve the same level of accuracy reported in the quantitative results above.

8 RELATED WORK

RFind is related to past work in three areas: localization of commercial RFID tags, ultra-wideband tag designs, and microscopic optical imaging. In contrast to all past work, RFind introduces the first system that emulates a large bandwidth on commercial tags, bringing the benefits of large bandwidth to billions of RFIDs already deployed. In doing so, it enables sub-centimeter 3D localization in multipath-rich environments. In what follows, we discuss how it relates to prior art.

(a) RFID Localization. The topic of RFID localization has gained much attention from the academic community over the past decade. Early proposals in this space relied on measuring the received signal strength (RSS) [16, 18, 41, 59], the angle of arrival (AoA) [14, 32, 38, 60], and the received signal phase [13, 35]. However, these proposals are based on line-of-sight assumptions and cannot deal with multipath. In particular, reflections off various objects in indoor environments (walls, ceilings, furniture) create constructive and destructive interference, making RSS and the phase of the received signal unpredictable. Moreover, since the strongest path between an RFID and reader may not always be the direct line-of-sight path but rather the one arriving off a side reflector, AoA can suffer from multi-meter errors in non-line-of-sight environments [53]. Moreover, in contrast to RFind, past multi-frequency techniques

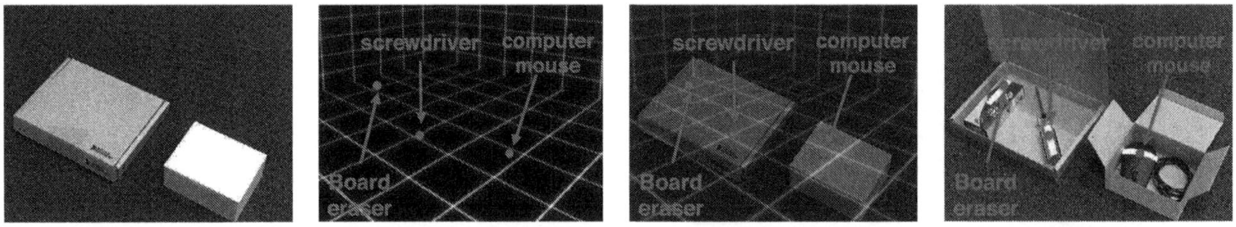

(a) Closed Box (b) RFind's Output (c) Overlayed Output (d) Opened box

Identifying and localizing items in closed boxes for packaging control and delivery services.

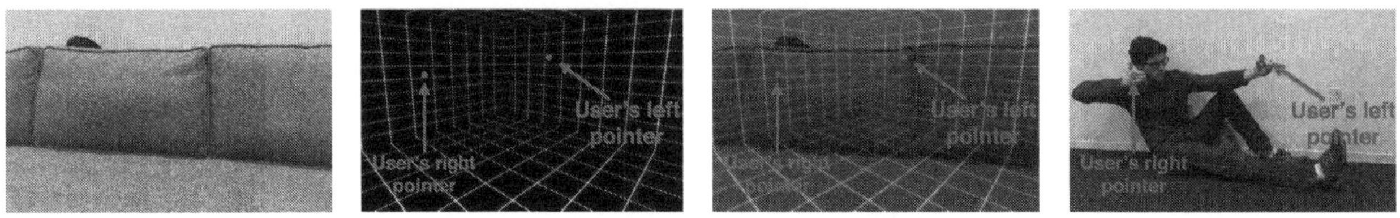

(e) Behind Couch (f) RFind's Output (g) Overlayed Output (h) Couch removed

Tracking user gestures behind occlusions such as furniture.

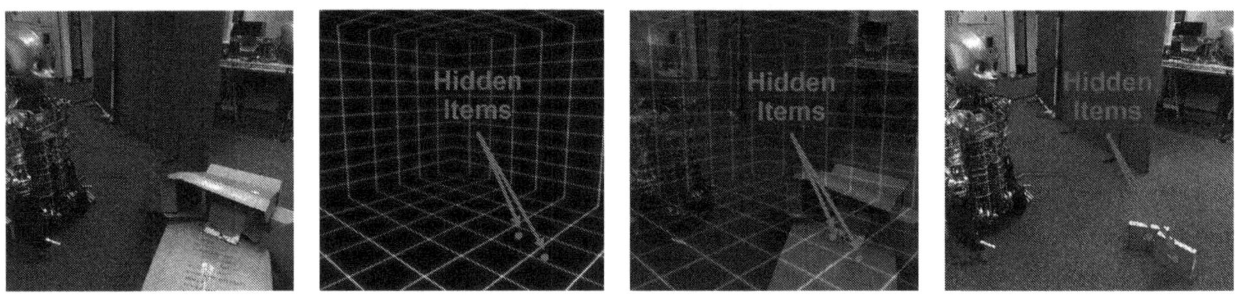

(i) Under Pile (j) RFind's Output (k) Overlayed Output (l) Pile removed

Robotic manipulation in cluttered environments.

Figure 12: RFind in Real-World Applications. (a) shows closed boxes containing RFID-tagged objects. (e) shows a gamer whose fingers are tagged with RFIDs. (i) shows a pile of clutter under which lay two items the robot needs to find. (b), (f), and (j) show RFind's output in identifying and localizing the objects. (c), (g), and (k) overlay our output over the images. After removing the occlusions in (d), (h), and (l), we can see that RFind's localization is very accurate.

are restricted to the ISM band, and hence lack the ability to tease apart multipath from the line-of-sight path.

Recent proposals that can address multipath fall under two main categories: reference-based and motion-based techniques. Reference-based proposals require manually deploying a dense, surveyed grid of reference tags throughout the area of interest and localize a tag by matching it to the grid [17, 26, 53]. Motion-based proposals either require moving a reader's antenna over multiple wavelength (2-3 meters) [48, 52] or they require prior knowledge of the exact trajectory and exact speed of a tag and match it to a location on that trajectory, by leveraging inverse synthetic aperture radar (ISAR) or holographic techniques [40, 46, 57]. In contrast, RFind neither requires mechanical motion nor the deployment of reference tags in the environment. In particular, because RFind can directly measure the time-of-flight, it has intrinsic mechanisms that enable it to accurately localize RFIDs and eliminate multipath.

Finally, some recent proposals such as RFIDraw [36, 42, 54] demonstrate very high *tracking* accuracy but a *localization* accuracy of tens of centimeters. In particular, by measuring phase changes over time, these proposals can track small changes in the *relative* location of a tag and recover its trajectory. Hence, they can recover a tag's trajectory but cannot know exactly where that trajectory was traced. In contrast, RFind enables sub-centimeter localization accuracy using time-of-flight measurements, demonstrating 21× localization improvement over these past proposals as we empirically demonstrated in §6.

(b) Ultra-wideband RFID tags. Past research has explored designing ultra-wideband tags. Due to their large bandwidth, these tags enable estimating the time-of-flight, and hence can deal with multi-path and achieve high accuracy localization [31, 37, 47, 58]. However, these proposals require building new hardware and, as a result, have multiple drawbacks: they are expensive, they are non-compliant with the RFID standard, and most of these proposals are not compliant with FCC regulations. More importantly, these proposals require replacing the billions of tags already produced and deployed annually.

In contrast to these past proposals, RFind leverages a realization that RFID backscatter communication is frequency agnostic, enabling us to emulate ultrawide bandwidth on the billions off-the-self tags already deployed. In particular, RFind can sense an RFID tag's response even outside the ISM band by transmitting signals below FCC spurious emission limits, making it both EPC-Gen2 and FCC compliant. Moreover, RFind introduces multi-path filtering and super-resolution algorithms that enable it to zoom in on a tag's location with sub-centimeter precision, i.e., at a finer granularity than enabled by its sensing bandwidth.

(c) Two photon microscopy. RFind is inspired by a technique from optical physics called two-photon microscopy [21, 27], which is used for deep tissue imaging. The technique fires one photon to excite the layer of interest inside the tissue, and uses a second photon to perform imaging. These photons may be at the same or different visible-light frequencies. Similarly, RFind leverages a frequency inside the ISM band to excite or power up a tag and another frequency outside the ISM to perform sensing. However, RFind differs from two-photon microscopy in both techniques and problem domain. Specifically, in contrast to two-photon microscopy which was designed for improve fluorescence imaging in thick specimens, RFind is designed for RFID localization and makes a realization about RFID backscatter that enables it to accurately localize RFIDs.

9 CONCLUSION

We present RFind, a system that enables emulating a large virtual bandwidth on off-the-shelf passive RFIDs. In this paper, we use the large virtual bandwidth to estimate the time-of-flight and achieve centimeter-scale localization accuracy without reference tags or reader/tag motion. However, we believe that the implications of such large bandwidth extend beyond localization and pave way for exciting new avenues for exploration in RFID communication and security.

Appendix A: Sensing Reflectivity Changes over a Wide Bandwidth.
The reflection of an RFID can be expressed as a function of the tag's electromagnetic (EM) reflection co-efficient γ [43]. Assume the incident electric field to the tag is E_{in}, we can express the reflected electric field E_{ref} as:

$$E_{ref} \propto E_{inc} \times \gamma \tag{10}$$

γ is a complex number which a function of the frequency dependent antenna impedance $Z_a(f)$ and the effective chip input impedance $Z_c{}^{eff}(f)$, and can be expressed as follows [43]:

$$\gamma = \frac{R_a(f)}{Z_a(f) + Z_c(f)^{eff}} \tag{11}$$

where $Z_a(f) = R_a(f)+jX_a(f)$. $R_a(f)$ and $X_a(f)$ are the frequency dependent real and imaginary parts of antenna impedance. The effective chip input impedance is affected by the switching transistor. Specifically, when the switch is open $Z_c{}^{eff}(f) = Z_c(f)$; when it is closed, $Z_c^{eff}(f) \approx 0$. Hence, γ switches between:

$$\gamma_{open} = \frac{R_a(f)}{Z_a(f) + Z_c(f)} \quad \text{and} \quad \gamma_{closed} = \frac{R_a(f)}{Z_a(f)} \tag{12}$$

A RFind reader senses the reflected field difference in the complex domain which can be expressed as:

$$E_{diff} \propto E_{in}(\gamma_{closed} - \gamma_{open}) \propto E_{in}\frac{R_a(f)Z_c(f)}{Z_a(f)(Z_a(f) + Z_c(f))}$$

Typically, RFIDs are designed such that the field difference is maximized at the desired antenna center frequency. Outside the design bandwidth, the differential field gradually decreases due to impedance mismatch. Note that in RFID tag designs, matching is much more critical for power delivery on the downlink rather than it is for the backscatter response on the uplink. Since RFind powers up an RFID tag using one carrier inside ISM band, the tag would always power up and switch the impedance. Such complex impedance switching can be sensed outside the optimal frequency.

To illustrate this concept, consider the following simple practical model [50]: Assume $Z_c = R$ which is purely resistive and an equivalent RLC circuit model for antenna, $Z_a = R + j\omega L + \frac{1}{j\omega C}$. The antenna center frequency is $f_c = 900$MHz and the quality factor of the antenna is $Q = 10$. So

$$\gamma_{closed} - \gamma_{open} = \frac{1}{(2 - jQ(1-(\frac{f}{f_c})^2))(1 - jQ(1-(\frac{f}{f_c})^2))} \tag{13}$$

The resultant SNR degradation from 900 MHz to 750 MHz is 17dB which is about the same amount of SNR degradation shown as measured from our experiment with a real tag in Fig. 4.

Appendix B: Recovering Phase While Mitigating Multi-path. We show that Eq. (6) reinforces the LOS path component and suppress leakages from multi-paths. Assume there are L multi-paths whose distances are $d_1, d_2, ..., d_L$, and that d_0 is the real LOS distance. The channel h_k can be expressed as:

$$h_k = a_0 e^{-j\frac{2\pi}{c}f_k d_0} + \sum_{l=1}^{L} a_l e^{-j\frac{2\pi}{c}f_k d_l} \tag{14}$$

where $\tilde{d}_0^c$ is the coarse LOS distance estimate derived from IFRFT. By factoring in h_k, we rewrite Eq. (6) as:

$$\theta_k = \angle a_0 e^{-j\frac{2\pi}{c}f_k d_0}\sum_{i=1}^{K} e^{j\frac{2\pi}{c}(i-k)\Delta f(\tilde{d}_0^c - d_0)} + \angle \sum_{l=1}^{L} a_l e^{-j\frac{2\pi}{c}f_k d_l}\sum_{i=1}^{K} e^{j\frac{2\pi}{c}(i-k)\Delta f(\tilde{d}_0^c - d_l)} \tag{15}$$

Since $(\tilde{d_0}^c - d_0)\Delta f/c << 1$:

$$\sum_{i=1}^{K} e^{j\frac{2\pi}{c}(i-k)\Delta f(\tilde{d}_0^c - d_0)} \approx K \tag{16}$$

while $\tilde{d}_0^c - d_l$ is large, resulting in

$$\left|\frac{\sum_{i=1}^{K} e^{j\frac{2\pi}{c}(i-k)\Delta f(\tilde{d}_0^c - d_l)}}{K}\right| \approx |sinc(B(\tilde{d}_0^c - d_l)/c)| \ll 1 \tag{17}$$

Thus, LOS is reinforced while multipath leakage is suppressed.

Acknowledgments. We thank Omid Abari, Dina Katabi, Zach Kabelac, our shepherd Shyam Gollakota, and the anonymous MobiCom reviewers for their insightful comments. This research is partially supported by NSF and the MIT Media Lab.

REFERENCES

[1] Calculating radiated power and field strength for conducted power measurements. http://www.semtech.com.
[2] CDA2990. http://www.ettus.com. Ettus Inc.
[3] EPC UHF Gen2 Air Interface Protocol. http://www.gs1.org/epcrfid/epc-rfid-uhf-air-interface-protocol/2-0-1.
[4] Laser Measuring. http://www.boschtools.com. Bosch Inc.
[5] LFRX daughterboard. http://www.ettus.com. ettus inc.
[6] MTI RFID antenna. http://www.mtiwe.com. MTI Wireless Edge.
[7] SBX daughterboard. http://www.ettus.com. ettus inc.
[8] usrp n210. http://www.ettus.com. ettus inc.
[9] *Understanding the Fcc Regulations for Low-power, Non-licensed Transmitters.* Office of Engineering and Technology Federal Communications Commission, 1993.
[10] The State of RFID Implementation and Its Policy Implications: An IEEE-USA White Paper. IEEE USA, 2009.
[11] F. Adib, Z. Kabelac, D. Katabi, and R. C. Miller. 3d tracking via body radio reflections. In *Usenix NSDI*, 2014.
[12] Alien Technology Inc. ALN-9640 Squiggle Inlay. www.alientechnology.com.
[13] D. Arnitz, K. Witrisal, and U. Muehlmann. Multifrequency continuous-wave radar approach to ranging in passive uhf rfid. *IEEE Transactions on Microwave Theory and Techniques*, 57(5):1398–1405, 2009.
[14] S. Azzouzi, M. Cremer, U. Dettmar, R. Kronberger, and T. Knie. New measurement results for the localization of uhf rfid transponders using an angle of arrival (aoa) approach. In *RFID (RFID), 2011 IEEE International Conference on*, pages 91–97. IEEE, 2011.
[15] D. H. Bailey and P. N. Swarztrauber. The fractional fourier transform and applications. *SIAM review*, 33(3):389–404, 1991.
[16] M. Bouet and A. L. Dos Santos. Rfid tags: Positioning principles and localization techniques. In *Wireless Days, 2008. WD'08. 1st IFIP*, pages 1–5. IEEE, 2008.
[17] M. Bouet and G. Pujolle. A range-free 3-d localization method for rfid tags based on virtual landmarks. In *Personal, Indoor and Mobile Radio Communications, 2008. PIMRC 2008. IEEE 19th International Symposium on*, pages 1–5. IEEE, 2008.
[18] K. Chawla, C. McFarland, G. Robins, and C. Shope. Real-time rfid localization using rss. In *Localization and GNSS (ICL-GNSS), 2013 International Conference on*, pages 1–6. IEEE, 2013.
[19] M. Chu, P. Jacob, J.-W. Kim, M. R. LeRoy, R. P. Kraft, and J. F. McDonald. A 40 gs/s time interleaved adc using sige bicmos technology. *IEEE Journal of Solid-State Circuits*, 45(2):380–390, 2010.
[20] D. Dardari, R. D'Errico, C. Roblin, A. Sibille, and M. Z. Win. Ultrawide bandwidth rfid: The next generation? *Proceedings of the IEEE*, 98(9):1570–1582, 2010.
[21] W. Denk, J. H. Strickler, W. W. Webb, et al. Two-photon laser scanning fluorescence microscopy. *Science*, 248(4951):73–76, 1990.
[22] K. Finkelzeller. The rfid handbook, 2003.
[23] L. Gang et al. Bandwidth dependence of cw ranging to uhf rfid tags in severe multipath environments. In *IEEE RFID 2011*.
[24] S. Gezici, Z. Tian, G. B. Giannakis, H. Kobayashi, A. F. Molisch, H. V. Poor, and Z. Sahinoglu. Localization via ultra-wideband radios: a look at positioning aspects for future sensor networks. *IEEE signal processing magazine*, 22(4):70–84, 2005.
[25] P. R. Gray and R. G. Meyer. *Analysis and design of analog integrated circuits.* John Wiley & Sons, Inc., 1990.
[26] J. Han, C. Qian, X. Wang, D. Ma, J. Zhao, W. Xi, Z. Jiang, and Z. Wang. Twins: Device-free object tracking using passive tags. *IEEE/ACM Transactions on Networking*, 24(3):1605–1617, 2016.
[27] F. Helmchen and W. Denk. Deep tissue two-photon microscopy. *Nature methods*, 2(12):932–940, 2005.
[28] HTC. HTC Vive. https://www.vive.com/us/.
[29] IEEE. *A new TX leakage-suppression technique for an RFID receiver using a dead-zone amplifier*, 2013.
[30] N. Kargas, F. Mavromatis, and A. Bletsas. Fully-coherent reader with commodity sdr for gen2 fm0 and computational rfid. *IEEE Wireless Communications Letters*, 4(6):617–620, 2015.
[31] N. C. Karmakar et al. Chipless rfid tag localization. *IEEE Transactions on Microwave Theory and Techniques*, 61(11):4008–4017, 2013.
[32] R. Kronberger, T. Knie, R. Leonardi, U. Dettmar, M. Cremer, and S. Azzouzi. Uhf rfid localization system based on a phased array antenna. In *Antennas and Propagation (APSURSI), 2011 IEEE International Symposium on*, pages 525–528. IEEE, 2011.
[33] I. Kwon, Y. Eo, H. Bang, K. Choi, S. Jeon, S. Jung, D. Lee, and H. Lee. A single-chip cmos transceiver for uhf mobile rfid reader. *IEEE Journal of Solid-State Circuits*, 43(3):729–738, 2008.
[34] N. Levanon. Radar principles. *New York, Wiley-Interscience, 1988, 320 p.*, 1988.
[35] X. Li, Y. Zhang, and M. G. Amin. Multifrequency-based range estimation of rfid tags. In *RFID, 2009 IEEE International Conference on*, pages 147–154. IEEE, 2009.
[36] T. Liu, L. Yang, Q. Lin, Y. Guo, and Y. Liu. Anchor-free backscatter positioning for rfid tags with high accuracy. In *INFOCOM, 2014 Proceedings IEEE*, pages 379–387. IEEE, 2014.
[37] Y. Ma, X. Hui, and E. C. Kan. 3d real-time indoor localization via broadband nonlinear backscatter in passive devices with centimeter precision. In *Proceedings of the 22nd Annual International Conference on Mobile Computing and Networking*, pages 216–229. ACM, 2016.
[38] G. Mao, B. Fidan, and B. D. Anderson. Wireless sensor network localization techniques. *Computer networks*, 51(10):2529–2553, 2007.
[39] A. McWilliams. RFID: Technology, Applications, and Global Markets. BCC Research, 2016.
[40] R. Miesen, F. Kirsch, and M. Vossiek. Holographic localization of passive uhf rfid transponders. In *RFID (RFID), 2011 IEEE International Conference on*, pages 32–37. IEEE, 2011.
[41] L. M. Ni, Y. Liu, Y. C. Lau, and A. P. Patil. Landmarc: indoor location sensing using active rfid. *Wireless networks*, 10(6):701–710, 2004.
[42] P. V. Nikitin, R. Martinez, S. Ramamurthy, H. Leland, G. Spiess, and K. Rao. Phase based spatial identification of uhf rfid tags. In *RFID, 2010 IEEE International Conference on*, pages 102–109. IEEE, 2010.
[43] P. V. Nikitin and K. S. Rao. Theory and measurement of backscattering from rfid tags. *IEEE Antennas and Propagation Magazine*, 48(6):212–218, 2006.
[44] Occulus. Occulus Rift. https://www.oculus.com/rift/.
[45] Omni-ID. Omni-ID Exo. www.omni-id.com.
[46] A. Parr, R. Miesen, and M. Vossiek. Inverse sar approach for localization of moving rfid tags. In *RFID (RFID), 2013 IEEE International Conference on*, pages 104–109. IEEE, 2013.
[47] M. Pelissier, J. Jantunen, B. Gomez, J. Arponen, G. Masson, S. Dia, J. Varteva, and M. Gary. A 112 mb/s full duplex remotely-powered impulse-uwb rfid transceiver for wireless nv-memory applications. *IEEE Journal of Solid-State Circuits*, 46(4):916–927, 2011.
[48] L. Shangguan and K. Jamieson. The design and implementation of a mobile rfid tag sorting robot. In *Proceedings of the 14th Annual International Conference on Mobile Systems, Applications, and Services*, pages 31–42. ACM, 2016.
[49] Smartrac Group. Smartrac Shortdipole Inlay. www.smartrac-group.com.
[50] W. L. Stutzman and G. A. Thiele. *Antenna theory and design.* John Wiley & Sons, 2012.
[51] D. Vasisht, S. Kumar, and D. Katabi. Decimeter-level localization with a single wifi access point. In *Usenix NSDI*, 2016.
[52] J. Wang, F. Adib, R. Knepper, D. Katabi, and D. Rus. RF-Compass: Robot Object Manipulation Using RFIDs. In *ACM MobiCom*, 2013.
[53] J. Wang and D. Katabi. Dude, where's my card? rfid positioning that works with multipath and non-line of sight. In *ACM SIGCOMM*, 2013.
[54] J. Wang, D. Vasisht, and D. Katabi. Rf-idraw: virtual touch screen in the air using rf signals. In *ACM SIGCOMM*, 2015.
[55] Y. Xie, Z. Li, and M. Li. Precise power delay profiling with commodity wifi. In *Proceedings of the 21st Annual International Conference on Mobile Computing and Networking*, pages 53–64. ACM, 2015.
[56] J. Xiong, K. Sundaresan, and K. Jamieson. Tonetrack: Leveraging frequency-agile radios for time-based indoor wireless localization. In *Proceedings of the 21st Annual International Conference on Mobile Computing and Networking*, pages 537–549. ACM, 2015.
[57] L. Yang, Y. Chen, X.-Y. Li, C. Xiao, M. Li, and Y. Liu. Tagoram: Real-time tracking of mobile rfid tags to high precision using cots devices. In *Proceedings of the 20th annual international conference on Mobile computing and networking*, pages 237–248. ACM, 2014.
[58] C. Zhou and J. D. Griffin. Accurate phase-based ranging measurements for backscatter rfid tags. *IEEE Antennas and Wireless Propagation Letters*, 11:152–155, 2012.
[59] J. Zhou and J. Shi. Rfid localization algorithms and applicationsâĂŤa review. *Journal of intelligent manufacturing*, 20(6):695–707, 2009.
[60] J. Zhou, H. Zhang, and L. Mo. Two-dimension localization of passive rfid tags using aoa estimation. In *Instrumentation and Measurement Technology Conference (I2MTC), 2011 IEEE*, pages 1–5. IEEE, 2011.

RIO: A Pervasive RFID-based Touch Gesture Interface

Swadhin Pradhan
UT Austin
swadhin@cs.utexas.edu

Eugene Chai
NEC Labs America
eugene@nec-labs.com

Karthikeyan Sundaresan
NEC Labs America
karthiks@nec-labs.com

Lili Qiu
UT Austin
lili@cs.utexas.edu

Mohammad A. Khojastepour
NEC Labs America
amir@nec-labs.com

Sampath Rangarajan
NEC Labs America
sampath@nec-labs.com

ABSTRACT

In this paper, we design and develop RIO, a novel battery-free touch sensing user interface (UI) primitive for future IoT and smart spaces. RIO enables UIs to be constructed using off-the-shelf RFID readers and tags, and provides a unique approach to designing smart IoT spaces. With RIO, any surface can be turned into a touch-aware surface by simply attaching RFID tags to them. RIO also supports custom-designed RFID tags, and thus allows specially customized UIs to be easily deployed into a real-world environment.

RIO is built using the technique of *impedance tracking*: when a human finger touches the surface of an RFID tag, the impedance of the antenna changes. This change manifests as a change in the phase of the RFID backscattered signal, and is used by RIO to track fine-grained touch movement over both off-the-shelf and custom-built tags. We study this impedance behavior in-depth and show how RIO is a reliable UI primitive that is robust even within a multi-tag environment. We leverage this primitive to build a prototype of RIO that can continuously locate a finger during a swipe movement to within 3*mm* of its actual position. We also show how custom-design RFID tags can be built and used with RIO, and provide two example applications that demonstrate its real-world use.

KEYWORDS

RFID; Touch Interface; Mutual Coupling; Impedance Tracking

1 INTRODUCTION

The future of IoT demands seamless, intuitive interaction between users and smart devices. The vision is one of *smart spaces* (Fig. 1a), where sensing and actuation interfaces are embedded into common objects, and can be controlled through touch, voice command, or gestures. Examples of such input modalities include wireless gesture sensing [1–3] which converts everyday body motions into input, and capacitive touch [4, 5] which recognizes physical actuation between a user and the IoT device. Imagine if all these input modalities operate without the need for any built-in battery or power source, and are integrated into everyday devices such as cups, bowls, door knobs, mattresses, and built upon hardware so cheap and simple that it can be installed or discarded easily. Any physical space can be converted into a smart space simply by embedding such input interfaces. The possibilities for such an input primitive are clearly endless.

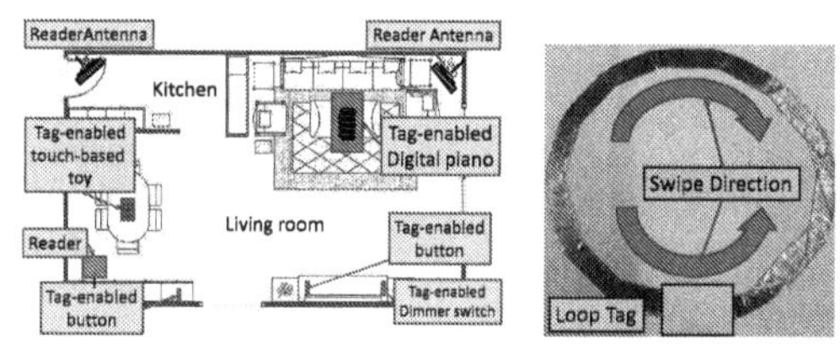

(a) RIO-enabled home setup. **(b) Custom RIO tag for volume control.**

Figure 1: Example applications of RIO.

Battery-Free Touch UI. We explore the design of a battery-free fine-grained touch gesture input interface using Radio Frequency IDentification (RFID) technology. RFIDs provide a low-cost, battery-free communication platform and have been used to develop sensing, activity recognition and localization solutions [6–11]. Among these notable works, machine learning techniques using the PHY-layer features of both off-the-shelf [8] and custom-built tags [9] have been successful in classifying several well-defined gestures such as hand waving, touching and swiping. Other approaches such as [12], have also designed custom backscatter capacitive measurement circuits to detect touch events on the tag antenna.

We note that these works only detect isolated, coarse-grained interactions and not fine-grained ones, such as the path traced by a finger over the surface of a tag. Machine learning approaches [8, 9] also demand a high training overhead that limits its deployability. For example, [8] uses 600 annotated interaction events to train and evaluate its classifier. and thus increase the cost and difficulty of large-scale integration into smart-spaces.

In this paper, we improve upon existing works by asking and answering an important question: *Can we use commercial off-the-shelf (COTS) RFIDs as a battery-free, low-cost, fine-grained touch-based user input primitive?*

We design and build such an input primitive using COTS RFID readers and tags. We call this primitive RIO, for **R**FID-based **I**nput / **O**utput. RIO turns COTS RFID tags into touch interfaces: a user interacts with RIO by touching the tag, and RIO accurately tracks the touch as it moves over the surface of a tag. RIO uses a novel technique of *impedance tracking* in backscatter communications. The human body is conductive, with a capacitance on the order

MobiCom '17, October 16-20, 2017, Snowbird, UT, USA

ACM ISBN 978-1-4503-4916-1/17/10...$15.00
https://doi.org/.1145/3117811.3117818

of hundreds of pico-Farads (*pF*) and a resistance of hundreds to thousands of Ohms [13, 14]. When a user touches an RFID tag, his/her body conductivity changes the effective *impedance* of the tag antenna. This impedance change manifests as a change in phase of the backscattered signal. Rio tracks this phase change to determine the location of the finger within a tag. By accurately modeling the relationship between impedance and RF phase, this fine-grained tracking can be achieved with minimal training overhead. Our evaluations show a tracking error of under 4% with only 4 training events (vs. 600 training events for IDSense [8]).

Rio offers three key features that make it ideal for IoT setting:

(i) Fine-Grained Accuracy. Rio detects finger taps on RFID tags with 100% accuracy, and tracks finger swipe positions to within 3*mm* of its true position (validated using a camera and OpenCV for finger tracking). This is achieved using off-the-shelf RFID tags, thus enabling a new battery-free, fine-grained and accurate UI primitive for smart-spaces.

(ii) Low-cost Hardware. Rio makes use of COTS RFID tags. We have tested Rio with a variety of tags, an example of which is the Monza 4D Dogbone tag [15]. These tags are extremely low-cost, and can be purchased for as low as 14-cents each. The low-cost nature of RFID tags lowers the barrier to smart spaces as large numbers of tags can be installed within an area easily.

(iii) Customizable User Interface. Rio also supports custom-designed RFID tags. We build tags with custom-shaped antennas by laying out the antennas with copper metal tape and inductively couple them to small near-field RFID tags. Rio tracks touch gestures over these custom antennas, and thus enables custom, application-specific interfaces to be built.

Applications. These features of Rio offer a novel primitive for future IoT UI design. As an example, RFID tags can be placed throughout a room to be used as dimmer switches — a user swipes his/her finger up and down a tag to increase/decrease the lighting brightness. A similar Rio interface can be used to increase/decrease the volume of audio systems. Rio also enables multiple tags to be arranged into an array. Such an array can be affixed to any table or wall to serve as a battery-free, wireless touch-pad to interact with home automation/entertainment systems.

Rio supports custom tags with antennas designed into application-specific control shapes. For example, a custom tag shown in Fig. 1b can be installed on a sofa to allow users to adjust the volume of the TV by swiping (anti-)clockwise over the tag. Such applications require fine-grained continuous touch tracking, which is now enabled by Rio. Rio thus opens up a whole new selection of such intuitive, battery-free interfaces that can be embedded into every-day spaces.

Contributions. In developing Rio as a practical, battery-free user-interface primitive, we address several challenges and make the following contributions:

(1) Rio as a Reliable Primitive for Touch Sensing. To validate the reliability of Rio's primitive, we present a detailed measurement study of RFID backscatter signals in response to physical touch across the RFID antenna. We use both over-the-air and Vector Network Analyzer (VNA) measurements, to show how (a) the impedance of the RFID antenna will vary in response to physical touch; (b) the amount of variation depends on the location of the physical contact with the antenna; and (c) the variations in antenna impedance form the dominant factor (compared to other artifact like multi-path) contributing to a corresponding change in the magnitude and phase of the backscattered signal. Equipped with this understanding, Rio uses this touch-dependent phase change behavior of RFID tags as a primitive to detect touches on a RFID tag, as well as to track the location of the finger during a swipe over the tag surface.

(2) Making Rio Resilient in a Multi-Tag Environment. Previous works have identified that *mutual coupling* between tags [16–19] has a significant impact on backscattered signal phase. Hence, when multiple RFID tags are deployed close together on the same surface, the backscattered phase is affected by both the physical contact with the RFID antenna, as well as mutual coupling affects, thereby substantially affecting the tracking accuracy. While previous works have made similar observations [16–19], the impact of such coupling has been overcome largely by building tolerance into the solution. In contrast, we take a more active approach to model and understand the impact of inter-tag coupling on our primitive. With the help of our measurement campaign and supporting model, we show that while coupling can affect the phase change behavior on a desired tag and hence its tracking accuracy, it contributes to a stable, predictable phase-change pattern in the neighboring tags. Thus, by leveraging the joint phase-change behavior across multiple tags, Rio translates the challenge of coupling into an opportunity to enhance the tracking accuracy even in multi-tag scenarios.

(3) Leveraging Rio's Primitive. We design algorithms that leverage the touch-based phase-change primitive in Rio as well as the inter-tag coupling behavior to track touches to an median error of only 3 and 7 *mm* in single and multi-tag settings respectively. Rio's algorithms provide the flexibility to operate at various points in the accuracy-latency trade-off curve, allowing for a reasonable loss in accuracy for a more responsive real-time tracking.

(4) Exploring Rio's Potential. The ability to go beyond COTS tags expands the scope of applications possible with Rio. Custom-designed RFID tags mimicking different shapes, characters, etc. allow battery-free interfaces to be customized for specific smart spaces use cases in Rio. We describe how these tags can be constructed, and extend the touch/gesture tracking algorithms in Rio to support tracking applications with these custom-designed tags.

(5) Realizing Rio in Practice. We develop a prototype of Rio, and demonstrate its touch and gesture tracking accuracy using both COTS and custom-designed RFID tags. We demonstrate the robustness of Rio through exhaustive real-world evaluations, and show that accurate tracking is maintained even at different tag angles and distances to the RFID reader. We also develop two sample applications using custom-designed RFID tags to highlight the flexibility and practicality of Rio.

Our evaluations demonstrate that Rio (a) detects a human touch event with 100% accuracy and (b) tracks the location of a human finger during a swipe gesture across the surface of a COTS RFID tag to within 3*mm* (less than 4% of the length of the RFID tag).

In the rest of this paper, we begin with a background on RFIDs in §2, followed by a quantitative and qualitative study of the RFID touch primitive in §3. We describe the algorithms for touch and swipe gesture tracking in §4, and extend it to support custom-designed RFID tags in §5. We then evaluate the Rio primitive in §6 and demonstrate two example applications in §6.4. Next, we discuss a few points regarding the extensions and limitations of RIO in §7 and finally conclude in §9 after reviewing related works in §8.

2 PASSIVE RFID PRIMER

Passive RFID system communicates using a backscatter radio link, as shown in Fig. 2. The reader supplies a Continuous Wave (CW) periodic signal that persists indefinitely. The passive tags purely harvest energy from this CW signal. The tag then modulates its data on the backscatter signals using ON-OFF keying through changing the impedance on its antenna.

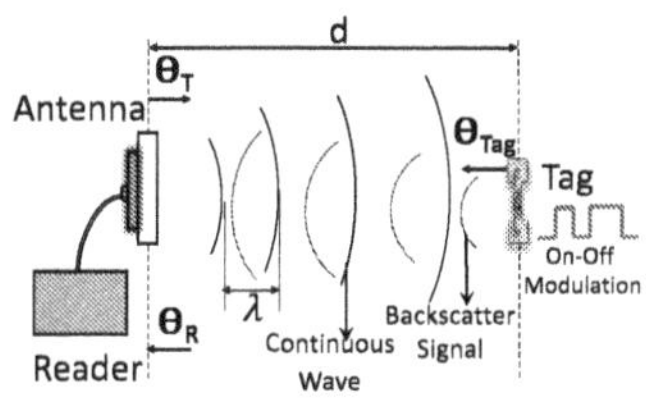

Figure 2: Operation of a RFID reader antenna and a tag.

Passive RFID tag: A typical passive RFID tag, as shown in Fig. 3b, consists of an antenna and an integrated circuit (chip). According to [20], passive RFID tag absorbs the most energy when the chip impedance and the antenna impedance are conjugately matched, *i.e.*, $Z_c = Z_a^*$ [21].

COTS RFID reader: COTS RFID reader [22] uses linear or circular polarized antennas for both transmitting and receiving. They generally provide facilities to access lower level information [23] like RSS and phase values etc. through SDK [24]. A COTS reader employs an open-loop estimation (*e.g.*, preamble correlation) or a closed-loop estimation technique for acquiring phase and RSS [25].

3 HUMAN TOUCH PRIMITIVE

Human touch on the RFID tag changes the effective impedance of the antenna, and will, in turn, influence the phase of the backscattered signal. In this section, we show how this phase-change behavior is used as a reliable and robust primitive for touch/gesture tracking in both single tag and multi-tag settings, and in the presence of artifacts such as multi-path and inter-tag coupling. We accomplish this with the help of both controlled and over-the-air measurements, and an analytical model that highlights the fundamental relationship between impedance change and RF phase.

3.1 How Does Human Touch Change the Backscatter Phase of a Single RFID Tag?

Fig. 3a illustrates the measurement setup that is used to study the touch-induced performance of the RFID tag. We attach a single RFID tag that is 1.5 × 10*cm* in size (shown in Fig. 3b) on a flat surface, and place a 9*dBi* circularly polarized RFID antenna 50*cm* directly below it. The antenna is powered by an Impinj R420 RFID reader. The camera in Fig. 3a only used in later sections for accuracy measurements. For clarity, we divide the tag into 9 equal subsections, as shown in Fig. 3b. Position 5 corresponds to the middle, while 1 and 9 are at the two ends of the tag.

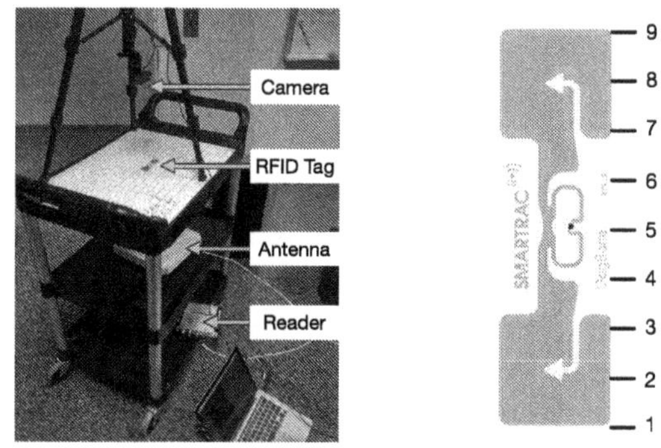

(a) Equipment setup. **(b) Monza R6 Dogbone RFID tag.**

Figure 3: Equipment and tags used in the swipe experiment.

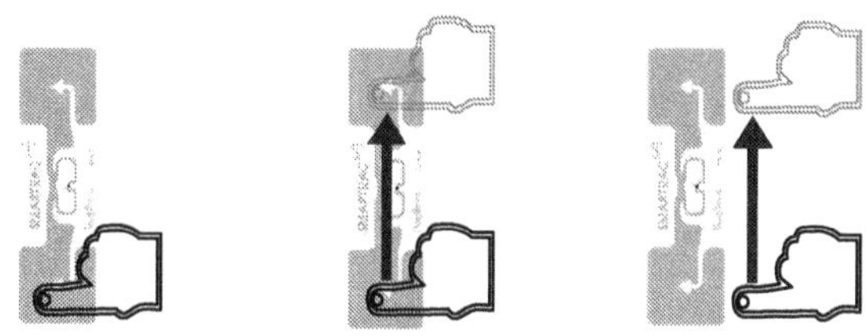

(a) Simple touch. **(b) Swipe on surface.** **(c) Swipe along edge.**

Figure 4: Touch gestures.

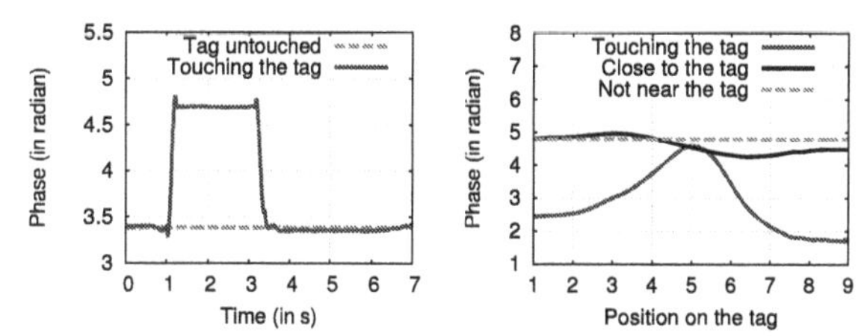

(a) Simple touch at 1 to 3 sec. **(b) Swipe gesture.**

Figure 5: Phase of backscattered RFID signals.

We perform three gestures, as illustrated in Fig. 4: a simple touch gesture where we touch one end of the tag (Fig. 4a), a swipe gesture where we start with a finger on one end of the RFID tag and move across the length of the tag at constant speed (Fig. 4b), and a swipe gesture that is performed along the edge of the tag but without touching the tag itself (Fig. 4c). The RFID reader continuously queries the RFID tag during the entire swipe gesture at a rate of ~200 reads/second. We use the Octane SDK [24] together with the Impinj R420 reader to obtain the phase and magnitude of the backscattered responses from the RFID tag. We make four observations from our experiments:

(1) Human touch induces significant phase changes in the backscattered response. Fig 5a shows the backscattered phase of the RFID tag when a simple touch is applied from 1 to 3 seconds after the start of the experiment. Observe that during this time interval, the backscattered phase jumps from 3.5 to 4.8 radians. The signal phase returns to 3.5 radians once the touch is removed. This demonstrates that a simple touch will induce a significant phase

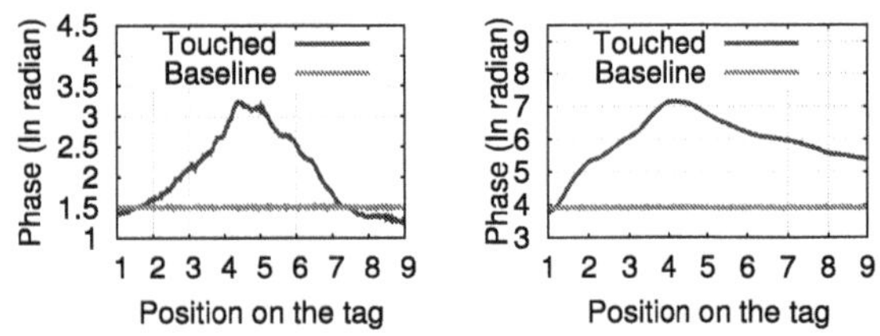

(a) Tag behind a wall. (b) Tag behind door.

Figure 6: Phase-change pattern of backscatter signals with tag in NLOS locations.

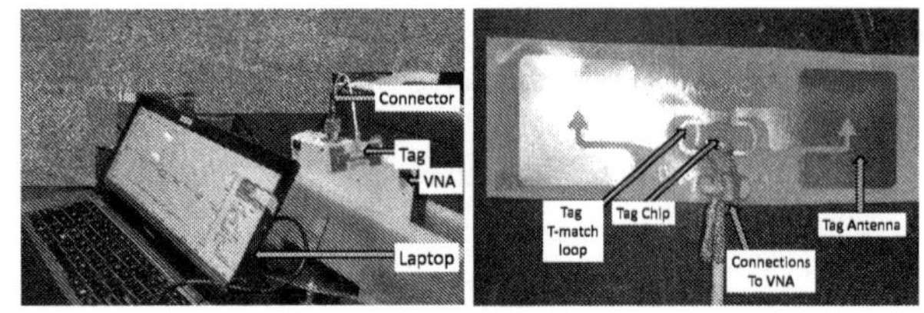

(a) VNA experimental setup. (b) Customized Dogbone RFID tag for VNA experiment.

Figure 7: Vector Network Analyzer (VNA) measurement.

change (1.3 radians in this experiment), and is a simple method to detect a touch gesture on an RFID tag. This amount of phase change varies between tags, and can either increase or decrease in response to human touch.

(2) A swipe gesture induces different phase changes as the finger moves over the tag. Fig. 5b shows the absolute backscattered phase under the two different swipe gestures. Observe that with the swipe gesture over the RFID tag, the amount that the phase changes compared to an untouched tag varies depending on the position of the finger. This phase trend follows a symmetrical bell-shape, with about 3 radians between the highest and lowest phases, and starting from one end of the tag, the largest phase-change is seen when the swipe crosses its middle.

(3) Human touch is the dominant cause of phase changes. Fig. 5b also shows the phase of the backscattered signal when the swipe gesture is performed without touching the antenna on the tag. Observe that *while some phase changes are present, they are much less significant than when the touch gesture is performed directly on the tag*. This observation, together with the measurement under NLOS conditions, shows that the dominant effect due to human touch can be measured under varying channel conditions.

(4) Phase behavior is resilient to multipath. In order to study the effect of non-line-of-sight (NLOS), we repeat the swiping gesture but with the tag and reader in different positions by separating them with (a) a wall, and (b) a door. The reader and tag are 2*m* apart. Under such conditions, the indirect signal paths and associated multi-path distortion has a greater impact on the backscatter signal. Note that the maximum range at which an RFID tag can be read depends on both the RFID reader and the tag. Our Monza R6 tags have a theoretical maximum read range of over 6*m*, but practically, this limit is close to the 2*m* used in our NLOS experiment.

Fig. 6 shows the phase of the backscattered signal under these two conditions (labeled *Touched*). The *baseline* plot shows the RF phase of the RFID tag without any human contact. Observe that *even in NLOS situations, the bell-shaped phase change behavior seen earlier is maintained.* Hence, even though multipath and NLOS effects can influence the RF phase readings, the impact of human touch on the phase of the backscattered signal is dominant.

3.2 Why Does the Backscatter Phase Change with Human Touch?

The human body can be modeled as an electrical circuit with an equivalent resistance and capacitance [26]. In particular, the human skin has a capacitance equivalent to hundreds of picofarads (*pF*) [14]. When a human touch is established with the RFID antenna, *capacitive coupling* [27] is established between the human and the RFID antenna at the point of contact. We explain the impact of this coupling and verify its influence on the backscatter phase through real-world VNA circuit measurements.

3.2.1 *Capacitive Coupling.*

The radiation of RF signals from the RFID tag antenna is the result of time-varying current induced within the antenna. A change in the phase of this current will induce a corresponding phase change in the associated RF radiation [28, 29]. Hence, in order to understand how the phase of the backscattered signal changes, it is helpful to know how the phase of this induced current is affected by touch. The RFID tag in our experiments uses a *dipole antenna* [30] for backscatter communications. Using a simplified model of dipole antennas, the current induced in the RFID antenna can be mathematically expressed as [29]

$$I_m = -\frac{E_{\text{inc}}}{(Z_C + Z_A)\gamma\cos^2(\gamma L/4)} \tag{1}$$

where Z_C and Z_A are the impedances of the RFID chip and antenna, respectively, E_{inc} is the incident electric field on the RFID antenna, L is the length of the antenna, and γ is the free-space phase constant. If the effective impedance of the antenna Z_A is changed, (1) shows that the induced current, and by extension, the backscattered electric field and signal, will undergo a corresponding change in phase and magnitude [30]. However, *how does human touch change the antenna impedance?*

Through capacitive coupling, the human body becomes an extension of the RFID antenna. The effective impedance of the RFID antenna, Z_A, as presented to the RFID chip, is now a sum of the impedance of the antenna without human touch and the impedance introduced by the human finger. A change in phase in this effective impedance will cause a corresponding phase change in the current distribution within the antenna. As a result, the phase of the backscattered signal changes in response to human touch.

3.2.2 *VNA Measurements.*

We directly measure this the impedance change due to human touch using an Array Solutions Vector Network Analyzer (VNA) [31]. We use the same RFID tag from Fig. 3b, but disconnect the RFID chip from the antenna, and solder the feed points of the RFID antenna directly to the electrical leads of the VNA. Fig. 7b shows the modified tag used for our VNA measurements. Using this setup, we can induce electrical currents within the RFID antenna, and directly measure the impedance in the antenna.

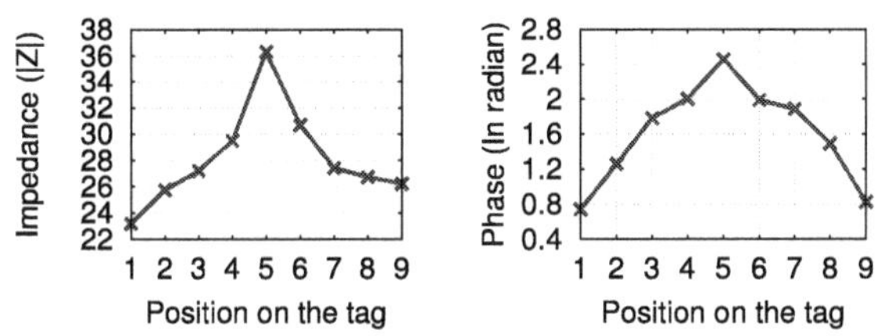

(a) Magnitude.

(b) Phase.

Figure 8: Tag impedance change due to human touch.

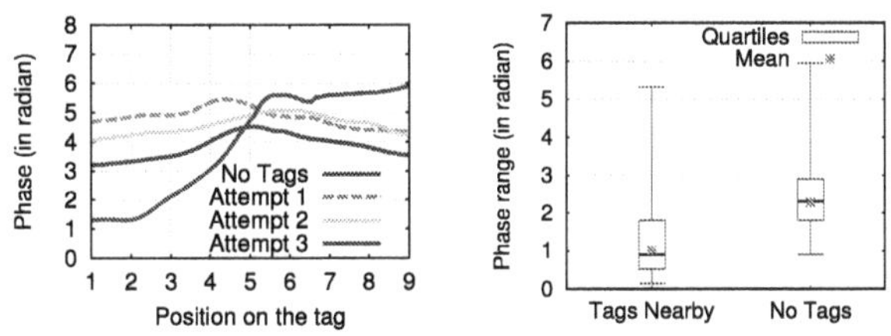

(a) Mutual coupling distorts swipe phase behavior.

(b) Mutual coupling reduces dynamic range of phase change.

Figure 9: Phase behavior with or without nearby tags.

We again divide the tag into 9 equal subsections, and measure the impedance of the antenna when human touch is applied to each of the 9 points. Fig. 8 shows the magnitude and phase of this measured impedance. Observe that the impedance change also follows a symmetric bell-shaped pattern, with the largest magnitude and phase changes occurring when the human touches the middle of the tag.

3.3 Human Touch on a Multi-Tag Array

Mutual coupling between one or more RFID tags in close proximity can distort the phase and magnitude of the backscattered signal during a swipe gesture [16, 32]. For example, Fig. 9a shows the phase trends of four swipe events over a single RFID tag when (a) there are no other tags in close proximity, and (b) three examples when there is one other tag placed 5*mm* away from it.

Observe that due to mutual coupling, the phase can even be almost invariant at several tag locations when one other tag is adjacent (e.g. positions 6 to 9 in Fig.9a for "w/ adj tag 3"). In the other two swipes with adjacent tags, the dynamic ranges of phase changes reduce to around 0.9 radian. This is equivalent to a reduction in the signal-to-noise ratio (SNR) of the phase data obtained by the RFID reader. Furthermore, Fig. 9b illustrates that dynamic range of phase change in both halves of the curve for mutual coupling scenarios is on an average 1 radian less than the case when no tag is nearby. This poses a challenge for RIO as a low SNR phase data is correlated with worse finger tracking accuracy.

To overcome this challenge, we now try to understand how mutual coupling between tags affects our primitive.

3.3.1 ***Inverted Phase Behavior.*** Our experiments show that due to mutual coupling, when human touch is applied to a tag,

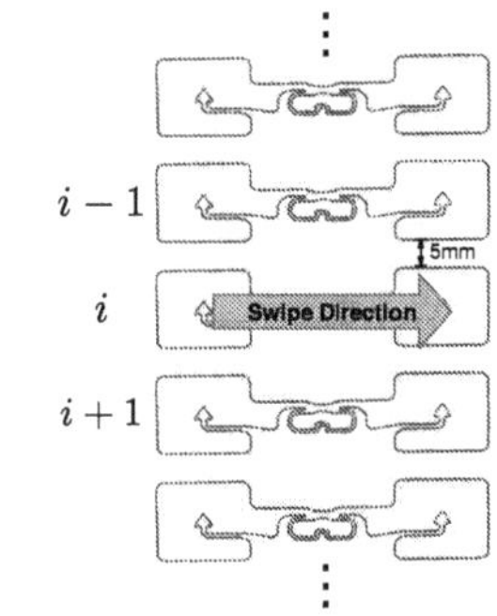

Figure 10: Tag array for coupling measurement.

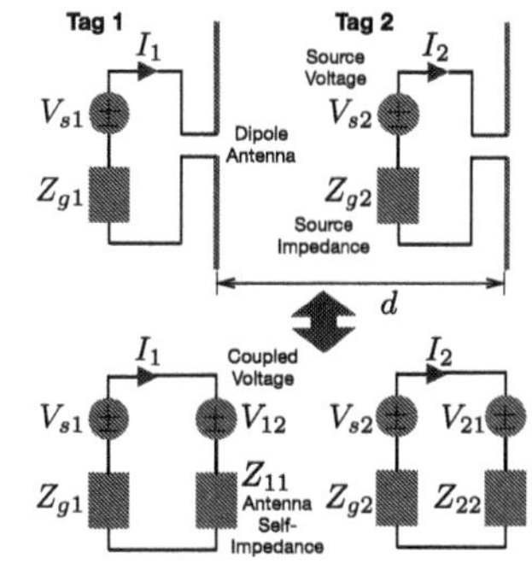

Figure 11: Equivalent circuit of tags 1 and 2.

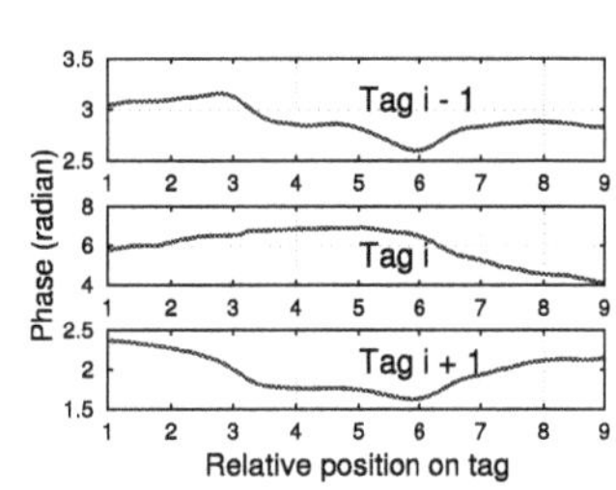

Figure 12: Phase change trends in tags $i-1$ and $i+1$ are the inverse of tag i.

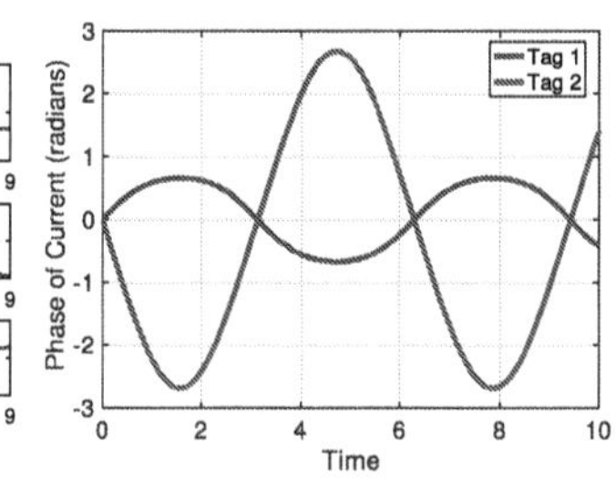

Figure 13: Phase of induced current in tags 1 and 2.

the *trend* of its own phase change is the *opposite* of those seen in adjacent tags.

Fig. 10 shows the tag layout used in this experiment, with each pair of adjacent tags separated by 5*mm*. To highlight the effect of mutual coupling, we consider only three tags in this array, labeled $i-1$, i and $i+1$. We swipe across tag i and record the phase of tags $i-1$, i and $i+1$.

Fig. 12 shows the phase of the backscatter signal measured from these three tags. Observe that due to mutual coupling, tag i experiences a smaller range (around 2 radian lesser) of phase variations during the swipe gesture. However, the trend of the phase changes show an interesting pattern: observe that as the swipe gesture moves across tag i, a increase in its phase coincides with a decrease in the phase of tags $i-1$ and $i+1$. We refer to this phenomenon as the *inverted phase behavior of adjacent tags.* The impact of such mutual coupling diminishes as we consider tags that are farther away than the adjacent tags.

3.3.2 ***Why is the trend of phase changes in adjacent tags inverted?*** **Model:** To understand the impact of mutual coupling on tag interaction, we model the basic scenario of coupling between two tags. The equivalent circuit of the two tags can be represented as shown in Fig. 11. Here, V_{s1} and V_{s2} are the equivalent source voltages induced by the reader's signal on the tag antenna, with Z_{s1} and Z_{s2} being the corresponding chip impedances, and Z_{11} and Z_{22} being their respective antenna self-impedances.

The current in tag 1, I_1 induces a magnetic field, which couples tag 1 and tag 2, thereby inducing a coupled voltage in tag 2, V_{21}, where $V_{21} = I_1 Z_{21}$, and Z_{21} is the mutual impedance in tag 2 due to tag 1. Similarly, we have the coupled voltage in tag 1 as $V_{12} = I_2 Z_{12}$. Now, taking mutual coupling into account, the resulting voltages, for tag 1 and tag 2 respectively, can be written as,

$$\begin{aligned} I_1(Z_{11} + Z_{s1}) &= V_{s1} + I_2 Z_{12} \\ I_2(Z_{22} + Z_{s2}) &= V_{s2} + I_1 Z_{21} \end{aligned} \tag{2}$$

When a tag is interrogated, the back-scattered field (signal) from a tag is a function of the current in the tag. Hence, it suffices for the analysis to focus on the currents in the two tags to understand how interacting with one tag changes the current in the mutually coupled tag. Solving for the two currents in Equation 2, we get,

$$I_1 = \frac{V_{s1}\tilde{Z}_{22} + V_{s2}Z_{12}}{\tilde{Z}_{11}\tilde{Z}_{22} - Z_{12}Z_{21}};\ I_2 = \frac{V_{s2}\tilde{Z}_{11} + V_{s1}Z_{21}}{\tilde{Z}_{11}\tilde{Z}_{22} - Z_{12}Z_{21}} \tag{3}$$

where $\tilde{Z}_{11} = Z_{s1} + Z_{11}$ and $\tilde{Z}_{22} = Z_{s2} + Z_{22}$.

Phase Change during Tag Interaction: Note that we are interested in modeling the *change in phase* of the signal received by the reader when a user is interacting with the tag being interrogated or a nearby tag. When a tag is interrogated, the signal received by the reader is a combination of the backscattered signal from the desired tag as well as the scattered signal from the other tags (which serve as simple scatterers). We will assume that the contribution of the scattered signals is negligible relative to that of mutual coupling from nearby tags. In this case, the phase of the received signal can be estimated from the phase of the current of the backscattered signal, while accounting for mutual coupling with nearby tags. The phase of the currents in the two tags, I_1 and I_2, can be written as,

$$\angle I_1 = \phi_1 - \phi_m, \text{ and } \angle I_2 = \phi_2 - \phi_m \tag{4}$$

where ϕ_1, ϕ_2 and ϕ_m are the phases of $(V_{s1}\tilde{Z}_{22} + V_{s2}Z_{12})$, $(V_{s2}\tilde{Z}_{11} + V_{s1}Z_{21})$, and $(\tilde{Z}_{11}\tilde{Z}_{22} - Z_{12}Z_{21})$ respectively.

Now, let us consider the case when the user interacts (touching or swiping) with tag 2. This will change the self impedance of Z_{22} as well as its coupled impedance Z_{12} on tag 1, while the chip impedances Z_{s1}, Z_{s2} and tag 1's self (Z_{11}) and induced (Z_{21}) impedances will not change. Hence, while phases ϕ_1 and ϕ_m will change, ϕ_2 will remain constant. The phase-change behavior can now be captured as,

$$\begin{aligned} \angle I_1(t) &= \phi_1(t) - \phi_m(t) \\ \angle I_2(t) &= \phi_2 - \phi_m(t) \\ \text{where, } \phi_1(t) &= \angle(V_{s1}Z_{s2} + V_{s1}Z_{22}(t) + V_{s2}Z_{12}(t)) \\ \phi_m(t) &= \angle\big(\tilde{Z}_{11}Z_{s2} + \tilde{Z}_{11}Z_{22}(t) - Z_{21}Z_{12}(t)\big) \end{aligned}$$

From the above equation, it can be observed that $\phi_1(t)$ and $\phi_m(t)$ are essentially functions of the same impedance changes, namely $Z_{22}(t)$ and $Z_{12}(t)$. However, the change in $Z_{12}(t)$ has an opposite effect in $\phi_1(t)$ compared to that in $\phi_m(t)$. This contributes to a counter-acting effect on the phase change of $I_1(t)$ compared to $I_2(t)$ (i.e. tag being touched), and results in the inverted phase-change behavior between the tags. To highlight this impact, we plot the phase evolution of $I_1(t)$ and $I_2(t)$ in Fig. 13. Here, $Z_{22}(t)$ is assumed to vary as a sine function during human interaction (for illustration), while $Z_{12}(t)$ is assumed to vary proportionally to $Z_{22}(t)$ (in both magnitude and phase), and rest of the non-varying complex quantities are assumed to be real with unit magnitude.

Thus, while leveraging the primitive for tracking could lead to reduced accuracy in the presence of mutual coupling, the above measurements and analysis highlight the predictable impact of mutual coupling on our primitive. Hence, by leveraging the phase-change behavior across neighboring tags jointly, our primitive can be made robust to mutual coupling in multi-tag settings.

4 RIO DESIGN

Leveraging the above characteristics of the primitive, we now design the algorithms needed to track the path of the human finger during a swipe gesture across a single isolated tag, and across any individual tag within a tag array. Note that for the sake of simplicity, RIO only tracks a continuous, one-direction swipe across a tag starting from location 1 and ending at 9, as shown in Fig. 4b. This is not a fundamental limitation of RIO, and the algorithms can be extended to support arbitrary touch movement within a tag.

4.1 Finger Tracking on a Single RFID Tag

Single-tag swipe tracking is done in two stages. RIO first detects a touch event on the tag. Once a touch is detected, RIO uses an online tracking algorithm, RIO-SINGLE, to track the position of a human finger across the single tag. A simple, low-overhead calibration is first performed on a tag that is attached to a surface to determine the precise characteristics of the bell-shaped phase trend. This calibration overhead is small and needs to be performed only once after the tag is first installed. RIO then uses a tracking algorithm based on *segmental dynamic time warping (SDTW)* [33–35] that allows for good tracking accuracy with only limited calibration overhead.

4.1.1 ***Low-Overhead Tag Calibration.*** Tag calibration has to be conducted once after the tag is installed on a surface. During tag calibration, the user swipes his/her finger across the surface of the RFID tag at constant speed (as constant as possible), while the Impinj R420 RFID reader continuously reads the tag at a rate of 200 reads/second, and records the phases of all backscatter responses. RIO *normalizes* the phase responses w.r.t. the lowest value:

$$p(x) = r(x) - \min_x r(x), \quad 0 \le x \le L \tag{5}$$

where $r(x)$ is the unnormalized (i.e. raw) phase values at location x from the calibration swipe across a tag of length L. RIO then uses polynomial curve-fitting to find the fourth-order polynomial that best describes the normalized calibration data.

Overhead. This calibration is repeated four (4) times. RIO uses the average of the four polynomial curves in the next touch detection/tracking step. This low-overhead calibration step is (a) *not* user-specific, and (b) only specific to the installed location of the tag. Hence, each installed tag only needs to be calibrated once before touch tracking is enabled for all users thereafter. Due to human limits, it is not possible to replicate a swipe with a human finger precisely. We have empirically determined that the average of four swipes is sufficient to capture the key behavior of an actual human swipe. We have validated this by having one person calibrate the tag, and evaluating the tracking accuracy of RIO with fifteen (15) other human individuals. Our tracking error remains under 4% for all the sixteen (16) individuals. Note that, we do not need to re-calibrate RIO if only the reading angle of the antenna or the tag

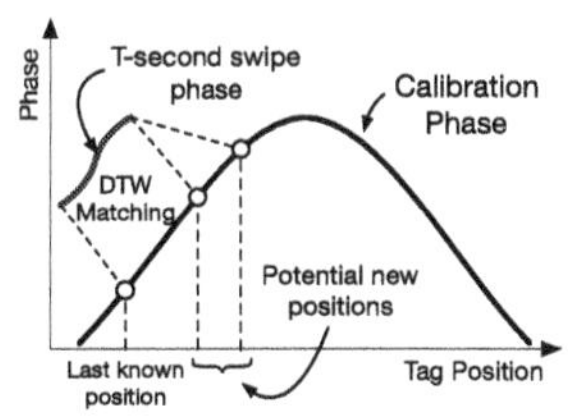

Figure 14: DTW search is applied to each window of samples during a swipe.

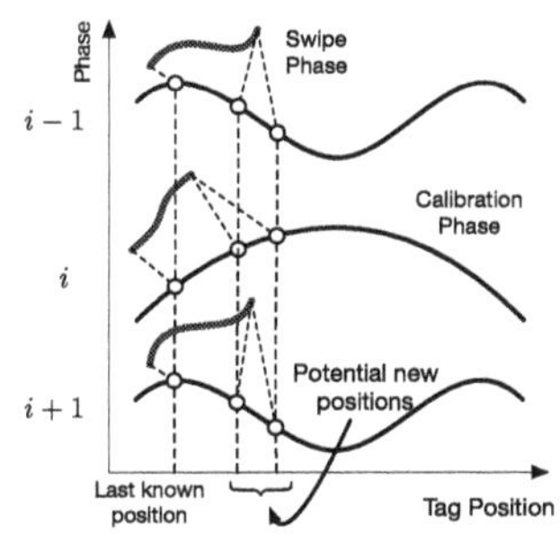

Figure 15: DTW search across adjacent tags.

changes. However, if there is some considerable change in the environment (e.g., introduction of more blockage due to new furnitures or more dynamic paths due to increased movements of people), we need to recalibrate to create the basic phase trend to achieve accurate tracking.

4.1.2 *Rio-Single Algorithm.*

Rio uses a two stage approach to finger tracking. Rio continuously reads the RFID tag until it detects a touch event. Once a touch has been detected, Rio switches to a tracking stage where it tracks the position of the finger as it is swiped across the RFID tag.

Touch Detection. A touch event results in a significant change in the phase of the response signal from the tag. Rio queries the tag continuously and finds the average signal phase over every time interval of T seconds. If a significant change is seen from one time interval to the next (a change larger than a threshold C), then a touch event has occured and Rio switches to a tracking mode. Rio uses a threshold of $C = 0.9$ radians, which is empirically determined to provide 100% detection accuracy in real-world conditions.

Touch Tracking. Rio updates the location of the finger during a swipe gestures using a segmental dynamic time warping (SDTW) search algorithm. A good overview of SDTW can be found in [35]. Broadly speaking, SDTW compares two sequence segments by stretching and squeezing (*i.e.*, warping) one of the sequences until an optimal match between them is found. The measure of similarity of between these two sequences at this optimal match is returned by the SDTW algorithm.

Fig. 14 illustrates how Rio updates the estimated location of the finger in real-time. Rio first collects a sequence of phases of all backscatter responses over a time window of T seconds. Starting from the previously estimated position of the finger, Rio begins a DTW matching by warping the collected sequence and comparing it against multiple *segments* of the calibration phase data. These segments start from the last known position of the finger, and have varying lengths that span the range of potential new positions, as shown in Fig. 14. The segment with the best match is chosen, and its corresponding end position is taken as the new position of the finger.

This search-and-update step is continuously repeated as Rio tracks the finger over the surface of the tag. The details of the touch detection and tracking algorithms are described in Algorithm 1.

Rio estimates the finger location after every time interval T seconds. The choice of T determines the latency and processing overhead of each location estimate. In our implementation of Rio, we use $T = 0.5s$ as we have empirically determined it to be suitable for a typical swiping speed. We have evaluated the performance of Rio for other values of T and found the performance to be similar.

Algorithm 1 Rio-Single

```
x0 ← current finger location;
xmax ← max finger location w.r.t. x0;
xmin ← min finger location w.r.t. x0;
p(x) ← calibration data (from Eq. (5));
procedure DTW(a, b)
    return DTW distance between sequences a and b;
procedure MINDTW(x0, x1, w, p(x))
    p ← {p(x) | x0 ≤ x ≤ x1}; ▷ Segment of calibration phase data between x0 and x1
    return DTW(w, p − p(x0));
procedure GETPHASEDATA
    t0 ← CURRENTSYSTEMTIME;
    t ← t0; w ← EMPTYVECTOR;
    while t ≤ t0 + T do
        t ← CURRENTSYSTEMTIME;
        w ← APPEND(w, CURRENTPHASEREADING);
    return w − min(w);
procedure UPDATELOCATION(x0, w)
    xnew ← arg min_{xmin<x<xmax} MINDTW(x0, x, w);
    return xnew;
procedure TOUCHDETECTION
    while True do
        w ← GETPHASEDATA;
        if mean(w) > C then return True;
procedure TOUCHTRACKING
    while True do
        w ← GETPHASEDATA;
        x0 ← UPDATELOCATION(x0, w);
TOUCHDETECTION(); TOUCHTRACKING();
```

In Algorithm 1, Rio performs a DTW search over a range of segment sizes, as specified by x_{min} and x_{max} in Algorithm 1. x_{min} and x_{max} determine the lower and upper ranges of swipe gesture speeds that will be accurately tracked by Rio. The greater the value of x_{max} the higher the upper bound of this speed limit. Similarly, the smaller the value of x_{min}, the slower the lower bound on the speed limit. We select x_{min} and x_{max} to correspond to $0.5T$ and $1.5T$ seconds of calibration data respectively, which is equivalent to a swiping speed of 10 to $15mm/s$.

4.1.3 *Computation Overhead.*

The computational overhead of finger tracking is dominated by the the DTW algorithm, which has a complexity of $O(N^2)$. In practice, Rio samples M equally spaced sample sizes from the range of x_{min} and x_{max}, and performs a location update (procedure UPDATELOCATION in Algorithm 1) over these M samples. The larger the number of samples M, the finer the tracking resolution. However, the overhead of the corresponding search will also be significantly greater. By default, Rio uses $M = 200$ to achieve high accuracy. However, our empirical evaluations, as shown in Fig. 24, show that we can reduce M to 50 with only a slight reduction in accuracy, but gain a 4× reduction in computation delay. With $M = 50$, each full tracking update step can be accomplished in under a second, thus enabling real-time tracking of the finger position. Hence, an interface that is built with Rio can tune M to match the desired accuracy-overhead trade-off.

4.2 Finger Tracking on a Multi Tag Array

We consider the tag array layout as illustrated in Fig. 10. Rio tracks a finger on a multi-RFID tag array with two steps. Rio first identifies the tag that the finger is touching, while accounting for mutual coupling. Once Rio determines the tag that is touched, it uses a multi-tag tracking algorithm (using neighboring tags) to continuously localize the finger during the swipe gesture.

4.2.1 ***Tag Calibration.*** As in the single tag case of §4.1.1, calibration has to be performed on the tag array only once after installation. Rio collects and normalizes the phases as the user swipes his/her finger across each tag in the array, as shown in Fig. 10. We use $p_1(x), \ldots, p_N(x)$ to refer to the normalized phases from the N tags in the array.

Algorithm 2 Rio-Multi: Touch Detection

```
procedure PHASEDIFF(w)
    s ← LINEARREGRESSION(w)
    return max{s} − min{s}
procedure TOUCHDETECT(w_1, ..., w_N, L)
    for i = 1, ..., N do
        d_i ← PHASEDIFF(w_i)
    for i = 1, ..., N do
        if i = 1 then
            m_i ← αd_i − βd_{i+1}
        else if i = N then
            m_i ← αd_i − βd_{i−1}
        else
            m_i ← αd_i − β(d_{i−1} + d_{i+1})
    i^(1) ← arg max_{i∈{1,...,N}} m_i
    return i^(1)
```

4.2.2 ***Rio-Multi Algorithm.*** **Touch Detection.** Touch detection operates on the backscatter phase from all N tags over a time window T. We use $\mathbf{w}_1, \ldots, \mathbf{w}_N$ to refer to these N vectors of phase data. Informally, Rio determines the total change in phase encountered by each tag over this time window. It then searches for the tag triple (or tag pair, in the case of the tags at either ends of the array) that best demonstrates the *inverted phase behavior* as described in §3.3: for a given tag i, the change in phase of its neighboring tags $i-1$ and $i+1$ are the inverse of its own.

Algorithm 2 shows the pseudo-code for touch detection. The PhaseDiff procedure determines the phase changes over the window of phase data. Rio smooths out the noise in the phase data by fitting the best line through the phase data using linear regression. The phase change of each tag, d_i, is the difference between the two extreme points on the line. Rio computes a weighted sum of the phase change of each tag i and its neighboring tags as $m_i = \alpha d_i - \beta(d_{i-1} + d_{i+1})$. By selecting weights α and β with opposite polarity, Rio can capture the effect of the inverse phase behavior of tag triples (or tag pairs). Empirically, we have found that the touch and tracking accuracy of Rio is best when $\alpha = 0.8$ and $\beta = 0.2$.

Touch Tracking. Once Rio has determined the specific tag that is being touched, it immediately begins reading phase data from that tag i, along with tags that are directly adjacent to it, tags $i-1$ and $i+1$ (if any). Fig. 15 illustrates how the segmental DTW search is extended to support two adjacent RFID tags. Rio conducts concurrent DTW searches on these three tags (or two tags, if i is an edge tag), using the same segment sizes for each step in the DTW search. The segment size that best matches the phase data from the three tags will indicate the new finger location.

Algorithm 3 shows the multi-tag tracking algorithm. The MaxMultiDTW procedure performs the multi-tag DTW search jointly on sets of three adjacent tags and combines the results using the weighted metric $h = \alpha g_i + \beta(g_{i-1} + g_{i+1})$ where g_i, g_{i+1} and g_{i-1} is the DTW distance of tag i, $i-1$ and $i+1$ respectively. This metric identifies segments that not only match the phase pattern in the desired tag but also the inverted phase pattern in the adjacent tags, to boost the tracking accuracy. The segment identified in the updateLocation procedure is used to update the new location of the finger during the swipe. As before, Rio runs this search-and-update procedure continuously to track the location of the finger.

Algorithm 3 Rio-Multi: Touch Tracking

```
x_0 ← 0                                              ▷ Current finger location
w_1, ..., w_N ← GETALLPHASEDATA
i_max ← TOUCHDETECT(w_1, ..., w_N, L)
procedure MINMULTIDTW(x_0, x, w_{i−1}, w_i, w_{i+1})
    g_i ← MINDTW(x_0, x, w_i, p_i)
    g_{i−1} ← MINDTW(x_0, x, w_{i−1}, p_{i−1})
    g_{i+1} ← MINDTW(x_0, x, w_{i+1}, p_{i+1})
    h ← αg_i + β(g_{i−1} + g_{i+1})
    return h
procedure UPDATELOCATION(x_0, w_{i−1}, w_i, w_{i+1})
    x_new ← arg min_{x_min≤x≤x_max} MINMULTIDTW(x_0, x, w_{i−1}, w_i, w_{i+1})
    return x_new
while TRUE do
    x_0 ← UPDATELOCATION(x_0, w_{i_max−1}, w_{i_max}, w_{i_max+1})
    w_{i_max} ← GETPHASEDATA
    w_{i_max−1} ← GETPHASEDATA
    w_{i_max+1} ← GETPHASEDATA
```

4.2.3 ***Scaling to Larger Multi-Tag Arrays.*** RFID readers achieve a constant number of reads/second (200 in case of our Impinj reader), regardless of the number of tags within the read range. Hence, when the array size is very large, the read rate per tag decreases, which reduces the fidelity of the phase data, and consequently the accuracy of both touch and gesture tracking. Rio addresses this by utilizing the PHY-layer filtering feature [36] of the RFID Class 1 Generation 2 (C1G2) protocol to read only subsections of the array at a time. After Rio-Multi detects the tag that is being touched, Rio applies the RFID filter to read up to eight tags around the tag that is touched (four on either side). The Rio-Multi touch tracking then tracks the swipe gesture on the touched tag.

5 EXTENDING RIO WITH CUSTOM DESIGNED RFID TAGS

COTS RFID tags are designed primarily for communications, and hence, the antennas are typically dipole antennas, and have sizes and shapes that are carefully tuned to match the electrical impedance of the RFID chip [21]. The limited variety in antenna designs restricts the range of user interfaces that can be built using COTS tags. In this section, we discuss Rio's potential by exploring how it can operate with custom-built RFID tags of varying shapes and sizes. This will allow the user interfaces built using our touch primitive to be better customized to the specific demands of smart spaces.

Constructing Custom RFID Tags. We extend Rio to support custom-designed RFID tags, two of which are shown in Fig. 16.

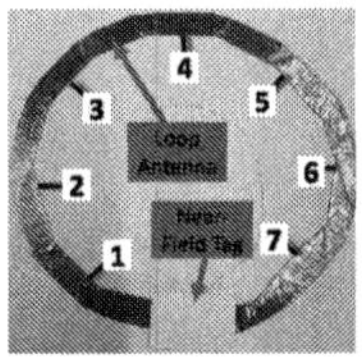

(a) Circle custom tag.

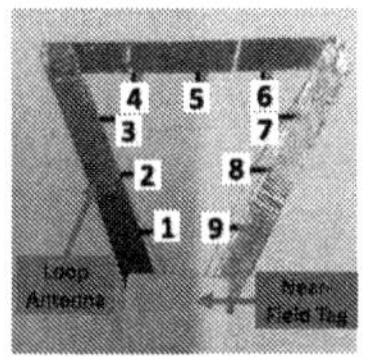

(b) Triangle custom tag.

Figure 16: Custom-designed RFID tags.

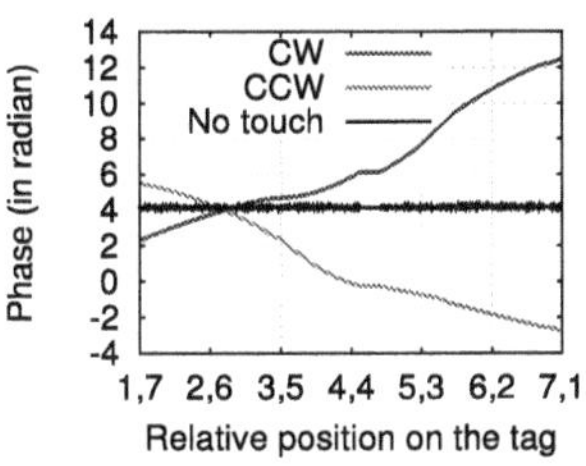

(a) Circle tag.

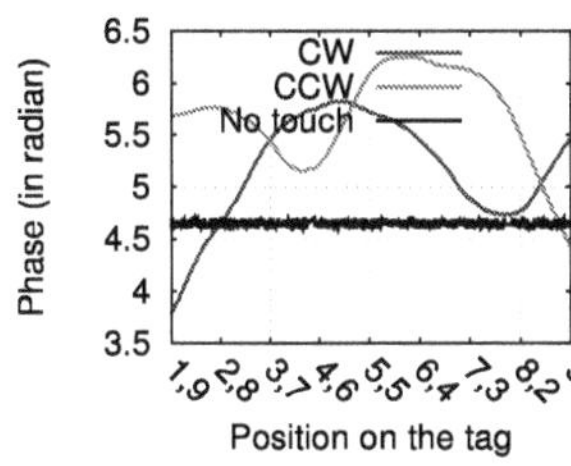

(b) Triangle tag.

Figure 17: Phase trends when a clockwise (CW) and counter-clockwise (CCW) swipe gestures are performed on the custom circle and triangle-shaped RFID tags.

The antenna of the tags are constructed using copper metal tape, arranged in shapes that can better mimic familiar control interfaces. For example, Fig. 16a shows a circle RFID antenna that resembles a round control knob. A user can swipe in either clockwise or counter-clockwise directions to adjust the music volume, or light brightness etc. Owners of the iPod Classic with the click wheel [37] will find this interface familiar. A small near-field RFID tag [38] with an adhesive side is attached to the custom-built antenna, as shown. The antenna forms an inductively coupled connection with the near-field RFID tag, and touching the antenna will result in a familiar phase change in the backscattered signal.

Antenna Design Space. The antennas shown in Fig. 16 are examples of *loop antennas* [39]. We use loop antennas because they have the advantage of being easy to construct in various shapes and sizes. Our demonstration only uses basic shapes (a circle and a triangle), but many other antenna structures such as folded dipoles [40], coil [41] and cloverleafs [42] can be used as building blocks for more complex interfaces.

In order for the antenna to operate at maximum efficiency, the antenna layout must be tuned such that its impedance matches the impedance of the RFID chip. Our custom RFID antennas are designed primarily to mimic real-world control interfaces, and are not impedance-matched to the RFID chip. However, even with this sub-optimality, our experiments show that our custom tags can be read at ranges of up to $1.5m$, which is comparable to the performance of COTS RFID tags $2.4m$.

Tracking on Custom Tags. Fig. 17 shows the phase trends when clock-wise and counter-clockwise swipes are performed on the tags (Fig. 16). Observe that the phase trends show distinctive patterns and large phase variations (similar to those seen in COTS RFID tags) that can aid in accurately locating a finger even in the presence of noise. Thus, the single tag tracking algorithm (Algorithm 1) in Rio can also be used to track touch/gesture with these custom tags.

6 RIO EVALUATION

In this section, we evaluate Rio using the setup shown in Fig. 3a. We show the performance of Rio with COTS tags, as well as custom-designed tags and highlight its robustness as a battery-free UI primitive. We also propose and evaluate two proof-of-concept applications to demonstrate the utility of Rio.

The RFID setup operates as before, where the Impinj R420 reader continuously queries the tags in range (at ~200 reads/second), and records the RF phase of all RFID responses. We thus have time series of phase readings for each individual tag. The camera is time synchronized with the reader control software, so that the video recording is time synchronized with the RF phase measurements. This video footage is used to determine the tracking accuracy.

COTS Tag Layout. We demonstrate the swipe tracking accuracy of Rio using the COTS tags. We use two different tag layouts: a single isolated tag, and a multi-tag array, as shown in Fig. 10. This tag layout has two parameters: Tag angle, and distance. *Tag angle:* Fig. 3a shows a setup where the tags are place flat on a surface, which is parallel to the plane of the RFID reader antenna. We tilt the reader antenna by elevating one edge of the antenna to vary the angle of the tag(s) w.r.t. the reader antenna. *Tag distance:* We also elevate the entire tag(s) shown in Fig. 3a to vary the distance of the tags to the reader antenna. Experiment result with different tag angle and distance serve to demonstrate the performance of Rio under real-world conditions, when the tag is not perfectly aligned with the antenna.

Custom Tags. We also evaluate Rio on custom tags, as described in §5. These custom tags are arranged $50cm$ away from, and parallel to the surface of the reader antenna.

Accuracy Measure. We use OpenCV [43] on the time-synchronized video footage to visually track the finger during the swipe and touch gestures. At any point in time, we compare the location of the finger as indicated by Rio to its actual finger position as shown by the camera. The tracking accuracy of Rio is reflected in the offset distance (in mm) between these two measurements (Rio and camera).

6.1 RIO with COTS Tags

6.1.1 ***Touch Detection.*** **COTS Single Tag.** For single-tag detection, we use the phase change threshold $C = 0.9$ as described in §4.1.2. With this threshold, Rio achieves perfect touch detection, even under varying tag angles (from 0 to 60°, w.r.t. the reader antenna surface) and tag distances (up to $2.4m$ from the reader).

COTS Multi-Tag Array. Fig. 20 shows the detection accuracy when we touch each tag in an array of eight tags. Observe that Rio correctly detects the tag being touched more than 92% of the time. Touch events on tags closer to either ends of the array are even correctly detected 100% of the time. Hence, *Rio provides close to perfect tag detection under real-world conditions, with RFID tags deployed in positions within an envisioned smart space.* We expect this accuracy to increase if multiple receive antennas, together with spatial diversity processing (*i.e.*, a multi-static setup) is used.

6.1.2 ***Touch Tracking.*** **COTS Single Tag.** Fig. 18 shows the tracking accuracy distribution of a swipe gesture when the tags are parallel to and at a distance of $50cm$ from the reader antenna. The swipe is performed at three different speed ranges: slow (less than $10mm/s$), medium (10 to $15mm/s$) and fast (quicker than $15mm/s$).

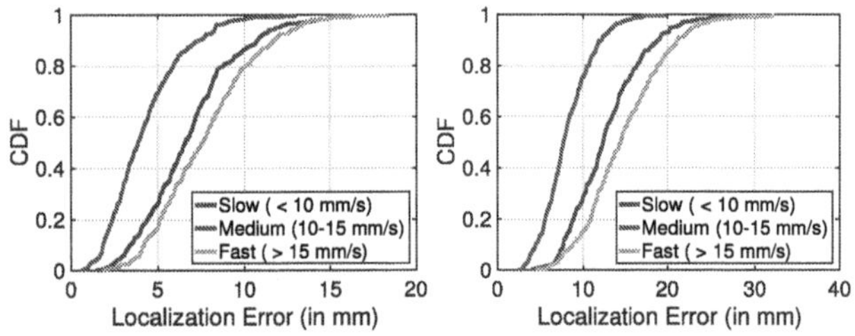

(a) RIO-SINGLE. (b) RIO-MULTI.

Figure 18: RIO tracking accuracy with swipes of different speeds.

(a) Smartrac Monza R5 RFID tag (Tag1). (b) Smartrac Monza R6 G2IL RFID tag (Tag2).

(c) Alien-9640, Higgs-3 short-dipole paper tag (Tag3). (d) Alien-9730, Higgs-4 short-dipole paper tag (Tag4).

Figure 19: RIO is tested on four other tag types.

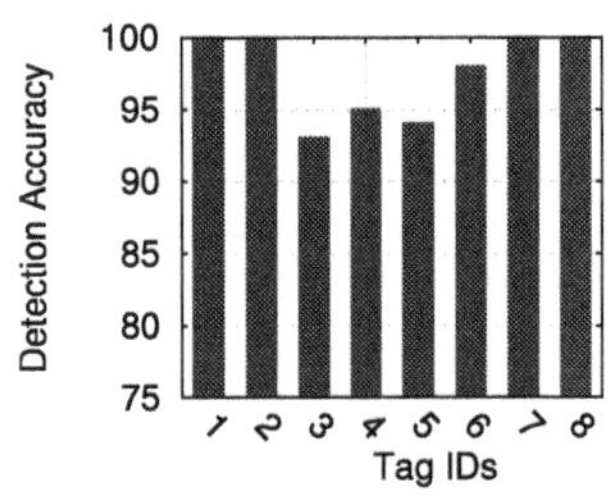

Figure 20: Touch detection on multi-tag array.

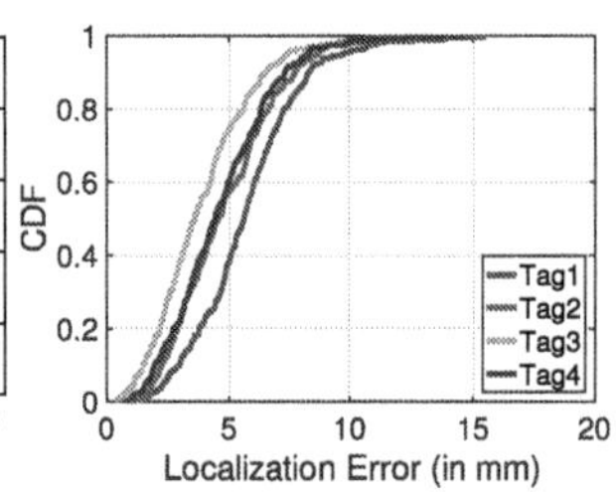

Figure 21: Swipe error distribution for 4 other tags(Tag1, Tag2, Tag3, Tag4).

A swipe at each speed range is repeated 100 times on each tag to obtain this distribution. Recall that the DTW window of $0.5T$ to T is chosen for swiping speeds of up to $15mm/s$. Observe that the median location error at medium speed over a single tag, as shown in Fig. 18a, is $3mm$. Given that the tag is $80mm$ in length, this median error is a mere 3.8% of the tag length. The median error with slow and fast swipes is greater, at 7 and $8mm$ respectively, but is still within 10% of the tag length.

This good single tag performance is not limited to our specific RFID tag. To demonstrate this fact, we perform the medium-speed swipe gesture over four other types of tags with different antenna designs and RFID chips, as shown in Fig. 19. Fig. 21 shows that the median tracking error lies between 3 and $6mm$, less than 10% of the tag length.

COTS Multi-Tag Array. Fig. 18b shows the tracking error distribution in an array of eight (8) tags. These results assume perfect touch detection accuracy. Observe that the results show similar behavior to the single-tag case, where the medium speed swipe has this lowest median error of $7mm$, while the slow and fast speeds have median errors of 12 and $14mm$. Hence, even in the presence

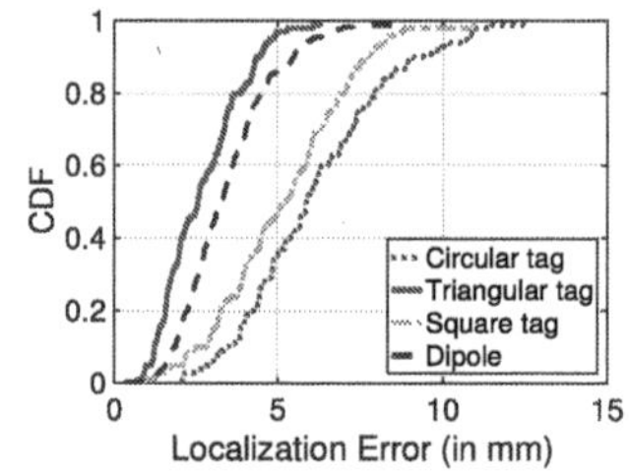

Figure 22: Tracking error distribution of custom tags.

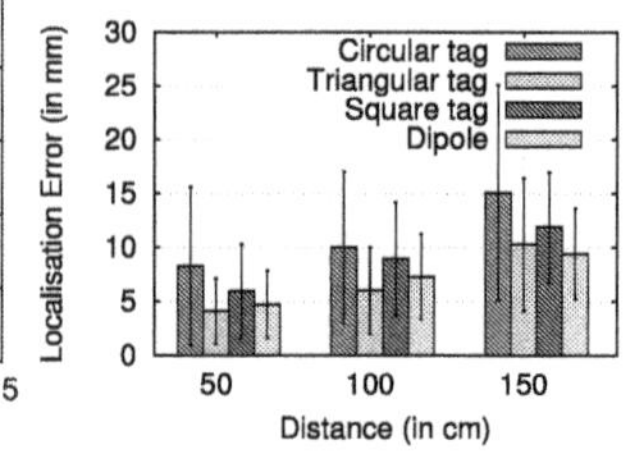

Figure 23: Tracking accuracy of custom tags at different distances from reader.

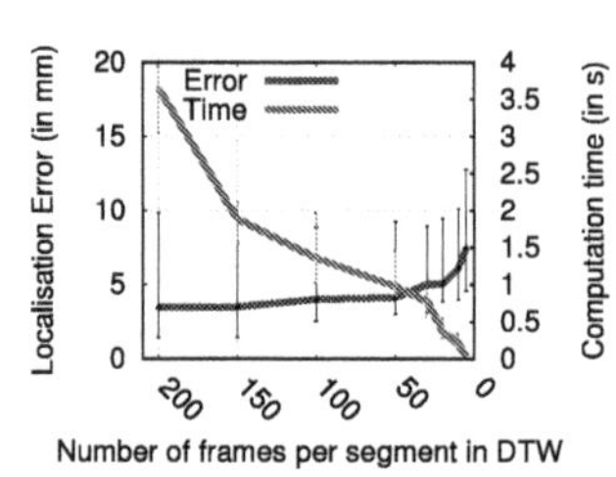

Figure 24: Tracking resolution vs computational overhead.

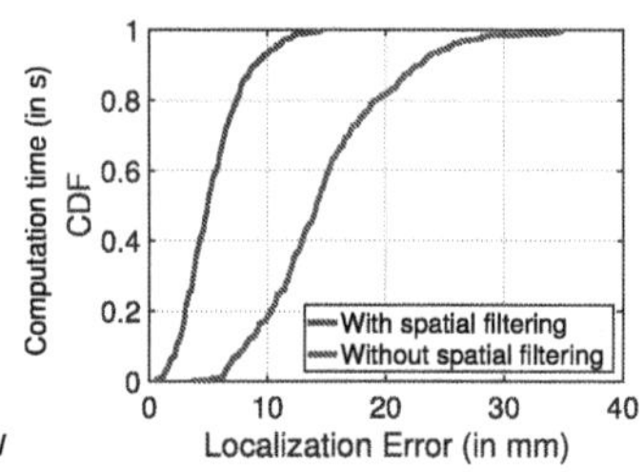

Figure 25: Swipe tracking accuracy over an array of 30 RFID tags.

of mutual coupling effects, RIO can localize the finger to within 10% of the overall tag length. The experiments on both the single and multi-tag arrays demonstrate that *RIO can accurately track the location of a finger during a swipe gesture.*

6.2 RIO with Custom-Designed Tags

We evaluate RIO with four different types of custom tags: the circle and triangle, as shown earlier in Fig. 16, along with a square and dipole that are constructed with the same techniques. We place the smart tags $50cm$ away from the reader antenna, and perform a medium-speed swipe gesture. Fig. 22 shows the tracking accuracy distribution when a swipe a performed on each of these four custom tags. Observe that the median tracking error of all four tags is less than $8mm$, which is comparable to that obtained using COTS RFID tags. Fig. 23 shows the localization error distribution when the custom tags are placed at distances up to $1.5m$ away from the reader. Observe that even at this distance, the median tracking error is no more than $15mm$, or less than 19% of the tag length. Hence, *RIO readily supports custom designed RFID tags that are purpose built for specific smart spaces.*

6.3 RIO is a Robust Touch-Sensing Primitive

6.3.1 ***Tracking Resolution vs Computation Overhead.*** RIO trades off finger tracking resolution and computational overhead through the number of segments, M, used for each location update (procedure UPDATELOCATION in Algorithm 1) and Algorithm 3. For RIO, we run the data processing and pattern recognition module at an Intel desktop with a 2.93GHz Core i7 CPU and 16GB of memory, running Ubuntu 14.04 and JDK8.

Fig. 24 shows this trade-off for several values of M. Observe that M can be chosen to be as low as 50 with only a slight increase

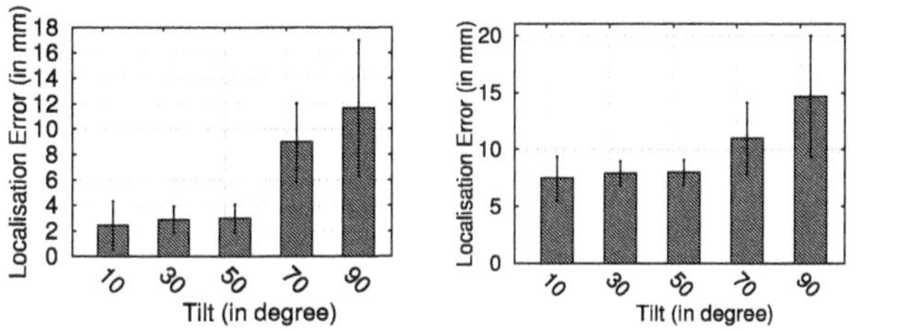

(a) Single tag. (b) Multi-tag array.

Figure 26: Tracking accuracy with varying tilt angle of the tag with respect to antenna.

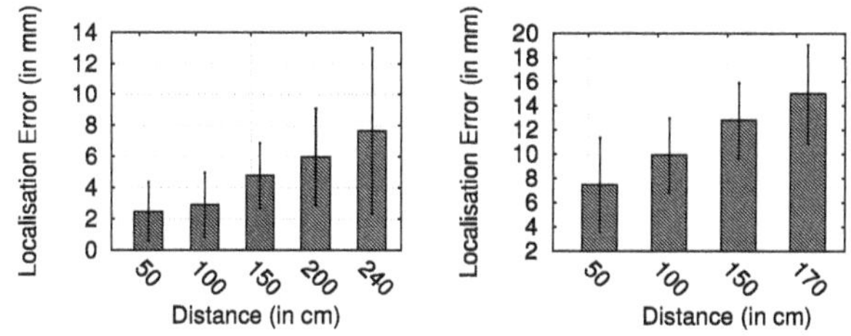

(a) Single tag. (b) Multi-tag array.

Figure 27: Tracking accuracy with varying distance of the tag from the reader antenna.

in median error (from 3 to 4*mm*), while achieving an almost 4× reduction in computation time. At this chosen level of accuracy, RIO has a touch location tracking response time of one second. This computational overhead applies to both single and multi-tag setups. We note that these latencies relates to *motion tracking* only. A simple single-point touch-event can be detected within several milliseconds.

6.3.2 ***RIO on Large Multi-RFID Tag Arrays.*** We evaluate the performance of Rio-Multi with 30 RFID tags, using the same experimental setup as that in §6. Fig 25 shows the tracking accuracy distribution of Rio with and without RFID spatial filtering. Observe that the median tracking error reduces from 14*mm* when no spatial filtering is used, to 6*mm* when filtering is enabled.Due to the large number of tags, when no filtering is used, there are time windows of *T* seconds when only a small number of phase data is obtained from the tag being touched. This results in poor tracking accuracy. However, no such abnormalities are observed when PHY-layer tag filtering is used.

6.3.3 ***Robust Tracking under Varying Tag Tilt Angles.*** Fig. 26 shows the tracking accuracy of a medium speed swipe when the tags are placed at varying angles w.r.t. the plane of the RFID reader antenna. Observe that in both the single and multi-tag array, Rio can track the finger location with a very small error (at 3 and 8*mm* respectively) when the tag is within 50°, of the reader antenna. This is because the RFID tags have linearly polarized directional antennas that focus the backscatter signals within a 120°, beam-width [44]. This result shows that *battery-free touch or gesture sensing is robust over a large range of incident angles to the RFID reader.* As the tilt angle increases to greater than half the beam-width and the reader antenna moves outside the beam edge of the RFID tag, the tracking accuracy decreases. Note that changing the relative tilt angle of the tag is analogous to the change of the relative angle of the RFID antenna, and will thus yield similar accuracy results.

6.3.4 ***Robust Tracking at Varying Distances from Reader.*** Fig. 27 shows the tracking accuracy when a medium-speed swipe is performed on a tag that is at varying distances from the RFID reader. Observe that in the single tag case, a low error of no more than 8*mm* (10% error) is achievable up to 2*m* from the reader. This demonstrates that *battery-free touch/swipe tracking is robust at varying distances from the reader.* However, if we change multiple factors simultaneously (e.g. reading angle, tag tilt, blockage etc.) or we change one of the impacting factor drastically (e.g. sudden increase of people in the room or introducing a new blockage between the

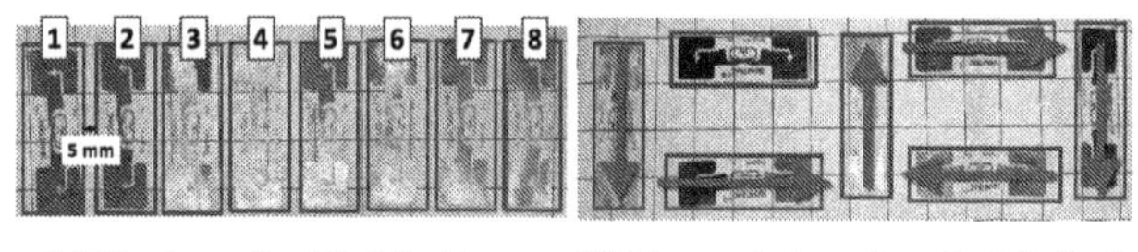

(a) Keyboard with 8 buttons. (b) Numeric touchpad with digit "6" traced (shown rotated 90°).

Figure 28: Example applications.

tag and the antenna), we need to re-calibrate RIO to create the reference phase pattern to achieve mm-level accuracy.

6.4 Proof-of-Concept Applications

Rio is a touch sensing primitive for battery-free UI design. In this section, we describe and evaluate two proof-of-concept UI applications that are built using Rio.

Battery-Free Keyboard. A keyboard directly uses the touch-detection capability of RIO in a multi-tag environment. We use Rio to develop an 8-key musical keyboard (as shown in Fig. 28a), along with an accompanying GUI. We can touch multiple keys simultaneously in this musical keyboard application. Fig. 29a shows the false positive (tag is mistakenly detected as being touched) and false negative (a touch event on a tag is missed). Observe that our simple threshold based touch detection algorithm achieves high accuracy in this battery-free key detection system, with a total false positive and negative rates below 10%.

2D Numeric Touchpad. We have constructed a 2D numeric touch-pad, as shown in Fig. 28b, using 7 COTS RFID tags. Each numeric digits is formed by tracing its shape over the RFID tags. Fig. 28b illustrates the outline of the number "6" (shown rotated 90°) traced on the touch-pad.

Fig. 29b shows the accuracy results when numbers 0 to 9 are drawn on this touch-pad. Each number is repeated 50 times, and the false positive and negative rates are reported here. Observe that all individual numbers can be detected with total errors of less than 15%. This shows that RIO with COTS tags can be used to design a general-purpose UI.

7 POINTS OF DISCUSSION

Naturally there is much room for further work and possible improvements. We discuss a few points here.

Cost of Rio system: Rio can support multiple tags simultaneously for single point touch tracking using single antenna and single RFID reader. Currently, this combined unit with one antenna, one RFID reader, costs approximately $1600. We expect that

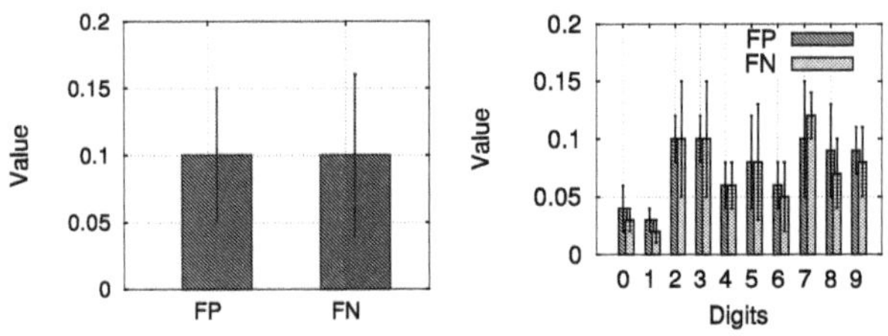

(a) Key press detection. (b) Numeric digit sensing.

Figure 29: False positive and negative rates for applications.

dedicated RFID sensing platforms built upon lower-cost hardware (e.g. ThinkMagic reader hardware [45]), together with low-cost off-the-shelf tags will eventually be available to consumers.

Comparison with touch-based sensing: Capacitive touch screens [46] found in smartphones, tablets, laptops and the recently introduced PixelSense [47] offer a readily-available multi-touch interface. However, smart spaces demand low-cost, low-powered, flexible touch interfaces that can be readily integrated into existing off-the-self items. Current capacitive touch screen technology cannot be easily and cost-effectively integrated into our envisioned smart spaces. We note that Rio offers a touch primitive to enable smart spaces and does not replace capacitive touch technology in all applications. Rather, we expect that Rio will integrate with and extend existing capacitive touch interfaces. For example, while Rio detects our direct interactions with the environment, these interactions can be managed through capacitive touch interfaces on our mobile devices.

Multi-touch tracking: Rio is basically a single touch-tracking system and in near future, we plan to extend it to multi-touch tracking interface. This extension will broaden Rio's potential use-cases. However, for this, we have to model more complex mutual coupling phenomenon to provide accurate impedance tracking.

Impact of different blockage scenarios: Although we have shown in Fig. 6 that the phase pattern maintains its shape even in the presence of obstacles like door or wall, the experiments are not exhaustive for different static or dynamic blockage scenarios. In near future, we plan to conduct more experiments in different types of blockage scenarios and different environment conditions to better understand the performance of Rio.

8 RELATED WORK

The core idea of using RFID tag as an input mechanism is not new. Researchers have used either tags with micro-controllers [48] or passive tags in a COTS or custom setup. In the following, we explore main research trends.

RFID-based gesture and activity recognition: RFID tags are used to recognize gestures or activities based on distinct phase and RSS signatures. Researchers [7, 49] have implemented a matrix of RFID tags with multiple antennas to detect gestures. Recently, a few systems [6, 50–52] have used machine learning to mine the phase data for predicting fine-grained exercising or shopping activities. Rio is orthogonal to such works as it targets fine-grained swipe tracking over a smaller area. In fact, Rio can be deployed in conjunction with such activity recognition techniques for a comprehensive IoT environment.

RFID-based fine-grained tracking: Wang *et al.* [10] track tag movement with 8cm median error by using customized 8 antennas. Moreover, *PolarDraw* [53] uses two linearly polarized COTS antennas and exploits polarization property to track a RFID tag. However, *Tagball* [54] employs extended kalman filtering (EKF) [55] technique on collected phase information to create a 3D mouse with 12 tagged object. Furthermore, *Tagyro* [19] exploits phase information of multiple tags to get the orientation of the object with a median error of 4 degrees. Rio is an evolution of such systems into one that enables robust fine-grained tracking on 2D surfaces using only a single antenna.

RFID-based sensing: Marocco *et al.* [56] observes that the change in tag signal RSS and phase due to change in tag antenna performance is related to the change in the environment. This observation underpins RFID tag designs used to measure temperature [57, 58], relative humidity [59–61], and gas presence [62]. Smith *et al.* [63] proposes building switches by connecting ICs with different IDs to the tag antennas. The authors in [12] design a custom backscatter circuit to use the tag antenna as both an RF antenna and a low-frequency capacitance induced electric field sensor simultaneously. This custom circuit enables battery-free detection of singular touch events. Rio is a further development of these works and shows that fine-grained touch and swipe tracking is feasible even with off-the-shelf hardware through the use of our novel impedance tracking techniques.

RFID-based UI: Early works [64, 65] use active tags as power-free buttons. Li *et al.* [8] use a single antenna to enable motion detection in their object interaction detection system called ID-Sense. It uses a Support Vector Machine (SVM) with a Radial Basis Function (RBF) kernel to detect five classes of tag interactions using PHY-layer features (RF Phase, RSSI, read rate, etc.). The SVM is trained using 600 interaction instances and achieves up to 97% accuracy. PaperID [9] is a similar work that uses supervised machine learning to detect 5 types of on-tag and free-air interactions with custom-designed RFID tags. It achieves a 94% accuracy (testing done by 5 users) by using the trained model from 150 instances at different locations. Rio improves upon these works by achieving high accuracy (4% error rate) using off-the-shelf hardware and an extremely low training overhead (only 4 swipe instances required).

9 CONCLUSION AND FUTURE WORK

In this paper, we develop and evaluate Rio, a touch and gesture UI primitive for smart spaces. Rio enables fine-grained touch tracking using COTS RFID reader and tags, and low-overhead training and installation. Rio is designed to be easily embedded into existing environments to turn them into smart spaces. Our evaluations demonstrate that Rio is a robust touch and gesture sensing primitive under various real-world situations. Rio also supports custom-designed RFID tags for a fully integrated UI design and our proof-of-concept applications highlight possible interfaces that can be built with Rio.

Rio is a first step towards a novel battery-free interface design, and presents many opportunities for future exploration into this space. Some extensions of our work that include two-dimensional gesture tracking, multi-touch tracking, tracking in different environment conditions (i.e. rain, snow etc.) and custom interfaces built using different materials. These and more are left to future work.

REFERENCES

[1] Q. Pu, S. Gupta, S. Gollakota, and S. Patel, "Whole-home gesture recognition using wireless signals," in *Proceedings of the 19th Annual International Conference on Mobile Computing & Networking*, MobiCom '13, (New York, NY, USA), pp. 27–38, ACM, 2013.

[2] L. Sun, S. Sen, D. Koutsonikolas, and K.-H. Kim, "Widraw: Enabling hands-free drawing in the air on commodity wifi devices," in *Proceedings of the 21st Annual International Conference on Mobile Computing and Networking*, MobiCom '15, (New York, NY, USA), pp. 77–89, ACM, 2015.

[3] S. Yun, Y.-C. Chen, and L. Qiu, "Turning a mobile device into a mouse in the air," in *Proceedings of the 13th Annual International Conference on Mobile Systems, Applications, and Services*, MobiSys '15, (New York, NY, USA), pp. 15–29, ACM, 2015.

[4] S. Kim, W. Choi, W. Rim, Y. Chun, H. Shim, H. Kwon, J. Kim, I. Kee, S. Kim, S. Lee, and J. Park, "A highly sensitive capacitive touch sensor integrated on a thin-film-encapsulated active-matrix oled for ultrathin displays," *IEEE Transactions on Electron Devices*, vol. 58, pp. 3609–3615, Oct 2011.

[5] M. Kranz, P. Holleis, and A. Schmidt, "Embedded interaction: Interacting with the internet of things," *IEEE Internet Computing*, vol. 14, pp. 46–53, March 2010.

[6] H. Ding, L. Shangguan, Z. Yang, J. Han, Z. Zhou, P. Yang, W. Xi, and J. Zhao, "Femo: A platform for free-weight exercise monitoring with rfids," in *Proceedings of the 13th ACM Conference on Embedded Networked Sensor Systems*, SenSys '15, (New York, NY, USA), pp. 141–154, ACM, 2015.

[7] Y. Zou, J. Xiao, J. Han, K. Wu, Y. Li, and L. M. Ni, "Grfid: A device-free gesture recognition system using cots rfid device," *IEEE Transactions on Mobile Computing*, vol. PP, no. 99, pp. 1–1, 2016.

[8] H. Li, C. Ye, and A. P. Sample, "Idsense: A human object interaction detection system based on passive uhf rfid," in *Proceedings of the 33rd Annual ACM Conference on Human Factors in Computing Systems*, CHI '15, (New York, NY, USA), pp. 2555–2564, ACM, 2015.

[9] H. Li, E. Brockmeyer, E. J. Carter, J. Fromm, S. E. Hudson, S. N. Patel, and A. Sample, "Paperid: A technique for drawing functional battery-free wireless interfaces on paper," in *Proceedings of the 2016 CHI Conference on Human Factors in Computing Systems*, CHI '16, (New York, NY, USA), pp. 5885–5896, ACM, 2016.

[10] J. Wang, D. Vasisht, and D. Katabi, "Rf-idraw: Virtual touch screen in the air using rf signals," in *Proceedings of the 2014 ACM Conference on SIGCOMM*, SIGCOMM '14, (New York, NY, USA), pp. 235–246, ACM, 2014.

[11] L. Yang, Y. Chen, X.-Y. Li, C. Xiao, M. Li, and Y. Liu, "Tagoram: Real-time tracking of mobile rfid tags to high precision using cots devices," in *Proceedings of the 20th Annual International Conference on Mobile Computing and Networking*, MobiCom '14, (New York, NY, USA), pp. 237–248, ACM, 2014.

[12] A. P. Sample, D. J. Yeager, and J. R. Smith, "A capacitive touch interface for passive rfid tags," in *2009 IEEE International Conference on RFID*, pp. 103–109, April 2009.

[13] K. Aga, H. Tarao, and S. Urushihara, "Calculation of human body resistance at power frequency using anatomic numerical human model," *Energy Procedia*, vol. 89, pp. 401 - 407, 2016. CoE on Sustainable Energy System (Thai-Japan), Faculty of Engineering, Rajamangala University of Technology Thanyaburi (RMUTT), Thailand.

[14] N. Jonassen, "Human body capacitance: static or dynamic concept? [esd]," in *Electrical Overstress/ Electrostatic Discharge Symposium Proceedings. 1998 (Cat. No.98TH8347)*, pp. 111–117, Oct 1998.

[15] "Smartrac dogbone rfid paper tag (monza 4d)." https://www.atlasrfidstore.com/smartrac-dogbone-rfid-paper-tag-monza-4d/a, 2017. [Online] Last Accessed : 07/12/2017.

[16] Y. Tanaka, Y. Umeda, O. Takyu, M. Nakayama, and K. Kodama, "Change of read range for uhf passive rfid tags in close proximity," in *2009 IEEE International Conference on RFID*, pp. 338–345, April 2009.

[17] S. E. Asl, M. T. Ghasr, M. Zawodniok, and K. E. Robinson, "Preliminary study of mutual coupling effect on a passive rfid antenna array," in *2013 IEEE International Instrumentation and Measurement Technology Conference (I2MTC)*, pp. 138–141, May 2013.

[18] P. V. Nikitin and K. V. S. Rao, "Theory and measurement of backscattering from rfid tags," *IEEE Antennas and Propagation Magazine*, vol. 48, pp. 212–218, Dec 2006.

[19] T. Wei and X. Zhang, "Gyro in the air: Tracking 3d orientation of batteryless internet-of-things," in *Proceedings of the 22Nd Annual International Conference on Mobile Computing and Networking*, MobiCom '16, (New York, NY, USA), pp. 55–68, ACM, 2016.

[20] K. V. S. Rao, P. V. Nikitin, and S. F. Lam, "Impedance matching concepts in rfid transponder design," in *Proceedings of the Fourth IEEE Workshop on Automatic Identification Advanced Technologies*, AUTOID '05, (Washington, DC, USA), pp. 39–42, IEEE Computer Society, 2005.

[21] P. V. Nikitin, K. V. S. Rao, S. Member, and S. Lazar, "An overview of near field uhf rfid," 2007.

[22] "Impinj speedway uhf rfid reader." https://www.impinj.com/products/readers/, 2017. [Online] Last Accessed : 07/12/2017.

[23] "Epc/rfid llrp standards." http://www.gs1.org/epcrfid/epc-rfid-llrp/1-1-0, 2017. [Online] Last Accessed : 07/12/2017.

[24] "Octane sdk for impinj." https://support.impinj.com/hc/en-us/articles/202755268-Octane-SDK, 2017. [Online] Last Accessed : 07/12/2017.

[25] "Speedway revolution reader application note low level." http://bit.ly/2geiFVA, 2017. [Online] Last Accessed : 07/12/2017.

[26] N. Cho, J. Yoo, S. J. Song, J. Lee, S. Jeon, and H. J. Yoo, "The human body characteristics as a signal transmission medium for intrabody communication," *IEEE Transactions on Microwave Theory and Techniques*, vol. 55, pp. 1080–1086, May 2007.

[27] L. Baxter, *Capacitive Sensors: Design and Applications*. IEEE Press Series on Electronics Technology, John Wiley & Sons, 1996.

[28] R. A. A. Rodrigues, E. C. Gurjão, and F. M. de Assis, "Radar cross-section and electric field analysis of backscattering elements of chipless rfid tag," in *2014 IEEE RFID Technology and Applications Conference (RFID-TA)*, pp. 103–108, Sept 2014.

[29] B. D. Braaten, G. J. Owen, and R. M. Nelson, "Design of space-filling antennas for passive uhf rfid tags," INTECH Open Access Publisher, 2010.

[30] W. Stutzman and G. Thiele, *Antenna Theory and Design*. Antenna Theory and Design, Wiley, 2012.

[31] "Array Solutions VNA-UHF - Two Port Vector Network Analyzer, 5 kHz to 1200 MHz." https://www.arraysolutions.com/vna-uhf, 2017. [Online] Last Accessed : 07/12/2017.

[32] "Mutual coupling in antenna arrays." https://nus.edu/2o5J8IN, 2017. [Online] Last Accessed : 07/12/2017.

[33] A. Park and J. R. Glass, "Towards unsupervised pattern discovery in speech," in *IEEE Workshop on Automatic Speech Recognition and Understanding*, pp. 53–58, Nov 2005.

[34] Y. Zhang and J. R. Glass, "Unsupervised spoken keyword spotting via segmental dtw on gaussian posteriorgrams.," in *ASRU*, pp. 398–403, IEEE, 2009.

[35] A. S. Park and J. R. Glass, "Unsupervised pattern discovery in speech," *IEEE Transactions on Audio, Speech, and Language Processing*, vol. 16, pp. 186–197, Jan 2008.

[36] "Specification for rfid air interface epc radio-frequency identity protocols class-1 generation-2 uhf rfid protocol for communications at 860 mhz–960 mhz." http://bit.ly/2gem5Ie, 2017. [Online] Last Accessed : 07/12/2017.

[37] "ipod click wheel." http://bit.ly/2gfTW2z, 2017. [Online] Last Accessed : 07/12/2017.

[38] "Alien 9613 higgs-3 loop near-field rfid tag." https://www.atlasrfidstore.com/alien-sit-rfid-white-wet-inlay-aln-9613-higgs-3/, 2017. [Online] Last Accessed : 07/12/2017.

[39] K. V. S. Rao, P. V. Nikitin, and S. F. Lam, "Antenna design for uhf rfid tags: a review and a practical application," *IEEE Transactions on Antennas and Propagation*, vol. 53, pp. 3870–3876, Dec 2005.

[40] N. Ma and L. Chen, "The design of folded dipole antenna," in *2008 4th International Conference on Wireless Communications, Networking and Mobile Computing*, pp. 1–3, Oct 2008.

[41] "Rfid coil antennas." http://bit.ly/2h8wLZI, 2017. [Online] Last Accessed : 07/12/2017.

[42] M. Deng and D. Campbell-Wilson, "The cloverleaf antenna: A compact wide-bandwidth dual-polarization feed for chime," in *2014 16th International Symposium on Antenna Technology and Applied Electromagnetics (ANTEM)*, pp. 1–2, July 2014.

[43] "Opencv python 3.1.0.3." https://pypi.python.org/pypi/opencv-python, 2017. [Online] Last Accessed : 07/12/2017.

[44] "Monza r6 datasheet." https://support.impinj.com/hc/en-us/articles/202765328-Monza-R6-Product-Datasheet, 2017. [Online] Last Accessed : 07/12/2017.

[45] "Thinkmagic rfid redaer." http://bit.ly/2tZeZ3w, 2017. [Online] Last Accessed : 07/12/2017.

[46] L. Du, "An overview of mobile capacitive touch technologies trends," *CoRR*, vol. abs/1612.08227, 2016.

[47] "Microsoft pixelsense - higher than 4k resolution." https://www.microsoft.com/en-us/surface/devices/surface-studio/innovation, 2017. [Online] Last Accessed : 07/12/2017.

[48] A. P. Sample, D. J. Yeager, P. S. Powledge, and J. R. Smith, "Design of a passively-powered, programmable sensing platform for uhf rfid systems," in *2007 IEEE International Conference on RFID*, pp. 149–156, March 2007.

[49] P. Asadzadeh, L. Kulik, and E. Tanin, "Gesture recognition using rfid technology," *Personal Ubiquitous Comput.*, vol. 16, pp. 225–234, Mar. 2012.

[50] S. Amendola, L. Bianchi, and G. Marrocco, "Movement detection of human body segments: Passive radio-frequency identification and machine-learning technologies.," *IEEE Antennas and Propagation Magazine*, vol. 57, pp. 23–37, June 2015.

[51] J. Han, H. Ding, C. Qian, W. Xi, Z. Wang, Z. Jiang, L. Shangguan, and J. Zhao, "Cbid: A customer behavior identification system using passive tags," *IEEE/ACM Transactions on Networking*, vol. 24, pp. 2885–2898, Oct 2016.

[52] L. Shangguan, Z. Zhou, X. Zheng, L. Yang, Y. Liu, and J. Han, "Shopminer: Mining customer shopping behavior in physical clothing stores with cots rfid devices," in *Proceedings of the 13th ACM Conference on Embedded Networked Sensor Systems*, SenSys '15, (New York, NY, USA), pp. 113–125, ACM, 2015.

[53] L. Shangguan and K. Jamieson, "Leveraging electromagnetic polarization in a two-antenna motion tracking system," *ACM CoNext*, 2016.

[54] Q. Lin, L. Yang, Y. Sun, T. Liu, X. Y. Li, and Y. Liu, "Beyond one-dollar mouse: A battery-free device for 3d human-computer interaction via rfid tags," in *2015 IEEE Conference on Computer Communications (INFOCOM)*, pp. 1661–1669, April 2015.

[55] S. Sarkka, V. V. Viikari, M. Huusko, and K. Jaakkola, "Phase-based uhf rfid tracking with nonlinear kalman filtering and smoothing," *IEEE Sensors Journal*, vol. 12, pp. 904–910, May 2012.

[56] G. Marrocco and F. Amato, "Self-sensing passive rfid: From theory to tag design and experimentation," in *2009 European Microwave Conference (EuMC)*, pp. 001–004, Sept 2009.

[57] S. Amendola, G. Bovesecchi, A. Palombi, P. Coppa, and G. Marrocco, "Design, calibration and experimentation of an epidermal rfid sensor for remote temperature monitoring," *IEEE Sensors Journal*, vol. 16, pp. 7250–7257, Oct 2016.

[58] S. Milici, S. Amendola, A. Bianco, and G. Marrocco, "Epidermal rfid passive sensor for body temperature measurements," in *2014 IEEE RFID Technology and Applications Conference (RFID-TA)*, pp. 140–144, Sept 2014.

[59] R. Bhattacharyya, C. Floerkemeier, and S. Sarma, "Rfid tag antenna based sensing: Does your beverage glass need a refill?," in *2010 IEEE International Conference on RFID (IEEE RFID 2010)*, pp. 126–133, April 2010.

[60] S. Manzari, A. Catini, G. Pomarico, C. D. Natale, and G. Marrocco, "Development of an uhf rfid chemical sensor array for battery-less ambient sensing," *IEEE Sensors Journal*, vol. 14, pp. 3616–3623, Oct 2014.

[61] S. Manzari, C. Occhiuzzi, S. Nawale, A. Catini, C. D. Natale, and G. Marrocco, "Humidity sensing by polymer-loaded uhf rfid antennas," *IEEE Sensors Journal*, vol. 12, pp. 2851–2858, Sept 2012.

[62] C. Occhiuzzi, A. Rida, G. Marrocco, and M. Tentzeris, "Rfid passive gas sensor integrating carbon nanotubes," *IEEE Transactions on Microwave Theory and Techniques*, vol. 59, pp. 2674–2684, Oct 2011.

[63] M. Philipose, J. R. Smith, B. Jiang, A. Mamishev, S. Roy, and K. Sundara-Rajan, "Battery-free wireless identification and sensing," *IEEE Pervasive Computing*, vol. 4, pp. 37–45, Jan 2005.

[64] D. Avrahami and S. E. Hudson, "Forming interactivity: A tool for rapid prototyping of physical interactive products," in *Proceedings of the 4th Conference on Designing Interactive Systems: Processes, Practices, Methods, and Techniques*, 2002.

[65] N. Marquardt, A. S. Taylor, N. Villar, and S. Greenberg, "Rethinking rfid: Awareness and control for interaction with rfid systems," in *Proceedings of the SIGCHI Conference on Human Factors in Computing Systems*, CHI '10, (New York, NY, USA), pp. 2307–2316, ACM, 2010.

FlipTracer: Practical Parallel Decoding for Backscatter Communication

Meng Jin
School of Information and Technology, Northwest University
mengj@stumail.nwu.edu.cn

Yuan He
School of Software and TNLIST, Tsinghua University
heyuan@tsinghua.edu.cn

Xin Meng
School of Information and Technology, Northwest University
mengxin@stumail.nwu.edu.cn

Yilun Zheng
School of Software and TNLIST, Tsinghua University
zhengyl15@mails.tsinghua.edu.cn

Dingyi Fang
School of Information and Technology, Northwest University
dyf@nwu.edu.cn

Xiaojiang Chen
School of Information and Technology, Northwest University
xjchen@nwu.edu.cn

ABSTRACT

With parallel decoding for backscatter communication, tags are allowed to transmit concurrently and more efficiently. Existing parallel decoding mechanisms, however, assume that signals of the tags are highly stable, and hence may not perform optimally in the naturally dynamic backscatter systems. This paper introduces FlipTracer, a practical system that achieves highly reliable parallel decoding even in hostile channel conditions. FlipTracer is designed with a key insight: although the collided signal is time-varying and irregular, transitions between signals' combined states follow highly stable probabilities, which offers important clues for identifying the collided signals, and provides us with an opportunity to decode the collided signals without relying on stable signals. Motivated by this observation, we propose a graphical model, called one-flip-graph (OFG), to capture the transition pattern of collided signals, and design a reliable approach to construct the OFG in a manner robust to the diversity in backscatter systems. Then FlipTracer can resolve the collided signals by tracking the OFG. We have implemented FlipTracer and evaluated its performance with extensive experiments across a wide variety of scenarios. Our experimental results have shown that FlipTracer achieves a maximum aggregated throughput that approaches 2 Mbps, which is 6× higher than the state-of-the-art.

CCS CONCEPTS

• **Networks** → *Network architectures*; *Wireless access networks*;

KEYWORDS

Backscatter; Wireless; Parallel Transmission

MobiCom '17, October 16–20, 2017, Snowbird, UT, USA

ACM ISBN 978-1-4503-4916-1/17/10...$15.00
https://doi.org/10.1145/3117811.3117828

1 INTRODUCTION

Backscatter provides the benefits of energy harvesting and low-power communication, making it attractive to a broad class of applications [16, 17, 20–23]. These applications, such as warehouse inventories, object tracking, and industry surveillance, involve large volumes of data carried by a large number of deployed tags. Therefore, how to fully utilize the channels and enhance network throughput, turns to be a crucial problem in the relevant area.

One potential solution to provide high throughput is to parallelize multiple backscatter transmissions. This however leads to an important challenge in parallel transmission: how collided signals can be decoded. Existing work proposed to use network coding, but it incurs computational overhead on the tags, which may not be realistic. More recent works [6, 7, 13] propose to shift the workload from tags to backscatter readers. Specifically, the reader can *separate* the interleaved signal edges from different tags using its capability to sample at a much higher rate than a tag. Then, according to the signals' locations in the In-phase and Quadrature (IQ) domain, the reader can *decode* the transmitted signals of tags.

Unfortunately, in order to distinguish signals from different tags, the above parallel decoding proposals rely on *stable* and *distinct* features of signals in the time and/or the IQ domain. On the contrary, in our real-world experiments, we have observed that signal features are likely to be highly *dynamic* and *unpredictable*. As a result, applying the existing proposals in practice usually results in unacceptably high decoding error rates, which in turn affects transmission efficiency and network throughput negatively.

It is therefore highly desirable to design practical protocols for parallel backscatter transmissions with hostile channel conditions. In our experiments, we have made a surprising observation. Despite the lack of stable features in the time and IQ domains, transitions between the *combined states* of these signals follow highly *stable* probabilities. To be more specific, due to the intrinsic asynchronism of signals from different tags, a higher transition probability between two combined states indicates higher similarity between their corresponding signals. Tracking these transition probabilities may help to distinguish signals' states, offering plenty of information for parallel decoding.

Towards the design of a practically usable solution, we still need to address the following challenges. First, factors like noise and frequency drifts of antennas may negatively affect signals' states, which need to be identified in a consistently correct fashion. Second, it is challenging to capture the stable transition probabilities in unstable signals, and to design a new model to represent these probabilities. Last but not the least, signal processing and counting are often error-prone, which must be taken into account when designing a practical decoding scheme.

In order to address the above challenges, we in this paper propose FlipTracer, a practical system that uses the observed *transition probabilities* between signals' combined states as input, and based on this information alone, achieves highly reliable parallel decoding. To realize this vision, we construct a graphical model, called *one-flip-graph (OFG)*, to capture the signals' transition pattern across the combined states, and provides fine-grained information about the similarity between signals' combined states. Based on the one-flip-graph, FliperTracer can decode the collided signal without relying on the stability of signal features, and is highly efficient and robust in a wide variety of practical scenarios. To the best of our knowledge, FlipTracer is the first practical solution that achieves highly reliable parallel decoding in practical scenarios.

In summary, our key contributions are two-fold:

- With a new graphical model (OFG) that translates the transition probability between combined states to the similarity between their corresponding signals, we are able to guarantee high efficiency under parallel decoding in hostile channel conditions.
- In practice, we have designed and implemented FlipTracer, a practical system that integrates two main techniques: reliable OFG constructing based on the trajectory of the signals in the IQ domain, and collided signal identification by tracking the constructed OFG. Our experimental results have shown that its achievable aggregate throughput approaches 2Mbps, which is 6× higher than the state-of-the-art [13].

In the rest of the paper, we discuss related work in Section 2, and describe the motivation of our design in Section 3. The design details of FlipTracer are introduced in Sections 5~7. Sections 8 and 9 evaluate the performance analytically and empirically. We conclude the paper in Section 10.

2 RELATED WORK

There have been many efforts made to enable multiple accesses in backscatter communication. The existing commodity backscatter systems typically adopt the slotted aloha scheme [1]. This scheme however incurs high coordination overhead and low throughput, especially when collision occurs. Although some recent methods [2] can deal with the collision problem, the throughput is bounded at one packet per time slot. To further improve the throughput, recent works try to parallelize multiple backscatter transmissions:

Using coding mechanisms. A direct method for parallel transmission is to exploit coding mechanisms [5, 9, 11, 12, 14] on tags to facilitate collision recovery. In these methods, each tag exploits an orthogonal code for encoding data where each bit is converted to a long PN sequence. Although such methods enable concurrent transmission, they incur unaffordable overhead on the tag side.

To solve this problem, some recent works propose to decode concurrent transmissions by extending the decoding capacity at the reader-side [3, 4, 6, 7, 10, 13, 18, 19]. Specifically, in these works, the reader decode the collided signals according to the signals' features in time and/or IQ domain:

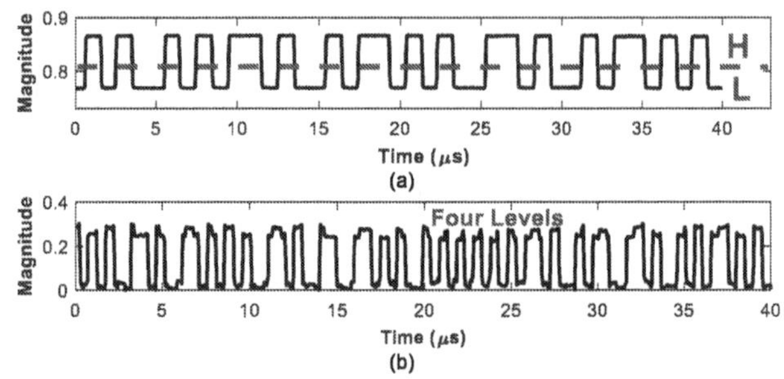

Figure 1: Signals in time domain: (a) a single tag. (b) two tags.

Using tags' IQ domain features. Theoretically the channel coefficients of the colliding tags are *stable* and collided signal is the *linear combination* of these tags' channel coefficients. Thus the collided signals with specific combined states will exhibit specific positions on the IQ plane. Under this assumption, designs like [7, 18, 19] propose to identify the collided signals based on their IQ domain positions.

Using tags' time domain features. An alternative method that has been considered in prior works is separation in the time domain [7, 13]. They assume that the signal edges of the same tag will come at a relatively fixed interval (i.e., *stable bit duration*). Thus they can separate the signal edges of different tags in the time domain, and connect with the signal clusters in the IQ domain for collision decoding. For example, LF-Backscatter [7] applies folding to extract the periodical signal edges of individual tags. BiGroup [13] achieves this using the linear regression model.

Although the above methods enable parallel decoding, our study reveals that they cannot provide satisfactory performance in practical backscatter systems. The reason is that they have to rely on the stability of the tags' signals. In practice, however, signals from the tags never exhibit stable patterns. According to our experiment, the dynamics induced by the low-cost hardware components and the ambient environment severely undermines signal features in both the time and the IQ domains. Hence, applying the above methods in practice generally results in high decoding error rates, which in turn hurts the transmission efficiency and throughput.

Different from all the above works, FlipTracer neither requires modifications on the tag side, nor assumes stable features of the collided signals. FlipTracer exploits the transition pattern among the signals which is fairly stable and robust against the dynamics in both the time and the IQ domains. Our experimental results show that FlipTracer is able to achieve highly reliable parallel decoding under various conditions.

3 BACKGROUND AND MOTIVATION

3.1 Preliminary

In backscatter systems, the tag encodes its data by reflecting or absorbing the carrier waves, resulting in two possible states: "High (H)" and "Low (L)", which can be decoded using a magnitude threshold (as shown in Figure 1(a)). When N tags transmit concurrently, their signals add up at the reader, and the collided signal will have 2^N combined states, forming 2^N signal levels. One combined state is theoretically a *linear* combination of all the N tags' signal state,

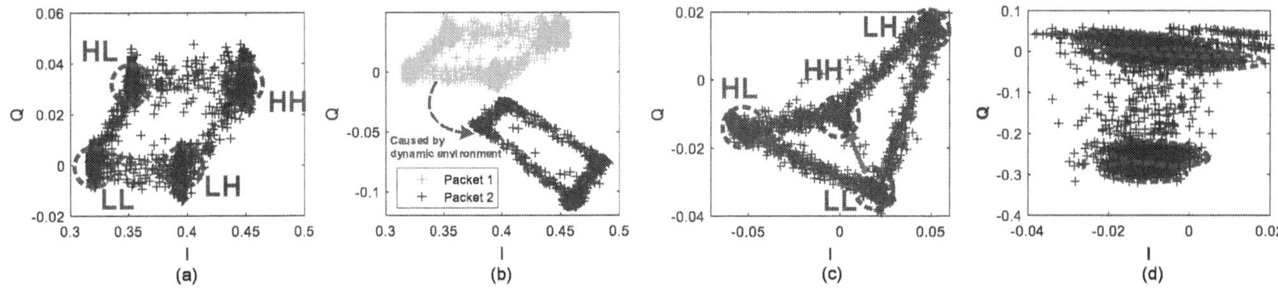

Figure 2: Symbol clusters: (a) a 2-tag collision example. (b) collided signal from two sequential packets under dynamic working condition. (c) 2-tag collision with non-linear dependency. (d) overlapped clusters.

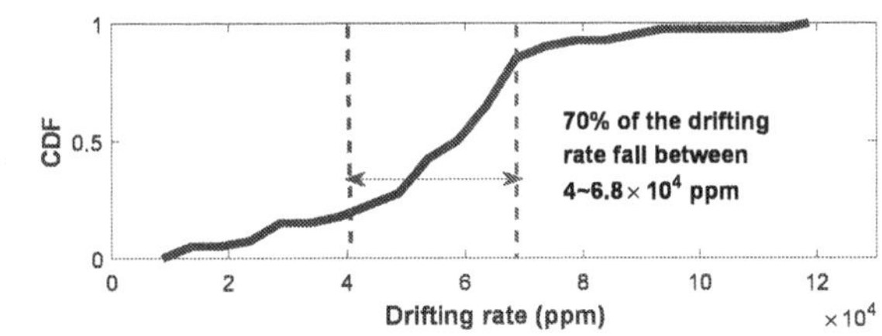

Figure 3: CDF of the measured drifting rate of 20 tags.

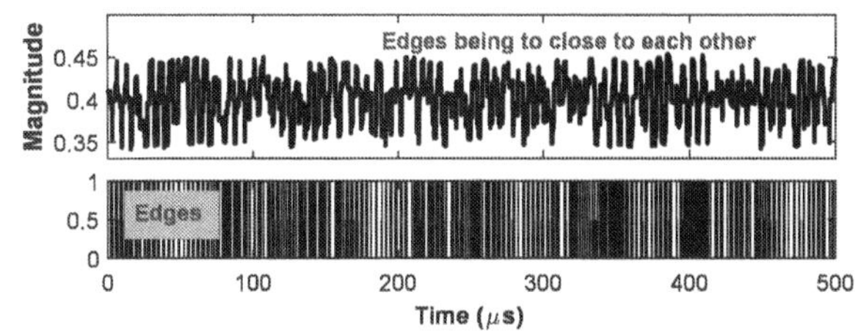

Figure 4: Signal series of a 4-tag collision.

denoted as $S = [S_1, S_2, ..., S_N]$, where $S_i = H_i$ or L_i indicates the state of tag i. Figure 1(b) shows the example of a 2-tag collision case. We find that we cannot determine the threshold to detect the states of either individual tag.

We further show the IQ signals received from 2 tags in Figure 2(a). We find that the symbols form four separable clusters, each represents a combined state of the tags. Therefore, if we can identify the combined state of each cluster, we can know whether an individual tag i's transmission state $S_i = H_i$ or L_i for each $i = 1, ..., N$. Then the collision is decoded. However, this is a challenging task due to the dynamics in the backscatter signals.

3.2 Signal Dynamics

The challenges for collision decoding in practical backscatter systems mainly lie in the highly dynamic signal of tags, in both the IQ and the time domains.

Dynamics in the IQ domain. Theoretically, the combined states of the clusters can be identified based on their locations in the IQ domain if the channel coefficients of tags are stable and are linearly combined when collision occurs. However, we observe both *dynamic* and *non-linear depended* signals in the IQ domain:

1) The positions of the clusters in the IQ plane will change with the dynamic environment. Figure2(b) shows the IQ symbols collected from two sequential packets (0.2s apart) when an obstacle moves around the reader. We can observe great difference between the positions of the two packets' symbol clusters. In this case, the decoding methods [19] which rely on channel coefficients have to conduct channel measurements frequently to deal with the changing environment. This significantly increases the protocol overhead.

2) The locations of clusters may sometimes exhibit non-linear dependence. In practice, when multiple tags coexist, tags may backscatter the signals from nearby tags, resulting in the non-linear dependency in the combined signals received at the reader [13]. Figure 2(c) gives an 2-tag collision case. In such a scenario, the reader cannot identify the clusters based on their position on the IQ plane.

3) The clusters may be too close to be separated. When the number of tags increases, the number of clusters will increase exponentially, resulting in clusters being closer to (or even overlap with) each other. What is worse, in a low SNR scenario, noise from the environment will increase the radius of the clusters, which incurs overlap even in 2-tag collision scenarios (as shown in Figure 2(d)). In such scenarios, we can not even separate different clusters.

Dynamics in the time domain. Distinguishing the collided signals in time domain is also challenging. Specifically, to map each signal edge to the flipping of each tag, an important assumption is that the tags have relatively stable bit durations. This requires the built-in oscillators have low drifting rate (less than 200*ppm* is tolerable [7]). However, due to the low cost design, the oscillators used in backscatter tags typically exhibit high drifting rates [7, 8, 24]. Figure 3 shows the CDF of the measured drifting rates of 20 tags. We can observe that 70% of tags' clock drifting rates fall between 40,000 ppm and 68,000 ppm. Consider a concrete example where tags transmit 100-bit packets at 100Kbps. Such high drifting rates can lead to 40 ~ 68μs time offsets within one-packet duration. Since the bit duration is only 10μs, 40 ~ 68μs offsets will inevitably incur excessive errors in the edge identification process.

Some schemes [13] propose to address this problem by using linear regression. Such schemes work only if the signal flips infrequently. Under this assumption, the long distance between edges can be used to gain confidence in edge detection. However, when multiple tags transmit concurrently at high bitrates (as shown in Figure 4), signal edges are stacked side by side. In this situation, the reader can hardly distinguish the edges from different tags.

3.3 Transition Probabilities Between Clusters

The above experimental results present a conundrum that: how to identify the combined states of each cluster based on such dynamic and irregular signals? Our idea is to leverage signals' *transition probabilities* between clusters. Specifically, Figure 5 shows the transfer trajectories of collided signals from two tags under different

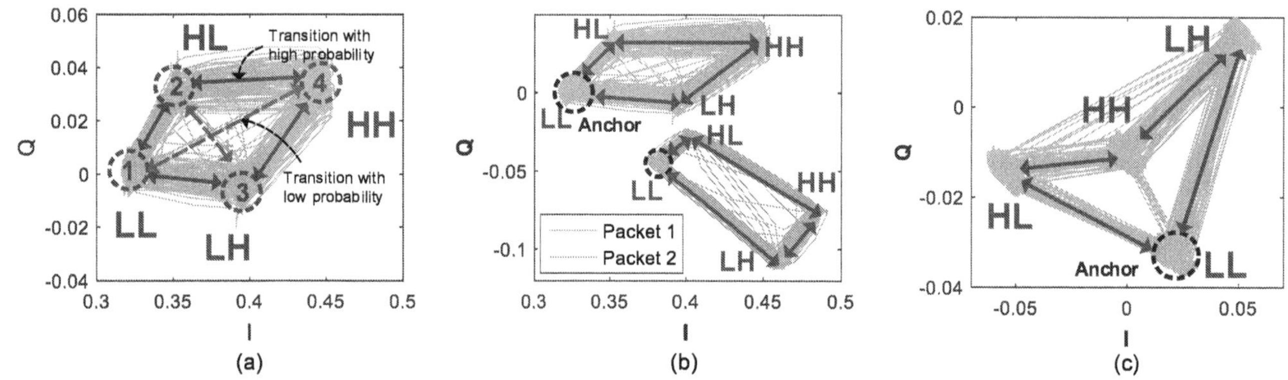

Figure 5: Transition pattern among clusters: (a) a 2-tag collision example. (b) collision under a dynamic working condition. (c) collision with non-linear dependency

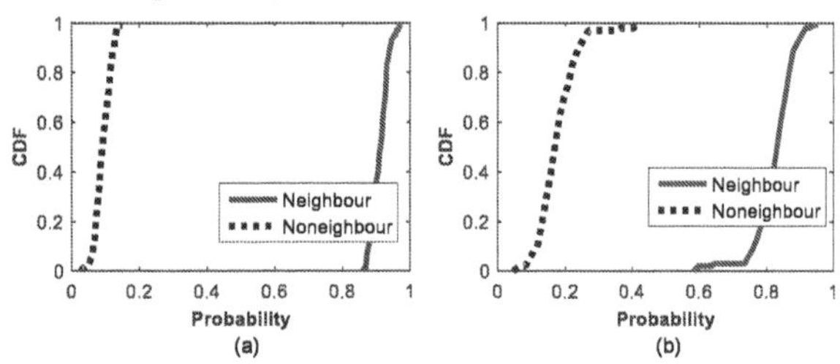

Figure 6: The CDF for the transition probability between both neighbor and non-neighbor clusters: (a) two tags; (b) five tags.

scenarios. We find that although the signals are dynamic and irregular, signals' transition probabilities between different clusters are highly *stable* and *traceable*. Indeed, a higher transition probability between two clusters implies the higher similarity between their corresponding combined states.

Let us explain the reason behind. In practice, flipping of tags makes the collided signal to transfer among clusters. Specifically, the flipping of a single tag causes the transition between two clusters whose combined states have only one different state (e.g., "L_1L_2" and "L_1H_2"), while the concurrent flipping of multiple tags causes the transition between two clusters whose combined states have multiple different states (e.g., "L_1L_2" and "H_1H_2"). We term the former cluster pair as *neighbor clusters* and the latter as *non-neighbor clusters*. Given that the state flipping of different tags are interleaved most of the time [7, 13], the transition probabilities between the neighbor clusters are obviously higher than those between the non-neighbor clusters.

As a concrete example, consider the transition probability between non-neighbor clusters in a 2-tag collision case where each tag transmits at 100Kbps and the USRP reader samples at 25 MHz (i.e. the reader samples 250 times for each bit duration). An edge has a width of 3 samples at the reader's sampling rate, which means that we can stack at most $\frac{250}{3} = 83$ separated edges in one bit duration. Thus the probability for the two tags to flip their state at exactly the same time can be calculated as: $1-(83\cdot82)/(83\cdot83) = 1.2\%$. Moreover, even under high concurrency scenarios, we can still observe very low transition probability between non-neighbor clusters (detailed discussion is given in Section 8.2).

We further conduct experiments to show the *distinctness* and *consistency* of the transition probability between neighbor clusters.

Distinctness. We plot the CDFs of the transition probabilities between both neighbor and non-neighbor clusters in Figure 6(a), which is calculated based on more than 100 collided packets of two concurrent tags (bitrate of the tags is 100Kbps). We can see that the transition probability between neighbor clusters is almost 8× higher than that between non-neighbor clusters. This ensures that we can correctly find the neighbors for each cluster.

Consistency. We have shown in Figure 5 that the signal's transition pattern is stable under dynamic scenarios, now let us look at its stability when the concurrency level is high. Figure 6(b) plots the CDFs of the transition probabilities between neighbor and non-neighbor clusters in a 5-tag collision case. We can see that when the concurrency level is high, the transition probabilities between neighbor and non-neighbor clusters are still distinguishable.

4 FLIPTRACER OVERVIEW

FlipTracer is a practical parallel decoding approach in which the collided signals are identified based on the transition probabilities between symbol clusters. In this system, the tags transmit packets concurrently when they receive a query from the reader. The collided packets will be resolved on the reader-side after every transmission. The FlipTracer system architecture is shown in Figure 7:

- **OFG construction.** FlipTracer first clusters the physical symbols in the IQ plane. Then, based on the observed signal transition probabilities among symbol clusters, FlipTracer constructs a graph, termed as *one flip graph (OFG)*, which connects all the neighbor clusters. The OFG acts as an important reference for the cluster identification component.
- **Cluster identification.** By tracking the OFG, FlipTracer identifies the combined states of all the clusters in the OFG. Then, by examining the identified combined states, FlipTracer outputs N sequences of binary states that represent the transmitted signals of the N colliding tags.
- **Decoding.** For each tag, FlipTracer applies a Conditional Random Field based decoder on the binary sequence to identify the most likely sequence of bits.

The next few sections elaborate on the above components, providing the technical details.

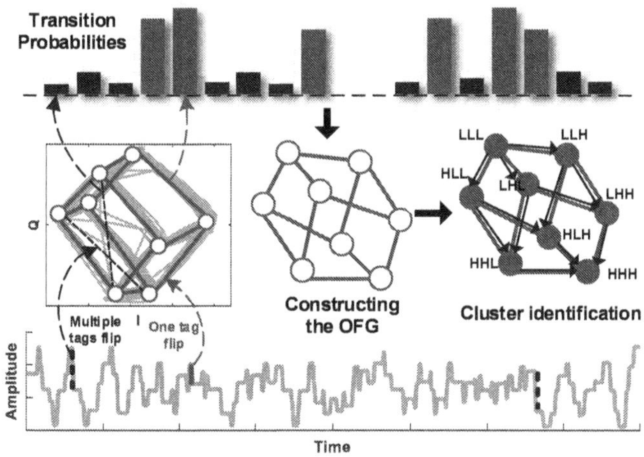

Figure 7: Workflow of FlipTracer.

5 THE ONE-FLIP-GRAPH

The One-Flip-Graph (OFG) is denoted as $\mathbf{OFG} = (\mathrm{C}, \mathrm{E})$, where $\mathrm{C} = \{C_1, ..., C_{Nc}\}$ denotes the $Nc = 2^N$ symbol clusters and if C_i and C_j ($C_i, C_j \in \mathrm{C}$) are neighbor clusters, we have $< C_i, C_j > \in \mathrm{E}$. In this section, we describe how to construct the OFG based on the collected IQ symbols.

5.1 Symbol Clustering

The first challenge we face is reliable symbol clustering. Although symbol clustering methods have been proposed in some recent works [7, 13], they can not separate overlapping clusters which are common in noisy environments. To separate the overlapping clusters, we need to first find their centers. Hence we employ *local densities*[1] based clustering methods. Specifically, a cluster center typically has high local density and is surrounded by symbols with lower local densities. Although clusters overlap with each other, we can still find their centers by finding the density peaks.

Our clustering approach is designed based on the algorithm introduced in [15] (we call it LDBC in this paper). We first use the idea in LDBC to find the Nc cluster centers, and estimate for each symbol i the probability that it belongs to each cluster C_k ($C_k \in \mathrm{C} = \{C_1, ..., C_{Nc}\}$) as $\mathbf{Pd}(i) = \{pd_i^k \mid 1 \le k \le Nc\}$, where pd_i^k is determined by the location and the local density of symbol i.

Then it seems that we can directly classify symbol i to C_k if pd_i^k is the maximum in $\mathbf{Pd}(i)$. However, since the symbols located at the overlapping area (termed as *confused symbols*) may exhibit similar pd_i^k for the corresponding clusters, classifying the confused symbols based only on their $\mathbf{Pd}(i)$ may incur errors. We propose to leverage the time domain information to address this problem.

In practice, the signal will dwell on a certain cluster for a while between two transitions, thus successive symbols are likely to belong to the same cluster. We propose a parameter $\mathbf{Pt}(i) = \{pt_i^k \mid 1 \le k \le Nc\}$ to describe from time domain that how likely symbol i belongs to cluster C_k. We have $pt_i^k = \frac{\#C_k}{w_c}$, where $\#C_k$ denotes the number of symbols belonging to cluster k in the time window centered at symbol i. The length of the window is set according to the bit duration of the tags and the sampling rate of the reader.

[1]The local density of a symbol is defined as the number of symbols located within a cutoff distance.

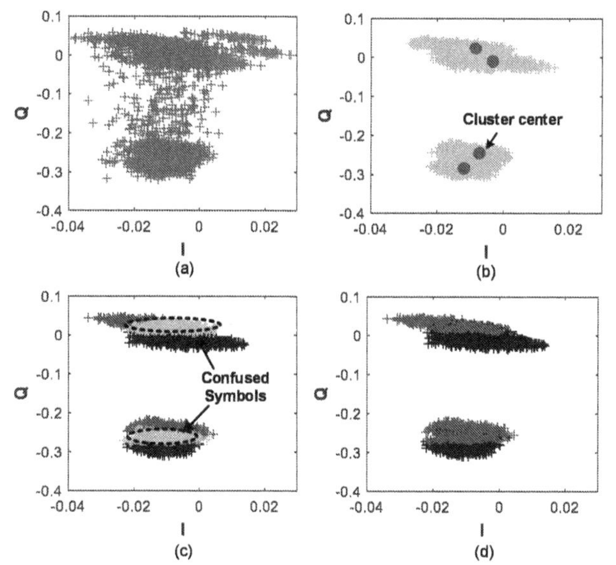

Figure 8: Symbol clustering: (a) received symbols. (b) identified cluster centers. (c) confused symbols. (d) symbols are finally classified to each cluster.

Now we can classify the confused symbols based on a joint consideration of **Pd** and **Pt**. Specifically, we calculate the $\mathbf{P}_{\mathbf{cluster}}(i) = \{pd_i^k \cdot pt_i^k \mid 1 \le k \le Nc\}$ for each symbol i, and classify symbol i to cluster C_k if $pd_i^k \cdot pt_i^k$ is the maximum in $\mathbf{P}_{\mathbf{cluster}}(i)$.

FlipTracer goes through three steps to classify the symbols (Figure 8 gives an example of the symbol clustering process for a 2-tag collision):

- It uses the idea in LDBC to estimate the **Pd** for each symbol (as shown in Figure 8(b)).
- It classifies each symbol i to the cluster which achieves $pd_i^k > PD_{th}$ (we empirically set $PD_{th} = 0.4$). If there are multiple (or no) clusters achieve $pt_i^k > PD_{th}$, it denotes symbol i as a confused symbol (as shown in Figure 8(c)).
- It estimates $\mathbf{P}_{\mathbf{cluster}}$ for the confused symbols, and classifies the confused symbols based on $\mathbf{P}_{\mathbf{cluster}}$. The final clustering result is shown in Figure 8(d).

Now each symbol is marked by the label of its cluster.

5.2 Building connections in the OFG

Now we have the symbol clusters (the nodes in the OFG), and the next step is to build the connections, namely, to form the neighbor relationships between clusters. Based on our observations in Section 3, the transition probabilities between neighbor clusters are significantly higher than those between non-neighbor clusters. Thus we can recognize neighbor clusters based on the transition probabilities between clusters.

However, we face a problem that due to the reader's query, signal edges of different tags might be aligned during the initial period of a concurrent transmission (as shown in Figure 9(d)). It results in high transition probabilities between non-neighbor clusters, in the initial period (as shown in Figure 9(a)). If such alignment lasts

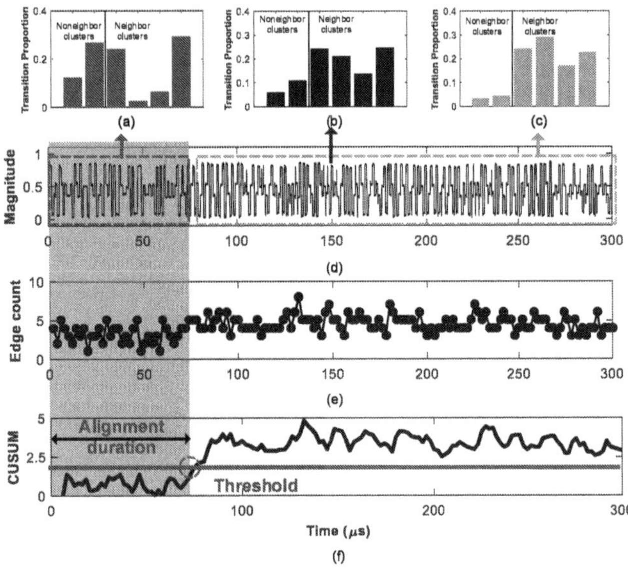

Figure 9: Impact of aligned signal flipping on the transition probabilities: (a)-(c) are the transition probabilities between clusters during the alignment period, the entire signal series and the misalignment period, respectively. (d) signal series. (e) the number of the state flipping. (f) CUSUM of the state flipping number.

for a long period of time (which is caused by very similar clock rates between tags), the gaps between the transition probabilities for neighbor and non-neighbor clusters will be small. This may incur errors in the neighbor identification process. Therefore, for reliable neighbor identification, we would like to first filter out those aligned signals, then calculate the transition probabilities based on only the misaligned signals.

Filter out the aligned signal flipping. The intuition of our method for detecting the aligned signals is that state flipping occurs more frequently in the misaligned signals than in the aligned signals. Figure 9(e) shows the number of state flipping counted over successive windows. Obviously, signal alignment leads to less frequent signal flipping. However, we cannot find an appropriate threshold to separate the aligned and misaligned signals.

To solve this problem, we use the Cumulative Sum (CUSUM) test, a method designed to detect the change in data distribution, to detect the change in flipping frequency. We apply the CUSUM on top of the series in Figure 9(e), and show the cumulative sum in Figure 9(f). We can see that now the aligned and misaligned signals are separable. After filtering out the aligned signals, the transition probabilities between neighbor clusters are highly distinct from those between non-neighbor clusters (as shown in Figure 9(c)).

Finding the neighbors. We first calculate the transition probabilities between clusters. For each cluster $C_i \in \mathbf{C}$, we can calculate the transition probability between C_i and every other cluster C_j as:

$$P_{trans}(C_i, C_j) = \frac{\#(C_i \leftrightarrow C_j)}{\sum_{C_k \in \mathbf{C}} \#(C_i \leftrightarrow C_k)} \quad (1)$$

where $\#(C_i \leftrightarrow C_j)$ denotes the number of transitions between C_i and C_j, and $\sum_{C_k \in \mathbf{C}}(C_i \leftrightarrow C_k)$ denotes the total number of transitions between C_i and all the other clusters in $\mathbf{C}$. Transitions between clusters can be detected using the method given in [13].

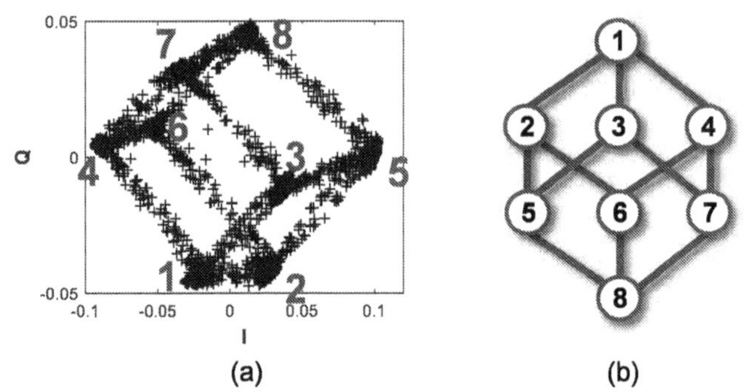

Figure 10: OFG example: (a) received symbol samples of a 3-tag collision. (b) constructed OFG for the received symbol clusters.

In a N-tag collision case, each cluster C_i has n neighbors, denoted as $\mathbf{C_{nei}}(C_i)$. Theoretically, the N neighbors of C_i should be the N clusters leading to the N highest $P_{trans}(C_i, C_j)$, termed as *potential neighbors* of C_i (denoted as $\mathbf{C_{pos}}(C_i)$). In practice, however, burst noise may result in wrong cluster labels, bringing deviations to the measured transition probabilities. An extreme case is that, for a cluster C_i, the measured transition probabilities between C_i and its non-neighbor clusters might be even higher than that between C_i and its neighbors. Thus, directly identifying $\mathbf{C_{pos}}(C_i)$ as $\mathbf{C_{nei}}(C_i)$ may incur errors. To solve this problem, we propose a new metric $Conf(C_i)$ for each cluster C_i to describe the *confidence* for identifying $\mathbf{C_{pos}}(C_i)$ as C_i's neighbors:

$$Conf(C_i) = \frac{min\{P_{trans}(C_i, \mathbf{C_{pos}}(C_i))\}}{max\{P_{trans}(C_i, \mathbf{C_{nopos}}(C_i))\}} \quad (2)$$

where $\mathbf{C_{nopos}}(C_i)$ denotes the clusters that do not belong to $\mathbf{C_{pos}}(C_i)$. A larger gap between $P_{trans}(C_i, \mathbf{C_{pos}})$ and $P_{trans}(C_i, \mathbf{C_{nopos}})$ indicates a higher confidence.

To improve neighbor identification robustness, we propose to first sort the clusters in descending order of their $Conf$, and identify the neighbors for the clusters sequentially. This allows us to process the clusters that have the higher $Conf$ earlier. Specifically, for the k-th cluster, if m of its N neighbors have been covered by the previous $k-1$ clusters (which have higher $Conf$), we only need to identify its other $(N-m)$ neighbors based on P_{trans}.

5.3 Correcting false connections

Now we have both the symbol clusters (nodes in the OFG) and the connections between neighbor clusters, so we can get the OFG. As an example, Figure 10(a) shows the received symbols of a 3-tag collision case, and Figure 10(b) shows the corresponding OFG. One problem we face, however, is how to handle the false connections (the connections which connect two non-neighbor clusters) in the OFG. Although it is a fairly rare occurrence, when it occurs, the following cluster identification process will be seriously affected. Thus we propose a false-tolerance design to avoid forming such false connections when constructing the OFG.

We propose such a design based on our intuition that the false connections will lead to abnormal structures in the OFG. In practice, *if all the connections in the OFG are correctly formed, there will be no odd-node loops in the OFG.* Specifically, a loop with an odd number of nodes implies that for an arbitrary cluster on the loop, its combined

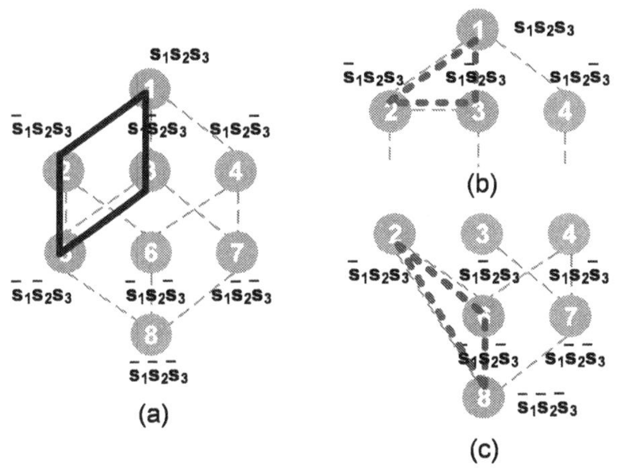

Figure 11: Loops in the OFG of a 3-tag collision case: (a) an example of a correct loop. (b) and (c) are two examples of the abnormal loops.

state can transfer to the initial state through an odd number of transitions, which is however impossible. The reason is that for a combined state $[S_1, ..., S_N]$, its each state S_i has to experience two transitions to transfer to its initial state (i.e., $S_i \rightarrow \overline{S}_i \rightarrow S_i$). Thus the combined state $[S_1, ..., S_N]$ has to experience an even number of transitions to transfer to the initial combined state. Figure 11(a) shows an example of the loop with four nodes.

However, a false connection will inevitably form a loop with an odd number of nodes. As an example, consider a false connection $< C_i, C_j >$ connecting two clusters whose combined states have two different states (denoted as States S_p and S_q). Thus, the combined states of C_i and C_j will have at least one common neighbor cluster (denoted as C_k) which have one different state (S_p or S_q) with C_i and C_j. Clusters C_i, C_j, and C_k form a 3-node loop. Figures 11(b) and 11(c) show two examples of such abnormal loops.

The above observation indicates that we can avoid forming false connections by detecting such *abnormal loops*. Specifically, before forming a connection $< C_i, C_j >$, we will first check whether $< C_i, C_j >$ leads to an abnormal loop. If it does, we will label C_j as a non-neighbor cluster of C_i [2].

6 CLUSTER IDENTIFICATION

In this section, we introduce how to identify the combined state of each cluster by tracking the OFG. We assume that there is an anchor cluster, whose combined state is known. This is reasonable because we can always identify the cluster representing all "L" states when all tags are being charged.

To describe the cluster identification process more clearly, we have to first layer the OFG. Specifically, the anchor cluster is the root (Layer 0) of the OFG, denoted as C_{root}. We define the neighbors of C_{root} as its child nodes, which form the first layer of the OFG. For each Layer l cluster (denoted as C_l^i, and $l > 0$), we define its neighbors, that is not in Layer $(l-1)$, as its child nodes. The child nodes of the Layer l clusters form the $(l+1)$-th Layer of the OFG.

Now we can identify the clusters in the OFG layer by layer, starting from C_{root}.

[2]Note that this process assumes the connects that formed earlier (which exhibit higher $Conf$) are more likely to be correct.

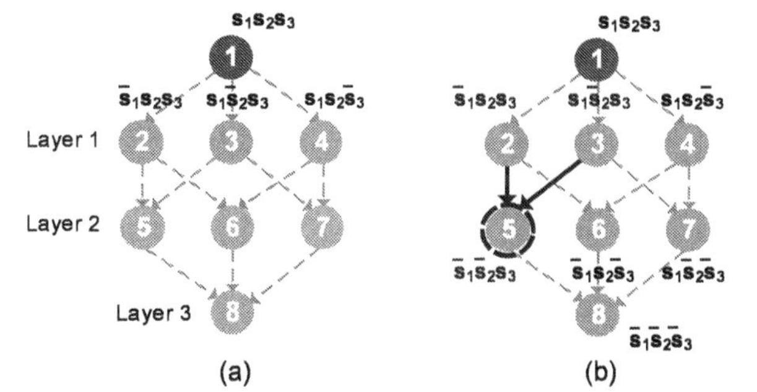

Figure 12: The process of decoding a 3-tag collision: (a) Identify the first layer clusters. (b) Identify the clusters in Layer $l-1$.

Claim 1. *We can identify the combined states of the Layer-1 clusters based on the combined state of* C_{root}.

If the combined state of C_{root} is $[S_1, S_2, ..., S_N]$, we can identify its neighbor clusters (i.e., the Layer 1 clusters) as $[\overline{S}_1, S_2, ..., S_N]$, $[S_1, \overline{S}_2, ..., S_N]$, ..., $[S_1, S_2, ..., \overline{S}_N]$. Figure 12(a) gives an example of the above process, in a 3-tag collision case. In this example, if we denote the tags that cause transitions between Clusters 1 and 2, 1 and 3, 1 and 4 as Tag 1, Tag 2, and Tag 3, respectively[3], the Clusters 2, 3, and 4 can be identified as $[\overline{S}_1, S_2, S_3]$, $[S_1, \overline{S}_2, S_3]$, and $[S_1, S_2, \overline{S}_3]$, respectively. We will show in the appendix with a concrete example that different assignments of the Layer 1 nodes do not affect the decoding result.

Claim 2. *There are l different states between the combined states of* C_{root} *and each Layer l cluster.*

We define the distance between two clusters C_a and C_b as the number of different states between their combined states, denoted as $d(C_a, C_b)$. Obviously, the distance between C_{root} and each Layer 1 cluster C_1^i is 1. Denote the k-th child node of C_1^i as $Ch(C_1^i, k)$, we have i) $d(Ch(C_1^i, k), C_1^i) = 1$, and ii) $d(Ch(C_1^i, k), C_{root}) > d(C_1^i, C_{root}) = 1$. Thus, we can derive that $d(Ch(C_1^i, k), C_{root}) = d(C_1^i, C_{root}) + 1 = 2$, namely $d(C_2^i, C_{root}) = 2$. Iteratively, we can derive that $d(C_l^i, C_{root}) = l$.

Now we can provide a set of candidate combined states for the Layer l ($l > 1$) clusters. Taking the 3-tag collision case in Figure 12 as an example, we can provide a set of candidate combined states for the Layer 2 clusters as $[\overline{S}_1, \overline{S}_2, S_3]$, $[\overline{S}_1, S_2, \overline{S}_3]$ and $[S_1, \overline{S}_2, \overline{S}_3]$. The next task is to map each combined state in the candidate set to each cluster.

Claim 3. *We can identify the combined states of the Layer-l clusters based on those of the Layer-$(l-1)$ clusters.*

As discussed in Claim 2, the distance between C_l^i and C_{root} is l. Thus, there are l different states between the combined states of C_{root} and C_l^i. We denote these states as $S_{k_1}, S_{k_2}, ..., S_{k_l}$, where $k_1, k_2, ..., k_l$ are the indexes of the states. Its easy to understand that C_l^i have l fathers in Layer $(l-1)$, and the different states between C_{root} and its fathers are $\{[S_{k_2}, S_{k_3}, ..., S_{k_{l-1}}, S_{k_l}], [S_{k_1}, S_{k_3}, ..., S_{k_{l-1}}, S_{k_l}], ..., [S_{k_1}, S_{k_2}, ..., S_{k_{l-2}}, S_{k_{l-1}}]\}$. Thus if the combined states of

[3]Such IDs are the "temporary IDs" which are used to distinguish (rather than to denote) the signals from different tags. What we essentially care about are the IDs (or data) embedded in the payloads of the packets.

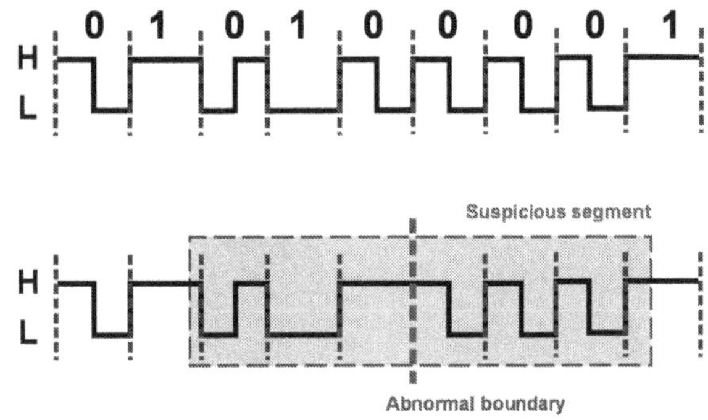

Figure 13: FM0 coding: (a) A correct state sequence. (b) A state sequence with errors.

the Layer-$(l-1)$ clusters have been identified (which means that $k_1, k_2, ..., k_l$ are known), the combined state of C_l^i can be identified accordingly. As the example shown in Figure 12(b), the combined state of Cluster 5 can be identified as $[\overline{S}_1, \overline{S}_2, S_3]$ if Clusters 2 and 3 are identified as $[\overline{S}_1, S_2, S_3]$ and $[S_1, \overline{S}_2, S_3]$, respectively.

The process of cluster identification can be concluded as follow:

- identify the combined state of an anchor cluster;
- identify the Layer 1 clusters based on Claim 1;
- identify the clusters in Layer 2~ N based on Claim 3;

Then the combined states of all the clusters can be identified.

7 RELIABLE DECODING

Now the combined states of all the clusters are identified. By examining those combined states, FlipTracer outputs a sequence of "H" and "L" states to represents the transmitted signal for each tag. The sequence can be decoded using the conventional single tag decoder.

Unlike the single tag transmission scenario, however, in the collision scenario, wrong labels in the symbol clustering process may increase the BER (bit error rate) of individual tags. Thus, we would like to correct the errors in the state sequence before inputting it to the decoder. The predictable state flipping pattern of the standardized FM0 and Miller codes suggests a possible solution - we can simply leverage the fact that certain state sequences are not possible. For brevity, we will later use FM0 code as a vehicle to describe our error correction method. Our method can be generalized to handle Miller codes as well with slight modifications.

FM0 code inevitably inverts the signal state at every bit boundary (as shown in Figure 13(a)). Thus it is a obvious error if two chips[4] on the opposite sides of a bit boundary have the same state. We term such a bit boundary as an *abnormal bit boundary* and the state sequence with a length of K chips ($K = 6$ in our implementation) centered at this abnormal boundary as a *suspicious segment* (as shown in Figure 13(b)). Once we detect an abnormal bit boundary, we use a Conditional Random Field based decoder to correct the errors in the corresponding suspicious segment.

For a tag i, suppose that we detect a suspicious segment with a sequence of $k = 1, 2, ..., K$ chips in the state sequence. For each chip, we introduce a random variable S_k ($S_k = H$ or L) to represent its state. The joint probability of assigning a sequence of states $\{S_1, S_2, ..., S_K\}$ to all the chips $k = 1, 2, ..., K$ is given as follows:

$$P(\mathrm{S}) = \beta \prod_{k} \phi(S_k) \prod_{k,k+1} \psi(S_k, S_{k+1}) \quad (3)$$

where β serves as a normalization constant. The factor $\phi(S_k)$ represents the emission probability of assigning S_k to k, which is highly related to the confidence of the clustering process (i.e., $\mathrm{P_{cluster}}$). Thus $\phi(S_k)$ can be given by the $\mathrm{P_{cluster}}$ of the symbols in $\mathrm{C_{S_k}}$, where $\mathrm{C_{S_k}}$ represents the clusters indicating a S_k state of tag i. The factor $\psi(S_k, S_{k+1})$ in equation (3) presents the transition probability between S_k and S_{k+1}. Specifically, if the transition between S_k and S_{k+1} indicates a bit boundary, we have $\psi(S_k, S_{k+1}) = 1$ if $S_{k+1} = S_k$, and $\psi(S_k, S_{k+1}) = 0$ if $S_{k+1} = \overline{S}_k$. Otherwise, we have $\psi(S_k, S_{k+1}) = 0.5$.

We calculate $P(\mathrm{S})$ for all possible state assignments and identify the one which the maximum $P(\mathrm{S})$ as the correct assignment for the corresponding sequence.

8 ANALYSIS

In this section, we provide theoretical analysis on the performance of FlipTracer.

8.1 Computation Overhead and Latency

The computation overhead of FlipTracer is dominated by the symbol clustering, OFG construction and cluster identification components.

In the symbol clustering component, to reduce the input size for faster clustering, FlipTracer aggregates received symbols into grids (which are much fewer than symbols) and cluster those grids (similar with BiGroup [13]). This reduce the computation overhead to $O(k \cdot logk + M)$, where k is the number of grids and M is the number of confused samples. In FlipTracer, k is around 200 and M is influenced by the SNR of the collided signals (the average number is 80 according to our experiments).

Let N be the number of the tags. The computation overheads of the OFG construction and cluster identification components are $O(N^2 + 2^{N-1} \cdot N)$ and $O(2^{N-1} \cdot N)$, respectively. Since the sampling capacity of the reader is limited, the aggregated throughput cannot increase infinitely with the number of tags. We find through experiments that the performance of FlipTracer peaks at $N = 5$.

We implement FlipTracer on an USRP N210 connected to a general PC equipped with 3.6GHz CPU and 16G memory. FlipTracer takes 180~320μs to decode the collided packet when $N = 5$. Our theoretical analysis tells that the upper bound of aggregated throughput that FlipTracer can achieve is "8 tags transmit at 500Kbps". In this case, we can still keep the time overhead in *ms* level.

8.2 Upper Bound Throughput

The aggregated throughput of FlipTracer is determined by two factors: the number of tags and the bitrate of each individual tag. Since the sampling capacity of the reader is limited, when the number of tags scales or the tags transmit at higher bitrates, signal edges of different tags may be aligned with each other with a higher probability. When the proportion of the aligned edges reaches a certain level, FlipTrace is likely to build false connections when constructing the OFG. This leads to errors in the decoding process.

[4]The FM0 code uses two chips to represent one bit

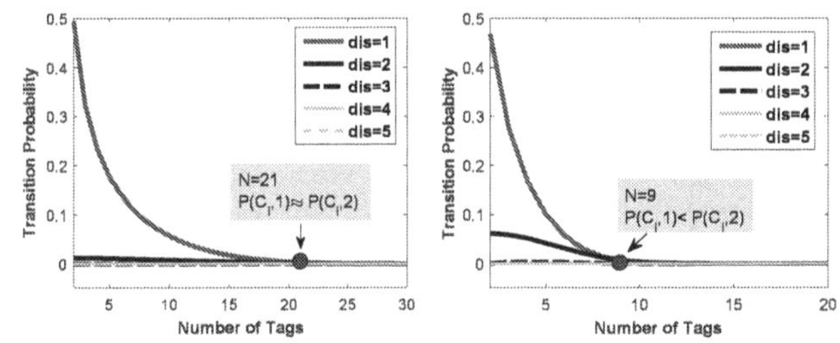

(a) Bitrate=100Kbps (b) Bitrate=500Kbps

Figure 14: Transition probability vs. number of tags

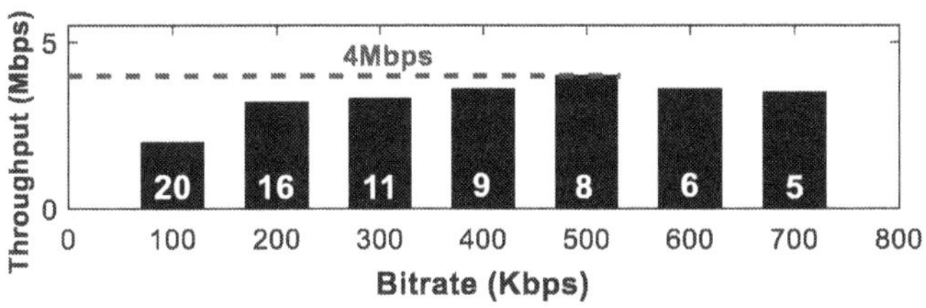

Figure 15: Maximum throughput vs. bitrates.

As noted earlier, if the transition probabilities between a cluster C_i and its neighbors are higher than that between C_i and other clusters, we can correctly find all the neighbors for C_i. Assume that N tags transmit concurrently with the same bitrate B and the sampling rate of the reader is S. Further assume that the signal edge has a width of e samples at the reader's sampling rate. The transition probability between C_i and another cluster C_j, can be calculated as follows, where $d(C_i, C_j) = dis$[5]:

$$P(C_i, dis) = \frac{\binom{\frac{S}{B\cdot e}}{1} \cdot \binom{\frac{S}{B\cdot e}-1}{N-dis} \cdot (N-dis)!}{\frac{S}{B\cdot e}^{N}} \tag{4}$$

If we have $P(C_i, 1) > P(C_i, dis)$ and $dis \geq 2$ for each C_i, we can correctly construct the OFG.

Figures 14(a) and 14(b) show the transition probability vs. the number of concurrent tags (under different dis), with the bitrates of the tags set at 100Kbps and 500Kbps, respectively. We find in Figure 14(a) that when $N \geq 21$, the transition probabilities between neighbor and non-neighbor clusters are too close to be differentiated. In this case ($B = 100Kbps$), the maximum throughput is 2.4Mbps. Similarly, Figure 14(b) shows that the maximum throughput is 4Mbps for $B = 500Kbps$. We also find that the transition probabilities between non-neighbor clusters decrease as N increases. This is because the number of clusters increases exponentially with that of the tags. Therefore, the transition probability between each two clusters will decrease accordingly.

We further show the maximum throughput of FlipTracer under different bitrates in Figure 15. Figure 15 presents the theoretical upper bound of the throughput that FlipTracer can achieve, i.e., 4Mbps (concurrent transmissions from 8 tags at 500Kbps)

[5]Note that $d(C_i, C_j) = dis$ means the transition between C_i and C_j is caused by the aligned edges from dis tags. Clearly, $d(C_i, C_j) = 1$ means that C_i and C_j are neighbors.

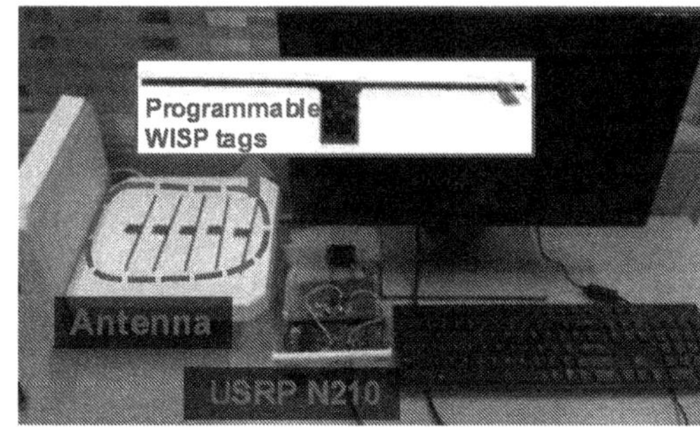

Figure 16: Experimental setup.

9 EVALUATION

9.1 Experiment Setting

The hardware platform is shown in Figure 16.

USRP Reader. FlipTracer is built based on the USRP N210 software radio reader with UBX RF daughterboards and two 900 MHz circular antennas. By default, the sampling rate is set as 20MHz, and the Tx-Gain is 20dBm.

Backscatter tags. Since COTS RFID manufacturers only provide limited interfaces to developers, we implement FlipTracer on programmable WISP tags. This only requires a slight modification to the EPCglobal C1G2 protocol. Specifically, we just remove the elements for Slot Aloha operation and thus the tags will respond concurrently. The packets are encoded with FM0 encoding scheme. The default bitrate is set as 100Kbps and the default packet length is set as 100 bits.

We compare FlipTracer with the following three schemes:

- **Cluster-based parallel decoding (CB).** This approach assumes that tags' channel coefficients are static and can be linearly combined when collision occurs.
- **BiGroup.** BiGroup [13] assumes that the signal edges of a tag come with a relatively fixed interval. It extracts the sequence of each tag's signal transitions in the time domain, and connects with the symbol clusters in the IQ plane for parallel decoding.

9.2 Evaluation of OFG construction

We first focus on the OFG construction component. As a core component of FlipTracer, it has a significant impact on the overall performance.

Two factors can affect the performance of this component - the number of concurrent tags and the SNR. In practice, a higher concurrency means a higher probability for multiple tags to flip their states concurrently, which may lead to higher error rate when identifying neighbour clusters. On the other hand, a lower SNR will incur more errors in both the symbol clustering and the neighbour identification processes.

In the experiments, we increase the number of tags from 2 to 5. For each concurrency level, we change the SNR of the signals by adjusting the gain of the transmitting antenna from 0 to 20dBm. We collect 100 collided packets for each setting and show the corresponding error ratio of the OFG construction component in Figure 17. The error ratio is calculated as the number of wrong OFGs over the constructed 100 OFGs. We find that: i) when the number of

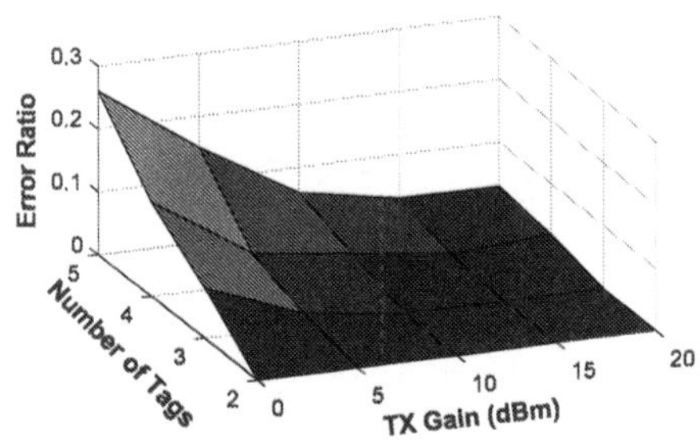

Figure 17: Error ratio of the OFG construction component.

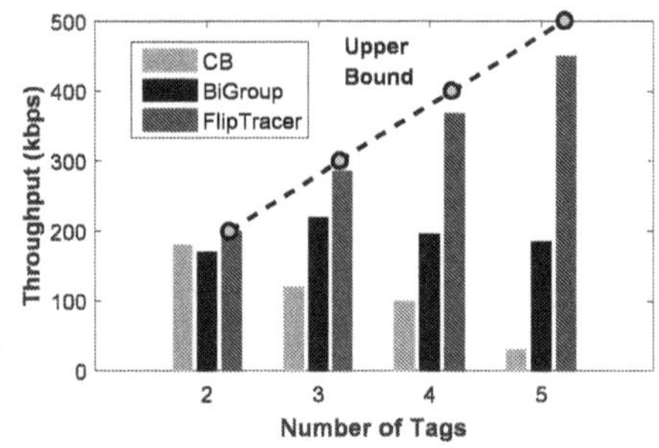

Figure 18: Aggregated throughput with different numbers of tags.

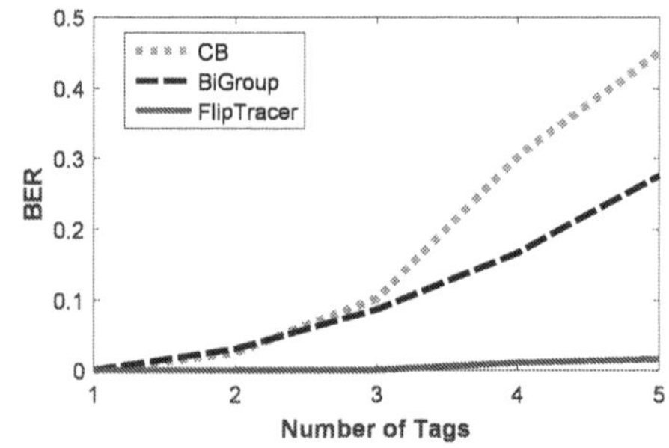

Figure 19: BERs with different numbers of colliding tags.

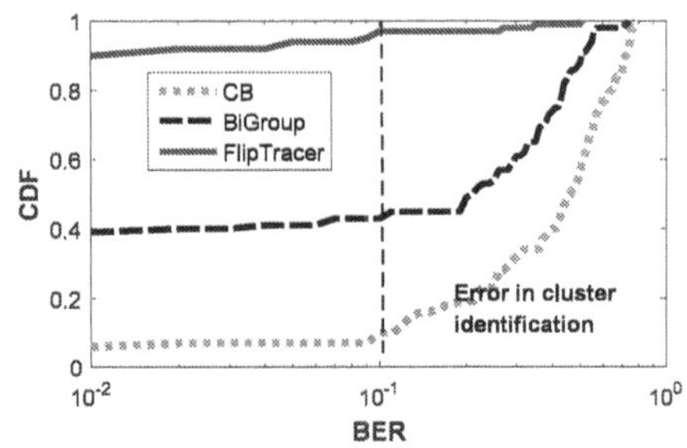

Figure 20: CDFs of BERs for different schemes when the number of tag is 5.

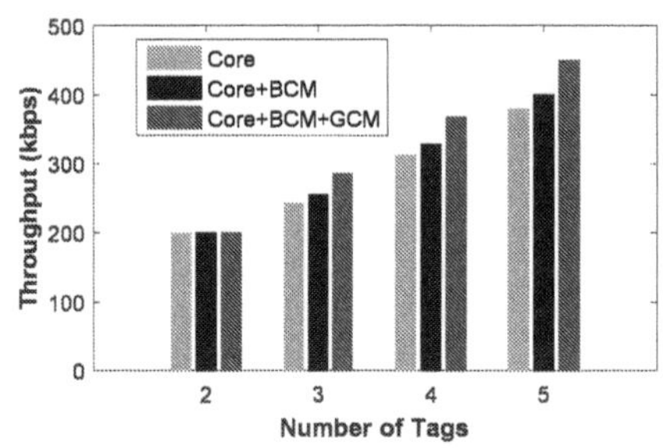

Figure 21: Breakdown of each component's contribution to throughput.

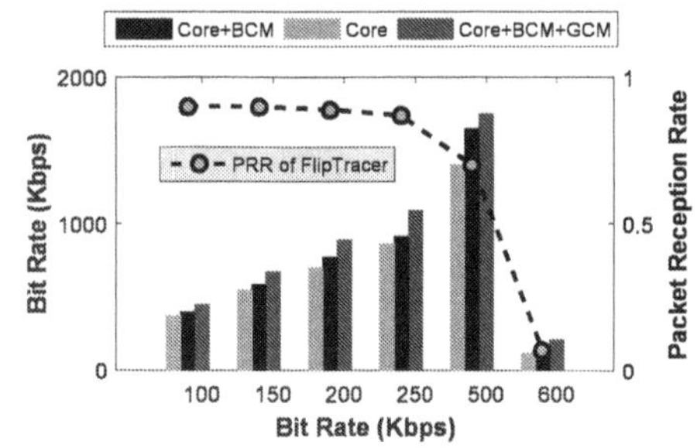

Figure 22: Throughput under different bitrates.

tags ≤ 4, the error ratio can be controlled under 5% even when the TX Gain is 0dBm; and ii) when the TX Gain ≥ 10dBm, the error ratio can be controlled under 10% (the TX Gain of the commercial RFID reader is 30dBm). Clearly, FlipTracer can correctly construct an OFG with high reliability.

9.3 FlipTracer Goodput

In this section, we look at the benefit of FlipTracer in terms of throughput and BER.

Aggregated throughput. Figure 18 compares the aggregated throughput achieved by different schemes for different numbers of colliding tags. We can see that the throughput of FlipTracer is very close to the maximum possible throughput in all cases. The throughput gain of FlipTracer is big: in the 5-tag collision case, FlipTracer is 2.5× better than BiGroup and 15× better than CB.

BER. Figure 19 plots the BERs of different schemes. When collision occurs, the decoding scheme may output multiple packets. Average BERs are record by comparing each output packet and the transmitted counterpart.

In Figure 19, we see that FlipTracer greatly outperforms CB and BiGroup. In the 5-tag collision case, the BER of FlipTracer is 28× lower than that of CB and 17× lower than that of BiGroup. We also find that for all three schemes, the BERs rise rapidly if the number of tags is larger than 4. This is because the error probability for cluster identification increases with the number of tags, which leads to excessive bit error in the decoding process.

To further investigate the major reason of the bit errors, in Figure 20 we plot the CDFs of BERs for the three schemes in the 5-tag collision case. The BERs above 0.1 are caused by errors in the cluster identification process, which generally results in excessive bit errors. We can see that the cluster identification error of FlipTracer is much lower than that of BiGroup and CB.

Breaking down the benefits. Let us now break down the aggregated throughput by different components of our design to see how much each of them matters. Figure 21 shows the result. We start with the approach that only uses the core design of FlipTracer[6]. Then we add bit error correction module (BCM). Finally we add the OFG correction module (GCM).

We see that each of these benefits the overall throughput: the core design of FlipTracer does really well by itself, but there are more errors as the number of tags increases. For example, when the number of the colliding tag is 5, the core design of FlipTracer causes about 20% of throughput reduction, compared to what is achieved by FlipTracer. Bit error correction component improves the throughput by about 5% and adding the OFG correction component further improves it by another 15%. We can see that the OFG correction component leads to more performance gain than the bit error correction component.

9.4 Impacts of Practical Factors

To understand the impacts of some practical factors on FlipTracer, we conduct the following experiments.

Bitrate. As shown in Section 8, besides the concurrency level, bitrate is another factor that can affect the performance of FlipTracer. In this experiment, we vary the bitrate of the 5 tags from 100Kbps to 600Kbps, and observe the aggregated throughput. Since the WISP platforms currently support only a 256Kbps bitrate, we conduct simulations to see the performance of FlipTracer with 500~600 Kbps

[6]FlipTracer that is not integrated with the OFG correction module and the bit error correction module

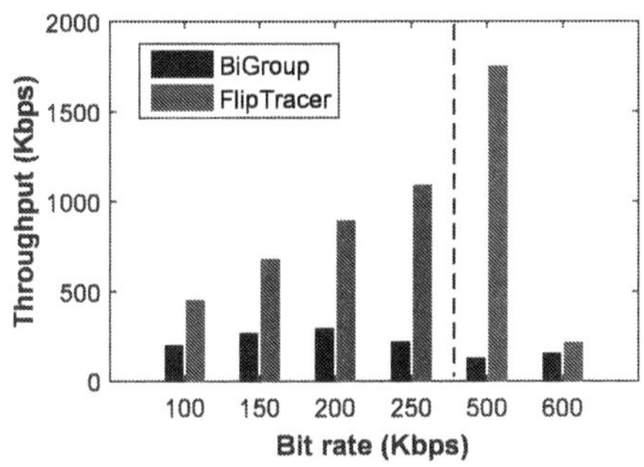

Figure 23: Throughput comparison under different bitrates.

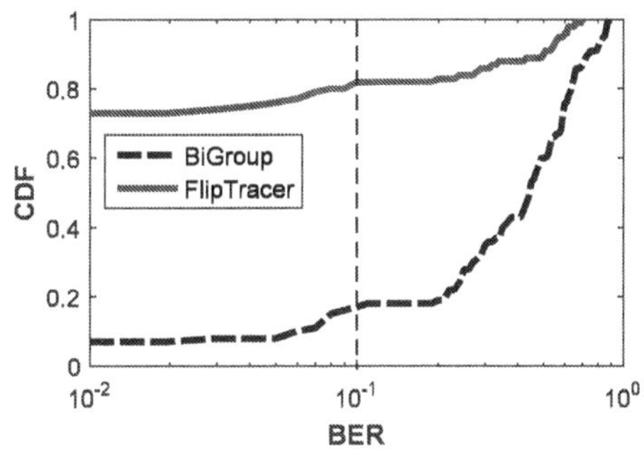

Figure 24: BERs when bitrate is 500Kbps and the number of tag is 5.

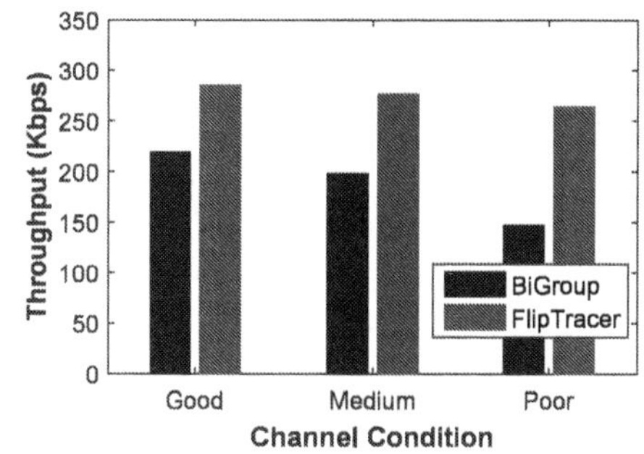

Figure 25: Throughput comparison under different channel condition.

bitrate. Figure 22 shows that the aggregated throughput crash at 600Kbps. This gives us an empirical upper bound on the aggregated throughput FlipTracer can support - **concurrent transfer from 5 tags at 500Kbps**. The crash is not surprising. Our reader samples at 20 MHz, and tags transmit at 600Kbps, so we can stack at most 12 separated edges in one chip (half bit) duration. Our deployment have 5 nodes, so there is a large number of aligned signal edges, which may overthrow our assumption that "the signal edges from different tags are separated most of the time".

In Figure 23, We compare the aggregated throughput for 5 concurrent tags achieved by BiGroup and FlipTracer (since CB can not support more than 4 tags) under different bitrates. We observe that the throughput of BiGroup crash after 200Kbps. The reason is that a high bitrate will make the signal edges from different tags be too close to each other. Given that the bit duration for each tag is not stable, the reader can hardly distinguish the edges of different tags. This results in excessive errors in the decoding process of BiGroup. Figure 23 also shows that the maximum aggregated throughput of BiGroup is 300Kbps. Compared with BiGroup, FlipTracer is more robust to the high bitrate: when tags transmit at 500Kbps, the throughput of FlipTracer is 14× higher than that of BiGroup.

In Figure 24, we plot the CDFs of BERs for FlipTracer and BiGroup when the bitrate is 500Kbps and the number of tags is 5. By comparing Figures 20 and 24, we find that a high bitrate can seriously affect the cluster identification accuracy of BiGroup, which results in the throughput crash of BiGroup after 200 Kbps.

Channel condition. Channel condition can also affect the performance of FlipTracer. To evaluate the impact of channel condition, in this experiment, we use three tags (each transmit at 100Kpbs) and keep moving the tags further and further away from the reader to worsen the channels of all tags. Figure 25 compares the aggregated throughput of BiGroup and FlipTracer under different channel conditions. We can see that when the channel quality is good, both FlipTracer and BiGroup achieve good throughput. When the channel worsens, the aggregated throughput of BiGroup decreases significantly. The reason behind is that under a poor channel condition, clusters become closer to or even overlap with each other, which brings errors in symbol clustering process of BiGroup. What's worse, noise spike occurs frequently in poor channel conditions, which will be confused as signal edges, making it more difficult to separate and extract the signal edges of different tags. This incurs excessive errors in BiGroup. By contrast, FlipTracer is highly robust to poor channel conditions.

We further plot the CDFs of BERs for BiGroup and FlipTracer under the poor channel condition in Figure 26. We find that the channel condition can affect the accuracy in both symbol clustering and cluster identification components, leading to high BERs even when the number of the concurrent tags is 3.

9.5 FlipTracer in "bad" working condition

This subsection evaluates the performance of FlipTracer under some "bad" working conditions.

Dynamic environment. Figure 27 shows the impact of dynamic working conditions. Four cases are compared: i) the stable working condition; ii) the tags and the reader are fixed, but there is a moving obstacle in the vicinity of the tags and the reader; iii) the reader is fixed but the locations of the tags keep changing; and iv) the reader is fixed but the tags' orientations keep changing.

We find in Figure 27 that the throughput of FlipTracer under dynamic scenarios is slightly lower than that in the static scenario. The reason behind is that although the obstacle, rotation and mobility will change the channel coefficients of the tags, FlipTracer is able to decode the collided signals without channel coefficient information.

Co-existence of fast and slow tags. One of the key benefits of FlipTracer is that it can support widely different bitrates among tags. To evaluate this benefit, we use three tags (denoted as Tags 1, 2, and 3) and evaluate the aggregated throughput in three different scenarios: i) we let all the three tags transmit at 100Kbps; ii) we let the three tags transmit at different bitrates (i.e., 100Kbps, 150Kbps and 200Kbps). iii) we let Tags 1 and 2 transmit very slow (50Kbps) and Tag 3 transmit very fast (250Kbps).

Figure 28 shows the packet reception rate achieved by each tag under different scenarios. The results show that: i) the throughput achieved in the second case is almost the same as that achieved in the first case. ii) even in the third case where the bitrate of the fast tag is 5× as that of the slow tags, the throughput only slightly decreases. The above results imply that FlipTracer can support concurrency tags with widely different bitrates.

9.6 Impact of unstable clocks

Another key benefit of FlipTracer is its ability to decoding without stable clocks. Since clock drifting rates of the tags are uncontrollable

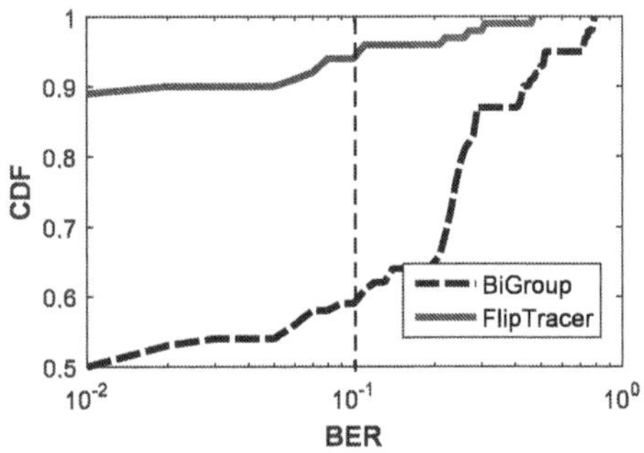

Figure 26: CDF for BERs under poor channel condition.

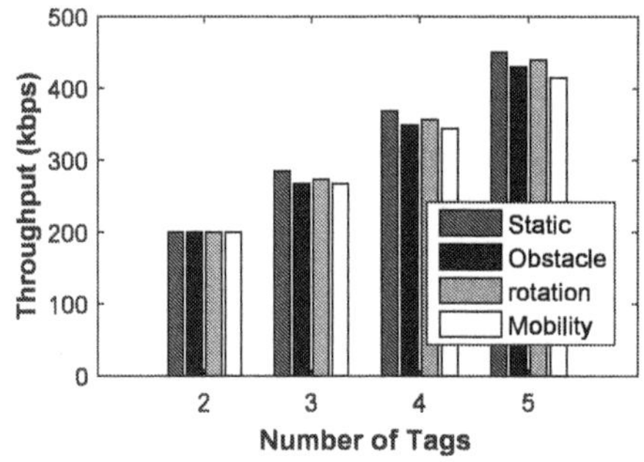

Figure 27: Throughput of FlipTracer under different working conditions.

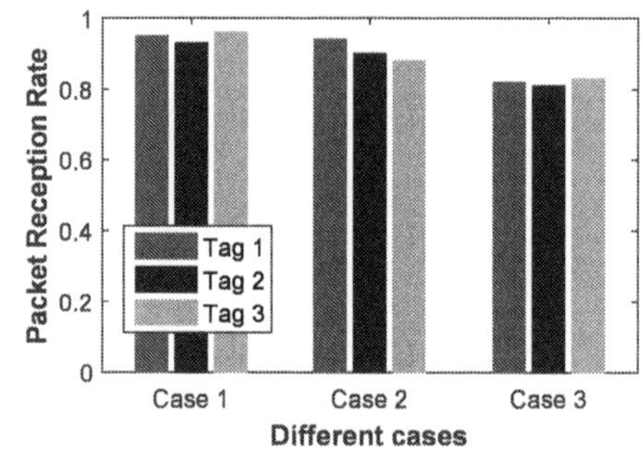

Figure 28: Throughput of FlipTracer when tags transmit at different bitrates.

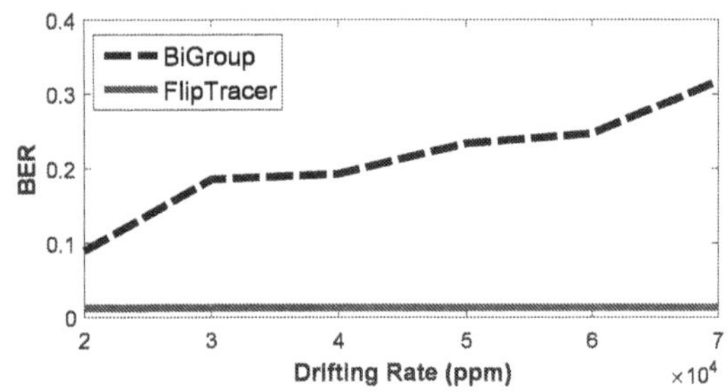

Figure 29: Impact of clock drifting rate.

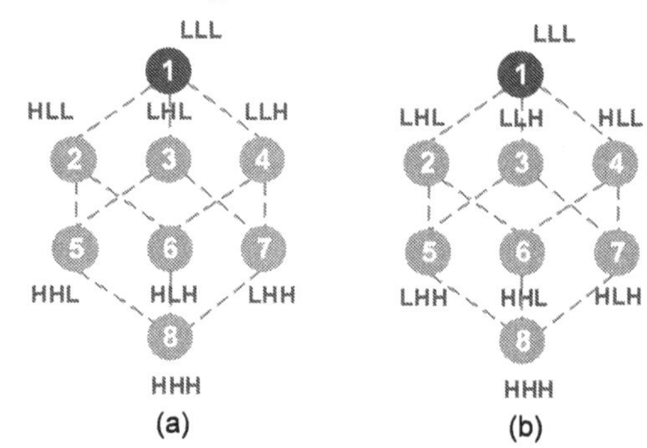

Figure 30: Two different assignments of the Layer 1 clusters on the same OFG.

in the real-world experiment, we conduct simulations to evaluate the impact of the clock drifting rate. Our simulation inherits the settings from our experiments.

Figure 29 shows the BER comparison of BiGroup and FlipTracer under different clock drifting rates, when the number of colliding tags is 5. We can see that the BER of BiGroup increases rapidly when the drifting rate increases. In comparison, the increase in the BER of FlipTracer is almost imperceptible.

10 CONCLUSIONS

We have presented FlipTracer, a practical parallel decoding approach that is designed to work under highly dynamic backscatter system. FlipTracer achieves this by leveraging the stable transition pattern of the signals, rather than the dynamic and irregular IQ and time domain features of the signals. The experimental results show that FlipTracer is robust in various scenarios and achieves a nearly 2Mbps maximum aggregate throughput. In the future works, we would like to explore the scalability of FlipTracer as well as hardware speedup for better time efficiency.

ACKNOWLEDGMENT

We would like to thank the shepherd Prof. Prasun Sinha, as well as Prof. Baochun Li, Prof. Bin Wu, Prof. Zheng Wang, Prof. Longfei Shangguan, and the anonymous reviewers for their valuable feedbacks on this paper. This work was supported by National Basic Research Program (973 program) under Grant of 2014CB347800, National Natural Science Fund of China for Excellent Young Scientist No.61422207, the NSFC (61572402, 61672428, 61672427), and the Program for Innovative Research Team in University No. IRT13090.

A APPENDIX

We explain why different assignments of the first layer clusters of OFG do not affect the decoding results. In fact, the assignments only determine the "temporary IDs" of the tags. All the assignments will eventually output N *uniquely determined* 'HL' sequences (where N is the number of tags). In other words, different assignments only lead to different mappings between the N "temporary IDs" and the N sequences. Note that what we essentially care about is not the "temporary IDs" (which are used to distinguish different tags in the decoding process), but the IDs (or data) embedded in the packets (these IDs are physically associated the tags).

Here we use a concrete example to clearly explain the above point. Figures 30(a) and 30(b) illustrate two different assignments of the Layer 1 clusters on the same OFG. In Figure 30(a), we denote Cluster 2 as HLL (that is to say, we denote the tag which causes the transition between cluster 1 and cluster 2 as Tag 1), Cluster 3 as LHL, and Cluster 4 as LLH. Assuming the reader receives Clusters 0, 1, and then 5, the output sequences are: Tag1: 'LHH'; Tag2: 'LLH'; Tag3: 'LLL'. If we use the assignments in Figure 30(b), the output sequences will be: Tag1: 'LLL'; Tag2: 'LHH'; Tag3: 'LLH'. As noted above, the temporary IDs of the tags are just used for distinguishing these tags (but not used for denoting the tags) in the decoding process. Once we know there are three tags transmitting LLL, LLH, and LHH, respectively, such information is sufficient for correct decoding. After the whole packets of the three tags are decoded, we can know the IDs (or data which are embedded in the payloads of the packets) of the tags.

REFERENCES

[1] Radio-frequency identity protocols class-1 generation-2. http://www.gs1.org/gsmp/kc/epcglobal/uhfc1g2.
[2] O. Abari, D. Vasisht, D. Katabi, and A. Chandrakasan. Caraoke: An e-toll transponder network for smart cities. In *SigComm*, 2015.
[3] C. Angerer, R. Langwieser, and M. Rupp. Rfid reader receivers for physical layer collision recovery. *IEEE Transactions on Communications*, 58(12):3526–3537, 2010.
[4] A. Bletsas, J. Kimionis, A. G. Dimitriou, and G. N. Karystinos. Single-antenna coherent detection of collided fm0 rfid signals. *IEEE Transactions on Communications*, 60(3):756–766, 2012.
[5] A. Gudipati and S. Katti. Strider: Automatic rate adaptation and collision handling. In *SIGCOMM*, 2011.
[6] P. Hu, P. Zhang, and D. Ganesan. Leveraging interleaved sig-nal edges for concurrent backscatter. In *HotWireless*, 2014.
[7] P. Hu, P. Zhang, and D. Ganesan. Laissez-faire: Fully asymmetric backscatter communication. In *SIGCOMM*, 2015.
[8] S. Jana and S. K. Kasera. On fast and accurate detection of unauthorized wireless access points using clock skews. In *MobiCom*, 2008.
[9] L. Kang, K. Wu, J. Zhang, and L. M. Ni. Ddc: A novel scheme to directly decode the collisions in uhf rfid systems. *IEEE Transactions on Parallel and Distributed Systems*, 23(2):263–270, 2012.
[10] R. Khasgiwale, R. Adyanthaya, and D. Engels. Extracting information from tag collisions. In *RFID*, 2009.
[11] L. Kong, L. He, Y. Gu, M.-Y. Wu, and T. He. A parallel identification protocol for rfid systems. In *INFOCOM*, 2014.
[12] C. Mutti and C. Floerkemeier. Cdma-based rfid systems in dense scenarios: Concepts and challenges. In *RFID*, 2008.
[13] J. Ou, M. Li, and Y. Zheng. Come and be served: Parallel decoding for cots rfid tags. In *MobiCom*, 2015.
[14] A. N. Parks, A. Liu, S. Gollakota, and J. R. Smith. Turbocharging ambient backscatter communication. In *SIGCOMM*, 2014.
[15] A. Rodriguez and A. Laio. Clustering by fast search and find of density peaks. *Science*, 344(6191):1492–1496, 2014.
[16] L. Shangguan, Z. Li, Z. Yang, M. Li, and Y. Liu. Otrack: Order tracking for luggage in mobile rfid systems. In *INFOCOM*, 2013.
[17] L. Shangguan, Z. Yang, A. Liu, Z. Zhou, and Y. Liu. Relative localization of rfid tags using spatial-temporal phase profiling. In *NSDI*, 2015.
[18] D. Shen, G. Woo, D. P. Reed, A. B. Lippman, and J. Wang. Efficient and reliable low-power backscatter networks. In *RFID*, 2009.
[19] J. Wang, H. Hassanieh, D. Katabi, and P. Indyk. Efficient and reliable low-power backscatter networks. In *SIGCOMM*, 2012.
[20] J. Wang and D. Katabi. Dude, where's my card? rfid positioning that works with multipathand non-line of sight. In *SIGCOMM*, 2013.
[21] J. Xiong and K. Jamieson. Arraytrack: A fine-grained indoor location system. In *NSDI*, 2013.
[22] L. Yang, Y. Chen, X.-Y. Li, C. Xiao, M. Li, and Y. Liu. Tagoram: real-time tracking of mobile rfid tags to high precision using cots devices. In *MobiCom*, 2014.
[23] L. Yang, Q. Lin, X.-Y. Li, T. Liu, and Y. Liu. See through walls with cots rfid system! In *MobiCom*, 2015.
[24] D. Zanetti, B. Danev, and S. Capkun. Physical-layer identification of uhf rfid tags. In *MobiCom*, 2010.

TagScan: Simultaneous Target Imaging and Material Identification with Commodity RFID Devices

Ju Wang†, Jie Xiong♯, Xiaojiang Chen†,
Hongbo Jiang‡, Rajesh Krishna Balan♯, Dingyi Fang†

†Northwest University, ♯Singapore Management University,
‡Huazhong University of Science and Technology
†{wangju,xjchen,dyf}@nwu.edu.cn, ♯{jxiong,rajesh}@smu.edu.sg, ‡hongbojiang2004@gmail.com

ABSTRACT

Target imaging and material identification play an important role in many real-life applications. This paper introduces TagScan, a system that can identify the material type and image the horizontal cut of a target *simultaneously* with cheap commercial off-the-shelf (COTS) RFID devices. The key intuition is that different materials and target sizes cause different amounts of phase and RSS (Received Signal Strength) changes when radio frequency (RF) signal penetrates through the target. Multiple challenges need to be addressed before we can turn the idea into a functional system including (i) indoor environments exhibit rich multipath which breaks the linear relationship between the phase change and the propagation distance inside a target; (ii) without knowing either material type or target size, trying to obtain these two information simultaneously is challenging; and (iii) stitching pieces of the propagation distances inside a target for an image estimate is non-trivial.

We propose solutions to all the challenges and evaluate the system's performance in three different environments. TagScan is able to achieve higher than 94% material identification accuracies for 10 liquids and differentiate even very similar objects such as Coke and Pepsi. TagScan can accurately estimate the horizontal cut images of more than one target behind a wall.

CCS CONCEPTS

• **Computer systems organization** → **Sensors and actuators**;

KEYWORDS

Horizontal cut imaging; Material identification; Multipath suppression; Phase and RSS measurements; RFID

MobiCom'17, October 16–20, 2017, Snowbird, UT, USA

ACM ISBN 978-1-4503-4916-1/17/10...$15.00
https://doi.org/10.1145/3117811.3117830

1 INTRODUCTION

Device-free passive sensing, where no device is attached to the target, has recently received considerable attentions. Many compelling applications are enabled by device-free passive sensing, such as human motion tracking [2, 45], gesture and activity recognition [35, 37], elderly fall detection [38], and even localizing a person behind a wall [3, 41]. Diverse technologies have been employed for these applications including camera [48], infrared [18], audio [36] and RF signal [47].

Among the technologies for device-free passive sensing, RF-based approaches [22, 28, 31, 37] offer two appealing advantages: (i) functioning in the dark environments and (ii) RF signals can penetrate non-metal walls. More importantly, RF-based solutions are promising due to their ubiquity and low cost. In particular, RFID is evolving as a major candidate for object identification and localization in indoor environments. RFID has been used for localization [32, 34], baggage sorting [25, 44], gesture recognition [10, 26], and even tracing a user's handwriting in the air without a physical touch screen [16, 33]. RFID tags are everywhere and commonly used for bus cards, car keys, pass cards, etc. One main reason for the widespread of usage is the simplicity and extremely low cost of the RFID tags (each tag costs 5 –10 cents USD).

Though a success in localization and gesture recognition, a missing research component of existing device-free sensing technology is using cheap commodity RF devices, such as RFID, to perform target imaging and material identification. Many applications would benefit from knowing the shape and material type of a target. For example, a robot can automatically adjust its grip strength if it knows the object is an egg instead of a stone by using material identification. Detecting concealed weapons at a security checkpoint would be possible by knowing the target shape and the material type. It will be possible to differentiate Pepsi from Coke without labels or a taste test.

Existing target imaging and material identification systems, such as Radar [19], X-Ray [21], CT/MRI [49] and B-scan ultrasonography [7], use dedicated hardware with high frequency signal, large bandwidth and antenna arrays, which are extremely expensive and usually large in size. Moreover, X-Ray and CT employ very high frequency signals which are harmful to the human body [23].

Recently, some researchers attempt to use the RF signals to image a target's shape [1, 8, 11] or identify a target's material [46, 50].

RF-Capture [1] can capture the skeleton of a human target using special-purpose hardware with larger than 1 GHz bandwidth Frequency Modulated Continuous Wave (FMCW) signals. However, commodity Wi-Fi and RFID devices have much smaller bandwidths. Wision system [11] with a two-dimensional antenna array, employs the reflected Wi-Fi signal from the target for imaging. However, its imaging performance is still coarse. Moreover, the above systems employ the reflection signals bounced off the target. Thus, these systems can only obtain the surface image and the surface material of a target – they are not able to obtain the internal horizontal cut image and the internal material of a target. Overall, imaging a target's shape and identifying its material type with cheap commodity devices remain challenging.

This paper introduces TagScan, a system that can both identify the material type and image the internal horizontal cut of a target *simultaneously* with cheap COTS RFID devices. Unlike existing systems which employ dedicated hardware or special-purpose large bandwidth signals to extract the reflectivity and permeability parameters for material identification [40], TagScan exploits the phase and RSS changes when the signal penetrates inside a target for material identification and imaging. The phase and RSS measurements are widely available on commodity devices and TagScan works well with a small 4 MHz bandwidth. We believe this work introduces a new direction for performing material identification and imaging with COTS devices. TagScan's material identification and imaging are based on the key observation that different materials and target sizes will cause different amounts of phase and RSS changes when the RF signal penetrates through a target. Further, if there is no multipath, the phase change values exhibit a linear relationship with the propagation distances inside the target.

Though the basic idea sounds straightforward, it is non-trivial to realize TagScan due to the following challenges:

- **Challenge 1**: In an indoor environment, the rich multipath signals break the linear relationship between the phase changes and the propagation distances inside a target.
- **Challenge 2**: Determining the size of a target given the material type or identifying the material given the target size is relatively easy. Without knowing either material type or target size, trying to identify these two pieces of information at the same time is much more challenging.
- **Challenge 3**: Even if the propagation distances inside a target at different directions are obtained, stitching them together to create the image is still challenging as the starting points of the propagation distances are unknown.

To deal with the first challenge, we propose a multipath suppression scheme based on the following observations: (i) the phase measurements change linearly over the carrier frequencies if the direct-path signal dominates; (ii) for nearby tags and adjacent channels, the direct-path signals are similar while the multipath signals are usually quite different. Based on the first observation, TagScan picks data from relatively "clean" channels that are not greatly affected by multipath for processing. With the second observation, TagScan further reduces the multipath effect by applying carefully chosen weights on the signals received from different tags and at different channels, so that the power of the direct-path signals increases greatly while the power of the reflection signals is averaged out to a small value.

To address the second challenge, although the RSS change and phase change are dependent on both the target material and the target size, we discover a parameter that related to the ratio of *RSS change* and *phase change* (denoted as RP-rate) is a unique feature for each material type and independent of the target size. By removing one variable, we are able to obtain the target material and size/shape at the same time.

To deal with the third challenge, the key intuition is that the target images estimated from two different arrays will align well when all the starting points of the propagation distances are correctly selected. We thus model the imaging problem as an optimization problem and search the starting points by minimizing the difference of two images estimated from the two arrays.

We build a prototype of TagScan using just one Impinj RFID reader [14] and 16 cheap Alien RFID tags [12]. The 16 tags form two linear tag-arrays with 8 tags in each. We evaluate the material identification and imaging performance in three typical indoor environments: a library, a lab-office and an empty hall corresponding to high, medium and low multipath environments. In the lab-office environment, the material identification accuracies of TagScan are higher than 94% and 91% for 10 types of liquids and 6 types of solid targets, respectively. Note that we employ very similar liquids such as Pepsi, Coke and sweet water with different sugar concentrations to make our material identification problem challenging. TagScan can also estimate the cut image of a human body accurately which has attractive authentication application. In a more challenging scenario, TagScan can estimate the cut images of a cube and a cylinder behind a wall simultaneously when they are not close to each other.

Contributions: The main contributions of this paper are summarized as follows:

(1) To the best of our knowledge, this is the first RFID-based system which utilizes the widely available phase and RSS information on COTS devices to perform material identification and target imaging simultaneously.
(2) We propose a multipath suppression method so that even in a rich multipath environment, the phase and RSS changes can be used to identify the material type and image the target shape at a high accuracy.
(3) We discover a feature that is unique for each material type and independent of the target size, and also can be easily calculated from the RSS and phase readings. We observe that this feature is sensitive enough to help differentiate between Pepsi and Coke.
(4) Without knowing the ground truth image beforehand, TagScan is able to estimate the cut image of a target based on one observation: the images estimated from two different arrays align well if they are estimated correctly.
(5) We design and implement TagScan with COTS RFID devices. Comprehensive experiments demonstrate the effectiveness of TagScan under varying conditions.

Paper outline: We introduce the preliminary studies in Section 2. We detail TagScan's design in Section 3. The implementation is described in Section 4 followed by the evaluations in Section 5. We discuss limitations and other related issues in Section 6. The related work is shown in Section 7 and we conclude this paper in Section 8.

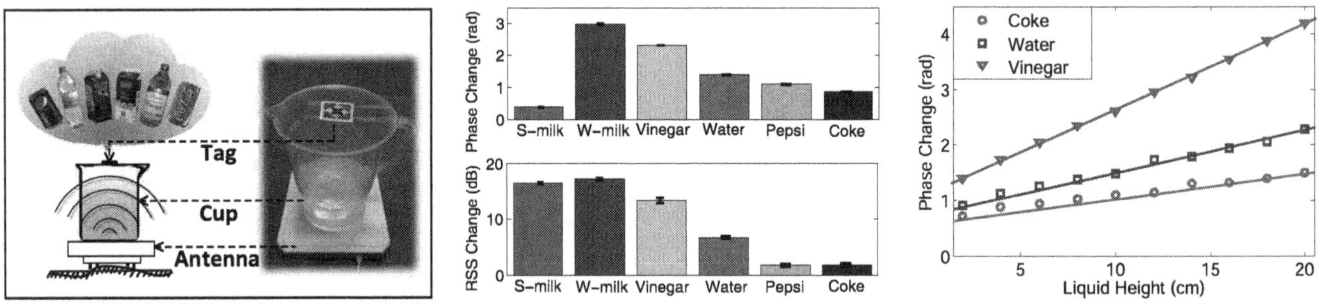

(a) Experimental setup. (b) Phase/RSS changes in different materials. (c) Phase changes *vs* liquid heights.

Figure 1: Preliminary studies of the phase and RSS changes inside targets with different materials and different sizes.

2 PRELIMINARY

We present the preliminary studies of the phase and RSS changes inside a target and the effect of multipath on the phase change measurements in this section.

2.1 Phase Changes Inside a Target

To illustrate TagScan's basic idea for material identification, Fig. 1(a) shows an example where a directional antenna of an RFID reader is placed on the ground in an open space to minimize the amount of multipath. A plastic measuring cup with a height of 28.5 cm and a diameter of 19.7 cm is placed on top of the antenna. We place an RFID tag on top of the cup and pour the same amount (8 cm of height) of purified water, vinegar, skimmed milk, whole milk, Coke and Pepsi into the cup. We measure the phase and RSS readings before and after each liquid is poured into the cup, and then calculate the changes shown in Fig. 1(b).

We observe that the phase changes for water, vinegar, skimmed milk and whole milk are quite different. For Coke and Pepsi, the result is surprising since there is still around 0.2 radians phase change difference,[1] which is clear enough for us to differentiate them. The RSS changes for Coke and Pepsi are very similar but are quite different from other liquids. The observation implies that it is possible to employ the phase and RSS changes for material identification. Note that the commodity RFID reader eliminates the directly reflected signal from a target and only keeps the signal from the tags [14].

To illustrate TagScan's basic idea for imaging, we use three different types of liquids (purified water, Coke, and vinegar) and run the following benchmark experiment. We vary the amount of liquid in the cup and measure the phase changes with respect to the empty cup. During the process, the gap distance between the tag and the liquid surface is decreased from 26.5 cm to from 8.5 cm in a step of 2 cm and the liquid height is increased from 2 cm to 20 cm. Fig. 1(c) shows a clear linear relationship between the phase change and the distance that the signal travelled inside the liquid. Further, the slopes of different materials are distinct. Based on this observation, if the material of a target is known, TagScan can get the propagation distance inside the target with the phase change measurement. This propagation distance is the "width" information of the target at one angle. By stitching those "widths" from many angles, TagScan can obtain the target's cut image.

2.2 Phase Changes in Multipath Environment

We show the intuition behind our multipath suppression method using both the theoretical analysis and the benchmark experiments. In an ideal open space without any multipath, the measured phase difference between frequency f_p and frequency f_q at a reader can be written as:

$$\Delta\phi_{f_p,f_q} = \frac{4\pi L}{C}(f_p - f_q), \quad (1)$$

where C is the speed of light and L is the distance between the tag and antenna. Since L is a constant for a given deployment, the slope $4\pi L/C$ of the phase change is also a constant. So the phase value changes linearly with frequency when there is only direct path. In reality, the linear relationship is broken by multipath. We run benchmark experiments in three different environments: a hall environment (little multipath), a lab-office environment (medium multipath), and a library environment (rich multipath). An RFID tag is placed 5 m away from the reader antenna, and the reader is programmed to hop over 16 adjacent channels.[2]

Observation 1: Fig. 2 shows the phase measurements over 16 channels in four different environments with different amounts of multipath. We can see that in the hall environment with little multipath, the linear relationship between phases and channels can still be observed. One reason behind this is that commodity RFID devices usually employ directional antennas to increase the transmission range, which reduces the amount of multipath. However, even with directional antenna, in a rich-multipath environment such as a library, the linear relationship does not exist any more.

Observation 2: Fig. 3 shows the phase measurements of 6 nearby tags (the spacing between adjacent tags is about 10 cm) in the hall environment. We can see that the slopes of the phase changes are similar for closely placed tags. As direct path is dominant in the hall environment, we conclude that the direct-path signals are similar at closely placed tags.

These results convince us to select phase readings from the relatively "clean" channels based on the linear property when multipath is not strong. The selection pool is large as we have multiple tags and each tag has multiple channels. When multipath is strong, it is difficult to find these kind of "clean" channels and thus we propose a multipath suppression scheme (Section 3.2) to address the multipath issue.

[1] Impinj R420 reader [14] has an analog to digital converter of 12-bit which achieves a phase resolution of 0.0015 radians.

[2] The frequency range of Impinj R420 reader in China is 920.625 – 924.375 MHz and each channel has a bandwidth of 250 KHz.

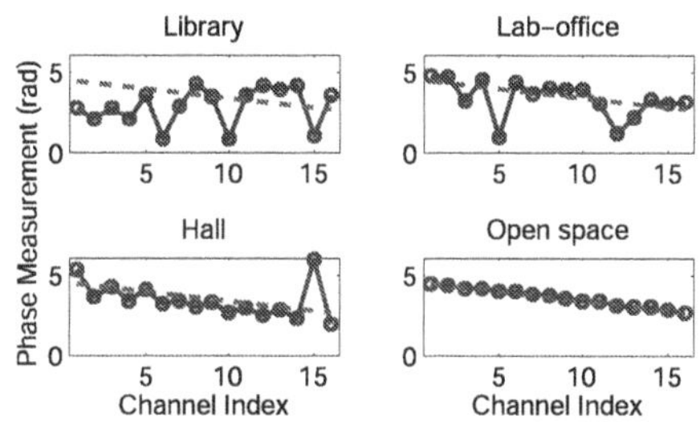

Figure 2: Phase changes linearly when the direct-path signal dominates.

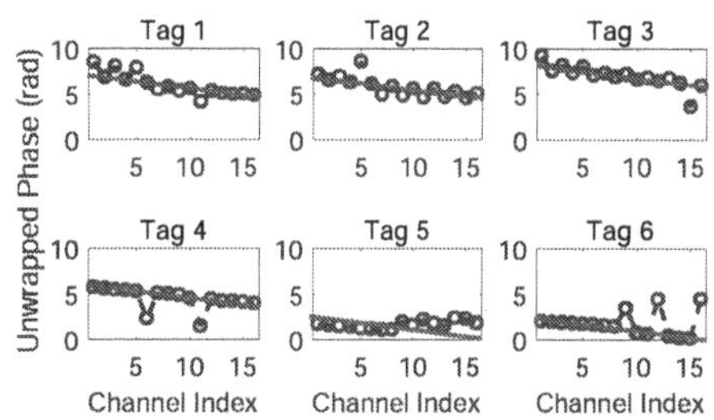

Figure 3: Unwrapped phase data over 16 channels in the hall environment.

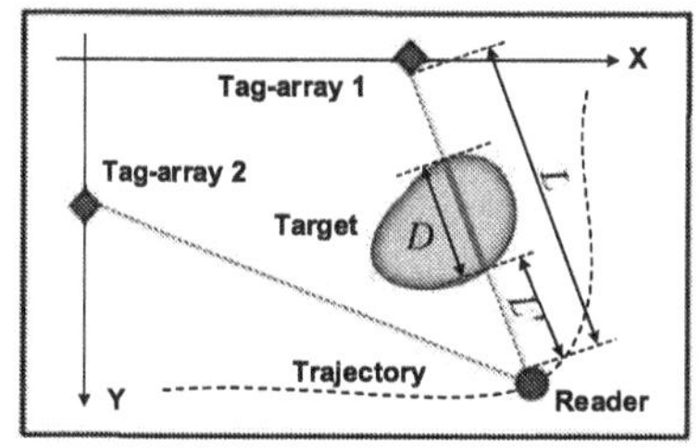

Figure 4: An overview of TagScan's system deployment setup.

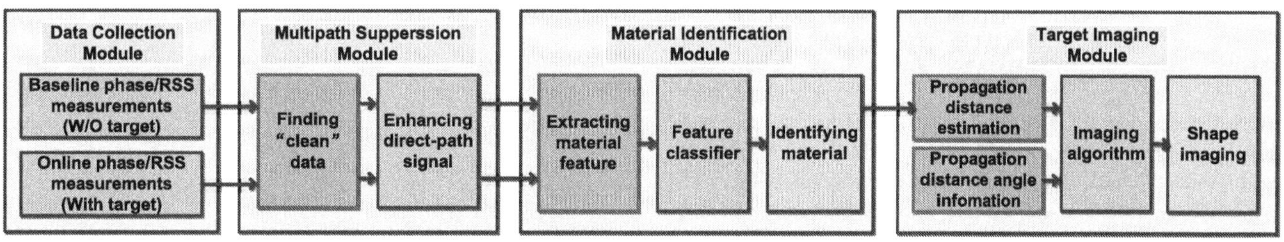

Figure 5: System architecture of TagScan.

3 DESIGN

3.1 Overview

TagScan is a material identification and imaging system built on COTS RFID devices. It only uses one RFID reader with one antenna and multiple tags which form two linear tag-arrays as shown in Fig. 4. The reader communicates with the tags across different frequency channels.[3] For imaging, we let the reader move along a given trajectory. When the target blocks the direct path between the reader and tag-array, phase and RSS changes can be observed and are utilised for material identification and target image. Fig. 5 shows the system architecture which has four modules:

- **Data Collection Module:** TagScan collects a set of phase and RSS measurements as the baseline data[4] when there is no target. TagScan then acquires another set of measurements when the target appears.
- **Multipath Suppression Module:** TagScan first identifies the relatively "clean" channels which are not greatly affected by multipath. TagScan then strengthens the power of the direct-path signal and reduces the power of reflection signals by assigning carefully chosen weights to the measured signals at different channels and different tags as discussed in Section 3.2.
- **Material Identification Module**: TagScan extracts the feature parameter *RP-rate* which is only dependent on the target material and employs the "K Nearest Neighbor" (KNN) [9] classifier to identify the target's material as described in Section 3.3. Note that for material identification, only one tag-array is needed and the reader does not need to move.
- **Target Imaging Module:** Once the target material is identified, TagScan estimates the signal propagation distance inside the target along a specific direction. This propagation distance is the "width" information of the target at one angle. TagScan stitches together the "widths" from many angles to obtain the horizontal cut image of the target as described in Section 3.4.

[3]RFID systems use frequency hopping for security reason.

[4]The baseline measurements only need to be measured once.

3.2 Multipath Suppression

TagScan relies on the linear relationship between the distance travelled inside the target and the phase/RSS changes for material identification and target imaging. However, multipath reflections break the linear relationship. To deal with multipath, we introduce a two-stage multipath suppression method. In stage 1, we identify the relatively "clean" channels that are not greatly affected by multipath. In stage 2, we further reduce the effect of multipath by assigning carefully chosen weights to the measured signals at different channels and different tags. By doing this, the power of direct-path signals increases greatly while the power of the reflection signals is averaged out to a small value.

3.2.1 Identifying the relatively "clean" channels. Using "Observation 1" and "Observation 2" in Section 2.2, we identify the relatively "clean" channels whose direct-path signal dominates with a simple linear fit. However, this works well only in the environment with little multipath such as the hall environment and is much less reliable in medium and rich multipath environments.

3.2.2 Enhancing the direct-path signal. Using the method described above, we are able to remove "dirty" data in environments with little multipath. However, there is always residual multipath noise left in the relatively "clean" data. Furthermore, in a rich multipath environment, it is difficult to identify such "clean" channels. Thus, we propose a method to strengthen the direct-path signal and reduce the power of multipath reflection signals.

At a high level, we combine signals measured from different channels and different tags by assigning each signal a different weight to enhance the direct-path signal and reduce the multipath

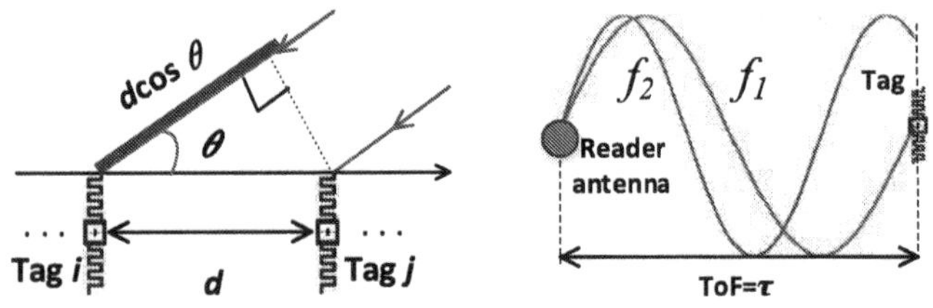

(a) Phase shift of $\frac{4\pi f}{C} d\cos(\theta)$ at two adjacent tags.

(b) Phase shift of $4\pi\tau\Delta f$ at two adjacent channels.

Figure 6: Phase shifts of measured direct-path signals at two adjacent tags and two adjacent channels.

effect. The intuition is that the direct-path signals measured at nearby tags and adjacent channels are similar. Thus, we can align these direct-path signals by compensating the phase shifts with carefully chosen weights. Then, we sum up the compensated signals so the direct-path signals are aligned and added constructively, while the reflected path signals are reduced to a small value.

Formally, we consider a tag-array with M tags and a reader working in frequency hopping mode across K adjacent channels. We take the first tag as the reference tag and the first channel with frequency f as the reference channel. The tags are placed with a distance of d and the frequency spacing between adjacent channels is Δf. There are two types of phase shifts in the direct-path signals. First, the phase shift between tags is due to the propagation distance difference. As shown in Fig. 6(a), when two direct-path signals arrive at the tags at a same angle-of-arrival (AoA) θ, the two direct-path signals have a propagation distance difference of $d\cos(\theta)$ and thus a phase difference of $\frac{4\pi f}{C} d\cos(\theta)$. Second, the phase shift between channels is due to the carrier frequency difference. As shown in Fig. 6(b), two direct-path signals with slightly different frequencies arrive at a same tag with a very similar propagation time τ. Thus, the two direct-path signals have a phase shift of $4\pi\tau\Delta f$.

To model the multipath reflection signals, suppose there are P copies (one direct-path and $P-1$ reflection paths) of a transmission, i.e., $S=[s_1, s_2, \cdots, s_P]^T$, arriving at the array from P different AoA angles $\theta=[\theta_1, \theta_2, \cdots, \theta_P]$ with P different time-of-flights (ToFs) $\tau = [\tau_1, \tau_2, \cdots, \tau_P]$. For M tags and K channels, we have a total of $M \times K$ measured signals. The measured signal $x_{m,k}$ at m-th tag and k-th channel is:

$$x_{m,k} = \sum_{p=1}^{P} s_p \cdot e^{-j\cdot[\omega(m,k,\theta_p)+\mu(m,k,\tau_p)]}, \tag{2}$$

$$\omega(m,k,\theta_p) = \frac{4\pi[f+(k-1)\Delta f]}{C}(m-1)dcos(\theta_p), \tag{3}$$

$$\mu(m,k,\tau_p) = 4\pi(k-1)\Delta f[\tau_p - \frac{(m-1)dcos(\theta_p)}{C}], \tag{4}$$

where, $\omega(m,k,\theta_p)$ and $\mu(m,k,\tau_p)$ represent two types of phase shifts due to the propagation distance difference and the carrier frequency difference. With respect to the direct-path signal at the reference tag and the reference channel, the phase shifts of direct-path signal at m-th tag and k-th channel are calculated using Eq. (3) and Eq. (4). Thus, we can align the direct-path signals by compensating the calculated phase shifts for measured signals at all tags and all channels, so the direct-path signals have a same phase and thus can be added constructively. Specifically, the weight for compensating the phase shift of signal $x_{m,k}$ at m-th tag and k-th channel is: $e^{j\cdot\omega(m,k,\theta_1)} \cdot e^{j\cdot\mu(m,k,\tau_1)}$.

Without loss of generality, we assume $s_1 \in S$ is the direct-path signal and $\{s_2, \cdots, s_P\}$ are the reflection-path signals. We can now sum the weighted signals as follows:

$$\begin{aligned}
\Gamma &= \sum_{m=1}^{M}\sum_{k=1}^{K} x_{m,k} \cdot e^{j\cdot\omega(m,k,\theta_1)} \cdot e^{j\cdot\mu(m,k,\tau_1)} \\
&= \left(s_1 + \sum_{p=2}^{P} s_p\right) + \cdots + \\
&\left(s_1 + \sum_{p=2}^{P} s_p e^{j\cdot[\omega(M,K,\theta_1)-\omega(M,K,\theta_p)+\mu(M,K,\tau_1)-\mu(M,K,\tau_p)]}\right) \\
&= \underbrace{MK\cdot s_1}_{\text{Direct-path signal increased}} + \underbrace{\sum_{p=2}^{P}\left[s_p\left(\sum_{m=1}^{M}\sum_{k=1}^{K} e^{j\cdot\Psi(m,k,\theta_p,\tau_P)}\right)\right]}_{\text{Reflection signals add up with random phase shifts}},
\end{aligned} \tag{5}$$

where, $\Psi(m,k,\theta_p,\tau_p) = \frac{4\pi[f+(k-1)\Delta f](m-1)d}{C}[\cos(\theta_1) - \cos(\theta_p)] + 4\pi(k-1)\Delta f(\tau_1 - \tau_p)$. As shown in the above equation, the direct-path signal s_1 adds constructively and its power is increased by MK times. The reflection-path signals are relatively random, i.e., their angle θ_p and propagation time τ_p ($p \neq 1$) are quite different from θ_1 and τ_1 of direct-path signal and are usually very different from each other. Thus, when we align the direct-path signals, the reflection signals add with random phases and their power averages out to a small value. Note that this "averaging out" happens when angles and propagation delays of different reflection signals are randomly distributed which is usually true in reality. With a relatively large value of M and K, the power of the combined direct-path signals is much stronger than the power of the reduced reflection-path signals. Thus, the direct-path signal now dominates and the linear relationship holds. We can then estimate the direct-path signal $\hat{s}_1$, and its corresponding phase ϕ and RSS R as:

$$\hat{s}_1 \approx \Gamma/(MK), \ \phi = \angle(\hat{s}_1), \ R = 20\log|\hat{s}_1|, \tag{6}$$

where $\angle(\cdot)$ and $|\cdot|$ represent the angle and absolute value of a complex number. In this paper, we employ the JADE [30] algorithm to jointly estimate the angle θ_1 and propagation time τ_1 of the direct-path signal. Specifically, JADE is a subspace-based technique which is an extension of the well known MUSIC algorithm [24]. MUSIC is utilized for one-dimensional parameter estimation while JADE is capable of multi-dimensional parameter estimation. We use the method introduced in SpotFi [15] to identify the direct path.

In the rest of this paper, we use the strengthened direct-path signal's phase and RSS value, i.e., ϕ and R in Eq. (6), for material identification and target imaging.

3.3 Target Material Identification

We first introduce the phase and RSS changes caused by a target and then describe our material identification method.

Phase changes after a target shows up. The wavelength of RF signal changes when the signal travels from one material into another while the frequency does not change [6]. As a result, the phase changes are different when the RF signal travels inside different materials, even if the propagation distances are the same. Considering the direct path between the reader and "Tag-array 1" as shown in Fig. 4, where the RF signal penetrates through a target. Let L and L' denote the distances along the direct path from the reader to tag-array and to target, respectively. D is the propagation distance inside the target. Let ϕ^{air} and ϕ^{tar} be the measured signal phase before and after the target blocks the direct path. The phase change $\Delta\phi = \phi^{tar} - \phi^{air}$ after the target shows up is given by:

$$\begin{aligned}\Delta\phi &= [2(L-D)\frac{2\pi}{\lambda_{air}} + 2D\frac{2\pi}{\lambda_{tar}} - 2L\frac{2\pi}{\lambda_{air}}] \mod 2\pi \\ &= [2D(\frac{2\pi}{\lambda_{tar}} - \frac{2\pi}{\lambda_{air}})] \mod 2\pi \\ &= [2D(\beta_{tar} - \beta_{air})] \mod 2\pi, \end{aligned} \tag{7}$$

where λ_{air} and λ_{tar} are signal wavelengths in the air and in the target. The $\beta_{air} = \frac{2\pi}{\lambda_{air}}$ and $\beta_{tar} = \frac{2\pi}{\lambda_{tar}}$ are defined as the signal's *phase constant* in the air and in the target.

RSS changes. The RSS measurement also changes when the RF signal travels through different target materials. Specifically, the amplitude has an $e^{-\alpha}$ attenuation over a unit prorogation distance, where α is the attenuation constant which only depends on the target material [6]. Let R^{air} and R^{tar} be the RSS measurements before and after the target blocks the direct path. Then, the RSS change $\Delta R = R^{tar} - R^{air}$ is given as:

$$\begin{aligned}\Delta R &= 20\log(\frac{A_{tar}}{A_{air}}) \\ &= 20\log\frac{A_S \cdot e^{-\alpha_{air}2L'}e^{-\alpha_{tar}2D}e^{-\alpha_{air}2(L-L'-D)}}{A_S \cdot e^{-\alpha_{air}2(L'+D+L-L'-D)}} \\ &= 20\log[e^{-2D(\alpha_{tar}-\alpha_{air})}], \end{aligned} \tag{8}$$

where A^{air} and A^{tar} are the measured signal amplitudes before and after the target blocks the direct path, A_S is the amplitude of the transmitted signal, α_{air} and α_{tar} are the signal's *attenuation constants* in the air and in the target. Note that Eq. (7) and Eq. (8) also show that the distance L between tags and reader does not affect TagScan's performance, since it is cancelled out when calculating the phase change and RSS change measurements.

3.3.1 Material feature extraction. To identify the material type, we need to extract features that are uniquely related to the material. The phase and RSS changes can not be used directly, since they are also related to the target size, i.e., the propagation distance D. Compared with the phase and RSS changes, the phase constant β and attenuation constant α are more promising candidates to serve as features for material identification. Different materials have different β and α values [6]. However, it is a challenge to estimate the values of β and α at the same time since there are three unknown parameters including the propagation distance D in the two equations Eq. (7) and Eq. (8). Employing multiple reader-tag pairs or frequency-hopping to increase the number of equations does not solve this problem, because the created additional equations are redundant. We address this problem with a novel method. Instead of seeking the absolute values of phase constant β and attenuation constant α, we prove that the relative relationship of β and α calculated by the RSS change and phase change is a parameter independent of target size, and also is unique for each material.

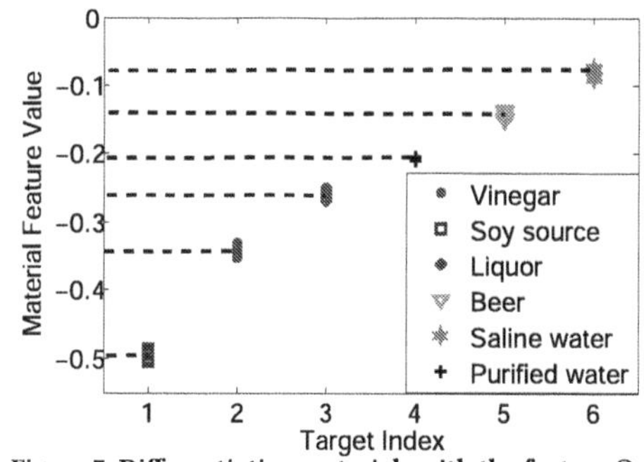

Figure 7: Differentiating materials with the feature Ω.

Specifically, based on Eq. (7) and Eq. (8), we have:

$$2D = \frac{\Delta\phi + 2\zeta\pi}{\beta_{tar} - \beta_{air}} = \frac{\ln 10^{\Delta R/20}}{\alpha_{air} - \alpha_{tar}}, \tag{9}$$

where, ζ is an integer.[5] Based on Eq. (9), we define a feature, i.e., RP-rate Ω, which is related to the ratio of RSS change and phase change as:

$$\Omega = \frac{\ln 10^{\Delta R/20}}{\Delta\phi + 2\zeta\pi} = \frac{\alpha_{air} - \alpha_{tar}}{\beta_{tar} - \beta_{air}}. \tag{10}$$

Note that (i) β_{air} and α_{air} are constants, since they are the phase constant and attenuation constant in the air; (ii) the values of β_{tar} and α_{tar} are also fixed for a given material. Thus, the right side of Eq. (10) is a constant and Ω is unique for a particular material. To this end, we successfully avoid solving β_{tar} and α_{tar} but employ Ω estimated by Eq. (10) for material identification. The feature Ω is independent of the signal propagation distance inside a target which enables material identification without a need of knowing the target size. We show through benchmark experiments that Ω is a fine-grained feature sensitive enough to identify different target materials. We test 6 liquid materials, i.e., "Vinegar", "Soy source", "Liquor", "Beer", "Saline water" and "Purified water". We conduct experiments in the lab-office environment based on the deployment shown in Fig. 1(a). We run the experiments 40 times and calculate the values of Ω based on Eq. (10). The results in Fig. 7 show that the Ω values of 6 liquids are clearly different from each other. It implies that Ω can be employed to effectively identify the target's material type.

3.3.2 Material identification. TagScan has two steps for material identification. First, TagScan builds a feature database which maps the materials to feature (Ω) values. Specifically, for each material, we collect the phase and RSS change measurements in an open space, and then calculate its feature value according to Eq. (10). Note that this process happens only once. Second, based on the phase and RSS change measurements of a test material, TagScan calculates the new feature value and employs the KNN classifier [9] to identify the material type with the database.

3.3.3 Distinguish between similar materials. The feature value Ω is a fine grained parameter to differentiate materials. We can even employ Ω to differentiate Pepsi and Coke as shown in Section 5.3. In rare cases when the Ω values are similar, the phase and RSS

[5] ζ=0 for relatively small objects. The propagation distance inside the water needs to be more than 84.25 cm to cause a phase change of more than 2π.

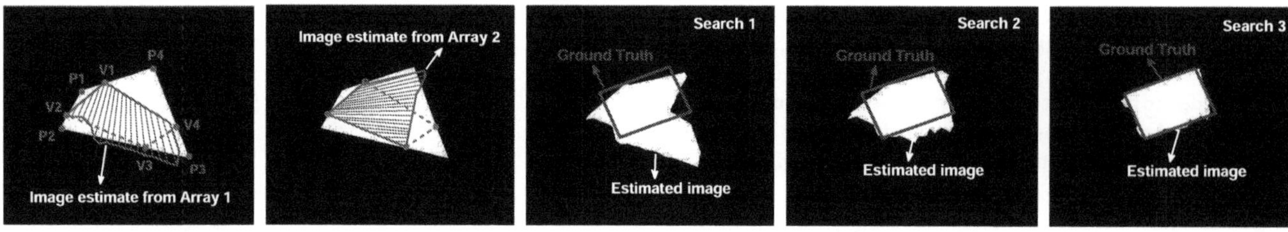

(a) Image from Array 1. (b) Image from Array 2. (c) Union set of images. (d) Another image estimate. (e) Final image estimate.

Figure 8: An illustration of target imaging. (a) and (b) show the target image estimates from Array 1 and Array 2, respectively. (c) is the union set of the two estimated images in (a) and (b). (d) shows another image estimate. (e) shows the output of final image estimate when the difference of images estimated from the two arrays is smaller than a pre-defined threshold.

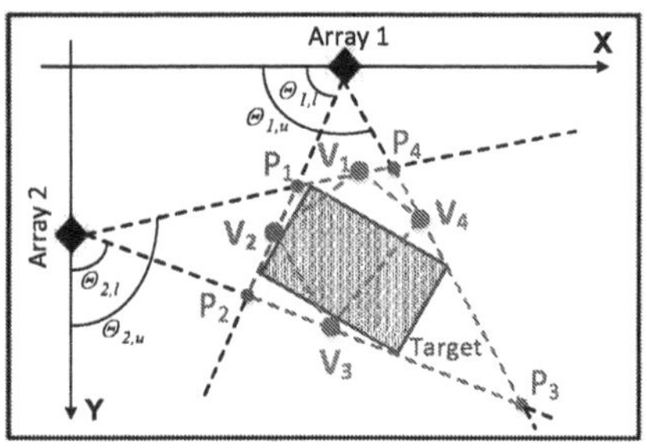

Figure 9: Boundary detection and starting points selection.

change values of each individual may be quite different and can also be employed to further differentiate two materials. For example, we find that sweet water with a 6% sugar concentration has a similar Ω with Coke but their phase change values are very different.

3.3.4 Propagation distance estimation. After identifying the target's material, we can acquire the material's phase constant β either via experiment or from handbook [6]. Then, the propagation distance D can be estimated from Eq. (7) for imaging. We employ the phase measurement but not the RSS measurement to estimate D since the resolution of phase data is higher and the phase readings are usually more stable than the RSS readings.

3.4 Target Shape Imaging

TagScan utilizes the propagation distances inside a target for imaging. Specifically, each propagation distance represents one piece of target width information at one angle. By stitching together these width information at many angles, TagScan can obtain the horizontal cut image of the target. Note that TagScan can obtain the propagation distances at different angles after the target's material is identified. However, the challenge here is that we have no idea about the starting points of the propagation distances. To address this challenge, the key intuition is that the target images estimated by two different arrays will align well when the starting points are correctly selected. Thus, we model the imaging problem as an optimization problem and search the starting points by minimizing the difference of two images estimated from the two arrays.

To narrow down the search space, we first detect the angles of the target boundaries based on the phase change measurements. As shown in Fig. 9, TagScan detects the angles for the lower boundary $\theta_{1,l}$ and the upper boundary $\theta_{1,u}$ at "Array 1" by comparing the phase changes with a threshold. However, the phase changes may be small when the target's boundary part is thin and the propagation distance inside the target is small. In this scenario, the phase noise will confuse the boundary detection. Traditionally, the Cumulative Sum (CUSUM) method [17] is used to address this type of boundary detection problem. However, this method needs a priori knowledge of the phase change distribution, which is not available in our design. To deal with this problem, we have two observations: (i) the phase variation caused by noise is random, which can be averaged out over a time window; (ii) phase changes caused by a target will be accumulated over the time window. We thus introduce a sliding window based cumulative phase change method to detect the angles of the target boundaries.

Formally, when the reader with antenna moves along a trajectory, let $\{\Delta\phi_1, \cdots, \Delta\phi_N\}$ be the phase changes at N successive angles $\{\theta_1, \cdots, \theta_N\}$ with respect to an array. If the indices of the lower and upper boundary angles are l and u, their corresponding estimated indexes $\hat{l}$ and $\hat{u}$ are:

$$\hat{l} = \inf\{n|J(n) > h\}, \ \hat{u} = \sup\{n|J(n) > h\}, \tag{11}$$

$$J(n) = |V(n) - \frac{\sum_{i=1}^{n-1} V(n-i)}{n-1}|, \ n \geq 2, \tag{12}$$

$$V(n) = \frac{1}{W} \sum_{j=n}^{n+W} \Delta\phi_j, \ n \geq 1, \tag{13}$$

where, W is a robust window size used to reduce the false alarms, $V(n)$ is the mean phase change of current window, $J(n)$ calculates the difference between mean phase change values of the current window and the past windows, h is an empiric threshold defined for boundary detection.

Once the angles of the target boundaries are detected, we have a polygon formed by the four intersection points of the four angle boundaries obtained from two arrays, i.e., the polygon $P_1P_2P_3P_4$ shown in Fig. 9. Next, TagScan estimates the target's cut image in the polygon area by searching the true starting points. Initially, TagScan randomly picks a point at each edge of the polygon $P_1P_2P_3P_4$, such as the points V_1, V_2, V_3 and V_4 in Fig. 9, and connects these points to form the initial candidate target edges. Then, each array chooses the closest candidate target edges and takes these edges as the *starting points* of the propagation distances estimated. For example, the "Array 1" chooses the edge V_1V_2 and edge V_1V_4 as the target edges and assumes the starting points are located on the two edges. TagScan can now stitch together the propagation

Table 1: Test liquids for material identification.

Liquids	Vinegar	Soy Source	Coke	Liquor	Beer
Compositions	Acetate 50%; Carbohydrate 4.9 g/100 ml.	Amino acids 0.4 g/100 ml; Carbohydrate 6.7 g/100 ml.	Carbohydrate 3.5 g/100 ml.	Ethyl alcohol 50% vol.	Ethyl alcohol 3.1% vol.
Liquids	Purified Water	Saline Water	Sweet Water	Whole Milk	Skimmed Milk
Compositions	——	Salt 10.9 g/100 ml.	Sugar 25.3 g/100 ml.	Fat 4.0 g/100 ml.	Fat 0 g/100 ml.

Table 2: Test targets for cut imaging.

Horizontal cut of target	Size (cm)	Material
Triangular	Edge: 20	Plastic, wood, water.
Hexagonal	Edge: 20	
Quadrangular	43.5 × 34	
Quadrangular	81 × 81	Concrete.
Circular	Diameter: 25	Plastic, water.
Circular	Diameter: 20	
Human target	40 × 20	Water, fat, bone, etc.

distances along different angles and obtain the coarse estimated images with respect to the two arrays, as shown in Fig. 8(a)-(b).

To combine the two images estimated from the two arrays, TagScan employs the union set of the two estimated images as the output. Fig. 8(c) shows the union set of two estimated images in Fig. 8(a)-(b). The estimated image in Fig. 8(c) is still quite different from the ground truth image which means the starting points of the propagation distances selected are not accurate. In reality, we do not know the ground truth so how can we know the estimated image is accurate? The key observation is that the images estimated from the two arrays will align well when all the starting points are selected accurately. While the starting points are located at the target edges, we search different combinations of target edge points on the four edges (e.g., P_1P_2, P_2P_3, P_3P_4 and P_4P_1) and then calculate the difference between the two estimated images from the two arrays. For example, Fig. 8(c) and (d) show another two image estimates when we search two different combinations of target edge points. The image estimated in Fig. 8(d) is better than the image estimated in Fig. 8(c) since the difference between two estimated images is smaller. In reality, finding the minimum difference is not time efficient so as long as the difference is smaller than a pre-defined threshold, the search stops and the union set of the two images is output as the final target image estimate, as shown in Fig. 8(e). We utilize the MATLAB Genetic Algorithm toolbox to speed up this searching process. Based on the experimental results, the proposed imaging method can usually converge within one second and the average processing time is around 200 ms. Note that this method does not need to know if the target shape is triangle, rectangle or circle beforehand and will automatically use the propagation distances inside a target to determine the shape. However, we do find that the imaging performance of TagScan is worse for complex shapes such as a target with sawtooth edges.

4 IMPLEMENTATION

Hardware implementation: The system setup is shown in Fig. 10. An Impinj Speedway R420 reader [14] is employed in our experiments without any hardware or firmware modification. The R420 reader operates in frequency range of 920.625 – 924.375 MHz, which is divided into 16 channels with a channel bandwidth of 250 KHz. The default antenna used by R420 reader is a directional antenna with a 9 dBi gain and 70° elevation and azimuth beam widths. In

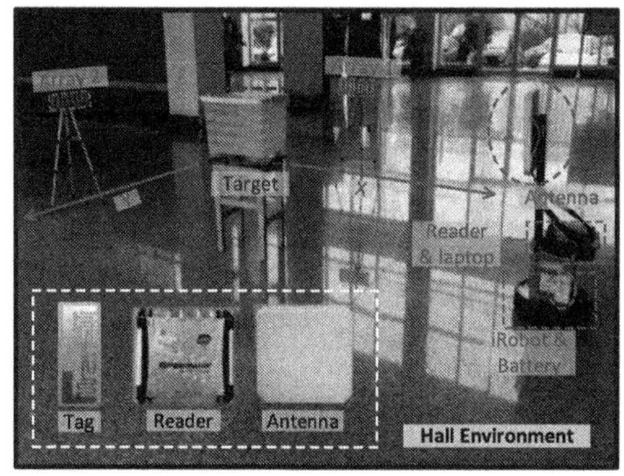

(a) Hall environment and system setup.

(b) Lab-office and library environment.

Figure 10: System setup and experimental environments.

the target imaging experiments, the reader together with the antenna is carried by an iRobot to move around the target for a half cycle. The moving speed is about 20 cm/s. Note that for material identification, we do not require the reader to move since the measurements at one location are enough. The cheap Alien General Purpose tags [12] are used in our experiments. Each tag costs 5 cents and is shown in Fig. 10(a). We place multiple tags (e.g., 8 tags) to form a linear tag-array and the spacing between adjacent tags is 4 cm. The heights of the tag-arrays and the reader antenna are the same, i.e., both of them are 44.5 cm above the ground.

Backend implementation: The proposed algorithms are implemented in C# and MATLAB code. The server is a laptop with a 2.6 GHz CPU (Intel i7-6700HQ) and 16 GB memory. The server communicates with the RFID reader using the low level reader protocol [13]. All the tags' backscatter packets received at the reader are forwarded to the server through an Ethernet cable. The size of the RFID backscatter packet is small (12 bytes) [14] since the packet only contains the tag's ID.

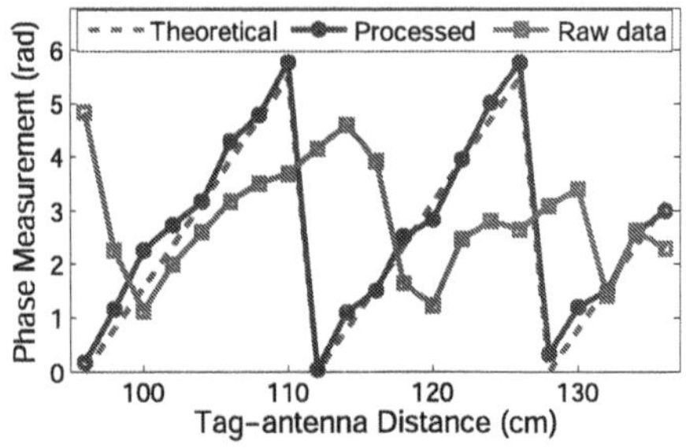

Figure 11: Phase change with the increasing distance between tag and antenna.

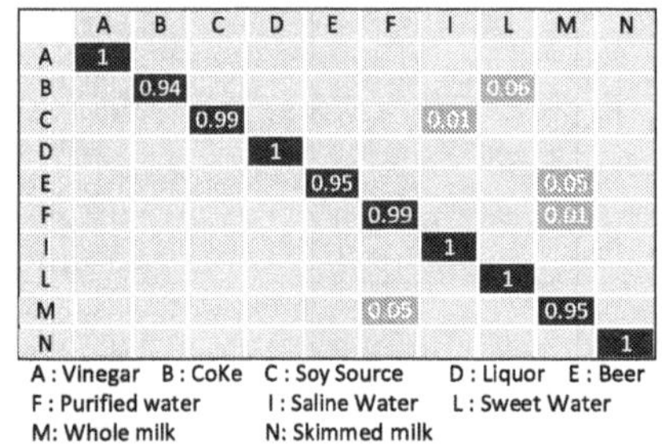

Figure 12: Confusion matrix: material identification results for the 10 liquids.

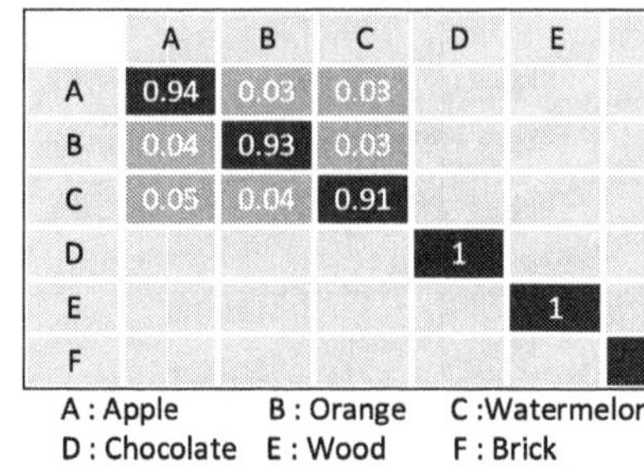

Figure 13: Confusion matrix: material identification results for the 6 solid targets.

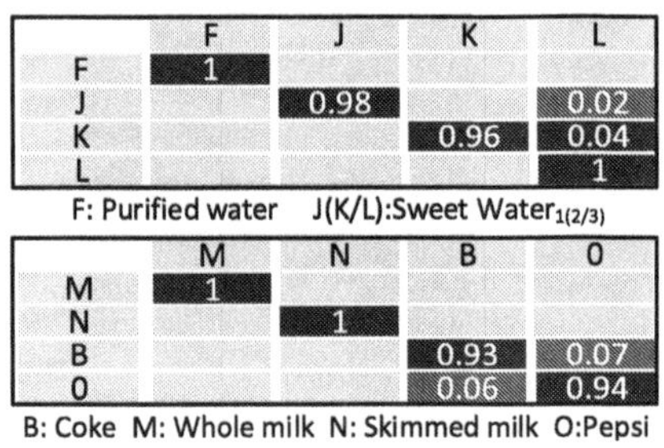

Figure 14: Confusion matrix: material identification results for the similar liquid materials.

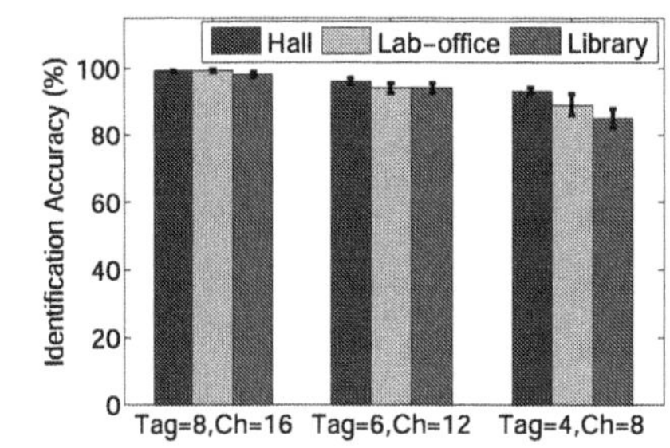

Figure 15: Material identification accuracy with varying number of tags and channels.

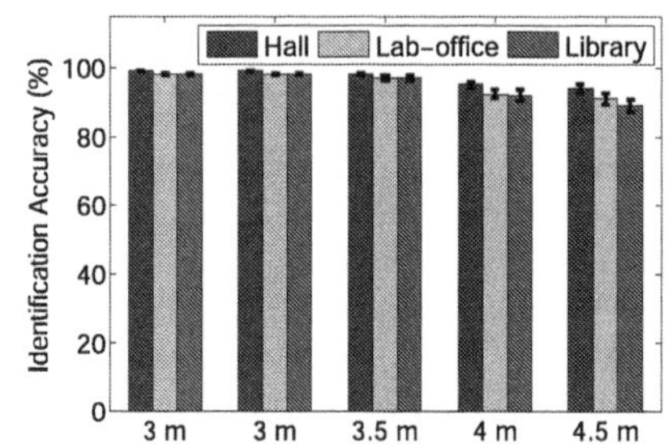

Figure 16: Material identification accuracy with varying tag-antenna distances.

Default deployment setup: In the experiment, we deploy one reader with one antenna and two tag-arrays. Each array has 8 tags for accurate AoA estimation [42]. The reader is programmed to hop over 16 channels. When we evaluate the impact of the number of tags and channels, we change the default setup. Unless specifically mentioned, we use this default setup for evaluation.

Tag diversity calibration: Accurate AoA estimation is highly dependent on the phase value measured from each tag. However, each tag has a random phase offset introduced by the hardware diversity [44] and the coupling effect [39]. This random phase offset needs to be carefully addressed before accurate AoA estimation. We employ the method proposed in [34] to calibrate the phase offsets among tags.

System requirements: In the current implementation, TagScan requires the target to be static for imaging. TagScan also requires the reader to move at a relatively low speed (i.e., below 0.5 m/s). When the reader moves fast, the Doppler shift effect will change the phase readings which will affect TagScan's performance accordingly.

5 PERFORMANCE EVALUATION

In this section, we evaluate the material identification and target imaging performance of TagScan. We first introduce the experimental environments and the tested targets, followed by the detailed experimental results.

5.1 Experimental Environments and Targets

Experimental environments: we conduct experiments in three typical indoor environments: a library, a lab-office, and an empty hall corresponding to high, medium and low multipath environments as shown in Fig. 10. For each experimental environment, we choose a 3.2 m × 3.2 m area as the test area and deploy TagScan based on the layout shown in Fig. 4.

Tested targets: To evaluate the material identification performance of TagScan, we use 10 different liquids and 6 different types of solid objects as test targets. The liquids are listed in Table 1. The solid objects are "Apple", "Orange", "Watermelon", "Chocolate", "Wood" and "Brick". To evaluate the imaging performance of TagScan, we test targets with different shapes, sizes and materials. The details are shown in Table 2.

5.2 Effect of Multipath Suppression

In the lab-office environment, we deploy one reader with just one antenna and one tag-array. When the direct-path signal dominates, the phases change linearly with the distance between the tag-array and reader antenna. Fig. 11, shows that compared with the raw phase values, the processed values after applying the multipath suppression scheme have a linear pattern and match the theoretical values well. This demonstrates the effectiveness of the proposed multipath suppression scheme.

5.3 Material Identification Performance

Material identification accuracy: In the lab-office environment, we evaluate the material identification accuracy of TagScan. For each identification, we repeat the experiments 30 times by using 30 different targets with the same material, e.g., 30 apples of a same brand. For each target, we collect 100 samples and set the number of "Nearest Neighbors" as 12 in the KNN classifier based on our empirical knowledge. Fig. 12 shows the identification accuracy is more than 94% for 10 liquid materials. Fig. 13 shows the identification accuracy is also high for solid targets although the

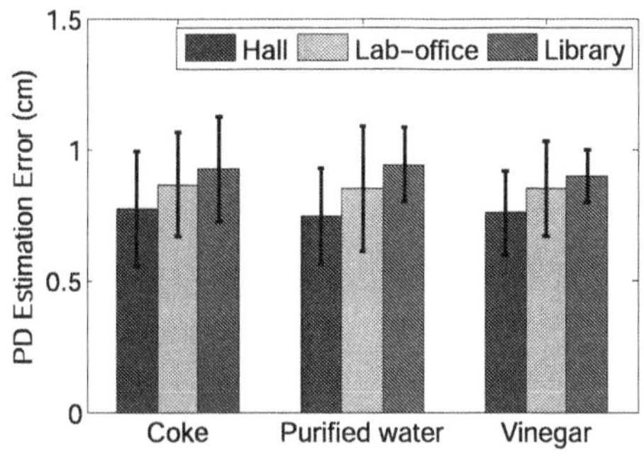

Figure 17: PD estimation errors in different environments.

performance is slightly worse than liquids, since even two apples of the same brand have slightly different feature values. We run additional experiments to identify the same type of liquids with slightly different concentrations, e.g., sweet water with sugar concentration 8.3 g/100ml, 16.7 g/100ml and 25.3 g/100ml. Fig. 14 (up) shows that TagScan still achieves a high accuracy of at least 96%. Finally, we attempt to differentiate between "Coke", "Pepsi", "Whole milk" and "Skimmed milk". Fig. 14 (below) shows that TagScan achieves 100% accuracies in differentiating the two types of milk since their phase difference is big as shown in Fig. 1(b). The difference between "Coke" and "Pepsi" is relatively small but TagScan still achieves a higher than 90% accuracy.

Effect of the number of tags and channels: More tags and channels are helpful to suppress the multipath and increase the phase estimation accuracy of direct-path signal. We run the material identification experiments on the 10 liquids with varying number of tags and channels in different environments. Fig. 15 shows that (i) the identification accuracy does increase with more tags and channels; (ii) even in a rich multipath environment such as a library, TagScan still achieves a high accuracy with 8 tags and 16 channels. This further demonstrates the effectiveness of the proposed multipath suppression scheme.

Effect of the distance between antenna and tags: When the distance between the antenna and the tag-array is larger, the signal becomes weaker and the multipath effect is stronger, which decrease the identification accuracy. We run material identification experiments on 10 liquids with varying distances between the antenna and the tag-array. Fig. 16 shows that the identification accuracy of TagScan does not decrease much. TagScan achieves an accuracy of higher than 90% in all the three environments when the tag-antenna distance is no larger than 4 m.

5.4 Shape Imaging Performance

5.4.1 Accuracy of propagation distance estimation. In this section, we evaluate the accuracy of the propagation distance (PD) estimation. Under the deployment setup shown in Fig. 1(a), we conduct experiments in the three environments using purified water, Coke and vinegar. We acquire the phase constant via the experimental measurement, i.e., we calculate the phase constant based on the phase value for a given liquid height. Fig. 17 shows that for a liquid target with a height of 10 cm, the mean propagation distance estimation errors are smaller than 1 cm.

(a) Imaging of a triangle shape target with plastic & water.

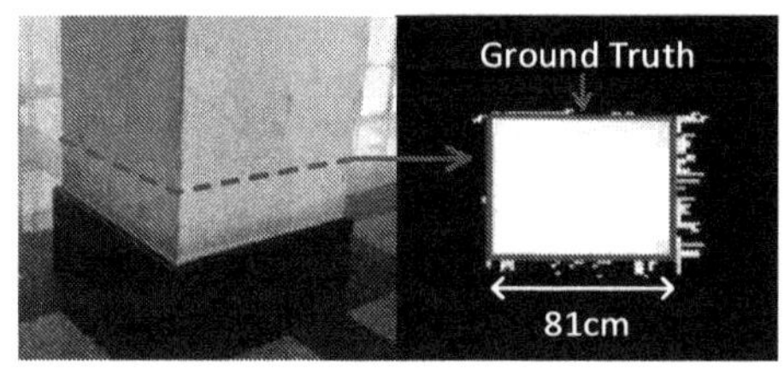

(b) Imaging of a rectangular shape cement pillar.

Figure 18: Cut imaging of a triangular target and a rectangular target with material of plastic & water and cement.

5.4.2 Single target imaging. Next, we evaluate TagScan's imaging performance for the 7 targets listed in Table 2 in the lab-office environment. Fig. 18 demonstrates that TagScan can estimate the cut image of a triangular shape and a rectangular shape accurately with only two arrays. Fig. 18(b) also shows that TagScan achieves a high accuracy when the target material is cement.

When the cut shape of the target is a hexagon or a circle, the imaging performance of TagScan degrades as shown in Fig. 19(a)-(b), because the constraints (i.e., the propagation distances) from the two arrays are not enough to achieve a fine-grained image. To achieve a better accuracy, we increase the number of arrays from 2 to 4. As shown in Fig. 19(c), the imaging performance improves significantly with more arrays. However, the computational load also increases with more arrays.

5.4.3 See-through the wall imaging. Next, TagScan is tested to image one and two targets behind a wall made of plywood.[6] We first carry out one round of baseline measurements when there is no target behind the wall. Then, TagScan performs another round of measurements when the target appears behind the wall and estimates the cut image of the target. Fig. 20(a) shows that the wall is not affecting the imaging performance and TagScan still accurately obtains the target image behind a wall.

5.4.4 Human target imaging. We test if TagScan can accurately obtain the cut image of a human target as this information can be employed for human identification. However, estimating the propagation distance inside a human body is more challenging, as the human body is composed of different materials that are in both liquid and solid forms. To overcome this challenge, TagScan first calculates the average phase constant using 15 different human targets (all volunteers are from the lab). Then, one human target is randomly selected for the imaging evaluation. Fig. 20(b) shows that TagScan can estimate the cut image of a human body at a relatively

[6]The thickness of the plywood wall is about 6 cm for easy of construction but the RFID signal can penetrate through a much ticker wall as demonstrated in Fig. 18(b).

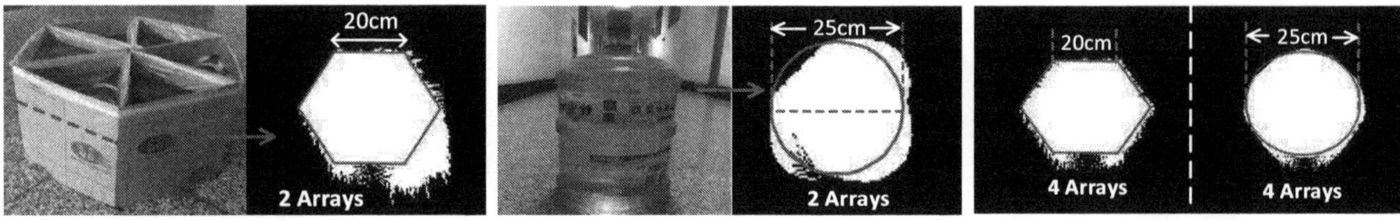

(a) Hexagonal shape imaging. (b) Circular shape imaging. (c) Imaging with 4 tag-arrays.

Figure 19: Cut imaging for a hexagonal target and a circular target with two and four arrays.

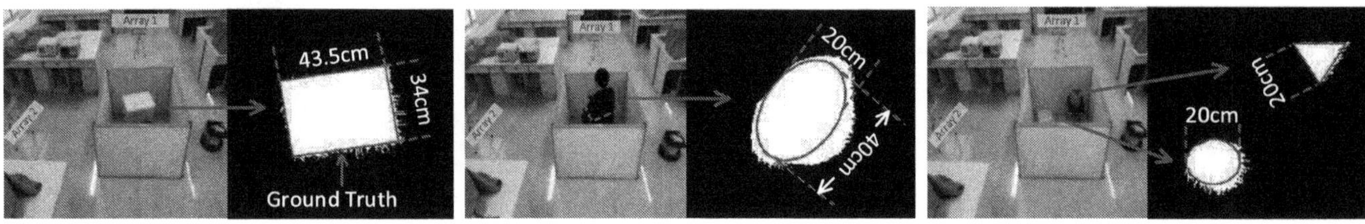

(a) Single target through wall imaging. (b) Human target through wall imaging. (c) Two-target through wall imaging.

Figure 20: See-through wall imaging for a single target, human target and two targets.

high accuracy. Note that a person's different clothes on different days may lead to small changes in estimated cut image. For the current experiments, the human target wears the same cloth.

5.4.5 Two-target imaging. Finally, TagScan is evaluated in a challenging scenario where there are two targets. The intuition allows TagScan to succeed is that the two targets will affect the direct-path links separately when the targets are not located close to each other. In this case, as shown in Fig. 20(c), TagScan images both targets accurately. When targets are very close to each other, TagScan will image them as one large target.

6 DISCUSSION

Maximum propagation distance inside a target: The transmission power of a COTS RFID reader is limited to 32.15 dBm and the weakest signal power that a reader can hear is around -90 dBm [14]. We measure and find that the maximum propagation distance that a RFID reader can still read a signal sent back by a tag through purified water is around 4 m. However, this is not a fundamental limitation of TagScan but the limit of hardware. By using directional antenna with thinner transmission beam, TagScan should have no problem for imaging even larger target.

Target mobility: When a target is moving, TagScan can still identify its material as long as the target passes through the direct-path link formed by the tag-array and the reader antenna. However, it is challenging to estimate a moving target's image since TagScan needs to match the baseline phase/RSS readings (without the target) with the online measurements (with the target) at the exact same target location to calculate the phase/RSS changes. When the target is moving, it is difficult to match the measurements with the appropriate baseline values.

End-to-end system latency: The system latency includes data collection time and the processing time of the algorithms to identify the material and image the target. The processing time is around 50 ms for material identification and 200 ms for imaging. For material identification, TagScan needs one round of measurements over 16 channels, which takes about 350 ms. Thus, the latency is below 0.5 s. The packet collection time for imaging depends on the size of the monitoring area. For example, TagScan takes 40 s to collect packets in a 4 m × 4 m area when the robot moves around the target for a half cycle at a speed of 20 cm/s. The data collection rate of the Impinj R420 reader is about 45 samples per second. So the number of samples collected for imaging is about 1800.

Identifying hybrid materials. In reality, a lot of targets consist of hybrid materials. It is a challenging problem to identify each component material and the corresponding percentage. We leave this interesting problem as the future work.

Imaging hollow targets. Imaging hollow targets has a lot of applications but is also challenging for TagScan. With holes inside the target, one propagation distance obtained may be divided into several segments which makes imaging much more difficult.

Impact of container on material identification. In the current experiments, the empty container (i.e., cup) is included when we carry out the baseline measurements. Thus, the effect caused by the container is totally removed, i.e., the material and the thickness of the container will not affect the identification of the internal material. In real-life applications, we may not always have the chance to carry out baseline measurement with the empty container beforehand. In these scenarios, the container's material and thickness do affect TagScan's performance.

7 RELATED WORK

Commodity imaging systems. These systems including Radar[19], X-Ray[21], CT/MRI [49] and B-scan [7], employ dedicated hardware with high frequencies, large bandwidths and antenna arrays, which are extremely expensive and usually large in size. For example, a medical MRI system [49] can cost 200000-1000000 USD. MRI [49] requires the target to be placed inside a large coil and then uses the resonance signal reflected by the target for imaging. Moreover,

X-Ray and CT employ very high frequency signals which are harmful to the human body [23]. The ultrasonic systems, like B-scan [7], can only work within a short distance range (e.g., sub-meters) and are easily disrupted by the background noise. TagScan is built on cheap commodity RFID devices (around 1000 USD) that works for a relatively long distance range of 10 meters.

Camera and infrared based systems. Thermal infrared sensor or visible light camera is widely used for target imaging [48] and material identification [4, 20, 27]. Specifically, they acquire a target's millions of reflectance and/or fluorescence spectra for material identification [4]. The thermal infrared sensor works in the night but it requires the target to have a temperature above a specific threshold to be detected. The visible light camera requires good lighting conditions and has privacy issues. Moreover, both of them cannot work in non-line-of-sight scenarios where the target is blocked from line-of-sight (LoS) view. TagScan has the advantages of working at day and night, not affected by heat sources, and can also penetrate non-metallic walls.

RF-based imaging systems. Previous imaging work relies on RF tomography technique [2, 41, 45]. However, they only obtain a very coarse-grained image and do not capture the target's fine-grained shape information. The RF-Capture system [1] captures the coarse skeleton information of a human target behind a wall using 20 antennas with a 1.78 GHz bandwidth. In contrast, TagScan is built using low-cost commodity RFID devices and only requires one antenna and a 4 MHz bandwidth. The Wision [11] system based on Wi-Fi infrastructure requires a large two-dimensional antenna array and uses the reflected signals from a target for imaging. Its imaging performance is coarse due to the small bandwidth of commodity Wi-Fi devices. Moreover, all the above systems only obtain the vertical cut image and the surface material of a target, since they use the reflection signals bounced off the target. TagScan uses the signals that penetrate through a target and thus is able to obtain the horizontal cut image and the internal material of the target. Depatla *et al.* [8] build a Wi-Fi imaging system by using the RSS attenuation caused by a target. However, the RSS readings from Wi-Fi cards are coarse, limiting its imaging accuracy. It also requires two Wi-Fi transceivers to move simultaneously and know each other's position at all time, severely limiting its practical application. TagScan only needs one moving antenna and uses much more fine-grained phase information for imaging.

RF-based material identification systems. The RSA system [50] uses 60 GHz radios to identify a nearby target's surface material and image its boundaries. However, 60 GHz signals have a short transmission range and require LoS view to the target. On the contrary, the wavelength of the RFID signal is relatively large (i.e., about 32 cm), which allows TagScan to identify a target's material and image its shape through a wall. RadarCat [46] also uses 60 GHz signals for accurate material and object classification. However, RadarCat requires to touch the target, which may not be convenient in some scenarios. While, TagScan can passively identify a target's material even when the target is away (1-5 m) from the devices (i.e., tag and antenna). Moreover, RFID's frequency band is much smaller than the 60 GHz signal. As a result, the sampling interval is much larger and the distance estimate is coarse. Thus, it is more challenging to carry out imaging and material identification with RFID signals. Sarma *et. al* [5] build an RFID based liquid volume detection system by mapping the RSS measurements with the level of liquid in the glass. However, this system can not identify the liquid material. TagScan not only can identify the target material, but also can estimate the liquid height accurately.

Multipath suppression approaches. Many methods have been proposed to address the multipath problem indoors [2, 15, 29, 42, 43]. ArrayTrack [42] employs the property that the direct path is more stable when the target is moving to identify the direct path. Chronos [29], ToneTrack [43] and WiTrack [2] identify the ToF of the direct-path signal based on the property that ToF of direct path has the minimum value. Specifically, they either combine the Wi-Fi signals of multiple channels [43] or use the FMCW signal with a large bandwidth (i.e., sweeping from 5.46 GHz to 7.25 GHz) [2] to separate different signals in the time domain. SpotFi [15] combines the two ideas and identifies the AoA and ToF of direct-path signal at the same time. Unlike previous methods that extracting the AoA or ToF information to identify the direct-path signal, this paper tries to strengthen the direct-path signal and average out the multipath signals. So our method is actually able to obtain the raw direct-path signal rather than just differentiating which AoA/ToF is corresponding to the direct-path signal.

8 CONCLUSION

This paper presents TagScan, the first RFID-based system which utilizes the phase and RSS changes to perform material identification and target imaging at the same time. Comprehensive real-world experiments show that TagScan can achieve high accuracies for target material identification and is sensitive enough to differentiate even Pepsi and Coke. TagScan can also image more than one targets of different shapes, sizes behind a wall.

ACKNOWLEDGMENT

This work is supported by National Natural Science Foundation of China (61572402, 61672428, 61672427). This research is also supported by the National Research Foundation, Prime Minister's Office, Singapore under its IDM Futures Funding Initiative. We also would like to thank the shepherd Prof. Lili Qiu, as well as Prof. Baochun Li and the anonymous reviewers for their valuable feedbacks on this paper. Xiaojiang Chen and Dingyi Fang are the corresponding authors.

REFERENCES

[1] Fadel Adib, C Hsu, Hongzi Mao, Dina Katabi, and Fredo Durand. 2015. Capturing the human figure through a wall. *ACM Transactions on Graphics* 34, 6 (2015), 219–231.

[2] Fadel Adib, Zach Kabelac, Dina Katabi, and Robert C Miller. 2014. 3d tracking via body radio reflections. In *Proc. USENIX NSDI.* 317–329.

[3] Fadel Adib and Dina Katabi. 2013. See through walls with WiFi. In *Proc. ACM SIGCOMM.* 75–86.

[4] Costas Balas, George Epitropou, Athanasios Tsapras, and Nikos Hadjinicolaou. 2016. A novel hyperspectral camera and analysis platform for the non-destructive material identification and mapping: An application in paintings by El Greco. In *IEEE International Conference on Imaging Systems and Techniques.* 211–215.

[5] Rahul Bhattacharyya, Christian Floerkemeier, and Sanjay Sarma. 2010. RFID tag antenna based sensing: Does your beverage glass need a refill?. In *IEEE International Conference on RFID.* 126–133.

[6] K Cheng David. 1983. Field and wave electromagnetics. *Addison-Wesley publications* (1983).

[7] Bats F De, B Wolff, M Mauget-Faysse, C Scemama, and L Kodjikian. 2013. B-scan and "en-face" spectral-domain optical coherence tomography imaging for the

diagnosis and followup of acute retinal pigment epitheliitis. *Case Reports in Medicine* 13, 2 (2013), 260–237.

[8] Saandeep Depatla, Lucas Buckland, and Yasamin Mostofi. 2015. X-Ray Vision With Only WiFi Power Measurements Using Rytov Wave Models. *IEEE Trans. on Vehicular Technology* 64, 4 (2015), 1376–1387.

[9] Gongde Guo, Hui Wang, David Bell, Yaxin Bi, and Kieran Greer. 2003. *KNN Model-Based Approach in Classification*. Springer Berlin Heidelberg. 986–996 pages.

[10] Jinsong Han, Ding Han, Qian Chen, Dan Ma, Xi Wei, Zhi Wang, Zhiping Jiang, and Longfei Shangguan. 2014. CBID: A Customer Behavior Identification System Using Passive Tags. In *Proc. IEEE ICNP*. 47–58.

[11] Donny Huang, Rajalakshmi Nandakumar, and Shyamnath Gollakota. 2014. Feasibility and limits of wi-fi imaging. In *Proc. ACM SenSys*. 266–279.

[12] Alien Inc. 2008. Alien Tags. (mar 2008). Retrieved June 27, 2017 from http://www.Alientechnology.com/tags/

[13] EPCglobal Inc. 2007. Low Level Reader Protocol, Version 1.0. 1. (2007).

[14] Impinj Inc. 2010. R420 Readers. (mar 2010). Retrieved June 27, 2017 from http://www.Impinj.com/products/readers/

[15] Manikanta Kotaru, Kiran Joshi, Dinesh Bharadia, and Sachin Katti. 2015. Spotfi: Decimeter level localization using wifi. In *Proc. ACM SIGCOMM*. 269–282.

[16] Kyle Jamieson Longfei Shangguan. 2016. Leveraging Electromagnetic Polarization in a Two-Antenna Whiteboard in the Air. In *Proc. ACM CoNEXT*. 443–456.

[17] James M Lucas and Michael S Saccucci. 1991. Exponentially weighted moving average control schemes: Properties and enhancements. *Quality Engineering* 36, 1 (1991), 31–32.

[18] G Marin, F Dominio, and P Zanuttigh. 2014. Hand gesture recognition with leap motion and kinect devices. In *Proc. IEEE International Conference on Image Processing*. 1565–1569.

[19] S. M. J Mortazavi, S Taeb, and N Dehghan. 2013. Alterations of visual reaction time and short term memory in military radar personnel. *Iranian Journal of Public Health* 42, 4 (2013), 428–435.

[20] Susmit Nanda, Sourav Manna, Arup Kumar Sadhu, Amit Konar, and Diptendu Bhattacharya. 2015. Real-time surface material identification using infrared sensor to control speed of an arduino based car like mobile robot. In *International Conference on Computer, Communication, Control and Information Technology*. 210–216.

[21] Koichi Ogawa, Tatsuma Hirokawa, and Shota Nakamura. 2010. Identification of a material with a photon counting x-ray CT system. In *IEEE Nuclear Science Symposium Conference Record*. 2582–2586.

[22] Qifan Pu, Sidhant Gupta, Shyamnath Gollakota, and Shwetak Patel. 2013. Whole-home gesture recognition using wireless signals. In *Proc. ACM MobiCom*. 27–38.

[23] Savithiri Ratnapalan, Yedidia Bentur, and Gideon Koren. 2008. Doctor, will that x-ray harm my unborn child? *Canadian Medical Association Journal* 179, 12 (2008), 1293–1296.

[24] Ralph O Schmidt. 1986. Multiple emitter location and signal parameter estimation. *IEEE Trans. on Antennas and Propagation* 34, 3 (1986), 276–280.

[25] Longfei Shangguan and Kyle Jamieson. 2016. The Design and Implementation of a Mobile RFID Tag Sorting Robot. In *Proc. ACM MobiSys*. 31–42.

[26] Longfei Shangguan, Zimu Zhou, Xiaolong Zheng, Lei Yang, Yunhao Liu, and Jinsong Han. 2015. ShopMiner: Mining Customer Shopping Behavior in Physical Clothing Stores with COTS RFID Devices. In *Proc. ACM SenSys*. 113–125.

[27] Juraj Števek, Svetozár Katuščák, Lenka Dubinyová, and Miroslav Fikar. 2016. An automatic identification of wood materials from color images. In *Cybernetics & Informatics (K&I)*. 111–116.

[28] Li Sun, Souvik Sen, Dimitrios Koutsonikolas, and Kyu-Han Kim. 2015. WiDraw: Enabling Hands-free Drawing in the Air on Commodity WiFi Devices. In *Proc. ACM MobiCom*. 77–89.

[29] Deepak Vasisht, Swarun Kumar, and Dina Katabi. 2016. Decimeter-level localization with a single WiFi access point. In *Proc. USENIX NSDI*. 165–178.

[30] A. J. Van Der Veen, M. C. Vanderveen, and A. Paulraj. 1997. SI-JADE: an algorithm for joint angle and delay estimation using shift-invariance properties. In *Proc. Signal Processing Advances in Wireless Communications*. 161–164.

[31] Ju Wang, Hongbo Jiang, Jie Xiong, Kyle Jamieson, Xiaojiang Chen, Dingyi Fang, and Binbin Xie. 2016. LiFS: Low Human-Effort, Device-Free Localization with Fine-Grained Subcarrier Information. In *Proc. ACM MobiCom*. 243–256.

[32] Jue Wang and Dina Katabi. 2013. Dude, where's my card? RFID positioning that works with multipath and non-line of sight. In *Proc. ACM SIGCOMM*. 51–62.

[33] Jue Wang, Deepak Vasisht, and Dina Katabi. 2014. Rf-idraw: virtual touch screen in the air using rf signals. In *Proc. ACM SIGCOMM*. 235–246.

[34] Ju Wang, Jie Xiong, Hongbo Jiang, Chen ? Xiaojiang, and Dingyi Fang. 2016. D-Watch: Embracing "bad" Multipaths for Device-Free Localization with COTS RFID Devices. In *Proc. ACM CoNEXT*. 413–425.

[35] Wei Wang, Alex X Liu, Muhammad Shahzad, Kang Ling, and Sanglu Lu. 2015. Understanding and Modeling of WiFi Signal Based Human Activity Recognition. In *Proc. ACM MobiCom*. 65–76.

[36] Wei Wang, Alex X Liu, and Ke Sun. 2016. Device-free gesture tracking using acoustic signals. In *Proc. ACM MobiCom*. 82–94.

[37] Yan Wang, Jian Liu, Yingying Chen, Marco Gruteser, Jie Yang, and Hongbo Liu. 2014. E-eyes: device-free location-oriented activity identification using fine-grained wifi signatures. In *Proc. ACM MobiCom*. 617–628.

[38] Yuxi Wang, Kaishun Wu, and Lionel M Ni. 2016. WiFall: Device-free Fall Detection by Wireless Networks. *IEEE Trans. on Mobile Computing* 12, 5 (2016), 11–22.

[39] Teng Wei and Xinyu Zhang. 2016. Gyro in the air: tracking 3D orientation of batteryless internet-of-things. In *Proc. ACM MobiCom*. 55–68.

[40] William B Weir. 1974. Automatic measurement of complex dielectric constant and permeability at microwave frequencies. *Proc. IEEE* 62, 1 (1974), 33–36.

[41] Joey Wilson and Neal Patwari. 2011. See-through walls: Motion tracking using variance-based radio tomography networks. *IEEE Trans. on Mobile Computing* 10, 5 (2011), 612–621.

[42] Jie Xiong and Kyle Jamieson. 2013. ArrayTrack: a fine-grained indoor location system. In *Proc. USENIX NSDI*. 71–84.

[43] Jie Xiong, Karthikeyan Sundaresan, and Kyle Jamieson. 2015. ToneTrack: Leveraging frequency-agile radios for time-based indoor wireless localization. In *Proc. ACM MobiCom*. 537–549.

[44] Lei Yang, Yekui Chen, Xiang Yang Li, Chaowei Xiao, Mo Li, and Yunhao Liu. 2014. Tagoram: real-time tracking of mobile RFID tags to high precision using COTS devices. In *Proc. ACM MobiCom*. 237–248.

[45] Lei Yang, Qiongzheng Lin, Xiangyang Li, Tianci Liu, and Yunhao Liu. 2015. See Through Walls with COTS RFID System. In *Proc. ACM MobiCom*. 487–499.

[46] Huishyong Yeo, Gergely Flamich, Patrick Schrempf, David Harrisbirtill, and Aaron Quigley. 2016. RadarCat: Radar Categorization for Input and Interaction. In *Proc. ACM UIST*. 833–841.

[47] Moustafa Youssef, Matthew Mah, and Ashok Agrawala. 2007. Challenges: device-free passive localization for wireless environments. In *Proc. ACM MobiCom*. 222–229.

[48] Zhengyou Zhang. 2012. Microsoft Kinect Sensor and Its Effect. *IEEE Multimedia* 19, 2 (2012), 4–10.

[49] Hua Zhou, Yi Xiang J. Wang, Haiyan Lou, Xiaojun Xu, and Minming Zhang. 2014. Hepatic Sinusoidal Obstruction Syndrome Caused by Herbal Medicine: CT and MRI Features. *Korean Journal of Radiology* 15, 2 (2014), 218–225.

[50] Yanzi Zhu, Yibo Zhu, Ben Y. Zhao, and Haitao Zheng. 2015. Reusing 60GHz Radios for Mobile Radar Imaging. In *Proc. ACM MobiCom*. 103–116.

Analog On-Tag Hashing: Towards Selective Reading as Hash Primitives in Gen2 RFID Systems

Lei Yang*, Qiongzheng Lin*, Chunhui Duan*†, Zhenlin An*
*Department of Computing, The Hong Kong Polytechnic University
† School of Software, Tsinghua University
{young,lin,hui,an}@tagsys.org

ABSTRACT

Deployment of billions of Commercial off-the-shelf (COTS) RFID tags has drawn much of the attention of the research community because of the performance gaps of current systems. In particular, hash-enabled protocol (HEP) is one of the most thoroughly studied topics in the past decade. HEPs are designed for a wide spectrum of notable applications (e.g., missing detection) without need to collect all tags. HEPs assume that each tag contains a *hash function*, such that a tag can select a *random* but *predicable* time slot to reply with a *one-bit* presence signal that shows its existence. However, the hash function has never been implemented in COTS tags in reality, which makes HEPs a 10-year untouchable mirage. This work designs and implements a group of analog on-tag hash primitives (called *Tash*) for COTS Gen2-compatible RFID systems, which moves prior HEPs forward from theory to practice. In particular, we design three types of hash primitives, namely, *tash function*, *tash table function* and *tash operator*. All of these hash primitives are implemented through *selective reading*, which is a fundamental and mandatory functionality specified in Gen2 protocol, without any hardware modification and fabrication. We further apply our hash primitives in two typical HEP applications (i.e., cardinality estimation and missing detection) to show the feasibility and effectiveness of Tash. Results from our prototype, which is composed of one ImpinJ reader and 3,000 Alien tags, demonstrate that the new design lowers 60% of the communication overhead in the air. The tash operator can additionally introduce an overhead drop of 29.7%.

CCS CONCEPTS

• **Networks → Cyber-physical networks;** • **Computer systems organization → Embedded and cyber-physical systems;**

KEYWORDS

RFID; Hash Function; Hash Table Function; EPCGlobal Gen2

MobiCom '17, October 16–20, 2017, Snowbird, UT, USA

ACM ISBN 978-1-4503-4916-1/17/10...$15.00
https://doi.org/10.1145/3117811.3117835

1 INTRODUCTION

RFID systems are increasingly used in everyday scenarios, which range from object tracking, indoor localization [60], vibration sensing [61], to medical-patient management, because of the extremely low cost of commercial RFID tags (e.g., as low as 5 cents per tag). Recent reports show that many industries like healthcare and retailing are moving towards deploying RFID systems for object tracking, asset monitoring, and emerging Internet of Things [12].

1.1 The State-of-the-Art

The Electronic Product Code global is an organization established to accomplish the worldwide adoption and standardization of EPC technology. It published the Gen2 air protocol [1] for RFID system in 2004. A Gen2 RFID system consists of a reader and many passive tags. The passive tags without batteries are powered up purely by harvesting radio signals from readers. This protocol has become the mainstream specification globally, and has been adopted as a major part of the ISO/IEC 18000-6 standard.

Embedding Gen2 tags into everyday objects to construct ubiquitous networks has been a long-standing vision. However, a major problem that challenges this vision is that the Gen2 RFID system is not efficient [55]. First, the RFID system utilizes simple modulations (e.g., ON-OFF keying or BPSK) due to the lack of traditional transceiver [9], which prevents tags from leveraging a suitable channel to transmit more bits per symbol and increase the bandwidth efficiency. Second, tags cannot hear the transmissions of other tags. They merely reply on the reader to schedule their medium access with the Framed Slotted ALOHA protocol, which results in many empty and collided slots. This condition also retards the inventory process. These two limitations force a reader to go through a long inventory phase when it collects all the tags in the scene.

1.2 Ten-Year Mirage of HEP

Motivated by the aforementioned performance gaps, the research community opened a new focus on HEP design approximately 10 years ago. The key idea that underlies HEPs is that each tag selects a time slot according to the hash value of its EPC and a random seed. It then replies a one-bit presence signal rather than the entire EPC number in the selected slot. HEPs treat all tags as if they were a virtual sender, which outputs a gimped hash table (i.e., a *presence bitmap*) when responding to a challenge (i.e., a random seed). Most importantly, HEPs assume the backend server and every tag share a *hash function*, and the resulting bitmap is random but predicable when the EPCs and seeds are known.

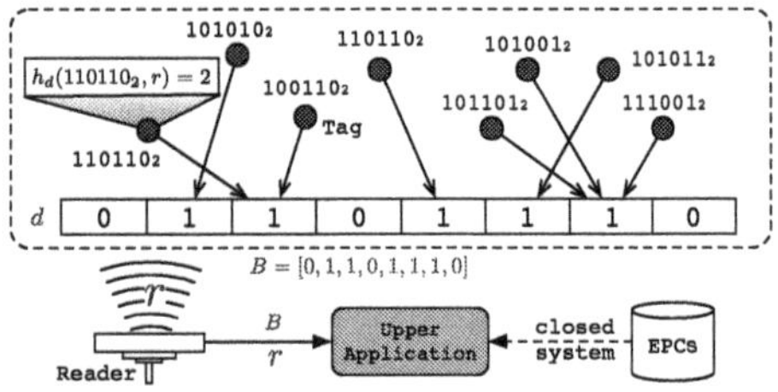

Fig. 1: Hash enabled protocol illustration. In the figure, 8 tags emit one-bit signals in the $h_d(\mathtt{EPC}, r)^{th}$ time slots respectively, which are challenged by the random seed r and the frame length d. Finally, the reader abstracts tags' responses as a presence bitmap.

Fig. 1 shows a toy example with $n = 8$ tags, each of which contains a unique EPC number presented in binary format (e.g., 101010_2), to illustrate the HEP concept. The reader divides the time into d time slots (e.g., $d = 8$.) and challenges these tags with the random seed r. Each tag selects the $(h_d(\mathtt{EPC}, r))^{th}$ time slot to reply the one-bit signal, where $h(\cdot)$ is a common hash function (e.g., MD5, SHA-1) and $h_d(\cdot) = h(\cdot) \bmod d$. The reader can recognize two possible results for each time slot, namely, *empty* and *non-empty*[1]. The reader abstracts the reply results into a bitmap (i.e., $B = [0, 1, 1, 0, 1, 1, 1, 0]$), where each element contains two possible values, that is, 0 and 1, that corresponds to empty and non-empty slots, respectively. The upper layer then utilizes this returned bitmap to explore many notable applications. We show the following two typical applications as examples to drive the key point:

- *Cardinality estimation.* Estimating the size of a given tag population is required in many applications, such as privacy sensitive systems and warehouse monitoring. Kodialam et al. [18] presented a pioneer estimator. Given that tags select the time slots uniformly because of hashing, the expected number of '0's equals $n_0 = d(1-1/d)^n \approx de^{-n/d}$. Counting n_0 in an instance yields a "zero estimator", i.e., $\widehat{n} \approx -d\ln(n_0/d)$. For example, $\widehat{n} = -8\times\ln(3/8) = 7.8$ in our toy example.
- *Missing detection.* Consider a major warehouse that stores thousands of apparel, shoes, pallets, and cases. How can a staff *immediately* determine if anything is missing? Sheng and Li [53] conducted the early study on the fast detection of missing-tag events by using the presence bitmap. They assumed all EPCs were known in a closed system. Given that hash results are predicable, the system can generate an *intact* bitmap at the backend. We can identify the missing tags in a probabilistic approach by comparing the intact and instanced bitmaps. For example, if the second entry equals 0 (which is supposed to be 1), the the tag 101010_2 must be missing in our toy example.

HEPs are advantageous in terms of speed and privacy. HEPs are faster than all prior per-tag reading schemes for two reasons. First, collecting all the EPCs of the tags is time consuming because of the aforementioned low-rate modulation, whereas one-bit presence signals of HEPs save approximately 96× of the time (i.e., the EPC length equals 96 bits in theory [2]). Second, collisions are considered as one of the major reasons that drag down the reading. On the contrary, HEPs tolerate and consider collisions as informative. When privacy issues are considered, the tag's identification may be unacceptable in certain instances. HEPs allow tags to send out non-identifiable information (i.e., one-bit signals).

HEPs are very promising. However, after 10 years of enthusiastic discussion about the opportunities that HEPs provide, the reality is beginning to settle: the functionality of hashing (i.e., hash function and hash table function) has never been implemented in any Gen2 RFID tags and considered by any RFID standard. No hint shows that this function will be widely accepted in the near future.

[1]Some work assume the reader can recognize the signal collision, obtaining three results: empty, single and collision.

1.3 Why Not Support Hashing?

A large number of recent work have attempted to supplement hash functionality to RFID tags, which can be categorized into three groups. First group, like [11, 39], modifies the common hash functions to accommodate resource-constrained RFID tags. The second group [5, 5, 14, 16, 24, 39, 44, 63, 66] designs new lightweight and efficient hash functions dedicatedly for RFID tags. The third group seeks new design of RFID tags like WISP[38] and Moo [67], which gives tags more powerful computing capabilities (e.g., hashing [37]). Unfortunately, as far as we know, none of these work has been really applied in COTS RFID systems yet.

Why is the hash function unfavored? A term called as *Gate Equivalent* (GE) is widely used to evaluate a hardware design with respect to its efficiency and availability. One GE is esquivalient to the area which is required by the two-input NAND gate with the lowest deriving strength of the corresponding technology. A glance at Table. 1 shows the available designs of hash functions for RFID tags require a significant number of GEs, which are completely unaffordable by current COTS tags. For example, the most compact hash functions requires thousands of GEs (e.g., 1,075 GEs for PRESENT-80), which incur extremely high energy consumption and manufacture cost. Thus, relatively few RFID-oriented protocols that appeal to a hash function can be utilized. RFID was expected to be one of the most competitive automatic identification technologies due to its many attractive advantages (e.g., simultaneous reading, NLOS, etc.) compared with others (e.g., barcode). However, this progress has been hindered for many years by the final obstacle that the industry is attempting to overcome (i.e., the price). The industry is extremely sensitive to the cost being doubled or tripled by the hash, although HEPs actually introduce significant outperformance.

1.4 Our Contributions

This work designs a group of hash primitives, *Tash*, which takes advantage of existing fundamental function of *selective reading* specified in Gen2 protocol, *without* any hardware modification and fabrication. Our design and implementation both strictly follow the Gen2 specification, so it can work in any Gen2-Compatible RFID system. These mimic (or analog) hash primitives act as we embedded real hash circuits on tags[3], while we actually implement

[2]Actual case in practice would be less than this estimate due to other extra jobs, such as setup time, query time, etc.

[3]This work does not target at designing any analog circuit on readers or tags, but offers a mimic hash function acting as we embed a hash circuit on each tag.

them in application layer. Specifically, we design the following three kinds of hash primitives to revive prior HEPs:

• We design a hash function (aka tash function) over existing COTS Gen2 tags. The hash function outputs a hash value associated with the EPC of the tag and a random seed, as HEPs require.

• We design a hash table function (aka tash table function) over all tags in the scene. It can produce a hash table (aka tash table), which is more informative than a bitmap, over the all tags in the scene. In particular, each entry indicates the exact number of tags hashed into this entry.

• Major prior HEPs require multiple acquisitions of bitmaps to meet an acceptable confidence. We design three tash operators (i.e., tash AND, OR and XOR) to perform entry-wise set operations over multiple tash tables on tag in the physical layer, which offers a one-stop acquisition solution.

Summary. It has been considered that HEPs are hardly applied in practice because of the 'impossible mission' of implementing hash function on COTS Gen2 tags [6]. In this work, our main contribution lies in the practicality and usability, that is, enabling billions of deployed tags to benefit performance boost from prior well-studied HEPs, with our hash primitives. To the best of our knowledge, this is the first work to implement the hash functionality over COTS Gen2 tags. Second, we provide an implementation of Tash and show its feasibility and efficiency in two typical usage scenarios. Third, we investigate several leading RFID products in market including 18 types of tags and 10 types of readers, in terms of their compatibility with Gen2, and conduct an extensive evaluation on our prototype with COTS devices.

2 RELATED WORK

We review the related work from two aspects: the designs of hash functions and hash enabled protocols.

Design of hash function. Feldhofer and Rechberger [11] firstly point that current common hash functions (e.g., MD5, SHA-1, etc.), are not hardware friendly and unsuitable at all for RFID tags, which have very constrained computing ability. Such difficulty has spurred considerable research [5, 5, 11, 14, 16, 24, 39, 39, 44, 63, 66]. We sketch the primary designs and their features in Table. 1. For example, Bogdanov et al. [5] propose a hardware-optimized block cipher, PRESENT, designed with area and power constraints. The follow-up work [44] presents three different architectures of PRESENT and highlights their availability for both active and passive smart devices. Their implementations reduce the number of GEs to 1,000 around. Lim and Korkishko [24] present a 64-bit hash function with three key size options (64 bits, 96 bits and 128 bits), which requires about 3,500 and 4,100 GEs. In summary, despite these optimized designs, majority are still presented in theory and none of them are available for the COTS RFID tags. On contrary, our work explores hash function from another different aspect, that is, leveraging selective reading to mimic equivalent hash primitives.

Design of hash enabled protocol. To drive our key point, we conduct a brief survey of previous related works. We list several key usage scenarios that we would like to support. Our objective is not to complete the list, but to motivate our design. (1) *Cardinality estimation.* Dozens of estimators [8, 13, 17, 19, 28, 29, 40, 41, 45, 47, 51, 52, 56, 71, 72] have been proposed in the past decade. For example, Qian et al. [41] proposed an estimation scheme called lottery frame. Shahzad and Liu [47] estimated the number based on the average run-length of ones in a bit string received using the FSA. In particular, they claimed that their protocol is compatible with Gen2 systems. However, their scheme still requires modifying the communication protocol, and thus, it fails to work with COTS Gen2 systems. By contrast, our prototype can operate in COTS Gen2 systems as demonstrated in this study. (2) *Missing detection.* The missing detection problem was firstly mentioned in [53]. Thereafter, many follow-up works [21, 22, 27, 31–33, 36, 48, 49, 54, 59, 64, 65, 68, 73] have started to study the issue of false positives resulting from the collided slots by using multiple bitmaps. (3) *Continuous reading.* The traditional inventory approach starts from the beginning each time it interrogates all the tags, thereby making it highly time-inefficient. These works [25, 50, 58] have proposed continuous reading protocols that can incrementally collect tags in each step using the bitmap. For example, Sheng et al. [50] aimed to preserve the tags collected in the previous round and collect only unknown tags. Xie et al. [58] conducted an experimental study on mobile reader scanning. Liu et al. [25] initially estimated the number of overlapping tags in two adjacent inventories and then performed an effective incremental inventory. (4) *Data mining.* These works [26, 34, 35, 51, 57] discuss how to discover potential information online through bitmaps. For example, Sheng et al. [51] proposed to identify the popular RFID categories using the group testing technique. Xie et al. found histograms over tags through a small number of bitmaps[57]. Luo et al. [34, 35] determined whether the number of objects in each group was above or below a threshold. Liu et al. [26] proposed a new online classification protocol for a large number of groups. (5) *Tag searching.* These works[30, 70] have studied the tag searching problem that aims to find wanted tags from a large number of tags using bitmaps in a multiple-reader environment. Zheng et al. [70] utilized bitmaps to aggregate a large volume of RFID tag information and to search the tags quickly. Liu et al. [30] first used the testing slot technique to obtain the local search result by iteratively eliminating wanted tags that were absent from the interrogation region. (6) *Tag polling.* [20, 42, 43] consider how to quickly obtain the sensing information from sensor-augmented tags. The system requires to assign a time slot to each tag using the presence bitmap. In summary, all the aforementioned HEP designs have allowed RFID research to develop considerably in the past decade. All the work can be boosted by our hash primitives.

Table 1: Performance overview of current hash functions [4]

Hash functions	Key size	GE	Power	Clock cycles
SHA-256[11]	256	10,868	$15.87\mu A$	1,128
SHA-1 [11]	160	8,120	$10.68\mu A$	1,274
AES [10]	128	3,400	$8.15\mu A$	1,032
MAME[63]	256	8,100	$5.16\mu A$	96
MD5 [11]	128	8,400	-	612
MD4 [11]	128	7,350	-	456
PRESENT-80 [5]	80	1,570	-	32
PRESENT-80 [44]	80	1,075	-	563
PRESENT-128 [6]	128	1,886	-	32
DES [39]	56	2,309	-	144
mCrypton [24]	96	2,608	-	13
TEA [66]	128	2,355	-	64
HIGHT [16]	128	3,048	-	34
DESXL [39]	184	2,168	-	144
Grain & Trivium[14]	80	2,599	-	1

3 OVERVIEW

Tash provides a group of hash primitives for HEPs. This section presents the scope and formally defines our hash primitives.

3.1 Scope

Despite clear and certain specifications, the implementation of the Gen2 protocol still varies with readers and manufacturers because of firmware bugs or compromises, especially in early released reader devices, according to our compatibility report presented in §7. Here, we firmly claim that our design and implementation strictly follow the specifications of the Gen2 and LLRP protocols (refer to §6). The framework works with any Gen2-compatible readers and tags. The performance losses caused by defects in devices are outside the scope of our discussion.

3.2 Definitions of Hash Primitives

Before delving into details, we formally define the hash primitives that the HEPs require, from a high-level.

Definition 1 (Tash function). *An l-bit tash function is actually a hash function $f_l(t,r) : \mathcal{T} \times \mathcal{R} \rightarrow 2^l$, where $\mathcal{T}$ and $\mathcal{R}$ are the domains of EPCs of the tags and random seeds.*

Tash function and tash value. As the above definition specifies, an l-bit tash function takes an EPC t and a random seed r as input and outputs an l-bit integer i, denoted by:

$$i = f_l(t,r) \quad (1)$$

We call l the *dimension* of tash function (i.e., $l = 0, 1, 2, \dots$). The tash value i is an integer $\in [0, 2^l - 1]$. Similar to other common hash function, the tash function has three basic characteristics. First, the output changes significantly when the two parameters are altered. Second, its output is uniformly distributed within the given range, and predicable if all inputs are known. Third, the hash values are accessible.

Definition 2 (Tash table function). *An l-bit tash table function can assign each tag t from a given set into the ith entry of a hash table (aka tash table) with a random seed r, where $i = f_l(t,r)$. Each entry of the tash table is the number of tags tashed into it.*

Tash table function and tash table. Let B and $\mathcal{F}_l$ denote a tash table and a tash table function respectively. The tash table function takes a set of tags (i.e., $T = \{t_1, t_2, \dots, t_n\}$) and a random number r as input and outputs a tash table B, denote by:

$$B = \mathcal{F}_l(T,r) \quad (2)$$

where $B[i] = |\{t|f_l(t,r) = i\}|$ (i.e., the number of tags tashed into the ith entry) for $\forall t \in T$. Let $L = 2^l$, which is defined as the *size* of the tash table. The tash table function is the core function that HEPs expect. HEPs consider the reader as well as all tags as a black box equipping with tash table function. When inputing a random seed, the box would output a tash table. HEPs then utilize such table to provide various services (e.g., missing detection or cardinality estimation.). It worths noting that superior to the bitmap employed in prior HEPs, our tash table is a perfect table that contains the exact number of tags tashed into each entry. Clearly, the table is completely backward compatible with prior HEPs because it can be forcedly converted into a presence bitmap.

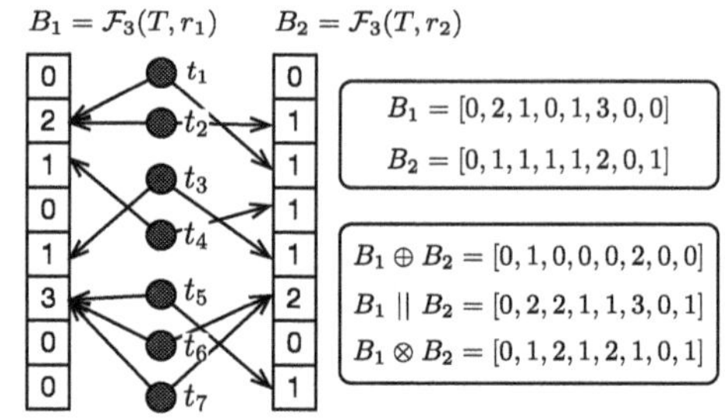

Fig. 2: Illustration of tash operators. The left shows two independent tash tables, while the right shows the results of the two tash tables with tash AND, OR and XOR.

Tash operators. Most prior HEPs adopt probabilistic ways and their results are guaranteed with a given confidence level. To meet the level, they usually combine multiple bitmaps, which are acquired through multiple rounds and challenged by different seeds. We abstract such combination into three basic tash operators, namely, tash AND, OR and XOR. These operators can comprise other complex operations. Let $B_1 = \mathcal{F}_l(T, r_1)$ and $B_2 = \mathcal{F}_l(T, r_2)$ denote two tash tables acquired twice with two different seeds, r_1 and r_2.

Definition 3 (Tash AND). *The tash AND (denoted by $\oplus$) of two tash tables is to obtain the intersection of two corresponding entry sets. Formally, $B = B_1 \oplus B_2$, where $B[i] = |\{t|f_l(t,r_1) = i \& f_l(t,r_2) = i\}|$.*

The tash AND is aimed at obtaining the common intersection of corresponding entries from two tash tables. For example, as shown in Fig. 2, $B_1[1]$ and $B_2[1]$ count $\{t_1, t_2\}$ and $\{t_2\}$ respectively. However, $(B_1 \oplus B_2)[1] = |\{t_2\}| = 1$, which counts t_2 only.

Definition 4 (Tash OR). *The tash OR (denoted by $||$) of two tash tables is to merge two corresponding entry sets. Formally, $B = B_1||B_2$, where $B[i] = |\{t|f_l(t,r_1) = i || f_l(t,r_2) = i\}|$.*

The tash OR is aimed at obtaining the total number of tags mapped into the corresponding entries in two tash tables. Note tash OR is not the same as the entry-wise sum, i.e., $B_1||B_2 \neq B_1 + B_2$ because the tags twice mapped into a same entry are counted only once. As shown in Fig. 2, $(B_1||B_2)[5] = |\{t_5, t_6, t_7\}| = 3$ although $B_1[5] + B_2[5] = 5$ because t_6 and t_7 appear twice in the two tash tables.

Definition 5 (Tash XOR). *The tash XOR (denoted by $\otimes$) is to remove the intersection of two corresponding entry sets from the first entry set. Formally, $B = B_1 \otimes B_2$ such that $B[i] = |\{t|f_l(t,r_1) = i \,\&\, f_l(t,r_2) \neq i\}|$.*

The tash XOR is aimed at obtaining the total number of the set difference. As Fig. 2 shows, $B_1[5] = |\{t_5, t_6, t_7\}|$ and $B_2[5] = |\{t_6, t_7\}|$. Then $(B_1 \otimes B_2)[5] = |\{t_5\}| = 1$.

The above operators can be applied in a series of tash tables with the same dimension for a hybrid operation, e.g., $B_1 \oplus B_2||B_3$. Tash AND and OR satisfy operational laws such as associative law and commutative law, e.g., $B_1 \oplus B_2 = B_2 \oplus B_1$. The design of tash operators is one of the attractive features of the tash framework, and it has never been proposed before. More importantly, we design and implement these operators in the physical layer to provide one-stop acquisition solution.

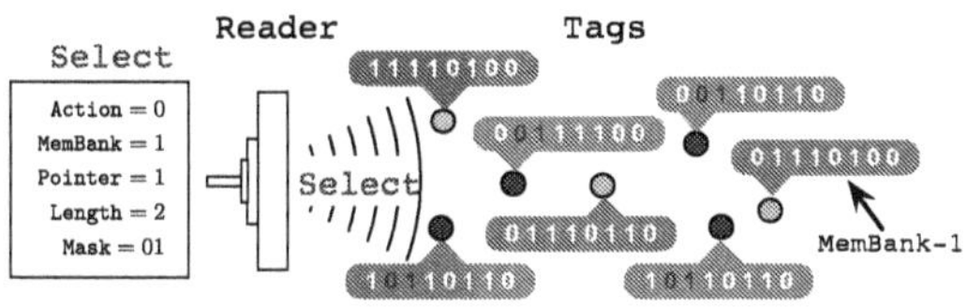

Fig. 3: Illustration of selective reading in Gen2. There are total 7 tags covered by a reader. The reader initiates a selective reading using a `Select` command, which let these tags (highlighted with dark red) whose data starting at the first bit with a length of 2 bits in the `MemBank-1` equals 01_2, participate in the incoming inventory, while other tags (with gray color) that do not meet the condition remain silent.

3.3 Solution Sketch

Tash is designed to reduce the overhead for air communications. It runs in the middle of the reader and upper application. The upper application passes a pair of arguments (i.e., r and l), or pairs of arguments (as well as operators) to Tash. On the basis of the arguments, Tash generates one or more configuration files to manipulate the reader's reading. Finally, Tash abstracts the reading results to a tash table, which is returned to the upper application.

The rest of the paper is structured as follows. We firstly present the tash design in §4. We next demonstrate the usage of our hash primitives in two classic applications in §5. We then introduce the tash implementation using LLRP interfaces in §6. In §7 and §8, we present the microbenchmark and the usage evaluation. Finally, we conclude in §9 and present future directions.

4 TASH DESIGN

In this section, we introduce the background of Gen2 protocol, and then present the technical details of our designs.

4.1 Background of Gen2 Protocol

The Gen2 standard defines air communication between readers and tags. On the basis of [1, 69], we introduce its four central functions we will employ:

F1: Memory Model. Gen2 specifies a simple tag memory model (pages 44 ~ 46 of [1]). Each tag contains four types of non-volatile memory blocks (called *memory banks*): (1) `MemBank-0` is reserved for password associated with the tag. (2) `MemBank-1` stores the `EPC` number. (3) `MemBank-2` stores the `TID` that specifies the unchangeable tag and vendor specific information. (4) `MemBank-3` is a customized storage that contains user-defined data. We can use `Read` or `Write` commands to read or write data into these banks.

F2: Selective Reading. Gen2 specifies that each inventory must be started with `Select` command (pages 72~73 of [1]). The reader can use this command to choose a subset of tags that will participate in the upcoming inventory round. In particular, each tag maintains a flag variable `SL`. The reader can use the `Select` command to turn the `SL` flags of tags into `asserted` (i.e., true) or `deasserted` (i.e., false). The `Select` command comprises six mandatory fields and one optional field apart from the constant cmd code (i.e., 1010_2). The following fields are presented for this study.

• `Target`. This field allows a reader to change `SL` flags or the inventoried flags of the tags. The inventoried flags are used when multiple readers are present. Such scenario is irrelevant to our requirements. Thus, we aim to change `SL` flags of tags.

• `Action`. This field specifies an action that will be will performed by the tags. Table. 2 lists eight action codes to which the tag makes different responses. For example, the matching or not-matching tags assert or deassert their `SL` flags when `Action=0`. We leverage this useful feature to design tash operators.

• `MemBank`, `Pointer`, `Length` and `Mask`. These four fields are combined to compose a *bitmask*. The bitmask indicates which tags are matched or not-matched for an `Action`. The `Mask` contains a variable length binary string that should match the content of a specific position in the memory of a tag. The `Length` field defines the length of the `Mask` field in bits. The `Mask` field can be compared with one of the four types of memory banks in a tag. The `MemBank` field specifies which memory bank the `Mask` will be compared with. The `Pointer` field specifies the starting position in the memory bank where the `Mask` will be compared with. For example, if we use a tuple (b, p, l, m) to denote the four fields, then only the tags with data starting at the pth bit with a length of l bits in the bth memory bank that is equal to m are matched.

To visually understand the selective reading, we show an example in Fig. 3 in which 4 out of 7 tags are selected to participate in the incoming inventory. Complex and multiple subsets of tags can be facilitated by issuing a group of `Select` commands to choose a subset of tags before an inventory round starts. For example, we can issue two `Select` commands: one for division and another for one-bit reply. Note the `Truncate` enabled `Select` command must be the last one if multiple selection commands are issued [1].

F3: Truncated Reply. Gen2 allows tags to reply a *truncated* reply (i.e., replying a part of `EPC`) through a special `Select` command with an enabled `Truncate` field, making a one-bit presence signal possible. When `Truncate` is enabled (i.e., set to 1), then the corresponding bitmask is not used for the division of tags, but lets tags reply with a portion of their `EPC`s following the pattern specified by the bitmask. Note that when `Truncate` is enabled, the `MemBank` must be set to the `EPC` bank (i.e., `MemBank = 1`) and such `Select` command must be the last one.

F4: Query Model. Followed by a group of `Select` commands, `Query` command (see page 76~80 of [1].) starts a new *inventory round* over a subset of tags, chosen by the previous `Select` commands.

4.2 Design of the Tash Function

An l-bit tash function is essentially a hash function that is indispensable to HEPs. We design the tash function while following the three principles outlined as follows. The first principle requires that

Table 2: Actions in the `Select` command

Action code	Tag matching	Tag not-matching
0	assert SL	deassert SL
1	assert SL	do nothing
2	do nothing	deassertSL
3	negate SL	do nothing
4	deassert SL	assert SL
5	deassert SL	do nothing
6	do nothing	assert SL
7	do nothing	negate SL

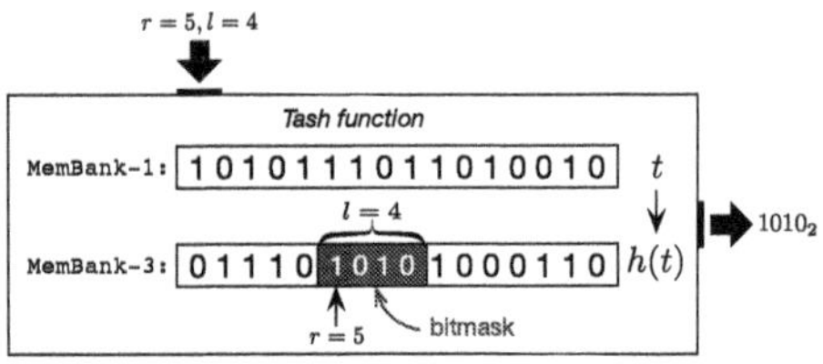

Fig. 4: Illustration of a tash function. The result of a tash function of $f_4(t, 5)$ is equal to 1010_2.

the tash result must be dependent on the input EPC and the seed. Moreover, it must be predictable as long as all the input parameters are known. The second principle requires the output values to be random, i.e., uniformly distributed in $[0, 2^l - 1]$. Even a one bit difference in the input will result in a completely different outcome. The third principle requires a method that can access the tash result of a tag directly or indirectly.

We have constructed the tash function as follows by applying the aforementioned principles: given a tag with an EPC of t, we firstly calculate the *hash value* of the EPC offline, using a common perfect hash function like 128-bit MD5 or SHA-1. Let $h(t)$ denote the calculated hash value. We then write $h(t)$ into the tag's user-defined memory bank of the tag, i.e., MemBank-3, for later use.

Definition 6 (Tash value). *The l-bit tash value of tag t challenged by seed r is defined as the value of the sub-bitstring starting from the rth bit and ending at the $(r+l-1)^{th}$ bit in the MemBank-3 of the tag.*

Evidently, $f_l(t, r)$ is actually a portion of $h(t)$, and thus, the parameter $r \in [0, \mathcal{L} - 1]$ and $l \in [1, \mathcal{L} - r]$, where $\mathcal{L}$ is the length of the hash value (e.g., 128 bits). Fig. 4 shows an example wherein the MemBank-1 and MemBank-3 of the tag store its EPC t and the hash value $h(t)$, respectively. When $r = 5$ and $l = 4$ are inputted, the tash value that this tag outputs is 1010_2, which is the sub-bitstring of $h(t)$ starting from the 5th bit and ending at the 8th bit in MemBank-3, i.e., $f_4(t, 5) = 1010_2$.

Our design does not require a tag to equip a real hash function or the engagement of its chip. It clearly applies the preceding principles. First, $f_l(t, r)$ is evidently repeatable, predicable and dependent on the inputs. Second, the randomness of $f_l(t, r)$ is derived from $h(t)$ and r, which are supposed to have a good randomness quality. Third, we have two ways to access the tash value. We can use the memory Read command to access MemBank-3 of a tag directly, or use the selective reading function to access the tash value indirectly (discussed later). Due to space limit, more discussions about the design are presented in our technical report [62].

4.3 Design of the Tash Table Function

The tash table function treats a reader and multiple tags as if they were a single virtual node, outputting a tash table. For simplicity, we use

$$S(\underbrace{a}_{\texttt{Action}}, \overbrace{b}^{\texttt{MemBank}}, \underbrace{p}_{\texttt{Pointer}}, \overbrace{l}^{\texttt{Length}}, \underbrace{m}_{\texttt{Mask}}, \overbrace{u}^{\texttt{Truncate}})$$

to denote a selection command (i.e., Select) with an Action (a), a MemBank (b), a Pointer (p), a Length (l), a Mask (m) and a Truncate (u). The command aims to select a subset of tags with a sub-bitstring that starts from the pth bit and ends at the $(p + l - 1)^{th}$ bit in the bth memory bank that is equal to m. These selected tags are requested to take an action a. The action codes are shown in Table. 2. In particular, if $u = 1$, then each tag will reply with a truncated EPC number.

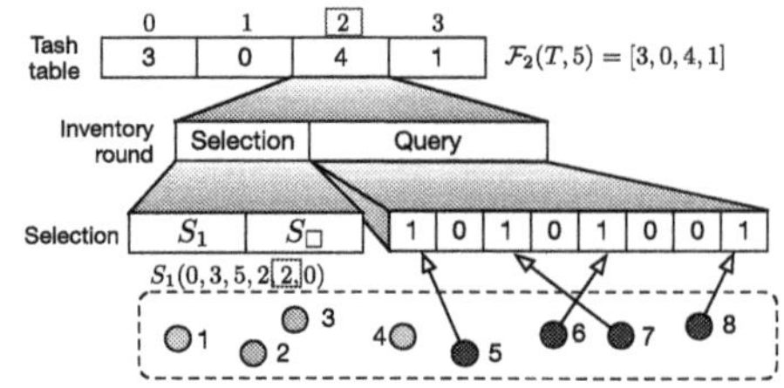

Fig. 5: Illustration of creating a tash table. Given that $r = 5$ and $l = 2$, $\mathcal{F}_2(T, 5) = [3, 0, 4, 1]$. Zooming into the 3rd entry-inventory, tags t_5, t_6, t_7 and t_8 are selected to join the inventory. $S_\square$ means this is the end command.

The tash table function is designed as follows. An l-bit table B consists of a total of 2^l entries, each of which contains the amount of tags mapped into it. In particular, the index number of each entry, which ranges from 0 to $2^l - 1$, is actually the tash values of the tags mapped into this entry, i.e., $B[\underline{i}] = |\{t | f_l(t, r) = \underline{i}\}|$. When constructing the ith entry, the reader performs selective reading with two selection commands as follows:

$$S_1(0, 3, r, l, i, 0) \text{ and } S_\square(1, 1, 1, 1, 1, 1)$$

Command S_1 selects a subset of tags with a sub-bitstring that starts from the rth bit and ends at the $(r+l-1)^{th}$ bit in the MemBank-3 that is equal to i. Notably, the involved sub-bitstring is the tash value of a tag, i.e., $f_l(t, r)$, which refers to Definition. 6. Consequently, only tags with tash values equal to i are selected to participate in the incoming inventory, i.e., counted by the ith entry. The second command $S_\square$ enables the selected tags to reply with the first bit of their EPC numbers for the one-bit signals. We call such inventory round as an *entry-inventory*. In this manner, we can obtain the whole tash table by launching 2^l entry-inventories.

To visually understand the procedure, we illustrate an example in Fig. 5, where $r = 5$ and $l = 2$. The tash table contains 2^2 entries; hence, four entry-inventories are launched. Their selection commands are defined as follows:

❶ $S_1(0, 3, \underline{5}, \underline{2}, \underline{0}, 0)$ and $S_\square(1, 1, 1, 1, 1, 1)$
❷ $S_1(0, 3, \underline{5}, \underline{2}, \underline{1}, 0)$ and $S_\square(1, 1, 1, 1, 1, 1)$
❸ $S_1(0, 3, \underline{5}, \underline{2}, \underline{2}, 0)$ and $S_\square(1, 1, 1, 1, 1, 1)$
❹ $S_1(0, 3, \underline{5}, \underline{2}, \underline{3}, 0)$ and $S_\square(1, 1, 1, 1, 1, 1)$

For the third entry-inventory, the Mask field is set to 2 because the index of the third entry is 2. Four tags (i.e., t_5, t_6, t_7 and t_8) are selected to join in this entry-inventory. Thus, $\mathcal{F}_2(T, 5)[2] = 4$.

For a tash table, note that (1) the sum of all its entries is equal to the total number of tags, and (2) it allows an application to selectively construct the entries of a tash table becaues each entry-inventory are independent of each other and completely controllable. For example, we can skip the inventories of these entries that are predicted to be empty.

4.4 Design of Tash Operators

A tash operator is connected to two tash tables, which have the same dimensions but are constructed using two different seeds. When two seeds, r_1 and r_2, are given, we can obtain two l-bit tash tables: $B_1 = \mathcal{F}_l(T, r_1)$ and $B_2 = \mathcal{F}_l(T, r_2)$. Our objective is to obtain a final tash table B by performing one of the subsequent tash operators on B_1 and B_2.

Tash AND. If $B = B_1 \oplus B_2$, then each entry of B denotes the number of tags that are concurrently mapped into the corresponding entries of B_1 and B_2. The selection commands for the ith entry-inventory are defined as follows:

$$S_1(\underline{0}, 3, r_1, l, i, 0), S_2(\underline{2}, 3, r_2, l, i, 0), S_\square$$

From the action codes shown in Table. 2, the purpose of S_1 with action code of 0 is to select tags $\in B_1[i]$ and deselect tags $\notin B_1[i]$. S_2 with action code of 2 deselects tags $\notin B_2[i]$ and results in tags $\in B_2[i]$ doing nothing. After S_1 is received, each tag exhibits one of two states, i.e., selected or deselected. Then, S_2 will make the selected tags remain in their selected states if they match its condition (i.e., doing nothing); otherwise, it changes their states to the deselected states (i.e., selected $\longrightarrow$ deselected), which is equivalent to removing tags $\notin B_2[i]$ from tags $\in B_1[i]$. Meanwhile, the tags deselected by S_1 remain in their states regardless of whether they match (i.e., do nothing) or not match (i.e., deselected $\longrightarrow$ deselected) the condition of S_2. Finally, $S_\square$ is reserved for the one-bit presence signal.

Tash OR. If $B = B_1 || B_2$, then each entry of B is the number of tags that mapped into the corresponding entry of either B_1 or B_2. The selection commands for the ith entry-inventory are defined as follows:

$$S_1(\underline{0}, 3, r_1, l, i, 0), S_1(\underline{1}, 3, r_2, l, i, 0), S_\square$$

Similarly, S_1 selects tags $\in B_1[i]$ and deselect tags $\notin B_1[i]$. S_2 with action code of 1 (see Table. 2) allows tags $\in B_2[i]$ to be selected as well, but tags $\notin B_2[i]$ remain in their states (i.e., do nothing), some of these tags may have been selected by S_1. The process is equivalent to holding the tags selected by S_1 and incrementally adding the new tags selected by S_2.

Tash XOR. If $B = B_1 \otimes B_2$, then each entry of B is the number of tags that are mapped into the corresponding entry of B_1 but not into the entry of B_2. The selection commands for the ith entry-inventory are defined as follows:

$$S_1(\underline{0}, 3, r_1, l, i, 0), S_2(\underline{5}, 3, r_2, l, i, 0), S_\square$$

Similarly, S_2 allows tags $\in B_2[i]$ to be deselected (i.e., removed from tags $\in B_1[i]$) and tags $\notin B_2[i]$ to do nothing. This process is equivalent to removing tags $\in B_2[i]$ from tags $\in B_1[i]$.

Tash hybrid. The aforementioned three operators can be further applied to a hybrid operation. When k seeds (i.e., $r_1, \cdots, r_k$) are given, we can obtain k tash tables. The selection commands for the ith entry-inventory can be designed as follows:

$$S_1(0, 3, r_1, l, i, 0), S_2(\mathtt{AC}, 3, r_2, l, i, 0),$$
$$\cdots, S_k(\mathtt{AC}, 3, r_k, l, i, 0), S_\square$$

where AC represents the `Action` code, which is set to 2, 1 and 5 for tash AND, OR and XOR, respectively. The action code of the first command is always set to 0. For example, the selection commands in the ith entry-inventory for $\mathcal{F}_l(T, r_1) \oplus \mathcal{F}_l(T, r_2) || \mathcal{F}_l(T, r_3) \otimes \mathcal{F}_l(T, r_4)$ are given by:

$$S_1(\underline{0}, 3, r_1, l, i, 0), S_2(\underline{2}, 3, r_2, l, i, 0),$$
$$S_3(\underline{1}, 3, r_3, l, i, 0), S_4(\underline{5}, 3, r_4, l, i, 0), S_\square$$

We leverage the action of a selection command to perform an operation in the physical layer before an entry-inventory starts, therefore, we introduce minimal additional communication overhead, i.e., broadcasting multiple `Select` commands. Compared with the multiple acquisitions of bitmaps used by prior HEPs, our solution provides a one-stop solution that can significantly reduce the total overhead in such situation.

4.5 Discussion

Comparison with bitmap. A tash table evidently takes a considerably longer time to obtain than a bitmap because a bitmap requires only one round of inventory, whereas a tash table requires multiple rounds. The additional time consumption is the trade-off for practicality because the reply of a COTS tag at the slot level is out of control. Nevertheless, this additional cost brings an additional benefit, i.e., a tash table has the exact number of tags mapped onto its each entry, which cannot be suggested by a bitmap. Moreover, a one-stop operator service can save more time.

Embedded pseudo-random function. Qian et al. [40] and Shahzad et al. [47] proposed a similar concept of utilizing a prestored random bit-string to construct a lightweight pseudo-random function. These studies have inspired our work. However, their main objective of these previous researchers is to accelerate the calculation of a random number, which still requires the engagement with the chip of a tag, and thus, has never been implemented in practice. In the present work, we do not require additional efforts on changing the logics of a tag chip and we associate this concept with the function of selective reading, moving the main task from a tag to a reader. Our design not only preserves the good features of the hash function but also gives a practical solution. This process has never been performed before.

5 TASH USAGE

This section revisits two classic problems of HEPs for usage study. We propose two practical solutions that use tash primitives for these problems. Note that in spite of two demonstration presented in this section, our tash primitives especially the tash table can serve any kind of HEPs.

5.1 Usage I: Cardinality Estimation

Cardinality estimation aims to estimate the total number of tags by using one-bit presence signals that are received without collecting each individual tag. The problem is formally defined as follows:

PROBLEM 1. *When a tag population of an unknown size n, a tolerance of $\beta \in (0, 1)$, and a required confidence level of $\alpha \in (0, 1)$ is given, how can the number of tags $\widehat{n}$ be estimated such that* $\Pr(|\widehat{n} - n| \leq \beta n) \geq \alpha$*?*

A naive method would be to add all the entries of a tash table together or let all tags reply at the first entry. Since each tag participates in one and only one entry-inventory, the final number is exactly equal to n. Keep in mind that our each entry corresponds to a complete round inventory. The naive method is equivalent to collecting them all, which is extremely time-consuming. We subsequently provide a reliable solution in a probabilistic way.

Proposed Estimator. We leverage the number of tags mapped into the first entry of a tash table to estimate n. Let X be the random variable to indicate the value of the first entry of a tash table. Since n tags are randomly and uniformly assigned into 2^l entires, we have

$$\Pr(X = m) = \binom{n}{m} p^m (1-p)^{n-m} \tag{3}$$

where $p = 1/2^l$. Evidently, variable X follows a standard Binomial distribution with the parameters n and p, i.e., $X \sim B(n, p)$. Therefore the expected value $\mu = np$ and variance $\delta = np(1-p)$. By equating the expected value and an instanced value m, our estimator $\widehat{n}$ is given by:

$$\widehat{n} = m/p = m2^l \tag{4}$$

The estimator only requires the first entry of the hash table, so it skips inventories of other entries. We can choose an appropriate l to ensure the estimation error within the given tolerance level β with a confidence of greater than α according to Theorem 1.

THEOREM 1. *The optimal dimension of the tash table is equal to* $\lceil \log_2 \frac{\sqrt{2}\cdot erf^{-1}(\alpha)}{\sqrt{2}\cdot erf^{-1}(\alpha)-\beta} \rceil$, *which results in an estimation error* $\leq \beta$ *with a probability of at least* α.

PROOF. Please refer to [62] for the proof. □

5.2 Usage II: Missing Tag Detection

The purpose of missing tag detection is to quickly find out the missing tags without collecting all the tags in the scene. Such detection is very useful, especially when thousands of tags are present. We formally define the problem of detecting missing tags in Problem 2. We assume that the EPCs of all the tags in a closed system are stored in a database and known in advance. This assumption is reasonable and necessary, because it is impossible for us to tell that a tag is missing without any prior knowledge of its existence.

PROBLEM 2. *How to quickly identify* m *missing out of* n *tags with a false positive rate of* γ *at most?*

Proposed detector. The underlying idea is to compare two tash tables B and $\widehat{B}$. B is an *intact tash table* created by tashing all the known EPCs which are stored in the database, while $\widehat{B}$ is an *instance tash table* obtained from the tags in the scene. We can detect the missing tags through comparing the difference between B and $\widehat{B}$. If the residual table $B - \widehat{B}$ (i.e., entry-wise subtraction) equals 0, no missing tag event happens. Otherwise, the tags mapped into the non-zero entries of the residual table are missing. Fig. 6(a) illustrates an example in which three tags, t_1, t_2 and t_3, are mapped into the intact tash table B. $\widehat{B}$ is an instance table where tag t_2 is missing, and thus $\widehat{B}[4] = 1$. Consequently, $(B - \widehat{B})[4] = 1$, we can definitely infer that one tag is missing. However, it is impossible for us to tell which tag is missing because t_2 and t_3 are simultaneously mapped into the fourth entry.

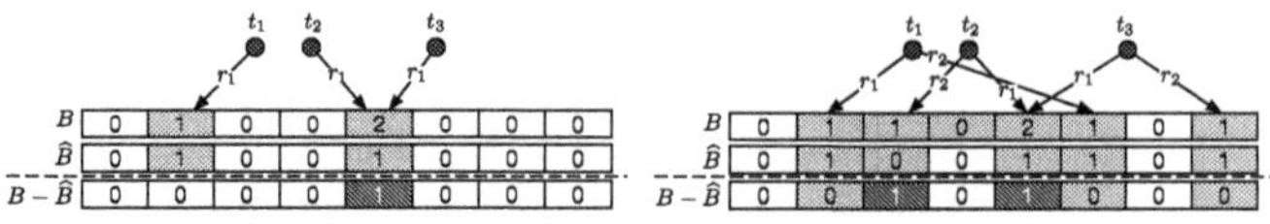

(a) Tashing once (b) Tashing twice

Fig. 6: An example of missing detection. B is the intact tash table generated using the known EPCs while $\widehat{B}$ is an instance over the tags in the current scene.

Inspired by the Bloom filter[7], we perform k tashings to identify the missing tags as follows:

$$B = \mathcal{F}_l(T, r_1) || \dots || \mathcal{F}_l(T, r_k) \tag{5}$$

The final B after tash ORs is considered to use k independent hash functions (i.e., induced by k random seeds) to map each tag into B for k times, as shown in Fig. 6(b). The residual table of $B - \widehat{B}$ is therefore viewed as a Bloom filter which represents the missing tags. Thereafter, to answer a query of whether a tag t is missing, we check whether all entries set by $f_l(t, r_1), \cdots$ and $f_l(t, r_k)$ in the residual table have a value of non-zero. If the answer is yes, then tag t is the missing one. Otherwise, it is not the missing tag. Fig. 6(b) illustrates an example in which each tag is tashed twice. The missing tag t_2 can be identified because both the 2rd and the 4th entry in the residual table have value of non-zero. Despite multiple tashings, the query may yield a *false positive*, where it suggests a tag is missing even though it is not.

Analysis. To lower the rate of false positive rate, it is necessary to answer two questions.

(1) *How many tash functions do we need?* Given the table dimension l, we expect to optimize the number of tash functions. There are two competing forces: using more tash functions gives us more chance to find a zero bit for a missing tag, but using fewer tash functions increases the fraction of zero bits in the table. After m missing tags are tashed into the table, the probability that a specific bit is still 0 is $(1 - \frac{1}{L})^{km} \approx e^{-km/L}$ where $L = 2^l$. Correspondingly, the probability of a false positive p is given by

$$p = (1 - e^{-km/L})^k \tag{6}$$

Namely, a missing tag falls into k non-zero entries. Lemma. 1 suggests that the optimal number of tash functions is achieved when $k = \ln 2 \cdot (L/m)$.

LEMMA 1. *The false positive rate is minimized when* $p = (1/2)^k$ *or equivalently* $k = \ln 2 \cdot (L/m)$.

PROOF. Please refer to [7] for the proof. □

(2) *How large tash table is necessary to represent all* m *missing tags?* Recall that the false positive rate achieves minimum when $p = (1/2)^k$. Let $p \leq \gamma$. After some algebraic manipulation, we find

$$L \geq \frac{m \log_2(1/\gamma)}{\ln 2} = m \log_2 e \cdot \log_2(1/\gamma) = 1.44m \log_2(1/\gamma) \tag{7}$$

Finally, putting the above conclusions together, we have the subsequent theorem.

THEOREM 2. *Setting the table dimension to* $\lceil \log_2(1.44m \log_2(1/\gamma)) \rceil$ *and using* $\lceil \ln 2 \cdot (2^l/m) \rceil$ *random seeds allow the false positive rate of identifying* m *missing tags lower than a given tolerance* γ.

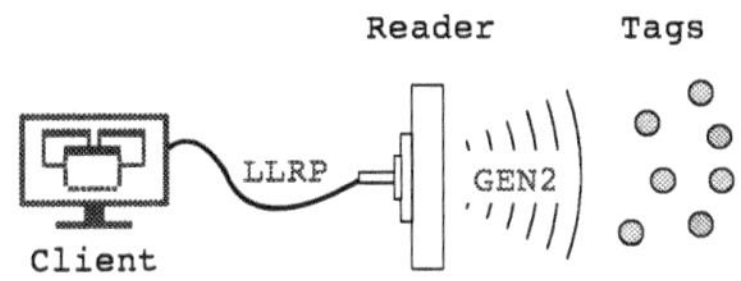

Fig. 7: Gen2 vs. LLRP. Gen2 is the air protocol between a reader and tags while LLRP is the driver protocol between a client computer and a reader. Our framework leverages LLRP to manipulate a reader to broadcast Gen2 commands that we need.

6 TASH IMPLEMENTATION

Our implementation involves two kinds of protocols: UHF Gen2 air interface protocol (Gen2) and Low Level Reader Protocol (LLRP). As shown in Fig. 7, Gen2 protocol defines the physical and logical interaction between readers and passive tags, while LLRP allows a client computer to control a reader. Each client computer connects one ore more RFID readers via Ethernet cables. LLRP is the *driver program (or driver protocol)* for Gen2 readers. We leverage LLRP to manipulate a reader to broadcast Gen2 commands that we need. Notice that we do not need particularly implement Gen2 protocol, which has been implemented in the COTS RFID devices that we are using. Specifically, LLRP specifies two types of operations: reader operation (RO) and access operation (AO). Both operations are represented in XML document form and transported to a reader through TCP/IP.

Reader operation. RO defines the inventory parameters specified in the Gen2 protocol, such as bitmask, antenna power, and frequency. Fig. 8 shows a simplified instance of an `ROSpec`. An `ROSpec` is composed of at least one `AISpec`. Each `AISpec` is used for an antenna setting. An `AISpec` consists of more than one `C1G2Filters`. The filter functions as a bitmask. We can set multiple selection commands by adding multiple `C1G2Filters`.

Access operation. AO defines the access parameters for writing or reading data to and from a tag. We leverage the `C1G2Write` inside an `AOSpec` to write the hash value of the `EPC` into a user-defined memory bank. As the `EPC`s are highly related to the products the tags attached, the writing of hash values should be accomplished by the product manufactures or administrators. There is almost no overhead to write data into `MemBank-3` since it is allowed to write a batch of tags simultaneously using `Write` commands specified in one `AOSpec`, without physically changing tags' positions.

7 MICROBENCHMARK

We start with a few experiments that provide insight to our hash primitives.

7.1 Experimental Setup

We evaluate the framework using COTS UHF readers and tags. We use a total of 3 models of ImpinJ readers (R220, R420 and R680), each of which is connected to a 900MHz and 8dB gain directional antenna. In order to better understand the feasibility and effectiveness of Tash in practice, we test a total of 3, 000 COTS tags with different models. We divide these tags into 10 groups of 300 tags each. The tags of each group are densely attached to a plastic board which is placed in front of a reader antenna. Three hundreds is the maximum number of tags that can be covered by one directional antenna in our laboratory. We store the 3, 000 `EPC` numbers in our database as the ground truth. The 128-bit MD5 is employed as the common hash function to generate the hash values of `EPC`s. The experiments with the same settings are repeated across the 10 groups, and the average result is reported.

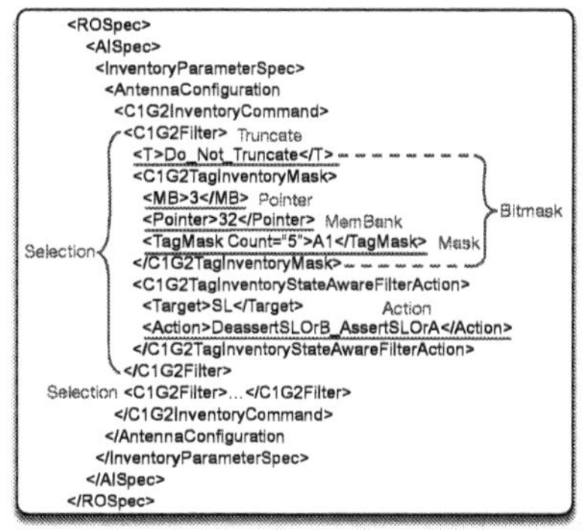

Fig. 8: LLRP RO specification. The XML document defines various parameters that are required for `Select` command.

7.2 Compatibility Investigation

First, we investigate the compatibility of Gen2 across 10 different types of readers and 18 different types of tags in terms of the functions or commands that Tash requires. The readers and tags may come from different manufacturers but work together in practice. These investigated products are all publicly claimed to be completely Gen2-compatible.

Reader compatibility. We investigate the R220, R420, and R680 models from ImpinJ [3], the Mercury6, Sargas and M6e models from ThingMagic [4], as well as the ALR-F800, 9900+, 9680 and 9650 models from Alien [2]. We perform the investigation through real tests for the first three models of readers (i.e., the ImpinJ series), and investigate the other readers through their data sheets or manuals (because we are limited by the lack of hardware). The Gen2-compatibility of readers is briefly summarized in Table. 3. Consequently, we have the subsequent findings. (1) All the readers do support `Write/Read` command, which Tash uses for writing or reading hash values of `EPC` numbers. (2) All the readers do support the `Select` command, which Tash uses for the selective reading. (3) However, our practical tests suggest that none model of the ImpinJ series supports the `Truncate` command, which Tash uses to hear the one-bit presence signal. The serviceability of other readers is not clearly indicated in the manuals of those readers. (4) The Gen2 protocol does not specify how many `C1G2Filters`

Table 3: Summary of Gen2-compatibility on reader

Commands or functions	ImpinJ	ThingMagic	Alien
`Write/Read`	✓	✓	✓
`Select`	✓	✓	✓
`Truncate`	×	–	–
Max No. of `C1G2Filters`	4	–	–
Max No. of `AISpecs`	16	–	–

Table 4: Summary of Gen2-compatibility on tag.

	ImpinJ Monza									Alien ALN								
Commands	5	D	E	QT	X-2K	X-8K	R6	R6-P	R6-C	9840	9830	9662	9610	9726	9820	9715	9716	9629
`MemBank1` (bits)	128	128	496	128	128	128	96	128/96	96	128	128	480	96-480	128	128	128	128	96
`MemBank3` (bits)	32	32	128	512	2176	8192	×	32/64	32	128	128	512	512	128	128	128	128	512
`Write` cmd	✓	✓	✓	✓	✓	✓	×	✓	✓	✓	✓	✓	✓	✓	✓	✓	✓	✓
`Select` cmd	✓	✓	✓	✓	✓	✓	✓	✓	✓	✓	✓	✓	✓	✓	✓	✓	✓	✓
`Truncate` cmd	–	–	–	–	–	–	–	–	–	–	–	–	–	–	–	–	–	–

and `AISpecs` that a reader should support. Our practical tests suggest that the ImpinJ series supports 4 `C1G2Filters` and 16 `AISpecs`, which means that we can only use a maximum of four tash operators each time.

Tag compatibility. We investigate 9 chip models from ImpinJ Monza series and 9 additional models from Alien ALN series. The majority of tags on the market contain these 18 models of chips and customized antennas. Table. 4 summarizes the result of our investigation, from which we have the subsequent findings. (1) Tags reserve 96 ~ 480 bits of memory for storing `EPC` numbers, among which the size of 96 bits has become the de facto standard. (2) Tash requires `MemBank-3` to store the hash values. The results of the investigation show that almost all tags allow to write to and read from the third memory bank, with an exception of ImpinJ Monza R6, which does not have the user-defined memory. The size of the third memory bank fluctuates around 32 ~ 512 bits. The de facto standard has become 128 bits. (4) All tags are claimed to support the `Truncate` command according to their public data sheets. However, we have no idea about their real serviceability due to the lack of `Truncate`-supportable reader available for practical tests. In our future work, we plan to utilize USRP for further tests.

Summary. Despite positive and public claims, our investigation shows that current COTS RFID devices, regardless of readers or tags and models, have some defects in their compatibility with Gen2, especially with regard to `Truncate`. The reason, we may infer, is that these commands are seldom used in practice and therefore never receive attention from manufacturers. The partial compatibility of such devices cannot fully achieve the performance Tash brings. Even so, we are obliged to make the claim, again, that our design strictly follows the Gen2 protocol. We hope this work can encourage manufacturers to upgrade their products (e.g., reader firmware) to achieve full compatibility.

7.3 Tash Function

Second, we evaluate the tash function with respect to the randomness and the accessibility.

Randomness. Randomness is the most important metric for a hash function. It requires that the outputs of a hash function must be uniformly distributed. To validate the randomness of the tash function, we collect 99, 886 real `EPC` numbers from our partner (i.e., an international logistics company), which introduced RFID technology for sorting tasks five years ago. Each `EPC` number has a length of 96 bits and encodes the basic information about the package, such as sources, destinations, serial numbers, and so on. We employ the 128-bit MD5 to create the hash values of these `EPC`s. As the minimum size of the `MemBank-3` is 32 bits (see Table. 3), we choose to use only the first 32 bits for our tests. We traverse r and l from 0 ~ 31 and 1 ~ $32 - r$ respectively. For each pair of r and l, we obtain 99, 886 tash values over all the `EPC`s. Across these tash values, we further conduct the following two analysis: (1) We merge 100 tash values, which are randomly selected from the above results, into a long bit string. We then calculate the percents of '0' and '1' emerged in that bit string. This operation is repeated for 100 times. Finally, totally 100 pairs of percents are obtained. Their CDFs are plotted in Fig. 9(a). Ideally, each bit has a equal probability of 0.5 to be zero or one if a hash function makes a good randomicity. From the figure, we can figure out that the percents distributed between 0.4 and 0.6. In particular, percents of '0' and '1' have means of 0.49 and 0.50 with standard deviations of 0.043 and 0.044 respectively. (2) We shuffle these values into 100 groups, and employ the χ^2-test with a significance level of 0.05 to test each group's goodness-of-fits of the uniform distribution (i.e., passed or failed). Then, we finally calculate the pass rate for a pair of setting. In this manner, we totally obtain 496 pass rates. More than 60% of the pass rates are over than 0.95. In particular, three sets of the results with $r = 16$, 20 and 26 and a variable l, are selected to show in Fig. 9(b). We find that 90% of the pass rates exceed 0.95 for the three cases, and their median pass rates are around 0.97. Thus, the two above statistical results suggest that our tash function has a very good quality of randomness.

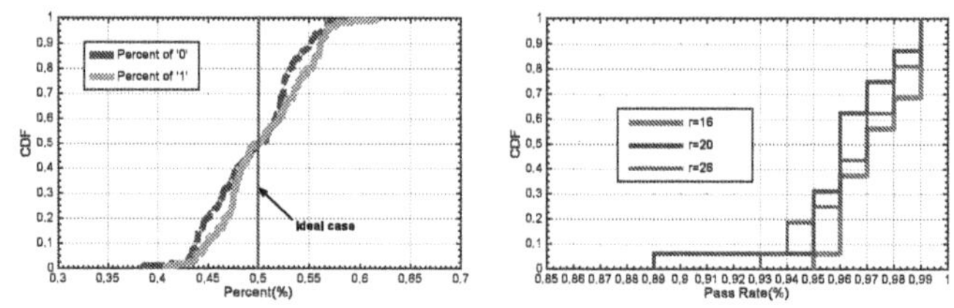

(a) Distributions of percents of '0' and '1'　　(b) Results of random test

Fig. 9: Evaluation of tash function. (a) shows the CDF of percents of '0' and '1' appearing in the tash values. (b) shows the CDF of pass rates of random ness tests.

Accessibility. Accessibility refers to the ability to get access to a tash value from a tag. As aforementioned, we have two ways to acquire the tash values. The first way is to use the `Read` command. The second way is to indirectly access a tash value through a selective reading. We choose the second method since it is the basis of our design. Specifically, we perform a selective reading to determine whether the tags are collected as expected, when given random inputs and a possible tash value. We intensively and continuously perform such readings across the 10 × 300 tags using three 4-port ImpinJ readers for three rounds of 24 hours in a relatively isolated environment (e.g., an empty room without disturbance). Surprisingly, we find all the reading results faithfully conform to

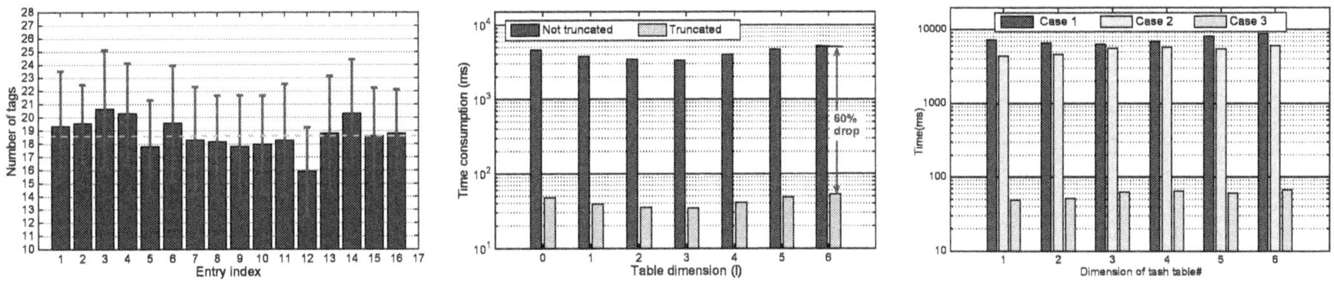

(a) Balance of tash table (b) Performance of tash table function (c) Performance of tash operator

Fig. 10: Evaluation of tash table function and tash operator. (a) shows the balance of a 4-bit tash table across 300 tags using 100 different random seed. (b) shows the time consumption on gathering 6 tash tables with different dimensions. **(c) shows the time consumption on performing OR on two tash tables.**

our benchmarks without any exceptions. This shows that the selective reading is well supported by the manufactures and is both stable and reliable.

7.4 Tash Table Function

Third, we evaluate the performance of the tash table function in terms of its balance and gathering speed.

Balance. A good hash table function will equally assign each key to a bucket. We expect the output tash table to be as balanced as possible. To show this feature, we generate 100 different 4-bit tash tables (i.e., each includes 16 entries) across 300 tags using 100 different random seeds. If the tash table is well balanced, the expected number of each entry should be very close to 300/16 = 18.7. Fig. 10(a) shows the mean number of tags in each entry as well as their standard deviations. The average number across 16 entries equals 18.75, which is very close to the expected theoretical value. The average standard deviation equals 0.44. Thus, the good randomness quality of tash functions results in output tash tables being well balanced.

Gathering speed. We then consider the time consumption of gathering a tash table. Fixing the random seed, we vary the table dimension l from 0 to 6. We then measure the time taken on gathering a tash table with the deployed 300 tags. Fig. 10(b) shows the resulting time as a function of the table dimension. From the immediately above-mentioned figure, we can observe the subsequent findings. (1) When $l = 0$ without truncating reply, the result is equivalent to collecting 300 complete `EPC`s of all the tags. Such time consumption (i.e., 4, 524*ms*) is viewed as our baseline. (2) By contrast, when $l > 0$ without truncating a reply, the collection amounts to dividing all the tags into 2^l groups "equally" and then collecting each group independently. In this manner, when $l \leq 4$, such "divide and conquer" approach is better than "one time deal", i.e., a drop in overhead of about 10%. The Gen2 reader uses a Q-adaptive algorithm for the anti-collision. This algorithm is able to adaptively learn the best frame length from the collision history. Due to the division, a smaller number of tags can make reader's learning relatively quicker and improve the overall performance. (3) However, when $l > 4$, the performance of "divide and conquer" approach starts to deteriorate. The ImpinJ reader supports 16 `AISpecs` at most (see Table. 3). We have to re-send another `ROSpec` for the remaining selective readings when the number of entry-inventory is above 16 (i.e., $l > 4$), which introduces additional time consumption. (4) We then consider the case where the reply is truncated to a one-bit presence signal as assumed by HEPs. Due to the defects of ImpinJ readers in the implementation of the `Truncate` command, we cannot measure the actual time spent on collecting truncated `EPC`s. We can only utilize the least-square algorithm to estimate the transmission time for a one-bit presence signal. Our fitting results show that truncating reply would introduce about 60% drop of the overhead at least.

7.5 Tash Operators

Finally, we investigate the performance of tash operators. Superior to existing HEPs, these operators allow us to perform set operations on-tag and conduct a one-stop inventory. In particular, we show the performance of OR as a representative across 300 tags. The tests for other operators are similar and omitted due to the space limitation. In the experiments, we fix the two random seeds but change the dimension of tash table. Fig. 10(c) shows the results of three cases. In Case 1, we independently produce 2 tash tables without truncating a reply and conduct the OR in the application layer. In Case 2 and Case 3, we conduct on-tag OR function as Tash provides without and with truncating a reply respectively. Consequently, when the dimension equals 2, Case 1 takes 6, 511*ms* on collecting two tables. On the contrary, the amount of time taken is reduced to 4, 578*ms* (i.e., 29.7% drop) if we perform an on-tag OR function even without truncation (Case 2). Ideally, the amount of time taken could be further reduced to 50.97*ms* by using a truncating reply (Case 3), which offers a staggering drop in time usage by 99.22%. Our experiments relate only to the amount of time spent on ORing two tables. It may be predicted that much more outperformance will be gained if multiple tables are involved. The tash operators that we design in this work have never been proposed before.

8 USAGE EVALUATION

We then use our prototype to demonstrate the benefits and potentials of Tash in two typical applications.

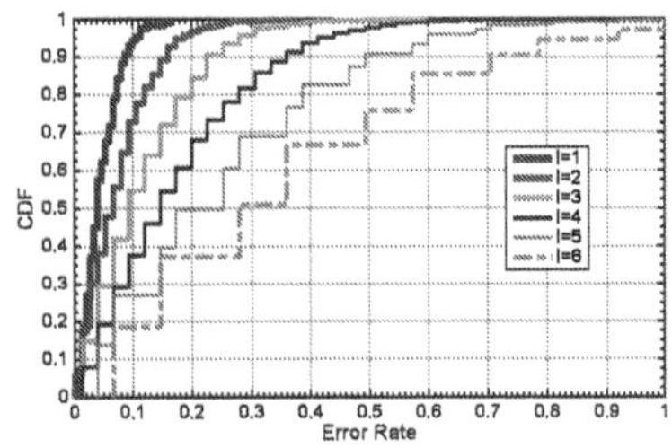

(a) Testbed

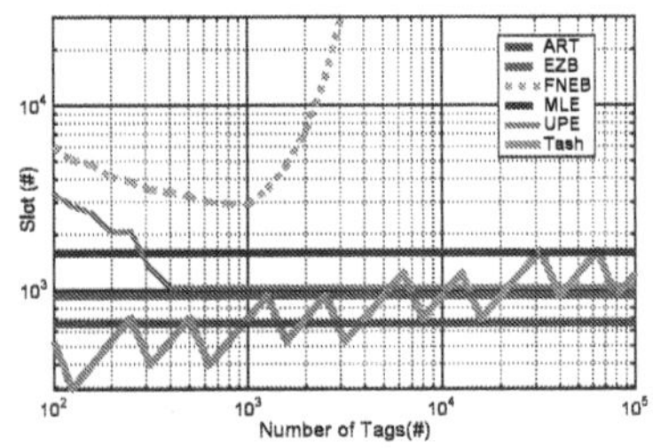

(b) Large-scale simulation

Fig. 11: Cardinality estimation. (a) shows the CDF of error rates for estimating 300 tags with our testbed. (b) shows the estimation comparisons with other theoretical algorithms with simulation.

8.1 Usage I: Cardinality Estimation

We evaluate our estimation scheme through the testbed as well as large-scale simulations.

Testbed based. Our scheme only uses the first entry of the tash table for the estimation, thereby we only need one entry-inventory. Fig. 11(a) shows the CDF of estimation results across 300 tags. We define the error rate as $|n - \widehat{n}|/n$ where $\widehat{n}$ is the estimated number. As a result, 90% of the estimations have an error rate less than 0.1 and a median of 0.04 when setting the dimension $l = 1$. In this case, almost half tags follow into the first entry so the rate could be pretty high, at the price of longer inventory time. As l increases, the error rate also increases because less samples are acquired for the estimation. These experiments show the feasibility of using tash table for cardinality estimation.

Simulation based. We then perform the evaluation through large-scale simulations for two reasons: (1) ensuring its scalability when meeting a huge number of tags. (2) making comparisons with prior work, which are all simulation-based. We numerically simulate in Matlab using tash scheme as well as other five prior RFID estimation schemes: UPE[18], EZB[19], FNEB[15], MLE[23], ART[47]. We implement these schemes by referring to the RFID estimation tool developed by Shahzad[46]. Fig. 11(b) shows the time cost with a varying n given $\alpha = 0.9$ and $\beta = 0.08$. We observe that our scheme is 5× faster than the others on average when $n < 1000$. Thus our scheme is suitable for the estimation with a small number of tags. When $n > 1000$, the performance of our scheme starts to vibrate between ART and MLE, due to two reasons. First, our scheme is not collision-free so that more efforts are required to deal with the collisions incurred by more tags. Second, the size of a tash table can only increase in the power of two, making the size always vibrate around the optimal one. Even so, the advantage of our scheme is still clear: it is the first RFID estimation scheme that can work in real life. Notice that ART claimed to work with RFID systems because they are theoretically compatible with ALOHA protocols. Actually, the current COTS RFID systems do not allow user to control the low-level access, like fined-grained adjustment of frame length and obtaining slot-level feedback, which are necessary to implement ART. Thus, there is no way for ART to implement their algorithms over COTS RFID systems without any hardware modification and fabrication.

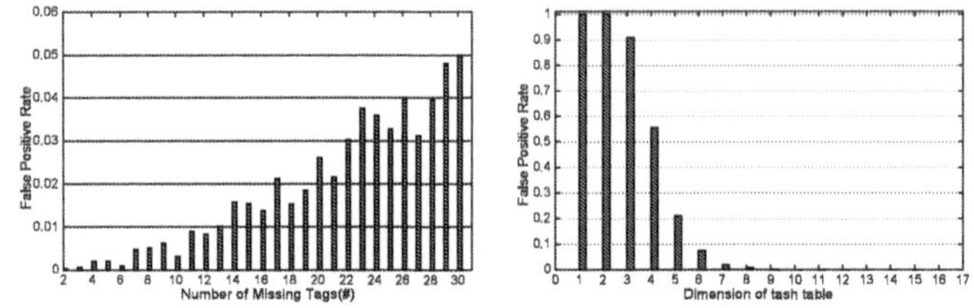

(a) $k = 2$ and $l = 8$ (b) $k = 2$ and $m = 10$

Fig. 12: Missing detection with 300 tags. (a) The resulted FPRs as function of the missing number (b) as function of the dimension of tash tables.

8.2 Usage II: Missing Detection

Finally, we evaluate the effectiveness of missing detection in real case. We randomly remove m tags from the testbed. Since we only have 300 tags in total, we fix the number of random seeds to 2, i.e., $k = 2$. The performance is evaluated in term of the false positive rate (FPR), which is the ratio of number of mistakenly detected as missing tags to the total number of really missing tags. Our scheme is able to successfully find out all the missing tags because the residual table always contains the entries that missing tags are tashed into. Fig. 12(a) shows the results of the first case in which we use an 8-bit hash table (i.e., $l = 8$) to detect the missing tags. Consequently, the FPR is maintained around 0.01 when $m < 14$ (i.e., 5% of the tags are missing). Fig. 12(b) shows the second case in which we remove 10 tags and detect the missing tags by changing the dimension of tash table. As Theorem. 2 suggests, we should set $l = 5, 6, 7$ to guarantee the FPR $\gamma < 0.2, 0.1, 0.01$. From the figure, we can find that the results of our experiments completely conform to this theorem. The real FPRs equal 0.21, 0.07 and 0.008 in the three cases. Tash enabled missing detection works well in practice.

9 CONCLUSION

This work discusses a fundamental issue that how to supplement hash functionality to existing COTS RFID systems, which is dispensable for prior HEPs. A key innovation of this work is our design of hash primitives, which is implemented using selective reading. Tash not only makes a big step forward in boosting prior HEPs, but also opens up a wide range of exciting opportunities.

Acknowledgments. The research is supported by GRF/ECS (NO. 25222917), NSFC General Program (NO. 61572282) and Hong Kong Polytechnic University (NO. 1-ZVJ3). We thank all the reviewers for their valuable comments and helpful suggestions, and particularly thank Eric Rozner for the shepherding.

REFERENCES

[1] 2004. EPCglobal Gen2 Specification. www.gs1.org/epcglobal. (2004).
[2] 2017. Alien. http://www.alientechnology.com. (2017).
[3] 2017. ImpinJ, Inc. http://www.impinj.com/. (2017).
[4] 2017. ThingMagic. http://www.thingmagic.com. (2017).
[5] Andrey Bogdanov, Lars R Knudsen, Gregor Leander, Christof Paar, Axel Poschmann, Matthew JB Robshaw, Yannick Seurin, and Charlotte Vikkelsoe. 2007. PRESENT: An ultra-lightweight block cipher. In *CHES*, Vol. 4727. Springer, 450–466.
[6] Andrey Bogdanov, Gregor Leander, Christof Paar, Axel Poschmann, Matt JB Robshaw, and Yannick Seurin. 2008. Hash functions and RFID tags: Mind the gap. In *Proc. of IACR CHES.*
[7] Andrei Broder and Michael Mitzenmacher. 2004. Network applications of bloom filters: A survey. *Internet Mathematics* 1, 4 (2004), 485–509.
[8] Binbin Chen, Ziling Zhou, and Haifeng Yu. 2013. Understanding RFID counting protocols. In *Proc. of ACM MobiCom.*
[9] Daniel M Dobkin. 2012. *The RF in RFID: UHF RFID in Practice.* Newnes.
[10] Martin Feldhofer, Sandra Dominikus, and Johannes Wolkerstorfer. 2004. Strong authentication for RFID systems using the AES algorithm. In *CHES*, Vol. 4. Springer, 357–370.
[11] Martin Feldhofer and Christian Rechberger. 2006. A case against currently used hash functions in RFID protocols. In *On the move to meaningful internet systems 2006: OTM 2006 workshops.* Springer, 372–381.
[12] Frost and Sullivan. 2011. Global RFID healthcare and pharmaceutical marke. *Industry Report* (2011).
[13] Wei Gong, Kebin Liu, Xin Miao, and Haoxiang Liu. 2014. Arbitrarily accurate approximation scheme for large-scale rfid cardinality estimation. In *Proc. of IEEE INFOCOM.*
[14] Tim Good and Mohammed Benaissa. 2007. Hardware results for selected stream cipher candidates. *State of the Art of Stream Ciphers* 7 (2007), 191–204.
[15] Hao Han, Bo Sheng, Chiu C Tan, Qun Li, Weizhen Mao, and Sanglu Lu. 2010. Counting RFID tags efficiently and anonymously. In *Proc. of IEEE INFOCOM.*
[16] Deukjo Hong, Jaechul Sung, Seokhie Hong, Jongin Lim, Sangjin Lee, Bonseok Koo, Changhoon Lee, Donghoon Chang, Jesang Lee, Kitae Jeong, et al. 2006. HIGHT: A new block cipher suitable for low-resource device. In *CHES*, Vol. 4249. Springer, 46–59.
[17] Yuxiao Hou, Jiajue Ou, Yuanqing Zheng, and Mo Li. 2015. PLACE: Physical layer cardinality estimation for large-scale RFID systems. In *Proc. of IEEE INFOCOM.*
[18] Murali Kodialam and Thyaga Nandagopal. 2006. Fast and reliable estimation schemes in RFID systems. In *Proc. of ACM MobiCom.*
[19] Murali Kodialam, Thyaga Nandagopal, and Wing Cheong Lau. 2007. Anonymous tracking using RFID tags. In *Proc. of IEEE INFOCOM.*
[20] Binbin Li, Yuan He, Wenyuan Liu, Lin Wang, and Hongyan Wang. 2016. LocP: An efficient Localized Polling Protocol for large-scale RFID systems. In *Proc. of IEEE ICNP.*
[21] Tao Li, Shigang Chen, and Yibei Ling. 2010. Identifying the missing tags in a large RFID system. In *Proc. of ACM MobiHoc.*
[22] Tao Li, Shigang Chen, and Yibei Ling. 2013. Efficient protocols for identifying the missing tags in a large RFID system. *IEEE/ACM Transactions on Networking* 21, 6 (2013), 1974–1987.
[23] Tao Li, Samuel Wu, Shigang Chen, and Mark Yang. 2010. Energy efficient algorithms for the RFID estimation problem. In *Proc. of IEEE INFOCOM.*
[24] Chae Hoon Lim and Tymur Korkishko. 2005. mCrypton-a lightweight block cipher for security of low-cost RFID tags and sensors. In *WISA*, Vol. 3786. Springer, 243–258.
[25] Haoxiang Liu, Wei Gong, Xin Miao, Kebin Liu, and Wenbo He. 2014. Towards adaptive continuous scanning in large-scale rfid systems. In *Proc. of IEEE INFOCOM.*
[26] Jia Liu, Bin Xiao, Shigang Chen, Feng Zhu, and Lijun Chen. 2015. Fast RFID grouping protocols. In *Proc. of IEEE INFOCOM.* 1948–1956.
[27] Xiulong Liu, Keqiu Li, Geyong Min, Yanming Shen, Alex X Liu, and Wenyu Qu. 2014. A multiple hashing approach to complete identification of missing RFID tags. *IEEE Transactions on Communications* 62, 3 (2014), 1046–1057.
[28] Xiulong Liu, Keqiu Li, Heng Qi, Bin Xiao, and Xin Xie. 2014. Fast counting the key tags in anonymous RFID systems. In *Proc.of IEEE ICNP.*
[29] Xiulong Liu, Bin Xiao, Keqiu Li, Jie Wu, Alex X Liu, Heng Qi, and Xin Xie. 2015. RFID cardinality estimation with blocker tags. In *Proc. of IEEE INFOCOM.*
[30] Xuan Liu, Bin Xiao, Shigeng Zhang, Kai Bu, and Alvin Chan. 2015. STEP: A time-efficient tag searching protocol in large RFID systems. *IEEE Trans. Comput.* 64, 11 (2015), 3265–3277.
[31] Wen Luo, Shigang Chen, Tao Li, and Shiping Chen. 2011. Efficient missing tag detection in RFID systems. In *Proc. of IEEE INFOCOM.*
[32] Wen Luo, Shigang Chen, Tao Li, and Yan Qiao. 2012. Probabilistic missing-tag detection and energy-time tradeoff in large-scale RFID systems. In *Proc. of ACM MobiHoc.*
[33] Wen Luo, Shigang Chen, Yan Qiao, and Tao Li. 2014. Missing-tag detection and energy–time tradeoff in large-scale RFID systems with unreliable channels. *IEEE/ACM Transactions on Networking* 22, 4 (2014), 1079–1091.
[34] Wen Luo, Yan Qiao, and Shigang Chen. 2013. An efficient protocol for RFID multigroup threshold-based classification. In *Proc. of IEEE INFOCOM.* 890–898.
[35] Wen Luo, Yan Qiao, Shigang Chen, and Min Chen. 2016. An efficient protocol for RFID multigroup threshold-based classification based on sampling and logical bitmap. *IEEE/ACM Transactions on Networking* 24, 1 (2016), 397–407.
[36] Cunqing Ma, Jingqiang Lin, and Yuewu Wang. 2012. Efficient missing tag detection in a large RFID system. In *Proc. of IEEE TrustCom.*
[37] Christian Pendl, Markus Pelnar, and Michael Hutter. 2012. Elliptic curve cryptography on the WISP UHF RFID tag. *RFID. Security and Privacy* (2012), 32–47.
[38] Matthai Philipose, Joshua R Smith, Bing Jiang, Alexander Mamishev, Sumit Roy, and Kishore Sundara-Rajan. 2005. Battery-free wireless identification and sensing. *IEEE Pervasive computing* 4, 1 (2005), 37–45.
[39] Axel Poschmann, Gregor Leander, Kai Schramm, and Christof Paar. 2007. New Light-Weight DES Variants Suited for RFID Applications, proceedings of Fast Software Encryption 14. *Lecture Notes in Computer Science, Springer (to appear)* (2007).
[40] Chen Qian, Yunhuai Liu, Hoilun Ngan, and Lionel M Ni. 2010. Asap: Scalable identification and counting for contactless rfid systems. In *Proc. of IEEE ICDCS.*
[41] Chen Qian, Hoilun Ngan, Yunhao Liu, and Lionel M Ni. 2011. Cardinality estimation for large-scale RFID systems. *IEEE Transactions on Parallel and Distributed Systems* 22, 9 (2011), 1441–1454.
[42] Yan Qiao, Shigang Chen, and Tao Li. 2013. Tag-ordering polling protocols in RFID systems. In *RFID as an Infrastructure.* Springer, 59–82.
[43] Yan Qiao, Shigang Chen, Tao Li, and Shiping Chen. 2011. Energy-efficient polling protocols in RFID systems. In *Proc. of ACM MobiHoc.*
[44] Carsten Rolfes, Axel Poschmann, Gregor Leander, and Christof Paar. 2008. Ultra-lightweight implementations for smart devices–security for 1000 gate equivalents. In *CARDIS*, Vol. 5189. Springer, 89–103.
[45] Vahid Shah-Mansouri and Vincent WS Wong. 2011. Cardinality estimation in RFID systems with multiple readers. *IEEE Transactions on Wireless Communications* 10, 5 (2011), 1458–1469.
[46] Muhammad Shahzad. [n. d.]. RFID estimation tool. http://www4.ncsu.edu/~mshahza/publications.html. ([n. d.]).
[47] Muhammad Shahzad and Alex X Liu. 2012. Every bit counts: fast and scalable RFID estimation. In *Proc. of ACM MobiCom.*
[48] Muhammad Shahzad and Alex X Liu. 2015. Expecting the unexpected: Fast and reliable detection of missing RFID tags in the wild. In *Proc. of IEEE INFOCOM.*
[49] Muhammad Shahzad and Alex X Liu. 2016. Fast and Reliable Detection and Identification of Missing RFID Tags in the Wild. *IEEE/ACM Transactions on Networking* 24, 6 (2016), 3770–3784.
[50] Bo Sheng, Qun Li, and Weizhen Mao. 2010. Efficient continuous scanning in RFID systems. In *Proc. of IEEE INFOCOM.*
[51] Bo Sheng, Chiu Chiang Tan, Qun Li, and Weizhen Mao. 2008. Finding popular categories for RFID tags. In *Proc. of ACM MobiHoc.*
[52] W-K Sze, W-C Lau, and O-C Yue. 2009. Fast RFID counting under unreliable radio channels. In *Proc. of IEEE ICC.*
[53] Chiu C Tan, Bo Sheng, and Qun Li. 2008. How to monitor for missing RFID tags. In *Proc. of IEEE ICDCS.*
[54] Chiu C Tan, Bo Sheng, and Qun Li. 2010. Efficient techniques for monitoring missing RFID tags. *IEEE Transactions on Wireless Communications* 9, 6 (2010), 1882–1889.
[55] Jue Wang, Haitham Hassanieh, Dina Katabi, and Piotr Indyk. 2012. Efficient and reliable low-power backscatter networks. In *Proc. of ACM SIGCOM.* ACM, 61–72.
[56] Qingjun Xiao, Bin Xiao, and Shigang Chen. 2013. Differential estimation in dynamic RFID systems. In *Proc. of IEEE INFOCOM.*
[57] Lei Xie, Hao Han, Qun Li, Jie Wu, and Sanglu Lu. 2014. Efficiently collecting histograms over rfid tags. In *Proc. of IEEE INFOCOM.*
[58] Lei Xie, Qun Li, Xi Chen, Sanglu Lu, and Daoxu Chen. 2013. Continuous scanning with mobile reader in RFID systems: An experimental study. In *Proc. of ACM MobiHoc.* ACM, 11–20.
[59] Wei Xie, Lei Xie, Chen Zhang, Qiang Wang, Jian Xu, Quan Zhang, and Chaojing Tang. 2014. RFID seeking: Finding a lost tag rather than only detecting its missing. *Journal of Network and Computer Applications* 42 (2014), 135–142.
[60] Lei Yang, Yekui Chen, Xiang-Yang Li, Chaowei Xiao, Mo Li, and Yunhao Liu. 2014. Tagoram: real-time tracking of mobile RFID tags to high precision using COTS devices. In *Proc. of ACM MobiCom.*
[61] Lei Yang, Yao Li, Qiongzheng Lin, Xiang-Yang Li, and Yunhao Liu. 2016. Making sense of mechanical vibration period with sub-millisecond accuracy using backscatter signals. In *Proc. of ACM MobiCom.*
[62] Lei Yang, Qiongzheng Lin, Chunhui Duan, and Zhenlin An. 2017. Analog On-Tag Hashing: Towards Selective Reading as Hash Primitives in Gen2 RFID Systems. *Technical Report (arXiv:1707.08883)* (2017).
[63] Hirotaka Yoshida, Dai Watanabe, Katsuyuki Okeya, Jun Kitahara, Hongjun Wu, Özgül Küçük, and Bart Preneel. 2007. MAME: A compression function with reduced hardware requirements. In *International Workshop on Cryptographic Hardware and Embedded Systems.* Springer, 148–165.

[64] Jihong Yu, Lin Chen, and Kehao Wang. 2015. Finding Needles in a Haystack: Missing Tag Detection in Large RFID Systems. *arXiv preprint arXiv:1512.05228* (2015).

[65] Jihong Yu, Lin Chen, Rongrong Zhang, and Kehao Wang. 2016. On Missing Tag Detection in Multiple-group Multiple-region RFID Systems. *IEEE Transactions on Mobile Computing* (2016).

[66] Y Yu, Y Yang, Y Fan, and H Min. [n. d.]. Security Scheme for RFID Tag: Auto-ID Labs white paper WP-HARDWARE-022. http://www.autoidlabs.org/. ([n. d.]).

[67] Hong Zhang, Jeremy Gummeson, Benjamin Ransford, and Kevin Fu. 2011. Moo: A batteryless computational RFID and sensing platform. *University of Massachusetts Computer Science Technical Report UM-CS-2011-020* (2011).

[68] Rui Zhang, Yunzhong Liu, Yanchao Zhang, and Jinyuan Sun. 2011. Fast identification of the missing tags in a large RFID system. In *Proc. of IEEE SECON*.

[69] Yan Zhang, Laurence T Yang, and Jiming Chen. 2009. *RFID and sensor networks: architectures, protocols, security, and integrations*. CRC Press.

[70] Yuanqing Zheng and Mo Li. 2013. Fast tag searching protocol for large-scale RFID systems. *IEEE/ACM Transactions on Networking* 21, 3 (2013), 924–934.

[71] Yuanqing Zheng and Mo Li. 2013. ZOE: Fast cardinality estimation for large-scale RFID systems. In *Proc. of IEEE INFOCOM*.

[72] Yuanqing Zheng and Mo Li. 2014. Towards more efficient cardinality estimation for large-scale RFID systems. *IEEE/ACM Transactions on Networking* 22, 6 (2014), 1886–1896.

[73] Yuanqing Zheng and Mo Li. 2015. P-mti: Physical-layer missing tag identification via compressive sensing. *IEEE/ACM Transactions on Networking* 23, 4 (2015), 1356–1366.

Cardiac Scan: A Non-contact and Continuous Heart-based User Authentication System

Feng Lin
CSE, University at Buffalo, SUNY
flin28@buffalo.edu

Chen Song
CSE, University at Buffalo, SUNY
csong5@buffalo.edu

Yan Zhuang
CSE, University at Buffalo, SUNY
yanzhuan@buffalo.edu

Wenyao Xu*
CSE, University at Buffalo, SUNY
wenyaoxu@buffalo.edu

Changzhi Li
ECE, Texas Tech University
changzhi.li@ttu.edu

Kui Ren
CSE, University at Buffalo, SUNY
kuiren@buffalo.edu

ABSTRACT

Continuous authentication is of great importance to maintain the security level of a system throughout the login session. The goal of this work is to investigate a trustworthy, continuous, and non-contact user authentication approach based on a heart-related biometric that works in a daily-life environment. To this end, we present a novel, continuous authentication system, namely *Cardiac Scan*, based on geometric and non-volitional features of the cardiac motion. Cardiac motion is an automatic heart deformation caused by self-excitement of the cardiac muscle, which is unique to each user and is difficult (if not impossible) to counterfeit. *Cardiac Scan* features intrinsic liveness detection, unobtrusiveness, cost-effectiveness, and high usability. We prototype a remote, high-resolution cardiac motion sensing system based on the smart DC-coupled continuous-wave radar. Fiducial-based invariant identity descriptors of cardiac motion are extracted after the radar signal demodulation. We conduct a pilot study with 78 subjects to evaluate *Cardiac Scan* in *accuracy, authentication time, permanence, evaluation in complex conditions*, and *vulnerability*. Specifically, *Cardiac Scan* achieves 98.61% balanced accuracy (BAC) and 4.42% equal error rate (EER) in a real-world setup. We demonstrate that *Cardiac Scan* is a robust and usable continuous authentication system.

KEYWORDS

Non-contact Sensing; Continuous Authentication; Biometrics.

1 INTRODUCTION

Continuous authentication improves upon one-pass validation by continuously verifying over the lifetime of a session that the system is operated by the same user as at initial login. It can prevent access by adversaries when the legitimate user is away or overwhelmed. Governments and private companies [14, 15] increasingly demand more secure authentication, because of credential compromises due to weak cryptographic mechanisms (hacking, password theft, etc.) and user carelessness. In 2014 alone, more than one billion personal records were illegally accessed including, health, financial, email and home address data, and other personal information like social security numbers [85].

Existing solutions for continuous authentication have certain limitations. Specifically, traditional methods demand the user to intentionally engage with the authentication system, such as scan a fingerprint or enter in a password after a certain period. Regardless of the vulnerability, these methods hurt the usability in practice. Several studies also have proposed advanced continuous authentication mechanisms based on the user's behavioral biometrics, such as keystroke dynamics and gaze pattern. However, keystroke dynamics [63, 73] require the user to keep typing on the keyboard, while gaze patterns [23, 54] requires the user to face and continuously look at the screen. Other methods, such as continuous face recognition [9] on Windows 10 Hello [20], are also reported to be vulnerable to spoofing or replay attacks [1]. Recently, the physiological biometrics-based approaches are emerging for continuous authentication, such as pulse response [67], however, they all require the human body to make contact with certain devices.

As a live individual trait, heart-based biometric is unique (i.e., distinguishable across subjects), measurable (i.e., hard to hide), non-volitional (i.e., unknown to the user), secure (i.e., difficult to counterfeit), and present in all living individuals (i.e., intrinsic liveness). Different from electrocardiogram (ECG) [70], we explore the cardiac motion, which is a heart-based functional behavior determined by the intrinsic geometric structure of the heart. We aim to develop a cardiac-motion-based continuous authentication scheme in a non-contact way. Specifically, there are three challenges involved: 1) how to obtain the high-resolution cardiac motion information unobtrusively? 2) how to extract invariant geometric-based features for each heart with regard to the cardiac motion mechanism? 3) how to examine the usability and security of the continuous authentication scheme?

To this end, we propose Cardiac Scan, a secure and trustworthy continuous user authentication scheme via non-contact cardiac motion sensing. Fig. 1 shows the working paradigm of transformative Cardiac Scan. The authentic user's credential is stored in the database prior to authentication, a new incoming cardiac motion will be matched to the stored credential to make the decision as to whether the access request is from an authorized user or a malicious adversary. Specifically, our work focuses on: 1) developing a smart DC-couple continuous-wave (CW) Doppler radar sensor to

*W. Xu is the corresponding author. F. Lin and C. Song contribute equally to this paper.

MobiCom '17, October 16-20, 2017, Snowbird, UT, USA

ACM ISBN 978-1-4503-4916-1/17/10...$15.00
https://doi.org/.1145/3117811.3117839

continuously capture the high-resolution cardiac motion information from the distance; 2) identifying fiducial descriptors of cardiac motion based on the heart geometric characteristics; 3) conducting intensive evaluations (e.g., accuracy performance, usability and complex use conditions) to validate its performance and examine its security against replay attacks. Through a pilot study with 78 subjects, Cardiac Scan achieves 98.61% balanced accuracy (BAC) and 4.42% equal error rate (EER). All these studies demonstrate that Cardiac Scan is a robust and usable continuous authentication system. *Moreover, Cardiac Scan can be conveniently integrated with existing one-pass user verification techniques (e.g., personal identification number [PIN], fingerprint, iris scan, and face) to enhance the continuous authentication capability of existing systems.*

In sum, our contribution in this work is two-fold:

1) We explore new cardiac motion-based biometrics for continuous authentication. Cardiac Scan exploits the unique and non-volitional components of individual cardiac motion and identifies users in a non-contact, unobtrusive, and secure manner. This approach holds the potential to transform existing authentication systems into a more undeceivable, disclosure-resistant and user-friendly solution.

2) We evaluate Cardiac Scan through a set of multi-scene evaluations, including authentication with unaligned sensors, authentication with different emotional states, authentication in motion, and authentication under replay attack.

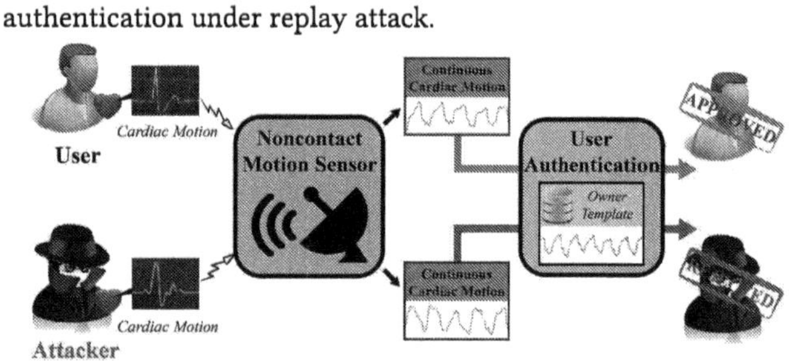

Figure 1: A novel continuous authentication method using cardiac motion captured by a non-contact radar.

2 DESIGN CONSIDERATIONS

2.1 Design Goals

A successful biometric system should possess some necessary properties. When designing our Cardiac Scan system, we have taken into account the following aspects.

Intrinsic Liveness: An essential requirement for a biometric system is intrinsic liveness detection, i.e., it should be able to distinguish if the authentication sample is a "live" user or a replay attack. Cardiac motion exists only in a "live" user and represents heart deformation when the heart is in contraction and relaxation states.

Unobtrusive Authentication: The authentication system should identify an authentic user in an unobtrusive way so that the user has no obligation to change his/her behavior to adapt to the system. Continuous authentication further requires the authentication process to be unobtrusive so that the user does not need to interrupt current work to authenticate. Cardiac Scan can perform unobtrusive authentication through a human-safe radio signal.

Highly Secure: The biometrics should be highly secure and unique, making it difficult to be forged and stolen. Cardiac Scan measures the live cardiac motion, which depends on the cardiac muscle structure of the user and therefore is impossible to completely mimic.

Cost-effective and Easy-to-Use: Some biometrics seem to have reliable and robust features, but the information acquisition requires expensive devices and specific conditions, such as an iris/retina authentication system. Cardiac Scan uses low-cost off-the-shelf components to build the radar sensor and is easy to use at a distance because of the propagation of the radio signal.

Resilient to Background Noise and Use Conditions: The biometric system should also be resilient to background noise and use conditions, no matter what the surrounding environmental conditions are. Camera-based systems, including face and iris recognition, usually have deteriorated performance with either too strong or too weak illuminations. Cardiac Scan uses a radio signal that is robust to the environmental change and can penetrate through obstacles to accurately sense the cardiac movement. Also, due to the essence that the sensing relies on the Doppler effect, static surrounding materials barely have an impact on the system performance.

2.2 Non-contact Cardiac Motion Sensing

2.2.1 *Rationale.* This work investigates cardiac motion as a new biometric to secure user authentication. Cardiac motion is a 3D automatic heart deformation caused by the self-excitement of the cardiac muscle [27]. As shown in Fig. 2(a), the human heart contains two upper cavities (atria) and two bottom chambers (ventricles) [33]. The successive contraction (systole) and relaxation (diastole) of both atria and ventricles circulate the oxygen-rich blood throughout the whole human body. The contraction and relaxation comprise the cardiac motion. In one cardiac cycle, ventricles relax and passively fill with the blood in approximately 70% of their total volume from atria through the open mitral valve. Then atria contract with heart muscles and pump blood. At the same time, ventricles continuously fill blood with the remaining 20%. (Ventricles, at least, free up 10% of the volume for the contraction.) After that, ventricles start to contract with all valves closed, and the blood volume remains unchanged. When the intraventricular pressures exceed the pressures within the aorta or pulmonary artery, blood is ejected and the heart volume reduces rapidly [8].

As shown in Fig. 2(b), one cardiac motion cycle consists of five distinct stages including: 1) ventricular filling (VF), 2) atrial systole (AS), 3) isovolumetric ventricular contraction (IC), 4) ventricular ejection (VE), and 5) isovolumetric ventricular relaxation (IR) [8]. These cycle stages are significantly different in volumes, surface shape, moving dynamics (speed, acceleration, etc.) and 3D deformation of the heart [12]. These stages vary from person to person due to the change in size, position, anatomy of the heart, chest configuration and various other factors [43]. No two persons have exactly the same heart, blood circulation system and other related tissues. Therefore, the cardiac motion is a unique identity marker for each individual [27]. Moreover, since cardiac motion is intrinsically connected to multiple biological functions, it is extremely difficult to counterfeit or to be hidden for a living individual.

2.2.2 *Feasibility.* Non-contact monitoring of human body motion, such as respiration and heartbeat rates using a Doppler radar motion sensor, has gone through a few decades of scientific study

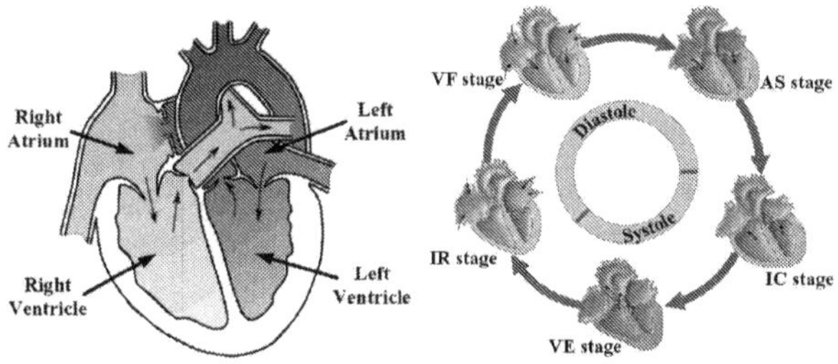

(a) Heart structure. (b) Cardiac motion stages.

Figure 2: Heart structure and dynamics.

[16, 21, 41, 48, 49]. Efforts have been devoted to the development of radar front-end hardware, signal processing algorithms, and system on-chip/on-board integration. Compared with other techniques such as non-contact laser vibrometer [72] and infrared imager [53] that can only detect motion at body surface, it has been shown that the Doppler radar sensor can directly measure the motion of internal organs [62] and heart [68, 92]. However, research results in those works are incomprehensive for a real authentication system, e.g., the impact of random body movement is not considered. Although random body movement and clutter noise still require significant efforts to resolve, some progress has been achieved [40, 82] and preliminary clinical studies have been reported [35]. However, existing cancellation approaches either compromise the quality of the baseband signals [40] or require sweeping the carrier frequency and adjusting the target position [82], which is not applicable to capture the high-fidelity cardiac motion in a real-world setup. Because of the sensitivity required for the detection along with difficulty in maintaining the original motion pattern during demodulation, most research using biomedical radar sensors have focused on detecting heart rate [49]. Recently, some of our research results have proved that DC-coupled interferometry radar and Doppler radar with digital-IF architecture can avoid frequency-selective signal distortion and thus make it possible to recover accurate motion patterns using continuous-wave (CW) Doppler radar sensors.

3 CARDIAC SCAN PROTOTYPE

3.1 System Overview

By measuring the signal phase shift caused by physiological motion, biomedical radar can reveal heartbeat and respiration information. Compared with conventional biomedical radars that can only measure the rate of the heartbeat signal, the main novelty of the radar sensor developed in this work is using distortion-free front-end architecture and demodulation to measure cardiac motion pattern. A smart DC-coupled radar architecture was employed in the radar front-end to eliminate undesired DC offset and preserve the desired cardiac motion characteristic information.

3.2 Architecture with Dynamic DC Tuning

To monitor cardiac motion pattern, a smart DC-coupled CW radar sensor was employed by taking advantage of real-time signal processing and mixed-signal design in modern devices. For cardiac motion sensing, the DC offset due to reflection from other parts of the body not related to cardiopulmonary activities may easily saturate the receiver and create frequency-dependent distortion, and is an important factor for the central intelligence unit to handle. Details of hardware innovation are discussed below.

3.2.1 Smart DC tuning. As shown in Fig. 3, the DC-coupled adaptive tuning architecture includes RF coarse-tuning and baseband fine-tuning. For RF tuning, the electronically controlled phase shifter and attenuator add a portion of the transmitted signal to the receiver signal to cancel most of the DC offset caused by clutter reflections. However, due to quadrature imbalance, the phase variation of the received signals, and the limited resolution of the phase shifter and the attenuator, the RF tuning cannot completely remove all the DC offsets. To further eliminate the remaining DC offsets, a baseband fine-tuning block was implemented to dynamically adjust the amplifier bias to the desired level that allows the maximum dynamic range. With the above DC tuning realized by a smart center in real time, the radar will precisely measure cardiac motion pattern. The integration of the DC-tuning technique into portable devices will be addressed with the help of logic control circuits coordinated by the I2C bus and CMOS-integrated calibration DACs.

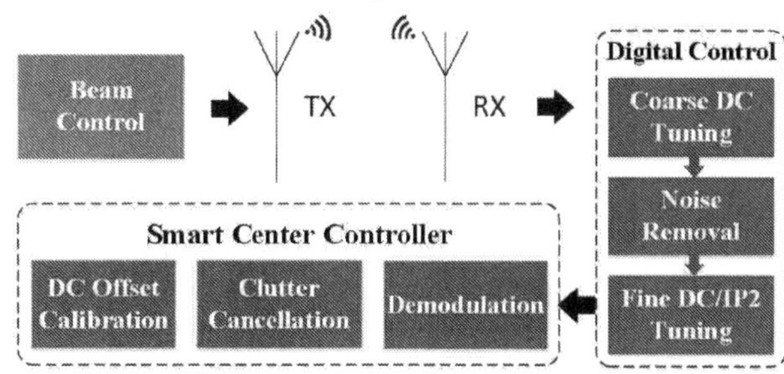

Figure 3: Doppler radar sensor with adaptive DC tuning.

3.2.2 Optimal carrier frequency. Besides manipulating the penetration depth, radar carrier frequency also determines the modulation sensitivity. Experiments were first carried out to compare the performance of carrier frequencies ranging from 2.4 GHz to 40 GHz. It should be noted that increasing the carrier frequency beyond 40 GHz may not help because as the wavelength approaches physiological motion amplitude, strong nonlinear phase modulation will generate harmonic interference [38] .

3.2.3 Electronic beam control. In this work, cardiac sensing will be realized from different angles to obtain sufficient information for biometrics applications. Also, multiple radars around a subject may "probe" cardiac signals simultaneously. To achieve this, it is essential that a radar can configure the radiation beam to precisely point at the location of interest. As shown in Fig. 3, digital beam control was implemented on the radar front-end. Conventional beamforming systems directly adjust the phase and amplitude of the signal of each element antenna. We demonstrated that it is much more convenient to simultaneously adjust the phase and amplitude in the complex domain than to adjust them separately. For a complex signal $x = \exp(-j2\pi ft)$ sent into each element antenna (where f is the signal frequency), a vector multiplier was used to realize phase and amplitude modulation by first splitting the signal into in- and out-of-phase components and then by multiplying each one using a variable gain amplifier. Finally, by adding the amplified in- and out-of-phase components together, complex modulation to the original signal can be achieved thus effectively realizing radar

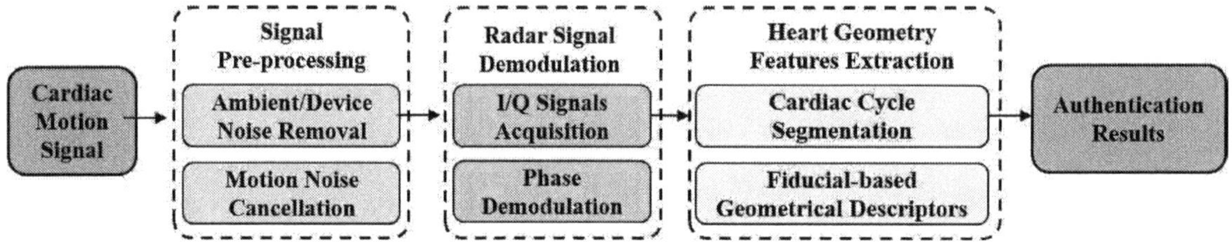

Figure 4: The flowchart of Cardiac Scan, a heart-biometric-based continuous user authentication system.

beam control. To align the radar beam with the user, a laser pointer can be used to indicate the beam direction.

4 RADIO SIGNAL PROCESSING SCHEMES

4.1 Scheme Overview

In this section, we elaborate on the radio signal processing schemes and correspondingly investigate user authentication methods to achieve secure and usable authentication results. As depicted in Fig. 4, our proposed approach is mainly comprised of three modules. First, the original sequential signal was preprocessed for noise reduction. Second, we performed de-noising aware radar signal demodulation. Third, we extracted fiducial-based descriptors using heart geometry features. Lastly, we obtained authentication results. Note that the existing heart-based biometrics, such as ECG, are recording the electrical activity of the heart, whose descriptors are extracted on the basis of the QRS complex [10]. As a new biometric modality, our non-contact cardiac motion is substantially different from the typical ECG signal in that it is a direct heart motion activity measured by an RF sensor. Therefore, it is crucial to explore new approaches in the non-contact cardiac motion authentication. To the best of our knowledge, no such work exists in the literature.

4.2 Pre-processing

Pre-processing is to reduce the noise level in the cardiac signal and simultaneously prevent the waveform from distortion. The noise includes low-band components (e.g., baseline wander), high-band components (e.g, power-line interference) and unpredictable-band components (e.g., arbitrary motion in the scene). Considering diverse and known frequency bands of the noise spectrum, we have addressed the noise level reduction in two areas: 1) one-pass noise reduction techniques (e.g., a Butterworth bandpass filter) and 2) adaptive noise canceling techniques [86] (e.g., a normalized least mean square adaptive filter [87]). These techniques have also been successfully applied in bio-artifact reduction [19, 87].

4.3 De-noising-aware Radar Demodulation

A novel signal demodulation is critical for distortion-free cardiac motion sensing because traditional Doppler radar is optimized for speed detection, which faces challenges when the movement pattern has very low frequency or stationary components [93].

4.3.1 Challenges in signal demodulation. The Doppler radar sensor transmits the continuous-wave signal $T(t)$:

$$T(t) = A_T \cos(\omega t + \phi(t)). \quad (1)$$

Then, the received signal is represented as $R(t)$:

$$R(t) = A_R \cos[\omega t - \frac{4\pi d_0}{\lambda} - \frac{4\pi x(t)}{\lambda} + \phi(t - \frac{2d_0}{c})], \quad (2)$$

where A is the amplitude, λ is the wavelength. c is the speed of light. ω represents the angular velocity. $\phi(t)$ is the time-varying phase. d_0 is the distance between the Doppler radar and the subject. $x(t)$ denotes the time-varying displacement caused by cardiac motion. Then two baseband signals, the in-phase signal $I(t)$ and quadrature signal $Q(t)$ can be derived from $R(t)$ [47]:

$$I(t) = A_I \cos[\frac{4\pi x(t)}{\lambda} + \frac{4\pi d_0}{\lambda} - \phi(t - \frac{2d_0}{c})] + DC_I, \quad (3)$$

$Q(t)$ is the quadrature signal:

$$Q(t) = A_Q \sin[\frac{4\pi x(t)}{\lambda} + \frac{4\pi d_0}{\lambda} - \phi(t - \frac{2d_0}{c}) + \phi_0)] + DC_Q, \quad (4)$$

where A_I and A_Q are the amplitude of the in-phase signal and the quadrature signal, respectively. DC_I and DC_Q are the DC offsets in I/Q channels, respectively. ϕ_0 is the phase offset between $I(t)$ and $Q(t)$. The baseband radar signals, $I(t)$ and $Q(t)$, are sampled by NI USB-6008 at 100 Hz.

For simplicity, we neglect the constant phase offset $4\pi d_0/\lambda + \phi(t - 2d_0/c)$ in Eq. (3) and Eq. (4). We assume that the gain imbalance is 1 (i.e., the ratio of A_I and A_Q is 1), and phase imbalance (ϕ_0) is 0. Thus, Eq. (3) and Eq. (4) can be simplified as:

$$\begin{cases} I(t) = A_0 cos(\frac{4\pi x(t)}{\lambda}) + DC_I \\ Q(t) = A_0 sin(\frac{4\pi x(t)}{\lambda}) + DC_Q \end{cases}. \quad (5)$$

According to trigonometric identities, we can transform Eq. (5) into Eq. (6)

$$(\frac{I(t) - DC_I}{A_0})^2 + (\frac{Q(t) - DC_Q}{A_0})^2 = 1, \quad (6)$$

which can be interpreted that the samples of I/Q channels stay on a circle whose center is (DC_I, DC_Q) with a radius of A_0. Then the least squares optimization [89] is employed to obtain the circle and obtain the three unknown parameters: DC_I, DC_Q, and A_0.

After identifying the DC component offsets, the displacement signal $x(t)$ can be derived using the arctangent demodulation method:

$$x(t) = arctan(\frac{Q(t) - DC_Q}{I(t) - DC_I}) \times \frac{4\pi}{\lambda}. \quad (7)$$

Traditionally, to detect the *weak* physiological signal $x(t)$, the small-angle approach was used [21, 40, 41, 48], which suffers from two inherent problems. First, when the distance between the target and the radar sensor changes, the detection sensitivity will also change, resulting in alternating *optimum* and *null* points [21]. Second, nonlinear harmonics and intermodulation products would appear when movement amplitudes are comparable to the carrier wavelength [37]. To solve this problems, an arctangent demodulation approach was proposed by calculating arctan$[\frac{Q(t)}{I(t)}]$, assuming DC_I and DC_Q can be properly calibrated [61]. Unfortunately, a direct arctangent function has a co-domain range of $(-\frac{\pi}{2}, \frac{\pi}{2})$. Once the demodulation exceeds this range, phase unwrapping is required, which is challenging in practical detection when noise is strong and the movement amplitude is large [29]. This is especially a problem when random body motion exists, which introduces a significant phase change that could easily go beyond multiples of 2π.

4.3.2 Phase demodulation solution. To overcome the limit of arctangent demodulation, we have investigated an extended differentiate and cross-multiply (DACM) algorithm to avoid the phase unwrapping problem. The algorithm computes a derivative to the arctangent-demodulated phase information first:

$$\omega(t) = \frac{\mathrm{d}}{\mathrm{d}t}[\arctan \frac{Q(t)}{I(t)}] = \frac{I(t)\dot{Q}(t) - \dot{I}(t)Q(t)}{I(t)^2 + Q(t)^2}, \tag{8}$$

where $\omega(t)$ is related to the velocity function of the cardiac motion, and $\dot{Q}(t)$ and $\dot{I}(t)$ denote the time derivative of $Q(t)$ and $I(t)$, respectively. To reconstruct the desired phase information, which represents cardiac motion, integration can be applied to the above result. Therefore, the signal phase can be recovered in the digital domain as:

$$\Phi_\theta[n] = \sum_{k=2}^{n} \frac{I[k]\Delta Q[k] - \Delta I[k]Q[k]}{I^2[k] + Q^2[k]}, \tag{9}$$

where $I[k]$ and $Q[k]$ are the discrete samples of the I/Q channel outputs. $\Delta I[k] = I[k] - I[k-1]$ and $\Delta Q[k] = Q[k] - Q[k-1]$. The operation block diagram is also included in the "smart center" of Fig. 3. By introducing an accumulation procedure, noises can be effectively suppressed. Once $\Phi_\theta[n]$ is obtained, the cardiac motion $x[n]$ can be linearly obtained based on a single scale calibration.

5 CONTINUOUS AUTHENTICATION

5.1 Heart Geometric Features

5.1.1 Segmentation. To extract the invariant descriptors from the cardiac motion signal of the subject, we segmented the periodical signal sequence into discrete frames. For fiducial descriptors, there exist literature [3, 44, 50, 64] where multiple cardiac cycles were used. We have investigated the performance with various numbers of cardiac motion cycles. Though each segment (see Fig. 5) includes all five heartbeat motion stages, the variations across individuals within one cardiac cycle may not be sufficient for differentiation. This segmentation with disparate cardiac motion cycles benefits the signal alignment because it associates the segment with the physiological cardiac motion in one or multiple cycles.

5.1.2 Fiducial descriptors. The fiducial-based method extracts intrinsic geometrical descriptors (e.g., temporal, amplitude, area or angle) from fiducial points in the cardiac motion signal. Specifically, fiducial points are the biomarkers with physical meanings in clinics during the cardiac motion cycle. Fiducial points contain the biological information that is unique and non-volatile for individuals, and are also independent of the sensor location or state of the individual such as anxiety, nervousness, or excitement [28]. On the other hand, non-fiducial-based methods focus on the non-physical attribute features, which fails to reflect the intrinsic geometric features of the heart. Also, they are computationally demanding [5] and apt to be interfered with by parameters setting [79], making non-fiducial-based methods inapplicable for continuous real-time authentication.

In the fiducial-based method, the cardiac displacement signal is well matched to the cardiac activity rationale in Section 2. The first stage, Ventricular Filling (VF), is when the semilunar valves (SV) close and the atrioventricular valves (AV) open. The whole heart is relaxed and the blood charges into atria as well as ventricles, resulting in the outward expansion of the heart. The second stage, Atrial Systole (AS), is when atria contract to pump their contained blood into ventricles. The heart will contract inward first due to the emptying of atria. It will expand outward again because the extra blood in atria is squeezed into ventricles (SV will close to prevent blood from flowing into arteries). The third stage, Isovolumetric Ventricular Contraction (IC), is when ventricles begin to contract and SV/AV close. Since there is no change in volume, no significant displacement occurs. Lastly, Ventricular Ejection (VE), is when SV opens and ventricles are contracting and forcing blood into arteries. As a result, the heart will contract inward. During the fifth stage, Isovolumetric Ventricular Relaxation (IR), ventricles finish the blood ejection, stop contracting and begin to relax. This cycle ends and begins anew.

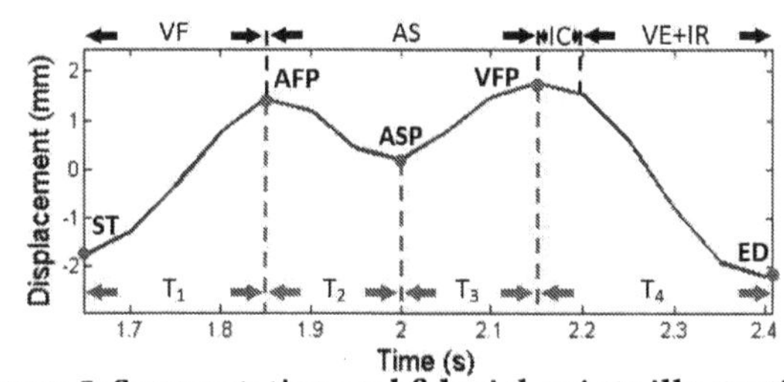

Figure 5: Segmentation and fiducial points illustration.

Fig. 5 is a complete segment which shows the changes of the cardiac displacement. Based on the cycle description above, the signal is typically further split into four sub-frames, each of which is labeled with the corresponding stage. We will refer to *ST* and *ED* as the starting point and ending point of the segment. The fiducial points that we plan to select are *AFP*, *ASP* and *VFP*, described as :
AFP: the first maximum point in the segment, which indicates the end of the VF stage and the onset of the AS period where the atrial muscles contract to squeeze the blood into the ventricles.
VFP: the second maximum point in the segment, which locates at the end of the AS stage. The blood flows into the ventricles and reaches the largest volume.
ASP: the local minimum point between *AFP* and *ASP*. It represents the end of atria contraction and the start of ventricles expansion.

Table 1 lists the descriptors based on the above fiducial points. Note that all the time descriptors T_i are normalized by the duration of one cardiac cycle, such that these descriptors are *independent* of heart rate.

Fiducial point extraction is of great importance to accurately locate the feature point. Due to the potential clutter noise, the radius of curvature is more robust than the more straight-forward local extreme point or signal derivatives. Specifically, we selected three points X, Y and Z with a fixed time interval along the time sequence. The minimum (maximum) radius of curvature in the corresponding region is found by maximizing (minimizing) the value of δ using the vector cross product between the two directed line segments, as shown in Fig. 6.

5.2 Continuous Authentication Protocol

One time validation of a user's identity, referred to as static authentication, has shown its vulnerability to attacks. Specifically, malicious adversaries may access the system that has been logged in by an authentic user when the authentic user is not nearby. Unlike static authentication, continuous authentication represents a new security mechanism which continuously monitors the user's trait and use it as a basis to re-authenticate periodically throughout the login session. Therefore, continuous authentication significantly enhances the security level of systems. Cardiac Scan enables unobtrusive and non-contact continuous authentication with the radio frequency (RF) interrogation, during which RF signals transmit and measure the human target continuously. By demodulating the received echo signal, the cardiac motion pattern of the user can be extracted. In what follows, we will discuss continuous authentication parameters and three typical scenarios.

Table 1: Fiducial-based descriptors.

List	Descriptor Definition
T_1	Normalized Time interval between ST and AFP.
T_2	Normalized Time interval between AFP and ASP.
T_3	Normalized Time interval between ASP and VFP.
T_4	Normalized Time interval between VFP and ED.
H_1	Displacement difference between ST and AFP.
H_2	Displacement difference between AFP and ASP.
H_3	Displacement difference between ASP and VFP.
H_4	Displacement difference between VFP and ED.

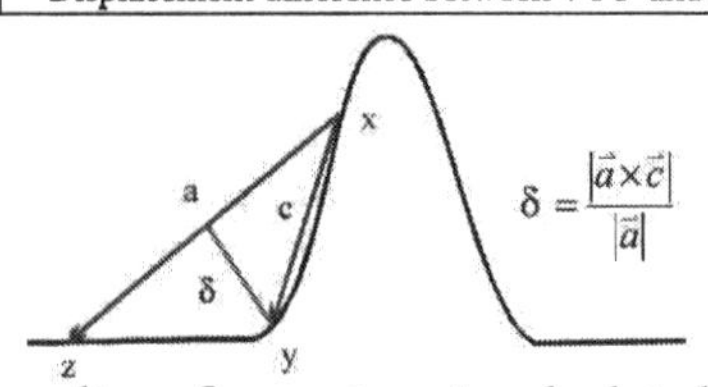

Figure 6: The radius of curvature is calculated as the vector cross product between the two directed line segments.

5.2.1 Continuous Authentication Parameters. Two parameters, refreshing interval T_r and negative tolerance threshold Th_{nt}, are important in continuous authentication, which are unique compared to static authentication.

Refreshing interval T_r: It is defined as the interval between two consecutive authentications. The appropriate choice of T_r has an impact on the performance and usability of continuous authentication. If T_r is too large, malicious adversaries may not be detected in time, thus may lead to severe security issues. On the other hand, if T_r is too small, some random activities (e.g., making phone calls, drinking water, turning around) or rhythmical body movement (e.g., listening to music) may compromise the system's recognition accuracy due to false alarms. Considering these random activities usually take about several seconds, we have set the refreshing interval as 5 sec. Note that the refreshing interval should be differentiated from the authentication time T_a. The latter is defined as the time duration for a single authentication process and will be discussed in subsection 7.2.

False negative tolerance threshold Th_{nt}: Usability is carefully considered in continuous authentication to make sure the authentic user will not frequently be interrupted by mistakenly logging out of the system. In other words, we aim to avoid the false negative event, which is the incorrect classification of an authentic user as an adversary due to motion artifacts. We noticed that false negative events are rare and appear sparsely in Cardiac Scan, which means there is a low probability that more than one "classified as adversary" event occurs consecutively when the authentic user is present. On the other hand, when the adversary is present, the "classified as adversary" event will occur consecutively. After observing such phenomena, we define the false negative tolerance threshold as the number of permitted consecutive "classified as adversary" events. Empirically, the value for this threshold can be 1 or 2. The larger value setting is more tolerant to false negative and the smaller value setting is more sensitive to risk. In the following scenarios, we adopt the threshold setting of 1 because the usability of continuous authentication will not be compromised given the low false negative rate of Cardiac Scan. In the mean time, this setting maintains a high sensitivity to unauthorized access.

5.2.2 Continuous Authentication Scenarios. We devise three scenarios in particular for Cardiac Scan enabled continuous authentication, including *Authentic user is present, Authentic user leaves*, and *Adversary is present.*

Authentic user is present: When an authentic user has logged into the system and is present within the range of the radar sensor, Cardiac Scan is able to detect whether cardiac motions are from the same person who was initially authorized. Thus, the permission of using the system for the user can be continuously granted without any interruption, unless the user logs off intentionally or leaves, as shown in Fig. 7 (a). By designing the false negative tolerance, Cardiac Scan allows one single "classified as adversary" event given that the classification results just before and after this event are both positive as "classified as authentic user". In case two or more than two consecutive "classified as adversary" events occur, though it has a low probability, Cardiac Scan will log out the initial user. Under such a circumstance, the user has to be re-authenticated by confirming his identity again using other complementary existing biometrics approaches, such as PIN, or fingerprint. Note that, for the scenario which has a specific requirement, the system tolerance level can be adjusted by changing the value of Th_{nt}.

Authentic user leaves: When the authentic user is away from the system and the radar sensor has detected the user's absence, as shown in Fig. 7 (b), Cardiac Scan will first check whether the user has logged off and the system has been locked up. If so, Cardiac Scan will classify the user's absence as a legitimate action and no further action needs to be taken. Otherwise, the system is at risk of unauthorized access, hence necessary actions such as locking the session, logging out the original user, or notifying the administrator [67], which depend on the system policy, have to be considered to address the security risks.

Adversary is present: In this scenario, an unauthorized adversary (the dark one in Fig. 7 (c)) is present and close to the system, and the system has been logged in initially by an authentic user. This can happen when the authentic user is under the coercion attack and being forced to be present or the adversary takes over the system before the system automatically locks up when the authentic user leaves. Therefore, immediate action is demanded to keep the adversary outside the system and prevent the leakage of sensitive information. In this case, Cardiac Scan will immediately log out the initial user and lock up the system once Th_{nt} is exceeded.

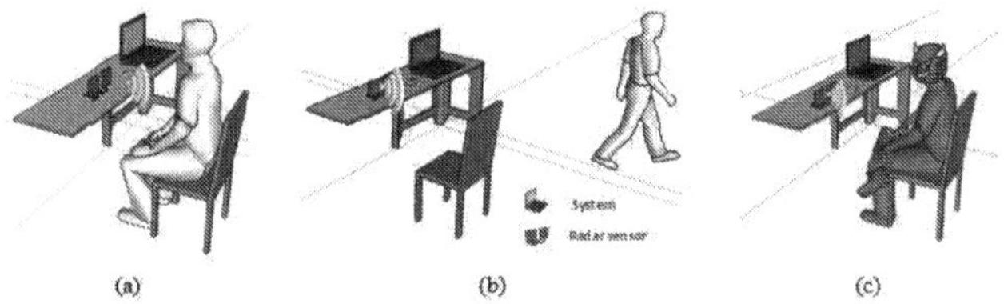

Figure 7: Three scenarios: (a) Authentic user is present, the system remains unlocked. (b) Authentic user leaves, the system locks up. (c) Adversary is present, the system locks up. Green screen: system is unlocked. Red screen: locked.

6 EXPERIMENTS AND VALIDATION

6.1 Experimental Setting

We conducted a pilot study to prove identifiability in cardiac motion. The Cardiac Scan system has been developed for the study, which works at the frequency of 2.4 GHz with the bandwidth of 5 kHz. The sampling frequency of 40 Hz. Though WiFi and Bluetooth also work at 2.4 GHz, our cardiac motion signal will not be interfered with because the motion information to be detected is only a few Hertz, which means both received signals and transmitted signals are only separated by a few Hertz, while other signals from potential interferences (e.g., WiFi and Bluetooth) have a much higher frequency separation and are conveniently rejected by the baseband signals. In other words, both transmitted signals and received signals are "coherent", whereas other signals are not coherent with transmitted signals. The Doppler radar has two antennas with the beam width of 45 degrees, i.e., one for transmitter and one for receiver. The power consumption of our radar is only 650 mW with 5 V voltage and 130 mA current. Note the transmission power level is within the human safety range because it is almost a thousand times less than the peak power of an ordinary global system for mobile communications (GSM) cellphone. The experimental setup is shown in Fig. 8, a subject sat in a chair in a relaxed condition. The customized Doppler radar sensor was placed in front of the subject with a distance of 1 m. A smartphone was placed close to a radar to record the subject identity and label the ground truth. The radar signal demodulation is done in a laptop equipped with Intel i7-3770 CPU @ 3.4 GHz. Motion compensation was carried out for the baseband complex signal obtained from subjects who breathed normally but randomly moved their body. A pulsed sensor (UFI 1010 pulse transducer) was attached to the subject's finger to provide a heartbeat reference. A chest belt (UFI 1132 piezo-electric respiration transducer) was used to provide a respiration reference.

6.2 Data Collection

As described above, our project evaluation relies on a strategically developed experiment that will involve a cohort of participants. We hold an existing active IRB protocol (# 502984/503753, Texas Tech University) that allows for recording body motion from adult human participants user identification. All the evaluations tightly follow the rule of IRB regulation. Seventy eight healthy subjects (46 males and 32 females) with their ages in the range of 16 - 54 participated in

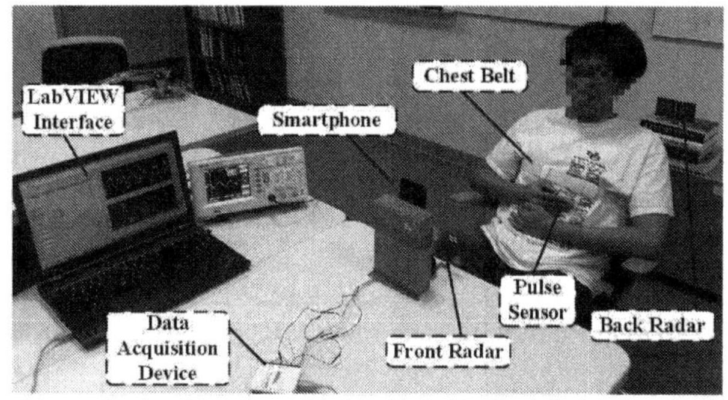

Figure 8: Experimental setup for cardiac motion sensing. A subject is sitting one meter away from both radar sensors, a chest belt and a pulsed sensor is attached to the subject.

the study. Their weights are between 42 - 83 kg. None of them have any heart disease. Each subject has 20 trials, and each trial lasts eight seconds including 8 to 10 cardiac cycles. In each trial, all subjects are required to sit in front of the radar, unless specified in the evaluation, to get the cardiac motion signals collected. Therefore, in total there are 20 sets of data containing 14,886 cardiac cycle samples in the evaluation. Currently, our work focuses on healthy people, the evaluation on subjects with pathologies or heart surgeries (e.g., heart diseases) is out of the scope of this work.

6.3 User Classification

To prove the identifiability in cardiac motion, dynamic time warping (DTW) [81] is used as the similarity matching metric. Support vector machine (SVM) with a radial basis function (RBF) kernel classifier and 10-fold cross validation were employed for the 20 sets of data in the evaluation, among which 18 are for the training and 2 for the testing. The choice of the classifier will be further discussed in Section 7.1.4. In authentication, initially, the owner's cardiac motion template is stored in the system. Then, unknown users attempt to access the system by keeping still in front of the radar. Since there are total 78 participants, and each participant acts as an owner once while remaining participants act as attackers.

6.4 Body Movement Interference Suppression

Compared with cardiac motion, body movement may result in a large perturbation to the output DC offset, and thus confuse the radar demodulation algorithm or even saturate the baseband circuit. In the experiment, the time-domain signal had fluctuations due to the random body motion as shown in Fig. ??(a). Strong near-DC spectral components were observed and the heartbeat was invisible in the spectrum (see Fig. ??(b)). Simply reducing the front-end gain, as adopted in some communication systems, does not work because the radar will lose the sensitivity to the weak cardiac motion signal.

Because biomedical radar can detect cardiac motion from four sides of a human body, multiple radars can be installed at different locations around the human body to cancel out random body motion based on the different patterns of body motion and cardiac motion [40]. In the view of the two radars, the heartbeat-and-respiration-caused body movements are in phase, while the random body movements are out of phase. In the current setting, two radars are detecting from the front and the back of the body. When the body is drifting toward one radar, it is moving away from the other; whereas heartbeat presents similar expansion/contraction patterns to the two radars [39]. Therefore, random body motion creates an opposite Doppler frequency shift to the signals of the radars, while cardiac motion leads to the same polarity. By properly combining the low-speed baseband signals from the radars, one type of motion can be canceled and the other type will be enhanced [40]. Note that although the random body movement can exist in the direction perpendicular to the radar direction, our body movement cancellation method still works effectively because only the movement in the radar direction is critical for the cardiac motion detection.

6.5 Signal Validation

We verified the validity of the collected data from our system. When the radar sensor detects the cardiac motion, the fingertip sensor simultaneously collects a signal as the ground truth signal. Both the radar sensor and fingertip pulse sensor were sampled at 40 Hz. We observed that the cardiac motion cycles are well aligned, each of which closely match the peaks in the fingertip signal. So we verified that our system could accurately detect the cardiac motion signal in a non-contact way.

7 EVALUATION RESULTS

As a potential breakthrough technology, it is necessary to evaluate the performance, flexibility, and vulnerabilities in practice of Cardiac Scan. Note that all the performance results are obtained after random body movement suppression except the one specified as "before random body movement suppression" in the evaluation of subjects in motion. We employed several statistics to describe the performance of Cardiac Scan.

7.1 Accuracy

7.1.1 Balanced Accuracy and F-measure. We provided the F-measure accuracy (F1 score) and balanced accuracy (BAC) for the accuracy measurement, both of which are non-sensitive to class distribution and can avoid misleading accuracy measurement when the true class distribution is unbalanced. F1 score is known as the harmonic mean of precision and recall, precision p is the number of true positive (TP) divided by the number of positive calls (TP+FP) while recall r (a.k.a. true positive rate) is the number of true positive (TP) divided by the number of condition positives (TP+FN) where FP is false positive and FN is false negative. F1 score reaches its best value at 1 and worst at 0. Simply, F1 score is defined as follows:

$$F_1(\%) = 2 \cdot \frac{precision \cdot recall}{precision + recall} = \frac{2TP}{2TP + FP + FN}. \quad (10)$$

And BAC is the equal combination of true positive rate (TPR) and true negative rate (TNR), which is defined as:

$$\begin{aligned} BAC(\%) &= 0.5 * TPR + 0.5 * TNR \\ &= \frac{0.5 * TP}{TP + FN} + \frac{0.5 * TN}{TN + FP}, \end{aligned} \quad (11)$$

where TN is true negative.

Table 2 shows the average F1 and BAC accuracies of the authentication with different configurations. BAC achieve 95.56%, 97.27% and 98.61% with the standard deviation (STD) of 0.92%, 0.65% and 0.38% for 1 cycle, 2 cycles and 4 cycles, respectively. F1 values are exactly mean values of BAC, which are 95.56%, 97.27% and 98.61% for 1 cycle, 2 cycles and 4 cycles. The results indicate that the increase of segment length improves accuracies. Furthermore, the performance benefits from the longer segment length and achieves the best accuracy of 98.61%. Note that the false positive events are not produced by the same pairs.

Table 2: Accuracy comparison for different cardiac cycles.

	1 cycle	2 cycles	4 cycles
F1 (%)	95.56	97.27	98.61
BAC (%)	95.56 ± 0.92	97.27±0.65	98.61±0.38

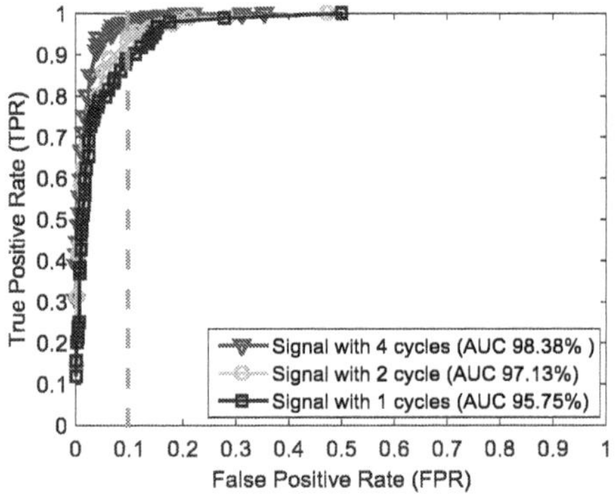

Figure 9: The average ROC curves with AUC of 78 subjects with different number of cardiac cycles.

7.1.2 Receiver Operating Characteristic. Receiver operating characteristic curve is created by plotting the true positive rate (TPR) against the false positive rate (FPR) at various threshold settings, which illustrates the performance of a binary classifier system as its discrimination threshold is varied. Fig. 9 depicts the average ROC curves of 78 subjects with different segment lengths. The signal with 4 cycles exhibits the best performance among three different segmentation configurations, which is consistent with the results of BAC and F1. Specifically, the corresponding area-under-curve (AUC) for each curve is also calculated as 98.38%, 97.13% and 95.75% for signals with 4 cycles, 2 cycles and 1 cycle, respectively.

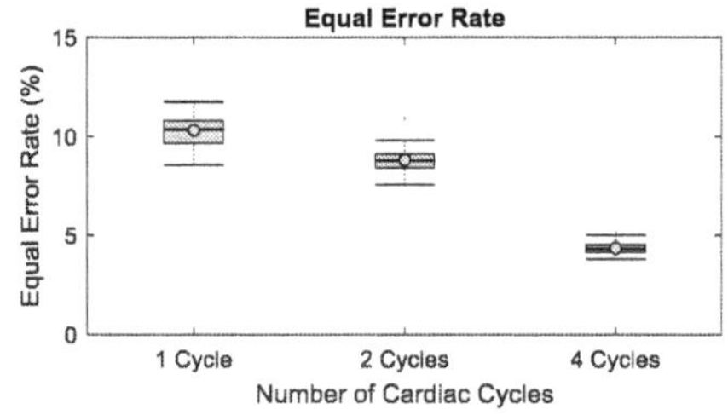

Figure 10: The EER with a different number of cardiac cycles. Four cardiac cycles configuration has the lowest EER.

7.1.3 Equal Error Rate. The equal error rate (EER) is a performance metric for authentication systems. It is a rate when the operating threshold for the accept and reject decision is adjusted such that the acceptance error (false positive rate, FPR) and rejection error (false negative rate, FNR) becomes equal. The lower the

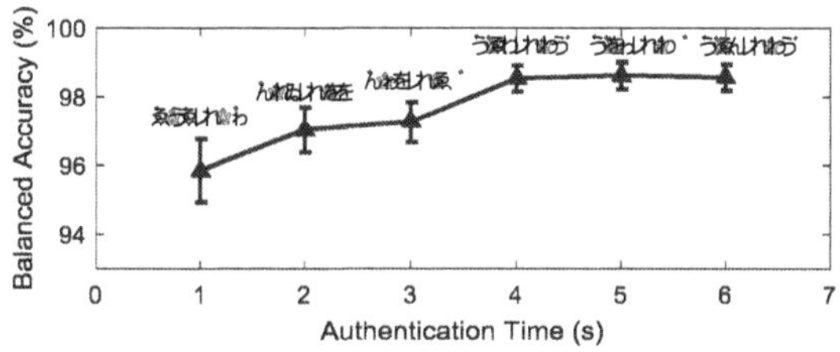

Figure 11: The balanced accuracy of 78 subjects with different authentication time. Authentication with 4 sec duration is the optimal choice.

equal error rate value, the higher the accuracy. Fig. 10 depicts the EER of 78 subjects with different segment lengths. The mean of EER is 10.37%, 8.79% and 4.42% for 1, 2, and 4 cycles, respectively.

Table 3: The different classifiers comparison.

	kNN	SVM (linear)	SVM (polynomial)	SVM (RBF)
BAC (%)	90.85	95.17	96.65	98.61
EER (%)	12.27	9.13	6.39	4.42

7.1.4 Classifier Impact. We compared two different classification techniques to select the best classifier for our application, including support vector machine (SVM) and k nearest neighbors (kNN). A linear, a polynomial, and a radial basis function (RBF) kernel are adopted for SVM. Parameters of each classifier are tuned to achieve the best performance. The number of nearest neighbors $k = 4$, and γ and C of RBF function are 0.001 and 10000, respectively. Four cycles of cardiac motion are employed in this evaluation. The BAC and EER results are shown in Table 3. KNN has the lowest BAC of 90.85% and highest EER of 12.27%. SVM with RBF kernel has the highest BAC of 98.61% and lowest EER of 4.42%. SVM with linear and polynomial kernel have BAC of 95.17% and 96.65%, EER of 9.13% and 6.39%. The SVM with RBF kernel showed the best performance, which will be adopted in this paper for the classification.

7.2 Authentication Time

Another important performance metric for the user authentication system is the authentication time. Generally, a practical user authentication mechanism should not only be accurate in identifying the legitimate owners and the invalid attackers, but also time-efficient in processing authentication. We specifically defined the authentication time in terms of the total time elapsed, T_a, to make a final prediction for each user access attempt:

$$T_a = T_{cardiac\_motion\_sensing} + T_{processing}, \tag{12}$$

where $T_{cardiac\_motion\_sensing}$ is the minimum time that Cardiac Scan needs to collect the cardiac motion signals with the smart radar device. This depends on the number of cardiac cycles required to identify users. $T_{processing}$ is the time needed to process cardiac motion signals, including demodulation, denoise, feature extraction and user authentication.

To evaluate the authentication time efficiency, we applied different time restrictions on authentication time. Twenty subjects repeated the experiment with six different duration setups from 1 s to 6 s with increments of 1 s. The balanced accuracy with different authentication time is illustrated in Fig. 11. The error bars are the STD of BAC among 78 subjects. We observed that the authentication duration less than 3 sec are not long enough for reliable authentication, with low BAC (95.85% for 1 s, 97.04% for 2 s, 97.26% for 3 s) and high STD (0.92% for 1 s, 0.66% for 2 s, 0.59% for 3 s). The performance is improved when the duration is increased to 4 s with BAC of 98.53% and STD of 0.38%. Generally speaking, the accuracy increases with the longer authentication time. However, when the duration is greater than 4 s, the performance improvement is not significant. To be specific, BAC of 98.62% and 98.57%, and STD of 0.39% and 0.38% are for 5s and 6s, respectively.

We also provided the growth rate for different authentication duration to find the optimal duration in Table 4. The growth rate is calculated by the accuracy in the current duration and the previous duration. The growth rates for each second are 1.23%, 0.23%, 1.29%, 0.09% and -0.05%. Note that the duration of 4 s has the largest growth rate, and seems to be a significant turning point.

Table 4: The BAC and growth rate.

Duration	1 sec	2 sec	3 sec	4 sec	5 sec	6 sec
BAC (%)	95.85	97.04	97.26	98.53	98.62	98.57
Growth (%)	-	1.23	0.23	1.29	0.09	-0.05

7.3 Evaluation in Complex Conditions

Another critical evaluation aspect is user experience. Typically, the user experience can be defined as: a person's perceptions and responses that result from the use and/or anticipated use of a product, system or service [36]. Therefore, the evaluation of user experience mainly focuses on the attitude/feeling of a person towards a product/system during its intended practical use. Traditionally, several methods have been widely adopted to maximally collect the feedback of a person on the product/system, such as interview, observation or survey. One unique aspect of the Cardiac Scan from many conventional authentication methods is that it is completely non-contact and passive to the user. Under normal conditions, the cardiac motion is not controllable or visible (even though it may be felt) to the user, which means that in most cases, the user will not be conscious of the interaction with the system in daily use. We also plan to evaluate usability with four variations: sensor distance, sensor alignment, emotional state, and subject in motion.

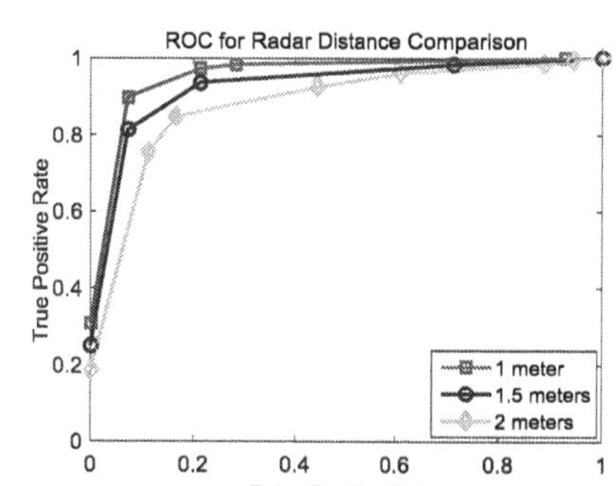

Figure 12: The ROC of different radar distances.

Distance Impact: We evaluated the impact of distance on the accuracy of cardiac motion authentication. The distance is defined as the length between the subject and the antenna of Doppler radar sensor. To make the Doppler radar sensor safe for human applications, we have restricted the transmission power, so that the effective distance for the Doppler radar is 2 meters. Based on our observation, the amplitude of the baseband radar I/Q signal is inversely proportional to the distance between the subject and Doppler radar sensor. When the subject is far away from the Doppler radar sensor, the amplitude diminishes because it is difficult for the sensor to capture the slight cardiac motion. Fig. 12 illustrates the ROC of different radar distance comparison. Not surprisingly, the closest distance of 1 m has the best recognition performance. The accuracy decreases with the increasing distance between radar and subject.

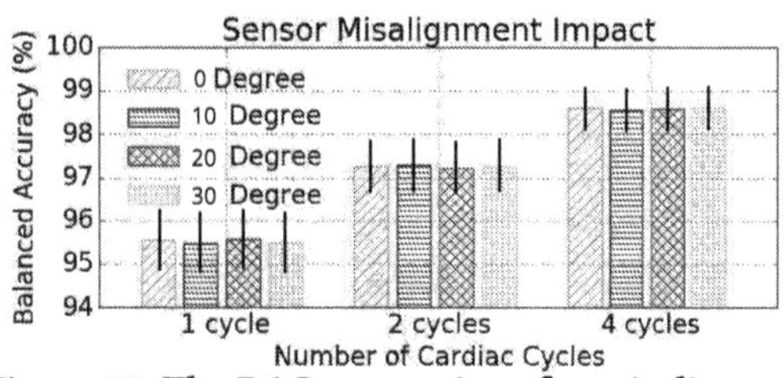

Figure 13: The BAC comparison for misalignment.

Location Sensitivity: As part of our understanding of how well non-contact cardiac motion can be utilized for identifying individuals, we investigated the relationship between various radar sensor orientation and identification performance. The hypothesis is that the extracted cardiac feature is insensitive to direction or orientation of the sensor beam. To test this hypothesis, we have collected a set of cardiac motion signals with a certain degree (10~30°) of orientation misalignment. Specifically, multiple radar sensors were used during the collection. One was placed in front of the subject, and others were placed out of alignment. The BAC comparison of each cycle length for different orientation misalignment is shown in Fig. 13. The BAC results for disparate misalignment with 0°, 10°, 20°, 30° are stable as observed from the figure which supports our argument that the extracted cardiac feature is insensitive to direction or orientation of the sensor beam.

Emotional State: A user's emotional state can change and is unknown to the identification system. The changes in emotional state will affect the cardiac motion (e.g, noise, heartbeat strength/cycle). The hypothesis is that the individualized features in cardiac motion are invariant to the user's emotional state. Research in heart-based biometrics [26, 28, 59] have demonstrated promising results for this hypothesis. To prove the usability and stability of Cardiac Scan under an unknown emotional state, we have conducted a set of experiments examining subjects in different emotional states. We have designated a special protocol to collect cardiac motion signals from low stress to high stress conditions. Specifically, selected subjects will perform two different task groups before collecting the data. The low stress tasks are meditation and listening to peaceful music. The high stress tasks are reading aloud, mathematical manipulation, driving in virtual reality, and intensive exercise. The BAC and EER comparison among all emotional tasks are shown in Fig. 14. The red bars with texture represent BAC and blue bars represent EER. The BAC and EER exhibit consistent performance across six different activities, including low stress and high stress conditions, which verifies that the emotional state will not impact the system performance.

Subject in Motion: Body movement may result in large perturbations to the output DC offset, and thus confuse the radar demodulation algorithm or even saturate the baseband circuit as described in detail in subsection 6.4. In this case, the recognition accuracy may be compromised, thus, the present user will experience logging out of the system. We investigated random movements in four activities ranging from tiny to large-range motions, including writing, drinking water, making phone calls, and one rhythmical movement when listening to music, to show the impact of body movement to the system performance. Twenty subjects participated in the experiment and each one performed all four body movement activities 10 times, a total of 200 trials for each activity are performed. Two radars are deployed in the front and at the back of the human body, and the measurement has to be performed simultaneously from both sides to cancel out the random frequency drift. With the current system setting, we evaluated how many times the authentic user is mis-classified as an unauthorized user before and after the body movement suppression approach described in subsection 6.4 is applied. The comparison results are shown in Fig. 15. Before body movement suppression, the mis-classified occurrence is 7 for making a phone call, 6 for drinking water, 5 for writing, and 18 for rhythmic movement. The rhythmic movement is more readily misclassified because it is periodic to some extent. The corresponding results after suppression are reduced to 2 for making a phone call, 1 for drinking water, 1 for writing, and 3 for rhythmic movement.

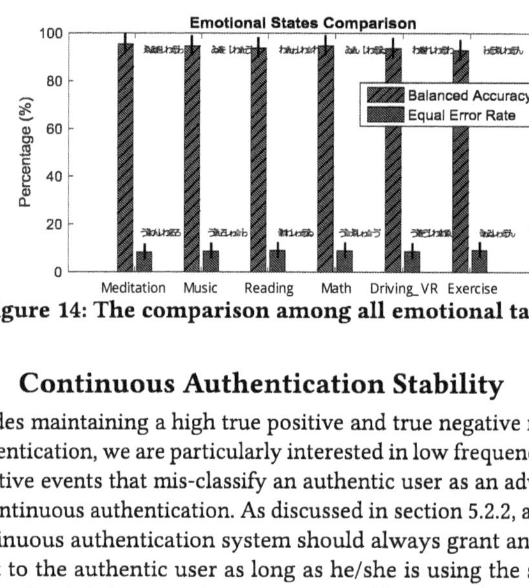

Figure 14: The comparison among all emotional tasks.

7.4 Continuous Authentication Stability

Besides maintaining a high true positive and true negative rate for authentication, we are particularly interested in low frequency false negative events that mis-classify an authentic user as an adversary in continuous authentication. As discussed in section 5.2.2, a usable continuous authentication system should always grant an access right to the authentic user as long as he/she is using the system. Otherwise, it is inconvenient even impossible to use the system if the user is being interrupted and asked to login again frequently. We conducted an evaluation on a continuous authentication session with four cardiac cycles setting. Under such configuration, the mean of false negative rate is as low as 0.4%. All 78 subjects participated in this evaluation and each session for each user lasts 40 minutes. Specifically, subject in turn acts as the user to login to the system and sit in front the system, browsing webpages or reading papers, until 40 minutes are reached or be logged out by the continuous authentication system. Not surprisingly, none of the subjects is forced to log out of the system due to a false negative, which is attributed to our continuous authentication protocol and parameters setting to maintain a satisfactory usability as described in Section 5.2.2.

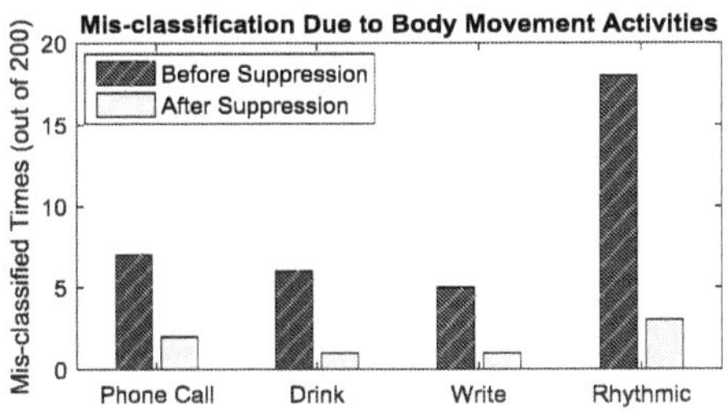

Figure 15: Body movement suppression before and after.

7.5 Longitudinal Study

It is important to prove the permanence of biometrics [30]. The permanence of heart-based biometrics was discussed in early experiments in many short-term studies [4, 25, 55]. In addition, each cardiac motion is independent, which means a prior result has no impact on the current result, so subsequent sessions study in short-term periods is not necessary. However, there are currently no longitudinal studies that establish this long-term persistence in any heart-based biometrics. Our generated dataset has included multiple sessions as part of a longitudinal approach to establish a baseline comparison of long-term persistence. 40 subjects (22 males and 18 females) participated in the longitudinal study lasting two months. Particularly, this study has two phases: enrollment phase and authentication phase. In the enrollment phase, training data were collected for each subject at the first day of this longitudinal study. Each subject finishes 20 trials in data collection events with the duration of each trial set as eight seconds. After that, the long-term authentication phase is carried out in the following two months. Each subject performed 20 authentication trials and each authentication duration is four seconds in this study. The BAC measurement is depicted in Fig. 16. In the 60-day duration, mean values of BAC measurement are between 98% and 99%, STDs are between 0.37 and 0.39. We concluded the BAC has no significant performance decreasing or ascending tendency, which demonstrates cardiac motion is robust against time change.

8 VULNERABILITY STUDY

Investigating the vulnerability of Cardiac Scan is crucial. Although cardiac motion is invisible and might possess better safety and security than other authentication approaches (e.g, PIN, fingerprint), it could become fallible under direct or spoofing attacks [51]. One immediate attack approach is the presentation of human characteristics to the acquisition device, including different living traits (i.e., zero-effort impostor attempts that try to take advantage of the false acceptance rate (FAR) of biometric systems) [31].

8.1 Replay Attack

One major risk of using biometrics is the danger that the biometric token can be intercepted and replayed by an unauthorized party. Compared to visual-based still biometrics (face/fingerprint/iris), the cardiac signal is more complex and dynamic to fake or replicate. However, there is still a chance to compromise cardiac signal under some extreme scenarios. Recently, Eberz *et al.* used a

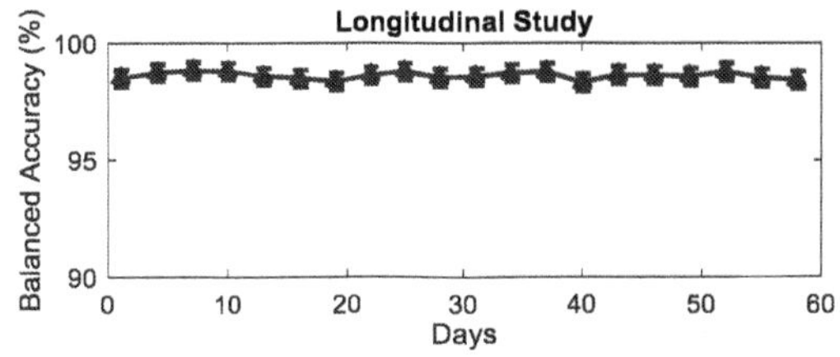

Figure 16: The 2-month longitudinal BAC performance.

hardware-based arbitrary waveform generator (AWG) and a sound card based AWG software to encode and emulate a set of pulse signals for attacking heart-based biometrics on the Nymi band [22]. Attackers might also hack into the database and obtain cardiac motion patterns or engineer the same cardiac motion sensing device to extract a user's cardiac signals. This work is to prove the possibility of a replay attack on Cardiac Scan if a legitimate user's cardiac signals are obtained by attackers. Our team has investigated the method of synthesizing cardiac motion and developed a programmable actuator to imitate the cardiac motion. As shown in Fig. 17, a linear actuator (ZABER TNA08A50) and a linear translational stage (i.e., ZABER TSB28-1) were placed 30 cm from the cardiac motion-sensing device. The actuator was programmed to perform a harmonic back-and-forth motion toward the radar for mimicking cardiac motion patterns.

8.2 Anti-Spoofing: Liveness Artifacts

Our team has also investigated a set of anti-spoofing approaches against a replay attack. The general idea of anti-spoofing is liveness detection [52, 80]. Liveness detection has been applied to existing biometrics systems by using affiliated living traits of humans by considering that it is relatively challenging to emulate multiple human traits at the same time during one spoofing attack section. For example, Pan *et al.* proposed the method to extract liveness information through eye blinks in face recognition [60]. Wei *et al.* detected counterfeit iris through texture analysis [84]. In this work, we have exploited the uniqueness of living traits in human cardiac motion to defend the above adversarial model. Specifically, we have tackled this challenge from two dimensions: hardware-based and software-based approaches. First, we integrated assisted sensors in Cardiac Scan, so that we can leverage additional information from these sensors to examine the legitimacy of subjects and capture the characteristics of multi-dimensional cardiac motions for liveness simultaneously. Specifically, as proposed in Section 6.4, the system employed multi-channel radars for noise reduction. Since the linear actuator only moves in rectilinear directions, the direction of arrival (DoA) [46] measurements with the linear actuator on these radars are different from DoA measured with real cardiac motion. Second, we have investigated software-based approaches. Because the sensor data from a live subject inevitably include vital sign (e.g., respiration) and other motion artifacts (e.g., body sway). These artifacts are not stored in the system database as credentials, so they are unable to be replicated and emulated for attack. Utilizing these vital sign detection and motion artifacts, liveness detection is conducted against the replay attack [26]. We programmed the actuator working with different moving amplitudes and frequencies to imitate cardiac motions of 12 subjects. *All replay attacks were rejected by our liveness detection method.*

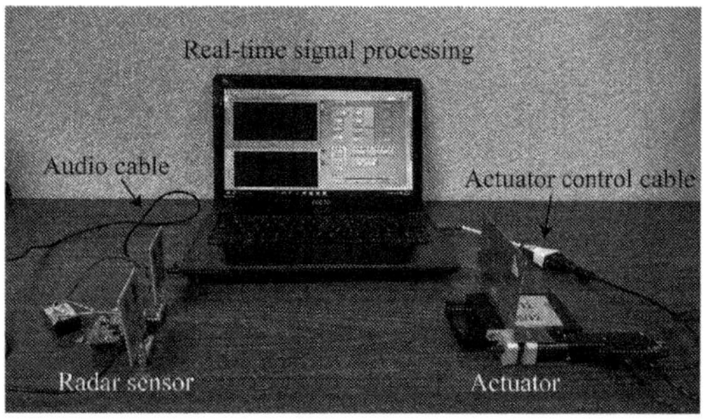

Figure 17: A linear actuator imitates cardiac motion.

9 RELATED WORK

Heart-based Identification: Heart-based identification has a long and rich research history in biometrics. There is sizable literature on user identification by analyzing heart-based signals. The most studied heart biosignals in identification application are the multi-lead electrocardiogram (ECG) body signals. Singh used both the analytical method of extracting fiducial features and the appearance method of extracting morphological features from the ECG trace for individual identification. The linear projection to a low-dimensional subspace is later applied to select the most significant features [74]. Zhao *et al.* extracted ECG feature for a human identification system by decomposing ECG signal into intrinsic mode functions using ensemble empirical mode decomposition [91]. Singh *et al.* delineated ECG waveform and extracted end fiducials from the heartbeat for individual authentication. The system is also evaluated in combination with face and fingerprint biometrics [75]. Silva *et al.* collected ECG from fingers for user authentication [18]. Safie *et al.* generated ECG features for authentication by using a pulse active ratio (PAR) technique [70]. To improve usability, other heart-related biosignals, such as Photoplethysmogram (PPG) [71, 78, 88], carotid pulse [17, 32], and finger pulse response [67], were investigated for human identification. Recently, there are some off-the-shelf user authentication products (e.g., the Nymi band [57]) using heart signatures from wrist pulse signals. However, these biosignals are not related to cardiac motion, in which case indirect or incomplete cardiac characterization will compromise the advantages of cardiac motion as a biometric. Moreover, these biosignals have to be obtained through skin contact, which is inconvenient and limits their applications for continuous authentication.

Continuous User Authentication: Most user authentication procedures, such as fingerprint or facial identification, only demand a one-pass session, which enables imposters to access the system until the user logs out. To address this security flaw, methods of continuous user authentication are explored. There are three categories. One category is to use soft biometric traits. Niinuma *et al.* used the color of user's clothing and facial skin for continuous monitoring [56]. This approach is readily counterfeited to confuse the system. The second category is to use behavioral biometrics. Keystroke dynamics, especially the rollover pattern, have been used for continuous authentication (e.g., Pinto *et al.* [63], Shepherd [73], Ali *et al.* [6]). Saevanee *et al.* utilize a text-based multimodal biometric including linguistic analysis, keystroke dynamics and behavioural profiling [69]. Behavioral screentouch features have also been explored for continuous authentication (e.g., Frank *et al.* [24] and Chan *et al.* [13]). Some studies leveraged eye movement biometrics (e.g., Eberz *et al.* [23], Mock *et al.* [54] and Song *et al.* [77]). Sitova *et al.* used hand gestures for continuous smartphone authentication [76], however, these methods require users to be obligated to continuously interact with systems for authentication. Khan *et al.* developed an implicit authentication (IA) framework for Android smartphone based on behavioral biometrics [34], yet there is no new biometrics proposed in this work. The third category is to use physiological biometrics. Rasmussen *et al.* utilized human body pulse-response as a continuous authentication mechanism[67]. However, this method demands the human body to make contact with electrodes, which is not user-friendly.

Radio-based Human Sensing: In recent years, there is a large wave of research work on radio-based (e.g., WiFi) human sensing applications. Pu *et al.* investigated gesture recognition by using radio signals [66]. Wang *et al.* studied radio signal analysis for people localization and motion tracking [83]. Li and Zhu explored the possibility of extracting fine-grained gait parameters from radio signals [45]. Adib *et al.* showed that a radio-based sensing system can collect physiological information, such as respiration, heartbeat, for health monitoring [2]. Obeid *et al.* obtained heart rate and heart rate variability (HRV) via microwave Doppler radar [58]. Boric *et al.* separated two subjects through multiple antenna systems [11]. Zhao *et al.* proposed EQ-Radio to infer a person's emotions from RF signals reflected off the body [90]. Scientists at Argonne National Laboratory have devised a millimeter-wave (mmW) system to remotely measure heartbeat, respiration and body motion [7]. However, little work exists for radio-based sensing identification. Identification is very challenging because it requires obtaining high-fidelity biometric information through non-contact radio sensing.

10 CONCLUSION AND FUTURE WORK

Existing biometric-based authentication systems are far from satisfactory. In this paper, we introduced a novel biometric system, Cardiac Scan, for non-contact continuous authentication. Specifically, Cardiac Scan can measure the unique cardiac motion of individuals with regard to the cardiac moving dynamics (e.g., speed, acceleration, etc.) and heart-blood circulation functionality in individuals. The system is unobtrusive, difficult to counterfeit, and easy to use. Our pilot study with 78 subjects showed that the system has a high balanced accuracy and low equal error rate. We evaluated the system in different complex conditions. As demonstrated in the longitudinal study, the cardiac motion biometric is robust

In the future work, we plan to evaluate Cardiac Scan with people of cardiovascular diseases, such as cardiac arrhythmia or using a cardiac pacemaker. Also, other methods, such as wavelet transformation [42] and area calculation upon phase portraits [65], will be further explored improve the system accuracy.

ACKNOWLEDGEMENT

We thank our shepherd Lakshminarayanan Subramanian and anonymous reviewers for their insightful comments on this paper. This work was in part supported by the National Science Foundation under grant No. 1718483/1718375, No. 1564104, and No. CNS-1421903.

REFERENCES

[1] 2016. Friends hacked into Windows using Windows Hello/camera-login. https://www.reddit.com/r/Surface/comments/4d9ykj/friends_hacked_into_windows_using_windows/. (April 2016). Accessed by August 2, 2017.

[2] Fadel Adib, Hongzi Mao, Zachary Kabelac, Dina Katabi, and Robert C Miller. 2015. Smart Homes that Monitor Breathing and Heart Rate. In *Proceedings of the 33rd Annual ACM Conference on Human Factors in Computing Systems*. ACM, Seoul, Republic of Korea, 837–846.

[3] Foteini Agrafioti and Dimitrios Hatzinakos. 2008. ECG based recognition using second order statistics. In *Communication Networks and Services Research Conference, 2008. CNSR 2008. 6th Annual*. IEEE, 82–87.

[4] Foteini Agrafioti and Dimitrios Hatzinakos. 2010. Signal validation for cardiac biometrics. In *Acoustics Speech and Signal Processing (ICASSP), 2010 IEEE International Conference on*. IEEE, 1734–1737.

[5] Foteini Agrafioti, Dimitrios Hatzinakos, and Jiexin Gao. 2011. *Heart biometrics: Theory, methods and applications*. INTECH Open Access Publisher.

[6] Zaire Ali, Jamie Payton, and Vincent Sritapan. 2016. At Your Fingertips: Considering Finger Distinctness in Continuous Touch-Based Authentication for Mobile Devices. In *Security and Privacy Workshops (SPW), 2016 IEEE*. IEEE, 272–275.

[7] Argonne National Laboratory. 2012. Millimeter-Wave Systems Track Biometrics; Detect Chemicals, Gases and Radiation. https://www.anl.gov/sites/anl.gov/files/millimeter_wave_detector.pdf. (November 2012). https://www.anl.gov/sites/anl.gov/files/millimeter_wave_detector.pdf Accessed by August. 2, 2017.

[8] Kim E Barrett, Susan M Barman, and Scott Boitano. 2010. *Ganong's review of medical physiology*. New Delhi: McGraw Hill, 2010.

[9] Joe Belfiore. 2015. Making Windows 10 More Personal and More Secure with Windows Hello. https://blogs.windows.com/windowsexperience/2015/03/17/making-windows-10-more-personal-and-more-secure-with-windows-hello/ #tK-BXz8oqEQBUXG4q.97. (March 2015). Accessed by March 10, 2017.

[10] Lena Biel, Ola Pettersson, Lennart Philipson, and Peter Wide. 2001. ECG analysis: a new approach in human identification. *Instrumentation and Measurement, IEEE Transactions on* 50, 3 (2001), 808–812.

[11] Olga Boric-Lubecke, Victor M Lubecke, Anders Host-Madsen, Dragan Samardzija, and Ken Cheung. 2005. Doppler radar sensing of multiple subjects in single and multiple antenna systems. In *TELSIKS 2005-2005 uth International Conference on Telecommunication in ModernSatellite, Cable and Broadcasting Services*, Vol. 1. IEEE, 7–11.

[12] Marcus Carlsson, Peter Cain, Catarina Holmqvist, Freddy Stahlberg, Stig Lundback, and Hakan Arheden. 2004. Total heart volume variation throughout the cardiac cycle in humans. *American Journal of Physiology-Heart and Circulatory Physiology* 287, 1 (2004), H243–H250.

[13] Alexander Chan, Tzipora Halevi, and Nasir Memon. 2014. Touchpad input for continuous biometric authentication. In *IFIP International Conference on Communications and Multimedia Security*. Springer, 86–91.

[14] Chaos Computer Club (CCC). 2013. Chaos Computer Club Breaks Apple TouchID. https://www.ccc.de/en/updates/2013/ccc-breaks-apple-touchid. (September 2013). Accessed by November 10, 2016.

[15] Chaos Computer Club (CCC). 2014. Fingerprint Biometrics Hacked Again. http://www.ccc.de/en/updates/2014/ursel. (Dec. 2014). Accessed by November 10, 2016.

[16] Kunmu Chen, Yong Huang, Jianping Zhang, and Adam Norman. 2000. Microwave life-detection systems for searching human subjects under earthquake rubble or behind barrier. *Biomedical Engineering, IEEE Transactions on* 47, 1 (2000), 105–114.

[17] Mei Chen, Joseph A O?Sullivan, Alan D Kaplan, Po-Hsiang Lai, Erik J Sirevaag, and John W Rohrbaugh. 2009. Biometrics with physical exercise using laser doppler vibrometry measurements of the carotid pulse. In *International Conference on Biometrics, Identity and Security (BIdS)*. 1–6.

[18] Hugo Plácido Da Silva, Ana Fred, Andre Lourenco, and Anil K Jain. 2013. Finger ECG signal for user authentication: Usability and performance. In *Biometrics: Theory, Applications and Systems (BTAS), 2013 IEEE Sixth International Conference on*. IEEE, 1–8.

[19] Carlo J De Luca, L Donald Gilmore, Mikhail Kuznetsov, and Serge H Roy. 2010. Filtering the surface EMG signal: Movement artifact and baseline noise contamination. *Journal of biomechanics* 43, 8 (2010), 1573–1579.

[20] J. Decker. 2016. Windows Hello biometrics in the enterprise. https://technet.microsoft.com/en-us/itpro/windows/keep-secure/windows-hello-in-enterprise. (September 2016). Accessed by November 10, 2016.

[21] Amy D Droitcour, Olga Boric-Lubecke, Victor M Lubecke, Jenshan Lin, and Gregory TA Kovacs. 2004. Range correlation and I/Q performance benefits in single-chip silicon Doppler radars for noncontact cardiopulmonary monitoring. *Microwave Theory and Techniques, IEEE Transactions on* 52, 3 (2004), 838–848.

[22] Simon Eberz, Nicola Paoletti, Marc Roeschlin, Marta Kwiatkowska, I Martinovic, and A Patané. 2017. Broken hearted: How to attack ECG biometrics. In *NDSS*.

[23] Simon Eberz, Kasper Bonne Rasmussen, Vincent Lenders, and Ivan Martinovic. 2015. Preventing Lunchtime Attacks: Fighting Insider Threats With Eye Movement Biometrics.. In *NDSS*.

[24] Mario Frank, Ralf Biedert, Eugene Ma, Ivan Martinovic, and Dawn Song. 2013. Touchalytics: On the applicability of touchscreen input as a behavioral biometric for continuous authentication. *IEEE transactions on information forensics and security* 8, 1 (2013), 136–148.

[25] Jiexin Gao, Foteini Agrafioti, Hoda Mohammadzade, and Dimitrios Hatzinakos. 2011. ECG for blind identity verification in distributed systems. In *Acoustics, Speech and Signal Processing (ICASSP), 2011 IEEE International Conference on*. IEEE, 1916–1919.

[26] Changzhan Gu and Changzhi Li. 2015. Assessment of Human Respiration Patterns via Noncontact Sensing Using Doppler Multi-Radar System. *Sensors* 15, 3 (2015), 6383–6398.

[27] John E Hall. 2010. *Guyton and Hall textbook of medical physiology*. Elsevier Health Sciences.

[28] Steven A Israel, John M Irvine, Andrew Cheng, Mark D Wiederhold, and Brenda K Wiederhold. 2005. ECG to identify individuals. *Pattern recognition* 38, 1 (2005), 133–142.

[29] Kazuyoshi Itoh. 1982. Analysis of the phase unwrapping algorithm. *Applied Optics* 21, 14 (1982), 2470–2470.

[30] Anil Jain, Brendan Klare, and Arun Ross. 2015. Guidelines for best practices in biometrics research. In *Biometrics (ICB), 2015 International Conference on*. IEEE, 541–545.

[31] Peter Johnson, Richard Lazarick, Emanuela Marasco, Elaine Newton, Arun Ross, and Stephanie Schuckers. 2012. Biometric liveness detection: Framework and metrics. In *International biometric performance conference*, Vol. 1.

[32] Alan D Kaplan, Joseph A O'Sullivan, Erik J Sirevaag, and John W Rohrbaugh. 2009. Laser Doppler vibrometry measurements of the carotid pulse: biometrics using hidden Markov models. In *SPIE Defense, Security, and Sensing*. International Society for Optics and Photonics, 730624–730624.

[33] Arnold M Katz. 2010. *Physiology of the Heart*. Lippincott Williams & Wilkins.

[34] Hassan Khan, Aaron Atwater, and Urs Hengartner. 2014. Itus: an implicit authentication framework for android. In *Proceedings of the 20th annual international conference on Mobile computing and networking*. ACM, 507–518.

[35] John E Kiriazi, Olga Boric-Lubecke, and Victor M Lubecke. 2012. Dual-frequency technique for assessment of cardiopulmonary effective RCS and displacement. *Sensors Journal, IEEE* 12, 3 (2012), 574–582.

[36] Effie Lai-Chong Law, Virpi Roto, Marc Hassenzahl, Arnold POS Vermeeren, and Joke Kort. 2009. Understanding, scoping and defining user experience: a survey approach. (2009), 719–728 pages.

[37] Changzhi Li and Jenshan Lin. 2007. Non-Contact Measurement of Periodic Movements by a 22-40GHz Radar Sensor Using Nonlinear Phase Modulation. In *Microwave Symposium, 2007. IEEE/MTT-S International*. IEEE, 579–582.

[38] Changzhi Li and Jenshan Lin. 2007. Optimal carrier frequency of non-contact vital sign detectors. In *Radio and Wireless Symposium, 2007 IEEE*. IEEE, 281–284.

[39] Changzhi Li and Jenshan Lin. 2008. Complex signal demodulation and random body movement cancellation techniques for non-contact vital sign detection. In *Microwave Symposium Digest, 2008 IEEE MTT-S International*. IEEE, 567–570.

[40] Changzhi Li and Jenshan Lin. 2008. Random body movement cancellation in Doppler radar vital sign detection. *IEEE Transactions on Microwave Theory and Techniques* 56, 12 (2008), 3143–3152.

[41] Changzhi Li and Jenshan Lin. 2013. *Microwave noncontact motion sensing and analysis*. John Wiley & Sons.

[42] Cuiwei Li, Chongxun Zheng, and Changfeng Tai. 1995. Detection of ECG characteristic points using wavelet transforms. *Biomedical Engineering, IEEE Transactions on* 42, 1 (1995), 21–28.

[43] Ming Li and Xin Li. 2014. Verification based ECG biometrics with cardiac irregular conditions using heartbeat level and segment level information fusion. In *Acoustics, Speech and Signal Processing (ICASSP), 2014 IEEE International Conference on*. IEEE, 3769–3773.

[44] Ming Li and Shrikanth Narayanan. 2010. Robust ECG biometrics by fusing temporal and cepstral information. In *Pattern Recognition (ICPR), 2010 20th International Conference on*. IEEE, 1326–1329.

[45] Yan Li and Ting Zhu. 2016. Gait-Based Wi-Fi Signatures for Privacy-Preserving. In *Proceedings of the 11th ACM on Asia Conference on Computer and Communications Security*. ACM, 571–582.

[46] Adrian Lin and Hao Ling. 2007. Doppler and direction-of-arrival (DDOA) radar for multiple-mover sensing. *IEEE transactions on aerospace and electronic systems* 43, 4 (2007), 1496–1509.

[47] Feng Lin, Yan Zhuang, Chen Song, Aosen Wang, Yiran Li, Changzhan Gu, Changzhi Li, and Wenyao Xu. 2017. SleepSense: A Noncontact and Cost-Effective Sleep Monitoring System. *IEEE transactions on biomedical circuits and systems* 11, 1 (2017), 189–202.

[48] James C Lin. 1992. Microwave sensing of physiological movement and volume change: A review. *Bioelectromagnetics* 13, 6 (1992), 557–565.

[49] Bram Lohman, Olga Boric-Lubecke, VM Lubecke, PW Ong, and MM Sondhi. 2002. A digital signal processor for Doppler radar sensing of vital signs. *Engineering in*

Medicine and Biology Magazine, IEEE 21, 5 (2002), 161–164.
[50] Justin Leo Cheang Loong, Khazaimatol S Subari, Rosli Besar, and Muhammad Kamil Abdullah. 2010. A new approach to ECG biometric systems: a comparative study between LPC and WPD systems. *World Academy of Science, Engineering and Technology* 68 (2010), 759–764.
[51] Sébastien Marcel, Mark S Nixon, and Stan Z Li. 2014. *Handbook of Biometric Anti-Spoofing.* Springer.
[52] Gian Luca Marcialis, Aaron Lewicke, Bozhao Tan, Pietro Coli, Dominic Grimberg, Alberto Congiu, Alessandra Tidu, Fabio Roli, and Stephanie Schuckers. 2009. First international fingerprint liveness detection competition??ivdet 2009. In *International Conference on Image Analysis and Processing.* Springer, 12–23.
[53] Manel Martinez and Rainer Stiefelhagen. 2012. Breath rate monitoring during sleep using Near-IR imagery and PCA. In *Pattern Recognition (ICPR), 2012 21st International Conference on.* IEEE, 3472–3475.
[54] Kenrick Mock, Bogdan Hoanca, Justin Weaver, and Mikal Milton. 2012. Real-time continuous iris recognition for authentication using an eye tracker. In *Proceedings of the 2012 ACM conference on Computer and communications security.* ACM, 1007–1009.
[55] Gary Garcia Molina, Fons Bruekers, Cristian Presura, Marijn Damstra, and Michiel van der Veen. 2007. Morphological synthesis of ECG signals for person authentication. In *15th European Signal Processing Conference (EUSIPCO 2007).* Poznan, Poland.
[56] Koichiro Niinuma, Unsang Park, and Anil K Jain. 2010. Soft biometric traits for continuous user authentication. *IEEE Transactions on information forensics and security* 5, 4 (2010), 771–780.
[57] Nymi. 2017. The Nymi band. https://nymi.com/product_overview. (August 2017). Accessed by August 2, 2017.
[58] Dany Obeid, Gheorghe Zaharia, Sawsan Sadek, and Ghaïs El Zein. 2012. Microwave doppler radar for heartbeat detection vs electrocardiogram. *Microwave and Optical Technology Letters* 54, 11 (2012), 2610–2617.
[59] Ikenna Odinaka, Po-Hsiang Lai, Alan D Kaplan, Joseph A O'Sullivan, Erik J Sirevaag, and John W Rohrbaugh. 2012. ECG biometric recognition: A comparative analysis. *Information Forensics and Security, IEEE Transactions on* 7, 6 (2012), 1812–1824.
[60] Gang Pan, Lin Sun, Zhaohui Wu, and Shihong Lao. 2007. Eyeblink-based anti-spoofing in face recognition from a generic webcamera. In *2007 IEEE 11th International Conference on Computer Vision.* IEEE, 1–8.
[61] Byung-Kwon Park, Olga Boric-Lubecke, and Victor M Lubecke. 2007. Arctangent demodulation with DC offset compensation in quadrature Doppler radar receiver systems. *Microwave Theory and Techniques, IEEE Transactions on* 55, 5 (2007), 1073–1079.
[62] Florian Pfanner, Joscha Maier, Thomas Allmendinger, Thomas Flohr, and Marc Kachelrieß. 2013. Monitoring internal organ motion with continuous wave radar in CT. *Medical physics* 40, 9 (2013), 091915.
[63] Paulo Pinto, Bernardo Patrão, and Henrique Santos. 2014. Free typed text using keystroke dynamics for continuous authentication. In *IFIP International Conference on Communications and Multimedia Security.* Springer, 33–45.
[64] Konstantinos N Plataniotis, Dimitrios Hatzinakos, and Jimmy KM Lee. 2006. ECG biometric recognition without fiducial detection. In *Biometric Consortium Conference, 2006 Biometrics Symposium: Special Session on Research at the.* IEEE, 1–6.
[65] Emil Plesnik, Olga Malgina, Jurij F Tasič, and Matej Zajc. 2011. Detection of the electrocardiogram fiducial points in the phase space using area calculation. *Electrotechnical. Review* 78, 5 (2011), 257–262.
[66] Qifan Pu, Sidhant Gupta, Shyamnath Gollakota, and Shwetak Patel. 2013. Whole-home gesture recognition using wireless signals. In *Proceedings of the 19th annual international conference on Mobile computing & networking.* ACM, 27–38.
[67] Kasper Bonne Rasmussen, Marc Roeschlin, Ivan Martinovic, and Gene Tsudik. 2014. Authentication Using Pulse- Response Biometrics. In *The Network and Distributed System Security Symposium (NDSS).* San Diego, CA.
[68] Dan Rissacher and Dan Galy. 2015. Cardiac radar for biometric identification using nearest neighbour of continuous wavelet transform peaks. In *Identity, Security and Behavior Analysis (ISBA), 2015 IEEE International Conference on.* IEEE, 1–6.
[69] Hataichanok Saevanee, Nathan Clarke, Steven Furnell, and Valerio Biscione. 2015. Continuous user authentication using multi-modal biometrics. *Computers & Security* 53 (2015), 234–246.
[70] Sairul I Safie, John J Soraghan, and Lykourgos Petropoulakis. 2011. Electrocardiogram (ECG) biometric authentication using pulse active ratio (PAR). *IEEE Transactions on Information Forensics and Security* 6, 4 (2011), 1315–1322.
[71] NSGR Salanke, Andrews Samraj, N Maheswari, and S Sadhasivam. 2013. Enhancement in the design of biometric identification system based on photoplethysmography data. In *Green High Performance Computing (ICGHPC), 2013 IEEE International Conference on.* IEEE, 1–6.
[72] Lorenzo Scalise, Ilaria Ercoli, Paolo Marchionni, and Enrico Primo Tomasini. 2011. Measurement of respiration rate in preterm infants by laser Doppler vibrometry. In *Medical Measurements and Applications Proceedings (MeMeA), 2011 IEEE International Workshop on.* IEEE, 657–661.
[73] SJ Shepherd. 1995. Continuous authentication by analysis of keyboard typing characteristics. In *Security and Detection, 1995., European Convention on.* IET, 111–114.
[74] Yogendra Narain Singh. 2014. Individual identification using linear projection of heartbeat features. *Applied Computational Intelligence and Soft Computing* 2014 (2014), 8.
[75] Yogendra Narain Singh and Sanjay Kumar Singh. 2011. Evaluation of electrocardiogram for biometric authentication. *Journal of Information Security* 3 (2011), 39.
[76] Zdeňka Sitová, Jaroslav Šeděnka, Qing Yang, Ge Peng, Gang Zhou, Paolo Gasti, and Kiran S Balagani. 2016. HMOG: New Behavioral Biometric Features for Continuous Authentication of Smartphone Users. *IEEE Transactions on Information Forensics and Security* 11, 5 (2016), 877–892.
[77] Chen Song, Aosen Wang, Kui Ren, and Wenyao Xu. 2016. "EyeVeri: A Secure and Usable Approach for Smartphone User Authentication". In *IEEE International Conference on Computer Communication (INFOCOM'16).* San Francisco, California, 1 - 9.
[78] Petros Spachos, Jiexin Gao, and Dimitrios Hatzinakos. 2011. Feasibility study of photoplethysmographic signals for biometric identification. In *Digital Signal Processing (DSP), 2011 17th International Conference on.* IEEE, 1–5.
[79] Fahim Sufi, Ibrahim Khalil, and Jiankun Hu. 2010. ECG-based authentication. In *Handbook of Information and Communication Security.* Springer, 309–331.
[80] Xiaoyang Tan, Yi Li, Jun Liu, and Lin Jiang. 2010. Face liveness detection from a single image with sparse low rank bilinear discriminative model. In *European Conference on Computer Vision.* Springer, 504–517.
[81] N Venkatesh and Srinivasan Jayaraman. 2010. Human electrocardiogram for biometrics using DTW and FLDA. In *Pattern Recognition (ICPR), 2010 20th International Conference on.* IEEE, 3838–3841.
[82] Fu-Kang Wang, Tzyy-Sheng Horng, Kang-Chun Peng, Je-Kuan Jau, Jian-Yu Li, and Cheng-Chung Chen. 2011. Single-antenna Doppler radars using self and mutual injection locking for vital sign detection with random body movement cancellation. *Microwave Theory and Techniques, IEEE Transactions on* 59, 12 (2011), 3577–3587.
[83] Guanhua Wang, Yongpan Zou, Zimu Zhou, Kaishun Wu, and Lionel M Ni. 2014. We can hear you with wi-fi!. In *Proceedings of the 20th annual international conference on Mobile computing and networking.* ACM, 593–604.
[84] Zhuoshi Wei, Xianchao Qiu, Zhenan Sun, and Tieniu Tan. 2008. Counterfeit iris detection based on texture analysis. In *Pattern Recognition, 2008. ICPR 2008. 19th International Conference on.* IEEE, 1–4.
[85] Zack Whittaker. 2016. These companies lost your data in 2015's biggest hacks, breaches. http://www.zdnet.com/pictures/biggest-hacks-security-data-breaches-2015/. (January 2016). Accessed by August, 2016.
[86] Bernard Widrow, John R Glover Jr, John M McCool, John Kaunitz, Charles S Williams, Robert H Hearn, James R Zeidler, Eugene Dong Jr, and Robert C Goodlin. 1975. Adaptive noise cancelling: Principles and applications. *Proc. IEEE* 63, 12 (1975), 1692–1716.
[87] Chenxi Yang. 2015. *MOTION NOISE CANCELLATION IN SEISMOCARDIOGRAM OF MOVING.* Ph.D. Dissertation. STEVENS INSTITUTE OF TECHNOLOGY.
[88] Jianchu Yao, Xiaodong Sun, and Yongbo Wan. 2007. A pilot study on using derivatives of photoplethysmographic signals as a biometric identifier. In *2007 29th Annual International Conference of the IEEE Engineering in Medicine and Biology Society.* IEEE, 4576–4579.
[89] Mari Zakrzewski, Harri Raittinen, and Jukka Vanhala. 2012. Comparison of center estimation algorithms for heart and respiration monitoring with microwave Doppler radar. *IEEE Sensors Journal* 12, 3 (2012), 627–634.
[90] Mingmin Zhao, Fadel Adib, and Dina Katabi. 2016. Emotion recognition using wireless signals. In *Proceedings of the 22nd Annual International Conference on Mobile Computing and Networking.* ACM, 95–108.
[91] Zhidong Zhao, Lei Yang, Diandian Chen, and Yi Luo. 2013. A human ECG identification system based on ensemble empirical mode decomposition. *Sensors* 13, 5 (2013), 6832–6864.
[92] Yan Zhuang, Chen Song, Feng Lin, Yiran Li, Changzhi Li, and Wenyao Xu. 2016. On the feasibility of Non-contact Cardiac Motion Sensing for emerging heart-based biometrics. In *2016 IEEE Radio and Wireless Symposium (RWS).* IEEE, 204–206.
[93] Yan Zhuang, Chen Song, Aosen Wang, Feng Lin, Yiran Li, Changzhan Gu, Changzhi Li, and Wenyao Xu. 2015. SleepSense: Non-invasive sleep event recognition using an electromagnetic probe. In *Wearable and Implantable Body Sensor Networks (BSN), 2015 IEEE 12th International Conference on.* IEEE, 1–6.

Automating Visual Privacy Protection Using a Smart LED

Shilin Zhu*
University of California-San Diego
shz338@eng.ucsd.edu

Chi Zhang*
University of Wisconsin-Madison
czhang296@wisc.edu

Xinyu Zhang
University of California-San Diego
xiz368@eng.ucsd.edu

ABSTRACT

The ubiquity of mobile camera devices has been triggering an outcry of privacy concerns, whereas privacy protection still relies on the cooperation of the photographer or camera hardware, which can hardly be guaranteed in practice. In this paper, we introduce LiShield, which automatically protects a physical scene against photographing, by illuminating it with smart LEDs flickering in specialized waveforms. We use a model-driven approach to optimize the waveform, so as to ensure protection against the (uncontrollable) cameras and potential image-processing based attacks. We have also designed mechanisms to unblock authorized cameras and enable graceful degradation under strong ambient light interference. Our prototype implementation and experiments show that LiShield can effectively destroy unauthorized capturing while maintaining robustness against potential attacks.

CCS CONCEPTS

• **Computer systems organization** → **Special purpose systems**; • **Security and privacy** → **Security services**; *Systems security*; • **Human-centered computing** → **Ubiquitous and mobile devices**; • **Computing methodologies** → **Computer vision**;

KEYWORDS

Privacy Protection, Visible Light, Camera, Computer Vision

1 INTRODUCTION

Cameras are now pervasive on consumer mobile devices, such as smartphones, tablets, drones, smart glasses, first-person recorders [53], *etc.* The ubiquity of these cameras, paired with pervasive wireless access, is creating a new wave of visual sensing applications, *e.g.*, autonomous photographer [54], quantified-self (life-logging) [24, 95], photo-sharing social networks, physical-analytics in retail stores [64], and augmented reality applications that navigate users across unknown environment [55, 96]. Zooming in the photo-sharing application alone, statistics report that 350 million photos/videos are uploaded to Facebook every day, majority of which are from mobile users [76]. Many of these applications automatically upload batches of images/videos online, with a simple one-time permission from the user. While these technologies bring significant convenience to individuals, they also trigger an outcry of privacy concerns.

Privacy is ultimately a subjective matter, and often varies with context. Yet many of the privacy-sensitive scenes occur in indoor environment, and are bound to specific locations. For example, recent user studies [17] showed that people's acceptability of being recorded by augmented reality glasses has a strong correlation with location. User studies of life-logging cameras [37] also indicate that 70.2% of the cases when the user disables capturing is associated with specific locations. In numerous real-world scenarios, cameras are forbidden, *e.g.*, concerts, theaters, museums, trade shows, hospitals [34], dressing rooms and exam rooms [57], manufacturing plants [6], *etc.* However, *visual privacy protection in such passive physical spaces still heavily relies on rudimentary approaches* like warning signs and human monitors, and there is no way to automatically enforce the requirements. In personal visual sensing applications like life-logging, even if a user were to disable the camera in private space (*e.g.*, bedroom and washroom), malware could perform remote reconnaissance and targeted visual theft by hijacking the victim's camera [81, 98].

In this paper, we propose LiShield, a system that deters photographing of sensitive indoor physical space, and automatically enforces location-bound visual privacy protection. LiShield protects the physical scenes against undesired recording without requiring user intervention, and without disrupting the human visual perception. Our key idea is to illuminate the environment using smart LEDs, which are intensity-modulated following specialized waveforms. We design the waveform in such a way that its modulation pattern is imperceptible by human eyes, but can interfere with the image sensors on mobile camera devices.

More specifically, our basic waveform follows an ON-OFF modulation, which causes the reflection intensity of the scene to "flicker" at high frequency. Digital cameras commonly adopt rolling-shutter image sensors, which sample the scene row by row during capturing. Consequently, LiShield will impose a striping effect on the captured image, as long as its flickering frequency exceeds the camera frame rate. To protect against a wide range of camera settings, we build a numerical model to explore the relation between the image quality degradation and the (uncontrollable) camera configurations (*e.g.*, exposure time). Accordingly, we derive common guidelines to maximize the effectiveness through waveform parameter configurations (*e.g.*, frequency, peak intensity, duty cycle). To further enhance the protection, we take two measures: *(i.)* scramble the color patterns, taking advantage of the array of multi-channel RGB chips commonly available on commercial smart LEDs; *(ii.)* randomize the waveform frequency to counteract exposure time manipulation that may circumvent the striping effect, while ensuring no low-frequency components are generated that affect human perception.

*Co-primary authors.

MobiCom '17, October 16-20, 2017, Snowbird, UT, USA

ACM ISBN 978-1-4503-4916-1/17/10...$15.00
https://doi.org/10.1145/3117811.3117820

In addition, LiShield can tailor the waveform for two special use cases: *(i.)* allowing an authorized camera, which shares secret configuration information with the LED, to recover the image or video frames it captures. *(ii.)* when strong ambient light interferes with the smart LED, LiShield cannot ensure full protection, but it can still emit structured light which embeds invisible "barcode" into the physical environment. The embedded information can convey a "no distribution" message, allowing online servers (*e.g.*, from Facebook and Instagram) to block and prevent the image from being distributed.

We have implemented LiShield based on a customized smart LED, which allows reconfiguration of intensity modulation waveforms on each color channel. Our experiments on real world scenes demonstrate that LiShield can corrupt the camera capturing to an illegible level, in terms of the image brightness, structure, and color. The impact is resilient against possible post-processing attacks, such as multi-frame combining and denoising. On the other hand, it enables authorized cameras to recover the image perfectly, as if no modulation is present. Even under strong sunlight/flashlight interferences, LiShield can still sneak barcode into the physical scenes which can be decoded with around 95% accuracy.

Preventing all privacy leaks, particularly those by determined attackers with professional global-shutter cameras, is likely impossible. Instead, LiShield aims for preventing ad-hoc capturing from benign camera-phone holders, by simply installing customized smart LEDs to fully cover the target environment. Our main contributions can be summarized as follows:

(i.) Proposing a new concept of automating privacy protection against cameras by modulating an LED's waveforms, and deriving general guidelines for optimizing the waveforms against possible camera settings and image recovery.

(ii.) Designing mechanisms to authorize desired capturing, and to embed protection information into the scene under strong ambient light interference.

(iii.) Verifying the system through a full-fledged testbed implementation and experiments in real environments.

2 ADVERSARY MODEL AND PROTECTION GOALS

LiShield's end goal is to prevent camera recording in protected indoor physical areas, without affecting normal human perception. The scene can be static or dynamic. In either case, we assume one or multiple LiShield-enabled smart LEDs can cover the whole area, while providing illumination similar to normal office lighting without human-perceptible flickering. Whereas conventional lighting and sunlight may co-exist with LiShield's smart LEDs (as to be verified in our experiments), covering the entire target scene with LiShield will ensure the strongest protection.

Now consider an unauthorized user (attacker) who wants to take pictures or videos within the protected space, with cameras and flashes embedded in smartphones, but no professional equipment such as global shutter cameras, filters or tripods. The attacker has full control over the camera parameters (*e.g.*, exposure time, capturing time, white-balancing), and can run any post processing on the captured images. Nonetheless, with LiShield's protection, the image frames are corrupted, so that major fraction of each frame is either blank or overexposed while colors are distorted (Sec. 3), which deters image viewing/sharing. In addition, LiShield should maintain its protection while allowing authorized users to capture the same scene simultaneously without distortion (Sec. 4). In case strong ambient interference may degrade LiShield's protection, LiShield embeds barcodes in images/videos captured by the attacker to convey privacy policies and ensures they are detectable even after common post-processing (Sec. 5).

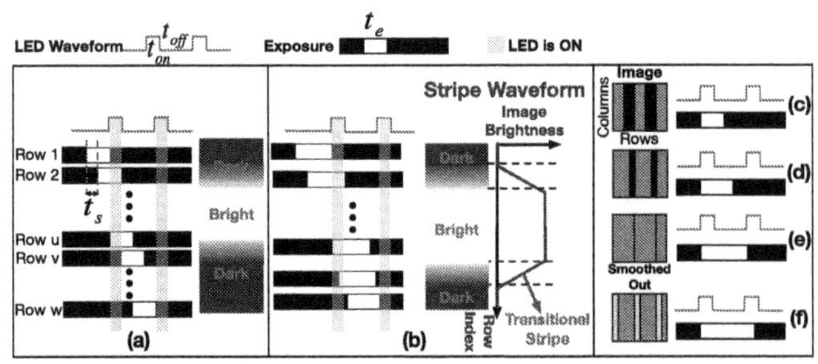

Figure 1: (a)-(b) Bright, dark and transitional stripes and their width changing with exposure time; (c)-(f) Stripe pattern of image changes under different exposure times.

3 PHYSICAL SCENE DISRUPTION

3.1 A Primer on Camera Image Disruption in LiShield

Cameras and human eyes perceive scenes in fundamentally different ways. Human eyes process continuous vision by accumulating light signals, while cameras slice and sample the scene at discrete intervals. Consequently, human eyes are not sensitive to high frequency flickers beyond around 80 Hz either in brightness or chromaticity [4, 41, 87, 104], while cameras can easily pick up flicker above a few kHz [44, 102]. Equally importantly, human eyes perceive brightness in a non-linear fashion [77], which gives them huge dynamic range, while cameras easily suffer from overexposure and underexposure when signals with disparate intensities mix in the same scene [66].

Unlike professional or industrial cameras which may have global shutters that mimic human eyes to some degree, nearly all consumer digital cameras, pinhole cameras, and smartphones use the rolling shutter sampling mechanism [49, 62], which is the main contributor to their high-frequency sensitivity. When capturing an image frame, a *rolling shutter camera exposes each row sequentially.*

LiShield harnesses the disparity between cameras and eyes to disrupt the camera imaging without affecting human vision. It modulates a smart LED to generate high-frequency flickering patterns. The reflection intensity (or brightness) of target scene also flickers following the same pattern as the LED's illumination, albeit at reduced intensity due to reflection loss. LiShield uses the On-Off Keying (OOK) as the basic modulation waveform (Fig. 1), which does not require complicated analog front-ends and is widely supported by smart LEDs [25, 26]. Due to rolling-shutter sampling, the rows of pixels that are fully exposed in the ON period will be bright, and rows in the OFF period become dark, thus causing striped patterns on the captured image (Fig. 1(a)(b)). Partially exposed rows experience moderate brightness. Meanwhile, human eyes can only perceive the smooth averaged intensity, as long as the OOK frequency goes beyond 80 Hz [4, 41, 87, 104].

In addition, commercial LED fixtures often comprise multiple LED bulbs/chips, and sometimes separate RGB channels to allow color adjustments [60]. LiShield can turn different numbers of LED bulb/chip on to generate different intensities, and control the RGB channels of the LEDs to vary the color. Therefore, LiShield's flickering waveform is staircase-shaped on-off patterns, running independently in 3 color channels. In what follows, we will show how such flickering corrupts the spatial patterns captured by a camera.

3.2 Maximizing Image Quality Degradation

LiShield aims to *minimize the image capturing quality by optimizing the LED waveform, characterized by modulation frequency, intensity, and duty cycle.* To explore the optimization space and to provide guidelines for designing the basic waveform, we derive a model to predict the image quality as a function of the LiShield's waveform and attacker's camera parameters. For simplicity, we start with monochrome LED (equivalent to one with a single color channel) that illuminates the space homogeneously. We denote P as the reference image taken under a non-flickering LED, and Q as the one taken under LiShield's LED with the same average brightness. We assume each image has m rows and n columns, and the light energy received by each pixel is denoted by $P(i,j)$ and $Q(i,j)$, respectively. Our model focuses on two widely adopted image quality metrics: *PSNR*, which quantifies the disruption on individual pixel intensity levels; and *SSIM* [91], which measures the structural distortion to the image (*i.e.*, deformation effects such as stretching, banding and twisting). In general, the minimum PSNR and SSIM corresponding to acceptable viewing quality are in the range of 25∼30 and 0.8∼0.9, respectively [3, 5, 12, 29].

3.2.1 Decomposing the Image. To compute the image quality, we need to model the intensity and width of each stripe caused by LiShield. As illustrated in Fig. 1, we use $t_{\text{on}}, t_{\text{off}}, I_p$ to denote the on/off duration and peak intensity of the flickering light source, and t_e, t_s are the exposure time (controllable by software) and sampling interval (fixed in hardware) of the rolling shutter camera. For convenience, denote the period of the light source as $t_l = t_{\text{on}} + t_{\text{off}}$, and duty cycle as $D_c = t_{\text{on}}/t_l$. For pixel j in row i which starts exposure at time t_i, its light accumulation would be:

$$Q(i,j) = \alpha_{i,j} \int_{t_i}^{t_i+t_e} \pi_l(\tau)d\tau \tag{1}$$

where $\alpha_{i,j}$ is the aggregated path-loss for pixel (i,j), including attenuation and reflection on the photographed object, and $\pi_l(\tau)$ represents the illumination waveform of the LED:

$$\pi_l(\tau) = \begin{cases} I_p, & 0 < \tau \bmod t_l \leqslant t_{\text{on}} \\ 0, & t_{\text{on}} < \tau \bmod t_l \leqslant t_l \end{cases} \tag{2}$$

When the camera's exposure time is equal or shorter than the LED's OFF period ($t_e \leqslant t_{\text{off}}$), the image will contain rows that are completely dark (Fig. 1(c)). On the other hand, when $t_e > t_l$, one row-exposure period of the camera will overlap multiple ON periods of the LED, accumulating higher intensity (Fig. 1(f)). The special case happens when $t_e = t_l$ where the integration of LED waveform and exposure has fixed value, which eventually smooths out dark stripes (Fig. 1(e)). Without loss of generality, assume the exposure starts right at the beginning of the ON period. Let $N = \lfloor t_e/t_l \rfloor$ which

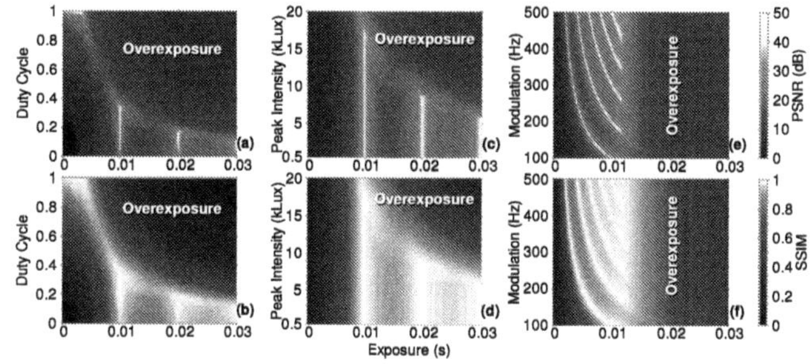

Figure 2: PSNR and SSIM with respect to exposure time, LED intensity, duty cycle, and modulation frequency.

is the number of whole flicker cycles covered by exposure time, and $t_{\text{rem}} = (t_e \bmod t_l)$ which is the remaining duration after multiple whole cycles, the light accumulation of the brightest rows Q_B is:

$$Q_B(i,j) = \begin{cases} \alpha_{i,j} I_p (N t_{\text{on}} + t_{\text{rem}}), & 0 < t_{\text{rem}} \leqslant t_{\text{on}} \\ \alpha_{i,j} I_p (N+1) t_{\text{on}}, & t_{\text{on}} < t_{\text{rem}} \leqslant t_l \end{cases} \tag{3}$$

Since the brightest rows appear when the exposure captures most ON periods possible (*e.g.*, row 2 to row u in Fig. 1 (a)), and rolling shutter effect converts temporal variation into pixels with sampling interval t_s, the width of Q_B is:

$$W_B = |t_{\text{rem}} - t_{\text{on}}|/t_s \tag{4}$$

Likewise, when the exposure captures least ON periods possible (*e.g.*, from row v to row w in Fig. 1 (a)), we get the darkest rows with light accumulation Q_D:

$$Q_D(i,j) = \begin{cases} \alpha_{i,j} I_p N t_{\text{on}}, & 0 < t_{\text{rem}} \leqslant t_{\text{off}} \\ \alpha_{i,j} I_p (N t_{\text{on}} + t_{\text{rem}} - t_{\text{off}}), & t_{\text{off}} < t_{\text{rem}} \leqslant t_l \end{cases} \tag{5}$$

and the width of Q_D is:

$$W_D = |t_{\text{rem}} - t_{\text{off}}|/t_s \tag{6}$$

We refer to a collection of consecutive brightest rows as "bright stripe" and consecutive dark rows as "dark stripe", as shown in Fig. 1(b). In addition, there exist intermediate rows containing linear intensity transition between dark and bright, referred to as "transitional stripe".

Meanwhile, if the LED were not flickering and provided the same average brightness, the pixel intensity would be:

$$P(i,j) = \alpha_{i,j} I_p \cdot D_c \cdot t_e \tag{7}$$

Since $D_c \cdot t_e$ remains constant within each frame, *the image captured under LiShield is equivalent to the original image multiplied by a piecewise function* (cf. Eqs. (3) and (5)).

Other common camera parameters (*i.e.*, ISO, white balance, and resolution) do not affect the structure of the stripe pattern, since they are unrelated to rolling shutters and they only affect the average pixel intensity. By default, we assume the attacker sets the ISO to its minimum (usually 100) to maximally suppress noise.

3.2.2 Optimizing the LED Waveform. Since the stripe pattern follows a piecewise function, a closed form expression of PSNR and SSIM becomes infeasible. We thus use numerical simulation to evaluate the impact of LiShield, based on the above model. We generate the piecewise function with $Q_B(i,j)$, W_B, $Q_D(i,j)$, W_D and multiply it on a reference image to obtain the disrupted image Q just like the process inside real cameras. We use the well-known Lena image as a reference, and stitch the original 512×512 version into a 3264×2448 (8-mega-pixel) image, assuming $t_s = 1/75000$ s, which matches the capability of a Nexus 5 camera. The quality metrics are calculated between the reference image P and LiShield-corrupted image Q, which are set to the same average intensity by scaling pixel values in Q. Note that if P and Q are both overexposed into the same white image, PSNR = ∞ and SSIM = 1 can no longer reflect image quality. Thus, we make P's pixel intensity range infinite, which allows quantifying quality loss caused by overexposure.

By default, we use OOK waveform with frequency $f = 100$ Hz, peak intensity $I_p = 10$ kLx and duty cycle $D_c = 0.5$. We vary one parameter while keeping others to the defaults. Note that the typical light intensity is ~ 700 Lx in office environments (considering energy efficiency), $\sim 5,000$ Lx for overcast sky and $\sim 100,000$ Lx for sunny days [33]. Our numerical results (Fig. 2 show a few general trends, which lead to the following design choices for LiShield.

(i) A single frequency cannot ensure robust protection. Fig. 2(e) and (f) show that for a given waveform frequency f, there exist several exposure time settings that lead to high-quality images. This is because when $t_e \approx Nt_l$, the stripes become smoothed out (Fig. 1(e)). Although the waveform parameters are unknown to the attacker, a determined attacker may launch a brute-force search for the t_e that satisfies this condition, thus circumventing the protection. To counteract such attackers, *LiShield includes a countermeasure called frequency randomization*, which we discuss in Sec. 3.3.1.

(ii) LiShield must prevent attackers from using long exposures. The image quality increases with exposure time t_e, until overexposure happens (Fig. 2(a) and (b)), because longer exposure leads to more waveform cycles being included as a constant base in the brightness of the stripes (larger N in Eqs. (3) and (5)), making the contrast of stripes Q_B/Q_D lower and weakening the quality degradation. Since overexposure limits the maximum exposure time, *LiShield should leverage overexposure to limit attacker's exposure time.*

(iii) LiShield should keep a high peak intensity to expand the overexposure zone. We observe that when t_e falls below a threshold ($\approx 1/100$ s in Fig. 2(c) and (d)), the image is always corrupted due to the dominance of dark stripes (Fig. 1 (c)). On the other hand, when t_e goes beyond a threshold, the image always suffers from overexposure. A larger I_p leads to a smaller overexposure threshold for t_e, which limits the attacker's ability to tune t_e to improve image quality. When $I_p \geq 10$ kLx (Fig. 2(c)), there almost exists only a single t_e setting ($t_e \approx 1/100$ s) that can avoid overexposure and dark stripes simultaneously. But even this setting fails under LiShield's frequency randomization mechanism (Sec. 3.3.1). With power efficiency and eye health in mind (Sec. 8), *LiShield sets I_p to 20 kLx by default.*

(iv) Duty cycle should be kept at a moderate level. Without overexposure, a lower D_c yields lower PSNR and SSIM (Fig. 2(a) and (b)), as it widens the dark stripes (Eq. (6)). On the other hand, a larger D_c means more light accumulation, resulting in overexposure across a wider range of t_e settings. Since higher I_p has the same impact given a fixed D_c, we design the LED waveform *to have maximum peak intensity with moderate duty cycle, empirically set to $D_c = 0.5$.*

The above conclusions hold for all scenes since the trend of quality does not vary with scenes (Sec. 7). Optimal parameters may vary slightly across different scenes (*e.g.* different reflectivity), and can be easily obtained by taking one photo of the scene and running the aforementioned simulation.

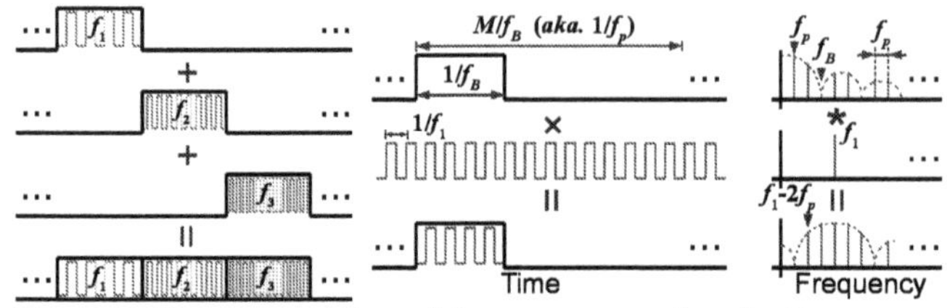

Figure 3: Decomposition of frequency randomization waveform and modulation generating side lobes.

3.2.3 Adding Color to the Model. Occasionally sensitive information is in the color channel of images, which requires LiShield to distort color for protection. LiShield extends to multi-channel setup by generating waveforms for each of the RGB channels independently, turning white stripes in the previous model into colored ones. To compensate the intensity loss compared with the white stripes, we need to make the new peak intensity $I'_p = 3I_p$, assuming R, G and B appear with equal probability.

3.3 Circumventing Potential Attacks

Based on the foregoing analysis, we identify the following potential holes that can be exploited by attackers to overcome the striping effect. *(i) Manual exposure attack.* If an attacker can configure the t_e to satisfy $t_e \approx Nt_l$, it can guarantee every row receives almost the same illumination, thus eliminating the stripes during a capture (Fig. 1(e)). In practice, t_l is unknown to the attacker, but it can try to capture images with different t_e, until seeing a version without obvious stripes[1]. *(ii) Multi-frame attack.* When the scene is static, an attacker may also combine multiple frames (taking a video and playback) to mitigate the stripes with statistical clues, *e.g.* by averaging or combining rows with maximum intensities from multiple frames. Note that the attacker must keep the camera highly stable, otherwise even pixel-level shift will cause severe deformation when combining multiple frames. *(iii) Post-processing attack.* Common post-processing techniques (*e.g.*, denoising and de-banding) might be used to repair the corrupted images.

In what follows, we introduce countermeasures to the first two attacks. In Sec. 7.4, we will verify that LiShield's distortion does not fit empirical noise or banding models, so the common post-processing schemes become ineffective.

3.3.1 Frequency Scrambling. To thwart the manual exposure attack, we design a *frequency scrambling*[2] mechanism, which packs multiple waveforms with randomly selected frequencies within each image frame duration. Since the camera exposure time t_e is always fixed within each frame, no single t_e can circumvent all the frequency components.

However, we cannot choose and switch the flickering frequencies in an arbitrary manner, for three reasons. *(i)* Multiple frequency values that share a common divisor can satisfy $t_e = Nt_l$ under the same t_e (recall N can be an arbitrary integer). We need to ensure the common divisor is small enough (*i.e.*, least common multiplier of t_l large enough), so that overexposure occurs even for the smallest N. *(ii)* Frequencies should be kept low to maximize image corruption,

[1]Digital camera's exposure time cannot be set arbitrarily due to hardware limitation. On Nexus 5, the granularity is around 13μs, *e.g.*, the actual exposure time is 1/1950 when the attacker needs 1/2000. Note that exposure time must be fixed within each frame.

[2]Scrambling and randomization are exchangeable in this paper.

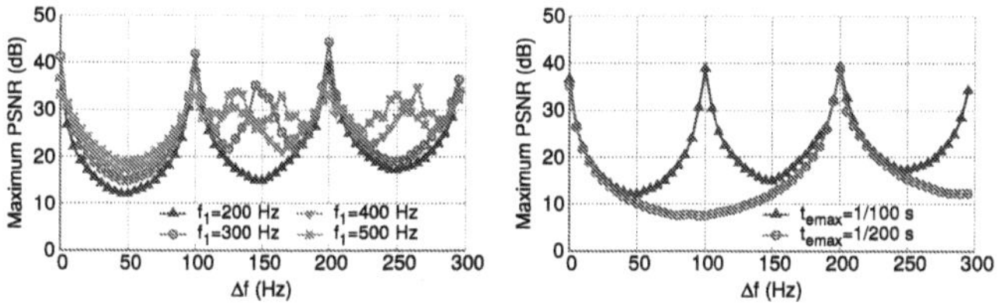

Figure 4: Worst-case PSNR with different frequency increment Δf under different (a) f_1 (b) t_{emax}.

as evident in Fig. 2(e) and (f), since camera's analog gain decreases at high frequencies [102]. *(iii)* Switching between different frequencies may create an additional level of modulation, which will spread the spectrum and generate unexpected low frequency components that become perceivable by eyes.

To explore the design space under these constraints, suppose we switch among M frequencies $f_1, f_2, \ldots, f_M$ (in ascending order) at a switching rate f_B. The whole pattern thus repeats itself at rate $f_p = f_B/M$. To pack at least M different frequencies in an image frame, we need $f_B > (M-1)f_r$, or preferably, $f_B > Mf_r$, where f_r is the frame rate, typically around 30 Hz (fps). Note that the switching rate cannot be higher than the lowest scrambling frequency, *i.e.* $f_B \leq f_1$, otherwise the waveforms of f_1 will be truncated. To maximize image corruption, we choose the smallest value for f_1 (*i.e.*, $f_1 = f_B$), and empirically set $f_n = f_B + (n-1)\Delta f, n \in 2, 3, \ldots, M$, where Δf is frequency increment, set to $\Delta f \neq f_B$ to lower the common divisor frequency.

The frequency scrambling can be considered as an M-FSK modulation: essentially, we multiply the waveform corresponding to each frequency with a rectangular wave of frequency f_p and duty cycle $1/M$, which convolves harmonics of the pattern repetition frequency f_p to the spectrum, creating side lobes around each scrambling frequency, spacing f_p apart, as shown in Fig. 3. These side lobes might appear at low-frequency region and become perceptible by human eyes.

To tackle this challenge, note that for waveforms with frequencies $f_2, f_3, \ldots$, their side lobes are dampened more at lower frequencies compared with f_1, so we only need to focus on f_1. The side lobes of f_1 are located at $f_1 + kf_p$, where k is an integer. For the side lobe with the lowest frequency, $k = \lfloor f_1/f_p \rfloor$. Since we selected $f_1 = f_B = Mf_p$, the lowest non-DC side lobe is at $f_p = f_B/M$. Therefore, to ensure no side lobe exists below the perceivable threshold $f_{th} \approx 80$ Hz, we need a small M and large f_B, and hence higher flickering frequency components f_n. Yet increasing the flickering frequencies may weaken LiShield's protection. Fortunately, since LiShield does not require large M (which leads to high f_M) to circumvent the manual exposure attack, the degradation should be tolerable.

To find the optimal Δf and showcase the effectiveness of the frequency scrambling, we choose the case $M = 2$ and $f_1 = f_B$ under 20 kLx peak intensity (to be consistent with our testbed setup in Sec. 6). We then repeat the numerical simulation (Sec. 3.2) to evaluate the attacker's maximum image quality. Fig. 4(a) shows that the quality has two peaks at $\Delta f = 0$ and 100 Hz, as well as a valley at $\Delta f = 50$ Hz. Note that the positions of these peaks/valleys are independent of f_1 and M, because quality always reaches the maximum at the longest t_e before overexposure happens (denoted as t_{emax} in Fig. 4(b)). Thus, we set $\Delta f = (1/2)/t_{emax} = 50$ Hz to maximize image disruption. The optimal Δf for other peak intensity settings can be obtained following a similar procedure. Fig. 4 also shows that, once set to the optimal Δf, *frequency randomization can significantly improve LiShield's robustness against manual exposure attacks.* Sec. 7 will show more evidence through testbed experiments.

3.3.2 Illumination Intensity Randomization. If attackers repetitively capture a static scene for a sufficiently long duration, they may eventually find at least one clean version for each row across all frames, thus *recovering* the image. LiShield does not guarantee complete protection against such brute-force attacks. However, it can increase the number of frames needed for image recovery, so that the attack becomes infeasible unless the camera can stay perfectly still over a long period of time, during which the attackers may have already been discovered by the owners of the physical space. LiShield achieves the goal by employing illumination intensity randomization, where it randomly switches the magnitude of each ON period across multiple predefined levels, which extends the attacker's search space. We note that the intensity randomization adds another level of modulation, but similar analysis in Sec. 3.3.1 still applies and can ensure imperceptible operation.

To understand the effectiveness of this scheme, we build a statistical model to estimate the number of frames needed to perfectly recover the image, as if LiShield did not function at all. Suppose the LED waveform has K intensity levels, and the camera has m rows. For simplicity, we assume the intensity levels of each row become uncorrelated after the randomization. Then the probability that one row gets any illumination is $p = t_{\text{on}}/(t_{\text{on}} + t_{\text{off}}) = D_c$. Observe that on average same intensities would reappear approximately every K frames, the possibility of combining L frames to fully recover an image of the static scene is thus:

$$P_{\text{rec}} = \begin{cases} \left[1 - (1 - D_c)^{L/K}\right]^m & \text{(monochrome)} \\ \left[1 - (1 - D_c)^{L/K}\right]^{3m} & \text{(RGB)} \end{cases} \tag{8}$$

Therefore, achieving a given level of P_{rec} becomes increasingly difficult as D_c and K increases, and for higher camera resolution (larger m). For example, to have $P_{\text{rec}} = 90\%$ for $D_c = 0.5$ and $m = 2448$ for 8-mega-pixel cameras, the attacker needs $L = 300$ frames under $K = 10$, and ~ 3000 frames under $K = 100$. For lower duty cycles, recovery becomes even more challenging (*e.g.*, ~ 7000 frames are needed for $D_c = 0.2$, $K = 100$). As we will show later (Sec. 7), in practice, the attackers cannot keep cameras completely still and all frames aligned at pixel level, even with a tripod and across a short duration. So Eq. (8) gives the best performance for such attacks. Note that *if the target scene is mobile, then the multi-frame attack becomes impossible, as long as the scene has certain variation across K frames.* The effectiveness of intensity randomization will be further justified in our testbed experiments (Sec. 7).

4 SCENE RECOVERY WITH AUTHORIZED CAMERAS

To allow authorized users to capture the scene while maintaining protection against unauthorized attackers, we need to impose additional constraints on the LED waveform. LiShield's solution leverages a secure side channel (*e.g.* visible light communication [16] or Wi-Fi) between authorized users and the smart LED, which

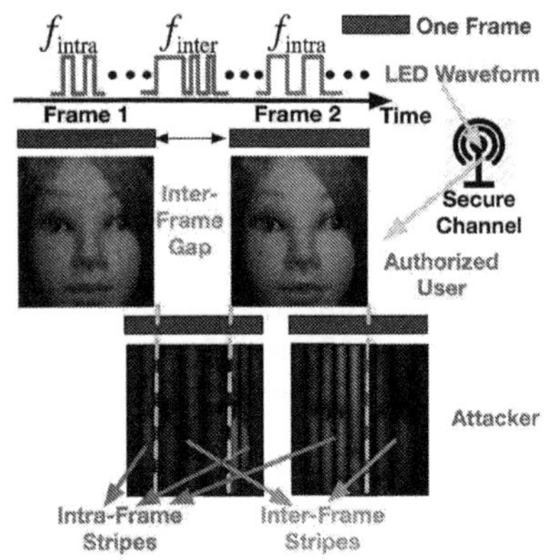

Figure 5: Enabling authorized users to capture dynamic scenes while corrupting unauthorized users.

conveys secret information such as frame timing and waveform parameters[3].

A naive solution is to stop flickering when authorized users are recording. However, since attackers may be co-located with the authorized users, this enables them to capture one or more frames that have part of the clean scene, which compromises privacy and security. To counteract such cases, we design special waveforms for the LED to minimize the flicker-free duration.

4.1 Authorized Video Recording

To authorize a camera to capture a dynamic scene, each individual frame within the video must be recoverable. To achieve this, the authorized camera needs to convey its exposure time setting t_e^u to the smart LED via the secure side channel, and synchronize its clock (for controlling capturing time) with the smart LED's clock (for controlling the waveform), so the smart LED can send recoverable waveforms precisely during the capture of the authorized camera. State-of-the-art time synchronization mechanisms through visible light [48] or wireless side-channels [23, 69, 74] can already achieve μs of accuracy, sufficient to synchronize the LiShield smart LED with camera at a resolution that is finer than the rolling shutter period (typically tens of μs).

Recall that the camera can evade the striping effects if $t_e = Nt_l$ (phase does not matter, see Sec. 3.3). So to authorize the user with exposure t_e^u, LiShield simply needs to set its flickering frequency $f_a = 1/t_l = N/t_e^u$ ($N = 1, 2, \ldots$) and maintain its peak intensity within each frame. In addition, the t_e^u and corresponding flickering frequency f_a can be varied on a frame by frame basis, making it impossible for an attacker to resolve the correct exposure time by trial-and-error (Sec. 3.3).

Meanwhile, when the authorized camera is not recording at its maximum possible rate (*e.g.*, a 30 fps camera recording at 25 fps), there will be an interval (*i.e.*, inter-frame gap) where the camera pauses capturing. LiShield packs random flickering frequencies other than f_a into the inter-frame gap, so as to achieve the same scrambling effect as described in Sec. 3.3.1, without compromising the authorized capturing. Fig. 5 depicts one example, where f_{intra} and f_{inter} denote intra-frame and inter-frame frequencies, respectively.

[3] Such information can be protected by existing encryption algorithms and systems, which are already mature and thus beyond the scope of this paper.

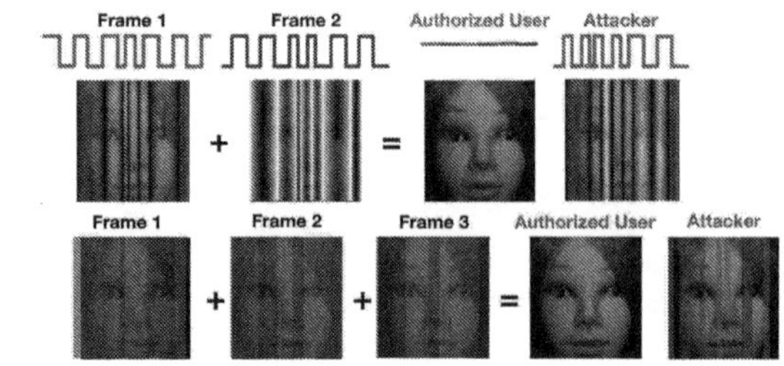

Figure 6: The impact of multi-frame recovery on authorized user and attacker, respectively.

4.2 Static Scene Recovery

When the target scene is static, the authorized user may capture a few complementary frames at a specific time to recover the scene as depicted in Fig. 6, where frequency and intensity randomization (Sec. 3.3) are employed in each frame to ensure robustness. While it does require recording a very short video, the process is extremely short (200ms at most) and barely noticeable to the authorized user. Meanwhile, an out-of-sync attacker will still receive corrupted images that cannot reconstruct the original scene even after combined.

Suppose a static scene is to be recovered using L_f frames, referred to as *critical frames*. To prevent attackers from launching the multi-frame attack, the timing of the critical frames is negotiated only between the smart LED and the authorized user through the secure side channel. These L_f frames together must contain the information of the entire scene, *i.e.* they must be complementary, as shown in Fig. 6. Meanwhile, all other frames will follow the normal flickering pattern as discussed in Sec. 3. Since the attackers cannot identify nor predict the timing of the critical frames , the best they can do is to launch the brute-force multi-frame attack, which has been discussed in Sec. 3.3.2.

5 AUTOMATIC PHYSICAL WATERMARKING FOR PRIVACY ENFORCEMENT

High-intensity ambient light sources (*e.g.* sunlight, legacy lighting, flash lights) can create strong interference to LiShield's illumination waveform, degrading the contrast by adding a constant intensity to both the bright and dark stripes, which may weaken LiShield's protection. In such scenarios, LiShield degrades itself to a *barcode mode*, where it embeds barcode in the physical scene to convey privacy policies. The barcode forms low-contrast stripes, which may not fully corrupt the images of the scene, but can still be detected by online photo-distributing hubs (*e.g.*, social website servers) who automatically enforce the policies, without cooperation of the uploader or evidence visible by naked eye. LiShield forms the watermark with just a single light fixture, instead of active displays (*e.g.*, projectors) that are required by conventional systems. The key challenge here is: how should LiShield encode the information, so that it can be robustly conveyed to the policy enforcers, despite the (uncontrollable) attacker camera settings? We now describe how LiShield's barcode design meets the challenge.

Embedding. LiShield's barcode packs multiple frequencies in every image (or in every frame of a video) following Sec. 3.3.1, but aims to map the *ratios between frequencies* into digital information. Suppose LiShield embeds two waveforms with frequencies F_0 and F_1, it chooses the two frequency components such that F_1/F_0 equals

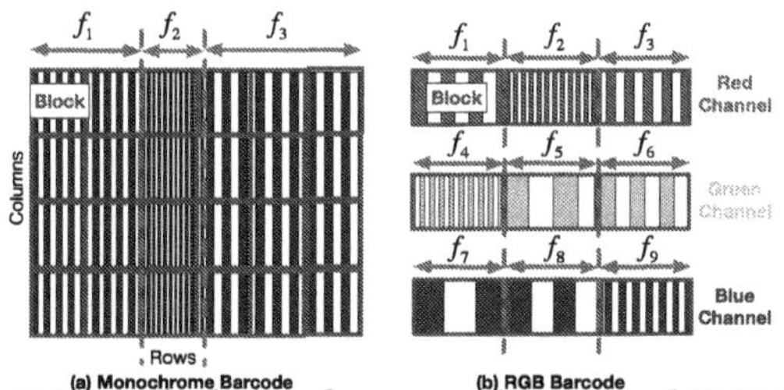

Figure 7: Barcode design for monochrome and RGB LED.

to a value R_p well known to the policy enforcers. In other words, the presence of R_p conveys "no distribution/sharing allowed". This encoding mechanism is robust against camera settings [4].

Since physical scenes usually comprise a mix of spatial frequencies, and spectral power rolls off in higher spatial frequencies thanks to camera lenses' limited bandwidth [31] while temporal frequencies are unaffected, LiShield's barcode uses frequencies that are much higher than the natural frequencies (> 400Hz) in the scene to avoid interference. It is worth noting that since the rolling-shutter sampling rate of all cameras falls in a range (30 kHz to slightly over 100 kHz [102]), LiShield limits its highest flickering frequency to 15 kHz, which respects the Nyquist sampling theorem so that the barcode can eventually be recovered without any aliasing effect.

To further improve robustness, LiShield leverages redundancy. It embeds multiple pairs of frequency components to make multiple values of R_p. In this way, LiShield can pack different R_p either at different rows of the image or in different color channels, further mitigating interference caused by intrinsic spatial patterns within the scene. Fig. 7 illustrates an example of monochrome ($C_3^2 = 3$ R_p values) and RGB LEDs ($C_{3\times3}^2 = 36$ R_p values). Note that the same mechanism can be used to increase the amount of information in the barcode, but this is beyond the scope of the present work.

Detection. Since the barcode contains M frequencies, *i.e.* $f_n = f_B + (n-1)\Delta f, n \in 2, 3, \dots, M$ (Sec. 3.3.1), there are $M_R = C_M^2$ possible frequency ratio values across the image for monochrome barcode ($M_R = C_{M\times3}^2$ for RGB barcode). Δf must be set large enough to avoid confusion ($\Delta f = 200$ Hz in experiments). The barcode decoder, running on the policy enforcer, recognizes the image as protected if there are at least M_b values that roughly match the known ratio R_p, *i.e.*, when the value falls within T_b of R_p. We empirically set $M_b = \lceil \gamma M_R + M_{\text{att}} \rceil$ where M_{att} is number of R_p removed by manual exposure attack (Sec. 3.3). γ and T_b are determined by bounding the false positive rate following an empirical procedure (to be discussed in Sec. 7.3).

To detect the frequency ratios, LiShield first partitions the image into $n_{b_r} \times n_{b_c}$ blocks, across both rows and columns, either within the monochrome channel or among all 3 RGB channels. Dividing image by columns provides LiShield multiple copies of the same frequency block, in case some of them are interfered by spatial patterns in the scene. For example, in Fig. 7, $n_{b_r} = 6$ and $n_{b_c} = 4$. For each block, LiShield averages the intensity of each row to get a one-dimension time series s_r of length $L_f = m/n_{b_r}$, given total m rows on the image. LiShield then runs FFT over each series to extract the M_p strongest frequencies. Note that LiShield's detector

[4]Although width of stripes is affected by sampling interval t_s and exposure time t_e (Fig. 1(a) and (b)), ratio of stripe widths resulted from two frequencies (which equals to R_p) remains constant.

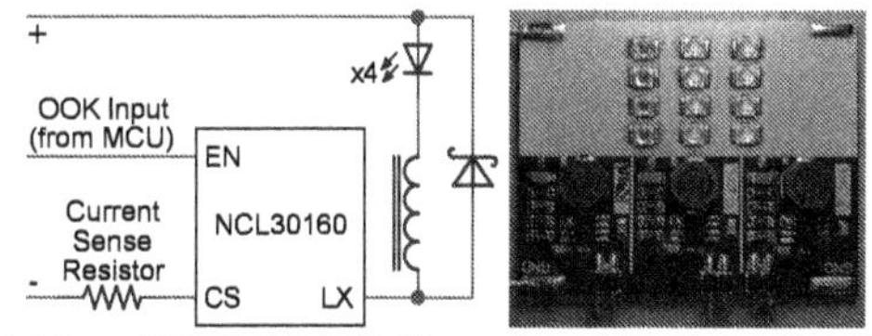

Figure 8: Simplified circuit diagram and photo for the smart LED module.

allows more than one frequencies to appear in one block. Finally, LiShield combines all unique frequencies extracted from each block and computes all frequency ratios (within and across color channels in the case of RGB barcode). Algorithm 1 describes the procedure of barcode detection.

Algorithm 1: Barcode Detection

Input: image I $(m \times n)$, n_{b_r}, n_{b_c}, T_b, S_b, M_b, $m_b = 0$, $F = \varnothing$, $D_p = \varnothing$, $B = \varnothing$, $f_s = 30$ kHz
Output: whether I is protected
crop I to $n_{b_r} \times n_{b_c}$-size blocks, store in set B;
for $b \in B$ **do**
  $s_r \leftarrow n_{b_r} \times 1 \leftarrow \text{mean}(n_{b_r} \times n_{b_c})$;
  $F_D \leftarrow \text{detrend}(FFT(s_r, f_s))$;
  pick M_p maximum peaks $F_p \in F_D$, 400 Hz $\leqslant F_p \leqslant$ 15 kHz;
  $F \leftarrow F \cup F_p$;
end
$D_p \leftarrow D_p \cup (f_i/f_j), \forall f_i, f_j \in F$;
for $d_p \in D_p$ **do**
  if $d_p \in [R_p - T_b, R_p + T_b], \forall R_p \in S_b$ **then**
    $m_b \leftarrow m_b + 1$;
  end
end
if $m_b \geq M_b$ **then**
  I is protected;
end

LiShield's redundancy in barcode ensures that the barcode cannot be completely destroyed, unless nearly all frequencies are distorted by processing the image, which will in turn cause strong deformation on the scene. We will verify the robustness of this scheme through testbed experiments (Sec. 7.4).

6 IMPLEMENTATION

Testbed setup. Fig. 9 shows our smart LED prototype, and the target scenes containing 5 capture-sensitive objects (document and painting are 2-D objects and others are all 3-D objects). We mount the LED inside a diffusive plastic cover similar to conventional ceiling light covers. We use a programmable motor [13] to hold the camera and control its distance/orientation, in order to create static or dynamic scene setup in a repeatable manner.

Smart LED modules. Commercial-of-the-shelf (COTS) household LED bulbs rely on integrated drivers to regulate LED's current [51, 88]. A dimming input is usually available on these drivers for controlling the current dynamically. We build our smart bulb based on the same topology as these COTS LED bulbs. For safety, we use 19V DC laptop power supplies instead of wall AC power, and NCL30160 [58] LED drivers which allow dimming at nearly 100

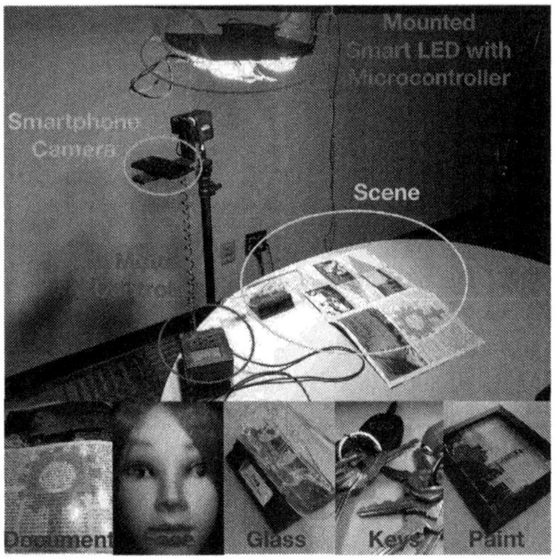

Figure 9: Experimental setup and multiple scenes we used.

kHz with arbitrary OOK waveform. The smart bulb has built-in independent RGB/white channels for controlling color/intensity. Each channel can be controlled by a separate waveform, with 4 LED chips in series, at driving current of 800 mA. In total, the 3 channels consume approximately 25 W peak power, close to common office LED troffer fixtures. However, since LiShield's OOK waveform has a duty cycle much lower than 1 (Sec. 3), the actual perceptible brightness is significantly lower. As a result, multiple LED modules can be used to improve light intensity. Fig. 8 depicts the circuit for each color channel and shows a photo of the whole module.

The dimming input signals of each channel are controlled by an STM32 [78] micro-controller unit (MCU), which generates the OOK waveform as specified by LiShield. For flexible reconfiguration, we generate digitized waveforms in MATLAB on a laptop or Android app on a smartphone instead, which are then passed to the MCU via USB.

Android app for normal, authorized and attacker's cameras. Unless otherwise noted, we use Nexus 5 [46] with stock ROM as our benchmark device. We assume that normal users use the stock camera app with default settings (including auto exposure), while a malicious attacker can manually tune the camera parameters (*e.g.*, using the Open Camera app [35]). By default, the camera ISO is set to the lowest value (100) since it is the most beneficial for attackers, as it allows longer exposure to smooth out the stripes without causing overexposure. To implement the authorization mechanism (Sec. 4), we develop a specialized app for the authorized smartphone, which uses Android's Camera2 API [32] to precisely control the exposure time, as well as communicating with the smart LED's MCU via USB. Since current Android camera APIs do not support precise frame timing, the app requests the smart LED to synchronize with the camera by altering its waveform.

Attacker's image processing. We have implemented the attacking algorithms in Sec. 3.3, which are specifically designed to combine/process the captured image, aiming to eliminate LiShield's stripe distortion. In addition, we implement classical image processing techniques, including denoising and debanding, which may be attempted by attackers. For denoising, we use the Haar-wavelet thresholding [14], non-local-means (NLmeans) [9] and BM3D [15],

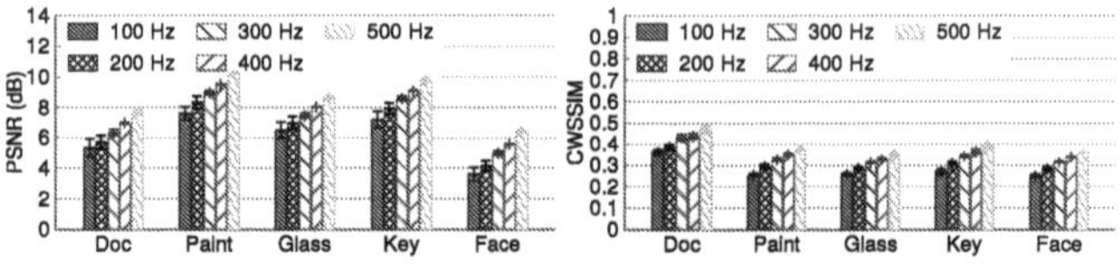

Figure 10: Impact of flickering frequency on quality.

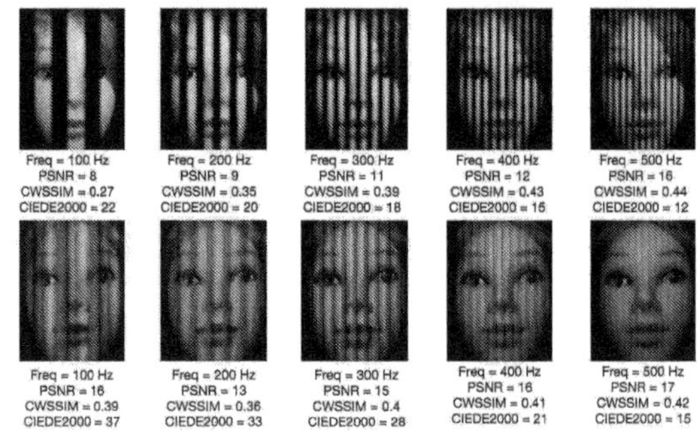

Figure 11: Image quality levels on a benchmark image.

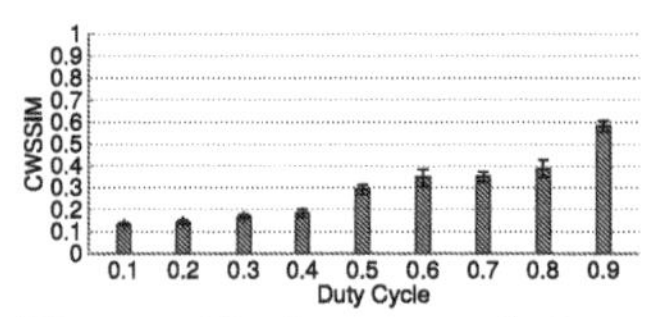

Figure 12: Impact of duty cycle on quality with auto-exposure.

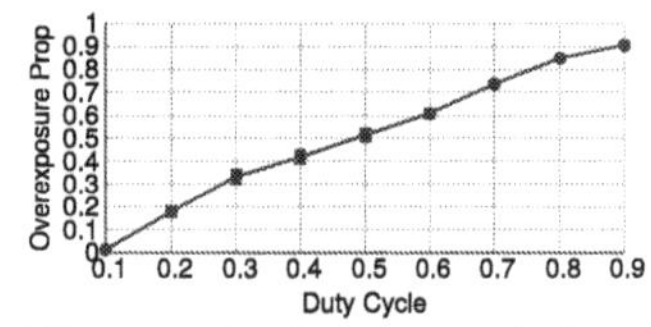

Figure 13: Impact of duty cycle on overexposure area with fix-exposure.

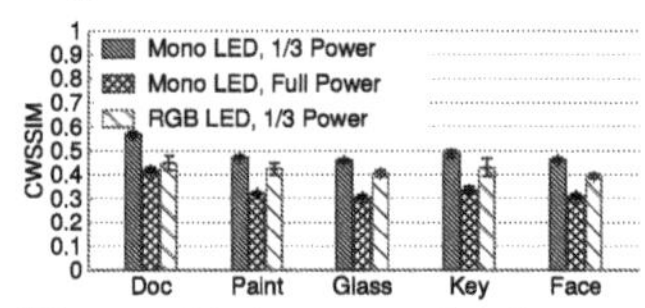

Figure 14: Impact of color on quality.

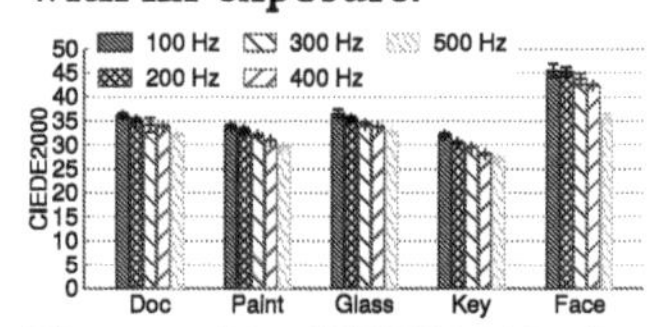

Figure 15: CIEDE2000 for color distortion.

which are among the most popular algorithms [70]. For Haar-wavelet and NLmeans, we use the G'MIC [40] plugin of the GIMP [83] image processing program. For BM3D, we use a CUDA implementation [36] since it is significantly faster and practical than CPU-base implementations. As for debanding, we use the Banding Denoise [22] and Unstrip [8] in the G'MIC [40] plugin.

Metrics. Small displacement and vibration of the camera are inevitable in physical environment, which is known to affect the SSIM of captured images significantly [92]. Thus, we quantify the image quality degradation with the enhanced CW-SSIM [67], which is insensitive under such translations, but similar to SSIM otherwise. Since PSNR shows similar trends with SSIM, we omit it in the experiments except for a few cases. Besides, we employ the CIEDE2000 [50] to compute the degradation of the images' color quality when the RGB LED is used.

7 EXPERIMENTAL EVALUATION

7.1 Effectiveness of Physical Scene Disruption

Impact of flickering frequency. We first verify LiShield's basic protection scheme (Sec. 3) with 5 static scenes, monochrome LEDs, and OOK waveform without frequency randomization, while attacker's camera uses auto-exposure. Without LiShield, the measured

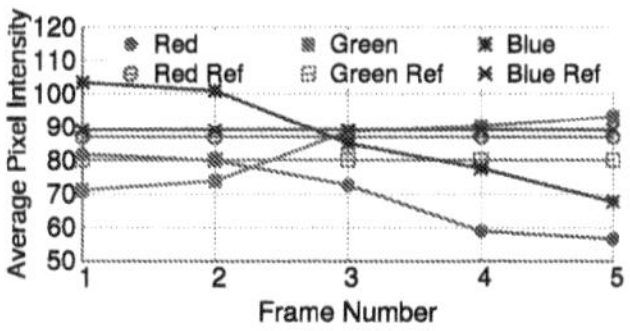

Figure 16: Impact on automatic white balance.

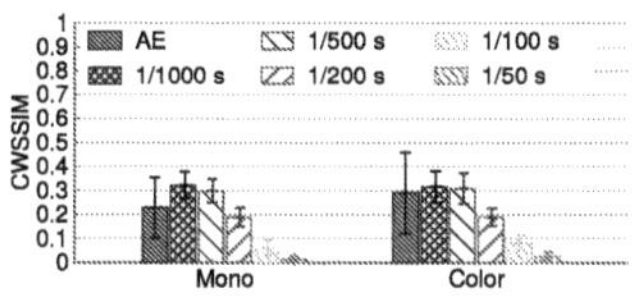

Figure 17: Impact on dynamic scene.

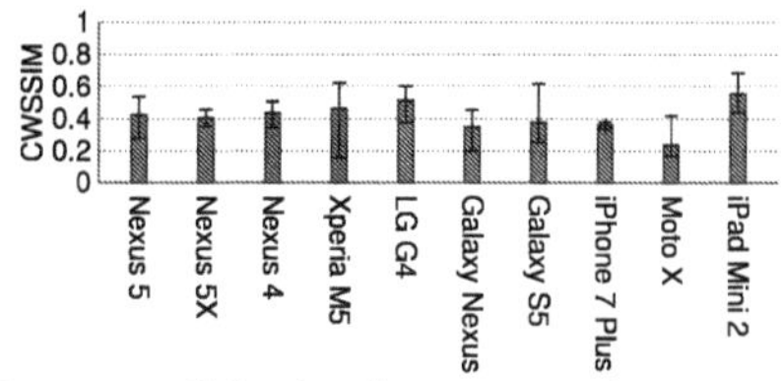

Figure 18: Impact of device heterogeneity. Error bars show *std.* across OOK waveforms with different frequencies (100 Hz to 500 Hz).

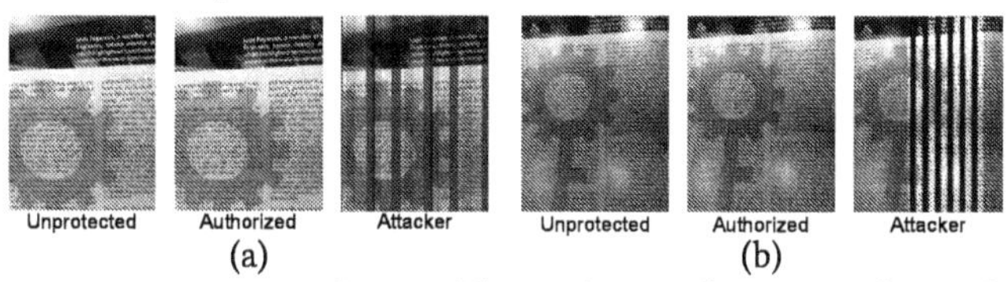

Figure 19: Frames observed by authorized users and attackers for (a) static scene (b) dynamic scene.

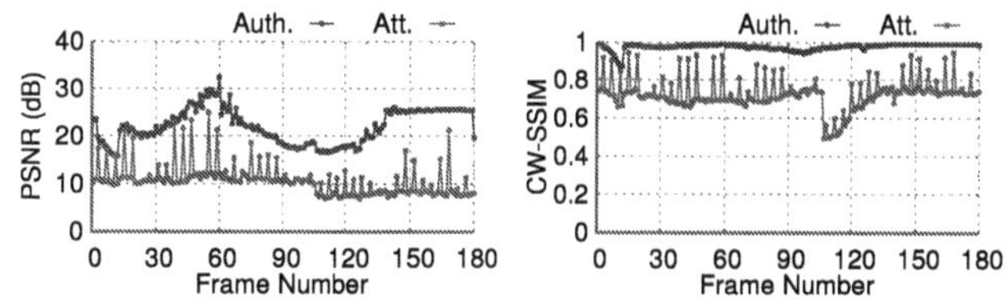

Figure 20: Video quality with and without authorization.

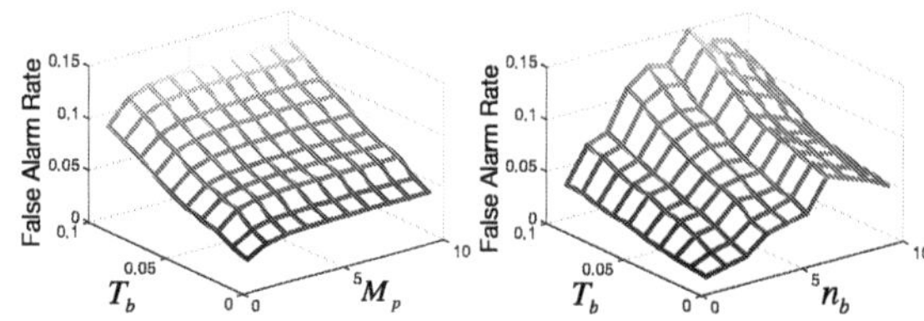

Figure 21: False alarm ratio across detector settings.

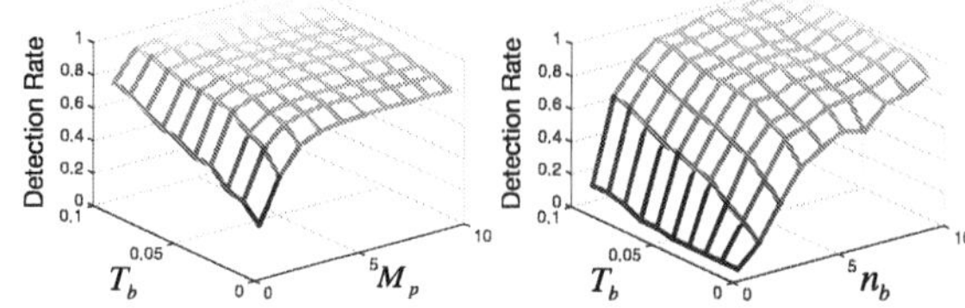

Figure 22: Detection rate across detector settings.

image quality stays high, with PSNR> 30 dB and CW-SSIM> 0.9 (slightly lower than simulation results due to digital noises in real cameras). Despite the use of a basic configuration, LiShield degrades the image quality by 3 to 10 dB for PSNR and 0.25 to 0.45 for CW-SSIM (Fig. 10). We notice that *the quality worsens slightly as flickering frequency decreases* from 500 Hz to 100 Hz, as the image sensor has higher analog gain at lower flickering frequencies [102]. In addition, *different scenes suffer from different levels of disruption*, depending on the scene's structure and reflection rate. As a visual *quality benchmark*, Fig. 11 plots the same scene with different qualities under flickering.

Impact of waveform duty cycle. We use 100 Hz flickering frequency on the document scene as a representative setup [5] to study the impact of duty cycle of emitted waveform. Here we enable auto-exposure to study the stripes' impact alone. Fig. 12 shows that lowering the duty cycle from 0.9 to 0.1 degrades the image quality dramatically, with CW-SSIM from nearly 0.6 to just over 0.1. However, higher duty cycle leads to more light influx and larger overexposure area (Fig. 13) when fix-exposure is used by attacker (here $t_e = 1/200$ s). To leverage both types of quality degradations (*i.e.*, flickering stripes and overexposure), *the LED should adopt a relatively moderate duty cycle but high peak intensity*, which echoes our model in Sec. 3.2.

Impact of RGB color distortion. We further verify the color-distortion impact when the RGB flickering is turned on. The results (Fig. 14) demonstrate slightly weaker quality degradation when its peak intensity is the same as monochrome LED (and thus average intensity is only 1/3). But *the quality degradation is stronger if the RGB LED has the same average intensity with monochrome LED.* Besides, the color distortion makes an additional independent impact. The corresponding CIEDE2000 metric (Fig. 15) escalates up to 45, way beyond the *human-tolerable threshold 6* [50]. This implies *the scene is no longer considered viewable by average viewers.*

Two *bonus effects* from our RGB LED are observed: *(i)* The structural distortion from the stripes disrupts the camera's auto-focus function, often *making the captured scene extremely blur.* This is because under LiShield, contrast of bands no longer depend on focusing accuracy, which breaks the assumption of auto-focus mechanism. *(ii) The color bands also mislead the automatic white balance function across all 5 different scenes*, since the camera can no longer identify a clean region in the image to calibrate itself and thus hesitates as shown in Fig. 16.

Impact on dynamic scenes. To create a dynamic scene, we use the motor to rotate the smartphone, creating relative motion at three different speeds (45, 100 and 145 degrees/second). Fig. 17 shows the average quality among all 3 speeds, which indicates that *dynamic scene experiences worse quality under LiShield* due to motion blur. Moreover, if the exposure time is larger than 1/100 s, then overexposure and motion blurs together further reduce the quality (PSNR < 6, CW-SSIM < 0.1). Thus, *dynamic objects further decrease the adjustment range of exposure time and make manual exposure attack more ineffective.*

Impact of device heterogeneity. We cross-validate the impact of LiShield on 10 common smartphone cameras. Fig. 18 shows the image quality varies slightly, due to different sampling rates across devices resulting in stripes of different widths. However, the quality remains at an intolerably low level across devices. Thus *LiShield's protection mechanism works across typical smartphone camera models.*

[5]Unless otherwise noted, the rest of experiments use the same setup.

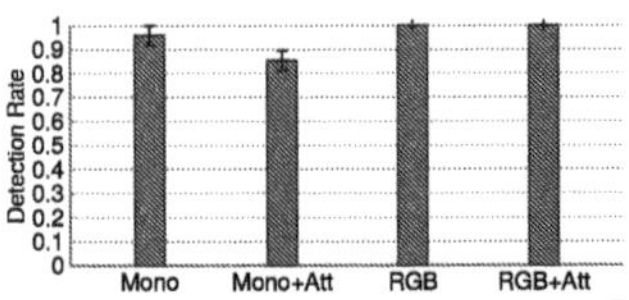

Figure 23: Detection rate of monochrome and RGB barcode design.

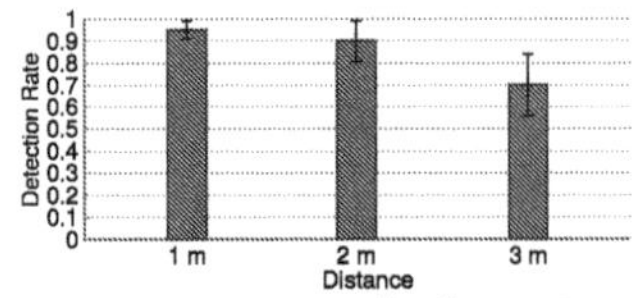

Figure 24: Barcode detection rate across distance under a single LED.

Table 1: Flicker-free configurations for monochrome barcode.

Seq	f_1 (Hz)	f_2 (Hz)	f_3 (Hz)	t_{att} (s)
1	400	600	800	1/400, 1/600, 1/800
2	1000	1200	1400	1/1000, 1/1200, 1/1400
3	1600	1800	2000	1/1600, 1/1800, 1/2000

Table 2: Flicker-free configurations for RGB barcode.

Color	f_1 (Hz)	f_2 (Hz)	f_3 (Hz)	t_{att} (s)
Red	400	600	800	1/2000 ~ 1/400
Green	1000	1200	1400	1/2000 ~ 1/400
Blue	1600	1800	2000	1/2000 ~ 1/400

7.2 Effectiveness of User Authorization

We developed an app (Sec. 6) that allows a user to capture critical frames on static scene protected by our RGB LED, and then recover the scene following Sec. 4. The resulting image quality (PSNR = 25dB, CW-SSIM = 0.9, CIEDE2000 = 5) is comparable to the ideal setting when we disable LiShield's LED modulation (Fig. 19 shows example frames extracted from a recorded video). In contrast, the attacker suffers intolerable image corruption (PSNR = 13dB, CW-SSIM = 0.56, CIEDE2000 = 34) by combining same number of randomly selected frames (Sec. 3.3.2).

For the dynamic scene, we set f_{intra} =1 kHz and f_{inter} =300 Hz (Sec. 4.1). From Fig. 20, we can see the authorized user has much higher quality (PSNR=25dB, CW-SSIM=0.98 in average) compared with attacker (PSNR = 10dB, CW-SSIM = 0.6 in average). This can be seen by resulting image frames in Fig. 19 where attacker suffers from both intra-frame and inter-frame stripes. Thus *LiShield's authorization scheme is effective in unblocking specific users while maintaining protection against attackers.*

7.3 Effectiveness of Barcode Embedding

We first determine general optimal parameters for LiShield's barcode detector (γ, T_b, n_{b_r} and n_{b_c} in Sec. 5), based on the following metrics. *(i)* False alarm rate. We run the detector on 200 images (random real-world scenes) in the SIPI database [93], and measure the probability that a barcode is detected from clean image. *(ii)* Detection rate. We embed monochrome barcodes with different f_1 from 400 Hz to 10 kHz with 200 Hz switching frequency. For each f_1, we embed 3 frequencies (*i.e.*, $M_R = 3$ in Sec. 5) with $\Delta f = 200$ Hz interval and capture 300 images with these barcodes over a benchmark scene (without loss of generality) to obtain detection rate. For simplicity we set $n_b = n_{b_r} = n_{b_c}$. Fig. 21 plots the fraction of falsely detected frequency ratios (*i.e.*, R_p in Sec. 5) over total number of ratios, while Fig. 22 shows successful detection rate under the same set of parameters. Considering the trade-off between false alarm and detection, we choose $T_b = 0.05$, $M_p = 2$ and $n_b = 4$ to bound the false alarm rate below 5%, and set $M_b = \lceil 2 \times 5\% \times M_R + M_{\text{att}} \rceil = 3$ to guarantee no false alarm for barcodes with 3 frequencies ($M_{\text{att}} = 2$ since manual exposure attack can remove two R_p), while ensuring around 90% detection rate for monochrome barcode.

Table 3: Flicker-free configurations for frequency randomization. f_c, t_{att} represent center frequency and attacker's exposure time.

M	$f_B = f_1$ (Hz)	Δf (Hz)	f_c (Hz)	t_{att} (s)
2	200	50	225	1/225
3	300	50	350	1/350
4	400	50	475	1/475
5	500	50	600	1/600
6	600	50	725	1/725

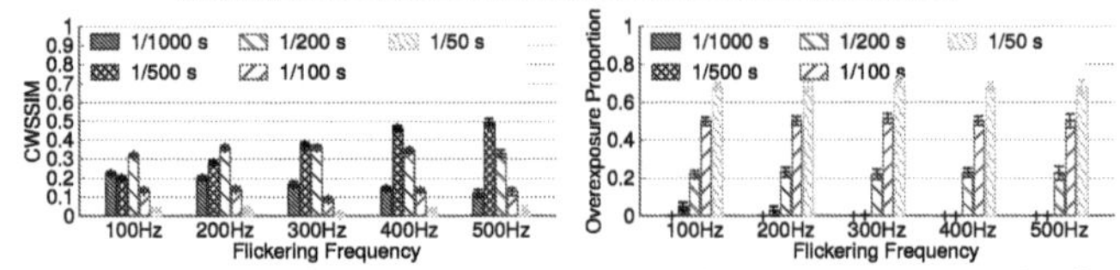

Figure 25: Quality and overexposed proportion with fix-exposure camera.

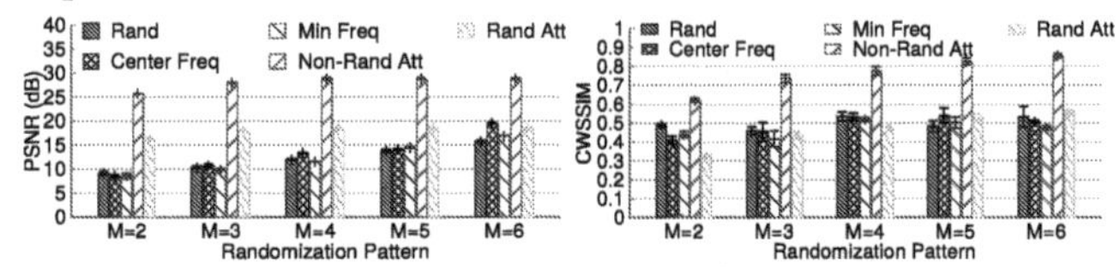

Figure 26: Quality with and without frequency randomization.

Using the above configuration and frequencies in Tables 1 and 2, Fig. 23 shows that detection rate for RGB barcodes is close to 100% with or without manual exposure attack, while being slightly below 90% for monochrome barcodes if attacked. We conclude that *LiShield's barcode detector provides reliable detection, while RGB barcodes are more detectable and robust than monochrome ones,* thanks to extra redundancy provided by color channels.

An attacker may post-process the image in attempt to remove the watermark. However, thanks to the redundancy of the barcode, the attacker will have to deform most parts of the image, which greatly reduces the image quality and makes the attack nonviable.

7.4 Robustness and Counteracting Attacks

Manual exposure attack. One possible attack against LiShield is to manually set the exposure time t_e to smooth out the flickering patterns (Sec. 3.3). Fig. 25 shows that although the image quality first increases with t_e, it drops sharply as overexposure occurs. Therefore, *LiShield traps the attacker in either extremes by optimizing the waveform* (Sec. 3.2), and *thwarts any attempts through exposure time configuration.*

We further test the effectiveness of randomization as configured in Table 3 with auto-exposure (except for attacker). Fig. 26 shows that the image quality with scrambling is comparable with single frequency of f_1 and f_c, thus *frequency randomization does not cause much difference in image quality.* Note that the image quality varies only slightly with number of frequencies, implying *it is insensitive to LiShield's frequency randomization pattern.* We assume the exposure time is $t_{\text{att}} = 1/f_c$, which is optimistic for the attacker. Results show that image quality does not vary significantly (compared with attacks to stripes without randomization), showing *LiShield's robustness against such attacks.*

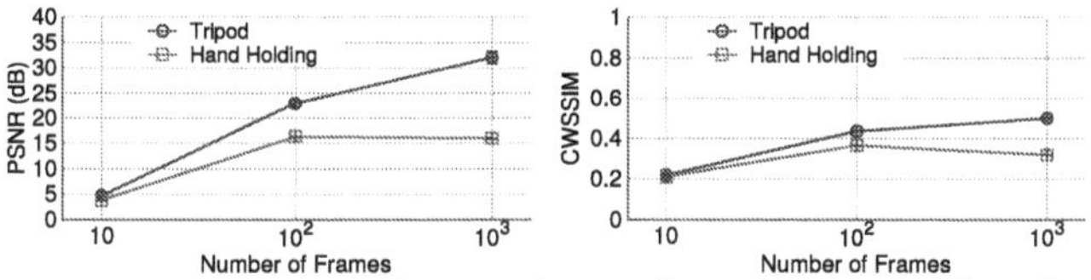

Figure 27: Image quality with number of frames of multi-frame attack.

Multi-frame attack. Fig. 27 plots the recovered scene's quality under the multi-frame attack. Here we set t_e to be 1/500 s to avoid overexposure and then record a video in 30 fps. When a tripod is used, PSNR goes to 30 dB but CW-SSIM remains low at 0.5 using 1000 frames, which means *the impact of stripes on structure of scene is still strong although intensity does not differ substantially, making quality still unacceptable for professionals who spend such a great cost.* We also ask 5 volunteers to hold the smartphone as stable as they can on a table, and Fig. 27 shows the quality is even lower, because it is impossible to completely avoid dithering with hands even with anti-shake technology, making recovered scene unviewable. Extending the recording duration increases the number of frames recorded by the attacker, but it also increases disturbance and probability of being identified by the protected user, making it risky and impractical for the attacker to pursue higher quality.

Image recovery processing attack. Fig. 28 shows the image quality after post-processing with denoising or de-banding (Sec. 6). The denoising methods fail to improve the quality significantly as the disruption pattern of LiShield does not fit any known noise model (*e.g.* the commonly used Gaussian model). BM3D can improve the CW-SSIM slightly because it decreases contrast slightly, but the PSNR remains low. The deformation removal methods (*i.e.*, de-banding and unstriping) do not help either, since interpolation process cannot bring back the correct pixel values. The CIEDE2000 color metric also shows a low quality (well above 6). Thus, *it is practically impossible to remove LiShield's impact by image processing, despite some unnoticeable increase of the image quality.* More advanced computer vision techniques may provide better recovery, but even they will not recover the *exactly original scene* since information is already lost at capture time.

Impact of ambient light. We evaluate LiShield's performance under different types of ambient lights and LED power to verify LiShield's robustness. As shown in Fig. 29, the stripes are almost completely removed under direct sunlight due to its extremely high intensity, making the quality comparable with the unprotected case (PSNR>30dB, CW-SSIM>0.9). However, CIEDE2000 remains relatively high as LED's light affects the scene's color tone significantly, which explains unexpected image quality degradation under diffused sunlight and office light in Fig. 29. Flash light can increase the quality slightly thanks to its close distance to the scene, but the improvement is marginal and far from unprotected. In addition, Fig. 30 shows a slight decrease of detection rate of barcode under direct sunlight, but the decrease is marginal in every case. Thus, we conclude that *LiShield is robust against ambient light, and still guarantees protection with barcode under direct sunlight.*

Impact of distance. We vary the distance between camera and *a single LED* from 1 m to 3 m. The scene resolution lowers at longer distance. Fig. 24 shows the barcode detection rate remains high (> 90%) at 2 m range (where the bright area is only 1/4 on the image compared with 1 m case). However only 70% rate can be achieved at 3 m range, since the bright area is too small on the image (1/9). But multiple LEDs may be distributed to increase the coverage. To make a fair comparison on quality, we tailor the same scene from image to avoid interference from surrounding objects. Fig. 31 shows that even under 3 m, CW-SSIM is still way below 0.9 and the quality only increases slightly with distance. Thus, *LiShield's working range can cover most of common applications with only a single smart LED.* With multiple smart LEDs, LiShield's coverage can be scaled up just like normal lighting (Sec. 8).

8 DISCUSSION

Considerations for high peak intensity. Considering the hardware capability and energy costs, we estimate the optimal LED peak intensity to be 20 kLux, and average intensity is 10 kLux with 0.5 duty cycle, which is an order of magnitude lower than outdoor intensity in a sunny day [85], and generally considered safe even for long activities [82]. Our smart LED is brighter than typical indoor lighting, which is usually less than 1 kLux. But we found the intensity is always acceptable by perception in our experiments, likely because the brightness perceived by human eyes and actual light intensity follow a logarithmic relationship. Since the privacy protection has higher priority than power savings, we expect slight increase of illumination brightness is acceptable in the target use cases.

Multiple LEDs and multiple cameras. When a large indoor environment needs LiShield's protection, the smart LEDs can be deployed pervasively to cover the whole area, just like regular lighting. Availability of multiple LEDs can also increase the diversity of the protection, since each of them can be controlled independently. We leave the optimization of such multi-LED setup for future work.

With the presence of multiple unauthorized cameras, LiShield needs to ensure no additional information can be recovered by combining images across them, which may impose extra constraints on waveform design. Meanwhile, when multiple authorized cameras (Sec. 4) are present, LiShield can serve them in a round-robin manner. Better strategies may require synchronization between cameras and we leave them for future work.

Attacker with special equipment. Global shutter cameras, ND filters (optical attenuators) and similar professional devices may compromise LiShield's protection. While this is inevitable, we note that such devices are usually bulky and costly, which makes them obtrusive and less accessible by everyday photographers. Thus, LiShield may still protect the privacy of its users by demotivating such attacks. An advanced version of LiShield that fully prevents such attacks will be left for our future work.

Recording a high speed video (*e.g.*, 120 FPS) by advanced cameras will not significantly weaken LiShield's protection, as stripes across frames will be similar. High FPS also requires shorter exposure, which actually amplifies LiShield's effect. Along with the backup barcode protection, which is not affected by the camera's frame rate, the threat posed by high speed camera is limited.

9 RELATED WORKS

Anti-piracy and capturing-resistant technologies. Camera recording of copyright screen-displayed videos (*e.g.*, in a movie theater) accounts for 90% of pirated online content [104]. Since

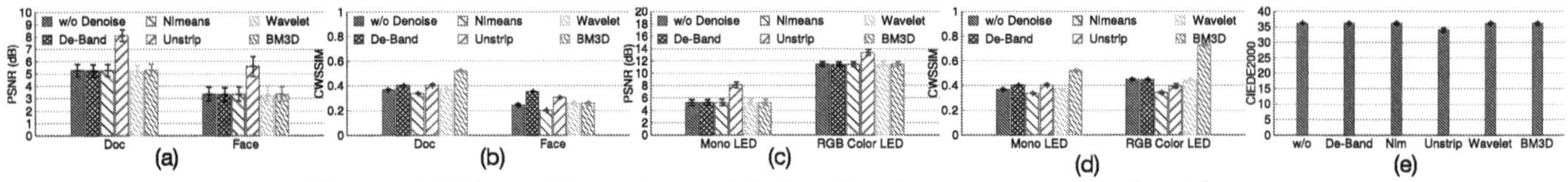

Figure 28: Effects of denoising and de-banding image processing algorithms.

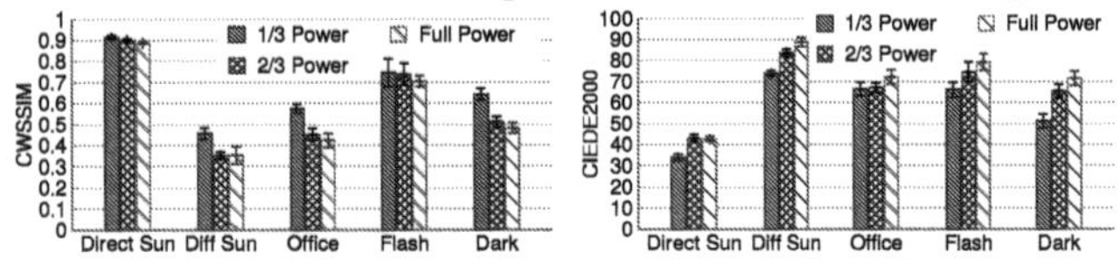

Figure 29: Image Quality under ambient lights.

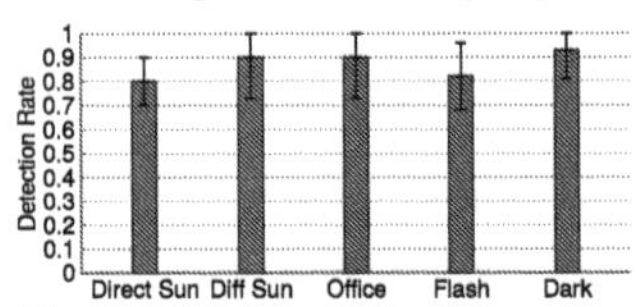

Figure 30: Barcode detection rate with ambient light intensity.

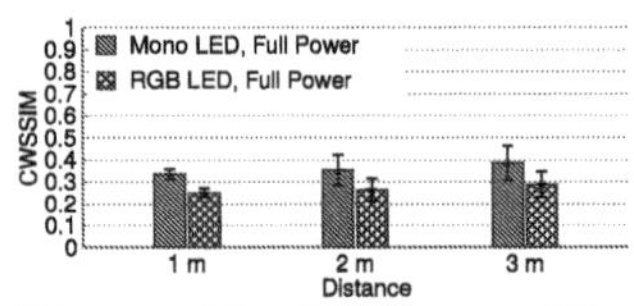

Figure 31: Image quality with different distances under a single LED.

screen refresh rate is much higher than video frame rate, Kaleido [104] scrambles multiple frames within the frame periods to deter recording, while preserving viewing experience by taking advantage of human eyes' flicker fusion effects. Many patented technologies addressed the same issue [10, 11, 20, 21, 30, 43, 61, 68, 71–73, 75, 79, 94, 100]. In contrast, the problem of automatic protection of private and passive physical space received little attention. Certain countries [19, 28] dictate that smartphone cameras must make shutter sound to disclose the photo-capturing actions, yet this does not enforce the compliance, cannot block the photo distribution, and cannot automatically protect against video recording.

Certain optical signaling systems can remotely ban photography in concerts, theaters and other capturing-sensitive sites. Courteous Glass [42] and a recent Apple patent [84] augment wearable devices with near-infrared LEDs, which are invisible to human but can be captured by camera, to convey hidden privacy appeal of the wearers. These LEDs cannot enforce protection (*e.g.*, through image corruption as in LiShield), and convey information only when they fall in the camera's field of view. BlindSpot [86] adopts a computer vision approach to locate retro-reflective camera lenses, and pulses a strong light beam towards the camera to cause overexposure. Despite its sophistication, approach fails when multiple cameras coexist with arbitrary orientations.

Invisible screen-camera communications. Recent research also explored novel ways of screen-to-camera visible light communication, by hiding information behind the display. VRCodes [97] carries information through high frequency changes of selected color, which can be decoded by rolling-shutter cameras. Hilight [47] conveys information by modulating the pixel translucency change in subtle ways. ARTcode [99] embeds data into images by modifying the pixels' colors, which is imperceptible due to human eyes' limited pixel resolution. This line of research is also related with the classical watermarking which hides copyright and authentication information in images/videos through spatial/frequency domain re-encoding [1, 59]. These mechanisms are applicable when the users have full control over the image/video source, but cannot prevent malicious capturing/distribution of physical scenes. On the other hand, conventional luminaries bear natural flickering effects that have been leveraged for localization purposes [102, 103, 106], but the frequencies are too high to cause visible corruption on the camera images.

Privacy protection for images/videos. Conventional visual privacy-protection systems have been replying on post-capture processing. Early efforts employed techniques like region-of-interest masking, blurring, mosaicking, *etc.* [56], or re-encoding using encrypted scrambling seeds [18]. There also exists a vast body of work for hiding copyright marks and other information in digital images/videos [27, 38, 39, 45, 52, 63, 89, 90, 97, 101]. LiShield's barcode protection is inspired by these schemes, but it aims to protect physical scenes prior to capturing.

One common challenge in visual privacy protection is to identify the privacy preference. Location-bound privacy expression can be achieved in everyday life using special signs. Privacy.Tag [7] allows people to express their privacy preference by wearing QR codes. I-Pic [2] allows people to broadcast their privacy preferences using Bluetooth. COIN [105] matches a user's face to a prescribed privacy preference, and can automatically detect and mask people who do not want to be captured. P3 [63] protects photo-sharing privacy by encoding an image into a private, encrypted part, and a public, standards-compatible part. PrivacyEye [65] allows a user to manually mark regions on an image that permit access from mobile apps. PlaceAvoider [80] allows first-person camera users to capture and blacklist sensitive spaces *a priori*, and use image matching to block subsequent pictures containing such spaces. These systems only work when the user has full control over the camera.

10 CONCLUSION

Privacy protection in passive indoor environment has been an important but unsolved problem. In this paper we propose LiShield, which uses smart-LEDs and specialized intensity waveforms to disrupt unauthorized cameras, while allowing authorized users to record high quality image and video. We implemented and evaluated LiShield under various representative indoor scenarios, which demonstrates LiShield's effectiveness and robustness. We consider LiShield as a first exploration of automatic visual privacy enforcement and expect it can inspire more research along the same direction.

ACKNOWLEDGEMENT

We would like to thank the anonymous reviewers and our shepherd Marco Grutester for their valuable comments and feedback. This project was partially supported by the NSF under Grant CNS-1343363, CNS-1350039, CNS-1506657, CNS-1518728, and CNS-1617321.

REFERENCES

[1] 2010. Digital Image Steganography: Survey and Analysis of Current Methods. *Signal Processing* 90, 3 (2010).
[2] Paarijaat Aditya, Rijurekha Sen, Peter Druschel, Seong Joon Oh, Rodrigo Benenson, Mario Fritz, Bernt Schiele, Bobby Bhattacharjee, and Tong Tong Wu. 2016. I-Pic: A Platform for Privacy-Compliant Image Capture. In *Proceedings of ACM Annual International Conference on Mobile Systems, Applications, and Services (MobiSys)*.
[3] Saeed Al-Mansoori and Alavi Kunhu. 2012. Robust watermarking technique based on DCT to protect the ownership of DubaiSat-1 images against attacks. *International Journal of Computer Science and Network Security (IJCSNS)* 12, 6 (2012), 1.
[4] Stephen J. Anderson and David C. Burr. 1985. Spatial and temporal selectivity of the human motion detection system. *Vision Research* 25, 8 (1985), 1147 – 1154.
[5] Mauro Barni. 2006. *Document and Image compression*. CRC press.
[6] BBC. 2004. The Camera Phone Backlash. (2004). http://news.bbc.co.uk/2/hi/uk_news/magazine/3793501.stm
[7] Cheng Bo, Guobin Shen, Jie Liu, Xiang-Yang Li, YongGuang Zhang, and Feng Zhao. 2014. Privacy.Tag: Privacy Concern Expressed and Respected. In *ACM Conference on Embedded Network Sensor Systems (SenSys)*.
[8] Jérôme Boulanger. [n. d.]. jboulanger.gmic. ([n. d.]). https://github.com/jboulanger/jboulanger-gmic
[9] Antoni Buades, Bartomeu Coll, and J-M Morel. 2005. A non-local algorithm for image denoising. In *Computer Vision and Pattern Recognition, 2005. CVPR 2005. IEEE Computer Society Conference on*, Vol. 2. IEEE, 60–65.
[10] Herschel Clement Burstyn. 2009. Cinema anti-piracy measures. (2009). US Patent 7,634,089.
[11] Herschel Clement Burstyn, George Herbert Needham Riddle, Leon Shapiro, and David Lloyd Staebler. 2008. Method and apparatus for film anti-piracy. (2008). US Patent 7,324,646.
[12] Tung-Shou Chen, Chin-Chen Chang, and Min-Shiang Hwang. 1998. A virtual image cryptosystem based upon vector quantization. *IEEE transactions on Image Processing* 7, 10 (1998), 1485–1488.
[13] Cinetics. [n. d.]. Axis360 Pro. http://cinetics.com/axis360-pro/. ([n. d.]).
[14] Ronald R Coifman and David L Donoho. 1995. *Translation-invariant de-noising*. Springer.
[15] Kostadin Dabov, Alessandro Foi, Vladimir Katkovnik, and Karen Egiazarian. 2006. Image denoising with block-matching and 3D filtering. In *Electronic Imaging*. International Society for Optics and Photonics.
[16] Christos Danakis, Mostafa Afgani, Gordon Povey, Ian Underwood, and Harald Haas. 2012. Using a CMOS camera sensor for visible light communication. In *Proc. of IEEE Globecom Workshops*.
[17] Tamara Denning, Zakariya Dehlawi, and Tadayoshi Kohno. 2014. In Situ with Bystanders of Augmented Reality Glasses: Perspectives on Recording and Privacy-mediating Technologies. In *SIGCHI Conference on Human Factors in Computing Systems (CHI)*.
[18] F. Dufaux and T. Ebrahimi. 2008. Scrambling for Privacy Protection in Video Surveillance Systems. *IEEE Transactions on Circuits and Systems for Video Technology* 18, 8 (2008).
[19] Engadget. 2016. Japan's noisy iPhone problem. (2016). https://www.engadget.com/2016/09/30/japans-noisy-iphone-problem/
[20] Michael Epstein and Douglas A Stanton. 2003. Method and device for preventing piracy of video material from theater screens. (2003). US Patent 6,529,600.
[21] James A Fancher, David H Sitrick, and Gregory P Sitrick. 2003. Movie film security system utilizing infrared patterns. (2003). US Patent 6,559,883.
[22] Iain Fergusson. [n. d.]. External Filters by Iain Fergusson. ([n. d.]). https://github.com/dtschump/gmic-community/blob/master/include/iain_fergusson.gmic
[23] Federico Ferrari, Marco Zimmerling, Lothar Thiele, and Olga Saukh. 2011. Efficient network flooding and time synchronization with glossy. In *Proc. of ACM/IEEE IPSN*. 73–84.
[24] Forbes. 2011. Adventures in Self-Surveillance, aka The Quantified Self, aka Extreme Navel-Gazing. (Apr. 2011).
[25] Nobuhiro Fujimoto and Hikari Mochizuki. 2013. 477 Mbit/s visible light transmission based on OOK-NRZ modulation using a single commercially available visible LED and a practical LED driver with a pre-emphasis circuit. In *National Fiber Optic Engineers Conference*. Optical Society of America, JTh2A–73.
[26] Nobuhiro Fujimoto and Shohei Yamamoto. 2014. The fastest visible light transmissions of 662 Mb/s by a blue LED, 600 Mb/s by a red LED, and 520 Mb/s by a green LED based on simple OOK-NRZ modulation of a commercially available RGB-type white LED using pre-emphasis and post-equalizing techniques. In *Optical Communication (ECOC), 2014 European Conference on*. IEEE, 1–3.
[27] Zhongpai Gao, Guangtao Zhai, and Chunjia Hu. 2015. The invisible qr code. In *Proceedings of the 23rd ACM international conference on Multimedia*. ACM, 1047–1050.
[28] Golf News Net. 2015. Why is it illegal in South Korea to silence mobile phone camera sounds? (2015). https://thegolfnewsnet.com/golfnewsnetteam/2015/10/07/illegal-south-korea-silence-mobile-phone-camera-sounds-13503/
[29] Rafael L Gomes, Luiz F Bittencourt, Edmundo RM Madeira, Eduardo Cerqueira, and Mario Gerla. 2015. QoE-Aware dynamic virtual network resource adaptation for EaaS environment. In *Communications (ICC), 2015 IEEE International Conference on*. IEEE, 6836–6841.
[30] Dean K Goodhill and Ty Safreno. 2011. Method and apparatus for inhibiting the piracy of motion pictures. (2011). US Patent 8,018,569.
[31] Joseph W Goodman. 2005. *Introduction to Fourier optics*. Roberts and Company Publishers.
[32] Google. [n. d.]. android.hardware.camera2. ([n. d.]). https://developer.android.com/reference/android/hardware/camera2/package-summary.html
[33] Phil Green and Lindsay MacDonald. 2011. *Colour engineering: achieving device independent colour*. Vol. 30. John Wiley & Sons.
[34] Stacey L. Gulick. 2004. Preventing Unauthorized Audio and Video Recording at Your Practice. (2004). http://medicaleconomics.modernmedicine.com/medical-economics/content/tags/hipaa/preventing-unauthorized-audio-and-video-recording-your-practice?page=full
[35] Mark Harman. [n. d.]. Open Camera. ([n. d.]). http://opencamera.sourceforge.net/
[36] David Honzátko. [n. d.]. CUDA implementation of BM3D. ([n. d.]). https://github.com/DawyD/bm3d-gpu
[37] Roberto Hoyle, Robert Templeman, Steven Armes, Denise Anthony, David Crandall, and Apu Kapadia. 2014. Privacy Behaviors of Lifeloggers Using Wearable Cameras. In *ACM International Joint Conference on Pervasive and Ubiquitous Computing (UbiComp)*.
[38] Chin-Wei Hsu, Kevin Liang, Hung-Yu Chen, Liang-Yu Wei, Chien-Hung Yeh, Yang Liu, and Chi-Wai Chow. 2016. Visible light encryption system using camera image sensor. In *OptoElectronics and Communications Conference (OECC) held jointly with 2016 International Conference on Photonics in Switching (PS), 2016 21st*. IEEE, 1–3.
[39] Chunjia Hu, Guangtao Zhai, and Zhongpai Gao. 2015. Visible light communication via temporal psycho-visual modulation. In *Proceedings of the 23rd ACM international conference on Multimedia*. ACM, 785–788.
[40] Image Team of the GREYC laboratory. [n. d.]. G'MIC - GREYC's Magic for Image Computing. ([n. d.]). http://gmic.eu/
[41] Yi Jiang, Ke Zhou, and Sheng He. 2007. Human visual cortex responds to invisible chromatic flicker. *Nature Neuroscience* 10, 5 (2007), 657–662.
[42] Jaeyeon Jung and Matthai Philipose. 2014. Courteous Glass. In *ACM International Joint Conference on Pervasive and Ubiquitous Computing (UbiComp)*.
[43] Masayuki Karakawa. 2006. Laser video projection system and method with anti-piracy feature. (2006). US Patent 7,103,074.
[44] Ye-Sheng Kuo, Pat Pannuto, Ko-Jen Hsiao, and Prabal Dutta. 2014. Luxapose: Indoor Positioning with Mobile Phones and Visible Light. In *Proc. of ACM MobiCom*.
[45] Hui-Yu Lee, Hao-Min Lin, Yu-Lin Wei, Hsin-I Wu, Hsin-Mu Tsai, and Kate Ching-Ju Lin. 2015. Rollinglight: Enabling line-of-sight light-to-camera communications. In *Proceedings of the 13th Annual International Conference on Mobile Systems, Applications, and Services*. ACM, 167–180.
[46] LG Electronics. [n. d.]. Nexus 5. ([n. d.]). http://www.lg.com/ca_en/cell-phones/lg-D820-White-nexus5
[47] Tianxing Li, Chuankai An, Xinran Xiao, Andrew T. Campbell, and Xia Zhou. 2015. Real-Time Screen-Camera Communication Behind Any Scene. In *Annual International Conference on Mobile Systems, Applications, and Services (MobiSys)*.
[48] Zhenjiang Li, Cheng Li, Wenwei Chen, Jingyao Dai, Mo Li, Xiang-Yang Li, and Yunhao Liu. 2012. Clock Calibration Using Fluorescent Lighting. In *Proceedings of International Conference on Mobile Computing and Networking (MobiCom)*.
[49] C. K. Liang, L. W. Chang, and H. H. Chen. 2008. Analysis and Compensation of Rolling Shutter Effect. *IEEE Transactions on Image Processing* 17, 8 (2008).
[50] M Ronnier Luo, Guihua Cui, and B Rigg. 2001. The development of the CIE 2000 colour-difference formula: CIEDE2000. *Color Research & Application* 26, 5 (2001), 340–350.
[51] Maxim Integrated Products, Inc. 2004. Why Drive White LEDs with Constant Current? https://www.maximintegrated.com/en/app-notes/index.mvp/id/3256. (Aug. 2004).
[52] Moni Naor and Adi Shamir. 1995. Visual Cryptography. In *Proceedings of the Workshop on the Theory and Application of Cryptographic Techniques (EUROCRYPT)*.
[53] Narrative. 2016. Narrative Clip 2 Wearable HD Video Camera. (2016). http://getnarrative.com/
[54] T. Naseer, J. Sturm, and D. Cremers. 2013. FollowMe: Person Following and Gesture Recognition With a Quadrocopter. In *IEEE/RSJ International Conference on Intelligent Robots and Systems*.
[55] Alaeddin Nassani, Huidong Bai, Gun Lee, and Mark Billinghurst. 2015. Tag It!: AR Annotation Using Wearable Sensors. In *SIGGRAPH Asia Mobile Graphics and Interactive Applications*.
[56] Elaine M. Newton, Latanya Sweeney, and Bradley Malin. 2005. Preserving Privacy by De-Identifying Face Images. *IEEE Transactions on Knowledge and Data Engineering* 17, 2 (2005).
[57] S. John Obringer and Kent Coffey. 2007. Cell Phones in American High Schools: A National Survey. *Journal of Technology Studies* 33, 1 (2007).

[58] ON Semiconductor. [n. d.]. NCL30160: LED Driver, Constant Current Buck Regulator, 1.0 A. ([n. d.]). http://www.onsemi.com/PowerSolutions/product.do?id=NCL30160
[59] F. A. P. Petitcolas, R. J. Anderson, and M. G. Kuhn. 1999. Information Hiding–a Survey. *Proc. IEEE* 87, 7 (1999).
[60] Philips Lighting B.V. [n. d.]. Philips Hue. ([n. d.]). http://meethue.com
[61] John D Price. 2009. Methods and apparatus for detection of motion picture piracy for piracy prevention. (2009). US Patent App. 12/322,915.
[62] QImaging. 2014. Rolling Shutter vs. Global Shutter. (2014). https://www.qimaging.com/ccdorscmos/pdfs/RollingvsGlobalShutter.pdf
[63] Moo-Ryong Ra, Ramesh Govindan, and Antonio Ortega. 2013. P3: Toward Privacy-preserving Photo Sharing. In *USENIX Conference on Networked Systems Design and Implementation (NSDI)*.
[64] Swati Rallapalli, Aishwarya Ganesan, Krishna Chintalapudi, Venkat N. Padmanabhan, and Lili Qiu. 2014. Enabling Physical Analytics in Retail Stores Using Smart Glasses. In *Annual International Conference on Mobile Computing and Networking (MobiCom)*.
[65] Nisarg Raval, Animesh Srivastava, Ali Razeen, Kiron Lebeck, Ashwin Machanavajjhala, and Lanodn P. Cox. 2016. What You Mark is What Apps See. In *Annual International Conference on Mobile Systems, Applications, and Services (MobiSys)*.
[66] Erik Reinhard, Wolfgang Heidrich, Paul Debevec, Sumanta Pattanaik, Greg Ward, and Karol Myszkowski. 2010. *High dynamic range imaging: acquisition, display, and image-based lighting*. Morgan Kaufmann.
[67] Mehul P Sampat, Zhou Wang, Shalini Gupta, Alan Conrad Bovik, and Mia K Markey. 2009. Complex wavelet structural similarity: A new image similarity index. *IEEE transactions on image processing* 18, 11 (2009), 2385–2401.
[68] Yosef Sanhedrai, Ariel Schwarz, Liad Ben Yishai, and Zeev Zalevsky. 2007. System and method for preventing photography. (2007). US Patent App. 12/308,525.
[69] Oren Shani. [n. d.]. Precise Time Synchronization Over WLAN. ([n. d.]). http://www.ti.com/lit/an/swaa162a/swaa162a.pdf
[70] Ling Shao, Ruomei Yan, Xuelong Li, and Yan Liu. 2014. From heuristic optimization to dictionary learning: A review and comprehensive comparison of image denoising algorithms. *IEEE Transactions on Cybernetics* 44, 7 (2014), 1001–1013.
[71] David H Sitrick and James A Fancher. 2004. Anti-piracy protection system and methodology. (2004). US Patent 6,771,349.
[72] David H Sitrick and James A Fancher. 2007. Targeted anti-piracy system and methodology. (2007). US Patent 7,170,577.
[73] David H Sitrick and James A Fancher. 2011. System and methodology for validating compliance of anti-piracy security and reporting thereupon. (2011). US Patent 8,006,311.
[74] Fikret Sivrikaya and Bülent Yener. 2004. Time Synchronization in Sensor Networks: a Survey. *IEEE network* 18, 4 (2004), 45–50.
[75] Vincent So. 2009. Anti-piracy image display methods and systems. (2009). US Patent 7,634,134.
[76] Social Pilot. 2016. 125 Amazing Social Media Statistics You Should Know. (2016). https://socialpilot.co/blog/125-amazing-social-media-statistics-know-2016/
[77] S.S. Stevens. 1975. *Psychophysics: introduction to its perceptual, neural, and social prospects*. Transaction Publishers.
[78] STMicroelectronics. [n. d.]. STM32F103C8. ([n. d.]). http://www.st.com/en/microcontrollers/stm32f103c8.html
[79] Emil Tchoukaleysky. 2013. Digital cinema anti-piracy method and apparatus for liquid crystal projection systems. (2013). US Patent 8,559,791.
[80] Robert Templeman, Mohammed Korayem, David J. Crandall, and Apu Kapadia. 2014. PlaceAvoider: Steering First-Person Cameras away from Sensitive Spaces. In *Network and Distributed System Security Symposium (NDSS)*.
[81] R. Templeman, Z. Rahman, D. Crandall, and A. Kapadia. 2013. PlaceRaider: Virtual Theft in Physical Spaces With Smartphones. In *Network and Distributed System Security Symposium (NDSS)*.
[82] Michael Terman and Jiuan Su Terman. 2005. Light therapy for seasonal and nonseasonal depression: efficacy, protocol, safety, and side effects. *CNS spectrums* 10, 08 (2005), 647–663.
[83] The GIMP Team. [n. d.]. GIMP - GNU Image Manipulation Program. ([n. d.]). https://www.gimp.org/
[84] Victor Tiscareno, Kevin Jonhson, and Cindy Lawrence. 2011. Systems and Methods for Receiving Infrared Data with a Camera Designed to Detect Images. (2011).
[85] PR Tregenza. 1980. The daylight factor and actual illuminance ratios. *Lighting Research & Technology* 12, 2 (1980), 64–68.
[86] Khai N. Truong, Shwetak N. Patel, Jay W. Summet, and Gregory D. Abowd. 2005. *Preventing Camera Recording by Designing a Capture-Resistant Environment.*
[87] Christopher W. Tyler. 1985. Analysis of visual modulation sensitivity. II. Peripheral retina and the role of photoreceptor dimensions. *Journal of the Optical Society of America A* 2, 3 (1985), 393–398.
[88] H. van der Broeck, G. Sauerlander, and M. Wendt. 2007. Power driver topologies and control schemes for LEDs. In *Annual IEEE Applied Power Electronics Conference and Exposition*.
[89] Anran Wang, Zhuoran Li, Chunyi Peng, Guobin Shen, Gan Fang, and Bing Zeng. 2015. Inframe++: Achieve simultaneous screen-human viewing and hidden screen-camera communication. In *Proceedings of the 13th Annual International Conference on Mobile Systems, Applications, and Services*. ACM, 181–195.
[90] Anran Wang, Chunyi Peng, Ouyang Zhang, Guobin Shen, and Bing Zeng. 2014. Inframe: Multiflexing full-frame visible communication channel for humans and devices. In *Proceedings of the 13th ACM Workshop on Hot Topics in Networks*. ACM, 23.
[91] Zhou Wang, A. C. Bovik, H. R. Sheikh, and E. P. Simoncelli. 2004. Image quality assessment: from error visibility to structural similarity. *IEEE Transactions on Image Processing* 13, 4 (2004), 600–612.
[92] Zhou Wang and Eero P Simoncelli. 2005. Translation insensitive image similarity in complex wavelet domain. In *Acoustics, Speech, and Signal Processing, 2005. Proceedings.(ICASSP'05). IEEE International Conference on*, Vol. 2. IEEE, ii–573.
[93] Allan G Weber. 1997. The USC-SIPI image database version 5. *USC-SIPI Report* 315 (1997), 1–24.
[94] Donald Henry Willis. 2008. Method, apparatus and system for anti-piracy protection in digital cinema. (2008). US Patent App. 12/736,774.
[95] H. James Wilson. 2012. You, By the Numbers. *Harvard Business Review* (Sep. 2012).
[96] W. Winterhalter, F. Fleckenstein, B. Steder, L. Spinello, and W. Burgard. 2015. Accurate Indoor Localization for RGB-D Smartphones and Tablets Given 2D Floor Plans. In *IEEE/RSJ International Conference on Intelligent Robots and Systems (IROS)*.
[97] Grace Woo, Andy Lippman, and Ramesh Raskar. 2012. VRCodes: Unobtrusive and Active Visual Codes for Interaction by Exploiting Rolling Shutter. In *IEEE International Symposium on Mixed and Augmented Reality (ISMAR)*.
[98] Nan Xu, Fan Zhang, Yisha Luo, Weijia Jia, Dong Xuan, and Jin Teng. 2009. Stealthy Video Capturer: a New Video-Based Spyware in 3G smartphones. In *Proceedings of the ACM conference on Wireless Network Security (WiSec)*.
[99] Zhe Yang, Yuting Bao, Chuhao Luo, Xingya Zhao, Siyu Zhu, Chunyi Peng, Yunxin Liu, and Xinbing Wang. 2016. ARTcode: Preserve Art and Code in Any Image. In *ACM International Joint Conference on Pervasive and Ubiquitous Computing (UbiComp)*.
[100] Hong Heather Yu and Prabir Bhattacharya. 2006. Methods and apparatus for digital content protection. (2006). US Patent 7,006,630.
[101] Guangtao Zhai and Xiaolin Wu. 2014. Defeating camcorder piracy by temporal psychovisual modulation. *Journal of Display Technology* 10, 9 (2014), 754–757.
[102] Chi Zhang and Xinyu Zhang. 2016. LiTell: Robust Indoor Localization Using Unmodified Light Fixtures. In *Proc. of ACM MobiCom*.
[103] Chi Zhang and Xinyu Zhang. 2017. Pulsar: Towards Ubiquitous Visible Light Localization. In *Proc. of ACM MobiCom*.
[104] Lan Zhang, Cheng Bo, Jiahui Hou, Xiang-Yang Li, Yu Wang, Kebin Liu, and Yunhao Liu. 2015. Kaleido: You Can Watch It But Cannot Record It. In *ACM International Conference on Mobile Computing and Networking (MobiCom)*.
[105] Lan Zhang, Kebin Liu, Xiang-Yang Li, Cihang Liu, Xuan Ding, and Yunhao Liu. 2016. Privacy-friendly Photo Capturing and Sharing System. In *ACM International Joint Conference on Pervasive and Ubiquitous Computing (UbiComp)*.
[106] Shilin Zhu and Xinyu Zhang. 2017. Enabling High-Precision Visible Light Localization in Today's Buildings. In *Proc. of ACM MobiSys*.

Continuous Authentication for Voice Assistants

Huan Feng*, Kassem Fawaz*, and Kang G. Shin
University of Michigan
Ann Arbor, Michigan 48109
{huanfeng,kmfawaz,kgshin}@umich.edu

ABSTRACT

Voice has become an increasingly popular User Interaction (UI) channel, mainly contributing to the current trend of wearables, smart vehicles, and home automation systems. Voice assistants such as Alexa, Siri, and Google Now, have become our everyday fixtures, especially when/where touch interfaces are inconvenient or even dangerous to use, such as driving or exercising. The open nature of the voice channel makes voice assistants difficult to secure, and hence exposed to various threats as demonstrated by security researchers. To defend against these threats, we present VAuth, the first system that provides *continuous* authentication for voice assistants. VAuth is designed to fit in widely-adopted wearable devices, such as eyeglasses, earphones/buds and necklaces, where it collects the body-surface vibrations of the user and matches it with the speech signal received by the voice assistant's microphone. VAuth guarantees the voice assistant to execute *only* the commands that originate from the voice of the owner. We have evaluated VAuth with 18 users and 30 voice commands and find it to achieve 97% detection accuracy and less than 0.1% false positive rate, regardless of VAuth's position on the body and the user's language, accent or mobility. VAuth successfully thwarts various practical attacks, such as replay attacks, mangled voice attacks, or impersonation attacks. It also incurs low energy and latency overheads and is compatible with most voice assistants.

1 INTRODUCTION

Siri, Cortana, Google Now, and Alexa are becoming our everyday fixtures. Through voice interactions, these and other voice assistants allow us to place phone calls, send messages, check emails, schedule appointments, navigate to destinations, control smart appliances, and perform banking services. In numerous scenarios such as cooking, exercising or driving, voice interaction is preferable to traditional touch interfaces that are inconvenient or even dangerous to use (e.g., while driving). Furthermore, a voice interface is even essential for the increasingly prevalent Internet of Things (IoT) devices that lack touch capabilities [29].

With sound being an open channel, voice as an input mechanism is inherently insecure as it is prone to replay attacks, sensitive to noise, and easy to impersonate. Recent studies have even demonstrated that it is possible to inject voice commands stealthily and remotely with mangled voice [9, 39], wireless signals [17], or through public radio stations [26] without raising the user's attention. Existing voice authentication mechanisms, such as Google's "Trusted Voice" and Nuance's "FreeSpeech", used by banks [33], fail to provide the security features for voice assistant systems. An adversary can bypass these voice-as-biometric authentication mechanisms by impersonating the user's voice (a feature already enabled by commercial software [5]) or simply launching a replay attack. Researchers have already shown that voice morphing techniques can defeat human and machine-based speaker verification systems [30]. Even Google warns against its voice authentication feature as being insecure,[1] and some security companies [6] recommend relinquishing voice interfaces all together until security issues are resolved. The implications of attacking voice-assistant systems can be frightening, ranging from information theft and financial loss [25] all the way to inflicting physical harm via unauthorized access to smart appliances and vehicles.

To defend against these threats, we propose VAuth, a novel system that provides *continuous* authentication for voice assistant systems. Designed as a wearable security token, it supports on-going authentication by introducing an additional channel that provides physical assurance. Specifically, VAuth collects the body-surface vibrations of a user and continuously matches them to the voice commands received by the voice assistant. This way, VAuth ensures that the voice assistant executes *only* the commands that originate from the voice of the owner.

In this paper, we choose to implement VAuth using an accelerometer because of its extremely low energy footprint and its ability to collect on-body vibrations (the direct product of user's speech) which the attacker cannot readily compromise or alter. This, however, does not preclude utilizing other sensors (e.g., specialized microphones), in VAuth, that can achieve a similar functionality and security guarantees as for the accelerometer. VAuth offers the following salient features.

Continuous Authentication. VAuth specifically addresses the problem of continuous authentication of a speaker to a voice-enabled device. Most authentication mechanisms, including all smartphone-specific ones such as passwords, PINs, patterns, and fingerprints, provide security by proving the user's identity *before* establishing a session. They hinge on one underlying assumption: the user retains exclusive control of the device right after the authentication. While such an assumption is natural for touch interfaces, it is unrealistic for the case of voice assistants. Voice

*Co-primary authors.

[1]When a user tries to enable Trusted Voice on Nexus devices, Google explicitly warns that it is less secure than password and can be exploited by the attacker with a very similar voice.

MobiCom '17, October 16–20, 2017, Snowbird, UT, USA.

ISBN 978-1-4503-4916-1/17/10...$15.00
DOI: https://doi.org/10.1145/3117811.3117823

allows access for any third party during a communication session, rendering pre-session authentication insufficient. VAuth provides ongoing speaker authentication during an entire session by ensuring that every speech sample recorded by the voice assistant originates from the speaker's throat. Thus, VAuth complements existing mechanisms of initial session authentication and speaker recognition.

Improved Security Features. VAuth overcomes a major security problem of voice biometric authentication schemes: the possibility of the voice biometric information to be leaked or compromised. A voice biometric (akin to a fingerprint) is a long term property of an individual, and compromising it (e.g., through impersonating the owner's voice) renders the voice authentication insecure. Automated speech synthesis engines can construct a model of the owner's voice (thereby impersonating him/her) using a very limited number of his/her voice samples [30]. On the other hand, when losing VAuth for any reason, the user has to just unpair the token and pair a new one.

Many of the existing biometric-based authentication approaches try to reduce time-domain signals to a set of vocal features. Regardless of how descriptive the features are of the speech signal, they still represent a projection of the signal to a reduced-dimension space. Therefore, collisions are bound to happen; two different signals can result in the same feature vector. Such attacks weaken the security guarantees provided by almost all voice-biometric approaches [35]. In contrast, VAuth depends on the instantaneous consistency of the entire signal from the accelerometer and the microphone. Thus, it can identify even minor changes/manipulations of the signal.

Usability. A user can use VAuth out-of-the-box as it does not require any user-specific training, a drastic departure from existing voice biometric mechanisms. It only depends on the instantaneous consistency between the accelerometer and microphone signals. Therefore, VAuth is immune to voice changes over time and different situations, such as sickness (a sore throat) or tiredness – a major limitation of voice biometrics. VAuth provides its security features as long as it touches the user's skin at any position on the facial, throat, and sternum[2] areas. This allows us to incorporate VAuth into wearables that people are already using on a daily basis, such as eyeglasses, Bluetooth earbuds and necklaces/lockets. Our usability survey of 952 individuals revealed that users are willing to accept the different configurations of VAuth when it comes in the forms with which they are already comfortable.

Another issue that affects the usability of VAuth is the quality of the accelerometer and voice signals. In the real world, the microphone and accelerometer do not pick up clean signals, rendering their matching non-trivial. VAuth is equipped with a matching algorithm that can handle the noise and other artifacts in both the accelerometer and voice signals without sacrificing its security features.

We have built a prototype of VAuth using a commodity accelerometer and an off-the-shelf Bluetooth transmitter. Our implementation is integrated into the Google Now system in Android, and could easily extend to other voice-based platforms such as Cortana, Siri, or even phone banking services. VAuth can thus be utilized by individuals in enterprises and organizations with high-security requirements such as financial institutions. To demonstrate the effectiveness of VAuth, we recruited 18 participants and asked each of them to issue 30 different voice commands using VAuth. We repeated the experiments for three wearable scenarios: eyeglasses, earbuds and necklace. We found that VAuth:

- delivers results with 97% detection accuracy and close to 0.1% false positives. This indicates most of the commands are correctly authenticated from the first trial and VAuth only matches the command that originates from the owner;
- works out-of-the-box regardless of variation in accents, mobility (still vs. jogging), or even languages (Arabic, Chinese, English, Korean, Persian);
- effectively thwarts mangled voice attacks and blocks unauthenticated voice commands replayed by an attacker or impersonated by other users; and
- incurs low latency (an average of 300ms) and energy overhead (requiring re-charging only once a week).

The rest of the paper is organized as follows. Sections 2 and 3 discuss the related work and background. Section 4 states the system and threat models and Section 5 details the design and implementation of VAuth. We discuss our matching algorithm in Section 6, and conduct a phonetic-level analysis on the matching algorithm in Section 7. We evaluate VAuth's effectiveness in Section 8. Section 9 discusses different aspects of VAuth, and finally, the paper concludes with Section 10.

2 RELATED WORK

Smartphone Voice Assistants. Many researchers have studied the security issues of smartphone voice assistants [13, 17, 36, 39]. They have also demonstrated the possibility of injecting commands into voice assistants with electromagnetic signals [17] or with a mangled voice that is incomprehensible to humans [39]. These practical attack scenarios motivate us to build an authentication scheme for voice assistants. Petracca *et al.* [36] proposed a generic protection scheme for audio channels by tracking suspicious information flows. This solution prompts the user and requires manual review for *each* potential voice command. It thus suffers from the habituation and satisficing drawbacks since it interrupts the users from their primary tasks [14].

Voice Authentication. Most voice authentication schemes involve training on the user's voice samples and building a voice biometric [4, 10, 12, 18]. The biometric may depend on the user's vocal features or cultural backgrounds and requires rigorous training to perform well. There is no theoretical guarantee that they provide good security in general. Approaches in this category project the signal to a reduced-dimension space and collisions are thus inherent. In fact, most companies adopt these mechanisms for the usability benefits and claim they are not as secure as passwords or patterns [31]. Moreover, for the particular case of voice assistants, they all are vulnerable to simple replay attacks.

Mobile Sensing. Researchers have studied the potential applications of accelerometers for human behavior analysis [3, 24, 34, 42]. It has been shown possible to infer keyboard strokes [3], smartphone touch inputs [42] or passwords [3, 34] from acceleration

[2] The sternum is the bone that connects the rib cage; it vibrates as a result of the speech.

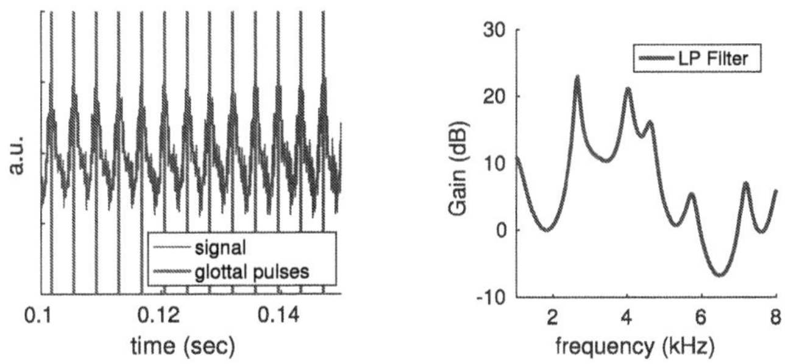

(a) Source (b) Filter

Figure 1: The source–filter model of human speech production using the vowel {i:} as an example.

information. There are also applications utilizing the correlation between sound and vibrations [20, 28] for health monitoring purposes. Doctors can thus detect voice disorder without actually collecting the user's daily conversations. These studies are very different from ours which focuses on *continuous* voice assistant security.

3 BACKGROUND

We introduce some basic concepts and terminology regarding the generation and processing of human speech, which will be referenced throughout the paper.

3.1 Human Speech Model

The production of human speech is commonly modeled as the combined effect of two separate processes [16]: a voice source (vibration of vocal folds) that generates the original signal and a filter (determined by the resonant properties of vocal tract including the influence of tongue and lips) that further modulates the signal. The output is a shaped spectrum with certain energy peaks, which together map to a specific phoneme (see Fig. 1(b) for the vowel {i:} – the vowel in the word "see"). This process is widely used and referred to as the *source-filter* model.

Fig. 1(a) shows an example of a female speaker pronouncing the vowel {i:}. The time separating each pair of peaks is the length of each glottal pulse (cycle). It also refers to the *instantaneous fundamental frequency* (f_0) variation while the user is speaking, which is the pitch of speaker's voice. The value of f_0 varies between 80 to 333Hz for a human speaker. The glottal cycle length (being the inverse of the fundamental frequency) varies 0.003sec and 0.0125sec. As the human speaker pronounces different phonemes in a particular word, the pitch changes accordingly, which becomes an important feature of speaker recognition. We utilize the fundamental frequency (f_0) as a reference to filter signals that fall outside of the human speech range.

3.2 Speech Recognition and MFCC

The most widely used features for speech recognition tasks are Mel-frequency cepstral coefficients (MFCC) [21], which models the way humans perceive sounds. In particular, these features are computed on short-term windows when the signal is assumed to be stationary. To compute the MFCCs, the speech recognition system computes the short-term Fourier transform of the signal, then scales the frequency axis to the non-linear Mel scale (a set of Mel bands). Then, the Discrete Cosine Transform (DCT) is computed on the log of the power spectrum of each Mel band. This technique works well in speech recognition because it tracks the invariant feature of human speech across different users. However, it also opens the door to potential attacks: by generating mangled voice segments with the same MFCC feature, an attacker can trick the voice assistant into executing specific voice commands without drawing any attention from the user.

4 SYSTEM AND THREAT MODELS

4.1 System Model

VAuth consists of two components. The first is wearable, housing an accelerometer that touches the user's skin at any position on the facial, throat, and sternum areas. This allows us to incorporate it into wearables that people are already using on a daily basis, such as eyeglasses, Bluetooth earbuds and necklaces/lockets. It constitutes a specialized "microphone" that only registers the user's voice via his body, providing a physical security guarantee. The second component is an extended voice assistant that issues voice commands after correlating and verifying both the accelerometer signal from the wearable device and the microphone signal collected by the assistant. VAuth is not only compatible with smartphone voice assistants such as Siri and Google Now, but also applies to voice systems in other domains such as Amazon Alexa and phone-based authentication systems used by banks.

We assume the communications between the two components are encrypted. Attacks to this communication channel are orthogonal to our work. We also assume the wearable device serves as a secure token that the user will not share with others. The latter is known as *security by possession*, which is widely adopted in the security field in the form of authentication rings [40], wristbands [23], or RSA SecurID. Thus, the problem of authenticating the wearable token to the user is orthogonal to VAuth and has been addressed elsewhere [11]. Instead, we focus on the problem of authenticating voice commands, assuming the existence of a trusted wearable device.

4.2 Threat Model

We consider an attacker who is interested in stealing private information or conducting unauthorized operations by exploiting the voice assistant of the target user. Typically, the attacker tries to hijack the voice assistant of the target user and deceive it into executing mal-intended voice commands, such as sending text messages to premium phone numbers or conducting bank transactions. The results can be much more serious considering voice is becoming the most promising UI interface for controlling smart home appliances and vehicles. The adversary mounts the attack by interfering with the audio channel. This does not assume the attacker has to be physically at the same location as the target. It can utilize equipment that can generate a sound on its behalf, such as radio channels or high-gain speakers. Specifically, we consider the following three categories of attack scenarios.

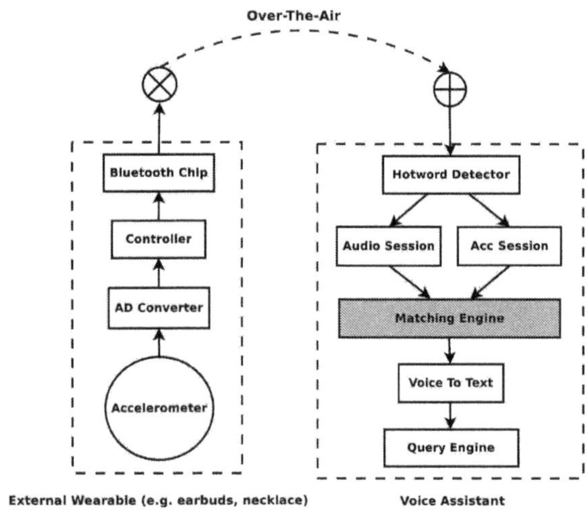

Figure 2: The high-level design of VAuth, consisting of the wearable and the voice assistant extension.

Scenario A – Stealthy Attack. The attacker attempts to inject either inaudible or incomprehensible voice commands through wireless signals [17] or mangled voice commands [9, 39]. This attack is stealthy in the sense that the victim may not even be aware of the on-going threat. It is also preferable to the attacker when the victim has physical control or within proximity of the voice assistant.

Scenario B – Biometric-override Attack. The attacker attempts to inject voice commands [35] by replaying a previously recorded clip of the victim's voice, or by impersonating the victim's voice. This attack can have a very low technical barrier: we found that by simply mimicking the victim's voice, an attacker can bypass the Trusted Voice feature of Google Now within five trials, even when the attacker and the victim are of different genders.

Scenario C – Acoustic Injection Attack. The attacker can be more advanced, trying to generate a voice that has a direct effect on the accelerometer [38]. The intention is to override VAuth's verification channel with high energy vibrations. For example, the attacker can play very loud music which contains embedded patterns of voice commands.

5 VAUTH

We present the high-level design of VAuth, describe our prototype implementation with Google Now, and elaborate on its usability aspects.

5.1 High-Level Overview

VAuth consists of two components: (1) a wearable component, responsible for collecting and uploading the accelerometer data, and (2) a voice assistant extension, responsible for authenticating and launching the voice commands. We chose to employ an accelerometer instead of an additional microphone because the accelerometer does not register voice (vibrations) through the air, thus providing a better security guarantee. The first component easily incorporates into existing wearable products, such as earbuds/earphones/headsets, eyeglasses, or necklaces/lockets.

When a user triggers the voice assistant, for example, by saying "OK, Google" or "Hey, Siri", our voice assistant extension collects accelerometer data from the wearable component, correlates it with signals collected from microphone and issues the command only when there is a match. It is worth noting that the wearable component of VAuth stays in an idle mode (idle connection and no accelerometer sampling) and only wakes up when it receives a trigger from the voice assistant extension. After the command finishes, the wearable component goes back to its idle mode. This helps reduce the energy consumption of VAuth's wearable component by reducing its duty cycle.

Fig. 2 depicts the information flows in VAuth. To reduce the processing burden on the user's device, the matching does not take place on the device (that runs the voice assistant), but rather at the server side. The communication between the wearable component and the voice assistant takes place over Bluetooth BR/EDR [7]. Bluetooth Classic is an attractive choice as a communication channel, since it has a relatively high data rate (up to 2Mbps), is energy-efficient, and enables secure communication through its pairing procedure. Upon losing the wearable component of VAuth, the user has to just unpair it with the voice assistant. This unpairing prevents an attacker from misusing a stolen wearable component to access the user's voice assistants.

5.2 Prototype

To build the wearable component, we use a Knowles BU-27135 miniature accelerometer with the dimension of only 7.92×5.59×2.28mm so that it can easily fit in any wearable design. The accelerometer uses only the z-axis and has an *analog* bandwidth of 11kHz, enough to capture the bandwidth of a speech signal, as opposed to the accelerometers available in commercial wearables with typical bandwidth of 200Hz. We utilize an external Bluetooth transmitter that provides Analog-to-Digital Conversion (ADC) and Bluetooth transmission capabilities to the voice assistant extension. To reduce energy consumption, VAuth starts streaming the accelerometer signal only upon request from the voice assistant. Our prototype communicates the microphone and accelerometer signals to a Matlab-based server which performs the matching and returns the result to the voice assistant. Fig. 3 depicts our wireless prototype standalone and attached to a pair of eyeglasses.

Our system is integrated with the Google Now voice assistant to enable voice command authentication. VAuth starts execution immediately after the start of a voice session (right after "OK Google" is recognized). It blocks the voice assistant's command execution after the voice session ends until the matching result becomes available. If the matching fails, VAuth kills the voice session. To achieve its functionality, VAuth intercepts both the `HotwordDetector` and the `QueryEngine` to establish the required control flow.

We implement our voice assistant extension as a standalone user-level service. It is responsible for retrieving the accelerometer signals from the wearable device and sending both accelerometer and microphone to our Matlab-based server for analysis. The user-level service provides two RPC methods, `start` and end, which are triggered by the events generated when the hotword "OK Google"

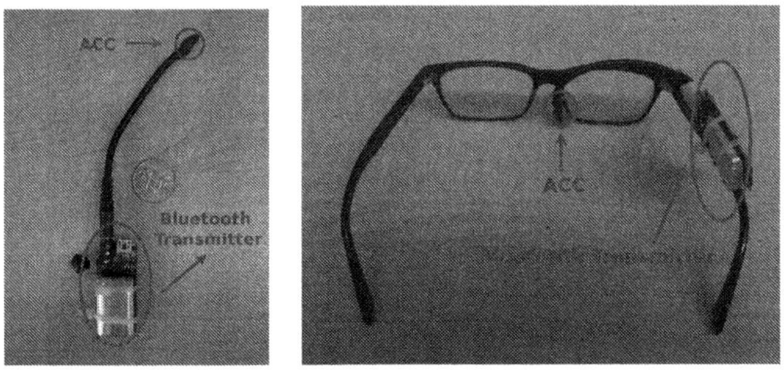

(a) Wireless (b) Eyeglasses

Figure 3: Our prototype of VAuth, featuring the accelerometer chip and Bluetooth transmitter, (a) compared to US quarter coin and (b) attached to a pair of eyeglasses belonging to one of the authors.

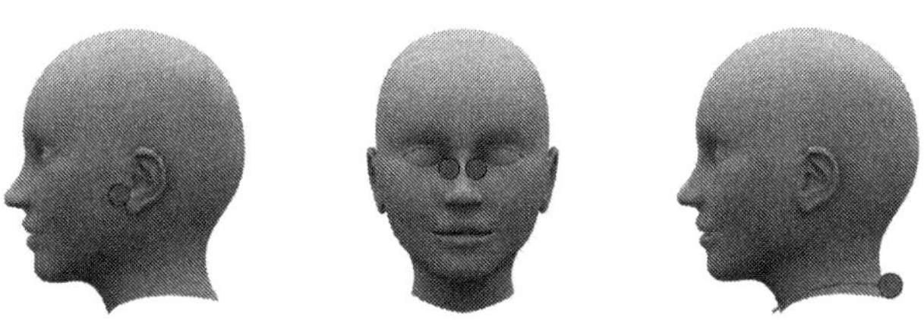

(a) Earbuds (b) Eyeglasses (c) Necklace

Figure 4: The wearable scenarios supported by VAuth.

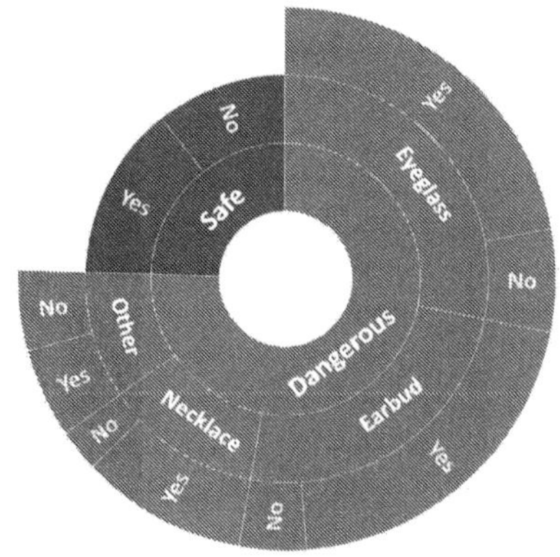

Figure 5: A breakdown of respondents' wearability preference by security concern and daily wearables. *Dangerous* and *Safe* refer to participants' attitudes towards the attacks to voice assistants after they've been informed; the *Dangerous* category is further split according to the wearables that people are already wearing on a daily basis; *Yes* and *No* refer to whether participants are willing to use VAuth in at least one of three settings we provided.

is detected, and when the query (command) gets executed, respectively. The first event can be observed by filtering the Android system logs, and we intercept the second by overriding the Android IPC mechanisms, by filtering the Intents sent by Google Now.

Note that the above modifications and interceptions (in the Android framework) are necessary only because Google Now is closed source. The incorporation of VAuth is straightforward in the cases when developers try to build/extend their voice assistant.

5.3 Usability

VAuth requires the user to wear a security-assisting device. Since security has always been a secondary concern for users [41], we design VAuth in a way such that it can be easily embedded into existing wearable products that the users are already comfortable with in their daily lives. Our prototype supports three widely-adopted wearable scenarios: earbuds/earphones/headsets, eyeglasses, and necklace/lockets. Fig. 4 shows the positions of the accelerometer in each scenario. We select these areas because they have consistent contact with the user's body. While VAuth performs well on all facial areas, shoulders and the sternal surface, we only focus on the three positions shown in Fig. 4 since they conform with widely-adopted wearables.

We have conducted a survey to evaluate the users' acceptance of the different configurations of VAuth with 952 participants using Amazon Mechanical Turk. We restricted the respondent pool to those from the US with previous experience with voice assistants; 58% of them reported using a voice assistant at least once a week. We follow the USE questionnaire methodology [22] to measure the usability aspects of VAuth. We use a 7-point Likert scale (ranging from Strongly Disagree to Strongly Agree) to assess the user's satisfaction with a certain aspect or configuration of VAuth. We pose the questions in the form of how much the respondent agrees with a certain statement, such as: *I am willing to wear a necklace that contains the voice assistant securing technology.* Below, we report a favorable result as the portion of respondents who answered a question with a score higher than 4 (5,6,7) on the 7-point scale. Next to each result, we report the portion of those surveyed, between brackets, who answered the question with a score higher than 5 (6 or 7).

We first asked the respondents about their opinion regarding the security of voice assistants. Initially, 86% (63%) of the respondents indicate that they think the voice assistants are secure. After being primed about the security risks by iterating the attacks presented in Section 4, the respondents' perceptions shifted considerably. 71% (51%) of the respondents indicate that attacks to voice assistants are dangerous, and 75%(52%) specified that they would take steps to mitigate the threats. This suggests that serious efforts remain to be made to raise the public awareness of the security concerns of voice assistants.

Then, we study the perception of using VAuth from individuals who are already aware of the security problems of voice assistants. We ask the participants about their preferences for wearing VAuth in any of the three configurations of Fig. 4. We have the following takeaways from the analysis of survey responses.

- 70%(47%) of the participants are willing to wear at least one of VAuth's configurations to provide security protection.

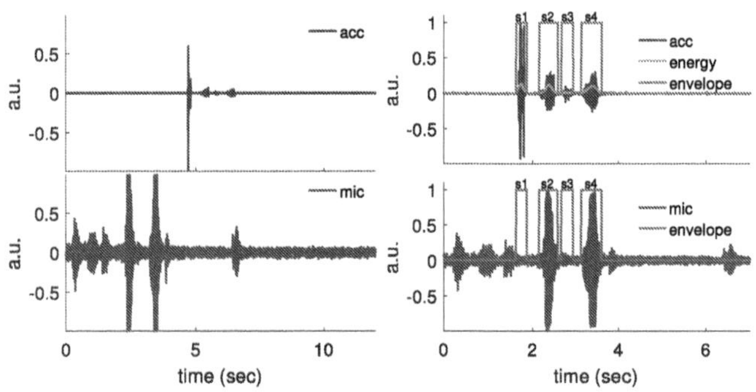

(a) Raw input signals (b) Energy envelopes

Figure 6: Pre-processing stage of VAuth's matching.

Specifically, 48% (29%) of the respondents favored the earbuds/earphone/headset option, 38% (23%) favored the eyeglasses option and 35% (19%) favored the necklace/locket option.

- As expected, the findings fit the respondents' wearables in their daily lives. 71% of the respondents who wear earbuds on a daily basis favored that option for VAuth, 60% for eyeglasses and 63% for the necklace option.
- There is no discrepancy in the wearable options among both genders. The gender distribution of each wearable option followed the same gender distribution of the whole respondent set.
- 75% of the users are willing to pay $10 more for a wearable equipped with this technology while more than half are willing to pay $25 more.

Fig. 5 presents a breakdown of the major findings from our usability survey. These results demonstrate that users are willing to accept the different configurations of VAuth, when they are well-educated about the privacy/security threats and when VAuth comes in the form with which they are already comfortable.

6 MATCHING ALGORITHM

To enable the useful scenarios we described in the previous section, the matching algorithm of VAuth (highlighted in Fig. 2) needs to be (1) resilient to the different placements of the accelerometer, while being (2) sensitive enough to identify even minor discrepancies of potentially modified microphone signals.

The matching algorithm of VAuth takes as input the speech and vibration signals along with their corresponding sampling frequencies. It outputs a decision value indicating whether there is a match between the two signals as well as a "cleaned" speech signal in case of a match. VAuth performs the matching in three stages: *pre-processing*, *speech segments analysis*, and *matching decision*. In what follows, we elaborate on VAuth's matching algorithm using a running example of a male speaker recording the two words: "cup" and "luck" with a short pause between them. The speech signal is sampled by an accelerometer from the lowest point on the sternum at 64kHz and recorded from a built-in laptop (HP workstation) microphone at a sampling frequency of 44.1kHz, 50cm away from the speaker.

6.1 Pre-processing

First, VAuth applies a highpass filter which removes all the artifacts of the low-frequency movement to the accelerometer signal (such as walking or breathing) and negates the effect of other environmental vibrations (such as the user being on a subway platform). We use 100Hz as a cutoff threshold because humans cannot generate more than 100 mechanical movements per second. VAuth then re-samples both accelerometer and microphone signals to the same sampling rate while applying a low-pass filter to prevent aliasing.

Second, VAuth normalizes the magnitude of both signals to have a maximum magnitude of unity, which necessitates removal of the spikes in the signals. Otherwise, the lower-energy components referring to the actual speech will not be recovered. The matching algorithm computes a running average of the signal's energy and enforces a cut-off threshold, keeping only the signals with energy level within the moving average plus six standard deviation levels.

After normalizing the signal magnitude, as shown in the top plot of Fig. 6(b), VAuth aligns both signals by finding the time shift that results in the maximum cross correlation of both signals. Note that VAuth does not utilize more sophisticated alignment algorithms such as Dynamic Time Warping (DTW), since they remove timing information critical to the signal's pitch and require a higher processing load. Fig. 6(b) shows both accelerometer and microphone signals aligned and normalized.

The next pre-processing step includes identification of the energy envelope of the accelerometer signal. VAuth identifies the parts of the signal that have a significant signal-to-noise ratio (SNR). These are the "bumps" of the signal's energy as shown in the top plot of Fig. 6(b). This results in four energy segments of the accelerometer signal of Fig. 6(b). The thresholds for energy detection depend on the average noise level (due to ADC chip's sampling and quantization) when the user is silent.

Finally, VAuth applies the accelerometer envelope to the microphone signal so that it removes all parts from the microphone signal that did not result from body vibrations, as shown in the bottom plot of Fig. 6(b). This is the first real step towards providing the security guarantees. In most cases, it avoids attacks on voice assistant systems when the user is not actively speaking. Inadvertently, it improves the accuracy of the voice recognition by removing background noise and sounds from the speech signals that could not have been generated by the user.

6.2 Per-Segment Analysis

Once it identifies high-energy segments of the accelerometer signal, VAuth starts a segment-by-segment matching. For each segment, VAuth normalizes the signal magnitude to unity to remove the effect of other segments, such as the effect of the segment *s1* in Fig. 6(b). VAuth then applies the approach of Boersma [8] to extract the glottal cycles from each segment. The approach relies on the identification of periodic patterns in the signal as the local maxima of the auto-correlation function of the signal. Thus, each segment is associated with a series of glottal pulses as shown in Fig. 7. VAuth uses information about the segment and the corresponding glottal pulses to filter out the segments that do not correspond to human speech. Specifically, we keep only those segments with the average

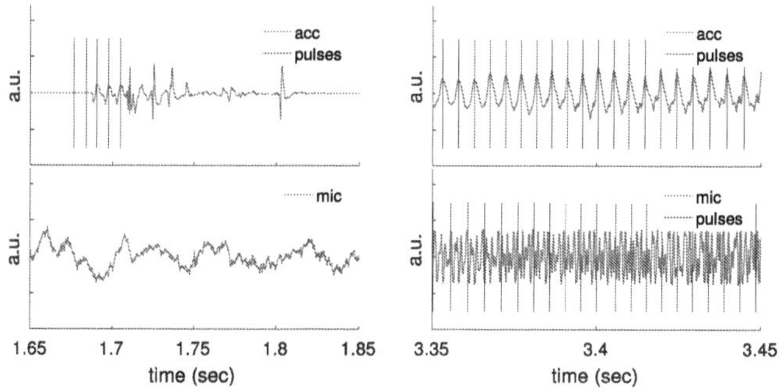

(a) Non-matching segment *s1* (b) matching segment *s4*

Figure 7: Per-segment analysis stage of VAuth.

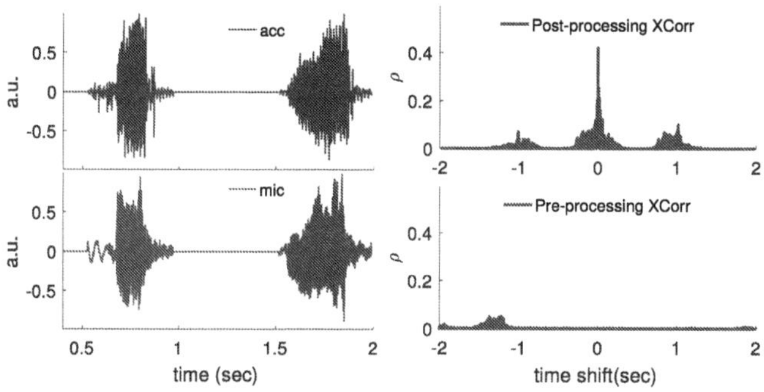

(a) Output signals (b) Cross correlation

Figure 8: Matching decision stage of VAuth's matching.

fundamental frequency falling into the human speech range ([80Hz, 333 Hz]).

Also, if the average relative distance between glottal pulse sequence between the accelerometer and microphone segments is higher than 25%, then VAuth removes the segment from both signals. This refers to the case of interfered speech (e.g., attacker trying to inject speech); the instantaneous pitch variations should be similar between the accelerometer and microphone [27] in the absence of external interference. For example, it is evident that the pitch information is very different between the accelerometer and microphone of Fig. 7(a).

After performing all the above filtering steps, VAuth does a final verification step by running a normalized cross correlation between the accelerometer and microphone segments. If the maximum correlation coefficient falls inside the range [-0.25,0.25], then the segments are discarded. We use this range as a conservative way of specifying that the segments do not match (correlation coefficient close to zero). The correlation is a costlier operation but is a known metric for signal similarity that takes into consideration all the information of the time-domain signals. For example, the segment "s4" depicted in Fig. 7(b) shows matching pitch information and a maximum cross-correlation coefficient of 0.52.

6.3 Matching Decision

After the segment-based analysis finishes, only the "surviving" segments comprise the final accelerometer and microphone signals. In Fig. 8(a), only the segments "s2" and "s4" correspond to matching speech components. It is evident from the bottom plot that the microphone signal has two significant components referring to each word.

The final step is to produce a matching decision. VAuth measures the similarity between the two signals by using the normalized cross-correlation, as shown in the top plot of Fig. 8(b). VAuth cannot just perform the cross-correlation on the input signals before cleaning. Before cleaning the signal, the cross-correlation results do not have any real indication of signal similarity. Consider the lower plot of Fig. 8(b), which corresponds to the cross-correlation performed on the original input signals of Fig. 6(a). As evident from the plot, the cross-correlation shows absolutely no similarity between the two signals, even though they describe the same speech sample.

Instead of manually constructing rules that map the cross-correlation vector to a *matching* or *non-matching* decision, we opted to utilize a machine learning-based classifier to increase the accuracy of VAuth's matching. Below, we elaborate on the three components of VAuth's classifier: the feature set, the machine learning algorithm and the training set.

Feature Set. The feature vector comprises the normalized cross-correlation values ($h(t)$) of the final accelerometer and microphone signals. However, we need to ensure that the structure of the feature vector is uniform across all matching tasks. To populate the feature vector, we identify the maximum value of $h(t)$, and then uniformly sample 500 points to the left and another 500 to the right of the maximum. We end up with a feature vector containing 1001 values, centered at the maximum value of the normalized cross-correlation.

Classifier. We opted to use SVM as the classifier thanks to its ability to deduce linear relations between the cross-correlation values that define the feature vector. We utilize Weka [15] to train an SVM using the Sequential Minimal Optimization (SMO) algorithm [37]. The SMO algorithm uses a logistic calibrator with neither standardization nor normalization to train the SVM. The SVM utilizes a polynomial kernel with the degree equal to 1. We use the trained model in our prototype to perform the online classification.

Training Set. We recorded (more on that in Section 7) all 44 English phonemes (24 vowels and 20 consonants) from one of the authors at the lower sternum position using both the accelerometer and microphone. Hence, we have 44 accelerometer and microphone pair of recordings corresponding for each English phoneme. To generate the training set, we ran VAuth's matching over all 44 × 44 accelerometer and microphone recordings to generate 1936 initial feature vectors and labeled them accordingly.

Here, it is critical to specify that VAuth's classifier is trained *offline*, only *once* and *only* using a single training set. The classifier is thus agnostic of the user, position on the body and language. In our user study and rest of the evaluation of Section 8, this (same) classifier is used to perform all the matching. To use VAuth, the user *need not* perform any initial training.

Table 1: The IPA chart of English phonetics.

Vowel	Examples	Consonants	Examples
ʌ	CUP, LUCK	b	BAD, LAB
ɑː	ARM, FATHER	d	DID, LADY
æ	CAT, BLACK	f	FIND, IF
e	MET, BED	g	GIVE, FLAG
ə	AWAY, CINEMA	h	HOW, HELLO
ɜː^{r}	TURN, LEARN	j	YES, YELLOW
ɪ	HIT, SITTING	k	CAT, BACK
iː	SEE, HEAT	l	LEG, LITTLE
ɒ	HOT, ROCK	m	MAN, LEMON
ɔː	CALL, FOUR	n	NO, TEN
ʊ	PUT, COULD	ŋ	SING, FINGER
uː	BLUE, FOOD	p	PET, MAP
aɪ	FIVE, EYE	r	RED, TRY
aʊ	NOW, OUT	s	SUN, MISS
eɪ	SAY, EIGHT	ʃ	SHE, CRASH
oʊ	GO, HOME	t	TEA, GETTING
ɔɪ	BOY, JOIN	tʃ	CHECK, CHURCH
eə^{r}	WHERE, AIR	θ	THINK, BOTH
ɪə^{r}	NEAR, HERE	ð	THIS, MOTHER
ʊə^{r}	PURE, TOURIST	v	VOICE, FIVE
-	-	w	WET, WINDOW
-	-	z	ZOO, LAZY
-	-	ʒ	PLEASURE, VISION
-	-	dʒ	JUST, LARGE

After computing the matching result, VAuth passes the final (cleaned and normalized) microphone signal to the voice assistant system to execute the speech recognition and other functionality.

7 PHONETIC-LEVEL ANALYSIS

We evaluate the effectiveness of our matching algorithm on phonetic-level matchings/authentications. The International Phonetic Alphabet (IPA) standardizes the representation of sounds of oral languages based on the Latin alphabet. While the number of words in a language, and therefore the sentences, can be uncountable, the number of phonemes in the English language are limited to 44 vowels and consonants. By definition, any English word or sentence, as spoken by a human, is necessarily a combination of those phonemes [19]. Our phonetic-level evaluation represents a baseline of VAuth's operation.

We study if VAuth can correctly match the English phoneme between the accelerometer and microphone (true positives), and whether it mistakenly matches phoneme samples from accelerometer to other phoneme samples from the microphone (false positives). We recruited two speakers, a male and a female, to record the 44 examples listed in Table 1. Each example comprises two words, separated by a brief pause, both representing a particular phoneme. We asked the speaker to say both words, not just the phoneme, as it is easier for the speaker to pronounce the phoneme in the context of a word. Both speakers were wearing VAuth, with the accelerometer taped to the sternum.

7.1 Accelerometer Energy & Recognition

Phonemes originate from a possibly different part of the chest-mouth-nasal area. In what follows, we show that each phoneme results in vibrations that the accelerometer chip of VAuth can register, but does not retain enough acoustic features to substitute a microphone speech signal for the purpose of voice recognition. This explains our rationale for employing the matching-based approach.

All phonemes register vibrations, with the minimum relative energy (accelerometer relative to microphone) coming from the ɔɪ (the pronunciation of "oy" in "boy") phoneme of the male speaker.

Table 2: The detection accuracy for the English phonemes.

microphone	accelerometer	TP (%)	FP (%)
consonants	consonants	90	0.2
consonants	vowels	-	1.0
vowels	consonants	-	0.2
vowels	vowels	100	1.7
all	all	94	0.7

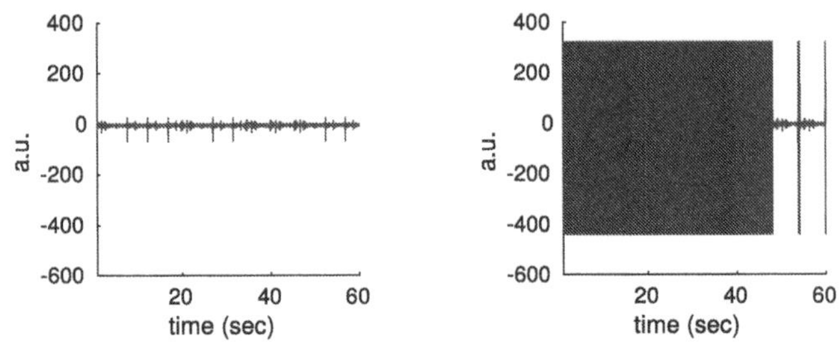

(a) Low energy and white noise (b) High energy and periodic noise

Figure 9: Examples of tested noise signals.

While the accelerometer chip senses considerable energy from the chest vibrations, it cannot substitute for the microphone. To confirm this, we passed the recorded and cleaned accelerometer samples of all phonemes for both speakers to the Nuance Automatic Speaker Recognition (ASR) API [32]. The state-of-the-art ASR engine fails to identify the actual spoken words. In particular, for about half of the phonemes for both speakers, the ASR fails to return any result. For the rest of the phonemes, Nuance API returns three suggestions for each accelerometer sample. The majority of these results do not match any of the spoken words. In only three cases for consonants phonemes for both speakers, the API returns a result that matches at least one of the spoken words.

The above indicates that existing ASR engines cannot interpret the often low-fidelity accelerometer samples, but it does not indicate that ASR engines cannot be retrofitted to recognize samples with higher accuracy. This will, however, require significant changes to deploying and training these systems. On the other hand, VAuth is an entirely client-side solution that requires no changes to the ASR engine or the voice assistant system.

7.2 Phonemes Detection Accuracy

We then evaluate the accuracy of detecting each phoneme for each speaker as well as the false positive across phonemes and speakers. In particular, we run VAuth to match each accelerometer sample (88 samples — corresponding to each phoneme and speaker) to all the collected microphone samples; each accelerometer sample must match only one microphone sample. Table 2 shows the matching results.

First, we match the consonant phonemes across the two speakers as evident in the first row. The true positive rate exceeds 90%, showing that VAuth can correctly match the vast majority of consonant phonemes. We also report the false positive rate which indicates the instances where VAuth matches an accelerometer sample to the inappropriate microphone sample. As shown in the same figure, the false positive rate is very low. Using the Hoeffding bound, it is easy to show (we do not provide this proof because of space constraints) that the false positive rate of a sentence comprising more phonemes decays exponentially fast in the number of phonemes. As such, the false positive rate of phonemes matching is only a (loose) upper bound of the whole sentence matching. Our evaluation in Section 8 further supports this property of VAuth. We also show that this non-zero false positive rate does not constitute a viable attack vector.

Moreover, a phoneme contains speaker-independent features. VAuth overcomes these similar features to successfully distinguish the same phoneme across the two speakers. The fourth row of Table 2 shows comparable results when attempting to match the vowel phonemes for both speakers.

The second and third rows complete the picture of phoneme matching, showing the matching results of the vowel to the consonant phonemes for both speakers. Both rows do not contain true positive values as there are no phoneme matches. Finally, the fifth row shows results of matching all the accelerometer samples to all the microphone samples. The true positive rate is 93%, meaning that VAuth correctly matched 82 accelerometer samples matched to their microphone counterparts. Moreover, the false positive rate was only 0.6%.

7.3 Idle Detection Accuracy

Last but not least, we evaluate another notion of false positives: VAuth mistakenly matches external speech to a silent user. We record idle (the user not actively speaking) segments from VAuth's accelerometer and attempt to match them to the recorded phonemes of both participants. We considered two types of idle segments: the first contains no energy from speech or other movements (Fig. 9(a)), while the other contains significant abrupt motion of the accelerometer resulting in recordings with high energy spikes (similar to the spike of Fig. 6(a)). We also constructed a high energy noise signal with periodic patterns as shown in Fig. 9(b).

We executed VAuth over the different idle segments and microphone samples and recorded the false matching decisions. In all of the experiments, we did not observe any occurrence of a false matching of an idle accelerometer signal to any phoneme from the microphone for both speakers. As recorded phonemes are representative of all possible sounds comprising the English language, we can be confident that the false positive rate of VAuth is zero in practice for silent users.

8 EVALUATION

We now evaluate the efficacy of VAuth in identifying common voice assistant commands, under different scenarios and for different speakers. VAuth is shown to achieve a matching accuracy exceeding 95% (True Positives, TPs) regardless of its position on the body, user accents, mobility patterns, or even across different languages except for the Korean language — which we will describe later. Since the TP rate is high, the False Negative rate is very low (less than 5%), meaning that the user need not repeat the command to get a positive match in the absence of an attacker. Moreover, we elaborate on the security properties of VAuth, demonstrating its effectiveness in thwarting various attacks. Finally, we report the delay and energy consumption of our wearable prototypes.

Table 3: The list of commands to evaluate VAuth.

Command	Command
1. How old is Neil deGrasse Tyson?	16. Remind me to buy coffee at 7am from Starbucks
2. What does colloquial mean?	17. What is my schedule for tomorrow?
3. What time is it now in Tokyo?	18. Where's my Amazon package?
4. Search for professional photography tips	19. Make a note: update my router firmware
5. Show me pictures of the Leaning Tower of Pisa	20. Find Florence Ion's phone number
6. Do I need an umbrella today? What's the weather like?	21. Show me my bills due this week
7. What is the Google stock price?	22. Show me my last messages.
8. What's 135 divided by 7.5?	23. Call Jon Smith on speakerphone
9. Search Tumblr for cat pictures	24. Text Susie great job on that feature yesterday
10. Open greenbot.com	25. Where is the nearest sushi restaurant?
11. Take a picture	26. Show me restaurants near my hotel
12. Open Spotify	27. Play some music
13. Turn on Bluetooth	28. What's this song?
14. What's the tip for 123 dollars?	29. Did the Giants win today?
15. Set an alarm for 6:30 am	30. How do you say good night in Japanese?

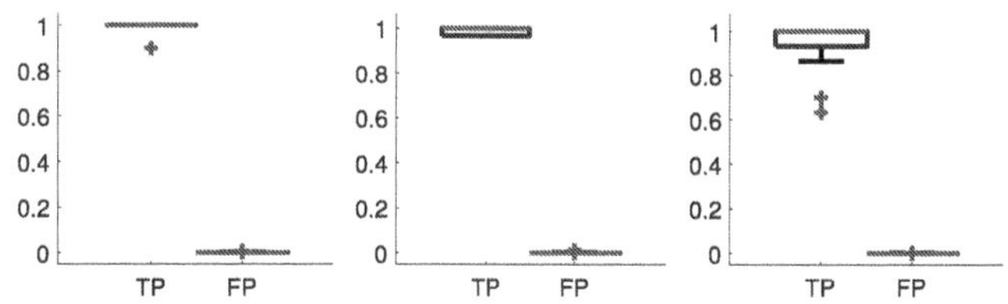

(a) earbuds (b) eyeglasses (c) necklace

Figure 10: The detection accuracy of VAuth for the 18 users in the still position.

8.1 User Study

To support the conclusions derived from our model, we conducted a detailed user study of the VAuth prototype with 18 users and under six different scenarios. We tested how VAuth performs at three positions, each corresponding to a different form of wearable (Fig. 4) eyeglasses, earbuds, and necklace. At each position, we tested two cases, asking the user to either stand still or jog. In each scenario, we asked the participants to speak 30 phrases/commands (listed in Table 3). These phrases represent common commands issued to the "Google Now" voice assistant. In what follows, we report VAuth's detection accuracy (TPs) and false positives (FPs) when doing a pairwise matching of the commands for each participant. We collected no personally identifiable information from the individuals, and the data collection was limited to our set of commands and posed no privacy risk to the participants. As such, we obtained non-regulated status from the IRB of our institution.

Still. VAuth delivers an overall detection accuracy rate (TPs) that is very close to 100% (97% on average). This indicates most of the commands are correctly authenticated from the first trial, and VAuth does not introduce a usability burden to the user. The false positive rate is 0.09% on average, suggesting that very few signals will leak through our filtering. Note that the non-zero false positive rate does not constitute a viable attack vector.

These false positive events occurred because after our matching algorithm removes all non-matching segments from both signals, the remaining segments of the microphone signal and accelerometer

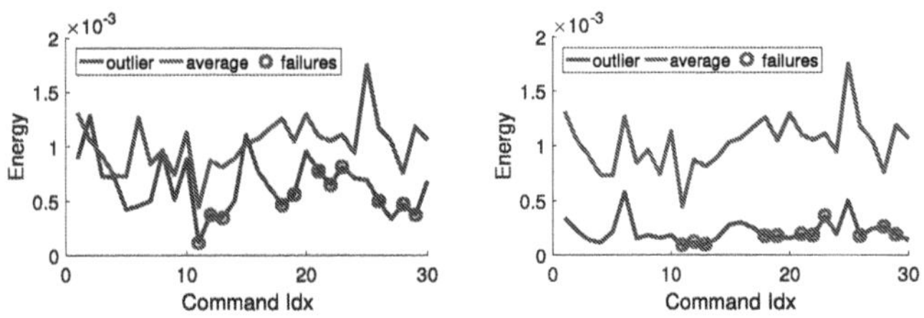

Figure 11: The energy levels of the outlier users (in Fig. 10(c)) compared to average users. The circles represent commands of the outlier users that VAuth fails to match.

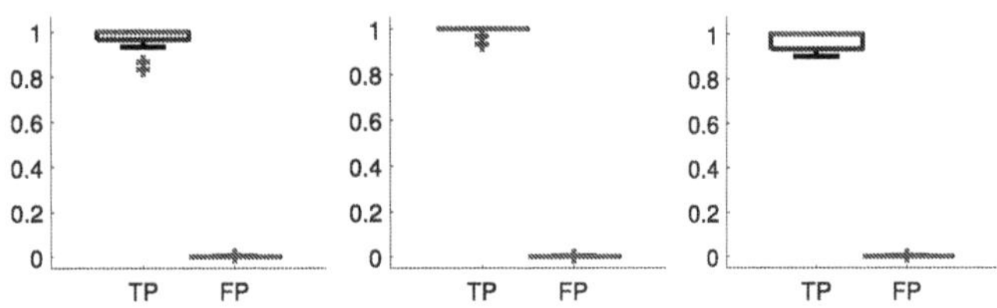

Figure 12: The detection accuracy of VAuth for the 18 users in the moving position.

signal accidentally match. In fact, what was eventually received by the voice assistants contains no semantic information and sounds very like random noise. The voice recognition system (Voice-to-Text) fails to pick them up as sensible voice commands. Fig. 10 shows the overall distribution of detection results for each scenario.

VAuth presents with a median detection accuracy of 100% in two wearable scenarios, eyeglasses and earbuds, but has two significant outliers in the case of the necklace. We investigated the commands that VAuth fails to recognize and found they happen when there are significant energy dips in the voice level. Fig. 11 reports the energy levels of the voice sessions for the two outlier users compared to the average across users. This suggests both participants had a lower (than average) voice when performing the experiments which did not generate enough energy to achieve the authentication.

Mobility. We asked the participants to repeat the experiments at each position while jogging. Our algorithm successfully filters the disturbances introduced by moving, breathing and VAuth's match accuracy remains unaffected (see Fig. 12). In fact, we noticed in certain cases, such as for the two outliers observed in our previous experiments, the results are even better. We studied the difference between their samples in the two scenarios and found both accelerometer and microphone received significantly higher energy in the jogging scenario even after we filtered out the signals introduced by movement. One explanation is that users are aware of the disturbance introduced by jogging and try to use louder voice to compensate. This observation is consistent across most of our participants, not just limited to the two outliers.

Table 4: The detection accuracy of VAuth for the 4 different languages.

Scenario	Language	TP (%)	FP (%)
earbuds	Arabic	100	0.1
	Chinese	100	0
	Korean	100	0
	Persian	96.7	0.1
eyeglasses	Arabic	100	0
	Chinese	96.7	0
	Korean	76.7	0
	Persian	96.7	0
necklace	Arabic	100	0
	Chinese	96.7	0
	Korean	96.7	0
	Persian	100	0

Table 5: The protections offered by VAuth.

Scenario	Adversary	Example	Silent User	Speaking User
A	Stealthy	mangled voice, wireless-based	✔	✔
B	Biometric Override	replay, user impersonation	✔	✔
C	Acoustic Injection	direct communication, loud voice	distance cut-off	distance cut-off

Language. We translated the list of 30 commands into four other languages — Arabic, Chinese, Korean and Persian — and recruited four native speakers of these languages. We asked the participants to place and use VAuth at the same three positions. As shown in Table 4, VAuth performs surprisingly well, even though the VAuth prototype was trained on English phonemes (Section 6.3). VAuth delivers detection accuracy of 97% (100% in some cases), except for one case, with the user speaking Korean when wearing eyeglasses. The Korean language lacks nasal consonants and thus does not generate enough vibrations through the nasal bone [43].

8.2 Security Properties

In Section 4, we listed three types of adversaries against which we aim to protect the voice assistants. Table 5 lists the protections offered by VAuth, when the user is silent or actively speaking, for each attack scenario.

Silent User. When the user is silent, VAuth completely prevents any unauthorized access to the voice assistant. In Section 7.3, we evaluate the false positive rate of VAuth mistakenly classifying noise while the user is silent for all English phonemes. VAuth is shown to have a zero false positive rate. When the user is silent, the adversary *cannot inject* any command for the voice assistant, especially for scenarios A and B of Section 4. There might be an exception, however, for scenario C; an adversary can employ a very loud sound to induce vibrations at the accelerometer chip of VAuth. Note that, since the accelerometer only senses vibrations at the z-axis, the attacker must make the extra effort to direct the sound wave perpendicular to the accelerometer sensing surface. Next, we will show that beyond a cut-off distance of 30cm, very loud

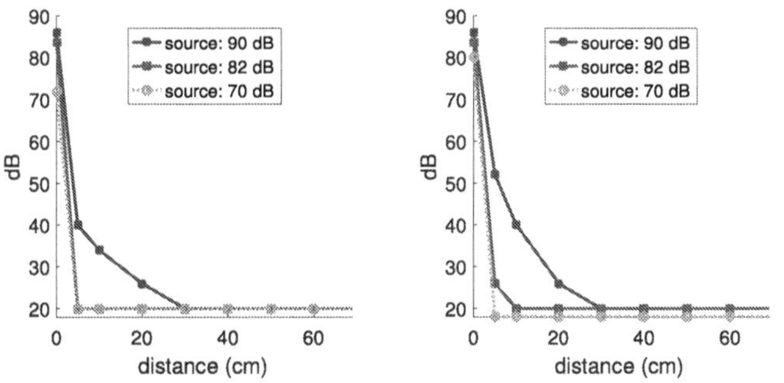

(a) Exposed accelerometer (b) Covered accelerometer

Figure 13: The magnitude of the sensed over-the-air vibrations by the accelerometer as a function of the distance between the sound source and the accelerometer.

sounds (directed at the z-axis of the accelerometer) do not induce accelerometer vibrations. Therefore, to attack VAuth, an adversary has to play a very loud sound within less than an arm's length from the user's body — which is highly improbable.

We conduct experiments on two scenarios: the first with VAuth exposed and the second with VAuth covered with cotton clothing. Fig. 13 reports how the accelerometer chip of VAuth reacts to over-the-air sound signals of different magnitudes at different distances. In each of these scenarios, we played a white noise at three sound levels: 2x, 4x and 8x the conversation level at 70dB, 82dB and 90dB, respectively [2]. The noise is directed perpendicularly to the sensing surface of the accelerometer. Fig. 13(a) shows the recorded magnitude of the accelerometer signal as a function of the distance between the sound source and VAuth when it is exposed. As evident from the plots, there is a cut-off distance of 30cm, where VAuth's accelerometer cannot sense even the loudest of the three sound sources. Beyond the cut-off distance, the magnitude of the recorded signal is the same as that in a silent scenario. This indicates that an adversary cannot inject commands with a high sound level beyond some cut-off distance. These results are consistent with the case of VAuth covered with cotton, as shown in Fig. 13(b).

Speaking User. The adversary may try to launch an attack on the voice assistant when the user is actively speaking. As we will show, VAuth matches signals in their entirety, thus can detect even minor discrepancies of the injected voice command compared to the authentic voice session. First, we show how VAuth can successfully thwart the stealthy attacks of scenario A. Vaidya *et al.* [9, 39] presented an attack that exploits the gap between voice recognition system and human voice perception. It constructs mangled voice segments that match the MFCC features of an injected voice command. An ASR engine can recognize the command, but not the human listener. This and similar attacks rely on performing a search in the MFCC algorithm parameter space to find voice commands that satisfy the above feature.

Fig. 14 shows the evaluation flow. For each of the recorded command of the previous section, we extract the MFCCs for the full signal and use them to reconstruct the voice signal. We vary the number Mel filter bands between 15 and 30. At 15 Mel filter bands, the reconstructed voice command is similar to what is reported in existing attacks [39]. At 30 Mel filter bands, the reconstructed voice command is very close to the original; it shares the same MFCCs and is easily identifiable when played back. Finally, we execute VAuth over the reconstructed voice segment and the original accelerometer sample to test for a match.

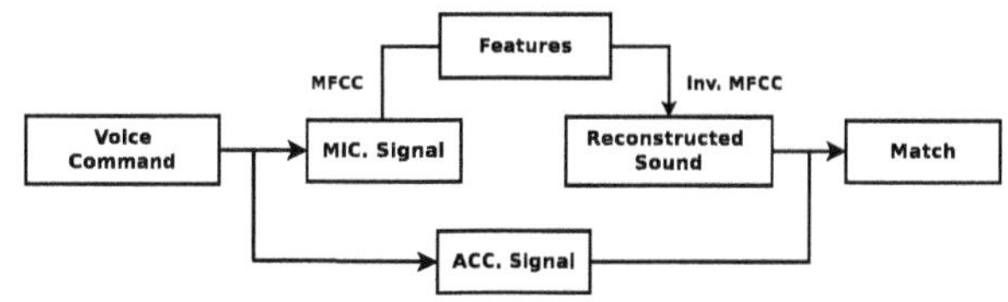

Figure 14: The flow of the mangled voice analysis.

In all cases, while the original microphone signal matches accelerometer signals near perfectly as indicated before, the reconstructed sound failed to match the accelerometer signal in 99% of the evaluated cases. Of 3,240 comparisons (2 Mel filter band lengths per command, 90 commands per user and 18 users), the reconstructed sound matched only a handful of accelerometer samples, and only in cases where we used 30 Mel filter bands. Indeed, those sound segments were very close to the original sound segment that corresponds to the matched accelerometer samples and are not stealthy at all. To constitute a practical attack, the mangled voice segment is not supposed to originate from the sound the user is speaking, let alone preserving discernible acoustic features. This demonstrates that VAuth matches the signals in their entirety, even subtle changes which are indistinguishable to human ears can result in discrepancies of our matching/authentication results.

In scenario B, an attacker also fails to overcome VAuth's protection. We indicated earlier in Section 7.2 and in this section that VAuth successfully distinguishes the phonemes and commands of the same user. This indicates 'sounds like' the user does not help the attacker much — it must inject the same command the user is saying using the same voice. Moreover, even if the user is speaking and the adversary is replaying another sound clip of the same user, VAuth can differentiate between the microphone and accelerometer samples and stop the attack.

Finally, the matching algorithm of VAuth might result in some false positives (albeit very low). Even though these false positives indicate the remaining segments after the "per-segment" stage of VAuth match, useful information in these accelerometer and microphone signals have already been filtered by our algorithm. What gets delivered to the voice assistant is practically random noise. Note that VAuth could use a more stringent classifier tuned to force the false positive rate to be 0. Such a classifier comes at the cost of usability but could be preferable in high-security situations.

8.3 Delay and Energy

We measure the delay experienced at the voice assistant and the energy consumption of the wearable component, using our prototype. As shown in Fig. 2, VAuth incurs delay only during the matching phase: when VAuth uploads the accelerometer and microphone signals to the remote service and waits for a response. According to our evaluation over the same list of 30 commands, we found that a

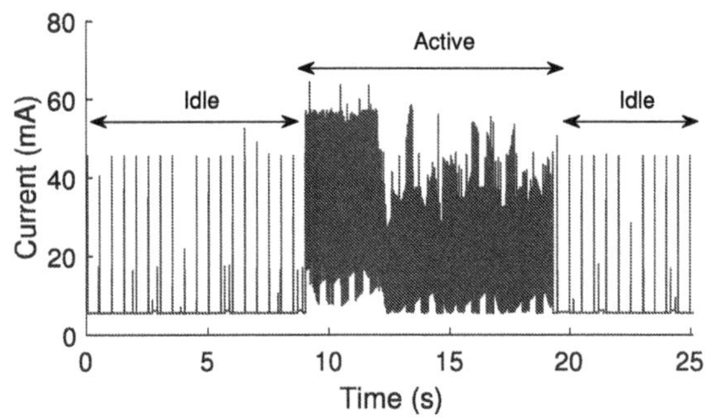

Figure 15: Current levels of the prototype in the idle and active states.

successful match takes 300–830ms, with an average of 364ms, while an unsuccessful match takes 230–760ms, with an average of 319ms. The response time increases proportionally with the length of the commands. Still, matching a command containing 30 words still takes less than 1 second. We expect the delay to decrease further with a more optimized server implementation.

When the wearable component transmits accelerometer signals, it switches between an *idle* state that keeps the connection alive and an *active* state to transmit the data. We connected our prototype to the Monsoon power monitor and recorded the current levels of the prototype in these two states when powered by a fixed voltage (4V). Fig. 15 illustrates the changes of the current levels when our prototype switches from idle to active and then back to idle. In the active state, our prototype consumes as much as 31mA, while in the idle state, it only consumes an average of 6mA. Most of the energy is used to keep the Bluetooth connection and transmit data (in the active state) — the energy consumed by the accelerometer sensor is almost negligible (3 μA).

Assuming the user always keeps the wearable open at daytime and sends 100 voice commands per day (10 seconds per voice command). Our prototype consumes 6.3mA on average. This might even be an over-estimation since 90% of the users issue voice commands at most once per day according to our survey. A typical 500mAh Li-Ion battery used by wearables (comparable to a US quarter coin) can power our prototype for around a week. 80% of the participants in our usability survey think they have no problem with recharging the wearable on a weekly basis. We conducted all the analyses on our prototype which directly utilizes off-the-shelf hardware chips without any optimization, assuming that VAuth is provided as a standalone wearable. If incorporated into an existing wearable device, VAuth will only introduce an additional energy overhead of less than 10mAh per day (to power the additional accelerometer).

9 DISCUSSION

VAuth requires the user to wear an additional device that is in continuous contact with his/her body. This requirement restricts our design options to embedding VAuth within wearables that maintain constant contact with the user's body. In this paper, we presented a proof-of-concept implementation of VAuth where we investigated three possible wearable scenarios: eyeglasses, earbuds, and necklaces. With more engineering effort, we can expand the use of VAuth to cover more wearables, such as watches and wristbands.

VAuth's energy consumption is another issue that affects its usability and practicality. In Section 8, our prototype was shown to deliver a week worth of battery life under a usage scenario of 100 commands per day. This overhead constitutes the energy consumption of the entire prototype of VAuth, most of which is spent on keeping the Bluetooth connection alive (between the matching and wearable components of VAuth). Integrating VAuth within existing Bluetooth-equipped wearables (such as a Bluetooth earbud or smartwatch) can limit its additional energy overhead to that needed to collect and communicate the vibrations from the user's body to the matching component. The latter only takes place when the user is issuing a voice command.

In its core, VAuth consists of the matching and wearable components. The wearable component collects the speech signal as it traverses the user's body (not injected through the air or another medium) and communicates them to the matching engine. In this paper, we presented a proof-of-concept implementation of the wearable component. This implementation, however, does not preclude other realizations of VAuth, as long as they meet both requirements: securely collect and communicate speech from the body to the matching component. We have used an accelerometer which captures vibrations through contact with the skin, as opposed to an on-body microphone, for instance, which captures voice through the air making it susceptible to voice injection. Even with a reasonably tuned sensitivity threshold, an attacker could always use higher power (louder voice) inject speech signals over the air for the on-body microphone. On the other hand, the human skin reflects most of the energy (95% to 99%) of the voice signal [1]; the accelerometer will only collect 1% to 5% of the over-air voice signal. We evaluated this property of the accelerometer in Section 8.2.

10 CONCLUSION

In this paper, we have proposed VAuth, a system that provides continuous authentication for voice assistants. We demonstrated that even though the accelerometer information collected from the facial/neck/chest surfaces might be weak, it contains enough information to correlate it with the data received via microphone. VAuth provides extra physical assurance for voice assistant users and is an effective measure against various attack scenarios. It avoids the pitfalls of existing voice authentication mechanisms. Our evaluation with real users under practical settings shows high accuracy and very low false positive rate, highlighting the effectiveness of VAuth. In future, we would like to explore more configurations of VAuth that will promote wider real-world deployment and adoption.

ACKNOWLEDGEMENTS

The authors would like to thank the anonymous reviewers, and the shepherd Marco Gruteser, for their constructive suggestions. They would also like to thank Timothy Trippel for his help in building VAuth's prototype and Mariam Fawaz for her comments on the earlier drafts of this manuscript. The work reported in this paper was supported in part by NSF under Grants CNS-1505785 and CNS-1646130.

REFERENCES

[1] Eugene Ackerman and Fujio Oda. 1962. *Acoustic absorption coefficients of human body surfaces.* Technical Report MRL-TDR-62-36. Pennsylvania State University, University Park.

[2] IAC Acoustics. 2017. Comparative Examples Of Noise Levels. http://www.industrialnoisecontrol.com/comparative-noise-examples.htm. (2017). Accessed: 2017-03-16.

[3] Adam J Aviv, Benjamin Sapp, Matt Blaze, and Jonathan M Smith. 2012. Practicality of accelerometer side channels on smartphones. In *Proceedings of the 28th Annual Computer Security Applications Conference.* ACM, 41–50.

[4] Mossab Baloul, Estelle Cherrier, and Christophe Rosenberger. 2012. Challenge-based speaker recognition for mobile authentication. In *Biometrics Special Interest Group (BIOSIG), 2012 BIOSIG-Proceedings of the International Conference of the.* IEEE, 1–7.

[5] BBC News. 2016. Adobe Voco 'Photoshop-for-voice' causes concern. http://www.bbc.com/news/technology-37899902. (2016). Accessed: 2017-07-26.

[6] Yuval Ben-Itzhak. 2014. What if smart devices could be hacked with just a voice? http://now.avg.com/voice-hacking-devices/. (Sep. 2014).

[7] Bluetooth SIG. 2014. *Specification of the Bluetooth System.* Version 4.2. https://www.bluetooth.org/en-us/specification/adopted-specifications.

[8] Paul Boersma. 1993. ACCURATE SHORT-TERM ANALYSIS OF THE FUNDAMENTAL FREQUENCY AND THE HARMONICS-TO-NOISE RATIO OF A SAMPLED SOUND. *Institute of Phonetic Sciences - University of Amsterdam* 17 (1993), 97–110.

[9] Nicholas Carlini, Pratyush Mishra, Tavish Vaidya, Yuankai Zhang, Micah Sherr, Clay Shields, David Wagner, and Wenchao Zhou. 2016. Hidden Voice Commands. In *25th USENIX Security Symposium (USENIX Security 16).* USENIX Association, Austin, TX, 513–530. https://www.usenix.org/conference/usenixsecurity16/technical-sessions/presentation/carlini

[10] Cory Cornelius, Zachary Marois, Jacob Sorber, Ron Peterson, Shrirang Mare, and David Kotz. 2014. Vocal resonance as a passive biometric. (2014).

[11] Cory Cornelius, Ronald Peterson, Joseph Skinner, Ryan Halter, and David Kotz. 2014. A Wearable System That Knows Who Wears It. In *Proceedings of the 12th Annual International Conference on Mobile Systems, Applications, and Services (MobiSys '14).* ACM, New York, NY, USA, 55–67. DOI: http://dx.doi.org/10.1145/2594368.2594369

[12] Amitava Das, Ohil K Manyam, Makarand Tapaswi, and Veeresh Taranalli. 2008. Multilingual spoken-password based user authentication in emerging economies using cellular phone networks. In *Spoken Language Technology Workshop, 2008. SLT 2008. IEEE.* IEEE, 5–8.

[13] Wenrui Diao, Xiangyu Liu, Zhe Zhou, and Kehuan Zhang. 2014. Your Voice Assistant is Mine: How to Abuse Speakers to Steal Information and Control Your Phone. In *Proceedings of the 4th ACM Workshop on Security and Privacy in Smartphones & Mobile Devices (SPSM '14).* ACM, New York, NY, USA, 63–74. DOI: http://dx.doi.org/10.1145/2666620.2666623

[14] Adrienne Porter Felt, Serge Egelman, Matthew Finifter, Devdatta Akhawe, and David Wagner. 2012. How to Ask for Permission. In *Proceedings of the 7th USENIX Conference on Hot Topics in Security (HotSec'12).* USENIX Association, Berkeley, CA, USA, 7–7. http://dl.acm.org/citation.cfm?id=2372387.2372394

[15] Mark Hall, Eibe Frank, Geoffrey Holmes, Bernhard Pfahringer, Peter Reutemann, and Ian H. Witten. 2009. The WEKA Data Mining Software: An Update. *SIGKDD Explor. Newsl.* 11, 1 (Nov. 2009), 10–18. DOI: http://dx.doi.org/10.1145/1656274.1656278

[16] Haskins Laboratories. 1999. The Acoustic Theory of Speech Production: the source-filter model. http://www.haskins.yale.edu/featured/heads/mmsp/acoustic.html. (1999).

[17] Chaouki Kasmi and Jose Lopes Esteves. 2015. IEMI Threats for Information Security: Remote Command Injection on Modern Smartphones. *Electromagnetic Compatibility, IEEE Transactions on* 57, 6 (2015), 1752–1755.

[18] Max Kunz, Klaus Kasper, Herbert Reininger, Manuel Möbius, and Jonathan Ohms. 2011. Continuous Speaker Verification in Realtime.. In *BIOSIG.* 79–88.

[19] Mark Liberman. 2016. Linguistics 001 – Sound Structure of Language. http://www.ling.upenn.edu/courses/ling001/phonology.html. (2016). Accessed: 2016-05-23.

[20] Yu-An S Lien, Carolyn R Calabrese, Carolyn M Michener, Elizabeth Heller Murray, Jarrad H Van Stan, Daryush D Mehta, Robert E Hillman, J Pieter Noordzij, and Cara E Stepp. 2015. Voice Relative Fundamental Frequency Via Neck-Skin Acceleration in Individuals With Voice Disorders. *Journal of Speech, Language, and Hearing Research* 58, 5 (2015), 1482–1487.

[21] Mumtaj Begam Lindasalwa Muda and I. Elamvazuthi. 2010. Voice Recognition Algorithms using Mel Frequency Cepstral Coefficient (MFCC) and Dynamic Time Warping (DTW) Techniques. *Journal Of Computing* 2, 3 (2010), 138–143.

[22] A. M. Lund. 2001. Measuring usability with the USE questionnaire. *Usability Interface* 8 (2001), 3–6. Issue 2.

[23] Shrirang Mare, Andrés Molina Markham, Cory Cornelius, Ronald Peterson, and David Kotz. 2014. ZEBRA: zero-effort bilateral recurring authentication. In *Security and Privacy (SP), 2014 IEEE Symposium on.* IEEE, 705–720.

[24] Philip Marquardt, Arunabh Verma, Henry Carter, and Patrick Traynor. 2011. (sp) iPhone: decoding vibrations from nearby keyboards using mobile phone accelerometers. In *Proceedings of the 18th ACM conference on Computer and communications security.* ACM, 551–562.

[25] Arnold Martin and Greenhalgh Hugo. 2016. Banking biometrics: hacking into your account is easier than you think. https://www.ft.com/content/959b64fe-9f66-11e6-891e-abe238dee8e2. (2016). Accessed: 2017-07-26.

[26] Rachel Martin. 2016. Listen Up: Your AI Assistant Goes Crazy For NPR Too. http://www.npr.org/2016/03/06/469383361/listen-up-your-ai-assistant-goes-crazy-for-npr-too. (Mar. 2016).

[27] D. D. Mehta, J. H. Van Stan, and R. E. Hillman. 2016. Relationships Between Vocal Function Measures Derived from an Acoustic Microphone and a Subglottal Neck-Surface Accelerometer. *IEEE/ACM Transactions on Audio, Speech, and Language Processing* 24, 4 (April 2016), 659–668. DOI: http://dx.doi.org/10.1109/TASLP.2016.2516647

[28] Daryush D Mehta, Matías Zañartu, Shengran W Feng, Harold A Cheyne, and Robert E Hillman. 2012. Mobile voice health monitoring using a wearable accelerometer sensor and a smartphone platform. *Biomedical Engineering, IEEE Transactions on* 59, 11 (2012), 3090–3096.

[29] Rachel Metz. 2014. Voice Recognition for the Internet of Things. https://www.technologyreview.com/s/531936/voice-recognition-for-the-internet-of-things/. (Oct. 2014).

[30] Dibya Mukhopadhyay, Maliheh Shirvanian, and Nitesh Saxena. 2015. *All Your Voices are Belong to Us: Stealing Voices to Fool Humans and Machines.* Springer International Publishing, Cham, 599–621. DOI: http://dx.doi.org/10.1007/978-3-319-24177-7_30

[31] Lisa Myers. 2004. An Exploration of Voice Biometrics. https://www.sans.org/reading-room/whitepapers/authentication/exploration-voice-biometrics-1436. (April 2004).

[32] Nuance Cloud Services. 2013. HTTP Services 1.0 Programmer's Guide. https://developer.nuance.com/public/Help/HttpInterface/HTTP_web_services_for_NCS_clients_1.0_programmer_s_guide.pdf. (Dec. 2013).

[33] Nuance Communications, Inc. 2017. Authentication via conversation. http://www.nuance.com/for-business/customer-service-solutions/voice-biometrics/freespeech/index.htm. (2017). Accessed: 2017-07-26.

[34] Emmanuel Owusu, Jun Han, Sauvik Das, Adrian Perrig, and Joy Zhang. 2012. ACCessory: password inference using accelerometers on smartphones. In *Proceedings of the Twelfth Workshop on Mobile Computing Systems & Applications.* ACM, 9.

[35] Saurabh Panjwani and Achintya Prakash. 2014. Crowdsourcing Attacks on Biometric Systems. In *Tenth Symposium on Usable Privacy and Security, SOUPS 2014, Menlo Park, CA, USA, July 9-11, 2014.* 257–269. https://www.usenix.org/conference/soups2014/proceedings/presentation/panjwani

[36] Giuseppe Petracca, Yuqiong Sun, Trent Jaeger, and Ahmad Atamli. 2015. AuDroid: Preventing Attacks on Audio Channels in Mobile Devices. In *Proceedings of the 31st Annual Computer Security Applications Conference (ACSAC 2015).* ACM, New York, NY, USA, 181–190. DOI: http://dx.doi.org/10.1145/2818000.2818005

[37] John Platt. 1998. Fast Training of Support Vector Machines Using Sequential Minimal Optimization, In Advances in Kernel Methods - Support Vector Learning. (January 1998). https://www.microsoft.com/en-us/research/publication/fast-training-of-support-vector-machines-using-sequential-minimal-optimization/

[38] Timothy Trippel, Ofir Weisse, Wenyuan Xu, Peter Honeyman, and Kevin Fu. WALNUT: Waging Doubt on the Integrity of MEMS Accelerometers with Acoustic Injection Attacks. In *In Proceedings of the 2nd IEEE European Symposium on Security and Privacy (EuroS&P 2017). To appear.*

[39] Tavish Vaidya, Yuankai Zhang, Micah Sherr, and Clay Shields. 2015. Cocaine noodles: exploiting the gap between human and machine speech recognition. In *9th USENIX Workshop on Offensive Technologies (WOOT 15).*

[40] Tam Vu, Akash Baid, Simon Gao, Marco Gruteser, Richard Howard, Janne Lindqvist, Predrag Spasojevic, and Jeffrey Walling. 2012. Distinguishing Users with Capacitive Touch Communication. In *Proceedings of the 18th Annual International Conference on Mobile Computing and Networking (Mobicom '12).* ACM, New York, NY, USA, 197–208. DOI: http://dx.doi.org/10.1145/2348543.2348569

[41] Ryan West. 2008. The Psychology of Security. *Commun. ACM* 51, 4 (April 2008), 34–40. DOI: http://dx.doi.org/10.1145/1330311.1330320

[42] Zhi Xu, Kun Bai, and Sencun Zhu. 2012. Taplogger: Inferring user inputs on smartphone touchscreens using on-board motion sensors. In *Proceedings of the fifth ACM conference on Security and Privacy in Wireless and Mobile Networks.* ACM, 113–124.

[43] Kenji Yoshida. 2008. Phonetic implementation of Korean denasalization and its variation related to prosody. *IULC Working Papers* 8, 1 (2008).

NICScatter: Backscatter as a Covert Channel in Mobile Devices

Zhice Yang
SIST, ShanghaiTech University
& CSE, Hong Kong University of
Science and Technology
yangzhc@shanghaitech.edu.cn

Qianyi Huang
CSE, Hong Kong University of
Science and Technology
qhuangaa@connect.ust.hk

Qian Zhang
CSE, Hong Kong University of
Science and Technology
qianzh@cse.ust.hk

ABSTRACT

Today's mobile devices contain sensitive data, which raises concerns about data security. This paper discusses a covert channel threat on existing mobile systems. Through it, malware can wirelessly leak information without making network connections or emitting signals, such as sound, EMR, vibration, etc., that we can feel or are aware of.

The covert channel is built on a communication method that we call NICScatter. NICScatter transmitter malware forces mobile devices, such as mobile phones, tablets or laptops, to reflect surrounding RF signals to covertly convey information. The operation is achieved by controlling the impedance of a device's wireless network interface card (NIC). Importantly, the operation requires no special privileges on current mobile OSs, which allows the malware to stealthily pass sensitive data to an attacker's nearby mobile device, which can then decode the signal and thus effectively gather the guarded data. Our experiments with different mobile devices show that the covert channel can achieve 1.6 bps and transmit as far as 2 meters. In a through-the-wall scenario, it can transmit up to 70 cm.

CCS CONCEPTS

• **Security and privacy → Mobile and wireless security**; • **Networks → Cyber-physical networks**;

KEYWORDS

Backscatter; Commercial Devices; Covert Channel; Wireless

1 INTRODUCTION

Mobile devices, including laptops, smartphones, wearables, etc., have become essential tools in modern life. We rely on them for social activities, document processing as well as health status monitoring. As these devices contain sensitive personal information, various security mechanisms, like firewalls, traffic monitors, and information flow control systems [15], have been developed for mobile devices to prevent unauthorized data leakage.

Nevertheless, our data is not safe enough. Covert channels remain an open threat to data security. A covert channel allows an attacker to leak information from a compromised system even without establishing explicit networked or logical connections. Covert channels exploit media that are usually not treated as data communication channels, and thus they are stealthy and hard for security systems to detect. For example, electromagnetic radiation (EMR) from a display interface [37], EMR from a CPU-to-memory bus [17], the magnetic field from a hard disk [33], etc. are feasible media to establish covert channels. Existing discussions on covert channels usually focus on desktops or servers and cannot be easily extended to mobile situations.

We thus introduce NICScatter, a covert communication method in which a mobile device backscatters surrounding radio frequency (RF) signals with different intensities, surreptitiously leaking out sensitive data from the mobile device's storage. A nearby receiver can then decode the leaked data from the reflected RF signals. Transmitting data through backscattered RF signals is not a new idea, but in conventional wisdom, such a form of communication relies on dedicated hardware to manipulate the impedance of the RF circuits. However, we show that NICScatter can work on a normal commercial mobile device with a wireless transceiver.

Specifically, NICScatter is based on the observation that the impedance of a Wi-Fi Network Interface Card (NIC) varies in different working states, which can be easily modulated via software commands. In this way, like conventional backscatter transmitters, the host mobile device reflects incident RF signals with different intensities, which can be used to covertly convey information to the receiver. Importantly, we can show that in current Linux and Android OSs, the operation of a NICScatter transmitter does not require special privileges. For example, in Linux, NICScatter requires no root privileges. In Android, apps using NICScatter only require a normal permission `CHANGE_WIFI_STATE` [1], which is treated as low risk and will not trigger a message to notify the user during the app installation. These features in current OSs make communication through NICScatter stealthy.

We have prototyped NICScatter transmitter malware in both laptops and smartphones. In addition, we have successfully tested two types of receivers for NICScatter. One is based on Received Signal Strength Indicator (RSSI)/Channel State Information (CSI) measurement ability, which covers many common wireless devices, like laptops and UAVs [30]. This type of receiver can achieve a 0.3bps data transmission rate and up to 0.4m communication range. Another type is based on a software-defined radio (SDR) platform which covers devices with a strong ability to capture wireless signals, like emerging wireless sensing platforms [10, 11, 41]. This type of receiver can achieve a data transmission rate of 1.6bps and a communication range of up to 2m from the transmitter. Through our prototype system, we can demonstrate that our malware can leak data from mobile devices without generating any network

MobiCom '17, October 16-20, 2017, Snowbird, UT, USA.

ISBN 978-1-4503-4916-1/17/10...$15.00
DOI: https://doi.org/10.1145/3117811.3117814

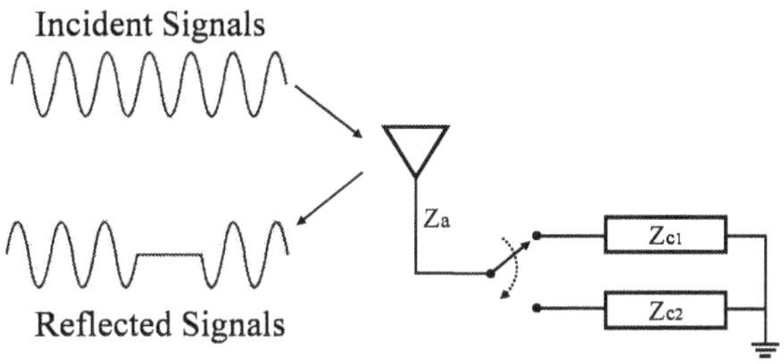

Figure 1: Backscatter Communication. The switch of a transmitter toggles its antenna's load to different impedances. As a result, the RF signals reflected by the antenna have different amplitudes, which are used to convey information, *e.g.*, a stream of encoded data, to the receiver.

traffic or any signals, such as EMR, sound, vibration, heat, etc., that users can feel or be aware of.

We summarize contributions of our work as follows:

1. We introduce a new form of backscatter communication, NICScatter, which uses software control instructions to change the impedance of NICs. In this way, a mobile device can reflect RF signals for communication. NICScatter is the first publicly discussed backscatter design that requires no dedicated hardware and works on today's Wi-Fi NICs.

2. We investigate the vulnerability of current Linux and Android mobile OSs to covertly communicate through NICScatter. By showing that covertly transmitting a stream of encoded data through NICScatter requires no special privileges, we expose the threat of unauthorized information leakage.

3. We evaluate the practicality of implementing a transmitter and receiver for NICScatter. Based on our prototype, we use extensive experiments under realistic settings to validate the feasibility of using NICScatter for covert communication.

The remaining parts of this paper are arranged as follows: we first give the overview for NICScatter in §2. Then we introduce the transmitter and receiver design of NICScatter in §3 and §4, respectively. §5 evaluates the practicality of implementing a covert channel in mobile devices through NICScatter. Related works about covert channels and backscatter communication are presented in §6. We discuss countermeasures, limitations and future work in §7. In §8, we conclude the work.

2 OVERVIEW

This section first gives the background and motivation of the NICScatter design. Then, it introduces a data exfiltration attack on mobile devices based on the NICScatter transmitter.

2.1 Backscatter Communication

Backscatter is a wireless communication method. A backscatter transmitter reflects surrounding RF signals to convey information. It is very power-efficient since the transmitter does not consume power in actively generating RF signals, like conventional RF transmitters do. As a result, it has been widely used in communication scenarios with ultra low power constraints, such as with RFID tags [39].

Model	Off state	Unstable state	On state
AR9380, ant1	$22.5 + j9.2$	$36.3 - j10.0i$	$22.5 + j9.2$
BCM1045, ant1	$12.4 + j14.4$	N/A	$106.9 - j9.8$
Intel5300, ant1	$119.0 + j137.0$	N/A	$80.3 + j66.8$
Intel5300, ant2	$54.3 + j122.7$	N/A	$57.7 + j78.4$

Table 1: NIC Impedance (Ω). Wi-Fi NICs have different impedances in different working states. BCM 1045 and Intel 5300 have different impedances in on and off states. Atheros AR9380 has different impedances in the unstable state when it is switched from the off state to the on state.

The working mechanism of backscatter is shown in Figure 1. When an incident RF signal encounters the antenna, a fraction of the signal is reflected/scattered off the antenna. When the chip impedance Z_c is in different states Z_{c1} or Z_{c2}, the amplitude of the reflected signal is also different. This property allows a backscatter transmitter to convey information, *e.g.*, a stream of encoded data, to a receiver. Given the power of the incident signal $P_{incident}$, the power of the backscatter signal $P_{reflected}$ is determined by:

$$P_{reflected} = P_{incident} \cdot \frac{|\rho_1 - \rho_2|^2}{4}, \qquad (1)$$

where $\rho_{1,2} = \frac{Z_{c1,c2} - Z_a^*}{Z_{c1,c2} + Z_a}$. $\frac{|\rho_1 - \rho_2|^2}{4}$ quantifies the efficiency in transforming the received signal into the backscatter signal[27, 34]. Since most Wi-Fi antennas are typically manufactured to $Z_a = 50\Omega$, the reflection efficiency is determined by the chip impedances of the two states. For example, when $Z_{c1} = 0$ and $Z_{c2} = \infty$, $\frac{|\rho_1 - \rho_2|^2}{4}$ reaches its maximum efficiency of 0dB loss.

2.2 NICScatter: Backscatter through NIC

As consumer mobile devices have no dedicated hardware to control the impedance of the RF circuits, backscatter is typically not considered as a possible communication method for them. NICScatter challenges such conventional wisdom. Its design is based on the interesting property that commercial Wi-Fi NICs have different circuit impedances in different working states.

We measured the impedance of Wi-Fi NICs from some major manufacturers. The measurement was done by connecting the RF port of each NIC to a Roche & Schwarz Vector Network Analyzer [5]. The measurement frequency and power were set to 2.4GHz and -40dBm, respectively. During the measurement, the NIC was switched between on and off states. The impedance readings are recorded in Table 1. We observe that the impedance of all these NICs changes when they are switched from the off state to the on state. BCM 1045 and Intel 5300 hold two different impedances in the two states. The impedance of Atheros AR9380 experiences a temporary change from the off to the on state.

The design of NICScatter is based on this observation. Similar to the impedance switch in Figure 1, NICScatter uses software instructions to switch the commercial Wi-Fi NICs between on and off states. Different circuit impedances in the two states result in different amplitudes of the reflected RF signals by the mobile

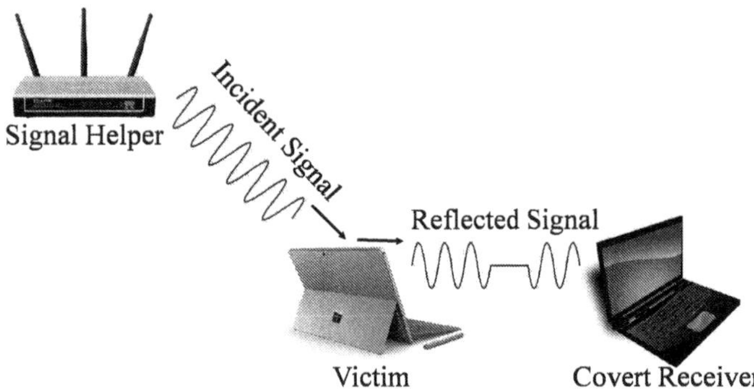

Figure 2: Attack Scenario. The malware in the victim leverages NICScatter to reflect the RF signal from the Signal Helper to covertly leak sensitive information, *e.g.*, a user password, to the Covert Receiver.

device. In this way, NICScatter enables backscatter communication in mobile devices equipped with a Wi-Fi NIC.

As we will show later in §3, the operation of NICScatter does not require root access privileges in Linux systems and only requires a normal access permission in Android systems. The special wireless communication ability combined with the stealthy nature makes NICScatter an ideal choice for a covert channel. In the following subsection, we describe a data exfiltration attack on mobile devices through NICScatter.

2.3 Attack Model

Figure 2 shows the attack scenario. We assume that the mobile devices, *e.g.*, smartphones or laptops, have somehow been compromised by the attacker and have had malware installed with NICScatter capability. The malware has access to certain sensitive data of interest but avoids using the network, because network traffic, as a major information flow, is normally under severe monitoring by many security mechanisms [15]. Moreover, if an application with access to the sensitive data also requires public network connections, it will raise serious attention and awareness of users. Leveraging NICScatter instead of network connections to leak information makes the malware inconspicuous and stealthy.

The covert receiver is positioned close to but isolated from the compromised mobile device; there are no physical or logical connections between them. We assume that the covert receiver can exploit the RF signals generated by a signal helper, *e.g.*, a nearby neutral access point, to enable backscatter from the victim. We also assume that the covert receiver can detect and decode the reflections from the victim. Attacks are likely to occur in public places, like cafes, libraries, transportation stations, *etc.* The attacker uses his/her laptop/AP as the receiver to gather information from neighboring victims. In another case, as modern mobile machines like UAVs [30] also have the capability to receive and decode covert information, they could be abused to gather information from victims in a dense residential environment.

The covert receiver could also be an emerging wireless sensing device, which is designed to perform localization, gesture recognition, *etc.* [10, 11, 41]. Some of these sensing platforms have a strong ability to identify changes in wireless signals, and thus could be used to receive signals reflected by victims. With more and more sensing platforms being developed and accessible, the attacker gains a powerful tool to receive covert information from the victims.

In the examples above, the receiver is not necessarily connected to the Internet. The attacker owns the receiver and collects data from the receiver directly. In a more complicated model, the receivers, such as public APs, may also be compromised by the attacker so that the gathered information is also covertly sent to the remote attacker through the Internet.

3 TRANSMITTER

The NICScatter transmitter changes the circuit impedance of the Wi-Fi NIC to reflect RF signals with different intensity for communication. In this section, we introduce its detailed design.

3.1 The Backscatter Properties of Wi-Fi NIC

To exploit the properties of NIC hardware, we conduct experiments to show how the working states affect the reflection. The topology is similar to Figure 2. A USRP is used as the signal helper to generate a sine wave with constant amplitude at 2.4GHz. The antenna of the Wi-Fi NIC of the victim is placed 1m from the signal helper. Another USRP is placed 1m from the victim to capture the reflections. The Wi-Fi NIC is turned on and off every 0.5 seconds. The captured signals are shown in Figure 3. The periodic switching of the NIC impedance results in periodic patterns in the reflected RF signals. Note that once we turn off the signal helper, the periodic patterns disappear immediately at the receiver. Thus, the periodic patterns are generated by the reflections of the Wi-Fi NICs. Our detailed observations are summarized in the following regarding hardware, software and phase diversity:

Hardware Diversity. The impedance changes are quite diverse in different Wi-Fi NICs. According to the waveforms of the reflected signals, NICs can be classified into two types. The impedance of the first type is almost static in the on or off state. Intel 5300 and BCM1045 belong to this type. We term them as *static type.* The impedance of the second type only changes in a short period when turning from on to off or turning from off to on. The corresponding waveform in the reflected RF signals is like a pulse or a bump wave. AR9380 and AR9285 belong to this type. In Figure 3 (a), when the NIC is switched from off to on, it has a square bump lasting for 0.1 seconds. When the NIC is switched from on to off, it has a very short pulse. We term NICs of this type as *pulse type.*

Although AR9380 and AR9285 belong to the same type, and their reflected signals are quite similar, this does not suggest that NICs from the same manufacturer have similar features. Another NIC from Intel (Intel 6300), which is not shown in Figure 3, shows different reflection features from Intel 5300. Intel 6300 is *pulse type*, but Intel 5300 is *static type.* Not surprisingly, NICs of the same model have the same features. We get this conclusion from 4 pieces of Atheros AR9380. Also, different RF ports of the same NIC have similar features, which can be seen from Figure 3 (d) and 3 (e). Therefore, NICs of the same model and RF ports of the same NIC have very similar reflection features, but NICs of different manufacturers and NICs of different models from the same manufacturer do not necessarily have similar features.

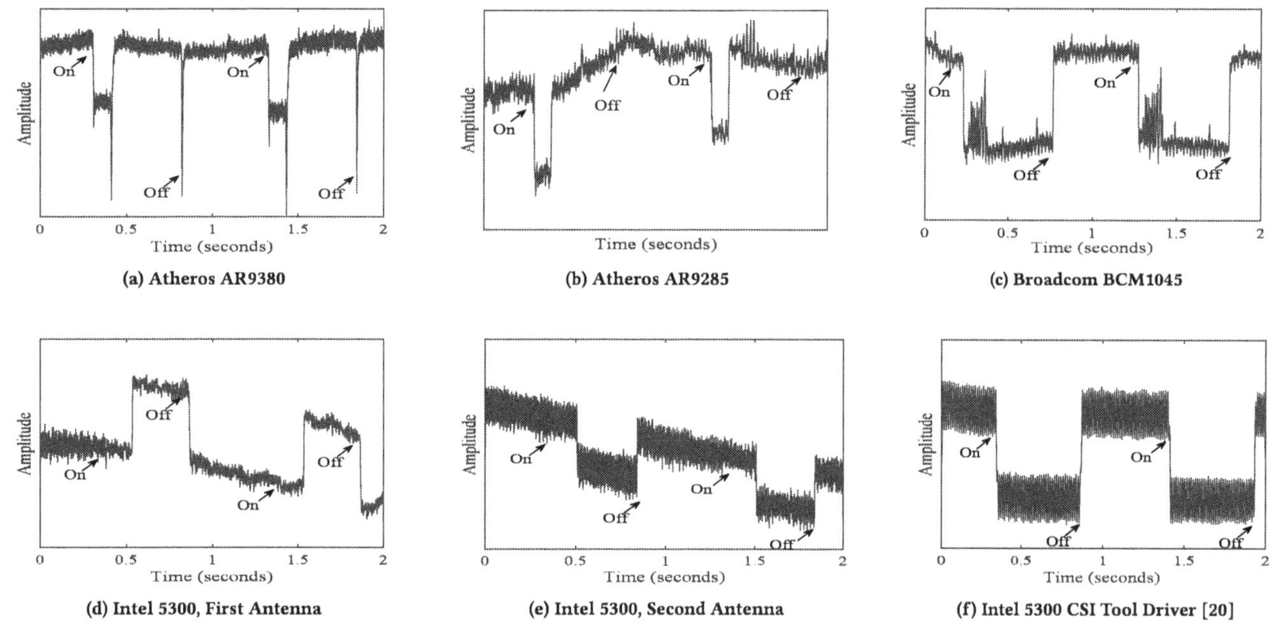

(a) Atheros AR9380 (b) Atheros AR9285 (c) Broadcom BCM1045

(d) Intel 5300, First Antenna (e) Intel 5300, Second Antenna (f) Intel 5300 CSI Tool Driver [20]

Figure 3: Waveforms of the Reflected RF Signals. A sine signal at 2.4GHz is reflected by commercial NICs when they are turned on and off every 0.5 seconds. The amplitude changes in the reflected RF signals are caused by the different NIC impedances in different working states. The results are consistent with our impedance readings recorded in Table 1.

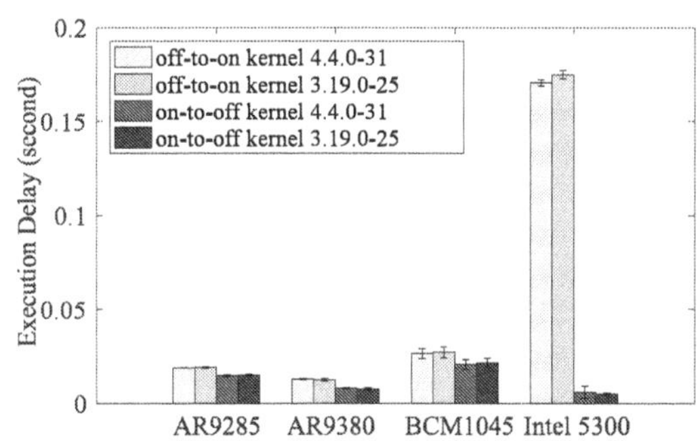

Figure 4: Software on/off Execution Delay of Different NICs. The on/off delay is measured with the same desktop by replacing its WiFi NIC. The software on/off execution time of different NICs is different.

Another important hardware feature is the reflection efficiency. For the ease of comparison, the y-axis of each subfigure in Figure 3 is shifted and scaled to make the waveforms have similar display sizes. However, their absolute amplitudes are quite diverse and are consistent with the impedance readings in Table 1. According to formula (1), the backscatter loss of AR9380, BCM1045 and Intel 5300 is -12dB, -6dB and -18dB, respectively.

Software Diversity. The reflection features also depend on the driver software. Intel 5300 is a NIC of *static type*, but the duty cycle of the reflected RF signals in Figure 3 (d) does not match the duty cycle of the on/off command. This is caused by the execution delay of the NIC driver. To investigate the execution delay of different drivers, we timestamp the instant when we issue commands, *e.g.*, `ifconfig up/down` to turn on/off the NIC, and the instant when the interface is really on/off by checking the `IFF_UP` flag. The execution delay for each NIC is measured 100 times. Results in Figure 4 show that the on-to-off or off-to-on delay is normally around 0.025s. One exception is Intel 5300. Its off-to-on delay is about 10 times higher than that of other NICs. However, in Figure 3 (f), we replace the stocked 5300 driver with the Intel 5300 CSI tool driver [20] and keep other conditions unchanged. The off-to-on delay can be reduced to 0.04s, which is close to that of other NICs. The underlying reason is uncertain for us since its driver uses closed-source firmware. One thing we can conclude is that the reflection features are highly related to the NIC driver.

Phase Diversity. The incident signal and the reflected signal superpose at the receiver's antenna. The final amplitude is related to the location of the receiver. Specifically, if the signal from signal helper is $E_h \sin(\omega t)$ and the signal reflected by the NIC is $E_r \sin(\omega t + \delta)$. The received signal is given by:

$$\sqrt{E_h^2 + E_r^2 + 2E_hE_r \cos\delta} \sin(\omega t + \phi), \qquad (2)$$

where δ represents the phase difference in the two received signals. The value of δ is determined by the location of the transmitter and the frequency of the RF signal. The two received signals may either superpose constructively or destructively, leading to an increase or decrease in signal amplitudes, respectively. This explains why the direction of the pulses in Figure 3 (d) is different from that of other subfigures.

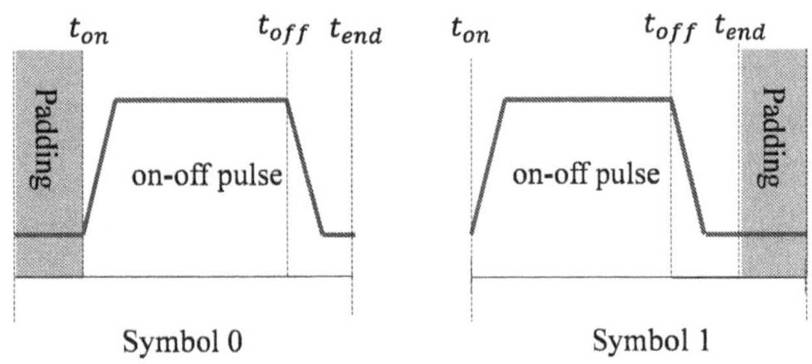

Figure 5: On-off Position Modulation (OOPM). Issuing a pair of off-to-on and on-to-off instructions to the Wi-Fi NIC results in a pulse in the reflected signals. OOPM divides time into equal time slots and uses the location of the on-off pulse in the slot to represent information. In this example, two on-off pulses with different time shifts in the slot are used to represent "0" and "1".

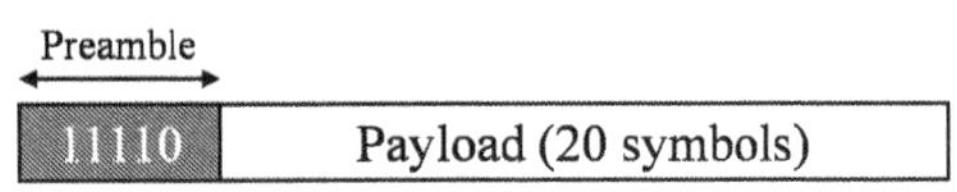

Figure 6: Packet Structure

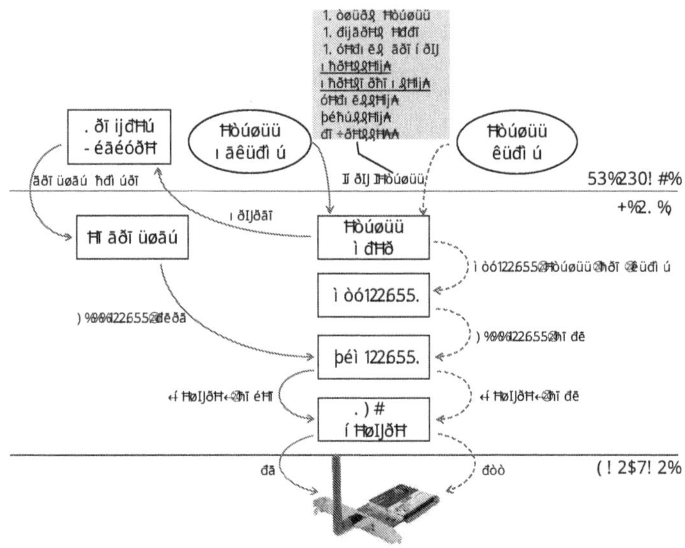

Figure 7: `rfkill` Call Map. `rfkill` is a subsystem in the Linux kernel for switching radio devices. Userspace programs can switch radio devices on and off through the `rfkill` device file at `/dev/rfkill`. The write permission of `/dev/rfkill` is open to the user without root privileges.

3.2 Encoding Schemes

Given the reflection properties of different NICs, especially the *pulse type*, it is intuitive to refer to pulse the position modulation (PPM) for the encoding scheme. In PPM, time is divided into equal time slots of duration L, and a single pulse is transmitted during each time slot. The position of the pulse in each time slot determines the symbol being transmitted. If there are M possible position values in one time slot, one symbol represents $\log_2 M$ bits. The corresponding bit rate is $\frac{1}{L}\log_2 M$.

NICScatter uses on-off position modulation (OOPM) to modulate the reflected signal. OOPM is a variant of PPM. Similar to PPM, OOPM divides time into slots and uses the position of a pulse in that slot to represent information. NICScatter generates a pulse in the reflected signal by giving on-off instructions to the NIC. We consider NICs of different types. For NICs of *pulse type*, a single off-to-on or on-to-off instruction is enough to generate a pulse in the reflection. For NICs of *static type*, we need an immediate off-to-on and on-to-off pair to generate a pulse. Note that, in both types, we can use the quick off-to-on and on-to-off pair to generate the pulse in the reflection.

Specifically, NICScatter uses the simplest version of OOPM, where two possible time shifts in one time slot are used to represent one bit. In Figure 5, t_{on} and t_{off} are the time instant when the on and off commands are issued respectively. t_{end} is the finishing time of the on-to-off instructions. $t_{off} - t_{on}$ and $t_{end} - t_{off}$ are the time reserved for the execution delay. The padding period is used to distinguish the position of the on-off pulse in the time slot. The NIC hardware treats the padding period the same as the off state.

We choose t_{on}, t_{off}, t_{end} according to our measurement in Figure 4. Our goal is to unify the transmission scheme among different NICs. So we fix $t_{off} - t_{on}$ to 0.3s and $t_{end} - t_{off}$ to 0.1s to incorporate Intel 5300, which has the largest off-to-on delay of 0.2s. The padding period is set to 0.1s. Thus, the duration of each symbol is 0.5s. Of course, the choice of these parameters can be adjusted to satisfy specific design goals. For example, the symbol period can be much smaller, and rate can be increased by 10× if we exclude Intel 5300.

The packet structure is shown in Figure 6. We use five symbols to transmit the preamble, which contains four consecutive "1"s and one "0". The four "1"s are used for packet detection. The following "0" is used for symbol synchronization, which we will explain later in the receiver design in §4. We use 20 symbols to form the payload, which includes data and the checksum.

Next, we consider implementation issues of the NICScatter transmitter in two popular mobile operating systems: Linux and Android. Our goal is to make the NICScatter transmitter stealthy, and thus we try to avoid the dependency on any sensitive privileges.

3.3 Transmitter in Linux

Linux is widely used on desktops, workstations and laptops. The Ubuntu distribution even has a mobile version for smartphones and tablets [6]. Linux uses privilege control to guarantee the system security. Normally, turning a Wi-Fi NIC on or off is treated as an important system action. To do so, a userspace program must have the root privileges. However, we have found a way to bypass the privilege requirement to enable NICScatter in current Linux systems.

We leverage the vulnerability in the `rfkill` subsystem [4]. `rfkill` is an interface that resides in the Linux kernel to switch radio devices. Drivers for radio devices, such as Wi-Fi, Bluetooth, WAN, GPS, *etc.*, provide interfaces for calls from `rfkill`. Meanwhile,

Algorithm 1 Transmitter

```
procedure TRANSMITTER()
    do
        t = 0.1s seconds;                    ▷ 5t is one time slot
        wait_for_data();
        while tx_buffer is not empty do
            data ←dequeue(tx_buffer)
            if data==1 then
                "unblock wifi"; sleep(3t);
                "block wifi"; sleep(2t);
            else
                sleep(t);
                "unblock wifi"; sleep(3t);
                "block wifi"; sleep(t);
            end if
        end while
    while True
end procedure
```

rfkill responds to events from the user. One typical event is the radio button/airplane mode button on many laptops. The `rfkill` subsystem turns radios on or off according to the voltage of the hardware button. The `rfkill` subsystem also responds to software events. Its interface is exposed to userspace through the device file at /dev/rfkill. Writing structured command, *e.g.*, "block wifi", to `/dev/rfkill` turns off the Wi-Fi radio. Note that writing the reverse command "unblock wifi" to `/dev/rfkill` will not turn on the Wi-Fi NIC directly. But as Figure 7 shows, another program, `network_manager`, in the system will automatically turn on the Wi-Fi NIC once the Wi-Fi is unblocked by `rfkill`. By default, `network_manager` is a startup system service. Therefore, applications can write a block or unblock Wi-Fi command to `/dev/rfkill` to turn on or off the Wi-Fi NIC.

We note that the write permission of the `/dev/rfkill` does not require root privileges in many Linux desktop distributions. The vulnerability is caused by Gnome-Bluetooth, which is an application shipped with the Gnome desktop environment. The application installs `61-gnome-bluetooth-rfkill.rules` to release the write permission of `/dev/rfkill` to normal users. The vulnerability is verified in Ubuntu-based distributions with Gnome-Bluetooth version 3.12.0-2 to 3.20.0-1. For newer distributions, the same vulnerability is caused by another application called gnome-settings-daemon [3]. Therefore, any program can use the Algorithm 1 to launch NICScatter transmissions.

3.4 Transmitter in Android

Android is widely used in modem smartphones and wearables. Its transmitter implementation is quite similar to that of Linux. One difference is that the `rfkill` subsystem in Android requires root privileges. To apply NICScatter in non-rooted devices, we propose to use `wifiManager` to control the on-off of the Wi-Fi NIC. Accessing `wifiManager` in an Android app only requires `CHANGE_WIFI_STATE` permission. Note that Android classifies app permissions into two categories. One is the dangerous level, which will explicitly notify users during app installation. The other is

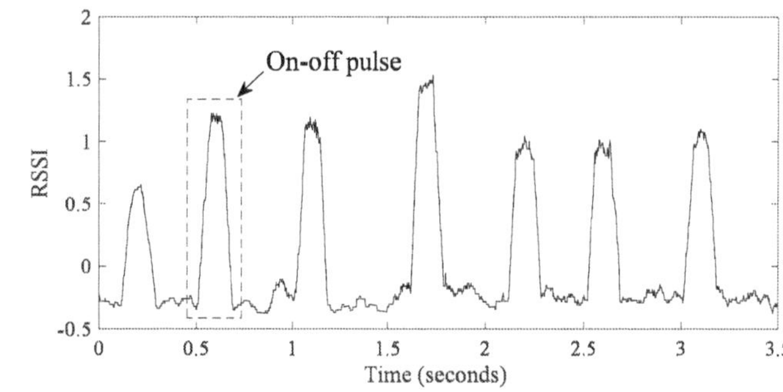

Figure 8: On-off Pulses in a Smoothed RSSI Trace.

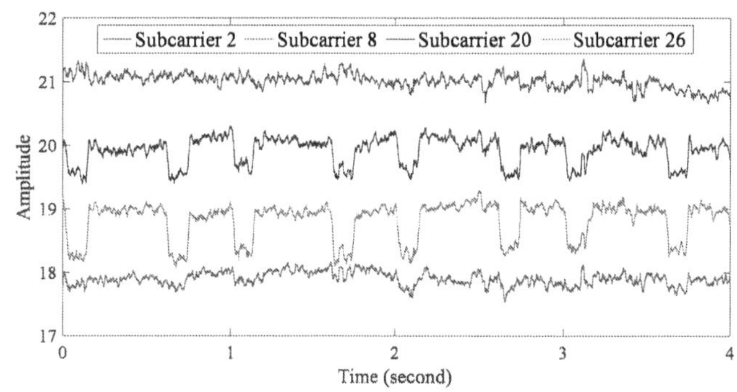

Figure 9: Subcarrier Diversity in CSI Traces.

normal level, which is treated as low risk and will not notify the user by default. `CHANGE_WIFI_STATE` belongs to the normal level. Malware can take this advantage to hide its NICScatter capability during the installation.

The transmitter program in Android is similar to Algorithm 1 except the on-off instructions are issued through `wifiManager` rather than `rfkill`. Another difference is the off-to-on delay in Android smartphones is around 1.5 seconds, which is longer than that of Linux laptops. We thus extend the time unit in Algorithm 1 to 0.6 seconds for Android platforms.

4 RECEIVER

This section introduces the NICScatter receiver. Our attack model (§2.3) focuses on two types of receivers. One is based on commercial Wi-Fi NICs, and the other is based on SDRs.

4.1 Receiving with Wi-Fi NIC

To reveal the reflections from the transmitter, NICScatter receiver keeps monitoring Wi-Fi packets from the signal helper. These packets are reflected by the transmitter. As the transmitter is changing its impedance, the signal strength of the reflected packet is also changed accordingly. Like a sampling point in Figure 3, the signal strength of a packet reflected during the on-off pulse is different from that of a packet reflected in the other periods. NICScatter receiver makes use of RSSI and CSI of these Wi-Fi packets to capture

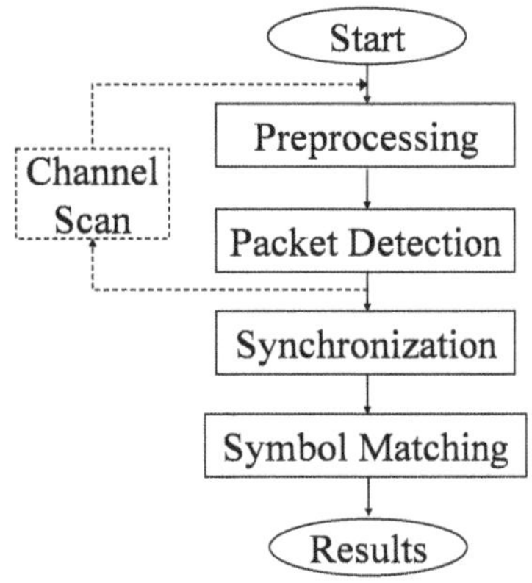

Figure 10: Receiver's Processing Flow.

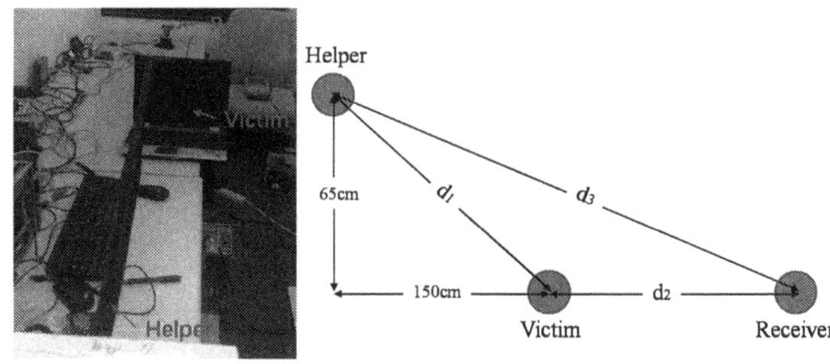

Figure 11: Evaluation Topology

Receiver	Victim	Helper	Result
USRP	Laptop	USRP	§5.1
	Phone		§5.1.7
Laptop	Laptop	Access Point	§5.2

Table 2: Evaluation Outline

the signal changes caused by the transmitter and then decode the information.

Receiving with RSSI. Most Wi-Fi NICs provide the RSSI information of the received packets. We first introduce the decoding method based on RSSI samples obtained from the packets received from the signal helper. An RSSI trace containing on-off pulses is shown in Figure 8. Bits in the trace are extracted with the following four steps:

1. Preprocessing. The recorded RSSI values are interpolated into even sampling intervals. Then, the DC is removed and the trace is smoothed.

2. Packet Detection. Similar to the packet detection process in IEEE 802.11, self-correlation is used to detect the occurrence of the NICScatter packets. Note that every packet starts with a preamble which contains four consecutive "1"s. We choose the duration of one symbol as the self-correlation window. A packet is detected if the self-correlation energy is higher than a threshold and lasts for 3 symbols. As the data payload may also contain four consecutive symbol "1"s, we buffer RSSI values for one packet length and treat every four "1"s as the start of a packet. False positive decoding can be detected through the checksum in the data payload.

3. Synchronization. One challenging problem in decoding PPM-like modulation is to find the exact boundary of the symbols. In our case, since different NICs have different shapes of on-off pulses, the shape of the preamble is unknown to the receiver. Thus, it is not possible to use a known correlation pattern like 802.11 to find the symbol boundary. Thus, the NICScatter receiver determines the symbol boundary through searching. Specifically, if the RSSI values have high self-correlation energy during $[t_1, t_2]$, we choose $T_0 = (t_1 + t_2)/2$, *i.e.*, the center of that period, as the initial boundary. Then, the RSSI samples from T_0 to $T_0 + L$ are treated as symbol "1". According the relation in Figure 5, Symbol "0" is estimated from the samples of the Symbol "1". Note that since the fifth symbol in the preamble is "0", we vary T_0 and fix it as the symbol boundary when the correlation of the estimated symbol "0" and the fifth symbol reaches the highest energy.

4. Symbol Matching. After the previous step, we obtain the template of the symbol "0" and the symbol "1" of the packet. The remaining RSSI samples are then sliced into the unit of one symbol length and correlated with the extracted reference symbol templates. The sliced samples are matched to "0" or "1" according to the correlation energy. The obtained bits are the information carried in the NICScatter packet.

Receiving with CSI. While the above discussion is based on RSSI, it can be easily extended to some Wi-Fi NICs having the CSI capability [20]. Compared with RSSI, CSI contains finer-grained channel information. It quantifies the amplitude and phase shift in subcarriers of the Wi-Fi channel.

One notable difference in the CSI information is the SNR of different subcarriers differs a lot. In Figure 9, subcarriers 20 and 26 have obvious on-off pulses, while the on-off pulses in subcarriers 2 and 8 are not obvious. This can be explained by Equation (2). Due to different wave paths and frequencies, the phase values of the received subcarriers are different, which results in different amplitudes of the received pulses. Therefore, we search the subcarrier of high SNR for decoding. The SNR value can be estimated after the self-correlation. The subcarrier searching process is called "channel scan." The decoding process of the NICScatter receiver with Wi-Fi NIC is summarized in Figure 10.

4.2 Receiving with SDR

We use a USRP N210[7] with XCVR2450[9] as the SDR platform. Using the topology from Figure 2, one USRP is used as the signal helper to generate a sine tone in the 2.4GHz band with constant amplitude. Another USRP is used as the receiver. They use 250kHz as the step in the channel scan. Because the samples of the SDR can be thought of as fine-grained RSSI samples, the decoding process is the same as the one shown in Figure 10.

5 EVALUATION

In this section, we evaluate the communication performance of NICScatter, and its security threat to mobile devices. The evaluation experiments are designed according to the attack scenarios in §2.3.

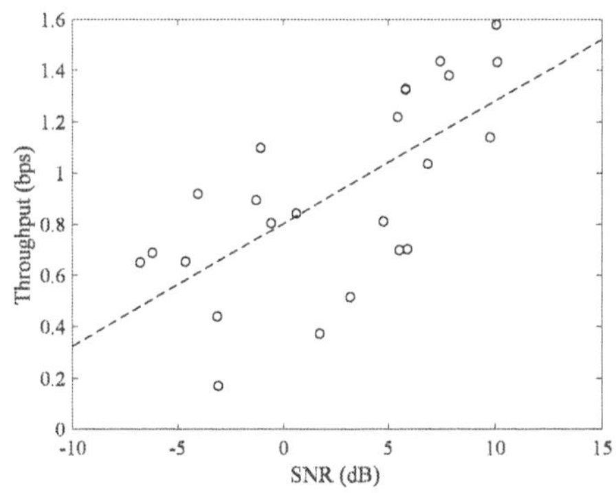

Figure 12: Throughput vs. SNR

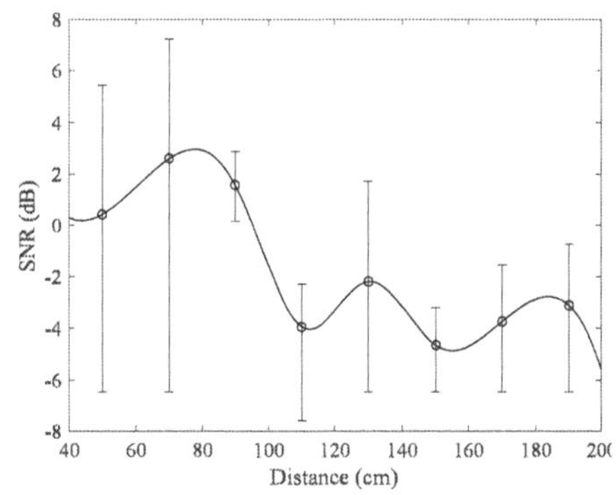

Figure 13: Laptop with Built-in Antenna.

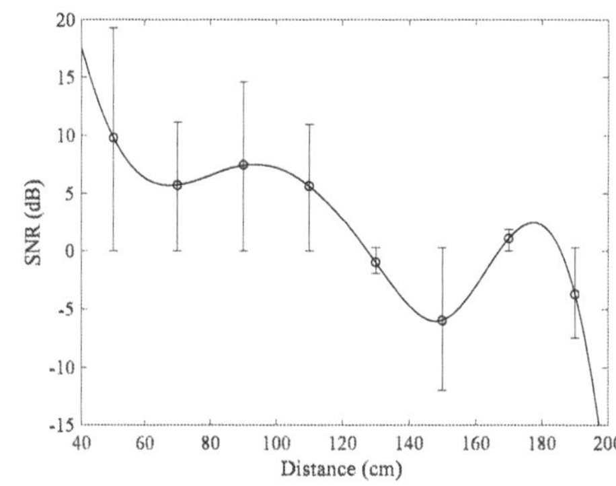

Figure 14: Laptop with External Omni-directional Antenna.

Specifically, we use commercial laptops and mobile phones as NICScatter transmitters, and normal WiFi devices and wireless sensing platforms as NICScatter receivers. Table 2 outlines corresponding evaluation subsections.

5.1 USRP as Receiver

5.1.1 Experiment Setup. The evaluation experiments are conducted in a typical office environment. The topology of the evaluation is shown in Figure 11. The evaluation with USRP as the receiver consists of two attack cases.

In first case, a laptop is the victim and two USRP N210s with XCVR 2450 daughter board are the attacker. This case is used to demonstrate the attack with wireless sensing platforms. Specifically, One USRP is used as the signal helper to generate a sine wave at 2.4GHz. It is equipped with a 5 dBi omni-directional antenna, and the transmit power is 0dBm. Another USRP is used as the receiver. It is equipped with a 2 dBi D-Link omni-directional antenna[2]. Its sampling rate is 250kHz and Rx gain is 45dB. The laptop is HP Elitebook 8530P, which is equipped with a built-in Intel 5300 Wi-Fi NIC.

Settings of the second case (§5.1.7) are the same as the first case, except that the laptop victim is replaced by a Samsung Galaxy S2 smartphone, whose Wi-Fi NIC is Broadcom BCM4330.

5.1.2 Throughput vs. SNR. We first evaluate the throughput under different channel conditions in Figure 12. Each measurement is conducted over a 6 minutes' period, containing 30 packets/600 bits. The payload of each packet is randomly generated. We change the channel condition by moving the receiver to 24 different distances from the victim. As expected, the throughput shows an increasing trend with SNR. Since the throughput is far less than the channel capacity, we can successfully decode packets when the SNR is as low as -5 dB. The maximum achievable throughput is 1.6 bps, which is a little bit lower than the transmission rate, *i.e.*, 2bps. Some bits are not received correctly, mainly due to the following two reasons. First, NICScatter transmits data at very low rates. Thus the mobility of nearby people will dramatically affect the multipath condition during the air time of one bit, resulting in the corruption of the received bits. The second reason is the interference from nearby wireless transmissions. There are about 10 active access points in our evaluation environment. Nearby wireless transmission would distort the received signals, leading to decoding failure.

5.1.3 SNR vs. Distance. The receiver is placed at different distance d_2 from the victim. Figure 13 shows the SNR of the received packets. As expected, the SNR curve has a decreasing trend with the increasing distance. Notice that there are some small fluctuations in the curve. As we described in Section 3, this is because, when the receiver is at different distance to the victim, the reflected signal may either superimpose constructively or destructively with the incident signal. When the receiver is 190 cm away from the victim, the SNR is -3 dB, which is close to the decodable bound in Figure 12. Thus, the effective receiving distance of this setting is about 2 meters.

As we notice the antenna design inside the laptop may affect the performance, we connect the Wi-Fi NIC with an external VERT 2450 3dBi omni-directional antenna[8]. The performance is shown in Figure 14. The overall performance of an external antenna is much better than the built-in antenna, especially when the receiver is close to the victim. This may be caused by the differences in the gain and polarization between the built-in and external antennas.

Note that the received signal is a combination of the backscatter signal and the helper's incident signal. The helper's signal contains no information and is the interference for receiving the backscatter signal. In our test settings, the helper's signal is 40dB to 50dB stronger than the backscatter signal. Since the USRP has 14bit ADC and 84dB dynamic range, the receiver is able to capture the backscatter signal under the presence of the interference. As the interference is a constant sine wave, it can be treated as the DC and easily removed in the received amplitude trace. When the receiver is 2m away from the victim, the power of the backscatter signal is far below the noise floor of the USRP receiver. Thus, given enough ADC dynamic range, increasing the sensitivity level of the USRP receiver is a direct way to increase the communication distance.

5.1.4 Performance of Different Wi-Fi NICs. In Figure 15, we show the performance of different Wi-Fi NICs. As laptops are normally not compatible with different models of Wi-Fi NICs, a desktop with a PCI-E adapter is used as the victim. Different Wi-Fi NICs

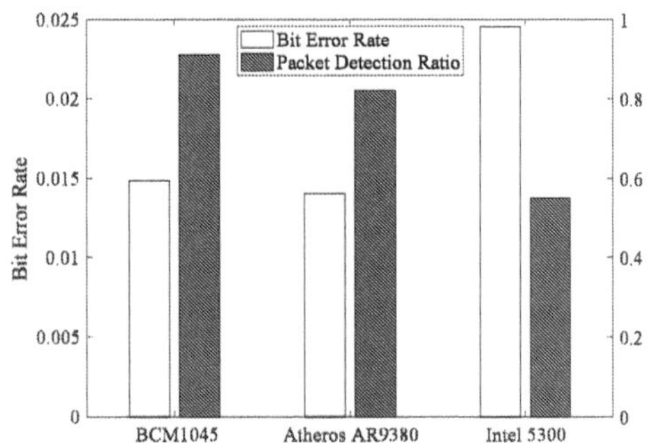

Figure 15: Performance of Different WiFi NIC Models.

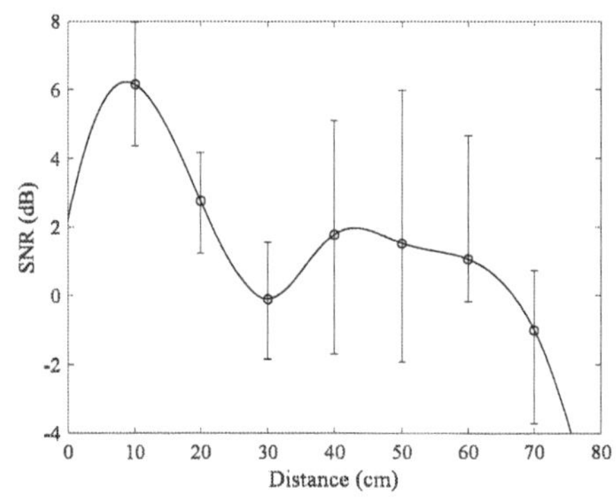

Figure 16: Receiving through the Wall.

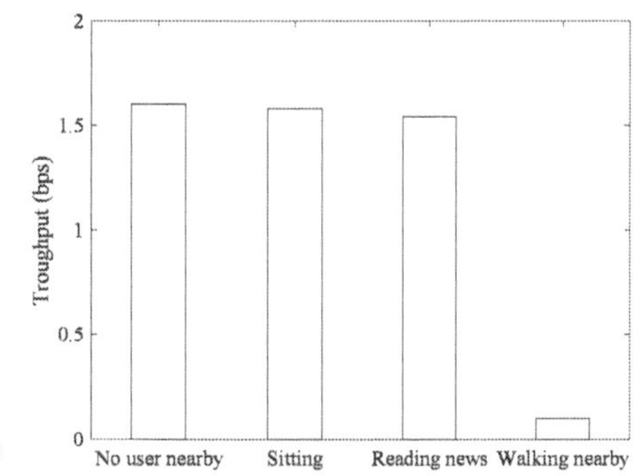

Figure 17: Impact of User Behaviours.

are installed on the PCI-E adapter and connected to a D-Link 2 dBi omni-directional antenna. This experiment covers the products from three major Wi-Fi NIC vendors, including Broadcom, Atheros, and Intel. The distance between the victim and the receiver is fixed to d_2=1m. From Figure 15, we can see that Intel 5300 shows the worst performance among the three. This result matches our impedance measurement in Table 1 and Equation 1. The impedances changes of the Intel 5300 NIC results in the largest backscatter loss among the three. Therefore, if a laptop is equipped with a Wi-Fi NIC from Broadcom or Atheros, its transmission range would likely be larger than 2 meters.

5.1.5 Through-the-Wall Performance. We also test the scenario when the receiver is behind the wall. We place the USRP receiver next to the wall in another room and increase the victim's distance to the wall from 10 cm to 80 cm. The results are shown in Figure 16. When the victim is 70cm away from the wall, the SNR is −1 dB. When the distance further increases to 80 cm, the receiver fails to receive packets. Thus, the communication distance is 70 cm in the through-the-wall scenario.

5.1.6 Throughput with Different User Behaviors. As we describe above, the nearby human movement would change the multipath conditions and affect the throughput. We evaluate the impact with four types of user behaviors: 1) nobody near the laptop; 2) a user sitting before the laptop, with no movement; 3) a user sitting before the laptop and reading news via a web browser; 4) a user walking around near the laptop. The results are shown in Figure 17. The first case is to test the static case, with no human movement; the second case is to see whether human breath/heartbeat would affect the performance; the third case is to show whether small user movement would degrade the performance; the last case is to show the system performance with significant human movement. From the figure, we can see that human breath or small movement would not degrade the system performance. However, significant movement such as walking will significantly degrade the throughput. The attacker may obtain information from the victim when the environment is stable.

5.1.7 Android Phone as Victim. We also evaluate the performance when using an Android phone as the victim. The Tx gain of the signal helper is increased to 10dB. The results are shown in Figure 18. When the receiver is 20 cm away from the victim, the SNR drops below −5 dB. The communication distance is less than that of the laptop. The major reason is the antenna of the mobile phone is more compact and has less gain than that of the laptop. Although the communication distance is limited, the smartphone is still under risks. There are many possible ways for the covert channel to leak information. For example, when making mobile payments, we need to put the smartphone close to a reader, which could be malicious. In another case, a QR code can pretend to be a coupon which in fact just intends to attract people to be close to the receiver.

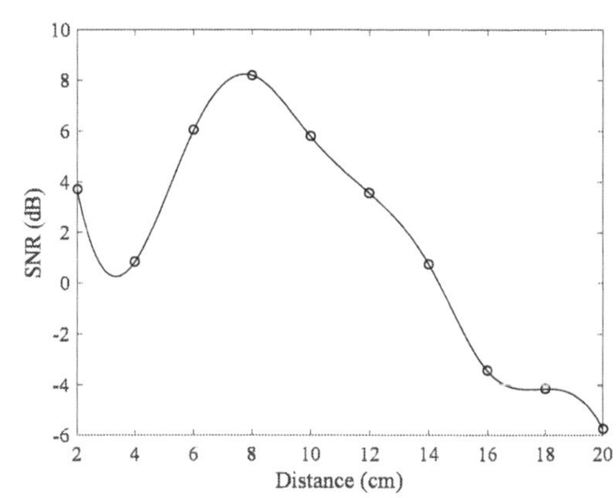

Figure 18: Android Phone as the Victim.

5.2 Laptop as Receiver

5.2.1 Experiment Setup. This scenario is used to demonstrate the attack using commercial Wi-Fi NIC as the receiver. The topology is the same as Figure 11. We uses laptops as the victim and the receiver. Both laptops are equipped with an Intel 5300 Wi-Fi NIC. A TP-Link TL-WDR4360 access point is used as the signal helper. The signal helper generates incident signals by transmitting UDP packets to the receiver. The receiver is running the CSI tool to capture the CSI trace of the received packets. On average, 1000 packets are received within one second. We also assume the attacker

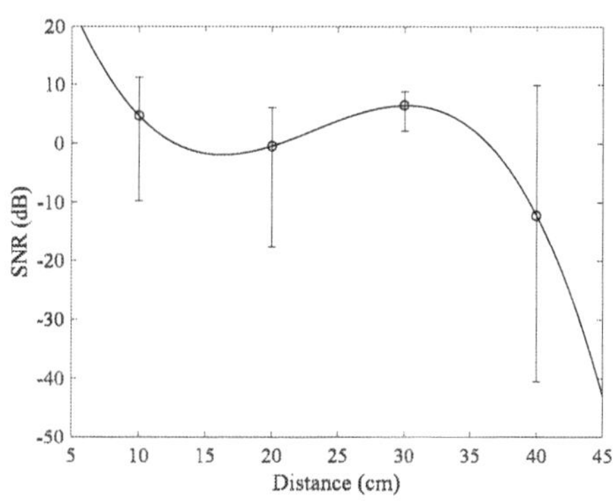

Figure 19: Receving with RSSI.

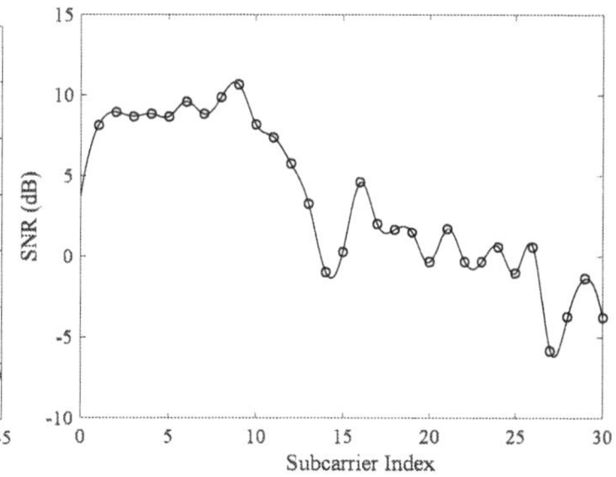

Figure 20: Subcarrier SNR.

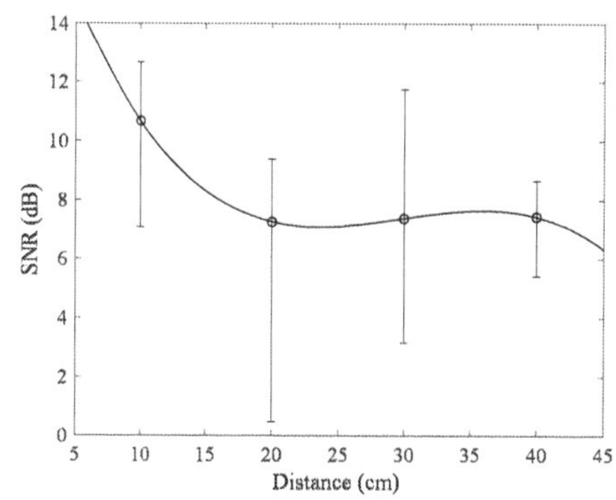

Figure 21: Receiving with CSI.

can improve the receiving ability of its devices. Thus, the receiver's internal antenna is replaced with an external 2dBi D-Link antenna.

5.2.2 Receiving with RSSI. We extract RSSI values from the CSI tool. Note this is not necessary, as RSSI value can also be extracted from the radio tap header in the captured packet. We decode the RSSI trace according to Figure 10, the SNR values are shown in Figure 19. When the victim is 40cm away from the receiver, the SNR drops below −11 dB. At this distance, the receiver can barely decode any packets. Thus, the effective decoding distance is about 30cm.

Compared with USRP, the laptop receiver must be closer to the victim. This is because the CSI tool exposes a smaller number of bits (also smaller dynamic range) than USPRs do. Recall that in our attack scenario the interference is 40dB to 50 dB stronger than the backscatter signal. The variation of the backscatter signal cannot be effectively quantified by the RSSI values. So even the backscatter signal is oversampled in the RSSI trace, the decoding distance is limited.

We note our performance agrees with existing work. The Wi-Fi backscatter transmitter[26] uses a 9dBi[40] directional antenna to reflect the incident signal and achieves 2m receiving distance. As we use a 3dBi antenna in the transmitter, their backscatter loss is 12dB higher than ours. In our evaluation topology, it can be calculated that the SINR at 30cm is 11dB higher than the SINR at 2m, which implies if we replace our transmitter's antenna with a 9dBi antenna, the two systems will have similar performance at 2m.

5.2.3 Receiving with CSI. We go further to analyze the CSI trace. The CSI tool provides channel information for adjacent subcarriers. We observe the same results as in [26] that there are large SNR variations among different subcarriers. Figure 20 shows the SNR for 30 subcarriers when the receiver is 10 cm away from the transmitter. The first to the 10th subcarriers have higher SNR than the remaining ones do. To eliminate the impact of the low SNR subcarriers, we use channel scan to select the high SNR subcarriers for decoding. We show the final results in Figure 21. Comparing Figure 21 with Figure 19, we can learn that CSI has better performance than RSSI. There are two main reasons. First, CSI values are expressed in linear unit and thus have higher resolution than RSSI values, which is expressed in dBm. Second, RSSI is an averaged value over all the subcarriers. Some subcarriers with low SNR may increase the noise in the corresponding RSSI value. With CSI, the communication distance can be larger than 40cm.

Data	bits	Laptop@30cm	USRP@90cm
MAC Address	48	49 sec	54 sec
Plain Password	64	1.09 min	1.20 min
MD5	128	2.18 min	2.40 min
GPS Coordinate	128	2.18 min	2.40 min
SHA1 Hash	160	2.72 min	3.00 min
Disk Encryption Key	256	4.35 min	4.80 min

Table 3: Transmission Time of Sensitive Information

5.3 Attack Summary

According to the above evaluation, we summarize the time needed to transmit the sensitive information in Table 3. In order to increase the effective distance, the attacker can choose to improve the sensitivity of the receiver devices. CSI values are more sensitive than RSSI values. Emerging wireless sensing platforms are more sensitive than commercial Wi-Fi NICs. Attacking small mobile devices, like a smartphone, may require close distance, since these devices use compact antennas, which have a small antenna gain. However, this does not suggest smaller mobile devices are safer. This is because we have more opportunities to carry them and they have more opportunities to be exposed to the risky public environment.

6 RELATED WORK

In this section, we review the related literature from two aspects: covert channels and backscatter communication.

6.1 Covert Channels

Covert channels have been a threat to security systems for a long time. The term was first introduced in 1973 by Lampson [29] to discuss the method through which a program leaks its private data to another process. After that, various covert channel techniques have been developed to bypass security measures to leak information. File locks [16], acoustic signals [36], vibrations [35], CPU temperature [32], *etc.* have all been used to transmit information between two processes. The concept also has been extended to networked systems, where patterns in network traffic are exploited to convey information [12].

Our work belongs to another type: the covert channel in air-gapped systems, where the victim is isolated from the receiver physically and has no network connections. As early as in the 1950s, the U.S. government became concerned about information leakage in such systems through the EMR emitted by computers' video display units or cables and thus started the TEMPEST program [28]. Over the past few decades, various air-gapped covert channels have been discussed in the public domain. Most of them assume that the victim is a desktop or a server. We compare our work with these covert channels below:

Electromagnetic Radiation. Among various computer components, the video display unit can generate significant EMR [37]. [23] shows how the display content from a laptop or pad can be captured remotely, but the process requires an SDR platform as the receiver. Another work uses a VGA port to generate FM signals [18] for mobile receivers, but not every mobile device has a VGA port. A recent work [33] shows that the EMR generated by the operations of the hard drive can be picked up by a smartphone's magnetic field sensor. However this technique cannot be applied to mobile devices with SSD drives. An interesting work, GSMem [17], leverages the bus operations to generate EMR at the cellular band, but it relies on SSE instructions, which are not available in mobile processors.

Acoustic channels. There are some work exploiting the sound from 18 to 20kHz to establish covert channels [13, 14, 21, 22]. However, one limitation is that the sound in this band can be heard by children or pets, which makes these methods less stealthy.

Thermal emanations. Guri [19] showed that by regulating different workloads on the CPU, they could manipulate the temperature level in the vicinity. These changes can be picked up by the temperature sensors in nearby PCs. However, due to the power constraints, this method cannot be applied to mobile devices.

6.2 Backscatter Communication

Backscatter communication works by reflecting RF signals. To transmit information, a backscatter device switches the load impedance of its antenna, which causes the incident RF signals to be reflected or absorbed. The receiver distinguishes between these two states to decode information. As backscatter devices do not actively generate signal waves, it consumes only microwatts of power. Thus, backscatter devices can be battery-free. RFID technology is an application of backscatter communication.

Recently, Liu *et al.* [31] proposed ambient backscatter, which takes advantage of TV signals in the air and no longer needs a dedicated reader. In a step forward, they [25, 27] enabled tags which can backscatter RF signals to 802.11b packets [25] for Wi-Fi receivers.

The work mostly related to ours is Wi-Fi backscatter [26]. The authors proposed a tag to backscatter Wi-Fi signals to a Wi-Fi reader, which could be an AP or a smartphone. Then, the Wi-Fi reader decodes the data through CSI or RSSI traces. NICScatter uses a Wi-Fi NIC rather than a tag to reflect the Wi-Fi signals. Thus, we have different design goals and constraints. With regard to the performance, their throughput and communication range is better than ours. This is because, as an attacker, we cannot switch the NICs as fast as dedicated tags can and the impedance difference between NICs' on/off states is much smaller than that of dedicated tags.

7 DISCUSSION

In this section, we discuss possible countermeasures against the covert channel enabled by NICScatter. We also discuss limitations and future work of the current NICScatter design.

7.1 Countermeasures

Since NICScatter is based on RF signals, one direct way to block it is shielding, *i.e.*, blocking the incident signal or the reflected signal. However, unlike shielding EMR signals from the display interface or the CPU, shielding a wireless NIC destroys its basic functionalities, which is not desirable for mobile devices.

Another way to disable NICScatter is through the software layer. For Linux systems, cutting off any transition path in Figure 7 will block the NICScatter transmitter. For example, releasing the write permission of a device file, like `/dev/rfkill`, to users without root privileges is usually weird and unnecessary. The Gnome maintainers should be aware of that and find other workarounds for the Bluetooth control application. Another example is to stop `network_manager` from bringing up any Wi-Fi interface automatically. This, however, adds burdens for users. They need to manually turn on Wi-Fi every time when the device leaves the airplane mode. For Android system, hiding the interface for Wi-Fi control may disable many useful applications and sacrifice usability. Thus, the Android society may consider increasing the permission of Wi-Fi control to the dangerous level, so that the permission requirement will be explicitly notified during the app installation. Nevertheless, it is still hard for users to be fully aware of its potential risks.

7.2 Limitations and Future Work

The communication distance of the current NICScatter system may not be sufficient to satisfy the attack from 2m away. In a customized receiver like USRP, if the dynamic range of the ADC is large enough, the distance is limited by the device's sensitivity level. One can adopt a narrow baseband filter and low noise components in the receiver to extend the receiving range. Further, a current NICScatter receiver cannot handle the situation where multiple victims present in the receiving range. The packets from different victims will collide at the receiver and become undecodable. The same problem exists in RFID systems for supporting concurrent transmissions. Similar to the existing work [24], it should be possible to leverage the properties of the oversampled trace and the features of OOPM modulation to decode the packets from multiple concurrent transmitters.

In addition to the covert nature, the insight of NICScatter also implies several interesting points that are worth exploring in the future work. Communicating via backscatter is a promising way to enable network access of low power wireless devices, such as IoTs. While today's discussion mainly focuses on hardware prototypes and PHY layer designs, NICScatter provides a possible way to leverage numerous conventional devices to understand the benefit and the impact of backscatter communication on the network level. Moreover, NICScatter also inherits the beneficial properties in backscatter signals. For example, as we already have knowledge on localizing RFID tags[38], it is possible to reuse the method to localize conventional wireless devices through NICScatter as well. Further, although we only verify NICScatter on Wi-Fi NICs in this paper, we believe the method we used, *i.e.*, modulating the impedance of the RF circuits through changing its working states, may exist in other RF transceivers, such as cellular, Bluetooth, etc., which may bring other communication opportunities and security issues.

8 CONCLUSION

This paper introduces NICScatter, a backscatter communication method relying on commercial Wi-Fi NICs. NICScatter's design is based on the property that the impedance of a Wi-Fi NIC varies in different working states. NICScatter transmitter thus switches NIC hardware between on and off states to modulate the RF signals reflected by its antenna. The NICScatter receiver extracts information from the transmitter by analyzing the amplitude of the reflected signals. We show that even an ordinary wireless device with RSSI/CSI measurement ability is capable of the decoding process.

As the communication form of NICScatter hasn't caused enough attention in current mobile systems, we show there are vulnerabilities to exploit NICScatter as a covert way to leak information. Our experiments show that the covert channel on a laptop can reach 2 meters away and it can even transmit through a wall. We, therefore, demonstrate a realistic threat of data exfiltration attack on mobile devices.

ACKNOWLEDGEMENT

We would like to thank our Shepherd Fadel Adib, and the anonymous MobiCom reviewers for their constructive comments. We also thank Ted Spaeth for help with proofreading and Shanpu Shen for help with impedance measurement. This work was supported in part by the 973 Project under Grant 2013CB329006, in part by the RGC under Contract CERG 16212714, 16203215, Contract ITS/143/16FP-A, and Contract R8015, in part by the Huawei-HKUST Joint Laboratory (by the IoT WiFi Key Technologies), in part by the ShanghaiTech University Startup Fund under Grant F-0203-17-010.

REFERENCES

[1] Android permissions. https://developer.android.com/reference/android/Manifest.permission.html.
[2] D-link 2dbi antenna. https://www.amazon.com/D-Link-2dbi-Antenna-Wireless-Router/dp/B002XENHB0.
[3] gnome-bluetooth source code. http://sources.debian.net/src/gnome-bluetooth/.
[4] rfkill. https://www.kernel.org/doc/Documentation/rfkill.txt.
[5] R&S®ZVB vector network analyzers. https://www.rohde-schwarz.com/us/product/zvb-productstartpage_63493-7990.html.
[6] Ubuntu mobile. https://www.ubuntu.com/mobile.
[7] Usrp n210. https://www.ettus.com/product/details/UN210-KIT.
[8] Vert 2450 3dbi antenna. https://www.ettus.com/product/details/VERT2450.
[9] Xcvr2450. https://kb.ettus.com/XCVR2450.
[10] F. Adib, Z. Kabelac, D. Katabi, and R. C. Miller. 3d tracking via body radio reflections. In *Proceedings of the 11th USENIX Conference on Networked Systems Design and Implementation*, pages 317–329. USENIX Association, 2014.
[11] F. Adib and D. Katabi. See through walls with wifi! *SIGCOMM Comput. Commun. Rev.*, 43(4):75–86, Aug. 2013.
[12] S. Cabuk, C. E. Brodley, and C. Shields. Ip covert timing channels: design and detection. In *Proceedings of the 11th ACM conference on Computer and communications security*, pages 178–187. ACM, 2004.
[13] B. Carrara and C. Adams. On acoustic covert channels between air-gapped systems. In *International Symposium on Foundations and Practice of Security*, pages 3–16. Springer, 2014.
[14] L. Deshotels. Inaudible sound as a covert channel in mobile devices. In *WOOT*, 2014.
[15] W. Enck, P. Gilbert, S. Han, V. Tendulkar, B.-G. Chun, L. P. Cox, J. Jung, P. McDaniel, and A. N. Sheth. Taintdroid: an information-flow tracking system for realtime privacy monitoring on smartphones. *ACM Transactions on Computer Systems (TOCS)*, 32(2):5, 2014.
[16] V. D. Gligor. *A guide to understanding covert channel analysis of trusted systems*. The Center, 1994.
[17] M. Guri, A. Kachlon, O. Hasson, G. Kedma, Y. Mirsky, and Y. Elovici. Gsmem: Data exfiltration from air-gapped computers over gsm frequencies. In *USENIX Security*, pages 849–864, 2015.
[18] M. Guri, G. Kedma, A. Kachlon, and Y. Elovici. Airhopper: Bridging the air-gap between isolated networks and mobile phones using radio frequencies. In *MALWARE*, pages 58–67. IEEE, 2014.
[19] M. Guri, M. Monitz, Y. Mirski, and Y. Elovici. Bitwhisper: Covert signaling channel between air-gapped computers using thermal manipulations. In *Computer Security Foundations Symposium*, pages 276–289. IEEE, 2015.
[20] D. Halperin, W. Hu, A. Sheth, and D. Wetherall. Predictable 802.11 packet delivery from wireless channel measurements. In *ACM SIGCOMM Computer Communication Review*, volume 40, pages 159–170. ACM, 2010.
[21] M. Hanspach and M. Goetz. On covert acoustical mesh networks in air. *Journal of Communications*, 8(11), 2013.
[22] M. Hanspach and M. Goetz. Recent developments in covert acoustical communications. In *Sicherheit*, pages 243–254. Citeseer, 2014.
[23] Y. Hayashi, N. Homma, M. Miura, T. Aoki, and H. Sone. A threat for tablet pcs in public space: Remote visualization of screen images using em emanation. In *Proceedings of the 2014 ACM CCS*, pages 954–965. ACM, 2014.
[24] P. Hu, P. Zhang, and D. Ganesan. Laissez-faire: Fully asymmetric backscatter communication. *acm special interest group on data communication*, 45(4):255–267, 2015.
[25] V. Iyer, V. Talla, B. Kellogg, S. Gollakota, and J. Smith. Inter-technology backscatter: Towards internet connectivity for implanted devices. In *SIGCOMM*, pages 356–369. ACM, 2016.
[26] B. Kellogg, A. Parks, S. Gollakota, J. R. Smith, and D. Wetherall. Wi-fi backscatter: Internet connectivity for rf-powered devices. *ACM SIGCOMM Computer Communication Review*, 44(4):607–618, 2015.
[27] B. Kellogg, V. Talla, S. Gollakota, and J. R. Smith. Passive wi-fi: Bringing low power to wi-fi transmissions. In *13th USENIX Symposium on Networked Systems Design and Implementation (NSDI 16)*, pages 151–164. USENIX Association, 2016.
[28] M. G. Kuhn and R. J. Anderson. Soft tempest: Hidden data transmission using electromagnetic emanations. In *International Workshop on Information Hiding*, pages 124–142. Springer, 1998.
[29] B. W. Lampson. A note on the confinement problem. *Communications of the ACM*, 16(10):613–615, 1973.
[30] B. Li, S. Zhang, and S. Shen. Csi-based wifi-inertial state estimation.
[31] V. Liu, A. Parks, V. Talla, S. Gollakota, D. Wetherall, and J. R. Smith. Ambient backscatter: wireless communication out of thin air. In *SIGCOMM*, pages 39–50. ACM, 2013.
[32] R. J. Masti, D. Rai, A. Ranganathan, C. Müller, L. Thiele, and S. Capkun. Thermal covert channels on multi-core platforms. In *USENIX Security*, pages 865–880, 2015.
[33] N. Matyunin, J. Szefer, S. Biedermann, and S. Katzenbeisser. Covert channels using mobile device's magnetic field sensors. In *Asia and South Pacific Design Automation Conference*, pages 525–532. IEEE, 2016.
[34] P. V. Nikitin and K. V. S. Rao. Antennas and propagation in uhf rfid systems. In *2008 IEEE International Conference on RFID*, pages 277–288, April 2008.
[35] E. Novak, Y. Tang, Z. Hao, Q. Li, and Y. Zhang. Physical media covert channels on smart mobile devices. In *Proceedings of the 2015 ACM International Joint Conference on Pervasive and Ubiquitous Computing*, pages 367–378. ACM, 2015.
[36] R. Schlegel, K. Zhang, X.-y. Zhou, M. Intwala, A. Kapadia, and X. Wang. Soundcomber: a stealthy and context-aware sound trojan for smartphones. In *NDSS*, volume 11, pages 17–33, 2011.
[37] W. Van Eck. Electromagnetic radiation from video display units: An eavesdropping risk? *Computers & Security*, 4(4):269–286, 1985.
[38] J. Wang and D. Katabi. Dude, where's my card?: Rfid positioning that works with multipath and non-line of sight. *acm special interest group on data communication*, 43(4):51–62, 2013.
[39] R. Want. An introduction to rfid technology. *IEEE pervasive computing*, 5(1):25–33, 2006.
[40] P. Zhang, M. Rostami, P. Hu, and D. Ganesan. Enabling practical backscatter communication for on-body sensors. pages 370–383, 2016.
[41] M. Zhao, F. Adib, and D. Katabi. Emotion recognition using wireless signals. In *Proceedings of the 22nd Annual International Conference on Mobile Computing and Networking*, pages 95–108. ACM, 2016.

Spurring Mobile Systems Research Into The Next Decade

Thyaga Nandagopal
National Science Foundation
Alexandria, VA 22314
tnandago@nsf.gov

ABSTRACT

Wireless and mobile systems are becoming an ubiquitous part of everyday life. Some of the most common systems have become commoditized, enabling higher-layer application-driven research while at the same time inhibiting lower-layer research. On the other hand, new frontiers of wireless communications are opening up in various spectrum bands hitherto not used for wireless data communications. This talk will cover the future of wireless systems-driven research and contributions to science & technology from the vantage point of the National Science Foundation.

CCS Concepts/ACM Classifiers

休General and reference 休Networks

Author Keywords

Wireless systems; ubiquitous computing; wireless spectrum; PAWR

BIOGRAPHY

Dr. Thyaga Nandagopal is a Program Director at the National Science Foundation in the Directorate of Computer & Information Science and Engineering (CISE), where he manages mobile systems and wireless networking research across multiple funding programs with an annual budget of over $50M. At NSF, he leads the Platforms for Advanced Wireless Research (PAWR) program, a $100M public-private partnership launched in July 2016. He also serves as the co-chair of the Wireless Spectrum Research and Development Senior Steering Group (WSRD SSG), which co-ordinates spectrum-related research and development activities across the Federal government. He is an IEEE Fellow, and a member of ACM SIGMOBILE. Thyaga Nandagopal holds a Ph.D. degree in Electrical Engineering from the University of Illinois at Urbana-Champaign.

MobiCom伕7, October 16-20, 2017, Snowbird, UT, USA.

ACM ISBN 978-1-4503-4916-1/17/10.
DOI: https://doi.org/10.1145/3117811.3130260

UIWear: Easily Adapting User Interfaces for Wearable Devices

Jian Xu*
Stony Brook University
jianxu1@cs.stonybrook.edu

Qingqing Cao*
Stony Brook University
qicao@cs.stonybrook.edu

Aditya Prakash
Stony Brook University
adiprakash@cs.stonybrook.edu

Aruna Balasubramanian
Stony Brook University
arunab@cs.stonybrook.edu

Donald E. Porter
The University of North Carolina at Chapel Hill
porter@cs.unc.edu

ABSTRACT

Wearable devices such as smartwatches offer exciting new opportunities for users to interact with their applications. However, the current wearable programming model requires the developer to write a custom *companion app* for each wearable form factor; the companion app extends the smartphone display onto the wearable, relays user interactions from the wearable to the phone, and updates the wearable display as needed. The development effort required to write a companion app is significant and will not scale to an increasing diversity of form factors. This paper argues for a different programming model for wearable devices. The developer writes an application for the smartphone, but only specifies a UI design for the wearable. Our UIWear system abstracts a logical model of the smartphone GUI, re-tailors the GUI for the wearable device based on the specified UI design, and compiles it into a companion app that we call the UICompanion app. We implemented UIWear on Android smartphones, AndroidWear smartwatches, and Sony SmartEyeGlasses. We evaluate 20 developer-written companion apps from the AndroidWear category on Google Play against the UIWear-created UICompanion apps. The lines-of-code required for the developer to specify the UI design in UIWear is an order-of-magnitude smaller compared to the companion app lines-of-code. Further, in most cases, the UICompanion app performed comparably or better than the corresponding companion app both in terms of qualitative metrics, including latency and energy, and quantitative metrics, including look-and-feel.

1 INTRODUCTION

After decades of largely homogeneous personal computing devices, the range of device form factors and user interfaces has widened dramatically. Wearable devices, such as smartwatches and smartglasses, provide user interfaces that decouple the benefits of computer assistance from constantly holding a phone or sitting at a computer. For example, a GPS heads-up display helps skiers navigate a difficult slope [11]. The *Spotify* smartwatch app [20] allows the user to control the music easily, freeing the user's hands from constantly holding the phone.

A key bottleneck in leveraging these wearable form factors is the developer effort involved in adapting an application to a wearable device. The dominant model for wearable apps is a *companion app*, that essentially mirrors the smartphone application onto the wearable form factor. The companion app maps a subset of the smartphone app's graphical user interface (GUI), and *re-tailors* the GUI to suit the wearable device. For example, a button on a smartphone might be enlarged and placed on a *card* [7] surface on the smartwatch so that the user can tap anywhere on the watch surface to toggle the button. Our study of the top 100 smartwatch applications in the AndroidWear category [23] on Google Play shows that, for 78% of the apps, the watch app simply mirrors the phone (§2).

For each application and form factor, developers need to write a unique companion app—each requiring thousands of lines of code (§8). As a result, only a small fraction of smartphone apps have companion apps. Moreover, without source code, third-party developers cannot design new companion apps for an existing smartphone app.

In this work, we present a different programming model for wearable devices, where the developer writes the smartphone application *once*, and writes a simple *meta program* to specify how the application should be extended to a given form factor. Our system, UIWear, automatically creates companion apps, that we call *UICompanion* apps, for different form factors based on the meta program. The developer effort in writing the meta program is an order-of-magnitude lower than writing the companion app. UIWear is transparent to the application, does not require source code or changes to the original application, can re-tailor the GUI to suit the wearable interface, and is well-suited for mobile and wearables.

The overarching principle of UIWear is to decouple application management from application design. The human designer (developer or end-user) only specifies what parts of the smartphone GUI are mapped to the wearable and how the GUI is re-tailored, encoded as a meta program.

UIWear's *UI virtualization architecture* manages all other aspects of extending the app to the wearable device. UIWear abstracts a logical model of the GUI and uses this abstraction to re-tailor and render the GUI on the wearable. UIWear also performs all underlying synchronization at the GUI layer. All user interactions on the wearable device are captured by the GUI abstraction and sent to the phone. The UIWear proxy on the phone emulates the

*Primary authors with equal contribution.

MobiCom '17, October 16–20, 2017, Snowbird, UT, USA

ACM ISBN 978-1-4503-4916-1/17/10...$15.00
https://doi.org/10.1145/3117811.3117819

user interaction as though it occurred locally, and the resulting update is mirrored on the wearable device.

One essential contribution of UIWear is identifying the "pinch-point" to extract a logical model of the GUI. Existing works on cross-device display, including RDP [59], and others [25, 27, 44, 60, 62], extract GUI at the hardware frame buffer level. Unfortunately, the frame buffer already composites the UI elements into a bitmap, losing any semantic information that is required for re-tailoring. Instead, UIWear uses the *UI tree* abstraction, which is commonly used across operating systems to represent the GUI as individual UI elements and their relationships [2, 4]. UIWear essentially splices the UI tree, tailors it according to the meta program, and compiles it into the UICompanion app. Although prior approaches [12, 30, 38, 55, 67] have shown how to transparently extract the UI tree without requiring application support, they are only able to extract the UI tree partially. UIWear augments the underlying UI tree mechanism to transparently extract the complete tree.

Another key challenge is in synchronizing at the GUI layer. Smartphones only allow a *single* active GUI at a given time; in fact, the graphics stack of background apps is destroyed. The consequence is that the wearable app can only synchronize as long as the phone app is in the foreground. We observe that, while maintaining the full graphics stack of each background application is power consuming, the logical GUI model (in our case the UI tree) can be kept active even for background apps with minimal effect on power. In UIWear, we modify the operating system to keep the UI tree of a background application active. This simple change allows us to multiplex I/O events to and from background applications with minimal effect on power.

There has been related work both in the systems and the human-computer interaction (HCI) communities for designing cross-device applications. However, related systems either only work in homogenous environments that do not require UI re-tailoring [24–26, 44, 59, 60], or support UI retailoring, but only for specific applications and devices [30, 50, 53, 65, 70]. UIWear combines the advantages of the two approaches.

UIWear is implemented over Android, AndroidWear (for smartwatches), and the Sony SmartEyeglass [17]. The meta program is specified as an XML. We built an easy-to-use overlay visual tool for the designer to mark parts of the GUI that are mapped to the wearable. UIWear then provides XML based templates for the designer to easily write the GUI layout for the wearable device.

We evaluate 20 developer-written companion apps from the AndroidWear category on Google Play. In each case, we create a UICompanion app to mimic the existing companion app functionality. The meta program used to create these UICompanion apps is an order-of-magnitude smaller compared to the AndroidWear companion app. Our evaluation shows that UICompanion apps perform similarly or better for most of the 20 apps in terms of update and response latencies, as well as CPU consumption. Further, UICompanion apps significantly reduce the energy consumption on the watch, in some cases by more than 5 times, by offloading most of the tasks to the more powerful phone. Interestingly, despite offloading the tasks to the phone, UIWear does not increase energy consumption on the phone when compared to companion apps.

We show that UIWear can also be extended to create companion apps on smartglasses. On the Sony SmartEyeglass [17], we create

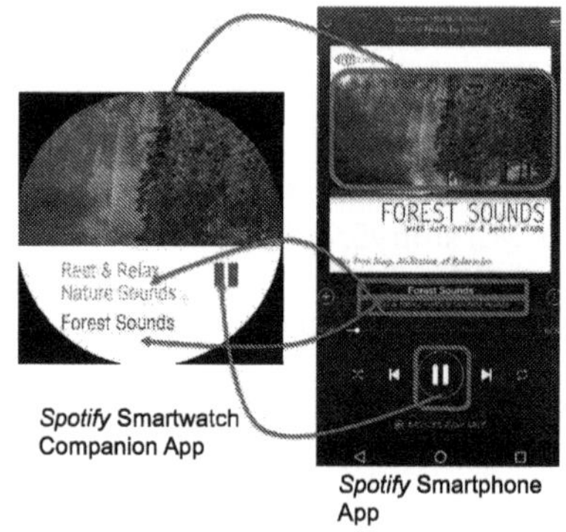

Figure 1: The *Spotify* smartphone and the corresponding smartwatch companion app. A subset of the smartphone GUI (marked within the *red* box) is re-tailored for the watch.

UICompanion apps for two apps, Spotify and MyShoppingList, with less than 30 lines of meta program.

Finally, we conduct a small scale user study to show the effectiveness of UICompanion apps in terms of functionality and look-and-feel. In our study, 20 subjects evaluated five applications using A/B testing techniques. The subjects reported that the UICompanion app was equal or better that the companion version 74% of the times in terms of functionality and 78% of the times in terms of look-and-feel. We also asked 10 of the 20 subjects to write a meta program for two applications. The subjects were able to write the meta program in under 16 minutes.

2 COMPANION APPLICATIONS

Companion apps are a common programming paradigm used by wearable operating systems and vendors including AndroidWear [23], Apple [5], Tizen [18], Pebble [15], and Google glass. A companion app is a GUI projection of the original smartphone app, where parts of the smartphone UI are re-tailored and displayed on the wearable. In most cases, the companion app does not operate independently but synchronizes with the smartphone app.

Figure 1 shows the *Spotify* companion app from the AndroidWear [23] category on Google Play. The companion app exports a view of the Spotify smartphone app to the watch. Events, such as pausing the song, are synchronized with the smartphone.

2.1 AndroidWear Apps

We studied the top 100 applications (as of March 2017) in the AndroidWear category on Google Play to categorize them in Table 1 on a spectrum from (A) completely independent of any smartphone interaction, to (D) Apps whose GUI is a subset of the smartphone GUI, and the wearable device completely mirrors changes on the phone. Between (A) and (D) are two categories: (B) apps that collect local data such as sensors, and (C) apps whose GUI is not a perfect mirror of the phone. Some apps in category (C) allow the two GUIs to drift out-of-sync in order to save energy. Our work focuses on the largest category of apps—category (D) at 78%—which mirror a subset of the GUI. We believe that (C) could likely also be subsumed by UIWear, and (B) would be possible in future work with some extensions.

We arrived at this categorization by manual inspection of the 100 applications to determine if they are standalone apps. To determine if the application uses local data, we look at permissions, since obtaining local sensor or GPS data requires explicit permission. To check if the app mirrors the smartphone UI, we perform various activities on both the phone and the watch and check for UI updates. Some apps also provide settings to allow users to choose between syncing with the phone or updating locally. Any app with this setting is marked *C*. The remaining apps, i.e., where the smartphone and the watch UIs mirror each other are marked *D*. *Watch Faces* are excluded in this study since they only change the watch background.

Category	% Apps	Examples
A	10%	Google Translate, TalkBack
B	6%	Fit, WeChat
C	6%	Outlook, Google Music
D	78%	Spotify, Weather

Table 1: Top 100 smartwatch apps in the AndroidWear category on Google Play divided among four subgroups.

Table 1 shows the percentage of apps and examples in each category. Over 78% of the applications fall under category *D*. This large number is attributable to a number of factors, including the small energy and CPU budgets on wearable devices, the fact that most users have a smartphone nearby at all times, and a desire to give users a consistent experience and data access on both devices. Even the newer Android 2.0 [3] OS which has about 25 (non watch face) applications on Google Play, only has 7 standalone apps. Although our manual categorization may miss some caveats in app functionality, the trend is clear. We expect that the companion app pattern will remain a common design pattern for wearable applications.

Spotify companion app: To analyze the principal implementation tasks for a companion app in category *D*, we analyze the Spotify companion app shown in Figure 1. The Spotify smartwatch app is about 10,000 lines of code (LoC), excluding libraries and comments. The app performs the following tasks (with the corresponding lines of code for each task): (1) creates native widgets to display on the wearable GUI and updates the GUI (> 4000 LoC) (2) implements a custom RPC protocol to exchange user input and other application data with the smartphone (> 4000 LoC), (3) creates basic data structures and classes (< 1000 LoC).

The Spotify companion app is a relatively simple adaptation of the smartphone GUI, yet this app is complicated by entangling the wearable GUI design problem with network protocol design to synchronize application state across devices. Our experience is that the Spotify app is representative of other companion apps. The current body of companion apps include one-off implementations of highly-similar management sub-tasks, including positioning GUI widgets on the remote device, synchronizing GUI state with the smartphone, and capturing user input. The goal of UIWear is to decouple GUI design from GUI management.

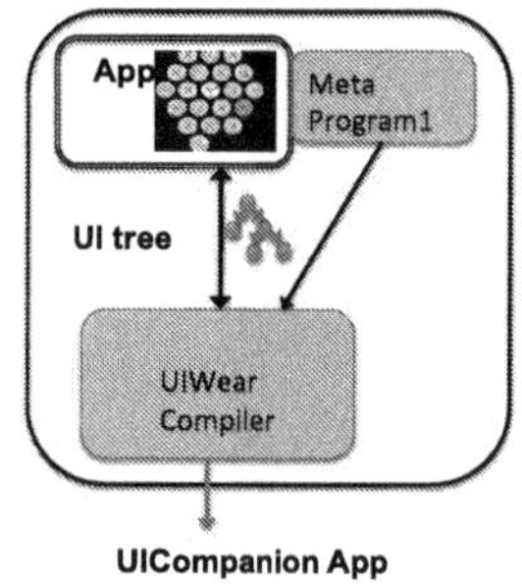

(a) UIWear Compiler and Meta program: UIWear compiles the meta program specification to create the UICompanion app.

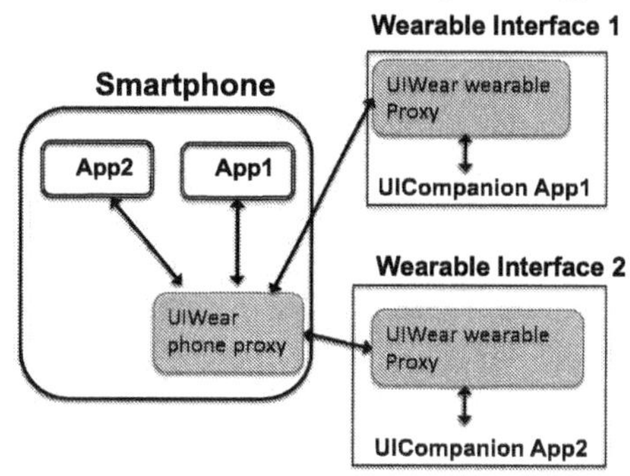

(b) UIWear Runtime: The UICompanion app on the wearable device synchronizes state with the smartphone app to relay user interactions and get UI updates.

Figure 2: UIWear Architecture

3 UIWEAR ARCHITECTURE

UIWear consists of both compile time and runtime components, depicted in Figure 2. At compile time, the human designer writes a meta program and UIWear compiles this into a UICompanion app. The UICompanion app is similar to a developer-written companion app, except that the app is automatically generated by UIWear, based on the design specified by the meta program. At runtime, UIWear synchronizes the application state between the companion app and the phone app, so that a user can access, control, and modify the application from the wearable device.

UIWear meta program: This is the only step of UIWear that requires a human-in-the-loop. Given an application, a developer writes a custom translation of the application UI to the wearable device. The custom translation includes decisions about what parts of the UI are to appear on the wearable device and how the UI is re-tailored. The designer writes a separate meta program for each wearable form factor, such as a smartwatch or a smartglass.

UIWear compiler: The UIWear compiler compiles the meta program to the UICompanion app and ships the app to the wearable device. This compilation step requires that UIWear extracts a logical model of the application GUI and re-tailors the GUI. UIWear uses the *UI tree* as the logical abstraction of the GUI.

A natural point at which to extract the UI tree is at the accessibility and UI automation interface. Current accessibility interfaces

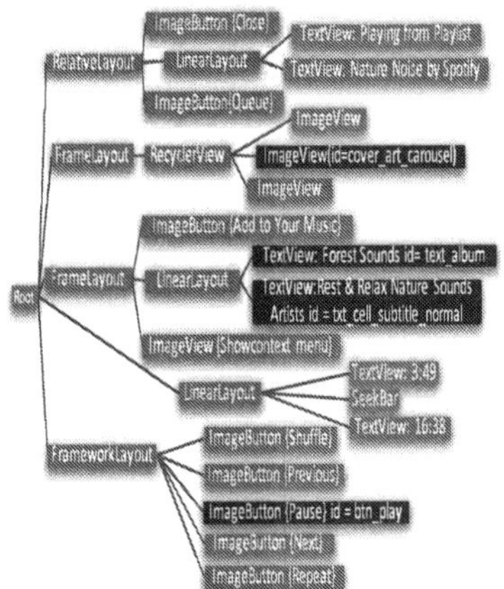

Figure 3: The UI tree corresponding to the Spotify phone GUI shown in Figure 1. The parts marked in *black* show the parts of the UI tree that are chosen by the human designer for display on the wearable device.

are designed only for extracting textual content of the GUI, primarily for applications for the visually impaired that may not require graphical content. UIWear augments this existing technique so that the complete UI tree, including text and visual data are extracted.

UIWear runtime: At run time, UIWear synchronizes the UI states of the wearable app and the corresponding phone app. UIWear's synchronization protocol relays input events from the wearable device to the UIWear phone proxy, which emulates the user input on the phone. The resulting GUI update is relayed to the wearable device using the UI tree abstraction. This synchronization requires no support from the phone application, unlike existing companion apps that need to write a custom remote procedure call interface. One constraint is that, in several smartphone OSes, only a single GUI (of the foreground application) is active at any given time. In UIWear we show how we can multiplex I/O events to and from several applications, including those in the background, at little-to-no marginal cost on the phone.

4 UI TREE EXTRACTION

UIWear uses *UI trees* to represent the logical model of the GUI. The UI tree is effectively a high-level, intermediate representation of the GUI. Both mobile and desktop operating systems use some variation of a UI tree to represent GUI state before it is rendered on the display frame buffer [2, 4, 30].

In Android, the key element required to construct the UI tree is the *view node*. The view node is an intermediate layer residing between the application and the graphics stack (other operating systems have a similar layer). The view node maintains information about each UI element in the application GUI. The view node then calls the graphics stack to composite the UI into a bitmap to render on the screen.

The UI tree is constructed by querying the view node for information about each UI element. Figure 3 shows an example UI tree representation corresponding to the Spotify app shown in Figure 1. Each vertex in the tree is a *UI element* such as a button, a scroll bar, a background image, or a text view. The attributes of these

Figure 4: The left shows the original UI and the right shows the UI reconstructed with the UI tree extracted using the accessibility service. Accessibility services are the state-of-the-art for transparently extracting the UI tree, but only extract the textual content.

elements include text, image information, location, and available UI actions, such as whether the element can be *clicked*.

Limitations of current UI tree extraction techniques: The state-of-the-art technique for extracting UI trees transparently, without application support, is through an *accessibility service*. The intended purpose of an accessibility service is to create accessible applications or assistive software for users with visual or other impairments [21]. These interfaces are more general and powerful than just accessibility, and have been used for software testing, UI automation, and other purposes [30, 38, 55, 67].

However, current accessibility APIs are insufficient for UIWear, since they only extract textual information, primarily motivated for helping users with visual impairments. Figure 4 is the reconstructed UI using current accessibility APIs, showing that the UI tree extraction is incomplete. Some tools such as UI Automator Viewer [67] and HierarchyViewer [12] show the complete UI tree either by superimposing the UI tree with the bitmap image, or only allow the UI tree to be accessed from a desktop. Neither of these approaches are suitable for UIWear.

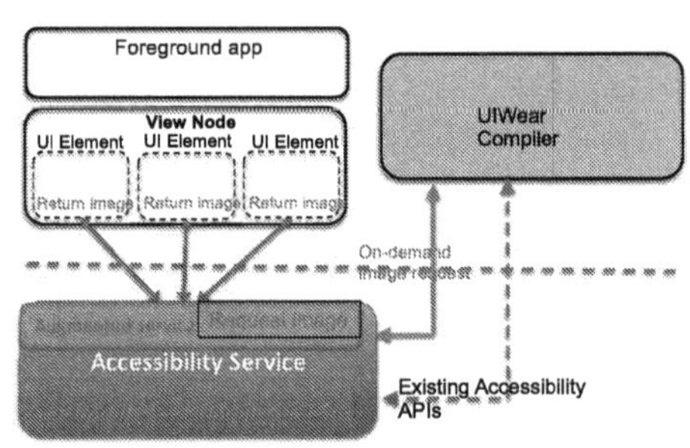

Figure 5: Augmenting the accessibility service to extract the application UI tree. The parts marked in orange show UIWear's augmentation.

UIWear's Augmented Service: UIWear augments the accessibility service to extract the complete UI tree. The default accessibility service works by creating an inter-process communication (IPC) channel between the accessibility service and the view node, which stores the UI tree. Figure 5 shows the UIWear augmented accessibility service. UIWear adds a new query/response API, to request

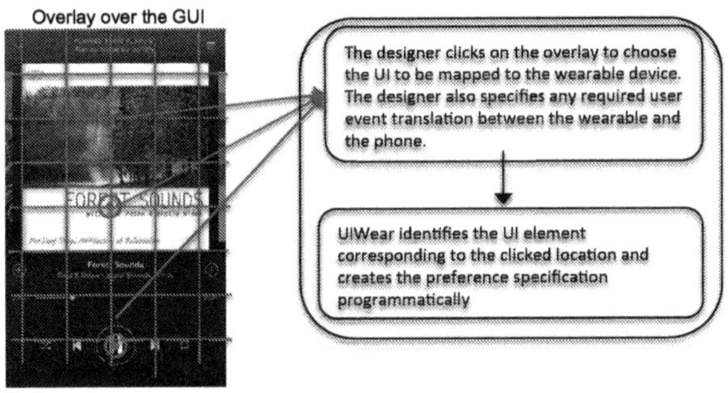

Figure 6: UIWear creates an overlay over the application GUI so that the designer can choose UI elements to map to the wearable using simple clicks.

and receive the image information available at the UI element. To reduce overhead, UIWear requests images on-demand only if the image is going to be used by the UICompanion app.

Beyond the scope of UIWear, a wider range of needs could be met with the augmented accessibility service. For instance, users with lowered vision, but not complete blindness, use screen magnifiers, such as MAGic [35] and ZoomText [22], which enlarge a small portion of the screen in addition to reading GUI contents. These magnifiers must currently resort to other hacks such as hooking the VGA pixel buffers, but could instead use the augmented accessibility service. Similarly, a number of projects have worked on automatically generating text describing images [45, 54]—an enhancement for blind users—and would benefit from the augmentation.

5 META PROGRAM AND COMPILER

The UIWear compiler creates the UICompanion app by combining the meta program and the UI tree. The goal of the meta program specification is to be expressive and yet be simple for a designer to write. The meta program specification consists of two parts: *(i) the preference specification:* containing the subset of UI elements from the original application GUI to be mapped to the wearable. UIWear provides an easy-to-use overlay visual tool for the designer to specify the preference, and *(ii) the wearable layout specification:* specifying how the UI elements on the phone are re-tailored for the wearable UI. We distill a small set of *templates* to make it simpler for designers to specify the wearable layout. Both the preference and the wearable layout specifications are in XML format.

5.1 Preference Specification

The designer creates the preference specification by choosing parts of the GUI to be mapped to the wearable by simply clicking on the objects on the phone UI (illustrated in Figure 6). UIWear combines the location of the click and the UI tree to extract the UI elements to be mapped.

When required, the designer also specifies a translation between the user events on the watch and the phone. For instance, a wrist gesture on the smartwatch is used to scroll the screen, but the same wrist gesture is not meaningful on the phone and needs to be converted to a "scroll" event. When the user event on the wearable input is sent to the phone, the input is translated so that the corresponding action is performed on the phone. In this paper, we focus on relatively simple translations, but the framework is generic enough to add more complex interactions, such as replacing a textbox with a voice-input class. We are exploring more complex translations as ongoing work.

5.2 Wearable Layout Specification

The wearable layout is used to specify how the phone UI is re-tailored to the wearable device.

Examples. We describe three examples of existing smartwatch companion apps that show the need for re-tailoring the GUI. The *ShoppingList* app on the phone uses a *ListView* to store items in the shopping list. However, the list is not easy to view on a watch. Instead, the corresponding companion app uses the *card* [7] UI design pattern. This pattern groups related information in a container resembling a playing card. Each card contains one shopping item and the user browses the list by swiping through the cards. The *WaterDrinkReminder* app on the smartphone displays the water consumption levels in text. The corresponding companion app transforms text to a progress bar for easy glanceability. Finally, the Spotify companion app, shown in Figure 1, maps four independent UI elements on the phone onto the *card* design pattern. The entire card is *clickable*, and the user can click on any part of the card to play and pause the song.

Wearable layout for Spotify. Figure 7 shows an example wearable layout specification for the Spotify app. The four UI elements from the Spotify phone app (marked in red box in Figure 1) are identified with IDs: backgroundID, titleID, iconID, and textID. On the wearable device, the layout specifies how these four UI elements are laid out using the card design pattern.

The wearable layout adheres to responsive application design [16], where the layout adjusts to different screen sizes and screen shapes. For example, the layout in Figure 7 uses directives such as *match_parent* and *wrap_content* to specify a relative layout according to the parent layout and the screen width respectively. The specification can also include other directives supported by wearable OSes, for example, to adapt the layout for a square screen versus a circular screen [7].

Easing designer effort using templates: To ease designer effort in creating the wearable layout, UIWear provides templates. Most wearable operating systems provide a set of pre-defined UI patterns for designing wearable applications [19]. Developers may also create custom designs. For the 20 AndroidWear applications that we consider for evaluation, only one application used a custom design; the rest used pre-defined templates. For example, the Spotify AndroidWear app uses a pre-defined card template provided by AndroidWear. With the UIWear templates, the designer only needs to fill in the data, such as the ID and position of the UI elements.

By using the template, subjects in our user study without prior experience in wearable programming were able to write the wearable layout specification in under 16 minutes (§8.6).

5.3 UIWear Compiler

The preference file and the wearable layout are combined to create the wearable UI tree, similar to the UI tree shown in Figure 3. UIWear creates the UICompanion app using the wearable UI tree. Creating a UICompanion app involves (1) converting the wearable UI tree

```
<wearable.view.CardScrollView>
    id="@+id/backgroundID"
    layout_width="match_parent"
    layout_height="wrap_content"
    layout_box="bottom">
    <wearable.view.CardFrame>
        <TextView
        id="@+id/titleID"
        layout_width="match_parent"
        layout_height="wrap_content"/>
      <ImageView
        id="@+id/iconID"
        layout_width="30dp"
        layout_height="30dp"/>
      <TextView
        id="@+id/albumID"
        layout_width="match_parent"
        layout_height="wrap_content" />
   </wearable.view.CardFrame>
</wearable.view.CardScrollView>
```

Figure 7: The Spotify wearable layout xml that specifies how the four phone UI elements (marked in the red square in Figure 1) are laid out on the watch. The UI element IDs are backgroundID, titleID, iconID, and albumID.

into a GUI of the proper size to display on the wearable device by detecting the target screen size, and (2) creating appropriate *call backs* to capture user interactions. The new companion app is created *completely* programmatically and does not require manual effort.

UIWear first inflates[1] the UI tree through the corresponding XML. For each UI element, UIWear extracts from the UI tree its image information, textual data, and events associated with it. The image and text information are used to fill the inflated GUI. For each event, for example, a *click* or a *long press*, UIWear creates a callback. The callback simply captures the user interaction, possibly translates the interaction to be meaningful on the phone, and sends the interaction and the UI element ID to the phone.

6 UIWEAR RUNTIME

In the default, non-UIWear companion app model, the application synchronizes its own state across devices using a custom protocol over network sockets. This approach to synchronizing application state requires developers to write a significant amount of error-prone code, as well as reason about and prevent potential concurrency bugs. Instead, UIWear performs an application-independent inter-device synchronization at the UI level. UIWear synchronization is based around the UI tree abstraction.

UIWear phone proxy: Upon changes to the phone GUI (as indicated by an accessibility event), the phone proxy parses the changed UI tree. When applicable, the phone proxy also fetches embedded images associated with certain UI elements in the tree using the augmented accessibility service (Figure 5). UIWear checks if the subset of the UI elements that appear on the wearable device have changed, by comparing them with a previous cached version. If no previous version exists or if there are changes, the proxy ships the *diff* to the wearable device. UIWear also maintains a small cache at the wearable side so that the same image does not have to be shipped repeatedly.

UIWear wearable proxy: On receiving an update, the wearable proxy forwards the update to the corresponding UICompanion application, which applies this update to its layout and renders the new UI. If the user interacts with the UICompanion app, the wearable proxy captures the interaction and serializes the information to the phone proxy. Example user events include clicks, long press, swiping, and gestures such as wrist movements. The phone proxy then delivers the user event to the application using the accessibility service, as though the event occurred locally on the phone. No change to the application is required. In some cases, the user event needs to be translated from the wearable to the phone, as specified in the meta program (§5). A few user events, such as zoom, are performed locally and not delivered to the phone.

If a user interacts with both the phone and watch interfaces simultaneously and very quickly (or the network is very slow), it is possible to have conflicting updates. In general, the UIWear protocol will serialize events in the order they are received by the application on the phone. We expect that, in the common case, these events will be serialized and processed faster than most humans can input them across devices.

Overcoming smartphone I/O restrictions: A current limitation of most smartphone OSes (including Android, on which we implement UIWear) is that they only allow a single GUI to be active at a given time. The OS shuts down the graphics stack for an application when it is no longer a foreground process. Not maintaining the graphic stack for background apps is a reasonable optimization to save power required for rendering and display. However, the implication of this design is that the GUI synchronization can only work with a foreground app. In order for background apps to be able to receive events from a UICompanion app, and respond to those events, we must keep the UI alive for background apps.

We observe that most of the savings from putting an app in the background are from not *rendering* the composite (pixel-level) display image in the graphics stack. The marginal cost of maintaining the logical UI structure in the view node is relatively low. Therefore, UIWear modifies the OS to disable the graphics stack for background apps, but keeps the view node active. UIWear will only keep the view node active if the app that moves to the background was previously interacting with a wearable device; non-UIWear applications are not affected by this change.

Thus, UIWear can multiplex I/O events to multiple applications, even if these applications are in the background on the phone. §7 discusses additional implementation details, and §8 measures the incremental energy of maintaining the view node for multiple background apps —showing that the costs are indeed negligible.

7 IMPLEMENTATION

We implement UIWear on the Android ecosystem: Android phone OS, AndroidWear smartwatch OS, and the Sony SmartEyeglass that runs over a version of Android [17]. We implemented UIWear on version 6.0 of Android, although there are no version-specific dependencies that would prevent porting UIWear to other versions of Android.

[1]Inflation is a term used in Android for parsing the XML and turning it into a representation that can be rendered.

7.1 Compiler Implementation

From the end-user's perspective, an Android application is made up of multiple **activities** or "windows". For example, viewing the playlist is one activity, and viewing the playback controls is another activity. The designer writes a meta program for each application activity to be mapped to the wearable, and UIWear compiles the meta programs and bundles them into a single UICompanion app. In rare cases, an activity may dynamically generate a UI, in which case we need to write a meta program for the dynamic UI. We did not encounter this case in our experiments.

UIWear uses the standard Android toolchain to create the UICompanion application. The application consists of the source file, the AndroidManifest file, the layout, and a set of resources that are created programmatically. We create templates for the meta program using FreeMarker [10].

7.2 UIWear Synchronization Implementation

We implement the UIWear phone proxy as a client to the accessibility service on Android, and the wearable proxy as a service on the wearable device. The phone and wearable proxies together are implemented in 5,300 lines of code.

For each application, the phone proxy keeps track of preference files and the wearable UI tree for each activity of the application. When the user switches between applications or activities on the wearable device, the phone proxy can identify this switch and perform the necessary action on the corresponding UI. The UIWear watch and phone proxy exchange information over the Google Messaging Service (GMS). GMS encapsulates the data and performs the low-level communication tasks, and can use Bluetooth or WiFi.

7.3 I/O Multiplexing Implementation

To multiplex I/O between several UICompanion apps and background apps, UIWear modifies Android to allow the graphics stack to sleep, but keep the intermediate UI representation (i.e., the view node state) active.

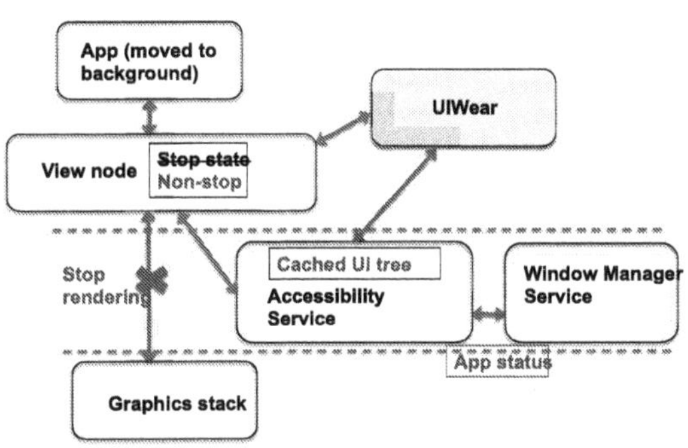

Figure 8: Implementing I/O multiplexing in UIWear: When an application moves to the background, as indicated by the Window manager service, UIWear performs a series of steps to keep the view node and the corresponding accessibility node active. UIWear changes are shown in red.

Figure 8 shows the UIWear implementation. The Window Manager Service indicates if an application is in the background or foreground. Typically, when the app moves to the background, it changes the status of its view node to *stop*, destroys the UI tree maintained by the accessibility service, and makes the graphics stack inactive. Instead, UIWear moves the view node state back to *nonstop* and caches the UI tree of the background application. This simple change makes it possible to multiplex I/O events to background apps.

The Android OS uses a *Low Memory Killer (LMK)* mechanism to kill background applications [1]. There is always a chance that a background app that is supporting a companion application will be killed. However, the LMK mechanism prioritizes background applications that remain inactive for long periods of time. Because the UIWear background applications send and receive events, they are not considered inactive, and are thus less likely to be killed. UIWear applications can also be relaunched by the proxy, if needed.

Our current implementation does not require any OS changes to AndroidWear and Sony SmartEyeglass. Our implementation does change the Android OS, but all changes are in the framework layer. This makes UIWear installation relatively simple as long as the phone is rooted. Further, we believe that there are good technical reasons for mobile OSes to incorporate the augmentations described in UIWear. §4 explains how our augmentations to the accessibility service would benefit other accessibility technologies. Similarly, as wearables and other small computing devices become increasingly ubiquitous, the ability to synchronize updates with multiple (background) apps is fundamentally useful. This functionality has been proposed independently for integrating with automotive displays [43].

7.4 Other Use Cases

While the primary purpose of UIWear is to help designers easily create UICompanion apps, a tech-savvy user can also create their own UICompanion apps even without application source code. We create UICompanion apps for *Yahoo Mail* and *Facebook messenger* (both of which do not have companion apps) in under 25 lines of developer-written XML code. We decompile both the applications using *JADX* [8] and extract the layout XML that specifies the UI. We load the app and use it to specify the preference (Figure 6), and write a layout XML file to re-tailor the phone GUI to the watch.

The Yahoo mail UICompanion app shows the top few emails on the watch and allows the users to read their emails from the watch and the *Facebook Messenger* UICompanion app allows users to read their messages on the watch.

7.5 Limitations and Future work

Wearable apps can perform additional tasks, such as collecting sensor data or running some computation locally; UIWear cannot currently match this functionality. Further, UICompanion apps are completely dependent on having network connectivity to a smartphone, although this problem also extends to most current companion apps. To address these issues, a future extension to UIWear would be to push some amount of computation to the device, such as running small tasks like spell checking or sensor data collection. Other computations, such as a calculator executing the computation on the wearable will require more invasive changes. For this case, we expect that UIWear meta programming model can be extended to annotate classes that should run remotely. We believe that the general approach to streamlining GUI adaptation will still be useful to these applications.

Further, the current implementation only supports touch and gesture inputs on the wearable, and does not yet support voice. If these additional user events can be encapsulated as a UI widget in the graph, such a translation is relatively straightforward. For instance, one can define an extended text box widget type that includes a voice-to-text synthesis.

UIWear's UI extension does not work for applications such as 3D games that are rendered using OpenGL, since they do not create intermediate UI trees, and instead composite the bitmap directly on the hardware. It is possible that we can intercept some commands at the OpenGL level, but transparently adapting the interface to a large body of graphics-intensive code will be more challenging.

8 EVALUATION

We compare UIWear's UICompanion apps with existing companion apps from the Android Wear category on Google Play using both quantitative measurements (§8.3) and qualitative user studies (§8.6). The evaluation seeks to answer the following questions:

(1) Does the meta programming framework lower development effort to create a wearable app? (§8.1)
(2) How does the end-user latency, CPU utilization, energy usage, and network costs for a UICompanion app compare with the companion app version? (§8.3)
(3) Does maintaining the view tree for multiple background applications affect performance or power? (§8.4)
(4) Can UIWear support heterogeneous form factors? (§8.5)
(5) Do users find the UICompanion app experience comparable to a companion app? How quickly can a new user proficiently write a meta program? (§8.6)

8.1 Applications

We experiment with 20 applications listed in Table 2. We chose companion applications from the top 150 trending apps (as of December 2016). The apps are chosen randomly from among the apps that are in category D (§2), and have diverse popularity, measured in downloads, ranging from 5 thousand to one billion (indicated in parenthesis in the Table).

For each companion app, we write a meta program to create a functionally-identical UICompanion app. Each companion app has between one and nine activities. Our UICompanion apps are written to implement the same number of activities, writing a meta program for each activity. Recall that Android applications encompass one or more activities and the meta program is written at the granularity of an activity (§7).

We are able to create these meta programs without access to source code, as described in §7.4. The LoC for the UICompanion metaprogram shown in Table 2 is for all activities combined, and includes the wearable layout XML, and any lines specified in the preference file to translate user events.

We conservatively estimate the lines of code in each companion app by first decompiling the application using *JADX* [8]. We exclude libraries and blank spaces, and do not count the lines of supporting code on the phone.

App (downloads)	Companion LoC*	Meta prog. LoC
4Sound (100K)	732	21
Anghami (10M)	2,263	79
BandLab (500M)	1,802	8
Counter (100K)	663	15
Endomondo (10M)	6,522	18
Ghostracer (10K)	5,324	95
HydroCoach (1M)	4,022	12
iHeartRadio (50M)	7,926	96
LensGuage (500K)	3,403	24
myTunerFree (5M)	1,535	56
MDPlayer (10K)	1,894	23
MusicPlayer (10M)	540	12
MyShoppingList (50K)	941	42
Parrot (100K)	3,711	9
PlayMusic (1B)	10,851	103
PodcastRepublic (1M)	808	24
Quitter'sCircle(5K)	2,517	17
Spotify (100M)	10,215	47
WaterDrinkReminder(10M)	1,408	18
WorkoutTrainer (10M)	2,265	36

Table 2: 20 companion applications from the AndroidWear category on Google Play used in our evaluations and their downloads in thousands (K), millions (M), and billions (B). The table shows the Lines of Code (LoC) for the smartwatch companion app and UICompanion meta program. **The companion application LoC is a conservative estimate and does not include the LoC at the phone required to support the companion app.*

A UICompanion app requires an order-of-magnitude fewer developer-written code than a comparable companion apps. A meta program ranges from 9–103 lines, and the size is proportional to the complexity of the number of elements and activities in the UI. In total, UIWear represents a significant reduction in effort for wearable app developers.

8.2 Experimental Setup and Methodology

The experiments are performed on two Nexus 5 phones running Android version 6.0.1, and two smartwatches: Sony Smartwatch 3 and Huawei smartwatch running AndroidWear 1.5. All experiments use Bluetooth for communication. In the interest of brevity, we present data from the Huawei smartwatch; the Sony Smartwatch results are very similar.

For fine-grained timing measurement of user events, rendering events, network activities, and CPU measurements, we use recent augmentations [46] to the systrace [69] tool. When needed, we synchronize the clocks on the phone and the watch using ntpd [14]. For apps with more than one activity, we evaluate the activity with the largest number of UI elements. For each activity, we choose all user events on the watch and the phone that generate a GUI update and automate the user events using the adb tool. Each set of user events is repeated 10 times and we report the average and standard deviation.

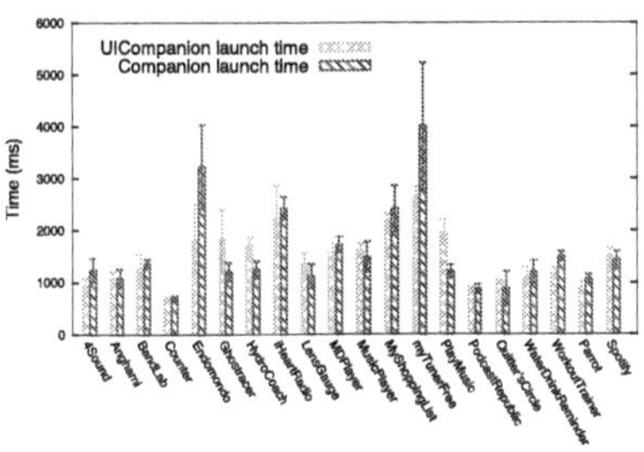

Figure 9: Comparing launch times, the time for the watch GUI to be rendered when it is first launched. The launch time is typically longer compared to response and update times because all images need to be loaded on the watch.

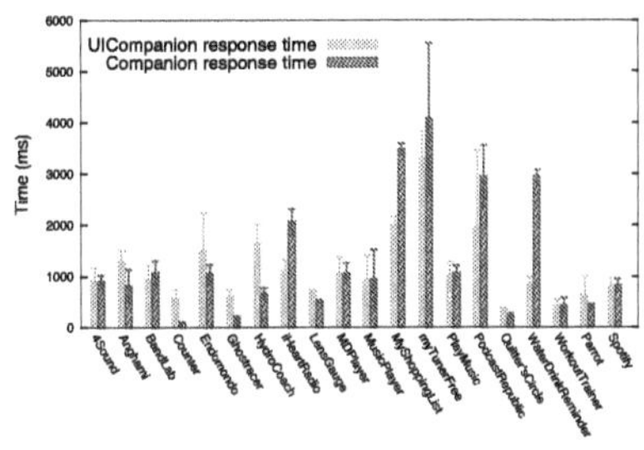

Figure 10: Comparing response times, the time taken for the watch GUI to update in response to a watch user event. The response time requires a round trip, to deliver the user event to the phone and then update the corresponding GUI.

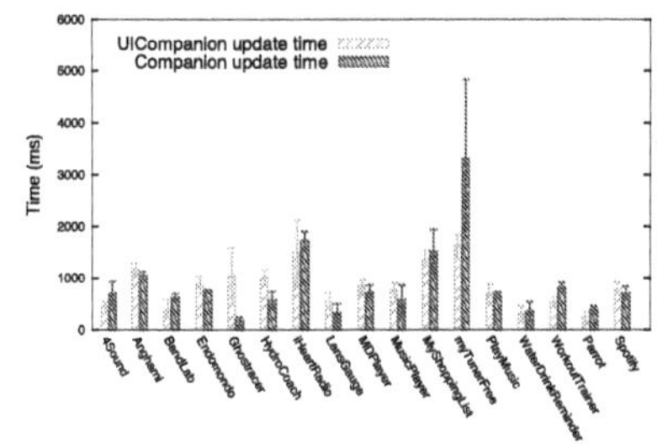

Figure 11: Comparing update times, the time to update the watch GUI in response to an update on the phone. The update times are shorter compared to the response times because the phone only needs to send diffs.

For power measurements on the phone, we use *BattOR*, a small, noninvasive hardware device that interposes between a device and its battery [63]. BattOR collects power measurements on the order of tens of microseconds and is known for high accuracy. Importantly, BattOR can measure power for phones without removable batteries, unlike the more popular Monsoon Power Monitor [13]. We also performed measurements on a Galaxy Nexus phone with the Monsoon Power Monitor, and our results were similar for both monitors. The energy consumption is measured over a period of 1 minute with 10 repeated GUI changes and user interactions. On the smartwatch, we use the dumpsys battery status tool [9]. In the default case, the phone application is in the foreground. §8.4 measures costs when the phone app is in the background.

8.3 Quantitative Comparisons

Although UIWear is not primarily designed to improve performance or resource consumption, UIWear apps perform comparably to (and in some cases even better than) hand-written companion apps.

Latency:

We compare AndroidWear companion and UIWear's UICompanion apps, measuring: (1) launch time, (2) update time, and (3) response time. Launch time is the time from starting an app until all text and image data are fetched from the phone. After initial launch, both the companion and UICompanion apps only need to send *diffs*. The update time is the time for the GUI update on the phone to be reflected on the watch. The response time is the time between a user event at the watch and the corresponding GUI update on the watch. The response time is typically larger than the update time because the response time requires a round trip; the user event is first shipped from the watch to the phone, and the corresponding GUI update on the phone is mirrored back on the watch.

Launch time: In most cases (16/20), the average launch times of companion and UICompanion apps are similar, shown in Figure 9. For three applications, *HydroCoach*, *Ghostracer*, and *PlayMusic*, UICompanion is 30% slower. We discuss why the *HydroCoach* and *Ghostracer* UICompanion apps perform poorly in the next section. With *PlayMusic*, our hypothesis is that the application is heavily optimized for the launch time due to high popularity of the app. In contrast, *MyTunerFree* and *Endomondo* companion apps are nearly 50% slower than UIWear. In case of *MyTunerFree*, the companion app did not perform well in general.

Response times: For about half of the cases (9/20), UIWear and the AndroidWear companion apps have comparable response times; for about a quarter, UIWear has faster responses, and for the other quarter the hand-written companion app has better response time. The average response times are shown in Figure 10. In general, the apps with comparable response times have comparable network costs (Figure 14).

For five apps, the UIWear response time is much better compared to the AndroidWear version, with an average reduction of 50%. Commiserate with the high response times, the companion app version for these five apps consume more power on the smartwatch compared to UIWear (Figure 15).

On the other hand, apps that can handle some updates locally tend to out-perform UIWear. *Ghostracer* and *Counter* companion apps have lower response times since they update the smartwatch GUI based on local computation (corroborated by network usage in Figure 14). We will investigate how to push modest computation to the watch to improve UIWear performance for such cases. The *Hydrocouch* application requires a lot of items to be fetched from the phone: UIWear extracts each item from the UI tree, whereas the companion app gets the items from the app. This results in higher response time for the *Hydrocouch* UICompanion app.

Update times: For 14 of 20 apps, the average update times were similar for the companion and UICompanion apps, listed in Figure 11. Three companion apps, *Counter*, *PodcastRepublic*, and *QuitterCircle* simply did not update the watch GUI in sync with the phone, so we were not able to compare them with UIWear. As before, the *myTunerFree* companion app is 50% slower than the UIWear version, and the *Ghostracer* and *Hydrocouch* companion apps are faster.

To understand where most of the time is spent, Figure 12 shows the breakdown of the update times for five UICompanion apps. We do not have the source code for the companion apps, and therefore cannot compute such a break down. The network contributes 50% to 80% of the total time. The next biggest bottleneck is the UIWear processing on the phone, to parse the UI tree and create diffs. Rendering contributes little to the overall latency.

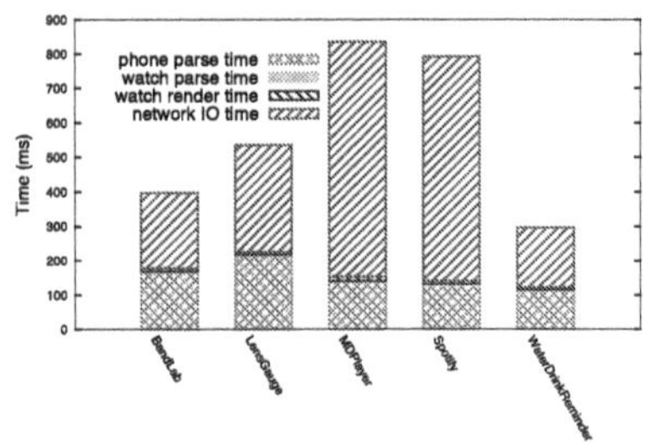

Figure 12: Breaking down the response times latency.

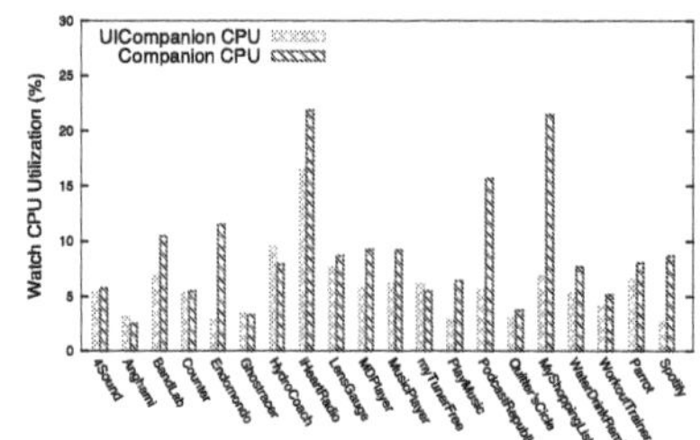

Figure 13: Comparing CPU consumption on the watch.

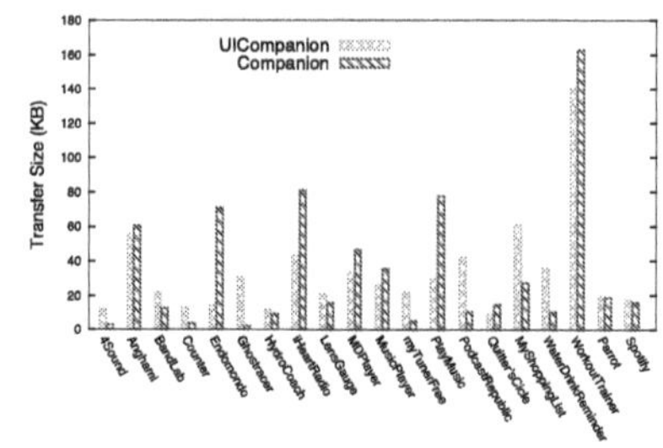

Figure 14: Comparing network data transfer from phone to watch.

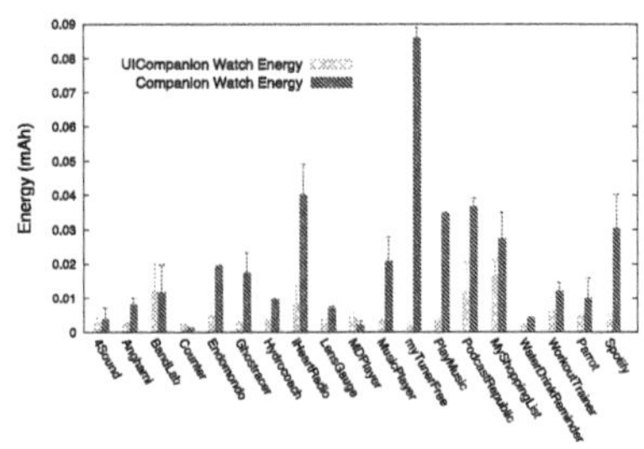

Figure 15: Comparing energy consumption on the watch UICompanion offloading more computation to the phone, reducing energy.

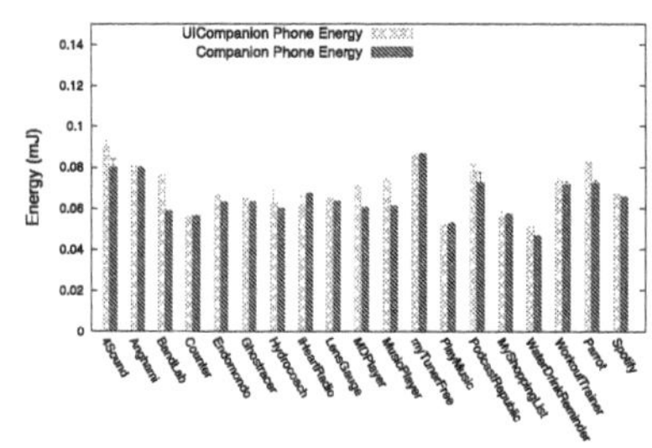

Figure 16: Comparing energy consumption on the phone. UICompanion and the companion counterpart consume have comparable energy consumptions.

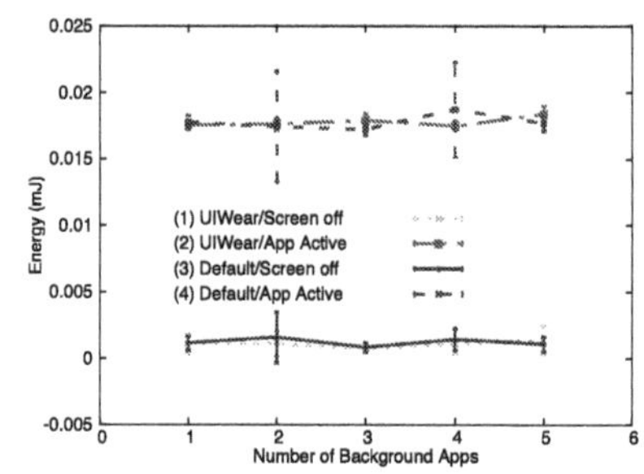

Figure 17: Comparing energy under UIWear and under default behavior where the view node is destroyed.

CPU, Energy, and Network Resources

CPU usage: Figure 13 shows that watch CPU consumption for both the UICompanion and the companion apps. For 3 apps, UICompanion app reduces CPU consumption by over 3 times by offloading most of the computation to the phone.

On the phone, the CPU consumption of UICompanion and companion apps is comparable across all 20 apps (2% lower for UICompanion on average). We omit a detailed listing in the interest of brevity.

Energy consumption: UICompanion apps consume *significantly* less energy on the watch than companion apps, depicted in Figure 15. In the case of *myTunerFree* app, UICompanion reduces energy by *20 times.* UIWear essentially shifts processing to the phone, reducing energy usage on the watch.

Even though work is offloaded to the phone, UICompanion apps generally do not increase phone energy consumption, shown in Figure 16. In the worst cases, 4 apps increase phone energy consumption by 3%. We believe this is because the phone is more powerful and the incremental costs of performing the additional work on the phone is lower.

Network usage: Figure 14 shows the amount of data transferred from the phone to the watch. For 9 of the 20 apps, the amount of data transferred by UICompanion and companion apps are similar. In other words, the developers of these 9 apps are also writing companion apps as GUI subsets of the original app, and synchronizing image and other data between the wearable and phone app at run time. UIWear simply streamlines this process to reduce developer effort. For 5 of the 20 apps, the companion app transfers a large amount of data to the watch; without source code, we are unable to determine the reason for this data transfer. The companion apps that perform more local computation (e.g., *Ghosttracer*, and *Counter*) require less data to be transferred.

8.4 Effect of Multiple Background Applications

One potential concern about UIWear is the incremental cost of having multiple active apps in the background on the phone, responding to I/O from the watch. Figure 17 shows the energy consumption as the number of background applications increases from one to five. We measure this under four conditions: (1) the view nodes are active, but the screen is off, (2) the view nodes are active, and an application is running in the foreground, (3) the view nodes are inactive and the screen is off, and (4) the view nodes are inactive with a foreground app. Cases (1) and (3) represent the UIWear design, and (2) and (4) are Android defaults.

Figure 17 shows that the energy cost of keeping view nodes active with the screen off (1) is comparable to making them inactive (3), and that having additional active view nodes running (2) along side a foreground application is comparable to having no background view nodes (4). In the interest of brevity, we omit performance figures; in summary, there is no difference in performance of the foreground application as the number of background apps increases. There was also no difference in performance on the watch whether the phone app is in the background or foreground.

Metric	UICompanion better or equal	AndroidWear better
Functionality	78%	22%
Look and feel	74%	26%

Table 3: Qualitative comparison of UIWear's UICompanion app and the AndroidWear playstore companion app in terms of functionality and look-and-feel. The results show the percentages across 20 subjects and 5 applications.

8.5 Sony SmartEyeglass

We demonstrate the ability for UIWear to support multiple form factors by also creating UICompanion apps for the smartglass form factor for two applications: Spotify and MyShoppingList. For both applications, the UICompanion app required less than 30 lines of meta program.

On the Spotify UICompanion app on the glass, users can pause or play the song. On the MyShoppingList app, users can delete items. The response time is *74ms* for the Spotify application and *24ms* for the MyShoppingList application, averaged over 10 runs. Since the Sony SmartEyeglass ecosystem does not have existing companion applications, we have no good baseline for comparison. This case study does demonstrate that UIWear can accelerate development of companion apps for a new platform.

8.6 User Study

We conducted an IRB-approved user study to (i) qualitatively compare the AndroidWear playstore companion app and the UIWear generated UICompanion app, and (ii) measure the time taken for a designer to write a meta program specification for a given application.

We recruited twenty subjects from the University: four undergraduate and sixteen graduate students. 30% of the students were female and 70% were male, 30% of the students were from outside the computer science department and the remaining were computer science students.

Qualitative comparisons: We use two qualitative measures for comparison: *look-and-feel* and *functionality*. The experiments are conducted on the following apps: Counter, LensGauge, MusicPlayer, MyShoppingList and Spotify. For each application, we let the subjects interact with the two versions of the app for one minute each. We use A/B testing and record the subjects responses in terms of whether they preferred A, B, or if the two versions were equal. The results of the comparison are shown in Table 3. Subjects found UICompanion version to be equivalent or better than the companion version 78% of the time in terms of functionality and 74% of the time in terms of look-and-feel.

We studied the cases when UICompanion apps performed worse than the AndroidWear companion apps in terms of look-and-feel and functionality. We find that this was likely because the UICompanion app did not port the progress-bar widget and did not support animations. The subjects found the animation and the widgets more appealing. We believe these issues can be addressed in a more fully-featured version of UIWear.

Estimating designer effort: We asked ten subjects to write a meta program to mimic two companion applications: Spotify and Music Player. Before the start of the study, we gave all subjects a ten minute introduction to the procedure. We provide the template for both applications and the preference file as described in §5.

The subjects had to first identify which UI element each ID in the preference file corresponded to and create the layout XML to specify the location and size of each UI element. The subjects were able to view the visual layout. *Each subject created a working meta program in under 16 minutes per application.* Of the ten, five were from the Computer Science department and five were from other departments. Six subjects considered themselves strong programmers and the other four rated themselves as novice programmers.

These results indicate that, from the end-user's perspective, UIWear can generate apps that are competitive with hand-written companion apps. Moreover, the meta programming process is accessible even to novice programmers.

9 RELATED WORK

Broadly speaking, related *systems* research on extending UIs to remote devices do not re-tailor the UI for the remote screen [24, 26, 34, 44, 59–61, 68]. As a result, these works are largely applicable only to homogenous settings where no UI retailoring is needed. Existing *HCI* work on designing cross-device UI focus on (1) designing UIs that are consistent across devices and (2) authoring tools for cross-device UI design. However, these HCI techniques cannot be applied to off-the-shelf applications and they do not solve the systems challenges of extracting and synchronizing UI elements. UIWear fills this void by addressing both the HCI and the systems challenges in extending UI across devices.

9.1 Systems Approaches

Supporting Remote Access

A number of protocols and systems have been designed for remote access to a server or desktop, including RDP [59], VNC [60], ICA [39], PCoIP [66] and many others [25, 27, 44, 62]. In general, these protocols simply relay the hardware framebuffer contents, as well as mouse and keyboard events, between systems. Research proposals have also extended remote access protocols with some semantic information, to cope with high resolution graphics [34], lower-bandwidth remote access connections [27], or to modify gestures [56]. These approaches do not support GUI re-tailoring to suit small form factor devices.

The main remote access protocol that uses semantic objects is X [61]; to our knowledge, X has not been previously used for adapting GUIs to heterogeneous and small form factors. In fact, there are no implementations of an *X client* on phones, although some smartphones do support an X server. The UIWear design is inspired by the X protocol, but is designed specifically for small form factor devices.

Porting Applictations

A number of solutions port applications from one platform to another, that includes porting the UI. A subset of related work in this category [28, 33, 41, 42, 57] port screen access through a virtual frame buffer, which, as stated above, does not solve the problems addressed by UIWear.

Flux [68] ports UI across devices *without* transferring the screen buffer, and instead migrates the application from one device to another. Flux does account for device heterogeneity and can run a smartphone application on a more powerful tablet and vice versa. Flux assumes that architectures of the devices have some differences, but largely provide similar functionality. However, wearable devices only support a small subset of functionalities of a smartphone, making app migration from a smartphone to a wearable device infeasible.

Cider [24] and Apportable [26] port phone applications that are designed for one OS to another. For instance, Cider [24] designs core libraries and compile-time code adaptation to support applications designed for iOS to run on Android. However, similar to the app migration above [68], these systems cannot be extended to highly heterogenous devices.

Most similar to UIWear is Sinter [30], which also mines a UI tree using accessibility interfaces. The goal of Sinter is to make accessibility tools, such as screen readers, work across different OSes and on remote or virtual desktops. Sinter is not sufficient to create a companion app, as it cannot extract or manipulate image or other visual data, does not address heterogeneity in form factors, and does not work when the smartphone application is no longer in the foreground.

9.2 HCI Approaches

Cross-Device UI Authoring tools

UIWear is inspired by the pioneering work in the model-based user interface design paradigm that allows developers to specify the UI using higher-level abstractions, rather than programming a specific UI layout [32, 32, 58, 64].

While the model-based design makes authoring UIs simpler, an abstraction layer has to specified for each concrete device, OS, and UI look-and-feel. As a result, recently, most works use a hybrid method that simplifies some elements of cross-device UI design, but ultimately maintains a WYSIWYG approach for each device type, requiring some manual effort per device type. Gummy [48], PageTailor [29], WinCuts [65] and Jelly [47] start off from a given UI and allow developers to choose pieces of this UI to be reused on a different device. Highlight [53] uses a middleware proxy to compile HTML from PCs to mobile phones rather than requiring a UI abstraction.

However, these projects do not solve the problems addressed in UIWear. While Gummy [48] and Jelly [47] provide developers a platform to *design* UIs for each device type, they do not automatically create the companion application. Specifically, these works do not address the systems challenges of extracting, transferring, and updating the UI.

On the other hand, WinCuts [65], PageTailor [29] and Highlight [53] work only for Web pages. In general, cross-device Web page authoring is a better-studied problem, in part because Web page compilers and Web browsers are more standardized across devices than the runtime environment for mobile applications. For example, recent work on *Responsive UI* platforms [6] allow developers to write a single Web page that can be modified for different screens. However, the ideas used for cross-device Web page designs do not translate to other mobile applications.

Co-designing cross-device UI

UI co-design research focuses on building platforms and tools for developers to simultaneously design UIs for different devices for consistent look-and-feel. Nguyen et al. [52] provides a platform to create a fully-abstracted UI that compiles to concrete UIs on different devices. Weave [31] uses a Javascript-based scripting framework for a developer to concurrently visualize UI on multiple devices. WatchConnect [40] is a toolkit and an emulation platform for users to easily design smartwatch UI. Ghiani *et al.* [36] lets a developer annotate an abstract UI and select which segments of the UI will be rendered on different devices

All of these works make it easy to design cross-device UIs, but they only work for custom applications that are designed using the tool. They do not work for off-the-shelf applications and do not handle any of the systems challenges of sharing the UI.

Distributing the UI across devices

Since wearable computers became mainstream, UI researchers are creating interactions that involve multiple devices working at the same time. In effect, a single application UI is split into different parts and shown on different device screens for the best viewing experience for the user.

The XDBrowser system [50, 51] allows web page authors to distribute the UI across the smartphone, smartwatch, and the PC. Recently, the XDBrowser system was extended for email clients [49]. Similarly, the Panelrama system [70] uses a novel annotation and distribution technique. The developer annotates the Web page and Panelrama automatically renders different parts of the Web page on different devices based on the annotation.

However, existing systems focus on a single application, most commonly Web pages. They do not work for diverse, off-the-shelf, applications. The Conductor [37] system designs new interaction methods for users to migrate between a smartphone and a wearable screen. This work makes it easier to move between UIs, but does not provide techniques to share the UI itself.

10 CONCLUSION

In the near future, we expect to see an increasing abundance of smaller, network-connected devices with diverse form factors and limited computing power. UIWear can dramatically simplify the development effort to export user interfaces to this broad array of devices. The developer writes an application for the smartphone, and UIWear extends the application to any wearable device with minimal effort from the developer, without sacrificing performance or power. UIWear contributes a new design point that decouples the concerns of application logic and UI design.

ACKNOWLEDGMENTS

We thank the anonymous reviewers and our shepherd, Sharad Agarwal, for their insightful comments. We thank Syed Masum Billah for his help with understanding and using intermediate UI representations. We thank Roy Shilkrot for his help in reviewing literature on cross-device user interfaces. We thank our user study participants. This work was supported in part by NSF grant CNS-1405641, CNS-1551909, and VMware.

REFERENCES

[1] Android Internals: A Confectioners Cookbook. http://newandroidbook.com/index.php.
[2] Android View Hierarchy. http://developer.android.com/guide/topics/ui/overview.html.
[3] Androidwear 2.0. http://www.wareable.com/android-wear/.
[4] Apple View Hierarchy. https://developer.apple.com/library/ios/documentation/General/Conceptual/Devpedia-CocoaApp/View%20Hierarchy.html.
[5] Apple watchos. http://www.apple.com/watchos/.
[6] Bootstrap. http://getbootstrap.com/.
[7] Card layout. https://developer.android.com/training/wearables/ui/cards.html.
[8] Dex to Java decompiler. https://github.com/skylot/jadx.
[9] Dumpsys battery status. https://source.android.com/devices/tech/power/batterystats.html.
[10] Freemarker. http://freemarker.org/.
[11] GPS Heads Up Display. http://www.reconinstruments.com/products/snow2/.
[12] Hierarchy Viewer. http://developer.android.com/tools/help/hierarchy-viewer.html.
[13] Monsoon Power Monitor. https://www.msoon.com/LabEquipment/PowerMonitor/.
[14] ntpd. http://doc.ntp.org/4.1.0/ntpd.htm.
[15] Pebble. https://www.pebble.com/.
[16] Responsive ui design. https://medium.com/google-developers/building-a-responsive-ui-in-android-7dc7e4efcbb3#.bi9jk1rdy.
[17] Sony SmartEyeglass SDK. https://developer.sony.com/develop/wearables/smarteyeglass-sdk/.
[18] Tizen. https://www.tizen.org/.
[19] Ui patterns for wearables. https://developer.android.com/design/wear/patterns.html.
[20] Wear Spotify for Android Wear. https://play.google.com/store/apps/details?id=wearablesoftware.wearspotifyplayer&hl=en.
[21] Android Accessibility Service. http://developer.android.com/reference/android/accessibilityservice/AccessibilityService.html.
[22] Ai Squared. Zoomtext magnifier. http://www.aisquared.com/zoomtext/more/zoomtext_magnifier.
[23] Google Android Wear Market. https://play.google.com/store/apps/category/ANDROID_WEAR?hl=en.
[24] J. Andrus, A. Van't Hof, N. AlDuaij, C. Dall, N. Viennot, and J. Nieh. Cider: Native execution of ios apps on android. In *Proceedings of the ACM International Conference on Architectural Support for Programming Languages and Operating Systems (ASPLOS)*, pages 367–382, 2014.
[25] Apple. Airplay—play content from ios devices on appletv. https://www.apple.com/airplay/.
[26] Apportable. http://www.apportable.com/.
[27] R. A. Baratto, L. N. Kim, and J. Nieh. Thinc: A virtual display architecture for thin-client computing. In *Proceedings of the ACM SIGOPS Symposium on Operating Systems Principles (SOSP)*, pages 277–290, 2005.
[28] A. Baumann, D. Lee, P. Fonseca, L. Glendenning, J. R. Lorch, B. Bond, R. Olinsky, and G. C. Hunt. Composing OS extensions safely and efficiently with Bascule. In *Proceedings of the ACM European Conference on Computer Systems (EuroSys)*, 2013.
[29] N. Bila, T. Ronda, I. Mohomed, K. N. Truong, and E. de Lara. Pagetailor: reusable end-user customization for the mobile web. In *Proceedings of the 5th international conference on Mobile systems, applications and services*, pages 16–29. ACM, 2007.
[30] S. M. Billah, D. E. Porter, and I. V. Ramakrishnan. Sinter: Low-bandwidth remote access for the visually-impaired. In *Proceedings of the ACM European Conference on Computer Systems (EuroSys)*, 2016.
[31] P.-Y. P. Chi and Y. Li. Weave: Scripting cross-device wearable interaction. In *Proceedings of the 33rd Annual ACM Conference on Human Factors in Computing Systems*, pages 3923–3932. ACM, 2015.
[32] K. Coninx, K. Luyten, C. Vandervelpen, J. Van den Bergh, and B. Creemers. Dygimes: Dynamically generating interfaces for mobile computing devices and embedded systems. In *International Conference on Mobile Human-Computer Interaction*, pages 256–270. Springer, 2003.
[33] J. R. Douceur, J. Elson, J. Howell, and J. R. Lorch. Leveraging legacy code to deploy desktop applications on the web. In *Proceedings of the USENIX Symposium on Operating Systems Design and Implementation (OSDI)*, 2008.
[34] C. D. Estes and K. Mayer-Patel. Moving beyond the framebuffer. In *Proceedings of the 21st International Workshop on Network and Operating Systems Support for Digital Audio and Video*, NOSSDAV '11, pages 93–98, New York, NY, USA, 2011. ACM.
[35] Freedom Scientific. Magic screen magnification software. http://www.freedomscientific.com/products/lv/magic-bl-product-page.asp.
[36] G. Ghiani, M. Manca, and F. Paternò. Authoring context-dependent cross-device user interfaces based on trigger/action rules. In *Proceedings of the 14th International Conference on Mobile and Ubiquitous Multimedia*, pages 313–322. ACM, 2015.
[37] P. Hamilton and D. J. Wigdor. Conductor: Enabling and understanding cross-device interaction. In *Proceedings of the SIGCHI Conference on Human Factors in Computing Systems*, CHI '14, pages 2773–2782, New York, NY, USA, 2014. ACM.
[38] S. Hao, B. Liu, S. Nath, W. G. Halfond, and R. Govindan. Puma: Programmable ui-automation for large-scale dynamic analysis of mobile apps. In *Proceedings of the 12th Annual International Conference on Mobile Systems, Applications, and Services*, MobiSys '14, pages 204–217, New York, NY, USA, 2014. ACM.
[39] J. Harder and J. Maynard. Technical deep dive: Ica protocol and acceleration. http://s3.amazonaws.com/legacy.icmp/additional/ica_acceleration_0709a.pdf.
[40] S. Houben and N. Marquardt. Watchconnect: A toolkit for prototyping smartwatch-centric cross-device applications. In *Proceedings of the 33rd Annual ACM Conference on Human Factors in Computing Systems*, pages 1247–1256. ACM, 2015.
[41] J. Howell, B. Parno, and J. R. Douceur. Embassies: Radically refactoring the web. In *Proceedings of the USENIX Symposium on Networked Systems Design and Implementation (NSDI)*, pages 529–546, 2013.
[42] J. Howell, B. Parno, and J. R. Douceur. How to run POSIX apps in a minimal picoprocess. In *Proceedings of the USENIX Annual Technical Conference*, pages 321–332, 2013.
[43] Intel. Intel atom e3800 processor series: Android multi-display features in automobiles. http://www.intel.in/content/www/in/en/embedded/products/bay-trail/atom-e3800-android-display-vehicles-paper.html, 2014.
[44] J. Kim, R. A. Baratto, and J. Nieh. pTHINC: A Thin-client Architecture for Mobile Wireless Web. In *Proceedings of the 15th International Conference on World Wide Web (WWW)*, pages 143–152, 2006.
[45] G. Kulkarni, V. Premraj, V. Ordonez, S. Dhar, S. Li, Y. Choi, A. C. Berg, and T. L. Berg. Babytalk: Understanding and generating simple image descriptions. *IEEE Trans. Pattern Anal. Mach. Intell.*, 35(12):2891–2903, Dec. 2013.
[46] R. Liu and F. X. Lin. Understanding the characteristics of android wear os. In *Proceedings of the 14th Annual International Conference on Mobile Systems, Applications, and Services*, MobiSys '16, pages 151–164, New York, NY, USA, 2016. ACM.
[47] J. Meskens, K. Luyten, and K. Coninx. Jelly: A multi-device design environment for managing consistency across devices. In *Proceedings of the International Conference on Advanced Visual Interfaces*, pages 289–296. ACM, 2010.
[48] J. Meskens, J. Vermeulen, K. Luyten, and K. Coninx. Gummy for multi-platform user interface designs: shape me, multiply me, fix me, use me. In *Proceedings of the working conference on Advanced visual interfaces*, pages 233–240. ACM, 2008.
[49] M. Nebeling. Xdbrowser 2.0: Semi-automatic generation of cross-device interfaces. In *Proceedings of the 2017 CHI Conference on Human Factors in Computing Systems*, CHI '17, pages 4574–4584, New York, NY, USA, 2017. ACM.
[50] M. Nebeling and A. K. Dey. Xdbrowser: User-defined cross-device web page designs. In *Proceedings of the 2016 CHI Conference on Human Factors in Computing Systems*, pages 5494–5505. ACM, 2016.
[51] M. Nebeling, T. Mintsi, M. Husmann, and M. Norrie. Interactive development of cross-device user interfaces. In *Proceedings of the 32nd annual ACM conference on Human factors in computing systems*, pages 2793–2802. ACM, 2014.
[52] T.-D. Nguyen, J. Vanderdonckt, and A. Seffah. Generative patterns for designing multiple user interfaces. In *3rd IEEE/ACM International Conference on Mobile Software Engineering and Systems MobileSoft'2016*, 2016.
[53] J. Nichols, Z. Hua, and J. Barton. Highlight: a system for creating and deploying mobile web applications. In *Proceedings of the 21st annual ACM symposium on User interface software and technology*, pages 249–258. ACM, 2008.
[54] V. Ordonez, W. Liu, J. Deng, Y. Choi, A. C. Berg, and T. L. Berg. Learning to name objects. *Commun. ACM*, 59(3):108–115, Feb. 2016.
[55] E. F. Oriana Riva, Suman Nath. Appstract: On-the-fly app content semantics with better privacy. In *ACM Mobicom*. ACM, July 2016.
[56] Parallels. Parallels access. http://www.parallels.com/products/access/.
[57] D. E. Porter, S. Boyd-Wickizer, J. Howell, R. Olinsky, and G. Hunt. Rethinking the library OS from the top down. In *Proceedings of the ACM International Conference on Architectural Support for Programming Languages and Operating Systems (ASPLOS)*, pages 291–304, 2011.
[58] A. R. Puerta. A model-based interface development environment. *IEEE Software*, 14(4):40–47, 1997.
[59] Remote Desktop Protocol. https://en.wikipedia.org/wiki/Remote_Desktop_Protocol.
[60] T. Richardson, Q. Stafford-Fraser, K. Wood, and A. Hopper. Virtual network computing. *Internet Computing, IEEE*, 2(1):33–38, Jan 1998.
[61] R. W. Scheifler and J. Gettys. The x window system. *ACM Trans. Graph.*, 5(2):79–109, Apr. 1986.
[62] B. K. Schmidt, M. S. Lam, and J. D. Northcutt. The interactive performance of slim: A stateless, thin-client architecture. In *Proceedings of the ACM SIGOPS Symposium on Operating Systems Principles (SOSP)*, pages 32–47, 1999.
[63] A. Schulman, T. Thapliyal, S. Katti, N. Spring, D. Levin, and P. Dutta. Battor: Plug-and-debug energy debugging for applications on smartphones and laptops. Technical report, Stanford University, 2015.

[64] P. Szekely, P. Sukaviriya, P. Castells, J. Muthukumarasamy, and E. Salcher. Declarative interface models for user interface construction tools: the mastermind approach. In *Engineering for Human-Computer Interaction*, pages 120–150. Springer, 1996.

[65] D. S. Tan, B. Meyers, and M. Czerwinski. Wincuts: Manipulating arbitrary window regions for more effective use of screen space. In *CHI '04 Extended Abstracts on Human Factors in Computing Systems*, CHI EA '04, pages 1525–1528, New York, NY, USA, 2004. ACM.

[66] Teradici. Pc-over-ip technology explained. http://www.teradici.com/pcoip-technology.

[67] UIAutomater Viewer. http://www.bdtool.net/third/android-doc/web-docs/tools/testing/testing_ui.html.

[68] A. Van't Hof, H. Jamjoom, J. Nieh, and D. Williams. Flux: Multi-surface computing in android. In *Proceedings of the Tenth European Conference on Computer Systems*, EuroSys '15, pages 24:1–24:17, New York, NY, USA, 2015. ACM.

[69] Systrace. https://developer.android.com/studio/profile/systrace-commandline.html.

[70] J. Yang and D. Wigdor. Panelrama: Enabling easy specification of cross-device web applications. In *Proceedings of the SIGCHI Conference on Human Factors in Computing Systems*, CHI '14, pages 2783–2792, New York, NY, USA, 2014. ACM.

TinyLink: A Holistic System for Rapid Development of IoT Applications

http://tinylink.emnets.org

Gaoyang Guan, Wei Dong*, Yi Gao, Kaibo Fu, Zhihao Cheng
College of Computer Science, Zhejiang University
Emails: {guangy, dongw, gaoy, fukb, chengzh}@emnets.org

ABSTRACT

Rapid development is essential for IoT (Internet of Things) application developers to obtain first-mover advantages and reduce the development cost. In this paper, we present TinyLink, a holistic system for rapid development of IoT applications. The key idea of TinyLink is to use a *top-down* approach for designing both the hardware and the software of IoT applications. Developers write the application code in a C-like language to specify the key logic of their applications, without dealing with the details of the specific hardware components. Taking the application code as input, TinyLink automatically generates the hardware configuration as well as the binary program executable on the target hardware platform. TinyLink provides unified APIs for applications to interact with the underlying hardware components. We implement TinyLink and evaluate its performance using real-world IoT applications. Results show that: (1) TinyLink achieves rapid development of IoT applications, reducing 52.58% of lines of code in average compared with traditional approaches; (2) TinyLink searches a much larger design space and thus can generate a superior solution for the hardware configuration, compared with the state-of-the-art approach; (3) TinyLink incurs acceptable overhead in terms of execution time and program memory.

CCS CONCEPTS

• **Computer systems organization → Embedded and cyber-physical systems**; • **Networks → Cyber-physical networks**;

KEYWORDS

Internet of Things; Rapid Development

1 INTRODUCTION

Over the past years, the Internet of Things (IoT) [1] has evolved from a vague concept to practical systems connecting lots of network devices, and it is considered as a promising future computing technology [2]. IoT platforms are tightly coupled to their applications [3–5]. This coupling makes it difficult for general-purpose platforms to address application-specific needs [6].

The lack of general-purpose IoT platforms causes difficulties in developing IoT applications. Developers have to know all aspects of an IoT system including the requirements of target application as well as the hardware components and the software components. They typically follow a *bottom-up* approach from building an appropriate hardware platform (consisting of appropriate microcontrollers and different sensors) to writing application software that can run on the platform [7–9]. This bottom-up approach is time consuming [10]: an individual application developer has to learn and build a hardware platform first, then construct the software libraries, and finally write the application code; an application developer in a team has to wait for others to complete the hardware platform and the software system before he/she can write application code.

In this paper, we advocate a *top-down* approach: an application developer can first write the application code as if there exists a virtual platform which *possesses* all hardware components in the market. An intelligent system takes the application code as input and will: (1) automatically generate concrete configurations for hardware platforms (e.g., which components to select and how they connect); (2) translate the hardware-independent application code into hardware-dependent code which can directly execute on the generated hardware platform. This top-down approach greatly *accelerates* the developing process. While our previous position paper suggested the promise of this top-down approach [11], it fell short of answering several practical challenges, which we address in this paper.

First, how to select the most appropriate hardware components in order to satisfy application requirements? User desired functionalities can be inferred from the application code. How to select the hardware components accomplishing all the desired functionalities? Considering different costs and different characteristics of these hardware components, how to formulate this hardware selection problem and which optimization criterion should be chosen?

Second, how to embrace a diverse set of commercially available hardware components in a compatible manner? Significant hardware innovation has occurred recently, particularly in the Maker domain around Arduino and Raspberry Pi platforms. There has been a move from fixed platforms towards platforms with high extensibility. For example, mainboards already offer many interfaces, e.g., port and physical pin. Shield (a.k.a. expansion board) offers more flexibility for peripherals to interface with the mainboard. How to consider complex connections between peripherals and the mainboard?

* Corresponding author.

MobiCom '17, October 16–20, 2017, Snowbird, UT, USA

ACM ISBN 978-1-4503-4916-1/17/10...$15.00
https://doi.org/10.1145/3117811.3117825

Finally, how to express application logic in a hardware-independent manner and translate it into the executable code for the corresponding hardware configuration? Abstracting a unified programming environment is difficult as different platforms support different environments, e.g., Arduino supports AVR programming environment, and Raspberry Pi supports ARM-based Linux programming environment. How to implement a holistic system so that application developers need not care about low-level details such as device drivers, cross-compilers and so on?

In order to address the above challenges, we present TinyLink, a holistic system for rapid development of IoT applications. With TinyLink, developers can specify application logic in a C-like language, without dealing with the details of the underlying hardware, drivers, compilers, etc. Taking the application code as input, TinyLink automatically generates hardware configurations as well as the hardware-dependent code executable on the target hardware platform.

TinyLink includes a hardware database containing commercial-off-the-shelf (COTS) hardware components as well as their characteristics (e.g., costs, interfaces, required voltage, etc.). Based on the hardware database, TinyLink explicitly formulates possible compositions as hardware constraints. TinyLink carefully considers possible connections between ports and physical pins provided by mainboards and shields, and thus can embrace a diverse set of COTS hardware components. TinyLink also extracts the user constraints from the code, e.g., the invocation of a TinyLink API `TL_GPS.read()` means that one GPS sensor is required. TinyLink explores the design space by considering both hardware constraints and user constraints. Currently, TinyLink adopts an optimization criterion to minimize the cost. Other criteria (e.g., extensibility, energy, and performance) can also be adopted. TinyLink seeks the best solution by solving the optimization problem and outputs the hardware configuration (consisting of the set of hardware components and their connections).

TinyLink reuses easy-to-use Arduino-like environment for application programming. TinyLink provides unified APIs for the application to interface with the underlying hardware components. The APIs are fully implemented on four mainboards, including Arduino UNO, Raspberry Pi 2, BeagleBone Black and LinkIt ONE. To minimize the implementation overhead, TinyLink heavily reuses existing libraries. Glue code is implemented in TinyLink, serving a binding from the APIs to existing libraries TinyLink builds upon.

TinyLink is a holistic system: besides generating hardware configurations and providing easy-to-use APIs, TinyLink also includes: (1) Cloud-based compiling architecture; (2) Web-based application programming interface; (3) commonly used benchmarks for system validation.

We evaluate TinyLink using real-world IoT applications. Results show that: (1) TinyLink achieves rapid development of IoT applications, reducing 52.58% of lines of code in average compared with existing programming approaches for Arduino UNO, Raspberry Pi 2, BeagleBone Black and LinkIt ONE; (2) TinyLink searches a much larger design space and thus can generate a superior solution for the hardware configuration, compared with CodeFirst [12]; (3) TinyLink incurs acceptable overhead in terms of execution time and program memory. Moreover, we present three concrete case

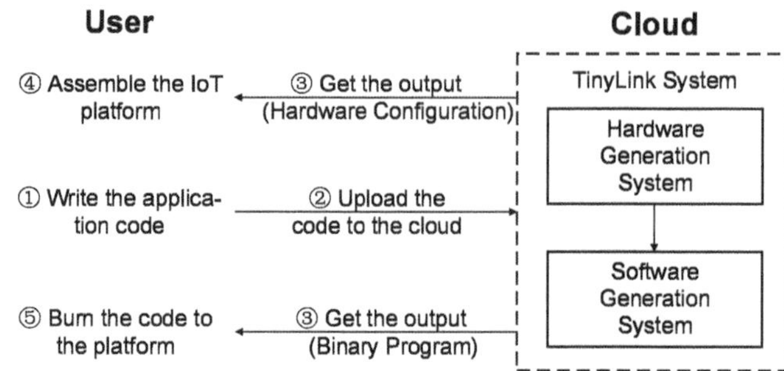

Figure 1: Workflow overview of TinyLink.

studies which illustrate how TinyLink can help us quickly develop real-world IoT applications.

The contributions of this work are summarized as below:

- We present TinyLink, a *holistic* system for developing IoT applications. TinyLink transforms IoT development process from *bottom-up* to *top-down*, enabling *rapid* development of IoT applications. TinyLink abstracts away the IoT hardware, so developers can focus on the application logic without experience in embedded systems.
- We formulate the hardware selection problem as an optimization problem. We carefully consider *hardware constraints* and *user constraints* so that a wide range of COTS hardware components can be used in a compatible manner and application requirements can be satisfied.
- We design unified APIs for applications to interface with COTS hardware components. We implement the APIs on four mainstream platforms so that application developers need not deal with low-level hardware details.
- We carefully evaluate TinyLink using benchmarks and three concrete case studies. Results show that TinyLink achieves rapid development of IoT applications and generates optimal solutions for hardware configuration, while incurring acceptable overhead.

The rest of this paper is structured as follows. Section 2 introduces how to use TinyLink. Section 3 shows TinyLink's design overview. Section 4 and Section 5 describe the hardware generation system and the software generation system, respectively. Section 6 shows the evaluation results. Section 7 discusses some important open issues. Section 8 describes the related work, and finally, Section 9 concludes this paper and gives future directions of work.

2 TINYLINK USAGE

In this section, we will describe how to use TinyLink for IoT application development. We first present an application example using TinyLink, followed by describing its syntax details.

2.1 Example

In this example, we present the development of an IoT application using TinyLink for monitoring the moisture and ambient light of a houseplant. As shown in Figure 1, a developer needs to perform the following five steps:

① **Write the application code.** Developers can directly write the application code in a *hardware-independent* way. For example,

```
1  void upload();
2  void setup() {
3    TL_WiFi.init();
4    TL_WiFi.join("SSID","PASSWORD");
5    TL_Light.setMeasuringRange(1,30000,"LUX");
6    TL_Light.setADCResolution(10);
7  }
8
9  void loop() {
10   TL_Light.read();
11   TL_Soil_Moisture.read();
12   upload();
13   TL_Time.delayMillis(60000);
14 }
15
16 void upload() {
17   double light = TL_Light.data();
18   double sm = TL_Soil_Moisture.data();
19   String url = "http://hostname/ul.php?";
20   url += String("light=") + String(light);
21   url += String("&sm=") + String(sm);
22   TL_WiFi.get(url);
23 }
```

Figure 2: Application code example.

Figure 2 shows our implementation. First, the `setup()` function is executed for the initialization of the required modules (i.e., the WiFi module). Second, the `loop()` function is continuously executed for reading the sensor data and uploading the data via the WiFi module. Applications can directly invoke functions of the modules via TinyLink built-in APIs which are prefixed with "`TL_`".

② **Upload the code to the cloud.** The TinyLink system runs at the cloud. Taking the application code as input, TinyLink executes multiple tasks and the results will be returned back to the developer.

③ **Get the outputs.** The developer gets the following two outputs: (1) the hardware configuration which includes the selected hardware components as well as their connections. TinyLink visualizes the result so that developers can easily follow the configuration to assemble the hardware platform. For example, Figure 3 shows the visualization of the hardware configuration which includes an Arduino UNO, a Base Shield V1.3, a Grove Light Sensor, a Soil Moisture Analog Sensor and an ESP8266 ESP01 WiFi module; (2) the hardware-dependent code. TinyLink transforms the hardware-independent application code into hardware-dependent binary code which can directly run on the target hardware platform.

④ **Assemble the IoT platform.** Given the visualization of the hardware configuration (e.g., Figure 3), developers can easily assemble the selected components into an IoT platform.

⑤ **Burn the code to the platform.** The developer can then burn the hardware-dependent code onto the hardware platform to execute the desired functionalities.

It is worth noting that this top-down development approach differs drastically from the traditional bottom-up approaches and can greatly accelerate the entire IoT developing process. With TinyLink, developers can easily express the application logic without dealing with hardware details. Also, the hardware engineering efforts can greatly be reduced since TinyLink automatically handles complex hardware compatibility issues.

2.2 TinyLink Programming

We consider ease of programming as a primary design goal of TinyLink. TinyLink borrows the program structure from Arduino programming. This is because: (1) it is fairly simple; (2) it is already very familiar to a large community. As shown in Figure 2, the application code built on top of TinyLink includes two primary functions.

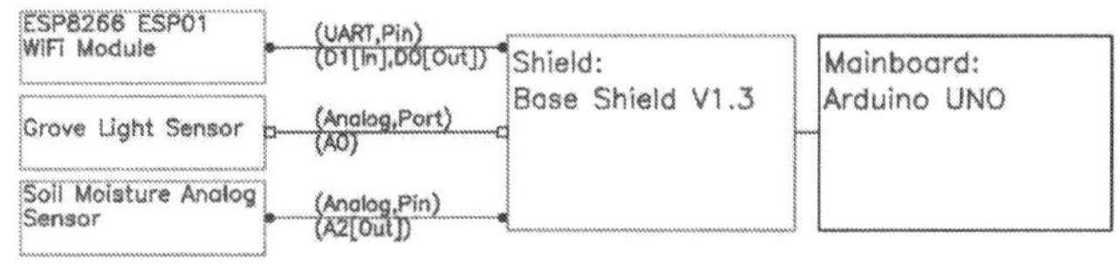

Figure 3: Hardware connection for the example.

`setup()`. The `setup()` function runs only once when the program starts. Developers can put the initialization of the required components or other one-shot tasks in this function. As shown in Figure 2, the program first initiates the WiFi module (line 3), and configures it by setting the SSID and the password of the AP (line 4). Developers can also specify additional features of hardware components, e.g., the measurement range (line 5) and the ADC resolution (line 6) of a light sensor.

`loop()`. The `loop()` function will be continuously executed after the `setup()` function. The `loop()` function usually includes some periodical tasks. As shown in Figure 2, the program reads data from the light sensor and the soil moisture sensor. Then the program invokes the function `upload()` to upload the data to the cloud server. Finally, the program invokes a built-in API to sleep for one minute (line 13) and then the loop restarts again.

TinyLink provides a keyword, `REQUIRE`, for explicitly specifying a required module. In the following, we give two examples.

(1) `REQUIRE Light;`—This statement specifies that the IoT platform must include the light sensor even if the light sensor is not used in the application code;
(2) `REQUIRE DBGPrint;`—This statement specifies that IoT platform must include an additional UART interface for printing out debugging information.

TinyLink provides many hardware-independent APIs for developers. The details will be described in Section 5.2.

3 TINYLINK DESIGN OVERVIEW

We describe TinyLink's design goals and the corresponding approaches we have adopted.

- **Rapid IoT application development.** To achieve this goal, TinyLink: (1) adopts the *top-down* development model for IoT applications; (2) generates the hardware configuration and the binary program *at the cloud* so that there is no installation of local developing environments.
- **Ease of programming.** To achieve this goal, TinyLink borrows the simple program structure of Arduino programming. In addition, TinyLink provides *hardware-independent* APIs to facilitate application programming.
- **Little hardware engineering efforts.** TinyLink incorporates a hardware database with clear specifications of hardware components and their characteristics. The generation of the hardware configuration is formulated as an optimization problem with constraints inferred from the application code. By solving the optimization problem, TinyLink *automatically* generates the best hardware configuration.

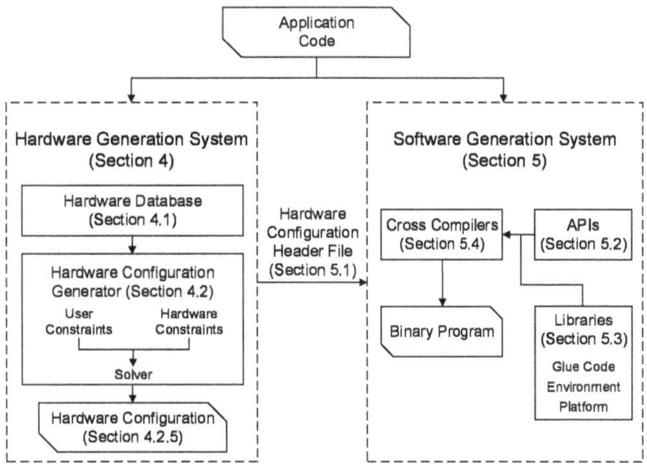

Figure 4: TinyLink system architecture.

- **High extensibility to accommodate many hardware components.** TinyLink is designed to embrace a set of COTS hardware components. Unlike CodeFirst [12], we do not assume a fixed mainboard. In addition, we need to consider complex connections between interfaces on hardware components. Finally, we need to carefully consider the implementations of libraries so that developers can easily interface with the underlying hardware components.

Figure 4 depicts the TinyLink system architecture, including the hardware generation system (Section 4) and the software generation system (Section 5). The application code serves as the input of TinyLink and is passed to both generation systems:

- Inside the hardware generation system, the hardware configuration generator automatically generates the hardware configuration by analyzing the application code and considering the information from the hardware database. The hardware generation system also generates the hardware configuration header file.
- Inside the software generation system, the cross compiler takes three sources as inputs, namely the application code, the generated hardware configuration header file and libraries. Finally, the binary program for the target platform is generated.

4 HARDWARE GENERATION SYSTEM

In this section, we will describe the TinyLink hardware generation system from two aspects, the hardware database (Section 4.1) and the hardware configuration generator (Section 4.2).

4.1 Hardware Database

TinyLink includes a hardware database containing COTS hardware components and their characteristics. This hardware database serves as the key information source to automatically generate hardware configurations. We look for popular and widely-used COTS hardware components for embedded and IoT development and find that many platforms consist of three kinds of components:

- Mainboard. A mainboard contains key electronic components of a system, e.g., MCU and memory. It also provides interfaces (in the forms of physical pin or port) for other peripherals.
- Shield. A shield can be plugged onto the mainboard to transform or extend the types or number of interfaces. Also, shields with built-in modules will consume interfaces and provide functionalities, e.g., WiFi Shield V2.0 consumes UART pins and provides WiFi functionality. Moreover, some shields containing MCUs can provide extra interfaces, e.g., GrovePi+ [13] has an ATmega328 MCU and provides three extra Analog pins for Raspberry Pi.
- Peripherals. A peripheral can connect to a mainboard or a shield via interfaces. Peripherals include input devices (e.g., sensors), output devices (e.g., display modules) and input/output devices (e.g., communication modules).

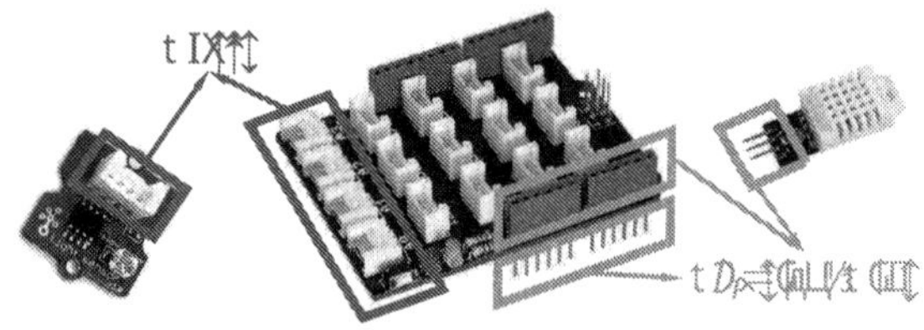

Figure 5: Physical pins and ports.

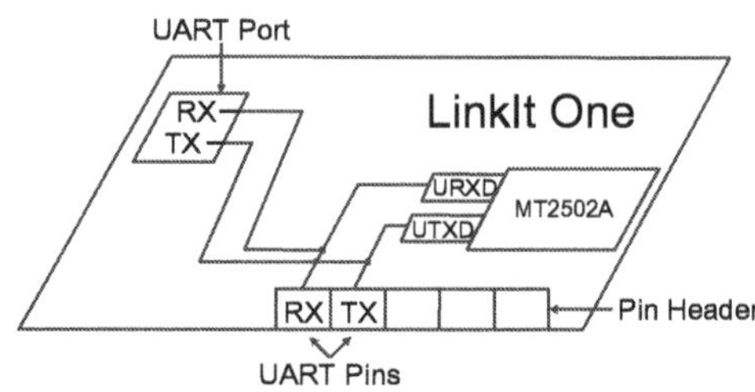

Figure 6: Internal connections of UART pins, UART ports and UART MCU pins on LinkIt One.

Correspondingly, our database includes three tables. Table 1 shows a simplified table which contains the following key fields: ID, cost, provided interface, consumed interface, provided MCU pin, consumed MCU pin and functionality. For LinkIt One, it: (1) costs 59 dollars; (2) has three Analog pins and two UART pins (the example only shows two types); (4) has one UART port; (5) has exposed three Analog MCU pins and two UART MCU pins; (6) occupies none of the interfaces and MCU pins; (7) has functionalities of GPRS, GPS, SD, WiFi, BLE integrated into the mainboard.

As shown in Figure 5, physical pins and ports are two major kinds of interfaces on IoT components. Besides, MCU or System on Chip (SoC) usually contains from several to dozens of general-purpose input/output pins (GPIO), which we call MCU pins. The physical pins and ports are wiring to MCU pins. For example, in Figure 6, the UART pins (i.e., RX and TX) and the UART port are wiring to the UART MCU pins (i.e., URXD and UTXD).

4.2 Hardware Configuration Generator

IoT has a diverse set of applications for different scenarios. Although some applications can use a powerful mainboard with abundant inferences, others cannot. Considering form factors, cost and other factors, the most appropriate hardware component may be resource constrained. The generation process intends to address the problem

Table 1: Database example.

Component	ID	Cost	Provided Interface				Consumed Interface				Provided MCU Pin		Consumed MCU Pin		Functionality
			Analog Pin	UART Pin	Analog Port	UART Port	Analog Pin	UART Pin	Analog Port	UART Port	Analog	UART	Analog	UART	
Arduino UNO	1	$21.99	6	2	0	0	0	0	0	0	6	2	0	0	LED
LinkIt One	2	$59.00	3	2	0	1	0	0	0	0	3	2	0	0	LED, GPRS, GPS, Storage, WiFi, BLE
BetaBlocks	3	$75.00	0	0	2	1	0	0	0	0	4	2	0	0	LED
WiFi Shield V2.0	4	$39.95	6	2	1	0	6	2	0	0	0	0	0	2	WiFi
Base Shield V1.3	5	$8.90	6	2	2	1	6	2	0	0	0	0	0	0	-
Grove Light Sensor	6	$2.90	0	0	0	0	0	0	1	0	0	0	2	0	Light
Soil Moisture Analog Sensor	7	$3.98	0	0	0	0	1	0	0	0	0	0	1	0	Soil_Moisture
Grove Moisture Sensor	8	$4.90	0	0	0	0	0	0	1	0	0	0	2	0	Soil_Moisture
ESP8266 ESP01 WiFi Module	9	$6.95	0	0	0	0	0	2	0	0	0	0	0	2	WiFi
Grove UART WiFi Module	10	$13.90	0	0	0	0	0	0	0	1	0	0	0	2	WiFi

of how to assemble COTS hardware components in an effective and compatible way.

We first describe the conditions for a valid/compatible hardware configuration. We then formulate the hardware selection problem, i.e., which hardware components should be selected to form the IoT platform. Finally, we generate the hardware connections and visualize the final results for the developers.

4.2.1 Valid Hardware Configuration. In TinyLink, it is important to clearly define a valid hardware configuration before we can search for a valid hardware configuration. We first define a valid connection between two hardware components via interfaces. A valid connection should satisfy the following conditions: (1) the two interfaces must be in the same form (i.e., physical pin or port); (2) the two interfaces must be type compatible. Usually, it means that the two interfaces has the same type, e.g., UART. In practice, we also consider the special case in which an interface can have two or more alternative types; (3) the interfaces must be power compatible, i.e., the supplied voltage level of an interface is compatible with the working voltage level of the other interface, and the drawn current should be smaller than the maximal allowable current of both interfaces.

In a valid hardware configuration, all connections must be valid. To simplify the configuration, we first assume that there is only one mainboard. In addition, it should satisfy the following conditions: (1) the configuration must satisfy all the application requirements; (2) a connection is a one-to-one mapping. In other words, an interface cannot connect to multiple interfaces of another component since it will cause signal interference. It also means that the provided number of interfaces must be no smaller than the consumed number of interfaces with respect to a particular interface type (e.g., UART); (3) only one connection can be established on interfaces which are wired to the same MCU pin. As shown in Figure 6, either the UART port or the UART pins can be connected at a time. A detailed example will be described in Section 4.2.4.

Table 2 summarizes the conditions we have considered in the current implementation of TinyLink.

There are several important points worth emphasizing. First, TinyLink has a much larger design space than previous approaches like CodeFirst [12]. For example, CodeFirst only allows connections between ports while TinyLink allows connections between pins which are common cases for many peripherals such as Soil Moisture Analog Sensor and ESP8266 WiFi module. Second, the conditions we have considered for a valid configuration are never exhaustive [14]. It is possible that a valid hardware configuration generated by TinyLink could not work due to conditions we have not considered,

Table 2: Implemented constraints in TinyLink.

Constraint	Description
Mainboard	Only one mainboard exists in a hardware configuration.
Interface	For each type of the interface, the number of consumed ones should be smaller than the number of the provided.
Power Supply	The supplied voltage level should be compatible with the working voltage level.
Drawn Current	The total drawn current of all components should be smaller than the input current; the drawn current of an interface should be smaller than the maximal allowable current.
MCU Pin	The number of consumed MCU pins should be smaller than the number of the provided.
Compatibility	All components should be compatible with each other in terms of form factor, communication, etc.
Alternative Type	All the interfaces which have alternative types can use at most one type at a time.

e.g., incompatible baud rate of UART. Nevertheless, TinyLink is valuable since it help developers avoid numerous invalid hardware configurations. In addition, TinyLink can be easily extended to accommodate additional conditions in the future.

4.2.2 Problem Formulation. We first introduce the following notations.

- M, S, P. We use them denote the sets of mainboard, shield, and peripheral, respectively. In the database example in Table 1, $M = \{1, 2, 3\}, S = \{4, 5\}, P = \{6, 7, 8, 9, 10\}$.
- U, F. We use F to denote the set of all functionalities. We use U to denote the set of user required functionalities. U can be inferred from the application code. U is included in F.
- i, d_i, c_i, f_i^u. We use d_i to denote the indicator variable. $d_i = 1$ indicates that hardware component i is present in the final IoT platform, where $i \in \{M \cup S \cup P\}$, while $d_i = 0$ indicates that it is not. c_i is the cost of the component i. f_i^u is the boolean value (i.e., 1 and 0) indicating whether the component i has the required functionality of $u \in U$ or not.
- t, T. We use t to denote the type of an interface, where t is in the interface type set T={UART, Analog, SPI, I^2C, PWM, USB, Digital}.
- $NO_i^+(t), NO_i^-(t)$. $NO_i^+(t)$ represents the number of interfaces with the type t in the form of port provided by the component i, while $NO_i^-(t)$ represents the number of interfaces with the type t in the form of port consumed by the component i.
- $NI_i^+(t), NI_i^-(t)$. Similar to the notations for ports, where NI represents the number of physical pins.
- $NM_i^+(t), NM_i^-(t)$. Similar to the notations for ports and physical pins, where NM represents the number of MCU pins.

With the above definitions, the hardware selection problem can be formulated as follows with the optimization criterion being the total cost.

$$\text{Find the values of } d_i \ (\forall i \in \{M \cup S \cup P\})$$
$$\min \sum_{i \in \{M \cup S \cup P\}} d_i c_i \quad (1)$$
$$\text{s.t.} \begin{cases} \text{User Constraints} \\ \text{Hardware Constraints} \end{cases}$$

Component i is selected iff $d_i = 1$. We call a set of is as a feasible set if they satisfy all the constraints. In the following, we describe how we carefully setup constraints and conduct validations to ensure that feasible solutions are valid ones.

4.2.3 User Constraint. TinyLink first *preprocesses* the application code and infers the user requirement U. User constraints are automatically generated:

$$\sum_{i \in \{M \cup S \cup P\}} f_i^u d_i \geq 1, \quad \forall u \in U \quad (2)$$

Example. We revisit the example shown in Figure 2. Also assume the hardware database is shown in Table 1. TinyLink automatically infers U as U={Light, Soil_Moisture, WiFi}. Thus three user constraints are generated:

$$\begin{cases} d_6 \geq 1 & \text{(Light)} \\ d_7 + d_8 \geq 1 & \text{(Soil\_Moisture)} \\ d_2 + d_4 + d_9 + d_{10} \geq 1 & \text{(WiFi)} \end{cases}$$

4.2.4 Hardware Constraint. While the user constraints are fairly simple, the hardware constraints are much more complicated. Due to space limit, we describe three important constraints.

1) ***Port Constraint.*** TinyLink allows the use of shields to extend the capability of mainboard. As such, for a particular type, the number of ports provided by the mainboard plus the number of ports provided by the shield, minus the number of ports consumed by the shield, should be no smaller than the number of ports consumed by the peripherals. The port constraint for TinyLink is shown below:

$$\sum_{i \in M} NO_i^+(t) d_i + \sum_{i \in S} (NO_i^+(t) d_i - NO_i^-(t) d_i) \geq \sum_{i \in P} NO_i^-(t) d_i, \forall t \in T \quad (3)$$

2) ***Physical Pin Constraint.*** TinyLink allows connections via physical pins. Similar to the port constraint, the physical pin constraint for TinyLink is shown below:

$$\sum_{i \in M} NI_i^+(t) d_i + \sum_{i \in S} (NI_i^+(t) d_i - NI_i^-(t) d_i) \geq \sum_{i \in P} NI_i^-(t) d_i, \forall t \in T \quad (4)$$

3) ***MCU Pin Constraint.*** Nevertheless, the actual number of *usable* ports and physical pins is not as easy as calculating their sum. This is because some ports and physical pins are mapped to the same MCU pins, which means that they actually share the same interface and will interfere with each other if they are used simultaneously. For example, in Figure 6, the UART physical pin RX in the pin header and the pin inside the UART port (i.e., RX pin of the UART port) are *wiring* to the same MCU pin URXD on MT2502A, the SoC of LinkIt One. It is the same case for the UART physical pin TX and the TX pin in the UART port.

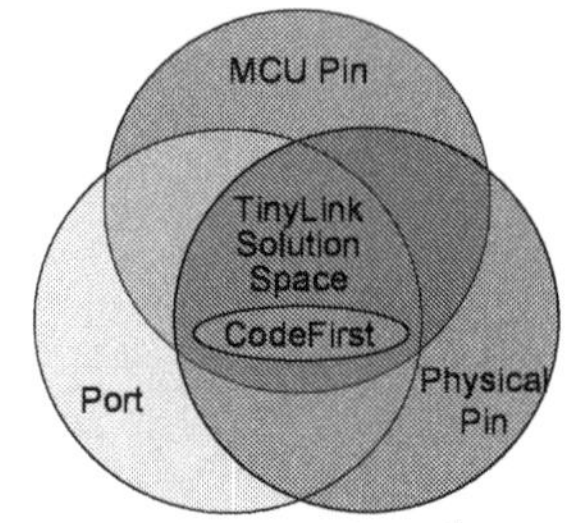

Figure 7: Solution space comparison between TinyLink and CodeFirst.

As a result, we need to constrain the number of usable interfaces at the MCU pin level. The total number of consumed MCU pins should be no larger than the total number of provided ones. The MCU pin constraint is generated as follows:

$$\sum_{i \in M} NM_i^+(t) d_i + \sum_{i \in S} (NM_i^+(t) d_i - NM_i^-(t) d_i) \geq \sum_{i \in P} NM_i^-(t) d_i, \forall t \in T \quad (5)$$

Example. We revisit the example in Figure 2. TinyLink generates the following constraints:

$$\begin{cases} 0d_1 + 0d_2 + 2d_3 + (1d_4 + 2d_5 - 0d_4 - 0d_5) \geq \\ \quad d_6 + 0d_7 + d_8 + 0d_9 + 0d_{10} \quad \text{(Port Cons. for Analog)} \\ 0d_1 + d_2 + d_3 + (0d_4 + d_5 - 0d_4 - 0d_5) \geq \\ \quad 0d_6 + 0d_7 + 0d_8 + 0d_9 + d_{10} \quad \text{(Port Cons. for UART)} \\ 6d_1 + 3d_2 + 0d_3 + (6d_4 + 6d_5 - 6d_4 - 6d_5) \geq \\ \quad 0d_6 + d_7 + 0d_8 + 0d_9 + 0d_{10} \quad \text{(PHY Pin Cons. for Analog)} \\ 2d_1 + 2d_2 + 0d_3 + (2d_4 + 2d_5 - 2d_4 - 2d_5) \geq \\ \quad 0d_6 + 0d_7 + 0d_8 + 2d_9 + 0d_{10} \quad \text{(PHY Pin Cons. for UART)} \\ 6d_1 + 3d_2 + 4d_3 + (0d_4 + 0d_5 - 0d_4 - 0d_5) \geq \\ \quad 2d_6 + d_7 + 2d_8 + 0d_9 + 0d_{10} \quad \text{(MCU Pin Cons. for Analog)} \\ 2d_1 + 2d_2 + 2d_3 + (0d_4 + 0d_5 - 2d_4 - 0d_5) \geq \\ \quad 0d_6 + 0d_7 + 0d_8 + 2d_9 + 2d_{10} \quad \text{(MCU Pin Cons. for UART)} \end{cases}$$

Together with the mainboard constraint (i.e., $d_1 + d_2 + d_3 = 1$) and user constraints in Section 4.2.3, we can get 19 feasible sets.

Comparison with CodeFirst. The CodeFirst [12]: (1) does not allow the use of shield; (2) does not allow connections via pins; (3) does not consider the MCU pin constraints.

With the following port constraints,

$$\sum_{i \in M} NO_i^+(t) d_i \geq \sum_{i \in P} NO_i^-(t) d_i, \quad \forall t \in T$$

CodeFirst generates the following concrete constraints for the example shown in Figure 2:

$$\begin{cases} 2d_3 \geq d_6 + 0d_7 + d_8 + 0d_9 + 0d_{10} & \text{(Port Cons. for Analog)} \\ d_3 \geq 0d_6 + 0d_7 + 0d_8 + 0d_9 + d_{10} & \text{(Port Cons. for UART)} \end{cases}$$

Assuming a fixed mainboard of BetaBlocks, CodeFirst gets only one feasible solution $\{3, 6, 8, 10\}$, which is included in the set of TinyLink's feasible solutions.

Figure 7 shows the solution space of TinyLink and CodeFirst. Under the three constraints we have described, the set of all

Table 3: API call frequency summarized from real-world projects.

LED	Tempe-rature	WiFi	Display	Humidity	Motor	Light	Speaker	Distance	Soil Moisture	Accele-rometer	BLE	Buzzer	GPS	Switch	Motion	Baro-metric	Joystick	RFID	Storage	Others
23.11%	10.22%	10.22%	9.78%	4.89%	4.44%	3.56%	2.67%	2.67%	2.22%	2.22%	2.22%	1.78%	1.78%	1.78%	1.78%	1.33%	1.33%	1.33%	1.33%	9.33%

CodeFirst feasible solutions is a subset of TinyLink feasible solutions. The search space of TinyLink is much larger since it allows complex connections between components.

4.2.5 Implementation. The generation of hardware configuration consists of three main steps.

First, we solve the optimization problem described above and look for the most appropriate hardware components. In real implementations, we use complete set of constraints listed in Table 2. We further consider the compatibility constraint. The compatibility constraint: (1) forbids physically incompatible hardware components to be connected, e.g., Base Shield V1.3 and Raspberry Pi 2 are not physically compatible due to their different form factors; (2) restrains hardware components from being connected to those they cannot work with in a compatible way during run time, e.g., a Grove Temperature and Humidity Sensor Pro on a LinkIt One frequently fails to read the temperature data though their connection via ports is valid. Since the formulated problem is a classical integer linear programming problem, we utilize the ILP solver, lp_solve [15], to solve this optimization problem.

Second, TinyLink will show developers how to assemble these hardware components after generating the hardware component list. The connection is generated by correctly allocating interfaces on the mainboard and the shields to hardware components. Given the selected mainboard and shields, TinyLink calculates all the available interfaces, and then allocate them by priority. First, TinyLink allocates the pin interfaces occupied by built-in modules on mainboards and shields, e.g., UART pins on WiFi Shield V2.0. Afterwards, TinyLink allocates non-occupied ports and non-occupied physical pins to peripherals, because ports usually occupy consecutive MCU pins shared with physical pins. Based on the allocation, TinyLink utilizes OpenCV to generate a simple visualization for the generated hardware configuration, e.g., Figure 3 visualizes the recommended hardware configuration for the application code shown in Figure 2.

Finally, TinyLink employs an additional validation procedure to verify that the recommended hardware configuration is a valid one, according to definitions described in Section 4.2.1. If the hardware configuration happens to be invalid due to invalid connections (which is rare from our experience), TinyLink invokes the ILP solver again to seek for a different solution which is valid by our definition. In the future, we would like to borrow the crowdsourcing idea for IoT application development. If the current developer selects a hardware configuration that was used and reported successfully by others, the developer has a high chance of getting the correct one.

5 SOFTWARE GENERATION SYSTEM

This section describes how to generate hardware-dependent binary program from the application code. Section 5.1 describes the generation of hardware configuration header file. Section 5.2 and Section 5.3 present TinyLink API design and the library implementations in detail. Section 5.4 describes the cross compilers, followed by Section 5.5 which discusses interactive debugging in TinyLink.

```
1  #include "TL_DeviceID.h"
2
3  #define MAINBOARD ARDUINO_UNO
4  #define WIFI ESP8266_ESP01
5  #define LIGHT GROVE_LIGHT
6  #define SOIL_MOISTURE SOIL_MOISTURE_ANALOG
7
8  #define WIFI_UART_RX 1
9  #define WIFI_UART_TX 0
10 #define LIGHT_ANALOG_OUTPUT A0
11 #define SOIL_MOISTURE_ANALOG_OUTPUT A2
```

Figure 8: Hardware configuration header file.

5.1 Hardware Configuration Header File

From the perspective of developers, the application code is hardware-independent. However, from the perspective of cross compilers, the code should be hardware-dependent, e.g., link to the correct libraries corresponding to the underlying hardware. Therefore, we translate the hardware configuration information (see Figure 3) to the hardware configuration header file in C language (see Figure 8).

The hardware configuration header file is composed of three sections. The first section includes other important header files (line 1), such as the device ID header file. The second section describes which hardware components are used via macros (line 3-6). In each line, an abstract component (e.g., `MAINBOARD` in line 3) is defined by a specific hardware component (e.g., `ARDUINO_UNO` in line 3), which relates the hardware-independent functionality to the hardware-dependent components. The third section describes the hardware connection information (line 8-11). This hardware configuration header file is generated by the hardware generation system and is essential for compiling the application code for the target platform.

5.2 API Design

Unlike traditional IoT programming, programming with TinyLink is hardware-independent, i.e., the developers are unaware of the underlying hardware components. APIs play an important role in relating high-level semantics to low-level details. TinyLink provides generalized APIs to facilitate application programming.

In order to provide developers with widely-used APIs, we investigate 116 projects from popular IoT online forums [16, 17] and websites [18, 19]. We extract 225 commonly used APIs from them, and group them into 39 categories by the functionalities they provide. As shown in Table 3, we list the twenty mostly used categories and their call frequency, where the most popular one is the LED, accounting for about 23%. In the current implementation of TinyLink, we encapsulate and implement 24 categories, covering 89.78% of the total APIs we have investigated. The remaining 10.22% (i.e., uncovered) of the APIs are left unimplemented, including those controlling DIY devices, transmitting and receiving infrared signals, etc. Given a limited development time, we have decided to implement the most important and commonly used APIs while skipping those infrequently invoked ones.

We say that TinyLink supports a project if all the APIs used in this project have corresponding TinyLink APIs. 67.24% of the projects are supported by TinyLink and can be ported to TinyLink with little modifications. The remaining 32.76% of the projects have at least one uncovered API and thus cannot be easily ported to TinyLink in the current stage. We plan to implement more TinyLink APIs to support more IoT applications in the future.

How to exchange messages over unreliable networks in an energy-efficient manner is an important issue in IoT development. Message Queue Telemetry Transport (MQTT) protocol is a lightweight messaging protocol [20] which builds on top of the TCP protocol. It has been adopted as a primary protocol for IoT communications by major IoT cloud providers (e.g., IBM, Amazon and Microsoft). To support this widely-used protocol in IoT development, we provide MQTT APIs in TinyLink. Once a TCP connection is established, a TinyLink node with MQTT can connect to a broker (i.e., MQTT client at the server side) upon it, and then publish/subscribe their information. We have tested our TinyLink MQTT APIs on IBM Bluemix and China Mobile IoT Open Platform. All four mainboards, i.e., Arduino UNO, LinkIt One, Raspberry Pi 2 and BeagleBone Black, can connect to MQTT brokers of the two cloud platforms using ESP8266 WiFi module and Grove UART WiFi module, as well as the built-in WiFi module of LinkIt One and the built-in Ethernet modules of Raspberry Pi 2 and BeagleBone Black.

In addition, we provide basic debugging APIs for developers. They can write `REQUIRE DBGPrint` to indicate that they require printing out debugging information. In this case, the TinyLink hardware system will occupy an additional serial interface on the mainboard. All debugging information will be transmitted via this serial interface. Developers can use `TL_Debug.print()` to print out their own debugging information.

5.3 Library Implementation

Libraries are the actual implementations of TinyLink APIs. We are facing practical implementation challenges since each library implementation requires developing efforts and the number of required implementations may grow rapidly with increasing number of hardware components. We address these challenges in the following ways.

First, we implement the most commonly used libraries according to our experience so that we can benefit more number of users given a limited development time. With the increasing use of TinyLink, we could get more feedbacks about which libraries should be implemented with a higher priority.

Second, we try to reuse existing libraries and only add *glue* code to implement TinyLink APIs. Writing glue code includes abstracting the unified input/output interfaces, replacing hardware-dependent code with macros, adding conditional syntax in the API header file and so on.

Figure 9 illustrates how we implement the TinyLink API `TL_LED.turnOn()` by reusing libraries on four mainboards. For these four mainboards, we use the function `pinMode()` to configure LED pin behavior and use `digitalWrite()` to turn the LED on. These APIs are implemented differently for different platforms. On Arduino and LinkIt platforms (Arduino programming environment and VM on Linux), they can be easily implemented using the

```
void TL_LED::turnOn() {
  pinMode(LED_DIGITAL_OUTPUT, OUTPUT);
  digitalWrite(LED_DIGITAL_OUTPUT, HIGH);
}
```

Figure 9: Glue code example of implementing an LED function.

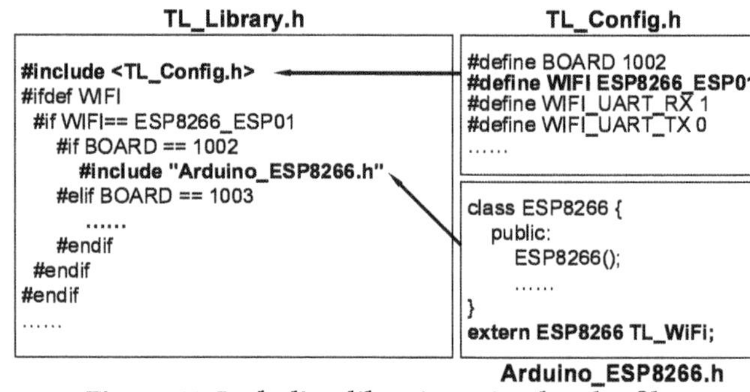

Figure 10: Including libraries using header files.

system library. On Raspberry Pi and BeagleBone platforms (Debian-based Linux operation systems), they can be implemented using third-party libraries, e.g., wiringPi [21] and wiringBone [22]. The implementation overhead for glue code is relatively small when we carefully choose the existing libraries.

Finally, we will allow for crowdsourcing the library implementations by application developers. We will release TinyLink libraries to be open source online, and in the long term, we hope that more and more IoT developers will join us to implement the useful libraries which can be shared among other developers. As an initial effort, we provide component templates written in C++ for developers to implement TinyLink libraries for a new device. For example, in order to implement a library for a simple sensor, a developer can use the sensor template we have developed, inherit the `Sensor` class and implement abstract interfaces like `virtual int _read()=0`.

It is also worth noting that it is possible for TinyLink to generate a hardware configuration which misses some software implementations. To address this issue, we provide two options for the developers: (1) provide the best IoT hardware configuration and the application developers have to implement the required library code; (2) provide the suboptimal solution with complete software implementations.

5.4 Cross Compiler

The preprocessed code needs to be cross compiled on the cloud to the binary code for the target platform. There are two key problems that TinyLink needs to address: (1) Which libraries to link? (2) Which cross compiler to use?

TinyLink relies on a header file `TL_Config.h` which encodes the hardware configuration. The type of mainboards defined in `TL_Config.h` determines the specific cross compiler.

Figure 10 shows how TinyLink links hardware-independent application code with hardware-dependent libraries. TinyLink libraries include two headers files, which are `TL_Library.h` and `<mainboard>_<peripheral>.h`, for transforming hardware-independent APIs to hardware-dependent APIs. For the example shown in Figure 10, `TL_Library.h` will include `TL_Config.h` to include necessary function modules, e.g., `ESP8266_ESP01`, which

Table 4: Cross compilers of four mainboards.

Mainboard	MCU Architecture	Cross Compiler
Arduino UNO	AVR ATmega	avr-gcc, avr-g++
LinkIt One	ARM7 EJ-S	arm-none-eabi-gcc, arm-none-eabi-g++
Raspberry Pi 2	ARM Cortex-A7	arm-linux-gnueabihf-gcc,
BeagleBone Black	ARM Cortex-A8	arm-linux-gnueabihf-g++

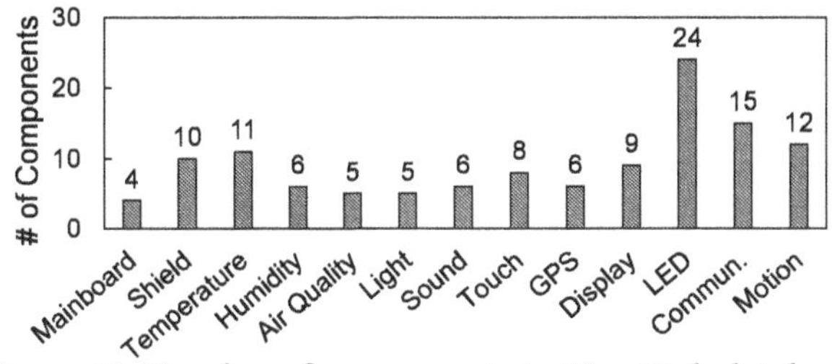

Figure 11: Number of components in TinyLink database.

again includes `Arduino_ESP8266.h` according to the hardware configuration defined in `TL_Config.h`.

We list cross compilers for four mainboards in Table 4. The Arduino UNO based on AVR ATmega utilizes avr-gcc and avr-g++ compilers. LinkIt One, which is based on ARM7, leverages arm-none-eabi-gcc and arm-none-eabi-g++ compilers. The Raspberry Pi 2 and BeagleBone Black, with ARM Cortex-A7 and Cortex-A8 respectively, both use arm-linux-gnueabihf-gcc and arm-linux-gnueabihf-g++ compilers.

5.5 Interactive Debugging

TinyLink supports interactive debugging if the native system supports it. In the current stage, TinyLink supports interactive debugging using gdb for the Debian systems on Raspberry Pi and BeagleBone Black. If gdb debugging is required by writing `REQUIRE GDB`, TinyLink will compile the application code to include necessary debugging information. In addition, developers are provided with the source code of the whole project, including high-level application code as well as low-level hardware-dependent library code. Based on these, developers can log into the platform and debug the source code with functions provided by gdb, e.g., breakpoints, watchpoints and stepped execution.

6 EVALUATION

In this section, we present the evaluation of TinyLink. Section 6.1 presents the experiment setup. Section 6.2 shows the overall evaluations in terms of ease of programming, feasible solutions and overhead. We study three real-world cases using both TinyLink and CodeFirst [12] in Section 6.3.

6.1 Experiment Setup

Hardware Component. In Figure 11, we list the number of components in our hardware database grouped by functionalities. There are four mainboards, ten shields and more than one hundred peripherals recorded in our database. The four mainboards include Arduino UNO (UNO for short), LinkIt ONE (ONE for short), Raspberry Pi 2 (RP2 for short) and BeagleBone Black (BBB for short). The characteristics (e.g., resolution and sensing range) of these components are also stored in our database.

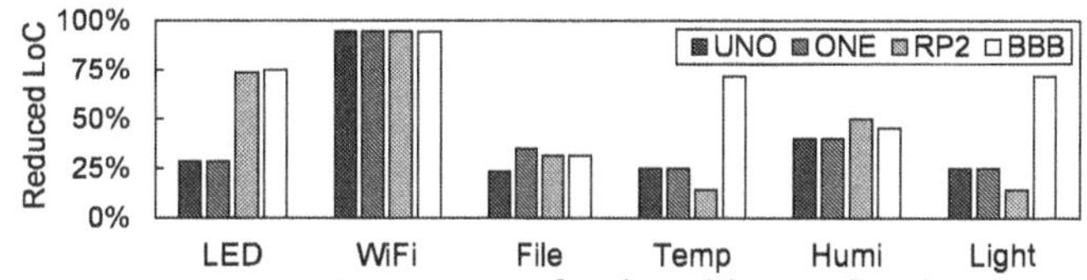

Figure 12: Percentage of reduced lines of code.

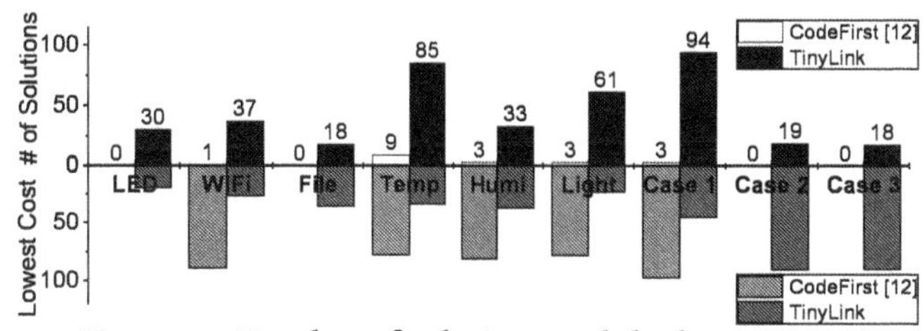

Figure 13: Number of solutions and the lowest cost.

Benchmark. We use six frequently used benchmarks according to Table 3 for evaluation, which are: (1) LED Write (LED for short), which turns on an LED; (2) WiFi GET (WiFi for short), which sends an HTTP GET request to a website in the local area network and retrieves the response; (3) File Write & Read (File for short), which writes data to a file on a storage module and then reads the data; (4) Temperature Read (Temp for short), which reads temperature data from a sensor; (5) Humidity Read (Humi for short), similar to Temp; (6) Light Read (Light for short), similar to Temp.

Case Study. We use three real-world case studies, which are an indoor smart houseplant node which has been described in Section 2, an air quality monitoring node and a voice controlled LED lamp node. More details are presented in Section 6.3.

6.2 Overall Evaluation

6.2.1 Ease of Programming. First, we compare lines of code needed to implement the benchmarks between using TinyLink APIs and using original APIs (e.g., APIs provided by hardware manufacturers). We implement the six benchmarks on four mainboards and report the reduced lines of code. In Figure 12, we can see that using TinyLink reduces the lines of code by 14.29% to 94.67%. The average percentage of reduced lines of code on four mainboards is 52.58%. In particular, for implementing the WiFi GET benchmark, using TinyLink APIs reduces more than 94.40% of lines of code on all mainboards. This is due to the simple API design and a large amount of glue code implementations for the WiFi library.

Second, we compare the lines of code between TinyLink and CodeFirst [12]. CodeFirst uses 27 lines of code to implement an example of reading data from a temperature sensor, displaying data on an LCD screen and transmitting data via Bluetooth. This is the only example which has the source code in CodeFirst. In TinyLink, developers can implement an application with the same functionalities only using 15 lines of code.

6.2.2 Feasible Solution. TinyLink can generate many feasible solutions after exploring the hardware database and choose the best one according to the given optimization criterion (e.g., the total cost). A larger searching space will provide more opportunities to generate more feasible solutions, as well as a better solution. We evaluate the feasible solutions for six small benchmarks and three case studies, and compare the results with CodeFirst [12]. Figure 13

Table 5: Relative execution overhead.

API From Benchmark	LED Write	UART Write	UART Read	File Write	File Read	Temp Read	Humi Read	Light Read
UNO	13.79%	0.00%	0.00%	1.10%	1.26%	0.01%	0.01%	7.56%
ONE	6.25%	0.02%	0.63%	0.38%	0.48%	0.02%	0.04%	1.15%
BBB	10.86%	0.76%	2.73%	15.68%	14.16%	0.03%	0.04%	8.90%
RP2	12.86%	10.74%	7.50%	0.71%	1.94%	0.43%	0.48%	2.13%

Table 6: Program space overhead (Bytes).

Benchmark	LED	WiFi	File	Temp	Humi	Light
UNO	166	184	2178	374	278	414
ONE	4372	2780	31000	3328	3320	3636
BBB	78224	63668	82311	79428	79428	77504
RP2	30713	11039	33317	27016	27016	26332

Table 7: Memory space overhead (Bytes).

Benchmark	LED	WiFi	File	Temp	Humi	Light
UNO	21	170	56	23	23	23
ONE	1272	1384	21384	1200	1208	1248
BBB	82591	99511	85193	82756	82627	82257
RP2	30713	11039	33317	27016	27016	26332

shows the results. For each benchmark and case study, we count the number of feasible solutions, as well as the lowest cost in the set of the feasible solutions. We can observe that TinyLink generates far more feasible solutions than CodeFirst and much lower total cost for each benchmark and case study. In the LED write and the File Write & Read benchmarks, CodeFirst fails to generate any feasible solutions, because it only use ports which are usually not supported by peripherals with the storage functionality.

6.2.3 Overhead. The implementations of glue code on existing libraries introduce overhead to the generated IoT applications. In the following, we evaluate the execution overhead, program space overhead and memory space overhead.

Execution Overhead. Most implementations of unified TinyLink APIs are the encapsulations of existing ones, and the overhead comes from the glue code. We take experiments on the execution time of API calls in our benchmarks. Table 5 shows the relative execution overhead of using TinyLink APIs compared with using original APIs. Considering the magnitude of the execution overhead is μs (e.g., 0.75μs for LED benchmark on UNO), the overhead is acceptable.

Program Space Overhead. The program space overhead is proportional to the amount of implemented glue code. Due to different MCU architectures, we take different methods to measure the program space. For the UNO with an AVR MCU, the program space is calculated by the sum of `.text` and `.data` segments. For the other three with ARM MCU, the program space is the size of their cross compiled binary programs.

Table 6 shows the program space overhead. The program space overhead of UNO and ONE is no more than 3KB and 31KB respectively. Considering their program flash are 32KB and 16MB respectively, the overhead is small and acceptable. The reasons why the overhead of BBB and RP2 is much larger is that they run on a Debian Linux system and their binary programs are in ELF format. But considering their program flash are at least 4GB, the overhead within 100KB is negligible.

Memory Space Overhead. The measured memory space overhead is composed of the overhead from static memory overhead (i.e., `.text`, `.data`, etc.) and run-time memory overhead (i.e., stack and heap). Table 7 shows that the memory space overhead is small

Table 8: Hardware configurations of smart houseplant nodes.

	TinyLink	CodeFirst [12]
Mainboard	Arduino UNO	BetaBlocks
Shield	Base Shield V1.3	-
Peripheral	Grove Light Sensor	Grove Light Sensor
	Soil Moisture Analog Sensor	Grove Moisture Sensor
	ESP8266 ESP01 WiFi Module	Grove UART WiFi Module
Total Cost	$44.72	$96.70

Table 9: Hardware configurations of air quality nodes.

	TinyLink	Mosaic Node V1 [23]	CodeFirst [12]
Mainboard	LinkIt ONE	Arduino UNO	No Solutions
Shield	Base Shield V1.3	Base Shield V1.3	
	-	GPRS Shield V2.0	
	-	SD Card Shield V4	
Peripheral	Dust Sensor (PPD42NS)	Dust Sensor (PPD42NS)	
	Grove Temperature and Humidity Sensor (DHT11)	Grove Temperature and Humidity Sensor (DHT11)	
	-	Grove GPS (SIM28)	
Total Cost	$89.70	$150.99	N/A

for UNO and is negligible for the other three. For UNO, the overhead of all benchmarks are within 171B, 8.35% of its RAM size (i.e., 2KB). For ONE, the overhead of all benchmarks is within 21KB, 1.03% of its RAM size (i.e., 2MB). For BBB and RP2, the overhead of benchmarks is within 100KB, which are negligible since their RAM are 512MB and 1GB, respectively.

6.3 Case Study

Smart Houseplant Node. This case has been described in Section 2. Figure 2 shows the application code. Under the criterion of the lowest cost, the best hardware configurations for both TinyLink and CodeFirst [12] are shown in Table 8. In the TinyLink solution, the Base Shield V1.3 is selected, because it can provide ports (required by the Grove Light Sensor) which UNO does not contain. The fixed platform of CodeFirst, BetaBlocks, contains ports so that it does not need shields. It is obvious that the cost of TinyLink's solution is much lower than the cost of CodeFirst's solution. This is because BetaBlocks's characteristic of only using ports limits the searching space for feasible solutions. The assembled node of TinyLink is shown in Figure 14(a).

Air Quality Node. Mosaic is a mobile sensor network system for city scale sensing [23]. The requirement of a mosaic node is measuring PM2.5, PM10, position, temperature and humidity every 30 seconds. Then the sampled data are uploaded to a cloud server via GPRS. Besides, output log data are stored in the SD card for further debugging and developing.

We intend to build such nodes using both TinyLink and CodeFirst. The generated hardware configurations are shown in Table 9. Mosaic Node V1 is the original node used in [23], which is very expensive. TinyLink generates a hardware configuration that reduces about 41% of the total cost, due to the built-in components on LinkIt One. In Table 10, we can observe that TinyLink achieves all functionalities provided by Mosaic Node V1. CodeFirst cannot generate a feasible solution, since there are no suitable interfaces for storage modules. The assembled node of TinyLink is shown in Figure 14(b).

Voice Controlled LED Lamp Node. TinyLink is suitable for building smart home applications. We intend to control home appliances (e.g., LED lamps) via smart devices which take voice commands as input. We have implemented a voice controlled LED

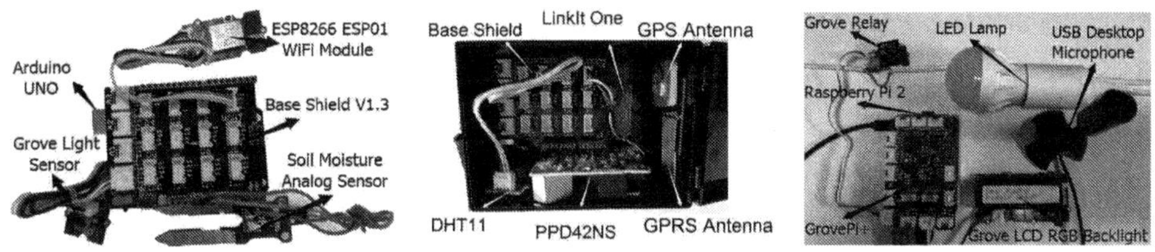

(a) (b) (c)

Figure 14: Assembled TinyLink nodes for three real-world case studies.

Table 10: Functionalities of implemented air quality nodes.

Functionality	TinyLink	Mosaic Node V1 [23]
PM2.5 Monitoring	✓	✓
PM10 Monitoring	✓	✓
Temperature Monitoring	✓	✓
Humidity Monitoring	✓	✓
GPS Sampling	✓	✓
Storing Data to the SD Card	✓	✓
Uploading Data to the Cloud	✓	✓
Periodically Executing Tasks	✓	✓

Table 11: Hardware configurations of voice controlled LED lamp nodes.

	TinyLink	CodeFirst [12]
Mainboard	Raspberry Pi 2	No Solutions
Shield	GrovePi+	
Peripheral	Grove Relay	
	USB Desktop Microphone	
	Grove LCD RGB Backlight	
Total Cost	$89.20	N/A

lamp node via TinyLink. The source code only contains 51 lines of code. The requirements extracted from the code are recording user's voice periodically using a sampling rate of 16kHz, recognizing voice commands (e.g., "Light On" and "Light Off"), printing commands on an LCD screen and controlling the corresponding home appliance.

Table 11 lists the generated hardware configurations. The hardware configuration for TinyLink contains a USB desktop microphone directly attached to a USB port on a Raspberry Pi 2, a Grove relay module and a Grove LCD RGB backlight module which are attached to ports on a shield, GrovePi+. Figure 14(c) shows the assembled node. There are no solutions for CodeFirst because its mainboard lacks interfaces for voice recording modules.

The library implementations for the recording API and the voice recognition API are based on PocketSphinx, a CMU's speaker-independent continuous speech recognition engine [24].

7 DISCUSSION

In this section, we discuss several important open issues.

Optimization Criteria. Currently, TinyLink's optimization criterion is to minimize the cost. However, other optimization criteria (e.g., extensibility, energy consumption, etc.) can also be adopted. For extensibility, it is possible to define an extensibility metric as the number of non-occupied interfaces which could be used in the future. For energy consumption, however, it is a non-trivial task to estimate accurately for a particular platform during design-time given the application code. One possible approach for optimizing energy consumption is described as follows. First, we should estimate the execution time and energy consumption of each TinyLink API for different components on different platforms by well-designed benchmarks (or values reported in datasheets). Second, we should carefully analyze the application code for information such as which TinyLink APIs it has invoked. Using the above information, we can roughly estimate the energy consumption of the entire code for different components on different platforms. Finally, we can look for the platform with minimum energy consumption by setting energy consumption as an optimization criterion and other factors like the cost as constraints.

TinyLink's Extensibility. Due to TinyLink's high level abstraction, the application code is hardware-independent. TinyLink can incorporate other MCUs by including their features into the hardware database as well as glue code for the new platforms. Therefore, other MCUs (e.g., MSP430) can also be supported by TinyLink in the future. TinyLink uses COTS hardware components and deals with the issues on how to assemble them in a compatible way. In the current stage, we think that TinyLink is primarily targeting for rapid prototyping. We think that the TinyLink's approach for rapid prototyping can have important implications and guidance to the final production.

Code Migration. For developers who are familiar with embedded systems (especially the hardware), code transformation is indeed a good feature for porting their existing code from one platform to another. For other developers, we believe that TinyLink is a good approach since it significantly reduces the developing efforts. With TinyLink abstraction, the code is hardware-independent and is also easy to migrate between platforms with the cross-compilation on the cloud. Moreover, TinyLink reuses the Arduino programming style heavily to prevent a steep learning curve. Since code transformation is another direction of work, we will consider it as possible future work of TinyLink.

8 RELATED WORK

TinyLink borrows heavily from three large areas of prior work: hardware platform design, hardware/software co-design and IoT rapid development. Each of these topics has made key implications which TinyLink incorporates into its design and structure.

Hardware Platform Design. With the development of MEMS technology, we have seen significant advances in the hardware industry. Early in 2003, the well-known sensor network platform, Telos, was released along with the TinyOS operating system by researchers at UC Berkeley [25].

The most important considerations for a sensor network platform are energy efficiency and small form factor. The design of such dedicated, small platform is difficult and requires expert knowledge. For example, Dutta *et al.* present a building block approach [6] to hardware platform design based on a decade of collective experience, arriving at an architecture in which general-purpose modules that incorporate commonly-used functionality are integrated with application-specific carriers that satisfy the unique sensing, power supply, and mechanical constraints of an application.

Andersen *et al.* present the design of a new hardware and software platform [26] by bringing together Mobile, Wearable, Maker and Wireless Sensor Network technologies to achieve a high degree of synergy and energy efficiency.

Sutton *et al.* present a design methodology [27] for adaptive event-triggered acoustic sensing systems, with the careful consideration for adaptability, responsiveness, and energy efficiency. All the work aims to design an energy-efficient hardware platform with good system performance. However, *expert knowledge* on the hardware experience and embedded software have created a barrier for upper-layer application development. TinyLink intends to remove this barrier by incorporating hardware knowledge into our system design.

Recent years have also witnessed significant innovations in the Maker domain around Arduino [28] and Raspberry Pi [29]. These platforms are characterized by powerful processors with rich interfaces. This development trends have important implications for our designs: (1) the COTS hardware components and their compositions have already enabled a wide range of innovative applications; (2) we need to carefully consider the complex connections among hardware components and the API implementations on different platforms.

Hardware and Software Co-design. Hardware/software co-design approaches use synthesis strategies to generate efficient hardware and software partitions.

The most relevant to our work is Platform Based Design (PBD) [30]. The goal of PBD is to select and compose a subset of available components (i.e., the configuration), from the design space of possible platform configurations. A good and implementable configuration satisfies the system constraints as well as all component-imposed assumptions. PBD is a meet-in-the-middle process which maps an abstracted top layer description to a more detailed lower layer implementation as well as building a platform by defining the library that allows performance estimation.

Peter *et al.* propose a component-based description language CoDeL [31] that allows system designers to express components as reusable building blocks of the system with parameterizable models, properties, and interconnectivity. The automatic mapping from the higher layer to the lower layer is the process of exploration of complex design spaces which is frequently fostered by satisfiability (SAT) [32] solvers or Integer Linear Programming (ILP).

Similar to PBD, TinyLink also adopts an automatic mapping process from the application logic to a concrete hardware configuration. While PBD addresses a general problem, TinyLink addresses specific and practical challenges such as hardware-independent APIs, compatibility among COTS hardware components, implementations of glue code on different platforms.

IoT Rapid Development. The rapid development of IoT systems have attracted much research attentions from both industrial and academic communities.

Shayne Hodge proposes a general idea [33] which is to build an architecture like that of a modern web application. At a very high level in this model, the IoT hardware sends data over a network (or the Internet) to the backend software for storage and processing. The user interface is built as a web application, which allows it to be viewed on a broad range of devices. The details on how to build the IoT hardware, however, are not given.

The Matrix project [34] was launched on Kickstarter in 2015. The platform contains up to 15 sensors, so that users only need to create IoT Apps, without caring about the hardware. However, the platform is fixed, it is not flexible to create customized IoT Apps.

IOTIFY [35] is the virtualization engine for the IoT to help build IoT applications. IOTIFY reduces the complexity of dealing with hardware, and large networks by virtualizing IoT endpoints in the cloud. Different from IOTIFY, TinyLink generates real hardware components and application software.

.NET Gadgeteer [36] is an integrated platform from Microsoft to support developing with customized components. Developers can quickly build devices with the help of Gadgeteer modules, .NET Micro Framework and 3D design tools. Wio Link [37] is a similar approach which builds upon the Wio Link board. TinyLink focuses on how to rapidly develop IoT applications using a variety of COTS components, instead of using customized components.

A recent approach is the code-first design to prototype wearable devices [12]. The hardware configuration would be generated from the analysis of the application code, because one software module is directly mapped to one hardware component and hardware dependencies can be determined by analyzing software dependencies. However, it assumes a fixed mainboard, limiting its capability to embrace a diverse set of COTS components.

The design of TinyLink is much more complex since it supports different mainboards and provides pin level abstractions with a careful consideration for shields. TinyLink also includes software libraries to facilitate upper layer application programming.

9 CONCLUSION

In this paper we present TinyLink, a holistic system for rapid development of IoT applications. TinyLink uses a top-down approach for both hardware and software designs. Developers only need to specify key application logic with TinyLink APIs, without dealing with the underlying hardware. TinyLink takes their code as input, automatically generates the hardware configuration and the binary program executable on the target platform. We implement TinyLink and evaluate its performance using benchmarks and three real-world case studies. Results show that TinyLink achieves rapid development of IoT applications, reducing 52.58% of lines of code in average for implementations, while incurring acceptable overhead.

The future work of TinyLink includes two directions. First, we will further extend the supported hardware components of TinyLink. Second, we will extend TinyLink to other optimization goals, e.g., energy, performance and extensibility.

ACKNOWLEDGMENTS

This work is supported by the National Basic Research Program of China (No. 2015CB352400), the National Science Foundation of China (No. 61472360 and No. 61502417), Alibaba-Zhejiang University Joint Institute of Frontier Technologies, Zhejiang Provincial Key Research and Development Program (No. 2017C02044), and the Fundamental Research Funds for the Central Universities (No. 2017FZA5013). We thank all the reviewers and the shepherd for their valuable comments and helpful suggestions.

REFERENCES

[1] Michael Chui, Markus Löffler, and Roger Roberts. The internet of things. *McKinsey Quarterly*, 2(2010):1–9, 2010.

[2] Rui Luis Aguiar, Nora Benhabiles, Tobias Pfeiffer, Pablo Rodriguez, Harish Viswanathan, Jia Wang, and Hui Zang. Big data, iot,.... buzz words for academia or reality for industry? In *Proc. of ACM MobiCom*, 2015.

[3] Biyi Fang, Qiumin Xu, Taiwoo Park, and Mi Zhang. Airsense: an intelligent home-based sensing system for indoor air quality analytics. In *Proc. of ACM UbiComp*, 2016.

[4] Hsin-Ruey Tsai, Shih-Yao Wei, Jui-Chun Hsiao, Ting-Wei Chiu, Yi-Ping Lo, Chi-Feng Keng, Yi-Ping Hung, and Jin-Jong Chen. ikneebraces: knee adduction moment evaluation measured by motion sensors in gait detection. In *Proc. of ACM UbiComp*, 2016.

[5] Mehrdad Hessar, Vikram Iyer, and Shyamnath Gollakota. Enabling on-body transmissions with commodity devices. In *Proc. of ACM UbiComp*, 2016.

[6] Prabal Dutta, Jay Taneja, Jaein Jeong, Xiaofan Jiang, and David Culler. A building block approach to sensornet systems. In *Proc. of ACM SenSys*, 2008.

[7] Deepak Vasisht, Zerina Kapetanovic, Jongho Won, Xinxin Jin, Ranveer Chandra, Sudipta N Sinha, Ashish Kapoor, Madhusudhan Sudarshan, and Sean Stratman. Farmbeats: An iot platform for data-driven agriculture. In *Proc. of USENIX NSDI*, 2017.

[8] Yi Gao, Wei Dong, Kai Guo, Xue Liu, Yuan Chen, Xiaojin Liu, Jiajun Bu, and Chun Chen. Mosaic: A low-cost mobile sensing system for urban air quality monitoring. In *Proc. of IEEE INFOCOM*, 2016.

[9] Lan Zhang, Xiang-Yang Li, Wenchao Huang, Kebin Liu, Shuwei Zong, Xuesi Jian, Puchun Feng, Taeho Jung, and Yunhao Liu. It starts with igaze: Visual attention driven networking with smart glasses. In *Proc. of ACM MobiCom*, 2014.

[10] Steve Hodges, Stuart Taylor, Nicolas Villar, James Scott, Dominik Bial, and Patrick Tobias Fischer. Prototyping connected devices for the internet of things. *IEEE Computer*, 46(2):26–34, 2013.

[11] Gaoyang Guan, Wei Dong, Yi Gao, and Jiajun Bu. Towards rapid and cost-effective prototyping of iot platforms. In *Proc. of IEEE ICNP Workshop on Hot Topics in Internet of Things (Hot-IoT)*, 2016.

[12] Daniel Graham and Gang Zhou. Prototyping wearables: A code-first approach to the design of embedded systems. *IEEE Internet of Things Journal*, 3(5):806–815, 2016.

[13] Port Description of GrovePi+. https://www.dexterindustries.com/GrovePi/engineering/port-description/.

[14] Rohit Ramesh and Prabal Dutta. Embedded development tools revisited: Verification and generation from the top down. *GetMobile: Mobile Computing and Communications*, 20(2):5–10, 2016.

[15] Michel Berkelaar, Kjell Eikland, and Peter Notebaert. lp_solve 5.5, open source (mixed-integer) linear programming system, 2004.

[16] Arduino Forum. https://forum.arduino.cc/.

[17] Raspberry Pi Forum. https://www.raspberrypi.org/forums/.

[18] Instructables. http://www.instructables.com/.

[19] Electronic Hub. http://www.electronicshub.org/iot-project-ideas/.

[20] Ala Al-Fuqaha, Mohsen Guizani, Mehdi Mohammadi, Mohammed Aledhari, and Moussa Ayyash. Internet of things: A survey on enabling technologies, protocols, and applications. *IEEE Communications Surveys Tutorials*, 17(4):2347–2376, 2015.

[21] Gordon Henderson. Wiring Pi GPIO Interface library for the Raspberry Pi. http://wiringpi.com/.

[22] Abhraneel Bera. Wiring/Arduino style library for BeagleBone Black Platform. http://beagleboard.org/project/wiringBone/.

[23] Wei Dong, Gaoyang Guan, Yuan Chen, Kai Guo, and Yi Gao. Mosaic: Towards city scale sensing with mobile sensor networks. In *Proc. of IEEE ICPADS*, 2015.

[24] David Huggins-Daines, Mohit Kumar, Arthur Chan, Alan W Black, Mosur Ravishankar, and Alexander I Rudnicky. Pocketsphinx: A free, real-time continuous speech recognition system for hand-held devices. In *Proc. of IEEE International Conference on Acoustics, Speech and Signal Processing*, 2006.

[25] Philip Levis, Sam Madden, Joseph Polastre, Robert Szewczyk, Kamin Whitehouse, Alec Woo, David Gay, Jason Hill, Matt Welsh, Eric Brewer, et al. Tinyos: An operating system for sensor networks. In *Ambient intelligence*, pages 115–148. 2005.

[26] Michael P. Andersen, Gabe Fierro, and David E. Culler. System design for a synergistic, low power mote/ble embedded platform. In *Proc. of ACM/IEEE IPSN*, 2016.

[27] Felix Sutton, Reto Da Forno, David Gschwend, Tonio Gsell, Roman Lim, Jan Beutel, and Lothar Thiele. The design of a responsive and energy-efficient event-triggered wireless sensing system. In *Proc. of ACM EWSN*, pages 144–155, 2017.

[28] Arduino. https://www.arduino.cc.

[29] Raspberry Pi. https://www.raspberrypi.org.

[30] Kurt Keutzer, A Richard Newton, Jan M Rabaey, and Alberto Sangiovanni-Vincentelli. System-level design: orthogonalization of concerns and platform-based design. *IEEE Transactions on Computer-Aided Design of Integrated Circuits and Systems*, 19(12):1523–1543, 2000.

[31] Steffen Peter and Tony Givargis. Component-based synthesis of embedded systems using satisfiability modulo theories. *ACM Transactions on Design Automation of Electronic Systems*, 20(4):49:1–49:27, 2015.

[32] Clark W Barrett, Roberto Sebastiani, Sanjit A Seshia, and Cesare Tinelli. Satisfiability modulo theories. *Handbook of satisfiability*, 185:825–885, 2009.

[33] Shayne Hodge. A Rapid IoT Prototyping Toolkit, 2016.

[34] MATRIX. https://www.kickstarter.com/projects/2061039712/matrix-the-internet-of-things-for-everyonetm.

[35] IOTIFY. http://iotify.io/.

[36] Nicolas Villar, James Scott, Steve Hodges, Kerry Hammil, and Colin Miller. .net gadgeteer: a platform for custom devices. In *Proc. of Pervasive Computing*, 2012.

[37] Wio Link. https://iot.seeed.cc/.

BlueMountain: An Architecture for Customized Data Management on Mobile Systems

Sharath Chandrashekhara, Taeyeon Ki, Kyungho Jeon, Karthik Dantu, Steven Y. Ko
Department of Computer Science and Engineering
University at Buffalo, The State University of New York
{sc296,tki,kyunghoj,kdantu,stevko}@buffalo.edu

ABSTRACT

In this paper, we design a pluggable data management solution for modern mobile platforms (e.g., Android). Our goal is to allow data management mechanisms and policies to be implemented independently of core app logic. Our design allows a user to install data management solutions as apps, install multiple such solutions on a single device, and choose a suitable solution each for one or more apps. It allows app developers to focus their effort on app logic and helps the developers of data management solutions to achieve wider deployability. It also gives increased control of data management to end users and allows them to use different solutions for different apps.

We present a prototype implementation of our design called BlueMountain, and implement several data management solutions for file and database management to demonstrate the utility and ease of using our design. We perform detailed microbenchmarks as well as end-to-end measurements for files and databases to demonstrate the performance overhead incurred by our implementation.

1 INTRODUCTION

Mobile systems have gradually become the predominant platform for everyday computing, and their computational, memory, network, and storage capabilities are getting powerful by the day. Apps on mobile systems span diverse categories such as games, personal activity, banking, productivity, and business applications. Consequently, mobile apps employ sophisticated data management solutions, including local file and database storage as well as cloud services for user/app data. These solutions enable desirable features such as backup, sync, and sharing.

However, data management in mobile apps is currently rigid, and does not provide enough flexibility for their developers and users. Specifically, individual app developers need to make policy and mechanism decisions on how user and app data should be managed. Examples include, but not limited to, which cloud provider to use for data backup (e.g., Dropbox vs. Google Drive), what policies to use when transferring data over the Internet (e.g., only when re-charging, only over Wi-Fi, etc.), and what mechanisms to use for synchronization (e.g., delta update, de-duplication, etc.). As a result, developers have to spend additional effort in putting their data management logic into each app, and users do not have any control over how their data is managed. Some app developers expose these decisions to users as configuration options, but those options are typically limited. In short, current mobile apps have a tight coupling between data management and app logic, which leads to added development time for developers and inflexibility for users.

In order to overcome this problem, we envision a new ecosystem where there are two kinds of apps. The first kind of apps are regular apps that one can find currently from online app stores such as Google Play. The second kind is what we call *data management apps* that are also downloaded from online app stores. However, these data management apps are meant to be *pluggable* and always used in conjunction with regular apps for the purpose of managing their data. A regular app delegates all its data management decisions to a data management app, and users choose a data management app to use for each regular app depending on their needs. For example, a user in this ecosystem could install a regular note-taking app with a data management app that backs up all notes to a public cloud. At the same time, another user could install the same note-taking app, but with a different data management app that uses a private cloud instead of a public cloud. This new ecosystem achieves decoupling of data management and app logic, and overcomes the current limitation of rigid data management in mobile apps.

In order to make this vision a reality, we have built BlueMountain, a framework for pluggable data management apps on Android that has three distinctive features. First, BlueMountain defines a clean interface for data management apps, which mimics the interface for Android's filesystem, database, and key-value storage (`SharedPreferences`). Using this interface, separate data management apps can be written solely for the purpose of data management such as backup, sync, and sharing. Second, BlueMountain enables dynamic binding between a data management app and a regular app, so that a user can choose which data management app to use for each regular app the user has. BlueMountain achieves this by dynamically loading a data management app's code into a regular app, and redirecting the regular app's storage calls to the data management app's code. Third, BlueMountain automatically transforms existing apps to leverage BlueMountain's functionality via Java bytecode instrumentation. BlueMountain's instrumentation finds all uses of local storage APIs in an Android app (filesystem APIs, database APIs, and `SharedPreferences` APIs) and translates them, so that it automatically uses BlueMountain-injected code. This means that regular app developers do not need to bother integrating BlueMountain for their local app data. Users can also benefit from BlueMountain immediately as legacy apps can be

MobiCom '17, October 16–20, 2017, Snowbird, UT, USA

ACM ISBN 978-1-4503-4916-1/17/10...$15.00
https://doi.org/10.1145/3117811.3117822

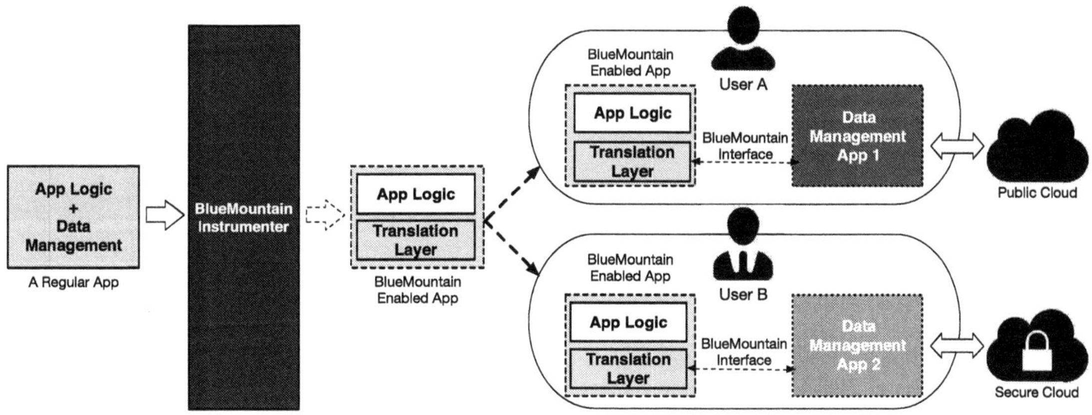

Figure 1: BlueMountain Workflow Example

BlueMountain-enabled automatically. Figure 1 shows a visualization of the envisioned workflow with BlueMountain.

To demonstrate the usefulness of our system, we have built five different data management apps, each of which implements one strategy for managing regular app data. The first data management app implements a personal data storage system, inspired by PSCloud [2], which uses all of the user's devices to store data. We use WiFi Direct [40], local network, and the Internet to communicate with a user's mobile devices, desktop, and cloud, respectively. The second data management app implements an efficient data synchronization mechanism, inspired by QuickSync [8] and implements file chunking to improve network utilization and reduce storage footprint. Further, we implement three mechanisms to provide database backup in the cloud. The first strategy locally logs all database operations and remotely replays the log for data backup. The second strategy divides a database file into multiple chunks, keeps track of modifications made to each chunk, and backs up individual chunks with new changes. This is inspired by the rsync library [31]. The last strategy automatically performs database sharding on Android, i.e., storing and managing each database table as a separate file. This strategy can be used in conjunction with other strategies for more efficient database backup.

In order to evaluate BlueMountain, we measure the overhead using microbenchmarks as well as the five data management apps described above. Our results show that the performance degradation is minimal (<10%) in most of the cases and stays less than 30% even in the worst case. This can be further reduced by using a more efficient memory management in our system.

We also have downloaded 400 apps from Google Play and automatically transformed them to leverage BlueMountain. Our instrumentation results show that BlueMountain's instrumentation does not incur much overhead in terms of code size increase (<12%), heap usage (<16%), and energy usage (<3.5%). We have also tested the correctness of our instrumentation via an automated UI testing system and verified that BlueMountain's instrumentation neither crashes apps nor throws new exceptions.

In summary, we make the following contributions:

- We show that it is *feasible* to decouple data management and app logic for mobile apps. We do this by proposing a new framework that enables the decoupling, as well as showing that the framework incurs minimal overhead.
- We demonstrate that the decoupling is *useful* by creating five data management apps and showing their practical performance. This includes re-implementing two file-based solutions previously proposed for mobile systems.
- We show that our approach *supports existing apps* by automatically transforming 400 apps downloaded from Google Play to leverage our framework and verifying the correctness of their functionality.

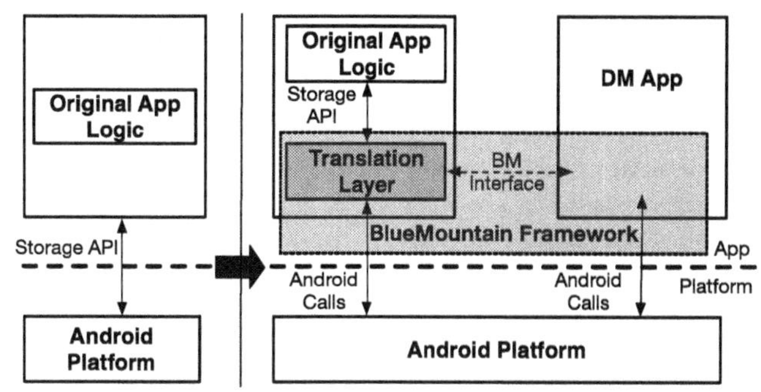

Figure 2: BlueMountain System Overview

2 BLUEMOUNTAIN DESIGN OVERVIEW

BlueMountain is designed with three goals in mind—*decoupling of data management and app logic, supporting widespread deployment,* and *supporting legacy apps.* We overview these goals and our design in this section.

2.1 Data Management and App Decoupling

Figure 2 shows how BlueMountain decouples data management and app logic. Shown on the left is a regular Android app that uses the Android storage APIs to store data locally. Shown on the right is the architecture enabled by BlueMountain that has a separate data management app. BlueMountain defines a clean interface (which we call the BlueMountain interface) that data management app developers use to provide their data management solutions. BlueMountain also has the translation layer, which translates all

Android storage APIs into the BlueMountain interface and redirects all storage API calls to a data management app. We note that for each regular app, we dynamically load a data management app's code into the same address space of the regular app. Figure 2 shows a regular app and a data management app side-by-side only to highlight our logical decoupling. It is not meant to show that they run as separate processes. Section 3 details the BlueMountain interface as well as the translation layer.

This design provides two benefits that overcome the limitation of the rigid data management that current mobile apps experience. First, it *simplifies development* for regular app developers since they do not need to implement various policies and mechanisms for data management. They can focus on their app logic and delegate the complexity of data management to separate data management apps. Second, it provides *flexibility* to users since users can choose different data management apps depending on their needs. This is possible since BlueMountain allows the binding between a regular app and a data management app to occur at *use time* instead of development time.

2.2 Supporting Widespread Deployment

BlueMountain supports widespread deployment by restricting all its implementation to take place within individual apps. This means that we do not modify anything in the Android platform—this is because modifications to the Android platform are tightly regulated by Google as well as other mobile platform vendors such as Samsung and Amazon. If any platform modification were to be required for BlueMountain, we would need to rely on Google or other vendors to approve the use of our system and properly distribute it, which is impractical. In contrast, if all modifications were restricted to individual apps, we could widely distribute our system by using an online app store such as Google Play. Therefore, BlueMountain restricts *all modifications to be self-contained in individual apps* and makes no changes to the Android platform.

2.3 Supporting Legacy Apps

Android is a popular platform for app development, and many app developers are now used to its programming model and interfaces for app design. If we were to require app developers to use a new storage interface for BlueMountain, it would involve learning and hinder the pace of development. Further, previously-developed apps would need to be re-written using the new interface, which puts an excess burden on the developers. To mitigate both of these challenges, we use Java bytecode instrumentation to automatically transform an app to leverage BlueMountain. For this purpose, we use Reptor [23], a tool that enables automated API class replacement for Android apps. Reptor takes an app binary, decompiles it, performs program analysis, correctly replaces Android API classes with custom classes, and recompiles it into a new app. This makes the process of replacing Android storage APIs with BlueMountain APIs seamless and transparent to regular app developers.

We now describe the BlueMountain system implementation.

3 SYSTEM IMPLEMENTATION

The BlueMountain architecture is shown in Figure 3. Any app that wishes to use our system has to include our framework within the app and use our interface for all data storage functionality. For this, we provide a modular implementation of our framework that can be used as a library. Given such a library, we use an instrumentation tool (Reptor [23]) to automatically inject the whole BlueMountain framework into existing apps without developer's intervention. This allows the existing apps to easily benefit from BlueMountain.

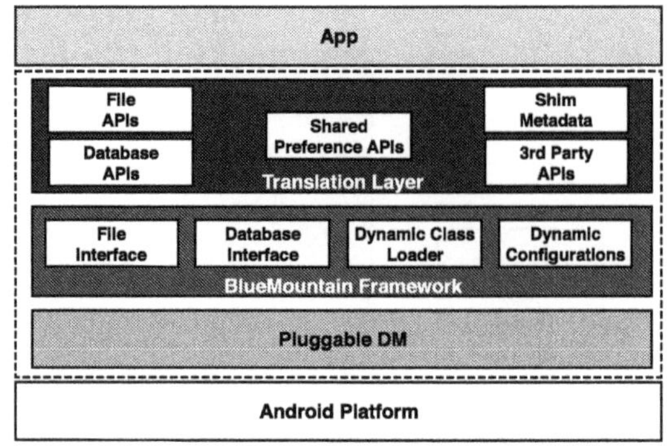

Figure 3: BlueMountain System Architecture

As described earlier, the BlueMountain framework dynamically loads a data management app's code. We define a clean interface for a data management app to implement, and our translation layer translates all Android storage API calls to the calls to our own interface. Below, we first describe our BlueMountain interface. We then describe our translation layer. Lastly, we describe how we inject the BlueMountain framework and dynamically load a data management app's code.

3.1 The BlueMountain Interface

We define a clean interface for data management apps which mimics the three storage options that Android provides. They are (a) files, (b) databases, and (c) key-value stores called `SharedPreferences`. The reason why we mimic Android's storage options for our interface design is to allow data management app developers to provide customized solutions for different storage options available on Android. BlueMountain intercepts all calls to these storage options and translates them into our own interface calls, so that the data management apps can handle them.

Table 1 describes our interface for data management apps. We design our interface using *objects* as our storage abstraction instead of files, which helps us keep our interface design simple. Our data objects are of a fixed size, but it can be configured by the individual data management apps. By default, we use 4MB, which is a typical choice for cloud vendors like Dropbox [11]. This means that if an app stores a single file, BlueMountain divides into multiple 4MB chunks. Below, we discuss how we use the object abstraction in our interface that mimics the Android storage APIs.

Files: We provide a simple CRUD interface for the data management apps that wish to manage files. Our read and update interfaces include two optional parameters to indicate the offset within the object and the requested length. This allows our interface to mimic Android APIs when apps want to optimize operations on files. Generally, the flush operation on a `FileIOStream` is a NOP. However, apps can force a `fsync` using low level Java constructs like `FileChannel` or `FileDescriptor`. To support this behavior, we add

Type	Interface	In	Out	Description
File: CRUD	fcreate	id, buffer[], length	none	Creates an object id of size length from buffer bytes
	fread	id, buffer[], [offset, length]	buffer[]	Reads data from object id into buffer. offset and length are optional parameters indicating the offset within the object and the length to read
	fupdate	id, buffer[], [offset, length]	none	Updates the object id with buffer bytes. offset and length are optional parameters indicating the offset within the object and the update length
	delete	list: id	none	Deletes all objects in the list
File: State	close	list: id	none	Indicates operations on all objects in the list is completed
	flush	list: id	none	Flushes all objects in the list to a persistent storage
	initFS	none	none	Initializes the system
	clearFS	none	none	Deletes all the data and formats the system
DB: State	open	db-path, flags	cnx-id	Opens the database in db-path with the provided access flags in flag and returns the connection id cnx-id
	close	cnx-id	none	Closes the previously opened connection cnx-id
	cancel	cnx-id	none	Cancels the current operation on the connection cnx-id
DB: Execute	executeWrite	cnx-id, SQL-String, args[]	rows	Executes statement SQL-String which modifies database, with args an Object array of bind arguments, on connection cnx-id. Returns rows, a row id or number of rows modified
	executeQuery	cnx-id, SQL-String, args[]	Cursor	Executes SQL-String query with args as an Object array of bind arguments, on the connection cnx-id. Returns Cursor for the result.
DB: Info	statementInfo	cnx-id, SQL-string	Info	Returns information about statement SQL-String on connection cnx-id in an Info Object

Table 1: BlueMountain Interface for Data Management Apps

flush to our interface. Since the app calls flush at the file level, this may affect all the objects belonging to a file, including the metadata file. Therefore, our flush operation takes a list of object ids which have to be flushed. Similarly, we include close as part of our interface. This provides a mechanism to indicate to the data management app that the app is done operating on the object, it can release the resources and flush it to a persistent storage.

Databases: To support databases, we provide open, close and cancel methods in our interface. Open returns a connection ID which all the subsequent calls should use to perform operations on the same database. For the execution of a database operation (e.g., insert, update, delete, query, etc.), we provide two methods—`executeWrite` and `executeQuery`. `executeQuery` is used in queries, `executeWrite` is used for insert, delete, and update operations and all other SQL operations. These two methods accept a raw SQL statement string as a parameter, which provides the most flexibility for a data management app in handling SQL operations. The `statementInfo` method allows us to get useful information about a SQL string from the database such the number of columns, the column name, or if a particular query is a read-only query.

There are certain types of database APIs that our current interface does not support—(1) APIs for controlling database queries issued from multiple threads, (2) APIs for compiled SQLite statements, and (3) APIs that use an app-provided `CursorFactory`, which handles query results in a customized fashion. These features are *not essential* for using a database but rather provide more support for app programmers. For example, multi-threading support provides an easier way to control queries that are executed in parallel from different threads; compiled SQLite statements make it easier to reuse frequently-issued queries; and `CursorFactory` provides support for customized output access. For each of these features, there are alternative ways for app programmers to accomplish the same tasks.

We can still support these features by adding them to our interface. However, our current prototype does not support them in the interest of keeping our interface clean and simple. Adding these features to our interface means that each data management app will need to support the features. For example, in order to support multiple threads, a data management app should be able to handle queries properly even if they are issued by multiple threads. Similarly, in order to support compiled SQLite statements, a data management app should be able to generate compiled SQLite statements even when it does not use a SQLite database underneath.

In Section 5.4, we present our detailed analysis on how many apps use these features.

SharedPreferences: `SharedPreferences` on Android is implemented as an XML file and is typically a small file where apps store key-value pairs like user settings. We can treat the XML file as any regular file and use our file interface to read and write the `SharedPreferences` file through the data management app. Thus, we do not provide a new interface to deal with `SharedPreferences`.

3.2 BlueMountain Translation Layer

The translation layer translates the Android Storage API calls into the BlueMountain interface calls. It is either directly built into an app (for newly-developed, BlueMountain-aware apps) or injected into it at a later stage (for legacy apps). Architecturally, we separate the translation layer from the rest of the framework. This is because this design enables third party data management libraries to be plugged into our system if they can provide a translation from their APIs into BlueMountain APIs. Below, we discuss the strategies for translation we have used for Android storage APIs.

Files: The translation layer needs to translate the Android file operations into the CRUD interface shown in Table 1. The files on Android are accessed through the following classes—`FileInputStream`, `FileOutputStream`, `FileReader` and `FileReader` for sequential access; `RandomAccessFile` for random file access; `File` for metadata, `FileDescriptor`, `FileChannel` as low level representations of a file and `FileLock` for locking. This requires us to translate the streaming I/O model into an object-based model. We have developed wrappers around the `FileInputStream` and `FileOutputStream`, which translates the calls to an object based I/O. As mentioned earlier, we have chosen the default object size to be *4 MB*, but this is a configuration parameter. Therefore, the translation layer also needs to break down files larger than 4MB into objects of 4MB chunks.

This also requires us to maintain mappings from files to objects as metadata. The metadata itself can be treated as an object and stored persistently using the same data management app that is plugged into the app. Since object size could have a significant impact on performance, we allow the data management app to change the default object size according to its design.

Our current interface translation supports most file operations on Android. However, there are some obscure lower-level representations of files through the `FileChannel` and `FileDescriptor` classes that we currently do not handle. Our preliminary examination of real apps suggests that most apps do not use these interfaces for data management. Therefore, we leave the handling of these interfaces as part of our future work.

File Metadata: Apart from metadata file which maintains the mapping from files to objects, we need a mechanism to deal with the system metadata as well. This includes all the operations from the Java `File` interface. Moving the management of this metadata to the data management app makes the design more complex, and is not particularly advantageous. Therefore, in our design, we let the Android framework deal with the filesystem metadata. For example, operations such as creating directories, empty files, maintaining access times of files, directory structures, permissions, etc., are left to the Android system. We do this by creating the entire directory structure with empty files using the Android platform interface whenever a file is accessed through the BlueMountain translation layer. Thus, while the translation layer through the BlueMountain framework delegates the responsibility of handling the file data to the data management app, the associated metadata is maintained locally.

Databases: In order to use a SQLite database, apps use the `SQLiteOpenHelper` and the `SQLiteDatabase` classes to open and issue requests to the database. These app-facing classes provide a variety of functionality not just to read and write from the database but also to perform database management. In our design, we intercept calls to these classes and translate them into our own.

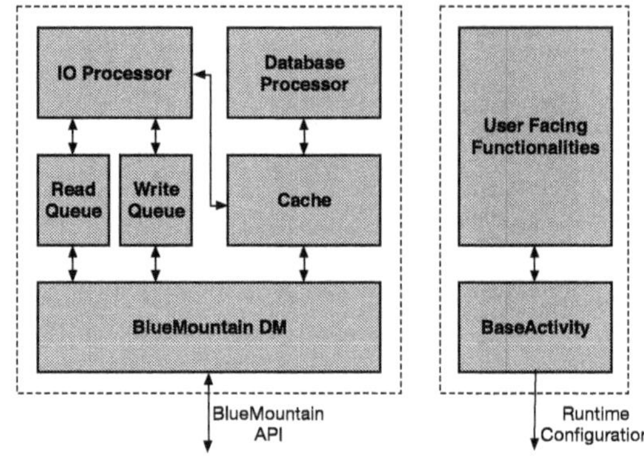

Figure 4: BlueMountain Data Management App SDK

For the Android database APIs that ultimately issue a database operation (e.g., insert, update, delete, query, etc.), we interpret and translate them into raw SQL strings and invoke either `executeWrite` or `executeQuery` (which we discuss in Section 3.1).

SharedPreferences: To handle SharedPreferences, we provide wrappers to access and edit the SharedPreferences and notify the data management app of any changes made to the corresponding XML file. While serving the reads, we check if the SharedPreferences file has been updated outside of the app, and if it is, we simply reload the SharedPreferences file.

3.3 BlueMountain Data Management App SDK

In order to support the development of a data management app, we have developed an SDK which provides common functionality and a base implementation for all APIs. Any data management solution that wishes to override the default behavior can override one or all the methods of the SDK or can simply extend the functionality that is provided. Figure 4 shows an overview of the SDK and the modules. For files, the base implementation writes all operations to the local storage cache with a FIFO policy, and adds them to the write queue. It also serves the reads from the cache, raising an exception when data is not found. The requested object is then added to the read queue. A background thread dispatches these requests to the I/O processing queue. The data management apps need to extend the I/O processor to handle these requests. For databases, the base implementation uses a local database as a cache and the data management apps have to override this behavior to provide additional functionality.

The SDK also provides a `BaseActivity`—a UI which identifies a set of BlueMountain enabled apps installed in the system and lets the user choose a regular app to which the data management app has to be plugged. A data management app can extend this functionality to enable runtime configurations. The data management apps can pass on these runtime configurations to the BlueMountain framework (running within the regular apps) using Androids `Intents`. The data management app might also implement other user functionality that allows users to modify some of these configurations—for instance, an interface that allows users to provide access to a particular cloud account or an interface to set the network data limit.

Our current version of SDK provides an implementation to handle object chunking, data caching, and a client to access cloud servers over a REST-based interface. In the future releases, we intend to add more functionality to the SDK to aid the development of data management apps.

3.4 Dynamic Loading and Instrumentation

At run time, we enable the data management apps to be plugged into any regular app having the BlueMountain framework. We achieve this by dynamically loading the data management app's code into the regular app. We use `DexClassLoader`, a Java class that Android provides, which allows an app to dynamically load another app's code. Once loaded, we use Java reflection to invoke data management app code. Such a mechanism binds the data management app with the regular app at runtime allowing the user to configure any regular app with a data management app of her choice. The overhead due to reflection can be mitigated by using a pre-defined interface and invoking the data management app methods through this interface. As we show in Section 5, the overhead due to reflection did this way is fairly minimal.

If a regular app is not compiled with the BlueMountain framework, we need to inject the BlueMountain framework into the app before a data management app can be plugged into it. We use Reptor [23] for this purpose. Reptor enables *API class replacement* for an Android app—a developer can replace an API class (such as `FileInputStream`) with a custom class that the developer writes. Thus, we use Reptor to replace all storage API classes with our own classes, which redirect all storage API calls to our translation layer.

4 PLUGGABLE DATA MANAGEMENT APPS

In this section, we discuss the design and implementation of five pluggable data management solutions built using our SDK and BlueMountain framework. We discuss two solutions that handle files and three solutions that handle databases. Our intent is to demonstrate the ease of implementing data management solutions using BlueMountain. Our first two data management apps are based on two previously published systems, PSCloud [2] and QuickSync [8]. For databases, we implement three strategies for efficiently synchronizing an Android app database with the cloud as separate data management solutions for databases. The key-value store is stored as a file. One of the two data management solutions for files can be used for the key-value store as well.

4.1 Personal-Device Cloud

Our first use case system is a data management solution for personal storage cloud inspired by PSCloud [2]. Briefly, PSCloud envisions the use of storage on all mobile devices of a single user, along with home servers and cloud storage services. It creates a single unified personal storage system where data is automatically cached, replicated, and placed to enable reliable access across all devices. It also minimizes network access and storage costs using a per-device network context graph that tracks connectivity relationships between a user's devices.

Inspired by the design of PSCloud, we have implemented a data management app that is capable of performing file transfers using three mechanisms—WiFi Direct (i.e., peer-peer wireless link between devices), desktop sync (i.e., local network access to desktop when possible), and Dropbox sync (i.e., cloud access when network connectivity is available). Our current implementation employs a simple file placement algorithm—a file is copied to other devices based on a device priority list. Currently, we give other mobile devices the highest priority. If no device is found, the system attempts to copy the file to a desktop. If that is also not available, the user's Dropbox account is used for backup (when network is available). Although we have implemented this policy based on the brief description from PSCloud [2], the file placement algorithm itself is orthogonal to our objectives and more sophisticated techniques can be implemented using our framework for improved efficiency. Once again, our intent is to demonstrate the feasibility of implementing previously proposed mobile data management systems using the BlueMountain framework.

4.2 Efficient Data Synchronization

Our second data management app is an efficient cloud data syncing system inspired by QuickSync [8]. QuickSync uses strategies such as chunking, bundling, delta encoding, de-duplication, and data compression to create an adaptive chunking and de-duplication strategy based on network conditions. Its goal is to reduce network traffic and have uninterrupted data syncing. It uses separate data and control servers. Inspired by QuickSync, we have implemented a data management app that efficiently syncs files by breaking them into finer chunks, and use a local Desktop as a control server to store metadata and Dropbox as a public cloud data server. Though chunking is just one of the optimizations provided in QuickSync, our simplified implementation demonstrates the ability to develop a system like QuickSync as a pluggable data management app for BlueMountain framework. Again, we do not attempt to replicate all of the advanced algorithms described in the original work as they are orthogonal to our design objectives.

When QuickSync is implemented as a data management app, it receives explicit notifications from the BlueMountain framework whenever an object is modified or read. In our implementation, when we receive a create notifications from the BlueMountain framework, we split the object into multiple chunks, update the metadata server with this information, and upload the chunks to the cloud. On read notifications, we first fetch the metadata and then fetch the required chunks if it is not present in the local cache. This differs from the library implementation where the reads will be directly handled by the Android framework. Similarly, on update notifications, only the affected chunk is uploaded and the metadata is updated.

4.3 Database Management

Our next set of data management apps are implementations of efficient backup mechanisms for databases. There are various libraries which assist in backing up databases ranging from transferring the database as a JSON string to using a rsync-like library to continuously back it up in the cloud. A sync library should be fast and efficient in using network bandwidth and energy. We implement three approaches for backing up the database with the cloud, each one designed as a data management app.

Log and Replay: Our first app for backing up a database to a server is to log all SQL statements on the mobile device and reconstruct the database on a server by replaying the logs. On the execution of every SQL statement, we synchronously log the SQL statement into a journal file. A background thread which monitors this file uploads file updates to a server. The server, after reading the statements, replays them on its SQLite server to recreate the database. Whenever there is data loss or when the user wants to restore to a previous version of the database, we can simply download it from the server and use it. Our current implementation of this works as a sync-only system, where we still maintain a local copy of the database and serve all the queries through it.

Backing Up The Database File: In our second database management app, we implement an approach similar to librsync, where we break up the database file into multiple virtual chunks. We monitor the database for every change, identify the chunk that was modified using a hashing function and upload that chunk. On the server side, we reconstruct the original database by merging the chunks. While we have used this approach as an example for database backup, this can be a light-weight solution to backing up any file between the device and the cloud.

Multiple Databases: In our third database management app, we split the database into multiple databases, each containing just one table. This is commonly referred to as database sharding in web services domain. Separate database files are created whenever a new table is created with the corresponding table in it. SQLite supports the SQL ATTACH which lets multiple databases to be accessed as one virtual database through a single connection. Using this, we attach all the databases, each containing one table and access it through a single virtual connection. SQLite can support up to 10 attached databases and can transparently handle modifications to the table.

The biggest advantage of this approach is that an update on a table will modify only the corresponding database file, and other database files will be untouched. This would enable us to use other back up mechanisms more efficiently as the database files are now smaller and updated independently. To enable this, our implementation starts with one database for the first table created and examine the SQL operations. On every create table operation, we create a new database and attach it to the existing database. One complication in our implementation is that this approach cannot handle foreign keys from different tables due to limitations of SQLite; tables with a foreign key relationship cannot be placed in two different database files. Thus, our implementation detects foreign key relationships between any two tables, and whenever a new table is created, we insert the table to the same database file that has the corresponding foreign key table.

5 EVALUATION

We evaluate BlueMountain in four aspects. The first is performance—we use microbenchmarks to show that BlueMountain incurs very little overhead (Section 5.1). The second is usefulness—we measure the performance of our prototype data management solutions for both files and databases, and show that they provide comparable performance to current Android storage APIs (Section 5.2). The third is support for automation—we inject BlueMountain into 400 existing apps, show that they work correctly under our testing scenarios, and report instrumentation statistics as well as energy and heap consumption for some of the well-known apps (Section 5.3). Lastly, we analyze 2000 apps and provide an insight into improvising the support for databases (Section 5.4). All our experiments, except when noted, were conducted on Google Nexus 5 phone, running Slim Rom [30] version of Android 6.0.1 (API 23).

5.1 Microbenchmarks

We first measure the performance of BlueMountain using microbenchmarks. As BlueMountain framework introduces multiple layers, we expect some performance degradation compared to directly using the Android APIs. The overhead can occur at two layers. First, due to our API translation layer, every storage API gets translated to our APIs. We call this overhead the *framework* overhead ("B framework" in the plots). In order to quantify this overhead, we intercept all storage APIs and translate it into our APIs, but instead of redirecting the calls to a pluggable data management app, we directly perform local I/O within our system. This also serves as a default data management policy when a user does not install any data management apps.

The second overhead is due to invoking a pluggable data management app. As we use Java reflection in this layer, we expect to have some overhead. We call this the *pluggable system* overhead. In order to quantify this overhead, we create a data management app which just uses the local storage on the phone through the Android Storage APIs and perform our measurements. This overhead indicates the base overhead incurred by any pluggable data management app ("DM App" in the plots).

Sequential I/O: In this section, we evaluate the overhead of BlueMountain for sequential file I/O. Figures 5 and 6 shows the total time taken for writing and reading files of 5 different sizes plotted as a CDF. [1] "Native" is the I/O performance through Android storage API classes, `FileInputStream` and `FileOutputStream`. Once again, "B Framework" indicates the performance of the BlueMountain framework and the translation layer, and "DM App" indicates the performance over a plugged in data management app. We conducted the experiments by measuring the average time taken for write/read for files of different sizes over 1000 iterations. We have used an object size of 4MB for our translation layer. This parameter can be configured by the pluggable data management app and our system used 4MB as the default settings. We study the impact of this object size in Section 5.1. Our write tests include flushing the data to persistent storage, while we use warm cache for our read performances. Photos and videos which are the most common type of data on mobile apps mainly use sequential I/O. Thus our tests are reflective of the performance we can expect on real apps. The performance numbers show that BlueMountain incurs minimal overhead over the native storage APIs. Further, we can see that the pluggable layer barely has any overhead above the framework overhead and has an almost-identical performance. This is because the two experiments are functionally equivalent as the

[1]We have also conducted the same experiments for file sizes up to 100MB, and the performance had the same pattern; thus, we do not include the results here.

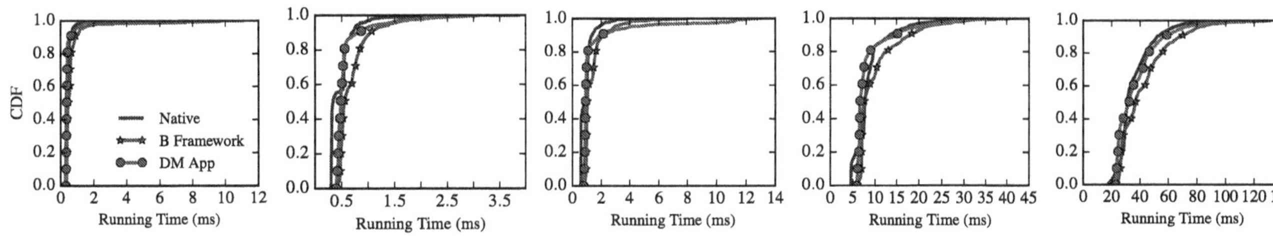

Figure 5: CDF: Sequential Writes with Various File Sizes, 4KB, 20KB, 100KB, 1MB, and 4MB (left to right)

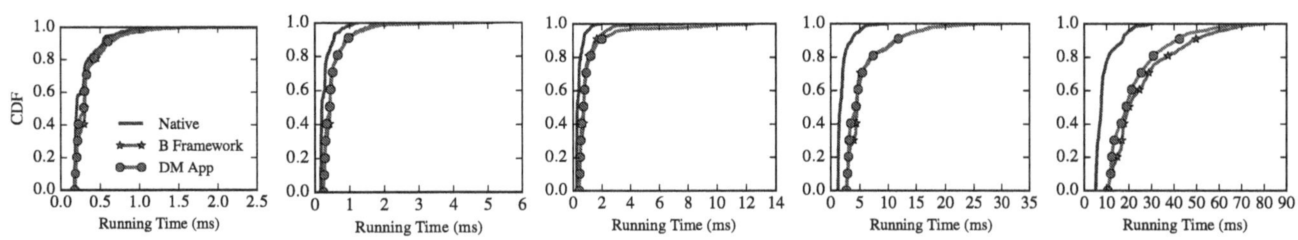

Figure 6: CDF: Sequential Reads with Various File Sizes, 4KB, 20KB, 100KB, 1MB, and 4MB (left to right)

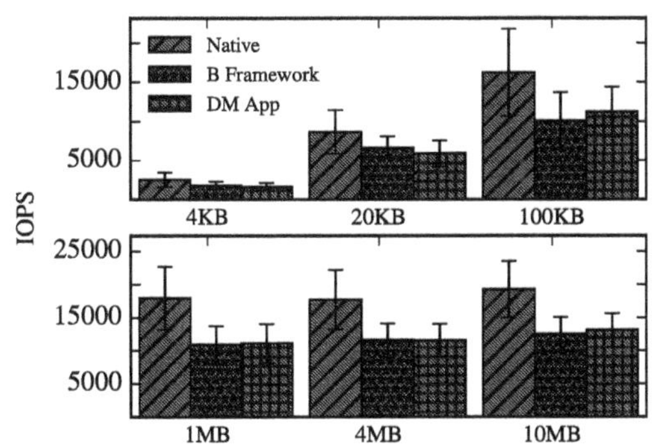

Figure 7: 4K IOPS for Random Writes

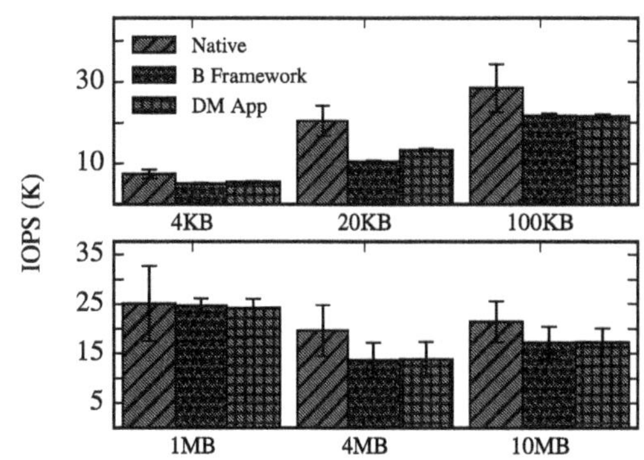

Figure 8: 4K IOPS for Random Reads

overhead of reflection is mitigated due to the use of our pre-defined interface as described in Section 3. The higher overhead for larger files is likely due to a higher memory pressure on the system; our current implementation allocates one large memory chunk for all data and does not perform any optimization. We expect that our future implementation can optimize this further.

Random I/O: In our next measurement, we evaluate our system against random I/O operations. We measure the number of IOPS by issuing I/O operations at a size of 4KB, which is typically the smallest size an app would read/write from/to a filesystem (4KB is the default block size of the ext4 filesystem—Android's default filesystem). Like the previous experiment, we measure the IOPS for files of different sizes over 1000 iterations and then calculate the average and standard deviation. Although random file access is not as common as streaming I/O, they are still used by plenty of apps, typically for accessing a documents or data files. BlueMountain's random access interface is based on Android's `RandomAccessFile` API. We measure the overhead of our system and compare it with the performance of when `RandomAccessFile` is directly used. Figure 7 and Figure 8 shows write and read IOPS respectively and compare Android's native performance, BlueMountain framework performance and the pluggable data management's performance. We incur some overhead on random access compared to the native performance. This is because Android's `RandomAccessFile` directly uses the low level file primitives while we build the random access support on top of a object based model. This means random writes on BlueMountain will results in updates to the object, which are typically slower. This is an optimization problem rather than an architectural limitation. For instance, in a app which primarily uses random I/O a much more optimized `update` which can handle small random I/O can be implemented by using techniques like chunking. The performance can also be improved by tuning the object size of the BlueMountain layer. As this parameter configurable, it enables the data management app to choose the best size depending on the targeted workload.

Effect on Object Size: As discussed in our system architecture, we divide large files into smaller objects of a particular block size. The choice of this block size will have an impact on the I/O performance. To measure the impact of the block size on the system performance, we vary the block size between 256KB and 8MB and

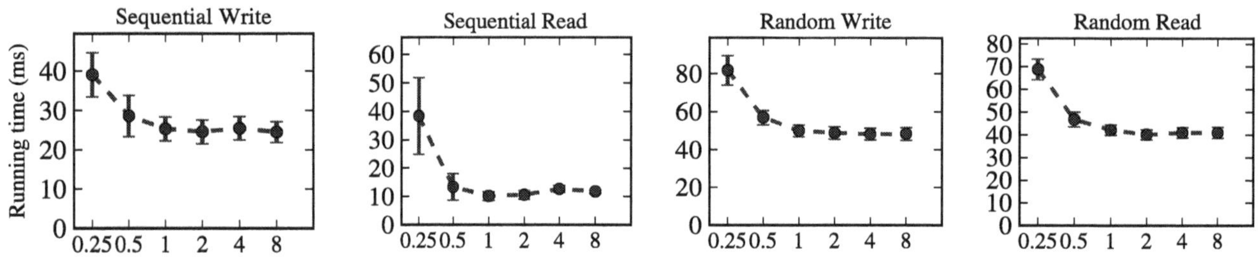

Figure 9: I/O performance of 4MB file for various block sizes (The x-axis shows block size in MB)

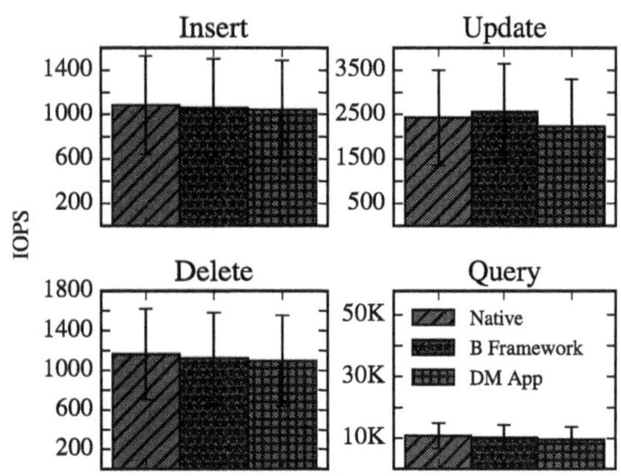

Figure 10: Database Microbenchmark

measure the I/O latency for a file of 4MB, for both sequential and random I/O. For random I/O, we issue I/O at 4KB chunks.

Figure 9 shows the performance for sequential and random I/O. With smaller block sizes, BlueMountain has to create multiple objects for the same file and I/O involves reading and writing to multiple objects. This adds additional overhead in our translation layer and degrades the performance. For instance, when the object size is 512KB, our system creates eight objects for a 4MB file. Hence, the overhead is higher compared to the case where we use the object size of 4MB—this is due to the difference in the number of objects that need to be created. With the object size of 8MB, there is no improvement as we still end up creating only one object. However, smaller objects might be beneficial with an app that issues many random I/O operations with frequent updates, since each update operation only needs to affect an object of a small size. Smaller object sizes can also reduce the network sync traffic if the app frequently updates the files after they are created.

Database operations: We have measured the overhead for database operations on Android's native database interface, with BlueMountain framework, and with a pluggable data management app. Just as in files, for framework experiments, the database operations go through our translation layer, and instead of redirecting the database operations to the data management app, we execute these operations on a local database. Similarly, to measure the pluggable overhead, we have developed a data management app for database which just uses a local database and Android's `SQLiteDatabase` interface to access it. Figure 10 shows the measurements in operations per second and for the four basic database operations—insert, update, delete and query. We have performed these operations on a table with 5 columns and having 10 rows to start with. We run 1000 iterations for each operation and measure the average and standard deviation. As we can see from the measurements, the overhead due to our framework and pluggable system is fairly minimal.

System	Throughput (write)
Native Android	68
Personal Device Syncing app (4.1)	52
Efficient Cloud Syncing app (4.2)	60

Table 2: Full Stack File Throughput (MB/s)

5.2 End-to-End BlueMountain Evaluation

We have measured the end-to-end throughput by plugging in the different data management solutions we have created as explained in Section 4. When the data management systems are plugged in, the app might experience slowdown due to two reasons. First is a combination of the "framework" and "pluggable" overhead as evaluated in our microbenchmarks. Second is due to the slowdown of the system when the data management apps are working in background. To quantify these, we have measured the throughput of our system, as MB/s writes for files and as the number of database operations per second for databases. We compare both these measurements with the corresponding measurements obtained from directly using the Android file/database APIs for local I/O—the goal here is to measure the maximum performance degradation that an app can experience when a data management app with cloud syncing abilities is plugged in.

Files: Table 2 shows the throughput for the two file data management systems we discussed in Section 4.1 and 4.2 and compare them with the native file throughput. We plugged in the two data management systems to our test suite app, one at a time, and enabled syncing to Dropbox and a private server which was hosted on our local network. We issued a large write from our test app, so the data management apps were continuously syncing the data to the cloud in the background. When the app is under full load, we measure the time taken to write a 1GB file. As we can see in the table, there is a slight degradation in the throughput compared to the native on both our file data management systems. We attribute this to the overhead caused by a background task which was actively syncing data to Dropbox and local server as described in Section 4.

Database Syncing Systems: Next, we show the performance of the three database syncing systems we have developed for BlueMountain, as previously described in Section 4.3. The goal of these systems is to synchronize the database with a remote server in the

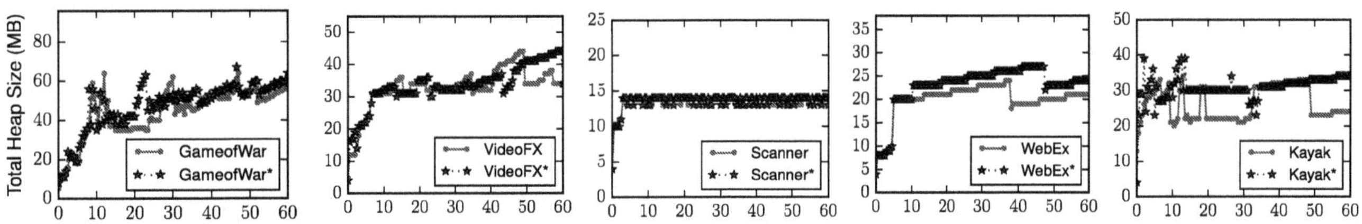

Figure 11: Heap Usage (*Instrumented apps): The x-axis shows elapsed time in seconds.

System	Insert	Query	Update	Delete
Native Android	1782	6300	1865	1835
File-Sync	764	6245	803	486
Log and replay	1367	6106	1485	1374
Multiple Databases	444	5188	417	407

Table 3: Full Stack Database Throughput (IOPS)

background and we capture the performance overhead of these systems when they are under full load and syncing data in the background.

For these measurements, we have a similar experimental setup for all three systems. We create eight tables, each having five columns and fifty rows. Our testing app, for which we plug in one database management app at a time, will run the four database operations—insert, update, delete and query, for 1,000 iterations. We then repeat the same experiment by directly using the Android's database APIs. All our database management systems synchronize data with a server. For our measurements, we used a local server hosted on our local network. Table 3 shows the throughput of four database operations using the three data management systems discussed in Section 4.3 along with the Android's native database APIs. We can see the throughput for write operations with these data management apps are considerably lower than that of the native database. In the next three paragraphs, we explain the possible reasons for this.

Log and replay: The log and replay system (described in Section 4.3) will synchronously log SQL operations to a persistent log-file on every database write operation. Since the log file is synchronously updated, we can observe a noticeable overhead for operations that modify the database—insert, update and delete. As queries are not logged, there is no additional overhead and the performance is comparable to the native performance. We also have a background task that continuously syncs the log-file to our server. When the system is under full load, this would affect the performance as well.

File sync: The file sync system (described in Section 4.3) has to notify a background task whenever a database write operation is issued. This, along with the computationally intensive background task of identifying the file chunks that are updated on each database operation, adds to the overhead. Like the log and replay, the queries are relatively unaffected by this and is comparable to the native system.

Multiple databases: In the multiple database system (described in Section 4.3), the overhead mainly comes from using multiple databases through a single connection. Due to this reason, the way database is accessed is changed and we can observe a higher penalty on queries as well. Like the previous two systems, this system is also continuously syncing the database files, but in this case, only the file which was affected by the operation. Thus, like the previous two database systems, we observe that the background sync slows down the system in this case well. The trade-off in this system is that we can achieve lower network traffic while the operations are slower.

5.3 Large Scale Instrumentation

In order to evaluate our support for automation, we inject BlueMountain interface into 400 existing apps by bytecode instrumentation. This means that these 400 apps, after our instrumentation, can leverage BlueMountain automatically without any involvement from their original developers. By default, BlueMountain uses the local filesystem for all storage calls if there is no pluggable data management app. We use this default setting to evaluate our instrumentation.

Instrumentation Correctness: To verify the correctness of our instrumentation, we have used the following three methods:

(1) **Robustness Testing:** In our first experiment, we have run all 400 apps using our automated UI testing system. This system uses Android UI Automator [15] to generate random UI events such as button clicks and text input. We have run each app (unmodified version and BlueMountain instrumented version) for 10 times and 30 seconds each time. With every run, we have recorded all the exceptions an app throws. Then, we have compared the exceptions thrown by the unmodified app with the exceptions thrown by the same app *with* BlueMountain instrumentation. If there were any exception with BlueMountain that does not appear in the unmodified app, we consider it a result of incorrect instrumentation. For all 400 apps, we have verified that there is no app that throws new exceptions with BlueMountain.
(2) **Log Analysis:** For our second experiment, we have modified our framework to track the number of I/O related calls that are invoked and successfully handled by our framework. This was done to make sure that our automated tests were indeed resulting in I/O calls. With the logs enabled, we have re-run the automated tests previously described and observed that every method in the BlueMountain interface was triggered during our runs. Table 6 summarizes the number of calls our framework handled in the course of the testing 400 apps. These results show that our tests successfully triggered many I/O calls which were successfully handled by our system.
(3) **Manual Testing:** Lastly, we selected five apps (a camera app, a video editor, a text editor, a shopping list manager, and a game) and manually tested each one of them. Through

Category	Examples	Inst. Time Avg. (Min./Max.)	DEX Size Avg. (Min./Max.)	DEX Size Increase Avg. (Min./Max.)	Lines of Code Avg. (Min./Max.)	Lines of Code Increase Avg. (Min./Max.)
Game	Game of War - Fire Age, Fruit Slice	27.7s (5.5s/53.4s)	2.6M (169.7K/4.4M)	330.1K (16.3K/818.9K)	231.34K (9.44K/379.40K)	3.65K (3.65K/3.70K)
Entertainment	VideoFX Music Video Maker, ESPN Fantasy Sports	31.7s (2.8s/74.9s)	3.6M (293.5K/9.8M)	404.3K (37.1K/1.3M)	294.75K (7.51K/748.96K)	3.67K (3.65K/3.73K)
Media	Radi Music, Google News & Weather	27.4s (1.8s/63.2s)	3.2M (17.9K/8.5M)	348.0K (31.5K/1.5M)	259.40K (0.97K/676.75K)	3.66K (3.65K/3.75K)
Education	NASA, ABC Preschool Free	19.3s (2.3s/52.3s)	2.0M (159.1K/6.5M)	289.0K (14.1K/980.1K)	160.69K (5.06K/537.00K)	3.65K (3.65K/3.69K)
Personalization	Asteroids 3D live wallpaper, Twemoji	18.0s (1.6s/57.9s)	1.9M (18.6K/7.1M)	246.5K (5.5K/553.9K)	164.80K (0.23K/559.70K)	3.65K (3.65K/3.68K)
Productivity	Google Now Launcher, Barcode Scanner	16.1s (1.5s/71.8s)	1.7M (4.9K/8.8M)	272.8K (30.1K/1.3M)	145.22K (0.16K/803.07K)	3.65K (3.65K/3.71K)
Business	Cisco WebEx Meetings, Indeed Job Search	29.4s (1.9s/56.7s)	3.5M (38.2K/7.7M)	362.1K (21.5K/1.2M)	282.34K (1.72K/607.75K)	3.67K (3.65K/3.87K)
Social	KAYAK Flights, Hotels & Cars, Airbnb	32.9s (8.5s/64.7s)	3.8M (1.2M/8.0M)	439.4K (59.6K/952.1K)	315.21K (66.94K/650.81K)	3.66K (3.64K/3.72K)
Total	N/A	25.3s (1.5s/74.9s)	2.8M (4.9K/9.8M)	336.5K (5.5K/1.5M)	231.72K (0.16K/803.07K)	3.66K (3.64K/3.87K)

Table 4: Instrumentation Results for 400 Popular Apps (50 apps in each category)

App Name	Average (J)	Std Dev (J)
Game of War	1340.7J	26.3J
Game of War*	1381.2J	30.5J
VideoFX	949.3J	15.6J
VideoFx*	939.0J	22.9J
Barcode Scanner	666.7J	8.1J
Barcode Scanner*	678.4J	8.6J
Cisco WebEx	767.1J	21.5J
Cisco WebEx*	787.0J	8.5J
Kayak	494.9J	10.0J
Kayak*	496.0J	10.1J

Table 5: Energy Consumption (*Instrumented apps)

API	Number of Calls
Files	331,759
Databases	28,660
Shared Preferences	100,052

Table 6: API Invocation Count

this experiment, we have verified that (1) the experience of using these apps was the same as using the unmodified app, (2) there was no noticeable lag when using these apps, and (3) all the I/O was successfully redirected to a preconfigured location.

From these experiments, we conclude with reasonable confidence that there was no error in the functionality of the apps we tested after instrumenting them with BlueMountain.

Instrumentation Overhead: Table 4 shows the apps and their code metrics of our instrumentation. As shown, injecting BlueMountain's framework code (which uses the local filesystem by default) does not have significant overhead in terms of instrumentation time and code size increase.

Heap and Energy Usage: Figure 11 shows the heap usage of five well-known apps—Game of War [44], VideoFX [12], Barcode Scanner [37], Cisco WebEx [6], and Kayak [21]. Even in terms of heap usage, BlueMountain does not incur much overhead compared to the original apps. Table 5 shows energy consumption of the five apps with and without BlueMountain. We have used a Nexus S phone, connected with a Monsoon Power Monitor for measurement, and run the five apps for ten minutes five times. The averages are all within the standard deviation, which indicates that there is little statistical difference in energy consumption.

Database Feature	Percentage of Apps Using
Thread control calls	1.6%
Compiled statements	19.2%
Custom `CursorFactory`	7.8%

Table 7: Unsupported Database Features

5.4 Unsupported Database APIs

As we discuss in Section 3, our current prototype does not support non-essential database APIs—APIs for control over parallel queries, APIs for compiled SQLite statements, and APIs for customized output access—in the interest of keeping our interface clean and simple. In order to understand how popular these unsupported APIs are, we have downloaded 2000 popular Android apps from Google Play, statically analyzed them, and gathered statistics on how many apps use the APIs. Through this experiment, we have found out that 511 out of 2000 apps use at least one of the APIs. Further, Table 7 shows the percentage of apps that use the features. As shown, compiled SQLite statements are the most popular feature. As mentioned earlier, there are alternative ways for app programmers to accomplish the same tasks for these features and we can still support them by including them in our interface.

6 DISCUSSION

Security: While our system enables flexibility of data management for end users, one important challenge is security, where a malicious app pretends to be a data management app and potentially compromises user data. Although our current work does not directly address security questions, mishandling of user data has been one of the biggest and known concerns for malicious apps on Android [17]. Moreover, techniques for mitigating such a concern are already in place [3] and will be applicable for malicious data management apps as well.

Switching Data Management Apps: A potential feature of interest is the ability to hot-swap different data management apps at run time. Since each data management app would implement their own way of managing data, enabling hot-swap between data management apps would require an ability to export from one data management app and importing to another. We are currently investigating various ways to provide this feature.

Extending Coverage: In our current implementation, we still depend on Android to manage the filesystem metadata and structure for a data management app. This can be a limitation when a user wants to use a highly secure data management system without leaking any information to the platform. We plan to address this issue in our future work by providing wrappers around the Android metadata management APIs.

7 RELATED WORK

Integrating Cloud Services: Previous work has tackled various challenges with mobile devices accessing cloud storage services. This ranges from optimizing data sync mechanism and providing better consistency models to providing more user functionality. In our own previous work, which laid the foundation for this work, we have explored the possibility of automatically integrating various cloud services into existing apps [5]. Many other systems provide libraries to be integrated with the apps or suggest modifications to underlying operating system/framework or to the cloud servers; our focus is complementary to these approaches, as we provide a mechanism through which some of these solutions can be easily deployed and used by the end user.

Call Interception: Our mechanism of intercepting Android storage calls and redirecting them is similar to FUSE [22]. GlusterFS [28] also uses `LD_PRELOAD` to intercept the POSIX filesystem calls and replace them with a custom implementation of GlusterFS core libraries. Recently, other techniques, such as Java bytecode rewriting and instrumentation, are utilized to change the behavior of applications without modifying their source code [4, 9, 10, 20, 25, 29, 32, 33, 38]. In the following, we discuss lines of research in data management issues arising from mobile apps and cloud-based storage services.

Cloud-Based File Synchronization Services: As cloud-based file synchronization services become popular, their shortcomings, challenges, and solutions have been discussed in the literature. Viewbox [43] proposes a design that integrates local file systems with cloud-based storage services to detect and recover from both inconsistency and data corruption that may happen in loosely coupled file synchronization services. QuickSync [8] and UDS [24] improve the efficiency of data synchronization in mobile devices using a variety of techniques. Metasync [18] implements a secure and reliable file synchronization mechanism by utilizing multiple cloud storage services.

Novel Data Management in Mobile Apps: A line of work discusses issues arising from how modern mobile apps utilize both filesystems and databases at the same time. Pebbles [35] argues that mobile apps do not correctly delete related data stored in filesystems and database and designs a system that can find the implicit relationships in an app's data stored in mobile devices. Simba [13] is a data-sync service for mobile apps and provides stronger consistency guarantees than file-based synchronization service. Diamond [42] designs a data management platform for reactive applications. Additionally, many commercial platforms such as Firebase [16] and Kinvey [34], enable app developers to link their apps to cloud backend which provides functionality like user management, push notifications, data management etc., through an emerging trend known as *Mobile Backend as a Service (MBasS)*. However, to take advantage of these services, the client components have to be integrated into the app at development time.

Context and Constraint-Based Data Management: Procrastinator [27], analyses and rewrites app binaries to do context based pre-fetching of the data. PSCloud [2] and Wherestore [36] create a location based data storage model which lets the users store their data on multiple devices. Cimbiosys [26] proposes partial replication of content shared among mobile devices and cloud services. WearDrive [19] is a storage system for wearable devices that offloads energy intensive tasks on the phone to improve the performance of apps and battery life of wearable devices.

Providing Flexibility and Cloud Adaptability for Mobile Data Management: Modern web/mobile applications rely on cloud-based storage services and there are various such services with different APIs. SPANStore [41] and Cloudlib [1] unify multiple cloud storage services with a single, key-value store interface. BlueMountain can easily transform an existing mobile application from using a single cloud storage provider to utilizing a layer like them. Zumero [45] provides a extension to SQLite database which enables database files to be synced across many devices. Lastly, to support the trend of employees using their personal mobile devices at workplace (BYOD), various Enterprise Mobility Management (EMM) systems, dedicated to manage user-owned devices, have come into existence. Systems like Airwatch [39], XenMobile [7], Android for Work [14], etc., provide a suite which includes device management, access control, data management (e.g. Airwatch Content Locker), etc., enabling personal devices to securely access corporate data. These platforms typically require a custom enterprise app to take advantage of their solutions while BlueMountain targets general apps which can be used by any user.

8 CONCLUSION

In this paper, we have presented a novel approach for customized data management on mobile devices. We have made a case for a new kind of app ecosystem where data management apps and regular apps exist. Our approach lets app developers focus on app logic while providing a way for data management app developers to provide innovative data management mechanisms. Our approach also gives end users better control over their data.

We demonstrate the usefulness of our approach by creating five data management apps. Each of the apps implements a unique mechanism for mobile data management, showcasing the flexibility of our approach. Our results show that our prototype system, BlueMountain, incurs only modest overhead in terms of read/write latency and throughput.

9 ACKNOWLEDGMENTS

We would like to acknowledge the works of Ajay Pratap Singh Chhokar, Ramanpreet Singh Khinda, and Aniruddh Ramesh Adkar who helped us immensely in developing the initial prototype of our data management apps. We would also like to thank the anonymous reviewers and our shepherd, Aruna Balasubramanian, for their valuable feedback. Lastly, we want to thank everyone working in our lab (Reliable Mobile Systems), for providing timely feedback. This work was supported in part by the generous funding from the National Science Foundation, CNS-1350883 (CAREER) and CNS-1618531.

REFERENCES

[1] Apache. 2017. Apache Libcloud. (Jan 2017). Retrieved July 10, 2017 from http://libcloud.apache.org

[2] Sobir Bazarbayev, Matti Hiltunen, Kaustubh Joshi, William H Sanders, and Richard Schlichting. 2013. Pscloud: a durable context-aware personal storage cloud. In *Proceedings of the 9th Workshop on Hot Topics in Dependable Systems*. ACM, 9.

[3] Google blog. 2017. Shielding you from Potentially Harmful Applications. (Feb 2017). Retrieved July 10, 2017 from https://goo.gl/KosA6d

[4] A. Chander, J.C. Mitchell, and Insik Shin. 2001. Mobile Code Security by Java Bytecode Instrumentation. In *DARPA Information Survivability Conference and Exposition II, 2001. DISCEX '01. Proceedings*, Vol. 2. 27–40.

[5] Sharath Chandrashekhara, Kyle Marcus, Rakesh GM Subramanya, Hrishikesh S Karve, Karthik Dantu, and Steven Y Ko. 2015. Enabling Automated, Rich, and Versatile Data Management for Android Apps with BlueMountain.. In *HotStorage*.

[6] Cisco. 2017. Cisco WebEx Meetings. (Jan 2017). Retrieved July 10, 2017 from https://play.google.com/store/apps/details?id=com.cisco.webex.meetings&hl=en

[7] Citrix. 2017. XenMobile. (Jan 2017). Retrieved July 10, 2017 from https://www.citrix.com/products/xenmobile/

[8] Yong Cui, Zeqi Lai, Xin Wang, Ningwei Dai, and Congcong Miao. 2015. QuickSync: Improving Synchronization Efficiency for Mobile Cloud Storage Services. In *Proceedings of the 21st Annual International Conference on Mobile Computing and Networking*. ACM, 592–603.

[9] Benjamin Davis and Hao Chen. 2013. RetroSkeleton: Retrofitting Android Apps. In *Proceeding of the 11th Annual International Conference on Mobile Systems, Applications, and Services (MobiSys '13)*.

[10] Benjamin Davis, Ben Sanders, Armen Khodaverdian, and Hao Chen. 2012. I-ARM-Droid: A Rewriting Framework for In-App Reference Monitors for Android Applications. In *Proceedings of the IEEE Mobile Security Technologies (MoST '12)*.

[11] Dropbox. 2014. Streaming File Synchronization. (Jul 2014). Retrieved July 10, 2017 from https://blogs.dropbox.com/tech/2014/07/streaming-file-synchronization/d

[12] FuzeBits. 2017. VideoFX Music Video Maker. (Jan 2017). Retrieved July 10, 2017 from https://play.google.com/store/apps/details?id=com.videofx&hl=en

[13] Younghwan Go, Nitin Agrawal, Akshat Aranya, and Cristian Ungureanu. 2015. Reliable, Consistent, and Efficient Data Sync for Mobile Apps. In *FAST'15*. USENIX Association. https://www.usenix.org/conference/fast15/technical-sessions/presentation/go

[14] Google. 2017. Android for Work. (Jan 2017). Retrieved July 10, 2017 from https://www.android.com/work

[15] Google. 2017. Android UI Automator. (Jan 2017). Retrieved July 10, 2017 from https://developer.android.com/topic/libraries/testing-support-library/index.html

[16] Google. 2017. Firebase. (Jan 2017). Retrieved July 10, 2017 from https://firebase.google.com/

[17] Google. 2017. The Google Android Security Team's Classifications for Potentially Harmful Applications. (Feb 2017). Retrieved July 10, 2017 from https://source.android.com/security/reports/Google_Android_Security_PHA_classifications.pdf

[18] Seungyeop Han, Haichen Shen, Taesoo Kim, Arvind Krishnamurthy, Thomas Anderson, and David Wetherall. 2015. MetaSync: File synchronization across multiple untrusted storage services. In *2015 USENIX Annual Technical Conference (USENIX ATC 15)*. 83–95.

[19] Jian Huang, Anirudh Badam, Ranveer Chandra, and Edmund B Nightingale. 2015. WearDrive: fast and energy-efficient storage for wearables. In *2015 USENIX Annual Technical Conference (USENIX ATC 15)*. 613–625.

[20] Galen Hunt and Doug Brubacher. 1999. Detours: Binary Interception of Win32 Functions. In *Proceedings of the 3rd Conference on USENIX Windows NT Symposium - Volume 3 (WINSYM '99)*.

[21] Kayak. 2017. KAYAK Flights, Hotels & Cars. (Jan 2017). Retrieved July 10, 2017 from https://play.google.com/store/apps/details?id=com.kayak.android&hl=en

[22] Linux Kernel. 2017. FUSE. (Jan 2017). Retrieved July 10, 2017 from http://fuse.sourceforge.net/

[23] Taeyeon Ki, Alex Simeonov, Bhavika Jain, Chang Min Park, Keshav Sharma, Karthik Dantu, Steven Y. Ko, and Lukasz Ziarek. 2017. Reptor: Enabling API Virtualization on Android for Platform Openness. In *Proceedings of the 15th annual International Conference on Mobile Systems, Applications, and Services (MobiSys '17)*. ACM.

[24] Zhenhua Li, Christo Wilson, Zhefu Jiang, Yao Liu, Ben Y Zhao, Cheng Jin, Zhi-Li Zhang, and Yafei Dai. 2013. Efficient batched synchronization in dropbox-like cloud storage services. In *ACM/IFIP/USENIX International Conference on Distributed Systems Platforms and Open Distributed Processing*. Springer, 307–327.

[25] Microsoft. 2017. Windows Hooks. (Jan 2017). Retrieved July 10, 2017 from http://goo.gl/r32d7B

[26] Venugopalan Ramasubramanian, Thomas L. Rodeheffer, Douglas B. Terry, Meg Walraed-Sullivan, Ted Wobber, Catherine C. Marshall, and Amin Vahdat. 2009. Cimbiosys: A Platform for Content-based Partial Replication. In *NSDI'09*. USENIX Association. http://dl.acm.org/citation.cfm?id=1558977.1558995

[27] Lenin Ravindranath, Sharad Agarwal, Jitendra Padhye, and Chris Riederer. 2014. Procrastinator: Pacing mobile apps' usage of the network. In *Proc. ACM MobiSys*.

[28] RedHat. 2017. GlusterFS. (Jan 2017). Retrieved July 10, 2017 from https://www.gluster.org/

[29] Jonathan Rentzsch. 2016. Mach Inject. (Nov 2016). Retrieved July 10, 2017 from https://github.com/rentzsch/mach_inject

[30] Slim Roms. 2017. Slim Roms. (Jan 2017). Retrieved July 10, 2017 from https://slimroms.org/

[31] Rsync. 2017. Lib Rsync. (Jan 2017). Retrieved July 10, 2017 from http://librsync.sourceforge.net/

[32] Algis Rudys and Dan S. Wallach. 2003. Enforcing Java Run-time Properties Using Bytecode Rewriting. In *Proceedings of the 2002 Mext-NSF-JSPS International Conference on Software Security: Theories and Systems (ISSS '02)*.

[33] Haichen Shen, Aruna Balasubramanian, Anthony LaMarca, and David Wetherall. 2015. Enhancing Mobile Apps to Use Sensor Hubs Without Programmer Effort. In *Proceedings of the 2015 ACM International Joint Conference on Pervasive and Ubiquitous Computing (UbiComp '15)*. ACM, New York, NY, USA, 227–238. https://doi.org/10.1145/2750858.2804260

[34] Progress Software. 2017. Kinvey BaaS. (Jan 2017). Retrieved July 10, 2017 from https://www.kinvey.com/

[35] Riley Spahn, Jonathan Bell, Michael Lee, Sravan Bhamidipati, Roxana Geambasu, and Gail Kaiser. 2014. Pebbles: Fine-Grained Data Management Abstractions for Modern Operating Systems. In *OSDI'14*. USENIX Association. https://www.usenix.org/conference/osdi14/technical-sessions/presentation/spahn

[36] Patrick Stuedi, Iqbal Mohomed, and Doug Terry. 2010. Wherestore: Location-based data storage for mobile devices interacting with the cloud. In *Proceedings of the 1st ACM Workshop on Mobile Cloud Computing & Services: Social Networks and Beyond*. ACM, 1.

[37] ZXing Team. 2017. Barcode Scanner. (Jan 2017). Retrieved July 10, 2017 from https://play.google.com/store/apps/details?id=com.google.zxing.client.android&hl=en

[38] Raja Vallée-Rai, Phong Co, Etienne Gagnon, Laurie Hendren, Patrick Lam, and Vijay Sundaresan. 1999. Soot - a Java bytecode Optimization Framework. In *Proceedings of the 1999 Conference of the Centre for Advanced Studies on Collaborative Research (CASCON '99)*.

[39] VmWare. 2017. Air-Watch Enterprise mobility platform. (Jan 2017). Retrieved July 10, 2017 from https://www.air-watch.com/

[40] Wi-Fi.org. 2017. Wi-Fi Direct. (Jan 2017). Retrieved July 10, 2017 from http://www.wi-fi.org/discover-wi-fi/wi-fi-direct

[41] Zhe Wu, Michael Butkiewicz, Dorian Perkins, Ethan Katz-Bassett, and Harsha V. Madhyastha. 2013. SPANStore: Cost-effective Geo-replicated Storage Spanning Multiple Cloud Services. In *Proceedings of the Twenty-Fourth ACM Symposium on Operating Systems Principles (SOSP '13)*. ACM, New York, NY, USA, 292–308.

[42] Irene Zhang, Niel Lebeck, Pedro Fonseca, Brandon Holt, Raymond Cheng, Ariadna Norberg, Arvind Krishnamurthy, and Henry M. Levy. 2016. Diamond: Automating Data Management and Storage for Wide-Area, Reactive Applications. In *12th USENIX Symposium on Operating Systems Design and Implementation (OSDI 16)*. USENIX Association, GA, 723–738. https://www.usenix.org/conference/osdi16/technical-sessions/presentation/zhang-irene

[43] Yupu Zhang, Chris Dragga, Andrea C. Arpaci-Dusseau, and Remzi H. Arpaci-Dusseau. 2014. ViewBox: Integrating Local File Systems with Cloud Storage Services. In *FAST'14*. USENIX. https://www.usenix.org/conference/fast14/technical-sessions/presentation/zhang

[44] Machine Zone. 2017. Game of War - Fire Age. (Jan 2017). Retrieved July 10, 2017 from https://play.google.com/store/apps/details?id=com.machinezone.gow&hl=en

[45] Zumero. 2017. SQL Datasync for Mobile Apps. (Jan 2017). Retrieved July 10, 2017 from http://zumero.com

Furion: Engineering High-Quality Immersive Virtual Reality on Today's Mobile Devices

Zeqi Lai*
Tsinghua University
laizq13@mails.tsinghua.edu.cn

Y. Charlie Hu
Purdue University
ychu@purdue.edu

Yong Cui
Tsinghua University
cuiyong@tsinghua.edu.cn

Linhui Sun
Tsinghua University
lh.sunlinh@gmail.com

Ningwei Dai
Tsinghua University
lemondnw@gmail.com

ABSTRACT

In this paper, we perform a systematic design study of the "elephant in the room" facing the VR industry – is it feasible to enable high-quality VR apps on untethered mobile devices such as smartphones? Our quantitative, performance-driven design study makes two contributions. First, we show that the QoE achievable for high-quality VR applications on today's mobile hardware and wireless networks via local rendering or offloading is about 10X away from the acceptable QoE, yet waiting for future mobile hardware or next-generation wireless networks (*e.g.*, 5G) is unlikely to help, because of power limitation and the higher CPU utilization needed for processing packets under higher data rate.

Second, we present Furion, a VR framework that enables high-quality, immersive mobile VR on today's mobile devices and wireless networks. Furion exploits a key insight about the VR workload that foreground interactions and background environment have contrasting predictability and rendering workload, and employs a split renderer architecture running on both the phone and the server. Supplemented with video compression, use of panoramic frames, and parallel decoding on multiple cores on the phone, we demonstrate Furion can support high-quality VR apps on today's smartphones over WiFi, with under 14ms latency and 60 FPS (the phone display refresh rate).

KEYWORDS

Virtual Reality; Mobile Devices; Untethered; Measurement

1 INTRODUCTION

The consumer virtual reality (VR) revolution started around 2012 when Palmer Luckey launched the now legendary Kickstarter campaign for Oculus Rift, which was acquired by Facebook in 2014. Since then, VR systems have been gaining growing market penetration, and are estimated to generate $30 billion annual revenue by 2020 [24].

Despite the growing market penetration, today's high-end VR systems such as Oculus Rift [16] and HTC Vive [9] that offer high quality and accurate positional tracking and handheld controllers remain tethered, where high-quality frames are rendered on a powerful server and streamed to the headset via a multi-Gbps HDMI cable. The cable not only limits users' mobility and hence VR experience but also creates a safety hazard as the user may trip and fall.

In this work, we perform a systematic design study to tackle this "elephant in the room" facing the VR industry – *is it feasible to enable high-quality VR apps on untethered mobile devices such as smartphones?*

We carry out our study in three steps. First, we profile the performance of two extreme design points on the latest Pixel phone which was dubbed by Google as "VR ready" [5], local rendering which performs rendering entirely on the phone, and remote rendering which renders frames entirely on a server and streams them over the best wireless network available on today's commodity smartphones, 802.11ac.

Our profiling study shows that the QoE achievable for high-quality VR apps on today's high-end mobile hardware (Pixel) and wireless networks (802.11ac) is about 10X away from the acceptable QoE. In particular, rendering a frame in a high-quality VR app on Pixel takes about 63-111ms and exhausts the phone CPU and GPU with utilization at about 60% and 100%, while on-demand streaming a frame rendered at the server over 802.11ac takes about 230ms.

Second, given neither local rendering nor remote rendering can support untethered VR on today's mobile hardware and wireless networks, we ask the question – will waiting for tomorrow's mobile hardware and next-generation wireless networks help?

Through analyzing the technology trend of mobile hardware and wireless networks we show that waiting for future mobile hardware or next-generation wireless networks (*e.g.*, 5G, 802.11ad) is unlikely to help. First, the CPU/GPU of mobile handsets will not grow significantly more powerful because of the power constraint. In fact, the technology trend shows the CPU capability of high-end phones has largely converged to using quad-cores at 2-2.5 GHz, with aggressive temperature control and hence frequency capping. Second, the multi-Gbps bandwidth promised by the next generation of wireless networks will not make remote rendering readily feasible, because packet processing at 10X higher data rate

*Work done while a visiting student at Purdue University.

MobiCom'17, October 16–20, 2017, Snowbird, UT, USA.

ACM ISBN 978-1-4503-4916-1/17/10...$15.00
https://doi.org/10.1145/3117811.3117815

will far exceed the mobile CPU capability, which as just discussed is unlikely to improve significantly. We show packet processing of 4 Gbps TCP flows would require 16 equivalent cores on PIXEL running at the capped frequency.

The above observation and reasoning suggest that the likely path to support untethered high-quality VR, *i.e.*, meeting its QoE requirements, is via software innovation. Furthermore, if such a software solution exists, following the same reasoning above, it should work on today's mobile hardware and wireless networks. In the third step of our study, we develop such a software solution, called FURION. FURION is a VR framework that enables high-quality, immersive mobile VR on today's mobile device and wireless networks.

The first thing FURION exploits is the classic technique for trading off computation time for reduced network transfer time: compression. However, we show directly applying the video compression scheme H.264 to compress the on-demand rendered frames on the server requires 32ms to get the frame and 16ms to decode it on the phone, for a total of 48ms end-to-end delay, which is about 3X beyond the 16ms per-frame interval on a 60 FPS display.

To bridge this 3X gap, the FURION design exploits several key insights about the VR workload: (1) a frame in high-quality VR apps consists of foreground interactions and background environment, (2) background environment is fairly predictable as it is incrementally updated as the user moves around in the virtual world, but has a much heavier rendering load due to rich details and complex textures, and hence is ideally suited for pre-rendering on and prefetching from the server, (3) foreground interactions are much lighter weight but unpredictable and hence are suited for rendering on the phone.

Motivated by the above insight, FURION employs a *cooperative renderer* architecture that renders less predictable, lighter-load interactions on the phone to *avoid network latency delay* while prefetching pre-rendered environment frames viewed from adjacent locations in the virtual world during the time it takes the user to walk to the adjacent location to *hide network transfer delay*.

While the cooperative renderer architecture is necessary to reduce end-to-end frame rendering time to under 16ms, making it to work requires solving a few remaining engineering challenges: (1) At a location in the virtual world, the user may still change orientation abruptly. How to render a new environment corresponding to any orientation without fetching new frames from the server on-demand? (2) How to prefetch the needed pre-rendered environment frames from the server just in time to be used for the next frame?

To tackle the first challenge, we prefetch pre-rendered panoramic frame of the environment for adjacent locations in the virtual world, which can be used to render an environment frame of any orientation by cropping. To tackle the second challenge, we use video compression to drastically cut down the panoramic frame size, and we further cut each panoramic frame into multiple segments to enable parallel decoding on multiple cores of the phone.

We have implemented the complete FURION platform on top of Unity [21] and Google Daydream [8]. We further show the FURION platform is easy to use – VR apps developed with Unity can be easily augmented to run on top of FURION.

Finally, we evaluate FURION using three open-source high-quality VR apps from Unity ported to Google Daydream, Viking Village [22], Corridor [4] and Nature [13]. We show FURION can support high-quality VR apps on today's smartphone (*e.g.*,PIXEL) over WiFi (802.11ac), by providing under 14ms latency and 60 FPS (the phone display refresh rate), under diverse user interactions including controller, rotation, and movement in the virtual world, for the three high-quality VR apps. We also show that FURION scales well with app features, in terms of the number of dynamic objects which enhance the immersive experience of VR apps. We further show that FURION supports the above QoE while incurring acceptable resource usage (under 37% GPU usage and 65% CPU utilization), which allows it to sustain long running of VR apps without being restricted by temperature control and frequency capping. Finally, by moving on-demand fetching of frames from the server out of the end-to-end delay critical path, *i.e.*, turning it into prefetching which just needs to finish in the prefetching window, FURION is robust to transient network bandwidth fluctuations. In summary, our evaluation shows that FURION's cooperative renderer design presents a viable solution to support high-quality VR apps on today's mobile hardware and wireless networks.

2 MOTIVATION

2.1 VR background

A typical VR system consists of three key components: a VR *headset*, a *controller* and a *renderer*. The headset serves two purposes: tracking user *pose* (including both 3D position and 3D orientation) and presenting the VR content to the headset display for user viewing. The controller integrates several physical buttons, touchpads and sensors to receive user interactions other than user pose. Additionally, some VR systems that contain social elements and support multiple online players can also receive remote interactions from other players via the Internet. The renderer then renders new frames according to new pose and interactions, which are updated on the head-mounted display.

2.2 QoE requirements of VR apps

VR apps impose a heavy computation workload on the system since they have to track user pose and interactively render high-quality graphics in real time. Any performance degradation can result in user discomfort or motion sickness due to the near-eye display characteristics of VR systems [31]. Specifically, to support acceptable user experience, which is dictated by the human biology, modern VR systems have to meet three critical performance and feature requirements:

1. **Responsiveness:** The motion-to-photon latency should be low enough, *e.g.*, under 10-25ms [26], in order to sustain good user experience.
2. **High-quality visual effects:** The VR system should not only render photo-realistic scenes in presenting the immersive virtual environment for users, but also ensure seamless playbacks by offering high frame rates (*e.g.*, 60 FPS is a minimum target [31]).
3. **Mobility:** A tethered VR headset presents a potential tripping hazard for the user. The VR system or at least the headset component should be untethered in order to provide the ultimate VR experience [28, 29].

(a) PolyRunner (b) Viking Village (c) Corridor (d) Nature

Figure 1: A subset of VR apps used in our study: PolyRunner is low-quality, and the rest are high-quality.

2.3 High-quality mobile VR is delay limited

Accomplishing the first two QoE requirements simultaneously for high-quality VR apps, however, has remained unattainable today on mobile systems due to the limited capability of mobile hardware and wireless technologies. As a result, all current high-end VR systems (*e.g.*, OculusRift [16], HTC Vive [9]) are *tethered*, providing good visual quality and responsiveness at the cost of mobility. In particular, these systems execute the heavy workload on powerful servers, and stream rendered frames to the headsets over high bandwidth cables.

Cutting the cord of high-quality VR systems is challenging because of the mismatch between their strict QoE requirements and mobile computation/network capability. To understand the gap between the two QoE requirements of high-quality VR apps (latency and FPS) and what today's mobile hardware and networking capability can deliver, we experimentally measure the achievable QoE under two straight-forward approaches to support mobile VR: local rendering and remote rendering.

2.3.1 Approach 1: Local rendering. The straight-forward approach to enable untethered VR systems is to perform rendering entirely on the mobile device, or local rendering for short. In fact, local rendering has been recently made available on commercial mobile VR systems such as Google Daydream [8] and Samsung Gear VR [7] to interactively render VR contents via the CPU/GPU on the smartphone. However, today's mobile VR systems can only support VR apps with low graphical quality which often breaks the illusion of immersion [31, 51], as they cannot satisfy the minimum QoE in running high-quality VR apps due to the constrained computation resource.

To quantify the resource usage and achieved QoE of popular VR apps on today's high-end mobile device, we experimented with seven popular VR apps on Google Daydream, as listed in Table 1: PolyRunner [18], Lego [10], vTime [25] and Overlord [17] are popular but low-quality Android VR apps available in Google Play which all have controller interactions, and Viking Village [22], Corridor [4] and Nature [13] are high-quality virtual-world Unity apps with more complex, realistic and immersive environments as shown in Figure 1. Because Viking, Corridor and Nature are three high-quality Unity apps originally designed for high-end PCs, we used Google Daydream SDK to port them to run on Android and added support for rendering virtual reality as well as controller interactions.

We ran the seven VR apps on a Pixel smartphone running Android 7.1. We used FPS and the BRISQUE value [46] to quantify the QoE, where the BRISQUE value is a well-known non-reference image quality access (IQA) metric. A lower BRISQUE value indicates better image quality and higher visual complexity for an app.[1]

Table 1: QoE and CPU/GPU load when running different VR apps on Pixel. A lower BRISQUE value of an app indicates better visual quality.

App Name	BRISQUE[46] Score	FPS	CPU Load	GPU Load
Low-quality VR apps				
PolyRunner [18]	89.19	60	36.2%	68.9%
Lego [10]	59.31	52	39.3%	74.4%
vTime [25]	54.48	47	41.7%	70.3%
Overlord [17]	50.10	41	44.8%	84.9%
High-quality VR apps				
Viking [22]	24.37	11	55.8%	99.9%
Corridor [4]	26.67	9	55.5%	99.8%
Nature [13]	26.67	16	59.9%	99.8%

The results in Table 1 show that (1) even the first four, low-quality VR apps incur up to 85% GPU utilization, while driving the CPU at 40% utilization[2] on average, and yet could only achieve 41 to 60 FPS; (2) the three high-quality VR apps, Viking, Corridor and Nature, exhausted both the GPU (100% utilization) and CPU (55-59% utilization), yet could achieve only 9-16 FPS, which makes the apps not usable. These results suggest that the VR rendering workload is simply too heavy for today's high-end mobile systems such as Pixel and as a result the VR apps suffer a rendering delay of 63-111ms which is far longer than the required 16ms per-frame rendering interval.

To summarize, under local rendering, the time to render a frame (roughly the inverse of each app's FPS) is:

$$T_{phone\_render} = 63 \sim 111ms \quad (1)$$

2.3.2 Approach 2: Remote rendering. The overwhelming CPU/GPU demand of local rendering on mobile devices motivates the alternative approach to support untethered VR of offloading the high rendering load to a powerful server and streaming the newly rendered frames to the headset via the wireless network, or remote rendering for short. In essence, this approach trades off computation workload for network workload. Under remote rendering, the time to render a frame is:

$$T_{remote\_render} = T_{req} + T_{server\_render} + T_{transfer} \quad (2)$$

[1] There is no well-defined threshold BRISQUE value for defining acceptable image qualities.
[2] Throughout the paper, phone CPU utilization refers to the average utilization of all cores.

Table 2: Latency breakdown when we stream high-quality VR content from a strong desktop to a smartphone via 802.11ac WLAN. The average FPS of each app is about 5. The peak network throughput is about 400Mbps.

App	Server Render	Network Delay (req/Xfer)	Frame Size
Viking	11ms	3/208 ms	10*MB*
Corridor	10ms	3/216 ms	10*MB*
Nature	8ms	3/214 ms	10*MB*

To quantify the resource usage and latency achieved of such an approach, we developed and profiled remote rendering versions for the three high-quality, open-source apps in Table 1. Specifically, we used Google Daydream SDK to split each app into a client app and a server counterpart where the client app running on the phone sends new user pose and controller interactions to the server app running on the PC, and the server app performs rendering of all objects and sends the rendered new frames back to the client app over the wireless network.

In our experiment, we ran the server of each app on a strong desktop, which has an Intel 6-core i7-6850K CPU, EVGA GTX1080 graphic card, and 256GB SSD, and ran the client of each app on Pixel, and the server sends rendered frames via an 802.11ac WLAN. We used 802.11ac because it provides the highest wireless bandwidth (about 400 Mbps in TCP) on current commodity smartphones.

The results, shown in Table 2, identified two QoE bottlenecks in supporting mobile VR apps using remote rendering over today's wireless networks:

(1) Long transfer delay $T_{transfer}$. We measured the QoE when the server streams raw frames in uncompressed format (Bitmap). The three VR apps use up the available network bandwidth (367-384 Mbps) yet still can only achieve on average 5 FPS. This is because transferring the raw data of one high-resolution frame (*i.e.*, 2560*1440 pixels, about 10 MB) over 802.11ac already takes between 208-216 ms. To support 60 FPS or higher requires streaming each high-quality frame well under 16ms, and would require at least 4 Gbps or 10X that of today's WiFi bandwidth, or about 200X that of today's LTE bandwidth (which is about 20 Mbps). A recent study [28] also confirmed multi-Gbps bandwidth is needed for supporting high-quality VR apps in remote rendering.

(2) Network latency delay T_{req}. Even if the wireless network has infinite bandwidth and hence the transfer time is insignificant, sending a request for the new frame and receiving the rendered frame from the server suffers a minimum round-trip delay. To measure the delay, we wrote a simple benchmark that performs back-to-back RTT measurements by sending and receiving 20-byte requests and replies from the server (to avoid the periodical SDIO bus sleep which inflates RTT [44]). Figure 2 shows the CDF of the measured RTTs from the Pixel to the LinkSys EA6350 AP over 802.11 b/g/n/ac, respectively. We see that the latency varies between 2ms minimum to 4ms at the 80th percentile, with a long tail reaching beyond 6ms. These results are consistent with those observed in [44]. The RTT can be explained by about 2ms base latency of PHY layer transfer (RTS/CTS/DATA/ACK) and the 1ms (median) delay in traversing the hardware/driver/kernel stack on the phone, which is again limited by the phone hardware capability.

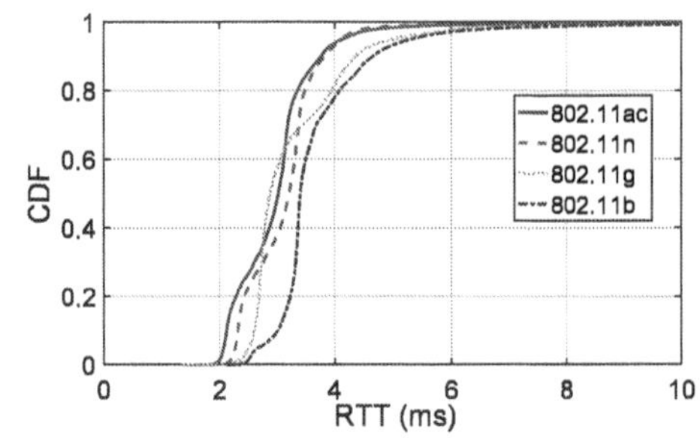

Figure 2: App-level RTT in different WiFi networks.

In summary, on today's high-end handset and highest bandwidth wireless network 802.11ac, the time to render a frame under on-demand remote rendering is:

$$\underset{(230ms)}{T_{remote\_render}} = \underset{(3ms)}{T_{req}} + \underset{(11ms)}{T_{server\_render}} + \underset{(216ms)}{T_{transfer}} \quad (3)$$

Summary: Supporting mobile VR on today's mobile hardware and wireless networking is *fundamentally delay limited* due to the wide gap (at least 10X) between the strict QoE requirements of VR apps dictated by human biology (*i.e.*, visual perception) and the long rendering delay due to limited mobile CPU/GPU hardware and wireless network bandwidth.

3 WILL FUTURE HARDWARE/NETWORKS HELP?

Given neither local rendering nor remote rendering can support untethered VR on today's mobile hardware and wireless networks, we ask the question – will waiting for tomorrow's mobile hardware and wireless networks help?

Mobile hardware are power limited. We argue that *the CPU/GPU of mobile handsets will not grow significantly more powerful because of the power constraint.* First, just like their counterpart in desktops and servers, the CPUs in mobile handsets are not getting faster, due to temperature and power limitation in the chip design. Second, since mobile handsets are fundamentally energy constrained, the CPUs on mobile devices are made to be less powerful (though often more power efficient), and come with far fewer cores, than their counterparts on desktops and servers.

In fact, the improvement of CPU/GPU capability of mobile handsets in high-end mobile handsets has already tapered off in recent years. Table 3 lists the CPU/GPU frequency and number of cores for the high-end Android handsets in the past five years and the upcoming S8+ (at the time of paper submission). We observe that (1) the CPU in these high-end phones has more or less converged to quad cores; although Nexus 6P comes with Octa cores, the upper four cores are rarely turned on due to temperature control; (2) the CPU frequency appears to have converged to between 2-2.5 GHz; (3) while the GPU frequency appears to be slowly increasing, we believe its provision benefited from larger batteries that come with larger phones adopted by the consumers in the past few years; the phone size clearly will not forever increase.

The stagnating improvement of CPU/GPU capabilities in mobile handsets suggests that local rendering will unlikely become a viable solution to support untethered VR apps.

Table 3: Evolution of CPU/GPU in high-end mobile handsets. Higher frequency benefited from larger batteries.

Phone (year)	Battery (size)	CPU	GPU
Nexus 4 (2012)	2100 mAh (4.7 inches)	Quad-core 1.5 GHz Krait	Adreno 320 400 MHz
Nexus 5 (2013)	2300 mAh (5.0 inches)	Quad-core 2.3 GHz Krait	Adreno 330 450 MHz
Nexus 6 (2014)	3220 mAh (6.0 inches)	Quad-core 2.7 GHz Krait	Adreno 420 500 MHz
Nexus 6P (2015)	3450 mAh (5.7 inches)	Octa-core 2.0+1.55 GHz Cortex-A57+A53	Adreno 430 600 MHz
Pixel XL (2016)	3450 mAh (5.5 inches)	Quad-core 2.15+1.6 GHz Kryo (2 sm, 2 lg)	Adreno 530 650 MHz
Galaxy S8+ (2017)	3500 mAh (6.2 inches)	Octa-core 2.45 GHz Kryo	Adreno 540 710 MHz

Table 4: Evolution of wireless technologies. We plot both theoretical peak bandwidth and achieved peak throughput of different cellular and WiFi networks.

Type	EDGE	UMTS	HSPA	LTE
Theoretical	1 Mbps	7.2 Mbps	42 Mbps	100 Mbps
Practical	384 Kbps	2 Mbps	10 Mbps	20 Mbps
Type	**802.11b**	**802.11g**	**802.11n**	**802.11ac**
Theoretical	11 Mbps	54 Mbps	600 Mbps	1.3 Gbps
Practical	6 Mbps	20 Mbps	100 Mbps	400 Mbps

Will next-generation wireless networks help? Compared to mobile CPU/GPU evolution, WiFi and cellular networking technologies have seen continuous and more rapid improvement. Table 4 lists the peak bandwidth provided by the generations of WiFi and Cellular. We see that in the past 10 years, the deployed cellular networks have evolved from 2.5G to 3G to LTE/4G, with achieved peak throughput growing from 384Kbps in 2.5G to 20 Mbps in LTE. Development of 5G started in year 2012 and wide deployment is estimated to happen in 2020. 5G is promised to deliver up to 1Gbps peak bandwidth [15], or 10X that of LTE/4G. Similarly, WiFi has evolved from 802.11a/b to 802.11ac which has a theoretical peak bandwidth of 1.3 Gbps and delivers up to 400 Mbps TCP throughput in practice, with 802.11ad promising a theoretical peak bandwidth of 7 Gbps.

However, we argue *the multi-Gbps bandwidth promised by the next-generation wireless networks will not make remote rendering readily feasible*, for the following reason.

Packet processing will exhaust the mobile CPU.

Packet processing at high throughput, which includes interrupt-driven packet receiving and stack processing, consumes a significant amount of CPU [39]. Since mobile CPUs will not become much faster or employ many more cores as discussed above, they will not be able to keep up with the 10X throughput increase.

To quantify how much the CPU is already consumed by packet processing, we measured the CPU utilization of Pixel when running a microbenchmark that performs downloading from a server connected via an 802.11ac WiFi AP under TCP. We ran the Linux tool `tc` on the server to control the peak throughput between the phone and server.

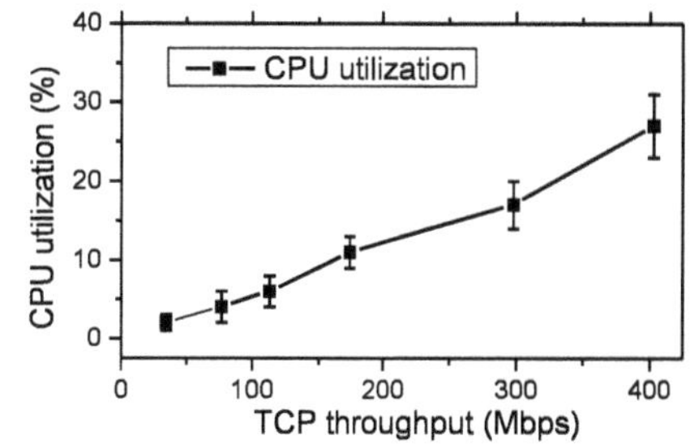

Figure 3: CPU utilization of Pixel from packet processing under varying downloading throughput.

Figure 3 plots the CPU utilization as the TCP throughput varies. We observe that (1) at 400 Mbps, the average utilization of the 4 cores of Pixel is already at 27%; (2) the CPU utilization scales roughly linearly with the TCP throughput; (3) under linear extrapolation, the CPU utilization would reach an unrealistic 270% at 4 Gbps (or 70% on 16 equivalent cores of Pixel).

Need software innovation. Given that waiting for the future mobile hardware or next-generation wireless networks is unlikely to help, we argue that the likely path to support untethered high-quality VR apps is via software innovation. In fact, following the same reasoning above, if such a software solution exists, it should work on today's mobile hardware and wireless networks.

4 EXPLORING VIDEO COMPRESSION

We start our quest for a software solution to support untethered VR apps today with the remote rendering approach discussed in §2.3.2, by exploring a classic technique for trading off computation time for reduced network transfer time: compression.

It is well known that for transferring consecutive frames that exhibit significant redundancy, as is the case with consecutive frames in a VR app, video compression gives high compression ratio. This is achieved by encoding the reference frame into an I frame which is relatively large and self-contained, and encoding the subsequent frames as much smaller, dependent P frames which encode the delta relative to the reference I frame and proceeding P frames.

Recall the original remote rendering approach suffers about 200ms transfer delay due to the large frame size, about 10 MB. We implemented three state-of-the-art video compression schemes: MJPG (a JPEG-based video encoding scheme), H.264 [27] and VP9 [23], to encode each on-demand requested frame rendered at the server relative to a reference frame previously rendered which is already streamed to the phone. Specifically, in each implementation, we use the mjpeg tool [12], libx264 [27] or libx-vp9 [11] to encode the frame on the server and leverage Android MediaCodec [2] to decode frames on the phone.

We then reran the three high-end VR apps on Pixel and measured the QoE when the server streams compressed frames in MPEG, H.264 or VP9. Table 5 shows that (1) MJPG compression incurs an encoding time of up to 17ms and reduces the average frame size to about 400KB for the three VR apps which cuts down the frame transfer time to 14ms, but it also incurs a high decoding delay of 128-137ms on the phone, which makes the end-to-end delay in remote rendering a new frame on-demand stay at about 179ms (3ms + 11ms + 17ms + 11ms + 137ms). (2) Although VP9 achieves the highest compression ratio and smallest per-frame size,

Table 5: Latency breakdown when we stream high-quality VR content from a strong desktop to a smartphone via 802.11ac WLAN, with video compression. M:MJPG. H:H.264. V:VP9. In each case the peak network throughput is about 400Mbps.

App (Format)	Server (render/ encode)	Phone decode	Network Delay (req/Xfer)	Frame Size
Viking (M)	11ms/16ms	134 ms	3/11 ms	407KB
Corridor (M)	10ms/17ms	128 ms	3/11 ms	379KB
Nature (M)	8ms/17ms	137 ms	3/10 ms	369KB
Viking (H)	11ms/9ms	15 ms	3/8 ms	286KB
Corridor (H)	10ms/10ms	16 ms	3/8 ms	277KB
Nature (H)	8ms/9ms	14 ms	3/7 ms	272KB
Viking (V)	11ms/193ms	72 ms	3/7 ms	228KB
Corridor (V)	10ms/188ms	83 ms	3/7 ms	209KB
Nature (V)	8ms/202ms	67 ms	3/6 ms	215KB

it also has the highest encoding/decoding time. (3) In contrast, H.264 compression not only cuts down the frame size to be under 286KB and the server encoding time and frame transfer time to be under 10ms and 8ms, it also cuts down the phone decoding time to be under 16ms. Overall, H.264 presents the most effective tradeoff between network bandwidth reduction and phone decoding time.

Under H.264 compression, the end-to-end time to remotely render a frame on demand for the three apps is bounded by:

$$\underset{(48ms)}{T_{remote\_render}} = \underset{(3ms)}{T_{req}} + \underset{(11ms)}{T_{render}} + \underset{(10ms)}{T_{encode}} + \underset{(8ms)}{T_{transfer}} + \underset{(16ms)}{T_{phone\_decode}} \quad (4)$$

Examining each of the five components of the end-to-end delay of 48ms, we see none of the components will easily improve: while higher bandwidth wireless network will reduce $T_{transfer}$, its effect will likely be limited by the CPU capability of the phone as discussed in §3. Therefore, although the end-to-end delay of 48ms is only 3X from the per-frame interval of 16ms, the gap appears very challenging to bridge.

5 KEY INSIGHT

The five components of the end-to-end time to render a frame in Equation (4) can be separated into two groups. The first group, consisting of the first four components, includes the delay in on-demand requesting, server rendering and encoding the new frame, and transferring the new frame over the network. The second group consists of the time to decode the compressed frame on the phone.

To gain insight on how to reduce the delay in the first group, we studied more than 50 popular VR apps collected from Google Daydream platform and Unity Store to understand the VR rendering workload. From the study, we derived four VR-specific insights:

(1) For most VR apps, the VR content rendered can be divided into *foreground interactions* and *background virtual environment*. For example, for the VR app we have tested in Figure 1, the interaction is the flyer in Figure 1a, the axe in Figure 1b, the gun or enemies in Figure 1c, or the animals in Figure 1d, which interact with the user via the controller. The environment refers to the background virtual world that covers the majority of the space in the display.

(2) Interactions are triggered by operating the controller or signals from other players. As a result, their animations are random and hard to predict.

(3) In contrast, the background environment is updated according to the user movement and thus changes continuously and is predictable. However, at a given location, the user may change orientation abruptly, *e.g.*, from turning, and the environment seen from the new viewing angle may change significantly, although the environment itself did not change.

Table 6: Resource usage when rendering only foreground interactions or background environment. TPF is average rendering time per frame.

App	Interaction only (TPF/CPU/GPU)	Environment only (TPF/CPU/GPU)
Viking	13ms / 29% / 22%	82ms / 42% / 95%
Corridors	13ms / 40% / 22%	104ms / 53% / 83%
Nature	12ms / 32% / 20%	61ms / 56% / 82%

Next, we break down the cost of rendering foreground interactions and background environment for the three high-quality VR apps in Figure 1 on Pixel. Specifically, for each app we build two new versions that disable the call for drawing foreground interactions and the background environment, respectively. We then measure the frame rendering time and CPU and GPU utilization of each version. Table 6 shows the results. We see that rendering interactions only takes 12-13ms, which is 7X shorter than rendering both interactions and environment (§2.3.1), and consumes only 29-40% CPU utilization and under 22% GPU utilization on the Pixel phone. In contrast, rendering only the environment takes 61-104ms which is about 90% of the delay in rendering both interactions and environment (§2.3.1). Thus we draw our next insight about VR rendering workload:

(4) In terms of rendering workload, foreground interactions are much more lightweight compared to the background environment. This is because the realistic, immersive environment in high-quality VR apps contains rich details and complex textures (*e.g.*, the sophisticated buildings and shadows in Figure 1) which incur significant rendering overhead.

6 COOPERATIVE RENDERING

6.1 Phone/server cooperative rendering

The above insights on the predictability and workload in rendering interactions and environment in VR suggest an effective way to enable high-quality mobile VR is to:

(1) divide VR rendering workload into foreground interactions and background environment,
(2) leverage the local mobile GPU to render foreground interactions,
(3) leverage the remote rendering engine on the server to pre-render and pre-fetch the background environment, and finally,
(4) combine them on the phone to generate the final frames.

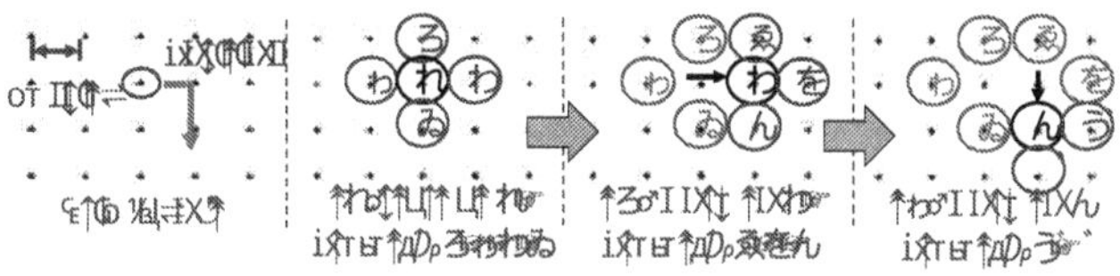

Figure 4: The prefetching process.

The key advantages of such a *cooperative rendering approach* between the phone and the server are (1) offloading a majority of the rendering load significantly reduces the computation overhead on the phone; (2) pre-rendering and pre-fetching environments hide the delay from on-demand rendering of environments (first four components in group 1 in Equation (4)); (3) rendering interactions locally avoids the network latency from on-demand rendering of interactions (which cannot be pre-rendered due to unpredictability).

With such cooperative rendering, the time to render a new frame is reduced to:

$$T_{co\_render} = max(T_{phone\_render\_intr}, T_{phone\_decode\_env}) + T_{integrate} \quad (5)$$

Constraint: environment frames are pre-fetched in time

The split architecture design requires an integration step that integrates the locally rendered interactions with remotely rendered environment into the final frame for displaying. Following the typical rendering framework (*e.g.,* OpenGL ES), where the pixel data of each object are rendered and integrated in a frame buffer before being sent to display, in cooperative rendering, the pixel data from the interaction renderer and the prefetched environment frame will be integrated in the frame buffer.

Thus, barring the following two remaining challenges, the above cooperative renderer design holds the promise to render a frame within the per-frame rendering interval of 16ms:

Q1: How to pre-render and pre-fetch environment frames just in time to be used for rendering the new frame?

Q2: How to speed up phone decoding time to be within the 16ms interval?

6.2 Prefetching panoramic frames

In the basic cooperative renderer design, we assume the next frame to be rendered can be pre-rendered and prefetched. However, straightforwardly applying prefetching in VR would face two challenges: (1) There are almost infinite possibilities for the next pose since a user can freely change position and orientation; (2) Delivering a large number of high-quality frames pre-rendered by the server to the client will incur significant bandwidth overhead and accordingly high CPU utilization on the client (from packet processing).

We tackle these challenges with a set of VR-specific optimizations as follows.

Leveraging movement delay to prefetch frames. In a VR system, the virtual world is discretized into grid points or grid locations, as shown in Figure 4, and rendering the faraway environment at any location in between grid points is approximated with rendering from the nearest grid point. We define the distance between two adjacent positions as *density (d)*. Effectively the grid density determines the smoothness of rendering during user movement in the virtual world. Previous studies (*e.g.,* [31]) have shown that for high-end VR apps, setting the density to 0.02 Unity units (which corresponds to about 2cm) is sufficient to sustain smooth rendering during user movement.

Table 7: Cutting down pre-rendered and pre-fetched frames.

Method	Data to fetch (In a time window (d/v))
Naive prefetching	5*N frames (5*10*N MB)
Panorama	≤ 3 panoramas (3*31 MB)
Panorama+ +Video compression	1 video (300-400 KB)

The discretization of the virtual world and delay in user movement to the next grid location provides us the opportunity to prefetch the frame for the next location. In particular, the time it takes the user to move from one grid point to an adjacent point is determined by the movement speed v. We make an observation that for realism, the typical user movement speed (*e.g.,* walking) in the virtual world is similar to in the real world, at about 1m/s. Dividing the grid density by this speed gives 20ms as the time interval for a user to move between adjacent grid points. This is the time window for prefetching the frame for the next grid location.

Using a panoramic frame to encapsulate all possible orientations. In a VR system, a user pose is composed of a position and an orientation. While there are only a few adjacent grid locations the user can move to next, at the next grid location, the user can freely change to any orientation (by turning the headset) abruptly which is difficult to predict, and hence pre-rendering and prefetching the frame with the right orientation is hard.

To overcome this challenge, we pre-render a *panoramic frame* for each grid location which conceptually aggregates or encodes all possible orientations at that fixed position, *i.e.,* a frame with any orientation from that location can be easily cropped from the panoramic frame. Whenever the user moves to one location, we can start prefetching the panoramic frame for the next grid location.

Prefetching frames for all adjacent positions. Since there are four grid locations surrounding each grid location, prefetching one panoramic location for only one adjacent grid location requires predicting which grid location the user will next move to, which is not always easy. To avoid complicated prediction and miss-predictions, at each grid location, we prefetch panoramic frames for all adjacent grid locations.

Since prefetching is done incrementally as the user moves, the number of frames to prefetch at each grid point is up to three, as shown by the example in Figure 4. Assume initially the user stands at position 0, and panoramic frames 1-4 are already prefetched. Then at t1 the user starts to move to position 3, and at the same time we prefetch panoramic frames for positions 5, 6, and 7. Similarly at t2, the users starts moving to position 7 and only frames in 8 and 9 are prefetched. Note in moving between positions 3 and 7, since the phone already prefetched panoramic views for both positions, it can decode a frame with any orientation locally.

Encoding multiple panoramic frames. Fetching a single panoramic frame for each grid location instead of many possible frames (for N possible orientations) already significantly cuts down the total frame size, from 5*N*10MB down to 3*31MB when without video compression, as shown in Table 7. With video compression,

Table 8: Latency of each step when we prefetch the background environment for Viking Village. Latencies of other two VR apps are similar.

On-demand	$T_{phone\_render\_intr}$	T_{phone_decode}	
	13ms	45ms	
Prefetching	T_{req}	$T_{transfer}$	T_{walk}
	3ms	10ms	20ms

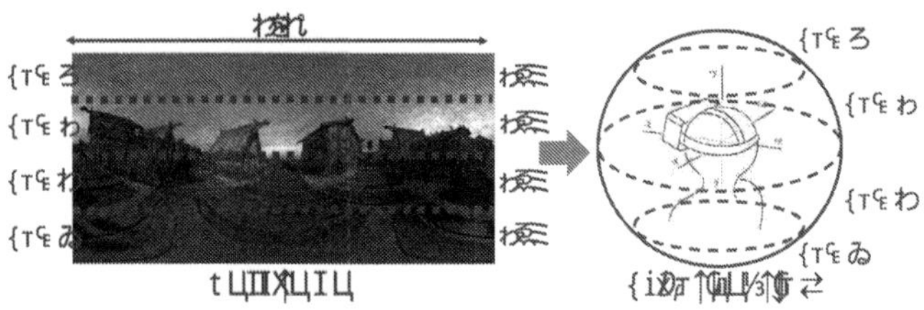

Figure 5: Parallel decoding: leveraging multi-core to decode frame segments in parallel.

one panoramic frame can be compressed down to a P-frame of under 133KB on average (using the panoramic frame at the current grid point as reference).

Encoding the three panoramic frames incrementally (*i.e.*, into three dependent P-frames) potentially gives higher compression ratio, but this can significantly increase the decoding time, to about 110ms, as decoding the last of the three panoramic frame in the video requires decoding the first two. For this reason, we encode each of the three panoramic frames (*e.g.*, for position 5, 6, and 7) as an independent P frame relative to the reference frame that the phone already has (*e.g.*, for position 3). Making the three P-frames not dependent this way reduces the decoding time of any P-frame (panoramic frame) to 45ms on average, at the cost of a slightly decreased compression ratio (about 9% reduction). We denote this non-successive variation of video encoding as *direct encoding*.

Delay reduction. We measured the delay reduction on the three reference VR apps from prefetching panoramic frames and video compression discussed above on the Pixel phone, over 802.11ac WiFi. Table 8 shows five components of the process. On one hand, sending the request for and transferring of three panoramic frames can be finished in 13ms, which is less than the 20ms delay for the user to walk from one grid location to the next, and hence satisfying the prefetching constraint in Equation (5):

$$Constraint: \underset{(3ms)}{T_{req}} + \underset{(10ms)}{T_{transfer}} \leq \underset{(20ms)}{T_{walk\_to\_next\_grid\_point}} \quad (6)$$

On the other hand, decoding any one of the three panoramic frames in the compressed video takes about 45ms, much higher than the 16ms for decoding a compressed regular frame (Table 5).

6.3 Parallel decoding on the phone

We observe that decoding a panoramic frame is an inherently sequential process, and hence does not employ the parallelism offered by the multiple cores on modern handsets. To exploit the hardware parallelism, we cut each panoramic frame into N segments, each at $1/N$ of the original size, encode the corresponding segments of the three panoramic frames into N videos. Since the redundancy

Table 9: Latency of each step with parallel decoding for Viking.

On-demand	$T_{phone\_render\_intr}$	T_{phone_decode}
	13ms	12ms

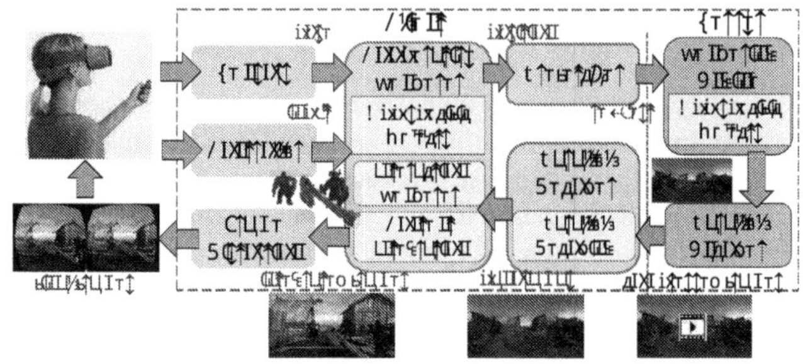

Figure 6: Furion system architecture.

remains between the corresponding segments and that of the reference panoramic frame (on the phone), the video compression ratio should remain high. More importantly, decoding on the phone of the N segments of each panoramic frame can now be done on N cores in parallel. Since Pixel comes with four cores, we experimented with different N (between 2 and 8) and found $N = 4$ gives the best decoding time. Figure 5 shows how a panoramic frame is segmented into 4 segments.

Table 9 shows parallel decoding of four segments reduces the phone decoding time from 45ms to 12ms, and the end-to-end time to render a new frame to $max(13ms, 12ms) + 1ms = 14ms$, which allows the VR apps to achieve 60 FPS.

6.4 Putting it together: Furion architecture

Incorporating the above ideas, we have developed Furion, a VR framework that enables high-quality, immersive mobile virtual reality on today's mobile device and wireless networks, by providing high visual quality, high frame rate, and low latency.

Figure 6 shows the system architecture and the workflow of Furion. At a high level, Furion includes the client part and the server part which cooperatively render VR contents to the user. The sensor module on the client tracks pose changes, including both position and orientation changes of the user headset, together with additional user inputs from the controller. The key component on the client is the *cooperative renderer*, which splits the VR workload into a local part and a remote part, and offloads the remote part to the server. Specifically, for each user pose, it renders locally the interactions and requests the parallel decoder to decode the background environment from a pre-fetched panoramic frame (4 subframes), combines the rendered interactions and decoded environment and sends it to the frame distortion module, which generates the final frame for each eye and displays to the user. Whenever the user moves to a new grid location, the prefetcher sends a request to the server to request for panoramic frames corresponding to up to three new adjacent grid locations.

The server part is a generic environment rendering engine that is initialized with app-specific objects, and pre-renders panoramic frames for each grid location. At runtime, the parallel encoder engine loads up to 3 panoramic frames specified in the client request,

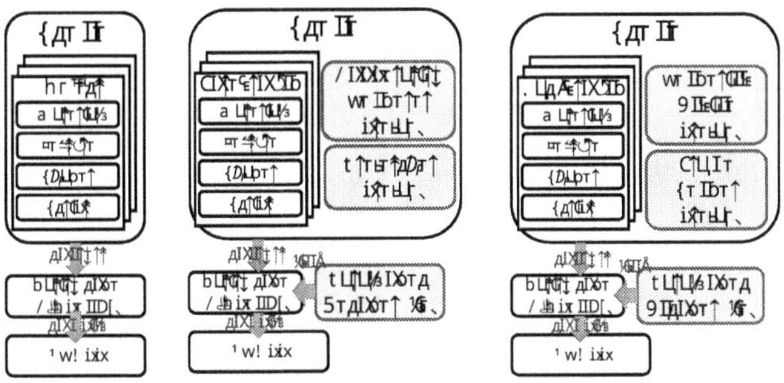

(a) Unity (b) Building the client. (c) Building the server.

Figure 7: Developing VR apps with FURION.

cuts each panoramic frame into 4 segments, encodes them with reference to the panoramic frame (subframes) in the last grid point using H.264 codec, and transfers the encoded video to the phone over the wireless network.

7 DEVELOPING VR APPS WITH FURION

We have implemented FURION on top of Unity and Google Daydream SDK. Before discussing the implementation details, we first describe the user interface of FURION, *i.e.*, how a developer uses FURION to develop VR apps.

Quick primer of Unity. Typically a VR app is developed by some virtual scene creation tools or game creation IDE, such as Unity and Unreal. We build our FURION system on Unity. Figure 7a shows the basic workflow of building apps with Unity. Specifically, Unity provides a WYSIWYG editor that allows a developer to work on a *scene* that describes the interactions and virtual environment in the app. A scene contains a number of objects that represent the basic unit at the development time, and the developer can change the property of an object by adding new material and texture to it. In addition, the developer can also write a script for each object to add animation and game logic. Unity then converts the visible scene to native codes and finally compiles the code to generate the executable app.

Developing VR with FURION. FURION provides an easy-to-use way for developers to augment VR apps developed using Unity. Figures 7b and 7c show the process to build the client and server part of a VR app with FURION. Specifically, we implement and export the cooperative renderer, the prefetcher and the rendering engine as specific prefabs in Unity, which can be imported and used in the app at the development time. In addition, we implement the parallel codec module as a library which is linked at the compiling time. For developers, augmenting a VR app with FURION only requires adding FURION prefabs in the scene and configuring app-specific parameters (*e.g.*, the reachable area in the scene) in the prefab.

8 IMPLEMENTATION

We describe a number of practical issues in implementing FURION.

Cooperative Renderer. In FURION, the cooperative renderer renders interactions using the mobile GPU and fills the surrounding environments with the panoramic frame rendered by the server. We leverage the native Unity API to write a Unity prefab called *EnvTexture* that can load frames generated from an external player and draw surrounding environments. With EnvTexture, FURION composes interactions and environments rendered on the client and server respectively. The cooperative renderer is implemented in around 1900 lines of C# code.

Prefetcher. We implement the prefetcher module in FURION as a prefab in Unity to calculate the user position and determine the time and data of a prefetching operation, according to the current user position. We build a series of rendering cameras in the rendering engine on the server to pre-render panoramic frames, each containing 3840*2160 pixels. The prefetcher together with the rendering engine on the server are implemented in around 2100 lines of C# code.

Parallel Codec. The basic requirement of our Parallel Codec is to encode the 4 segments per panoramic frame on the server and to quickly decode them to display a specific frame on the mobile client. We implement the parallel codec module by extending existing ffmpeg [6] and x264 [27] libraries. We extend the encoding/decoding module in the x264 library to support direct encoding and modify the sequential playback logic in ffmpeg to support parallel decoding. To synchronize all segments during the playback in ffmpeg, we build one decoding thread for each segment and a master thread to send the entire frame to the display hardware once all segments are decoded. In addition, we build a separate network process to deliver the compressed video to the client over TCP. Collectively, we modified about 1100 lines of C code in the ffmpeg and x264 libraries.

Sensing and Distortion. We leverage the Google Daydream SDK to (1) build the sensor module to read pose and additional user inputs from the controller and (2) perform distortion on the frame generated by the cooperative renderer.

9 PERFORMANCE EVALUATION

In this section, we evaluate the end-to-end performance and system overhead of VR apps built upon FURION.

9.1 Experiment setup

We run the FURION server on a strong desktop as we described in Section 2. We run the client app on a PIXEL smartphone running Android 7.1 with Google Daydream support. The client communicates with the server via an 802.11ac AP which supports up to 400Mbps TCP throughput for a single device. We augment the three high-quality apps as we described previously (Viking [22], Corridor [4], and Nature [13]) with FURION to support high-quality virtual reality.

We build three implementations of each app in our experiment: (1) *Mobile*: a local rendering version that renders all VR content locally; (2) *Thin-client:* a remote rendering version that offloads all rendering workloads to the server and encodes frames with H.264; (3) FURION*:* built on FURION which leverages both client and server to cooperatively render VR content. We do not compare our solution with MoVR [28, 29] because there is no 60GHz WiFi support in current commodity smartphones, or with FlashBack [31] which does not support user interactions.

Table 10: Visual quality and FPS of each VR app under different implementations.

App (Implementation)	Visual Quality (Average SSIM)	Average FPS
Viking (Mobile)	0.812	11
Corridor (Mobile)	0.834	9
Nature (Mobile)	0.833	15
Viking (Thin-client)	0.927	36
Corridor (Thin-client)	0.933	34
Nature (Thin-client)	0.944	37
Viking (FURION)	0.927	60
Corridor (FURION)	0.933	60
Nature (FURION)	0.944	60

In the FURION versions of the three VR apps, the total size of the panoramic frames pre-rendered by the server are 74 GB, 71 GB, and 53 GB, respectively.

9.2 Visual quality, frame rate, responsiveness

Image quality. We use Structural Similarity (SSIM) [59] to quantify the image quality of different schemes. SSIM is a standard metric from the video processing community used to assess the user-perceived loss in frame quality between the original version A and a distorted version B. SSIM has a value between 0 and 1; a larger SSIM value indicates higher fidelity to the original frame. In our experiment, we use SSIM to compare each final frame rendered by each scheme with the corresponding original frame rendered by the strong desktop (before encoding). All final frames are rendered with 2560*1440 pixels.

Table 10 shows the visual quality results. The SSIM value of the mobile rendering system is about 0.812, which falls short of high graphics quality. The visual quality decreases because the quality manager inside the Android rendering system automatically disables some functions that provide immersive visual effects (*e.g.*, anti aliasing and color grading) but are too computation intensive on mobile devices. The SSIM values under FURION and Thin-client are identical as both go through H.264 encoding and decoding, and integration of rendered interactions and decoded environment under FURION does not affect image quality. Further, the SSIM values are above 0.927. A SSIM value higher than 0.9 indicates that the distorted frame well approximates the original high-quality frame and provides "good" visual quality [37].

Frame rate. To enable a smooth immersive experience, it is necessary for the VR system to deliver at least 60 FPS. Table 10 shows across the three high-quality VR apps, the mobile system delivers the lowest FPS, between 9-15, the thin-client version delivers between 34-37 FPS, while FURION comfortably delivers 60 FPS. We note that the 60 FPS frame rate of FURION is not limited by our implementation, but by the 60Hz refresh rate of the display hardware on PIXEL.

Responsiveness. Following [31], we define app responsiveness as the latency or elapsed time from when the last pose or user action is received from the device until when the corresponding frame is sent to the display. We note the latency thus defined does not include the latency contributed by the input subsystem and the display hardware, which are difficult to measure and equally present when VR apps execute under any of the three schemes. We evaluate the app responsiveness under three user interaction scenarios: (1) *controller latency* for clicking the controller; (2) *rotation latency* for rotating the headset (orientation); and (3) *motion latency* for changing the position.

Figure 8 shows FURION achieves far better responsiveness than the other two systems. In particular, it achieves under 14ms controller latency, under 1ms rotation latency, and under 12ms motion latency for the three apps, respectively. In FURION, the rotation latency is much lower than the controller and motion latency because FURION can quickly generate a final frame for a given orientation by cropping the in-memory, already decoded panoramic frame.

Table 11: System overhead of VR apps upon FURION.

App	CPU Utilization (Pixel/6P)	GPU Utilization (Pixel/6P)	Average Bandwidth (Pixel/6P)
Viking	64% / 76%	37% / 63%	127 Mbps / 131 Mbps
Corridor	62% / 71%	34% / 61%	132 Mbps / 122 Mbps
Nature	65% / 73%	33% / 64%	130 Mbps / 128 Mbps

9.3 Scalability with app features

Next, we evaluate the scalability of different schemes in terms of different app features, in particular, in terms of the number of dynamic objects, which enhances the immersive experience of the VR apps.

We modify the three VR apps with an increasing number of dynamic objects in foreground interactions and measure the frame rate of each implementation. Figure 9 shows the result for Viking Village; results of the other two apps are similar and omitted due to the page limit. We see as the number of dynamic objects increases, the local rendering workload increases and as a result the FPS of the mobile version decreases. The FPS of the thin-client version does not change because adding more dynamic objects only increases the workload on the server. Finally, FURION can maintain high FPS when supporting up to 10 interactive dynamic objects.

9.4 Resource usage

We next evaluate the resource usage of FURION in supporting the three VR apps.

CPU/GPU usage. We first measure the CPU/GPU utilization together with the network usage in Table 11. We see FURION incurs up to 65% CPU utilization and 37% GPU utilization on the PIXEL phone in supporting the three high-quality VR apps with target low latency and 60 FPS.

Since Google labeled the PIXEL phone as VR-ready with its introduction [5], we were curious what new capability made the most difference, compared to a previous generation phone, Nexus 6P. We evaluated FURION on Nexus 6P and compared its resource usage with that on PIXEL. Table 11 shows that running the three apps on Nexus 6P incurs much higher CPU and GPU utilization, up to 76% for CPU and 64% for GPU, suggesting the VR-readiness of PIXEL mainly comes from the upgraded GPU (Table 3).

CPU usage and temperature over time. Today's high-end phones such as PIXEL have built-in temperature control to avoid phone overheating. For example, by default the thermal limit of PIXEL is 58 Celsius (from reading /system/etc/thermal-engine.conf on the phone). When the thermal limit is reached, *e.g.*, from long

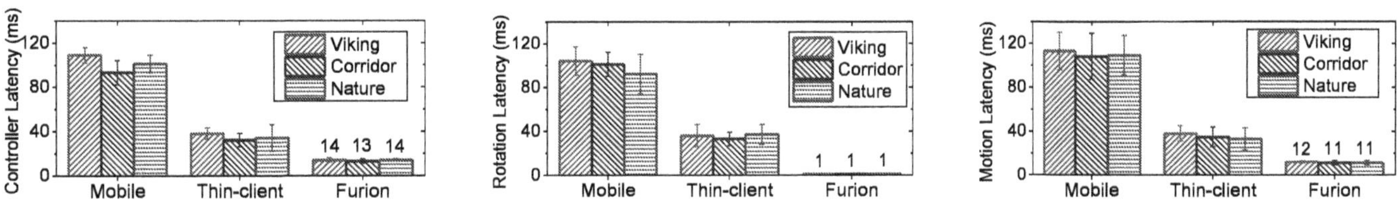

(a) Controller latency. (b) Rotation latency. (c) Motion latency.

Figure 8: Responsiveness of different VR implementations.

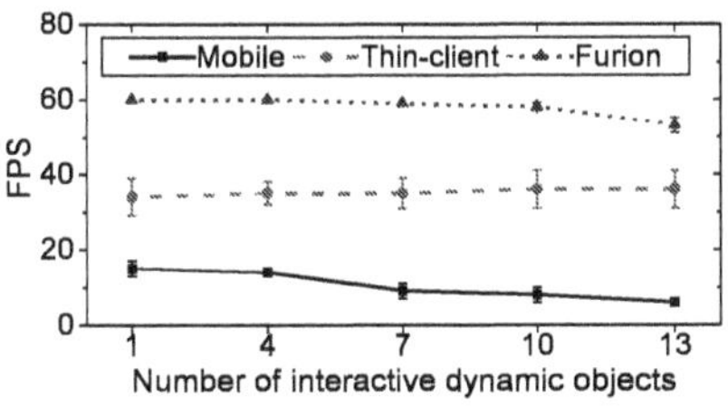

Figure 9: FPS as the number of interactive dynamic objects varies.

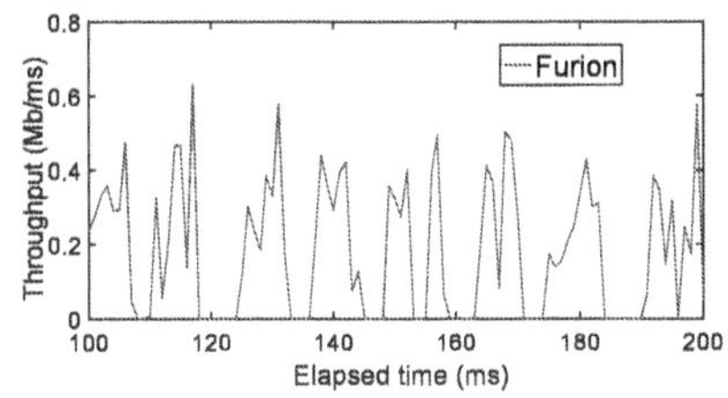

Figure 10: Bandwidth usage in each 20ms window.

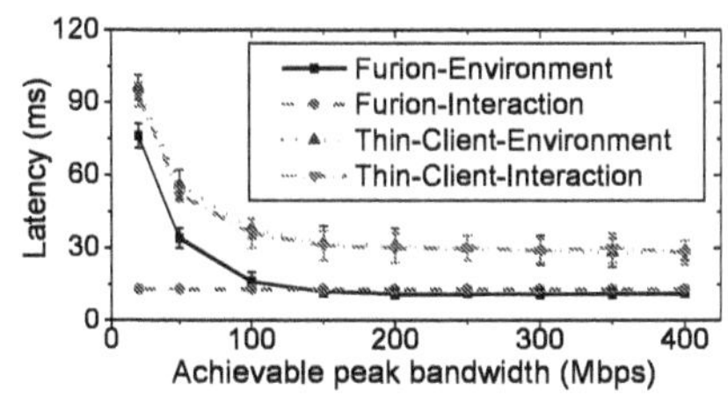

Figure 11: Rendering latency under bandwidth capping.

running, power-intensive apps, the power control manager will cap or reduce the CPU/GPU frequency to avoid overheating the phone.

Since VR apps present a new class of power-intensive apps, and in fact Google proposed explicit thermal requirement [20] that "your Daydream app must not hit the device's thermal limit during 30 minutes of usage", we measured the phone SoC temperature when running the three VR apps under Furion for 30 minutes. Figure 12(a)(b) shows during the 30-minute runs, the CPU frequency and utilization remain steady, and the SoC temperature increases gradually but stays under the thermal limit.

Power drain over time. We leverage the Google Battery Historian tool [3] to inspect the power drain of the Android device over time. Figure 12(c) shows that the power draw stays steady at 410 mA on average in running the three VR apps over the extended half-hour period. Given Pixel's battery capacity of 2770 mAh, at such a power level, the three VR apps can last for about 6 hours.

9.5 Robustness to network instability

Table 11 further shows that supporting the three VR apps in Furion requires on average 132 Mbps network throughput, well below the 400Mbps peak throughput supported by 802.11ac. Figure 10 shows this is because prefetching panoramic frames of adjacent positions in the virtual world can quickly complete in a short burst (about 8ms per Equation (4)) within each 20ms interval of moving between two adjacent positions. The throughput value in Figure 10 starts from 100ms to exclude the slow start stage.

In fact, the cooperative renderer design of Furion which turns on-demand fetching of frames from the server into prefetching pre-rendered frames, effectively moves fetching frames from the server outside the end-to-end delay path of rendering a new frame. As a result, prefetching pre-rendered panoramic frames just needs to finish within the 20ms window. This property suggests Furion can tolerate transient bandwidth fluctuations as long as the network provides 130Mbps bandwidth on average (in each window). To confirm this property, we used the tc tool to control the maximal available bandwidth on the AP and ran the three VR apps. Figure 11 shows under Furion the delay in rendering of interactions and in decoding environment stays constant when the average peak bandwidth is reduced from 400Mbps to 150Mbps.

10 DISCUSSIONS

We now discuss how Furion design can be extended to handle more complicated VR app features.

Handling drastic movement. In a VR system, the virtual world is discretized into grid points and Furion leverages the movement delay between adjacent points to prefetch future frames in time. As discussed in Section 6.2, the movement delay is about 20ms under a normal user movement. However, there can be cases where the user moves more quickly and the movement delay is too low to prefetch the adjacent panoramic frame in time. In practice, such drastic user movement implies there is no need to render frames at consecutive grid positions, and it can be handled by selective-prefetching, *i.e.*, prefetching frames from further grid points. For example, at moment t1 in Figure 4, if the user moves at twice the normal speed, we just need to prefetch the frames from 2 grid positions away.

Dynamic objects in background environment. For some VR apps, the background environment may contain several dynamic objects, *e.g.*, floating clouds in the sky, or flowing creeks in the mountain. These dynamic objects are typically small and have similar workloads as foreground interactions. Furion can support dynamic objects in the environment by rendering them on the local GPU and superimposing them on the rest background environment.

Multi-player support. Some latest VR apps such as vTime [25] and Altspace VR [1] contain social elements and enable multiple users playing in the same virtual environment, *e.g.*, chatting in the same office. A key feature of multi-player VR apps is that some foreground interactions are updated according to inputs (*e.g.*, pose or controller changes) from other players. In our future work, we plan to extend the split renderer of Furion to support multiple players by addressing the higher demand on network bandwidth and latency.

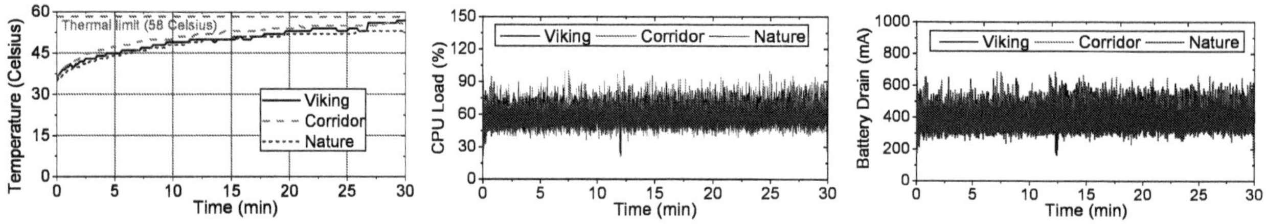

(a) Temperature of three VR apps.
(b) CPU utilization over time.
(c) Battery power.

Figure 12: Resource usage of Furion over time. During the experiment, the CPU frequency of all four cores is capped by the default CPU governor of Pixel at 1.44GHz. The thermal limit on Pixel is 58 Celsius.

Applicability to non-VR apps. Finally, the local-remote cooperative rendering architecture of Furion can be applied to non-VR mobile apps such as 3D games which similarly contain foreground interactions and continuously changing background environment to enhance their responsiveness and visual quality and reduce their battery drain.

11 RELATED WORK

We discuss closely related work in several areas.

Mobile virtual reality: Several recent work studied understanding and improving the performance on current VR systems. Chang *et al.* [32] experimentally quantified the timing and positioning accuracy of existing VR head-mounted hardware. To enable high-quality VR on mobile devices, Flashback [31] pre-renders all possible views for different positions and orientations and stores them on a local cache. At runtime, it fetches frames on-demand from the cache according to current orientation and position. Flashback has two limitations: (1) Since all frames are pre-rendered, it does not support interactions which update animation/behavior based on user actions; (2) Pre-caching all possible views locally incurs overwhelming storage overhead (*e.g.*, 50GB for one app) on the phone. More recently, MoVR [28, 29] tries to cut the cord in high-quality VR by using mmWave technology to enable multi-Gbps wireless communication between VR headsets and the server, but it relies on specialized hardware support not present in current VR headsets or smartphones. In early 2017, Qualcomm introduced the newest premium-tier mobile platform Snapdragon 835, together with a new virtual reality development kit (VRDK) [19] which is designed to meet the demanding requirements of mobile VR and expected to be available in Q2 2017. Such hardware enhancement complements our work.

Cloud offloading and cloud gaming: The mobile computing community has a long history of leveraging cloud offloading to supplement the capabilities of resource-constrained mobile handsets (*e.g.*, [35, 36, 40, 42, 47, 48]). However, these works focus on general computation workloads and cannot meet the strict latency requirement specific to VR systems. Similarly, several recent studies focus on real-time rendering/cloud gaming for mobile devices [37, 43, 52–56, 60]. Again, the latency requirement of VR systems (*e.g.*, under 25ms) is much more stringent than computer games (*e.g.*, 100-200ms [54]) due to the near-eye setting.

Graphics and video processing: The graphics and video community has also studied efficient rendering on resource-constrained devices. For example, Image-Based Rendering (IBR) [45, 51] is a well studied technology that renders new frames based on a previous image and extra information (*e.g.*, a new angle). More recently, the authors in [51] propose a new IBR algorithm to mask the latency of the rendering task while providing the client with coverage for filling disocclusion holes. However, IBR-like methods do not support well dynamic objects (*e.g.*, interactions that change due to user actions) which may lead to visual artifacts. Parallel codec for traditional video playback has been studied in recent years [30, 33, 34]. Furion makes a special optimization by modifying the codec scheme to support direct encoding/decoding. In addition, several previous studies leverage the viewpoint-adaptive mechanism [14, 38, 49, 50, 57], which reduces the resolution for the pixels outside the field of view (FOV) to cut down the bitrate of the stream. Similarly, foveated rendering leverages eye-tracking to cut down resolution outside the eye gaze [41, 58, 61]. These approaches do not perform well when the user quickly and randomly turns the headset and changes the FOV.

12 CONCLUSION

We presented a quantitative, performance-driven design study that shows (1) the QoE achievable for high-quality VR apps on today's mobile hardware and wireless networking is about 10X away from the acceptable QoE; (2) waiting for future mobile hardware or next-generation wireless networks (*e.g.*, 5G) is unlikely to help. Guided by the quantitative, performance-driven design study, we developed Furion, a VR framework that enables high-quality, immersive mobile VR on today's mobile devices and wireless networks. Furion employs a split renderer architecture running on both the phone and the server to exploit a key insight about the high-quality VR workload that foreground interactions and background environment have contrasting predictability and rendering workload. We implemented Furion on top of Unity and Google Daydream and our evaluation shows it can support high-quality VR apps on today's smartphones over WiFi, with 60 FPS and under 14ms, 1ms, and 12ms responsiveness to controller, rotation, and movement interactions, respectively.

13 ACKNOWLEDGEMENTS

We thank our shepherd, Robert LiKamWa, for helpful feedback that greatly improved our paper. We also thank the anonymous reviewers for their valuable comments. This project is supported by NSF CCF-1320764 and NSFC of China (No. 61422206).

REFERENCES

[1] Altspace vr. https://play.google.com/store/apps/details?id=com.altvr.AltspaceVR&hl=en.
[2] Android mediacodec. https://developer.android.com/reference/android/media/MediaCodec.html.
[3] Battery historian tool. https://github.com/google/battery-historian.
[4] Corridor. https://www.assetstore.unity3d.com/en/#!/content/33630.
[5] Daydream-ready smartphones. https://vr.google.com/daydream/phones/.
[6] ffmpeg. https://ffmpeg.org/.
[7] Gear vr. http://www.samsung.com/global/galaxy/gear-vr/.
[8] Google daydream. https://vr.google.com/daydream/.
[9] Htc vive. https://www.vive.com/us/.
[10] Lego. https://play.google.com/store/apps/details?id=com.lego.brickheadz.dreambuilder&hl=en.
[11] libx-vp9. https://trac.ffmpeg.org/wiki/Encode/VP9.
[12] mjpeg tool. http://mjpeg.sourceforge.net/.
[13] Nature. https://www.assetstore.unity3d.com/en/#!/content/52977.
[14] Next generation video encoding for 360 video. https://code.facebook.com/posts/1126354007399553/next%2Dgeneration%2Dvideo%2Dencoding%2Dtechniques%2Dfor%2D360%2Dvideo%2Dand%2Dvr/.
[15] Ngmn 5g white paper. https://www.ngmn.org/uploads/media/NGMN_5G_White_Paper_V1_0.pdf.
[16] Oculus rift. https://www3.oculus.com/en-us/rift/.
[17] Overlord. https://play.google.com/store/apps/details?id=com.otherside.underworldoverlord&hl=en.
[18] Polyrunner vr. https://play.google.com/store/apps/details?id=com.lucidsight.polyrunnervr&hl=en.
[19] Qualcomm snapdragon 835. https://www.qualcomm.com/news/releases/2017/02/23/qualcomm%2Dintroduces%2Dsnapdragon%2D835%2Dvirtual%2Dreality%2Ddevelopment%2Dkit.
[20] Thermal requirement. https://developers.google.com/vr/distribute/daydream/performance-requirements.
[21] Unity 3d. https://unity3d.com.
[22] Viking village. https://www.assetstore.unity3d.com/en/#!/content/29140.
[23] Vp9. https://www.webmproject.org/vp9/.
[24] Vr and augmented reality will soon be worth $150 billion. here are the major players. https://www.fastcompany.com/3052209/tech-forecast/vr%2Dand%2Daugmented%2Dreality%2Dwill%2Dsoon%2Dbe%2Dworth%2D150%2Dbillion%2Dhere%2Dare%2Dthe%2Dmajor%2Dpla.
[25] vtime. https://play.google.com/store/apps/details?id=net.vtime.cardboard&hl=en.
[26] What vr could, should, and almost certainly will be within two years. http://media.steampowered.com/apps/abrashblog/Abrash%20Dev%20Days%202014.pdf.
[27] x264library. http://www.videolan.org/developers/x264.html.
[28] O. Abari, D. Bharadia, A. Duffield, and D. Katabi. Cutting the cord in virtual reality. In *Proceedings of the 15th ACM Workshop on Hot Topics in Networks*, pages 162–168. ACM, 2016.
[29] O. Abari, D. Bharadia, A. Duffield, and D. Katabi. Enabling high-quality untethered virtual reality. In *NSDI*, pages 531–544. USENIX, 2017.
[30] M. Alvarez-Mesa, C. C. Chi, B. Juurlink, V. George, and T. Schierl. Parallel video decoding in the emerging hevc standard. In *Acoustics, Speech and Signal Processing, 2012 IEEE International Conference on*, pages 1545–1548. IEEE, 2012.
[31] K. Boos, D. Chu, and E. Cuervo. Flashback: Immersive virtual reality on mobile devices via rendering memoization. In *Proceedings of the 14th Annual International Conference on Mobile Systems, Applications, and Services*, pages 291–304. ACM, 2016.
[32] C.-M. Chang, C.-H. Hsu, C.-F. Hsu, and K.-T. Chen. Performance measurements of virtual reality systems: Quantifying the timing and positioning accuracy. In *Proceedings of the 2016 ACM on Multimedia Conference*, pages 655–659. ACM, 2016.
[33] C. C. Chi, M. Alvarez-Mesa, B. Juurlink, G. Clare, F. Henry, S. Pateux, and T. Schierl. Parallel scalability and efficiency of hevc parallelization approaches. *IEEE Transactions on Circuits and Systems for Video Technology*, 22(12):1827–1838, 2012.
[34] J. Chong, N. Satish, B. Catanzaro, K. Ravindran, and K. Keutzer. Efficient parallelization of h. 264 decoding with macro block level scheduling. In *Multimedia and Expo, 2007 IEEE International Conference on*, pages 1874–1877. IEEE, 2007.
[35] B.-G. Chun, S. Ihm, P. Maniatis, M. Naik, and A. Patti. Clonecloud: elastic execution between mobile device and cloud. In *Proceedings of the sixth conference on Computer systems*, pages 301–314. ACM, 2011.
[36] E. Cuervo, A. Balasubramanian, D.-k. Cho, A. Wolman, S. Saroiu, R. Chandra, and P. Bahl. Maui: making smartphones last longer with code offload. In *Proceedings of the 8th international conference on Mobile systems, applications, and services*, pages 49–62. ACM, 2010.
[37] E. Cuervo, A. Wolman, L. P. Cox, K. Lebeck, A. Razeen, S. Saroiu, and M. Musuvathi. Kahawai: High-quality mobile gaming using gpu offload. In *Proceedings of the 13th Annual International Conference on Mobile Systems, Applications, and Services*, pages 121–135. ACM, 2015.
[38] V. R. Gaddam, M. Riegler, R. Eg, C. Griwodz, and P. Halvorsen. Tiling in interactive panoramic video: Approaches and evaluation. *IEEE Transactions on Multimedia*, 18(9):1819–1831, 2016.
[39] A. Garcia-Saavedra, P. Serrano, A. Banchs, and G. Bianchi. Energy consumption anatomy of 802.11 devices and its implication on modeling and design. In *Proceedings of the 8th international conference on Emerging networking experiments and technologies*, pages 169–180. ACM, 2012.
[40] M. S. Gordon, D. A. Jamshidi, S. Mahlke, Z. M. Mao, and X. Chen. Comet: code offload by migrating execution transparently. In *USENIX Symposium on Operating Systems Design and Implementation*, pages 93–106, 2012.
[41] B. Guenter, M. Finch, S. Drucker, D. Tan, and J. Snyder. Foveated 3d graphics. *ACM Transactions on Graphics*, 31(6):164, 2012.
[42] K. Ha, Z. Chen, W. Hu, W. Richter, P. Pillai, and M. Satyanarayanan. Towards wearable cognitive assistance. In *Proceedings of the 12th annual international conference on Mobile systems, applications, and services*, pages 68–81. ACM, 2014.
[43] K. Lee, D. Chu, E. Cuervo, J. Kopf, Y. Degtyarev, S. Grizan, A. Wolman, and J. Flinn. Outatime: Using speculation to enable low-latency continuous interaction for mobile cloud gaming. In *Proceedings of the 13th Annual International Conference on Mobile Systems, Applications, and Services*, pages 151–165. ACM, 2015.
[44] W. Li, D. Wu, R. K. Chang, and R. K. Mok. Demystifying and puncturing the inflated delay in smartphone-based wifi network measurement. In *Proceedings of the 12th International on Conference on emerging Networking EXperiments and Technologies*, pages 497–504. ACM, 2016.
[45] W. R. Mark, L. McMillan, and G. Bishop. Post-rendering 3d warping. In *Proceedings of the 1997 symposium on Interactive 3D graphics*, pages 7–ff. ACM, 1997.
[46] A. Mittal, A. K. Moorthy, and A. C. Bovik. No-reference image quality assessment in the spatial domain. *IEEE Transactions on Image Processing*, 21(12):4695–4708, 2012.
[47] D. Narayanan and M. Satyanarayanan. Predictive resource management for wearable computing. In *Proceedings of the 1st international conference on Mobile systems, applications and services*, pages 113–128. ACM, 2003.
[48] B. D. Noble, M. Satyanarayanan, D. Narayanan, J. E. Tilton, J. Flinn, and K. R. Walker. Agile application-aware adaptation for mobility. In *Proc. of ACM Symposium on Operating System Principles*, 1997.
[49] D. Ochi, Y. Kunita, K. Fujii, A. Kojima, S. Iwaki, and J. Hirose. Hmd viewing spherical video streaming system. In *Proceedings of the 22nd ACM international conference on Multimedia*, pages 763–764. ACM, 2014.
[50] F. Qian, L. Ji, B. Han, and V. Gopalakrishnan. Optimizing 360 video delivery over cellular networks. In *Proceedings of the 5th Workshop on All Things Cellular: Operations, Applications and Challenges*, pages 1–6. ACM, 2016.
[51] B. Reinert, J. Kopf, T. Ritschel, E. Cuervo, D. Chu, and H.-P. Seidel. Proxy-guided image-based rendering for mobile devices. *Computer Graphics Forum*, 35(7):353–362, 2016.
[52] R. Shea, D. Fu, and J. Liu. Rhizome: Utilizing the public cloud to provide 3d gaming infrastructure. In *Proceedings of the 6th ACM Multimedia Systems Conference*, pages 97–100. ACM, 2015.
[53] R. Shea and J. Liu. On gpu pass-through performance for cloud gaming: Experiments and analysis. In *Proceedings of Annual Workshop on Network and Systems Support for Games*, pages 1–6. IEEE Press, 2013.
[54] R. Shea, J. Liu, E. C.-H. Ngai, and Y. Cui. Cloud gaming: architecture and performance. *IEEE Network*, 27(4):16–21, 2013.
[55] S. Shi and C.-H. Hsu. A survey of interactive remote rendering systems. *ACM Computing Surveys*, 47(4):57, 2015.
[56] S. Shi, C.-H. Hsu, K. Nahrstedt, and R. Campbell. Using graphics rendering contexts to enhance the real-time video coding for mobile cloud gaming. In *Proceedings of the 19th ACM international conference on Multimedia*, pages 103–112. ACM, 2011.
[57] K. K. Sreedhar, A. Aminlou, M. M. Hannuksela, and M. Gabbouj. Viewport-adaptive encoding and streaming of 360-degree video for virtual reality applications. In *International Symposium on Multimedia*, pages 583–586. IEEE, 2016.
[58] N. T. Swafford, J. A. Iglesias-Guitian, C. Koniaris, B. Moon, D. Cosker, and K. Mitchell. User, metric, and computational evaluation of foveated rendering methods. In *Proceedings of the ACM Symposium on Applied Perception*, pages 7–14. ACM, 2016.
[59] Z. Wang, A. C. Bovik, H. R. Sheikh, and E. P. Simoncelli. Image quality assessment: from error visibility to structural similarity. *IEEE transactions on image processing*, 13(4):600–612, 2004.
[60] J. Wu, C. Yuen, N.-M. Cheung, J. Chen, and C. W. Chen. Enabling adaptive high-frame-rate video streaming in mobile cloud gaming applications. *IEEE Transactions on Circuits and Systems for Video Technology*, 25(12):1988–2001, 2015.
[61] L. Zhang, X.-Y. Li, W. Huang, K. Liu, S. Zong, X. Jian, P. Feng, T. Jung, and Y. Liu. It starts with igaze: Visual attention driven networking with smart glasses. In *Proceedings of the 20th annual international conference on Mobile computing and networking*, pages 91–102. ACM, 2014.

RAVEN : Perception-aware Optimization of Power Consumption for Mobile Games

Chanyou Hwang*
chanyou@nclab.kaist.ac.kr
School of Computing - KAIST

Saumay Pushp*
saumay@nclab.kaist.ac.kr
School of Computing - KAIST

Changyoung Koh
changyoung@nclab.kaist.ac.kr
School of Computing - KAIST

Jungpil Yoon
jdsp@nclab.kaist.ac.kr
School of Computing - KAIST

Yunxin Liu
yunxin.liu@microsoft.com
Microsoft Research

Seungpyo Choi
spchoi@nclab.kaist.ac.kr
School of Computing - KAIST

Junehwa Song
junesong@nclab.kaist.ac.kr
School of Computing - KAIST

ABSTRACT

High-end mobile GPUs are now becoming an integral part of mobile devices. However, a mobile GPU constitutes a major portion of power consumption on the devices, and mobile games top as the most popular class of graphics applications. This paper presents the design and implementation of RAVEN, a novel, on-the-fly frame rate scaling system for mobile gaming applications. RAVEN utilizes human visual perception of graphics change to opportunistically achieve power saving without degrading user experiences. The system develops a light-weight frame comparison technique to measure and predict perception-aware frame similarity. It also builds a low resolution virtual display which clones the device screen for performing similarity measurement at a low-power cost. It is able to work on an existing commercial smartphone and support applications from app stores without any modifications. It has been implemented on Nexus 5X, and its performance has been measured with 13 games. The system effectively reduces the overall power consumption of mobile devices while maintaining satisfactory user experiences. The power consumption is reduced by 21.78% on average and up to 34.74%.

CCS CONCEPTS

• **Human-centered computing** → *Ubiquitous and mobile computing systems and tools*; • **Computing methodologies** → *Perception*;

KEYWORDS

Perception-aware processing; Energy-efficient processing; Frame-rate scaling; Mobile games; Experiments; Measurement; Mobile systems

*Co-primary authors, order chosen alphabetically.

MobiCom '17, October 16-20, 2017, Snowbird, UT, USA.

ACM ISBN 978-1-4503-4916-1/17/10...$15.00
https://doi.org/.1145/3117811.3117841

1 INTRODUCTION

Over the past three years, the processing power of mobile GPUs has increased more than double [5][6]. In response, mobile game application developers have begun to capitalize on the modern GPU's processing power to make their game graphics look crispier and more appealing. However, those visually appealing mobile games come at a high energy cost. Each high-resolution frame consumes a large amount of system resources, especially the GPU computation, and results in high system power consumption.

Mobile games top as the most popular class of graphics applications (apps) on smartphones [18] and are frequently the major sources of energy drain. Depending upon the amount of graphics contents inside a game app, the GPU power consumption increases almost linearly. However, few power management studies have been performed for mobile games [23]. In this paper, we explore the potential to optimally use limited computing resources and energy by delving into the computation process from the perspective of human perception, i.e., game player's perception in this case. We specifically look into the rendering process of gaming apps considering perceptual sensitivity of human, and re-organize the process, emphasizing sensitive moments while de-emphasizing the rest.

Upon the above idea, we present RAVEN[1], a novel system for scaling the rate of rendering frames which leverages human visual perception. RAVEN introduces perception-aware scaling of frame-rendering rates (PAS) while a user is engaged in a game-play. In detail, PAS reduces an application's rate of rendering game frames whenever succeeding frames are predicted to be perceptually similar enough. For this, we set a side channel to track the rendered frame sequences which can tailor user's perception with graphics changes in a game-play. In this way, RAVEN opportunistically reduces power consumption of a GPU. Existing methods to measure user's perception of visual changes such as structural similarity (SSIM) [33] are computationally expensive and not adequate for a system to maintain quality user experiences during game-play. We leverage **YUV** color space [12] to develop a simple, but effective way to track user's perception on-the-fly.

There have been efforts to reduce battery consumption in playing games or other apps on mobile systems. User configuration-based

[1] RAVEN is a DC comics character, from whom we would like to signify the ability to 'sense and alter'.

approaches have been adopted in many systems, e.g., Samsung-Game-Tuner [9]. They allow users to pre-set manually parameters related to display resolutions or frame rates. They could lead to energy savings; however, it is difficult to match consistently users' desires for quality experiences which potentially require different configurations depending on game contents such as scene changes or graphics changes during plays. Approaches for user interaction-based rate control have also been attempted [27][34]. They make systems respond with high resolutions or frame rates upon user interactions assuming that users pay higher attention at those moments. However, moments of high visual attention do not always overlap with those of user interactions. In addition, user interactions frequently come as responses to game flows intended in a game design. To provide a truly immersive game-play and energy saving, the system needs to consider visual fidelity, i.e., the game-play should be seamless to the eyes of a user.

There are several challenges in building the RAVEN system. First, it is important to measure the perceptual similarity efficiently. As mentioned, inferring the perceptual similarity with existing methods incur high computational cost. The system should be able to approximate such computation-intensive methods at a very low cost. Second, while saving energy, degradation of user experiences caused by the system should be minimal. Third, mobile gaming apps and GPU drivers are closed source. This asks for building a system that is transparent to the apps, and avoids low-level system optimization.

To overcome the above challenges, we have developed an energy-efficient method to measure perceptual similarity exploiting the susceptibility of human eyes to color difference. The proposed method leverages the difference in the luminance components (in **YUV** color space) between frames. We extensively evaluated the method by comparing it with the well-known SSIM method under various settings, and show that the proposed luminance-based method can efficiently measure perceptual similarity with low computational costs. Also, we build in the RAVEN system a virtual display, cloned from the main screen of the device but with a much lower resolution. The system reads the graphical contents of the small virtual display for the similarity measurement with low computational and energy overhead. In addition, RAVEN realizes the idea of perception-aware rate scaling by interfering and impeding the rendering loop of a game app. For frames that are perceptually similar to the current frame, the loop skips its operation, i.e., rendering of those frames. Instead, a delay for the amount of corresponding frames' periods, is inserted to the loop. Afterwards, it jumps to the next frame to be rendered. In this way, the rate of frame rendering is effectively scaled. The RAVEN system is designed and implemented by customizing an Android framework as Android's system services, which makes itself transparent to apps and avoids the complication of accessing closed source.

We have implemented the RAVEN system on a Nexus 5X smartphone. We conduct comprehensive experiments and a user study to evaluate our implementation with 13 real mobile games. Experimental results show that all 13 games can run successfully with per-frame, real-time perception-aware scaling of frame rendering rates. The energy per game session can be reduced by 21.78% in average and up to 34.74% while maintaining quality user experiences. To the best of our knowledge, RAVEN is the first system designed and implemented to achieve rate scaling and energy savings based on perceptual similarity for mobile games. The main contributions of this paper are:

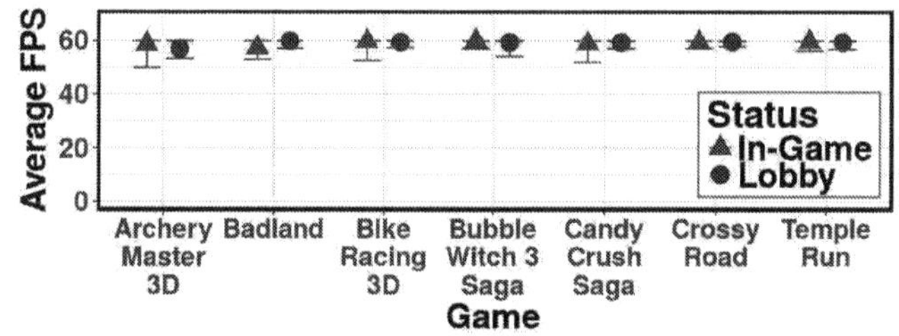

Figure 1: Frame rates in a game-play and while standing in a game lobby.

- We present a novel rate-scaling technique for rendering app frames based on the human visual perception to game's graphics to reduce energy consumption on-the-fly.
- We explore and develop a novel, energy-efficient perceptual similarity measurement method leveraging the differences in luminance values between frames.
- We present the design and implementation of the RAVEN system with its application transparency.
- We adopt a user-tunable approach which provides an on-demand access to tune power drain and user experience.
- We conduct experiments and a user study to confirm the effectiveness of our system for quality user experience and power saving.

The rest of this paper is organized as follows. Section 2 motivates the need of RAVEN and set our goals. It also introduces the graphics processing flow of Android. Section 3 gives an overview of RAVEN's system architecture and defines its key components. Section 4 and Section 5 present how to perform frame comparison for regulating the applications' rates of rendering frames, and our rationale behind building a low-power virtual display. Section 6 describes some details on RAVEN's implementation and Section 7 reports the evaluation results. Section 8 surveys the related work and Section 9 discusses the limitations of our system, while Section 10 concludes the paper.

2 MOTIVATION AND BACKGROUND

Motivation. A high frame rate is beneficial if it provides a good user experience. However, we have observed that a high frame rate may not always be necessary in mobile games. We have played a set of mobile games (see Figure 1) and measured their frame rates. We provide description on the types of the games used in our study in Section 7. We have intercepted `eglSwapBuffer()` function in OpenGL ES/EGL [13] which gives accurate numbers on how fast games generate new frames. In a game-play, the game may enter different states, depending on user interactions and game stages. We focus on two cases: "In-Game" where we play a game actively and graphics contents on the screen change quickly; and "Lobby" where a game is in a session-transition stage or shows setting menus and thus we perceive few or zero changes on the screen.

Figure 1 presents the results. It shows that no matter the states of the games, they always ran at a high frame rate of 60 FPS. Even in the

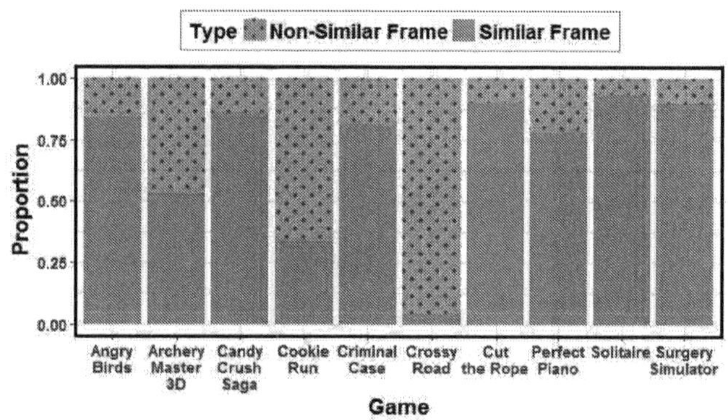

Figure 2: Proportions of similar and non-similar adjacent frames in different gaming apps.

"Lobby" case where the screen showed relatively-static contents, they still kept generating 60 new frames per second. The same observation was also reported in a previous study [34].

We have further studied similarity between consecutive frames in playing games. We have employed SSIM [33] to calculate the similarity between frames. A SSIM index is a number between 0 and 1, and a value higher than 0.97 is considered as a strong level of similarity in mobile games [22]. We have chosen 0.975 as the threshold to decide whether two frames are similar or not. Figure 2 shows how many frames are similar in playing the selected games. On average, we have recorded 15,035 frames for each game. That is, the average game-play time was 4.2 minutes. Up to 93.5% of the total frames generated by the games are indeed very similar. This strong similarity existed not only for "Lobby" frames but also "In-Game" frames.

The observations show that 1) the game apps maintain high frame rates irrespective of their game states, and 2) large portions of consecutive frames of the game apps show strong similarity. These findings give an opportunity to save energy without compromising user experiences by regulating redundant frame renderings. Specifically, when consecutive frames are highly similar, we may bypass rendering the frames and reduce the power consumption. Thanks to strong frame similarity, the user experiences will not be compromised much. These findings motivate us to seek for a system to optimize power consumption of mobile games using perception-aware frame rate scaling.

Goals. We set the following goals and requirements in designing a target system: 1) Automatically change the rates of rendering application frames on-the-fly without requiring any user efforts; 2) Be able to run on commercial smartphones without requiring any special hardware or re-building a device driver; 3) Support legacy apps without requiring any app-side modifications; 4) Effectively achieve significant power savings.

2.1 Graphics Processing on Android

We briefly describe some background information on Android graphics operations and OpenGL ES/EGL [13] related to our design. Android applications use OpenGL ES API [17] to leverage GPU acceleration for rendering their graphics contents and to draw their

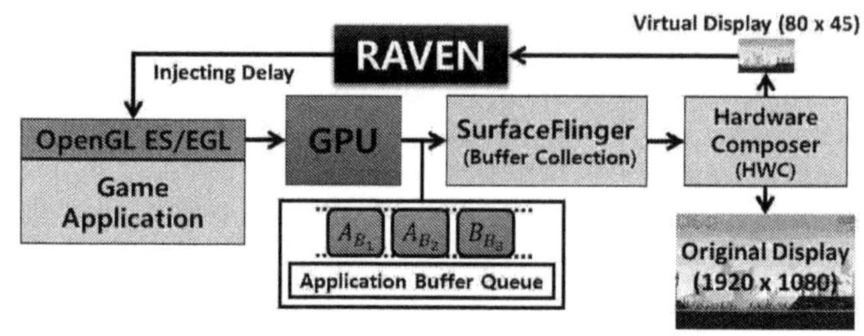

Figure 3: Flow of graphics processing on a Nexus 5X running Android 6.0.1. OpenGL ES/EGL is paddled by RAVEN, and the frame-rendering process of GPU is regulated.

User Interface (UI) objects. Rendered results are stored in a **BufferQueue**[3], which consists of graphics buffers. Each app has its own, separate **BufferQueue**. The Android system uses a system service called **SurfaceFlinger**[10] to coordinate all rendered graphics contents of foreground apps and the Android UI subsystem. On a smartphone, the display driver typically refreshes the screen at 60 Hz and generates a **VSYNC** (Vertical Synchronization) signal for each frame period. Upon receiving a **VSYNC** signal, **SurfaceFlinger** collects the graphics buffers (from multiple apps) and sends them to **Hardware Composer**. Hardware Composer composes the final graphics contents which will be displayed on a device screen. A detailed flow of Android graphics processing is shown in Figure 3.

3 SYSTEM OVERVIEW

The idea of RAVEN can be described in high level with its major components and their interactions. The system consists of three major components which collectively perform scaling the rates of game-frame rendering (Figure 4): **FrameDiff Tracker** (F-Tracker), **Rate Regulator** (R-Regulator), and **Rate Injector** (R-Injector). The system works in a pipelined fashion. First, F-Tracker measures perceptual similarity between two recent frames at a low energy cost. Then, R-Regulator predicts the level of similarity between the current and the next frame(s). If the next frames are similar to the current one, it notifies R-Injector to limit frame-rendering rates by injecting some delay in a rendering loop and skip graphics processing for unnecessary frame(s). Presently, RAVEN is able to skip up-to the maximum of three frames, and thus, inflict frame-rate drop down to 15 FPS. The continuous regulation of the rates results in opportunistic energy savings. Figures 5 and 7 show three different system states of current implementation, i.e., No-skipping, 1-Skipping, and 3-Skipping states, and their transitions corresponding to different rates. Note that the system is not limited to the above and could be generalized to include other skipping states.

F-Tracker measures perceptual similarity between frames on-the-fly. To compute the perceptual similarity efficiently, the system takes a twofold strategy. First, RAVEN leverages a light-weight, low-resolution virtual display supported by Android system. Constructing a virtual display is lighter weighted than reading a display frame buffer as the latter involves a higher resolution (equivalent to the native resolution of the screen). Second, to measure perceptual similarity between frames, RAVEN utilizes an approximation of SSIM based on the **Y**(luminance) component in the **YUV** color space. SSIM is a well-known index to measure perceptual similarity, but computationally expensive and hard to compute for every

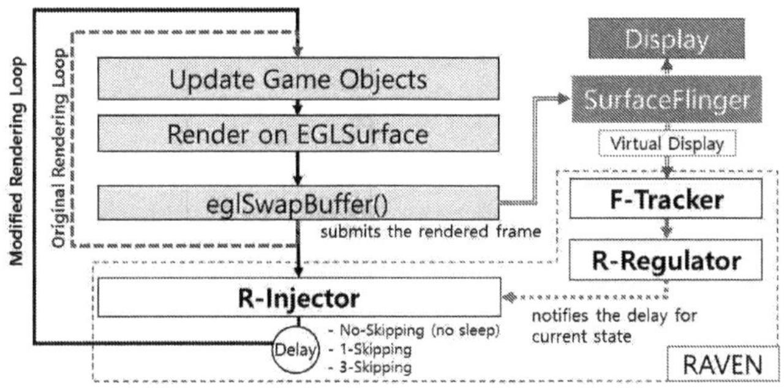

Figure 4: Modified rendering loop for delay injection and rate scaling. White-colored blocks are RAVEN's components.

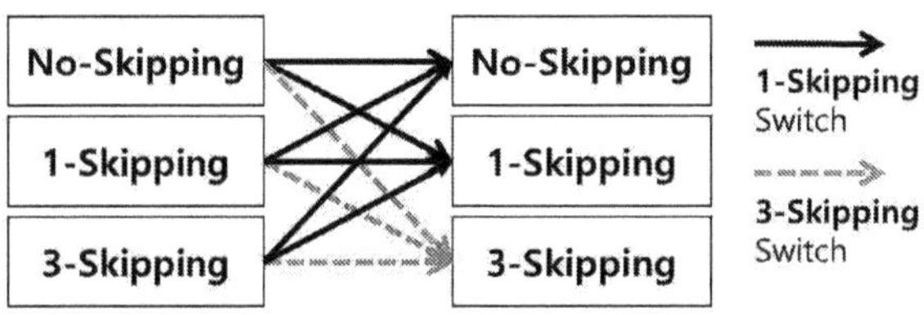

Figure 5: Different system states and their transitions in RAVEN: 1-Skipping skips a frame and results in 30 FPS, and 3-Skipping does three and results in 15 FPS.

frame at 60 FPS. In Section 4.1, we show the design rationale and the performance of our approximation method.

The system forces apps to skip perceptually similar frames by applying a proper frame rendering rate. Consider the following three frames (Section 4): the current frame (f_N), the frame which is expected to arrive after 16.7ms (f_{N+1}) , and the one, expected after 50ms (f_{N+3}). R-Regulator predicts the similarity scores of (f_N, f_{N+1}) and (f_N, f_{N+3}), and compares them with thresholds τ_1 and τ_3 (used as scaling factors), respectively. Each threshold stands for the minimum required similarity level for skipping f_{N+1} or f_{N+1}~f_{N+3}. If the predicted scores exceed their threshold values, the system applies the corresponding rate scaling by skipping the frames.

For rate scaling, RAVEN interferes and modifies the rendering loop of a gaming app (see Figure 4). Upon skipping decision of some frames, it inserts into the loop a delay for the duration of the corresponding frames' periods and have the system sleep for the duration without performing the rendering operations. The loop awakens after the delay and jumps to the next frame to render. This ensures the rate of frame rendering to be effectively scaled.

RAVEN is designed and implemented by customizing an Android framework, i.e., `FrameDiff Tracker` and `Rate Regulator` as Android's system services as well as `R-Injector` by adjusting the system function, `eglSwapBuffer`. The rendering loop in a mobile game runs in a separate thread from the main thread of the game. The operating system ensures that the rendering loop processes each frame to attain the maximum frame rate of 60 FPS. The RAVEN system successfully hooks into the rendering loop as above by customizing an Android framework, more specifically `eglSwap-Buffer()` function is called in the rendering loop and swaps the graphical content inside `EGLSurface`'s buffer (an off-screen buffer

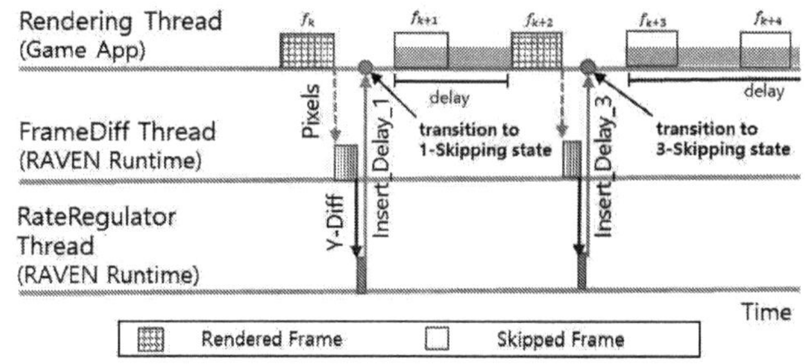

Figure 6: Flow of operations at a thread level.

which stores SurfaceView, SurfaceTexture etc. of an app). We modify the `eglSwapBuffer()` function in Android's EGL API and inject delay in this function through `R-Injector`. Thereafter, the operation of the loop is regulated with the inserted delay, and enforces the desired frame rate.

At the thread level, three threads play important roles in the operation of RAVEN: game app's rendering thread, RAVEN's `FrameDiff Tracker` thread, and `Rate Regulator` thread. Figure 6 presents how these threads communicate with each other to work together. At runtime, the rendering thread generates the pixels of the current frame. The `FrameDiff` thread reads the down-scaled pixels through a virtual display in a synchronous way, and compares **Y**−values of consecutive frames and sends the result to the `Rate Regulator` thread. Finally, the `Rate Regulator` thread calculates the appropriate delay to adjust the frame rendering rates, and then send the delay value to the rendering thread. The successful implementation of RAVEN based on the customization of an Android framework as above leads the system to be transparent to apps, enabling it to effectively support commercial gaming apps from app stores without any modifications.

4 PERCEPTUAL SIMILARITY AND REGULATION OF FRAME RENDERING RATES

The idea of regulating rendering rates without degrading user experiences is to skip rendering frames whenever adjacent frames are perceptually similar. However, without actually rendering a frame, we do not know how similar it is with the previous one, and thus, cannot decide whether to render it or not. Therefore, RAVEN compares the recently rendered frames, measures their perceptual similarity, and uses the result to decide whether to skip future one(s). Figure 7 depicts the prediction scheme as well as the rendering process on a sequence of frames.

The discussion in this section focuses on the case of developing two different skipping states capitalizing on four frames; however, the idea of perception-aware optimization (or rate scaling) could easily be generalized in diverse ways. Importantly, the similarity among consecutive frames is prevalent, and there is a broad spectrum of potential to utilize such similarity. Particularly, it would be feasible to develop many different levels of frame skipping transitions and rate regulations.

Consider the four frames, f_{N-k}, f_N, f_{N+1}, and f_{N+3}, where f_{N-k} is the previously rendered frame, f_N is the currently rendered one, and f_{N+1} and f_{N+3} are the future frames to be rendered.

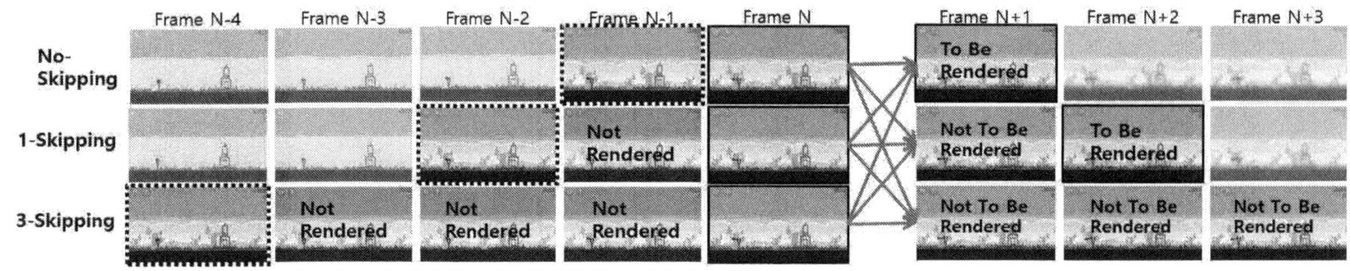

Figure 7: Process of rendering a sequence of frames in RAVEN (Best viewed in color).

Without RAVEN, these frames will be sequentially rendered, however, with RAVEN, the system first predicts the perceptual similarity scores of the future frames, i.e., f_{N+1} and f_{N+3} from those of the previously rendered ones. If the result of prediction for f_{N+1} is sufficiently similar to f_N, the system skips the rendering of f_{N+1}. If f_{N+3} is also predicted to be similar, the system skips f_{N+1}, f_{N+2}, and f_{N+3}. The user-perceived experience is maintained as if the frame rate is still 60 FPS, even though the system has reduced the rates to 30 FPS or 15 FPS.

4.1 Building a Perceptual Similarity Score

To build a perceptual similarity score for frame comparison, we leverage ***Y–Difference*** (or ***Y–Diff***). **Y**–Diff is the difference in **Y**(luminance) values of two images in the **YUV** color space. It takes into account the human perception associated with perceiving brightness as human vision is sensitive to brightness changes. In the human visual system, a majority of visual information is conveyed by patterns of contrasts from its brightness changes[35]. Furthermore, the luminance is a major input for the human perception of motion[30]. Since people perceive a sequence of graphics changes as a motion, consecutive images are perceptually similar if people do not recognize any motions from the image frames. From this perspective, **Y**–Diff could be suitable for measuring perceptual similarity. Also, as we discuss later in Sections 4.2 and 5, **Y**–Diff is a good, energy-efficient approximation of SSIM.

Our primary interest in using **Y**–Diff is on its low overhead. Its computation requires $O(N)$ comparisons (N is the number of pixels) as well as a single matrix multiplication to transform a color space, from **RGB** to **YUV**. The overhead is low enough to compute it for every frame while matching the rate of 60 FPS. SSIM requires a relatively heavy computational cost. Regarding the limited computing resource of mobile devices, computing SSIM for every frame is impractical.

Why not grid-based comparison with RGB? A straightforward approach in measuring graphics difference between image frames would be to compare them in RGB space. However, as shown in Figure 8, when it comes to measuring structural similarities, SSIM shows a linear relationship with **Y**–Diffs while not with RGB distances.

Why not SSIM scores on a low-resolution virtual display of RAVEN? Computing SSIM indices of consecutive frames on a mobile environment is expensive from the view of both computation and energy costs. We measured the cost of calculating SSIM indices for every pair of frames on a Nexus 5X smartphone. Comparing frames with a low resolution of 192×108 pixels continuously took power drain of 332mW, and computation time of 87ms. This result shows that we could only calculate SSIM indices of up to 10 frames per second on single-thread settings, and the extra power consumption makes it impractical to save power.

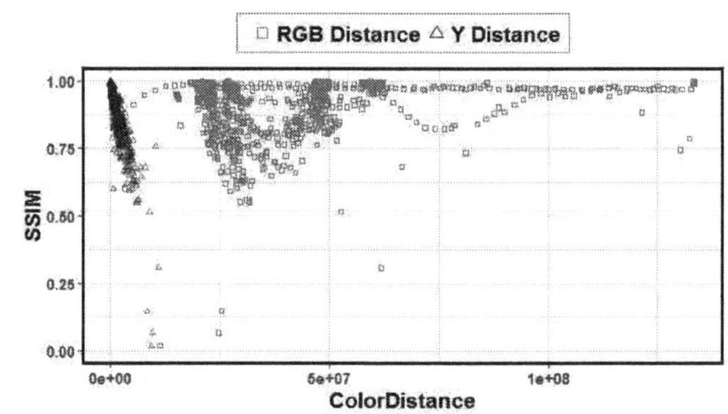

Figure 8: Comparison of RGB distances and Y distance with respect to SSIM.

Would it be reasonable to focus on luminance component? Chrominance components (U and V) may show dramatic changes while luminance does not change significantly. In such cases, the system's performance would get affected if only **Y**–Diff is used. To see if such cases occur frequently, we analyzed the videos recorded while playing Cookie Run and extracted **Y**–Diff, **U**–Diff, and **V**–Diff of consecutive frames. We observed that for the pairs of frames with small **Y**–Diff values (within the low 10%), 99.95% of them had also small **U**–Diff and 99.9%, small **V**–Diff values (and belonged to the low 20%). From the observation, it is not highly likely that abrupt changes occur in chrominance values when luminance show gradual changes. Therefore, it would be reasonable to focus on luminance in estimating perceptual similarity for energy-efficient processing.

*4.1.1 Using **Y**–Diff for perceptual similarity.*

We look into the performance of the approximation by **Y**–Diff in comparison to SSIM. For this, we calculate the correlation between the two.

Performing a fair comparison between **Y**–Diff and SSIM is difficult in the case of gaming apps. Game-plays are not reproducible because of their non-deterministic nature. Therefore, we take a record and replay based approach. We first recorded the screen using a screen recording application. Then, we used the OpenCV

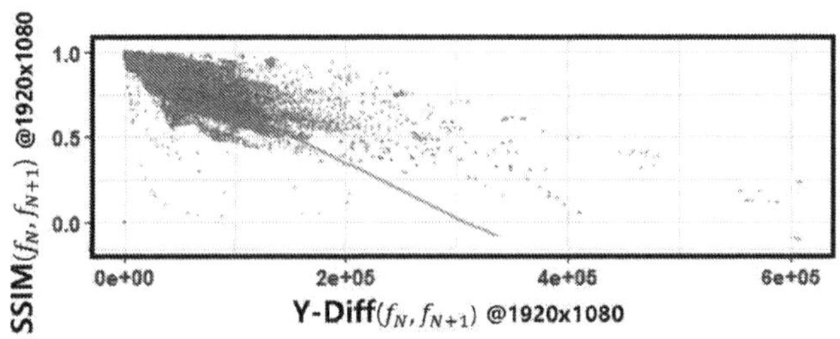

Figure 9: Correlation between Y–Diff and SSIM (Best viewed in color).

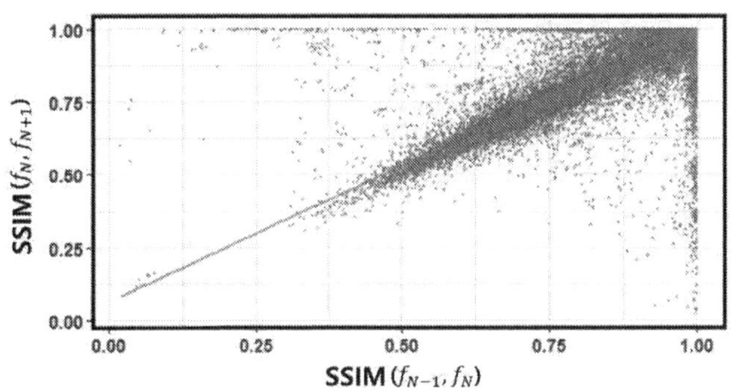

Figure 10: (Best viewed in color) Correlation between SSIM(f_{N-1}, f_N) and SSIM(f_N, f_{N+1}) (Pearson's correlation coefficient: 0.93). The correlation between SSIM(f_{N-1}, f_N) and SSIM(f_N, f_{N+3}) has also been explored (Pearson's correlation coefficient: 0.90), but the graph is omitted to save space.

library [8], and extracted each frame of a game-play. Thereafter, we iteratively calculated the **Y–Diff** and SSIM values for every frame f_N with respect to its previous four frames. In total, we analyzed 16 recorded plays of 13 games.

Figure 9 shows the relation between SSIM and **Y–Diff** values. Each color in the figure represents a game app. SSIM and **Y–Diff** values are strongly correlated and shows a linear relationship (Pearson's correlation coefficient of -0.926). We thus approximate SSIM with **Y–Diff** by linear regression. We denote the approximation as *Estimated Perceptual Similarity (EPS)*.

4.2 Estimating Frame Rendering Rates

Predicting perceptual similarity: To make decisions on whether to skip a future frame(s), we first look into the perceptual similarity of the current frame with the previously rendered one, and then predict the similarity with future one(s) to be rendered.

Figure 10 shows the relationship between the similarity scores of consecutive game frames from the 13 games. They show a linear relationship with a Pearson's correlation coefficient value of 0.93. This fact motivates us to use linear regression for predicting similarity scores between two frames. That is, the similarity score with a future frame in-line is predicted from that with a previous one. Let EPS(f_N, f_{N+l}) represent the prediction of perceptual similarity between frames f_N and f_{N+l}. It is basically predicted from **Y–Diff**

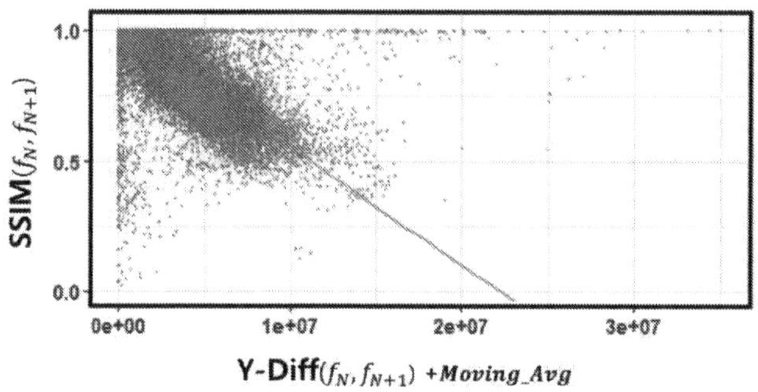

Figure 11: Correlation between SSIM(f_N, f_{N+1}) and the Y–Diff(f_{N-1}, f_N) + 'moving average' of Y–Diff (Best viewed in color).

of previous frames. Currently, the system implements two different levels of rate reduction, 30 FPS and 15 FPS, corresponding to 1-skipping and 3-skipping, respectively, and utilizes EPS(f_N, f_{N+1}) and EPS(f_N, f_{N+3}). To improve the performance of similarity prediction, it leverages the moving average of previous **Y–Diff** values to reflect their past history.

Figure 11 shows the correlation between the SSIM and the predicted similarity scores using both **Y–Diff** and the moving average of **Y–Diff** with the window size 10. The resulting equation of regression is:

$$\text{EPS}(f_N, f_{N+l}) = 1 - c_{kl_1} \times \text{D}_\text{Y}(f_{N-k}, f_N) - c_{kl_2} \times ma_w. \quad (1)$$

In the equation, the index k of the previous frame f_{N-k} depends on the current state, i.e., $k = 1$, 2 and 4 if the state is No-Skipping, 1-Skipping, and 3-Skipping, respectively. Also, there are two possible l values, i.e., 1 or 3, to predict EPS(f_N, f_{N+1}) or EPS(f_N, f_{N+3}). $\text{D}_\text{Y}(f_i, f_j)$ is the **Y–Diff** between f_i and f_j. ma_w is the moving average of the recent **Y–Diff** scores between consecutive frames over window size w. c_{kl_1} and c_{kl_2} are regression coefficients to predict EPS(f_N, f_{N+l}) with $\text{D}_\text{Y}(f_{N-k}, f_N)$. These values are obtained from the videos of the selected games.

The window size of moving average affects the performance of the regression. We compared R^2 (*R-squared*) values while varying the window sizes to 1, 2, 5, and 10 frames. R^2 is a measure of goodness of fit to the regression model. For each size, the R^2 values are obtained as 0.417, 0.467, 0.559, and 0.622, respectively. This result shows that the R^2 value increases with the window size. In the current study, the size is set to 10 frames, and finding the optimal size is left as a future work.

Determining state transitions: The system determines the state to transit, i.e., No-Skipping, 1-Skipping, or 3-Skipping, from the predictions of similarity scores, i.e., EPS(f_N, f_{N+1}) and EPS(f_N, f_{N+3}). It uses separate threshold values (or *scaling factors*), τ_1 and τ_3, to look for the opportunity to skip either one frame or three consecutive frames, respectively. The system compares EPS(f_N, f_{N+1}) and EPS(f_N, f_{N+3}) with respect to τ_1 and τ_3. If EPS(f_N, f_{N+1}) is not greater than τ_1, no frame skipping takes place, and the system shifts to No-Skipping state. If EPS(f_N, f_{N+1}) is greater than τ_1, it further checks EPS(f_N, f_{N+3}) with τ_3. If EPS(f_N, f_{N+3}) is also greater than

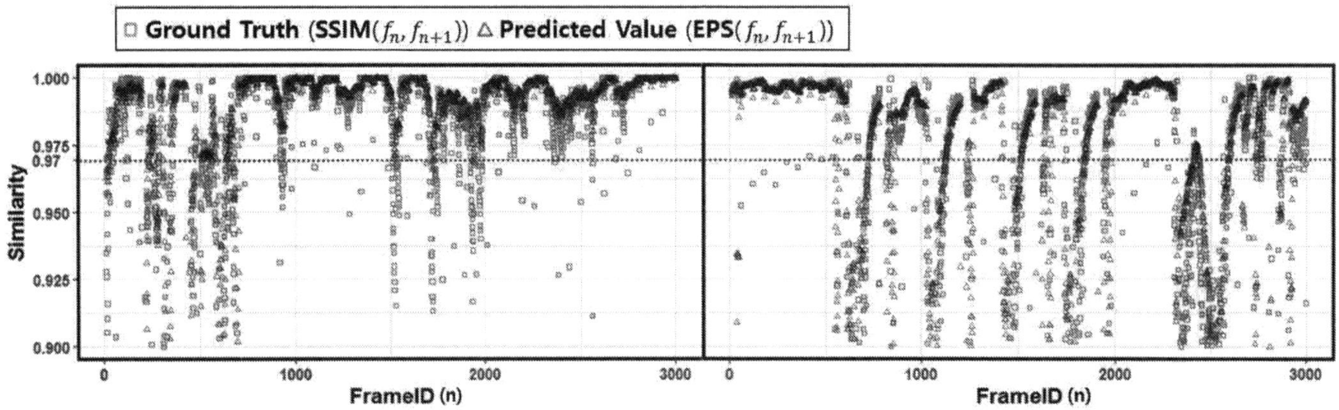

Figure 12: Comparison between the ground truths and the predicted values of SSIM(f_N, f_{N+1}) in Candy Crush Soda Saga (Left) and Archery Master 3D (Right). In total, ~50,000 frames were recorded. For brevity, predictions up-to 3000 frames are shown.

τ_3, it skips 3 frames and moves to 3-Skipping. Otherwise, it moves to 1-Skipping while skipping only one frame.

Determining scaling factors: A raw SSIM score of greater than 0.97 indicates a strong level of similarity between two images in mobile games [22]. Since our concept of predicting perceptual similarity thrives on the scale of actual SSIM scores, we look for threshold values between 0.97 to 1.

Figure 12 shows the comparison between the ground truths, i.e., SSIM(f_N,f_{N+1}) and the predicted similarity scores, i.e., EPS(f_N, f_{N+1}) over two game-play scenarios. We simulated game-play scenarios with an oracle (Section 7.1), which replays identically the recorded game-plays of gaming apps. The predictions were more accurate within the potential range of threshold values (> 0.97) than below it. This implies that the selection of threshold values in the range would result in inclusion of the areas in which EPS potentially makes correct skipping decisions; that is, it is likely that decisions to skip frames would be made (e.g., EPS(f_N, f_{N+1}) > τ_1) when the SSIM values are in reality greater than 0.97.

To maintain quality user experiences, the determination of threshold values should reduce potential of wrong skipping (or state transition) decisions, i.e., skipping decisions should not be made when no skipping should occur in reality. This means that the decision on the similarity assessed by EPS should be consistent with that made by SSIM:

$$\text{EPS}(f_N, f_{N+1}) > \tau_1 \ \textit{only if}\ \text{SSIM}(f_N, f_{N+1}) > 0.97$$
$$\text{EPS}(f_N, f_{N+3}) > \tau_3 \ \textit{only if}\ \text{SSIM}(f_N, f_{N+3}) > 0.97$$

The errors in making state transition decisions could cause significant loss in user experience. We experimented with different threshold values in our lab environment in the range of 0.97 to 1 and figured out τ_1 and τ_3 which best satisfy the above conditions. The system also provides users with a UI to customize the selection of the scaling factors on their own as shown in Figure 15.

To assess the frequency of false skipping decisions, we looked into the cases when a given threshold value is lower than predicted EPS (i.e., a skip decision occurs) but higher than actual SSIM (i.e., not to be skipped in reality). As for 1-Skipping transitions, the false decisions accounted for 4.1% of the total 1-Skipping transitions when τ_1 is set to 0.97. In the case of 3-Skipping with τ_3 set to 0.97, 27% of the total 3-Skipping transitions were false. To reduce the number of the false decisions, we increased the threshold values. To be conservative with user experiences, the 90th percentile of the EPS which makes the false skipping with threshold values set to 0.97 is taken as the revised values. For example, τ_3 is set to 0.9945, which is the 90th percentile of the EPS(f_N, f_{N+3}) such that SSIM(f_N, f_{N+3}) $\leq$ 0.97 and EPS(f_N, f_{N+3}) > 0.97. The ratio of false transitions with this new value is reduced to 2.7%

5 CLONING THE PRIMARY DISPLAY

In this section, we describe why and how RAVEN clones the primary display of an Android device into a small virtual display.

The processes of graphics and display on Android could be viewed from two perspectives, i.e., that of apps and that of system display. In its rendering loop, a gaming app draws its game frame on `EGLSurface` using OpenGL ES. From the system's view, each frame is stored as `Surface` in a graphics memory area. The display process is initiated by `SurfaceFlinger`. It takes the `Surface` from each app or UI object as a display `layer`. When a VSYNC signal arrives, `SurfaceFlinger` arranges display layers from multiple applications or UI objects for the primary display output. Usually, `Hardware Composer` composes all the collected graphics buffers (or layers) and sends the result to the primary display.

A simple approach to read a rendered game frame is to intercept and read it from an app's `EGLSurface` upon its generation. However, this approach has a limitation; an access to `EGLSurface` occurs in a blocking fashion, and would cause the whole rendering pipeline to be delayed. Moreover, it contains a frame in its full-resolution (in the case of Nexus 5X, 1920×1080), which is heavy to process for 60 times per second. According to our preliminary experiment, reading a single frame from an `EGLSurface` takes 0.49 seconds on average. Thus, this approach could be performed for less than 3 frames per second, and is not feasible to match usual frame rates.

A different approach would be to read it from a (display) frame buffer (e.g., `/dev/graphics/fb0`). It is well-known and has been used in other works [27]. However, recent Android OS versions do not allocate display frame buffers[10].

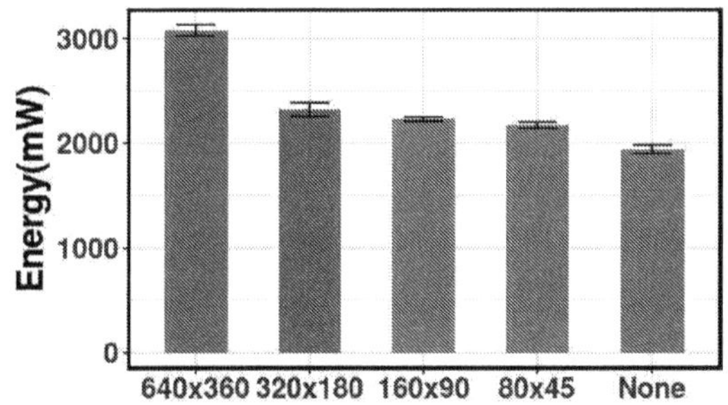

Figure 13: Total system power consumption according to the resolution of a virtual display (width×height; *None* implies no virtual display), measured with Candy Crush Saga.

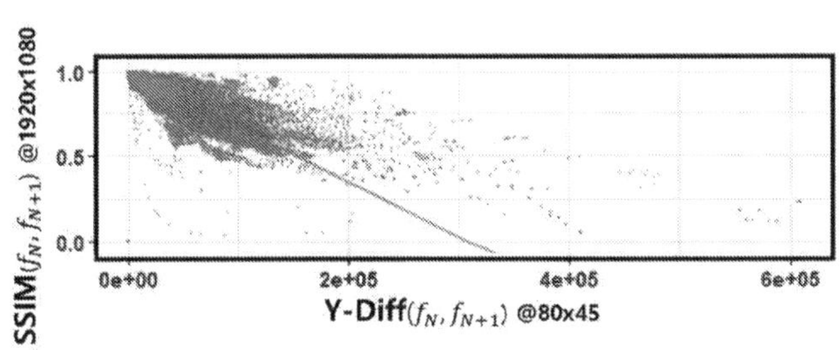

(a) Correlation between SSIM at 1080p and Y–Diff at 45p.

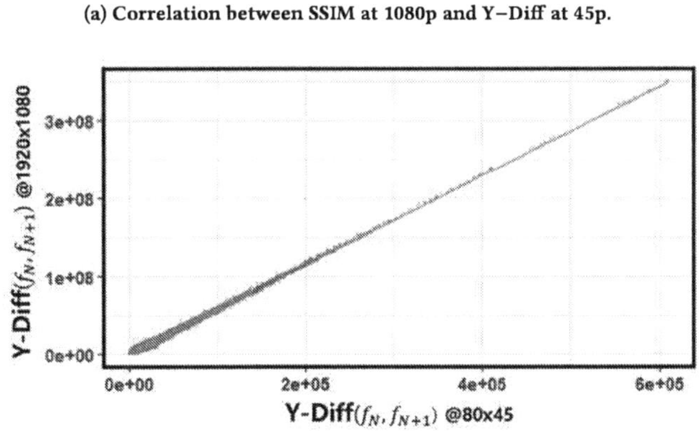

(b) Correlation between Y–Diff at 1080p and Y–Diff at 45p.

Figure 14: 80×45 resolution and 1920×1080 resolution are nearly identical in (a) SSIM and (b) Y–Diff (Best viewed in color).

RAVEN leverages the virtual display of Android. A virtual display could be allocated and maintained by SurfaceFlinger and used to side-track the screen data for various purposes, e.g., screen sharing or capturing. Upon generation, HWC fills up the virtual display while it composes the display for the physical screen. While allocated separately in graphics memory, the overhead to compose its content is small because it piggybacks the process of physical screen composition. As mentioned earlier, HWC also reduces the buffer-composition overhead.

The overhead of a virtual display is primarily proportional to the resolution of the display. In Figure 13, we show the total system power while running FrameDiff Tracker with different virtual display resolutions. It indicates that using the resolution of 80×45 can effectively reduce the energy overhead. From extensive trials

Type	Component	LoC
Java based System Service	Rate Regulator	570
Native C/C++ based System Service	Frame Difference Tracker	847
OpenGL/ES	Rate Injector	161

Table 1: RAVEN's code breakdown for AOSP modification.

with different resolutions, we figured out that the resolution of 80×45 for the virtual display is optimal for attaining minimum energy overhead while preserving the performance. The **Y–Diff** results with 80×45 and 1920×1080 are nearly identical with the selected game-play data, scoring a 0.9989 Pearson's correlation coefficient, as shown in Figure 14.

6 IMPLEMENTATION

We have implemented a prototype of RAVEN as a system service by customizing Android (AOSP) 6.0.1 upon Google Nexus 5X. The implementation is in C++ and Java, consisting of 1,578 lines of code in total as shown in Table 1.

Rate Injector: To inject a delay into the rendering loop of a game app, `eglSwapBuffer()` function in OpenGL/ES is modified, so that it lets the rendering loop sleep and adjust the frame rendering rates. For this, a `sleep()` function call is inserted right after submitting the rendered frame, stored in `EGLSurface`, to `BufferQueue`. (See Figure 4, Section 3.) The sleep duration is decided by considering the time for the next rendering (after skipping renderings), T_r, decided by `Rate Regulator` and the estimation of a rendering duration D_r, i.e., T_r - D_r. The rendering duration can be estimated by capturing the system times at the end of a sleep and at the completion of the next round rendering.

The three major components are implemented in different processes, i.e., `Rate Injector` as a part of the game app process, and `Rate Regulator` as well as `FrameDiff Tracker` as parts of system services, requiring a medium for inter-process communication. Current implementation uses a UNIX Local Socket.

FrameDiff Tracker: As mentioned, `SurfaceFlinger` service is used to clone the primary display, which offers the concept of a virtual display [10]. In reality, `SurfaceComposerClient` is used, which acts as an interface for `SurfaceFlinger` since `FrameDiff Tracker` and `SurfaceFlinger` are in different processes. `SurfaceComposerClient` calls `createDisplay()` function to create a virtual display as a newly allocated Surface.

To access thus constructed virtual display, `FrameDiff Tracker` also creates a new `BufferQueue` to connect to the `Surface`, i.e., the virtual display. Thereafter, `FrameDiff Tracker` can extract the cloned frames from the `Surface` successively. The RGB values in the frames are converted into **Y**–values.

`FrameDiff Tracker` utilizing the virtual display faces a slight delay in tracking the most recently rendered frame. Upon rendering a frame, it needs to be composed by the `SurfaceFlinger`, and thus, would not yet be available to `FrameDiff Tracker`. The rendering time of a frame usually overlaps with the display composition time of its previous one. We currently use the most recently composed frame from the virtual display for similarity prediction. This could

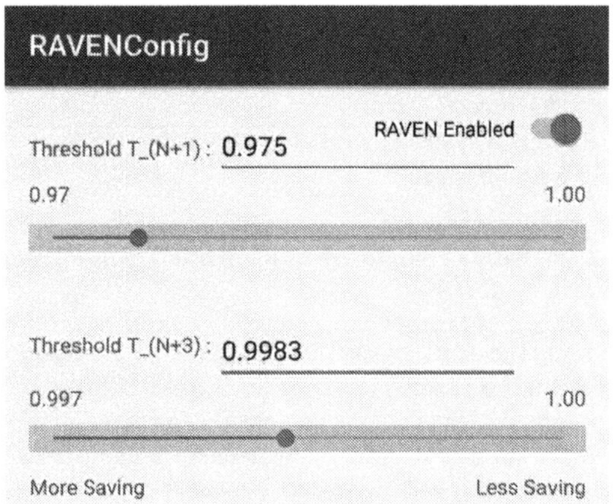

Figure 15: Screen-shot of RAVENConfig, an app to scale threshold values. If τ_3 is moved leftward, frame rates from GPU will lean more towards 15 FPS. Users are also provided with a switch to enable or disable RAVEN to tune the rates or keep the original rates following developer's intention.

incur some errors but within an acceptable range. Our measurements show that the errors were negligible. A better approach would be to slightly tune the regression model in Equation 1.

RAVENConfig: We implemented RAVENConfig, an app for personalized configuration. Figure 15 shows the layout of the RAVENConfig. It allows users to tune the RAVEN parameters according to their own subjective perception on the degree of experience degradation caused by the system. The users are allowed to change the threshold values (τ_1 and τ_3) to inject different rates of game-frame renderings to their game-play. For instance, tuning τ_3 below 0.997, will result in a more frequent usage of the 15 FPS mode, which may affect the user experience in return of higher energy savings. In Section 7, we evaluate the impact of tuning the threshold values with two cases, denoted as PAS and PAS++. PAS++ acts more aggressively to save energy, i.e., it enforces 3-skipping more often than in PAS. PAS sets τ_1 to 0.9975 and τ_3 to 0.9993. PAS++ uses 0.975 and 0.9983 for $\tau 1$ and τ_3.

7 EVALUATION

We evaluated the performance of RAVEN in terms of video quality scores, amount of skipped frames, energy savings in different settings (i.e., PAS and PAS++), and system overheads. We also explored RAVEN's impact on user experiences with two rounds of user studies.

Game Apps used for Experiments. We selected 13 commercial game apps with various graphical characteristics for the evaluation. They are grouped into three categories based on their graphics design and game mechanics: **(A)** Static, **(B)** Dynamic, and **(C)** Hybrid group. The static group includes puzzles and board games (e.g. Solitaire), which are mainly turn-based games that utilize simple graphical effects for visual feedback. The dynamic group consists of games that have *continuous graphical changes* (e.g. racing games). The games that belong to the hybrid group mostly have turn-based flows with clear separation between two phases: the input and the response phase. The input phase tends to be graphically static while displaying basic UI objects. The response phase incorporates dynamic, graphically intense visualizations without user interactions.

	PAS		PAS++		30 FPS		
Game	VMAF	SSIM	VMAF	SSIM	VMAF	SSIM	Type
Perfect Piano	99.98%	99.87%	99.47%	98.65%	99.77%	98.89%	A
Solitaire	99.94%	99.92%	99.68%	99.71%	99.06%	99.57%	
Cookie Run	99.92%	95.60%	99.89%	95.45%	90.35%	94.30%	B
Crossy Road	99.96%	98.24%	99.65%	98.00%	78.87%	90.29%	
Race the Traffic Moto	99.76%	98.21%	99.42%	97.91%	87.81%	93.33%	
Subway Surfers	99.94%	99.71%	99.70%	99.45%	79.46%	87.50%	
Angry Birds	99.80%	99.40%	98.85%	99.08%	97.31%	98.44%	C
Archery Master 3D	99.94%	98.23%	99.01%	97.40%	95.12%	95.60%	
Candy Crush Saga	99.93%	99.09%	99.56%	98.85%	99.09%	98.74%	
Candy Crush Soda Saga	99.97%	99.11%	99.46%	98.44%	98.50%	97.93%	
Criminal Case	99.71%	99.33%	99.32%	99.07%	97.74%	98.40%	
Cut the Rope	99.86%	99.12%	99.81%	98.51%	98.87%	98.57%	
Surgery Simulator	99.96%	99.63%	99.70%	99.24%	99.41%	99.14%	

Table 2: Video quality scores in percentage, higher is better. A, B, and C represents respective game types.

7.1 Objective Quality Assessment

To measure the number of skipped frames and to understand its effect on visual quality across different settings, identical game-play data should be provided for each measurement. Since gaming apps are non-deterministic in their nature, we first recorded game-plays at 60 FPS (for three minutes each) and then extracted each frame as an image from the recorded game-play videos. Thereafter, we applied the perception-aware rate scaling logic on the extracted image sequences, and re-encoded the resulting image sequences as separate videos for the assessment. For comparison, we also prepared constant 30-FPS scenarios; for this, we generated videos by re-encoding the image sequences, constructed by skipping alternate images from the original sequences.

We evaluated the performance of RAVEN using objective video quality metrics. The metrics give video quality scores which collectively indicate perceptual similarity across a sequence of frames from a video. We measured video quality scores for two different frame rendering rate scaling policies (PAS and PAS++) as well as for the constant 30-FPS setting. We used two objective video quality metrics: SSIM, and VMAF[11][2].

Table 2 presents the results of the video quality assessment. The results show that PAS and PAS++ achieve high video-quality scores, which means they do not make significant perceptual differences, compared to the original 60 FPS game-play videos. Also, in each case, PAS and PAS++ produce better results than 30-FPS. In the case of the games in the Static and the Hybrid groups like Criminal Case, Cut The Rope, Candy Crush Saga and Angry bird, 30-FPS also performs decently. On the other hand, for the games in the Dynamic group like Crossy Road and Cookie Run, both PAS and PAS++ scored notably higher, compared to 30-FPS. This indicates that 30-FPS would cause more negative impacts on human visual perception. Figure 16 shows the proportion of the different skipping states that the RAVEN system applied in the re-composed videos.

[2]Unlike SSIM which can give per image based similarity score, VMAF is a newly introduced state-of-the-art video quality metric which gives video quality score across a video stream. It shows a better correlation with device specific Mean Opinion Score (MOS).

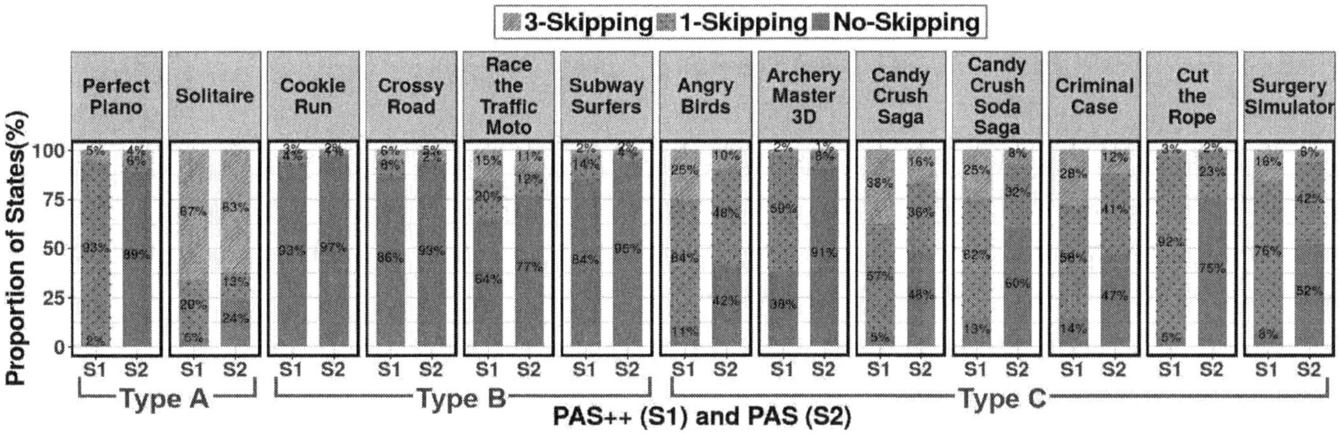

Figure 16: Comparison of PAS and PAS++ in terms of frame skipping (Best viewed in color).

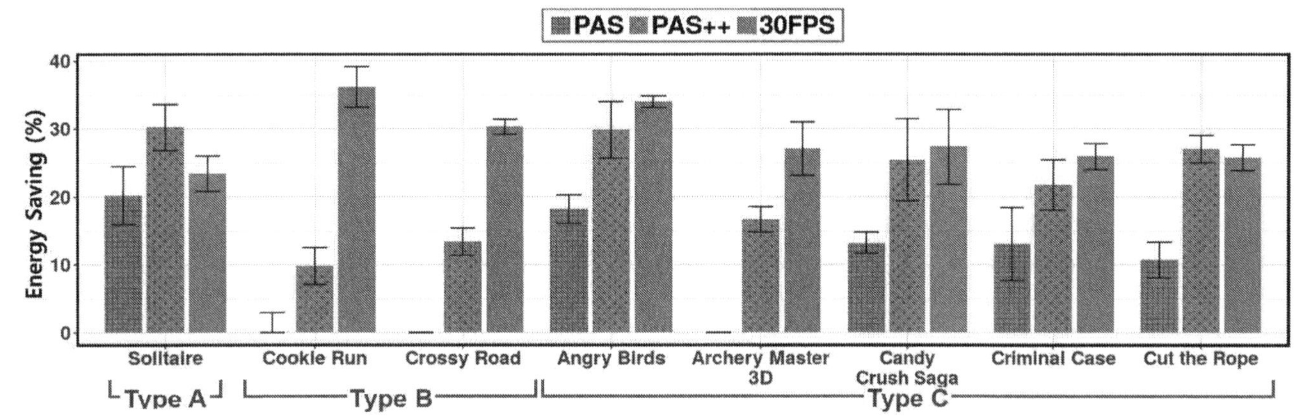

Figure 17: Percentage of energy savings while playing each game for 3 minutes (averaged on five repeated measurements).

In 7 out of the 12 cases, PAS++ skipped as many frames as `30-FPS` setting while achieving better video quality scores.

7.2 Energy Saving

We measured energy consumption on Nexus 5X running our customized Android (AOSP) 6.0.1 with a Monsoon Power Monitor[7]. We configured the device brightness to 30% and activated the airplane mode except for Cookie Run which requires a network connection. To prevent CPU/GPU throttling caused by overheating, we ensured that the devices were cooled before each measurement.

We evaluated and compared the energy consumption of four settings: `Stock` is the baseline setting that uses the stock Android, which does not change frame rendering rates. `30-FPS`, PAS++, and PAS are the same as described above. The evaluation covers 8 game apps, including at least one game from each game category to reflect various gaming behaviors. For each game app, we tried to repeat the same play (or interaction) sequence for measurement. We measured the energy consumption for three minutes, and recorded the average after repeating the session five times.

Figure 17 shows the proportion of energy savings in each setting compared to `Stock`. PAS does not save substantial amount of energy in the games that show continuous movements of characters or changes of scenes such as Cookie Run, Archery Master 3D, and Crossy Road. Except those games, PAS saves at least half the amount of energy saved by `30-FPS`. PAS++ saves at least 10% more energy than `Stock`. Notably, PAS++ saves 5% more energy than `30-FPS` in Solitaire since there are many perceptually similar frames as seen in Figure 2 (Section 2).

7.3 System Overhead

Energy overhead: We measured the energy overhead of RAVEN under the same experiment configurations as in Section 7.2 while playing Candy Crush Saga. The measurements were performed for each major component of RAVEN, namely `FrameDiff Tracker`, `Rate Regulator`, and `Rate Injector`. In total, the RAVEN system consumes 173 mW in average. This accounts for only 8% of total device power consumption (2186 mW) while playing the game. 96% of total energy overhead (165.5 mW) is taken by `FrameDiff Tracker` for managing a virtual display and calculating **Y–Diffs** from it. The other components consume negligible amounts of energy (3.7 mW by `Rate Regulator` and 3.9 mW by `Rate Injector`), since they are engaged in light-weight computations.

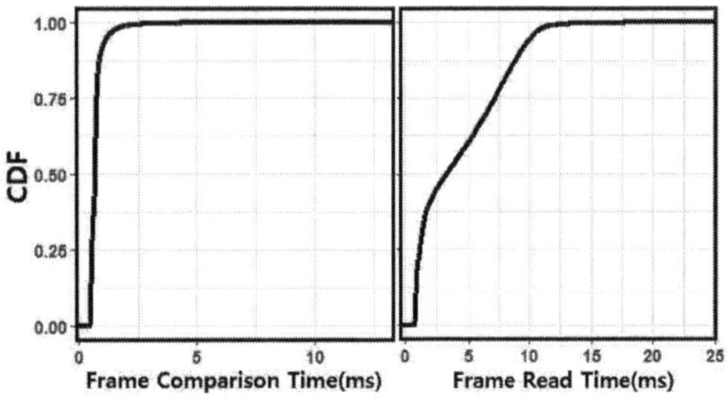

Figure 18: Times taken for frame read and comparison in the games Candy Crush Saga, and Cut the Rope (combined).

Application overhead: Since RAVEN requires modifications in `eglSwapBuffer()` function, it could incur extra overhead in the rendering thread of gaming apps. We measured the processing time of RAVEN's code block in the `eglSwapBuffer()` function. The code block takes only 4.88μs on average. Thus, RAVEN does not impose significant overheads to the rendering threads of game apps.

Frame reading and comparison overhead: The bottleneck of RAVEN's processing pipeline lies in reading frames and calculating Y–Diffs by comparing them. We measured the time taken to read each frame and to compute Y–Diff between two frames for all gaming apps. Figure 18 shows the results with two games.

7.4 User Study

To explore the impact of RAVEN on user experiences, we conducted a user study with 12 participants (7 males and 5 females are recruited, all were in the ages from 20 to 30). To assess the game-play experience, we used Double Stimulus Impairment Scale(DSIS) and Double Stimulus Continuous Quality Scale (DSCQS), which are widely used as specifications for quality assessment of systems [2][27].

DSIS uses a discrete five-point impairment scale in two variants, i.e., stimulus A and B. Both stimuli are sequentially presented to each participant and the participant is asked to rate the quality of each stimulus. The participants are informed of the device setting. Unlike DSIS, DSCQS aims at assessing the differences in perceived visual qualities among different device settings without informing participants the setting of each task. Also, the order of the assessment tasks is randomly arranged. This could mitigate potential contextual biases (e.g. effects caused by the names of settings). The participants score the perceived quality of each test setting on a [0-100] scale.

DSIS: The participants were asked to play three games: 1) Cookie Run, 2) Solitaire, and 3) Candy Crush Saga for 2 minutes each. The participants are informed of RAVEN with PAS++ before the test. Figure 19(a) shows the impairment rating result. Most of the participants scored either "imperceptible" or "perceptible but not annoying" on all three games. However, some scored "slightly annoying" with Cookie Run. Those participants observed slight stuttering from repetitive movements of a character. The character stayed at the same position and made short, repetitive movements, which made even slight changes in the frame rendering rate noticeable to the participants.

DSCQS: The participants were asked to play the same three games. They played them for four sessions, three minutes each, with different FPS manipulation settings including 1) `Stock` (60-FPS fixed), 2) `30-FPS` fixed, 3) PAS, and 4) PAS++. During each session, they are allowed to play the game freely without game content-related instructions. Figures 19(b) and (c) show the results. The participants could not discriminate the tested settings against `Stock`. The difference in the scores between `Stock` and PAS++ was 4.5 points in average, which could be considered as negligible.

The results above show that the RAVEN system provides similar levels of user experience compared to the reference system, i.e., `Stock`. However, considering the diversity of mobile game apps and their player groups, we plan to evaluate the system more extensively over a broader set of games and participant groups.

8 RELATED WORKS

`dJay` [25] utilized the concept of predictive SSIM-based approach to dynamically tune client GPU rendering workloads in order to, first, ensure all clients get satisfactory frame rates, and second, provide the best possible graphics quality across clients. The system builds a *utility* optimizer in the cloud gaming server which defines *cost* in terms of GPU time and *benefits* in terms of graphics visual quality. On the other hand, RAVEN is the first system which performs rendering rate scaling on a commodity smartphone while maintaining satisfactory user experiences.

Apogee [31] made a low-overhead pre-fetcher that adapts to address patterns found in graphics memory. This approach reduces the degree of multi-threading and thus, resulting in higher energy efficiency. The whole process involves highly complicated processing and needs access to GPU driver source code.

There was an effort to utilize the knowledge on display contents on a screen [27][26]. The work used the RGB differences of the contents and controlled the refresh rates from the display driver. The approach incurs considerable deterioration in quality without a touch-boosting technique, which enforces the refresh rates to the maximum upon a touch event. On the contrary, RAVEN leverages human perception by measuring perceptual similarity, and thus, provides good performance without any extra hints like touch.

Vatjus-Anttila et al.[32] built a GPU power model based on three render complexity characteristics 1) number of triangles, 2) render batches, and 3) addressed texels. It mostly focuses on relating the power consumption to hardware events by observing hardware performance counters of the GPU. Such techniques require low-level hardware modifications and also cannot cope with different graphics designs of gaming apps. There have been several other works on GPU power modeling [28][29][36], but most of them targeted the concept of dynamic frequency scaling. Though these techniques could be applicable on smartphones, they require vendor-side modifications of GPU drivers.

The power consumption of display increases with its pixel brightness [19][21] [24]. In recent years, vendors are exploring methods to reduce power consumption by darkening the least important contents on the screen [20]. On the similar note, Chen et al.[21]

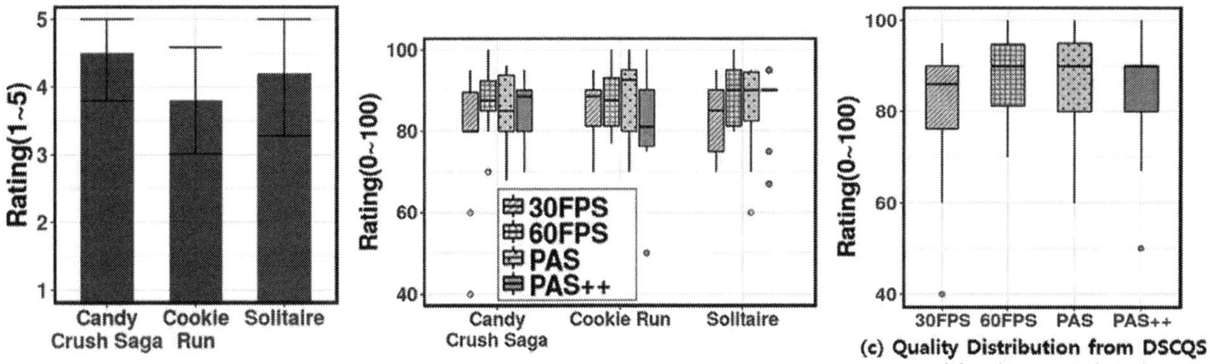

(a) Quality rating from DSIS (b) Quality rating from DSCQS (c) Quality Distribution from DSCQS (result from the games Candy Crush Saga, Cookie Run, and Solitaire)

Figure 19: Results from the user study.

introduced a software technique which could perform local dimming for the screen areas covered by users' fingers to save more power, without compromising their visual experiences. Anand et al.[19] and Dong et al.[24] utilized the brightness index of pixels to save significant amounts of power while preserving image qualities. Though these works are motivational, they are subjected to external factors, e.g., lighting conditions. To the contrary, RAVEN's approach is independent of such external factors. Moreover, the works focused more on power consumption rather than retaining the quality of user experience.

Software plug-ins have been provided for desktop computers in recent years [1][15][4][16], which attempt to optimize the rendering power of a GPU. Such plug-ins transfer the information on their graphics objects to the video cards (GPUs) and adopt Dynamic Resolution Rendering [14]. Upon complex graphics contents, they exert slow changes in resolution while trying to maintain high frame rates.

9 DISCUSSION AND FUTURE WORK

As shown in Figure 17, there are cases where the PAS do not lead to energy saving, e.g., Archery Master 3D. Such situations may occur when a game scene continuously changes throughout the play, and RAVEN does not skip frames. Those situations are not prevalent as the design as well as the play of a game vary across its different stages or sessions. While playing Archery Master 3D, we found that there are cases in which RAVEN saved about $\sim 15\%$ of energy with the PAS setting. This shows that RAVEN is designed to understand the importance of having a good game-play experience, and does not try to greedily skip frames to achieve higher energy savings.

The current implementation has been built and tested on a Nexus 5X smartphone. We think that it would work on other modern smartphones running latest versions of Android OS. As for GPUs, RAVEN has been tested with an Adreno 418 GPU. More work needs to be performed to see how much energy it saves on other types of GPUs.

`Hardware Composer(HWC)` is a specialized hardware component, generating the final frames for display on a screen. An idea to save more energy would be to extend HWC to include parts or all of perceptual similarity computation. This approach seems feasible since it touches every frame to be displayed. With such extension, tasks of `FrameDiff Tracker` can be offloaded to the HWC, which incur 96% of total energy overhead.

We plan to continue to improve the current design and implementation to explore ways to further optimize power consumption. A potential direction would be to develop a technique for resolution scaling, which could be used in combination with the current approach. Also interesting is to build a tool, based on RAVEN, to assist developers in optimizing power consumption of their gaming apps.

10 CONCLUSION

This paper presents RAVEN, a system for mobile gaming apps to opportunistically save power consumption without degrading user experiences. It introduces a new, on-the-fly perception-aware rate scaling technique, which utilizes human visual perception of graphics changes, and helps reduce power consumption by smartphone GPUs. It develops a light-weight frame comparison technique to measure and predict perception-aware frame similarity. It also builds a low resolution virtual display which clones the device screen for performing similarity measurement at a low-power cost. It is able to work on an existing commercial smartphone and support applications from app stores without any modifications. The experiments in the paper show that RAVEN saves up-to 35% of total device energy consumption without causing any substantial user experience degradation while playing mobile games.

11 ACKNOWLEDGMENT

We are thankful to our shepherd Prof. Robert LiKamWa and the anonymous reviewers for their valuable comments and suggestions that helped bring the paper to its current form. We would also like to thank Joo Ho Lee for all the valuable discussions during the writing of this paper. This work was supported by Basic Science Research Program through the National Research Foundation of Korea (NRF) funded by the Ministry of Science, ICT & Future Planning (2017R1A2B3010504) and the Ministry of Education (2016R1D1A1B03930311).

REFERENCES

[1] 2017. Boost. http://www.hialgo.com/TechnologyBOOST.html. (2017). [Online; accessed Aug-1-2017].
[2] 2017. BT.500 : Methodology for the subjective assessment of the quality of television pictures. https://www.itu.int/rec/R-REC-BT.500-13-201201-I/en. (2017). [Online; accessed Aug-1-2017].
[3] 2017. BufferQueue and gralloc. https://source.android.com/devices/graphics/arch-bq-gralloc. (2017). [Online; accessed 7-July-2017].
[4] 2017. LucidLogix. http://www.lucidlogix.com/powerxtend/overview/. (2017). [Online; accessed Aug-1-2017].
[5] 2017. Mali-G71 ARM GPUs. https://www.arm.com/products/multimedia/mali-gpu/high-performance/mali-g71.php. (2017). [Online; accessed Aug-1-2017].
[6] 2017. Mali-T760 ARM GPUs. https://www.arm.com/products/multimedia/mali-gpu/high-performance/mali-t760.php. (2017). [Online; accessed Aug-1-2017].
[7] 2017. Monsoon Power Monitor. https://www.msoon.com/LabEquipment/PowerMonitor. (2017). [Online; accessed Aug-1-2017].
[8] 2017. Open CV. http://docs.opencv.org/2.4.13/. (2017). [Online; accessed Aug-1-2017].
[9] 2017. Samsung Game Tuner. https://play.google.com/store/apps/details?id=com.samsung.android.gametuner.thin&hl=en. (2017). [Online; accessed Aug-1-2017].
[10] 2017. SurfaceFlinger and Hardware Composer. https://source.android.com/devices/graphics/arch-sf-hwc. (2017). [Online; accessed 7-July-2017].
[11] 2017. Toward A Practical Perceptual Video Quality Metric . http://techblog.netflix.com/2016/06/toward-practical-perceptual-video.html. (2017). [Online; accessed Aug-1-2017].
[12] 2017. YUV - Wikipedia. https://en.wikipedia.org/wiki/YUV. (2017). [Online; accessed Aug-1-2017].
[13] February 11, 2013. Khronos Native Platform Graphics Interface. https://www.khronos.org/registry/EGL/specs/. (February 11, 2013). [Online; accessed Aug-1-2017].
[14] July 13, 2011. Dynamic Resolution Rendering Article. https://software.intel.com/en-us/articles/dynamic-resolution-rendering-article. (July 13, 2011). [Online; accessed Aug-1-2017].
[15] March 17, 2013. HiAlgoBoost. http://semiaccurate.com/2013/04/17/hialgo-boost-for-far-cry-3/. (March 17, 2013). [Online; accessed Aug-1-2017].
[16] March 23, 2012. DynamiX, LucidLogix. http://semiaccurate.com/2012/03/23/lucid-releases-dynamix-software/. (March 23, 2012). [Online; accessed Aug-1-2017].
[17] May 12, 2009. OpenGL ES Common Profile Specification. https://www.khronos.org/files/opengles_shading_language.pdf. (May 12, 2009). [Online; accessed Aug-1-2017].
[18] October 29, 2012. The Truth About Cats and Dogs: Smartphone vs Tablet Usage Differences. http://flurrymobile.tumblr.com/post/113379683050/the-truth-about-cats-and-dogs-smartphone-vs. (October 29, 2012). [Online; accessed Aug-1-2017].
[19] Bhojan Anand, Karthik Thirugnanam, Jeena Sebastian, Pravein G. Kannan, Akhihebbal L. Ananda, Mun Choon Chan, and Rajesh Krishna Balan. 2011. Adaptive Display Power Management for Mobile Games. In *Proceedings of the 9th International Conference on Mobile Systems, Applications, and Services (MobiSys '11)*. ACM, New York, NY, USA, 57–70. https://doi.org/10.1145/1999995.2000002
[20] J. Betts-LaCroix. 2010. Selective dimming of oled displays. (June 17 2010). https://www.google.com/patents/US20100149223 US Patent App. 12/538,846.
[21] Xiang Chen, Kent W. Nixon, Hucheng Zhou, Yunxin Liu, and Yiran Chen. 2014. FingerShadow: An OLED Power Optimization Based on Smartphone Touch Interactions. In *Proceedings of the 6th USENIX Conference on Power-Aware Computing and Systems (HotPower'14)*. USENIX Association, Berkeley, CA, USA, 6–6. http://dl.acm.org/citation.cfm?id=2696568.2696574
[22] Eduardo Cuervo, Alec Wolman, Landon P. Cox, Kiron Lebeck, Ali Razeen, Stefan Saroiu, and Madanlal Musuvathi. 2015. Kahawai: High-Quality Mobile Gaming Using GPU Offload. In *Proceedings of the 13th Annual International Conference on Mobile Systems, Applications, and Services (MobiSys '15)*. ACM, New York, NY, USA, 121–135. https://doi.org/10.1145/2742647.2742657
[23] B. Dietrich and S. Chakraborty. 2014. Forget the battery, let's play games!. In *2014 IEEE 12th Symposium on Embedded Systems for Real-time Multimedia (ESTIMedia)*. 1–8. https://doi.org/10.1109/ESTIMedia.2014.6962338
[24] Mian Dong and Lin Zhong. 2011. Chameleon: A Color-adaptive Web Browser for Mobile OLED Displays. In *Proceedings of the 9th International Conference on Mobile Systems, Applications, and Services (MobiSys '11)*. ACM, New York, NY, USA, 85–98. https://doi.org/10.1145/1999995.2000004
[25] Sergey Grizan, David Chu, Alec Wolman, and Roger Wattenhofer. 2015. dJay: Enabling High-density Multi-tenancy for Cloud Gaming Servers with Dynamic Cost-benefit GPU Load Balancing. In *Proceedings of the Sixth ACM Symposium on Cloud Computing (SoCC '15)*. ACM, New York, NY, USA, 58–70. https://doi.org/10.1145/2806777.2806942
[26] Dongwon Kim, Nohyun Jung, and Hojung Cha. 2014. Content-centric Display Energy Management for Mobile Devices. In *Proceedings of the 51st Annual Design Automation Conference (DAC '14)*. ACM, New York, NY, USA, Article 41, 6 pages. https://doi.org/10.1145/2593069.2593113
[27] D. Kim, N. Jung, Y. Chon, and H. Cha. 2016. Content-Centric Energy Management of Mobile Displays. *IEEE Transactions on Mobile Computing* 15, 8 (Aug 2016), 1925–1938. https://doi.org/10.1109/TMC.2015.2467393
[28] J. Lee, V. Sathisha, M. Schulte, K. Compton, and N. S. Kim. 2011. Improving Throughput of Power-Constrained GPUs Using Dynamic Voltage/Frequency and Core Scaling. In *2011 International Conference on Parallel Architectures and Compilation Techniques*. 111–120. https://doi.org/10.1109/PACT.2011.17
[29] Jingwen Leng, Tayler Hetherington, Ahmed ElTantawy, Syed Gilani, Nam Sung Kim, Tor M. Aamodt, and Vijay Janapa Reddi. 2013. GPUWattch: Enabling Energy Optimizations in GPGPUs. In *Proceedings of the 40th Annual International Symposium on Computer Architecture (ISCA '13)*. ACM, New York, NY, USA, 487–498. https://doi.org/10.1145/2485922.2485964
[30] Margaret S Livingstone. 2002. *Vision and Art: The Biology of Seeing*.
[31] Ankit Sethia, Ganesh Dasika, Mehrzad Samadi, and Scott Mahlke. 2013. APOGEE: Adaptive Prefetching on GPUs for Energy Efficiency. In *Proceedings of the 22Nd International Conference on Parallel Architectures and Compilation Techniques (PACT '13)*. IEEE Press, Piscataway, NJ, USA, 73–82. http://dl.acm.org/citation.cfm?id=2523721.2523735
[32] J. M. Vatjus-Anttila, T. Koskela, and S. Hickey. 2013. Power Consumption Model of a Mobile GPU Based on Rendering Complexity. In *2013 Seventh International Conference on Next Generation Mobile Apps, Services and Technologies*. 210–215. https://doi.org/10.1109/NGMAST.2013.45
[33] Zhou Wang, Alan C Bovik, Hamid R Sheikh, and Eero P Simoncelli. 2004. Image quality assessment: from error visibility to structural similarity. *IEEE transactions on image processing* 13, 4 (2004), 600–612.
[34] Yu Yan, Songtao He, Yunxin Liu, and Longbo Huang. 2015. Optimizing Power Consumption of Mobile Games. In *Proceedings of the Workshop on Power-Aware Computing and Systems (HotPower '15)*. ACM, New York, NY, USA, 21–25. https://doi.org/10.1145/2818613.2818746
[35] Semir Zeki. 1993. *A Vision of the Brain*. Blackwell scientific publications.
[36] Y. Zhu, A. Srikanth, J. Leng, and V. J. Reddi. 2014. Exploiting Webpage Characteristics for Energy-Efficient Mobile Web Browsing. *IEEE Computer Architecture Letters* 13, 1 (Jan 2014), 33–36. https://doi.org/10.1109/L-CA.2012.33

Advertising-based Measurement: A Platform of 7 Billion Mobile Devices

Mark D. Corner, Brian N. Levine, Omar Ismail, and Angela Upreti
College of Information and Computer Sciences
University of Massachusetts Amherst, MA, USA
mcorner,levine,oismail,aupreti@cs.umass.edu

ABSTRACT

The most important step in an empirical computer scientist's research is gathering sufficient real-world data to validate a system. Unfortunately, it is also one of the most time-consuming and expensive tasks: placing measurement tools in remote networks or end-clients requires one to marshal resources from different administrative domains, devices, populations, and countries. Often such efforts culminate in a trace that is deficient in multiple ways: a small set of test subjects, a short time frame, missing ground truth for device IDs, networking environments lacking in diversity and geographic spread, or highly biased sampling.

We present a method of addressing these challenges by leveraging the most open and globally accessible test and measurement platform: digital advertising. Digital advertising instantly provides a window into 7 billion devices spanning every county for an extremely low cost. We propose *Advertising as a Platform* (AaaP), an ad-based system to perform massive-scale mobile measurement studies. In contrast with measurements made by large media companies who own platforms, ad networks, and apps, we concentrate on the opportunities and challenges for researchers that are end-users of advertising systems. We evaluate a prototype system, discuss ethical guidelines, and demonstrate its use in four scenarios: IP2Geo databases, bandwidth measurement, energy management, and the identifiability of mobile users. We show the efficacy and ease-of-use of AaaP, and illuminate key challenges and the great promise of using AaaP to study a wide variety of mobile phenomena.

CCS CONCEPTS

• **Networks** → **Network measurement**; **Mobile networks**;

KEYWORDS

Mobile measurement;Mobile advertising

1 INTRODUCTION

Empirical research on mobile systems is a process that ideally involves the placement of measurement tools in varied domains, on a variety of devices, for users with diverse demographics, and in many countries. The reality for many studies is that some or all of these ideals fail. In this paper, we show that this challenge can be met by leveraging the most open and globally accessible test and measurement platform: digital advertising.

Digital advertising provides a window into virtually every Internet-connected device on the planet, instantly, at an extremely low cost. U.S. users are exposed to an estimated 100 to 1,300 ads *per day* [31, 58]. Advertisements not restricted demographically; for instance black and white American adults were equally likely to own a smartphone [65]. Ads are cheap, often less than $0.0005 per displayed ad (i.e., per *impression*). And ads possess the resources of a full browser. Accordingly, advertisements have access to some native sensors, such as the accelerometer and the state of the device's battery, without special privilege. Ads can fetch images and run javascript. Ads have access to a unique identifier and device location. And all of these capabilities are available without user interaction, such as clicking.

Such data is already available, collected, and analyzed by a variety of actors. Handset and platform creators have access to all data. A large media company, such as Google or Twitter, that distributes an SDK to thousands of publisher's has access to similar data. These parties all collect measurements as a matter of course. Outside of these organizations, researchers sit in a less privileged position. This paper concentrates on the opportunities for designing and executing experiments for researchers that are end-user of advertising systems.

Consider a researcher who requires bandwidth measurements at many geographic locations through multiple providers. It is highly unlikely that ISPs would provide that information, so there is no choice but to directly measure it. The researcher could travel and measure bandwidth using phones from each provider; e.g., [67]. Or the researcher could recruit users to install a bandwidth measurement application; e.g., [4, 32]. Both options are time consuming and expensive.

In contrast, by purchasing advertisements a researcher can gather data about bandwidth, with GPS information, by measuring how long a client takes to download an image. One million data points can be generated from $100 without recruitment, without leaving their desks, and without deployment. The infrastructure is already in place on more than 7 billion mobile devices spanning the globe [17] and permits experimentation and measurement at unprecedented scale and at diminutive costs.

To leverage the opportunities of **advertising-based measurement**, we have developed a system called *Advertising as a Platform (AaaP)*, which places ads on mobile devices and can measure a wide variety of phenomena. In contrast to measurements made by larger

MobiCom '17, October 16–20, 2017, Snowbird, UT, USA.

ACM ISBN 978-1-4503-4916-1/17/10...$15.00
https://doi.org/10.1145/3117811.3117844

media companies, we introduce and quantify the power of this paradigm from the perspective of a research scientist. We evaluate our approach along many dimensions, including ethics, scalability, cost, and efficiency. All told, for this paper, after a careful IRB process, we took measurements from more than 553,043 distinct devices on 276,214 IP addresses, with 991,485 ads — yet the total cost was less than $1000 and we set up minimal infrastructure. All countries are within AaaP's scope, but it can also target specific geographic areas. We gathered data from as much as 6% of the mobile devices in a small town in 20 days. AaaP can also gather repeated measurements from specific devices. In a week-long experiment that targeted ads to a specific set of 8,358 devices, AaaP gathered measurements from 16% of the devices at least once a day for the entire week. When an experiment requires even more granular results, AaaP could gather more than 10 data points in one day for 20% of devices.

While these results show that AaaP has many advantages in deployability and cost over *direct measurement*, it is also clear that there are many challenges. Thefi rst challenge is to examine the ethics of conducting ad-based experiments. Hence we prioritize this concern as Section 2, where we examine human subjects concerns and draw a boundary around acceptable experiments.

The remaining challenges are technical, and methods for confronting them are best demonstrated through a series of example experiments:

- **Ads provide inaccurate location information from devices.** Can AaaP measure and utilize location data of sufficientfi delity and reliability to be useful in experiments? We demonstrate how to discriminate reliable location information from estimated location and use it to examine the accuracy of a popular IP2Geo database. Further we show how data from advertisements can reduce error in geolocation by a factor of 53*x*.
- **Advertising networks have access to exact data from native calls in mobile devices, but often return less specific information to advertisers.** Can AaaP overcome limited specificity in measurements, such as model information, when comparing performance of systems in situ? We show the results of an experiment to measure if the two chipsets available for the iPhone 7 affect bandwidth.
- **Ads provide only samples of phenomena.** As AaaP can only take measurements when the device is displaying an advertisement, it is inherently a sampling-based system. We demonstrate techniques for prediction and interpolation through an experiment that gathers battery and charge state information from devices.
- **Ground truth identities are sometimes unavailable and may change over time.** Advertising systems return a unique device identifier, but it is sometimes unavailable, such as when iOS is set to turn on "limit ad tracking". Fingerprinting techniques can overcome this mechanism, and we replicate previous work quantifying identifiability with very little effort.

We selected these examples because they span a broad range of mobile systems research, and the last two are reproductions of results that were originally conducted using methods other than AaaP (e.g., [18, 28]).

2 HUMAN SUBJECTS CONCERNS

Strict adherence to a set of ethical standards was of paramount importance to us during this work. Because the ethical issues raised by AaaP are not unprecedented, we consulted heavily with existing ethical guidelines. In particular, we followed the 2012 Menlo report [25], which is an update of the 1979 Belmont Report [62] that focuses on technology. Here we summarize the most relevant aspects of the Menlo report and related work.

Thefi rst concern is, does it qualify as human subjects research? As advertisements do not contain any personally identifiable information, they cannot be linked to a real-world identity, and such research is technically not subject to IRB approval. Other IRBs have reached the same conclusion for similar studies [18, 33, 39, 52].

Nonetheless, we asked for guidance from our board, which was very helpful in crafting protocols, especially those dealing with location information, under numbers 2016-3112 and 2016-3141. Obtaining certification of these protocols required a written proposal, several deeply technical discussions with members of the board, as well as an in-depth presentation to the full board to explain how advertisements work, what data was being collected, and the expected scientific gain. The board's purpose is to weigh these risk factors against the scientific gain to approve, modify, or reject a protocol; see [33]. The interactive, multi-round, in-person IRB process, allows for a deeper discussion of ethics than might be had during a non-interactive blind review process; see [19, 52].

The second concern is, do such experiments require explicit consent? U.S. federal guidelines permit studies that lack explicit consent under circumstances where the research carries no more than minimal risk for the participants, it is impractical to obtain written consent, and the probability and magnitude of harm or discomfort is not greater than that encountered in their daily life. These were the guidelines we followed in designing experiments for which we received IRB approval. (See [52] for a discussion on Internet-scale consent.)

For instance, we are not increasing the number of advertisements users see (another ad would be shown in its place) thus we are not creating additional discomfort. Another example is testing bandwidth with multi-megabytefi les (see Section 6.2). We have studied mobile advertisements beyond this work and it is extremely common for ads to request high definition imagery, complex javascript, streaming video, and even fully playable mini-games. Ads can use as much as 79% of a user's bandwidth [16]. Users may not welcome ads using bandwidth, but AaaP ads do not create greater harm than typically encountered. We explored these and other issues with our board before receiving approval.

Even with community guidelines and IRB approval, some experiments can prove controversial during peer review. For example, though our IRB approved an AaaP-based study of censorship, we do not include one here. The community is split over the studies that we could replicate on a much larger scale [18, 19, 39, 52].

Another question is whether such advertisements fall outside of the terms of service of advertising platforms. The terms of service that we have found do not explicitly preclude the kinds of advertisements AaaP uses. Advertising networks typically prohibit *misrepresentation*, but the definition of misrepresentation is in a business

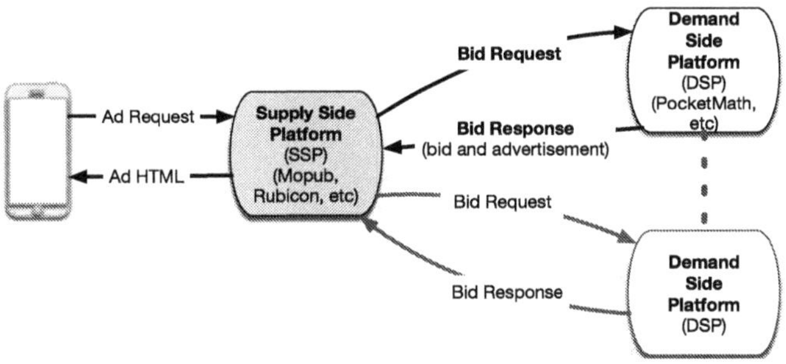

Figure 1: Auctions: Device requests ad from SSP. Each DSP bids, a winner is selected, and the ad HTML is shown.

sense (fake offers for products, impersonating user interface elements, etc.). Many ad tracking platforms will measure bandwidth, battery levels, etc. for the purposes of delivering different ads or digitalfi ngerprinting, thus such uses are not unprecedented.

3 BACKGROUND

The two primary entities involved in digital advertising are the *publishers*, who show ads in their own web page or mobile app; and the *advertisers*, who purchase advertising space. For instance, a car company (an advertiser) buys advertising space from an online newspaper (a publisher) and the newspaper will show ads for the car company.

A large fraction of digital advertisements are bought through a process called *Real Time Bidding* (RTB). In RTB, both the publisher and the advertiser are intimately involved in showing ads. We show this process in Figure 1. When a device starts the publisher's app or website, a request is made to an RTB *Supply Side Platform* (SSP). The SSP then forwards all of the information it has about that ad opportunity to a large set of *Demand Side Platforms* (DSPs) that are acting on behalf of advertisers. Each of the DSPs bid for that one advertising impression and the SSP selects the highest bid and shows that DSP's ad. This process all takes place in less than 200ms and typical DSPs may receive several million opportunities per second. Note that very large publishers, such as Facebook or Twitter, typically do not use RTB to sell their own ad inventory.

To alleviate an advertiser having to act as a DSP, there are relatively easy to use *self-service* RTB DSP platforms. These self-service platforms allow advertisers to setup advertisements with targeting parameters and then collect data about their advertisements, in real-time, through two mechanisms: *macros* that arefi lled in with data available in the bid requests from the SSP; and data collected via an *ad-tag* using HTML and javascript of the advertiser's choosing. These two sources of data are complimentary in the context of our work.

Macros. Self-service platforms allow an advertiser to set up ad targeting and upload imagery for the ad (known as the *creative*) and configure the click destination. The self-service platform then formats a small HTML document containing the image with the click destination. This document is displayed in an embedded *WebView* in a mobile app or an *iframe* on a website.

As shown in Figure 2, self-service DSPs also allow an advertiser to configure an impression beacon that will be inserted into the advertising document. This tracking pixel or *beacon* is a URL for a

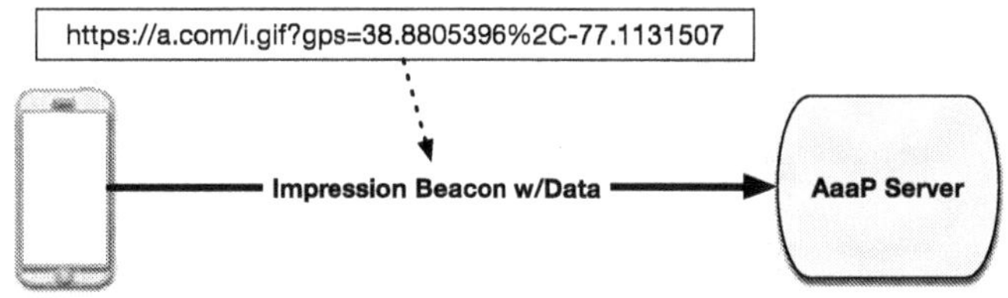

Figure 2: Impression Beacons: The HTML contains an impression beacon that requests additional javascript and HTML from the AAAP server, adding to the Ad DOM.

`page_url`	The URL of the page
`device_identifier`	Value of device identifier, may be SHA1-hashed
`device_isp`	Name of ISP
`device_model`	Device model
`device_os`	Device operating system (i.e. "ios", "android")
`os_version`	Device operating system version number.
`ip_add`	IP address of the ad viewer
`source_id`	Plain text name for the site or app
`timestamp`	UNIX timestamp of RTB auction
`exchange`	Name of RTB exchange where impression is won
`gps`	GPS coordinates, up to 6 decimals
`user_agent`	User-agent string for the user device
`campaign_id`	Campaign identification number
`gender`	Gender of the ad viewer "male" and "female"

Figure 3: Sample macros from publisher platforms that can recover information via advertisements.

1×1 invisible image served by the advertiser's servers, which will be requested by the device when the ad is shown. The impression beacon may also contain *macros* that the DSP substitutes with real values when the ad is shown using the data contained in the bid request from the publisher's app. For instance, if the bid request contains a GPS location determined by the publisher's app and sent to the SSP and then the DSP, then the DSP can substitute this data into the ad markup. A beacon URL such as https://advertiser.com/i.gif?gps={GPS} will cause the device's browser or app to request https://advertiser.com/i.gif?gps=38.8805396%2C-77.1131507 when the ad is shown. Through impression beacons, an advertiser can gather a multitude of information. Figure 3 shows a sample list of macros available on the DSP platform we have been using.

Ad Tags. A more complex form of interaction between the DSP and the advertiser uses *ad tags*. This process is shown in Figure 4. Ad tags are a javascript HTML tag that the advertiser gives to the DSP who inserts it into the markup causing the mobile device to retrieve and run the advertiser's javascript. Thus, instead of adding a single beacon URL, the advertiser can control the entire ad markup. Anything that is available through javascript is available to the advertiser. For instance, through a javascript callback on the image load, one can collect the amount of time the client took to download the image, thus computing bandwidth. Javascript and HTML5 provide a multitude of other information; e.g., the Android Browser provides the Battery Status API.

Note that the impression alone invokes javascript and gathers data; no clicking is needed.

Ad Targeting. Through RTB platforms, one can target ads on a variety of criteria: country, publisher showing the ad, IP addresses and ranges, and *advertising identifiers*. Both iOS and Android use an advertising identifier that is a random UUID shared across all

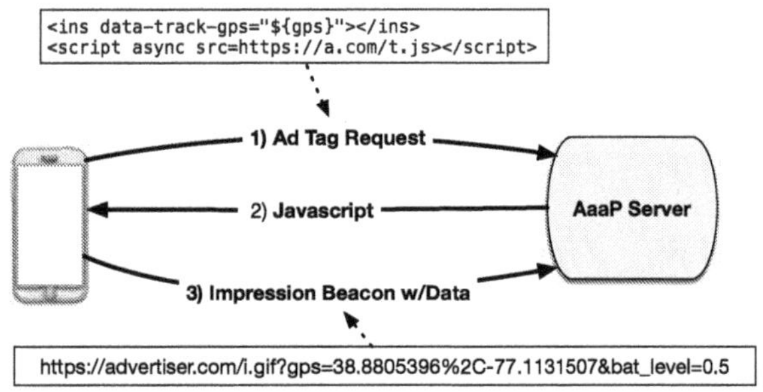

Figure 4: Ad Tags: HTML contains a *tag* that requests additional javascript and HTML from the AAAP server. Any data gathered (e.g. battery level) by the javascript is added to the impression beacon URL for our AAAP server.

apps on the device (though not available in the native browsers MobileSafari and Chrome). Targeting specific advertising identifiers enables our system to collect longitudinal data by targeting ads to specific devices. For instance, if we are interested in the behavior of devices assigned a certain IP address or are located in a certain geographic area, we can collect research data even when they change IP addresses or move from that location. We can answer questions such as, "Among mobile devices that are observed in a particular location, in which other locations where they also observed?".

4 IMPLEMENTATION

We have constructed a functioning AaaP service in Ruby on Rails, running on Amazon Web Services (AWS). Our prototype places ads, serves ad tags, gathers data via macros and javascript, and analyzes the results. Our AaaP service runs experiments based on a script, including a cron system for making regular changes to the experiment, such as increasing a bid or adding advertising identifiers to the set of targeted devices.

AaaP controls experiments programmatically through APIs provided by the self-service DSP. AaaP adjusts the targeting of advertisements, controls the starting and stopping times, and changes the amount the experiment is bidding for an advertisement. The system also uploads lists of advertising identifiers to target.

AaaP works through the API of a self-service Real-Time Bidding platform to place ads. As the self-service platform handles the bidding, the AaaP server only interacts with advertisements when an ad impression occurs (i.e., only when the ad is displayed on a device). Using a self-service platform avoids a great deal of work and expense that would be involved in our building of an RTB bidder capable of handling over 500k bid requests per second.

Our AaaP service uses macros and ad tags as explained in Section 3 and our custom javascript fetches and displays the creative and sets up the DOM for the advertisement and all measurements. We have developed a number of javascript functions that gather data and post it back to our server to be stored in a database and later analyzed. The system is scalable to large amounts of traffic and permits easy post-experiment analysis.

Because our system is based on a self-service platform, our server's work increases with the number of impressions per second, rather than the number of bids per second. Therefore, we can support many experiments with a handful of lightweight machines.

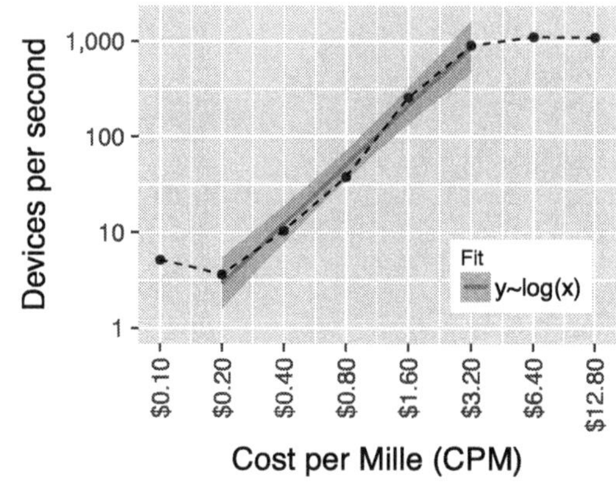

Figure 5: The relationship between the bid price (CPM=dollars/1000 impressions) and the number of new devices per second an experiment can measure. (Log-log scale. Points represent observed data. Fit includes only CPMs greater than $0.10 and less than $6.40.) Total cost = $95.58; Impressions = 19,764; Efficiency = 100%

The current system uses an AWS Elastic Load Balancer, one to four *t2.micro* EC2 servers in an autoscale group, one *t1.small* RDS Postgresql database, and the AWS Cloudfront CDN, backed by S3. The entire backend system costs less than $100 per month to run, well within the reach of most researchers.

5 CHARACTERIZATION

In this section, we characterize the efficacy, cost, and granularity of data that is measurable using AaaP. For instance, if an experiment requires single measurements from a multitude of unique devices, how fast can those devices be discovered and at what cost? Or if an experiment requires not just one, but many samples from particular devices, typically how long is it before they are seen again? The driving factors for all the questions we pose in this section are the *cost* and *time* incurred.

We have taken a simple approach in this section, bidding only on the smallest ad size available (320×50 pixels) and only on one of the self-service platform's Supply Side Platform (SSP) partners, Mopub, though there are more than a dozen additional exchanges such as Rubicon, Nexage, and Smaato.

5.1 Device Discovery

Question 1. At what rate can AaaP obtain at least one measurement from unique mobile devices, given an offered spend? Without other constraints, we have found that a massive amount of opportunity is available, even at very low bids. The minimum RTB bid is approximately $0.10 Cost Per Mille (CPM) — that is, cost per one thousand impressions — which is $0.0001 per ad shown. To provide a picture of the number of unique devices (as defined by unique advertising identifiers), we bid different amounts and measured the number of unseen and unique devices we could discover. Unfortunately, even at low bids, the scale is so massive that we used a sampling approach to estimate the actual scale. Note, our goal isn't to measure the exact amount of traffic available at different costs as it is highly dependent on all of the targeting factors, including: ad size, ad exchange, country, IP address targeting, time of day or day of week, etc.

We sampled one out of every 10,000 IP addresses in the US by targeting a random selection of 629 class C subnets. These subnets may not have any mobile devices, but we sampled uniformly at random, and should therefore be reasonably representative of activity on US IP addresses. We bid from a set of CPMs at random for 10 minutes at a time throughout the day to eliminate diurnal effects and measured the number of unique mobile advertising identifiers. We then scaled the results by 10,000 to determine the expected rate at which we could gather data. The results are shown in Figure 5 and covers two weeks of experimentation and approximately 20K impressions. As thefi gure shows, without constraints on where to place the ad, we were able to discover about 5 new devices *per second* at a $0.10 CPM. The results for $0.10 are slightly lower than those at $0.20. We do not know the exact reason, but we suspect it is either due to the higher variance at lower traffic levels or due to market effects where lower priced traffic is actually less desirable due to quality.

In this and all subsequentfi gures we report the number of impressions, the cost, the number of unique devices, and efficiency (percentage of impressions used to produce the plot). Note that sometimes the data is reused across plots. For example, we measured battery charge and bandwidth with the same impressions. In sum, we spent approximately $400 on more than 500k ads to produce this paper.

5.2 Geographic Fencing

Question 2. What is the cardinality of available devices in a limited geographic area? Many experiments can be conducted when accurate location information is available, such as studies of context-based behavior and local bandwidth conditions. Location information is often passed from mobile applications to SSPs then to bidders. Our self-service provider also allows us to target geographic areas (called *fences*). The fencing is often based on an IP2Geo database which can lead to errors; fortunately, we can often get highly accurate locations in a macrofi eld so we canfi lter all results by that location. Additionally, in the U.S. there is a mismatch between the name of a city in a postal address, which is used in targeting, and the administrative boundaries of a town. For instance, many postal address are labeled "Buffalo, NY" that are not within the administrative boundaries of Buffalo.

We conducted two experiments: *(a)* 70 days in Amherst, MA; and *(b)* 20 days in Amherst, MA, Charlottesville, VA, and New City, NY starting on a later date. Amherst, MA is a town of approximately 60k residents and 30k students; Charlottesville, VA is a town of 40k residents and 20k students; and New City, NY has a population of 30k residents. We limited the advertisement to exactly one impression for each unique device. We thenfi ltered the results to only permit data that: *(i)* included accurate location information, which is detectable on the SSP we used by the macrofi eld used, and *(ii)* truly within each city using *PostGIS* and *OpenStreetMap's* administrative boundaries for the town. The experiment used a CPM bid of $2 and the resulting cost of the experiment was $169.73, including impressions outside of the cities. The results of the experiment are shown in Figure 6. Due to the mismatch in addresses and boundaries, and missing GPS information, the overall efficiency was 14%.

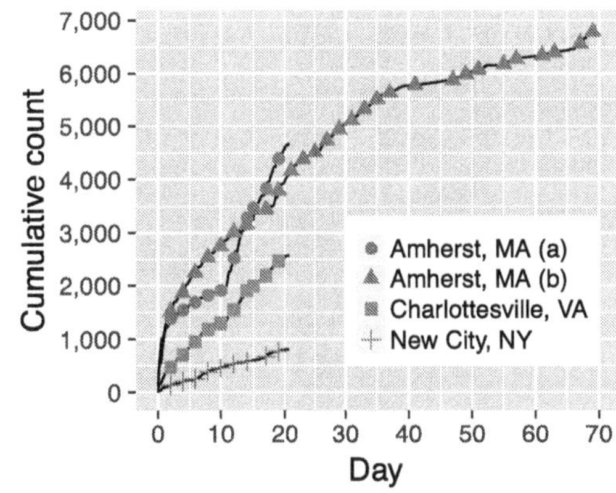

Figure 6: The rate at which AaaP can discover distinct devices in a limited geographic area. Total cost = $169.73; Impressions = 82,860; Efficiency = 14%. Efficiency is low as targeting is based on city name, not administrative boundaries and impressions lacking accurate location information are thrown out. (Points are a visual guide for legend; lines represent all data.)

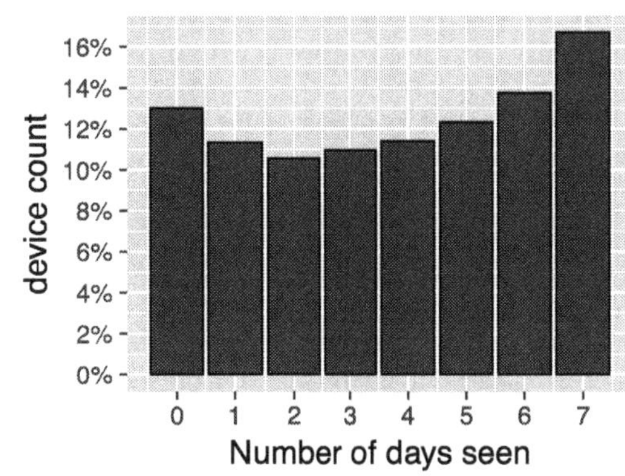

Figure 7: How often AaaP sees the same devices. Over a period of 7 days we added devices we saw to a target list. This graph shows the number of days following the device's first day that we saw them again. For instance we saw 50% of devices on at least 4 of the days. Total cost = $74.49; Impressions = 37,118; Efficiency = 94%. Imperfect impression cap per device leads to lowered efficiency.

The experiment demonstrates that, as expected, after an initial burst offi nding new devices, new devices are discovered at a steady rate with returns diminishing after two months. Increases in this rate are possible by targeting more RTB exchanges (provided that we canfi nd exchanges that provide honest location data) as well as targeting more ad sizes (factoring in that larger ad sizes are more expensive). There is also a burst of new devices found starting at day 11 in experiment (b). This occurred after US "Black Friday", a large shopping day and it is likely that students returned to town with new devices. This also occurred shortly after the release of a new iPhone.

As a very rough estimate, if we assume that Amherst, MA has about as many devices as people (60k), then we reached approximately 6% of the devices after 20 days and 12% of the devices after 60 days. The result is impressive considering how little effort is involved compared to any other methodology.

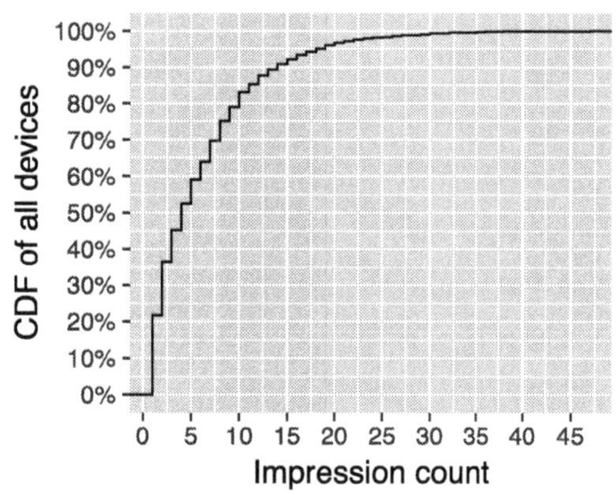

Figure 8: The count of impressions per device, as a CDF, when place a cap of 40 impressions per day, per device. Some devices see many, many ads in a short period, permitting high fidelity traces. Total cost = $12.88; Impressions = 9,921; Efficiency = 100%.

5.3 Repeat Observations

Question 3. With what frequency are devices observed multiple times? Experimenters may want to take multiple measurements from particular devices to see a pattern of behavior. Some devices will be seen frequently and others very infrequently. We measured how often devices in our Amherst, MA study were seen in a week. We limited it to one impression per day, per device, and targeted all of the devices that appeared in Amherst, MA, which was 8,358 devices . From that data we extracted the fraction of days we saw each device. The results are shown in Figure 7.

The experiment shows that more than half of the devices were seen on at least 4 of the days and 16% of the devices were seen all 7 days. This means that a large fraction of devices can provide measurements on a large fraction of days.

Experimenters may also be interested in even higherfi delity data from devices that appear very frequently. For instance if a device is contained in a traveling vehicle, would it be possible to get a continuous stream of locations? We conducted a similar experiment on approximately 10k Android devices (we reuse these results as part of section 6.3), but allowed 10 impressions per device during each of 4 six-hour periods in a day. The cumulative distribution function of the impressions seen is shown in Figure 8. While most devices only saw a few ads, many devices saw large numbers of ads, with 20% of devices seeing at least 10 ads and several devices seeing the maximum of 40. To collect highfi delity data, it may be necessary to target larger numbers of devices andfi lter the results accordingly for devices that present that opportunity. How such filtering influences sampling bias depends on what is measured. Optimizing the cost of discovery we leave as future work.

6 CHALLENGES AND TECHNIQUES

While AaaP exhibits superior scale, deployability, and cost when compared to direct measurement, it introduces new challenges, which we detail in this section. In this section, we demonstrate techniques for mitigating four primary deficiencies related to measuring location, bandwidth, batteries, and device identifiability. Through four studies, we address these issues and show how AaaP is relevant to the broad mobile systems topics of geography, networking, energy management, and security and privacy. Our intention is not to fully explore each, but to demonstrate how these challenges can be addressed.

6.1 Unreliable Location Information

Challenge 1: Location information provided by advertisements may be inaccurate. When an app is permitted access to a device's location APIs, advertisers learn a device's precise location. Otherwise, coarse estimates of the device location are sourced from IP-to-location databases (IP2Geo). Through a measurement study, we show that such databases are inaccurate for mobile device, as past work has found in small scale studies [10, 57, 70]. And we show that with carefulfi ltering, ads with precise location information can be leveraged by experimenters to greatly improve existing geolocation services.

RTB standards definefi elds that pass the source of location information to the advertiser, so that the quality may be considered. Unfortunately, the self-service advertising system we used provided no such labeling. Through trial and error using ads targeted at our own devices on a single SSP (Mopub) with location access permitted or denied, we determined which apps return high-quality location information. The simple rule we discovered and verified is that when a devices permits an app to access location, the *lat* and *lon* impression macros receive the correct location (and the *gps* macro). Without permission, those two macros are null, and a IP2Geo-based location is supplied by the *gps* macro only. On other exchanges, the mapping can be different, resulting in some manual work to determine the origin of the location.

The most reliable apps appear in Table 1, along with the fraction of ads that were returned in our study with non-null *lat/lon* macros. Not surprisingly, apps that require a device's location to work, like casual dating and weather apps, are among the list. The Weather Channel app and TuneIn self-report having 50 million [3] and 60 million [9] monthly active users, respectively. Whereas Grindr, Growlr, and MeetMe self-report relatively smaller audiences of 5 million [38], 4 million [36], and 2 million [2] monthly active users, respectively.

By targeting the publishers shown in Figure 1, and restricting advertisements to non-cellular US-based IPs, we constructed our own geolocation lookup service for each IP we observed with ads. We omitted cellular IPs because they are shared across many devices and wide geographic areas [70]. In total we measured device-native locations for 112k distinct IP addresses and 350k devices. We used these locations as ground-truth as they came directly from the device; in truth, they are only as accurate as the method used by device's location API (e.g., GPS, Cellular).

For each IP address k, each of D devices sees n ads that generate a set of n locations $L_{i,k} = (x_1, y_1), \ldots, (x_n, y_n)$. We calculate the centroid for the dth device seen at k as

$$C_{k,d} = (\frac{x_1 + \cdots + x_n}{n}, \frac{y_1 + \cdots + y_n}{n}) = (x_d, y_d). \quad (1)$$

We then estimate the location of k as C_k, the centroid of all of the D centroids as

$$C_k = (\frac{x_1 + \cdots + x_D}{n}, \frac{y_1 + \cdots + y_D}{n}) = (x_k, y_k). \quad (2)$$

App Name	Perc.	Notes
GROWLr Android	99%	Required
GROWLr iOS	99	Required
Grindr iOS	98	Required
Weather Mood	97	For weather
Grindr Android	96	Required
The Weather Channel iOS	84	For weather
My Clock Android	81	For weather
The Weather Channel Android	78	For weather
MeetMe: Chat Android	76	Encouraged
TextNow Android	71	Asks at install
My Clock Free Android	67	For weather
TuneIn Radio iOS	61	Local stations
TuneIn Android	61	Local stations
MB3: Mixer Box	61	Asks at install

Table 1: Apps that provide accurate GPS information based on non-null *lat/lon* macros. The percentage of devices (and thus users who gave the app permission) with access to device-native location information is shown.

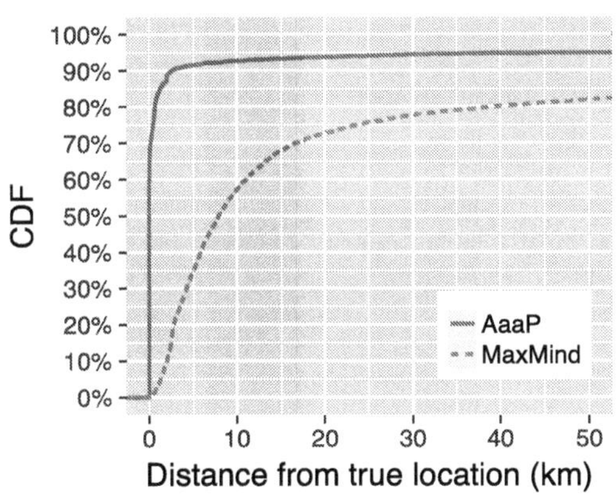

Figure 9: AaaP provides significantly lower error from true geographic location than using a commercial IP2Geo database. However, not all IPs can be geolocated with AaaP. Total cost = $40; Impressions = 396,382 ; Efficiency = 68%.

For each trial we left one device l out, and computed the Haversine distance between $C_{k\setminus l}$ and $C_{k,l}$; and also the distance between MaxMind's geographic location and $C_{k,l}$. We did not include any IP addresses where there weren't at least two devices as this test requires one to leave out and one to test.

As Figure 9 shows, using ads is tremendously more accurate than MaxMind: our AaaP approach is within 0.15 km 50% of the time, and within 1.0 km 85% of the time. In contrast, MaxMind is off by at least 8.0 km 50% of the time, and within only 40 km 85% of the time. The median error for AaaP is a 53*x* improvement. We investigated the places where AaaP made large errors and found devices from drastically different locations using the same IP address. We believe this is caused by devices using proxy/VPN servers at those IPs.

The union of the tens of millions of users of weather and dating apps (as well as the many, many other publishers we did not target), provides high levels of coverage of IPs, but ads will not be available at every IP. The best of use of such data is to augment, not replace, databases such as MaxMind or to provide high resolution location information to other experiments.

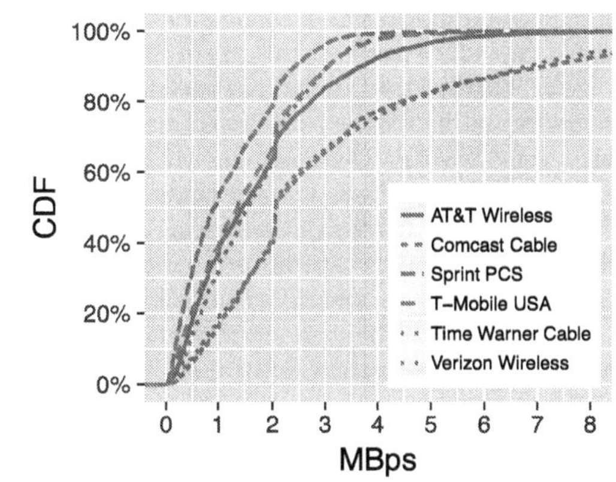

Figure 10: The bandwidth we observed for US-based carriers. Total cost = $26.72; Impressions = 45,581; Unique IPs: 21,193; Efficiency = 46%.

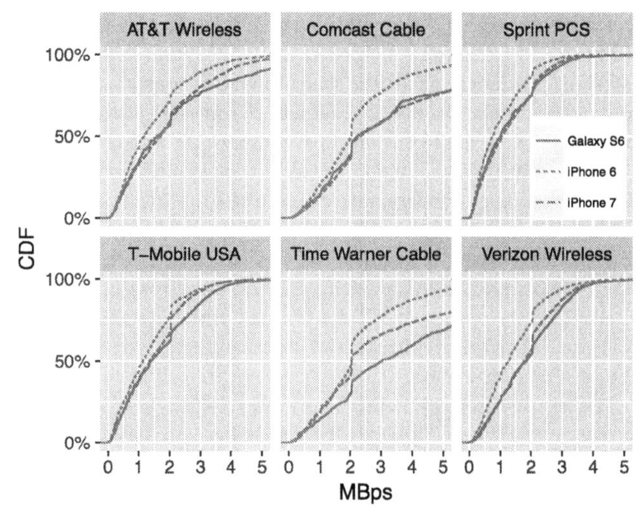

Figure 11: The bandwidth we observed for US carriers, per device model. (Uses same data as Figure 10.)

6.2 Abstracted Information and Bandwidth

Challenge 2: Information in advertisements is abstracted and aggregated. Similarly to location information, other, detailed information about a device may be abstracted by different actors between the experimenter and the end device's native components. For instance, in-app advertisements have access to the model of the device via native components and ad macros provided by the native components of the ad library. However, the model supplied via ad-macros for iOS yields the model of the phone at the level of iPhone 7 or iPhone 5s, but does not reveal the exact Apple model number, such as A1453 versus A1457, which are both iPhone 5s and would be available through direct measurement.

Even with these challenges we sought to measure mobile bandwidth provided to mobile devices, both over WiFi and cellular by timing how long it takes to fetch data from a server. In contrast with other techniques, AaaP measurements are precisely geolocated and attributed to mobile carriers and can scale quickly to millions of end-hosts.

There are a great number of questions that can be answered about bandwidth, but we chose to study the Apple iPhone 7. Popular press has highlighted the fact that Apple chose to produce two different versions of the iPhone 7 for the US market, one with an Intel modem and one with a Qualcomm modem. The Intel version did not support CDMA and was sold primarily through US carriers AT&T and T-Mobile and the Qualcomm version that supports GSM and CDMA was sold through Verizon and Sprint. Independent testing has shown that there are performance differences between these two models [1], but these are limited trials performed in a laboratory-like setting. We wanted to see what the practical effects of these differences are by studying the bandwidth achieved by in situ phones. Due to the abstracted information supplied to advertisements we do not know which model an ad is shown on, but we can detect which carrier they are using. Using this we can assume that the majority of devices on AT&T are of the Intel variant.

Our bandwidth test consisted of having the advertisement serially download three images sized 0.5,1, and 4 MB. Thesefi les are typical of the largerfi les downloaded on phones and are not dissimilar in size to some video advertisements. We found that 1MB and 4MBfi les resulted in about the same download speeds, suggesting both overcame startup effects. Thefiles: *(i)* consisted of compressed image data to eliminate the effects of compressing proxies, *(ii)* were placed on a well-distributed CDN (AWS Cloudfront), and *(iii)* used a cache-busting query parameter to eliminate the effects of caching proxies. We targeted ads to iPhone7s in 7 major US cities to give a more consistent environment to the measurements. We also measured the bandwidth achieved by phones on two major US cable Internet ISPs, Comcast and Time Warner, which demonstrate an upper bound on the performance of downloadingfi les of these sizes. The results of this test are shown in Figure 10.

The results show that AT&T consistently provides better performance to iPhone 7 devices than does Verizon. (We noted the performance bump at 2MB for all carriers and model and believe it was caused by the CDN.) If anything the Intel modem could be faster than the Qualcomm one, however given the limitations of targeting we cannot completely separate the effects of the ISP from the effects of the phone. If we were to bring the Qualcomm version to AT&T, would we achieve even higher bandwidths than the average because AT&T can achieve higher speeds than Verizon? To help answer this question, we repeated the test with the iPhone 6, which does not have the same bifurcation in chipsets and the Galaxy S6 to compare with Android. The results are shown in Figure 11 and demonstrate the same ordering of carriers. This provides strong evidence that the performance gap shown in the iPhone 7 experiment is largely due to differences in the network itself and not the device — consumers should feel comfortable purchasing either.

6.3 Sampled Data and Batteries

Challenge 3: AaaP can only collect data when an advertisement is shown, leading to varying numbers and irregular intervals of samples for each device. One of the advantages to AaaP is that it can target a subset of devices based on their advertising identifiers and bid relatively high to capture more data per user. However, even if AaaP bids very high, it can collect data only when

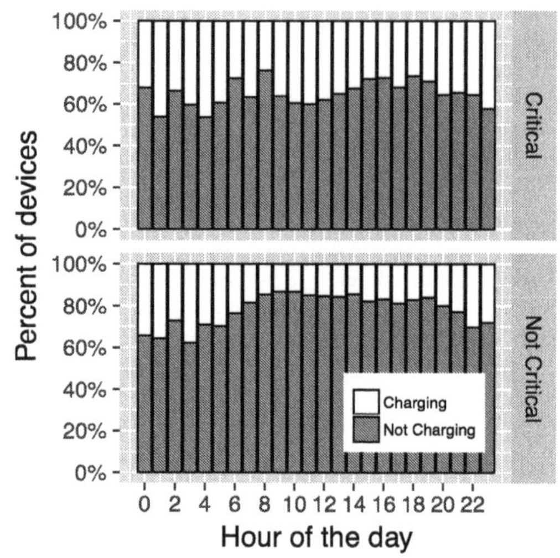

Figure 12: Battery level data we collected from Android devices by hour of the day, localized to their time zone. Critical battery level is defined as <20%. Impressions=142,706 ads; Unique devices=38,265; Total cost=Approximately $75 (reused data from other experiments). Efficiency=100%.

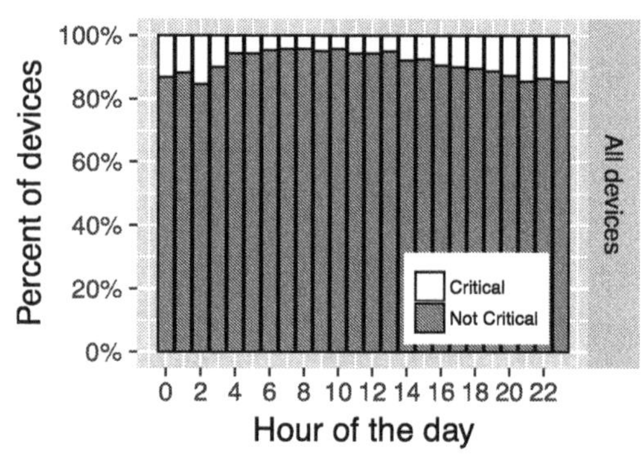

Figure 13: Most mobile phone batteries are not allowed to become critical, but the most frequent times are in late evening, among devices shown ads. (Same data as Fig.12.)

the ad is being shown. AaaP experiments can interpolate missing data and predict values based on past measurements.

To demonstrate this technique we deliberately picked a difficult, yet important example: battery state and the time at which the device was plugged in or unplugged. Using javascript and HTML5 it is possible to query the state of a mobile device's battery using the Battery Status API. This API is currently supported on Android devices and some laptop browsers. We can query *(i)* the fraction of the battery remaining, *(ii)* whether the device is charging, and the *(iii)* discharging and *(iv)* charging rates. We used only the battery remaining and charging state — the two rates *(iii)* and *(iv)* are often incorrect or unavailable. Results from this data are shown in Figures 12 and 13.

The results show a clear diurnal pattern with the majority of mobile device use occurring in the afternoon and evening. One can also see that it is much more common for devices to be plugged in when the battery is above 20% and a small proportion of devices are used when the battery is below 20%, though this is most likely in the

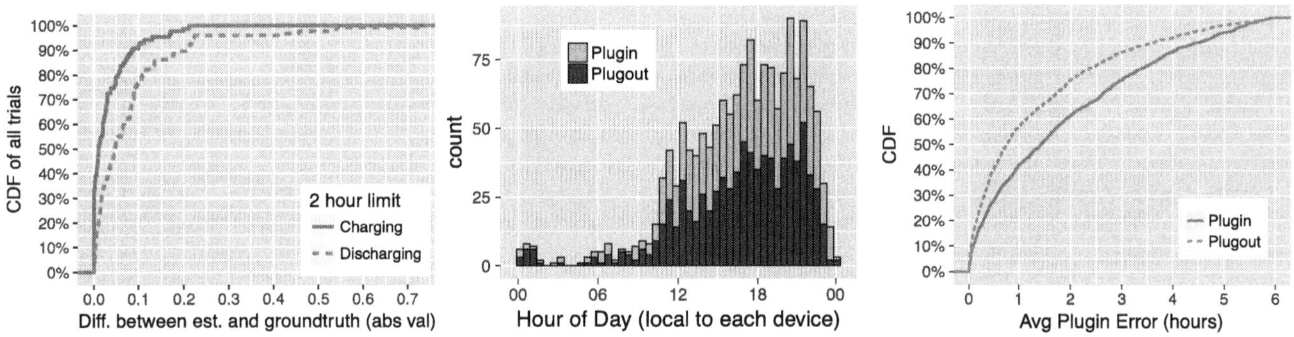

Figure 14: (Left) Error predicting battery level using measured ground truth. (Middle) Estimation of plug-in/unplug. (Right) Estimated error from using sampled data. Impressions=86,389; Unique devices=7,613; Cost=$80; Efficiency=48% (some devices show no plug in or out).

evening. However, this experiment brings up one of the unavoidable biases in our methodology. The data is solely derived from devices when they are being used and we have no ability to gather data while the device is idle (for instance while the user is asleep or the device is in a pocket.). In exchange for massive experimental scale, we incur some bias in the data and our conclusions must be couched in those biases.

Our goal is to infer information about what happened with the devices in between, or after measurements. To that end, we can use the pattern of a device's measurement to predict the state of the battery into the future and to estimate when the device may have been plugged in or unplugged. To do that we conducted an experiment using AaaP where we targeted devices for two days to gather battery information including the fraction the battery is charged ([0,1.0]) and the charging state (true or false). We targeted ads to 38k devices over two days. While we cannot ask the RTB platform to pace impressions, we did create four advertising campaigns per day, each one 6-hours long, and limited each to show up to 10 advertisements to each device.

Level Prediction. We can accurately predict the future state of the battery a short time into the future using a simple linear model of battery behavior. For each device, we have a sequence of observations; the ith observation $b_i = (t_i, c_i, s_i)$ has timestamp t_i, battery charge c_i, and charging state s_i. We then segment the sequence into observations that are of the same charging state. We then compute the linear regression over the segment (i.e., the values b_0 and b_1 such that $c_k = b_0 + b_1 t_k$ has the least sum square error for all observations, $k = 0 \ldots$, in the segment).

We measure accuracy by removing the last point in each segment (for segments with at least 3 points) and measure the error as the fraction of the battery the prediction is off by. This last, removed, point is the ground truth for measuring the prediction error. If the linear model intersects 100% or 0% battery, then we assume the battery stays in that state. We limit results to predictions less than two hours into the future, as accuracy degrades rapidly otherwise.

The results, shown in Figure 14(Left), demonstrate that within two hours, 90% of the time a linear model can predict the state of the battery to within 10% of the battery capacity when charging, and within 20% when discharging. The errors result from our use of a simple model; in practice, batteries behavior is more complicated. In our measurements we observed battery levels decreasing even while charing (perhaps due to high CPU activity), and devices that discharge much more rapidly than typical (perhaps due to faulty batteries).

Plug-in times. These same measurements also reveal when devices are plugged in or are operating on battery. While ads are not active long enough to usefully measure the exact time when the device was plugged in, AaaP can book-end such times by looking for points where the device was plugged in and then later not-plugged in, and vice versa. During this period, the state of charging must have changed *at least* once — we assume it was the midpoint. By excluding periods longer than 2 hours, we can estimate the histogram of when devices around the world were plugged in or unplugged, shown as Figure 14(Middle) and localized to the users' timezones.

Figure 14(Right) shows the error for this estimate. The maximum error would be the full duration of each period; since we use the midpoint as the plug-in (or -out) time, we assume the average error of half the period. Under this assumption, about 50% of our plugin periods are within 60 minutes, and 50% of our unplugged periods are within 90 minutes. (Doubling the minutes gives the maximum error.)

Prediction and interpolation are powerful tools for compensating for AaaP's sampling. More is possible: e.g., AaaP can measure location or the context of a user, such as using Wi-Fi or a particular application, take later measurements, and interpolate behaviors and movements that occurred between those points. All sampling-based systems make such inferences, and AaaP can leverage any such algorithms.

6.4 Longitudinal Data and Identifiability

Challenge 4: Solid, longitudinal, identifiers are not always available in advertisements. We heavily use advertising identifiers to target devices to focus data collection and to establish which measurements came from the same device, for instance when taking a trace of battery levels. However *(i)* some publishers apply a one-way hash to advertising identifiers before forwarding them to the SSP, *(ii)* advertising identifiers can be rotated through the operating systems settings, and *(iii)* for advertisements on the web we can apply cookies and read them, but the cookies are only available when the impression is shown, not when targeting. In AaaP we can deal with *(i)* by "unhashing" the identifiers and *(ii)* and *(iii)* by re-identifying devices based on *digitalfingerprinting* techniques.

Approximately 17k data points (7% of data) that we received carried a hashed device identifier. If overlooked, we might attribute data to two different devices when there is actually only one. To disambiguate devices, AaaP unhashes the identifiers by creating a dictionary of all advertising identifiers it sees, and hashes them with both MD5 and SHA-1. Using the dictionary we unhashed 8.4k devices (49% of the 17k) and use this identity in our other experiments. The remaining 51% remain hashed; and while none of them are the same as unhashed device identifiers, it is possible that some are different hashes of the same identifier, though this is less likely.

Other sources of ambiguity arise because devices can be configured to block their advertising identifier from being used or it can be rotated. When "limit ad tracking" is set in iOS, the advertising identifier is all zeros and the do not track (DNT)fl ag is set; we observed that no more than 7% of iOS devices had enabled this feature.[1]

However, when an identifier is reset or masked, devices can be re-identified based on persistent characteristics of their device or its connection to the network, e.g., device model and IP address. Many studies have been performed to measure identifiability from device metadata. For example, the Javascript AudioContext API can be leveraged to return a signature (without actually playing sound) [72]. To measure the entropy of this technique, the authors of a recent study created a web page and recruited visitors with 18,500 distinct cookies, resulting in 713 distinctfi ngerprints. All told, they measured 5.4 bits of entropy in the audio context. Other privacy researchers have also built javascript libraries [68, 77] and websites [15, 26] to expose as manyfi ngerprinting techniques as possible. And most new capabilities added to browsers often engender a discussion of privacy [42].

To demonstrate the efficiency of our platform we set up a experiment — using ads rather than a web page or new app — that measured several features available to advertisers. Several features are already returned by ad impressions: IP address, timezone, GPS and/or IP-based geo-location, model, and OS version. As a simple method of aggregating GPS information, we used Zip Code. In our ads, we used the same javascript as the previous study [28]. Our goal was to repeat the experiment and quantify the identifiability of these features, using the advertising identifier as ground truth.

Building and deploying the ad code took only hours. We placed 142,592 ads on 40,001 distinct devices, and measured the entropy of features alone and in combination. For example, we gathered 728 distinct audio signatures, with a measured entropy of 5.5 bits, which is similar to the previous study [28]. In comparison, the entropy of the OS version is 2.8 bits; device model is 7.5 bits; and IP address is 16.7 bits of entropy. Combinations are more powerful. For example, an IP and audio signature is 20.4 bits; and the combination of ISP, Model, TZ, IP, Audio, OS version, Zip code was the highest at 22.8 bits. Obviously, some features are overlapping in terms of information.

To gain additional clarity, we ran a series of experiments that quantified device identifiability given these features and a decision tree classifier.[2] We performed 66 trials with a 80%/20% train and test split for each feature/combination. The advertising identifier forms the ground-truth for the experiment. Accuracy results for a variety of non-overlapping features are shown in Figure 15 as boxplots. There exists some controls over IP address (by using Tor) and over geographic information (by turning of GPS and by using Tor to thwart geo-location). Therefore, the results are show in groupings: neither geographic nor IP address features available; geographic available but not IP address; both geographic and IP address information available. In this study, without IP and geographic information, the most accurate identification was fairly low at 15% from a combination of audio signature, device model, ISP, and timezone. With the addition of geographic information (making timezone obvious), the combination of audio signature, device model, ISP, and zip code is 34% accurate. Finally, with IP information and without zip code, we see that the combination of the IP and model is the most identifying; adding audio as a third component actually lowers accuracy. This shows that in many cases AaaP can collect longitudinal data even without the use of platform supplied identifiers.

7 LIMITATIONS

AaaP is not appropriate for all experiments. Particularly, when compared to native applications, AaaP suffers from two limitations: *(i)* the uncontrolled nature of the platform, and *(ii)* the substrate is a web browser without direct access to native APIs.

AaaP cannot sample with a precise rate nor interact with users who never use applications that show advertisements—by its nature AaaP can only gather data when advertisements can be purchased for a device. While we have provided some guidance in the paper, the individual experiment will dictate the statistical conclusions. What AaaP does provide is a population of devices orders of magnitude larger than any research experiment based on native apps, with a very low level of selection bias, which we believe can often counteract the lack of sampling control.

AaaP is also limited to the capabilities provided by browser implementations, outlined in Figure 3. There is always a tension between the availability of data and the scale of an experiment, and researchers will naturally pick the substrate that provides the required data at the largest scale. AaaP exists in a *hierarchy* of environments, starting from lab-bench experiments that have direct access to hardware; to rooted devices that remove sandboxing restrictions and yield access private APIs; to native applications that have access to a subset of that information; to advertising that has access to a combination of native and browser information; and finally a pure browser environment. For the same level of effort, each method provides less access, but perhaps greater scale. And all methods are complimentary, with AaaP providing some of the broadest and most diverse measurements that are easiest to gather. We suggest that AaaP be an experimenter'sfi rst step; and if needed, code deployed natively on the device as a second step.

[1]Specifically, we placed ads on 43,620 iOS 10 *devices* that *did not* have the DNTflag set, and we placed on 3,095 *ads* on devices that *did* have it set; i.e., as an upper bound, only 7% of iOS devices limit tracking.

[2]See http://scikit-learn.org/stable/modules/tree.html.

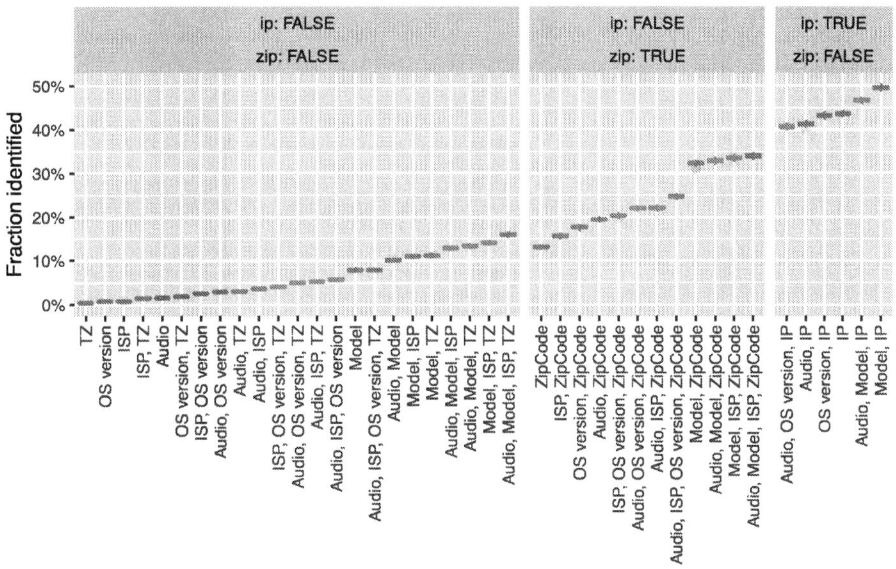

Figure 15: Identifying devices based on one or more features available from data returned from impressions. Each boxplot is the result of 66 trials, i.e., 2,706 trials total. Total cost = Approximately $75 (we reused data from a variety of experiments), Impressions = 142,592; Unique Devices: 40,010; Efficiency = 100%.

8 RELATED WORK

Measurement of mobile systems is a richfi eld. To our knowledge, AaaP is thefi rst to leverage advertisements as a platform for measurement and experimentation. Below we provide comparisons of AaaP to the most relevant related work. See also Section 2 [25, 33, 39, 52].

Testbeds and their characterization (Section 5). AaaP can be viewed as the largest-ever mobile measurement testbed. Past testbed efforts include indoor wireless testbeds, WinLab [46], outdoor mobile testbeds [66], and related efforts such as LiveLab [64], PhoneLab [51], and PhantomNet [12]. Unlike these past approaches, AaaP requires no installation, maintenance, or major infrastructure. Code on devices is maintained by third parties who have a deep interest in ensuring ads are displayable and richly featured.

Measuring Location (Section 6.1). There are two primary methods to determine the location of a mobile device: *(i)* use the device-native capabilities or W3C Geolocation API in the browser, or *(ii)* approximate the location based on the IP address of the device using a commercial IP2Geo database [5–8]. The accuracy of such databases vary, and the sources of their data is mostly opaque. Several studies have attempted to quantify the accuracy using native apps [10, 70] or estimates of ground truth from POP locations [57]. AaaP can be used to both quantify the accuracy of such databases and greatly enhance their accuracy in a focused, inexpensive, and highly scalable manner.

Bandwidth Measurement (Section 6.2). Bandwidth measurement is a core task of networking research, and it is impractical to list all related work. In contrast to selected works, our study requires no carrier assistance [55] and is not limited to a single geographic area or country [71]. On the other hand, AaaP would be a challenging platform to gather statistics from base stations or to evaluate gains from delayed scheduling of requests [43], or from using two carriers at once [11]. An alternative is to recruit users to install a mobile app [4, 32]; however, such recruitment takes time and will inevitably be biased by geography and other factors.

Device Battery Behavior (Section 6.3). Many studies have looked at measuring battery power patterns in mobile devices, all using native measurements. Less recent studies were limited to less than 100 users [13, 21, 40, 40, 59, 60, 75]. These studies look to correlate battery usage with the processes running on the device, including background tasks [21, 75], which is not something that AaaP could measure. The OpenBattery project proposed a piecewise linear model for battery charging and discharging patterns [40]. We do the same, but we also contribute predictions about battery levels. Falaki et. al. [29] makes similar observations about approximating discharge and charge patterns as linear in a study of 255 users. Context aware battery management [60] attempts to control battery based on the user's context—AaaP can measure location, which could provide a greatly expanded study.

Carat is a recent native measurement tool, used by more than 300k users [37, 54]; see also Device Analyzer [78]. Carat was able to access the list of processes running and the battery level and identify energy intensive apps. AaaP cannot list processes on a device; but unfortunately, as of iOS 9.3.3, neither can native applications like Carat. The larger point is that recruiting tens or hundreds of thousands of users to a study relies on a massive effort or perhaps publicity in the popular press [23]. We were able to take battery measurements from 38k distinct users without recruitment. Further, we believe that an AaaP-base study can be far less biased in sampling than a self-selecting participant pool.

Identifiability (Section 6.4). Numerous papers have sought to evaluate distinguishing features of web browsers [27, 48–50, 74]. These studies are primarily restricted to the web, whereas mobile advertising libraries, and thus DSPs and advertisers, have access to many additionalfi ngerprinting features, such as location, device names, storage sizes, etc. Such data has not been considered in otherfi ngerprinting work, to our knowledge, and many studies are small.

Advertising. Past work has concentrated on measurements of ads themselves, including: consumer privacy [20, 34, 45, 56, 61, 63, 69]; algorithms to optimizing ad placement and delivery [22, 30, 41, 44, 47, 80]; and measurement of what ads users are shown [14, 24, 35, 53, 73, 76, 79].

9 CONCLUSIONS

We believe that AaaP is just the beginning in using ads to measure phenomena across mobile systems by researchers. While we have developed a number of techniques that solidify AaaP's capabilities, there will be more efficient methodologies — we reiterate that ethics discussions must keep pace with such innovations. Given the incredibly low effort needed to build new collection methods, the negligible costs, and the time required for deployment, this paper only scratches the surface of what is possible. Here we have made very little use of a wealth of location information, the access to the accelerometer, and the upcoming APIs that will be built to access numerous sensors on mobile devices. We expect that all of these willfi nd their way into advertising-based measurement systems.

ACKNOWLEDGEMENTS

We are thankful to the anonymous reviewers for their insightful comments and suggestions, especially our shepherd Matt Welsh. We also thank Simson Garfinkel for insightful discussions about the IRB process. Our deployment was supported by the Amazon Web Services (AWS) Cloud Credits for Research program as well as high performance computing equipment obtained under a grant from the Collaborative R&D Fund managed by the Massachusetts Technology Collaborative.

REFERENCES

[1] iPhone 7 Plus: A Tale of Two Personalities. http://cellularinsights.com/iphone7/. (Oct 2016).
[2] MeetMe Reports U.S. Mobile CPMs Increased 14for November; Reiterates Fourth Quarter and Full Year 2016 Guidance. http://www.snl.com/irweblinkx/file.aspx?IID=4392695&FID=36970855. (December 05 2016).
[3] The Weather Company Fact Sheet. http://www.theweathercompany.com/weather-company-fact-sheet. (Oct 24 2016).
[4] http://www.eecs.umich.edu/3gtest (dead link). (2017).
[5] https://www.maxmind.com/. (2017).
[6] https://www.neustar.biz/risk/compliance-solutions/ip-intelligence. (2017).
[7] http://www.ip2location.com/. (2017).
[8] http://www.ipligence.com/. (2017).
[9] TuneIn Set to Deliver Coverage of Super Bowl LI to Global Audience. http://tunein.com/press-releases/TuneIn-Set-to-Deliver-Coverage-of-Super-Bowl-LI-to-Global-Audience/. (Jan 30 2017).
[10] Mahesh Balakrishnan, Iqbal Mohomed, and Venugopalan Ramasubramanian. 2009. Where's that phone?: geolocating IP addresses on 3G networks. In *Proc. ACM Internet measurement conference.* 294–300.
[11] Dziugas Baltrunas, Ahmed Elmokashfi, and Amund Kvalbein. 2014. Measuring the Reliability of Mobile Broadband Networks. In *Proc. ACM Internet Measurement Conference.* 45–58. http://doi.acm.org/10.1145/2663716.2663725
[12] Arijit Banerjee, Junguk Cho, Eric Eide, Jonathon Duerig, Binh Nguyen, Robert Ricci, Jacobus Van der Merwe, Kirk Webb, and Gary Wong. 2015. Phantomnet: Research infrastructure for mobile networking, cloud computing and software-defined networking. *GetMobile: Mobile Computing and Communications* 19, 2 (2015), 28–33.
[13] Nilanjan Banerjee, Ahmad Rahmati, Mark D Corner, Sami Rollins, and Lin Zhong. 2007. Users and Batteries: Interactions and Adaptive Energy Management in Mobile Systems. In *International Conference on Ubiquitous Computing (UbiComp).* Springer, Innsbruck, Austria, 217–234.
[14] Paul Barford, Igor Canadi, Darja Krushevskaja, Qiang Ma, and S Muthukrishnan. 2014. Adscape: Harvesting and analyzing online display ads. In *Proceedings of the 23rd international conference on World wide web.* ACM, 597–608.
[15] Benoit Baudry. Am I unique? https://amiunique.org/. (2017).
[16] Karl Bode. Why Are People Using Ad Blockers? Ads Can Eat Up To 79% Of Mobile Data Allotments. https://www.techdirt.com/articles/20160317/09274333934/why-are-people-using-ad-blockers-ads-can-eat-up-to-79-mobile-data-allotments.shtml. (March 2016).
[17] Zachary Davies Boren. There are officially more mobile devices than people in the world. http://www.independent.co.uk/life-style/gadgets-and-tech/news/there-are-officially-more-mobile-devices-than-people-in-the-world-9780518.html. (Oct 7 2014).
[18] Sam Burnett and Nick Feamster. 2015. Encore: Lightweight measurement of web censorship with cross-origin requests. *ACM SIGCOMM Computer Communication Review* 45, 4 (2015), 653–667.
[19] John W. Byers. 2015. *Encore: Lightweight Measurement of Web Censorship with Cross-Origin Requests – Public Review,.* Technical Report http://conferences.sigcomm.org/sigcomm/2015/pdf/reviews/226pr.pdf. Department of Computer Science, Boston University.
[20] Claude Castelluccia, Mohamed-Ali Kaafar, and Minh-Dung Tran. 2012. Betrayed by your ads!. In *International Symposium on Privacy Enhancing Technologies Symposium.* Springer, 1–17.
[21] Hui Chen. 2016. *User-Centric Power Management For Mobile Operating Systems.* Ph.D. Dissertation. Wayne State University.
[22] Ye Chen, Pavel Berkhin, Bo Anderson, and Nikhil R Devanur. 2011. Real-time bidding algorithms for performance-based display ad allocation. In *Proc. ACM SIGKDD international conference on Knowledge discovery and data mining.* ACM, 1307–1315.
[23] Josh Constantine. Carat: The Brilliant App That Increases Your Battery Life By Showing What Other Apps To Kill. https://techcrunch.com/2012/06/14/carat-battery/. (June 14 2012).
[24] Amit Datta, Michael Carl Tschantz, and Anupam Datta. 2015. Automated experiments on ad privacy settings. *Proceedings on Privacy Enhancing Technologies* 2015, 1 (2015), 92–112.
[25] David Dittrich, Erin Kenneally, et al. 2012. *The Menlo Report: Ethical Principles Guiding Information and Communication Technology Research.* Technical Report https://www.caida.org/publications/papers/2012/menlo_report_actual_formatted/menlo_report_actual_formatted.pdf. U.S. Department of Homeland Security Science and Technology Directorate, Cyber Security Division.
[26] Peter Eckersley. 2010. How unique is your web browser?. In *Privacy Enhancing Technologies (https://panopticlick.eff.org/).* Springer, 1–18.
[27] Peter Eckersley. 2010. How unique is your web browser?. In *International Symposium on Privacy Enhancing Technologies Symposium.* Springer, 1–18.
[28] Steven Englehardt and Arvind Narayanan. 2016. Online tracking: A 1-million-site measurement and analysis. In *Proc. ACM Conference on Computer and Communications Security.*
[29] Hossein Falaki, Ratul Mahajan, Srikanth Kandula, Dimitrios Lymberopoulos, Ramesh Govindan, and Deborah Estrin. 2010. Diversity in smartphone usage. In *Proc. ACM Mobisys.* 179–194.
[30] Ayman Farahat and Michael C Bailey. 2012. How effective is targeted advertising?. In *Proc. international conference on World Wide Web.* ACM, 111–120.
[31] Jay Friedman. How do I estimate the total number of online ad impressions that might be seen by internet users over a 30-day period for a given U.S. DMA? https://www.quora.com/How-do-I-estimate-the-total-number-of-online-ad-impressions-that-might-be-seen-by-internet-users-over-a-30-day-period-for-a-given-U-S-DMA. (February 2015).
[32] Zhaoyu Gao, Arun Venkataramani, James F. Kurose, and Simon Heimlicher. 2014. Towards a Quantitative Comparison of Location-independent Network Architectures. In *Proc. ACM Sigcomm.* 259–270.
[33] Simson L. Garfinkel. 2008. *IRBs and Security Research: Myths, Facts and Mission Creep.* Technical Report https://calhoun.nps.edu/bitstream/handle/10945/40330/garfinkel_IRBs_and_Security_Research.pdf?sequence=1. Naval Postgraduate School.
[34] Michael C Grace, Wu Zhou, Xuxian Jiang, and Ahmad-Reza Sadeghi. 2012. Unsafe exposure analysis of mobile in-app advertisements. In *Proceedings of thefifth ACM conference on Security and Privacy in Wireless and Mobile Networks.* ACM, 101–112.
[35] Saikat Guha, Bin Cheng, and Paul Francis. 2010. Challenges in measuring online advertising systems. In *Proc. ACM Internet measurement conference.* ACM, 81–87.
[36] Stuart Haggas. Grindr & Scruff & Hornet… Oh My! Using Gay Social Networking Apps When Traveling. http://passportmagazine.com/grindr-scruff-hornet-oh-my-using-gay-social-networking-apps-when-traveling/. (retrieved March 14 2017).
[37] Mohammad A. Hoque and Sasu Tarkoma. 2016. Characterizing Smartphone Power Management in the Wild. In *International Conference on Ubiquitous Computing (UbiComp).* 1279–1286.
[38] Gustavo Inciarte. 2014. Grindr Turns Five! http://queermeup.com/lgbt-community-2/grindr-turns-five (March 2014).
[39] Ben Jones, Roya Ensafi, Nick Feamster, Vern Paxson, and Nick Weaver. 2015. Ethical concerns for censorship measurement. In *Proc. ACM SIGCOMM Workshop on Ethics in Networked Systems Research.* ACM, 17–19.

[40] Gareth L. Jones and Peter G. Harrison. 2012. Collecting battery data with Open Battery. In *2012 Imperial College Computing Student Workshop (OpenAccess Series in Informatics (OASIcs))*, Andrew V. Jones (Ed.), Vol. 28. Schloss Dagstuhl–Leibniz-Zentrum fuer Informatik, Dagstuhl, Germany, 75–80.
[41] Azeem J Khan, Kasthuri Jayarajah, Dongsu Han, Archan Misra, Rajesh Balan, and Srinivasan Seshan. 2013. CAMEO: A middleware for mobile advertisement delivery. In *Proc. ACM Mobisys*. ACM, 125–138.
[42] Anssi Kostiainen and Mounir Lamouri. 2016. *Battery Status API W3C Candidate Recommendation*. Technical Report.
[43] Kyunghan Lee, Joohyun Lee, Yung Yi, Injong Rhee, and Song Chong. 2013. Mobile Data Offloading: How Much Can WiFi Deliver? *IEEE/ACM Trans. Netw.* 21, 2 (April 2013), 536–550.
[44] Kuang-chih Lee, Burkay Orten, Ali Dasdan, and Wentong Li. 2012. Estimating conversion rate in display advertising from past performance data. In *Proc. ACM SIGKDD international conference on Knowledge discovery and data mining*. 768–776.
[45] Ilias Leontiadis, Christos Efstratiou, Marco Picone, and Cecilia Mascolo. 2012. Don't kill my ads!: balancing privacy in an ad-supported mobile application market. In *Proc. Workshop on Mobile Computing Systems & Applications*. ACM, 2.
[46] Zoran Miljanic, Ivan Seskar, Khanh Le, and Dipankar Raychaudhuri. 2007. The WINLAB network centric cognitive radio hardware platform-WiNC2R. In *Proc. International Conference on Cognitive Radio Oriented Wireless Networks and Communications*. IEEE, 155–160.
[47] Prashanth Mohan, Suman Nath, and Oriana Riva. 2013. Prefetching mobile ads: Can advertising systems afford it?. In *Proc. ACM European Conference on Computer Systems*. ACM, 267–280.
[48] Keaton Mowery, Dillon Bogenreif, Scott Yilek, and Hovav Shacham. 2011. Fingerprinting information in JavaScript implementations. *Proceedings of W2SP* 2 (2011), 180–193.
[49] Keaton Mowery and Hovav Shacham. 2012. Pixel perfect: Fingerprinting canvas in HTML5. *Proceedings of W2SP* (2012).
[50] Martin Mulazzani, Philipp Reschl, Markus Huber, Manuel Leithner, Sebastian Schrittwieser, Edgar Weippl, and FC Wien. 2013. Fast and reliable browser identification with javascript enginefi ngerprinting. In *Web 2.0 Workshop on Security and Privacy (W2SP)*, Vol. 5.
[51] Anandatirtha Nandugudi, Anudipa Maiti, Taeyeon Ki, Fatih Bulut, Murat Demirbas, Tevfik Kosar, Chunming Qiao, Steven Y Ko, and Geoffrey Challen. 2013. Phonelab: A large programmable smartphone testbed. In *Proc. International Workshop on Sensing and Big Data Mining*. ACM, 1–6.
[52] Arvind Narayanan and Bendert Zevenbergen. 2015. *No Encore for Encore? Ethical Questions for Web-Based Censorship Measurement*. Technical Report https://ssrn.com/abstract=2665148. SSRN.
[53] Suman Nath. 2015. Madscope: Characterizing mobile in-app targeted ads. In *Proc. ACM Mobisys*. ACM, 59–73.
[54] Adam J Oliner, Anand P Iyer, Ion Stoica, Eemil Lagerspetz, and Sasu Tarkoma. 2013. Carat: Collaborative energy diagnosis for mobile devices. In *Proc. ACM Conference on Embedded Networked Sensor Systems*. 10.
[55] U. Paul, A. P. Subramanian, M. M. Buddhikot, and S. R. Das. 2011. Understanding traffic dynamics in cellular data networks. In *2011 Proceedings IEEE INFOCOM*. 882–890. https://doi.org/10.1109/INFCOM.2011.5935313
[56] Paul Pearce, Adrienne Porter Felt, Gabriel Nunez, and David Wagner. 2012. Addroid: Privilege separation for applications and advertisers in android. In *Proc. ACM Symposium on Information, Computer and Communications Security*. 71–72.
[57] Ingmar Poese, Steve Uhlig, Mohamed Ali Kaafar, Benoit Donnet, and Bamba Gueye. 2011. IP geolocation databases: Unreliable? *ACM SIGCOMM Computer Communication Review* 41, 2 (2011), 53–56.
[58] David Raab. How Many Ads Do You See Each Day? Fewer Than It Seems (I Think). http://customerexperiencematrix.blogspot.com/2015/09/how-many-ads-per-day-do-you-see-fewer.html. (September 2015).
[59] Ahmad Rahmati, Angela Qian, and Lin Zhong. 2007. Understanding Human-battery Interaction on Mobile Phones. In *Proc. International Conference on Human Computer Interaction with Mobile Devices and Services*. ACM, 265–272.
[60] Nishkam Ravi, James Scott, Lu Han, and Liviu Iftode. 2008. Context-aware battery management for mobile phones. In *IEEE International Conference on Pervasive Computing and Communications*. 224–233.
[61] Franziska Roesner, Tadayoshi Kohno, and David Wetherall. 2012. Detecting and defending against third-party tracking on the web. In *Proc. USENIX conference on Networked Systems Design and Implementation*. 12.
[62] Kenneth John Ryan et al. 1979. *The Belmont Report*. Technical Report http://www.hhs.gov/ohrp/humansubjects/guidance/belmont.html. U.S. Department of Health and Human Services.
[63] Shashi Shekhar, Michael Dietz, and Dan S Wallach. 2012. Adsplit: Separating smartphone advertising from applications. In *Proc. USENIX Security Symposium*. 553–567.
[64] Clayton Shepard, Ahmad Rahmati, Chad Tossell, Lin Zhong, and Phillip Kortum. 2011. LiveLab: measuring wireless networks and smartphone users in thefield. *ACM SIGMETRICS Performance Evaluation Review* 38, 3 (2011), 15–20.
[65] Aaron Smith. African Americans and Technology Use. http://www.pewinternet.org/2014/01/06/african-americans-and-technology-use/. (January 2014).
[66] Hamed Soroush, Nilanjan Banerjee, Mark Corner, Brian Levine, and Brian Lynn. 2011. A retrospective look at the UMass DOME mobile testbed. *ACM SIGMOBILE Mobile Computing and Communications Review* 15, 4 (October 2011), 2–15.
[67] Hamed Soroush, Keen Sung, Erik Learned-Miller, Brian Neil Levine, and Marc Liberatore. 2013. Turning Off GPS is Not Enough: Cellular location leaks over the Internet. In *Proc. Privacy Enhancing Technologies Symposium (PETS)*. 103–122.
[68] Jack Spirou. Clientjs. https://github.com/jackspirou/clientjs. (2017).
[69] Ryan Stevens, Clint Gibler, Jon Crussell, Jeremy Erickson, and Hao Chen. 2012. Investigating user privacy in android ad libraries. In *Workshop on Mobile Security Technologies (MoST)*. 10.
[70] Sipat Triukose, Sebastien Ardon, Anirban Mahanti, and Aaditeshwar Seth. 2012. Geolocating IP addresses in cellular data networks. In *International Conference on Passive and Active Network Measurement*. Springer, 158–167.
[71] Fung Po Tso, Jin Teng, Weijia Jia, and Dong Xuan. 2010. Mobility: A Double-edged Sword for HSPA Networks: A Large-scale Test on Hong Kong Mobile HSPA Networks. In *Proc. ACM MobiHoc*. 81–90.
[72] Liam Tung. Think you're not being tracked? Now websites turn to audiofinger-printing to follow you. http://www.zdnet.com/article/think-youre-not-being-tracked-now-websites-turn-to-audio-fingerprinting-to-follow-you/. (May 20 2016).
[73] Imdad Ullah, Roksana Boreli, Mohamed Ali Kaafar, and Salil S Kanhere. 2014. Characterising user targeting for in-app mobile ads. In *IEEE Infocom Workshops*. IEEE, 547–552.
[74] Thomas Unger, Martin Mulazzani, Dominik Frühwirt, Markus Huber, Sebastian Schrittwieser, and Edgar Weippl. 2013. Shpf: Enhancing http(s) session security with browserfi ngerprinting. In *Proc. International Conference on Availability, Reliability and Security (ARES)*. IEEE, 255–261.
[75] Narseo Vallina-Rodriguez, Pan Hui, Jon Crowcroft, and Andrew Rice. 2010. Exhausting Battery Statistics: Understanding the Energy Demands on Mobile Handsets. In *Proc. ACM Workshop on Networking, Systems, and Applications on Mobile Handhelds*. 9–14.
[76] Narseo Vallina-Rodriguez, Jay Shah, Alessandro Finamore, Yan Grunenberger, Konstantina Papagiannaki, Hamed Haddadi, and Jon Crowcroft. 2012. Breaking for commercials: characterizing mobile advertising. In *Proc. ACM Internet Measurement Conference*. ACM, 343–356.
[77] Valentin Vasilyev.fi ngerprintjs2. https://github.com/Valve/fingerprintjs2. (Retreived June 2017).
[78] Daniel T Wagner, Andrew Rice, and Alastair R Beresford. 2013. Device analyzer: Understanding smartphone usage. In *International Conference on Mobile and Ubiquitous Systems*. Springer, 195–208.
[79] Jun Yan, Ning Liu, Gang Wang, Wen Zhang, Yun Jiang, and Zheng Chen. 2009. How much can behavioral targeting help online advertising?. In *Proc. International conference on World Wide Web*. ACM, 261–270.
[80] Weinan Zhang, Shuai Yuan, and Jun Wang. 2014. Optimal real-time bidding for display advertising. In *Proc. ACM SIGKDD international conference on Knowledge discovery and data mining*. 1077–1086.

NutShell: Scalable Whittled Proxy Execution for Low-Latency Web over Cellular Networks

Ashiwan Sivakumar
Purdue University
West Lafayette, IN, USA

Chuan Jiang
Purdue University
West Lafayette, IN, USA

Yun Seong Nam
Purdue University
West Lafayette, IN, USA

Shankaranarayanan P.N.
AT&T Labs – Research
Bedminster, NJ, USA

Vijay Gopalakrishnan
AT&T Labs – Research
Bedminster, NJ, USA

Sanjay G Rao
Purdue University
West Lafayette, IN, USA

Subhabrata Sen
AT&T Labs – Research
Bedminster, NJ, USA

Mithuna Thottethodi
Purdue University
West Lafayette, IN, USA

T.N. Vijaykumar
Purdue University
West Lafayette, IN, USA

ABSTRACT

Despite much recent progress, Web page latencies over cellular networks remain much higher than those over wired networks. Proxies that execute Web page JavaScript (JS) and push objects needed by the client can reduce latency. However, a key concern is the scalability of the proxy which must execute JS for many concurrent users. In this paper, we propose to scale the proxies, focusing on a design where the proxy's execution is solely to push the needed objects and the client completely executes the page as normal. Such *redundant execution* is a simple, yet effective approach to cutting network latencies, which dominate page load delays in cellular settings. We develop *whittling*, a technique to identify and execute in the proxy only the JS code necessary to identify and push the objects required for the client page load, while skipping other code. Whittling is closely related to program slicing, but with the important distinction that it is acceptable to approximate the program slice in the proxy given the client's complete execution. Experiments with top Alexa Web pages show *NutShell* can sustain, on average, 27% more user requests per second than a proxy performing fully redundant execution, while preserving, and sometimes enhancing, the latency benefits.

CCS CONCEPTS

• **Networks** → **Transport protocols**; *Network measurement*; *Cloud computing*; • **Information systems** → *Browsers*;

KEYWORDS

Mobile Web, Cloud computing, Proxy-assisted browsing, Program Slicing, Whittling

MobiCom '17, October 16–20, 2017, Snowbird, UT, USA

ACM ISBN 978-1-4503-4916-1/17/10...$15.00
https://doi.org/10.1145/3117811.3117827

1 INTRODUCTION

Web pages have, over the years, evolved from simple and relatively static pages to ones that are feature rich and customized to individual user preferences. This evolution, however, has made them significantly more complex [17, 33], with most pages comprising of tens to hundreds of static and dynamic objects (images, cascading style-sheets (CSS), JavaScript (JS) files, etc.) downloaded from multiple domains. Consequently, today's Web page download process involves many HTTP request-response interactions, each triggered due to the parsing of, or interpretation of one or more objects on the page. When network latencies go up, as is typically the case with cellular networks, the page load times increase significantly degrading user experience. Users, on the other hand, have come to expect an interactive experience to the point where studies show revenue losses due to poor responsiveness [1, 3, 4, 24].

Many recent attempts [27, 44], most notably SPDY [27] which has shaped the recent HTTP/2 standard [32], has attempted to address protocol level limitations with traditional HTTP. HTTP/2 and SPDY seek to accelerate page loads by allowing for multiple outstanding requests in parallel on a single connection, and supporting out-of-order delivery of responses. However, the performance improvements of these protocols in the real world are mixed [25, 55]. A key reason is that the objects needed for the page to load cannot be requested in parallel because of complex dependencies in pages (Figure 1b). To overcome this limitation, the protocol allows the server to push objects to the client without waiting for explicit client requests. However, server push requires explicit identification of objects that can be pushed. This constraint is non-trivial since many Web pages require parsing/executing HTML, CSS and JS to identify the associated objects.

Recent proposals suggest the use of a powerful, well-connected proxy that can emulate (part of the) client functionality, including JS execution, and push the required objects to the client. The proxy's functionality (and hence complexity) can vary depending on the solution. In one approach [42, 52], the client performs all of the functions of a traditional client, while proxies perform *redundant execution*, merely to identify and push objects needed by the client. In another approach, the proxy generates a "rendered" page that the client can display with minimal work [6, 11, 56, 62]. Here, proxy computation is not redundant, and client-side processing is completely [6, 11, 62], or partially [56] eliminated. Results show that both redundant and non-redundant execution can significantly reduce page load times. While non-redundant execution promises additional benefits by reducing or eliminating client-side compute, it may result in additional latencies on client interactions [51] for the complete elimination approaches, or additional complexity associated with migrating execution state mid-flight from the proxy to the client for the partial elimination approaches.

Regardless of the proxy design choice, their benefits are at the cost of significant additional computational overheads, a dominant component of which is JS execution. Deploying such proxies at carrier-scale to millions of users requires that the computational overheads of the approach be economized (our measurements indicate a server with 32 cores and 128 GB RAM can support 2000 users, which translates to $2.5 Million in CAPEX alone for a million users assuming $5000 per server). Motivated by this scaling challenge, in this paper we focus on minimizing the proxy computational overheads in general, and JS execution in particular. We tackle this challenge in the context of redundant execution, since it is simple, allows for responsive client interactions and is well-suited for cellular settings where the network constitutes more than half the client latency (§2).

We present the design of *NutShell*, a system to tackle these challenges. *NutShell* leverages two key observations. First, the proxy need not execute all JS code (e.g., UI-related code need not be executed). Instead, only the subset of code necessary to identify and fetch the objects to be pushed is executed (see Fig. 2 for a detailed example). In other words, using terminology used in the programming language community, only the *backward slice* of the code [53, 58] related to URL fetching must be executed. Second, while static analysis of JS code is a hard, open research problem (e.g., [26, 34, 48, 54]), proxies can approximate the backward slice since only the redundant proxy execution is affected. Because the client performs the actual full execution, the client would directly fetch any objects not pushed by the proxy, trading off client latency for computation at the proxy without any correctness problems.

Since statement-level slicing is time-consuming, our approach, called *whittling*, works at JS function granularity, turning off entire functions that do not affect the set of fetched objects. Thus, whittling *dynamically learns* the slices by turning off function definitions – *i.e.* all the invocations of a function, whereas conventional slicing selectively turns off individual invocations. The approach is complicated by two issues. First, examining all JS functions would be time-consuming. Second, owing to inter-function dependencies, turning off two functions simultaneously may impact object fetching, although turning them off individually may not. We tackle the first issue by exploiting the fact that a majority of JS execution time is spent in a small fraction of heavy functions. We identify the heavy functions via profiling and examine only those functions. Because identifying the optimal set of independent functions would be time-consuming, we tackle the second issue with a greedy approach of examining functions in the decreasing order of their execution times, to grow a set of functions that may be turned off together. Finally, despite the above optimizations, whittling at every page load would be too slow to be effective. To that end, we exploit the fact that although objects in a page change, the code is stable over a period of several hours to allow profitable reuse of the same slice over several loads of a given page.

Our contributions are:

- presenting the first effort to our knowledge for scaling execution-based Web proxy designs.
- proposing a dynamic learning scheme, called *whittling*, to compute approximate backward slices of object fetches at function granularity; and
- proposing several optimizations to make whittling computationally efficient, practical and effective.

We conducted experiments with 78 pages from the Alexa Top 100 Web-sites. Our key results are:

- *NutShell* reduces JS computation by 1.33X in the median case, and up to 4X for some pages. Further, the user requests per second increases on average by 27% for a range of web page popularity models, and upto 4X for some pages.
- The scalability benefits can be achieved while preserving, and even exceeding the latency gains of a redundant execution approach. By combining redundant execution and whittling, *NutShell* achieves speedups in median page load times of 1.5 compared to SPDY and speedups of 20% compared to fully redundant execution for 15% of the pages.
- Whittling can be computed in an online fashion. Through a longitudinal study we show that for 92% of the Web pages *NutShell*'s whittling remain accurate (i.e., it pushes all the needed objects) over 3-hour windows. Further, the whittled JS can be reused across users due to large code overlap.

2 MOTIVATION

The overall client latency comprises compute delay (for parsing and executing HTML, CSS and JS, and for rendering) and network delay to fetch the required objects. For mobile devices over cellular networks, which is our focus, the network component is a dominant component of the overall latency. To see this, consider Fig. 1a which shows the reduction in the Onload time for a mobile phone when moving from a cellular LTE connection to a Wi-Fi connection for 20 top Alexa pages. The Onload time (OLT) is a common measure of page load latency, and is the time from request initiation until when the browser triggers an onLoad() event. Fig. 1a shows that the OLT reduces by more than 50% for 53% of the pages, and by more than 40% for 82% of the pages. Since the compute activity in both cases is the same, these percentages directly relate to the network component of the overall client latency. The network component may in fact be higher because a portion of the latency with WiFi could also be attributed to network activity.

A commonly used technique to reduce the network component is push (which controls what objects are pushed to the client without explicit requests). A key difficulty with any push technique is that owing to dependencies inherent in Web pages (Figure 1b), objects required later in the page load process can be identified only after the execution of prior objects (e.g., JS). A common approach then is to push objects whose URLs are embedded in the root HTML (often referred to as *embedding level 1* (or simply L1) objects [55]). However, the approach is limited by the fact that L1 objects only constitute a subset of all objects. Further, since the HTML may include objects from multiple domains, in practice not

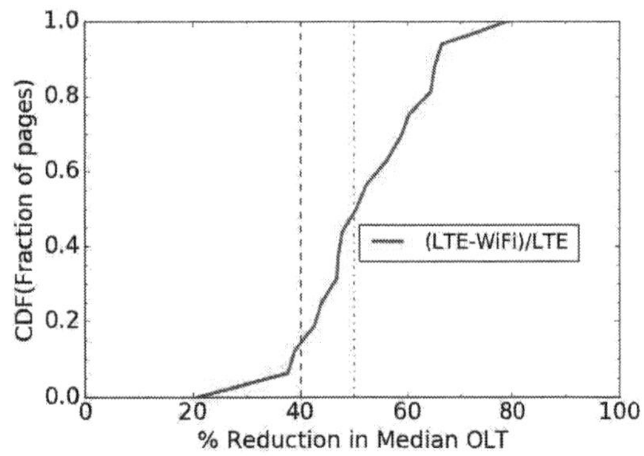

(a) % reduction in OLT for mobile page loads when moving from LTE to Wi-Fi.

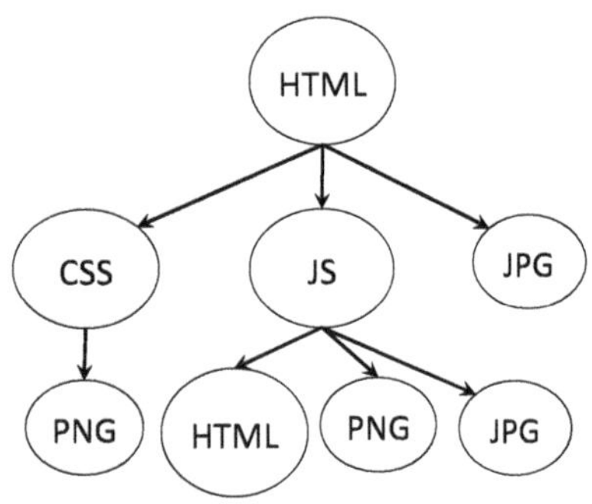

(b) Dependency graph of a page load – JS execution may trigger further object fetches.

Figure 1: Motivation

all L1 objects can be pushed. In an *execution-based* approach, a proxy [5, 6, 11, 42, 52, 56, 62] identifies all objects that the client needs by parsing HTML and CSS, and executing JS. The proxy, with much faster network connectivity, and secondarily faster compute, can quickly identify and fetch the objects needed for a client's page load, and proactively push *all* the objects to the client, so the network delay associated with explicit client requests can be avoided (§6.3 experimentally shows the latency benefits).

An alternative to a proxy-based execution approach is to observe which objects are fetched across users of a page load, and push those objects. Given that pages are often personalized, such an approach can only push content common across users. To evaluate the potential of this approach, we conducted a user study with 8 real users simultaneously downloading a series of landing pages from Alexa top 100 (refer §6.4 for further details) and assume only common objects fetched across downloads of the same page by the 8 different users are pushed, with all other objects explicitly pulled by each user. For 29% of the pages, the median % of objects that must be pulled across user loads exceeds 55%, while for 50% of the pages, the median % of objects that must be pulled across user loads is 31%. This indicates that relying on historical observations of objects across page loads can miss out on latency savings offered by proxy-based execution since only a subset of objects can be pushed by the proxy. That said, it may be possible to combine such an approach with proxy-based execution as we discuss in §8.

Execution based approaches themselves differ based on whether they eliminate client JS execution. Eliminating client JS execution

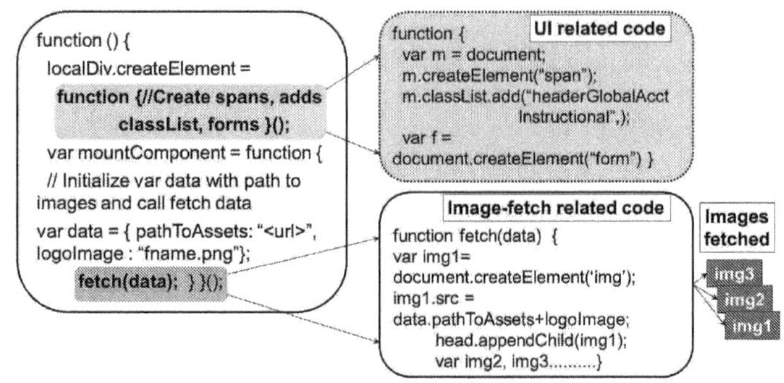

Figure 2: Whittling Example

has the advantage of reducing client computation related delays, but has associated trade-offs that we detail in §7. Regardless of these differences, a common unaddressed challenge to all these designs is the computation scaling bottlenecks associated with execution based approaches. In this paper, we focus on tackling the proxy computation bottlenecks in the context of *redundant execution* approaches [42, 52] which do not eliminate any client-side execution. Instead, the proxy executes redundantly only for identifying objects needed by the client. As such, the client execution remains unchanged except for seeing faster object fetches. We focus on redundant execution given its simplicity and effectiveness in reducing network delay which dominates cellular client latencies.

Finally, a potential approach to reducing the computation requirements at the proxy is to only perform redundant execution for a subset of the most popular pages. However, such an approach can lose out on the latency benefits of redundant execution for a large number of pages (as we show in §6.1). In contrast, our goal in this paper is to reduce the proxy computation requirements, while still preserving the latency benefits of redundant execution for a larger set of pages.

3 NUTSHELL DESIGN

NutShell seeks to scale proxies based on redundant execution by addressing their primary computation bottlenecks. Given that browser functionality such as rendering and display are not replicated at the proxy, and parsing HTML and CSS is relatively light-weight, the dominant portion of proxy computation is the execution of JS [12]. *NutShell* leverages the key insight that since proxy execution is redundant, it suffices for the proxy to execute only the JS code necessary to fetch objects. *NutShell*'s central mechanism – whittling – effectively removes JS code that does not affect the URLs fetched.

To illustrate the opportunity for whittling, Fig. 2 shows a concrete example of the JS from an Alexa Top 100 Web page. A top-level function (left side of Fig. 2) calls two functions (right half of Fig. 2). One of the functions sets up the UI-related aspects of the page such as span creation, button creation and addition of event listeners to handle button clicks. This function does not affect the fetching of objects. The second function fetches a number of images which are displayed in the UI panels. The UI-related function (shaded rectangle with dotted outline in the top-right corner of Fig. 2) can be whittled at the proxy without affecting the set of fetched objects. The top-level function and the image fetching functions (clear boxes with solid outlines in Fig. 2) are in the backward slice of the fetched objects, and hence must be preserved.

NutShell's use of whittling is related to the area of program slicing, which has seen much research in the programming languages and compiler community in the last couple of decades [53, 58]. Despite promising advances (e.g., [26, 34, 48, 54]), computing program slices for JS code using *static analysis* techniques remains a hard problem in general. Specifically, JS's use of dynamic typing and `eval` could result in backward slices whose sizes approach the size of the original program, diminishing their effectiveness in reducing computation overheads – one of our key goals.

Instead, *NutShell* employs dynamic learning of backward slices, which involves comparing URLs fetched before and after statements of code are dropped. Although such an approach has been explored in other contexts (e.g., finding language-independent program slices and for fault isolation) [15, 23, 61], *NutShell*'s context presents unique opportunities. Unlike fault isolation where false negatives (i.e., missing a fault) are unacceptable, in *NutShell*'s context it is acceptable to approximate the backward slice. Such acceptability arises from slicing being performed only on the redundant *NutShell* proxy execution. Since the client performs the actual full execution, any objects not pushed by the *NutShell* proxy could be fetched directly by the client, trading off client latency reduction opportunities for computation savings at the proxy.

We next describe *NutShell*'s whittling strategy which uses a dynamic approach, but with the ability to tolerate imperfect (approximate) slicing.

3.1 Whittling individual functions

NutShell makes the design choice to whittle code at the function granularity. The choice of function granularity is driven by the opportunity-overhead trade-off; choosing fine-granularity (e.g., statements) may provide the ability to whittle additional code, but may increase the overhead because each statement may have to be individually tested. On the other hand, coarse-grained whittling of entire JS files results in minimal benefits as most files cannot be whittled if even a single function affects object loading. Further, the relatively-few JS files that can be whittled are typically rarely-executed files that do not result in significant savings even if whittled. Note that whittling eliminates all dynamic invocations of the function. This implies that we are conservative in function whittling; if even one invocation of the function affects URL fetches, the function will not be whittled.

NutShell uses automated two-version testing to determine if a function can be safely whittled while ensuring that all objects needed for page load are fetched. Our mechanism generates two versions of a page: (i) an unmodified *full* version 'F'; and (ii) a *partial* version 'P' produced by eliding the function under test by rewriting the function to be an empty function. If both versions identify the same set of objects for downloading, then the function under test can be whittled because eliding it does not affect the objects fetched.

Determining the set of objects fetched by the baseline 'F' version itself poses interesting issues, since multiple interpretations are possible regarding when a page load is considered complete. Nominally, one can consider a page load to be complete based on time bounds (e.g., after 30 seconds). Alternately, recognizing that objects needed for an initial acceptable rendering of a page are more critical to user experience than other objects, a page may be viewed complete based on browser events (e.g., when the browser onLoad event fires), when all above-the-fold content is loaded [7] or when content with the highest utility to users is received[18, 35].

NutShell is agnostic about the metric of page load completion; however, for any chosen metric, an appropriate *signature*, must be extracted, which is the subset of objects fetched by the 'F' version that serve as a baseline of comparison for the whittling tests. To be concrete, we use the browser onLoad event to determine page completion. We run the 'F' version many times till onLoad and use the intersection set of objects fetched in each run as the *signature* of the page. Doing so ensures the signature only contains objects always fetched before onLoad (note that in any given run, additional URLs may be fetched incidentally as a consequence of asynchronous JS). *NutShell* may be extended in the future to accommodate other notions of page completeness.

Our two-version test outcome determines whether the function may be safely whittled (i.e., the signature matches) or not (i.e., there is a mismatch). Note that even in cases where there is a match, there may be other side-effects due to function whittling. For example, whittling a function may give rise to errors because some objects (which would be defined in the whittled function) are undefined. Such errors impose some minimal overheads as the errors must be caught/handled (often with a nominal error message output to the console). Such errors do not affect our technique as (1) our focus is solely on whether all the objects in the signature are fetched, and (2) we fully include the overheads of error handling in our measurements.

All of *NutShell*'s two-version testing is performed in a recorded environment. The first access to the page by the proxy (where all JS is executed) is recorded, and all testing of JS subsets occurs by replaying the recorded page in a deterministic manner [8, 42, 52]. Doing so ensures the whittling tests are not impacted by randomization, and date/time-dependent code which may complicate ascertaining whether the differences between the F and P versions are because of whittling or because of variability.

3.2 Whittling across functions

With the above mechanism, we can test any individual function to determine if it may be whittled. However, directly using the approach to test *all* functions has two weaknesses. First, Web pages often have hundreds of JS functions, many of which are rarely invoked. Testing them all increases overheads without commensurate benefits. Second, there are often dependencies among JS functions that prevent collective whittling of multiple functions even though each function may be whittled individually.

To avoid testing all functions, *NutShell* employs a greedy heuristic by sorting functions in the order of their computational work (captured by execution time). We measure the work done in each function by profiling a full JS execution. By testing functions in the order of computational effort, we maximize the potential savings from whittling. The greedy order is especially effective because we observed that on an average 20% of JS functions account for 80% of JS execution time across all Alexa top 100 pages. Fig. 3a shows the percentage of functions that account for 80% of JS CPU-time for the

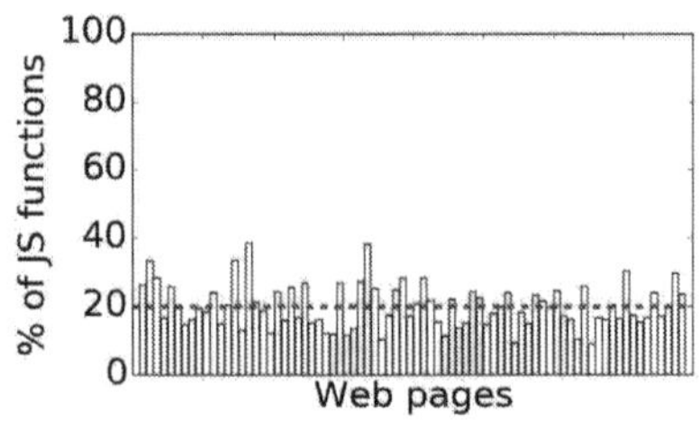

(a) Percentage of functions accounting for 80% of total JS execution time.

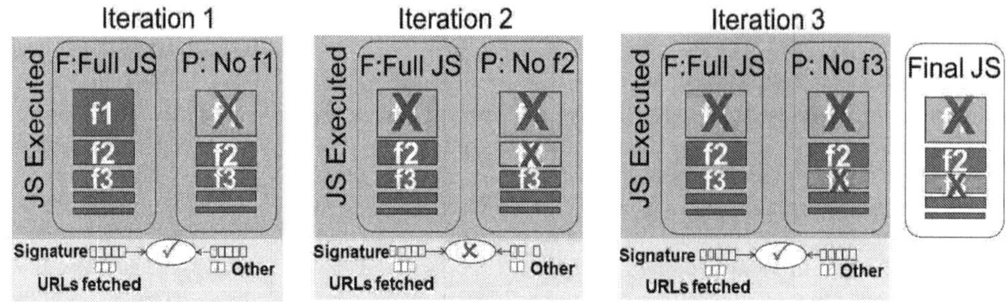

(b) Walk-through example of NutShell's Greedy Whittling.

Figure 3: NutShell's Whittling Method

Alexa Top 100 pages(X-axis). Uniformly, we observe that a small percentage (9%-38%) is enough to cover 80% of execution time. This 80-20 rule enables us to limit whittling to this percentage.

Handling Dependencies: Consider the following example taken from an Alexa Top 100 Web page. The JS code contains two functions (say A and B) both of which invoke the jQuery initializer. The jQuery initializer invocation impacts other URL-fetching code and hence is needed. The other work in functions A and B are not relevant for any URL fetch. When doing the basic whittling test, we find that each function is individually safe to whittle because jQuery initializer is still invoked in the other function. However, when both functions are whittled, the jQuery initializer is never invoked, which affects other parts of the JS code which fetch URLs.

The above example is one of many possible dependencies that prevent whittling of large collections of functions. Because such dependencies are hard to analyze, we take an empirical approach. Specifically, we use the greedy order of function testing to grow a set of functions that may be turned off together. We describe this greedy algorithm using an example (Fig. 3b).

Fig. 3b assumes a Web page with the JS functions pre-sorted in decreasing order of computation effort (f1, f2, f3, and so on). We start with a two-version test against the full Web page load which includes execution of all JS ('F' version in iteration 1 of Fig. 3b). If the 'P' version which whittles f1 results in the same signature as that of the 'F' version, the function f1 is whittled/dropped from future runs. Subsequent functions are further tested to see if they can be whittled in conjunction with all the previously-whittled functions. These secondary tests are an alternative two-version test in which the F version is the JS code *without* all previous functions that can be safely whittled (as determined by previous tests) and the P version which drops the new function that is under test. (For example, in iteration 2, the 'F' version whittles f1 because f1 is known to be safe to drop from the previous iteration. The 'P' version additionally drops f2 to test if f2 may be safely whittled.) Functions that can be dropped without impacting the page signature are marked for whittling; others must remain in the executed JS. In Fig. 3b, f2 cannot be whittled (because of signature mismatch when f2 is dropped), but f3 can be whittled. This process continues to whittle the JS code until all functions under consideration for whittling are tested. *NutShell*'s greedy approach has the added advantage that it minimizes the overheads of dynamic learning as the heavier functions are whittled for a large fraction of tests. As a practical matter, implementations may choose to filter the set of functions that are considered based on (a) minimum work threshold, to avoid examining light functions that do not provide significant benefits, and (b) numerical limits, to bound the time overheads of whittling. (In practice, *NutShell* tests up to 200 of the top functions till we account for 80% of CPU work.)

NutShell's greedy heuristic strategy does not allow for backtracking (e.g., by bringing back a dropped function); the set of dropped functions starts with the heaviest function that can be whittled and can only grow by adding other functions that can be whittled without dependency problems. As such, the result may not be optimal. However, we show later that the greedy heuristic is effective in practice. More sophisticated techniques to identify collections of functions that may be simultaneously whittled, which we leave for future work, can only improve *NutShell*'s results.

3.3 Amortizing overheads across page loads

The process of dynamically learning the whittled JS depends on (1) the number of functions, which ranges from the low 10s to 200, and (2) the time for each per-function two-version test, which is typically a few seconds because each test is a page load (0.3-4s) followed by signature comparison (<10 ms). For our evaluation set of Web pages from Alexa Top 100 (§5), the average learning time is 213 seconds across pages.

The dynamic learning of JS whittling is not done for every page load. Rather, *NutShell* performs whittling for the first page load, and then re-uses the whittled code for all the common JS content in a new load. §4 discusses how we implement such reuse. In this section, we present an empirical study showing the feasibility of such reuse. The study is based on a recording of 25 pages from the Alexa Top 100 obtained every hour over a 24 hour period using the approach described in §5.

For each page, we whittled JS based on the version recorded at time $t = 0$. We extract the signature (the set of objects needed for page load) for the $t = 24hr$ recording based on a full execution of all JS in that recording. We then determine the fraction of objects in the signature fetched by the whittled JS code using whittling learnt at $t = 0$. Fig. 4 shows the corresponding fractions. For all but 2 pages, 99% of the signature or higher can be fetched, indicating whittling reuse is effective even over a 24 hour period for most pages.

Note that while the JS is stable the page content is not. Fig. 5 shows the incremental differences in the page signatures at time $t = 0$ and $t = 24hr$ for the pages on the Y-axis. Objects that are

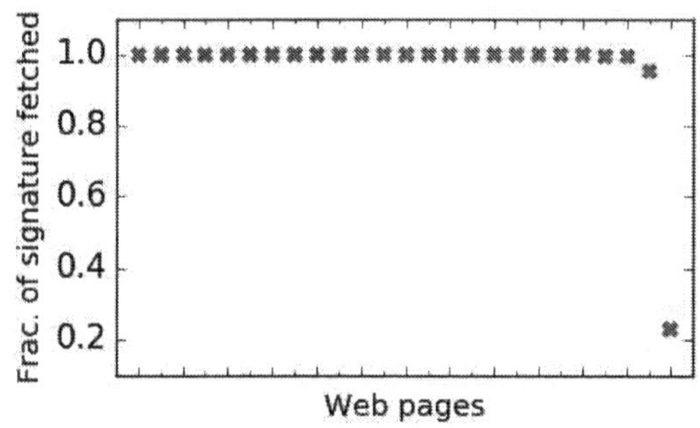

Figure 4: Fraction of signature URLs fetched by whittled JS at time t=24hr using whittling learnt at t=0.

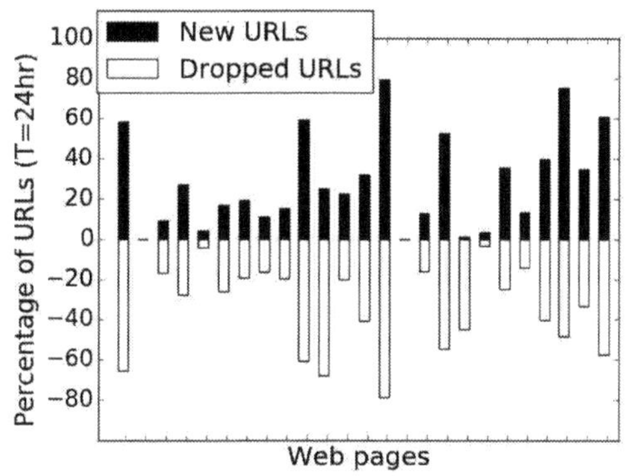

Figure 5: Percentage of new and dropped URLs in the page signature at t=24hr compared to t=0.

fetched at $t = 24hr$ that were not present at $t = 0$ are shown on the positive side. Objects that were fetched at $t = 0$ that were absent at $t = 24hr$ are shown on the negative side. Even though there is significant churn in the Web page content over a period of 24 hours, executing the same 24-hour-old whittled JS is effective at fetching the changed content.

In practice, it is acceptable to relearn whittling over more frequent time intervals. For instance, reusing whittled code over a 3-hour window results in under 2% overhead ($2\% = 213s/(3hr \times 3600secs/hr)$), for a learning time of 213s discussed above. Even for the page which had more frequent changes (rightmost bar in Fig. 4), changing *NutShell*'s learning frequency to once every 3 hours results in a larger fraction of objects being fetched.

For pages with dynamically changing JS, *NutShell* may lose some of the CPU savings from whittling (and the resulting throughput improvement at the proxy) because the functions identified for whittling may not be present in the changed JS. To evaluate this concern, we consider the fraction (%) of functions (X-Axis) that can be whittled based on the $t = 0$ version, which are still relevant for whittling at a later time across the pages. For the $t = 3hr$ page load, for 75% of pages, all functions can be whittled, while for another 15% of pages over 70% of functions can be whittled. Note however that as Fig. 4 shows, client latency is not affected for most pages because the proxy fetches and pushes all objects obtained from its JS execution. Overall, these results show that it is viable to reuse

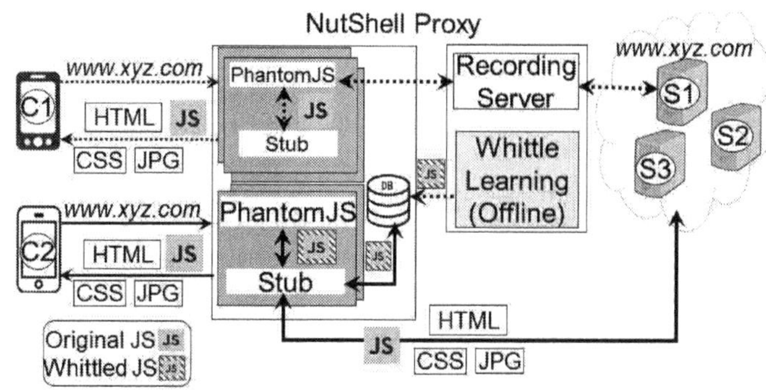

Figure 6: NutShell proxy architecture.

whittling over a 3-hour window of time while still retaining most of the benefits.

We close with two comments. First, it is important to consider reuse across users. We evaluate this further in §6.4. Second, rather than relearning over fixed time intervals, *NutShell* may be augmented to re-learn whittling based on feedback from clients – e.g., the client may report the fraction of objects needed for page load that was successfully received from the proxy. A low fraction across multiple loads is an indication that the slices must be relearnt. We do not further consider such feedback mechanisms given the effectiveness of a simple 3-hour reuse window in our evaluations above.

4 IMPLEMENTATION

Proxy implementation: *NutShell* involves extending the implementation of a proxy based on fully redundant execution to support whittling. Prior fully redundant execution schemes, Cumulus [42] and Parcel [52], use PhantomJS and Firefox respectively to parse and evaluate HTML and CSS, and execute JS. A comparison of these options indicated that PhantomJS has better scaling characteristics as it is a headless browser, which led us to employ PhantomJS in *NutShell*. To reduce computational overheads at the proxy, we disable the rendering and painting functionality which are not essential for identifying and pushing objects. We henceforth refer to this baseline fully redundant proxy as *FullRedEx*.

Fig. 6 shows our *NutShell* proxy architecture, which extends *FullRedEx* to support whittling. For each page that has undergone whittling, *NutShell* maintains (i) the JS file name; (ii) the MD5 hash of the file content; and (iii) the actual whittled version of the file. We implement a separate stub module that intercepts requests sent by the PhantomJS proxy to the server, as well as responses from the server to the proxy. When a JS file is fetched, the stub code intercepts the server response, and computes an MD5 hash of the fetched object. The index is looked up to see if there is a whittled JS file with the same hash associated with that main page. If so, the whittled version of the file is retrieved and forwarded to the PhantomJS proxy, which executes this version. The stub also pushes the unwhittled code to the client.

We use an MD5 hash rather than just the file name to (i) ensure JS content associated with that file name did not change; and (ii) to maximize the reuse of whittling in cases where the same content is fetched across runs but with slightly different URLs (a common scenario in web downloads). In some cases, a JS file may have undergone minor changes and functions that can be whittled in the original JS code may still be whittled. As an optimization, the index stores the list of functions that can be whittled for each JS file. When the stub code receives a JS file that shares the same name as an indexed file but with a different hash, it simply whittles away functions listed in this index. While this involves some online modifications to the JS file, the overheads of such modifications is modest.

Like any execution-based proxy [6, 11, 52, 56], *NutShell* must emulate the client environment including parameters such as the User-Agent, screen width and height, viewport settings, and CSS3 media query parameters like devicePixelRatio [59] since the requested URLs may depend on these parameters. To achieve this, we use the page APIs [31] (e.g., page.settings.userAgent, and page.viewportSize) supported by PhantomJS. This is supported by most modern browsers today. The client sends these parameters when it connects to the proxy and requests the URL. The proxy dynamically creates a page object, and sets these parameters as object properties. Further, the proxy tracks the state of the objects (cache and cookies) stored at the client. This enables us to fetch the right objects and avoid transferring objects cached at the client. Like any proxy-based approach [6, 11, 52, 56], we handle HTTPS requests by assuming users trust the proxy. Such trust may be facilitated by personalized proxies [19]. Alternately, recent proposals [39, 49] that extend HTTPS to allow middleboxes to read or modify parts of the data could be adopted as part of *NutShell*.

Client implementation: We implement the client as a custom-built browser using Chromium WebView for Android 5.1.1 (rendering engine used by popular browsers). The browser accepts URLs from the user and forwards the request to the main html alone to the *NutShell* proxy. Further requests are intercepted and queued at the client. The *webview* client waits for responses pushed by the proxy, and when a response is received, matches it with a queued request if it exists. The proxy sends a flag to the client once it is done pushing all the objects required for the initial page load (§3.1). Upon receiving the flag, the client then contacts the server to obtain any remaining objects for the page load. We chose to implement a custom-built browser rather than a standard browser to facilitate the interception of client requests and to serve responses pushed by the proxy.

5 EVALUATION METHODOLOGY

Our evaluations compare *NutShell* with *FullRedEx*, a proxy that does *fully redundant execution* of all JS code (§4). We evaluate the effectiveness of *NutShell* in supporting more user requests per second by reducing JS computation at the proxy through whittling, and its ability to preserve the latency benefits of *FullRedEx*.

Test set: Since web pages change over time, and to minimize the impacts of variable server load, we used an open source record and replay tool called web-page-replay(WPR) [8] to emulate real web server. We recorded entire web pages including all constituent objects using WPR by downloading from the actual webserver(s). We then replayed the recording across all our experiments. We recorded the pages using a phone to ensure that the mobile version of the page is recorded. Note that many pages do not have separate

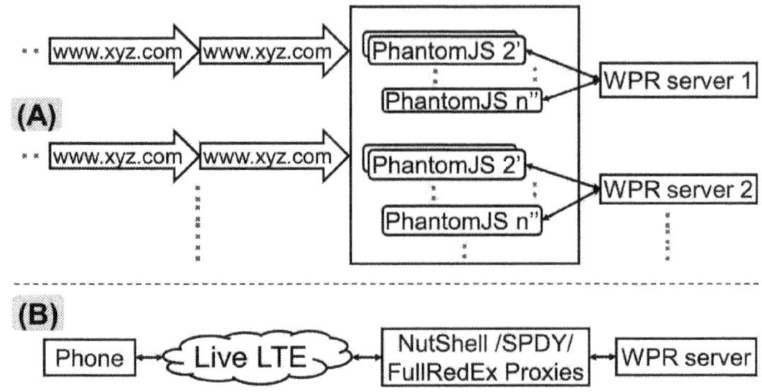

Figure 7: Experimental setup to measure (A) request throughput improvement; and (B) latency savings. For meaningful measurements, throughput experiments were performed under load, and latency measurements under a lightly loaded setup.

desktop and mobile pages, but use CSS3 media queries [59] to tailor the rendering of the page content for different devices. In either case, the right version of the page for the mobile device is recorded. For *NutShell*, we use a commonly used JS formatting tool [2] to ensure that functions (including anonymous ones) can be unambiguously identified by their line numbers to facilitate whittling.

We chose the Alexa top 100 US sites [13] for our evaluation. However, our final evaluation used 78 web pages for two reasons. First, we conducted a large number of experiments with each of our web pages, and found that ten pages did not trigger onLoad in a large fraction of experiments. Given one of our evaluation metrics depends on the onLoad event, we excluded these pages from our evaluation. Second, recall that the first step in whittling is to identify the most computationally intensive JS. While our proxy implementation is based on PhantomJS (for reasons described in §4), we are not aware of native profiler support for PhantomJS. Consequently, we employed the Chrome V8 profiler [10]. Using Chrome for profiling, and PhantomJS for slice testing and proxy implementation sometimes resulted in differences in files fetched and functions executed. Consequently, functions indicated by the profiler sometimes could not be matched to appropriate functions in the JS code.

This resulted in two issues: First, for 12 pages, none of the functions identified by the profiling step matched those actually executed by phantomJS. We excluded these pages from our analysis. Second, for all pages, a subset of functions identified by the profiler step could not be tested for whittling, limiting the amount of computation that can be saved through whittling (see §6.2). Fortunately, the issues here are not fundamental to our whittling approach. The availability of native phantomJS profiling support can both expand the set of pages we can test, as well as potentially improve the fraction of compute saved for all pages.

Measuring scaling benefits of *NutShell*: We measure the request throughput (user requests per second) under load that can be served by each of *NutShell* and *FullRedEx*. Fig. 7(A) shows our evaluation setup. Since we did not have enough mobile clients to generate sufficient load for meaningful request throughput measurements, we synthetically generated simultaneous user requests to saturate the proxy CPU by running many parallel instances of

PhantomJS. The requests from the PhantomJS instances were load balanced across five WPR servers. We made a pragmatic choice to use a commodity desktop with Intel i7 CPU @ 3.60GHz and 16 GB RAM to run the proxies, so that the number of WPR servers needed to handle the load was small. We accounted for impacts of initial ramp up and the final ramp down times by running the experiment for a sufficient duration. We ran this experiment across all the 78 web pages. We tuned the number of instances of PhantomJS and the number of requests served by each instance for each web page to ensure that the CPU was saturated for both *NutShell* and *FullRedEx*.

Setup for latency comparisons: To capture real-world impacts of cellular networks, our latency comparison experiments are done using a Google Nexus 5 phone downloading web pages over a live LTE network. In this experiment, we compared *NutShell* not only to *FullRedEx*, but also to HTTP/1.1 browser (which we refer to as *Baseline*) and to SPDY using a proxy [29] (which we refer to as SPDY). The proxy honored the default SPDY priorities (HTML > CSS & JS > images) set by our browser (Google Chrome).

We also compare *NutShell* to an approach that parses only the main HTML of a web page and pushes all objects embedded in the main HTML (which we refer to as *Push_HTMLEmbed*). We use *Push_HTMLEmbed* to generalize SPDY's server push when configured with the commonly used *embedding level 1* policy (§2). *Push_HTMLEmbed* provides an upper bound on the latency benefits of the above SPDY push approach because it also allows for pushing objects spread across multiple domains whereas a SPDY server can push objects only in its domain.

Ideally, our proxies would run in the packet core of cellular networks. Since this was not feasible, we ran an instance of each proxy on an Internet-facing server in a university campus (see Fig. 7(B)). To account for the delay from the cellular core to a typical web server, we emulate a round trip delay of 20*ms* between our proxies and the WPR server. To account for the fact that cellular networks use HTTP proxies [25], we also emulated the same delay for *Baseline* at the WPR end. We selected this 20*ms* delay based on measurements of delay when fetching the top 100 web pages from a desktop client in a university campus.

We ensured that only a single user request is served at anytime with all the schemes. We use a lightly loaded setup since our focus was on evaluating the impact on latency by reducing JS computation work at the proxy through whittling. Unlike request throughput measurements before, latency measurements require light loading to be meaningful. We expect that, in practice, these schemes would be provisioned with sufficient proxy servers to ensure small queuing delays.

We compared schemes both with respect to their Onload time (OLT) (§2), and Speed Index [7]. Speed Index is a measure of how quickly a web page's content renders on the screen. It works by calculating the completeness of a page at various points during the page load. The completeness itself is measured by comparing the distribution of colors at any instant with the final distribution after the page load. We capture a video of the page load in each of our experiments using the Android 5.1 screenrecord utility. Then we use WebPageTest's visualmetrics tool [60], to analyze the videos and generate the Speed Index metric.

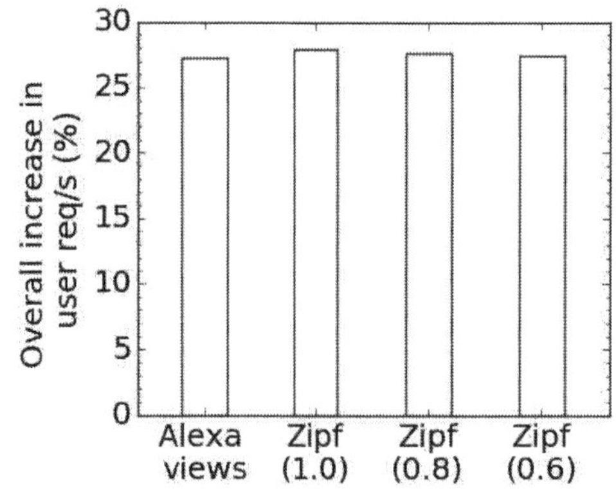

Figure 8: Overall increase in user requests per second with NutShell across page popularity models.

6 RESULTS

6.1 Scaling benefits of NutShell

We begin by presenting the effectiveness of *NutShell* in supporting more user requests per second than *FullRedEx* (§4), whose performance is representative of prior fully redundant execution schemes [42, 52].

Since a proxy would be serving multiple web pages in practice, the scaling benefits of *NutShell* depend on a combination of (i) the popularity of pages; and (ii) the savings with *NutShell* for each page. Formally, the overall benefits with *NutShell* may be computed as:

$$(\sum_i f_i \times (1/R_{if}))/(\sum_i f_i \times (1/R_{in})) \quad (1)$$

where, f_i is the fraction of requests for page i, while R_{if} and R_{in} are the number of requests per second that can be served for page i under load with *FullRedEx* and *NutShell* respectively. We obtain R_{if} and R_{in} through experiments with the setup described in Fig. 7(A).

Fig. 8 shows the increase in user requests per second with two different models for web page popularity (f_i). The first model (Alexa views) uses statistics on the number of requests to each web page estimated monthly from Alexa traffic data [9]. The second model (Zipf(α)) uses a Zipf distribution based on the Alexa rank of the page as suggested by studies on web page popularity [14, 16], where the number of accesses to a page of rank i is $1/i^{\alpha}$. We also study sensitivity to different values of the exponent α (a larger α increases the fraction of requests to the most popular page). Fig. 8 shows that across all models *NutShell* achieves fairly consistent average improvement ranging from 27.2% to 27.89%.

To further understand these benefits, Fig. 9 shows the increase in user requests per second achieved by *NutShell* over full JS execution (Y-axis) for individual pages (X-axis), sorted by the access frequency of the page. While *NutShell* provides benefits for most pages (with a 12% improvement for the median page), the benefits exceed 34% for 25% of the pages, and is as high as 100-300% for a few pages.

Further investigation shows the benefits with *NutShell* are most pronounced for pages with (i) significant JS computation, and (ii) where whittling can achieve significant reduction in such computation. For example, for *www.facebook.com*, the JS compute is significant, and whittling reduces JS computation by a factor of 2, which translates to an increase in user requests per second by

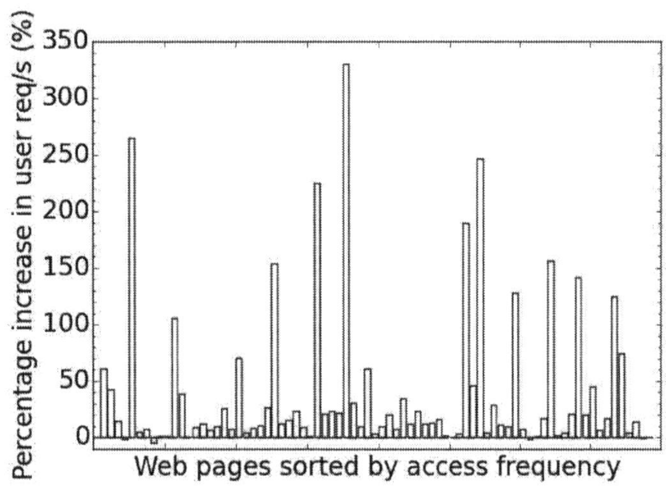

Figure 9: Increase in user requests per second with NutShell for each web page.

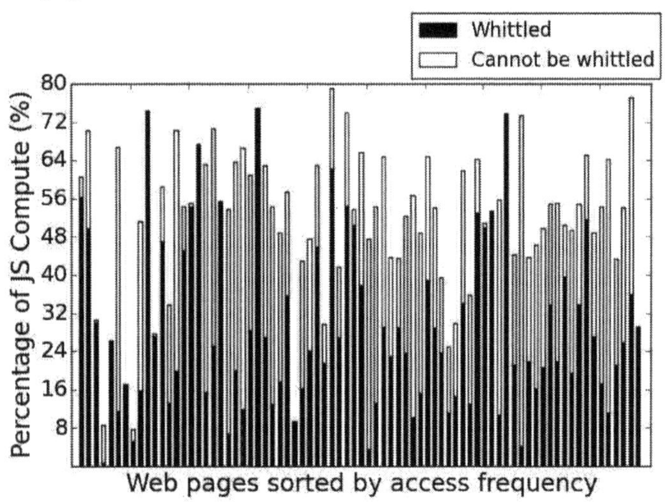

Figure 10: Percentage JS compute contributed by all the functions tested by *NutShell*, split as fraction that can and can not be whittled.

a factor of 1.43 compared to *FullRedEx*. *NutShell* achieves these benefits while still pushing all objects in the signature (§3).

A potential alternative to *NutShell* that can provide equivalent scaling benefits, is to only perform JS execution for a subset of the most popular pages. However, this approach gives up latency savings associated with proxy execution for other pages. Specifically, an analysis of Alexa web page popularities [9] indicates that the top 23 pages account for 73% of accesses of the top 100, and the top 112 pages account for 73% of accesses of the top 1000 pages. This suggests that to achieve the same 27% computation reduction that *NutShell* provides, the selective execution approach can only perform JS execution, and hence provide the associated latency benefits for 23 (112) pages. In contrast, *NutShell* can provide latency benefits for 100 (1000) pages for the same computation requirements.

6.2 Effectiveness of whittling

Fig. 10 shows the percentage of JS computation (Y-axis) that can be whittled for each page. Each bar corresponds to a page (sorted by page frequency). The lower dark and upper unshaded portions respectively correspond to the fraction of JS compute that can and cannot be whittled based on whether the associated functions were necessary for object fetches. Note that the numbers do not add up to 100% – the remainder corresponds to functions that were not tested by *NutShell* for reasons described in the next paragraph. For the left most page, the lower and upper portions are 56% and 4% respectively. *NutShell* saves more than 25% of the overall JS computation for half the pages and as much as 50-75% for 15% of the pages (thereby incurring 2X-4X lower JS computation times).

While the benefits are already substantial, these reported savings are conservative because they are based only on functions we were able to test. There are two factors that limit tested functions: (i) only heaviest functions that account for 80% of compute and at most 200 functions are tested for any page (§3); and (ii) mismatches between the browsers used for the profiling and whittling steps implied functions identified by the profiler could not be tested for whittling (§5). The first factor was relatively minor – for 85% of the pages, functions accounting for 80% of compute could be tested, while for all pages, functions accounting for at least 62% of compute could be tested. The second factor while more significant is not fundamental to our approach, and can be handled in the future through better profiler support (§5). Despite this factor, *NutShell* is still able to achieve significant savings already. For half the pages, *NutShell* can whittle over 50% of compute corresponding to the tested functions. Further, we find the overall increase in user reqs. per second by *NutShell* goes up to 40% if we only consider pages where functions corresponding to at most 20% of JS compute cannot be tested due to the second factor.

Finally, we have also considered JS computation that cannot be whittled, and investigated the extent to which dependencies required the function to be retained, though individual function testing indicated the function could be whittled. Overall, we find that savings lost due to function dependencies is not significant – *NutShell* loses JS computation savings of under 10% for 90% of the pages and at most 25% across all pages. Overall our results indicate that whittling is effective in eliminating significant fraction of the JS computation at the proxy without impacting objects fetched.

6.3 Impact of NutShell on client latency

We next present results comparing the latency of *NutShell*, with *FullRedEx* as well as other schemes – *Baseline*, SPDY and *Push_HTMLEmbed* (setup shown in Fig. 7(B)). To minimize the impact of LTE network variability, we conduct multiple rounds of experiments, with each round involving running latency experiments with all the schemes back-to-back. For each scheme, we summarize results by the median OLT and Speed Index metrices (§5) across the runs.

Fig. 11 shows *NutShell*'s speedup over each of these schemes (ratio of median OLT with a scheme to median OLT with *NutShell*). Fig. 12 shows the absolute reduction in median OLT with *NutShell* We make several points. First, *NutShell* provides a speedup of 1.7 over *Baseline* and a speedup of more than 1.5 over SPDY for half

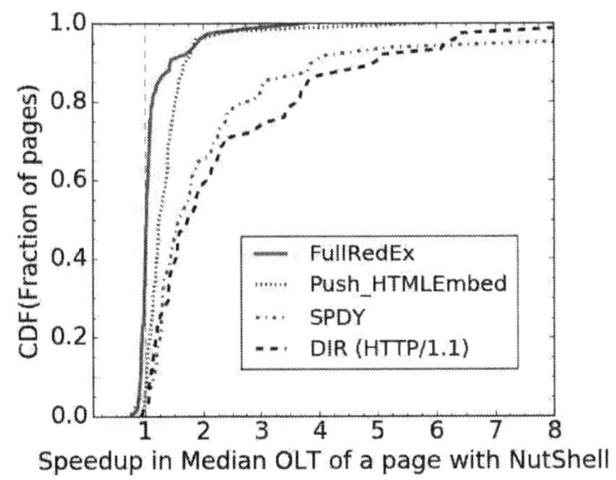

Figure 11: Speedup in median client OLT with *NutShell* compared to other schemes.

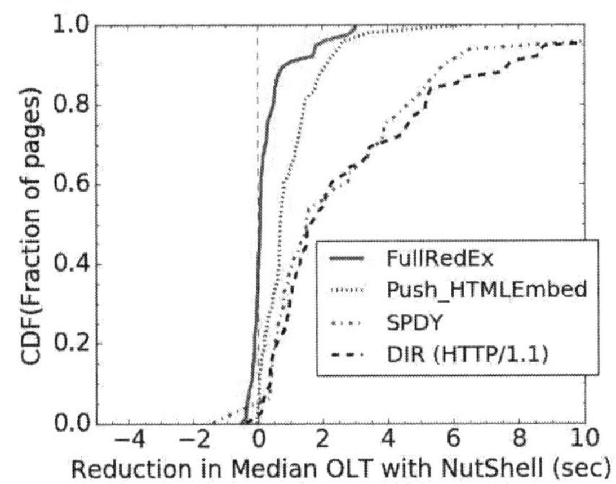

Figure 12: Reduction in median client OLT with *NutShell* compared to other schemes.

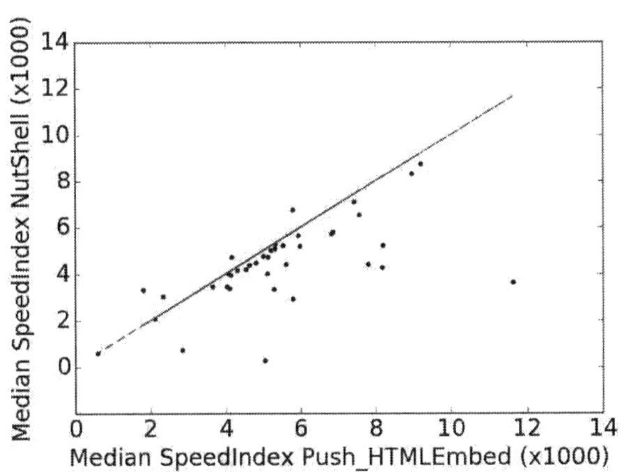

Figure 13: Median Speed Index with Push_HTMLEmbed and *NutShell*. Each dot corresponds to a page.

the pages, and latency reductions of more than 2 seconds for 45% of the pages compared to both schemes. Further analysis shows the benefits over SPDY are more pronounced for pages with deeper dependency graphs while the benefits are more limited for pages with more shallow dependency graphs. This makes sense since with SPDY the task of identifying object dependencies is still with the client.

Second, *NutShell* provides a speedup of 1.24 over *Push_HTMLEmbed* for the median page but the speedups exceed 1.5 for more than 15% of the pages. In absolute terms, this translates to latency reductions of over 1 second for 25% of the pages, with some pages seeing reductions of 6 seconds. These benefits may be attributed to *NutShell* pushing all objects as opposed to a subset.

Finally, while *NutShell* and *FullRedEx* perform comparably for the majority of pages, *NutShell* achieves speedups higher than 1.2 for 15% of the pages, and absolute latency reductions of over 1 second for 10% of the pages. The differences arise since *NutShell* lowers the OLT at the proxy since less JS computation is needed, which in turn results in objects being pushed to the client earlier. Observe that *NutShell* performs slightly worse for 34% of the pages, but only 10% of the pages see median OLT higher by 200*ms*, and no page sees median OLT higher than 515*ms*. Likewise, *NutShell* achieves latency benefits of under 500*ms* for 45% of the pages. We attribute these minor performance differences to LTE network variability.

While the results above are based on the OLT metric, we found trends generally consistent with the Speed Index metric. For example, Fig. 13 shows a scatter plot, with each point corresponding to a page, and the X-axis and Y-Axis representing the median Speed Index across the runs with *Push_HTMLEmbed* and *NutShell* respectively. A majority of points lie below the y=x line indicating *NutShell* achieves a smaller Speed Index (lower values represent better performance), and a faster visual page load from a user perspective.

Likewise, comparing *NutShell* and *FullRedEx*, the Speed Index metric results are generally consistent with OLT (not shown). *NutShell* achieves a lower Speed Index for 65% of the pages, while the Speed Index is smaller with *FullRedEx* for 35% of the pages, with the differences relatively small. Further, for most pages where *NutShell* achieves significantly lower OLT than *FullRedEx*, the Speed Index is lower as well. An exception is *www.reddit.com*, where *NutShell* achieves lower OLT but a higher Speed Index. Further analysis shows that page contains images that are shown above-the-fold, yet fetched after onLoad. Since our current *NutShell* implementation derives a signature based on objects needed for a page load event (as discussed in §3.1), *NutShell* whittles away a function responsible to fetch one of the images. Consequently, this object is not pushed by the *NutShell* proxy, and must be fetched directly by the client from the server. This issue is not inherent to whittling itself – for instance, if a signature were based on above-the-fold content, then, *NutShell* would retain necessary code, and ensure all necessary objects are pushed. Interestingly, for a few pages, notably *www.ups.com*, we found that the same phenomenon led *NutShell* to whittle code that fetched an asynchronous JS object and not push that object. In this case, *NutShell* performed better in both OLT and Speed Index by avoiding compute delays associated with the JS, since the object did not impact above-the-fold content.

Overall, these results show that beyond the primary benefit of achieving higher throughput compared to *FullRedEx*, *NutShell* can not only match the latency benefits but provide substantial latency improvements for some pages.

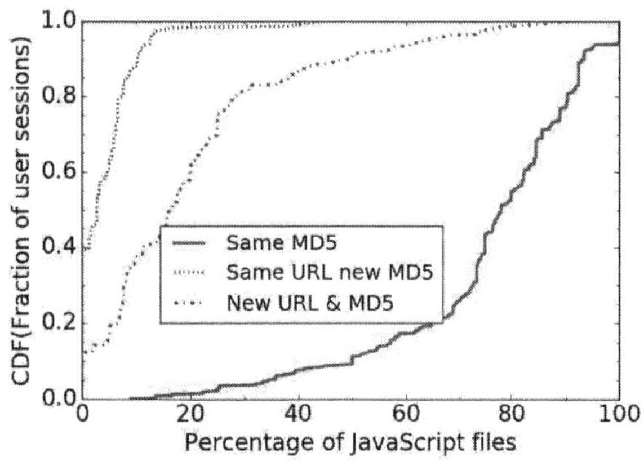

Figure 14: JavaScript code overlap across users.

6.4 Re-using whittling across users

§3.3 has shown the feasibility of reusing whittling across page loads. In this section, we study the feasibility of reusing whittling across users by analyzing common JS content among users. To this end, we conduct a user study with 14 landing pages from the Alexa top 100 pages. Each of these pages were downloaded simultaneously by 8 real users, all using the Chrome browser, but with diverse browsing profile. Further, the users corresponded to 4 different <OS,location,devicetype> settings, where the OS was Linux or Windows, location was within Purdue University, or external, and the devicetype was either a desktop or a laptop. Choosing one user as a baseline, we compare the JS files of all other users to this baseline classifying them into three categories: (i) files whose MD5 hashes match the MD5 hash of a JS file of the baseline user; (ii) files that share the same file name as the baseline user, but with a different MD5 hash; and (iii) files for which neither the MD5 hash nor file name match any JS file for the baseline user. As discussed in §4, *NutShell* can obtain full benefits with whittling for class (i) files, and a significant fraction of the benefits for class (ii) files. We repeat the analysis choosing different users as the baseline resulting in 56 user session data points for each of the 14 pages.

Fig. 14 shows a CDF of the % of JS that falls under the 3 classes across all users sessions and all pages. More than 80% of JS files have the same content across users (right-most curve) for half of the user sessions allowing full reuse of whittling. Further, the middle curve shows that for half of the user sessions, less than 18% of JS files belong to class (iii), where whittling cannot be reused. Overall, these results indicate significant common JS code across users and the potential for significant reuse of whittling across users.

6.5 Redundantly pushed data

With any redundant execution approach [42, 52] including *NutShell*, there may be differences in the URLs requested by the proxy and the client (a) if the proxy does not emulate the client (§4) faithfully, or (b) if the web page uses functions like Math.random() in JS to generate a different URL in each run. In particular, the proxy may push objects whose URLs are not requested by the client, thereby resulting in wasted bandwidth. We measure the wasted data (*WD*) as the percentage of bytes pushed by the proxy which are unused by the client. We report average *WD* across all pages weighted by the popularity of the pages (refer to §6.1). The weighted average *WD* is 18.4% with *FullRedEx*, and 18.3% with *NutShell* for the 'Alexa views' model (§6.1), with similar results for other models. Further investigation shows a key factor impacting the results is that PhantomJS currently does not support several HTML5 features (e.g. srcset attribute). This resulted in the proxy sometimes requesting different URLs than the mobile client even though we emulated the mobile user environment as described in §4. We believe that *WD* would be lower as support for these features is implemented in PhantomJS, or with an alternate browser choice for the proxy implementation. To confirm this, we repeated the above measurements using a desktop PhantomJS client and our results show that the weighted average *WD* is modest with both *FullRedEx* and *NutShell* (8% and 7%) respectively. *NutShell* sees slightly lower *WD* than *FullRedEx* because the proxy only executes the code required to fetch the signature (§3.1), which sometimes excludes URLs that vary in back-to-back runs.

Table 1: Implications of proxy execution architecture choice

	No Execution	Non-Redundant	Redundant
Prioritization	√	√	√
Compression	√	√	√
Push	Subset	All	All
Reduce Client JS	×	√	×
Complexity	Low	High	Low
Scalability bottleneck	None	Compute	Compute

7 RELATED WORK

Existing approaches to improving web page load can be classified along two dimensions: (a) proxy based execution and (b) optimizations such as content push, prioritization (controlling the order in which objects are sent) [18, 35, 41], and object compression [12, 50]. We discuss these below.

Non-redundant execution: As Table 1 shows, proxy execution based approaches themselves may be classified into (i) non-redundant execution; and (ii) redundant execution. Non-redundant proxy-based execution can reduce the compute delay at the client. Some implementations [6, 11, 62] eliminate all client side execution by getting the proxy to render the page and pushing the rendered page to the client. Though these approaches can reduce initial page load times, eliminating client execution incurs latency on user interactions (*e.g.*, mouse hover, clicks) since the JS processing of these interactions must be done in the cloud [51].

A more recent approach [56] involves partial-elimination of client-side JS code. Here, the proxy executes JS in a web page to a point and then migrates state to the client. The client continues the process from that point. Since the migrated state can become large, these approaches re-execute part (idempotent operations) of the CSS and JS code at the client. The migration of execution mid-flight from the proxy to the client makes partial elimination fairly complex. It is further complicated by issues such as modifications to the underlying JavaScript engine, browser consistency at the proxy and client, and not supporting widely-used JS constructs such as `eval` [43] prior to page load. A recent emulation-based study [40] posits that mobile web latencies are compute-bound. Our measurements on real LTE networks with mobile clients show that the network is a significant component of latency (see Fig. 1a). Consequently, the benefit of reduced compute delay while adding network delay may be relatively small in latency-dominated cellular networks.

Content Push: The benefits of server push over basic SPDY are well known [55]. Klotski [18] does a limited form of push where only static objects (invariant across users and multiple runs) are pushed, with other objects pulled by the client. Recent works [30, 37] augment server push to ensure that the server does not push objects already in the client's cache. In contrast, we seek to solve the harder problem of identifying *all* the objects relevant to the client (including personalized content), and push those objects. With *NutShell*, we improve the scaling of redundant execution proxies to fully derive the advantages of push. Wang *et al.* [57] show the benefits of pre-loading resources of a page through speculative prefetching - we derive similar benefits through proxy-based push.

Compression, transformation and prioritization: Several popular browsers [5, 6, 12] reduce the size of data transferred by including support for data transformation and compression in the cloud. However, compression by itself does not always lower latencies [12, 50, 51]. Klotski [18] reprioritizes content so that critical content is delivered early by using a dependency structure of objects and user preferences. Incorporating user preferences may not be easy in practice. Polaris [41] proposes dynamic re-prioritization of object fetches by tracking fine-grained dependencies in Web pages. For best results with Polaris, the page has to be served from a single server. WebGaze [35] employs user gaze tracking to automatically identify critical content. Requiring users to submit to gaze tracking may not be easy in practice, and it is unclear how the approach will extend to highly personalized pages where users see varying content. That said, *NutShell* is complementary to all these above approaches, and all the mechanisms above may be readily combined with *NutShell*.

Other related work: Beyond web pages, researchers [20, 21, 36, 38, 45–47] have investigated offloading code of generic applications (*e.g.*, compute intensive face recognition applications) to the cloud, primarily to reduce computation time and save device energy. In contrast, we explore redundant execution for networking-intensive Web download. Tango [28] replicates execution at the client and the cloud, and allows either replica to lead the execution depending on which is faster during different phases of the application. Because either replica may affect user-visible content, Tango is unable to leverage approximation or to execute only a subset of JS code, which are the two key optimizations that *NutShell* employs. *NutShell*'s two-version testing has similarities to A/B testing. However, while A/B testing is typically used to measure the impact of user-visible changes on user behavior [22]. *NutShell*'s approach is an internal method to determine if a function can be whittled; end users see a single unmodified view of the Web page.

8 CONCLUSION

In this paper, we have presented *NutShell*, a proxy design that can simultaneously (i) achieve low latency over cellular networks by pushing all objects needed for a page load through redundant execution; and (ii) scale to support more simultaneous users by reducing JS computation overheads at the proxy. *NutShell* achieves the above through *whittling* – a novel technique to dynamically identify and execute only a portion of the JS code necessary to identify and push objects required for a page load. Whittling exploits the fact that approximation is acceptable at the proxy, given the client executes the full JS code. Experiments with 78 popular Alexa web sites reveal that *NutShell* sustains 27% higher user requests per second on average than *FullRedEx*. Further, by combining redundant execution and whittling, *NutShell* achieves speedups in median page load times of 1.5 compared to SPDY, and speedups of 20% compared to *FullRedEx* for 15% of the pages.

In the future, we plan to investigate ways to achieve more scaling for *NutShell* while keeping latency penalties small. A potential direction is to tune our whittling technique to eliminate functions only responsible for fetching a small number of objects. Another interesting direction is to analyze the extent of personalization in a page, and employ redundant execution for more personalized pages, and push objects based on historical accesses for less personalized pages. Finally, we also hope to further validate *NutShell* through real-world deployments.

9 ACKNOWLEDGMENTS

We thank our shepherd Matt Welsh and the anonymous reviewers for their constructive feedback and comments. This work was supported by the National Science Foundation (NSF) Award CNS-1618921. Any opinions, findings and conclusions or recommendations expressed in this material are those of the authors and do not necessarily reflect the views of NSF.

REFERENCES

[1] 2008. The Psychology of Web Performance. (2008). http://www.websiteoptimization.com/speed/tweak/psychology-web-performance.
[2] 2009. JavaScript beautifier. (2009). http://jsbeautifier.org.
[3] 2009. Latency - it costs you. http://highscalability.com/latency-everywhere-and-it-costs-you-sales-how-crush-it. (2009).
[4] 2009. Slow pages lose users. http://radar.oreilly.com/2009/06/bing-and-google-agree-slow-pag.html. (2009).
[5] 2011. Amazon Silk Split Browser Architecture. (2011). https://s3.amazonaws.com/awsdocs/AmazonSilk/latest/silk-dg.pdf.
[6] 2011. Opera Mini Architecture and JavaScript. (2011). http://dev.opera.com/articles/view/opera-mini-and-javascript/.
[7] 2012. Google Speed-index. https://sites.google.com/a/webpagetest.org/docs/using-webpagetest/metrics/speed-index. (2012).
[8] 2014. Record and play back web pages with simulated network conditions. (Oct 2014). https://github.com/chromium/web-page-replay/.
[9] 2015. Alexa Traffic Data. (2015). http://www.rank2traffic.com.
[10] 2015. Chrome devtools JavaScript CPU profiler. (2015). https://tinyurl.com/yb8uxpxl.
[11] 2017. SkyFire - Cloud based Mobile Optimization Browser (Now Opera). (2017). http://www.skyfire.com/operator-solutions/whitepapers.
[12] Victor Agababov, Michael Buettner, Victor Chudnovsky, Mark Cogan, Ben Greenstein, Shane McDaniel, Michael Piatek, Colin Scott, Matt Welsh, and Bolian Yin. 2015. Flywheel: Google's Data Compression Proxy for the Mobile Web. In *Proceedings of the 12th USENIX Conference on Networked Systems Design and Implementation (NSDI'15)*. USENIX Association, Berkeley, CA, USA, 367–380. http://dl.acm.org/citation.cfm?id=2789770.2789796
[13] Alexa. 2017. (2017). Available at http://www.alexa.com/topsites.
[14] Virgílio Almeida, Azer Bestavros, Mark Crovella, and Adriana de Oliveira. 1996. Characterizing Reference Locality in the WWW. In *Proceedings of the Fourth International Conference on on Parallel and Distributed Information Systems (DIS '96)*. IEEE Computer Society, Washington, DC, USA, 92–107. http://dl.acm.org/citation.cfm?id=382006.383200

[15] David Binkley, Nicolas Gold, Mark Harman, Syed Islam, Jens Krinke, and Shin Yoo. 2014. ORBS: Language-independent Program Slicing. In *Proceedings of the 22Nd ACM SIGSOFT International Symposium on Foundations of Software Engineering (FSE 2014)*. ACM, New York, NY, USA, 109–120. https://doi.org/10.1145/2635868.2635893

[16] L. Breslau, Pei Cao, Li Fan, G. Phillips, and S. Shenker. 1999. Web caching and Zipf-like distributions: evidence and implications. In *INFOCOM '99. Eighteenth Annual Joint Conference of the IEEE Computer and Communications Societies. Proceedings. IEEE*, Vol. 1. 126–134 vol.1. https://doi.org/10.1109/INFCOM.1999.749260

[17] Michael Butkiewicz, Harsha V Madhyastha, and Vyas Sekar. 2011. Understanding website complexity: measurements, metrics, and implications. In *Proceedings of the 2011 ACM SIGCOMM conference on Internet measurement conference*. ACM, 313–328.

[18] Michael Butkiewicz, Daimeng Wang, Zhe Wu, Harsha V. Madhyastha, and Vyas Sekar. 2015. Klotski: Reprioritizing Web Content to Improve User Experience on Mobile Devices. In *12th USENIX Symposium on Networked Systems Design and Implementation (NSDI 15)*. USENIX Association, Oakland, CA, 439–453. https://www.usenix.org/conference/nsdi15/technical-sessions/presentation/butkiewicz

[19] Ramón Cáceres, Landon Cox, Harold Lim, Amre Shakimov, and Alexander Varshavsky. 2009. Virtual Individual Servers As Privacy-preserving Proxies for Mobile Devices. In *Proceedings of the 1st ACM Workshop on Networking, Systems, and Applications for Mobile Handhelds (MobiHeld '09)*. 37–42. https://doi.org/10.1145/1592606.1592616

[20] Byung-Gon Chun, Sunghwan Ihm, Petros Maniatis, Mayur Naik, and Ashwin Patti. 2011. CloneCloud: Elastic Execution Between Mobile Device and Cloud. In *Proceedings of the Sixth Conference on Computer Systems (EuroSys '11)*. 301–314. https://doi.org/10.1145/1966445.1966473

[21] Eduardo Cuervo, Aruna Balasubramanian, Dae-ki Cho, Alec Wolman, Stefan Saroiu, Ranveer Chandra, and Paramvir Bahl. 2010. MAUI: Making Smartphones Last Longer with Code Offload. In *Proceedings of the 8th International Conference on Mobile Systems, Applications, and Services (MobiSys '10)*. 49–62. https://doi.org/10.1145/1814433.1814441

[22] Pete Koomen Dan Siroker. 2013. *A/B Testing: The Most Powerful Way to Turn Clicks Into Customers*. Wiley.

[23] Richard A. DeMillo, Hsin Pan, and Eugene H. Spafford. 1996. Critical Slicing for Software Fault Localization. In *Proceedings of the 1996 ACM SIGSOFT International Symposium on Software Testing and Analysis (ISSTA '96)*. ACM, New York, NY, USA, 121–134. https://doi.org/10.1145/229000.226310

[24] KIT EATON. 2012. How One Second Could Cost Amazon 1.6 Billion In Sales. (2012). https://www.fastcompany.com/1825005/how-one-second-could-cost-amazon-16-billion-sales.

[25] Jeffrey Erman, Vijay Gopalakrishnan, Rittwik Jana, and K. K. Ramakrishnan. 2013. Towards a SPDY'Ier Mobile Web?. In *Proceedings of the Ninth ACM Conference on Emerging Networking Experiments and Technologies (CoNEXT '13)*. 303–314. https://doi.org/10.1145/2535372.2535399

[26] Stephen J. Fink and Julian Dolby. 2012. WALA-The T. J. Watson Libraries for Analysis. (2012). http://wala.sourceforge.net/.

[27] Google. 2009. Whitepaper – SPDY: An experimental protocol for a faster web. (Dec 2009). http://www.chromium.org/spdy/spdy-whitepaper.

[28] Mark S. Gordon, David Ke Hong, Peter M. Chen, Jason Flinn, Scott Mahlke, and Zhuoqing Morley Mao. 2015. Accelerating Mobile Applications Through Flip-Flop Replication. In *Proceedings of the 13th Annual International Conference on Mobile Systems, Applications, and Services (MobiSys '15)*. ACM, New York, NY, USA, 137–150. https://doi.org/10.1145/2742647.2742649

[29] Ilya Grigorik. 2013. Node SPDY proxy. (2013). https://github.com/igrigorik/node-spdyproxy.

[30] Bo Han, Shuai Hao, and Feng Qian. 2015. MetaPush: Cellular-Friendly Server Push For HTTP/2. In *Proceedings of the 5th Workshop on All Things Cellular: Operations, Applications and Challenges (AllThingsCellular '15)*. ACM, New York, NY, USA, 57–62. https://doi.org/10.1145/2785971.2785972

[31] Ariya Hidayat. 2010. PhantomJS APIs. (2010). http://phantomjs.org/api/

[32] IETF. 2015. Hypertext Transfer Protocol Version 2. (June 2015). https://tools.ietf.org/html/rfc7540.

[33] Sunghwan Ihm and Vivek S Pai. 2011. Towards understanding modern web traffic. In *Proceedings of the 2011 ACM SIGCOMM conference on Internet measurement conference*. ACM, 295–312.

[34] Vineeth Kashyap, Kyle Dewey, Ethan A. Kuefner, John Wagner, Kevin Gibbons, John Sarracino, Ben Wiedermann, and Ben Hardekopf. 2014. JSAI: A Static Analysis Platform for JavaScript. In *Proceedings of the 22Nd ACM SIGSOFT International Symposium on Foundations of Software Engineering (FSE 2014)*. ACM, New York, NY, USA, 121–132. https://doi.org/10.1145/2635868.2635904

[35] Conor Kelton, Jihoon Ryoo, Aruna Balasubramanian, and Samir R. Das. 2017. Improving User Perceived Page Load Times Using Gaze. In *14th USENIX Symposium on Networked Systems Design and Implementation (NSDI 17)*. https://www.usenix.org/conference/nsdi17/technical-sessions/presentation/ryoo

[36] Roelof Kemp, Nicholas Palmer, Thilo Kielmann, and Henri E. Bal. 2010. Cuckoo: A Computation Offloading Framework for Smartphones.. In *MobiCASE (Lecture Notes of the Institute for Computer Sciences, Social Informatics and Telecommunications Engineering)*, Martin L. Gris and Guang Yang 0001 (Eds.), Vol. 76. Springer, 59–79. https://doi.org/10.1007/978-3-642-29336-8_4

[37] Junaid Khalid, Sharad Agarwal, Aditya Akella, and Jitendra Padhye. 2054. Improving the performance of SPDY for mobile devices (POSTER). In *Proceedings of the 16th Workshop on Mobile Computing Systems and Applications (HotMobile '15)*. ACM, New York, NY, USA.

[38] Sokol Kosta, Andrius Aucinas, Pan Hui, Richard Mortier, and Xinwen Zhang. 2012. ThinkAir: Dynamic resource allocation and parallel execution in the cloud for mobile code offloading. In *INFOCOM, 2012 Proceedings IEEE*. 945–953. https://doi.org/10.1109/INFCOM.2012.6195845

[39] David Naylor, Kyle Schomp, Matteo Varvello, Ilias Leontiadis, Jeremy Blackburn, Diego R. López, Konstantina Papagiannaki, Pablo Rodriguez Rodriguez, and Peter Steenkiste. 2015. Multi-Context TLS (mcTLS): Enabling Secure In-Network Functionality in TLS. In *Proceedings of the 2015 ACM Conference on Special Interest Group on Data Communication (SIGCOMM '15)*. ACM, New York, NY, USA, 199–212. https://doi.org/10.1145/2785956.2787482

[40] Javad Nejati and Aruna Balasubramanian. 2016. An In-depth Study of Mobile Browser Performance. In *Proceedings of the 25th International Conference on World Wide Web (WWW '16)*. International World Wide Web Conferences Steering Committee, Republic and Canton of Geneva, Switzerland, 1305–1315. https://doi.org/10.1145/2872427.2883014

[41] Ravi Netravali, Ameesh Goyal, James Mickens, and Hari Balakrishnan. 2016. Polaris: Faster Page Loads Using Fine-grained Dependency Tracking. In *13th USENIX Symposium on Networked Systems Design and Implementation (NSDI 16)*. Santa Clara, CA. https://www.usenix.org/conference/nsdi16/technical-sessions/presentation/netravali

[42] Ravi Netravali, Anirudh Sivaraman, Somak Das, Ameesh Goyal, Keith Winstein, James Mickens, and Hari Balakrishnan. 2015. Mahimahi: Accurate Record-and-Replay for HTTP. In *2015 USENIX Annual Technical Conference (USENIX ATC 15)*. 417–429. https://www.usenix.org/conference/atc15/technical-session/presentation/netravali

[43] Gregor Richards, Christian Hammer, Brian Burg, and Jan Vitek. 2011. The Eval That Men Do: A Large-scale Study of the Use of Eval in Javascript Applications. In *Proceedings of the 25th European Conference on Object-oriented Programming (ECOOP'11)*. Springer-Verlag, Berlin, Heidelberg, 52–78. http://dl.acm.org/citation.cfm?id=2032497.2032503

[44] Jim Roskind. 2013. QUIC: Design Document and Specification Rationale. (Dec 2013). http://goo.gl/p2mbcf.

[45] Aki Saarinen, Matti Siekkinen, Yu Xiao, Jukka K. Nurminen, Matti Kemppainen, and Pan Hui. 2012. Can Offloading Save Energy for Popular Apps?. In *Proceedings of the Seventh ACM International Workshop on Mobility in the Evolving Internet Architecture (MobiArch '12)*. 3–10. https://doi.org/10.1145/2348676.2348680

[46] Aki Saarinen, Matti Siekkinen, Yu Xiao, Jukka K. Nurminen, Matti Kemppainen, and Pan Hui. 2012. SmartDiet: Offloading Popular Apps to Save Energy (POSTER). In *Proceedings of the 2012 ACM Conference of the Special Interest Group on Data Communications (SIGCOMM '12)*. 297–298. https://doi.org/10.1145/2342356.2342418

[47] Mahadev Satyanarayanan, Paramvir Bahl, Ramón Cáceres, and Nigel Davies. 2011. The Case for VM-based Cloudlets in Mobile Computing. *Pervasive Computing, IEEE* PP, 99 (2011), 1–1. https://doi.org/10.1109/MPRV.2009.64

[48] Max Schaefer, Manu Sridharan, and Julian Dolby. 2014. Analyzing JavaScript and the Web with WALA. (2014). http://wala.sourceforge.net/files/WALAJavaScriptTutorial.pdf.

[49] Justine Sherry, Chang Lan, Raluca Ada Popa, and Sylvia Ratnasamy. 2015. BlindBox: Deep Packet Inspection over Encrypted Traffic. In *Proceedings of the 2015 ACM Conference on Special Interest Group on Data Communication (SIGCOMM '15)*. ACM, New York, NY, USA, 213–226. https://doi.org/10.1145/2785956.2787502

[50] Shailendra Singh, Harsha V. Madhyastha, Srikanth V. Krishnamurthy, and Ramesh Govindan. 2015. FlexiWeb: Network-Aware Compaction for Accelerating Mobile Web Transfers. In *Proceedings of the 21st Annual International Conference on Mobile Computing and Networking (MobiCom '15)*. ACM, New York, NY, USA, 604–616. https://doi.org/10.1145/2789168.2790128

[51] Ashiwan Sivakumar, Vijay Gopalakrishnan, Seungjoon Lee, Sanjay Rao, Subhabrata Sen, and Oliver Spatscheck. 2014. Cloud is Not a Silver Bullet: A Case Study of Cloud-based Mobile Browsing. In *Proceedings of the 15th Workshop on Mobile Computing Systems and Applications (HotMobile '14)*. ACM, New York, NY, USA, Article 21, 6 pages. https://doi.org/10.1145/2565585.2565601

[52] Ashiwan Sivakumar, Shankaranarayanan P N, Vijay Gopalakrishnan, Seungjoon Lee, Sanjay Rao, Subhabrata Sen, and Oliver Spatscheck. 2014. PARCEL: Proxy Assisted BRowsing in Cellular networks for Energy and Latency reduction. In *Proceedings of the Tenth ACM Conference on Emerging Networking Experiments and Technologies (CoNEXT '14)*.

[53] Frank Tip. 1995. A Survey of Program Slicing Techniques. *Journal of Programming Languages* 3 (1995), 121–189.

[54] Qi Wang, Jingyu Zhou, Yuting Chen, Yizhou Zhang, and Jianjun Zhao. 2013. Extracting URLs from JavaScript via Program Analysis. In *Proceedings of the 2013 9th Joint Meeting on Foundations of Software Engineering (ESEC/FSE 2013)*. ACM,

New York, NY, USA, 627–630. https://doi.org/10.1145/2491411.2494583
[55] Xiao Sophia Wang, Aruna Balasubramanian, Arvind Krishnamurthy, and David Wetherall. 2014. How Speedy is SPDY?. In *Proceedings of the 11th USENIX Conference on Networked Systems Design and Implementation (NSDI'14)*. 387–399. http://dl.acm.org/citation.cfm?id=2616448.2616484
[56] Xiao Sophia Wang, Arvind Krishnamurthy, and David Wetherall. 2016. Speeding up Web Page Loads with Shandian. In *13th USENIX Symposium on Networked Systems Design and Implementation (NSDI 16)*. USENIX Association, Santa Clara, CA, 109–122. https://www.usenix.org/conference/nsdi16/technical-sessions/presentation/wang
[57] Zhen Wang, Felix Xiaozhu Lin, Lin Zhong, and Mansoor Chishtie. 2012. How Far Can Client-only Solutions Go for Mobile Browser Speed?. In *Proceedings of the 21st International Conference on World Wide Web (WWW '12)*. ACM, New York, NY, USA, 31–40. https://doi.org/10.1145/2187836.2187842
[58] Mark Weiser. 1981. Program Slicing. In *Proceedings of the 5th International Conference on Software Engineering (ICSE '81)*. IEEE Press, Piscataway, NJ, USA, 439–449. http://dl.acm.org/citation.cfm?id=800078.802557
[59] W3C working group. 2012. Media Queries : W3C. (2012). https://www.w3.org/TR/css3-mediaqueries/
[60] W3C working group. 2014. WPO-Foundation/visualmetrics. (2014). https://github.com/WPO-Foundation/visualmetrics
[61] Andreas Zeller. 2002. Isolating Cause-effect Chains from Computer Programs. In *Proceedings of the 10th ACM SIGSOFT Symposium on Foundations of Software Engineering (SIGSOFT '02/FSE-10)*. ACM, New York, NY, USA, 1–10. https://doi.org/10.1145/587051.587053
[62] Bo Zhao, Byung Chul Tak, and Guohong Cao. 2011. Reducing the Delay and Power Consumption of Web Browsing on Smartphones in 3G Networks. In *Proceedings of the 2011 31st International Conference on Distributed Computing Systems (ICDCS '11)*. 413–422. https://doi.org/10.1109/ICDCS.2011.54

Demo: The Sound of Silence: End-to-End Sign Language Recognition Using SmartWatch

Qian Dai
University of Science and Technology of China
Hefei, China
dq620@mail.ustc.edu.cn

Jiahui Hou
Illinois Institute of Technology
Chicago, Illinois
jhou11@hawk.iit.edu

Panlong Yang
University of Science and Technology of China
Hefei, China
panlongyang@gmail.com

Xiangyang Li*
University of Science and Technology of China
Hefei, China
xiangyangli@ustc.edu.cn

Fei Wang
University of Science and Technology of China
Hefei, China
wf314159@mail.ustc.edu.cn

Xumiao Zhang
University of Science and Technology of China
Hefei, China
zxm0112@mail.ustc.edu.cn

ABSTRACT

Sign Language is a natural and fully-fledged communication method for deaf and hearing-impaired people. In this demo, we propose the first SmartWatch-based American sign language (ASL) recognition system, which is more comfortable, portable and user-friendly and offers accessibility anytime, anywhere. This system is based on the intuitive idea that each sign has its specific motion pattern which can be transformed into unique gyroscope and accelerometer signals and then analyzed and learned by using Long-Short term memory recurrent neural network (LSTM-RNN) trained with connectionist temporal classification (CTC). In this way, signs and context information can be correctly recognized based on an off-the-shelf device (*e.g.* SmartWatch, Smartphone). The experiments show that, in the Known user split task, our system reaches an average word error rate of 7.29% to recognize 73 sentences formed by 103 ASL signs and achieves detection ratio up to 93.7% for a single sign. The result also shows our system has a good adaptation, even including new users, it can achieve an average word error rate of 21.6% at the sentence level and reach an average detection ratio of 79.4%. Moreover, our system performs real time ASL translation, outputting the speech within 1.69 seconds for a sentence of 12 signs in average.

CCS CONCEPTS

• **Human-centered computing → Natural language interfaces**; **Gestural input**; **Mobile computing**;

KEYWORDS

Wearable computing; activity recognition; mobile sensing

*Xiangyang Li is the corresponding author.

MobiCom '17, , October 16–20, 2017, Snowbird, UT, USA.

ACM ISBN ISBN 978-1-4503-4916-1/17/10.
https://doi.org/10.1145/3117811.3119853

1 INTRODUCTION

Sign language composed of a series of gestures is a form of communication which is mainly used by the hearing-impaired or deaf mutism. However, there exists a language barrier between the deaf signers with non-verbal behavior and the speakers with verbal language. To facilitate the communication between the hearing-impaired and people with normal hearing, automatic sign language recognition (ASLR) has been addressed and widely studied.

Existing methods can be classified into two categories based on the kinds of devices: image-based and sensor-based. Image-based methods usually use a camera [7, 8] or depth-camera like Kinect or Leap Motion [2, 4], which are cumbersome and not applicable for outdoor uses. Sensor-based methods usually use sensory gloves [9, 10] and Cyber Gloves [12], which are not desirable for resource-constrained devices and have bad portability.

In this paper, we propose a novel American Sign Language recognition system using a lightweight and portable device – SmartWatch, which is much less constrained by the environment and can be used anytime, anywhere. The system is based on the motion sensors embedded in the SmartWatch, which track the users' wrists and have certain ability to track the users' hands. Long-short Term Memory (LSTM) [6] recurrent network trained with connectionist temporal classification (CTC)[5] loss is used in the end-to-end sentence-level training.

Specifically, in the first place, the system collects sensory data from accelerometer and gyroscope embedded in the SmartWatch as input. Then, the data are transmitted to the Smartphone and transformed into the spectrogram after that. Next, the pre-trained end-to-end sentence-level recurrent neural network recognizes the sign language sentences out of the spectrogram. Finally, the texts are translated into voice via a fully-fledged Text-to-Speech (TTS) technique.

To the best of our knowledge, we first propose the SmartWatch-based ASLR method. In this paper, we explore the recurrent neural network to model the sequential data and build a high-accuracy American sign language recognition system. However, to achieve this goal, we face challenges as follows:

- **Features Extraction and Selection**: In this work, there are only two sensors - accelerometer and gyroscope in the

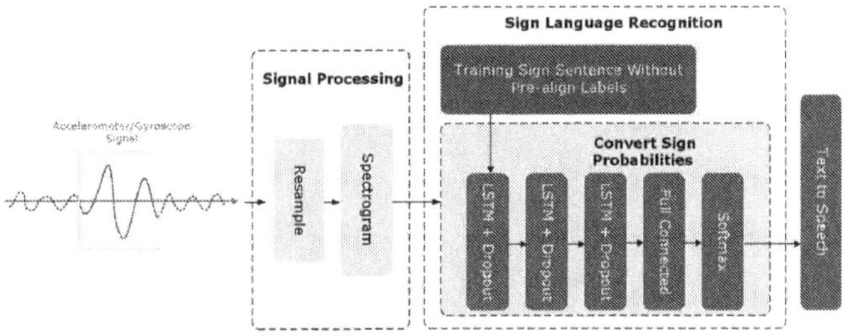

Figure 1: Architecture of our system.

(a) initial (b) YOUR (c) FATHER (d) NAME (e) end position

Figure 2: The way of user performing a sign sentence.

SmartWatch, whose insufficient, noisy sensory data make 3D position recovery infeasible. Hence, it is challenging to recognize continuous sign language precisely.

- **Segmentation**: Efficiently achieving the segmentation of the continuous input sign language is requisite but difficult due to movement epenthesis, which is the transition that connects two successive signs.
- **Low energy consumption and real-time performance**: The predicting process on mobile device consumes both memory and large quantity of energy. The actual communication scenario requires system to be real-time, which needs to address these challenges.

Our contributions:

- As far as we know, we propose the first SmartWatch-based end-to-end sentence-level sign language recognition system, which has a good performance. It provides a non-invasive, anytime-anywhere service for the signer to express himself/herself without heavy devices and strict environmental requirements.
- High quality features are extracted and learned for the SmartWatch-based ASLR system. We present a LSTM-CTC network to train a model which has a good performance on recognition and is robust for sign language recognition.
- Our system achieves a word error rate of 21.6% on our test set of 73 predefined sentences which is formed by 103 signs. Specially, our system achieves a word error rate of 7.3% on those persons that it *knows*[1]. Besides, our system is user-independent and can be implemented on smartwatch and smartphone, which achieves the goal of low energy consumption at 80 milliwatts and low delay within 1.69 seconds on average for a 12-sign 16-second sentence[2].

2 SYSTEM OVERVIEW

Our system utilizes commercial SmartWatch and SmartPhone and deep neural network to achieve sequential American Sign Language Recognition. Figure 1 illustrates the architecture of our system.

For the first part, a SmartWatch collects all the necessary sensory data and makes some simple detection. A signer wears a SmartWatch on his/her right hand (dominant hand) wrist and performs the signs continuously. The SmartWatch captures the sequential signals of accelerometer, gyroscope and linear accelerometer. The SmartWatch monitors the sensory data to see if the signals consist of meaningful signs, and if so, the SmartWatch transmits them to the SmartPhone. Then the subsequent energy-consuming computation is left for the SmartPhone with a larger battery capacity.

In the second part, a SmartPhone utilizes a deep neural network to do the prediction. SmartPhone receives the signals from the SmartWatch, realigns the signals to the same time steps, compresses the signals with Short-Time Fourier Transformation (STFT) with proper parameters and feeds the signals to the pre-trained deep neural network. The neural network contains 4 hidden layers, where the first three layers are LSTM layers with 128 LSTM neurons for each layer, and the last layer is a linear transformation with a softmax activation function. A CTC decoder is used to translate the probability sequence into the most probable label output. During training procedure, the CTC loss function is used to help handle the epenthesis and remove the need of pre-aligned labels, thus provides end-to-end sentence-level training.

In the third part, the SmartPhone translates the text sequences into voice. We utilize the mature Text-to-Sound technique to translate the text sequences output by the neural network into voice for the hearing people.

3 IMPLEMENTATION AND EVALUATION

3.1 Hardware and Software

We build our system based on Huawei Watch (Android Wear based on Android 6.0) and Huawei Nexus 6P smartphone (Android 7.0). All data are collected from Huawei Watch at a sampling rate of 100 Hz. We use TensorFlow [1] (version 1.0.1) to train the neural network model on a desktop computer. We are aware that the binarized network technique [3] can reduce the training computation cost and memory consumption, however the spectrogram input and intermediate result of the training of LSTM still exceed the memory of smartphone. Besides, the full precision model is not so large that suits the prediction phase on mobile phone. Thus, binarized technique is not suitable here. So we train the model on a desktop computer instead of a mobile phone.

3.2 Dataset

We select 103 words which can well perform the diversity of the ASL actions (including moving up and down, rotate, sway, making a fist *etc.*) from a widespread american sign language learning website - Lifeprint[11]. Based on selected words, we structure 73 sentences, which follow the grammar of ASL. We recruited 15 volunteers – 5 women and 10 men aging from 20 to 30. The volunteers were told to perform each of the sentence in ASL for 10 times.

[1]Our system knows a person means that the training set of our system contains this person's samples.
[2]This is the longest sentence in our dataset.

The dataset is divided into training set and test set, and the test set will be further divided into *known* and *unseen*. The training set consists of 80% of randomly-selected 11 (out of 15) people's data. The known set consists of the rest 20% of these 11 people's data. The unseen set consists of the rest 4 out of 15 people's all data. Indeed, the unseen set is used for testing the performance of model adaptation.

3.3 Evaluation

In the field of language recognition, there are generally three types of errors: *deletion* (labeled as *D*), which represents missing a word; *insertion* (*I*), which implies recognize a non-existent word; and *substitution* (*S*), which means false classification.

We define three metrics, Detection Ratio (*DR*), Reliability Ratio (*RR*) and Word Error Rate(*WER*), for evaluation as follows.

$$\mathrm{DR} = \frac{\mathbf{C}}{\mathbf{D}+\mathbf{C}+\mathbf{S}},\ \mathrm{RR} = \frac{\mathbf{C}}{\mathbf{C}+\mathbf{I}},\ \mathrm{WER} = \frac{\#\mathbf{D}+\#\mathbf{I}+\#\mathbf{S}}{\#\mathbf{D}+\#\mathbf{C}+\#\mathbf{S}},$$

where C refers to the number of correct signs.

Performance on single signs. The total detection ratio on the Known and the Unseen test set is 93.7% and 71.5% respectively, while the total reliability on the Known and the Unseen test set is 96.2% and 83.7% respectively. The average reliability ratio is higher than the average detection ratio for both test sets. Indeed, reliability means that when our system recognize a sign, we have a high confidence that it is right.

Performance on sentence. We choose sliding window size of 128, cut-off frequency at 25 Hz and training samples of 8. We calculate the mean word error rate of the whole test set and the separated part of the test set. The result shows that our model performs well when it "knows" the person, which can achieve a low word error rate of 7.29%, while its generalization ability to a person it does not see before is limited as the word error rate of the Unseen test set is 29.43%. The total word error rate of the test set is 21.57%.

Processing Delay and Energy Consumption. In our implementation, the mobile device needs an average processing delay of 1.69 second to give a prediction on a 16-second 12-sign sentence. This means that our system can realize real-time working. We evaluate our system's energy overhead. We run our system on a Huawei Nexus 6P SmartPhone and a Huawei Watch SmartWatch, and the power consumption for SmartWatch and SmartPhone is $19mW$ and $61mW$ respectively.

4 DEMONSTRATIONS

We develop an application called Deep Sign (shown in Fig 3), which enables a user to wear an Android Wear SmartWatch and perform continuous sign sentences and get the corresponding voice output in English.

The demonstration consists of one Android Wear, which collects the sensory data, and one Android mobile phone, where all the energy-consuming computation takes place. Both two devices need to install Deep Sign on them. We will bring our own smartphone and smartwatch. We do need a small desk to hold the smartphone to show to others. No other special space, setup time or additional facility is needed. We hope to inspire future researchers to utilize the SmartWatch to design more advanced interactions for the disabled.

Figure 3: Illustration of the Deep Sign app.

ACKNOWLEDGMENTS

The research is partially supported by China National Funds for Distinguished Young Scientists with No. 61625205,Key Research Program of Frontier Sciences, CAS, No. QYZDY-SSW-JSC002, NSFC with No. 61520106007, NSF ECCS-1247944, and NSF CNS 1526638.

REFERENCES

[1] Martín Abadi, Ashish Agarwal, Paul Barham, Eugene Brevdo, Zhifeng Chen, Craig Citro, Greg S Corrado, Andy Davis, Jeffrey Dean, Matthieu Devin, et al. 2016. Tensorflow: Large-scale machine learning on heterogeneous distributed systems. *arXiv preprint arXiv:1603.04467* (2016).

[2] Xiujuan Chai, Guang Li, Xilin Chen, Ming Zhou, Guobin Wu, and Hanjing Li. 2013. Visualcomm: A tool to support communication between deaf and hearing persons with the kinect. In *Proceedings of the 15th International ACM SIGACCESS Conference on Computers and Accessibility*. ACM, 76.

[3] Matthieu Courbariaux, Itay Hubara, Daniel Soudry, Ran El-Yaniv, and Yoshua Bengio. 2016. Binarized neural networks: Training deep neural networks with weights and activations constrained to+ 1 or-1. *arXiv preprint arXiv:1602.02830* (2016).

[4] Cao Dong, Ming C Leu, and Zhaozheng Yin. 2015. American sign language alphabet recognition using microsoft kinect. In *Proceedings of the IEEE Conference on Computer Vision and Pattern Recognition Workshops*. 44–52.

[5] Alex Graves, Santiago Fernández, Faustino Gomez, and Jürgen Schmidhuber. 2006. Connectionist temporal classification: labelling unsegmented sequence data with recurrent neural networks. In *Proceedings of the 23rd international conference on Machine learning*. ACM, 369–376.

[6] Sepp Hochreiter and Jürgen Schmidhuber. 1997. Long short-term memory. *Neural computation* 9, 8 (1997), 1735–1780.

[7] Daniel Kelly, Jane Reilly Delannoy, John Mc Donald, and Charles Markham. 2009. A framework for continuous multimodal sign language recognition. In *Proceedings of the 2009 international conference on Multimodal interfaces*. ACM, 351–358.

[8] Oscar Koller, O Zargaran, Hermann Ney, and Richard Bowden. 2016. Deep Sign: Hybrid CNN-HMM for Continuous Sign Language Recognition. In *Proceedings of the British Machine Vision Conference 2016*.

[9] Kehuang Li, Zhengyu Zhou, and Chin-Hui Lee. 2016. Sign transition modeling and a scalable solution to continuous sign language recognition for real-world applications. *ACM Transactions on Accessible Computing (TACCESS)* 8, 2 (2016), 7.

[10] Noor Tubaiz, Tamer Shanableh, and Khaled Assaleh. 2015. Glove-based continuous Arabic sign language recognition in user-dependent mode. *IEEE Transactions on Human-Machine Systems* 45, 4 (2015), 526–533.

[11] William Vicars. 2017. Basic ASL: First 100 Signs. (May 2017). Retrieved May 15, 2017 from http://www.lifeprint.com/asl101/pages-layout/concepts.htm

[12] Honggang Wang, Ming C Leu, and Cemil Oz. 2006. American Sign Language Recognition Using Multi-dimensional Hidden Markov Models. *Journal of Information Science and Engineering* 22, 5 (2006), 1109–1123.

Demo: FlexRAN – A Software-Defined RAN Platform

Xenofon Foukas
The University of Edinburgh
x.foukas@ed.ac.uk

Navid Nikaein
Eurecom
Navid.Nikaein@eurecom.fr

Mohamed M. Kassem
The University of Edinburgh
M.M.M.Kassem@sms.ed.ac.uk

Mahesh K. Marina
The University of Edinburgh
mahesh@ed.ac.uk

Kimon Kontovasilis
"NCSR" Demokritos
kkont@iit.demokritos.gr

ABSTRACT

Although SDN is considered as one of the key technologies behind the impending 5G evolution of mobile networks, the opportunity of reaping its benefits is largely still untapped on the Radio Access Network (RAN) side due to the lack of a software-defined RAN (SD-RAN) platform. In this work we demonstrate the capabilities of FlexRAN, an open-source SD-RAN platform developed to fill this void. FlexRAN separates the RAN control and data planes with a custom-tailored southbound API. Besides it features a hierarchical control plane architecture that enables programmability, flexible and dynamic control function placement (allowing different degrees of coordination within and among base stations) and real-time control. Virtualized control functions and control delegation are two key features in FlexRAN that makes these capabilities possible. This demo illustrates the capabilities and the performance of FlexRAN based on a prototype implementation, while its applicability is highlighted through a Mobile Edge Computing use case, where it acts as an enabler of a video bitrate adaptation application based on the radio conditions at the network edge.

KEYWORDS

5G architecture; 5G RAN; software-defined RAN; SD-RAN; RAN softwarization

1 INTRODUCTION

The Radio Access Network (RAN) is a significant part of the mobile infrastructure, responsible for managing the air interface. In particular, the RAN needs to efficiently manage the limited wireless spectrum, performing various complex operations like radio resource allocation, load balancing and mobility management. The recent dramatic increases in mobile data traffic pose a significant strain to the underlying infrastructure and make the optimized management of resources a necessity. This is led in part by the rapid adoption of smartphones and their support of new types of data-hungry services like video streaming and by the emergence of new communications paradigms like machine-to-machine and device-to-device, which are characterized by high control signaling to data ratios. Current mobile networks were not designed with such scenarios in mind and are therefore unable to efficiently cope with them. With respect to the RAN, many solutions have been considered to deal with such issues, including an increased cell density and advanced radio resource management techniques like Coordinated Multipoint and enhanced Inter-Cell Interference Coordination. While such techniques can enhance the network efficiency, they require a high level of coordination among base stations, leading to further increases in the signaling complexity and the capex/opex. These changes, in combination with the requirements of future 5G networks, are necessitating innovation towards newer, more flexible RAN architectures [1].

Software Defined Networking (SDN) is among the key technologies considered in the context of evolving mobile networks [4]. This is brought about by paradigm shifting ideas underlying SDN, which are the separation of the control from the data plane via a well-defined API and the consolidation of the control plane. The same SDN ideas that have proved fruitful in the wired domain could also be seen as a key element in the solution mix to address the aforementioned RAN challenges and this is why there has recently been a significant interest both in the research community and industry on bringing SDN ideas to mobile networks. However, despite the plethora of conceptual proposals for re-architecting the mobile RAN based on SDN principles, there is still a lack of implementable solutions and suitable prototyping/experimentation platforms [3]. Moreover, even the existing designs lack certain desirable features, like the support for real-time control which is essential for many RAN-related operations, the capability to easily implement new control functions and the means to dynamically adapt the control scheme (local vs centralized) to the network requirements following NFV principles.

FlexRAN is a novel software defined RAN (SD-RAN) platform we have developed [2], with the aim of overcoming the aforementioned limitations. In the following, we give an overview of its design and implementation. The focus of this demo is two-fold: (1) showcase the unique capabilities of FlexRAN; (2) demonstrate its potential benefit in the context of emerging 5G mobile networks via the Mobile Edge Computing (MEC) oriented use case of adaptive video streaming over the network edge based on the radio conditions.

2 FLEXRAN

2.1 Design Overview

Figure 1 provides a high-level schematic of the FlexRAN platform, which as shown is made up of two main components: **FlexRAN Control Plane** and **FlexRAN Agent API**. The FlexRAN control plane follows a two-layered design and is in turn composed of a **Master Controller** that is connected to a number of FlexRAN **Agents**, one for each eNodeB. The agents can either act as local

MobiCom'17, October 16–20, 2017, Snowbird, UT, USA.
 ISBN 978-1-4503-4916-1/17/10.
DOI: https://doi.org/10.1145/3117811.3119852

controllers with a limited network view and control delegated by the master, or in concert with other agents and the master controller. The control and data plane separation is provided by the FlexRAN Agent API which acts as the southbound API with FlexRAN control plane on one side and eNodeB data plane on the other side.

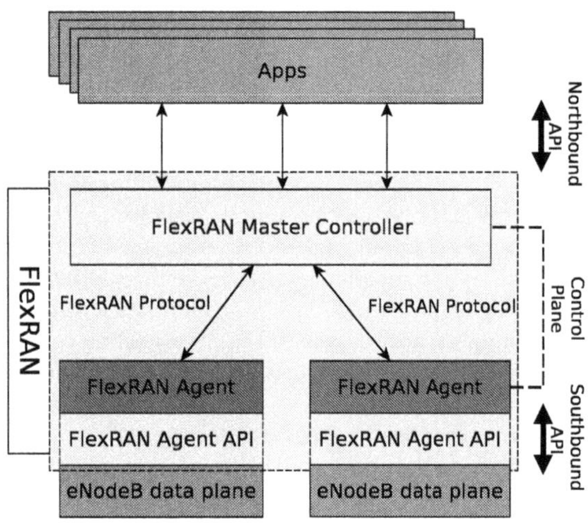

Figure 1: High-level schematic of the FlexRAN platform.

The FlexRAN **Protocol** facilitates communication between the master controller and the agents. As shown in the figure, it allows a two-way interaction between the master and the agents. In one direction, the agent sends relevant messages to the master with eNodeB statistics, configurations and events, while in the other direction the master can issue appropriate control commands that define the operation of the agents. In contrast to typical SDN controllers found in the wired domain, the FlexRAN controller has been designed with support for time critical RAN operations (e.g., MAC scheduling) in mind.

On top of the FlexRAN master controller lies a northbound API, which allows RAN applications to control and modify the state of the underlying network infrastructure (eNodeBs and UEs) based on the statistics and events gathered from the eNodeBs in the FlexRAN control plane. Such applications could greatly vary from simple monitoring applications that obtain statistics reporting which can be used by other apps, to more sophisticated applications that involve control-related RAN functions that modify its state (e.g., MAC scheduler).

2.2 Salient Features

Here we outline the salient features of FlexRAN:

Control and data plane separation - FlexRAN decouples the RAN control and data plane operations, towards reducing the complexity of developing new control solutions, promoting openness and innovation and allowing operators to open their RAN service environment to authorized third-parties to rapidly deploy innovative applications and service endpoints for mobile subscribers, enterprises and vertical segments.

Centralized & real-time control - FlexRAN consolidates the control plane into a single logically centralized controller, enabling easier coordination among the base stations of a region, effectively simplifying the development of new and more sophisticated control applications. Moreover, the FlexRAN platform has been designed in a way that enables support for the deployment of real-time control applications with very stringent time constraints, which is essential for many radio resource management related operations. An example of such a time-critical application would be the MAC scheduler of the LTE RAN, that needs to make and apply scheduling decisions with a very fine time granularity (1ms).

Virtualized Control Functions - FlexRAN allows the flexible and programmable control of the underlying RAN infrastructure through the introduction of a number of virtualized control functions that have a clean structure and well-defined interfaces and are responsible for performing the various control operations of the base station. This allows part of the system's logic, like the mobility manager or the MAC scheduler, to be easily upgraded by replacing or extending the corresponding function without affecting the rest of the system.

Control delegation & policy reconfiguration - The virtualized control functions of FlexRAN are exploited in a more dynamic way through a set of mechanisms designed to allow the delegation of control functions from the master controller to the base stations at runtime and the reconfiguration of their behavior and parameters on-the-fly in a simple and seamless manner. This feature makes the system very flexible and adaptable to the underlying networking conditions and to the specific requirements of the network operator, e.g., by enabling actions like the switching of scheduling from a centralized to a distributed scheme on-the-fly.

User Equipment (UE) transparency - The whole design is completely transparent to the UEs attached to the network. This is a key feature for deploying the system in existing networks and avoiding backwards compatibility problems.

The virtualization of control functions and the control delegation capabilities offered by FlexRAN follow the NFV principles and indeed bring runtime service function chaining capabilities to the RAN, as they add a virtualization layer over the RAN infrastructure and allow the flexible placement of RAN control functions closer or further away from the base station based on the networking conditions, the available computing resources and the requirements of the operator in terms of performance. However, it should be noted that these capabilities relevant to the RAN are yet to be considered by NFV standards specifications, like that of ETSI NFV.

2.3 Implementation Outline

As a proof of concept, we have developed an open source prototype implementation of the FlexRAN platform. The FlexRAN controller is built from scratch using C++ with support for x64 Linux systems. The implementation supports both a real-time and non real-time mode of operation to cater for different time criticalities of the deployed applications and the requirements of the network operator. The FlexRAN agent was implemented in C on top of the open source LTE/LTE-A implementation of OpenAirInterface (OAI)[1]. The platform offers full transparency to UEs (incl. commercial UEs). FlexRAN Agent has been integrated into the most recent

[1] http://www.openairinterface.org/

(a) Basic FlexRAN demonstration setup

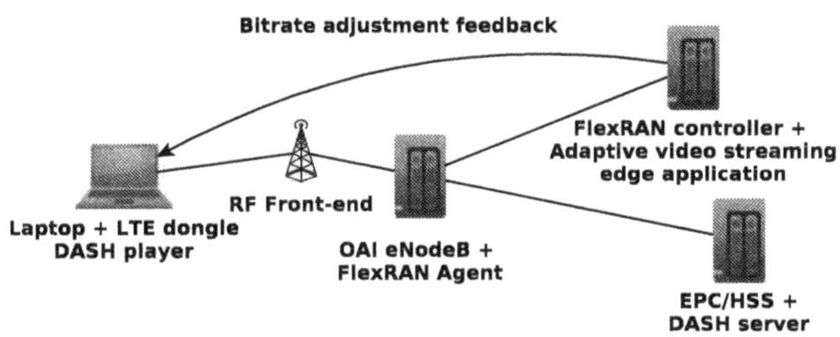

(b) MEC use case setup

Figure 2: Demonstration setup

versions of OAI. The rest of FlexRAN has also been made publicly available[2] and is already being used by around 15 research groups from academia and industry worldwide.

3 DEMONSTRATION

The goal of this demonstration is twofold:

- Firstly, to demonstrate the feasibility of realizing flexible software defined control in an LTE RAN using FlexRAN while maintaining full transparency for the attached UEs.
- Secondly, to highlight the value of FlexRAN as an enabler of emerging 5G use cases by demonstrating the use of FlexRAN in a scenario of adaptive bitrate video streaming at the network edge in the context of MEC.

For the first part of the demonstration, we use an LTE network testbed setup similar to Fig 2a, composed of a commercial LTE-enabled smartphone and 3 nodes; one acts as the eNodeB and is connected to a Software-Defined Radio (SDR) RF front-end, one acts as the EPC of the LTE network and the other acts as the FlexRAN controller. The eNodeB has two versions of OAI installed, a vanilla version and a modified version that provides support for the FlexRAN agent. Through this setup we demonstrate the feasibility of the FlexRAN-enabled LTE architecture and its transparency for the UE, by running in turn the vanilla and the modified version of OAI at the eNodeB and streaming in both cases an online video at the UE, noting the seamlessness for the user. Moreover, we show the control delegation and virtualized control function capabilities of FlexRAN by swapping a remote downlink MAC scheduler running at the master controller with a local one running at the FlexRAN agent while the UE is streaming an online video. This experiment

[2] http://networks.inf.ed.ac.uk/flexran/

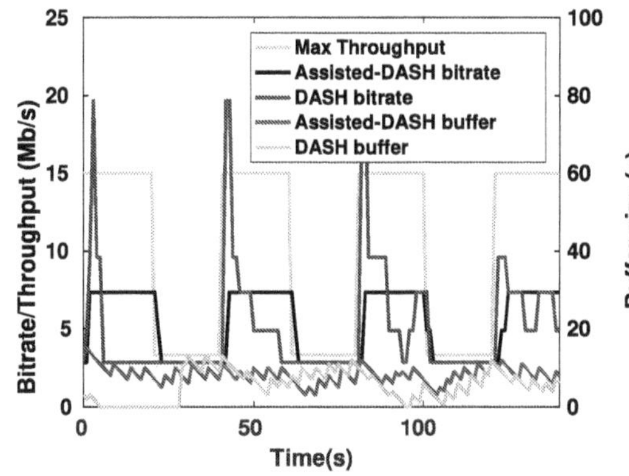

Figure 3: Rate adaptation of DASH vs controller-assisted DASH and corresponding buffer sizes

demonstrates the flexibility of placing control functions closer or further away from the base station, while the service at the UE remains uninterrupted.

For the second part of the demonstration, the testbed is slightly modified by replacing the smartphone with a laptop-based UE, equipped with an LTE dongle (Fig 2b). The relevant scenario demonstrates how FlexRAN can be used as an edge computing application deployment platform, using as a concrete example the use case of adaptive bitrate video streaming. More specifically, we consider the case of MPEG-DASH as a streaming service, where a DASH server is deployed at the EPC and a DASH player is running at the laptop-based UE. An edge computing application is deployed over the FlexRAN controller and uses the FlexRAN protocol to obtain network information from the MAC layer of the eNodeB (CQI measurements, throughput per UE, etc) at a fine time granularity (1ms). This information allows the edge application to react in the changes observed at the radio link conditions between the eNodeB and the UE in real-time by re-adjusting the bitrate of the UE DASH player accordingly. As a result, we show (Figure 3) that the edge computing enabled video streaming is more reactive to changes in the network conditions, leading to an improved streaming quality compared to the conventional DASH streaming (no video freezes and buffer stalls).

ACKNOWLEDGMENTS

This work was partly funded by the European FP7 FLEX project (612050) and H2020 COHERENT project (671639).

REFERENCES

[1] Shanzhi Chen and Jian Zhao. 2014. The requirements, challenges, and technologies for 5G of terrestrial mobile telecommunication. *Communications Magazine, IEEE* 52, 5 (2014), 36–43.
[2] Xenofon Foukas et al. 2016. FlexRAN: A Flexible and Programmable Platform for Software-Defined Radio Access Networks. In *Proceedings of ACM CoNEXT*. ACM, 427–441.
[3] Aditya Gudipati et al. 2013. SoftRAN: Software defined radio access network. In *Proceedings of the second ACM SIGCOMM workshop on Hot topics in software defined networking*. ACM, 25–30.
[4] Li Erran Li et al. 2012. Toward software-defined cellular networks. In *Software Defined Networking (EWSDN), 2012 European Workshop on*. IEEE, 7–12.

Demo: Orion – A Radio Access Network Slicing System

Xenofon Foukas
The University of Edinburgh
x.foukas@ed.ac.uk

Mahesh K. Marina
The University of Edinburgh
mahesh@ed.ac.uk

Kimon Kontovasilis
"NCSR" Demokritos
kkont@iit.demokritos.gr

ABSTRACT

Emerging 5G mobile networks are envisioned to support the dynamic deployment of services with diverse performance requirements, accommodating the needs of mobile network operators and verticals. Virtualizing the mobile network components in a flexible and cost-effective way is therefore of paramount importance. In this work, we highlight the capabilities of Orion, a novel RAN slicing architecture that enables the dynamic virtualization of base stations and flexible customization of slices to meet their respective service needs. Our demonstration of Orion's capabilities is based on a prototype implementation employing a modified version of the OpenAirInterface software LTE platform. Using this prototype, we demonstrate the functional and performance isolation, and the efficient sharing of radio hardware and spectrum that can be achieved among Orion RAN slices. Moreover, we show how Orion can be used in an end-to-end network slicing setting and demonstrate the effects of the slices' configuration and placement of virtual functions in the overall quality of the deployed services.

KEYWORDS

5G mobile networks; network architecture; RAN slicing; RAN virtualization; abstractions

1 INTRODUCTION

The rapid increase in the usage of mobile devices in recent years has placed a big strain on the current mobile network architecture is paving the way for next generation (5G) mobile networks. Apart from the performance and efficiency improvements that 5G is expected to bring, another equally significant aspect of the 5G vision is the support of a *service-oriented* mobile network architecture [4]. This service-oriented approach envisions network support for a wide range of services, differing significantly in their performance requirements and supported device types. A one-size fits all architecture is unlikely to be suitable for such diverse use cases. Therefore, it is of paramount importance to find ways for increasing the flexibility of the architecture, so that the underlying physical infrastructure may be turned into multiple logical networks or *slices* that are tailored in terms of resources (computing, network, storage, radio, access hardware and virtual network functions (VNFs)) to meet the requirements of the service in question [5]. In this context, network softwarization via Software Defined Networking (SDN) and Network Functions Virtualization (NFV), and virtualization are seen as key enablers that can be used to create end-to-end network instances spanning both the core and the radio access network (RAN).

For mobile core slicing, research prototypes and operational systems using virtualization technologies and SDN/NFV principles have already started to appear. On the other hand, RAN slicing is at a more premature stage, with the main challenge being that apart from computing, storage and network resources, the limited radio resources need to also be virtualized and efficiently assigned to slices. This must be achieved while guaranteeing the functional and performance isolation between tenants and the infrastructure provider, and among tenants themselves, so that these tenants can maintain full control and independence of their slices to tailor them to the respective service requirements. State-of-the-art RAN slicing solutions solve this problem only partially, by focusing on some aspects of RAN slicing while sacrificing others. Specifically, approaches with origins in RAN sharing focus mainly on the efficient sharing of radio resources with no support for functional isolation, giving the infrastructure provider full visibility and control over all slices (e.g. FlexRAN [1]). On the other end of the spectrum, the isolation is put at the center stage without considering the efficient and adaptive use of resources (e.g. FLARE [3]).

We attempt to balance these objectives through Orion [2], which in our knowledge is the first RAN slicing system that provides full functional and performance isolation while also facilitating efficient sharing of radio and spectrum resources. The focus of this demo (elaborated in Section 3) is on showcasing the unique capabilities of Orion, as well as on demonstrating how Orion can fit in the emerging 5G paradigm as a key component of an end-to-end mobile network slicing architecture. The next section gives an overview of Orion's design and implementation.

2 ORION

2.1 Design

Orion's design (Fig. 1) explicitly distinguishes the infrastructure provider from the service providers, who own the slices. The infrastructure provider is the owner of physical base stations, comprising of hardware resources (i.e., radio equipment, memory, CPU and network) and a chunk of spectrum. Regardless of its realization, either via dedicated specialized hardware or in a cloud environment using re-programmable hardware (e.g., C-RAN baseband processing unit and remote radio heads), each physical base station supports a single Radio Access Technology (RAT), meaning that all radio and spectrum resources available at the base station can be exploited through a *shared* physical layer.

The `Base Station Hypervisor` that sits over the physical layer is the heart of Orion's design. It is the component used for managing RAN slices, enforcing resource segregation among slices (for performance isolation) and segregation in terms of control

MobiCom '17, October 16–20, 2017, Snowbird, UT, USA.
 ISBN 978-1-4503-4916-1/17/10.
DOI: https://doi.org/10.1145/3117811.3119860

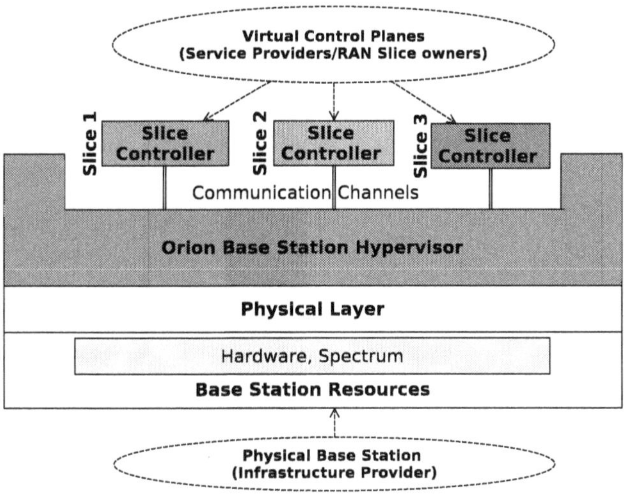

Figure 1: High-level architecture of Orion.

logic segregation (for functional isolation) and for facilitating efficient sharing of underlying physical resources. Essentially, the Hypervisor is the liaison that binds the individual (and mutually isolated) slices to the physical infrastructure, providing them with a virtual view of the underlying radio resources and data plane state, and maintaining a mapping between virtual and physical resources so that slice state changes may be applied over the physical data plane. The Hypervisor is part of the infrastructure provider's software infrastructure to support RAN slicing. The infrastructure provider is also responsible for admission control.

Service providers (e.g., MVNOs and verticals) in Orion realize their RAN slices through the creation of virtual base stations over the Hypervisor. Each virtual base station is a composition of a virtual control plane, responsible for managing the data plane state revealed to it by the Hypervisor. Following SDN principles, Orion's design assumes control-data plane separation, where the virtual control plane of a slice is effectively a local RAN-level slice controller running as a *separate process*, responsible to tailor the functionality and manage the allocation of resources to the mobile devices associated with the slice as if the slice was operating using its own dedicated infrastructure. The virtual control plane is also responsible for implementing the control protocols required for the communication and coordination of the virtual base station with the rest of the mobile infrastructure (e.g., S1 and X2 interfaces in LTE). This means that all operations defined for a given mobile network architecture can be supported by slices so long as the appropriate interfaces and messages are implemented as part of the respective virtual control planes.

2.2 Key Properties of Orion

The design of Orion provides strong isolation guarantees while allowing efficient resource sharing.

First, since each of the slice controllers runs as a separate process, isolation among controllers in terms of memory and CPU can leverage well known OS and process virtualization techniques, like virtual machines (e.g., KVM) or containers (e.g., Docker).

Second, the Hypervisor is the sole entity responsible for handling actual radio resources which it virtualizes and distributes among slices in an abstract form, ensuring isolation from a radio resource perspective. The isolation properties of Orion are illustrated in the example of Fig. 2 for 2 slices, where the throughput of the UEs in one slice remains unaffected from the changes in the state of the other slice. More specifically, the addition of more UEs in one slice at $t1$-3 only affects the throughput of the UEs co-existing in the same slice, leaving the other slice unaffected (indicating performance isolation). Similarly, a change in the scheduling policy of slice 2 at $t4$, from proportional fair to class-based only affects the performance of the UEs in that slice, having no effect for slice 1 (reflecting functional isolation).

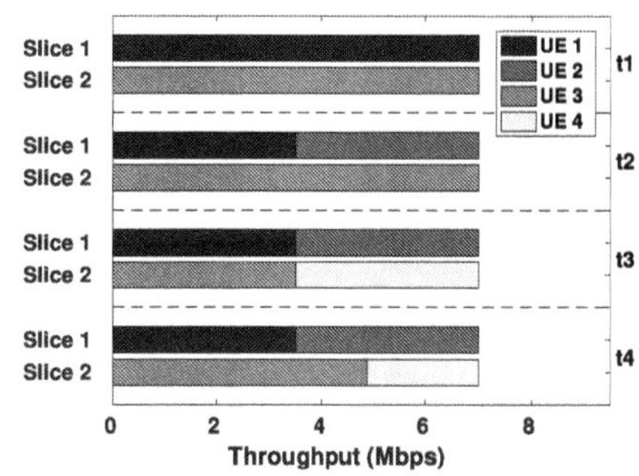

Figure 2: Isolation of RAN slices in terms of radio resources and control functions (scheduling).

Third, it can internally facilitate efficient use of the spectrum pool via a suitable allocation algorithm that considers the slices' SLAs and current state as well as the underlying physical conditions. This flexible allocation of radio resources to slices can lead to an improved performance compared to a static allocation mechanism, as illustrated in the example of Fig. 3 (slice 2 borrowing the unused resources of slice 1).

Finally, from a UE perspective, the whole slicing operation is transparent with each slice appearing as a different MVNO like in RAN sharing.

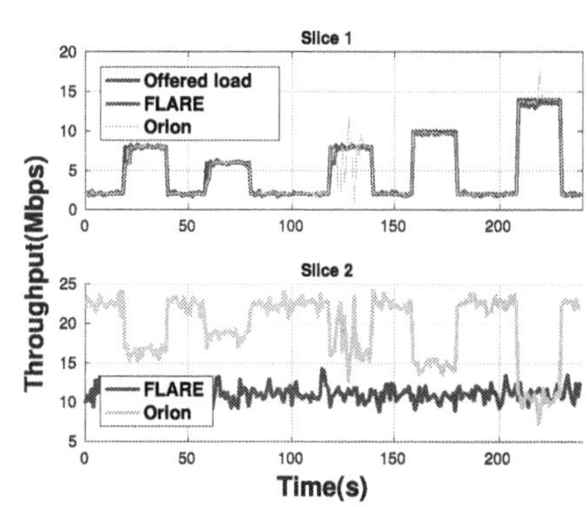

Figure 3: Instantaneous throughput of two slices in static (FLARE) vs dynamic (Orion) resource allocation.

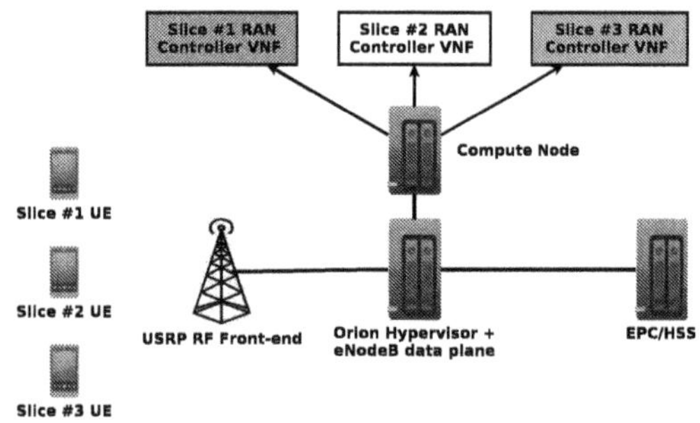

Figure 4: Basic Orion demonstration setup with shared core network among slices

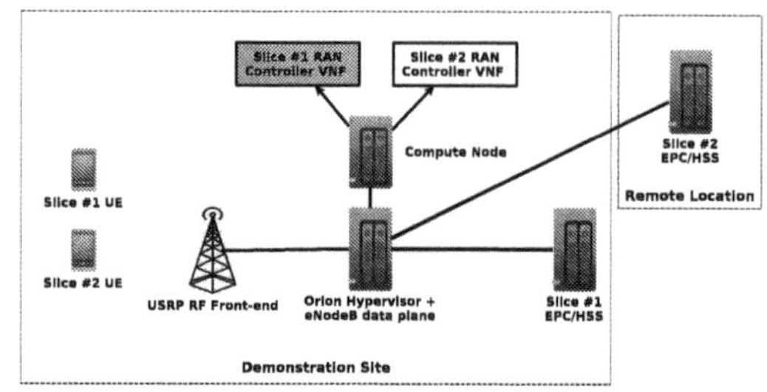

Figure 5: End-to-end Orion demonstration setup with local and remote core network

2.3 Implementation

Following the aforementioned design, we developed a prototype implementation of Orion considering LTE as the supported RAT, providing full support for the virtualization of downlink radio resources. The Orion Hypervisor was implemented completely from scratch in C. For the separation of the control and the data plane required by Orion, we leveraged the API and controller of the publicly available FlexRAN platform [1], which is based on the well known open-source LTE software implementation of OpenAirInterface (OAI).

3 DEMONSTRATION

The demonstration of Orion has three main goals:

- To show how the Orion architecture accommodates the dynamic creation of RAN slices sharing the underlying common radio hardware and spectrum, while providing functional and performance isolation among the co-located tenants (MVNOs and verticals).
- To highlight the efficiency and flexibility of Orion's mechanisms in distributing the available radio resources among slices based on the service requirements and corresponding SLAs of the latter.
- To show how Orion can be integrated into an end-to-end network slicing architecture composed of virtualized RAN and core network functions and how the configuration of the slices and the placement of the virtual functions composing the network can impact the characteristics of the provided service.

For the first and the second part of this demonstration, we will use the testbed setup illustrated in Fig. 4, including three commercial LTE smartphones (LG and Samsung), 3 Intel-based mini PCs (Intel i7 at 3.4GHz and 8GB RAM) and 1 Ettus USRP B210 RF front-end. The USRP is connected to one of the PCs, over which the eNodeB data plane and the Orion Hypervisor is deployed. The Hypervisor communicates through an Ethernet connection with a compute node that is used for the deployment of the virtual control planes (RAN controllers) of three RAN slices. The controllers are deployed in the form of virtual network functions, running in isolation by employing Docker containers. The Hypervisor also communicates with the third PC, which acts as an EPC (MME and SP-GW) and HSS shared among all three RAN slices.

Through this setup, we demonstrate the capability of Orion to create RAN slices on-the-fly through a simple set of tools and configuration files. We show how each UE can be mapped dynamically to a slice through Orion during its attachment process, based on the configuration provided by the slice owner. Moreover, we show the functional and performance isolation that Orion enables, by using different downlink scheduling functions with different radio resource allocation policies on each of the slices' RAN controllers, streaming video flows and observing how the introduction of new slices leaves the performance of other co-located slices completely unaffected. Finally, we demonstrate the flexibility of sharing the available spectrum among slices in an efficient way, by creating slices with services differing in their requirements for radio resources (some slices asking a fixed number of radio resource blocks and others specifying throughput guarantees in ideal conditions) and by showing how the unused radio resources of one slice can be dynamically assigned to other slices running over the same physical base station to improve their performance.

For the final goal of this demonstration, the testbed is slightly modified (Fig. 5) so that, instead of having a shared core for all slices, two EPCs are connected with the eNodeB, each associated with a different slice. One EPC is co-located with the base station at the demonstration site (direct Ethernet connection), while the other is deployed in a remote location. Based on this setup, we show how the various EPC components can be deployed as virtual network functions in different physical locations (at the network edge or in a central cloud) and how they interact with the RAN slices of Orion to create an end-to-end network slicing setting. Additionally, we show how the placement of these virtual functions and the radio resource allocation policies used by the Orion Hypervisor can affect the service provided by the slices, using latency of the slices' traffic as a concrete example.

REFERENCES

[1] Xenofon Foukas et al. 2016. FlexRAN: A Flexible and Programmable Platform for Software-Defined Radio Access Networks. In *Proceedings of ACM CoNEXT*. ACM, 427–441.
[2] Xenofon Foukas et al. 2017. Orion: RAN Slicing for a Flexible and Cost-Effective Multi-Service Mobile Network Architecture. In *Proceedings of ACM MobiCom*. ACM.
[3] Akihiro Nakao et al. 2017. End-to-end Network Slicing for 5G Mobile Networks. *Journal of Information Processing* 25 (2017), 153–163.
[4] NGMN-Alliance. 2015. 5G White Paper. (Feb 2015).
[5] Peter Rost et al. 2017. Network Slicing to Enable Scalability and Flexibility in 5G Mobile Networks. *IEEE Communications magazine* (2017).

Demo: Sensor Fusion Localization and Navigation for Visually Impaired People

Giovanni Galioto,
Ilenia Tinnirello, Daniele Croce
DEIM, Università di Palermo & CNIT
Viale delle Scienze, 9
Palermo, Italy 90128
giovannigalioto@gmail.com
ilenia.tinnirello@tti.unipa.it
daniele.croce@unipa.it

Federica Inderst,
Federica Pascucci
DI, Università Roma Tre
Via della Vasca Navale, 79
Roma, Italy 00146
federica.inderst@uniroma3.it
federica.pascucci@uniroma3.it

Laura Giarré
DIEF, Università di Modena
e Reggio Emilia
Via P. Vivarelli, 10
Modena, Italy 41125
giarre@ieee.org

ABSTRACT

We present an innovative smartphone-centric tracking system for indoor and outdoor environments, based on the joint utilization of dead-reckoning and computer vision (CV) techniques. The system is explicitly designed for visually impaired people (although it could be easily generalized to other users) and it is built under the assumption that special reference signals, such as painted lines, colored tapes or tactile pavings are deployed in the environment for guiding visually impaired users along pre-defined paths. Thanks to highly optimized software, we are able to execute the CV and sensor-fusion algorithms in run-time on low power hardware such as a normal smartphone, precisely tracking the users movements.

Figure 1: Exemplary installation of the ARIANNA system.

1 INTRODUCTION

The pervasive availability of technologies for localization and user interfaces (such as GPS, WiFi networks, smartphones, etc.) is originating a proliferation of interesting solutions devised to improve the independence and social inclusion of visually impaired people. Some of these solutions, as discussed in [1], also consider the design of special-purpose devices that enables specific activities such as pattern identification, perception of spatial layout, control of locomotion with respect to the *near* environment, for facilitating mobility, and *large scale* environment, for facilitating orientation. A survey on solutions for supporting navigation of blind persons is reported in [2].

In this demo, we focus our attention on navigation, localization, and orientation of visually impaired people, primarily indoor, but also outdoor. Differently, from previous works, which are focused on the utilization of inertial sensors integrated into the smartphones, we exploit the smartphone camera as an additional sensor that, on one side, can help the visually impaired user to identify the paths and, on the other side, can provide direction estimates to the tracking system. While today outdoor navigation is generally based on GPS (which, already, may produce errors in the order of several meters), the situation is more complex in indoor environments, where GPS is not available at all and other localization solutions have to be considered for supporting user orientation. Examples of these solutions are triangulation of RF signals (mainly WiFi), direct sensing of reference points (with RFIDs, ultrasound, bluetooth, etc.), estimates of relative user movements by means of odometry readings provided by *Inertial Measurement Units* (IMU), i.e. accelerometers, magnetometers, compasses, and gyroscopes. This last approach is accurate in low-medium range, but in long distance, it suffers by a drift due to noise [3]. Many solutions have been proposed to eliminate such bias. For example, *Pedestrian Dead Reckoning* (PDR) uses the knowledge of the walking patterns to reset velocity when the pedestrian is not moving [4], or exploits extended Kalman filtering to compensate such drift [5, 6]. More examples of indoor localization techniques may be found in [7]. Obviously, indoor navigation systems for blind users have stricter requirements than general systems, in terms of accuracy and reaction times. Moreover, apart from the need of retrieving direction information towards the desired destination, visually impaired people are used to a continuous reference signal, currently provided by tactile pavings, which *accompany* the users along the path to the destination. Recently, an interesting solution for providing this signal by means of flexible, economic, and easy-to-deploy traces has been proposed with the design of the ARIANNA system (pAth Recognition for Indoor Assisted NavigatioN with Augmented perception), whose practical feasibility has been demonstrated in [8] and [9]. The system is based on a common smartphone camera and lightweight CV algorithms for detecting colored tapes deployed

MobiCom '17, October 16–20, 2017, Snowbird, UT, USA

ACM ISBN 978-1-4503-4916-1/17/10.
https://doi.org/10.1145/3117811.3119858

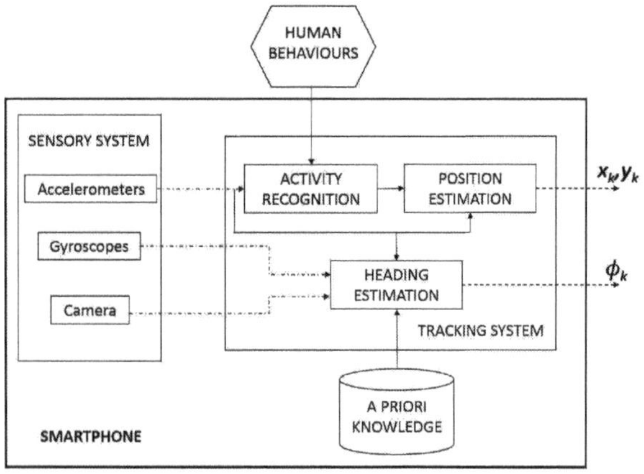

Figure 2: Navigation system architecture: enabling integration of computer vision and dead-reckoning techniques.

on the floors, and on an innovative user interface, providing user feedback in terms of vibration signals. Figure 1 summarizes the main features of the system, by showing an exemplary bi-colored tape deployed in a room, the thick blue line recognized by the smartphone application, and the typical orientation of the smartphone (parallel to the floor) adopted for utilizing the system.

The idea on the basis of this work is to integrate classic PDR techniques with the ARIANNA system, in order to provide a tracking system explicitly designed for visually impaired users. To this purpose, we defined a position estimation technique able to work simultaneously on the data provided by the IMU system embedded in the smartphone, and on the additional information (when available) that can be extracted from the images captured by the smartphone camera. The key features of the system stand in the use of low a priori information, pervasive devices already available for most users (i.e. common smartphones) and low infrastructures in the environment. The algorithms are particularly optimized and present low computational burden in order to be run on commonly used smartphones.

2 SYSTEM ARCHITECTURE

Figure 2 summarizes the main functional components of the navigation system: i) the sensory system, for acquiring inertial data and images of the floor; ii) the tracking system for processing and aggregating the data into a position estimate; iii) the maps of the environment, which represent the a-priori knowledge of the available paths and relevant orientation. The sensory system is implemented by exploiting the IMU and camera embedded in the smartphone. In our implementation, sensor measurements are sampled at higher frequency than camera images and therefore, in general, multiple measurements are linked to the same image of the floor. The tracking system is implemented directly in the smartphone: in each update interval, it is enough to sample a few images (e.g. 2 images/s) and use low resolution (e.g. 144x192 pixels), thus resulting in a limited amount of data to be processed (typically, images are only 10 kB each). The smartphone extracts heading information from the sequence of images and from the map of the paths and runs the tracking operations presented in Sec. 3. To extract the heading information from the ARIANNA system, the basic idea is to identify the painted lines in the acquired images, quantify the slope of the lines seen by the camera, and convert this slope in an absolute orientation of the user, on the basis of a rough positioning of the user on the map.

To identify the slope of the line seen by the camera, we implemented three different steps: i) filtering the image, for reducing the noise and the details of the image background; ii) applying the Canny algorithm, for detecting the edges of the objects in the image; iii) identifying the sub-set of edges which can be considered as a line, by means of the Hough transform. The first step is performed by using a Gaussian smoothing filter, whose main goal is defocusing the image for avoiding that some regular patterns of the floor, such as the edges of squared tiles, can be erroneously considered as a path trace. Since the lines deployed on the floor are much thicker than the typical tiles' edges, such a filtering operation does not affect the identification of the line edges. The second step is given by the application of the well-known Canny scheme to identify the pixels corresponding to paths' edges. Finally, the Hough transform is used for mapping each edge point in a set of parameters (ρ, θ) representing the bundle of lines passing through that point. When multiple edge points are aligned, there is a common (ρ, θ) value representing the line passing through all the points. Therefore, the scheme simply works by counting the maximum number of occurrences (called votes) of quantized (ρ, θ) values computed for each edge point. The quantization compensates noise effects in the identification of the alignments. We chose to consider the global maximum in the parameter space, i.e. a single (ρ, θ) value receiving the greatest number of votes, because we assume that the greatest number of aligned points always corresponds to the painted line.

For optimizing the configuration of the above scheme, we have considered the effects of the image resolution, the smoothing factor of the Gaussian filter, and the threshold values of the Canny schemes on the accuracy of line detection. In proximity of a turning point, such as L-like junction points, the number of path segments with different orientation is at least equal to two. However, by always choosing the line with the highest number of votes, which usually correspond to the longest detected line, we avoid ambiguity in the reference orientation for the user.

3 TRACKING SYSTEM

The tracking system is composed of three different modules: the *Activity Recognition*, the *Heading Estimation* and the *Position Estimation*. The first module identifies the type of motion performed by the user. In the addressed scenario, the user moves in a planar environment, therefore only 2 activities, i.e., *standing still* and *walking*, have been considered. The classification problem is regarded as a sequential decision problem and the solution is found by exploring a decision tree. A time window is applied to select and analyze data from the accelerometer measures.

The Heading Estimation is performed using data from gyroscopes and accelerometer merged with the information provided by the camera. The estimate is computed by a prediction-correction filter: in the prediction step, we use the Extended Kalman Filter (EKF) presented in [10] to compute the rotation matrix $\mathbf{R}_b^n$ from the Body frame to the Navigation frame, the heading γ_k and its uncertainty Γ_k. Then, the heading γ_k and the related uncertainty Γ_k

feed the correction step: the output of the image processing is used to update the heading and bound the drift error. During *staying still*, the measurements collected from gyroscope and accelerometer are used to update the bias, that slowly changes over time. Moreover, the attitude is reset by using the above mentioned procedure to retrieve the initial condition for the filter.

Finally, the Position Estimation is devoted to compute the position (x, y) of the user with respect to the Navigation frame. This module exploits data from the accelerometer and the rotation matrix R_b^n provided by the Heading Estimation. The accelerometer data is projected in the Navigation frame by using R_b^n: in this way, the acceleration along the z-axis of the Navigation frame corresponds to the acceleration on the vertical axes of the user. The initial position is supposed known while the position of the user during *walking* is recursively computed, by estimating the length of the stride on step event detection i

$$\begin{bmatrix} x_i \\ y_i \end{bmatrix} = \begin{bmatrix} x_{i-1} \\ y_{i-1} \end{bmatrix} + l_i \begin{bmatrix} \sin \bar{\phi}_i \\ \cos \bar{\phi}_i \end{bmatrix} \tag{1}$$

where l_i is the displacement of the user between two step events with respect to the Navigation frame and $\bar{\phi}_i$ is the average heading in the same time interval. The step detection is obtained using the human body dynamic associated with the human gait cycle, detected by analyzing the local minima and the local maxima of the vertical acceleration signal. To this end, both peak detection and zero crossing algorithms are applied to identify the sharp changes to the vertical acceleration associated with the heel strike. During *walking* activity, the displacement l_i is estimated as proposed in [11]. Finally, the user displacement is null when the output of the classification phase is *standing still*.

4 EXPERIMENTS

In the demo, the goal is to show the tracking of the user exploiting the handheld smartphone. The device used is a Samsung Galaxy S6 (SM-G920F), running Android version 6.0.1 Marshmallow. The sensors embedded in this smartphone and used by the tracking system are the IMU unit MPU6500 by Invensense and the rear camera IMX240 by Sony. IMU data is available at sampling frequency 100 Hz, while images from the camera are acquired by ARIANNA at a sampling frequency of approximately 15 Hz. During the test, the measurements are processed in real-time on the smartphone and the users can evaluate the accuracy of the proposed system by comparing the PDR alone or the complete tracking system (TS), including the use of ARIANNA.

The envisioned trial is a short Q shaped path (a rectangle sized 5x2 m), and Fig. 3 shows an example in our office environment. The Q-path test is used to estimate the accuracy when a closed loop is considered: the user can repeat the path several times without stops (5 in the figure, with overall length of 70 m). The size of the rectangle can be easily changed at will and other shapes/tests are also possible. In Fig. 3(a), we show some results obtained in our office using the PDR, compared with the ground truth. At the end of the experiment the error accumulated along the path using PDR-only is relevant, considering that the path is short and the drift is partially compensated by the opposite curves. The TS instead suitably reduces the error, that is limited in this experiment to only 0.54 m in the worst case.

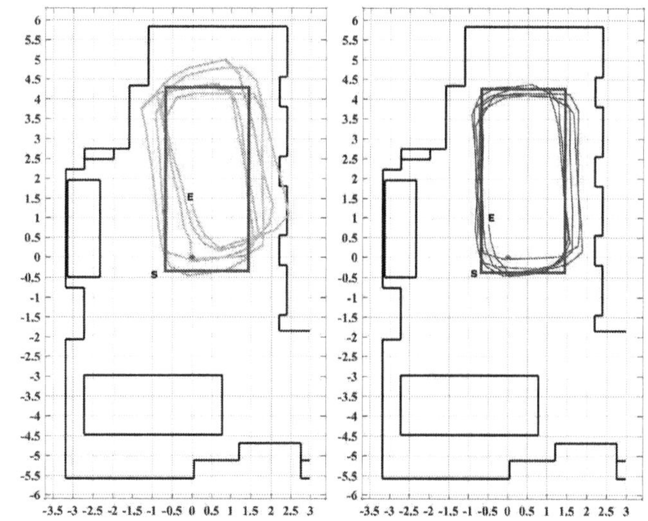

(a) Q-path estimated using the PDR. (b) Q-path updated w/ Camera Correction.

Figure 3: Path estimated by the PDR (Fig. 3(a)) and path corrected by the TS (Fig. 3(b)). The Q path is represented in blue, S and E are the starting and the ending point respectively.

We are currently quantifying the battery energy drained by the processing operations, although preliminary results show that a full battery can last over 4 hours of continuous use (indeed, it is the screen which consumes the most in a smartphone). Future development of the system will include also a model of the hand movement and possibly the design of a vibration feedback to tell the user how to correct its location.

REFERENCES

[1] Loomis, J. M., Klatzky, R. L., Giudice, N. A. Sensory substitution of vision: Importance of perceptual and cognitive processing. In Assistive Technology for Blindness and Low Vision, pp. 162-191. CRC Press 2012.
[2] R. Velázquez, Wearable Assistive Devices for the Blind. Chapter 17 Smart Environment: Issues and Characterization, LNEE 75, Springer, pp 331-349, 2010.
[3] A. R. Jiménez, F. Seco, J. C. Prieto, and J. Guevara Rosas. Indoor pedestrian navigation using an INS/EKF framework for yaw drift reduction and a foot-mounted IMU. Workshop on Positioning Navigation and Communication, Dresden, 2010.
[4] L. Filardo, F. Inderst, F. Pascucci. C-IPS: a Smartphone based Indoor Positioning System. International Conference on Indoor Positioning and Indoor Navigation (IPIN), 4–7 October 2016, Alcala de Henares, Madrid, Spain, 2016.
[5] A. R. Jiménez, F. Seco, F. Zampella, J. C. Prieto, and J. Guevara Rosas. Improved Heuristic Drift Elimination (iHDE) for pedestrian navigation in complex buildings. Int. Conf. on Indoor Positioning and Indoor Navigation, Guimaraes, 2011.
[6] F. Montorsi; F. Pancaldi; G. M. Vitetta. Design and implementation of an inertial navigation system for pedestrians based on a low-cost MEMS IMU. 2013 IEEE International Conference on Communications (ICC 2013) - Budapest, Hungary - June, 9-13, 2013.
[7] N. Fallah, I. Apostolopoulos, K. Bekris, E. Folmer, Indoor Human Navigation Systems; A survey, Interacting with Computers, Oxford Journals. 25:1 Pages 21-33, February 2013.
[8] Croce D., Gallo P., Garlisi D., Giarré L., Mangione S., Tinnirello I. ARIANNA: A smartphone-based navigation system with human in the loop 22nd Mediterranean Conference of Control and Automation (MED), Page(s): 8 - 13, 2014.
[9] D. Croce, L. Giarré, F. G. La Rosa, E. Montana, I. Tinnirello. Enhancing tracking performance in a smartphone-based navigation system for visually impaired people, 24th Mediterranean Conference of Control and Automation (MED), 2016.
[10] L. Faramondi, F. Inderst, F. Pascucci, R. Setola, and U. Delprato, An Enhanced Indoor Positioning System for First Responders, International Conference on Indoor Positioning and Indoor Navigation (IPIN), 2013.
[11] H. Wienberg,Using the ADXL202 in Pedometer and Personal Navigation Applications, *Analog Devices AN-602 application note, 2002.*

Demo: A Cell-level Traffic Generator for LoRa Networks

Michele Gucciardo
University of Palermo
Palermo, Italy
michele.gucciardo@unipa.it

Ilenia Tinnirello
University of Palermo
Palermo, Italy
ilenia.tinnirello@unipa.it

Domenico Garlisi
University of Palermo
Palermo, Italy
domenico.garlisi@unipa.it

ABSTRACT

In this demo we present and validate a LoRa cell traffic generator, able to emulate the behavior of thousands of low-rate sensor nodes deployed in the same cell, by using a single Software Defined Radio (SDR) platform. Differently from traditional generators, whose goal is creating packet flows which emulate specific applications and protocols, our focus is generating a combined radio signal, as seen by a gateway, given by the super-position of the signals transmitted by multiple sensors simultaneously active on the same channel. We argue that such a generator can be of interest for testing different network planning solutions for LoRa networks.

1 INTRODUCTION

In recent years, we have assisted to an impressive proliferation of wireless technologies and mobile-generated traffic, which is now the highest portion of the total internet traffic and will continue to grow with the emergence of IoT applications [1]. Understanding how wireless networks would respond to the increasing capacity demand is therefore of crucial importance. High-density deployments of wireless networks are difficult to study in real testbeds or installations, especially when we can expect that hundreds or even thousands of mobile devices (not limited to traditional user terminals, but including smart objects and sensors) are simultaneously active in the same environment.

In this demo we consider the case of LoRa technology, which represents a critical example of wireless technology working with high-density devices. Indeed, LoRa technology has been conceived for Low Power Wide Area Networks (LPWAN), characterized by low data rate requirements per single devices, large cells and heterogeneous application domains, which may lead to extremely high numbers of devices coexisting in the same cell. Despite of the robustness of the LoRa PHY [2], patented by Semtech, in WAN scenarios where multiple gateways can be installed, the scalability of this technology is still under investigation [3]. Current studies are mostly based on simulation results [4] and assume that the utilization of multiple transmission channels and spreading factors lead to a system that can be considered as the simple super-position of independent (single channel, single spreading factor) sub-systems. This is actually a strong simplification, especially because the spreading factors adopted by LoRa are pseudo-orthogonal [5] and therefore, in near-far conditions, collisions can prevent the correct reception of both the overlapping transmissions using different spreading factors.

For characterizing these phenomena on real gateways, we designed and implemented a cell traffic generator for LoRa-based networks on top of the well known USRP software-defined-radio (SDR) platform. While traditional traffic generators are limited to the generation of packet flows emulating specific applications and protocols [6, 7], our focus is on the generation of a *combined* radio signal given by the super-position of the signals, generated by multiple devices operating in the same cell, as seen by a gateway.

Similar approaches have been recently proposed for studying high-density WiFi networks [8], resulting from installations in a stadium, a conference hall, an airport, etc. Commercial solutions try to emulate multiple devices by means of a special contention scheduler working on a single radio interface [9, 10] or by embedding multiple radio interfaces in the same traffic generator [11]. SDR-based solutions, summing overlapping signals in software before generating the resulting aggregated signal on the air, have also been explored in [12] for studying high-density cognitive networks.

Also our solution is based on SDR and software-based combination and scheduling of signals to be transmitted in real-time, according to a desired traffic and cell scenario. To this purpose, we modeled LoRa modulation (based on chirp spread spectrum) and LoRa access mechanism (based on aloha and duty cycle enforcement). Simple models for traffic sources and physical channels are also included. We also provide a software receiver, able to process the trace produced by the traffic generator and evaluate low-level statistics to be compared with the statistics of a real gateway.

2 LORA TRANSCEIVER IN SDR

An important component of our Traffic Generator is obviously the software-defined implementation of a LoRa transceiver. Indeed, this block is essential for producing elementary LoRa-modulated signals, as a function of the traffic source schedules, which are then translated on time and attenuated according to the physical channel model of each node.

LoRa modulation. It is derived from *Chirp Spread Spectrum (CSS)*, which makes use of *chirp signals*, i.e. frequency-modulated signals obtained when the modulating signal varies linearly in the range $[f_0, f_1]$ (upchirp) or $[f_1, f_0]$ (downchirp) in a symbol time T. Binary modulations, mapping 0/1 information bits in upchirps/downchirps, have been demonstrated to be very robust against in-band or out-band interference [2]. LoRa employes a M-ary modulation scheme based on chirps, in which symbols are obtained by considering different circular shifts of the basic upchirp signal. The temporal shifts, characterizing each symbol, are slotted into multiples of time

MobiCom '17, October 16–20, 2017, Snowbird, UT, USA

ACM ISBN 978-1-4503-4916-1/17/10.
https://doi.org/10.1145/3117811.3119862

$T_{chip} = 1/BW$, called chip, being $BW = f_1 - f_0$ the bandwidth of the signal. It results that the modulating signal for a generic n-th LoRa symbol can be expressed as:

$$f(t) = \begin{cases} f_1 + k \cdot (t - n \cdot T_{chip}) & \text{for } 0 \leqslant t \leqslant n \cdot T_{chip} \\ f_0 + k \cdot (t - n \cdot T_{chip}) & \text{for } n \cdot T_{chip} < t \leqslant T \end{cases}$$

where $k = (f_1 - f_0)/T$ is the slope of the frequency variations. The total number of symbols (coding SF information bits) is chosen equal to 2^{SF}, where SF is called spreading factor. The symbol duration T required for representing any possible shift is $2^{SF} \cdot T_{chip} = 2^{SF}/BW$. It follows that, for a fixed bandwidth, the symbol period increases with SF, enlarging the temporal occupancy of the signal. Figure 1 shows the modulating signal used for a basic upchirp and three examples of circular shifts obtained for $SF = 9$: the symbol time is 512 T_{chip}, while the three examplary shifts code the symbols 128, 256 and 384. The preamble of any LoRa frame is obtained by sending a sequence of at least eight upchirps, followed by two coded upchirps, used for network identification (sync word), and two and a quarter base downchirps. Payload data are then sent by using the M-ary modulation symbols.

LoRa provides three BW settings (125, 250 or 500 KHz) and seven different SF values (from 6 to 12). In general, a larger bandwidth translates in a data rate increase and a receiver sensitivity deterioration. Conversely, higher spreading factors can be used for improving the link robustness at the cost of a lower data rate. The computation of the signal samples has been implemented in MATLAB and sent to the DAC of the USRP board, by also considering the preamble format of LoRa PHY. No channel coding has been currently considered.

LoRa demodulation. An interesting feature of LoRa modulation is the pseudo-orthogonality of signals modulated under different spreading factors. This feature allows the receiver to easily separate multiple concurrent transmissions because of the cross-energy between symbols modulated at different spreading factors is almost zero. In general, a single-user receiver multiplies the received signal with the base downchirp. This leads to a signal with only two frequencies: $f_n = -k \cdot n \cdot T_{chip}$ and $f_n - BW = -(f_1 - f_0) - k \cdot n \cdot Tchip$. They will be both aliased to the same frequency f_n by downsampling at rate BW. The position of the peak at the output of an iFFT will correspond to the estimated symbol $\hat{n}$, as described in [13] and [14]. An example output of this workflow is shown in figure 4, when a reference signal at $SF = 9$ is overlapped to an interferer at $SF = 8$ with equal power. A clear peak reveals the reference symbol, whereas the interfering signal results in a wide-band spectrum with low spectral density. We exploited these considerations for implementing a LoRa demodulator in MATLAB, working on the signal samples generated by the modulator.

3 DEMONSTRATION DESCRIPTION

Goal of our demo is analyzing the cell-level performance of a LoRa network under different network plannings, i.e. under different allocations of per-node spreading factors and transmission powers. Indeed, rather than working with random spreading factors and uniform transmission powers, more robust configurations can be reserved for users experiencing bad channel qualities. We assume that all the nodes emulated by our traffic generator are configured for working on the same channel, while the number of nodes and their distribution within the cell can be configured in each experiment.

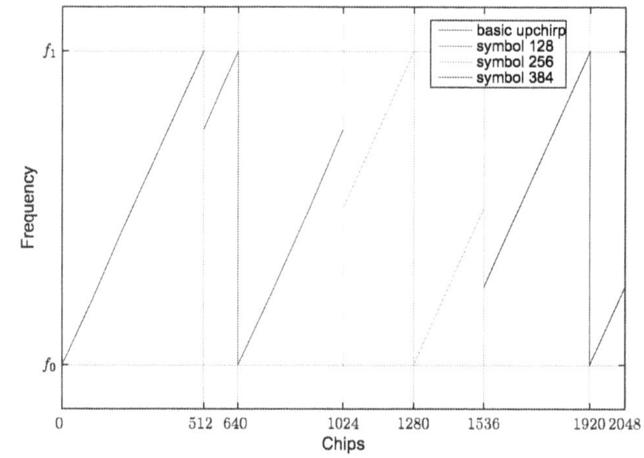

Figure 1: Modulating signal with $SF = 9$ for one basic upchirp and three symbols: 128, 256 **and** 384.

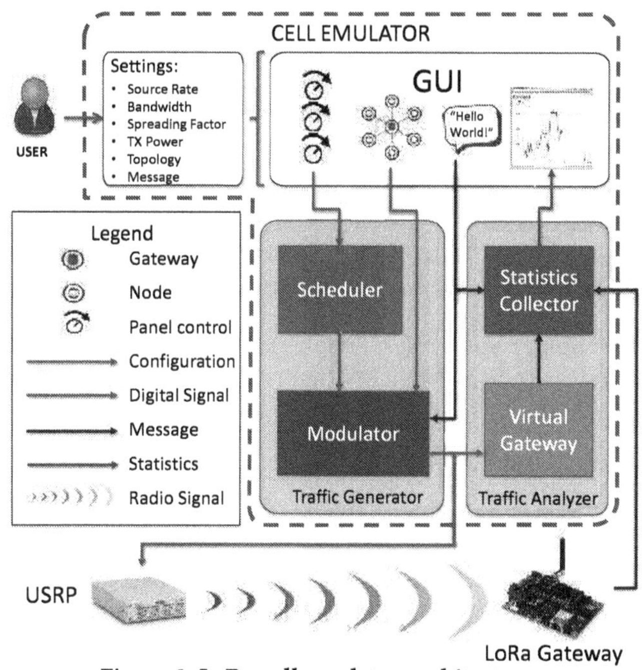

Figure 2: LoRa cell emulator architecture.

Figure 2 summarizes the software architecture of the LoRa cell emulator and the hardware used for the demo set-up: a real *LoRa Gateway*, implemented by using a Raspberry Pi 3 piloting the iC880A gateway transceiver, receives over-the-air the signal produced through a *USRP B210*, which results from the super-position of multiple LoRa-modulated signals generated by the cell nodes simultaneously active. Two additional monitors (HDMI), keyboards and mouses, not shown in the figure, will be utilized for visualizing the configuration interface and results.

The LoRa cell emulator is composed of three main software modules: (a) a *Traffic Generator*, (b) a *Traffic Analyzer* and (c) a *Graphical*

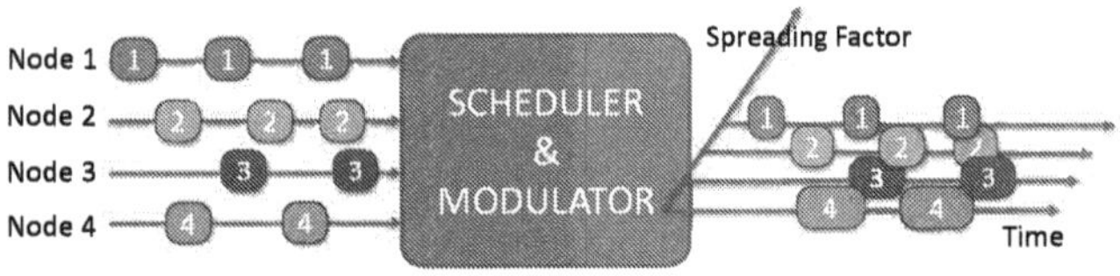

Figure 3: An example of per-node LoRa modulated signals, which are scheduled on time before being combined into the cell-level aggregated signal.

User Interface (GUI). The first two modules are written in MATLAB, whereas the GUI is Python based. The traffic generator, in turn, is composed of: a *Scheduler*, which is responsible of generating the activity intervals of each node according to the source rate and duty-cycle constraints; a *Modulator*, which receives the schedule of the nodes involved in transmission and generates the cell-level aggregated signal by summing up the LoRa modulated signals of the nodes simultaneously active, as shown in figure 3. Before combing the signal generated by each node into the cell-level signal, a path-loss attenuation model is applied by scaling and delaying the relevant chirps.

The digital signal is sent to both the USRP, for being transmitted over the air, and the Traffic Analyzer. The Traffic Analyzer is composed of a *Virtual Gateway* and a *Statistics Collector*. The former implements a LoRa demodulator working in parallel on multiple spreading factors, for identifying message preambles and then correlating each message with the corresponding basic upchirp. The latter compares the symbols demodulated in each message with the ones sent by the nodes, in order to produce low-level error statistics. The signal transmitted over the air is demodulated also by a real gateway, whose packet error statistics are sent to the statistic collector module for comparison with the results obtained by the virtual gateway.

The cell configuration, specified by means of the GUI, includes the tuning of the following parameters: number of nodes, nodes distribution (uniform, uniform in a given area), source rates, bandwidth, spreading factor allocation (random, distance-based), transmission power (uniform, distance-based). The parameters can be differentiated for groups of nodes, thus facilitating the planning for large cells.

Figure 4 shows an example of digitally overlapped signal generated by two nodes using different spreading factor: one signal modulated with SF equal to 9 (blue line) is overlapped to two symbols modulated with SF equal to 8 (red line). The figure also shows the output of the iFFT, after multiplication with the base downchirp at $SF = 9$ and downsampling, in two different scenarios: the two nodes are equally distant from the gateway and employ uniform transmission powers (middle figure); the distances of the two nodes are heterogeneous and results in one signal power 20dB greater than the other one (bottom figure). In this second case, although the two signals are in principle orthogonal, the interference between the two nodes can prevent the correct demodulation of the symbol modulated with $SF = 9$, that we assume is received at lower power (being higher spreading factors usually allocated to farer users). In

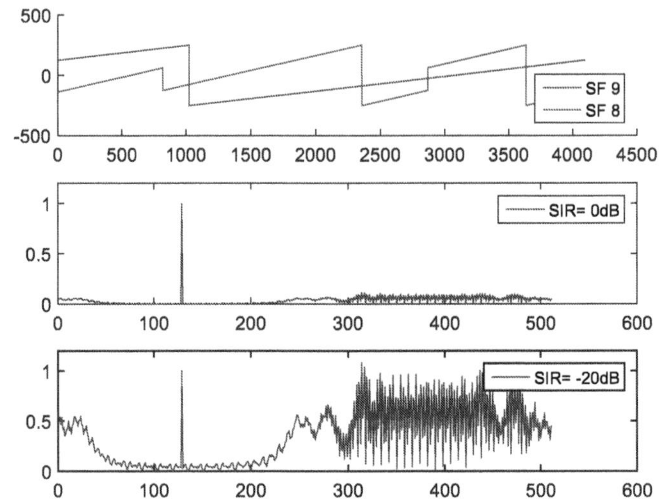

Figure 4: An example of collision between signals modulated with different SF. A LoRa symbol with SF equal to 9 (solid line) and two overlapping interfering symbols with SF equal to 8 (dashed line) received at different SIR levels, and iFFT output after multiplication with the base downchirp and downsampling.

fact, correlation peaks can occur in positions different from 128, as evident from the figure in the interval [300 − 450].

4 ACKNOWLEDGEMENTS

This work has been partially supported by EU funded research project symbIoTe, H2020-ICT-2015 grant agreement number 688156.

REFERENCES

[1] Worldwide connected devices forecast www.statista.com
[2] Semtech. LoRa Modulation Basics. AN1200.22, Revision 2, May 2015. www.semtech.com
[3] M. C. Bor, U. Roedig, T. Voigt, and J. M. Alonso, "Do LoRa Low-Power Wide-Area Networks Scale?", In Proc. of MSWiM 2016. ACM, New York, pp. 59-67.
[4] B. Reynders and S. Pollin, "Chirp spread spectrum as a modulation technique for long range communication", In SCVT 2016, Mons, pp. 1-5.
[5] B. Reynders, W. Meert and S. Pollin, "Range and coexistence analysis of long range unlicensed communication", In ICT 2016, Thessaloniki, pp. 1-6.
[6] L. Kelch, T. Pigel, L. Wolf, A. Sasse, "Traffic Generator for HSDPA Network Simulations", In ICCVE 2014, Vienna, 25-330.
[7] D. Kaulbars, F. Schweikowski, C. Wietfeld, "Spatially Distributed Traffic Generation for Stress Testing the Robustness of Mission-Critical Smart Grid Communication", In Proc. of GLOBECOM Workshops 2015, San Diego.
[8] G. A lvarez *et al.*, "Multi-client Emulation Platform for Performance Testing of High Density 802.11 Networks", In Wireless Days (WD) 2016, 1-6.
[9] CT520 LANforge WiFIRE 802.11a/b/g/n WiFi Traffic Generator. www.candelatech.com
[10] Multi-Client Traffic Generator/Performance Analyzer www.veriwave.com
[11] TM500 Network Tester www.cobhamwireless.com
[12] S. Papadakis, A. Makrogiannakis, M. Surligas, P. Papadakis, Single SDR Multiple Primary & Secondary Users Emulation Platform, in EuCNC 2015, Paris.
[13] O. Bernard, A. Seller, N. Sornin, "Low power long range transmitter", European Patent Application EP 2763321 A1 by Semtech Corporation, 2014
[14] C. Goursaud, J.M. Gorce, "Dedicated networks for IoT: PHY / MAC state of the art and challenges", in EAI endorsed transactions on Internet of Things, 2015.

Demo: DEMS: DEcoupled Multipath Scheduler for Accelerating Multipath Transport

Yihua Ethan Guo, Ashkan Nikravesh, Z. Morley Mao, Feng Qian†, Subhabrata Sen‡

University of Michigan †Indiana University ‡AT&T Labs – Research
{yhguo, ashnik, zmao}@umich.edu fengqian@indiana.edu sen@research.att.com

ABSTRACT

We present the demonstration of DEMS, a new multipath scheduler aiming at reducing the data chunk download time. DEMS consists of three key design decisions: (1) being aware of the chunk boundary and strategically decoupling the paths for chunk delivery, (2) ensuring simultaneous subflow completion at the receiver side, and (3) allowing a path to trade a small amount of redundant data for performance. We integrate the DEMS components into a holistic system and implement it on commodity mobile devices, where unmodified mobile applications can use DEMS to transmit data over multipath. We demonstrate the simple configuration of using DEMS over multipath, visualization of multipath scheduling, download time reduction of data chunks with DEMS over both emulated and real cellular/WiFi networks compared to default MinRTT scheduler, and application QoE improvement on mobile phones from DEMS.

1 INTRODUCTION

Simultaneously using multiple network paths such as cellular and WiFi to accelerate data transfer is an attractive feature on mobile devices. It is supported by many commercial products such as Apple Siri [3], Gigapath by Korean Telecom [1], and Samsung Download Booster [2]. Currently the most widely used multipath solution is MPTCP [4], which enables unmodified applications to leverage multipath by adding a shim layer to the TCP interface. MPTCP establishes a *subflow* over each network path. The MPTCP sender distributes the data onto the subflows; the receiver reassembles the data into the original byte stream and delivers it to the app transparently.

Multipath *scheduler* is an important component in multipath transport, which determines how the data is distributed onto the subflows. MPTCP supports different types of schedulers. For example, the *MinRTT* scheduler attempts to deliver the data as soon as possible by choosing a subflow with the smallest RTT unless its congestion window is full. Despite existing efforts on improving multipath scheduler [5, 7–11], we found that the multipath scheduler design is far from being optimal. In a pilot experiment, we observe that surprisingly, under representative WiFi/LTE network conditions, the MinRTT scheduler inflates the download time for a medium-sized file by up to 33% compared to the optimal scheduling decision derived offline. In real-world networks with fluctuating bandwidth or latency, MinRTT may perform even worse (up to 7.5x download time increase, 49% median increase compared to optimal scheduling). Regarding the root cause, our key insight is that for such a file download, oftentimes the subflows do *not* complete at the same time at the *receiver* side, leading to suboptimal performance.

MobiCom '17, October 16–20, 2017, Snowbird, UT, USA

ACM ISBN 978-1-4503-4916-1/17/10.
https://doi.org/10.1145/3117811.3119869

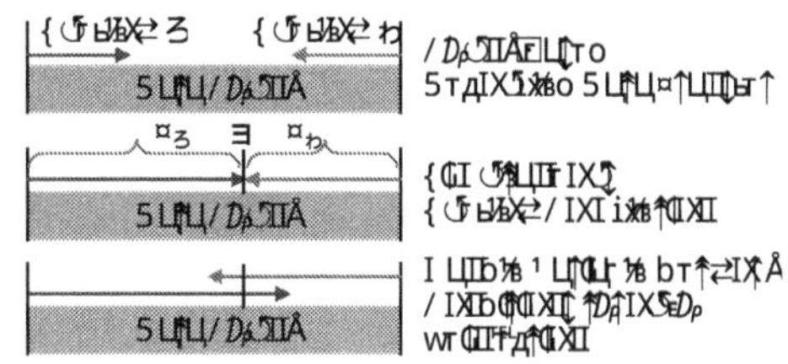

Figure 1: Key design decisions of DEMS.

This demonstration shows DEMS (**DE**coupled **M**ultipath **S**cheduler[1]) [6], a new multipath packet scheduler aiming at reducing the data chunk download time over multiple paths. A *data chunk* is simply a block of application-defined bytes, which is a very common data transfer workload in mobile applications, *e.g.*, fetching an image, JavaScript, MP3 file, or video chunk. The key idea behind DEMS is to *achieve simultaneous subflow completion at the receiver side through strategic packet scheduling over decoupled subflows* in order to minimize the chunk download time. To accomplish this, DEMS incorporates three design components: (1) chunk-based data transfer, (2) simultaneous subflow completion, and (3) dynamic reinjection. We demonstrate that DEMS is easy to use for unmodified applications, beneficial to both chunk downloads and real applications including web browsing.

2 DESIGN OVERVIEW

As shown in Figure 1, the key design decisions of DEMS include the following: (1) DEMS leverages a heuristic that treats all data in the meta buffer as a chunk, and it strategically decouples the paths for chunk delivery (§2.1). (2) DEMS ensures simultaneous subflow completion at the receiver side (§2.2). (3) DEMS allows a path to trade a small amount of redundant data for performance (§2.3). We further elaborate on how DEMS is integrated into a mobile multipath system (§2.4).

[1]Note here "decoupled scheduling" is different from the decoupled congestion control in MPTCP.

2.1 Chunk-based Data Transfer

In DEMS, by default, data is delivered to the application on a *per-chunk* basis. A (data) chunk consists of a block of bytes defined by the application, which can be, for example, an image, a Javascript, an audio snippet, or a video chunk. As long as a chunk can be correctly reassembled at the transport layer, bytes within the chunk can be delivered in any order. The data chunk is thus split into different parts that are distributed onto different paths for delivery. For the common scenario involving two paths, we design a "two-way" splitting approach: the two paths transfer the data in opposite directions, one from the beginning and the other from the end; when they "meet" each other, the chunk is fully downloaded. This approach is intuitive and parameterless. Furthermore, it helps improve the multipath performance by *decoupling* the two subflows. Each subflow freely and independently transfers the data until the very end when subflows meet and merge.

2.2 Simultaneous Subflow Completion

Having all subflows complete at the same time at the receiver side is a necessary condition for achieving the optimal performance. The reason can be easily shown through *proof by contradiction*: suppose in an optimal scheme, Subflow A finishes earlier than Subflow B; in that case Subflow B can further "offload" some bytes to Subflow A, leading to an even shorter download time. To achieve simultaneous subflow completion, the high-level idea is to introduce a timing offset at the sender to compensate the heterogeneous delay across both subflows. DEMS uses bandwidth and delay prediction to calculate the timing offset and dynamically decides the network path to transmit each packet.

2.3 Handling Variable Network Conditions

DEMS tolerates unbalanced completion of subflows under variable network condition by performing *reinjection*: instead of having a full stop when all bytes of a chunk are transmitted, a subflow may further "overshoot" its portion by sending a small number of bytes that are beyond the meeting point of the two subflows. These bytes are redundant because they have already been transmitted over the other subflow. The purpose of reinjection is to trade redundant data for better performance: under uncertain network conditions, if the reinjected (redundant) data arrives earlier than its original copy, the overall download time is reduced. In DEMS, reinjection only occurs near subflows' meeting point. We develop a method that adaptively determines the amount of the redundant data to strike a sweet spot between the performance and the additional data transmission due to reinjection.

2.4 System Design

We now elaborate on how to integrate the DEMS algorithm into a real system. Figure 2 plots the system diagram. At the sender side (right), the chunk data coming from the application is stored in the meta buffer, and is then split, scheduled, and transmitted by the packet scheduler. Working with the packet scheduler, the reinjection manager keeps track of packets' transmission states and makes decisions on adaptive reinjection. We also design a module for measuring and predicting network conditions (One-way delay difference between two subflows, i.e. ΔOWD, and bandwidth).

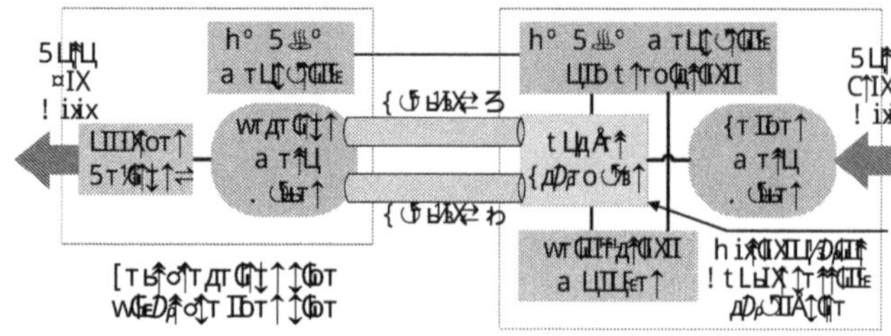

Figure 2: System diagram of DEMS.

The application can also optionally specify the chunk size through an API. The receiver side logic is much simpler. It passively receives/acknowledges the data, reassembles it in the receiver-side meta buffer, and delivers the in-order data to the application. Note that data over the (decoupled) subflows are acknowledged separately using the per-subflow ACK numbers. Meanwhile, similar to MPTCP, at the receiver meta buffer, the global sequence number carried by each packet is used to mark which portion within the chunk has been received. While Figure 2 illustrates one-way data transfer, our system supports full-duplex data transmission.

3 DEMONSTRATION

The demonstration consists of two Android phones and two Linux laptops. We use both the Android phones and Linux laptops to demonstrate the capability of running DEMS scheduler over multipath. The phones require access to both the cellular network (3G or 4G/LTE) and WiFi network. Both laptops require access to a WiFi network and power. One of the laptop serves as a multipath proxy for mobile devices and visualizes the multipath scheduling of both MinRTT and DEMS. We need one table to setup all equipments with an estimated time of 1 hour. We use these devices to demonstrate the following:

Simple configuration of using DEMS. We show how DEMS can be easily used by unmodified applications on commodity mobile devices. We leverage a customized multipath TCP proxy infrastructure. Between the proxy and the mobile device, multipath is realized as multiple conventional TCP connections each corresponding to a subflow established over a network path. For download traffic, the proxy makes the corresponding multipath scheduling decision for each data packet. A policy file on the mobile device configures the scheduler to be used for each application. We demonstrate that by using this proxy infrastructure and easily modifying the configuration file, DEMS can be enabled over multipath for unmodified mobile applications.

Visualization of multipath scheduling. This shows how different schedulers including MinRTT and DEMS makes scheduling decision for each packet over time, to better understand the design of multipath schedulers. We show that oftentimes the subflows in MinRTT do not complete at the same time at the receiver side, achieving sub-optimal download time. Instead, DEMS minimizes the data transfer time by achieving simultaneous subflow completion.

Improvement of data chunk download. This shows the performance improvement of DEMS on downloading data chunks over both emulated and real multipath environments of WiFi and cellular networks. We take a "record and replay" approach to realistically emulate the varying bandwidth. We collect multiple 5-minute bandwidth traces of both paths from different locations. In the demonstration, we compare the performance of DEMS and MinRTT under the same network conditions, by replaying the bandwidth traces or using real networks.

Application QoE benefits. This shows how DEMS helps improve the QoE of web browsing, one of the most popular applications on mobile devices. We use web page loading experiments using off-the-shelf Chrome browser (version 53.0.2785.124) on our Android phones. We picked 10 popular websites and use their mobile-version landing pages as the target web pages. We use the page load time (PLT), which is programmatically measured by the Chrome debugging interface, as the QoE metric. We demonstrate that PLT is improved with DEMS over multipath compared to default MinRTT scheduler.

REFERENCES

[1] 2015. In Korean, Multipath TCP is pronounced GIGA Path. http://blog.multipath-tcp.org/blog/html/2015/07/24/korea.html. (2015).

[2] 2016. Samsung Download Booster. http://www.samsung.com/uk/support/skp/faq/1061358. (2016).

[3] 2017. iOS: Multipath TCP Support in iOS 7. https://support.apple.com/en-us/HT201373. (2017).

[4] Alan Ford, Costin Raiciu, Mark Handley, and Olivier Bonaventure. 2013. TCP Extensions for Multipath Operation with Multiple Addresses. RFC 6824. (2013).

[5] Alexander Frömmgen, Tobias Erbshauser, Alejandro P. Buchmann, Torsten Zimmermann, and Klaus Wehrle. 2016. ReMP TCP: Low Latency Multipath TCP. In *IEEE ICC 2016*.

[6] Yihua Ethan Guo, Ashkan Nikravesh, Z. Morley Mao, Feng Qian, and Subhabrata Sen. 2017. Accelerating Multipath Transport Through Balanced Subflow Completion. In *ACM MobiCom 2017*.

[7] Bo Han, Feng Qian, Lusheng Ji, and Vijay Gopalakrishnan. 2016. MP-DASH: Adaptive Video Streaming Over Preference-Aware Multipath. In *ACM CoNEXT 2016*.

[8] Nicolas Kuhn, Emmanuel Lochin, Ahlem Mifdaoui, Golam Sarwar, Olivier Mehani, and Roksana Boreli. 2014. DAPS: Intelligent Delay-aware Packet Scheduling for Multipath Transport. In *IEEE ICC 2014*.

[9] Yeon-sup Lim, Erich M Nahum, Don Towsley, and Richard J Gibbens. 2017. ECF: An MPTCP Path Scheduler to Manage Heterogeneous Paths. In *ACM SIGMETRICS 2017 Abstracts*.

[10] Christoph Paasch, Simone Ferlin, Ozgu Alay, and Olivier Bonaventure. 2014. Experimental Evaluation of Multipath TCP Schedulers. In *ACM SIGCOMM Capacity Sharing Workshop (CSWS) 2014*.

[11] Yeon sup Lim, Yung-Chih Chen, Erich M. Nahum, Don Towsley, Richard J. Gibbens, and Emmanuel Cecchet. 2015. Design, Implementation and Evaluation of Energy-Aware Multi-Path TCP. In *ACM CoNEXT 2015*.

Demo: Atlas Thing Architecture 任Enabling Mobile Apps as Things in the IoT

Sumi Helal
School of Computing and Communication
Lancaster University, UK
s.helal@lancaster.ac.uk

Ahmed E. Khaled
Mobile and Pervasive Computing Lab
University of Florida, USA
aekhaled@cise.ufl.edu

Venkata Gutta
Mobile and Pervasive Computing Lab
University of Florida, USA
venkatagutta@ufl.edu

ABSTRACT

We make the case for mobile apps as crucial and influential things in the Internet of Things (IoT) and then present our Atlas Thing Architecture that provides the explicit support necessary for their inclusion. We present the World Cup demo scenario which involves media appliances and mobile app things, and which shows how we implemented it as an IoT application based on our architecture.

CCS CONCEPTS

休Ubiquitous and mobile computing → Ubiquitous and mobile computing systems and tools; 休Computer systems organization → Architectures; 休 Computer systems organization → Embedded and cyber-physical systems

KEYWORDS

Internet of Things; thing architecture; Mobile Apps as IoT things

1 INTRODUCTION

The success of the Internet of Things (IoT) will largely depend on how its main ingredient似the thing似s architected and prepared to match expectations, and to fulfill the big heroic role that will magically make blue-sky visions a reality. However, thing architectures explicitly designed with IoT scenarios in mind are direly needed. Today, embedded Linux is utilized conveniently thanks to the abundant power of embedded processors de jour. But Linux was never designed for the IoT and does not offer many of the elements and services that would better promote IoT application development. The ARM Mbed OS [7] offers a fresh redesign of embedded operating system especially designed for the IoT, and offering key services such as light-weight messaging protocols, energy-efficient encryption, and event based processing. It also offers thing 佰PIing佧known as device cloud services, which makes an embedded system connected to and accessible from the cloud by other things.

1.1 The Atlas thing architecture

In our ongoing Atlas Thing Architecture project [1][2][3], we go a step further in adding more IoT-specific functionalities over current embedded OS to address more IoT requirements. One such requirement is for things to be able to learn, prepare and plan for opportunistic and meaningful interactions serving the user and enriching her experience, but without requiring her intervention! Such requirement can empower thing佮ability to discover the existence of potentially useful social relations with its mates and to cue the user with possible app formation opportunities.

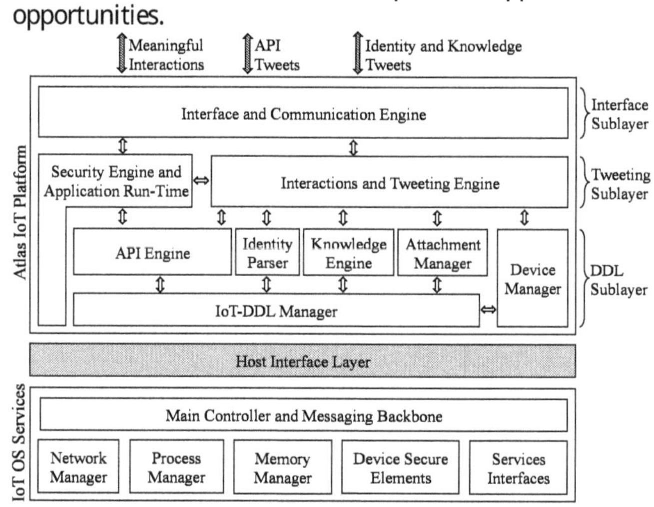

Figure 1: Atlas thing architecture.

Figure 1 above shows the various layers of our architecture starting with the IoT data description layer (IoT-DDL) that enables just-in-time APIing, identity management, device management (for a full life-cycle maintenance of thing), own- and learnt-knowledge management, and an extensibility feature we call thing

Mobicom 佅7, October 16-20, 2017, Snowbird, UT, USA

ACM ISBN 978-1-4503-4916-1/17/10.
https://doi.org/10.1145/3117811.3119856

attachment. A thing vendor may update its description, manage the revisions via standard device management standard (a version of OMA-DM), and also add cloud-hosted attachments overtime which are referenced and used by the thing description.

Our architecture recognizes that knowing and sharing API佮 are not enough to enable IoT scenarios, and that it needs to go beyond API佮 to offer paths to 佳meaningful interactions佅and new models of programming meaningful and opportune applications. The tweeting and interface layers in our architecture enable such meaningful interactions. More specifically, a thing in a smart space engages with thing mates through a set of information- and action-based interactions [2]. Information-based interactions (referred to as tweets) enable a thing to announce its presence, identity, capabilities, and knowledge as a way to describe what it is, what it does, what services it can offer to others, and what it knows. Such informational exchange leads to the creation of a set of social relationships among things that can then guide the formation of meaningful thing engagement opportunities. Action-based interactions, on the other hand, include device management commands for OEM software and IoT-DDL updates, and configurations and settings from authorized users.

It is worth mentioning that our IoT-DDL specifications are machine- and human-readable manifests of thing descriptions including identity, capabilities, interest, services, and other elements such as fetch interfaces to externally stored attachments. The architecture implementation to date [2][3] supports hardware and software things and utilizes light weight messaging protocols such as Rest-HTTP, MQTT, and CoAP, and ensures interoperable communication among things that speak different protocols. It also takes advantage of device management standards such as OMA-DM. It is also worth mentioning that the discovery of social relationships through ad-hoc social interactions (tweets) which enables the discovery of semantic similarity and affinity between Atlas thing mates is accomplished in our architecture with the help of WordNet [5]. WordNet is a lexical database that groups the English words into sets of synonyms words; measures the semantic similarity between them; and records relations between such sets. Our architecture also utilizes the inverse document frequency measure (IDF) [6], which is a numerical statistic intended to reflect how important a word is in a corpus.

2 THE WORLD CUP SCENARIO

In 2014, soccer fans around the world had many things, all smart, all connected, but no IoT! From smartphones with World Cup apps, to smart TV佮 to connected Digital Video Recorder (DVR), all in their homes, and even accessible remotely. Browsing the Semifinal games佮schedule on a mobile app revealed the historical Germany-Brazil game that a fan is unable to watch due to an urgent business meeting. The fan is forced to put down the smartphone, moves to the living room, search for the basket of remotes, and sits down to program the DVR to record the game. In 2018, or perhaps 2022, the cup watching experience could be much different 伻enhanced by IoT. A fan browsing the games佮schedule will be able to schedule a recording of the game directly from the app. Here, the app developer did not make assumptions about the availability of a DVR thing in the user佮佳smart space佅and did not write any code to enable such a recording. The DVR thing and the World Cup app chatted and exchanged interest and capability/interest lists, which resulted in the DVR thing initiating a meaningful interaction with the mobile app offering a recording service. The fan is presented with a toast or a pop-up screen (an asset part of the meaningful interaction) asking if she wants to record the game on its DVR. On answering Yes, she is asked if she wishes to have recording as a permanent feature of the app, which she happily accepts.

We use this IoT scenario to underscore three key requirements that we address in our Atlas thing architecture. First, things should socially interact to learn of potentially productive or useful relationships. Once relationships are discovered, applications or parts of applications can be recognized and suggested as opportunities to other things, or the smart space user. Second, mobile apps should be fully supported as future things in the IoT. This is a significant requirement because we have to find ways for apps to change behavior and deviate from their standard logic intended by their original developers. Changing behavior will be required to enable meaningful and spontaneous interactions. Another requirement is the use of attachments. It is unlikely that things host and maintain multiple up-to-date copies of meaningful interaction assets (e.g., copies for Android, for iOS, etc.). It may be more manageable to architect things in a way that allows additional elements to be 佳attached佅 to them but stored, hosted and managed in the cloud.

3 DEMONSTRATION

Our demo utilizes two Atlas things: a digital video recorder (DVR) and a mobile app. Given the lack of open DVR hardware, we used the Kodi open source DVR software [4] to build our DVR hardware thing 伻Thing A, as illustrated in Figure 2. It consists of four components: 1) Kodi: a media player software ported to a Raspberry-Pi, 2) TVheadend: a media streaming and recording software server ported to a second Raspberry-Pi and serves as a backend for Kodi, 3) RCA: an indoor flat HDTV multi-directional antenna, and 4) HDHomeRun: a network-attached digital TV tuner, with input signal connected to the RCA antenna and output digital TV signal connected to the TVheadend server. Kodi also offers a web dashboard that provides the user with a friendly interface to remotely control the DVR capabilities through a set of HTTP-REST APIs. The IoT-DDL for the DVR Thing A reflects its identity, its main programmatic services (and corresponding API佮 for pre-recording a TV program or playing a recorded program, and a thing attachment which is the Kodi web app as a user interface. Thing A IoT-DDL also includes a set of keywords that describes the DVR capabilities and interest. (e.g., listing available channels, recording specific channel).

The Android mobile app or Thing B, on the other hand, is a specialized seasonal app for the World Cup games offering the games佮 schedule, dynamically updated scoreboard, analyses and other information such as historical and players profiles. Thing B IoT-DDL for the mobile app reflects the app identity but does not reflect services it offers to others. It also includes a set of keywords that describes the app capabilities and interest.

When both things are 佴owered on佅 the Atlas thing architecture in each starts parsing and processing the uploaded IoT-DDL. Each thing now identifies itself, discovers the different services it can offer and starts generating its own APIs that reflect how other things may access such services. Each thing then starts looking for thing mates by broadcasting tweets that hold its identity and capability/interest keywords to other things in the smart space. Exchanging such tweets triggers the semantic similarity process described in section 1.1 on the received keywords for the possibility of mutually beneficial interactions that may take place, hence establishing 佴ocial relations佅 A high correlation is established between the keywords offered by the DVR as capability for recording soccer games (as TV programs) and those offered by the mobile app as capability for displaying World Cup games' schedule (also as TV programs). The DVR sends the API for the recording service to the mobile app to extend the app capability (and behavior) to also be able to prompt the user to record the games. Sending the API notifies the app user of such external service, asking if s/he would like to use it to record. Another follow on notification is possible which asks if the user wishes to keep the recording service as a permanent feature in his app. The app updates its UI layout dynamically according to the received tweets by adding new UI elements (views, buttons, notifications) to invoke the received APIs through a meaningful interaction.

Accepting the notification therefore extends the app layout with the recording feature that when "clicked" makes API call to the actual service residing in the DVR thing. An earlier tweet exchange about a DVR attachment supplies the app with the UI elements needed to extend itself. A pool of in-app chromeless browser views are used by the app to dynamically extend its function and behavior.

3.1 What will be demonstrated?

We will demonstrate the entire prototype operational and displayed on a demo table. We will also display the IoT-DDL files of both the DVR and mobile app things on big screens. We will also demonstrate the mobile app live and will display the live parsing of IoT-DDLs and the exchange of tweets, showing how meaningful interactions are shaped and formed, and how the mobile app begins to extend its logic to become a slightly different one with capabilities beyond what its original developer has intended and coded. We will also share with the community how we were able to facilitate dynamic app logic changes within the Android platform. An actual, off-the-air, live TV signal will be utilized during the demo.

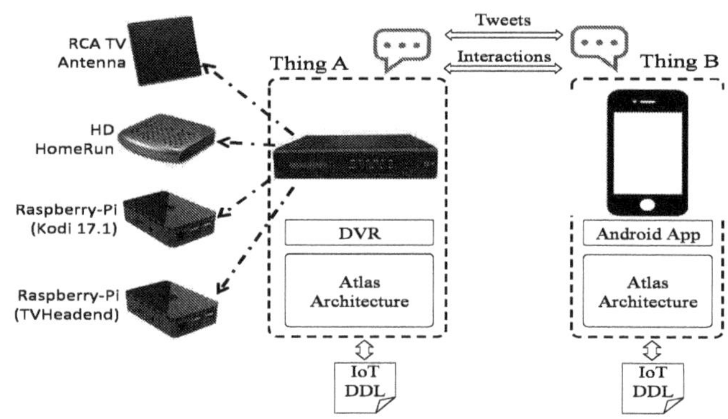

Figure 2: A DVR and a mobile app Atlas things seamlessly interacting to record a World Cup game.

4 CONCLUSIONS

We presented a demo of an IoT scenario that is not possible to achieve without explicit thing architectures like ours. We believe more work is needed in this area to empower future powerful scenarios that are easily talked about but difficult to implement.

REFERENCES

[1] J. King, R. Bose, H. Yang, S. Pickles and A. Helal, 佴tlas 伻A Service-Oriented Sensor Platform.佅 Proceedings of the first IEEE International Workshop on Practical Issues in Building Sensor Network Applications (SenseApp 2006). Tampa, Florida, 2006.

[2] A. E. Khaled and A. Helal, 佴nteroperable Communication Framework for Bridging RESTful and Topic-based Communication in IoT.佅n review. Technical Report available at: https://www.cise. ufl.edu/~aekhaled/Comm_Framework.pdf

[3] A. E. Khaled and A. Helal. IoT-DDL佡Device Description Language for the 佴佅in IoT. In review. Technical Report available at: https://www.cise.ufl.edu/~aekhaled/IoTDDL.pdf

[4] Kodi media player. https://kodi.tv/

[5] Wordnet. https://wordnet.princeton.edu/wordnet/

[6] J. Ramos, "Using tf-idf to determine word relevance in document queries." The first instructional conference on machine learning. 2003.

[7] ARM mbed OS. https://www.mbed.com/en/platform/mbed-os/

Demo: LL-MEC A SDN-based MEC Platform

Anta Huang and Navid Nikaein
Communication Systems Department, Eurecom
Sophia Antipolis, France 06410
firstname.name@eurecom.fr

ABSTRACT

Software-defined Networking (SDN) is seen as a promising solution that allows for a more distributed, flexible, and scalable network. Multi-access Edge Computing (MEC), initiated as an Industry Specification Group (ISG) within ETSI, is also emerging as a low-latency and high-throughput cloud environment at the edge of network. The noticeable success that aforementioned technologies made attracts massive research interests and the interplay between them on programmable network requires an open source platform to evaluate. In this work, we present a low-latency MEC platform (LL-MEC) providing the required flexibility and programmability to meet the expected performance gain following SDN and MEC principles. We also demonstrate an use case of real-time content caching application using LL-MEC platform and OpenAirInterface LTE implementation on commodity hardware.

KEYWORDS

MEC, OpenAirInterface, SDN, LTE, OpenFlow, Programmability.

1 INTRODUCTION

Recently, Multi-access Edge Computing (MEC), introduced and specified by European Telecommunications Standards Institute (ETSI)[5], has attracted huge interests among research communities due to the promising benefits at the network edge. MEC is a platform enabling applications with the function of clouds[1, 2] at the network edge and in close proximity to end-users. Besides, MEC is not only characterized by its proximity to Radio Access Network (RAN) but also by providing a real-time access to radio network information that can be exposed to applications; therefore *low latency* comes as one of the key features of MEC. The ETSI specifications also have rich set of functionalities to ensure that the MEC concept can be the solutions to the problems surfacing. Not only does MEC provide technical benefits, but it also creates a new market and value chain not seen before in mobile networks by opening the network to authorized third-parties, who can develop and rapidly install innovative applications, benefiting both the third-parties and the network owners. Having smart and diversified applications toward 5G mobile network requires pushing the boundaries of existing network and service infrastructure. Services desiring lower-latency are emerging and pushing network services to the edge has the potential to enhance user latency and experience, as well as to offload Internet traffic.

The noticeable success in non-mobile networks made by SDN gives the initiatives to apply it onto the core network (CN) of LTE [6]. With the separation of control and data plane, SDN provides the possibilities to program and virtualize the mobile network components, such as Mobility Management Entity (MME), control plane of Serving-Gateway (SGW-C), and control plane of Packet-Gateway (PGW-C) as potential MEC applications. The programmability of the CN provided by SDN is exactly where MEC can facilitate its programmability in RAN and further delegate control decisions. SDN and MEC are complementary concepts and SDN has the same objectives as MEC in the way of applying specific rules to data plane. Not surprisingly, there have been considerable research interests on SDN and MEC with most of them focusing on conceptual frameworks but no open source platform for researchers as a reference to evaluate the benefits of MEC and SDN enabled services. This gives the initiatives of LL-MEC to exploit SDN in providing an end-to-end network programmability through an ecosystem of network services and applications. Given the open specifications of MEC for vendor implementation, the SDN concept is applied in LL-MEC with OpenFlow and FlexRAN [3].

In this work, we present the first open source low latency multi-access edge computing platform (LL-MEC) with 3GPP and ETSI compliance, as a complete implementation of previous work[4] to fill the aforementioned void. LL-MEC incorporates data plane APIs to provide an end-to-end separation between control-plane and data-plane following the SDN principles. It features real-time application task manager and low-level application APIs to support low latency. Furthermore, practical use cases are provided to be deployed on

MobiCom '17, October 16–20, 2017, Snowbird, UT, USA.
 ISBN 978-1-4503-4916-1/17/10.
DOI: https://doi.org/10.1145/3117811.3119857

the top of LL-MEC. LL-MEC is built and evaluated upon a real-time LTE platform, OpenAirInterface [7] and LL-MEC along with its toolbox adopted in this work will soon be made available to the wide research community.

2 LL-MEC OVERVIEW

This section gives an overview of LL-MEC platform and describes how LL-MEC can operate over software-defined mobile network at the edge. We present a high-level schematic of LL-MEC in Figure 1, mainly composed of a three-layer design: *MEC Application*, *MEC Platform*, and *Abstraction*. This platform functions upon software-defined mobile network consisting of multiple LTE eNodeBs and OpenFlow-enabled switches, whether it is physical or software, and fully separates the data plane from control functions. Furthermore, the agent (refer to Figure 1) acts as a local controller on behalf of RAN or OpenFlow-enabled switches. The entities and interfaces we implement in this platform follow the ETSI MEC specifications[5] to support the full functionalities provided by the Mp1 and Mp2 interfaces while retaining the 3GPP compatibility.

2.1 Abstraction

The abstraction layer models and exposes the required operations for the underlying network through a unified interface. In LL-MEC, the *C-plane API* and *D-plane API* naturally comprise the abstraction layer for control plane and data plane of mobile network respectively by providing only the necessary information for the development of *MEC Applications* and *MEC Platform*. In addition to monitoring, they allow flexible and programmable control of the RAN infrastructure.

2.2 MEC Platform

MEC Platform resides in LL-MEC as a core entity between the MEC applications and the real network elements. It constitutes the brain of LL-MEC that controls the fundamental services such as events trigger and register, and provides low latency support, and library integration. Besides, MEC Platform also implements the necessary building blocks to create MEC applications by simplifying the reuse of core components and services. This gives the possibilities for application developers to focus on their specific MEC applications rather on the detailed functionalities of underlying network. It's also worth mentioning that the current implementation of LL-MEC does not support the Mp3 reference point used for the communication with the other MEC platforms.

2.3 MEC Application

MEC applications have limitless possibilities to be developed for any specific purpose without knowing the detailed knowledge of the underlying network. The Mp1 reference point enables the MEC applications to access the network information or delegate the control decision towards network. Multiple choices are provided as the Mp1 including REST API, message bus, and local APIs. Another pivotal feature LL-MEC has is that the application can be deployed in different scheduling recipes such as round robin, first-in-first-out, or deadline scheduler for having different time-scales and priority when executing the task behind the scene. Especially, the RAN-related applications can benefit from this feature to avoid further delay when interacting with radio network.

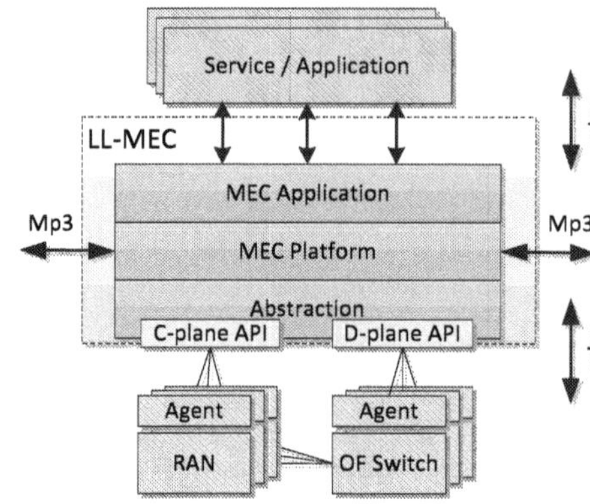

Figure 1: High-level schematic of LL-MEC

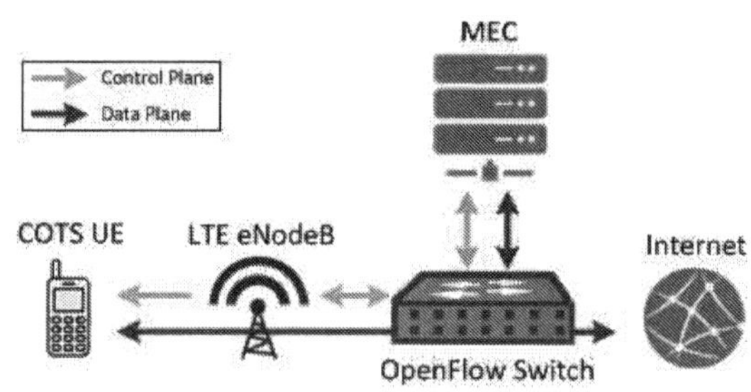

Figure 2: The deployment of LL-MEC demonstration

3 DEMO DESCRIPTION

The considered demonstration scenario is illustrated in Figure 2 and consists of 2 commercial LTE-enabled smart phones (Huawei Nexus 6p), National Instrument/Ettus USRP B210 as RF front-end, and 4 Linux-based PC running OAI eNodeB, OAI core network, Open vSwitch v2.7, and LL-MEC. The demonstration will be deployed in FDD SISO mode with 5MHz channel bandwidth. The target frequencies will be band 7 (Europe) radio environment. In the proposed demonstration, we will assess the following objectives.

- feasibility of low latency MEC framework based on SDN concept;
- ease of MEC application deployment at the network edge;
- gain in latency for content optimization use case.

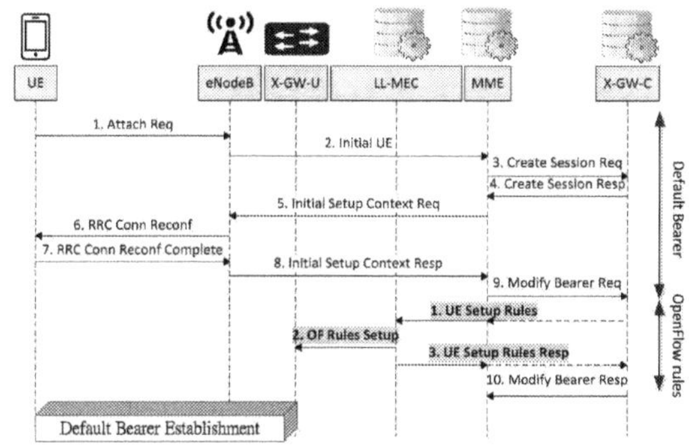

Figure 3: Sequence diagram of default bearers setup

3.1 Workflow to setup default bearers

Figure 3 shows the workflow of how an SDN-based mobile network operates and interacts with LL-MEC to handle UE initial attach procedures for bearers establishment. The main point of the sequence diagram starts from the message calls initiated all the way from X-GW-C through LL-MEC to X-GW-U. As soon as the UE is properly attached to the network with MME and X-GW-C knowing the GTP information, X-GW-C will initiate the procedure to transmit the UE information (*UE Setup Rules*) to LL-MEC and then based on the rules, LL-MEC is able to setup the OpenFlow rules (*OF Rules Setup*) in the corresponding switches. By introducing the concept of SDN into mobile network, the default bearer can be setup by configuring the OpenFlow rules when UE completes the initial attach procedure.

3.2 RAN-aware Content Optimization

As a showcase of mobile network slicing, RAN-aware content optimization is chosen as the representative use case to study the benefit of RAN information reported by the eNodeB on improving user quality of experience (QoE). For example, the application can monitor the cell load status and radio link quality in order to enforce a new resource allocation policy or change the content quality. In this work, we implement a video streaming over HTTP as one LL-MEC application and choose channel quality indicator (CQI) as a flag to reflect radio status of each UE. Besides, an Android video application developed in the context of one of the ETSI proof-of-concept[8] is utilized in this work in order to measure the uplink and downlink performance as well as the mean opinion score (MOS). When two UEs start the video streaming, LL-MEC has the ability to program the routing path so that the video application can be redirected to a relay server instead of the real server in Internet and further adapt the streaming rate according to the RAN status. In Table 1, we show the measurements of the maximum sustainable TCP bitrate of a video stream through the mapping between CQI index and bi-directional TCP throughput identified during experiments. Surely, CQI index is one of the meaningful parameters and any potential parameter can be involved easily to optimize video streaming and QoE.

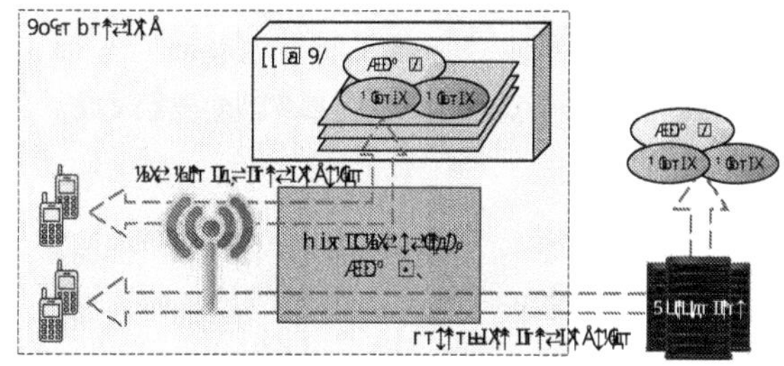

Figure 4: Video optimization setup schematic

Table 1: CQI index mapped as max TCP throughput

CQI	Downlink (Mb/s)	Uplink (Mb/s)
15	15.224	8.08
11	11.469	6.04
9	9.88	4.47
7	5.591	2.49
4	1.08	0.69

ACKNOWLEDGMENTS

Research and development leading to these results have received funding from the European Framework Program under H2020 grant agreement No. 671639 for the COHERENT project and No. 761913 for the SLICENET project.

REFERENCES

[1] Michael Till Beck, Sebastian Feld, Andreas Fichtner, Claudia Linnhoff-Popien, and Thomas Schimper. 2015. ME-VoLTE: Network functions for energy-efficient video transcoding at the mobile edge. In *Proceedings of the 18th International Conference on Intelligence in Next Generation Networks (ICIN 15')*.

[2] Mung Chiang and Tao Zhang. 2016. Fog and IoT: An Overview of Research Opportunities. *IEEE Internet of Things Journal* (2016).

[3] Xenofon Foukas, Navid Nikaein, Mohamed M. Kassem, Mahesh K. Marina, and Kimon Kontovasilis. 2016. FlexRAN: A Flexible and Programmable Platform for Software-Defined Radio Access Networks. In *Proceedings of the 12th International on Conference on Emerging Networking EXperiments and Technologies (CoNEXT '16)*.

[4] Anta Huang, Navid Nikaein, Tore Stenbock, Adlen Ksentini, and Christian Bonnet. 2017. Low Latency MEC Framework for SDN-based LTE/LTE-A Networks. In *Proceedinds of IEEE International Conference on Communications Conference (ICC '17)*.

[5] European Telecommunications Standards Institute. 2016. ETSI GS MEC 001-006 Mobile Edge Computing (MEC) Terminology. (2016).

[6] Xin Jin, Li Erran Li, Laurent Vanbever, and Jennifer Rexford. 2013. SoftCell: Scalable and Flexible Cellular Core Network Architecture. In *Proceedings of the Ninth ACM Conference on Emerging Networking Experiments and Technologies (CoNEXT '13)*.

[7] Navid Nikaein, Mahesh K. Marina, Saravana Manickam, Alex Dawson, Raymond Knopp, and Christian Bonnet. 2014. OpenAirInterface: A flexible platform for 5G research. *SIGCOMM Comput. Commun. Rev.* (2014).

[8] ETSI MEC Proof of Concept. 2016. Radio Aware Video Optimization in a Fully Virtualized Network. (2016). http://mecwiki.etsi.org/index.php?title=PoC_3_Radio_aware_video_optimization_in_a_fully_virtualized_network

Demo: BlueBee: 10,000x Faster Cross-Technology Communication from Bluetooth to ZigBee

Wenchao Jiang, Ruofeng Liu, Ling Liu†, Zhijun Li*, Tian He
jiang832@umn.edu,liu4189@umn.edu,liulingliuf@sjtu.edu.cn,lixx5427@umn.edu,tianhe@umn.edu
University of Minnesota, 200 Union Street SE, Minneapolis, MN, 55455

ABSTRACT

Cross-Technology Communication is an emerging research direction providing a promising solution to the coexistence problem of heterogeneous wireless technologies in the ISM bands. However, existing works use only the coarse-grained packet-level information for cross-technology modulation, suffering from a low throughput (e.g., 10bps). Our approach, called BlueBee, aims at achieving much higher CTC throughput thus extends CTC applications. We proposes a new direction by emulating legitimate ZigBee frames using a Bluetooth Low Energy (BLE) radio. Uniquely, BlueBee achieves dual-standard compliance (i.e., BLE and ZigBee) and transparency by selecting only the payload of Bluetooth frames, requiring neither hardware nor firmware changes at the BLE senders and ZigBee receivers. Our implementation on commodity device testbeds shows that BlueBee can achieve a more than 99% accuracy and a throughput 10,000x faster than the state-of-the-art CTC reported so far. Here we demonstrate using BlueBee on a smartphone to control several smart light bulbs attached with ZigBee radio.

KEYWORDS

Cross Technology Communication; Signal Emulation; Bluetooth Low Energy, ZigBee, Internet of Things

1 INTRODUCTION

The wireless devices under the Internet of Things (IoT) era, is anticipated to grow as large as 20 billion by 2020 [2]. The dense and heterogeneous network deployment inspires the study of the collaboration of heterogenous radios to reach beyond independent operation. For example, in ZiFi [5], ZigBee as a second radio can save huge amount of power consumed by power-hungry WiFi on mobile devices.

Deploying multi-radio gateways is a traditional way of communicating among heterogeneous devices. However, it suffers from several drawbacks including additional hardware cost, complicated network structure, and increased traffic overhead. In the literature, Cross-technology communication (CTC) provides light weight and promising solutions. CTC techniques commonly use packet-level modulations, where the combinations of timing [4] and durations [1]of packets convey the data. Despite their effectiveness, the bit rates are inherently limited as they adopt coarse-grained 'packets' as the basis for modulation. For example, the bit rate of BLE to ZigBee communication in the state of the art is limited to 18bps [4]. This not only constraints the usage, but also indicates spectrum inefficiency compared to 250kbps and 1Mbps if used for legacy ZigBee and Bluetooth.

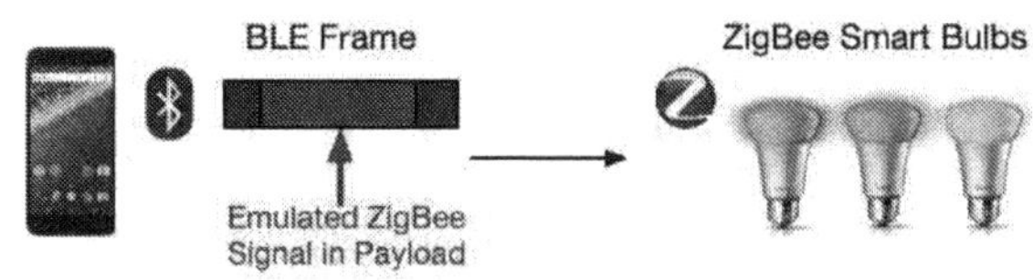

Figure 1: The system architecture of the BlueBee.

The BlueBee introduced in this paper is a practical CTC design via physical-layer emulation. As illustrated in Fig. 1, a legitimate ZigBee packet, including preamble, header, and payload, is fully encapsulated within a legitimate Bluetooth packet. In addition, the bit rate of the embedded ZigBee frame is the same as normal ZigBee frame, conceptually reaching 250*Kbps*. Note that such design is transparent to both the Bluetooth sender and ZigBee receiver. For the sender, the embedding of ZigBee frame is only by selecting the content (i.e., bytes) in the payload of a Bluetooth packet, without hardware or firmware change. For the receiver, a ZigBee receiver can not even notice it is an emulated packet due to the same ZigBee preamble, header, and payload as a normal ZigBee packet. BlueBee can be easily deployed on all kinds of commodity Bluetooth devices, including PCs, smartphones, and other Bluetooth IoT devices.

The direct communication from Bluetooth to ZigBee is surprising, because the bandwidth of Bluetooth (1MHz) is only half of that of ZigBee (2MHz). BlueBee makes it possible by two key technical insights: (i) similarity of (de)modulation techniques of Bluetooth and ZigBee and (ii) error tolerance of ZigBee demodulation (OQPSK/DSSS). More specifically, both Bluetooth and ZigBee signal can be demodulated through phase shifts, which is the phase difference between consecutive samples. In addition, BlueBee is optimally designed such that the emulation error is minimized and kept under the tolerance of ZigBee's OQPSK/DSSS modulation. Our experiments show that BlueBee can achieve a bit rate of 250kpbs at 90% frame reception ratio (FRR), 10,000 times faster than the state-of-art [4].

†Ling Liu is a visiting student at the University of Minnesota and officially affiliated with Shanghai Jiao Tong University, China.
*Zhijun Li is a visiting professor at the University of Minnesota and officially affiliated with Harbin Institute of Technology, China.

MobiCom '17, October 16–20, 2017, Snowbird, UT, USA

ACM ISBN 978-1-4503-4916-1/17/10
DOI: https://doi.org/10.1145/3117811.3119855

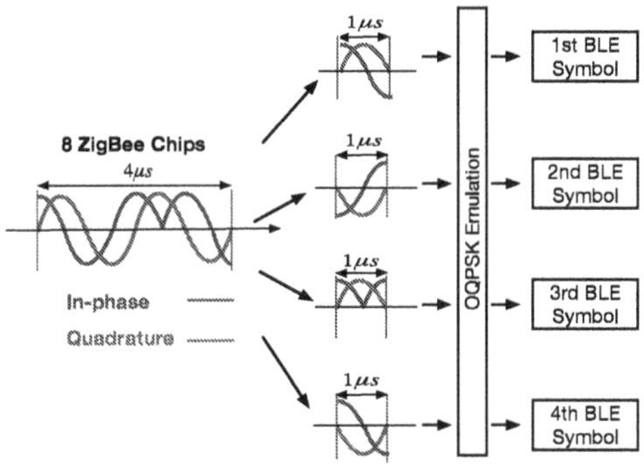

Figure 2: Emulating ZigBee with BLE

2 SYSTEM DESIGN

Here we introduce how we can use phase shift to establish CTC communication between Bluetooth, more strictly Bluetooth Low Energy (BLE), and ZigBee, as well as how ZigBee can tolerate inevitable errors due to incompatible bandwidth.

- **Signal Emulation** Here we will show how signal emulation works. According to the DSSS modulation, each 4-bit ZigBee symbol will be expanded to 32 chips, which lasts $16\mu s$. Without loss of generality, we only show 8 chips in Fig. 2. The time domain ZigBee signal will be cut into $1\mu s$ segments and one BLE symbol will be used to emulate each $1\mu s$ segment, denoted as OQPSK emulation.

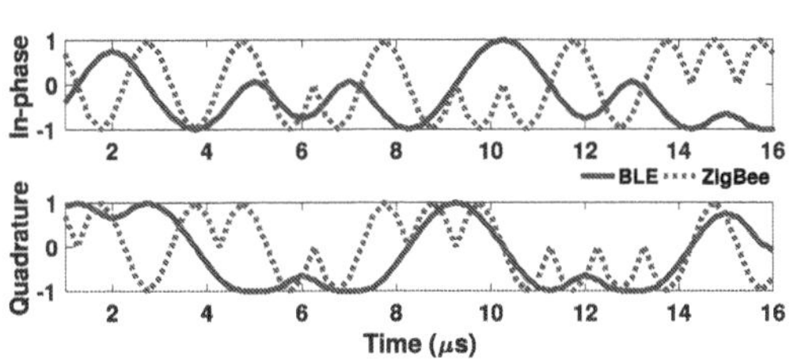

(a) Emulated signal in time domain

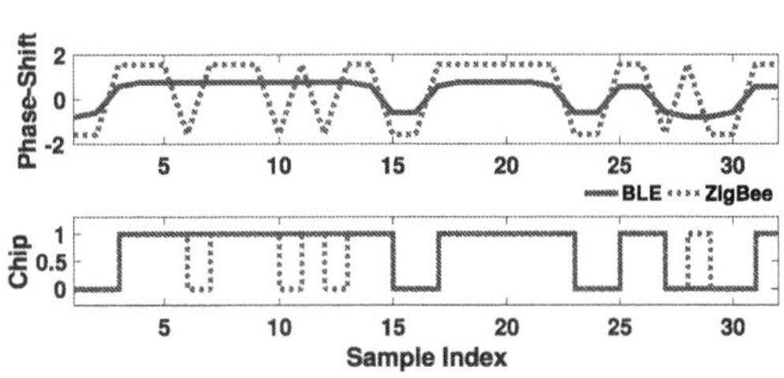

(b) Phase shifts and chips of emulated signal

Figure 3: Comparison between BLE emulated signal and the desired ZigBee signal

During the OQPSK emulation, we smartly choose the bytes of BLE payload so that the sign of the phase shift, the intrinsic nature of OQPSK (de)modulation, of the emulated signal is closest to that of the original signal. For exmaple Fig. 3a shows the time domain ZigBee signal and the constructed BLE signal in the In-phase and Quadrature signal. Although the time domain signals are quite different, their phase shifts and according decoded chips in Fig. 3b are quite similar. It shows the phase shifts of signal is intrinsic for signal emulaiton, even though the time-domain signals may be quite different.

- **Error Tolerance** Due to the narrow-band of BLE, there are some inevitable errors in signal emulation. However, the inevitable emulation error can be resolved by the error tolerance provided by ZigBee's DSSS modulation. In ZigBee's DSSS modulation, 4-bit symbol will be mapped to be 32 chips. We can still decode a ZigBee frame correctly if the number of erroroneous chips are within a default threshold of 12. We checked all the 4-bit symbols, and find the maximum number of chips in error is 8, fully tolerable by ZigBee's DSSS modulation. Note that the preamble of ZigBee frame consists of a constant string of some symbol "0"s followed by a symbol "7A" [3]. Since we are able to emulate *every* ZigBee symbol, we are able to emulate the whole ZigBee frame, including its preamble, header, and payload.

3 DEMO

For our demo, we will show a prototype BlueBee implementation on an off-the-shelf smartphone, i.e., Nexus 5X, with commodity BLE chips to control a smart bulb with commodity ZigBee chip. We developed an Android app to control the on/off, color, and brightness of multiple smart bulbs (up to 16), as shown in Fig. 4.

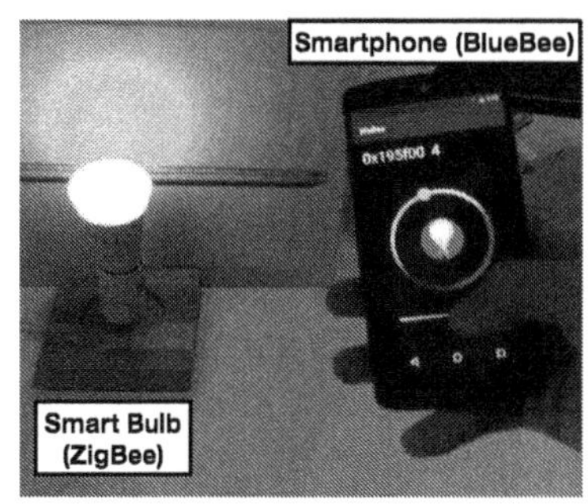

Figure 4: The demo of the BlueBee.

During the demo, the visitors are also able to try the demo by turning on/off the light bulbs and changing the color and brightness of the light bulbs from the Android app. They will immediately see the change they made.

The demo of controlling light bulbs is only an example. BlueBee has the potential of controlling all kinds of smart devices attached with ZigBee radio through the BLE radio on everyone's smartphone.

ACKNOWLEDGEMENT

This work was supported in part by the NSF CNS-1444021 and NSF CNS-1718456, and NSF China 61672196. We sincerely thank anonymous reviewers for their valuable comments and feedback.

REFERENCES

[1] Kameswari Chebrolu and Ashutosh Dhekne. 2009. Esense: communication through energy sensing. In *Proceedings MobiCom 2009*. ACM, 85–96.
[2] Inc Gartner. 2016. *Gartner Report*. Available at http://cloudtimes.org/2013/12/20/gartner-theinternet-of-things-will-grow-30-times-to-26-billion-by-2020/.
[3] Ieee802.org. 2012. IEEE 802.15.4. (2012).
[4] Song Min Kim and Tian He. 2015. FreeBee: Crosstechnology Communication via Free Sidechannel. In *MOBICOM, 2013 Proceedings ACM*.
[5] Ruogu Zhou, Yongping Xiong, Guoliang Xing, Limin Sun, and Jian Ma. 2010. ZiFi: wireless LAN disc overy via ZigBee interference signatures. In *Proceedings of MobiCom 2010*. ACM, 49–60.

Demo: Position Tracking for Virtual Reality Using Commodity WiFi

Manikanta Kotaru, Alexander Anemogiannis, Samuel Joseph, Sachin Katti
Stanford University
{mkotaru,anemogia,josamuel,skatti}@stanford.edu

ABSTRACT

Today, experiencing virtual reality (VR) is a cumbersome experience which either requires dedicated infrastructure like infrared cameras to track the headset and hand-motion controllers (*e.g.* Oculus Rift, HTC Vive), or provides only 3-DoF (Degrees of Freedom) tracking which severely limits the user experience (*e.g.* Samsung Gear VR). To truly enable VR everywhere, we need position tracking to be available as a ubiquitous service. This paper demonstrates WiCapture [5], a novel approach which leverages commodity WiFi infrastructure, which is ubiquitous today, for tracking purposes. We prototyped WiCapture using off-the-shelf WiFi radios and demonstrated that it achieves an accuracy of 0.88 cm compared to sophisticated infrared-based tracking systems like the Oculus Rift, while providing much higher range, resistance to occlusion, ubiquity and ease of deployment.

CCS CONCEPTS

• **Information systems → Location based services**; *Sensor networks; Global positioning systems*; • **Human-centered computing** → *Ubiquitous and mobile computing systems and tools*; • **Hardware** → *Emerging interfaces*;

KEYWORDS

Virtual reality; augmented reality; WiFi; positioning; indoor localization; OFDM; CSI

1 INTRODUCTION

Immersive experiences like virtual reality (VR) require accurate tracking of the headset and other accessories like hand-motion controllers. Current commercial VR systems like Oculus Rift [3] and HTC Vive [1] use outside-in tracking where the tracking is performed using infrastructure external to the VR accessories. The external infrastructure is specialized and typically uses infrared (IR) cameras along with sensors on the headset to perform the tracking. These systems are very accurate but have the following limitations:

- They require installing specialized hardware and dedicated infrastructure wherever user wants to experience VR. So if a user wishes to use VR headsets anywhere in her home, one would need IR cameras everywhere.

MobiCom '17, October 16–20, 2017, Snowbird, UT, USA

ACM ISBN 978-1-4503-4916-1/17/10.
https://doi.org/10.1145/3117811.3119865

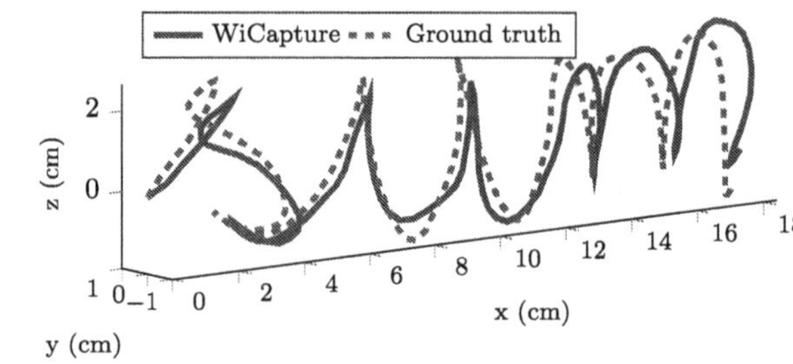

Figure 1: Solid blue path estimated by WiCapture is compared against the dotted red ground truth trajectory.

- These systems are not occlusion resistant. For example, if the camera is blocked by furniture or if the user turns away from the camera, then the tracking fails.
- These systems have limited range, typically around 2 m in front of the camera [4].

A competing technology to provide position tracking is inside-out position tracking found in systems like the Microsoft Hololens [2]. These systems use cameras (both RGB and depth sensing) and implement vision based tracking algorithms on the headset. These systems are both accurate and infrastructure-free; however they come with certain limitations. Specifically, they significantly increase the complexity of the headset since they require several cameras as well as complex algorithms running on the headset to provide tracking. Further they are not robust, tracking fails in environments with transparent or texture-less objects (*e.g.* a white wall) [6]. Finally and most importantly, these systems cannot be used for tracking peripherals such as hand-motion controllers; the complexity of inside-out tracking is too high to be implemented on such peripherals which are meant to be lightweight and cheap.

In this paper, we demonstrate WiCapture [5], a VR position tracking system which addresses the above limitations of existing systems. WiCapture is a WiFi based position tracking system. Headsets transmit standard WiFi packets which are received by standard WiFi access points (APs). Upon each packet reception, the APs obtain metadata called Channel State Information (CSI), which encodes the transformation that the environment has induced upon the transmitted WiFi signals. WiCapture employs novel algorithms that mine the CSI metadata to recover the position of the headset accurately. It has the following properties:

- WiCapture does not require special hardware, it uses commodity APs that can be bought in retail stores.
- WiCapture is occlusion resistant, it continues to work even when the APs and headsets are occluded due to furniture or other objects in between.

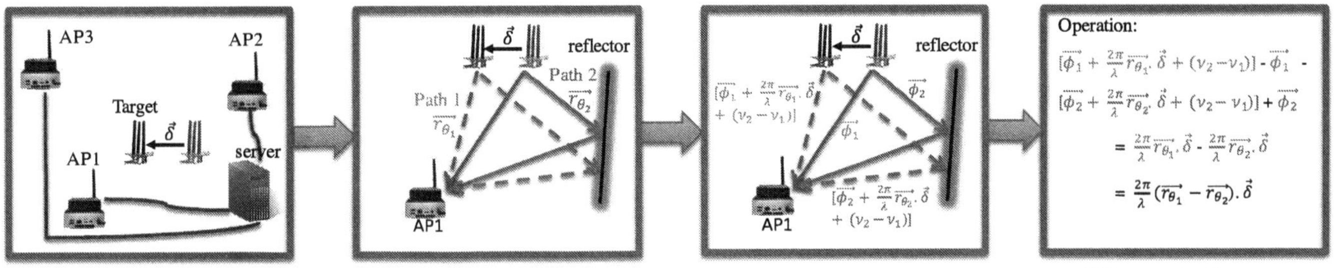

(a) Collect CSI from each AP and send it to a central server

(b) Resolve multipath

(c) Obtain the phase for each path for each packet

(d) Remove the distortion due to clock differences

Figure 2: Target moves by $\vec{\delta}$. The new position of the target is shown with solid target icon and the old position with shaded icon. In the first step, for each AP, WiCapture obtains unit vectors along the direction of departure of all the paths. Here, there are two paths, green and red paths, with directions $\vec{r}_{\theta_1}$ and $\vec{r}_{\theta_2}$. The paths for first packet are shown using solid lines and the paths for the second packet using dashed lines. Next, the phase of complex attenuation along both the paths for both the packets is calculated. Finally, the effect of frequency offset on the phase values, $\nu_2 - \nu_1$, is removed to obtain equations dependent on just $\vec{r}_{\theta_1}$, $\vec{r}_{\theta_2}$ and $\vec{\delta}$, which can be solved to estimate $\vec{\delta}$.

- WiCapture has larger range and operates across rooms.
- It is insensitive to room illumination or texture and it can work in the dark. Further, headset complexity is minimal, all the headset needs is a standard WiFi chip.

2 OVERVIEW

At a high level, WiCapture obtains the change in the position of the transmitter by using the change in the phase of the CSI between packets. The phase is distorted due to the signal received from reflectors; this phenomenon is called multipath propagation. The phase of WiFi signal is also distorted due to the lack of synchronization of clocks at the WiFi transmitter and receiver. WiCapture tackles these challenges using novel algorithms that compensate for these distortions and provides accurate phase measurement which in turn enables accurate position tracking. WiCapture's algorithm to track the position of a target that moves in an environment with two propagation paths is illustrated in Fig. 2.

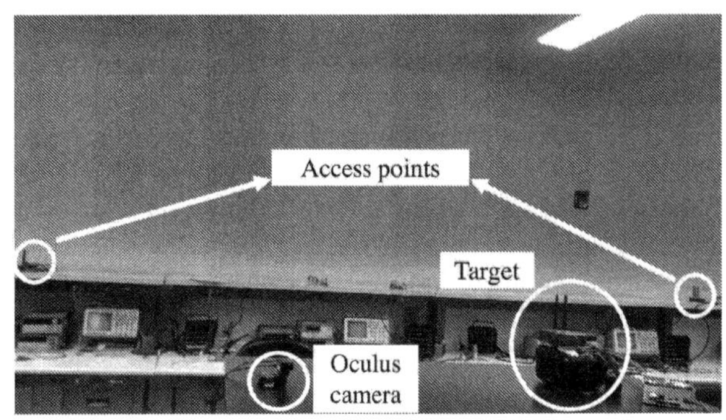

Figure 3: Typical deployment with two access points tracking a target WiFi device. The target WiFi device is mounted on a Oculus headset and a Oculus camera is placed in front of the headset to compare WiCapture's performance against that of Oculus DK2.

3 DEMONSTRATION

In this demonstration, we will show a prototype implemented using commodity Intel 5300 WiFi chips. The target device is tracked by using two access points. Each access point is equipped with Intel 5300 WiFi chip and collects CSI for the WiFi packets transmitted from the target device. All the WiFi chips operate in 5 GHz WiFi spectrum and use 40 MHz bandwidth. The target has a 3-antenna circular array, and the access points have a three-antenna uniform linear array with adjacent antennas separated by 2.6 cm both at the transmitter and the receiver. CSI is calculated once every 6 ms. So, position is estimated at an update rate of 167 Hz. Fig. 3 shows a typical deployment. Our prototype demonstrated a precision of 0.25 mm and position tracking error of 0.88 cm [5].

WiCapture's current prototype however has two limitations compared to existing systems. It has higher latency since the tracking is computed in the network and then provided as an update to the headset. Second, it is less accurate than current outside-in position tracking systems. Nonetheless, we believe that WiCapture's accuracy is acceptable for VR, especially considering the significant benefits that WiCapture provides around deployment, coverage and occlusion resistance.

ACKNOWLEDGMENTS

Manikanta Kotaru was supported by Thomas and Sarah Kailath Stanford Graduate Fellowship.

REFERENCES

[1] HTC Vive. https://www.vive.com/. Accessed: November 2016.
[2] Microsoft Hololens. https://www.microsoft.com/microsoft-hololens/. Accessed: November 2016.
[3] Oculus Rift. https://www.oculus.com/. Accessed: November 2016.
[4] Why virtual reality is not (just) the next big platform, Michael Abrash and Dov Katz of Oculus VR. https://www.youtube.com/watch?v=dxbh-TM5yNc. Accessed: November 2016.
[5] M. Kotaru and S. Katti. Position Tracking for Virtual Reality Using Commodity WiFi. In *The IEEE Conference on Computer Vision and Pattern Recognition (CVPR)*, July 2017.
[6] A. Yates and J. Selan. Positional tracking systems and methods, May 2016.

Demo: Ultra-Low Power Gaze Tracking for Virtual Reality

Tianxing Li, Emmanuel S. Akosah, Qiang Liu, and Xia Zhou
Department of Computer Science, Dartmouth College, Hanover, NH
tianxing@cs.dartmouth.edu,emmanuel.s.akosah.19@dartmouth.edu,{qliu,xia}@cs.dartmouth.edu

CCS CONCEPTS

•Computer systems organization → Embedded systems;

KEYWORDS

Gaze tracking; virtual reality; visible light sensing

1 EXTENDED ABSTRACT

Our work in this extended abstract focuses on a feature crucial to Virtual Reality (VR): gaze tracking, i.e., determining user's eye fixation direction. Not only does gaze tracking allow users to interact with the content just by glances, it also can greatly improve user's visual experience, reduce VR sickness, and save systems (display) energy. The energy saving can be achieved by foveated rendering [7, 10], which progressively reduces image details outside the eye fixation region. Such energy saving is particularly beneficial for mobile VR headsets, where the display is powered by a smartphone.

The dominating methodology to gaze tracking relies on (infrared) cameras, often accompanied by infrared (IR) LEDs to illuminate eyes. The combination of IR LEDs and cameras raises concern on energy consumption and form factor. Recent hardware advances have led to modular designs of eye tracker that can be included to mobile and wearable devices. These commercial eye trackers (e.g., Tobii), however, are still expensive (e.g., $10K for integrating Tobii eye tracker into a VR headset) and power-hungry (requiring external battery pack). As a result, most VR headsets today are shy away from integrating gaze tracking and resort to head direction as a coarse, often incorrect, estimate of user's gaze.

We seek a low-power, low-cost approach that can lower the barrier to integrate gaze tracking into various VR headsets including those for mobile VR. We consider a minimalist sensing approach, which eliminates active IR LEDs and replaces cameras with a few low-cost ($2 each), small (e.g., < 2 mm) photodiodes. Exploiting the fact that VR screen light is the sole and constant light source within the space of a VR headset, we reuse screen light to track user gaze. Specifically, we place a few (e.g., 16) photodiodes at the boundary of each VR lens (Figure 1), so that each photodiode senses screen light reflected by user's eyeball in certain direction. Given that our pupil is a hole in the iris center and absorbs incoming light rays, when screen light strikes the pupil region, most light rays are absorbed from the photodiode's point of view, weakening reflected light perceived by photodiodes in that direction. Thus,

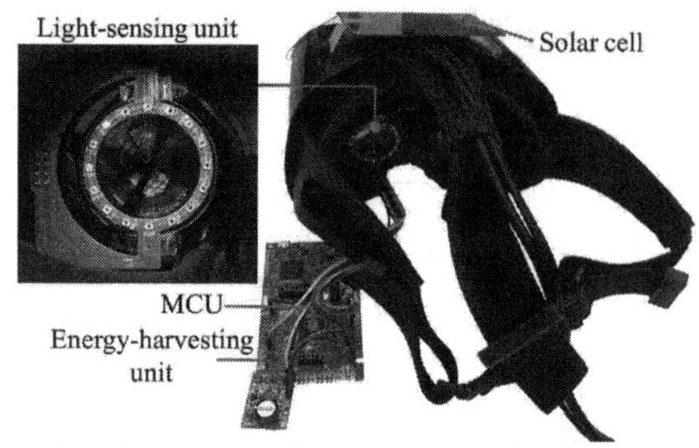

Figure 1: LiGaze integrated into a FOVE VR headset. LiGaze uses only passive photodiodes on a light-sensing unit to track user gaze. It can be powered by a solar cell harvesting energy from indoor lighting.

pupil position affects the spatial pattern of changes in reflected screen light. Such pattern can be exploited to infer gaze direction.

Although pupil's light absorption has been exploited by prior methods [5, 8], we face unique challenges in VR, mainly because of the uncontrolled nature of our light source (screen light). VR screen content is colorful and dynamic, resulting in screen light and reflected screen light that are spatially nonuniform and time-varying. Such inherent variations make it hard to identify reflected light changes related to pupil position. Furthermore, even with identified changes related to pupil position, inferring a 3D gaze vector is challenging given user diversity. Our experiments show eye and skin characteristics all affect the actual impact of pupil's light absorption on sensed reflected light. The gaze tracking algorithm needs to be customized for individual users. Additionally, blink can interfere with the sensing of reflected light and gaze tracking.

To address these challenges, we design LiGaze. The core of LiGaze is to estimate reflected light changes associated with screen content and then identify changes caused by pupil movement. To do so, we design a dual-side sensing circuit board with photodiodes embedded back to back on both sides, where one side faces the screen sensing incoming screen light in different directions and the other faces user's eyeball sensing reflected screen light. We characterize the relationship between the front and back sensors' readings assuming a center pupil. This characterization is then used to derive features related to changes of reflected light caused by pupil position. We leverage supervised learning (boosted trees [3, 6]) to learn the correlation between our features and the 3D gaze vector, and infer gaze vectors on the fly using regression. To deal with user diversity, we calibrate our characterization and apply bootstrap aggregating [2] atop boosted trees to allow quick adjustment of the trained model for a specific user. Furthermore, LiGaze detects blinks in a parallel process. Considering that a blink causes most photodiodes observing similar changes in reflected light, LiGaze leverages this spatial correlation to detect blink occurrence.

MobiCom '17, October 16–20, 2017, Snowbird, UT, USA.
 ISBN 978-1-4503-4916-1/17/10.
DOI: https://doi.org/10.1145/3117811.3119866

2 LIGAZE DESIGN

Based on photodiode data coming on the fly, LiGaze infers 3D gaze vectors represented as normalized 3D vectors. Next we first introduce our estimation of reflected screen light under a center pupil. We then describe our learning algorithm for gaze inference and the mechanism for blink detection.

2.1 Estimating Reflected Screen Light

Given N photodiodes on each side of the annulus sensing panel, we seek to model the relationship between screen light sensed by N front photodiodes (facing the screen) and the reflected screen light sensed by N back photodiodes (facing the eye), given an fixed pupil location (center). This relationship characterizes the impact of the reflections occurred after screen light rays strike the eyeball.

Interestingly, a strong linear correlation commonly exists between back photodiode in direction d and front photodiode in direction d' that is diagonally opposite to d. Front photodiodes in directions other than d' are also correlated with back sensor in direction d, and the correlation becomes weaker for front photodiodes further away from direction d'. Take the top-right (TR) back photodiode as an example, its perceived reflected light has the strongest linear correlation ($r = 0.91$) with that at the bottom-left (BL) front photodiode. For front photodiodes further away from BL, the correlation gradually decreases. This observation suggests that reflected light intensity is dominated by specular reflections (possibly due to eyeball's glossy surface), which direct each incoming screen light ray to a coplanar direction diagonally opposite to its incident direction. Diffuse reflections, on the other hand, scatter a light ray in a broad range of directions. Although they also contribute to the reflected light intensity perceived by a back photodiode, diffused light rays are much weaker and thus play a much less significant role.

Given the linearity of light transport [9] (i.e., contributions of individual light rays add up at a receiver location), we consider to model the relationship between back and front photodiodes' readings as a simple linear relation. Similar linear models have also been applied in prior works [4, 11, 9] in computer graphics and vision. Specifically, let $\mathcal{I}$ be the vector of N front photodiodes' readings. Assuming a center pupil, the estimated back photodiodes' readings, denoted as vector $\widetilde{\mathcal{R}}$, can be written as:

$$\widetilde{\mathcal{R}} = \mathbb{W} \cdot \mathcal{I}, \tag{1}$$

where $\mathbb{W}$ is a $N \times N$ weight matrix: $\mathbb{W} = \{w_{ij} | i, j \in [1, N]\}$. w_{ij} indicates the contribution of incoming light intensity $\mathcal{I}_j$ perceived by front photodiode j to the estimated reflected light $\widetilde{R}_i$ perceived by back photodiode i.

The weight matrix $\mathbb{W}$ can differ across users based on their eye and skin characteristics. Subtle offset of the headset to the eyes can also affect screen light's reflections and thus $\mathbb{W}$. To deal with user diversity and headset offsets, we determine $\mathbb{W}$ using a calibration phase (5 minutes) when a user first puts on the VR headset. During the calibration, the user is instructed to stare at a small white box on screen center while the rest of the screen is displaying video or various images. The readings of all front and back photodiodes are then used to calculate $\mathbb{W}$ using linear regression. Specifically, let $\mathcal{R}$ be the vector of measured back photodiodes' readings, we are seeking $\mathbb{W}$ that leads to the estimated vector best matching the measurement R:

$$\mathbb{W} = \underset{\mathbb{W}'}{\operatorname{argmin}} ||\mathcal{R} - \widetilde{\mathcal{R}}(\mathbb{W}')||^2. \tag{2}$$

With the calibrated $\mathbb{W}$, upon real-time readings $\mathcal{I}$ from front photodiodes, we can then estimate on the fly reflected light at each back photodiode using Eq. (1), assuming pupil is in the center.

2.2 Gaze Inference

The next step of LiGaze is to extract features related to pupil position and infer a 3D gaze vector. Given incoming screen light, our model in § 2.1 estimates the reflected light that each back photodiode would perceive if pupil is in the center. Thus, the difference between this estimate and the measured reflected light is caused by the offset between the actual pupil position and the center. Specifically, we consider normalized change, since the actual amount of change in reflected light can depend on the level of reflected light intensity. Hence, let $\mathcal{R} = \{R_1, ..., R_N\}$ denote the vector of measured reflected light at N back photodiodes, we compute $f_i = R_i/\widetilde{R}_i$ for each photodiode, and use the resulting set $\mathcal{F} = \{f_1, ..., f_N\}$ as the feature vector for later gaze inference.

We infer gaze using supervised learning. In particular, we choose boosted trees (or tree ensemble) [3, 6], which represent the relationship between features and prediction values as a set of regression trees. Here each tree is similar to a decision tree but differs in that it associates a weight to each leaf (i.e., decision). By summing the predictions of multiple trees, boosted trees improve the reliability and accuracy of the final prediction. Another important benefit is its lightweight computation. Once the tree ensemble is trained, online regression involves only comparison operations. Thus it is fast and entails low power, which is critical for real-time execution in low-power micro-controller.

2.3 Blink Detection

LiGaze detects a blink event based on a simple observation: when a blink occurs, the reflected light intensity around the eye experiences similar pulse changes in most directions. We observe that reflected light intensity in three directions exhibit similar pulse changes during a blink. When the eye is closed, the pupil is covered by the eyelid, which reflects light rays better than pupil. When the eye is opened, pupil continues absorbing incoming light rays, which decreases the reflected light intensity around the eye. Since the eyelash can block some light rays between the eyeball and photodiodes, this pulse change is not significant at the top photodiode. However, a blink still leads to noticeable patterns in most photodiodes. Thus, by counting the number of photodiodes concurrently perceiving pulses of reflected light intensity, we can detect the occurrence of blink.

3 LIGAZE PROTOTYPE

We build a LiGaze prototype using off-the-shelf hardware and attach it to an existing VR headset (FOVE). The prototype contains three main components:

Light-Sensing Unit. We design and fabricate a thin (0.8 mm), ring-shaped PCB (Figure 2(a)) that hosts 16 photodiodes (OPT3001)

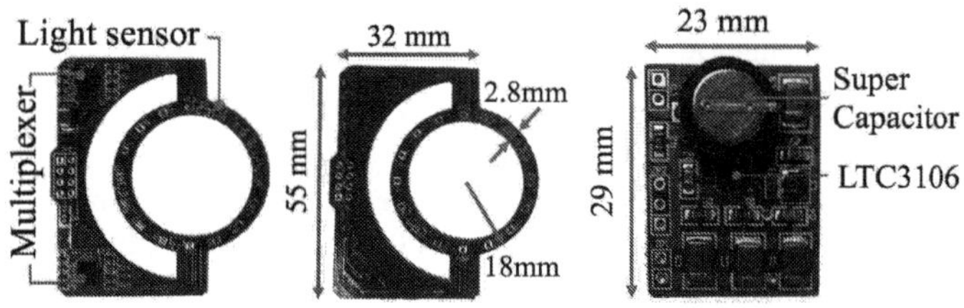

(a) Light-sensing unit (front and back) (b) Energy-harvesting Unit

Figure 2: Fabricated PCBs in LiGaze prototype.

on each side and their associated circuits (e.g., resistors, capacitors). The photodiode is 1.9 mm × 1.25 mm in size, so the PCB ring is narrow in width (2 mm), avoiding to affect user's view. The ring diameter is 36 mm, customized to fit the lens of the FOVE headset.

Photodiodes transmit raw data to a micro-controller through a hardware Inter-Integrated Circuit (I2C) interface at the clock of 400 kHz. Given that OPT3001 allows up to 4 serial bus addresses, one hardware I2C can only differentiate up to 4 photodiodes. To support fetching data from 32 (16 front and 16 back) photodiodes, we design a switch using two 4-channel analog multiplexers (74HC4052). The switch divides 32 photodiodes into 8 groups and lets each group transmit data to the micro-controller in turn. The switch consumes less than 2 μW, which is 1.5 times more energy-efficient than software simulation I2C interface for supporting the 32 sensors. The switch and its associated circuit are integrated in a side PCB board connecting to the PCB ring. The arc gap allows the rim of the VR lens to fit in.

Micro-Controller. The micro-controller periodically wakes up to receive data from photodiodes, computes the feature vector related to pupil position, and runs our gaze inference algorithm to derive the current 3D gaze vector. We choose MSP432 because of its ultra-low power according to the power benchmark ULPBench [1]. ULPBench is from the embedded micro-processor benchmark consortium (EEMBC) and is a standard way to compare power performance on micro-controllers.

Energy-Harvesting Unit. To demonstrate the ultra-low power of our system, we add a credit-card sized solar cell (AM-1816) atop the headset, which harvests energy from indoor lighting to power the entire system (sensing and computation). AM-1816 is a amorphous silicon solar cell and is sensitive only to visible light (wavelengths from 400 nm to 700 nm). Therefore, it is ideal for harvesting indoor light. We use a buck-boost DC/DC converter (LTC3016) to maintain the output voltage at 4V, which maximizes the output power at varying light conditions (e.g., 200 - 800 lux).

4 DEMO OVERVIEW

Our demo comprises two parts. In the first part, participants will wear our prototype (Figure 1) to experience a simple virtual reality scene and test our gaze tracking system. In the second part, the presenter will demonstrate the gaze tracking performance in complex virtual content using calibration data and a personalized model.

To present the demo, we need a table to place a desktop machine and a monitor. We need 2 m^2 space to let participants try our testbed. A chair is needed for the participants when they wear our headset. We also need a power cord to power the desktop and the monitor. The total setup time is about 15 – 20 minutes.

REFERENCES

[1] ULPBench. http://www.eembc.org/ulpbench/.
[2] Breiman, L. Bagging predictors. *Machine Learning 24*, 2 (1996), 123–140.
[3] Chen, T., and Guestrin, C. Xgboost: A scalable tree boosting system. In *Proceedings of the 22Nd ACM SIGKDD International Conference on Knowledge Discovery and Data Mining* (2016), ACM, pp. 785–794.
[4] Debevec, P., Hawkins, T., Tchou, C., Duiker, H.-P., Sarokin, W., and Sagar, M. Acquiring the reflectance field of a human face. In *Proc. of SIGGRAPH* (2000).
[5] Ebisawa, Y., and i. Satoh, S. Effectiveness of pupil area detection technique using two light sources and image difference method. In *Proc. of the 15th Annual International Conference of the IEEE Engineering in Medicine and Biology Societ* (1993), pp. 1268–1269.
[6] Friedman, J. H. Greedy function approximation: a gradient boosting machine. *Annals of statistics* (2001), 1189–1232.
[7] Guenter, B., Finch, M., Drucker, S., Tan, D., and Snyder, J. Foveated 3D Graphics. *ACM Trans. Graph. 31*, 6 (Nov. 2012).
[8] Morimoto, C., Koons, D., Amir, A., and Flickner, M. Pupil detection and tracking using multiple light sources. *Image and Vision Computing 18*, 4 (2000), 331 - 335.
[9] O'Toole, M. *Optical Linear Algebra for Computational Light Transport.* PhD thesis, University of Toronto, 2016.
[10] Patney, A., Salvi, M., Kim, J., Kaplanyan, A., Wyman, C., Benty, N., Luebke, D., and Lefohn, A. Towards foveated rendering for gaze-tracked virtual reality. *ACM Trans. Graph. 35*, 6 (Nov. 2016).
[11] Sen, P., Chen, B., Garg, G., Marschner, S. R., Horowitz, M., Levoy, M., and Lensch, H. P. A. Dual photography. In *Proc. of SIGGRAPH* (2005).

Demo: WEBee: Physical-Layer Cross-Technology Communication via Emulation

Zhijun Li*, Zhimeng Yin, Ling Liu†, Ruofeng Liu, Tian He
lixx5427@umn.edu,yinxx283@umn.edu,liulingliuf@sjtu.edu.cn,liu4189@umn.edu,tianhe@umn.edu
University of Minnesota, 200 Union Street SE, Minneapolis, MN, 55455

ABSTRACT

The applicability of existing Cross-Technology Communication (CTC) methods, which rely on packet-level modulation, is severely limited due to their very low throughput, e.g., tens of bps. Our work, named as WEBee, opens a promising direction for high throughput CTC via physical-level emulation. Specifically, WEBee synthesizes the time-domain signals by choosing appropriate frequency-domain components fed into the subcarriers of WiFi OFDM. WEBee can emulate the desired physical-layer ZigBee signals by manipulating only the data bits in WiFi packet payload, requiring neither hardware nor firmware changes in commodity technologies. Moreover, WEBee enables the parallel CTC, where one WiFi frame emulates two ZigBee frames simultaneously. To evaluate the performance, we implemented WEBee on commodity devices (the Atheros AR2425 WiFi card, BCM 4330 WiFi card and CC2420, CC2530 ZigBee devices). Our comprehensive evaluation reveals that WEBee can achieve the CTC between WiFi and ZigBee with a reliable throughput of 126Kbps in noisy environment, 16,000x faster than current state-of-the-art CTC methods.

CCS CONCEPTS

•**Networks** →Wireless Networks;

KEYWORDS

Cross Technology Communication; Signal Emulation; WiFi, ZigBee, Internet of Things

1 INTRODUCTION

According to Gartner[3], the number of Internet of Things (IoT) devices connected wirelessly will reach 20 billion by 2020. To connect these devices, different wireless technologies, such as Wi-Fi, ZigBee, Bluetooth Low Energy, etc., are utilized due to the specific requirements of IoT applications, and the unique features of wireless communication. As a result, the ISM band will experience a severe coexisting problem among these heterogeneities.

*Zhijun Li is a visiting professor at the University of Minnesota and officially affiliated with Harbin Institute of Technology, China.

†Ling Liu is a visiting student at the University of Minnesota and officially affiliated with Shanghai Jiao Tong University, China.

MobiCom '17, October 16–20, 2017, Snowbird, UT, USA

ACM ISBN 978-1-4503-4916-1/17/10.
https://doi.org/10.1145/3117811.3119859

However, the coexistence also provides new opportunities for improving the performance when different wireless technologies cooperate. For example, ZiFi[6] can significantly reduce the energy consumption of WiFi by adding one low-power ZigBee radio, and only waking up the WiFi card when necessary. To enable such cooperations, the communication among heterogeneous wireless devices is necessary.

Although a multi-radio gateway can bridge these wireless technologies, it introduces extra hardware cost, deployment complexity and the doubled traffic overhead. To avoid these drawbacks, a few pioneering works [1, 2, 4, 5] have proposed cross-technology communication (CTC) to enable *direct* communication (i.e., message/data exchange) among heterogeneous wireless devices by utilizing the packet-level modulation. However, these methods have a severe throughput limitation, since one packet can only modulate a few bits. As the state-of-the art, FreeBee [4] offers a throughput of only around 10bps with the side channel.

In this paper, we introduce a new direction for high-throughput CTC, a physical-level emulation technique named WEBee (for WiFi Emulated ZigBee). The basic architecture of WEBee is illustrated as Fig. 1. At the Wi-Fi sender, WEBee chooses the payload of a WiFi frame and transmits this frame through the commercial Wi-Fi chip. At the receiver, the commodity ZigBee devices recognize a portion of this WiFi frame as ZigBee physical-layer signals and demodulate it as a *legitimate* ZigBee frame.

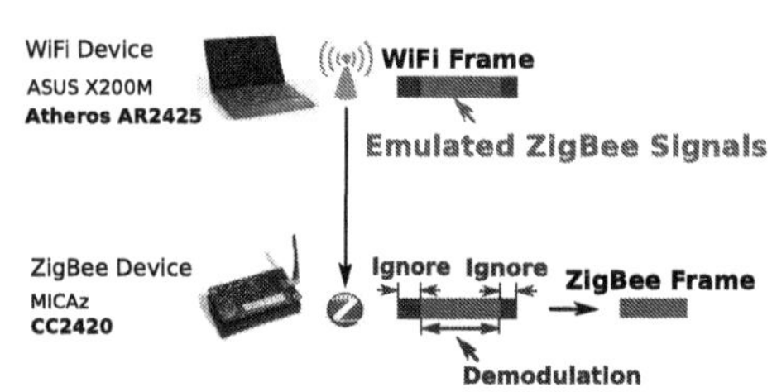

Figure 1: The system architecture of the WEBee.

In a nutshell, WEBee utilizes a Wi-Fi frame to emulate the ZigBee time-domain waveform closely, so that WEBee inherently provides much higher throughput capability other than previous packet-level emulation methods, where one CTC symbol is represented by several WiFi packets. To evaluate the performance, we implement WEBee on commodity devices, such as Atheros AR2425 WiFi card, and MicaZ nodes with CC2420 chip. Detailed experiments across various aspects demonstrate WEBee's high throughput, where WEBee achieves a throughput of 63Kbps data rate at a 99% reliability, 8,000x faster than the state-of-the-art (7.5bps@99%) [4]. In addition, WEBee is able to successfully emulate two ZigBee frames at different frequencies within a single WiFi frame, resulting in a 16,000x throughput and a much higher spectrum efficiency.

2 OVERVIEW OF WEBEE

This section presents the overview of WEBee, including the emulation path and the transmission path in Fig. 2. In the emulation path, first step of WEBee is to emulate the time-domain waveform of the legitimate ZigBee packet. This is done via the "Post-QAM Emulation" module, which computes the corresponding frequency-domain signals, i.e., the QAM constellation points in Wi-Fi OFDOM modulation. After this, the second step is to retrieve the coded bits which activate the computed QAM points via the "QAM Emulation". The final step is called "Channel Coding Emulation", where WEBee obtains the source bits matched with the coded bits, and synthesizes the corresponding WiFi frame.

For the transmission procedure, when this Wi-Fi frame is transmitted by commercial Wi-Fi cards, the source bits in the *selected* WiFi payload determine the specific coded bits in channel coding. After that, these coded bits activate the wanted QAM constellation points via QAM modulation. As a result, these frequency-domain points will generate the desired time-domain signals (i.e., ZigBee waveforms) through IFFT, while the commodity ZigBee devices demodulate these waveforms as a legitimate ZigBee frame.

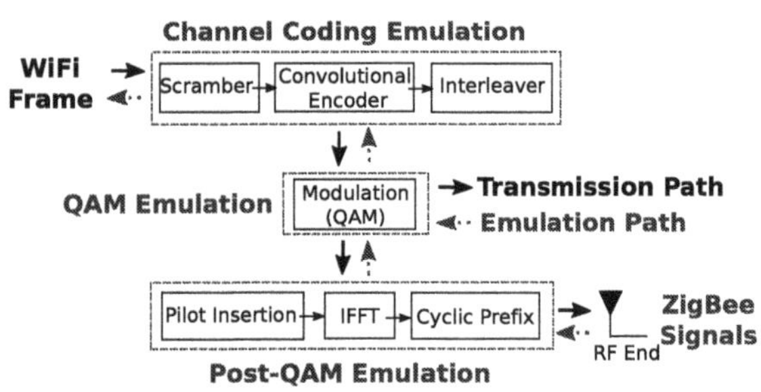

Figure 2: The Complete Procedure of WEBee Emulation.

3 EVALUATION & DEMO

We implement WEBee on commodity devices, such as Atheros AR2425 WiFi card, and MICAz motes without changing the hardware nor firmware. To evaluate its performance, test WEBee at various sites: a laboratory room, a hallway, and an outdoor site (Fig. 3). We evaluate the throughput of WEBee in hallway site and outdoor site, which is between 56Kbps and 68Kbps from 10 to 80 meters with 99% reliability (Fig. 4 and Fig. 5). In addition, WEBee performs stably in many scenarios, including mobile environments, low-duty-cycle receivers, etc.

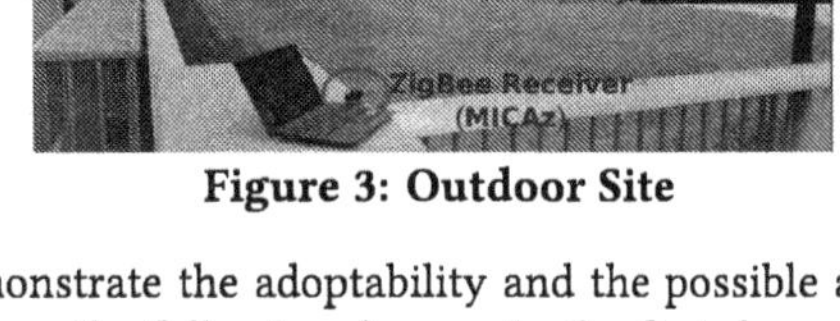

Figure 3: Outdoor Site

To demonstrate the adoptability and the possible applications, we introduce the following demos. In the first demo in Fig.6, we build WEBee on the following commodity devices, such as ASUS laptop equipped with a WiFi card Atheros AR2425, and MICAz.

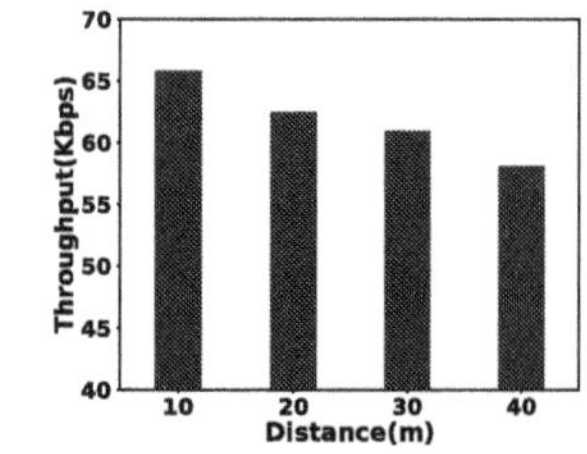

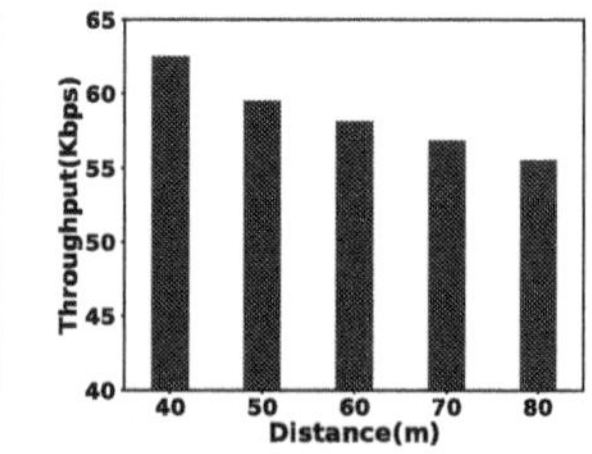

Figure 4: Frame Reception Ratio with Dist. (Hallway) **Figure 5: Frame Reception Ratio with Dist. (Outdoor)**

In the WiFi transmitter, we build a software to inject WEBee (i.e., WiFi) frames from the WiFi card. In commodity ZigBee receiver, a listening process based on TinyOS is used to capture and display the demodulated ZigBee packets.

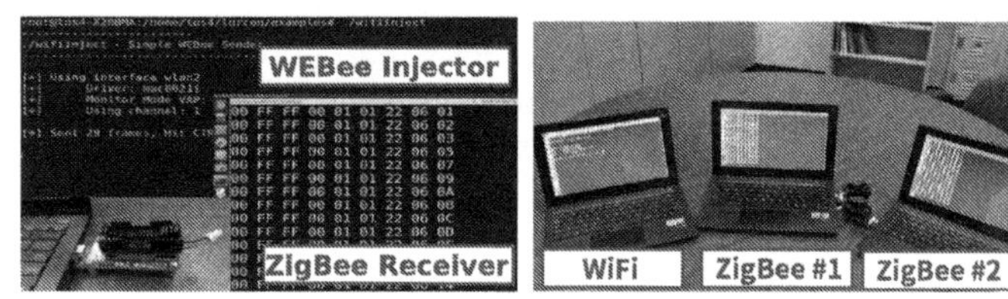

(a) unicast CTC communication (b) parallel CTC communication

Figure 6: Demo of WEBee Communication

We also demonstrate the WEBee used in real-life settings as Fig. 7. Specifically, we implement a WEBee in a LG Nexus 5 smart phone equipped with a Broadcom BCM4330 WiFi chip. ZigBee chip embedded in the light bulb receives the emulated ZigBee frame and turn on/off bulbs accordingly.

Figure 7: Demo of WEBee Light Bulb Control

ACKNOWLEDGEMENT

This work was supported in part by the NSF CNS-1444021, NSF CNS-1718456 and NSF China 61672196. We sincerely thank anonymous reviewers for their valuable comments and feedback.

REFERENCES

[1] K. Chebrolu and A. Dhekne. 2009. Esense: communication through energy sensing. In *In Mobicom*.
[2] Zicheng Chi, Yan Li, Hongyu Sun, Yao Yao, Zheng Lu, and Ting Zhu. 2016. B2W2: N-Way Concurrent Communication for IoT Devices. In *Sensys*. ACM.
[3] Inc Gartner. 2016. *Gartner Report*. Available at urlhttp://cloudtimes.org/2013/12/20/gartner-theinternet-of-things-will-grow-30-times-to-26-billion-by-2020/.
[4] Song Min Kim and Tian He. 2015. FreeBee: Cross-technology Communication via Free Side-channel. In *In Mobicom*.
[5] Zhimeng Yin, Wenchao Jiang, Song Min Kim, and Tian He. 2017. C-Morse: Cross-technology Communication with Transparent Morse Coding. In *INFOCOM 2017*.
[6] Ruogu Zhou, Yongping Xiong, Guoliang Xing, Limin Sun, and Jian Ma. [n. d.]. ZiFi: wireless LAN discovery via ZigBee interference signatures. In *Proceedings of Mobicom 2010*.

Demo: Towards Flexible and Scalable Indoor Navigation

Zhuqi Li
Peking University
lizhuqi@pku.edu.cn

Yuanchao Shu
Microsoft Research
yuanchao.shu@microsoft.com

Börje F. Karlsson
Microsoft Research
borje.karlsson@microsoft.com

Yiyong Lin
Microsoft Research
yiyolin@microsoft.com

Thomas Moscibroda
Microsoft Research
moscitho@microsoft.com

ABSTRACT

Bootstrapping efforts and scalability issues hinder large-scale deployment of indoor navigation systems. We present FollowUs, an easily-deployable (bootstrap-free) and scalable indoor navigation system. In addition to robust navigation through real-time trace-following, FollowUs integrates cloud services to process and combine traces at large scale. It can also leverage optional floor plans to further enhance navigation performance. We designed and implemented FollowUs, including a mobile app and cloud services on Azure, and validate its real-world usability.

KEYWORDS

Navigation; indoor; cloud; app; trace; map; scalability; flexibility

1 INTRODUCTION

Despite years of research attention, localization-based indoor navigation has not found wide-spread practical use, largely due to the high burden on deployment and bootstrapping. They are usually built upon full-fledge indoor localization systems, which rely on specialized infrastructure (e.g. beacons) or incur high bootstrap costs. On the contrary, recently proposed lightweight peer-to-peer navigation systems promise easy and incremental deployment, without the need for extra infrastructure or maps. Despite these promising advantages, peer-to-peer navigation suffers from poor scalability and flexibility as navigation is only possible over pre-collected leader paths.

In this demonstration, we present FollowUs, a new end-to-end indoor navigation system that combines the advantages of both localization-based and peer-to-peer navigation with increased flexibility and scalability. As in typical peer-to-peer navigation, users can walk along a path, share it with others and follow paths shared by others via a mobile client. During the navigation, FollowUs can provide timely instructions to help user walk from starting point to destination by synchronizing magnetic sequence between leader trace and follower trace. FollowUs also incorporates an intelligent cloud service to the lightweight navigation application to parse and combine ("stitch together") traces at scale. Based on the analysis of motion events and the matching results between sensor signals, FollowUs is able to split, concatenate, and generate new traces according to users' searching input. In addition, FollowUs can incrementally build the indoor trace graph and improve its quality with optional floor plan. In a nutshell, FollowUs can scale both horizontally — reaching as many users as possible without requiring much effort of them — as well as vertically by efficiently computing new paths from traces shared by users.

MobiCom'17, October 16–20, 2017, Snowbird, UT, USA.
 ISBN 978-1-4503-4916-1/17/10.
DOI: http://dx.doi.org/10.1145/3117811.3119854

2 OVERVIEW

It is important to highlight that FollowUs is completely plug-and-play, meaning it imposes no infrastructure requirements on buildings, no bootstrapping effort such as creating Wi-Fi fingerprint databases, and it requires minimal effort from users. This allows the system to scale out to reach as many potential users and to work in as many locations as possible. FollowUs traces *require* only readings from smartphones' magnetometer, accelerometer, gyroscope, and barometer sensors. Nevertheless, other signals (e.g. Wi-Fi RSSI, cellular signals) can easily be integrated into the system.

2.1 Usage scenarios

FollowUs allows users to record and follow paths using its mobile client app or conduct *app-less navigation* with web-based offline instructions.

Recording (as "leader"). During recording, the FollowUs client queries sensors and detects user motion events including steps, turns, and level changes (i.e., staircases, elevators, or escalators). When the leader arrives at the destination, sensor measurements and detection results are packed to build a reference trace and then sent to the cloud to be shared publicly or with specific users.

Navigation (as "follower"). Users can follow traces over any pre-generated path. Traces can either be pushed to the client app Inbox or pulled via Search functionality (e.g., from East Entrance to Room 1357). When following a trace, real-time navigation instructions including turns and floor/level changes are displayed in the app based on online synchronization between the reference trace and current ambient sensing information. Besides real-time navigation modes, FollowUs also provides a web interface featuring static *app-less navigation* — users can view trace summaries online in a browser and perform self-navigation without app installation on the client.

2.2 Architecture

Figure 1 shows the system architecture and its main modules: Recording Manager and Navigation Manager (client-side), and

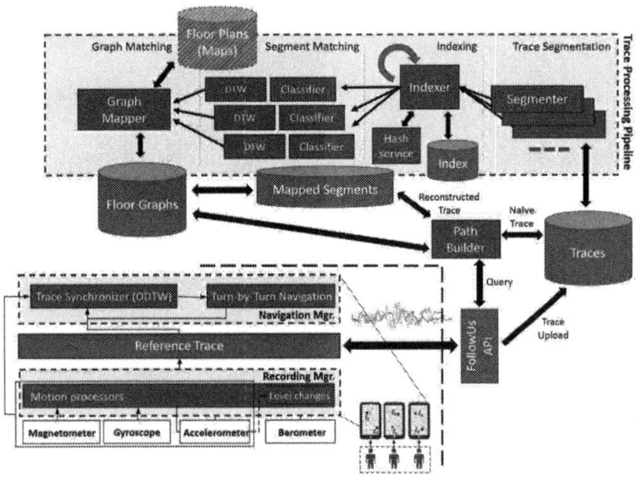

Figure 1: System diagram of FollowUs.

Service API, Trace Processing Pipeline (TPP), and Path Builder (cloud-side).

Recording Manager fuels the whole system by providing trace data recorded from mobile devices (e.g., smartphones) during a users' walk. This module collects and processes IMU data and location-specific geomagnetic signals [1–3] to extract user motion patterns and construct a trace. The output of this module can be directly used by the Navigation Manager to provide real-time plug-and-play navigation service. The processing results yielded by this module are also pushed to the cloud through the FollowUs Service API for storage and further processing by TPP, ensuring the scalability of the system.

Navigation Manager takes a reference trace as an input and navigates followers from the starting point to its selected destination from the database. A reference trace can be generated by either Recording Manager (local to the device) or Path Builder (queried from the backend service). During navigation, the module provide step-by-step navigation instructions, which is based on the synchronization result between geomagnetism readings from the reference trace and real-time measurements from the follower's Recording Manager[1]. The online dynamic time warping [2, 4] (ODTW) synchronization algorithm is designed to provide accurate navigation progress estimation with enhanced adaptability (capable to mitigate the effect of different walking speed) and efficiency (linear time complexity). To enhance navigation robustness, this module also contains a "deviation detection" component and the corresponding recovery mechanisms.

Service API handles trace and (media) annotation upload/download, data storage, user authentication, user notifications, and metadata search.

Trace Processing Pipeline ingests newly uploaded traces and is responsible for segmenting traces, identifying similarities between segments, and building logical graphs of building floor plans. Specifically, TPP will first split the incoming traces into trace segments by navigation events. Then trace segments will be organized by a high-efficient indexing structure to find the mutual matching candidates. Finally TPP utilizes the connectivity information and matching result between trace segments to build indoor trace graphs. Such graphs and mapped segments can later be used to produce new navigation paths. The pipeline design allows FollowUs to leverage cloud capabilities to dynamically scale processing power as more data arrives. If indoor floor-plans are available, this module can automatically find best match paths and improve graph building efficiency.

Path Builder receives user queries for paths between given start and end points. If a path is readily available, it is immediately returned. Otherwise, PB will find an optimal path by searching the floor plan graphs from TPP and combines corresponding segments to create a new trace for download.

2.3 Data flow

As shown in Figure 1, data flows from client (as a leader) to cloud, and then from cloud back to client (as a follower) in FollowUs. The cloud component not only provides storage, communication interfaces, telemetry, and account management, but also features an intelligent trace processing pipeline that makes FollowUs flexible and scalable. In "naïve" navigation, where one can only follow the exact same paths from others, each path recording produces and uploads a trace. To enable "cross-trace" navigation, FollowUs employs a novel *trace segmentation and indexing* technique. Segments are then efficiently matched, indexed, and persisted to allow the construction of *segment graphs*. A segment graph is incrementally built from trace segments and can eventually provide users with an exponentially increasing number of paths. Additionally, floor plans can naturally be leveraged to improve both performance and efficiency of the graph generation process.

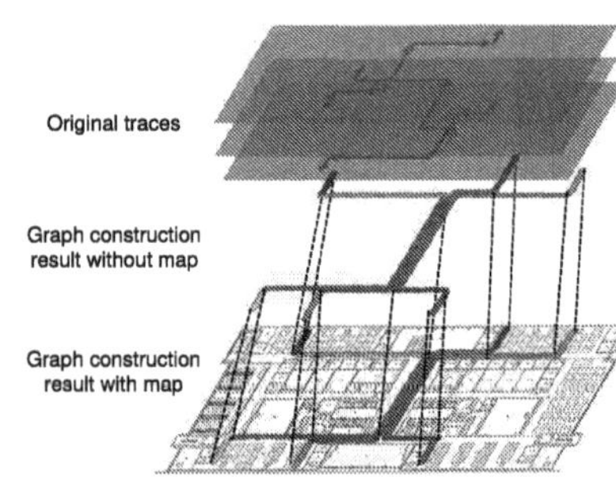

Figure 2: Graph construction visualization.

3 IMPLEMENTATION

We implemented FollowUs as an Android app and a set of backend cloud services on Azure[2]. The entire system consists of ≈ 56k lines of code (loc), broken into: Mobile Core 8.9kloc; FollowUs App 29kloc; Trace Processing Pipeline 13.6kloc; Path Builder 1.7kloc, and FollowUs Service API 2.5kloc. Mobile Core encompasses platform-independent algorithms and functions to be re-used by other applications and services. The FollowUs app makes use of the core modules to accomplish trace collection and real-time

[1]Note that other location-specific signals like Wi-Fi RSSI can also be naturally leveraged.

[2]A public version is available to download at https://aka.ms/mspathguide [5].

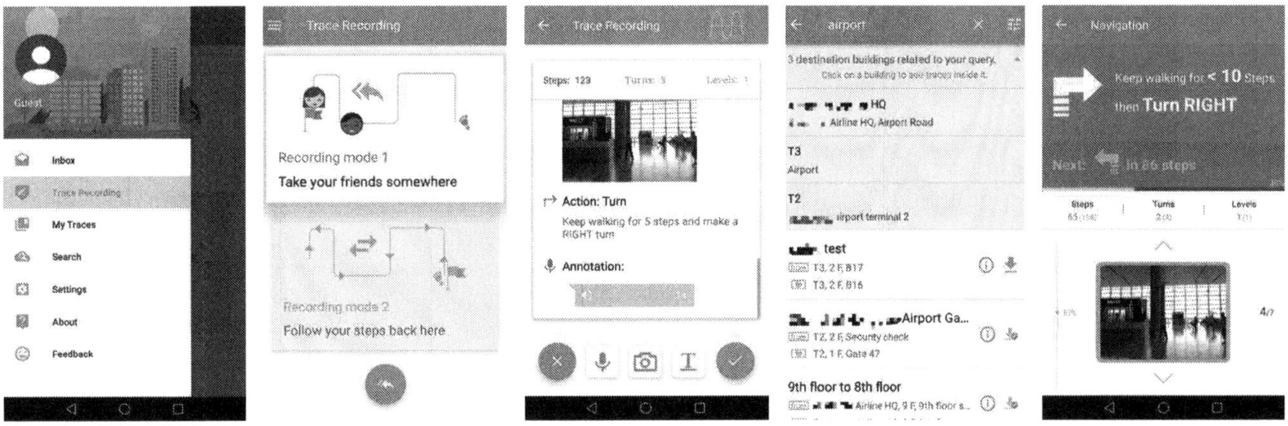

(a) Side menu (b) Two recording modes (c) Trace recording (d) Trace search (e) Real-time navigation

Figure 3: App screenshots.

navigation tasks. Basic implementation of data collection, motion detection, and trace synchronization in FOLLOWUS is generally similar to [2, 6], whereas details and improvements are omitted due to space limitations. Trace Processing Pipeline and Path Builder are implemented to split, match, concatenate, and generate traces at scale. Beyond the core modules, the app UI and user experience has been optimized throughout the development cycle and feedback from testing. Figure 3 shows app snapshots, and Figure 4 shows a web-based offline instructions summary that can be used if a user does not have the app on her phone.

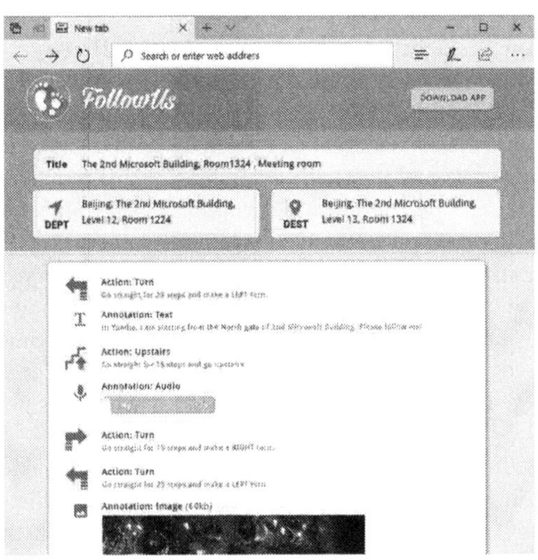

Figure 4: Offline (app-less) navigation.

4 DEMONSTRATION

In this demonstration, we will show the app and its capability of navigation. The demonstration will cover the three different modes under which FOLLOWUS can be used.

Ad-hoc navigation. In ad-hoc navigation demonstration, we will record an indoor trace with one smartphone and share it to another smartphone. Then we will use the second smartphone to follow the shared trace from the starting point to the destination. This mode can help subsequent visitors find a meeting room regardless of whether infrastructure and floor plans are available.

One-to-many navigation. In one-to-many navigation demonstration, we will record one indoor trace and share it to the public. Users can use the search function to find the trace and perform real-time navigation. This mode can help customers find desired stores in a shopping mall in an efficient way.

Reverse navigation. In reverse navigation demonstration, we will use a smartphone to record a trace from the starting point to the destination, and then navigate user back to the starting point. This mode can be used to record a trace from a parking spot to the elevator, and later follow it in reverse to find the car.

The demo only requires three Android smartphones (higher than 5.0). In ad-hoc navigation and one-to-many navigation mode, smartphones should be connected to Internet to allow trace uploading and downloading. In reverse navigation mode, no Internet access is required. The demo only needs few minutes to setup, including app installation and sensor calibration. This demo sets minimal requirements on the test sites. It can be demonstrated in any indoor environment.

REFERENCES

[1] Yuanchao Shu, Cheng Bo, Guobin Shen, Chunshui Zhao, Liqun Li, and Feng Zhao. Magicol: Indoor Localization Using Pervasive Magnetic Field and Opportunistic WiFi Sensing. *IEEE Journal on Selected Areas in Communications*, 33(7):1443–1457, 2015.

[2] Yuanchao Shu, Kang G Shin, Tian He, and Jiming Chen. Last-Mile Navigation Using Smartphones. In *ACM MobiCom*, 2015.

[3] Jaewoo Chung, Matt Donahoe, Chris Schmandt, Ig-Jae Kim, Pedram Razavai, and Micaela Wiseman. Indoor location sensing using geo-magnetism. In *ACM MobiSys*, 2011.

[4] Meinard Müller. Dynamic time warping. *Information retrieval for music and motion*, 2007.

[5] Microsoft. Microsoft Path Guide. https://aka.ms/mspathguide.

[6] Yuanqing Zheng, Guobin Shen, Liqun Li, Chunshui Zhao, Mo Li, and Feng Zhao. Travi-navi: Self-deployable Indoor Navigation System. In *ACM MobiCom*, 2014.

Demo : FROG : Optimizing Power Consumption of Mobile Games Using Perception-Aware Frame Rate Scaling

Chanyou Hwang*
chanyou@nclab.kaist.ac.kr
School of Computing - KAIST

Saumay Pushp*
saumay@nclab.kaist.ac.kr
School of Computing - KAIST

Changyoung Koh
changyoung@nclab.kaist.ac.kr
School of Computing - KAIST

Jungpil Yoon
jdsp@nclab.kaist.ac.kr
School of Computing - KAIST

Yunxin Liu
yunxin.liu@microsoft.com
Microsoft Research Asia

Seungpyo Choi
spchoi@nclab.kaist.ac.kr
School of Computing - KAIST

Junehwa Song
junesong@nclab.kaist.ac.kr
School of Computing - KAIST

ABSTRACT

A mobile GPU constitutes the majority of power consumption on a mobile device and mobile games top as the most popular class of graphics applications. In this demo, we present FROG, a novel frame rate optimization system for mobile gaming applications. FROG makes use of human visual perception to graphics and regulates application's frame rendering process on-the-fly for maximizing power saving without degrading the user experience. The system works on an existing commercial smartphone and support the legacy gaming applications from app stores without requiring any changes from applications.

CCS CONCEPTS

• **Human-centered computing** ⟶ *Ubiquitous and mobile computing systems and tools*; • **Computing methodologies** ⟶ *Perception*;

KEYWORDS

Perception-aware processing; Energy-efficient processing; Frame-rate scaling; Mobile games; Experiments; Measurement; Mobile systems

1 INTRODUCTION

Over the past three years, the processing power of mobile GPUs has increased more than double [1][2]. In response, mobile game application developers have begun to capitalize on the modern GPU's processing power to make their game graphics look crispier and appealing. However, those visually appealing mobile games come at a high energy cost. Each high-resolution frame consumes a large amount of system resources, especially the GPU computation, and thus, results in high system power consumption.

Mobile games top as the most popular class of graphics applications (apps) on smartphones [5] and are frequently the major sources of energy drain. Depending upon the amount of graphics contents inside a gaming app, the GPU power consumption increases almost linearly. However, few power management studies have been performed for mobile games [6]. In this demo, we explore the potential to optimally use the limited computing resources and energy by delving into the computation process from the perspective of human perception. i.e., game player's perception in this case. We specifically look into the rendering process of gaming apps considering the perceptual sensitivity of human, and re-organize the process, emphasizing sensitive moments while de-emphasizing the rest.

Upon the above idea, we present FROG [1], a novel system for scaling the rate of rendering frames which leverages human visual perception. FROG introduces perception-aware frame rate scaling (PAFS) while a user is engaged in a game-play. In detail, PAFS reduces an applications' rate of rendering frames whenever succeeding frames are predicted to be perceptually similar enough. For this, we set a side channel to track the rendered frame sequences which can tailor user's perception with graphics changes in a game-play. In this way, FROG opportunistically reduces power consumption of a GPU. Existing methods to measure user's perception of visual changes such as structural similarity (SSIM) [7] are computationally expensive and not adequate for a system to maintain quality user experiences during game-play. We leverage **YUV** color space [4] to develop a simple, but effective way to track user's perception on-the-fly.

There are several challenges in building the FROG system. First, it is important to measure the perceptual similarity efficiently. As mentioned, inferring the perceptual similarity with existing methods incur high computational cost. The system should be able to approximate such computation-intensive methods at a very low cost. Second, while saving energy, degradation of user experiences caused by the system should be minimal. Third, mobile gaming apps and GPU drivers are closed source. This asks for building a system that is transparent to the apps, and avoids low-level system optimization.

*Co-primary authors, order chosen alphabetically.

[1] Frame Rate Optimizer for mobile Games.

MobiCom '17, October 16–20, 2017, Snowbird, UT, USA.

ACM ISBN 978-1-4503-4916-1/17/10.
https://doi.org/10.1145/3117811.3119868

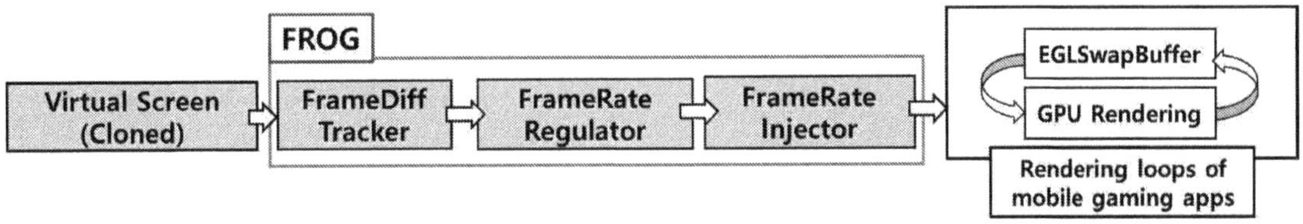

Figure 1: System architecture of FROG. Gray-colored blocks are FROG's components.

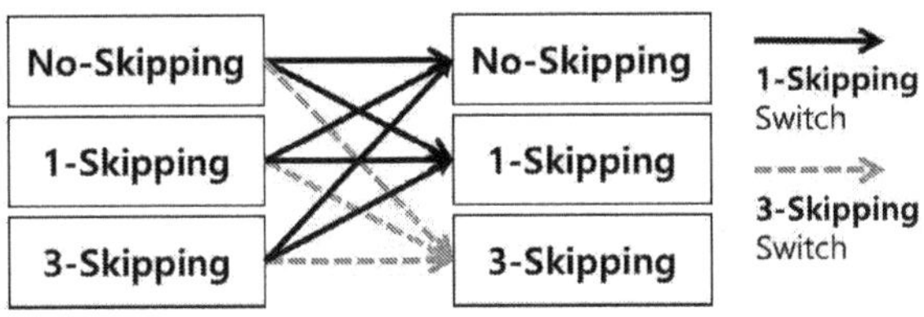

Figure 2: The system state transitions in FROG. 1-Skipping results in 30 FPS, and 3-Skipping results in 15 FPS.

To overcome the above challenges, we have developed an energy-efficient method to measure perceptual similarity exploiting the susceptibility of human eyes to color difference. The proposed method leverages the difference in the luminance components (in **YUV** color space) between frames. We extensively evaluated the method by comparing it with the well-known SSIM method under various settings, and show that the proposed luminance-based method can efficiently measure perceptual similarity with low computational costs. Also, we build in FROG system a virtual display, cloned from the main screen of the device but with a much lower resolution. The system reads the graphical contents of the small virtual display for the similarity measurement with low computational and energy overhead. In addition, FROG realizes the idea of perception-aware rate scaling by interfering and impeding the rendering loop of a game app. For frames that are perceptually similar to the current frame, the loop skips its operation, i.e., rendering of those frames. Instead, a delay for the amount of corresponding frame's periods is inserted to the loop. Afterwards, the loop jumps to the next frame to be generated. In this way, the rate of frame rendering is effectively scaled. The FROG system successfully hooks into the rendering loop as above by customizing the Android framework, and makes itself transparent to apps and avoids the complication of accessing closed source.

We have implemented the FROG system on a Nexus 5X smartphone. We conduct comprehensive experiments and a user study to evaluate our implementation with 13 real mobile games. Experimental results show that all 13 games can run successfully with per-frame, real-time perception-aware frame rate scaling. The energy per game session can be reduced by 21.78% in average and up to 34.74% while maintaining quality user experiences.

2 SYSTEM OVERVIEW

The idea of FROG can be described in high level with its major components and their interactions. The system consists of three major components which collectively perform frame rate scaling (Figure 1): **`FrameDiff Tracker`** (`F-Tracker`), **`FrameRate Regulator`** (`F-Regulator`), and **`FrameRate Injector`** (`F-Injector`). The system works in a pipelined fashion. First, `F-Tracker` measures perceptual similarity between two recent frames at a low energy cost. Then, `F-Regulator` predicts the level of similarity between the current and the next frame(s). If the next frames are similar to the current one, it notifies `F-Injector` to limit frame rates by injecting some delay in the rendering loop and skip graphics processing for unnecessary frame(s). Presently, FROG is able to skip up-to the maximum of three frames, and thus, inflict frame-rate drop up to 15 FPS. The continuous regulation of the frame rates results in opportunistic energy savings. Figure 2 show three different system states, i.e., No-skipping, 1-Skipping, and 3-Skipping states, and their transitions corresponding to different frame rates in FROG.

`F-Tracker` measures the perceptual similarity between consecutive frames on-the-fly. To compute the perceptual similarity efficiently, the system takes a twofold strategy. First, FROG leverages a light-weight, low-resolution virtual display via the operating system's graphics-composition library (i.e., `Hardware Composer`). Constructing a virtual display is lighter weighted than reading a frame buffer as the latter involves a higher resolution (equivalent to the native resolution of the screen). Second, to measure perceptual similarity between frames, FROG utilizes an approximation of SSIM based on the **Y**(luminance) component in the **YUV** color space. SSIM is a well-known way to measure perceptual similarity, but computationally expensive and hard to compute for every frame at 60 FPS.

The system forces apps to skip perceptually similar frames by appropriately regulating the rendering process. In determining the number of frames to skip, a set of three frames plays a key role: the current frame (f_N), the frame which arrives after 16.7ms (f_{N+1}) , and the frame which arrive after 50ms (f_{N+3}). `F-Regulator` predicts the perceptual similarity of (f_N, f_{N+1}) and (f_N, f_{N+3}) pairs, and compares them to thresholds T_{N+1} and T_{N+3} (used as scaling factors), respectively. Each threshold stands for the minimum required similarity for skipping either f_{N+1} or f_{N+3} frames.

Rendering loop in a mobile game runs in a separate thread from the main thread. The operating system tries to ensure that the rendering loop processes each frame in 16.7ms (to maintain 60 FPS). Moreover, game developers are less cautious and unaware about the fact that graphical contents from, e.g., game lobbies, incur additional energy drain, if rendered at 60 FPS. To regulate the rendering process (and thus frame rate), we leverage the **`eglSwapBuffer()`** function's system call [2] to the **`SurfaceFlinger`** which swaps the graphical content inside **`EGLSurface`**'s buffer (an off-screen buffer

[2]On Android, a game or game engine developer calls the **`eglSwapBuffer()`** function through EGL API to swap the buffer of current **`EGLSurface`** to the **`SurfaceFlinger`** in order to propagate the frame processing of the game.

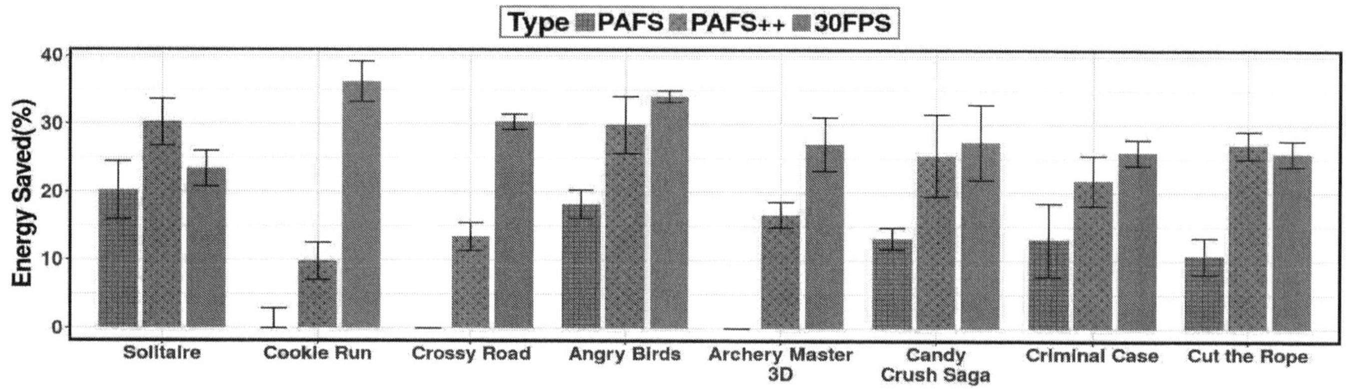

Figure 3: Percentage of energy saved while playing each game for 3 minutes (five times).

which stores SurfaceView, SurfaceTexture etc. of an app). We modified the **`eglSwapBuffer()`** function in Android's EGL API and injected delay in this function through **`F-Injector`**. Thereafter, the **`F-Injector`** enforces the desired frame rate.

In total, we used 8 games to measure the energy reduction from FROG to evaluate how much power can be saved in both PAFS and PAFS++ (a more aggressive version of PAFS, adds frequent 3-frame skipping). The device power consumption is measured with four settings: `30 FPS`, PAFS, PAFS++, and `Stock` Android settings. `Stock` setting is our baseline approach that is running a stock Android OS, which does not change frame rate.

Figure 3 shows the proportion of energy saved in each setting compared to the `Stock` setting. PAFS did not save any substantial amount of energy in games with high graphics motion such as `Cookie Run`, `Archery Master 3D`, and `Crossy Road`. Except those games, PAFS saves at least half the amount of energy saved by `30 FPS`. PAFS++ saves energy in every game with more than 10% with respect to `Stock`. Especially, it saves 5% more energy than `30 FPS` in `Solitaire`.

3 DEMONSTRATION

In this demo, we will show the power consumption optimization opportunity by using our FROG system as shown in Figure 4. We will provide each participant with a mobile phone running our prototype system, and let them play some mobile gaming applications. We will inject our PAFS and PAFS++ scaling policy and will ask the participants to see any perceived graphical differences while playing the games. Concurrently, we will also show the participants the relative power consumption from each game play sessions.

Equipment and Setup. We will bring mobile phones with our prototype system, two laptops, and two Monsoon Power Monitors [3] by ourselves. And the setup time of our demo is within 10 minutes. Our demo requires 4 power outlets, and a wifi connection.

4 CONCLUSION

This demo presents FROG, a system which utilizes perceptual similarity among frames to save power. FROG introduces a new on-the-fly frame rate scaling technique which helps in reducing energy consumption by the smartphone GPU. Moreover, FROG is the first system which actually can perform frame-rate changes without any external hints (e.g., touch inputs or sensor inputs).

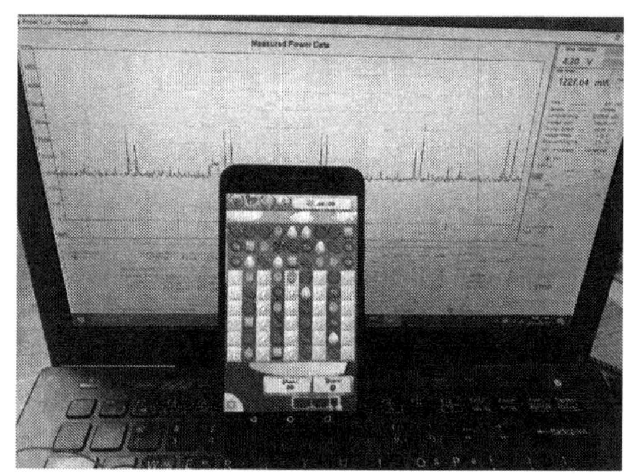

Figure 4: Demonstration System.

5 ACKNOWLEDGEMENT

This work was supported by the National Research Foundation of Korea (NRF) grant funded by the Korean Government (MSIP) (No.2017R1A2B3010504).

REFERENCES

[1] 2017. Mali-G71 ARM GPUs. https://www.arm.com/products/multimedia/mali-gpu/high-performance/mali-g71.php. (2017). [Online; accessed 21-July-2017].
[2] 2017. Mali-T760 ARM GPUs. https://www.arm.com/products/multimedia/mali-gpu/high-performance/mali-t760.php. (2017). [Online; accessed 21-July-2017].
[3] 2017. Monsoon Power Monitor. https://www.msoon.com/LabEquipment/PowerMonitor. (2017). [Online; accessed 21-July-2017].
[4] 2017. YUV - Wikipedia. https://en.wikipedia.org/wiki/YUV. (2017). [Online; accessed 21-July-2017].
[5] October 29, 2012. The Truth About Cats and Dogs: Smartphone vs Tablet Usage Differences. http://flurrymobile.tumblr.com/post/113379683050/the-truth-about-cats-and-dogs-smartphone-vs. (October 29, 2012). [Online; accessed 21-July-2017].
[6] B. Dietrich and S. Chakraborty. 2014. Forget the battery, let's play games!. In *2014 IEEE 12th Symposium on Embedded Systems for Real-time Multimedia (ESTIMedia)*. 1–8. https://doi.org/10.1109/ESTIMedia.2014.6962338
[7] Zhou Wang, Alan C Bovik, Hamid R Sheikh, and Eero P Simoncelli. 2004. Image quality assessment: from error visibility to structural similarity. *IEEE transactions on image processing* 13, 4 (2004), 600–612.

Demo: ArgosV3: An Efficient Many-Antenna Platform

Clayton Shepard[†‡], Rahman Doost-Mohammady[†], Ryan E. Guerra[†‡], and Lin Zhong[†]

[†]Department of Electrical and Computer Engineering, Rice University, Houston, TX

[‡]Skylark Wireless LLC, Houston, TX

cws@rice.edu, doost@rice.edu, ryan@skylarkwireless.com, lzhong@rice.edu

ABSTRACT

We present the third generation of Argos platforms, ArgosV3, intended for real-world applications and research. Developed from scratch specifically for many-antenna MU-MIMO, ArgosV3 is highly efficient in space, power, computation, and cost. While this new platform is highly configurable, featuring FPGA SoCs and frequency agile transceivers capable of operation from 50 MHz to 3.8 GHz, it is also highly compact and power efficient, enabling a complete 160 radio base station in less than 2 ft^3. ArgosV3 is currently being deployed in a campus-wide multi-cell many-antenna network. For our demonstration we will show a single ArgosV3 base station serving multiple clients using a realtime LTE stack.

1 INTRODUCTION

Many-antenna MU-MIMO, or Massive MIMO at large scales, can improve spectral efficiency by and order of magnitude, and is a key candidate technology for next-generation wireless systems. Over the past few years multiple experimental testbeds have been released [1–3, 5, 9, 10]. These testbeds have been instrumental in testing, validating, and improving many-antenna MU-MIMO technologies, however as initial prototypes and research equipment they are cumbersome, expensive, and limited to laboratory-scale experiments.

Leveraging our experience in building ArgosV1 and ArgosV2 [9, 10], we designed and built ArgosV3 from scratch to support real-world many-antenna MU-MIMO. ArgosV3 is very configurable and scalable, while being highly efficient in space, power, computation, and cost. The ArgosV3 base station is composed of three components: 1) a central controller, 2) a hub, and 3) multiple radio modules, which are capable of being daisy-chained. Notably, ArgosV3 fully implements the original Argos architecture [9], and as such is extremely scalable: from just a few base station antennas to hundreds, or even thousands. A single ArgosV3 hub currently supports over 300 radios, and multiple hubs can be used in a single base station. To enable mobile experiments, we also designed a compact battery-powered ArgosMobile, based on the same radio module as the base station.

MobiCom '17, October 16–20, 2017, Snowbird, UT, USA

ACM ISBN 978-1-4503-4916-1/17/10.
https://doi.org/10.1145/3117811.3119863

ArgosV3 supports multiple design flows, however for this demonstration we leverage the OpenAirInterface realtime LTE stack [6] to show an ArgosV3 base station serving multiple MU-MIMO clients simultaneously.

2 DESIGN

Based on our experience building two previous generations of many-antenna base stations, we designed ArgosV3 to be incredibly scalable, flexible, and usable. ArgosV3 fully supports the Argos architecture [9], and is provisioned to support streaming massive MIMO applications with up to 56 MHz of bandwidth. By employing frequency-agile transceivers and modular frontends, ArgosV3 enables high RF performance from 50 MHz to 3.8 GHz. Each component in ArgosV3 runs a full Linux OS, and the system supports multiple mature software-defined radio projects, including Pothos/SoapySDR, OpenAirInterface, the Argos channel measurement system, and GNU Radio [6–8, 11]. To support truly mobile experiments, ArgosV3 also provides updated battery-powered ArgosMobiles that feature integrated GPS.

2.1 Computational Design

The ArgosV3 base station is composed of three computational components: 1) a central controller, 2) a hub, and 3) multiple radio modules, shown in Figure 1.

The central controller is a standard server, or server cluster, that can be provisioned according to the application. For some design flows the central controller provides all of the processing in the system, and simply transmits IQ values to the radio modules. If required, the central controller can leverage optional PCIe FPGA co-processors, e.g., the Xilinx ZC706 or NetFPGA [12]. The central controller is connected to one or more hubs, each with up to four 10 GbE connections, for up to 40 Gbps of connectivity per hub.

The ArgosV3 hub is based on a Xilinx ZCU102 development board with a custom daughtercard to connect to the radio modules. This daughtercard provides high-precision clocking, power, GPIOs, and up to 13.2 Gbps of bi-directional connectivity to each chain of radio modules for coherent MIMO operation. The daughtercard is provisioned to support up to 8 chains of radio modules, and contains integrated GPS to enable global time-frequency synchronization. Additionally, the Xilinx ZCU102 supports Synchronous Ethernet (SyncE) and Precision Time Protocol (PTP) for network time-frequency synchronization.

The most complex and innovative component in ArgosV3 is the radio module, called an Iris, which provides 2 independent radios. Each Iris contains a Xilinx Zynq 7030 SoC, which provides significant computational capacity with two ARM cores and FPGA

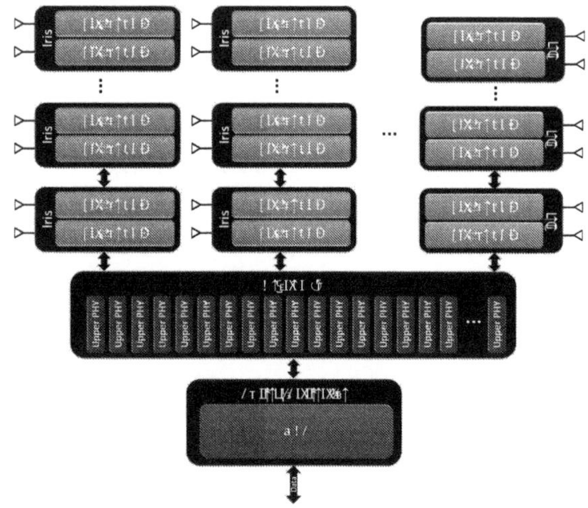

Figure 1: To enable extreme scalability, ArgosV3 can distribute computation across the central controller, hub, and radio modules.

Figure 2: ArgosV3 Iris radio modules. *(Left)* A coherent 18-radio array connected through a bus providing 13.2 Gbps connectivity, shared clocks, GPIOs, and power. *(Right)* A single ArgosV3 radio module with two antennas powered with PoE.

fabric. To fully support the Argos architecture [9], Irises can be daisy chained, either with a cable, or directly attached, as shown in Figure 2. This series connected bus provides clocking, power, GPIOs, and up to 13.2 Gbps of serial connectivity, completely eliminating the need for additional cabling. While the length of chains is only limited by power, which can be injected at multiple points, for streaming designs we typically limit the chain length to 10 to manage end-to-end latency. Conveniently, Irises can also be directly powered by barrel connectors, or via Power over Ethernet (PoE). Notably, individual Irises can also be used as standalone 2 antenna clients.

2.2 RF Design

The Iris radio modules in ArgosV3 employ a modular RF design. Each Iris contains a Lime Microsystems LMS7002M frequency-agile transceiver that supports two radio chains from 50 MHz to 3.8 GHz with up to 56 MHz channel bandwidth. However, to support high performance at a given frequency, e.g., in outdoor long-range environments, band-specific components such as filters, Low-Noise Amplifiers (LNAs), and Power Amplifiers (PAs), and antennas are required. Thus each Iris connects to an interchangeable RF frontend, designed to support the targeted bands. To date, we have designed two band-specific RF frontends for ArgosV3, the first supports 470-700 MHz UHF operation with 30 dBm transmit power, and the second supports 2.4-2.7 GHz and 3.5-3.8 GHz operation with 28 dBm transmit power. For development and testing on the full 50 MHz to 3.8 GHz frequency range, we also built an RF frontend that simply passes through the RF signals to the Lime transceiver, without filtering or amplification.

Additionally, to achieve a compact form-factor, as well as simplify design and cabling, we designed dual-polarized antennas for the UHF, 2.4-2.7 GHz, and 3.5-3.8 GHz bands, each with over 5 dBi gain across their target frequencies.

2.3 Mechanical Design

ArgosV3 was designed to be versatile and highly compact, as well as support outdoor deployments. Each Iris radio module is 1.55" wide, and thus can be spaced 1/2 wavelength apart at the highest supported frequency, 3.8 GHz, when daisy-chained. Since every Iris provides two radios, dual polarized antennas can be directly attached while maintaining this compact 1/2 wavelength spacing, as shown in Figure 4. For longer wavelengths Irises can be separated by cables or spacer boards, or RF cables can be used to attach the antennas.

While each Iris was designed to be very power efficient, consuming less than 15 W depending on design and transmit power, in dense configurations heat dissipation is a concern. Thermal considerations are even more challenging for outdoor deployments, where the base station needs to be weatherproofed. To address this issue we built a compact enclosure which provides two fully enclosed extruded heatsinks that span every chain of Irises, one for the Zynq processing unit, and one for the RF power amplifier. These heatsinks have fans at both ends to provide forced-air cooling. This weatherproof compact enclosure, containing a hub, 80 Irises, and antennas, is only 18"x14.5"x13", providing 160 radios in just 2 ft^3. A UHF version that is approximately 40"x20"x6", shown in Figure 3, is currently being finalized. This UHF enclosure contains 16 radios, and while it can be used standalone for small-scale deployments, to support massive MIMO multiple enclosures are deployed and connected to an ArgosHub.

2.4 Software Frameworks

ArgosV3 contains both CPUs and FPGA resources in all of its components, enabling it to support virtually any software framework. While not required, for convenience we typically run a full Linux OS on each radio module, as well as the hub and central controller. ArgosV3 supports multiple mature software-defined radio projects, including Pothos/SoapySDR, OpenAirInterface, the Argos channel measurement system, and GNU Radio [6–8, 11].

Pothos and GNU Radio provide similar features for rapid prototyping of research systems, including high-level language support, e.g., Python, a plethora of sample code, and even GUI interfaces. The Argos channel measurement system provides a framework for flexibly capturing and analyzing high time-frequency resolution

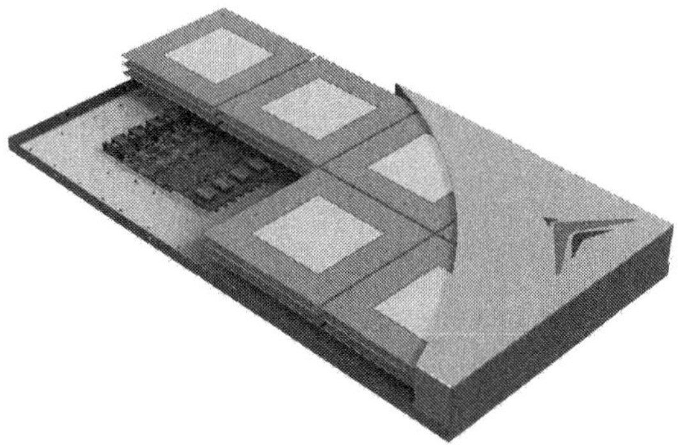

Figure 3: Rendering of UHF enclosure with 16 radios connected to 8 dual-polarized antenna elements. This enclosure is approximately 40"x20"x6" and is currently being finalized for production. To scale to massive MIMO, multiple UHF enclosures are deployed and connected to an ArgosHub.

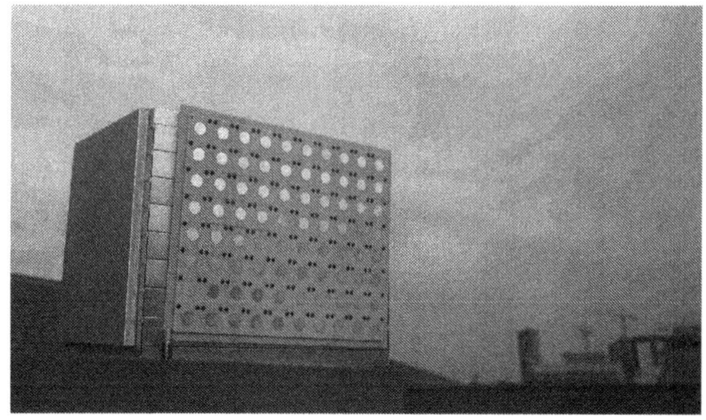

Figure 4: Complete ArgosV3 base station with 160 radios designed for 3.55 to 3.75 GHz operation. This compact cube is only 18"x14.5"x13". The plastic radome is removed to show the 80 dual-polarized antenna elements in a 10x8 configuration.

channel traces for many-antenna MU-MIMO. Finally, OpenAirInterface provides a production quality realtime LTE implementation entirely in software (C).

2.5 ArgosMobile

Since the capacity of MU-MIMO is fundamentally limited by mobility, ArgosV3 provides compact battery-powered clients to enable truly mobile experiments in diverse environments. This ArgosMobile is currently based on the same Iris radio module used in the base station, however it leverages a custom 3D printed enclosure that also contains 26650 Li-Ion batteries in a 3S2P configuration to provide roughly 8 hours of power in a 2"x2.5"x10" form-factor. A modified Iris that includes integrated GPS, a battery controller, and a USB WiFi bridge is currently being finalized.

3 DEMONSTRATION

In this demonstration we show an ArgosV3 base station running a realtime LTE stack serving multiple clients simultaneously. We ported the open-source OpenAirInterface LTE eNodeB and UE implementation [4, 6] to the ArgosV3 platform, and show that it is capable of serving 4 users simultaneously with up to 64 base station antennas, as supported by the LTE standard release 10.

For this demonstration we will need a medium sized table, e.g. 3'x6' and a standard power strip; internet access would be preferable, but is not required. We will provide all equipment, including a base station and multiple clients. It should take between 30 minutes and an hour for us to setup.

4 CONCLUDING REMARKS

We present ArgosV3, a novel many-antenna MU-MIMO platform designed from scratch to support real-world deployments of massive MIMO. ArgosV3 fully implements the Argos computational architecture, enabling unprecedented scalability and flexibility in a space, power, computation, and cost-efficient design.

ACKNOWLEDGEMENTS

ArgosV3 is developed as part of NSF CRI and SBIR projects: award numbers 1405937 and 1632565, respectively.

REFERENCES

[1] 2017. Bristol and BT collaborate on massive MIMO trials for 5G wireless. http://www.bris.ac.uk/news/2017/february/massive-mimo-trials.html. (2017).

[2] Neeraj Choubey and Ali Panah. 2016. Introducing Facebook's new terrestrial connectivity systems - Terragraph and Project ARIES. https://code.facebook.com/posts/1072680049445290. (2016).

[3] Xiang Gao, Fredrik Tufvesson, Ove Edfors, and Fredrik Rusek. 2012. Measured propagation characteristics for very-large MIMO at 2.6 GHz. In *IEEE Asilomar Conference on Signals, Systems, and Computers*. IEEE, 295–299.

[4] Xiwen Jiang and Florian Kaltenberger. 2017. Demo: an LTE compatible massive MIMO testbed based on OpenAirInterface. (2017).

[5] Nutaq. 2017. TitanMIMO. https://www.nutaq.com/5g-massive-mimo-testbed. (2017).

[6] OpenAirInterface: 5G software alliance for democratising wireless innovation. 2017. http://www.openairinterface.org/. (2017).

[7] Thomas W Rondeau. 2015. On the GNU Radio Ecosystem. *Opportunistic Spectrum Sharing and White Space Access: The Practical Reality* (2015), 25–48.

[8] Clayton Shepard, Jian Ding, Ryan E Guerra, and Lin Zhong. 2016. Understanding real many-antenna MU-MIMO channels. In *Signals, Systems and Computers, 2016 50th Asilomar Conference on*. IEEE.

[9] C. Shepard, H. Yu, N. Anand, E. Li, T. Marzetta, R. Yang, and L. Zhong. 2012. Argos: Practical Many-Antenna Base Stations. In *Proc. Ann. Int. Conf. Mobile Computing & Networking (MobiCom)*.

[10] Clayton Shepard, Hang Yu, and Lin Zhong. 2013. ArgosV2: A Flexible Many-Antenna Research Platform. In *Extended Demonstration Abstract in Proc. ACM MobiCom*.

[11] The SoapySDR Project. 2017. https://github.com/pothosware/SoapySDR/wiki. (2017).

[12] Noa Zilberman, Yury Audzevich, G Adam Covington, and Andrew W Moore. 2014. NetFPGA SUME: Toward 100 Gbps as research commodity. *IEEE Micro* 34, 5 (2014), 32–41.

Demo: WiFi-Assisted 60 GHz Wireless Networks

Sanjib Sur[∞,*], Ioannis Pefkianakis[¬], Xinyu Zhang[▷], Kyu-Han Kim[¬]
University of Wisconsin-Madison[∞], Hewlett Packard Labs[¬], University of California San Diego[▷]
sur2@wisc.edu, ioannis.pefkianakis@hpe.com, xiz368@eng.ucsd.edu, kyu-han.kim@hpe.com

ABSTRACT

Despite years of innovative research and development, multi-Gbps 60 GHz wireless networks are still not mainstream. The unfavorable propagation characteristics due to short wavelength and high directionality, makes the 60 GHz links highly vulnerable to blockage and mobility. However, the advent of multi-band chipsets opens the possibility of leveraging the more robust WiFi technology to assist 60 GHz in order to provide seamless, Gbps connectivity. In this demonstration, we will present *MUST*, an 802.11-compliant real-time system that provides seamless, high-speed connectivity over multi-band 60 GHz and WiFi devices. *MUST* has two key design components: (1) a WiFi-assisted 60 GHz link adaptation algorithm, which can instantaneously predict the best beam and PHY rate setting, with zero probing overhead at 60 GHz; and (2) a proactive blockage detection and switching algorithm which can re-direct ongoing user traffic to the robust interface within sub-10 ms latency. We have implemented *MUST* on off-the-shelf devices where our experiments show high throughput gain and almost 2 orders of magnitude cross-band switching latency improvement over state-of-the-art solutions.

CCS CONCEPTS

• **Networks → Wireless access networks; Network protocol design;**

KEYWORDS

60 GHz; Millimeter-Wave; IEEE 802.11ad; Session Transfer

1 INTRODUCTION

The multi-GHz unlicensed spectrum at the 60 GHz millimeter-wave frequency band, promises to shift today's WiFi-experience from "Wireless" to Gbps "Wire-like". With 14 GHz of free spectrum [1], 60 GHz offers foundation for next-generation bandwidth-intensive applications, such as uncompressed video streaming, snap wireless file synchronization, wireless virtual and augmented reality, wireless data centers, and Gbps Internet access. Multiple standardization efforts such as IEEE 802.11ad [9], 802.15.3c [5], ECMA [7] and millimeter-wave products [12] are tailored to support such applications, and promise upto 7 Gbps of wireless bit-rate. These advances and research demonstrations [8, 16, 19] have led millimeter-wave technology to be recommended as a key component in 5G multi-Gbps cellular networks [1–3].

However, the short wavelength (5 mm at 60 GHz) and weak reflection characteristics (compared to LTE/WiFi signals) render 60 GHz links highly vulnerable to channel propagation loss [13, 18]. In the same environment, a 60 GHz link suffers from around 1000× higher signal strength loss compared to typical LTE/WiFi [15]. Millimeter-wave devices overcome such challenge by focusing RF energy towards narrow spatial direction through beamforming using phased-array antennas. Maintaining beams from access point/base station toward mobile users is a challenging task and 60 GHz links formed via such narrow beams get highly affected during mobility and human blockage [6, 11, 15, 16].

Fortunately, the advent of multi-band WiFi chipsets [17] opens the possibility of leveraging the more robust WiFi interface in those scenarios where 60 GHz fundamentally performs poorly, to enable robust connectivity. Specifically, WiFi's omni-directional view of the wireless channel could be leveraged to design highly-adaptive 60 GHz beam and PHY rate selection. In the scenarios where 60 GHz link cannot be established due to obstacles, WiFi could provide admittedly lower speeds, but still a very robust communication anchor.

In this demonstration, we will present *MUST* [14], an 802.11-compliant real-time system which provides high-speed, robust connectivity over 60 GHz and WiFi multi-band devices, in dynamic indoor environments. *MUST* achieves its objective by introducing *two* key design components: (1) *Fast link adaptation:* A WiFi-assisted 60 GHz link adaptation module that can instantaneously predict the best 60 GHz beam and PHY rate setting, with zero 60 GHz probing, under blockage and mobility; (2) *Seamless switching:* A low-latency (sub-10 ms), proactive switching algorithm to reroute traffic from highly fragile 60 GHz links to WiFi, without breaking the existing connection. *MUST* design is built upon *two* key observations: (1) Human mobility and blockage affect the dominating path of the 60 GHz channel and thus best beam, at much slower pace (order of 100s of ms). While a small scale variation can still affect channel quality of the best beam, it does not necessarily change the entire best beam direction in a practical system. Thus, instead of relying on the existing method of link adaptation that itself can take hundreds of ms to converge, *MUST* use out-of-band information with appropriate modeling that provides the hint for the 60 GHz channel's most dominating path and best link settings. (2) When LOS is blocked, 60 GHz provides highly dynamic, rampant zero throughput connection that eventually degrades upper layer performance. In order to achieve smooth real-time response, it is far better to proactively move to WiFi interface and survive blockage. We have implemented entire *MUST* design in an off-the-shelf IEEE 802.11ac/ad multi-band AP platform (Figure 1) without any modifications to the end-user device or additional standards support. Our experiments show that *MUST* can accurately approximate the best performance link settings under various channel dynamics in enterprise environment. Even after including all out-of-band probing and interface switching related overheads, it stays within 10% of the optimum and achieves 25-60%

*Sanjib Sur interned at Hewlett Packard Labs, Palo Alto during this work.

MobiCom '17, October 16–20, 2017, Snowbird, UT, USA

ACM ISBN 978-1-4503-4916-1/17/10.
https://doi.org/10.1145/3117811.3119870

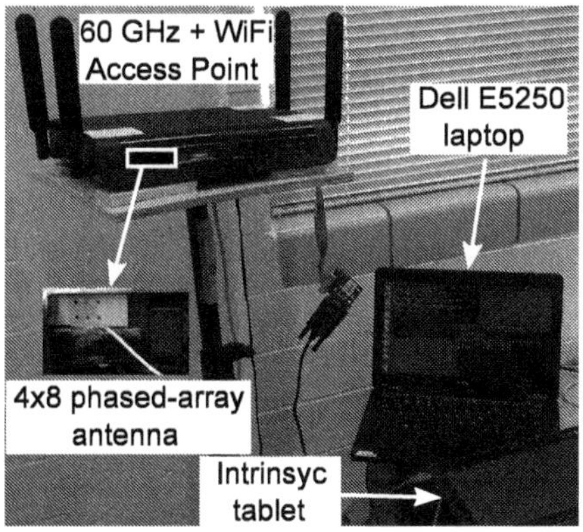

Figure 1: Off-the-shelf 60 GHz and WiFi multi-band platform.

throughput gain over state-of-the-art solutions. While proactively switching to WiFi can occasionally incur performance loss (less than 6% on average), *MUST* improves the switching latency by almost 2 orders of magnitude.

2 OVERVIEW

MUST is an 802.11-compliant system that provides seamless, high-speed 60 GHz connectivity in dynamic indoor wireless networks. The key idea is to leverage the existing robust WiFi technology to assist 60 GHz links. Practical challenges emerge when designing WiFi-assisted 60 GHz communication for *three* key reasons. *First,* while omni-directional WiFi Channel State Information (CSI) could provide a hint to the most dominant propagation path of wireless channel, it is very-coarse grained estimation, and often leads to erroneous beam and PHY rate selection. *MUST* builds a dominating LOS path tracking model [14] together with the non-uniformity of the practical phased-array antennas (Figure 2) to adapt to the best 60 GHz beam and PHY rate. *Second,* simultaneously transmitting data over highly heterogeneous-speed (*i.e.* 60 GHz and WiFi) interfaces can degrade applications' performance running over TCP by as much as 5×. This is due to out-of-order TCP sequences and congestion control over heteregeneous links [10, 14]. *MUST* thus adopts a fast switching from 60 GHz to WiFi during LOS blockage. *Finally,* designing seamless 60 GHz-WiFi interface switching, which meets the sub-10 ms latency requirements of many real-time applications, remains an open problem. Existing off-the-shelf multi-band devices adopt a reactive interface switching approach, which requires multiple seconds to identify and switch to the best interface. *MUST* employs a proactive solution for fast switching between wireless interfaces [14].

We have implemented *MUST* on the 60 GHz and WiFi AP (Figure 1) without any modification to the end-user devices. Our implementation spreads across our AP's kernel and firmware, as shown in Figure 3 and the software architecture follows open source OpenWrt [4] design. We modified kernel and firmware of the AP to periodically collect link statistics from both the 60 GHz and WiFi radios and extract them to a large DDR buffer. This statistics drive the 60 GHz prediction module to adapt the beam and PHY rates. Further, we adopt and modify the existing IEEE 802.11ad FST design [9] and appropriately modified the Linux's bonding driver to incorporate the practical interface switching. We refer interested readers to [14] for more detailed discussion on the design and implementation of *MUST*.

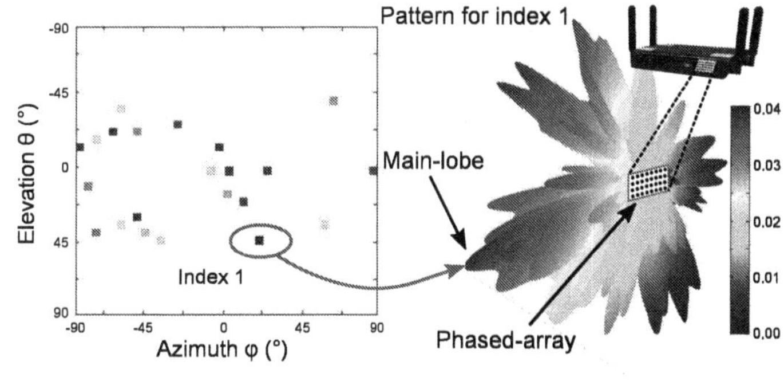

Figure 2: (*a*) Phased-array beam directions. (*b*) Measured 3D radiation pattern of beam index 1.

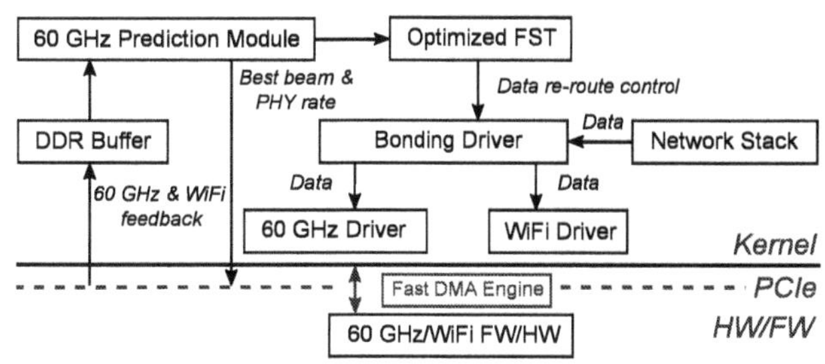

Figure 3: *MUST* system architecture. Refer [14].

3 DEMONSTRATION

In this demonstration, we will show real-time *MUST* system and its efficacy to enable robust, Gbps 60 GHz connectivity in dynamic indoor environment. In this system, we will demonstrate real-time 60 GHz beam-searching/steering with off-the-shelf phased-array devices, visualize transmit beam patterns, fast switching between 60 GHz and WiFi interfaces and run real-time ultra-HD stream under challenging and dynamic indoor environments. We will bring off-the-shelf multi-band 60 GHz and WiFi access points, laptops and tablets and our own visualization devices for the demonstration. However, we will need around 2m×2m space with a desk to place the equipments and power outlet for the devices. Our demonstration does not require any Internet access and the whole setup process should take less than half an hour.

4 CONCLUSION

By leveraging existing robust WiFi technology *MUST* enables high-performance, robust 60 GHz wireless networks. *MUST* is designed and implemented using standard, off-the-shelf hardware that provides seamless, high-speed connectivity in highly dynamic 60 GHz indoor environments. *MUST* introduces a WiFi-assisted 60 GHz link adaptation module that can instantaneously predict the best 60 GHz beam and PHY rate setting. It further designs a proactive switching algorithm to achieve sub-10 ms switch to WiFi, allowing latency-sensitive traffic to run seamlessly over existing network stack. This demonstration will showcase *MUST* in the *MobiCom'17* conference site, using off-the-shelf 60 GHz access points with unmodified commodity user devices. We believe this will trigger substantial interests and a strong push towards enabling mainstream Gbps 60 GHz wireless networks.

REFERENCES

[1] FCC Promotes Higher Frequency Spectrum for Future Wireless Technology. https://apps.fcc.gov. 2015.

[2] Verizon applauds FCC chairman's move to 5G spectrum. http://www.fiercewireless.com/tech/verizon-applauds-fcc-chairman-s-move-to-5g-spectrum. 2015.

[3] Unlocking the Promise of Broadband for All Americans. https://obamawhitehouse.archives.gov/blog/2016/07/15/unlocking-promise-broadband-generate-gains-all-americans. 2016.

[4] OpenWrt Wireless Freedom. https://openwrt.org/. 2017.

[5] IEEE Standards Association. IEEE Standards 802.15.3c-2009: Millimeter-wave-based Alternate Physical Layer Extension. 2009.

[6] Sylvain Collonge, Gheorghe Zaharia, and Ghais El Zein. Influence of the Human Activity on Wide-Band Characteristics of the 60 GHz Indoor Radio Channel. *IEEE Transactions on Wireless Communications* Vol. 3, No. 6. 2004.

[7] ECMA International. Standard ECMA-387: High Rate 60 GHz PHY, MAC and PALs. 2010.

[8] Daniel Halperin, Srikanth Kandula, Jitendra Padhye, Paramvir Bahl, and David Wetherall. Augmenting Data Center Networks with Multi-gigabit Wireless Links. In *Proc. of ACM SIGCOMM*. 2011.

[9] IEEE Standards Association. IEEE Standards 802.11ad-2012, Amendment 3: Enhancements for Very High Throughput in the 60 GHz Band. 2012.

[10] Costin Raiciu, Christoph Paasch, Sebastien Barre, Alan Ford, Michio Honda, Fabien Duchene, Olivier Bonaventure, and Mark Handley. How Hard Can It Be? Designing and Implementing a Deployable Multipath TCP. In *Proc. of USENIX NSDI*. 2012.

[11] Maryam Eslami Rasekh, Zhinus Marzi, Yanzi Zhu, Upamanyu Madhow, and Haitao Zheng. Noncoherent mmWave Path Tracking. In *Proc. of ACM HotMobile*. 2017.

[12] Grand View Research Report. Wireless Gigabit (WiGig) Market Size To Reach $7.42 Billion By 2024. http://www.grandviewresearch.com/press-release/global-wireless-gigabit-wigig-market. 2016.

[13] Peter F. M. Smulders. Statistical Characterization of 60-GHz Indoor Radio Channels. *IEEE Transactions on Antennas and Propagation* Vol. 57, No. 10. 2009.

[14] Sanjib Sur, Ioannis Pefkianakis, Xinyu Zhang, and Kyu-Han Kim. WiFi-Assisted 60 GHz Wireless Networks. In *Proc. of ACM MobiCom*. 2017.

[15] Sanjib Sur, Vignesh Venkateswaran, Xinyu Zhang, and Parmesh Ramanathan. 60 GHz Indoor Networking through Flexible Beams: A Link-Level Profiling. In *Proc. of ACM SIGMETRICS*. 2015.

[16] Sanjib Sur, Xinyu Zhang, Parmesh Ramanathan, and Ranveer Chandra. BeamSpy: Enabling Robust 60 GHz Links Under Blockage. In *Proc. of USENIX NSDI*. 2016.

[17] www.qualcomm.com. Qualcomm Atheros and Wilocity Announce Tri-band Wi-Fi: Industry's First Standards-compliant, Multi-Gigabit Wireless Chipset. https://www.qualcomm.com/news/releases/2011/05/31/qualcomm-atheros-and-wilocity-announce-tri-band-wi-fi-industrys-first. 2011.

[18] Hao Xu, Vikas Kukshya, and Theodore S. Rappaport. Spatial and Temporal Characteristics of 60-GHz Indoor Channels. *IEEE Journal on Selected Areas in Communications* Vol. 20, No. 3. 2002.

[19] Xia Zhou, Zengbin Zhang, Yibo Zhu, Yubo Li, Saipriya Kumar, Amin Vahdat, Ben Y. Zhao, and Haitao Zheng. Mirror Mirror on the Ceiling: Flexible Wireless Links for Data Centers. In *Proc. of ACM SIGCOMM*. 2012.

DEMO: Dynamic Adaptations of WiFi Channel Widths Without TX/RX Coordination

Alice Lo Valvo
University of Palermo
Palermo, Italy
alice.lovalvo@unipa.it

Ilenia Tinnirello
University of Palermo
Palermo, Italy
ilenia.tinnirello@unipa.it

Fabrizio Giuliano
University of Palermo
Palermo, Italy
fabrizio.giuliano@unipa.it

Giuseppe Santaromita
University of Palermo
Palermo, Italy
giuseppe.santaromita@unipa.it

ABSTRACT

Most modern standards for wireless communications support physical layer adaptations, in terms of dynamic selection of channel central frequency, transmission power, modulation format, etc., in order to increase link robustness under time-varying propagation and interference conditions. In this demo, we demonstrate that another powerful solution for extending physical layer flexibility in OFDM-based technologies is the dynamic adaptation of the channel width. Although some standards already define the possibility of utilizing multiple channel widths (e.g. 20MHz, 10MHz, 5MHz for IEEE 802.11a standards), such an utilization is limited to a static configuration of a value defined during the network set-up. Conversely, we demonstrate that channel width adaptations can be performed in real-time during network operation, even on a per-packet basis. To this purpose, we propose an innovative and efficient receiver design, which allows the transmitter to take decisions about the channel width without explicitly informing the receiver.

1 INTRODUCTION

Spectrum agility has been traditionally considered as the capability to set up a wireless communication link over different spectrum blocks, by shifting from one central frequency to another. This capability is of primary importance for cognitive radio systems or for systems working in ISM bands, which are usually unplanned and characterized by significant spatial variations of spectrum availability. Available spectrum portions can differ in size. Therefore, another desirable capability of spectrum-agile technologies is the possibility of adapting the channel width to the available spectrum bandwidth and/or aggregating independent (non-contiguous) spectrum portions into a single logical link.

In this demo we deal with channel width adaptations for OFDM-based systems. As a reference technology, we consider wireless nodes based on the IEEE 802.11a OFDM PHY and MAC specifications. The PHY of legacy 802.11a nodes includes the possibility of working with 5MHz and 10MHz channel widths, in addition to the usual 20MHz configuration. Indeed, the possibility of adapting the channel width has been demonstrated to be beneficial for different performance figures, such as energy consumption, link reliability, throughput and fairness, [1], by generalizing the concept of *rate adaptation*. Differently from usual rate adaptation, where modulation formats are specified in the PHY fields of each frame, requests for channel width adaptation are transmitted in special control frames which require a confirmation by the intended receiver. A similar adaptation of modulation formats and channel widths is proposed in [2] for OFDM systems. Rather than changing the transmitter clock as in [1], in this work bandwidth adaptations are supported by selecting a set of subcarrier groups for each frame transmission. The subcarrier group ordering is piggybacked by the receiver to the sender in each acknowledgement. Randomized hopping between different channel widths have been proved to increase robustness against jamming attacks of fixed bandwidths [3]. In this case, the hopping sequence used by the transmitter is known to the receiver, which recovers the per-packet channel width by means of a synchronization mechanism with the transmitter hopping sequence. In [4] the benefits of heterogeneous channel widths are achieved by configuring multiple coexisting networks working with different (static) channel widths. To speed-up the scanning of networks working on multiple channel widths, the authors propose to passively perform a temporal analysis of typical channel timings that can be related to the transmission bandwidth employed in each network (such as the duration of acknowledgement transmissions or the DIFS interval).

In our demo we do not focus on the logic for selecting the channel width, but rather on the receiver architecture which enables the possibility of implementing different decision logics at the transmitter side. Although the logic could in principle benefits on context information signaled by the receiver, our architecture allows the transmitter to take decisions about channel widths, without explicitly signaling the decision to the intended receiver. As in [1], channel width adaptations are implemented by changing the clock of the OFDM transmitter. The receiver architecture has been implemented on the well-known WARP [5] research board, which is a FPGA-based SDR platform, for which it is available a reference implementation of legacy 802.11 PHY (including 802.11a/g OFDM modulations). We demonstrate that a spectral analysis of the preamble of each incoming frame can be performed on time for

MobiCom '17, October 16–20, 2017, Snowbird, UT, USA

ACM ISBN 978-1-4503-4916-1/17/10.
https://doi.org/10.1145/3117811.3119861

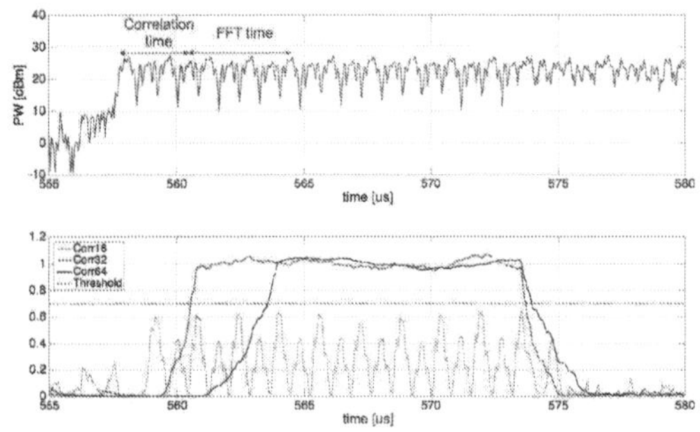

(a)

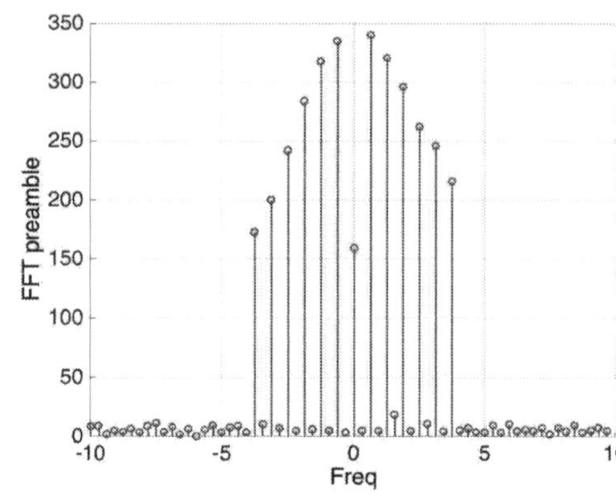

(b)

Figure 1: (a) Preamble time and correlations, (b) FFT shift of a preamble sent at 10MHz

reconfiguring the internal clock of the receiver consistently to the transmitter one.

2 TRANSCEIVER ARCHITECTURE

We designed a OFDM transceiver under the assumption that wireless nodes belonging to the same network work with a fixed central frequency, while the channel width used for transmissions can be arbitrarily selected by the senders in each transmission attempt, without explicitly signaling the choice to the receiver.

At the transmitter side, channel width adaptations are implemented by simply scaling the basic clock of the system (80MHz for the WARP board) to a desired output clock by means of a dynamic reconfiguration port. At the receiver side, we considered more general extensions of a typical OFDM receiver, devised to enable the correct identification of the channel width of an incoming frame within the reception of the short OFDM preamble. Specifically, we modified the peak detection block of a OFDM receiver working with fixed channel width, and we added an FFT block for performing a preliminary spectral analysis of the received signal when a preamble is detected.

Peak detection. The legacy 802.11 short preamble has a periodic structure with 10 identical symbols, each one lasting $0.8\mu s$, $1.6\mu s$ or $3.2\mu s$ in case the channel width is set to 20MHz, 10MHz or 5MHz. Usually, OFDM receivers detect the beginning of a short preamble by identifying this periodic structure, i.e. by correlating two windows of signal samples corresponding to two consecutive symbols. Working at a fixed sampling rate of 20Msample/s, a preamble symbol includes 16, 32 or 64 samples according to the channel width used in transmission. Therefore, rather than working with a correlator whose window value is statically configured, we replicated the correlator blocks, in order to perform three parallel correlations on windows of 16, 32 and 64 samples. The channel width of an incoming frame can be estimated by observing the minimum window size which gives an high correlation result. The total detection delay is 2 symbols, because two preamble symbols are enough for detecting the first correlation peak. For deciding if the correlation is positive or not, the correlation result is compared with a percentage of the sum of the modules of the first window W of samples used for correlation (i.e. with the theoretical correlation result in case of perfect periodic samples of the signal, $s(nT + WT) = s(nT)$ for $n = 0, \cdots W - 1$ and $T = 1/20MHz$).

Note that a positive detection of a short preamble with a given channel width does not necessarily imply that the incoming frame belongs to the receiver network and is transmitted at the network (static) central frequency. Indeed, by sampling the signal at 20Msamples/s, we can recognize valid preambles sent with a central frequency shifted of +/- 10MHz from the receiver one.

Spectral analysis. In case a valid short preamble is detected, a spectral analysis of the sub-sequent preamble symbols is performed by means of a 64-point FFT. The number of preamble symbols required for collecting 64 samples are obviously dependent on the channel width, and in particular are equal to 4 symbols transmitted at 20MHz, 2 symbols transmitted at 10MHz and 1 symbol transmitted at 5 MHz. In the worst case, such an analysis lasts 4 symbols of the preamble, thus leading to a total time of 6 symbols before taking a decision on the channel width. The results of the FFT allows to immediately reject preambles transmitted with a different central frequency. Moreover, they also provide an additional evidence of the channel width used for transmission. Indeed, because of the preamble structure, sub-carriers with non-null coefficient appear in contiguous positions, spaced of two sub-carriers or spaced of four sub-carriers when the channel width is, respectively, 5MHz, 10MHz, or 20MHz. In our implementation, the decision logic works by comparing the sub-carrier amplitude with a threshold calculated by averaging the amplitude of 12, 18 or 24 sub-carriers around the central frequency. We chose to limit the average operation to these sets of sub-carriers, rather than considering the whole set of 64 sub-carriers, in order to discard the power of interfering signals occupying adjacent bands. If six sub-carrier amplitudes are higher than the threshold in contiguous positions or spaced of a null sub-carrier or spaced of three null sub-carriers around the central frequency, the frame is recognized as a valid frame transmitted at 5MHz, 10MHz or 20MHz. This result is used for reconfiguring the clock of the system.

Clock Reset. After completing the reception of the frame, the receiver switches the clock to the basic value (i.e. switch to a reference bandwidth of 20MHz). In case the receiver is the destination of the frame, the clock reset is deferred until the completion of the ACK frame transmission.

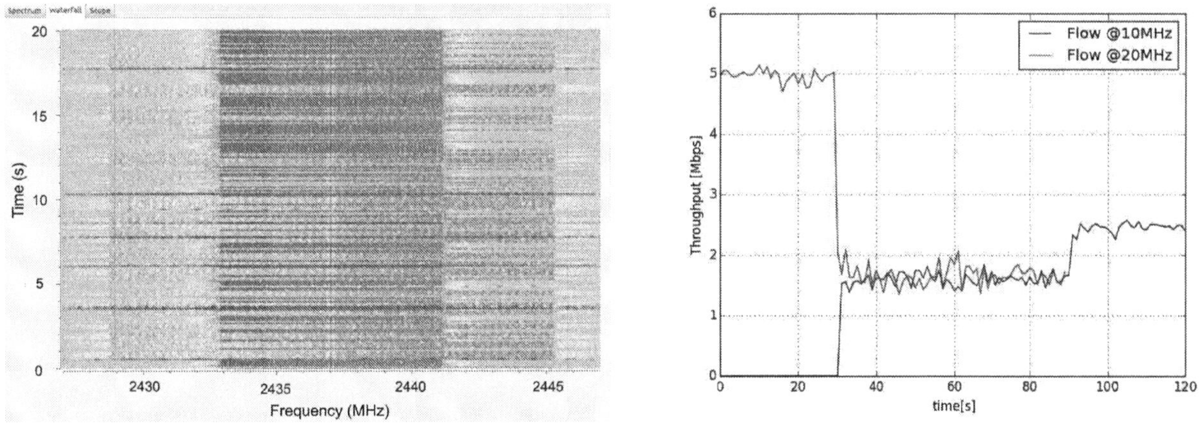

(a) (b)

Figure 2: Agile Receiver Performance: (a) waterfall and (b) throughput of two flows at 10 and 20MHz

Figure 1-a shows the temporal structure of a short preamble (top part of the figure) transmitted at 10MHz and the parallel correlations of windows with 16, 32 and 64 samples (bottom part of the figure). Figure 1-b shows the results of the 64-point FFT. Both the correlation results and the FFT analysis allows to identify that the channel width of the incoming frame is set to 10MHz; moreover, the FFT results indicate the position of the central frequency used in transmission.

3 DEMONSTRATION DESCRIPTION

We consider a simple network with three nodes only, devised to showcase the functionalities of our bandwidth-agnostic receiver: two senders, A and B, able to dynamically tune the channel width used for transmissions, act in proximity of a receiver C. All nodes are implemented on top of the WARP board, for which it is also available a complete implementation of the 802.11 DCF access scheme. A further monitoring node, implemented by using a USRP [6], acts as a spectrum analyzer for showing in real-time the spectrum occupancy of the network in an output monitor (which also displays the throughput results obtained by the receiver). The transmitter A is statically configured for working at the same central frequency f_c of the receiver C, while the transmitter B can be tuned on the same central frequency f_c or on a central frequency in the range $[f_c - 10MHz, f_c + 10Mz]$. On each transmitter, it is possible to configure the rate of the traffic source (implemented with an iperf client transmitting UDP packets of 1470 bytes) and the channel width mode (static, at a given value, or dynamic with random patterns).

In case both the transmitters A and B are configured for working on the frequency f_c, we can demonstrate that the receiver is able to correctly demodulate the frames transmitted without any a-priori knowledge about the used channel width. Indeed, in this scenario the sequence of channel widths used in consecutive frames is unpredictable, due to the fact that transmitters A and B randomly win consecutive contentions. Therefore, even pseudo-random sequences of channel widths adopted by A and B cannot be mapped into a deterministic sequence of channel widths for the receiver. In other words, random contention prevents the adoption of any signaling mechanism based, for example, on the possibility of pre-announcing in each frame the channel width used for the next transmission. Figure 2 shows the results obtained in a real experiment based on this scenario, in which nodes A and B are statically configured for transmitting, respectively, at 20MHz and 10MHz, with a data rate set to 6Mbps. The figure shows the temporal sequence of random spectrum occupancy due to the contention mechanism (Figure 2-a), and the throughput results (2-b) when only node A is active, both nodes A and B are active, and when only node B is active. The receiver is able to simultaneously works with both the transmitters, which achieve a similar throughput when simultaneously active, because of the performance anomaly phenomenon [7].

In case transmitter B is configured for working on a different (opportunistically spaced) f_c frequency, we will demonstrate that the receiver is still able to detect node A transmissions despite of node B interference.

For showing properly this demo, we need a desk and a monitor (at least 24 inches), which displays the waterfall plot and the throughput of two traffic flows.

ACKNOLEDGMENTS

This work is supported in part by the EU H2020 WiSHFUL project, Grant No. 645274, and in part by the Flex5Gware project, Grant No. 671563.

REFERENCES

[1] R. Chandra, R. Mahajan, T. Moscibroda, R. Raghavendra, and P. Bahl. A Case for Adapting Channel Width in Wireless Networks. SIGCOMM'08, Seattle, WA, Oct. 2008.
[2] V. Pejovic and E. M. Belding, Whiterate: A context-aware approach to wireless rate adaptation, IEEE Transactions on Mobile Computing, vol. 13, no. 4, April 2014
[3] M. Liechti, V. Lenders, and D. Giustiniano. Jamming mitigation by randomized bandwidth hopping. In Proc. of ACM CoNEXT 2015. ACM, New York, NY, USA-
[4] P. Bahl, R. Chandra, T. Moscibroda, R. Murty, and M. Welsh. White space networking with wi-fi like connectivity. In Proc. of ACM SIGCOMM 2009. ACM, New York, NY, USA, 27-38.
[5] A. Khattab, at al. WARP: A flexible platform for clean-slate wireless medium access protocol design. SIGMOBILE Mobile Computing Communication Review, vol. 12, no. 1, pp. 56-58, 2008.
[6] M. Ettus, "Universal Software Radio Peripheral", [online] Available: http://www.ettus.com.
[7] M. Heusse, et al. Performance Anomaly of 802.11b, INFOCOM 2003.

Demo: UIWear: Easily Adapting User Interfaces for Wearable Devices

Jian Xu*
Stony Brook University
jianxu1@cs.stonybrook.edu

Qingqing Cao*
Stony Brook University
qicao@cs.stonybrook.edu

Aruna Balasubramanian
Stony Brook University
arunab@cs.stonybrook.edu

Donald E. Porter
The University of North Carolina at Chapel Hill
porter@cs.unc.edu

ABSTRACT

Wearable devices, such as smart watches, offer exciting new opportunities for users to interact with their applications. The current state of the art for wearable devices is for a developer to write a custom *companion app*, which is a variant of the smartphone app, tailored to the wearable form factor. A developer puts a non-trivial amount of effort to write these companion apps and the programming model does not scale to an increasing diversity of form factors.

In this demo, we show a working prototype of our system UIWear that allows a developer to easily extend a smartphone application to other wearable interfaces. Our system, UIWear, extracts the application GUI as a UI tree, which preserves the semantics of the GUI. The developer (or the user) only writes a *metaprogram* to encode the GUI design for the wearable device; no effort is needed beyond the design phase. UIWear executes the metaprogram by performing all the underlying tasks to virtualize the application GUI, adapt it, and recreate it on the wearable. A metaprogram can create the same functionality as existing companion apps with an order-of-magnitude less programming effort.

1 INTRODUCTION

Wearable computing devices are a major growth sector for computing, and represent a step torward practical, ubiquitous computing. Wearable devices decouple the benefits of computer assistance from sitting at a computer or even holding a bulky phone. Wearable apps have applications in diverse areas, including healthcare, personal assistance, navigation, personal security, and many more. For example, GPS heads-up display helps skiers navigate a difficult slope [4]. Similarly, the *Spotify* smartwatch app allows the user to control the music easily, freeing the user's hands from repeatedly taking out the phone.

A prevailing programming model for wearable devices is to create *companion apps* that act as a companion for apps on the more powerful mobile phone. A companion app extends a subset of the smartphone app's graphical user interface (GUI) to the wearable device, adapting the GUI for a different form factor. For example, the *Spotify* companion app (see Figure 1) on the user's watch exports a view of the *Spotify* smartphone app to the watch, and events such as pausing the song are synchronized with the smartphone app.

Unfortunately, the programming model for wearable devices simply does not scale. For example, the *Spotify* app needs to be extended to the smartglass, a different companion app is required. These companion apps can be over a thousand lines of code (and tens of thousands of lines of code including libraries), and require the original app developer to manage the UI, emulate user interaction, and write an ad hoc RPC protocol to synchronize the wearable and the phone application [11]. Because of the significant developer effort required to create a companion app, only a small fraction of smartphone apps have companion apps. Even popular apps such as Facebook do not have a companion app. Worse yet, without source code, third-party developers cannot design new companion apps for an existing smartphone app nor adjust a companion app to better suit their needs.

In this demo, we present a different programming model for wearable devices, where the developer writes the smartphone application *once*, and writes a simple *meta program* to specify how the application should be extended to a given form factor. Our system, UIWear, automatically creates companion apps, that we call *UICompanion* apps, for different form factors based on the meta program. The developer effort in writing the meta program is an order-of-magnitude lower than writing the companion app. UIWear is transparent to the application, does not require source code or changes to the original application, can re-tailor the GUI to suit the wearable interface, and is well-suited for mobile and wearables.

The overarching principle of UIWear is to abstract application management from application design. The human designer (developer or end-user) only specifies what parts of the smartphone GUI are mapped to the wearable device and how the GUI is re-tailored, using a simple *metaprogram*. Writing a metaprogram requires substantially lower programming effort than writing a full-fledged companion app, as the developer needs only specify the interface design.

UIWear's *UI virtualization architecture* manages all other aspects of extending the app to the wearable device. UIWear abstracts a logical model of the GUI as a loose set of UI elements, and uses this abstraction to re-tailor and render the GUI on the wearable. UIWear also performs all synchronization at the GUI layer using the logical GUI model. All user interactions on the wearable device are

*Primary authors with equal contribution.

MobiCom '17, October 16–20, 2017, Snowbird, UT, USA

ACM ISBN 978-1-4503-4916-1/17/10.
https://doi.org/10.1145/3117811.3124769

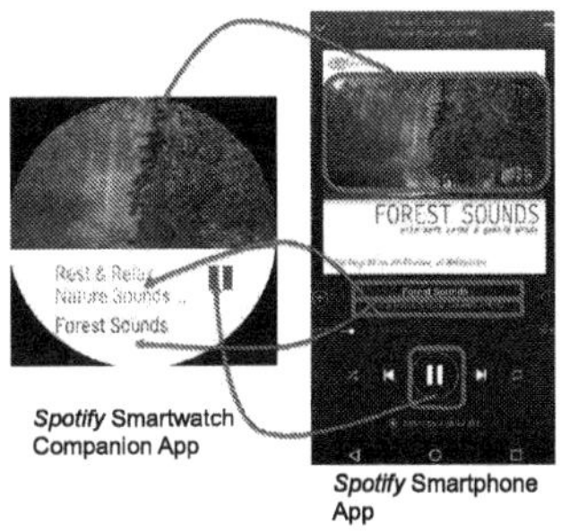

Figure 1: The *Spotify* smartphone and the corresponding smartwatch companion app. A subset of the smartphone GUI (marked within the *red* box) is re-tailored for the watch.

captured by the GUI abstraction and sent to the phone. The phone emulates the user interaction as though it was a local event, and the resulting update to the phone GUI is mirrored on the wearable.

One essential contribution of UIWear is identifying and extracting a logical model of the GUI. UIWear uses the *UI tree* abstraction, which is commonly used across operating systems to represent the GUI as individual UI elements and their relationships [1, 2]. UIWear essentially splices the UI tree, tailors it according to the metaprogram, and compiles it into the UICompanion app. A key contribution of UIWear is in extracting the UI tree from the applications transparently.

Another key challenge is in synchronizing at the GUI layer. Smartphones only allow a *single* active GUI at a given time; in fact, the graphics stack of background apps is destroyed. The consequence is that the wearable app can only synchronize as long as the phone app is in the foreground. We observe that, while maintaining the full graphics stack of each background application is power consuming, the logical GUI model (in our case the UI tree) can be kept active even for background apps with minimal effect on power. In UIWear, we modify the operating system to keep the UI tree of a background application active. This simple change allows us to multiplex I/O events to and from background applications with minimal effect on power.

There has been related work both in the systems and the human-computer interaction (HCI) communities for designing cross-device applications. However, related systems either only work in homogenous environments that do not require UI re-tailoring [7, 8], or only work for specific applications and devices while supporting UI tailoring [9, 10, 12]. UIWear combines the advantages of the two approaches.

2 UIWEAR

Companion app Background. Companion apps are a common programming paradigm used by wearable operating systems and vendors including AndroidWear, Apple, Tizen, Pebble, and the now defunct Google glass. A companion app is a GUI projection of the original smartphone app, where parts of the smartphone UI are re-tailored and displayed on the wearable.

Figure 1 shows the *Spotify* companion app from the AndroidWear playstore [6] for smartwatches. The companion app exports a view of the Spotify smartphone app to the watch, and events such as pausing the song are synchronized with the smartphone.

UIWear Architecture. The UIWear architecture has two stages: compile time and runtime, as shown in Figures 2(a) and (b). At compile time, the human designer writes a metaprogram and UIWear compiles this to the UICompanion app. The metaprogram is the only step that requires a human-in-the-loop. The developer writes a separate metaprogram for each wearable interface such as watch and a glass. The metaprogram includes decisions about what parts of the UI are to appear on the wearable device and how the UI is re-tailored.

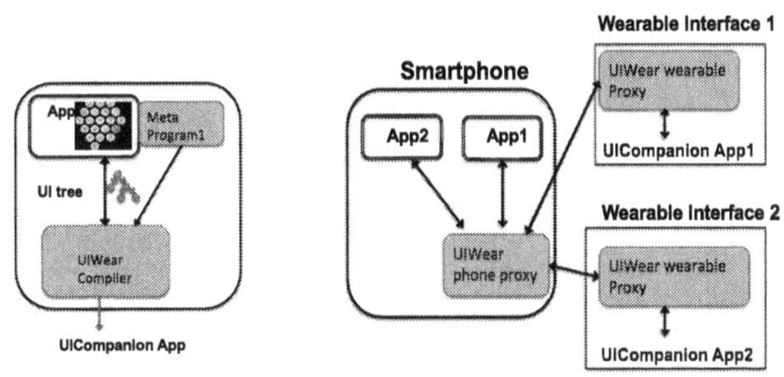

(a) UIWear Compiler and Metaprogram: UIWear compiles the metaprogram specification to create the UICompanion app.

(b) At UIWear Runtime: The UICompanion app on the wearable device synchronizes state with the smartphone app to relay user interactions and get UI updates.

Figure 2: UIWear Architecture

The UIWear compiler compiles the metaprogram to the UICompanion app and ships the app to the wearable device. UIWear extracts the UI tree to abstract and re-tailor the GUI. A natural point at which to extract the UI tree is at the accessibility and UI automation interface. Current accessibility interfaces are designed only for extracting textual content of the GUI, primarily for applications for the visually impaired that may not require graphical content. UIWear augments this existing technique so that the complete UI tree, including text and visual data are extracted.

At run time, UIWear synchronizes the UI states of the wearable app and the corresponding phone app. UIWear's synchronization protocol relays input events from the wearable device to the UIWear phone proxy, which emulates the user input on the phone. The resulting GUI update is relayed to the wearable device using the UI tree abstraction. This synchronization requires no support from the phone application, unlike existing companion apps that need to write a custom remote procedure call.

Implementation. We implement UIWear on the Android ecosystem: Android phone OS, AndroidWear smartwatch OS, and the Sony SmartEyeGlass that runs over a version of Android [5].

From the end-user's perspective, an Android application is made up of multiple "windows" or activities. The designer writes a metaprogram for each application window to be mapped to the wearable, and UIWear compiles the metaprograms and bundles them into a single UICompanion app. UIWear uses the standard Android toolchain to create the UICompanion application. The application consists of the source file, the AndroidManifest file, the layout, and a set of resources that are created programmatically. We create templates for the metaprogram using FreeMarker [3].

We implement the UIWear phone proxy as a client to the accessibility service on Android, and the wearable proxy as a service on the wearable device. The phone and wearable proxies together contain 5,300 lines of code. The phone proxy keeps track of preference files and wearable UI tree for different applications as well as different windows of the same application. The UIWear watch and phone proxy exchange information over the Google Messaging Service (GMS). GMS encapsulates the data and performs the low-level communication tasks, and can use Bluetooth or WiFi.

To multiplex I/O between several UICompanion apps and background apps, UIWear modifies Android to allow the graphic stack to sleep, but keep the intermediate UI representation active.

3 DEMO DETAILS

In this demonstration, we will show how the UICompanion app is generated by UIWear based on the metaprogram specification. We will also show the corresponding developer-written companion apps downloaded from AndroidWear Marketplace. The audience can interact with both versions of the app and compare the look-and-feel and functionality between two versions. We will also show how UIWear can create wearable applications for smartphone apps for which no wearable application currently exists. Specifically, we will demonstrate the companion app creation for *Facebook messenger* and *Yahoo Mail*, as well as companion app creation on Smartglasses. Interested audience members will be invited to write their own metaprogram for extending smartphone apps to wearables.

The demonstrations will be performed on a Nexus 5 smartphone running a customized Android Marshmallow 6.0.1 OS, a smartwatch running AndroidWear 1.5, the Sony SmartEyeglass, and a laptop, all of which will be bought to the venue by the authors. The demonstration requires a desk, power outlets, and WiFi. The demo setup will take less than 30 minutes.

REFERENCES

[1] Android View Hierarchy. http://developer.android.com/guide/topics/ui/overview.html.

[2] Apple View Hierarchy. https://developer.apple.com/library/ios/documentation/General/Conceptual/Devpedia-CocoaApp/View%20Hierarchy.html.

[3] Freemarker. http://freemarker.org/.

[4] GPS Heads Up Display. http://www.reconinstruments.com/products/snow2/.

[5] Sony SmartEyeGlass SDK. https://developer.sony.com/develop/wearables/smarteyeglass-sdk/.

[6] Google Android Wear Market. https://play.google.com/store/apps/category/ANDROID_WEAR?hl=en.

[7] J. Andrus, A. Van't Hof, N. AlDuaij, C. Dall, N. Viennot, and J. Nieh. Cider: Native execution of ios apps on android. In *Proceedings of the ACM International Conference on Architectural Support for Programming Languages and Operating Systems (ASPLOS)*, pages 367–382, 2014.

[8] Apportable. http://www.apportable.com/.

[9] S. M. Billah, D. E. Porter, and I. V. Ramakrishnan. Sinter: Low-bandwidth remote access for the visually-impaired. In *Proceedings of the ACM European Conference on Computer Systems (EuroSys)*, 2016.

[10] J. Nichols, Z. Hua, and J. Barton. Highlight: a system for creating and deploying mobile web applications. In *Proceedings of the 21st annual ACM symposium on User interface software and technology*, pages 249–258. ACM, 2008.

[11] J. Xu, Q. Cao, A. Prakash, A. Balasubramanian, and D. E. Porter. Uiwear: Easily adapting user interfaces for wearable devices. In *Proceedings of the 24th Annual International Conference on Mobile Computing and Networking*, MobiCom '18, 2018.

[12] J. Yang and D. Wigdor. Panelrama: Enabling easy specification of cross-device web applications. In *Proceedings of the SIGCHI Conference on Human Factors in Computing Systems*, CHI '14, pages 2783–2792, New York, NY, USA, 2014. ACM.

Demo: Coding with Superposed Reflection Light for LED-Camera Communication

Yanbing Yang, Jiangtian Nie, Jun Luo*
School of Computer Science and Engineering, Nanyang Technological University
Singapore
{yyang017,jnie001,junluo}@ntu.edu.sg

ABSTRACT

As a popular approach to implementing *Visible Light Communication* (VLC) on commercial-off-the-shelf devices, LED-Camera VLC has attracted substantial attention recently. While such systems initially used reflected light as the communication media, direct light becomes the dominant media for the purpose of combating interference. Nonetheless, the data rate achievable by direct light LED-Camera VLC systems has hit its bottleneck: the dimension of the transmitters. In this demo, we revisit the reflected light approach and propose a novel modulation mechanism, ReflexCode, which converts the potentially destructive interferences into collaborative transmissions. Essentially, our ReflexCode system codes information by superposing light emissions from multiple transmitters. It combines traditional amplitude demodulation with slope detection to "decode" the grayscale modulated signal, and it tunes decoding thresholds dynamically depending on the spatial symbol distribution. In addition, ReflexCode re-engineers the balanced codes to avoid flicker from individual transmitters. We implement ReflexCode as a prototype and demonstrate that it can achieve a promising throughput.

CCS CONCEPTS

• **Computer systems organization** → **Special purpose systems**; • **Networks** → *Wireless access networks*; • **Human-centered computing** → **Mobile computing**; • **Theory of computation** → Error-correcting codes;

KEYWORDS

Visible Light Communication; Collaborative Transmissions; Grayscale Modulation

1 INTRODUCTION

Deemed as a potential "role" in the 5G era, *Visible Light Communication* (VLC), using visible light spectrum as the communication media, has been attracting increasing attentions. While high-power *Light Emitting Diodes* (LEDs) and high-sensitivity *Photo-Diodes* (PD) may achieve a data rate at Gbit/s level within very short distance, readily deployable VLC systems need to be based on *commercial-off-the-shelf* (COTS) devices such as LED luminaires, screens, and smartphone cameras [5–9]. Among the latter category, the LED-Camera communication is particularly promising thanks to the widespread usage of LED lighting and smartphones [5, 6, 8, 9, 13]. On one hand, LED luminaires, of high efficiency and long lifespan, are becoming a mainstream lighting apparatus [11] and are thus good choices of VLC transmitters. On the other hand, smartphone cameras, with the rolling-shutter effect [4], are deemed as convenient VLC receivers. More importantly, as a smartphone camera has limited angle-of-view, using it as a receiver can largely avoid interference that severely challenges the potential implementation of LED-PD VLC [15].

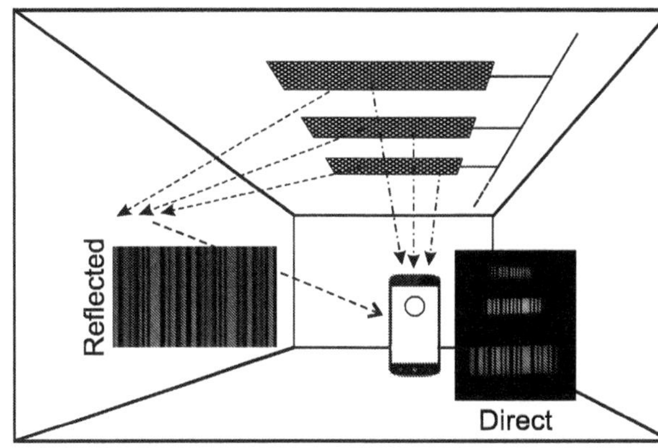

Figure 1: Two approaches of LED-Camera VLC: reflected vs. direct. One major difference is that, under direct light, the transmitters have a natural spatial division on the receiver side, i.e., the frame captured by a camera.

Many innovative systems have been proposed for realizing LED-Camera VLC [4–6, 8, 9, 12]. These systems initially made use of reflected light as their communication media, but reflections may blend emissions from various interfering LED transmitters and hence these early systems were confined to a single transmitter [4, 10]. Recent developments shifted to direct light, i.e., taking photos of LED luminaires directly, in order to avoid interference [8, 9] and also to take the advantage of collaborative transmissions [5, 6]. We illustrate and compare these two approaches qualitatively in Figure 1; it shows the spatial division advantage of direct light. However, direct light LED-Camera VLC has already hit its bottleneck of data rate [5]: as the data rate is strongly affected by the dimension of a transmitter, achieving a kbit/s level of data rate at a reasonable distance would require a luminaire dimensionally similar to the outdated fluorescent tube. Reflected light, on the

*This work was supported in part by the AcRF Tier 2 Grant MOE2016-T2-2-022 and the DSAIR Center at NTU.

MobiCom '17, October 16–20, 2017, Snowbird, UT, USA

ACM ISBN 978-1-4503-4916-1/17/10.
https://doi.org/10.1145/3117811.3124770

contrary, does not depend on the dimension of the transmitter, so it has the potential to serve as the stepping-stone for achieving higher data rates.

Therefore, we intend to answer the following question in this demo: *would it be possible to constructively use the multiple transmissions within a cell of a reflected light LED-Camera VLC system?* Apparently, a satisfactory answer would boost data rate for individual cells while extending the system to cover a large area in an interference-free manner through cell partition. To this end, we proposed ReflexCode that codes information by superposing light emissions from multiple transmitters. With a close synchronization among these transmitters, the new modulation, termed *Grayscale-Shift Keying* (GSK), achieves a higher bit-per-symbol ratio than the commonly used *On-OFF Keying* (OOK), thus potentially resulting in a high bit rate. In summary, our contributions can be summarized as:

- The innovative idea of GSK to constructively use multiple LED transmissions for boosting data rate.
- A robust demodulation algorithm to effectively extract information from GSK modulated transmissions.
- Novel balanced codes adapted to GSK for flicker mitigation and reliability improvement.
- Two prototypes for validating the effectiveness of ReflexCode, and extensive field experiments to show the promising performance of ReflexCode.

The remainder of this demo is organized as follows. We first introduce the concept of GSK and describe the system architecture of ReflexCode in Section 2. Section 3 presents the facilities requirements, and Section 4 quickly concludes this demo.

2 REFLEXCODE: MODULATION BY SUPERPOSING TRANSMISSIONS

2.1 Grayscale-Shift Keying (GSK)

The rolling shutter effect stems from the sequential exposure of CMOS cameras. As the pixels are exposed and sampled in a column-by-column manner, they may record time-varying information [4, 9]. In particular, if the light emitted from an LED luminaire (transmitter hereafter) flickers in a high frequency unnoticeable by human users, the rolling shutter will lead to bright-dark bands in a frame depending on the ON-OFF state of the transmitters when individual columns are exposed. The bit rate of such a transmission depends on several factors including the signal frequency and the camera features, mostly importantly on the *Region of Interest* (RoI) [3]. As shown in Figure 2, direct light LED-Camera VLC has spatially separated RoIs, yet the dimensions of individual RoIs are determined by those of the transmitters and their distances from the receiver [5]. This makes it quite easy to handle interference but extremely difficult to scale-up data rate.

However, the brightness of the bands within an RoI can actually be individually controlled: the brightness of a given band is proportional to the light intensity when the band is exposed. Using the level of brightness (hence grayscale in digital image) to form symbols, a special *Amplitude-Shift Keying* (ASK) can be constructed. We term this modulation Grayscale-Shift Keying (GSK); it extends OOK to have a higher bit-per-symbol ratio. Although GSK applies

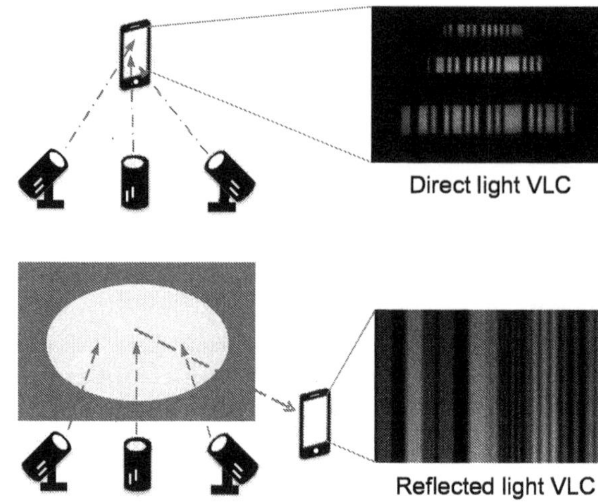

Figure 2: Rolling shutter under both direct and reflected VLCs.

to direct light VLC, it can be more complicated and less robust than OOK. However, as shown in Figure 2, the mutual-interfering transmissions under reflected light VLC naturally form bands with a various grayscale, albeit too messy to be demodulated without coordination. If we can constructively superpose these transmissions by re-designing the modulations for individual transmitters, we may end up with a GSK that potentially leads to a higher throughput.

2.2 GSK from Synchronized Emissions

Considering a common area on a reflector lit by N transmitters. Depending on how many transmitters are ON at a given moment, the reflected light intensity has $N + 1$ scales due to superposition. In conventional VLC systems, these transmitters may not be closely synchronized, hence the resulting superposition may not be decodable. However, synchronizing these transmitters is rather straightforward as they are connected to a common power grid. In our prototypes, these transmitters share the same drivers and are thus inherently synchronized. Consequently, each grayscale lasts for a fixed amount of time, causing a determined width of band on the receiver side. Therefore, we can treat each distinct grayscale as a symbol. We compare an asynchronous superposition with a synchronized one (hence GSK) in Figure 3. Although GSK may still lead to variations in the widths of bands due to consecutive identical symbols, asynchronous superposition results in a high

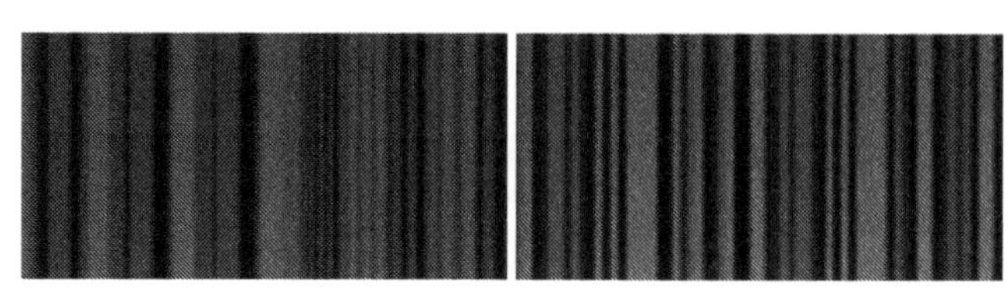

Figure 3: Superposition under asynchronous transmissions (left) and that under synchronized transmissions (right).

variance in width and also very blurred boundaries between bands, making it almost impossible to demodulate.

As GSK encodes bits to these $N + 1$ symbols, the bit-per-symbol ratio is $b = \log_2(N + 1)$ in theory. Note that b does not have to be an integer. For example, if $N = 2$, we can code information in a ternary system instead of binary. However, we currently only consider the cases where b is an integer, so as to simplify the system design. In particular, our prototype involves three transmitters to form at most a 4-GSK, with each symbol representing 2 bits in the following manner:

i) All three transmitters OFF to generate a totally dark band for 00, i.e., symbol-0 (or S-0),
ii) The middle transmitter tx_2 ON while others OFF for 01, i.e., symbol-1 (or S-1),
iii) The complement of symbol-1 (tx_1 and tx_3 ON and tx_2 OFF) for 10, i.e., symbol-2 (or S-2), and
iv) All ON to form symbol-3 (or S-3) for 11.

This balanced allocation aims to produce a symmetric tonal range within an RoI, thus facilitating the demodulation. The principle behind this allocation scheme can be readily extended to a larger N, yet we shall not dwell on this technique detail as we would most probably not have a very large N under normal lighting constraints.

2.3 System Architecture and Implementation

The system is partitioned by default into two parts, namely transmitter and receiver. As shown in Figure 2 (the lower part), the transmitter consists of a group of coordinated LED luminaires, while the receiver uses a smartphone camera as its front-end. Although the reflector is part of the communication media, we do not involve it in the design of ReflexCode. On the transmitter side, GSK is obtained by superposing different ON-OFF states of the synchronized transmitters as described in Section 2.2. Moreover, the emissions from individual transmitters have to be first encoded to achieve DC-balance and bounded disparity, so as to confine bit errors and avoid flicker. Finally, FEC is added to combat possible packet loss. On the receiver side, demodulation is proceeded by a tonal range identification process; this calibration is needed to cope with the nonuniform tone distribution. The demodulation process takes the dynamically calibrated thresholds and the local differentials as input to convert grayscale bands into bits. We omit the detailed demodulation/decoding in this demo due to page limitation, but refer to our full paper [14].

We implement a small-scale prototype using three LED spotlights [1]. This prototype is meant to emulate the reflected lighting [2], as the spotlights are facing directly to the reflector (a billboard). Due to the small dimension and the facing direction of these spotlights, direct light VLC is impossible, which is exactly the scenario where ReflexCode is supposed to work. Our current fixture puts those three spotlights at an adjacent distance of 7cm and a 30cm distance from the wall or a reflector. We employ the self-built LED driver consisting of low-cost transistors and a MSP430 MCU to drive the LED luminaires. The prototype runs at a transmission frequency of 6kHz. A ReflexCode packet has a preamble of five successive S-3 and a single S-0 to indicate the header, followed by 24 data bits (8-bit packet sequence number and 16-bit payload), and finally ends with a S-0. We employ a Nexus 6 smartphone as the receiver, and build an APP on it for demodulation/decoding . Basically, we configure the Nexus 6's camera to work in the preview mode so as to capture banded frames at a rate of 30fps.

3 FACILITY REQUIREMENTS

In this demonstration, we will setup a testbed with three LED luminaires which transmit messages with the proposed GSK modulation. We will bring our LED luminares, own laptops and smartphones, but we do need a desk as well as power outlets. Specifically, we need a plain wall perfecting in white or light color, and the available area should not be less than $0.6m \times 0.6m$ above the desk. In case there is no available walls, a white plastic panel with similar size of an A0 poster is needed. Our demonstration does not require special Internet access, yet the Wi-Fi connection might be required. The whole setup process should be less than half or an hour.

4 CONCLUSION

In this demo, we have presented ReflexCode, a novel yet practical LED-Camera VLC system that adopts reflected light as its communication media. Compared with the existing peers, Reflex has improved on throughput substantially, mainly due to its innovation on exploiting collaborative transmissions to form GSK, a modulation scheme based on grayscale. This demo will first showcase ReflexCode for public and demonstrate its efficacy in real lives.

REFERENCES

[1] *Low Cost LED Lamp.* https://item.taobao.com/item.htm?spm=a1z09.2.0.0.rUBQRc&id=520120735357&_u=95plk56ee7c.
[2] *Paulmann.* http://www.paulmann.com/en/all/all-about-light/led-strips/indirect-lighting.html.
[3] G. Corbellini, K. Aksit, S. Schmid, S. Mangold, and T. Gross. 2014. Connecting Networks of Toys and Smartphones with Visible Light Communication. *IEEE Communications Magazine* 52, 7 (2014), 72–78.
[4] C. Danakis, M. Afgani, G. Povey, I. Underwood, and H. Haas. 2012. Using a CMOS Camera Sensor for Visible Light Communication. In *Proc. of the 31th IEEE GLOBECOM Workshop.* 1244–1248.
[5] J. Hao, Y. Yang, and J. Luo. 2016. CeilingCast: Energy Efficient and Location-bound Broadcast through LED-Camera Communication. In *Proc. of the 35th IEEE INFOCOM.* 1–9.
[6] P. Hu, P. H. Pathak, X. Feng, H. Fu, and P. Mohapatra. 2015. Colorbars: Increasing Data Rate of LED-to-Camera Communication Using Color Shift Keying. In *Proc. of the 11th ACM CoNEXT.* 12.
[7] W. Hu, Z. Huang J. Mao, Y. Xue, K. Bian J. She, and G. Shen. 2014. Strata: Layered Coding for Scalable Visual Communication. In *Proc. of the 20th ACM MobiCom.* 79–90.
[8] Y.-S. Kuo, P. Pannuto, K.-J. Hsiao, and P. Dutta. 2014. Luxapose: Indoor Positioning with Mobile Phones and Visible Light. In *Proc. of the 20th ACM MobiCom.* 447–458.
[9] H. Lee, H. Lin, Y. L. Wei, H. I. Wu, H. M. Tsai, and K. Lin. 2015. RollingLight: Enabling Line-of-Sight Light-to-Camera Communications. In *Proc. of 13th ACM MobiSys.* 167–180.
[10] N. Rajagopal, P. Lazik, and A. Rowe. 2014. Hybrid Visible Light Communication for Cameras and Low-Power Embedded Devices. In *Proc. of the 1st ACM VLCS.* 33–38.
[11] B. Weir. 2012. Driving The 21st Century's Lights. *IEEE Spectrum* 49, 3 (2012).
[12] Y. Yang. 2017. Practical Visible Light Communication System Utilizing LED Sensing. In *Proc. of the 15th IEEE PerCom Workshops.* 109–110.
[13] Y. Yang, J. Hao, and J. Luo. 2017. CeilingTalk: Lightweight Indoor Broadcast Through LED-Camera Communication. *IEEE Transactions on Mobile Computing (to appear)* (2017). https://doi.org/10.1109/TMC.2017.2694834
[14] Y. Yang, J. Nie, and J. Luo. 2017. ReflexCode: Coding with Superposed Reflection Light for LED-Camera Communication. In *Proc. of the 23th ACM MobiCom (to appear).*
[15] R. Zhang, H. Claussen, H. Haas, and L. Hanzo. 2016. Energy Efficient Visible Light Communications Relying on Amorphous Cells. *IEEE Journal on Selected Areas in Communications* 34, 4 (2016), 894–906.

Demo: Stuffing Wi-Fi Beacons for Fun and Profit

Sven Zehl
Technische Universität Berlin
(TUB), Germany
zehl@tkn.tu-berlin.de

Anatolij Zubow
Technische Universität Berlin
(TUB), Germany
zubow@tkn.tu-berlin.de

Adam Wolisz
Technische Universität Berlin
(TUB), Germany
wolisz@tkn.tu-berlin.de

ABSTRACT

Ubiquitous Wi-Fi access points (APs) constantly send out beacon and probe response frames to inform potential stations (STAs) about their existence. Beacon and probe responses can be extended by adding additional information (so-called beacon stuffing) making it possible to deliver this information to mobile devices (e.g. smart-phones equipped with 802.11 interfaces) without the need for association with the local infrastructure. This feature can be used to support location-based information services (LBS) related for e.g. advertising local opportunities, temporary obstacles and traffic disturbances or emergency notifications.
In this paper we introduce a demonstrator for Location-based Wi-Fi Services (LoWS) based on beacon stuffing. The LoWS system can be easily installed within an existent 802.11 infrastructure while the receiver application can be installed on nearly all up-to-date commercial off-the-shelf smartphones, e.g. based on Android or iOS.

CCS CONCEPTS

•**Networks →Network experimentation; Local area networks; Location based services; Wireless access networks;** *Wireless access points, base stations and infrastructure;* Network architectures;

KEYWORDS

LoWS; Location-based Wi-Fi Services; LBS; IEEE 802.11; Beacon Stuffing

1 INTRODUCTION

Nowadays most urban and suburban areas are widely instrumented for Internet access by deployment of Wi-Fi access points (APs). Due to legal and security concerns, most of these APs are, however, secured and thus regular usage is available only to owners of proper credentials. In order to enable the Wi-Fi equipped devices (STAs) to search for the APs and in order to support the security verification, the 802.11 standard includes mechanisms for frame exchange between any STA and any AP in an unconstrained "pre-connection" mode.

MobiCom'17, October 16–20, 2017, Snowbird, UT, USA.
 ISBN 978-1-4503-4916-1/17/10.
DOI: http://dx.doi.org/10.1145/3117811.3119851

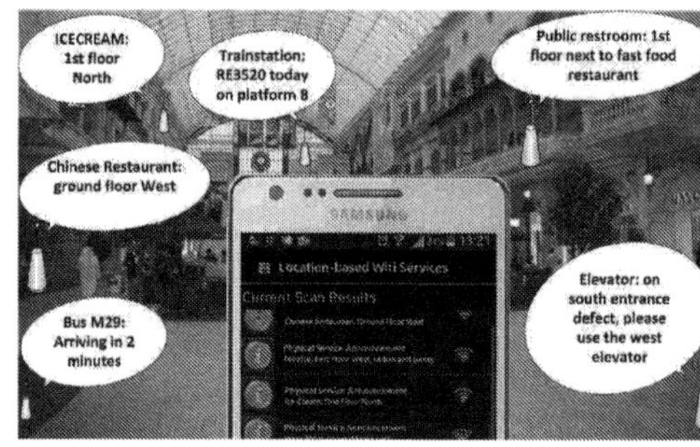

Figure 1: Examples of location based physical service announcements

Two of the frames used in this mode are beacon and probe response frames. Each AP broadcasts beacons periodically announcing information such as the name of the wireless network and some capabilities provided by this network. Client STAs collect beacons and extract the required information. To accelerate the collection process, clients have also the possibility to trigger an AP to transmit the information contained in beacons immediately by sending a probe request frame which causes the AP to reply with a probe response frame. The value of the option to piggyback in beacons information potentially relevant for the user, but not related to the operation of the network itself, has been for the first time discussed by Chandra et al. [1] who have established the term "beacon stuffing" for such information dissemination. This mechanism has in fact a huge application potential in context of offering so-called "location based services" (LBS) – information relevant in a rather limited proximity. The coverage of APs under usual operating conditions is limited, thus assuming the possibility to "feed" only selected APs (or groups of APs) with targeted information is very attractive. But the real potential of this technology can be exploited in the best way in combination with smartphones – which are actually omnipresent and by default equipped with Wi-Fi.

In general all kind of information which is normally visually or acoustically announced, e.g. bus or train schedule, advertisements, conference program, airport announcements, or emergency information, can be broadcasted using beacon stuffing, cf. Fig. 1 and Fig. 2.

2 SYSTEM DESIGN

Wi-Fi beacon and probe response frames are built up using some fixed and variable length fields. The variable length fields are called information elements (IEs). Beside a lot of predefined IEs, the 802.11 standard defines a special IE which carries the human readable name of the network called service set identifier (SSID) which is able to transport up to

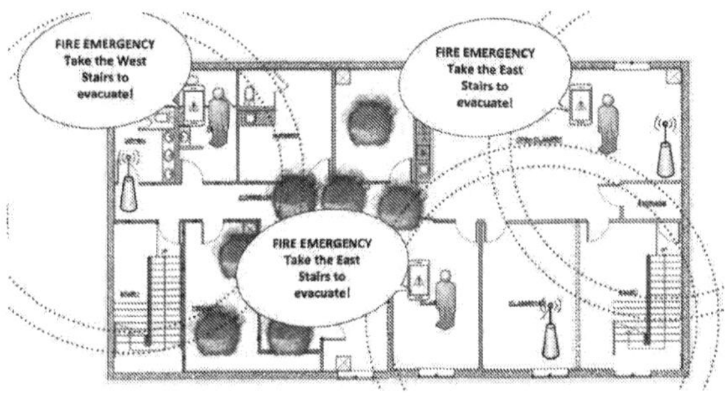

Figure 2: Providing location based emergency notifications and evacuation instructions

32 alphanumeric characters. Most of the literature relied on embedding LBS data into so-called vendor specific IE(s), e.g. [2, 3]. But, during our investigation, we found that this solution brings the drawback that the disseminated information cannot be received by all currently available smart-phone platforms without applying jail-break or rooting procedures. This problem can be solved by utilizing the SSID IE which is included within all beacon and probe responses.

But also this approach is challenging, e.g. using parts of the SSID IE to include additional information prevents the automatic connection establishment with already known 802.11 networks. Further, if not only information is appended to the SSID but rather the entire SSID is replaced, even manual connection is impossible, because without the SSID the user does not know which AP belongs to which network. As consequence, we utilize a different approach of exploiting the SSID IE.

Since nearly all up-to-date COTS Wi-Fi APs provide the possibility to enable multiple virtual SSIDs beside the standard SSID, an additional virtual SSID can be exploited to transport the additional LBS data. Virtual SSIDs are in most cases used to provide a second network with restricted access, e.g. for guests or visitors. In our case, we simply create an additional virtual SSID to broadcast LBS data. After the creation of an additional virtual SSID, the AP will broadcast beacon frames containing the new SSID embedded in a SSID IE and will respond to probe request frames with probe responses that also contain the new SSID IE.

As this additional broadcasted beacon and probe response frames consume lots of air-time, we keep the amount of additional sent data as low as possible and utilize a codebook (CB) approach to disseminate the LBS data. Different CBs can be used to map a code either to a human readable string which might be displayed at the receiver or to a unified resource identifier (URL) that then maps to the actual information. But, as every location may want to transmit different information, each location needs its own location dependent CB. To enable the download of a location dependent CB, we postulate to use local CB servers. For mapping the local CB servers to the different locations, a global address server is utilized which takes the globally unique MAC addresses of the APs and returns the address of the corresponding local CB server. The local CB is downloaded and cached in advance when a client enters a new location the first time or when an

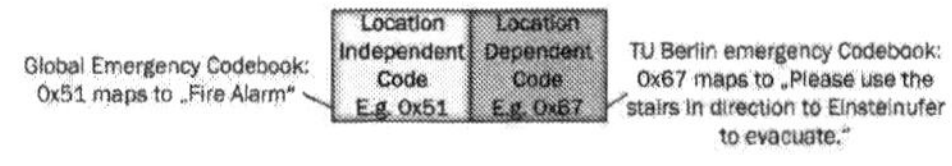

Figure 3: Example of the LoWS dichotomous code

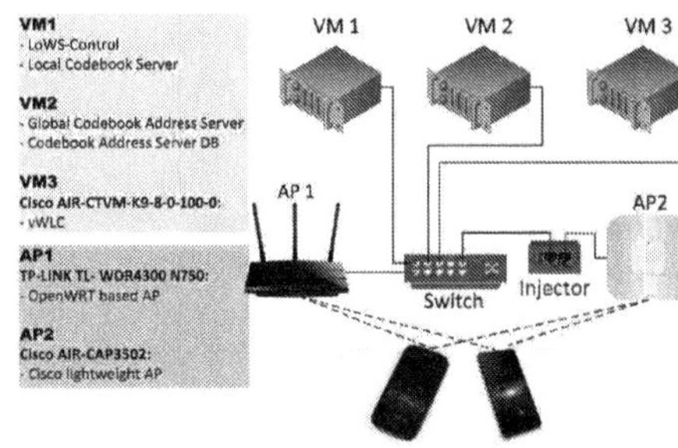

Figure 4: LoWS Demonstrator setup

unknown code is received. Also several location dependent CBs may be preinstalled in the receiver application. If the location dependent CB is not available, client devices need an Internet connection to be able to download the CB. As this is not always possible or not intended, e.g. the user wants to save his mobile data volume; we utilize a coding scheme that always allows decoding the general information of the broadcasted LBS without the location dependent CB. We named this scheme the dichotomous code which is shown in Fig. 3. In general all broadcasted codes consist of a location dependent code and a location independent code. The location independent code is more general, never maps to a URL, and the codebook for this code part is preinstalled on all receiver applications.

Fig. 6 describes the general Location-based Wi-Fi Services architecture (LoWS architecture) and its basic actors and entities that are needed to enable the aforementioned functionality. Each location provides its (logically) own local codebook server, while a global codebook server is used to map the different APs to the corresponding local codebook servers.

Once the embedded code has been received and decoded by the receiver application, it can be filtered, categorized, transformed or translated. For instance, the local application on the mobile end device can use the LBS data to notify a user if a pre-specified information is available, e.g. if a specific waiting ticket number is now "called out", if a particular train is arriving, a public restroom is in vicinity or a conference session will start soon. Moreover, the end devices can translate the information in other languages or can transform it from audio to text for deaf people or vice versa for blind people.

3 DEMONSTRATOR SETUP

We introduce our demonstrator for Location-based Wi-Fi Services (LoWS) which utilizes Beacon and Probe Response Stuffing to disseminate LBS data using already deployed Wi-Fi APs and Android based COTS unmodified smart-phones as receivers, Fig. 4. For the embedding of the dichotomous

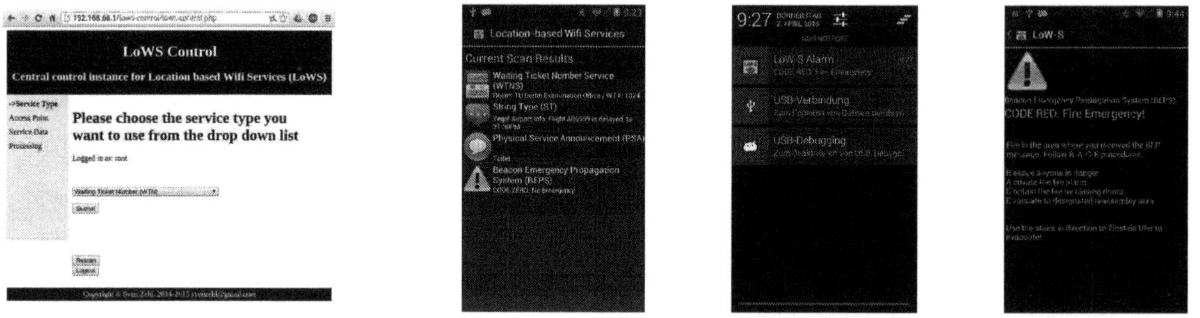

(a) LoWS Control (b) LBS List (c) Fire Warning (d) Detailed Warning

Figure 5: Screenshots of (a) LoWS Sending Entity and (b)-(d) LoWS Receiver Application (Android example)

code, we utilize the SSID field of the beacon and probe responses that are broadcasted by an additional virtual Wi-Fi network as described in the last section. As there are today mainly two kinds of 802.11 network architectures deployed, the centralized architecture and the autonomous architecture, we decided to use one representative from each kind for the LBS broadcasters. For the centralized architecture we use APs from the vendor Cisco. For the autonomous architecture the demonstrator utilizes an OpenWRT based AP from TP-Link (TL-WDR4300). The receiver devices consist of Android based smartphones running a LoWS receiver application. Moreover, the demonstrator uses virtual machines (VM) running in VMware Player on Ubuntu Linux as hypervisor. The first VM (VM1) comprises the LoWS control program used to program new LBS broadcast requests into specific AP(s), cf. Fig. 5(a), and the local codebook server responsible to provide the local codebook to the clients; both are implemented using the PHP: Hypertext Preprocessor scripting language and MySQL. The second VM (VM2) used in the demonstrator represents the global codebook server which is also implemented using PHP and MySQL. Finally VM3 implements the virtual Wireless LAN controller (vWLC) needed to control the centralized Cisco AP.

During the demo we show how easily various LBS data can be programmed into beacon and probe response frames using the LoWS Control unit (Fig. 5a) and how easily it can be received using the LoWS receiver application. As all LBS data is sent using probe responses and beacons which are sent before 802.11 association and before authentication, the receiver devices do not need any kind of network connection such as Wi-Fi or cellular to receive the messages. But of course the system also works if the device is connected to a Wi-Fi AP or a cellular base station.

To enable the conference attendees to participate interactively, we provide a possibility to download the LoWS receiver application via the official Android app store and enable therefore everyone to use his own smartphone. Moreover, the demonstrator is equipped with several smartphones to show the functionality also to people unwilling to install the application on their own device. Different scenarios such as simulating an emergency and broadcasting emergency notifications, cf. Fig. 5c-d, or broadcasting physical service announcements (presence of public-restroom, elevator) are

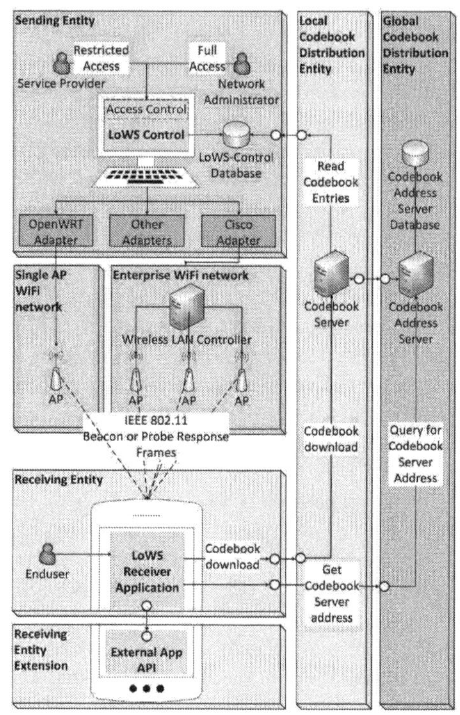

Figure 6: LoWS System Architecture

shown during the demo session. Moreover, during the whole conference, the demonstrator will be utilized to announce the conference program, e.g. additional APs in the refreshment area will be programmed to announce the current session, the currently presented paper and the beginning/end of a coffee break. Moreover, conference attendees in vicinity to one of our demonstrator APs can be notified when a new session or a specific talk starts.

REFERENCES

[1] R. Chandra, J. Padhye, L. Ravindranath, and A. Wolman. Beacon-stuffing: Wi-fi without associations. In *Mobile Computing Systems and Applications, 2007. HotMobile*, March 2007.

[2] S. Zehl, N. Karowski, A. Zubow, and A. Wolisz. Lows: A complete open source solution for wi-fi beacon stuffing based location-based services. In *IFIP/IEEE WMNC 2016*, July 2016.

[3] S. Zehl, A. Zubow, M. Döring, and A. Wolisz. Resfi: A secure framework for self organized radio resource management in residential wifi networks. In *IEEE WoWMoM 2016*, June 2016.

Demo: Acoustic Sensing Based Indoor Floor Plan Construction Using Smartphones

Bing Zhou[1], Mohammed Elbadry[2], Ruipeng Gao[3], Fan Ye[1]
[1]Department of Electrical and Computer Engineering, Stony Brook University
[2]Department of Computer Science, Stony Brook University
[3]School of Software Engineering, Beijing Jiaotong University
{bing.zhou,mohammed.salah,fan.ye}@stonybrook.edu
rpgao@bjtu.edu.cn

ABSTRACT

This demo presents *BatMapper*, an acoustics sensing technology for fast, fine-grained and low cost floor plan construction. BatMapper operates by emitting sound signal and capturing its reflections by two microphones on smartphones. We develop robust probabilistic echo-object association and outlier removal algorithms to identify the correspondence between distances and objects, thus the geometry of corridors. We compensate minute hand sway movements to identify small surface recessions, thus detecting doors automatically. Additionally, we leverage structure cues in indoor environments for user trace calibration. The demo will enable any person to hold the smartphone and walk along a corridor to map the corridor shape and detect doors in real-time.

CCS CONCEPTS

• **Networks → Location based services;** • **Human-centered computing → Mobile computing; Smartphones;**

KEYWORDS

Acoustic Sensing; Indoor Floor Plans; Smartphones

1 INTRODUCTION

Online digital maps (e.g., Google Maps) have provided great convenience for location based services (LBS) outdoors such as finding nearby point-of-interests (POIs) and navigation. However, for indoor environments, such maps are extremely scarce and unavailable in most buildings. This has become a huge obstacle to pervasive indoor LBS.

Accurate, scalable indoor floor plan construction at low costs is urgently needed. Autonomous robots equipped with high precision special sensors (e.g., laser rangers [6], depth cameras [4], sonars [7]) can produce high quality maps. However, the high manufacturing costs, operational and logistic obstacles make it difficult to deploy robots in large quantities. Recently some work [2, 3] have leveraged crowdsourced data (e.g., WiFi, inertial, images) from commodity mobile devices to achieve scalability. However, they require large amounts of data to combat inevitable errors and noises in crowdsourcing, hence expensive total efforts and long data collection times. Those using images also face common limitations in vision techniques: dark/changed lighting, blurry images, glass walls, and restrictions on photo-taking due to privacy concerns.

In this demo, we present BatMapper, a novel acoustic sensing based system for accurate floor plan construction using commodity smartphones. Unlike inertial [1] or Wi-Fi [5] data that are inherently noisy, acoustics is capable of producing very accurate (e.g., cm-level) distance measurements. Unlike images [3], its performance is not affected by lighting conditions or transparent objects, nor does it cause privacy concerns. A single person can finish the measurements of a floor in a few minutes, eliminating the long time needed to crowdsource large amounts of data from many users.

2 OVERVIEW

BatMapper leverages three sensing modalities: acoustic, gyroscope and accelerometer for fast, accurate floor plan construction. The user walks along corridors while holding the phone, which keeps emitting and recording sound signals. It detects sound reflections (i.e., echoes) and measures their distances/amplitudes, from which relative positions of objects (e.g., walls) are inferred, and combined with user traces for floor plans.

Acoustic Ranging. The acoustic ranging module in BatMapper consists of sound emitting, sound recording by two microphones, and a series of signal processing steps to produce distance/amplitude measurements for echo candidates in both microphones (Figure 1). The received signals will go through Butterworth bandpass filters for the bottom/top microphone to remove background noise. Without such filtering, weak reflections can be buried in the noise. This step is critical for collecting data in noisy environments. Next we cross-correlate the signal with its respective pulse, a common technique that produces a peak for each echo, and obtain the upper envelop for the signal. Then we chop the envelop into segments of small time windows of 35*ms*, each containing echoes from one pulse only. The first peak will always be the direct sound from the speaker to the microphone, and it has the highest amplitude. It will be used as the starting point. By measuring the time between the sound emission and echo reception, a series of ranging candidates to nearby objects are estimated.

Echo-Object Association. The ranging candidates are inherently noisy due to cluttered objects, multi-surface reflections, and lack direction information. *Echo-object association*, detecting which echo thus distance corresponds to which object (e.g., walls), is critical.

MobiCom '17, October 16–20, 2017, Snowbird, UT, USA

ACM ISBN 978-1-4503-4916-1/17/10.
https://doi.org/10.1145/3117811.3119864

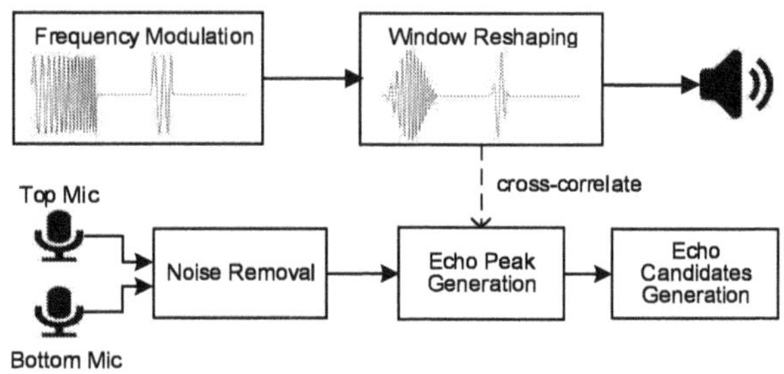

Figure 1: A particular sound signal and multiple signal processing steps produce echo candidates.

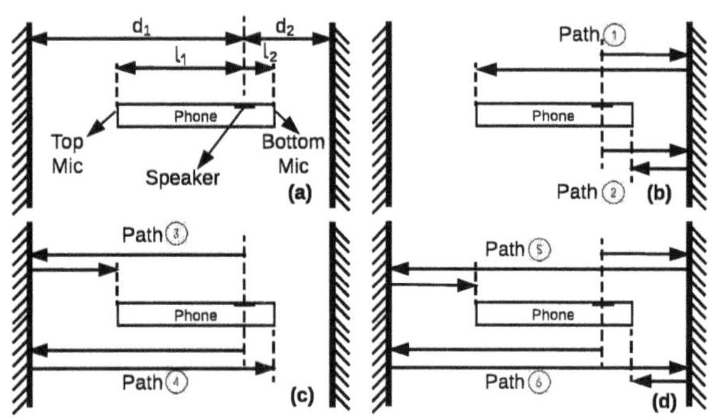

Figure 2: Position of speaker and microphones on the phone, and sound travelling paths of strong echoes in corridor.

We propose robust algorithms for echo-object association to derive geometries of corridors: a *probabilistic evidence accumulation* wall-distance association algorithm computes probabilities of echoes bouncing off different surfaces using relationships among various distances. Figure 2 shows a phone held perpendicular to both sidewalls in a corridor, and reflection paths of strong echoes received by microphones. In Figure 2(a), d_1, d_2 are distances from the speaker to the left/right wall (the width of corridor $d = d_1 + d_2$); l_1 and l_2 are the constant distances from speaker to the two microphones (the length of the phone $l = l_1 + l_2$). Certain distance relationships can be derived, such as echoes bounced from the same side wall have a certain difference (Figure 2(b&c)), and the multipath (Figure 2(d)) reflects the corridor width. Depending on how close these constraints are met, we assign probabilities for each echo candidate whether it's from left or right side walls.

A *recursive outlier removal* further eliminates residual incorrect associations caused by cluttered/moving objects. A *sway compensation* technique is designed to extract and compensate hand sway during walking and its disturbance to distance, thus small surface recessions caused by doors ($\sim 10cm$) are reliably identified and door locations detected. Distinct patterns in inertial and acoustics are combined to classify corridors, corners, open spaces and cluttered areas. Refer to [8] for further details.

User Trace Construction. We construct user's walking trace through step counting and orientation estimation from inertial sensors. However, the accumulation error with dead-reckoning from inertial sensors is a well known problem. Thus, several techniques are developed to suppress such errors: i) we minimize user's manipulation while walking; ii) we estimate orientation from sensor fusion instead of gyroscope only; iii) structure cues of indoor environments are leveraged to calibrate the orientation drifts.

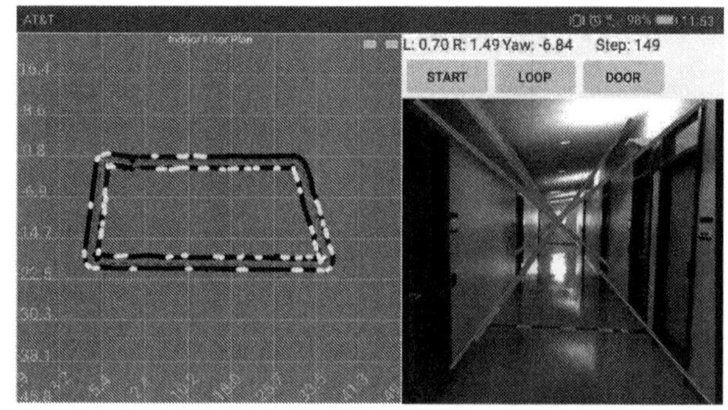

Figure 3: User interface of BatMapper demo application on Android.

First, BatMapper just requires the user to hold the phone and walk along a corridor. It does not require the user to take pictures every now and then, which involves a lot of phone rotations, thus introducing more errors in orientation estimation and step detection. Second, for more robust orientation measurement, we use the composite sensor game-rotation-vector in smart phones that leverages accelerometer and gyroscope, which proves to be more reliable than integrating gyroscope data for orientation. Finally, to combat the accumulation error, we leverage the structure cues (e.g., straight corridor, right-angle corners) in buildings for orientation calibration. As the user is supposed to walk along corridors, and make turns at corners, we detect major orientation changes instead of using instantaneous inertial sensor readings. That is, we "lock" the orientation to a constant value when there's no obvious rotation detected (e.g., the user is walking along a straight corridor). When the user makes turns, we detect such large orientation changes. If the orientation change is close to right-angle within a certain threshold, it will be calibrated to right-angle automatically. The trace is further calibrated when a walking loop closure is available to compensate step length error.

3 DEMO SETUP

A demo application on Android devices is developed for real-time mapping. Figure 3 shows the user interface and a sample corridor map. The constructed map sample is on the left, the red dotted line represents user's walking trace, and black lines are corridor walls with door locations marked as yellow segments. The camera view on the right side leverages computer vision techniques for straight corridor detection, which is used for map refinement.

Our demo setup just requires a smartphone and indoor environment (i.e., a long corridor) for experiment. Due to acoustic sensing range limitations, our demo is capable to produce reliable results in buildings with a reasonable corridor width(i.e., <3m, office building, hotel), but not those with extreme wide corridors (e.g., shopping malls). The demo will generate the corridor shape with door locations marked in real-time as the user walks along the corridor.

We may need a table to set our laptop (plus a monitor, if available) to show our off-line map generation from collected data. We also need a place to hang the poster and AC power for laptop. Setup is expected to be done within 10 minutes.

Acknowledgements: This work is supported in part by a 2016 Google Faculty Research Award, and BJTU funding R16RC00030.

REFERENCES

[1] Moustafa Alzantot and Moustafa Youssef. 2012. Crowdinside: automatic construction of indoor floorplans. In *Proceedings of the 20th International Conference on Advances in Geographic Information Systems*. ACM, 99–108.

[2] Jiang Dong, Yu Xiao, Marius Noreikis, Zhonghong Ou, and Antti Ylä-Jääski. 2015. imoon: Using smartphones for image-based indoor navigation. In *Proceedings of the 13th ACM Conference on Embedded Networked Sensor Systems*. ACM, 85–97.

[3] Ruipeng Gao, Mingmin Zhao, Tao Ye, Fan Ye, Yizhou Wang, Kaigui Bian, Tao Wang, and Xiaoming Li. 2014. Jigsaw: Indoor floor plan reconstruction via mobile crowdsensing. In *Proceedings of the 20th annual international conference on Mobile computing and networking*. ACM, 249–260.

[4] Kourosh Khoshelham and Sander Oude Elberink. 2012. Accuracy and resolution of kinect depth data for indoor mapping applications. *Sensors* 12, 2 (2012), 1437–1454.

[5] Hongbo Liu, Yu Gan, Jie Yang, Simon Sidhom, Yan Wang, Yingying Chen, and Fan Ye. [n. d.]. Push the limit of WiFi based localization for smartphones. In *ACM Mobicom 2012*.

[6] Hartmut Surmann, Andreas Nüchter, and Joachim Hertzberg. 2003. An autonomous mobile robot with a 3D laser range finder for 3D exploration and digitalization of indoor environments. *Robotics and Autonomous Systems* 45, 3 (2003), 181–198.

[7] Juan D Tardós, José Neira, Paul M Newman, and John J Leonard. 2002. Robust mapping and localization in indoor environments using sonar data. *The International Journal of Robotics Research* 21, 4 (2002), 311–330.

[8] Bing Zhou, Mohammed Elbadry, Ruipeng Gao, and Fan Ye. 2017. BatMapper: Acoustic Sensing Based Indoor Floor Plan Construction Using Smartphones. In *Proceedings of the 15th Annual International Conference on Mobile Systems, Applications, and Services*. ACM, 42–55.

Demo: LiShield: Privacy Protection of Physical Environment Against Photographing

Shilin Zhu*
University of California San Diego
shz338@eng.ucsd.edu

Chi Zhang*
University of Wisconsin-Madison
czhang296@wisc.edu

Xinyu Zhang
University of California San Diego
xiz368@eng.ucsd.edu

ABSTRACT

The ubiquity of mobile camera devices has been triggering an outcry of privacy concerns, whereas privacy protection still relies on the compliance of the photographer or camera hardware, which can hardly be guaranteed in practice. In this demo, we introduce LiShield, which automatically protects a physical scene against photographing, by illuminating it with smart LEDs flickering in a specialized waveform. We use a model-driven approach to optimize the waveform, so as to ensure protection against the (uncontrollable) cameras and potential image-processing based attacks. We have also designed mechanisms to unblock authorized cameras and enable graceful degradation under strong ambient light interference. This demo will show our prototype implementation, with simple on-site experiments that demonstrate how LiShield effectively destroys unauthorized photo capturing.

CCS CONCEPTS

• **Computer systems organization → Special purpose systems**; • **Security and privacy → Security services**; *Systems security*; • **Human-centered computing → Ubiquitous and mobile devices**; • **Computing methodologies → Computer vision**;

KEYWORDS

Privacy Protection; Visible Light; Camera; Computer Vision

1 INTRODUCTION

Cameras are now pervasive on consumer mobile devices, such as smartphones, tablets, drones, smart glasses, first-person recorders, *etc.* The ubiquity of these cameras, paired with pervasive wireless access, is creating a new wave of visual sensing applications, *e.g.*, autonomous photographer, quantified-self (life-logging), photo-sharing social networks, physical-analytics in retail stores, and augmented reality applications that navigate users across unknown environment. Zooming in the photo-sharing application alone, statistics report that 350 million photos/videos are uploaded to Facebook every day, majority of which are from mobile users [7]. Many of these applications automatically upload batches of images/videos online, with a simple one-time permission from the user. While these technologies bring significant convenience to individuals, they also trigger an outcry of privacy concerns.

Privacy is ultimately a subjective matter, and often varies with context. Yet many of the privacy-sensitive scenes occur in indoor environment, and are bound to specific locations. For example, recent user studies [2] showed that people's acceptability of being recorded by augmented reality glasses has a strong correlation with location. User studies of life-logging cameras [3] also indicate that 70.2% of the cases when the user disables capturing is associated with specific locations. In numerous real-world scenarios, cameras are forbidden, *e.g.*, concerts, theaters, museums, trade shows, hospitals, dressing rooms and exam rooms, manufacturing plants, *etc.* However, *visual privacy protection in such passive physical spaces still heavily relies on rudimentary approaches* like warning signs and human monitors, and there is no way to automatically enforce the requirements. In personal visual sensing applications like life-logging, even if a user were to disable the camera in private space (*e.g.*, bedroom and washroom), malware could perform remote reconnaissance and targeted visual theft by hijacking the victim's camera [8].

In this demo, we introduce LiShield, a system that thwarts photographing of sensitive indoor physical space, and automatically enforces location-bound visual privacy protection. LiShield safeguards the physical scenes against undesired recording without requiring user intervention, and without disrupting the human visual perception. Our key idea is to illuminate the environment using smart LEDs, which are intensity-modulated following specialized waveforms. We design the waveform in such a way that its modulation pattern is imperceptible by human eyes, but can disrupt the image sensors on mobile camera devices.

More specifically, our basic waveform follows an ON-OFF modulation, which causes the reflection intensity of the scene to "flicker" at high frequency. Digital cameras commonly adopt rolling-shutter image sensors, which sample the scene row by row during capturing. Consequently, LiShield will impose a striping effect on the captured image, as long as its flickering frequency exceeds the camera frame rate. To protect against a wide range of camera settings, we build a numerical model to explore the relation between the image quality degradation and the (uncontrollable) camera configurations (*e.g.*, exposure time). Accordingly, we derive common guidelines to maximize the effectiveness through waveform parameter configurations (*e.g.*, frequency, peak intensity, duty cycle). To further enhance the protection, we take two measures: *(i.)* scramble the color patterns, taking advantage of the array of multi-channel RGB chips commonly available on commercial smart LEDs; *(ii.)* randomize the waveform frequency to thwart exposure time manipulation that may circumvent the striping effect, while ensuring

*Co-primary authors.

MobiCom '17, October 16-20, 2017, Snowbird, UT, USA

ACM ISBN 978-1-4503-4916-1/17/10.
https://doi.org/10.1145/3117811.3119867

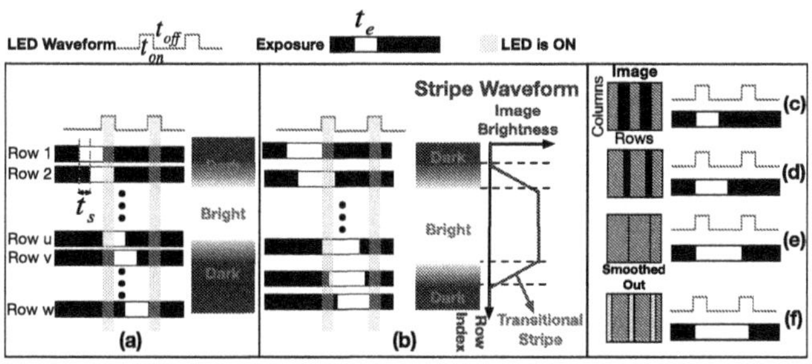

Figure 1: (a)-(b) Bright, dark and transitional stripes and their width changing with exposure time; (c)-(f) Stripe pattern of image changes under different exposure times.

no low-frequency components are generated that affect human perception.

In addition, LiShield can tailor the waveform for two special use cases: *(i.)* allowing an authorized camera, which shares secret configuration information with the LED, to recover the image or video frames it captures. *(ii.)* when strong ambient light interferes with the smart LED, LiShield cannot ensure full protection, but it can still emit structured light which embeds invisible "barcode" into the physical environment. The embedded information can convey a "no distribution" message, allowing online servers (*e.g.*, from Facebook and Instagram) to block and prevent the image from being distributed.

We have implemented LiShield based on a customized smart LED, which allows reconfiguration of intensity modulation waveforms on each color channel. Our experiments on real world scenes demonstrate that LiShield can corrupt the camera capturing to an illegible level, in terms of the image brightness, structure, and color. The impact is resilient against possible post-processing attacks, such as multi-frame combining and denoising. On the other hand, it enables authorized cameras to recover the image perfectly, as if no modulation is present. Even under strong sunlight/flashlight interferences, LiShield can still sneak barcode into the physical scenes which can be decoded with around 95% accuracy.

2 WORKING PRINCIPLE OF LISHIELD

Unlike professional or industrial cameras which may have global shutters that mimic human eyes to some degree, nearly all consumer digital cameras, pinhole cameras, and smartphones use the rolling shutter sampling mechanism [5], which is the main contributor to their high-frequency sensitivity. When capturing an image frame, a *rolling shutter camera exposes each row sequentially.* This effect has been leveraged to capture high-frequency optical signals for other purposes such as localization [4, 6, 9] and communication.

LiShield harnesses the disparity between cameras and eyes to disrupt the camera imaging without affecting human vision. It modulates a smart LED to generate high-frequency flickering patterns. The reflection intensity (or brightness) of target scene also flickers following the same pattern as the LED's illumination, albeit at reduced intensity due to reflection loss. LiShield uses the On-Off Keying (OOK) as the basic modulation waveform (Fig. 1), which does not require complicated analog front-ends and is widely supported by smart LEDs. Due to rolling-shutter sampling, the rows of pixels that are fully exposed in the ON period will be bright, and rows in the OFF period become dark, thus causing striped patterns on the captured image (Fig. 1(a)(b)). Partially exposed rows experience moderate brightness. Meanwhile, human eyes can only perceive the smooth averaged intensity, as long as the OOK frequency goes beyond 80 Hz [1]. LiShield aims to minimize the image capturing quality by optimizing the LED waveform, characterized by modulation frequency, intensity, and duty cycle.

In addition, commercial LED fixtures often comprise multiple LED bulbs/chips, and sometimes separate RGB channels to allow color adjustments. LiShield can turn different numbers of LED bulb/chip on to generate different intensities, and control the RGB channels of the LEDs to vary the color. Therefore, LiShield's flickering waveform is staircase-shaped on-off patterns, running independently in 3 color channels.

LiShield should still maintain its protection while allowing authorized users to capture the same scene simultaneously without distortion. LiShield's solution leverages a secure side channel (*e.g.*, visible light communication [10, 11]) between authorized users and the smart LED, which conveys secret information such as frame timing and waveform parameters. To authorize a camera to capture a dynamic scene (Fig. 2), each individual frame within the video must be recoverable. To achieve this, the authorized camera needs to convey its exposure time setting to the smart LED via the secure side channel, and synchronize its clock (for controlling capturing time) with the smart LED's clock (for controlling the waveform). State-of-the-art time synchronization mechanisms through visible light or wireless side-channels can already achieve μs of accuracy, sufficient to synchronize the LiShield smart LED with the camera at a resolution finer than the rolling shutter period (typically tens of μs). The corresponding flickering frequency can be varied on a frame by frame basis, making it impossible for an attacker to resolve the correct exposure time by trial-and-error. When the target scene is static, it requires the authorized user to capture a few complementary frames to recover the scene as depicted in Fig. 3. Meanwhile, frequency and intensity randomization can still be employed in each frame to ensure robustness. While it does require recording a very short video, the process is extremely short (200ms at most) and barely noticeable.

In case strong ambient interference may degrade LiShield's protection, LiShield embeds barcodes in images/videos captured by the attacker to convey privacy policies and ensures they are detectable even after common post-processing.

3 DEMO SETUP AND REQUIREMENT

In the demo, we will show our LiShield hardware prototype, and encourage the audience to take photos using their smartphones while experiencing the corruption effects under LiShield. We will also demonstrate how an authorized camera (which we bring by ourselves) can circumvent the corruption effects. Besides the AC power and a table, no other facility is needed. The setup time is around 10 minutes.

Fig. 5 shows our LiShield prototype, and the target scenes containing 5 capture-sensitive objects (document and painting are 2-D objects and others are all 3-D objects). We mount the LED inside a diffusive plastic cover similar to conventional ceiling light covers. We use a programmable motor to hold the camera and control

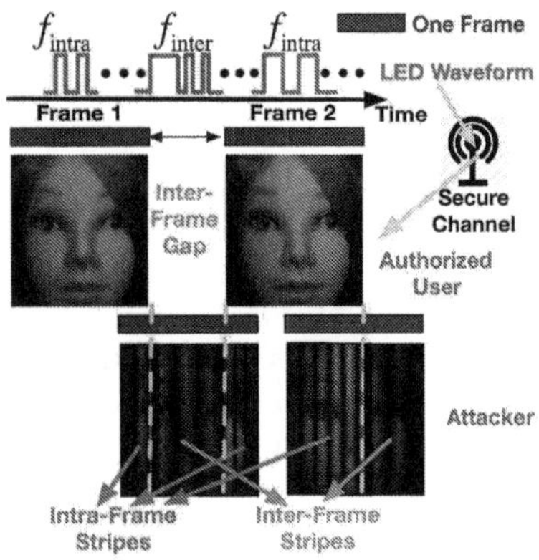

Figure 2: Enabling authorized users to capture dynamic scenes while corrupting unauthorized users.

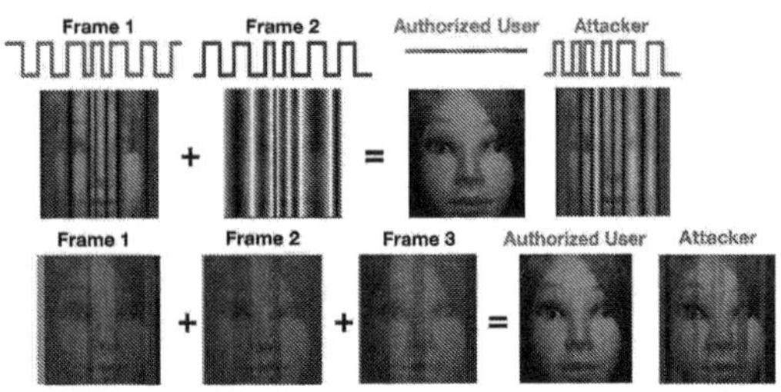

Figure 3: The impact of multi-frame recovery on authorized user and attacker, respectively.

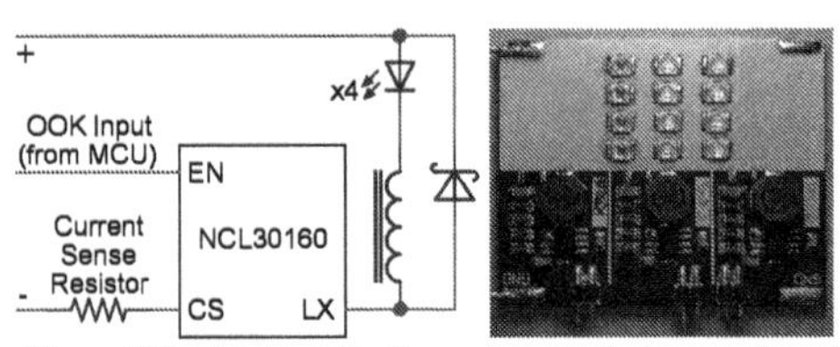

Figure 4: Simplified circuit diagram and photo for the smart LED module.

its distance/orientation, in order to create static or dynamic scene setup in a repeatable manner.

We build our smart bulb based on the same topology as those COTS LED bulbs. For safety, we use 19V DC laptop power supplies instead of wall AC power, and NCL30160 LED drivers which allow dimming at nearly 100 kHz with arbitrary OOK waveform. The smart bulb has built-in independent RGB/white channels for controlling color/intensity. Each channel can be controlled by a separate waveform, with 4 LED chips in series, at driving current of 800 mA. In total, the 3 channels consume approximately 25 W peak power, close to common office LED troffer fixtures. However, since LiShield's OOK waveform has a duty cycle much lower than 1, the actual perceptible brightness is significantly lower. As a result, multiple LED modules can be used to improve light intensity. Fig. 4 depicts the circuit for each color channel and shows a photo of the whole module. The dimming input signals of each channel are controlled by an STM32 micro-controller unit (MCU), which generates the OOK waveform as specified by LiShield. For flexible reconfiguration, we generate digitized waveforms in MATLAB on

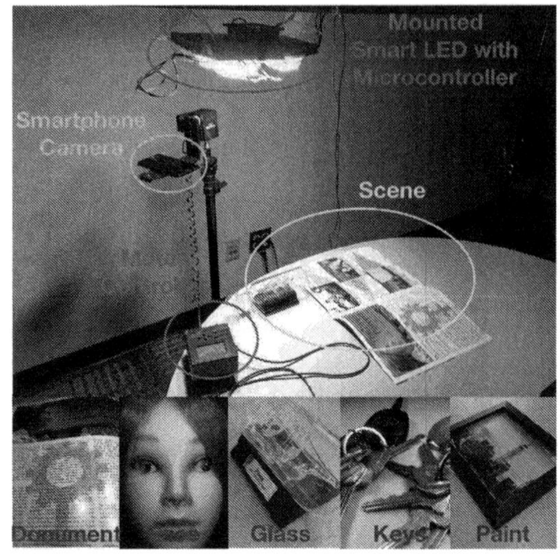

Figure 5: Experimental setup and multiple scenes we used.

a laptop or Android app on a smartphone instead, which are then passed to the MCU via USB.

4 CONCLUSION

Privacy protection in passive indoor environment has been an important but unsolved problem. In this demo we present LiShield, which uses smart-LEDs and specialized intensity waveforms to disrupt unauthorized cameras, while allowing authorized users to record high-quality image and video. We implemented and evaluated LiShield under various representative indoor scenarios, which demonstrates LiShield's effectiveness and robustness. We consider LiShield as the first exploration of automatic visual privacy enforcement and expect it can inspire more research along the same direction.

REFERENCES

[1] Stephen J. Anderson and David C. Burr. 1985. Spatial and temporal selectivity of the human motion detection system. *Vision Research* 25, 8 (1985), 1147 – 1154.
[2] Tamara Denning, Zakariya Dehlawi, and Tadayoshi Kohno. 2014. In Situ with Bystanders of Augmented Reality Glasses: Perspectives on Recording and Privacy-mediating Technologies. In *Proc. of ACM CHI.*
[3] Roberto Hoyle, Robert Templeman, Steven Armes, Denise Anthony, David Crandall, and Apu Kapadia. 2014. Privacy Behaviors of Lifeloggers Using Wearable Cameras. In *Proc. of ACM UbiComp.*
[4] Ye-Sheng Kuo, Pat Pannuto, Ko-Jen Hsiao, and Prabal Dutta. 2014. Luxapose: Indoor Positioning with Mobile Phones and Visible Light. In *Proc. of ACM MobiCom.*
[5] QImaging. 2014. Rolling Shutter vs. Global Shutter. (2014). https://www.qimaging.com/ccdorscmos/pdfs/RollingvsGlobalShutter.pdf
[6] Niranjini Rajagopal, Patrick Lazik, and Anthony Rowe. 2014. Visual Light Landmarks for Mobile Devices. In *Proc. of ACM/IEEE IPSN.*
[7] Social Pilot. 2016. 125 Amazing Social Media Statistics You Should Know. (2016). https://socialpilot.co/blog/125-amazing-social-media-statistics-know-2016/
[8] R. Templeman, Z. Rahman, D. Crandall, and A. Kapadia. 2013. PlaceRaider: Virtual Theft in Physical Spaces With Smartphones. In *Network and Distributed System Security Symposium (NDSS).*
[9] Chi Zhang and Xinyu Zhang. 2016. LiTell: Robust Indoor Localization Using Unmodified Light Fixtures. In *Proc. of ACM MobiCom.*
[10] Jialiang Zhang, Chi Zhang, Xinyu Zhang, and Suman Banerjee. 2016. Towards a Visible Light Network Architecture for Continuous Communication and Localization. In *Proc. of ACM VLCS.*
[11] Jialiang Zhang, Xinyu Zhang, and Gang Wu. 2015. Dancing with Light: Predictive In-frame Rate Selection for Visible Light Networks. In *Proc. of IEEE INFOCOM.*

Poster: Resource Allocation with Conflict Resolution for Vehicular Sidelink Broadcast Communications

Luis F. Abanto-Leon
Eindhoven University of Technology
Eindhoven, Netherlands
l.f.abanto@tue.nl

Arie Koppelaar
NXP Semiconductors
Eindhoven, Netherlands
arie.koppelaar@nxp.com

Sonia Heemstra de Groot
Eindhoven University of Technology
Eindhoven, Netherlands
sheemstradegroot@tue.nl

ABSTRACT

In this paper we present a graph-based resource allocation scheme for sidelink broadcast V2V communications. Harnessing available information on geographical position of vehicles and spectrum resources utilization, eNodeBs are capable of allotting the same set of sidelink resources to different vehicles distributed among several communications clusters. Within a communications cluster, it is crucial to prevent time-domain allocation conflicts since vehicles cannot transmit and receive simultaneously, i.e., they must transmit in orthogonal time resources. In this research, we present a solution based on a bipartite graph, where vehicles and spectrum resources are represented by vertices whereas the edges represent the achievable rate in each resource based on the SINR that each vehicle perceives. The aforementioned time orthogonality constraint can be approached by aggregating conflicting vertices into macro-vertices which, in addition, reduces the search complexity. We show mathematically and through simulations that the proposed approach yields an optimal solution. In addition, we provide simulations showing that the proposed method outperforms other competing approaches, specially in scenarios with high vehicular density.

KEYWORDS

resource allocation; vehicular communications; sidelink

1 INTRODUCTION

Vehicle–to–vehicle (V2V) communications is one of the novel use cases in 5G and has attracted much interest, specially for safety applications, since connected vehicles may have the potential to prevent accidents [1].

In V2V *Mode 3*, eNodeBs assign resources to vehicles for them to periodically broadcast CAM messages [2]. Once the allocation has been accomplished, data is disseminated directly between vehicles. Conversely, in conventional cellular communications, data traverse the eNodeB via uplink/downlink before it can be forwarded. Thus, since data traffic is controlled by the eNodeB, users can be allocated in the same time resource but different frequency subchannels. Nevertheless, in V2V *Mode 3* the flow of data is not controlled, thus it is fundamental to guarantee that vehicles will transmit in orthogonal time resources to prevent conflicts. On the other hand, assignment problems can be represented as weighted bipartite graphs, where the objective is to find a maximal matching. This classical problem is called herein *unconstrained weighted graph matching*. Resource allocation for V2V communications has a time orthogonality constraint which cannot be handled by the mentioned method. We have therefore envisaged a solution called *constrained weighted graph matching*, which incorporates the mentioned constraint.

The objective of this paper is two-fold: (i) prove that an optimal solution for the *constrained weighted graph matching* problem exists and (ii) discuss the suitability of such an approach for avoiding resource allocation conflicts in broadcast vehicular communications.

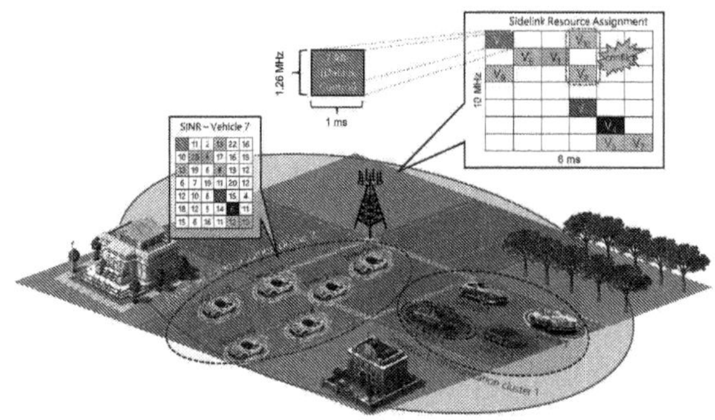

Figure 1: V2V Broadcast Communications via Sidelink

2 MOTIVATION AND CONTRIBUTIONS

Our motivation is to develop an approach capable of (a) preventing allocation conflicts—by enforcing constraints—and (b) maximizing the sum-rate capacity of the system. For instance, in one of the clusters of Fig. 1, a resource conflict can be observed between vehicles V_8 and V_{10} since they have been allotted resources in the same time subframe.

The contributions of our work are summarized:

- Kuhn-Munkres [3] is a computationally efficient method for solving matching problems in bipartite graphs. However, due to additional time orthogonality constraints, the resultant problem is not directly approachable by it. In our solution, vertices conflicting among each other

MobiCom '17, October 16–20, 2017, Snowbird, UT, USA

ACM ISBN 978-1-4503-4916-1/17/10.
https://doi.org/10.1145/3117811.3131260

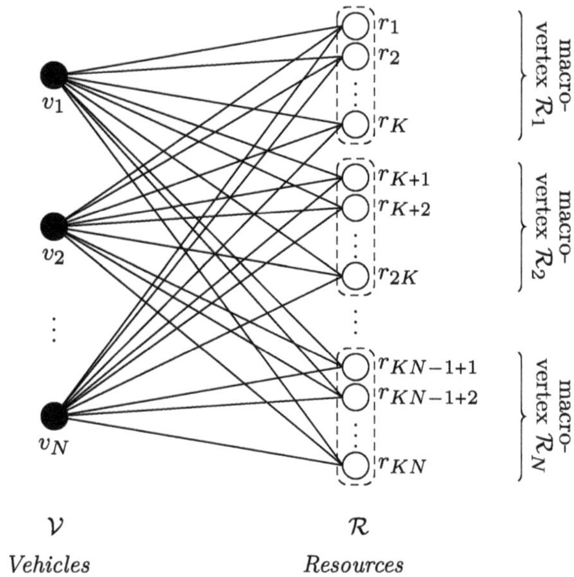

Figure 2: Constrained Weighted Bipartite Graph

have been aggregated into macro-vertices yielding a resultant graph which is solvable by Kuhn-Munkres.

- Vertex aggregation cuts down the number of effective vertices and therefore narrows the amount of potential solutions, without affecting optimality.
- We show through simulations that our approach is capable of providing fairness among all vehicles, especially in scenarios with high vehicle density.

3 PROPOSED APPROACH

Let $G = (\mathcal{V}, \mathcal{R}, \mathcal{E})$ be a bipartite graph such that $|\mathcal{R}| = K|\mathcal{V}| = KN$, as depicted in Fig. 2. In this scheme, the KN vertices in $\mathcal{R}$ are clustered into N disjoint groups $\{\mathcal{R}_\alpha\}_{\alpha=1}^{N}$ called macro-vertices, such that $\mathcal{R} = \cup_{\alpha=1}^{N}\mathcal{R}_\alpha$, $\mathcal{R}_\alpha \cap \mathcal{R}_{\alpha'} = \emptyset$, $\forall \alpha \neq \alpha'$. Each macro-vertex $\mathcal{R}_\alpha$ is an aggregation of K vertices, i.e., $|\mathcal{R}_\alpha| = K$. The target is to find a vertex-to-vertex (or vehicle-to-resource) matching with maximum sum of weights such that no two vertices in $\mathcal{V}$ are matched to any two vertices in the same macro-vertex $\mathcal{R}_\alpha$. This condition must be satisfied as it depicts the time orthogonality requirement that prevents allocation conflicts. We will show that the optimal solution is tantamount to finding the maximum vertex-to-macro-vertex matching.

In Fig. 2, vertices v_i represent the vehicles in cluster $\mathcal{V}$ whereas vertices r_j represent the allotable resources managed by the eNodeB. K represents the number of resources per subframe. N represents the amount of available subframes in which the resource allocation task can be accomplished. The problem is formulated by (1)

$$\max \ \mathbf{c}^T\mathbf{x} \qquad \text{subject to} \ \underbrace{\left[\frac{\mathbf{I}_{N\times N}\otimes \mathbf{1}_{1\times N}}{\mathbf{1}_{1\times N}\otimes \mathbf{I}_{N\times N}}\right]}_{\mathbf{A}} \otimes \mathbf{1}_{1\times K}\ \mathbf{x} = \mathbf{1} \tag{1}$$

where $\otimes$ represents the tensor product operator, $\mathbf{c} \in \mathbb{R}^M$, $\mathbf{x} \in \mathbb{B}^M$ with $M = KN^2$. The solution and weight vectors are $\mathbf{x} = [x_{1,1}, \dots, x_{N,N}]^T$ and $\mathbf{c} = [c_{1,1}, \dots, c_{N,N}]^T$, respectively. Also, $c_{ij} = B\log_2(1+\mathsf{SINR}_{ij})$. Because $\mathbf{x}$ exists on the binary subspace, the cost function can be equivalently expressed as $\mathbf{c}^T\mathbf{x} = \mathbf{x}^T diag(\mathbf{c})\mathbf{x}$ without affecting optimality. Also, we can add zero-valued terms $c_{ij}x_{ij}x_{ik}$ (with $r_j, r_k \in \mathcal{R}_\alpha$) to the cost function without affecting the solution. A more generalized expression is given by $\mathbf{x}^T(\mathbf{I}_{M\times M} \otimes \mathbf{1}_{K\times K} - \mathbf{I}_{K\times K}) diag(\mathbf{c})\mathbf{x} = 0$.

Now, the augmented cost function can be recast as

$$\begin{aligned}
&\mathbf{c}^T\mathbf{x}\\
&= \mathbf{x}^T diag(\mathbf{c})\mathbf{x} + \mathbf{x}^T\left(\mathbf{I}_{M\times M} \otimes [\mathbf{1}-\mathbf{I}]_{K\times K}\right) diag(\mathbf{c})\mathbf{x}\\
&= \mathbf{x}^T\left(\mathbf{I}_{M\times M} \otimes \mathbf{1}_{K\times K}\right) diag(\mathbf{c})\mathbf{x}\\
&= \mathbf{x}^T\left(\mathbf{I}_{M\times M}\mathbf{I}_{M\times M} \otimes \mathbf{1}_{K\times 1}\mathbf{1}_{1\times K}\right) diag(\mathbf{c})\mathbf{x}\\
&= \underbrace{\mathbf{x}^T\left(\mathbf{I}_{M\times M} \otimes \mathbf{1}_{K\times 1}\right)}_{\mathbf{y}^T} \underbrace{\left(\mathbf{I}_{M\times M} \otimes \mathbf{1}_{1\times K}\right) diag(\mathbf{c})\mathbf{x}}_{\mathbf{d}}
\end{aligned} \tag{2}$$

From (2), we obtain that $\mathbf{d} = (\mathbf{I}_{M\times M} \otimes \mathbf{1}_{1\times K}) diag(\mathbf{c})\mathbf{x}$ and $\mathbf{y} = (\mathbf{I}_{M\times M} \otimes \mathbf{1}_{1\times K})\mathbf{x}$. Similarly, we obtain that $\mathbf{x} = (\mathbf{I}_{M\times M} \otimes \mathbf{1}_{1\times K})^\dagger\mathbf{y}$. In the following, we use the previous relations to simplify the constraint in (1),

$$\begin{aligned}
&\left(\left[\frac{\mathbf{I}_{N\times N}\otimes \mathbf{1}_{1\times N}}{\mathbf{1}_{1\times N}\otimes \mathbf{I}_{N\times N}}\right] \otimes \mathbf{1}_{1\times K}\right)\left(\mathbf{I}_{M\times M} \otimes \mathbf{1}^\dagger_{1\times K}\right)\mathbf{y} = \mathbf{1}\\
&= \left(\left[\frac{\mathbf{I}_{N\times N}\otimes \mathbf{1}_{1\times N}}{\mathbf{1}_{1\times N}\otimes \mathbf{I}_{N\times N}}\right] \mathbf{I}_{M\times M}\right) \otimes \underbrace{\left(\mathbf{1}_{1\times K}\mathbf{1}^\dagger_{1\times K}\right)}_{1}\mathbf{y} = \mathbf{1}\\
&= \left[\frac{\mathbf{I}_{N\times N}\otimes \mathbf{1}_{1\times N}}{\mathbf{1}_{1\times N}\otimes \mathbf{I}_{N\times N}}\right]\mathbf{y} = \mathbf{1}
\end{aligned} \tag{3}$$

Thus, the problem in (3) can be recast as (4)

$$\max \ \mathbf{d}^T\mathbf{y} \qquad \text{subject to} \ \underbrace{\left[\frac{\mathbf{I}_{N\times N}\otimes \mathbf{1}_{1\times N}}{\mathbf{1}_{1\times N}\otimes \mathbf{I}_{N\times N}}\right]}_{\mathbf{A}}\mathbf{y} = \mathbf{1}. \tag{4}$$

Fig.3 shows the transformation process from (1) to (4). We notice that $\mathbf{d}$ depends on $\mathbf{x}$ which is not desirable. In order to eliminate this dependency, we state without a proof—due to space limitations—that

$$\mathbf{d} = \lim_{\beta\to\infty} \frac{1}{\beta} \overset{\circ}{\log}\{\mathbf{I}_{M\times M} \otimes \mathbf{1}_{1\times K} \mathrm{e}^{\circ\beta\mathbf{c}}\} \tag{5}$$

where $\overset{\circ}{\log}\{\cdot\}$ and $\mathrm{e}^{\circ\{\cdot\}}$ are the element-wise natural logarithm and Hadamard exponential [4], respectively.

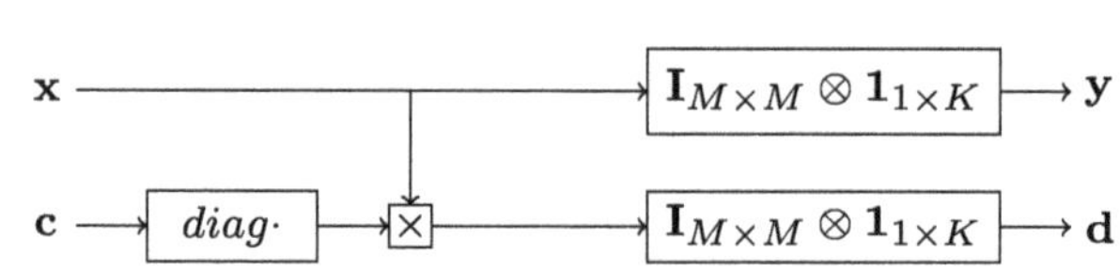

Figure 3: Transformation Process

4 SIMULATIONS

We consider a 10 MHz channel which is divided into several resource chunks, each with an extent of 1ms in time and 1.26 MHz in frequency. To wit, 1.26 MHz corresponds to 7 resource blocks (RBs), each consisting of data (5RBs) and control information (2RBs) [5]. In our model, we consider that clusters are independent from each other. Thus, resources used in a certain cluster can be repurposed by vehicles in other clusters. Since we consider a message rate of 10 Hz, the resource allocation task is carried out every 0.1 s and therefore the maximum number of allotable subframes is 100. We also assume that the sidelink channel conditions of each vehicle are reported to the eNodeB via uplink. The resource allocation is broadcasted to vehicles via downlink. Notice that sidelink resources are exclusively used for communications.

In Fig. 4, we compare 4 different algorithms in base of the average over 1000 simulations. We have considered $N = 100$ vehicles in each cluster. Through simulations, we show that our scheme is optimal since it achieves the same performance as exhaustive search. The greedy algorithm performs as good as the proposed approach when we examine the highest-rate vehicle only. This is logical as the premise of the greedy algorithm is to assign the best resources on first-come first-served basis. Considering the system average rate, our proposed approach has an advantage over the greedy algorithm. Also, when considering the worst-rate vehicle, our proposal excels as it is capable of providing a higher level of fairness. In all cases, the random allocation algorithm is outperformed by the other approaches. Fig. 5 shows the achievable rate for

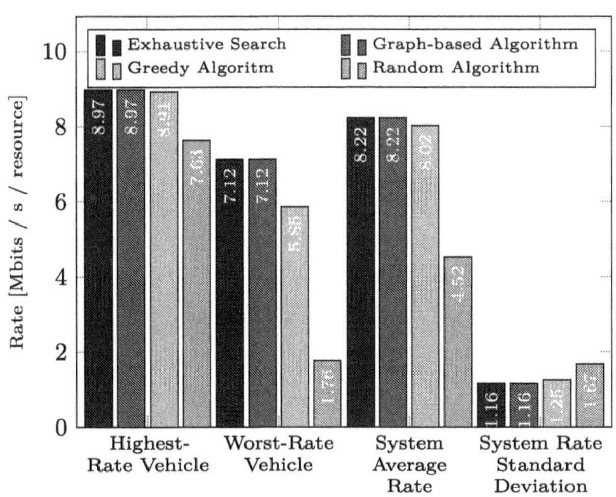

Figure 4: Vehicles Data Rate

the worst-rate vehicle. The proposed graph-based algorithm attains the same performance as the exhaustive search. We observe that when the vehicle density per cluster is low, the greedy approach attains near optimal solutions as there are far more resources than vehicles to serve. However, as the density increases, especially near the overload state, its performance drops. The random allocation algorithm performs worse than the other approaches.

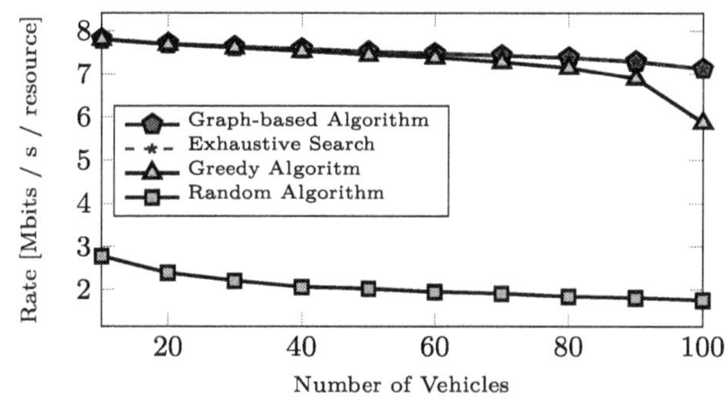

Figure 5: Worst-rate Vehicle

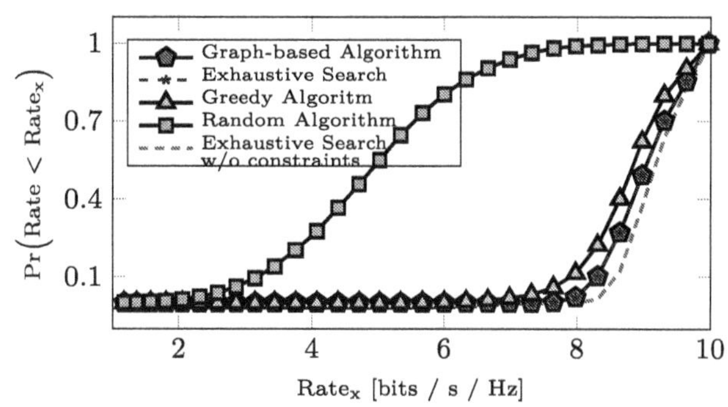

Figure 6: Cumulative Distribution Function

Fig. 6 shows the CDF of the achievable rates. We observe that the proposed approach outperforms the other two approaches. For the sake of comparison, we have included the results of the unconstrained system, which does not takes into account conflict avoidance constraints. This is of course not desirable but it serves as a comparison bound.

5 CONCLUSION

We have presented a novel resource allocation algorithm for V2V communications considering conflict constraints. We were able to transform the original problem into a simplified form. In our future work, we will consider (i) power control and (ii) the assumption that a subset of vehicles may belong to more than one cluster simultaneously.

REFERENCES

[1] Crash data analyses for vehicle-to-infrastructure communications for safety applications. Technical Report FHWA-HRT-11-040, U.S. Department of Transportation, November 2012.
[2] Intelligent transport systems (its); stdma recommended parameters and settings for cooperative its; access layer part. Technical Report ETSI TR 102 861, ETSI, January 2012.
[3] J. Munkres. Algorithms for the assignment and transportation problems. *SIAM J Appl Math*, 5(1):32–38, March 1957.
[4] Fumio Hiai. Monotonicity for entrywise functions of matrices. *Journal of Linear Algebra and its Applications*, 431(8):1125–1146, September 2009.
[5] Technical specification group radio access network; evolved universal terrestrial radio access (e-utra); physical layer procedures; (release 14) v14.2.0. Technical Report 3GPP TS 36.213, 3GPP, March 2017.

Poster Abstract: Link Line Crossing Speed Estimation with Narrowband Signal Strength

Alemayehu Solomon Abrar, Anh Luong, Peter Hillyard
University of Utah
Salt Lake City, UT 84112
{aleksol.abrar,anh.n.luong,peter.hillyard}@utah.edu

Neal Patwari
University of Utah and Xandem Technology
Salt Lake City, UT 84112
npatwari@ece.utah.edu

ABSTRACT

We present results from a system which uses received signal strength (RSS) measurements to estimate the speed at which a person is walking when they cross the link line. While many RSS-based device-free localization systems can detect a line crossing, this system estimates additionally the speed of crossing, which can provide significant additional information to a tracking system. Further, unlike device-free RF sensors which occupy tens of MHz of bandwidth, this system uses a channel of about 10 kHz. Experiments with a person walking from 0.3 to 1.8 m/s show the system can measure walking speed within 0.05 m/s RMS error.

1 INTRODUCTION

Radio frequency (RF) signals have been widely explored in device-free localization, including detection of line crossings and use of line crossing measurements to track people [3, 4]. In these applications, the speed of a person is a fundamental parameter to track a subject. Typical methods first perform RF-based device-free localization [3, 10] and then derive the speed from the coordinate estimates over time; however, such systems require many transceivers deployed around the area of interest. A few other techniques directly measure speed or range using a radar measurement system [2, 8]; however, such systems use multiple GHz of bandwidth to generate range-Doppler responses, and they become less effective in the presence of interfering communication systems. Similarily, Wang *et al.* [9] use channel state information (CSI) measurements from WiFi devices to determine human speed for activity recognition. Even though such CSI-based sensing might be convenient in terms of infrastructure by using the same channel for both communication and sensing, it still puts more strain on an increasingly crowded spectrum. In this poster abstract, we propose speed estimation using the spectrogram of single-channel RSS measurements. Our transceivers are narrowband, reducing the bandwidth requirement to 11 kHz.

When a person moves near a wireless link, the RSS changes due to their presence, but in ways that are challenging to model. The model of Rampa *et al.* [7] predicts the RSS as a function of a person's location with respect to the transceivers, modeling a human as a perfect cylinder and applying diffraction theory. Based on this model, as the person moves towards the link line, the peak frequency in the spectrogram of the RSS decreases, as shown in Fig. 2a, directly proportional to the speed and the distance from the crossing. However, an actual human is not like a cylinder as assumed in the model of [7]. Different body parts such as the legs, torso and hands move at different instantaneous velocities. In Fig. 2b, we show the spectrogram of the measured RSS during a time when an actual walking person crosses the link line, which differs visually from the spectrogram in Fig. 2a.

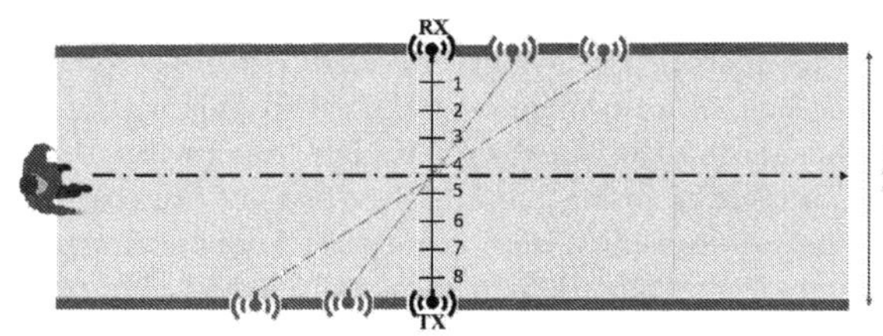

Figure 1: Experimental setup for line crossing.

We propose to estimate human walking speed based on the spectral components of RSS measured when a person approaches and crosses a link line. We envision a setup as shown in Figure 1 where two sensors on opposite sides of a hallway are deployed. A person walking through the hallway has his speed estimated as she crosses through the link line. One fundamental challenge in extracting speed from RSS measurement is that RSS measurements are typically quantized to 1 dB, which is not sufficient in tracking small changes in RSS due to a distant human in motion. To overcome this challenge, we use a high resolution RSS estimate [5] from a TI CC1200 transceiver. Other challenges stem from the fact that different people walk with different gaits, and each person's different body parts have different instantaneous speeds during their walk. As a result the RSS spectrogram for a given walking speed varies by person. We address this challenge by tracking a time-averaged frequency from the spectrogram of RSS measurements, which is then used to estimate the average body speed. We first predict a link line crossing when the RSS average frequency drops below a certain threshold. We then estimate the speed of crossing from the minimum of the time-averaged RSS frequency during the crossing. In this poster abstract, we show experimentally that the use of spectral information of RSS data provides a bandwidth-efficient and inexpensive means for human speed estimation.

MobiCom'17, October 16–20, 2017, Snowbird, UT, USA.
 978-1-4503-4916-1/17/10...$15.00
DOI: http://dx.doi.org/10.1145/3117811.3131253

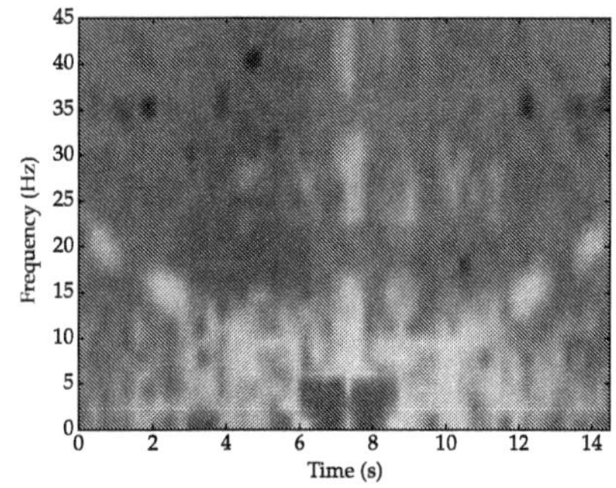

(a) **Simulated for cylinder crossing at t = 7 seconds**

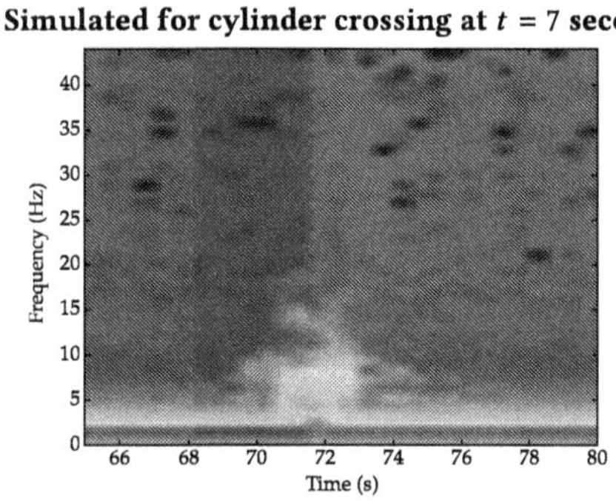

(b) **Measured from human crossing at t = 72 seconds**

Figure 2: Spectrogram of of (a) simulated and (b)measured RSS data.

2 HARDWARE AND RSS ESTIMATION

Our RF sensing hardware is composed of a pair of inexpensive wireless nodes. Each node includes a Beaglebone Green (BBG) platform connected to a TI CC1200 narrowband radio transceiver, its matching network for the 434 MHz band, and an SMA-connected antenna. The parts for each node cost less than 50 USD, compared to more than 1000 USD for a USRP N200 used in other RF sensing systems [1, 2, 6].

We reproduce a high resolution RSS measurement system described in [5] using the CC1200 transceiver. One device transmits a CW signal at 434 MHz, while the other captures its receiver's complex baseband samples and sends them to the BBG via SPI, at a sampling rate of 54 kHz. The BBG caluculates each RSS estimate, $r(t)$, from 100 samples of the 17-bit magnitude by summing the squared magnitude [5]. This process reduces the average sampling rate to 449 Hz, which is high enough for most RF sensing applications, including human speed estimation.

3 WALKING SPEED ESTIMATION

As described in Section 1, the spectrogram of RSS measured during a line crossing differs significantly from that predicted by model, and varies by person. The peak frequency in the spectrogram is not, as would be predicted by the model, strongly related to the speed of the walking person.

We propose instead to utilize the average frequency of the spectrogram of the mean-removed RSS waveform, which we denote $f_{av}(t)$ at time t. The value $f_{av}(t)$ is calculated as

$$f_{av}(t) = \frac{\sum_i f_i S_r(f_i, t)}{\sum_i S_r(f_i, t)}, \quad (1)$$

where $S_r(f_i, t)$ is the power of the spectrogram S_r of the mean-removed RSS at frequency f_i at time t. The spectrogram is computed from a 2 s sliding window.

The estimated average frequency is then smoothed using a moving-average filter. We call the output of the filter as $f_s(t)$. Fig. 3 shows $f_{av}(t)$ and $f_s(t)$. Note that the average frequency decreases as the person approaches the link line, is minimum at the instant the person crosses the link line, and then rises again.

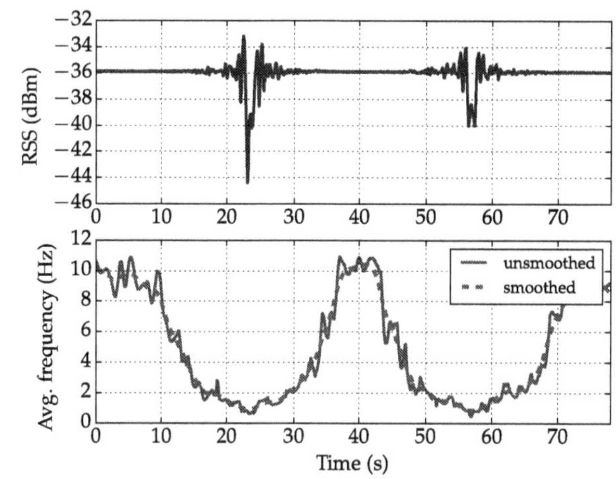

Figure 3: Average RSS frequency for measured line crossing with 2 second windows: The average frequency is smoothed using moving average filter before speed estimation.

We detect a line crossing by thresholding $f_s(t)$, i.e., when a person approaches a link line the smoothed average frequency drops below a certain threshold.

After detecting a crossing, we estimate the time of crossing as the minimum $f_s(t)$ within a wide window. Next, we estimate the speed by scaling the smoothed average frequency by a constant α,

$$\hat{v} = \alpha \min_t f_{av}(t),$$

where the minimum is taken over a set time interval.

4 RESULTS

We perform experiments in two different indoor hallways of width 3.2 m, with the nodes kept on either side of the hall way at 1 m high from the ground, as shown in Fig. 1. The person walks across the link line at a known speed. The person uses a metronome and distance markers to keep a constant speed over 14 m. We conduct the experiment while the subject walks in solitude through the hallway.

First, we evaluate human walking in the range of speeds from 0.30 m/s to 1.81 m/s. We determine the best linear fit between actual velocity and f_{av} and find that α = 0.88 for hallway 1 and α = 0.72 for hallway 2 during a training period. Clearly, the best linear fit α may vary per link.

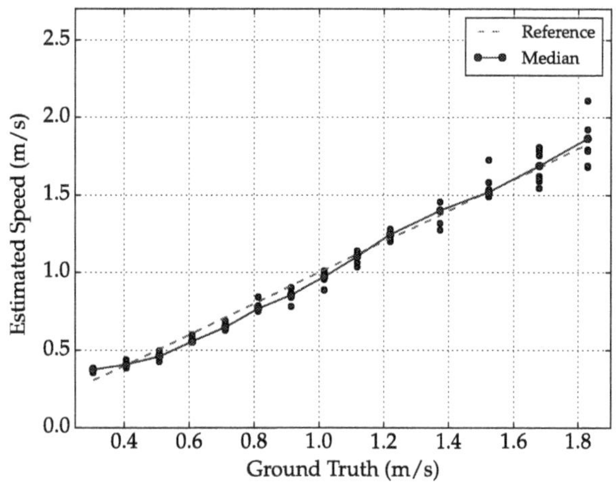

Figure 4: Estimated walking speed vs ground truth when a person crosses a link.

Fig. 4 shows the estimated speed $\hat{v}$ as a function of the ground truth walking speed, which has RMS error of 5.13 cm/s. For a person walking through a hallway at a constant rate, this means that we can accurately estimate a person's distance from the line over time and be off by less than 1 m for a period of 20 seconds, using measurements from only one link line.

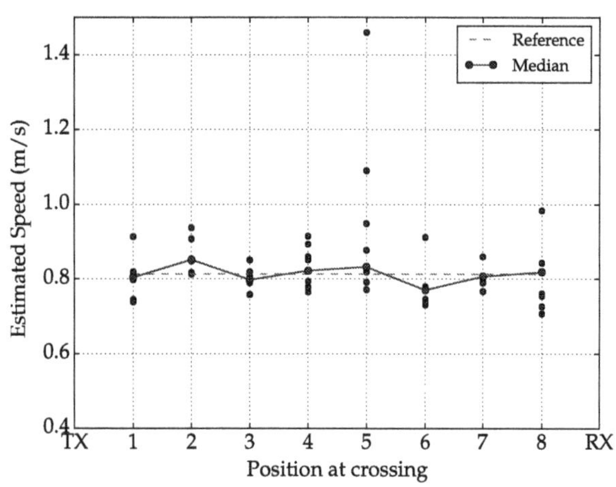

Figure 5: Estimated walking speed vs. ground truth when a person crosses a link at different position along the link line.

We also show the estimated speed for a person crossing the link line at different places, marked as 1 through 8 in Fig. 1, at a constant speed of 0.813 m/s. As shown in Fig. 5, the median of the estimated speed is within 0.05 m/s from the correct value. The physical model of [7] provides analytical justification for this result. In that model, assuming a transmitter and a receiver are located at $(0, 0)$ and $(0, d)$, for a person walking at a constant speed, the average RSS frequency at the link line crossing at y meters away from the transmitter is directly proportional to $\frac{1}{y(d-y)}$. This implies that the average RSS frequency is nearly constant with crossing position y unless the person is very close to either transceiver.

We have also experimentally found that the value of $\hat{v}$ is not a strong function of the angle between the person's walking path and the line between the transmitter and receiver, as shown in the green and red lines in Fig. 1. As the results are similar, they are omitted due to space limitations.

5 CONCLUSION

In this poster abstract, we present a human walking speed estimation method which is based on the frequency content of RSS measured from two low-cost single-carrier narrowband radio transceivers. We analyze the RSS spectral content and estimate speed from average frequency of the spectrogram of RSS measured when a person crosses a link line. Unlike other RF-based methods which require a few GHz of bandwidth to track human subjects, our RSS-based speed estimation approach utilizes only 11 kHz of RF bandwidth while maintaining accurate speed estimation with an error of 5 cm/s. The results indicate that RSS can be a rich source of information when it is provided without quantization to 1 dB step size.

We plan to explore the application of these speed estimates to improve device-free localization and tracking. Further, the work may have application in activity recognition and other context aware computing systems.

ACKNOWLEDGEMENTS

This material is based upon work supported by the U.S. National Science Foundation under Grants #1329755, 1407949, and 1622741.

REFERENCES

[1] 2017. USRP N210 . https://www.ettus.com/product/. (2017). [Online; accessed 30-Mar-2017].
[2] Fadel Adib, Zachary Kabelac, Dina Katabi, and Robert C Miller. 2014. 3D Tracking via Body Radio Reflections.. In *NSDI*, Vol. 14. 317–329.
[3] Maurizio Bocca, Ossi Kaltiokallio, Neal Patwari, and Suresh Venkatasubramanian. 2014. Multiple Target Tracking with RF Sensor Networks. *IEEE Transactions on Mobile Computing* 13, 8 (Aug 2014), 1787–1800.
[4] Peter Hillyard, Neal Patwari, Samira Daruki, and Suresh Venkatasubramanian. 2015. You're crossing the line: localizing border crossings using wireless RF links. In *Signal Processing and Signal Processing Education Workshop (SP/SPE), 2015 IEEE*. 249–254.
[5] Anh Luong, Alemayehu Solomon Abrar, Thomas Schmid, and Neal Patwari. 2016. RSS step size: 1 dB is not enough!. In *Proceedings of the 3rd Workshop on Hot Topics in Wireless*. ACM, 17–21.
[6] Qifan Pu, Sidhant Gupta, Shyamnath Gollakota, and Shwetak Patel. 2013. Whole-home gesture recognition using wireless signals. In *Proceedings of the 19th annual international conference on Mobile computing & networking*. ACM, 27–38.
[7] Rampa, Vittorio and Savazzi, Stefano and Nicoli, Monica and D'Amico, Michele. 2015. Physical modeling and performance bounds for device-free localization systems. *IEEE Signal Processing Letters* 22, 11 (2015), 1864–1868.
[8] Ph Van Dorp and FCA Groen. 2008. Feature-based human motion parameter estimation with radar. *IET Radar, Sonar & Navigation* 2, 2 (2008), 135–145.
[9] Wei Wang, Alex X Liu, Muhammad Shahzad, Kang Ling, and Sanglu Lu. 2015. Understanding and modeling of WiFi signal based human activity recognition. In *Proceedings of the 21st annual international conference on mobile computing and networking*. ACM, 65–76.
[10] Zheng Yang, Zimu Zhou, and Yunhao Liu. 2013. From RSSI to CSI: Indoor localization via channel response. *ACM Computing Surveys (CSUR)* 46, 2 (2013), 25.

Poster: Broadcast LTE Data Reveals Application Type

Arjun Balasingam
Stanford University
arjunvb@stanford.edu

Manu Bansal
Uhana Inc.
manub@uhana.io

Rakesh Misra
Uhana Inc.
rakesh@uhana.io

Rahul Tandra
Uhana Inc.
rahul@uhana.io

Aaron Schulman
UC San Diego
schulman@cs.ucsd.edu

Sachin Katti
Stanford University
skatti@cs.stanford.edu

ABSTRACT

The rapid growth in mobile connectivity is enabling phones to support a wide range of societally-important applications. In this work, we show that broad classes of popular mobile applications have distinct radio resource allocation signatures. Using this insight, we design a mobile application classifier, and demonstrate that (1) an application can infer its own type solely from its resource allocation patterns, and (2) *anyone* can accurately infer the type of application being served by each session on a particular cell tower. We present our findings by showing the breakdown of applications being served by an LTE base station belonging to a Tier 1 US provider in downtown Palo Alto. Our work encourages an open discussion about LTE standards, and whether they might need to be enhanced to mask features that can be exploited to infer application type from signals broadcast over the air.

CCS CONCEPTS

• **Networks** → **Network resources allocation**; **Security protocols**; **Mobile and wireless security**; *Mobile networks*; *Packet classification*;

KEYWORDS

Application Classification; Cellular; LTE; PHY; Resource Allocation

1 INTRODUCTION

Internet-connected mobile devices play indispensable roles in our lives today. From online educational content, to video streams carrying sports, news, and entertainment, consumers are increasingly accessing cloud-based data on their wireless mobile devices. The amount of traffic on wireless mobile networks is expected to increase sevenfold over the next five years [1].

Conventional downlink scheduling algorithms at LTE base stations (e.g. round-robin, proportional-fair) [2] are agnostic to application type. In this paper, we show that surprisingly, resource allocation signatures repeatably capture the traffic arrival patterns demanded by different types of applications. We use this insight to demonstrate that it is possible to *infer the type of application being hosted by any LTE session* from only its radio resource allocation patterns. We present the design of an application classifier and quantify application usage on eNB in a network-congested region of Palo Alto.

Prior work, such as LTEye [3] and piStream [6], has analyzed broadcast LTE data to study network characteristics like spectrum utilization and inter-cell interference, and improve user quality of experience for video streaming and web browsing applications. Previous attempts at application classification from network data have employed deep packet inspection (DPI) to analyze data within packets to select application type [4]. In this work, we present a technique to classify applications from broadcast radio-layer (LTE) data.

We make two signficant contributions:

(1) **Local application inference.** We show through controlled experiments that an application can infer its *own* type from local resource allocation data that it receives at the client phone's modem. We introduce the `PROMINENCE` metric, and use it to characterize different types of applications. We then present a heuristic based only on `PROMINENCE`, that can accurately identify file download, video streaming, video conferencing, and web browsing applications from one another.

(2) **Cell-wide application inference.** We extend the findings in (1), and demonstrate that *anyone* can identify the type of application being served by each live radio session on a cell tower, by passively sniffing a broadcast LTE channel, without any dependency on a cellular carrier, application type, or eNB vendor.

Our work has important consequences. It encourages a discussion about the privacy implications of having open access to application type without any privileged information from the network or application provider. Such information can be used to understand a user's application preferences; for instance, a classifier like the one presented in this work allows anyone to draw conclusions about the mix of applications run by a user over some timespan. Additionally, hackers can use application type to target attacks during particular segments of a session; for example, after inferring that a user is engaged in a video conference call, one could predict that account authentication or payment details will be transmitted at the beginning of a call or after a re-connection, which can be used to disrupt the session. Thus, discussions around improving the security of data broadcast over LTE are necessary to prevent malicious attacks on applications carrying user data.

MobiCom '17, October 16–20, 2017, Snowbird, UT, USA

ACM ISBN 978-1-4503-4916-1/17/10.
https://doi.org/10.1145/3117811.3131254

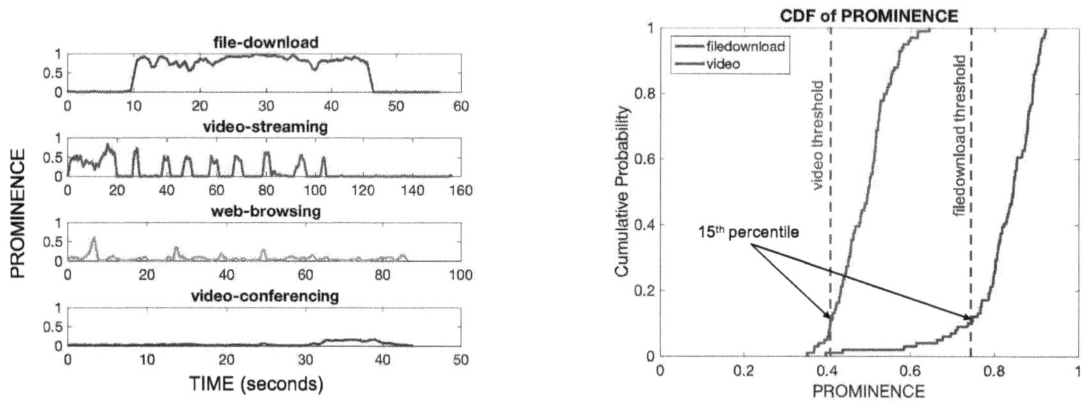

Figure 1: Different applications have unique PROMINENCE signatures. [left] PROMINENCE time series signatures for 4 different application types. [right] CDF of PROMINENCE showing reliability of metric.

2 DESIGN OF APPLICATION CLASSIFIER

We designed our application classifier using radio-layer data supplied by QXDM [5], a software package that logs messages received by a phone's modem. Our experimental setup consisted of an LG android phone (running one of the applications under investigation) connected to a PC running QXDM.

2.1 The PROMINENCE Metric

Our classifier is based on data transmitted on LTE's Physical Downlink Control Channel (PDCCH), a broadcast channel that carries Downlink Control Information (DCI) messages, specifying information about the encoding rate, modulation, and allocation of resource blocks scheduled in each millisecond of transmission.

We construct the following simple metrics for each session from the raw data exposed by the DCIs logged in QXDM:

- SCHEDTIME: the total number of milliseconds where that session was scheduled at least one resource
- SESSDUR: the total duration of that session in milliseconds
- PROMINENCE: schedule count normalized by session duration (i.e. SCHEDTIME/SESSDUR)

The PROMINENCE metric—a very simple quantity to compute—is surprisingly sufficient to classify broad categories of applications being run on mobile phones. It leverages the insight that different applications have distinct traffic arrival patterns (e.g. files are downloaded in a continuous stream, while videos are downloaded in segments), and abstracts out other session-specific quantities like the volume and modulation of the transmitted data. External factors that might affect the quality of experience a user sees at the application level, such as poor RF channel conditions, will not impact the overall PROMINENCE of a session[1]. In the rest of this section, we characterize different applications in terms of their PROMINENCEs and present the design of our classifier.

2.2 Classifier Design

As we see in Figure 1 on the left, different classes of applications have unique PROMINENCE signatures. A prominence signature is a timeseries of the PROMINENCE metric, computed in a moving window of 1 second.

We can characterize each application type in terms of their prominence signatures.

- **File download** sessions are full-buffer and consequently highly prominent—they are scheduled resources in on average 80% of the transmission intervals in a second.
- The PROMINENCE signature of a **video playback** session captures the fairly regular periodicity of video streaming algorithms, characterized by segment downloads (buffer building) followed by idle periods.
- **Web browsing** (loading a sequence of web pages) can be viewed as a stream of very brief file downloads.
- **Video conferencing** sessions have consistently low (nonzero) overall PROMINENCE, since data is transmitted as needed per millisecond (instead of as larger chunks).

The analysis of prominence signatures suggests that a simple thresholding of the PROMINENCE metric for sessions is sufficient to distinguish between file download and video sessions. We corroborate this observation by running 100 file download and 100 video sessions at different times of day and under different channel conditions. CDFs of the PROMINENCE metric are shown in Figure 1 on the right.

First, we see that both distributions are tight—the spread in PROMINENCE for each application type is less than 25%—indicating that the PROMINENCE score is a highly repeatable metric that can be used reliably to identify file download from video. Second, video and file downloads have clearly different distributions, suggesting that a very simple thresholding by the PROMINENCE metric is sufficient to distinguish between file downloads and videos. Even a highly conservative choice (e.g. 15th percentile) of PROMINENCE threshold allows us to separate file download traces from video traces accurately.

Expanding on this insight from the PROMINENCE metric, we can design an application classifier to identify file download, video streaming, video conferencing, and web browsing sessions. File downloads can be filtered based on high PROMINENCE scores (e.g. PROMINENCE > 0.4) and a large fraction of 1-second windows with

[1]We experimentally validate this claim, as discussed in Section 2.2.

nonzero PROMINENCE. Web browsing sessions also have a large fraction of 1-second windows with nonzero PROMINENCE, but have low overall PROMINENCE (e.g. PROMINENCE < 0.15). Video streaming has low overall prominence, but high prominence in 1-second windows (due to segment downloads), while video conferencing has low overall PROMINENCE as well as low PROMINENCE in 1-second windows (since data is encoded on a per-millisecond frame basis).

3 CELL-WIDE APPLICATION INFERENCE

In this section, we leverage the classifier presented in Section 2 and show that it is possible to tag each user connected to a particular cell tower with the category of application being run on their phone. We then show a breakdown of the types of applications being served by an eNB in downtown Palo Alto.

3.1 eNBsniffer

In order to get a cell-wide view of resource allocation, we built eNBsniffer, an LTE PHY-layer sniffer, similar to LTEye [3]. The eNBsniffer system consists of an off-the-shelf software-defined radio (USRP), a standard LTE decoder chain from MATLAB's LTE toolbox, and a series of heuristic filters that we designed. One of its advantages is that it is completely passive—it does not require any special handling or access to privileged information that only carriers can sanction. Further, it listens *only* on the PDCCH, which broadcasts metadata to all users, and does not sniff on any data sent to specific users.

From eNBsniffer, we process DCI messages sent to *all* users connected to the LTE band to which we tune the USRP. So, it provides us with the same information about the PDCCH that QXDM supplies, but for every user connected to the eNB, instead of for just our test user.

We ran several field experiments to verify the accuracy of DCIs recovered by eNBsniffer against the ground-truth DCI contents reported for our own users by QXDM. First, we added our own traffic on an LTE picocell that we deployed in our lab space; our false negative error was close to 0% and our false positive error was less than 1%. On multiple production LTE base-stations, we saw a false negative error of 5% and false positive error < 1% for moderately high SNR RF conditions. Given our performance on the picocell and from our analysis of the raw PDCCH symbols, we believe that most of the 5% false negative error can be made up for with better frontend hardware. Additionally, a 5% error in volume recovered will not affect the classification accuracy, for the broad class of applications discussed in Section 2.

3.2 Application Usage in Palo Alto

With eNBsniffer, we have a means to passively sniff the LTE PDCCH channel, and collect resource allocation patterns for all users connected to a cell tower—without any dependency on the network carrier. We can apply our application classifier to tag each session with its application type. We now show the results of this exercise on a base station in downtown Palo Alto.

Using eNBsniffer, we obtained the resource allocation signatures of all sessions being served by an eNB in Palo Alto for a few minutes during peak hours. We applied the classifier discussed in Section 2, and the results are shown in Figure 2. About 68% of the traffic was video (53% video streaming, 15% video conferencing). Six percent were file downloads and 18% were web browsing sessions. 8% of sessions could not be classified by our heuristic. This breakdown in usage on this one eNB is consistent with the application usage projected in Cisco's Virtual Networking Index (VNI) Forecast [1].

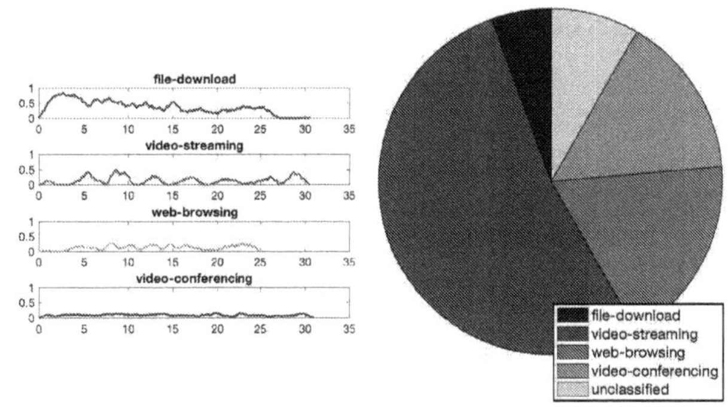

Figure 2: PROMINENCE analysis conducted using eNBsniffer. [left] PROMINENCE signatures for applications classified from eNBsniffer data. [right] Breakdown of application usage on a congested eNB in downtown Palo Alto.

4 CONCLUSIONS

This initial work shows us that a simple metric derived only from broadcast resource allocation data reveals the type of application supported by a radio session. We introduced the PROMINENCE metric, used it to describe popular classes of applications, and applied it on data sniffed over the air from a congested eNB in downtown Palo Alto.

As future work, we would like to further validate the accuracy of our heuristic on a broader class of applications, on different types of video and file download clients, and on eNBs with different schedulers. As we expand the application space for this heuristic, we might also consider machine learning-based approaches to identifying hidden patterns in PROMINENCE signatures. Additionally, we hope to more extensively discuss the privacy and security implications of our findings, and propose modifications to LTE standards that conceal features of application type from unencrypted signals broadcast over the air.

REFERENCES

[1] Cisco. Cisco Visual Networking Index: Global Mobile Data Traffic Forecast Update, 2016–2021 White Paper. http://www.cisco.com/c/en/us/solutions/collateral/service-provider/visual-networking-index-vni/mobile-white-paper-c11-520862.html, 2016],.

[2] M. Kawser, H. Farid, A. Hasin, A. Sadik, and I. Razu. Performance comparison between round robin and proportional fair scheduling methods for lte. In *International Journal of Information and Electronics Engineering*, 2012.

[3] S. Kumar, E. Hamed, D. Katabi, and L. E. Li. LTE Radio analytics made easy and accessible. In *Proc. ACM SIGCOMM*, 2014.

[4] S. Lee, H.-c. Kim, D. Barman, S. Lee, C.-k. Kim, and T. T. Kwon. Netramark: A network traffic classification benchmark. In *ACM SIGCOMM Computer Communication Review*, 2011.

[5] QUALCOMM. Qualcomm extensible diagnostic monitor. https://www.qualcomm.com/documents/qxdm-professional-qualcomm-extensible-diagnostic-monitor.

[6] X. Xie, X. Zhang, S. Kumar, and L. E. Li. piStream: Physical layer informed adaptive video streaming over lte. In *Proc. ACM Conference on Mobile Computing and Networking (MobiCom)*, 2015.

Poster: Toward a Better Monitoring of Air Pollution using Mobile Wireless Sensor Networks

Ahmed Boubrima, Walid Bechkit, Hervé Rivano
Univ Lyon, INRIA, INSA Lyon, CITI Villeurbanne F-69621
France

Lionel Soulhac
LMFA, Univ Lyon, CNRS UMR 5509 ECL, INSA Lyon,
Univ Claude Bernard Ecully 69134 France

ABSTRACT

Mobile wireless sensor networks (MWSN) are widely used for monitoring physical phenomena such as air pollution where the aim is usually to generate accurate pollution maps in real time. The generation of pollution maps can be performed using either sensor measurements or physical models which simulate the phenomenon of pollution dispersion. The combination of these two information sources, known as data assimilation, makes it possible to better monitor air pollution by correcting the simulations of physical models while relying on sensor measurements. The quality of data assimilation mainly depends on the number of measurements and their locations. A careful deployment of nodes is therefore necessary in order to get better pollution maps. In this ongoing work, we tackle the placement problem of pollution sensors and design a mixed integer programming model allowing to maximize the assimilation quality while ensuring the connectivity of the network. We perform some simulations on a dataset of the Lyon city, France in order to show the effectiveness of our model regarding the quality of pollution coverage.

KEYWORDS

Mobile wireless sensor networks; placement; air pollution monitoring; data assimilation.

1 INTRODUCTION AND RELATED WORK

Mobile wireless sensor networks (MWSN) are widely used in environmental applications where the aim is to sense a physical phenomenon such as temperature, humidity, air pollution, etc. Air pollution is one of the main physical phenomena that still need to be studied and characterized. According to the World Health Organization (WHO), exposure to air pollution is accountable to seven million casualties in 2012. Air pollution is therefore considered as a major issue of modern megalopolis, where the majority of world population lives. As a consequence, the effective monitoring of pollutant emissions is at the heart of many sustainable development efforts. The progress of electrochemical sensors, that are smaller and cheaper while keeping a reasonable measurement quality, makes the use of MWSN for air pollution monitoring viable (4). The aim of using MWSN for air pollution monitoring is usually to generate accurate pollution maps in real time (2). Unlike our work presented in (1) where we consider only sensor measurements in the generation of pollution maps, we propose in this abstract paper to perform pollution mapping based on physical models which simulate the phenomenon of pollution dispersion. Our aim is to focus on data assimilation in order to correct the simulations of the physical models based on sensor measurements, which would lead to better performances. In this context, we tackle in this paper the optimal deployment of mobile sensor nodes for effective data assimilation.

The deployment issue of wireless sensor networks has been extensively studied in the literature where several mathematical models, optimal algorithms and near-optimal heuristics have been proposed. The problem has been defined in multiple ways depending on the context of the deployment. The main issues targeted in the literature are coverage, connectivity, network lifetime and the network deployment cost. To the best of our knowledge, existing deployment approaches are either event-aware (like the work of (5)) or correlation-aware (like the work of (6)). In the first case, a sensor is assumed to have a detection range, usually circular, within which the sensor is capable of detecting any event that may happen. This cannot be applied to air pollution monitoring because a pollution sensor needs to take an air sample in order to evaluate the pollutant concentration. The second class of deployment approaches is based on the correlation that sensor measurements may present in order to select the minimum number of sensing nodes. In addition, non realistic properties of some phenomena like pollution being Gaussian are assumed in these works.

Novel application-aware deployment methods have been recently proposed to consider the characteristics of the application case in the design of the deployment approach; one example is the work of (3) on wind monitoring. Following the same direction, we propose in this abstract paper a mixed integer programming model (MILP) allowing to maximize the assimilation quality and hence minimize the error of assimilation while ensuring the connectivity of the mobile sensor network. Unlike most of the existing deployment approaches, we base on data assimilation to define an appropriate mathematical formulation of coverage quality in the context of air pollution mapping. We perform some simulations on a dataset of the Lyon city, France in order to show the effectiveness of our model regarding the quality of pollution coverage.

2 DEPLOYMENT MODEL

2.1 Main inputs and variables

We consider three types of nodes: 1) mobile sensors that are used to measure pollution concentrations and which are deployed on top of electric buses and trams; 2) relay nodes which are used for connectivity; and 3) sinks which are used to gather data from all

MobiCom'17, October 16–20, 2017, Snowbird, UT, USA.

DOI: 10.1145/3117811.3131249

the other nodes. We also consider as input the map of a given urban area that we call the deployment region. Let $\mathcal{P}$ be a set of discrete points approximating the deployment region at a high-scale ($|\mathcal{P}| = \mathcal{N}$). The set $\mathcal{P}$ can be obtained using a 2D or 3D discretization. Our goal in this paper is to be able to determine with a high precision the concentration value of pollution at each point $p \in P$. We ensure that for each point $p \in P$, either there is a mobile sensor which passes through p; or the pollution concentration can be estimated with a high precision based on the physical model simulations and the data gathered by the neighboring mobile sensors. In addition to pollution coverage, we also ensure that all the deployed sensors can send their data to at least one sink node while optimizing the positions of sinks and relay nodes.

We use decision variables r_p (respectively y_p) to specify if a relay node (respectively a sink) is deployed at point p or not. As for mobile sensor nodes, let first $\mathcal{I}$ be the set of lines of buses and trams. We consider each trajectory $i \in \mathcal{I}$ as a subset of $\mathcal{P}$. We use binary variables t_i to denote the fact that a mobile sensor is deployed on the trajectory i or not. In addition, let the binary variables x_p denote the fact that there is at least one mobile sensor which passes through the point p or not. A variable x_p is necessarily equal to 0 if no mobile sensor passes through it as formulated in constraint 1 where $\mathcal{I}_p$ denotes the set of trajectories that include the point p.

$$x_p \leq \sum_{i \in \mathcal{I}_p} t_i, \quad p \in \mathcal{P} \tag{1}$$

2.2 Deployment budget

We first denote by θ_i (respectively δ_p and ψ_p) the deployment cost of a sensor on trajectory i (respectively a relay node or a sink at point p). The network deployment cost should not exceed the deployment budget J as follows:

$$\sum_{i \in \mathcal{I}} \theta_i \cdot t_i + \sum_{p \in \mathcal{P}} \delta_p \cdot r_p + \sum_{p \in \mathcal{P}} \psi_p \cdot y_p <= J \tag{2}$$

2.3 Air pollution coverage

Using data assimilation, the estimated concentration $\widehat{\mathcal{Z}}_p$ at a given location $p \in \mathcal{P}$ where no mobile sensor passes through is formulated as the sum of $\mathcal{M}_p$, which is the physical model simulation value at p, and a weighted combination of the errors of the physical model at neighboring sensor nodes $m_q,\ q \in \mathcal{P}\ where\ x_q = 1$. The m_q values are determined with respect to the ground truth (or real) concentrations and can be estimated using sensors with high accuracy. The weights $\mathcal{W}_{pq}$ are called correlation coefficients and can be evaluated in a deterministic way based on the distance between the location of the measured concentration and the location of the estimated concentration. In this case, $\widehat{\mathcal{Z}}_p$ is evaluated using formula 3. The data assimilation equation in formula 3 is constrained by formula 4, which ensures that the denominator is never equal to 0. $\mathcal{B}_{pq}$ parameters define whether there is a correlation between points p and q or not. Given the formula of the assimilation estimated concentration $\widehat{\mathcal{Z}}_p$, the assimilation error with respect to the ground truth value can be derived as in formula 5 with m_p being the physical model simulation error at point p.

$$\widehat{\mathcal{Z}}_p = \mathcal{M}_p + \frac{\sum_{q \in \mathcal{P}} \mathcal{W}_{pq} \cdot x_q \cdot m_q}{\sum_{q \in \mathcal{P}} \mathcal{W}_{pq} \cdot x_q} \tag{3}$$

$$\sum_{q \in \mathcal{P}} \mathcal{B}_{pq} \cdot x_q \geq 1 \tag{4}$$

$$\mathcal{E}_p = m_p + \frac{\sum_{q \in \mathcal{P}} \mathcal{W}_{pq} \cdot x_q \cdot m_q}{\sum_{q \in \mathcal{P}} \mathcal{W}_{pq} \cdot x_q} \tag{5}$$

Using the already deployed pollution monitoring stations, the simulation errors can be estimated through rough comparison between the currently available real data and the outputs of the simulation model. In this paper, we consider the main cause of the simulation errors, which is in fact the inputs of the physical model. It is worth noting that simulated concentrations that are provided by the physical models are based on weather conditions and pollution emissions. Therefore, we consider multiple possibilities of simulation errors depending on the values of the inputs of the physical model. We first define a set of possible snapshots of simulation errors that we denote by $\mathcal{L}$. For a given $l \in \mathcal{L}$, let m_p^l (respectively $\mathcal{E}_p^l$) be the simulation error (respectively the assimilation error) at point p in the case of l. We formulate in formula 6 the coverage quality at point p as the maximum value among all possible errors. Then, we denote by the function $f(\{\mathcal{E}_p^*,\ p \in \mathcal{P}\})$, the overall coverage quality of a given sensor network topology. Without loss of generality, we consider that f is the mean function. The function f is defined using constraint 7 where $\mathcal{N} = |\mathcal{P}|$.

$$\mathcal{E}_p^* = Max_{l \in \mathcal{L}}\{|\mathcal{E}_p^l|\} = Max_{l \in \mathcal{L}}\{|m_p^l + \frac{\sum_{q \in \mathcal{P}} \mathcal{W}_{pq} \cdot x_q \cdot m_q^l}{\sum_{q \in \mathcal{P}} \mathcal{W}_{pq} \cdot x_q}|\} \tag{6}$$

$$f = \sum_{p \in \mathcal{P}} \mathcal{E}_p^* / \mathcal{N} \tag{7}$$

Formula 7 together with constraint 6 define the two main constraints of our pollution coverage model. However, in order to get a linear model, we need to linearize constraint 6 by eliminating the fraction and the absolute and maximum functions. Using state-of-the-are linearization techniques, we get the linear form of constraint 6 in constraints 8, 9, 10 and 11 where h_{pq} is an auxiliary variable and H is a big number used to ensure that when $x_q = 0$, h_{pq} is also equal to 0.

$$\sum_{q \in \mathcal{P}} \mathcal{W}_{pq} \cdot h_{pq} \geq \sum_{q \in \mathcal{P}} \mathcal{W}_{pq} \cdot x_q \cdot (m_q^l + m_p^l), \quad l \in \mathcal{L} \tag{8}$$

$$\sum_{q \in \mathcal{P}} \mathcal{W}_{pq} \cdot h_{pq} \geq -\sum_{q \in \mathcal{P}} \mathcal{W}_{pq} \cdot x_q \cdot (m_q^l + m_p^l), \quad l \in \mathcal{L} \tag{9}$$

$$-H \cdot x_q \leq h_{pq} \leq H \cdot x_q \tag{10}$$

$$-H \cdot (1 - x_q) + \mathcal{E}_p^* \leq h_{pq} \leq H \cdot (1 - x_q) + \mathcal{E}_p^* \tag{11}$$

2.4 Network connectivity

We formulate the connectivity constraint as a network flow problem. We first denote by $\Gamma(p),\ p \in \mathcal{P}$, the set of neighbors of a node located at point p. This set can be determined using sophisticated path loss models. It can also be determined using the binary disc model, in which case $\Gamma(p) = \{q \in P\ where\ q \in Disc(p, R)\}$ where R is the communication range of sensors. Then, we define the decision variables g_{pq} as the flow quantity transmitted from a node located at point p to another node located at point q. In addition, let

f_{ip} be the flow quantity transmitted from a mobile node deployed on trajectory i to a relay or sink node located at point p. We suppose that each mobile sensor of the resulting MWSN generates a flow unit in the network, and verify if these units can be recovered by sinks. We formulate constraint 12 to ensure the generation of the flow units by mobile sensors and constraints 13, 14 and 15 to ensure that relay nodes are flow conservative. As a result, sinks recover all the generated units and the MWSN is connected.

$$\sum_{p \in \Gamma(i)} f_{ip} = t_i,\ i \in \mathcal{I} \tag{12}$$

$$\sum_{i \in \mathcal{I}_p} f_{ip} + \sum_{q \in \Gamma(p)} g_{qp} - \sum_{q \in \Gamma(p)} g_{pq} \le (|\mathcal{I}| + 1) \cdot y_p,\ p \in \mathcal{P} \tag{13}$$

$$\sum_{i \in \mathcal{I}_p} f_{ip} + \sum_{q \in \Gamma(p)} g_{qp} - \sum_{q \in \Gamma(p)} g_{pq} \ge 0,\ p \in \mathcal{P} \tag{14}$$

$$\sum_{q \in \Gamma(p)} g_{pq} \le |\mathcal{I}| \cdot r_p, \quad p \in \mathcal{P} \tag{15}$$

3 SIMULATION RESULTS

We perform our simulations on a pollution map corresponding to the 2008 Nitrogen Dioxide (NO_2) concentrations in the Lyon district of La-Part-Dieu, which is the heart of the Lyon City. This Pollution map was generated by an enhanced physical model called SIRANE, which is designed for urban areas and takes into account the impact of street canyons on pollution dispersion. The dataset has been provided by LMFA, which is a research lab specialized in fluid mechanics in the Lyon city, France. We discretize the deployment region with a spatial resolution of 50 meters. We consider as potential positions of nodes all the grid points and as trajectories of mobile sensors all the lines and columns in the deployment grid. The physical model maximum errors have been generated through a comparison between the physical model results and the data of the currently deployed pollution monitoring stations. As a proof of concept, we consider that the error snapshots of the inputs of our model correspond to 10 different levels varying from 10% to 100% of the maximum errors of the physical model.

We evaluate the quality of air pollution monitoring depending on the deployment budget. We depict in Fig. 1 the assimilation error depending on the number of mobile nodes that can be deployed. The assimilation error of the obtained networks is evaluated based on a set of 100 randomly generated simulation error maps. We consider two cases: using uniform and Gaussian random distributions. Results show that the higher the number of mobile nodes, the less the assimilation error in both cases, which is reasonable since reducing the estimation error requires more information and hence more sensors. Also, we notice that the assimilation errors obtained using the Gaussian function are less than those obtained using the uniform distribution. Indeed, with the Gaussian distribution, most errors are located near the mean of the simulation error (which is equal to 0) whereas in the other case, the errors are distributed uniformly.

4 CONCLUSION AND ONGOING WORK

In this abstract paper, we target the deployment issue of mobile sensor networks and propose a mixed integer programming model allowing to improve air pollution monitoring through the correction of physical models. Our main idea is to define an appropriate coverage formulation for pollution data assimilation and then derive an optimal deployment model using integer linear programming. We applied our model on a dataset of the Lyon City, France in order to assess the impact of the deployment budget on the quality of pollution monitoring. We are currently working to extend our model while taking into account more coverage constraints like the calibration of sensor nodes and the drift in sensor measurements. We are also working on the design of some heuristics that are specific to our problem.

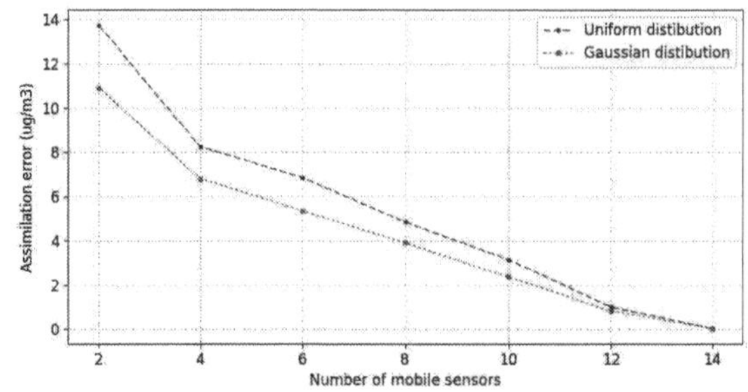

Figure 1: Coverage quality depending on the deployment budget (number of mobile nodes).

ACKNOWLEDGMENT

This work has been supported by the "LABEX IMU" (ANR-10-LABX-0088) of Université de Lyon, within the program "Investissements d'Avenir" (ANR-11-IDEX-0007) operated by the French National Research Agency (ANR).

REFERENCES

[1] Ahmed Boubrima, Walid Bechkit, and Hervé Rivano. 2016. Error-Bounded Air Quality Mapping Using Wireless Sensor Networks. In *Local Computer Networks (LCN), 2016 IEEE 41st Conference on*. IEEE, 380–388.

[2] Ahmed Boubrima, Walid Bechkit, and Hervé Rivano. 2017. Optimal WSN Deployment Models for Air Pollution Monitoring. *IEEE Transactions on Wireless Communications* 16, 5 (2017), 2723–2735.

[3] Wan Du, Zikun Xing, Mo Li, Bingsheng He, Lloyd Hock Chye Chua, and Haiyan Miao. 2015. Sensor placement and measurement of wind for water quality studies in urban reservoirs. *ACM Transactions on Sensor Networks (TOSN)* 11, 3 (2015), 41.

[4] MI Mead, OAM Popoola, GB Stewart, P Landshoff, M Calleja, M Hayes, JJ Baldovi, MW McLeod, TF Hodgson, J Dicks, et al. 2013. The use of electrochemical sensors for monitoring urban air quality in low-cost, high-density networks. *Atmospheric Environment* 70 (2013), 186–203.

[5] Maher Rebai, Hichem Snoussi, Faicel Hnaien, Lyes Khoukhi, et al. 2015. Sensor deployment optimization methods to achieve both coverage and connectivity in wireless sensor networks. *Computers & Operations Research* 59 (2015), 11–21.

[6] Venkat Roy, Andrea Simonetto, and Geert Leus. 2016. Spatio-temporal sensor management for environmental field estimation. *Signal Processing* 128 (2016), 369–381.

Poster: DeepTFP: Mobile Time Series Data Analytics based Traffic Flow Prediction

Yuanfang Chen, Falin Chen, Yizhi Ren, Ting Wu, Ye Yao
Cyberspace School, Hangzhou Dianzi University
Hangzhou, China
yuanfang.chen.tina@gmail.com,cyuanfang@acm.org
0linsrz@gmail.com
{renyz,wuting,yaoye}@hdu.edu.cn

ABSTRACT

Traffic flow prediction is an important research issue to avoid traffic congestion in transportation systems. Traffic congestion avoiding can be achieved by knowing traffic flow and then conducting transportation planning. Achieving traffic flow prediction is challenging as the prediction is affected by many complex factors such as inter-region traffic, vehicles' relations, and sudden events. However, as the mobile data of vehicles has been widely collected by sensor-embedded devices in transportation systems, it is possible to predict the traffic flow by analysing mobile data. This study proposes a deep learning based prediction algorithm, DeepTFP, to collectively predict the traffic flow on each and every traffic road of a city. This algorithm uses three deep residual neural networks to model temporal closeness, period, and trend properties of traffic flow. Each residual neural network consists of a branch of residual convolutional units. DeepTFP aggregates the outputs of the three residual neural networks to optimize the parameters of a time series prediction model. Contrast experiments on mobile time series data from the transportation system of England demonstrate that the proposed DeepTFP outperforms the Long Short-Term Memory (LSTM) architecture based method in prediction accuracy.

CCS CONCEPTS

• **Mathematics of computing → Time series analysis**; • **Information systems → Data analytics**; • **Computer systems organization → Neural networks**; *Sensor networks*; • **Theory of computation →** *Machine learning theory*;

KEYWORDS

Mobile data analytics; deep learning; neural networks; time series prediction models; traffic flow prediction

ACM ISBN 978-1-4503-4916-1/17/10.
https://doi.org/10.1145/3117811.3131269

1 INTRODUCTION

Traffic flow prediction is an important research issue, and it is a feasible method to be able to solve or alleviate some serious problems in an Intelligent Transportation System (ITS), for example, energy saving and emission reduction problems caused by traffic congestion. Traffic congestion is a serious problem in the traffic management of big cities across the world. Moreover, the public safety caused by traffic congestion is another serious problem. For example, in a study of 471 U.S. urban areas of 2014 [4], the extra energy cost due to traffic congestion was $160 billion (3.1 billion gallons of fuel). In addition, long periods of traffic congestion force the release of more carbon dioxide (CO_2) greenhouse gases into the atmosphere, and increase the number of accidents. Predicting citywide traffic flow patterns can help reduce traffic congestion by planning and controlling the traffic, and therefore reduce the amount of CO_2 emissions as well as save lives.

It is possible to predict the citywide traffic flow by analysing mobile time series data, because of the traffic flow correlation between different traffic roads, as shown in Figure 2.

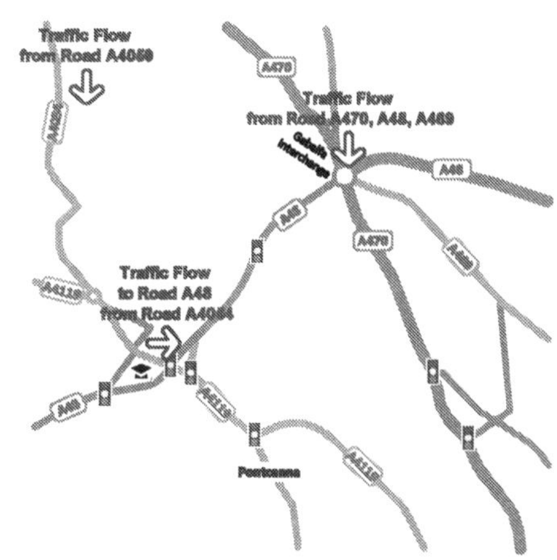

Figure 1: Traffic flow relationship between different traffic roads.

The traffic flow of a traffic road is the total number of vehicles driving on the road during a given time interval. It is estimated by counting the passing vehicles with various wireless devices, e.g., Automatic Number Plate Recognition (ANPR) cameras, in-vehicle Global Positioning System (GPS), and inductive loops built into road surfaces. The spatio-temporal relevance of the traffic flow between different traffic roads makes the prediction possible.

Many kinds of techniques have been proposed to address the traffic flow prediction problem in different situations, and traditionally there is no single best method for every situation. It is better to combine several suitable techniques to improve the accuracy of prediction under considering different situations. It means that the traditional traffic flow prediction methods are not able to satisfy most real-world application requirements. During the last five years, some studies have tried to use data analytics to solve the traffic flow prediction problem, and the results demonstrate that such schemes are feasible and are able to improve the accuracy of prediction, as the method proposed in [3]. Such kind of data analytics based prediction method is able to satisfy the requirements of different applications by analyzing the data from each corresponding specific application.

This paper proposes an algorithm DeepTFP to predict the traffic flow of a city. DeepTFP consists of two modules: (i) deep learning module. It designs three residual neural networks to model the temporal closeness, period, and trend properties of citywide traffic flow; (ii) time series function module. DeepTFP dynamically aggregates the outputs of the three residual neural networks to optimize the parameters of the time series prediction function $\hat{X}_{t+1} = c + \varepsilon_{t+1} + \sum_{i=1}^{n} \theta_i X_t$.

2 DEEPTFP

DeepTFP consists of two parts: (i) residual neural network framework, and (ii) parameter optimized time series model. Figure 2 illustrates the architecture of DeepTFP.

DeepTFP has three components to model the temporal closeness, trend, and period properties of the traffic flow from different roads. The three components have the same network structure. Such structure captures the spatial dependency between traffic roads. To capture the spatial dependency of connecting traffic roads, a residual neural network with convolutions and residual units is designed. The convolution is formulated as: $Con^{(1)}_{c/t/p} = f(W^{(1)}_{c/t/p} * Con^{(0)}_{c/t/p} + b^{(1)}_{c/t/p})$, where $*$ denotes the convolutional process, f is an activation function, e.g., the rectifier $f(z) := max(0, z)$, and $W^{(1)}_{c/t/p}$, $b^{(1)}_{c/t/p}$ are the parameters of the convolution.

The outputs of the three components are fused as X_{Con}, and the outputs are used as the input of the time series prediction function to be used to optimize the parameters of the function by minimizing the mean squared error between the predicted flow values and the true flow values: $\mathcal{L}(\theta) = ||X_t - \hat{X}_t||_2^2$, where θ denotes the set of learnable parameters of the time series prediction function $\hat{X}_{t+1} = c + \varepsilon_{t+1} + \sum_{i=1}^{n} \theta_i X_t$.

Algorithm 1 presents the steps of DeepTFP.

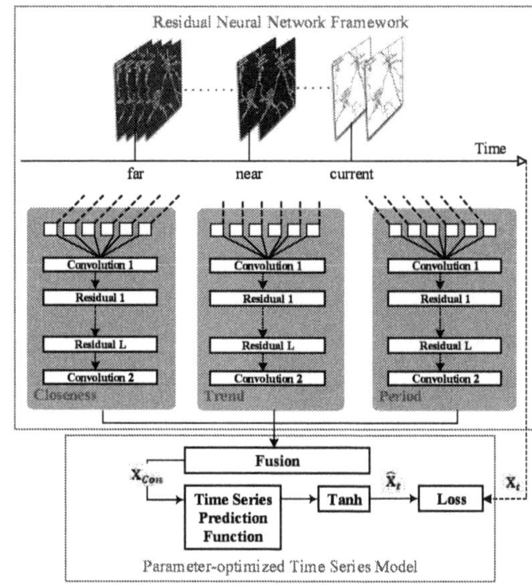

Figure 2: Architecture of DeepTFP.

Algorithm 1 Deep Learning based Traffic Flow Prediction

Input: Time series observations: $\{X_1, ..., X_n\}$; lengths of closeness, period, trend sequences: l_c, l_p, l_q; period p; trend span: q.
Output: Predicted traffic flow value X_{t+1}.
▷ construct training instances
$\mathcal{D} \leftarrow \emptyset$
for all `available time interval` $t (1 \le t \le n)$ **do**
    $\mathcal{S}_c = [X_{t-l_c}, ..., X_t]$
    $\mathcal{S}_p = [X_{t-l_p \cdot p}, ..., X_{t-p}]$
    $\mathcal{S}_q = [X_{t-l_q \cdot q}, ..., X_{t-q}]$
    put an training instance $(\{\mathcal{S}_c, \mathcal{S}_p, \mathcal{S}_q\}, X_t$ into $\mathcal{D}$
▷ train the model
initialize all learnable parameters θ in the time series prediction function
repeat
    randomly select a batch of instances $\mathcal{D}_b$ from $\mathcal{D}$
    input $\mathcal{D}_b$ into residual convolutional units to get $\hat{X}_t^{'}$
    input $\hat{X}_t^{'}$ into the time series prediction function as the X_t to get $\hat{X}_t$
    find θ by minimizing the objective $\mathcal{L}(\theta) = ||X_t - \hat{X}_t||_2^2$ with $\mathcal{D}_b$
until stopping criteria is met
▷ predict the traffic flow value X_{t+1}
input the traffic flow X_t into trained time series prediction function
return $\hat{X}_{t+1}$

3 EVALUATION RESULTS

This section compares the performance of DeepTFP and Long Short-Term Memory (LSTM) architecture based method.

LSTM is a type of recurrent neural network [2]. It is capable of learning order dependence in sequence prediction problems.

3.1 Experimental Data

In this study, trajectory data of vehicles is used, which is a kind of series transportation data. This data can be used to calculate and predict the traffic flow of a transportation system. It is collected from the transportation system of England. This transportation system has 2501 traffic roads[1] covering 300 miles of England highways and arterial roads, which is illustrated in Figure 3.

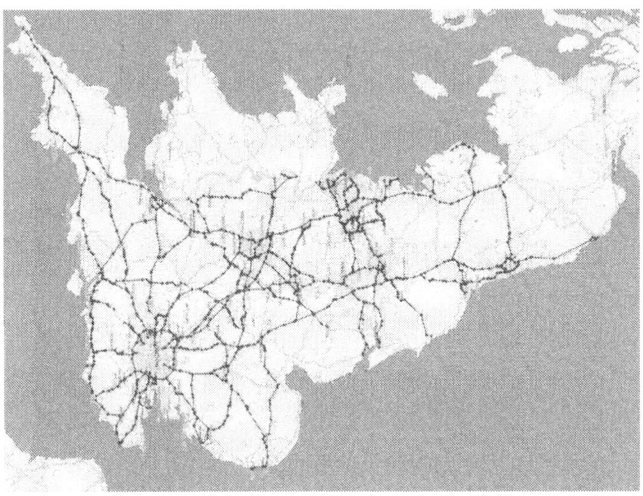

Figure 3: Flow information of traffic roads is acquired by analyzing the trajectory data of the vehicles driving on these traffic roads. The update period of this information is 15 minutes. Highways and arterial roads are marked by blue lines and dots, where the dots denote the beginnings and ends of roads.

3.2 Comparative Results

Comparative experiments measure and compare average prediction results. Each line is the average of 2501 traffic roads and 31 days of one month.

The Root-Mean-Square Error (RMSE) [1] is used to measure the differences between the values actually observed and the values predicted by methods. It is defined as the square root of the mean square error: $\text{RMSE}(\hat{\theta}) = \sqrt{MSE(\hat{\theta})} = \sqrt{E((\hat{\theta} - \theta)^2)}$, where θ is the values actually observed, and $\hat{\theta}$ is used to denote the values predicted by a method.

The results are illustrated in Figure 4.

These are two important observations which can be used to direct algorithm design to improve the performance of a prediction algorithm:

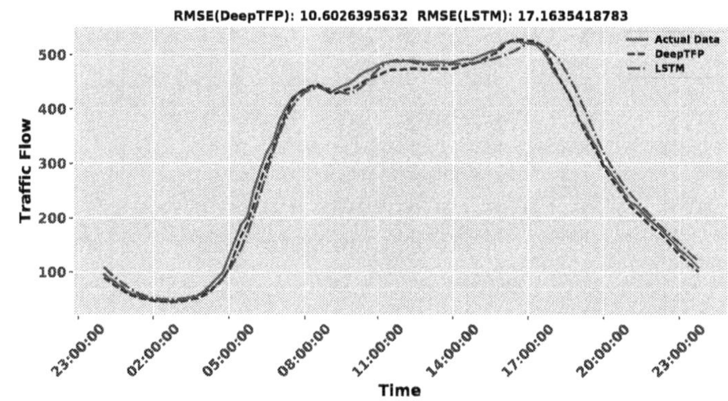

(a) Two months of training data (October and November) are used to train the model. One month (December) is predicted with the trained model.

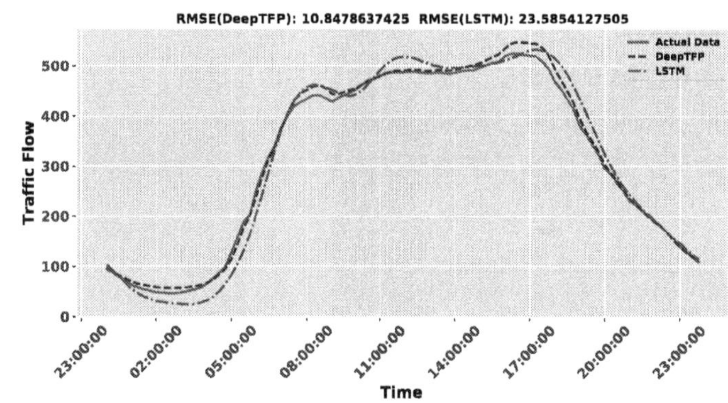

(b) One month of training data (November) is used to train the model. One month (December) is predicted with the trained model.

Figure 4: Predicted values with DeepTFP and the LSTM architecture based prediction method, and comparative results with actual values.

(1) The performance of prediction does be improved by training the model with the actual data;
(2) Increasing the volume of training data is able to improve the performance of prediction. The deep learning framework is effective for organizing high-volume data to train a prediction model.

REFERENCES

[1] Tianfeng Chai and Roland R Draxler. 2014. Root mean square error (RMSE) or mean absolute error (MAE)? *Geoscientific Model Development Discussions* 7 (2014), 1525–1534.

[2] Felix A Gers, Jürgen Schmidhuber, and Fred Cummins. 2000. Learning to forget: Continual prediction with LSTM. *Neural computation* 12, 10 (2000), 2451–2471.

[3] Yisheng Lv, Yanjie Duan, Wenwen Kang, Zhengxi Li, and Fei-Yue Wang. 2015. Traffic flow prediction with big data: a deep learning approach. *IEEE Transactions on Intelligent Transportation Systems* 16, 2 (2015), 865–873.

[4] David Schrank, Bill Eisele, Tim Lomax, and Jim Bak. 2015. 2015 Urban Mobility Scorecard. (2015).

[1] A two-way highway/arterial road is counted as two traffic roads.

Poster: A New Scalable, Programmable and Evolvable Mobile Control Plane Platform

Junguk Cho
University of Utah
junguk.cho@utah.edu

Jacobus Van der Merwe
University of Utah
kobus@cs.utah.edu

ABSTRACT

We propose a new scalable, programmable and evolvable mobile control plane platform running on realtime stream frameworks for future mobile networks. We build our prototype and show its feasibility by using Cellular Internet of Things (CIoT) as an example use case in a realistic mobile networking testbed.

CCS CONCEPTS

• **Networks → Mobile networks;**

KEYWORDS

Mobile Network; Mobility Management Entity (MME); Realtime Stream Frameworks

1 INTRODUCTION

5G networks need flexible service-based abstractions to support various services which have different network requirements. To support this, several new mobile network architectures have proposed, for example, Mobile Edge Computing (MEC) [10] for latency sensitive services, Cellular IoT (CIoT) Serving Gateway Node (C-SGN) [2] for IoT and M2M and Control and User Plane Seperation of EPC nodes (CUPS) using SDN-based approaches for better scalability and flexibility [1].

To successfully support new services in future mobile networks, the Mobility Management Entity (MME) is one of the most important components. MME is a key control plane component in mobile networks and manages the connectivity and mobility of user devices. In addition, it communicates to other mobile network control plane components (e.g., eNB, SGW, and HSS), based on user device's activities (e.g., initial attachments, handover, etc) and using standard protocols.

MobiCom '17, October 16–20, 2017, Snowbird, UT, USA

ACM ISBN 978-1-4503-4916-1/17/10.
https://doi.org/10.1145/3117811.3131247

As a key enabler for future mobile networks, MME faces two emerging concerns: massive traffic volumes and the need to support versatile functionality. First, around 26 billion IoT devices will be connected to mobile networks in 2020 [7]. These devices will generate a huge volume of control traffic, which might lead to signalling storms [6]. This phenomenon will require highly scalable MME designs. Second, a recent 3gpp specification [4] proposes that the MME would be used for control plane *as well as* data plane functionality, even supporting IP and non-IP data traffic, while it is only used for control plane functionality in current LTE/EPC networks. This change is mainly for optimizing the delivery of small size messages generated by IoT and M2M devices. In general, MME is the first component to be updated for new protocols or interfaces when new mobile network architectures or services are proposed. Hence, future mobile networks need a new software-based scalable and evolvable MME to adress these requirements.

This paper proposes a new MME architecture which is scalable, programmable and evolvable by leveraging a realtime stream framework. It first provides basic building blocks (e.g., S1AP and NAS message handlers and security functions) for building basic MME functionality and executes it on a realtime stream framework in a cloud environment. In addition, it allows users to add their own functions and plug them in on top of these basic building blocks to support new services which require new protocols and interfaces. We develop an MME library to support the basic building blocks and combine it with Apachc Storm [11] which is a production-grade realtime stream framework. We evaluate our prototype and show its feasibility by using Cellular Internet of Things (CIoT) as an example use case in a realistic mobile networking testbed.

2 DESIGN

2.1 Design Insights

The key insights of our design are based on requirements of the MME and the characteristics of control messages. First, the MME should be scalable to handle massive numbers of control messages and run continuously to avoid mobile service unavailability. In addition, it should be easily extensible to enable new services or architectures. Second, the size of control messages is small on average, as shown in Table 1, and generated by mobile events (e.g., an initial attachment, mobility, etc). The number of these messages may be burst when a large number of IoT devices start using mobile networks at the same time. In addition, control messages have latency requirements, e.g., 5 to 15 seconds defined for EPS mobility management (MM) timers [3], to deal with the retransmissions of failed messages.

Events	Mean / std (Bytes)	# of msgs
Initial attach	91.61 / 89.04	13
Service request	125 / 119.41	4
S1 release	23.33 / 3.21	3
Tracking area update (TAU)	70 / 24.24	3
Paging	108.6 / 121.72	5
Setup dedicated bearer	56 / 15.52	3

Table 1: Control message statistics

Realtime stream frameworks meet these requirements very well. They are used for continuous processing of unlimited big data which has three characteristics: *volume*, *velocity* and *variety*. Stream frameworks specialize in processing large volumes of event-based data streams and offer low-latency (e.g., msec or sec level) and high throughput by using computation parallelisms in cloud platforms. So, they are inherently designed to be scalable, fault tolerant and programmable. Based on these observations, we split MME functionality into small tasks (e.g., S1AP, NAS, security etc.) and run them as realtime stream applications to function as MME on a realtime stream framework.

2.2 Challenges

While the capabilities of realtime stream frameworks meet MME requirements, there are several challenges to leverage them for MME applications. First, the abstractions are different. Stream applications are generally represented as Direct Acyclic Graph (DAG) which means one direction communication or support cycles for iterative computations for machine learning or graph analysis in the stream applications. However, MME is highly interactive, interacting directly with eNBs and indirectly with UEs through S1AP and NAS protocols respectively. Second, MME needs to manage complex states (e.g., S1 bearer, IMSI, GUTI, security keys, etc.) based on each event and multiple EPS MM timers for retransmissions per UE. Third, in terms of framework functionality, it needs to provide basic MME functions and interfaces to enable easy programmability. Existing realtime stream frameworks do not have these capabilities.

2.3 Architecture

Figure 1 shows the proposed MME architecture. It consists of a realtime stream framework to process messages and key-value storage to store UE contexts in a cloud platform. The MME runs as a stream application which consists of

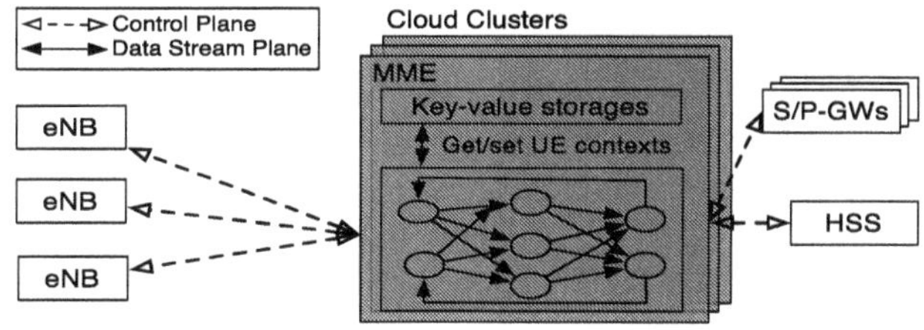

Figure 1: Architecture overview

multiple computation nodes. The first nodes get control messages from eNBs and forward them to the next nodes. Each computation node processes a small part of the MME functionality and forwards an output to a next node. If required, after processing the incoming messages, the responses will be forwarded back to the first nodes which received the incoming messages. The first nodes transfer the responses to target eNBs. Whenever each node needs to read or update UE contexts, it contacts the key-value store. In the proposed architecture, the other mobile network components (i.e., eNB, S/P-GWs and HSS), protocols and interfaces do not need to be modified.

2.4 Use Case

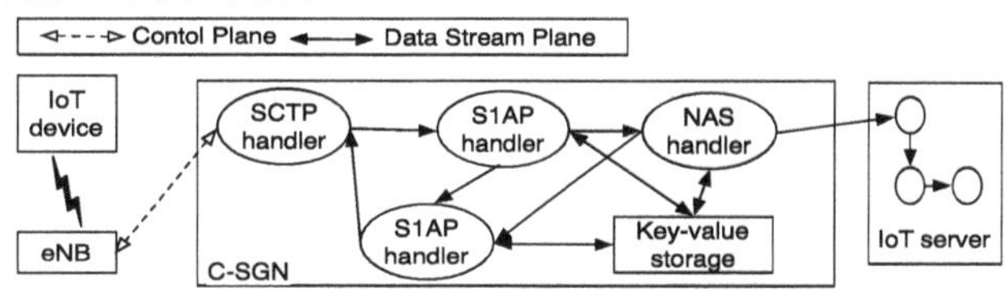

Figure 2: C-SGN architecture

The proposed architecture can be used for new mobile architectures. One compelling use case is CIoT Serving Gateway Node (C-SGN) [2] which is a new logical component and specializes in IoT and M2M traffic. It consists of the necessary functionalities from MME and S/P-GWs for CIoT devices. Thus, it supports both control and data plane functionality to deliver small size IoT messages. Specifically, IoT data can be included in control messages during an initial attach procedure and delivered over a control plane to avoid heavy control message overheads (e.g., set up data bearers in S/P-GWs). Figure 2 shows C-SGN architecture consisting of multiple computation nodes based on protocol-level partitions. Since the data from an IoT device is included in a NAS message, NAS handler node extracts and forwards it to IoT server nodes.

3 PROTOTYPE AND PRIMINARY RESULTS

Prototype: We have implemented an MME library which supports S1AP, NAS, and security functions for an initial

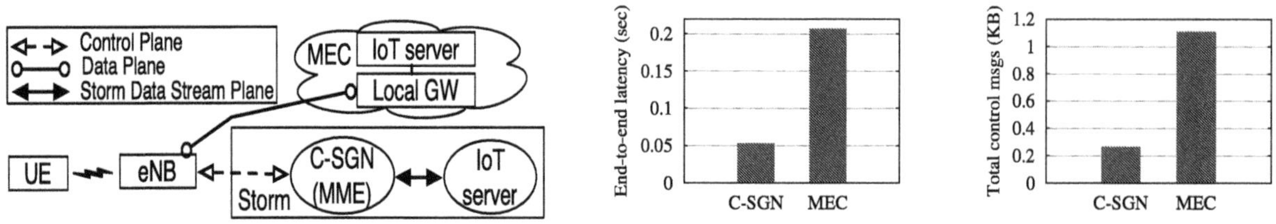

(a) Evaluation topology (b) Latency (c) Message size

Figure 3: C-SGN vs MEC comparisons

attachment with IMSI/GUTI based on srsLTE [8] in the PhantomNet [5] testbed. With the MME library, we build the MME stream application running on Apache Storm [11]. To use the MME library in Storm which supports clojure and JAVA languages, we use the Java Native Interface (JNI). Our evaluation setup is depicted in Figure 3(a).

Validating MME's standards compliance: We verify our MME's standards compliance by testing its inter-operability with several open source projects and commercial hardware with the evaluation topology shown in Figure 3(a). When a UE successfully finishes an initial attachment procedure and can send data to an IoT server in MEC, we count it as success. Table 2 shows successfully tested combinations with our MME prototype.

UE	eNB
srsUE [8]	srsENB [8]
srsUE	OpenAirInterface [9] eNB
srsUE	commercial ip.access small cell
Nexus 5	srsENB
Nexus 5	OpenAirInterface eNB
Nexus 5	commercial ip.access small cell

Table 2: MME inter-operability evaluation

Perfomance evaluation: We evaluate the C-SGN and MEC architecture using the CIoT use case. For C-SGN, a stream application on Storm consists of two nodes: C-SGN and IoT server. A UE sends small data in an initial attach request on a control plane (i.e., non-IP communication) to G-SGN in Storm. When C-SGN node gets an initial attach request message, it extracts IoT data and forwards it to an IoT server node in Storm. In case of MEC, as soon as the normal LTE/EPC initial attach procedure completes, excluding S/P GW's bearer setup, it sends a small amount of data to an IoT server on a data plane (i.e., IP communication) in an MEC cloud. We use srsUE and srsENB as UE and eNB respectively and intentionally insert 10 ms one-way delay in the link between eNB and MME for a realistic setup. We modify srsUE to send small messages over both control and data plane and measure the latency from srsUE log file and exchanged data size using tcpdump. Figure 3 shows the results. C-SGN shows better performance than MEC in terms of latency and the total size of control messages since it avoids a complex intial attach procedure.

4 FUTURE DIRECTIONS

In the future, we will first build several MME stream applications consisting of multiple nodes running on a large cluster in a cloud platform. Each node handles a small part of the MME role, based on protocol, function or UE's state machine. This would allow us to evaluate its performance with massive contol plane traffic. Second, we will extend a realtime stream framework to support dynamic reconfigurations of running MME stream applications (e.g., auto-scaling operations based on traffic loads and adding new functions for new control plane functionality) and manage EPS MM timers for retransmissions. In addition, we will investigate failure handling when active nodes fail. Finally, we will explore the feasibility of using our design for the control and data planes of S/P-GWs.

Acknowledgements: This work is supported by the National Science Foundation under grant number 1305384.

REFERENCES

[1] 3GPP Ref #: 23.714. 2015. Study on control and user plane separation of EPC nodes. (2015).
[2] 3GPP Ref #: 23.720. 2015. Study on architecture enhancements for Cellular Internet of Things. (2015).
[3] 3GPP Ref #: 24.301. 2015. Non-Access-Stratum (NAS) protocol for Evolved Packet System (EPS). (2015).
[4] 3GPP Ref #: 24.401. 2016. GPRS enhancements for E-UTRAN Access. (2016).
[5] A. Banerjee et al. 2015. PhantomNet: Research Infrastructure for Mobile Networking, Cloud Computing and Software-Defined Networking. *GetMobile: Mobile Computing and Communications* 19, 2 (2015), 28–33.
[6] A. Banerjee et al. 2015. Scaling the LTE control-plane for future mobile access. In *Proceedings of the 11th ACM Conference on Emerging Networking Experiments and Technologies*. ACM, 19:1–19:13.
[7] Gartner. 2013. Gartner Says the Internet of Things Installed Base Will Grow to 26 Billion Units By 2020. (2013).
[8] I. Gomez-Miguelez et al. 2016. srsLTE: an open-source platform for LTE evolution and experimentation. In *Proceedings of the Tenth ACM International Workshop on Wireless Network Testbeds, Experimental Evaluation, and Characterization*. ACM, 25–32.
[9] N. Nikaein et al. 2014. OpenAirInterface: A flexible platform for 5G research. *ACM SIGCOMM CCR* 44, 5 (2014), 33–38.
[10] M. Patel et al. 2014. Mobile-Edge Computing Introductory Technical White Paper. *White Paper, Mobile-edge Computing (MEC) industry initiative* (2014).
[11] A. Toshniwal et al. 2014. Storm @Twitter. In *Proc. of ACM SIGMOD*.

Poster: Conservative Modulation and Coding for Low-latency Robust Transmission of Scalable ECG over LTE MTC

Yongwoo Cho
Hanyang University
Ansan, Korea
ywc@hanyang.ac.kr

Hyo-Joong Suh
The Catholic University of Korea
Bucheon, Korea
hjsuh@catholic.ac.kr

Kyungtae Kang*
Hanyang University
Ansan, Korea
ktkang@hanyang.ac.kr

ABSTRACT

This study introduces a novel conservative modulation and coding scheme to minimize and stabilize the delay incurred during the process of electrocardiogram (ECG) transmission over a wireless medium, while maintaining the desired level of the ECG pattern quality required for improving the chance of its interpretation. A machine-type communication system is adopted for the delivery of ECG data to benefit from its inherent reliability, pervasiveness, security, and performance of 4G long-term evolution technologies with reduced cost and enhanced coverage. Extensive evaluations indicate that the proposed system provides a sufficient level of service for medical-grade instantaneous ECG monitoring even under significantly deteriorated channel conditions.

CCS CONCEPTS

• **Networks** → **Error detection and error correction**; **Cyber-physical networks**; *Layering*; • **Information systems** → *Data streaming*; • **Human-centered computing** → *Mobile computing*;

KEYWORDS

Electrocardiography; low-latency; conservative modulation and coding; machine-type communications

1 INTRODUCTION

A crucial issue pertaining to electrocardiogram (ECG) data transmission over long-term evolution (LTE) machine-type communication (MTC) for remote monitoring is the delay between the real-time status of the patient and the information displayed on the remote monitor. According to the latest recommendation of the American heart association (AHA) [1], recent observations by healthcare providers indicate that most wireless hospital telemetry systems used for monitoring patients' heart rhythms tend to exhibit clinically significant delays between the current heart condition and the displayed ECG pattern. This temporal inconsistency of real-time cardiac information can compromise the safety of the patient in clinical situations that demand instantaneous monitoring. Therefore, the advisory recommended the use of hard-wired telemetry systems instead of wireless systems for instantaneous ECG monitoring.

We propose a novel approach focusing on the latency aspect, which is an enhanced spatio-temporal scalable system with a novel conservative modulation and coding scheme for low-latency delivery of ECG data over LTE MTC to meet two crucial QoS considerations for instantaneous monitoring: 1) extremely short delay and 2) effective representation and robust delivery of ECG data to enhance its interpretation.

First, the timing aspects for the overall process of real-time ECG monitoring systems, from ECG signal acquisition and sampling steps to the entire communication procedure of LTE MTC systems, was analyzed. Consequently, major elements that can lead to nondeterministic and significant delays in the systems were successfully identified, and unnecessary buffers and delays from those elements were eliminated. Initially, any ECG data encoding steps that demand a considerable level of the buffering process were bypassed. Then, by adopting a dedicated channel allocation scheme, the latency of the packet scheduling process was made negligible and deterministic. Finally, the retransmission steps of hybrid automatic repeat request (HARQ) were eliminated to achieve a satisfactory level of the end-to-end latency.

Subsequently, a novel scalable media encoding and communication error control scheme was introduced to cope with the limitations induced by those system-level restrictions. By analyzing the exact amount of physical information that is required using various clinical environments, ECG service profiles were categorized into three levels: mandatory profile for real-time LCD display, standard profile for diagnostic printout, and high-precision profile to provide more sophisticated accuracy for high-end medical services. Then, a spatio-temporal scalable ECG coding scheme that covers these levels of service profiles in a versatile fashion without any extra system delays was introduced.

Finally, the channel quality indicator (CQI) mapping process of LTE MTC systems was modified to provide additional protection against channel errors to the mandatory part of the ECG stream at the cost of the total channel efficiency and throughput. Thus, the provision of a minimum margin for medically required level of service in real-time monitoring services under various channel conditions is guaranteed with extremely short system delays. It was observed that by protecting the essential portions of ECG signals, the proposed system surpasses the original ones in terms of the total signal distortion, especially under poor channel conditions.

2 SYSTEM ARCHITECTURE

A wearable wireless ECG sensor, which consists of multiple electrodes, a wireless transmitter, and a receiver, is used to continuously

*Author to whom correspondence should be addressed.

MobiCom'17, October 16–20, 2017, Snowbird, UT, USA

ACM ISBN 978-1-4503-4916-1/17/10.
https://doi.org/10.1145/3117811.3131267

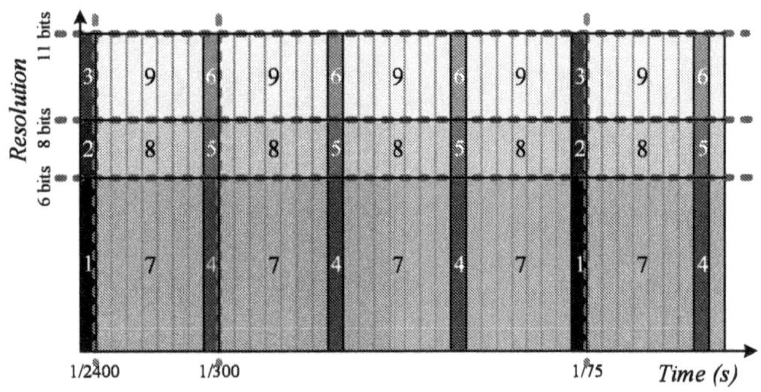

Figure 1: Sequence order of spatio-temporal scalable coding.

measure the heart activity of a mobile patient. The ECG sensor uses different combinations of electrodes to monitor signals from the heart. If the electrical signals from the heart are sampled to be ε electrodes and the signal from each lead is digitized at a rate of f samples per second with a sample size of η bits, the resulting data rate of the wireless ECG application is $\mu_{ECG} = \varepsilon f \eta$. The digital stream is packed into frames using a packetization process and transmitted wirelessly to remote nodes in real-time over a secure LTE MTC channel.

2.1 Spatio-Temporal Scalable ECG Coding

Fig. 1 presents the sequential order of the proposed spatio-temporal scalable coding. The marked numbers on each code segment denote their transmission priority, which increases along the spatial axis preferentially and then along the temporal way. In this case, the required bitrate to deliver the i-th temporal level and the j-th spatial level $B(i, j)$ can be calculated as

$$B(i,j) = f_D(i-1)\max(\eta_D) + \{f_D(i) - f_D(i-1)\}\,\eta_D(j), \quad (1)$$

where $f_D(i)$ denotes the sampling frequency of the i-th temporal level, $\eta_D(j)$ denotes the number of bits for the j-th spatial level, and $\max(\eta_D)$ is the maximum bit count for the highest spatial level.

2.2 Conservative Modulation and Coding

LTE systems adopt link adaptation technology by varying the modulation scheme and the code rate according to the channel conditions, called adaptive modulation and coding. Higher order modulation schemes, such as m-ary quadrature amplitude modulation have higher spectral efficiency, whereas lower order schemes, such as binary phase-shift keying (BPSK), are more robust under error-prone conditions. In a standard MTC system, the base station estimates the uplink channel quality of the user equipment (UE) using sounding reference signals and assign the highest possible modulation and coding scheme (MCS). The standard intentionally retains errors, targeting the block error rate (BLER) of up to 10%, which can be handled by retransmission combined with the incremental redundancy of the forward error correction technique to maximize the spectral efficiency and the data rate.

This study introduces a novel conservative CQI to MCS mapping scheme, which minimizes the end-to-end latency while maintaining adequate quality of ECG patterns by providing extra protection to higher prioritized layers by sacrificing the total spectral efficiency

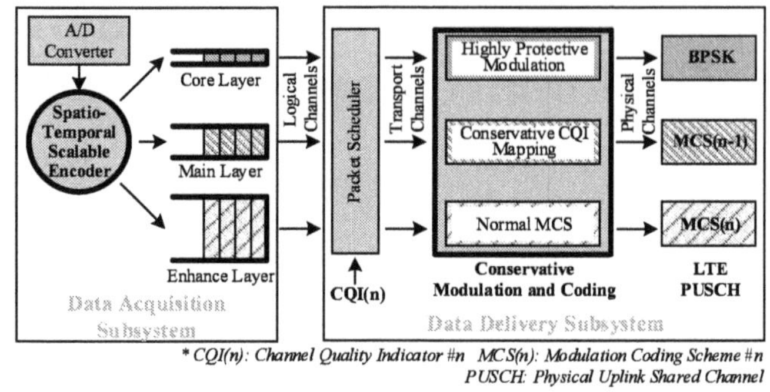

Figure 2: System architecture using conservative modulation and coding.

and throughput. The previously introduced spatio-temporal scalable encoder classifies scalable data layers according to their profile levels. The data layers can be categorized in three groups: a *core layer* to deliver the mandatory portion of total signals, *main layers* for transferring up to a temporal standard profile level, and *enhance layers* for beyond the temporal standard profile.

Fig. 2 shows the overall signal processing steps for the proposed CQI mapping scheme. Retransmission is eliminated from the error control process to minimize the latency in the system. Instead, the scheme utilizes the reserved channel bandwidth for retransmission to higher prioritized layers, such as core or main layers. Because the bitrate of the *core layer* is approximately 1-2% of the total ECG data, the BPSK modulation scheme was used for delivering all bits of the core layer data with *highly protective modulation*, which provides the best protection. This scheme enables a dramatic increase in the probability of perfect delivery of mandatory profiled data in extremely error-prone situations, without any further means of error control.

Then, the data of the *main layers* are handled with lower MCS for a given CQI. This scheme is called *conservative CQI mapping*. As shown in Fig. 6, by shifting one MCS, the received BLER can be reduced by an approximate order of 10^{-3}. In contrast, the bandwidth reduction is 7.91% when used with MCS #14, which has an efficiency of 5.1152, compared to MCS #15 with an efficiency of 5.5547. Similarly, the maximum bandwidth reduction is 37.82%, when MCS #3 is substituted with MCS #2.

By adopting highly protective modulation for the core layer and conservative CQI mapping to the main layer, the proposed conservative modulation and coding scheme makes use of retransmission-purpose bandwidth to successfully provide more protection of high-priority layers.

3 PERFORMANCE EVALUATION

Simulations were performed on the Vienna LTE-A uplink link-level simulator [2], using ECG data from PhysioBank [3]. The main simulation parameters of the simulated LTE MTC are listed in Table 1.

Fig. 3 compares the differences between a conventional real-time streaming system and the proposed scheme under significantly poor air conditions. Although the conventional real-time streaming system is capable of reducing the communication latency, it cannot

Table 1: Simulation Parameters

Parameter	Value
Carrier Frequency	2.4 GHz
MTC channel bandwidth	1.4 MHz
Antenna configuration	SISO
Channel model	AWGN/WINNER phase II [4]
Number of UEs	1
UE speed	3 km/h
Number of HARQ processes	0
TTI duration	1 ms
Number of slots per subframe	2
Number of subframes per frame	10
Number of ECG electrodes	2
ECG Sampling frequency	2400 Hz
Bit resolution of ECG data	11-bits

AWGN: Additive White Gaussian Noise
TTI: Transmission Time Interval

mitigate accidental episodes of transient errors that cause signal skipping. However, with the help of highly protective modulation, the proposed system can usually successfully deliver the mandatory part of the ECG signal, which ensures the basic readability of the transmitted ECG pattern

Fig. 4 compares the weighted diagnostic distortion (WDD) [5] for a standard best-effort MTC uplink, real-time streaming without

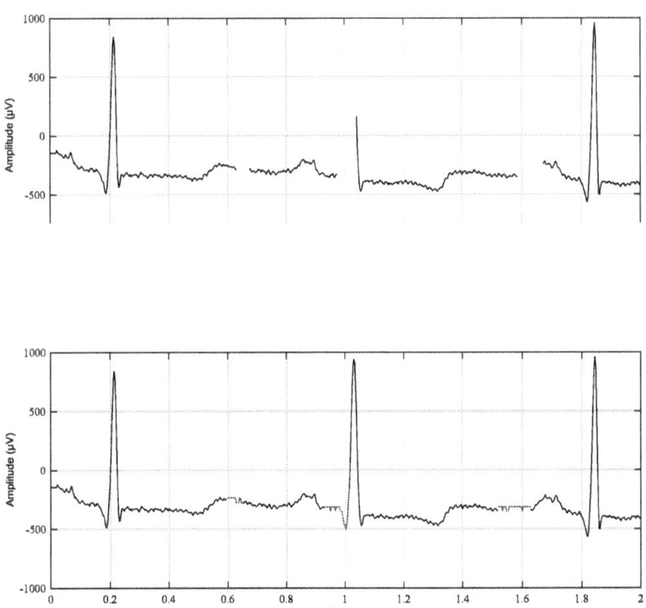

(b)

Figure 3: Difference of delivered ECG pattern under deteriorated channel condition (PER 5%). (a) Signal skip in real-time streaming. (b) Peaceful in-time quality degradation in the proposed scheme.

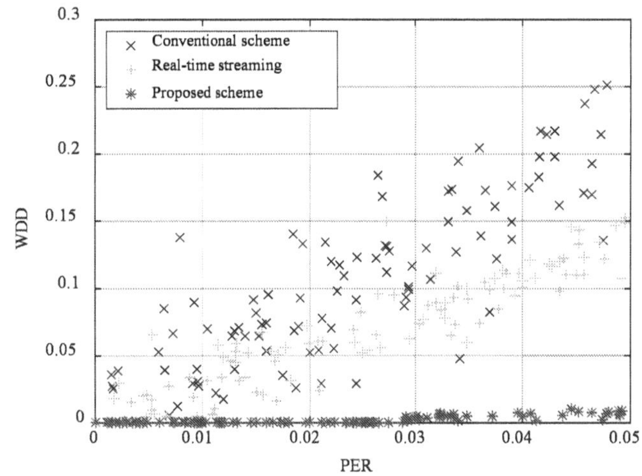

Figure 4: WDD comparison.

It segments ECG data into layers, and provides enhanced protection by adopting a conservative CQI mapping scheme for the core data which is essential to clinical interpretation of the signal.

4 CONCLUSIONS

This study introduced a novel, conservative modulation and coding scheme based on LTE MTC combined with spatio-temporally scalable representations of ECG data for instantaneous wireless monitoring. The proposed scheme successfully reduced the end-to-end latency, while maintaining adequate signal quality over a severely deteriorated wireless medium. Various simulation results ensured the validity of the proposed system.

ACKNOWLEDGMENTS

This work was partly supported by IITP (Institute for Information & Communications Technology Promotion) grant funded by the Korean government (Ministry of Science and ICT) (2014-0-00065, Resilient CPS Research). This work was also partly supported by Basic Science Research Program through the National Research Foundation of Korea (NRF) funded by the Ministry of Education (2016R1D1A1B01006716).

REFERENCES

[1] M. P. Turakhia, N. M. Estes, B. J. Drew, C. B. Granger, P. J. Wang, B. P. Knight, and R. L. Page. 2012. Latency of ECG displays of hospital telemetry systems a science advisory from the American Heart Association. *Circulation* 126, 13 (Sept. 2012), 1665–1669. https://doi.org/10.1161/CIR.0b013e31826ae459

[2] M. Rupp, S. Schwarz, and M. Taranetz. 2016. The Vienna LTE-Advanced Simulators: Up and Downlink, Link and System Level Simulation. Springer, Singapore.

[3] A. L. Goldberger, L. A. Amaral, L. Glass, J. M. Hausdorff, P. C. Ivanov, R. G. Mark, J. E. Mietus, G. B. Moody, C.-K. Peng, and H. E. Stanley. 2000. Physiobank, PhysioToolkit, and PhysioNet: Components of a new research resource for complex physiologic signals. *Circulation* 101, 23 (June 2000), e215–e220. https://doi.org/10.1161/01.CIR.101.23.e215

[4] P. Kyösti, J. Meinilä, L. Hentilä, X. Zhao, T. Jämsä, C. Schneider, M. Narandzić, M. Milojević, A. Hong, J. Ylitalo, and V.-M. Holappa. 2007. WINNER II Channel Models (IST-4-027756 WINNER II D1.1.2 V1.1). (Sept. 2007). Retrived August 8, 2017 from http://projects.celtic-initiative.org/winner+/phase_2_model.html

[5] Y. Zigel, A. Cohen, and A. Katz. 2000. The weighted diagnostic distortion (WDD) measure for ECG signal compression. *IEEE Transactions on Biomedical Engeering* 47, 11 (Nov. 2000), 1422–1430. https://doi.org/10.1109/TBME.2000.880093

Poster: DRIZY- Collaborative Driver Assistance Over Wireless Networks

Nakul Garg*[1], Ishani Janveja*, Divyansh Malhotra*, Chetan Chawla*, Pulkit Gupta*,

Harshil Bansal*, Aakanksha Chowdhery†, Prerana Mukherjee††, Brejesh Lall††

* Bharati Vidyapeeth's College of Engineering Delhi, †Princeton University, †† IIT Delhi
[1]nakulgarg.2208@gmail.com, † aakanksha@princeton.edu, †† {eez138300, brejesh}@ee.iitd.ac.in

ABSTRACT

Driver assistance systems, that rely on vehicular sensors such as cameras, LIDAR and other on-board diagnostic sensors, have progressed rapidly in recent years to increase road safety. Road conditions in developing countries like India are chaotic where roads are not well maintained and thus vehicular sensors alone do not suffice in detecting impending collisions. In this paper, we investigate a collaborative driver assistance system "DRIZY:DRIve eaSY" for such scenarios where inference is drawn from on-board camera feed to alert drivers of obstacles ahead and the cloud uses GPS sensor data uploaded by all vehicles to alert drivers of vehicles in potential collision trajectory. Thus, we combine computer vision and vehicle-to-cloud communication to create comprehensive situational awareness. We prototype our system to consider two types of collisions: vehicle-to-vehicle collisions based on uploading GPS sensor data of vehicles to cloud and vehicle-to-pedestrian collisions based on detecting pedestrians from vehicle's dashboard camera feed. Sensor data processing in each vehicle occurs on smartphone for GPS values which are then uploaded to cloud and on raspberry pi3 for video feeds to make a cost-effective solution. Experiments over both 4G and wireless networks in India show that collaborative driver assistance is feasible in low traffic density within acceptable driver reaction time of <5 sec, but can be limited by the time to process compute-intensive video feeds in real-time. We investigate novel ways to optimize the processing tofi nd an acceptable trade-off.

CCS CONCEPTS

• **Networks** → **Location based services**; • **Computing methodologies** → **Image processing**; • **Computer systems organization** → *Sensor networks*; *Real-time system architecture*;

KEYWORDS

Driver assistance system; vehicle-to-cloud communication; edge computing; pedestrian detection; HOG+SVM sliding-window optimization

MobiCom '17, October 16–20, 2017, Snowbird, UT, USA

ACM ISBN 978-1-4503-4916-1/17/10.
https://doi.org/10.1145/3117811.3131255

1 INTRODUCTION

Road accidents continue to be a major cause of human fatalities, resulting in as many as 1.2 million fatalities each year [2]. In developing countries, such as India, two major causes of road accidents are vehicle-to-vehicle collisions at road intersections and vehicle-to-pedestrian collisions when drivers are distracted. Such accident prone areas are referred to as "accident blackspots".
Advanced driver assistance systems (ADAS) intend to increase the road safety by assisting in crucial decision-making using vehicular sensors, such as CMOS vision sensors, LIDARs, etc. Road conditions in developing countries, such as India, include chaotic traffic on unmaintained roads. Pedestrian behavior is particularly unpredictable and people cross roads anywhere without crosswalk. Such conditions make the design of driver assistance systems particularly challenging and on-board vehicular sensors alone do not suffice to predict impending collisions.
In this paper, we propose a collaborative driver assistance system DRIZY in which vehicular sensor data and inference drawn from the data is uploaded over a wireless network to the cloud which alerts the vehicles of obstacles in potential collision trajectory. The objective of our system is twofold: i) to detect the presence of pedestrians in the specific region of interest around the host vehicle using dashboard camera feed and alert the driver, and ii) to predict and alert vehicles on a collision course using GPS sensor data uploaded by all vehicles. We delegate pedestrian detection processing to an embedded platform and a dedicated application in the smartphone in each vehicle handles the impending collision alerts. The key challenges in our system design are ensuring low latency in estimating and sending alerts about vehicle-to-vehicle collisions and ensuring real-time processing to detect pedestrians. Our system design solves these challenges by pre-processing the sensor data locally on smartphone/embedded platform and minimizing overhead processing on the cloud. Experiments over 4G and WiFi networks in India show that collaborative driver assistance is feasible in low traffic density within acceptable driver reaction time of <5 sec.Further, we optimize the pedestrian detection module on embedded platforms to achieve real-time processing at 9.8 fps.

2 SYSTEM DESIGN

We discuss key components of the system architecture below and illustrate the same in Fig. 1.
Sensing on the vehicle. The driver installs DRIZY app which processes GPS values obtained from smartphone to infer the vehicle location, speed and direction of travel. In addition, the vehicle can be equipped with a dashboard camera that captures video-feed of

the view in front of the car and relays it to an embedded platform to provide real-time assistance warnings when a pedestrian is in collision trajectory.

Cloud database and server. DRIZY app uploads processed vehicular data to the cloud database. The cloud server processes data for each accident prone area to predict vehicles in collision trajectory and ping alerts to the app in case of impending danger.

Local processing vs cloud processing. DRIZY app pre-processes the vehicular GPS data to identify if the vehicle is close to an accident prone area and to add it to a "cluster" of vehicles present in the same area, also called accident blackspot. Thus, the cloud only needs to process data captured in each accident blackspot in real-time to predict potential collisions.

Alarm Unit. The embedded platform and cloud server generate alerts for vehicle and pedestrian collisions respectively. In a with-camera system, both alerts are sounded from a piezo-buzzer attached to the embedded system. Whereas the vehicle collision alerts are received on the smartphone itself for users using app only. We next discuss how we infer the two type of collisions: a) vehicle-to-vehicle collisions at road intersections, and b) vehicle-to-pedestrian collision on roads.

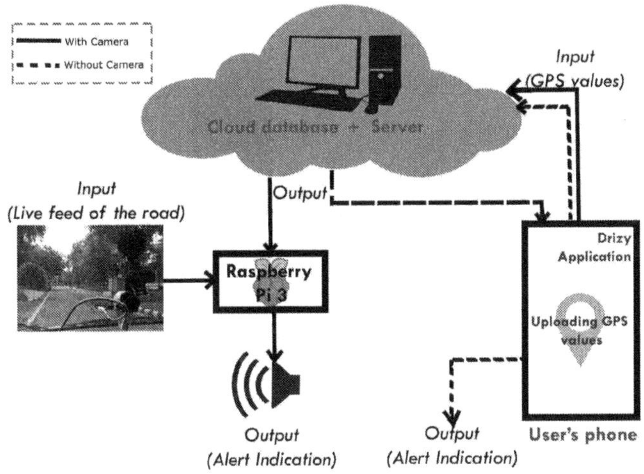

Figure 1: Workflow of the DRIZY Framework with and without camera.

2.1 Vehicle-to-vehicle collisions at road intersections

The cloud maintains a database representation of all accident blackspots in the form of hierarchical representation. DRIZY app uploads processed GPS data collected by smartphone to the respective blackspot in database. This data includes GPS coordinates, road number, speed and direction of motion towards or away from intersection point. For each accident blackspot, the cloud then predicts the collisions of vehicles approaching the same road intersection. Algorithm 1 discusses how the server predicts impending collisions and calculates time for each vehicle to reach the intersection point. If the difference in estimated time of any two vehicles to approach the intersection is less than a threshold set to 5 secs, then the cloud sends an alert to vehicles of interest. The algorithm adapts its threshold according to the speed of the vehicle. For example, if the vehicle is travelling too fast, then the threshold is doubled to 10 secs and prior alerts are generated, thereby giving the driver sufficient time to apply brakes after alert reception.

Algorithm 1: Server Code Algorithm

```
foreach pair of vehicles in Accident Black Spot do
    Get vehicle's GPS, speed, road number from Cloud
    if roadofvehicle1 != roadofvehicle2 then
        if direction of both vehicles is toward intersection then
            Find the distance of two vehicles from intersection
              using Haversine formula [5]
            Predict times t1 and t2 to reach the intersection
              using linear predictive model
            if |t1 - t2| < threshold then
                Send collision alert to vehicles
            end
        end
    end
end
```

2.2 Vehicle-to-pedestrian collisions

The embedded platform uses computer vision to detect pedestrians in the video feed collected from dashboard camera. This is done in real-time on using sliding window algorithm with HOG+SVM classifier. This feature is aimed specifically to help distracted drivers stay aware. Computationally intensive classifiers in computer vision algorithms limit the video processing speed on embedded platforms, such as Raspberry Pi 3. We optimize this processing using several steps. We select region of interest based on known geometric constraints and reduce the number of sliding windows where we detect pedestrians. Thus, the processing time for each frame is reduced by a factor of 7x (from 1.4 fps to 9.8 fps). Next, we use multithreading to parallelize the capture of camera frames and pedestrian detection for multiple frames. Finally, we speed up the input of video feed by using Raspberry Pi camera module that connects directly to GPU instead of relying on USB camera. Thus, novelty of this feature lies in the optimisations performed to minimize computation and increase available reaction time for drivers.

3 EVALUATION

3.1 Vehicle-to-vehicle collisions at road intersections

This section evaluates 2 parameters: (i) available time for driver to apply brake before collision (ii) frequency of alerts generated by DRIZY. We compare DRIZY with an "Always On" system that gives alerts to every vehicle in the accident blackspot.

Experiment. We perform an experiment at IIT Delhi campus roads to analyze the reaction time with 50 test drives and 2 vehicles approaching an intersection point. With DRIZY installed in them wefi nd the available reaction time after reception of alerts. Figure 2 shows a plot between speed and reaction time available. For speeds limits between 20-25 kmph the system generates alerts with available reaction time >20s and for speed limits reaching 40-45

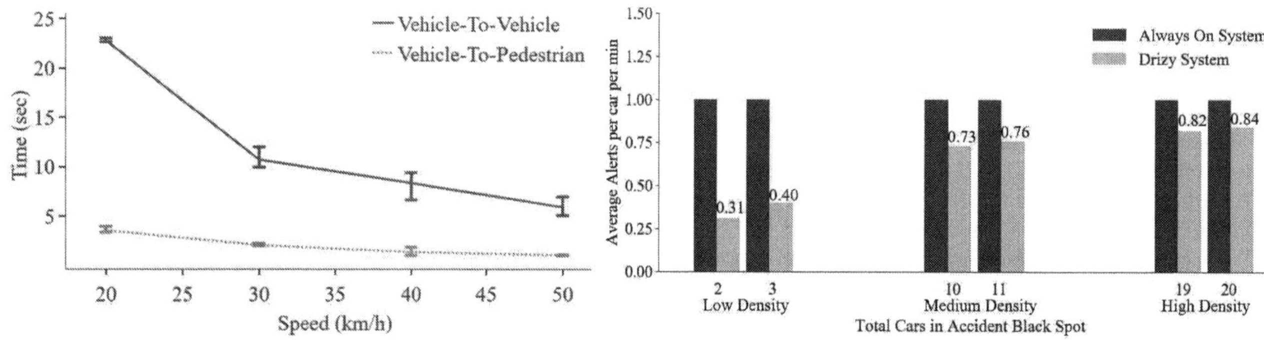

Figure 2: Left: Available Reaction time before collision with pedestrians and vehicles. It shows maximum and minimum values of time obtained during test-runs. Right: Comparative analysis of a system that gives alerts to every vehicle in the accident prone area with DRIZY that predicts collisions before giving alerts. The values were obtained using simulation and spawning of vehicles with random attributes in an accident blackspot.

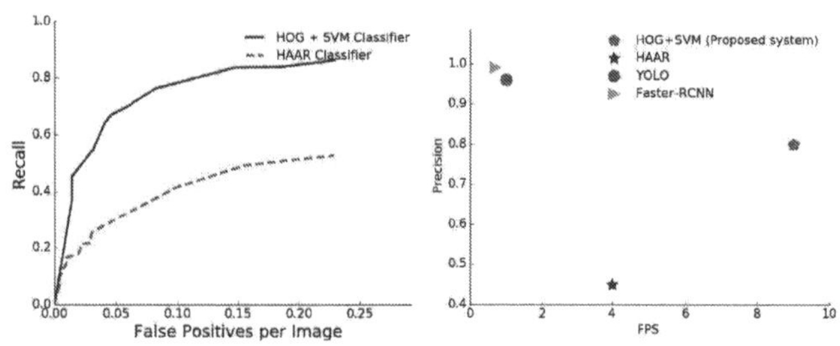

Figure 3: Left: Recall vs FPPI for pedestrian classifiers at varying thresholds. Right: Precision vs frames processed per second for various detection techniques.

kmph, it is found to be close to 8s. Latencies associated with upload, download and server processing over 4G and WiFi networks are shown in in Table 1. Due to the small packet size of the data being uploaded, the throughput of the system does not dependent on the network bandwidth and just requires connectivity.

Simulation. In order to study the frequency of collision alerts in different traffic densities, we simulate an experiment. We generate synthetic data with uniform distribution for 'N'vehicles which includes vehicle distance from intersection ranging between 0-400m, road number from 0-4, vehicle speed in range 1-36kmph and direction of motion of vehicle. This data is then accessed by the server to predict collisions. Figure 2 shows the comparison of DRIZY with an Always On system at low, medium and high density traffic levels. The proposed system reduces the redundant warnings by 80%, 50% and 10% in low, medium and high traffic density, respectively.

	4G Time	WifiTime
Upload/Download	258/746 ms	229/678 ms
Server processing	30 ms	30 ms

Table 1: Average latencies in Collaborative Assistance workflow over different network types

3.2 Vehicle-to-pedestrian collisions on roads

This section addresses the question of how well Drizy can detect pedestrians keeping sufficient reaction time for the driver.

Experiment. We analyze the accuracy of proposed technique against various state of the art pedestrian detection techniques on video dataset collected on Indian roads with 5500 positive images (pedestrian) and 4500 negative (non-pedestrian/background) images. Similar set of test drives as in the case vehicle-to-vehicle collision are repeated for determining the trend of available reaction time after vehicle-to-pedestrian collision alerts.

Result. The plots of obtained results are shown in Fig. 2, 3. HOG[1]+SVM classifier (proposed system) provides a speedup 10x over faster RCNN[4] and YOLO[3] at high precision rates. It is observed that HOG+SVM classifier performs better over HAAR[6] with a gain of 0.4% recall at 0.1 FPPI (false positives per image).The pedestrian detection module is capable of successful detection upto a range of 18 to 23m in varied lighting conditions during the day. The system warns the driver 4-5 seconds prior to approaching a pedestrian ahead at 10-40 kmph speed limit.

4 CONCLUSIONS

Results validate that a collaborative driver assistance system is feasible in low and medium traffic density. While video feed based assistance turns out to be useful in clear weather conditions the alerts inferred on processing GPS sensor data over cloudfi nd their utility even in bad weather conditions. They are also capable of avoiding collisions at unsupervised intersections especially in low traffic areas where drivers tend to drive carelessly. In our future work we aim to implement forward collision alert to avoid tailgating and embed the concept of a "Green Corridor" to assist an approaching ambulance. We would also consider peer-to-peer interactions to further reduce the latency in generating assistance warnings.

REFERENCES

[1] Navneet Dalal and Bill Triggs. [n. d.]. Histograms of oriented gradients for human detection. In *CVPR 2005*.
[2] World Health Organization. 2015. *Global status report on road safety 2015*. World Health Organization.
[3] Joseph Redmon, Santosh Divvala, Ross Girshick, and Ali Farhadi. [n. d.]. You only look once: Unified, real-time object detection. In *CVPR 2016*.
[4] Shaoqing Ren, Kaiming He, Ross Girshick, and Jian Sun. [n. d.]. Faster R-CNN: Towards real-time object detection with region proposal networks. In *NIPS 2015*.
[5] C Carl Robusto. 1957. The cosine-haversine formula. *The American Mathematical Monthly* 64, 1 (1957), 38–40.
[6] Paul Viola and Michael Jones. [n. d.]. Rapid object detection using a boosted cascade of simple features. In *CVPR 2001*.

Poster: Emotion-Aware Smart Tips for Healthy and Happy Sleep

Yanxiang Guo[1,2], Xiaoyi Yang[3], Jiao Zhang[1,4], Chunbin Zhong[1,2], Yilong Li[5], *Xiping Hu[1,2], *Bin Hu[6], *Jun Cheng[1,2], Zhaolong Ning[7]

[1] Shenzhen Institutes of Advanced Technology, Chinese Academy of Sciences, China | [2] The Chinese University of Hong Kong, Hong Kong | [3] Carnegie Mellon University, USA | [4] National University of Defense Technology, China | [5] University of Wisconsin-Madison, USA | [6] Lanzhou University, China | [7] Dalian University of Technology, China

yanxiang.gyx@gmail.com, xp.hu@siat.ac.cn, bh@lzu.edu.cn, jun.cheng@siat.ac.cn

ABSTRACT

People spend up to one-third of lives asleep, and healthy sleep habits can make a big difference in their quality of life. But in modern society, many people have unhealthy sleep diaries and suffer from various sleep disorders, which may result in irregular mood fluctuations or even mental health problems such as anxiety and depression. We propose the Emotion-Aware Smart Tips (EAST), a novel approach that could help to inform users about their irregular emotional states with smart tips to improve their sleep qualities. EAST aims at helping users keep healthy sleep schedules and emotional states by providing smart tips through a novel model that combines multivariate regression, random forest, and neural network to quantify the relations between sleep patterns and emotional states. Prototype implementation and initial experiments of EAST in mobile phones have demonstrated its desired functionality and practicality for real-world deployment.

CSS CONCEPTS

• **Human-centered computing → Ubiquitous and mobile computing**; Ambient intelligence; Smartphones

KEYWORDS:

Mobile application; emotion-aware; smart tip

1 INTRODUCTION

Nowadays, many people are suffering from sleep disorders, and the statistics published by The Institute of Medicine (US) indicate that about 50-70 million of American has chronic sleep problems [1]. Lack of sleep correlates with many chronic medical diseases, and results in many unhealthy behaviors, such as nodding off while driving and accidentally falling asleep during daytime [1, 2]. Not only does sleep deprivation affect cognitive and motor performance, but it also has more negative impacts on mood [3]. Without properly regulating moods, a person is more likely to have mental health problems such as depression. Thus, we propose emotion-aware smart tips (EAST).

EAST aims to provide a seamless and practical solution to improve users' sleep quality and emotions conveniently, and it can be deployed in most contemporary mobile phones. EAST interprets sleep features through processing the raw data collected by accelerometer sensors integrated in smartphones. Also, EAST uses a novel model which can analyze these sleep features and explore their emotional patterns on arousal-valence model [4] through artificial neutral network based methods in the cloud. Furthermore, EAST recommends smart tips to users based on their emotional states in order to improve their sleep qualities and moods. For example, this mechanism may help user to relax before sleep, such as avoiding bright light or reading a book, if it finds out this user has hard time falling asleep in the previous nights. This feature could help users more easily get high quality sleep, and maintain healthy emotional states.

Currently, a variety of mobile applications based approaches have been proposed for improving users' sleep quality or tracking sleep patterns [5, 6, 7, 8]. In [5], authors try to predict users' sleep quality via context mining data from users' mobile phones. A method using smartphones' sensors to capture sleep stage transitions and evaluate sleep quality is proposed in [6]. Both research only focuses on analyzing users' sleep patterns. There are also some research works via mobile phones to identify users' emotions, such as MoodMagician [7], which uses Galvanic Skin Response (GSR) signals from a wearable device to infer users' emotions on Android phones. Different from these approaches, EAST not only analyzes users' sleep patterns so as to quantify the relations between sleep and moods, but it also aims at helping users improve healthy sleep and emotional states through recommending smart tips to them.

2 SYSTEM DESIGN

As shown in Fig. 1, the work flow of EAST consists of three parts, Sleep Features Extraction, Moods Prediction, and Tips Recommendation.

Sleep Features Extraction: At present, accelerometer sensors or microphones in mobile phones or wearable devices are commonly used to detect users' movements during sleep so as to analyze their sleep patterns. For our design, we use accelerometer sensors integrated in smartphones to collect acceleration data in 3-Dimentions at a frequency of 10 Hz. The acceleration data will be periodically transmitted to the cloud server for data processing.

MobiCom '17, October 16–20, 2017, Snowbird, UT, USA

ACM ISBN 978-1-4503-4916-1/17/10.
https://doi.org/10.1145/3117811.3131256

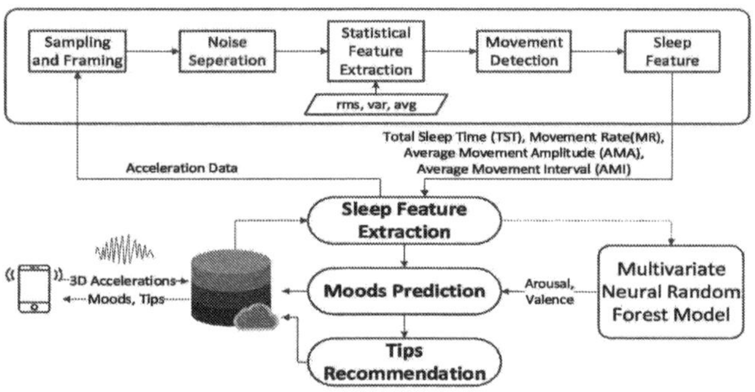

Figure 1: System model design

To analyze these data, first, we continuously sample and segment signals into frames for sleep features extraction. In order to detect movements from these signals, we collect a short period of noise signals to determine the noise threshold of each phone. Then, based on these noise thresholds, we are able to separate movement events from the noise. After that, the statistical features such as root mean square (rms), variance (var), and mean (avg) of the accelerations are extracted from the frames, and based on these extracted features, we adopt lower-pass filter to detect the movement events. Finally, after we find the movement events, sleep features, such as total sleep time (TST), movement rate (MR), average movement amplitude (AMA), and average movement interval (AMI), can be obtained and used to measure the quality of sleep through the night.

Moods Prediction: We build a classification model to predict users' arousal and valence coordinates of the arousal-valence model with the sleep indicators that we collect every night. Since the size of dataset is not fixed and will keep increasing, and any change may cause the traditional tree to fall apart necessitating the reconstruction of the tree, the traditional decision trees is not efficient enough once the model needs to be updated. Therefore, one of the idea is to implement the tree structure into a deep structure, such as a neural network model. Similar empirical studies by [9] have already proved the practicality of this approach.

The theoretical idea of neural random forest has been studied in recent years, which focuses on how to covert a tree structure's threshold decisions boundaries into a stochastic and differentiable model [10]. An even simpler idea comes from [11], which claims that every CART classification tree can be converted into a neural network with two hidden layers and a threshold activation function approximated by the hyperbolic tangent function. Even though we still use decision tree for classification, the structure of the model will change. When more data are collected, the structure of the model will be relatively stable and only the weight values in the network will be adjusted. Each of such neural trees provides a prediction for the data and the final result of neural random forest will be the average of all trees.

In our case, the number of the repetitions or the number of trees in such random forest will be selected through cross validation at the beginning of the model training. In addition, since we have multiple response variables to predict for the mood coordinates, we implement multivariate regression into the neural random forest and estimate the two coordinates at the same time by also considering the correlation between two coordinates. We call this model as the multivariate neural random forest. This approach can be easily extended to higher dimensional spaces if we can identify more indicators for the emotional states.

Tips recommendation: After moods are inferred from our model, smart tips could be provided corresponding to both the sleep features extracted before and the moods predicted, a function that could help users be aware of their irregular emotion fluctuations and improve sleep quality. For instance, if a user has low valence and high arousal values of emotions, and he has difficulty in falling asleep, then he may receive a tip to perform some exercises at regular times to relax his body.

3 IMPLEMENTATION AND EVALUATION

To demonstrate the desired functionalities of EAST, we implement it on the iSmile platform we have developed recently [12]. The prototype version of EAST mainly contains two parts, the mobile side and the cloud side. The mobile side is developed on Android system, and it is used to collect users' sleep data through the accelerometer sensors when users are sleeping. The cloud side performs all the calculations for sleep quality examinations to predict users' emotional states and recommend tips. Besides, users could track their sleep data and mood trends in day, week, or month intervals.

Before the alarm sound, EAST sends the sleep data (accelerations) to the cloud server for data processing such as sleep features extraction and moods prediction. After that, the result of predicted emotions and smart tips will be sent back to the mobile side. As shown in Fig. 2 (a), users will see the predicted moods after they turn off their alarms. Moods are shown on the arousal-valence coordinates, and the highlight circle indicates the predicted mood of the day. If users are unsatisfied with the moods predicted, they are also able to manually update their arousal and valence values to the cloud side to enhance our EAST method. After that, as shown in Fig. 2 (b) and (c), once the smart tips are inferred through the analysis of sleep patterns and the predicted emotions, they are delivered to users both in the application page and in the notification bar. In addition, as shown in Fig. 2 (d), we display the results of our predicted moods in days, weeks, and months intervals so that users could easily trace their emotion tendencies and be aware of their irregular emotional fluctuations.

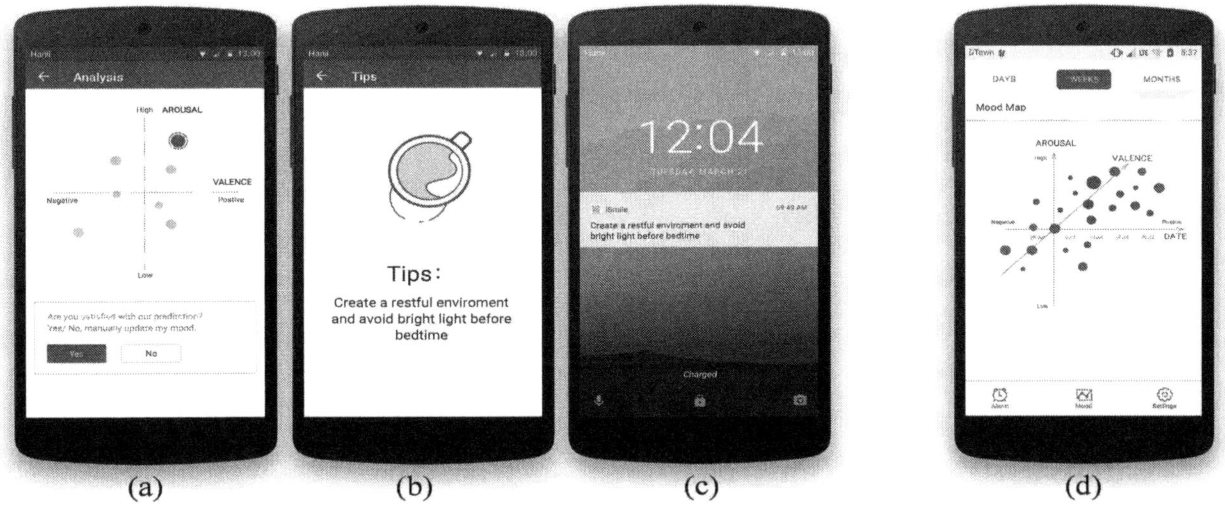

Figure 2: EAST user interfaces

We conduct an initial experiment with 20 users to demonstrate the feasibility of the EAST. We use some data to train our model, and the others to give comparisons of the predicted values and the ones given by the users on the arousal-valence coordinates separately. The result is summarized in Table 1. Both arousal and valence values are ranged from 0 to 10. The minimum distance between the predicted moods and the real values inputted by the users is 0.5, and the standard deviation of the distance is 1.27, which means that the accuracy rate of our solution is up to 87.3%. In addition, as we get more data for training, our model will become more reliable. Our initial result demonstrates that it is feasible to deploy EAST in popular smartphones and predict users' emotion states through their sleep patterns in practice.

Table 1: Experimental results

	Real(v.)	Real(a.)	Pred(v.)	Pred(a.)	Error
Min.	4	3	2.53	4.49	0.50
Max.	6	6	8.26	7.00	3.82
Mean.	4.83	4.83	5.03	5.60	1.82
SD.	0.98	1.17	2.22	0.95	1.27

4 CONCLUSIONS AND FUTUREWORK

In this project, we have firstly proposed, designed and implemented Emotion-Aware Smart Tips (EAST) that could remind users of their emotional problems caused by irregular sleep, and then provided smart tips to improve their sleep qualities via mobile phones. EAST uses multivariate neural random forest model to predict users' moods on the arousal-valence model by quantifying the relations between sleep patterns and emotional states. We have implemented a prototype version of EAST on the iSmile platform and set up an initial experiment to demonstrate its functionality and feasibility in real world. In the future, we plan to explore the usage of new algorithms to enhance the prediction accuracy. Also, we shall conduct systematic experiments to find out how the smart tips EAST recommends may influence users' sleep behaviors and emotions. More details will be introduced in full paper version.

ACKNOWLEDGMENTS

This work is partially supported by the Shenzhen Engineering Laboratory for 3D Content Generating Technologies (NO. [2017]476), Guangdong Technology Project (2016B010108010, 2016B010125003), National Basic Research Program of China (973 Program) (No.2014CB744600), National Nature Science Foundation of China (61403365, 61402458, 61632014, 61210010), Program of International S&T Cooperation of MOST (No.2013DFA11140).

REFERENCES

[1] I. of Medicine, Sleep Disorders and Sleep Deprivation: An Unmet Public Health Problem, H. R. Colten and B. M. Altevogt, Eds. *Washington, DC: The National Academies Press*, 2006.
[2] J. M. Parish, "Sleep-related problems in common medical conditions," 2009. [Online]. Available: http://dx.doi.org/10.1378/chest.08-0934
[3] J. J. Pilcher and A. I. Huffcutt, "Effects of sleep deprivation on performance: a meta-analysis," *Sleep*, vol. 19, no. 4, pp. 318–326, 1996.
[4] J. A. Russell, "Affective space is bipolar." *Journal of personality and social psychology*, vol. 37, no. 3, p. 345, 1979
[5] Y. Bai, B. Xu, Y. Ma, G. Sun, and Y. Zhao, "Will you have a good sleep tonight?: sleep quality prediction with mobile phone," *in Proc. BodyNets*, 2012, pp. 124–130.
[6] W. Gu, Z. Yang, L. Shangguan, W. Sun, K. Jin, and Y. Liu, "Intelligent sleep stage mining service with smartphones," *in Proc. ACM Ubicomp*, 2014, pp. 649–660.
[7] S. Li, R. Guo, L. He, W. Gao, H. Qi, and G. Owens, "Moodmagician: A pervasive and unobtrusive emotion sensing system using mobile phones for improving human mental health," *in Proc. ACM SenSys*, 2014, pp. 310–311.
[8] J. Liu, Y. Wang, Y. Chen, J. Yang, X. Chen, and J. Cheng, "Tracking vital signs during sleep leveraging off-the-shelf wifi," *in Proc. ACM MobiHoc*, 2015, pp. 267–276
[9] J. Welbl, "Casting random forests as artificial neural networks (and profiting from it)," *in German Conference on Pattern Recognition*, 2014, pp. 765–771.
[10] P. Kontschieder, M. Fiterau, A. Criminisi, and S. Rota Bulo, "Deep neural decision forests," *in Proc. IEEE ICCV*, 2015, pp. 1467–1475.
[11] G. Biau, E. Scornet, and J. Welbl, "Neural random forests," *arXiv preprint arXiv:1604.07143*, 2016.
[12] X. Hu, J. Cheng, M. Zhou, B. Hu, X. Jiang, Y. Guo, K. Bai, and F. Wang, "Emotion-aware cognitive system in multi-channel cognitive radio ad hoc networks," *IEEE Communications Magazine*, to appear.

Poster – IoTURVA: Securing Device-to-Device Communications for IoT

Ibbad Hafeez
University of Helsinki
ibbad.hafeez@helsinki.fi

Aaron Yi Ding
Technical University of Munich
aaron.ding@tum.de

Markku Antikainen
University of Helsinki
Helsinki Institute for Information Technology (HIIT)
markku.antikainen@helsinki.fi

Sasu Tarkoma
University of Helsinki
Helsinki Institute for Information Technology (HIIT)
sasu.tarkoma@helsinki.fi

ABSTRACT

In this poster we present IoTURVA, a platform for securing Device-to-Device (D2D) communication in IoT. Our solution takes a black-box approach to secure IoT edge-networks. We combine user and device-centric context-information together with network data to classify network communication as *normal* or *malicious*. We have designed a dual-layer traffic classification scheme based on fuzzy logic, where the classification model is trained remotely. The remotely trained model is then used by the edge gateway to classify the network traffic. We have implemented a proof-of-concept prototype and evaluate its performance in a real world environment. The evaluation shows that IoTURVA causes very small overhead while it works with minimal hardware, and that our model training and classification approach can improve system efficiency and privacy.

KEYWORDS

IoT; Access control; Security; Network;

1 INTRODUCTION

With growing popularity of Internet-of-Things (IoT) and online services, edge networks are becoming even more densely populated. Latest generation of IoT devices are developed to cooperate with each other to improve automation in smart homes and industries.

IoT devices are potentially vulnerable and could be compromised by a malicious actor [6, 7]. In a typical edge network, there are no security measures to detect and prevent a malicious from talking to other devices in the network. External attackers can use these compromised devices as a foothold and attack other benign devices in the same network. These infected IoT devices can then be used, for example, as a part of a larger DoS campaign [8]. Therefore, it is crucial to monitor and control device-to-device (D2D) traffic in the edge networks to identify and isolate malicious devices, and prevent them from infecting larger parts of the network.

Unfortunately, due to their constrained nature, traditional security solutions do not help with IoT devices. For example, automated software patching, anti-virus solutions, and host-based firewalls are very rarely seen on constrained IoT devices. On the other hand, traditional network perimeter security systems, such as IDS, IPS, and firewalls, are deployed at the edge of the network and thus do not necessarily help in scenarios where an infected device connects and spreads malware to devices connected to same network [4].

We propose IoTURVA to address the aforementioned security problems in IoT networks. Our solution is an easy to deploy, low cost, and scalable approach for securing one of the most vulnerable pieces in the of network security puzzle, such as the SOHO edge networks. Our proposal classifies the network activity of any user device, namely network host, as *normal* or *malicious*, and updates network configuration at runtime in order to prevent a malicious device from communicating with other devices in the same network. We use context information to improve our classification model for detecting misuse attacks where a seemingly *normal* D2D interaction between two hosts is in fact untrusted and a potential attack.

IoTURVA prototype evaluation shows that our solution is easy to deploy and effective in securing edge networks. The fuzzy dual-layer classification model classifies traffic efficiently in real-time and is suitable for a small–medium sized edge networks ($\leq$ 20 connected to an AP) without significantly affecting user experience.

2 SYSTEM DESIGN

The high level system design is shown in Fig. 1. IoTURVA consists of two primary components i.e. Turva Gateway and Turva Service. The Turva Gateway serves as an access point typically deployed in edge network and is responsible for traffic classification as well as enforcement of security policies in the IoT network. Turva Gateway offloads intensive tasks such as model training, training data collection, and mobility support to Turva Service. The Turva Service is a logically centralized entity supporting one or more Turva Gateway installations across edge networks.

2.1 Turva Gateway

We designed Turva Gateway as an improvised gateway or access point typically used to setup SOHO edge networks. The lightweight design allows us to deploy it using minimal hardware resources e.g. Raspberry PI or legacy APs. The primary tasks of Turva Gateway include traffic monitoring and enforcement of security policies required to prevent any malicious communications in the network.

Figure 1 shows three major operations performed by Turva Gateway. First, it monitors all the traffic passing flowing through the network. Second, it classifies every network interaction using a set

MobiCom '17, October 16–20, 2017, Snowbird, UT, USA.
 ISBN 978-1-4503-4916-1/17/10.
DOI: https://doi.org/10.1145/3117811.3131262

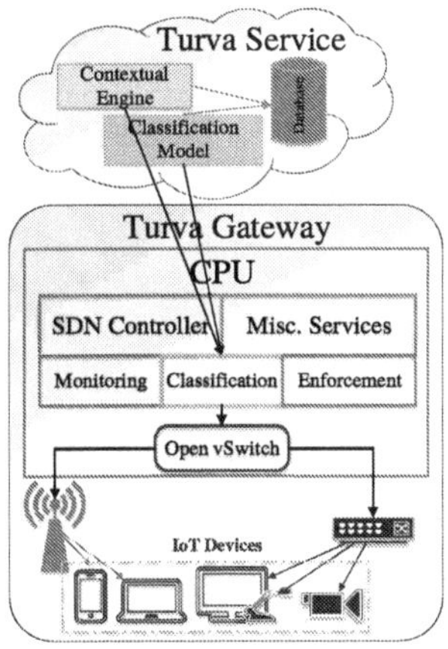

Figure 1: System design for IoTURVA.

of rules (security policies) to be either malicious or normal traffic flow. Finally, once classified, it updates network rules to block any malicious traffic flows in the network.

The monitoring and enforcement mechanism are implemented using *software-defined networking* technologies, where Turva Gateway runs an OpenFlow-switch and a lightweight SDN-controller. The SDN-controller uses classification module to classify every unique network traffic flow it monitors. Based on classification results, it generates OF-rules necessary to allow or block (when classified as malicious) the given traffic flow(s). The rules used for traffic classification are obtained from Turva Service.

In IoT networks, Turva Gateway also acts as a sensor, which aggregates network statistics, traffic signatures and other network data to be shared with Turva Service, if required. Sharing this information, in aggregated and anonymous form, can protect user privacy and improve training process of traffic classifier.

2.2 Turva Service

The logically centralized Turva Service can be deployed as a single service or a set of services colluding together to generate classification model for classifying network traffic data. Two main components of Turva Service are 1) *classification model training engine*, which is responsible for feature extraction, feature analysis, and model training; and 2) the *contextual engine*, which is responsible for collecting context information from user devices.

In order to improve the classification accuracy and generalization of classification model, Turva Service should get data from multiple sources to develop a global view. Its design allows to easily plug-in data from 3rd party sources e.g. network middleboxes, perimeter security solutions, and device logs to improve model accuracy.

2.2.1 Training data collection. : A primary source of data collection can be Turva Gateway(s) as they provide insights of most commonly observed attacks, device usage patterns, and ratio of classification model hit/miss. Incentivized crowd-sourcing campaign can be used to collect signatures for normal and malicious device activity. Anonymized submissions, threshold-based acceptance criteria, user reputation, voting mechanism, etc., can also be used to overcome issues related to data quality and user privacy [3, 5]. Furthermore, public CVE [1], CWE [2] and malware databases are reliable sources for obtaining information about latest vulnerabilities. Besides, device and service manuals also offer a lot of details about related services and features for any IoT devices. This information gives valuable information about cross device interactions and dependencies which are used in our training classification model.

In addition, the testbeds developed by researchers working on IoT security and communications can provide in-depth data about device vulnerability and cross-device dependencies. These testbeds can also be used to individually monitor device behavior and interaction mode in several states. IoTURVA can use such data to model device behaviors and identify (signatures of) abnormal device interactions. A combination of these models can be further used to capture multi-level attacks using cross-device interactions.

2.2.2 Model training. We use Fuzzy C-means clustering technique to develop network traffic classification model. We obtain a set of clusters from the training data and each of these clusters can be represented as a security rule. The set of rules are transferred to Turva Gateway devices where they are used for traffic classification.

Feature extraction and selection: In model training, we first extract a set of features from training data. In this work, we mainly use network communication related features including network and transport protocol headers (port numbers, transport protocols, etc.). We also use features related to the context of the user and device including geo-location, user actions, and device state. We use Pearsons correlation coefficient to measure linear dependency among features and remove one of every two strongly linearly dependent features. All the features are normalized in range $[0, 1]$ to avoid any effects over clustering algorithm.

Classification engine: After feature selection, we assign each sample data point $X_j (j = 1, 2, ..., n)$ (in training data) to cluster $C_i (i = 1, 2, ..., c)$. Each of these clusters represents either *normal* or *malicious* traffic class. During training, we randomly assign each sample X_j to a cluster with random membership value μ_{ij} and iteratively update Eq. 2 and Eq. 3 to minimize objective function given in Eq. 1, where $1 \leq i \leq c$ and $1 \leq j \leq n$.

$$J_m = \sum_{i=1}^{c} \sum_{j=1}^{n} \mu_{ij}^{m} \left\| V_i - X_j \right\|^2 \tag{1}$$

$$\mu_{ij} = \left(\sum_{d=1}^{c} \left(\frac{\left\| V_i - X_j \right\|}{\left\| V_d - X_j \right\|} \right)^{\frac{2}{m-1}} \right)^{-1} \tag{2}$$

$$V_i = \frac{\sum_{j=1}^{n} (\mu_{ij})^m \times X_j}{\sum_{j=1}^{n} (\mu_{ij})^m} \tag{3}$$

For each cluster i, clustering is performed n times with goal to minimize *within-cluster-sum of distances* to best fit the data. In the end, each cluster can be represented as a rule e.g.

R_i: if $F_1 \in A_1, F_2 \in A_2, ..., F_k \in A_k, ..., F_h \in A_h \implies y \in B_i$

where A_k is subset of distribution for possible values of F. Set of these rules are sent to Turva Gateway for traffic classification.

3 EVALUATION

We have implemented a prototype for IoTurva to evaluate its performance in real world scenario. We setup Turva Gateway using a Raspberry PI (R-PI) model B running Raspbian OS. We use hostapd to setup R-PI as WiFi access point. R-PI is connected to Internet and wired network using on board ethernet port. All wired and wireless interfaces are bridged to OVS running on R-PI and OVS is managed by our customized version of Floodlight controller performing network monitoring, classification and enforcement tasks. Turva Service runs on a HP Core i5 Laptop running Ubuntu 16.04LTS connected to a remote network. We implemented feature extraction and clustering using Python and scikit-fuzzy library and a RestAPI for communcations between Turva Gateway and Turva Service. The test network contains 15 different devices including smart phones, tablets, file server, PC, laptops and IoT devices.

For training data collection, we outlined different scenarios portraying normal and malicious network communication among devices connected to same network. We repeated same scenario for $n = 10$ times for data collection, to avoid any biases or artifacts.

During evaluation, we followed same scenario using different set of devices to check the robustness of classification model. We use 11 devices with 10 interactions for each pair of devices to get a total of $10 \times 10 \times 10$ test scenarios. Table 1 shows that we accurately classify malicious flows and normal flows with 96% and 93.4%, achieving overall accuracy of 93.7%. Our classification model achieves F1-score of 0.753% with 96% sensitivity and 93.4% specificity and classification precision of 0.62%.

Table 1: Confusion matrix

		Predicted class		
		Malicious	Normal	Total
Actual class	Malicious	96	4	100
	Normal	59	841	900
	Total	155	845	1000

With increasing popularity of streaming and video on demand services, minor deterioration in network performance can seriously affect user experience and cause business losses. Therefore, we have tested our system in real world setup to examine the impact on user experience in terms of latency and throughput. The results plotted in Figure 2 show that the traffic monitoring and classification procedures introduce minor overhead on the latency.

Table 2 shows the effect on network throughput with IoTurva in comparison with traditional network setup. We used local and remote servers (deployed in Amazon and FUNET cloud) for this test where *S1: localserver,S2: iperf.funet.fi, S3:iperf.scottlinux.com, S4:bouygues.testdebit.info.*

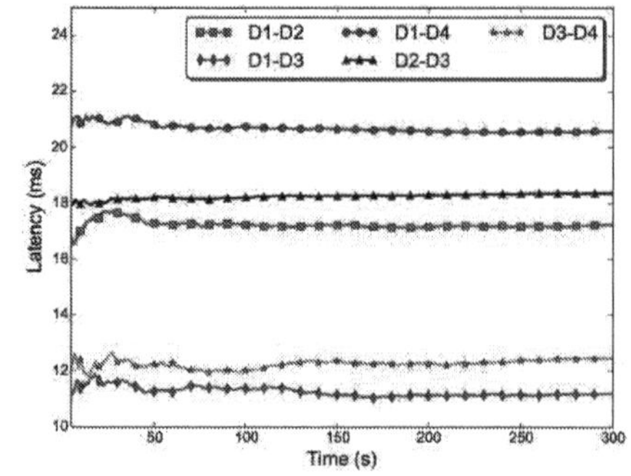

Figure 2: D2D communications latency using IoTurva

Table 2: Throughput (Mbps) achieved when using IoTurva.

Server	D1	D2	D3	D4
S1	25.1 (±0.3)	33.5 (±0.1)	33.1 (±0.1)	42.9 (±0.1)
S2	16.4 (±0.9)	14.4 (±0.9)	14.1 (±1.3)	32.7 (±0.8)
S3	9.6 (±10.7)	8.9 (±12.1)	9.5 (±11.1)	16.1 (±6.3)
S4	17.7 (±3.1)	15.8 (±3.9)	16.6 (±3.2)	30.9 (±2.1)

4 DISCUSSION

The evaluation shows that IoTurva can efficiently secure edge networks by identifying and blocking malicious D2D communications in real time with high accuracy. The seggregation of training and classification phases allows us to take the advantage of advanced anomaly detection mechainsm without requiring special hardware deployment in edge network. Currently, our model training focuses on minimizng *false-negatives* to remove any exploitable weak links in the network. However, our future work focuses on minimizing *false-positives* as they affect user experience by obstructing normal device operations (e.g. user is not able to use his smartphone to unlock the door because system thinks its an attack). To support incremental and easy deployment, Turva Gateway is designed to have minimal resource footprint to enable deployment using PC-on-a-card devices or legacy access points/gateways with OF support. We will extend this work with improved data collection, data processing schemes and improve our model to support classification of multi–level D2D interactions by incorporating state and other device–based features.

REFERENCES

[1] 2017. Common Vulnerabilities and Exposures. https://cve.mitre.org/. (2017). [Online; accessed 04-June-2017].
[2] 2017. Common Weakness Enumeration. https://cwe.mitre.org/. (2017). [Online; accessed 04-June-2017].
[3] Yves-Alexandre de Montjoye, Erez Shmueli, Samuel S. Wang, and Alex Sandy Pentland. 2014. openPDS: Protecting the Privacy of Metadata through SafeAnswers. *PLoS ONE* 9, 7 (07 2014), e98790. DOI:http://dx.doi.org/10.1371/journal.pone.0098790
[4] Ibbad Hafeez, Aaron Yi Ding, Lauri Suomalainen, Alexey Kirichenko, and Sasu Tarkoma. 2016. Securebox: Toward Safer and Smarter IoT Networks. In *Proceedings of the 2016 ACM Workshop on Cloud-Assisted Networking (CAN '16)*. ACM, New York, NY, USA, 55–60. DOI:http://dx.doi.org/10.1145/3010079.3012014
[5] Hiroshi Kajino, Hiromi Arai, and Hisashi Kashima. 2014. Preserving worker privacy in crowdsourcing. *Data Mining and Knowledge Discovery* 28, 5 (2014), 1314–1335. DOI:http://dx.doi.org/10.1007/s10618-014-0352-3
[6] Markus Miettinen, Samuel Marchal, Ibbad Hafeez, N. Asokan, Ahmad-Reza Sadeghi, and Sasu Tarkoma. 2016. IoT Sentinel: Automated Device-Type Identification for Security Enforcement in IoT. *CoRR* abs/1611.04880 (2016). http://arxiv.org/abs/1611.04880
[7] H. Ning, H. Liu, and L. T. Yang. 2013. Cyberentity Security in the Internet of Things. *Computer* 46, 4 (April 2013), 46–53. DOI:http://dx.doi.org/10.1109/MC.2013.74
[8] Nicky Woolf. 2017. DDoS attack that disrupted internet was largest of its kind in history, experts say. https://www.theguardian.com/technology/2016/oct/26/ddos-attack-dyn-mirai-botnet. (2017). [Online; accessed 04-June-2017].

Poster: A Portfolio Theory Approach to Edge Traffic Engineering via Bayesian Networks*

Mary Hogan
Computer Science Department
Saint Louis University
mhogan26@slu.edu

Flavio Esposito
Computer Science Department
Saint Louis University
espositof@slu.edu

ABSTRACT

One of the main goals of mobile edge computing is to support new generation latency-sensitive networked applications. To manage such demanding applications, a fine-grained control of end-to-end paths is imperative. End-to-end delay estimation and forecast techniques were essential traffic engineering tools even before the mobile edge computing paradigm pushed the cloud closer to the end user. In this paper, we model the path selection problem for edge traffic engineering using a risk minimization technique inspired by portfolio theory in economics, and we use machine learning to estimate the risk of a path.

In particular, using real latency time series measurements, collected with and without the GENI testbed, we compare four short-horizon latency estimation techniques, commonly used by the finance community to estimate prices of volatile financial instruments. Our initial results suggest that a Bayesian Network approach may lead to good latency estimation performance and open a few research questions that we are currently exploring.

1 INTRODUCTION

Mobile Edge Computing is a fairly novel computing paradigm in which node processing and traffic engineering decisions may be offloaded from processes on mobile devices to the edge of the network. This approach has been shown to improve user experience by reducing the perceived latency, and is growing in popularity because of the Internet of Things (IoT) and the vast amount of data that sensors generate. It is inefficient to transmit all the data that a bundle of sensors creates to the cloud for processing and analysis; doing so requires a great deal of bandwidth and all the back-and-forth communication between the sensors and the cloud can negatively impact performance. Traffic engineering at the edge is critical not only to support future Internet of (medical) Things applications, but also to support delay-sensitive applications whose traffic spans across 5G customers or across several Points of Presence, *i.e.*, servers located at the edge of the network of application providers, see, *e.g.*, the Facebook's [2] or the Google's edge networks [4].

*This work has been supported by the NSF award CNS-1647084.

MobiCom '17, October 16–20, 2017, Snowbird, UT, USA

ACM ISBN 978-1-4503-4916-1/17/10.
https://doi.org/10.1145/3117811.3131250

Most mobile edge computing applications orchestrate multiple processes that compete for network resources, causing data transmissions to become inefficient, or data paths to become congested or unreliable. This problem is exacerbated in mobile and challenged environments, where network connectivity is scarce, unavailable, and latency-sensitive applications need to pre-process real time data captured from IoT devices, *e.g.*, images captured by drones or by first responder devices in a natural or man-made disaster scenario. Existing forecast-based path management solutions for mobile and delay-sensitive applications are often tailored to specific protocols or applications [3, 6], they focus on link bandwidth [3] or switch queue size estimation [6], they are not designed to dynamically steer traffic in a multi-path network [3, 4], or they focus on maximizing performance of a single flow [2, 3].

Our Contributions: In this paper, we present a path management solution that, leveraging results from portfolio theory and stochastic learning theory, helps edge traffic engineers identify end-to-end paths (routes) whose future estimated latency is minimized in a given horizon. In particular, leveraging a portfolio theory formulation [7], we first introduce an analytic model for the path selection problem in edge traffic engineering, capturing the risk-return factor associated with a network path choice and its latency. In our model, selecting a set of low-latency paths is equivalent to the problem of selecting a portfolio of assets, maximizing the expected return subject to a given level of (volatility) risk. Since our model captures the risk of a path with its predicted latency value, we need a valuable short-horizon latency estimation technique. To this end, we measured end-to-end latencies using the ICMP protocol over the GENI testbed [1], and compared the performance of (four) latency estimation techniques commonly used to predict future prices of a volatile financial instrument: a Bayesian network model [5], an autoregressive model, a moving average model, and an AutoRegressive Moving Average (ARMA) model. Our initial results show that the Bayesian network approach is the best latency (peak) predictor *i.e.*, it has the lowest relative error, as long as there are statistical dependencies among the latency measurements, and such measurements do not have latency variance too small.

The rest of the paper is organized as follows: In § 2 we present our model inspired by portfolio theory; in § 3 we describe how we applied the Bayesian network model to predict latencies and in § 4 we present our initial evaluation results. Finally, in § 5 we present the limitations of our study, the lesson learned and our ongoing and future work.

2 MODELING RISKY PATHS USING PORTFOLIO THEORY

Aside from its applications for financial asset allocation, we argue that portfolio theory [7] is a valuable resource allocation tool also for traffic engineering problems, especially in mobile edge computing, where latency is as crucial as stock prices. In this section we first give a background on portfolio theory, applied to a standard financial portfolio selection problem and then we describe how we use it to model risky paths for an edge traffic engineering problem.

Background: Portfolio Theory. Maximizing the return is undoubtedly the first goal of every investor. The second main characteristic of an investment is the level of perceived risk to obtain such return, compared to the average over the investment period. Portfolio theory [7] formalizes the problem of selecting a portfolio *i.e.*, the set of items (*e.g.*, financial instruments) that maximizes the expected return given some level of risk. The problem can be alternatively formulated as a risk minimization problem, given an expected value of return.

The classical portfolio problem considers n assets held over a period of time. Let us denote with z_i the dollar amount of asset i held throughout the investment period, at the price obtained at the beginning of the investment period. The simplest formulation does not consider obligations to buy assets at the end of the period, that would yield $z_i < 0$, so asset i always corresponds to $z_i > 0$; We let p_i denote the relative price change of asset i over the period, *i.e.*, its change in price over the period divided by its price at the beginning of the period. The overall dollar return on the portfolio is hence given by $r = p^T z$, where the optimization variable is the portfolio vector $z \in \mathbb{R}^n$. A wide variety of constraints on the portfolio can be considered. Let us consider $1^T z = B$, that is, the total budget to be invested is B, which is often normalized to one.

Considering a stochastic model for price (or latency) changes, we have that $p \in \mathbb{R}^n$ is a random vector, with known mean $\bar{p}$ and covariance Σ on the assets (paths) in the portfolio. Therefore, with portfolio $z \in \mathbb{R}^n$, the return r is a (scalar) random variable with mean $\bar{p}^T z$ and variance $z^T \Sigma z$. The choice of portfolio z involves a trade-off between the mean of the return and its variance. The portfolio optimization problem is the following quadratic program:

$$\begin{aligned} \underset{z}{\text{minimize}} \quad & z^T \Sigma z \\ \text{subject to} \quad & \bar{p} z \geq r_{min} \\ & 1^T z = 1, \\ & z_i > 0 \quad \forall i = 1, \dots, n. \end{aligned} \tag{1}$$

The risk of a small or large loss, *i.e.*, a change in portfolio values below its expected value, is directly related to the standard deviation, and increases with it. For this reason, the standard deviation (or the variance) is used as a measure of the risk associated with the portfolio.

Modeling Risky Paths in Mobile Edge Computing. We model the domain of financial instruments to be selected as physical paths, and the portfolio to be invested as virtual paths (or flows) connecting two end-points. We then model the expected return of our portfolio over a period of time (the time during which we hold the assets) as the throughput during the considered lifetime of a flow. The availability of all resources composing the portfolio (in our case physical links) fluctuates due to edge user mobility, failures, and the statistical multiplexing nature of connectionless networks. Packets corrupted or lost due to queuing delays or congestion increase throughput variance across each flow and the mobile and prone to failures nature of edge computing applications exacerbate such variations. For each path (flow) j, we model its risk (volatility) with z_{ij}, that is, as the probability of obtaining a given latency variance if we select z_{ij}. We now describe a method that we used to estimate such path latency, that can be in turn used as input of our optimization problem.

3 PREDICTING RISKY PATHS

Bayesian Networks. A Bayesian network is a probabilistic graphical model containing random variables and their conditional dependencies, expressed by a directed acyclic graph. The edge $x_j \rightarrow x_i$ represents the dependency of the random variable x_i on the random variable x_j, in which x_j is the parent of child x_i. Each random variable (a latency value) has a corresponding conditional probability table that is used to determine the conditional probability $P(x_i|x_j)$, *i.e.*, the probability of x_i given x_j, where:

$$P(x_i|x_j) = \frac{P(x_i \cap x_j)}{P(x_j)}. \tag{2}$$

We define the set of parents for the random variable x_i to be $\text{Pa}(x_i)$. To construct a Bayesian network from discretized data, we follow the constraint-based approach outlined by Koller and Friedman [5]. We omit such description in this paper for lack of space.

Our approach is based on three steps: (1) Discretize latency measurements using k-means clustering, (2) construct a Bayesian network with discretized latency data, and (3) predict latency using the Bayesian network by maximizing conditional probability $P(x_t \mid \text{Pa}(x_t))$. We use k-means clustering to discretize path latency measurements. The k-means clustering algorithm partitions observations $(y_1, y_2, \dots, y_n)$ into sets $S = \{S_1, S_2, \dots, S_k\}$ by minimizing the within-cluster sum of squares:

$$\underset{S}{\text{argmin}} \sum_{i=1}^{k} \sum_{y \in S_i} ||y - \mu_i||^2, \tag{3}$$

where μ_i is the mean of the observations in S_i. We define the set of discrete latency values as $\{a_1, \dots, a_n\}$, where n is the total number of clusters.

Constructing the Latency Bayesian Network. We construct a Bayesian network using the collected discretized latency measurements. Each node in the network represents the latency at a point in time relative to time t, with the aim of predicting the latency at time t. The set of nodes in the network is $\{x_{t-n}, x_{t-n+1}, \dots, x_{t-1}, x_t\}$. The set of possible states for a node is composed by the means of the clusters.

Predicting Latency. Once the Bayesian network is constructed, we use it to predict path latency at time t, given the latency measurements for all nodes in the set $\text{Pa}(x_t)$. Similar approaches have been used to predict daily stock price fluctuations [8]. We first obtain the discrete latency values for parent nodes of x_t, and then predict the discrete latency by computing the conditional probability $P(x_t \mid \text{Pa}(x_t))$ for each of the possible states of x_t. The predicted latency a_t is the state a_l of node x_t in which the conditional probability is maximized: $a_t = \text{argmax}_{a_l} P(a_l|Pa(x_t))$, where each state a_l is

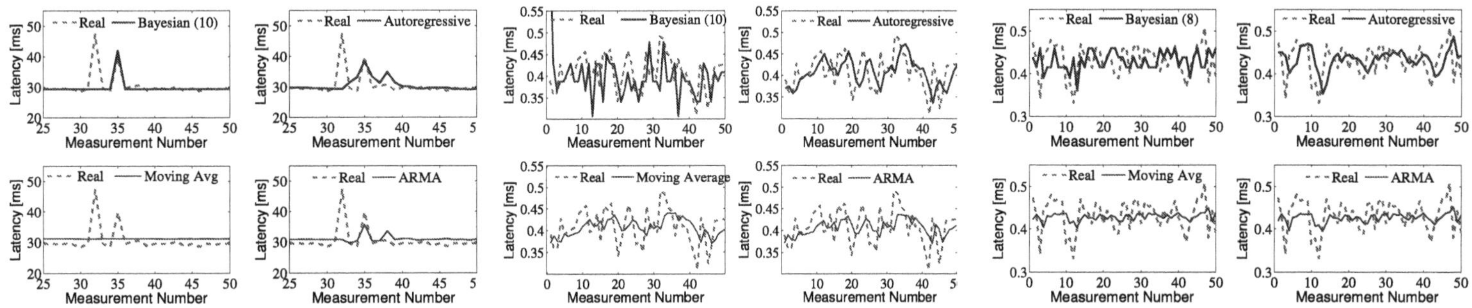

(*a*) SLU - Stanford (*b*) GENI: GPO Rack (*c*) GENI: GPO - University of Washington

Figure 1: The Bayesian Network approach predicts e2e latencies more accurately w.r.t. Autoregressive, Moving Average and Autoregressive moving average: (a) ICMP traffic from Saint Louis to Stanford.edu (b) ICMP traffic across VMs in the same GENI rack. (c) ICMP traffic across two East-coast GENI racks.

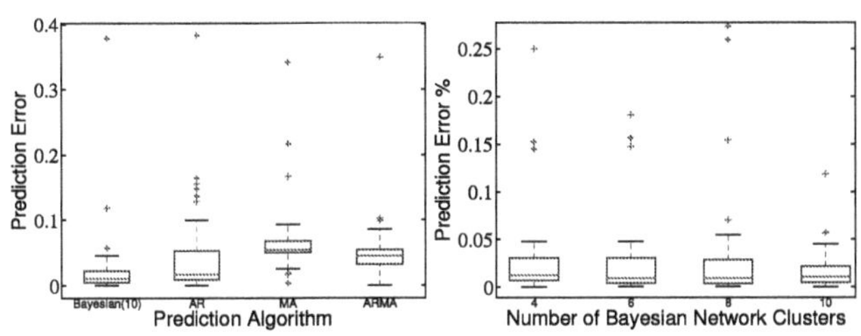

(*a*) Predictors Comparison (*b*) Clusters Impact

Figure 2: (a) The Bayesian network prediction with 10 clusters has the lowest latency prediction error w.r.t. Autoregressive, Moving Average and Autoregressive moving average. (b) Impact of the number of clusters in the Bayesian network on the prediction error.

the mean of cluster S_l. To construct a portfolio, we predict the next value of latency for each available path in a network. We then select the set of paths (portfolio) that minimize the overall predicted latency (the risk).

4 EVALUATION

We evaluate our method against an autoregressive model, a moving average model, and an ARMA (autoregressive moving average) model. These methods captures the time series of latency values. Unlike Bayesian networks, they do not model the dependencies within a dataset. Forecasts are made by these time series models by combining past values. Consistent with the Bayesian network method, each predicted latency value is a one-step-ahead forecast. Although an extensive evaluation campaign would be needed to draw more meaningful conclusions, our initial results suggest that the Bayesian network approach predicts e2e latencies more accurately w.r.t. autoregressive, moving average and autoregressive moving average models (Figure 1). Our measurements include ICMP traffic (*i.e.* ping) from Saint Louis to the `Stanford.edu` web server, and within the GENI testbed [1]; we emulated an edge network pinging VMs in the same GENI rack as well as across two close enough East-coast GENI racks. To quantify the superior behavior of the Bayesian network approach, we show the distribution of errors across the tested methods in Figure 2*a*. Finding the optimal number of clusters that minimize the prediction error is still an open question, but our initial results suggest that, as long as there is dependency among latency measurements, 8 or 10 clusters produce the best accuracy, especially for latency peaks (Figure 2*b*).

5 LIMITATIONS, LESSON LEARNED AND FUTURE WORK

Our finding are far from ideal for several reasons. The accuracy of the Bayesian network is limited by its ability to correctly identify and model dependencies in the data. If the variance within a dataset is small, or the dependencies between variables are weak, the Bayesian network is likely to miss the dependencies. Additionally, the clustering process is likely to hide small dependencies because the variance between two data points can be lost when they belong to the same cluster, as we use the cluster mean as input to the Bayesian network. Our results were also limited by the consistency of the latency values in our data. We found that this resulted in the cluster means having a small spread. When the Bayesian network predicted the incorrect cluster, the value of the predicted cluster was close to the actual latency value, resulting in low errors despite the erroneous prediction.

In future work, we plan to explore improvements to our Bayesian network prediction method. We also plan to continue investigating the dependencies in latency data through alternative methods. We also intend to expand our latency prediction method to a multipath network in order to implement a more complete path management solution.

REFERENCES

[1] 2010. Global Environment for Network Innovations http://www.geni.net. (2010).
[2] B. Schlinker et al. 2017. Engineering Egress with Edge Fabric: Steering Oceans of Content to the World. In *In Proc. of ACM SIGCOMM.*
[3] K. Winstein et al. 2013. Stochastic Forecasts Achieve High Throughput and Low Delay over Cellular Networks. In *NSDI 13*. USENIX, Lombard, IL, 459–471.
[4] Kok-Kiong Yap at al. 2017. Taking the Edge off with Espresso: Scale, Reliability and Programmability for Global Internet Peering. In *Proceedings of ACM SIGCOMM.*
[5] Daphne Koller and Nir Friedman. 2009. *Probabilistic Graphical Models: Principles and Techniques.* MIT Press, Cambridge, MA.
[6] M.Alizadeh et al. 2010. Data Center TCP (DCTCP). In *Proceedings of the ACM SIGCOMM Conference (SIGCOMM).* 63–74.
[7] Harry M. Markowitz. 1987. *Mean-variance analysis in portfolio choice and capital markets.* Blackwell, Oxford.
[8] Yi Zuo and Eisuke Kita. 2012. Stock price forecast using Bayesian network. *Expert Systems with Applications* 39, 8 (June 2012), 6729–6737. https://doi.org/10.1016/j.eswa.2011.12.035

Poster: Interacting Data-Intensive Services Mining and Placement in Mobile Edge Clouds

Yuze Huang, Jiwei Huang*, Bo Cheng, Tianxiang Yao, Junliang Chen
State Key Laboratory of Networking and Switching Technology
Beijing University of Posts and Telecommunications, Beijing 100876, China
Email: {huangyz, huangjw, chengbo, hdyao2010, chjl}@bupt.edu.cn

ABSTRACT

With the rapid growth of cloud computing and mobile computing, it is commonplace for users to request cloud services from mobile devices. Mobile edge clouds (MECs) allow the users to access the cloud services seamlessly. Although cloudlets provide a promising technique to reduce the service access latency, how to place the data-intensive service in MECs to reduce the communication overhead between different services is yet to be addressed. To attack this challenge, this paper proposes an approach for mining interacting services and placing the services on the cloudlets by optimizing the communication overhead. In this approach, a frequent itemsets mining algorithm is proposed to obtain the fine-grained frequent 2-itemsets by analyzing the cookies. This algorithm determines the minimum support threshold automatically, based on which FP-tree with FP-matrix is constructed to avoid traversing the FP-tree during the process of frequent 2-itemsets discovery, then a searching algorithm is presented to mine the discriminative frequent 2-itemsets with interestingness measure. Furthermore, the communication overhead is optimized with the capacity constraints of cloudlets. Finally, we validate the efficacy of our approach by real-world data based simulations. The results show our approach can reduce the communication overhead for service placement in MECs.

CCS CONCEPTS

• **Computer systems organization** → **Cloud computing**; • **Human-centered computing** → **Mobile computing**;

KEYWORDS

Data-Intensive Service, Interacting Services, Service Placement, Mobile Edge Clouds

*Jiwei Huang is the corresponding author.

MobiCom '17, October 16–20, 2017, Snowbird, UT, USA

ACM ISBN 978-1-4503-4916-1/17/10.
https://doi.org/10.1145/3117811.3131263

1 INTRODUCTION

With the proliferation of smart phones in recent years, more and more people request cloud services from their mobile devices. The application of cloud services in the mobile ecosystem enables a newly emerging mobile computing paradigm, namely mobile edge clouds (MECs). Mobile edge clouds are cloud-like infrastructures, which enable the users to access the cloud services seamlessly [1]. In mobile edge clouds, the services are deployed on edge servers to reduce the latency, which is caused by the long RTTs and possible congestions in WAN. Cloudlet is a middle tier between end devices and traditional Internet data centers, which is a promising technique for service placement to reduce the service accessing latency [2].

Data-intensive services are interacting with each other to complete the collaboration works, which may produce lots of communication overhead. Communication overhead is an non-negligible factor for service placement. Some efficient approaches have been proposed to reduce the services accessing latency [1, 3], but most of them ignored the communication overhead between different services. Although the most straightforward approach for reducing the communication overhead is placing the interacting data into data centers, with the increasing of data processed by services, it is a time-consuming and resource-consuming process for data placement. Therefore, how to design an approach for service placement to reduce the communication overhead is an interesting and unexplored problem in MECs.

To solve this problem, the services in data-intensive systems should be treated differently according to involved activities. Therefore, as a fundamental step, interacting services should be precisely discovered, and then the interacting services are placed on cloudlets by optimizing the communication overhead. In this paper, we propose an approach for interacting services mining and placement, named ISMP. In this approach, a frequent itemset mining algorithm named PISMine is designed at first, which mine the fine-grained frequent 2-itemsets by interestingness measure. With the frequent 2-itemsets discovered, the interacting services are placed on edge servers by optimizing the communication overhead with the capacity constraints of the cloudlets. Specifically, the contribution of this paper is fourfold as follows.

- This interacting services mining algorithm determines the minimum support threshold based on the statistical distribution of data items, which requires no training data for initialization.

- In order to reduce traverse the FP-tree, we constructs the FP-matrix, recording the support count and interestingness value of data item pairs, with FP-tree, which is helpful to control the space complexity increased significantly without increasing the time complexity than the traditional algorithm for constructing the FP-tree.
- The mining algorithm adopts the interestingness measure technique to mine the discriminative itemsets directly without complete frequent itemsets generation. In this algorithm, we estimate the interestingness measure value of each FP-tree node with its parents to mine the fine-grained frequent 2-itemsets.
- With the fine-grained frequent 2-itemsets discovered, the interacting services are placed on edge servers by optimizing the communication overhead with the capacity constraints of cloudlets.

2 INTERACTING SERVICES MINING AND PLACEMENT

In this paper, we put forward an approach for interacting services mining and placement in mobile edge clouds, named ISMP, which discovers the interacting services by mining algorithm at first, and then the interacting services are placed on cloudlets. Specifically, our approach can be decomposed into the following four steps, illuminated by Fig. 1.

Step 1 Initially, we analyze the cookies which record the information of services usage to obtain the original dataset.

Step 2 The minimum support threshold is determined based on the statistical distribution of data items, which requires no training data for initialization. Then, the FP-tree with FP-matrix is constructed to reduce the traverse of FP-tree during the procedure of following mining steps. The matrix records the support count and interestingness measure value of frequent item pairs.

Step 3 A mining algorithm is applied on the FP-tree for searching fine-grained frequent 2-itemsets by interestingness measure technique.

Step 4 Finally, interacting services are placed in edge servers, and then we optimize the communication overhead with the capacity constraints of cloudlets.

A precise support threshold is the foundation of our approach for effective frequent pattern mining. In our approach, we propose a mechanism of automatic threshold calculation which is designed based on the statistical distribution of data items and requires no training data for initialization. In light of the statistic character of cookies, we suggest the frequency of the data is followed by general distribution. During the procedures for determining the minimum support threshold, we analyze the distribution characteristic of original dataset at first, and then the proportion of the minimum support threshold p is calculated by the Cumulative Distribution Function (CDF) of the distribution for the dataset, so the minimum support threshold min_sup can be calculated by $min\_sup = F_{\lfloor pN \rfloor}$, where $F_{\lfloor pN \rfloor}$ represents the frequency of item $\lfloor pN \rfloor$, and N is the number of data items.

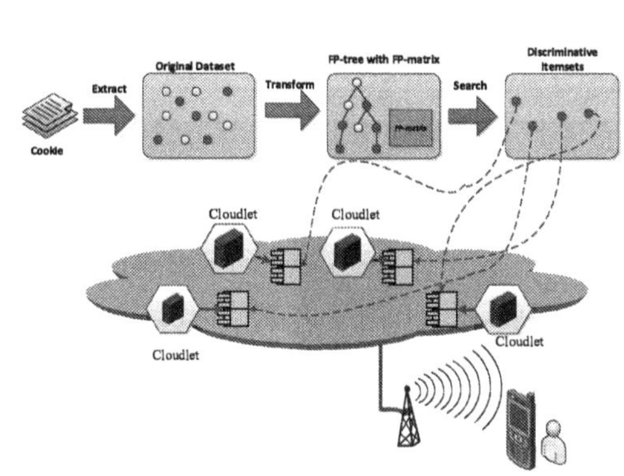

Figure 1: Framework of ISMP

With the minimum support threshold determined, we construct the FP-tree and FP-matrix. The FP-matrix is an echelon form matrix, whose size is $\frac{m(m-1)}{2}$. In this matrix, each element of the matrix records the frequency information and interestingness measure value of item pairs. Using such data structure, our algorithm can avoid traversing the FP-tree during frequent itemsets discovery. After constructing the FP-tree and FP-matrix, a searching algorithm is designed for directly mining discriminative itemsets, which selects the positively correlated items with interestingness measure. During this process, we construct a frequent item queue that stores frequent items according to their support count in an increasing order, and search the positively correlated itemsets from the node with minimum support. Comparing with other Apriori-like algorithms, although these algorithm can produce the frequent 2-itemsets by join arithmetic, they may generate huge number of candidate sets, which are useless in reality and cost plenty of time and resources. Another exponent distinguish is that our algorithm can obtain the fine-grained frequent 2-itemsets other than the frequent patterns produced by traditional FP-growth algorithm. We believe that our approach can help significantly reduce the communication overhead between different services in MECs.

With the frequent 2-itemsets obtained by our parallel mining algorithm, we should place the interacting services on Cloudlets. Due to the fine-grained frequent itemsets obtained by our approach, the interacting services are stored into a same cloudlet as much as possible, during this procedure, we should optimize the communication overhead with the capacity constraints of cloudlets.

3 EVALUATION

In this section, we adopt three real-life datasets with different characteristics to evaluate the efficacy of our approach. Table 1 illustrates the characteristics of these three datasets, which are selected from Entree Chicago Recommendation Data [1]. This data is a real-world dataset containing detailed

[1] http://infolab.cs.uchicago.edu/entree

Table 1: Datasets Characteristics

Datasets	#Items	Avg.Length	#Transactions
Atlanta	125	13.27	267
Los Angeles	142	11.47	447
New York	155	8.47	1200

Table 2: Communication Overhead

Datasets	Algorithm	Average	Differentials
Atlanta	PISMine	50.2356	24.5427
	FP-growth	74.7783	
Los Angeles	PISMine	100.6247	49.2627
	FP-growth	149.8873	
New York	PISMine	261.4717	137.2960
	FP-growth	399.1007	

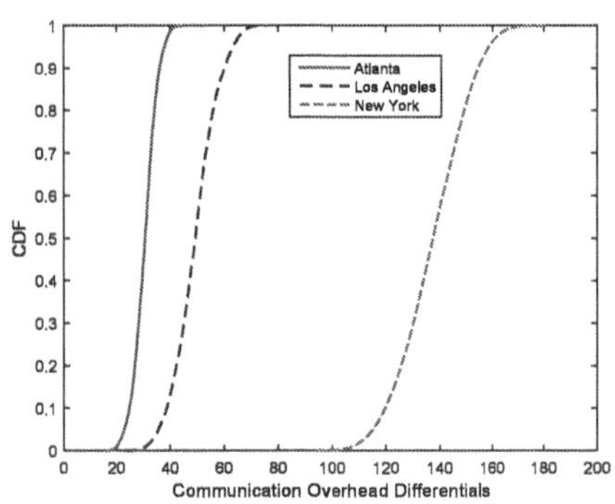

Figure 2: CDF of Communication Overhead Differentials

user online ordering information of several restaurants in 8 cities across the United States. Among them, we pick three groups of data from different locations with different scales, namely Atlanta, Los Angeles and New York. We expect that all the results can provide the reference value for location s-election for restaurants according to the different preference of different throngs.

To illuminate the advantages of our PISMine algorithm for interacting services placement compared with tradition-al FP-growth algorithm, we implement PISMine and FP-growth to mine the frequent itemsets respectively, furthermore, we place the services using the same placement strategy. Finally, we conduct the experiment with uniformly distributed communication overheads between cloudlets with random values ranged from 0 to 1. After 30 random runs, we show the experimental results as follows. Table. 2 shows the simulation results using our approach and FP-growth to mine the frequent itemsets, and optimize the placement for data-intensive services. From the experimental results, we know that the communication overhead using our approach is much lower than using traditional FP-growth algorithm. With the scale of datasets is enlarged, the results seem to be more evident. Fig. 2 demonstrates the CDF of communication overhead differentials on three different datasets, which indicates the communication overhead differentials between our algorithm and FP-growth have different characteristics on different datasets.

4 CONCLUSION

In this paper, we propose an approach for mining interacting services and placing the services on the cloudlets by optimizing the communication overhead between different services. In this approach, a mining algorithm is designed to obtain the fine-grained frequent 2-itemsets by analyzing the cookies, which determines the support minimum support threshold based on the statistical distribution of data items, and then we construct FP-matrix to reduce the need to traverse the FP-trees. Furthermore, the mining algorithm adopts interestingness measure technique to mine the discriminative itemsets directly without complete frequent itemsets generation. With the frequent 2-itemsets discovered, we designed an approach for optimizing the communication overhead with the capacity constraints of cloudlets. Finally, we evaluate the efficacy of our approach by real-word data based simulations. The results show that our approach can reduce the communication overhead for service placement effectively. One of the directions of future work is to optimize our approach and evaluate the efficiency by large-scale real-world data based experiments.

ACKNOWLEDGMENT

This work is supported by Beijing Natural Science Foundation (No. 4162042), National Natural Science Foundation of China (No. 61502043), and BeiJing Talents Fund (No. 2015000020124G082).

REFERENCES

[1] Andrew Machen, Shiqiang Wang, Kin K. Leung, Bongjun Ko, and Theodoros Salonidis. 2016. Migrating running applications across mobile edge clouds: poster. In *Proceedings of the 22nd Annual International Conference on Mobile Computing and Networking, MobiCom 2016*. ACM, New York City, NY, USA, 435–436.

[2] Mahadev Satyanarayanan, Paramvir Bahl, Ramón Cáceres, and Nigel Davies. 2009. The Case for VM-Based Cloudlets in Mobile Computing. *IEEE Pervasive Computing* 8, 4 (2009), 14–23.

[3] Lei Yang, Jiannong Cao, Guanqing Liang, and Xu Han. 2016. Cost Aware Service Placement and Load Dispatching in Mobile Cloud Systems. *IEEE Transations on Computers* 65, 5 (2016), 1440–1452.

Poster: Connecting Simulation and Real World: IEEE 802.11p in the Loop

Florian Klingler, Gurjashan Singh Pannu, Christoph Sommer, Falko Dressler
Heinz Nixdorf Institute and Dept. of Computer Science
Paderborn University
Paderborn, Germany
klingler@ccs-labs.org, pannu@ccs-labs.org, sommer@ccs-labs.org, dressler@ccs-labs.org

ABSTRACT

We present LAN Radio, an Open Source prototyping system to couple simulation and real world for the wireless channel of IEEE 802.11p based communication. Our main focus is the use in a vehicular networking environment, where field testing and real world experimentation is becoming more relevant these days. Large Field Operational Tests (FOTs) are expensive and difficult to handle in terms of reproducibility and controllability – particularly for application development and integration tests for automotive Electronic Control Units (ECUs). To support such experiments, we developed an approach to integrate a real system to test into a large scale simulation scenario without the need to change the physical and access layer parts of the communication stack of this system. We closely followed the Hardware In The Loop (HIL) simulation concept but also integrated a wireless communication channel into the picture. LAN Radio is building upon the well established and Open Source development platform OpenWRT to provide optimal extensibility.

ACM Reference Format:

Florian Klingler, Gurjashan Singh Pannu, Christoph Sommer, Falko Dressler. 2017. Poster: Connecting Simulation and Real World: IEEE 802.11p in the Loop. In *Proceedings of MobiCom '17, Snowbird, UT, USA, October 16–20, 2017,* 3 pages.
https://doi.org/10.1145/3117811.3131265

1 INTRODUCTION

Research in the context of vehicular communication has evolved from pure theoretical studies to fully integrated prototypes ready for deployment on the road [2]. Many manufacturers have developed systems to allow inter-vehicle communication for safety and efficiency applications, however their operation is only evaluated in terms of simulation studies. In order to validate the correct behavior of such prototypes, realistic experiments are necessary, which can be scaled both in terms of abstraction detail and traffic density. One approach to such validation is to deploy a large set of vehicles in real world field tests [1], each equipped with prototype hardware for vehicular communication. This has two major downsides: first, the setup is very cost intensive; second, the environment is very difficult to control in terms of reproducibility. Another option is to first record traces of real wireless traffic of communicating vehicles [5], and to then replay those traces on the system under test. However, most of the time this is no option, as other vehicles depend on the behavior of the target system, i.e., the surrounding traffic and the target system form a closed-loop control system.

HIL simulation can fill this gap between field tests and simulation by bidirectionally coupling the simulation framework together with the system under test [4, 6]. It has all the advantages of simulation studies (such as scalability, debug-ability, and reproducibility) and can integrate the system under test as a participant in the simulation study. This enables the system under test to participate in the network traffic available in the simulation, react to information received, and transmit own information to vehicles inside the simulation framework. Yet, current implementations of HIL simulations either have a special focus in mind, e.g., investigating lower layer characteristics of communication devices [4], or require specialized hardware with custom developed software like Software Defined Radios (SDRs) [3, 6]. Recently, investigations have been made to develop a framework for interoperability testing of ECUs used for cooperative ITS systems to allow over the Internet conformance tests [8]. However, a fundamental limitation is that the physical and access layers of the network stack need to be replaced at the system under test.

In this paper, we present *LAN Radio,*[1] a system which fills this gap by coupling the wireless channel modeled in a simulation framework with the wireless channel in the real world without the need to change the physical and access layers of the system under test. We therefore call it IEEE 802.11p in the Loop following the HIL terminology. The simulation and prototype hardware can be physically separated by a network, potentially even the Internet, simplifying field trials. The goal is to offer a flexible framework to allow prototypes in hardware to interact with nodes in a simulated environment using standardized IEEE 802.11p based protocol suites such as ETSI ITS-G5 and IEEE WAVE. Our implementation is using low cost hardware and will be made available as Open Source to the research community.

In brief, our main contributions can be summarized as follows.

- We introduce a new interface for realizing an IEEE 802.11p in the Loop system.
- We primarily focus on the higher layer protocols to enable investigation of application layer performance without the need to modify the system under test.
- Our system is easily extensible, based on commodity WLAN hardware, and freely available as Open Source.

MobiCom '17, October 16–20, 2017, Snowbird, UT, USA

ACM ISBN 978-1-4503-4916-1/17/10.
https://doi.org/10.1145/3117811.3131265

[1] http://www.ccs-labs.org/software/

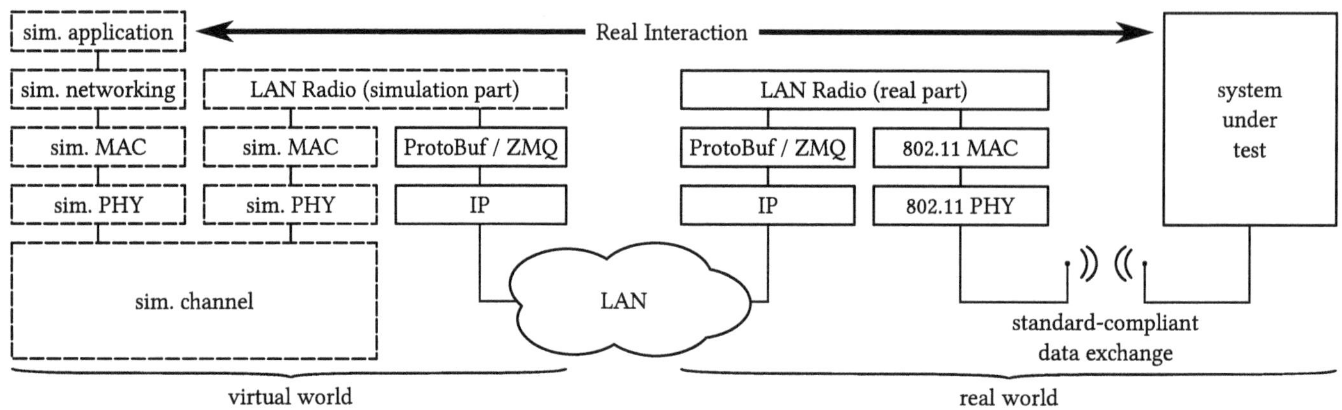

Figure 1: System model of LAN Radio

2 IEEE 802.11p IN THE LOOP

The system model of our LAN Radio system in outlined in Figure 1. The objective of our system is to allow applications running in a simulation environment to interact in real time with an application in the real world (e.g., running on an ECU equipped with radio communication) while providing a standard-compliant interface for data exchange to the *system under test*. Our system consists of two parts, namely *(a)* a model in the simulation framework to represent an *external* wireless network interface which connects to *(b)* a prototype in the real world to receive and transmit the information via an IEEE 802.11 compatible wireless interface. We want to highlight that the communication between the simulation and the real world is bidirectional, therefore, we can both receive frames from the real world in the simulation, as well as transmit information from the simulation to the real world.

2.1 Challenges

Combining the wireless channels of a virtual world (simulation) with the real world brings up two main challenges.

First, wireless signals exchanged inside the simulation have to be modeled to exhibit a realistic behavior by using adequate path loss models for signal propagation as well as realistic models for frame reception and decoding. The decoded messages then need to be sent to the real world side via our hardware prototype in order to be transmitted over the air using the standardized IEEE 802.11p communication protocol. We solve this first challenge by integrating LAN Radio into a discrete event simulation framework to model the wireless communication in a realistic way, and use encoding and decoding functionality to generate standards-compliant payload for frames transmitted via a dedicated hardware prototype.

Second, to transfer radio messages from the real world into the simulation, it is necessary to change the simulation state upon an external event. In our case, that means that whenever the hardware prototype sends a decoded frame from the real world to the simulator, the internal state of the simulation needs to be modified to process the frame. LAN Radio approaches this challenge by using a separate thread in the simulation model dedicated to listening for received messages from the hardware, and then interacting with the simulation kernel to update the state of the simulation.

2.2 Messaging

We rely on Google Protocol buffers (Protobuf) for serialization of messages sent between the simulation model and the hardware prototype. In particular, we include the standards-compliant encoded payload of the frame to be transmitted as well as meta information like source and destination MAC addresses in each Protobuf message. Further, we use ZeroMQ (ZMQ) as a messaging library to exchange the Protobuf encoded messages with the hardware.

The advantage of our approach is that all payload sent via the LAN Radio system is generated in the simulation framework as a MAC service data unit (MSDU). The generation of an MSDU within the simulation leads to full flexibility in protocol design, and allows easy testing of new applications, since the hardware prototype can be reused without modification. The MSDU, together with protocol control information like addressing information as well as optionally data rate and transmit power, is then transmitted via an IP based network to our prototype, which transmits the MSDU to the system under test. When receiving information from our system under test, the LAN Radio prototype decodes the frame and sends the information as a MAC SDU together with lower layer protocol information back to the LAN Radio model inside the simulation framework. This lower layer information includes addressing information as well as optional received signal strength and data rate information.

3 SIMULATION WORLD

For our implementation of LAN Radio on the simulation side, we selected the Veins vehicular network simulation framework [7]. Veins is based on the OMNeT++ discrete event simulator and provides realistic models for signal propagation and medium access according to the IEEE 802.11p standard, and evolved to a widely accepted toolkit in the vehicular networking research community. Moreover, Veins connects to SUMO to provide realistic modeling of road traffic. LAN Radio extends Veins by providing a module such that a node can connect its radio interface to be coupled with the real world. This way, all messages received by this node in the simulation world are forwarded to the hardware connecting to the real world prototype and transmitted over the air to the system under test. Further, the simulation model provides an interface to configure the hardware prototype to the needs of the system under test such as the used carrier frequency and channel bandwidth.

In the following, we outline the operation of LAN Radio in detail using a simple example. In particular, we consider a scenario of some nodes inside a simulation, each within communication distance and running an example application generating beacon messages at periodic intervals (as used, for example, for cooperative awareness messages). All nodes are configured to use IEEE 802.11p in combination with realistic channel modeling as supported by the Veins framework.

The transmission of frames from the simulation to the real world is modeled as follows:

(1) Whenever a node generates a message, it is handed down to the simulated networking layer, and then further to the MAC for transmission. After competing for channel access, the frame is handed to the PHY module of all nodes within interference range to detect (but not necessarily decode) the frame.

(2) Any node that detects this frame tries to decode it, and if successful hands it up to the networking layer, and then further to the application. If this receiving node is configured to use our LAN Radio interface, a copy of this frame is handed to the LAN Radio module as well, which then encodes the message according to the protocol specifications of the respective message. The encoding is done using the corresponding ASN.1 packet encoding rules.

(3) Additional information such as higher layer message headers are prepended to the frame, such that it corresponds to a standards-compliant MSDU. This MSDU together with protocol control information, e.g., source and destination MAC Address and Ethertype, is then embedded inside a Protobuf message and sent via ZMQ to the hardware prototype for transmission.

The transmission of frames from the real world to the simulation is modeled as follows:

(1) A dedicated thread within the simulation model continuously listens for incoming messages from the hardware prototype. Whenever the hardware prototype receives an IEEE 802.11p frame, the MSDU is encoded inside a Protobuf/ZMQ message together with protocol control information and sent to our simulation model.

(2) Within the simulation model, the payload is decoded according to the ASN.1 specification. Then a message is generated following the standard procedure of the underlying network simulator. The corresponding frame is then inserted by the LAN Radio thread into a queue of frames to be processed by the simulation scheduler for transmission.

(3) Our model periodically checks for the presence of frames in this queue. If available, they are handed down to the PHY layer, which delivers it to all nodes within the simulation environment. Receiving nodes which are able to decode the frame then hand it up to the networking layer for further processing.

4 REAL WORLD

Our hardware prototype implementation builds upon the *LEDE* fork of *OpenWRT* for developing embedded systems based on Linux. OpenWRT allows to develop small firmware images for a variety of embedded systems (such as many cheap Wi-Fi routers) as well as commodity x86/x64 platforms. These firmware images contain the operating system adapted to unattended operation as well as all necessary applications for simple deployment and maintenance. Images are usually no larger than a few MB.

At boot time, our application listens for configuration information from the simulation model via the Protobuf/ZMQ interface in order to correctly set up all wireless interfaces. Finally, one thread each is created to send and to receive IEEE 802.11p frames. Upon the successful reception of a frame from the wireless interface, it is encapsulated into a Protobuf message together with status information, e.g., addressing, and sent via Protobuf/ZMQ to the simulation model. When receiving a Protobuf message via ZMQ from the simulation, its MSDU is decapsulated and sent via the wireless interface to the system under test.

Based on the Outside the Context of a BSS (OCB) mode functionality of IEEE 802.11p our platform supports standard vehicular network on 5.9 GHz using 10 MHz channels.

5 CONCLUSION AND FUTURE WORK

We presented LAN Radio, a system to bidirectionally couple the wireless channel of a simulation framework with the wireless channel of the real world. Applications of such a system can be found in the validation of automotive ECUs for vehicular networking (or ECUs interacting with such). This way, the test of application behavior becomes better controllable in fully user customizable scenarios. Our system builds upon the OpenWRT framework and allows transmission and reception of data frames based on the IEEE 802.11p protocol as used in vehicular communication standards. In future work we will investigate the effects when integrating the system with a complete ETSI ITS G5 networking stack.

ACKNOWLEDGEMENTS

This work has been supported in part by the EU/EFRE.NRW Hy-Nets project.

REFERENCES

[1] Bin Cheng, Ali Rostami, and Marco Gruteser. 2016. Experience: Accurate Simulation of Dense Scenarios with Hundreds of Vehicular Transmitters. In *22nd ACM International Conference on Mobile Computing and Networking (MobiCom 2016)*. ACM, New York, NY, 271–279. https://doi.org/10.1145/2973750.2973779

[2] Falko Dressler, Hannes Hartenstein, Onur Altintas, and Ozan K. Tonguz. 2014. Inter-Vehicle Communication – Quo Vadis. *IEEE Communications Magazine* 52, 6 (June 2014), 170–177. https://doi.org/10.1109/MCOM.2014.6829960

[3] Norman Franchi, Georg Fischer, and Robert Weigel. 2013. Radio Hardware In-the-Loop Emulation for Testing Vehicular Communication Systems. In *5th IEEE International Symposium on Wireless Vehicular Communications (WiVeC 2013)*. IEEE, Dresden, Germany. https://doi.org/10.1109/wivec.2013.6698242

[4] Paul Fuxjaeger and Stefan Ruehrup. 2015. A Software-Defined Radio Testbed for Car-to-X Communication Devices and Protocols. In *3rd GI/ITG KuVS Fachgespräch Inter-Vehicle Communication*. Ulm University, Ulm, Germany, 5–8.

[5] Javier Gozalvez, Miguel Sepulcre, and Ramon Bauza. 2012. IEEE 802.11p Vehicle to Infrastructure Communications in Urban Environments. *IEEE Communications Magazine* 50, 5 (May 2012), 176–183. https://doi.org/10.1109/MCOM.2012.6194400

[6] Matej Kloc, Robert Weigel, and Alexander Koelpin. 2016. Making Real-Time Hardware-in-the-Loop Testing of Automotive Electronic Control Units Wireless. In *International Conference on Advanced Technologies for Communications (ATC 2016)*. IEEE, Hanoi, Vietnam, 407–412. https://doi.org/10.1109/ATC.2016.7764816

[7] Christoph Sommer, Reinhard German, and Falko Dressler. 2011. Bidirectionally Coupled Network and Road Traffic Simulation for Improved IVC Analysis. *IEEE Transactions on Mobile Computing* 10, 1 (Jan. 2011), 3–15. https://doi.org/10.1109/TMC.2010.133

[8] Alexey Voronov, Cristofer Englund, Hoai Hoang Bengtsson, Lei Chen, Jeroen Ploeg, Jan de Jonhg, and Jacco van de Sluis. 2015. Interactive Test Tool for Interoperable C-ITS Development. In *18th IEEE International Conference on Intelligent Transportation Systems (ITSC 2015)*. IEEE, Las Palmas, Spain, 1713–1718. https://doi.org/10.1109/ITSC.2015.278

Poster – FooDNet: Optimized On Demand Take-out Food Delivery using Spatial Crowdsourcing

Yan Liu, Bin Guo, He Du, Zhiwen Yu
Northwestern Polytechnical University, China
guob@nwpu.edu.cn

Daqing Zhang
Telecom SudParis, France
daqing.zhang@itsudparis.eu

Chao Chen
Chongqing University, China
cschaochen@cqu.edu.cn

ABSTRACT

This paper builds a Food Delivery Network (FooDNet) that investigates the usage of urban taxis to support on demand take-out food delivery by leveraging spatial crowdsourcing. Unlike existing service sharing systems (e.g., ridesharing), the delivery of food in FooDNet is more time-sensitive and the optimization problem is more complex regarding high-efficiency, huge-number of delivery needs. In particular, we study the food delivery problem in association with the Opportunistic Online Takeout Ordering & Delivery service (O-OTOD). Specifically, the food is delivered incidentally by taxis when carrying passengers in the O-OTOD problem, and the optimization goal is to minimize the number of selected taxis to maintain a relative high incentive to the participated drivers. The two-stage method is proposed to solve the problem, consisting of the construction algorithm and the Large Neighborhood Search (LNS) algorithm. Preliminary experiments based on real-world taxi trajectory datasets verify that our proposed algorithms are effective and efficient.

KEYWORDS

Spatial crowdsouring; food delivery; optimization

1 INTRODUCTION

In recent years, with the prevalence of the mobile Internet, Online Takeout Ordering & Delivery (OTOD) using smart phones has become an emerging service (e.g., KFC delivery). In the OTOD service, the user could get the take-out food delivered by the restaurant staff after ordering online. In addition, some online delivery platforms are developed as the new model of the OTOD service (e.g., ele.me[1]). Different from the traditional delivery method that take-out food is delivered independently by staffs of different restaurants, multiple merchants registered in these platforms could share the resources of professional delivery staffs to reduce the delivery cost. In general, the OTOD service is convenient and time-saving especially for people who are taking rest at home or busy working.

[1] http://www.ele.me

MobiCom'17, October 16-20, 2017, Snowbird, UT, USA.

ACM ISBN 978-1-4503-4916-1/17/10.
DOI: https://doi.org/10.1145/3117811.3131268

Though having rising development in the last few years, existing OTOD services still have some limitations. First, food delivery is usually completed by using bicycles or electric motorcars rather than cars in view of the delivery cost, which reduces the delivery efficiency and results in the limited delivery range because of the slow speed. Second, most of food orders appear in the same time period (e.g., lunch and dinner times), which could lead to a lot of delivery requests in a short time duration. Therefore, it becomes difficult to deliver the food on time during the rush hour because of a fixed number of delivery staffs. In addition, the resources of professional delivery staffs may be wasted when there are few delivery requests during the most part of a day. So a new method is under investigated to tackle these challenges.

Spatial Crowdsourcing (SC) is an emerging paradigm that extends traditional crowdsourcing to the physical world, by assigning location-based tasks to moving workers to complete [3, 4]. In this paper, we view the OTOD service as a special type of SC task, which refers to object delivery that delivers objects from one place (i.e., restaurants) to another place (i.e., food orders). Recently, there have been several works that try to combine SC and object delivery. For example, Chen *et al.* [1] proposed a package delivery system, namely CROWDDELIVER, where packages share the resources of vehicles with passengers. Inspired by previous studies, we devote to building a food delivery network that uses an abundance of taxis in the road network to deliver food packages. For taxi drivers, extra income from the food delivery service can be obtained to promote the long-term engagement. For passengers, sharing the resources of taxis with food could reduce the taxi fare, and increase the riding comfort without sharing the limited space of the taxi with other strangers in ridesharing. For restaurants, delivering food using existing resources of urban taxis can decrease the cost on recruiting extra delivery staffs, and enable the long-distance food delivery.

To the best of our knowledge, this is the first work that studies the efficient delivery network by sharing rides of passengers and food packages using taxis. Most of current works mainly focus on the package delivery [2], which is significantly different from the food delivery as investigated in this work. First, food delivery has more strict 'pick-up' (the restaurant) and 'arrival' (the food order) time constraints to ensure the quality of food and meet users' dining demands. Second, the food package is usually smaller in size compared with other types of packages, and a taxi could serve more food orders to increase the delivery efficiency and lower the cost. Third, a taxi may be required to visit multiple locations to deliver the food because of various food orders with different restaurants and users, which could result in a more complicated optimization problem on delivery task assignment. Therefore, the solution of food delivery using SC is still to be further explored.

To address the above challenges, we propose FooDNet, which is a novel food delivery network that achieves the OTOD service based on spatial crowdsourcing. In particular, we solve the Opportunistic OTOD (O-OTOD) problem by leveraging pervasive taxis running in cities. In O-OTOD, taxis with carrying passengers deliver the food with low cost using spatial crowdsourcing. Specifically, we define the places of the restaurant and the requester in the food order as starting and destination areas. If the order happens in the frequent-interaction areas (i.e., there are more taxis running between the starting and destination areas), the taxi can deliver the food package opportunistically. In general, we have made the following contributions.

1. We present a novel system to deliver the take-out food by leveraging existing resources of taxis. To the best of our knowledge, it is the first work that applies spatial crowdsourcing in the OTOD field.
2. We elaborate the O-OTOD problem that the food is delivered incidentally by taxis when carrying passengers, and the optimization goal is to minimize the number of selected taxis.
3. We propose the two-stage method to solve the O-OTOD problem, which consists of the construction algorithm and the Large Neighborhood Search (LNS) algorithm. Specifically, the construction algorithm constructs an initial solution, and LNS optimizes the original solution by removing and inserting food requests.
4. We have conducted initial experiments using real-world taxi trajectory datasets to test the performance of FooDNet. The results indicate that our proposed algorithms are effective and efficient compared to baseline methods.

2 SYSTEM DESIGN

2.1 System Overview

The proposed FooDNet framework is shown in Fig. 1.

Pre-ordering food: The system has three stakeholders, namely restaurants, taxi drivers, and users. Specifically, it provides some information of restaurants for users to order the food, including the location, the business hour, and the food category. Meanwhile, information of taxis is also collected, i.e., the current location, the historical trajectory, and the passenger's request. When users start to order the food, they should provide the request information, including the location, the mealtime, and the kind of food.

Accepting food-delivery request: When the user starts an order, the system then determines whether to accept it. Based on the information of restaurants and taxis, as well as the user's food request, the system will accept the food-delivery request if it satisfies constraints (e.g., the time of ordering food can be 30 minutes earlier than the mealtime).

Selecting taxi for food delivery: For the accepted requests, the system will select proper taxis to deliver the food. The selection method is mainly divided into two steps. First, we apply the heuristic algorithm to construct the initial feasible solution. Second, LNS optimizes the original solution by removing and inserting food requests. Finally, the optimized solution is obtained, i.e., the planned route of each selected taxi to deliver the food.

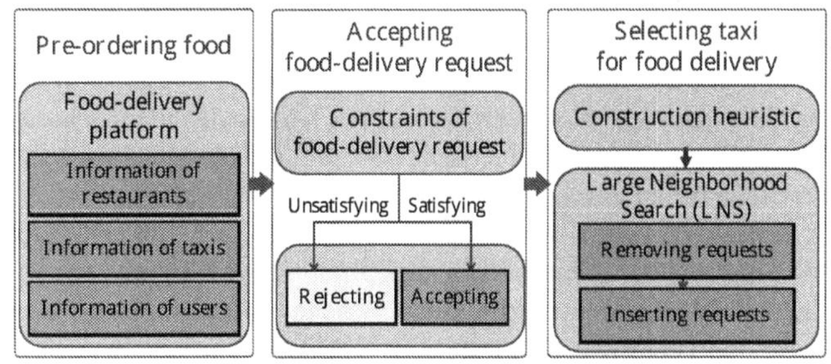

Figure 1: An overview of FooDNet.

2.2 Problem Statement

Food is delivered in the O-OTOD problem incidentally when taxis carry passengers. For the taxi, in view of the priority of the passenger, the taxi should pick up all food packages before picking up the passenger, and deliver the food after the passenger takes off. We assume that the passenger is willing to wait for a relatively short time period (e.g., 10 minutes) cost on picking up food packages as we can give her/him discounts for shared-riding.

Assume that there are a number of available taxis with passenger demands in the system, and a sequence of food orders with different time requirements that need to be delivered on time. Note that the food-delivery request is associated with two spatial points where the taxi has to visit: its *origin*, where the food is picked up at the restaurant, and its *destination*, where the taxi delivers the food package to the user. The *optimization goal* of the problem is to minimize the number of selected taxis in order to increase the income of each taxi driver and attract more drivers to participate over the long-term running. In addition, the optimal route of each selected taxi should be planned to deliver the passenger and food. Note that the planned route of the taxi have to satisfy the time constraints of passengers and food-delivery requests, such as any food request must be delivered within a given time period, and the extra time of the taxi to pick up food should be less than the maximum waiting time of the passenger.

2.3 The Algorithm Design

Obviously, the O-OTOD problem is known to be an NP-hard problem [5]. Moreover, many constraints of food requests and passengers make the problem more complicated. In general, there are two challenging issues to be addressed. One is to assign food-delivery requests to appropriate taxis among plenty of taxis with different passenger demands. The other is to plan the best route of the taxi to deliver the food under different constraints. Therefore, we propose the two-stage method to solve the O-OTOD problem, consisting of the construction algorithm and the LNS algorithm.

2.3.1 The construction algorithm. The construction algorithm obtains the initial feasible solution by selecting proper taxis for each food-delivery request. In general, we propose three greedy methods to get the feasible solution of the problem: First Taxi (FT), Best Taxi (BT) and Best Delivery (BD). FT inserts the food-delivery request in the route of first appropriate taxi while satisfying all constraints of food packages and the passenger. BT selects the best taxi among all available taxis that minimizes the increase in the cost of the solution after the insertion process. BD chooses the best food-delivery request whose insertion causes the least increase in the overall cost of solution among all the un-delivered food requests.

2.3.2 The LNS algorithm. LNS optimizes the initial solution obtained by the construction algorithm, and it can move from one promising area of the solution space to another to jump from local optimal solution and guide the search in global solutions. In general, LNS includes two parts: one is removing a number of food requests delivered by the taxi from the current solution, the other is reinserting these requests in the current routes of taxis again. Specifically, we propose two methods to remove and insert food-delivery requests: Shaw Removal (SR) and Best Insertion (BI). SR removes some similar food-delivery requests, because there is a little influence among different requests, and we may reinsert the removed requests at original positions or some bad positions which could lead to small change or no change of the initial solution. In addition, BI selects the best position which has the minimum increasing cost from all available positions of multiple available taxis' routes to insert the food-delivery request.

3 PRELIMINARY EVALUATION

We evaluate our system based on three kinds of real-world datasets: the taxi trajectory data, the restaurant data with food orders, and the cell tower data to simulate the distribution of users. Note that we simulate a sequence of food-delivery requests based on Gaussian distribution in advance which should arrive as a data stream in one day. The preliminary results are shown in Fig.2.

We compare the performance of proposed algorithms under different number of food-delivery requests. It is clear that the number of selected taxis grows gradually with the increasing number of food-delivery requests. Note that FTBI, BTBI and BDBI are baseline methods based on the construction algorithm, and LNS optimizes these baselines by SR. For example, FTBI-SR means that it selects the proper taxi for the request by FT and plans the route of the taxi to deliver the food by BI, then optimizes the solution by SR. We can find that LNS (i.e., FTBI-SR, BTBI-SR and BDBI-SR) can improve the initial solution to some extent. In addition, we investigate the number of selected taxis of six algorithms under the different time to deliver the food. In general, the peak hours of taxis to carry passengers during the day are about 12:00 and 18:00, which means that there are more available taxis visiting from restaurant areas to user areas. Therefore, the number of taxis to deliver the food at 12:00 is less than 11:30 and 18:00 is less than 17:30.

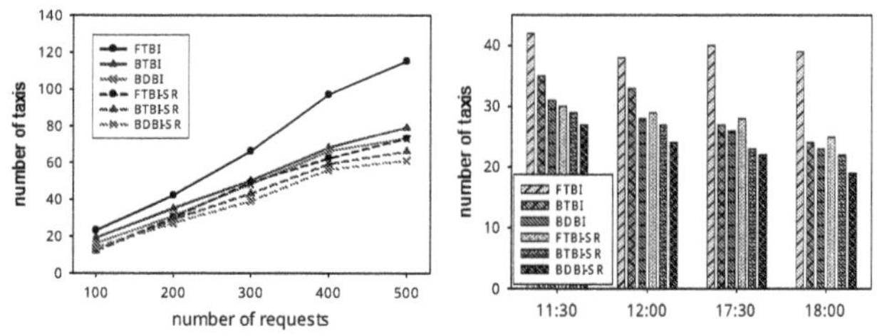

(a) Different number of requests (b) Different delivery time

Figure 2: Performance comparison under different situations.

4 CONCLUSIONS AND FUTURE WORK

In this paper, we presents a novel framework called FooDNet for food delivery by using existing resources of taxis, which can save the human resource, reduce the delivery cost, and improve the delivery efficiency. We also recognize some issues that are not reported in this work due to space and time constraints, which will be considered in our future work. First, we plan to solve the food delivery problem when there are few taxis running between the restaurant and user areas (e.g., infrequent-interaction areas), and taxis need to deliver the food specially without taking passengers. Second, we attempt to support real-time food delivery once users order the food based on the predicted movement of taxis and the predicted time of each restaurant for preparing the food. Third, we intend to make large-scale user studies over FooDNet, and test the performance of the system to solve the dynamic food-delivery requests. Finally, to apply our work in practice, it is important to study the complementary features and combination issues of the long-distance food delivery by FooDNet and the existing short-distance food delivery systems.

ACKNOWLEDGMENTS

This work is supported by the National Natural Science Foundation of China (grant nos. 61332005, 61373119 and 61602067), the National Basic Research Program of China (grant no. 2015CB352400), the Open Research Fund Program of the Shenzhen Key La-boratory of Spatial Smart Sensing and Services, and the Seed Foundation of Innovation and Creation for Graduate Students in NWPU (grant no. Z2017039).

REFERENCES

[1] Chao Chen, Daqing Zhang, Xiaojuan Ma, Bin Guo, Leye Wang, Yasha Wang, and Edwin Sha. 2017. Crowddeliver: planning city-wide package delivery paths leveraging the crowd of taxis. IEEE Transactions on Intelligent Transportation Systems 18, 6 (2017), 1478–1496.

[2] Aashwinikumar Devari. 2016. Crowdsourced last mile delivery using social network. Ph.D. Dissertation. State University of New York at Buffalo.

[3] Bin Guo, Yan Liu, Wenle Wu, Zhiwen Yu, and Qi Han. 2017. ActiveCrowd: A Framework for Optimized Multi-Task Allocation in Mobile Crowdsensing Systems. IEEE Transactions on Human-Machine Systems 47, 3 (2017), 392-403.

[4] Bin Guo, Zhu Wang, Zhiwen Yu, Yu Wang, Neil Yen, Runhe Huang, and Xingshe Zhou. 2015. Mobile Crowd Sensing and Computing: The Review of an Emerging Human-Powered Sensing Paradigm. ACM Computing Surveys 48, 1 (2015) 1-31.

[5] Jan Karel Lenstra and AHG Kan. 1981. Complexity of vehicle routing and scheduling problems. Networks 11, 2 (1981), 221–227.

Poster – RQL: REST Query Language for Converting Firebase to a Mobile Cloud Computing Platform

www.RQL.io

Saqib Rasool
University of Gujrat, Gujrat
Information Technology University
Lahore, Pakistan
saqib@ieee.io

Afshan Saleem
University of Gujrat
Gujrat, Pakistan
afshan@ieee.io

Adnan Noor Mian
Information Technology University
Lahore, Pakistan
adnan.noor@itu.edu.pk

ABSTRACT

MCC (Mobile Cloud Computing) performs computation offloading from mobile edge devices to centralized cloud services for achieving the reduction in resource consumption of mobile devices. MBaaS is considered as a new service model within the range of MCC and firebase by Google has been accepted as the most popular MBaaS. However, firebase has not made the efforts for performing computation offloading, as it is expected from an MCC platform. We have contributed in two folds by 1) identifying the limitations of firebase as an MCC platform and by 2) proposing RQL (REST Query Language) as a wrapper over firebase to improve its services for achieving computational offloading. RQL is used for requesting data in the form of JSON instead of using URLs for making REST requests. We have also explained different case studies to evaluate the effectiveness of RQL for converting firebase to an MCC platform.

CCS CONCEPTS

•Information systems → Query representation; *Query languages for non-relational engines;* RESTful web services; **•Software and its engineering → API languages;**

KEYWORDS

MBaaS; MCC; REST Services; Firebase; RQL; GraphQL; RQL.io.

1 INTRODUCTION

Although the capabilities of mobile devices are increasing rapidly but the computation shifted to these devices is far more than the increase in their computational capacity. This is due to the exponential increase in number of applications and operations shifted to mobile devices and therefore, efforts must be done to reduce the computational burden of mobile devices. MCC (Mobile Cloud Computing) deals with this issue by offloading computation from mobile devices to centralized cloud services. MCC not only helps in improving battery life of mobile devices but also improves the user experience by executing major chunk of computation at centralized cloud. It allows the mobile devices to act as a representational layer for displaying the output generated at cloud services [2].

MobiCom'17, October 16–20, 2017, Snowbird, UT, USA.
 ISBN 978-1-4503-4916-1/17/10.
DOI: http://dx.doi.org/10.1145/3117811.3131244

MBaaS (Mobile Backend as a Service) or more generally BaaS (Backend as a Service) is a term used for providing cloud storage equipped with many other features to mobile application developers. MBaaS is considered as a new service model within the range of MCC [2]. Firebase is the most popular commercial MBaaS and it has been used for implementing over a million mobile applications just within a period of about one year between Google I/O 2016 and Google I/O 2017 [5]. This is due to the popularity of firebase that we have focused our study on firebase and from now to onwards, we will be using the terms of MBaaS and firebase interchangeably.

Although firebase is very popular among the community of mobile application developers but it has few limitations that are discussed in third section of evaluation. These limitations are increasing the computational burden of mobile devices. Facebook has introduced GraphQL [1] to improve its web and mobile applications and same concepts can be applied to firebase for achieving computational offloading. However, firebase is based on REST and JSON [3] while GraphQL is not designed for REST services and its input queries are also not JSON compatible [1]. We have contributed by introducing RQL (REST Query Language) [1] based on the same concepts of GraphQL. However, in contrast to GraphQL, RQL is JSON compatible query language for REST services [4] and it allows the smooth integration of RQL with REST based firebase services.

Our contributions include the identification of firebase limitations from the prospective of an MCC platform and introduction of RQL as a wrapper over firebase services for converting it to an MCC platform. Moreover, RQL is not limited to firebase and it can be used as a wrapper over any platform based on REST services. RQL is also fully compatible with GraphQL queries as it takes input from mobile developers in JSON format and translates it to a valid GraphQL query. It results in the compatibility of RQL with existing GraphQL clients and also makes it vendor agnostic by supporting available GraphQL clients like Relay, Apollo etc. Introduction of RQL eliminates the need of learning GraphQL and the knowledge of REST services is the only prerequisite of learning RQL.

Next section contains the introduction and comparison of RQL with related tools and technologies, its syntax and the execution flow of RQL queries. Section three is based on the comparison of RQL with Firebase and multiple scenarios have been discussed to explain the effectiveness of RQL for converting firebase to an MCC platform by shifting the computation to the centralize cloud services. Last section concludes our work along with some future directions for improvements.

[1] www.RQL.io

2 RQL

There are three different ways of interacting with a web service using 1) events, 2) commands or 3) queries [7]. Commands are non-idempotent actions and are used for making changes in system states. Events are triggers along with some information about what has happened. Queries are idempotent and are used for looking something from remote services. Query language of RQL is also designed for querying data from REST services of MBaaS and is targeted for idempotent operations. REST services of firebase are event driven while RQL is a query language that abstracts the interaction with event driven REST services of MBaaS through JSON based queries. Although we have evaluated RQL with firebase but it is a generic language that can be used for abstracting interaction with any REST based BaaS.

2.1 RQL vs existing tools and technologies

RQL is based on the idea of GraphQL and its few constructs like limit, offset etc. are derived from SQL. It is based on JSON and is designed for REST services to ensure its smooth integration with firebase. Figure 1 shows that RQL is based on the features of four different tools/technologies and following discussion is based on the comparison of RQL with each of these four:

RQL and SQL: RQL is inspired from SQL (Structure Query Language) as it provides the interaction with REST services through a query language similar to SQL which supports the interaction with databases through a query language. RQL has also borrowed few constructs from SQL like offse, limit, etc.

RQL and JSON based REST services: REST is the most popular way of implementing web services and JSON is the most popular data representation format and is also best supported option for REST services. Therefore, RQL is also based on REST concepts and is written in JSON. More details of RQL syntax are in section 2.2.

RQL and MBaaS: As most of the MBaaS (including firebase) are based on REST therefore, existing mobile application developers, that are already familiar with REST/JSON, can easily start using RQL without learning any other concept or language.

RQL and GraphQL: Although GraphQL is not designed for REST services and also not supports the JSON based input queries but JSON based RQL presents the GraphQL features to the developers that are only aware of JSON based REST services. This enables the developers to achieve the strengths of both GraphQL and firebase. RQL abstracts the GraphQL queries and developers can use GraphQL without learning it. Only the knowledge of JSON based REST services is required for calling firebase through RQL which automatically utilizes the strengths of GraphQL underneath.

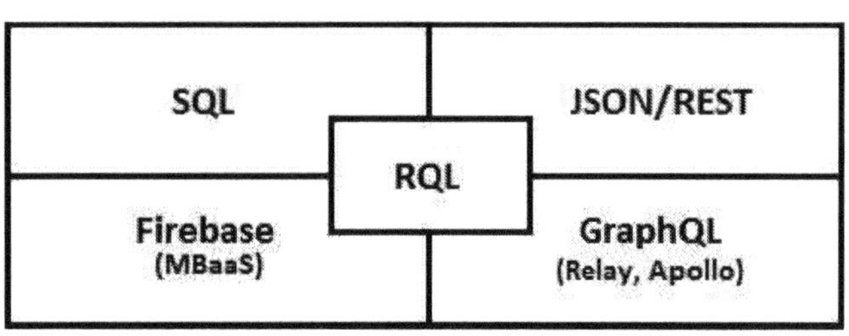

Figure 1: RQL vs existing tools and technologies

2.2 Syntax of RQL Queries

Each RQL query is based on a single JSON object where keys of that object are representing the resources of REST services. Each key is further having an array type value containing the names of states that are required against the resource mentioned in key, as it is given in line 2 and 4 of Listing 1. Each array may have nested objects of following three types:

Nested entity: If the nested object is further having an array type value then its key is considered as another resource of REST service (as shown at line 5 of Listing 1).

Search parameters: Nested object with key-value pairs are considered as searching parameters. Line 4 of Listing 1 is containing two search parameters of *id* and *name* with values of *3* and *Saqib*.

Extra features: Key-value pairs of nested objects may contain keywords for pagination (offset,limit) and sorting (sort) where + and - are for descending and ascending respectively (line 3).

```
1 {
2   "post": ["title","description",{
3   "offset":30, "limit":10, "sort":"-date"}],
4   "user":[{"id":3, "name", "Saqib"},{
5   "post":["title","description","body"]}]
6 }
```

Listing 1: Example of an RQL query

For the RQL query of Listing 1, all posts are sorted in ascending order based on date attribute and then posts from 31 to 40 will be returned (line 3) with only the attributes of title and description (line 2). However, for the posts of user with *id=3* and *name=saqib*, all posts will be returned with attributes of title, description and body of the post (line 5).

2.3 Execution flow of an RQL query

Each RQL query is invoked from a mobile application for reading data from MBaaS of firebase. This query is initially converted from JSON based RQL format to text based format of a valid GraphQL query. This GraphQL query is then passed to a GraphQL client that forwards it to the GraphQL runtime. We have used the Apollo client of GraphQL for testing purpose. GraphQL runtime receives the query and invokes the firebase services within the resolve functions. Resource information in RQL query is used for the service discovery and response is returned in the form of JSON which is formatted according to the requested format in RQL query.

3 CASE STUDY BASED EVALUATION

We have explained five case studies where each is having three further portions. First portion elaborates the limitations of firebase as an MCC platform, second portion presents RQL as a solution for overcoming identified limitations of firebase and third portion explains the importance of RQL improvements for mobile devices.

3.1 Case study 1: Fetching different data from same resource multiple times

RQL query in Listing 1 is reading the resource of *post* in two different ways by 1) fetching 10 posts with pagination (line 3) and by 2) reading all posts of user with *id=3* and *name=Saqib* (line 4 and 5).

Limitation of Firebase: Firebase is not capable of fetching same resource in different ways through a single request. It needs to initiate one request for each representation of a single resource.

Solution by RQL: RQL can query a single resource in unlimited ways through a single request by considering each key-value pair of RQL query as independent representation of the resource.

Impact on mobile applications: RQL can reduce the number of requests between MBaaS and mobile clients.

3.2 Case study 2: Querying multiple resources

RQL query in Listing 1 is looking up data of two resources independently. It is fetching that of resource post at line 2 and data of resource user at line 4.

Limitation of Firebase: Firebase requires one round-trip for fetching data of one independent resource and thus requires two round-trips for fetching data of two resources in Listing 1.

Solution by RQL: RQL is capable of reading data from unlimited independent resources through a single request by considering each key-value pair of level one as independent resource to handle.

Impact on mobile applications: RQL is again reducing the multiple round-trips to a single round-trip.

3.3 Case study 3: Request selected attributes

RQL query in Listing 1 is requesting only two attributes at line 2 and three attributes at line 5. No attribute is defined against user resource so all attributes of user resource are requested.

Limitation of Firebase: Firebase does not support the feature of selecting limited attributes of a resource and it returns all the attributes of the requested resource.

Solution by RQL: RQL is capable of requesting only the selected attributes as it is clear from Listing 1.

Impact on mobile applications: Requesting only the required attributes reduces the payload size and thus optimally uses the network resources. It also reduces the computation required at mobile end for filtering the required attributes out of all the delivered attributes.

3.4 Case study 4: Pagination and Sorting

RQL query in Listing 1 has requested the posts from 31 to 40 to display the data in the pagination format.

Limitation of Firebase: Firebase can only perform pagination against the id values and is not capable of returning data by skipping few entries like it is done against offset in SQL. Moreover, firebase does not support sorting in descending order.

Solution by RQL: RQL fetches the data in ascending order from firebase and converts it to descending order before shifting to mobile clients, if required. It can also perform the pagination by skipping number of records mentioned through offset.

Impact on mobile applications: While using firebase, developers need to run the algorithm on mobile devices for converting data from ascending to descending order. Developers also need to maintain the id information to achieve the pagination at mobile clients. Both of these requirements are eliminated by the RQL for reducing the code complexity of mobile applications. RQL also reduces resource consumption of mobile devices by offloading computation for both features of descending sorting and pagination using offset.

3.5 Case study 5: Multiple search terms

RQL query in Listing 1 has requested the user resource with two parameters of id and name and these are treated as multiple search parameters for fetching the results.

Limitation of Firebase: Firebase does not support search against multiple search terms simultaneously.

Solution by RQL: RQL supports multiple search terms against the firebase services. Server first checks the count value for each search term from firebase independently, which returns the total number of records available against each search term. Based on the count values of all search terms, data is fetched against the term having least count value. All the other terms are applied over that data at server side of RQL layer and only those records are returned that are satisfying the criteria of all requested search terms.

Impact on mobile applications: As there is no built-in option available for multiple search terms in firebase, hence developers need to fetch all the data at mobile devices against any single search term and execute an algorithm in mobile applications for filtering the received data based on multiple search terms. In this scenario, firebase increases both the computation and bandwidth consumption and both of these result in more power consumption of mobile devices. Studies have been conducted to improve the battery consumption of mobile devices [6] and RQL also helps in reducing the battery consumption by offloading the execution of algorithm at server and sending only the required data to the mobile devices. It also reduces the bandwidth consumption by limiting the size of payload to only the requested data. Hence, firebase equipped with RQL is acting as an MCC platform by reducing the consumption of both bandwidth and computational resources.

4 CONCLUSION AND FUTURE WORK

This study has presented a new query language for REST services that we call as RQL. It is inspired from SQL and it abstracts the communication with REST services by using a JSON based syntax. RQL is also fully compatible with GraphQL and it can be used with different GraphQL clients. However, current paper is only based on the comparison with most popular MBaaS of firebase and the evaluation is done through multiple case studies. Extensive experiments can be performed in future to evaluate and report the extent to which RQL is reducing the consumption of both bandwidth and computational resources of mobile devices.

REFERENCES

[1] Samer Buna. 2016. *Learning GraphQL and Relay.* Packt Publishing Ltd.
[2] Igor Costa, Jean Araujo, Jamilson Dantas, Eliomar Campos, Francisco Airton Silva, and Paulo Maciel. 2016. Availability Evaluation and Sensitivity Analysis of a Mobile Backend-as-a-service Platform. *Quality and Reliability Engineering International* 32, 7 (2016), 2191–2205.
[3] Documentation. 2017. Firebase Database REST API – Firebase. (2017). https://firebase.google.com/docs/reference/rest/database/
[4] Documentation. 2017. RQL Documentation – RQL. (2017). https://rql.io/docs
[5] Firebase. 2017. Firebase on Twitter: "#GoogleNext17 shout out to our momentum - Mobile developers have created One Million+ #Firebase projects since #io16!". (2017). https://twitter.com/firebase/status/839902027543044096
[6] Saqib Rasool and Hamid Mukhtar. 2013. Adaptive switching of traffic between WebRTC and WebSocket based on battery status of portable devices. In *Advances in Information Technology for the Holy Quran and Its Sciences (32519), 2013 Taibah University International Conference on.* IEEE, 345–351.
[7] Ben Stopford. 2017. Build Services on a Backbone of Events – Confluent for Microservices. (2017). https://www.confluent.io/blog/build-services-backbone-events/

Poster: EasyDefense: Towards Easy and Effective Protection Against Malware for Smartphones

Bingfei Ren, Chuanchang Liu*, Bo Cheng, Yimeng Feng, Junliang Chen
State Key Laboratory of Networking and Switching Technology
Beijing University of Posts and Telecommunications, Beijing, China
{rbf, lcc3265, chengbo, fyimeng, chjl}@bupt.edu.cn

ABSTRACT

As the dominant mobile operating system in the markets of smartphones, Android platform is increasingly targeted by attackers. Besides, attackers often produce novel malware to bypass the conventional detection approaches, which are largely reliant on expert analysis to design the discriminative features manually. Therefore, more effective and easy-to-use approaches for detection of Android malware are in demand. In this paper, we design and implement EasyDefense, a lightweight defense system that is integrated with Android OS for easy and effective detection of Android malware utilizing machine learning methods and the ensemble of them. Besides universal static features such as permissions and API calls, EasyDefense also employs the N-gram features of operation codes (opcodes). These N-gram features are extracted and learnt automatically from raw data of applications. Experimental results on 204,650 applications show that users can easily and effectively protect the privacy and security on their smartphones through this system.

CCS CONCEPTS

• Security and privacy → Mobile platform security; • Human-centered computing → Mobile computing;

KEYWORDS

Security, Privacy, N-gram, Machine learning

1 INTRODUCTION

With the rapid development of Android platform, more and more attackers turn their eyes on it owing to its openness. Besides, applications in Android often have the ability of accessing sensitive resources on mobile devices to provide new or enhanced services, which makes it easier for malware to breach the security and privacy of users. Consequently, there is an increasingly volume of work on effective detection of malware, and machine learning is a buzzword in this area [1]. Various methods have been proposed based on static features (API calls, Permissions) analyzing approach that utilize machine learning methods [2][3]. However, these approaches require specifying static features beforehand through expert analysis, and most of them can be rendered largely ineffective due to the producing of novel malware or new forms of attacking with the use of sophisticated detection avoidance techniques.

As new malware tends to have the most same malicious codes as previous versions, hence we propose EasyDefense, a lightweight defense system that is integrated with Android OS in this paper. Besides conventional static features analysis, like API calls and Permissions, we investigate N-gram features of opcodes (n-opcodes) analysis for Android malware detection through utilizing machine learning methods to automatically learning features from raw data of applications. In addition, we integrate the learning model with Android OS after the learning phase, which enable smartphones with Android to extract features (conventional static features and n-opcodes) and to predict whether the application is benign or malicious at the time of installation.

2 ARCHITECTURE

To give a clear description, the overall architecture of EasyDefense is shown in Fig. 1, which can be divided into two phases: training model phase and smartphone defense phase.

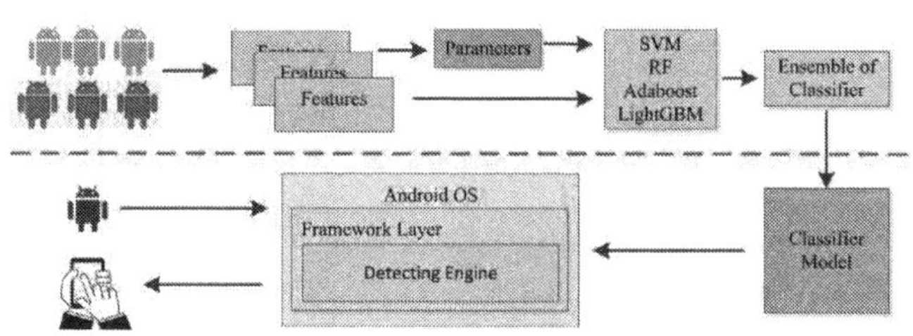

Figure 1: Architecture of EasyDefense System.

2.1 Training model phase

This phase mainly focuses on learning classifier model using sample datasets. First of all, collecting a large scale of real applications and extracting features from these samples that have already been labeled with benign or malicious applications, and then using part of these features to choose the best parameters of multiple classifiers. At last, training the whole set

*Chuanchang Liu is the corresponding author

MobiCom '17, October 16–20, 2017, Snowbird, UT, USA

ACM ISBN 978-1-4503-4916-1/17/10. https://doi.org/10.1145/3117811.3131261

of datasets with multiple machine learning classifiers and the ensemble of them to get a classifier model.

Collect Data, In order to get a more effective training model, we collect 204,650 Android application package (apk) files consisting of 183,341 benign applications crawled from google market and other third-part markets in China and 21309 malware in the wild. We use VirusTotal1 to re-label each sample in our datasets to ensure that our samples are correctly split.

Extract Features, more than 2,000 features utilized in EasyDefense comprise conventional static features and n-opcodes. We use androguard2 to extract features of permissions and API calls from apk files, and to disassemble the Dalvik executable (dex) files compressed in apk files to get smali files wherein opcodes are contained, then n-gram of opcodes from all classes of one application can be extracted. Below is an example of 3-opcodes used in our system.

('invoke-virtual/range', 'new-instance', 'invoke-direct')

...

('const-string', 'move-object/from16', 'invoke-virtual')

...

('if-eqz', 'iget-object', 'invoke-static')

Choose Parameters, the selection of parameters in each machine learning classifier determines the accuracy and stability of the training results. As the most popular method to choose parameters, we adopted 5-fold cross validation based on grid search to find the suitable parameters of classifiers used in EasyDefense, which are Support Vector Machine (SVM), Random Forest (RF), Adaboost and Gradient Boosting Machine (GBM).

Training Data, with the leverage of the whole features and parameters, we choose four classifiers to training our model. To facilitate the accuracy of detection, we employ the ensemble of multiple classifiers with Deny-overrides rule, which means ensemble of classifiers will treat an application as a benign one only if all the four classifiers identify it as a benign application, otherwise the application will be treated as a malware.

2.2 Smartphone defense phase

We integrate the learning model obtained in the training phase into Android OS, and port the customized Android OS to smartphones. Users can choose to detect the application when installing it, which is not supported by inherent installation mechanism of Android. The Detecting Engine working in the framework layer of Android OS will detect and predict whether this app is malware or not, and show the result to users.

Integrate with Android, we integrate the learning model with Android OS based on LineageOS, a third-part open-source project of Android. In order to guarantee the sustained effectiveness of EasyDefense, this learning model can be upgraded through over-the-air (ota) technology once a new and more effective model being trained aiming at novel malware.

Detecting Engine, once users choose to detect the application when installing it, Detecting Engine starts to analyze the apk file and extract features including n-opcodes features from it, and then to transform these features into shapes that beforehand learning model can process. After the prediction of ensemble of classifiers, the detection result will be shown to the users of smartphones in order to help them decide whether this application should be installed further.

1 https://www.virustotal.com/

2 https://github.com/androguard/androguard

3 PRELIMINARY RESULTS

We conduct the following two experiments to evaluate EasyDefense: Detection performance and Run-time performance.

3.2 Detection performance

The computing environment that we used for detection performance is a PC that runs under Ubuntu 14.04 (64 bit) with an Intel® Xeon(R) CPU E5620 @ 2.40GHz x 16 and 132GB of main memory.

We collect 204,650 Android applications consisting of 183,341 benign applications and 21309 malware as the dataset to learning model.

First, we leverage SVM, RF and Adaboost classifier provided by scikit-learn [4] and GBM classifier provided by LightGBM framework [5]. We adopt 5-fold cross validation approach based on grid search to choose parameters, and we obtain the parameters after the process.

- SVM classifier, we choose the rbf-kernel function, and set the parameter wi to "balanced". The penalty parameter of the error C is set as 2. Another parameter gamma is set as 2-4.
- RF classifier, the parameters of random_state, max_depth, min_samples_leaf and criterion is important for RF. Therefore we set them as 14, 18, 2 and "entropy" respectively.
- Adaboost classifier, to balance the efficiency and accuracy of the detection performance, we set the best estimator of Adaboost as Decision Tree, whose parameters of criterion and splitter are set as 'gini' and 'random'. Meanwhile, set the number of estimators of Adaboost to 18.
- GBM classifier, the number of leaves and the max depth are important parameters for the best split. After cross validation, we set them as 35 and 13.

Next, we randomly split the dataset into train-data (70%) and test-data (30%). Then training these samples using classifiers mentioned above, and the result is depicted in Fig. 2. We can easily find that each of the four classifiers achieves a high accuracy and stability in malware detection.

Last, we employ the ensemble of these four classifiers with Deny-overrides rule and compare its performance against other four classifiers. The result is shown in Table 1.

Our ensemble of multiple classifiers outperforms the four classifiers and achieves the accuracy of 98.70% in the detection of malicious applications.

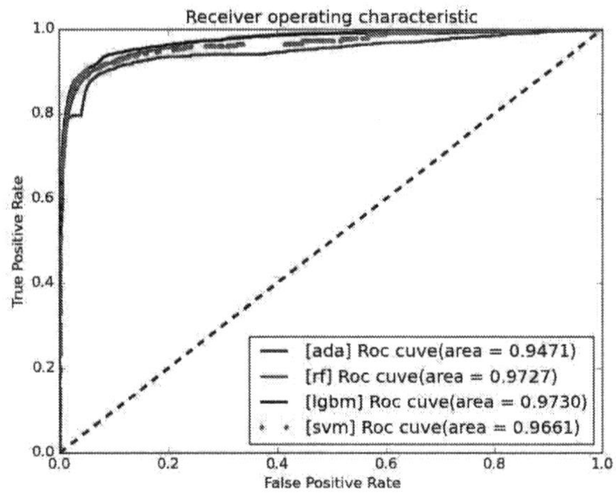

Figure 2: Roc-curve of four classifiers

Table 1. The detection performance of multiple classifiers and ensemble of them

Classifier	SVM	RF	Ada	GBM	Ensemble
Accuracy	96.48%	96.28%	96.73%	96.76%	98.70%

3.2 Run-time performance

We evaluate the usability of EasyDefense after integrating it with Android6.0 and porting the customized Android OS to Xiaomi4 smartphone, whose codename is cancro. Furthermore, as it is the most time-consuming part during the detection on smartphones, we conduct two experiments to evaluate the time consumption of feature extracting by using different size of apk files: the relationship between the size of apk files and time consumption (TC-test1); the relationship between the size of the raw data in class dex files and time consumption (TC-test2).

As the result shown in Fig. 3, we can surprisingly realize that the size of apk files have no directly influence on time consumption of feature extracting, it can be affected by the size of classes dex file of apks. The reason is that an apk file contains not only the manifest file which is used to extract conventional static features and the class dex files which are used to extract n-opcodes features, but also contains resource files which are useless in extracting features, and those resource files may occupy the biggest part of size in most situation.

4 CONCLUSIONS AND FUTURE WORK

In this paper, we design and implement a lightweight defense system that is integrated with Android OS for easy and effective detection of Android malware by users. Except conventional static features analysis, like API calls and Permissions, we

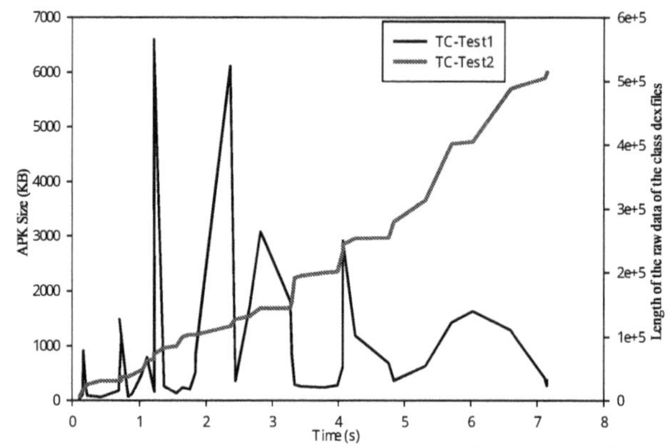

Figure 3: Time consumption of EasyDefense in Smartphones

investigate N-gram features of opcodes (n-opcodes) analysis for Android new malware detection through utilizing machine learning methods to automatically learning features from raw data of applications.

We also recognize the limitations of our study, and plan to work on the following challenges and extensions:

- N-gram features of opcodes extraction. This system is currently selected 3-opcodes as features to malware classification, and next we plan to evaluate other values of n-opcodes (4-opcodes, 5-opcodes, etc.) to choose one that can optimize malware detection.
- Feature extraction. We use a python tool named androguard to extract features from apk files. It converts each raw data to python object beforehand feature extraction, which will increase the time consumption to a great extent. Therefore, we plan to use a replacement approach for feature extraction.

ACKNOWLEDGMENTS

This work is supported by National Natural Science Foundation of China under Grant No. U1536112.

REFERENCES

[1] D. Arp, M. Spreitzenbarth, M. Hübner, H. Gascon, and K. Rieck. 2014. DREBIN: Effective and Explainable Detection of Android Malware in Your Pocket. In Proceedings of the Annual Symposium on Network and Distributed System Security (NDSS), 2014.

[2] S. Roy, J. Deloach, Y. Li, N. Herndon, D. Caragea, and X. Ou, et al. 2015. Experimental Study with Real-world Data for Android App Security Analysis using Machine Learning. Computer Security Applications Conference 81-90

[3] Arvind Mahindru and Paramvir Singh. 2017. Dynamic Permissions based Android Malware Detection using Machine Learning Techniques. In Proceedings of the 10th Innovations in Software Engineering Conference. ACM, New York, NY, USA, 202-210

[4] Scikit-learn. http://scikit-learn.org/stable/

[5] LightGBM. https://github.com/Microsoft/LightGBM

Poster: Can MPTCP Improve Performance for Dual-Band 60 GHz/5 GHz Clients?

Swetank Kumar Saha[1], Roshan Shyamsunder[1], Naveen Muralidhar Prakash[1], Hany Assasa[2,3], Adrian Loch[2], Dimitrios Koutsonikolas[1], Joerg Widmer[2]
[1]University at Buffalo, SUNY, Buffalo NY, USA, [2]IMDEA Networks Institute, Madrid, Spain, [3]Universidad Carlos III de Madrid, Spain
{swetankk,roshansh,naveenmu,dimitrio}@buffalo.edu,{hany.assasa,adrian.loch,joerg.widmer}@imdea.org

ABSTRACT

This work conducts one of the first experimental studies of Multipath TCP (MPTCP) in dual-band 60 GHz/5 GHz WLANs using off-the-shelf hardware. We consider both uncoupled and different coupled congestion control algorithms, compare their performance and their potential to improve throughput over single path TCP, and uncover their limitations. In contrast to a recent study that reports reduced throughput with MPTCP compared to single path TCP over 60 GHz, our results show that significant performance improvements are possible, especially in the case of uncoupled congestion control. On the other hand, performance gains with coupled congestion control are lower as these algorithms often fail to fully utilize the capacity of both paths simultaneously. We also observe a pathological case that can lead to significantly reduced throughput with MPTCP regardless of the congestion control algorithm.

1 INTRODUCTION

The almost 7 GHz of unlicensed spectrum centered around 60 GHz has attracted ample attention from both academia and industry as a solution for providing multi-gigabit indoor WLAN connectivity. Over the last couple of years, devices compliant with IEEE 802.11ad such as access points and laptops have been released commercially. In the future, 802.11ad (and eventually 802.11ay) devices will likely become as ubiquitous as legacy WiFi WLANs.

To overcome the high attenuation at millimeter wavelengths, 60 GHz radios use directional communication, typically enabled via phased array antennas. Directional communication, however, introduces new challenges as narrow beams are highly fragile under mobility and human blockage, and current beam training algorithms typically take 100s of milliseconds to converge. While several recent works have explored ways to reduce beamforming overhead (e.g., [3, 5, 12, 13]), client mobility and human blockage are still considered major challenges to the realization of 60 GHz WLANs.

The recent advent of tri-band chipsets (supporting 2.4, 5, and 60 GHz) by major chipset manufacturers [8] offers an attractive solution to mitigate these challenges; one can leverage the legacy WiFi interfaces (2.4/5 GHz) to maintain connectivity in cases 60 GHz connectivity is lost. In fact, the 802.11ad standard supports an optional Fast Session Transfer (FST) feature that allows traffic to migrate from 60 GHz to legacy WiFi and vice versa in a way transparent to higher layer protocols. Even more attractive is the possibility of using both interfaces (60 GHz and legacy WiFi) simultaneously when both networks are available, while seamlessly falling back to WiFi when the 60 GHz network becomes unavailable. This is possible via Multipath TCP (MPTCP) [2], a transport layer protocol that allows applications to exchange data over multiple paths, without any modification.

However, caution is needed in using MPTCP in practice. In fact, a large number of studies in datacenters and smartphones (e.g. [10], [1]) have shown that the protocol performs poorly over heterogeneous paths, due to interactions among out of order TCP packets, congestion control, and limited receiver buffer size. Given the large bandwidth disparity between WiFi and 60 GHz interfaces, it is likely that MPTCP will suffer from similar problems in hybrid 60 GHz/5 GHz WLANs. Hence, it is important to study the use of MPTCP in such WLANs, understand its potential to improve performance and robustness, and uncover its pitfalls and limitations.

Surprisingly, this is an aspect of 60 GHz networking which has remained largely unexplored. To our best knowledge, the only work that has briefly studied MPTCP performance in 60 GHz WLANs is [11]; it reports that using the 60 GHz interface alone achieved 7%-45% higher throughput compared to MPTCP but it does not explore the causes of the observed performance. The only other related work is [7], which explores the use of MPTCP in 5G cellular networks, over 28 GHz and LTE using simulations. The authors find that MPTCP with uncoupled congestion control performs better than single path TCP (SPTCP) by up to 100%; on the other hand, MPTCP with the recently proposed coupled congestion control *balia* algorithm [6] in many cases performs worse than SPTCP. Nonetheless, the use of a simulator instead of experiments with real hardware and the fundamental differences between outdoor cellular networks and indoor WLANs make it unclear if the these findings are still valid in the context of 60 GHz WLANs.

This work fills this gap by conducting an experimental study of the MPTCP performance in dual-band 802.11ac/802.11ad WLANs using off-the-shelf hardware. Our study considers both uncoupled and coupled congestion control and different Tx-Rx distances. In contrast to the results in [11], our study shows that MPTCP with uncoupled congestion control can significantly boost performance, often yielding throughput equal to the sum of the SPTCP throughputs over the two interfaces. On the other hand, performance with recently proposed coupled congestion control algorithms is typically much lower. We also found a few cases where large RTT inflation over both subflows results in significantly reduced throughput,

MobiCom '17, October 16–20, 2017, Snowbird, UT, USA

ACM ISBN 978-1-4503-4916-1/17/10.
https://doi.org/10.1145/3117811.3131248

even lower than the throughput of SPTCP over the best path. We are currently investigating the causes of this.

2 EXPERIMENTAL METHODOLOGY

2.1 Devices

Our setup consists of a Netgear Nighthawk® X10 Smart WiFi Router and an Acer Travelmate P446-M laptop. Both devices have chipset(s) supporting 802.11ac and 802.11ad.

60 GHz (802.11ad) The router has the QCA9008-SBD1 module housing the QCA9500 chipset from Qualcomm, supporting all the single-carrier 802.11ad data rates (from 385 Mbps up to 4.6 Gbps). The laptop carries the client-version of the module: QCA9008-TBD1, which houses the 802.11ac, 802.11ad and BT chipsets. It runs a typical Linux OS (kernel 4.x) and uses the open source wil6210 wireless driver to interface with the chipset. Both the router and the laptop use a 32-element phased antenna array on a separate chipset and connected to the main chipset using a MHF4 cable. The 60 GHz radios on both devices use their own rate adaptation and beamforming algorithms to select MCS and control beam properties, respectively. In case the link is blocked, the radios automatically search for an alternative NLOS path through a reflection to re-establish the connection. On the laptop, the wil6210 driver exports detailed connection parameters, including Tx and Rx MCS, MAC layer throughput, signal quality indicator (SQI), beamforming (BF) status (OK/Failed/Retrying), and sectors in use both by itself and the AP. We log all the parameters every 150 ms.

WiFi (802.11ac) Although the router supports up to 4 MIMO spatial streams, our client only supports 2. Hence, our effective link configuration for WiFi is 802.11ac, 2x2 MIMO, 80 MHz, SGI, and default rate adaptation.

Traffic Generation and Maximum Goodput A high-end desktop is connected to the router through a 10G LAN SFP+ interface to generate/receive TCP traffic. This setup should ideally allow us to take achieve multi-Gigabit speeds, we found that the maximum goodput is limited to ~2.3 Gbps and ~550 Mbps, with 802.11ad and 802.11ac, respectively.

2.2 MPTCP

We use MPTCP version v0.92 with the *fullmesh* path manager that creates a subflow over all available network interfaces for each established TCP connection, and the *default* RTT-based scheduler that sends packets over the available path with the lowest RTT. We experiment with both uncoupled congestion control (TCP Cubic) and three coupled congestion control algorithms, *lia* [9], *olia* [4], and *balia* [6]. We consider both interfaces for the primary subflow and the results are similar (which is expected given that the RTT is similar for both interfaces). In Section 3, we only present results with the primary subflow over the 60 GHz interface.

2.3 Environment and Methodology

Our experiments are conducted in an open Lobby thinly populated by some desks and chairs. The ceiling height is rather high and thus it does not serve as a viable reflector. We select this location to emulate near-free space propagation. Each experiment consists of a 10-second backlogged iperf3 TCP session from the desktop behind the router to the laptop. All the results are the average of 5 sessions. We further capture all the packets on the receiver side using tcpdump and calculate the throughput of each subflow over each 100-ms interval in order to study the evolution of throughput over time for each run and the interaction between the two subflows.

All our measurements are done during night time to make sure there is no WiFi (802.11ac) interference from other users in the building. Further, we ensure that the entire 80 MHz bandwidth is indeed available exclusively to our link by continuously checking, in between our actual measurement runs, that the maximum throughput (with 2x2 MIMO, 80 MHz, SGI, and high SNR) is achievable when using single-path TCP.

3 RESULTS

Figure 1a compares the performance of different versions of MPTCP against SPTCP for two Tx-Rx distances. In contrast to the observations in [11], we observe that *MPTCP has the potential to improve performance compared to SPTCP over 60 GHz.* The average throughput improvement of MPTCP with *cubic*, *lia*, *olia*, and *balia* compared to SPTCP over 60 GHz is 29%, 9%, 9%, and 2%, respectively at 10 ft, and 32%, 27%, 5%, and 14%, respectively, at 70 ft. Note that these performance differences are not due to different channel conditions or due to different MAC layer decisions over different runs. We observed that the same sector was used 100% of the time at each experiment at both distances. Further, MCS 8 was used at least 99% of the time in all experiments at 10 ft and MCS 6 was used 88-90% of the time in all experiments at 70 ft. Hence, any performance differences can be attributed to decisions made at the transport layer (congestion control and scheduler).

Interestingly, MPTCP with uncoupled congestion control performs the best at both distances, achieving a throughput roughly equal to the sum of the SPTCP throughputs over WiFi and 60 GHz alone. Figures 1b, 1c show two examples of the evolution of throughput over time separately for each interface in the case of MPTCP with uncoupled congestion control, at 10 ft and 70 ft, respectively. This *ideal* behavior is very similar for 4 out of 5 runs with uncoupled congestion control at each of the two distances. In spite of this promising result (which is similar to the result in [7] for 5G cellular networks over LTE and 28 GHz), we note that previous studies [4, 6, 9] showed that MPTCP with uncoupled congestion control can be unfriendly to SPTCP flows and proposed coupled congestion control algorithms to address this issue.

Nonetheless, Figure 1a shows that the performance improvements with coupled congestion control are in most cases much lower than with uncoupled congestion control; in fact, the most recently proposed *balia* algorithm performs the worst among the three algorithms at 10 ft. The *ideal* behavior is observed only 1, 0, 0 out of 5 times with *lia*, *olia*, and *balia*, respectively, at 10 ft, and 3, 0, and 1 out of 5 times, respectively, at 70 ft. In contrast, the most common behavior with all three algorithms is the one shown in Figures 1d and 1e. At 10 ft (Figure 1d), the throughput of the 60 GHz subflow is initially lower than its maximum value (below 1.5 Gbps); after some time (between 0.5 and 4 s for different runs), it obtains its maximum value but at the same time, the throughput of the WiFi subflow drops to a lower level (100 Mbps in Figure 1d, anywhere between 50-400 Mbps in different runs). At 70 ft, this transition

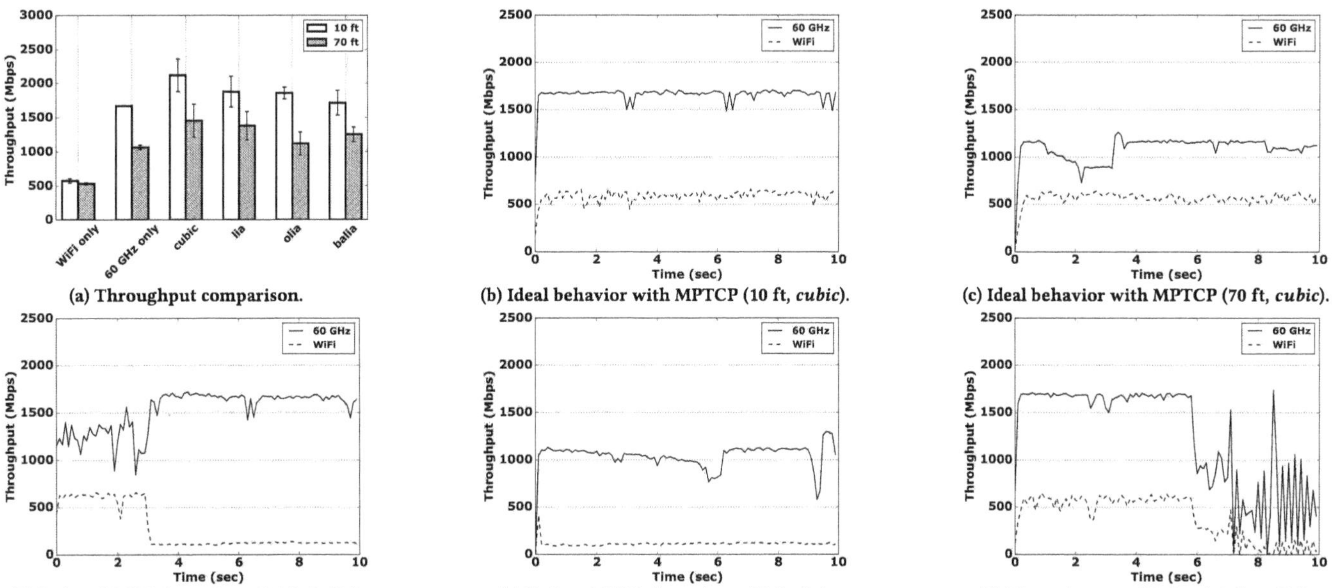

(a) Throughput comparison.

(b) Ideal behavior with MPTCP (10 ft, *cubic*).

(c) Ideal behavior with MPTCP (70 ft, *cubic*).

(d) Reduced WiFi throughput (10 ft, *balia*).

(e) Reduced WiFi throughput (70 ft, *lia*).

(f) Throughput oscillation (10 ft, *cubic*).

Figure 1: Experimental results.

happens much faster (within 0.2 s), as shown in Figure 1c. In other words, MPTCP with coupled congestion control fails to fully utilize the capacity of both paths simultaneously in most runs. The varying WiFi throughput over different runs and the different times at which the 60 GHz subflow achieves its maximum throughput are among the reasons for the large standard deviations observed for *lia*, *olia*, and *balia* in Figure 1a.

We are currently investigating the causes of this behavior. Note that the work in [7] also found *balia* to perform worse than *cubic* in 5G cellular networks because it perceives losses over the mmWave link as congestion, and consequently shifts all the traffic to the low-rate LTE link. In contrast, we do not observe any TCP timeouts or duplicate ACKs and the RTTs are similar over both subflows in our experiments exhibiting the behavior shown in Figures 1d, 1e.

Figure 1a shows that throughput with *cubic* also features large standard deviations, similar to *lia*, *olia*, and *balia*, even though *cubic* never exhibited the behavior shown in Figures 1d, 1e. On the other hand, note that the standard deviations for SPTCP performance over both interfaces are negligible, suggesting again a stable wireless channel. The reason for the large standard deviations with *cubic* is that, in one of the 5 runs for each distance, both subflows with *cubic* experienced significantly reduced throughput and very large oscillations over time for a fraction of the 10-second interval. One such example is shown in Figure 1f. We observed a similar behavior in one of the 5 runs with *lia* and *balia* at 10 ft and one run with *olia* at 70 ft. In all these runs, RTT is significantly inflated during the throughput oscillation intervals – up to 40-60 ms for the 60 GHz subflow and up to 150 ms for the WiFi subflow. In spite of the RTT inflation, in most of these runs there are no TCP retransmissions. Further, the RTT inflation is not caused due to ACKs being lost in the channel or delayed due to congestion. The receiver simply delays to send the ACKs, albeit without following the standard rule of one ACK for every two segments. In several cases, it receives multiple segments before sending an ACK.

In our future work, we plan to investigate the causes of the observed performance and look into the effectiveness and responsiveness of MPTCP in mobility and blockage scenarios. We also plan to study the impact of simultaneously using both interfaces on power consumption which will be important as smartphones become the next target of 802.11ad.

REFERENCES

[1] Simone Ferlin, Thomas Dreibholz, and Özgu Alay. 2014. Multi-Path Transport Over Heterogeneous Wireless Networks: Does It Really Pay Off?. In *Proc. of IEEE Global Telecommunications Conference (GLOBECOM)*.

[2] A. Ford, C. Raiciu, M. Handley, and O. Bonaventure. 2013. TCP Extensions for Multipath Operation with Multiple Addresses. (2013). RFC 1546.

[3] Muhammad Kumail Haider and Edward W. Knightly. 2016. Mobility Resilience and Overhead Constrained Adaptation in Directional 60 GHz WLANs: Protocol Design and System Implementation. In *Proc. of ACM MobiHoc*.

[4] Ramin Khalili, Nicolas Gast, Miroslav Popovic, and Jean-Yves Le Boudec. 2013. MPTCP Is Not Pareto-Optimal: Performance Issues and a Possible Solution. *IEEE/ACM Transactions on Networking* 21, 5 (2013).

[5] Thomas Nitsche, Adriana B. Flores, Edward W. Knightly, and Joerg Widmer. 2015. Steering with Eyes Closed: mm-Wave Beam Steering without In-Band Measurement. In *Proc. of IEEE INFOCOM*.

[6] Qiuyu Peng, Anwar Walid, Jaehyun Hwang, and Steven H. Low. 2016. Multipath TCP: Analysis, Design, and Implementation. *IEEE/ACM Transactions on Networking* 24, 1 (2016).

[7] Michele Polese, Rittwik Jana, and Michele Zorzi. 2017. TCP in 5G mmWave Networks: Link Level Retransmissions and MP-TCP. In *Proc. of IEEE Workshop on 5G New Radio Technologies*.

[8] Qualcomm. 2017. Qualcomm Technologies' Tri-Band Solution. https://www.qualcomm.com/products/features/80211ad. (2017).

[9] Costin Raiciu, Mark Handley, and Damon Wischik. 2011. Coupled Congestion Control for Multipath Transport Protocols. (2011). RFC 6356.

[10] Costin Raiciu, Christoph Paasch, Sebastien Barre, Alan Ford, Michio Honda, Fabien Duchene, Olivier Bonaventure, and Mark Handley. 2012. How Hard Can It Be? Designing and Implementing a Deployable Multipath TCP. In *Proc. of USENIX NSDI*.

[11] Sanjib Sur, Ioannis Pefkianakis, Xinyu Zhang, and Kyu-Han Kim. 2017. WiFi-Assisted 60 GHz Wireless Networks. In *Proc. of ACM MobiCom*.

[12] Sanjib Sur, Xinyu Zhang, Parameswaran Ramanathan, and Ranveer Chandra. 2016. BeamSpy: Enabling Robust 60 GHz Links Under Blockage. In *Proc. of USENIX NSDI*.

[13] Anfu Zhou, Xinyu Zhang, and Huadong Ma. 2017. Beam-forecast: Facilitating Mobile 60 GHz Networks via Model-driven Beam Steering. In *Proc. of IEEE INFOCOM*.

Poster: X60: A Programmable Testbed for Wideband 60 GHz WLANs with Phased Arrays

Swetank Kumar Saha[1*], Yasaman Ghasempour[2*], Muhammad Kumail Haider[2*], Tariq Siddiqui[1], Paulo De Melo[1], Neerad Somanchi[1], Luke Zakrajsek[1], Arjun Singh[1], Owen Torres[1], Daniel Uvaydov[1], Josep Miquel Jornet[1], Edward Knightly[2], Dimitrios Koutsonikolas[1], Dimitris Pados[1], Zhi Sun[1]
[1]University at Buffalo, SUNY, Buffalo NY, USA, [2]Rice University, Houston TX, USA
{swetankk,tariqsid,paulodem,neeradso,lukezakr,asingh29,owentorr,danieluv,jmjornet,dimitrio,pados,zhisun}@buffalo.edu,{ghasempour,kumail.haider,knightly}@rice.edu

ABSTRACT

We introduce X60, the first SDR-based testbed for 60 GHz WLANs, featuring fully programmable MAC/PHY/Network layers, multi-Gbps rates, and a user-configurable 12-element phased antenna array. These features provide us with an unprecedented opportunity to revisit the most important aspects of 60 GHz signal propagation and obtain new insights on performance expected from practical 60 GHz systems. X60's unique capabilities make it an ideal platform for experimentation and prototyping across layers.

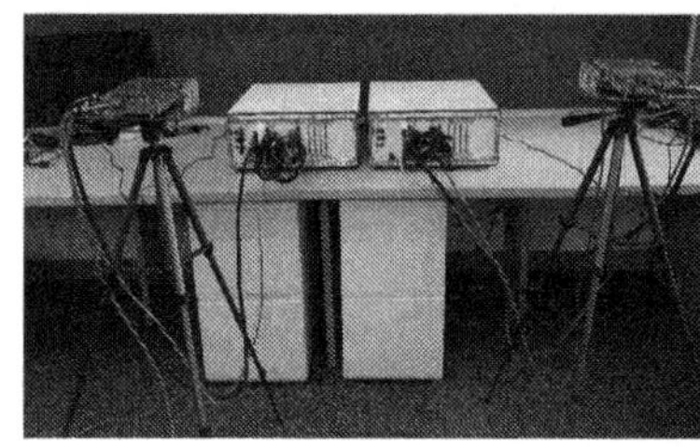

Figure 1: Two X60 nodes, each attached to a SiBeam phased array module.

1 INTRODUCTION

The IEEE 802.11ad standard, using 2.16 GHz wide channels in the unlicensed band centered around 60 GHz and directional transmissions, provides data rates of up to 6.7 Gbps in an indoor WLAN setting. Realizing high-speed directional links, however, comes with challenges, sparking off research for the design of efficient link adaptation techniques. Nonetheless, most available experimental platforms either offer very limited access to the PHY/MAC layers (commercial devices) or use narrow band transmissions (USRP/WARP combined with a 60 GHz frontend) coupled with horn antennas (e.g., [2, 5]) deviating significantly from 802.11ad's use of ultra-wide channels and phased array antennas. This leaves a vacuum for a testbed that can offer the best of both worlds: a realistic PHY *and* programmability of PHY/MAC layers.

This poster introduces **X60**, the first highly configurable software defined radio (SDR) 60 GHz testbed, featuring fully *programmable PHY, MAC, and Network* layers, ultra-wide channels, and phased arrays. Based on the National Instrument's (NI) millimeter-wave (mmWave) Transceiver System [3] and equipped with *user-configurable* 12-element phased array antennas from SiBeam, X60 nodes (Figure 1) enable communication over **2 GHz** wide channels using realistic Tx and Rx beams that can be steered in **real-time** and support multi-gigabit data rates.

X60 offers several advantages over existing mmWave experimental platforms. Unlike commercial 802.11ad devices, X60 with its SDR/FPGA based architecture allows access to and complete control over the PHY and MAC layers. This not only enables experimentation that can obtain a full view of the often complex interaction among multiple layers of the networking stack, but also allows for prototyping and testing of new techniques at multiple layers. In contrast to most existing SDR mmWave platforms, X60 provides high reconfigurability without limiting baseband bandwidth to a few hundred MHz, enabling us to study the impact of extra wide channels supported by 802.11ad. Further, X60's phased arrays generate beam patterns that are configurable and steerable in real time, overcoming a basic limitation of horn-antenna based platforms.

The only testbeds capable of wide-band transmission with phased array antennas are OpenMili [6] and the testbed in [1]. OpenMili supports a channel width of 1 GHz and uses 4-element phased-arrays, with two possible values for each element's weight. The testbed in [1] uses 8-element phased arrays but operates in the 24 GHz band. In contrast, X60 has antenna 12 elements, 4 discrete possible phase values per element, and supports a 2 GHz channel width, enabling higher rate and higher resolution experiments.

X60's design and capabilities, for the first time, provide an opportunity to re-examine the current understanding of the most important aspects of 60 GHz WLAN signal propagation and performance. To this end, we summarize in this poster the results from an extensive measurement campaign across four characteristic indoor environments in a typical academic building. Our measurements encompass a range of propagation scenarios (dominant LoS, non-LoS only, reflections from multiple obstacles, LoS propagation with side-lobes) and Tx and Rx orientations.

*Primary co-author

MobiCom '17, October 16–20, 2017, Snowbird, UT, USA

ACM ISBN 978-1-4503-4916-1/17/10.
https://doi.org/10.1145/3117811.3131251

2 X60 TESTBED

In the following, we describe the different components of the testbed. All the modules are programmed using NI LabVIEW.

Baseband Tx/Rx. Each X60 node is based on the NI mmWave Transceiver System. All modules involved in the baseband signal generation are assembled inside a NI PXIe-1085 PXI Express chassis. Most of the inter-module signaling and data transfer happens over the chassis's high-speed backplane using FIFO queues or DMA. The Tx/Rx chains consist of one or more high-performance FPGAs which handle the majority of the transmit/receive operations including encoding/decoding and modulation/demodulation. The FPGA outputs feed into an ultra-wideband DAC/ADC module which generates/samples the baseband signal. In addition, the chassis holds a high-end controller (host machine) that generates the source bits for transmission and is the sink for the receive operation. It controls different Tx/Rx parameters (MCS, uplink/downlink, etc.) and logs system information for user-display and debugging.

PHY/MAC Structure. The current reference PHY implementation supports the following MCS: 1/5 BPSK, 1/4 QPSK, 1/2 QPSK, 3/4 QPSK, 1/2 16QAM, 3/4 16QAM, 7/8 16QAM, resulting in theoretical bit rates from 300 Mbps to 4.75 Gbps. Data transmission takes place in 10 *ms frames* which are divided into 100 *slots* of 100 *μs* each. Both the MCS and operation type (uplink/downlink/sync) can be configured on a *per-slot* basis. A slot is made up of 92 codewords, each of which has an attached CRC block.

Antenna Array and Beam Patterns. The SiBeam mmWave module, in the Tx path, takes as input the baseband signal (as differential I/Q), up-converts, and transmits over the air a 2 GHz wide waveform centered around one of the 802.11ad channel center-frequencies. The Tx power is 30 dBm EIRP at channel 2. The in-built phased array has 24 elements; 12 for Tx and 12 for Rx. The module connects to the baseband chassis over an additional dedicated control path that allows different phase values for the antenna elements through the use of codebooks. The phase of each antenna element can be set to one of four values: 0, $\pi/2$, π, $3\pi/2$.

SiBeam's reference codebook defines 25 such beams spaced roughly 5° apart (in their main lobe's direction). The beams cover a sector of 120° (in the azimuthal plane) centered around the antenna's broadside direction. We refer to the beams using index range -12 (-60°) to +12 (+60 °), with index 0 corresponding to the broadside beam. The 3 dB beamwidth for the beams ranges from 25 to 30 degrees for Tx and from 30 to 35 degrees for Rx.

We computed the idealized beam patterns using COMSOL Multiphysics. Figs. 2a-2d depict examples of 2D and 3D radiation patterns for select beam indices. These patterns highlight how, in contrast to beams generated by horn antennas, phased-array generated beams often have strong side-lobes. Moreover, as beams are steered away from the main lobe, patterns become more imperfect with even stronger side lobes and a considerably weaker main lobe. For instance, comparing beam index 3 (Fig. 2b) and 12 (Fig. 2c) shows how practical phased-arrays can have *non-uniform steerability* along different directions as opposed to mechanically rotated horn antenna beams. Surprisingly, beam indices equally apart from the broadside beam (e.g., +3 (Fig. 2b) and -3 (Fig. 2d) can have radiation patterns that are *not* necessarily mirror images of each other.

These particular characteristics of the beam patterns result both out of the discretization of the individual antenna element phase weights and the particular geometry in which the elements are arranged in the 2D array. Nitsche et al. [4] also found the beam patterns of commercial WiGig devices to be imperfect with strong side lobes. Also, an inspection of the open source wil6210 driver targeting Qualcomm 802.11ad chipsets suggests 2 bits for phase control of the antenna elements, allowing for 4 possible values.

2.1 Enhancements for Measurements

We made the following modifications to the reference code to enable logging of all the required PHY/MAC parameters and to allow for more realistic measurements. **Automatic Gain Control (AGC):** We implemented an AGC block running on the host machine (every 100 ms) that adjusts the receiver's gain value based on the energy calculated from the raw I/Q samples to achieve an experimentally determined optimal target energy value that ensures best ADC operation. Through a separate set of experiments, we verified that our implementation is throughput optimal (as compared to exhaustive-search manual gain control) for different MCS and channel conditions. **Thin Control Channel:** We added an external legacy WiFi radio to all four nodes to implement a reliable control path. This allows us to implement certain features like Tx-Rx beam selection or MCS selection and to automate parts of our measurements with only few modifications to the existing code base, without the burden of maintaining tight timing requirements of the code running the mmWave channel. The scripts that implement this control path run on the host machine and communicate with the LabVIEW process via IPC over TCP to control parameters like MCS and beam index, and collect link metrics for further processing. **Instrumentation:** We instrumented the host side LabVIEW code base to log a range of PHY/MAC layer parameters. Given that the host is an active part of the Tx/Rx flow and needs to maintain strict timing guarantees, we selected different logging frequency for each parameter to minimize overhead. Some parameters (Signal Power Estimation, Noise Power Mean, Throughput, CRC pattern) are logged on a per-frame basis (every 10 ms), while others (RSSI, SNR, Carrier-to-Noise, Phase, Power Delay Profile) are logged at a lower frequency (every 40 ms).

3 MEASUREMENT STUDY

3.1 Methodology

Our measurement campaign is aimed at collecting key PHY and MAC layer parameters across multiple indoor environments. Four indoor measurement locations – a narrow corridor, a lab with cardboard partitions and metal cabinets, a conference room with various metallic/shiny surfaces, and a lobby with large glass panels as walls – are selected to characterize static 60 GHz channels, as well as emulate typical mobility patterns like translation and rotation.

At each location, we collect channel measurements in two steps: *(i) Beam Sweep:* This step encompasses channel estimation for all possible beam pairs in an exhaustive search. The transmitter and receiver co-ordinate their beam switching (over the control channel) to generate all 625 (25x25) beam-pair combinations. For each beam pair, 25 frames are transmitted at MCS 0 and SNR is logged for the channel estimation slot in each frame (every 40*ms*). *(ii) MCS sweep:* In this step, we select a small subset of (Tx,Rx) beam pairs

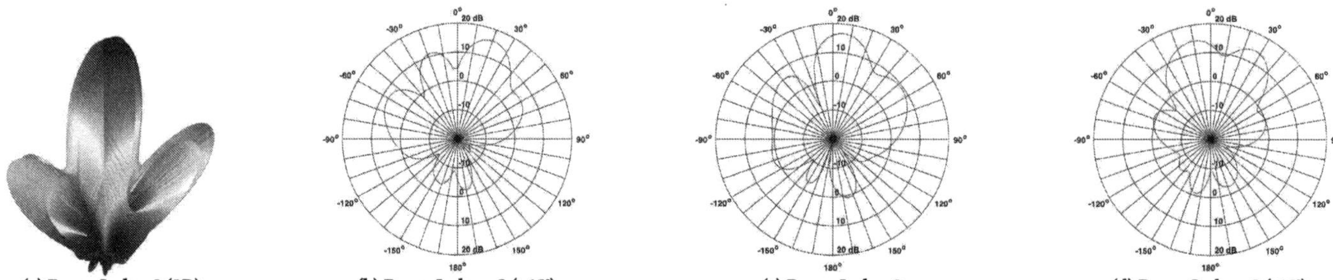

(a) Beam Index 0 (3D) (b) Beam Index +3 (+15°) (c) Beam Index 0 (d) Beam Index -3 (-15°)

Figure 2: Antenna array beam patterns.

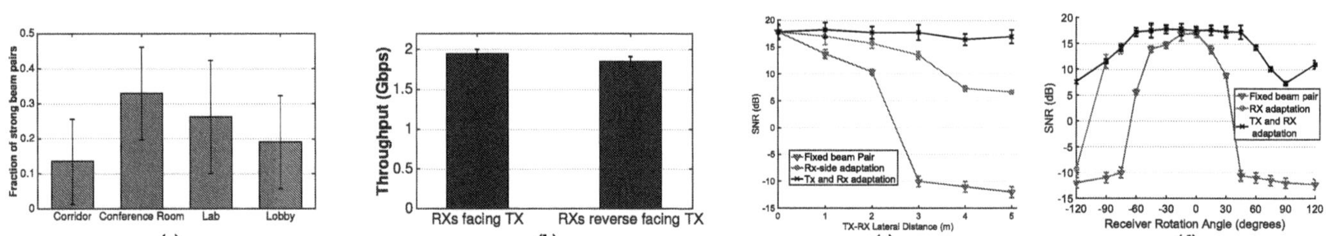

(a) (b) (c) (d)

Figure 3: Experimental results: (a) Richness of strong beam pairs, (b) Throughput in LoS and NLoS positions, (c) Beam adaptation strategies for lateral translation, (d) Beam adaptation strategies for rotation.

for which we repeat measurements at all seven achievable MCS levels. We select the 3 strongest beam pairs out of all 625 beam pairs, based on average SNR computed during beam sweep in step (i). Further, to study the impact of selecting neighboring beams, we also include the immediate neighbors of the Rx beam in each of the three (Tx,Rx) pairs, for a total of nine (Tx,Rx) beam pairs. For each MCS, we log all channel parameters for 500 frame transmissions.

3.2 Experimental results

We summarize the most important findings in Figs. 3a-3d.

Richness of Strong Beam Pairs. Fig. 3a shows that the average (over all measurement positions) ratio of strong beam pairs (at least 10 dB SNR) is above 0.13 for all four environments, i.e., more than 80 beam pairs provide at least 1 Gbps of throughput. Hence, in contrast to the common belief, there are several beam pairs that are able to provide Gbps data rates for 60 GHz communication. The richness of strong beam pairs implies that beam adaptation algorithms might be able to avoid time-expensive exhaustive search through all beam combinations. Another implication is that interference between simultaneous transmissions may not be negligible in 60 GHz.

Performance of NLoS links. We consider the conference room since it has many reflectors such as whiteboard and TV screen and measure throughput in six positions. In three of them, there is a LoS path between the Tx and Rx; in the other three, the Tx and Rx face away from each other and can only communicate through a NLoS path (via reflections). Fig. 3b shows that the throughput is close to 1.9 Gbps in either case, with and without the LoS path, confirming that Gbps communication is feasible via reflections.

Beam Misalignment and Nodal Mobility. We analyze two typical mobility scenarios, lateral translation and rotation, in Figs. 3c, 3d, respectively. We consider three possible adaptation strategies: (i) fixed beams – we use beam pair (0,0), the default pair when the Tx and Rx face each other, (ii) Tx and Rx adaptation, and (iii) Rx-only adaptation. Fig. 3c plots the SNR with each strategy at 6 different Rx positions in the lobby, emulating a path taken by a node as it moves perpendicularly to the Tx in steps of 1m. We observe that the gradient for the Rx-only adaptation curve is significantly better than the no-adaptation curve, and a link is sustained across all positions, indicating that a local search at the Rx, though sub-optimal, may be sufficient to maintain the link.

Fig. 3 plots the results for a scenario where the Rx was placed directly in front of Tx, 6.3 m apart, and the SiBeam antenna was rotated mechanically. Again, Rx-only adaptation achieves similar SNR as Tx-and-Rx adaptation, although the maximum achievable SNR diminishes for higher Rx angles on one side – a consequence of non-uniform angular spread of beam patterns and diminishing directivity gain of beam indices farther from the central beam, both limitations of practical phased array antennas. On the other hand, we found (graph omitted due to space limit) that, when the Tx and Rx are placed at a relative angle of 30°, Rx-only adaptation alone is not enough to sustain high SNR; this shows the importance of identifying different mobility scenarios for appropriate adaptation.

REFERENCES

[1] Omid Abari, Haitham Hassanieh, Michael Rodriguez, and Dina Katabi. 2016. Millimeter Wave Communications: from Point-to-Point Links to Agile Network Connections. In *Proc. of ACM HotNets*.

[2] Muhammad Kumail Haider and Edward W. Knightly. 2016. Mobility Resilience and Overhead Constrained Adaptation in Directional 60 GHz WLANs: Protocol Design and System Implementation. In *Proc. of ACM MobiHoc*.

[3] National Instruments. 2017. Introduction to the NI mmWave Transceiver System Hardware - National Instruments. http://www.ni.com/white-paper/53095/en/. (2017). (Accessed on 06/25/2017).

[4] Thomas Nitsche, Guillermo Bielsa, Irene Tejado, Adrian Loch, and Joerg Widmer. 2015. Boon and Bane of 60 GHz Networks: Practical Insights into Beamforming, Interference, and Frame Level Operation. In *Proc. of the 11th ACM CoNEXT*.

[5] Sanjib Sur, Vignesh Venkateswaran, Xinyu Zhang, and Parameswaran Ramanathan. 2015. 60 GHz Indoor Networking through Flexible Beams: A Link-Level Profiling. In *Proc. of ACM SIGMETRICS*.

[6] Jialiang Zhang, Xinyu Zhang, Pushkar Kulkarni, and Parameswaran Ramanathan. 2016. OpenMili: A 60 GHz Software Radio Platform With a Reconfigurable Phased-Array Antenna. In *Proceedings of the ACM MobiCom*.

Poster: A VLC Solution for Smart Parking

Yang Shen†, Guojun Chen†, Xieyang Xu†, Chenren Xu†, Guobin Shen§, Jiaji Li♯

†Peking University
{sy2006, leochan, xy.xu, chenren}@pku.edu.cn

§Zepp Labs, Inc.
jackyshen@zepplabs.com

♯The High School Affiliated to Renmin University of China
jimmylijiaji@sina.com

ABSTRACT

With the rapid growth of vehicle ownership, parking has become an issue, especially in metropolitan areas – the extra time for check-ins, check-outs and finding available parking spaces not only causes frustration and potential road rage on the driver side, but also increases the traffic congestion, gasoline waste and air pollution in consequence. In order to address these problems, the concept of "smart parking" is put forward. To make a parking lot "smart", we argue that three basic features, namely *Vehicle Identification*, *Parking Space Detection* and *Indoor Localization* are are critical and should be supported by the infrastructure. Herein, we present LightPark, a Visible Light Communication (VLC) solution to realize the vision of "smart parking". Building on top of the visible light backscatter communication primitive, LightPark is able to leverage the lighting infrastructure to perform scalable visible light communication and networking with the batter-free tag devices instrumented on the vehicles and parking spaces to manage the critical information such as identification and real-time location of vehicles, and status of parking spaces in a centralized and low-cost manner.

CCS CONCEPTS

• **Hardware** → **Wireless devices**; • **Computer systems organization** → *Embedded systems*;

KEYWORDS

Visible Light Communication; Backscatter; Smart Parking; Parking Space Detection; Indoor Localization

1 INTRODUCTION

In big cities, parking has become a potential societal problem. People waste a lot of time waiting for check-ins and check-outs, circling around looking for available parking spaces, as well as finding their cars when they forget where they park them. More importantly, these things not only frustrate drivers but can also lead to traffic congestion, gasoline waste, and air pollution.

MobiCom '17, October 16–20, 2017, Snowbird, UT, USA

ACM ISBN 978-1-4503-4916-1/17/10.
https://doi.org/10.1145/3117811.3131245

Aiming to resolve all these problems, the concept of "smart parking" is put forward in recent years. Imagine when you drive into a parking lot, a parking space will have been reserved for you in advance. The navigation system will give you, or even your autopilot system precise instructions to park your car into that specific parking space. There will be no problem if you forget where you park your car because your smart phone will be able to navigate you back. And you won't have to stop at the entrance or exit anymore because your car will be identified and the parking fee will be charged automatically. To realize the "vision" aforementioned, the following three features appear to be critical:

- **Vehicle Identification**, that is to say the parking lot should be able to identify the vehicles.
- **Parking Space Detection**, which means the parking lot should be able to detect whether a parking space is occupied and keep track of available parking spaces.
- **Indoor Localization**, which requires the parking lot infrastructure to provide vehicles and other smart devices the ability to locate themselves inside the parking lot.

To provide these features in a low-cost and easy-to-maintain manner, we propose LightPark.

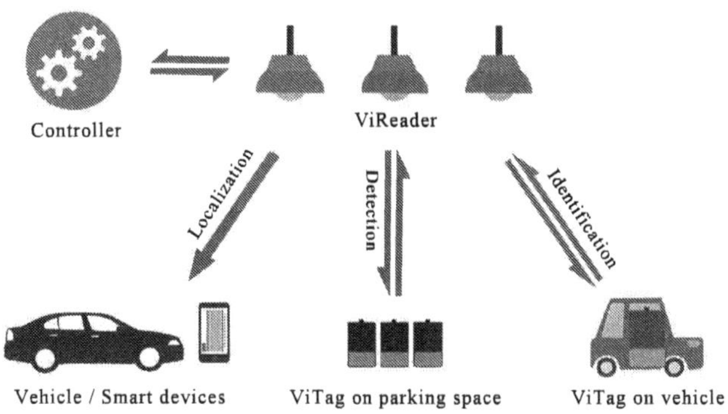

Figure 1: LightPark System Diagram

LightPark is based on a recently emerged technique called PassiveVLC [2, 4]. PassiveVLC is a low power visible light backscatter communication system, consisting of ViReaders and ViTags. ViReaders are LED light sources that can perform bidirectional communication with low-cost battery-free ViTags using visible light as carrier. More details about PassiveVLC can be found in §2.

Since PassiveVLC only specify the communication between one ViReader and one ViTag, a data link layer for it is designed and implemented to enable collaboration of multiple ViReaders and ViTags, making it possible to scale out. Without loss of flexibility, the data link layer is optimized for the needs of LightPark according to the characteristics of PassiveVLC. See §3 for details.

The key idea of LightPark is to replace the lighting facilities in the parking lot with ViReaders, thus lights will not only work for illumination but also act as medium to communicate with users, vehicles and parking spaces, enabling our desired features. §4.1 and §4.2 describe how LightPark supports *Vehicle Identification* and *Parking Space Detection*. We adopt *Epsilon* [3] as a subsystem to support *Indoor Localization*, which is briefly discussed in §4.3. Such system can be integrated into existing illumination infrastructure and be easily deployed.

2 BACKGROUD: PASSIVEVLC

PassiveVLC is a bidirectional communication system using visible light as its carrier. The system uses modified LED lights called ViReader to work as base stations, and the corresponding mobile devices are called ViTag, which are credit card size, battery-free tags built for IoT applications.

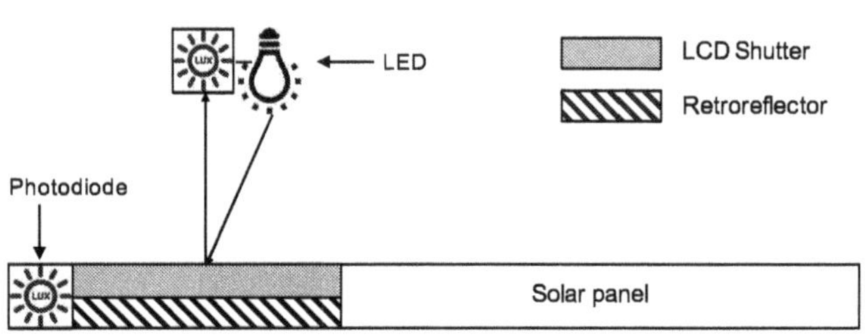

Figure 2: PassiveVLC design illustration.

Current communication systems for IoT applications are commonly based on RF techniques, *e.g.*, BLE and NB-IoT, *etc.*, while PassiveVLC shows another approach to achieve low-power, low-cost and practical networking and sensing. At a high level, PassiveVLC works as follows. For the downlink, the LED in ViReader switches on and off, turning the illuminating light into a communication carrier. The light signals are then picked up by the light sensor on the ViTag and decoded therein. For the uplink, the same carrier is leveraged via reflection. The ViTag uses a special material called retroreflector to concentrate and reflect the light from the lighting source and further carries information bits by toggling an LCD shutter. The modulated reflected light carrier is then picked up by a photodiode on the ViReader and further demodulated and decoded. PassiveVLC reported a maximum of $5kbps$ speed for downlink and $1kbps$ for uplink.

Meanwhile, such visible light link has another unique feature that it only performs line-of-sight communication. This feature, which is commonly treated as bad for communication, turns out to be critical to enable *Parking Space Detection*. *Indoor Localization* can also benifit from it to achieve higher accuracy.

3 SCALING OUT PASSIVEVLC

3.1 Logic Link Control

The Logic Link sublayer specifies communication mode, ID space, packet format and error control for the system. As the name suggests, ViTags perform passive communication, which means that ViTags will never actively send packets but respond to packets sent by ViReaders. The ViReader is able to unicast to a specific ViTag by ID, and broadcast to all ViTags within its work range.

Given the uplink speed being much slower than the downlink speed, we aim to reduce uplink packet overhead as much as possible. By taking advantage of the passive communication mode and offloading overheads to downlink packets, we manage to completely remove the header for uplink packets. Another trick that makes it possible is to XOR-encrypt the uplink packet with downlink checksum, so that only the sender can decode the uplink packet. As a result, our uplink packet consists of payload and CRC checksum only. The downlink packet is pretty ordinary, consisting of header, payload and CRC checksum.

3.2 Tag Discovery

The tag discovery protocol is responsible for discovering and identifying nearby ViTags within the range of a ViReader. The basic idea is to broadcast a query and let each ViTag respond its ID. The problem is that collision happens when multiple ViTags respond at the same time, in which case reader will not receive any useful information. To resolve these collisions, we adopt a binary tree based method. Compared to the slotted-ALOHA method used in EPC Gen 2[1] RFIDs, our method expects less uplink time.

3.3 Muliple Access of ViReaders

If two ViReaders' work ranges intersect, we say these two ViReaders interfere with each other. If they send at the same time, ViTags in their common coverage may not be able to decode the packet. Therefore, two ViReaders interfering with each other shouldn't be permitted to send at the same time. A MAC protocol for ViReaders is needed. Since the coverage of lights are relatively stable, and their position rarely change once installed, we can assume that the interference map is available in advance.

In our use case, the work load will be heavy as we frequently update the status of each parking space. Besides, concurrent sending for multiple ViReaders that do not interfere with each other should be allowed and utilized to gain better efficiency, since coverage of each light is relatively small.

With these properties taken into consideration, we come up with a centralized turn-taking Media Access Control protocol. In each turn, the centralized controller selects a set of pending ViReaders that do not interfere with each other, and permits them to send. It won't proceed to the next turn until all responses are received. The selection is done in a greedy manner, from the least recently sent ViReader to the most recently sent one, to guarantee fairness.

4 FEATURE DESCRIPTION

4.1 Vehicle Identification

Vehicle Identification requires a ViTag to be installed on each vehicle, usually on the front window by design. With these ViTags

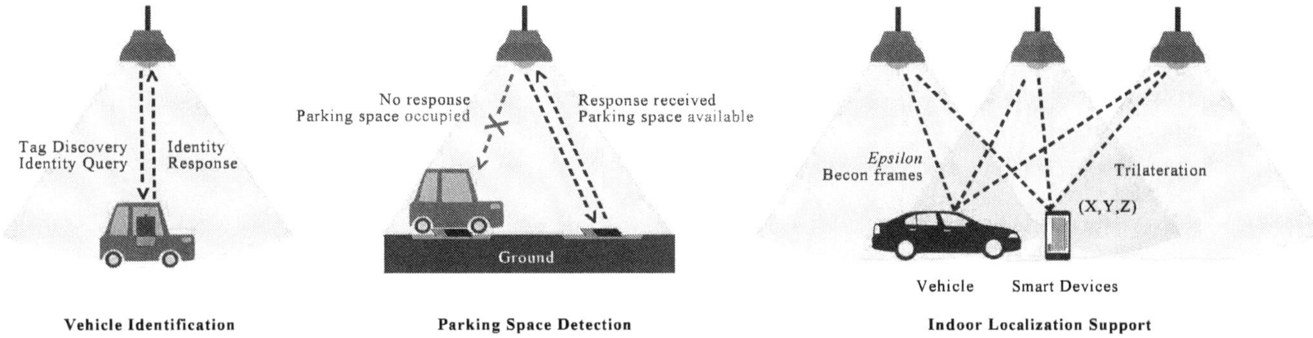

Figure 3: Illustration of LIGHTPARK features.

carrying vehicle identity information installed, *Vehicle Identification* is straight forward. The ViReader that needs to perform *Vehicle Identification* (e.g. the ones at the entrance or exit) simply runs tag discovery protocol and communicate with the discovered ViTags to obtain the corresponding vehicle identities.

4.2 Parking Space Detection

For *Parking Space Detection*, we have a ViTag installed onto the middle of each parking space.

Leveraging the fact that light travels in straight lines, we can indicate the occupancy of a parking space by reachability of the corresponding ViTag installed on it. Considering a ViTag within the work range of a ViReader, the ViReader should be able to get response from the ViTag if the corresponding parking space is available; otherwise if the parking space is occupied, the line-of-sight path between the ViReader and ViTag will be blocked, then the ViReader thus will never receive response from the ViTag.

For the parking-lot-wide detection, the solution is polling. At system start-up, each ViReader in the system runs tag discovery protocol to discover all the ViTags (representing parking spaces) it can manage. Then, once a ViReader is permitted to send according to Link Layer MAC (and there is no other packet pending to send on this ViReader), it sends to one of the ViTag within its work range to update the status of the corresponding parking space according to response. If there is more than one ViTag to choose from, the ViReader chooses the one that least recently got its status updated, for fairness.

4.3 Localization

Visible light based indoor localization has been well-studied in recent years. Among many works, *Epsilon* [3] provides a simple but powerful way for accurate localization. We adopt *Epsilon* as a subsystem of LIGHTPARK to support indoor localization. Note that in our system, in most of the time a ViReader is sending nothing but an empty carrier signal, due to asymmetric uplink/downlink rates and Media Access Control for ViReaders. We utilize these "wasted" time frames to send location beacons.

5 PRELIMINARY RESULTS

So far, we've built a prototype with 4 parking spaces and 2 ViReaders using the original PassiveVLC hardware for concept demonstration, shown in Fig. 4. We run the prototype under different configurations and measure the average status update period for all parking spaces. The results are shown in Tab. 1.

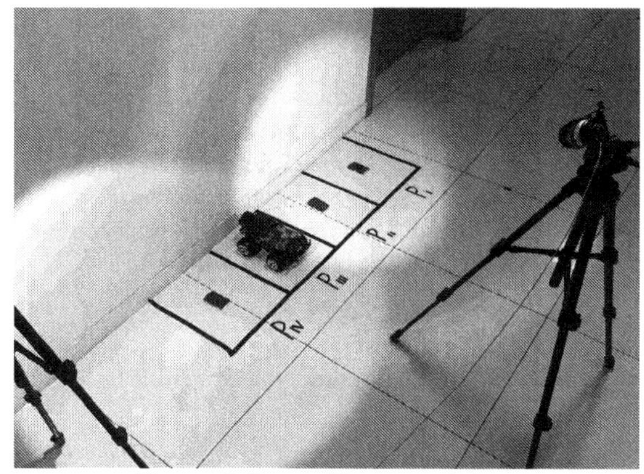

Figure 4: LIGHTPARK prototype

Configuration	Period
1 ViReader	0.45 s
2 ViReaders with interference	0.45 s
2 ViReaders without interference, each covering 2 parking spaces	0.23 s
2 ViReaders without interference, covering 1 and 3 parking spaces respectively	0.28 s

Table 1: Measurement result of average status update period under different configurations.

REFERENCES

[1] EPC Global. 2008. EPC Radio-Frequency Identity Protocols Class-1 Generation-2 UHF RFID Protocol for Communications at 860 MHz–960 MHz. *Version* 1, 0 (2008).

[2] Jiangtao Li, Angli Liu, Guobin Shen, Liqun Li, Chao Sun, and Feng Zhao. 2015. Retro-VLC: Enabling battery-free duplex visible light communication for mobile and iot applications. In *ACM HotMobile*.

[3] Liqun Li, Pan Hu, Chunyi Peng, Guobin Shen, and Feng Zhao. 2014. Epsilon: A Visible Light Based Positioning System.. In *NSDI*.

[4] Xieyang Xu, Yang Shen, Junrui Yang, Chenren Xu, Guobin Shen, Guojun Chen, and Yunzhe Ni. 2017. PassiveVLC: Enabling Practical Visible Light Backscatter Communication for Battery-free IoT Applications. In *ACM MobiCom*.

Poster: Battery-free Visible Light Sensing

Andreas Soleiman
Co-primary student author
Uppsala University
Sweden
andreas.soleiman@it.uu.se

Ambuj Varshney
Co-primary student author
Uppsala University
Sweden
ambuj.varshney@it.uu.se

Thiemo Voigt
Uppsala University and RISE SICS
Uppsala, Sweden
thiemo@sics.se

ABSTRACT

We present our efforts to design the first Visible Light Sensing (VLS) system that consumes only tens of µWs of power to sense and communicate. Our system requires no modification to the existing light infrastructure and uses unmodulated ambient light as sensing medium. We achieve this by designing a sensing mechanism that uses solar cells to achieve sub-µWs of power consumption. Further, we devise an ultra-low power backscatter based transmission mechanism we call *Scatterlight* that transmits digital readings without incurring the processing and computation overhead of existing sensors. Based on these principles we build a preliminary prototype. Our initial results demonstrate its ability to sense and communicate three hand gestures at 20 µWs of power.

KEYWORDS

Battery-free; Backscatter; Ultra-low power; Visible light sensing

1 INTRODUCTION

Visible light is a ubiquitous medium that can illuminate spaces or objects through low-cost fluorescent bulbs, light emitting diodes (LEDs) or natural light. Further, visible light can be sensed using simple and low-cost photodiodes or solar cells which requires minimal processing effort at the sensing device. Thus, visible light offers a significant advantage for sensing applications over mediums such as radio frequency (RF) signals which require complex processing and radios operating on licensed spectrum. However, despite the clear advantages there have only been limited deployments of visible light sensing (VLS) systems.

There are two main reasons for the lack of pervasive deployment of VLS systems: First, existing VLS system fail to take advantage of the ubiquitious nature of visible light. These systems combine visible light communication (VLC) together with sensing which requires retrofitting of the luminaries with specialized modulating circuits [3, 4]. This significantly increases the cost and the complexity of deployment. Second, these systems employ conventional light sensing mechanisms to sense changes in ambient light conditions [1, 3, 4]. Such mechanisms employ sensors with components that negatively affect pervasive deployment, as we discuss next.

MobiCom '17, October 16–20, 2017, Snowbird, UT, USA

ACM ISBN 978-1-4503-4916-1/17/10.
https://doi.org/10.1145/3117811.3131252

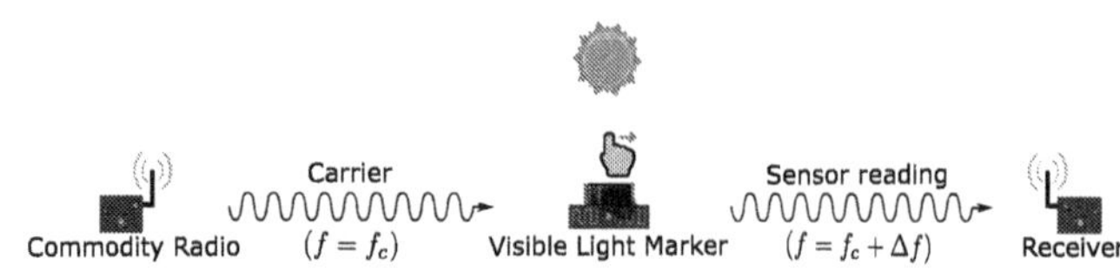

Figure 1: *Shadow sensing at* µWs *of power.* We can detect and communicate shadow events by reflecting RF signals at a peak power consumption of 20 µWs.

Conventional light sensing mechanisms amplify the signals from photodiodes using transimpedance amplifiers (TIA), sample them using analog to digital converters (ADC), and process them using computational blocks involving microcontrollers (MCU) or FPGAs. Further, the sampled values are communicated using traditional RF radios or external cables [3, 4]. This approach suffers from two main problems: *First*, it consumes significant power (mWs) and requires sensors that are battery-powered or powered through other external sources. *Second*, this approach increases the deployment cost due to increased complexity and cost of components.

We present our vision to design simple and ultra-low cost and power light sensors with the ability to sense changes in ambient light. Such sensors can operate on small amounts of energy harvested from ambient light or other harvesting sources, and transform any well-lit surface to a sensing medium. Their low cost enables deployment at a wide scale. Hence, such sensors could make VLS systems pervasive. To enable our vision, we use unmodulated light to sense shadows by building on recent systems [3, 4].

We introduce the first VLS system that can sense changes in unmodulated ambient light by tracking shadows at a power of 0.5 µWs and can communicate these events at peak power of 20 µWs. To achieve this, we make two key contributions over existing state-of-the-art systems [3, 4]: *First*, we design a mechanism that couples solar cells to a thresholding circuit to consume sub-µWs of power to sense shadow events. *Second*, we devise a mechanism we call *Scatterlight* that *offloads processing* from sensors to powerful end-devices using RF backscatter without involving energy-expensive computational blocks. This enables ultra-low power and inexpensive sensors, which we call visible light markers (VLMs).

2 DESIGN AND IMPLEMENTATION

The fundamental operation of our system is to detect and transmit changes in ambient light while consuming µWs in order to identify hand gestures. Towards this end, our system performs a series of steps: We first generate a carrier signal at a frequency of 868 MHz, and of strength 24 dBm using a TI CC1310 transceiver. Next, the VLM senses and backscatters a carrier signal to communicate the shadow events. The VLM leverages a solar cell to harvest

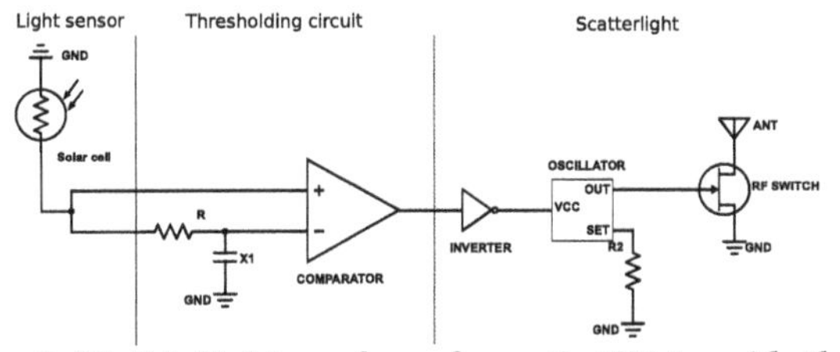

Figure 2: *Visible light marker schematic.* VLM avoids the use of energy expensive parts and local processing. VLM digitise and communicate shadow events at a power of 20 μW.

energy for its operation and to sense shadow events. The analog changes from the solar cell are digitised by an ultra-low power thresholding circuit, from which the output digital signals are mirrored onto backscattered signals by the *Scatterlight* mechanism. Finally, we receive *Scatterlight* transmissions from the VLM at the end-devices. To receive transmissions, we sample the RSSI at the transmit frequency of the VLM. As an end-device, we leverage a CC1310 transceiver.

2.1 Visible Light Marker

Solar cells as light sensors. Existing VLC-based systems commonly employ photodiodes to sense rapid changes in visible light [3, 4]. The photodiodes are coupled with a TIA to amplify the signal to a level required for further processing. The use of a TIA, however, increases the power consumption to mWs, which makes it difficult to operate on harvested energy.

To decrease the power consumption for visible-light sensing to μWs which is necessary for battery-free operation, we take advantage of solar cells to achieve the necessary amplification without energy-expensive amplifiers. Similar to photodiodes, solar cells transform variations in ambient light caused by, e.g., a shadow to a change in the electrical signal. Solar cells have been recently used to enable high-speed VLC using energy-hungry ADCs [8]. To the best of our knowledge, solar cells have not been explored for VLS.

Selecting solar cell for sensing. We evaluate six different commercial solar cells of different characteristics to select the one that is most responsive to sensing a shadow. We place a solar cell on the floor, and cast a shadow on it. We track its analog output using a logic analyser. We perform the experiment three times for each solar cell. Figure 4 demonstrates that all six solar cells observe a significant change (> 10 dB) in the signal-to-noise ratio (SNR) which confirms that solar cells can be used for passive sensing. Among the best performing solar cells, the thinfilm solar cell offers the highest short-circuit current which improves energy harvesting performance. Thus, we select the thin film (USD 4) solar cell.

Digitising at μWs of power. On existing sensing systems, processing the analog signals and converting them to the digital domain contributes significantly to the high energy consumption. Existing VLS systems use energy expensive ADCs [3, 4] to achieve this. We employ a thresholding circuit in place of commonly employed ADCs to convert changes in analog signals to binary values. A thresholding circuit, as shown in Figure 2 consists of a comparator and a low pass filter (LPF) composed of a resistor (R) and a capacitor (X1). Thresholding circuits are commonly employed in backscatter systems [5]. However, to the best of our knowledge, we are the *first* to use a thresholding circuit with a solar cell to achieve 0.5 μWs of power for VLS systems.

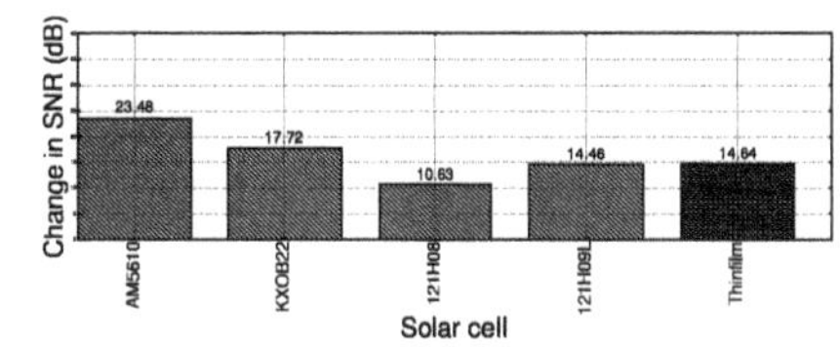

Figure 3: *Sensing using a solar cell.* A shadow cast on a solar cell causes a significant change in the SNR.

Scatterlight. A key bottleneck on existing sensors is the high energy consumption for the computational blocks involved [6, 9]. For example, existing VLS systems leverage platforms such as an Arduino to preprocess light samples, and transfer these to an end-device such as a workstation [3, 4]. We eliminate this overhead by building on the observation by Zhang et al. [9] that processing is significantly more energy expensive than backscatter transmissions. We devise a mechanism we call *Scatterlight* that causes changes in backscattered signals similar to the digital signals from the sensor without using energy-expensive computational blocks such as FPGAs or MCUs. We face two main challenges to realise this concept: *First,* the carrier adds significant interference to the weak backscatter signals. *Second,* we have to modulate the carrier signal with shadow events without using computational blocks. Next, we describe how we implement the *Scatterlight* mechanism.

We solve the first challenge by building on recent systems [2, 10] that keep the backscattered and the carrier signal at separate frequencies: If the ambient RF signal is present at a center frequency f_c, while the VLM backscatters at a frequency Δf, the backscattered signal appears at an offset Δf away from f_c. This displacement reduces interference from the carrier [2, 7, 10], and allows the receiver to detect backscattered signals. However, a crucial question is the choice of Δf, which is transceiver dependent. In this paper, we employ a transceiver that requires a Δf of 100 kHz.

To overcome the second challenge, we observe that a commodity radio transceiver enables fast RSSI sampling to determine the energy levels, e.g., due to the presence of backscatter transmissions [10]. If we can backscatter for the duration of the shadow event, the receiver by observing backscatter signals in the RSSI samples can detect the presence and the duration of the shadow event. We implement *Scatterlight* and achieve the above capability, by building on the fact that a digital signal from the thresholding circuit can directly control a backscatter switch, thus modulating the carrier with the information of the shadow event without requiring computational blocks. However, the key challenge with such a design is that backscatter signals are at the same frequency as the carrier signal which causes severe self-interference [6]. To overcome these challenges, as we illustrate in Figure 2, we instead control an ultra-low power oscillator (LTC 6906, USD 1.5) through the thresholding circuit. The oscillator controls the backscatter switch (NXP BFT25A, USD 0.2). We configure the oscillator to a frequency larger than Δf required to mitigate self-interference. Hence, when there is a shadow event, the thresholding circuit enables the oscillator to generate a backscatter signal at a frequency Δf from the center frequency f_c of the carrier signal.

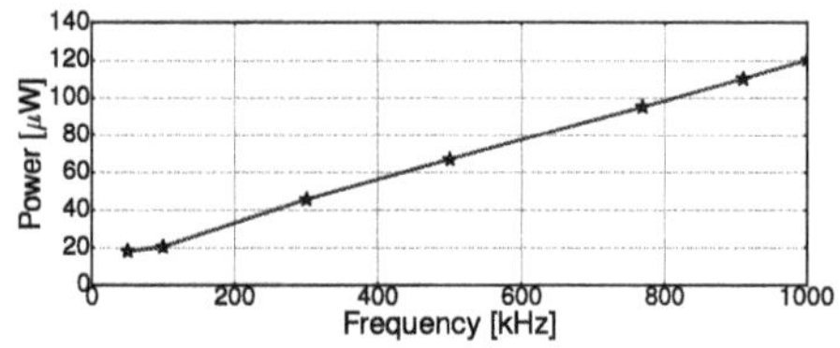

Figure 4: ***Power consumption of VLM at*** **2 V. At a 100 kHz frequency for transmission, the VLM consumes 20 μWs.**

Table 1: Power consumption breakdown of VLM at 2 V

Module	Power consumption
Solar cell	0
Thresholding circuit	0.5 μW
Scatterlight (100 kHz - 1 MHz)	19.5 μW - 120 μW

Scatterlight is similar to battery-free cellphones [6] in that it eliminates computational blocks. *Scatterlight* significantly improves the design presented by Talla et al. [6]. Their battery-free cellphones suffer severe self-interference since they backscatter on the same frequency as the carrier signal which requires extensive processing on expensive SDRs. On the other hand, *Scatterlight* frequency-shifts the backscatter transmissions away without requiring computational blocks which reduces self-interference and enables the use of inexpensive radios to receive the backscattered signals.

3 RESULTS

Experiment setup. We evaluate our system indoors under office lights which were 200 lx; a level much lower than typical indoor illumination. As an energy harvester, we use the TI BQ25570 because it can operate at very low input voltages. We use a capacitor of size 22 μF that is comparable to other energy harvesting platforms such as CRFIDs. We use a thin film solar cell for both sensing and harvesting. At the VLM, we keep track of the analog signal from the solar cell, and the output of the thresholding circuit.

Power consumption. To measure the power consumption, we first connect the VLM in series with a Fluke multimeter, then we vary the oscillator frequency. As the power consumption increases with voltage [10], we keep the voltage to the lowest level required to operate all the modules, which we found to be 2 V.

Table 1 demonstrates the power breakdown of the VLM. The thresholding circuit together with the solar cell consumes 0.5 μW of power to sense and digitise shadow events. In the presence of a shadow, the VLM enables the Scatterlight mechanism to communicate the shadow event, which increases the overall power consumption. Figure 4 shows that Scatterlight, when enabled, consumes power proportional to the backscatter frequency. The power consumption of Scatterlight varies between 19.5 μW to 120 μW when backscattering at frequencies between 100 kHz to 1 MHz. The energy harvested by the solar cell we employ is sufficient to power the VLM, even in darker light conditions (100 lx). Further, at a backscatter frequency of 100 kHz, the ultra-low-power nature of the VLM allows it to be operated on harvested energy from photodiodes [6].

Sensing and communicating gestures. We investigate the ability of our system to detect hand gestures. In this preliminary work, we focus on three gestures: swipe, two taps and four taps, which we illustrate in Figure 5. We perform the experiment indoors, and

Figure 5: *Supported hand gestures.* We support three hand gestures: Swipe is represented by a single and brief hand movement, Two and four taps are represented by fixed number of slower palm movements.

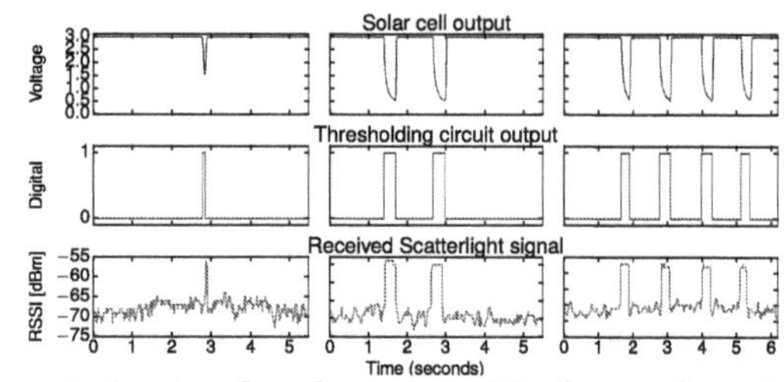

Figure 6: *Sensing hand gestures.* We detect three hand gestures (Swipe, Two taps, Four taps) at 20 μWs of power. The top two rows shows output at the VLM, the bottom row shows received signal at the end-device.

locate the carrier generator approx. 20 m from the VLM. The carrier generator is not in line-of-sight. We place the VLM at a distance of 1 m from the receiver, a typical distance for transmissions from smart clothes to a wearable device.

To conduct the experiment, we perform hand gestures over the VLM's solar cell. We track the digital and analog signal from the VLM, and also sample the RSSI at the RF receiver at an interval of 10 ms. Figure 6 shows the result of the experiment. The figure shows that each gesture causes unique patterns in the ambient light, as also observed by Kaholokula et al. [1]. However, unlike their design we use our energy efficient thresholding circuit to digitise shadow events, and communicate them at μWs of power. Figure 6 shows the distinct patterns caused by the gestures in the received RSSI samples at the CC1310 RF receiver.

4 ACKNOWLEDGEMENTS

This work has been funded by the Swedish Energy Agency (Energimyndigheten).

REFERENCES

[1] M Kaholokula. 2016. Reusing Ambient Light to Recognize Hand Gestures. Dartmouth college. (2016).
[2] Bryce Kellogg et al. Passive wi-fi: Bringing low power to wi-fi transmissions. In *USENIX NSDI 2016.*
[3] Tianxing Li et al. Human Sensing Using Visible Light Communication. In *ACM MOBICOM 2015.*
[4] Tianxing Li et al. Practical Human Sensing in the Light. In *ACM MOBISYS 2016.*
[5] Vincent Liu et al. Ambient Backscatter: Wireless Communication out of Thin Air. In *ACM SIGCOMM 2013.*
[6] Vamsi Talla et al. 2017. Battery-Free Cellphone. *Proc. ACM Interact. Mob. Wearable Ubiquitous Technol.* (2017).
[7] Ambuj Varshney et al. 2017. LoRea: A Backscatter Architecture that achieves a long communication range. In *ACM SenSys 2017.*
[8] Zixiong Wang et al. 2015. On the design of a solar-panel receiver for optical wireless communications with simultaneous energy harvesting. *IEEE JSAC 2015* (2015).
[9] Pengyu Zhang et al. Ekhonet: High speed ultra low-power backscatter for next generation sensors. In *ACM MOBICOM 2014.*
[10] Pengyu Zhang et al. Enabling practical backscatter communication for on-body sensors. In *ACM SIGCOMM 2016.*

Poster: Improving Multipath Resolution with MIMO Smoothing

Elahe Soltanaghaei
University of Virginia
Charlottesville, VA
es3ce@virginia.edu

Avinash Kalyanaraman
University of Virginia
Charlottesville, VA
ak3ka@virginia.edu

Kamin Whitehouse
University of Virginia
Charlottesville, VA
whitehouse@virginia.edu

ABSTRACT

Super-resolution subspace methods are popular in estimating multipath parameters such as angle of arrival and time of flight. However, they require decorrelation techniques to resolve coherent multipath components. The conventional decorrelation techniques reduce the effective aperture of the MIMO array, thus reducing the resolution and number of resolved paths. In this paper, we introduce *MIMO smoothing* as a new technique to bring decorrelation effect by leveraging the spacial and frequential diversity in MIMO transmitters and receivers. Via extensive experiments on WiFi links, we show that MIMO smoothing can increase the accuracy of multipath resolution.

KEYWORDS

MIMO smoothing, CSI, Multipath resolution, Spatial diversity

ACM Reference format:
Elahe Soltanaghaei, Avinash Kalyanaraman, and Kamin Whitehouse. 2017. Poster: Improving Multipath Resolution with MIMO Smoothing. In *Proceedings of MobiCom'17, October 16–20, 2017, Snowbird, UT, USA.*, , 3 pages.
https://doi.org/10.1145/3117811.3131244

1 INTRODUCTION

In wireless communications, signals from a transmitter arrive at the receiver in multiple paths after reflecting off the objects in the physical environment. Each of these paths have their own specifications which could be characterized by the Angle-of-Arrival (AoA), Angle-of-Departure (AoD), path delay or Time-of-Flight (ToF), and fading (shown in Figure 1). Many techniques have been proposed for estimating AoA in a MIMO array such as super-resolution subspace methods [4]. However, they assume that the received reflections are from different targets, thus uncorrelated with each other; while the wireless multipath reflections in indoor environments are emitted from a single source, thus phase-synchronized and highly correlated.

To address this issue, some signal processing methods such as spatial smoothing [5, 9] and forward-backward averaging [3] are proposed to decorrelate the multipath signals. However, they decrease the array aperture and the degree of freedom, resulting in lower accuracy and fewer number of resolved paths. Recent works try to overcome these limitations by developing joint estimation in both ToF and AoA dimensions [2, 8], but they still suffer from reduced effective aperture. In this paper, we propose a new smoothing algorithm called *MIMO Smoothing*, which leverages the recent advances in wireless techniques such as *MIMO-OFDM* to improve the accuracy of multipath estimation. MIMO arrays employ multiple transmitting antennas for emitting multiple data streams, and multiple receiving antennas for separating these signals. This results in spatial diversity both in transmitting and receiving antenna arrays. In addition, OFDM as a modulation format has been widely used in wireless communication for encoding data streams on multiple carrier frequencies, which provides frequential diversity due to multipath selective fading. MIMO smoothing combines the frequential and spatial diversity to accurately decorrelate coherent signals, without decreasing the effective aperture.

The basic idea in MIMO smoothing is that the signals transmitted from any of the transmitting antennas will be incident in any of the receiving antennas, provided they are in far field. However, each propagation path has to travel an additional distance if transmitted from the second antenna, introducing a constant phase shift on the received signal. Therefore, the propagation paths received from multiple transmitting antennas have similar steering vectors, while the superimposed received signals across receiving antennas are linearly independent. This is due to different phase shifts associated with multipath components from the transmitting antennas to the receiving antennas. As a result, the transmitting antennas could be successfully used to decorrelate the received signals and vice versa, which are explained in details in the next section.

To evaluate MIMO smoothing, we leverage the PHY layer Channel State Information (CSI) provided in off-the-shelf WiFi cards. The CSI values include the phase and amplitude shifts due to channel for multiple transmitting and receiving antennas at the granularity of OFDM subcarriers. We evaluate MIMO smoothing with 90 experiments in a large smart home lab with different link conditions. Our extensive analyses show that MIMO smoothing achieves higher

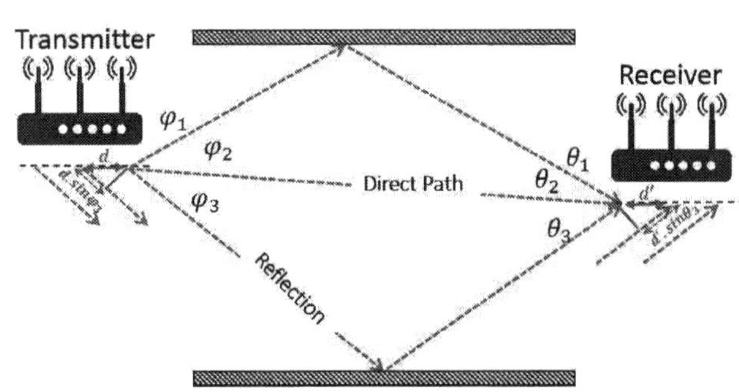

Figure 1: An illustration of multipath propagation in an indoor environment

MobiCom'17, , October 16–20, 2017, Snowbird, UT, USA.

ACM ISBN 978-1-4503-4916-1/17/10.
https://doi.org/10.1145/3117811.3131244

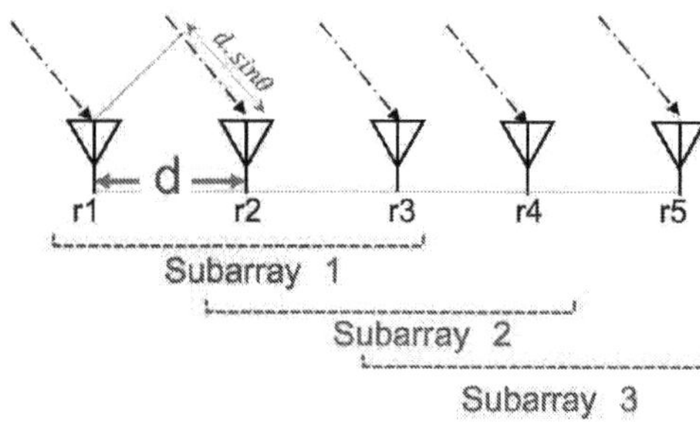

Figure 2: The Conventional spacial smoothing approach reduces the array aperture length and degree of freedom

$$\begin{bmatrix} x_{1,1} & x_{1,2} \\ x_{2,1} & x_{2,2} \\ x_{3,1} & x_{3,2} \end{bmatrix} = \begin{bmatrix} 1 & 1 \\ \phi_{\theta_1} & \phi_{\theta_2} \\ \phi^2_{\theta_1} & \phi^2_{\theta_2} \end{bmatrix} \begin{bmatrix} \alpha_1 & \alpha_1\Gamma_{\varphi_1} \\ \alpha_2 & \alpha_2\Gamma_{\varphi_2} \end{bmatrix}$$

Measurements at the two transmit virtual arrays — Same Steering Vector — Linearly Independent Gains

Figure 3: The transmit virtual subarrays share the same steering vector but linearly independent gains.

multipath resolution by achieving an average improvement of 6.9 degree in estimating AoA of the direct path between transmitters and receivers. In addition, its larger effective aperture resolves more paths compared to conventional sub-space methods.

2 METHODOLOGY

The super-resolution sub-space methods such as MUSIC [4] resolve multipath components by relying on extra phase shifts across sensor arrays due to additional travel distance. The introduced phase shift is a function of AoA and could be expressed as

$$\Phi(\theta_l) = e^{-j2\pi f d \sin(\theta_l)/c} \tag{1}$$

for l^{th} path due to AoA of θ_l, where d is the distance between antennas, c is the speed of light, and f is the frequency of the transmitted signal. Therefore, the received channel response X at the receiving antenna array can be expressed as

$$X(t) = [x_1(t), ..., x_M(t)]^T = a(\theta)s(t) + N(t) \tag{2}$$

where M is the number of receiving antennas, $s(t)$ is the received signal vector at the first antenna and $N(t)$ is the noise vector. $a(\theta)$ is called the steering vector and expresses the phase differences at the antenna array:

$$a(\theta) = [1, \phi(\theta), ..., \phi(\theta)^{M-1}]^T \tag{3}$$

The MUSIC algorithm calculates the eigenvectors of XX^H, and divides them into noise and signal subspace. Then, it searches for the AoAs whose steering vectors are orthogonal to the noise subspace. This method assumes that the incoming signals are from different sources and are uncorrelated with each other. However, the multipath signals are phased-synchronized, thus resulting in a reduction in the rank of the covariance matrix and superposition of coherent signals in the output of MUSIC. Therefore, a preprocessing scheme such as spatial smoothing [5] is required to convert the covariance matrix into a full rank matrix[5, 9]. In spatial smoothing, the receive antenna array is divided into a number of smaller overlapping sub-arrays as shown in Figure 2. Then, the covariance matrices of all sub-arrays are averaged. However, this smoothing method reduces the aperture of the sensor array from M to $M-r+1$, where $r = L + 1$ is the size of sub-arrays and L is the number of coherent paths.

To address this problem, we leverage the presence of multiple transmit and receive antennas in MIMO systems. The idea is that the incoming signals from different transmitting antennas can define the virtual subarrays required in spatial smoothing. The intuition behind this idea is that the signals emitted from a linear transmit array will be received with a phase shift $\Gamma(\varphi)$, which is a function of AoD

$$\Gamma(\varphi_l) = e^{-j2\pi f d \sin(\varphi_l)/c} \tag{4}$$

where φ_l is the AoD of the lth path. Since each received signal from different transmitting antennas has its own AoD, the virtual subarrays are linearly independent, thus increasing the rank of the covariance matrix. A MIMO radar with M receiving and N transmitting antennas can resolve $L = min(M, N)$ coherent paths using MIMO smoothing, while the effective aperture of the sensor array remains M. For more clarity, let's consider an example, where $L = 2$, $M = 3$, and $N = 2$. As shown in Figure 3, $x_{i,j}$ shows the received signal at antenna i from transmitting antenna j. The measurements of the two virtual transmit subarrays can be written as a linear combination of the same steering vectors, but with linearly independent complex gains due to AoD phase shift. Therefore, we can successfully apply MUSIC on the averaged covariance matrix of multiple transmitting antennas, while increasing the rank of the coveranice matrix.

We further improve the multipath resolution, by combining MIMO smoothing with joint estimation of multipath characteristics. The current WiFi standards such as 802.11 leverage MIMO-OFDM technology, in which data streams are transmitted over multiple antennas and multiple subcarriers. Therefore, instead of just estimating AoA of each propagation path, we can jointly estimate AoA and ToF while applying MIMO smoothing. For two consecutive OFDM subcarriers, the lth path with ToF τ_l introduces a phase shift as bellow

$$\Omega(\tau_l) = e^{-j2\pi f_\delta \tau_l} \tag{5}$$

where f_δ is the frequency difference between two consecutive subcarriers. It should be noted that AoA and AoD do not introduce any phase shift across subcarriers because of the small frequency differences. However, we can measure the phase shifts across subcarriers based on ToF (because of the absence of speed of light factor in the denominator). Considering the sensor array as all subcarriers in all receiving antennas, the new steering vector per transmitting antenna is formed by phase shifts due to AoA and ToF as

$$\begin{aligned} a(\theta, \tau) = [1..\Omega^{K-1}(\tau), \Phi(\theta), ..., \Omega^{K-1}(\tau)\Phi(\theta), ..., \\ \Phi^{M-1}(\theta), ..., \Omega^{K-1}\Phi^{M-1}(\theta)] \end{aligned} \tag{6}$$

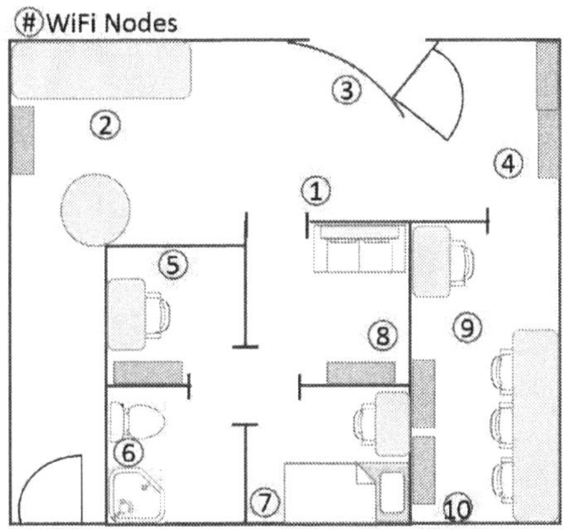

Figure 4: Floor plan and the experimental setup

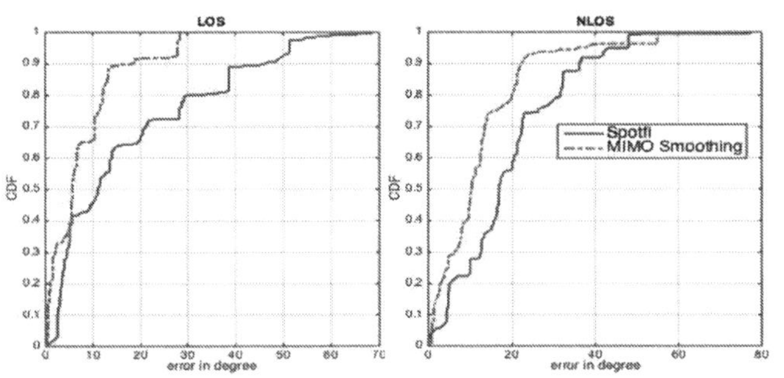

Figure 5: MIMO smoothing achieves an average improvement of 6.9 degree over SpotFi in AoA estimation

where M is the number of receiving antennas and K is the number of subcarriers. The new steering vector is of dimension $(MK) \times L$, and the measurement matrix X is of dimension $(MK) \times PN$, where P is the number of samples and N is the number of transmitting antennas. It should be noted that the MIMO smoothing could be applied for AoD-ToF estimation by defining virtual sub-arrays from receiving antennas.

3 PRELIMINARY RESULTS

Current commercial WiFi cards report the overall phase and amplitude shifts of the wireless channel as Channel State Information (CSI) for each subcarrier of each (tx-rx) antenna pair. Therefore, to evaluate MIMO smoothing, we use 10 mini-PCs that are equipped with Intel 5300 cards, CSI tool [1], and 3 antennas. Each of these nodes can work in transmitting or receiving modes. We conducted a round robin experiment in a smart home lab as shown in figure 4, where in each round one node is transmitting and the other nine nodes are receiving. The experiments are performed in the 5GHz frequency band by employing a 40MHz channel. The measured vector is of size 90×60 (or $(3 \times 30) \times (3 \times 20)$), for 3 tx and 3 rx antennas, 30 subcarriers, and 20 samples. Since we only have ground truth AoA for the direct path between the transmitter and receivers, we measure the accuracy of the AoA estimation as the minimum difference of the ground truth value and estimated AoAs. Figure 5 shows

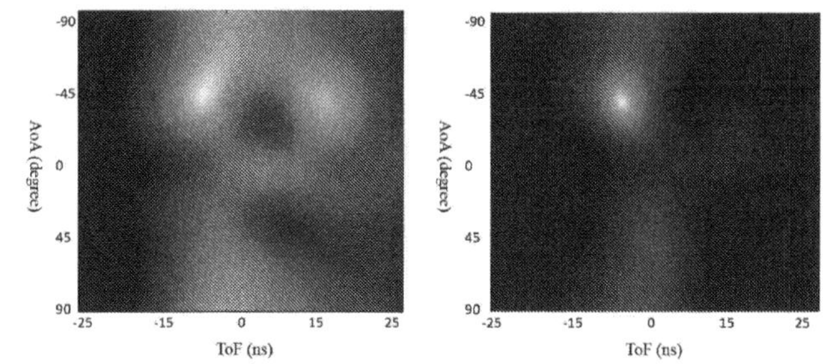

Figure 6: MIMO Smoothing (Left) can resolve more paths compared to SpotFi (Right)

the CDFs for AoA estimation error and compare MIMO smoothing with SpotFi which introduces a 2D smoothing for AoA-ToF estimation. In line-of-sight (LoS) cases, MIMO smoothing achieves median AoA accuracy of 7.1 degrees better than that achieved by SpotFi. In non-line of sight (NLoS) scenarios, we achieve an improvement of 6.8 degree in direct path AoA errors.

We further improve MIMO smoothing by combining it with SpotFi to define virtual arrays both from transmitting antennas and subcarriers, which results in a 45x48 matrix (or $(15 \times 3) \times (16 \times 3)$). Please refer to SpotFi paper [2] for more details. Our empirical analyses show that MIMO Smoothing can resolve more paths as shown in Figure 6. The higher resolution in addition to more accurate estimations provides the opportunity of using Wireless signals and commodity WiFi devices for reliable presence sensing [6, 7] and precise localization of people/robots in the physical environment even if the reflected signals from human body is so weak. However, to quantify the performance of MIMO smoothing in resolving more multipaths, the groundtruth of reflected paths are required which is not accessible with current techniques. In our future work, we address this requirement using synthetic data, and chamber analysis.

REFERENCES

[1] D. Halperin, W. Hu, A. Sheth, and D. Wetherall. Predictable 802.11 packet delivery from wireless channel measurements. In *ACM SIGCOMM Computer Communication Review*, volume 40, pages 159–170. ACM, 2010.
[2] M. Kotaru, K. Joshi, D. Bharadia, and S. Katti. Spotfi: Decimeter level localization using wifi. In *ACM SIGCOMM Computer Communication Review*, volume 45, pages 269–282. ACM, 2015.
[3] S. U. Pillai and B. H. Kwon. Forward/backward spatial smoothing techniques for coherent signal identification. *IEEE Transactions on Acoustics, Speech, and Signal Processing*, 37(1):8–15, 1989.
[4] R. Schmidt. Multiple emitter location and signal parameter estimation. *IEEE transactions on antennas and propagation*, 34(3):276–280, 1986.
[5] T.-J. Shan, M. Wax, and T. Kailath. On spatial smoothing for direction-of-arrival estimation of coherent signals. *IEEE Transactions on Acoustics, Speech, and Signal Processing*, 33(4):806–811, 1985.
[6] E. Soltanaghaei, A. Kalyanaraman, and K. Whitehouse. Occupancy state detection using wifi signals. In *Proceedings of the 15th Annual International Conference on Mobile Systems, Applications, and Services*, pages 161–161. ACM, 2017.
[7] E. Soltanaghaei, A. Kalyanaraman, and K. Whitehouse. Peripheral wifi vision: Exploiting multipath reflections for more sensitive human sensing. In *Proceedings of the 4th International on Workshop on Physical Analytics*, pages 13–18, 2017.
[8] M. C. Vanderveen, C. B. Papadias, and A. Paulraj. Joint angle and delay estimation (jade) for multipath signals arriving at an antenna array. *IEEE Communications letters*, 1(1):12–14, 1997.
[9] J. Xiong and K. Jamieson. Arraytrack: A fine-grained indoor location system. Usenix, 2013.

Poster: Combating Multipaths to Enable RFID Sensing in Practical Environments

Ge Wang†, Chen Qian*, Jinsong Han†, Haofan Cai*
†Xi'an Jiaotong University, China, * University of California Santa Cruz, California, USA
[gewang.cs,hanjinsong]@gmail.com,[cqian12,hcai10]@ucsc.edu

ABSTRACT

There have been increasing interests in exploring the sensing capabilities of RFID beyond its basic identification task, to reveal more information of tagged objects and the physical world. Phase is a crucial physical feature for many RFID sensing applications, such as tag localization. Most existing methods rely on a low multipath environment for accurate phase measurement. Unfortunately, practical environments are highly likely to be multipath-prevalent, especially for indoors. This paper presents the first work to extract "clean" phase measurement of RFID tags in multipath-prevalent environments. We propose CPEX (Clean Phase EXtraction) based on theoretical modeling, which is also validated via experimental results of our prototype implementation. We studied the performance of CPEX on tag localization. CPEX can achieve median errors of 4.3~6.4cm (in different setups), which is **the most accurate 3D tag localization result** in multipath-prevalent environments.

1 INTRODUCTION

As a cost- and energy-efficient solution for the Internet of Things, Radio Frequency IDentification (RFID) technology has been widely used to connect tagged objects to computer networks in ubiquitous applications, such as retailing, warehouse, transportation, and manufactures. Beside its basic identification task, recent research has discovered the sensing capability of RFID that reflects the relationship and information of a physical world to tags. Typical applications of RFID sensing include localization, human activity detection, and trajectory tracking. The majority of these applications rely on the measurement of the phase difference from the reader to tags (we use "phase" hereafter). Phase can help to derive the distance and angle of arrival (AoA) from the reader antennas to a tag and hence localize the tag [2]. A successive collection of phases from a mobile tag can help to determine the moving trajectory of the tagged object [6][7][4][8]. Phases have also been used for human activity sensing.

For all applications mentioned above, accurate measurement of *the phase from the line-of-sight backscatter signal* is a must for the correct operations of these applications. It is because only the line-of-sight phase difference can reflect the actual distance and relative location changes from a tag to the reader. We call the line-of-sight signal phase as the *clean phase*. Unfortunately in most practical RFID setups, signals may be reflected by various reflectors in the environment [5], including walls, furniture, and moving persons. We consider these environments as *multipath-prevalent* environments. The multiple reflected copies will combine at a reader antenna and result in phase measurement extremely different from the clean phase. Existing RFID sensing applications either assume low-multipath environments and no moving persons[6][2][7][4], or apply the following two approaches. 1) Collecting plenties of training data in the area of deployment to model the multipath [8]. This type of methods only considers the static reflectors but obviously does not work when moving persons exist. 2) Using special hardware including Software-Defined Radio (SDR) [5], moving antennas [5][3], and robots [3]. This type of methods increases the device cost significantly.

We propose CPEX for **C**lean **P**hase **EX**traction in multipath-prevalent environments. To our knowledge, CPEX is the first work of computing clean phases in the presence of rich multipath. The theoretical basis of CPEX is to find out the inner relationship among the measured phases of the multiple channels of the reader, and evaluate the impact of multipath signals in the received phase data. CPEX does not need extra hardware besides Commodity Off-The-Shelf (COTS) RFID readers and tags. It is fully compatible to standard RFID protocols [1]. We evaluate the performance of CPEX on tag localization. CPEX can achieve median errors of 4.3~6.4cm (in different setups), which is **the most accurate 3D tag localization result** in multipath-prevalent environments. The accuracy is also comparable to those in low-multipath lab environments by recent methods (some of them only apply to 2D) [2][7][4].

2 CPEX DESIGN

A passive RFID tag responses to a reader interrogation message by backscattering the electric waves generated by the reader. The received phase of a tag will change over the travel distance in a cycle of 2π. In addition to the rotation over distance (θ_D), the antenna's circuits (θ_A) and the tag's *reflection characteristic* (θ_T) will also introduce some additional rotations to the phase, *i.e.*:

$$\theta = (\theta_D + \theta_A + \theta_T) \ mod \ 2\pi \tag{1}$$

Besides the frequency and travel distance, in practice the measured phase is also determined by other external factors, such as multipath reflections. We perform three experiments

MobiCom '17, October 16–20, 2017, Snowbird, UT, USA

ACM ISBN 978-1-4503-4916-1/17/10.
https://doi.org/10.1145/3117811.3131258

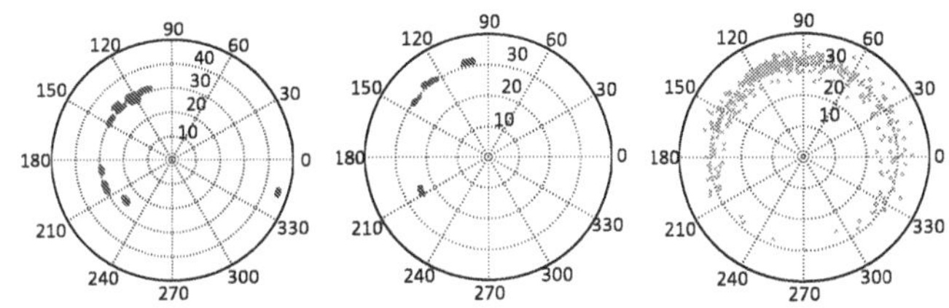

(a) Different static environments (b) Different reader antennas (c) With moving persons

Figure 1: Phase variation with different factors

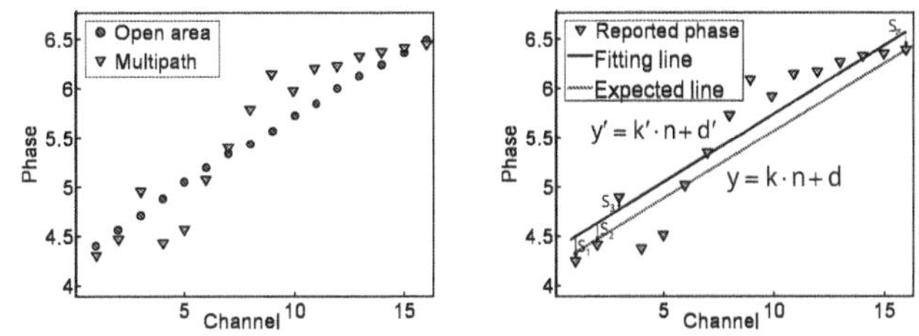

(a) The reported phases in two cases (b) The fitting line

Figure 2: The received phases in 16 channels

for validate that multipath reflections will make the measured phase completely unpredictable and deviated from the clean phase. As shown in Fig. 1(a), the received phase of the same tag will change according to its position (surrounding environments), different readers and moving objects. In most situations, we only need the "clean" phase, *i.e.*, θ in Eq. 1, which is purely determined by the line-of-sight signal.

To solve this problem, we present CPEX. In this section, we will introduce the design of CPEX.

We first make a conjecture that the received phase β_n in channel n can be expressed as:

$$\beta_n = \alpha_n + \theta + (n-1)\cdot\Delta\theta \qquad (2)$$

where θ refers to the received phase in the first channel. And α_n, $(n = 1, 2, 3, ..., N)$ is the multipath variable in each channel n ($N = 16$ for the commercial reader we use). When the channel is switched from n to $n+1$, the received phase increases $\Delta\theta$. Due to the change of frequency, the wavelength λ varies. Hence the received signal over a same distance will incur a phase change of $\Delta\theta_D$. In addition, the initial phases of the antenna and tag will change by $\Delta\theta_A$ and $\Delta\theta_T$, respectively. Therefore the phase difference $\Delta\theta$ is composed of three parts, including $\Delta\theta_D$, $\Delta\theta_A$, and $\Delta\theta_T$.

In this way, the reported phase β in each channel can be denoted as follows:

$$\begin{cases} \alpha_1 + \theta + 0\cdot\Delta\theta = \beta_1 \\ \alpha_2 + \theta + 1\cdot\Delta\theta = \beta_2 \\ \alpha_3 + \theta + 2\cdot\Delta\theta = \beta_3 \\ \dots \\ \alpha_N + \theta + (N-1)\cdot\Delta\theta = \beta_N \end{cases} \qquad (3)$$

Eq. 3 has $N+2$ unknown variables$(\alpha_1, \alpha_2, \alpha_3, ...\alpha_N, \theta, \Delta\theta)$ and N equations. So we should find out two more additional equations to solve the exact values of these unknown variables. Observing this equations, we find that if there is completely no multipath effects in the environments, *i.e.*, $\alpha_n = 0$, the received phases are exactly on a straight line y, which has a rake rate k and the intercept d as follows.

$$y = k\cdot n + d, where\ k = \Delta\theta, d = \theta - \Delta\theta \qquad (4)$$

To validate the conjecture, we collect the phase in all the 16 channels in both an open area and a narrow space. As shown in Fig. 2(a), the reported phases in the open area (the blue circles) indeed follow linear relationship, which is consistent to our conjecture. On the other hand, in a narrow space the multipath effect becomes severe. As a results, the phase fluctuates sharply from channel 1 to 16, as outlined by the orange triangles in Fig.2(a). We find that if we obtain the parameters of y, we can solve the "clean" phase θ ($\theta = k+d$). We call this the line y as an expected one. To calculate the parameters k and d, we try to fit the received phases in all the channels into a straight line y' with least square method. We find that the rake rate k' and the intercept d' of the fitting line y', both have differences with our expected parameters, *i.e.* k and d (as shown in Fig. 2(b)). Note that, we can obtain the values of k' and d' by fitting these received phases. However, we do not know the exact differences between k and k', or d and d'. If we can calculate the differences between them, we would know the parameters (both k and d) of the expected line y.

To reach this goal, we should find out two more additional equations according to the fitting line to solve the polynomial in Eq. 3. After our analysing and calculations (omit here), we find out two more equations as follows:

$$\begin{cases} k = \Delta\hat{\theta} + e_1 \\ (y_i + y_{N+1-i}) - \frac{\sum_{n=1}^{N} S_n}{N} = \theta + (n-1)\cdot\Delta\theta + \overline{\alpha_n}, \end{cases} \qquad (5)$$

where e_1 is the difference between k and k'. It can be denoted by the unknown variables in Eq. 3. And S_n represents the gap between the fitting line and the reported phase β_n. In this way, we can calculate the value of the mirror image phase $\hat{\theta}$ and obtain the solution of the clean phase θ.

3 IMPLEMENTATION

The CPEX prototype includes the basic components of a typical passive RFID system: an RFID reader, multiple directional antennas, a set of tags, and a server. In specific, we use an ImpinJ Speedway R420 RFID reader, four Laird S9028PCL directional antennas, and two types of mainstream UHF passive RFID tags: ImpinJ E41C and Alien 964X. The R420 reader operates at the UHF frequency band (920.625 $\sim$ 924.375 MHz) and is able to hop over 16 channels. The gaps between two adjacent channels are the same, *i.e.*, 0.25 MHZ.

In our evaluation, we collect two sets of phase data. One set of data are processed by CPEX and the other are from the COTS RFID reader's API, denoted as **CPEX phase** and **raw phase**, respectively. We then use the data as the

Table 1: Comparison of state-of-the-art RFID localization schemes

Localization works	Environment	People Moving	Dimension	Median error
PinIt (SIGCOMM'13) [5]	Multipath-prevalent	Mobility	Three	11cm
MobiTagbot (MobiSys'16) [3]	Multipath-prevalent	Mobility	Two	3.4cm
STPP (NSDI'15) [4]	Low multipath	Non-mobility	Two	8.6cm
RF-IDraw (SIGCOMM'14) [6]	Low multipath	Non-mobility	Three	3.7cm
Tagoram (MobiCom'14) [7]	Low multipath	Non-mobility	Two	5.6cm
BackPos (INFOCOM'14) [2]	Low multipath	Non-mobility	Two	12.8cm
CPEX (This work)	Multipath-prevalent	Mobility	Three	4.3∼6.4cm

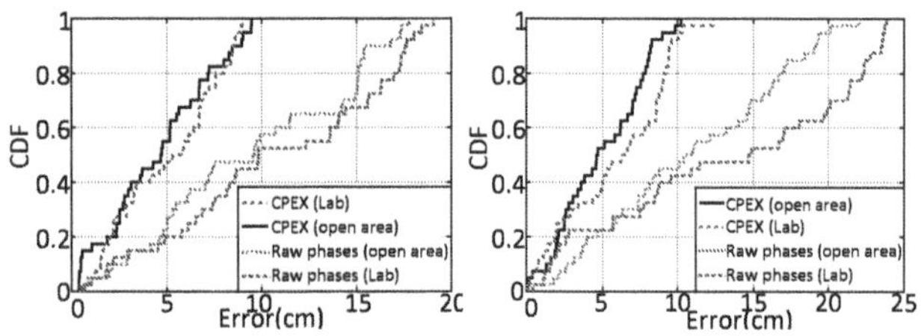

(a) no person walking around (b) 1 person walking around

Figure 3: CDF curve of CPEX and raw data

input in tag localization and evaluate the effectiveness and accuracy of CPEX.

4 CPEX EVALUATION

The most common RFID sensing application in which phase can be utilized is tag localization. To simulate the practical environments, we conduct experiments in two different scenes, *i.e.*, **open area** and **laboratory**. We deploy 10 passive R-FID tags in the two environments, respectively. In particular, all 10 tags are placed in different positions. In both environments, multipath reflection exists and could be a critical factor that impacts the localization accuracy. Intuitively, the laboratory environment is considered to include more multipath reflectors than the open area. In our experiment, four antennas form a square and work together. In each environment, we conduct two sets of experiments. One is without moving objects and another is having one volunteer keeping walking arbitrarily in the area. The walking speed is 1∼2m/s. We call these two setups as **non-mobility/mobility**. We evaluate the localization error using the CPEX phase and raw phase data. We choose the Hyperbola-based Localization (HL) method, which has been widely employed in tag localization approaches [6][2].

As shown in Fig. 3, we show the localization errors of HL when using the CPEX phase and raw phase data, respectively. As the figure shows, using the CPEX phases in the open area, the median localization error is 4.70cm (non-mobility) and 4.65cm (mobility), respectively, while the error of using raw phase are 9.57cm and 10.73cm. And CPEX improves the localization accuracy in the laboratory environment even more significantly. The median localization error becomes 5.58cm (non-mobility) and 6.39cm (mobility), which are much smaller than those when using the raw phase data (9.82cm and 14.79cm). Both the worst-case and median errors are reduced by more than 50%. Note the this error is **the smallest tag localization error in the literature** for 3D multipath-prevalent environments using COTS RFID devices.

We also compare the CPEX-enabled HL with some state-of-arts localization schemes, including PinIt [5], RF-IDraw [6], Tagoram [7], STPP [4], BackPos [2], and MobiTagbot [3]. Note some of them are not generalized solutions and may only be applied to certain applications. As shown in Tab. 1, most of those methods operate with low multipath environments. Obviously, CPEX based localization does not need any extra hardware deployment or training procedure and works well in multipath-prevalent environments.

5 ACKNOWLEDGMENT

This work was supported in part by National Basic Research Program of China (973 Program) under Grant No. 2015CB351705, NSFC Grant No.61190112, 61325013, 61572396, 61402359, China 863 Grant 2013AA014601, and National Science and Technology Major Project of the Ministry of Science and Technology of China JZ-20150910. Chen Qian is supported by National Science Foundation grants CNS-1701681 and CNS-1717948. We thank the valuable comments from anonymous reviewers.

REFERENCES

[1] EPCglobal. 2005. *EPC^{TM}* radio-frequency identity protocols class-1 generation-2 UHF RFID protocol for communications at 860 MHz–960 MHz. (2005).

[2] Tianci Liu, Lei Yang, Qiongzheng Lin, Yi Guo, and Yunhao Liu. 2014. Anchor-free backscatter positioning for RFID tags with high accuracy. In *Proceedings of IEEE INFOCOM.*

[3] Longfei Shangguan and Kyle Jamieson. 2016. The design and implementation of a mobile RFID tag sorting robot. In *Proceedings of ACM MobiSys.*

[4] Longfei Shangguan, Zheng Yang, Alex X. Liu, Zimu Zhou, and Yunhao Liu. 2015. Relative localization of RFID tags using spatial-temporal phase profiling. In *Proceedings of USENIX NSDI.*

[5] Jue Wang and Dina Katabi. 2013. Dude, where's my card?: RFID positioning that works with multipath and non-line of sight. In *Proceedings of ACM SIGCOMM.*

[6] Jue Wang, Deepak Vasisht, and Dina Katabi. 2014. RF-IDraw: Virtual touch screen in the air using RF signals. In *Proceedings of ACM SIGCOMM.*

[7] Lei Yang, Yekui Chen, XiangYang Li, Chaowei Xiao, Mo Li, and Yunhao Liu. 2014. Tagoram: Real-time tracking of mobile RFID tags to high precision using COTS devices. In *Proceedings of ACM MOBICOM.*

[8] Lei Yang, Qiongzheng Lin, Xiangyang Li, Tianci Liu, and Yunhao Liu. 2015. See through walls with COTS RFID system!. In *Proceedings of ACM MOBICOM.*

Poster–EasyApp: A Widget-based Cross-platform Mobile Development Environment for End-users

Zhaoning Wang, Bo Cheng, Ying Jin, Yimeng Feng, Junliang Chen
State Key Laboratory of Networking and Switching Technology
Beijing University of Posts and Telecommunications
asimoo@bupt.edu.cn,chengbo@bupt.edu.cn

ABSTRACT

The rapid development of mobile internet attracts end-users to creating mobile applications. Traditional development process cannot meet their needs. In this paper, we present a cross-platform mobile development environment, EasyApp. It provides a highly-integrated, UI-friendly and easily-operating environment. The architecture of this environment is based on OSGi framework. Users could create mobile applications with draggable widgets and package applications for multiple platforms. Native APIs could be invoked with native API plugins.

CCS CONCEPTS

• **Human-centered computing → Mobile computing**; • **Software and its engineering → Integrated and visual development environments**;

KEYWORDS

Mobile application; end-users development; widgets; OSGi

1 INTRODUCTION

The trend of mobile internet rapidly developing has inspired plenty of developers devoting to mobile developing. However, not only the professional developers have ideas about mobile applications, but many ordinary users and UI designers (called end-user) intend to create their own products. Traditional development process exists following problems:

- It demands professional development skills which most end-users don't have. End-users need a specific environment which could achieve their ideas immediately.
- It relies on the developing tools providing by officials which only supports single platform. Different platform follows completely different developing logic and techniques. End-users need an integrated environment.

Several research results or products aiming at end-users have been released. Mobimash [3] and MIT App Inventor [6] are typical two of them. Mobimash is an end-user development environment for the construction of mobile mashups. Users can create mobile application schema with light-weight visual template. This tool only provides designing environment and the final products could not directly transfer to actual applications. As for MIT App Inventor, It provides users an online visual designing environment with draggable components of Android applications and a logic editor is available to design the service logic. However, some problems still remain to solve. Firstly, only native components of Android SDK can be used in the visual designer and no components extending interface is provided, so there is not much personal customization for individual user. Secondly, the designer only supports Android applications developing. Other popular platform, such as iOS, which demands completely different SDK and developing framework, is not supported. Thirdly, the developing process is still not that simple.

Given these facts, we propose a widget-based cross-platform mobile application development environment in this paper, EasyApp. We implemented a WYSIWYG (What You See Is What You Get) visual editor based on draggable widgets. End-users could assemble their mobile applications with draggable widgets. The creation of application employs the web techniques following W3C standard which bridge the gap between different platform cooperating with middleware. This environment integrates build tools for iOS and Android platform (more platforms will be supported in the future.) which could help end-users create package with one-click button after designing. This environment provides several essential tools during development process. End-users could quickly start to design a mobile application using widget with multiple functions and build an installing package for major mobile platforms.

2 WIDGET-BASED MOBILE DEVELOPMENT ENVIRONMENT

Figure 1 shows the developing process of EasyApp. Firstly, choose widgets and native UI plugins to design the functions of applications. Widgets are basic components. Available widgets include basic UI components, Google and Baidu map, multiple charts, etc. Widgets are extensible and following the unified standard, which will be presented in detail below. More Javascript libraries could be imported in the future. Native API plugins provide Javascript APIs of native functions of mobile phone, such as GPS, Bluetooth, message, Wi-Fi, etc. The products of visual editor is several HTML, css and Javascript files. Through EasyApp Build, these file could be built and packaged into APK and IPA files.

The architecture of EasyApp is based on OSGi framework [2] following basic B/S model. To implement the draggable widgets, we design a widget model and a dynamically loading mechanism of widget libraries. Based on the widget model, various widgets with

*Bo Cheng is the correspongding author.

MobiCom'17, , October 16–20, 2017, Snowbird, UT, USA.

ACM ISBN 978-1-4503-4916-1/17/10.
https://doi.org/10.1145/3117811.3131242

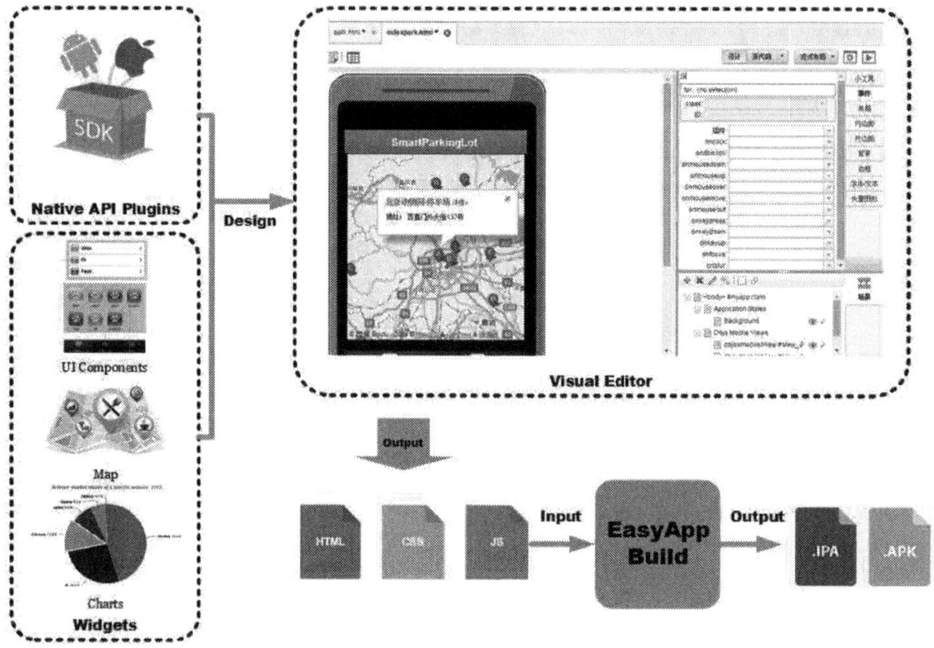

Figure 1: The developing process of EasyApp

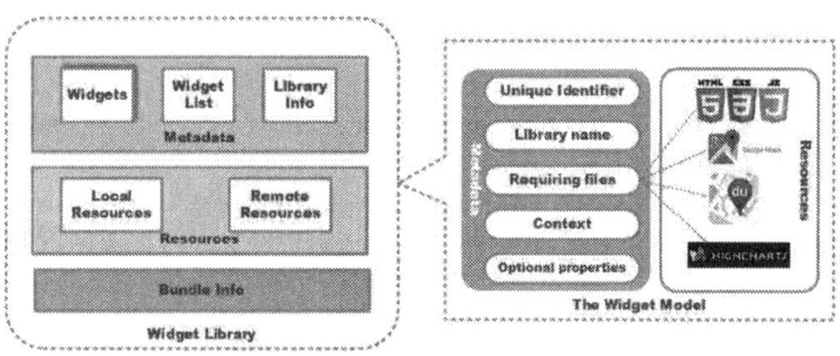

Figure 2: The widget model and widget library

multiple functions are created. In this section, we will present the widget model, the widget library, EasyApp Build and native API plugins in detail.

2.1 The Widget Model

A widget is a basic component of a mobile application[4]. Different widgets provide various functions. Users are supposed to drag the icons of the widgets onto the visual editor, at the same time, preset source codes will be added to the index file of the application. For applications are created with web techniques, a widget is a web component which demands web resources. Figure 2 shows the structure of the widget model. A widget consists of two major part, metadata[1] and resources.

Metadata describes the essential information to identify and construct a widget on the visual editor. The information mainly includes a unique identifier, library name, requiring files, context and other optional properties. The unique identifier acts as a handler of the widget. It must be the same as the identifier listed in the widget library, in other word, the widget library distinguishes and collects the essential materials with this identifier. The library name states the widget library that this widget belongs to. A widget library is a collection of the widgets, and it will be deeply introduced in next section. The requiring files include all necessary files to render the widgets on the visual editor and in the application. Similar with the usual web components, the widgets rely on css, Javascript and other image files. The type, relative path and library name of files are supposed to be declared. The context declares the HTML tag that the source codes of the widget will be surrounded by.

Resources provide all necessary scripts and images of the widget. There are two categories of resources according to the purpose. One is used to display the icons and descriptions in the widget palette of the main GUI. This category of resources mostly are icons and images . The other one is used to construct the mobile application in the visual editor and the applications. This category includes the requiring files declaring in the metadata and other essential files. For different kinds of widget, different resources are needed. For basic UI components and dynamic components, local and external Javascript files and css files are necessary. For web contents, remote resources should be imported (e.g. Google Map widget).

2.2 The Widget Library

As shown in Figure 2, the widget library is the collection of widgets. The widgets in the same library usually share the source files or provide similar functions. Through the library, widgets are located and loaded. A widget library is an individual OSGi bundle[5]. A standard widget library consists of three major parts, metadata, resources and bundle information.

Metadata of library consists of three parts. The first part is metadata of widgets. Each widget corresponds to a unique description file. The second part is a widget list including all available widgets

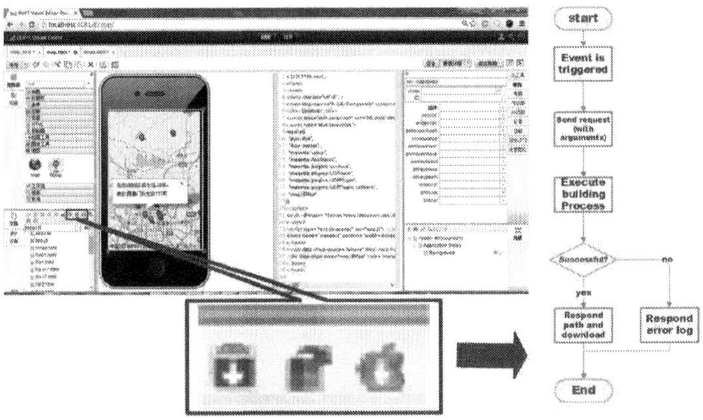

Figure 3: The GUI and procces of EasyApp Build

in this library. The essential information to identify and locate the widgets must be declared in this list. The third part is essential information of the library. In this part, library name, version number, directory path and depending libraries are required to declared. The widget list and library information are recorded in respective JSON files. Resources of library is the collection of widget resources. Local files are placed in the directory and the urls of remote files are recorded. Bundle information declares the activator and service interfaces. All materials mentioned above are placed in this OSGi bundle.

2.3 EasyApp Build

As shown in Figure 3, EasyApp Build includes two major part, GUI part and back-end part. GUI part include a group of buttons placed on the main GUI corresponding to respective platforms. These Buttons are bound with event listeners. When click event is triggered by users, a request with arguments will be sent. The arguments of the request cover the platform name, platform version and user name. The back-end part is responsible to building and packaging. It intercepts requests from the GUI part and execute the packaging process. The output files are embeded into webview of native project. If the package is successfully created, server-side will respond the path to GUI and it will be downloaded. If not, an error log will be responded.

2.4 Native API Plugins

Mobile web applications could not invoke native APIs of mobile phone directly, so a middleware is imported as communication tunnel. This tunnel intercepts the messages from Javascipt and transfers them to operating system. This middleware is embeded into applications during EasyApp Build creating process. Native API Plugins are created following the communication rules. A plugin requires a Javascript interface and a comparable Java handler. Two parts are communicating through middleware. When Javascript interfaces are invoked, Java handler will catch the messages and invoke native APIs. More powerful plugins could be created and uploaded to EasyApp following this standard.

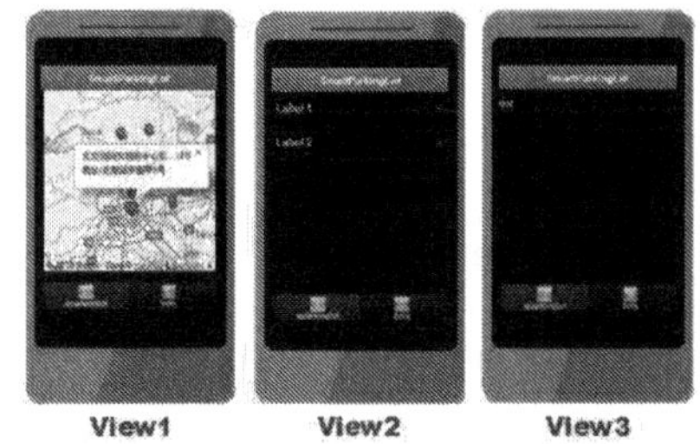

Figure 4: Three view of Smart Parking Lot

3 DEMONSTRATION

In this section, we demonstrate a complete development process of a mobile application, Smart Parking Lot. This application mainly implements the functions, that find the actual location, display the parking lot around and obtain the user's bills (https://youtu.be/AGnhxK8R-hE).

According these requirements, three page views are designed. On the bottom of every page view there is a navigation tab bar that links to two main page of the applications, service map and bills list. On the first view, we drag a BaiduMap widget on it. This widget integrated the functions of locating and searching service around. On the second page view is a list view widget which is bound data form URL. The third view shows the detail of bills. Clicking the item of list view leads to the detail page. Figure 5 shows the three page views.

4 CONCLUSIONS

Summing up the above, we implemented a widget-based cross-platform mobile applications development environment. However, there are still some problems to solve. Firstly, our widget libraries are not that abundant. Secondly, not all platforms are supported well. In the future, we will go step further to enrich the categories of widget libraries. More latest web libraries will be added. More popular platforms will be supported and we will continue improving characteristic of cross-platform.

5 ACKNOWLEDGMENTS

This work was supported by National Natural Science Foundation of China (61132001 and U1536111).

REFERENCES

[1] 2016. openajax metadata 1.0 specification. http://www.openajax.org/member/wiki/OpenAjax_Metadata_Specification. (2016).
[2] OSGi Alliance. 2009. OSGi-the dynamic module system for Java. *accessed, May 25* (2009).
[3] Cinzia Cappiello, Maristella Matera, Matteo Picozzi, Alessandro Caio, and Mariano Tomas Guevara. 2012. MobiMash: end user development for mobile mashups. In *Proceedings of the 21st International Conference on World Wide Web*. ACM, 473–474.
[4] Nassim Laga, Emmanuel Bertin, Roch Glitho, and Noel Crespi. 2012. Widgets and composition mechanism for service creation by ordinary users. *Communications Magazine, IEEE* 50, 3 (2012), 52–60.
[5] Jeff McAffer, Paul VanderLei, and Simon Archer. 2010. *OSGi and Equinox: Creating highly modular Java systems*. Addison-Wesley Professional.
[6] Shaileen Crawford Pokress and José Juan Dominguez Veiga. 2013. MIT App Inventor: Enabling personal mobile computing. *arXiv preprint arXiv:1310.2830* (2013).

Poster – RECO: A Reconfigurable Core Network for Future 5G Communication Systems

Chia-Han Wu
Department of Computer Science
National Chiao Tung University
Hsinchu 300, Taiwan
chiahan.cs04g@g2.nctu.edu.tw

Wei-Jen Chen
Department of Computer Science
National Chiao Tung University
Hsinchu 300, Taiwan
batx6.cs00@g2.nctu.edu.tw

Jyh-Cheng Chen*
Department of Computer Science
National Chiao Tung University
Hsinchu 300, Taiwan
jcc@cs.nctu.edu.tw

ABSTRACT

It is envisioned in the future that not only smartphones will connect to cellular networks, but all kinds of different wearable devices, sensors, vehicles, home appliances, VR headsets, robots, will also connect to cellular networks. Because the characteristics of these devices differ largely, people argue that future 5G systems should be designed to elastically accommodate to the different users. In this paper, we propose a reconfigurable core network called RECO that demonstrates how to implement customized virtual core network entities efficiently to suit for users with different characteristics. We then build a testbed to verify our proposed RECO architecture. Finally, we will open source our RECO in the near future so that the research community can take benefit out of it.

KEYWORDS

5G; Reconfigurable Networks; Network Function Virtualization; System Design and Experimentation

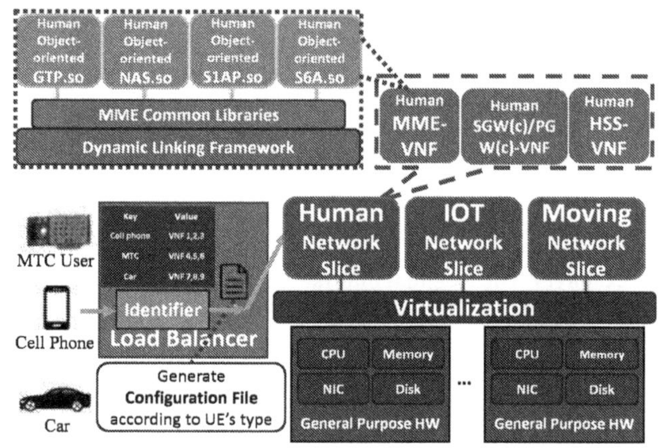

Figure 1: RECO Architecture

1 INTRODUCTION

The future 5G communications system is envisioned to transform from a human-oriented system into an *Internet of Things (IoT)* system. This new system will connect tens of billions of devices ranging from mobile phones, tablets, home appliances, wearable devices, VR headsets, sensors, vehicles, robots, and so on, making our lives smarter and more convenient. The NGMN 5G white paper shows new use cases that will emerge beyond 2020 [8]. The use cases range from delay-tolerant applications to extreme real-time communications, from high user mobility to pedestrian speed mobility, from best effort network applications to ultra-reliable ones, and from an average connection density network for smartphones to an extremely high connection density, low-cost, long-range, low-power network for sensors.

Due to the diverse characteristics of different use cases, the future 5G cellular networks should be designed to elastically accommodate such a heterogeneous environment. In other words, a 5G core network should be able to flexibly customize itself to serve different use cases. To achieve this goal, we propose **Re**configurable **Co**re (RECO) that can flexibly support different types of users with different characteristics. In addition, we have built a prototype and tested it with commercial User Equipment (UE) terminals and a real LTE base station. Please refer to our demo video [1]. We plan to release the whole source code of RECO to [2] soon. In the past, the cellular core network was very expensive and not easy to access the source code. With Object-Oriented Programming (OOP) design in our RECO testbed, however, researchers not only can get the source code for free, but also can add their own modules easily. For people doing research in this area, they usually could only conduct mathematical analysis and simulation to verify their ideas. In contrast, our RECO testbed provides a low-cost way for researchers to implement new ideas in a real core network environment. Professors teaching courses in cellular core networks can also design labs for students, which is not easy to achieve without open-source code with modularized design.

*Corresponding author: Prof. Jyh-Cheng Chen

MobiCom '17, October 16-20, 2017, Snowbird, UT, USA.
 ISBN 978-1-4503-4916-1/17/10.
DOI: http://dx.doi.org/10.1145/3117811.3131257

2 RECONFIGURABLE CORE (RECO)

To build a flexible 5G core network, we propose RECO and the architecture is shown in Fig. 1. RECO is designed based upon a virtualized core network environment using Network Function Virtualization (NFV) and has three key components:

(1) Modularized virtual network functions (VNFs) designed by OOP language: We split the code for virtual network functions (virtual network entities) into modules and compile them into shared libraries (.so). We then separate the modules into two groups: (i) ***common modules*** which are the same among different types of users, and (ii) ***customized modules*** which differ between different types of users. As shown in Fig. 1, the Mobility Management Entity (MME) common libraries are the common modules and GTP.so, NAS.so, S1AP.so, and S6A.so are the customized modules. Different customized VNFs on the same machine can share the same copy of common modules. For example, a human MME VNF, an IoT MME VNF and a vehicle MME VNF can all share the same copy of common modules. On the other hand, customized modules differ between different user types and should be implemented in OOP languages. The major benefit of implementing customized modules like this is that it can highly reuse existing code and promote the process of creating new customized VNFs. For example, suppose we have already implemented a human MME VNF. We can directly inherit most of the classes within the human MME VNF and just override particular mobility-related member functions to build a high-mobility MME VNF for vehicles.

(2) Dynamic linking framework which links customized modules during run-time: For each virtual network entity, there is a dynamic linking framework inside it. The framework's major job is to link customized modules during run-time according to the configuration file provided by the identifier to form a customized virtual network entity. The reason we choose to use dynamic linking is because it highly increases the flexibility to create a new network entity. When a new virtual network entity is needed, all we need is to create new corresponding customized modules for the particular type of users. The dynamic linking framework then will compose everything together to form a new network entity. This is somewhat similar to adding a plugin into the Chrome browser to generate a customized browser.

(3) An identifier which generates a configuration file to form customized virtual network entities: When a new user first tries to attach to the core network, the identifier inside the load balancer will identify the user's type by using some mechanism such as parsing an ***user type tag*** in the attach request packet. If this kind of user type has never attached to the core network before, the identifier will generate a ***configuration file*** including information about what customized modules are needed to form particular virtual network entities. The identifier then will pass it to the dynamic linking framework. Accordingly, the dynamic linking framework will compose these modules together and form customized VNFs to serve the type of users. The identifier also records a ***hash table*** with user types as the key and index of corresponding VNFs for particular user types as the value. In this manner, the load balancer can forward subsequent packets of the same user type to corresponding VNFs according to the hash table.

3 RECO MME AND RECO TESTBED

We built a reconfigurable virtual MME to demonstrate the proposed RECO architecture. It is modified from the MME of openair-cn [6], a simple core network developed by EURECOM [7]. We separated the highly bundled MME executable linked with many static libraries in openair-cn into a dynamic linking framework linked with shared libraries. Fig. 2 shows the architecture of our RECO MME. It is composed of four main components:

(1) Common modules: We modified the static libraries used in openair-cn's MME into two kinds of shared libraries: (i) *load-time shared libraries* shared among different types of users, and (ii) *run-time shared libraries* differing between types of users. The *load-time shared libraries* are common modules shared among different customized MMEs. When the MME executable (the dynamic linking framework) is executed and loaded into memory, these common modules will also be loaded into memory. Using common modules can reduce the disk and memory usage.

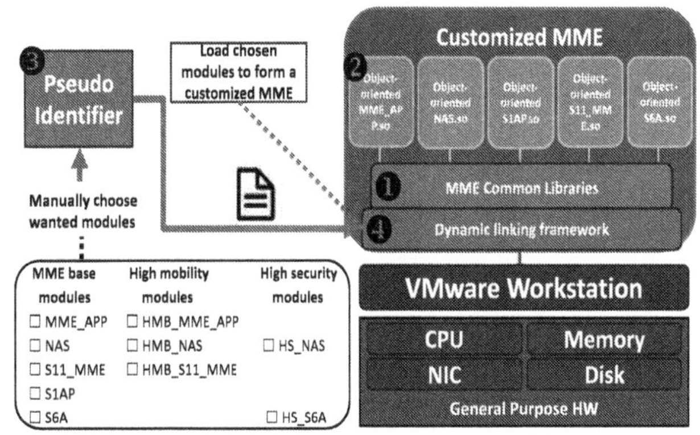

Figure 2: RECO Testbed

(2) Customized modules: We built five modules MME_APP, NAS, S1AP, S11_MME and S6A inside openair-cn from static libraries into *run-time shared libraries*. Building these customized modules into *run-time shared libraries* enables the MME to load and unload shared libraries during run-time. By doing so, the dynamic linking framework can load different customized modules according to the configuration file and form a customized MME. In addition, the source code inside these five modules are all refactored from C to OOP language C++. This was done by composing related functions and variables inside each module into classes. By doing so, a programmer can use the capabilities of OOP such as inheritance, override, polymorphism, etc. to extend the existing modules into new customized modules in a more efficient manner. This highly promotes the process of development.

(3) Pseudo Identifier: Currently, we simply implemented a checkbox list as a pseudo identifier to mimic the behavior of a real identifier as shown in Fig. 2. Programmers can choose particular modules for a type of user manually through the checkbox list. The pseudo identifier then will generate the corresponding configuration file and pass it to the dynamic linking framework.

(4) Dynamic linking framework: The dynamic linking framework is used to link customized modules at run-time according to the configuration file provided by the pseudo identifier. Its main functionalities are to provide a standard interface for customized modules, parse the configuration file, load and initialize corresponding customized modules according to the configuration file, and help resolve dependency relationships among customized modules.

4 EVALUATION

4.1 Verify Correctness of RECO

In order to verify the correctness of our RECO MME, we connected it with real commercial UEs and a real commercial LTE small-cell eNB along with S-GW, P-GW and HSS provided by openair-cn. Because the commercial UEs can successfully connect to the

Table 1: Testbed comparison

Testbed	Open source	Completeness	Status	Reduce disk&memory	Flexibility	OOP Design
Open5GCore [3]	Very Expensive	✓	Active	✓	✓	
OpenEPC [4]	Very Expensive	✓	Active	✓	✓	
nwEPC [5]	✓		Frozen			
openair-cn [6]	✓		Active			
RECO MME [2]	✓		Active	✓	✓	✓

Table 2: Performance Overhead for RECO MME

	MME Setup Time	S1 Setup Time	Initial Attach Time (1 PC)	Initial Attach Time (3 PCs)
RECO MME	57.64536 ms (+15.72%)	0.4717692 ms (+3.23%)	12.996 ms (+8.62%)	15.6608 ms (+4.19%)
openair-cn	49.81621 ms	0.457 ms	11.96421 ms	15.0304 ms

Internet through a commercial LTE eNB and our testbed, our RECO MME is implemented correctly.

4.2 Benefits of using RECO

Compared to other testbeds shown in Table 1, RECO has the benefits of reducing memory and disk space and can flexibly load and unload customized modules during run-time. This is because we build our RECO MME by using dynamic linking technologies just as commercial products OpenEPC and Open5Gcore do. However, OpenEPC and Open5Gcore are too expensive for most universities. Besides, as far as we know, RECO is the only testbed implemented in an object-oriented code structure. By doing so, developers can inherit many existing classes and override member functions with customized functionalities which improve the development process of building customized virtual network entities.

4.3 Performance Overhead of RECO

Although using dynamic linking and C++ programming have the benefits described in Sec. 4.2, there is performance overhead comparing to using static linking and C. To measure the performance overhead, we measured MME Setup Time, S1 Setup Time, and Initial Attach Time for our RECO MME compared to the original openair-cn MME. Table 2 shows that RECO MME takes 15.72% more time than openair-cn MME to finish initialization. This is because RECO MME needs additional linkage time on every execution due to the use of dynamic linking. Although this overhead seems excessive in proportion, it is actually only less than eight milliseconds, which is acceptable. As for S1 Setup Time, RECO MME costs only 3.23% more than the original openair-cn. For Initial Attach Time, we installed each core network entity in a virtual machine (VM) and deployed these VMs (RECO MME VM, openair-cn SPGW VM, openair-cn HSS VM) on 1 PC and 3 separate PCs. The results show that RECO MME costs only 8.62% and 4.19% more, respectively. The reason that the overhead decreases on 3 separate PCs is because the transmission delays between the 3 PCs reduce the impact of dynamic linking and C++ overhead. In a real cloud environment, there might be more than 3 physical machines. Thus, the delay caused by the distance between UE, eNB, and other network entities would make the dynamic linking and C++ overhead negligible.

5 FUTURE PLAN

We plan to release the whole source code of RECO to [2] soon. Besides, we will provide complete documentation including how to install RECO, how to add a new customized module, and how to program a real SIM card to connect to our core network. Thus, researchers can easily implement and test their proposed algorithms in a real testbed. For example, if a researcher propose a new paging algorithm, traditionally the researcher could only simulate the new algorithm. With RECO, the researcher can now inherit most of the classes developed by us and only modify paging-related member functions to form new customized modules. The dynamic linking framework then will automatically link these new customized modules together to generate a new customized MME with the newly proposed paging algorithm inside it. This would greatly benefit the research community.

ACKNOWLEDGMENTS

This work was supported in part by the Ministry of Science and Technology of Taiwan under grant numbers MOST 106-2221-E-009-046-MY3, MOST 106-2221-E-009-047-MY3, MOST 106-2218-E-009-016 and MOST 105-2218-E-009-008. We would also like to thank the people who contributed in different ways to this research, including Hong-Shiang Lan, Yu-Sen Hsueh, Jia-Ru Li, You-Min Lin, Yi-Hua Wu, Fu-Cheng Chen, Chia-Wei Chang, Ping-Fan Ho, Bo-Jun Qiu, Yi-Hao Lin, and Chia-Che Hsu.

REFERENCES

[1] https://youtu.be/6iuCq350LYM.
[2] https://github.com/RECONet/RECO.
[3] http://www.open5gcore.org/.
[4] http://www.openepc.com/.
[5] https://sourceforge.net/projects/nwepc/.
[6] https://gitlab.eurecom.fr/oai/openair-cn.
[7] http://www.eurecom.fr/en.
[8] NGMN Alliance. NGMN 5G white paper. *Next Generation Mobile Networks, White paper*, 2015.

Poster: Smart RF Table Enables IoT on a Desk

Yue Wu
Peking University
wuyue16@pku.edu.cn

Caihua Li
Peking University
peterli@pku.edu.cn

Jieqi Shi
Peking University
jaycee_sjq@pku.edu.cn

ABSTRACT

IoT has long been a hot topic, and many researchers have made great efforts especially in wireless charging and communication between smart furniture, recognization and localization. However, people always divide charging, communicating and sensing apart. In our paper, we put forward a simple but practical method to make use of NFC communication and resonance-type WPT to build up a system which can be used to locate, identify, charge devices while providing a platform for objects to communicate with each other. Our system acts as an intelligent controller, and it links all devices registered to it together to form a scalable network based on common furniture in daily life.

CCS CONCEPTS

• **Hardware** → **Networking hardware**; **Smart grid**; • **Networks** → *Sensor networks*;

KEYWORDS

NFC Network, Charging Network, IoT

1 INTRODUCTION

Imagine that you just come back from work and is too tired to make supper for you and your little daughter. Thus, you decide to relax in your bedroom for a while.

Slumping in your chair, you put your iphone on the table carelessly. Your smart table find that your phone is out of charge after a long day, and charges it for you. What's more, the table opens the lamb and plays cello for you on your laptop automatically. Half an hour later, the lamb begins to twinkle and informs you that according to the schedule on your phone, you should prepare for supper now.

MobiCom'17, October 16–20, 2017, Snowbird, UT, USA.
 ISBN 978-1-4503-4916-1/17/10.
DOI: http://dx.doi.org/10.1145/3117811.3131246

With the development of IoT, more and more attention is paid to smart furniture, and the imagination above is not only a scene in folks any more. However when we get down to it, we need to think about three basic questions that "how to sense", "how to charge" and "how to interact". Above those three basic questions we need to think about a software architecture which could use simple drivers to link smart gadget on table.

As a result, we have developed a system which

1. **Based on widely-used equipments.** We want to develop the system on which common people use most everyday. In our project we choose table to realize our idea, with your documents, lamp, laptop and phones on it. The modification should be realized within limited budget.
2. **Easy to change the size.** Different facilities may require different structure of hardware. However, if we do not want to limit the use of our system, we should ensure that our design is easy to change size. It will be ideal if we need to do nothing but increase or decrease number of elements in the system without changing its structure when applying to a different size.
3. **Act as an integrated controller.** As is mentioned above, we design our system to be an identifier, a charger, a controller of items on the desk, and even a communication media. It does not need to provide too much service for users, but take the advantage of link different device and provide a platform for them. Thus, We should be able to tell items on the desk apart, and decide which service we should provide to each user separately. We do not to make limitations on what device can be registered to our system and where items should be located.

2 SYSTEM DESIGN

2.1 Keypoints of System

Our system has made several differences in different aspects:

(1) Integrated Hardware

To identify and locate objects, we use NFC which works in the range of 4-10cm with less than 0.1s setup time[5]. Also NFC support data transmission between devices. With some modification it could even support charging for low-power devices[8], however to support higher power devices such as lamp, we use isolated resonance-type WPT coil beside the NFC coil[3].

(2) Simple but Powerful Principle

We use common NFC technology and resonance-type WPT, using antenna array to extend them in space. Other technology could also enable large range or multiple device wireless charging such as magnetic MIMO[4] and resonant coupling[7][2][1][6], however, our design based on table could also realize a convenient charging environment as well as sensing functions.

(3) Low Cost Realization

The whole system is of low cost, and users are not limited to only researchers in labs and universities. We have made sure that both chips and power needed to implement the system are reasonable.

2.2 Hardware Structure

Since we want our system to be scalable while able to locate every small component at the same time, we design a multi-level structure linked by a link-level switcher.

Above all small components is a host controller which take the responsibility of all calculations and decision making, such as which component should be activated, where message packets from devices should go to and what response should be made. In a word, it acts as CPU in our personal computers.

The middle layer between host and table is a link-level switcher. Components on table are divide to three levels. The first level is called "Big Group". Corresponding to rule 2(scalable), number of big groups can be easily changed when extending the ports of link-level switcher, thus changing the size of our system and adapting to different environments.

Each big group has two "sides": control side and coil side. They are similar to two sides of a coin, looking different but fixed closely.

On the coil side are twenty-one cells. A cell is the smallest hardware unit of our system, consisting of a NFC coil(hexagon) surrounded by a wireless charging coil(round). Every seven cells will be carefully arranged to form an "Element", and three "Element" will be put together to form coil side of big groups while providing the function of charging and identifying without gaps.

Control side is made up of one processor, three NFC transceiver IC and twenty-one WPT(Wireless Power Transmission) IC. Every NFC IC controls 7 NFC coils in an "Element" using multiplexing, while WPT IC and wireless charging coils are one-on-one. Such NFC IC will

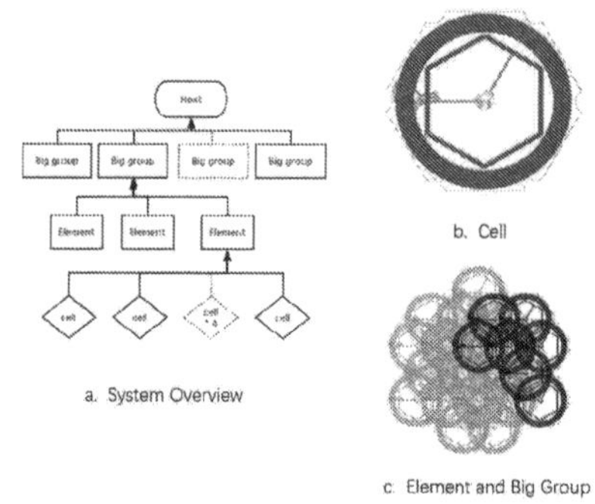

Figure 1: overview

also help to realize the function of P2P communication between our system and objects.2

2.3 Execution Logic

Users of RF table should make sure that their smart gadgets attaching NFC tag required before asking for any type of service we provide.

We urge the host to scan items on table surface every 200ms. Since interference between NFC chips will lead to fail of detection, we only activate one out of seven NFC coils at one time. Thus, it need 1.4s to scan thourght the whole table.

In this way, we are capable of keeping tabs on users entering or leaving our system. Through the information provided by NFC chips, we can locate and identify different items and provide targeted service. Host will decide which cells should be activated to act as a charger, which one should act as an identifier while others remain idle according to the driver of that device.

We provide some API to simplify the use of RF table, and will keep record of all sevices both from our system and devices registered to our system. What users should do is to realize their own drivers, and provide us with whether they want to be charged and what service they want and support. The system will locate articles and match them with specific service provided by our system itself or devices within our system. After that, meassages will be passed through switchers between host and cells, and detailed instructions will be sent and replied to.

3 EXPERIMENT

We designed a demo to show one senario with Smart RF Table. https://youtu.be/toLVdr9TUxQ

In the demo we found that the table could recogize a book, and the light detected the book and turned on. After some time the light blinking itself to remind user it's time to have a rest.

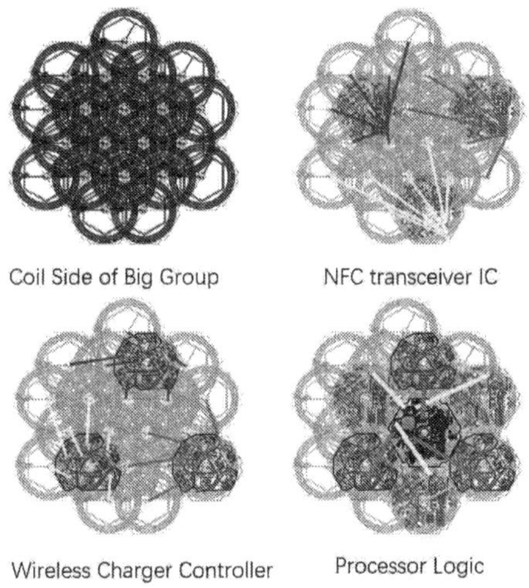

Figure 2: Illustration of Big group

The senario is very simple, however it demonstrate the flexibility of Smart RF Table. More applications such as study schedule recorder, document or book classifier, permission manager, cell-phone charger and so on, could just developed as plug-ins to our system. The combination of sensor, charger and interaction enables Smart RF Table as a smart IoT platform.

4 CONCLUSION

In this paper, we have put forward a smart table system, which acts as an integrated platform for sensing, charging and interacting. Our system is of low cost and low power consumption, and is proved to be scalable and robust.

REFERENCES

[1] AndrKursA KaralisR MoffattJD JoannopoulosP Fisher. 2007. Wireless Power Transfer via Strongly Coupled Magnetic Resonances. *Science* 5834 (2007), 83.
[2] BL CannonJF HoburgDD StancilSC Goldstein. [n. d.]. Magnetic Resonant Coupling As a Potential Means for Wireless Power Transfer to Multiple Small Receivers. *IEEE Transactions on Power Electronics* 7 ([n. d.]).
[3] C. F. Huang and C. L. Lin. 2014. Design of antennas and circuit for integrating RFID and wireless charging systems. In *The 8th European Conference on Antennas and Propagation (EuCAP 2014)*. 1580–1581. https://doi.org/10.1109/EuCAP.2014.6902086
[4] J JadidianD Katabi. [n. d.]. Magnetic MIMO: how to charge your phone in your pocket. *ACM MobiCom '14* ([n. d.]).
[5] V CoskunB OzdenizciK Ok. [n. d.]. A Survey on Near Field Communication (NFC) Technology. ([n. d.]).
[6] L ShiZ KabelacD KatabiD Perreault. 2015. Wireless Power Hotspot that Charges All of Your Devices. *ACM MobiCom '15 Proceedings of the 21st Annual International Conference on Mobile Computing and Networking* (2015), 2–15.
[7] AP SampleBH WatersST WisdomJR Smith. 2013. Enabling Seamless Wireless Power Delivery in Dynamic Environments. *Proceedings of the IEEE2013, 101(6):1343-1358* 6 (2013), 1343–1358.
[8] E. Strommer, M. Jurvansuu, T. Tuikka, A. Ylisaukko-oja, H. Rapakko, and J. Vesterinen. 2012. NFC-Enabled Wireless Charging. In *2012 4th International Workshop on Near Field Communication*. 36–41. https://doi.org/10.1109/NFC.2012.17

Poster: Enabling Secure Location Authentication in Drone

Feng Xiao, Man Zhou, Youcheng Liye, Jingxiao Yang, Qian Wang
{f3i,zhouman,liye97,yangjingxiao,qianwang}@whu.edu.cn
The State Key Lab of Software Engineering, School of Computer Science, Wuhan University, P. R. China

ABSTRACT

With the popularity of commodity drones in a wide variety of applications, significant security issues have been raised. One of the major problems is that a legal drone may be illegally hijacked by GPS spoofing attacks. Though some GPS anti-spoofing techniques have been proposed, no effective technique has been implemented in commodity drones yet due to practical limitations. Motivated by the ubiquitous WiFi signals around us, we propose WiDrone, a WiFi fingerprint location cross-check based anti-hijacking system on commodity drones in this poster. WiDrone still relies on GPS for navigation but it will authenticate the destination by comparing current WiFi fingerprint (CWF) with the destination WiFi fingerprint (DWF) when the drone receives a landing order. Furthermore, we propose a WiFi fingerprint authentication algorithm to decide whether CWF matches DWF. We have designed and implemented the prototype of WiDrone on DJI Matrice 100 to ascertain the practicability of proposed system.

CCS CONCEPTS

• **Security and privacy** → **Mobile and wireless security**; • **Networks** → **Location based services**;

KEYWORDS

Drone, Secure Location Authentication, WiFi

1 INTRODUCTION

Drones (or unmanned aerial vehicles) are aircraft without pilots on board. With the fast development of drone technology, commodity drones have been increasingly used in a wide variety of applications, such as aerial photography, search and rescue, environmental monitoring, electrical inspection and so on. In recent years, some e-commerce giants have proposed to employ drones for delivery services of packages (e.g., Amazon Prime Air [2] and JD.com Drone Delivery Program [3]). It is widely believed that the drone industry will experience an exponential growth in the near future.

However, the popularity of drones also raises a number of security issues. One of the major problems is that a legal drone may be illegally hijacked by adversaries. For example, an adversary may hijack the delivery drone on its way to the destination and take away the packages. The easy implementation of hijack mainly because drones only rely on civilian GPS navigation while civilian signals are not encrypted or authenticated. In civilian GPS, the signals are spread using publicly known spreading codes. Therefore, the adversary can cheat the drone's GPS receiver by broadcasting bogus signals (called GPS spoofing attacks [6]) and control the drone landing on the way. Researchers have shown how to successfully spoof GPS receivers of drones with COTS (commercial off-the-shelf) GPS signal simulator or software defined radios [1, 4, 8].

Some proposed GPS anti-spoofing techniques recently can be classified into four categories: signal processing defenses, cryptographic defenses, correlation with other GNSS sources and radio spectrum and antenna defenses [5]. These countermeasures monitor GPS signals and detect the abnormality, modify on satellite to encrypt civilian signals, cross-check with other timing or location sources, or use customized antenna receiver. However, due to some practical limitations, no effective technique has been implemented in commodity drones yet. Motivated by the ubiquitous WiFi signals around us, we propose WiDrone, an anti-hijacking system on commodity drones which leverages the WiFi fingerprint for location cross-check in this poster. WiDrone still relies upon GPS for navigation but it will authenticate the destination by comparing current WiFi fingerprint with that of the destination before the drone starts to land. We have designed and implemented the prototype of WiDrone on DJI Matrice 100 to ascertain the practicability of proposed system. Video of the conducted case study can be found in [9].

2 SYSTEM DESIGN

In this section, we present the design of WiDrone. To enable anti-hijacking on commodity drones which systems are always restricted and unprogrammable, it is crucial to build an extensible onboard platform that is able to authenticate the destination as well as automatically control the drone. Hence, we propose WiDrone, the extensible anti-hijacking platform for drones. Figure 1 elaborates the architecture of the proposed design.

Design goal. The goal of WiDrone is to protect drones from GPS-spoofing attack with WiFi fingerprint. Currently, there are two methods to spoof drone: 1) No-fly zone abuse: The firmware of commodity drones records the GPS information of areas over which drones are not permitted to fly, and these locations are called No-fly zone. Emitting No-fly zone GPS information might lead drones to fly back or land immediately. 2) Fine-grained GPS spoofing: Attackers emit false GPS

MobiCom '17, October 16–20, 2017, Snowbird, UT, USA

ACM ISBN 978-1-4503-4916-1/17/10.
https://doi.org/10.1145/3117811.3131259

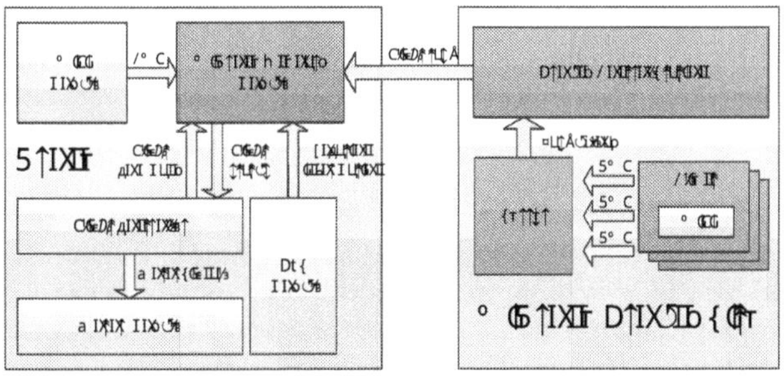

Figure 1: System architecture of WiDrone.

(a) DJI Matrice 100 (b) USRP

Figure 2: (a) is the drone prototype used in WiDrone, (b) is the GPS spoofing tool.

signals that slightly different from the real one, so as to gradually mislead the drone to the false location. The first one is not efficient because it is easy to be detected: Since legitimate flight routines will not fly over any no-fly zone, such attacks need to emit GPS signals that are far away from any location in the routine. Hence drones can easily detect the spoofing. In our poster, WiDrone mainly focuses on the fine-grained GPS spoofing, which is more efficient and commonly used [1].

WiDrone workflow. As shown in Figure 1, a user firstly submits an order along with its destination WiFi fingerprint via the client (e.g., a mobile app), then the server will gather orders from the user and submit them to the ground control station of drones. After the onboard platform receives the flight task with the destination WiFi fingerprint (DWF) from the ground site, it will navigate the vehicle to the destination.

Once WiDrone judges that it arrives at the destination according to GPS location information, it will perform the authentication algorithm in the air, to authenticate the destination by current WiFi fingerprint(CWF), and CWF only records the RSSI of APs. If CWF matches DWF, it will touch down and finish the task. Otherwise, it will decide that errors or attacks occur in the GPS locating, and thus climbs to a safe flying height and flies away from the wrong location. After that, it will be navigated by GPS module and perform the same authentication before landing.

Core algorithm design. The algorithm of WiDrone addresses two major challenges. First, unlike previous works [10] about high accuracy localization, WiDrone needs to perform the algorithm high from the air. The signals are very weak. In addition, objects in the city (e.g., bird, tree and car) can exert strong interference on the WiFi signals. However, our goal is to achieve high accuracy and robustness so that an attacker near the true destination could not hijack the drone. To achieve this goal, we employ WiFi fingerprint set V_d and V_c to describe DWF and CWF. All APs and its corresponding Received Signal Strength Indication (RSSI) are recorded ($V_d = \{Rd_1, Rd_2, ..., Rd_\alpha\}$, $V_c = \{Rc_1, Rc_2, ..., Rc_\beta\}$).

Even though APs are ubiquitous in the cities, they are sometimes unstable: Any AP near the destination can be established or removed at any time. To overcome this challenge, Client of WiDrone will ask the user to submit the latest DWF periodically. For example, a user who wants to deliver some goods to his side can submit the order with WiDrone mobile client, the client will collect DWF immediately. In addition, users can save some common delivery addresses in advance when they are at that place so that they can deliver goods from everywhere.

When drones are about to arrive at the destination, it will detect the CWF and calculate the WiFi fingerprint similarity s between V_d and V_c. We compute $V_u = V_d \bigcup V_c$, and thus obtain $V_u = \{Rd_1, Rd_2, ..., Rd_\varphi\}$. If there is an element in V_u that is not in V_d, corresponding element will be added into V_d and its value will be set to 0. The same operations will be performed on the set V_c. Then the number of elements in V_d and V_c will all be φ. Let R_{max} denote the max value of RSSI, and s is calculated as follows

$$s = 1 - \frac{\sum_{i=1}^{\varphi} |Rd_i - Rc_i| \cdot Rd_i/R_{max}}{\sum_{i=1}^{\varphi} Rd_i^2/R_{max}} \quad (1)$$

If s is larger than a threshold, WiDrone will permit the drones to land at the destination.

3 SECURITY ANALYSIS

WiDrone leverages AP fingerprint to achieve secure authentication before landing. Unlike civil GPS that are unencrypted and unauthenticated, APs can be encrypted. To cheat WiFi based location authentication system [7], attackers can only perform replay attack to counterfeit APs as well as jam original WiFi signals locally to avoid leaking genuine location information. However, WiFi jamming can be easily detected. Since cities are full of public/private APs, such jamming is unavoidable if attackers want to capture the drone flying in cities. To further mitigate such attacks, WiDrone can ask users to establish a temporary AP specialized for WiDrone authentication (e.g., personal hotspot on mobile phones), and then WiDrone performs secure landing by authenticating and connecting to this special AP.

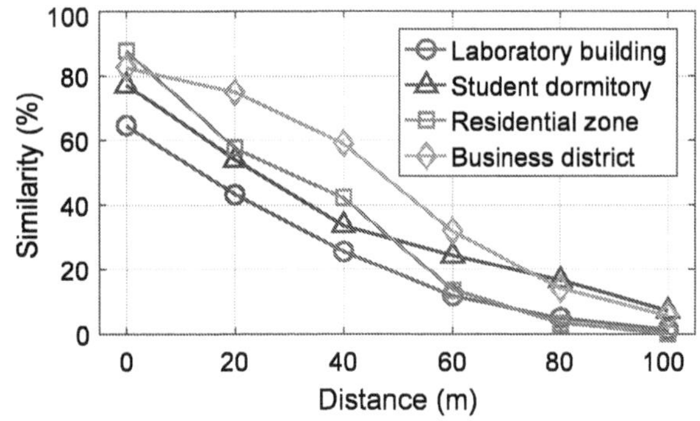

Figure 3: The WiFi fingerprint similarity s in different environment.

4 EVALUATION

4.1 Experiment Setup

In this poster, we implement our system on DJI Matrice 100. The core onboard module is implemented on a Raspberry Pi 3. We choose MT7601U wireless network card as the WiFi module to perform WiFi fingerprint collection. The Drone and the Raspberry Pi was connected via UART cable. Figure 2(a) shows our system, and we use USRP N210 as the GPS spoofing tool, as shown in Figure 2(b).

4.2 Result

To guarantee the usability of our system, we must ensure that WiDrone can accurately authenticate the CWF with DWF. Since drones will sample CWF in the air while DWF is always sampled on the ground or at indoor environments, the influence of distance between CWF and DWF on similarity is critical. Hence, we investigate the relationship of distance and similarity s in our algorithm. We conducted an experiment in which our drone is at different distance from the destination with a horizontal interval of ten meters and a total of 100 meters.

We choose four typical destinations for drones to validate our algorithm: a plaza in front of the laboratory building, a street between student dormitory, area inside residential zones and business districts. First, we collect DWF on the ground at the four places, and then we sample CWF from different distances above destinations. Figure 3 illustrates the relationship between fingerprint similarity and distance. As shown in Figure 3, s declines when the distance becomes larger. All four lines can be roughly divided into 2 periods: When the distance is less than 60 meters, declines are more rapid, however, declines becomes slower after 60 meters. This is because WiDrone will collect many other fingerprints that are not in DWF from 60 meters away that add up noises into similarity calculation, thus s becomes less sensitive with distance. To perform secure authentication, we should choose the distance in the first period where different WiFi fingerprints can be accurately differentiated. Hence we set the authentication distance at 50 meters, where WiDrone is able to authenticate WiFi fingerprints at all typical destinations. We deem that 50m is a suitable distance to perform authentication since sampling CWF from DWF 50m away can satisfy most landing scenarios in the cities.

5 CONCLUSION AND FUTURE WORK

In this poster, we designed and implemented WiDrone, an anti-hijacking system on commodity drones which leverages the WiFi fingerprint for location cross-check. The authentication algorithm is effective with our design, and its mitigation against spoofing attack is demonstrated. The design of WiDrone leverages WiFi infrastructure to perform city location authentication, and we deem that such design is stable enough because WiFi signals are ubiquitous in cities. However, it may fail to finish some special tasks if we wish WiDrone lands in particular scenarios (e.g., a mountain area without enough WiFi signals). In the future, we plan to add more kinds of signals (e.g., FM radio signals, GPRS signals) into consideration and design a dynamic algorithm to adaptively combine some of them to perform more robust authentication. The applications of WiDrone is not limited to the applications depicted in this paper but can be further expanded. For example, there is a growing concern that malicious drones may give rise to terrorist attacks or illegal spying by bypassing no-fly zone policy. WiDrone may provide a secure and low-cost solution against these problems (e.g., No-fly WiFi zone can be introduced in our further works).

6 ACKNOWLEDGMENT

Qian's research is supported in part by National Natural Science Foundation of China under Grant No. 61373167, National Basic Research Program of China under Grant No. 2014CB340600.

REFERENCES

[1] Researchers successfully spoof an 80-million yacht at sea, 2013. https://news.utexas.edu/2013/07/29/ut-austin-researchers-successfully-spoof-an-80-million-yacht-at-sea.
[2] Amazon prime air, 2016. https://www.amazon.com/b?node=8037720011.
[3] Jd.com drone delivery program, 2016. http://fortune.com/2016/11/14/jd-china-drone-delivery-singles-day/.
[4] Huang, L., and Yang, Q. Low cost gps simulator: Gps spoofing by sdr. *DEFCON* (2015).
[5] Schmidt, D., Radke, K., Camtepe, S., Foo, E., and Ren, M. A survey and analysis of the gnss spoofing threat and countermeasures. *ACM Computing Surveys (CSUR) 48*, 4 (2016), 64.
[6] Tippenhauer, N. O., Pöpper, C., Rasmussen, K. B., and Capkun, S. On the requirements for successful gps spoofing attacks. In *Proc. of CCS* (2011), ACM, pp. 75–86.
[7] Tippenhauer, N. O., Rasmussen, K. B., Pöpper, C., and Capkun, S. Attacks on public wlan-based positioning systems. In *Proc. of MobiSys* (2009), ACM, pp. 29–40.
[8] Wang, K., Chen, S., and Pan, A. Time and position spoofing with open source projects. *Black Hat Europe 148* (2015).
[9] Xiao, F., Zhou, M., Liye, Y., Yang, J., and Wang, Q. Poster: Enabling secure location authentication in drone. https://youtu.be/T1mA9tRDVz0.
[10] Yang, Z., Wu, C., and Liu, Y. Locating in fingerprint space: wireless indoor localization with little human intervention. In *Proc. of MobiCom* (2012), ACM, pp. 269–280.

Poster: An Efficient Control Framework for Supporting the Future SDN/NFV-enabled Satellite Network

Zhenning Zhang, Baokang Zhao, Wanrong Yu, Chunqing Wu
National University of Defense Technology
Changsha, China
{zhangzhenning12,bkzhao,wlyu,wuchunqing}@nudt.edu.cn

ABSTRACT

Control framework design is critical to future SDN/NFV-enabled satellite network. However, the current multi-layer constellation based solutions have drawbacks in terms of availability, latency, openness, etc. The key contribution in this work is the study of an efficient control framework, which logically consists of two parts: entity part and overlay part. The entity part is a novel heterogeneous single-layer LEO satellite network, while the overlay part implements a virtualized overlay network. We have implemented a lightweight prototype of our framework and compared it with a GEO satellite based solution (i.e. OpenSAN). We demonstrate proof-of-concept that our framework performs better than OpenSAN with respect to control latency and avoids potential system bottleneck.

CCS CONCEPTS

• **Networks** → **Network architectures**; *Mobile networks*; *Overlay and other logical network structures*;

KEYWORDS

Satellite network, SDN, NFV, Control framework

1 INTRODUCTION

Evolving from traditionally limited application scenarios (video broadcasting, network access in rural areas and terrestrial network backup) to an integrated part of the next generation 5G networks, advances in satellite network are being addressed from multiple angles such as seamless integration of satellite and terrestrial networks, flexible and agile network management and unified and open control interface. Despite the continued advances in satellite network technologies, there is a lack of prevalent standards and many functions are mainly deployed on vendor-specific network appliances. Hence, in this context, SDN/NFV technologies have been introduced in satellite network to overcome several existing limitations in terms of flexibility, evolvability and openness [2, 4].

MobiCom '17, October 16–20, 2017, Snowbird, UT, USA

ACM ISBN 978-1-4503-4916-1/17/10.
https://doi.org/10.1145/3117811.3131264

Terrestrial network architectures are taking advantages from SDN/NFV technologies. SDN has emerged as a novel technology for network programmability and management, where the centralized control plane logic is decoupled from the data forwarding plane. Whereas NFV advocates the virtualization of network functions (switching, routing and security services, etc.) as software modules running on general purpose commodity infrastructure rather than dedicated hardware. Although they are separate initiatives, it appears that both SDN and NFV need an efficient management and control entity to facilitate flexible monitoring, virtualization and programing of underlying physical network devices [3].

To this end, a software defined satellite network architecture referred to as OpenSAN [1] was proposed to investigate the design of a Geostationary Earth Orbit (GEO) satellites based control plane. The GEO satellites and several globally scattered ground stations constitute the control (and management) plane, which monitors the satellite network's status and operates the network functions in a software defined manner. Distinct from traditional control structure based only on ground stations, this "relay" based scheme takes advantage of the GEO satellite's ability of wide coverage, broadcasting and stationary relative to the ground to achieve a relatively low control latency. However, this scheme involving multi-layer satellite constellation and large ground stations has shown multiple drawbacks in supporting the future SDN/NFV-enabled satellite network.

Firstly, a limited number of GEO satellites may become the bottleneck of the overall control system under heavy control loads, even causing service degradation in satellite failure cases. Though increasing the number of GEO satellites would partially alleviate this issue, launching satellites to the higher orbit is a huge price to pay from economic perspective. Secondly, subject to meeting the antenna requirements of long distance communication with GEO satellites, control messages from the ground have to be firstly aggregated and then forwarded by a few chosen network control centers. Note that data plane interfaces are accessible and directly open to all the users, this imbalanced treatment significantly limits the application scenarios such as enabling separation of identifier from routable location in satellite network to enhance mobility [5]. Thirdly, every control packet must be routed via an indirection path though GEO satellites, causing significant control routing stretch. Moreover, growing with increasing path length, the consequent long propagation delay will inevitably affect the real-time control of underlying SDN/NFV infrastructure.

In this work, we address these issues by designing an efficient control framework for supporting the future SDN/NFV-enabled satellite network, which incorporates two parts: entity part and overlay part. The entity part is a novel heterogeneous single-layer LEO satellite network, which contains specific functional nodes to implement communication, control, computing, etc. The overlay part enabled by above entity part, consists of virtual and independently running control and data networks, and a hybrid combination of them. The key insight underlying our design is to tightly integrate function separated control plane and data plane just like the neural network embedded in the muscle tissue in human body.

2 DESIGN OVERVIEW

2.1 Entity Part

Advances such as programming and virtualization (i.e. SDN/NFV) based network function operation, programmable hardware (i.e. FPGA) based network function acceleration, laser link based inter-satellite communication and low-cost micro-satellites based LEO satellite constellation are changing the way future satellite network being designed. Therefore, we argue that next generation satellite network will be a SDN/NFV-enabled configurable and open platform constructed by massive LEO micro-satellite nodes.

The proposed heterogeneous single-layer LEO satellite network consists of two kinds of satellite nodes: control satellites and data satellites, respectively. They carry dedicated payloads to complete specific function: data switching or control forwarding. However, heterogeneous satellite nodes still constitute a unified single-layer LEO constellation in our design. The partial topology of proposed design is shown in Figure 1a. Note that control satellites (e.g. C:1-1, C:1-2, C:2-1 and C:2-2) and data satellites (e.g. D:1-1, D:1-2, D:2-1 and D:2-2) are alternately arranged in the same orbit. In addition to the conventional inter-satellite links (ISLs), we have also designed a "direct path" for control and data plane (e.g. ISLs between C:2-1 and C:2-2, D:2-1 and D:2-2), which is a special intra-orbit ISL. Driven by non-interferential laser channels, direct paths directly connect two adjacent homogeneous satellite nodes. Taken direct path into account, each satellite in our design is able to set up six ISLs connecting to its four immediately neighboring satellites (two heterogeneous nodes and two homogeneous nodes) and two adjacent homogeneous nodes in the same orbit.

2.2 Overlay Part

In overlay part, we create a virtual overlay model of entity part, consisting of an independent virtual control overlay network, an independent virtual data overlay network and a combination of them. Each node in virtual control overlay network is a SDN/NFV controller embodied by a control satellite; similarly, each node in virtual data overlay network is a SDN/NFV switch embodied by a data satellite. As illustrated in Figure 1b, C:1-1, C:1-2, C:2-1 and C:2-2 construct the virtual control overlay network, while D:1-1, D:1-2, D:2-1 and D:2-2 construct the virtual data overlay network. Note

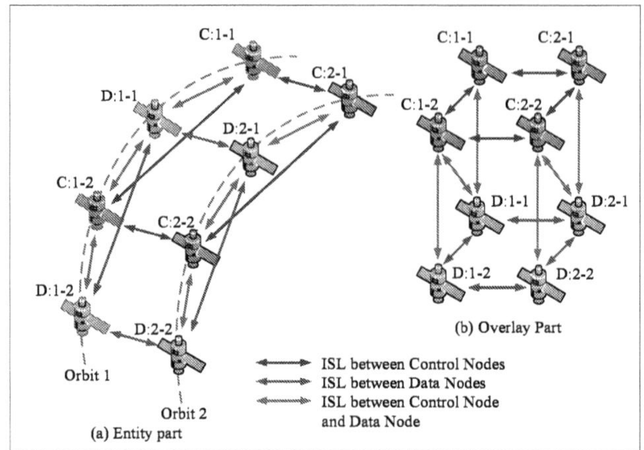

Figure 1: The structure of the heterogeneous single-layer LEO satellite network and virtualized two-layer overlay network

that controllers in virtual overlay network connect directly to the switches that serve as SDN/NFV infrastructure, e.g. D:1-1 is directly connected to C:1-1 and C:1-2; likewise, C:2-2 is directly connected to D:2-1 and D:2-2. This model can be used to control the route that different packets will take through the entity part: routing of data packets is performed with reference to the virtual data overlay network, and routing of control packets is performed with reference to the virtual control overlay network.

The highly topological dynamics characterizes the fundamental property of LEO satellite networks with respect to terrestrial ones. Consequently, the handicap is that existing entitative multi-layer satellite constellation based control framework suffers the relative movement between control plane (i.e. GEO/MEO satellites) and data plane (i.e. LEO satellites). Whereas in our virtualized two-layer overlay network, there is no such relative movement due to a data satellite and its associated control satellites are moving with identical direction and velocity in the same orbit. This relatively static characteristic would help the routing of control messages across different layers.

The control plane (a collection of interconnected controllers in virtual control overlay network) maintains a logically centralized control over data plane (realized by SDN/NFV capable switches on board LEO satellites). Specifically, the control plane consists of controllers in charge of managing different network partition or flow space. The terrestrial administrators can send policy update requests to the distributed controllers through the satellite-ground links. As an individual controller is unable to control the whole underlying physical switches, controllers within the control plane can communicate among themselves through the control overlay network in a reliable but asynchronous manner to operate a whole network from a global view. The distributed design is a trade-off between the system availability, network performance and control consistency. Furthermore, the massive

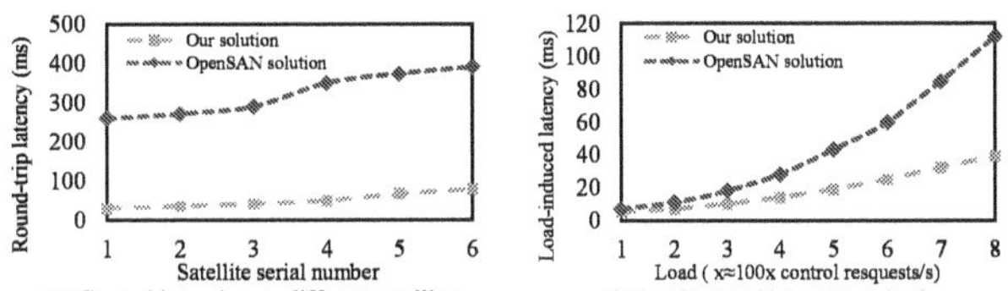

(a) Control latencies vs. different satellites (b) Load-induced latencies vs. load

Figure 2: The evaluation results

control satellites with more powerful computation and storage can be used to provide a space-based cloud computing and storage services to terrestrial users with low response latency.

3 PRELIMINARY EVALUATIONS

Good control framework performance, e.g. low control latency, is critical for achieving high network performance. The proposed control framework has been evaluated through a proof-of-concept implementation. Then we mainly compare our control framework with the OpenSAN solution in term of the control plane latency. In particular, we simulated a polar-orbiting satellite constellation with 12 orbits and each of which has 12 control satellites and 12 data satellites.

Due to the super-symmetrical characteristic of satellite network topology, the average round-trip latencies to some selected nodes including the nodes with shortest (satellite No.1)/farthest (satellite No.6) distance from terrestrial administrators at any location on the ground are shown in Figure 2a. Our solution has lower latencies over OpenSAN. This is mainly because the propagation delays between nodes in our control framework are much lower. Note that our solution also benefits from the advantages of other LEO features like low error rate, low power consumption, smaller communication payloads, etc. Figure 2b shows the load-induced latencies refer to the mean of the latencies introduced by control network congestion. OpenSAN gives low latencies at the small load levels, but shows high latencies at the high load levels; while our solution performs better, especially under high control loads. This is due to our design with mesh topology and massive nodes brings us higher system capacity, and avoids the potential bottleneck caused by star topology of traditional design in the meantime.

ACKNOWLEDGMENTS

The work is supported by the projects of National Natural Science Foundation of China under Grant No.61202488, No.61379147 and Guangxi Cooperative Innovation Center of Cloud Computing and Big Data under Grant No.YD16505.

REFERENCES

[1] Jinzhen Bao, Baokang Zhao, Wanrong Yu, Zhenqian Feng, Chunqing Wu, and Zhenghu Gong. 2014. OpenSAN: a software-defined satellite network architecture. In *ACM Conference on SIGCOMM*. 347–348.

[2] Lionel Bertaux, Samir Medjiah, Pascal Berthou, Slim Abdellatif, Akram Hakiri, Patrick Gelard, Fabrice Planchou, and Marc Bruyere. 2015. Software defined networking and virtualization for broadband satellite networks. *Communications Magazine IEEE* 53, 3 (2015), 54–60.

[3] Xavier Costa-Perez, Andres Garcia-Saavedra, Xi Li, Thomas Deiss, Antonio De La Oliva, Andrea Di Giglio, Paola Iovanna, and Alain Moored. 2017. 5G-Crosshaul: An SDN/NFV Integrated Fronthaul/Backhaul Transport Network Architecture. *IEEE Wireless Communications* 24, 1 (2017), 38–45.

[4] R. Ferrs, H. Koumaras, O. Sallent, G. Agapiou, T. Rasheed, M. A. Kourtis, C. Boustie, P. Glard, and T. Ahmed. 2016. SDN/NFV-enabled satellite communications networks: Opportunities, scenarios and challenges. *Physical Communication* 18, P2 (2016), 95–112.

[5] Zhenning Zhang, Baokang Zhao, Zhenqian Feng, Wanrong Yu, and Chunqing Wu. 2016. MSN: a mobility-enhanced satellite network architecture: poster. In *International Conference on Mobile Computing and Networking*. 465–466.

Poster: WiFi-based Device-Free Human Activity Recognition via Automatic Representation Learning

Han Zou
University of California, Berkeley
Berkeley, CA
hanzou@berkeley.edu

Yuxun Zhou
University of California, Berkeley
Berkeley, CA
yxzhou@berkeley.edu

Jianfei Yang
Nanyang Technological University
Singapore
yang0478@ntu.edu.sg

Weixi Gu
Tsinghua University
China
guweixigavin@gmail.com

Lihua Xie
Nanyang Technological University
Singapore
elhxie@ntu.edu.sg

Costas Spanos
University of California, Berkeley
Berkeley, CA
spanos@berkeley.edu

ABSTRACT

Existing human activity recognition approaches require either the deployment of extra infrastructure or the cooperation of occupants to carry dedicated devices, which are expensive, intrusive and inconvenient for pervasive implementation. In this paper, we propose SmartSense, a device-free human activity recognition system based on a novel machine learning algorithm with existing commercial off-the-shelf (COTS) WiFi routers. By exploiting the prevalence of existing WiFi infrastructure in buildings, we developed a novel OpenWrt based firmware for COTS WiFi routers to collect the CSI measurements from regular data frames. To identify different human activities, an automatic kernel representation learning method, namely auto-HSRL, is established to selection informative Hilbert space patterns from time, frequency, wavelet, and shape domains. A new information fusion tool based on multi-view kernel learning is proposed to combine the representations extracted from diverse perspectives and build up a robust and comprehensive activity classifier. Extensive experiments were conducted in an office and the experimental results demonstrate that SmartSense outperforms existing methods and achieves a 98% activity recognition accuracy.

CCS CONCEPTS

• **Human-centered computing → Ubiquitous and mobile computing**;

KEYWORDS

WiFi, human activity recognition, representation learning

1 INTRODUCTION

Human activity recognition plays an indispensable role in a myriad of emerging applications in smart buildings. Various human activity recognition systems, such as camera, Passive Infra-Red (PIR) sensor, and embedded sensors in mobile and wearable devices, have been proposed in recent years [1]. However, certain limitations hinder them from practical and pervasive implementation. They either require occupants to carry or wear the devices or need extra infrastructure for activity monitoring. With the pervasive and wide availability of WiFi infrastructure, leveraging WiFi signals to estimate the location of occupants and distinguish human activities becomes feasible [4, 5]. Channel State Information (CSI), a fine-grained channel measurement from the physical layer that describes how WiFi signals propagate from the transmitter (TX) to receiver (RX) through multiple paths at the granularity of OFDM subcarriers, has become available from commodity WiFi NIC [2]. CSI is able to reveal human activity in a non-intrusive manner because the body movements during different activities change the signal propagation paths and lead to the high variation of CSI. Identifying activities with high recognition accuracy can be feasible by analyzing the CSI measurement at RX. Although some CSI based activity recognition systems have been proposed in recent years [1], they only explore features in time and frequency domain, require expert feature engineering, and these features may not be transferable due to environmental and temporal dynamics. Therefore, it is still challenging to realize human activity recognition in an accurate, automatic and non-invasive manner.

In this paper, we propose SmartSense, a device-free human activity recognition scheme that is able to accurately distinguish common activities using only COTS WiFi routers. We developed a novel OpenWrt based firmware for WiFi routers so that the CSI measurements from regular data frames can be obtained directly from them. For the purpose of human activity recognition, a novel machine learning algorithm, namely automatic kernel representation learning (auto-HSRL), is established. The algorithm starts with a library based Hilbert space patterns generation from time, frequency, wavelet, and shape domains. Then an optimal kernel string representation is learned with an efficient greedy method. Finally, the representations obtained from diverse domains are combined together via a new information fusion tool in the form of multi-view kernel learning. Extensive

MobiCom '17, October 16–20, 2017, Snowbird, UT, USA

ACM ISBN 978-1-4503-4916-1/17/10.
https://doi.org/10.1145/3117811.3131266

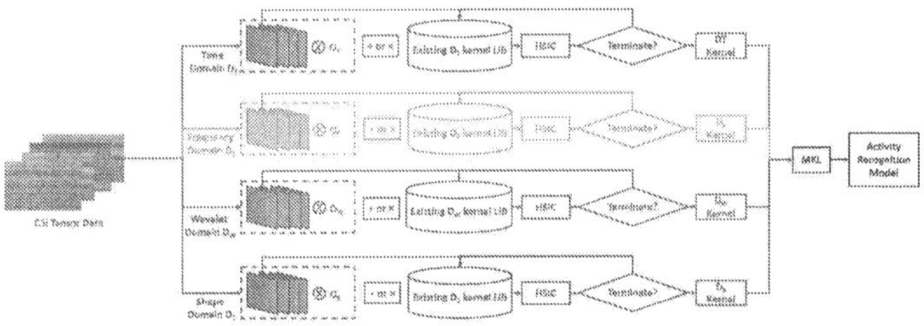

Figure 1: System architecture of auto-HSRL.

experiments were conducted in typical indoor environment and demonstrated that SmartSense can distinguish numbers of daily human activities with 97.9% recognition accuracy using only two COTS WiFi routers.

2 SYSTEM DESIGN

2.1 CSI enabled WiFi Router Platform

Conventional CSI-based sensing systems adopt either the Intel 5300 NIC tool or the Atheros 9390 tool to extract the CSI data from modified WiFi NIC card equipped with laptop or PC. The demand of laptops as receivers severely hinders them from large-scale implementation. To overcome this bottleneck, we upgrade the Atheros CSI Tool [2] and develop a new OpenWrt based firmware for COTS WiFi routers so that the CSI measurements from regular data frames transmitted in the existing traffic can be obtained directly from routers instead of using laptop or PC with external WiFi NIC adapter. Moreover, the traditional Intel 5300 NIC tool only provides CSI for 30 out of the 56 subcarriers. Our platform reports CSI data on all the 114 subcarriers for 40 MHz bandwidth on each TX-RX pair, which provides much more information than conventional CSI tools. SmartSense only requires two routers, one serves as TX and the other is adopted as RX, to perform device-free activity recognition. TX continuously transmits data packets and RX monitors the channels, captures and analyzes these packets. Suppose N_{TX} and N_{RX} represent the number of transmitting and receiving antennas. At each time instant, $N_{TX} \times N_{RX} \times 114$ CSI streams are available to analyze the variations of WiFi communication links caused by human presence and movement.

2.2 Automatic Hilbert Space Representation Learning

In order to recognize various human activities in an accurate, automatic and robust manner, we propose auto-HSRL, a novel automatic representation learning and multi-view learning scheme. Figure 1 illustrates its system architecture, which consists three stages. Firstly, we calculate various features based on the CSI measurements from time (mean, variance, skewness, kurtosis), frequency (FFT), wavelet (DTW), and shape (DTW) domains. Previous WiFi-based activity recognition approaches often resort to manual inspection, or simply combine all information together as the input of an ML algorithm, which leads to degraded recognition performance due to the suboptimal usage of extracted patterns. We propose auto-HSRL, a simple yet powerful tool to learn useful representation from data. Consider a possibly nonlinear mapping $\phi : \mathcal{X} \to \mathcal{H}$ from the raw data space $x \in \mathcal{X}$ to a feature space $\mathcal{H}$. The Mercer's theorem allows the expression of the inner product between the features via a positive definite (PD or Mercer's) kernel function, i.e., $k(x, x') = \langle \phi(x), \phi(x') \rangle_{\mathcal{H}}$ The kernel function $k(\cdot,\cdot)$ is uniquely determined by the respective reproducing kernel Hilbert space $\mathcal{H}$. Multiple Mercer's kernels are calculated and leveraged to offer more modeling capacity and performance improvement due to increased modeling flexibilities. Then, auto-HSRL learns a multiple kernel information representation for each domain. The combination structure is called "string kernel", which contains the multiplication and addition operations of base kernels. The Hilbert-Schmidt Independence Criterion (HSIC) is leveraged to learn the optimal string kernel. HSIC can be computed with statistical estimation techniques, such as

$$\frac{1}{m(m-1)}\left[\operatorname{tr}(KL) + \frac{\mathbf{1}^T K \mathbf{1} \mathbf{1}^T L \mathbf{1}}{(m-1)(m-2)} - \frac{2}{m-2}\mathbf{1}^T K L \mathbf{1}\right]$$
$$\triangleq \widehat{\mathrm{HSIC}}(K, L)$$

where K is the kernel matrix calculated by $K_{i,j} = k(x_i, x_j)$, and L is the kernel matrix of the target output space. In the current case dealing with activity recognition, the output kernel is computed with $L_{i,j} = m_{y_i}^{-1}\delta(y_i, y_j)$. We propose a greedy algorithm to learn the optimal string kernel based on HSIC. After that, we propose a multi-view learning based information fusion through multiple kernel learning (MKL). The key idea is to perform an overall regularized empirical risk minimization over the combined Hilbert space identified from the previous step, in order to find the classifier that takes all information sources into consideration. We substantiate information fusion by solving the following MKL problem:

$$\begin{aligned} &\min_{\{f_m\},b,\xi,d} \frac{1}{2}\sum_m \frac{1}{d_m}\|f_m\|^2_{\mathcal{H}_m} + C\sum_i \xi_i \\ &\text{s.t.} \quad y_i \sum_m f_m(x_i) + y_i b \geq 1 - \xi_i \quad \forall i \qquad \text{(Primal)} \\ &\qquad \sum_m d_m = 1, \quad d_m \geq 0 \quad \forall m, \quad \xi_i \geq 0 \quad \forall i \end{aligned}$$

The above Primal problem can be rewritten into a dual form that directly uses kernel representations learned from the last step. The Primal problem is equivalent to

$$\min_d J(d) \quad \text{s.t.} \quad \sum_m d_m = 1, \; d_m \geq 0$$

where

$$J(d) = \left\{ \begin{array}{l} \max_\alpha -\frac{1}{2}\sum_i\sum_j \alpha_i\alpha_j y_i y_j \sum_m d_m K_m + \sum_i \alpha \\ \sum_i \alpha_i y_i = 0, \quad 0 \leq \alpha_i \leq C \quad \forall i \end{array} \right.$$

$J(d)$ is a convex function of d, which can be solved with gradient based methods [3]. The kernel representations K_T, K_F, K_W, K_S obtained from auto-HSRL can be combined together within the above MKL learning framework.

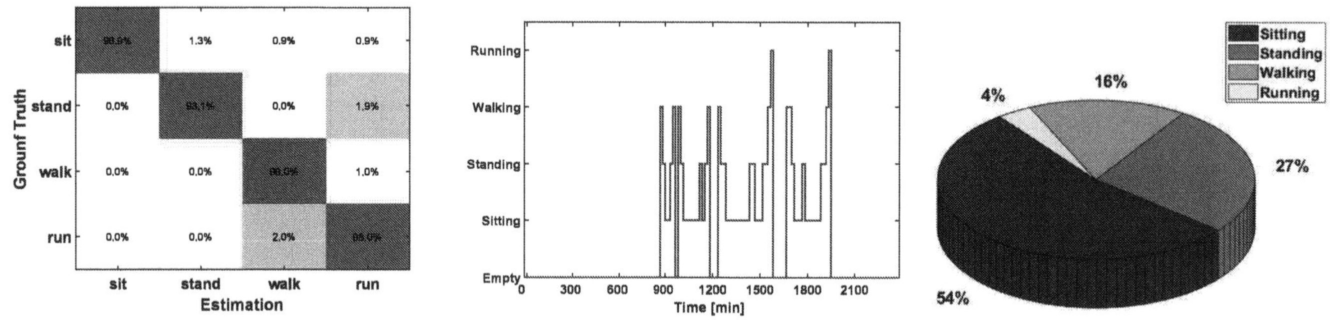

(a) Confusion matrix of human activity recognition accuracy.

(b) Occupant behavior profile in the office on one weekday.

(c) Occupant behavior profile in the office on one weekday.

Figure 2: Performance of SmartSense.

3 PERFORMANCE EVALUATION

We implemented SmartSense on 2 TPLINK N750 WiFi routers: one serves as TX and another one acts as RX. We upgraded their firmware to our CSI OpenWrt version so that the CSI measurements from regular data frames are reported directly from them. TX was operated on 5 GHz frequency band and we leveraged the 40 MHz channel bandwidth. We used 1 TX antenna to send data packets to 3 RX antennas at a transmission rate of 700 packets/s. 4 common activities, e.g. sitting, standing, walking and running, were performed by 10 volunteers to validate the activity recognition performance of SmartSense in an office ($50m^2$). Training and testing data were collected on different days to evaluate the performance of SmartSense under both temporal and environmental dynamics. Figure 2(a) depicts the confusion matrix of activity recognition accuracy using SmartSense. It achieves an average cross-validation activity recognition accuracy of 97.9% across all the four activities. As shown in Figure 2(a), its recognition accuracy for sitting, standing, walking and running is 96.9%, 98.1%, 99% and 98% respectively. SmartSense considers the features from four domains and combines them with an optimal representation, which can reveal the nature of each activity more clearly than existing approaches.

To validate its performance for practical implementation, we leveraged SmartSense to monitor one occupant's activities and analyzed his activity patterns in an office during one weekday. As presented in Figure 2(b), we can infer when the occupant arrived at the office, the duration of his lunch break and when he got off work with the measurements of SmartSense. With this fine-grained occupant activity information, the building management systems can adjust the light and ventilation accordingly to reduce the energy consumption in commercial buildings. As shown in Figure 2(c), the occupant spent more than 53% of the time sitting in the office. Thus, we can recommend him to exercise more in order to have a healthier lifestyle and also improve his productivity.

4 CONCLUSION

In this paper, we proposed SmartSense, a device-free human activity recognition scheme using only COTS WiFi routers. We designed a CSI enabled WiFi router platform and various features from time, frequency, wavelet, and shape domains were calculated based on the de-noised CSI data and developed a multi-view kernel learning model to select the most representative subset of features to build up a robust activity classifier. Extensive experiments were conducted and demonstrate that SmartSense can distinguish numbers of daily human activities with 97.9% recognition accuracy by leveraging only two WiFi routers. It has great potential to serve as a fundamental service to facilitate a broad range of emerging applications in smart buildings.

ACKNOWLEDGEMENT

This research is funded by the Republic of Singapore National Research Foundation (NRF) through a grant to the Berkeley Education Alliance for Research in Singapore (BEARS) for the Singapore-Berkeley Building Efficiency and Sustainability in the Tropics (SinBerBEST) Program. BEARS has been established by the UC Berkeley as a center for intellectual excellence in research and education in Singapore.

REFERENCES

[1] Wei Wang, Alex X Liu, Muhammad Shahzad, Kang Ling, and Sanglu Lu. 2015. Understanding and modeling of wifi signal based human activity recognition. In *MobiCom 2015*. ACM, 65–76.

[2] Yaxiong Xie, Zhenjiang Li, and Mo Li. 2015. Precise power delay profiling with commodity wifi. In *MobiCom 2015*. ACM, 53–64.

[3] Yuxun Zhou, Ninghang Hu, Costas J Spanos, et al. 2016. Veto-Consensus Multiple Kernel Learning.. In *AAAI*. 2407–2414.

[4] Han Zou, Baoqi Huang, Xiaoxuan Lu, Hao Jiang, and Lihua Xie. 2016. A robust indoor positioning system based on the procrustes analysis and weighted extreme learning machine. *IEEE Transactions on Wireless Communications* 15, 2 (2016), 1252–1266.

[5] Han Zou, Yuxun Zhou, Hao Jiang, Baoqi Huang, Lihua Xie, and Costas Spanos. 2016. A transfer kernel learning based strategy for adaptive localization in dynamic indoor environments: poster. In *Proceedings of the 22nd Annual International Conference on Mobile Computing and Networking*. ACM, 462–464.

Author Index

NOTES

www.ingramcontent.com/pod-product-compliance
Ingram Content Group UK Ltd.
Pitfield, Milton Keynes, MK11 3LW, UK
UKHW051417290926
15471UKWH00009B/1655

9 781450 356763